Who's Who
in
Scotland

2022

Carrick Media

Published by Carrick Media
89 Mount Pleasant Way, Kilmarnock KA3 1HJ
01563 521839

Copyright 2022 Carrick Media

Printed in Great Britain by Biddles Books Limited

British Library Cataloguing-in-Publication Data
A catalogue record for this book is available from the British Library

ISBN 978-1-3999-2862-5

Preface

Welcome to Who's Who in Scotland 2022, Scotland's dictionary of contemporary biography. First appearing in 1986, it is simultaneously a useful address book, a mine of information, and an essential guide to the establishments of Scotland (academic, ecclesiastical, legal, commercial, professional, political, artistic and literary) as well as to individuals who conform to no known category or establishment. Also, the book can be a source of amusement and miscellaneous interest.

Many new entries have been added, and great care has been taken to ensure that information given is accurate and up to date. Thank you to everyone who co-operated in the compilation of this book.

The Editor
Kilmarnock
June 2022

ADVERTISEMENTS

With a strong sense of purpose and mission as the University for the Common Good, we are committed to sustainability and have a platinum-award winning eco-friendly campus (EcoCampus, 2019), in Glasgow and London.

Highlands and Islands Enterprise
Iomairt na Gàidhealtachd 's nan Eilean

HIGHLANDS AND ISLANDS ENTERPRISE
An Lòchran, 10 Inverness Campus, Inverness IV2 5NA

Tel: 01463 245245
E-mail: corporate.relations@hient.co.uk
Web: www.hie.co.uk

HIE is an ambitious organisation with a remit from the Scottish Government that integrates economic and community development across the Highlands and Islands of Scotland. HIE supports businesses, communities and social enterprises across a diverse region covering more than half of Scotland's land mass. HIE's three priorities are to: build successful, productive and resilient businesses; create the conditions for growth and a green recovery; and enable strong, capable and resourceful communities. We help build a prosperous, inclusive and sustainable economy across the Highlands and Islands to attract more people to live, work, study, invest and visit.

INSTITUTE OF DIRECTORS SCOTLAND
10 Charlotte Square, Edinburgh EH2 4DR

Tel: 0131 557 5488
E-mail: iod.scotland@iod.com
Web: www.iod.com/events-community/regions/scotland
Contact: Louise Macdonald, National Director.

Providing personal and professional development for directors and senior management, members and non-members, from private, public and third sector organisations. We aim to assist individuals and Boards acquire the skills and knowledge required to fulfil their Corporate Governance and Leadership responsibilities. Our wide variety of courses and workshops run year-round and include the Chartered Director Programme; Role of the Non-Executive Director; Role of the Chair; Role of the Trustee workshops; a variety of Boardroom Skills workshops and Board Evaluation & Development Services.

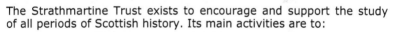

Biographies

An A to Z of prominent people in Scotland

A

Abbas, Malath, MA (Hons). Creative Producer, Game Designer and Director; b. 3.82. Educ. Liverpool John Moores University. Career history: PC support and web developer, Rundum Meir UK, 2007-08; Freelance 3D Artist, Milky Tea, 2009-2010; Team Leader/3D Artist/Game Designer, Dare To Be Digital, 2011-12; 3D Artist, NoodlFroot/Motoblox, Dundee, 2011-12; Freelance 3D Artist, Bigyama, Dundee, 2012; Technical Artist, Interface3, Edinburgh, 2012; Founding Partner/Artist/Producer/Client Relations, Quartic Llama, Dundee, 2012-15; Director: NEoN, 2015-2021; IGDA Scotland, since 2015; Member of Advisory Board, BGI (British Games Institute), since 2018; Trustee, Scottish Games Developers Association, since 2019; Board Member, Creative Scotland (part-time), since 2021; Founder/Game Designer, Biome Collective, since 2015. Address: Biome Collective, Unit 5, 20 Greenmarket, Dundee DD1 4QB; e-mail: info@biomecollective.com

Abbot, Grant. Head Teacher, Linlithgow Academy, since August 2021. Career: PE and Guidance Teacher; Depute Head Teacher, Linlithgow Academy. Head Teacher, Bathgate Academy, 2012-2021. Address: Linlithgow Academy, Braehead Road, Linlithgow, West Lothian EH49 6EH; T.-01506 280180.

Abbott-Halpin, Professor Edward, MA, PhD. Principal, Orkney College, since 2019; Professor of Social and Human Rights Informatics, University of the Highlands and Islands, since 2019; b. 1959. Educ. Blessed Humphrey Middlemore, Birmingham; University of Central Lancashire; Leeds Metropolitan University. Career: Leeds Metropolitan University: Associate Dean, Director, The Senator George Mitchell Centre for Peace and Conflict Resolution, 2006-09, Professor for Peace Education, 2009-2012; Chair/President, HURIDOCS, Geneva, Switzerland, 2008-2018; Professor of Social and Human Rights Informatics, Leeds Beckett University, 2012-2018. Publications: Human Rights and the Internet (Co-Author), 2000; Human Rights and Information Communication Technologies: Trends and Consequences of Use (Co-Editor), 2012. Address: Orkney College, East Road, Orkney, Kirkwall KW15 1LX.
E-mail: Edward.Abbott-Halpin@uhi.ac.uk

Abercrombie, Ian R., QC, LLB (Hons). Sheriff Principal, South Strathclyde, Dumfries and Galloway, 2015-2020; formerly Sheriff of Tayside, Central and Fife at Dunfermline; b. 7.7.55, Bulawayo. Educ. Milton High School; Edinburgh University. Recreations: travelling; walking.

Abernethy, Rt. Hon. Lord (John Alastair Cameron), PC 2005. Senator, College of Justice, 1992-2007; b. 1.2.38, Newcastle-upon-Tyne; m., Elspeth Mary Dunlop Miller; 3 s. Educ. Clergy House School, Khartoum; St. Mary's School, Melrose; Glenalmond College, Perth; Pembroke College, Oxford. National Service, 2nd Lt., RASC, Aldershot and Malta, 1956-58. Called to the Bar, Inner Temple, 1963; admitted Member, Faculty of Advocates, 1966; Advocate-Depute, 1972-75; Standing Junior Counsel to Department of Energy, 1976-79, Scottish Development Department, 1978-79; QC (Scotland), 1979; Vice-Dean, Faculty of Advocates, 1983-92; President, Pensions Appeal Tribunals for Scotland, 1985-92 (Legal Chairman, 1979-85); Chairman, Faculty Services Ltd., 1983-89 (Director, 1979-83); Hon. Fellow, Pembroke College, Oxford, 1993;

International Bar Association: Vice Chairman, Judges' Forum, 1993-94, Chairman, 1994-98, Member, Council, Section on Legal Practice, 1998-2002, and Member, Council, Human Rights Institute, 1998-2000 and 2002-05; Trustee, Faculty of Advocates 1985 Charitable Trust, since 1985; Member, Executive Committee, Society for the Welfare and Teaching of the Blind (Edinburgh and South East Scotland), 1979-92; Trustee, Arthur Smith Memorial Trust, 1975-2001, Chairman, 1990-2001; President, Scottish Medico-Legal Society, 1996-2000; Governor, St. Mary's School, Melrose, 1998-2012, Vice-Chairman, 2004-2012; Member, International Legal Assistance Consortium, since 2002; Commissioner, Northern Ireland (Remission of Sentences) Act 1995, since 2008; Trustee, Southern Africa Litigation Centre, 2008-2015; Justice of Appeal, Botswana, 2009-2018; Judge of Interim Independent Constitutional Dispute Resolution Court, Kenya, 2010. Publications: Medical Negligence: an introduction, 1983; Reproductive Medicine and the Law (ed A A Templeton and D J Cusine, 1990) (Contributor). Club: New, Edinburgh. Recreations: travel; nature conservation; Africana. Address: (b.) 4 Garscube Terrace, Edinburgh EH12 6BQ; T.-0131-337 3460.

Abram, Henry Charles, LLB, WS. Chairman, Hunter Reim Ltd; Company Director, Tods Murray LLP, 2008-2012; Solicitor, Tods Murray WS, 1973-2008; b. 11.8.51, Glasgow; m., Leslie Anne Hamilton; 2 s.; 1 d. Educ. Merchiston Castle School; Aberdeen University. Articled Tods Murray WS; qualified, 1976; Partner, 1978; Chairman, Management Board, 1994-97; Chairman, 1998-2002. Member, Council of Law Society of Scotland, 1983-86; Chairman of Governors, Merchiston Castle School, 2000-07; Member, High Constables and Guard of Honour of Holyroodhouse, 2012-15; former Chairman, Chiene + Tait LLP; Chairman, Cuthbert White Ltd; Trustee, Corra Foundation (formerly Lloyds TSB Foundation for Scotland), 2013-19; Chairman, St Columba's Hospice Rebuild Campaign; Past Member, Audit and Risk Management Committee of The National Trust for Scotland, 2008-2011. Recreations: shooting; stalking; golf; skiing; running. Address: (b) 107 George Street, Edinburgh EH2 3ES; T.-0131-240-0900; e-mail: hcabram@gmail.com

Ace, Jeff. Chief Executive, Dumfries and Galloway NHS Board. Address: (b.) Mid North, Crichton Hall, Dumfries DG1 4TG.

Adair, Ian. Headteacher, Inverkeithing High School, since 2016. Formerly Rector, Whitburn Academy (2007-2016). Address: Inverkeithing, Hillend Road, Fife KY11 1PL; T.-01383 602403.

Adam, George. Lord Provost of Aberdeen, 2012-17; b. 26.1.57. Educ. Brechin High School; Duncan Jordanstone College of Art, Dundee. Career: worked in the corporate communications sector for more than 30 years, as a designer, event organiser and video producer; Format Communications, Aberdeen (produced programmes and events for a wide range of companies and organisations, including the Oil & Gas and Retail sectors), 1979-90; The Presentation Business, Aberdeen (ran own production company, mainly involved in corporate video and digital imaging projects), 1999-2012; elected member for Hilton, Stockethill and Woodside Ward, 2007-2017. Honorary Patron of Aberdeen Performing Arts; Aberdeen's member of the World Energy Cities Partnership; membership of outside bodies includes Commissioner of the Northern Lighthouse Board. Recreations: gardening; visual arts; music; cinema; theatre.

Adam, George. MSP (SNP), Paisley, since 2011; Minister for Parliamentary Business, since 2021; SNP Chief Whip; Councillor for Paisley South: Ward 5 in Renfrewshire Council, 2007-2012; m., Stacey. Active with the SNP in Paisley since the 1980s. Worked in the motor industry as a sales manager. Member: Multiple Sclerosis Society of Scotland; Scottish Parliament: member of the Cross-Party Group on Carers; Social Security Committee; Convener: CPG MS, CPG End of Life Choices; Patron, SDEF; former Political Liaison Officer to the Cabinet Secretary for Education and Lifelong Learning. Recreations: passionate supporter of St Mirren FC, Chair, SMISA (St Mirren Independent Supporters Association); Honorary President, Paisley Pirates. Address: Scottish Parliament, Edinburgh EH96 1SP; Paisley Constituency Office: 4 Johnston Street, Paisley PA1 1XG.

Adam, Ian Clark. Non-Executive Director, Britannia Building Society, 1998-2008 (Non-Executive Chairman, 2004-08); b. 2.9.43; m., Betty; 1 d.; 1 s. Educ. Harris Academy. Trainee Accountant, Henderson & Logie, 1962-67; Price Waterhouse: Audit Senior and Assistant Manager (Rio de Janeiro), 1967-70, Manager, Bristol, 1970-76, Partner, Edinburgh, 1976-86, Senior Partner, Scotland, 1986-95; Financial Director, Christian Salvesen plc, 1995-98; Non-Executive Director: Fishers Holdings Ltd, 1996-2004, St. Leonards School, 2009-2016, St. Columbas Hospice, Edinburgh (Chairman), 2009-2016; Member, Council, Scottish Further and Higher Education Funding Council (2003-2011); Old Master Co of Merchants of the City of Edinburgh; MICAS 1967. Recreations: reading; golf; travel. Address: Gowanfield, 2 Cammo Road, Edinburgh EH4 8EB; T.-0131 339 6401.

Adam, Karen, MSP (SNP), Banffshire and Buchan Coast, since 2021. Carer and advocate for people with additional support needs; elected as a councillor in the Mid-Formartine ward of Aberdeenshire in 2017. Address: The Scottish Parliament, Edinburgh EH99 1SP.
E-mail: Karen.Adam.msp@parliament.scot

Adams, Professor Colin Ean, BSc (Hons), PhD. Professor of Freshwater Ecology, University of Glasgow, since 2009, Director, Scottish Centre for Ecology and The Natural Environment, since 1995; b. 21.06.59, Dumfries; 2 d. Educ. Annan Academy; University of Glasgow. Lecturer in Ecology, University of Glasgow, since 1995; Professor in Freshwater Biology, University of Tromsø, 2006. Member, Science Advisory Committee to Scottish Natural Heritage; Trustee, Loch Lomond Fishery Trust. Recreations: sailing; game shooting. Address: (b.) Scottish Centre for Ecology and Natural Environment, University of Glasgow, Rowardennan, Glasgow G63 0AW; T.-01360 870 271; e-mail: colin.adams@glasgow.ac.uk

Adams, Professor David, MA, MCD, PhD, FAcSS, FRTPI, FRICS, FRSA. Emeritus Professor in Urban Studies, University of Glasgow, since 2019; Board Member of the Scottish Land Commission, since 2016; b. 10.9.54, Menston, England; m., Judith Banks; 1 s.; 1 d. Educ. Rossall School; University of Cambridge; University of Liverpool. Planning Assistant, Leeds City Council, 1978-83; Research Assistant, University of Reading, 1983-84; Lecturer, University of Manchester, 1984-93; University of Aberdeen: Senior Lecturer, 1993-95, Reader, 1995-97, Professor of Land Economy, 1997-2004; Ian Mactaggart Professor of Property and Urban Studies, University of Glasgow, 2004-19. Publications: Urban Planning and the Development Process, 1994; Land for Industrial Development (Co-Author), 1994; Greenfields, Brownfields and Housing Development (Co-Author), 2002; Planning, Public Policy and Property Markets (Co-Editor), 2005; Urban Design in the Real Estate Development Process (Co-Editor), 2011; Shaping Places: Urban Planning, Design and Development (Co-Author), 2013. Recreations: walking; gardening; classical music.
E-mail: david.adams@glasgow.ac.uk

Adams, James, BA (International Relations). Director, RNIB Scotland (Royal National Institute of Blind People), since 2018. Educ. University of Reading. Career history: Scottish Labour Party: Trainee Organiser, 2000-01, Regional Organiser, 2001-03, Scottish Organiser, 2004-07; Councillor, Glasgow City Council (Govan Ward), 2012-17; Trustee, SCVO (Scottish Council for Voluntary Organisations), since 2020; Deputy Director/Head of Public Affairs, RNIB Scotland, 2007-2018. Address: RNIB Scotland (Head Office), 12-14 Hillside Crescent, Edinburgh EH7 5EA; T.-0131 652 3140.
E-mail: rnibscotland@rnib.org.uk

Adams, Kaye, MA (Hons). Scottish television presenter and journalist; b. 28.12.62, Falkirk; 2 d. Educ. University of Edinburgh. Started media career as a graduate trainee at Central Television; moved to Scottish Television in 1988, hosted Scottish Women, 1993-99; anchored the ITV talk show Loose Women, 1999-2006, co-anchor, since 2013; regular guest host of Channel 5 panel show The Wright Stuff, 2007-2010; guest co-host of The Hour on STV, 2009; joined BBC Radio Scotland in 2010; guest presenter of Channel 5's LIVE with... programme, since 2011; co-hosted the daytime chat show Sunday Scoop, 2013. Co-patron of Kindred, a Scottish based charity supporting families of young people with disabilities. Address: BBC Radio Scotland, 40 Pacific Quay, Glasgow G51 1DA; T.-0141 422 6000.

Adamson, Clare, BSc. MSP (SNP), Motherwell and Wishaw, since 2016 (Central Scotland, 2011-16); b. Motherwell; m., John Adamson; 1 s.; 3 stepchildren. Educ. Glasgow Caledonian University. Career: European Development Manager (IT) at a Glasgow-based software house; worked for four years at the SNP HQ Campaign Unit as Project Manager of the SNP's 'Activate Project'. Currently serves as Convenor of Education and Skills Committee; Member, National Union of Journalists; Board Member, Scottish Schools Education Research Centre (SSERC); qualified as a Member of the British Computer Society; Convener, Parliamentary Cross Party Group on Accident Prevention and Safety Awareness; Co-Convener on Cross Party Group on Science and Technology. Recreations: painting; watching live music, especially folk music. Address: (b.) Scottish Parliament, Edinburgh EH99 1SP.

Addison, Beverley, LLB, PGDipPLP. Family and Fertility Law Senior Solicitor, BTO Solicitors LLP, Glasgow, since 2020. Educ. Inverclyde Academy; University of Glasgow. Career history: Adviser, Citizens Advice, Glasgow, 2012-13; Legal Research Assistant, McGlashan MacKay Solicitors, Glasgow, 2013; Legal Intern, The Women's Support Project, Glasgow, 2013; student, Scottish Law Commission, 2013; Summer Intern, Simpson & Marwick, Edinburgh, 2013; President, Glasgow University Law Society, 2013-14; Youth Development Worker, Inverclyde Community Development Trust, 2014-15; BTO Solicitors LLP, Glasgow: Trainee Solicitor, 2015-17; Family Law Solicitor, 2017-2020. Member: Law Society of Scotland's Family Law Policy Committee; Family Law Association; Scottish Young Lawyers Association and Consensus Scotland. Recreations: current Captain of Greenock Wanderers Ladies Rugby Team; enjoys running with the dog; dabbling in interior design. Address: BTO Solicitors LLP, 48 St. Vincent Street, Glasgow G2 5HS; T.-0141 221 8012; e-mail: bea@bto.co.uk

Agnew of Lochnaw, Sir Crispin Hamlyn. 11th Baronet (created 1629); Chief of the Agnews; Advocate 1982; Queen's Counsel (1995); FRGS (1969); Deputy Social Security Commissioner (2000-08); Deputy Judge of the

Upper Tribunal, 2008-19; Chairman, Pension Appeal Tribunal, 2002-2012; Convenor, Mental Health Tribunal for Scotland, 2016-20; Unicorn Pursuivant of Arms, 1981-86; Rothesay Herald of Arms, since 1986; Trustee, John Muir Trust, 1989-2005; Chairman, Crofting Law Group; Council, SYHA, 2008-2012 and Board Member, SYHA, 2010-2012; President, Royal Highland Agricultural Society of Scotland (2018); b. 13.5.44, Edinburgh; m., Susan Rachel Strang Steel, PgDip, Careers Adviser (daughter of J.W. Strang Steel); 1 s.; 3 d. Educ. Uppingham School; Royal Military Academy, Sandhurst. Commissioned Royal Highland Fusiliers, 1964, as 2nd Lieutenant; Major, 1977; retired, 1981. Member: Royal Navy Expedition to East Greenland, 1966; Joint Services Expedition to Elephant Island, Antarctica, 1970-71; Army Nuptse Himal Expedition, 1975; Army Everest Expedition, 1976; Leader: Army East Greenland Expedition, 1968; Joint Services Expedition to Chilean Patagonia, 1972-73; Army Api Himal Expedition, 1980. Publications: Licensing (Scotland) Act 1976 (5th edition 2002) (Co-Author); Agricultural Law in Scotland, 1996; Connell on the Agricultural Holdings (Scotland) Acts (Co-Author) 1996; Land Obligations, 1999; Crofting Law, 2000; articles in various newspapers and journals. Recreations: mountaineering; sailing and mountain biking. Address: 6 Palmerston Road, Edinburgh EH9 1TN; T.-0131-668 3792.

Agnew, Denis, DipDA, MPhil, PhD; b. 1950, Clydebank; m., Carole (née Rowan); 1 d. (Julie); 1 s. (Julian). Educ. Royal Scottish Academy of Music & Drama; University of Glasgow; Queen Margaret University College, Edinburgh; Leverhulme Scholar (2001). Theatre practitioner (1972-2003) as actor, director & tutor. Published in international Journal of Scottish Theatre; compiled and edited booklet The Hospice: A History of St Margaret of Scotland Hospice, 2015. Chair of Equity Scottish Committee (1999-2003). Elected Councillor, West Dunbartonshire Council, 2003-2022; elected Leader of Council, 2007; elected Provost and Chair of Council, 2007-2012. Made Bailie (2017-2022). Awarded The Knight's Cross of the Order of Merit of The Republic of Poland in August 2013; made Honorary Patron of the Polish Combatants Memorial Group, September 2018.

Agnew, Ian, MA (Hons) (Cantab). Rector, Perth High School, 1975-92; b. 10.5.32, Newcastle-upon-Tyne; m., Gladys Agnes Heatherill; 1 d. Educ. King's College School, Wimbledon; Pembroke College, Cambridge. Assistant Teacher of Modern Languages, Melville College, Edinburgh, 1958-63; Assistant Teacher of Modern Languages, then Principal Teacher of Russian, George Heriot's School, Edinburgh, 1964-70; Housemaster, Craigmount Secondary School, Edinburgh, 1970-73; Deputy, Liberton High School, Edinburgh, 1973-75. Non-Executive Director, Perth and Kinross Healthcare NHS Trust, 1994-98; Minute Secretary, Headteachers Association of Scotland, 1979-81; Committee Member, SCCORE; President: Perthshire Musical Festival, 1978-88, Perth Chamber Music Society, 1982-89; Past President, Rotary Club of Perth St. John's; Past Chairman: Barnton and Cramond Conservative Association and West Edinburgh Conservative and Unionist Association; Serving Officer (OStJ), Priory of Scotland of the Most Venerable Order of St. John; Member, Society of High Constables, City of Perth; Governor: Balnacraig School, Perth, 1981-2007, Kilgraston School, 1990-99, Convent of the Sacred Heart, Bridge of Earn; Secretary, Friends of Perth Festival of the Arts, 1996-99; Member, Advisory Group, Perth College Development Trust; Chairman, Friends of St. John's Kirk, Perth, 1996-2008; Past President, Fair City Probus Club, Perth. Recreations: music (opera); reading; tennis; gardening. Address: (h.) Northwood, Heughfield Road, Bridge of Earn, Perthshire PH2 9BH; T.-01738 81 2273; e-mail: I.agnew576@btinternet.com

Agnew, Rosemary. Scottish Public Services Ombudsman. Address: (b.) Bridgeside House, 99 McDonald Road, Edinburgh EH7 4NS.

Ahmad, Mushtaq, OBE, BA, MA. Lord-Lieutenant for Lanarkshire, 2010-2017; b. India; 3 s.; 2 d. Educ. Murray College; JI College, Sialkot; University of Punjab; University of Glasgow. Teacher training, Jordanhill College of Education; taught Economics and Modern Studies for 2 years in Scotland; spent 3 years in London heading an East London school's large department, before returning to Lanarkshire working as Specialist Organiser for the largest Adult Basic Education Programme in Scotland for 17 years. Over several years, has served the community in Lanarkshire as a Councillor in Hamilton District and South Lanarkshire Councils, holding a number of posts; also served a term as Provost of South Lanarkshire, 2003-07; voluntary work through the Citizen's Advice Bureau and other bodies.

Ahmed-Sheikh, Tasmina, OBE. MP (SNP), Ochil and South Perthshire, 2015-2017; former SNP Trade and Investment spokesperson and former Deputy Shadow Leader of the House in the House of Commons; former SNP National Women's and Equalities Convener; founder and formerly chaired the Scottish Asian Women's Association; b. 5.10.70, Chelsea; m., Zulfikar Sheikh; 4 c. Educ. University of Edinburgh; University of Strathclyde. Former Partner, Hamilton Burns (Glasgow law firm); co-owner, Slainte Media Limited.

Ainsley, Sam, BA (Hons), PGDip. Artist and teacher; former Head of the Master of Fine Art (MFA) programme, The Glasgow School of Art; b. 1950, North Shields. Educ. Jacob Kramer College of Art, Leeds; Newcastle Polytechnic; Edinburgh College of Art. Career: taught on the Environmental Art programme (1985-1991) under David Harding's leadership and co-founded the Master of Fine Art course and was the programme Director from its inception until 2006; artwork is in a number of public and private collections nationally and internationally; contributed to a broad range of visual art initiatives in Scotland and has served as a Board member on The Scottish Sculpture Trust, The Arts Trust of Scotland, and many others; appointed to the Council of the Scottish Arts Council in 1998 and Chaired the Visual Art Committee at the SAC for two terms of office; informal position as an "International Ambassador" for Scottish Art and Artists (extensive International travel and invited role as a visiting artist and curator). Exhibited in and curated independent exhibitions and undertaken residencies in numerous institutions and arts organisations across the USA, Australasia, Europe and the UK. External advisor to many MFA courses including Liverpool John Moores & Newcastle University and is the Visitor to the Royal Academy Schools. Presentations include 'New Scots', RSA Edinburgh, 2008 and a recent two person show "Atlas of Encounters" at I Space Gallery, Chicago in February 2009. Undertook a collaborative 3 year residency at Glasgow Sculpture Studios alongside David Harding and Sandy Moffat.

Airlie, 13th Earl of (David George Coke Patrick Ogilvy), KT, GCVO, PC, KStJ; b. 17.5.26, London; m., Virginia Fortune Ryan; 3 s.; 3 d. Educ. Eton College. Lieutenant, Scots Guards, 1944; serving 2nd Bn., Germany, 1945; Captain, ADC to High Commissioner and C-in-C Austria, 1947-48; Malaya, 1948-49; resigned commission, 1950; Chairman, Ashdown Investment Trust Ltd., 1968-82; Director, J. Henry Schroder Wagg & Co. Ltd., 1961-84 (Chairman, 1973-77); Chairman, Schroders plc, 1977-84; Scottish and Newcastle Breweries plc, until 1983; Director,

Royal Bank of Scotland Group, 1983-94; Director, Royal Bank of Scotland plc, 1991-93; Chairman, General Accident Fire & Life Assurance Corporation plc, 1987-97; Chancellor of the Royal Victorian Order, 1984-97; Trustee, Royal Collection Trust, 1993; Ensign, Queen's Body Guard for Scotland (Royal Company of Archers) (President, Council, since 2001), Captain General, 2004-2011; Chancellor of the Most Noble and Ancient Order of the Thistle, November 13th 2007; Royal Victorian Chain and Chancellor, Royal Victorian Order; former Lord Chamberlain of Queen's Household; Chancellor, University of Abertay, Dundee, 1994-2009; President, National Trust for Scotland, 1997-2002; Hon. President, Scottish Council, The Scout Association; Chairman, Historic Royal Palaces, 1998-2002. Address: (h.) Airlie House, Cortachy, Kirriemuir, Angus DD8 4QJ.

Airlie, Countess of (Virginia Fortune Ryan), DCVO. Lady in Waiting to HM The Queen, since 1973; Chairman, National Galleries of Scotland, 1997-2000; b. 9.2.33, London; 3 s.; 3 d. Educ. Brearley School, New York City. Commissioner, Royal Fine Arts Commission; Trustee, Tate Gallery, 1983-95; Trustee, National Gallery, London, 1989-95; Member, Industrial Design Panel, British Rail, 1974-91. Founder/Governor, Cobham School; President, Angus Red Cross; Chairman, American Museum in Britain, Bath. Address: (b.) Airlie House, Cortachy, Kirriemuir, Angus DD8 4QJ; T.-01575 540231.

Aitchison, James Douglas, MA (Hons), MEd (Hons). Director, Scotland - Malawi School Improvement Programme, 2005-08 (Adviser to Schools Inspectorate, Uganda, 2003-05); Head Teacher, Boclair Academy, Bearsden, 1991-2002; Head Teacher, Gleniffer High School, Paisley, 1984-91; b. 2.7.47, Glasgow. Educ. High School of Glasgow; Glasgow University; University of Marburg. Teacher, Lycee Faidherbe, Lille; Principal Teacher, Bearsden Academy; Assistant Head Teacher, Gryffe High School, Houston. Recreations: curling; walking; travel. Address: (h.) 2/2 8 Crossveggate, Milngavie, Glasgow G62 6RA; T.-0141-956 6693.

Aitken, Hugh, CBE. Senior Industry Consultant, Aitken's Office, since 2019; Chairman of the Board, Dundee Science Centre, 2019-2021; Strategic Advisor, CBI Scotland, 2018 (Director, 2015-18). Educ. Woodside Secondary School. Career: European Distribution Manager, Digital Equipment Corporation, 1979-1985; European Logistics and Materials Manager, Apollo Computers, 1985-89; Sun Microsystems: Manager, European Logistics and Materials, 1989-1999, Director, European Logistics and Materials, 1992-94, Director of Business Strategy, 1994-95, Director of European Manufacturing, 1995-98, VP European Operations, 1998-2001, VP WW Customer Fulfillment, 2001-05; Chairman, Electronics Scotland, 2000-06; Sun Microsystems: VP WW Customer Fulfillment, 2006-08, Vice President, WW Manufacturing, 2008-09; VP WW Manufacturing, Oracle Corporation, 2009-2010; Microsoft, 2011-2013; President, ASCC INC (Aitken's Supply Chain Consultancy), 2013-2014.

Aitken, Cllr Susan. Leader of Glasgow City Council, since 2017; representing Langside ward (SNP), since 2012. Educ. University of Glasgow; Strathclyde University. Leader of the SNP Group, Glasgow City Council, since 2014; SNP's Local Government Convener. Address: Glasgow City Council, George Square, Glasgow G2 1DU; T.-0141 287 2000.

Aitken, William Mackie. JP, DL. MSP (Conservative), Glasgow, 1999-2011 (Conservative Justice Spokesman,

2001-03 and 2007-2011; Convener, Justice Committee, 2007-2011; Parliamentary Business Manager and Chief Whip, 2003-07; Housing Spokesman, 1999-2001); b. 15.4.47, Glasgow. Educ. Allan Glen's School, Glasgow. Chairman, Scottish Young Conservatives, 1975-77; Councillor, City of Glasgow, 1976-99: Convenor, City Licensing Committee and Vice-Convenor, Personnel Committee, 1977-79, Leader of the Opposition, City Council, 1980-84 and 1992-96, Bailie of the City, 1980-84, 1988-92, 1996-99; Magistrate, Deputy Lord Lieutenant, City of Glasgow. Recreations: football; reading; foreign travel. Address: (h.) 35 Overnewton Square, Glasgow G3 8RW; T.-0141-357 1284.

Akers, Fiona Moira, LLB (Hons), DipLP. Partner, Dickson Minto W.S., Solicitors, since 1999, Head of IP/Technology; b. 5.5.65, Paisley; m. Educ. Craigholme School; Edinburgh University. Trained with McGrigor Donald (now Pinsent Masons), Partner, 1997-99. Address: (b.) 16 Charlotte Square, Edinburgh EH2 4DF; T.-0131-225-4455; e-mail: fiona.akers@dmws.com

Alberti, Dr Sam, FRSE. Director of Collections, National Museums Scotland, since 2021; Honorary Professor in Cultural Heritage, University of Stirling. Career history: worked in and with museums for 20 years, first at the University of Manchester, then as Director of Museums and Archives at the Royal College of Surgeons of England; appointed Keeper of Science & Technology, National Museums Scotland, since 2016, then Interim Keeper of Art & Design in 2019. Former Visiting Professor at the University of Edinburgh College of Medicine and Veterinary Medicine; curated exhibitions on race, museum history, and the First World War. Publications include: Nature and Culture: Objects, Disciplines and the Manchester Museum, 2009; Morbid Curiosities: Medical Museums in Nineteenth-Century Britain, 2011. Address: National Museums Scotland, Chambers Street, Edinburgh EH1 1JF; T.-0131 247 4415; e-mail: s.alberti@nms.ac.uk

Alcorn, Dr. Rhona, PhD, MSc, MA (Hons). Chief Executive and Editor-in-Chief, Scottish Language Dictionaries, since 2017; Honorary Fellow, University of Edinburgh; extensive management experience from earlier public sector career (1984-2001). Address: 9 Coates Crescent, Edinburgh EH3 7AL; T.-0131 220 1294.

Alderson, Dr Michael, BA, PGCE, MA, PhD, FRSA. Warden, Glenalmond College, since 2020. Educ. Durham University; University of Cambridge. Career history: Head of Sixth Form & German Master, Derby Grammar School, 2000-03; Tutor, Durham University, 2003-09; Assessment Associate & Team Leader, Pearson, 2005-2011; Deputy Head, Durham School, 2003-2020. Boarding, Compliance & Educational Quality Inspector, Independent Schools Inspectorate, since 2011. Address: Glenalmond College, Back Avenue, Glenalmond, Perth PH1 3RY; T.-01738 842000.

Alessi, Dario Renato, FRS, FRSE. Principal Investigator, Honorary Professor and Director of the MRC Protein Phosphorylation and Ubiquitylation Unit, University of Dundee, since 2012; b. 23.12.67, Strasbourg, France; 1 s. Educ. European School of Brussels; University of Birmingham. Discovered and characterised PDKI protein Kinase; discovered and characterised the mechanism of activation and function of the LKBI tumour suppressor; identified two physiological substrates of the WNKI and WNK4 Kinase that control blood pressure; described the mechanism by which PKB/AKT enzyme is activated; identified ERM proteins as potential substrates for the

LRRK2 Parkinson's Disease Kinase. Colworth Medal, 1999; Eppendorf Young European Investigator Award, 2000; Makdougall Brisbane Prize, 2002; Philip Leverhulme Prize, 2002; Embo Gold Medal, 2005, Francis Crick Prize, 2006; elected Fellow of Royal Society, 2008; elected Fellow of the Academy of Medical Sciences, 2012. Recreations: running; watching football and collecting stamps. Address: MRC Protein Phosphorylation Unit, College of Life Science, University of Dundee, Dundee DD1 5EH; T.-01382 385602.
E-mail: d.r.alessi@dundee.ac.uk

Alexander, Professor Alan, MA, OBE, FRSE, FAcSS. Chair, Audit Scotland, since 2020; General Secretary, Royal Society of Edinburgh (RSE), 2013-18; Chair, Scottish Water, 2002-06 (Chair Designate, 2001-02); Chairman, West of Scotland Water Authority, 1999-2002; Professor of Local and Public Management, Strathclyde University, 1993-2000, now Emeritus Professor (Head, Department of Human Resource Management, 1993-96, Professor of Local Government, 1987-93); Visiting Professor, University of Edinburgh Management School, since 2006; b. 13.12.43, Glasgow; m., Morag MacInnes (Morag Alexander, qv); 1 s.; 1 d. Educ. Possil Secondary School, Glasgow; Albert Secondary School, Glasgow; Glasgow University. Lecturer/Assistant Professor, Political Science, Lakehead University, Ontario, 1966-71; Lecturer in Politics, Reading University, 1971-87. Member of Board, Housing Corporation, 1977-80; Member, Standing Research Committee on Local and Central Government Relations, Joseph Rowntree Memorial Trust, 1988-92; conducted inquiry into relations between Western Isles Islands Council and BCCI, 1991; Director, Scottish Local Authorities Management Centre, 1987-93; Member, Commission on Local Government and the Scottish Parliament, 1998-99; Chair, Glasgow Regeneration Fund, 1998-2001; Trustee, Quarriers, 1995-2000; Trustee, WaterAid, 2001-06; Trustee, David Hume Institute, 2012-18; Member, Council, Royal Society of Edinburgh, 2012-18; Chair, Scottish Council, Outward Bound, 2012-15; Vice-Chair, Royal Society of Edinburgh enquiry 'Digital Scotland: Spreading the Benefits', 2012-14; Member, Accounts Commission, 2002-08; Member, Economic and Social Research Council, 2003-09. President, Institution of Water Officers, 2005-06; Chair: Postwatch Scotland, 2007-08, Distance Lab Ltd., 2006-2010, RCUK/UUK Review of Full Economic Costing of University Research, 2008-09, Waterwise, 2010-2015, Data Access Committee, Understanding Society, 2010-2015; Chair, Advisory Board, School of Management, University of St Andrews, 2016-2021; Independent Member, Board of Audit Scotland, since 2018. Publications: Local Government in Britain since Reorganisation, 1982; The Politics of Local Government in the UK, 1982; L'amministrazione locale in Gran Bretagna, 1984; Borough Government and Politics: Reading, 1835-1985, 1985; Managing the Fragmented Authority, 1994; The Future of DLOs/DSOs in Scotland, 1998; articles in learned journals. Recreations: theatre; cinema; walking; avoiding gardening.

Alexander, Professor Michael Joseph, BA, MA (Oxon). Professor Emeritus of English Literature, St. Andrews University; b. 21.5.41, Wigan; m., 1, Eileen Mary McCall (deceased); 2, Mary Cecilia Sheahan; 1 s.; 2 d. Educ. Downside School; Trinity College, Oxford; Perugia University; Princeton University. Editor, William Collins, London, 1963-65; Lecturer, University of California, 1966-67; Editor, André Deutsch, London, 1967-68; Lecturer: East Anglia University, 1969, Stirling University, 1969; Senior Lecturer, 1977; Reader, 1985; Berry Professor of English Literature, St Andrews University, 1985-2003. Represented Scotland on 'Round Britain Quiz' for 17 years. Publications: Earliest English Poems (Translator), 1966; Beowulf (Translator), 1973; Twelve Poems, 1978; The

Poetic Achievement of Ezra Pound, 1979; History of Old English Literature, 1983; Macmillan Anthology of English Literature, 1989; Beowulf (Editor), 1995; Sons of Ezra (Editor), 1995; The Canterbury Tales – The First Fragment (Editor), 1996; The Canterbury Tales: Illustrated Prologue (Editor), 1996; A History of English Literature, 2000, 2007, 2013; Medievalism: the Middle Ages in Modern England, 2007, 2017; Old English Riddles from the Exeter Book (Translator), 2007; The First Poems in English (Translator), 2008; Geoffrey Chaucer, 2012; Reading Shakespeare, 2013, 2019; The Wanderer: Elegies, Epics, Riddles (Translator), 2013; The Wanderer and other Old-English Poems (Translator), 2018. Address: School of English, St. Andrews University, St. Andrews KY16 9AL; T.-01865-741774; e-mail: michael.j.alex@gmail.com

Alexander, Morag, BA (Hons), OBE. Co-Chair, Scottish Commission on Older Women, since 2015; Commissioner, East Lothian Poverty Commission, 2016; Lay member, General Optical Council, 2007-2014; Scotland Commissioner, Equality and Human Rights Commission, 2007-2010; Convener, Scottish Social Services Council, 2001-07; Director, Equal Opportunities Commission, Scotland, 1992-2001; Trustee, Turning Point Scotland, 2000-07; b. 10.10.43, Kilwinning; m., Professor Alan Alexander (qv); 1 s.; 1 d. Educ. Lourdes Secondary School, Glasgow; Glasgow University; Lakehead University, Ontario. Research Assistant, ASTMS, 1971-73; Editor and Researcher, RIPA, 1973-82; freelance journalist and consultant, 1982-90; Founding Editor, Women in Europe, 1985-89, and UK Correspondent, Women of Europe, 1987-92; Founding Director, Training 2000 (Scotland) Ltd., Scottish Alliance for Women's Training, 1990-92; Member, Policy Committee, Children in Scotland, Chair, Early Years Advisory Group, 1995-2003; Board Member, Scottish Commission for the Regulation of Care, 2001-07; Member, Board, Partnership for a Parliament, 1997; Member, Scottish Senate, the Windsor Meetings, 1997-2000; Member, Expert Panel on Procedures and Standing Orders, Scottish Parliament, 1997-98; Member, Committee of Inquiry into Student Finance, 1999; Member, Governing Body, Court, Queen Margaret University, 2001-08; Trustee and Board Member, ELCAP, since 2010, Chair, 2015-19. Recreations: music; opera; visiting art galleries and museums; walking.
E-mail: morag.alexander@virginmedia.com

Alexander, Wendy, MA (Hons), MA (Econ), MBA, FRSE (2016). MSP (Labour), Paisley North, 1999-2011; Vice-Principal (International), University of Dundee, since 2015; Associate Dean, Global Business, Degree Programmes and Career Services, London Business School, since 2012; b. 27.6.63, Glasgow; m., Prof. Brian Ashcroft; 1 s.; 1 d. Educ. Park Mains School, Erskine; Pearson College, Canada; Glasgow University; Warwick University; INSEAD, France. Research Officer, Scottish Labour Party, 1988-92; Senior Associate, Booz Allen & Hamilton Int., 1994-97; Special Adviser to Secretary of State for Scotland, 1997-98; Minister for Communities, 1999-2000; Minister for Enterprise and Lifelong Learning, 2000-01; Minister for Enterprise, Transport and Lifelong Learning, 2001-02; Leader, Labour in Scottish Parliament, 2007-08. Visiting Professor, University of Strathclyde, 2002-2012. Address: (b.) Nethergate, Dundee DD1 4HN.

Allan, Dr Alasdair James, MA, PhD. MSP (SNP), Western Isles, since 2007; Minister for International Development and Europe, 2016-18; Minister for Learning, Science and Scotland's Languages, Scottish Government, 2011-16; b. 6.5.71, Edinburgh. Educ. Selkirk High School; University of Glasgow; University of Aberdeen. Senior Vice President, Students Representative Council, Glasgow University, 1991-92; Researcher, SNP Headquarters, 1998-

99; Parliamentary Assistant: Michael Russell MSP, 1999-2002, Alex Salmond MP, 2002-03; Policy and Parliamentary Affairs Manager, Carers Scotland, 2003-04; Senior Media Relations Officer, Church of Scotland, 2004-06; Parliamentary Assistant to Angus B MacNeil MP, 2006-07. National Secretary, SNP, 2003-06; Scottish Parliament Local Government and Communities Committee, 2007-2010; former Vice President, Scots Language Society; currently a member of Parliament's Social Security Committee and Education Committee. Recreations: Scottish languages and literature; hill walking; travel; promoting Scottish independence; singing in a Gaelic choir and learning Norwegian. Address: (b.) 20 Kenneth Street, Stornoway, Isle of Lewis HS1 2DR; T.-01851 700357; e-mail: alasdair.allan.msp@parliament.scot

Allan, Angus, BSc (Hons), MBA (2002). Depute Principal, South Lanarkshire College, 2006-2020; Board Member, Loch Lomond and the Trossachs National Park Authority, 2012-2019; Convener, Environmental Association of Colleges and Universities, 2015-17; HM Inspector of Education; b. 28.3.60, Glasgow. Educ. Larkhall Academy; Edinburgh University. Lecturer in Agriculture, Kirkley College, Northumberland, 1982-85; farming, Ross-shire, 1985-88; Elmwood College, Cupar, 1988-2001 (latterly as Assistant Principal); Principal, Oatridge Agricultural College, 2001-02. Church of Scotland Elder. Recreation: sailing.

Allan, Charles Maitland, MA, MUniv (Aberdeen). Journalist, Economist and Farmer; b. 19.8.39, Stirling; m., Fiona Vine; 2 s.; 2 d. Educ. Dartington Hall; Aberdeen University. Lecturer in Economic History, Glasgow University, 1962-63; Lecturer in Economics, St. Andrews University, 1963-65; Lecturer and Senior Lecturer, Strathclyde University, 1965-74; Producer/Presenter, BBC, 1982-86; Managing Editor, Ardo Publishing Co. Publications: Theory of Taxation; Death of a Papermill; Farmer's Diary I, II, III, IV, V; Neeps and Strae; The Truth Tells Twice; Them That Live The Longest. Recreations: cycling; cricket; turning off television sets; World Caber Tossing Champion, 1972. Address: (h.) Ythan Cottage, Methlick, Ellon, Aberdeenshire; T.-01651 806 218.

Allan, Gary James Graham, QC, LLB (Hons); b. 21.1.58, Aberdeen; m., Margaret Muriel Glass; 1 s.; 1 d. Educ. Aberdeen Grammar School; University of Aberdeen. Legal apprenticeship, McGrigor Donald & Co., Solicitors, Glasgow and Edinburgh, 1980-82; Hughes Dowdall, Solicitors, Glasgow: Assistant Solicitor, 1982-1986, Partner, 1986-93; Admitted as a Member of the Faculty of Advocates, 1994; Appointed Queen's Counsel, 2007; Senior Advocate Depute (Crown Counsel), 2007-11; Advocate Depute ad hoc, since 2011. Executive Member, Glasgow Bar Association, 1983-93; Member, Management Committee, Castlemilk Law Centre, 1985-87; Local Parliamentary Liaison Officer, Law Society of Scotland, 1986-88; President, Aberdeen Grammar School Former Pupils' Club, 2007-08; Director, Hillhead High School War Memorial Trust Limited, 2000-2012; Director, Casus Omissus: The Aberdeen Law Project, since 2010; Appeal Chair member of the Judicial Panel of the Scottish Football Association, since 2011. Address: (b.) Optimum Advocates, Glasgow High Court, 1 Mart Street, Saltmarket, Glasgow G1 5NA; T.-0141 553 4890.

Allan, George Alexander, MA (Hons). Headmaster, Robert Gordon's College, Aberdeen, 1978-96; b. 3.2.36, Edinburgh; m., Anne Violet Veevers; 2 s. Educ. Daniel Stewart's College, Edinburgh; Edinburgh University. Teacher of Classics, Glasgow Academy, 1958-60; Daniel Stewart's College: Teacher of Classics, 1960-63, Head of

Classics, 1963-73 (appointed Housemaster, 1967); Schoolmaster Fellow Commoner, Corpus Christi College, Cambridge, 1972; Deputy Headmaster, Robert Gordon's College, 1973-77. Former Chairman and former Secretary, Headmasters' Conference (Scottish Division) (Member, National Committee, 1982 and 1983); Governor, Welbeck College, 1980-89; Council Member, Scottish Council of Independent Schools, 1988-96 and 1997-2002; Director, Edinburgh Academy, 1996-2003; Governor, Longridge Towers School, Berwick-upon-Tweed, 2004-08. Recreations: gardening; music. Address: 5 Abbey View, Kelso, Roxburghshire TD5 8HX.

Allan, Sheriff John Douglas, OBE, BL, DMS. Sheriff of Lothian and Borders at Edinburgh, 2000-08; b. 2.10.41, Edinburgh; m., Helen E.J. Aiton; 1 s.; 1 d. Educ. George Watson's College, Edinburgh; Edinburgh University. Solicitor in private practice, Edinburgh, 1963-67; Procurator Fiscal Depute, Edinburgh, 1967-71; Solicitor, Crown Office, Edinburgh, 1971-76; Assistant Procurator Fiscal, then Senior Assistant Procurator Fiscal, Glasgow, 1976-79; Solicitor, Crown Office, Edinburgh, 1979-83; Procurator Fiscal for Edinburgh and Regional Procurator Fiscal for Lothians and Borders, 1983-88; Sheriff of Lanark, 1988-2000. Part-time Lecturer in Law, Napier College, Edinburgh, 1963-66; Sheriffs' Association: Secretary, 1991-97, Vice-President, 1997-2000, President, 2000-2002; Chairman, Judicial Commission, General Assembly of the Church of Scotland, 1998-2003, Member, since 2009; Member, Board, Scottish Children's Reporter Administration, 1995-2003 (Deputy Chairman, 2002-03); Regional Vice-President, Commonwealth Magistrates' and Judges' Association, 2003-09 (Council Member, 2000-03, Member, 2009-2021); Member, Judicial Appointments Board for Scotland, 2002-08; Chairman, Executive Committee of Scottish Council, Scout Association, 2009-2013; Vice President, South East Scotland Regional Scout Council, since 2013; Holder, Scout "Medal of Merit". Recreations: Scouts; youth leadership; walking; Church. Address: 80 Greenbank Crescent, Edinburgh EH10 5SW; T.-0131-447-2593; e-mail: jdouglasallan80@gmail.com

Allan, Tim, MA (Hist), FRSA. President, Scottish Chambers of Commerce, since 2017; Chief Executive, Unicorn Property Group, since 2006. Educ. Robert Gordon's College; University of St Andrews. Career: Major, British Army, 1988-98; VP - Private Bank, Citi, 1998-2003; Director, UBS Wealth Management, 2003-05; Scotland Chair, Young Enterprise UK, 2006-09; Scotland Committee Member, Big Lottery Fund, 2007-2014; Director, Scorpion PFS, 2008-2015; Director, Dundee and Angus Chamber of Commerce, 2014-16, President, 2014-16; Deputy Chair, Campaign Board, Victoria and Albert Museum of Design, since 2011; Non Executive Director, Motor Fuel Group/Murco, since 2011; Non Executive Board Member of the University Court, University of St Andrews, since 2015; Member of the Board, Scottish Chambers of Commerce, since 2016. Chairman, Young Enterprise Scotland, 2006-09. Address: Scottish Chambers of Commerce, Strathclyde Business School, 199 Cathedral Street, Glasgow G4 0QU; T.-0141 444 7500.

Allan, Lesley, LLB (Hons). Partner: Kennedys, since 2022, Clyde & Co LLP, Glasgow, 2015-2022; b. 10.71. Educ. University of Glasgow. Career history: Trainee Solicitor/Solicitor, Strathclyde Regional Council, 1993-96; Solicitor, North Lanarkshire Council (Litigation Department), 1996-97; Assistant: Wilson Chalmers & Hendry, Glasgow, 1997-98; Reid Cooper Partnership, 1998-99; Simpson & Marwick, Glasgow: Assistant, 1999-2005, Associate, 2006-2012, Partner, 2012-15. Address: Kennedys, The Mercantile Building, Fifth floor, 53 Bothwell Street, Glasgow G2 6TS; T.-0141 370 2949.

Allard, Cllr Christian. Member of the European Parliament for Scotland (SNP), 2019-2020; former MSP (SNP), North East Scotland region (2013-16); Councillor, Aberdeen City Council, since 2017; b. 31.3.64, Dijon, Côte-d'Or, France; m.; 3 c. Educ. Lycee Montchapet Dijon. Career history: worked in the fishing industry for over 30 years; Scottish Development Manager, Tradimar (STEF-TFE) (European seafood transport and logistics network), 1987-93; Export Manager, Charles & Caie (seafood exporting company), 1994-2013; Constituency Officer for Dennis Robertson MSP, The Scottish Parliament, 2011-13. Address: Aberdeen City Council, Town House, Broad Street, Aberdeen AB10 1FY; T.-01224 346642. E-mail: callard@aberdeencity.gov.uk

Allardyce, Jason, MSc. Editor, The Sunday Times Scotland, since 2012; b. 23.10.71, Greenock; m., Aine; 1 d. Educ. Greenock Academy; Queen Margaret University. Reporter: West Highland Free Press, 1990-95, The Scotsman, 1995-97; Political Correspondent, Scotland on Sunday, 1997-98; Political Reporter, The Times, 1998-99; Assistant Editor, Scotland on Sunday, 1999-2004; The Sunday Times Scotland: Assistant Editor, 2004-06, Associate Editor, 2006-2010, then Political Editor. UK Daily News Journalist of the Year, 1997; Scottish Journalist of the Year, 2003; Scottish Political Journalist of the Year, 2002, 2003, 2004, 2010. Recreations: walking; golf; rescuing spiders. Address: (b.) The Sunday Times, Fifth Floor, Guildhall, 57 Queen Street, Glasgow G1 3EN; T.-0141 4205338; e-mail: jason.allardyce@sunday-times.co.uk

Allen, Ann. Chair, Architecture and Design Scotland, since 2018. Educ. Oswestry Girls High School; University of Reading. Career history: Surveyor, Slough Estates plc, 1989-94; Head of Estate and Facilities, HBOS plc, 2005-08; Head of Asset Management, John Lewis, 2008-2012; Trustee, Ethical Property Foundation, 2012-2016; Non Executive Director, Gentoo Sunderland, 2015-16; University of Glasgow: appointed Director of Estates and Buildings in 2012, then Executive Director, Estates and Commercial Services, 2017-2020. Board Member, Scottish Futures Trust, since 2019; Board Trustee, National Museum of Scotland, since 2017; appointed CEO, Chartered Institute of Civil Engineering Surveyors, since 2020; Board Member, Water Commission Scotland, since 2020; Chair, Scottish Board, Women in Property, since 2019. Address: Architecture and Design Scotland, 9 Bakehouse Close, 146 Canongate, Edinburgh EH8 8DD; T.-0131 556 6699.

Allen, Martin Angus William, MA, BD (1st Class Hons), ThM. Retired Minister, Chryston Parish Church of Scotland (1977-2007); b. 5.8.42, St. Andrews; m., Ann; 2 s. Educ. St. Andrews University; Edinburgh University; Covenant Seminary, St. Louis, USA. Assistant Education and Training Officer, Scottish Gas Board, 1964-71; Student in Theology, Edinburgh University, 1971-74; Assistant Minister, Church of Scotland, Wester Hailes, Edinburgh, 1974-75; Post Graduate Student, St. Louis, USA, 1975-76. Former Trustee, Rutherford House, Edinburgh - Theological Study Centre; former Trustee and Chairman, Crieff Trust - (Ministers' Fellowship). Recreations: golf; walking; reading. Address: (h.) 5 Marguerite Grove, Lenzie G66 4HD; e-mail: annmartinallen@gmail.com

Allison, Barbara, CBE (2018), MBA, BAcc. Director of Communications & Ministerial Support, Scottish Government, 2015-2020. Educ. Lanark Grammar School; Glasgow University; Edinburgh University. Previously Director of People, 2009-15, Head of HR, 2008-09, Director of Human Resources, Scottish Prison Service, 2003-08 and held roles in Finance, Manufacturing and Strategy and Corporate Services; Non-Executive Director, Scottish Ballet. Recreations: walking; reading; music.

Allison, Charles William, MBChB, FRCA. Consultant Anaesthetist, Stracathro Hospital, Brechin, 1982-2012

(retired); Consultant, Ninewells Hospital, Dundee; Honorary Senior Lecturer, Dundee University; b. 1.7.52, Newport on Tay; m., Elspeth Stratton; 2 d. Educ. Madras College, St. Andrews; Dundee University. Training grades in anaesthesia, Dundee, 1976-81; Clinical Research Fellow, Hospital for Sick Children, Toronto, 1982. Editor, Annals of the Scottish Society of Anaesthetists, 1999-2003; President, NESSA, 2004-05; Secretary, DMGS, since 1982 and Captain, 2018-19; Dean, Guildry of Brechin, 2007-09; President: Rotary Club of Brechin, 2010-11, Scottish Society of Anaesthetists, 2012-13, Dundee Medical Club, 2012-13. Publications: papers and book chapter. Recreations: golf; photography. Address: Summerbank House, Brechin, Angus DD9 6HL; T.-01356 623624.

Alstead, Brigadier (Francis) Allan (Littlejohns), CBE, DL, MPhil, FCILT, FCMI, FCIPD, FInstD, FBISA. Director: Alstead Consulting Ltd, 2000-18, Launchsite Ltd, 2000-17; Chief Executive, sportscotland (formerly Scottish Sports Council), 1990-2000; Chef de Mission for Scottish Team, Commonwealth Games 2002; Chairman, Mercy Corps Scotland, 2001-08; Board Member, Mercy Corps International, USA, 2001-08; Board Member, CRP (Bosnia), 2005-08; Chairman, Scottish Target Shooting Federation, 2011-15; b. 19.6.35, Glasgow; m., Joy Veronica Edwards (deceased 20 July 2019); 2 s. Educ. Glasgow Academy; Royal Military Academy, Sandhurst; Royal Naval Staff College; Joint Services Staff College; Edinburgh University; University of Wales, Aberystwyth. Commissioned into King's Own Scottish Borderers, 1955; commanded 1st Bn., KOSB, 1974-76 (Mention in Despatches, Northern Ireland); Military Assistant to Quarter-Master-General, 1976-79; Instructor, Army Staff College, Camberley, 1979-81; Assistant Chief of Staff, BAOR, 1981-84 (Colonel); Commander, 51st Highland Brigade, 1984-87 (Brigadier); NATO Research Fellow, Edinburgh University, 1987-88; NATO HQ Reinforcement Co-ordinator, 1988-90. Member, Royal Company of Archers (Queen's Bodyguard in Scotland); Deputy Lieutenant, City of Edinburgh; Regimental Trustee, KOSB, 1980-2006; Trustee, KOSB Association, 2006-2019; Trustee, Youth Sport Trust, 1992-99; Deputy Hon. Colonel, City of Edinburgh Universities OTC, 1990-99; Governor, Moray House College, 1991-97; Governor, Glasgow Academy, 1995-2001; Member, Executive, Scottish Council, Development and Industry, 1995-2008; Member, Lowland RFCA, since 1995; Trustee, Council for the Advancement of Arts, Recreation and Education, 2003-2014; Director and Trustee, Seagull Trust, 1995-2007; Non-Executive Director, JRG Ltd, 1996-2007; Trustee, Erskine Hospital, 2001-2012; Member, General Council, Erskine Hospital, since 2012; Member, Council, National Playing Fields Association, 2001-07; President, SSAFA, Edinburgh, East and Midlothian, 1990-98 and then Edinburgh and Lothians, 2003; FRSA, 1994-2002; Mercy Corps, Humanitarian Hero Award, 2008; DUniv (Glasgow Caledonian), 2009. Publications: Ten in Ten; The Reinforcement of Europe in Crisis and War. Recreations: walking; archery. Address: (h.) 49 Moray Place, Edinburgh EH3 6BQ.

Alston, Dr. David. Historian; Chair, NHS Highland, 2016-19. Career history: teacher, then organiser for the Workers Education Association in the Highlands; helped establish Cromarty Courthouse Museum and was its Curator/Manager; elected councillor representing the Black Isle in 1999, stood down in 2017. Non-executive member, NHS Highland, 2003-2011 and Highland Council nominee to Board, 2012-2016. Freelance historian with a special interest in Scotland's involvement in slavery.

Amner, Neil, LLB (Hons), DipLP, NP, FCILT. Director, Anderson Strathern LLP, since 2017; President, Glasgow

Chamber of Commerce, 2016-18 (Board Member, 2012-2020, Director since 2006); Board Member, Scottish Chambers of Commerce, since 2017 (Member of Scottish Business Advisory Group, since 2019; Chairman of Economic Advisory Board, 2016-19); Director and Company Secretary, Scottish Maritime Cluster, since 2017. Educ. Glasgow Academy; University of Glasgow. Career: Partner, MacRoberts LLP, 2015-16; Partner and Head of Infrastructure, Environment & Transport: Biggart Baillie LLP, 1995-2012, DWF LLP, 2012-15. Member, Law Society of Scotland Environmental Law and Maritime Law Sub-Committees and Climate Change Working Group; Chartered Fellow of Chartered Institute of Logistics & Transport (UK); Member, Rail Freight Group; Member, European Aviation Law Association; Member, United Kingdom Environmental Law Association; Board Member, Glasgow Building Preservation Trust, 2015-17; Visitor, Incorporation of Maltmen in Glasgow, 2004-05. Recognised as leader in fields of transport, environmental and Scottish parliamentary law in both Legal 500 and Chambers directories of the legal profession. Recreations: triathlon; watersports; running; cycling and skiing.

Amyes, Professor Sebastian Giles Becket, BSc, MSc, PhD, DSc, Drhc, FRCPath, FIBiol. Professor Emeritus of Microbial Chemotherapy, Edinburgh University; b. 6.5.49, Stockton Heath; 1 s.; 1 d; m. Hilary-Kay Young, 2010. Educ. Cranleigh School; University College, London. London University, Teaching Fellow in Bacteriology 1974; Edinburgh University Medical School, since 1977; Reader, 1988; Professor, 1992; Head of Medical Microbiology Dept., 1997-2000; Emeritus Professor, 2013. Research speciality: Antibiotic Resistance. Royal Pharmaceutical Society annual conference award, 1984; C.L. Oakley lectureship, Pathological Society, 1987; Doctor honoris causa, Semmelweis University, Hungary, 2004; Honorary life member of the Hungarian Society of Microbiology, 2007. Author: Bacteria VSI; Antibacterial Chemotherapy - Theory, Problems and Practice; Magic Bullets: Lost Horizons. Recreations: fly fishing; opera; Renaissance cartography. Address: (b.) Biomedical Sciences, Chancellor's Building, Little France, Edinburgh EH16 4SB; e-mail: s.g.b.amyes@ed.ac.uk

Anderson, Professor Annie S., BSc, PhD, SRD, FRCP (Edin), FRSE. Professor of Public Health Nutrition, Ninewells Medical School, University of Dundee; Director, Centre for Public Health Nutrition Research, since 1996; b. 24.12.57, Torphins; m., Professor Robert Steele. Educ. Cults Academy, Aberdeen; RGIT; University of Aberdeen. Dietitian, Cambridge Area Health Authority, 1979-81; Research Assistant, Medical School, University of Cambridge, 1982-84; Research Dietitian, Grampian Health Board, 1985-86; Postgraduate Research Student, Department of Obstetrics, University of Aberdeen, 1987-91; Research Fellow (Human Nutrition), University of Glasgow, 1991-96; Member, Dundee University Court, 1999-2001; Editor, Journal of Human Nutrition and Dietetics (2001-06); Member, Scientific Advisory Committee on Nutrition, 2001-04, 2004-08, 2009-11; Observer (on behalf of UICC), WCRF/AICR Review Fund, Nutrition and Physical Activity; Chair, MRC Scientific Committee of National Prevention Initiative, 2012-2015; Workstream Lead on Health and Sustainability for Scottish Government National Food and Drink Policy, 2003-2011; Director, Scottish Cancer Foundation, since 2006; Co Director, Scottish Cancer Prevention Network (www.cancerpreventionscotland.org.uk), since 2008; Policy Adviser: Bowel Cancer UK, since 2006. Chair/member World Cancer Research Fund International grants committee, 2018-2022; Chair, Norwegian Cancer Society Research Committee, 2021; Advisor, Breast Cancer Now-Science Strategy Committee, 2021-2023; Vice-President, President, UK Society for Behavioural Medicine, 2018-

2021; Chair, Scottish Government Steering Group on Cancer Prehabilitation, 2021-2022. Recreations: archaeology; orchards. Address: Centre for Research into Cancer Prevention and Screening, Centre for Public Health Nutrition Research, Division of Cancer Research, Level 7, Mailbox 7, Ninewells Medical School, Dundee DD1 9SY; T.-01382 383299; e-mail: a.s.anderson@dundee.ac.uk

Anderson, Christopher. Senior Partner, Stuart & Stuart; Head of the Private Client team, advising on Wills, Powers of Attorney and asset protection; nominated officer for Anti Money Laundering. Recreations: enjoys golf; watching rugby; dog walking. Address: Stuart & Stuart, 25 Rutland Street, Edinburgh EH1 2RN; T.-0131 222 9975. E-mail: canderson@stuartandstuart.co.uk

Anderson, David, LLB, LLM, FCIArb. Partner, Shepherd and Wedderburn, since 1998; Solicitor, 1992-97; Associate, 1997-98; b. 8.67. Educ. Boroughmuir High School; University of Edinburgh. Address: Edinburgh Office: 1 Exchange Crescent, Conference Square, Edinburgh EH3 8UL; T.-0131 473 5102.

Anderson, Dorothy Elizabeth, BSc (Hons), MB, ChB (with Commendation), MRCP(UK), DMRD, FRCR, FRCP(Glas). Consultant Radiologist, Glasgow Royal Infirmary, 1981-2010; Honorary Clinical Lecturer, then Senior Lecturer, Glasgow University, 1982-2010; b. 1950, Glasgow; m., David Anderson; 1 s.; 1 d. Educ. Glasgow High School for Girls; Glasgow University. Pre-registration posts, Stobhill Hospital and Glasgow Royal Infirmary; post-registration year, Respiratory Unit, Knightswood Hospital; trained in radiology, Western Infirmary, Glasgow (Registrar, then Senior Registrar). Recreations: choral singing; walking; reading; history; piano; travel. E-mail: deanderson@doctors.org.uk

Anderson, Douglas Kinloch, OBE, MA. Chairman, Kinloch Anderson (Holdings) Ltd., Edinburgh, since 1975; b. 19.2.39, Edinburgh; m., Deirdre Anne; 2 s.; 1 d. Educ. George Watson's Boys College; St. Andrews University. Joined Kinloch Anderson Ltd., 1962 (fifth generation in family business); Assistant on Master's Court, Edinburgh Merchant Company, 1976-79; elected Honorary Member, St. Andrew's Society of Washington DC, 1985; Board Member, Scottish Tourist Board, 1986-92; Member, Edinburgh Festival Council, 1988-90; President, Edinburgh Royal Warrant Holders Association, 1987-88; former Member, Scottish Committee, Institute of Directors; President, Edinburgh Chamber of Commerce, 1988-90; Master, Edinburgh Merchant Company, 1990-92; Deputy Chairman, Edinburgh Marketing Ltd., 1990-92; Director, Lothian and Edinburgh Enterprise Ltd., 1990-95; elected Leith High Constable, 1993, Moderator, 2010; Freeman, City of London; Past President, Royal Warrant Holders Association. Recreations: golf; fishing; watching rugby; travel (non-business). Address: (b.) Commercial Street/Dock Street, Leith, Edinburgh EH6 6EY; T.-0131-555 1355; e-mail: douglaska@kinlochanderson.com

Anderson, Gavin John, LLB (Hons), DipLP. Advocate, since 2001; b. 22.8.71, Edinburgh; m., Lynne Ann Montgomery; 2 s. Educ. St Thomas of Aquin's High Sch., Edinburgh; Aberdeen University. Solicitor, 1995-2000; awarded Faculty of Advocates Scholarship, 2000; admitted to Faculty, 2001; Member, Compass Chambers. Recreations: golf; classic cars. Address: (b.) Advocates' Library, Parliament House, Edinburgh EH1 1RF; T.-0131 226 5071. E-mail: gavin.anderson@compasschambers.com

Anderson, Gillian, LLB, DipLP. Senior Associate, Pinsent Masons, since 2004; specialises in intellectual property dispute resolution. Educ. Aberdeen Grammar School; University of Aberdeen; Glasgow Graduate School of Law; College of Law, London. Address: Pinsent Masons, 141

Bothwell Street, Glasgow G2 7EQ; T.-0141 249 5458.
E-mail: gillian.anderson@pinsentmasons.com

Anderson, Iain Buchanan, MA, DipEd, LGSM. Music Presenter/Sports Commentator, BBC, since 1985; m., Marion Elizabeth; 3 s.; 1 d. Educ. Bellahouston Academy, Glasgow; Glasgow University; Guildhall School. Lecturer in Speech and Drama, Jordanhill College, 1967; Arts Editor/Presenter, Radio Clyde, 1974. Former Rugby Correspondent, Scotland on Sunday. Address: (h.) Elmhurst, Station Road, Langbank PA14 6YA; T.-01475-54 1226; e-mail: iain53@btinternet.com

Anderson, John, BSc (Hons), PGCE, PGCert. Rector, Jordanhill School, Glasgow, since 2020. Educ. University of Strathclyde; University of Glasgow. Career history: Teacher of Chemistry: Port Glasgow High School, 2001-02, Woodfarm High School, 2003-07; Fitness to Teach Panel Member, General Teaching Council for Scotland (Freelance), 2014-18; Jordanhill School, Glasgow: Principal Teacher of Chemistry, 2007-2012, Depute Head Teacher, 2012-18; HM Inspector of Education, Education Scotland, 2018-19; Depute Head Teacher (Academic Leadership), St Aloysius' College, Glasgow, 2019-2020. Address: (b.) 45 Chamberlain Road, Glasgow G13 1SP; T.- 0141 5762500.

Anderson, Kathryn, MB, ChB, FRCPE. Associate Medical Director, NHS Lothian, since 2020. Educ. Boroughmuir High School, Edinburgh; University of Aberdeen; Royal College of Physicians of Edinburgh. Career history: Associate Lecturer, Flinders University, 1999-2000; Consultant in Medicine of the Elderly, NHS Lanarkshire, 2001-04; Clinical Lead for hospital based complex clinical care, Edinburgh Health and Social Care Partnership, 2012-2018; NHS Lothian: Clinical Director in Medicine of the Elderly, 2017-2020, Consultant Physician in Medicine of the Elderly, since 2004. Address: Lothian NHS Board, Waverley Gate, 2-4 Waterloo Place, Edinburgh EH1 3EG.
E-mail: Kathryn.anderson@nhslothian.scot.nhs.uk

Anderson, Keith, BA, CA. Chief Executive, ScottishPower, since 2018. Educ. Edinburgh Napier University; ICAS. Audit Manager, Standard Life, 1991-93; Audit Manager, Insurance, Royal Bank of Scotland, 1993-98; Senior Consultant, Ernst & Young, 1998-2000; Director of Strategy - UK, ScottishPower, 2003-05; Chairman, Wise Group, 2010-12; appointed to the Board of ScottishPower in 2012; appointed Chief Executive, ScottishPower Renewables in 1998. Address: Cathcart Business Park, Spean Street, Glasgow G44 4BE; T.-0141 568 2000.

Anderson, Kenneth, MBChB, MD, FRCP (Glas & Edin). Consultant Physician with special interest in respiratory medicine; b. Glasgow; m., M. Ruth Adamson. Educ. Allan Glen's School; Glasgow University. Visiting Physician, University of Colorado Hospitals, Denver; President, Scottish Thoracic Society, 2016; past Chairman, British Lung Foundation Scotland. Awarded the medal of the Royal Environmental Health Institute of Scotland for research on organic aerosols and building related diseases. Recreations: golf at Barassie and St Andrews; gardens, and listening to saxophone practice.

Anderson, Lin. Crime novelist and screenwriter; b. Greenock. Worked in the Nigerian bush for five years during the 1980s, and later wrote an African short story which was broadcast on BBC Radio Four; another of her African stories was published in the 10th Anniversary Macallan/Scotland on Sunday Short Story Collection.

Before turning full time to writing, taught maths and computing at George Watson's College, Edinburgh. A film of her screenplay Small Love was shown at London Film Festival and Edinburgh International Film Festival in 2001, and broadcast on Scottish Television in 2001 and 2002. Graduated from the newly founded Screen Academy Scotland, and has further screenplays in production. Member of the Femmes Fatales crime writing trio, together with Alanna Knight and Alex Gray. Co-founder with Alex Gray of Bloody Scotland, Scotland's International Crime Writing Festival; Chair of the Society of Authors in Scotland. Publications: Rhona MacLeod series: Driftnet (2003), Torch (2004), Deadly Code (2005), Blood Red Roses (2005), Dark Flight (2007), Easy Kill (2008), Final Cut (2009), Reborn (2010), Picture Her Dead (2011), Paths of the Dead (2014), The Special Dead (2015), None But the Dead (2016), Follow the Dead (2017), Sins of the Dead (2018), Time for the Dead (2019); Patrick de Courvoisier series: The Case of the Black Pearl (2014), The Case of the Missing Madonna (2015); screenplays: Small Love (2001), River Child (2006), The Incredible Lightness of Brian (2006); non-fiction: Braveheart: From Hollywood to Holyrood (2004). Address: Jenny Brown Associates, 31 Marchmont Road, Edinburgh EH9 1HU.

Anderson, Professor Michael, OBE, MA, PhD, Dr hc, HonDLitt, FBA, FRSE, FRHistSoc, Hon FFA. Professor (Emeritus, since 2007) of Economic History, University of Edinburgh, since 1979; b. 21.2.42, Woking; m. (1), Rosemary Elizabeth Kitching; 1 s.; 1 d.; m. (2), Elspeth MacArthur. Educ. Kingston Grammar School; Queens' College, Cambridge. University of Edinburgh: Assistant Lecturer, 1967-69, Lecturer, 1969-75, Reader, 1975-79, Dean of Faculty of Social Sciences, 1985-89, Vice-Principal, 1989-93, and 1997-2000, Acting Principal, 1994, Senior Vice-Principal, 2000-07. Member: Scottish Records Advisory Council, 1984-93, Economic and Social Research Council, 1990-94, Follett Committee on Libraries and Follett Implementation Group, 1993-97, British Library Board, 1994-2003, Council of British Academy, 1995-98, Research Information Network Advisory Board, 2005-2011, National Statistics Centre for Demography Advisory Board, 2006-2012, ONS UK Population Theme Advisory Board, since 2012, HEFCE Research and Innovation Strategic Advisory Committee, 2006-09; Scottish Census Steering Committee, 2009-2011; Curator, Royal Society of Edinburgh, 1997-99; Trustee, National Library of Scotland, 1998-2012, Chairman, 2000-2012; National Library of Scotland Foundation, Chairman, 2013-2017; Chairman, Research Support Libraries Programme, 1998-2003. Publications: Family Structure in Nineteenth Century Lancashire, 1971; Approaches to the History of the Western Family, 1981; Population Change in North-Western Europe 1750-1850, 1988; Scotland's Populations from the 1850s to Today, 2018; many papers on family sociology and history and historical demography. Recreations: natural history; gardening; the rise and fall of ancient civilisations. Address: (b.) School of History, Classics and Archaeology, Doorway 4, Teviot Place, Edinburgh EH8 9AG.

Anderson, Moira, OBE. Singer; b. Kirkintilloch; m., Dr. Stuart Macdonald. Educ. Ayr Academy; Royal Scottish Academy of Music, Glasgow. Began with Kirkintilloch Junior Choir, aged six; made first radio broadcast for BBC in Scotland, aged eight; was Teacher of Music in Ayr before becoming professional singer; made first professional broadcast, White Heather Club, 1960; has toured overseas, had her own radio and TV series; has introduced Stars on Sunday, ITV; appeared in summer shows, cabaret, pantomime and numerous other stage shows; several Royal Variety performances.

Anderson, Neil Robert, LLB (Hons), DipLP, NP. Consultant, BTO Solicitors LLP, since 2021; Head of Student Services for DipPLP in the School of Law, University of Edinburgh, since 2021; Partner, Rooney

Nimmo, Solicitors, 2020-21; b. 10.5.71, Edinburgh; m., Jill Shaw Andrew. Educ. Dalkeith High School; University of Aberdeen. Trained, Fyfe Ireland WS, Edinburgh, 1994-96; Biggart Baillie, Glasgow: Assistant, 1996-99, Associate, 1999-2003, Partner, 2003-08; Partner, Ledingham Chalmers LLP, 2008-2020. Recreations: cinema/film; orchid cultivation; travel to anywhere. Address: BTO Solicitors LLP, One Edinburgh Quay, 133 Fountainbridge, Edinburgh EH3 9QG; T.-0131 222 2939.

Anderson, Peter David, MA, PhD, FIRMS, FSA Scot, FRHistS. Deputy Keeper, National Archives of Scotland (formerly Scottish Record Office), 1993-2009; b. 10.3.47, Greenock; m., Jean Johnstone Smith; 1 d.; 1 s. (deceased). Educ. Hutchesons' Grammar School, Glasgow; Glasgow School of Art; St. Andrews University; Edinburgh University. Teacher of History, Cranhill Secondary School, Glasgow, 1972-73; Research Assistant, Scottish Record Office, 1974-80; Registrar, National Register of Archives (Scotland), 1980-83; Secretary, NRA(S), 1984-85; Conservation Officer, 1985-89; Head, Records Liaison Branch, 1989-93. Chair, International Council on Archives Committee on Archive Buildings and Equipment, 1996-2004; Chair, Society of Archivists, 2005-07; External Examiner, Dundee University Centre for Archive and Information Studies, 2005-09; Secretary, Scottish Oral History Group, 1984-88, Deputy Convener, 1988-2008; Chair, Linlithgow Heritage Trust, 2008-2017. Publications: Robert Stewart, Earl of Orkney, Lord of Shetland, 1533-93, 1982; Black Patie, 1993; The Stewart Earls of Orkney, 2012; articles on archival and historical subjects. Recreations: writing; historical research. Address: (h.) 74 Burghmuir Court, Linlithgow EH49 7LL; T.-01506-844663.

Anderson, Robert Alexander, MA, BD (Glas), DPhil (Oxon). Minister, Blackburn and Seafield Church, 1998-2017; b. 3.4.47, Kilwinning; m., Christine Main; 2 step s.; 1 step d. Educ. Kilwinning High School; Irvine Royal Academy; Glasgow University; Hertford College, Oxford. Missionary of The Church of Scotland as Tutor in Theology at St. Paul's United Theological College, Limuru, Kenya, 1980-86; Head of Theology and Philosophy, 1984-86; Dean of Studies, 1982-83 and 1984-85; Minister, Overtown Parish Church, 1986-89; P/T Chaplain, Shotts Prison, 1988-89; Chaplain, Edinburgh University, 1989-94; Development Officer, Carberry Tower, 1994-96. Publications: Intimations of Love Divine, 1996; Stop The World, I Want To Think, 1998; Who Cares Wins, 2000; Changes in Spiritual Freedom in the Church of Scotland, 2005; The Church of Scotland Ministry Disciplinary Proceedings, the New Testament, Natural Justice and Human Rights, 2011; Grains of Gold, 2012, 2nd Edition, 2015; Could The Church of Scotland Become Christian In The Twenty First Century?, 2018. Recreations: golf; cycling; music; reading. Address: Aiona, 8 Old Auchans View, Dundonald KA2 9EX; T.-01563 850554.
E-mail: robertanderson307@btinternet.com

Andrew, Hugh, BA (Oxon), FSA Scot. Managing Director, Birlinn Ltd (incorporating John Donald, Polygon, Mercat and Tuckwell Press); Director, Compass Independent Publishing Services; b. 8.4.62. Educ. Glasgow Academy; Magdalen College, Oxford. Set up own publishing company, Birlinn Ltd., 1992; Joint Managing Director, Canongate Books, 1994-99. Chairman, Ossian Trust; Trustee, The Great Tapestry of Scotland; Vice Chair, Auchindrain Trust. Recreations: reading; music; travel; archaeology; history; islands. Address: (b.) West Newington House, 10 Newington Road, Edinburgh EH9 1QS; T.-0131-668 4371. E-mail: hugh@birlinn.co.uk

Andrews, Professor June, OBE, FRCN, RMN, RGN, MA (Hons), FCGI. Professor Emeritus, University of Stirling (former Director, Dementia Services Development Centre); Adviser to The Dementia Services Development Trust;

former Director, Centre for Change and Innovation, Health Department, Scottish Executive; b. Kilwinning. Educ. Ardrossan Academy; Glasgow University; Nottingham University. NHS nursing and management posts, Nottingham and London; Director of Nursing, Forth Valley Acute Hospitals NHS Trust; Royal College of Nursing: adviser on ethics and Aids, Assistant Director Policy and Research, Scottish Board Secretary. Address: (b.) c/o Morton Fraser, Quartermile Two, 2 Lister Square, Edinburgh EH3 9GL.

Andrews, Kieran. Scottish Political Editor, The Times, since 2018; Convener, Scottish Parliamentary Journalists' Association, since 2019. Educ. University of Dundee. Career history: Reporter, Brechin Advertiser, 2008-09; DC Thomson: News Reporter, 2009-2010; Crime Reporter, Evening Telegraph, 2010-12; Political Editor, The Courier, 2012-17; Politics and Investigations Reporter, Sunday Post, 2017-18; Investigations Editor, The Courier, 2018.

Andrews, Professor Richard, BA, PhD, PGCE. Head of the Moray House School of Education and Sport, The University of Edinburgh, since 2019. Educ. University of Oxford; University of Hull; University of Leeds. Career history: Professor of Education, University of York, 2000-07; Professor in English, Institute of Education, University of London, 2007-2014; Deputy Vice-Chancellor (Research and Innovation), Anglia Ruskin University, 2014-15; Professor in English Education, University of East Anglia, 2016-19. Volunteer, Beverley Food Bank, 2016. Fellow of the Royal Society of Arts and an elected Fellow of the Academy of Social Sciences; member of the All Souls Group (Oxford) on education policy and an associate of the Centre for Science and Policy at the University of Cambridge; external examiner for the Chinese University of Hong Kong and Hong Kong University. Publications: A Prosody of Free Verse: explorations in rhythm, 2016; The Sage Handbook of E-Learning Research (Co-Editor), 2016; Multimodality, Poetry and Poetics, 2018; Co-Series Editor of the Cambridge School Shakespeare. Address: Moray House School of Education and Sport, Old Moray House, University of Edinburgh (Holyrood Campus), Edinburgh EH8 8AQ; T.-0131 651 6167.
E-mail: richard.andrews@ed.ac.uk

Angus, Morag, MA (Hons), DipLS, FRICS. Deputy Director, Head of Property and Construction and Chief Surveyor, Scottish Government, since 2016; m.; 2 c. Educ. University of Aberdeen; Glasgow University. Career: Estates Advisor, Defence Estates, 2001-06; Community Land Advisor, Community Land Advisory Service, 2012-13; Principal Estates Surveyor, Scottish Government, 2013-16. Publication: Guide for Landowners (Joint Author). Recreations: enjoys sailing; cycling; walking and singing. Address: Scottish Government, Victoria Quay, Edinburgh EH6 6QQ.

Annand, David Andrew, DA, ARBS. Sculptor; b. 30.1.48, Insch, Aberdeenshire; m., Jean; 1 s.; 1 d. Educ. Perth Academy; Duncan of Jordanstone College of Art, Dundee. Lecturer, Sculpture Department, Duncan of Jordanstone College of Art, Dundee, 1972-74; Art Department, St. Saviour's High School, Dundee, 1975-88; full-time sculptor, since 1988; RSA Latimer Award, 1976; RSA Benno Schotz Award, 1978; RSA Ireland Alloys Award, 1982; Scottish Development Agency Dundee Technology Park Competition, 1986, "Deer Leap", Sir Otto Beit Medal, 1986; Royal Botanic Garden, Edinburgh "Ardea Cinerea", 1987; Winner, Almswall Road Sculpture Competition, Irvine Development Corporation, "The Ring", 1989; Winner, Perth High Street Sculpture Competition, Perth Partnership "Nae Day Sae Dark", 1989; Baxters of Speyside

"Royal Stag" cast by Powderhall Bronze, 1993; Tranent Massacre Memorial bronze casting by Powderhall Bronze, 1995; Winner, competition to design sculpture for Lord Street, Wrexham, 1995, "Y Bwa" Civic Society Award, 1995; Winner, competition to design sculpture, Ashworth Roundabout, Blackpool, "Helter-skelter", 1995; Strathcarron Hospice composition, 1996; British High Commission, Hong Kong, "Three Cranes in Flight", 1997; Hamilton Town Square "Strongman", 1998; Aberdeen Angus Bull, Alford, 2001; The Declaration of Arbroath, Arbroath, 2001; Civic Pride, Barnet, London, 2001; other commissions completed in 2001 for BT Brentwood and Maidstone Borough Council; Winner of project to create a memorial to the poet Robert Fergusson, 2002; Sir Jimmy Shand Memorial, 2003; completed commissions in Redruth, Poole, Belfast, Mansfield, Hawick, Wirral, Republic of Ireland, 2004-09. Recreations: music; bird watching; wine and food. Address: Pigscrave Cottage, The Wynd, Kilmany, Cupar, Fife KY15 4PT; T.-01382 330 714.
Web: www.davidannand.com

Annandale and Hartfell, 11th Earl of (Patrick Andrew Wentworth Hope Johnstone of Annandale and of That Ilk). 27th Chief, Clan Johnstone; Baron of the Barony of the Lands of the Earldom of Annandale and Hartfell, and of the Lordship of Johnstone; Hereditary Steward, Stewartry of Annandale; Hereditary Keeper, Keys of Lochmaben Castle; Deputy Lieutenant, Dumfriesshire, 1987-92, Vice-Lieutenant, 1992-2016; b. 19.4.41, Auldgirth, Dumfriesshire; m., Susan Josephine; 1 s.; 1 d. Educ. Stowe School; Royal Agricultural College, Cirencester. Member: Dumfriesshire County Council, 1970-75, Dumfries and Galloway Regional Council, 1975-85, Scottish Valuation Advisory Council, 1982, Solway River Purification Board, 1973-85; Underwriter, Lloyds, London, 1976-2004. Address: (b.) Annandale Estates Office, St. Anns, Lockerbie DG11 1HQ.

Anwar, Aamer, LLB, PGDip (LP). Scottish lawyer; Rector, University of Glasgow, 2017-2020; b. 30.12.67, England. Educ. University of Glasgow; University of Strathclyde; University of Liverpool. Career: Solicitor & Criminal Defence, since 2000; Principal Solicitor, Aamer Anwar & Co, Solicitors & Notaries, since 2007; Freelance Writer, since 2014; Columnist for Scottish Sun, 2012-14. "Lawyer of the Year", Scottish Legal Awards, 2017; "Solicitor of the Year, Herald's Law Awards of Scotland, 2016. Address: Aamer Anwar & Co., 63 Carlton Place, Glasgow, Lanarkshire G5 9TW; T.-0141 429 7090.
E-mail: office@aameranwar.com

Anwar, Sheriff Aisha. Sheriff Principal, South Strathclyde, Dumfries and Galloway, since 2020. Appointed as a Resident Sheriff at Glasgow Sheriff Court and as a designated Family Law and Commercial Law Sheriff in 2014; appointed as a part-time Sheriff in 2011; Admitted as a solicitor in 2000; Co-Author of the Civil Bench Book for Sheriffs', and a contributor to MacPhail, Sheriff Court Practice; appointed to Board of the Scottish Courts and Tribunals Service in 2018; appointed to the Judicial Appointments Board for Scotland in 2021. Address: Hamilton Sheriff Court, 4 Beckford Street, Hamilton ML3 0BT.

Arbuthnott, 17th Viscount of (John Keith Oxley); b. 18.7.50; m.; 1 s.; 2 d. Scottish farmer and businessman. Address: (h.) Kilternan, Arbuthnott, by Laurencekirk, Kincardineshire AB30 1PA.

Archer, Gilbert Baird. Vice Lord-Lieutenant for Tweeddale, 2008-2017 (DL, Tweeddale, 1994); Chairman, Tods of Orkney Ltd (oatcake and biscuit manufacturers), 1970-2016; b. 24.8.42, Edinburgh; m., Irene Conn; 2 d. Educ. Melville College. Chairman: John Dickson & Son Ltd, 1985-97, Borders 1996 Ltd, 1996-98; Director, EPS Moulders Ltd, 1985-88, Scottish Council for Development and Industry, 1993-96; Chairman, Leith Chamber of Commerce, 1986-88; President, Edinburgh Chamber of Commerce, 1990-92; Chairman, Association of Scottish Chambers of Commerce, 1993-96; Deputy President, British Chambers of Commerce, 1995-96; Chairman, Edinburgh Common Purpose, 1991-94; Director, Scottish Council of Independent Schools, 1988-91; Member, Council, Governing Bodies Association of Independent Schools, 1988-91; Chairman, St. Columba's Hospice, 1998-2004 (now Vice President); Vice Convenor, George Watson's College, 1978-80; Governor, Fettes College, 1986-90; Napier University, 1991-97; Master: Company of Merchants of the City of Edinburgh, 1997-99, Gunmakers' Company, 2006-07; Moderator, High Constables of Port of Leith, 1990-91. Recreation: previously flying, now country pursuits. Clubs: Army and Navy, New (Edinburgh). Address: 10 Broughton Place Lane, Edinburgh EH1 3RS; T.-0131-556 4518; Fax: 01856-850213.

Archer, Janet. Chief Executive Officer, Edinburgh Printmakers, since 2021; Director, Festival and City Events, The University of Edinburgh, 2019-2021; Chief Executive, Creative Scotland, 2013-18. Career history: work in Scotland includes chairing the artist-led organisation, The Work Room; supported the British Council in programming their showcases in Edinburgh and as a former dancer, choreographer, founder and Artistic Director of the Nexus Dance Company, touring into Scotland as well as attending the Scottish Youth Dance Festivals held in Stirling in the 1980's; 16 years with the Newcastle based National Dance Agency, Dance City as Chief Executive and Artistic Director were instrumental to the organisation's growth, and included the project management of a large scale capital development working with a Scottish design team led by Malcolm Fraser Architects; formerly Dance Director, Arts Council England working as part of the national strategy team; has a broad knowledge of the wider arts and creative industries having been involved in developing Arts Council England's 10 year framework for the arts: Achieving Great Art For Everyone; also led the team that delivered the State of the Arts 2012 conference: Artists Shaping the World.

Archer, John William, BA (Hons). Independent film and television producer; b. 19.9.53, Evesham; 4 s. Educ. Dean Close School, Cheltenham; University of Birmingham; University College, Cardiff. Researcher, Nationwide, 1975-77; Director, BBC TV, London: Writers and Places, Global Report, Omnibus; Producer, The Book Programme, Did You See...?; Editor, Saturday Review, A Week of British Art; Head of Music and Arts, BBC Scotland, 1989, including editing Edinburgh Nights; Executive Producer, The Bigger Picture, Billy Connolly's World Tour of Scotland/Australia; producing and directing Stevenson's Travels; BAFTA Award, best programme/ series without a category for Did You See...?, 1983; Chief Executive, Scottish Screen, 1996-2001; Managing Director, Hopscotch Films Ltd., since 2002; Producer, 'Writing Scotland'. Recreations: walking; tree planting; mountain biking; necessary gardening; novels. Address: (b.) Hopscotch Films, Film City Glasgow, 401 Govan Road, Glasgow G51 2QJ; T.-0141-440-6740.
E-mail: john@hopscotchfilms.co.uk

Archibald, Grant. Chief Executive, NHS Tayside, since 2018. Career: worked for NHS Scotland for over 30 years and held a series of senior posts, most recently as Chief Operating Officer of NHS Greater Glasgow and Clyde's

Acute Services. Address: NHS Tayside, 230 Clepington Road, Dundee DD2 1UB; T.-01382 660111.

Argyll, Duke of (Torquhil Ian Campbell); b. 29.5.68. Succeeded to title, 2001. Chief of Clan Campbell.

Arkless, Richard, BA (Hons), LLB. MP (SNP), Dumfries and Galloway, 2015-17; b. 1975, Stranraer. Educ. Glasgow Caledonian University, Glasgow; School of Law, University of Strathclyde.

Armes, Right Rev. Dr. John, BA, MA, PhD. Bishop, Diocese of Edinburgh, since 2012; formerly Dean, Diocese of Edinburgh, 2010-12; Rector, St John the Evangelist Church, Edinburgh, 1998-2012; b. 1955; m., Clare; 4 c. Educ. Cambridge University; University of Manchester; Salisbury–Wells Theological College. Deaconed 1979. Priested 1980. Formerly Area Dean, Rossendale in the Manchester Diocese; priest-in-charge, Goodshaw & Crawshawbooth, 1994-98; Anglican Chaplain to University of Manchester; Team Vicar and then Team Rector, Parish of Whitworth (University Parish), Convener of Chaplaincy Ecumenical Team, 1986-94; Chaplain, Agriculture and Rural Life in Cumbria (two-thirds time) and Team Vicar in Greystoke Team Ministry, looking after Watermillock Parish, 1982-86. Curate, Walney, Barrow in Furness; Chaplain, Barrow Sixth Form College, 1979-82. Recreations: theatre; cinema; walking; reading novels; watching sport; travel and humour. Address: Diocesan Office, 21a Grosvenor Crescent, Edinburgh EH12 5EL; T.-0131 538 7044.

Armour, Robert Malcolm, OBE, MBA, LLB (Hons), DipLP, WS, NP, FEI. Chair, Brockwell Energy Group, since 2019; Director, Opportuneo Limited, since 2019; Director, Albion Community Power plc, Nuclear Liabilities Fund Ltd, Eneus Energy Ltd; Senior Counsel, Gowlings UK LLP; Chair, Regenerco Renewable Energy; Smarter Grid Solutions, 2011-16; Deputy Chair, NuGeneration Limited, 2015-17; Non Executive Director, Oil and Gas Authority, since 2015; b. 25.9.59, Edinburgh; m., Anne Ogilvie White. Educ. Daniel Stewart's and Melville College, Edinburgh; Edinburgh University. Solicitor, Haldanes McLaren and Scott, WS, Edinburgh, 1983-86; Partner, Wright, Johnston and MacKenzie, Edinburgh, 1986-90; Scottish Nuclear Limited: Company Secretary, 1990-95, Director, Performance Development, 1993-95; Director, Corporate Affairs, British Energy, 1999-2009; General Counsel and Company Secretary, British Energy plc, 1995-2009; Director, Network Project, EDF Energy, 2009-2010; Past Chair, SCDI (2009-2013); Energy Regulation Commission (2013-14). Recreations: golf; curling.

Armstrong, Lord (Iain Gillies Armstrong), QC. Senator of the College of Justice, since 2013; b. 26.5.56; m., Deirdre Elizabeth Mary MacKenzie (deceased); 1 d.; 1 s. Educ. Inverness Royal Academy; University of Glasgow. Admitted to the Faculty of Advocates in 1986; Clerk of Faculty, 1995-99; Standing Junior Counsel for the Department of Social Security, 1998-2000; appointed Queen's Counsel in 2000; full-time Advocate Depute (Crown Office), 2000-03; Vice-Dean of the Faculty of Advocates, 2008-2013. Member of the Standing Committee on Legal Education in Scotland, 1995-99; Governor of Fettes College, Edinburgh, 1991-2011; Member of the Advisory Panel to the School of Law of the University of Glasgow, 2009-2015. Address: (b.) Supreme Courts, Parliament House, Edinburgh EH1 1RQ; T.-0131 226 2595.

Armstrong, Pat, OBE, MBA. Chief Executive, Association of Chief Officers of Scottish Voluntary Organisations, since 2003. Educ. Broughton High School; Heriot Watt University. Career history: Bank Officer, Clydesdale Bank plc, 1977-83; Assistant Financial Controller, Ferranti plc, 1983-88; Information Worker, Pilton Health Project, 1989-

90; Administrator, Women and New Direction, 1991-98; Development Officer, Lintel Trust, 1997-98; Financial Administrator/Deputy Manager, Moving On (Edinburgh) Ltd, 2000-02; Manager, Drylaw Neighbourhood centre, 2000-02; Network Development Officer, Scottish Adult Learning Partnership, 2003; Consultant, Chameleon Consultancy Service Ltd, 2003-2010; Board Member, OSCR (Office of the Scottish Charity Regulator), since 2014. Address: ACOSVO, Thorn House, 5 Rose Street, Edinburgh EH2 2PR; T.-0131 243 2755; e-mail: office@acosvo.org.uk

Arnold, Andy, MA (Hons), DipEd and D.Litt (Honorary Degree – Strathclyde Uni.) Artistic Director of Tron Theatre Glasgow, since 2008; Founder and Artistic Director, The Arches, Glasgow (1991-2008); Director, Bloomsbury Theatre, London (1986-89); Artistic Director, Theatre Workshop, Edinburgh, 1980-85; Community Artist, Punk Poet, and Cartoonist, since 1974; b. Southend-on-Sea. Directing Credits include: The Drawer Boy, Translations, Bailegangaire, Metropolis - The Theatre Cut, Caligari, The Devils, The Crucible, Waiting for Godot; The Caretaker, first British production of Ballyturk by Ends Walsh, Juno and the Paycock, stage adaptations of Tam O'Shanter, Dante's Inferno, and Beowulf, world premier stage production of Ulysses by James Joyce which toured internationally including mainland China; then directed three productions in mandarin with Chinese actors in Beijing. Two Paper Boat awards; Spirit of Mayfest Award; Arts & Business Arts Leadership award. Recreations: family; tennis; motorcycling; improving my French.

Arnott, Ian Emslie, DA, DipTP, RSA, RIBA, FRIAS, OStJ. Retired Architect; Chairman, Saltire Society, 2001-04; b. 7.5.29, Galashiels. Educ. Galashiels Academy; Edinburgh College of Art. Flying Officer, RAF, 1955-57; Founding Partner, then Chairman, Campbell and Arnott, 1962-94; External Examiner, Dundee University, 1989-93. RSA Gold Medal for Architecture, 1981; nine Civic Trust Awards; one RIBA Award; two EAA Awards. Publication: The Hidden Theatres of the Marche, 2013. Recreations: music; painting; reading; resting. Address: The Rink, Gifford, East Lothian EH41 4JD; T.-01620 810278.

Arran, 9th Earl of (Arthur Desmond Colquhoun Gore). British peer and an elected hereditary member of the House of Lords for the Conservative Party; b. 14.7.38; m., Eleanor van Cutsem; 2 d. Educ. Eton College and Balliol College, Oxford. Served in the Grenadier Guards, gaining the rank of Second Lieutenant; Assistant Manager of the Daily Mail, then Assistant General Manager of the Daily Express and the Sunday Express in the 1970s; formerly a director of Waterstone's; active in the Lords for the Conservatives, serving in several junior ministerial roles. Succeeded as 9th Earl of Arran, 1983.

Arshad, Rowena, CBE, EdD (Edin), EdD (Edinburgh Napier University) (Honorary), MEd (Community Education), OBE. Former Head of the Moray House School of Education; Director, Centre for Education for Racial Equality in Scotland (CERES), since 1994; Senior Lecturer in Equity and Rights; Equal Opportunities Commissioner for Scotland, 2001-07; Member of the Scotland Committee of the Equality and Human Rights Commission; Member (first ever black woman Member), Scottish Trades Union Congress General Council, 1997-2003; b. 27.4.60, Brunei Town, Brunei; m., Malcolm Quarrie Parnell; 1 s.; 1 d. Educ. Methodist Girls School, Penang, West Malaysia; Moray House Institute of Education; Edinburgh University. Education and Campaigns Organiser, Scottish Education and Action for Development, 1985-88; Director, Edinburgh Multicultural Education Centre, 1988-90. Currently, on the board of Her Majesty's Inspectorate of Education; the Scottish Funding Council; Chair of Equality Forward, first equality unit for Scottish Colleges and Universities; Member of the Scottish Advisory Group of the British Council; Member, Editorial Board of the Journal of Race Equality Teaching. Formerly, Chair of the Equality Advisory Group, COPFS (2003-05); Chair of Linknet Mentoring Initiative, Edinburgh (2000-03); Chair of the Widening Access to Council Membership Progress Group (2004-05); first Honorary President of the Institute of Contemporary Scotland; Member of the Independent Committee of Inquiry into Student Finance (Cubie Committee); Member of the Working Party on Guidelines in Sex Education in Scottish Schools (Section 2A); Convenor of the Education Institute of Scotland Anti-Racist Committee; Member, STUC Black Workers Committee; Member of the Race Equality Advisory Forum. Author of numerous chapters to publications on equality; principal writer of the first anti-sectarian education resource for teachers and youth workers in Scotland. Recreations: keen reader of crime novels; border collies and animal issues; international cuisine and baroque music. Address: (b.) CERES, Moray House School of Education, Room 2:13, St. John's Land, School of Education, Holyrood Road, Edinburgh EH8 8AQ; T.-0131 651 6446.

Arthur, Adrian, BL. Hon. Fellow, University of Abertay Dundee; Editor, The Courier, Dundee, 1993-2002; b. 28.9.37, Kirkcaldy; m., Patricia Mill; 1 s.; 2 d. Educ. Harris Academy, Dundee; St. Andrews University. Joined staff of People's Journal; through the editorial ranks of The Courier (Deputy Editor, 1978-93). Recreations: golf; travel; Rotary. Address: (h.) 33 Seaforth Crescent, West Ferry, Dundee DD5 1QD; T.-01382 776842.
E-mail: adrianarthur33@blueyonder.co.uk

Arthur, Lt. General Sir Norman, KCB (1985), CVO (2007). Lord Lieutenant, Stewartry of Kirkcudbright, Dumfries and Galloway Region, 1996-2006; b. 6.3.31, London (but brought up in Ayrshire, of Scottish parents); m., Theresa Mary Hopkinson (deceased 2011); 1 s.; 1 d.; 1 s. (adopted); m., Jillian C. Andrews, née Summers. Educ. Eton College; Royal Military Academy, Sandhurst. Commissioned Royal Scots Greys, 1951; commanded Royal Scots Dragoon Guards, 1972-74, 7th Armoured Brigade, 1976-77, 3rd Armoured Division, 1980-82; Director, Personal Services (Army), 1983-85; commanded Army in Scotland, and Governor of Edinburgh Castle, 1985-88; retired, 1988; Honorary Colonel, Royal Scots Dragoon Guards, 1984-92; Col. Comdt. Military Provost Staff Corps, 1983-88; Honorary Colonel, 205 (Scottish) General Hospital, Territorial Army, 1988-93; Colonel, The Scottish Yeomanry, 1992-97; mentioned in Despatches, 1974. Officer, Royal Company of Archers; President, Scottish Conservation Projects Trust, 1989-93; Vice President, Riding for the Disabled Association, Edinburgh and the Borders, 1988-94; Chairman: Army Benevolent Fund, Scotland, 1988-2000, Leonard Cheshire Foundation, SW Scotland, 1994-2000; Member, Committee, Automobile Association, 1990-98; humanitarian aid work, Croatia and Bosnia, 1992-2015; Knights of Malta decoration "pro Merito Melitensi", 1987; President, Reserve Forces and Cadet Association, Lowlands, 2000-06; Member, British Olympic equestrian team (three-day event), 1960. Recreations: riding; country sports; country life; reading. Address: (h.) Newbarns, Dalbeattie, Kirkcudbrightshire DG5 4PY; T.-01556 630227, and The Garden House, Sparsholt, Winchester, Hants SO21 2NS; T.-01962 776279.

Arthur, Tom. MSP (SNP), Renfrewshire South, since 2016; Minister for Public Finance, Planning and Community Wealth, since 2021; b. 1985, Paisley. Educ.

Cross Arthurlie Primary; Barrhead High School; University of Glasgow. Joined the SNP in 2009. Address: Scottish Parliament, Edinburgh EH99 1SP; 49 High Street, Johnstone PA5 8AJ.

Arthurson, Hon. Lord (Paul Arthurson), QC. Senator of the College of Justice, since 2017. Educ. University of Edinburgh. Career history: became an advocate in 1991, specialising in civil practice, principally in the Court of Session, latterly in high value reparation and clinical negligence actions; served as a chair of tribunals for the Mental Health Tribunal for Scotland and on the Parole Board for Scotland; appointed as a sheriff in 2005, Queen's Counsel in 2005 and a Temporary Judge of the Court of Session in 2013; served as a member of the Sheriff Appeal Court, since 2015. Address: Parliament House, 11 Parliament Square, Edinburgh EH1 1RQ.

Asher, George Russell. Lord-Lieutenant for Nairnshire, since 2017; b. 1965; m.; 3 s. Joint Managing Director of Ashers Bakery Ltd in Nairn, since 1992.

Aspden, Professor Richard Malcolm, PhD, DSc, FIPEM. Emeritus Professor of Orthopaedic Science, Aberdeen University, since 2016; b. 23.9.55, Malta; m., Anne Maclean; 3 s.; 2 d. Educ. Bosworth College, Desford; University of York; University of Manchester (postgraduate). Research Associate, University of Manchester; Wellcome Research Fellow: University of Lund, University of Manchester, University of Aberdeen; MRC Senior Fellow, University of Aberdeen. Editorial Consultant, Journal of Biomechanics. Publications: 2 books; 170 research papers. Recreations: woodworking; music; hill-walking. Address: (b.) University of Aberdeen, School of Medicine, Medical Sciences and Nutrition, IMS Building, Foresterhill, Aberdeen AB25 2ZD; T.-01224 437445; e-mail: r.aspden@abdn.ac.uk

Atack, Alison Mary, LLB, FRSA, FICS. Lawyer; Non-Practising member and Fellow of Law Society of Scotland; President of the Law Society of Scotland, 2018-2019; Convener of various LSS Professional Regulatory Committees including Professional Conduct, The Regulatory Committee and Audit; presently a member of the Client Protection Sub-Committee; b. 23.2.53, Richmond; m., Iain; 1 d.; 1 s. Educ. Larbert High School; Glasgow University. Legal training, Biggart Baillie & Gifford, Solicitors, Glasgow; pursued career in private practice specialising in property and private client; set up own legal practice as a sole practitioner, thereafter merged with large Scotland-wide firm, becoming Head of Office based in Glasgow; formerly Governor of Jordanhill College of Education and involved with its merger with University of Strathclyde; Honorary member of the Royal Faculty of Procurators, Glasgow; former Director of the Diploma in Professional Legal Practice, Edinburgh University; presently on Editorial Board of newly launched UK-wide publication "Legal Women Magazine". Recreations: hillwalking; skiing; gym; music, especially opera; enjoys life in rural Stirlingshire.
E-mail: alisonatack@icloud.com

Atholl, 12th Duke of (Bruce George Ronald Murray); b. 6.4.60, South Africa; m., Charmaine Myrna (née Du Toit); 2 s.; 1 d. Succeeded to the title, 2012. Has the right to raise Europe's only legal private army, named the Atholl Highlanders (a unique privilege granted to his family by Queen Victoria after visiting Blair Atholl in 1844). Educated at Saasveld Forestry College before serving two years' National Service with the South African Infantry Corps. Currently a volunteer member of the Transvaal Scottish Regiment, holding the rank of Lieutenant. Previously managed a tea plantation, then ran a signage business producing signs for commercial buildings. Commissioned into the Atholl Highlanders in 2000, being appointed as Lieutenant Colonel.

Atkinson, Professor The Rev. David, BSc, PhD, FRSB, CBiol, MIEEM, FHEA, FRSA, FRCP (Edin), MISoilSci. Emeritus Professor of Land Resources and former Vice Principal, Scottish Agricultural College; b. 12.9.44, Blyth; m., Elisabeth Ann Cocks (deceased 2012); 1 s.; 2 d. Educ. Newlands County Secondary Modern School; Hull University; Newcastle-upon-Tyne University; Theological Institute of Scottish Episcopal Church (TISEC). East Malling Research Station, Maidstone, 1969-85; Macaulay Institute for Soil Research, 1985-87; Macaulay Land Use Research Institute, 1987-88; Professor of Agriculture, Aberdeen University, and Head, Land Resources Department, Scottish Agricultural College, 1988-93; Deputy Principal (R. & D.) and Dean, Edinburgh Centre, Scottish Agricultural College, 1993-2000, Vice Principal, 2000-04. Honorary Professor, University of Edinburgh, 1994-2006; Visiting Professor, Washington State University, 1983, Michigan State University, 1986, University of Michigan Biological Station, 1987-92; Member, BCPC Council, 1994-2016, Vice Chairman, 2002-2009, Trustee, 2009-2016, BCPC Medal, 2001; Member, Advisory Group, Royal College of Physicians (Edinburgh), 2004-2012; Member, Management Board, MRCP, 2005-2011; Member, Scottish Government Food and Drink Forum and Convenor of Committee on Food Affordability, Access and Security, 2008-2010; Chair, ACTS Rural Committee, 2005-2012, 2014-15 and 2018-19, Committee Member, since 2012; Ordained Deacon, 2005; Priest, 2006; Associate Curate, Aberdeen Cathedral, 2005-07; Interim Priest, St Devenick's, Aberdeen, 2007-09; Associate Minister, St. Mary Inverurie with St Anne Kemnay and St Mary Auchindoir, since 2009; Information Officer, Diocese of Aberdeen and Orkney, 2005-2018; Chair, TISEC Board of Studies, 2007-08; Editor, Northern Light, 2007-2014; Convenor: SEC Church in Society Committee, 2014-19, SEC Rural Network, 2014-18; Director, Falkland Rural Enterprises Limited, 2006-2016, Chair, 2012-16; Chair, Scottish Pilgrim Routes Forum management committee, 2012-17; Board Member, Nourish, 2013-2015; Chair, SCI Horticulture Committee, since 2020. Publications: Author/Editor: The Science Beneath Organic Production, 2020; Editing Humanity, 2020. Recreations: discussing organic agriculture and GM issues; music; reading thrillers; quotations. Address: (b.) SAC, Craibstone Estate, Bucksburn, Aberdeen AB21 9YA.
E-mail: atkinson390@btinternet.com

Atkinson, Kate, MBE. Writer of novels, plays and short stories; b. 20.12.51, York; m.; 1 d. Educ. University of Dundee. Created the Jackson Brodie series of detective novels, which has been adapted into the BBC series Case Histories; won the Whitbread Book of the Year prize in 1995 in the Novels category for Behind the Scenes at the Museum, winning again in 2013 and 2015 under its new name the Costa Book Awards. Novels published: Behind the Scenes at the Museum, 1995; Human Croquet, 1997; Emotionally Weird, 2000; Life After Life, 2013; A God in Ruins, 2015; Transcription, 2018. Novels featuring Jackson Brodie: Case Histories, 2004; One Good Turn, 2006; When Will There Be Good News?, 2008; Started Early, Took My Dog, 2010; Big Sky, 2019. Plays: Nice, 1996; Abandonment, 2000. Story collections: Not the End of the World, 2002. Lives in Edinburgh.

Atkinson, Peter. Chief Executive, Macfarlane Group PLC, since 2003. Career: Procter & Gamble and S.C. Johnson; Senior Executive roles, GKN PLC and its joint venture partners, 1988-2001; successful track record of both business turnarounds and business development with extensive exposure to international business, having worked in the UK, Continental Europe and the USA; responsible for the US automotive and materials handling businesses of Brambles Industries PLC, 2000-03. Non-Executive Director of Speedy Hire PLC, 2004-2011. Address: (b.) Macfarlane Group PLC, 21 Newton Place, Glasgow G3 7PY; T.-0141 333 9666.

Auchincloss, Matthew, MA, LLB, DipLP, Solicitor-Advocate. Director of The Public Defence Solicitors' Office, since 2005; b. 16.10.71, Edinburgh. Educ. Sandhurst School; Linlithgow Academy; University of Glasgow. Admitted as a Solicitor in Scotland, 1997; Partner in Gordon McBain and Company, Solicitors, Edinburgh, 1999; joined Public Defence Solicitors' Office, 2003; joined the College of Justice as a Solicitor with extended rights of audience, 2005. Tutor for Central Law Training. Recreations: music; horse riding. Address: (b.) Public Defence Solicitors' Office, 50 St. Mary's Street, Edinburgh EH1 1SX; T.-0131 557 1222; e-mail: mauchincloss@pdso.org.uk

Audain, Irene, MBE, MA (Hons), MEd, AdvDip (Educ), DipInfoScience. Chief Executive, Scottish Out of School Care Network, since 1993; b. 10.7.56, Glasgow. Educ. University of Glasgow; University of Strathclyde; The Open University. Voluntary sector work: promoting school age childcare, children's rights, has also been involved in promoting equality. Recreation: travel. Address: (b.) Level 2, 100 Wellington Street, Glasgow G2 6DH; T.-0141 564 1284.

Austin, Lloyd, BSc (Hons). Freelance environmental professional, since 2018; Chair (since 2021) and Trustee (since 2020), Environmental Rights Centre Scotland; Head of Conservation Policy, RSPB Scotland, 1999-2018; b. 5.10.60, Haddenham; divorced; 1 s.; 2 d. Educ. Peter Symond's School, Winchester; Edinburgh University. Scientific Officer, Department of Environment (NI), 1985-86; Conservation Officer: Cleveland Wildlife Trust, 1986-88, Lincolnshire Wildlife Trust, 1988-90; Conservation Planning Officer (Scotland), RSPB, 1990-99. Trustee, Scottish Environment Link, 2000-14, Chair of Trustees, 2004-07; Trustee, Stop Climate Chaos Scotland, 2006-15; Hon. Fellow, Royal Scottish Geographical Society. Recreations: natural history; travel; current affairs. Contact via @lloydaustin3 on twitter or via linkedin

Avila, Martin, BSc (Sociology). Group Chief Executive Officer, Community Enterprise in Scotland (CEIS), since 2021; b. 6.81. Educ. Abertay University. Career history: Deafblind Scotland: Guide Communicator, 2009-2011, Project Manager, 2010-11; Xchange Scotland: Development Coordinator, 2007-2012, Director, 2012-15; Kinning Park Complex SCIO: Development Director, 2015-19, Director, 2019-2021. Board Member: Community Land Scotland, SURF - Scotland's Regeneration Forum; former Treasurer of the Alliance of European Voluntary Service Organisations. Address: CEIS, Moorpark Court, 5 Dava Street, Glasgow G51 2JA; T.-0141 425 2900.

B

Bachell, Andrew, BSc (Ecol), MPhil. Chief Executive, John Muir Trust, 2017-19. Educ. University of Edinburgh. Career history: 35 years of experience working on environmental and conservation issues having previously worked for the National Trust for Scotland as Director of Countryside and Director of Conservation, and at the Woodland Trust as Director in Scotland; Director of Operations, Scottish Natural Heritage, 2010-2015; Director of Policy and Advice, Scottish Natural Heritage, 2015-17. Board Member, Traditional Music Forum, 2013-2021; Director/Trustee, Traditional Arts and Culture Scotland (TRACS), since 2016, Chair, since 2021; Member, UK Statutory Conservation Agencies Scientists Group. Volunteer experience: Convenor, Blackford Fiddle Group (Community music group).

Bacon, Professor Liz, PhD, CEng, CSci, CITP, FBCS, PFHEA. Principal and Vice-Chancellor, Abertay University, since 2022; Deputy Principal and Deputy Vice-Chancellor, 2020-22; Professor of Computing Science; b. 27.9.63; m., Stuart Kabler. Educ. University of Greenwich. Career history: Vice-President, Trustee, Chair of the BCS Academy of Computing, British Computer Society, 2010-2013; BCS, The Chartered Institute for IT: Deputy President, 2013-14; President, 2014-15; Past President, 2015-16; University of Greenwich: Professor and Dean of School of Computing and Mathematical Sciences, 2011-13; Deputy Pro Vice-Chancellor and Professor, 2013-18; Member of the Board of Trustees, Bletchley Park, since 2017; President, European Quality Assurance Network for Informatics Education - EQANIE, since 2018; Vice-Principal and Deputy Vice-Chancellor (Academic), Abertay University, 2018-2020. Became a Principal Fellow of the HEA in 2015; identified as the 35th Most Influential Woman in UK Technology, 2015 by Computer Weekly. Recreations: horse jumping; skiing; scuba diving. Address: Abertay University, Bell Street, Dundee DD1 1HG; T.- 01382 308000; e-mail: l520309@abertay.ac.uk

Bagshaw, Stuart Neville, Dip (Arch). Director/Sole Proprietor, SBA Architects Ltd, since 2009; b. 2.12.48; m., Lesley; 2 s.; 1 d. Educ. Whitcliffe Mount Grammar School; Leicester Polytechnic. Career: Project Architect/Team Leader, Warrington New Town Development Corporation; Senior Architect, Western Isles Council; Director/Sole Proprietor, Stuart Bagshaw & Associates, 1982-2009. RIAS Fellow; RIBA Member; Registered Chartered Architect; Member, Scottish Society of Architect Artists; various awards. Address: (b.) SBA Architects Ltd, Marybank Lodge, Lews Castle Grounds, Isle of Lewis HS2 0DD; T.-01851-70-4889.
E-mail: sbaarchitects@btconnect.com

Baillie, Jackie. MSP (Labour), Dumbarton, since 1999; Scottish Labour Deputy Leader, since 2020; Scottish Labour Spokesperson on Health and Social Care, and Spokesperson on COVID-19 recovery, since 2021; Scottish Labour Spokesperson for Finance, 2019-2021; Shadow Labour spokesperson for Economy, Jobs and Fair Work, 2016-2018; Shadow Cabinet Secretary for Finance, Constitution and Economy, 2014-16; Social Justice, Equalities and Welfare, 2013-2014; Wellbeing and Cities Strategy, 2010-2013; Minister for Social Justice, 2000-01; Deputy Minister for Communities, 1999-2000; b. 15.1.64, Hong Kong. Co-ordinator, Gorbals Unemployed Workers Centre, 1987-90; Resource Centre Manager, Strathkelvin District Council, 1990-96; Community Economic Development Manager, East Dunbartonshire Council, 1996-99. Board Member, Volunteer Development Scotland, 1997-99; Chairperson, Scottish Labour Party, 1997-98. Address: (b.) Dumbarton Constituency Office, 6 Church Street, Dumbarton G82 1QL; T.-01389 734214.

Baillie, John, MA, CA. Board Member, Gambling Commission, 2016; Visiting Professor of Accountancy: Heriot-Watt University, Edinburgh, 1989-99, University of Glasgow, 1996-2012, University of Edinburgh, 2013-2019; Member, Reporting Panel, Competition Commission, 2002-2011; Chair, Accounts Commission, 2007-2013; Member, Accounts Commission, 2003-07; Chair, Audit Scotland, 2008-2011; Board Member, Audit Scotland, 2003-2013; Member, Local Government Finance Review Committee, 2004-07; m.; 1 s.; 1 d. Johnstone-Smith Professor of Accountancy, Glasgow University, 1983-88; Partner, KPMG, 1978-93; Partner, Scott-Moncrieff, 1993-2001. Trustee, ICAS Foundation, 2005-2017; Institute of Chartered Accountants of Scotland: Convenor, Research Committee, 1994-99, member, various technical and professional affairs committees; member, Institute of Chartered Accountants of Scotland, 1967. Recreations: keeping fit; reading; music; golf.

Bain, Aly, MBE. Fiddler; b. 1946, Lerwick. Co-founder, Boys of the Lough, 1972; Soloist; TV and radio anchorman.

Bain, Professor Andrew David, OBE, FRSE; b. 21.3.36, Glasgow; m., Eleanor Riches; 3 s. Educ. Glasgow Academy; Cambridge University. Various posts, Cambridge University, 1959-67; Professor of Economics: Stirling University, 1967-77, Strathclyde University, 1977-84; Group Economic Advisor, Midland Bank, 1984-90. Member: Committee to Review the Functioning of Financial Institutions, 1977-80, Monopolies and Mergers Commission, 1980-81; Visiting Professor, Glasgow University, 1991-97; Board Member, Scottish Enterprise, 1991-97; Chairman of Trustees, Scottish Enterprise Pension Scheme, 1995-2004; Member, Competition Appeals Tribunal, 2000-2011. Publications: The Control of the Money Supply, 1970; The Economics of the Financial System (2nd Edition), 1992.

Bain, Dorothy, QC. Lord Advocate, since 2021; Senior Counsel Member, Ampersand stable of advocates at the Faculty of Advocates, Edinburgh, since 2011. Career history: Solicitor, Dundas & Wilson CS Edinburgh, Litigation Department; Personal Injury Law, Clinical Negligence Law, Professional Negligence Law, Public and Fatal Accident Inquiries, 1990-94; Called to the Bar, 1994; Advocate Depute, November 2002-December 2003; Senior Advocate Depute, January 2004-2005; Assistant Principal Advocate Depute, January 2006-May 2009. Appointed QC in 2007; Commissioned by the Lord Advocate & Solicitor General to report on and make recommendations in relation to the prosecution of Sexual Crime in Scotland, which in turn resulted in the creation of the National Sex Crimes Unit: February-October 2008; Principal Advocate Depute, June 2009-July 2011; November 2011, nominated to the list of Special Counsel by the Lord President in terms of the Criminal Justice & Licensing (Scotland) Act 2010; Advocacy Skills Instructor on the Advocates training course for Devils. Address: Advocates' Library, Parliament House, Edinburgh EH1 1RF.

Bain, Iain Andrew, MA. Editor and Proprietor, The Nairnshire Telegraph, 1987-2021; b. 25.2.49, Nairn; m., Maureen Beattie; 3 d. Educ. Nairn Academy; Aberdeen University. Joined The Geographical Magazine, 1974, Editor, 1981-87. Chairman, Nairn Museum Ltd. Recreations: reading; writing; photography; golf.

Bain, Marion, BSc, MB, ChB, FFPH, FRCPE, MBA. Senior Public Health Advisor to Scottish Government, since 2021; previously Deputy Chief Medical Officer for

Scotland, Scottish Government, 2020-2021. Qualified from Edinburgh University in 1988, then worked across a range of clinical areas and hospitals in Scotland before specialising in Public Health Medicine. Career developed increasingly over time into clinical leadership roles and medical management. Holder of a wide range of senior medical leadership roles at strategic and national levels in Scotland including as: Medical Director of Information Services Division of NHS National Services Scotland (2003-09), Delivery Director and Senior Medical Adviser for Public Health Reform in Scottish Government (2017-2019), Director of Infection Prevention and Control in NHS Greater Glasgow and Clyde (2019-2020). Elected Chair of the Scottish Association of Medical Directors, 2014-17. Honorary Professor, University of Edinburgh, with particular research expertise around the use of routine health information for public health and clinical research. Address: Scottish Government, St. Andrew's House, Regent Road, Edinburgh EH1 3DG.

Baird, Gareth. Chairman, The Moredun Foundation, since 2020; Kelso based farmer; previous Chairman of the Pentlands Science Park; b. 5.57. Career history: Scottish Commissioner for the Crown Estate, 2004-2019; Chair of the Scottish Enterprise South of Scotland Advisory Board, 2008-2015; Scotland Food and Drink, Director, 2007-2019; Vice Chairman, Grainco Ltd, since 2005; Fellow: the Royal Agricultural Societies, RSA; Deputy Lieutenant for Roxburgh, Ettrick and Lauderdale. Address: The Moredun Foundation, Pentlands Science Park, Bush Loan, Penicuik EH26 0PZ; T.-0131 445 5111.

Baker, Christopher. Director, European and Scottish Art and Portraiture, National Galleries of Scotland; Director, Scottish National Portrait Gallery, 2012-17. Career history: Curator, Christ Church Picture Gallery, Oxford; Deputy Director, Scottish National Gallery, 2003-2012. Enjoys an international reputation as a scholar-curator and has organised some of the Scottish National Gallery's most successful exhibitions, such as The Discovery of Spain (2009) and Turner and Italy (2009). Address: National Galleries of Scotland, 73 Belford Road, Edinburgh EH4 3DS; e-mail: pginfo@nationalgalleries.org

Baker, Claire. MSP (Labour), Scotland Mid and Fife, since 2007; Shadow Secretary for Culture, Tourism, Europe and External Affairs; formerly Justice spokesperson; b. 4.3.71, Fife; m., Richard Baker, MSP; 1 d. Career history: worked in a variety of research and policy posts including Research Officer for the Scottish Parliamentary Labour Group, Research Officer for the trade union Amicus and a similar role for the Royal College of Nursing; Policy Manager for the Scottish Council for Voluntary Organisations; former Shadow Minister for Education; Shadow Cabinet Secretary for Culture, Europe and External Affairs, 2014-16. Address: Scottish Parliament, Edinburgh EH99 1SP.

Baker, Richard. MSP (Labour), North East Scotland, 2003-2016; Head of Policy, Public Affairs and Research, Sight Scotland and Sight Scotland Veterans, since 2017; Policy and Communications Manager, Age Scotland, 2016-17; b. 29.5.74, Edinburgh. Educ. Aberdeen University. Member, Board of Trustees, Faith in Older People, since 2017. Address: (b.) Sight Scotland, 2A Robertson Avenue, Edinburgh EH11 1PZ.

Baker, Emeritus Professor Thomas Neville, BMet, PhD, DMet (Sheffield), DSc (Strathclyde), DEng (Sheffield), FIMMM, FInstP, CEng, CPhys. Research Professor,

Department of Mechanical and Aerospace Engineering – Metallurgy and Engineering Materials Group, Strathclyde University; b. 11.1.34, Southport; m., Eileen May Allison (deceased). Educ. King George V School, Southport; Sheffield University. National Service, Royal Corps of Signals; Research Metallurgist, Nelson Research Laboratories, English Electric Co., Stafford, 1958-60; Scientist, Project Leader, Tube Investments Research Laboratories, Hinxton Hall, Cambridge, 1961-64; Department of Metallurgy, Strathclyde University: SRC Research Fellow, 1965, Lecturer, 1966, Senior Lecturer, 1976, Reader, 1983, Professor, 1990, Professor of Metallurgy (1886 Chair), 1992-99, Vice Dean, School of Chemical and Materials Science, 1979-82, Head, Department of Metallurgy, 1986-87, Head, Division of Metallurgy and Engineering Materials, 1988-90; President, University of Strathclyde Staff Club, 1976-77; University of Strathclyde representative as a Governor of the Renfrewshire Educational Trust, 1989-97; Committee Member, Institute of Materials, Minerals and Mining (IoM3) (formerly Institute of Metals), Metal Science Committee, 1980-94, Materials Technology Committee, 1994-96, Process Science and Technology Committee, 1996-99, Integrated Processing and Manufacturing Committee, 1999-2006, High Temperature Materials Committee, 2007-2016; Chairman of Organising Committee of Annual Conference on 'Metals and Materials', 1982-92 and conference series on 'Erosion and Wear of High Temperature Materials used in Aerospace and Power Generation', 1998, 2001, 2010, 2015; Member, Council, Scottish Association for Metals (SAM), 1975-79 and 1997-2003, Vice-President, 1999-2000, President, 2001. Awards: IoM3 Vanadium Medal, 2009; IoM3 Tom Colclough Medal & Prize, 2010; Williams Award, 2017; SAM, The James Riley Medal, 2020; Leverhulme Trust Visiting Professorship, 2012. Publications: Yield, Flow and Fracture in Polycrystals (Editor), 1983; Titanium Technology in Microalloyed Steels (Editor), 1997; over 210 learned society publications. Recreations: music; collecting books; creating a garden. Address: (b.) Department of Mechanical and Aerospace Engineering, Strathclyde University, Glasgow; T.-0141-548 3101; (h.) Clovelly, Rowantreehill Road, Kilmacolm PA13 4NW.

Balfour of Burleigh, The Dowager Lady (Janet Morgan), MA, DPhil, FRSAS, Hon LLD (Strathclyde), Hon DLitt (Napier), FRSE, CBE. Member, American Philosophical Society; Chevalier de l'Ordre Grand Ducale de la Couronne de Chêne; Writer; Company Director; b. 5.12.45, Montreal; m., Lord Balfour of Burleigh (deceased). Educ. Newbury County Girls' Grammar School; Oxford University; Sussex University; Harvard University. Member: Central Policy Review Staff, Cabinet Office, 1978-81, Board, British Council, 1989-99; Special Adviser to Director-General, BBC, 1983-86; Chairman: Espirito Ltd, 2010-2014, Cable & Wireless Flexible Resource Ltd., 1993-97; Non-Executive Director: Cable & Wireless, 1988-2004, W.H. Smith, 1989-95, Midlands Electricity, 1990-96, Scottish American Investment Co., 1991-2008, Scottish Oriental Smaller Companies Investment Trust, 1994-2017, Albion Enterprise VCT plc, 2007-2021; Chairman, Board Level Partners Ltd, since 2020; Non-Executive Director: The Scottish Life Assurance Company, 1995-2001, Nuclear Generation Decommissioning Fund Ltd, 1996-2005, Nuclear Liabilities Fund, 2005-2017, Nuclear Liabilities Financing Assurance Board, 2008-2015, New Medical Technologies plc, 1997-2004, BPB plc, 2000-05, Stagecoach plc, 2001-2010, Murray International plc, 2003-2016; Non-Executive Director, NDA Archives Ltd, since 2014; Scottish Medical Research Fund, 1992-94; Member: Scottish Museums Council Development Resource, 1988-97, Ancient Monuments Board for Scotland, 1990-97, Book Trust Scotland, 1992-99, Scottish Economic Council, 1993-95, Scottish Hospitals Endowment Research Trust, 1992-98, Dorothy Burns Charity, 1994-2002; Chairman, Scotland's Book Campaign, 1994-96, Scottish Cultural

Resources Access Network, 1995-2004, Scottish Museum of the Year Award, 1999-2004; Trustee: Carnegie Endowment for the Universities of Scotland, 1993-2016, National Library of Scotland, 2002-2010, Stewart Ivory Foundation, 2001-08, Trusthouse Charitable Foundation, 2006-2018, The Royal Anniversary Trust, 2010-2020. Publications: Diaries of a Cabinet Minister 1964-70 by Richard Crossman (4 volumes) (Editor); The Future of Broadcasting, (Co-Editor, 1982); Agatha Christie: a biography, 1984; Edwina Mountbatten: a life of her own, 1991; The Secrets of rue St. Roch, 2004. Recreations: music of JS Bach and GF Handel; sea bathing; pruning; ice skating out of doors.

Balfour of Burleigh, Lady (Victoria Bruce-Winkler); b. 7.5.73; m., Michail Winkler; 1 d. Succeeded to title, 2019.

Balfour, Ian Leslie Shaw, MA, LLB, BD, PhD, SSC, NP. Solicitor in private practice with Balfour & Manson, Edinburgh, 1957-97; b. 16.6.32, Edinburgh; m., Joyce Margaret Ross Pryde; 3 s.; 1 d. Educ. Edinburgh Academy; Edinburgh University. Qualified as Solicitor, 1955; commissioned, RASC, 1955-57; Partner, then Senior Partner, Balfour & Manson, 1959-97; Secretary, Oliver & Son Ltd., 1959-89; Fiscal to Law Society of Scotland, 1981-1997. Baptist Union of Scotland: President, 1976-77, Law Agent, 1964-97, Secretary, Charlotte Baptist Chapel, Edinburgh, 1980-2000, Secretary, Scottish Baptist College, 1983-2003; Secretary, Elba Housing Society Ltd., 1969-92; Council, Society for Computers and Law, 1988-92; Director, Edinburgh Medical Missionary Society; Honorary Vice-President, Lawyers Christian Fellowship, 1997. Publication: Author, "Revival in Rose Street: Charlotte Baptist Chapel, 1808-2008", 2007. Recreations: gardening; home computing; lay preaching. Lecturer in Church History, Edinburgh Faith Mission Bible School and Institute of Biblical Studies, since 2008 and Edinburgh Bible College, 2011-16. Joint Auditor, Edinburgh Sheriff Court, 1991-2021. Address: (h.) 32 Murrayfield Avenue, Edinburgh EH12 6AX; T.-0131-337 2880; e-mail: I_Balfour@msn.com; web: ianbalfour.co.uk

Balfour, Jeremy Ross. MSP (Scottish Conservative), Lothian Region, since 2016; b. 11.3.67. Educ. Edinburgh Academy; Edinburgh University; London Bible College. Elected to Edinburgh City Council, representing Corstorphine/Murrayfield. Address: Scottish Parliament, Edinburgh EH99 1SP.

Balfour, Robert William, FRICS. Lord-Lieutenant of Fife, since 2014; b. 25.3.52, Edinburgh; m., Jessica McCrindle; 4 s. (1 deceased). Educ. Eton; Edinburgh University (BSc Hons). Managing Partner, Balbirnie Home Farms, 1991-2017; Management trainee, Ocean Group, 1974-78; Surveyor, Bell-Ingram, Perth, 1978-88; Bidwells Chartered Surveyors, Perth, 1988-94, Associate Partner, 1991; Chairman, RICS RPD (Scotland), 1990-91; Convenor, Scottish Landowners Federation, 1999-2002; Member, Board of Management, Elmwood College, 2000-08; Member, East Area Board, Scottish Natural Heritage, 2003-07, Area Advisor, 2007; Director, Fife Coast and Countryside Trust, since 2003, Chairman, 2007-2015; Chairman, Association of Deer Management Group, 2005-2011; Director, Paths for all Partnership, 2005-2013; Chairman, Kettle Growers Ltd., 2006-2011. General Trustee, Church of Scotland, since 2012; Vice Lord-Lieutenant of Fife, 2013-14; DL (Fife), 1994; Elder, Markinch Parish Church; Member, Royal Company of Archers (Officer, 2017); Vice President, Black Watch Association, since 2015. Recreations: shooting; skiing; music; arts; travel. Address: Little Kinloch, Ladybank, Fife KY15 7UT; T.-07774 833620.
E-mail: robertwbalfour@gmail.com

Balfour, William Harold St. Clair. Solicitor (retired); b. 29.8.34, Edinburgh; m., 1, Patricia Waite (m. dissolved); 1

s.; 2 d.; 2, Alice Ingsay McFarlane; 2 step. d. Educ. Hillfield, Ontario; Edinburgh Academy; Edinburgh University. Partner, Balfour & Manson, 1962-98; Clerk to Admission of Notaries Public, 1971-92; Prison Visiting Committee, 1965-70; Chairman, Basic Space Dance Theatre, 1980-86; Friends of Talbot Rice Art Centre, 1982-97, Garvald Trustees, 1980-2004, Wellspring Management, 1990-97, Tekoa Trust, since 1990; Council Member: Scottish Association of Marine Science, 2002-2010, Audit Committee, 2009-2013. Recreations: walking; current affairs; charities. Address: (h.) Flat 15, 50 Annandale Street, Edinburgh EH7 4FA; T.-0131-556 7298.
E-mail: w.whsbalfour@btopenworld.com

Balharry, David, PhD. Chief Executive, John Muir Trust, since 2020; b. 10.64. Educ. Aberdeen University. Career history: former Director of Rewilding Britain; previously worked for six years for the Crofters Commission (latterly as acting Chief Executive), and as Technical Director of the Deer Commission for Scotland; was working on rural policy post 2024 with Scottish Government. Former Director of the Strathglass and Affric Community Company and promotes Community Action Planning that links with land management. Recreations: enjoys mountaineering; sea kayaking and woodwork. Address: John Muir Trust, Tower House, Station Road, Pitlochry PH16 5AN; T.-07786 190912.

Ballantyne, Professor Colin Kerr, MA, MSc, PhD, DSc, FRSE, FRSA, FRSGS, FGS, FBSG. Emeritus Professor in Physical Geography, St Andrews University, since 2015; b. 7.6.51, Glasgow; m., Rebecca Trengove; 1 s.; 1 d. Educ. Hutchesons' Grammar School; Glasgow University; McMaster University; Edinburgh University. Lecturer in Geography, St Andrews University, 1980-89, Senior Lecturer in Geography and Geology, 1989-94, Professor in Physical Geography, 1994-2015, Emeritus Professor in Physical Geography, since 2015. Gordon Warwick Award Medal, British Geomorphological Research Group, 1987; Presidents' Medal, Royal Scottish Geographical Society, 1991; Newbigin Prize, Royal Scottish Geographical Society, 1992; Scottish Science Award, Saltire Society, 1996; Wiley Award, British Geomorphological Research Group, 1999; Clough Medal, Edinburgh Geological Society, 2010; Coppock Research Medal, Royal Scottish Geographical Society, 2015; Lyell Medal, Geological Society, 2015. Visiting Professor, UNIS, Svalbard, 2000-2019; Erskine Fellow, University of Canterbury, New Zealand, 2003, 2013 and 2019. Publications: The Quaternary of the Isle of Skye, 1991; The Periglaciation of Great Britain, 1994; Classic Landforms of the Isle of Skye, 2000; Paraglacial Geomorphology, 2002; The Quaternary of Skye, 2016; Periglacial Geomorphology, 2018; Scotland's Mountain Landscapes: a geomorphological perspective, 2019; Landscapes and Landforms of Scotland, 2021. Recreations: music; travel; mountaineering; skiing; naval history; writing. Address: (h.) Birchwood, Blebo Craigs, Fife KY15 5UF; T.-01334 850567; e-mail: ckb@st-andrews.ac.uk

Ballantyne, Fiona Catherine, OBE, MA, FCIM. Director, RIO Ltd, 2014-19; Director, 4Consulting Ltd., 2001-2011; Member, Board, Queen Margaret University College, Edinburgh, 1995-2005, Vice Chair, 2002-05; Director, The Audience Business Ltd., 1998-2004; Member, Scottish Committee, Institute of Directors, 1996-2006; Member, Audit Committee, Scottish Further and Higher Education Funding Councils, 2000-02; b. 9.7.50, Bristol; m., A. Neil Ballantyne. Educ. Marr College, Troon; Edinburgh University. Former Market Researcher and Market Research Manager; Research and Planning Manager, Thistle Hotels Ltd., 1975-77; Assistant Marketing Manager, Lloyds & Scottish Finance Group, 1977-79; Scottish

Development Agency: Marketing Manager, Small Business Division, 1979-84, Head of Small Business Services, 1984-88, Director, Tayside and Fife, 1988-90; Managing Director, Ballantyne Mackay Consultants, 1990-2012; Vice-Chair: BBC Broadcasting Council for Scotland, 1991-96, Duncan of Jordanstone College of Art, 1988-94; Director, Edinburgh Healthcare Trust, 1994-96; Director, The Essentia Group (formerly Network Scotland Ltd.), 1991-2001, Chairman, 1997-2001; Member, Board, Scottish Campaign for Learning, 1997-98; Member, Ofcom Consumer Panel, 2004-2012; Board Member, Museums Galleries Scotland, 2004-2012; Chair, MGS, 2007-2012; Board Member, Edinburgh Printmakers, 2004-08; Trustee: OSCR, 2008-2016, Love Music Productions Ltd., 2009-2018, Water Customer Forum, 2012-17, Scottish Trust for Underwater Archaeology, since 2018, Vice Chair, since 2020. Governor, Royal Conservatoire of Scotland, 2015-2018. Recreations: walking; swimming; gardening; painting.

Ballantyne, Michelle. Former MSP (South Scotland region): Reform UK, 2021; Independent, 2020-2021; Conservative, 2017-2020; Leader of Reform UK Scotland, 2021-22; b. 28.11.62, Ashton-under-Lyne; m., Neil; 6 c. Educ. Royal London Hospital; Heriot-Watt University. Career history: staff nurse and health service manager in London; moved to the Scottish Borders in 1990 and established a manufacturing business in Walkerburn; began managing an acute medicine department in Edinburgh in 2000, and took a position in 2005 at a charity supporting people struggling with drugs and alcohol; elected to Scottish Borders Council (2012-17); Convener of the Economy, Energy and Fair Work Committee, Scottish Parliament, 2020; Scottish Conservative Spokesperson for Social Security, 2018-2020. Candidate in the February 2020 Scottish Conservative leadership election. Managing trustee of The Haining; a patron of a foodbank in Penicuik and a council member of Friends at the End.

Ballard, Mark, MA (Hons). Head of Policy and Influencing for Scotland, National Deaf Children's Society, since 2022; Director of Strategic Planning and Campaigns, Children 1st, 2019-2022, Policy Manager, 2019; Head of Save the Children in Scotland, 2017-18; Editor-in-Chief, Bright Green (blog); MSP (Scottish Green Party), Lothian Region, 2003-07; Lord Rector, University of Edinburgh, 2006-09; b. 27.6.71, Leeds; m., Heather Stacey; 2 s. Educ. Lawnwood Comprehensive, Leeds; Edinburgh University. Worked for European Youth Forest Action, 1994-98; Editor, Reforesting Scotland, 1998-2001; Director, EMBE Environmental Communications, 2002-03; Assistant Director, Policy, Barnardo's Scotland, 2009-2016; Director of Strategy and Communications, Chest Heart & Stroke Scotland, 2016-17. Publication: Scotlands of the Future (Contributor). Recreations: cycling; Indian cookery.

Bamford, Linda. Convener of the Mobility and Access Committee for Scotland, The Scottish Government, since 2017; Convener for Disability Equality Scotland; previously Chair, Spinal Injuries Scotland. Career spanning over 30 years with NHS Scotland, initially as a psychiatric and general nurse before moving into paramedicine with the Scottish Ambulance Service (SAS); 13 years as a frontline paramedic in Glasgow, then moved into management with SAS (held various senior posts for over 15 years before retiring due to a spinal cord injury). Recipient of two Queen's medals, "Long service and good conduct" to the NHS and "Dedication to the NHS". Panel practice advisor with the Children's Hearing Scotland and a qualified counsellor. Experience and qualifications in Operational Management and Service Delivery, Corporate Governance, Strategy Development, Risk Management, Change Management, Team Building and Leadership; recently

appointed by Scottish Ministers as a Commissioner with the new statutory Scottish Poverty and Inequality Commission. Address: Mobility and Access Committee for Scotland, The Scottish Government, Victoria Quay, Area 2F-North, Edinburgh EH6 6QQ; T.-0131 244 0923. E-mail: macs@gov.scot

Banks, Gordon, BA (Hons). MP (Labour), Ochil and Perthshire South, 2005-2015; Shadow Scotland Office Minister, 2012-2015; Shadow Business Minister, 2010-2011; b. 1955, Acomb, Northumberland; m.; 2 c.

Banks, Lang, BSc (Hons). Director, WWF Scotland, since 2013, Deputy Executive Director, Advocacy and Campaigns. Educ. University of Paisley. Address: WWF Scotland, The Tun, 4 Jackson's Entry, Holyrood Road, Edinburgh EH8 8PJ; T.-0131 659 9100.
Web: www.wwfscotland.org.uk

Banks, Professor William McKerrell, BSc, MSc, PhD, CEng, FIMechE, FREng, FRSE. Emeritus Research Professor of Advanced Materials, Strathclyde University (Professor, since 1991); formerly Director, Centre for Advanced Structural Materials; formerly Co-Director, Scottish Polymer Technology Network; President, SCOTETA, 2010-11; Past President and Chairman, Board of Trustees, IMechE; formerly Chairman, Qualifications and Membership Board, IMechE; formerly Chairman, Trustee Board Awards Committee, IMechE; former member, EC (UK) Council (now Engineering Council); former Member, Engineering and Technology Board (now Engineering UK); Past Chairman and Vice Chairman, Engineering Professors' Council; former Director of Research and Training, Faraday Plastics; b. 28.3.43, Dreghorn; m., Martha Ruthven Hair; 3 s. Educ. Irvine Royal Academy; Strathclyde University. Senior Research Engineer, G. & J. Weir Ltd., 1966-70; Lecturer, Senior Lecturer, Reader, Professor, Strathclyde University, since 1970. Recipient of James Alfred Ewing Medal (Royal Society and ICE), 2007; recipient of James Clayton Prize (IMechE), 2011; 150th Anniversary Gold Medal Award from IMechE, 1998; Member of SQA "Qualifications Design Team" for Technological Studies/Engineering (Rep RSE), 2010-14. Recreations: family; Bible teaching; gardening; travel. Address: (h.) 19 Dunure Drive, Hamilton ML3 9EY; T.-01698 823730.

Bannatyne, Hon. Lord (Iain Alexander Scott Peebles). Senator of the College of Justice, since 2008; b. 8.54. Educ. University of Strathclyde. Admitted to the Faculty of Advocates in 1979, and appointed Queens' Counsel in 1993; appointed as a temporary Sheriff in 1991, a full-time Sheriff in 1995, and began sitting as a commercial sheriff in 1999; appointed a temporary High Court judge in 2003, serving until being elevated to the Bench in 2008. Member of the Sheriff Courts Rules Council, 2001-07, and joint-chairman of the IT Committee of the Sheriff and Court of Session Rules Council. Address: (b.) Parliament House, 11 Parliament Square, Edinburgh EH1 1RQ.

Bantick, Allan David, OBE. Chairman, Scottish Wildlife Trust, 2008-2014; b. 22.12.39, London; m., Heather Susan; 1 d. Educ. Kingsbury County Grammar School. RAF Physical Education specialising in aircrew survival, mountain rescue and outdoor pursuits, 1957-83; Record Producer, 1984-2005; 1990-: Founder Member: Scottish Badgers, Scottish Beaver Network; Founding Chairman, Boat of Garten Wildlife Group; regular contributor to Radio and TV Wildlife Programmes including Nature's Calendar and Spring Watch. Joined the Council of The Scottish Wildlife Trust in 2005; became a Trustee of The Royal

Society of Wildlife Trusts in 2006. Appointed OBE in the 2015 New Years Honours List. Recreations: golf; hill walking. Address: (h.) 23 Craigie Avenue, Boat of Garten, Inverness-shire PH24 3BL; T.-01479 831768.
E-mail: allanbantick@yahoo.co.uk

Barbenel, Professor Joseph Cyril, BDS, BSc, MSc, PhD, LDS RCS(Eng), CBiol, FIBiol, CPhys, FInstP, CEng, FIPEM, FEAMBES, FRSE. Emeritus Professor, University of Strathclyde; b. 2.1.37, London; m., Lesley Mary Hyde Jowett; 2 s.; 1 d. Educ. Hackney Downs Grammar School, London; London Hospital Medical College; Queen's College, Dundee (St. Andrews University); Strathclyde University. Dental House Surgeon, London Hospital, 1960; National Service, RADC, 1960-61 (Lieutenant, 1960, Captain, 1961); general dental practice, London, 1963; student, University of St Andrews, 1963-67; Lecturer, Department of Dental Prosthetics, Dental School, Dundee, 1967-69; Senior Lecturer, Reader, Professor, Bioengineering Unit, Strathclyde University. Recreations: music; art; theatre. Address: (b.) University of Strathclyde, Centre for Ultrasonic Engineering, 204 George Street, Glasgow G1 1XW; T.-0141-552 4400.
E-mail: j.c.barbenel@strath.ac.uk

Barclay, Rev Dr Grant, DipLP, MSc, BD (Theology), LLB. Chaplain to Her Majesty The Queen, since 2022; Presbytery Clerk, University of Glasgow, since 2021; Minister, Orchardhill Parish Church, Giffnock, 2016-2021; m., Karen; 3 c. Educ. Armadale Academy; University of Glasgow; Lancaster University; The University of Edinburgh. Practiced law in Sneddons Solicitors in Whitburn and Armadale before training for the ministry; Convener, Council of Assembly, Church of Scotland, 2012-16; Minister, St Kentigern's Church, 1995-2016; Depute Clerk, Presbytery of Irvine and Kilmarnock, 2011-16; Board Trustee, Action of Churches Together in Scotland, 2017-19. Recreation: walking. Address: Presbytery of Glasgow, 260 Bath Street, Glasgow G2 4JP.

Barclay, Rev Iain Cameron, MBE, MStJ, TD, MA, BD, MTh, MPhil, PhD, FRSA. Awarded the Territorial Decoration, 1994; Admitted to the Most Honourable Order of the British Empire as Member in the Military Division, 2003; Admitted to the Order of St John in the grade of Member, 2006; Minister of the Church of Scotland, Licensed at Glasgow Cathedral by the Presbytery of Glasgow, 1975 and Ordained in The Highland, Tolbooth, St John's Church by the Presbytery of Edinburgh, 1976; b. 13.9.47, Giffnock, Renfrewshire; m., Carilon Dene Barclay (formerly Wilmot). Educ. Queen's Park Senior Secondary School, Glasgow; University of Edinburgh; University of Glasgow; University of Aberdeen. Served Royal Army Chaplains' Department, 1976-1979; Regular Army - Chaplain to The Royal Scots (The Royal Regiment), 1983-2007, TA&VR Group A - Chaplain to 205 (Scottish) General Hospital RAMC (Volunteers); Staff Chaplain Headquarters Scotland; Staff Chaplain Headquarters 2nd Division; Chaplain to 306 Field Hospital (Volunteers) and (1996-2012) TA&VR Group B - Chaplain to The Black Watch (Royal Highland Regiment) Army Cadet Force; Minister of Edinburgh: New Restalrig, 1979-1988; Dunoon: Kilfinan with Kyles, 1988-1996; Assistant at Aberdeen: Beechgrove, 1996-1999; Minister of Aberdeen: Torry St Fittick's, 1999-2012; Admitted as Minister of the Presbyterian Church of Australia and Inducted Minister of the Scots Church, Sydney, 2012-2015; re-admitted to the Church of Scotland and Inducted Minister of Appin with Lismore, 2015-2020 and thereafter appointed to The Robin Chapel, Edinburgh as Chaplain, from 2020. The first Church of Scotland Chaplain to be mobilised since the 2nd World

War when his unit 205 (Scottish) General Hospital RAMC (Volunteers) deployed to Riyadh for the Gulf War of 1990/1991 as 205 General Evacuation Hospital (Volunteers); Chairman, The Society of Friends of Kilfinan Parish Church, 1990-1996; Chaplain to The Moderator of the General Assembly of the Church of Scotland, 2003-2004; Chaplain, Scottish Prison Service, HMP Aberdeen, 2007-2012; Chairman, The Torry Trust, 2010-2015; Chaplain, New South Wales Police, 2012-2015; Chaplain, New South Wales Regimental Association, 2012-2015; Chairman, City Community Care, 2014-2018; Patron, City Community Care, 2018-2021; appointed Fellow of the Royal Society of Arts (2012). Clubs: Edinburgh: New and Royal Scots; Aberdeen: Royal Northern & University; Sydney, New South Wales: Australian Club. Address: (b.) The Thistle Foundation, Edinburgh EH16 4EA; T.-07393232736; e-mail: chaplain@robinchapel.org.uk. Address: (h.) Ashburn Villa, Taigh-na-bruaich PA21 2BE; e-mail: iaincbarclay@gmail.com

Bardell, Hannah. MP (SNP), Livingston, since 2015; SNP Spokesperson for Digital, Culture, Media and Sport, 2018-19; Business, Innovation and Skills Spokesperson, 2015-18; b. 1.6.83, Craigshill, Livingston. Educ. Broxburn Academy; University of Stirling. Career: SNP election campaign for the Scottish Parliament election, 2007; worked for Alex Salmond and Ian Hudghton MEP for 3 years; joined the US State Department in their Edinburgh Consulate; subsequently worked in the oil and gas industry initially with Subsea 7 and later as Head of Communications & Marketing for the UK, Africa & Norway with Oil & Gas Service company Stork. Address: House of Commons, London SW1A 0AA.

Barker, Emeritus Professor John Reginald, BSc, MSc, PhD, FBIS, FRAS, FRSE. Honorary Senior Research Fellow, University of Glasgow, Professor of Electronics (1985-2008); b. 11.11.42, Stockport; m., Elizabeth Carol Maguire; 2 s.; 1 d. Educ. New Mills Grammar School; University of Edinburgh; University of Durham; University of Warwick. University of Warwick: SRC Personal Research Fellowship, 1969-70, Lecturer in Theoretical Physics, 1970-84, Senior Lecturer, 1984-85; Affiliate Professor, Colorado State University, 1979-83; Distinguished Science Lecturer, Yale University, 1992; Irvine Lectures in Chemistry, St. Andrews, 1994; TV/broadcasting: History of the Microchip, 1982; The Magic Micro Mission, 1983. Member, various SERC/DTI committees, 1987-93: Devices Committee, Electronic Materials Committee, National Committee for Superconductivity, Materials Commission, Molecular Electronics Committee (Chairman, 1990-93). Fellow of the Royal Society of Edinburgh (1990): served as Convenor of the Mathematics section and Convenor of the Electronics and Electrical Engineering Section. Royal Philosophical Society of Glasgow: Council Member (2010-2018), Vice-President (2014-2017). Nomads Club (2006-2017). Publications: over 370 scientific papers; Physics of Non-Linear Transport in Semi-conductors (Co-Author), 1979; Granular Nanoelectronics (Co-Author), 1991. Recreations: hill-walking; astronomy; reading; photography. Address: (b.) Rankine Building, School of Engineering, College of Science and Engineering, University of Glasgow, Glasgow G12 8LT; T.-0141 338 6026.
Website: http://johnreginaldbarker.co.uk
E-mail: John.Barker@glasgow.ac.uk

Barley, Nick. Director, Edinburgh International Book Festival, since 2009. Ran his own publishing company, August Publications, before becoming Editor of The List (2003-06); then became Director of The Lighthouse,

Scotland's National Centre for Architecture and Design. As Director of the Book Festival he has introduced several innovations including Unbound, a new strand of late night events, a Reader's First Book Award for debut novelists and the 2012 Edinburgh World Writers' Conference. Publications: Lost and Found: critical voices in new British design, 1999; Breathing Cities: the architecture of movement, 2000. Address: (b.) Edinburgh International Book Festival, 5 Charlotte Square, Edinburgh EH2 4DR; T.-0131 718 5666.

Barlow, Nevile Robert Disney, OBE, DL, FRICS. Chartered Surveyor and Farmer; Chairman, Scottish Borders Valuation Appeal Panel, 1995-2015; b. 3.2.41, Bagshott, Surrey; m., Myfanwy Louise Kerr-Wilson; 3 s. Educ. Winchester College; Royal Agricultural College, Cirencester. Assistant Agent, Bathurst Estate, Cirencester, 1963-95; Resident Sub-Agent, Bletchingdon Park, 1966-67; Head Factor, National Trust for Scotland, 1986-91; Vice-President, Scottish Landowners' Federation, 1995-2003 (Convener, 1991-94); Member, Board, East of Scotland Water, 1995-99; Member, East Region Board, Scottish Environmental Protection Agency, 1996-2000. Recreations: shooting; fishing; sailing; rowing. Address: Parkcroft House, Redpath, Earlston TD4 6AD; T.-01896 849267.

Barnard, Professor Alan John, BA, MA, PhD, FBA, FSAScot, FRAI. Professor Emeritus; formerly Professor of the Anthropology of Southern Africa, Edinburgh University, 2001-2015 (retired); Honorary Consul of Namibia in Scotland, 2007-2018; b. 22.2.49, Baton Rouge, USA; m., Dr Joy E. Barnard. Educ. New Providence High School; George Washington University; McMaster University; University College London. Junior Lecturer in Social Anthropology, University of Cape Town, 1972-73; Field Research with Bushmen in Botswana, 1974-75 and later; Lecturer in Social Anthropology, University College London, 1976-78; Lecturer in Social Anthropology, 1978-90, Senior Lecturer, 1990-94, Reader, 1994-2001, Edinburgh University. Hon. Secretary, Association of Social Anthropologists, 1985-89. Publications include: Hunters and Herders of Southern Africa, 1992; Kalahari Bushmen (children's book), 1993; Encyclopaedia of Social and Cultural Anthropology (Co-Editor), 1996; History and Theory in Anthropology, 2000; Social Anthropology, 2000; The Hunter-Gatherer Peoples, 2001; Africa's Indigenous Peoples (Co-Editor), 2001; Self- and Other Images of Hunter-Gatherers (Co-Editor), 2002; Hunter-Gatherers in History (Editor), 2004; Anthropology and the Bushman, 2007; Social Anthropology and Human Origins, 2011; Genesis of Symbolic Thought, 2012; Language in Prehistory, 2016; Bushmen: Kalahari Hunter-Gatherers and Their Descendants, 2019; Hunters and Gatherers: What Can We Learn from Them, 2020; History and Theory in Anthropology (second edition), 2021. Recreations: walking; cooking; watercolour painting. Address: (b.) School of Social and Political Science, Edinburgh University, Chrystal Macmillan Building, George Square, Edinburgh EH8 9LD.
E-mail: A.Barnard@ed.ac.uk

Barnes, David. Chief Agricultural Officer for Scotland, since 2015; formerly Deputy Director, Department for Agriculture and Rural Affairs, Scottish Government. Address: (b.) St. Andrew's House, Regent Road, Calton Hill, Edinburgh EH1 3DG.

Barnes, Eddie, MA. Former Director of Strategy and Communications, Scottish Conservative Party; b. 10.6.72, Ormskirk, Lancashire; m., Malini Geeta; 1 s.; 1 d. Educ. St.

Bede's Comprehensive, Ormskirk; Glasgow University. Scottish Catholic Observer Reporter, 1997, Editor, 1998-2000; Scottish Daily Mail, Political Reporter, 2000-02; Political Editor, 2002-04; Political Editor, Scotland on Sunday, 2004-2013.

Barnes, James David Kentish. Director, Dobbies Garden Centres plc, 1994-2006; b. 18.4.30, Cheshire; m., 1, Julie Pinckney; 1 s.; 1 d.; m. 2, Susan Mary Leslie. Educ. Eton College; Royal Military Academy Sandhurst. Commissioned 5th Innis Dragoon Guards, 1948-57. Served Germany, Korea, Middle East. Joined John Waterer Sons & Crisp (Horticulture), 1957. Managing Director, 1968-84; Managing Director (Owner), Dobbie and Co Edinburgh, 1968-94; National Trust for Scotland member of Council and Chairman of Gardening committee, 1996-2000; Chairman, NTS Enterprise Company, 2000-05; Director, Grimsthorpe and Drummond Castle Trust Ltd., since 2005. Recreations: cricket; golf; shooting; fishing; gardening; clubs: cavalry & guards, MCC, Muirfield. Address: (h.) Biggar Park, Biggar, Lanarkshire ML12 6JS.

Barr, Ian Mason, DA, BA, PGCE. Artist; Educationalist; b. 16.3.46, Glasgow; m., Joan Sinclair; 2 s.; 1 d. Educ. Rutherglen Academy; Glasgow School of Art; University of Strathclyde. Teacher, Strathclyde Regional Council Education Department, 1969-82; National Development Officer, Scottish Curriculum Development Service, 1982-85; Member of Staff, Jordanhill College of Education, 1985-87; Director, Curriculum Evaluation Advisory Service, 1991-93; Director, Scottish Consultative Council on the Curriculum, 1993-2000; Specialist Adviser in Values Education, UNESCO, 1993-95; Founder, Ian M Barr Consultancy, since 2001. Founder Member, Strathclyde Environmental Education Group, 1975; Member, Secretary of State's Education for Sustainable Development Group, 1997-99; Board Member, Scottish Council for Research in Education, 1998-2003; Founder Member, European Educational Design Group, 1988; Board Member, Centre for Creative Communities, 1998-2000; Chair, Independent Television Commission Education Advisory Committee, 2000-03; Member, Scottish Arts Council Forum on the Arts and Education, 2002-03; Member, Campaign for Drawing Advisory Committee; Trustee, National Galleries of Scotland, 2005-2013; Convener, Art Fund Highland Branch, 2014. Authored and edited several publications on aspects of education and the curriculum; numerous exhibitions in UK and Europe. Recreations: gardening; music; reading; cinema; hill walking. Address: Whitefield, Ordhill, Fortrose IV10 8SH; T.-01381 622545; e-mail: ianmbarr@btinternet.com

Barraclough, David Rex, BSc, DSc, FRAS. Chairperson, Enable (formerly Scottish Society for the Mentally Handicapped), 1998-2001; b. 7.3.40, Halifax; m., Christine; 1 s.; 1 d. Educ. Crossley and Porter Boys' School, Halifax; Imperial College, London University. Research Physicist, AEI Ltd., 1962-64; Research Assistant, Bradford University, 1964-68; Geophysicist, British Geological Survey, 1969-2000. Vice-President, Royal Astronomical Society, 1999-2000. Recreations: walking; reading; listening to music. Address: (h.) 49 Liberton Drive, Edinburgh.
E-mail: drbarraclough@hotmail.com

Barrett, John Andrew. MP (Liberal Democrat), Edinburgh West, 2001-10; b. 11.2.54, Hobart, Australia; m., Carol; 1 d. Educ. Forrester High School; Telford College; Napier Polytechnic. Company Director, ABC Productions, 1985-2001; Member, City of Edinburgh Council, 1995-2001;

Director, The EDI Group, 1995-99; Board Member, Edinburgh International Film Festival, 1995-2001; Board Member, Lothian and Borders Screen Industry Office, 1998-2001; Member, Edinburgh Filmhouse Board, 1999-2001. Recreations: cinema; travel; music.

Barrie, Andrew, BSc, BD. Minister of St. Serf's Church, Tullibody, since 2016; Minister of Rothesay: Trinity, Church of Scotland, 2010-16; m., Sheila. Educ. Muiredge Primary; Uddingston Grammar; Strathclyde University; Aberdeen University. Minister: Lochranza and Pirnmill with Shiskine (Isle of Arran), 1984-2000, Denny: Westpark, 2000-2010. Address: 22 The Cedars, Tullibody FK10 2PX. E-mail: dbarrie@churchofscotland.org.uk

Barrie, Ken, BA Hons (Psych), CQSW, PGDip (Alcohol Studies). Senior Lecturer in Alcohol and Drug Studies, University of the West of Scotland, since 1983; b. 13.4.52, Edinburgh; m., Nancy Docherty; 1 s. Educ. Royal High School, Edinburgh; Strathclyde University; Edinburgh University; Paisley University. 1975-83: Social Worker, Strathclyde Regional Council; full range of social work tasks; specialism in addiction; contributor to MSc Contemporary Drug and Alcohol Studies and BA Hons Criminal Justice programmes. Recreations: swimming; cycling; canoeing. Address: (b.) University of the West of Scotland, High Street, Paisley PA1 2BE; T.-0141 848 3140; e-mail: ken.barrie@uws.ac.uk

Barry, Dr Yahya, BA, PGDip, MA, PhD. Executive Director, Olive Tree Madrasah, since 2018; Board Member, Creative Scotland, since 2021; b. 9.83. Educ. Islamic University of Madinha; Institute for Religious Leaders, The Muslim World League, Mecca, KSA; University of Copenhagen; Uppsala University; University of Edinburgh. Career history: Arabic-English Translator, Al-Qabas, Madinha, Saudi Arabia, 2006-08; Secondary School Teacher, West African Secondary School, Kanifing Industrial Estate, The Gambia, 2010; Research Intern, Open Skane - Internship, Malmo, Sweden, 2015; Minister of Religion, Edinburgh Central Mosque, 2015-17; University of Edinburgh: Arabic Language Tutor, 2016; Islamic Law and Shariah MOOC Tutor, 2019; PhD Candidate and Outreach Assistant, 2013-19; Muslim Belief Contact, 2018-2020; Postdoctoral Visiting Scholar, 2019-2020; Senior Visiting Researcher, University of Copenhagen, since 2020; Chair, The Board of Trustees, BE United, since 2020. Address: Flat 12, 16 Hopetoun Street, Edinburgh EH7 4GH.

Bartlett, Professor Robert John, CBE (2019), MA, DPhil, FRHS, FBA, FSA, FRSE. Professor Emeritus, St Andrews University (appointed Professor of Mediaeval History in 1992); b. 27.11.50, London; m., Honora Hickey (deceased 2016); 1 s.; 1 d. Educ. Battersea Grammar School; Peterhouse, Cambridge; St. John's College, Oxford. Lecturer in History, Edinburgh University, 1980-86; Professor of Medieval History, University of Chicago, 1986-92. Presenter, "Inside the Medieval Mind", BBC4, 2008; "The Normans", BBC2, 2010; "The Plantagenets", BBC2, 2013. Publications: Gerald of Wales 1146-1223, 1982; Trial by Fire and Water: the medieval judicial ordeal, 1986; The Making of Europe, 1993; England under the Norman and Angevin Kings, 2000; Medieval Panorama (Editor), 2001; The Hanged Man: A Story of Miracle, Memory and Colonization in the Middle Ages, 2004; The Natural and the Supernatural in the Middle Ages, 2008; Why can the dead do such great things? Saints and Worshippers from the Martyrs to the Reformation, 2013; Blood Royal: Dynastic Politics in Medieval Europe, 2020. Recreations: walking; squash. Address: (b.) Department of Mediaeval History, St Andrews University, St Andrews KY16 9AL; T.-01334 463308.

Barton, Professor Geoffrey John, BSc (Manchester), PhD (London). Head of Computational Biology and Professor of Bioinformatics, School of Life Sciences, University of Dundee, since 2001; b. 01.11.60, Glenelg, Australia; m., Julia; 3 s. Educ. Challney High School; Luton VIth Form College; University of Manchester; Birkbeck College, University of London. Imperial Cancer Research Fund Fellow, Lincoln's Inn Fields, London, 1987-89; Royal Society University Research Fellow, Laboratory of Molecular Biophysics, University of Oxford, 1989-97; Research and Development Team Leader and Head of European Macromolecular Structure Database, EMBL European Bioinformatics Institute, Hinxton, Cambridge, 1997-2001. Fellow of the Royal Society of Biology (FRSB), Fellow of the Royal Society of Edinburgh (FRSE). 130+ peer reviewed publications. Recreations: family; DIY; writing music; swimming/running. Address: (b.) School of Life Sciences, University of Dundee, Dow Street, Dundee DD1 5EH; T.-01382 385860.
E-mail: g.j.barton@dundee.ac.uk
Web: www.compbio.dundee.ac.uk

Batchelor, Louise Mary, BA (Hons). Retired Journalist; Environment Correspondent, BBC Scotland, 1994-2008; freelance, 2009-2017; b. 23.2.53, Swanage; m., David Batchelor; 2 s. Educ. Dorchester Grammar School; Reading University. Milton Keynes Gazette, 1974; Oxford Mail, 1977; BBC Radio Scotland, 1978; Presenter/Reporter, Reporting Scotland, 1980; Presenter, Newsnight, 1981-82; Presenter, Breakfast News (Scotland), 1982-83; presenter, various programmes, including Voyager, Fringes of Faith; Presenter, Newsroom South East, 1989. Media Natura Award, 1996, for environment reporting; British Environment and Media Award for TV News and Current Affairs coverage of the environment, 2003; Member, Steering Group, Portmoak Community Woodlands; Member, Scottish Green Party. Recreations: walking; bird watching; playing cello; swing dancing; jazz; saxophone; tennis. Address: The Old Manse, Scotlandwell, Kinross KY13 9HY; e-mail: louise@louisebatchelor.co.uk

Bate, Beth, MA, BA (Hons). Director, Dundee Contemporary Arts, since 2016; b. 5.77. Educ. University of Birmingham (BA Hons English with History of Art, 1999); University of Leicester (MA, Museum Studies, 2002). Career history: Programme Assistant, Fierce Festival, 2000-02; Assistant Curator, The Public, 2002-04; Director and Studio Manager, Platform Projects, 2004-07; Project and Event Manager, AV Festival, 2006-2010; Chair of Board, Wunderbar Festival, 2008-2014; Director, Press Play Festival, 2009-2014; Clore Leadership Programme, 2014/15 Fellow; Director, Great North Run Culture, Newcastle upon Tyne, 2004-2015; Senior Project Manager, Digital Events (Clore Secondment), British Museum, London, 2015; Freelance Culture Consultant, 1999-2016; Board Member, Culture Bridge North East, Newcastle upon Tyne, 2015-16; Board Member, British Council Scotland; Honorary Research Fellow, University of Dundee, 2021; Board Member, V & A Dundee, since 2020; Trustee, Mount Stuart Trust, since 2020. Address: Dundee Contemporary Arts, University of Dundee, 152 Nethergate, Dundee DD1 4DY; T.-01382 432462.

Bateman, Derek Walls. Former Presenter, BBC Radio Scotland (1995-2013); b. 10.5.51, Selkirk; m., 1, Alison Edgar (deceased); 2 d.; 2, Judith Mackay; 1 d. Educ. Selkirk High School; Edinburgh College of Commerce. Scotsman Publications; Glasgow Herald; BBC Scotland; Scotland on Sunday; freelance (Sunday Times, STV). Publication: Unfriendly Games (Co-Author), 1986. Recreation: wine.

Bateman, Professor Meg (Vivienne Margaret), MA (Hons), PhD. Gaelic poet; b. 13.4.59, Edinburgh; 1 s. Educ. Mary Erskine School, Edinburgh; University of Aberdeen. Poetry collections: Orain Ghaoil (1990); Aotromachd is

Dàin Eile (Lightness and Other Poems) (1997); Soirbheas/Fair Wind, 2007; (both shortlisted for Scottish Book of the Year Award); Transparencies, 2013; translations of Gaelic poetry published in An Anthology of Scottish Women Poets, Gàir nan Clàrsach (The Harps' Cry); Duanaire na Sracaire/Songbook of the Pillagers, 2007; The Glendale Bards, 2014; Window to the West (Co-Author), 2020 (e-book). Recreations: walking; geology; the arts in general. Address: (b.) Sabhal Mòr Ostaig, Sleat, Isle of Skye IV44 8RQ; T.-01471 888310.
E-mail: meg.smo@uhi.ac.uk

Bates, Damian, BA (Hons). Chairman, Fifth Ring Communications, since 2016; Director of Communications, Well-Safe Solutions, 2017-19; Managing Director, Abraitis & Company, since 2017; former Editor-in-Chief, Aberdeen Journals (2013-17) and former Editor, Press and Journal (2011-17); b. 9.4.69, Blackpool, Lancashire. Educ. Cardinal Allen RC High School, Fleetwood; St. Mary's VIth Form, Blackpool; Reading University. Trainee Reporter; Business Reporter; Deputy Business Editor; Crime Reporter - all Evening Gazette, Middlesbrough; Assistant News Editor; Deputy News Editor - The News, Portsmouth; News Editor; Assistant Editor (News) - Telegraph and Argus, Bradford; Deputy Editor, then Editor, Evening Express, Aberdeen; Visiting Professor, Robert Gordon University. Publication: No More I Love Yous - The Nikki Conroy Story.

Baughan, Mike, OBE. Former Chief Executive, Learning and Teaching Scotland (formerly Scottish Consultative Council on the Curriculum), 2000-2004; b. 11.6.44, Dumfries; m., Anna; 1 s.; 1 d. Educ. St. Joseph's College, Dumfries; Dundee University; Dundee College of Education. RAF Air Radar; brief career in industrial banking; English Teacher, secondary schools, Dundee, 1975-82; Churchill Fellow, 1977; Adviser in Education, Tayside Regional Council, 1982-87; Rector, Webster's High School, Kirriemuir, 1987-97; Scottish Consultative Council on the Curriculum: Development Fellow, 1997-98, appointed Chief Executive, 1998. Chair/Member, various national education committees, including "Curriculum for Excellence"; Fellow, Education Institute of Scotland; Past Council Member, Save the Children Scotland; Past Member of Ancient Monuments Board for Scotland; Ex Director and Board Member of Young Enterprise Scotland. Recreations: 6 grandchildren; hill-walking; member of the Munro Society and the Grampian Club; golf; gardening; fishing; theatre; travel. Address: (b.) 6 Shepherd's Road, Newport-on-Tay, Fife DD6 8HJ.

Bauld, Professor Linda C., OBE, BA, PhD, FRCPE, FRSE, FAcSS, FFPH. Chief Social Policy Adviser, Scottish Government, since 2021; Bruce and John Usher Chair of Public Health in The Usher Institute, University of Edinburgh, since 2018; CRUK/BUPA Chair in Behavioural Research for Cancer Prevention, Cancer Research UK, 2014-2021; b. 2.6.70, Edinburgh; m.; 1 s.; 1 d. Educ. Glenlyon Norfolk School; University of Toronto; University of Edinburgh. Career history: postdoctoral fellow, University of Kent, 1997-2000; appointed Lecturer, Department of Social Policy, University of Glasgow in 2000; appointed as Reader (2006) and subsequently Professor and Head of Department of Social and Policy Sciences, University of Bath; the Government of the United Kingdom's scientific adviser on tobacco control, UK Government, 2006-2010; University of Stirling, 2011-2018. Regular contributor to UK and international media debate on public health responses during the Covid-19 pandemic, as well as serving as adviser to the Covid-19 Committee of the Scottish Parliament, 2020-2021. Address: Usher Institute – University of Edinburgh, Doorway 1, Old Medical School, Teviot Place, Edinburgh EH8 9AG; T.-0131 650 3213; e-mail: Linda.Bauld@ed.ac.uk

Baxter, Jayne, MSP (Labour), Mid Scotland and Fife, 2012-16; b. 5.11.55. Educ. Edinburgh Napier University. Background in local government with a particular interest in social care, young people, economic development and community planning. Former Member of the Education and Culture Committee, Scottish Parliament.

Baxter, Peter R., DHE. Curator, Edinburgh Botanic Garden (Sibbald) Trust; Curator, Benmore Botanic Garden, since 1995; b. 30.6.58, Irvine; m.; 1 s.; 1 d. Address: (b.) Arboretum Place, Edinburgh EH3 5NZ; T.-0131 248 2909.

Beamish, Claudia, MSP (Labour and Cooperative), South Scotland, 2011-2021; former Shadow Minister for Environment and Climate Change; b. 9.8.52; partner, Michael Derrington; 1 d.; 1 s. Chair of the Scottish Labour Party, 2008-10, former Chair of Socialist Environmental Resources Association; Member of the Cooperative Group of MSPs. Taught part-time in South Lanarkshire Primary Schools and has also run a community theatre company. Awarded the RSPB Environment Politician of the Year in the Nature of Scotland Awards, 2014.

Beat, Janet Eveline, BMus, MA. Composer; Lecturer, Glasgow University, 1996-2004; Artistic Director and Founder, Soundstrata (electro-acoustic ensemble); Honorary Research Fellow, Music Department, Glasgow University, 1996-2016; Affiliate, Glasgow University, since 2016; b. 17.12.37, Streetly. Educ. High School for Girls, Sutton Coldfield; Birmingham University. Freelance Orchestral Player, 1960s; Lecturer: Madeley College of Education, 1965-67, University of Worcester, 1967-71, Royal Scottish Academy of Music and Drama, 1972-96; music published by Furore Verlag, Kassel; wrote musical criticism for The Scotsman; G.D. Cunningham Award, 1962; her works have been performed throughout the UK as well as in Switzerland, Germany, Poland, North America, South America, Greece, Australia, Japan, Austria, Portugal, Spain and Africa. Prize winner in Zweiter Internationaler Wettbewerb für Komponistinnen in conjunction with the Mariann-Steegmann Stiftung, 2016; 2021 Release of 1st album by Trunk Records: Janet Beat - Pioneering KnobTwidler. Received the Lifetime Achievement Award, Scottish Women Inventing Music 2019 (SWIM). Recreations: travel; reading; art. Address: The Gait, Candleriggs, Glasgow G1 1NQ; T.-0141 552 5222.

Beath, Professor John Arnott, OBE, MA, MPhil, FRSE, FRSA, FAcSS. Member, Competition Appeal Tribunal, 2013-19; Emeritus Professor of Economics, St. Andrews University; b. 15.6.44, Thurso; m.; Dr. Monika Schroder. Educ. Hillhead High School; St. Andrews, London, Pennsylvania and Cambridge Universities. Research Officer, Department of Applied Economics, Cambridge University; Fellow, Downing College, Cambridge; Lecturer, then Senior Lecturer in Economics, Bristol University. Member, Research Priorities Board, Economic and Social Research Council, 1996-2000; Chair, Conference of Heads of University Departments of Economics, 1997-2003; RAE Panellist, 1996, 2001; Chair, Economic Research Institute of Northern Ireland, 2003-09; Member, Review Body on Doctors' and Dentists' Remuneration, 2003-09; Council member, Economic and Social Research Council, 2009-14; Secretary-General, Royal Economic Society, 2008-15; Member, Prison Service Pay Review Body, 2010-16; Member, Competition Appeal Tribunal, 2011-19. Publication: The Economic Theory of Product Differentiation. Recreations: gardening; golf; music. Address: (h.) Simonden, Ceres, Cupar KY15 5PP.

Beattie, Alistair Duncan, MD (Hons), FRCPGlas, FRCPLond. Consultant Physician, Southern General Hospital, Glasgow, 1976-2002; Honorary Clinical Lecturer, Glasgow University, 1977-2002; Chairman, Medical and Dental Defence Union of Scotland, 2002-2012; b. 4.4.42, Laurencekirk; m., Gillian Margaret McCutcheon; 3 s.; 2 d.

Educ. Paisley Grammar School; Glasgow University. Junior hospital appointments, Royal Infirmary and Western Infirmary, Glasgow, 1965-69; Department of Materia Medica, Glasgow University: Research Fellow, 1969-73, Lecturer, 1973-74; MRC Research Fellow, Royal Free Hospital, London, 1974-75. Recreations: golf; music. Address: (h.) Flat 3/2 Lauderdale Mansions, 47 Novar Drive, Glasgow G12 9UB; T.-0141-334 0101.

Beattie, Andrew Watt, LLB (Hons), DipLP, NP. First Scottish Parliamentary Counsel, since 2012; Scottish Parliamentary Counsel, 2008-2012; Depute Scottish Parliamentary Counsel, 1999-2008; b. 16.11.72, Aberdeen; m., Claire Louise. Educ. Elgin Academy; Edinburgh University. Solicitor, Shepherd & Wedderburn, WS, 1995-99. Recreations: hillock-walking; squash; camping. Address: (b.) Office of the Scottish Parliamentary Counsel, Victoria Quay, Edinburgh EH6 6QQ; T.-0131-244 1665.

Beattie, Bryan William, JP, BA, FRSA. Honorary Fellow, Queen Margaret University. Chairman, Eigg Box, since 2014; Chairman and Founder, Tappstory Ltd, since 2015; Chairman, Centre for Rural Creativity Advisory Group, since 2016; Interim Director, Eden Court Theatre, 2021-22; Creative Director, Inverness Castle, since 2019; Expert Adviser to Minister for Tourism, Culture and Sport, 2003-05; Special Adviser to Royal Scottish Academy of Music and Drama, 2005-08; Chairman, Board of Governors, Eden Court Theatre, 1996-2002; Board Member, Scottish Screen, 1998-2003; b. 3.5.60, Dundee; m., Emer Leavy; 3 d.; 1 s. Educ. High School of Dundee; Stirling University. Director, Stirling Festival, 1984-86; Arts Development Officer for Scotland, Scottish Council on Disability, 1986-87; Principal, Creative Services (arts consultancy), since 1992; Director, Big Sky (publisher and event producer), since 2011; Chairman, Scottish Youth Theatre, 1993-99; Councillor, Highland Regional Council, 1994-96, and Highland Council, 1995-99 (Chairman, Cultural and Leisure Services Committee, 1995-99); Board Member, Ross and Cromarty Enterprise, 1996-2002, Vice-Chairman, 1999-2002; Chairman: Feis Rois, 2006-2011, Booth Scotland, 2007-2012; Trustee, Dewar Arts Awards, 2011-2013; Member, University of Highlands and Islands Foundation, 1996-99 and 2008-10; Founder Member, Highlands and Islands Alliance, 1998; author of plays for tv, radio and theatre; Editor, "ImagiNation: Stories of Scotland's Future", 2011; Producer, "The Boy and the Bunnet", "Infinite Scotland", "Scotland Inspired"; "Arrest This Moment"; broadcaster; columnist, Press and Journal, 1994-2008. Recreations: music; books; sport. Address: (h.) Drumderfit, North Kessock, by Inverness IV1 3ZF; T.-01463 731596.
E-mail: bryan@creativeservicesscotland.co.uk

Beattie, Carol, MA (Hons). Chief Executive Officer, Stirling Council, since 2019. Educ. Falkirk High School; The University of Edinburgh; International People's College. Career history: Senior Manager, Scottish Enterprise, 1997-2013; Scottish Development International: Senior Manager, 2009-2013, International Sector Head Technology and Engineering, Creative Industries and Construction, 2013-14; Managing Director, Beattie International Trade Ltd, 2014; Stirling Council: appointed Senior Manager Economic Development in 2014; appointed Director Children, Communities and Enterprise in 2017; appointed Depute Chief Executive in 2018, then Interim Chief Executive in 2018. Honorary Fellow of the Institute of Export, May 2012. Address: Stirling Council, Viewforth, 14-20 Pitt Terrace, Stirling FK8 2ET; T.-01786 404040.

Beattie, Colin. MSP (SNP), Midlothian North and Musselburgh, since 2011; b. 17.10.51. Has had a career in national and international finance, working in both the UK and overseas. Served as a councillor in Midlothian, 2007-2012. SNP Treasurer. Address: Scottish Parliament, Edinburgh EH99 1SP.

Beaty, Professor Robert (Bob) Thompson, OBE, BSc (Hons), FREng, FIEE, CEng. Managing Director, GlenCon Ltd., 1996-2007; Chairman, Scottish Enterprise Renfrewshire, 1999-2003; b. 13.10.43, Kilmarnock; m., Anne Veronica; 2 s. Educ. Hamilton Academy; Glasgow University. Hoover Scholar, 1961-65; Test Engineer, Hoover Ltd., Cambuslang, 1965-68; IBM, 1968-96, latterly Director of Personal Computer Manufacturing and Development Site at Greenock. Former Chair of Court, University of the West of Scotland; former Vice-Chairman, Board of Management, James Watt College; Visiting Professor in Product Design, Glasgow University; former Board Member, SIDAB; Honorary Doctorate received from the University of the West of Scotland, 2010. Recreations: cycling; hill-walking; golf; travel; France. Address: (h.) Glenside, 89 Newton Street, Greenock PA16 8SG; T.-01475 722027/07961 068614.
E-mail: bob.beaty@btopenworld.com

Beaumont, Professor Paul Reid, LLB, LLM, FRSE. Professor of Private International Law, University of Stirling, since 2019; b. 27.10.60, Hamilton; 1 s.; 1 d. Educ. Claremont High School, East Kilbride; Glasgow University; Dalhousie University, Canada. University of Aberdeen: Lecturer in Public Law, 1983-91, Senior Lecturer in Public Law, 1992-95, Professor, European Union and Private International Law, 1995-2019. Adviser to UK and Scottish Governments on private international law (1996-2013). Author and editor of several books. Recreations: golf; stamp collecting. Address: School of Law, University of Stirling, Stirling FK9 4LA.
E-mail: paul.beaumont@stir.ac.uk

Beaumont, Professor Steven Peter, OBE, MA, PhD, FRSE, FREng, CEng, MIET. Professor of Nanoelectronics, Department of Electronics and Electrical Engineering, Vice Principal Emeritus, University of Glasgow; b. 20.2.52, Norwich; m., Joanne Mary; 1 s.; 2 d. Educ. Norwich School; Corpus Christi College, Cambridge University. Research Fellow, Glasgow University, 1978-83; Barr and Stroud Lecturer in Electronics, Glasgow University, 1983-86, Senior Lecturer, 1986-89, Head of Department of Electronics and Electrical Engineering, 1994-98, Vice Principal (Research & Enterprise), 2005-2014; Director: Institute for System Level Integration, 1999-2004, Intellemetrics Ltd., 1982-90, System Level Integration Ltd, Electronics Scotland, 1998-2004, Photonix Ltd, 2005-2010, Kelvin Nanotechnology Ltd., 1999-2020, Saw Dx Ltd, 2014-2020, Smart Crofting Ltd, Aon-Flow Ltd, Multicorder Dx Ltd, Semiwise Ltd, Vector Photonics Ltd, III-V EPI Ltd; Solasta Bio Ltd; Awards Convener, Royal Society of Edinburgh, 2008-2015; Enterprise Committee, Royal Academy of Engineering, since 2013. Recreations: walking; crofting. Address: (h.) 13 Kelvinside Terrace South, Glasgow G20 6DW; T.-0141-330 2112.

Becher, Mark, MA (Hons), PGCE. Headteacher, The Compass School, Haddington, since 1997; b. Ayr; m., Agnieszka; 3 d. Educ. Queen Margaret Academy, Ayr; University of Dundee: Craigie College of Education; University of Strathclyde. Primary Teacher: The Edinburgh Academy, 1988-93; Primary Teacher/Senior Teacher, The Mary Erskine and Stewart's Melville Junior School, 1993-97. Member, Scottish Council of Independent Schools Governing Board, 2004-2013 and since 2018; Lay Assessor, Scottish Qualification for Headship, since 2010. Recreations: theatre; rugby; hillwalking. Address: (b.) The Compass School, West Road, Haddington EH41 3RD; T.-01620 822642; e-mail: office@thecompassschool.com

Beck, Jon. Chair, Sacro, since 2022; b. 4.68. Chartered Accountant with more than 30 years' experience in financial services, investing and charity sectors; particular interest in community, education and medical research causes. Address: Sacro National Office, 29 Albany Street, Edinburgh EH1 3QN; T.-0131 624 7270.

Beckett, Rev. David Mackay, BA, BD. Minister, Greyfriars Tolbooth and Highland Kirk, Edinburgh, 1983-2002; b. 22.3.37, Glasgow; m., Rosalie Frances Neal; 2 s. Educ. Glenalmond; Trinity Hall, Cambridge; St. Andrews University. Assistant Minister, Dundee Parish Church (St. Mary's), 1963-66; Minister, Clark Memorial Church, Largs, 1966-83; Moderator, Presbytery of Ardrossan, 1974. Convener, Committee on Public Worship and Aids to Devotion, General Assembly, 1978-82; President, Church Service Society, 1986-88; Secretary, General Assembly Panel on Doctrine, 1987-95; Moderator, Presbytery of Edinburgh, 1999-2000. Publication: The Lord's Supper, 1984. Address: (h.) 31 (1F1) Sciennes Road, Edinburgh EH9 1NT.

Beckett, Hon. Lord (John), QC. Senator of the College of Justice, since 2016; All-Scotland Floating Sheriff, since 2008; Solicitor General for Scotland, 2006-07. Educ. University of Edinburgh. Elected to the Faculty of Advocates, 1993; Advocate Depute and a Senior Advocate Depute, since 2003; Principal Advocate Depute, 2006. Address: (b.) Scottish Courts, Parliament Square, Edinburgh.

Bedford, Professor Tim, BSc (Hons), MSc, PhD. Associate Principal (Research and Innovation), University of Strathclyde, since 2016, Associate Deputy Principal (Knowledge Exchange and Research Enhancement), since 2010, Professor of Decision Making and Risk Analysis, since 2001; b. 14.4.60, London. Educ. Oulder Hill, Rochdale; Warwick University. Fellow, Kings College, Cambridge, 1984-87; Lecturer in Probability, Delft University of Technology, Netherlands, 1987-94; Senior Lecturer in Applications of Decision Theory, Delft University of Technology, 1994-2000. Hon Doctorate, Faculté Polytechnique de Mons, Belgium, 2008. Fellow of the Royal Society of Edinburgh. Publication: Probabilistic Risk Analysis: Foundations and Methods. Recreations: jazz music; gardening; family. Address: (b.) Department of Management Science, Sir William Duncan Building, 130 Rottenrow, Glasgow G4 0GE; T.-0141-548 2394.

Beedham, Dr. Christopher, BSc, PhD. Lecturer in German, St. Andrews University, 1984-2018 (now retired but still research active); b. 29.12.52, Cleethorpes; m., Barbara H. Chruscik; 2 d. Educ. Barton-upon-Humber Grammar School; Salford University; Leipzig University. Research Assistant in Applied Linguistics, University of Aston in Birmingham, 1979-81; Teaching Assistant, English Dept. of the Philological Faculty, Moscow State University, 1982-84. Publications: The Passive Aspect in English, German and Russian, 1982; German Linguistics: An Introduction, 1995; *Langue* and *Parole* in Synchronic and Diachronic Perspective (Editor), 1999; Language and Meaning, 2005; Rules and Exceptions (Co-Editor), 2014; Letter to Times Higher Education, 3.7.2014. Recreations: hill-walking; jogging; yoga; travel; music. Address: (b.) Dept. of German, School of Modern Languages, University of St. Andrews, St. Andrews, Fife KY16 9PH.
E-mail: c.beedham@st-andrews.ac.uk

Beevers, Professor Clifford, OBE, DSc, PhD, MILT. Professor Emeritus, Heriot Watt University, since 2005, Professor of Mathematics, 1993-2005; b. 4.9.44, Castleford; m., Elizabeth Ann; 2 d. Educ. Castleford Grammar School; Manchester University. Senior Lecturer, 1985; Director, CALM, 1985; Chairman of the e-Assessment Association, 2006-12, Vice Chairman, 2012-13; Past Chairman, Edinburgh Branch, British Retinitis Pigmentosa Society, 1977-97; Past Chairman of the Juniper Green Community Council, 2009-17; Chairman of Pentlands Book Festival, 2015-2021; Chairman of Pentlands Community Space, 2019-2021. Recreations: walking; reading; theatre. Address: School of Mathematical and Computer Sciences, Heriot Watt University, Riccarton, Edinburgh EH14 4AS; T.-0131-453 4115; e-mail: c.e.beevers@gmail.com

Begbie, Alexander (Sandy), CBE, MBA, FCIBS. Chief Executive Officer, Scottish Financial Enterprise, since 2020; b. 13.04.66, Edinburgh; m., Carolann; 2 d. Educ. Musselburgh Grammar School; Edinburgh University. Awarded the CBE for services to Business and Social Inclusion. Career: The Royal Bank of Scotland plc, 1983-2000; Scottish Power plc, 2000-2007; Director, Human Resources and Corporate Responsibility, Aegon, 2007-2010; Chief People Officer and Lead Executive for China, Standard Life plc, 2010-2017, Transformation Director, Standard Life plc, 2010-2012, Chief Operations Officer, 2012-2015; Chief Transformation Officer, Tesco Bank, 2019-20. Global Director of People, Organisation and Culture Integration, Standard Life Aberdeen, 2017-2018. Chairman, the Board of Career Ready for the UK; Chairman, Place2Be Scotland. Former Chair, Centre for Moving Imagine; former Non-Executive Director, Scottish Government; former Chairman of the Scottish Government Remuneration Group; former Non-Executive Advisory, Wharton Executive Board, Philadelphia, USA; former Non-Executive Director with KPMG; Chair for Scotland of Career Ready, 2014-2019; Chairman, the Regional Invest in Youth Board, Edinburgh and the Lothians; Non-Executive Director to the Open University, 2016-2020. Recreations: reading; running; travelling.
E-mail: sandybegbie@icloud.com

Begg, Dame Anne, DBE, MA. MP (Labour), Aberdeen South, 1997-2015; b. 6.12.55, Forfar. Educ. Brechin High School; University of Aberdeen; Aberdeen College of Education. Teacher of English and History, Webster's High, Kirriemuir, 1978-88; Assistant Principal Teacher, then Principal Teacher of English, Arbroath Academy, 1988-97. Disabled Scot of the Year, 1988. Chair, Work and Pensions Select Committee, 2010-15. Recreations: cinema; theatre; reading.

Begg, Professor Hugh MacKemmie, MA, MA, PhD, DipTP, FRTPI. Consultant Economist and Chartered Planner; Visiting Professor, University of Abertay, Dundee; Associate, Cambridge Economic Associates; b. 25.10.41, Glasgow; m., Jane Elizabeth Harrison; 2 d. Educ. High School of Glasgow; St. Andrews University; University of British Columbia; Dundee University. Lecturer in Political Economy, St. Andrews University; Research Fellow, Tayside Study; Lecturer in Economics, Dundee University; Assistant Director of Planning, Tayside Regional Council; Visiting Professor, Technical University of Nova Scotia; Consultant, UN Regional Development Project, Egypt and Saudi Arabia; Consultant, Scottish Office Industry Department, Scottish Office Agriculture and Forestry Department; Head, School of Town and Regional Planning, Dundee University; Dean of Faculty of Environmental Studies, Dundee University. External Adjudicator, Scottish Enterprise; Convener, The Standards Commission for Scotland; Member, Private Legislation Procedure (Scotland) Extra-Parliamentary Panel; Member, Local Government Boundary Commission for Scotland; Honorary Professor of Economics, University of Abertay Dundee; Reporter, Directorate for Environmental and Planning Appeals; Assessor for Private and Hybrid Bills, Scottish Parliament; Honorary Fellow, Patrick Geddes Institute, Dundee University. Recreations: Scottish history; hill walking; watching rugby; puppy walking for guide dogs for the blind. Address: (h.) 4 The Esplanade, Broughty Ferry, Dundee; T.-01382 779642.
E-mail: hughbegg@blueyonder.co.uk

Begg, William Kirkwood, OBE. Retired former Chairman and Managing Director, Begg, Cousland Holdings Ltd.; former Chairman, Begg Cousland & Co. Ltd.; b. 5.2.34; m., Thia St Clair; 2 s.; 1 d. Educ. Glenalmond College. Former Chairman, Scottish Advisory Committee on Telecommunications; former Member, CBI SME Council; former Privy Council Nominee to General Convocation, Strathclyde University; former Director, Weavers' Society of Anderston; Founder Trustee, Dallas Benevolent Fund; former Chairman of Trustees, James Paterson Trust; former Director (and former Vice Chairman), The Wise Group; former Director, Commercially Wise Ltd.; former Director, Merchants' House of Glasgow; former Member, Scottish Industrial Development Advisory Board; former Member, CBI Council for Scotland; former Convener of Trustees, the George Craig Trust Fund. Recreations: sailing; shooting; DIY. Address: (h.) 58A Cleveden Drive, Glasgow G12 0NX.

Beggs, Professor Jean Duthie, CBE, PhD, BSc, FRS, FRSE, Hon DSc (St Andrews). Emeritus Professor of Molecular Biology, Edinburgh University, since 2019 (appointed Professor in 1999); Royal Society Darwin Trust Research Professor, 2005-2016; b. 16.4.50, Glasgow; m., Dr Ian Beggs; 2s. Educ. Glasgow High School for Girls; Glasgow University. Post-doctoral Fellow, University of Edinburgh, 1974-77; Post-doctoral Fellow, ARC Plant Breeding Institute, Cambridge, 1977-79; Lecturer, Department of Biochemistry, Imperial College of Science and Technology, London, 1979-85; Royal Society University Research Fellow, Edinburgh University, 1985-89; Royal Society Cephalosporin Fund Senior Research Fellow, University of Edinburgh. 1989-99; Edinburgh University Professorial Research Fellow, 1994-99; Beit Memorial Fellowship, 1976-79; Elected Member, EMBO, 1991; Member, Council and various committees of Royal Society (London and Edinburgh), Biochemical Society, RNA Society; Royal Society Gabor Medal, 2003; Biochemical Society Novartis Medal, 2004; University of Edinburgh Chancellor's Award, 2005; Vice President, Royal Society of Edinburgh, 2009-2012. Recreations: walking; dogs; pilates. Address: (b.) Institute of Cell Biology, Wellcome Trust Centre for Cell Biology, Edinburgh University, King's Buildings, Max Born Crescent, Edinburgh, EH9 3BF; T.-0131-650 5351.

Belch, Professor Jill J. F., MD (Hons), FRCP, FMEdSci, FRSE, OBE. Professor of Vascular Medicine, University of Dundee; b. 22.10.52, Glasgow. Educ. Morrison's Academy, Crieff; University of Glasgow. University of Glasgow and Royal Infirmary: Research Fellow, 1980, Lecturer, 1984; University of Dundee and Ninewells Hospital: Senior Lecturer, 1987, Reader, 1990, Professor, 1996, Director of Research, 2012, Dean of Research, 2014-15; Co-Dean, Medical School, 2015; NHS Tayside R&D Director, 2009-2015. Council member, Royal Society of Edinburgh, 2016-20; President, Section of Vascular Medicine, Royal Society of Medicine, 2014-2018; President, European Society of Vascular Medicine, since 2018. Chair, short term charity, Masks for Scotland, 2020-21. Saltire Outstanding Woman of Scotland, 2019; Evening Times Scotswoman of the Year, 2021; The Sun Covid Hero, 2021. Publications: over 400 peer-reviewed articles in scientific journals. Recreations: family; skiing. Address: (b.) Division of Molecular and Clinical Medicine, Medical Research Institute, Ninewells Hospital and Medical School, Dundee DD1 9SY; T.-01382 383092.

Belhaven and Stenton, 14th Lord (Frederick Carmichael Arthur Hamilton); b. 1954. Succeeded to title, 2020.

Bell, Christopher Philip, BMus, MMus. Conductor/Chorusmaster; Chorus Director; b. 1.5.61, Belfast. Educ. Royal Belfast Academical Inst.; Edinburgh University. Chorus Master/Director: Edinburgh University Musical Society Choir, 1984-88, Edinburgh Royal Choral Union, 1987-90, Royal Scottish National Orchestra Chorus, 1989-2004, Royal Scottish National Orchestra Junior Chorus, since 1995, Belfast Philharmonic Choir, 2005-2011. Chorus Director, Grant Park Chorus, Chicago, USA, since 2002; Artistic Director: Total Aberdeen Youth Choir, 1992-96, National Youth Choir of Scotland, since 1996, Ulster Youth Choir, 1999-2003, Children's Classic Concerts, 2002-08. Associate Conductor, BBC Scottish Symphony Orchestra, 1987-89; Principal Guest Conductor, State Orchestra of Victoria, Melbourne, 1997-99; Associate Conductor, Ulster Orchestra, since 2009. Guest conductor with various orchestras and choirs annually. Publications: Author, My Voice is Changing; Co-Author: Go for Bronze; Go for Silver, Go for Gold; General Editor, SingBronze, Sing Silver, SingGold. Recordings: Mahler *Symphony no 3*, Chandos; Paray *Joan of Arc Mass*, Reference. Grammy Nomination 1999; Britten Ceremony of Carols (Signum); The Pulitzer Project (Cedille); *Burns Sequence: There's Lilt in the Song*, NYCoS; Holst *The Planets, Naxos;* A Family Christmas (Signum). Scotsman of the Year - Creative Talent, 2001; Charles Groves Prize, 2003. Master of the University (Open Univ, hon) 2009. Address: 2F1/143 Warrender Park Road, Edinburgh EH9 1DT; T.-07712 050295; e-mail: bellman@ednet.co.uk

Bell, Malcolm John. Honorary Sheriff, Sheriffdom of Grampian, Highlands and Islands at Lerwick, since 2010; b. 10.01.64, Lerwick; m. Moira Simpson; 2 s. Educ. Anderson High School, Lerwick; The Open University; University of Edinburgh; Scottish Police College. Convener, Shetland Islands Council, 2012-2022; Councillor for Lerwick North and Bressay (Independent), 2012-2022; President, Scottish Provosts Association, 2017-2022; Non-Executive Director and Vice-Chair, NHS Shetland, 2010-2022; General Manager, COPE Ltd, Shetland, 2010-12; Police Officer in Northern Constabulary, 1980-2009; Chief Inspector and Area Commander Shetland, 2006; Deputy Divisional Commander, Northern Constabulary, 2008; Member, Amnesty International. Recreations: reading; photography; travel; cooking. Address: (b.) Town Hall, Lerwick, Shetland ZE1 0HB; T.-07777 607741.
E-mail: mj.bell@btopenworld.com
Twitter: @malcolm_bell

Bell, Patrick Ian, BA (Hons). Partner, Shepherd and Wedderburn LLP, since 2007; b. 22.3.67, Edinburgh; m., Karen Jane (nee White); 2 s.; 1 d. Educ. The Edinburgh Academy; Trinity College, Glenalmond; St. Chad's College, University of Durham; Guildford Law College. Linklaters & Paines, London: Trainee Solicitor, 1991-93, Assistant Solicitor, 1993-95; Assistant Solicitor, Linklaters & Paines, Singapore, 1995-98; Managing Associate, Linklaters & Alliance, London, 1998-2001; Partner: Linklaters, Warsaw, 2001-05, McClure Naismith, Solicitors, 2005-07. Finance Law Specialist with wide banking, project finance and capital markets experience; Member: Law Society of England and Wales (1996), Court of Directors, The Edinburgh Academy (2006-2012), Salmon & Trout Association (Scotland) (1993), New Club (2006), Wooden Spoon Society (2007), Pilotlighter (2018). Recreations: fishing; tennis; skiing; history. Address: (b.) 1 Exchange Crescent, Conference Square, Edinburgh EH3 8UL; T.-0131 473 5355.
E-mail: patrick.bell@shepwedd.com

Bell, Robin, MA, MSc. Writer, Broadcaster and Artist; b. 4.1.45, Dundee; m. (1), Suzette Von Feldau (divorced 1996) (2), Eirwen Bengough (deceased 2014); 2 d.; 5 gc. Educ. Morrison's Academy, Crieff; St. Andrews University; Perugia University, Italy; Union College, New York; Columbia University, New York. Formerly: Director of Information, City University of New York, Regional Opportunity Program; Assistant Professor, John Jay College of Criminal Justice, City University of New York; Member,

US Office of Education Task Force in Educational Technology; Audio-Visual Editor, Oxford University Press; Editor, Guidebook series to Ancient Monuments of Scotland; Secretary, Poetry Association of Scotland. Television and Radio Industries of Scotland Award for Best Radio Feature, 1984; Sony Award, Best British Radio Documentary, 1985; Creative Scotland Award, 2005; Scottish Heritage Angel Awards, 2016; Chairman, Strathearn Heritage Trust; Founder, Robin and Eirwen Bell Trust. Publications: The Invisible Mirror, 1965; Culdee, Culdee, 1966; Collected Poems of James Graham, Marquis of Montrose (Editor), 1970; Sawing Logs, 1980; Strathinver: A Portrait Album 1945-53, 1984; Radio Poems, 1989; The Best of Scottish Poetry (Editor), 1989; Bittersweet Within My Heart: collected poems of Mary Queen of Scots (Translator/Editor), 1992; Scanning the Forth Bridge, 1994; Le Château des Enfants, 2000; Chapeau!, 2001; Civil Warrior, 2002; Tethering a Horse, 2004; How To Tell Lies, 2006; Auchterarder, Strathearn's Royal Burgh, 2008; Behind You, 2011; Ruchill Linn (with music by Gabriel Jackson), 2012; Set On A Hill: A Strategic View Over Scottish History, 2012; The Architecture of Human Needs, 2021; Art exhibitions: My River, Your River (following the 2005 Gleneagles G8); Drawing The Tay (Travelling solo exhibition); Strathearn: A Celebration (permanent heritage exhibition at Gleneagles Station), 2015. Address: (h.) The Orchard, Muirton, Auchterarder PH3 1ND.

Bell, Tom, MSc, FREHIS, MIFEH. Secretary, The Royal Environmental Health Institute of Scotland (REHIS), 2020 (retired); Chief Executive, REHIS, 2004-2020; b. 15.9.58, Edinburgh; m. Angela, 2 d. Educ. Leith Academy, Edinburgh; Napier College, Edinburgh; The University of Edinburgh. Qualified as an Environmental Health Officer, 1980; Corporate Membership of REHIS gained, 1983; gained MSc in Environmental Health, University of Edinburgh, 1993; Training Adviser to REHIS, 1998; Director of Professional Development to REHIS, 1999; Chartered Environmental Health Officer 2004-2020. Elected Fellow of REHIS, 2008. Honorary Fellow, The University of Edinburgh, 1994-98; Elected Honorary Member, Malawi Environmental Health Association, 2010; Member of the International Federation of Environmental Health, 2013-2020; Elected Honorary Member, Environmental Health Association of Ireland, 2015; Director, Specialist in Land Contamination Register Limited, 2011-2018; Elected Honorary Member of REHIS, 2020; Elected Member of The Council, REHIS, 1994-98; Elected Hon. Treasurer, REHIS, 1995-98. Recreations: Hibernian FC; travel; family life; learner gardener, beekeeper and mole catcher. E-mail: MontyTom2021@gmail.com

Belton, Professor Valerie, PhD, MA, BSc (Hons). Emeritus Professor of Management Science, University of Strathclyde (appointed Professor in 1999), former Associate Deputy Principal (Education); President, EURO (European Federation of Operational Research Societies), 2009-2010; President, UK Operational Research Society, 2004-06; b. 9.8.56, Rotherham. Educ. Wath upon Dearne School; Durham University; Lancaster University, Cambridge University. Operational Research Analyst, Civil Aviation Authority; Academic, University of Kent, 1984-88; Academic, University of Strathclyde, since 1988. Chair, International Society of Multicriteria Decision Making, 2000-04; Editor, Journal of Multicriteria Decision Analysis; author of a book and many academic articles. Recreations: orienteering; mountain biking. Address: (b.) University of Strathclyde, Management Science, 40 George Street, Glasgow G1 1QE; T.-0141-548 3615; e-mail: val.belton@strath.ac.uk

Benedetti, Nicola, MBE, CBE. Scottish classical violinist; Director, Edinburgh International Festival, from October 2022; b. 20.7.87, West Kilbride. Educ. Wellington School,

Ayr; Yehudi Menuhin School, Surrey. Started learning to play the violin at the age of four; became the leader of the National Children's Orchestra of Great Britain at age eight. Won the BBC Young Musician of the Year competition in May 2004, performing Karol Szymanowski's First Violin Concerto in the final at the Usher Hall in Edinburgh, with the BBC Scottish Symphony Orchestra. Awarded honorary doctorate from Glasgow Caledonian University in November 2007, and Heriot-Watt University in 2010; honorary degree from the University of Edinburgh in November 2011. Presented with the Queen's Medal for Music in 2017, the youngest of the twelve people to receive the award since it was established in 2005. Founder of the Benedetti Foundation in January 2020. Won the GRAMMY for best classical instrumental solo for Marsalis: Violin Concerto; Fiddle Dance Suite, 2020.

Bennett, David, MA (Econ). Chairman, Virgin Money UK, since 2020; b. 3.62. Educ. King's College School, Wimbledon; University of Cambridge; Harvard Business School. Career history: Alliance & Leicester: Group Treasurer, 1999-2001, Group Finance Director, 2001-07, Chief Executive, 2007-08; Executive Director, Abbey Plc, 2008-09; Non-Executive Director, Clarity Commerce Solutions Ltd, 2010-2011; Chairman of Audit & Risk Committee and Non-Executive Director, CMC Markets, 2010-2012; Chairman, Financial Services Knowledge Transfer Network, 2010-2014; Chairman of Audit Committee and Finance Committe, Non-Executive Director, easyJet plc, 2005-2014; Chairman of Remuneration Committee and Non-Executive Director, Pacnet Ltd, 2009-2014; Non-Executive Director, Bank of Ireland UK Ltd, 2013-15; Chairman, Homeserve Membership Ltd, 2012-17; Chairman Retail, Together - loans, mortgages and finance, 2010-19; Non-Executive Director and Chairman of Audit and Risk Committee, Paypal (Europe) S.a.r.l et Cie, S.C.A., since 2014; Non Executive Director, Department for Work and Pensions (DWP), since 2021; Chairman, Ashmore plc, since 2014; joined Virgin Money UK in 2015. Address: Virgin Money UK, UK Governance, 30 St. Vincent Place, Glasgow G1 2HL.

Bennett, Professor Mark, BA, PhD, AcSS. Emeritus Professor of Developmental Psychology, University of Dundee; b. 12.10.56, Bangkok, Thailand; m., Ann Warren; 1 s. Educ. Farnborough Grammar School; University of Reading; LSE. Lecturer: University of Durham, 1982-85, Roehampton Institute, London, 1985-91, University of Dundee, since 1991, also Reader, then Professor since 2004. Editor of the journal Infant & Child Development, 2001-2010; elected to the Academy of Social Sciences, 2006. Major Publications: The Child as Psychologist, 1993; Developmental Psychology: Achievements & Prospects, 1999; The Development of the Social Self (Co-Author), 2004. Recreations: hill-walking; cycling; music; Qigong. Address: School of Psychology, University of Dundee, Dundee DD1 4HN; T.-01382 384631. E-mail: m.bennett@dundee.ac.uk

Bennett, Robin Alexander George, MA, LLB. Retired solicitor; b. 6.6.40, Edinburgh; m., Mary Funk; 2 d. Educ. Hillhead High School, Glasgow; Glasgow University. Assistant, Harrisons and Crosfield, Malaysia and Brunei, 1965-78; Solicitor, Drummond Johnstone and Grosset, Cupar, 1978-80; Partner: Drummond Cook and Mackintosh, Cupar, 1980-90, Wallace and Bennett, 1990-92, Bennetts, Cupar, 1992-2010. Consultant with Murray Donald Drummond Cook LLP, 2010-11. Member of the Executive, then Director, Scottish Legal Action Group, 1980-2011 (Vice Chair, 1989-95); Chairman, Ceres and District Community Council, 1980-82 and 1993-98; Founder/Secretary, Scottish TSB Depositors Association,

1986; Chairman, Tranquilliser Addiction Solicitors Group, 1988-90; Honorary Sheriff, Cupar, 1991-2014; Trustee, The Lady Margaret Skiffington Trust, 2004-2015 (Chair, 2004-2013); Elder, Ceres, Kemback & Springfield Parish Church, since 2006. Recreations: water gardening; listening to organ music. Address: (h.) Sandakan, Curling Pond Road, Ceres, Fife KY15 5NB; T.-01334 828452.
E-mail: ragbennett@yahoo.com

Bennison, Dr Jennifer Marion, MA, MSc, MBBChir, FRCGP. General Practitioner, Niddrie Medical Practice, Edinburgh, since 2015; Executive Officer (Quality), Scottish Council, Royal College of General Practitioners, 2012-14; Vice Chair, Scottish Intercollegiate Guideline Network, 2014-2020; b. Essex; divorced; 2 s.; 2 d. Educ. Hertfordshire and Essex High School for Girls; Corpus Christi College, Cambridge; Royal Free Hospital School of Medicine, London. GP Principal, Leith Walk Surgery, Edinburgh, 1993-98; GP Partner, Rose Garden Medical Centre, Edinburgh, 1998-2015; Director, Phased Evaluation Programme, RCGP Scotland, 1999-2002; Assistant Director of Postgraduate General Practice Education, South East Scotland, 2006-2014; Deputy Chairman (Policy), Scottish Council, Royal College of General Practitioners. Recreations: children; walking; singing. Address: (b.) Rose Garden Medical Centre, 4 Mill Lane, Leith, Edinburgh EH6 6TL; T.-0131-554 1274; e-mail: Jenny.Bennison@nhslothian.scot.nhs.uk

Bentley, Professor Michael, BA, PhD, FRHistS. Emeritus Professor of Modern History, St Andrews University; b. 12.8.48, Rotherham; 1 s.; 1 d. Educ. Oakwood School, Rotherham; Sheffield University; St John's College, Cambridge. Lecturer, Senior Lecturer and Reader in History, Sheffield University, 1971-95. Publications: The Liberal Mind; Politics without Democracy; Climax of Liberal Politics; Companion to Historiography; Modern Historiography; Lord Salisbury's World; Modernizing England's Past; The Life and Thought of Herbert Butterfield. Recreations: reading; piano. Address: (b.) Christ Church, Oxford OX1 1DP; T.-01865 286077.
E-mail: michael.bentley@history.ox.ac.uk

Berk, Very Rev'd Dr Dennis. Dean of the Diocese of Aberdeen & Orkney, since 2020; Rector of St James the Less in Cruden Bay and St Mary-on-the-Rock in Ellon, since 2018; b. USA. Educ. Wheaton College. Career history: moved to Canada where he took a degree in theology from Trinity College in Toronto; Ordained in the Anglican Church of Canada in 1990; served his curacy in the Diocese of Ontario; returned to the United States and engaged in parish ministry in Pennsylvania whilst pursuing a doctorate at Lancaster Theological Seminary; selected by the Episcopal Church in the USA for a three-year missionary appointment in Zambia, Africa in 2003; came to the UK to join the Community of the Resurrection, an Anglican monastic community in West Yorkshire in 2009; drawn to their life of prayer, he resided in their monastery from 2009 until 2018. Naturalised as a British citizen in 2016, and holds dual nationality. Address: Ellon - St Mary's Church, 1 South Road, Ellon AB41 9NP; T.-01358 720366.
E-mail: rector@stmarystjames.org.uk

Berry, Professor Christopher Jon, BA, PhD, FRSE. Honorary Professorial Research Fellow, (Emeritus Professor [Political Theory]), Glasgow University; b. 19.6.46, St. Helens; m., Christine; 2 s. Educ. Upholland Grammar School; Nottingham and LSE. Lecturer, then Senior Lecturer, then Reader, then Professor, Department of Politics, University of Glasgow. Author of 9 books and over 50 other academic publications. Recreation:

contemporary literature. Address: (b.) Adam Smith Building, The University, Glasgow G12 8RT; T.-0141 330 5064; e-mail: christopher.berry@glasgow.ac.uk

Berry, David S., BSc (Hons) Phys (Edin). Leader, East Lothian Council, 2007-2010; b. 13.4.48, London. Educ. North Berwick High; University of Edinburgh. Honeywell Information Systems, London, 1971-73; Siemens AG, Munich, Germany, 1973-77; Applied Computer Systems, Sunnyvale, California, 1977-82; Product Planning Manager, AMD, Sunnyvale, California, 1982-88; Marketing Manager, Adaptec, Milpitas, California, 1988-93; Loch Moy Ltd., Database Consultancy, Edinburgh, since 1993; Proprietor, GoForth Tours, since March 2013. Elected Member, East Lothian Council, since 1999. Board Member, SEPA, 2002-09; Convener, Association of Nationalist Councillors, 2005-2010; Member, National Executive, SNP, 2006-2013 (resigned from SNP, March 2013). Nominated Herald Local Politician of the Year, 2010. Recreations: film; history; marine watersports.

Berry, William, MA, LLB, DL, WS. Formerly Senior Governor and Chancellor's Assessor, St. Andrews University; Partner and Chairman, Murray Beith Murray, WS, Edinburgh, 1967-2004; formerly Chairman: Scottish Life Assurance Co., Inchcape Family Investments Ltd; Director: Scottish American Investment Co. Plc, Fleming Continental European Investment Trust Plc, Alliance Trust plc, Second Alliance Trust plc, Dawnfresh Holdings Ltd, and other companies; b. 26.9.39, Newport-on-Tay; m., Elizabeth Margery Warner; 2 s. Educ. Ardvreck, Crieff; Eton College; St. Andrews University; Edinburgh University. Interests in farming, forestry, etc. Depute Chairman, Edinburgh Festival Society, 1985-89; Deputy Lieutenant, Fife, 2007-2014; formerly Chairman, New Town Concerts Society Ltd; Trustee/Board Member of many charities and cultural bodies. Performer in three records of Scottish country dance music. Recreations: music; shooting; forestry; conservation. Address: Newhouse of Tayfield, Kilnburn, Newport-on-Tay, Fife DD6 8DE.

Bevan, Mark. Chief Executive, Leuchie House, since October 2018; Chief Executive Officer, Scottish Council for Development and Industry, 2017-18. Educ. Altrincham Boys. Career history: Specialist Residential Care Officer, Aberlour Childcare Trust, 1992-95; Youth Strategy, City of Edinburgh Council, 1995-2000; Capability Scotland: Business Development Manager, 2000-08, Head of Children's Services, 2008-2011; The Scottish Government: National Review Member - Strategic Review of Services for Disabled Children, 2010-2011, Chair - Sub group, 2011, National Review Member - Doran Review of Learning Provision for Children with ASN, 2010-12, Group Member - National Implementation Group - Self Directed Support, 2012; Director of Services, Capability Scotland, 2011-12; General Secretary, Secretariat to the Scottish Parliament Cross Party Group on Human Rights, 2013; Programme Director, Amnesty International, 2013; Advisor, Advisory Council to the Scottish Human Rights Commission, 2013-14; Director (Operations, Campaigns & Advocacy), Keep Scotland Beautiful, 2013-15; Chair, Business engagement, Clean Europe Network, 2014-15; Director: Scottish Centre for Children with Motor Impairement, 2010-2015, Children in Scotland, 2015-16; Secretary, West Bay Moorings Association, 2013-16; Advisor, R S McDonald Charitable Trust, 2014-16; Business in the Community Scotland: Operations Director and Deputy Chief Executive, 2015-17, Scotland Director - HRH The Prince Charles' Responsible Business Network, since 2017. Address: (b.) Leuchie House, North Berwick, East Lothian EH39 5NT; T.-01620 892864.

Beveridge, Stuart Gordon Nicholas, LLB (Hons), DipLP, NP. Partner, Grant Smith Law Practice, since 2001; b. 19.3.68, Edinburgh. Educ. George Heriot's School; Daniel Stewart's and Melville College; Edinburgh University.

Traineeship, Campbell Smith and Co., Solicitors, Edinburgh; Legal Adviser, Citizen's Advice Bureau, Edinburgh; Oddbins Wine Merchants; Aberdein Considine and Co., Aberdeen (Partner, 1998-2001). President, Aberdeen Bar Association, 2001-02 (Committee Member, 1995-2003). Recreations: wine; cooking; chicken wrangling; failing to finish DIY projects. Address: (b.) Amicable House, 252 Union Street, Aberdeen AB10 1TN; T.-01224 621620.

Bewsher, Colonel Harold Frederick, LVO, OBE. Vice-President, The Atlantic Salmon Trust (Chairman, 1995-2005); Chairman, Scottish Venison Partnership, since 2016; Vice Chairman, Association of Deer Management Groups in Scotland, 2001-2012 (Member, Executive Committee, since 1998); Chairman, The Airborne Initiative (Scotland) Ltd., 1995-98; Lieutenant, The Queen's Bodyguard for Scotland (Royal Company of Archers) (Secretary, 1982-94); Captain of Shooting, 2003/06/09, Queen's Prize Winner, 2001, 2006; b. 13.1.29, Glasgow; m., Susan Elizabeth Cruickshank; 2 s. Educ. Merchiston Castle School; Royal Technical College; Glasgow University; Royal Military Academy, Sandhurst. The Royal Scots, 1949-72; Operational Service in Korea, Port Said and Suez, South Arabia, Radfam and Aden, Staff College, 1961, Joint Services Staff College, 1966; DS Staff College, 1967-69, CO Scottish Infantry Training Regiment, 1969-71; Colonel GS Military Operations, MOD, 1971-72. Director-General, Scotch Whisky Association, 1973-94. Chairman, New Club, Edinburgh, 1981-82; Chairman, Scottish Society for the Employment of Ex-Regular Soldiers, Sailors and Airmen, 1973-83; Freeman, City of London, 1992; Liveryman, Worshipful Company of Distillers, 1993. Rugby Football: Rhine Army XV, 1952/53, London Scottish XV, 1955/56; Cricket: Rhine Army XI, 1953/59/60, Army XI, 1962. Clubs: Free Foresters, I Zingari. Recreations: outdoors — salmon fishing, field sports, deer stalking. Address: 33 Blacket Place, Edinburgh EH9 1RJ; T.-0131-667 4600.

Bezuidenhout, Willem Jacobus, BA, BD, NHED, MEd. Minister, St Oran's Connel, Dunbeg & Coll Church of Scotland, since 2019; formerly Minister, Parish of Barlanark-Greyfriars, Glasgow; b. 14.8.53, Johannesburg, South Africa; m., Hazel; 1 s.; 1 d. Educ. Hartswater High School, South Africa; Pretoria University; Johannesburg University. Ordination as Minister, Dutch Reformed Church, 1977; Senior Liaison Officer, Foreign Office, Namibia, 1989-90; Senior Liaison Officer, State President's Office, Cape Town, South Africa, 1990-92; English Teacher, Vorentoe High School, Johannesburg, 1992-2000; Minister, St Andrews Presbyterian Church, Pretoria, 2000-07. University of Pretoria: Dux Awards: 1976, 1977; University of Johannesburg, 1994: Gold Medal; South African Education Association: Top Student, RSA. Recreations: photography; hiking; volleyball; music; film. Address: St Oran's Manse Church of Scotland, Connel, Oban PA37 1PJ; e-mail: macwillem@btinternet.com

Bhopal, Professor Raj Singh, CBE, DSc (hon), BSc, MBChB, MD, MPH, FFPH, FRCP (Edin). Emeritus Professor of Public Health, since 2018; Bruce and John Usher Chair of Public Health, University of Edinburgh, 1999-2018 (Head, Division of Community Health Sciences, 2000-03); Honorary Consultant in Public Health Medicine, Lothian Health Board, 1999-2018; b. 10.4.53, Moga, Punjab, India; m., Roma; 4 s. Educ. University of Edinburgh; University of Glasgow. House Officer/Senior House Officer, medicine and surgery, 1978-82; Trainee GP, 1980; Registrar/Senior Registrar/Lecturer in Public Health Medicine, 1983-88; Senior Lecturer/Honorary Consultant in Public Health Medicine, 1988-91; Professor of Epidemiology and Public Health, University of Newcastle upon Tyne, 1991-99 (Head, Department of Epidemiology and Public Health); Non-Executive Director (Vice-Chairman), Newcastle and North Tyneside Health Authority, 1992-96; Non-Executive Director, Health Education Authority, 1996-99; Chairman, Steering Committee, National Resource Centre on Ethnic Minority Health, 2002-08; Member, MRC Health Services Research and Public Health Board, 1999-2003; Chairman, Executive Committee of the World Congress of Epidemiology 2011; Chairman, Executive Committee of the First World Congress on Migration, Ethnicity, Race and Health 2018; Member, Expert Reference Group on Covid-19 and Ethnicity, Scottish Government, since 2020. Publications: Books: Concepts of Epidemiology, 2002, 2008, 2016 (3rd edition); Public Health, Past, Present and Future, 2004; The Epidemic of Coronary Heart Disease in South Asians, 2003; Ethnicity, race and health in multicultural societies, 2007 (second edition in 2014 as Migration, Ethnicity, Race and Health); Epidemic of Cardiovascular Disease and Diabetes: Explaining the Phenomenon in South Asians Worldwide, 2018; about 300 papers in academic journals and chapters in books on Legionnaires' disease, environmental epidemiology, primary care, ethnicity and health, Covid-19 pandemic, and application of epidemiology in public health and health care. Recreations: chess; golf; hill climbing; photography; travel; music; reading. Address: (b.) Usher Institute, University of Edinburgh, College of Medicine and Veterinary Medicine, Teviot Place, Edinburgh EH8 9AG; T.-0131-283 4108; e-mail: raj.bhopal@ed.ac.uk

Bibby, Neil. MSP (Labour), West Scotland (Region), since 2011; Shadow Cabinet Secretary for Transport, since 2021; Chief Whip, 2014-16; b. 6.9.83, Paisley. Educ. Glasgow University. Became a local councillor in Renfrewshire in 2007. Former chair of Young Labour UK. Address: Scottish Parliament, Edinburgh EH99 1SP.

Bibby, Vicki. Chief Operating Officer, Audit Scotland, since 2022. Educ. University of Aberdeen; University of Glasgow. Career history: COSLA: Chief Officer Finance, 2007-2018, Head of Resources, 2018-2020; Director of Strategic Planning and Performance, Public Health Scotland, 2020-2022. Address: Audit Scotland, Head office, 4th Floor, 102 West Port, Edinburgh EH3 9DN; T.-0131 625 1500.

Biberbach, Petra Elke, MSc, FRSA. CEO, PAS (Planning Aid Scotland), since 2005; Vice Chair, Link Group, since 2017; b. Germany, Nuremburg; 1 s.; 1 d. Educ. Glasgow University. Panel Member, Review of Planning in Scotland, 2015-16; Member of the independent review of the Planning system to inform changes to the forthcoming Planning Bill. Recreations: golf coach level 1; gardening; cycling; choir. Address: (b.) 3rd Floor, 125 Princes Street, Edinburgh EH2 4AD; T.-07812 103967. E-mail: petra@pas.org.uk

Biddulph, 5th Lord (Anthony Nicholas Colin). Interior Designer and Sporting Manager; b. 8.4.59; m., Hon. Sian Gibson-Watt (divorced); 2 s. Educ. Cheltenham; RAC, Cirencester. Recreations: shooting; design; fishing; skiing; racing; painting. Address: Address: (h.) Makerstoun, Kelso TD5 7PA; T.-01573 460 234. E-mail: nickbiddulph@makerstoun.com

Bingham, James Alexander, KStJ, FSAScot. Retired Civil Servant; Director, St John Scotland; Director of Ceremonies, the Most Venerable Order of the Hospital of St John of Jerusalem in Scotland, 2016-2021; b. 22.5.54, Airthrey Castle. Commander, the Military and Hospitaller Order of St Lazarus of Jerusalem in Scotland. Baron-Marshal of Miltonhaven, Sei-i Tai Shogun, Order of the

Scottish Samurai. Companion, the Sovereign Military Order of Malta. Member, the Sacra Militia Foundation of Malta. Deacon, Govan Weavers Society, 2014. Member of the Incorporation of Tailors in Glasgow; Burgess, Guild Brother and Freeman of the City of Glasgow. Member, Heraldry Society of Scotland, and Heraldry Society (England). Author: A Handbook for Directors of Ceremonies and Ceremonial Officers of the Priory of Scotland; Stall Plates of the Knights and Dames of the Priory of Scotland of the Order of St John, 2020. Recreations: heraldry; local history; book collecting; ceremonial; reading; walking; classical music. Address: 43 Anderson Crescent, Queenzieburn, Kilsyth G65 9EW; T.-01236 824903; e-mail: jabingham@talktalk.net

Bird, Professor Colin C., CBE, Drhc (Edin), MBChB, PhD, FRCPath, FRCPE, FRCSE, FRSE, FAMS, Knight's Cross, Order of Merit (Poland) 2006. Dean, Faculty of Medicine, Edinburgh University, 1995-2002; b. 5.3.38, Kirkintilloch; m., Ailsa M. Ross; 2 s.; 1 d. Educ. Lenzie Academy; Glasgow University. McGhie Cancer Research Scholar, Glasgow Royal Infirmary, 1962-64; Lecturer in Pathology: Glasgow University, 1964-67, Aberdeen University, 1967-72; MRC Goldsmiths Travelling Fellow, Chicago, 1970-71; Senior Lecturer in Pathology, Edinburgh University, 1972-75; Professor and Head, Department of Pathology, Leeds University, 1975-86; Professor of Pathology and Head, Department of Pathology, Edinburgh University, 1986-95. Recreations: golf; hill walking; music.

Bird, Jackie, DLitt. Journalist; former Presenter, Reporting Scotland (1989-2019); b. 31.7.62, Bellshill; 1 s.; 1 d. Educ. Earnock High School. Music/Film/Television Editor, Jackie Magazine; Radio News Reporter and Presenter, Radio Clyde; Reporter, Evening Times; Reporter, Sun; Reporter/Presenter, TVS; Presenter: BBC Scotland's Hogmanay Live and Children in Need programmes.

Bird, Stephen, MBA. Chief Executive Officer, abrdn plc (formerly Standard Life Aberdeen), since 2020; b. 2.67. Educ. Cardiff University. Management postion at British Steel; Director of UK Operations, GE Capital, 1996-98; joined Citigroup in 1998; held a number of leadership roles in banking, operations and technology across its Asian and Latin American businesses; former Chief Executive for all of Citigroup's Asia Pacific business lines across 17 markets in the region, including India and China; Chief Executive Officer, Global Consumer Banking, Citigroup, 2015-19 (responsibilities encompassed all consumer and commercial banking businesses in 19 countries, including retail banking and wealth management, credit cards, mortgages, and operations and technology supporting these businesses. Honorary Fellow, University College Cardiff. Address: abrdn plc, 1 George Street, Edinburgh EH2 2LL; T.-0131 225 2552; e-mail: stephen.bird@abrdn.com

Birley, Tim(othy) Grahame, BSc(Eng), MSc, ACGI, FRTPI, FRSA. Independent adviser on sustainable development and public policy, since 1995; b. 13.3.47, Kent; m., Catherine Anne; 1 s.; 2 d. Educ. Sir Roger Manwood's Grammar School; Imperial College, London University; Edinburgh University. Local government, 1965-71; academic appointments, 1973-81; Director, Energy and Environment Research, 1982-85; Scottish Office: Inquiry Reporter, 1985-87, Principal Inquiry Reporter, 1987-88, Deputy Director, Scottish Development Department, 1988-90, Head, Rural Affairs Division, 1990-95, pioneered a joined-up approach to rural policy (Rural Framework) and inter-agency working (Rural Focus Group) in support of Ministers, since 1995. Facilitator for government, local government, companies, NGOs and community organisations, including SNIFFER and SSN, on many

aspects of sustainable development, tackling climate change and organisational development, 1995-2015. Author or co-author of numerous reports including Reality Check, 2001/2 (for WWF); Mainstreaming sustainable development in regional regeneration, 2004 (for ESEP), and in structure and local plans (including for Glasgow and Clyde Valley, North Lanarkshire and Ayrshire); Mourne National Party Working Party report, 2007; Towards a Step Change in Sustainable Development Education in Scottish Schools, 2011 (for WWF). Recreation: family outings. Address: (b.) 6 Malta Terrace, Edinburgh EH4 1HR; T.-0131-332 3499.

Birss, Rev. Alan David, DL, MA (Hons), BD (Hons); b. 5.6.53, Ellon; m., Carol Margaret Pearson; 1 s. Educ. Glenrothes High School; St. Andrews University; Edinburgh University. Assistant Minister, Dundee Parish Church (St. Mary's), 1978-80; Minister, Inverkeithing Parish Church of St. Peter, 1982-88; Minister, Paisley Abbey, 1988-2020. Deputy Lieutenant of Renfrewshire, 2015-2020. Past President, Church Service Society; Past President, Scottish Church Society. Address: 36 Marquis Drive, Aboyne, Aberdeenshire AB34 5FD; T.-01339 886 231; e-mail: alan.birss@btinternet.com

Bishop, Mark. Chief Executive Officer, Dynamic Earth, since 2022. Career history: worked in book publishing, television and internet-start ups; Head of Corporate Fundraising, Leonard Cheshire, 2004-09; Director of Fundraising, Prostate Cancer UK, London, 2009-2015; Director of Customer and Cause, The National Trust for Scotland, since 2015. Address: Dynamic Earth, Holyrood Road, Edinburgh EH8 8AS.

Bisset, David W., FAMS, MCLIP, FSA (Scot), DEAB, FEAB. Secretary, Scottish Esperanto Association, since 1997; b. 8.8.38, Motherwell; m., Jean; 1 s.; 1 d. Educ. Dalziel High, Motherwell; University of Strathclyde. Librarian, Coatbridge Technical College, 1962-72; Head of Library Services, Bell College of Technology, Hamilton, 1972-95. Various positions within the Esperanto Movement in Scotland and Britain; Hon. Vice-President, Hamilton Civic Society. Recreations: cultural tourism; town walking; architectural history. Address: (h.) 47 Airbles Crescent, Motherwell ML1 3AP; T.-01698 263199.

Bisset, Raymond George, OBE. Provost, Aberdeenshire Council, 2003-07 (Convener, 1999-2003); Non-executive member, Aberdeen Harbour Board, 2008-10; Chair, North East of Scotland Fisheries Partnership, 2000-07; b. 16.8.42, Ellon; m., Heather Bisset. Educ. Inverurie Academy; Aberdeen University; College of Education. Chemistry/Physics Teacher, Ellon Academy, 1963-64; Maths/General Science Teacher, Insch School, 1965-74; Head Teacher: Keithall Primary School, 1975-76; Kintore Primary and Secondary School, 1977-81; Kintore Primary School, 1981-94. Provost, Gordon District Council, 1992-96; Member, North of Scotland Water Authority (NOSWA), 1995-99; Chair, Gordon Area Tourist Board, 1986-89, 1991-96; Hon. President, University for Children and Communities, 1999-2007; former Chair, Inverurie and District Round Table; Founder Chair, North East Scotland Anglers' Federation; former Hon. President, Inverurie Arthritis Society; Member, NHS (Grampian), 2001-07 and 2009-2017; Chair, Nestour (VisitScotland), 2005-08; Chair of NHS (Grampian) Clinical Governance Committee, 2002-07; Chair, NHS (Grampian) Patient Focus Public Involvement Committee, 2011-12; Member, Garioch Probus Club; Chair, NHS (Grampian) Endowments Committee, 2009-2017; Co-Chair, Aberdeenshire Transitional Leadership Group in Adult Health and Social Care, 2013-2016; Chair of Aberdeenshire Integrated Joint Board in Adult Health and

Social Care, until 2016; Chair, Aberdeenshire Community Health Partnership, 2013-15; Member, Aberdeenshire Community Planning Board, 2013-16; past Chair, Grampian Houston Association; Member, Garioch Probus Club; Honorary Member, Inverurie Angling Association and Inverurie Cricket Club; former President, Inverurie Angling Association. Recreations: angling; golf; hill walking; reading; amateur writing. Address: (h.) The Schoolhouse, Keithhall, Inverurie, Aberdeenshire AB51 0LX; T.-01467 621015.

E-mail: raymond_bisset@yahoo.co.uk

Bissett, Alan. Author and playwright; b. 17.11.75. Educ. Falkirk High School; University of Stirling. After a short spell as a secondary school teacher at Elgin Academy, gained a Masters degree in English from the University of Stirling; wrote his first novel, Boyracers (2001); lectured in creative writing at Bretton Hall College, now part of the University of Leeds, and tutored the creative writing MLitt at the University of Glasgow; became a full-time writer in December 2007, then a playwright shortly after. His various novels and plays have been shortlisted for numerous awards, and in 2011 he was named Glenfiddich Spirit of Scotland writer of the year. Address: A M Heath & Company Limited, Authors' Agents, 6 Warwick Court, Holborn, London WC1R 5DJ.

Bissett, Sheriff Colin John, LLB, DipLP. Sheriff of North Strathclyde at Kilmarnock, since 2021; b. 04.01.78, Glasgow; m., Elaine Roanna (née Perera); 1 s.; 1 d. Educ. Greenfaulds High School; University of Dundee. Career history: Solicitor - Partner, Bell, Russell & Co., 2009-12; Principal, Bissett Solicitors, 2012-15; Partner and Head of Regulatory, DAC Beachcroft Scotland LLP, 2015-21. Member of the Royal Faculty of Procurators in Glasgow. Recreations: time with family; hillwalking; literature; history; motor cars. Address: Sheriff Court House, St. Marnock Street, Kilmarnock KA1 1ED.

Bissett, Graeme. Non-Executive Director, Smart Metering Systems, since 2016; Chairman, Macfarlane Group, 2012-2017. Joined the Board of Macfarlane Group in 2004 as a Non-Executive Director; former Finance Director of International Groups and former Partner with Arthur Andersen. Currently holds non-executive appointments with Cruden Group Limited, Anderson Strathern LLP and Aberforth Split Level Income Trust plc and undertakes a number of pro bono appointments, including as a member of court at the University of Glasgow, trustee of Citizens Advice Scotland and director and trustee of Entrepreneurial Scotland Foundation. Address: (b.) Smart Metering Systems PLC, Bell Lawrie, 48 St Vincent Street, Glasgow G2 5TS.

Black, Rev. Archibald Tearlach, BSc. Chairman of Council, The Saltire Society, 1997-2001; retired Church of Scotland minister, formerly at Ness Bank Church, Inverness; b. 10.6.37, Edinburgh; m., Bridget Mary Baddeley; 2 s.; 1 d. Elected Member of Council, National Trust for Scotland, 1991-96, 1997-2002 and 2003-08; Chairman, Sorley MacLean Trust, 2000-2011. Recreations: Eden Court Theatre; all the arts; the enjoyment of Scotland's natural and cultural heritage. Address: (h.) 16 Elm Park, Inverness IV2 4WN; T.-01463 230588.

E-mail: a.black236@btinternet.com

Black, Elspeth Catherine, LLB, NP. Solicitor, since 1973; formerly Honorary Sheriff, Dunoon; b. 25.10.50, Kilmarnock; m., James Anthony Black; 1 s.; 1 d. Educ. Kilmarnock Academy; Glasgow University. Apprentice, then Assistant, Wright, Johnston and McKenzie, Glasgow, 1971-74; Assistant, Messers Wm. J. Cuthbert and Hogg,

Fort William, 1974-75; Assistant, then Partner, Kenneth W. Pendreich and Co. Dunoon, 1975-87; Partner, Elspeth C. Black and Co., Dunoon and Anderson Banks and Co., Oban, Fort William and Balivanich, 1987-98; Partner, Corrigall Black, Dunoon, since 1998. Recreations: swimming coaching (Chief Coach, Dunoon ASC); running/fitness training. Address: (b.) 20 John Street, Dunoon; T.-01369 704777.

Black, Mhairi. MP (SNP), Paisley and Renfrewshire South, since 2015; SNP Shadow Secretary of State for Scotland, since 2020; b. 12.9.94. Educ. University of Glasgow. Baby of the House (2015-19) and the youngest MP since the Reform Act of 1832. Address: House of Commons, London SW1A 0AA.

Black, Professor Robert, QC, LLB (Hons), LLM, FRSA, FRSE, FFCS, FHEA. Professor of Scots Law, Edinburgh University, since 1981 (Emeritus, since 2005); Temporary Sheriff, 1981-94; b. 12.6.47, Lockerbie. Educ. Lockerbie Academy; Dumfries Academy; Edinburgh University; McGill University, Montreal. Advocate, 1972; Lecturer in Scots Law, Edinburgh University, 1972-75; Senior Legal Officer, Scottish Law Commission, 1975-78; practised at Scottish bar, 1978-81; QC, 1987; General Editor, The Laws of Scotland: Stair Memorial Encyclopaedia, 1988-96 (formerly Deputy and Joint General Editor). Publications: An Introduction to Written Pleading, 1982; Civil Jurisdiction: The New Rules, 1983; various articles on the Lockerbie disaster. Recreation: blogging on Lockerbie: http://lockerbiecase.blogspot.com. Address: (h.) 6/4 Glenogle Road, Edinburgh EH3 5HW; T.-0131-557 3571; Gannaga Lodge, Agterkop, Middelpos 8193, Northern Cape, South Africa; T.-+27 (0)799 221688.

Black, Robert William, CBE, MA (Hons, Econ), MSc (Town Planning), MSc (Public Policy), LLD, FRSE. Auditor General for Scotland, 2000-2012; b. 6.11.46, Banff; m., Doreen Mary Riach; 3 s.; 1 d. Educ. Robert Gordon's College, Aberdeen; Aberdeen University; Heriot-Watt University; Strathclyde University. Nottinghamshire County Council, 1971-73; City of Glasgow Corporation, 1973-75; Strathclyde Regional Council, 1975-85; Chief Executive: Stirling District Council, 1985-90, Tayside Regional Council, 1990-95; Controller of Audit, Accounts Commission for Scotland, 1995-99. Former Fellow, Royal Statistical Society (resigned in 2012); Hon. Doctor of Law, University of Aberdeen, 2004; Hon. Doctor of Business Administration, Queen Margaret University College, 2006; Fellow of the Royal Society of Edinburgh (FRSE), 2006; Honorary Member of the Chartered Institute of Public Finance; Lay Member of Court, University of Edinburgh, 2012; Public Interest Member, Institute of Chartered Accountants of Scotland (ICAS), 2012; Board Member, The British Library, 2012; Chairman, Scottish Commission on Housing and Wellbeing, since 2013; Honorary Vice President of Shelter Scotland, 2017. Recreations: the outdoors and the arts. E-mail: robertwblack@me.com

Black, Stuart. PhD. Chief Executive, Highlands and Islands Enterprise, since 2022. Educ. University of Edinburgh; University of Glasgow. Career history: Lecturer in Land Economy, University of Aberdeen, 1990-96; Director of Global Connections, Highlands and Islands Enterprise, 1996-2008; Director of Planning and Development, then Executive Chief Officer for Transformation and Economy, Highland Council, 2008-2020; Highlands and Islands Enterprise Area Manager, Moray, 2020-22. Board member, EDAS (Economic Development Association Scotland). Address: An Lòchran, 10 Inverness Campus, Inverness IV2 5NA; T.-01463 245240; e-mail: stuart.black@hient.co.uk

Black, Tracy, MA (Hons). Director Scotland, CBI (Confederation of British Industry), since 2018. Educ. University of Aberdeen. Career: VP Sales and Marketing, Edinburgh Financial Publishing/Bara Inc, 1995-98; UK Sales Manager, AutEx, Thomson Financial, 1998-2000; Executive Director, USB Investment Bank, 2000-09; MD, Portfolio & Electronic Execution, ICAP, 2009-2010; VP, Electronic Trading - Sales, Goldman Sachs, 2010-12; Consultant: Pohjola Asset Management Execution Services Ltd, 2012-14, TradingScreen, 2014, ParkWalk Advisors Ltd, 2013-17; Founder, Interactive Partners Limited, 2012-17; Director, The Evolution Dog Wash, 2015-17; Deputy Director - Scotland, CBI (Confederation of British Industry), 2017. Address: CBI Scotland, 160 West George Street, Glasgow G2 2HQ; T.-0141 222 2184.

Blackford, Ian. MP (SNP), Ross, Skye and Lochaber, since 2015; Leader of the SNP Westminster Group, since 2017; b. 14.5.61; m., Ann. Educ. The Royal High School, Edinburgh. Career: 20 years in the financial industry; analyst with NatWest Securities, before moving to a managerial role; ran Deutsche Bank's operations in Scotland and the Netherlands; formed consultancy business First Seer in 2002; joined the Dutch banking products company CSM in 2005 as an investor relations manager; appointed non-executive chairman of the Edinburgh-based telecommunications firm Commsworld in 2006. Trustee, Golden Charter Trust; formerly chairman of the Glendale Trust; formerly a member of the FlySkye group, campaigning to bring commercial air services back to Skye; formerly National Treasurer of the Scottish National Party. Address: House of Commons, London SW1A 0AA.

Blackie, Professor John Walter Graham, BA (Cantab), LLB (Edin). Professor of Law, Strathclyde University, since 1991, Emeritus, since 2009; Advocate, since 1974; b. 2.10.46, Glasgow; m., Jane Ashman. Educ. Uppingham School; Peterhouse, Cambridge; Harvard; Merton College, Oxford; Edinburgh University. Open Exhibitioner, Peterhouse, Cambridge, 1965-68; St. Andrews Society of New York Scholar, Harvard, 1968-69; practised at Scottish bar, 1974-75; Edinburgh University: Lecturer, 1975-88, Senior Lecturer in Scots Law, 1988-91. Director, Blackie & Son Ltd., publishers, 1970-93. Recreations: music, particularly horn playing; sailing, particularly classic boats (Convenor, Gairloch One Design Class Association). Address: (h.) 23 Russell Place, Edinburgh EH5 3HW.

Blacklock, Telfer George, MA, LLB, DipLP, NP, SSC. Partner, Blacklocks Solicitors, since 1992; b. 3.3.58, Edinburgh; m., Mairead; 4 s. Educ. St. Marks, Swaziland; George Heriots, Edinburgh; Edinburgh University. Balfour & Manson, 1982-92. Recreations: golf; bridge; cinema; cooking. Address: (b.) 34 Bernard Street, Edinburgh EH6 6PR; T.-0131 555 7500; e-mail: tgb@blacklocks.co.uk

Blackman, Kirsty. MP (SNP) Aberdeen North, since 2015; SNP Deputy Westminster Leader, 2017-2020; b. 1986; m., Luke Blackman; 2 c. Elected to Aberdeen City Council as an SNP councillor in the Hilton/Stockethill ward, 2007, re-elected in 2012; became Convenor of the SNP group in Aberdeen City Council; SNP Spokesperson for the Economy, 2017-19. Address: 46 John Street, Aberdeen, AB25 1LL.

Blackmore, Professor Stephen, CBE, BSc, PhD, CBE, FRSE, FLS, FRSB, CBiol. Chair, Darwin Initiative, Darwin Expert Committee, 2013-19; Her Majesty's Botanist in Scotland, since 2010; Visiting Professor, Glasgow University, since 1999; Honorary Professor, University of Edinburgh, since 2003; Honorary Professor, Kunming Institute of Botany, since 2003; Board of Governors, Edinburgh College of Art, 2003-2010; Trustee, Seychelles Islands Foundation, since 1996; Trustee, Little Sparta Trust, 2001-09; Trustee, Botanic Gardens Conservation International, since 2001; b. 30.7.52, Stoke on Trent; m., Patricia Jane Melrose; 1 s.; 1 d. Educ. St George's School, Hong Kong; Reading University. Royal Society Aldabra Research Station, Seychelles, 1976; Lecturer and Head of National Herbarium, University of Malawi, 1977; Palynologist, British Museum (Natural History), 1980; Keeper of Botany, Natural History Museum, 1990; Regius Keeper, Royal Botanic Garden Edinburgh, 1999-2013. Awarded the Victoria Medal of Honour (VMH) by the Royal Horticultural Society, 2012. Publications: Gardening the Earth, 2009; Green Universe, 2012; How Plants Work, 2019; author of numerous research papers on plant taxonomy and palynology. Recreations: photography; hill-walking; blues guitar music. Address: (b.) Royal Botanic Garden, 20A Inverleith Row, Edinburgh EH3 5LR; T.-0131-248 2930.
E-mail: S.Blackmore@rbge.org.uk

Blaikie, Professor Andrew, MA, PhD, FAcSS, FRHistS. Emeritus Professor of Historical Sociology, University of Aberdeen; b. 30.11.56, St. Anne's. Educ. Kirkham Grammar School; Downing College, Cambridge; Queen Mary College, London. Lecturer, Birkbeck College, University of London, 1986-91; Department of Sociology, University of Aberdeen: Lecturer, 1991, Senior Lecturer, 1995, Professor 1999, Nuffield Foundation Research Fellow, 1998, Director of Research in Social Sciences and Law, 1999-2001, Head of Sociology, 2002-04; Secretary, Economic and Social History Society of Scotland, 1994-99 and Member of Council, 2010-2016; Executive Committee, British Sociological Association, 1997-2001 (Vice Chair), Member of Council, 2007-2010. Publications: Illegitimacy, Sex and Society, 1994; Ageing and Popular Culture, 1999; The Scots Imagination and Modern Memory, 2010. Recreations: swimming; hillwalking; travel. Address: (h.) 5 Pilot Square, Aberdeen AB11 5DS; T.-01224 588313; e-mail: a.blaikie@abdn.ac.uk

Blair, Anna Dempster, DPE. Writer and Lecturer; b. 12.2.27, Glasgow; m., Matthew Blair; 1 s.; 1 d. Educ. Hutchesons' Girls Grammar School, Glasgow; Dunfermline College. Novels: A Tree in the West; The Rowan on the Ridge; Short Stories: Tales of Ayrshire; Scottish Tales; The Goose Girl of Eriska; Seed Corn; social history: Tea at Miss Cranston's; Croft and Creel; More Tea at Miss Cranston's; Old Giffnock. Recreations: film-making; travel; reading; friendship.

Blair, John Samuel Greene, OBE (Mil), TD, TAVRD, KStJ, BA, Hon. DLitt (St. Andrews), ChM, FRCSEdin, FRCP, FICS, D(Obst)RCOG, FSAScot, FRHistS, Diploma in History of Medicine, Society of Apothecaries (Honorary), 2004. Honorary Senior Teacher, Faculty of Medicine, University of Dundee, 2004-2015; Vice-President, International Society for the History of Medicine, 2000-04; Editorial Manager, International Journal of Medical History, 2002-06; Honorary Reader, History of Medicine and Apothecaries Lecturer, St. Andrews University, 1997-2002 (Senior Lecturer, 1993-97); Honorary Senior Lecturer in Surgery, Dundee University, 1967-90; Apothecaries Lecturer, Worshipful Society of London, since 1991; Member, Editorial Board, Vesalius, since 1994; Member, Organising Committee, International Society for the History of Medicine, Cyprus Congress, 2009; b. 31.12.28, Wormit, Fife; m., Ailsa Jean Bowes, MBE; 2 s.; 1 d. Educ. Dundee High School (Harris Gold Medal for Dux of School, 1946, Intermediate Athletics

Champion, 1944, School Golf Champion, 1945, Runner-up, School Athletics Championship, 1946); St. Andrews University (Harkness Scholar, 1946-50). National Service, RAMC, 1952-55 (member of RAMC four-man team finalists in Army Golf Championship, 1954); Tutor, Department of Anatomy, St. Salvator's College, St. Andrews, 1955; surgical and research training, Manchester, Dundee, Cambridge, London, 1957-65; Member, Court of Examiners, Royal College of Surgeons of Edinburgh, 1964-93; Consultant Surgeon, Perth Royal Infirmary, 1965-90; postgraduate Clinical Tutor, Perth, 1966-74; first North American Travelling Fellow, St. Andrews/Dundee Universities, 1971; Secretary, Tayside Area Medical Advisory Committee, 1974-83; Member, Education Advisory Committee, Association of Surgeons, 1984-88; Secretary, Perth and Kinross Division, British Medical Association, 1982-90; Member, Scottish Council and Chairman's Sub-Committee, BMA, 1985-89; Fellow of the BMA, 1990; Chairman, Armed Forces Committee, BMA, 1992-98; President: British Society for the History of Medicine, 1993-95, Scottish Society for the History of Medicine, 1990-93; Captain, Royal Perth Golf Club, 1997-99; British National Delegate, International Society for the History of Medicine, 1999-2001; Honorary Colonel (TA), RAMC; Member, Principal's Council, St Andrews University, 1984-99; Elder, Church of Scotland; Hospitaller, Priory of Scotland, Order of St. John of Jerusalem; Mitchiner Lecturer, Army Medical Services, 1994; Haldane Tait Memorial Lecturer, 1998; Osler Club Lecturer, 1998; Birmingham Medical History Society Lecturer, 1998; Douglas Guthrie Memorial Lecturer, 1998; Brigadier Ian Haywood Lecturer, 1999; Haywood Society Lecturer, 1999; Pybus Society Lecturer, 2001; International Blood Transfusion Society Lecturer, 2004; Invited Speaker, International Congress on High Technology Medicine and Doctor-Patient Relationship, Istanbul, 2006; Invited speaker, Division of Medical Humanities, University of Arkansas, 2007; Annual Osler Oration, 2007. Publications: books on medical history and anatomy including the history of medicine at St. Andrews University, 1987, the centenary history of the RAMC, 1998, The Conscript Doctors – Memories of National Service, 2001 and History of Medicine in Dundee University, 2007. Recreations: golf; travel. Address: (h.) 143 Glasgow Road, Perth; T.-Perth 623739; e-mail: jgb143@btinternet.com

Blair, Robin Orr, CVO, MA, LLB, WS. Angus Herald Extraordinary; Lord Lyon King of Arms and Secretary, Order of the Thistle, 2001-08. Educ. Rugby School; St. Andrews University; Edinburgh University. Partner, Dundas & Wilson, 1967-97 (Managing Partner, 1976-83 and 1988-91); Partner, Turcan Connell WS, 1997-2000. Purse Bearer to the Lord High Commissioner to General Assembly of Church of Scotland, 1989-2002; Chairman, Inches Carr Trust, since 1997; Chairman, Scotland's Churches Trust, 1997-2016, President, since 2017. Address: 2 Blacket Place, Edinburgh EH9 1RL; T.-0131-667 2906.

Blakey, Rev. Ronald Stanton, MA, BD, MTh. Editor, Church of Scotland Year Book, 2000-2011; b. 3.7.38, Glasgow; m., Kathleen Dunbar; 1 s. Educ. Hutchesons' Boys' Grammar School, Glasgow; Glasgow University. Minister: St. Mark's, Kirkconnel, 1963-67; Bellshill West, 1967-72; Jedburgh Old Parish with Edgerston and Ancrum, 1972-81. Member, Roxburgh District Council, 1974-80 (Chairman of Council, 1977-80); Religious Adviser, Border Television, 1973-81; Member, Borders Region Children's Panel, 1974-80; JP, 1974-80; Church of Scotland: Deputy Secretary, Department of Education, 1981-88; Secretary, Assembly Council, 1988-98; Israel Project Secretary, Board of World Mission, 1998-2000. Publication: The Man in the Manse, 1978. Recreation: collecting antiquarian books on Scotland. Address: (h.) 24 Kimmerghame Place, Edinburgh EH4 2GE; T.-0131 343 6352.

Blaxter, Professor John Harry Savage, MA (Oxon), DSc (Oxon), HonDUniv (Stirling), FRSB, FRSE. Hon. Professor, Stirling University; b. 6.1.29, London; m., Valerie Ann McElligott; 1 s.; 1 d. Educ. Berkhamsted School; Brasenose College, Oxford. SO, then SSO, Marine Laboratory, Aberdeen, 1952-64; Lecturer, Zoology Department, Aberdeen University, 1964-69; PSO, 1969, SPSO, 1974, DCSO, 1985-91, Hon. Research Fellow, 1992-2001, Scottish Marine Biological Association, later Scottish Association for Marine Science, Oban; Hon. Professor, St. Andrews University, 1990-99; President, Fisheries Society of the British Isles, 1992-97 (Beverton Medal, 1998); Individual Achievement Award, American Institute of Fisheries Research Biologists, 1998; Editor, Advances in Marine Biology, 1980-98; Editor, ICES Journal of Marine Science, 1991-97; Member, Editorial Board, Encyclopaedia of Ocean Sciences, 1998-2001; Trustee, Argyll Fisheries Trust, 1999-2010. Recreations: golf; gardening. Address: (h.) Lag-an-Tobair, Old Shore Road, Connel, Oban, Argyll PA37 1PT; T.-01631 710588.

Blow, Professor Julian, FRSE, FMEdSci, BSc, PhD. Vice-Principal (Academic Planning and Performance), University of Dundee. Educ. Perse School for Boys, Cambridge; The University of Edinburgh; University of Cambridge. Career history: ICRF Clare Hall Laboratories: Research Scientist, 1991-96, Senior Scientist, 1996-97; appointed Principal Investigator, University of Dundee in 1997. Address: University of Dundee, Nethergate, Dundee DD1 4HN; T.-01382 385797; e-mail: j.j.blow@dundee.ac.uk

Bloxwich, Janet Elizabeth. Principal Bassoon, Orchestra of Scottish Opera, since 1980; b. 11.4.56, Brentwood; m., Alan J. Warhurst. Educ. Belfairs High School; Southend Technical College; Royal College of Music, London. Two years freelancing in London; on staff at Royal Conservatoire of Scotland, since 1997. Recreations: hillwalking; painting; wood-turning; instrument repairs; cooking. Address: 91 Fotheringay Road, Pollokshields, Glasgow G41 4LH; T.-0141-423 2303.

Blunden, Martin, QFSM, MIFireE, MBA, DMS, CertEd. Chief Officer, Scottish Fire and Rescue Service, since 2019; b. 3.68. Educ. Universities of Bedfordshire, Warwickshire. Career history: Buckinghamshire Fire and Rescue Service, 1992-2006; Area Commander: Hereford & Worcester Fire and Rescue Service, 2006-08; Hertfordshire County Council, 2008-15; Assistant & Deputy Chief Fire Officer, South Yorkshire Fire and Rescue, 2015-19. Address: Scottish Fire and Rescue Service Headquarters, Westburn Drive, Cambuslang G72 7NA; T.-0141 646 4500.

Blyth, Emeritus Professor Thomas Scott, BSc, DèsSc, DSc, FIMA, FRSE, Corr. Member, Soc.Roy.Sc. Liège. Emeritus Professor, Pure Mathematics, St Andrews University (appointed Professor of Pure Mathematics in 1977); b. 3.7.38, Newburgh, Fife; m., Jane Ellen Christine Harman; 1 d. Educ. Bell-Baxter High School, Cupar; St Andrews University. NATO Research Scholar, Sorbonne, 1960-63; St Andrews University: Lecturer in Mathematics, 1963-72, Senior Lecturer, 1972-73, Reader, 1973-77, Dean, Faculty of Science, 1994-98; Chairman, British Mathematical Colloquium, 1987; President, Edinburgh Mathematical Society, 1979-80. Publications: more than 130 research papers and ten books. Address (b.) Mathematical Institute, North Haugh, St Andrews KY16 9SS.
E-mail: tsb@st-and.ac.uk or tsblyth.prof@btinternet.com

Blythe, Graham, MA. Head of the European Commission Office in Scotland, 2012-2020; b. 6.7.61; m., Catherine Ross; 1 d.; 1 s. Educ. Universities of Aberdeen; Leeds Polytechnic; Université de Nice. Career history: University of Bradford, 1987-89; University of Bristol, 1989-93; appointed a European Commission Official in 1993.

Blythe, Professor Richard, MSci Hons (Physics), PhD (Physics). Professor, University of Edinburgh, since 2019; Personal Chair of Complex Systems. Educ. University of Bristol; University of Edinburgh. Career history: EPSRC Postdoctoral Research Fellow, University of Manchester, 2001-04; University of Edinburgh: RSE/Scottish Executive Research Fellow, 2004-07; RCUK Fellow/Lecturer, 2007-2012; Lecturer, 2012-14; Reader, 2014-19. Divisional Associate Editor of Physical Review Letters, 2011-17; currently an Academic Editor of PLOS ONE. Address: James Clerk Maxwell Building, Room 2505, University of Edinburgh; T.-0131 650 5105; e-mail: r.a.blythe@ed.ac.uk

Boa, Rev Ian. Interim General Secretary, Action of Churches Together in Scotland, since 2018. Address: Jubilee House, Stirling, Stirlingshire FK8 1QZ; T.-01259 222361.

Bogle, Very Rev. Albert Orr. Pioneer Minister of Falkirk Presbytery and founder of Sanctuary First, the Church of Scotland's On-line Worshipping Community creating and developing alternative ways for church to offer worship opportunities, since 2016; Minister of Church of Scotland, St. Andrew's Parish Bo'ness, 1981-2015; Moderator of the General Assembly of the Church of Scotland, 2012-13; b. 3.2.49, Glasgow; m., Martha; 1 s.; 1 d. Educ. Woodside Senior Secondary School; Glasgow University; Edinburgh University. Moderator of Falkirk Presbytery, 1993; Founder Chairman, The Vine Trust, 1985 (an international development and medical agency working in Peru and Tanzania); Convener, Church of Scotland's Church Without Walls, 2004; Director of Branches, 1985; Director, Sanctus Media, 2009; Project Director, World Without Walls, 2005. Pioneering the use of media and internet within the structure of the Church of Scotland; helping the Church nationally and internationally to see the benefits of technology to communicate; Founder of Branches Charity Shop, 1985; Co-founder and Director of Sanctus Media, a not for profit company working to serve the Third Sector. Regular broadcaster, blogger and podcaster; Music singles released: When Grace comes into town, Jubilee Hope. Publications: Book: Pray Today, 1987; 5 albums of songs - Lamplighter, Run Scared No More, Brave, Cardboard House, Cries In The Dark. Recreations: music; songwriting; walking; film making; writing.
E-mail: albertbogle@mac.com

Bolander, Cllr Eva. Lord Provost of Glasgow, 2017-19; representing Anderston/City/Yorkhill ward (SNP), since 2015; b. Stockholm, Sweden. Educ. University of Stockholm; Glasgow College of Building and Printing (now Metropolitan College). Career: Museum Education Officer, National Historical Museums, Sweden, 1981-90; Editor, Project Coordinator, EduMedia AB, Sweden, 1993-94; Web Designer, Scottish Accessible Information Forum, 2002-07; Web Editor, John Wheatley College, 2006-2013; Owner, Hayburn House, 2009-2013; Web Services Officer, Glasgow Kelvin College, 2013-15; Web Consultant, design and accessibility, Bestla Design (owner), since 2002; appointed Office Manager, Carol Monaghan MP in 2015. Member, Partick Community Council, since 2009. First visited Glasgow in the 1980s, competing in the World Pipe Band Championships.

Bolland, Alexander, QC (Scot), BD, LLB; b. 21.11.50, Kilmarnock; m., Agnes Hunter Pate Moffat; 1 s.; 2 d. Educ. Kilmarnock Academy; St. Andrews University; Glasgow University. Admitted Faculty of Advocates, 1978; Captain, Army Legal Services, 1978-80; Standing Junior Counsel to Department of Employment in Scotland, 1988-92; QC (Scot), since 1992; Temporary Sheriff, 1988-99. Dental Vocational Appeal Tribunal, since 2011; Judicial Proceedings Panel, Church of Scotland, since 2013; Military Chaplains Committee, Church of Scotland, since 2016; Part Time Chairman, Pensions Appeal Tribunal, 2008-2017; Part Time Chairman, Employment Tribunals, since 2016. Recreations: Hellenistics; walking; reading. Address: (h.) 60 North Street, St. Andrews, Fife; T.-01334 474599.

Bond, Maurice Samuel, BA, MSc, MTh, MEd, PhD, PGCE. Minister of St. Michael's Church, Dumfries, since 1999; Hon. Chaplain, Glasgow University, Crichton Campus, Dumfries, since 2002; Ceremonial Burgh Chaplain to Dumfries Cornet Club, since 1999; b. 25.6.52, Augher, Northern Ireland; 1 s.; 1 d. Educ. Limavady High School; Universities of Nottingham, Cambridge, Dublin and Belfast. Joiner, 1967-71; Teacher, 1978-79; Minister of the Presbyterian Church in Ireland, 1981-91; Minister of the Church of Scotland, Downfield South Church, Dundee, 1991-99. Dumfries and Galloway NHS Medical Research Ethics Committee, 2005-2008; Research Ethics Committee of Glasgow University, Crichton Campus, 2005-08. Publications: Reconciliation of Cultures in Reconciling Memories, 1998; Presence: in Theology in Scotland, 1998. Recreation: rugby. Address: Braemar, 15 Pleasance Avenue, Dumfries DG2 7JJ; T.-01387 253849.
E-mail: mauricebond399@btinternet.com

Bond, Professor Sir Michael R., MD, PhD, FRSE, FRCSEdin, FRCA (Hon), FRCPsych, FRCPSGlas, DPM, DSc (Leics, Hon), DUniv (Glas, Hon). Hon. Fellow, Faculty of Pain Medicine, Royal College of Anaesthetists (2013); Emeritus Professor of Psychological Medicine, Glasgow University; President, International Association for the Study of Pain, 2002-05; b. 15.4.36, Balderton, Nottinghamshire; m., Jane; 1 s.; 1 d. Educ. Magnus Grammar School, Newark; Sheffield University. Professor of Psychological Medicine, Glasgow University, 1973-98 (former Vice-Principal, Glasgow University, former Administrative Dean, Faculty of Medicine); Member, Medical Committee, UGC 1983-89; Chairman, Medical Committee, UFC, 1989-92; Member, Council, SHEFC, 1992-96; Chair, Joint Medical Advisory Committee for UK Funding Councils, 1991-95; Member, London Inquiry Group, 1992/93; former Director (former Chairman), Head Injuries Trust for Scotland 1988-99; former Member, Council, St. Andrews Ambulance Association, 1995-2001; Past President, British Pain Society, 1999-2001, Interim President, 2009/10; former Director, Prince and Princess of Wales Hospice, 1997-2002, Glasgow; Governor, 1990-2001, Glasgow High School, Chairman, 2001-06; Trustee, Lloyds TSB Foundation, 1999-2005; Fellow, Royal Society of Arts; Knight Bachelor, 1995; Deacon, Incorporation of Bakers of Glasgow, 2011-12; Late Deacon, 2012-13. Recreations: reading; music; painting (President, Bearsden Art Club, 2014/16). Address: (b.) No. 2 The Square, University of Glasgow, University Avenue, Glasgow G12 8QQ; T.-0141-330 3692; e-mail: m.bond@admin.gla.ac.uk

Bone, David James, LLB (Hons), DipLP, NP. Partner and Head of Energy and Natural Resources Sector Group, Harper Macleod LLP, since 2010 and Senior Partner, since 2017. Educ. Paisley Grammar School; University of Glasgow. Career history: Partner, Wright, Johnston & Mackenzie, 1988-2010 (including Head of Renewable Energy and two spells as Managing Partner); Partner and Head of Energy and Natural Resources Sector Group, Harper Macleod, 2010-17. Won the prestigious 'Partner of the Year', Award at the Scottish Legal Awards in 2006 (for work in Renewable Energy); one of the Band One ranked Scottish Energy lawyers in each of Chambers and Legal 500's 2021 guides to the legal profession; led the Harper Macleod team to Energy Team of the Year Award at the Scottish Law Awards, 2011, 2013 and 2016. Company

Secretary and Legal adviser, Scottish Renewables Forum Limited, 2000-2020. Non-executive Director, The Natural Power Consultants Limited, since 2008. Writes and speaks extensively on renewable energy in Scotland, including a series of annual reviews on developments in the sector. Address: Harper Macleod LLP, The Ca'd'oro, 45 Gordon Street, Glasgow G1 3PE; T.-0141 227 9599; e-mail: david.bone@harpermacleod.co.uk

Bone, Professor Sir (James) Drummond, MA (Glas), MA (Oxon), HonDLitt (Ches, Lanc, Liv, Bucharest), Hon DUniv (Glas), HonDEd (Edin), HonArtD (XJTLU Suzhou), FRSE, FRSA. Master, Balliol College, Oxford, 2011-18; Pro-Vice-Chancellor, Oxford University, 2016-18; Chair, Arts and Humanities Research Council, 2014-2021; Chair, Advisory Board, Laureate Inc., 2008-2011 with ongoing advisory role, until 2018; Chair, i-graduate, 2005-15; Trustee, The Shirley Foundation (for autism), 2011-17; Chair, The Wordsworth Trust, since 2017; Board Member of Oxford-Suzhou Centre for Advanced Research, since 2017; Chair, The National Library of Scotland, since 2021; b. 11.7.47, Ayr; m., Vivian. Educ. Ayr Academy; Glasgow University; Balliol College, Oxford. Lecturer in English and Comparative Literary Studies, Warwick University; Lecturer, Senior Lecturer, and Professor, English Literature, Glasgow University (Vice-Principal, 1995-99); Principal, Royal Holloway, University of London, 2000-02; Vice-Chancellor, University of Liverpool, 2002-08; President, Universities UK, 2005-07; Honorary Fellow, Royal Holloway, 2004; Honorary Fellow, Balliol College, Oxford, 2018. Knighted, Queen's Birthday Honours, 2008. Freeman of the Worshipful Company of Coachmakers and Coach Harness Makers. Publications: Byron (Writers and their Work); The Cambridge Companion to Byron; Internationalisation of Higher Education: A 10-Year View, report commissioned by DIUS, 2008. Recreations: music; skiing; Maseratis. Address: (h.) The Old Manse, Bow of Fife, Cupar, Fife.

Bone, Professor Thomas R., CBE, MA, MEd, PhD, FCCEA, FSES, FRSGS. Professor and Deputy Principal, Strathclyde University, until 1996; b. 2.1.35, Port Glasgow; m., Elizabeth Stewart; 1 s.; 1 d. Educ. Port Glasgow High School; Greenock High School; Glasgow University; Jordanhill College. Teacher of English, Paisley Grammar School, 1957-62; Lecturer in Education: Jordanhill College, 1962-63, Glasgow University, 1963-67; Jordanhill College: Head of Education Department, 1967-71, Principal, 1972-92. Member, Dunning Committee, 1975-77; Chairman, Educational Advisory Council, IBA, 1985-88; Vice-Chairman: Scottish Examination Board, 1977-84; Scottish Tertiary Education Advisory Council, 1984-87; Chairman: Scottish Council for Educational Technology, 1981-87, Standing Conference on Studies in Education, 1982-84, Council for National Academic Awards Board for Organisation and Management, 1983-87, Council for National Academic Awards Committee for Teacher Education, 1987-89, General Teaching Council for Scotland, 1990-91; Member, Complaints Committee, Law Society of Scotland, 1996-2000. Publication: School Inspection in Scotland, 1968; chapters in books and articles in journals. Clubs: Paisley Burns; Paisley Probus. Recreations: golf; bridge. Address: (h.) 7 Marchbank Gardens, Ralston, Paisley.

Bonnar, Anne Elizabeth, MA, FRSA. Director, Bonnar Keenlyside; arts management consultant; Chair, Collective Gallery; b. 9.10.55, St. Andrews; 2 s.; 2 d. Educ. Dumbarton Academy; Glasgow University; City University, London; Transition Director, Creative Scotland, 2008; Trustee, National Galleries of Scotland, 2002-2010; Director, National Theatre of Scotland, 2004-08; General Manager, Traverse Theatre, 1986-91; Publicity Officer,

Citizens' Theatre, Glasgow, 1981-85. Address: (b.) 15 Old Fishmarket Close, Edinburgh EH1 1AE; T.-0131-225 7677; e-mail: anne@b-k.co.uk

Bonnar, David James, OBE; b. 20.10.50, Dunfermline; m., Sally Elizabeth Armour; 2 s. Educ. Dunfermline High School. Royal Bank of Scotland, 1968-73; Theatre Royal, Glasgow, 1975-80; Theatre Royal, Newcastle upon Tyne, 1980-84; General Manager, Perth Repertory Theatre, 1984-94; Director (National Lottery), Scottish Arts Council, 1994-99, Artisanat Gallery, 2000-09; Board Member: Foxtrot Theatre Co., 2000-06, craftscotland, 2007-08; Trustee, Tim Stead Trust, 2015-19. Recreations: gardening; opera; architecture. Address: (h.) 12 Queen Street, Perth PH2 0EQ; T.-01738 633424.

Bonnar, Sheriff Gerard. Sheriff, Glasgow and Strathkelvin, since 2020. Qualified as a solicitor in 1993; partner in a large high street firm for 6 years before joining South Lanarkshire Council Legal Services in 2002, then the Scottish Government Legal Department (SGLD) in 2005; appointed as a resident summary sheriff in Glasgow in 2017. Address: Glasgow High Court, 1 Mart Street, Saltmarket, Glasgow G1 5JT.

Bonnar, Steven. MP (SNP), Coatbridge, Chryston and Bellshill, since 2019. Educ. Cardinal Newman High. Career history: Loss Prevention Manager, BHS, 2000-03; Loss Prevention Supervisor, Debenhams, 2003-2011; Internal Auditor, John Lewis Partnership, 2011-15; Councillor (SNP), North Lanarkshire Council, 2015-2020. Address: Houses of Parliament, Westminster, London SW1A 0AA. E-mail: steven.bonnar.mp@parliament.uk

Bonomy, Angela, LLB. Executive Director, Sense Scotland, since 2020. Educ. Dalziel High School, Motherwell; University of Glasgow. Career history: Senior Manager, Boots UK, 1993-2003; National Audiology Manager, NHS Scotland, 2003-2012; The Scottish Government: Programme Lead - Sensory Impairment, 2012-14, Specialist Advisor, 2014-16; Director, National Deaf Children's Society, Glasgow, 2016-18; Head of Charity, ENABLE Scotland, 2019; Sense Scotland: Interim Director, 2019-20, Director of Corporate Affairs, 2020. Address: Sense Scotland, 43 Middlesex Street, Kinning Park, Glasgow G41 1EE; T.-0300 330 9292.

Bonomy, Rt. Hon. Lord (Iain Bonomy). Senator of the College of Justice, 1997-2012; permanent judge of the UN International Criminal Tribunal for the Former Yugoslavia, 2004-09; judge of the International Residual Mechanism for Criminal Tribunals, since 2020; b. 15.1.46, Motherwell; m., Jan; 2 d. Educ. Dalziel High School; University of Glasgow. Apprentice Solicitor, East Kilbride Town Council, 1968-70; Solicitor, Ballantyne & Copland, 1970-83; Advocate, 1984-93; Queen's Counsel, 1993-96; Advocate Depute, 1990-93; Home Advocate Depute, 1993-96. Surveillance Commissioner, 1998-2004 and 2010-2017; Judicial Commissioner, 2017-2022; LLD (Strathclyde). Address: (b.) Parliament House, Edinburgh EH1 1RF.

Booth, Martin, BA, FCPFA, MBA. Executive Director of Finance, Glasgow City Council, since 2018; b. 12.66. Educ. St Aloysius College; Glasgow Caledonian University. Career history: Assistant Director, Admin and Finance, Premier Prison Services, 1998-2000; Management Consultant, PwC, 2001-04; Senior Management Consultant, IBM, 2004-06; Managing Director, Isoplan, Glasgow, 2006-08; Head of Finance, COSLA, Edinburgh, 2008-2010; Director of Finance and Governance and Company Secretary, Glasgow Life, 2010-2018; Interim Chief Executive, Jobs and Business Glasgow, 2016-18; Trustee of Enable Scotland; Captain of The Whitecraigs Golf Club, 2017 and 2020; Chair, CIPFA Scottish Branch, 2021/22. Address: Glasgow City Council, City Chambers, Glasgow G2 1DU; e-mail: martin.booth@glasgow.gov.uk

Borthwick of that Ilk, Lord (John Hugh Borthwick), DL. 24th Lord Borthwick; Hereditary Falconer to the Kings and Queens of Scotland; b. 14.11.40; m. Adelaide; 2 d. Educ. Gordonstoun; Edinburgh School of Agriculture. Recreations: stalking; wild trout fishing. Club: Edinburgh New Club. Address: (h.) The Garden Flat, Crookston, Heriot, Midlothian EH38 5YS.

Borthwick, Professor George Cooper, CBE, FRSE, CEng, DEng, DBA, BSc (Hons), FIMechE, FIET, CCMI, FRCSEd (Hon), FRCPS (Glas), FRCOG (Hon), FRCOphth (Hon). Former Chairman, Non Executive Director, Touch Bionics (2011-2015); Chairman, Surgeons Quarter Limited, since 2009; former Chairman, Scottish Business in the Community; former Chairman, Tayside Flow Technologies Ltd.; former Chairman, Nova Science Ltd.; former Member, Scottish Higher Education Review Panel; former Chairman, Edinburgh Napier University Court (2008-2012); former Chairman, Mpathy Medical Devices Ltd.; Director, Surgeons' Hall Trust Ltd, since 2005; b. 17.8.44, Glasgow; m., Milly Chalmers Redfern; 2 s.; 1 d. Educ. Lourdes Senior Secondary School, Glasgow; Strathclyde University. Worked for Ethicon for 33 years; former President, Ethicon Europe, former Managing Director, Ethicon Ltd UK, and former Member, Ethicon Global Council. Visiting Professor, Napier University, since 1993; former Chairman, Breast Cancer Institute (2001-2012); former Lay Member, Senate of Surgery of Great Britain and Ireland; former Lay Member, Joint Committee on Higher Surgical Training; former President, European Association of the Surgical Suture Industry; Hon. Fellow, Association of Surgeons of East Africa, since 1995; Hon. Member, James IV Association of Surgeons; Patron, Royal College of Surgeons in Ireland, since 1997; Patron, Royal College of Surgeons of England; Master, Worshipful Company of Needlemakers, 2012-13; Regent, Royal College of Surgeons of Edinburgh, since 2004; Freeman, City of London. Recreations: golf; antiques; art; theatre. Address: (h.) Hillside, 28 St John's Road, Edinburgh EH12 6NZ; T.-0131 334 6945.

Boswell, Philip. MP (SNP), Coatbridge, Chryston and Bellshill, 2015-17; b. 23.7.63, Coatbridge; m.; 3 c. Career as a quantity surveyor and contracts engineer in the oil industry.

Bouchier, Professor Ian Arthur Dennis, CBE, MB, ChB, MD, FRCP, FRCPEdin, FFPHM, Hon. FCP (SAf), FRSBiol, FMedSci, MD h.c., FRSE, FRSA. Professor of Medicine, Edinburgh University, 1986-97 (now Emeritus Professor); b. 7.9.32, Cape Town, South Africa; m., Patricia Norma Henshilwood; 2 s. Educ. Rondebosch Boys High School; Cape Town University. Instructor in Medicine, School of Medicine, Boston University, 1964; London University: Senior Lecturer in Medicine, 1965; Reader in Medicine, 1970; Professor of Medicine, Dundee University, 1973-86. Member: Court, Dundee University, Council, Royal Society, Edinburgh, Medical Research Council; former Chief Scientist, Scotland; Past President, World Organization of Gastroenterology; former Dean, Faculty of Medicine and Dentistry, Dundee University; Past President, British Society of Gastroenterology. Publications: Clinical Skills (2nd edition), 1982; Gastroenterology (3rd edition), 1982; Gastroenterology: clinical science and practice (2nd edition), 1993. Recreations: music; history of whaling; cooking. Address: (h.) 8A Merchiston Park, Edinburgh EH10 4PN.

Boulton, Professor Geoffrey Stewart, OBE, FRS, FRSE, BSc, PhD, DSc, FGS, Hon D.Technol (Chalmers), Hon D.Science (Heidelberg, Birmingham, Keele). General Secretary, Royal Society of Edinburgh, 2007-2011; Regius Professor Emeritus of Geology and Mineralogy and Senior Honorary Professorial Fellow, Edinburgh University (appointed Professor in 1986, Vice-Principal, 1999-2008,

Provost and Dean, Faculty of Science and Engineering, 1994-99); b. 28.11.40, Stoke-on-Trent; m., Denise Bryers; 2 d. Educ. Longton High School; Birmingham University. Geological Survey of GB, 1962-64; Demonstrator, University of Keele, 1964-65; Research Fellow, Birmingham University, 1965-67; Hydrogeologist, Water Supply Department, Kenya, 1968; University of East Anglia, 1968-81; Extraordinary Professor, University of Amsterdam, 1981-86. President, Quaternary Research Association, 1991-94; President, British Glaciological Society, 1989-91; President, Geological Society of Edinburgh, 1991-94; Member: Nature Conservancy Council for Scotland Science Board, 1991-92, Natural Environmental Research Council, 1993-98 (Chair, Earth Science and Technology Board, 1993-98), Royal Commission on Environmental Pollution, 1993-2000, Scottish Higher Education Funding Council, 1997-2003, Scottish Association for Marine Science Council, 1998-2003, Royal Society Council, 1997-99 and 2012-2015, Prime Minister's Council for Science and Technology, 2004-2011; Chair, Scottish Knowledge Transfer Taskforce, 2003-07; Chair, Research Committee, League of European Research Universities, 2003-2009; Scottish Science Advisory Committee, 2002-2008; Chair, Royal Society Science Policy Advisory Group, 2011-2015; President, Scottish Association for Marine Science, 2013-19; Seligman Crystal, International Glaciological Society, 2001; Kirk Bryan Medal, Geological Society of America, 1982; Lyell Medal, The Geological Society, 2006; Tedford Award for Science, Institute for Contemporary Scotland, 2006; Honorary Fellow, International Union for Quaternary Research, 2007; James Croll Medal of the Quaternary Research Association, 2011; Commandeur dans l'Ordre des Palmes Academiques, Government of France; Royal Gold Medal of the Royal Geographical Society, 2014; Chair, Academic Council of the University of Heidelberg, since 2007; Member, Strategic Council of the University of Geneva, since 2009; President, Commission of the International Council for Science & Technology Data, 2014-18; Member of the Governing Board of the International Science Council, since 2018; UK Polar Medal, 2015. Clubs: New Club, Edinburgh; Arctic Club. Recreations: violin; sailing; mountaineering. Address: (b.) School of Geosciences, University of Edinburgh, Grant Institute, Kings Buildings, West Mains Road, Edinburgh EH9 3JW; e-mail: g.boulton@ed.ac.uk

Bourhill, Peter. Owner, Edinburgh Life magazine. Educ. Leeds University. Address: Edinburgh Life Magazine, PO Box 28948, Gorebridge EH22 9BD; T.-07850 938407. E-mail: editorial@edinburghlifemagazine.com

Bowden, Frederick A.W. Former Chairman, Tullis Russell Group; b. 20.1.47, Aberdeen; m., Sheila; 2 s.; 1 d. Educ. Robert Gordon's Institute of Technology. Production Management Trainee, Inveresk Paper Company, 1964-68; held several management positions, Arjo Wiggins Appleton, 1968-91; appointed Operations Director/Managing Director/Chief Executive, Tullis Russell Group in 1991.

Bowen, Sheriff Principal Edward Farquharson, CBE, TD, QC, LLB. Advocate; Sheriff Principal, Lothian and Borders, 2005-2011; Sheriff Principal, Glasgow and Strathkelvin, 1997-2005; Temporary Judge of the Court of Session, 2000-2015; Chairman, Commissioners of Northern Lighthouses, 2003-05; Visiting Professor of Law, University of Strathclyde, 1999-2004; b. 1.5.45, Edinburgh; m., Patricia Margaret Brown; 2 s.; 2 d. Educ. Melville College, Edinburgh; Edinburgh University. Admitted Solicitor, 1968; Advocate, 1970; Standing Junior Counsel, Scottish Education Department, 1976; Advocate Depute, 1979-83; Sheriff of Tayside, Central and Fife, at Dundee, 1983-90; Partner, Thorntons WS, 1990-91; resumed practice at Scottish Bar; QC, 1992; Chairman (Part-time) Industrial Tribunals, 1995-97;

Member, Criminal Injuries Compensation Board, 1996-97; Chairman, Independent Review of Sheriff & Jury Procedure, 2009-2010; Governor, Dundee Institute of Technology, 1987-90; Chancellor's Assessor, University of Edinburgh, 2011-19; served RAOC TA/TAVR, 1964-80. Recreation: golf. Address: (h) The Old Manse, Lundie, Angus DD2 5NW.

Bowie, Allan. Former President, NFU Scotland (2015-17); m., Christine; 2 s.; 1 d. Farms in North East Fife and Clackmannanshire; former Chairman of the North East Fife branch and served two years as Chairman for East Central region; Vice President, NFU Scotland, 2009-2015.

Bowie, Andrew, MA. MP (Conservative), West Aberdeenshire and Kincardine, since 2017; b. 28.5.87, Arbroath. Educ. Inverurie Academy; University of Aberdeen. Junior Warfare Officer, The Royal Navy, 2007-2010; Military Projects Co-ordinator, Divex, 2013; North Scotland Campaign Manager, The Conservative Party, 2014-15; Parliamentary Assistant and Rural Affairs Policy Advisor, European Parliament, 2015-16; Head of Office to Liam Kerr MSP, The Scottish Parliament, 2016-17. Member, House of Commons Work & Pensions Select Committee, October 2017-February 2018; Parliamentary Private Secretary, Department of Culture, Media and Sport, February 2018-December 2018; Parliamentary Private Secretary to The Prime Minister, December 2018-July 2019; Vice Chairman of The Conservative Party, since 2019. Address: House of Commons, London SW1A 0AA.

Bowie, Lesley. Chair, NHS Ayrshire and Arran Health Board, since 2020. Worked within the IT sector for more than 30 years, all of which were with major Global companies; Non-Executive Board Member of NHS Ayrshire & Arran Board, 2014-2020. Address: NHS Ayrshire & Arran, Eglinton House, Ailsa Hospital, Dalmellington Road, Ayr KA6 6AB.

Bowler, David P., BA, MPhil, FSA Scot, MCIfA. Director, Alder Archaeology Ltd., since 2009. Educ. McGill University, Montreal; Lincoln College, Oxford. Address: Alder Archaeology Ltd., 55 South Methven Street, Perth PH1 5NX; T.-01738 622393. E-mail: director@alderarchaeology.co.uk

Bowman, Professor Adrian William, BSc (Hons), DipMathStat, PhD, FRSE. Emeritus Professor of Statistics, University of Glasgow, since 2020; b. 3.1.55, Ayr; m., Janet Edith Forster; 2 s.; 1 d. Educ. Prestwick Academy; Ayr Academy; University of Glasgow; University of Cambridge. Lecturer in Mathematical Statistics, University of Manchester, 1981-86; University of Glasgow: Lecturer in Statistics, 1986-90, Senior Lecturer in Statistics, 1990-92, Reader in Statistics, 1992-95, Professor of Statistics, 1995-2020. Publications: Applied Smoothing Techniques for Data Analysis, (Co-Author), 1997; Statistics and Problem Solving (Co-Editor), 1999. Recreations: music, particularly singing. Address: (b.) School of Mathematics and Statistics, University of Glasgow, Glasgow G12 8QQ; T.-0141-330 2940.

Bowman, (Bernard) Neil, LLB, NP. Formerly Consultant (retired, 2008), previously Senior Partner, Bowman Scottish Lawyers, Solicitors, Dundee and Forfar, 1984-98; b. 11.11.43, Dundee; m. (1967), (Sheriff) Pamela Margaret Munro Wright (divorced 2010); 2 d.; 3 grandsons; m., Karin Boehm (2011). Educ. High School of Dundee where he captained the Cricket XI in 1961 & 1962, the Rugby XV in 1961/2, the Debating Team in 1962 and was CSM in the CCF; Edinburgh University; St. Andrews University. Apprenticeship, Sturrock Morrison & Gilruth, Solicitors, Dundee, 1967-69; admitted Solicitor, 1969; Notary Public, 1970; assumed Partner, Gray Robertson & Wilkie (subsequently Bowman Gray Robertson and Wilkie, now Bowmans) 1971. Secretary: Dundee Institute of Architects,

1970-96, Dundee Building Trades (Employers) Association, 1970-89, Dundee Construction Industry Group Training Association, 1970-93, Tayside Construction Safety Association, 1975-89; Joint Secretary, Local Joint Council for Building Industry, 1970-89, and Local Joint Apprenticeship Committee for the Building Industry, 1970-89; Clerk, Three United Trades of Dundee and to Mason Trade, Wright Trade and Slater Trade of Dundee, 1997-2000; Lord Dean of Guild of Dundee, 1987-90; first Lord President, Court of Deans of Guild of Scotland, 1989; Director, High School of Dundee, 1980-90; Chairman, High School of Dundee Scholarship Fund, 1987-90; Co-opted Member, Law Society of Scotland Committees - Public Relations and Conference, 1982-90, Complaints, 1987-90; Member: Working Party on "Corporate Conveyancing", 1989, School Age Team Sports Enquiry, 1989; Committee Member and National Selector, Scottish Cricket Union, 1974-83; Selector, 1990; President: Scottish Counties Cricket Board, 1981, Scottish Cricket Union, 1989; Sometime Highland Cattle Breeder - Champion Male, Oban, 1991; Best Male Calf, Oban, 1991; Best Male, Angus Show, 1996. Recreations: family; cricketophile; travel; golf; music; opera. Address: (h.) 96 Dunnichen Avenue, Gowanbank, Forfar, Angus DD8 2EJ. E-mail: bnb551@gmail.com

Bowman, Bill. MSP (Scottish Conservative and Unionist), North East Scotland region, 2016-2021; b. 30.5.50. Chartered Accountant.

Bownes, Professor Mary, OBE (2006), BSc, DPhil. Emerita Professor of Developmental Biology, University of Edinburgh, since 2014, Vice-Principal (Community Development), 2015-16; b. 14.11.48, Drewsteignton, Devon. Educ. Univ. of Sussex. Career: postdoctoral associate, Univ. of Freiburg and Univ. of California, Irvine, 1973-76; Lecturer in genetics and Developmental Biology, Univ. of Essex, 1976-79; Univ. of Edinburgh, Lecturer in Molecular Biology, 1979-89, Senior Lecturer, 1989-91, Reader 1991-94, Personal Chair in Developmental Biology, since 1994, Associate Dean for Postgraduates Faculty of Science and Engineering, 1997-98, Head, Institute of Cell and Molecular Biology, 1998-2001, Vice-Principal, 2003-2006, Senior Vice-Principal; Member, numerous university committees and groups; Director, Scottish Initiative for Biotechnology Education, since 2002; Member, Editorial Advisory Board, Journal of Embryology and Experimental Morphology/Development, 1982-88; Member, Editorial Board, Insect Molecular Biology, since 1990; Associate Editor, Developmental Biology, 1992-95; Member, Editorial Board, Journal of Endocrinology, since 2000. Author of numerous papers in journals, book chapters and review articles; external examiner, Univ. of Sussex, 1996-2000, Univ. of Oxford, 2001-03, Univ. of York, 2004-06, Univ. of Glasgow, 2005-09, Univ. of Leicester, 2007-09; Chair, Steering Committee, Science and Plants for Schools (SAPS) Biotechnology Scotland Project, 2000-09, Member, 1998-2000; Chair, Board, Edinburgh Centre for Rural Research, 2003-2011 (Member, 1999, Member, Executive Committee, 2000-03); Chair, Strategy Board, BBSRC, 2004-07, Students and Fellowships Strategy Panel, BBSRC, 2004-08; Chair, Young People's Committee, RSE, 2003-2011; Member: Board, Genetics Society, 1980-83, Committee, Br Society for Developmental Biology, 1982-87 (Treasurer, 1984-89), Advisory Board Institute for Science Education Scotland, 2002-03, Advisory Board, MRC, 2002-03, Cell and Molecular Biology Section Committee, RSE, 2004-06, public eng on Educ Committee, RSE, since 2009, Meetings Committee, RSE, 2005-09, Skills Committee 2011 SFC, 2006-09, Board, Highlands and Islands Enterprise, 2008; Member, Executive Committee, RSE, since 2008; Board of Scot Association of Marine Sciences and Chair of Education Committee; CBiol, FIBiol, FRES, FRSE, FRSA 2009. Publications:

Metamorphosis (jt ed, 1985); Ecdysone from Metabolism to Regulation of Gene Expression (ed, 1986). Style – Prof Mary Bownes, OBE. Address: (b.) The University of Edinburgh, Charles Stewart House, Room 2.2, 9-16 Chambers Street, Edinburgh EH1 1HT.

Boyack, Sarah. MSP (Labour), Lothian region, since 2019 and 2011-16, Edinburgh Central, 1999-2011; Spokesperson for Local Government, since 2019; Shadow Cabinet Secretary for Environmental Justice, 2015-16. Former Lecturer in Planning; Minister for Transport and Environment, 1999-2000; Minister for Transport and Planning, 2000-01; Convener, Environment and Rural Development Committee, 2003-07; Deputy Minister for Environment and Rural Development, 2007; Shadow Cabinet Secretary for Rural Development, Environment and Climate Change, 2007-2011; Shadow Cabinet Secretary for Local Government and Planning, 2011-14; Shadow Cabinet Secretary for Rural Affairs, Food and Environment, 2014-15; Visiting Lecturer, Heriot Watt University, 2016-17; Head of Public Affairs, Scottish Federation of Housing Associations, 2017-19. Address: Scottish Parliament, Edinburgh EH99 1SP.

Boyd, Alan Robb, LLB, BA. Director, Public Law, McGrigors LLP (formerly McGrigor Donald), 1997-2010; Consultant, Pinsent Masons LLP, 2010-2014; b. 30.7.53, Glasgow; m., Frances Helen; 2 d. Educ. Irvine Royal Academy; Dundee University. Principal Solicitor, Shetland Islands Council, 1979-81; Principal Solicitor, Glenrothes Development Corporation, 1981-84; Legal Advisor, Irvine Development Corporation, 1984-97. Law Society of Scotland: Member, Council, 1985-97, Convener, Finance Committee, 1992-94, Vice-President, 1994-95, President, 1995-96; President, European Company Lawyers' Association, 1992-94; Convenor, Association for Scottish Public Affairs, 1998-2000. Recreations: golf; reading; gardening; music. Address: (h.) 26, Hannah Wynd, St Quivox, Ayr KA6 5HB; T.-01292 521936.

Boyd of Duncansby, Rt Hon Lord (Colin David Boyd), PC, BA (Econ), LLB. Senator of the College of Justice, since 2012; Member of the Inner House of the Court of Session, since 2022; Life Peer; Lord Advocate, 2000-06; Solicitor General for Scotland, 1997-2000; Member of the Scottish Executive, 1999-2006; Head of Public Law, Dundas & Wilson LLP, 2007-2012; b. 7.6.53, Falkirk; m., Fiona Margaret MacLeod; 2 s.; 1 d. Educ. Wick High School; George Watson's College, Edinburgh; University of Manchester; University of Edinburgh. Solicitor, 1978-82; called to Bar, 1983; Advocate Depute, 1993-95; took Silk, 1995; Solicitor Advocate, 2007-2012; Honorary Fellow, Society of Advanced Legal Studies; Honorary Professor of Law, University of Glasgow, 2007-2012; Member, Commission on Scottish Devolution, 2008-09; Chairman, Northern Lighthouse Heritage Trust, 2008-2012; Deputy Chair, Scottish Civil Justice Council, since 2020 (Member, since 2016); Vice President, Investigatory Powers Tribunal, since 2019; Writer to the Signet (WS), since 2007. Publication: The Legal Aspects of Devolution (Contributor), 1997. Recreations: hill-walking; reading; watching rugby. Address: (b.) Court of Session, Parliament House, Parliament Square, Edinburgh EH1 1RQ.

Boyd, Dr Donald MacLeod, MB, ChB, DipTheol. Medical Practitioner; Highlands and Islands Campaign Manager, Scottish Christian Party "Proclaiming Christ's Lordship", 2006-07, Chairman, 2007-2010; Leader, Scottish Christian Party, since 2010; Nomination Officer, Christian Party "Proclaiming Christ's Lordship", since 2013; Chairman, Westhill Community Council, Inverness, 2011-2014; Webmaster, since 2013; Vice Chair of Highland Friends of Israel, since 2015; Minister, Inverness Free Presbyterian Church of Scotland, 1989-2000 (Clerk, Northern Presbytery, 1991-2000); Church Tutor in Systematic Theology, 1995-2000; b. Glasgow; m., Elizabeth Schouten;

1 s.; 3 d. Educ. Glasgow Academy; Glasgow University. Southern General Hospital, 1978; Stobhill General Hospital, 1979; Vale of Leven Hospital, 1979; ordained Free Presbyterian Church of Scotland, 1983; Clerk of Religion and Morals Committee, 1984-92 and Convener, 1992-94; Deputy to Australia and New Zealand, 1988; Member, Churches Liaison Committee on AIDS, Highland Health Board, 1992-94; Member, Highland Regional Council Education Committee, 1994-96; Moderator of Synod of Free Presbyterian Church of Scotland, 1997-98; Church delegate to the European Court of Human Rights, February 2000. Publications: Popular History of the Origins of the Free Presbyterian Church of Scotland, 1987; "What's that Tune? A Melody Index of Sol-fa Tunes", 2009. Blog: donaldboyd.org. Twitter: @DonaldBoyd7. Recreations: reading; writing; Street Pastor, 2007–2017; gardening; walking; photography; British Sign Language; historical research; advanced driving; astrophysics; genealogy. Address: Inverness.

Boyd, Professor Sir Ian L., BSc, PhD, DSc, FRSB, FRSE, FRS. Chief Scientific Adviser, Department for Environment, Food and Rural Affairs, 2012-19; Professor in Biology, University of St Andrews, since 2001; Director, Sea Mammal Research Unit, 2001-2012; Director, Scottish Oceans Institute, 2009-2012; Chief Executive, SMRU Ltd., 2006-09; b. 9.2.57, Kilmarnock; m., Sheila M.E. Aitken; 1 s.; 2 d. Educ. George Heriot's School, Edinburgh; Aberdeen University; Cambridge University. Churchill Fellow, 1980; Institute of Terrestrial Ecology, Monks Wood, 1982-87; British Antarctic Survey, 1987-2001; Antarctic Service Medal of the United States, 1995; Bruce Medal, Royal Society of Edinburgh, 1995; Honorary Professor, Birmingham University, 1997; Scientific Medal, Zoological Society of London, 1998; Fellow of the Royal Society of Edinburgh since 2002; Editor-in-Chief, Journal of Zoology, 2006-08; Marsh Award for Marine and Freshwater Conservation, 2006. Member, Council, Hebridean Trust and Seamark Trust; Chair, Marine Alliance for Science and Technology for Scotland, 2005-2010; Member, Scottish Science Advisory Council, 2010-2014; Member, Natural Environment Research Council, 2013-19; Member, Biotechnology and Biological Sciences Research Council, 2013-19; Chair, UK Food Research Partnership, 2013-15; Chair, Governance Board for UK Climate Projections, 2015-19; Member, Royal Society Science Policy Advisory Group, since 2015; Reviewing Editor, Science, since 2011; Non-Executive Director, Fera Science Ltd, since 2015; Fellow, Royal Society of Biology, since 2011; Chairman, Oil & Gas UK Advisory Board on Decommissioning, 2010-12; Chair, UK Research Integrity Office, since 2019; Trustee, National Oceanography Centre, since 2019; Honorary Doctorate, University of Exeter, 2017, University of Plymouth, 2021; Polar Medal, 2017; Knight Bachelor, 2019; Fellow of the Royal Society, since 2021; Co-Chair with First Minister of Scotland, Scottish Environment Council; Member COVID-19 Scientific Advisory Group for Emergencies (SAGE), since 2020. Publications: seven books; over 170 papers. Recreations: walking; photography. Address: College Gate, North Street, St Andrews University, St Andrews KY16 9AJ; T.-01334 462553.

Boyle, Professor Alan Edward, LLD, MA, BCL. Emeritus Professor of Public International Law, University of Edinburgh (Professor, since 1995); Barrister, since 1977; b. 28.3.53, Belfast; m., Caroline. Educ. Royal Belfast Academical Institution; University of Oxford (Pembroke College). Queen Mary College, University of London, Faculty of Law, 1978-94; University of Texas, School of Law, 1988 and 1994; Paris II and X, 2000-01; LUISS,

Rome, 2009; Essex Court Chambers, London, since 2006; General Editor, International and Comparative Law Quarterly, 1998-2006. Publications: International Law and The Environment (Co-author), 2009; The Making of International Law (Co-author), 2007. Recreations: gliding; music; theatre. Address: (b.) School of Law, University of Edinburgh, Old College, South Bridge, Edinburgh EH8 9YL.

Boyle, James, FRSE. Former Chair, National Library of Scotland; b. 29.3.46; m., Marie; 3 s. Head of BBC Radio Scotland when it was named UK Radio Station of the Year; former Controller of BBC Radio 4; has had several public service posts, including Chair of the Scottish Arts Council and Chair of the Scottish Cultural Commission; founder and first Chair of Edinburgh UNESCO City of Literature; founder of Glasgow UNESCO City of Music.

Boyle, Stephen, BAcc, FCPFA. Auditor General for Scotland, since 2020; m.; 2 c. Educ. Glasgow University. Career history: Senior Associate, PricewaterhouseCoopers, 1997-2001; Audit Manager, Audit Scotland, 2002-07; Financial Analysis Manager, Scottish Housing Regulator, 2007-08; Head of Finance and Corporate Services, Cube Housing Association (Wheatley Group), 2008-2010; Assistant Director of Finance, Glasgow Housing Association (Wheatley Group); Audit Director, Audit Scotland, 2010-2020. Address: Audit Scotland, 4th Floor, 102 West Port, Edinburgh EH3 9DN; T.-0131 625 1617.

Boyne, Professor George, MA, MLitt, PhD, AcSS. Principal and Vice-Chancellor, University of Aberdeen, since August 2018. Career history: spent most of academic career in Wales; Pro Vice-Chancellor, Head of College of Arts, Humanities and Social Sciences, Member of University Executive Board, Cardiff University from 2012; previously Dean of Cardiff University's Business School. Former pupil of Aberdeen Grammar School. Address: University of Aberdeen, King's College, Aberdeen AB24 3FX; T.-01224 272000.

Braat, Bailie Philip, LLB (Hons), DipLP, MSc. Lord Provost and Lord Lieutenant, Glasgow City Council, since 2020. Educ. University of Glasgow; Glasgow Graduate School of Law; University of Strathclyde. Career history: Trainee Solicitor, Mitchells Roberton Solicitors, 2000-02; Solicitor: Dundas & Wilson, 2002-04, Wright, Johnston & Mackenzie LLP (WJM), 2004-07; Board Member: City of Glasgow Licensing Board, 2007-09, Glasgow Housing Association (GHA), 2009-2012; Chair, Strathclyde Police Authority, 2012-13; Non-Executive Director, Scottish Exhibition and Conference Centre (SECC), 2007-2013; Chair, Regeneration and the Economy Policy Development Committee, 2015-16; Director, Clydeside Action on Asbestos (CAA), 2011-16; Trustee, Kelvin Hall Sports Trust, 2007-2017; Board Member, The Advocacy Project, 2007-2017; Chair, Local Government Pension Schemes (Scotland) Conveners Forum, 2010-17; Board Member, Legal Services Agency Limited (Brown & Co. Solicitors), 2012-17; Director, West of Scotland Loans Fund Limited, 2014-17; Strathclyde Pension Fund: Chair, 2010, Vice Convener, 2010-16, Convener, 2016-17; Trustee, Glasgow City Heritage Trust (GCHT), 2012-17; Glasgow City Council: ward 10 Anderston/City/Yorkhill (Labour), since 2007, City Treasurer, 2016-17, Depute Lord Provost, 2017-2020. Address: Glasgow City Chambers, 82 George Square, Glasgow G2 1DU; T.-0141 287 5788.

Bracadale, The Hon. Lord (Alastair P. Campbell), MA, LLB. Retired senior Scottish judge; b. 18.9.49, Skye. Educ. George Watson's College; University of Aberdeen. English Teacher, Vale of Leven Academy, Dunbartonshire, 1973-75 before returning to study law at the University of Strathclyde; admitted as a solicitor in 1979 and entered the Procurator Fiscal service as a prosecutor; admitted to the Faculty of Advocates in 1985; called to the English Bar at the Inner Temple in 1990; Advocate Depute, 1990-93; Senator of the College of Justice, 2003-2017; Judge of the Court of Session and High Court of the Justiciary, 2003-2017; Standing Junior Counsel in Scotland to HM Customs and Excise, 1995; appointed Queen's Counsel, 1995; served as Home Advocate Depute, 1997-98; Member: Criminal Justice Forum, 1996-97, Scottish Criminal Rules Council 1996-98, Criminal Injuries Compensation Board, 1997; Home Advocate Depute (Scotland's senior prosecutor), 1997-1999; Senior Crown Counsel in Lockerbie trial, Camp Van Zeist, the Netherlands, 1999-2001.

Bradley, Andrea, PGDip. General Secretary, Educational Institute of Scotland (EIS), since 2022. Educ. University of Strathclyde. Career history: began teaching in 1995 as an English teacher in Inverclyde; became Principal Teacher of English in South Lanarkshire; appointed as National Officer (Education and Equality), EIS in 2014; EIS Assistant Secretary (Education and Equality), 2015-2022. The first woman to hold the post of General Secretary in the 175-year history of the EIS. Address: The Educational Institute of Scotland, 46 Moray Place, Edinburgh EH3 6BH; T.-0131 225 6244.

Bradley, Monsignor Hugh, BA. Diocesan Administrator, Archdiocese of Glasgow, since 2021; Parish Priest, Holy Cross, Crosshill. Educ. Pontifical Gregorian University in Rome (ecclesiastical degrees in philosophy, theology and Church history); University of Strathclyde. Ordained by the late Cardinal Tom Winning in 1989; former official at the Congregation for Catholic Education at the Vatican; served as General Secretary of the Bishops' Conference of Scotland, and latterly as Vicar General of the Archdiocese of Glasgow. Address: Archdiocese of Glasgow, 196 Clyde Street, Glasgow G1 4JY; T.-0141 226 5898.

Bradley, Professor Ian Campbell, MA, BD, DPhil. Emeritus Professor of Cultural and Spiritual History, St. Andrews University; Writer and Broadcaster; b. 28.5.50, Berkhamsted; m., Lucy Patricia; 1 s.; 1 d. Educ. Tonbridge School, Kent; New College, Oxford; St. Andrews University. Research Fellow, New College, Oxford, 1971-75; Staff Journalist, The Times, 1976-82; ordained into Church of Scotland, 1990; Head, Religious Broadcasting, BBC Scotland, 1990-91; Lecturer in Practical Theology, Aberdeen University, 1992-99; Reader in Church History and Practical Theology, University of St Andrews, 1999-2016; Principal of St Mary's College, St Andrews University, 2013-2017; appointed Professor of Cultural and Spiritual History, University of St Andrews, 2017. Vice President of the Sir Arthur Sullivan Society. Trustee of the D'Oyly Carte Opera Trust and the Scottish Pilgrim Routes Forum. Publications: The Call to Seriousness, 1974; William Morris and his World, 1975; The Optimists, 1976; The Penguin Annotated Gilbert & Sullivan, 1980; The Strange Rebirth of Liberal Britain, 1982; Enlightened Entrepreneurs, 1986; The Penguin Book of Hymns, 1989; God is Green, 1990; O Love That Wilt Not Let Me Go, 1990; Marching to the Promised Land, 1992; The Celtic Way, 1993; The Power of Sacrifice, 1995; The Complete Annotated Gilbert and Sullivan, 1996; Columba, Pilgrim and Penitent, 1996; Abide with Me – the World of the Victorian Hymn, 1997; Celtic Christianity: Making Myths and Chasing Dreams, 1999; The Penguin Book of Carols, 1999; Colonies of Heaven: Celtic Models for Today's Church, 2000; God Save the Queen – The Spiritual Dimension of Monarchy, 2002; You've Got to Have a Dream: The Message of the Musical, 2004; Oh Joy! Oh

Rapture! The Enduring Phenomenon of Gilbert and Sullivan, 2005; The Daily Telegraph Book of Hymns, 2005; The Daily Telegraph Book of Carols, 2006; Believing in Britain, 2006; Pilgrimage - A cultural and spiritual journey, 2009; Water Music: Music Making in the Spas of Europe and North America, 2010; Grace, Order, Openness and Diversity: Reclaiming Liberal Theology, 2010; God Save the Queen - The Spiritual Heart of Monarchy, 2012; Water: A Spiritual History, 2012; Lost Chords and Christian Soldiers: The Sacred Music of Arthur Sullivan, 2013; Argyll - The Making of a Spiritual Landscape, 2015; The Complete Annotated Gilbert and Sullivan (20th Anniversary Edition), 2016; Following the Celtic Way, 2017; The Fife Pilgrim Way, 2019; Health, Hedonism and Hypochondria: The Hidden History of Spas, 2020; God is Green (new edition), 2021; Columba: Politician, Penitent and Pilgrim, 2021; Arthur Sullivan, A Life of Divine Emollient, 2021; The Quiet Haven: An Anthology of Readings on Death and Heaven (2021); The Coffin Roads: Journeys to the West (2022). Recreations: music; walking; family; spas; tennis; singing. Address: (h.) 4 Donaldson Gardens, St Andrews KY16 9DN.
E-mail: icb@st-andrews.ac.uk

Brady, Adrian J.B, BSc, MB, ChB, MD, FRCP (Glasg), FRCPE, FBHS, FESC, FAHA. Honorary Professor and Consultant Cardiologist, Glasgow Royal Infirmary, since 1996; b. 27.5.61, Edinburgh; 1 s.; 2 d. Educ. Edinburgh Academy; Scotus Academy; Edinburgh University. Trained in Cardiology at Hammersmith Hospital and National Heart and Lung Institute, London; Winner, American Heart Association Young Investigator Award, 1993; Winner, British Cardiac Society Young Investigator Award, 1993; President, British Hypertension Society, 2015-17; Chairman, Guidelines Committee, British Cardiovascular Society; Visiting Professor of Cardiology, Mayo Clinic and Cleveland Clinic; Faculty Member, American Heart Association. Recreations: skiing; golf; piano. Address: (b.) Cardiology Department, Walton Building, Glasgow Royal Infirmary, Glasgow G4 0SF; T.-0141-211 4727.

Brady, John, BSc Hons (Open), MBA with Distinction. Head of Fundraising, St Andrew's Hospice (Lanarkshire), since 2015; b 10.03.65, Glasgow. Educ. Craigmount High School; Glasgow University; Open University; Strathclyde University. Advertising Sales Manager, Angel Publishing, 1986-91; Financial Adviser, City Financial Partners, 1991-95; Field Sales Executive, Daily Record, 1995-97; Field Sales Executive, The Scotsman, 1997-98; Scottish Manager, British Lung Foundation, 1998-2000; Donor Development Manager, Sense Scotland, 2000-02; Community Investment Programme Manager, BT Scotland, 2002-03; Fundraising and Communications Manager, Alcohol Focus Scotland, 2003-05; Head of Fundraising, Sense Scotland, 2005-10; Director, Business Development, Erskine, 2010-12; Chief Executive Officer, OneKind (formerly Advocates for Animals), 2012-15. Recreations: family; films; football; reading. Address: (b.) St. Andrew's Hospice Ltd, Henderson Street, Airdrie, Lanarkshire ML6 6DJ; T.-01236 766951.

Braid, The Hon Lord (Peter John), LLB (Hons), WS. Senator of the College of Justice, since 2020; Sheriff, Edinburgh, since 2015 (formerly Sheriff, Haddington); Solicitor Advocate, 1995-2005; Partner, Morton Fraser, Solicitors, 1985-2005; b. 6.3.58, Edinburgh; m., Heather McIntosh; 2 s. Educ. George Watson's College, Edinburgh; University of Edinburgh. Recreations: golf; bridge; cycling. Address: Parliament House, Parliament Square, Edinburgh EH1 1RQ.

Brailsford, Hon. Lord (Sidney) Neil Brailsford. Senator of the Royal College of Justice in Scotland, since 2006; b. 15.8.54, Edinburgh; m., Elaine Nicola Robbie; 3 s. Educ. Daniel Stewart's College, Edinburgh; Stirling University;

Edinburgh University. Admitted Scottish Bar, 1981, English Bar, 1990; Standing Junior Counsel, Department of Agriculture and Fisheries, 1987-92; QC, 1994; Advocate Depute, 1999-2000. Treasurer, Faculty of Advocates, 2000; Member, Court, Stirling University, 2001-05; Part-time Chairman, Discipline Committee, Institute of Chartered Accountants of Scotland, 2002-06. Recreations: food; wine; travel; reading; American history and politics; baseball; fishing; supporting Heart of Midlothian Football Club. Address: (b.) Parliament House, Edinburgh EH1 1RF; Kidder Hill Road, Grafton, Vermont 05146, USA.

Brankin, Rhona, Hon. FRIBA. MSP (Labour), Midlothian, 1999-2011; Shadow Cabinet Secretary for Education and Lifelong Learning, 2007-2010; Minister for Communities, 2007; Deputy Minister for Environment and Rural Development, 2005-07; Deputy Minister for Health and Community Care, 2004-05. Educ. Aberdeen University; Northern College. Former teacher and lecturer on special educational needs; Deputy Minister for: Culture and Sport, 1999-2000, for Environment and Rural Development, 2000-01; former Chair, Scottish Labour Party; Honorary Member of Chartered Institute of Library and Information Professionals in Scotland.

Brannen, Roy. Interim Director-General Net Zero, Scottish Government, since 2021; Chief Executive, Transport Scotland, 2015-2021 (previously Director of Trunk Roads and Bus Operations). Career history: Transport Scotland and Transport Directorate since joining the then Scottish Executive in 1999. Chartered Civil Engineer with over 25 years' experience in highways and transportation and a Fellow of both the Institution of Civil Engineers and the Chartered Institution of Highways and Transportation. Address: The Scottish Government, St Andrew's House, Regent Road, Edinburgh EH1 3DG.
E-mail: DGNetZero@gov.scot

Bray, Professor Francesca Anne, PhD. Professor Emerita of Social Anthropology, University of Edinburgh (Professor, since 2005); b. 18.12.48, Cairo, Egypt; m., A.F. Robertson. Educ. Collège Sévigné, Paris; Girton College, Cambridge. Career: East Asian History of Science Library, Cambridge, 1973-84; Centre National de la Recherche Scientifique (CNRS), Paris, 1985-87; Professor of Anthropology, UCLA, 1988-93; University of California Santa Barbara, 1993-2004. Publications: Science and Civilisation in China: Agriculture (1984); The Rice Economies (1986); Technology and Gender: Fabrics of Power in Late Imperial China (1997); Rice: Global Networks and New Histories (2015); Moving Crops and the Scales of History (2022); Cambridge History of Technology (in progress). Prix Bordin for History, Académie des Inscriptions et Belles-Lettres, 1985; Dexter Prize (Society for the History of Technology), 1999; Leonardo da Vinci Medal for History of Technology, 2019; Fellow, Royal Society of Arts. Address: (b.) Social Anthropology, Crystal Macmillan Building, 15a George Square, University of Edinburgh, Edinburgh EH8 9LD.
E-mail: francesca.bray@ed.ac.uk

Breeze, David John, OBE, BA, PhD, HonDLitt (Glasgow), HonFSA Scot, FRSE, HonMIFA. Chief Inspector of Ancient Monuments, Scotland, 1989-2005; Head of Special Heritage Projects, Historic Scotland, 2005-09; Visiting Professor, Department of Archaeology, Durham University, since 1993; Honorary Professor, Edinburgh University, since 1996; Honorary Professor, Newcastle University, since 2003; Honorary Professor, Stirling University, since 2016; b. 25.7.44, Blackpool; m., Pamela Diane Silvester; 2 s. Educ. Blackpool Grammar School; Durham University. Inspector of Ancient Monuments, Scotland, 1969-88;

Principal Inspector of Ancient Monuments, Scotland, 1988-89. Member: International Committee of the Congress of Roman Frontier Studies, since 1983, International Committee on Archaeological Heritage Management, 1997-2009, Council, Society of Antiquaries of London, 1984-86 and 2009-2013, Council, Royal Society of Edinburgh, 1997-2000; Trustee, Senhouse Roman Museum, since 1985; Chairman: 1989, 1999, 2009 and 2019; Hadrian's Wall Pilgrimages, British Archaeological Awards, 1993-2009; President: South Shields Archaeological and Historical Society, 1983-85, Society of Antiquaries of Scotland, 1987-90, Society of Antiquaries of Newcastle, 2008-11, Royal Archaeological Institute, 2009-2011, Cumberland and Westmorland Antiquarian and Archaeological Society, 2011-14; Corresponding Member, German Archaeological Institute; Current Archaeology "Archaeologist of the Year 2009"; recipient of the European Archaeological Heritage Prize 2010; recipient of the British Academy's Kenyon Medal 2021 awarded for contributions to classical studies and archaeology. Publications: The Building of Hadrian's Wall, The Army of Hadrian's Wall, Hadrian's Wall, and Roman Officers and Frontiers (all Co-author); Roman Scotland: a guide to the visible remains; Roman Scotland: some recent excavations (Editor); The Romans in Scotland (Co-author); The Northern Frontiers of Roman Britain; Roman Forts in Britain; Studies in Scottish Antiquity (Editor); Hadrian's Wall, a souvenir guide; A Queen's Progress, an introduction to the buildings associated with Mary Queen of Scots in Scotland; The Second Augustan Legion in North Britain; Service in the Roman Army (Co-editor); Invaders of Scotland (Co-author); Roman Scotland: Frontier Country; The Stone of Destiny: Symbol of Nationhood (Co-author); Historic Scotland, 5000 Years of Scotland's Heritage; Historic Scotland, People and Places; Stone of Destiny, artefact and icon (Co-editor); The Antonine Wall; Frontiers of the Roman Empire (Co-author); Handbook to the Roman Wall; Roman Frontiers in Britain; Edge of Empire, Rome's Scottish Frontier, The Antonine Wall; Frontiers of the Roman Empire, The European Dimension of a World Heritage Site (Co-editor); The Frontiers of Imperial Rome; The First Souvenirs, Enamelled Vessels from Hadrian's Wall (editor); 200 Years: The Society of Antiquaries of Newcastle upon Tyne, 1813-2013 (editor); Hadrian's Wall: A History of Archaeological Thought; Understanding Roman Frontiers (Co-editor); The Roman Army; Bearsden: A Roman Fort on the Antonine Wall; Hadrian's Wall: Paintings by the Richardson Family; Maryport: A Roman Fort and its Community; The Crosby Garrett Helmet (editor); Hadrian's Wall. A study in archaeological exploration and interpretation; Hadrian's Wall. A Journey Through Time; The Pilgrimages of Hadrian's Wall, 1849-2019: A History; The Antonine Wall (Co-editor). Recreations: reading; walking; travel. E-mail: davidbreeze@hotmail.co.uk

Bremner, Colin. Partner, Burnett & Reid; b. 1968. Educ. Cults Academy; Aberdeen University. Joined Burnett & Reid in 1996, becoming a partner in 2001; many years of experience specialising in all aspects of property law and can assist with buying or selling residential property, title transfers, security work and re-mortgaging, boundary disputes and servitudes. Notary Public; Director of Aberdeen Solicitors Property Centre. Address: Burnett & Reid, 15 Golden Square, Aberdeen AB10 1WF; T.-01224 644333; e-mail: csbremner@burnett-reid.co.uk

Brennan, Ian, BA, FCCA, MBA. Director of Regulation, Scottish Housing Regulator, since 2018; Director of Finance & Risk, Scottish Housing Regulator, 2013-18; Head of Business Analysis, 2009-2013; b. 20.6.59, Glasgow; m., Carolyn; 1 s.; 1 d. Educ. Holyrood, Glasgow; Strathclyde University; Glasgow University. Early career in the utility sector in finance and IT; worked in a variety of audit posts in the public and private sectors, latterly as an IT

audit specialist with the Accounts Commission for Scotland in the late 1980's and early 1990's; joined Ayrshire and Arran Health Board as Chief Internal Auditor; left the NHS to join the University of Glasgow, serving as Head of Internal Audit and Head of Management Services; became Risk Manager for the Medical and Dental Defence Union of Scotland (MDDUS). Board Member & Audit Committee Chair, Historic Environment Scotland, since 2016; Board Member, Cardonald College, 2005-2013; Chair, Council of Higher Education Internal Auditors, 1996-98. Recreations: squash; tennis; writing. Address: (b.) Buchanan House, 58 Port Dundas Road, Glasgow G4 0HF; T.-0141 242 5642. E-mail: ian.brennan@shr.gov.scot

Brennan, Dr Janet. Lecturer and Author. Spent twenty-five years in The Netherlands, latterly as Head of Faculty of Behavioural Sciences at an American University in Leiden; returned to Scotland and oversaw the restoration of Barholm Castle, Galloway from a ruinous state, 2003-05; former Chair of the Scottish Castles Association; gives regular lectures on restoring Scottish castles and castles at risk. Trusteeships in the arts, heritage, education and tourism; Member of the Board of Management, Dumfries and Galloway College; Board Member, Historic Environment Scotland, since 2017. Publication: Scotland's Castles: Rescued, Rebuilt and Reoccupied, 2014. Address: Historic Environment Scotland, Longmore House, Salisbury Place, Edinburgh EH9 1SH; T.-0131 668 8600.

Brett Young, Michael Jonathan, DL. Manager, East Sutherland Village Advisory Service, 1986-99; Director: Voluntary Groups, East Sutherland, 1996-99, and 2001-2020, Highland Advice and Information Network Ltd., 1994-99; Deputy Lieutenant, Sutherland, 1995-2012; Chairman, Voluntary Groups, East Sutherland, 2011-14; b. 18.10.37, Salisbury; m., Helen Dorothy Anne Barker; 2 s. Educ. Dartmouth. Royal Australian Navy, 1956-69; Sales and Marketing Manager, 1969-79; Senior Account Manager, 1979-84. Chairman, PR Committee, Retread Manufacturers Association, 1975-79; Executive Member, Community Organisations Group, Scotland, 1990-93; Chairman: East Sutherland Council of Social Service, 1991-94, East Sutherland Local Community Care Forum, 1993-99; Chairman, SSAFA, Sutherland, 2002-2017; Chairman, Dornoch Cricket Club, 1991-2005. Recreations: cricket; naval history; music. Address: (h.) West Shinness Lodge, Lairg, Sutherland; T.-01549 402495.

Brew, David Allan, BA, MSc. Head of Fisheries, Marine Scotland, 2009-2011; b. 19.2.53, Kettering. Educ. Kettering Grammar School; Heriot-Watt University; Strathclyde University; European University Institute, Florence. Administration Trainee and HEO(D), Scottish Office, 1979-81; Administrator, DGV, Commission of the EC, 1981-84; Principal, Scottish Office, Glasgow, 1984-88, Edinburgh, 1988-90; Head: Electricity Privatisation Division, 1990-91, European Funds and Co-ordination Division, 1991-95, Sea Fisheries Division, 1995-98; Cabinet Office, Constitution Secretariat, 1998-99; Chief Executive, Institute of Chartered Accountants of Scotland, 2000-03; Scottish Government, Head: Cultural Policy Division, 2004-06, Rural Communities Division, 2006-09. Member, Court, Heriot-Watt University, 1985-91 and 2000-06; Member, AUC (Air Transport Users Council), 2004-2011; Board Member: Creative Scotland, since 2015, MG Alba, 2012-2020, Robert Gordon University, 2012-15; Public Member, Network Rail, 2012-15. Recreations: languages; music; film; gastronomy. Address (h.) 1 Dundas Street, Edinburgh EH3 6QG; T.-0131-556 4692.

Breward, Professor Chris, FRSE. Director, National Museums Scotland, since 2020. Educ. The Courtauld

Institute and the Royal College of Art. Taught the history of design, Royal College of Art, 1994-99 before becoming Research Director at the London College of Fashion; moved to the V&A as Head of Research in 2004; Principal, Edinburgh College of Art, University of Edinburgh, 2011-17; Director, Collection & Research, National Galleries of Scotland, 2017-2020. Currently Visiting Professor at the University of Edinburgh, Fellow of the Royal Society of Arts and an Honorary Fellow of the Royal College of Art; Governor of the Pasold Foundation; Advisory Board Member, Glasgow School of Art Collections. Address: National Museums Scotland, Chambers Street, Edinburgh EH1 1JF.

Brewis, Aileen. Lord Lieutenant of Wigtown, since 2020; m., Christopher Brewis; 2 c (Catherine and David); 2 grandchildren (William Mowat and Lucy Mowat). Career history: journalist on local newspapers and communications advisor for local government; has worked with service organisations, various veterans' groups and charities. Trustee of Ardwell Community Kirk; heavily involved with many local charities and active member of Stoneykirk Scottish Women's Institute.

Brian, Simon, MA (Hons), PGCE. Head, St Leonards School, St Andrews, since 2021; m., Veronique; 3 s. Educ. Quarry Bay School, Hong Kong; Ripon Grammar School; The University of Edinburgh; University of London. Career history: taught in France and Austria; Teacher, 2 i/c French, Dulwich College, 2003-07; Head of French, Highgate School, 2007-2011; Deputy Head: Cheltenham College, 2011-18, Charterhouse, Surrey, 2018-2021. Address: St Leonards School, St Andrews, Fife KY16 9QJ; T.-01334 472126.

Bridle, Nikki. Chief Executive, Clackmannanshire Council since May 2018; b. Halifax. Career history: worked for the Council for 8 years, starting as Finance and Corporate Services Director and rising to Depute Chief Executive; previously worked for Audit Scotland, Audit Commission and KPMG. Address: Clackmannanshire Council, Kilncraigs, Greenside Street, Alloa, Clackmannanshire FK10 1EB; T.-01259 452002.

Briggs, Colin, MA (Hist). Chair, NHS Scotland Directors of Planning, since 2019; Director of Strategic Planning, NHS Lothian, since 2016; Chair, Penumbra; b. 3.77. Educ. The University of Edinburgh; University of Birmingham; Harvard Business School; Edinburgh Napier University; Harvard Business School. Career history: National Management Trainee, NHS Graduate Management Training Scheme, West Midlands, 2000-02; Planning Manager, NHS Greater Glasgow and Clyde, 2002-03; Project Manager, NHS Forth Valley, Falkirk, 2003-05; Program Manager, NHS Tayside, Dundee, 2005-07; Chief Strategy and Performance Officer, Edinburgh Integration Joint Board, 2017-19; NHS Lothian: Service Manager, Women's and Children's Services, 2007-08, Head of Service, WCN, 2008-2011, Associate Director of Operations - Women's, Children's and Neurosciences, 2011-12, General Manager, Edinburgh CHP, 2012-13, Hospital Director, 2013-15, Associate Director of Strategic Planning (Acute), 2015-16. Recreations: comics nerd; cyclist. Address: Lothian NHS Board, Waverleygate, 2-4 Waterloo Place, Edinburgh EH1 3EG; T.-0131 242 1000.

Briggs, Miles Edward Frank. MSP (Scottish Conservative), Lothian region, since 2016; Shadow Cabinet Secretary for Social Justice, Housing and Local Government, since 2021; Scottish Conservative Chief Whip, 2020-2021; Shadow Cabinet Secretary for Health and Sport, 2017-2020; Scottish Conservative Spokesman for Mental Health and Public Health, 2016-17. Educ. Auchtergaven Primary School; Perth Grammar School; Robert Gordon University. Stood as the Conservative candidate in United Kingdom general election, 2010 for the North East Fife constituency, then in the Scottish Parliament election, 2011 for North East Fife, then in the Scottish Parliament election, 2016 and 2021 for Edinburgh Southern. Address: Scottish Parliament, Edinburgh EH99 1SP.

Brittain, Christopher Neil, BSc, MB, ChB, MBA, MRCGP, DRCOG, DipIMC, RCS (Edin.), FRSocMed, MInstD; b. 3.3.49, Birmingham; m., Rosemary; 1 s.; 1 d. Educ. Bishop Vesey's Grammar School, Sutton Coldfield; St. Andrews University; Dundee University; Heriot Watt University. Senior Partner, Anstruther Medical Practice, 1978-97; Co-ordinator for Scotland, Sargent Cancer Care for Children, 1997-99. Executive Director, Scottish Science Trust, 1999-2003; Chairman, British Association of Immediate Care, 1994-97; Director, Resuscitation Council UK, 1995-1997; Member, East Board, Scottish Environment Protection Agency, 2002-07; Board Member, SSERC, 2001-04. Executive Committee, Association for the Protection of Rural Scotland, 2011-14; Trustee/Treasurer, Fife Folk Museum, 2014-16. Recreations: the countryside; walking. Address: (h.) The White House, Smithy Brae, Kilrenny, Anstruther, Fife KY10 3JN; T.-01333 310191.

Britton, Professor David, BSc, MSc, PhD, FInstP. Professor of Physics, University of Glasgow, since 2007; Project Leader, GRIDPP (UK Computing for LHC), since 2007; b. 25.2.60, Colwyn Bay; m., Linda Barclay; 1 s.; 1 d. Educ. Rydal School; University of Nottingham; University of Victoria. Research Associate, McGill University, Montreal, Canada, 1989-96; Lecturer, Imperial College London, 1996-2001, Senior Lecturer, 2001-04, Reader of Physics, 2004-07. Member: CMS Experiment, 1996-2006, ATLAS Experiment, since 2007; Project Manager, GRIDPP Project, 2001-07. Recreations: running; sailing. Address: (b.) Kelvin Building, University of Glasgow, Glasgow G12 8QQ; T.-0141 330 5454.
E-mail: david.britton@glasgow.ac.uk

Broadhurst, Paul Anthony, MBChB, MD, FRCP, FESC, FHRS. Consultant Cardiologist, Aberdeen Royal Infirmary, since 2002; Clinical Director for Cardiology, NHS Grampian, 2017-19; Training Programme Director for Cardiology, 2013-17; b. 19.12.58, Ashford, Middx; m., Amanda Jayne Powe; 2 s. Educ. Ashford Grammar School; University of Dundee. Research Fellow in Cardiology, Northwick Park Hospital, Harrow, 1987-90; Registrar then Senior Registrar in Cardiology, St. Bartholomew's Hospital, London, 1990-97; Consultant Cardiologist, Borders General Hospital and Royal Infirmary of Edinburgh, 1997-2002. Previous Secretary, Scottish Cardiac Society; Member, Scottish Executive CHD Advisory Committee, 2010-19. Publication: Cardiology Explained (Joint Author), 1997. Recreations: fishing; playing the piano (ATCL); skiing; playing golf. Address: Department of Cardiology, Aberdeen Royal Infirmary, Foresterhill, Aberdeen AB21 2ZB; T.-01224 559308; e-mail: paul.broadhurst@nhs.scot

Broadie, Professor Alexander, MA, MLitt, PhD, DLitt, Hon DUniv, FRSE. Professor of Logic and Rhetoric, Glasgow University, 1994-2009; Hon. Professorial Research Fellow, since 2009; m., Patricia Stewart Martin. Educ. Royal High School, Edinburgh; Edinburgh University; Balliol College, Oxford; Glasgow University. Henry Duncan Prize Lecturer in Scottish Studies, Royal Society of Edinburgh, 1990-93; Gifford Lecturer, Aberdeen

University, 1994; Doctor honoris causa (Blaise Pascal), 2007; Saltire Society Scottish History Book of the Year, 2009; Leader, Leverhulme International Network on 17c Scottish Philosophy, 2010-14; Co-investigator, RSE-funded project 'Scotland, France and Existentialist Philosophy', 2017-19; Lifetime Achievement Award, 18th-Century Scottish Studies Society, 2018; Hon. Vice-President, Saltire Society, 2020. Publications: A Samaritan Philosophy, 1981; George Lokert: Late-Scholastic Logician, 1983; The Circle of John Mair, 1985; Introduction to Medieval Logic, 1987, 2nd edn., 1993; Notion and Object, 1989; The Tradition of Scottish Philosophy, 1990, rev. edn., 2011; Paul of Venice: Logica Magna, 1990; Robert Kilwardby O.P.: on time and imagination, 1993; The Shadow of Scotus, 1995; The Scottish Enlightenment: an anthology, 1997; Why Scottish Philosophy Matters, 2000; The Scottish Enlightenment: The Historical Age of the Historical Nation, 2001; The Cambridge Companion to the Scottish Enlightenment, 2003, Chinese edn., 2010, 2nd edn., 2019; George Turnbull: Principles of Moral and Christian Philosophy, 2004; Thomas Reid on Logic, Rhetoric and the Fine Arts, 2005; A History of Scottish Philosophy, 2009; Agreeable Connexions: Scottish Enlightenment Links with France, 2012; Studies in Seventeenth-Century Scottish Philosophers and their Philosophy, 2017; Scottish Philosophy in the Seventeenth Century, 2020. Address: (h.) 2/2, 15 Naseby Avenue, Glasgow G11 7JQ.
E-mail: alexander@broadie.scot

Brock, Deidre, BA. MP (SNP), Edinburgh North and Leith, since 2015; Shadow SNP Spokesperson on Environment, Food and Rural Affairs, since 2018; Shadow SNP Spokesperson on COP26, since 2021; Shadow SNP Spokesperson (Devolved Government Relations), 2015-18; Shadow SNP Spokesperson on Northern Ireland, 2017-18; Shadow SNP Spokesperson on Fair Work and Employment, 2017-18; Shadow SNP Westminster Group Leader (Scottish Parliament/Scottish Government Liaison), 2015-17; b. Western Australia; 2 d. Educ. Curtin University; Western Australian Academy of Performing Arts. Worked for Rob Gibson MSP before being elected as SNP Councillor on the City of Edinburgh Council for the Leith Walk ward in 2007; formerly Convenor of Culture and Leisure; re-elected in the 2012 elections; formerly Deputy Lord Provost of Edinburgh. Select committees in Parliament: Public Accounts Commission, 2015-16, Public Accounts Committee, 2015-16, Scottish Affairs Committee, since 2016. Recreations: theatre; netball; cinema; traditional Scottish music and arts. Address: House of Commons, London SW1A 0AA.

Brock, Tom, OBE, BSc (Hons). Chair, Keep Scotland Beautiful, since 2021; b. 9.60. Educ. The High School of Glasgow; Langside College, Glasgow; University of Aberdeen; University of Glasgow; Sir Winston Churchill Travelling Fellowship; Common Purpose (Birmingham). Career history: Head of Special Initiatives; Waterway Manager, British Waterways, 1984-98; Chairman, Tourism Environment Forum, 2002-05; Board Member, Association of Scottish Visitor Attractions, 2000-09; Chairman, National Sustainable Tourism Partnership, 2005-09; Director, Scottish Seabird Centre Trading Ltd, 1999-2018; Chief Executive, Scottish Seabird Centre, North Berwick, 1998-2018; Trustee, Forth Estuary Forum, 2014-19; Keep Scotland Beautiful: Trustee, 2010-2019, Interim Chief Executive, 2019-2020; Trustee, 2020-21. Awarded an OBE for services to tourism in 2006. Recreations: wildlife and the natural environment; keen cyclist; walker; photographer. Address: Keep Scotland Beautiful, Glendevon House, The Castle Business Park, Stirling FK9 4TZ; e-mail: board@keepscotlandbeautiful.org

Brockie, Rev. Colin Glynn Frederick, BSc (Eng), BD, SOSc. Minister, Kilmarnock: Grange, 1978-2007; Clerk to Presbytery of Irvine and Kilmarnock, 1992-2011; Hon. Chaplain: Air Training Corps, 1971-78, 1143 (Portobello)

Squadron, 327 (Kilmarnock) Squadron, 1978-2018, West Scotland Wing, 2001-2018; Secretary, Society of Ordained Scientists, since 2013; b. 17.7.42, Westcliff on Sea; m., Barbara Katherine Gordon; 2 s.; 1 d. Educ. Musselburgh Grammar School; Aberdeen Grammar School; University of Aberdeen. Probationary year, Aberdeen: Mastrick, 1967-68; Minister, St. Martin's, Edinburgh, 1968-78. Recreations: billiards; photography; computing. Address: 36 Braehead Court, Kilmarnock, Ayrshire KA3 7AB.

Brocklebank, Ted. MSP (Conservative), Mid Scotland and Fife, Scottish Parliament, 2003-2011; Shadow Minister for Europe, External Affairs and Culture, 2007-2011; formerly Scottish Conservative Rural Development and Fisheries Spokesman; b. 24.9.42, St. Andrews; 2 s. Educ. Madras College, St. Andrews. D.C. Thomson, Dundee, 1960-63; Freelance Journalist, 1963-65; Scottish TV, 1965-70; Grampian Television: Reporter, 1970-76, Head of News and Current Affairs, 1977-85, Head of Documentaries and Features, 1985-95; M. D., Greyfriars Prods, St. Andrews, 1995-2003. BAFTA Award for What Price Oil?; Radio Industries Club of Scotland Special Award (Documentary) for Tale of Two Cities; Norwegian Amanda award for Oil, eight-part series on world oil business, networked on Channel 4 and throughout USA on PBS; BMA Award for Scotland the Grave. Recreations: Life Member, St. Andrews Preservation Trust; Trustee, Kinburn Trust (St. Andrews) Charitable Trust.

Brodie, Chic, BSc. MSP (SNP), South Scotland, 2011-16. Educ. Morgan Academy, Dundee; University of St Andrews. Has run several companies and been an advisor to small and start-up companies in Scotland. Stood as a Liberal Democrat candidate in the 1992, 1997 and 2001 UK General Elections; then switched parties to the Scottish National Party, standing for them in the 2010 UK general election for Ayr, Carrick and Cumnock and the 2011 Scottish Parliament general election for Ayr.

Brodie, Iain, BSc (Hons), AdvDip, PGDip. Director for Scotland/Deputy Director, Field Operations Division, Health and Safety Executive, since 2017. Educ. Dunoon Grammar School; Glasgow Caledonian University; Bell College; Heriot-Watt University. Career: Scottish Environment Protection Agency: Research Assistant, 1994-97, Environmental Protection Officer, 1997-99; Health and Safety Executive: HM Inspector of Health and Safety, 1999-2009, HM Principal Inspector of Health and Safety, 2009-13, Head of Operations (Construction Division), Scotland, Yorkshire and North East England, 2013-17. Address: (b.) Cornerstone, 107 West Regent Street, Glasgow G2 2BA.

Brodie, James, OBE, FFCS. National Chairman, Victim Support Scotland, 1998-2003; Director, The Ayrshire Hospice, 1987-2008; b. 29.4.38, Elderslie; m., Anne Tweedie; 1 s. Educ. Ayr Academy. Joined Ayrshire Constabulary, 1955, and retired as Superintendent; during career was: Chairman, West of Scotland Security Association; Chairman, Ayrshire and Arran Review Committee on Child Abuse; National Secretary, SASD; Director, Strathclyde Police Crime Prevention courses; Member, National Council, SACRO; Member, Home Office Working Party on vandalism caused by fires; Member, Secretary of State's Working Party on Police Community courses; Member, Executive Committee, Strathclyde Federation of Boys' Clubs; Member, West of Scotland Committee, Institute of Contemporary Scotland; Co-Chairman, Joint Management Committee, 1st Ayr Company, BB; Elder, St Columba Church. Recreations: reading; music; gardening. Address: (h.) 3 Portmark Avenue, Doonbank, Ayr KA7 4DD; T.-01292 443553.

Brodie, John, MBE. Chairman, Scottish Retail Consortium, since 2018; Chief Executive, Scotmid (the largest independent co-operative in Scotland with around 350 retail outlets employing more than 4,000 people in Scotland, Northern Ireland and Northern England). Trained and qualified as a Chartered Accountant; worked eight years in practice before joining Scotmid in 1993 as Financial Controller. Scottish Retail Consortium Board member, since 2015; previously represented Scotmid in a number of Board capacities; member of the Audit Committee for the Institute of Chartered Accountants Scotland (ICAS); Board member, Edinburgh Children's Hospital Charity (formerly SKFF). Address: (b.) Box 122, 12 Southbridge, Edinburgh EH1 1DD; T.-07880 039 743.

Brodie, Penny, FRSA. Executive Director, Lead Scotland, 2007-2015; b. Calgary, Canada; 1 s.; 1 d. Educ. James Fowler High School; Dundee College. Administrator, Maxwelltown Information Centre, Dundee, 1995-99; Co-ordinator (Programme), Visual Research Centre, Dundee University, 1999-2001; Chief Executive, Perth and Kinross Association of Voluntary Services (PKAVS), 2001-07. Director: Scotland's Garden Trust; Board Member/Chairman, Perth College UHI, 2004-2014; former Member, Soroptimist International Perth, 2005-2012, having served as Regional Representative, Vice-President, President Elect, President (two terms of office) and Immediate Past President; also having served as Vice-President, President Elect, President and Immediate Past President for Soroptimist International Scotland North Region. Recreations: travel; reading. Address: (h.) Blairgowrie, Perthshire. E-mail: pbrodie8@gmail.com

Brodie, Rt. Hon Lord (Philip Hope Brodie); QC, PC, LLB, LLM. Senator of the College of Justice in Scotland, 2002-2020; Chairman, Judicial Studies Committee, 2006-2012; b. 14.7.50; m.; 2 s.; 1 d. Educ. Dollar Academy; Edinburgh University; University of Virginia.

Brooke, (Alexander) Keith, FRAgS. Farmer; b. 11.2.46, Minnigaff; m., Dilys K. Littlejohn; 1 s.; 3 d. Educ. George Watson's College, Edinburgh. President, Blackface Sheep Breeders Association, 1985-86, Hon. President, 1989-90 and since 2007. Awarded Connachan Salver for Services to the Breed by Blackface Sheep Breeders' Association, 2007; Chairman, Royal Highland and Agricultural Society of Scotland, 2016-17 (Director, 1986-93 and since 1994), formerly Convener, Public Relations and Education Committee; Inaugural Chairman, Royal Highland Education Trust, 1998-2001, Honorary Treasurer and Chief Steward, Press Radio and Television; Animal Diseases Research Association, now Moredun Foundation for Animal Health and Welfare, 1981-96, Wallets Marts PLC, 1989-91, Scottish, English and Welsh Wool Growers Ltd., 1988-95, Wigtownshire Quality Lamb Ltd., 1991-96; Chairman, Blackface Sheep Breeders' Development Board, 1996-99; Member: Council of Awards of Royal Agricultural Societies, since 1997 and RHASS Representative on Scottish Panel; Council, British Rouge de l'Ouest Sheep Society, 1986-97 (Chairman, 1990-92, Treasurer, 1994-97); formerly Chairman of Stewartry Western District Agricultural Club; Chairman of Stewartry District Association of YFCs and Final Chairman of Old South West Area of YFCs; member of winning Scottish International Beef Judging Team, 1966, and member of winning Stewartry Team, 1970 at the Royal Highland Show Stockjudging Competition for the Glasgow Herald Trophy; member of winning team from Stewartry Western in 1966 Scottish National Beef Judging Competition. Address: (h.) Carscreugh, Glenluce, Newton Stewart DG8 0NU; T.-01581 300334.

Brooke, Hazel, MBE, DSc (Hon), MA. Executive Director, Scottish Cot Death Trust, 1988-2005; b. 31.7.45, Forfar; m., Anthony Brooke; 2d. Educ.

Inverness Royal Academy; Edinburgh University; Strathclyde University. Unilever, London; The Rank Organisation, London; Scottish Council, Development and Industry, Edinburgh; Glasgow University; Member, Merchant's House, Glasgow; Chair of Court, Glasgow Caledonian University, 2015-2018. Recreations: reading; singing. Address: (h.) 9 Campbell Drive, Bearsden G61 4NF; T.-0141-942 7942.

Brooks, Dr. Naomi, BSc (Hons), PhD. Senior Lecturer (Sport), University of Stirling, since 2016 (Lecturer, since 2012); b. Glasgow. Educ. Shawlands Academy, Glasgow; Ohio University. Post-doctoral Fellow, Human Nutrition Research Centre for Aging, Tufts University, Boston, MA, USA, 2005-06; Post-doctoral Associate, Stellenbosch University, South Africa, 2007-09, Lecturer, 2010-12. Presented invited seminars at universities in the USA and South Africa and given research presentations at various international conferences, one of which achieved the Health and Wellness Award: Best Oral Presentation on Sport at the Physiological Society of Southern Africa, Annual Meeting, 2008. Published numerous research papers in peer-reviewed journals; written chapters for books and spoken at various international conferences. Address: (b.) School of Sport, University of Stirling, Stirling FK9 4LA; T.-01786 466 478; Fax: 01786 466 477; e-mail: n.e.brooks@stir.ac.uk
Web: www.stir.ac.uk/sport

Brooks, Stuart. Head of Conservation and Policy, The National Trust for Scotland, since 2018, Head of Natural Heritage Policy, 2017-18; Chairman, IUCN UK National Committee, since 2011. Educ. Stamford School. Career history: Director of Conservation, Scottish Wildlife Trust, 1995-2009; Director and Chief Executive, John Muir Trust, 2009-2017. Address: The National Trust for Scotland, Hermiston Quay, 5 Cultins Road, Edinburgh EH11 4DF.

Brown, Alan. MP (SNP), Kilmarnock and Loudoun (elected 2015, re-elected 2017); SNP Spokesperson for Energy and Climate Change, since 2020; b. 12.8.70, Kilmarnock; m.; 2 s. Educ. Loudoun Academy; Glasgow University. Worked in both the public and private sectors, as a Civil engineer. Elected SNP councillor in the 2007 East Ayrshire Council election (Irvine Valley ward); re-elected in 2012; held positions in Housing and Strategic Planning & Resources. Address: House of Commons, London SW1A 0AA.

Brown, Alan David Gillespie, MBChB, FRCOG, FRCSEd. Consultant Obstetrician and Gynaecologist, initially at Eastern General Hospital, then at the Royal Infirmary, Edinburgh, 1983-2004; b. 27.5.39, Falkirk; m. Elizabeth Ballantyne; 2 step-s; 1 step-d.; 5 grandsons; 1 granddaughter. Educ. Dalhousie School, Fife; Merchiston Castle School, Edinburgh; Medical Faculty, Edinburgh University. MRC Research Fellowship, Middlesex Hospital, London; appointed Senior Lecturer/Hon. Consultant in O & G, University Hospital of South Manchester, 1975; returned to Edinburgh, 1983. Previously, Hon. Gynaecologist and later, Vice-Chair, Caledonia Youth (1987-2004); President, Edinburgh Obstetrical Society, 2002-04. For University of Edinburgh: elected member of Business Committee, General Council, since 2005, Convener, 2009-2012; a Regent, since 2012; elected General Council Assessor to Court (the governing body), from 2015-19, including member of three sub-committees. Trustee of Pleasance Theatre Trust Ltd., London and Edinburgh, 2011-2020. Publications: over 50 articles and textbook chapters. Recreations: golf; bridge; theatre; opera; travel. Address: (h.) 32 Queen Street, Edinburgh EH2 1JX; T.-0131 225 1418; e-mail: alanbrown179@btinternet.com

Brown, Alastair Nigel, LLB (Hons), PhD. Sheriff of Tayside, Central and Fife at Dunfermline; b. 3.5.55, Kirkcaldy; m., Dr Susan Brown; 2 s.; 1 d. Educ. Royal Grammar School, Newcastle-upon-Tyne; University of Edinburgh. Solicitor (Scotland), 1979; Advocate Depute, 2003-09; Solicitor (England & Wales), 1992-2009; Advocate, 2010; Sheriff, 2011; Council of Europe expert on Corruption Law, since 2001. Publications: "Money Laundering" (2009); Criminal Evidence and Procedure: An Introduction, 3rd ed. (2011); Annotated Statutes: Human Rights Act, 1998; Proceeds of Crime Act, 2002; Extradition Act, 2003; Sexual Offences (Scotland) Act, 2009; Bribery Act, 2010. Address: (b.) Dunfermline Sheriff Court, 1/6 Carnegie Drive, Dunfermline KY12 7HJ.

Brown, Professor Alice, MA, PhD, CBE, FRSE, FRCP Edin, FRSA, AcSS, Cipfa (Hon). Chancellor, Abertay University, since 2019; Chair, Scottish Funding Council, 2013-17; General Secretary, Royal Society of Edinburgh, 2011-2013; Scottish Public Services Ombudsman, 2002-2009; b. 30.9.46, Edinburgh; m., Alan James Brown; 2 d. Educ. Boroughmuir High School, Edinburgh; Stevenson College, Edinburgh; University of Edinburgh. Lecturer in Economics, University of Stirling, 1984; University of Edinburgh: Lecturer, Departments of Economics, Continuing Education and Politics, 1985-92, Senior Lecturer in Politics, 1992-97, appointed Head of Politics Department, 1995, appointed Head, Planning Unit, 1996, Personal Chair, 1997; Co-Director, Institute of Governance, 1998-2002, Vice Principal, 1999-2002, Professor Emeritus, 2008. Honorary Degree (Doctor of the University), University of Stirling, 2004; Fellow of Stevenson College, Edinburgh, 2006; Honorary Degree (Doctor of Laws), Edinburgh Napier University, 2009; Honorary Degree (Honoris Causa), University of Edinburgh, 2010; Honorary Degree (Doctor of Letters), Glasgow Caledonian University, 2012; Honorary Degree (Doctor of Social Science Honoris Causa), Queen's University Belfast, 2014; Honorary Degree (Honoris Causa), University of Aberdeen, 2016; Honorary Degree, Doctor of Education (Honoris Causa), Robert Gordon University, 2018; Honorary Degree, Doctor of the University, University of Strathclyde, 2018. Received Special Recognition Award from the Political Studies Association, 2009; Lifetime Achievement Award from The Herald Higher Education Awards, 2017; Lifetime Achievement Awards from the Scottish Public Services Awards, 2017. Council Member, Administrative Justice and Tribunals Council (AJTC), 2008-2013; Trustee, David Hume Institute; Chair, Lay Advisory Group, Royal College of Physicians of Edinburgh, 2009-2013; Member, Advisory Board, Institute for Advanced Studies in the Humanities, University of Edinburgh, 2011-2013; Member, Scottish Resource Centre Steering Committee, Edinburgh Napier University, 2011-2013. Fellow, Sunningdale Institute, 2008-2012; Executive Member, British and Irish Ombudsman Association (BIOA), 2006-2009; Member, Architects Registration Board, 2006-2009; Member, Committee on Standards in Public Life, 1999-2003; ESRC Research Grants Board and other committees, 1997-2001; Board Member, Scottish Higher Education Funding Council (SHEFC), 1998-2002; Chair, Community Planning Taskforce, 2000-02; Member, Public Sector Finance Taskforce, 2001; Member, Scottish Committee, British Council, 1998-2002; Member, Hansard Society Scotland and other committees, 1998-2002; Member, Advisory Group to the EOC in Scotland, 1995-2002; Member, Advisory Group to the CRE in Scotland, 2003-07; Member, Consultative Steering Group in Scotland, 1997-98; Executive Member, Political Studies Association, 1996-1999; Executive Member, Centre for Scottish Public Policy; Assistant Editor, Scottish Affairs journal, 1992-2002; Co-Editor, The Scottish Government Yearbook, 1989-1991. Member, Board of Governors, Public Policy, Institute for Wales, 2014-18; Member, Strategic Group on Women and Work, Scottish Government, 2013-17; Member of Programme Board of Scotland's Futures Forum, 2016-17; Member, Advisory Group, Wales Centre for Public Policy, since 2018; Member, Education Committee, Royal Society of Edinburgh, 2018-2021. Publications: The MSC in Scotland (Joint Editor and Contributor) 1989; Restructuring Education in Ireland (Joint Author), 1993; A Major Crisis: The Politics of Economic Policy in Britain in the 1990s (Joint Author), 1996; Gender Equality in Scotland (Joint Author), 1997; Politics and Society in Scotland (Joint Author), 1996 and 1998; The Scottish Electorate (Joint Author), 1999; New Scotland, New Politics (Joint Author), 2001; The Changing Politics of Gender Equality in Britain (Joint Editor), 2002; Author of numerous book chapters, articles, papers and reports. Recreations: reading; music; cooking. E-mail: alajbrown@hotmail.com

Brown, Andrew Stewart, BArch (Hons), RIBA, ARIAS. Partner, Simpson and Brown Architects, 1977-2009; b. 7.6.45, Northwood; m., Morven Islay Helen Gibson; 1 s.; 1 d. Educ. Bradfield College, Berkshire; Edinburgh University. Architect with Sir Basil Spence Glover and Ferguson, Edinburgh, 1970-73; Architect with Andrew Renton, Edinburgh, 1973-77; Founding Partner, Simpson and Brown Architects, 1977; Director and Company Secretary, Addyman Associates, Building Research, Building Archaeologists and Archaeologists. Trustee, Scotland's Churches Scheme, 1997-2012; Trustee, Scotland's Churches Trust, 2012-2014; Trustee, The Willow Tea Rooms Trust, since 2015; former Chairman, Traverse Theatre, Edinburgh. Recreations: restoring vintage motorcars and older buildings. Address: (h.) 49 Stirling Road, Edinburgh EH5 3JB; T.-(b.) 0131 555 4678. E-mail: stewart.morven@blueyonder.co.uk

Brown, Rev. Colin Campbell, BD. Principal Clerk to General Assembly, since 2004; Minister, Darnley United Free Church, Glasgow, 1979-2021; Moderator, General Assembly, United Free Church of Scotland, 2002; Teacher (part-time) of Religious Education, Williamwood High School, Glasgow, 1987-2019; b. 30.8.54, Perth; m., Mairi; 1 s. Educ. Perth High School; University of Edinburgh; Moray House College of Education. Convener, United Free Church Youth Committee, 1985-89; Moderator, Presbytery of Glasgow and the West, 1990-91; Convener, Action of Churches Together in Scotland Education Group, 1992-94; Convener, United Free Church Ministry and Home Affairs Committee, 1997-2002; part-time Religious Education Teacher, Renfrew High School, 1980-87. Address: 37 Warrack Street, St Andrews, Fife KY16 8DR.

Brown, Professor David William, MA (Edin/Oxon), PhD (Cantab), DPhil (Oxon), DLitt (Edin), FBA, FRSE. Professor of Theology, Aesthetics and Culture, St. Andrews University, 2007-2015, Wardlaw Professor, 2008-2015, Professor Emeritus, since 2015; b. 1.7.48, Galashiels. Educ. Keil School, Dumbarton; University of Edinburgh; University of Oxford; University of Cambridge. Fellow and Tutor in Theology and Philosophy, Oriel College, Oxford and University Lecturer in Philosophical Theology, Oxford, 1976-90; Van Mildert Professor of Divinity, Durham University and Canon of Durham Cathedral, 1990-2007. Fellow of British Academy, since 2002, Member of its Council (Governing Body), 2008-2012. Publications: The Divine Trinity, 1985; Continental Philosophy and Modern Theology, 1987; Tradition and Imagination, 1999; Discipleship and Imagination, 2000; God and Enchantment of Place, 2004; God and Grace of Body, 2007; God and Mystery in Words, 2008; Divine Humanity, 2011; Durham Cathedral: Community, Fabric and Culture, 2015; Gospel as Work of Art, 2022; 7 other books. Recreation: gardening. E-mail: dwb21@st-andrews.ac.uk

Brown, Derek. Deputy Chief Executive, North Lanarkshire Council, since 2022, Executive Director of Education and Families, 2019-2022. Career: Senior Depute, Jordanhill School, then Headteacher, Oldmachar Academy, 2009-

2014; Head of Education, Fife Council, 2014-17; Improvement Manager (Seconded), The Scottish Government, 2018; Head of Education, Youth and Communities, North Lanarkshire Council, 2018. Address: North Lanarkshire Council, 7 Scott Street, Motherwell ML1 1PN; T.-01698 274220.

Brown, Douglas. Head Teacher, Boclair Academy. Address: Inveroran Drive, Bearsden G61 2PL; T.-0141 955 2358; e-mail: office@boclair.e-dunbarton.sch.uk

Brown, Sir Ewan, CBE, MA, LLB, DL (St Andrews), DUniv (Heriot-Watt), CA, FRSE, FCIBS, FRSA, Hon FRZS (Scot). Director: Stagecoach Holdings Plc, until 2019; James Walker (Leith) Ltd (Chairman); b. 23.3.42, Perth; m., Christine; 1 s.; 1 d. Educ. Perth Academy; St. Andrews University. CA apprentice with Peat Marwick Mitchell, 1964-67. Senior Governor of Court, St Andrews University, 2007-2016; Board Member, Entrepreneurial Scotland, 2013-18; Trustee, Royal Scottish Academy Foundation; Deputy Chair, Edinburgh International Festival Society, 2006-2014; Director, Scottish Financial Enterprise (Chairman, 2012-16); Honorary Professor in Finance, Heriot Watt University, 1988-2010; Treasurer, Royal Society of Edinburgh, 2008-12; Trustee, National Youth Orchestras of Scotland, 2006-2011; Member, Council of Assembly, Church of Scotland, 2004-07; Chair of Trustees, IMPACT Scotland, since 2016; Chairman, University Court, Heriot-Watt University, 1996-2002; Master, The Company of Merchants of the City of Edinburgh, 1994-95; Lord Dean of Guild, City of Edinburgh, 1995-97; Council Member: Institute of Chartered Accountants of Scotland, 1988-91, Scottish Business School, 1974-80; previous directorships: Scottish Transport Group, 1983-88, Scottish Development Finance, 1983-93, Harrison Lovegrove Plc, Lloyds Banking Group, 1999-2009, John Wood Group plc, 1983-2006, Pict Petroleum plc, 1973-95, Scottish Widows Bank plc, 1994-97; Trustee, Carnegie Trust for the Universities of Scotland, 1988-2005; Chairman: Lloyds TSB Scotland, 1998-2008, Dunedin Income Growth Investment Trust Plc, 1996-2001, Transport Initiatives Edinburgh Ltd, 2002-06, Scottish Knowledge Plc, 1997-2002; Governor, Edinburgh College of Art, 1986-89; Chair, Creative Scotland 2009 Ltd, 2008-2010. Knighted in 2014 for services to business, public life and philanthropy. Recreations: family; golf; Scottish art; Mah Jongg.

Brown, Gavin. MSP (Conservative), Lothian, 2011-16, Lothians, 2007-2011; Shadow Minister for Enterprise, Energy and Tourism, 2007-2011; Shadow Minister for Finance, Employment and Sustainable Growth, 2011-16; b. 4.6.75, Kirkcaldy; m., Hilary Jane Brown (nee Fergus); 1 d.; 2 s. Educ. Fettes College; Strathclyde University. Solicitor, McGrigor Donald, 1998-2002; Director, Speak with Impact Ltd, since 2002. Finance Committee; JCI Most Outstanding Trainer in the World Award, 2004. Recreations: tae kwon-do (1st Degree Black Belt).

Brown, Hamish Macmillan, MBE, D.Litt, D.Uni, Open, FRSGS. Author, Lecturer, Photographer and Mountaineer; b. 13.8.34, Colombo, Sri Lanka. Educ. several schools abroad; Dollar Academy. National Service, RAF, Middle East/East Africa; Assistant, Martyrs' Memorial Church, Paisley; first-ever full-time appointment in outdoor education (Braehead School, Fife); served many years on Scottish Mountain Leadership Board; has led expeditions world-wide for mountaineering, skiing, trekking, canoeing, botanising, etc. Publications: Hamish's Mountain Walk, 1979 (SAC award); Hamish's Groats End Walk, 1981 (Smith's Travel Prize shortlist); Time Gentlemen, Some Collected Poems, 1983; Eye to the Hills, 1982; Five Bird Stories, 1984; Poems of the Scottish Hills (Editor); 1982;

Speak to the Hills (Co-Editor), 1985; Travels, 1986; The Great Walking Adventure, 1986; Hamish Brown's Scotland, 1988; Climbing the Corbetts, 1988; Great Walks Scotland (Co-author), 1989; Scotland Coast to Coast, 1990; Walking the Summits of Somerset and Avon, 1991; From the Pennines to the Highlands, 1992; The Bothy Brew & Other Stories, 1993; The Fife Coast, The Last Hundred, 1994; 25 Walks Fife; Seton Gordon's Scotland (anthology); Fort William and Glen Coe Walks, 1996; Compendium: Hamish's Mountain Walks/Climbing the Corbetts, 1997; Fife in Focus, Photographs of the Fife Coast; 25 Walks, Skye and Kintail, 2000; Billy Black's Dog/The Lost Hogmanay (stories), 2002; Travelling Hopefully (poems), 2003; Along the Fife Coastal Path, 2004; Seton Gordon's Scotland (anthology), 2005; Exploring the Edinburgh to Glasgow Canals, 2006; The Mountains Look on Marrakech (Atlas traverse), 2006 (shortlisted for Boardman-Tasker Prize, 2007); A Scottish Graveyard Miscellany, Achnashellach (poems); Seton Gordon's Cairngorms (Anthology), 2009; Hamish's Mountain Walk, 2010; Hamish's Groat's End Walk, 2011; Walking the Mull Hills, 2011; The High Atlas; Peaks and Climbs (200 photographs); The Oldest Post Office in the World and Other Scottish Oddities, 2012; Climbing the Corbetts, 2012; Three Men on the Way Way (West Highland Way), 2013; Tom Weir, An Anthology, 2013; Fantasies, Fables, Fibs and Follies (stories), 2014; Canals Across Scotland, 2015; Walking the Song, 2017; East of West, West of East, 2018; Chasing the Dreams, 2019; Exploring the Fife Central Path: Kincardine to Newburgh. Recreations: books; music; Morocco; alpine gardening. Address: 8 Links Place, Burntisland, Fife KY3 9DY; T.-01592 873546.

Brown, Professor Ian James Morris, MA (Hons), MLitt, PhD, DLitt, DipEd, FRSE, FRSA, FHEA, FFCS. Professor in Drama, Kingston University, 2010-14, Emeritus Professor, since 2014; Freelance scholar, arts and education consultant, 2002-2010; Playwright and poet, since 1969; b. 28.2.45, Barnet; m., 1, Judith Sidaway; 2, Nicola Axford; 1 s.; 1 d. Educ. Dollar Academy; Edinburgh University; Crewe and Alsager College; Glasgow University. Schoolteacher, 1967-69, 1970-71; Lecturer in Drama, Moray House College; Lecturer, Dunfermline College, 1971-76; British Council: Assistant Representative, Scotland, 1976-77, Assistant Regional Director, Istanbul, 1977-78; various posts, Crewe and Alsager College, 1978-86, latterly Leader, BA (Hons) Drama Studies; Programme Director, Alsager Arts Centre, 1980-86; Drama Director, Arts Council of Great Britain, 1986-94; Queen Margaret University College, Edinburgh: Reader, 1994-95, Professor of Drama, 1995-2002, Head, Drama Department, 1996-99, Dean, Arts Faculty, 1999-2002, Director, Scottish Centre for Cultural Management and Policy, 1996-2002. British Theatre Institute: Vice Chairman, 1983-85, Chairman, 1985-87; Member, International Advisory Committee, O'Neill Theatre Center, 1994-2012; Chair, Scottish Society of Playwrights, 1973-75, 1984-87, 1997-99 and 2010-13; Scottish Society of Playwrights Council Member, 1999-2007 and 2009-2010; Chair, Highlands and Islands Theatre Network, 2005-09; President, Association for Scottish Literary Studies, 2010-2015, Publications Convener, since 2012; Cultural Consultant, Rose Theatre, Kingston, 2012-14; Visiting Professor, Centre for the Study of Media and Culture in Small Nations, University of Glamorgan, 2007-13; Honorary Senior Research Fellow (Visiting Professor), Department of Scottish Literature, University of Glasgow, since 2007; plays include Mother Earth, The Bacchae, Carnegie, The Knife, The Fork, New Reekie, Mary, Runners, Mary Queen and the Loch Tower, Joker in the Pack, Beatrice, First Strike, The Scotch Play, Bacchai, Wasting Reality, Margaret, A Great Reckoning; An Act o Love; Translating Lies; books include Poems for Joan, 2001 (Author), and Journey's Beginning: the Gateway building and company, 2004 (Editor); General Editor, The Edinburgh History of Scottish Literature, 2007; Joint Series

Editor and Contributor, Edinburgh Companions to Scottish Literature, since 2007 (renamed International Companions, from 2014); Co-Editor, Edinburgh Companion to Twentieth-Century Scottish Literature, 2009; Editor, From Tartan to Tartanry (2010); Co-Editor, International Journal of Scottish Theatre and Screen, 2000-17; Editor, Edinburgh Companion to Scottish Drama (2011); Editor, Literary Tourism, the Trossachs and Walter Scott (2012); Co-Editor and contributor, Lion's Milk: Turkish Poems by Scottish Poets, 2012 (Author); Scottish Theatre: Diversity, Language, Continuity, 2013; Co-Editor, Roots and Fruits of Scottish Culture: Scottish Identities, History and Contemporary Literature (2014); Author, Collyshangles in the Canopy (2015); Author, History as Theatrical Metaphor: History, Myth and National Identities in Modern Scottish Drama (2016); Co-Editor, Taking Liberties: Scottish Literature and Expressions of Freedom (2016); Author, Performing Scottishness: Enactment and National Identities (2020); Co-Editor, Performing Robert Burns: Enactments and Representatives of the 'National Bard' (2021); Saltire Society: Council member, 2010-16 and since 2019, Executive Board member, 2010-16, Convenor, 2014-16; Vice-Chair, Standing Committee of University Drama Departments, 2013-16. Recreations: theatre; sport; travel; cooking. Address: 34 Dalmeny Avenue, Giffnock G46 7QF.

Brown, J. Craig, CBE, DUniv, DA, BEd (Hons), BA. Non-Executive Director, Aberdeen FC, 2013-19, formerly Manager, 2010-2013; Manager, Motherwell FC, 2009-2010; Football Consultant, Derby County FC, 2005-07; International Representative, Fulham FC, 2004-05; Manager, Preston North End, 2001-04; Technical Director and International Team Manager, Scottish FA, 1993-2001; Assistant National Coach and Under 21 Team Manager, 1986-93; Manager, Clyde FC, 1977-86; Assistant Manager, Motherwell FC, 1975-77; b. 1.7.40, Glasgow; 2 s.; 1 d. Educ. Hamilton Academy; Scottish School of Physical Education; Open University. Teacher, Head Teacher, Lecturer in Education, 1962-86; Professional footballer: Rangers F.C., 1958-60, Dundee F.C., 1960-65 (League Champion 1962), Falkirk F.C., 1965-68. FIFA Instructor; Ex-Co Member, AEFCA (Alliance of European Football Coaches' Associations); Patron, Scottish Disability Sport; Sports Photographers' Personality of the Year, 1989, 1996; City of Glasgow Sportsperson of the Year, 1997; Bells Manager of the Month on 7 occasions; Clydesdale Bank Premier League Manager of the Month on 4 occasions; Hall of Fame - Scottish Football Association, 2010, Clyde FC, 2012, Strathclyde University, 2013; Show Racism the Red Card, 2004. Publications: Activity Methods in the Middle Years, 1975; Craig Brown, The Autobiography, 1998; The Game of My Life, 2001, 2003. Recreation: golf. Address: (b.) Aberdeen Football Club plc, Pittodrie Stadium, Aberdeen AB15 4BE.

Brown, Sheriff Jack. Sheriff of Grampian, Highland and Islands at Aberdeen, since 2016. Educ. University of Dundee. Career history: following a traineeship with Dundee City Council, worked with Messrs J&J Hunter before becoming a partner in Messrs Shaw and Co.; Principal of own practice, Jack Brown and Company, since 1996; appointed as a solicitor advocate in 2003; appointed as a fee-paid part-time sheriff in 2005. Address: Sheriff's Chambers, Sheriff Court, Aberdeen AB10 1WP.

Brown, Rt. Hon. (James) Gordon, PC, MA, PhD, MP. Prime Minister and First Lord of the Treasury, 2007-10; Leader of the Labour Party, 2007-10; Chancellor of the Exchequer, 1997-2007; MP (Labour), Kirkcaldy and Cowdenbeath, 2005-2015, Dunfermline East, 1983-2005; UN Special Envoy for Global Education, since 2012; Chair, International Commission on Financing Global Education Opportunity, since 2016; WHO Ambassador for Global Health Financing, since 2021; Honorary Fellow, Royal Society of Edinburgh; b. 20.2.51; m., Sarah; 2 s. Educ. Kirkcaldy High School; Edinburgh University. Rector, Edinburgh University, 1972-75; Temporary Lecturer, Edinburgh University, 1976; Lecturer, Glasgow College of Technology, 1976-80; Journalist and Current Affairs Editor, Scottish Television, 1980-83. Contested (Labour) South Edinburgh, 1979; Chairman, Labour Party Scottish Council, 1983-84; Opposition Chief Secretary to the Treasury, 1987; Shadow Minister for Trade and Industry, 1989; Shadow Chancellor, 1992. Publications: The Red Paper on Scotland (Editor), 1975; The Politics of Nationalism and Devolution (Co-Editor), 1980; Scotland: The Real Divide, 1983; Maxton, 1986; Where There is Greed, 1989; John Smith: Life and Soul of the Party (Co-Author), 1994; Values, Visions and Voices: An Anthology of Socialism (Co-Editor), 1994: Maxton: A Biography, 2002; Speeches, 1997-2006, 2006; Moving Britain Forward, Selected Speeches, 1997-2006, 2006; Courage: Eight Portraits, 2007; Wartime Courage, 2008; Beyond the Crash, 2010; My Scotland, Our Britain, 2014; Britain: Leading, Not Leaving, 2016; My Life, Our Times, 2017; Seven Ways to Change the World: How to Fix the Most Pressing Issues We Face, 2021. Recreations: reading and writing; football; golf; tennis.

Brown, Janet Marjorie, BSc, PhD, FInstP, FRSE, FRSA. Non Executive Director, Edinburgh Science, since 2019; Chief Executive, Scottish Qualifications Authority, 2007-2019; b. 31.07.51, Sheffield. Educ. High Storrs Grammar School for Girls, Sheffield; University of Birmingham. Visiting Assistant Professor, University of Illinois, Urbana, IL USA, 1981-84; Member of Technical Staff, Bell Laboratories, AT & T, Murray Hill, NJ USA, 1984-90; Director of Process Architecture & Characterisation, SEMATECH, Austin, TX USA, 1990-93; Director, Reliability & Quality Assurance, Motorola, Austin, TX USA, 1993-97; European Operations Director, Smartcard Division, Motorola, East Kilbride, 1997-98; Director of Operations, Networking Systems Memories, Motorola, Austin TX, 1998-2000; Managing Director, Industries, Scottish Enterprise, Glasgow, 2000-07.

Brown, Jenny, MA (Hons), Hon FRSL, FRSE. Literary agent; b. 13.5.58, Manchester; m., Alexander Richardson; 4 s. Educ. George Watson's College; Aberdeen University; Open University (Honorary Doctorate), 2015; Aberdeen University (Honorary Doctorate), 2017; St Andrews University (Honorary Doctorate), 2018. Assistant Administrator, Edinburgh Festival Fringe Society, 1980-82; Director, Edinburgh Book Festival, 1983-91; Presenter, Scottish Television book programmes, 1989-94; National Co-ordinator, Readiscovery Campaign, 1994-95; Head of Literature, Scottish Arts Council, 1996-2002. Commissioner, Press Complaints Commission, 1993-97; Non-Executive Director, Scottish Television (Regional) Ltd., 1998-2004; Governor, George Watson's College, 1999-2005; Board Member, Edinburgh International Book Festival, since 2003; Company Secretary, Edinburgh UNESCO City of Literature Trust, 2004-07; Chair, Association of Scottish Literary Agents, 2009-11; Chair, Bloody Scotland (Scotland's Crime Writing Festival), 2010-2021. Recreations: Founder member, Pizza Cats cycling club; hill walking; ceilidh dancing. Address: (b.) 31-35 Marchmont Road, Edinburgh EH9 1HU.
E-mail: jenny@jennybrownassociates.com

Brown, Jock (John Winton), MA (Cantab), DUniv (Strathclyde). Fellow of the Law Society of Scotland; Chairman, Children's University Trust, Scotland, 2013-18; Ambassador, Children's University, England; Freelance Sports Commentator; b. 7.5.46, Kilmarnock; m., Ishbel; 3 d. Educ. Hamilton Academy; Cambridge University (Sidney Sussex College). The Glasgow Herald, and D.C. Thomson & Co. Ltd. (The Sunday Post), 1967-68; Assistant Secretary, The Scottish Football League, 1968-70;

Journalist, D.C. Thomson & Co. Ltd. (The Sunday Post), 1970-73; Ballantyne & Copland, Solicitors, Motherwell (Partner from 1977), 1973-93; Consultant, Ballantyne & Copland, and Director, Caledonian Television Ltd., 1993-95; Sports Law Consultant, Harper Macleod, Solicitors, Glasgow, 1995-97; General Manager, Football, Celtic F.C., 1997-98; Partner: Winton Brown, Solicitors, Hamilton, 1999-2005, Bishops Solicitors LLP, Glasgow, 2005-06; Brodies LLP, Glasgow, 2006-2010. Consultant, Brodies LLP, Glasgow, 2010-2016. Part-Time: Sports Broadcaster, BBC Radio Scotland, 1977-80; Football Commentator: Scottish Television plc, 1980-90, BSkyB, 1989-95, BBC Scotland Television, 1990-97; Current Affairs Radio Broadcaster, Scot FM, 1999-2000; Football Commentator: ITV On Digital, 1999-2001, ntl, 2001-02, Setanta Sports, 2003-09, BT Vision and Scottish Televison, 2009-10, Sky Sports, 2010-2012. Publication: Celtic-Minded, 1999. Recreation: golf.

Brown, John, CBE, MBA. Chairman, NHS Greater Glasgow and Clyde, since 2015; Interim Chairman, NHS Tayside, 2018-19; Chairman, NHS Scotland Global Citizenship Programme, since 2017. Educ. University of Glasgow. Senior Civil Servant, Central Government, 2000-2013; Member, Lay, Advisory Board, Royal College of Physicians and Surgeons of Glasgow, 2014-15; Company Secretary, Student Loans Company, 2014-15; Managing Director, JJ Brown Consulting Ltd, since 2014. Associate, Chartered Institute of Management Accountants; Fellow, Institute of Leadership & Management; Fellow, Institute of Credit Management; Member, Institute of Chartered Secretaries & Administrators. Address: NHS Greater Glasgow and Clyde, 1055 Great Western Road, Glasgow G12 0XH; T.-0141 201 4444.

Brown, John Caldwell, DA, RSW. Painter; Member, Board, Leith School of Art, 1991-2007; b. 19.10.45, Irvine; m., Elizabeth Ann (deceased); 3 s. Educ. Ardrossan Academy; 1967 David Murray Scholarship, Royal Academy; Glasgow School of Art. RSA Carnegie Travelling Scholarship and GSA Cargill Travelling Scholarship, 1968; Director of Art, Fettes College, 1971-86; Director of Art, Malvern College, 1986-88; Head of Art, Edinburgh Academy, 1988-97; former Lecturer (part-time): Edinburgh College of Art, Leith School of Art; solo exhibitions: GSA, 1970, Moray House, 1989, Torrance Gallery, 1992, Open Eye Gallery, 1996, 1998, 2000, 2002, Duncan Miller Fine Art London, 1996, 1997, 1999, 2000, 2001, 2005, 2007, 2008, 2010, 2013, 2014, John Davies Gallery, 2001, 2003, Richmond Hill Gallery, 2003, 2005, The Scottish Gallery, 2004, 2006, 2009, 2011, 2014, 2018, 2022, Lemon Street Gallery, 2009, 2011, Rendezvous Gallery, 2010, Stafford Gallery, 2015, 2016, 2019, Leith School of Art, 2019. James Torrance Award, RGI, 1970; Scottish Arts Club Award SAAC, 1993; Scottish Provident Award, 1993; Heinzel Gallery Award SAAC, 1994; 2010 RSW Council Award; commissioned to make Prestigious Print Edition for Art in Healthcare; Mackintosh Residency in Collioure; Plein-Air Prize PA1; elected Member: Visual Arts Scotland, 1994, Royal Scottish Society of Painters in Watercolour, 1996; Alexander Graham Munro Award, RSW, 2004. Corporate purchase: Kuwait Royal Family; Hugh Martin Partnership; Royal Bank of Scotland; Aida Cherfan Gallery, Beirut; Robert Fleming Holdings Ltd; Scottish Life Assurance Co Ltd; John Menzies plc; Korean Embassy; Lillie Art Gallery; University of Edinburgh; British Steel; Dunfermline Building Society; Aberdeen Assets. Address: (b.) 163B Craigleith Road, Edinburgh EH4 2EB; T.-07816592760.

Brown, John Souter, MA (Hons), FCIPR. Public Relations Consultant; Fellow, Chartered Institute of Public Relations (CIPR); Accredited PR practitioner; b. 15.10.48, Glasgow; m., Angela McGinn; 1 s.; 1 d. Educ. Kirkcaldy High School; Edinburgh University. Statistics and Information Officer, Lanark County Council, 1970-72; Senior Officer

(Research, Planning Publicity), Manchester City Social Services Department, 1972-75; Press Officer, Strathclyde Regional Council, 1975-80; Journalist and Presenter, Scottish Television, 1980-82; Editor, What's Your Problem?, 1982-84; Editor, Ways and Means, 1984-86; Senior Producer (Politics), Scottish Television, 1986-91; North of Scotland TV Franchise Team, 1991; Managing Director, Lomond Television, 1992-93; Head of Public Relations, Strathclyde Regional Council, 1993-96; Head of Public Relations and Marketing, Glasgow City Council, 1996-2004; PR and Marketing Consultant, since 2005; Consultant, Notamvis (Brand Asset Management), since 2017. Chair, Volunteer Centre, Glasgow, 1996-98; Director, Scottish Foundation, 1990-2002; Member, BAFTA Scotland; Member, NUJ; Scotland CIPR Chair, 2004-05; CIPR Council and Board Member, 2008-2012; Chair, CIPR Professional Practices Committee, 2012; National CIPR Treasurer, 2008; Trustee, Radio Clyde Cash for Kids, 2009-2014; Trustee (2005-2017) and Chair (2010-15) of Iprovision CIPR Benevolent Fund; Trustee, Association of Charitable Organisations, 2017-2023. Awarded Stephen Tallents Medal by CIPR, 2007. Publication: PR and Communication in Local Government and Public Services, 2013 (Co-Author with Pat Gaudin and Wendy Moran). Mobile: 07881 818474; e-mail: johnbrownpr@gmail.com

Brown, Keith James, MA (Hons). MSP (SNP), Clackmannanshire and Dunblane, since 2011, Ochil, 2007-2011; Cabinet Secretary for Justice and Veterans, since 2021; Cabinet Secretary for Economy, Jobs and Fair Work, 2016-18; SNP Deputy Leader, since 2018; Cabinet Secretary for Infrastructure, Investment and Cities, 2014-16; Minister for Transport and Veterans, 2012-14; Minister for Housing and Transport, 2011-2012; Minister for Transport and Infrastructure, 2010-2011; Minister for Schools and Skills, 2009-2010; b. 20.12.61, Edinburgh; divorced; 2 s.; 1 d. Educ. Tynecastle High School; Dundee University. Royal Marines, 1980-83; local government administrative officer, since 1988. Member, Association of Electoral Administrators. Recreations: astronomy; hill-walking; football. Address: (b.) Scottish Parliament, Edinburgh EH99 1SP.

Brown, Professor Kenneth Alexander, BSc, MSc, PhD, CBE, FRSE. Emeritus Professor of Mathematics, Glasgow University; Vice-President, London Mathematical Society, 1997-99 and 2009-2017; b. 19.4.51, Ayr; m., Irene M.; 2 s. Educ. Ayr Academy; Glasgow University; Warwick University. Recreations: reading; running. Address: (b.) School of Mathematics and Statistics, Glasgow University, Glasgow G12 8QW; T.-0141-330 5180.

Brown, Professor Kenneth J., BSc, PhD, FRSE. Professor Emeritus in Mathematics, Heriot-Watt University (Professor, 1993-2007); b. 20.12.45, Torphins; m., Elizabeth Lobban; 1 s.; 2 d. Educ. Banchory Academy; Robert Gordon's College; Aberdeen University; Dundee University. Lecturer in Mathematics, Heriot Watt University, 1970-81, Senior Lecturer, 1981-91, Reader, 1991-93. Publications: 50 papers. Recreations: tennis; theatre; reading; bridge. Address: (h.) 3 Highlea Grove, Balerno, Edinburgh EH14 7HQ; T.-0131-449 5314; e-mail: mthkjb@gmail.com

Brown, Lynn, OBE, MA Hons (Edin). Chief Executive, Scottish Police Authority, since 2021 (Interim Chief Executive, 2019-2021). Educ. University of Edinburgh. Executive Director of Financial Services of Glasgow City Council and Strathclyde Pension Fund, 2003-2016. Member of the Chartered Institute of Public Finance and Accountancy (CIPFA); former Chair of CIPFA in Scotland.

Ian Doig Award for services to CIPFA in Scotland, 2009; UK Director of Finance of the Year, 2008; Public Sector Director of Finance of the Year, 2008. Address: The Scottish Police Authority, 1 Pacific Quay, Glasgow G51 1DZ; T.-01786 896630.

Brown, Sheriff Paul. Sheriff at Tayside, Central and Fife, since 2021. Educ. University of Glasgow. Career history: trained with Davidson Chalmers in Edinburgh; a solicitor in private practice latterly with JC Hughes in Glasgow, 2003-09; became an Advocate in 2009 specialising in criminal trials and appeals; appointed as an Advocate Depute in 2015; worked in the Crown Office National Sex Crimes Unit, then the prosecution of Serious and Organised Crime; became a Summary Sheriff in 2018. Address: Dundee Sheriff Court, 6 West Bell Street, Dundee DD1 9AD; T.-01382 229961.

Brown, R. Iain F, MBE, MA, MEd, ABPsS, ChPsychol, ERC (Hon). Senior Lecturer in Psychology, University of Glasgow (retired); b. 16.1.35, Dundee; m., Catherine G.; 2 d. Educ. Daniel Stewart's College, Edinburgh; St. Andrews University; Edinburgh University; Glasgow University. Education Department, Corporation of Glasgow; Department of Psychological Medicine, Glasgow University; Senior Lecturer, Department of Psychology, University of Glasgow 1968-2000. Honorary Senior Research Fellow, University of Glasgow, until 2005. National Training Advisor, Scottish Council on Alcohol, 1979-94; Member, Executive, Scottish Council on Alcohol, 1980-94 and Alcohol Focus Scotland, 1998-2007; Chairman, Society for the Study of Gambling, London, 1987-92; Founding Chairman, European Association for the Study of Gambling, 1992-95; Chairman, Glasgow Council on Alcohol, 1985-2014; Founding Chairman, Confederation of Scottish Counselling Agencies, 1989-93; Lecturer/tutor for Post Graduate Diploma in Cognitive Behavioural Therapy for Addictions (validated by The University of The West of Scotland), since 2011; President, Scottish Unitarian Association, 2005-09; Vice-Convener, Scottish Inter Faith Council, 2009-2011; Chairman, Glasgow Anniesland Lib-Dems; Candidate: Glasgow Anniesland (Holyrood) 2000, Motherwell (Westminster) 2001. Various publications, mainly on addictions, in scientific books and journals. Recreations: travel; music. Address: (h.) 13 Kirklee Terrace, Glasgow G12 0TH; T.-0141-339 7815; mobile: 07742653305; e-mail: iain.brown13@gmail.com

Brown, Robert, LLB (Hons). Councillor, Rutherglen South Ward on South Lanarkshire Council, since 2012; Leader of Liberal Democrat Group on South Lanarkshire Council, since 2019; Convener, Association of Scottish Liberal Democrat Councillors and Campaigners (ASLDC), since 2017; MSP (Liberal Democrat), Glasgow, 1999-2011; Spokesperson in Justice and Civil Liberties, 2008-2011; Liberal Democrat Group Business Manager, 2007-08; Convener, Scottish Parliament Education Committee, 2003-05; Deputy Minister for Education and Young People, 2005-07; b. 1947, Newcastle upon Tyne; m.; 1 s.; 1 d. Educ. Gordon Schools, Huntly; Aberdeen University. Former Solicitor (1972-2011); former Senior Civil Partner, Ross Harper and Murphy; former Glasgow District Councillor (Leader, Lib Dem Group, 1977-92). Address: Council Offices, Beckford Street, Hamilton ML3 0AA; T.-01698 453609.

Brown, Russell Leslie. MP (Labour), Dumfries and Galloway, 2005-2015, Dumfries, 1997-2005; b. 17.9.51, Annan; m., Christine Margaret Calvert; 2 d. Educ. Annan Academy. Employed by ICI for 23 years in variety of positions; Local Councillor, 1986-1997. Recreations: walking; sport, especially football.

Brown, Sarah Laura, BSc (Hons), PGCE, MA (EdMgmt), PGDipEd and Leadership, SQH. Headteacher, Kinross High School. Address: Loch Leven Community Campus, Muirs KY13 8FQ; T.-01577 867100.
E-mail: kinrosshigh@pkc.gov.uk

Brown, Simon Thomas David, LLB (Hons), DipLP, WS, FRSA. Partner and Head of Corporate, Anderson Strathern Solicitors, since 1997; b. 22.4.60, Edinburgh; m., Karen Ivory; 2 s.; 1 d. Educ. Royal High School, Edinburgh; Edinburgh University. Dundas and Wilson CS, 1983-89; Partner, Steedman Ramage WS, 1989-97. Director, Publishing Scotland. Recreations: golf; football; family; travel; literature. Address: (b.) 1 Rutland Court, Edinburgh EH3 8EY; T.-0131 270 7700.
E-mail: simon.brown@andersonstrathern.co.uk

Brown, Siobhian. MSP (SNP), Ayr, since 2021; 3 c. Founded the South Ayrshire Babybank in 2016 and remains a volunteer for the organisation; councillor for the Ayr West ward of South Ayrshire Council, 2017-2022. Address: The Scottish Parliament, Edinburgh EH99 1SP; T.-0131 348 5089; e-mail: Siobhian.Brown.msp@parliament.scot

Brown, Professor Stewart J., BA, MA, PhD, FRHistS, FRSE. Professor of Ecclesiastical History, Edinburgh University, since 1988; Dean, Faculty of Divinity, 2000-04; Head of the School of Divinity, 2010-2013; b. 8.7.51, Illinois; m., Teri B. Hopkins-Brown; 1 s.; 1 d. Educ. University of Illinois; University of Chicago. Fulbright Scholar, Edinburgh University, 1976-78; Whiting Fellow in the Humanities, University of Chicago, 1979-80; Assistant to the Dean, College of Arts & Sciences, and Lecturer in History, Northwestern University, 1980-82; Associate Professor and Assistant Head, Department of History, University of Georgia, 1982-88; Visiting Lecturer, Department of Irish History, University College, Cork, 1986; Editor, Scottish Historical Review, 1993-99. Publications: Thomas Chalmers and the Godly Commonwealth in Scotland, 1982 (awarded Agnes Mure Mackenzie Prize from Saltire Society); Scotland in the Age of the Disruption (Co-Author), 1993; William Robertson and the Expansion of Empire (Editor), 1997; Piety and Power in Ireland 1760-1960 (Co-Editor), 2000; Scottish Christianity in the Modern World (Co-Editor), 2000; The National Churches of England, Ireland and Scotland, 1801-1846, 2001; Cambridge History of Christianity, vol. 7: Enlightenment, Reawakening, and Revolution 1660-1815 (Co-Editor), 2006; Providence and Empire: Religion, Politics and Society in the United Kingdom 1815-1917, 2008; The Union of 1707: New Dimensions (Co-Editor), 2008; The Oxford Movement: Europe and the Wider World, 1830-1930 (Co-Editor), 2012; Religion, Identity and Conflict in Britain: From the Restoration to the Twentieth Century (Co-Editor), 2013; The Oxford Handbook of the Oxford Movement (Co-Editor), 2017; The Church and Empire (Co-Editor), 2018; W. T. Stead: Nonconformist and Newspaper Prophet (2019). Recreations: swimming; hill-walking. Address: (h.) 160 Craigleith Hill Avenue, Edinburgh EH4 2NB; T.-0131-539 2863.
E-mail: s.j.brown@ed.ac.uk

Brown, Very Rev Susan. Minister, Dornoch Cathedral, since 1998; Moderator of the General Assembly of the Church of Scotland, 2018-19; Honorary Chaplain to the Queen in Scotland; b. 12.12.58, Edinburgh; m., Derek. First woman to take charge of a cathedral in the United Kingdom; officiated at the weddings of Madonna, Guy Ritchie, Ashley Judd and Dario Franchitti; previously minister at Killearnan Church, near Muir of Ord in Ross-Shire. Address: Dornoch Cathedral, Dornoch IV25 3SJ; T.-01862 810575.

Brown, Professor Tom, BSc, PhD. Vice-Principal (Research and Innovation), University of St Andrews, since 2019. Educ. Imperial College London; University of Southampton. Career history: Scientific Officer, Defence Research Agency, 1993-94; Analyst, Dresdner Kleinwort Benson, 1999-2000; University of St Andrews: appointed Senior Lecturer in 2009, then Reader in Photenics in 2014, then Professor of Physics and Astronomy in 2017, then Dean of Science in 2018. Research interests are in the development of laser systems and related technologies for applications in biology and medicine, working in collaboration with colleagues within the University and further afield. Address: University of St Andrews, College Gate, St Andrews KY16 9AJ; T.-01334 46 2542.
E-mail: vpresearch@st-andrews.ac.uk

Browne of Ladyton, Rt. Hon. Lord (Desmond Browne), LLB (Hons). Former Labour MP, Kilmarnock and Loudoun (1997-2010); Secretary of State for Defence, 2006-08; Secretary of State for Scotland, 2007-08; Chief Secretary to the Treasury, 2005-06; Minister for Immigration and Citizenship, 2004-05; Minister for Work, 2003-04; Under Secretary of State, Northern Ireland Office, 2001-03; b. 22.3.52; m., Maura; 2 s. Educ. St Michael's Academy, Kilwinning; Glasgow University. Partner, Ross Harper and Murphy, 1980-85; Senior Partner, McCluskey Browne, Kilmarnock, 1985-92; called to the Bar, 1993; Member, Council, Law Society of Scotland, 1988-91; Chair, Children's Rights Group, 1981-86; Member, Sheriff Court Rules Council, 1990-92; Member, Dean's Council, Faculty of Advocates, 1994-97. Recreations: football; swimming; reading. Address: House of Lords, London SW1A 0PW.

Browning, Derek, Very Rev Dr, MA, BD, DMin. Minister, Morningside Parish Church, Edinburgh, since 2001; Moderator of the 2017 General Assembly of the Church of Scotland; b. 24.5.62, Edinburgh. Educ. North Berwick High School; Corpus Christi College, Oxford; St. Mary College, St. Andrews; Princeton Theological Seminary. Minister, Cupar Old Parish Church, 1987-2001; Moderator, Presbytery of St. Andrews, 1996-97; Convener, Prayer and Devotion Committee, Panel on Worship, 2000-04; Convener of Assembly Arrangements Committee and the Business Committee of the General Assembly, 2015-16; Moderator, Presbytery of Edinburgh, 2021-22. Recreations: reading; cooking; croquet; travel; the arts. Address: (h.) 20 Braidburn Crescent, Edinburgh EH10 6EN; T.-0131 447 1617; e-mail: derek.browning@churchofscotland.org.uk

Browning, Professor George Gordon, MD, ChB, FRCS(Ed.), FRCPS(Glas). Professor of Otolaryngology, Head and Neck Surgery, University of Glasgow, 1991-2002; Visitor, Scottish Section, MRC/CSO Hearing Sciences, Nottingham University; Honorary Consultant Otolaryngologist, Glasgow Royal Infirmary, 1978-98, now Emeritus Professor; Senior Consultant Otologist to British MRC Institute of Hearing Research, 1992-2002; Editor in Chief, Clinical Otolaryngology, 2004-2014; b. 10.1.41, Glasgow; m., Annette; 1 s.; 2 d. Educ. Kelvinside Academy; University of Glasgow. Resident House Surgeon, Western Infirmary, Glasgow, 1964-65; West of Scotland General Surgical Training Scheme, 1965-75; West of Scotland Otorhinolaryngological Training Scheme, 1975-78; MRC Wernher-Piggot Travelling Fellow, Harvard University, 1976-77. President, Otorhinolaryngological Research Society UK, 1992-94; Chairman, British Society of Academics in Otolaryngology, UK, 1995-99; Vice-Chairman, Specialist Advisory Committee in Otolaryngology, 1997-99; President, Section of Otology, Royal Society of Medicine, 1999-2000; Chairman, Academic Board, Royal Society of Medicine, 2001-03

(Vice-Chairman, 2000-01); Vice-President, Royal Society of Medicine, 2005-07; Member, Post-Graduate Examining Boards, FRCS Edinburgh, since 1997, and FRCPS Glasgow, since 1987. Publications: Updated ENT (3rd Edition), 1994; Picture Tests in Otolaryngology (Co-Author), 1998; Clinical Otology and Audiology (2nd Edition), 1998; Otoscopy – A Structured Approach (Co-Author), 1995; Scott Brown's Otolaryngology Head & Neck Surgery (7th Ed., Co-Editor), 2008; over 140 scientific articles. Recreations: Conservation (Chairman, Great Western Road Defense Committee, 1971-74; Founder Chairman, Glasgow West Conservation Society, 1975; Chairman, Kew Terrace Association); cycling; gardening; glasswork; silversmithing; skiing; swimming. Address: (b.) MRC/CSO Institute of Hearing Sciences, Scottish Section, Glasgow Royal Infirmary, New Lister Building, 16 Alexandra Parade, Glasgow G31 2ER; T.-0141-242 9665.

Brownlee, Derek. MSP (Conservative), South of Scotland, 2005-2011; b. 10.8.74. Formerly Conservative Finance Spokesman; Head of Research & Content, Royal Bank of Scotland, 2011-2013.

Brownlie, Alistair Rutherford, OBE, MA, LLB, SSC, FCSFS, NP; b. 5.4.24, Edinburgh; m., Martha Barron Mounsey. Educ. George Watson's; Edinburgh University. Served as radio operator in 658 Air O.P. Squadron RAF, Europe and India; apprenticed to J. & R.A. Robertson, WS; qualified Solicitor, 1950; in private practice, until 1995; Member, Committee on Blood Grouping (House of Lords); Solicitor for the poor, 1955-64, in High Court of Justiciary; Secretary, SSC Society, 1970-95, now Archivist; former Member, Council, Law Society of Scotland; Legal Aid Central Committee; Chairman, Legal Aid Committee, Scottish Legal Aid Board, 1986-90; founder Member, Past President, now Hon. Fellow, Chartered Society of Forensic Sciences; Member, Vice-Chairman, Scottish Council of Law Reporting, 1975-97; Chairman, Edinburgh Diabetes Research Trust; Fellow, RSA; Hon. Fellow, Cancer Research UK; Member, 1124 Society of St. Giles; Elder, Church of Scotland and United Reformed Church. Publications: The Universities and Scottish Legal Education; Drink, Drugs and Driving (Co-author); Crime Investigation: art or science (Editor); HM Advocate v Preece - A Judicial Fiasco; autobiography: "The Treasured Years"; various papers on forensic science, criminal law, legal aid and local history. Recreations: the pen and the mouse. Address: (h.) 8 Braid Mount, Edinburgh; T.-0131-447 4255; e-mail: a.brownlie@icloud.com

Bruce, Adam Robert. WS. Marchmont Herald of Arms at the Court of the Lord Lyon, since 2012; Global Head of Corporate Affairs, Mainstream Renewable Power, since 2008; b. 1968; m., Donna Maria-Sofia Granito Pignatelli di Belmonte; 2 s. Educ. Glenalmond College; Balliol College, Oxford University (MA Hons) (President, Oxford Union, 1989); Edinburgh University (LLB). Formerly a solicitor in private practice (Writer to HM Signet, 2001); Member, Council, WS Society (2016-19); Chairman, RenewableUK (2007-2010); Chairman, Offshore Wind Programme Board (2012-2015). Formerly Finlaggan Pursuivant to Clan Donald, and Unicorn Pursuivant at the Court of the Lord Lyon; Trustee: National Museums of Scotland, since 2017, St Andrew's Trust for Scots Heraldry; FRSA; FSA (Scot); OStJ. Address: c/o The Court of the Lord Lyon, HM New Register House, Edinburgh EH1 3YT.

Bruce of Crionaich (Major General Alastair Andrew Bernard Reibey Bruce), OBE, VR, DL. Governor, Edinburgh Castle, since 2019; British Army reservist, journalist and television commentator; b. 25.6.60, Winchester; m., Stephen James Michael Knott. Educ.

Milton Abbey School; The Royal Military Academy Sandhurst (RMAS). Career history: joined the British Army in 1979; gained the rank of Lieutenant in the 2nd Battalion of the Scots Guards in 1980; served as a regular officer for four years, and saw active service in the Falklands War of 1982; served as an Army Reserve Brigadier, Deputy Commander of 3rd Division (United Kingdom) and Colonel of the London Scottish Regiment; Assistant Vice-President, Merrill Lynch, 1983-89. Recognised in the name of Bruce of Crionaich by Lord Lyon King of Arms in 1984; appointed as one of The Queen's heralds on 7 October 1998 as Fitzalan Pursuivant; member of the Royal Company of Archers, the Queen's ceremonial bodyguard in Scotland, since 1990; appointed Officer of the Order of St John in 1991; promoted to Commander in 1997; took command of the reserve unit, Media Operations Group, co-ordinating media representation of military activity in 2004; mobilised on active operations in Iraq, serving in Operation TELIC in 2004; promoted Colonel in the Territorial Army, and became the Equerry to Prince Edward; appointed Knight of St John in 2008. Worked as a historical advisor to Oscar-winning films such as The King's Speech (2010) and The Young Victoria (2009), and of the BAFTA-winning television series Downton Abbey (2010–2015); lectured widely in Britain, Europe and the United States (subjects range from the last Tsars of Russia to Britain's monarchy and the Vatican in Rome); appointed Honorary Professor of Media at the University of Winchester in 2011; appointed Honorary Colonel, 5th Military Intelligence Battalion in 2020; appointed Tayforth Officers' Training Corps in 2021; appointed British Army Race Advocate, 2020. Written many books, and worked with several independent production companies in the preparation of television documentaries which are regularly aired on the BBC, America's PBS network, Discovery Channel and A&E channels. Address: Edinburgh Castle, Castlehill, Edinburgh EH1 2NG; e-mail: abofc@abofc.org.uk

Bruce, Alistair James, LLB. Retired Solicitor; Partner, Director, Lows Solicitors, Kirkwall, 1985-2016, Consultant, 2016-18; currently supports the solicitors and paralegals in complex conveyancing issues, including corrective conveyancing and crofting matters; b. 4.12.58, Perth; m., Jane; 2 s. Educ. Perth Academy; University of Dundee. Apprenticeship with A.C. Morrison and Richards, Advocates, Aberdeen, 1980-82; Assistant Solicitor, T.P. and J.L. Low, Kirkwall, 1982-85. Member, Council, Law Society of Scotland, 1996-98. Past President, Rotary Club of Kirkwall; Chair, Orkney Theatre; Chair, Age Scotland Orkney; Past Captain, Orkney Golf Club; Secretary of the Rotary Club of Orkney. Recreations: golf; drama; St. Magnus Cathedral Choir. Address: (b.) 5 Broad Street, Kirkwall, Orkney; T.-01856 873151.
E-mail: Alistair.bruce@lowsorkney.co.uk

Bruce, Andy, BA (Hons) Eng. Director of Communications and Ministerial Support, The Scottish Government, since 2021; m.; 2 c. Educ. Bishop's Stortford College; University of Cambridge. Career history: Fast Stream Programme, UK Ministry of Defence, London and Cyprus, 2000-05; Team Leader, Skill Force, Edinburgh, 2005-07; The Scottish Government: Team Leader, Social Work Services, 2007-09, Team Leader, Health Improvement and Health Inequalities Team, 2009-2012, Head of Tobacco, Alcohol and Diet, 2012-2013, Deputy Director, Community Justice Division, 2013-16, Deputy Director, Curriculum, Qualifications and Gaelic, 2016-19, Principal Private Secretary to the Permanent Secretary, 2019-2021. Address: Scottish Government, St Andrew's House, Regent Road, Edinburgh EH1 3DG.

Bruce, David, MA, FRPS, Chevalier de L'Ordre des Arts et des Lettres. Writer and Consultant; Director, Scottish Film Council, 1986-94; b. 10.6.39, Dundee; m., Barbara; 1 s.; 1 d. Educ. Dundee High School; Aberdeen Grammar School; Edinburgh University. Freelance (film), 1963; Assistant Director, Films of Scotland, 1964-66; Director, Edinburgh International Film Festival, 1965-66; Promotions Manager, Mermaid Theatre, London, 1966-67; Executive Officer, British Universities Film Council, 1967-69; joined Scottish Film Council as Assistant Director, 1969; Depute Director, SFC and Scottish Council for Educational Technology, 1977-86. Chairman, Mental Health Film Council, 1982-84; Chairman, Scottish Society for History of Photography, 1983-86 and 2003-2014; Chairman, Association of European Film Institutes, 1990-94; Director, David Octavius Hill Bicentenary Festival, 2002; Glasgow Film Theatre, Chairman, 2002-08; Chairman, Regional Screen Scotland, 2008-2010; Chairman, Historical Group, Royal Photographic Society, 2018; Partner, Renaissance Press, Edinburgh, since 2003. Various publications, including Sun Pictures, 1973; Scotland–the Movie, 1996; Greatrex - Forger and Photographer, 2013. Recreations: movies; music; photo-history. Address: (h.) Rosebank, 150 West Princes Street, Helensburgh G84 8BH.
E-mail: david@bruce150.me.uk

Bruce, Fraser Finlayson, RD, MA (Hons), LLB, FSA(Scot). Regional Chairman, Industrial Tribunals for Scotland, 1993-97 (Permanent Chairman, 1982-93); Solicitor, since 1956; b. 10.10.31, Kirkcaldy; m. (1), Joan Gwendolen Hunter (deceased); 2 step-s; m. (2), Violet Margaret Ross MacGregor; 1 step-d. Educ. St. Andrews University. National Service, Royal Navy, 1956-58, commissioned Sub-Lieutenant, RNVR; Legal Assistant: Lanark County Council, 1958-60, Inverness County Council, 1960-66; Depute County Clerk: Argyll County Council, 1966-70, Inverness County Council, 1970-72; County Clerk, Inverness County Council, 1972-75; Joint Director of Law and Administration, Highland Regional Council, 1975-82; Temporary Sheriff, 1984-92. Served RNVR, 1956-76, retiring as Lieutenant-Commander RNR. Recreations: hill walking; reading (in philosophy and naval/military history). Address: (h.) Arlberg, Mossie Road, Grantown-on-Spey PH26 3HW; T.-01479 873969.

Bruce of Bennachie, Baron (Sir Malcolm Gray Bruce), Kt, PC, MA, MSc. Liberal Democrat Scotland Spokesman in the House of Lords, since 2017, Spokesman on Northern Ireland, 2019-2020; MP (Liberal Democrat, formerly Liberal), Gordon, 1983-2015; Deputy Leader, Liberal Democrat Party, 2014-15; President, Scottish Liberal Democrats, 2000-2015; Liberal Democrat Shadow Secretary of State for the Department of Trade and Industry, 2003-05; Liberal Democrat Shadow Secretary of State for the Department of the Environment, Food and Rural Affairs, 2001-02; Liberal Democrat Treasury Spokesman, 1995-2000; Chairman, Liberal Democrat Parliamentary Party, 1999-2001; b. 17.11.44, Birkenhead; m., 1, Jane Wilson; 1 s.; 1 d; m., 2, Rosemary Vetterlein; 1 s.; 2 d. Educ. Wrekin College; St. Andrews University; Strathclyde University. Trainee Journalist, Liverpool Daily Post & Echo, 1966-67; Section Buyer, Boots the Chemist, 1968-69; Fashion Retailing Executive, A. Goldberg & Sons, 1969-70; Research and Information Officer, NESDA, 1971-75; Marketing Director, Noroil Publishing, 1975-81; Director, Aberdeen Petroleum Publishing; Editor/Publisher, Aberdeen Petroleum Report, 1981-83; Co-Editor, Scottish Petroleum Annual, 1st and 2nd editions; Called to the Bar (Gray's Inn), 1995. Vice Chairman, Political, Scottish Liberal Party, 1975-84; Rector, Dundee University, 1986-89; Privy Councillor, 2006; Chair, Globe UK - APPG dialogue on climate change, 2004-06; President, Globe International, 2004-06; Trustee, RNID, 2004-2010; Honorary National Vice President of National Deaf Children's Society (NDCS); Honorary Vice President, Action on Hearing Loss. Member of the Privy Council, since 2006. Recreations: reading; music; theatre; hill-walking; cycling; travel. Address: House of Lords, Westminster, London SW1A 0PW.

Bruce, Professor Steve, BA, PhD, FBA, FRSE. Professor of Sociology, Aberdeen University, since 1991; b. 1.4.54, Edinburgh; m., Elizabeth S. Duff; 1 s.; 2 d. Educ. Queen Victoria School, Dunblane; Stirling University. Variously Lecturer, Reader and Professor of Sociology, Queen's University of Belfast, 1978-91. Publications: author of numerous books on religion, and on the Northern Ireland conflict. Recreation: shooting. Address: (b.) Department of Sociology, Aberdeen University, Aberdeen AB24 3QY; T.-01224 272761.

Bruce, Dame Susan, DBE, MPhil, LLB, Dip, FRSA, DUniv. Non Executive Director, SSE plc, since 2013; Chairperson, Expert Panel on Environmental Charging and Other Measures (EPECOM), since 2018; Convener of Court, University of Strathclyde, since 2017; Electoral Commissioner - Scotland, since 2017; Director, Bruce Consultancy, since 2015; m. Educ. Jordanhill College of Education; University of Strathclyde; JFK School of Government, Harvard. Career: local government, 1976; appointed to the Director role in East Dunbartonshire covering Education, Social Work, Housing and Cultural Services in 2000 and then Chief Executive in 2004; Chief Executive of Aberdeen City Council from 2008 before joining City of Edinburgh Council; Chief Executive, City of Edinburgh Council, 2011-15; Partner, Aurum Resolution LLP, 2015-17. First public sector leader to receive the Prince's Ambassador in Scotland Award, 2010 and again in 2011; Scottish Business Insider Public Sector Leader of the Year Award, 2010; HR Network Chief Executive of the Year, 2013; MIPIM UK City Leader of the Year, 2014; Board Chair, RSNO, since 2015; Independent Chair of Nominations Committee, The National Trust for Scotland, since 2017. Recreations: the arts; reading; gardening. Address: SSE plc, Inveralmond House, 200 Dunkeld Road, Perth PH1 3AQ.

Brumpton, Jane, BEd (Hons), PGCE. Chief Executive, Early Years Scotland, since 2020. Educ. Turnbull High School, Bishopbriggs; St Andrew's Teaching College/Glasgow University; University of Strathclyde. Career history: Primary Teacher (Early Stages), Kuwait National English School, 1993-95; Rome International School, 1995-98; Primary Teacher, St Aloysius Primary School, 1998-99; Primary One Teacher, St Helen's Primary School, Bishopbriggs, 2000; Nursery Teacher, Hilltop Nursery School, 2000-04; Learning and Teaching Scotland: Early Years Development Officer, 2008-2010, Early Years Team Leader (Acting) on Secondment, Glasgow, 2010-2011; Nursery School Head Teacher, Woodacre Nursery School, Glasgow, 2005-2014; Depute Head Teacher, St. Philomena's Enhanced Nurture Unit, 2014-15; Deputy Chief Executive Officer, Early Years Scotland, 2014-2020. Address: Early Years Scotland, 21 Granville Street, Glasgow G3 7EE; T.-0141 221 4148.

Bruntisfield, 3rd Baron (Michael John George Warrender); b. 9.1.49; succeeded to title, 2007.

Brunton, Rodger James Horne, DipArch, RIBA, FRIAS, MaPS. Consultant, Brunton Design Studio; b. 11.7.51, Dundee; m., Sheila; 1 s.; 1 d. Educ. Morgan Academy, Dundee; School of Architecture, Duncan of Jordanstone College of Art. Dundee District Council, 1975-80; Robbie and Wellwood Architects, 1980-85; Brunton Voigt Partnership, 1985-99. Past President, Dundee Institute of Architects; Secretary, Dundee Institute of Architects;

Chairman, Morgan Academy Former Pupils Association; Past Chairman, School Board, Carnoustie High School; Past Chairman, Carnoustie Centre Action Group; Past President and Senator of Junior Chamber Dundee. Recreations: after-dinner speaking; amateur operatics. Address: (b.) 95 Dundee Street, Carnoustie DD7 7EW; T.-01241 858153. E-mail: rodger@bruntondesign.com

Brunton, Sandy, DipY and BM. Director, Connecting Scotland CiC, since 2014; Trustee/Board Member, Development Trusts Association Scotland, since 2021; Convenor, Mull and Iona Community Trust, since 2008; b. 22.7.59, Oban; m., Jane; 1 s.; 2 d. Educ. Oban High School; James Watt, Greenock; Southampton College of Higher Education. Shipwright/Boatbuilder, Southampton, 1983-86; Retailer and Subpostmaster, Fionnphort, Mull, since 1986. Member of the Management Board, Scottish Rural Parliament, since 2013. Address: The Ferry Shop, Fionnphort, Isle of Mull PA66 6BL; T.-01681 700470. E-mail: bruntonmull@aol.com

Bruton, Annette. Former Principal, Edinburgh College (2015-18); former Chief Executive, Care Inspectorate (2012-15); b. East Lothian. Career: trained and worked as a Geography teacher before moving into Learning Support and Special Educational Needs; joined HM Inspectorate of Education in 2001 and was appointed as Chief Inspector in 2005 playing a key role in developing the successful multi-agency child protection inspections; Director of Education, Culture and Sport, Aberdeen City Council, 2009-2011. Student, Open College of the Arts, since 2018.

Bryce, Professor Charles F.A., BSc, PhD, DipEdTech, EurBiol, CBiol, FIBiol, CSci, CChem, FRSC, FHEA. Emeritus Professor at Edinburgh Napier University, since 1983; b. 5.9.47, Lennoxtown; 2 s. Educ. Lenzie Academy; Shawlands Academy; Glasgow University; Max Planck Institute, Berlin. Former Executive Editor, Computer Applications in the Biosciences; Editor of Biotechnology; Vice President, European Federation of Biotechnology (EFB); Member, EFB Task Group on Public Perceptions of Biotechnology; Chairman, EFB Task Group on Education and Mobility; Member, EFB Executive Board; Adviser to the Committee on Science and Technology in Developing Countries (India); former Chairman, UK Deans of Science Committee; Secretary General, European Association for Higher Education in Biotechnology; President, Academic Board, CSM International, Singapore; actively involved in quality audit and quality assessment in biomedical sciences and forensic science in UK, Eire, Bosnia and Hertzegovina, Australia, Bangladesh and Zambia; Visiting Professor, Zhengzhou University, China; Director, TopoSphere; Chair of Accreditation Panels for the Chartered Society of Forensic Sciences; External Examiner for the Pre-Employment Assessment of Competence (PEAC) for the Chartered Society of Forensic Sciences. Appointed by the Scottish Minister to membership of the Children's Hearing System. Recreations: competitive bridge; collecting wine. Address: (b.) 75 Carnbee Avenue, Edinburgh EH16 6GA.

Bryce, Colin Maxwell, DA (Edin), CertEd, FCSD, LRPS. Artist/Photographer, since 2011; Special Advisor to the Vice Principals, Napier University, 2006-08, Dean, Faculty of Arts and Social Science, 1997-2006; b. 14.9.45, Edinburgh; m., Caroline Joy; 2 s. Educ. Royal High School, Edinburgh; Edinburgh College of Art; Moray House College of Education. Art and Design Teacher, Portobello High School, 1968-75; Head of Art and Design, Wester Hailes Education Centre, 1975-85; Education Advisory Officer/Senior Education Officer/Chief Executive, The Design Council Scotland, 1985-90; Managing Director, Quorum Graphic Design, 1990-91; Head, Department of

Design, Napier University, 1992-97. Board Member/Chair, Craigmillar Opportunity Trust, 2001-11; Director/Chair, Creative Edinburgh, 2000-11; Trustee, Scottish Historic Buildings Trust, 2008-2018. Recreations: looking and listening. Address: 126 Willowbrae Road, Edinburgh EH8 7HW; e-mail: colinmbryce@mac.com

Bryce, Dr Rosalind, BSc (Hons), PhD. Director, Centre for Mountain Studies, Perth College, University of the Highlands and Islands. Educ. University of Glasgow; University of Aberdeen. Joined the Centre for Mountain studies in January 2014 as a researcher; teaches on the online MSc in Sustainable Mountain Development and supervises postgraduate researchers. Address: Top Floor, Webster Building, Crieff Road, Perth College, Perth PH1 2NX; T.-01738 877217.
E-mail: rosalind.bryce.perth.uhi.ac.uk

Bryce, Professor Tom G.K., BSc, MEd, PhD. Emeritus Professor of Education, University of Strathclyde, Professor, since 1993; Vice-Dean (Research), 1997-2002; b. 27.1.46, Glasgow; m., Karen Douglas Stewart; 1 d.; 1 s.; 3 grandchildren. Educ. King's Park Secondary School, Glasgow; Glasgow University. Teacher of Physics, Jordanhill College School, 1968-71; P.T. of Physics, King's Park Secondary School, 1971-73; part-time Lecturer in Psychology, Glasgow University, 1972-75; Open University Tutor, 1979-84; Lecturer, 1973, Head of Psychology, 1983, Head, Division of Education and Psychology, 1987-93, Jordanhill College of Education; Head, Department of Educational Studies, University of Strathclyde, 1993-94. Chairman, Editorial Board, Scottish Educational Review, 1988-2002. Publications include: Scottish Education (Co-Editor), 1999 (2nd edition: Post-devolution, 2003; 3rd edition: Beyond Devolution, 2008; 4th edition: Referendum, 2013; 5th edition, 2018) and numerous articles in the international literature on science education. Recreations: moutaineering (Munro completer); badminton. Address: (b.) School of Education, Faculty of Humanities and Social Sciences, University of Strathclyde, Lord Hope Building, 141 St James Road, Glasgow G4 0LT; e-mail: t.g.k.bryce@strath.ac.uk

Bryden, Duncan Mackenzie, BSc (Hons), MSocSc, CBiol. Rural Development Consultant, since 2002; Past Convener, Cairngorms National Park Authority; b. 22.01.59, Edinburgh; m., Michelle; 3 s. Educ. Glenalmond College; Edinburgh University; Birmingham University. Visitor Services Manager, Rothiemurchus Estate, Aviemore, 1986-91; Senior Tourism Executive, Highlands and Islands Enterprise, 1991-92; Head of Planning and Research, Ross and Cromarty Enterprise, 1992-94; Director, Tourism and Environment Forum, 1994-2000; Director, Scottish Wildlife Trust, 2000-02. Lecturer, University of The Highlands and Islands; Director: Outdoor Access Trust Scotland, Strathdearn Community Developments. Recreations: mountaineering; mountain biking; fishing; carpentry. Address: (h.) Corry View, Tomatin, Inverness IV13 7ZB; T.-01808 511777.

Buccleuch and Queensberry, Duke of (Richard Walter John Montagu Douglas Scott), KT, KBE, FRSE. Lord High Commissioner to the General Assembly of The Church of Scotland, 2018 and 2019; Lord-Lieutenant for Roxburgh, Ettrick and Lauderdale, since 2016; High Steward of Westminster Abbey, since 2017; President, National Trust for Scotland, 2002-2012; b. 14.2.54; m., Lady Elizabeth Kerr; 2 s.; 2 d. Member, Millennium Commission, 1994-2003; Deputy Chairman, Independent Television Commission, 1996-98; President, Royal Scottish Geographical Society, 1999-2005; Member, National Heritage Memorial Fund, 2000-05; President: Royal Blind,

since 2008, St Andrew's First Aid, since 2008; Trustee, Royal Collection, since 2011. Address: (h.) Bowhill, Selkirk TD7 5ET.

Buchan-Hepburn, 8th Baronet of Smeaton-Hepburn (Sir John James Christopher Thomas Buchan-Hepburn); b. 1.12.92. Suceeded to title in 2022.

Buchanan, Alan. Director of Operations, Police Investigations & Review Commissioner (PIRC), since 2018. Career: extensive experience as an investigator in both the public and private sectors; Investigation Manager with the Royal Bank of Scotland (responsible for the investigation of misconduct and financial crime, nationally and internationally); previously investigated numerous major crimes as a police officer within Strathclyde Police and Police Scotland; as Detective Superintendent, investigated several complex murder investigations; also led a team which had governance oversight of all murder investigations throughout Scotland and reviewed historical and unsolved murders. Address: (b.) Hamilton House, Hamilton Business Park, Caird Park, Hamilton ML3 0QA; T.-01698 542900.

Buchanan, Prof. Bill, OBE, PhD, FBCS. Professor, School of Computing, Edinburgh Napier University, since 1986; leads the Centre for Cybersecurity and Cryptography, and the Blockpass ID Lab; b. 6.3.61, Falkirk. Educ. Graeme High School, Falkirk; Edinburgh Napier University. Regularly appears on TV and radio related to computer security, and has given evidence to both the UK and Scottish Parliament; recent work on Secret Shares received "Innovation of the Year" at the Scottish Knowledge Exchange Awards, for a research project which involves splitting data into secret shares, and can then be distributed across a public Cloud-based infrastructure; received an "Outstanding Contribution to Knowledge Exchange" at the Scottish Knowledge Exchange Awards, 2018; led work that has created 3 successful spin-out companies (Zonefox, Symphonic Software and Cyan Forensics); Principal Fellow of the HEA; Director of Blockpass Identity Lab (BIL). Received OBE in 2017 for services to cyber security; Fellow of the BCS. Published 29 academic books and over 300 academic papers. Created Asecuritysite.com (https://asecuritysite.com) and the BrightRed Digital Zone. Address: School of Computing, Merchiston Campus, Edinburgh Napier University, 10 Colinton Road, Edinburgh EH10 5DT; T.-0131 455 2706.

Buchanan, Cameron R.M. Non-Executive Director of Angus Energy PLC; Regional Member of the Scottish Parliament (Conservative), 2013-16; b. 1946, Edinburgh; 2 s.; 2 d. Educ. St Edward's School, Oxford; Sorbonne, Paris. Lived and worked in France, Germany and Italy; Managing Director, Harrisons of Edinburgh, 1985-97; Entrepreneur of the Year, 1992; Textile Consultant, since 1997. High Constable of Leith; Hon. Co. Edinburgh Golfers. Recreations: skiing; tennis; golf. T.-0131 629 6476.
E-mail: cameron@cameronbuchanan.com

Buchanan, Jan. Director of Finance, Glasgow Life, since 2018. Educ. Glasgow Caledonian University; University of the West of Scotland. Career history: UK Ministry of Defence: Finance roles, 1999-2004, Head of Finance and Business, 2004-06, Head of Finance, 2006-07; Inverclyde Council: Head of Finance, 2013-14, Finance Manager, 2007-2015; Head of Finance, University of the West of Scotland, 2015-19. Address: Glasgow Life, 38 Albion Street, Glasgow G1 1LH; T.-0141 287 4350.

Buchanan, John Michael Baillie-Hamilton, CEng, MICE. Chief of Clan Buchanan, since 2018; Manager, Cambusmore Estate; b. 14.9.58; m., Paula Frances

Hickman; 3 s.; 1 d. Educ. Oxford University. First Chief of Scottish Buchanan Clan, since 1681. Address: Cambusmore, Callander, Perthshire FK17 8LJ.

Buchanan, Malcolm. Managing Director, Corporate and Commercial Banking, Scotland and Chairman, Scotland Board, The Royal Bank of Scotland, since 2015; Vice Chair, Scotland Leadership Board, Business in the Community Scotland; b. 11.67. Educ. Braidhurst High School, Motherwell. Career history: early career in retail/branch banking; various corporate and commercial banking roles in Scotland, Manchester and London over 25 years; joined Clydesdale Bank in Glasgow in 1984 before moving to NatWest in 1998 and Royal Bank of Scotland in 2000; completed Chartered Banker qualifications with the Chartered Institute of Bankers in Scotland, 1987; completed an MBA (Dist), Edinburgh Business School, 1998; Certified Bank Director, The Institute of Banking, 2019. Member, Board of Scottish Financial Enterprise. Address: The Royal Bank of Scotland, 24-25, St. Andrew Square, Edinburgh EH2 1AF.

Buchanan, Cllr Tony. Leader, East Renfrewshire Council, since 2017; representing Neilston, Uplawmoor and Newton Mearns North (SNP), since 2007. Current roles and responsibilities: Convener for infrastructure and sustainable growth; COSLA: member of regeneration and sustainable development executive group; delegate/member of the European Committee of the Regions; Vice President & Treasurer, The European Alliance Group, Committee of Regions, EU; Chair/Director - Supplier Development Programme; Director/Chair, West of Scotland Loan Fund; Director, WSLF Management Services; member, West Regional Advisory Board; Chair, West of Scotland European Forum; City Deal Cabinet (substitute); SPT Board member; Director, Business Loans Scotland; member, Glasgow Airport Consultative Committee. Address: (b.) 29 Sunnyside Place, Barrhead, East Renfrewshire G78 2RT; T.-07976 360398.
E-mail: tony.buchanan@eastrenfrewshire.gov.uk

Buckland, Roger, MA, MBA, MPhil. Emeritus Chair of Finance & Accountancy, University of Aberdeen (Head of Business School, Chair of Accountancy, 1993-2015); b. 22.04.51, Swallownest, England; m., Professor Lorna McKee; 2 d. Educ. Aston High School, South Yorkshire; Selwyn College, University of Cambridge. Research Assistant, University of Aston, 1972-74; Research Fellow, University of York, 1974-78; Lecturer in Finance, University of Aston, 1978-93; Visiting Professor, Bordeaux Business School, 1989-90, Michigan State University, 2011. Address: University of Aberdeen Business School, Edward Wright Building, Dunbar Street, Old Aberdeen AB24 3QY; T.-01224 272206; e-mail: acc040@abdn.ac.uk

Buckland, Professor Stephen T., BSc, MSc, PhD, CStat. Professor of Statistics, St. Andrews University, since 1993 (Director, Centre for Research into Ecological and Environmental Modelling, 1999-2004 and 2009-2014); Co-Director, National Centre for Statistical Ecology, 2005-2019; b. 28.7.55, Dorchester; 1 d. Educ. Foster's School, Sherborne; Southampton University; Edinburgh University; Aberdeen University. Lecturer in Statistics, Aberdeen University, 1977-85; Senior Scientist, Tuna/Dolphin Program, Inter-American Tropical Tuna Commission, San Diego, 1985-87; Senior Consultant Statistician, Scottish Agricultural Statistics Service, 1988-93, Head, Environmental Modelling Unit, 1991-93. Publications: The Birds of North-East Scotland (Co-editor), 1990; Distance Sampling: estimating abundance of biological populations (Co-author), 1993; Introduction to Distance Sampling (Co-author), 2001; Estimating Animal Abundance (Co-author), 2002; Advanced Distance Sampling (Co-editor), 2004; Modelling Population Dynamics (Co-author), 2014;

Distance Sampling: Methods and Applications (Co-author), 2015. Recreations: wildlife photography; natural history; walking; reading. Address: (b.) St. Andrews University, The Observatory, Buchanan Gardens, St. Andrews KY16 9LZ; T.-01334 461841.

Bullock, Michael Peter, OBE, MA, FCILT. Chief Executive, Northern Lighthouse Board, since 2014; b. 7.1.61, Liverpool; m., Clare Diana (nee Fairbairn); 1 s.; 1 d. Educ. Scarisbrick Hall School, Lancashire; Britannia Royal Naval College; Royal College of Defence Studies; King's College London. Royal Navy, 1980-2014; Commander Logistics, HMS Illustrious, 1998-99; Career Manager, 1999-02; British Defence Staff, Washington DC, 2002-05; Head of Supply Chain Policy, Defence Logistics Organisation, 2005-07; UK Liaison Officer, Directorate of Logistics, United States Joint Staff, Pentagon, 2007-10; Royal College of Defence Studies, 2010-11; Commodore, 2011; Assistant Chief of Staff Logistics and Infrastructure, Navy Command HQ, 2011-14; Trustee of Northern Lighthouse Heritage Trust; Trustee of Museum of Scottish Lighthouses; Non-executive Director, Scottish Maritime Cluster. High Constabulary of the Port of Leith. Hammermen of Edinburgh. Recreations: family; classic cars. Address: (b.) 84 George Street, Edinburgh EH2 3DA; T.-0131-473-3100; e-mail: mike.bullock@nlb.org.uk

Bunch, Antonia Janette, OBE, MA, FCLIP, FSAScot, FRSA. Librarian (retired); b. 13.2.37, Croydon. Educ. Notting Hill and Ealing High School; Strathclyde University. Assistant Librarian, Scottish Office; Librarian, Scottish Health Service Centre; Lecturer, Strathclyde University; Director, Scottish Science Library. Founding Chairman, Association of Scottish Health Sciences Librarians; Member: Standing Committee on Science and Technology Libraries, IFLA, 1987-91, Advisory Committee, British Library Science Reference and Information Service, 1987-96, Advisory Committee on Telematics for the Scottish Parliament, 1996-97; Chairman: Friends of St. Cecilia's Hall and the Russell Collection of Early Keyboard Instruments, 1997-2003; Trustee, Scottish Homeopathic Research and Education Trust, 1998-2008. Publications: Libraries in Hospitals (Co-author), 1969; Hospital and Medical Libraries in Scotland: an Historical and Sociological Study, 1975; Health Care Administration: an Information Sourcebook, 1979; The Temple of Harmony: a new architectural history of St Cecilia's Hall, Edinburgh (Co-author), 2011. Recreations: gardening; music. Address: Dove Cottage, Garvald, Haddington, East Lothian EH41 4LL.

Buncle, Tom, BA, MA. Managing Director, Yellow Railroad Ltd. International Destination Consultancy; b. 25.6.53, Arbroath; m., Janet; 2 s. Educ. Trinity College, Glenalmond; Exeter University; Sheffield University; London Business School. Various overseas posts (North America, Europe, Asia), British Tourist Authority, 1978-91; International Marketing Director, then Chief Executive, Scottish Tourist Board, 1991-2000. Independent Member: Scottish Prison Service Risk Monitoring and Audit Committee, 2007-2014; Fellow, UK Tourism Society; Experts' Committee of World Tourism Cities Forum (China); Fellow, UK Tourism Management Institute; Member, United Nations World Tourism Organization (UNWTO) Panel of Experts; Member, Place Brand Observer International Virtual Research Panel; National Committee Member, UK Tourism Consultants Network; Hon. Professor, Heriot-Watt University, since 2017. Recreations: wind-surfing; scuba diving; cycling; sailing; hill-walking. E-mail: tom@yellowrailroad.com

Bundy, Professor Alan Richard, CBE, BSc, PhD, FRS, FREng, FRSE, FAAAI, FECCAI, FBCS, FIET. Professor, University of Edinburgh; b. 18.5.47, Isleworth; m., D. Josephine A. Maule; 1 d. Educ. Heston Secondary Modern School; Springgrove Grammar

School; Leicester University. Tutorial Assistant, Department of Mathematics, Leicester University, 1970-71; University of Edinburgh: Research Fellow, Metamathematics Unit, 1971-74; Lecturer, Department of Artificial Intelligence, 1974-84; Reader, 1984-87; Professorial Fellow, 1987-90; Professor, since 1990. Editorial Board: AJ & Society Journal, Communications of the ACM. IJCAI Donald E. Walker Distinguished Service Award, 2003; IJCAI Research Excellence Award, 2007; CADE Herbrand Award, 2007. Publications: Artificial Intelligence: An Introductory Course, 1978; The Computer Modelling of Mathematical Reasoning, 1983; The Catalogue of Artificial Intelligence Tools, 1984; Rippling: Meta-level Guidance for Mathematical Reasoning. Recreation: walking. Address: (b.) School of Informatics, Edinburgh University, Informatics Forum, Crichton Street, Edinburgh EH8 9AB; T.-0131 650 2716.

Burberry, Very Revd. Frances Sheila. Dean, Diocese of Edinburgh, Scottish Episcopal Church, since 2017; Chaplain, University of Edinburgh, since 2006; Rector, St Ninian's Church, Edinburgh, since 2011; b. 1960. Synod Clerk to the diocese, 2016-17. Address: The Diocese of Edinburgh, 21a Grosvenor Crescent, Edinburgh EH12 5EL; T.-0131 5387033.
E-mail: dean@dioceseofedinburgh.org

Burden, Claire, BSc, DMS, MBA, MSc. Chief Executive Officer, NHS Scotland, since 2022. Educ. The Open University; Norwich City; Anglia Ruskin University; Chartered Management Institute; NHS Leadership Academy; University of Leicester. Career history: Paramedic, Norfolk Ambulance Service, 1989-95; Director - EMCC, East Anglian Ambulance Service NHS Trust, 1995-2000; National Network Support, NHS Direct, London and Anglia, 2000-03; Associate Director, Commissioner, South Cambridgeshire PCT, 2003-06; Chief Operating Officer, Primary Care - Out of Hours Services, 2006-07; Operations Programme Director, Cambridge University Hospitals NHS Foundation Trust, 2007-09; Director of Strategy, Scarborough General Hospital, 2010; Emergency Care Intensive Support Team (ECIST), NHS, National Role, 2009-2012; Director of Productivity, Kingston Hospital NHS Foundation Trust, Kingston on Thames, 2012; Deputy Chief Operating Officer, Birmingham Children's Hospital NHS Foundation Trust, 2012-15; Barts Health NHS Trust: Hospital Director, The Royal London; Whitechapel, London, 2015-17, Director of Emergency Care Improvement, Whitechapel, 2017-19, Deputy Chief Executive Officer, Whipps Cross Hospital, 2019-2022.

Burgess, Ariane, BA (Hons), MSc. MSP (Scottish Green Party), Highlands and Islands (Region), since 2021. Educ. Kingston University; Wimbledon School of Art; Institute for Popular Education; The Mother Hand Society; Findhorn Foundation; New York Open Center; Gaia University. Career history: Production Designer/Producer/Writer, Freelance Filmmaker, New York City, 1988-97; Commission on Sustainable Development, Women's Caucus, United Nations, New York, 2007-09; Adviser, Gaia University, 2012-16; Co-Facilitator and Trainer, Gaia Education, Thailand and Findhorn, 2008-2019; Founder (1995) and Designer, Camino de Paz, Global; Regenerative Leadership Strategy and Training, Regenerative Living and Leading, Global, from 2006. Publication: Life Design for Women: Conscious Living as a Force for Positive Change (Author), 2020. Address: The Scottish Parliament, Edinburgh EH99 1SP; T.-0131 348 6330.
E-mail: Ariane.Burgess.msp@parliament.scot

Burgess, Margaret. Former MSP (SNP), Cunninghame South (2011-16); former Minister for Housing and Welfare (2012-16); b. 7.12.49, Ayrshire. Served as a Councillor in Dreghorn and as SNP group leader on Cunninghame District Council. Previously worked as the Manager of East Ayrshire Citizens Advice Bureau and as a Director of Citizens Advice Scotland.

Burgess, William George, MA, PhD. Director of Agriculture and the Rural Economy (interim), The Scottish Government, since 2022; b. 8.5.70, Aberdeen; m., Adrienne Kirk; 1 d. Educ. Keith Grammar School; Churchill College, Cambridge University. Social Work Services Group, Scottish Office, 1994-96; Finance Group, Scottish Office, 1996-97; Referendum Bill Team, Scotland Bill Team, Scotland Act Implementation, 1997-2000; Private Secretary to Deputy First Minister, 2000-02; Head of Sustainable Development Team, Scottish Executive, 2002-04; Deputy Director, Criminal Law and Licensing, Scottish Government, 2004-2010, Facilities and Estates Services, 2010-11, Environmental Quality, 2011-16, Trade Policy, Food & Drink, 2016-18, Head of Food & Drink, 2018-2022. Session Clerk, St Andrews and St George's West Church, Edinburgh, 2013-2017. Scottish Young Scientist of the Year, 1988; CEGB Prize, Cambridge University, 1991. Recreations: choral music; historical research. Address: (b.) Saughton House, Broomhouse Road, Edinburgh EH11 3XD; T.-0131-244 0240.

Burke, Florence. National Head - Scotland, BBC Children in Need, since 2017. Development Manager, CEiS, 1997-2008; Director for Scotland, Carers Trust, 2008-2016; Chief Executive Officer, Music in Hospitals Scotland, 2016-17. Address: BBC Scotland, 40 Pacific Quay, Glasgow G51 1DA.

Burley, Lindsay, CBE, MBChB, FRCPE, FRCGP, FRSA. Partner, Eskhill & Co; formerly Chair, NHS Education for Scotland; formerly Chair, National Waiting Times Centre Board; formerly Chief Executive, NHS Borders; b. 2.10.50, Blackpool; m., Robin Burley. Educ. Queen Mary School, Lytham; University of Edinburgh. Address: (b.) Green House at Eskhill, 15A Inveresk Village, Musselburgh EH21 7TD; T.-0131 271 4000; e-mail: lindsay@eskhill.com

Burman, Professor Michele Jane, BA (Hons), MSc, PhD. FRSE, FAcSS, CBE. Professor of Criminology, University of Glasgow, since 2003; Founding Co-Director, Scottish Centre for Crime and Justice Research (SCCJR); b. London; m., Neil Hutton; 2 d. Educ. Springfield Convent, Cape Town; University of Cape Town; University of Edinburgh. Director, Women's Support Project, Scottish Womens Rights Centre. Publications: academic articles and papers on gender and justice. Recreations: gardening; cooking; travelling. Address: (b.) University of Glasgow, Ivy Lodge, 63 Gibson Street, Glasgow G12 8RT.
E-mail: michele.burman@glasgow.ac.uk

Burman, Professor Peter Ashley Thomas Insull, MBE, MA, FSA, Dr hc, Brandenburg Technical University, Cottbus, Germany. Director of Conservation & Property Services, The National Trust for Scotland, 2002-07; Professor of Cultural Management, World Heritage Studies, Cottbus University, 2007-2012; Independent Arts and Cultural Heritage Consultant; b. 15.9.44, Solihull. Educ. Kings College, Cambridge; ICCROM, Rome. Assistant Secretary, Deputy Secretary, Secretary (Chief Executive), Church of England, Council for the Care of Churches and the Cathedrals Fabric Commission for England, 1968-90; Director, Centre for Conservation Studies, University of York, 1990-2002; Visiting Professor, Department of Fine Arts, University of Canterbury, Christchurch, New Zealand, 2002. Publications include: Books: Chapels and Churches: Who Cares?, 1977; St. Paul's Cathedral, 1987; 7 book

chapters; Refereed articles: Reflections on the Lime Revival, 1995; The Ethics of Using Traditional Building Materials, 1997; The Study and Conservation of Nineteenth Century Wall Paintings, 2003. Esher Award, SPAB. Memberships include: Community Councillor, Falkland, since 2015; Trustee, Falkland Stewardship Trust (responsible for Educational Relationships and Crafts); Trustee and Archivist, Hopetoun House; Fabric Advisory Committee, St George's Chapel, Windsor Castle (2015-2020); SPAB Scotland; Companion, Guild of St. George (with two portfolios, for International Relationships and for Craftspeople & Craftsmanship); Scotland's Garden and Landscape Heritage; Ancient Monuments Society; Georgian Group; Twentieth Century Society. Recreations: music; playing keyboard instruments and recorders; walking, especially in remote upland areas; reading, especially books relating to the Buddhist Dharma; cooking (attended one of Alastair Little's cookery courses in Umbria). Address: (h.) Brunton House, Brunton Street, Falkland KY15 7BQ; T.-01337 857610.
E-mail: peterburman@btinternet.com

Burnet, George Wardlaw, LVO, BA, LLB, WS, KStJ, JP. Lord Lieutenant, Midlothian, 1992-2002; b. 26.12.27, Edinburgh; m., Jane Elena Moncrieff; 2 s.; 1 d. Educ. Edinburgh Academy; Lincoln College, Oxford; Edinburgh University. Senior Partner, Murray Beith & Murray, WS, 1983-91; Chairman, Life Association of Scotland Ltd., 1985-93; Chairman, Caledonian Research Foundation, 1988-99. Captain, Queen's Bodyguard for Scotland (Royal Company of Archers); former Midlothian County Councillor; Elder, Church of Scotland, since 1962; Convenor, Church of Scotland Finance Committee, 1980-83; Hon. Fellow, Royal Incorporation of Architects in Scotland. Address: (h.) Rose Court, Inveresk, Midlothian EH21 7TD.

Burnett, Alexander, LLB. MSP (Scottish Conservative), Aberdeenshire West, since 2016; Energy spokesperson; b. 30.7.73; m., Lavinia Cox; 1 s.; 2 d. Educ. Eton College; Newcastle University. The son of James Comyn Amherst Burnett of Leys and Fiona Mercedes Phillips; 4th great grandson of Nicholas I of Russia on his mother's side. Address: Scottish Parliament, Edinburgh EH99 1SP.

Burnett, Charles John, KStJ, DA, AMA, FSAScot, FHSS, MLitt. Ross Herald of Arms, 1988-2010, Ross Herald Extraordinary, 2011-2016; Chamberlain, Duff House, Banff, 1997-2004; Curator of Fine Art, Scottish United Services Museum, Edinburgh Castle, 1985-96; President, Heraldry Society of Scotland, 2004-2015, President Emeritus, since 2015; Vice-Patron, Genealogical Society of Queensland, 1986-2010; Chairman, Banff Preservation and Heritage Society, 2002-2010; b. 6.11.40, Sandhaven, by Fraserburgh; m., Aileen E. McIntyre; 2 s.; 1 d. Educ. Fraserburgh Academy; Gray's School of Art, Aberdeen; Aberdeen College of Education; University of Edinburgh. Advertising Department, House of Fraser, Aberdeen, 1963-64; Exhibitions Division, Central Office of Information, 1964-68 (on team which planned British pavilion for World Fair, Montreal, 1967); Assistant Curator, Letchworth Museum and Art Gallery, 1968-71; Head, Design Department, National Museum of Antiquities of Scotland, 1971-85. Heraldic Adviser, Girl Guide Association in Scotland, 1978-2010; Librarian, Priory of the Order of St. John in Scotland, 1987-99; Vice President, Society of Antiquaries of Scotland, 1992-95; Honorary Citizen of Oklahoma, 1989; Chevalier, Order of St. Maurice and St. Lazarus, 1999; Knight of the Royal Order of Francis I, 2002; President, 27th International Congress of Genealogical and Heraldic Sciences at St. Andrews University, 2006; Chairman, Pitsligo Castle Trust, 2010-2014; Honorary President, The Moray Burial Ground

Research Group, since 2012; Member of the Spanish Noble Company of Ballesteros, 2010. Published Officers of Arms in Scotland 1290-2016, 2016. Recreations: reading; visiting places of historic interest. Address: (h.) Seaview House, Portsoy, Banffshire AB45 2RS; T.-01261 843378.
E-mail: charles@rossherald.co.uk

Burnett of Leys, James Comyn Amherst. Chief of the Name and Arms of Burnett; b. 7.41. Address: Banchory Business Centre, Burn O'Bennie Road, Banchory AB31 5ZU.

Burnett, Rodney Alister, MBChB, FRCP, FRCPath. Lead Clinician in Pathology, University Department of Pathology, Western Infirmary, Glasgow, 1985-2007 (retired); b. 6.6.47, Congleton; m., Maureen Elizabeth Dunn; 2 d. Educ. Sandbach School; St. Andrews University. Lecturer in Pathology, Glasgow University, 1974-79; Consultant in administrative charge, Department of Pathology, Stobhill Hospital, Glasgow, 1979-85. Specialist Adviser, Royal Institute for Public Health and Hygiene, and Chairman, Board of Education and Examination for Anatomical Pathology Technology, 1994-2012; Vice President, Association of Clinical Pathologists, 2001-03. Address: (h.) 77 Blairbeth Road, Burnside, Glasgow G73 4JD; T.-0141-634 4345.

Burnie, Joan Bryson. Columnist, Daily Record, 1987-2014, formerly Associate Editor; b. 19.12.41, Glasgow; 1 s.; 1 d. Educ. Hutchesons' Girls' Grammar School. Filed pix, Herald; married; had children; freelanced; Contributing Editor, Cosmopolitan, 1977-81; You (Mail on Sunday), 1984-90; "Just Joan", Daily Record, since 1979; hacks around the air waves for BBC Radio 5 and BBC Scotland. Publications: Scotland The Worst; Post Bus Country. Recreations: lunch; walking dogs; gardening.

Burns, Andrew. Chair, The Scottish Council for Voluntary Organisations, since 2018; former Leader, The City of Edinburgh Council (2012-17); b. 1965; m.; 1 s. Educ. University of Ulster. Career: professional background in personnel and training, and worked for several years in a variety of personnel and training roles in both manufacturing industry and the service sector; became a Graduate of the Chartered Institute of Personnel and Development (CIPD) in 1990, gaining Full Member status of the CIPD in 2003; first elected to The City of Edinburgh Council in May 1999 and has represented the Fountainbridge/Craiglockhart ward; previously had responsibility for the transport and education portfolios while in administration. Chair of the Electoral Reform Society, 2008-2011. Recreations: walking; cycling; films; music; reading.

Burns, The Hon. Lord (David Burns), QC. Senator of the College of Justice, since 2012; b. 1952. Career: legal assistant in New York and California; admitted to the Faculty of Advocates in 1977; became a Queen's Counsel in 1991; practiced family, personal injury and planning; full-time Advocate Depute, 1989-91; Deputy Commissioner of Social Security; one of the advocates representing Abdelbaset al-Megrahi during the Lockerbie trial (2000-02); served as a temporary judge, 2002-05; became a part-time sheriff in 2007.

Burns, John. Chief Operating Officer, NHS Scotland, since 2021; Chief Executive, NHS Ayrshire & Arran, 2012-2021; m.; 2 c. NHS career started at Tayside Health Board in 1983; held several positions throughout Scotland before taking up the post as Chief Executive of Dumfries and

Galloway Acute and Maternity Hospitals NHS Trust in 2001; formerly Director of Health Services, then Chief Executive, NHS Dumfries & Galloway. Chaired a range of national work programmes including Financial Shared Services, review of Cervical Cytology Laboratory Services and the Implementation Board for the Managed Services Network for Children and Young People's Cancer.

Burns, Paul, BA. Head of Dance, Creative Scotland, since 2018. Educ. University of Manchester. Career history: General Manager, Punch Records, 2003-06; DanceXchange/International Dance Festival Birmingham: Programme Manager, 2007-12; Director of Programming and Production, 2012-14; Interim Artistic Director, Yorkshire Dance, 2015; freelance consultancy, from 2015; Associate Director, Greenwich Dance, 2016-17; Interim Administrative Director, The Place, 2017; Associate Director, Dance4, 2017-18. Address: Creative Scotland, Waverley Gate, 2-4 Waterloo Place, Edinburgh EH1 3EG; T.-0131 523 0052.
E-mail: paul.burns@creativescotland.com

Burnside, David Melville, LLB, NP. Managing Director, Burnside Legal Services (Aberdeen) Ltd, since 2013; Consultant, Burness Paull LLP, 2009-2015; b. 5.3.43, Dumfries; m., Gill; 3 s.; 2 d. Educ. Dumfries Academy; University of Edinburgh. Apprentice Solicitor, Melville & Lindesay W.S., Edinburgh, 1964-67; Assistant Solicitor: National Coal Board Legal Department, 1967-70, Clark & Wallace, Advocates, Aberdeen, 1970-71 (Partner, 1971-89); formed Burnside Advocates (later Burnside Kemp Fraser), 1989 (firm merged with Simpson and Marwick, 2004), thereafter Partner, then Consultant until 2009; acted for families in Chinook, Brent Spar and Cormorant Alpha helicopter crashes and Piper Alpha explosion (joint lead negotiator for Piper Alpha settlement); Member, Executive Committee, and Scottish Convenor, Association of Personal Injury Lawyers, 1990-96; certified by Law Society of Scotland as an employment law specialist, 1990-2015; Treasurer, Employment Law Group; Past President: Aberdeen Bar Association, Junior Chamber, Aberdeen; Member, Board of Directors, Legal Defence Union; President, Society of Advocates in Aberdeen, 2000-01 (Treasurer, 1999-2000); Member, Edinburgh Town Council, 1967-70; Chairman, Board of Governors, Albyn School for Girls, 2001-05; Chairman, Organising Committee, Aberdeen FC Centenary, 2003; Board Member, Aberdeen Performing Arts, since November 2014; Chairman, Royal Northern and University Club, Aberdeen, 2014-15; Free Burgess and Guild Member of Burgh of Aberdeen; Consultant, Paull and Williamsons (later Burness Paull), 2009-2015. Recreations: family; music; theatre; following the Dons; spending time in France. Address: (b.) 31 Albert Terrace, Aberdeen AB10 1XY; T.-01224 636645.

Burnside, John. Writer; b. 19.3.55, Dunfermline. Scottish Arts Council Book Award, 1988, 1991, 1995, 2006; Geoffrey Faber Memorial Prize, 1994; Whitbread Poetry Prize, 2000; Saltire Book of the Year, 2006, 2013; Prix Zepter, 2009; The Forward Poetry Prize, 2011; TS Eliot Prize for Poetry, 2011; Petrarca-Preis, 2011; CORINE International Zeit Publishing Literature Award, 2011; Prix Virgin-Lire, 2011. Publications: poetry: The hoop, 1988; Common Knowledge, 1991; Feast Days, 1992; The myth of the twin, 1994; Swimming in the flood, 1995; A Normal Skin, 1997; The Asylum Dance, 2000; The Light Trap, 2002; The Good Neighbour, 2005; Selected Poems, 2006; Gift Songs, 2007; The Hunt in the Forest, 2009; Black Cat Bone, 2011; All One Breath, 2014; Still Life with Feeding Snake, 2017; fiction: The Dumb House, 1997; The Mercy Boys, 1999; Burning Elvis, 2000; The Locust Room, 2001; Living Nowhere, 2003; The Devil's Footprints, 2007; Glister, 2008; A Summer of Drowning, 2011; Something

Like Happy, 2013; Ashland & Vine, 2017; Havergey, 2017; non-fiction: Wild Reckoning, 2004; A Lie About My Father (memoir), 2006; Wallace Stevens: poems/selected by John Burnside, 2008; Waking Up In Toytown, 2010; I Put A Spell On You, 2014; On Henry Miller, 2018; The Music of Time: Poetry in the Twentieth Century, 2019. Address: (b.) c/o Anna Webber, United Agents, 12-26 Lexington Street, London W1F 0LE.

Burr, Malcolm, LLB (Hons), DipLP, LLM (Hons), NP, FSA Scot. Chief Executive, Comhairle nan Eilean Siar, since 2005; b. 24.3.66, Edinburgh; m., Chrissie Kennedy. Educ. Edinburgh University; Cambridge University (Sidney Sussex College). Trainee Solicitor, later Solicitor, Strathclyde Regional Council, Glasgow, 1990-94; Principal Solicitor, Comhairle Nan Eilean, Stornoway, 1994-97; Chief Administrative Officer, 1997-2000, Assistant Chief Executive, 2000-05, Orkney Islands Council; Office-bearer, Society of Local Authority Chief Executives in Scotland (SOLACE Scotland), 2011-17; Member, Standing Council on Europe; Convener, Electoral Management Board for Scotland. Recreations: current affairs; history; walking; following football and rugby. Address: (b.) Council Offices, Sandwick Road, Stornoway, Isle of Lewis HS1 2BW; T.-01851 822600.
E-mail: m.burr@cne-siar.gov.uk

Burt, John Clark, OBE, MA (Hons), CertEd. Education management consultant, since 2013; Principal, Angus College, 1996-2013; b. 25.4.51, Dunfermline; m., Dory; 1 s.; 1 d. Educ. Dunfermline High School; Edinburgh University; Moray House College. Marketing Economist, Lloyds and Scottish Finance, 1974-76; Lecturer/Senior Lecturer in Economics and Marketing, Fife College, 1976-96. Member, Scottish Welfare to Work Advisory Task Force; Member, East of Scotland European Partnership; Director, FE Development, Scottish Further Education Funding Council (seconded); Chair of "Differences College Make Group", Scottish Executive; awarded OBE for services to Further Education in Scotland, 2006. Recreations: golf; hill-walking; running; Italian language.

Burt, Professor Steven Leslie, BA, PhD, FRSA. Professor of Retail Marketing, University of Stirling, since 1998, Deputy Principal, 2007-2015, Senior Deputy Principal, 2011-2014; b. 23.3.60, Chorley, Lancashire; m., Wendy Hayes; 2 s. Educ. Bolton School; Queen's College, Oxford University; University of Wales; University of Stirling. University of Stirling: currently Professor of Retail Marketing, Stirling Management School and Head, Division of Marketing & Retailing; previously Research Fellow, then Lecturer, then Senior Lecturer, 1984-98, Head, Department of Marketing, 1993-95, 2000-06, 2017-18; Director, Institute for Retail Studies, 1993-96, 1999-2003; Acting Dean, 2012-13; Associate Dean (Research), Stirling Management School, 2017-2021; Visiting Professor, Lund University, Sweden, 2000-2013; Visiting Professor, Queens University, Kingston, Ontario, 2003-04; Visiting Professor, IGR-IAE Universite de Rennes 1, France, 2006-07. President, European Association for Education and Research in Commercial Distribution. Recreation: watching Stirling Albion Football Club. Address: University of Stirling, Stirling FK9 4LA; T.-01786 467399.

Burton, Tony, OBE, BA (Hons) Keele. Vice President, Which?; Council Member and Hon. Sec. of the Royal Philosophical Society of Glasgow; Director and Hon. Sec. of the Planning Exchange Foundation. Board Member, Scottish Opera, 2015-2020. Executive Producer of the documentary film A Symphony in Stone on Glasgow's

historic townscape and architecture. Interests include sailing his vintage yacht Talisker of Lorne and opera.
E-mail: pefinfo1@gmail.com

Bush, Paul Anthony, OBE (2007), BEd, DipSC, FISC. Chief Operating Officer, EventScotland, 2007-2013; Chair, Commonwealth Games Scotland, since 2015; Chair, Cycling World Championships, 2023; Chair, East of Scotland Institute of Sport, 2007-2016; Member, UK Sport Major Events Panel, 2008; b. 11.6.57, Leicester; m., Katriona Christine. Educ. Gateway Sixth Form College, Leicester; Borough Road College; Moray House College. Professional Swimming Coach, Bradford and Leicester; Sports/Swimming Development Officer, Leeds City Council; Technical Director, Amateur Swimming Association; Assistant Head of Development, English Sports Council; Director, Sporting Initiatives Sports Marketing and Media Consultancy. Leicestershire County Swimming Coach; Swimming Team Manager, Olympic, World, European, Commonwealth Games; Chef de Mission, BOA, European Youth Olympics; General Team Manager, Scottish Commonwealth Games Council, Manchester, 2002; Fellow, BISA; General Secretary, British Swimming Coaches Association; Member, English Sports Council Task Force – Young People and Sport; Event Director, World Cyclo Cross Championships, Leeds; school governor; Chef de Mission, Scottish Commonwealth Game Team, Melbourne, 2006; 2011 Scottish Event Professional of the Year. Recreations: golf; walking the dogs; sport in general; travel. Address: Ochil Paddocks, Burnfoot, Dollar FK14 7JY; Paul.Bush@eventscotland.org; pbush@bushsport.co.uk

Busuttil, Professor Anthony, OBE, MOM, KCHS, MD, FRCPath, FRCP (Glasg), FRCPE, FRCS (Edin), DMJ (Path), FBAFM, FFSS, FRSSA, FRSM, FFFLM (Lond). Emeritus Regius Professor of Forensic Medicine, Edinburgh University, since 2006; Past Chairman, European Council for Legal Medicine; Honorary Consultant Pathologist, Edinburgh Universities NHS Trust, since 1976; Clinical Lead, Forensic Medical Examiner Service, NHS Lothian; Forensic Physician, Lothian and Borders Police Force, since 1980; b. 30.12.45, Rabat, Malta; m., Angela; 3 s. Educ. St. Aloysius' College, Malta; Royal University of Malta. Junior posts, Western Infirmary, Glasgow; Lecturer in Pathology, Glasgow University. Address: (h.) 78 Hillpark Avenue, Edinburgh EH4 7AL; T.-0131-336 3241; e-mail: tony@busuttil.org.uk

Bute, 8th Marquess of (John Bryson Chrichton-Stuart); Scottish peer; b. 21.12.89. Styled Lord Mount Stuart, 1989-1993 and Earl of Dumfries, 1993-2021. Succeeded to title, 2021.

Butler, Cllr Bill. MSP (Labour), Glasgow Anniesland, 2000-2011; Councillor, Glasgow City Council Garscadden/Scotstounhill, since 2017, Greater Pollok ward, 2012-17; b. 30.3.56, Glasgow; m., Patricia Ferguson (qv). Educ. Stirling University; Notre Dame College of Education. English teacher, 20 years; elected Glasgow City Councillor, 1987 (Convener, Policy and Resources (e-Glasgow) Working Group; Vice-Convener, Policy and Resources Committee; Secretary, Labour Group). Address: City Chambers, George Square, Glasgow G2 1DU; T.-0141 287 5735.
E-mail: bill.butler@glasgow.gov.uk

Butlin, Ron, MA, DipAECD. Poet, Novelist, Opera Librettist, Children's Author, Playwright; b. 1949, Edinburgh. Educ. Dumfries Academy; Edinburgh University. Appointed Edinburgh Makar (Poet Laureate),

2008, reappointed, 2011-2014; made Honorary Writing Fellow by Edinburgh University, 2009; Specialist Advisor to Scottish Arts Council, 2009; Writer in Residence, Lothian Region Education Authority, 1979, Edinburgh Univ., 1981, 1984-85; Scottish/Canadian Writing Exchange Fellow, University of New Brunswick, 1983-84; Writer in Residence for Midlothian, 1989-90; Writer in Residence, Craigmillar Literacy Trust; Novelist in Residence, St. Andrews University, 1998-99. Publications: poetry: Stretto, 1976; Creatures Tamed by Cruelty, 1979; The Exquisite Instrument, 1982 (Scottish Arts Council Book Award); Ragtime in Unfamiliar Bars, 1985 (SAC Book Award, Poetry Book Society recommendation); Histories of Desire, 1995; prose: The Tilting Room (short stories), 1983 (SAC Book Award); The Sound of My Voice (novel), 1987; Blending In (play), 1989; Mauritian Voices (Editor), 1996; Night Visits (novel), 1997; When We Jump We Jump High!, 1998; Faraway Pictures (opera), 2000; Our Piece of Good Fortune (poetry), 2002; Vivaldi and the Number 3 (short stories), 2004; Without a Backward Glance - New and Selected Poems, 2005; Good Angel, Bad Angel (Opera), 2005; Belonging (novel), 2006; No More Angels (short stories), 2007; The Perfect Woman (Opera), 2008. Awarded the Prix MillePages, 2004 and the Prix Lucioles, 2005 (both for Best Foreign Novel); The Money Man (Opera), 2010; Sweet Dreams (play), 2012; The Magicians of Edinburgh (poetry), 2012; Ghost Moon (novel), 2014 (nominated for the International IMPAC Award, 2016); Wedlock (opera), 2014; The Magicians of Scotland (poetry), 2015; Here Come The Trolls! (verse for children), 2015; Billionaires' Banquet (novel), 2017; Steve & FranDan Take on the World (young adult novel), 2017; Day of the Trolls! (verse for children), 2017; The Sound of My Voice (novel, new and revised edition), 2018; The Little Book of Scottish Rain (poetry), 2018; The Lost Poets: Found (poetry), 2019. Recreation: music.
Website: www.ronbutlin.co.uk

Butt, Professor John, OBE, MA, PhD, FBA, FRSE, FRCO(CHM), ADCM. Gardiner Professor of Music, University of Glasgow, since 2001; b. 17.11.60, Solihull; m., Sally Cantlay; 4 s.; 1 d. Educ. Solihull School; King's College, University of Cambridge. Temporary Lecturer, University of Aberdeen, 1986-87; Research Fellow, Magdalene College, Cambridge, 1987-89; University Organist and Professor of Music, UC Berkeley, California, 1989-97; University Lecturer and Fellow, King's College Cambridge, 1997-2001. Eleven CD recordings on organ and harpsichord; Director, Dunedin Consort (Edinburgh), three recordings; Gramophone and Midem awards for recording of Handel's Messiah. Publications: five books. Recreations: reading; walking; tai chi. Address: (b.) Music Department, University of Glasgow, 14 University Gardens, Glasgow G12 8QQ; T.-0141-330 4571.
E-mail: j.butt@music.gla.ac.uk

Byng, Jamie. Publisher, Canongate Books, since 1994; b. 27.6.69, Winchester; m. (1), Whitney Osborn McVeigh (divorced); m. (2), Elizabeth Sheinkman (divorced); m. (3), Silvia Gimenez Varela; 5 c. Educ. Winchester College; Edinburgh University. Recreations: tennis; cooking; deejaying; reading; drinking. Address: (b.) 14 High Street, Edinburgh EH1 1TE; T.-0131-557 5111.

Byrne, John. Dramatist and stage designer; b. 1940, Paisley. Plays include: The Slab Boys, Cuttin' A Rug, Still Life (trilogy); Normal Service; Cara Coco; television series: Tutti Frutti; Your Cheatin' Heart. Associate of the Royal Scottish Academy, 2004; Honorary Doctorate: University of Paisley, 1997, Robert Gordon University Gray's School of Art, Aberdeen, 2006, University of Dundee, 2011.

Byrne, Kate (Kathleen) Frances, MBE, MA, MSc, PhD, CEng, MBCS, CITP. Commissioner, The Royal Commission on the Ancient and Historical Monuments of Scotland, 2004-2015; b. 2.12.59, London; m., Peter Emrys

Williams. Educ. St. Catherine's, Twickenham; University of Edinburgh. Various posts in the Scottish Office Computer Service, 1985-91; MIS Manager, Heriot-Watt University, 1991-92; Information Systems Manager, RCAHMS, 1992-98; Infrastructure Manager at Tullis Russell Papermakers, 1998-99; Head of Computer Services and Deputy Director of ICT, The National Library of Scotland, 1999-2002; Research in Computational Linguistics, University of Edinburgh, 2002-2019. Data Scientist at Brainwave Ltd, 2016-17; Data Wrangler to the National Gallery, London, 2017-19. Director of Scran and The Scran Trust, 2008-16; Scottish Government non-executive director, 2010-13; Director of The Wildlife Information Centre, 2012-13; Director of The Scottish Gliding Union, 2005-08; Member of "Walking On Air" (Gliding for the Disabled); CFI of Scottish Gliding Centre. Recreations: gliding; hill-walking; learning the piano. Address: (h.) 5 Kirkhill Way, Penicuik EH26 8HH; T.-01968 674114; e-mail: katefbyrne@gmail.com

Byrne, Laurie, MA (Hons). Former Headteacher, Holyrood RC Secondary School, Glasgow (2012-17); b. 7.6.56, Glasgow; m., Helen; 1 s.; 1 d. Educ. St. Patrick's High School, Dumbarton; University of Glasgow; Notre Dame College. Teacher of Modern Languages, St. Margaret's HS, Airdrie, 1980-85; Assistant Principal Teacher of Guidance, Holy Cross, Hamilton, 1985-89; Principal Teacher of Guidance, St. Aidan's HS, Wishaw, 1989-96; Assistant Head, Cardinal Newman HS, Bellshill, 1996-2000; Deputy Head, St. Ninian's HS, Giffnock, 2000-04; Head Teacher, St. Maurice's HS, Cumbernauld, 2004-12. Past Chair, Catholic Headteachers' Association of Scotland, 2009-2011; Member of Catholic Education Commission Executive, 2011-2014. Recreations: football; travel.

Byrne, Rosemary, Dip Ed, DipSen. MSP (Solidarity), South of Scotland, 2003-07; b. 3.3.48, Irvine; m., James; 1 s. Educ. Irvine Royal Academy; Craigie College, Ayr. Primary teacher, Ayrshire, 1977-88; Learning Support Teacher, 1988-96; Senior Teacher, North Ayrshire Network Support Team, 1996-99; Principal Teacher, Pupil Support, Ardrossan Academy, 1999-2003. Address: (h.) Williamsfield, Irvine; T.-01294 311105.

C

Cable, Clare. Chief Executive and Nurse Director of The Queen's Nursing Institute Scotland, since 2014. Educ. Sutton High School; University of Southampton. Trained as a children's nurse in Oxford and in 1993 joined the Royal College of Nursing as Research and Development Officer, completing a Masters degree a year later; Director, Quality Improvement Programme, Royal College of Nursing, 2003-2007; Policy Adviser, RCN Scotland, 2007-2014. Address: The Queen's Nursing Institute Scotland, 31 Castle Terrace, Edinburgh EH1 2EL; T.-0131 229 2333.
E-mail: office@qnis.org.uk

Cackette, Paul, LLB (Hons), DipLP, NP. Former Acting Director of Legal Services, Chief Reporter and Head of Directorate for Planning and Environmental Appeals (DPEA), Scottish Government (2016-18); b. 26.3.60, Edinburgh; m., Helen Thomson; 1 s.; 2 d. Educ. George Heriot's School, Edinburgh; Edinburgh University. Admitted as a Solicitor, 1985; Solicitor, Kirkcaldy District Council, 1985-88; Office of Solicitor to Secretary of State for Scotland, 1988-99; Office of Solicitor to the Scottish Government, 1999-2003 and 2008-2016; Legal Secretary to Lord Advocate (2008-09) and Deputy Solicitor to the Scottish Government (2009-2016). Recreations: literature; athletics.

Caddy, Professor Brian, BSc, PhD, CChem, MRSC, FCSFS. Professor of Forensic Science, Strathclyde University, 1992-99, now Emeritus Professor; b. 26.3.37, Burslem, Stoke-on-Trent; m., Beryl Ashworth; 1 s.; 1 d. Educ. Longton High School, Stoke-on-Trent; Sheffield University. MRC Research Fellow, 1963-66; Strathclyde University: Lecturer in Forensic Science, 1966-77, Senior Lecturer in Forensic Science, 1977-92. Founder Member, European Network of Forensic Science Institutes; President, Forensic Science Society, 1999; Member, Executive Committee, Council for the Registration of Forensic Practitioners, 1999; appointed Commissioner to the Scottish Criminal Cases Review Commission, 2006-2015; Review of the Damilola Taylor case for the Home Secretary, 2007; appointed external verifer for the Council for the Regulation of Forensic Practitioners, 2004, 2006 and 2007. Publications: three books; over 90 papers/articles. Editor, Science and Justice (Forensic Science Society journal), 1993-1999. Recreations: reading; painting; walking the dog; dining with friends; good food and wine. Address: (h.) 5 Kings Park, Torrance, Glasgow G64 4DX; T.-01360 622 358; e-mail: B.Caddy@strath.ac.uk

Caie, Professor Graham Douglas, CBE, MA, PhD, FEA, FRSA, FRSE, FFCS. Honorary Research Professor, Glasgow University; Dean of Faculties, Glasgow University; Vice President, Royal Society of Edinburgh, 2009-14; formerly Clerk of Senate and Vice-Principal, Glasgow University; Professor of English Language, Glasgow University, 1990-2012; Independent Governor, Glasgow School of Art; Senate Assessor, Glasgow University Court, 1998-2003; b. 3.2.45, Aberdeen; m., Ann Pringle Abbott; 1 s.; 1 d. Educ. Aberdeen Grammar School; Aberdeen University; McMaster University, Canada. Teaching Assistant, McMaster University, 1968-72; Amanuensis and Lektor, Copenhagen University, 1972-90. Chairman, Medieval Centre, Copenhagen University, 1985-90; Visiting Professor: McMaster University, 1985-86, Guelph University, 1989; Associate Fellow, Clare Hall, Cambridge, 1977-78; Court of Queen Margaret University, 2015-2021; Member, British Council Scottish Advisory Committee, 2016-2021; former posts: Faculty of Advocates Abbotsford Book Trust; Scottish Arts Council Advisory Panel; Vice-President, Scottish Texts Society; Secretary, European Society for the Study of English; Trustee and

Vice-Chairman, National Library of Scotland; Member, Council, Dictionary of Older Scottish Tongue; Board, Scottish Language Dictionaries; English Panel, AHRC; English Panel, RAE; Board, English Subject Centre (HEA); SQA English Panel. Publications: Transitional States: Change, Tradition and Memory in Medieval Literature and Culture (2018); Medieval Manuscripts in Context; Judgement Day II edition 1, The Theme of Doomsday in Old English Poetry; Beowulf; Bibliography of Junius XI MS; numerous articles. Address: (h.) 12B Upper Glenburn Road, Bearsden, Glasgow G61 4BW.
E-mail: G.Caie45@gmail.com

Caimbeul, Aonghas Phàdraig, MA. Sgrìobhadair; Fearnaidheachd (òraidiche agus craoladair); r. Uibhist-a-Deas; p., Liondsaidh; 1. m.; 5 n. Foghlam: Ard-Sgoil an Obain; Oilthaigh Dhùn Eideann. Treis aig: A' Phàipear Bheag, BBC Rèidio, Grampian Telebhisean; Sgrìobhaiche an t-Sabhail Mhòir, 1990-92; Oraidiche an sin on uairsin; Crìosdaidh; ag obair air nobhal mòr an-dràsda. Air foillseachadh: 2 leabhar bàrdachd; nobhal dheugairean; dà nobhal eile tighinn a-mach am bliadhna. Cuir-seachad: bhith ris an teaghlach agus leughadh Tolstoy. Seòladh: Sabhal Mòr Ostaig, An Teanga, Slèite, an t-Eilein Sgitheanach; F.-01471 844373.

Cairns, Professor Douglas Laidlaw, MA (Hons), PhD, FHEA, FRSE, FBA, MAE. Professor of Classics, University of Edinburgh, since 2004; b. 10.1.61, Glasgow; widowed; 1 s. Educ. Eastbank Academy, Glasgow; University of Glasgow. Temporary Lecturer in Greek, University of St. Andrews, 1986; Lecturer in Classics, University of Otago, New Zealand, 1988-92; Lecturer/Senior Lecturer in Classics: University of Leeds, 1992-99, University of Glasgow, 1999-2004. Research Fellow, Georg-August Universität, Göttingen, 1987-88, 1993-95; Humboldt Universität, Berlin, 2011; University of Oxford, 2012-13; Technische Universität, Dresden, 2016; Visiting Professor: Kyoto University, 2008, Florida State University, 2012; University of Pisa, 2017; University of Tokyo, 2017; Fu Jen University, Taiwan, 2018; elected member, Academia Europaea, 2013; FRSE 2018; FBA 2018. Publications: Author of Aidôs: The Psychology and Ethics of Honour and Shame in Ancient Greek Literature, 1993; Bacchylides: Five Epinician Odes, 2010; Sophocles: Antigone, 2016. Recreations: music; travel; cinema; food and wine. Address: (b.) School of History, Classics and Archaeology, University of Edinburgh EH8 9JX; T.-0131 651 1647; e-mail: douglas.cairns@ed.ac.uk

Cairns, Very Rev. John Ballantyne, KCVO, KStJ, LTh, LLB, DD, LLD. Chaplain, then Extra Chaplain to the Queen, since 1997; Dean of the Chapel Royal, 2006-13; Chaplain, The Queen's Bodyguard for Scotland, Royal Company of Archers, since 2007; Moderator, General Assembly of the Church of Scotland, 1999-2000; Dean of the Order of St. John Scotland, 2011-2021; b. 15.3.42, London; m., Dr. Elizabeth Emma Bradley; 3 s. Educ. Sutton Valence School, Kent; Bristol University; Edinburgh University. Messrs Richards, Butler & Co., Solicitors, City of London, 1964-68; Administrative Assistant, East Lothian County Council, 1968-69; Assistant Minister, St. Giles, Elgin, 1973-75; Minister, Langholm, Ewes and Westerkirk Parish Churches, 1975-85, also linked with Canonbie, 1981-85; Clerk, Presbytery of Annandale and Eskdale, 1980-82; Minister, Riverside Church, Dumbarton, 1985-2001; Parish Minister, Aberlady and Gullane Parish Churches, 2001-09; Locum Minister, St. Columba's Church, Pont Street, London, 2010-2012; St. Mary's Church, Haddington, 2017-19; Convener, Maintenance of the Ministry Committee and Joint Convener, Board of Ministry and Mission, Church of Scotland, 1984-88; Chairman, Judicial Commission of General Assembly, 1993-98; Convener, General Assembly Committee on Chaplains to Her Majesty's Forces, 1993-98; General Trustee of the Church of Scotland, 1995-2017;

Moderator, Presbytery of Dumbarton, 1993-94; Chaplain to Moderator of General Assembly, 1995; Chaplain to Lord High Commissioner (HRH Duke of York), 2007; Chaplain to the Lieutenancy of Dumbarton, 1997-2019; Divisional Chaplain, Strathclyde Police, 1987-2001; Chairman of Governors, Compass School, 2008-2015; President, Dumbarton Burns Club, 2002; President, Friends of St Andrew's, Jerusalem, 2005-2011; DD, University of Aberdeen, 2003; LLD, University of Bristol, 2004; KCVO, 2013. Publications: Keeping Fit for Ministry, 1988; Democracy and Unwritten Constitutions, 1989. Recreations: golf; gardening; music; Robert Burns. Address: Bell House, Roxburghe Park, Dunbar, East Lothian EH42 1LR.

Cairns, Professor John William, LLB, PhD, FRSE, FSA Scot. Professor of Civil Law, University of Edinburgh, since 2012; b. 17.8.55, Crieff; partner, Donald Jardine. Educ. Hutchesons' Boys' Grammar School; University of Edinburgh. Lecturer in Jurisprudence, Queen's University of Belfast; Lecturer, Senior Lecturer, Reader, Professor of Legal History (2000-2012), University of Edinburgh; Visiting Professor: Southern Methodist University, Dallas, 1986, Miami, 1988, 1991, 1995, École normale supérieure Paris, March-April 2017. Chairman, Council, The Stair Society, 1998-2015; President, Eighteenth-Century Scottish Studies Society, 2006-08. Recent Publications: Enlightenment, Legal Education, and Critique, 2015; Law, Lawyers, and Humanism, 2015; Codification, Transplants, and History: Law Reform in Louisiana (1808) and Quebec (1866), 2015. Recreations: cooking; reading. Address: (b.) University of Edinburgh, School of Law, Old College, South Bridge, Edinburgh EH8 9YL; T.-0131-650 1000. E-mail: john.cairns@ed.ac.uk

Cairns, Joyce, PRSA, DEd (hc), HRA, HRHA, HRWA, HRBA, RSW. President, The Royal Scottish Academy of Art and Architecture, since 2018; painter; b. 1947, Edinburgh. Educ. Mary Erskine School for Girls; Gray's School of Art, Aberdeen; Royal College of Art, London; Goldsmiths, University of London. Career history: exhibiting since 1969, work is held in numerous private and public collections throughout the world; taught drawing and painting at Grays School of Art, Aberdeen, 1976-2004; took early retirement to complete the vast body of work which culminated in 'War Tourist' (exhibited for 3 months in 2006 at Aberdeen Art Gallery). Address: The Royal Scottish Academy of Art and Architecture, The Mound, Edinburgh EH2 2EL; T.-0131 225 6671.

Cairns, Professor Robert Alan, BSc, PhD, FInstP, FRSE. Emeritus Professor of Applied Mathematics, School of Mathematics and Statistics, St. Andrews University; Visiting Professor of Physics, University of Strathclyde; b. 12.3.45, Glasgow; m., Ann E. Mackay. Educ. Allan Glen's School, Glasgow; Glasgow University. Lecturer in Applied Mathematics, St. Andrews University, 1970-83; Senior Lecturer, 1983-85; Reader, 1985-91; Professor, 1991-2010. Member, SERC Laser Committee, 1990-93; Member, SERC Atomic and Molecular Physics Sub-Committee, 1990-93; Chairman, Plasma Physics Group, Institute of Physics, 1999-2001 (Committee Member, 1981-84); Member, Editorial Board, Plasma Physics, 1983-85; Editor, Journal of Plasma Physics, 1995-2006. Publications: Plasma Physics, 1985; Radiofrequency heating of plasmas, 1991. Recreations: music; golf; walking; gardening. Address: (b.) Seaview, Boarhills, St Andrews KY16 8PP; T.-01334880354.

Cairns Speitel, Pauline. Senior Editor, Scottish Language Dictionaries. Editor managing the Word Collection programme. Began career in publishing with Chambers in Edinburgh, then spent twenty years with the Scottish National Dictionary Association, as lexicographer on all of their dictionary projects. Directed lexicographical projects with a range of community groups in Scotland. Address:

Scottish Language Dictionaries, 9 Coates Crescent, Edinburgh EH3 7AL; T.-0131 220 1294; e-mail: pcspeitel at scotsdictionaries.org.uk

Caithness, 20th Earl of (Malcolm Ian Sinclair), PC; b. 3.11.48; 1 s.; 1 d. Educ. Marlborough; Royal Agricultural College, Cirencester. Succeeded to title, 1965; Parliamentary Under Secretary of State, Department of Transport, 1985-86; Minister of State, Home Office, 1986-88; Minister of State, Department of the Environment, 1988-89; Paymaster General and Minister of State, HM Treasury, 1989-90; Minister of State, Foreign and Commonwealth Office, 1990-92; Minister of State, Department of Transport, 1992-94; Trustee, Queen Elizabeth Castle of Mey Trust, 1996-2006, Honorary Patron, since 2017; Trustee and Chief Executive, Clan Sinclair Trust, since 1999; elected Member, House of Lords, since 1999.

Calder, Professor Andrew Alexander, MBE, MD, FRCS (Edin), FRCP (Glas), FRCP (Edin), FRCOG, HonFCOG (SA), FSAScot. Professor Emeritus, University of Edinburgh, Professor of Obstetrics and Gynaecology, 1987-2009; Honorary Professor in the School of Medicine, University of St Andrews, 2012-17; Chairman, Scotland's Churches Trust, 2015-19; Chairman, Tenovus Scotland, 2011-19; formerly Director, Jennifer Brown Research Laboratory and Tommy's Centre for Fetal and Maternal Health Research, Queen's Medical Research Institute; b. 17.1.45, Aberdeen; m., Valerie Anne Dugard; 1 s.; 2 d. Educ. Glasgow Academy; Glasgow University. Clinical training posts, Glasgow, 1968-72; Research Fellow, Nuffield Department of Obstetrics and Gynaecology, University of Oxford, 1972-75; Lecturer/Senior Lecturer, Obstetrics and Gynaecology, University of Glasgow, 1975-86; Consultant Obstetrician and Gynaecologist: Glasgow Royal Infirmary and Royal Maternity Hospital, 1978-86, Royal Infirmary of Edinburgh and Simpson Centre for Reproductive Health, 1987-2009; British Exchange Professor, University of California, Los Angeles, 1992. Blair Bell Memorial Lecturer, RCOG, 1977; WHO Travelling Fellow, Uruguay, 1985. Recreations: music; golf; curling; history of medicine. Address: Department of Obstetrics and Gynaecology, Royal Infirmary of Edinburgh, Little France, Edinburgh; e-mail: a.a.calder@ed.ac.uk

Calder, Rev. Bryce, MA (with Merit) (Hist), BD (First Class Hons) (OT Stud). Parish Minister, Motherwell St. Mary's Parish Church, since 2017; b. 26.12.66, Bo'ness; m., Helen Calder (nee Miller); 1 s.; 1 d. Educ. Bo'ness Academy; Edinburgh University. Metropolitan Police Officer, 1985-87; Candidate for Church of Scotland Ministry, 1988-93; Assistant Minister of Troon: St. Meddan's, 1994; Parish Minister, Buckhaven Parish Church and Manager, Buckhaven Theatre, 1995-2000; Parish Minister, Kirkintilloch St. David's Memorial Park Church, 2001-2016; Founder Member, Levenmouth YMCA; retired Company Director, Cutting Edge Theatre Company; recently retired Chairman of Friends of SYCAM (A Charity that supports Children's Aid work in India); Member of Presbytery of Hamilton Superintendence Committee and Safeguarding Group; Church of Scotland Safeguarding Committee. Recreations: football (supporter of Motherwell FC); reading; listening to music; playing Rickenbacker bass guitar; dog walking; reading and reciting Burns poetry. Address: 19 Orchard Street, Motherwell ML1 3JE; T.-01698-328665; e-mail: BCalder@churchofscotland.org.uk

Calder, Finlay, OBE; b. 20.8.57, Haddington; m., Elizabeth; 1 s.; 1 d. Educ. Daniel Stewart's and Melville College. Played rugby for Scotland, 1986-90; captained Scotland, 1989; captained British Isles, 1989.

Calder, George, BA (Hons) (Cantab), LLB; b. 20.12.47; 2 d. Educ. George Watson's College, Edinburgh; Cambridge University; Edinburgh University. Joined

Civil Service (Department of Employment), 1971; worked in European Commission (cabinet of George Thomson), 1974-76; Treasury, 1977-79; Manpower Services Commission, 1979-87; Scottish Office/Scottish Government (Head of European Funds and Co-ordination Division, Head of Personnel, Head of Water Services Unit), 1987-99; Head, Scottish Government EU Office, 1999-2004. Recreations: military history guide; football; book club; hill-walking; gardening.

Calder, Jenni, BA, MPhil. Freelance Writer; b. 3.12.41, Chicago, Illinois; 1 s.; 2 d. Educ. Perse School for Girls, Cambridge; Cambridge University; London University. Freelance writer, 1966-78; taught and lectured in Scotland, England, Kenya and USA; Lecturer in English, Nairobi University, 1968-69; successively Education Officer, Head of Publications, Head of Museum of Scotland International, National Museums of Scotland, Edinburgh, 1978-2001. Publications: Chronicles of Conscience: a study of George Orwell and Arthur Koestler, 1968; Scott (with Angus Calder), 1969; There Must be a Lone Ranger: the Myth and Reality of the American West, 1974; Women and Marriage in Victorian Fiction, 1976; Brave New World and Nineteen Eighty Four, 1976; Heroes: from Byron to Guevara, 1977; The Victorian Home, 1977; The Victorian Home from Old Photographs, 1979; RLS, A Life Study, 1980; The Robert Louis Stevenson Companion (Editor), 1980; Robert Louis Stevenson and Victorian Scotland (Editor), 1981; The Strange Case of Dr Jekyll and Mr Hyde (Editor), 1979; Kidnapped (Editor), 1981; Catriona (Editor), 1981; The Enterprising Scot (Editor), 1986; Island Landfalls (Editor), 1987; Bonny Fighters: The Story of the Scottish Soldier, 1987; Open Guide to Animal Farm and Nineteen Eighty Four, 1987; The Wealth of a Nation (Editor), 1989; St. Ives, a new ending, 1990; Scotland in Trust, 1990; Treasure Islands (Editor), 1994; Mediterranean (poems, as Jenni Daiches), 1995; Tales of the South Seas (Editor), 1996; The Nine Lives of Naomi Mitchison, 1997; Everyman's Poetry: Robert Louis Stevenson (Editor), 1997; Present Poets anthology, Editor), 1998; Translated Kingdoms (anthology, Editor), 1999; A Beleaguered City and Other Tales of the Seen and the Unseen (Editor), 2000; Scots in Canada, 2003; Not Nebuchadnezzar: In Search of Identities, 2005; Scots in the USA, 2005; Smoke (poems, as Jenni Daiches), 2005; Letters from the Great Wall (fiction, as Jenni Daiches), 2006; Frontier Scots: The Scots Who Won the West, 2009; Lost in the Backwoods: Scots and the North American Wilderness, 2013; Waverley by Walter Scott, adapted for the modern reader, 2014; Forgive (fiction, as Jenni Daiches), 2014; Borrowed Time (fiction, as Jenni Daiches), 2016; Essence of Edinburgh: An Eccentric Odyssey, 2018; The Burning Glass: The Life of Naomi Mitchison, 2019. Recreations: music; films; walking the dog. Address: (h.) 31 Station Road, South Queensferry, West Lothian; T.-0131-331 1287.

Calder, Dame Muffy, OBE, BSc, PhD, FRSE, FREng, FBCS. Professor of Formal Methods (Computer Science), Glasgow University, since 1999; Chief Scientific Adviser, Scottish Government, 2012-2014; Vice-Principal, Head of College of Science and Engineering, University of Glasgow, since 2015; b. 21.5.58, Shawinigan, Quebec, Canada; m., David Calder. Educ. Stirling University; St Andrews University. Research Fellow, Edinburgh University and Stirling University, 1983-87; Lecturer/Senior Lecturer, Computing Science, Glasgow University, 1988-99. Recreations: road running; hill-running. Address: (b.) Department of Computer Science, Glasgow University. T.-0141-330 4969.

Calder, Robert Russell, MA. Critic, Philosophical Writer, Historian of Ideas, Poet, Freelance Journalist, Book Reviewer, Performer and Singer; b. 22.4.50, Burnbank. Educ. Hamilton Academy; Glasgow University; Edinburgh University. Co-Editor, Chapman, 1974-76 and 1986-91; Editor, Lines Review, 1976-77; Theatre Critic and Feature Writer, Scot, 1983-86; Staff Writer, Popmatters (Chicago), Journal of Global Culture; Staff writer, All About Jazz. Books: A School of Thinking, 1995; Narcissism, Nihilism, Simplicity (Editor), 1992; poetry: Il Re Giovane, 1976, Ettrick & Annan, 1981; Serapion, 1996; Urlaubsgedichte, 2009. Recreations: music - opera singing; jazz piano. Address: (h.) 23 Glenlee Street, Burnbank, Hamilton ML3 9JB; T.-01698 824244; e-mail: serapion@btinternet.com

Calderwood, Dr Catherine, MA (Cantab), FRCOG, MBChB, FRCP (Edin), FRCP (Glasg), FRCS (Ed), HonFFPH. National Clinical Director, Centre for Sustainable Delivery, Golden Jubilee Hospital, Clydebank, since 2021; former Chief Medical Officer, Scottish Government; Hon Colonel, 205 (Scottish) Field Hospital; consultant obstetrician and gynaecologist, NHS Lothian; 3 c. Educ. University of Cambridge; University of Glasgow. Career: national clinical director for maternity and women's health, NHS England; formerly Acting Deputy Chief Medical Officer, Scottish Government. Fellow of the Royal College of Obstetricians and Gynaecologists; Honorary Fellow of the Royal College of Physicians of Edinburgh; Honorary Fellow, Royal College of Physicians and Surgeons of Glasgow; Honorary Fellow, Royal College of Surgeons of Edinburgh; Honorary Fellow, Faculty of Public Health. Address: Golden Jubilee National Hospital, Agamemnon Street, Clydebank G81 4DY; T.-0141 951 5000.

Calderwood, Robert. Former Chief Executive, Greater Glasgow and Clyde NHS Board (2009-2017). Career history: joined Argyll and Clyde Health Board in 1974 having previously been an NHS Administrative Trainee; became Hospital Administrator for Greenock Royal and Associated Hospitals in 1978; appointed Administrator, Acute Services, for Inverclyde District in 1981; became Deputy Unit Administrator for all acute services within Renfrewshire in 1984; joined Greater Glasgow Health Board in 1985 as Unit Administrator for Western Infirmary/Gartnavel General Hospital Unit; appointed as Director of Property and Strategic Planning at Greater Glasgow Health Board in 1988; became Unit General Manager for the Southern General Hospital Unit in April 1991 and became its first Chief Executive on achieving Trust status in 1993; appointed Chief Executive for both the Southern General Hospital and Victoria Infirmary NHS Trusts in 1997, and appointed Chief Executive of the South Glasgow University Hospitals NHS Trust in 1999; Programme Director for the implementation of the Board's Acute Services Strategy in 2003; appointed as Chief Operating Officer for Greater Glasgow Acute Division; role was expanded to include the acute elements of Clyde in April 2006 when NHS Greater Glasgow and Clyde was formed; key member of NHSGGC's most senior executive team.

Caldwell, David Hepburn, MA, PhD, FSA, FSAScot. Former Keeper of Scotland and Europe; Keeper of Archaeology; Director, Finlaggan Archaeological Project, National Museums of Scotland; Trustee of the National Trust for Scotland; Chairman, Fife Cultural Trust; b. 15.12.51, Kilwinning, Ayrshire; m., Margaret Anne McGovern; 1 s.; 2 d. Educ. Ardrossan Academy; Edinburgh University. Joined staff, National Museum of Antiquities, 1973. Publications: The Scottish Armoury, 1979; Scottish Weapons and Fortifications, 1981; Scotland's Wars and Warriors, 1998; Islay, Jura and Colonsay, A Historical Guide, 2001 and 2011; Islay Land of the Lordship, 2008; (Co-Author) The Lewis Chessmen Unmasked, 2010; (Co-

Author) The Lewis Chessmen, New Perspectives, 2014; Mull and Iona: A Historical Guide, 2018. Recreations: travelling; table tennis; dressmaking. Address: (h.) 3 James Park, Burntisland, Fife KY3 9EW; T.-872175.

Caldwell, Miller H., MA, CQSW, DipSocWk, DipRS, FFCS. Guest Speaker, Writer and Film Script Writer; Camp Manager, Mundihar NWFP Pakistan 2006 Post Earthquake; former Dumfries and Galloway Authority Reporter; b. 6.10.50, Glasgow; m., Jocelyn M. France; 2d. Educ. Glasgow Academy; London University; Moray House College; Jordanhill College. Fraternal Worker, Ghana, West Africa, Overseas Council, Church of Scotland, 1972-78; Postgraduate student, 1978-80; School Social Worker, Central Regional Council, 1980-83; Kilmarnock and Loudon Reporter, 1983-88; Area Reporter, Kyle and Carrick, Cumnock and Doon Valley, 1988-92; Principal Reporter, Dumfries and Galloway, 1992-95; Regional Reporter, 1995. President, Dumfries Burns Club, 2020 (200th anniversary year); Past President, Dumfries and Galloway Burns Club (direct descendent of Robert Burns). Publications: Operation Oboe (Historical Novel); Have You Seen My ...Umm...Memory (Self Help Memory Book); Poet's Progeny (Editor) (A line of descent from the Bard); Ponderings - poems and short stories in large print; Restless Waves (Novel); 7 Point 7 (On the Richter Scale) The Diary of the Camp Manager (Biography); Untied Laces (Autobiography), 2009; Miss Martha Douglas (Novel); The Last Shepherd (Novel); The Parrot's Tale (Novel); Jim's retiring Collection; The Crazy Psychologist; Take the Lead (Biography); The Trials of Sally Dunning (Novel); A Clerical Murder (Novel); childrens books: Lawrence The Lion; The Spotless Dalmation; Chaz The Friendly Crocodile; A Reluctant Spy (now a documentary; an ARTE French/German film); Caught in a Cold War Trap; The Arran Trilogy; Murders at Blackwaterfoot; Seaweed In My Hair; Dementia Adventure; Ruffled Feathers at Blackwaterfoot. Penned poetry for Parkinson's Research (all proceeds going to Parkinson's Research). Recreations: all things West African; piano; clarinet. Address: (h.) Netherholm, Edinburgh Road, Dumfries. E-mail: netherholm6@yahoo.com
Web: www.millercaldwell.com

Callaghan, Amy, BA (Politics). MP (SNP), East Dunbartonshire, since 2019; SNP Spokesperson for Pensions and Intergenerational Affairs, since 2020; b. 21.5.92. Educ. University of Strathclyde. Career history: Personal Support Assistant, University of Strathclyde, 2014-15; The Scottish Parliament: Intern for Aileen McLeod MSP, 2015, Parliamentary Assistant, 2015-16, Senior Caseworker, 2016-18, Office Manager, 2018-19. Volunteer Research Assistant, CLIC Sargent, 2015; Volunteer, Glasgow Life, 2014; Panel Member, Children's Hearings Scotland, 2016-19; Research Volunteer, James Lind Alliance, 2015-18; Volunteer Fundraiser, Teenage Cancer Trust, since 2011. Member of the House of Commons Health and Social Care Select Committee, since 2020. Address: Houses of Parliament, Westminster, London SW1A 0AA.

Callaghan, Stephanie, MSP (SNP), Uddingston and Bellshill, since 2021; b. 1971. Elected to South Lanarkshire Council in 2016 (by-election for the Hamilton North and East ward). Address: The Scottish Parliament, Edinburgh EH99 1SP; T.-0131 348 5493.
E-mail: Stephanie.Callaghan.msp@parliament.scot

Calman, Professor Sir Kenneth Charles, KCB 1996, DL, MD, PhD, FRCP, FRCS, FRSE. Chancellor, University of Glasgow, 2006-2020; Chairman, National Trust for Scotland, 2010-2015; Chairman, Commission on Scottish Devolution, 2008-09; Vice-Chancellor and Warden, Durham University, 1998-2007; b. 25.12.41, Glasgow; m., Ann; 1 s.; 2 d. Educ. Allan Glen's School, Glasgow; Glasgow University. Lecturer in Surgery, Western Infirmary, Glasgow, 1968-72; MRC Clinical Research Fellow, London, 1972-73; Professor of Oncology, Glasgow University, 1974-84; Dean of Postgraduate Medicine, 1984-89; Chief Medical Officer, Scottish Home and Health Department, 1989-91; Chief Medical Officer, Department of Health, 1991-98. Chairman, Executive Board, World Health Organisation, 1998-99; Deputy Chair, The British Library, 2010-15; Chairman, National Library of Scotland, 2016-20. Written 12 books; most recent is "It Started in a Cupboard" (autobiography), 2019. Recreations: golf; Scottish literature; gardening; cartoons; sundials. Address: (b.) University of Glasgow G12 8QQ.

Cameron of Lochbroom, Rt. Hon. Lord (Kenneth John Cameron), Life Baron (1984), PC (1984), MA (Oxon), LLB, QC, FRSE, Hon. FRIAS. Senator of the College of Justice, 1989-2003; Chairman, Royal Fine Art Commission for Scotland, 1995-2005; b. 11.6.31, Edinburgh; m., Jean Pamela Murray; 2 d. Educ. Edinburgh Academy; Corpus Christi College, Oxford; Edinburgh University. Advocate, 1958; Queen's Counsel, 1972; President, Pensions Appeal Tribunal for Scotland, 1976; Chairman, Committee of Investigation Under Agricultural Marketing Act 1958, 1980; Advocate Depute, 1981; Lord Advocate, 1984; Hon. Bencher, Lincoln's Inn; Hon. Fellow, Corpus Christi College, Oxford; Hon. Fellow, RIAS; Hon Fellow, RSA. Recreation: fishing. Address: (h.) Stoneyhill House, Musselburgh.

Cameron, Right Rev. Andrew Bruce. Primus of the Scottish Episcopal Church, 2000-06; Bishop of Aberdeen and Orkney, Scottish Episcopal Church, 1992-2006; b. 2.5.41, Glasgow; m., Elaine Cameron; 2 s. Educ. Eastwood Secondary School; Edinburgh Theological College. Curate, Helensburgh and Edinburgh, 1964-70; Chaplain, St. Mary's Cathedral, Edinburgh, 1970-75; Diocesan and Provincial Youth Chaplain, 1969-75; Rector, St. Mary's Church, Dalmahoy, and Anglican Chaplain, Heriot Watt University, 1975-82; Churches Development Officer, Livingston Ecumenical Parish, 1982-88; Rector, St. John's Episcopal Church, Perth, 1988-92; Convener, Mission Board, Scottish Episcopal Church, 1988-92; Resident Scholar, Bruton Parish Church, Williamsburg, USA, 2006-07; Int. Warden, Scottish Churches House, Dunblane, 2008. Recreations: music; theatre; various sports; gardening. Address: (h.) 21/1 Barossa Place, Perth PH1 5HH; T.-01738 441172; e-mail: bruce2541@gmail.com

Cameron, Colin. Freelance Television Producer; Managing Director, Lion Television Scotland, 2004-07; Controller, Network Development, BBC Nations and Regions, 2001-04; b. 30.3.50; m., Christine Main; 2 s. Educ. Glasgow Academy; Duke of York School, Nairobi; Polytechnic of Central London. Journalist, Current Affairs, BBC Scotland, 1973-76; Film Director, That's Life, 1976-77; Producer/Director, Everyman and Heart of the Matter, 1977-85; Editor, Brass Tacks, BBC North, 1985-88; Head of Documentary Features, BBC Television, 1988-91; BBC Scotland: Head of Television, 1991-96, Head of Production, 1997-2000, Head of Network Programmes, 2000-01. Controller Network Development, BBC Nations & Regions 2001-04. Chair, Balfron Community Council, since 2013; Chair, Strathendrick Singers, since 2016; RTS International Current Affairs Award, 1984; UN Association Media Peace Prize, 1984. E-mail: cc@colincameronmedia.com

Cameron, Colin, BL. Retired Solicitor; b. 24.8.33, Lanark; m., Rachel Weir Allison Cameron; 3 s.; 1 d. Educ. Uddingston Grammar School (School Captain and Dux in 1951); National Service, RASC, 1952-54;

Commissioned 2nd Lieutenant, 1954-57; TA Service, Platoon Commander, Amphibians, Beach Brigade, Glasgow; Glasgow University (graduated Bachelor of Law in 1957). Solicitor, Wilson and Morgan, Blantyre, Malawi, 1957-61; Minister of Transport and Communications, Malawi, 1961-64; Solicitor, Allan Black and McCaskie, Elgin, 1964-66; Solicitor to Cumbernauld and Irvine Development Corporations, 1966-70; own Legal practice in Irvine, 1970-2000. Council Member, Law Society of Scotland, 1976-82; served as VSO Volunteer in Solomon Islands, 1988-90; Hon. Consul to Republic of Malawi, 1994-2010); Member of Scotland/Malawi Partnership, since 2010; Past President, Irvine Rotary Club; Past Secretary, Abbeyfield Irvine and District Society Ltd; Hon. Vice President, Clan Cameron Association; Elder and Member, Church of Scotland; Member, Scottish National Party, and stood twice in Ayrshire as parliamentary candidate in Westminster Elections. Recreations: hill-walking; swimming; music; reading; family.

Cameron, Professor David, MA (Maths), MMBS (Medicine). Professor of Oncology and Director of Cancer Services, NHS Lothian, University of Edinburgh, since 2009. Educ. University of Cambridge; St. George's, University of London. Professor of Medical Oncology, University of Leeds, 2006-09. Address: Cancer Research UK Edinburgh Centre, Institute of Genetics and Cancer, The University of Edinburgh, Western General Hospital, Crewe Road South, Edinburgh EH4 2XR; T.-0131 651 8510.
E-mail: d.cameron@ed.ac.uk

Cameron, David Roderick Simpson, FRIAS, MRTPI, FSAScot. Retired consultant architect-planner; b. 2.6.41, Inverness; m., Filitsa Boulton; 1 s.; 2 d. Educ. George Watson's College; Edinburgh College of Art; Newcastle University; Leith School of Art. Trainee, then project architect, Rowand Anderson, Kininmonth & Paul; Depute Director of Planning, City of Edinburgh District Council, 1983-96; ECOS Project Manager for revival of Kazimierz, Krakow, 1993-96. Curator, exhibition on Charles Cameron (1745-1812); architect to Russian Court, held in Edinburgh and Achnacarry, 1995; Hon. Chieftain, Clan Cameron Association Scotland, since 2012; Elder, Corstorphine Old Parish Church, since 1981; Chairman: Saltire Society, 1990-95, Patrick Geddes Memorial Trust, 1991-99; Convener, Historic Burghs Association of Scotland, 1993-99; Hon. Secretary, Edinburgh Architectural Association, 1972-75; Membership Secretary, Scottish Society of Architect Artists, 2008-2015; Member, Council, National Trust for Scotland, 1994-99, Grants Council, Scottish Community Foundation, 1996-2006, Council, Cockburn Association, 2003-2012, Royal Celtic Society, since 2019, Mapa Scotland Trust, since 2010 and Chair, 2021-22; awarded Polish "Pro Patria" Medal, 2018. Recreations: art; angling; conservation; heritage; trees. Address: 4 Dovecot Road, Edinburgh EH12 7LE.

Cameron, Donald Andrew John Cameron. MSP (Scottish Conservative), Highlands and Islands region, since 2016; Shadow Cabinet Secretary for the Constitution, External Affairs and Culture, since 2021; Shadow Cabinet Secretary for Health and Sport, 2016-17 and 2020-21; Shadow Cabinet Secretary for Europe and External Affairs, 2019-20; Shadow Cabinet Secretary for the Rural Economy, 2018-19; Scottish Conservative and Unionist 2021 Policy Co-ordinator, 2017-20; Shadow Cabinet Secretary for the Environment, Climate Change and Land Reform, 2017-18; b. 26.11.76, Lochaber. Educ. University of Oxford; City University London. Advocate. Conservative candidate in the Ross, Skye and Lochaber constituency, in

the United Kingdom general election, 2010; Standing Junior Counsel to the Scottish Government, 2009-2016. Son of Donald Cameron, the 27th Lochiel, Chief of the Clan Cameron. Address: Scottish Parliament, Edinburgh EH99 1SP.

Cameron of Lochiel, Donald Angus, CVO, MA, FCA, DL. 27th Chief of the Clan Cameron; Lord-Lieutenant of Inverness, 2002-2021; JP, Highland Region, 2002-08; Director, J. Henry Schroder & Co. Limited, 1984-99; President, Highland Society of London, 1994-97; b. 2.8.46; m., Lady Cecil Kerr; 1 s. 3 d. Educ. Harrow; Christ Church, Oxford. 2nd Lieutenant, Queen's Own Cameron Highlanders (TA), 1966-68; Chartered Accountant, 1971. Address: (h.) Achnacarry, Spean Bridge, Inverness-shire.

Cameron, Rt. Rev. Douglas M. Bishop of Argyll and the Isles, 1993-2003; b. 23.3.35, Natal; m., Anne Patricia Purnell; 2 d. Educ. Eastwood Grammar School; Edinburgh Theological College; University of the South, Sewanee, Tennessee. Curate, Christ Church, Falkirk, 1962-65; Priest, Papua New Guinea, 1965-74, Archdeacon, 1972-74; Rector: St. Fillan's and St. Hilda's, Edinburgh, 1974-88, St. Mary's, Dalkeith, and St. Leonard's, Lasswade, 1988-92; Canon and Synod Clerk, Diocese of Edinburgh, 1990-92; Dean of Edinburgh, 1991-92. Recreations: walking; music; cooking. Address: (h.) 23 Craigs Way, Rumford, Falkirk FK2 0EU; T.-01324 714137.

Cameron, Professor Dugald, OBE, DA, FCSD, DSc (hc) Strathclyde, DLitt (hc) Glasgow. Former Chairman, Glasgow Prestwick International Airport Consultative Committee (retired); Director, Glasgow School of Art, 1991-99; Visiting Professor, University of Strathclyde, since 1999; Visiting Professor, Department of Aerospace Engineering, University of Glasgow, 2000; Companion, Royal Aeronautical Society, 1996; Industrial Design Consultant, since 1965; Hon. President, R. Aero Soc. Prestwick Branch; b. 4.10.39, Glasgow; m., Nancy Inglis. Educ. Glasgow High School; Glasgow School of Art. Industrial Designer, Hard Aluminium Surfaces Ltd., 1962-65; Visiting Lecturer, Glasgow School of Art, 1963-70; Head of Product Design, Glasgow School of Art, 1970-82; Head of Design, 1982-91. Hon. Professor, Glasgow University, 1993-99; Director, Squadron Prints, 1977-2000; Member: Engineering Advisory Committee, Scottish Committee, Council of Industrial Design, since 1966, Industrial Design (Engineering) Panel and 3D Design Board, CNAA, since 1978, Scottish Committee of Higher Education, Design Council; commission RAFVR (T), 1974; Adviser, Railway Heritage Trust, since 2003; Patron: Universities of Glasgow and Strathclyde Air Squadron, 2001; Trustee, Baird of Bute Society; Hon. President, North British Locomotive Preservation Group. Publications: Glasgow's Own (a history of 602 City of Glasgow Squadron, Royal Auxiliary Air Force), 1987; Glasgow's Airport, 1990; compiler of 'Central to Glasgow', 2006; compiler of 'From the Karoo to the Kelvin', 2010; 'Personal Passions', 2013 - Baird of Bute Award, 2013; Memoir, 'A Home For Lost Dogs', 2018. Recreations: railways; flying (lapsed private pilot); aviation history (particularly Scottish). Address: (h.) Achnacraig, Skelmorlie, Ayrshire.

Cameron, Duncan Graham, MStJ, KGOEG, KGOPRH, KHT, KLJ, OMLJ, MBA, MA, MA, BA, PGCE, DipEd Mgt, FIH, FRSA, FSA Scot. Hon President of Clan Cameron Association: immediate past Commissioner for Scotland, UK & Europe; one of the founding members of the Association of Highland Clan Societies; retired Principal Lecturer (Management Studies). Educ. 2010 MA Scottish Cultural Studies, University of Aberdeen; 2007 Degree Level Award in Medieval and Early Modern History and 2002 Modern Scottish History, University of Dundee; 1993 Diploma in Education Management, Sheffield Hallam University; 1990 MA Education, The

University of Lancaster; 1985 MEd in Educational Administration (year one), The University of Birmingham; 1982 MBA, Master of Business Administration, The University of Aston Management Centre; 1978 Certificate in Administrative Management, Dudley Technical College; 1975 Post Graduate Certificate in Education, Brunel University; 1974 BA Economics (Hons) CNAA, City of Birmingham Polytechnic, Commerce Centre; 1970 Final Membership Examination, Hotel & Catering Institute and 3-year Hotel Management Diploma, Birmingham College of Food and Domestic Arts (Now University College Birmingham); 1969 General Catering Diploma, BCFDA. Grant of arms by the Lord Lyon King of Arms in Scotland. Member, The Order of St John. Knight Grand Officer of the Eagle of Georgia and the Seamless Tunic of Our Lord Jesus Christ. Knight Grand Officer, Portuguese Royal Household & Honorary Member of the Honour Guard. Knight of the Confraternity of the Knights of the Most Holy Trinity. Knight of The Military and Hospitaller, Order of St Lazarus of Jerusalem & Officer of the Order of Merit. Fellow, Institute of Hospitality; Fellow, Royal Society for the Encouragement of Arts, Manufactures and Sciences; Fellow, Society of Antiquaries of Scotland (until retirement); Member, The Institute of Management; Member, Chartered Institute of Marketing; Affiliate, Chartered Institute of Personnel & Development; Fellow, The College of Preceptors; Member, The Tourism Society. Address: 22 Glamourhaugh Avenue, Huntly, Aberdeenshire AB54 8AS.

Cameron, Brigadier Ewen Duncan, OBE; b. 10.2.35, Bournemouth; m., Joanna Margaret Hay (deceased); 2 d. Educ. Wellington College; Royal Military Academy, Sandhurst. Commissioned The Black Watch, 1955; DS, The Staff College, 1972-75; Commanding Officer, 1st Bn., The Black Watch, 1975-78; Commander, Royal Brunei Armed Forces, 1980-82; Indian College of Defence Studies, Delhi, 1983; Divisional Brigadier, Scottish Division, 1984-86; Director of Administration and Personnel, National Trust for Scotland, 1986-98, Deputy Director, 1998-2000. Member, Queen's Bodyguard for Scotland (Royal Company of Archers). Recreations: opera; bridge; bird-watching; travel; golf; gardening. Address: (h.) The Old Manse, Arngask, Glenfarg, Perth PH2 9QA; T.-01577 830394.

Cameron, John Angus, MBChB, MRCGP, MBA. Chair, West of Scotland Clinical Board; works part-time as medical advisor to regional planning in the West of Scotland, and part-time as a hill sheep farmer in the Borders; Medical Director, NHS Dumfries and Galloway, 2003-2017 (retired); b. Bath. Educ. Marlborough College; Edinburgh University. GP, Biggar, 1982-99; Medical Director, Dumfries and Galloway Primary Care Trust, 2001-02. Non Executive Director, Lanarkshire Health Board, 1992-99. Recreations: hill farming; hill-walking.

Cameron, John Bell, CBE, FSAC, AIAgricE. Director, South West Trains, since 1995; Chairman, Scottish Beef Council, since 1997; Farmer, since 1961; b. 14.6.39, Edinburgh; m., Margaret Clapperton. Educ. Dollar Academy. Vice President, National Farmers' Union, 1976-79, President, 1979-84; Member, Agricultural Praesidium of EEC, 1979-84; Chairman, EEC Advisory Committee for Sheepmeat, 1982-90; Chairman, World Meats Group, (IFAP), since 1983; Chairman, Board of Governors, Dollar Academy, 1985-2015 (retired); Chairman, United Auctions Ltd., since 1985; President: Scottish Beef Cattle Association, since 2006, National Sheep Association (Scotland), since 2004; Vice President, National Sheep Association, since 2014; Member, Board of Governors, Macaulay Land Use Research Institute, since 1987; Chairman, British Railways (Scottish) Board, 1988-93; Member, British Railways Board, 1988-94; Honorary

Doctorate of Technology, Napier University, 1998; Honorary Doctorate of Law, St Andrews University, 2017. Long Service Award, Royal Observer Corps. Recreations: flying; shooting; travelling. Address: (h.) Balbuthie Farm, by Leven, Fife; T.-01333 730210.

Cameron, Rev. Dr. John Urquhart, BA, BSc, PhD, BD, ThD. Parish Minister, Broughty Ferry, 1974-2008; b. 10.6.43, Dundee; m., Jill Sjoberg; 1 s.; 1 d. Educ. Falkirk High School; St. Andrews University; Edinburgh University; University of Southern California. Marketing Executive, Beechams, London, 1969-73; Assistant Minister, Wellington Church, Glasgow, 1973-74; Chaplain, Royal Naval Reserve, 1976-81; Marketing Consultant, Pergamon Press, Oxford, 1977-81; Religious Education Department, Dundee High School, 1980-87; Sports Journalist and Travel Writer, Hill Publications, Surrey, 1981-2006; Physics Department, Dundee College of Further Education, 1987-95; Moderator, Presbytery of Dundee, 1993-94; Chaplain, Royal Caledonian Curling Club, 1980-95; Chaplain, Black Watch ACF, 1994-99. National and international honours in both summer and winter sports, 1960-85; sports scholarship, University of Southern California, 1962-64. Recreations: golf; skiing; curling. Address: 10 Howard Place, St. Andrews, Fife KY16 9HL; T.-01334 474 474. E-mail: jucameron43@yahoo.co.uk

Cameron, Sheriff Lewis, MA, LLB. Retired Solicitor; Sheriff of South Strathclyde Dumfries and Galloway at Hamilton, 1994-2002, at Dumfries, 1988-94; b. 12.8.35, Glasgow; m., Sheila Colette Gallacher; 2 s.; 2 d. Educ. St. Aloysius College; Blairs College; St. Sulpice, Paris; Glasgow University. RAF, 1954-56; admitted Solicitor, 1962. Member, Legal Aid Central Committee, 1970-80; Legal Aid Secretary, Airdrie, 1978-87; Chairman, Social Security Appeal Tribunals, 1983-88; Dean, Airdrie Society of Solicitors, 1984-85; Tutor, Strathclyde University, 1981-88; Treasurer, Monklands Victim Support Scheme, 1983-88; Chairman: Dumfries and Galloway Family Conciliation Service, 1988-92, Dumfries and Galloway, Scottish Association for the Study of Delinquency, 1988-92; Member, Scotland Committee, National Children's Homes; Trustee, Oscar Marzaroli Trust; Chairman, PHEW, 1994-2000. E-mail: cameron.lewis@virgin.net

Cameron, Dr. Lisa. MP (SNP), East Kilbride, Strathaven and Lesmahagow, since 2015; b. 8.4.72, Glasgow; m., Mark; 2 d. Educ. Duncanrig Secondary School, East Kilbride; Strathclyde University; Glasgow University. NHS Consultant working with clients who have mental health problems and learning difficulties. Served the public at Hairmyres Hospital, Wishaw General Hospital, Dykebar Hospital and the State Hospital. Expert Witness within the Scottish Court system working in cases of childhood sexual abuse and domestic violence. Active local Union Representative, campaigning for workers' rights, pay, pensions and issues of discrimination and equality. Address: Room 510, 1 Parliament Street, House of Commons, London SW1A 0AA.

Cameron, Dr Liz, OBE. Chief Executive & Director, Scottish Chambers of Commerce, since 2004; Member, UK Government Strategic Trade Advisory Group since 2018; Member, Director & Trustee, Inverclyde Leisure Trust, since 2020; GlobalScot since 2014; Scottish Government, Enterprise & Skills Strategic Board, 2018-2021; Chair & Board Trustee, Wevolution, 2016-2020; Vice-Chair, Scottish National Lottery Fund, 2007-2015; Chief Executive/Director, Renfrewshire Chamber of Commerce, 1996-2004. Educ. University of Strathclyde. Address: (b.) 199 Cathedral Street, 3rd Floor, University of Strathclyde, Glasgow G4 0QU; T.-0141 444 7500.

E-mail: lcameron@scottishchambers.org.uk
Web: scottishchambers.org.uk

Cameron, Michael. Chief Executive, Scottish Housing Regulator. Address: (b.) Buchanan House, 58 Port Dundas Road, Glasgow G4 0HF; T.-0141 242 5642; e-mail: michael.cameron@scottishhousingregulator.gsi.gov.uk

Cameron, Sandy, CBE. Educ. Strathclyde University; Aberdeen University. Social worker in Clackmannanshire, 1973-75; Principal Officer, Research and Planning Fieldwork, 1975-81; Assistant Director of Social Work in Central Region, 1981-87; Director of Social Work, Borders Regional Council, 1987-95; Executive Director, Social Work, South Lanarkshire Council, 1995-2006; Chairman, Parole Board for Scotland, 2006-2013. Chair, Management Board of the Institute for Research and Innovation in Social Services, 2000-2013; Chair of Executive Governance Group, Centre for Youth and Criminal Justice, University of Strathclyde; Panel Member, Independent Jersey Care Inquiry; Chair, SASO (Scottish Association for the Study of Offending); former Trustee, Lloyds TSB Foundation in Scotland; former Chair, Sacro; Chair, Capability Scotland; Visiting Professor, Strathclyde University, since 1998. Former Secretary and President, Association of Directors of Social Work; former Non-Executive Director, The State Hospitals Board for Scotland; Non Executive Director, Care Visions Group; Trustee, Why Not? Trust. Address: (b.) Glencairn Gattonside, Melrose TD6 9NB; T.-01896 820088.

Campbell, Aileen, MA Hons (Soc Sci). Chief Executive, Scottish Women's Football, since 2021; MSP (SNP), Clydesdale, 2011-2021, South of Scotland, 2007-2011; Cabinet Secretary for Communities and Local Government, 2018-2021; Minister for Public Health and Sport, 2016-18; Minister for Children and Young People, 2011-16; formerly Minister for Local Government and Planning, 2011; b. 18.5.80, Perth. Educ. Collace PS; Perth Academy; University of Glasgow. Press Officer for Shona Robison MSP and Stewart Hosie MP, 2006-07; PA to Nicola Sturgeon MSP, 2005-06; Editorial Assistant, Scottish Standard, 2005; Editor, Construction Magazine, Keystone, 2004-05. Address: Scottish Women's Football, Hampden Park, Glasgow G42 9DF; T.-0141 620 4580.

Campbell of Airds, Alastair Lorne, OStJ. Former Chief Executive, Clan Campbell; Archivist, Inveraray Castle, 1984-97; H.M. Unicorn Pursuivant of Arms, Court of the Lord Lyon, 1986-2008; Islay Herald of Arms Extraordinary, 2008-2014; b. 11.7.37, London; m., Mary-Ann Campbell-Preston; 3 s.; 1 d. Educ. Eton; R.M.A., Sandhurst. Regular Army, 1955-63 (commissioned Argyll and Sutherland Highlanders); Reid Pye and Campbell, 1963-71 (Managing Director, 1970-71); Waverley Vintners Ltd., 1972-83 (Marketing Director, 1972, Managing Director, 1977). Member: Queen's Bodyguard for Scotland (Royal Company of Archers), Chapter of Scottish Priory, Order of St John; FSA Scot; Patron, Armorial and Heraldry Society of Australasia; Chairman, Advisory Committee on Tartan to the Lord Lyon; Member, Council, National Trust for Scotland, 1996-2001; Honorary Research Fellowship, University of Aberdeen, 1996-2001. Publications: Two Hundred Years — The Highland Society of London; The Life and Troubled Times of Sir Donald Campbell of Ardnamurchan; The History of Clan Campbell – Vol. I. Recreations: painting; fishing; walking. Address: (h.) Inverawe Barn, Taynuilt, Argyll PA35 1HU; T.-01866 822207.

Campbell, Calum, BA (Hons), MBA, RGN, HV. Chief Executive, NHS Lothian, since 2020; b. 7.11.65, Erskine; m., Fidelma; 3 s. Educ. St. John Bosco; Trinity High School; Paisley University; Glasgow Caledonian University. Director of Strategic Change, NHS Grampian, 2001-04; Director of Governance and Delivery, NHS Argyll

& Clyde, 2004-06; Acting Chief Executive: Swansea NHS Trust, 2006-08, ABM University NHS Board Wales, 2008-09; Chief Executive, NHS Borders, 2010-2015; Chief Executive, NHS Lanarkshire, 2015-2020. Address: (b.) NHS Lothian, 2-4 Waterloo Place, Edinburgh EH1 3EG; T.-0131 242 1000.

Campbell, Christopher. Managing Director, Campbells Prime Meat, since 1994; b. 1965. Address: Campbells Prime Meat Ltd, The Heatherfield, Lathallan, by Linlithgow EH49 6LQ.

Campbell, Professor Colin, BSc, PhD. Chief Executive Officer, The James Hutton Institute, since 2015. Educ. University of Strathclyde. Post-doctoral researcher, Hill Farming Research Organisation, University of Edinburgh, 1986-87; Science Leader, Macaulay Land Use Research Institute, 1987-2011; Director of Science Excellence, The James Hutton Institute, Aberdeen, 2011-15. Director, James Hutton Institute's Post-Graduate School; Visiting Professor at Soil and Environment Department, Swedish Agricultural Sciences University (SLU), Uppsala, Sweden. Address: The James Hutton Institute, Craigiebuckler, Aberdeen AB15 8QH; T.-0344 928 5428.
E-mail: colin.campbell@hutton.ac.uk

Campbell, Colin MacIver, MA (Hons). MSP (SNP), West of Scotland, 1999-2003; SNP Defence Spokesperson, 1995-2003; National Secretary, SNP, 1997-99; b. 31.8.38, Ralston, Paisley; m., Evelyn; 3 s. Educ. Paisley Grammar School; Glasgow University; Jordanhill College of Education. Teacher: Hillhead High School, 1961-63; Paisley Grammar School, 1963-67; Principal Teacher, Greenock Academy, 1967-73; Depute Head Teacher, Merksworth High, 1973-77; Head Teacher, Westwood Secondary, 1977-89; Tutor (part-time), Strathclyde University Senior Studies Institute, 1995-98. Member, Renfrewshire Council, 1995-99; General Election Candidate: 1987, 1992, 1997; Euro Candidate: 1989, 1994. Elder, Church of Scotland; Former Chairman, Kilbarchan Civic Society and Kilbarchan Community Council; Former Convener, Kilbarchan SNP; Past Convener, Renfrew West SNP; Past Chairman, Kilbarchan Pipe Band, 2009-2011; Member, Lowlands Reserve Forces and Cadets Association, 1997-2003. Publication: co-author, Can't Shoot a Man With a Cold, 2004; author, 'Engine of Destruction. The 51st (Highland) Division in the Great War', 2013; Listen Closely: An oral history of Kilbarchan 1900-2000, 2020 (Co-Author). Recreation: military history. Address: (h.) Braeside, Shuttle Street, Kilbarchan PA10 2PR.

Campbell, David Ross, CBE, FInstD. Director, The Wise Group of Companies, 2009-2016; Public Member, Network Rail Ltd, 2009-2015; Chairman, NHS National Services Scotland, 2004-08; Chairman and Director of a number of private companies; Chairman, Health Education Board for Scotland, 1995-2001; b. 27.9.43, Glasgow; m., Moira. Educ. Whitehill Senior Secondary School, Glasgow; James Watt Memorial College, Greenock. Officer, Merchant Navy, 1961-68; Sales Executive, 1968-69; various management positions, George Outram & Co. Ltd., 1969-73; Managing Director, Scottish & Universal Newspapers Ltd., 1974-84; Executive Director, Scottish & Universal Investments Ltd.; Chief Executive, Clyde Cablevision Ltd., 1982-84; Chairman and Chief Executive, West Independent Newspapers Ltd., 1984-94; Chairman, Saltire Holdings Ltd., 1991-93. Past President: Scottish Newspaper Proprietors Association, Glasgow Chamber of Commerce; Liveryman and Freeman, City of London; Past Regional Chairman, PSYBT. Recreations: golf; theatre; travel; reading. Address: (h.) Summerlea, Summerlea Road, Seamill KA23 9HP.

84 WHO'S WHO IN SCOTLAND

Campbell, Doris Margaret, MD, FRCOG. Honorary Reader, Obstetrics and Gynaecology, Aberdeen University; b. 24.1.42, Aberdeen; m., Alasdair James Campbell; 1 s.; 1 d. Educ. Aberdeen High School for Girls; Aberdeen University. Resident house officer posts, Aberdeen, 1967-69; Research Fellow, Aberdeen University, 1969-73; Registrar in Obstetrics and Gynaecology, Aberdeen Hospitals, 1973-74; Lecturer in Obstetrics and Gynaecology and Physiology, Aberdeen University, 1974-84, Reader, Obstetrics and Gynaecology, 1984-2007. Former Member, Scottish Women's Hockey Council. Recreations: bridge; walking; guiding. Address: (h.) 77 Blenheim Place, Aberdeen; T.-01224 639984.
E-mail: d.m.campbell@abdn.ac.uk

Campbell, Cllr Douglas. Leader, South Ayrshire Council, 2017-2020; representing Ayr North Ward (SNP), since 1995. Educ. Belmont Academy. Address: County Buildings, Wellington Square, Ayr KA7 1DR; T.-07767 380298; e-mail: douglas.campbell@south-ayrshire.gov.uk

Campbell, Edward James, MA, LLB. Managing Director, Campbell's Prime Meat Ltd., 1970-2006; b. 18.3.37, Edinburgh; m., Ellen; 2 s.; 2 d. Educ. Daniel Stewart's College, Edinburgh; Edinburgh University. Worked in family business (Campbell Brothers Ltd); started Campbell's Prime Meat Ltd., 1970. Recreations: reading; cinema; bridge; travel. Address: 6 Easter Belmont Road, Edinburgh EH12 6EX;T.-0131-337 7698; e-mail: ellen_campbell@btinternet.com

Campbell, Fiona, BA (Hons), BMus. Freelance fundraiser, project manager, trainer, consultant and dance tutor in the voluntary and cultural sectors; formerly Development Manager, Voluntary Arts (2013-17); formerly Executive Officer, Voluntary Arts Scotland (2001-2012); b. 9.10.70, Wellington, New Zealand. Educ. Wellington East Girls College; Victoria University of Wellington. Press and Marketing Officer, National Association of Youth Orchestras, 1996-97, 1999; Project Administrator, SEAD, 1998-2000. Convener & Board Member, TMSA; Board Member, Traditional Dance Forum of Scotland (TDFS); Board Director, Neo Productions; Board Director, Scottish Fiddle Festival; Board Member, SEAD; Postgraduate Cert. in Cultural Policy and Management (Heriot-Watt University, 2004). Recreations: traditional music, song and dance; musical theatre and opera; reading; craftwork; swimming and historical interests. Address: (b.) 5 Appin Lane, Edinburgh EH14 1JL; T.-07951918366; e-mail: thefabspot@yahoo.com

Campbell, Glenn. Scottish news and current affairs broadcaster; Political Editor, BBC Scotland, since 2021; b. 1976, Islay. Educ. Islay High School; University of Glasgow. Career: Head of news and sport; news reporter, Scot FM, 1997-2001; Correspondent, BBC, since 2001. Notable credits: Newsnight Scotland; The Politics Show. Address: BBC Scotland, 40 Pacific Quay, Glasgow G51 1DA.

Campbell, Hugh Hall, QC (retd), BA (Hons), MA (Oxon), LLB (Hons), FCIArb. Queen's Counsel, since 1983; b. 18.2.44, Glasgow; m., Eleanor Jane Hare; 3 s. Educ. Glasgow Academy; Trinity College, Glenalmond; Exeter College, Oxford; Edinburgh University. Called to Scottish Bar, 1969; Standing Junior Counsel to Admiralty, 1976; Hon. Citizen of Antigua and Barbuda, 2010. Recreations: carnival, wine, music. Address: (h.) 12 Ainslie Place, Edinburgh EH3 6AS; T.-0131-225 2067.

Campbell, Professor Ian, MA, PhD, DLitt. Emeritus Professor of Scottish and Victorian Literature, Edinburgh University (Professor, since 1992); b. 25.8.42. Lausanne, Switzerland. Educ. Lausanne; Findochty; Buckie; Mackie Academy, Stonehaven;

Aberdeen University; Edinburgh University. Joined staff, English Department, Edinburgh University, 1967; Visiting Professor, Guelph, Duke, UCLA; Europa Professor, Mainz; Visiting Lecturer, United States, Canada, France, Germany, Switzerland, Italy, Japan, China. Publications: editorial team of Carlyle Letters, numerous books and articles on Scottish and Victorian Literature. Recreations: music; sport. Address: (b.) Department of English, Edinburgh University, 50 George Square, Edinburgh EH8 9LH.
E-mail: Ian.Campbell@ed.ac.uk

Campbell, Sir Ian, CBE, OStJ, VRD, JP. Deputy Chairman, Heath (Scotland) Ltd., 1987-95; Chairman, Select Assured Properties PLC, 1989-96; b. 3.2.23, Edinburgh; m., Marion Kirkhope Shiel; 1 d. Educ. Daniel Stewart's College, Edinburgh. Royal Navy, 1942-46; Royal Naval Reserve, 1946-64 (retired with rank of Commander); John Line & Sons, 1948-61 (Area Manager, West of England); Managing Director, MacGregor Wallcoverings Ltd., 1965-77; Finance Director, Scottish Conservative Party, 1977-89. Director, Travel System Ltd., 1987-90; Councillor, City of Edinburgh, 1984-88; Member, Transport Users Consultative Committee for Scotland, 1981-87; Freeman, City of Glasgow, 1991. Recreations: golf; vintage cars; water colour painting. Address: (h.) Merleton, 10 Boswall Road, Edinburgh EH5 3RH; T.-0131-552 4825.

Campbell, John David, FCIArb, Hon FRIAS. QC, Scotland, since 1998; b. 1949, Inverness; 2 s.; 3 d.; m., Kate Knight (2009). Educ. Gordonstoun; Edinburgh University. Former Solicitor, 1972-78, Advocate, since 1981; Barrister, Lincoln's Inn, since 1990; Arbitrator; Trustee, Scottish Historic Buildings Trust, since 2007; Trustee, The Ross Trust, since 2017; Director, Planning Aid Scotland, since 2018; Trustee, Berwickshire Housing Association, since 2020. Publication: Scottish Planning Encyclopaedia (Contributor), 2001. Recreations: family; music; gardening; building conservation. Address: (b.) Advocates Library, Parliament House, Edinburgh EH1 1RF.
E-mail: jcampbellqc@advocates.org.uk

Campbell, Jonathan, LLB (Hons), DipLP. Director, Capital Defence Lawyers, since 2019; b. 4.85. Educ. Currie Community High School; University of Glasgow; University of Strathclyde. Career history: Solicitor, Capital Defence Lawyers, 2008-2014; Associate Solicitor, George More and Company, 2014-16; Criminal Solicitor Advocate, Society of Solicitor Advocates, since 2017; Tutor, Diploma in Professional Legal Practice, University of Edinburgh Law School, since 2018. Member: Law Society of Scotland, Society of Solicitor Advocates, Edinburgh Bar Association, University of Edinburgh. Address: Capital Defence Lawyers, 9-10 St Andrew Square, Edinburgh EH2 2BH; T.-0131 553 4333.

Campbell, Sheriff Kenneth, QC. Sheriff of Lothian and Borders, since 2020. Educ. Glasgow University; University of London. Career history: trained with Dickson Minto, then worked as a civil litigation solicitor with Brodies; joined the Bar in 1996; Director of Training and Education, Faculty of Advocates, 2002-05; practised in a number of areas of civil law, and appeared in courts and tribunals at all levels across Scotland, as well as before the UK Supreme Court; served as an ad hoc Advocate Depute, prosecuting criminal trials in the High Court of Justiciary. Legal Member of the First-tier Tribunal for Scotland (Tax Chamber), 2015-2020; Legal Member of the Mental Health Tribunal for Scotland, 2017-2020. Address: Edinburgh Sheriff & Justice of the Peace Court, Sheriff Court House, 27 Chambers Street, Edinburgh EH1 1LB; T.-0131 225 2525.

Campbell, Mary Theresa MacLeod, OBE, BA, CA. Chief Executive Officer, Blas Limited in Edinburgh and

Manhattan, since 2002; b. 24.2.59, Glasgow; 2 d.; 2 s. Educ. Lochaber High School; University of Stirling. Ernst and Young, 1980-86; Noble Group Limited, 1986-98; British Linen Bank Ltd., 1998-99. Founding Director, British Linen Advisers Ltd., 1999-2002. Recreations: literature; theatre; opera; Barra. Address: (b.) Blas Limited, 1 Rutland Square, Edinburgh EH1 2AS; e-mail: mary@blasltd.co.uk

Campbell, Melfort Andrew, OBE, FRSA. Chairman, Imes Group Holdings Ltd., since 1997; b. 6.6.56, Exeter; m., Lucy Nickson; 3 d. Educ. Ampleforth College, York. Director, OGTC; past Chairman, CBI Scotland; Director, NSRI; Visiting Professor, University of Strathclyde. Recreations: fishing; shooting; rugby; tennis. Address: (b.) Old School, Maryculter, Aberdeen AB12 5GN; T.-01224 734106.

Campbell, Morag. Governor, Royal Conservatoire of Scotland, since 2019; b. 2.58. Formerly Assistant Principal (Creative Industries), Stevenson College, Edinburgh; Chief Executive, National Youth Choir of Scotland, 2012-19. Chair, Enterprise Music Scotland; Trustee, IMPACT (Scotland). Address: Royal Conservatoire of Scotland, 100 Renfrew Street, Glasgow G2 3DB.

Campbell, Rev. Murdo Macdonald, BD (Hons), DipMin. Minister, Strathblane Parish Church of Scotland, since 2017; formerly Minister, Brightons Parish Church of Scotland (2007-2017); formerly Minister, Carloway, Isle of Lewis (1997-2007); b. 13.5.60, Stornoway, Isle of Lewis; m., Lorraine Anne Campbell (nee McLeod); 2 s. Educ. Bayble Junior Secondary; Nicolson Institute, Stornoway; Aberdeen University. Probationer, Martins Memorial Church, Stornoway; Elder, St. Columbas Church; Divinity Student Attachment: Ruthrieston South and Ruthrieston West Churches, Aberdeen, Aberdeen Royal Infirmary Chaplaincy; Inducted and Ordained to Carloway Church of Scotland; Chairperson, Carloway Youth Initiative; Convener, Presbytery Parish Appraisal Committee; Chairperson, Carloway School Board; Moderator of Presbytery. Member, Church of Scotland National Mission Committee. Recreations: hill walking. Address: Strathblane Parish Church of Scotland, Campsie Road, Strathblane G63 9AB; T.-01360 770418.

Campbell, Niall Gordon, BA. Under Secretary, Civil and Criminal Law Group, Scottish Executive Justice Department, (formerly Scottish Office Home Department) 1997-2001; b. 9.11.41, Peebles; m., Alison M. Rigg; 3 s. Educ. Edinburgh Academy; Merton College, Oxford. Entered Scottish Office 1964; Assistant Secretary, 1978; various posts in Scottish Education Department and Scottish Development Department; Under Secretary, Social Work Services Group, 1989-97. Member, Parole Board for Scotland, 2003-09; Chairman, SACRO, 2002-07; Chairman, Scottish Association for the Study of Offending, 2001-06; Council of the British Trust for Ornithology, 2006-2011; Company Secretary, Citizens Advice Edinburgh, since 2008. Address: (h.) 15 Warriston Crescent, Edinburgh.

Campbell, Nicholas Andrew Argyll (Nicky), OBE. Scottish radio and television presenter and journalist; b. 10.4.61, Edinburgh; m. (1), Linda Larnach (divorced); m. (2), Tina Ritchie; 4 d. Educ. Edinburgh Academy; University of Aberdeen. Career history: jingle writer, then breakfast show host, Northsound Radio, 1981-85; Capital Radio, London, 1986-87; BBC Radio 1, 1987-97; joined BBC Radio 5 Live in 1997; TV presenter: Wheel of Fortune, 1988-96, Watchdog, 2001-09, BBC One's Sunday morning show The Big Questions, 2007-2021; co-host,

Long Lost Family, since 2011; Radio presenter, BBC Radio 5 Live breakfast programme, since 2003. Won seven Sony Awards, including a Gold Award in 2007 for the Radio 5 Live Breakfast programme as "Best News and Current Affairs Programme" (with Shelagh Fogarty); received an Honorary Doctorate from the Robert Gordon University, Aberdeen in 2008; won a Royal Television Society Award for best 'Popular Factual' programme for Long Lost Family in 2013; Television BAFTA award for best "Features Programme" in 2014. Publication: Blue Eyed Son, 2004.

Campbell, Paul, MCIAT. Director, Pollock Hammond Ltd, since 2001; b. 6.73. Educ. South Queensferry High. Architectural Technician, WN Thomson & Co., 1990-2001. Member, Institute of Architectural Technologists. Address: Pollock Hammond Ltd, Grange West, Linlithgow EH49 7RH; T.-01506 847829.
E-mail: paul@pollockhammondarchitects.co.uk

Campbell, (Robert) Mungo (McCready), BA, MPhil, FRSA. Deputy Director, Hunterian Museum & Art Gallery, University of Glasgow, since 1997; b. 8.10.59, Newcastle upon Tyne; m., Teresa Margaret Green; 1 s.; 1 d. Educ. Royal Grammar School, Newcastle upon Tyne; University of Durham; University of Glasgow. Assistant Keeper, National Gallery of Scotland, Edinburgh, 1987-97; Member, Scottish Arts Council Visual Arts Committee, 1998-2003; Board Member: SCRAN, 2004-06, Scottish Museums Council, 2001-07; Chair: VAGA Scotland, 2005-07, The Skateraw Foundation, 2009-2010. Recreations: island life; walking with my children; cooking good food; eating good food. Address: (b.) Hunterian Museum, University of Glasgow, Glasgow G12 8QQ; T.-0141-330 4735.

Campbell, Roderick, BA (Hons), LLM. MSP (SNP), North East Fife, 2011-16; b. 15.6.53, Edinburgh. Educ. Reading School; Exeter University; University of Glasgow; University of Strathclyde. Has a degree in politics and qualified as a solicitor in both England, Wales and Scotland. Formerly a partner in an international law firm based in London. Qualified as an Advocate in 2008.

Campbell, Shirley, BSc Hons (Psyc). People and Organisational Development Director, Scottish Water, since 2011; b. 3.66. Educ. Marr College; University of Strathclyde; INSEAD; Wharton Business School. Career history: Human Resources graduate/generalist, Xerox, 1990-94; UK Human Resources Director, Aviva General Insurance, Aviva plc, 1994-2005; UK Organisational Development Director, Aviva, 2005-06; UK Human Resources Director, RSA, 2007-08; People and Organisational Development Director, Heriot-Watt University, 2009-2011. Scottish Water: member of the Remuneration Committee, the Business Ethics Committee and leads International business; Non Executive Director, BT (Scotland); Lay Member of Court, University of Dundee; member, University of Dundee's Remuneration Committee and Chairs the University of Dundee's Human Resources Committee. Address: Scottish Water, Head Office, 6 Castle Drive, Carnegie Campus, Dunfermline KY11 8GG.

Campbell, Stewart, BSc, DipSH. Member: Scottish Criminal Cases Review Commission, 2007-2015, Parole Board for Scotland, since 2015; formerly Health and Safety Executive Director, Scotland, 2001-08; b. 9.4.48, Bridge of Allan; m., Susan; 2 s. Educ. McLaren High School, Callander; Glasgow University. Nuffield and Leverhulme Travelling Fellowship, 1983-84. Publication: Labour Inspection in the European

Community. Recreations: golf; hill-walking; genealogy.
E-mail: stewart.campbell18@googlemail.com

**Campbell of Pittenweem, Rt. Hon. Lord (Walter)
Menzies Campbell,** CH (2013), CBE (1987), Kt (2003),
PC, MA, LLB, LLD, QC, FRSE. MP (Liberal Democrat),
North East Fife, 1987-2015; Advocate, 1968-2017; Queen's
Counsel (1982); Leader, Liberal Democrats, 2006-07;
Liberal Democrat Shadow Foreign Secretary, 2001-06;
Deputy Leader, Liberal Democrats, 2003-06; Member,
Parliamentary Assembly of OSCE, 1992-1997; Vice
President, NATO Parliamentary Assembly, since 2017; b.
22.5.41, Glasgow; m., Elspeth Mary Urquhart. Educ.
Hillhead High School, Glasgow; Glasgow University;
Stanford University, California. President, Glasgow
University Union, 1964-65; took part in Olympic Games,
Tokyo, 1964; AAA 220-yards champion, 1964, 1967;
Captain, UK athletics team, 1965, 1966; 1966
Commonwealth Games, Jamaica; UK 100-metres record
holder, 1967-74. Advocate Depute, 1977-80; Standing
Junior Counsel to the Army in Scotland, 1980-82.
Parliamentary candidate (Liberal): Greenock and Port
Glasgow, February, 1974, and October, 1974, East Fife,
1979, North East Fife, 1983; Chairman, Scottish Liberal
Party, 1975-77; Member, Select Committee on Defence,
1992-99; Party Spokesman on Defence, Foreign Affairs and
Sport, until 1997, Foreign Affairs and Defence, 1997-2001;
Member: Select Committee on Foreign Affairs, 2008-2015,
Parliamentary Committee on Intelligence and Security,
2008-2015, UK Sports Council, 1965-68, Scottish Sports
Council, 1971-81, Broadcasting Council for Scotland,
1984-87, Joint Committee on National Security Strategy,
2006-2021; Member of the House of Lords International
Relations and Defence Committee, since 2021; Chairman,
Royal Lyceum Theatre, Edinburgh, 1984-87; Leader, UK
delegation to the NATO Parliamentary Assembly, 2010-
2015. Honorary Degrees: DUniv Glasgow University, 2001;
LLD Strathclyde University, 2005; LLD St. Andrews 2006;
Chancellor of St. Andrews University, since 2006.
Recreations: all sports; music; theatre.

Campbell, William Kilpatrick, MA (Hons). Director,
Mainstream Publishing, 1978-2013; b. 1.3.51, Glasgow; 2
d. Educ. Kilmarnock Academy; Edinburgh University.
Postgraduate research, Universities of Edinburgh and
California; world travel, 1975; Publications Manager,
Edinburgh University Student Publications, 1976-78.
Publications: Alternative Edinburgh (Co-Editor), 1972;
Another Edinburgh, 1976. Recreations: soccer; rugby; wine;
books; people. E-mail: billcampbell450@gmail.com

Campbell-Jones, Anna, BA, PG Cert. Interior Design
Consultant; Director, Habitus Design Ltd, Glasgow, since
2016; b. 1.69, London. Educ. The Glasgow School of Art;
University of Glasgow. Career history: Senior Interior
Designer, Imagination, London, 1995-97; Associate, Morey
Smith Limited, London, 1997-99; Director, Rehab Interiors
Limited, 2007-2016; Lecturer, Glasgow School of Art,
2000-2018. TV presenter on Hire My Home, Channel 4;
Judge on Scotland's Home of the Year, BBC Scotland.
Address: Habitus Design Ltd, 6th Floor, Gordon Chambers,
90 Mitchell Street, Glasgow G1 3NQ.

Canavan, Dennis, BSc (Hons), DipEd, DUniv, LLD. MSP
(Independent), Falkirk West, 1999-2007; b. 8.8.42,
Cowdenbeath. Educ. St. Bride's and St. Columba's Schools,
Cowdenbeath; Edinburgh University. Principal Teacher of
Mathematics, St. Modan's High School, Stirling, 1970-74;
Assistant Head, Holyrood High School, Edinburgh, 1974;
Leader, Labour Group, Stirling District Council, 1974; MP,
West Stirlingshire, 1974-83; MP, Falkirk West, 1983-2000;
Chair: Scottish Parliamentary Labour Group, 1980-81, PLP
Northern Ireland Committee, 1989-97; Member: Foreign
Affairs Select Committee, 1982-97, British–Irish Inter-
Parliamentary Body, 1992-2000, International Development
Select Committee, 1997-99; Scottish Parliament European

and External Relations Committee, 1999-2007; Convener,
Cross-Party Sports Group, Scottish Parliament, 1999-2007;
President, then Convener, Ramblers Scotland, 2007-2012,
Vice-President, since 2012; Trustee of the Scottish Mining
Museum, since 2007; Honorary President, Milton Amateurs
Football Club; Honorary Doctorates from University of
Strathclyde and University of Stirling. Chair of St. Mary's
Primary School Bannockburn Parent Council, 2009-2014;
Chair of Falkirk Football Community Foundation, 2010-
2016; Patron of Falkirk & District Association for Mental
Health, since 2007; Patron of The Driving Force,
Bonnybridge, since 2009; Patron of Wiston Lodge Outdoor
Adventure Centre, since 2012; Honorary President of
Rivers Forth & Teith Anglers' Association, since 2008;
Chair of Yes Scotland Advisory Board, 2012-2014;
Member of Advisory Group appointed by the Scottish
Government in 2018 to review the impact of policing on
communities affected by the 1984-85 Miners Strike;
Secretary of Scottish Parliament Cross-Party Group on St.
Andrew's Day, since 2018. Publication: Author of
Autobiography, "Let the People Decide", 2009.
Recreations: hill-walking; swimming; football (former
Scottish Universities football internationalist). Address:
Ardsonas, Sauchieburn, Bannockburn FK7 9PZ; T.-01786
812581; e-mail: canavan897@btinternet.com

Cannon, Malcolm Stewart Graham, BSc (Hons).
Managing Director of Property Services, Simpson &
Marwick, since 2021; b. 5.62. Educ. Dulwich College;
University of St Andrews. Career history: Sales rep, LEO
Pharma, 1985-89; Marketing Manager, Fisons plc, 1989-95;
International Marketing Manager, Fisons Pharmaceuticals,
1989-95; Business Development Manager, Highland
Distillers, 1995-99; The Edrington Group: Director of
Corporate Affairs, 1999-2001, Director of E-Business,
2001-04; Business Development Manager, Maclay Murray
& Spens LLP, 2006; Chief Executive Officer: Hunter Boot
Ltd, 2006-08, ESPC, 2009-2013; Chief Executive
Edinburgh, Lomond Lettings, 2013-14; CEO, Braemore,
2014-15; Non Executive Director, The Property
Ombudsman Scotland Ltd, 2015-16; Director (Scotland),
Asset Skills, 2011-16; Board Member, The Building
Futures Group, 2013-17; CEO, Cricket Scotland, 2015-19;
Board Member, Scottish Sports Association, 2017-19; Non-
Executive Director, Partick Thistle Football Club, 2019;
Director Scotland, The Institute of Directors, 2019-2021.
Address: Simpson & Marwick, 23 Alva Street, Edinburgh,
EH2 4PS; T.-0131 581 5700.
E-mail: malcolm.cannon@simpsonmarwick.com

Cantlay, Michael Brian, OBE, BA, MBA, DUniv
(Stirling). Chair, Scottish Funding Council; Chair,
NatureScot; CEO, William Glen and Son Ltd; President,
William Glen and & Son Inc, San Francisco; Chair,
William Glen Canada Ltd, Toronto; Board Member,
CrossReach; Chair, Highlands and Islands Airports Ltd,
2016-17; Director, Dundee Airport Ltd, 2016-17; Director,
Airport Management Services Ltd, 2016-17; Chair,
VisitScotland, 2010-2016; Board Member, VisitBritain,
2010-2016; CEO, "The Whisky Shop", 1992-2004, CEO,
Hector Russell Ltd, 1993-2005; Chair, Callander
Community Council, 1992-93; Chair, Scottish Enterprise
Forth Valley, 1995-2001; Advisory Board Member,
Scottish Enterprise, 2000-02; Deputy Chair, VisitScotland,
2001-05; Chair, Forth Valley College, 2005-09; Convener,
Loch Lomond and Trossachs National Park Authority,
2006-2010; Non Executive-Director, Highlands and Islands
Airports Ltd, 2008-2014; b. 2.2.64, Galashiels; m., Linda.
Educ. McLaren High School, Callander; Strathclyde
University. Address: Callandrade, Callander, Perthshire
FK17 8HW.

Caplan, Lady (Joyce Caplan). President, Friends of
University Library, Edinburgh, since 2002; Chair, Poetry
Association of Scotland, since 2002; Chair, Scottish
Poetry Library, 2004-09; m.,1. David Leigh (d. 1970); 2.

Lord Caplan (deceased); 1 d. Member of Children's Panel, 1978-81; Governor, Lomond School, Helensburgh, 1985-89; Chairman: Play in Scottish Hospitals, 1990-96, Smiths Place Group, 1992-95, Scottish Play Council, 1992-95; Chair, Children's Classic Concerts, since 2010; Chair, Snowball Trust, since 2000; Chairman, Couple Counselling Scotland, 1997-2001; Teaching Fellow, Edinburgh University, since 2018; Edinburgh Burns Club Council, 2010; Committee of PEN, 2012 (Scotland); Muriel Spark Society Committee, 2012; Member, the John P. Mackintosh Memorial Committee, since 2013; Member of Business Committee, Edinburgh University General Council, since 2019; Chair, Scottish Centre of Tagore Studies, since 2019; Jewish Literary Committee, 2016; clubs: Scottish Arts Club, New Club, Oyster Club, Fair Intellectuals, Tuesday Club, since 2013. Recreations: books; music; friends; paintings; poetry. Address: (h.) Nether Liberton House, Old Mill Lane, Edinburgh EH16 5TZ.

Cardownie, Steve. Former Depute Lord Provost of the City of Edinburgh Council; b. 1.6.53, Leith; m.; 2 s. Educ. Leith Academy; Telford College. Civil service; National Executive Committee Member, CPSA, five years; Councillor, Edinburgh, 1988-2017; Director, Edinburgh Jazz and Blues Festival; Employment Tribunal Member, since 1981; former Member, Culture & Sport Committee and Transport & Environment; Director, Community Football Academy, Spartans FC. Recreations: hill-walking; running; Heart of Midlothian FC; theatre; reading; fine wines and travelling.

Carey, Professor Frank A., BSc, MD, FRCPath. Professor and Consultant Pathologist, since 1995; Lead Clinician, Scottish Pathology Network, 2005-2010; b. 5.7.61, Cork, Ireland; m., Dr Julie Curran; 1 s.; 1 d. Educ. University College, Cork. Senior House Officer, Cork University Hospital, 1986-87; Registrar in Pathology, Royal Infirmary of Edinburgh, 1987-89; Senior Registrar, Royal Infirmary of Edinburgh, 1989-95; Consultant, Tayside University Hospitals, since 1995. Member, Scottish Council, Royal College of Pathologists. Address: (b.) Department of Pathology, Ninewells Hospital and Medical School, Dundee DD1 9SY; T.-01382 632548.

Carlaw, Jackson. MSP (Scottish Conservative), Eastwood, since 2016 (West Scotland, 2007-2016); former Leader of the Scottish Conservatives (February 2020-July 2020); b. 12.4.59; m.; 2 s. Educ. Glasgow Academy. Career history: worked in the retail motor industry for 25 years; held various voluntary positions including National Chairman of the Scottish Young Conservatives, 1984-86, Chairman of Eastwood Conservatives, 1988-92; appointed Vice, then Deputy Chairman of the Scottish Conservatives, 1992-98 and 2005-06; Deputy Leader of the Scottish Conservatives, 2011-2020; former Shadow Cabinet Secretary for Europe and External Affairs. Recreations: theatre; film; reading; walking. Address: (b.) Constituency Office: Spiersbridge House, 1 Spiersbridge Way, Thornliebank, Glasgow G46 8NG.

Carlin, Audrey, BSc (Hons), MRTPI. Chief Executive Officer, Wasps Studios, since 2017; b. 1.69. Educ. University of Dundee. Career history: Planning Assistant, Renfrew District Council, 1992-94; Planning Officer, Glasgow City Council, 1994-99; Development Officer, Glasgow Alliance, 1999-2003; Clydebank Urban Regeneration Company: Planning Manager, 2003-08, Senior Manager, 2008-2015; appointed Senior Executive Director, Wasps Studios in 2015; appointed to the Board of The National Galleries of Scotland in 2018; appointed Chair of Major Capital Projects Committee in 2020. Address: Wasps Studios, The Briggait, 141

Bridgegate, Glasgow G1 5HZ; T.-0141 553 5890. E-mail: info@waspsstudios.org.uk

Carloway, Rt. Hon. Lord (Colin John MacLean Sutherland), PC 2008, FRSE 2020. Lord President of the Court of Session, since 2015; Senator of the College of Justice, since 2000; Lord Justice Clerk and President of the Second Division of the Court of Session, 2012-15; b. 20.5.54; m., Jane Alexander Turnbull; 2 s. Educ. Edinburgh Academy; Edinburgh University (LLB Hons). Advocate, 1977; Advocate Depute, 1986-89; QC (Scot), 1990. Treasurer, Faculty of Advocates, 1994-2000. Address: (b.) Parliament House, Edinburgh EH1 1RQ.

Carlyle, Robert, OBE. Actor and Director; b. 14.4.61; m., Anastasia Shirley; 3 c. Trained, RSAMD; Duncan Macrae Memorial Prize for Scots verse. Credits include: (film) The Full Monty, Carla's Song, Trainspotting, Riff Raff (European film of the year), Priest, Plunkett and MacLeane, Ravenous, The Beach, Angela's Ashes, The World Is Not Enough, There's Only One Jimmy Grimble, To End All Wars, 51st State, Once Upon a Time in the Midlands, Black and White, Dead Fish, Marilyn Hotchkiss Ballroom Dancing and Charm School, The Mighty Celt, Eragon, 28 Weeks Later, Flood, Stone of Destiny, The Meat Trade, Summer, I Know You Know, The Tournament, California Solo, The Legend of Barney Thomson, Trainspotting 2, Yesterday; (television) Hitler: The Rise of Evil, 2003, Gunpowder, Treason and Plot, 2004, Class of '76, 2005, Human Trafficking, 2005, Hamish Macbeth (title role), 2005, Born Equal, 2006, The Last Enemy, 2008, 24: Redemption, 2008, Stargate Universe, 2009-2011, Once Upon a Time, 2011-18, The War of the Worlds, 2019, Cobra, 2019; (theatre) Twelfth Night, Cuttin' A Rug, Othello; (television and theatre) Go Now, Face; as Director of Rain Dog Theatre Company: Wasted, One Flew Over the Cuckoo's Nest (Paper Boat Award), Conquest of the South Pole, Macbeth (Paper Boat Award); Best Actor: Evening Standard Film Awards, 1998; Film Critics' Circle Awards, 1998, Bowmore Whisky/Scottish Screen Awards, 2001, Michael Elliott Awards, 2001; David Puttnam Patrons Award. Patron of School For Life Romania, Charity No. 1062953.

Carmichael, Alexander Morrison (Alistair), MP. Liberal Democrat MP, Orkney and Shetland, since 2001; Liberal Democrat Spokesperson for Home Affairs, since 2020; Deputy Leader, Scottish Liberal Democrats, 2012-2021; Secretary of State for Scotland, 2013-15; b. 15.7.65; m., Kathryn Jane; 2 s. Educ. Islay High School; Aberdeen University. Hotel manager, 1984-89; Procurator Fiscal Depute, Crown Office, Edinburgh and Aberdeen, 1993-96; solicitor in private practice, 1996-2001. Address: (b.) House of Commons, London SW1A 0AA; e-mail: carmichaela@parliament.uk

Carmichael, (Katharine) Jane, MA (Mod Hist). Governor, Hospitalfield Trust, since 2015; former Director of Collections, National Museums of Scotland (2003-2015); b. 12.3.52; m., Adrian Craxton; 1 step son; 2 d.; 2 step daughters. Educ. St. Leonards; St. Andrews; Edinburgh University. Imperial War Museum, 1974-2003: Keeper of Photographic Archive, 1982-95, Director of Collections, 1995-2003. Served various committees of National Museums Directors Conf., since 1995. FRSA, 2000; FSA (Scot). Publications: 1st World War Photographers, 1989; contributed to various journal articles. Recreations: the family; country walking; going to the ballet.

Carmichael of Carmichael (Richard John). 26th Baron of Carmichael, since 1980; 30th Chief of Name and Arms of Carmichael, since 1981; has held 12 international Clan gatherings at Carmichael since 1983. Most recently 2017. Farmer producing venison beef and lamb from own abattoir on farm selling at Carmichael farm shop and Glasgow/Edinburgh farmers markets, since 2001. Chartered

88 WHO'S WHO IN SCOTLAND

Accountant; b. 1.12.48, Stamford; m., Patricia Margaret Branson; 1 s.; 2 d.; 4 gs.; 1 gd. Educ. Hyton Hill Preparatory School; Kimbolton School; Coventry College of Technology. Audit Senior, Coopers and Lybrand, Tanzania, 1972; Audit Manager, Granger Craig Tunnicliffe, Tauranga, New Zealand, 1974; ACA, 1971; FCA, 1976; Factor/Owner, Carmichael Estate, 1980; Director: Carmichael Heritage Leisure Ltd.; claims family titles: Earldom of Hyndford, Viscountcies of Inglisberry and Nemphlar, and Lordship Carmichael of Carmichael. Member, Standing Council of Scottish Chiefs; New Zealand Orienteering Champion, 1977; International Orienteering Federation Senior Event Advisor, 1996-2018 including World Masters Games Alberta 2005 and Race The Castles Scotland, 2014. Director & Chairman, Scottish Six Day Orienteering Event Company Ltd, 1986-2001. Recreations: orienteering; skiing; Clan Carmichael Association. Address: Carmichael House, Carmichael, by Biggar, Lanarkshire ML12 6PG; T.-01899 308336; e-mail: chiefcarm@aol.com; web: www.carmichael.co.uk

Carr, Professor Chris, MA, PhD, DMS, ACMA, CEng, MIMechE. Professor of Corporate Strategy, Edinburgh University, since 1999; b. 13.8.51, Brentwood; m., Jennifer Munro; 1 s.; 1 d. Educ. Harrow; Trinity Hall, University of Cambridge; Warwick University. Early career in industry with British Aerospace, GKN; Lecturer: Buckingham University; Warwick University; Bath University; Senior Lecturer/Associate Research Director, Manchester Business School; Visiting Professor, Moscow State University; Visiting Professor, International Business, Witten-Herdecke University, Germany; teaching/research overseas: Harvard Business School; Zhejiang University; Shenzen University; IIMB, Bangalore; St Petersburg University; Sao Paulo University; HEC; University of Carlos III; Bicocca University; Bilgi University. Publications: Britain's Competitiveness, 1990; Strategic Investment Decisions, 1994; numerous articles in academic journals including the Strategic Management Journal and Sloan Management Review. Recreations: politics; tennis; sailing. Address: (b.) Edinburgh University Management School, 29 Buccleuch Place, Edinburgh EH8 9JS; T.-0131-650 6307; e-mail: Chris.Carr@ed.ac.uk

Carruthers, Professor Gerard Charles, BA, PGCE, MPhil, PhD, FRSE. Francis Hutcheson Professor of Scottish Literature, University of Glasgow; b. 4.7.63, Lennoxtown, Stirlingshire. Educ. St. Andrew's High School, Clydebank; University of Strathclyde; University of Glasgow. Temporary Lecturer, Department of Scottish Literature, University of Glasgow, 1992-93; Research Fellow, Department of English, University of Aberdeen, 1993-95; Lecturer, Department of English, University of Strathclyde, 1995-2000; Lecturer, then Senior Lecturer, then Reader, then Professor, Department of Scottish Literature, University of Glasgow, since 2000; Founder (2007) & Co-Director of The Centre for Robert Burns Studies; Member, Abbotsford Library Joint-Advisory Committee; Hon. Advisor, National Trust for Scotland; Member, Research and Ethics Committee, Paisley Museum; Secretary and Board Member, Ellisland Museum and Farm; Convenor, Scottish Catholic Historical Association; Trustee, Scottish Catholic Heritage Collections Trust; Honorary Fellow, Association for Scottish Literary Studies, 2021; Visiting Professor of English, UESTC, Chengdu, China 2017; Fellow of the Royal Society of Edinburgh, 2013; Visiting Research Fellow, All Souls College, Oxford, 2012; Visiting Professor of English, University of Wyoming, 2011-12; Visiting Stuart Scholar, University of Otago, New Zealand, 2012; W. Ormiston Roy Memorial Research Fellow, University of South Carolina, 2002; Principal Investigator, 2 major AHRC grants (£2M FEC) both under the rubric of 'Editing

Robert Burns for the 21st Century', since 2011; President of the Newman Association of the United Kingdom, 2009-2011. Publications include: General Editor, Oxford University Press Edition of The Collected Works of Robert Burns, since 2008; Scottish Literature, A Critical Guide, 2009; Robert Burns, 2006; Editor: The Edinburgh Companion to Robert Burns, 2009; The Devil To Stage: Five Plays by James Bridie, 2007; Burns: Selected Poems, 2006; Co-Editor: Performing Robert Burns: Enactments and Representations of the National Bard, 2021; Literature and Union: Scottish Texts, British Contexts, 2018; The International Companion to John Galt, 2017; Thomas Muir of Huntershill: Essays for the Twenty First Century, 2016; The Burns Encyclopaedia, 2013; The Cambridge Companion to Scottish Literature, 2012; Scotland and the 19th Century World, 2012; Fickle Man: Robert Burns for the 21st Century, 2009; Walter Scott, Reliquiae Trotcosienses, 2004; Beyond Scotland, 2004; English Romanticism and the Celtic World, 2003. Recreations: playing guitar; watching football. Address: Scottish Literature, 7 University Gardens, University of Glasgow; T.-0141 330 4286. E-mail: gerard.carruthers@glasgow.ac.uk

Carruthers, Tomás, MA (Hons). Chief Executive Officer, Project Heather, since 2017. Educ. Royal Grammar School, Newcastle upon Tyne; University of Cambridge. Career history: Co-founder, Director, E*TRADE, 1994-97; founder, Managing Director, Interactive Markets Limited, 1997-98; Chief Executive, Interactive Investor International PLC, 1998-2001; Director, AMP International & Technology Ventures, 2001-03; Chairman, Angelbourse Group PLC, 2003-05; Council Member, The 800 Appeal, University of Cambridge, 2006-2012; Founder and CEO, Interactive Investor, 2003-2012; Co-Founder, SharePrice, 2008-2012; Trustee and British Treasurer, Institute for War and Peace Reporting, 2010-2015; Chief Executive, Social Stock Exchange, 2013-17; Ambassador, Home-Start UK, 2010-19; Trustee: The Tom Bowdidge Youth Cancer Foundation, 2014-19, NEST - National Employment Savings Trust, 2016-19. Address: Bourse Scot Limited, 83 Princes Street, Edinburgh EH2 2ER.

Carslaw, Neil, MA, LLB. Senior Associate Lawyer, Pinsent Masons (Litigation/Dispute Resolution), since 2020. Educ. Kelvinside Academy; University of Aberdeen; University of Law; Law Society of Scotland; The Open University. Career history: Internship Program, Advocacy Forum, Internship, Nepal, 2004; Sales Administrator, ScottishPower, Glasgow, 2004; Irwin Mitchell: Senior Fundraiser, British Red Cross, 2005-07; Legal Administrator, Glasgow, 2007-08; Summer Student, Internship, Sheffield, 2008; Summer Student, DLA Piper, Internship, London, 2008; Pinsent Masons: Internship, London, 2008; Trainee Solicitor, 2010-2012; Solicitor (Litigation/Dispute Resolution), 2012-15; Solicitor (Litigation/Corporate Crime), 2015-16; Associate (Litigation/Corporate Crime), 2016-2020. Address: Pinsent Masons, Princes Exchange, 1 Earl Grey Street, Edinburgh EH3 9AQ; T.-0131 777 7000. E-mail: neil.carslaw@pinsentmasons.com

Carson, Finlay Hamilton, BSc. MSP (Scottish Conservative), Galloway and West Dumfries, since 2016; Convenor of Scottish Parliament committee of Rural Affairs, Island and Natural Environment; b. 18.10.67, Twynholm; 2 c. Educ. Kirkcudbright Academy; University of Aberdeen. Conservative candidate, UK Parliament, for the Dumfries and Galloway constituency in 2015. Address: Scottish Parliament, Edinburgh EH99 1SP.

Carson, Steve, BA (Hons). Director, BBC Scotland, since 2020; b. 1968, Belfast; m., Miriam O'Callaghan. Educ. University of Manchester. Career history: runner and researcher, then Assistant Producer, Manchester and London, BBC Television, 1990-94; Producer/Director, BBC News and Current Affairs, London, 1994-97; Producer/Director, Freelance, Dublin and London, 1997-2000; Managing Director, Mint Productions, Dublin and Belfast, 2000-09; Director of Programmes, RTÉ Television, Dublin, 2009-2013; Head of BBC Northern Ireland Production, Belfast, BBC, 2013-17; Head of Multiplatform Commission, BBC Scotland, 2017-2020. Address: BBC Scotland, 40 Pacific Quay, Glasgow G51 1DA; T.-0141 422 600.

Carswell, William Steven, MA, LLB. Chairman, General Trustees of the Church of Scotland, 1999-2003; retired Director, Association for the Relief of Incurables; former Trustee, Ferguson Bequest Fund (retired); b. 13.7.29, Manchester; m., Jean Lang Sharpe; 2 s. Educ. Hutchesons' Boys' Grammar School; Glasgow University. Legal Assistant, Dunbarton County Council, 1953-56; Legal Assistant, Stirling County Council, 1956-59; Partner, McGrigor Donald, 1960-89. Recreations: golf; walking; cycling. Address: (h.) 37 Hilltree Court, 96 Fenwick Road, Giffnock, Glasgow G46 6AA; T.-0141-638 1286.
E-mail: billcarswell29@gmail.com

Carter, Professor Alan, DPhil (Oxon), MA (Sussex), BA Hons (Kent). Emeritus Professor of Moral Philosophy, University of Glasgow; b. 5.7.52, Lincolnshire. Educ. Monkwearmouth Grammar School; St. Cross College, Oxford. Lecturer in Political Theory, University College Dublin, 1987; Lecturer in Philosophy, Heythrop College, University of London, 1988; Professor of Philosophy and Environmental Studies, University of Colorado at Boulder, 2001; Professor, University of Glasgow, since 2005. Former Board Member of Friends of The Earth Scotland. Publications: 3 books; over 50 articles in academic journals. Recreations: hiking; playing electric guitar; movies. Address: (b.) 69 Oakfield Avenue, Glasgow G12 8LT; T.-0141 330 5692; e-mail: acr@arts.gla.ac.uk

Carter, Professor Sir David Craig, MB, ChB, MD, FRCSEdin, FRCPEdin, FRCSIre (Hon), FACS (Hon), FRCGP (Hon), FCS HIC (Hon), FRACS (Hon), LLD (Hon), FRSEd, FRCGP (Hon), FAcadMedSci, FFPHM, DSc (Hon), LLD (Hon). Chairman, Board for Academic Medicine, Scotland, 2005-2016; Chairman, Managed Service Network for Neurosurgery in Scotland, 2009-13; Chairman, BMA Board of Science, 2002-05; Vice Principal, Edinburgh University, 2000-02; Member, Scientific Executive Board, Cancer Research UK, 2002-04 (Chairman, Programmes and Projects Committees, 2000-04); Trustee, Cancer Research UK, 2004-07; Vice Chairman, Cancer Research UK, 2005-07; President, British Medical Association, 2001-02; Chief Medical Officer (Scotland), 1996-2000; Surgeon to the Queen in Scotland, 1993-97; b. 1.9.40, Penrith; m., Ilske; 2 s. Educ. St. Andrews University. Lecturer in Clinical Surgery, Edinburgh University, 1969-74; 12-month secondment as Lecturer in Surgery, Makerere University, Kampala, Uganda, 1972; Senior Lecturer in Surgery, Edinburgh University, 1974-79; 12-month secondment as Associate Professor of Surgery, University of California, 1976; St. Mungo Professor of Surgery, Glasgow University, 1979-88; Honorary Consultant, Glasgow Royal Infirmary, 1979-88; Regius Professor of Clinical Surgery, Edinburgh University, 1988-96; Honorary Consultant Surgeon, Edinburgh Royal Infirmary, 1988-96. Former Council Member, Royal College of Surgeons of Edinburgh; former Member, Broadcasting Council for Scotland; former Chairman, Scottish Council for Postgraduate Medical and Dental Education; former Co-editor, British Journal of Surgery; Member, Medical Advisory Committee, Higher Education Funding Council, 1994-97; Non-executive Director, Lothian Health Board, 1994-96; President, Surgical Research Society, Association of Surgeons (Great Britain and Ireland), 1996-97; Vice President, Royal Society of Edinburgh, 2000-03; Chairman: The Health Foundation, 2002-08, Queens Nursing Institute, Scotland, 2002-2010. Moynihan Prize, 1973 (Association of Surgeons); James IV Association of Surgeons Travelling Fellow, 1975; Gold Medal, British Medical Association, 2006; Royal Medal, Royal Society of Edinburgh, 2007. Recreation: music. Address: (h.) 19 Buckingham Terrace, Edinburgh EH4 3AD.

Carter, Professor Sara, OBE, FRSE. Vice-Principal and Head of the College of Social Sciences, University of Glasgow, since 2019; Professor of Entrepreneurship; previously Associate Principal (Learning & Teaching), University of Strathclyde; former Head of the Hunter Centre for Entrepreneurship. Holds a number of external appointments as a Board member of the South of Scotland Enterprise Agency; Non-Executive Director of Women's Enterprise Scotland; member of the Enterprise & Skills Strategic Board; served on the Leverhulme Trust Research Awards Advisory Committee; former editor of Entrepreneurship Theory & Practice, 2006-2012; member of the UK Government's Women's Enterprise Taskforce, 2007-09. Awarded OBE for services to women's enterprise in 2008. Publication: Companion to Makers of Modern Entrepreneurship, 2016 (contributor). Address: University of Glasgow, Florentine House, 53 Hillhead Street, Glasgow G12 8QF; T.-0141 330 2943.

Cartwright, Bruce, BCom (Hons). Chief Executive, Institute of Chartered Accountants of Scotland (ICAS), since 2018. Educ. University of Edinburgh. Career: Senior Manager, Corporate Restructuring Team, PwC, 1986-2000; Director, EY, 2000-01; Member of ICAS Council, Institute of Chartered Accountants of Scotland, 2008-2014; Partner, Head of Scottish Corporate Restructuring team, PwC, 2001-2016; Chairman of the ICAS Lothian Borders and Central Area Committee, ICAS - The Professional Body of CAs, 2014-17; Executive Director, Policy Leadership, Institute of Chartered Accountants of Scotland (ICAS), 2017-18. Member of Scottish Committee, Wooden Spoon Charity, since 2002. Address: CA House, 21 Haymarket Yards, Edinburgh EH12 5BH; T.-0131 347 0100.

Carty, Gillian, LLB (Hons). Chair, Shepherd and Wedderburn, since 2020; Partner, since 2001; previously led the firm's Commercial Disputes and Regulation Division and, as a board member, sponsored the firm's People Strategy. Educ. University of Edinburgh; Cranfield University - Cranfield School of Management. Career history: Shepherd and Wedderburn: Trainee Solicitor, Edinburgh, 1993-95, Assistant Solicitor, 1995-99, Associate Solicitor, 1999-2001. Licensed insolvency practitioner; accredited by the Law Society of Scotland as a specialist in insolvency law. Member of Audit Committee, Joint Management Board, Scotland Office/Office of the Advocate General for Scotland, 2015-2021; Member of Audit and Risk Committee, Scottish Fiscal Commission, since 2017. Address: Shepherd and Wedderburn, 1 Exchange Crescent, Conference Square, Edinburgh EH3 8UL; T.-0131 228 9900.

Carwood-Edwards, Jean, MEd. Professional Advisor (Part-time), The Scottish Government, since 2021; former Chief Executive, Early Years Scotland. Educ. University of Glasgow; Jordanhill College. Career: Head of School of Education, James Watt College of Further and Higher Education, 2002-07; Early Years Team Leader, Learning and Teaching Scotland, 2007-2010; Programme Director and Area Adviser, Education Scotland, 2010-2012.

Casely, Gordon, KStJ, FRSA, FHSS, FSAScot. Journalist and heraldist; Baron-Baillie of Miltonhaven; personal herald to the Chief of Irvine; b. 29.6.43, Glasgow; 1 s.; m., Janet McPherson. Educ. Hutchesons' Boys' Grammar School. Reporter, D.C. Thomson & Co. Ltd., Dundee, Aberdeen and Elgin, 1966-68; Evening Express, Aberdeen, 1968-73; PRO, Greater Glasgow Passenger Transport Executive, 1973-78; public affairs posts in banking, local government, offshore and energy industries, 1978-95 (Assistant Director, CBI Scotland, 1988-91). Director, Herald Strategy Ltd., since 1999; Founder Member, Heraldry Society of Scotland, 1977; Press Officer, Commonwealth Games Council for Scotland, 1989-93; Member: Scottish Commonwealth Games Team, Auckland, 1990, Guild Burgess of Aberdeen, 1992; Hon. Vice-President, Lonach Highland and Friendly Society, since 1990; Member, Lonach Pipe Band, 2002-10; President, Aberdeen Welsh Society, 1997-98; Governor, Scottish Tartans Authority, 2003-2011; sub-3 marathoner (London 1991). Publications: magazine contributor and obituarist; I Belong To Glasgow (human history of the Subway), 1975; ed. Who Do You Think You Are? (heraldry in modern Scotland), 2006. Recreations: piping; painting; promoting heraldry; pedalling the continents; poking fun at Abellio ScotRail. Address: (h.) Westerton Cottage, Crathes, Kincardineshire AB31 6LA; T.-07785-333301; e-mail: gcasely@herald-strategy.co.uk

Caskie, Rev. J. Colin, BA, BD. Minister at Rhu and Shandon, 2002-2012; b. 17.8.47, Glasgow; m., Alison McDougall; 2 s.; 1 d. Educ. Knightswood Secondary School; Strathclyde University; Glasgow University. Minister, Penilee: St Andrew, 1977-83; Minister, Carnoustie, 1983-2002; Moderator, Presbytery of Angus, 1995; Chairman, The Duncan Trust, 1992-2002; Vice-Convenor, General Assembly's Board of Stewardship and Finance, 1998-2001, Convenor, 2001-05; Clerk to Presbytery of Dumbarton, 2005-2012; Moderator, Presbytery of Dumbarton, 2011-2012; Clerk to the Presbytery of Perth, 2015-19. Recreations: stamp collecting; gardening. Address: (h.) 13 Anderson Drive, Perth PH1 1JZ.

Casot, Lucy, BA (Hons). Chief Executive Officer, Museums Galleries Scotland, since 2019. Educ. Boroughmuir High School; University of Sheffield. Career history: Archaeologist, The British School at Rome, 1993-98; Curator, Archeological Archives, Royal Commission on the Ancient and Historical Monuments of Scotland, 1999-2001; Head of Heritage Lottery Fund, Scotland, 2001-2018. Address: Museums Galleries Scotland, 2-4 Waterloo Place, Edinburgh EH1 3EG; T.-0131 550 4122.
E-mail: LucyC@museumsgalleriesscotland.org.uk

Catterall, Nicola Jane, BA, ACA, FRSA. Chief Operating Officer, National Galleries Scotland, 2007-2018; Director and Trustee, Dewar Arts Awards; Director and Trustee, National Galleries of Scotland Foundation; former Director and Trustee, Glasgow Sculpture Studios; Faculty & Centre for Visual Arts & Culture (CVAC) Advisory Boards, Durham University; former Director, Artists' Collective Gallery; b. 14.12.58, Holmfirth; 2 d. Educ. George Stephenson High; University of Durham (St. Mary's College). Chartered Accountant, Ernst & Young, 1980-84; various roles in Investment Banking, J.P. Morgan, 1985-98;

Investment Management, Standard Life Investments, 1998-2003; Programme Director for Demutualisation of Standard Life, 2003-2006; Director of Finance, National Galleries of Scotland, 2007. Address: 73 Belford Road, Edinburgh EH4 3DS; T.-0131 624 6202.

Catto, Professor Sir Graeme, FAoP (2020), R.D., Kt, MB, ChB (Hons), MD (Hons), DSc, FRCP, FRCPE, FRCPGlas, FRCGP (Hon), FRSE, FFPM, FMedSci, FRCSE (Hon), FHEA, FAcadMEd. Emeritus Professor of Medicine, Universities of London and Aberdeen, since 2009; Professor of Medicine, University of Aberdeen, 2005-09; Vice-Principal, King's College London, and Dean, Guy's, King's and St. Thomas' Hospitals Medical and Dental Schools, 2000-05; Professor of Medicine, University of London, 2000-05; Pro Vice Chancellor, University of London, 2003-05; President, General Medical Council, 2002-09; Chairman, Robert Gordon's College, 1995-2005; b. 24.4.45, Aberdeen; m., Joan Sievewright; 1 s.; 1 d. Educ. Robert Gordon's College; Aberdeen University. Research Fellow/Lecturer/Senior Lecturer/Reader in Medicine, Aberdeen University, 1970-88; Harkness Fellow of Commonwealth Fund of New York, 1975-77 (Fellow in Medicine, Harvard Medical School and Peter Bent Brigham Hospital, Boston); Aberdeen University: Professor in Medicine and Therapeutics, 1988-2000, Dean, Faculty of Clinical Medicine, 1992-98, Vice-Principal, 1995-2000; Vice Chairman, Aberdeen Royal Hospitals NHS Trust, 1992-99; Chief Scientist, NHS in Scotland, 1997-2000; Member, Scottish Higher Education Funding Council, 1996-2002; Member, General Medical Council, Education and Standard Committees, 1994-2002 (Chairman, Education, 1999-2002); Treasurer, Academy of Medical Sciences, 1998-2001; Governor, PPP Medical Foundation, 2000-02; Member, SE London Strategic Health Authority, 2002-05; Member, Council for the Regulation of Healthcare Professionals; Hon. DSc, St Andrews University, 2003; Hon. LLD, Aberdeen University, 2002; Hon. MD, University of Southampton, 2004; Hon. DSc, Robert Gordon University, 2004; Hon. FRCGP, 2000; Hon. FRCSE, 2002; Fellow, King's College London, 2005; Hon. DSc, University of Kent, 2007; Hon. DSc, South Bank University, 2008; Hon DSc, University of London, 2009; Hon. MD, University of Brighton, 2010; Hon MD, University of Buckingham, 2015; President, College of Medicine, 2010-14; Chairman, Scottish Stem Cell Network, 2008-2011; Chairman, Higher Education Better Regulation Group, 2009-2012; President, Association for the Study of Medical Education, 2009-2013; Member, Qatar Council for Healthcare Practitioners, since 2013; Co-Chair, Review Group on Medical and Dental School Intakes in England, 2011-2012; Member, Commission on Assisted Dying, 2010-11; Chairman, Dignity in Dying, 2012-15; Chairman, Lathallan School, 2012-2017; Member, Joint Advisory Board, Weill Cornell Medicine - Qatar, since 2017; Trustee, iMedTrust, since 2012; Fellow, Association of Physicians, 2021. Recreations: hills and glens. Address: Maryfield, Glenbuchat, Strathdon, Aberdeenshire AB36 8TS; T.-0197 56 41317.

Catto, Joan, MBE, DL, MUniv, LLB, NP; b. 30.4.46, Aberdeen; m., Sir Graeme Catto; 1 s.; 1 d. Educ. Aberdeen High School for Girls; Aberdeen University. Qualified as a solicitor in 1968; career in Aberdeen (apart from two years in the US); Partner, Burnett & Reid, 1990-2002; Partner, Ledingham Chalmers, 2002-08, Consultant, 2008-10; Chairman, Social Security Appeal Tribunal, 1983-98; Chairman, Child Support Appeal Tribunal, 1998-2002; Founder member, Scottish Family Law Association, 1980-2008; Founder board member, Scottish Children's Reporter Administration, 1992-98; Safeguarder in Sheriff Courts (including 1990s Orkney cases) and Children's Panels, 1980-99; Court reporter, Aberdeen Sheriff Court re contact & custody cases, 1980-2002; Member, Scottish Legal

Group of British Agencies for Adoption & Fostering, 1980-2008; listed as a Leader in the field of Family Law, Chambers' Legal Directory, 1995-2005; Vice-Chairman, Grampian Healthcare NHS Trust, 1993-1999; Assessor, Dean of Guild, City of Aberdeen, 1999-2007; Member, Group of Friends, Mither Kirk Project, Aberdeen, 2000-2010; Member, University Court, University of Aberdeen, 2002-10; Convener, formerly Member, Business Committee, University of Aberdeen, 1994-2010; Local Chairman, RSNO Circle, 2004-2012; Board Member, then Chair, Voluntary Service Aberdeen, 2010-16, Honorary Vice President, since 2016; Committee Member, Grampian Hospitals Arts Trust, since 2017; President, Granite City Ladies Probus Club, 2018-19, Past President, since 2019; Member, Board of Friends, Aberdeen Cyrenians (charity for the homeless); Member, fund-raising team, Red Cross, Aberdeen; commissioned as Deputy Lieutenant for City of Aberdeen, November 2015; Accredited specialist in Child Law, 1993, and in Family Law, 1994; awarded MUniv by University of Aberdeen, June 2016; appointed MBE, June 2016 (for services to disadvantaged children and young adults in Scotland). Recreations: needlework of all kinds; English setters; R&R in Glenbuchat. Address: (h.) 4 Woodend Avenue, Aberdeen AB15 6YL; T.-01224 310509; e-mail: joancatto@btinternet.com

Catto, Simon James Dawson, LLB (Hons), DipLP, NP. Head of Litigation (Scotland), Addleshaw Goddard LLP, since 2017; Solicitor-Advocate, since 2007; b. 21.5.72, Aberdeen; m., Caroline; 1 d. Educ. Robert Gordon's College, Aberdeen; Edinburgh University. Ledingham Chalmers, Aberdeen: Trainee Solicitor, 1995-97, Solicitor, 1997-2002; Partner, Ledingham Chalmers, Edinburgh, 2002-06. Burgess of Guild of The City of Aberdeen. Recreations: music; sport; travel. Address: (b.) Addleshaw Goddard LLP, Exchange Tower, 19 Canning Street, Edinburgh EH3 8EH; T.-0131 228 2400.

Cawdor, 7th Earl of (Colin Robert Vaughan Campbell); b. 30.6.62; m., Lady Isabella Stanhope; 1 s.; 3 d. Succeeded to title, 1993. Educ. Eton; St. Peter's College, Oxford.

Cha, Sang Y., BTh, MTh, FRSA. Parish Minister, St. Mungo's, Alloa, since 2011; b. 2.2.77, Seoul, South Korea. Educ. University of Cambridge, Selwyn College; University of Edinburgh. New College; University of Cambridge, Fitzwilliam College. Coordinated client public relations, logistics and planning in film/TV projects, William Morris Agency, Inc., Beverly Hills, CA, USA, 1999-2000; Vice-President of Talent and Development, JS Entertainment, Inc., Studio City, CA, USA, 2001-2002; instructed English grammar and writing (basic and advanced), Americorps National Service Project, Anchorage, AK, USA, 2002-03; Church of Scotland, Cambridge, Edinburgh, Alloa, since 2006. University of Cambridge Divinity Faculty Board, 2007-08; Member of the Board of Trustees, Presbytery of Stirling Strategy Committee; Voting Member of the Council, Clackmannanshire Council's Education, Sport and Leisure Committee, since 2012; Member: Clackmannanshire County Cricket Club; Scottish Conservative Party; Chaplain to: Redwell Primary School, Alloa Academy, Park Primary School; Board of Trustees to Clackmannanshire County Cricket Club; Moderator of Presbytery of Stirling for 2019; ABC Nursery Chaplain; Church of Scotland supervisor for candidates in training; Board of Trustees: Connect Alloa, Forth Valley Welcome. Recreations: jazz; saxophone; certified bow hunter and archery enthusiast; tennis; staying busy with 2 border collies; love to work with children and the elderly. Address: The Manse, 37A Claremont, Alloa FK10 2DG; T.-01259 723004; e-mail: syc@cantab.net

Chalmers, Douglas, PhD, MA (Hons), FHEA. Caledonian Scholar; President of University and College Union Scotland, June 2015-June 2017; President of University and College Union (UK), June 2019-2020;

Senior Lecturer, Department of Media and Journalism, Glasgow Caledonian University, since 2002; Member of Mercator European Research Centre Database of Experts on Scottish Gaelic and Economic and Social Impact of language, arts and culture; b. 22.6.57, Dundee; m., Mhairi McGowan; 2 s.; 1 d. Educ. Kirkton High School, Dundee; Dundee University. National Organiser, Young Communist League, 1981-83; General Secretary, Young Communist League, 1983-85; Scottish Organiser, Communist Party, 1985-88; Scottish Secretary, Communist Party, 1988-91; Convener, Democratic Left Scotland, 1991-95; Researcher, Glasgow Caledonian University, 1996-2002; Executive Member, Scottish Constitutional Convention, 1989-95; Secretary, Campaign for a Scottish Parliament 1992-1993; Member, Council, Scottish Civic Forum, 2001-05, Board Member, 2001-05; Member, Broadcasting Council for Scotland, 2005-07, Audience Council Scotland, 2007-2010; Member, University Senate, 2012-2020; Member, University Court, since 2013. Recreations: politics; community; family; sport; musician; languages. Address: (b.) Glasgow Caledonian University, 70 Cowcaddens Road, Glasgow G4 0BA; T.-0141 331 3350 (GCU); 07989 477570 (UCU); e-mail: d.chalmers@gcu.ac.uk or dchalmers@ucu.org.uk
http://www.gcu.ac.uk/gsbs/staff/drdouglaschalmers/

Chalmers, John, LLB, DipLP. Partner, Ledingham Chalmers, since 2004; b. 11.63. Educ. Elgin Academy; University of Aberdeen. Career history: trained with Cochrane & Blair Paterson SSC; qualified in 1987; Solicitor, Cochrane & Blair Paterson SSC, 1987-94; A&WM Urquhart WS, 1994-2001; joined Ledingham Chalmers in 2001. Extended Rights of Audience (Civil) granted in 2008; Member of the Scottish Law Agents Society and the British Insurance Law Association. Recreations: modern history; Scottish art; golf; hill walking; skiing. Address: Ledingham Chalmers, 3rd Floor, 68-70 George Street, Edinburgh EH2 2LR; T.-0131 200 1052.
E-mail: john.chalmers@ledinghamchalmers.com

Chalmers, Very Rev. John Pearson, BD, DD (Hon). Convener of the Church of Scotland Assembly Trustees, since 2019; Principal Clerk to the General Assembly of the Church of Scotland (2010-2017); Moderator of the General Assembly of the Church of Scotland (2014-2015); Chaplain in Ordinary to HM The Queen; Patron of Donaldson's School; Patron of Place for Hope; b. 5.6.52, Bothwell; m., Elizabeth; 2 s.; 1 d. Educ. Marr College; Strathclyde University; Glasgow University. Minister, Renton Trinity, 1979-86; Clerk, Dumbarton Presbytery, 1982-86; Minister, Palmerston Place, Edinburgh, 1986-95; Deputy General Secretary, Board of Ministry, Church of Scotland, 1995-2001; Pastoral Adviser and Associate Secretary, Ministries Council, Church of Scotland, 2001-2010. Recreations: golf; bee-keeping. Address: (b.) 121 George Street, Edinburgh EH2 4YN; T.-0131-225 5722.
E-mail: jchalmers@churchofscotland.org.uk

Chalmers, Michael, LLB (Hons), DipLP, LLM. Director for Children and Families, The Scottish Government, since 2017. Educ. University of Edinburgh. Career: Solicitor, Dundas & Wilson, 1997-2005; Branch Head, Litigation, The Scottish Government, 2007-09; Solicitor (Scotland) to HM Revenue & Customs, 2009-11; Director of the Office of the Advocate General and Solicitor to the Advocate General, 2012-17. Address: Scottish Government, Children & Families Directorate, Victoria Quay, Edinburgh EH6 6QQ; T.-0131 244 5444.

Chamberlain, Wendy, MA (Hons). MP (Liberal Democrat), since 2019; 20.12.76, Greenock; m., Keith; 2 c. Educ. Greenock Academy; University of Edinburgh. Career history: Lothian and Borders Police: Police Constable, 1999-2005, Investors in People Coordinator,

2005-07; Part-time Communications Lecturer, Carnegie College, 2006-07; Business Support Manager - HR and Development Business Area, Association of Chief Police Officers in Scotland, 2007-2010; Business Management Unit Project Officer, Scottish Police Services Authority, 2010-2011; Regional Employment and Training Manager (Scotland), Career Transition Partnership (Right Management), 2013-15; Diageo, Capability Development Manager, 2015-18; Capability Specialist, 2018-19. Address: Houses of Parliament, Westminster, London SW1A 0AA.

Chambers, Professor Helen Elizabeth, MA, PhD. Emeritus Professor of German, St Andrews University; b. 4.3.47, Glasgow; m., Hugh Rorrison; 2 s. Educ. Hutchesons' Girls' Grammar School, Glasgow; Glasgow University; Freiburg University. Lecturer, then Senior Lecturer in German, Leeds University, 1972-99; Visiting Lecturer in German, Melbourne University, 1998. Publications: Supernatural and Irrational Elements in the Works of Theodor Fontane, 1980; Co-existent Contradictions: Joseph Roth in Retrospect (Editor), 1991; Theodor Fontane: The London Symposium (Co-Editor), 1995; T. Fontane, Effi Briest (Co-Translator), 1995; The Changing Image of Theodor Fontane, 1997; Theodor Fontane and the European Context (Co-Editor), 2001; Violence, Culture and Identity (Editor), 2006; Humor and Irony in Nineteenth-Century German Women's Writing, 2007; T. Fontane, No Way Back (Co-Translator), 2010; Fontane-Studien, 2014. Recreations: theatre; film; travel. Address: (b.) School of Modern Languages, St Andrews University, St Andrews KY16 9PH; T.- 01334 463670.

Chambers, Rev. Samuel John, OBE, BSc. Retired Church of Scotland Minister; b. 3.4.44, Banbridge, Co. Down, Northern Ireland; m., Anne; 2 s.; 1 d. Educ. Banbridge Academy; Annadale Grammar School, Belfast; Queen's University Belfast; Presbyterian College, Belfast. Minister, Presbyterian Church in Ireland, 1972-84, Belfast, Donegal and Comber, Co. Down; Chairman, East Belfast Youth Council, 1972-73; Chief Executive, Relate, Northern Ireland, 1984-98; Chairman, International Commission on Marriage and Interpersonal Relationships, 1994-98; Church of Scotland Minister, Ness Bank Church of Scotland, Inverness, 1998-2009. Contributions to Journal of Sexual and Marital Therapy; presenter 'Thought for the day', Radio Ulster, 1979-98, Radio Scotland, 1998-2009. Recreations: golf; travel; hill walking. Address: (h.) Bannlagan Lodge, 4 Earls Cross Gardens, Dornoch, Sutherland IV25 3NR; T.-01862 811520.

Chandler, Glenn. Playwright and novelist; b. 1949, Edinburgh. Educ. Royal High School, Edinburgh. Written plays for theatre and radio, original screenplays for television and films, television series, and novels. Moved from Scotland to London and began writing for the Soho Poly, where his early plays were produced; went on to write for BBC Television and Radio, and for Granada Television (including its series Crown Court (TV series)) before creating and writing his own series Taggart for STV Productions (ITV Network). Awards: BAFTA (1991), Taggart (winner of Best Drama Serial Award); Writers' Guild of Great Britain Award (1993) (winner of Best Original Drama Serial); BAFTA (1995), nominated Best TV Writer; BAFTA (1997), Taggart nominated for Best Drama Serial Award. Address: MBA Literary Agents, 62 Grafton Way, London W1T 5DW.

Chaplain, Professor Mark Andrew Joseph, BSc (Hons), PhD, FRSE. Gregory Chair of Mathematics, University of St Andrews, since 2015; b. 1.5.64, Dundee; m., Fiona; 3 s. Educ. St John's RC High School, Dundee; Dundee University. Lecturer, School of Mathematical Sciences, Bath University, 1990-96; Senior Lecturer, Department of Maths, Dundee University, 1996-98; Reader in Mathematical Biology, Dundee University, 1998-2000; former Ivory Chair of Applied Mathematics, Dundee University, Head of Mathematics Division, 2006-2012. Whitehead Prize, London Mathematical Society, 2000; recipient of 2014 Lee Segel Prize from The Society of Mathematical Biology. Publications: On Growth and Form: Spatio-Temporal Pattern Formation in Biology; Polymer and Cell Dynamics: Multiscale modelling and numerical simulations. Recreations: golf; squash; badminton; tennis. Address: (b.) School of Mathematics and Statistics, University of St Andrews, Mathematical Institute, North Haugh, St Andrews KY16 9SS.

Chapman, Douglas. MP (SNP), Dunfermline and West Fife, since 2015; SNP Small Business, Enterprise and Innovation spokesperson; b. 5.1.55; m.; 2 c. Educ. West Calder High; Edinburgh Napier University. Career history: worked for 18 years in financial services before getting involved in politics; has lived in the Dunfermline area since 1990, serving as a councillor for Rosyth and North Queensferry ward on Fife Council for eight years where he held the role of Chair of Education and Children's Services and latterly COSLA Spokesperson on Education, Children and Young People, 2007-2015; worked for Bruce Crawford MSP, 1999-2005; Campaign Manager, SNP HQ, 2006-07. As an MP, served on the Public Accounts Committee, Defence Select Committee and was a member of the NATO Parliamentary Assembly. Currently Chairs the APPG on the Nordic Council and Arctic Council. Address: House of Commons, London SW1A 0AA; T.-020 7219 6888; Constituency Office - 16 Cromarty Campus, Rosyth Europarc, Rosyth KY11 2WX T.-01383324775.
E-mail: douglas.chapman.mp@parliament.uk

Chapman, Professor John N., MA, PhD, FInstP, FIEEE, FRSE. Emeritus Vice Principal and Professor, Physics and Astronomy, Glasgow University, since 2014; formerly Vice Principal and Head of College of Science and Engineering; b. 21.11.47, Sheffield; m., Judith M.; 1 s.; 1 d. Educ. King Edward VII School, Sheffield; St. John's College and Fitzwilliam College, Cambridge. Research Fellow, Fitzwilliam College, Cambridge; Lecturer, Glasgow University. Recreations: photography; walking; tennis. Address: (b.) Kelvin Building, Glasgow University, Glasgow G12 8QQ; T.-0141-330 4462.
E-mail: john.chapman@glasgow.ac.uk

Chapman, Maggie. MSP (Scottish Green Party), North East (Region), since 2021; Scottish Greens spokesperson for Justice, Equality, Human Rights and Economy; Vice-Convener of the Scottish Parliament Equalities, Human Rights and Civil Justice Committee; member of the Scottish Parliament Economy and Fair Work Committee; member of the Scottish Parliament Corporate Body; former Rector, Aberdeen University, 2015-2021; former Convener, Scottish Independence Convention, 2019-2021; b. 27.6.79, Harare, Zimbabwe. Educ. University of Edinburgh; Stirling University. Career history: Lecturer in cultural geography, environmental ethics and social justice, Edinburgh Napier University, 2006-2015; former Vice President of the Educational Institute of Scotland's University Lecturers' Association; Councillor for the Leith Walk Ward in Edinburgh, 2007-2015; first-ever convener of the Petitions Committee; Co-convener, Scottish Green Party, 2013-19; Chief Executive, Scottish Council on Visual Impairment (SCOVI), 2017-19; Chief Operating Officer, Edinburgh Rape Crisis Centre, 2020-2021. Recreations: plays the fiddle; violin and accordion; enjoys exploring Scotland. Address: The Scottish Parliament, Edinburgh EH99 1SP;

T.-0131 348 6332.
E-mail: Maggie.Chapman.msp@parliament.scot

Chapman, Peter John, MSP (Scottish Conservative), North East Scotland region, 2016-2021; Shadow Cabinet Secretary for Rural Economy and Connectivity, 2016-18; b. 13.5.50. Conservative candidate in Banffshire and Buchan Coast in the 2016 Scottish Parliament election.

Chapman, Phil. Director of Operations, Police Investigations and Review Commissioner, since 2021. Career history: Police Officer, Grampian Police/Police Scotland, 1991-2021; Police Scotland: DCS, Senior Investigating Officer (Misconduct), Scotland, 2014-15, Detective Chief Superintendent, Senior Investigating Officer, Northern Ireland, 2015-2021, Detective Chief Superintendent, Head of Organised Crime and Counter Terrorism, Scotland, 2019-2021. Address: Hamilton House, Hamilton Business Park, Caird Park, Hamilton ML3 0QA; T.-01698 542900.

Chapman, Professor Robert, BSc, PhD, CPhys, FInstP. Emeritus Professor of Physics, University of the West of Scotland, since 2011; b. 10.8.41, Holytown; m., Norma Gilchrist Hope; 3 d. Educ. Bellshill Academy; University of Glasgow. UKAEA Research Fellow, AWRE, Aldermaston, and AERE, Harwell, 1966-70; University of Manchester: Lecturer, 1970-75, Senior Lecturer, 1975-87, Reader in Physics, 1987-93; Paisley University: Head, Department of Physics, 1993-96, Head, Department of Electronic Engineering and Physics, 1996-2000, Head, School of Information and Communication Technologies, 2000-03, Acting Vice Principal, Research and Commercialisation, 2004-06. Publications: in excess of 200 research papers. Recreations: walking; gardening; listening to music. Address: (b.) University of the West of Scotland, Paisley PA1 2BE; T.-0141-848 3600.
E-mail: robert.chapman@uws.ac.uk

Charlesworth, Professor Brian, BA, PhD, FRS, FRSE, Foreign Associate, US National Academy of Sciences. Senior Honorary Professorial Fellow, Edinburgh University, since 2007; b. 29.4.45, Brighton; m., Deborah Maltby; 1 d. Educ. Haberdashers' Aske's Elstree School; Queens' College, Cambridge. Post-doctoral Fellow, University of Chicago, 1969-71; Lecturer, Genetics, University of Liverpool, 1971-74; Lecturer, Biology, Sussex University, 1974-82; Reader in Biology, Sussex University, 1982-84; Professor of Biology, University of Chicago, 1985-92; G.W. Beadle Distinguished Service Professor of Ecology and Evolution, University of Chicago, 1992-97; Royal Society Research Professor, Edinburgh University, 1997-2007. Darwin Medal, The Royal Society, 2000. Publications: Evolution in Age-structured Populations, 1994; co-author, Evolution: A Very Short Introduction, 2003; co-author, Elements of Evolutionary Genetics, 2010. Recreations: walking; listening to classical music. Address: (b.) Institute of Evolutionary Biology, Edinburgh University, The King's Buildings, Edinburgh EH9 3FL; T.-0131-650 5751.

Charteris, Ruth, QC, LLB (Hons), DipLP. Solicitor General for Scotland, since 2021; b. 1973. Educ. University of Glasgow. Career history: admitted as an advocate in 2000, then a Queen's Counsel (QC) in 2020; an Ad hoc Advocate Depute, 2010-2016; served as an Advocate Depute, since October 2020; legally qualified Chair of the Scottish Social Services Council, since 2017; served as the Legal Assistant to the Lord President; a Standing Junior to the Scottish Government, since 2012; Chair of the Fitness to

Practice Panel of the SSSC, since 2017. Address: Crown Office, 25 Chambers Street, Edinburgh EH1 1LA; T.-0300 020 3000.

Cherry, Joanna. MP (SNP), Edinburgh South West, since 2015; Deputy Chair, Joint Lords and Commons Committee on Human Rights; Justice and Home Affairs spokesperson in the House of Commons, 2015-2021; b. 18.3.66. Educ. University of Edinburgh. Worked as a research assistant with the Scottish Law Commission (1990) before practising as a solicitor with the Edinburgh legal firm Brodies until 1995; worked as a part-time tutor in constitutional law, family law and civil court practice at the University of Edinburgh, 1990-1996; admitted as an advocate in 1995, with a particular interest in employment and industrial relations, health and safety, mental health, personal injury and professional negligence; served as a Standing Junior Counsel to the Scottish Government, 2003-2008, and as an Advocate Depute and Senior Advocate Depute, 2008-2011; appointed a Queen's Counsel in 2009; limited practice as an Advocate with the Arnot Manderson stable within the Faculty of Advocates. Set up the "Lawyers for Yes" campaign group in 2014. Lead litigant in the successful 'Cherry Case' against the unlawful prorogation of parliament in 2019. Hon Bencher, Middle Temple. Address: House of Commons, London SW1A 0AA.

Cheyne, George Martin Frazer, BSc, DUniv. Chair, NHS 24, since 2020; Chair, NHS Ayshire & Arran Health Board, 2012-19; Chair, Grameen in the UK, 2011-15; b. 17.5.44, Ayr; m., Beatrice; 1 s.; 1 d. Educ. Ayr Academy; Strathclyde University. Over 30 years with ICI of which 20 years abroad managing ICI businesses in Dubai, Zambia, Chile, Hong Kong, and Mexico as CEO or MD; Chair of Court, Glasgow Caledonian University, 2005-2011. Past Vice Chair, Lloyds TSB Foundation for Scotland; Past Chair, Ayrshire Council on Alcohol, former Board Member; Captain, Royal Troon Golf Club, 2015-17. Recreation: golf. Address: (h.) 65 Gailes Road, Troon KA10 6TB; T.-01292 317442.
E-mail: mcheyne17@yahoo.co.uk

Chick, Jonathan Dale, MA (Cantab), MBChB, MPhil, DSc (Edin), FRCPE, FRCPsych. Consultant Psychiatrist, Royal Edinburgh Hospital and Senior Lecturer, Dept. of Psychiatry, Edinburgh University, 1979-2010; Honorary Professor, Queen Margaret University, 2009-2016; Visiting Professor, Edinburgh Napier University, 2016-2019; Medical Director, Castle Craig Hospital Scotland; b. 23.4.45, Wallasey; 2 s. Educ. Queen Elizabeth Grammar School, Darlington; Corpus Christi College, Cambridge; Edinburgh University. Posts in Edinburgh teaching hospitals, 1971-76; scientific staff, MRC Unit for Epidemiological Studies in Psychiatry, 1976-79. Chief Editor, Alcohol and Alcoholism; Hon. Life Fellow, Soc. Study Addiction and French Society for Addictology; awarded Royal College of Psychiatrists Research Medal and Prize. Publications: numerous research papers; two books. Recreation: music.

Chillingworth, David Robert, BA (Mod), TCD, MA (Oxon), DD (Hon) (Univ of The South, Sewanee). Bishop of St. Andrews, Dunkeld and Dunblane, 2005-2017; Primus of the Scottish Episcopal Church, 2009-2017; b. 23.6.51, Dublin, Ireland; m., Alison; 2 s.; 1 d. Educ. Portora Royal School, Enniskillen; Royal Belfast Academical Institution; Trinity College, Dublin; Oriel College, Oxford; Ripon College, Cuddesdon. Curate Assistant, Holy Trinity, Joanmount, Belfast (Connor), 1976-79; Church of Ireland Youth Officer, 1979-83; Curate Assistant, Bangor Abbey (Down and Dromore), 1983-86; Rector, Seagoe Parish Church, Portadown, 1986-2005; Dean of Dromore, 1995-2002; Archdeacon of Dromore, 2002-05. Recreations: music; sailing; cycling; reading; travel. Address: 9 Almondhill Steading, Kirkliston EH29 9LA; e-mail: david@chillingworth.org.uk

Chisholm, Duncan Fraser, OStJ, JP (Retd). Director, Duncan Chisholm & Sons Ltd., Inverness; President, Inverness Nairn Badenoch Scout District, 2021; Member of Clan Council of The Clan Chisholm Association; Chairman, The Kiltmakers Association of Scotland Ltd., 2000-2014; Justice for Sheriffdom of Grampian, Highlands and Islands, 1989-2011; Member, Order of St. John, since 2003; Member, Inverness St. Columba New Charge Commission of Church of Scotland, 2009-2021; Member, The Highland Society of London; Director, Inverness City Business Improvement District Ltd., 2009-2012; b. 14.4.41, Inverness; m., Mary Rebecca MacRae (deceased 2018); 1 s.; 1 d. Educ. Inverness High School. Member, Inverness District Council, 1984-92; Member, Board of Governors, Eden Court Theatre, Inverness, 1984-88; President, Inverness and Highland Chamber of Commerce, 1983-84 (Vice-President, 1982-83); Member, Highland TAVRA Committee, 1988-92; Vice-Chairman, Inverness, Loch Ness and Nairn Tourist Board, 1988-96; President, Clan Chisholm Society, 1978-89; Chairman, Inverness Town Twinning Committee, 1992-98; Member, Management Committee: Highland Export Club, 1998-2008, Inverness Project Board Member, 1997-2007; GSL, Scout Association, 1969-2021 (Scout Leader, 1960-69); Session Clerk, St. Columba High Church, Inverness, 2001-2010. Recreations: swimming; music; painting. Address: (b.) 47-51 Castle Street, Inverness; T.-01463 234599; e-mail: Duncan@kilts.co.uk

Chisholm, Malcolm. MSP (Labour), Edinburgh North and Leith, 1999-2016; Minister for Health and Community Care, 2001-04, Minister for Communities, 2004-06; MP (Labour), Edinburgh North and Leith (formerly Edinburgh Leith), 1992-2001; b. 7.3.49; m.; 2 s.; 1 d. Former teacher. Parliamentary Under-Secretary of State, Scottish Office (Minister for Local Government, Housing and Transport) 1997 (resigned over cuts).

Choudhury, Foysol, MBE. MSP (Scottish Labour), Lothian (Region), since 2021; Shadow Minister for Culture, Europe and International Development; b. 5.1.69, Bangladesh; m., Tahmina; 1 s.; 1 d. Educ. Drummon High School; Habiganj Government High School. Career history: charity fundraiser and organiser, since 1990; Joint GS, Zukta-Razya Nabigonj Education Trust UK, since 1990; Chairman, Guild of Bangladeshi Restauranteurs of Scotland, since 1995; Founding Member, Edinburgh Mela Ltd, since 1995; Chairman, Bangladesh Samity Edinburgh, since 2010; General Secretary of the Council of Bangladeshis in Scotland. Parliamentary Candidate, Labour Party, 2017 United Kingdom general election; Chair, Edinburgh and Lothians Regional Equality Council (ELREC), since 2000; Councillor, New Town and Broughton Community Council, 2016-2020. Worked on several successful fundraising campaigns raising over 1 million for causes including Bangladesh Cyclone Appeal in Scotland, St Columba's Hospice, Leukaemia & Cancer appeal, Sick Kids Hospital appeal, British Heart Foundation, Indian Earthquake appeal, Tsunami appeal, Cycling for refugees and many others. Appointed a Member of the Order of the British Empire (MBE) in the 2004 New Year Honours for services to the community. Recreations: avid sports enthusiast and is involved in several sporting events and sponsored sports uniforms to schools; active footballer, snooker and badminton player and has won several trophies and medals; supporter of Heart of Midlothian FC and Manchester United FC. Address: The Scottish Parliament, Edinburgh EH99 1SP; T.-0131 348 6761; e-mail: Foysol.Choudhury.msp@parliament.scot

Christie, John, MTheol, DipEd. Educational consultant, since 2002; Director of Lifelong Learning, Scottish Borders Council, 2001-02 (Director of Education, 1995-2001); Non-Executive Director, Learning and Teaching Scotland, 2000-04; b. 25.12.53, Edinburgh; m., Katherine; 2 d. Educ. Daniel Stewart's College; St. Andrews University;

Edinburgh University; Moray House College of Education. Teacher, 1977-83; Principal Assistant, Stockport MBC, 1983-85; Assistant Director of Education, then Depute Director of Education, Tayside Regional Council, 1985-95. Hon. Treasurer, Association of Directors of Education in Scotland, 1995-2002; Member: Health Education Board for Scotland, 1991-97, Advisory Committee on Scottish Qualification for Headship, since 1999, Scotland Against Drugs Primary School Initiative, COSLA/SEED Group on Value-Added in Schools; Non-Executive Director, Scottish Consultative Council on the Curriculum, 1995-2000. E-mail: jchristie@tinyworld.co.uk

Christie, Very Rev. John Cairns, BSc, BD (Hons), PGCertEd, CBiol, MRSB. Clerk to the Presbytery of Dumbarton, 2018; Moderator of the General Assembly of the Church of Scotland, 2011-2012; Interim Minister, Old Cumnock: Trinity; Kilmacolm: Old Kirk; Arisaig and the Small Isles linked with Mallaig St. Columba's and Knoydart; West Kilbride; Lausanne: St. Andrew; Greenock: Finnart St Paul's; Paisley: Oakshaw Trinity; Church of Scotland Minister, Hyndland Parish Church, Glasgow, 1990-2004; Convener: Church of Scotland Board of Parish Education, 2001-05, Joint Committee for Safety and Protection of Children, 2001-05, Safeguarding Committee, 2005-2010; Teacher, 1972-86; b. 9.7.47, Glasgow; m., (1) Elizabeth McDonald McIntosh (died 1993); 1 d. Elizabeth Margaret; (2) Annette Cooke Carnegie Evans (nee Hamill). Educ. Hermitage School, Helensburgh; University of Strathclyde; Jordanhill College; University of Glasgow. Teacher, Albert Secondary School, Springburn, Glasgow, 1973-76, Assistant Principal Teacher, Guidance, 1976-78; Principal Teacher of Science, Tiree High School, 1978-84; Warden, Dalneigh Hall of Residence, 1984-86; Upper Second Honours Degree in New Testament and Systematic Theology, University of Glasgow, 1986-90; Probationer Assistant Minister, Mosspark Parish Church, 1989-90; Qualified Church Mediator; regular contributor to BBC Scotland 'Thought for the Day'. Recreations: hill-walking; reading; radio; tv; DIY; gardening.

Chrystie, Kenneth, LLB (Hons), PhD. Trustee, Hugh Fraser Foundation (former Chairman); Depute Chair, Glasgow School of Art Development Board; Past President, Royal Glasgow Institute of the Fine Arts; b. 24.11.46, Glasgow; m., Mary; 1 s.; 2 d. Educ. Duncanrig Senior Secondary; University of Glasgow; University of Virginia. Joined McClure Naismith, 1968. Publications: contributor to Encyclopedia of Scots Law, Labour Law Handbook and other legal publications. Recreations: golf (Prestwick, Glasgow and Boat of Garten Golf Clubs); curling; tennis. Address: 2 Redlands Road, Glasgow G12 0SJ; T.-0141 339 2757; e-mail: kgchrystie@icloud.com

Churchill, Professor Robin, LLB, LLM, PhD. Emeritus Professor of International Law, University of Dundee (Professor, since 2006); b. 02.02.47, Pulham Market, Norfolk; m., Margaret Churchill (nee Powell); 1 s.; 1 d. Educ. King Edward VI, Norwich; University College London. Research Officer in International Law, British Institute of International and Comparative Law, London, 1970-77; Lecturer, Senior Lecturer, Reader and Professor of Law, Cardiff University, 1977-2006; Visiting Professorial Fellow, University of Wollongong, Australia, 2005-06; Lecturer, University of Tromsø, Norway, 1983-84. Publications: Author of 4 books and nearly 150 papers on International and EU Law. Recreations: walking; cycling; bird watching; music; campanology. Address: 3, Balmanno Entry, Auchterarder, Perthshire PH3 1FW; T.-01764 662650; e-mail: r.r.churchill@dundee.ac.uk

Clancy, Rev. P. Jill, BD, DipMin. Full-Time Prison Chaplain at HMP Barlinnie, since July 2017; b. 10.7.70, Irvine; m., Frank J. Clancy. Educ. Kilwinning Academy; Aberdeen University. YTS, Cunningham District Council; Rating Clerk, Northern Ireland Trailers; Distribution

Assistant, Caledonian Paper Mill; Minister of Religion, St. John's Church of Scotland, Gourock, 2000-08; Tron St. Mary's Church of Scotland, Balornock, Glasgow, 2008-2013; Annbank linked with Tarbolton Parish Church of Scotland, 2013-17; Part-Time Chaplain, HMP Kilmarnock, 2013-2020. Recreations: plays piano; plays saxophone; sings and is a Musical Director of a Community Choir called 'Songs for All'.

Clapham, David Charles, LLB, SSC. Solicitor (qualified 1981, founded own legal practice 1984, sole principal of David C Clapham, 1984-2007, then partner in Claphams Solicitors, 2007-2015); Consultant to Claphams, since 2015; Fee paid Judge in the First Tier Tribunal in the Social Entitlement Chamber (1992-2021) and in the Immigration and Asylum Chamber (2001-2021); Part Time Sheriff (appointed 2007); Secretary of Local Valuation Panel for Glasgow, Dunbartonshire and Argyll and Bute (appointed 1996) and of the former Strathclyde Region Local Valuation Panel (1988-96); Legal Member of Mental Health Tribunal for Scotland (appointed 2005); Legal Assessor to Nursing and Midwifery Council (2011-2021); Legal Adviser to General Dental Council (appointed 2016); b. 16.10.58, Giffnock; m., Debra; 1 s.; 2 d. Educ. Hutchesons' Grammar School and the University of Strathclyde. Glasgow Bar Association: President, 1992-93. Address: 1B/1C Helena House, Clarkston Toll, Glasgow G76 7RA.

Clark of Calton, (Baroness M. Lynda Clark), QC, LLB, PhD. Judge of the Court of Session in Scotland, since 2006; Advocate-General for Scotland, 1999-2006; MP (Labour), Edinburgh Pentlands, 1997-2005; Life Peer; Admitted Advocate, 1977; Lecturer in Jurisprudence, Dundee University, 1973-76; Standing Junior Counsel, Department of Energy, 1984-89; called to English Bar, 1988; appointed QC, 1989; contested Fife North East (Labour), 1992. Former Member, Scottish Legal Aid Board and Edinburgh University Court. Address: (b.) House of Lords, London, SW1A 0AA.

Clark, Anita, MA, BA (Hons), FRSA. Director, The Work Room; former Head of Dance, Creative Scotland; b. 26.11.71, Dunfermline. Educ. Royal Scottish Academy of Music and Drama; London College of Dance; University of Buckinghamshire. Freelance community dance artist, 1992-96; Dance co-ordinator, Glasgow City Council, 1996-97; Education Officer, Birmingham Royal Ballet, 1998-2000; Artistic Director, Citymoves Dancespace, Aberdeen, 2001-04. Lisa Ullmann Fellowship awardee in 2004. Recreations: dance and performing arts. Address: (b.) Tramway, 25 Albert Drive, Glasgow G41 2PE; T.-0141 423 3864.

Clark, Professor Brian Drummond, BA, MA, MBE. Professor, Environmental Management and Planning, Aberdeen University, since 1994; Committee on Radioactive Waste Management (CORWM), since 2003; b. 22.1.38, Sherborne; m., Edwina Clegg; 1 s.; 2 d. Educ. Ashville College, Harrogate; Liverpool University. Board Member, Scottish Environment Protection Agency (SEPA), 2000-08; Chair, North Region Board, SEPA and Chair, Planning and Finance Committee, 2000-08; Commission Member, Local Government Boundary Commission Scotland, 2007-13; Governor, Macaulay Land Use Institute, Aberdeen, 2005-11; Governor, The James Hutton Institute, since 2010. UNEP Global 500 Award; Author of 10 books. Recreations: croquet; gardening; Aberdeen FC. Address: (h.) 'Farragon', 513 North Deeside Road, Cults, Aberdeen AB15 9ES; T.-01224 867159; e-mail: briandrummondclark@btinternet.com

Clark, Colin. MP (Conservative), Gordon, 2017-19; b. 20.5.69. Educ. Turriff Academy; Heriot-Watt University. MD and Owner, DGM Growers, 1993-2005; Serial investor, 2000-2012; Conservative Westminster Candidate (Gordon), General Election, 2015; Owner, R&M Clark Farmers, since 2005; Chairman, Nessgro Ltd, since 2005. Member of the Treasury Select Committee and the Environment, Food and Rural Affairs Backbench Committee.

Clark, Professor Craig Stewart, MBE, BEng, MSc. Professor of Practice, Space (Part-time), University of Strathclyde, since 2022; Chairman, Sylatech Limited, since 2021; Chair, Space Scotland, since 2021; Founder and CSO, Clyde Space, 2018-2021, CEO, 2005-2018; electronics engineer; b. 8.73. Educ. University of Glasgow; University of Surrey. Career history: Power Systems Team Leader, Surrey Satellite Technology Ltd, 1994-2005; Member, Space Leadership Council, 2010-16; Member of Council of Economic Advisors to Scottish Government, 2018-2021. Scotland's first satellite - UKube-1 - designed and built by Clyde Space, launched in Russia, 2014; opened a US subsidiary, Clyde Space Inc., 2016; inducted into the Scottish Engineering Hall of Fame, 2017; Honorary Fellow of IESIS. Address: Space Scotland, 2 Lochside View, Edinburgh EH12 1LB.

Clark, David Alexander, EurIng, BEng (Hons), CEng, MIET, ICIOB. Managing Director, Dalzell Consulting Ltd, since 2002; b. 01.11.65, Duns; m., Judith Miller Clark. Educ. Hamilton Grammar School; University of Strathclyde. Engineer and Manufacturing Manager, British Steel, Corus, 1987-98; Engineering Manager, Operations Development: Allied Distillers Ltd., 1998-2002; Chief Executive, Shetland Islands Council, 2009-2010. Scottish Chairman, Steel & Industrial Managers Association, 1992-98; Director, Allied Domecq First Pension Trust, 2000-02. Recreations: sports cars; Cuban cigars; malt whisky; hi-fi; Italian history & culture. Address: (h.) 3 Dalzell Castle, Dalzell Estate, Lanarkshire ML1 2SJ; T.-07919 274104; e-mail: david.clark@dalzell.org.uk

Clark, David Findlay, OBE, DL, MA, PhD, CPsychol, FBPsS, ARPS, FFICS. Deputy Lieutenant, Banffshire, 1992-2005; Consulting Clinical Psychologist; former Director, Area Clinical Psychology Services, Grampian Health Board; Clinical Senior Lecturer, Department of Mental Health, Aberdeen University; b. 30.5.30, Aberdeen; m., Janet Ann Stephen; 2 d. Educ. Banff Academy; Aberdeen University. Flying Officer, RAF, 1951-53; Psychologist, Leicester Industrial Rehabilitation Unit, 1953-56; Senior, then Principal Clinical Psychologist, Leicester Area Clinical Psychology Service, and part-time Lecturer, Leicester University and Technical College, 1956-66; WHO short-term Consultant, Sri Lanka, 1977; various lecturing commitments in Canada and USA, since 1968. Honorary Sheriff, Grampian and Highlands; former Governor, Aberdeen College of Education; Member, Grampian Children's Panel, 1970-85; Safeguarder (Social Work Scotland Act, 1969 and Children (Scotland) Act, 1995), 1985-2008; Past Chairman, Clinical Division, British Psychological Society. Publications: Help, Hospitals and the Handicapped, 1984; One Boy's War, 1997; Stand By Your Beds!, 2001; Stand By Your Beds!, 2nd Edition, 2006; Remember Who You Are!, 2007; Chancer, 2007; Against All Gods: The Way To Humanism, 2019; Secret Heroes: A Manse at War; book chapters and technical and magazine articles. Recreations: reading; writing; chess; guitar playing. Address: (h.) Glendeveron, 8 Deveron Terrace, Banff AB45 1BB; T.-01261 812624; e-mail: drdavidfindlayclark@btinternet.com

Clark, Derek John, BMus (Hons), DipMusEd (Hons), DRSAMD. Head of Music, Scottish Opera, since 1997; b. 22.8.55, Glasgow; m., Heather Fryer; 1 d. Educ. Dumbarton Academy; Royal Scottish Academy of Music and Drama; University of Durham; London Opera Centre. Debut as professional accompanist, 1976; joined music staff, Welsh National Opera, 1977, conducting debut 1982; Guest

Conductor, Mid Wales Opera, 1989-92; Guest Coach and Conductor, Welsh College of Music, 1990-97; Conductor, South Wales Opera, 1994-96; Guest Coach at major Conservatoires, National Opera Studio, since 1997; arranger/composer since late 1980s including work for radio and television; musicals for young people; Orchestral Reductions of Operas (Pocket Publications); choral music (Pub: Roberton/Goodmusic). Appointed Musical Director, Dundee Choral Union, 2011. Silver Medallist, Worshipful Company of Musicians, 1976. Recreation: reading. Address: (b.) Scottish Opera, 39 Elmbank Crescent, Glasgow G2 4PT; T.-0141-248 4567.

Clark, Gregor Munro, CB, LLB, FRSSA. Counsel to the Scottish Law Commission, 2006-2019; b. 18.4.46, Glasgow; m., 1, Jane Maralyn Palmer (deceased); 2, Alexandra Groves Miller or Plumtree; 1 s.; 2 d. Educ. Queen's Park Senior Secondary School, Glasgow; Queen's College, St Andrews University. Admitted Faculty of Advocates, 1972; Lord Advocate's Department, 1974-99 (Assistant Parliamentary Draftsman, then Deputy Parliamentary Draftsman, then Parliamentary Draftsman); Counsel to the Scottish Law Commission, 1995-2000; Scottish Parliamentary Counsel, Scottish Executive, 1999-2002 and 2004-06; Scottish Parliamentary Counsel (UK), 2002-04. Recreation: piano. Address: 18 Rocheid Park, Edinburgh EH4 1RU; T.-0131 315 4634.
E-mail: gregor.clark86@gmail.com

Clark, Guy Wyndham Nial Hamilton, CVO, JP. Lord Lieutenant of Renfrewshire, 2007-2019 (Vice Lord Lieutenant, Renfrewshire, 2002-07, Deputy Lieutenant, 1987-2002); JP Inverclyde, since 1987; b. 28.3.44; m., Brighid Lovell Greene; 2 s.; 1 d. Educ. Eton. Commd. Coldstream Guards, 1962-67; Investment Manager, Murray Johnstone Ltd., Glasgow, 1973-77; Partner, R.C. Greig & Co. (Stockbrokers), Glasgow, 1977-86; Director, Greig, Middleton & Co. Ltd., 1986-97; Managing Director, Murray Johnstone Private Investors Ltd., 1997-2001; Managing Director, Aberdeen Private Investors, 2001-06; Director, Bell Lawrie Investment Management, 2006-08. Member, Executive Committee, Erskine Hospital for Disabled Servicemen, 1986-97; Member, International Stock Exchange, 1983. Chairman, JP Advisory Committee, 1991-2002; President, The Reserve Forces and Cadets Association for the Lowlands of Scotland, 2014-2019; Vice President, Erskine Hospital; Patron, Accord Hospice, Paisley; Hon. President, St Columba's School, Kilmacolm; Vice President, Army Cadet Force League (West Lowland); President, Renfrewshire and Inverclyde Branch - SSAFA. Recreations: gardening and field sports. Address: (h.) Braeton, Inverkip PA16 0DU; T.-01475 520 619; Fax: 01475 521 030; e-mail: g.clark282@btinternet.com

Clark, Johnston Peter Campbell, LLB, DipLP, NP, MCISI. Managing Partner, Blackadders LLP Solicitors, since 1999; Chief Executive, Blackadders Wealth Management LLP; Director, Legal Defence Union Ltd; b. 29.10.62, Dundee; m., Sara Elizabeth Philp; 1 s.; 1 d. Educ. High School of Dundee; Aberdeen University. Trainee Solicitor, Blackadder Gilchrist and Robertson, 1984-86; Solicitor, Blackadder Reid Johnston, 1986-88; Partner, Blackadders LLP, since 1988. Past Dean, Faculty of Procurators and Solicitors, Dundee; Secretary, Dundee Disabled Children's Association; past Deacon, Baker Incorporation of Dundee. Recreations: watching football; playing golf; garden. Address: (b.) 34 Reform Street, Dundee DD1 1RJ; T.-01382 229222; (b.) 40 Torphichen Street, Edinburgh EH3 8JB; T.-0131 222 8000.

Clark of Kilwinning, Baroness (Katy Clark). MSP, West of Scotland (Region), since 2021; MP (Labour), North Ayrshire and Arran, 2005-2015; b. 3.7.67, Kilwinning. Educ. University of Aberdeen. Member of Scottish Affairs Committee, 2005-2010; Member of European Scrutiny Committee, 2005-2010; Member of the Procedure Committee, 2005-2010; Member of Business, Innovation and Skills Committee, 2010-15; Member of Environmental Audit Committee, 2010-15; Member of Speakers' Panel of Chairs, 2010-15. Address: Scottish Parliament, Edinburgh EH99 1SP.

Clarke, Alan, PGDip, MBA. Chief Executive, Quality Meat Scotland, since 2017. Educ. University of Ulster. Career: Chief Executive, Wholesale & Retail Training Council NI, 1992-2004; Director, Lifelong Learning UK, 2005-2010; Chief Executive, Scottish Bakers, 2010-2017. Address: (b.) The Rural Centre, West Mains, Ingliston, Newbridge EH28 8NZ; T.-0131 510 7920.

Clarke, Professor Andrew David, MA, PhD. Honorary Professor, University of Aberdeen, since 2015 (Senior Lecturer in New Testament, 1995-2015); b. 3.12.64, Bradford; m., Jane; 2 s.; 1 d. Educ. Dean Close School, Cheltenham; University of Cambridge (Girton College). Research Librarian, Tyndale House, Cambridge, 1990-95; Lecturer, then Senior Lecturer, New Testament, University of Aberdeen, since 1995. Chairman of Tyndale House Council, 2005-12; Trustee of Universities and Colleges Christian Fellowship, 2005-12; Member, Studiorum Novi Testamenti Societas. Publications: A Pauline Theology of Church Leadership, 2008; Serve the Community of the Church: Christians as Leaders and Ministers (First-Century Christians in the Graeco-Roman World), 2000; Secular and Christian Leadership in Corinth: A Socio-Historical and Exegetical Study of 1 Corinthians 1-6, 2nd Edition, 2006.

Clarke, (Christopher) Michael, CBE, BA (Hons), FRSE. Former Director, Scottish National Gallery (2000-2016); b. 29.8.52, York; m., Deborah Clare Cowling; 2 s.; 1 d. Educ. Felsted School, Essex; Manchester University. Art Assistant, York City Art Gallery, 1973-76; Research Assistant, British Museum, 1976-78; Assistant Keeper in charge of prints, Whitworth Art Gallery, Manchester, 1978-84; Assistant Keeper, National Gallery of Scotland, 1984-87; Keeper, 1987-2000. Visiting Fellow, Yale Center for British Art, 1985; Clark Art Institute, 2004; Chevalier de l'Ordre des Arts et des Lettres, 2004; Fellow of the Royal Society of Edinburgh, 2008; Commander of the British Empire, 2009; Commander of the Order of the Dannebrog, 2012. Publications include: The Tempting Prospect; A Social History of English Watercolours; The Arrogant Connoisseur: Richard Payne Knight (Co-Editor); Lighting Up the Landscape – French Impressionism and its Origins; Corot and the Art of Landscape; Eyewitness Art – Watercolours; Corot, Courbet and die Maler von Barbizon (Co-Editor); Oxford Concise Dictionary of Art Terms; Monet: The Seine and The Sea (Co-author); The Playfair Project. Recreations: listening to music; golf.

Clarke, Eric Lionel. MP (Labour), Midlothian, 1992-2001; b. 9.4.33, Edinburgh; m., June; 2 s.; 1 d. Educ. Holy Cross Academy; W.M. Ramsey Technical College; Esk Valley Technical College. Coal miner, 1949-77; General Secretary, NUM Scottish Area, 1977-89; County Councillor, Midlothian, 1962-74; Regional Councillor, Lothian, 1974-78. Recreations: fly fishing; gardening; carpentry. Address: (h.) 32 Mortonhall Park Crescent, Edinburgh; T.-0131-664 8214.

Clarke, Geoff, QC. Chairman, Faculty Services Ltd, 2018-2021; b. 1966. Educ. North Berwick High School; University of Edinburgh. Career: admitted as a member of the Faculty of Advocates in 1994; Member, Compass Chambers, since 2007; QC, since 2008; Member, Faculty

Council, since 2018. Address: Faculty of Advocates, Advocates Library, Parliament Square, Edinburgh EH1 1RF; T.-0131 226 5071.

Clarke, The Rt. Hon. Lord (Matthew Gerard Clarke), PC (2009). Senator of the College of Justice, 2000-2016. Educ. Holy Cross High School, Hamilton; Glasgow University (MA, LLB). Solicitor, 1972; Lecturer, Depatment of Scots Law, Edinburgh University, 1972-78; admitted, Faculty of Advocates, 1978; QC (Scot), 1989; a Judge, Courts of Appeal of Jersey and Guernsey, 1995-2000; Leader, UK Delegation, Council of the Bars and Law Societies of EC, 1992-96; Hon. Fellow, Europa Institute, Edinburgh University, since 1995.

Clarke, Steve. National Coach, Scottish Football Association, since 2019; b. 29.8.63, Saltcoats. Senior career: St Mirren, 1982-87; Chelsea, 1987-98; National team: Scotland U21, 1983-85, Scotland, 1987-94. Teams managed: West Bromwich Albion, 2012-13; Reading, 2014-15; Kilmarnock, 2017-19. Player Honours include: FA Cup, 1996-97; Football League Cup, 1997-98, UEFA Cup Winners' Cup, 1997-98; Full Members' Cup, 1989-90; Chelsea Player of the Year, 1993-94; Chelsea Centenary XI, 2004-05; Managerial Honours include: SFWA Manager of the Year: 2017-18, 2018-19; PFA Scotland Manager of the Year: 2018-19; SPFL Premiership Manager of the Year, 2018-19; Premier League Manager of the Month, November 2012; Scottish Premiership Manager of the Month: December 2017, February 2018, March 2018. Address: Scottish Football Association, Hampden Park, Glasgow G42 9AY.

Clarke, Rt. Hon. Sir Thomas, CBE, JP. MP (Labour), Coatbridge and Chryston and Bellshill, 1982-2015 (formerly Monklands West); Shadow Secretary of State for Scotland, 1992-93; b. 10.1.41, Coatbridge. Educ. Columba High School, Coatbridge; Scottish College of Commerce. Former Assistant Director, Scottish Council for Educational Technology; Provost of Monklands, 1975-82; Past President, Convention of Scottish Local Authorities; MP, Coatbridge and Airdrie, 1982-83; author: Disabled Persons (Services Consultation and Representation) Act, 1986, International Development (Reporting and Transparency) Act, 2006; elected four times to Shadow Cabinet; Minister for Film and Tourism, 1997-98; director, amateur film, Give Us a Goal. Recreations: films; walking; reading.

Clarkson, Erica. Chief Executive, The Judicial Appointments Board for Scotland, 2018-2021 (previously at the Creating Positive Futures Division in the Scottish Government's Children and Families Directorate). Career: previously responsible for a range of policies affecting Scotland's Children and Young People including Secure Care and Youth Justice, Scotland's National Parenting and Play Strategies, family support and has most recently led on the development and delivery of Scotland's Baby Box.

Clegg, David. Editor, The Courier, since 2019; b. 28.5.82. Previously Assistant Editor, Daily Record; Political Editor, The Courier, until 2012. Journalist of the Year, Scottish Press Awards, 2019; Political Journalist of the Year title four times. Address: The Courier, 2 Albert Square, Dundee DD1 1DD; T.-01382 575318.

Cleland, Lynsey, BSc. Director of Quality Assurance, Healthcare Improvement Scotland, since 2021. Educ.

University of Strathclyde. Career history: Royal Pharmaceutical Society of Great Britain: Head of Professional Ethics, London, 2004-07, Professional Standards Inspector, Scotland, 2007-08; General Pharmaceutical Council: Regional Lead Inspector, 2008-2011, Director for Scotland, 2011-19; Director of Community Engagement, Healthcare Improvement Scotland, 2019-2021. Address: Healthcare Improvement Scotland, Delta House, 50 West Nile Street, Glasgow G1 2NP; T.-0141 225 6999.

Clements, Angela. Chair, Sense Scotland, since 2020; b. 6.62. Career history: Chief Officer and Head of ICT & Business Development, Public Sector, Glasgow, 1994-2007; Interim IT and Programme Director, Private Sector, Edinburgh and Glasgow, 2007-2015; Director of Enterprise and IT, CalMac Ferries Limited, 2015-2017; ICT Management Consultant, ISCMS, since 2017; Sense Scotland: Trustee/Board Director/Deputy Treasurer, since 2014, Board Vice-Chair, 2019-2020, Acting Chair, 2020, Chair of Remuneration Committee, since 2020, Chair of Governance Committee, since 2020, Chair of Sustainability and Rapid Response Committee, since 2021. Address: TouchBase Business Centre/Sense Scotland, 43 Middlesex Street, Kinning Park, Glasgow G41 1EE; T.-0300 330 9292.

Clifford, Jo, MA, PhD. Writer, performer, poet and teacher; Founder, Teatro do Mundo (2000); b. 1951, North Staffordshire. Educ. University of St Andrews. Writer, Traverse Theatre Scotland, 1985-92; Professor of Theatre, Queen Margaret University, Edinburgh, 1996-2009. Author of over 100 plays, many of which have been translated into various languages and performed all over the world (they include: Losing Venice, Every One, Faust and The Tree of Knowledge); adaptation of Charles Dickens's Great Expectations makes her the first openly transgendered woman playwright to have had a play on in London's West End. Associate Artist of Chris Goode and Company; transition from John to Jo has enabled her to become an actor and performer.

Clifford, John Gilmore, R1 (AT), MA (Oxon), MSc (Edin), FRSA. Honorary Consul of Austria for Scotland aD, 2003-2016; Dean of Consular Corps in Edinburgh and Leith, 2014-2015; m. Elisa Trimby/Clifford, illustrator, engraver, artist, writer, taught at Glasgow School of Art (died 2001); 2 s.: Ben, actor; Adam, musician/actor. Educ. Henley on Thames Grammar School; St Catherine's College Oxford (Mod Langs); Goethe Institut, Germany; Europa Institute; University of Edinburgh, European Legal Studies, EU Environment Law. Hon Consul of Austria for Scotland, 2003; Dean, Consular Corps in Edinburgh and Leith, 2014-2015; Fellow, Royal Society of Art; Business Committee, General Council of University of Edinburgh; Consultant, Austrian Trade Commission and Austrian Cultural Forum; re-discovery in Edinburgh of ashes of Alfred Adler, Psychoanalyst/Founder, Individual Psychology; historic meeting of Scottish Freudians and Austrian Adlerians, Edinburgh, 2011; re-interment, Central Cemetery Vienna, 2011; European and international public affairs: political, cultural and ecological exchange; Quadro Europa, Edinburgh; Focus Scotland Ltd (delegations, study/cultural/professional programmes); Freudenstadt Symposium (Professor Chris Harvie, former MSP), Universities of Edinburgh & Tübingen; Associate, University of Edinburgh, former Centre for Human Ecology, 1990s; Lothian Regional Councillor, 1994-1996 (European Affairs, Environmental Strategy); election campaigns: candidate for European Parliament, 1999, local/regional elections; Council Member, Scottish Civic Forum (Environment/Europe), 2004-08; Community Councillor, Stockbridge/Inverleith, 2006-2011; Projects

Director, St Andrew Foundation, public/constitutional affairs - Russia, 1996-2000; Secretary, Scottish Council of Fabian Societies, 1987-1997; Secretary/Chairman, Edinburgh Fabian Society, 1987-1998; Member, sometime Committee Member, European Movement, Scottish Council; Member, Edinburgh Committee, Helsinki Citizens Assembly, 1996-2009; Member/contributor, British-Yugoslav Society, then Scotland - South Slav Society, 1990s; Oyster Club, Edinburgh; Chairman, Friends of Demarco Gallery, 1996-2000; Scottish Arts Club; Youth Music Theatre UK; Chairman, Friends of the Lyceum Youth Theatre, 2001-06. Publications/contributions/papers include: Joint translator, Earth Politics - Ernst Ulrich von Weizsäcker: Environmental Politics for the 21st century; Scottish Office report on sub-state legislation in Europe (reference Austria); Scotland's Place in Europe, John Wheatley Centre (CSPP); Freudenstadt Symposium, and papers, Regionalism in Europe, 2010 ongoing; low energy housing seminars, Scottish Parliament; regular renewable energy events, sustainable architecture with wood; seminars and exhibitions. Some interests: architecture; music; theatre and other performing arts; visual arts; cinema; reading and exchange of ideas; psychoanalysis; ecology; world/social affairs, especially Europe/Middle East (and beyond); political thought, cultures and anthropology - the Other: mountain walking; family and friends; conversation and laughter. Address: (h/w) 9 Howard Place, Edinburgh EH3 5JZ; T.-0131 558 1124; mobile: +44(0) 7968 97 57 83. E-mail: johnclifford@focusscotland.co.uk

Clift, Benedict, BMSc (Hons), MBChB, FRCSEd, FRCSOrth. Consultant Orthopaedic and Trauma Surgeon, Ninewells Hospital, Dundee, since 1995; Honorary Senior Lecturer, Dundee University; b. 22.7.62, Manchester; m., Alison; 1 s.; 2 d. Educ. Cardinal Langley Grammar School; Dundee University. Recreations: jazz; trees; Dante; Homer; classical piano; running. Address: (b.) Department of Orthopaedic and Trauma Surgery, Ninewells Hospital, Dundee DD1 9SY; T.-01382 660111; e-mail: ben.clift@nhs.scot

Clinton, Jacqueline. Governor, HMP YOI Cornton Vale. Address: Cornton Road, Stirling FK9 5NU. E-mail: jacqueline.clinton@sps.pnn.gov.uk

Clive, Eric McCredie, CBE, MA, LLB, LLM, SJD, Dr hc, FRSE; b. 24.7.38, Stranraer; m., Kay McLeman; 1 s.; 2 d. Educ. Stranraer Academy; Stranraer High School; Universities of Edinburgh, Michigan, Virginia. Lecturer, Senior Lecturer, Reader, Professor of Scots Law, Faculty of Law, Edinburgh University, 1962-81; Commissioner, Scottish Law Commission, 1981-99; Visiting Professor, School of Law, Edinburgh University, 1999-2014; Honorary Professor, School of Law, Edinburgh University, 2014-2020. Publications: The Law of Husband and Wife in Scotland (4th edition), 1997; Principles, Definitions and Model Rules of European Private Law (co-editor), 2009; legal articles. Address: (h.) 14 York Road, Edinburgh EH5 3EH; T.-0131-552 2875.

Clouting, David Wallis, BDS, MSc, LDSRCS (Eng), DDPH, FFPH. Clinical Director of Community Dental Services, Borders Primary Care NHS Trust, 2000-03, NHS Borders, 2003-2013; b. 29.3.53, London; m., Dr. Margaret M.C. Bacon; 3 s.; 1 d. Educ. Leyton County High School for Boys; University College Hospital Dental School, London; Institute of Dental Surgery, London; Joint Department of Dental Public Health, London Hospital Medical College and University College London. Senior Dental Officer for Special Needs, East and North Hertfordshire Health Authorities, 1983-90; Chief Administrative Dental Officer, Borders Health Board, 1990-

95; Community Dental Services Manager, Borders Community Health Services NHS Trust, 1995-99. Recreations: amateur radio; cooking; hill walking. Address: (h.) 36 Gallowhill, Peebles EH45 9BG.

Clugston, Dr. Carol, BSc (Hons), PhD, CMgr, FCMI, FLF. Chief Operating Officer, College of Medical, Veterinary & Life Sciences, University of Glasgow, since August 2010; b. 26.10.62, Glasgow; m., Ewan J. Graham; 1 s. Educ. Dumbarton Academy; University of Glasgow. Research Scientist, Cancer Research Campaign, Beatson Laboratories, 1989-94; Nanoelectronics Research Centre Administrator, University of Glasgow, 1994-98; Executive Assistant to Vice-Principal (Research), University of Glasgow, 1998-2000; Secretary to the Faculty of Medicine/Head of Division of Education and Administration, University of Glasgow, 2005-2010. Community Councillor, Stepps & District. Recreations: photography; painting. Address: (b.) MVLS College Office, Wolfson Medical School Building, University of Glasgow, University Avenue, Glasgow G12 8QQ; T.-0141-330-3142; e-mail: carol.clugston@glasgow.ac.uk

Clydesmuir, 3rd Baron (David Ronald Colville); b. 8.4.49; m.; 2 s.; 2 d. Educ. Charterhouse. Succeeded to title, 1996.

Coburn, David. Former Member of the European Parliament for Scotland (Independent, 2018-19, United Kingdom Independence Party, 2014-18); b. 11.2.59, Glasgow. Educ. High School of Glasgow; University of Leeds. Ran the Lexicon School of English in Kensington in 1993; worked as an art dealer and City of London trader before owning a freight company. Contested the seat of Old Bexley and Sidcup in 2010 and the seat of Kirkcaldy and Cowdenbeath in 2017; also stood in Bexley and Bromley in the 2012 London Assembly election.

Cochrane, Alan. Scottish Editor, The Daily Telegraph; b. Dundee. Educ. Grove Academy; m.; 4 c. Career history: entered journalism as a sub-editor and reporter for DC Thomson before joining the Daily Express in Glasgow; covered political issues across a number of newspapers in London, between the mid-1970s and the mid-1990s; appointed Editor of the Scottish Daily Express in 1994 before becoming Deputy Editor of Scotland on Sunday; became a columnist at the Daily Telegraph in the late 1990s. Publication: Alex Salmond: My Part in His Downfall - The Cochrane Diaries, 2014. Lives in Edinburgh.

Cochrane, Keith, CBE, FRSE. Chief Executive, Schenck Process, since 2019; Chairman, Score Group plc, since 2018; b. 2.65; m.; 2 c. Chartered Accountant (1989) and a member of Institute of Chartered Accountants of Scotland; Audit Manager, Arthur Andersen, 1990-93; Group Financial Controller and Co. Secretary, 1993-96, Group Financial Director, 1996-2000, Stagecoach Holdings plc; Chief Executive, Stagecoach Group, 2000-02; Director of Group Financial Reporting, 2003-04, Group Controller, 2004-05, Group Director of Finance, 2005-06, Scottish Power plc; Chief Executive, The Weir Group PLC, 2009-2016; Senior Independent Director, Carillion plc, 2015-17, Interim Chief Executive, 2017-18; UK Government Lead non-executive Director, Scotland Office and Office of Advocate General, since 2015; Member, Council, Glenalmond College, since 2013; Trustee, Duke of Edinburgh's Study Conferences (UK Fund) Board, since 2015. Fellow of the Royal Society of Edinburgh (FRSE), 2016. Commander of the Order of the British Empire

(CBE), 2016; Hon. DSc (Strathclyde), 2013. Recreations: golf; gardening; watching Scotland play rugby.

Cochrane of Cults, 5th Baron (Thomas Hunter Vere Cochrane), LLB; b. 7.9.57; m., Silke Quandt. Educ. Eton College, Windsor, Berkshire; Exeter College, Oxford University. Admitted to Inner Temple in 1980, entitled to practise as a barrister. Suceeded to title, 2017.

Cockburn, Dr Duncan, PhD, FRSA. Director of Planning and Policy, The Robert Gordon University, since 2013; Board Member, Creative Scotland. Educ. University of Aberdeen. Career history: Aberdeen City Council; currently the Chair of Culture Aberdeen – the network of cultural organisations within the city and is responsible for the implementation of Aberdeen's cultural strategy; former Chair of the Look Again visual arts and design festival (based in Aberdeen), 2015-2018; former Head of sparqs (Student Participation in Quality Scotland) and former President of the University of Aberdeen Students' Association; former Principal's Policy Advisor, The Robert Gordon University. Board member of Aberdeen Performing Arts. Recreations: enjoys reading history; attempting to run; listening to a wide range of music; cooking; fine dining. Address: The Robert Gordon University, Garthdee House, Garthdee Road, Aberdeen AB10 7AQ; T.-01224 262194. E-mail: duncan.cockburn@rgu.ac.uk

Cockburn, Professor Forrester, CBE, FRSE, MD, FRCPGlas, FRCPEdin, FRCPCH (Hon), FRCSEd (Hon), DCH. Past Chairman, Yorkhill NHS Trust; Emeritus Professor and Senior Research Fellow, Department of Child Health, Royal Hospital for Sick Children, Yorkhill, Glasgow; formerly Samson Gemmell Professor of Child Health, Glasgow University; b. 13.10.34, Edinburgh; m., Alison Fisher Grieve; 2 s. Educ. Leith Academy; Edinburgh University. Early medical training, Edinburgh Royal Infirmary, Royal Hospital for Sick Children, Edinburgh, and Simpson Memorial Maternity Pavilion, Edinburgh; Research Fellow in Paediatric Metabolic Disease, Boston University; Visiting Professor, San Juan University, Puerto Rico; Nuffield Fellow, Institute for Medical Research, Oxford University; Wellcome Senior Research Fellow, then Senior Lecturer, Department of Child Life and Health, Edinburgh University. Publications: a number of articles and textbooks on paediatric medicine, neonatal medicine, nutrition and metabolic diseases. Recreations: gardening and walking. Address: (b.) 53, Hamilton Drive, Glasgow G12 8DP; T.-0141 339 2973.

Cockburn, Dr. Hermione. British television and radio presenter; Scientific Director, Our Dynamic Earth, since 2014; b. 1973, Sussex; m.; 2 s. Educ. University of Edinburgh. Worked at various academic institutes including a two-year post-doctorate at the School of Earth Sciences at the University of Melbourne; has carried out extensive fieldwork in Antarctica, Australia, and Namibia; helped to establish the education service Our Dynamic Earth; presented BBC's Tomorrow's World and Rough Science; regular presenter of Resource Review on the Teachers' TV channel, 2005-2010. Associate lecturer with the Open University, teaching environmental science in Scotland. Publication: The Fossil Detectives: Discovering Prehistoric Britain (Co-Author), 2008. Address: 112-116 Holyrood Gait, Edinburgh EH8 8AS; T.-0131 550 7800.

Cockhead, Peter, BSc (Econ), MA, MSc, MRTPI, MZIP. Town Planning Adviser to Zambian Government (for VSO), 2008-2017; Teaching Fellow in Town and Regional Planning, University of Dundee, 2007-2017; Associate,

BusinessLab, Aberdeen, 2007-2010; b. 1.12.46, Beckenham; m., Diana Douglas; 2 s.; 1 d. Educ. Beckenham Grammar School; London School of Economics; University of Witwatersrand, South Africa; University of Edinburgh. Lecturer: University of Witwatersrand, 1970-71, University of Edinburgh, 1973-74; Consultant: OECD, Paris, 1974, Percy Johnson-Marshall and Associates, Edinburgh, 1974-75; Grampian Regional Council: Assistant Director of Planning, 1975-83, Depute Director of Planning, 1983-90, Regional Planning Manager, 1990-95; Director of Planning and Strategic Development, Aberdeen City Council, 1995-2001; Director, North East Scotland Transport Partnership (NESTRANS), 2002-07. Chairman, Scottish Society of Directors of Planning, 1997-98; Chairman, Scottish Planning Education Forum, 1999-2001; Executive Secretary, North Sea Commission, 1992-95; Member, Scottish Executive Committee, Royal Town Planning Institute, 2009-2011. Recreations: hillwalking; open water swimming; music.

Coffey, Willie, MSP (SNP), Kilmarnock and Irvine Valley, since 2011, Kilmarnock and Loudoun, 2007-2011; b. 24.5.58. Educ. University of Strathclyde. Formerly a councillor on East Ayrshire Council; Software Development Manager, then Quality and Risk Manager with Learning and Teaching Scotland. Address: (b.) Scottish Parliament, Edinburgh EH99 1SP.

Cogdell, Professor Richard John, BSc, PhD, FRS, FRSE, FRSA, FSB. Hooker Professor of Botany, Glasgow University, since 1993; b. 4.2.49, Guildford; m., Barbara; 1 s.; 1 d. Educ. Royal Grammar School, Guildford; Bristol University. Post-doctoral research, USA, 1973-75; Botany Department, Glasgow University, 1975-94, now Institute of Molecular, Cell and Systems Biology in the College of Medical, Veterinary and Life Sciences. Member, Board of Governors, Scottish Crop Research Institute, 1997-2005; Chairman, Trustees, Glasgow Macintyre Begonia Trust; Member, Council of the Biochemical Society, 2007-2010; Chairman of the Scientific Advisory Board of the Max Planck Institute for Bioinorganic Chemistry, Mülheim-an-der-Ruhr, 2007-2013; Trustee Director of The Genome Analysis Centre, 2009-2012; President of the International Society for Photosynthesis Research, 2013-2017; Council of BBSRC, 2013-2019. Recreations: cricket; aerobics; Scottish dancing; theatre. Address: (b.) Institute of Molecular, Cell and Systems Biology, GBRC, Glasgow University, Glasgow G12 8QQ; T.-0141-330 4232; e-mail: Richard.Cogdell@glasgow.ac.uk

Coggins, Professor John Richard, MA, PhD, OBE, FRSE, FRSB. Emeritus Professor of Molecular Enzymology, School of Biology, Glasgow University; b. 15.1.44, Bristol; m., Dr. Lesley F. Watson; 1 s.; 1 d. Educ. Bristol Grammar School; The Queen's College, Oxford; Ottawa University. Post-doctoral Fellow: Biology Department, Brookhaven National Laboratory, New York, 1970-72, Biochemistry Department, Cambridge University, 1972-74; Glasgow University: Lecturer/Senior Lecturer/Professor, Biochemistry Department, 1974-95, Director, Graduate School of Biomedical and Life Sciences, 1995-97, Head, Division of Biochemistry and Molecular Biology, 1997-98, Research Director, Institute of Biomedical and Life Sciences, 1998-2000, Director/Dean, Institute of Biomedical and Life Sciences, 2000-05; Vice-Principal, Life Sciences, Medicine & Veterinary Medicine, 2006-09; Pro Vice-Principal, 2009-10. Biochemical Society: Chair, Molecular Enzymology Group, 1982-85; Chair, Policy Committee, 2004-8; Chair, Portland Press, 2010-13. SERC: Chair, Biophysics & Biochemistry Committee, 1985-88; Managing Director, Biomac Ltd., 1988-94; Member, DTI-Research Councils Biotechnology Joint Advisory Board, 1989-94; AFRC Council, 1991-94; Biochemistry Adviser to

UFC, 1989-92; Governing Member, Caledonian Research Foundation, 1994-2007, Chair, 2008-09; Chair, HEFC Biochemistry Research Assessment Panel, 1995-96; Royal Society of Edinburgh: Research Awards Convener, 1999-2002, Vice President (Life Sciences), 2003-06; Chairman, RSE Scotland Foundation, 2009-12; Member, Scottish Science Advisory Committee, 2002-07; Chairman, Heads of University Biological Science Departments, 2003-07; Trustee, Glasgow Science Centre, 2004-16; BBSRC Council, 2008-14; RIN Advisory Board, 2005-11; Treasurer, Biosciences Federation, 2007-09; Royal Society of Biology Council, 2009-18. Recreations: gardening; travelling. Address: 5 Chapelton Gardens, Bearsden, Glasgow G61 2DH; T.-0141-942-5082.
E-mail: john.coggins@glasgow.ac.uk

Cohen, Professor Anthony Paul, CBE, BA, MSc (SocSc), PhD, HonDSc (Edin), D.Sc (h.c.) (St Andrews), FRSE. Honorary Professor of Social Anthropology, University of Edinburgh; Emeritus Professor, Queen Margaret University; b. 3.8.46, London; m., Professor Bronwen J. Cohen OBE; 3 s. Educ. Whittingehame College, Brighton; Southampton University. Research Fellow, Memorial University of Newfoundland, 1968-70; Assistant Professor, Queen's University, Kingston, Ontario, 1970-71; Lecturer/Senior Lecturer in Social Anthropology, Manchester University, 1971-89; Professor of Social Anthropology, Edinburgh University, 1989-2003 (Provost of Law and Social Sciences, 1997-2002); Principal and Vice-Chancellor, Queen Margaret University, Edinburgh, 2003-09. Convener, Scottish Forum for Graduate Education, 1996-98; Convener, Universities Scotland Health Committee, 2006-09. Publications: The Management of Myths; The Symbolic Construction of Community; Whalsay: Symbol, Segment and Boundary in a Shetland Island Community; Self Consciousness: an alternative anthropology of identity; Belonging (Editor); Symbolising Boundaries (Editor); Humanising the City? (Co-Editor); Questions of Consciousness (Co-Editor); Signifying Identities (Editor). Recreations: reflection; music; novels.

Cohen, Professor Sir Philip, BSc, PhD, FRS, FRSE, FFMedSci, FAA. Professor of Enzymology, University of Dundee, since 2010; Director of the Scottish Institute for Cell Signalling (SCILLS), 2008-2012; Honorary Director, Medical Research Council Protein Phosphorylation Unit, 1990-2012; Director, Wellcome Trust Biocentre, 1997-2007; b. 22.7.45, London; m., Patricia Townsend Wade (deceased); 1 s.; 1 d. Educ. Hendon County Grammar School; University College, London. Science Research Council/NATO postdoctoral Fellow, Department of Biochemistry, University of Washington, 1969-71; Dundee University: Lecturer in Biochemistry, 1971-78, Reader in Biochemistry, 1978-81, Professor of Enzymology, 1981-84 and since 2010; Royal Society Research Professor, 1984-2010; Wellcome Trust Senior Investigator, since 2013. Publications: over 500 papers and reviews, one book. Recreations: bridge; golf; natural history. Address: (h.) Inverbay Bramblings, Invergowrie, Dundee; T.-01382 562328; mobile: 07885-423623.

Cohen, Professor Stephen Douglas, BSc, PhD. Emeritus Professor, University of Glasgow (formerly Professor of Number Theory, 2002-09); b. 7.1.44, London; m., Yvonne Joy Roulet; 2 d. Educ. Allan Glen's School, Glasgow; University of Glasgow. Department of Mathematics, University of Glasgow: Lecturer, 1968, Senior Lecturer, 1988, Reader, 1992; visiting positions: Research Associate, University of Illinois, 1979, Lecturer, University of Witwatersrand, 1987, Professor, University of Limoges, France, 1994; Member, various editorial boards including: Finite Fields and Their Applications, since 1995, Applicable Algebra, 1996-2008, Glasgow Mathematical Journal, 1986-99 and 2002-07, Proceedings of Edinburgh Mathematical Society, 1991-97. Publications: over 120 articles in mathematics research journals. Address: (h.) 6 Bracken Road, Portlethen, Aberdeen AB12 4TA.
E-mail: Stephen.Cohen@glasgow.ac.uk

Cohn, Professor Samuel Kline, MA, PhD, FRHistS. Professor of History, Glasgow University, since 1995; b. 1949, Birmingham, Alabama; m., Genevieve Warwick; 2 s. Educ. Indian Springs School; Harvard University. Assistant Professor, Wesleyan University, Connecticut, 1978-79; Assistant Professor, Brandeis University, 1979-86; Associate Professor of History, Brandeis University, 1986-89; Visiting Professor, Brown University, 1990-91; Professor of History, Brandeis University, 1989-95. Publications include: Women in the Streets: Essays on Sex and Power in the Italian Renaissance, 1996; The Cult of Remembrance and the Black Death: Six Renaissance Cities in Central Italy, 1997; The Black Death and the Transformation of the West (Co-author), 1997; Creating the Florentine State: Peasants and Rebellion, 1348-1434, 1999; The Black Death Transformed: Disease and Culture in Early Renaissance Europe, 2002; Popular Protest in Late Medieval Europe; Lust for Liberty: The Politics of Social Revolt in Medieval Europe, 1200-1425, 2006; Cultures of Plague in Sixteenth-Century Italy, 2009. Recreation: hill-running. Address: (h.) 14 Hamilton Drive, Glasgow; T.-0141-330 4369.

Cole-Hamilton, Alex. MSP (Scottish Liberal Democrat), Edinburgh Western, since 2016; Scottish Liberal Democratic Leader and spokesperson for Health; b. 22.7.77; m., Gillian; 3 c. Educ. Madras College; University of Aberdeen (President of the Students' Association, 1999-2000). Worked in the voluntary sector; formerly a Convener and Director of "Together (Scottish Alliance for Children's Rights)". Liberal Democrat candidate: Scottish Parliament elections in 2003 for Kirkcaldy and 2007 for Stirling; United Kingdom general election in 2005 for Kirkcaldy and Cowdenbeath. Address: Scottish Parliament, Edinburgh EH99 1SP.

Cole-Hamilton, Anni, MA Hons (Eng Lang + Lit) Edin. Principal, Moray Firth Tutorial College, since 1999; Principal, Moray Firth School, 2002-2010; b. 24.9.49, Cupar, Fife; m., Simon Cole-Hamilton; 2 d. Educ. Craigholme, Glasgow; Hutchesons' Grammar, Glasgow; George Watson's, Edinburgh; Edinburgh University. Founder and Principal of Moray Firth School. Founder, Chairman (and worst player) of The Truly Terrible Orchestra, Inverness. Recreations: laughter with friends and family; reading; red wine; walking. Address: (b.) 94 Academy Street, Inverness IV1 1LU; T.-01463 716151; e-mail: ach@mfschool.co.uk

Cole-Hamilton, Professor David John, BSc, PhD, CChem, FRSC, FRSE. Emeritus Professor, University of St Andrews, since 2014; Irvine Professor of Chemistry, 1985-2014; b. 22.5.48, Bovey Tracey; m. (1), Elizabeth Ann Brown (diss. 2008) 2 s.; 2 d.; m. (2), Rosemary Elizabeth Macrae (née Semple). Educ. Haileybury and ISC; Hertford; Edinburgh University. Research Assistant, Temporary Lecturer, Imperial College, 1974-78; Lecturer, Senior Lecturer, Liverpool University, 1978-85. Sir Edward Frankland Fellow, Royal Society of Chemistry, 1984-85; Corday Morgan Medallist, 1983; Museums and Galleries Commission Award for Innovation in Conservation, 1995 (runner-up); Royal Society of Chemistry Award for Organometallic Chemistry, 1998; Tilden Lecturer, Royal Society of Chemistry, 2000-2001; Institute of Applied Catalysis, Award of the Institute of Chemical Engineers,

2001, Runner-up; Catalysis Society of South Africa, Eminent Visitor, 2004; Sir Geoffrey Wilkinson Prize Lecturer of the Royal Society of Chemistry, 2005-06; Foreign Member of the Russian Academy of Natural Sciences, 2017-2022 (resigned); Alwin Mittasch Prize, German Catalysis Society, 2017; President: Chemistry Section, British Association for the Advancement of Science, 1995, Chemistry Sectional Committee, Royal Society of Edinburgh, 1993-95; Royal Society of Chemistry Council, President, Dalton Division, Royal Society of Chemistry, 2013-16; President, 2014-17 and Vice-President, 2013-14, 2017-19 and President Elect, European Association of Chemical and Molecular Sciences (EuCheMs), 2013-14, President, since 2014; Vice President, Royal Society of Chemistry, Dalton Council, 1996-99, 2011-12, President, 2013-16; Royal Society of Chemistry Council (Elected Member), 2009-12; Chair, Royal Society of Chemistry Audit Committee, 2010-2012; Royal Society of Edinburgh Education Committee, 2012-18; Royal Society of Edinburgh Learned Societies Group for STEM Education, since 2016, Interim Chair, 2021; Royal Society of Edinburgh, European Strategy Group (Chair, Sub-Group for Research Innovation and Tertiary Education), since 2017; Scientific Editor, Journal of the Chemical Society, Dalton Transactions, 2000-03. Address: 22, Buchanan Gardens, St Andrews, Fife KY16 9LU; T.-+44-7979-711714.
E-mail: djc@st-and.ac.uk

Colella, Professor Anton, BA (Hons), DipEd. Global Chief Executive, Moore Global Network Limited, since 2018; Chairman Executive Board, Catholic Education Service for Scotland (SCES), since 2015; Trustee, International Valuation Standards Council (IVSC); Chairman, Salvesen Mindroom Centre, since 2017; Chief Executive, Institute of Chartered Accountants of Scotland, 2006-2018; Chairman, Scottish Council of Independent Schools, 2010-2016; Chairman, Global Accounting Alliance, 2011-2018; Chief Executive, Scottish Qualifications Authority, 2003-06 (Director of Qualifications, 2002-03); b. 25.5.61, Glasgow; m., Angela; 2 s.; 2 d. Educ. St Mungo's Academy, Glasgow; Stirling University. Teacher of Religious Education, Holyrood Secondary School, Glasgow, 1983-87; Principal Teacher of Religious Education, St Columba's High School, Gourock, 1987-92, Holyrood Secondary School, 1992-96; Assistant Head Teacher, Holyrood Secondary School, 1996-99; Depute Head Teacher, St Margaret Mary's Secondary, Glasgow, 1999-2001; seconded to Scottish Qualifications Authority, 2001; Board Member: Glasgow College of Nautical Studies, 1998, Quality Assurance Agency Scotland Committee, 2001, Scottish Further Education Unit, 2001, CBI Scotland, 2008, Columba 1400, 2008; Honorary Professor of Education, University of Glasgow, since 2012; Honorary Professor, University of Strathclyde Business School, since 2017; Honorary Doctorate, BPP University, 2014; Board Member, Adam Smith Business School, since 2013. Recreations: family life; music; rugby; eating out.

Colgan, Greg. Chief Executive, Dundee City Council, since 2020. Educ. University of Dundee; Chartered Institute of Management Accountants; Chartered Institute of Housing. Career history: Financial Analyst, NCR Analyst, NCR Corporation, Dundee, 2000-06; Finance and IT Manager, Servite Housing Association, Dundee, 2006-2009; Board Member, Cairn Housing Association, Edinburgh, 2013-18; Dundee City Council: Finance and Corporate Services Manager, 2009-2013; Head of Corporate Debt and Welfare Reform, 2014-15; Head of Customer Services and IT, 2015-2017; Executive Director of Corporate Services, 2017-2020. Address: Dundee City Council, Dundee House, 21 City Square, Dundee DD1

3BY; T.-01382 434431.
E-mail: gregory.colgan@dundeecity.gov.uk

Collins, Rev. Catherine E. E., MA (Hons), BD, CertEd, DipCounselling. Parish Minister, Broughty Ferry New Kirk, 2006-2021 (retired); b. 12.11.54, Hastings; m., Rev. David A. Collins; 2 s. Educ. Kelso High School; University of St. Andrews. Teacher of English, Full Time and Temporary in Borders and Renfrewshire, 1977-89; Parish Minister (Job Share), Greyfriars Parish Church, Lanark, 1993-2006. (Past) Moderator of Presbytery; Depute Presbytery Clerk; Convener, Pastoral Support, Church of Scotland's Board of Ministry; Moderator, Presbytery of Dundee, 2019-20. Recreations: gardening; walking; genealogy. Address: (h.) 16 Melville Road, Ladybank, Fife KY15 7LU.

Collins, Rev. David Arthur, BSc (Hons) Zoology, BD. Retired Parish Minister (Church of Scotland); b. 15.6.51, Dumbarton; m., Rev. Catherine E.E. Collins; 2 s. Educ. Clydebank High School; University of Glasgow; University of St. Andrews; Jordanhill College. Teacher of Biology, Selkirk High School, 1974-79; Assistant Education Officer, Glasgow Museum Education Service, 1979-88; Education Officer, Dundee Art Galleries and Museums, 1988-89; (BD/Ministry Training, 1989-93); Locum Minister, Westray & Papa Westray, Orkney, 1991; Parish Minister, Lanark: Greyfriars, 1993-2006; Auchterhouse linked with Murroes & Tealing, 2006-09; Auchterhouse linked with Monikie & Newbigging and Murroes & Tealing, 2009-16. Moderator, Presbytery of Lanark, 2001-02; Moderator, Presbytery of Dundee, 2015-16. Church of Scotland National Assessor, 2010-15. Recreations: photography; drawing and painting; reading; walking. Address: Eden Cottage, 16 Melville Road, Ladybank, Cupar, Fife KY15 7LU; T.-01337 830707; e-mail: dcollins@webartz.com

Collins, Sir Kenneth Darlingston, BSc (Hons), MSc; b. 12.8.39, Hamilton; m., Georgina Frances Pollard; 1 s.; 1 d. Educ. St. John's Grammar School; Hamilton Academy; Glasgow University; Strathclyde University. Steelworks apprentice, 1956-59; University, 1960-65; Planning Officer, 1965-66; WEA Tutor, 1966-67; Lecturer: Glasgow College of Building, 1967-69, Paisley College of Technology, 1969-79; Member: East Kilbride Town and District Council, 1973-79, Lanark County Council, 1973-75, East Kilbride Development Corporation, 1976-79; Chairman, NE Glasgow Children's Panel, 1974-76; European Parliament: Deputy Leader, Labour Group, 1979-84, Chairman, Environment Committee, 1979-84 and 1989-99 (Vice-Chairman, 1984-87), Socialist Spokesman on Environment, Public Health and Consumer Protection, 1984-89; Chairman, Conference of Committee Chairs, 1993-99; Member (Labour), European Parliament, 1979-99; Chairman, Scottish Environment Protection Agency, 1999-2007; Ambassador for the National Asthma Campaign, until 2007; Chairman, Advisory Committee, SAGES (Scottish Association of Geosciences, Environment & Society), 2008-2010. Fellow, Royal Scottish Geographical Society; Hon. Fellow, Chartered Institution of Water and Environmental Management; Hon. Fellow, Chartered Institution of Wastes Management; former Board Member, Institute for European Environmental Policy, London; Fellow, Industry and Parliament Trust; former Board Member, Energy Action Scotland; former Member, British Waterways Scotland Group; former Trustee, The Green Foundation; Board Member, Central Scotland Forest Trust, 2001-04 (Chairman, 1998-2001); Former Board Member, Forward Scotland; Chairman, Tak Tent Cancer Support, 1999-2002; former Member, Management Board, European Environment Agency; Honorary Vice President, Environment Protection UK, until 2009; Vice President, Royal Environmental Health Institute of Scotland, until

2009; Vice President: Town and Country Planning Association, The Trading Standards Institute, The Association of Drainage Authorities, until 2009; former Chairman, Health Equality Europe; Member, Advisory Board, ESRC Genomics Policy and Research Forum, until 2005; Member: European Public Affairs Consultancies Association (EPACA) Professional Practices Panel, until 2009, European Commission High Level Group on Competitiveness, Energy and the Environment, 2006-08. Knighthood in 2003 for services to Environmental Protection; Honorary Degree of Doctor, University of Paisley, 2004; Honorary Doctor of Science, University of Glasgow, 2009. Recreations: music; dogs; gardening. Address: (b.) 11 Stuarton Park, East Kilbride G74 4LA; T.- 01355 221345; e-mail: ken.collins@blueyonder.co.uk

Collins, Kenneth E., MPhil, PhD, FRCGP. President, Glasgow Jewish Representative Council, 1995-98 and 2004-07 (Hon. President, 1998-2001); Chairman, Scottish Council of Jewish Communities, 1999-2003 and 2007-08; Chairman, Scottish Jewish Archives Centre; b. 23.12.47, Glasgow; m., Irene Taylor; 1 s.; 3 d. Educ. High School of Glasgow; Glasgow University. General medical practitioner in Glasgow, 1978-2007; Medical Officer, Newark Lodge, Glasgow; Senior Research Fellow, Centre for the History of Medicine, Glasgow University; Visiting Professor, Hebrew University of Jerusalem, since 2007. Past Chairman, Glasgow Board of Jewish Education. Publications: Aspects of Scottish Jewry, 1987; Go and Learn: International Story of the Jews and Medicine in Scotland, 1988; Second City Jewry, 1990; Be Well!, Jewish Immigrant Health and Welfare in Glasgow, 1860-1914, 2001; ed., Scotland's Jews, 2nd Edition, 2008; Narrative editor, Jewish Glasgow, an Illustrated History (2013); The Jewish Experience in Scotland: from Immigration to Integration (2016); Zev's Children: An International Jewish Family (2021). Address: (b.) Centre for the History of Medicine, Lilybank House, University of Glasgow, Glasgow G12 8QQ.
E-mail: drkcollins@gmail.com

Collins, Simon, LLB (Hons), DipLP. Solicitor Advocate; Founding Partner, Collins & Co Defence Lawyers, Edinburgh, since 2016; b. 6.69. Educ. Daniel Stewart's and Melville College; University of Glasgow. Career history: Solicitor Advocate and Partner, Capital Defence Lawyers, 1992-2016. Legal representative for In Care Abuse Survivors (INCAS) assisting them in lobbying the Government for the now established Scottish Child Abuse Inquiry; heads the legal team representing INCAS as core participants in the Inquiry. Address: Collins & Co Defence Lawyers, 18 Cadzow Place, Edinburgh EH7 5SN; T.-0131 661 3210; e-mail: julie@collinsandcolawyers.com

Coltman, Professor Viccy, BA, MA, PhD, FSA (London), FSA (Scotland), FRHS. Professor of Eighteenth-Century History of Art, University of Edinburgh (Head of History of Art, 2010-13); b. 15.4.72, Leamington Spa. BA, University of Bristol, 1990-93; MA, Courtauld Institute of Art, 1994-95, PhD, 1996-99; appointed Lecturer, History of Art, University of Edinburgh, 2002, Senior Lecturer, 2006, Professor, 2015. Philip Leverhulme Prize, 2006. Recreation: yoga. Publications: Fabricating the Antique: Neoclassicism in Britain; Classical Sculpture and the Culture of Collecting; Art and Identity in Scotland: A cultural history from the Jacobite Rising of 1745 to Walter Scott (Author). Address: (b.) History of Art, Edinburgh College of Art, 74 Lauriston Place, Edinburgh EH3 GDF; T.-0131 650 8426; e-mail: viccy.coltman@ed.ac.uk

Coltrane, Robbie, DA. Actor/Director; b. 31.3.50, Glasgow. Educ. Trinity College, Glenalmond; Glasgow School of Art. Film credits: Subway Riders, 1979, Balham

Gateway to the South, 1980, Britannia Hospital, 1981, Scrubbers, 1982, Krull, 1982, Ghost Dance, 1983, Chinese Boxes, 1984, The Supergrass, 1984, Defense of the Realm, 1985, Revolution, 1985, Caravaggio, 1985, Absolute Beginners, 1985, Mona Lisa, 1985, Eat the Rich, 1987, The Fruit Machine, 1987, Slipstream, 1988, Bert Rigby, You're a Fool, 1988, Danny Champion of the World, 1988, Let It Ride, 1988, Henry V, 1988, Nuns on the Run, 1989, Perfectly Normal, 1989, Pope Must Die, 1990, Oh What A Night, 1991, Adventures of Huck Finn, 1992, Goldeneye, 1995, Buddy, 1996, Montana, 1997, Frogs for Snakes, 1997, Message in a Bottle, 1998, The World Is Not Enough, 1999, From Hell, 2000, Harry Potter and the Philosopher's Stone, 2001, Harry Potter and the Chamber of Secrets, 2002, Harry Potter and Prisoner of Azkaban, 2003, Harry Potter and the Goblet of Fire, 2004, Ocean's 12, Stormbreaker, 2005, Harry Potter and the Order of the Phoenix, 2006; The Brothers Bloom, 2007; Harry Potter and the Half Blood Prince, 2007; Harry Potter and the Deathly Hallows, 2010; Brave, 2011; Great Expectations, 2011; Arthur Christmas, 2011; Effie, 2014; theatre credits: The Bug, 1976, Mr Joyce is Leaving, 1978, The Slab Boys, 1978, The Transfiguration of Benno Blimpie, 1978, The Loveliest Night of the Year, 1979-80, Dick Whittington, 1979, Snobs and Yobs, 1980, Yr Obedient Servant (one-man show), 1987, Mistero Buffo (one-man show), 1990; television credits include: roles in several The Comic Strip Presents productions, lead role in Tutti Frutti (BBC Scotland), Alive and Kicking, 1991, Coltrane in a Cadillac, 1992, Cracker, 1993, 1994, 1995, Ebbtide, 1996, Coltrane's Planes and Automobiles, 1997, Alice in Wonderland, 1998, The Plan Man, Frazier, 2004, Cracker 9:11, 2005, B Road Britain, 2007, Murderland, 2009; Lead Balloon, 2010; Five Go to Rehab; The Hunt for Tony Blair; Yes Prime Minister; Crackanory; National Treasure (Channel 4); Critical Evidence (A&E); Urban Myths: F for Fakenham. Recreations: vintage cars; sailing; painting; reading; movies. Address: c/o CDA, 22 Astwood Mews, London SW7 4DE.

Colvin, Professor Calum Munro, DA, MA (RCA), RSA, OBE. Professor of Fine Art Photography, Dundee University, since 2001; artist, since 1985; b. 26.10.61, Glasgow. Educ. North Berwick High School; Duncan of Jordanstone College of Art and Design; Royal College of Art, London. Lecturer in Fine Art, Dundee University, from 1993; Creative Scotland Award, 2000; 13th Higashikawa Overseas Photographer Prize, 1997; has exhibited work internationally since 1986 with work in many collections; recent solo exhibitions include Scottish National Gallery of Modern Art, 1998; Kawasaki City Museum, 1998; UNESCO Headquarters, Paris, 2005; Royal Scottish Academy, 2009; Scottish National Portrait Gallery, 2015. Address: (h.) 1 Duddingston Park South, Edinburgh EH15 3NX; T.- 0131-669 0218; m. 0780 327 4694.
E-mail: calumcolvin@me.com

Comiskey, Patricia Bernadette, BSc, MSc, PhD, LLB, LLM, DipLP, FCIArb. Advocate, since 2001. Educ. Leicester Polytechnic; University of Minnesota; Edinburgh University; University of Aberdeen. Researcher in Textile Technology, University of Minnesota, 1981-83; Lecturer in Textile Technology, Leicester Polytechnic, 1983-88; Assistant Fabric Technologist, Marks and Spencer, London, 1988-90; Menswear Buyer Manager, Jenners Ltd, Edinburgh, 1990-95; Tutor Law School, University of Edinburgh, 2001-04; Clerk to the Examiners, Deputy Clerk of Faculty of Advocates, 2003-09; Board Member, Stepfamily Scotland, 2005-09; Member, Edinburgh Branch Committee, Royal Overseas League Club, 2007-2010; Member of the Council of The Stair Society, 2009-2015; Ad hoc Advocate Depute, since 2015;

Treasurer of The Tumbling Lassie Committee since 2015; External Counsel for Nursing & Midwifery Council, since 2017; Fellow of the Chartered Institute of Arbitrators, since 2018. Address: Parliament House, Edinburgh EH1 1RF.
E-mail: patricia.comiskey@advocates.org.uk

Conn, Stewart. Poet and playwright; b. 1936, Glasgow, brought up Kilmarnock. Educ. Glasgow University. Author of numerous stage plays, including The Burning, Herman, The Aquarium, By the Pool, Clay Bull; television work includes The Kite, Bloodhunt; poetry includes In the Kibble Palace, The Luncheon of the Boating Party, At the Aviary, In the Blood; Stolen Light; Distances: a personal evocation of people and places; l'Ànima del Teixidor; Ghosts at Cockcrow; The Loving-Cup; The Breakfast Room; Estuary; The Touch of Time: New & Selected Poems; Against the Light; Aspects of Edinburgh; his production of Carver (by John Purser) won Gold Medal Award, New York, International Radio Festival, 1991; left BBC, 1992; appointed to Edinburgh's poet laureateship, 2002-05. In 2006 received the Institute for Contemporary Scotland's Iain Crichton Smith Award for services to literature. Editor, 100 Favourite Scottish Poems, 2006; 100 Favourite Scottish Love Poems, 2008; Stolen Light shortlisted for Saltire Scottish Book of the Year; The Breakfast Room chosen as 2011 Scottish Mortgage Investment Trust Poetry Book of the Year. E-mail: stewartconn@btinternet.com
Web: www.stewartconn.com

Connaghan, John, CBE. Chair, Lothian NHS Board, since 2021; Chief Executive, NHS Scotland, 2020-21. Career history: printing and publishing with Wm Collins and Letts; three different 'career roles' firstly in industry, secondly in the NHS and now in the Civil Service; management trainee, became General Manager of production for Letts with responsibility for manufacturing plants in Scotland and Long Island, USA; joined the NHS as General Manager for the South of Glasgow in the late 1980s, responsible for the Victoria and Southern General; held positions as Chief Executive of the Victoria, the Western General and then Fife Acute Trusts; joined the Civil Service in 2006 as Director of NHS Delivery and then as Chief Operating Officer, NHS Scotland; filled the post of Director-General Health and Social Care and Chief Executive of NHS Scotland on an interim basis; joined the Health Service Executive for Ireland in 2017, serving latterly as Director General of the Irish Health Service based in Dublin with responsibilities for £16bn and 130,000 staff. Visiting Professor for Strathclyde University Business School. Recreation: hockey. Address: Lothian NHS Board, 2-4 Waterloo Place, Edinburgh EH1 3EG; T.-0131 536 9000.

Connal, Robert Craig, QC, LLB (Hons), SSC. Arbitrator; Freelance Litigator with Vario from Pinsent Masons, since 2020; Solicitor, since 1977; Partner, Pinsent Masons LLP, 2012-2020; Head of Advocacy (Litigation and Compliance), 2014-16; Partner, McGrigors, 1980-2012 (Head of Commercial Litigation, 2002-07); Senior Litigation Partner and UK Head of Advocacy, 2007-2012; Solicitor Advocate: Scotland (civil), 1996, (criminal), 2004, England and Wales, (all courts), 2006; b. 7.7.54, Brentwood; m., Mary Ferguson Bowie; 2 d. Educ. Hamilton Academy; University of Glasgow. Apprentice, Brown, Mair, Gemmill & Hislop, 1975-77; Assistant, McGrigor Donald, 1977-1980. Council Member, Royal Faculty of Procurators in Glasgow, 1995-98; appointed Scotland's first Solicitor Advocate QC, 2002; External Examiner, University of Aberdeen, 2001-05; Convenor, Law Society of Scotland Supreme Courts Training Course (Civil), since 2004; NITA Awarded Advocacy Trainer; Committee Member, Society of Solicitor Advocates; UK Chairman, BICBA; Member: Delos Arbitration, Arbitration Ireland,

Scotland Arbitration Centre; Law Society of England and Wales Solicitor Advocate of the Year, 2012. Publications: many articles in press and professional journals in print and online. Recreations: rugby referee; gardens (but not gardening). Address: Lethendy, 170 East Kilbride Road, Busby, Glasgow G76 8RU.
E-mail: RCCQC@protonmail.com

Connarty, Michael, BA, DCE. MP (Labour), Linlithgow and East Falkirk, 2005-2015, Falkirk East, 1992-2005; Board Member, Parliamentary Office of Science and Technology, 1996; Chair, European Scrutiny Select Committee, 2006-2010; b. 3.9.47, Coatbridge; m., Margaret Doran; 1 s.; 1 d. Educ. Stirling University; Jordanhill College of Education; Glasgow University. Member, Stirling District Council, 1977-90 (Council Leader, 1980-90); Member, Convention of Scottish Local Authorities, 1980-90 (Depute Labour Leader, 1988-90); Member, Scottish Executive, Labour Party, 1981-92; Vice-Chair, Socialist Educational Association, 1983-85; Council Member, Educational Institute of Scotland, 1984-85; PPS to Tom Clarke, MP, 1987-88; Chair, Labour Party Scottish Local Government Committee, 1988-90; Vice-Chairman, Scottish MAP, 1988-95; Secretary, PLP Science and Technology Comittee, 1992-97; Member, European Directives Committee on Agriculture, Environment and Health and Safety, 1993-96; Chair, Economy, Industry and Energy Committee, Scottish PLP Group, 1993-97; Scottish Co-ordinator, Labour Crime and Drugs Campaign, 1993-97; Scottish Task Force Leader on Skills and Training in Scotland and Youth and Students, 1995-97; Member, Select Committee on the Parliamentary Commissioner for Administration, 1995-97; Chairman, Scottish Parliamentary Labour Party Group, 1998-99. Recreations: family; hill-walking; reading; music.

Connolly, Liz, BA, MBA. Principal and Chief Executive, West College Scotland, since 2018. Educ. University of Strathclyde; Harvard University Graduate School of Education. Chief Executive: Scottish Enterprise Ayrshire, 1999-2000, Scottish Enterprise Lanarkshire, 2000-06; Scottish Enterprise: Senior Director Operations, 2006-08, Regional Operations Director - West, 2008-2010; Business Consultant, 2011-13; Member of Court, University of the West of Scotland, 2008-2017; Vice Principal, Corporate Development, West College Scotland, 2013-18. Board Member, Targeting Innovation; Board Member, Interface. Address: West College Scotland, Clydebank Campus, Queens' Quay, Glasgow GB1 1BF; T.-0300 600 60 60.

Connor, George. Board Member, Parole Board for Scotland, since 2015 (Chief Executive, 2014-15); b. 22.11.57, Glasgow; 1 s.; 1 d. Educ. St Mungo's Academy, Glasgow. Department of Health & Social Security, 1975-89; Ministry of Defence, 1989-2007; Criminal Injuries Compensation Authority, 2007-2012; Scottish Government, 2012-2014. Recreations: reading; live music. Address: (b.) Saughton House, Broomhouse Drive, Edinburgh EH11 3XD; T.-0131 244 3404.
E-mail: george.connor@scotland.gsi.gov.uk

Connor, James Michael, MD, DSc, BSc (Hons), MB, ChB (Hons), FRCP. Former Professor of Medical Genetics and Director, West of Scotland Regional Genetics Service (1987-2011) (Wellcome Trust Senior Lecturer and Honorary Consultant in Medical Genetics, Glasgow University, 1984-87); b. 18.6.51, Grappenhall, England; m., Dr. Rachel A.C. Educ. Lymm Grammar School, Cheshire; Liverpool University. House Officer, Liverpool Royal Infirmary; Resident in Internal Medicine, Johns Hopkins

Hospital, USA; University Research Fellow, Liverpool University; Instructor in Internal Medicine, Johns Hopkins Hospital, USA; Consultant in Medical Genetics, Institute of Medical Genetics, Yorkhill, Glasgow. Publications: Essential Medical Genetics (Co-author), 1984 (6th edition, 2011); Principles and Practice of Medical Genetics (Co-Editor), (5th edition, 2007); various articles on aspects of medical genetics. Recreations: fly fishing; sea kayaking and classic cars. Address: (h.) East Collarie Farm, by Fenwick, Ayrshire.

Conroy, Professor James Charles, FAcSS, BEd, MA, PhD. Director, European Institute for Advanced Studies, Lüneburg, Germany; Vice Principal (Emeritus), University of Glasgow; Professor of Religious and Philosophical Education, since 2004; formerly Dean for European Affairs and Strategy (2012-21); formerly Dean of Faculty of Education (2005-2010); b. 30.04.55, Portadown, Northern Ireland; m., Denise Frances (nee Meagher); 1 s. 2 d. Educ. St Patrick's College, Armagh; London (St Mary's and Institute of Education (UCL)); Lancaster; VU, Amsterdam. Accounts Controller, Chase Bank Ireland, 1973-76; Development Officer, Adult Education, Westminster Diocese, 1981-83; Teacher and Head of Department Theology, St Brendan's VIth Form, 1983-87; Senior Lecturer, Education and Theology, St Mary's College, Twickenham, 1987-90; Director, RE and Pastoral Care, St Andrews's College, Bearsden, 1990-99; Head of Department of RE, University of Glasgow, 1999-2004. Co-Founder: Guild of European Research-Intensive Universities; Board of Directors: Learning and Teaching Scotland, 2007-2011; President, Association for Moral Education (Based in US), 2007-2010; Chair, Philosophy of Education Society of Great Britain, 2013-2016; Chair, Journal of Moral Education Trust; Trustee, Hutchesons' School, Glasgow; Co-Chair: UUKi, PVC Network, 2016-2018. Elected to the Fellowship of the Academy of Social Sciences, 2012. Publications; Does Religious Education Work?, 2013; Catholic Education: Inside-Out/Outside-In, 1999; Betwixt and Between: The Liminal Imagination, Education and Democracy, 2004. Recreations: antique furniture; gardening; cooking and family. Address: St. Andrew's Building, Eldon Street, Glasgow G12 8QQ; T.-0141 3307375; e-mail: James.Conroy@glasgow.ac.uk

Constance, Angela. MA (Soc.Sci), MSc (Social Work). MSP (SNP), Almond Valley, since 2011, Livingston, 2007-2011; Minister for Drugs Policy, since 2020; Cabinet Secretary for Communities, Social Security and Equalities, 2016-18; Cabinet Secretary for Education & Lifelong Learning, 2014-16; Cabinet Secretary for Training, Youth & Women's Employment, 2014; Minister for Youth Employment, 2011-2014; Minister for Children and Young People, 2011; Minister for Skills and Lifelong Learning, 2010-11; b. 15.7.70; m., Garry Knox; 1 s. Educ. West Calder High; Boness Academy; Glasgow University; Stirling University. Social Worker, 1997-2007; Social Worker/Mental Health Officer, 2002-07; Social Worker/Mental Health Officer/Practice Teacher, 2005-07. Member, West Lothian Coun., 1997-2007. Recreations: jogging; reading; drawing. Address: Scottish Parliament, Edinburgh EH99 1SP.

E-mail: angela.constance.msp@parliament.scot

Conti, Most Rev. Mario Joseph, PhL, STL, DD, DLitt, FRSE. Archbishop Emeritus of Glasgow; Archbishop of Glasgow, 2002-2012; Bishop of Aberdeen, 1977-2002; Apostolic Administrator, Paisley, 2004-05; b. 20.3.34, Elgin. Educ. St. Marie's Convent; Springfield School, Elgin; Blairs College, Aberdeen; Pontifical Scots College, Pontifical Gregorian University, Rome. Ordained priest, Rome, 1958; Curate, St. Mary's Cathedral, Aberdeen, 1959-62; Parish Priest, St. Joachim's, Wick and St. Anne's, Thurso, 1962-77; President-Treasurer, SCIAF (Scottish Catholic International Aid Fund) 1977-85, Member of the Board, until 2012; President, National Liturgy Commission,

1981-85; Member, International Commission for English in the Liturgy, 1978-87; Founding Member and Chairman, Scottish Catholic Heritage Commission, 1980-2014; Member, Pontifical Council for the Promotion of Christian Unity, Rome, 1984-2014; President, (National) Commission for Christian Doctrine and Unity, 1986-2012; first Convener, Central Council, ACTS (Action of Churches Together in Scotland), 1990-93; Co-Moderator, Joint Working Group of the World Council of Churches and the Roman Catholic Church, 1996-2006; Head of Catholic Delegation to 8th General Assembly, World Council of Churches, Harare, 1998; a President, Churches Together in Britain and Ireland, 1999-2005; Chair, Scottish Bishops' Conference Committee for Inter-Religious Dialogue, 2012-2020; Member, Pontifical Commission for the Cultural Heritage of the Church, 1994-2004; Member, Historic Buildings Council of Scotland 2000-03; a founding Member of Mediaeval Glasgow Trust, 2014; Health Appointments Advisory Council, 1994-2000; Knight Commander with Star of the Order of the Holy Sepulchre, 1989 - Grand Prior, Scottish Lieutenancy, since 2013; Principal Chaplain to British Association of the Sovereign Military Order of Malta, 1995-2000 and 2005-2015, Conventual Chaplain, Grand Cross, since 2001; (Italian State honours): Commendatore, Order of Merit of the Italian Republic, Grande Ufficiale (1 Classe) dell'Ordine della Stella della Solidarietà Italiana, 2007; from the Associazione dei Lucchesi nel Mondo, il Medaglio d'oro, 2020; (Scottish University honours): DD honoris causa: Aberdeen 1989, Glasgow 2010, DLitt honoris causa: Glasgow Caledonian, 2015. Recreations: music; art; travel. Address: (h.) 40 Newlands Road, Glasgow G43 2JD. E-mail: Mario.conti@rcag.org.uk

Conway, Very Revd. John. Provost, St Mary's Cathedral, Edinburgh, since 2017; m.; 3 d. Began training for ordination at Lincoln Theological College; completed studies at TISEC and New College, Edinburgh University. Curacy at St Mary's Cathedral; Rector, St Martin of Tours Episcopal Church, 2001-2017 (helped establish the St Martin's Community Resource Centre; former Co-ordinator of Initial Ministerial Education in the Diocese; former Co-Convenor of Edinburgh Interfaith Association, and former Convenor of the Diocesan Mission & Ministry Committee). Address: St Mary's Cathedral, Palmerston Place, Edinburgh EH12 5AW; T.-0131 225 6293.

Cook, Colin. Director of Economic Development, Scottish Government, since 2021, Director of Digital, 2017-2021 (appointed Acting Director in 2016). Educ. University of Durham; International Management Centres; Institute of Directors. Career history: Marketing, Metal Box plc, 1997-2002; Marketing Director, Royal Mail, 1993-2003; Senior Civil Servant, Scottish Government, 2003-09; Marketing Director, British Army, 2009-2012; Trustee, Royal British Legion Poppy Factory, since 2011; appointed Head of Digital Strategy and Programmes, Scottish Government in 2012, then Head of Digital Public Services and Business Transformation in 2015. Trustee of Royal Caledonian Education Trust. Address: Scottish Government, St. Andrews House, Regent Road, Edinburgh EH1 3DG.

Cook, James. Scotland Editor, BBC Scotland, since 2022, Chief News Correspondent, The Nine, since 2019. Educ. Forfar Academy. Began career in journalism at local radio station in Dundee; held roles at BBC Scotland including sub-editor, duty editor, reporter, correspondent and presenter; joined the network BBC News team as a Scotland Correspondent in 2007. Address: BBC Scotland, 40 Pacific Quay, Glasgow G51 1DA.

Cook, Rev. James Stanley Stephen Ronald Tweedie, BD, DipPSS. Minister, Hamilton West Parish Church, 1974-2001; b. 18.8.35, Tullibody; m., Jean Douglas McLachlan; 2 s.; 1 d. Educ. Whitehill Senior Secondary

School, Glasgow; First violin in school orchestra; St Andrews University (Graduated 1973 - BD; 1974 - DipPSS). Apprentice quantity surveyor, Glasgow, 1953-54; regular soldier, REME, 1954-57; served in Cyprus during ENOSIS Terrorist Campaign. Assistant Preventive Officer, Waterguard Department, HM Customs and Excise, 1957-61; Officer, HM Customs and Excise, 1961-69; studied for the ministry, 1969-74. Chairman, Cruse (Lanarkshire), 1983-93, 1994-99; Chairman, Cruse - Scotland, 1991-95, Convener, 1999-2001; Member, Council, Cruse UK, 1988-94; Member, National Training Group, Cruse, 1987-94; Member, Action Research for Crippled Child Committee, 1977-94; Substitute Provincial Grand Master, Lanarkshire (Middle Ward), 1983-88; Honorary Provincial Grand Chaplain, since 1989; founder Member, Wishaw Victim Support Scheme, 1985; Member, Hamilton Rotary Club, 1980-2014, President, 1994-95; Member, Hamilton Crime Prevention Panel, 1976-2000, Chairman, 1986-87; Moderator, Presbytery of Hamilton, 1999-2000; Mental Health Chaplain, 1988-2010; Wishaw Probus Club, 2010-2020, President, 2013-14. Recreations: music; photography; DIY; computer enthusiast. Address: Mansend, 137a Old Manse Road, Netherton, Wishaw ML2 0EW.

Cooke, Anthony John, BA (Hons), MA (Manchester); b. 15.7.43, Salford, Lancashire; m., Judith Margaret; 2 s. Educ. Accrington Grammar School; Manchester University. Teacher, Bishops College, Carriacou, Grenada, West Indies; Lecturer, Dundee College of Commerce; Lecturer/Senior Lecturer, University of Dundee; Consultant, Historic Scotland. Publications: Stanley: From Arkwright Village to Commuter Suburb, 2003; From Popular Enlightenment to Lifelong Learning, 2006; The Rise and Fall of the Scottish Cotton Industry, 1778-1914 (2010); A History of Drinking. The Scottish Pub, since 1700 (2015). Recreations: walking; swimming; choral singing. Address: (h.) 424, Blackness Road, Dundee DD2 1TQ; T.-01382 668476.
E-mail: a_j_cooke@btinternet.com

Cooke, Nicholas Huxley, MA (Oxon), FRSA. Independent sustainability consultant, CLEAR Services Ltd; b. 6.5.44, Godalming, Surrey; m., Anne Landon; 2 s.; 3 d. Educ. Charterhouse School; Worcester College, Oxford University. Retail management, London; chartered accountancy training, London; British International Paper, 1972-78; Director (Scotland), British Trust for Conservation Volunteers, 1978-84; Director, Scottish Conservation Projects Trust, 1984-98; Member, Scottish Committee for European Year of the Environment, 1987-88; Policy Committee Member, Scottish Council for Voluntary Organisations, 1992-2002; Board Member: Youthlink Scotland, Falkirk Environment Trust, Dundee Waste and Environment Trust, 1996-99; Member, Scottish Employer Supported Volunteering Group, 1997-2002; Chair, Scottish Committee, Voluntary Sector NTO, 1997-2001, Gowanbank Historic Village Ltd, 2001-04; Director, Rockdust Ltd, 2005-08; Secretary, Scottish Senior Alliance for Volunteering in the Environment (SSAVE), 2001-03; Managing Director, Scottish Organic Producers Association, 2003-05 (Executive Chairman, 2002-03); Hon. President, Callander Youth Project Trust, 2009-17 (Chair, 2004-09); Member, WREN Scottish Advisory Panel, 2016-18 (Chair, 2017-18); ACTS Scottish Churches Rural Group and ACTS Fife Pilgrim Way Group (Convenor), 2013-2019. Secretary, Incorporated Glasgow, Stirlingshire and Sons of the Rock Society (forthgiving), since 2007 (Preses, 2003-04); Secretary, Scottish Pilgrim Routes Forum SCIO, since 2012; Treasurer, The Carse of Stirling Partnership SCIO, since 2019; Trustee, Northern Pilgrims' Way Group SCIO, since 2020; Member, Scottish Episcopal Church, St Andrews' Diocesan Administration Board, since 2011. Recreations: Lepidoptera surveys and field entomology; fly fishing; churches; pilgrimage walking routes. Address: (b.) The Old School House, 23 King Street, Doune, Perthshire FK16 6DN; T.-01786 841809.
E-mail: Nick@clearserv.co.uk

Cooper, Professor Christine, BA, MSc, PhD. Chair in Accounting, University of Edinburgh Business School, since 2018; Professor of Accounting, Strathclyde University, 1999-2018; b. 16.3.56, London; 1 d. Educ. Crown Woods, Eltham, London; Greenwich University; London School of Economics. Trustee, Association for Accountancy and Business Affairs. Publication: 'Critical Perspectives on Accounting' Journal (Co-Editor). Address: (b.) 29 Buccleuch Place, Edinburgh EH8 9JS.

Cooper, Professor Jonathan. Vice Principal for Knowledge Exchange, University of Glasgow, 2014-2019, Professor, since 1991. Career history: Dean of Graduate Studies, College of Science and Engineering, 2010-14; Head of Division of Biomedical Engineering, School of Engineering, 2010-14; University of Glasgow: The Wolfson Chair of Bioengineering, since 2009; ERC Advanced Investigator, since 2014. Fellow of the Royal Academy of Engineering; Fellow of the Royal Society of Edinburgh. Address: University of Glasgow, R726 Level 7, S&E College Office, Rankine Building, Glasgow G12 8LT; T.-0141 330 4931.
E-mail: Jon.Cooper@glasgow.ac.uk

Cooper, Penelope, BA, CMgr, FCMI. Director of Culture and Major Events, The Scottish Government, since 2021; b. Anglesey, North Wales; m.; 2 d. Educ. Ysgol Gyfun Llangefni. The Open University; The Open University Business School; Chartered Management Institute; Chartered Institute of Personnel and Development. Career history: Registered General Nurse, NHS, 1983-89; Life and Pensions Sales Trainer and Advisor, Citibank Life, London, 1989-93; Standard Life Germany: Corporate Change Manager, Edinburgh, 1994-97, Customer Service Manager, Pensions Servicing (Group Final Salary, Personal Pensions), Edinburgh, 1997-2002, Manager, Review of New Business Operations, Edinburgh, 2002-03, Operations Director, Frankfurt, Germany, 2003-04; Head of Customer Services, European Financial Services, HBOS, Maastricht, Netherlands; Heidelberg, Germany, 2004-08; Regional Director (Europe), World Association of Girl Guides and Girl Scouts, Brussels, Belgium, 2009-2012; Chief Operations Officer, OneLife, Luxembourg, 2012-17; Chief Executive, Scottish Public Pensions Agency (SPPA), 2017-2021; Director of Covid Coordination, The Scottish Government, 2020-2022. Address: The Scottish Government, St. Andrew's House, Regent Road, Edinburgh EH1 3DG.

Cooper, Professor Sally-Ann, OBE, BSc, MB, BS, MD, FRCPsych. Honorary Senior Research Fellow (Mental Health & Wellbeing), University of Glasgow; appointed Professor of Learning Disabilities, Institute of Health and Wellbeing, Glasgow University in 1999; Honorary Consultant in Learning Disabilities Psychiatry, NHS Greater Glasgow and Clyde, since 1999; b. 28.4.61, Lincoln; m., Mark Guy Venner Anderson. Educ. Medical College of St Bartholomew's Hospital, London. Address: (b.) Institute of Health and Wellbeing, Glasgow University, Mental Health and Wellbeing Group, 1st floor Administrative Building, Gartnavel Royal Hospital, 1055 Great Western Road, Glasgow G12 0XH; T.-0141-211 3701.

Cooper, Professor Thomas Joshua, BA, MA. Professor of Fine Art, Senior Researcher, Glasgow School of Art, since 2002; artist; b. 19.12.46, San Francisco; m., Catherine Alice Mooney; 2 d. Educ. Arcata High School, CA; University of New Mexico; Humboldt State University. Former Senior Lecturer, Trent Polytechnic, Nottingham; Head of Fine Art Photography, Glasgow School of Art, 1982-2000. Creative Scotland Award, 2005. Recreations: walking; music; wine; film; reading. Address: (b.) Glasgow School of Art, 167 Renfrew Street, Glasgow G3 6RQ; T.-0141 353 4500.

Corbett, Gavin. Special Advisor to the First Minister, since 2021; Councillor for Fountainbridge/Craiglockhart Ward in Edinburgh (Green), 2012-2021; b. 9.10.65, Cumnock; partner, Karen Robertson; 2 s. Educ. Cumnock Academy; Glasgow University. Joined Shelter Scotland as campaign worker, 1993-2000, former Policy Advisor. Recreations: climbing hills; cycling; campaigning. Address: (h.) 28 Briarbank Terrace, Edinburgh EH11 1SU; T.-0131-337 5227.
E-mail: karenandgavin@blueyonder.co.uk

Cormack, Arthur. CEO of Fèisean nan Gàidheal, since 1992; Gaelic Singer (professional as solo artist), since 1983; Gaelic Broadcaster, since 1987; Director of Macmeanmna Ltd., since 2004; Director of Aros Ltd, since 2016; b. 21.4.65, Portree, Isle of Skye; m., Shona (nee MacDonald); 2 s.; 1 d. Educ. Portree High School. Ran R Cormack Clothing (family business), 1985-92; established and ran EISD Music, 1987-2003; founder of Macmeanmna (Gaelic Music Recording Label), 1987; Chairman and Co-founder of Aros Ltd, 1991; Member of Bòrd na Gàidhlig, 2003-2009, Chair, 2009-2012; Member of the Board of Eden Court Theatre, 2000-05; Member of Scottish Arts Council, 2004-09; former Trustee and Vice Chair of Sabhal Mòr Ostaig, 2014-19. Appointed OBE, 2015. Recreations: music; graphic design. Address: (b.) Meall House, Portree, Isle of Skye IV51 9BZ; T.-01478 613355.
E-mail: arthur@feisean.scot

Cormack, James Shearer, QC, LLB (Hons), DipLP. Solicitor, Partner, Pinsent Masons LLP, since 2012; b. 11.11.68, Inverness; m., Emma; 1 s.; 2 d. Educ. Lochaber High School; University of Edinburgh. Trainee Solicitor, then Qualified Assistant, McGrigor Donald, 1991-95; Member, Faculty of Advocates, 1996-2001; Partner, McGrigors LLP, 2001-2012. Appointed Queen's Counsel in Scotland, 2018. Recreations: family; cinema; dogs; running. Address: (b.) Pinsent Masons LLP, Princes Exchange, 58 Morrison Street, Edinburgh EH3 8BP; T.-0131 777 7356.
E-mail: jim.cormack@pinsentmasons.com

Cormack, Professor Robert John, MA, FRSA, FRSE, DLitt (Cape Breton), Doctor honoris causa (Edin), Fellow (University of the Highlands and Islands); b. 14.12.46, Blantyre; divorced, 2009; m. (2010); 1 s.; 2 d. Educ. Montrose Academy; Aberdeen University; Brown University, USA. Queen's University of Belfast: Lecturer in Sociology, 1973-87, Senior Lecturer, 1987-92, Reader, 1992-96, Professor, 1996-2001, Head, Department of Sociology and Social Policy, 1991-93, Dean, Faculty of Economics and Social Sciences, 1993-95, Pro-Vice Chancellor, 1995-2001; Principal, UHI Millennium Institute (now the University of the Highlands and Islands), 2001-09. FRSE, 2008. Publications: numerous books and articles on Northern Ireland including Discrimination and Public Policy in Northern Ireland (Co-Author). Address: 1/15 Tower Wynd, Edinburgh EH6 7BA.
E-mail: rjc@fastmail.fm

Cornwell, Professor Keith, BSc, PhD, DEng, FIMechE. Emeritus Professor of Heat Transfer, Heriot-Watt University; b. 4.4.42, Abingdon; m., Sheila Joan Mott; 1 s.; 1 d. Educ. City University, London. Research Fellow, Middlesex Polytechnic; Lecturer, Head of Department, Dean of Engineering, Director of Quality, and Head, School of Mathematical and Computing Science, Heriot-Watt University; Head of Heriot-Watt Dubai Campus, UAE; Chairman, C-MIST Ltd, 2009-2014. Partner, A1 Classic Cars LLP, since 2010. Publications: The Flow of Heat; numerous journal papers. Recreations: classic cars; hillwalking. Address: (h.) Ivanlea, Main Road, Dirleton EH39 5EA; e-mail: cornwellmail@gmail.com

Corrie, John Alexander. Member (Conservative), European Parliament for West Midlands Region, 1999-2004 (for Worcestershire and South Warwickshire, 1994-99); Co-ordinator, Development Committee, 1999-2004; Member, Budgets Committee, 1999-2004; Co-President, ACP/EU Joint Parliamentary Assembly, 1999-2002, now Honorary Life President; Member of North South Forum, 2002-04; Vice-President, Working Group "A", Foreign Affairs and Development, 2002-04; Delegation Leader to Dafur (Sudan), 2004; Election Monitor in Malawi, Congo, Brazzaville, Solomon Isles, Madagascar, The Seychelles, Fiji, Peru, Tanzania, Chad and Rwanda, 2002-04; farms family farm in Galloway; b. 1935; m.; 1 s.; 2 d. Educ. Kirkcudbright Academy; George Watson's College, Edinburgh; Lincoln Agricultural College, New Zealand. Commissioned from the ranks of New Zealand Army, 2nd Lieutenant, 1956; Nuffield Farming Scholar, 1972; National Chairman, Scottish Young Conservatives, 1964; MP (Conservative): Bute and North Ayrshire, 1974-83, Cunninghame North, 1983-87; PPS to Secretary of State for Scotland, 1979-81; introduced Private Member's Bill to reduce upper limit on abortion, 1979; Member: European Assembly, 1975-76 and 1977-79, Council of Europe, 1983-87, Western European Union (Defence Committee), 1983-87; Chief Whip, Conservatives in Europe, 1997-99; Senior Instructor, British Wool Board, Agricultural Training Board, 1970-74; elected to Council, Belted Galloway Cattle Society, 1978; Chairman, Scottish Transport Users Consultative Committee, 1988-94; Vice Chairman, Central Transport Consultative Committee, 1988-94; Council Member, Royal Agricultural Society of England, 1992-2000; Industrial Fellowship with Conoco and Du Pont, USA, 1987; awarded Wilberforce Plaque for Humane Work, 1981; Belted Galloway Judge, Royal Show, 2006; won Supreme Belted Galloway Champion at Royal Highland in 2010; Patron: Kisumu Children's Trust, Kenya, since 2006, DTI Mine Clearing and Development Initiative, since 2006; Belted Galloway Society: Vice Chairman, 2008-2011, Chairman, 2011-2014, Vice President, since 2017; Executive Member, Westminster Former Members Committee and Member, Trustee Committee, 2016-2020; President, European Sustainable Project Group, 2004-2010; President, Rigget Galloway Cattle Society, 2009-2013; Vice Chair, Scottish Former Members of Parliament Association; 2012 Lecture on "Democracy Building" in Bishkek, Kirgyzstan; observer in Libya in 2012 on war situation; President of African European Parliamentarians Initiative (AEPI), since 2018. Publications: Forestry in Europe; Fish Farming in Europe; The Importance of Forestry in the World Today; Towards a Community Rural Policy (Co-author). Address: (h.) Park House Tongland, Kirkcudbright DG6 4NE; e-mail: j.corrie126@btinternet.com

Corry, Maurice. MSP (Scottish Conservative), West Scotland region, 2016-2021; b. 6.60. Former Argyll and Bute councillor, representing Lomond North; stood for the Scottish Parliament in 2016 as the Conservative candidate for Dumbarton.

Cosgrove, Rt. Hon. Lady (Hazel Josephine Aronson), CBE, LLD. Senator of the College of Justice in Scotland, 1996-2006; b. 12.1.46, Glasgow; m., John A. Cosgrove; 1

s.; 1 d. Educ. Glasgow High School for Girls; Glasgow University. Advocate at Scottish Bar, 1968-79; Sheriff: Glasgow and Strathkelvin at Glasgow, 1979-83, Lothian and Borders at Edinburgh, 1983-96; Temporary Judge, Court of Session and High Court, 1992-96; Past Chairman, Mental Welfare Commission for Scotland; Past Chairman, Expert Panel on Sex Offending; Past Depute Chairman, Boundaries Commission for Scotland. Recreations: walking; opera; foreign travel. Address: (b.) Parliament House, Edinburgh EH1 1RQ; T.-0131-225 2595; e-mail: hazelcosgrove1967@gmail.com

Cosgrove, Stuart, PhD. Journalist and broadcaster; Director of Creative Diversity, Channel Four Television, 2010-2015; b. 12.11.52, Perth. Educ. Hull University. Lecturer, film and television; cultural critic; Media Editor, NME; contributor, The Face, The Guardian, The Observer, Arena; regular presenter, The Late Show, BBC TV; joined Channel Four after period as independent producer; appointed Senior Commissioning Editor, then Controller of Arts and Entertainment, before returning to Scotland. Co-host, BBC Radio Scotland's popular comedy football phone-in, Off The Ball; co-host, BBC Scotland's Saturday football results show, Sportscene Results; Head of Programmes (Nations and Regions), Channel Four Television, 1997-2015. Recreation: supporter of St Johnstone F.C. Address: (b.) BBC Radio Scotland, 40 Pacific Quay, Glasgow G51 1DA.

Costello, Peter. Chief Executive, Money Advice Scotland, since 2021. Educ. The Open University. Career history: Telecomms Exchange manager, British Telecom, 1987-93; Youth Worker, local church, 1993-94; Telecommunications SpecialistEnergis systems, BT, 1995; Software Support Specialist, Simens Nixdorf, 1995; Network Administrator, SGI, 1996-97; IT Manager, Aylesbury Vale Mental Health Authority, 1998-2000; Director of Shared Services, Wycliffe UK, 2000-08; Chief Operations Officer, City Temple, London, 2009-2014; Deputy Chief Executive, DENS Ltd, Hemel Hempstead, 2014-15; Trustee, Freedom in Christ Ministries, Reading, 2003-2016; Chief Executive Officer, Heart of Bucks, Aylesbury, 2016-19; Chief Executive, River Garden Auchincruive, Ayr, 2019-2020. National Teaching Team, Freedom in Christ Ministries, since 2002. Address: Money Advice Scotland, 36 Washington Street, Glasgow G3 8AZ; T.-0141 572 0237.

Coton, Professor Frank Norman, BSc, PhD, CEng, FRAeS, AFAIAA. Professor of Low Speed Aerodynamics, University of Glasgow, since 2003, Senior Vice Principal and Deputy Vice Chancellor (Academic), since 2021, Vice Principal, 2010-21, Dean of Engineering, 2007-09; b. 25.05.63, Dumbarton; m., Caroline; 1 s.; 2 d. Educ. Vale of Leven Academy; University of Glasgow. Production Engineering Apprentice, Rolls Royce Ltd., 1980-84; Glasgow University: Research Assistant, 1987-89, Lecturer, Department of Aerospace Engineering, 1986-89, Senior Lecturer, 1986-2000, Reader, 2000-03. Recreations: travel; photography. Address: (b.) Office of the Vice Principals, Level 4, Main Building, East Quadrangle, University of Glasgow, Glasgow G12 8QQ; T.-0141 330 4305. E-mail: frank.coton@glasgow.ac.uk

Cottom, Professor Sonia, BA (Hons). Director, Pain Association Scotland, since 2010. Educ. Wigan & Leigh College; Nottingham University Business School; Nottingham Trent University. Career: Export Sales Co-ordinator, Macnaughton Holdings Linited, 1998-2001; Cost Analyst, Halifax, 2001-06; Capacity Planner, Aviva, 2006-2010. Winner: Institute of Directors Early Stage Business UK Director of The Year Award, Institute of Directors Scotland Emerging Director award,

2013 Sayer Vincent Financial Leadership Awards. Editor of The Journal of Strategy, Operations and Economics and The Journal of Hospital and Medical Management; Visiting Professor, York St John University. Address: Pain Association Scotland, Suite D, Moncrieffe Business Centre, Friarton Road, Perth PH2 8DG; T.-0800 783 6059.

Coull, Rev. Morris. Retired Minister, St. Margaret's Church, Greenock (2014-18); m., Ann. Career: two years as an assistant at Bearsden South Parish Church on the North side of Glasgow; first charge in New Cumnock Old Parish Church in Ayr Presbytery, 1974-83; inducted to Hillington Park Parish Church on the south side of Glasgow, 1983-96; during a sabbatical period in 1993 attached to Peachtree Presbyterian Church in Atlanta, Georgia, USA; linked charge of Allan Park South with the Church of the Holy Rude in Stirling, 1996-2006; retired from full-time ministry, 2006; Locum at Old Gourock and Ashton Parish Church, 2007; returned to full-time ministry in 2008; Minister at Skelmorlie and Wemyss Bay Parish Church, 2008-2011; retired from full-time ministry in April 2011; Interim Moderator, Greenock Westburn Church, 2012-14; Interim Moderator, Lyle Kirk, Greenock, 2014; returned to full-time Ministry in 2014 when inducted to Greenock St. Margaret's Church. Involved in taking 144 ministers, elders and their spouses over to Charlotte, North Carolina to see Team Ministry in action in four successful church locations in 2006.

Coulson, Neil. Chief Executive, St Andrews Links Trust, since 2021; b. 9.74. Educ. Upton-by Chester High School; Professional Golfers Association (British). Career history: IMG: Operations Director, Braemar Golf/PGA Golf Management, St Andrews, 2006-09, Senior Director, IMG, Singapore, 2009-2015, Director, Golf, IMG Academy, Bradenton, Florida, 2015-18; Senior Manager, KPMG, Budapest, Hungary, 2018-2019; Reignwood Investment UK, London: Vice-President, 2020-21, Member, Board of Directors, 2021; Wentworth Club Ltd, London: General Manager, 2019-2021, Member, Board of Directors, 2021. Address: Pilmour House, St Andrews, Fife KY16 9SF.

Couper, Jean, CBE, BSc, MCMI. Director: K3 Management Consultants, Catalyst Consulting; Member, The Merchants' House of Glasgow; Chair: Advisory Audit Board, Scottish Parliament Corporate Body, Glasgow Medical and Nursing Trust; Trustee: The Endrick Trust, Bellahouston Trust; b. 31.8.53, Kilmarnock; m., John Anderson Couper; 1 s.; 1 d. Educ. Kilmarnock Academy; University of Glasgow. Production Engineer and Foundry Manager, Glacier Metal Co., 1974-79; Materials Manager, Levi Strauss, 1979-81; Management Consultant: Arthur Young, 1982-87, Price Waterhouse, 1987-95; Chairman, Scottish Legal Aid Board, 1998-2006 (Member, 1994-98); Director, Ombudsman Services Ltd (2006-2012); Chair, Aberlour Child Care Trust (2008-2014); Deputy Chairman, Health Education Board for Scotland, 2000-01 (Member, 1994-2001); Member, Accounts Commission, 2002-08; Member, Police Advisory Board for Scotland, 2002-06; Vice-Chairman, Wise Group, 1988-96; Vice Chairman, Heatwise Glasgow Ltd., 1988-96; National President, Junior Chamber Scotland, 1983; former Chair, Community Justice Scotland; Senator, Junior Chamber International; former Chairman, Scottish Criminal Cases Review Commission. Recreations: gardening; skiing. Address: Glenesk House, 36 Sherbrooke Avenue, Pollokshields, Glasgow G41 4EP; T.-0141 427 3416. E-mail: jean.couper@k3consultants.co.uk

Coutts, Alister William, DQS, BA (Hons), MBA (Dist), MSc, PhD, FRICS, FCIOB, FCMI. Senior Partner, Dr Alister W Coutts and Partners LLP, Construction and Management Consultants, since 2011; b. 21.12.50,

Aberdeen; m., Sheelagh Anne Smith; 1 s.; 2 d. Educ. Robert Gordon's College, Aberdeen; Dundee College of Technology; Open University; University of Hong Kong; Heriot-Watt University. Armour and Partners, Chartered Quantity Surveyors: Assistant Quantity Surveyor, 1969-71, Quantity Surveyor, 1975-76; Senior Quantity Surveyor, Anderson Morgan Associates, Chartered Surveyors, 1976-78; Professional Officer, Public Works Department, Hong Kong Government, 1978-81; Project Co-ordinator, Hong Kong Mass Transit Railway Corporation, 1981-89; Project Management and Development Director, DCI (Holdings) Ltd., 1989-93; Director of Operations, Fife Health Board, 1993-98; Director of Property and Architectural Services and PPP Projects Director, The Highland Council, 1998-2007; Partner, Head of Public Sector Services, Robinson Low Francis LLP, Construction and Property Consultants, 2007-2011; External Examiner in Quantity Surveying and Contract Administration, Edinburgh Napier University, 2008-2012; Visiting Lecturer in Project Finance and Project Risk Management, Edinburgh Napier University, 2012-13; Associate, Edinburgh Institute, Edinburgh Napier University, 2015-17. Member, Children's Panel (Grampian), 1976-78; President, Scottish Football Association Referees (Angus and Perthshire), 1994-96; Member, Scottish Council, Royal Institution of Chartered Surveyors, 2005-2011. Recreations: travel; lecturing; academic research; watching soccer. Address: (b.) 29 Lady Nairne Drive, Perth PH1 1RF; T.-01738 634330.

Coutts, Herbert, KM, MBE, MStJ, AMA, FMA, FFCS, FSAScot, Bailie in Barony of Dolphinstoun; Cross of Merit of Order of Malta. Director of Culture and Leisure, Edinburgh City Council, 2001-07, retired 2007; b. 9.3.44, Dundee; m., Angela E.M. Smith; 1 s.; 3 d. Educ. Morgan Academy, Dundee. Assistant Keeper of Antiquities and Bygones, Dundee City Museums, 1965-68, Keeper, 1968-71; Superintendent, Edinburgh City Museums, 1971-73, City Curator, Edinburgh City Museums and Art Galleries, 1973-96, Head of Museums and Galleries, 1996-97, Head of Heritage and Arts, 1997-98, Director of Recreation, Edinburgh City Council, 1998-2001. Vice-President, Museum Assistants Group, 1969-70; Member: Government Committee on future of Scotland's National Museums and Galleries, 1979-80; Council, Museums Association, 1977-78, 1987-88; Council, Society of Antiquaries of Scotland, 1981-82; Board, Scottish Museums Council, 1985-88; Museums Adviser, COSLA, 1985-90; Member, Paxton House Trust, 1988-2002 and since 2007; External Examiner, St. Andrews University, 1994-97. Member, Board, Museums Training Institute, 1995-2004; Contested Angus South (Lab), 1970; Trustee, East Lothian Community Development Trust, 1989-2007; Member, Scottish Catholic Heritage Commission, 2006-2010; Trustee, Scottish Catholic Heritage Collections, since 2011; Trustee, National Galleries of Scotland, 2007-2011; Board Member, Order of Malta Dial-a-Journey Trust, 2007-2017, Chairman, 2011-2017; Chairman, Wheelchair Accessible Vehicle Enterprise Ltd, 2011-16; Member, Dunbar Community Council, since 2007; Member, Dunbar Community Development Company, since 2007; Trustee, Battle of Prestonpans (1745) Trust, since 2007; Chairman, Scottish Battlefields Trust, since 2014; Trustee, British Association of the Sovereign Military Order of Malta, 2016-18; major capital projects include: City of Edinburgh Art Centre, Museum of Childhood extension, People's Story Museum, City Art Centre extension, Scott Monument restoration, Usher Hall restoration and extension; Makars' Court (Scotland's Poets' Corner); Lauriston Castle Japanese Garden. Publications: Ancient Monuments of Tayside; Tayside Before History; Edinburgh Crafts (Co-Author); Aince a Bailie, Aye a Bailie; Amber in Polish History; Edinburgh: an illustrated history; Huntly House (guide book); Lady Stair's House (guide book); The Emperor's Warriors (Editor); The Pharaoh's Gold Mask (children's book); Gold of the Pharaohs (Editor); Dinosaurs Alive! (Editor); Sweat of the Sun — Gold of Peru (Editor); Golden Warriors of the Ukrainian Steppes (Editor); StarTrek – the exhibition (Editor); Quest for a Pirate (Editor); Gateway to the Silk Road – Relics from the Han to the Tang Dynasties from Xi'an, China (Editor); Faster, Higher, Stronger – The Story of the Olympic Movement (Editor); articles in archaeological and museums journals; Strategy Documents: Towards The New Enlightenment - A Cultural Policy for Edinburgh; Festivals Strategy; Theatre Strategy; Allotments Strategy; A Capital Commitment to Sport-Sport and Physical Recreation Strategy for Edinburgh. Recreations: family; gardening; opera; writing; reading; walking. Address: (h.) Kirkhill House, Queen's Road, Dunbar EH42 1LN; T.-01368 863113; e-mail: coutts826@btinternet.com

Coutures, Jean-Christophe. Chairman and Chief Executive Officer, Chivas Brothers, since 2018; b. 1966. Educ. Université Paris-Dauphine; ESCP Europe. Career history: Senior Consultant, Arthur Andersen Business Consulting, France, 1992-96; VP Finance, Pernod Ricard Asia, Hong Kong, 2000-04; Chief Executive Officer: Pernod Ricard Korea, 2005-08, Pernod Ricard Pacific, 2008-2010; Chairman and Chief Executive Officer: Pernod Ricard Winemakers, 2010-16, Irish Distillers Pernod Ricard, 2016-18. Address: Chivas Brothers Limited, 111-113 Renfrew Road, Paisley PA3 4DY.

Cowan, Sheriff Annella Marie, LLB (Hons), MSc. Sheriff of Grampian, Highland and Islands at Aberdeen, 1997-2016 (retired); b. 14.11.53, Sheffield; m., James Temple Cowan (marriage dissolved). Educ. Elgin Academy; University of Edinburgh. Admitted Solicitor, 1978; Procurator Fiscal Depute, 1978-86; seconded to Scottish Law Commission, 1984-86; admitted Faculty of Advocates, 1987; Sheriff, Tayside Central and Fife at Stirling, 1993. Recreations: equestrianism; foreign travel.

Cowan, Cathie. Chief Executive, NHS Forth Valley, since 2017. Career history: began NHS career in the 1980s as a nurse in Glasgow and held a number of clinical and managerial posts before taking up role as Director of Nursing in Fife; moved to Fife Health Board as Director of Service Development & Planning, played a key role in service transformation; Director in an integrated health and social care partnership, Glasgow City Council; Chief Executive, NHS Orkney, 2010-17. Deputy Chair, Innovation Partnership Board. Address: (b.) Stirling Road, Larbert FK5 4WR; T.-01324 566 000.

Cowan, John Mervyn, TD, MCIBS. Lt. Col. (Retd), RA/TA; b. 13.2.30, Oban; m., Marion Neilson Kidd; 1 s.; 2 d. Educ. Oban High School. National Bank of Scotland, National Commercial Bank of Scotland, Royal Bank of Scotland, 1946-90 (retired); TA commission, 1963; commanded 207 (Scottish) Battery RA(V), 1980-82; J.S.L.O., HQ Scotland, 1982-90; Chairman: The Sandilands Trust, 1993-2011, Royal Artillery Association Scottish Region, 1991-2002 (President, 2002-09), Earl Haig Fund (Scotland), 1993-99, SSAFA West Lothian, 2001-05; Patron, RA Council for Scotland; Trustee, 445 and City of Edinburgh RA Regimental Trusts. Recreations: travel; charitable works; sport. Address: (h.) 39 Kinloch View, Linlithgow, West Lothian EH49 7HT; T.-01506 671618.

Cowan, Margaret Morton (Lady Cowan), MA. Member, Council, National Trust for Scotland, 1989-94 and 1997-2002; former Member of Executive and of Highland Committee; b. 4.11.33, Newmilns; m., Sir Robert Cowan ; 2 d. Educ. St. George's School for Girls, Edinburgh; Edinburgh University. British Petroleum Company, 1955-59; Teacher, West Midlands Education Authority, 1965-76; Consultant and Lecturer in Use of Language, Hong Kong, 1976-81; Member, Justice of the Peace Committee, Inverness, 1985-2000; Member, Scottish Committee, British Council, 1991-2000; Convener, Highland Festival, 1992-97. Address: (h.) 1 Eyre Crescent, Edinburgh EH3 5ET; T.-0131-556 3379.

Cowan, Ronnie. MP (SNP), Inverclyde, since 2015; b. 6.9.59, Inverclyde. Manages IT company; worked with major companies all over the UK and Ireland. Son of Morton and Scotland football goalkeeper Jimmy Cowan. Address: House of Commons, London SW1A 0AA.

Cowie, Alan. Journalist and broadcaster; Media Training Consultant - Scotland and UK, Kazakhstan, Tunisia and United Arab Emirates, 2011-22; Digital UK, North of Scotland Liaison, 2008-2010; Head, Current Affairs, Grampian Television, 1998-2000; b. 28.4.48, Aberdeen; m., Evelyn; 2 d. Educ. Aberdeen Grammar School; Central School of Speech and Drama London; Jordanhill College of Education, Glasgow. Teacher, Glasgow, 1971-72; Reporter/Presenter, Radio Scotland, 1972-75; joined Grampian Television as News Reporter, 1975; Programme Editor, 1988; Freelance TV Producer, 2001-2010. Burgess, City of Aberdeen. Recreations: family (both in Scotland and Netherlands). E-mail: alancowietv@aol.com

Cowie, Neil. Principal and Chief Executive, North East Scotland College, since 2019. Career history: lecturer at Banff and Buchan College in 1999, then held a variety of roles, from school liaison to Assistant Principal; appointed Vice-Principal, following the merger of Aberdeen and Banff and Buchan Colleges in 2013. Address: North East Scotland College, Aberdeen City Campus, Gallowgate, Aberdeen AB25 1BN.

Cox, Gilbert Kirkwood, CVO, MBE, JP. Lord Lieutenant of Lanarkshire, 2000-2010; Honorary Sheriff, since 2002; Board Member, New Lanarkshire plc; Board Member, Lanarkshire, Prince's Trust, Scotland; Director/Trustee, Airdrie Savings Bank, 1987-2012 (President, 1996-98); retired General Manager Scotland, Associated Perforators & Weavers Ltd.; b. 24.8.35, Chapelhall, Airdrie; m., Marjory Moir Ross Taylor; 2 s.; 1 d. Educ. Airdrie Academy. National Coal Board, 1953-63; David A. McPhail & Sons Ltd., 1963-68; D.A. Monteith Holdings, 1968-71. Chair, Board of Management, Coatbridge College, 1997-2000; founder Member and Past President, Monklands Airdrie Rotary Club; currently Chair, St Andrew's Hospice Airdrie Capital Appeal. Recreations: golf; gardening; walking. Address: (h.) Bedford House, Commonhead Street, Airdrie ML6 6NS; T.-01236 763331. E-mail: coxgk@btinternet.com

Cox, Roy Frederick, OBE. Former Chairman, Sense Scotland; former Director, Old Mill Chimneys Scotland Ltd; b. 4.11.49, Leicester; m., Elizabeth; 1 s.; 1 d. Educ. New Parks Boys School; College of Textiles, Leicester. Engineering apprenticeship, Mellor Bromley; textile mechanical engineer, Corar's. Past President, Clydebank Rotary Club; Member, The Incorporation of Bonnetmakers and Dyers of Glasgow; a Freeman Citizen of Glasgow. Author of Children's book. Recreations: golf; gardening; travelling. Address: Craigmuir Farm, Greenock Road, Bishopton PA7 5NN; T.-07768723757. E-mail: roycoxs@aol.com

Coyle, Andrew, CMG, BA (Hons), PhD, FRSA, FKC. Emeritus Professor, London University, since 2011; President of the Howard League for Penal Reform in Scotland, since 2013; b. 17.6.44, Edinburgh. Educ. Edinburgh University. Scottish Prison Service, including Governor, Greenock, Peterhead and Shotts Prisons, 1973-91; Governor, Brixton Prison, 1991-97; Director, International Centre for Prison Studies and Professor of Prison Studies, Kings College, London University, 1997-2010; Visiting Professor, Essex University, 2011-14. Fellow: Royal Society for the Arts, since 1993; King's

College London, since 2010. Member: Foreign Secretary's Advisory Group on Torture Prevention, 2002-10; Billy Wright Inquiry Panel (NI), 2004-10; Judicial Appointments Board for Scotland, 2009-2014; Administrative Justice and Tribunals Council, 2009-13. Expert Adviser on prison issues to: Council of Europe, 1992-2012; UN High Commissioner for Human Rights, 1995-2004; European Committee for the Prevention of Torture, 1997-2004. Appointed by Scottish Government to review arrangements for independent monitoring of prisons, 2012-13. Advisory Board to UN Global Study on Children Deprived of their Liberty, 2017-20. Books include: Inside: Re-thinking Scotland's Prisons, 1991; The Prisons We Deserve, 1994; Understanding Prisons, 2005; A Human Rights Approach to Prison Management, 3rd edition 2018; Prisons of the World, 2021. E-mail: andrew.coyle@prisonstudies.org

Craig, Darren, LLB Hons, DipLP. Managing Partner, CMS Scotland, since 2016; b. 2.76. Educ. Glasgow Academy; University of Edinburgh. CMS Scotland: Senior Associate, 2006-2011, Partner, 2011-13, Partner, Edinburgh, since 2013; Director, The Montgomerie Arms Limited, Edinburgh, since 2008. Address: CMS Cameron McKenna Nabarro, Olswang LLP, Saltire Court, 20 Castle Terrace, Edinburgh EH1 2EN.

Craig, Sheriff Susan. Floating Sheriff of Lothian and Borders based at Livingston, since 2013; Interim Director, Judicial Institute for Scotland; Solicitor Advocate, since 1994; admitted, Faculty of Advocates, 2015. Educ. University of Aberdeen. Accredited Employment Law Specialist; Litigation partner in Brodies WS until 2001; Partner at Shepherd and Wedderburn until 2003; Employment Judge based in Edinburgh, since 2003; appointed a part-time Sheriff in 2011. Address: Livingston Sheriff Court, Sheriff Court House, The Civic Centre, Howden South Road, Livingston EH54 6FF; T.-01506 402 400.

Craigie, Cathie. MSP (Labour), Cumbernauld and Kilsyth, 1999-2011; b. 1954, Stirling; m.; 2 c. Councillor, Cumbernauld and Kilsyth District Council, 1984-96 (Council Leader, 1994-96); Member, North Lanarkshire Council, 1995-99; former Chair, Cumbernauld Housing Partnership.

Cramb, Auslan, MA (Hons). Former Scottish Correspondent, Daily Telegraph (1994-2020); b. 6.10.56, Dunoon; m., Catriona; 1 s.; 1 d. Educ. Perth Academy; Aberdeen University. Reporter, Press and Journal, 1979-82; Reporter, Press Association, Glasgow, 1982-85; The Herald, Glasgow, 1985-90; Environment Correspondent, The Scotsman, 1990-94. Scottish Specialist Writer of the Year, 1992 and 1993. Publications: Who Owns Scotland Now?, 1996; Fragile Land, 1998.

Cramb, Rev. Erik McLeish, LTh. Former National Co-ordinator, Scottish Churches Industrial Mission; former Convener, Church of Scotland Committee on Ecumenical Relations; b. 26.12.39, Glasgow; m., Elizabeth McLean; 2 s.; 3 d. Educ. Woodside Secondary School, Glasgow; Glasgow University and Trinity College. Minister: St. Thomas' Gallowgate, Glasgow, 1973-81, St. Paul's United Church, Kingston, Jamaica, 1981-84; Yoker, Glasgow, 1984-89; Organiser for Tayside, Scottish Churches International Mission, 1989-97. Socialist; Member, Iona Community, 1972-2009; former Chairman, Church Action on Poverty; Hon. Fellow, Al Maktoum Institute; Member, Dundee Pensioners' Forum. Recreation: supports Partick Thistle. Address: (h.) 1 Spence Place, Dundee DD5 1HL; T.-01382 480116; e-mail: erikcramb@blueyonder.co.uk

Crandles, Gillian, MA (Hons), LLB. Managing Partner (2019) & Head of Divorce and Family, Turcan Connell (Partner, since 2010). Educ. University of Edinburgh. Dual

Qualified in Scotland and England & Wales. Heavily involved in the introduction of Collaborative Law to Scotland; founder member and immediate past secretary of the Scottish Collaborative Family Law Group; interdisciplinary collaborative practitioner; immediate past secretary of FLAGS (Family Law Arbitration Group Scotland); one of the first solicitors in Scotland to undergo arbitration training for family law. Address: Turcan Connell, Princes Exchange, 1 Earl Grey Street, Edinburgh EH3 9EE.

Cranstoun of That Ilk and Corehouse, David Alexander Somerville, TD, MA, MSc, PhD, DL. Member, Queen's Bodyguard for Scotland (Royal Company of Archers); b. 19.12.43, Washington DC; m., Dr. iur. M.M. Glättli; 2 s. Educ. Winchester College; Trinity College, Oxford; Edinburgh University. National List Trials Officer, ESCA, 1973; Emeritus Fellow, SAC, 2003. Director, Scottish Quality Cereals; Director, Crop Evaluation Ltd; Member, AHDB Recommended List Project Board; Cereal Specialist, SAC, 1982-2003; Chairman, Scottish Society for Crop Research, 1996-2000; Board Member, Clyde River Purification Board, 1992-96; Member, Clyde Area Advisory Group, 2005-2010; Hon. Director, Lord Roberts Workshops (Edinburgh); Vice President, SSAFA Forces Help (Lanark); Commissioned Queens Own Lowland Yeomanry (TA), 1964, Lt. Col., 1982; Comd District Specialist Training Team, 1988, TA Col. Lowlands, 1990; Hon. Col. Glasgow and Lanarkshire Bn. ACF, 2001-06; Member, Lowland Reserve Forces and Cadets Association, 1969. Recreation: forestry. Address: (h.) Corehouse, Lanark ML11 9TQ.

Craven, Professor Alan James, MA, PhD, FInstP, CPhys, FRMS. Emeritus Professor and Senior Honorary Research Fellow, University of Glasgow, since 2012. Address: School of Physics and Astronomy, University of Glasgow, Glasgow G12 8QQ.

Crawford, Barbara Elizabeth, OBE, MA (Hons), PhD. Honorary Reader in Medieval History, St. Andrews University, since 2001; b. 5.4.40, Barnsley; m., Robert M.M. Crawford; 1 s. Educ. Queen Margaret's School; St. Andrews University. Carnegie Senior Scholarship, 1968; Temporary Lecturer, Department of History, Aberdeen University, 1969; Lecturer in Medieval History, St. Andrews University, 1972. Elected Fellow, Society of Antiquaries London, 1973; Fellow Society of Antiquaries of Scotland, 1964; Member Norwegian Academy of Science and Letters, 1997; Fellow, Royal Society of Edinburgh, 2001; Leverhulme Research Fellow, 2000-01; President of the Society of Antiquaries of Scotland, 2008-2011; awarded Hon. Professorship, University of the Highlands & Islands, 2015. Publications: Scandinavian Scotland, 1987; The Biggings, Papa Stour, Shetland, 1999; The Northern Earldoms: Orkney and Caithness from AD 870-1470, 2013. Recreations: exploring areas of Viking settlement in Scotland and North Atlantic. Address: (b.) The Strathmartine Centre, 2, Kinburn Place, St. Andrews KY16 9DT; T.-01334 478644.
E-mail: bec@strathmartinetrust.org

Crawford, Professor Dorothy H., OBE, MBBS, PhD, MD, DSc, FRCPath, FRSE, FAcadMedSci. Emeritus Professor of Medical Microbiology, University of Edinburgh, since 2010 (Professor, 1997-2010); b. 13.4.45, Glasgow; m., Dr. W.D. Alexander; 2 s. Educ. St. Thomas's Hospital Medical School. Senior Lecturer then Reader, Royal Post-graduate Medical School, London, 1985-90; Professor of Medical Microbiology, London School of Hygiene and Tropical Medicine, 1990-97. Publications: written several popular science books on microbes

including 'Deadly Companions' (latest edition 2018), 'Virus Hunt' (2015), 'Ebola: Profile of a Killer Virus' (2016), and 'Viruses: The Invisible Enemy' (latest edition 2021).

Crawford, Douglas James, LLB, DipLP, NP, CF, WS. Partner in Brodies LLP; formerly Partner in CMS Cameron McKenna LLP and Partner and Founder in the corporate group of Aberdeen office, Dundas & Wilson (1997-2014); b. 28.2.65, Ayr; m., Alison; 1 s.; 2 d. Educ. Belmont Academy, Ayr; Edinburgh University. Trained, Shepherd & Wedderburn WS, 1987-89; Assistant, Associate, Partner, Maclay Murray & Spens, 1989-97. Recreations: golf; winter sports. Address: (b.) Brodies House, 31-33 Union Grove, Aberdeen AB10 6SD; T.-07798 855 290; e-mail: douglas.crawford@brodies.com

Crawford, Professor Elizabeth Bryden, LLB (Hons), PhD. Emeritus Professor of International Private Law, University of Glasgow; b. 20.04.49, Glasgow; m., Robin Crawford; 1 s.; 1 d. Educ. Laurel Bank School, Glasgow; University of Glasgow. Admitted as Solicitor, 1974; successively since 1976, Lecturer, Senior Lecturer, Reader in the Conflict of Laws, Professor, University of Glasgow. Publications include: Crawford & Carruthers, International Private Law: A Scots Perspective, 4th edition, 2015. Recreations: golf; cooking. Address: (b.) School of Law, Stair Building, University of Glasgow, Glasgow G12 8QQ; T.-0141-330 4729; e-mail: e.crawford@law.gla.ac.uk

Crawford, Hugh William Jack, BArch, DipTP, RIBA, FRIAS, FRTPI. Part-time Inquiry Reporter (Local Plans), Scottish Executive, 1982-2005; Sir Frank Mears Associates, from 1985; b. 19.1.38, Dalry; m., Catherine Mary McIntyre; 1 s.; 2 d. Educ. Dalry High School; University of Strathclyde. Partner, Sir Frank Mears and Partners, 1965-85. Scottish Chairman, Royal Town Planning Institute, 1979, 1980, 1992; Past President, Committee of Liaison for Planning Practitioners in Member Countries of the European Union; President of Honour, European Council of Town Planners, Brussels, since 1985; former National Vice-President, Pedestrians Association; President, Association of Mediators. Recreations: walking; visiting historic buildings and towns; art galleries and museums. Address: (b.) 67 Ferry Gait Drive, Edinburgh EH4 4GJ; T.-0131 531 8455.
E-mail: hwjcrawford@gmail.com

Crawford, Professor Robert, MA, DPhil, FRSE, FBA, FEA. Emeritus Professor, University of St Andrews (appointed Professor, Modern Scottish Literature and Bishop Wardlaw Professor of Poetry, School of English in 1995; Head of School, 2002-05); Associate Director, St. Andrews Scottish Studies Centre, 1993-2009; Poet and Critic; b. 23.2.59, Bellshill; m., Alice Wales; 1 s.; 1 d. Educ. Hutchesons' Grammar School, Glasgow; Glasgow University; Balliol College, Oxford. Snell Exhibitioner & Carnegie Scholar, Balliol College, Oxford, 1981-84; Elizabeth Wordsworth Junior Research Fellow, St. Hugh's College, Oxford, 1984-87; British Academy Postdoctoral Fellow, Department of English Literature, Glasgow University, 1987-89; Lecturer in Modern Scottish Literature, School of English, St. Andrews University, 1989-95. Former Co-Editor, Verse Magazine; Co-Editor, Scottish Studies Review, 1999-2004. Publications: The Savage and the City in the Work of T.S. Eliot, 1987; A Scottish Assembly, 1990; Sharawaggi (Co-author), 1990; About Edwin Morgan (Co-Editor), 1990; Other Tongues: young Scottish poets in English, Scots and Gaelic (Editor), 1990; The Arts of Alasdair Gray (Co-Editor), 1991; Devolving English Literature, 1992; Talkies, 1992; Reading

Douglas Dunn (Co-Editor), 1992; Identifying Poets, 1993; Liz Lochhead's Voices (Co-Editor), 1993; Twentieth Century Literature of Scotland: a selected bibliography, 1995; Talking Verse (Co-Editor), 1995; Masculinity, 1996; Penguin Modern Poets 9 (Co-Author), 1996; Robert Burns and Cultural Authority (Editor), 1997; Launch-site for English Studies: Three Centuries of Literary Studies at the University of St. Andrews (Editor), 1997; Impossibility, 1998; The Scottish Invention of English Literature (Editor), 1998; The Penguin Book of Poetry from Britain and Ireland since 1945 (Co-Editor), 1998; Spirit Machines, 1999; The New Penguin Book of Scottish Verse (Co-Editor), 2000; Scottish Religious Poetry (Co-Editor), 2000; The Modern Poet, 2001; Heaven-Taught Fergusson, 2002; The Tip of My Tongue, 2003; Selected Poems, 2005; The Book of St. Andrews (Editor), 2005; Apollos of the North, 2006; Contemporary Poetry and Contemporary Science, 2006 (Editor); Scotland's Books, 2007; Full Volume, 2008; The Bard, Robert Burns, A Biography, 2009; The Best Laid Schemes (Co-Editor), 2009; New Poems, Chiefly in the Scottish Dialect (Editor), 2009; The Beginning and the End of the World, 2011; Simonides, 2011; On Glasgow and Edinburgh, 2013; Bannockburns: Scottish Independence and Literary Imagination, 1314-2014, 2014; Testament, 2014; Young Eliot, 2015; The Book of Iona (Editor), 2016; Chinese Makars, 2016; Fire, 2017; Holy Rood, 2017. Recreation: mischief. Address: (b.) School of English, University of St Andrews, St Andrews KY16 9AL; T.- 01334 476161, Ext. 2666.

Crawford, 29th Earl of, and Balcarres, 12th Earl of (Robert Alexander Lindsay), KT, GCVO, PC. Premier Earl of Scotland; Head of House of Lindsay; b. 5.3.27; m., Ruth Beatrice Meyer; 2 s.; 2 d. Educ. Eton; Trinity College, Cambridge. Grenadier Guards, 1945-49; MP (Conservative), Hertford, 1955-74, Welwyn and Hatfield, February to September, 1974; Opposition Front Bench Spokesman on Health and Social Security, 1967-70; Minister of State for Defence, 1970-72; Minister of State for Foreign and Commonwealth Affairs, 1972-74; Chairman, Lombard North Central Bank, 1976-80; Director, National Westminster Bank, 1975-88; Director, Scottish American Investment Co., 1978-88; Vice-Chairman, Sun Alliance & London Insurance Group, 1975-91; President, Rural District Councils Association, 1959-65; Chairman, National Association of Mental Health, 1963-70; Chairman, Historic Buildings Council for Scotland, 1976-83; Chairman, Royal Commission on Ancient and Historical Monuments of Scotland, 1985-95; First Crown Estate Commissioner, 1980-85; former Deputy Lieutenant, Fife; Chairman, National Library of Scotland, 1990-2000; Lord Chamberlain to HM Queen Elizabeth The Queen Mother, 1992-2002. Hon. Fellow, RIAS, NLS. Address: (h.) Balcarres, Colinsburgh, Fife KY9 1HN.

Crawford, Robert Hardie Bruce, JP. MSP (SNP), Stirling, 2007-2021, Mid Scotland and Fife, 1999-2007; Cabinet Secretary for Parliamentary Business and Government Strategy, 2011-2012; Minister for Parliamentary Business, 2007-2011; Chairman, SNP, 2004-07; Shadow Minister for Parliament, 2003-04; Shadow Minister, Environment and Energy, 2001-03; Shadow Minister, Transport and the Environment, 2000-01; Chief Whip, SNP Scottish Parliamentary Group, 1999-2001; b. 16.2.55, Perth; m., Jacqueline; 3 s. Educ. Kinross High School; Perth High School. Civil servant, Scottish Office, 1974-99; Leader, Perth and Kinross Council, 1995-99; Chairman, Kinross-shire Partnership Ltd., 1997-99; Chairman, Perth and Kinross Recreation Facilities Ltd, 1995-99; Member: Perthshire Tourist Board, Scottish Enterprise Tayside, Perth College, 1995-99. Recreations: golf; watching Dunfermline Athletic. Address: (h.) 12 Douglas Crescent, Kinross; T.-01577 863531.

Crawford, Robin, LLB, CA. Former Chairman, Erskine Hospital (2016-2021), former Trustee, 2006-2021; Member,

then Vice Chairman, Scottish Further and Higher Education Funding Council, 2009-2017; Director, Skills Development Scotland Ltd, 2013-2017; Chair, Scottish Government Review of Procurement in Construction, 2012-13; Member of Court, Strathclyde University, 2007-14; Director of The Merchants House of Glasgow (2010-16); Partner, KPMG, 1979-2003; Captain, Glasgow Golf Club, 2008; Chairman, Scottish Business Crime Centre Ltd., 2003-08; Member, Council, CBI Scotland, 2000-06; Governor, then Vice-Chairman, Laurel Bank and Laurel Park Schools, 1988-98; b. 2.10.48, Greenock; m., Elizabeth; 1 s.; 1 d. Educ. Greenock Academy; Glasgow University. Recreations: golf; fly fishing; hillwalking.

Crawford, Ruth, QC, LLB (Hons), DipLP. Admitted Faculty of Advocates, 1993; b. 17.7.65, Glasgow. Educ. Cranley School for Girls; George Heriot's School; Aberdeen University. Standing Junior Counsel to Keeper of the Registers of Scotland, 1998-2002; Second Standing Junior Counsel to Scottish Executive, 2002-08. Address: Advocate's Library, Parliament House, Parliament Square, Edinburgh EH1 1RF; T.-0131-226 5071.

Crawley, Angela, BA. MP (SNP), Lanark and Hamilton East, since 2015; SNP Shadow Attorney General, since 2021; former SNP Spokesperson for Women and Equalities and Young People and Community Resources; b. 3.6.87, Hamilton. Educ. University of Stirling; University of Glasgow. Worked in Brighton for the Educational Travel Group; elected to South Lanarkshire Council in the Hamilton Ward in 2012; National Convenor of the SNP's youth-wing, Young Scots for Independence, since 2014; sits on the National Executive Committee; former Parliamentary Assistant for a Government Minister and Member of the Scottish Parliament. Address: House of Commons, London SW1A 0AA.

Creally, Eugene P., LLB (Hons), DipLP, PhD. Appointed Queen's Counsel, 2011; Advocate, since 1993; Clerk of Faculty, Faculty of Advocates, 1999-2003; Standing Junior Counsel to Lord Advocate (1998-2005); Counsel to Billy Wright Inquiry; Vice Chairman of Faculty of Advocates Free Legal Services Unit; Member of the Court of Session Rules Council, 2004-2011; Standing Counsel to Advocate General for Scotland, 2009-2012; b. 3.2.61, Dungannon, Co. Tyrone; 1 s. Educ. St Patrick's Academy, Dungannon; Queens University, Belfast; Edinburgh University. Address: (b.) Advocates Library, Parliament House, Edinburgh EH1 1RF; T.-0131-226 5071.

Creegan, Chris, BA (Hons), MSc, FCIPD, FRSA. Chair, Scottish Association for Mental Health; Associate Director, CCPS - Coalition of Care and Support Providers in Scotland, since 2021; b. 3.61. Educ. Lancaster University; University of Bristol; Ashridge Business School. Career history: Unison, 1992-96; Senior Research Fellow, London Metropolitan University, 1999-2006; Independent Social Policy Research Consultant, Edinburgh, 2003-06; NatCen Social Research: Deputy Director, Qualitative Research, 2006-09, Director of Corporate Affairs, 2010-12; Chief Executive, Scottish Commission for People with a Learning Disability, 2013-19; Non-Executive Member, Executive Advisory Board, Social Security Scotland, since 2018; occasional columnist, Holyrood Communications, since 2019; Associate, The Diffley Partnership, since 2021. Address: CCPS, Norton Park, 57 Albion Road, Edinburgh EH7 5QY; T.-0131 475 2676.

Crerar, Lorne Donald, CBE, LLB (Hons), NP, FCIBS. Founding Partner and Chairman, Harper Macleod LLP, since 1987; Emeritus Professor in Banking Law, University

of Glasgow; b. 29.07.54, Renfrew. Educ. Kelvinside Academy, Glasgow; Glasgow University. Partner in Mackenzie Robertson & Co, 1979-87. Chairman, Discipline for Scottish Rugby Union, 1995-2017; International Rugby Board Judicial Officer, since 1995; Chairman, Discipline for European Rugby Cup Limited, 1999-2017; Chairman, Discipline for 6 Nations Limited, 1999-2017; Deputy Chairman, Scottish Enterprise Glasgow, 2000-2003; Chairman, Sub-Group Housing Improvement Task Force, 2001-03; Convener, Standards Commission for Scotland, 2003-07; Non-Executive Director, Scottish Government Justice Department, until 2011; Independent Member of the Purchasers Information Advisory Group, 2005-08; Chairman, Independent Review of Audit, Inspection, Regulation and Complaints Handling in the Public Sector ("The Crerar Review") (1 July 2006-August 2008). Board Member, Highlands & Islands Enterprise, 2007-2011; Chairman, Highlands & Islands Enterprise, since 2011; Chairman, Highlands and Islands Audit Committee, 2011-2012; Advisory Board Member, Scottish Investment Bank, 2011. Chairman, Implementation Board for Scottish Government regarding Enterprise and Skills Review, 2017; Trustee, Robertson Trust, since 2017; Co-Chair, National Council of Rural Advisors for Scottish Government, 2017; Panel Member, Independent Review of the Regulation of Legal Services, 2017-18. On Editorial Board of "World Sports Law Report"; elected "Fellow" of the Chartered Institute of Bankers, June 1999; listed in "Chambers Guide to the Legal Profession" as one of Scotland's very few "Sports Law Experts". Publications: "The Law of Banking in Scotland", 2nd edition, 2007; commissioned author for Stair Memorial Encyclopaedia (the leading Scottish Text) for financial institutions, banking and currency (2000); Independent Reviewer of Lending Code, 2010-11 which covers all personal and small business lending in the UK. Awarded CBE, 2019 and was awarded Lifetime Achievement Award at Scottish Legal Awards 2019. Elected Fellow of Royal Edinburgh Society 2021. Recreations: The West Highlands of Scotland and its history; hillwalking; fishing and sailing. Address: (b.) Harper Macleod LLP, The Ca'd'oro Building, 45 Gordon Street, Glasgow G1 3PE; T.-0414 227-9377.
E-mail: lorne.crerar@harpermacleod.co.uk

Crerar, Paddy. Chairman, Crerar Hotels Trust (Charitable), since 2005; Non Executive Director: Archerfield Estates Ltd, since 2015, Highlands and Islands Enterprise, since 2014, VisitScotland, 2009-2015; b. 21.10.68, Oban; m., Sheila. Educ. Rockfield, Oban; George Watson's, Edinburgh. Career: Commercial Union Assurance; North British Trust Group; Founding Director, North British Holidays, British Trust Hotels; Easy Breaks and Crerar Hotels; Founder of Crerar Management Ltd., CEO of Swallow Hotels; owner of Newmains Farm - Pedigree Luing & Highland Cattle. Thistle Award Winner; Trustee of Hospitality Industry Trust Scotland; Chairman, North British Hotels Trust; Director of Mull & Iona Enterprise. Recreations: field sports; sailing and shouting at kids; hockey; rugby. Address: (b.) 1 Queen Charlotte Lane, Edinburgh; T.-0131 561 1203.
E-mail: crerar@crerarhotels.com

Crewe, Martin Alistair, BSc, PhD, MBA, MSc. Director, Barnardo's Scotland, since 2007; b. 13.07.60, London; m., Jane; 3 s.; 1 d. Educ. Alleyn's School, London; Exeter University; Nottingham-Trent University; Stirling University. Regional Manager, NSPCC, 1989-97; Finance Director, Barnardo's Scotland, 1997-2007. Board Member, Office of The Scottish Charity Regulator (OSCR), 2006-2010; Board Member, Edinburgh College, 2012-2015. Recreation: running very slowly. Address: (b.) 111 Oxgangs Road North, Edinburgh EH14 1ED; T.-0131 446 7000; e-mail: martin.crewe@barnardos.org.uk

Crichton, David. Former Interim Chair, Scottish Police Authority; Chair, NHS Health Scotland, 2015-2020; former Vice-Chair, Scottish Police Authority; Member of Scotland Committee, Equality and Human Rights Commission, since 2017. International development adviser in Afghanistan, Montserrat, the Balkans and Tanzania, 2009-2015; Global Director of Country and Economic Research, Economist Intelligence Unit, 2007-09; Chief Executive: Confederation of Forest Industries, 2005-07, Scottish Enterprise Edinburgh and Lothian, 1998-2003. Board of Harakat (Afghanistan), 2011-2017, NHS Lothian, 2004-07.

Crichton, John Hugh McDiarmid, BMedSci (Hons), BMBS, PhD, FRC Psych, FHEA, MFFLM, FRCP(E). Consultant Forensic Psychiatrist, since 2000; Honorary Fellow in Law, since 2000; Honorary Professor, 2019; Honorary Senior Clinical Lecturer, 2011; Treasurer, Royal College of Psychiatrists, since 2021; Vice President of the Royal College of Psychiatrists, 2017-2021; Chair of the Royal College of Psychiatrists in Scotland, 2017-2021; Consultant to the International Committee of the Red Cross, since 2015; Chair of the Faculty of Forensic Psychiatry, 2012-2017, Royal College of Psychiatrists in Scotland; Clinical Director, Forensic Medicine and Psychiatry, Psychotherapy and Rehabilitation; Clinical Lead, Forensic Mental Health, NHS Lothian, 2009-2012; Medical Director, Forensic Mental Health Services managed Care Network and State Hospital's Board for Scotland, 2005-06; b. 8.9.66, Edinburgh; m., Dr. Anne-Marie Crichton; 3 d. Educ. Edinburgh Academy; Nottingham University; Trinity Hall, Cambridge. Nightingale Research Scholar, Institute of Criminology, Cambridge University, 1993; Lecturer in Developmental Psychiatry, Cambridge University, 1997; Lecturer in Forensic Psychiatry, Edinburgh University, 1998. Publications: Psychiatric Patient Violence: Risk and Response, 1995; Homicide, Mental Disorder and the Media, 2015; The Classical Origins of the Insanity Defence, 2016. Recreation: gardening. Address: (b.) Orchard Clinic, Royal Edinburgh Hospital, Edinburgh EH10 5HF; T.-0131-537 5857; e-mail: john.crichton@nhslothian.scot.nhs.uk
Twitter: @JohnHMCrichton

Crichton, Robin, Chevalier des Arts et des Lettres. Retired film producer and director; b. 14.5.40, Bournemouth; m., 1, Trish Dorrell, 2, Flora Maxwell Stuart; 3 d. Educ. Sherborne; Paris; Edinburgh. Built Scotland's first independent film studio, 1968; started film training scheme, now Napier University M.A., 1970; founded first animation studio in Scotland; managed first independent outside broadcast unit in Scotland; Founder Member: Scottish ACTT Committee, Scottish Film Archive; former UK Vice-Chair and Scottish Chair, Independent Programme Producers' Association; former Co-ordinator, Working Party, Scottish Screen; co-initiated Annual Co-production Conference; organised Scottish stand at international TV television markets; Churchill Fellowship, 1990 (to study models for Scottish Screen); Co-production Consultant to various European broadcasters and producers; former Project Leader, Eureka Audiovisual Federation; founder Director, Scottish Screen Locations; Consultant Programme Buyer, Gaelic Television Committee; President, L'Association Charles Rennie Mackintosh en Roussillon; Chairman, The Arthur Trail Association. Publications: On the Trail of Merlin in a Dark Age; On the Trail of King Arthur; Monsieur Mackintosh; Sara; The Curious Case of Santa Claus; Christmas Mouse. Recreations: writing; DIY. Address: Keeper's House, Traquair, by Innerleithen, Peebleshire EH44 6PP; T.-01896 831188; e-mail: crichton.efp@g.mail.com

Crockart, Mike, BSc (Social Services). Transformation Lead, The Scottish Government, since 2016; MP (Liberal Democrat), Edinburgh West, 2010-2015; b. 19.3.66; m.; 2 s. Educ. Perth High School; Edinburgh University. Career: contested Edinburgh North and Leith, 2005 general election; Convener, Edinburgh West Liberal Democrats,

2009; PPS to Michael Moore as Secretary of State for Scotland until 2010. Member: Joint Committee on Human Rights, 2011-12, Business, Innovation and Skills Select Committee, 2012, Scottish Affairs Select Committee, 2012; Liberal Democrat Parliamentary Party DECC Committee Co-Chair, 2012-2013; Founder of the APPG on Nuisance Calls. Recreations: photography; classical music.

Crockett, Cllr Barney, MA (Hons), MA (Post Grad), Dip (Race and Community Relations). Lord Provost of Aberdeen, Aberdeen City Council, since 2017; b. Aberdeen. Educ. Aberdeen Academy; Aberdeen University; Liverpool University; Open University. Career: Aberdeen City Council: Leader of the Opposition, 2009-12, Leader of the Council, 2012-14; Board Member, NHS Grampian, 2012-17; Councillor for Dyce/Bucksburn/Danestone, Aberdeen City Council, since 2007. Executive Committee Member, Local Authority Pension Fund Forum, since 2015; President, HyER (European Association for Hydrogen and fuel cells and Electro-mobility in European Regions), since 2015; HM Lord-Lieutenant of Aberdeen, since 2017; Vice President, World Energy Cities Partnership, since 2017. Recreations: reading; coaching Rugby. Address: Aberdeen City Council, Town House, Broad Street, Aberdeen AB10 1FY; T.-01224 522514.
E-mail: bcrockett@aberdeencity.gov.uk

Croft, Professor Amanda. Chief Nursing Officer, Scottish Government, since 2021; Chief Executive, NHS Grampian, 2019-20. Career history: qualified as a Registered Nurse at Sheffield and North Trent School of Nursing in 1992 and began clinical career in the medical domain; moved into clinical management, initially in Primary Care, before moving to Scotland and NHS Grampian in 2000; undertaken a number of different positions across Primary and Secondary Care, in both Professional Leadership and General Management roles. Obtained Masters of Science in Nursing from the University of Aberdeen in 2004. Visiting Professor, Robert Gordon University, since 2016. Address: Scottish Government, St. Andrew's House, Regent Road, Edinburgh EH1 3DG.

Crofts, Roger Stanley, CBE, BA, MLitt, CertEd, FRSE, FRSGS, FRGS, FCIEEM, FRCGS, Hon DSc (St Andrews), Hon DSc (Glasgow); Knight's Cross of the Icelandic Order of the Falcon; Icelandic Soil Conservation Medal; CIEEM Medal Winner, 2016; Fred Packard Award, 2016; Scottish Geographical Medal, 2021. Adviser, lecturer and writer; Chief Executive, Scottish Natural Heritage, 1991-2002; b. 17.1.44, Leicester; m. Lindsay Manson (deceased); 1 s.; 1 d. Educ. Hinckley Grammar School; Liverpool University; Leicester University. Research Assistant in Geography: Aberdeen University, 1966-72, University College, London, 1972-74; entered Scottish Office, 1974; Senior Research Officer, 1974-78; Principal Research Officer, 1978-84; Assistant Secretary, Highlands and Tourism Division, Industry Department, 1984-88; Assistant Secretary, Rural Affairs Division, Scottish Development Department, 1988-91. Chairman, IUCN UK Committee, 1999-2002; Chair, World Commission on Protected Areas (Europe), 2001-08; Emeritus World Commission on Protected Areas, since 2008; Chairman, Plantlife International, 2007-2010; Chairman, Royal Scottish Geographical Society, 2014-2020; Board Member: Scottish Agricultural College, 2002-2010, National Trust for Scotland, 2004-09, Fieldfare Ecological Development, since 2004, Crichton Carbon Centre, 2009-2014; Chair, Galloway and Southern Ayrshire Biosphere Reserve, 2012-15; Project Director, Watson Bird Centre and Celebration; Director: Esk Valley Trust, since 2014, Fieldfare International Ecological Development plc, since 2003; Patron, Scottish Association of Geography Teachers, 2002-2019; Visiting Professor in Geography and Environment, University of Aberdeen, 1998-2012;

Honorary Professor in Geoscience, University of Edinburgh, until 2011; Honorary Professor, Dundee University and Edinburgh University, since 2016; Vice President, Royal Scottish Geographical Society, since 2020; Patron, CIEEM; Royal Society of Edinburgh Councillor. Publications: Co-Author/Editor: 'Land of Mountain and Flood'; 'Scotland's Environment: the Future'; 'Conserving Nature: Scotland and the Wider World'; 'Scotland: The Creation of its Natural Landscape'; 'Ecosystems and Health: a UK Perspective'; 'Healing the Land: Soil Conservation and Land Restoration in Iceland'; Guidelines for geoconservation in protected and conserved areas. Recreations: gardening; choral singing; hill-walking; wildflower photography. Address: (h.) 6 Eskside West, Musselburgh EH21 6HZ; T.-07803 595267.
Web: www.rogercrofts.net

Cromartie, Earl of (John Ruaridh Grant Mackenzie), MIExpE. Land manager, since 1989; Executive Member, Mountaineering Council of Scotland, 1990-2007, and President, 2003-07; Explosives Consultant, since 1979; b. 12.6.48, Inverness; m. (1), Helen Murray; m. (2), Janet Harley; 2 s.; m. (3), Jane Margaret Eve Austin. Educ. Rannoch School; Strathclyde University. Research Geologist, New Quebec, 1970s; Chief of the Clan Mackenzie; Chair, Highland Clans Partnership Group; President, Scottish Mountaineering Club, 2012-2014. Many articles on mountaineering; co-author of guide books on mountaineering. Recreations: mountaineering; geology; art. Address: (h.) Castle Leod, Strathpeffer IV14 9AA.

Crombie, Sir Alexander (Sandy), FRSE, FFA. Chairman: Edinburgh Alternative Finance, Cameron Hume, Amiqus Resolution; b. 08.02.49; m., Margaret; 2 d. Educ. Buckhaven High School. President, The Cockburn Association, since 2009. Trustee of the Ross Development Trust. Joined Standard Life, 1966; Group Chief Investment Manager, 1996-98; Chief Executive, Standard Life Investments, 1998-2004; Group Chief Executive, Standard Life, 2004-09; Senior Independent Director, RBS Group plc, 2010-2017. Chairman, Creative Scotland, 2010-15; Chairman, UNESCO City of Literature Trust, 2006-11; Vice Chairman, The Board of Governors of The Royal Conservatoire of Scotland, 2007-2016.

Crompton, Professor David William Thomasson, OBE, MA, PhD, ScD, BSc (Open), FRSE, FRSB. Director, St Andrew's Clinics for Children, 1992-2019; b. 5.12.37, Bolton; m., Effie Mary Marshall; 1 s.; 2 d. Educ. Bolton School; Sidney Sussex College, University of Cambridge; Fellow, Sidney Sussex College, Cambridge, 1964-85; Lecturer, Parasitology, Cambridge University, 1968-85; Adjunct Professor, Nutritional Sciences, Cornell University, 1981-2004; John Graham Kerr Professor of Zoology, Glasgow University, 1985-2000; Visiting Professor, University of Nebraska, 1982; Chairman, Company of Biologists Ltd., 1994-2000; Scientific Medal, Zoological Society of London, 1977; Member, WHO Expert Committee on Parasitology; Hon. Member: Slovak Society of Parasitologists, 1999, American Society of Parasitologists, 2001, Helminthological Society of Washington, 2002. Honorary Fellow, University of Glasgow, 2005. Publications: author/editor, 10 books; Co-editor, Parasitology, 1972-82; author/co-editor, 250 scientific papers. Recreations: books; gardening. Address: (h.) 101A Clifton Hill, London NW8 0JR; T.-0207 625 1204; e-mail: dwtc101A@gmail.com

Crook, Emeritus Professor Jonathan Nicholas, BA, MSc (Econ), Hon DBA, FRSE, FAcSS. Emeritus

Professor of Business Economics, University of Edinburgh Business School, since 2021; Leverhulme Emeritus Fellowship, since 2021; m., Kate Vincent; 2 d. Educ. Cheltenham Grammar School; Lancaster University; University College, Cardiff. Research Assistant, Sheffield University, 1977-79; Lecturer, then Senior Lecturer, then Reader, Department of Business Studies, Edinburgh University, 1979-2002, Professor of Business Economics, 2002-2021; Director, Credit Research Centre, Edinburgh University, 1997-2021; Head of Management Science and Business Economics Group, 2005-09, Director of Research, 2014-20, Deputy Dean, 2016-2021. Joint winner, Goodeve Medal (OR Society). Fellow, Wharton Financial Institutions Center, University of Pennsylvania, USA; External Research Fellow, Centre for Finance, Credit and Macroeconomics, University of Nottingham; Fellow, Royal Society of Edinburgh; Fellow, Academy of Social Sciences. Publications: Managerial Economics (Co-Author); Economics of Modern Business (Co-Author); Credit Scoring and its Applications (Co-Author); Credit Scoring and Credit Control (Co-Editor); Readings in Credit Scoring (Co-Editor); Joint Editor, Journal of the Operations Research Society, 2010-19. Awarded Honorary Doctorate, University of Abertay, 2011. Recreations: singing; running. Address: (b.) University of Edinburgh Business School, Edinburgh University, 29 Buccleuch Place, Edinburgh EH8 9JS. E-mail: j.crook@ed.ac.uk

Cross, Mhairi. Chief Executive, National Mining Museum Scotland, since 2015. Wealth of experience in the cultural sector, spanning over 20 years. Set up the first contemporary art gallery in Falkirk, establishing artist in residence programmes across educational establishments in North Lanarkshire and developing the Arts and Museum Service in Renfrewshire; also successfully developed the visitor experience within Paisley Museum and the educational programme for children and young people. Board Trustee, Association of Independent Museums, since 2018. Recreations: cultural activities; canoeing; kayaking; cycling; running; swimming. Address: (b.) Lady Victoria Colliery, Newtongrange, Midlothian EH22 4QN; T.-0131 663 7519.

Cross, Professor Rod, BSc (Econ), BPhil. Emeritus Professor of Economics, University of Strathclyde (appointed Professor in 1991); Visiting Professor, University of Aix-Marseille, since 2003; b. 27.3.51, Wigan. Educ. Wigan Grammar School; London School of Economics; University of York. Research Assistant, University of Manchester, 1972-74; Temporary Lecturer, Queen Mary College, University of London, 1974-75; Lecturer, University of St. Andrews, 1975-91. Adviser to Governor, Polish National Bank, 1990-92; Occasional Member, H.M. Treasury Academic Panel. Publications: Economic Theory and Policy in the UK, 1982; Unemployment Hysteresis and the Natural Rate Hypothesis (Editor), 1988; The Natural Rate of Unemployment, 1995. Recreations: hillwalking; rugby league and union; fiction. Address: (b.) Department of Economics, University of Strathclyde, Sir William Duncan Building, 130 Rottenrow, Glasgow G4 0GE; T.-0141-548 3855/4555; e-mail: rod.cross@strath.ac.uk

Crotty, Professor Patrick. Emeritus Professor of Irish and Scottish Literature, University of Aberdeen (appointed Professor in 2005), Head of School of Language and Literature, 2009-2012; b. 18.04.52, Fermoy, Ireland; 3 s. Educ. St. Colman's College, Fermoy; University College Cork; University of Stirling. Primary Teacher, Lismore, Co. Waterford, Bishopstown, Cork, 1978-86; Senior Lecturer in English, Trinity College, Carmarthen, Wales, 1986-98; Head of English Department, St. Patrick's College, Dublin City University, 1998-2001; Professor of Irish and Scottish Literary History, University of Ulster, 2001-05; Director of Research Institute of Irish and Scottish Studies, University of Aberdeen, 2007-09. Director of Yeats International Summer School, Sligo, 2006-08. Publications: Modern Irish Poetry, 1995; Penguin Book of Irish Verse, 2010; Oxford Companion to English Literature (Associate Editor), 2009. Recreation: music. Address: (b.) Taylor Building, University of Aberdeen, King's College, Aberdeen AB24 3UB; T.-01224 272562; e-mail: p.j.crotty@abdn.ac.uk

Crowe, Sheriff Frank Richard, LLB. Secretary, Fairer Justice for Scotland Group, since 2019; Sheriff of Lothian and Borders at Edinburgh, 2008-2019; Solicitor Advocate; b. 15.3.52, Kirkcaldy; m., Alison Margaret Purdom (separated); partner, The Hon. Lady Scott; 2 d.; 1 s. Educ. Kirkcaldy High School; Royal High School, Edinburgh; University of Dundee. Law Apprentice, North of Scotland Hydro-Electric Board, 1973-75; Procurator Fiscal Depute: Dundee, 1975-78, Glasgow 1978-81; Senior Legal Assistant, Crown Office, 1981-83; Senior Depute Procurator Fiscal, Edinburgh 1983-87; Senior Depute i/c Crown Office Fraud Unit, 1987-88; Assistant Solicitor i/c High Court Unit, Crown Office, 1988-91; Procurator Fiscal, Kirkcaldy, 1991-96; Regional Procurator Fiscal, South Strathclyde, Dumfries and Galloway, 1996-99; Procurator Fiscal, Hamilton, 1996-99; Deputy Crown Agent, Crown Office, 1999-2001; Sheriff of Tayside Central and Fife at Dundee, 2001-04; Director of the Judicial Studies Committee, 2004-08. Member: Management Committee, Lothian Victim Support Scheme, 1983-89, Training Advisory Committee, Victim Support Scotland, 1994-98, Council, Law Society of Scotland, 1996-99, Scottish Executive Stephen Lawrence Steering Group, 1999-2001; Chairman, Advisory Committee, Zone Project Dundee, 2003-04; Consultant to Justice Oversight Commission for Northern Ireland, 2003-06; Member and latterly Chairman of Stockbridge Primary School Board, Edinburgh, 2003-07; Member of Antisocial Behaviour Expert Advisory Group, 2008-09; Member of the Council of the Sheriffs' Association, 2004-2008; contributor to "Sentencing Practice", since 2004; External Examiner for the Law Diploma at Edinburgh University, 2004-09 and since 2018; Member of Bail Project Board, 2007-2008; Member of Lay Justice Reform Group, 2007-08; Member of the Criminal Courts Rules Council, since 2008; Member of Advisory Committee into Research on Drug Treatment and Testing II Orders, 2009-2010; Member of Lothian and Borders Justice of the Peace Training Committee, 2011-19; President, The Royal High School FP Club, 2013-16; Member, Board of Apex Scotland, 2013-19; I/c, Edinburgh Alcohol Problem Court, 2016-19. Member of Scottish Government Restore Reform Transform (RRT) Advisory Group, 2020-2021; External Examiner for University of Edinburgh Diploma, since 2019. Publications: The Golfing Life of Jock Kirkcaldy, 2019; Criminal Appeals Chapter in the Stair Encyclopaedia; Co-Author of the JSC Bench Book for Justices of the Peace and Legal Advisers' Manual; Journal of the Law Society of Scotland Criminal Briefing, since 2013. Recreations: dog walking; racing; music. Address: 8 Malta Terrace, Edinburgh EH4 1HR. E-mail: frankrcrowe23@gmail.com

Crowe, Victoria Elizabeth, OBE, Drhc, MA (RCA), RSA, RSW. Artist, Painter and Printmaker; b. 8.5.45, Kingston-on-Thames; m., Michael Walton; 1 s.; 1 d. Educ. Ursuline Convent Grammar School, London; Kingston College of Art; Royal College of Art. Part-time Lecturer, Drawing and

Painting, Edinburgh College of Art, 1968-98; solo exhibitions: The Scottish Gallery, Edinburgh, 1970, 1973, 1977, 1982, 1995, 1998, 2001, 2004, 2008, 2010, 2012, 2014, 2016, 2018; Thackeray Gallery, London, 1983, 1985, 1987, 1989, 1991, 1994, 1999, 2001, 2003, 2005, 2007; Bruton Gallery, Bath and Leeds, 1989, 1993, 1998; Plant memory: Royal Scottish Academy, 2007; A Shepherd's Life, retrospective, Scottish National Portrait Gallery, 2000, touring throughout Scotland and to Mercer Art Gallery, Harrogate, and Hatton Art Gallery, Newcastle upon Tyne, 2001-02; Shepherd's Life, 2009 Fleming Collection, London; overview, retrospective solo show, Fine Art Society, London, 2009; solo show, Browse and Darby, London, 2012, 2015, 2017; exhibited throughout Europe and USA with Artists for Nature Foundation; significant portrait commissions, NPG, SNPG, universities and public bodies; work in public and private collections, 2003-07; Beyond Likeness, Scottish National Portrait Gallery, 2018 (retrospective); Invited Artist Residency, Dumfries House, 2015, 2017. Senior Visiting Scholar, St. Catherine's College, Cambridge University; Honorary doctorate, Aberdeen University, 2009; elected fellow of Royal Society Edinburgh, 2010. Address: (b.) c/o The Scottish Gallery, 16 Dundas Street, Edinburgh EH3 6HZ.

Crozier, Paul Vincent. Resident Sheriff of Glasgow and Strathkelvin based at Glasgow, since 2013; Solicitor Advocate, since 2002. Educ. Strathclyde University. Admitted as a solicitor in 1985; set up practice in Dumbarton in 1987; sat as a Relief Stipendiary Magistrate, 1993-98; Lecturer in criminal procedure in the Diploma in Legal Practice at Strathclyde University, 1998-2002; appointed as a part-time Sheriff in 2009; Shrieval Convenor of Mental Health Tribunals. Chairman of the Championship Committee of the Scottish Rugby Union, 2011-13. Address: 1 Carlton Place, Glasgow G5 9DA; T.-0141 429 8888.

Cruickshank, Alastair Harvey, LLB, WS, DL. Retired Solicitor and Consultant; b. 10.8.43, Perth; m., Moira E. Pollock (deceased); 2 s. Educ. Perth Academy; Edinburgh University. Apprentice, then Assistant, Shepherd & Wedderburn, WS, Edinburgh, 1964-67; Assistant, then Partner, then Consultant, Condie Mackenzie & Co. (now Condies), 1967-2007. Diocese of Brechin: Registrar, 1974-99, Chancellor, 2000-03; Member, Perth Society of High Constables; Captain, Royal Perth Golfing Society, 2001-2003; Deputy Lieutenant, Perth and Kinross, since 1995. Recreations: hill-walking; sailing; chamber music, opera and classical music generally. Address: 8 Kincarrathie Crescent, Perth PH2 7HH; T.-01738 628484.

Cruickshank, Sheena Carlin, CVO, JP. Lord Lieutenant, County of Clackmannan, 2001-2011; b. 26.3.36, Stirling; m., Alistair Booth Cruickshank; (qv); 2 s.; 1 d. Educ. High School of Stirling. Honorary Sheriff. Recreation: quilting.

Cubie, Sir Andrew, CBE, FRSE, LLD (Edinburgh, Glasgow, Glasgow Caledonian), DUniv (Edinburgh Napier), DBA (QMUC), FRCPS (Glas) (Hon), FCGI, LLB, NP, WS. Consultant; b. 24.8.46, Northallerton; m., Professor Lady Heather Ann Cubie, MBE; 1 s.; 2 d. Educ. Dollar Academy; Edinburgh University. Partner, Fyfe Ireland & Co., WS, 1971; Chairman, Bird Semple Fyfe Ireland WS, 1991-94; non-executive Director, Scotland's Futures Forum and Scottish Cancer Foundation. Chairman: Leith Trust, sparqs, Housing First Advisory Board for Scotland, Centre for Healthy Working Lives, Scotland's Garden Trust and Campaign Board of Edinburgh Napier University; Advisor to The World Bank, Washington; sometime Chairman, Quality Scotland Foundation, Northern Lighthouse Board, Education Scotland, Leadership Foundation for Higher Education, Scottish Credit & Qualification Framework, Joint Negotiating Committee of USS and Independent Committee of Inquiry into Student Finance (the "Cubie Committee"); Member: Ministerial Action Group on Standards in Scottish Schools and, Independent Commission on Local Government and the Consultative Steering Group on the Scottish Parliament; former Chairman: CBI Scotland, Governing Council, George Watson's College, Edinburgh Napier University, Committee of University Chairs for the UK (CUC); former Trustee of British Council and Chair in Scotland; Chair, VSO; Deputy Chairman, RNLI for the UK and Ireland and Chairman in Scotland. Recreations: sailing; gardening. Address: (b.) 4/4 The Cedars, Edinburgh EH13 0PL; e-mail: andrew@cubie-edinburgh.com

Cubie, Professor Lady Heather Ann, MBE, BSc, MSc, PhD, FRCPath, FRSE. Senior Advisor, University of Edinburgh Global Health Academy; b. 8.12.46, Dunfermline; m., Andrew Cubie; 1 s.; 2 d. Educ. Dunfermline High School; Edinburgh University. Honorary Professor of Research and Research Management, College of Medicine and Veterinary Medicine, University of Edinburgh, since 2006; Board of Scottish Malawi Partnership, since 2014 and Chair, since 2019. Previous posts: Director, Scottish HPV Reference Laboratory, 2008-2012; NHS Lothian R&D Director, 1996-2008; Head of Service, Scottish Training Scheme for Clinical Scientists in Microbiology, 1997-2011; Chairman, Association of Clinical Microbiologists, 1999-2002. In retirement, actively involved in cervical cancer screening and treatment programme in Malawi. Publications: in field of Human Papilloma Virus (HPV) and molecular diagnostics in clinical virology. Recreations: gardening; travel; walking. Address: (b.) Global Health Academy, Ground Floor-Doorway 3, Teviot Quad, Teviot Place, Edinburgh EH8 9AG; e-mail: Heather.Cubie@ed.ac.uk

Cullen of Whitekirk, Rt. Hon. Lord (William Douglas Cullen), KT, PC, LLD, DUniv, FRSE, HonFREng, Hon FRCSEd, FRCPEd. Chancellor, University of Abertay Dundee, 2009-2019; Lord President and Lord Justice General, 2001-05; b. 18.11.35, Edinburgh; m., Rosamond Mary Downer; 2 s.; 2 d. Educ. Dundee High School; St. Andrews University (MA); Edinburgh University (LLB). Called to the Scottish Bar, 1960; QC, 1973; Advocate-Depute, 1977-81; Lord Justice Clerk, 1997-2001; PC, 1997; Life Peer, 2003; Justice of Civil and Commercial Court of Qatar Financial Centre, 2007-2015; Chairman: Inquiry into the Piper Alpha Disaster, 1988-90, Inquiry into the Shootings at Dunblane Primary School, 1996, Ladbroke Grove Rail Inquiry, 1999-2001, Review of fatal accident inquiry legislation, 2008-09. Member, Royal Commission on the Ancient and Historical Monuments of Scotland, 1987-97; Member, Napier University Court, 1996-2005; Chairman: Cockburn Association, 1984-86, Board of Governors, St. Margaret's School, Edinburgh, 1994-2001; Honorary President, SACRO, 2000-2015; President, Saltire Society, 2005-2011. Recreations: gardening; natural history. Address: (b.) c/o Lord President's Private Office, Parliament House, Edinburgh EH1 1RQ.

Culley, Dr Ron. Chief Executive, Quarriers, since 2020; formerly Chief Officer, Health and Social Care, Convention of Scottish Local Authorities (COSLA), then Chief Officer with the Western Isles Health and Social Care Partnership, 2016-2020. Address: Quarriers, 20 St. Kenneth Drive, Govan, Glasgow G51 4QD; T.-01505 6122246.

Cumberford, Audrey, MBE, FRSE, BEd (Hons), MBA, FCIM, FCMI. Principal and Chief Executive, Edinburgh College, since 2018; Board Member, Enterprise and Skills Strategic Board, Scottish

Government, since 2017; Principal and Chief Executive, West College Scotland, 2012-18; Principal and Chief Executive, Reid Kerr College, 2011-2012; Member of Scottish Funding Council, 2009-2017; b. 25.07.65, Glasgow. Educ. Uddingston Grammar; Moray House College of Education (Edinburgh University); Open University. Career history: Graduate Assistant, Bristol University; Sales Executive with GSK (Glaxo) and Baker Norton Pharmaceuticals; Sales and Marketing Manager in Product Design and Manufacture Sector; Senior Lecturer, Business School, Edinburgh's Telford College; Head of Department, Reid Kerr College. Currently Vice Chair, Colleges Scotland's College Principals' Group. Address: Edinburgh College, 350 West Granton Road, Edinburgh EH5 1QE.

Cumming, Professor Allan David, BSc, MBChB, MD, FRCPE. Emeritus Professor of Medical Education, University of Edinburgh; b. 12.2.51, Buenos Aires, Argentina; m., Lindsay Cumming (nee Galloway); 1 s.; 1 d. Educ. Nairn Academy; University of Edinburgh. Training posts in medicine/nephrology, 1975-89; Clinical research fellowship, University of Western Ontario, 1984-85; Honorary Consultant Physician, Renal Medicine, Lothian Health, 1998-2012. Dean of Students, College of Medicine and Veterinary Medicine, University of Edinburgh, 2012-16. Chancellor's Award for teaching, University of Edinburgh, 2004; Chair, MEDINE2 Network for Medical Education in Europe, 2009-2013. Recreations: golf; curling; music. E-mail: allan.cumming@ed.ac.uk

Cumming, Grant Philip, BSc (Hons), MD, MBChB, FRCOG. Consultant, Obstetrician and Gynaecologist, Dr. Grays Hospital, Elgin, since 2000; Honorary Senior Lecturer, Grampian University Hospitals NHS Trust, since 2000; Honorary Professor, University of the Highlands and Islands; b. 8.5.61, Derby; m., Fiona; 1 s.; 2 d. Educ. George Heriots School, Edinburgh; St. Andrews University; Victoria University, Manchester. Aberdeen Royal Infirmary and Maternity Hospital, 1996-2000. Medical Director, The Menopause and You (CD Rom); Scientific Lead: menopausematters.co.uk, babyfeedingmatters.co.uk, health-e-space.com. Recreations: golf; conjuring. Address: (b.) Dr Grays Hospital, Elgin, Moray; T.-01343 543131; e-mail: grant.cumming@nhs.net

Cumming, Ian, MBE, MA. Chief Executive Officer, Erskine, since 2018; b. Glasgow. Educ. Daniel Stewart's & Melville College; Joint Services Command and Staff College; King's College London; Chartered Management Institute. Career history: Royal Air Force (RAF), 1998-2006; Graduate, UK Advanced Command and Staff Course, 2007-08; Director, Resilience Operations and Community Protection, ISAF, 2009; CEO of RAF Operational Resilience Centre, 2008-2010; Head of RAF Corporate Communication, 2010-12; UK Strategic Liaison Officer to Pentagon and White House, US Federal Government, 2012-13; Programme Manager, Corporate Security and Resilience, RAF, 2013-2014; Business Development and Resilience Consultant, Sage Rock Consulting, 2013-15; Director of Fundraising, Communication and Development, Guideposts Charity, 2015-17; Trustee and Director, Vale House, Oxford, 2015-18; Deputy Managing Director, Carewatch Care Services Ltd, 2017-18. Awarded an MBE in 2007 for work in Basra whilst Commanding Officer of No 51 Squadron, RAF Regiment. Address: Erskine, 7 West George Street, Glasgow G2 1BA.

Cumming, Sandy, CBE, BSc (Hons); b. 30.10.52, Dingwall; m., Rosemary; 2 d. Educ. Dingwall Academy; University of Edinburgh. Highlands and Islands Development Board, 1973-1991; Highlands and Islands Enterprise, 1991-2010 (HIE Chief Executive, 2000-2010); Chair, Scotland's Rural College; former Trustee, The Robertson Trust; former Member, the Accounts Commission; former Board Member, Cromarty Firth Port Authority. Address: (b.) 15 Cradlehall Meadows, Inverness IV2 5GD; T.-01463 795533.
E-mail: sandy.cumming@btopenworld.com

Cunningham, David Kenneth, CBE, BEd, MEd (Hons), DUniv, FRSA, FSQA. Independent Education Consultant; General Secretary, School Leaders Scotland (SLS) (formerly HAS), 2008-2015; Head Teacher, Hillhead High School, Glasgow, 1993-2008; b. 19.4.48, Saltcoats; m., Marion S. Shedden; 2 d. Educ. Ardrossan Academy; Glasgow University; Jordanhill College of Education. Principal Teacher of English, North Kelvinside Secondary, 1976-80; Assistant Head Teacher, Garthamlock Secondary, 1980-82; Adviser in English, Dunbarton Division, 1982-90, Education Officer (Acting), 1989-90; Inspector, Quality Assurance Unit, Strathclyde Regional Council, 1990-93; Examiner, Setter, Principal Examiner, SEB, 1979-90; Member, Board, Glasgow Area, Young Enterprise Scotland; Vice-Chair, Glasgow Board, Young Enterprise Scotland; Director and Vice Chair, National Board, Young Enterprise Scotland; Headteachers Association of Scotland: Executive Member, 1997-2005, Vice President, 2000-01, President, 2001-02; Member, UCAS Standing Committee, 1997-2007; Director, Notre Dame Centre for Children, Young People and Families, 1999-2012; Associate Assessor, HMI, 1999-2008; Member, New National Qualifications Steering Group, 2001-04; Member, English and Communications Higher Still Revision Group; Chair, revision of Mental Health Higher, 2010; Vice-Chair, Educational Broadcasting Council for Scotland, 2002-07, Chair, since 2007; Member, Minister's Group on Race Relations Amendment Act, 2002; Member, SQA Qualifications Committee, 2003-2017; Member, Advisory Board of SCHOLAR, 2005-2016; Member, SFEU Core Skills Advisory Group; Director, DKC Consulting Ltd; Trustee, Scottish Board, Children's University, 2013-18; Trustee, ICAS Foundation, since 2014; Adviser to Education Department, Isle of Man government, since 2014; Honorary DUniv. from Heriot Watt University, 2015; Ambassador, Girl Guides, since 2003; Governor, Belmont House School, since 2012, Chair, 2013-2021; Director, Flying Start Enterprises, 2010-14; co-optee, RSA Scottish committee, 2015-16; Trustee, Children 1st (RSSPCC), since March 2016, Chair, since September 2016; Member, Minister's Group on Assessment and Qualifications, since January 2016; Member, Scottish Education Leaders Forum, since 2018; University Scotland's Bridging Programmes Working Group, 2017; Senior Project Adviser, Giglets Education Ltd, 2018-2021; Chair, Trust Board, Wren and Fraser, since 2019. Publication: Reading for 'S' Grade English, 1988. Recreations: various sports; reading; photography; travel; family. Address: (h.) Hillbrae, 154 Glasgow Road, Nerston, East Kilbride, Glasgow G74 4PB; T.-01355 230335.
E-mail: ken.cunningham194@icloud.com

Cunningham, Maggie. Executive and Leadership Coach; former Chairwoman, MG Alba; Joint Head of Programmes and Services for BBC Scotland, 2005-09; Head of Radio, Scotland, 2000-05; m.; 2 c. Producer, BBC Highland, 1979; freelance journalist, 1982-89; BBC Radio nan Gaidheal: Executive Producer, 1989; Editor, 1992; BBC Scotland: Secretary, 1995, returned to production to set up BBC Scotland's Talent Pool, 1997, Head of Features, Education and Religion, 1999; Board Member: Vice-Chair, Sistema, Scotland; Vice-Chair, Columba 1400; Edinburgh Festivals Forum; WW100 Scotland; Skye and Lochalsh Young Carers.

Cunningham, Roseanna. MSP (SNP), Perthshire South and Kinross-shire, 2011-2021, Perth, 1999-2011; Cabinet

Secretary for the Environment, Climate Change and Land Reform, 2016-2021; Cabinet Secretary for Fair Work, Skills and Training, 2014-16; Minister for Community Safety and Legal Affairs, 2011-14; Minister for Environment, 2009-2011; SNP Deputy Leader, 2000-04; Shadow Minister for Rural Affairs, Environment, Culture and Sport, 2003-04; Shadow Minister for Justice, 1999-2003; Convener, Rural Affairs and Environment Committee, 2007-09; Convener, Health Committee, 2004-07; Convener, Justice and Home Affairs Committee, 1999-2000; MP (SNP), Perth, 1995-2001; b. 27.7.51, Glasgow. Educ. University of Western Australia. SNP Research Department, 1977-79; law degree, Edinburgh University; Trainee Solicitor, Dumbarton District Council, 1983-84; Solicitor, Dumbarton, 1984-86; Solicitor, Glasgow, 1986-89; called to the Scottish Bar, 1990. Recreations: folk festivals; reading; cinema; cats; novice hill-walker.

Cunningham, Stewart, BA (Law), DipLP, PhD (Law). Lawyer, The Scottish Government, since 2020. Educ. University of Strathclyde; Glasgow Graduate School of Law; University of Strathclyde. Career history: Solicitor, Ethnic Minorities Law Centre, Glasgow, 2004-2010; Support Program Manager, Youthco HIV and Hep C Society of BC, Vancouver, Canada, 2011-12; Research Assistant, University of Leicester, 2017; Research Associate, University of Strathclyde, 2015-17; Consultant, NSWP (Global Network of Sex Work Projects), Edinburgh, 2014-2020; Research Associate: Hertie School of Governance, Berlin, Germany, 2017-2020; University of Strathclyde, 2019-2020; Associate Lecturer (part-time), 2019-2020. Address: Scottish Government, St. Andrew's House, Regent Road, Edinburgh EH1 3DG.

Curran, Frances. MSP (SSP), West of Scotland, 2003-07; former co-chair, Scottish Socialist Party; b. 21.5.61, Glasgow; 1 s. Educ. St Andrews Secondary School, Glasgow.

Curran, James, MBE. Director, Green Purposes Company; Chair, Climate Ready Clyde; past Chair, The James Hutton Institute; past Chair, Isle of Man Climate Change Committee, now independent advisor; former Chief Executive, Scottish Environment Protection Agency (SEPA) (2012-15). Career history: worked in environmental science and environmental regulation for 35 years, with studies in meterology, hydrology, oceanography and numerical modelling, water resources managament, and direct regulation and enforcement with agricultural and industrial businesses; formerly consultant with the Scottish Office; Head of Science, then Head of Environmental Strategy, SEPA; co-founded and managed Entrading, the UK's first comprehensive eco-store in central Glasgow; Director of Science and Strategy, SEPA, 2009-2011. Honorary Fellow, James Hutton Institute; Honorary Fellow, Scottish Environment LINK; Fellow of The Royal Society of Edinburgh; Visiting Professor, Centre For Sustainable Development, University of Strathclyde. Recreation: rewilding. Address: 15 Brooklands Avenue, Uddingston, Glasgow G71 7AT; T.-01698 812441.
E-mail: jamescurran@hotmail.co.uk

Curran, Margaret. Consultant and trainer for political and women's affairs, since 2015; Co-designer, Political Leadership Programme, University of Edinburgh, since 2017; MP (Labour), Glasgow East, 2010-2015; MSP (Labour), Glasgow Baillieston, 1999-2011; Shadow Secretary of State for Scotland, 2011-2015; Shadow Minister for Disabilities, 2010-2011; Minister for Parliament, Scottish Executive, 2004-07; Minister for Communities, 2002-04. Educ. Glasgow University. Former Lecturer in Community Education; Deputy Minister for Social Justice, Scottish Executive, 2001.

Currie, Angela. Chief Executive, Hanover (Scotland), Housing Association Ltd, since 2021. Educ. Heriot-Watt University. Career history: Policy, East Ayrshire Council, 2000-02; Research and Development Manager, SHBVN, 2002-2011; Chairperson, Link Housing Association, Edinburgh, 2009-2015; Director, Scotland's Housing Network, 2011-15; Chairperson, Housing Support Enabling Unit, 2017; Board Member, CCPS - Coalition of Care and Support Providers in Scotland, 2017; Blackwood Homes, Care and Support, Edinburgh: Director of Housing and Care, 2015-2021, Director of Operations, 2019-2021. Address: Hanover Scotland, 95 McDonald Road, Edinburgh EH7 4NS; T.-0131 557 0598.

Currie, David. Scottish television presenter and journalist; Presenter, Sportscene, BBC TV; Presenter, Sportsound, BBC Radio Scotland; b. 1967. Former journalist with The Sunday Post; became a television reporter at Border Television and joined BBC Scotland in 1999. Address: BBC Scotland, Pacific Quay, Pacific Drive, Glasgow G51 1DA.

Currie, Rev. Ian Samuel, MBE, BD. Retired Minister (2010); b. 14.8.43, Glasgow; m., Jennifer; 1 s.; 1 d. Educ. Bellahouston Academy; Trinity College; University of Glasgow; Minister: Blairhill Dundyvan Church, Coatbridge, 1975-80, St John's Church, Paisley, 1980-91, Oakshaw Trinity Church, Paisley, 1991-2005, United Church of Bute, 2005-2010. Chair, Victim Support Scotland, 1993-98; former Director, Wynd Centre, Paisley. Recreation: chess. Address: 26 Old Bridge of Weir Road, Houston, Johnstone PA6 7EB; T.-01505 227027.
E-mail: ianscurrie@tiscali.co.uk

Currie, Ken. Painter; b. 1960, North Shields. Educ. Paisley College; Glasgow School of Art. Worked on two films about Glasgow and Clyde shipbuilding, 1983-85; specialises in political realism, including a series of murals for the People's Palace Museum, Glasgow, on the socialist history of the city.

Currie, Ken. Rector, Madras College, St Andrews, since 2021. Worked as a technology teacher in Stirling; various roles at Balwearie High School, Kirkcaldy, including principal guidance teacher, pupil support and depute rector; periods on secondment at Glenwood High School, Glenrothes, and St Andrews High School, Kirkcaldy. Address: Madras College, Bell Brae, St Andrews, Fife KY16 9BY; T.-01334 659401.

Currie, Cllr Robin. Leader of Argyll and Bute Council, since 2020; Councillor, Kintyre and the Islands (Liberal Democrats); b. 10.55. Councillor for more than 30 years, in roles as wide-ranging as planning and housing, and leisure, islands and roads services. Board Member: Ionad Chaluim Chille Ile, Iomairt Chille-Chomain. Address: (b.) 10 Burnside, Bruichladdich, Islay PA49 7UR; T.-01496 850517.
E-mail: robin.currie@argyll-bute.gov.uk

Currie, Susan, BSc, PhD, PGCert. Reader/Associate Professsor in Cardiovascular Physiology, University of Strathclyde, since 2021. Educ. University of Glasgow; University of Strathclyde. Career history: Postdoctoral Researcher, Eli Lilly and Company, Indianapolis, Indiana Area, 1992-94; University of Glasgow: Postdoctoral Researcher, 1994-99; Postdoctoral Fellow, 1999-2004; Principal Investigator, 2004; University of Strathclyde: Lecturer, 2005-2012; Senior Lecturer, MPharm Deputy Director and IMU Director, 2012-18; Senior Lecturer and Cardiovascular Research Group Leader, 2018-2021. Address: Strathclyde Institute of

Pharmacy and Biomedical Sciences, 161 Cathedral Street, Glasgow G4 0RE.
E-mail: susan.currie@strath.ac.uk

Curtice, Professor Sir John Kevin, MA (Oxon). Professor of Politics, Strathclyde University, since 1998; Senior Research Fellow, ScotCen Social Research, since 2015; Research Consultant, ScotCen Social Research, 2001-2015; President, British Polling Council, since 2008; b. 10.12.53, Redruth; m., Lisa; 1 d. Educ. Truro School; Magdalen and Nuffield Colleges, Oxford. Research Fellow, Nuffield College, Oxford; Lecturer in Politics, Liverpool University; Fellow, Netherlands Institute for Advanced Study, 1988-89; Senior Lecturer in Politics, Strathclyde University, 1989-96; Reader in Politics, Strathclyde University, 1997-98. FRSA 1992; FRSE 2004; FAcSS 2013, FBA 2014; Hon FSS 2016; Kt 2018; Hon FMRS 2021. Publications include: How Britain Votes; Understanding Political Change; Labour's Last Chance; On Message; New Scotland, New Politics; The Rise of New Labour; New Scotland, New Society; British Social Attitudes; Devolution – Scottish Answers to Scottish Questions?; Has Devolution Delivered?; Has Devolution Worked?; Revolution or Evolution? The 2007 Scottish elections; Personality Politics? The Role of Leader Evaluations in Democratic Elections. Recreations: music; gardening. Address: (b.) School of Government and Public Policy, Strathclyde University, 16 Richmond Street, Glasgow G1 1XQ; T.-0141-548 4223.

Cusine, Sheriff Douglas James, LLB. Sheriff, Grampian, Highland and Islands at Aberdeen, 2001-2011; All-Scotland Floating Sheriff based at Peterhead, 2000-01; b. 2.9.46, Glasgow; m., Marilyn Calvert Ramsay; 1 s.; 1 d. Educ. Hutchesons' Boys' Grammar School; Glasgow University. Solicitor, 1971, Lecturer in Private Law, Glasgow University, 1974-76; Aberdeen University: Lecturer in Private Law, 1977-82, Senior Lecturer, 1982-90, Professor, Department of Conveyancing and Professional Practice of Law, 1990-2000. Member: Council, Law Society of Scotland, 1988-99, Lord President's Advisory Council on Messengers-at-Arms and Sheriff Officers, 1989-97; Member, UK Delegation to CCBE, 1997-2000; Member, Council of the Sheriffs Association, 2006-09; Trustee, Newbattle Abbey College, since 2012. Publications: Marine Pollution: Law and Practice (Co-Editor), 1980, reprinted 2019; Cases and Materials in Commercial Law (Co-Editor), 1987; A Scots Conveyancing Miscellany (Editor), 1987; New Reproductive Techniques: A Legal Perspective, 1988; Law and Practice of Diligence (Co-Author), 1989; Reproductive Medicine and the Law (Co-Author), 1990; Standard Securities, 1990, 2nd ed., (Co-Author), 2002; Missives (Co-Author), 1993, 2nd ed., 1999; Requirements of Writing (Co-Author), 1995; Servitudes and Rights of Way (Co-Author), 1998; various articles on medico-legal issues and conveyancing. Recreations: swimming; walking; photography, bird-watching. Address: The Brae, Gurney Street, Stonehaven, Kincardineshire AB39 2EB.

Cuthbert, Mary, OBE. Chair: Alcohol Focus Scotland, since 2014, Action on Smoking & Health (Scotland) (ASH Scotland), since 2014; m.; 2 c. Career Civil Servant for nearly 40 years; extensive experience of public policy making and delivery gained across a range of Scottish Government Departments and on secondment to external agencies; formerly Head of Alcohol, Tobacco and Sexual Health Policy within the CMO and Public Health Directorate; at the forefront of a number of key public health policy and legislative developments in HIV/AIDS; sexual health; drugs misuse; alcohol and tobacco during 14 years in the Directorate (this included the ban on smoking in public places and alcohol minimum pricing). Currently on the Board of Directors of Young Scot, Alcohol Focus Scotland and ASH Scotland. Outstanding Contribution Award by INWAT Europe for the part played in helping Scotland to become a world leader in tobacco control in 2007; awarded an OBE in 2009 in recognition of service to the public and the voluntary sector. Address: ASH Scotland, 8 Frederick Street, Edinburgh EH2 2HB; T.-0131 225 4725.

Cuthbertson, Rev. Malcolm, BA, BD (Hons). Minister: Rutherglen West and Wardlawhill Church, since 2017, Mure Memorial Church, 2010-17; b. 3.4.56, Glasgow; m., Rena Fennel; 1 s.; 2 d. Educ. Grangemouth High School; Stirling University; Aberdeen University. Probationer Assistant, Crown Court Church, London, 1983-84; Minister, Easterhouse: St. George's and St. Peter's Church of Scotland, 1984-2010. Recreations: eating out; reading theology. Address: 3 Western Avenue, Rutherglen G73 1JQ.

Cuthell, Rev. Thomas Cuthbertson, MA, BD. Minister Emeritus, St. Cuthbert's Parish Church, Edinburgh, since 2007 (retired); b. 18.2.41, Falkirk. Educ. Bo'ness Academy; University of Edinburgh. Assistant Minister, St. Giles Cathedral, Edinburgh; Minister, North Church, Uphall. Recreations: travel; music; sailing. Address: Flat 10, 2 Kingsburgh Crescent, Edinburgh EH5 1JF.

Cutler, Timothy Robert (Robin), CBE, BSc, DSc. b. 24.7.34, India; m., Ishbel W.M.; 1 s.; 1 d. Educ. Banff Academy; Aberdeen University. Colonial Forest Service, Kenya, 1958-64; New Zealand Government Forestry, 1964-90, latterly Chief Executive, New Zealand Ministry of Forestry; Director General, Forestry Commission, 1990-95. Recreations: golf; travel. Address: 14 Swanston Road, Edinburgh EH10 7BB; T.-0131-445 5437.

Czerkawska, Catherine, MA (Hons), MA (Postgraduate). Novelist and Playwright; b. 3.12.55, Leeds; 1 s. Educ. Queen Margaret's Academy, Ayr; St. Michael's Academy, Kilwinning; Edinburgh University; Leeds University. Published poetry (White Boats and a Book of Men); taught EFL in Finland and Poland; thereafter, full-time freelance writer working on novels, short stories and plays. Pye Award for Best Radio Play of 1980, O Flower of Scotland; Scottish Radio Industries Club Award, 1983, Bonnie Blue Hen; Wormwood, and Quartz, Traverse Theatre, Edinburgh, 1997 and 2000; The Way It Was, a History of Gigha, 2016. Historical novels including The Physic Garden; The Jewel: a novel of the life of Jean Armour and Robert Burns; Bird of Passage; The Curiosity Cabinet; The Posy Ring; A Proper Person to be Detained: the true story of a murder in the family. Recreations: antique textiles; social history; gardening. Website: www.catherineczerkawska.co.uk
E-mail: catherine.czerkawska@gmail.com

D

Dale, Professor John Egerton, BSc, PhD, FRSE, FSB. Emeritus Professor of Plant Physiology, Edinburgh University, since 1993; b. 13.2.32, London; m., Jacqueline Joyce Benstock (deceased) 1 s.; 2 d.; m. (2), Kay. Educ. City of London School; Kings College, London. Plant Physiologist, Empire Cotton Growing Corporation, Uganda, 1956-61; Edinburgh University: Lecturer in Botany, then Reader, 1961-85, Professor of Plant Physiology, 1985-93, Head, Division of Biological Sciences, 1990-93. Secretary, Society for Experimental Biology, 1974-79; Secretary General, Federation of European Societies of Plant Physiology, 1978-84; Trustee, Peter Potter Gallery, 1994-99; Institute of Biology: Chairman, Scottish Branch, 1999-2001; Scottish Wildlife Trust: Acting Chairman, 2002, Vice Chairman, 1999-2002. Publications: 100 papers on growth of leaves and related topics. Recreations: the arts; travel; gardening. Address: (h.) 26 Tantallon Court, Heugh Road, North Berwick EH39 5QF; T.-01620 893332.

Dalhousie, Earl of (James Hubert Ramsay), DL, CStJ. Chairman, Brechin Castle Centre Ltd.; former Chairman: Jamestown Investments Ltd., Dunedin Smaller Companies Investment Trust plc (retired 2015); President: Caledonian Club; Vice-Chairman, Game and Wildlife Conservation Trust, 1987-2009; Director, Scottish Woodlands, 1993-2005; b. 17.1.48, London; m., Marilyn; 1 s.; 2 d. Educ. Ampleforth College. Commissioned, Coldstream Guards, 1968-71; Hambros Bank Ltd (Director, 1971); Co-Founder, Jamestown Investments, 1982. Captain, Royal Company of Archers; Vice Lord Lieutenant, County of Angus; President, Unicorn Preservation Society, 2001-2013; Hon. Captain, RNR; President, Angus Branch, Cdr of St John; Board Member, Deer Commission Scotland, 2005-2010; Lord Steward, since 2009. Address: (b.) Dalhousie Estates Office, Brechin DD9 6SG; T.-01356 624566.

Dalling, Ken, LLB (Hons), DipLP, NP, SSC. President, Law Society of Scotland, since 2021; Owner, Dalling Solicitors, Stirling, since 1992. Educ. Strathclyde Business School. Qualified as solicitor in 1988. Member of the Council of the Law Society of Scotland; elected to the Board of the Law Society in June 2017; former Vice-President; represented Stirling Faculty on the Standing Advisory Committee, Stirling Sheriff Court, since 2000; Secretary to the Society of Solicitors and Procurators of Stirling, since 2003 (past Dean). Convener: Law Society's Client Protection Fund Committee; Anti Money Laundering Committee; member of the Senior Solicitor Advocate Accreditation Committee and the Professional Practice Committee; participated in a number of Law Society Working Groups dealing with matters of professional practice and legal aid. Address: Dalling Solicitors, 83 Barnton Street, Stirling FK8 1HJ; T.-01786 448 111.

Dalrymple Hamilton, North John Frederick, OBE, TD, MA (Hons), DL. Farmer and Land Manager; b. 7.5.50, Edinburgh; m., Sally Anne How; 2 s.; 1 d. Educ. Aberdeen University. Scottish and Newcastle Breweries, 1972-82; certificate of farming practice, East of Scotland College of Agriculture, 1982-84; farming of Bargany Farms, 1984-2021 (retired). TA Commission, 1967-95; Member, Queen's Bodyguard for Scotland; Vice Lieutenant for Ayrshire and Arran; President, RBL(S), Maybole Branch; Chair, Lowland RFCA, 2003-07. Address: (h.) Houdston Farm, Girvan, Ayrshire KA26 9RF.

Dalyell, Kathleen Mary, DL, MA, FRSAS, OBE. Chairman, Royal Commission on Ancient and Historical Monuments of Scotland, 2000-05; Administrator, The Binns, 1972-2018; Director, Heritage Education Trust, 1987-2005; Director, Weslo Housing Association, 1994-

2003; Trustee, Carmont Settlement Trust, 1997-2013; Deputy Lieutenant, West Lothian, until 2012; b. 17.11.37, Edinburgh; m., Tam Dalyell (deceased) 1 s.; 1 d. Educ. Convent of Sacred Heart, Aberdeen; Edinburgh University; Craiglochart Teacher Training College. Teacher of History, St. Augustine's Secondary School, Glasgow, 1961-62; James Gillespie's High School for Girls, Edinburgh, 1962-63; Member, Historic Buildings Council for Scotland, 1975-87; Member, Lady Provost of Edinburgh's Delegation to China, 1987; Member, National Committee of Architectural Heritage Society for Scotland, 1983-89 (Vice-Chair, 1986-89); Chairman, Bo'ness Heritage Trust, 1988-93; Trustee, Paxton Trust, 1988-92; Member, Ancient Monuments Board for Scotland, 1989-2000; Member, Royal Fine Art Commission for Scotland, 1992-2000; Member, Lord Mackay's Panel on Governance, NTS, 2003; Member, Court of University of Stirling, 2002-08; Trustee, Hopetoun Preservation Trust, 2005-2016; Hon. Degree, University of Edinburgh, 2006; Hon. Degree, Stirling University, 2008; Trustee, National Museums of Scotland Charitable Trust. Recreations: reading; travel; hillwalking; chess. Address: The Binns, Linlithgow EH49 7NA; T.-01506 83 4255.

Dane, Graham Charles, BSc, BA, MEd, MCIL, MInstP, CPhys, FEIS. Educational Consultant, occasionally in Africa; formerly Principal Teacher of Physics, St Augustine's High School, Edinburgh, 1983-2010, seconded to International Relations Unit, Scottish Executive Education Department, 2002-03; b. 19.7.50. Educ. Saint Andrews University. Teacher of Science, Merksworth High School, Paisley, 1973-75; Information Scientist, The Electricity Council, London, 1975-77; Teacher of Physics, Forrester High School, Edinburgh, 1978-80; Assistant Principal Teacher of Science, Deans Community High School, Livingston, 1980-83. Elected Member, General Teaching Council for Scotland (Convener, Committee on Exceptional Admission to the Register), 1995-2001; holder of numerous trade union positions over the years, mainly in the EIS; Member of the Board, Scottish Council for Research in Education, 1992-98; Chair, Currie Community Council, 1998-2013; Treasurer, Socialist Educational Association Scotland, 2010-2015; Governor, Donaldson's College, 1996-2005; Trustee of Currie Community Centre and Chair, Management Committee of Currie Community Centre, 2013-2018; Member of Scottish Committee of WEA, 2009-2012; Chair, Currie Riding of the Marches Committee, since 2016; Director, Currie and Balerno News, since 2021; Delegate to the Labour Party Conference, 2016 and 2018. Recreations: travel; languages; skiing; learning new things; meeting people he likes; enjoying the arts; being a grandfather. Address: (h.) 25 Thomson Road, Edinburgh EH14 5HT.

Darling of Roulanish, Baron (Alistair Maclean Darling), PC, LLB (Labour), Edinburgh South West, 2005-2015, Edinburgh Central, 1987-2005; Member, Board of Directors, Morgan Stanley, since 2016; Chair of the Better Together Campaign, 2012-14; Chancellor of the Exchequer, 2007-10; Secretary of State for Trade and Industry, 2006-07; Secretary of State for Transport, 2002-06; Secretary of State for Scotland, 2003-06; Secretary of State for Work and Pensions, 2001-02; b. 28.11.53, London; m., Margaret Vaughan; 1 s.; 1 d. Educ. Loretto School; Aberdeen University. Solicitor, 1978-83; Advocate, 1984-2010; Member: Lothian Regional Council, 1982-87, Lothian and Borders Police Board, 1982-87; Governor, Napier College, 1985-87; Chief Secretary to the Treasury, 1997-98; Secretary of State for Social Security, 1998-2001. Chair of Trustees, Standard Life Foundation, since 2017; Hon. President, Chatham House, since 2016.

Darroch, Martin, BA, CA. Chief Executive, Harper Macleod LLP, since 2006. Educ. University of Strathclyde; Institute of Chartered Accountants of Scotland. Career: CA

Trainee, BDO LLP, 1995-98; Corporate Finance Executive: RMD, 1998-99, Deloitte, 1998-2000; Finance Director, Harper Macleod LLP, 2002-06. Chairman of the TPE Board, The Institute of Chartered Accountants of Scotland, 2008-2011; Chair, Managing Partners Forum Scotland Committee (MPF), 2010-2011; Institute of Chartered Accountants of Scotland: Member of Council, 2006-2017, Chairman of The Regulation Board, 2014-17, Oversight Board, 2014-17; Advisory Board Member, Entrepreneurial Spark, 2017-18. Shortlisted as Regional Director of the Year at the IoD Director of the Year Scotland Awards, 2015; won Young Finance Director of the Year at the Finance Director of the Year Awards, 2007 and was awarded the title of Managing Partner of the Year at The Law Awards of Scotland in 2009 (being the first non-lawyer to win the award) and again in 2011, 2012, 2013 & 2015; also shortlisted for Scotland's Young Business Leader of the Year award in 2012. Address: Harper Macleod, Ca'd'oro, 45 Gordon Street, Glasgow G1 3PE; T.-0141 221 8888.

Darwent, Dr Kirsty, BSc Hons (Psyc), MSc, AdvDip, PhD. Chair, The Scottish Fire and Rescue Service, since 2017; Director, The Family Therapy Training Network Co-operative, since 2012; Chair, Relationships Scotland, since 2015. Educ. Institute of Psychiatry, King's College London; University of Aberdeen; Scottish Institute of Human Relations; University of Stirling. Non-Executive Member of the Board, NHS Ayrshire and Arran, 2004-2016; Member, Midwifery Committee, The Nursing and Midwifery Council, 2009-2015; Member of the Board, The Scottish Fire and Rescue Service, 2012-17. Address: Scottish Fire and Rescue Service Headquarters, Westburn Drive, Cambuslang G72 7NA; T.-0141 646 4500.

Das, Dr Sachi Nandan, MB, BS, FRCR, DMRT. Chairman, Dudhope Multicultural Centre, a multicultural, multiethnic voluntary organisation, since 2007; b. 1.8.44, Cuttack, India; m., Dr. Subhalaxmi; 1 s.; 1 d. Educ. Ravenshaw Collegiate School; SCB Medical College, Cuttack, India; Utkal University. Senior House Officer in Radiotherapy, Plymouth General Hospital, 1969-70; Registrar in Radiotherapy and Oncology, then Senior Registrar, Mersey Regional Centre for Radiotherapy, Liverpool, 1970-77; Consultant in administrative charge, Ninewells Hospital, Dundee, 1987-91, Clinical Director, 1991-98; Regional Postgraduate Education Advisor in Radiotherapy and Oncology, 1987-2002. Member: Standing Scottish Committee, National Medical Consultative Committee, Scottish Paediatric Oncology Group, Joint Radiological Safety Committee, Radiation Hazards Sub-Committee, Unit Medical and Dental Advisory Committee; Council Member, Scottish Radiological Society, 1987-93; Head, Department of Radiotherapy and Oncology, Dundee University, 1987-2000; Chairman, Tayside Oncology Research Committee, 1987-2007. Recreations: gardening; walking; reading. Address: (h.) Grapevine, 42 Menzieshill Road, Dundee DD2 1PU; T.-Dundee 642915.

Davey, Andrew John, BSc (Hons), DipArch, RIBA, RIAS. Partner, Simpson & Brown Architects of Edinburgh; b. 6.6.52, Exmouth, Devon; m., Christina; 2 s.; 1 d. Educ. Queen Elizabeth's School, Devon; Bartlett School of Architecture; University College London. Publication: joint author, The Care and Conservation of Georgian Houses', 1978 (now in its 4th Edition). Address: (b.) Simpson and Brown Architects, St. Ninian's Manse, Quayside Street, Edinburgh EH6 6EJ; T.-0131 555 4678.
E-mail: admin@simpsonandbrown.co.uk

Davidge, Rev. Alison Elizabeth Shaw. Interim Moderator, Calton Parkhead Parish Church; b. 8.64. Address: 365

Hallhill Road, Barlanark, Glasgow G33 4RY; T.-0141 771 6477.

Davidson, Professor Donald Allen, BSc, PhD, FRSE. Emeritus Professor of Environmental Science, Stirling University; b. 27.4.45, Lumphanan; m., Caroline E. Brown; 1 s.; 2 d. Educ. Robert Gordon's College, Aberdeen; Aberdeen University; Sheffield University. Lecturer, St. David's University College, Wales, 1971-76; Lecturer, Senior Lecturer, Reader, Strathclyde University, 1976-86; Reader, Stirling University, 1986-91. Editor of journal Earth and Environmental Science Transactions of the Royal Society of Edinburgh. Publications include: The Evaluation of Land Resources, 1992; many papers. Recreations: exploring the countryside; maintaining a large garden. Address: (b.) Biological and Environmental Science, Stirling University, Stirling FK9 4LA; T.-01786 823599.

Davidson, Duncan Lewis Watt, BSc (Hons), MB, ChB, FRCPEdin. Chairman, Tweedsmuir Community Company; Consultant in Medical Education, 2002-05; Consultant Neurologist, Tayside; Honorary Senior Lecturer in Medicine, Dundee University, 1976-2002; b. 16.5.40, Kingston, Jamaica; m., Dr. Anne V.M. Maiden; 4 s.; 1 d. Educ. Knox College, Jamaica; Edinburgh University. House Officer, Senior House Officer, Registrar and Senior Registrar posts in medicine and neurology, Edinburgh, 1966-75; Peel Travelling Fellowship, Montreal, 1973-74; MRC clinical scientific staff, MRC Brain Metabolism Unit, Edinburgh, 1975-76. Recreations: gardening; photography. Address: (h.) Oliver, Tweedsmuir, Biggar ML12 6QN; T.-01899 880278.

Davidson, Gina. Scotland Political Editor, LBC, since 2021; Deputy Political Editor, The Scotsman, 2019-2022; Media and Communications Specialist, Gina Davidson Media, 2018-2021. Educ. James Gillespie's High School; Napier University. Career history: Reporter: Edinburgh Herald and Post, 1993-94, Edinburgh Evening News, 1994-97; Reporter and Producer with Edinburgh Live, Trinity Mirror, 1997-98; East of Scotland Reporter, Press Association, 1998; Home Affairs Editor, then Deputy Features Editor, Edinburgh Evening News, 1998-2000; Writer, Scotland on Sunday, 2000-01; Edinburgh Evening News: Features Editor, 2001-08, Associate Editor, 2008-2015; Owner, Gina Davidson Media, 2015-16; Director of Policy, Scottish Labour Party, The Scottish Parliament, 2016-17; Head of Communications, Scottish Labour Parliamentary Group, 2017-18; Political Communications Manager, SP Energy Networks, 2018. Scottish Journalist of the Year 2013.

Davidson, Ian. Head of Agriculture Policy Division, Scottish Government. Career history: long experience in policy and delivery; previously held posts in developing the current Common Agricultural Policy in Scotland and also in the Area Office network as part of the RPID; has responsibility for the Scottish Rural Development Programme, current CAP Pillar 1 policy, Agricultural Holdings legislation, GM policy, Climate Change in Agriculture policy, Crofting policy and the Scottish Agricultural Wages Board. Address: Scottish Government, St Andrew's House, Regent Road, Edinburgh EH1 3DG.

Davidson, Ian Graham, MA (Hons). MP (Labour and Co-op), Glasgow South West, 2005-2015 (Glasgow Pollok, 1997-2005, Glasgow Govan 1992-97); b. 8.9.50, Jedburgh; m., Morag Mackinnon; 1 s.; 1 d. Educ. Jedburgh Grammar School; Galashiels Academy; Edinburgh University; Jordanhill College of Education. Project Manager, Community Service Volunteers, 1985-92; Councillor,

Strathclyde Regional Council, 1978-92 (Chair, Education Committee, 1986-92); former Member, Public Accounts Select Committee; Member, Committee of Selection, 1997-99; Secretary, Trade Union Group of Labour MPs, 1998-2002.

Davidson, Rev. Ian Murray Pollock, MBE, MA, BD. Minister, Allan Park South Church and Church of the Holy Rude, Stirling, 1985-94; Chairman, General Trustees, Church of Scotland, 1994-99; b. 14.3.28, Kirriemuir; m., Isla; 2 s. Educ. Montrose Academy; St. Andrews University. National Service, 1949-51; Minister: Crieff North and West Church (St. Andrew's), 1955-61, Grange Church, Kilmarnock, 1961-67, Cambuslang Old Church, 1967-85; Convener, Maintenance of the Ministry Committee and Board, Church and Ministry Department, 1981-84; General Trustee, 1975-2003. Publications: At the Sign of the Fish (history of Cambuslang Old Parish Church), 1975; A Guide to the Church of the Holy Rude. Recreations: travel; photography; reading; writing. Address: (h.) 13/8 Craigend Park, Edinburgh EH16 5XX; T.-0131-664 0074.

Davidson, Professor Ivor John, MA, PhD, MTh. Professor of Systematic and Historical Theology, since 2009; b. 23.12.67, Glasgow; m., Dr. Julie Elaine Hunter (née); 1 d. Educ. Bradford Grammar School; University of Glasgow; University of Edinburgh. Part-time Lecturer, University of Glasgow, 1992-94; Temporary Lecturer, University of St Andrews, 1994-96; Lecturer, University of Otago, New Zealand, 1997-99, Senior Lecturer, 2000-04, Professor of Theology, 2005-09; Professor of Systematic and Historical Theology, University of St Andrews, 2009-16; Head of School, Dean of Faculty of Divinity and Principal, St Mary's College, St Andrews, 2010-13; Honorary Research Professor of Theology, University of Aberdeen, since 2016; higher education management consultant and international peer assessor in Arts and Humanities; member of Center of Theological Inquiry, Princeton, since 2006. Academic awards include Logan Prize (most distinguished graduate in Arts, University of Glasgow); Jeffrey, Cowan, Ramsay Medals, Kenmure Scholarship, Coulter Prize, Scott Scholarship, etc. Publications: books include Ambrose, De Officiis (2 vols.), 2002; The Birth of the Church, 2004; A Public Faith, 2005; God of Salvation, 2011; Salvation, 2017; numerous articles in learned journals; founding series editor, Bloomsbury T. & T. Clark Studies in Systematic Theology monographs. Recreations: walking; running; music; reading. Address: School of Divinity, History and Philosophy, King's College, University of Aberdeen, Aberdeen AB24 3UB; e-mail: ivor.davidson@abdn.ac.uk

Davidson, Jane. Former Chief Executive, NHS Borders (2015-19), previously Deputy Chief Executive, 2012-15. Began career in Lanarkshire, moving to the State Hospitals Board for Scotland, holding the post of Director of Finance; worked as a senior manager in the NHS in Scotland, since 1993; worked with the Scottish Government as Deputy Director of Health Finance; led the modernisation and integration of the health finance division of the Scottish Government Health Directorates with responsibility for the development and implementation of the financial planning strategy and the financial performance management of NHS Boards; appointed Director of Finance, NHS Borders in 2010, then Chief Operating Officer in 2010.

Davidson, John Knight (Jake), OBE, MD, FRCP (Edin), FRCP (Glas), FRCR, (Hon) FACR, (Hon) FRACR. Consultant Radiologist; expert adviser on bone disease in compressed air and diving medicine; b. 17.8.25, Edinburgh; m., Edith E. McKelvie; 2 s.; 1 d. Educ. George Watson's Boys College, Edinburgh; Edinburgh University. Adviser in Bone Disease in Divers MRC, Aberdeen, US Navy, 1970-92; Non Executive Director, Yorkhill NHS Trust, 1993-95; Member, Council, Medical and Dental Defence Union, 1971-95; Chairman, Health Policy, Council, Scottish Conservative and Unionist Association, 1991-95; Member, BBC Medical Advisory Group, 1988-95; Consultant Radiologist in Administrative Charge, Western Infirmary and Gartnavel General, Glasgow, 1967-90; Royal College of Radiologists: Member, Council, 1974-77, 1984-87, Chairman, Examining Board, 1976-79, Scottish Committee, 1985-89; Member, Council, Royal Glasgow Institute of Fine Arts, 1978-88; Deputy President, Glasgow and Renfrewshire, British Red Cross Society, 1988-93; Honorary Fellow: Royal Australian and New Zealand College of Radiology, 1981, Scottish Radiological Society, 1990, American College of Radiology, 1992, Medical and Dental Defence Union, Scotland, 1995; Honorary Fellow and Medallist, International Skeletal Society, 1995; Rohan Williams Professor, Australasia, 1977; Aggarwal Memorial Oration, India, 1988. Member: Royal and Ancient Golf Club, St Andrews; Pollok GC, Glasgow; Queen Anne Golfing Society; British Golf Collectors Society; Glasgow Art Club; RLS Club; Buchanan Bridge Club, Glasgow. Editor: Jake's Corner, Queen Anne Golfing Society, 1948-2008, Aseptic Necrosis of Bone and numerous publications. Recreations: golf; water colours; golf history; Robert Louis Stevenson; bridge; meeting people. Address: (h.) 1/1, 15 Beechlands Avenue, Netherlee, Glasgow G44 3YT; T.-0141-637 0290; e-mail: jaked15b@gmail.com

Davidson, Julie. Writer and journalist; freelance contributor to radio, television, books, newspapers and magazines, since 1981; b. 11.5.43, Motherwell; m., Harry Reid (qv); 1 d. Educ. Aberdeen High School for Girls. Trainee Journalist, D.C. Thomson Ltd., Dundee, 1961-64; Feature Writer and Sub-Editor, Aberdeen Press & Journal, 1964-67; The Scotsman: Feature Writer, 1967-77, Columnist, 1977-81; The Herald: Television Critic, 1981-95, Columnist, 1995-97. Columnist/Critic of the Year, Scottish Press Awards, 1985; Critic of the Year, Scottish Press Awards, 1988-89-92-94-95; Canada Travel Award, 1992; Travelex Travel Writers Award, 1999; Scottish Thistle Travel Media Award, 1999. Publications: Scots We Ken, 2007; Reflections of Scotland, 2009; Looking for Mrs Livingstone, 2012. Recreations: reading; cinema; walking; travelling; wildlife; lunching.
E-mail: julie.davidson3@talktalk.net

Davidson, Cllr Margaret. Leader, The Highland Council; represents 12 Aird and Loch Ness Ward (Independent). Address: Abriachan Nurseries, Kilianan, Loch Ness Side, Inverness IV3 8LA.
E-mail: margaret.davidson.cllr@highland.gov.uk

Davidson of Glen Clova, Lord (Neil Forbes Davidson), QC, BA, MSc, LLB, LLM, DUniv (Stirling). Advocate General for Scotland, 2006-10; Solicitor General for Scotland, 2000-01; b. 13.9.50; m. Educ. Stirling University; Bradford University; Edinburgh University. Admitted, Faculty of Advocates, 1979; Standing Junior Counsel to Registrar General, 1982, to Department of Health and Social Security, 1988; called to the Bar, Inner Temple, 1990; Director, City Disputes Panel, 1993-2000. Author, Davidson Review on UK Implementation of EU Regulation (2007); Judicial Review in Scotland (1986); Member, Advisory Council of International Monetary Institute, Renmin University, since 2017; Hon 5th Dan, International Taekwondo Federation. Address: Axiom Advocates, Faculty of Advocates, Parliament House, Edinburgh EH1 1RF; T.-0131 226 5071.

Davidson, Professor Roger, MA, CertEd, PhD, FRHistS. Emeritus Professor of Social History; b. 19.7.42, Guildford; m., Mo Townson; 1 s.; 1 d. Educ. King Edward VI School, Chelmsford; St Catharine's College, Cambridge. Teacher in History and Economics,

Watford Boys Grammar School, 1965-67; Research Graduate, St Catharine's College, Cambridge, 1967-70; Lecturer, 1970, Senior Lecturer, 1984, Reader, 1996, in Economic and Social History, Edinburgh University. Former Member, Scottish Records Advisory Council. Publications: Whitehall and the Labour Problem in Late-Victorian and Edwardian Britain, 1985; Dangerous Liaisons: A Social History of VD in 20th Century Scotland, 2000; The Sexual State: Sexuality and Scottish Governance 1950-80 (2012); Illicit and Unnatural Practices: The Law, Sex and Society in Scotland since 1900 (2019). Recreation: bird-watching. Address: 21 Eskfield Grove, Dalkeith EH22 3FA.
E-mail: Roger.Davidson@ed.ac.uk

Davidson of Lundin Links, Baroness (Ruth Elizabeth Davidson). MSP (Conservative) Edinburgh Central, 2016-2021 (Glasgow, 2011-16); Leader of the Conservative Party in the Scottish Parliament, 2020-2021; Leader of the Scottish Conservatives, 2011-19; b. 10.11.78, Edinburgh; 1 s. Educ. Buckhaven High School, Fife; University of Edinburgh; University of Glasgow. Career: worked as a presenter, journalist and documentary maker with the BBC and a number of newspapers and radio stations.

Davidson, Valerie, BA, CPFA. Chief Executive, Strathclyde Partnership for Transport (SPT), since 2021; b. East Kilbride; m., Alasdair Davidson; 1 s. Educ. St. Brides High School; Glasgow College of Technology. Career History: Trainee Accountant, Surrey Borough Council; Systems Auditor (Secondment), Surrey County Council; Contracts Auditor, Surrey Heath Borough Council; Internal Audit Manager, London Borough of Croydon; Depute Director, CIPFA Scotland/Secondment as Competition Consultant; Head of Finance, SPT, then Director of Finance. Consulting Author to Stairs Encyclopedia; contributing Author to CIPFA Publications. Recreations: cooking; golf. Address: Strathclyde Partnership for Transport, 131 St Vincent Street, Glasgow G2 5JF; T.-0141 332 6811.

Davies, Alan Graham, LLB(Hons), Dip. Legal Practice. Solicitor in private practice since 1983, Partner, since 1987; b. 4.2.59, Perth; m., Fiona; 2 s.; 1 d. Educ. Perth Grammar School; University of Edinburgh. Recreations: golf; football; skiing; tennis. Address: (b.) 25 South Methven Street, Perth; T.-01738 620451.

Davies, Professor Christine Tullis Hunter, OBE, MA, PhD (Cantab), FInstP, FRSE, FAPS. Professor of Physics, University of Glasgow, since 1999; b. 19.11.59, Clacton, Essex; m., John Davies; 2 d. Educ. Colchester County High School for Girls; Churchill College, University of Cambridge. Postdoctoral Research Associate, Cornell University, 1984-86; SERC Advanced Fellow, Glasgow University, 1987-93; Lecturer, 1993-96; Reader, 1996-99. Fulbright Scholar and Leverhulme Trust Fellow, University of California at Santa Barbara, 1997-98; PPARC Senior Fellow, 2001-04; Royal Society/Leverhulme Trust Senior Fellow, 2008; Rosalind Franklin Award, Royal Society, 2005. STFC Particle Physics Grants Panel (Theory), 2006-09; IOP Council and Chair of Diversity Committee, 2007-2011; RCUK (Wakeham) Committee, 2008; Royal Society Wolfson Research Merit Award, 2012-2017; STFC Science Board, 2015-18. Recreations: walking; photography. Address: (b.) School of Physics & Astronomy, University of Glasgow, Glasgow G12 8QQ; T.-0141 330 4710; e-mail: christine.davies@glasgow.ac.uk

Davies, Sir Howard John, MA, MS. Chairman, NatWest Group plc (formerly The Royal Bank of Scotland Group

plc), since 2015; Professor of Practice, The Paris Institute of Political Science (Sciences Po); b. 12.2.51; m., Prue Keely; 2 s. Educ. Bowker Vale County Primary School; Manchester Grammar School; Merton College, Oxford University; Stanford Graduate School of Business. Worked at the Treasury and the Foreign and Commonwealth Office, which included a posting of Private Secretary to the British Ambassador to France; McKinsey and Company, 1982-87; Special Advisor to Chancellor of the Exchequer Nigel Lawson, 1985-86; Controller of the Audit Commission, 1987-92; Director General of the Confederation of British Industry, 1992-95; Deputy Governor of the Bank of England, 1995-97; Chairman of the Financial Services Authority, 1997-2003; Director of the London School of Economics and Political Science, 2003-2011. Independent Director of Prudential plc and Chair of the Risk Committee; Member of the Regulatory and Compliance Advisory Board of Millennium Management LLC; Chair of the International Advisory Council of the China Securities Regulatory Commission; Member of the International Advisory Council of the China Banking Regulatory Commission; Council Member of the Asian Bureau of Finance and Economic Research in Singapore. Chair, UK Airports Commission, 2012-15. Writes regularly for The Financial Times, Times Higher Education, Project Syndicate and Management Today. Publications: Chancellors Tales (Co-Author), 2006; Global Financial Regulation: the Essential Guide, 2008; Banking on the Future: the fall and rise of central banking, 2010; The Financial Crisis: Who's to Blame, 2010; Can Financial Markets be Controlled?, 2015. Recreations: supporter of Manchester City Football Club and the Lancashire County Cricket Club; plays cricket for Barnes Common and Powerstock and Hooke cricket clubs. Address: NatWest Group plc, 36 St Andrew Square, Edinburgh EH2 2YB.

Davies (a.k.a. Glasse-Davies), Professor R. Wayne, MA, PhD, ScD. Hon. Professor, University of Edinburgh, since 2009; Director, Snowsport Scotland, 2014-2020 (Chair, 2014-17); Director, GB Snowsport, 2017-2019; CEO, Brainwave-Discovery Ltd., Edinburgh, since 2010; Scientific Director, Pathfinder Cell Therapy Inc, 2010-19; Director, Brainwave-Discovery Ltd., since 2007; Director, Age Analytics Ltd., 2011-2021; Director, Achronis Ltd., since 2017; Parkure Ltd: Director, since 2015, COO and CSO, since 2019; Robertson Professor of Biotechnology, Glasgow University, 1989-2009; b. 10.6.44, Cardiff; m., Victoria Glasse; 3 s.; 2 d. Educ. Queen Elizabeth's Hospital, Bristol; St. John's College, Cambridge. Research Fellow, University of Wisconsin, 1968-71; H3 Professor, Universität zu Köln, FRG, 1971-77; Lecturer, University of Essex, 1977-81; Senior Lecturer, UMIST, 1981-83; Vice-President, Scientific and Research Director, Allelix Biopharmaceuticals, Toronto, 1983-89; Neuropa Ltd.: Founding Director, 1996, CEO, 1997-2000; CEO Uman Genomics AB, Sweden, 2001-03. Recreations: poetry and literature; cello; skiing. Address: (b.) University of Edinburgh, Institute of Adaptive and Neural Computation, Informatics Forum, 10 Crichton Street, Edinburgh EH8 9AB.

Davies, Susan, BSc, MSc. Chief Executive, Scottish Seabird Centre, since 2019; Chair (voluntary), Venture Trust, since 2018, Director & Trustee (voluntary), 2015-18. Educ. University of St Andrews; University of Aberdeen. Career history: various positions, Joint Nature Conservation Committee, 1990-99; Scottish Natural Heritage: Director of Operations (North), 2006-2010, Director of Policy & Advice, 2010-13; Director, Langholm Moor Demonstration Project, 2010-13; Deputy Director, Rural & Environment Science & Analytical Services Division (Secondment), Scottish Government, 2013-14; Acting CEO, Scottish Natural Heritage, 2015-16; Director of Conservation, Scottish Wildlife Trust, 2016-19. Member, IUCN UK

National Committee; Fellow of Society of Biology (FSB). Address: Scottish Seabird Centre, The Harbour, North Berwick EH39 4SS.

Davila, Professor James R., BA, MA, PhD. Professor of Early Jewish Studies, University of St Andrews, since 2008; b. 08.08.60, San Diego, Ca., USA. Educ. Crawford High School; UCLA; Harvard University. Visiting Assistant Professor of Jewish Studies, Tulane University, 1988-89, Visiting Assistant Professor of Classics, 1989-91; Assistant Professor of Religion, Central College, 1991-95; Lecturer in Early Jewish Studies, University of St Andrews, 1995-2006; Reader in Early Jewish Studies, University of St Andrews, 2006-08. Member of the editorial team that published Dead Sea Scrolls. Publications: numerous articles and books on ancient Judaism and related matters. Blog: PaleoJudaica (paleojudaica.blogspot.com). Address: (b.) St. Mary's College, University of St Andrews, St Andrews, Fife KY16 9JU; T.-01334 462834; e-mail: jrd4@st-andrews.ac.uk

Davis, Isabel. Executive Director, Creative Scotland, since 2018; leads Screen Scotland; Head of International Affairs, The British Film Institute (BFI), 2011-18. Production executive/Executive Producer on several high profile UK co-productions; credits on films including Pawel Pawlikowski's Cold War which premiered at Cannes 2018 in Official Selection, winning Best Director; Haifaa Al Mansour's Mary Shelley; Yorgos Lanthimos's The Lobster, Claire Denis's Highlife and Victor Kossakovsky's Aquarela. Address: Creative Scotland, Waverley Gate, 2-4 Waterloo Place, Edinburgh EH1 3EG; T.-0141 302 0775. E-mail: Isabel.Davis@creativescotland.com

Davis, Lisa, MSc. Registrar of Companies for Scotland, since 2017. Educ. University of Stirling. Police Officer, West Yorkshire Police, 1994-98; Business Manager, West Yorkshire Police, 1998-2008; Sheriffdom Business Manager, Scottish Court & Tribunal Service, 2008-2017. Address: Registrar of Companies (Scotland), 4th Floor, Edinburgh Quay 2, 139 Fountainbridge, Edinburgh EH3 9FF; e-mail: enquiries@companies-house.gov.uk

Davis, Ray, DipArch, MSc, DipUD, RIBA, FRIAS. Retired Consultant Architect, McLean Architects; former Managing Director, Davis Duncan Architects; b. 11.2.48, Glasgow; m., Ruth; 3 d. Educ. Aberdeen Grammar School; Robert Gordon University; Heriot Watt University. Alison and Hutcheson and Partners: Architect, Edinburgh Office, 1973-79, Senior Architect and Office Manager, Glasgow, 1979-81; Visiting Lecturer, Planning Department, Mackintosh School, 1979-81; formed Ray Davis Architects and Urban Design Consultants, 1981; part-time Design Tutor, Department of Architecture, Strathclyde University, 1981-86; formed current practice, 1982. Convenor, Baptist Union Property Group, 1997. Recreations: golf; sketching; skiing; church. Address: (b.) 29 Eagle Street, Craighall Business Park, Glasgow G4 9XA; T.-0141 353 2040.

Dawson, Rev. Morag Ann, BD, MTh. Minister of Dalton linked with Hightae linked with St Mungo, since 2011; Minister, Galashiels, 2003-2011; b. 1.11.52, Gorebridge; 1 s.; 1 d. (twins). Educ. Greenhall High School; New College, School of Divinity, University of Edinburgh. Civil Servant (CO), Register House, Edinburgh, 1970-74; Strathclyde Police (HCO), Glasgow, 1974-79; Church of Scotland Minister, since 1999. Young Offenders Institution, Falkirk; P/T Chaplain, Kilmarnock Prison. Recreations: rugby; music; reading; walking. Address: (h.) The Manse, Hightae, Lockerbie DG11 1JL; T.-01387 811 499; e-mail: moragdawson@yahoo.co.uk

Dawson, Kathleen Mary, MBE. British backstroke swimmer; b. 3.10.97, Kirkcaldy. Educ. University of Stirling. Won gold in a world record time at the 2020

Tokyo Olympics in mixed 4 × 100 metre medley relay; European champion at the 2020 Budapest Championships; holder of the European record in 100 m backstroke (58.08); represented Scotland at the Commonwealth Games, since 2014. Observatory for Sport in Scotland ambassador; helps spotlight the benefits of community sport for all ages and abilities; Sportswoman of the Year, Scottish Women in Sport Awards, 2021.

Dawson, Peter, OBE, CBE, MA. Managing Director, The Old Course Hotel, Golf Resort & Spa, St Andrews, since 2022; Secretary, Royal and Ancient Golf Club of St Andrews, 1999-2015; b. 28.5.48, Aberdeen. Educ. Corpus Christi College, Cambridge.

Dawson, Thomas Christopher, BA (Hons), FSA (Scot). Archaeologist; Managing Director, The SCAPE Trust, since 2001; Research Fellow, University of St Andrews, since 2000; b. Oxford. Educ. University of Leicester. Senior Archaeologist, Museum of London, 1989-91; Archaeological site director with AFAN-sites in Lyon and Haute Savoie, 1992-94; Archaeological supervisor, Elms Farm Project, Essex, 1994; Archaeologist with the Department of Archaeology, Sri Lanka (VSO posting), 1995-98; Project Officer, Excavation of the Chateau de Mayenne, 1999; Director: The Bardsey Island Trust, 2002-08, The SCRAN Trust, since 2010, SCRAN Ltd, since 2010. Commissioner, Royal Commission on the Ancient and Historical Monuments of Scotland; Editor, Coastal Archaeology and Erosion in Scotland (Historic Scotland). Recreations: cycling; travel. Address: (b.) St Katharine's Lodge, St Andrews KY16 9AL; T.-01334 467172; e-mail: tcd@st-andrews.ac.uk

Dawson Scott, Robert, MA, MLitt. Chairman, Dance Base, since 2020; playwright; former Head of Engagement, STV (Web Editor, stv.tv); b. 24.7.56, London; 3 d. Educ. Oxford University; Strathclyde University. Formerly Theatre critic, The Times; formerly Head of Content, scotsman.com. Founder of Critics Awards for Theatre in Scotland (CATS). Recreations: music; hill-walking. Address: (b.) 14-16 Grassmarket, Edinburgh EH1 2JU; T.-0131 225 5525.

Day, Martyn. MP (SNP), Linlithgow and East Falkirk, since 2015; b. 1971, Falkirk. Educ. Linlithgow. Elected to West Lothian Council in the Scottish local elections, 1999 representing the Linlithgow ward; Development and Transport portfolio on the Council Executive, West Lothian Council, 2007-2012; served on over 40 committees and outside bodies; appointed spokesperson for Development and Transport and group whip in 2012. Address: House of Commons, London SW1A 0AA.

Day, Phillip. Director of Operations, Northern Lighthouse Board, since 2017 (Director of Marine Operations, 2007-2017). Educ. Warsash; South Tyneside College. Career history: Cadet, Chief Officer, Merchant Navy, 1986-2001; Master, Northern Marine Management, 2001-04; Berth Supervisor & Marine Team Leader, BP, 2004-07. Chair, ARM Committee, IALA_AISM, since 2010. Address: Northern Lighthouse Board, 84 George Street, Edinburgh EH2 3DA; T.-0131 473 3100.

Deacon, Professor Susan Catherine, CBE, MA (Hons), MBA, FRSA, CCMI, FIoD, Assoc CIPD. Chair: Home Scotland, since 2021; Edinburgh Festivals Forum, since 2016; Scottish Police Authority, 2017-19; Institute of Directors Scotland, 2015-18; ScottishPower Renewables,

2010-12 (previously non-executive director); Hibernian Community Foundation, 2008-12; Non-Executive Director: Home Group, since 2021; Lothian Buses, since 2015; ScottishPower, 2012-17; Special Adviser to the Principal and Vice Chancellor, since 2018, Professorial Fellow, since 2012, Assistant Principal (External Relations), 2012-18, Honorary Professor, School of Social and Political Science, 2010-12, University of Edinburgh; b. 2.2.64; m., John Boothman; 1 s.; 1 d. Educ. Musselburgh Grammar School; University of Edinburgh. Professor of Social Change, Queen Margaret University, 2007-10; Trustee: British Gas Energy Trust, since 2021; Iberdrola Foundation, 2009-14; Dewar Arts Awards Trust, 2008-10. Scottish Government Early Years' Champion and Author of 'Joining the Dots', 2010-11. Board member: Institute of Occupational Medicine (IOM), 2013-18; Pfizer UK Foundation, 2008-13; Traverse Theatre, 2007-10. Member of the Scottish Parliament (Labour), Edinburgh East & Musselburgh, 1999-2007; Cabinet Minister for Health and Community Care, 1999-2001; MBA Director of Programmes, Edinburgh Business School, Heriot-Watt University, 1994-98; local government officer research/management 1987-94. Awarded CBE in 2017 for services to business, education and public service.
E-mail: susan@susandeacon.com

Dean, Bonnie, OBE. Vice Principal (Corporate Engagement & Innovation), University of Glasgow, since 2018. Developed the first phase of the Bristol & Bath Science Park which opened in 2011 and which provides a supportive eco-system for knowledge exchange between entrepreneurs, academia and other stakeholders; worked for several decades in the advanced engineering sector for US research-led multinationals and had responsibility in the UK, Europe, Middle East, Africa, India and Asia. Council Member of the Engineering and Physical Sciences Research Council; Deputy Chair of Catalyst, Inc, the Northern Ireland science park; on the advisory boards of the Engine Shed and the Faculty of Business and Law at University of the West of England in Bristol; Chair of the EEF's Economic Policy Committee; Chair of Brandon Trust, a charity which cares for the learning disabled. Address: University of Glasgow, University Avenue, Glasgow G12 8QQ; T.-0141 330 3044.
E-mail: Bonnie.Dean@glasgow.ac.uk

Dean, (Catherine) Margaret, MA, CVO. Lord Lieutenant of Fife, 1999-2014; b. 16.11.39, Edinburgh; m., Brian Dean; 3 d. Educ. George Watson's Ladies' College; Edinburgh University. Teacher of English; Past Chairman, Dunfermline Heritage Trust. Recreations: bridge; theatre; family (grandchildren); walking. Address: (h.) Viewforth, 121 Rose Street, Dunfermline KY12 0QT; T.-01383 722488.

Dean, Michael, LLB (Hons), DipAdvEurStud (Bruges). Partner, Dentons UKMEA, since 2017; Honorary Consul for the Federal Republic of Germany in Glasgow and Port of Glasgow, since 2007; b. 15.01.60, Glasgow; m., Anne; 3 d. Educ. St. Aloysius' College, Glasgow; University of Glasgow; College of Europe, Bruges. Working in the area of European Law and competition law; heavily involved in competition law investigations, merger clearances, competition law export related matters, distribution, public law, procurement law, bribery and ethical compliance programmes, Competition and Markets Authority inquiries, FCA inquiries and European Commission cartel inquiries; presents regularly on competition law, international distribution and on Brexit related matters. Recreations: running; choir; theatre. Address: (b.) G1, 1 George Square, Glasgow G2 1AL; T.-0330 222 1713.
E-mail: michael.dean@dentons.com

Deans, Rev. Dr. Graham Douglas Sutherland, MA, BD (Hons), MTh (Oxon), MLitt, DMin, FBS, FGMS. Locum Minister at Auchtertool with Kirkcaldy: Linktown, since November 2020; Minister at Aberdeen: Queen Street, 2008-2017; b. 15.8.53, Aberdeen; m., Marina Punler. Educ. Mackie Academy, Stonehaven; University of Aberdeen; Westminster College, Oxford; Pittsburgh Theological Seminary; University of St Andrews. Winner of Richard J Rapp Memorial Prize, 2006. Assistant Minister, Craigsbank Parish Church, Corstorphine, 1977-78; Parish Minister: Denbeath with Methilhill, 1978-87, St. Mary's Parish Church, Dumfries, 1987-2002, South Ronaldsay and Burray, 2002-08. Depute Clerk and Treasurer, Presbytery of Kirkcaldy, 1981-87; Chaplain, Randolph Wemyss Memorial Hospital, 1980-87; Moderator, Presbytery of Dumfries and Kirkcudbright, 1994-95; Convener: Committee on Glebes, 1991-92, Committee on Music and Worship, 1993-96, Committee on the Maintenance of the Ministry, 1997-2000 (Vice-Convener, 1991-96), Committee on Ministry, 2000-02; Member: Assembly Committee on Probationers, 1991-97, Maintenance of the Ministry Committee, 1991-98, Board of Ministry, 1998-2002, Ministry Support Committee, 1998-2001, Ministry Development Committee, 2001-02; Trustee, Housing and Loan Fund, 1999-2004; Convener, Business and Finance Committee, Presbytery of Aberdeen, 2011-2014; Member, Executive Committee, Hymn Society of Great Britain and Ireland, 1998-2001, 2002-08, 2009-2015 and from 2017. Publications: A History of Denbeath Church, 1980; Children's Addresses in the Expository Times, 1983, 1987 and 1988; Presbyterian Praise, 1999; contributions to Bulletin of the Hymn Society; contributor to Christian Hymns (new edition), 2004; contributor to Come Celebrate (Contemporary Hymns), 2009; "Race Shall Thy Works Praise Unto Race": the Development of Metrical Psalmody in Scotland, 2012; contributor to Transactions of the Burgon Society (Volume 13), 2013; contributor to Thanks and Praise, 2015; Suitable for Singing? An Exploration of the Hymns of the Book of Revelation, 2019 and Discipleship in the Book of Revelation, 2019; "When mind and memory flee": Hymns and ministry to people with dementia, 2020. Elected to Fellowship of the Guild of Musicians and Singers, 2018. Recreation: music. Address: 38 Sir Thomas Elder Way, Kirkcaldy KY2 6ZS; T.-01592 641429; e-mail: graham.deans@btopenworld.com

Deans, Joyce Blair, CBE, DUniv, BArch, PPRIAS, RIBA, ACIArb, FRSA. Architect; President, Royal Incorporation of Architects in Scotland, 1991-93 (first woman President); b. 29.1.27, Glasgow; m., John Albert Gibson Deans; 2 s.; 2 d. Educ. Laurel Bank School for Girls; University of Strathclyde. Re-entered profession as Assistant, private practice, 1968; appointed Associate, 1972; established own practice, 1981. Elected Member, Council: Glasgow Institute of Architects, 1975-90 (Founded and Edited the 'GIA Newsletter', 1976-1984; first woman President, 1986-88); Royal Incorporation of Architects, 1979-95; first female Vice President, Royal Incorporation of Architects in Scotland, 1986-88; Member, Building Standards Advisory Committee, 1987-96; Chairman, BSAC Scottish Office (Research), 1988-96 (first woman); Chairman (first woman), Scottish Construction Industry Group, 1996-2001 (Member, since 1991); Director, Cairn Housing Association, 1988-99; Founder Member, Glasgow West Conservation Trust, 1987-2000; Governor: Laurel Bank School for Girls 1981-99, Board Member, Glasgow School of Art, 1986-98, (Vice Chairman (Estates) 1992-98); Vice Chairman of Court, Strathclyde University, 2000-03 (Member of Court, 1993-2003); elected to Management Council for Learning in Later Life Students' Association, Strathclyde University, 2003; elected President, Learning in Later Life Students' Association, 2004-06; elected Vice President, Royal Institute of British Architects, 1993-95, and 1999-2001; Member: RIBA Council, 1991-2001, Patrick Geddes Award Panel, since 1993; Industrial Assessor (Architecture), SHEFC, 1994-95; External Examiner, Part 3, since 1994; Member, Professors' Advisory Team, University of Strathclyde, since 1993;

Member, MSc Management Advisory Board, University of Northumbria at Newcastle, 1997-2003. Founder Member and Chairman, Brookwood Computer Group, 2006; Member, Executive Council of Friends of Loch Lomond and the Trossachs, since 2007, Trustees 'Membership' Chairman, since 2011; Consultant to the Development Group of Bearsden Cross Parish Church, 2007-2010; Member of The Church Board and Property Committee, since 2011. Hon. DUniv (University of Strathclyde), 1996; MBE, 1989; CBE, 1999; awarded Glasgow Institute of Architects Supreme Award, 2009; Author of 'The Time of Our Lives', 2012; lectured widely on 'The Time of Our Lives', since 2012; Member of Judging Panel for RIAS Awards, 2013. Recreations: gardening; golf; walking; reading; theatre. Address: 11 South Erskine Park, Bearsden, Glasgow G61 4NA; T.-0141-942 6795.

Deans, Mungo Effingham, BSc (Econ), LLB. Deputy Judge of the Upper Tribunal Immigration and Asylum Chamber (part time); former Resident Judge of the First-tier Tribunal, Immigration and Asylum Chamber (retired, 2017); Resident Senior Immigration Judge, Asylum and Immigration Tribunal, 2005-2010; Regional Adjudicator, Immigration Appellate Authority, 1996-2005; part-time Legal Member, Immigration Appeal Tribunal, 2000-05; b. 25.5.56, Lytham St. Annes; m., Kathryn Atkinson; 3 s. Educ. Fettes College, Edinburgh; London School of Economics; University of Edinburgh. Admitted as Solicitor, 1981; Lecturer, Department of Law: Napier University, 1981-82, Dundee University, 1983-96; Chairman: Social Security Appeal Tribunals, 1989-99, Disability Appeal Tribunals, 1992-99; Immigration Adjudicator, 1994. Publication: Scots Public Law, 1995. Recreations: Scottish history; fine art.

Deas, Sarah, BA Hons (Geog), MBA, MSc (Enterprise), PGCert (Executive Coaching), FRSA. Visiting Professor, Hunter Centre for Entrepreneurship, Strathclyde Business School, University of Strathclyde, since 2020; Trustee, WEAll Scotland (Wellbeing Economy Alliance), since 2019; Member of Sustainability Taskforce, The Institute of Directors, since 2019; Member of Glasgow and West Scotland Committee, The Institute of Directors, since 2021; Chair, Community Wealth Building Expert Advisory Panel, North Ayrshire Council, since 2020. Educ. Derby High School; University of Leeds; The Chartered Institute of Marketing; The Open University; Edinburgh Napier University; University of Strathclyde. Career history: Commercial Manager, Metal Box, 1982-85; Director, RBM Europa, RB Macmillan, 1985-87; Business Development Manager, LinPac Plastics International, 1987-89; Marketing Manager, Fort Stirling, 1989-92; Managing Director, Airport Advertising Europe, 1993-95; Senior Leadership roles, Scottish Enterprise, 1995-2019 including Chief Executive, Co-operative Development Scotland, 2008-2019; Business Mentor, The Prince's Scottish Youth Business Trust, 1995-98; Non-Executive Director, Scottish Youth Theatre, Glasgow, 2007-2014; Chair, Arts & Business Scotland, 2014-16; Trustee, Bank of Scotland Foundation, 2011-2020; Member of Scotland Advisory Committee, British Council, 2018-2021; Winner, Institute of Directors 'Non-Executive Director of the Year 2020'. Recreations: hill walking; cycling; gardening. Address: Strathclyde Business School, University of Strathclyde, 199 Cathedral Street, Glasgow G4 0QU. E-mail: sarah.deas@strath.ac.uk

Deighan, Susan. Chief Executive, Glasgow Life, since 2022; b. 5.64, Glasgow. Helped to establish Glasgow Life in 2007 and has held a number of senior positions, including Deputy Chief Executive, and Director of City Marketing and External Relations; worked in Glasgow's arts and culture sector for more than 30 years; began career in 1988 as part of preparations for Glasgow's 1990 Year of Culture celebrations; previous roles have included Performance Producer at Tramway. Address: Glasgow Life, 220 High Street, Glasgow G4 0QW; T.-0141 287 4350.

Delahunt, Jim, BA. Journalist/Broadcaster; Columnist, Scottish Sun, since 2010; b. 10.5.62, Irvine. Educ. St. Andrews Academy, Saltcoats; Glasgow Caledonian University. Reporter, Kilmarnock Free Press; Reporter, West Sound; Editor, Daily Winner; Night News Editor, Radio Clyde; Sub-Editor, The Sunday Times; Sub-Editor, Reporter, then Presenter, Scottish Television, 1990-2006; Presenter, Setanta Sports, 2006-09; Columnist, Sunday Herald, 1999-2010; Sports Editor/Presenter, Radio Clyde, 2010-2015. Currently Raceday presenter, Hamilton Park/Perth Racecourse. Recreations: horse-racing; ex-amateur jockey. E-mail: jjimmydel@aol.com

Della Sala, Professor Sergio F., MD, PhD, FRSE. Professor of Human Cognitive Neuroscience; Hon. Consultant in Neurology, Edinburgh; b. 23.9.55. Chair of Neuropsychology, Aberdeen; Milan. Senior Neurologist, Milan teaching hospital; Head, Neuropsychology Unit, Veruno, Italy. Address: (b.) University of Edinburgh, 7 George Square, Edinburgh.

Demarco, Professor Richard, CBE, RSW, SSA, Hon. FRIAS, FRSA, DA, Hon. DFA, ACA, Hon. LLD (Dundee). Artist and Writer; Director, Richard Demarco Gallery, 1966-92; b. 9.7.30, Edinburgh; m., Anne Muckle. Educ. Holy Cross Academy, Edinburgh; Edinburgh College of Art. National Service, KOSB and Royal Army Education Corps, 1954-56; Art Master, Scotus Academy, Edinburgh, 1957-67; Vice-Chairman, Board, Traverse Theatre Club, 1963-67; Director, Sean Connery's Scottish International Education Trust, 1972-73; Member: Board of Governors, Carlisle School of Art, 1970-74, Edinburgh Festival Society, 1971-86; Contributing Editor, Studio International, 1982-84; External Assessor, Stourbridge College of Art, 1988-90; Artistic Director, European Youth Parliament, since 1993; Professor of European Cultural Studies, Kingston University, 1993-2000, Emeritus Professor, since 2000; Director, Demarco European Art Foundation, since 1993; Trustee, Kingston-Demarco European Cultural Foundation, 1993-95; Honorary Member, Scottish Arts Club; Elected Member, L'Association International des Critiques D'Art (AICA), 1994. Awards: Gold Order of Merit, Polish People's Republic; Chevalier de L'Ordre des Arts et Lettres; Order of Cavaliere della Reppublica d'Italia; Scottish Arts Council Award for services to Scotland's visual arts, 1975; Medal, International Theatre Institutes of Great Britain and Poland, 1992; Honorary Doctorate, Atlanta College of Art, 1993; Arts Medal, Royal Philosophical Society of Glasgow, 1995; appointed Commander, Military and Hospitaller Order of St. Lazarus of Jerusalem, 1996; Honorary Fellow of the Institute of Contemporary Scotland, 2003; awarded silver 'Gloria Artis' Medal by the Minister of Culture for Poland; awarded Honorary Citizenship of Lodz, Poland, 2007; awarded Honorary Fellow of Edinburgh College of Art, 2007; Honorary President of the Society of Scottish Artists, 2007. Publications: The Road to Meikle Seggie; The Artist as Explorer; A Life in Pictures; Kunst=Kapital: The Adam Smith Lecture, 1995; Honouring Colmcille, 1997; Demarco: On the Road to Meikle Seggie, 2000; The Demarco Collection and Archive: an Introduction, 2009. Recreation: walking "The Road to Meikle Seggie".

Dempsey, Sheriff Colm. Sheriff, North Strathclyde and South Strathclyde, Dumfries and Galloway, since 2022; Director, Capital Defence Lawyers, 2006-2019; b. 1978. Educ. George Heriot's School; Rockwell College.

Discipline Panel Member, Scottish Rugby Union, since 2017. Address: Dumfries Sheriff Court, Buccleuch Street, Dumfries DG1 2AN.

Dennis, Dr Richard, MA, BA, DPhil, CPPI. Head of Accountant in Bankruptcy, since 2015. Career in the Civil Service, both in Scotland and at Whitehall; 17 years at the Scottish Government and 10 years at Whitehall before that. Worked with the European Commission in the Directorate General concerned with Environmental Policy; held a range of finance related posts including a five year spell at the UK HM Treasury; Head of Civil Law Policy, then Head of the Fire and Rescue Division, Scottish Government. Address: Accountant in Bankruptcy, 1 Pennyburn Road, Kilwinning KA13 6SA.

Dennis, Roy, MBE. Wildlife Consultant/Ornithologist; Specialist, species recovery & ecological restoration projects, satellite tracking, UK and overseas; Founder and Director, Roy Dennis Wildlife Foundation, since 1996; b. 4.5.40. Educ. Price's School. Migration Research Assistant, UK Bird Observatories, 1958-59; Warden, Lochgarten Osprey Reserve, 1960-63; Warden, Fair Isle Bird Observatory, 1963-70; Highland Officer, RSPB, 1971-87, Regional Officer (North Scotland), 1987-91; Main Board Member, Scottish Natural Heritage, 1992-97; Director, Cairngorms Partnership, 1995-97; Member, Deer Commission for Scotland, 1999-2002; President, Fair Isle Bird Observatory Trust; Honorary President, Scottish Ornithologists' Club. Publications: Ospreys and Speyside Wildlife; Birds of Badenoch and Strathspey; Puffins; Ospreys; Peregrine Falcons; Divers; The Loch; Golden Eagles; A Life of Ospreys, 2008. TV presenting, latest Autumnwatch 2011 & Springwatch 2012; podcasts on major platforms. Recreations: travel; photography; bird-watching. Address: Half Davoch Cottage, Dunphail, Forres, Moray IV36 2QR; e-mail: roydennis@aol.com; web: www.roydennis.org

Denniston, Rev. David William, BD, DipMin. Interim Minister (West Region), since 2019; Interim Minister (East Region), since 2018; Interim Minister (Central Region), 2016-18; Minister, St. Cuthberts, Edinburgh, 2008-2016; b. 23.4.56, Glasgow; m., Jane Ross; 2 s.; 1 d. Educ. Hutchesons' Boys Grammar School, Glasgow; University of Glasgow. Minister: Ruchazie Parish Church, Glasgow, 1981-86, Kennoway, Fife, 1986-96; Minister, North Church, Perth, 1996-2008. Recreations: hill-walking; fishing; music. Address: c/o Campsie Parish Church, 130 Main Street, Lennoxtown G66 7DD.
E-mail: denniston.david@gmail.com

Dent, John Anthony, MMEd, MD, FHEA, FRCS (Edin). International Relations Officer, AMEE (The Association for Medical Education in Europe), since 2011; Reader in Medical Education and Orthopaedic Surgery, University of Dundee, since 1990; b. 4.3.53, Kendal; m., Frances Jane Wyllie; 1 s.; 1 d. Educ. Haversham Grammar School, Cumbria; University of Dundee. Hand Research Fellow, Princess Margaret Rose Orthopaedic Hospital, Edinburgh; Christine Kleinert Hand Fellow, University of Louisville, Kentucky, USA; co-established Dundee Hand Surgery Service, Ninewells Hospital, Dundee; undergraduate teaching, Clinical Skills Centre; has worked in curriculum development and implementation, University of Dundee Medical School, since 1997; External Examiner: University of Brighton, 1995-98, University of Sunderland, 1998-2001, University of East Anglia, since 2003, University of Hong Kong, since 2010. Member, Examinations Committee, Royal College of Surgeons of Edinburgh, since 1997; Member, National Panel of Specialists for Training in Orthopaedic and Trauma Surgery, 1993-2000; Guest

Lecturer: University of Gezira, Sudan, 1996, and to Association of Surgeons of India, Bombay, 1996. Publications: papers on upper limb surgery and medical education; The Musculoskeletal System: Core Topics in the New Curriculum (Co-Author/Editor), 1997; Churchill's Mastery of Medicine: Surgery 2 (Co-Author/Editor), 3rd ed, 2008; A Practical Guide for Medical Teachers (Co-Editor), 3rd ed, 2008. Recreations: heraldry; history; gardens. Address: (b.) Tay Park House, 484 Perth Road, Dundee DD2 1LR; T.-01382 381991.
E-mail: j.a.dent@dundee.ac.uk

Deregowski, Professor Jan Bronislaw, BSc, BA, PhD, DSc, FBPsS, FRSE. Emeritus Professor of Psychology, Aberdeen University (appointed Professor in 1986, Reader, 1981-86); b. 1.3.33, Pinsk, Poland; m., Eva Loft Nielsen; 2 s.; 1 d. Educ. London University. Lecturer, then Senior Lecturer, Aberdeen University, 1969-81. Publications: Illusions, Patterns and Pictures: a cross-cultural perspective; Distortion in Art; Perception and Artistic Style (Co-author). Address: (b.) School of Psychology, King's College, Old Aberdeen AB24 2UB; T.-Aberdeen 272246.
E-mail: j.b.deregowski@abdn.ac.uk

Devine, Professor Emeritus Sir Thomas Martin, Kt, OBE, BA, PhD, DLitt (Strathclyde), Hon DLitt (Queen's Belfast), Hon DLitt (Abertay, Dundee), Hon DUniv (Strathclyde), FRHistS, FSA Scot, FRSE, HonMRIA, FRSA, FBA, MAE. Sir William Fraser Professor Emeritus of Scottish History and Palaeography, University of Edinburgh, since 2015; Sir William Fraser Professor of Scottish History and Palaeography, 2003-2011; Personal Senior Research Professor in History, 2011-15; Director, Scottish Centre for Diaspora Studies, 2008-2015; Head, School of History, Classics and Archaeology, University of Edinburgh, 2009-2010; Glucksman Research Professor in Irish and Scottish Studies and Director, Research Institute of Irish and Scottish Studies, Aberdeen University, 1998-2003; Director, Arts and Humanities Research Council, Centre for Irish and Scottish Studies, 2001-05, Aberdeen, Trinity College Dublin and Queen's Belfast; b. 30.07.45, Motherwell; m., Catherine Mary Lynas; 2 s. of whom 1 deceased; 3 d. Educ. Our Lady's RC High School, Motherwell; Strathclyde University. Strathclyde University: Lecturer, then Senior Lecturer and Reader, Department of History, 1969-88 (Head of Department, 1990-92), Dean, Faculty of Arts and Social Sciences, 1993-94, Deputy Principal, 1994-97, Professor of Scottish History, 1988-98, Director of Research Centre in Scottish History, 1994-98; Visiting Professor, University of Guelph, Canada, 1983 and 1988 (Adjunct Professor in History, since 1988); Adjunct Professor in History, University of North Carolina; Governor, St. Andrews College of Education, 1990-94. Joint Founding Editor with TC Smout, Scottish Economic and Social History, 1980-84 (now Journal of Scottish Historical Studies); British Academy/Leverhulme Trust Senior Research Fellow, 1992-93; Trustee, National Museums of Scotland, 1995-2002; Member, RAE Panel in History, 1992, 1996; Member, Council, British Academy, 1999-2001; Convener, Irish-Scottish Academic Initiative, 1998-2002; Chair, Joint Working Party, NMS and NTS, Museum of Scottish Country Life, 1999-2003; Member, Advisory Group, Glasgow City of Architecture and Design, 1999; Member, Secretary of State for Scotland's Advisory Committee, Friends of Scotland Initiative, 2001-03; Member, Scottish Council on Archives, 2002-08; Member, Advisory Committee on ESRC Devolution Programme; Member, Research Awards Advisory Committee, The Leverhulme Trust; Trustee, Edinburgh City of Literature, 2005-09; Winner: Senior Hume Brown Prize, 1977, Agnes Mure MacKenzie Prize for Scottish Historical Research, Saltire Society, 1992, Henry Duncan Prize, Royal Society of Edinburgh, 1995; Royal Gold Medal, Royal Society of Edinburgh (RSE), 2001; Hon. Fellowship, University of the West of Scotland, 2005; John Aitkenhead Medal, Institute of Contemporary Scotland, 2006; Member, Academy of

Merit, Institute of Contemporary Scotland, 2006; RSE/Beltane Senior Prize for Excellence in Public Engagement across all disciplines (2012); RSE Inaugural Sir Walter Scott Medal for Excellence in the Humanities and Creative Arts (2012); Wallace Prize, American-Scottish Foundation (2015). Knight Bachelor (2014) for services to the study of Scottish history; Lifetime Achievement Award of UK All Party Parliamentary Group on History and Archives, House of Commons and Lords, 2018; Honorary Membership of Scottish PEN ('rarely granted to those who have advanced and enriched out Scottish literary tradition', 2020). Publications (books only): The Tobacco Lords, 1975; Lairds and Improvement in Enlightenment Scotland, 1979; Ireland and Scotland 1600-1850 (Co-Editor), 1983; Farm Servants and Labour in Lowland Scotland 1770-1914, 1984; A Scottish Firm in Virginia 1767-77, 1984; People and Society in Scotland 1760-1830 (Co-Editor), 1988; The Great Highland Famine, 1988; Improvement and Enlightenment (Editor), 1989; Conflict and Stability in Scottish Sociey (Editor), 1990; Irish Immigrants and Scottish Society in the Eighteenth and Nineteenth Centuries (Editor), 1991; Scottish Emigration and Scottish Society, 1992; Scottish Elites, 1993; The Transformation of Rural Scotland, 1994; Clanship to Crofters' War, 1994; Industry, Business and Society in Scotland since 1700 (Co-Editor), 1994; Glasgow: I, Beginnings to 1830, 1995; St. Mary's, Hamilton: a social history; Exploring the Scottish Past, 1995; Scotland in the Twentieth Century (Co-Editor), 1996; Eighteenth Century Scotland: New Perspectives (Co-Editor), 1998; The Scottish Nation, 1700–2000, 1999; Celebrating Columba – Irish–Scottish Connections 597–1997 (Co-Editor), 1999; Scotland's Shame? – Bigotry and Sectarianism in Modern Scotland, 2000; Being Scottish – Personal Reflections on Scottish Identity Today, 2002; Scotland's Empire, 1600-1815, 2003; The Transformation of Scotland (Co-Editor), 2005; The Scottish Nation, 1700-2007, 2006; Clearance and Improvement: Land, Power and People in Scotland, 1600-1900, 2006; Scotland and the Union, 1707-2007 (Editor), 2007; To the Ends of the Earth: Scotland's Global Diaspora, 1750-2010, 2011; Scotland and Poland: Historical Connections, 1500-2010 (Co-Editor), 2011; Scotland and the British Empire (Co-Editor), 2011; The Oxford Handbook of Modern Scottish History, 1500-2010 (Co-Editor), 2012; Recovering Scotland's Slavery Past (Editor), 2015; Independence or Union: Scotland's Past and Scotland's Present, 2016; The Scottish Experience in Asia since 1700 (Co-Editor); Tea and Empire, 2017 (Co-Author); New Scots: Scotland's Immigrant Communities since 1945, 2018 (Joint Editor and Contributor); The Scottish Clearances: A History of the Dispossessed 1500-1900, 2018. Recreations: grandchildren; walking in and exploring the Hebrides; watching skilful football; travelling in the Mediterranean; France; flyting in the press and public events. Address: (b.) School of History, Classics and Archaeology, William Robertson Wing, Old Medical School, University of Edinburgh, Edinburgh EH8 9AG. E-mail: tmdevine1@aol.com

de Vink, Peter Henry John, BComm. Managing Director, Edinburgh Financial and General Holdings Ltd., since 1978; b. 9.10.40, Amsterdam; m., Julia Christine (Krista) Quarles van Ufford (deceased); m., Jean Murray-Lyon (dissolved); 1 d.; 1 s. Educ. Edinburgh University. National Service, Dutch Army, 1961-63; Edinburgh University, 1963-66; Ivory and Sime Investment Managers, 1966-78, latterly as Managing Director; Councillor (Independent) in Midlothian, 2012-2017. Address: (b.) The Office Huntly Cot Temple Midlothian EH23 4TF; T.-0131-225 6661; (h.) Huntly Cot, Temple, Midlothian EH23 4TS; T.-01875 830345; e-mail: PdeV@efgh.co.uk

Devlin, Liam, MA, BMus, MSc, LRAM, ARCM, FSA Scot, FRSA. Rothesay Herald, since 2021, having previously been Unicorn Pursuivant, from 2016 and Linlithgow Pursuivant Extraordinary, from 2014. Professional musician and teacher, having taught at the

Universities of Glasgow and Edinburgh, the former Royal Scottish Academy of Music and Drama and St Aloysius' College. Clothworker Fellow, New Hall, Cambridge, 2002, and holder of bye-fellowships at Trinity College and Pembroke College, Oxford. A Burgess of the City of Glasgow, Deacon of the Incorporation of Cordiners in Glasgow, 2014-2015, and a Burgess of the City of Edinburgh where he is an Honorary Member of the Incorporation of Candlemakers. A Trustee of Scotland's Churches Trust and a board member of the Children's Music Foundation of Scotland. He is a Knight of Malta.

Dewar, Alan Robert, LLB (Hons). Queen's Counsel, since 2002; Treasurer of the Faculty of Advocates, 2007-2011; Advocate, since 1989; b. 9.12.56, Edinburgh; m., Katherine Margaret Dewar; 1 s.; 2 d. Educ. Lasswade High School, Midlothian; Dundee University. Solicitor in private practice, 1982-88 (Partner in law firm, 1986-88); Writer to the Signet, since 1986; Advocate Depute, 1996-99; Standing Junior Counsel to various Government departments, including Scotland Office, 2000-02. Recreations: golf; football; jazz. Address: (h.) 6 Crawfurd Road, Edinburgh; T.-0131 667 1810; e-mail: AlanRDewar@aol.com

Dewar, Gordon. Chief Executive, Edinburgh Airport, since 2012. Career: started as a consultant with Halcrow, managing the company's transport business in Scotland; moved to First Group, and was Managing Director of the company's east of Scotland bus operations; became Commercial Director for First Group in Scotland and latterly Commercial Director for First Scotrail; joined Arriva as Commercial Director for the UK regions in 2006, and was appointed as Managing Director of Glasgow Airport (BAA) in 2007; Managing Director, Edinburgh Airport, 2008-2010; Chief Executive, Bahrain International Airport, 2010-12. Address: Edinburgh Airport Limited, EH12 9DN.

Dewar, Karen, MA (Hons), MBA. Head of Analytics and Decisioning for Retail Banking, NatWest Group, since 2018. Educ. Aberdeen University; Edinburgh Business School, Heriot-Watt University. Career history: RBS: Programme Lead, Operating Model Review, 2008-09; Head of Operations, Private Banking and Advice, Edinburgh/London, 2009-2010; Head of Transformation, Private Banking and Advice, Edinburgh/London, 2009-2012; Head of Multi-Channel Incentives, Edinburgh, 2012-16; Head of Customer Experience Planning and Execution, Edinburgh, 2016-17; Head of Customer Insight - Personal and Private, Edinburgh, 2017-18. Address: NatWest Group plc, 36 St Andrew Square, Edinburgh EH2 2YB.

Dewhurst, Professor David, BSc, PhD. Emeritus Professor of e-learning; Director of Learning Technology, College of Medicine and Veterinary Medicine, University of Edinburgh, 1999-2018, formerly Assistant Principal (e-learning and e-health); b. 27.2.50, Crewe; 2 s. Educ. Crewe County Grammar School; Sheffield University. Lecturer, University of Sheffield; Lecturer/Senior Lecturer, Sheffield Hallam University; Principal Lecturer/Professor of Health Sciences, Leeds Metropolitan University. Address: (b.) Learning Technology Section, College of Medicine and Veterinary Medicine, University of Edinburgh, 15 George Square, Edinburgh EH8 9XD; T.-0131 6511564; e-mail: d.dewhurst@ed.ac.uk

Dey, Graeme, MSP (SNP), Angus South, since 2011; Minister for Transport, since 2021; Minister for Parliamentary Business and Veterans, 2018-2021; b.

29.10.62, Aberdeen. Joined D C Thomson as a journalist in 1980 and became sports editor of the Dundee Courier. Election agent to Mike Weir MP, 2001-2010. Address: Scottish Parliament, Edinburgh EH99 1SP.

Dick, David, BA, PGDip. Editor in Chief (Nationals and Digital), Reach Scotland, since 2018; in charge of all editorial content at Media Scotland's national and digital titles which include Daily Record, Sunday Mail, dailyrecord.co.uk and glasgowlive.co.uk. Educ. University of Stirling; University of Strathclyde. Career history: Evening Times: Sub Editor, 1996-98, Design Executive, 1998-99; Sunday Herald: Sports Production Editor, 1999, Deputy Sports Editor, 1999-2000, Sports Editor, 2000-04, Deputy Editor, 2004-05; The Age: Executive Editor (Development), 2005-07, Deputy Editor (Saturday), 2007, Executive Editor (Sport), 2007-11, Tablet Editor, 2011-13; Executive Director of Sport, PlayUp, 2013-15; Digital Director, Media Scotland, 2015-18. Address: Reach Scotland, c/o Scottish Daily Record & Sunday Mail, 1 Central Quay, Glasgow G3 8DA; T.-0141 309 3000.

Dick, Rev. John Hunter Addison, MA, MSc, BD. Parish Minister, Aberdeen: Ferryhill, 1982-2012; Master, Christ's College, University of Aberdeen, 2005-2012; b. 27.12.45, Dunfermline; 3 s. Educ. Dunfermline High School; Edinburgh University. Research Assistant, Department of Geography, Edinburgh University, 1967-70; Senior Tutor, Department of Geography, Queensland University, 1970-78; student of divinity, 1978-81; Assistant Minister, Edinburgh: Fairmilehead, 1981-82. A Burgess of Guild of Aberdeen. Governor, Robert Gordon's College, 1993-2012; Trustee, Aberdeen Educational Endowments Trust, 1998-2012. Recreations: music; painting; walking. Address: 18 Fairfield Road, Kelty KY4 0BY.

Dickinson, Professor Harry Thomas, BA, DipEd, MA, PhD, DLitt, FHA, FHEA, FRHistS, FRSE. Professor of British History, Edinburgh University, 1980-2006, Emeritus Professor, since 2006; Professor of British History, Nanjing University, since 1987; b. 9.3.39, Gateshead; m., Jennifer Elizabeth Galtry; 1 s.; 1 d. Educ. Gateshead Grammar School; Durham University; Newcastle University. Teacher of History, Washington Grammar School, 1961-64; Earl Grey Fellow, Newcastle University, 1964-66; History Department, Edinburgh University: Assistant Lecturer, 1966-68, Lecturer, 1968-73, Reader, 1973-80, Associate Dean (Postgraduate), 1992-96, Convener, Senatus PGS Committee, 1998-2001; Visiting Professor, Nanjing University, China, 1980, 1983, 1985, 1987, 1994 and Peking University in Beijing, 2011; Fulbright Scholar, 1973; Huntington Library Fellowship, 1973; Folger Shakespeare Library Fellowship, 1973; Winston Churchill Fellow, 1980; Leverhulme Award, 1986-87 and 2006-07; Ahmanson Fellowship, UCLA, 1987; Anstey Lecturer, University of Kent, 1989; Douglas Southall Freeman Professor, University of Richmond, Virginia, 1987; Lewis Walpole Library Fellowship (Yale University), 2004; Honorary Professor, South East University, China, 2017-20; Honorary Professor, Sichuan University, 2019-2022; Chairman, Publications Committee, Historical Association, 1991-94; Vice-President, Royal Historical Society, 1991-95, 2003-05; President, Historical Association, 2002-05 (Vice President, 1995-97 and 2005-2014, Deputy President, 1997-98); Member, Humanities Committee, CNAA, 1991-93; National Auditor, Higher Education Quality Council, 1993-95; Team Assessor, History, TQA, SHEFC, 1995-96; Member, Marshall Aid Commonwealth Commission, 1987-96; Member, QAA History Subject Benchmarking Committee, 1998-99; Academic Auditor, QAA, 1997-2001; Academic Reviewer, QAA, 1998-2001; Chair, History Panel, Arts and Humanities Research Council, 2002-06; Member, History Panel, QCA, 2003-2010; Member, Lord Chancellor's Advisory Council on National Records and Archives, 2006-2014; Editor, History, 1993-2000. Publications: Bolingbroke; Walpole and the Whig Supremacy; Liberty and Property; British Radicals and the French Revolution; The Correspondence of Sir James Clavering; Politics and Literature in the 18th Century; The Political Works of Thomas Spence; Caricatures and the Constitution, 1760-1832; Britain and the French Revolution; The Politics of the People in Eighteenth-century Britain; Britain and the American Revolution; The Challenge to Westminster (Co-Author); A Companion to Eighteenth-Century Britain; Constitutional Documents of the United Kingdom, 1782-1835; British pamphlets on the American Revolution, 8 vols.; Reactions to Revolutions (Co-Author); La Révolution française vue des îles britanniques (Co-Author); Ireland in the Age of Revolution, 1760-1805, 6 vols.; over 200 pamphlets, articles, essays and reviews. Recreations: reading; films. Address: (h.) 44 Viewforth Terrace, Edinburgh EH10 4LJ; T.-0131-229 1379; e-mail: Harry.Dickinson@ed.ac.uk

Dickson, Dr. Belinda Jane, OBE, BEd. Self-employed businesswoman; b. 15.9.59, Glasgow; 2 d. Educ. Bearsden Academy; Dunfermline College. Marketing Telephone Rentals, 1981-87; self-employed, since 1987; Entrepreneur of the Year, 2000; Scottish Businesswoman of the Year, 1999; Member, Board, UK Fashion & Textiles Association; Honorary Degree, Napier University; Doctor of Letters, Caledonia University. Recreations: skiing; cycling; kayaking; swimming; walking. Address: (b.) Belinda Robertson & Cashmere Circle, Dunbar Business Centre, Spott Road, Dunbar, East Lothian EH42 1RS; T.-0131 557 8118. E-mail: belinda@belindarobertson.com

Dickson, Professor James Holms, BSc, MA, PhD, FLS, FRSE. Emeritus Professor, since 2002; Professor of Archaeobotany and Plant Systematics, Glasgow University, since 1998 (Reader in Botany, 1993-98); b. 29.4.37, Glasgow; m. Camilla A. Lambert, 1 s.; 1 d. Educ. Bellahouston Academy; University of Glasgow; University of Cambridge. Fellow, Clare College, University of Cambridge, 1963-70; Lecturer then Senior Lecturer in Botany, University of Glasgow, 1970-93. Leader, Trades House of Glasgow Expedition to Papua, New Guinea, 1987; Consultant, Britoil, Glasgow Garden Festival, 1988; currently working on plant remains found with 5,300 year old Tyrolean Iceman, and with 550 year old British Columbian iceman. Neill Medallist, Royal Society of Edinburgh, 1996; twice Past President, Glasgow Natural History Society; Past President, Botanical Society of Scotland; Leverhulme Emeritus Fellow, 2006-07: "Archaeobiology of Ancient Icemen". Northlight Heritage Dickson Laboratory for Bioarchaeology named in honour (shared with the late Camilla Dickson, eminent archaeobotanist), 2012. Publications: five books, including The Changing Flora of Glasgow, Plants and People in Ancient Scotland and Ancient Ice Mummies; many papers on Scottish flora, Ice Age plants, archaeobotany, the Tyrolean Iceman. Address: (b.) Graham Kerr Building, Glasgow University; T.-0141-330 4364.

Dickson, Jenny, LLB. Chair, Morton Fraser Lawyers, since 2021, Partner, since 2011; Solicitor Advocate. Educ. University of Aberdeen. Associate, HBJ Gateley, 2000-08; Associate, Morton Fraser, 2008-2011. Regularly represents clients in the Court of Session, and is recognised by The Legal 500 in Health and Safety, and Medical Negligence as well as listed as an elite 'Leading Lawyer' in Personal Injury. Address: Morton Fraser Lawyers, Quartermile Two, 2 Lister Square, Edinburgh EH3 9GL; T.-0131 247 1000. E-mail: jenny.dickson@morton-fraser.com

Dickson, John (Iain) Anderson, BSc, DipArch, RIBA, PPRIAS. Architect; formerly Senior Partner, George Watt & Stewart, Aberdeen; President, Royal Incorporation of Architects in Scotland, 1999-2001; b. 28.5.51, Hamilton; m., Patricia Frances Whyte. Educ. Aberdeen Grammar School; Scott Sutherland School of Architecture, Robert Gordon's Institute of Technology, Aberdeen. Architectural Assistant: Department of Housing and Construction, Darwin, Australia, 1973-74, W.G. Crerar & Partners, Inverness, 1976-77; Architect, George Watt & Stewart, Aberdeen, 1977-80. Chairman, Kincardine and Deeside Area, British Field Sports Society, 1995-98; Senior Under Officer, Aberdeen University Officer Training Corps, 1973; Chairman, RIAS Practice Board, 1995-99; Member, RIBA Council, 1999-2001; Director, Aberdeenshire Housing Partnership, 1999-2004; Member, Scottish Construction Industry Group, 1999-2001; Member, Leadership Group, Scottish Enterprise Forestry Cluster, 2000; Member, Sounding Board, Scottish Executive Review of Scotland's Cities, 2001; Director, RIAS Insurance Services Ltd., 2002-04; Member, Advisory Board, Centre for Timber Engineering, Napier University, 2002-04; Member, Executive RIAS Insurance Services, 2004-2011; Chair/Member, RIBA/RIAS Membership Liaison Group, 2009-2017; Member, RIAS Council, 2008-2017; Member, RIAS Education Committee, 2010-2017; Professional Studies Adviser, Scott Sutherland School of Architecture and the Built Environment, Robert Gordon University, 2009-2017; Member, Chair, Judging panel, RIAS/RIBA Awards in Scotland, 2015; Member, RIAS Doolan Awards, 2016. Recreations: field sports; fishing; shooting; racing; good food and wine. Address: (h.) Kentucky, Banchory, Kincardineshire AB31 4EQ. E-mail: kentuckybanchory@btinternet.com

Dickson, Malcolm Rae, QPM, MA, DipCrim. Campaigner for a Scottish Borders National Park, since 2015; Landowner/manager, since 2008; former Non-executive Director, NHS Borders Board; former Board Member, Scottish Children's Reporter Administration, 2008-2016; former Board Member, Children's Convenor and Tribunal Board, States of Guernsey, 2013-15; b. 1956, Galashiels; m., Anna; 1 s. Educ. Earlston High School; Berwickshire High School; University of St. Andrews; University of Cambridge. Joined Lothian and Borders Police as Graduate Entrant Constable in 1977; served in Uniform, CID and Drugs Squad through ranks to Inspector, then in Planning, East Lothian and Central Edinburgh to Chief Superintendent. Commanded many large public events including Edinburgh's Millennium Street Party and Open Golf Championship. Later Assistant Chief Constable and Deputy Chief Constable, then the Assistant Inspector of Constabulary for Scotland; responsible for several seminal reports which resulted in improved policing across a range of functions; completed Police career in 2008. Publications: Author of 'The Role of Policing in Modern Scotland' (A Chapter in 'Policing Scotland'), 2nd ed. 2010. Recreations: drawing and painting indifferent pictures; riding; fishing; reading.

Dickson, Mark. Director of Capital Investment, Scottish Water. Educ. University of Strathclyde. Career history: General Manager, Scottish Water, 2002-2013, then Director of Information Technology and Business Change. Address: Scottish Water, Castle House, 6 Castle Drive, Carnegie Campus, Dunfermline KY11 8GG.

Dickson, Michael. Chief Executive, NHS Shetland, since 2020; Interim Chief Executive, NHS Orkney, since 2020. Career history: Oncology/Orthopaedics Staff Nurse, 1994-95; Haematology/Oncology Senior Staff Nurse, Bristol University Hospital NHS Trust, 1995-96; Oncology Nurse Specialist, Australian Acute Health Service, 1996-97; Oncology Nurse Specialist, UCLH NHS Trust, 1997-2000; HCA International Ltd: Oncology Unit Manager, 2000-01, Deputy Director of Nursing/Director of Nursing, 2001-05; Executive Director of Nursing, Mayday Healthcare NHS Trust, 2005-07; Lead Programme Manager, Northern Ireland National Programme, 2008-09; Executive Director of Acute Services, Western Trust, 2009-2010; Lead Programme Manager, UK Department of Health, 2007-2010; Director of Clinical and Information Governance, Healthcare at Home, 2011-13; Interim Director of Nursing, Quality and People, Central Surrey Health, 2013-14; Head of Risk and Quality, West Herts NHS Trust, 2014-15; Deputy Controller Health and Social Care, SSAFA - The Armed Forces Charity, 2014-17; Hub Director, Getting it Right First Time (GIRFT), 2007-2020. Address: NHS Shetland, 26-32 Burgh Road, Lerwick, Shetland ZE1 0QB; T.-01595 743060.

Dickson, Rob. Director of Industry and Destination, VisitScotland, since 2021. Previously Executive Director, Scottish Borders Council. Address: VisitScotland, Shepherds Mill, Whinfield Road, Selkirk TD7 5DT. T.-0131 472 2222.

Dickson, Sheriff Robert Hamish, LLB, WS, DL. Sheriff of South Strathclyde, Dumfries & Galloway at Airdrie, 1988-2015; Sheriff (part-time), 1982-86; working retired Sheriff, 2015-2020; Deputy Lieutenant of Lanarkshire, since 2012; b. 19.10.45, Glasgow; m., Janet Laird Campbell (deceased 2004); 1 s. Educ. Glasgow Academy; Drumtochty Castle; Glenalmond; Glasgow University. Solicitor, Edinburgh, 1969-71, and Glasgow, 1971-86; Partner, Brown Mair Gemmill & Hislop, Solicitors, Glasgow, 1973-86; appointed floating Sheriff of South Strathclyde, Dumfries & Galloway at Hamilton, 1986; President, Sheriffs' Association, 2006-09. Publication: Medical and Dental Negligence, 1997. Recreations: golf; music; reading; bridge.

Dinning, Robert James (Fred), BSc (Eng), MBA, CEng, CEnv, FEI, FIET, FCMI; b. 16.12.52; m., Elizabeth Johnstone. Educ. Kilmarnock Academy; Glasgow University. Formerly Energy and Environment Director of the Scottish Power Group (retired at end of 2005). Main Board Member, Scottish Environment Protection Agency, 2006-2013; Court Member, University of the West of Scotland; Board Member (until 2019), Sustainable Development Panel; Board Member, SAC Commercial Ltd., 2013-15; Board Member, SRUC, since 2015; Chair, Carbon Trust Consultant Accreditation Board; Chair (until 2012), Edinburgh Research Partnership Energy JRI (until 2010); Member, Sustainable Development Panel (until 2010); Member, Church of Scotland Church and Society Council and Convenor of Council sub group on energy and environmental issues (2005-09). Member, Advisory Board, WWF Scotland (until July 2013). Fellow of the Energy Institute and member of its Scottish Committee. Delivered a wide range of lectures and speeches on energy and environment topics affecting the UK and Scotland. Recreations: keen cruising yachtsman (RYA Yachtmaster), kayaker, hillwalker and cyclist. Address: (h.) South Brae Farm, Dunlop, Ayrshire KA3 4BP.

Di Rollo, Alison, QC. Solicitor General for Scotland, 2016-2021. Joined Crown Office and Procurator Fiscal Service in 1985, following a legal traineeship in private practice, and worked in various PF Offices and Crown Office, before being appointed Deputy Head of the High Court Unit in Crown Office, and later Head of Operational Policy. Appointed Trial Advocate Depute in May 2008 and in February 2010 joined the COPFS

National Sexual Crimes Unit; Head, National Sexual Crimes Unit, 2013-15; Senior Advocate Depute, 2015-16.

Di Rollo, Simon Ronald, QC, LLB (Hons), FCIArb (2018). Advocate, since 1987; b. 28.10.61, Edinburgh; m. (1), Alison Margaret Lafferty (marr. diss. 2012); 1 s.; 1 d.; m. (2), Kim Louise Leslie (2013); 1 s. Educ. Holy Cross Academy; Scotus Academy; Edinburgh University. Admitted to Faculty of Advocates, 1987; Advocate Depute, 1997-2000; Lecturer (part-time) in Civil Procedure, University of Edinburgh 1999-2012. Member, Sheriff Court Rules Council, 2002-2011; Member, Parole Board for Scotland, since 2018; Director of Quality Assurance, Faculty of Advocates, since 2016. Recreations: Italian; cooking; walking; golf. Address: (b.) Advocates' Library, Parliament House, Edinburgh EH1 1RF.

Ditchburn, Liz. Director-General Economy, Scottish Government, 2016-2021. Career history: joined the civil service and DFID in 1998, and worked firstly as a technical specialist in Latin America and Africa on rural development, environment and economic growth, moving into management and leadership roles from 2003; Director, Value for Money, Department for International Development (DFID), 2010-14, Director of Policy, 2014-16 (led on international development policy for the UK across areas as diverse as girls and women, inclusive societies, governance and anti-corruption, youth, migration and climate change).

Dixon, Andrew, BSc. Freelance Director, Culture Creativity Place Ltd, since 2013; Visiting Professor, Warwick Business School and Coventry University; Chief Executive, Creative Scotland, 2010-13; Programme Director, Hull UK City of Culture, 2013-14; b. 1958. Educ. University of Bradford. Career: administrator and youth projects director of the Major Road Theatre Company; after five years as an arts officer in Local Government moved to Northern Arts, progressing to become its Chief Executive and was a member of the national executive team of Arts Council England for three years; Chief Executive, NewcastleGateshead Initiative, 2005-2010. Alternative Businessman of the year 2005, for his public sector work in North East England; honorary doctorate, Northumbria University, 2008; former member, North East Economic Forum. Address: (b.) 12A Great Stuart Street, Edinburgh EH3 7TN. Web: www.andrewdixon.org

Dixon, Dr. Richard, BSc (Hons), MSc (distinction), PhD. Director, Friends of the Earth Scotland, since 2013; b. 22.3.64, Dublin, Ireland. Educ. Exeter School; St. Andrews University; Edinburgh University; Glasgow Caledonian University. Development Officer, CSV Glasgow, 1992-94; Assistant Environmental Policy Officer, Strathclyde Regional Council, 1993-94; Head of Research, Friends of the Earth Scotland, 1994-2002; Head of Policy, WWF Scotland, 2002-05, Director, 2005-2013. Board Member: SNIFFER, SEPA, Postcode Culture Trust, Postcode Equalities Trust. Recreations: cycling; science fiction; computing. Address: (b.) Thorn House, 5 Rose Street, Edinburgh EH2 2PR; e-mail: rdixon@foe-scotland.org.uk

Dobie, Margaret G.C., OBE, MA, DipSocStud, FFCS. Hon. Vice President, Scottish Association for the Study of Delinquency, 1997-2005; b. Galloway; m., James T.J. Dobie; 3 s. Educ. Benedictine Convent, Dumfries; Dumfries Academy; Edinburgh University. Medical Social Worker; Chair, Dumfries and Galloway Regional Children's Panel, 1971-77; Member, Broadcasting Council for Scotland,

1987-91; Chair, Dumfries and Galloway Children's Panel Advisory Committee, 1982-89; Chair, Children's Panel Advisory Group, 1985-88; Member, Polmont Young Offenders' Institution Visiting Committee, 1992-99; Chair, Dumfries & Galloway Valuation Appeal Panel, 1987-2004. Recreations: travel; tennis; reading. Address: (h.) 6, Mountainhall Park, Dumfries, DG1 4YS T. 01387-254595; e-mail: mgcd3@btinternet.com

Docherty, Sadie. Former Lord Provost and Lord Lieutenant of Glasgow (2012-17); Linn Ward Councillor (Labour), 2007-2017; m.; 2 c. Migrated to Scotland in the mid 1950s; formerly Glasgow Council's Executive Member for Communities and Housing; also chaired Policy Development Committees responsible for Sustainability and the Environment, and Children and Families.

Docherty, Thomas, MP (Labour) Dunfermline and West Fife, 2010-2015; b. 28.1.75; m., Katie McCulloch; 1 s.; 1 d. Educ. Open Univ. Research Assistant to Scott Barrie MSP, 1999-2002; Public Affairs Officer, BNFL, 2002-05; Communications Manager, Network Rail, 2006-07; Account Dir, communications consultancy, 2007-10. Contested (Lab): Tayside N, 2001; S of Scotland, Scottish Parliament, 2003.

Docherty-Hughes, Martin John. MP (SNP), West Dunbartonshire, since 2015; SNP Spokesperson (Industries of the Future and Blockchain Technologies, since 2018, Industries for the Future, 2017-18); b. 21.01.71. Educ. Glasgow College of Food technology (now City of Glasgow College); University of Essex (BA Hons); Glasgow School of Art (MPhil). Worked for a decade for the West Dunbartonshire Community & Volunteering Services, worked for Volunteer Scotland as National Policy Officer; joined the SNP in 1991, and was elected first past the post one year later as Scotland's youngest Councillor to the-then Clydebank District Council in 1992, at the age of 21; elected City Councillor to the third seat of the Anderston/City Ward of Glasgow City Council and appointed Bailie of the City of Glasgow in the Scottish local government elections (2012-15). Elected Member of Parliament for West Dunbartonshire, May 2015, majority 14,171 (59%). Address: Constituency Office, Titan Enterprise Centre, Suite 1-11, 1 Aurora Avenue, Queens Quay, Clydebank, Dunbartonshire G81 1BF; T.-0141 952 2988; e-mail: martin.docherty.mp@parliament.uk Web: www.martindocherty.scot
Westminster Office: House of Commons, London SW1A 0AA.

Dodd, Marion Elizabeth, MA, BD, LRAM. Minister of Kelso Old and Sprouston Parish Church, 1989-2010 (retired); b. 19.4.41, Stirling. Educ. Glasgow High School; Burgh School/Knowepark Primary School (both in Selkirk); Selkirk High School; Esdaile School, Edinburgh; Edinburgh University. Foreign Office, London (Russian translator), 1962-64; Iron and Steel Institute, London, (Editor, Stahl translated from Russian), 1964-67; BBC Singers, 1967-84; Assistant Minister, Colinton Parish Church, 1987-89 (ordained in July 1988). Member, Board of Parish Education, 1989-94, Board of World Mission, 1994-98, Panel on Worship, 1993-2000 (Music Committee Member); Church Hymnary Revision Committee, 1995-2005; Liturgical Group, 2010-2013; Nomination Committee, 2011-15; Vice-Convener, Panel on Review and Reform, 2005-08; President, Church Service Society, 2004-06; Secretary, Dunkeld Fellowship, 2009-2019; Moderator, Jedburgh Presbytery, 1993-94 and 2007-08; Locum at Earlston; Interim Moderator from 2019, Lauder,

Caddonfoot linked with Galashiels: Trinity (Interim Moderator, 2011-14) and Oxnam; Chairperson, Abbeyfield Kelso Society Ltd., 1995-2009; President, Glasgow Society for the Sons and Daughters of Clergy of the Church of Scotland, 2016-2018, and from 2021; Chairperson, Kelso Churches Together, 1992-93, 1996-97, 2000-01, 2005-06. Musical Director, Kelso Amateur Operatic Society, 1990-93; Musical Director, Roxburgh Singers, 1996-2021; Conductor, Oxnam Valley Voices, since 2016; Founder and Musical Director, Border Pilgrims. Recreations: music; cooking; reading; interior design. Address: Esdaile, Tweedmount Road, Melrose TD6 9ST; T.-01896 822446. E-mail: mariondodd@btinternet.com

Dodd, Raymond Henry, PhD, MA, BMus, ARAM. Cellist and Composer; b. 31.3.29; m., Doreen Joyce; 1 s.; 1 d. Educ. Bryanston School; Royal Academy of Music; Worcester College, Oxford. Music Master, Sedbergh School, 1951-55; Aberdeen University: Lecturer in Music, 1956, Senior Lecturer in Music, 1971-91, Head of Department, 1981-88; Visiting Professor of Music, Wilson College, USA, 1972-73. As a cellist he has performed widely, particularly in Scotland where he is known as a soloist and chamber music player; was for many years a member of the Aberdeen Trio; compositions include orchestral, vocal and chamber music pieces with a number of broadcasts; awarded Szymanowski Medal, Polish Ministry of Art and Culture, 1982. Address: (h.) 14 Giffordgate, Haddington, East Lothian EH41 4AS; T.-01620 824618.

Dodds, Alistair Bruce, CBE, MA (Hons), MBA, FCIPD. Chairman, Board of Directors, Highlands and Islands Enterprise; former Depute Chairman, Board of Trustees, National Galleries of Scotland (until 31/12/21); retired Chief Executive, The Highland Council (2007-2013); b. 23.8.53, Kelso; 1 d.; m., Ann Clark. Educ. Glenrothes High School; Edinburgh University; Strathclyde University; Dundee University. Assistant Director of Personnel, Fife Regional Council, 1988; Depute Director of Manpower Services, Highland Regional Council, 1991; Director of Personnel Services, The Highland Council, 1995, Director of Corporate Services/Deputy Chief Executive, 1998. Awarded Honorary Fellowship, University of The Highlands and Islands (2014). Recreations: Scottish contemporary art; watching rugby; golf; walking dogs. Address: Moorlands, 11, Drummond Road, Inverness IV2 4NA. E-mail: doddsab@btinternet.com

Dodds, Blane. Chief Executive Officer, Tennis Scotland, since 2018; b. 12.66. Career history: Sports Management, Carnegie Sports International, 1992-93; Sales and Marketing Manager, David Lloyd Leisure, 1993-96; Founder and Managing Director, International Golf Network Ltd, 1996-2000; Chief Executive, NL Leisure Ltd, 2006-2016; President UK, European Capital of Sport Association, 2011-17; Chief Executive Officer, Scottish Golf, St Andrews, 2016-17; Chairman, Tennis Scotland, Edinburgh, 2016-17. Address: Tennis Scotland, Airthrey Castle, Hermitage Road, Stirling FK9 4LA; T.-01786 641716.

Dodds, Douglas. Provost, Stirling Council, since 2022; represents Dunblane and Bridge of Allan (Conservative), since 2017; m.; 2 c. Former Chair of Bridge of Allan Community Council; retired Police Officer, with extensive experience in Health & Safety with NEBOSH (The National Examination Board in Occupational Safety and Health). Recreations: country sports and outdoor activities. Address: Stirling Council, Old Viewforth, Stirling FK8 2ET; T.-01786 233113; e-mail: doddsd@stirling.gov.uk

Doherty (Hon. Lord Doherty) (J. Raymond Doherty). Senator of the College of Justice, since May 2010. LLB (Edinburgh), BCL (Oxon), LLM (Harvard); Advocate, since 1984; QC, since 1997; b. 1958, Stirling; m., Arlene Donaghy; 1 s.; 2 d. Educ. St. Mungo's Primary School, Alloa; St Joseph's College, Dumfries; Edinburgh University; Hertford College, Oxford; Harvard Law School. Standing Junior Counsel to Ministry of Defence (Army), 1990-91; Standing Junior Counsel to Scottish Office Industry Department, 1992-97; Advocate Depute, 1998-2001; Clerk of Faculty, Faculty of Advocates, 1990-95; Joint Editor, Armour on Valuation for Rating, since 1990, Editor, since 2022; Contributor, Stair Memorial Encyclopaedia of the Laws of Scotland; Trustee, Carmont Settlement, since 2011, Chairman of Trustees, since 2015; Lands Valuation Appeal Court, since 2011; Upper Tribunal (Tax and Chancery), since 2013; Commercial Reserve Judge, 2013-2014; Commercial Judge, 2014-2020; Principal Commercial Judge, 1 January 2018-11 May 2020; Exchequer Judge, 2014-2020; a Chairman of the Competition Appeal Tribunal, 2015-2020; Inner House (First Division), since 3 December 2020. Address: (b.) Supreme Courts, Parliament House, 11 Parliament Square, Edinburgh EH1 1RQ; T.-0131-225 2595.

Doherty, Una, LLB. Queen's Counsel, since 2018; b. Stirling; m., Douglas Fairley. Educ. High School of Stirling; Edinburgh University. Solicitor, 1988-98; Litigation Partner, Balfour and Manson, 1993-98; Advocate, since 1999. Address: (b.) Advocates' Library, Parliament House, Edinburgh EH1 1RF; T.-0131-226 5071.

Doig, Ian Peebles, CA, CPFA. Independent Consultant & Non-Executive Director, since 2004; m., Barbara; 1 d. Assistant Director of Finance, Central Regional Council, 1981-86; Director, CIPFA in Scotland, 1986-2004; range of independent consultancy projects, since 2004; SSSC Council Member, 2005-2011; SEPA Board Member, 2006-2013. National Records of Scotland Management Board Member & Chair of Audit & Risk Committee, 2011-17; Scottish Court Service Audit Committee Member, 2011-15; Care Inspectorate Board Member, 2012-19; The Scotland Office Audit Committee Member, 2008-2011; Board of Trustees Member and Chair of Audit and Risk Committee, National Trust for Scotland, 2013-2017; Merchiston Community Councillor, Chair; Edinburgh College - Audit Committee Member. Recreations: walking; music; Doig Family Society, Hon. Treasurer. E-mail: ianpdoig@yahoo.com

Doig, P. Michael R., MA (Hons). B. 2.5.48, Glasgow; m., Catherine; 2 s. Educ. High School of Glasgow; University of Glasgow. Teacher/Assistant Principal Teacher/Principal Teacher of Modern Languages, 1972-81; Assistant Head Teacher, Hermitage Academy, Helensburgh, 1981-85; Depute Head Teacher, Kirkintilloch High School, 1985-92; Head Teacher, Cumbernauld High School, 1992-2000; Head Teacher, Bearsden Academy, 2001-08. President, Headteachers' Association of Scotland, 2003; Elected Member, General Teaching Council Scotland, 2005-08; Panel Practice Adviser, East Dunbartonshire Children's Panel Area Support Team, 2009-2016; Lay Representative, NHS Education for Scotland, 2010-2016. Recreations: music; travel; walking. Address: (h.) 3 Moorfoot Way, Bearsden, Glasgow G61 4RL. E-mail doigmichael@hotmail.com

Dolezalek, Professor Gero R., Dr. Jur. (Frankfurt). Emeritus Professor of Civil Law, University of Aberdeen (Professor, 2005-09); b. 18.01.43, Poznan, Poland; m., Iva L. Dolezalek; 3 s.; 1 d. Educ. Schools in Austria, West-Berlin, Western Germany; Universities of Kiel,

Florence, Frankfurt, Modena. Researcher, Max-Planck-Institut for European Legal History, Frankfurt, 1971-85; Professor, Faculty of Law: Nijmegen, Netherlands, 1985-89, University of Cape Town, South Africa, 1989-95; Senior Researcher, School of Law, University of Aberdeen, 1995-96; Professor, Faculty of Law, University of Leipzig, Germany, 1996-2005. Guest professorships in Belgium, France, Germany, Italy. Publication: Scotland under Jus Commune. Census of manuscripts of Scottish legal literature mainly between 1500 and 1660, Edinburgh 2010 (The Stair Society volumes 55, 56, 57). Address: 17 Heriot Row, Edinburgh EH3 6HP.

Dominiczak, Professor Dame Anna F., DBE, MD, FRCP, FAHA, FMedSci, FRSE. Regius Professor of Medicine, University of Glasgow, since 2010; Honorary Consultant Physician and Endocrinologist, NHS Greater Glasgow and Clyde Health Board; Health Innovation Champion, Medical Research Council; b. 26.8.54, Gdansk, Poland; m., Professor Marek Dominiczak; 1 s. Educ. Copernicus High School, Gdansk; Medical School, Gdansk; University of Glasgow. Junior House Officer, Glasgow Royal Infirmary, 1982; Senior House Officer (and Registrar) in Medicine, Royal Alexandra Hospital, Paisley, 1983-1986; MRC Clinical Scientist and Honorary Registrar (and Senior Registrar), Western Infirmary, Glasgow, 1986-1992; British-American Research Fellow and Associate Professor, University of Michigan, Ann Arbor, USA, 1990-1991; University of Glasgow: Clinical Lecturer and Honorary Senior Registrar in Medicine and Endocrinology, 1992-1993, Senior Lecturer, then Reader in Medicine, 1993-1996, British Heart Foundation Senior Research Fellow, 1993-1998, Professor of Cardiovascular Medicine, Personal Chair, since 1997, British Heart Foundation Professor of Cardiovascular Medicine, 1998-2010, Director, BHF Glasgow Cardiovascular Research Centre, 2001-2010, Associate Dean for Research, Faculty of Medicine, 2003-2010, Head of Division of Cardiovascular and Medical Sciences, 2008-2010; Vice-Principal and Head of the College of Medical, Veterinary and Life Sciences, 2010-2020; Member, British Hypertension Society Executive Committee, 1999-2002; Member, MRC Physiological Medicine and Infections Board, 2000-2004; Member, British Heart Foundation Project Grant Committee, 2000-2004; Member, MRC & Wellcome Trust Protocol Development Committee for BioBank UK, 2001-2002; Secretary, International Society of Hypertension, 2002-2006; Member, Chief Scientist Office Advisory Group on Cardiovascular Disease and Stroke, 2002-2007; Member, Royal Society of Edinburgh International Committee, 2004-2008; Member, Royal Society of Edinburgh Research Fellowship Committee, 2005-2007; Member, Research Assessment Exercise 2008, Cardiovascular Sub-panel, 2005-2008; Member, Wellcome Trust Physiological Sciences Funding Committee, 2005-2008; Member, Foundation Leducq, Scientific Advisory Committee, 2006-2011, Vice President, 2009-2011; Chair, Royal Society of Edinburgh Sectional Committee, 2007-2009; Member, Max-Delbrück Centre for Molecular Medicine (MDC) Scientific Advisory Board, 2007-2016; Member, George Pompidou European Hospital (HEGP) Paris Scientific Advisory Board, since 2007; Member, Academy of Medical Sciences, Fellow Selection Panel for Clinical Medicine, 2008-2011; Member, Council, Royal Society of Edinburgh, 2009-2014; Member, MRC Clinical Training & Career Development Panel, 2010-2012; Member, Medical Schools Council, 2010-2020; Member, Board for Academic Medicine (Scotland), 2010-2020; Member, American Heart Association Leadership Committee, since 2010; Member, Health Committee, Universities Scotland, 2011-2013; Member, Health Science Scotland Oversight Board, 2011-2018; Non-Executive Member, NHS Greater Glasgow and Clyde Health Board, 2012-2021; Member, Council of the Academy of Medical Sciences, 2012-2014; Vice President,

Life Sciences, Royal Society of Edinburgh, 2012-2015; Member, Wellcome Trust Peer Review College, 2012-2016; Member, Research Excellence Framework, Clinical Medicine Panel, 2013-2014; President, European Society of Hypertension, 2013-2015; Member, MRC Stratified Medicine Panel, 2013-2018; Co-founder and Board Member, Stratified Medicine Scotland - Innovation Centre, 2013; Trustee, British Heart Foundation, 2014-2020; Chair, MRC Translational Research Group, since 2016; Member, MRC Strategy Board, since 2016; Member, Medical Schools Council Executive, 2016-2020; Chair, Equality & Diversity Working Group, Medical, Dental & Veterinary School Councils, 2016-2018; Member, Council, Academy of Medical Sciences, 2018-2022; Scottish Science Advisory Committee, since 2018, Scientific Advisory Board, Monash University, Australia, since 2018, REF Main Panel A (interdisciplinary role), 2018-2021; Member, Research Excellence Framework, Main Panel A, 2018-2022; Member, Research Excellence Framework, Interdisciplinary Panel, 2018-2022; Member, Health and Social Care Innovation Steering Group, 2020-2023; Chair, International Scientific Council at the Medical University of Gdansk, since 2020; Fellow, Royal College of Physicians (Glasgow), since 1995; Fellow, American Heart Association, since 1996; Fellow, Academy of Medical Sciences, since 2001; Fellow, Royal Society of Edinburgh, since 2003; Fellow, European Society of Cardiology, since 2008; Fellow, Society of Biology, since 2010; Fellowship of the Association of Physicians of Great Britain & Ireland, since 2021; Advisory Professor of Shanghai Jiao Tong University School of Medicine, since 2019; Editor in Chief, Clinical Science, 2004-2008; Editor in Chief, Hypertension, 2012-2022. Recreation: modern literature. Address: (b.) University of Glasgow, BHF Glasgow Cardiovascular Research Centre, 126 University Place, Glasgow G12 8TA; e-mail: anna.dominiczak@glasgow.ac.uk

Don, Natalie, MSP (SNP), Renfrewshire North and West, since 2021; b. 1989, Paisley; 1 d. Served as a local councillor for the Bishopton, Bridge of Weir and Langbank ward, 2017 Renfrewshire Council election. Recreation: video games. Address: The Scottish Parliament, Edinburgh EH99 1SP; T.-0131 348 5085.
E-mail: Natalie.Don.msp@parliament.scot

Don, Nigel, BA, MEng, LLB. Scottish composer, arranger and former politician; MSP (SNP), Angus North and Mearns, 2011-16, North East Scotland, 2007-2011; b. 16.4.54; m., Wendy; 2 c. Educ. King's College School; Pembroke College, Cambridge; University of London. Thirteen year career as a chemical engineer with Unilever; time out of working to stay at home and raise his children, which allowed his wife to continue working; later became a music teacher and a music publisher; formerly Director, Masterclass Music Ltd; former councillor for Ninewells ward; former SNP Group Convenor on Dundee City Council; elected in May 2007 to the multi-member Lochee ward but resigned as councillor in August 2007 to concentrate on role as MSP. Member: Performing Right Society, Mechanical Copyright Protection Society. Recreations: walking and music; member of the Musicians' Union.

Donald, George Malcolm, RSA, RSW, DA, ATC, MEd. Former Director of Summer School, Centre for Continuing Studies, ECA; former Keeper, Royal Scottish Academy; former Lecturer, Edinburgh College of Art; b. 12.9.43, Ootacamund, South India; 1 s.; 1 d. Educ. Robert Gordon's College; Aberdeen Academy; Edinburgh College of Art; Hornsey College of Art; Edinburgh University. Joined Edinburgh College of Art as Lecturer, 1969; Visiting Lecturer, five Faculties of Art in India, 1979; Visiting Professor: University of Central

Florida (Drawing and Anatomy, 1985 to present); Hon. Professor, Al Maktoum Institute, Dundee; Visiting Prof. University of Central Florida (Art Dept) and Florida Interactive Entertainment Academy Orlando, Florida. Strasbourg, 1986, Belgrade, 1987, Sechuan Fine Art Institute, China, 1989, Chinese Academy of Fine Art, 1994, Osaka and Kyoto Universities, Japan, 1999, 2002 and 2007; Visiting Tutor, The Royal Drawing School, London, since 2008; Latimer Award, RSA, 1970; Guthrie Award, RSA, 1973; Scottish Arts Council Bursary, 1973; RSA Gillies Bequest Travel Award to India, 1978, USA, 2003; SAC Travel and Study Award, Indiana, 1981; RSA Gillies Prize, 1982; RSW Mary Marshall Brown Award, 1983; RGI Cargill Award, 1987; Scottish RSW Arts Club Award, 2006, 2013; one man shows: Florida, 1985, Helsinki, 1985, Edinburgh Festival, 1985, 2011; Belgrade, 1987, Florida, 1987, Edinburgh, 1988, 1990, London, 1992-94, Edinburgh 1993, 1994, 1995, 1998, 1999, 2002, 2003, 2005, 2007, 2008, Bohun Gallery, Henley, 2009, 2011, Open Eye Gallery, Edinburgh, 2012, 2015, 2018. Address: (h.) Bankhead, by Duns, Berwickshire TD11 3QJ; T.-01361 883014; e-mail: georgedonaldstudio@gmail.com
Web: www.georgedonald.com
Instagram: georgedonaldpaintings

Donald, Marion Coats (nee McClure), DipArch (Abdn), MPhil, RIBA, FRIAS; b. 15.5.47, Aberdeen; m. John Donald; 1 s.; 1 d.; Educ. Aberdeen High School for Girls; Colchester County High School for Girls; Scott Sutherland School of Architecture, RGIT; Scott Sutherland School of Architecture, Robert Gordon University. Student architect, Lyster, Grillet & Harding, Cambridge, 1969-70; Sir Basil Spence, Glover and Ferguson, 1972; Architectural Assistant, SSHA, 1973-74; Architect, Jenkins and Marr, 1974-76; Principal, John and Marion Donald, Chartered Architects, 1976-2006; Professional Studies Advisor, Scott Sutherland School of Architecture, RGU, 2002-2009; retired 2009. Former Chairman, Aberdeen Soroptimist Housing Society Ltd; Elder, Queen's Cross Church, 1977-2017. RIBA Award, 1998; Aberdeenshire Design Award: 2004 (Housing), 2000 (Conservation); Association for Preservation of Scotland Award, 1995; Aberdeen Civic Society Award, 1984; Civic Trust Commendation, 1984. Recreations: family; gardening; music; art and architecture. Address: Forbes Lodge, Strathdon, Aberdeenshire AB36 8YA; T.-01975 651393; e-mail: mariondonald@ifb.co.uk

Donald, Rev. Peter Harry, MA, PhD, BD. Minister, Cairnlea Church, Airdrie and Calderbank, since 2018; b. 3.2.62, Edinburgh; m., Brigid Mary McNeill; 1 s.; 1 d. Educ. George Watson's College; Gonville and Caius College, University of Cambridge; University of Edinburgh. Scouloudi Research Fellow, Institute of Historical Research, University of London, 1986-87; Probationer Assistant, St. Michael's Church, Edinburgh, 1990-91; Minister: Leith St. Serf's Parish Church, 1991-98, Crown Church, Inverness, 1998-2018. Member, Faith and Order Commission, 1993-2014. Publication: An Uncounselled King: Charles I and the Scottish Troubles 1637-1641, 1990; God in Society (Co-editor), 2003. Recreations: golf; piano; singing; walking; family. Address: 31 Victoria Place, Airdrie ML6 9BU; T.-01236 753159.

Donaldson, Professor Iain Malcolm Lane, BSc, MB, ChB, MA, FRCPE, MRCP. Professor of Neurophysiology, Edinburgh University, 1987-2003; Emeritus Professor, Edinburgh University, since 2003; b. 22.10.37; m.; 1 s. Educ. Edinburgh University. House Physician and Surgeon, Research Fellow, Honorary Lecturer, Honorary Senior Registrar, Departments of Medicine and Surgical Neurology, Edinburgh University, 1962-69; Anglo-French Research Scholarship, University of Paris, 1969-70; Research Officer, University Laboratory of Physiology, Oxford, 1970-79; Fellow and Tutor in Medicine, St. Edmund Hall, Oxford, 1973-79; Professor of Zoology, Hull University, 1979-87; Honorary Librarian, Royal College of Physicians of Edinburgh, 2000-2017; Sibbald Bibliographer, Royal College of Physicians of Edinburgh, since 2017; Emeritus Fellow, St. Edmund Hall, Oxford, since 1979. Recreation: studying the past. Address: (b.) Royal College of Physicians of Edinburgh, 9 Queen Street, Edinburgh EH2 1JQ.

Donaldson, James Andrew, BDS, BA, DFM. Principal in general dental practice; Chairman, Dental Practitioners Association, 2009-2011; President, General Dental Practitioners Association, 2002-05 and 2011-2012; b. 28.2.57, Glasgow; divorced; 1 s.; 3 d. Educ. Coatbridge High School; Dundee University; Open University; Glasgow University. Dental Adviser, British Antarctic Survey, 1986-97; Member: National Council, General Dental Practitioners Association, 1989-2013, Scottish General Dental Services Committee, 1991-93, Aberdeen District Council, 1984-86, Grampian Regional Council, 1986-88; Director, "Open Wide" Dental Courses; contested Liberal Democrat, Aberdeen North, elections to Scottish Parliament, 1999, Westminster election, 2001; Burgess of Guild, City of Aberdeen, 2009. Recreations: golf; skiing; football. Address: (h.) 28/1 Rutland Street, Edinburgh EH1 2AN; T.-07721 453802.
E-mail: jimdonaldson1@btinternet.com

Doncaster, Neil, MBA. Chief Executive, Scottish Professional Football League, since 2013; b. 1970, Devon. Educ. Bristol University. Career: qualified as a solicitor and worked for four years for Burges Salmon, solicitors; joined Norwich City in November 1997 as company secretary and solicitor, promoted to Head of Operations in 1999, then Chief Executive, 2001-09. Director of The Football League, 2006-09; elected to The Football Association board as one of two representatives of The Football League, 2008-09; Chief Executive, Scottish Premier League, 2009-2013. MBA from the University of East Anglia, 2008. Address: Hampden Park, Glasgow G42 9DE; T.-0141 620 4140. Web: www.spfl.co.uk

Donegan, Kate, OBE, BA. Retired Prison Governor; b. 21.4.53, Newport on Tay; m., Dr Chris Donegan; 2 s. Educ. Kirkcaldy High School; Stirling University. Assistant Governor: Cornton Vale, 1977-84, Barlinnie Prison, 1984-87; Deputy Governor: Reading Prison, 1987-89; Deputy Governor, Perth Prison, 1989-91; Head, Operational Manpower, Planning Unit, 1991-93; seconded to Staffing Structure Review Team, 1993-94; Deputy Governor, Barlinnie Prison, 1994-95; Deputy Chief Inspector of Prisons, 1995-96; Governor, HM Prison and Institution, Cornton Vale, 1996-2001; Governor, HMP Glenochil, 2001-06; Governor, HMP, Perth, 2006-2010; Deputy Chief Inspector of Prisons, 2010-2011; Governor, HM YOI Polmont, 2011-2012; Governor, HMP and YOI Cornton Vale, 2012-2014. Awarded OBE in Queen's Birthday Honours, June 2014. Recreations: gardening; reading; computing.

Donnelly, Dougie, LLB. Presenter/commentator, Golf Channel USA and worldwide coverage of European Tour Golf; sports video writer and director; b. 7.6.53, Glasgow; m., Linda; 3 d. Educ. Hamilton Academy; Strathclyde University. Former Presenter, BBC Television Sport: Grandstand, World Championship snooker, Olympic Games (summer and winter), World Cup, Commonwealth Games, Ryder Cup, golf, Sportscene, Match of the Day;

Mid-Morning Show, Album Show, Radio Clyde, 1976-92. Chairman, Commonwealth Games Endowment Fund; after-dinner speaker, conference and seminar host. Recreations: sport; travel; reading; good food and wine. Address: (b.) David John Associates, 6 Victoria Crescent Road, Glasgow G12 9DB; T.-07774 248753.
E-mail: david@davidjohnassociates.co.uk

Donnelly, Frances. Head of Finance, Citizens Advice Scotland. Address: Citizens Advice Scotland, Spectrum House, 2 Powderhall Road, Edinburgh EH7 4GB; T.-0131 550 1000.

Donohoe, Sir Brian H. MP (Labour), Central Ayrshire, 2005-2015, Cunninghame South, 1992-2005; b. 10.9.48, Kilmarnock; m., Christine; 2 s. Educ. Irvine Royal Academy; Kilmarnock Technical College. Ailsa Shipbuilding, Troon: Apprentice, 1965-70, Draughtsman, 1970-77; Engineer, Hunterston Power Station, 1977-78; Draughtsman, ICI, Stevenston, 1978-81. Secretary, Irvine and District Trades Council, 1973-81; Chair: North Ayrshire and Arran LHC, 1977-79, Cunninghame Industrial Development Committee, 1975-79; former full-time trade union official (NALGO), 1981-1992. Transport Select Committee, 1993-2010; Chairman, Scottish group of Labour MPs, 1996-1998; Parliamentary Private Secretary to Minister then Secretary of State for Transport, 2002-2010; Honorary Secretary to the British American Parliamentary Group, 2010-15; Chairman, Parliamentary Pension Trustees Scheme, since 2010; Chairman of the Horticulture Charity THRIVE, 2010-2012; Special Constable, British Transport Police, 2004-2014. Recreations: flying model helicopters; gardening; cycling. Address: (h.) 5 Greenfield Drive, Irvine, Ayrshire.

Donovan, Professor Robert John, OBE (2007), BSc, PhD, DSc (Hon), CChem, FRSC, FRSE. Emeritus Professor of Chemistry, Edinburgh University (Professor, since 1979); b. 13.7.41, Nantwich; m., Marion Jacubeit; 1 d. Educ. Sandbach School; University College of Wales, Aberystwyth; Cambridge University. Research Fellow, Gonville and Caius College, 1966-70; Edinburgh University: Lecturer in Physical Chemistry, 1970-74, Reader in Chemistry, 1974-79. Member: Physical Chemistry Panel, Science & Engineering Research Council, 1977-80, Management Committee, SERC Synchrotron Radiation Source, Daresbury, 1977-80, SERC Synchroton Radiation Facility Committee, 1979-84; Chairman, SERC Laser Facility Committee, 1989-92; Member, SERC Science Board, 1989-92; Chairman, Facilities Commission, SERC, 1993-94; Coordinator, STFC, Synchrotron and Free-Electron Laser Science, 2006-09; awarded Corday-Morgan Medal and Prize, Royal Society of Chemistry, 1975; Member: Faraday Council, Royal Society of Chemistry, 1981-83, 1991-93; Vice President, Royal Society of Edinburgh, 1998-2001 (Member, Council, 1996-2001); Member of Council, CCLRC, 2004-06; Tilden Prize, Royal Society of Chemistry, 1995. Recreations: hill-walking; skiing; sail-boarding; cross-country skiing. Address: (b.) School of Chemistry, Edinburgh University, West Mains Road, Edinburgh EH9 3FJ; T.-0131-650 4817; e-mail: R.Donovan@ed.ac.uk

Doogan, David (Dave) Michael. MP (SNP), Angus, since 2019; b. 4.3.73, Perth. Educ. University of Dundee. Career history: former aircraft engineer with the Ministry of Defence; left his successful career in the civil service in 2007 to pursue a university degree graduating in 2011 with a First Class Honours with two Distinctions in International Relations & Politics; elected to Perth and Kinross Council as a councillor for Perth City North in 2012, became Convenor of Housing and Health, having responsibility for

council housing, social care, and a seat on the board of NHS Tayside; reelected to Perth and Kinross Council in 2017, became the leader of the SNP group on Perth and Kinross Council, and Leader of the Opposition. Address: Houses of Parliament, Westminster, London SW1A 0AA.

Dorans, Allan Hopkins. MP (SNP), Ayr, Carrick and Cumnock, since 2019; b. 30.7.55, Dailly. Career history: joined the Metropolitan Police and reached the rank of Detective Inspector by the age of 28; first elected to South Ayrshire Council in 2012 for the SNP in Ayr Ward West, then appointed in 2014 as SNP Group Leader. Address: Houses of Parliament, Westminster, London SW1A 0AA.

Dorchester, Martin, MBA, BSc (Hons). Non Executive Director, Office of the Secretary of State for Scotland and the Office of the Advocate General for Scotland (Part-time); Chief Executive Officer, Includem, since 2018; Non Executive Director, Transport for Wales, 2017-18; Chief Executive, David MacBrayne Ltd, 2012-18. Educ. Kingston University; The Open University. Career: Managing Director for Dixons B2B business; ran consultancy business with clients ranging from large private sector businesses to smaller third sector organisations. Address: Includem, Unit 6000, Academy Office Park, Gower Street, Glasgow G51 1PR; T.-0141 427 0523.

Doris, Bob, MA. MSP (SNP), Glasgow Maryhill and Springburn, since 2016 (Glasgow region, 2007-2016); Convener of the Social Security Committee in the Scottish Parliament; b. 11.5.73; b. Vale of Leven. Educ. University of Glasgow. Campaign manager to Bill Wilson for the SNP leadership in 2003. Formerly convener of the SNP Maryhill Constituency Branch and Glasgow Regional Association SNP (GRA). Has campaigned successfully on a number of issues including free school meals, kinship care payments, extending rail provision in Maryhill and Town Centre Regeneration Fund money for Glasgow. A leading campaigner against the Glasgow Labour Council's closure of 20 primary and nursery schools, and supported the parental occupation of Wyndford and St Gregory's primary schools in Maryhill. Address: (b.) Scottish Parliament, Edinburgh EH99 1SP.

Dornan, James, MSP (SNP), Glasgow Cathcart, since 2011; Deputy Convener of the Scottish Parliament Subordinate Legislation Committee; b. 17.3.53. Represented the Langside Ward, Glasgow City Council, 2007-2012 (SNP Group Leader until 2011). Address: (b.) Scottish Parliament, Edinburgh EH99 1SP.

Dorrian, Lady Leeona June, QC, LLB. Lord Justice Clerk, since 2016; Senator of the College of Justice, since 2005; b. 16.6.57, Edinburgh. Educ. Cranley Girls' School, Edinburgh; University of Aberdeen. Admitted to the Faculty of Advocates in 1981; Standing Junior Counsel to the Health and Safety Executive and Commission, 1987-1994, Advocate Depute, 1988-91, Standing Junior to the Department of Energy 1991-94; appointed Queen's Counsel, 1994; called to the English Bar in 1991, at the Inner Temple; Member of the Criminal Injuries Compensation Board, 1997-2001; appointed a Temporary Judge of the Court of Session, 2002. Address: (b.) Parliament House, 11 Parliament Square, Edinburgh EH1 1RQ.

Dougall, Rona. Freelance journalist; presenter, Scotland Tonight on STV, since 2011; b. 21.7.66; m., David Halliday; 2 d. Educ. Edinburgh University. Formerly with Radio Forth; became Scotland correspondent with Sky News (1996-2011). Address: STV, Pacific Quay, Glasgow G51 1PQ.

Douglas, Alan. Journalist and Broadcaster; b. 16.10.51, Dundee; m., Viv Lumsden (qv); 2 d. Educ. Forfar Academy. Local newspapers, 1970-74; BBC Local Radio Reporter and Producer, 1974-78; Reporter/Presenter, BBC TV Scotland, 1978-95; freelance broadcaster and journalist, BBC TV and Radio, corporate and Scottish TV; Director, The Broadcasting Business Ltd (media consultancy), 1989-2013; Director, Scotcars.co.uk (motoring website), 2009-2014; contributor to magazines, websites, newspapers, radio and tv on transport and travel. Former Guild of Motoring Writers' Regional Journalist of the Year. Recreations: cars; driving buses; walking; eating; drinking. Address: (b.) Pink Elephant Communications, Lochinch House, 86 Dumbreck Road, Glasgow G41 4SN.
E-mail: alan.doug@ntlworld.com

Douglas, Alison, BA. Chief Executive, Alcohol Focus Scotland, since 2015. Educ. University of Aberdeen. Career history: Director, UK Research Office, Brussels Area, Belgium, 1998-2001; Scottish Government: Head of Marine Environment, 2001-03, Head of Genetic Modification Policy, 2003-05, Head of Corporate Homicide & Prostitution, 2005-07; Panel Member, Edinburgh Children's Panel, 2004-08; Scottish Government: Head of Alcohol Policy & Delivery, 2007-2012, Head of Public Bodies & Public Service Reform, 2012-2015; Tutor, UK GRAD School, since 2000. Address: Alcohol Focus Scotland, 2nd floor, 166 Buchanan Street, Glasgow G1 2LW; T.-0141 572 6700.
E-mail: Alison.Douglas@alcohol-focus-scotland.org.uk

Douglas, Dr Lynne, BSc, MPhil, PhD. Chief Executive Officer, Bield Housing & Care, since 2019. Educ. Queen Margaret University; University of Edinburgh; Harvard Business School; Glasgow Caledonian University. Director, NHS, 2008-2019. Address: Bield Housing & Care, 79 Hopetoun Street, Edinburgh EH7 4QF; T.-0131 273 4000.
E-mail: hello@bield.co.uk

Douglas-Home, Lady (Lavinia) Caroline, MBE 2010, DL, FSA Scot. Deputy Lieutenant, Berwickshire, 1983-2012; b. 11.10.37 (daughter of Baron Home of the Hirsel, KT, PC). Educ. privately. Woman of the Bedchamber (Temporary) to Queen Elizabeth the Queen Mother, 1963-65; Lady-In-Waiting (Temporary) to HRH Duchess of Kent, 1966-67; Estate Factor, Douglas and Angus Estates, 1960-95; Trustee, National Museum of Antiquities of Scotland, 1982-85; President, Borders Branch, British Red Cross, 1998-2010, Chairman, Borders Volunteer Council, 2010-2017; Trustee, Scottish Episcopal Church Nominees, 1993-2020; Trustee, Scottish Redundant Churches Trust, 1995-2016; Governor, Longridge Towers School, 1995-2010; President, Berwick Citizens Advice Bureau, 1996-2014. Recreations: reading; antiquities. Address: (h.) Heaton Mill House, Cornhill-on-Tweed, Northumberland TD12 4XQ; T.-01890 882303.

Douglas-Scott, Susan, CBE, DipCOT, BSc (Hons), MSc (QMUC). Consultant in Health Equality and Social Care Issues and Humanist Celebrant, since 2010; Chair, ILF Scotland, since 2015; Chair, Board of Directors, Golden Jubilee Foundation, since 2018; Honorary Vice President, Leonard Cheshire Disability, since 2016; Non Executive Board Member, NHS Education for Scotland, 2010-18; Chief Executive, The Long Term Conditions Alliance Scotland (LTCAS), 2009-2010; b. 12.9.60, Glasgow; 1 s.; 1 d. Educ. Eastwood High School; Glasgow School of Occupational Therapy; Caledonian University.

Occupational therapist, NHS, 1981-82; social work, 1983-87; manager, social work, 1987-92; registration and inspection officer, 1992-98; Head of Service, Sense Scotland, 1998-2000; Director, fpa Scotland, 2000-03; Chief Executive, PHACE Scotland (Promoting Health and Challenging Exclusion), 2003-05; Chief Executive, Epilepsy Scotland, 2005-09. Recreations: yoga; crafts; singing; Reiki; cooking.

Dove, Rev. Giles Wilfred, MA, MPhil, BD, FSA Scot. Director of Development and Alumni Relations, The Edinburgh Academy, since 2019; Chaplain of Glamis Castle, since 2019; b. 25.1.62, Hendon; m., Katherine Ann MacCallum; 2 s.; 1 d. Educ. Winchester College; University of St. Andrews; University of Glasgow. Alumnus Relations Officer, University of St. Andrews, 1988-91, Development Officer, 1992-97; Director of Communications and Development, University of Stirling, 1998-2005; Director of Development, National Library of Scotland, 2005-2007; Chaplain and Head of Divinity, Glenalmond College, 2007-2019; Scottish Episcopal Church: Ordained Priest, 2006, Ordained Deacon, 2005, Non-Stipendiary Curate, St. Mary's Church, Dunblane, 2005-07; Convener, Standing Committee, General Synod, 2002-05, Trustee, Pension Fund, 2002-05, Convener, Budget Review Committee, General Synod, 2002-04, Convener, Resources Committee, General Synod, 1999-2002, Member, Board for Ministry, General Synod, 1999-2002; Trustee, Council for Advancement and Support of Education, 1999-2005; Governor, Aberlour Child Care Trust, 2001-04; Vice-Chairman, Board of Management, St. Mary's Episcopal Primary School, Dunblane, 2000-02; Director, Rymonth Housing Society Ltd., 1993-95; Trustee, St. Andrews Preservation Trust Ltd., 1991-94; Freeman of The City of London. Publications: "Alma Matters: A Guide To Alumni Relations"; "Pilgrimage Sites" (in "The Fife Book"); various articles in professional journals. Recreations: choral music; ecclesiastical history; good food and drink; Scottish islands. Address: (h.) "South Eden", 8A High Road, Strathkinness, St Andrews, Fife KY16 9XY.
E-mail: gileswdove@gmail.com

Dow, Douglas C. J., KStJ, LLB. Former Chancellor and Registrar, The Priory of Scotland of the Order of St. John; retired solicitor; b. 18.7.43, Johnstone; m., Alice Mackay; 1 s.; 2 d. Educ. Paisley Grammar School; Glasgow University. Partner, Stirling and Gilmour, Solicitors, West Dunbartonshire, 1969-2008. Town Clerk, Burgh of Cove and Kilcreggan, 1967-75. Past President, Helensburgh Rotary Club. Interests: arms and armour; medieval churches; history and art. Recreations: shooting; gardening. Address: (h.) Holyrood, Kilcreggan, Helensburgh G84 0HN; T.-01436 842405.

Dow, Rear-Admiral Douglas Morrison, CB, DL. Chief Executive, The National Trust for Scotland, 1992-97; b. 1.7.35; m., Felicity Margaret Mona Napier; 2 s.; Educ. George Heriot's School; BRNC Dartmouth. Joined RN, 1952; served HMS Sheffield, 1957-61; Staff of C-in-C Plymouth, 1959-61; HMS Plymouth, 1961-63; RN Supply Sch., 1963-65; Staff of Comdr FEF, 1965-67; HMS Endurance, 1968-70; BRNC Dartmouth, 1970-72; Cdr 1972; Assistant Director, Officer Appointments (S), 1972-74; Sec to Comdr British Navy Staff, Washington, 1974-76; HMS Tiger, 1977-78; NDC Latimer, 1978-79; Captain 1979; CSO(A) to Flag Officer Portsmouth, 1979; Sec to Controller of Navy, 1981; Captain, HMS Cochrane, 1983; Commodore, HMS Centurion, 1985; RCDS, 1988; Rear Admiral, 1989; Director General, Naval Personal Services, 1989-92. Vice-Chairman, George Heriot's Trust, 1996-2009; President, South Queensferry Sea Cadets, 1993-2009; President, Royal Naval Association Edinburgh, 1994-2017; appointed Deputy Lieutenant, City of Edinburgh in 1996.

Recreations: rugby union; fly fishing; golf; gardening. Address: (h.) Tor Lodge, 1 Eskbank Terrace, Dalkeith, Midlothian EH22 3DE.

Dow, Professor Julian Alexander Thomas, MA PhD, ScD, FRSE. Professor of Molecular and Integrative Physiology, Glasgow University, since 1999 (Chair of Integrative & Systems Biology, 2008-10); b. 1957; m., Shireen-Anne Davies; 3 s.; 2 d. Educ. King's School, Gloucester; St. Catharine's College, University of Cambridge. Glasgow University: Lecturer, 1984-94, Senior Lecturer, 1994-97, Reader, 1997-99; Nuffield Fellow, 1992-94. President's Medal, Society for Experimental Biology, 1992; Member, several committees, BBSRC. Recreations: skiing; diving. Address: (b.) Davidson Building, University of Glasgow, Glasgow G12 8QQ.
E-mail: julian.dow@glasgow.ac.uk

Dow, Professor Sheila Christine, MA (Hons), MA (Econ), PhD. Professor Emeritus in Economics, Stirling University (Professor, 1996-2009, Head of Department, 2002-04); Adjunct Professor of Economics, University of Victoria, Canada, since 2012; b. 16.4.49, Dumfries; m., Professor Alexander Dow; 2 d. Educ. Hawick High School; St. Andrews University; University of Manitoba; McMaster University; Glasgow University. Overseas Office, Bank of England, 1970-72; Economist, then Senior Economist, Department of Finance, Government of Manitoba, 1973-77; Lecturer, then Reader, Department of Economics, Stirling University, 1979-96. Chair, International Network for Economic Method, 2001-02; special advisor to House of Commons Treasury Select Committee, 2001-2010; Director of Stirling Centre for Economic Methodology, 2005-10; Member of Academic Advisory Board of the Independent Social Research Foundation, 2018-21; Member of Academic Council of Institute for New Economic Thinking, since 2018; Fellow of the Academy of Social Sciences, since 2020. Publications: Money Matters (Co-Author), 1982; Macroeconomic Thought, 1985; Financial Markets and Regional Economic Development, 1990; Money and the Economic Process, 1993; The Methodology of Macroeconomic Thought, 1996; Economic Methodology: An Inquiry, 2002; A History of Scottish Economic Thought (Co-Editor), 2006; Open Economics (Co-Editor), 2009; Foundations for New Economic Thinking, 2012; The General Theory and Keynes for the 21st Century (Co-Editor), 2018; Money, Method and Post-Keynesian Economics for the 21st Century (Co-Editor), 2018. Address: (b.) Division of Economics, Stirling University, Stirling FK9 4LA; T.-01786 467370; e-mail: s.c.dow@stir.ac.uk

Dow, Sylvia, MLitt, ALAM, LRAM, FRSA. Playwright, since 2010; Arts Education Consultant; Head of Education, Scottish Arts Council, 1994-2004; b. 19.7.39, Edinburgh; m., Ronald Dow; 1 s.; 1 d. Educ. James Gillespie's High School for Girls; Edinburgh College of Speech and Drama. Freelance radio actor/presenter, California, 1960-65; Tutor, Edinburgh College of Speech and Drama, 1969-70; Drama Teacher (Head of Drama), Bo'ness Academy, 1970-85; Education Officer, MacRobert Arts Centre, 1985-93; Arts Co-ordinator, Central Region Education Service, 1993-94. Recreation: arts. E-mail: sylvia.dow@btinternet.com

Dowey, Cllr Martin. Leader, South Ayrshire Council, since 2022; representing Ayr West (Scottish Conservative and Unionist), since 2017. Worked as a police officer across Ayrshire. Board Member, Ayrshire Valuation Joint Board; Scottish Conservative and Unionist candidate for Ayr, Carrick and Cumnock in the 2019 UK General Election.

Address: County Buildings, Wellington Square, Ayr KA7 1DR; T.-01292 612496.
E-mail: martin.dowey@south-ayrshire.gov.uk

Dowey, Sharon, MSP (Scottish Conservative), South Scotland (Region), since 2021; b. Girvan; m., Martin; 3 c. Former Senior Manager at the Morrisons supermarket chain. Address: The Scottish Parliament, Edinburgh EH99 1SP; T.-0131 348 6799.
E-mail: Sharon.Dowey.msp@parliament.scot

Downes, Bob, DipTP, BPhil. Chair, The Independent Oversight Board, Dublin, since 2019; Chair, Scottish Environment Protection Agency, since 2016; Non Executive Director, Grown, since 2018; Director, Kube Networks, 2015-2021; Director, CRYPTIC (arts production house), since 2016; Chairman, Global Surface Intelligence, 2012-17; Chair, CENSIS, Scottish Sensor Innovation Centre, 2013-19; Non Executive Director, Scottish Government, 2014-18; Director, Network Investment, Openreach, 2009-2011; b. 10.8.51, Belfast; m., Julie McGarvey; 2 s. Educ. Portora Royal School, Enniskillen; Dundee University; Duncan of Jordanstone College of Art, Dundee; BPhil, Open University. Local government, 1976-82; Dundee Project, 1982-84; SDA, 1984-87; Director: North East, SDA, 1987-90, Conran Roche Planning, London, 1990-92; independent consultant, 1992-93; Chief Executive, Dumfries and Galloway Enterprise, 1993-94; Director, Scottish Enterprise, 1994-99; BT Scotland: Director, Economic Development, 1999-2000; Director, e-business Development, 2000-01, National Manager, 2001-02, Director, 2002-05. Advisor, Flax Trust, Belfast, 1994-2001; Director: Wise Group, Glasgow, 1997-2000, Emerging Business Trust, Belfast, 1996-2004, Businesslab, 1996-2003; Director Scotland, Openreach, 2005-09; Member, President's Executive Committee, National Council for Urban Economic Development, Washington D.C., 1996-2001; Member, Advisory Board, The Competitiveness Institute, Barcelona, 1998-99; Director, Big Issue International, 2002-04; Director, Scottish Ensemble, 2012-16; Board Member, Scottish Arts Council, 2003-05; Advisory Board Group, DA Group, 2002-05; Glasgow University Adam Smith Business School Advisory Board, since 2005; Scottish Environmental Protection Agency: Deputy Chairman, non-executive director, since 2008; Glasgow School of Art, Trustee, 2009-2018; Care Visions Group, Advisor, 2010-13; ScotRail Advisory Board, 2008-2013. Recreations: biking; sea kayaking; live music; travelling; films; history; whisky collecting; biographies; Kelvin walkway. Address: (h.) 21 Cleveden Road, Kelvinside, Glasgow G12 0PQ.

Downie, Emeritus Professor Robert S., MA, BPhil, FRSE, FRSA. Honorary Professorial Research Fellow, Glasgow University; b. 19.4.33, Glasgow; m., Eileen Dorothea Flynn (deceased); 3 d. Educ. High School of Glasgow; Glasgow University; Queen's College, Oxford. Tutor, Worcester College, Oxford, 1958; Glasgow University: Lecturer in Moral Philosophy, 1959, Senior Lecturer, 1968, Professor of Moral Philosophy, 1969 (Stevenson Lecturer in Medical Ethics, 1984-88); Visiting Professor: Syracuse University, New York, 1963-64, Dalhousie University, Nova Scotia, 1976. Publications: Government Action and Morality, 1964; Respect for Persons, 1969; Roles and Values, 1971; Education and Personal Relationships, 1974; Caring and Curing, 1980; Healthy Respect, 1987; Health Promotion: models and values, 1990; The Making of a Doctor, 1992; Francis Hutcheson, 1994; The Healing Arts: an Oxford illustrated anthology, 1994; Palliative Care Ethics, 1996; Medical Ethics, 1996; Clinical Judgement – Evidence in Practice, 2000; The Philosophy of Palliative Care: Critique and Reconstruction, 2006; Bioethics and the Humanities, 2007;

End of Life Choices, 2009; Francis Hutcheson, new ed., 2019; Quality of Life: A Post-Pandemic Philosophy of Medicine, 2021. Recreation: music. Address: (b.) Department of Philosophy, Glasgow University G12 8QQ; T.-0141-339 1345; e-mail: Robert.Downie@glasgow.ac.uk

Dowson, William K., BSc, MSc. Agent for Scotland, Bank of England, since 2010; b. 3.3.71, Bridlington; m Sarah Laing; 2 s.; 1 d. Educ. Wycliffe College; University of London. Joined Bank of England, 1995; worked in policy and management roles in Banking, Financial Stability and Markets Directorates, before joining Agency Network. Assessor to the Executive Committee of the SCDI, and an Observer on the Council of CBI Scotland. Recreations: sailing; walking; reading. Address: (b.) Bank of England, Agency for Scotland, 2 West Regent Street, Glasgow G2 1RW; T.-0141 433 7165; e-mail: scotland@bankofengland.co.uk

Doyle, Rev. David Wallace, MA (Hons), BD (Hons). Retired Minister, St. Mary's Parish Church, Motherwell (1987-2015); b. 12.4.48, Glasgow; m., Alison W. Britton; 1 s.; 1 d. Educ. High School of Glasgow; University of Glasgow; Corpus Christi, University of Cambridge. Assistant Minister, East Kilbride Old Parish Church, 1973-74; Minister, Tulliallan and Kincardine Parish Church, Fife, 1977-87. Recreations: music; gardening.

Doyle, Gemma, MA. MP Labour (Co-op), West Dunbartonshire, 2010-2015; Shadow Minister for Defence, 2010-2015; b. 1981. Educ. Our Lady and St Patrick's High, Dumbarton; Glasgow University. Member: Select Committee on Armed Forces Bill, 2011; Energy and Climate Change, 2010; Administration, 2010; Chair, PLP Departmental Group for Defence, 2010.

Doyle, Roberta, BA. Board Director, Scottish Opera, since 2018; Trustee, Donald Dewar Arts Awards, since 2017, the National Autistic Society, since 2018; Director of External Affairs, National Theatre of Scotland, 2007-2017; b. 5.1.60, Glasgow; m., Cemal Ozturk; 1 s. Educ. Notre Dame High School, Glasgow; University of Strathclyde. Head of Publicity, Citizens Theatre Glasgow, 1986-1990; Director of Marketing, Scottish Ballet, 1990-1992; Head of Marketing and Press, Scottish Opera, 1992-2000; Director of Public Affairs, National Galleries of Scotland, 2000-2004; Director of External Affairs, Scottish Opera, 2005-2007. Tutor on Arts Council England/Theatrical Management Association/Scottish Arts Council/Arts Council Ireland Essentials of Arts Marketing courses. Chair of Scotland Reference Group, National Autistic Society; member, British Council UK Cultural Diplomacy group; Chair of the Arts Jury of the Royal Television Society Scotland Annual Awards 2020 and 2019; UK speaker at the St Petersburg International Cultural Forum in 2019 and the St Petersburg International Festivals Conference in November 2020; Speaker, City of Belgrade International Theatre Forum, December 2020. Chair, London-based CultureComms; guest lecturer and speaker worldwide on arts and cultural management policy. Justice of the Peace in the Sheriffdom of Glasgow and Strathkelvin. Recreations: theatre; opera; riding; Turkish culture and Italian cooking.

Drennan, Barry. Head Teacher, Portlethen Academy, since 2021; previously Depute Head, Aboyne Academy. Address: Bruntland Road, Portlethen, Aberdeenshire AB12 4QL; T.-01224 087880.

Driscoll, Professor Stephen T., BA, MSc, PhD. Professor of Archaeology, University of Glasgow, since 2005, Lecturer, Department of Archaeology, since 1992; b. 11.11.58, Monterey, California, USA; m., Katherine S. Forsyth; 3 d. Educ. St. Anselm's Abbey School, Washington, DC; University of Pennsylvania, Philadelphia. Founding Director of Glasgow Archaeological Research

Division (GUARD) - full contract unit, 1989-94; Research Director of GUARD, since 1994; Lecturer in Archaeology, University of Glasgow, 1992-97, Senior Lecturer, 1997-2005. Editor of Scottish Archaeological Journal, since 1998; Vice President, Glasgow Archaeological Society, since 2007. Publications: Excavations at Edinburgh Castle (Co-Author), 1997; Excavations at Glasgow Cathedral, 2002; Alba: Gaelic Kingdom of Scotland, 2002. Recreations: cycling; gaelic language. E-mail: s.driscoll@archaeology.gla.ac.uk

Drummond, Rev. John Whiteford, MA, BD. Retired Minister; b. 27.6.46, Glasgow; m., Barbara S. Grant; 1 s.; 3 d. Educ. Bearsden Academy; University of Glasgow. Probationer Assistant, St. Francis-in-the-East Church, Bridgeton, 1970-71; Ordained Assistant, King's Park Parish Church, Glasgow, 1971-73; Minister: Linwood Parish Church, 1973-86, Rutherglen West Parish Church, 1986-2007, Rutherglen West and Wardlawhill Parish Church, 2007-2011. Recreations: reading; television; family. Address: (h.) 25 Kingsburn Drive, Rutherglen G73 2AN; T.-0141 571 6002.

Drummond, Sheriff Lorna Allison, QC. Senator of the College of Justice, since 2022; b. 19.12.67. Educ. Glasgow and Cambridge Universities. Career history: appointed assistant parliamentary counsel before calling at the Bar in 1998; became a QC in 2011 after acting as standing junior to the Advocate General and Scottish Ministers; sat as a part-time Sheriff from 2009 and took up the role as resident Sheriff in Dundee in 2014 and commercial sheriff in 2017; Justice of Appeal for St Helena, Ascension and Tristan da Cunha, since 2015 and has served as an Appeal Sheriff and a Temporary High Court Judge since 2020. Address: Parliament House, 11 Parliament Square, Edinburgh EH1 1RQ.

Drummond, Rev. Professor Norman Walker, CBE, FRSE, DUniv. Chairman, Scottish Commemorations Panel, 2012-19; Special Representative for Scotland, UK Advisory Group, World War 1 Commemorations, 2012-18; Visiting Professor of Leadership in Education, University of Edinburgh; Chaplain to the Queen in Scotland, since 1993; Non-executive Director: J & J Denholm Ltd, 2002-2015, Denholm Energy Services, since 2014; Hon Colonel, The Black Watch ACF, since 2014; Chairman, Drummond International, since 1999; Founder and President, Columba 1400, Community and International Leadership Centre, Isle of Skye, since 1997; Chairman, Lloyds TSB Foundation for Scotland, 2003-09; Founder and non-executive Chairman, The Change Partnership Scotland, 1999-2003; Chairman, Community Action Network Scotland, 2001-03; b. 1.4.52, Greenock; m., Lady Elizabeth Kennedy; 3 s.; 2 d. Educ. Merchiston Castle School; Fitzwilliam College, Cambridge; New College, Edinburgh. Chaplain to the Forces, 1976-82; Depot, The Parachute Regiment and Airborne Forces, 1977-78; 1st Bn., The Black Watch (Royal Highland Regiment), 1978-82; Chaplain, Fettes College, 1982-84; Headmaster, Loretto School, 1984-95; Minister, Kilmuir and Stenscholl, Isle of Skye, 1996-98; BBC National Governor and Chairman, Broadcasting Council for Scotland, 1994-99; former Chairman, BBC Children in Need; Member, Queen's Bodyguard for Scotland (Royal Company of Archers); Past President: Victoria League for Overseas Students in Scotland, Edinburgh Bn., Boys' Brigade; former Governor, Gordonstoun School; former Chairman, Aiglon College, Switzerland; former Member, Scottish Committee for Imperial Cancer Research; former Trustee, Foundation for Skin Research; former Member, Scottish Committee, Duke of Edinburgh's Award Scheme; former Member, Court, Heriot-Watt University; former Chairman, Musselburgh and District Council of Social Services.

Publications: The First Twenty Five Years (the official history of the Black Watch Kirk Session); Mother's Hands; The Spirit of Success; The Power of Three; Step Back. Recreations: rugby football; cricket; golf; curling; traditional jazz. Address: 34a Great King Street, Edinburgh EH3 6QH.

Drummond, Robbie, BAcc (Hons), CA. Managing Director, CalMac Ferries Ltd, since 2018; other roles in the Group included Service Delivery Director, Group Finance Director (2012-2017), Bid Director and Transition Director; b. 8.6.69, Inverness; m., Amanda Drummond; 2 d. Educ. Morrisons Academy; Glasgow University. Early career spent with KPMG and Pricewaterhousecoopers (Corporate Finance); subsequently held senior finance positions with Thus plc, Invocas plc and HBOS plc. Scottish Council for Development and Industry (Highlands & Islands) Committee Member; Chairman of Stramash - an outdoor social enterprise. Recreation: ultra running. Address: (h.) 56 Braehead Avenue, Milngavie, East Dunbartonshire G62 6DY; T.-07766021415.
E-mail: robbie.drummond@davidmacbrayne.co.uk

Drummond, Sheriff Thomas Anthony Kevin, LLB, QC. Retired Sheriff, Lothian and Borders at Jedburgh, Selkirk and Duns (2000-2013); b. 3.11.43, Howwood, Renfrewshire; m., Margaret Evelyn Broadley; 1 d. (1 d. deceased). Educ. St. Mirin's Academy, Paisley; Blairs College, Aberdeen; Edinburgh University. Admitted, Faculty of Advocates, 1974; Advocate Depute, 1985-90; Member, Firearms Consultative Committee, 1989-97; Member, Criminal Injuries Compensation Board, 1990-96; Home Advocate Depute, 1996-97; Sheriff, Glasgow and Strathkelvin, 1997-2000. Joint Chairman, Institute of Chartered Accountants of Scotland, 1993-2000. Hon. US Deputy Marshal, 1998. Chair, Legislation Regulation and Guidance Committee, PAWS (Partnership for Action against Wildlife Crime Scotland). Publications (legal cartoons): The Law at Work; The Law at Play; Great Defences of Our Time. Recreations: fishing; shooting. Address: (h.) Pomathorn House, Penicuik, Midlothian; T.-01968 674046; e-mail: kdrummondqc@btinternet.com

Drummond Young, Hon. Lord (James Edward Drummond Young), QC. Senator of the College of Justice in Scotland, 2001-2020 (retired); former Chairman, Scottish Law Commission; b. 1950; m.; 1 d. Educ. Cambridge University; Harvard University; Edinburgh University. Admitted, Faculty of Advocates, 1976. Recreations: music; travel; member of The Speculative Society of Edinburgh.

Drysdale, Professor David Douglas (Dougal), BSc, PhD, MRSC, FIFireE, FSFPE, CEng, FRSE. Professor Emeritus (Fire Safety Engineering), Edinburgh University, since 2004; Chairman, International Association for Fire Safety Science, 2002-05; b. 30.9.39, Dunfermline; m., Judyth McIntyre; 3 s. Educ. Edinburgh Academy; Edinburgh University; Cambridge University. Post-doctoral Fellow, University of Toronto, 1966-67; Research Lecturer, Leeds University, 1967-74; Lecturer, Fire Engineering, Edinburgh University, 1974-90; Visiting Professor, Centre for Fire Safety Studies, Worcester Polytechnic Institute, Mass., USA, 1982; Reader, Fire Safety Engineering, Edinburgh University, 1990-98, Professor, Fire Safety Engineering, 1998-2004; Member of the Buncefield Major Incident Investigation Board, 2006-2009; SFPE Man of the Year (USA), 1983; BRE Fire Research Lecturer, 1995; SFPE Arthur B. Guise Medal for eminent achievement advancing the Science of Fire Protection Engineering, 1995; IAFSS Kawagoe Medal for lifelong career in and contribution to fire safety science, 2002; IFE Rasbash Medal, 2005;

International Forum for Fire Research Directors' Sjolin Award for "outstanding career in fire science", 2005; SFPE 2009 D. Peter Lund Award for "significant contribution to the advancement of the profession". Publications: Introduction to Fire Dynamics, 3rd Edn., 2011; Handbook of Fire Protection Engineering, 4th Edn. (co-ed.), 2008; Fire Safety Journal (ed.), 1988-2009. Recreations: music; hill walking; curling; cycling; reading. Address: (b.) Institute of Infrastructure and Environment, School of Engineering, Edinburgh University, King's Buildings, Edinburgh EH9 3JN; T.-0131-650 5710.

Drysdale, James Cunison, LLB. Partner, Ledingham Chalmers LLP, specialising in Rural, Private Client and Environmental Law, since 2013; b. 30.4.56, Edinburgh; m., Fiona Jean nee Duncan Millar; 1 s.; 3 d. Educ. Winchester College; Aberdeen University. Apprentice at Brodies, 1979-81; Assistant Solicitor: Murray Beith and Murray, 1981-83, J&F Anderson, 1983-86; Partner, J&F Anderson & Anderson Strathern, 1986-2013. Treasurer and Council Member, UKELA (UK Environment Law Association) until 1 July 2009, having served the full term; Legal Adviser to the Association of Salmon Fishery Boards, 1994-2009; Convener, Law Society Rural Affairs Committee; Member, Law Society Environmental Committee; Member, Scottish Land & Estates Legal Committee; Clerk of the Course, Fife Foxhounds Point To Point. Recreations: countryside pursuits. Address: (b.) Unit 2B, The Paddock, Stirling Agricultural Centre, Stirling FK9 4RW; e-mail: jim.drysdale@ledinghamchalmers.com

Drysdale, Thomas Henry, LLB, WS. Retired Solicitor; b. 23.11.42, Stirlingshire; m., Caroline Drysdale (nee Shaw); 1 s.; 2 d. Educ. Cargilfield and Glenalmond College; University of Edinburgh (LLB, 1964). Qualified as a Solicitor, 1966; Partner in Shepherd and Wedderburn WS, 1967-99 (Managing Partner, 1988-94); Partner in Olivers WS, 1999-2004; Chairman of Edinburgh Solicitors' Property Centre, 1981-88; Deputy Keeper of HM Signet, 1991-98; Part time Judge of the First Tier, the Tribunals Service, 2003-2013; Honorary Consul for Hungary, 2001-2012. Chairman of Council, The Stair Society (legal history), 2016-18 (Secretary and Treasurer 1998-2016); Chairman, Gullane Area Community Council, 2019-2022 (Vice Chairman, 2014-2018). Recreations: legal history; walking; gardening; reading. Address: 6 The Glebe, Manse Road, Dirleton, East Lothian EH39 5FB; T.-01620 850264. E-mail: tomdrysdale@btinternet.com

Duckett, Professor Jane, FRSE. Professor, Edward Caird Chair of Politics and Director of the Scottish Centre for China Research, University of Glasgow, since 1999. Educ. Universities of Leeds and London (SOAS); Nankai University; Fudan University. Lecturer, University of Manchester, 1995-97; Lecturer, University of York, 1997-99. President, British Association for Chinese Studies, 2014-17; International Dean for East Asia, University of Glasgow, 2014-18; Lord Provost of Glasgow Award for Education, 2011; Fellow of the British Academy, 2016. Publications: The Entrepreneurial State in China, 1998; The Open Economy and its Enemies, 2006; China's Changing Welfare Mix, 2011; The Chinese State's Retreat from Health, 2011. Address: University of Glasgow, R1202 Level 12, Adam Smith Building, Glasgow G12 8RT; e-mail: Jane.Duckett@glasgow.ac.uk

Duddy, Ian, BSc. Chair, Scottish Human Rights Commission, since 2022. Educ. Loughborough University; Universität Trier; The Australian National University; Saïd Business School, University of Oxford. Career history: English Language Teacher, JET Exchange Programme,

Miyazaki, Japan, 1996-98; Research Analyst, European Equities, Meijiseimei International, London, 1998-99; Diplomat and Team Leader, Foreign and Commonwealth Office, London and Argentina, 2000-08; Deputy Director, International Policy Directorate, UK IPO, London, 2008-2011; Political Counsellor; Head of Political, Human Rights and Press, UK Diplomatic Mission in Geneva, Switzerland, Foreign and Commonwealth Office, 2011-16; British Ambassador to Uruguay, Foreign and Commonwealth Office, 2016-2020; Foreign and Commonwealth and Development Office: British Ambassador (interim) to Chile, 2020-21, appointed Head of Human Rights and Rule of Law Department in 2021. Address: Scottish Human Rights Commission, Bridgeside House, 99 McDonald Road, Edinburgh EH7 4NS; T.-0131 297 5750.

Dudek, Pamela, BSc, RMN, BSc, MSc. Chief Executive Officer, NHS Highland, since 2020. Educ. Dundee School of Nursing; University of Abertay Dundee; University of Dundee. Career history: Head of Substance Misuse Services, NHS Tayside, 2003-08; NHS Grampian: Long Term Conditions Programme Manager, 2009-2012, Deputy General Manager, 2009-2012, Head of Aberdeenshire Community Health Partnership, 2014; Chief Officer, Health and Social Care, The Moray Council, 2014-2020; Deputy Chief Executive, NHS Highland, 2020. Address: NHS Highland, Assynt House, Beechwood Park, Inverness IV2 3BW; T.-01463 717123.

Duffin, Stuart, DA, RE, RSA. Studio Etcher, Glasgow Print Studio, 1984-1989; Studio Workshop Manager, 1989-2002; Etching Master, since 2002; b. 13.6.59. Educ. Gray's School of Art, Aberdeen. SAC award to study and travel in Italy, 1987; exchange visit to Senej Print Workshop, Moscow, 1992; British Council support to study at the Jerusalem Print Workshop, 1996 and 2012; Royal Scottish Academy Gillies Awards to Study in Belfast (2006) and Jerusalem (2016); solo exhibitions: Glasgow Print Studio, 1995, 2001, 2013, Gallery of Jerusalem Print Workshop, 1998 and 2019, Royal Scottish Academy, 2020, Djanogly Centre; Visiting lecturer tour and exhibition, New Zealand, 2002, 2007-2010. Address: c/o Glasgow Print Studio, Trongate 103, Glasgow G1 5HD.
E-mail: stuartduffin007@gmail.com
Website: www.stuartduffin.com

Duffus, John Henderson, BSc, PhD, DSc, CSci, CBiol, MRSB, CChem, FRSC. Professor, Chulabhorn Graduate Institute, Bangkok; Consultant, Edinburgh Centre for Toxicology (EdinTox). Educ. Arbroath High School (Dux); Edinburgh University; Heriot-Watt University. Research Fellow: Warwick University, 1965-67, Edinburgh University, 1967-70; Lecturer, Heriot-Watt University, 1970-80; Senior Lecturer in Environmental Toxicology, Heriot-Watt University, 1980-97; Hon. Fellow in Public Health Sciences, Edinburgh University, 1997; WHO Consultant, Toxicology and Chemical Safety, 1981-2006; Member, UK Department of the Environment Advisory Committee on Hazardous Substances, 1991-99; Titular Member, IUPAC Commission on Toxicology, 1991-2001, Chair, 1997-2001; Titular Member, IUPAC Committee on the Teaching of Chemistry, 1999-2001; Member, RSC Committee on Environment, Health and Safety, 2001-2016; Member, UK HSE Biocides Consultative Committee, 2001-06; Titular Member, IUPAC Division VII, Chemistry and Human Health Committee, 2004-08; Adjunct Professor, Asian Institute of Technology, 2005; Chair, IUPAC Subcommittee on Toxicology and Risk Assessment, 2001-2018; Scientific Advisor, EC, 2009-2014. Publications: Environmental Toxicology, 1980 (Author); Environmental Toxicology and Ecotoxicology, 1986 (Contributor); Magnesium in Mitosis and the Cell Cycle (Co-Author), 1987; Yeast: A Practical Approach (Co-Editor, Co-Author), 1988; The Toxicology of Chemicals, Series 1, Carcinogenicity, Vol III, Vol IV (Co-Editor/Co-Author), 1991-93; Toxic Substances in Crop Plants (Co-Editor/Co-Author), 1991; Cancer and Workplace Chemicals, 1995 (Author); IUPAC Glossaries of Terms Used in Toxicology, Pure and Applied Chemistry, 1993-2017 (Main Author); Carcinogenicity of Inorganic Substances (Chief Editor/Co-Author), 1997; Chemical Risk Assessment (Co-Author), 1999; Risk Assessment and Elemental Speciation, 2001, 2003, 2006 (with special attention to nickel and vanadium); Fundamental Toxicology (Editor, Co-Author), 2006; Concepts in Toxicology (Editor, Co-Author), 2009; NLM-SOT ToxLearn Multi-Module Toxicology Tutorial (Co-Editor, Co-Author), 2010-2015; Encyclopedia of Toxicology, 3rd and 4th Edition (Contributor), 2014; Regulatory Toxicology (Co-Author), 2014; Comprehensive Glossary of Terms Used in Toxicology, 2017 (Main Author); RSC/IUPAC Glossary of Terms Used in Molecular Toxicology, 2020 (Co-Author). Awards: US Society of Toxicology Education Award, 2012; Princess Chulabhorn Gold Medal, 2012; Emeritus Fellow, IUPAC Division VII, 2017. Address: Edinburgh Centre for Toxicology, 43 Mansionhouse Road, Edinburgh EH9 2JD.

Duffy, David, BBS, MA. Chief Executive, Virgin Money UK plc; b. 9.61, Hammersmith, London; partner, Carolyn; 2 d.; 1 s. Educ. Terenure College; Trinity College Dublin. Career: Goldman Sachs International, 1987-97, served as Business Manager of Information Technology, Head of General Services, Europe, 1988-93, Head of Human Resources, Europe, 1993-97; ING Group, 1998-2006, Global Head of Human Resources and Global Chief Operating Officer, President and Chief Executive Officer of the franchises in the US and Latin America, 2000-06, served at New York as the Head of the Global Wholesale Banking Network, based in Amsterdam, 2004-06; Chief Executive of Corporate and Investment Banking International, Standard International Holdings SA and Standard Bank Group Limited, 2006-2011, established Celtic Advisory International, which provides Capital Raising and Corporate Development Advisory Services to corporate and emerging companies; Chief Executive, Allied Irish Banks, 2011-2015; joined Clydesdale Bank in 2015 as Chief Executive Officer. Recreations: running; playing tennis; sailing. Address: (b.) 30 St Vincent Place, Glasgow, G1 2HL.

Duffy, Karen, BA, MSc. Delivery Director, Preventative and Proactive Care, The Scottish Government, since 2022. Educ. Lothian College of Nursing and Midwifery; Selkirk High School; Abertay University; Queen Margaret University. Career history: NHS Lothian, 1990-94; Health Visitor: NHS Fife, 1995-96, NHS Lothian, 1996-99; NHS Borders: Nurse Co-ordinator, 1999-2002, Public Health Practitioner, 2000-05, Programme Lead for Multiple and Complex Needs Project, 2005-08; Learning Disability Review Health Improvement Advisor, NHS Quality Improvement Scotland, 2008; The Scottish Government: National Programme Manager - Equally Well, 2008-2013, CPP Engagement and Support Manager, 2013; Interim Associate Director of Nursing - Primary and Community Services, NHS Borders, 2013-14; NHS Lothian: Clinical Nurse Manager, 2014-16, Strategic Programme Manager, Maternity, Children and Young People, 2016-18; NHS National Services Scotland: Interim Director of National Services Division (NSD), Edinburgh, 2020, Programme Associate Director - National Planning, 2018-2020; The Scottish Government: Deputy Director (working on the delivery programme for the Scottish Covid-19 Vaccination Programme), 2020-21, Delivery Director (Interim), 2021-22. Address: Scottish Government, St. Andrew's House, Regent Road, Edinburgh EH1 3DG.

Duffy, Nicholas, LLB. Senior Solicitor, The Scottish Government, since 2018. Educ. University of Glasgow. Career history: The Scottish Government: Solicitor,

Contracts, Procurement and Commercial Property Division, 2001-06; Solicitor, Police and Fire Service Division, 2006; Solicitor, Food and Environment Division, 2007-09; Solicitor, Health and Social Care Division, 2009-2012; Solicitor, Civil Law and Constitution Division, 2012-15; Senior Solicitor, 2015-16; Head of Human Trafficking, 2016-17; Deputy Solicitor to the Edinburgh Tram Inquiry, 2017-18. Address: Scottish Government, St. Andrew's House, Regent Road, Edinburgh EH1 3DG.

Duffy, Sean, MBA. Chief Executive, The Wise Group, since 2018. Educ. Strathclyde Business School. Career: Business Analyst/Project Manager, BskyB, 1992-2000; MGt plc: Projects Director, 2000-02, Sales & Marketing Director, 2002-04; Commercial Director, STV Group plc, 2004-07; Business Director, CBS Outdoor, 2008-2010; Commercial Consultant, Independent Consultancy, 2010; Group Commercial Director, Herald & Times Group, 2010-12; Commercial Director, FirstGroup PLC - ScotRail, 2012-15; Interim Franchise Change Director, National Express Ltd, 2015-16; Commercial Director, Newsquest, 2016-17; Council Member, GLG (Gerson Lehrman Group), since 2009. Board Member, South Lanarkshire College, since 2016; Advisory Board Member, Strathclyde Business School, since 2017; Board Member: Scottish Golf, since 2018, SCVO, since 2018. Address: The Wise Group, 72 Charlotte Street, Glasgow G1 5DW.

Dugdale, Kezia. Director, The John Smith Centre for Public Service, University of Glasgow, since 2019; MSP (Labour), Lothian, 2011-19; former Leader of the Scottish Labour Party (2015-17); b. 28.8.81, Aberdeen. Educ. Harris Academy, Dundee; University of Aberdeen; University of Edinburgh. Worked in public affairs, latterly with the National Union of Students; ran the parliamentary office of Lord Foulkes, 2007-2011; Shadow Cabinet Secretary for Education and Lifelong Learning, 2013-15; Deputy Leader, the Scottish Labour Party, 2014-15. Weekly columnist, Scottish Daily Record. Recreations: going to the cinema; reading Scottish crime novels; enjoying the City of Edinburgh. Address: The John Smith Centre for Public Service, Adam Smith Building, University of Glasgow, Glasgow G12 8RT.

Dugmore, Professor Andrew J., PhD, BSc. Professor of Geosciences, University of Edinburgh, since 2007; Adjunct Professor (Research), Graduate Center, City University of New York, USA, since 2002; m., Thelma (nee Williamson); 1 s.; 1 d. Educ. Denes High School, Lowestoft; University of Birmingham; University of Aberdeen. Lecturer, Senior Lecturer, University of Edinburgh, 1992-2004, Reader in Tephrochronology, 2004-07. Visiting Lecturer, University of Lund, Sweden, 1997; President's Award, Royal Scottish Geographical Society, 2002. Recreations: hill walking and mountaineering. Address: (b.) Institute of Geography, School of Geosciences, University of Edinburgh, Drummond Street, Edinburgh EH8 9XP; T.-0131 650 8156; e-mail: andrew.dugmore@ed.ac.uk

Duguid, David. MP (Conservative), Banff and Buchan, since 2017; Parliamentary Under Secretary of State, Scotland Office, since 2020; Government Whip, Lord Commissioner of HM Treasury, since 2020; b. 8.10.70, Turriff. Educ. Banff Academy; The Robert Gordon University. Chemical Sales/Service Engineer, Servo Oilfield Chemicals, 1992-93; Production Chemist, SGS, 1993-2001; BP: Production Efficiency Engineer/Ops Excellence Coach, 2001-03, Integrity Engineer, 2003-06, Common Process/Continuous Improvement Coach; Project Manager/Management Consulting/Oil & Gas Operations, Hitachi Consulting, 2011-2016; Managing Director, D & R

Duguid Limited, 2016-2020. Address: House of Commons, London SW1A 0AA.

Dumville, Professor David Norman, MA (Cantab), PhD (Edin), HonMA (Pennsylvania). Sixth-Century Professor in History, Palaeography and Celtic, University of Aberdeen, since 2005; Fellow, Girton College, Cambridge, since 1978; b. 5.5.49, Hillingdon, London. Educ. St Nicholas Grammar School, Northwood, Middlesex; Emmanuel College, Cambridge; Ludwig-Maximilians Universität München; University of Edinburgh. Career History: University of Wales Fellow, Department of Welsh, University College of Swansea; Assistant Professor, Department of English, University of Pennsylvania; Lecturer, Reader, then Professor, Department of Anglo-Saxon, Norse and Celtic, University of Cambridge; Sixth-Century Professor in History, Palaeography and Celtic, University of Aberdeen. Honorary Member, Royal Irish Academy. Publications: 15 books, about 150 scholarly articles. Recreations: politics and other arguments. Address: (b.) Department of History, University of Aberdeen, King's College, Old Aberdeen AB24 3FX; T.-01224-272455; e-mail: d.n.dumville@abdn.ac.uk

Dunbar, Jackie, MSP (SNP), Aberdeen Donside, since 2021; b. Peterhead. Educ. Elgin. Elected to the Northfield (later Northfield/Mastrick North) ward of Aberdeen City Council in 2007, and held some senior posts on the council. Address: The Scottish Parliament, Edinburgh EH99 1SP; T.-0131 3485067.
E-mail: Jackie.Dunbar.msp@parliament.scot

Dunbar, Professor Lennox Robert, RSA. Emeritus Professor of Fine Art, Grays School of Art; Painter and Printmaker; b. 17.5.52, Aberdeen; m., Jan Storie; 2 s.; 1 d. Educ. Aberdeen Grammar School; Grays School of Art. Part-time Lecturer, 1975-82; Etching Technician, Peacock Printmakers, 1978-82; Education Officer, Peacock Printmakers, 1982-86; appointed Lecturer in Painting and Printmaking, Grays School of Art, 1986; Visiting Lecturer, Duncan of Jordanstone College of Art, Dundee, and Newcastle University; Visiting Artist/Tutor, Louisiana State University; College of Santa FE, New Mexico; participated in many group and one-man exhibitions; numerous awards including Latimer Award, 1978, Guthrie Award, 1984, Shell Expro Premier Award, 1991, 1993 and 2006; work in many private and public collections.

Dunbar, Morrison Alexander Rankin, CBE, FRSAMD. Chairman: Royal Scottish Academy of Music and Drama Trust, 1992-2004, Westbourne Music, 1998-2008, Cantilena Festival, Islay, 2002-2011; b. 27.4.29, Glasgow; m., Sally Joan Sutherland; 2 s.; 1 d. Educ. Belmont House; Gresham House. Managing Director, Morrison Dunbar Ltd. Builders, 1957-81. President: Scottish Building Contractors Association, 1968, Scottish Building Employers Federation, 1975, Building Employers Confederation, 1980, Builders Benevolent Institution, 1987; Lord Dean of Guild, Merchants House of Glasgow, 1991-93; Chairman: Epilepsy Association of Scotland, 1990-93, Royal Scottish Academy of Music and Drama, 1987-91, Royal Scottish National Orchestra, 1993-97; Member, Trades House of Glasgow. Recreations: music; art galleries; golf. Address: (h.) 18 Devonshire Terrace Lane, Glasgow G12 9XT; T.-0141-357 1289.

Dunbar-Nasmith, Professor Emeritus Sir James Duncan, Kt (1996), CBE (1976), BA, DA, RIBA, PPRIAS, FRSA, FRSE. Partner, Law and Dunbar-Nasmith, Architects, Edinburgh and Forres 1957-99; b. 15.3.27,

Dartmouth. Educ. Lockers Park; Winchester College; Trinity College, Cambridge; Edinburgh College of Art (Hon. Fellow, 1997). Lt., Scots Guards, 1945-48; ARIBA, 1954; President: Edinburgh Architectural Association, 1967-69, Royal Incorporation of Architects in Scotland, 1971-73; RIAS Lifetime Achievement Award, 2012; Member, RIBA Council, 1967-73 (Vice-President and Chairman, Board of Architectural Education, 1972-73); Council, ARCUK, 1976-84, Board of Education, 1976-88 (Vice Chairman, 1977); Professor and Head, Department of Architecture, Heriot-Watt University and Edinburgh College of Art, 1978-88; President, Scottish Civic Trust (Chairman, 1995-2003); Vice-President, Europa Nostra, 1997-2005, Hon. Life Member, 2005. Member: Royal Commission on Ancient and Historical Monuments of Scotland, 1972-96, Ancient Monuments Board for Scotland, 1969-82 (interim Chairman, 1972-73), Historic Buildings Council for Scotland, 1966-93; Trustee, Architectural Heritage Fund, Theatres Trust, 1983-95; Deputy Chairman, Edinburgh Festival Society, 1981-85. Recreations: music; theatre; skiing; sailing. Address: (b.) Sandbank, Findhorn, Moray IV36 3YY; T.-0130 9690445; mobile: 0780 137 1515; e-mail: jdnasmith@fastmail.net

Duncan, Dr David, MA, PhD. Chief Operating Officer and University Secretary, University of Glasgow, since 2017. Educ. Daniel Stewart's and Melville College; University of Aberdeen; Queen's University, Canada. Career history: Research Fellow, University of the Witwatersrand, South Africa, 1991-92; Scottish Consultative Council on the Curriculum (became Director of Corporate Affairs), then Assistant Chief Executive, Learning & Teaching Scotland, 1992-2001; University Secretary, University of Dundee, 2001-08; Registrar, University of York, 2009-2017. Address: University of Glasgow, University Avenue, Glasgow G12 8QQ; T.-0141 330 4246. E-mail: David.Duncan@glasgow.ac.uk

Duncan, Elaine Margaret, BSc (Hons) Behavioural Sciences. Chief Executive, Scottish Bible Society, since 2006; b. 29.8.58, Whitehaven, Cumbria. Educ. Whitehaven Grammar School; Huddersfied Polytechnic. Universities and Colleges Christian Fellowship, 1981-95; Scripture Union Scotland, 1995-2006. Address: (b.) 7 Hampton Terrace, Edinburgh EH12 5XU; T.-0131-337-9701; e-mail: elaine.duncan@scottishbiblesociety.org

Duncan, Fiona. Chief Executive, Corra Foundation (formerly Lloyds TSB Foundation for Scotland), since 2014; Chair, Independent Care Review, since 2017; Director, THINK Consulting Solutions, 2009-2013; Deputy Chief Executive, Lloyds TSB Foundation for Scotland, 2013-14. Address: (b.) Riverside House, 502 Gorgie Road, Edinburgh EH11 3AF; T.-0131 444 4020.

Duncan, The Right Reverend Dr Gregor. Bishop of Glasgow and Galloway, 2010-18; b. 11.10.50. Educ. Allan Glen's School; University of Glasgow; Clare College, Cambridge. Studied for the priesthood at Ripon College Cuddesdon; ordained in 1984 and began career as an Assistant Curate at Oakham; Chaplain of Edinburgh Theological College, then Rector of St Columba's, Largs, then St Ninian's, Pollokshields in Glasgow; Dean of Glasgow and Galloway until elevation to the Episcopate in 2010. Consecrated and installed as Bishop of Glasgow and Galloway at St Mary's Cathedral in Glasgow on 23 April 2010 (retired 2018). Address: 3 Golf Road, Rutherglen G73 4JW; T.-0141 634 1167.

Duncan of Springbank, Baron (Ian James Duncan), PhD, FGS. Parliamentary Under Secretary of State: Scotland Office, 2017-19, Northern Ireland Office, 2017-2020; Honorary President, The English-Speaking Union (Chairman, 2014-17); b. 13.2.73. Educ. Alyth High School; Bristol University; University of St. Andrews. Policy Analyst BP, 1998-99; Deputy Chief Executive/Secretary, Scottish Fishermen's Federation, 1999-2003; Head of Policy & Communication, The Scottish Refugee Council, 2004-2005; Head of EU Office, The Scottish Parliament, 2005-2011; Parliamentary Under Secretary of State: Business, Energy and Industrial Strategy, since 2019; Minister for Climate Change: Scotland Office, 2017-19, Wales Office, 2017; Member of the European Parliament for Scotland (Scottish Conservatives), 2014-17. Publications include: Three-dimensionally mineralized insects and millipedes from the Tertiary of Riversleigh, Queensland, Australia, 1998 (Co-Author). Recreation: art.

Duncan, John. Lord-Lieutenant, Ayrshire and Arran, 2006-2017 (retired); m., Jess; 1 s.; 1 d.; 1 stepdaughter. Joined Renfrew and Bute Constabulary as a Police Cadet in 1959, retiring as Deputy Chief Constable of Strathclyde Police in 2001.

Duncan, Dr William, BSc (Hons), MCIPD, PhD. Visiting Professor, International Public Policy Institute, University of Strathclyde, since 2017; b. 6.12.50, Edinburgh. Educ. Linlithgow Academy; Edinburgh University. Greater London Council, 1975-78; Lothian Regional Council, 1978-85; Chief Executive, Royal Society of Edinburgh, 1985-2017. Secretary to Trustees, Scottish Science Trust, 1997-98; Board member, The Careers Research and Advisory Centre (CRAC) Ltd; Chair, George Street Association in Edinburgh; Trustee, Glasgow Science Centre (Chair, Audit Committee). Recreations: contemporary music; opera.

Duncan-Glancy, Pam, BSc (Psych), MSc (Health Psych), PGCert (Citizenship and Human Rights). MSP (Scottish Labour), Glasgow (Region), since 2021; Scottish Labour Spokesperson for Social Security and Social Justice, since 2021; b. 2.11.81. Educ. Milnes High; University of Stirling; Glasgow Caledonian University. Career history: Independent Living Advisor, GCIL, 2004-09; Policy Officer, ILiS, Glasgow, 2009-2015; Senior Communications and Engagement Officer, NHS Health Scotland, 2015-2020; Communications Team Manager, Public Health Scotland, 2020-2021. Sat on the Commission on Strengthening Local Democracy and on the Commission on Parliamentary Reform. Address: The Scottish Parliament, Edinburgh EH99 1SP; T.-0131 348 6389. E-mail: Pam.Duncan-Glancy.msp@parliament.scot

Duncan Millar, Ian, MBE, BScAg, MRICS, FRAgS. Chair, Moredun Foundation, 2012-2020; Farmer, since 1973; b. 1.6.51, Aberfeldy; m., Hazel; 1 s.; 1 d. Educ. Loretto School; Aberdeen University. Trainee Surveyor, Renton Finlayson, 1972-74; running family farms of Tirinie and Wester Tullich, since 1973; Chair, Highland Glen Producers, 1980-90 and 2000-09; Council of Scottish Agricultural Arbiters & Valuers, 2006-13, President, 2008-10; Agricultural Arbitrator, 2006 (ACIARB); Director: National Fallen Stock Cic, 2003-2012, Moredun Research Institute, 2003-2012. Fellow of Royal Agricultural Society, 2003; MBE, 2010; Member, Agricultural Rent Review Working Group, 2012. Recreations: ornithology & wildlife; curling. Address: Tirinie, Aberfeldy, Perthshire PH15 2ND; T.-01887 830394; e-mail: idmtirinie@aol.com

Dundas-Bekker, Althea Enid Philippa; b. 4.11.39, Gorebridge; m., Aedrian Ruprecht Bekker (deceased); 2 d. Business work abroad, in London, and with the National Trust for Scotland; inherited Arniston House, 1970, and restoring ever since. Recreations: Scottish history; Scottish songs; walking dogs. Address: (h.) Arniston House, Gorebridge, Midlothian EH23 4RY; T.-01875 830238.

Dundee, 12th Earl of (Alexander Henry Scrymgeour). Hereditary Royal Standard-Bearer for Scotland; b. 5.6.49; m.; 1 s.; 3 d. Educ. Eton; St. Andrews University. Address: Farm Office, Birkhill, Cupar, Fife.

Dundonald, 15th Earl of (Iain Alexander Douglas Blair); b. 17.2.61; m., Marie Beatrice Louise Russo (divorced, 2011); 2 s.; 1 d. Educ. Wellington College; Royal Agricultural College, Cirencester. Company Director; Hon. Chilean Consul to Scotland; Founder Director, Anglo Scientific and Associated Companies, 2001-2021 (retired); Co-Founded Scientific Venture Partners, 2020. Interests: marine and rural environment; rural housing; Scottish affairs; innovation. Address: Lochnell Castle, Benderloch, Argyll.

Dunion, Kevin Harry, OBE, MA (Hons), MSc (Dist), Hon. LLD, FRSA. Honorary Professor, Centre for Freedom of Information, Dundee Law School, University of Dundee; Convener, Standards Commission for Scotland, 2015-2021; Panel Member, International Finance Corporation Access to Information Appeals Panel, 2012-2020; Member, The World Bank Access to Information Appeals Board, 2012-2020; Visiting Professor, University of Northumbria, 2012-2017; Board Member, Scottish Legal Complaints Commission, 2013-2017; Chairperson, University of St Andrews Students Association Board, 2012-2014; Lord Rector, University of St Andrews, 2008-2011; Scottish Information Commissioner, 2003-2012; Chief Executive, Friends of the Earth Scotland, 1991-2003; Honorary Senior Research Fellow, University of Strathclyde, 1998-2004; b. 20.12.55, Bridge of Allan; m., Linda Dunion (qv); 2 s.; 1 step d. Educ. St Andrew's High School, Kirkcaldy; St Andrews University; Edinburgh University. HM Inspector of Taxes, 1978-80; Administrator, Edinburgh University Students Association, 1980-84; Scottish Campaigns Manager, Oxfam, 1984-91. Editor, Radical Scotland, 1982-85; Chair: Scottish Education and Action for Development, 1990-92, Friends of the Earth International, 1996-99 (Treasurer, 1993-96); Member: Secretary of State's Advisory Group on Sustainable Development, 1996-99, Scottish Executive Ministerial Group on Sustainable Scotland, 1999-2001, Scottish Executive Cabinet Sub-Committee on Sustainable Scotland, 2001-03, Board, Scottish Natural Heritage, 2000-03, United Nations Environment and Development International Advisory Board, 1999-2002; Trustee and Board Member, Scottish Fisheries Museum; Chair, Kilrenny and Anstruther Burgh Collection. Publications: Living in the Real World: An International Role for Scotland's Parliament, 1993; Troublemakers: the Struggle for Environmental Justice in Scotland, 2003; The Democracy of War, 2007; Freedom of Information in Scotland in Practice, 2011. Address: (h.) Johnston Lodge, Hadfoot Wynd, Anstruther KY10 3AD. E-mail: kevindunion@hotmail.com

Dunipace, Sheriff Colin, LLB (Hons), DipLP, DipIT, NP. Sheriff of South Strathclyde, Dumfries and Galloway, since 2019. Educ. University of Strathclyde. Career history: Solicitor, Barrowman and Partners, 1988-1993; Solicitor-Advocate and Owner, Dunipace Brown, 1993-2019; Quality Assurance Peer Reviewer, Scottish Legal Aid Board, 2012-2019; Tutor in Professional Ethics. University of Strathclyde, 2008-2019; Legal Member, Housing and Property Chamber, 2017-2019; Dean of Airdrie Society of Solicitors, 2017-2019; Part-time Summary Sheriff, 2016-2019; Commissioner of the Scottish Criminal Cases Review Commission, 2015-2019; Immigration Judge, HM Courts and Tribunal Service (HMCTS), 2019; Solicitor member of Law Society Regulatory Committee and Convenor of Law Society Professional Conduct Committee; Member of Police Appeals Tribunal; Member of Judicial Panel of the Scottish Football Association; Judicial member of Upper Tribunal for Scotland. Recreations: hillwalking; music; history; rugby; French cinema. Address: Hamilton Sheriff Court, 4 Beckford Street, Hamilton ML3 0BT; T.-01698 282957.

Dunlop, Alastair Barr, OBE (1989), FRICS. Deputy Chairman, Lothians Ethics of Medical Research Committee, 1984-2004; General Commissioner for Income Tax, 1991-2009; Member, NHS Complaints Panel; Chairman, Paintings in Hospitals Scotland, 1991-2004; b. 27.12.33, Calcutta; m., Catriona C.L.H. MacLaurin; 1 s.; 1 d. Educ. Radley. Member, British Schools Exploring Society Expedition, Arctic Norway, 1950. National Service, 1952-54 (active service, Malaya: 2nd Lt., 1st Bn., RWK); commerce, City of London, 1954-58; agricultural student, 1959-61; Land Agent, Inverness, 1962-71 (Partner, Bingham Hughes & Macpherson); Joint Founding Director, Martin Paterson Associates Ltd., 1971; ecology studies, Edinburgh University, 1973-74. Member, Lothian Health Board, 1983-91 (Vice-Chairman, 1989-91); Scottish Member, RICS Committee for Wilson Report on Financial Institutions, 1973-74; Chairman, Edinburgh and Borders Branch, RICS, 1977; Life Member, Institute of Directors; President and Past President, Edinburgh South Conservative Association; Chairman, South Edinburgh Conservative Association, 1980-84 and 1992-00, Central and South, Scottish Conservative and Unionist Association, 1985-88; Chairman, Edinburgh Branch, World Wildlife Fund, 1982-96; elected Member, Council, National Trust for Scotland, 1992-97. Recreations: golf; reading; fine arts. Address: (h.) 12B Corrennie Drive, Edinburgh EH10 6EG; T.-0131 447 5209.

Dunlop, Eileen. Biographer and Children's Writer; b. 13.10.38, Alloa; m., Antony Kamm (deceased). Educ. Alloa Academy; Moray House College. Publications: Robinsheugh, 1975; A Flute in Mayferry Street, 1976; Fox Farm, 1978; The Maze Stone, 1982 (SAC Book Award); Clementina, 1985 (SAC Book Award); The House on the Hill, 1987 (commended, Carnegie Medal); The Valley of Deer, 1989; Finn's Island, 1991; Tales of St. Columba, 1992; Green Willow's Secret, 1993; Finn's Roman Fort, 1994; Tales of St. Patrick, 1995; Castle Gryffe, 1995; Waters of Life, 1996; The Ghost by the Sea, 1997; Warrior's Bride, 1998; A Royal Ring of Gold, 1999; Ghoul's Den, 1999; The Haunting of Alice Fairlie, 2001; Nicholas Moonlight, 2002; Weerdwood, 2003; Queen Margaret of Scotland, 2005; Robert Louis Stevenson: The Travelling Mind, 2008; Sir Walter Scott: A Life in Story, 2016; Walter Scott's The Bride of Lammermoor, 2019; Co-Author, Scottish Verse to 1800, 1985; A Book of Old Edinburgh, 1983. Recreations: reading; gardening; theatre. Address: (h.) 46 Tarmangie Drive, Dollar FK14 7BP; T.-01259 742007.

Dunlop, Forbes. Chief Operating Officer, sportscotland, since 2019; Chief Executive, Scottish Swimming, 2013-19. Career: taught, coached and tutored swimming coach education courses and was part of the team that helped secure the National Swimming Academy at the University of Stirling as a location for one of British Swimming's Intensive Training Centres; held roles at sportscotland, since 2002, including Lead Manager, Achieving Excellence, 2004-09, then Partnership Manager, Achieving Excellence, 2002-04, then Head of Sporting Pathways until 2013. Served on the Board of Directors, recently as Chairman of the British Paralympic Performance Services in the lead into the

2012 Paralympic Games. Address: sportscotland, Doges, Templeton on the Green, 62 Templeton Street, Glasgow G40 1DA; T.-0141 534 6500.

Dunlop, Juliet. Scottish freelance broadcast journalist; Correspondent, Good Morning Britain, ITV. Career history: former Presenter for the BBC, appearing on the BBC News channel, BBC World News and BBC One daytime updates, 2008-2011; fronted the interactive news headlines for the BBC's red button news service; also presented daytime news updates on BBC One; co-anchored STV's overnight coverage of the Scottish Parliamentary elections in May 2011; presenter for STV News at Six, 2011-2013; former Scotsman columnist.

Dunlop, Steve. Chief Executive, Scottish Enterprise, 2018-2020; previously Chief Executive, Scottish Canals. Career: senior positions at Newcastle City Council and Falkirk Council. A finalist in Entrepreneurial Scotland's 'Entrepreneur of the Year' award for 2017.

Dunlop, Sheriff William, LLB, QC. Sheriff of North Strathclyde, 1995-2014; b. 7.3.44, Glasgow; m., Janina Marthe; 1 s.; 2 d. Educ. High School of Glasgow; Glasgow University. Solicitor, 1968-84; called to Scottish Bar, 1985; QC, 2011. Governor, The High School of Glasgow, 1999-2012; Member, Council, Sheriffs' Association, 2001-04; International Rugby Board Match Commissioner for European Cup and Six Nations matches, 1999-2012; Chairman, Scottish Rugby Union Championship Appeals Panel, since 2000; Emeritus member, SRU Championship Appeals Panel.

Dunn, Professor Douglas Eaglesham, OBE, BA, FRSL, Hon.LLD (Dundee, 1987), Hon.DLitt (Hull, 1995). Poet, academic and critic; Emeritus Professor, St Andrews University (Professor, School of English, 1991-2008, Head of School, 1994-99); formerly Director, St Andrews Scottish Studies Institute (1993-2008); b. 23.10.42, Inchinnan. Educ. Renfrew High School; Camphill Senior Secondary School, Paisley; Hull University. Books of poems: Terry Street, 1969, The Happier Life, 1972, Love or Nothing, 1974, Barbarians, 1979, St. Kilda's Parliament, 1981, Elegies, 1985, Selected Poems, 1986, Northlight, 1988, Dante's Drum-Kit, 1993, The Donkey's Ears, 2000, The Year's Afternoon, 2000; New Selected Poems, 2003; Secret Villages (short stories), 1985; Boyfriends and Girlfriends (short stories), 1995; Andromache (translation), 1990; Poll Tax: The Fiscal Fake, 1990; Editor: Choice of Lord Byron's Verse, 1974, The Poetry of Scotland, 1979, A Rumoured City: New Poets from Hull, 1982; Two Decades of Irish Writing: a Critical Survey, 1975; The Essential Browning, 1990; Scotland: an anthology, 1991; Faber Book of Twentieth Century Scottish Poetry, 1992; Oxford Book of Scottish Short Stories, 1995; 20th Century Scottish Poems, 2000; author of plays, and TV films using commentaries in verse. Gregory Award, 1968; Somerset Maugham Award, 1972; Geoffrey Faber Memorial Prize, 1975; Hawthornden Prize, 1982; Whitbread Award for Poetry and Whitbread Book of the Year Award, 1985; Cholmondeley Award, 1989; awarded the Queen's Gold Medal for Poetry, 2013. Honorary Visiting Professor, Dundee University, 1987; Fellow in Creative Writing, St. Andrews University, 1989-91; Honorary Fellow, Humberside College, 1987. Address (b.) School of English, St. Andrews University, St. Andrews KY16 9AL.

Dunning, Claire, BA, DipM, MCIM, MCSD, FCIM, FRSA. Board Director, Strategic Marketer & Social Media Advisor, The Communications Breakfast, since 2011; former Managing Director, Dunning Creating

Sparks (1996-2014); formerly President, Glasgow Chamber of Commerce; b. 26.08.65, Glasgow; m., Julian Westaby. Educ. Bearsden Academy, Glasgow; Grays School of Art, Aberdeen; Glasgow Central College of Commerce. Management Trainee, Retail Sector, 1988-90; Sales and Marketing in Design Sector, 1990-96. Board Director: The Chartered Institute of Marketing, 2010-2014, Glasgow Chamber of Commerce, 2002-2017, Scottish Chamber of Commerce, 2007-2010. Recreations: the arts; hillwalking; gardening; animals.

Dupree, Professor Marguerite Wright, BA, MA, DPhil, FRHistS, FAcSS. Honorary Professor (School of Social and Political Sciences), University of Glasgow; b. 18.04.50, Boston, MA, USA; m., Richard Hughes Trainor; 1 s.; 1 d. Educ. Skyline High School, Oakland, California, USA; Mount Holyoke College; Princeton University; University of Oxford. Research Officer, Nuffield College, Oxford, 1977-78; Research Fellow, Emmanuel College, Cambridge, 1978-82; Fellow, Wolfson College, Cambridge, since 1982; University of Glasgow: Research Fellow, 1986-97, Senior Lecturer, 1997-2003, Reader, 2003-06; Professor, 2007-2013. Publications: Lancashire and Whitehall: the diary of Sir Raymond Streat (Editor), 1987; Family Structure in the Staffordshire Potteries, 1840-1880, 1995; Medical Lives in the Age of Surgical Revolution (Co-Author), 2007. Recreation: tennis. Address: (b.) Centre for the History of Medicine, Economic and Social History Subject Area, University of Glasgow, Lilybank House, Bute Gardens, Glasgow G12 8RT; T.-0141-330-6072.
E-mail: marguerite.dupree@glasgow.ac.uk

Durie, Roy Ross, FRICS. Consultant, Ryden, Edinburgh; b. 11.5.48, Edinburgh; m., Dorothy; 1 s.; 3 d.; 9 gc. Educ. Edinburgh Academy; Britannia Royal Naval College, Dartmouth. Royal Navy Officer (Lt. R.N.), 1966-72; joined Ryden, 1973. Elder, St. Giles, Edinburgh. Recreations: walking; swimming; sailing; skiing; golf; rugby; baby sitting. Address: 12 Pentland Avenue, Edinburgh EH13 0HZ; mobile: 07836 347247; e-mail: royrdurie@gmail.com

Durrani, Professor Tariq Salim, OBE, FRSE, FREng, FIEEE, FIET, FTWAS. Research Professor, Department of Electronic and Electrical Engineering, Strathclyde University, since 1982; b. 27.10.43, Amraoti, India; m., Clare Elizabeth; 1 s.; 2 d. Educ. Marie Colaco High School, Karachi; Engineering University, Dacca; Southampton University. Research Fellow, Southampton University, 1970-76; joined academic staff, Strathclyde University, 1976, Chairman, Department of Electronic and Electrical Engineering, 1986-90, Deputy Principal, 1990-91, and 2000-06; Director, Scottish Electronics Technology Group, 1983-2000; President, IEEE Signal Processing Society, 1993-94; Chair, IEEE Periodicals Council, 1996-98; President, IEEE Engineering Management Society, 2006-07; Vice-Chair, Technical Activities, IEEE Region 8, 2003-06; Director: Glasgow Chamber of Commerce, 2003-09, Institute for System Level Integration, 2002-09; Vice President, Royal Society of Edinburgh, 2007-2010; Director, Equality Challenge Unit, 2008-2010; Member, Scottish Funding Council, 2005-09; Director, UK National Commission for UNESCO, 2011-17; Vice President, IEEE, 2010-2011; Vice President (International), Royal Society of Edinburgh, 2012-16; Member, International Committee, Royal Academy of Engineering, 2017-2020; Member, Research Committee, Royal Academy of Engineering, since 2022; Board Member, IEEE Technology & Engineering Management Society, 2017-19; International Member, US National Academy of Engineering, since 2018; Member, Helensburgh Community Council, since 2017; Member, Helensburgh Garelochside Rotary Club, since 2017 (President, since 2020). Publications: 7 books; over 360 technical research papers. Recreation: playing occasional golf badly. Address: (b.) Department of Electronic and Electrical Engineering, Strathclyde University, Glasgow; T.-0141-548 2540.

Duthie, Sheriff Euan, QC. Sheriff at Tayside, Central and Fife, since 2021. Educ. University of St Andrews; University of Edinburgh. Practised with Burness Solicitors until 2005; Lord Reid Scholar, calling to the Bar in 2006; as a Royal Naval Reserve officer in 2010, worked in Kenya on Somali piracy trials; joined Axiom Advocates in 2007; appointed Standing Junior Counsel to the Advocate General in 2012; appointed Fee-paid judge of the First-tier Tribunal in 2014; appointed Queen's Counsel in 2019. Scottish Editor of Mithani: Directors Disqualification. Address: Perth Sheriff Court House, Tay Street, Perth PH2 8NL; T.-01738 620546.

Duthie, Peter. Group Chief Executive, Scottish Event Campus Limited, since 2014; Director, Glasgow Chamber of Commerce; b. 4.59; m.; 2 d. Address: Scottish Event Campus, Glasgow G3 8YW.

Duthie, Sir Robert (Robin) Grieve, CBE (1978), CA, LLD, CBIM, FRSA, FRIAS, DTech (Napier). Chairman, RG Duthie & Co. Ltd., since 1984; b. 2.10.28, Greenock; m., Violetta Noel Maclean; 2 s.; 1 d. Educ. Greenock Academy. Apprentice Chartered Accountant, Thomson Jackson Gourlay and Taylor, CA, 1946-51; joined Blacks of Greenock, 1952; appointed Managing Director, 1962; Chairman, Black & Edgington, 1972-83. Chairman, Inverkip Society, 1966; Director, Greenock Chamber of Commerce, 1966; Member, Clyde Port Authority, 1971-83 (Chairman, 1977-80); Director, Royal Bank of Scotland plc, 1978-98; Director, British Assets Trust plc, 1977-98; Chairman, Scottish Development Agency, 1979-88; Chairman, Britoil PLC, 1988-90; Vice Chairman, BP Advisory Board Scotland, 1990-2001; Chairman, Neill Clerk Group plc, 1993-98; Director, Greenock Provident Bank, 1969-75 (Chairman, 1975); Director, Devol Engineering Ltd., 1993-2003; Member, Scottish Telecommunications Board, 1972-77; Council Member, Institute of Chartered Accountants of Scotland, 1973-78; Member: East Kilbride Development Corporation, 1976-78, Strathclyde Region Local Valuation Appeal Panel, 1976-83; CBI Tax Liaison Officer for Scotland, 1976-79; Chairman, Made Up Textile Association of Great Britain, 1972; Member: British Institute of Management Scottish Committee, 1976, Glasgow and West of Scotland Committee, Scottish Council (Development and Industry), 1975-79; Chairman, Greenock Club, 1972; Captain, Greenock Cricket Club, 1960-61; Commissioner, Queen Victoria School, Dunblane, 1972-89; Commissioner, Scottish Congregational Ministers Pension Fund, 1973-2003; Member, Scottish Economic Council, 1980-96; Member of Council, Royal Caledonian Curling Club, 1984-88; Treasurer, Greenock West URC, since 1970. Awarded Honorary Degree of Doctor of Laws, Strathclyde University, 1984. Recreation: golf. Address: (h.) Fairhaven, 181 Finnart Street, Greenock, PA16 8JA; T.-01475 722642.

Dye, Jonathan, BSc (Hons), CA. Head of Assurance Services, Heriot-Watt University, since 2017; Head of Finance, Citizens Advice Scotland, 2013-2016, Head of Financial Governance, 2009-2011; Deputy Chairman, English-Speaking Union of the Commonwealth, 2011-15; Chairman, English-Speaking Union, Scotland, 2003-09; Treasurer, Edinburgh City Youth Cafe, 1997-2003; Chartered Accountant, Pricewaterhousecoopers, 1993-2003, National Australia Bank, since 2003; Head of Sarbanes-Oxley Compliance, NAB UK, 2007-09; Member, Security Board, Association of Payment and Clearing Services (APACS), 2004-07; Board Member, LGBT Health and Wellbeing Scotland; b. 29.5.71, Dundee. Educ. Harris Academy, Dundee; St. Andrews University.

Dyer, Rt Rev Anne Catherine, MA (Oxon), MTh. Bishop of Aberdeen and Orkney, since 2018; b. 2.57, Bradford; m., Roger; 1 d. Educ. Bradford Girls' Grammar School; St Anne's College, Oxford. Career: worked as a business analyst/systems analyst at Unilever; entered Wycliffe Hall, Oxford, an Evangelical Anglican theological college, to train for ordained ministry in 1984; also studied theology; left theological college in 1987 to be ordained in the Church of England; continued theological studies, and completed a Master of Theology (MTh) degree at King's College, London in 1989; ordained in the Church of England as a deacon in 1987 and as a priest in 1994; appointed an associate adviser in evangelism for the diocese in 1993; also an NSM of St Barnabas' Church, Istead Rise, 1994-98; Ministry Development Officer for the Diocese of Rochester, 1998-2004; appointed an Honorary Canon of Rochester Cathedral in 2000; Warden, Cranmer Hall, Durham, a theological college of the Church of England, 2005-2011; Honorary Canon, Durham Cathedral, 2008-2011; Rector of Holy Trinity Church, Haddington, East Lothian in the Diocese of Edinburgh, 2011-2018. Address: Diocese of Aberdeen and Orkney, University of Aberdeen, Marischal College, Broad Street, Aberdeen AB10 1YS.

Dysart, 13th Earl of (John Peter Grant of Rothiemurchus), DL. Landowner; b. 22.10.46, Rothiemurchus; m., Philippa; 1 s.; 2 d. Educ. Gordonstoun. Chairman and Director, Scot Trout Limited, 1989-95; Past Chairman, Highland Region, Forestry, Farming and Wildlife Advisory Group; Patron, Highland Hospice; Vice-President, Scottish Landowners' Federation, 1991-2004; Deputy Lieutenant, Districts of Lochaber, Inverness, Badenoch and Strathspey, 1986-2001; Member: Council, National Trust for Scotland, 1990-95, Native Woodlands Advisory Panel to the Forestry Commission, 1993-97, National Access Forum, 1993-99, Cairngorm Partnership, 1995-2003; Chairman, Tourism and Enivronment Task Force, 1995-98; President, Royal Zoological Society of Scotland, 1996-2006. Recreations: skiing; hill walking. Address: (b.) Doune of Rothiemurchus, by Aviemore, Inverness-shire PH22 1QP.

E

Eadie, Jim. MSP (SNP), Edinburgh Southern, 2011-16; b. 10.2.68, Glasgow. Educ. Waverley Secondary School; University of Strathclyde. Career history: worked for the Royal College of Nursing and Scottish Television, before becoming head of the Scottish branch of the Association of the British Pharmaceutical Industry in 2002; started healthcare consulting business in 2007.

Eagles, Professor John Mortimer, MBChB, MPhil, FRCPsych. Retired Honorary Professor, Mental Health, Aberdeen University (2007-2011); Consultant Psychiatrist, Royal Cornhill Hospital, Aberdeen, 1985-2011; Honorary Reader, Mental Health, Aberdeen University, 2000-07; b. 21.10.52, Newport-on-Tay; m., Janette Isobel Rorke; 2 d. Educ. Bell-Baxter High School, Cupar; Aberdeen University; Edinburgh University. Resident House Officer posts, Aberdeen, 1977-78; Senior House Officer/Registrar in Psychiatry, Royal Edinburgh Hospital, 1978-82; Lecturer, Department of Mental Health, Aberdeen University, 1982-85; Honorary Senior Lecturer, Department of Mental Health, Aberdeen University, 1985-2000; Psychiatric Tutor for trainee psychiatrists, Aberdeen, 1987-92. Chairman, North-East Regional Postgraduate Medical Education Committee, 1990-95; former Chair, Scottish Division, Royal College of Psychiatrists Undergraduate Student Teaching and Recruitment Group; Non-Executive Director, Temple Medical, Aberdeen. Author of novel Starting To Shrink. Recreations: cricket; golf; travel; reading; creative writing. Address: (h.) 41 Binghill Park, Milltimber, Aberdeenshire AB13 0EE.

Eassie, Rt. Hon. Lord (Ronald Mackay). Senator of the College of Justice, 1997-2015; formerly Chairman, the Scottish Law Commission; b. 1945; m.; 1 s. Educ. Berwickshire High School; St. Andrews University; Edinburgh University. Admitted, Faculty of Advocates, 1972; QC, 1986.

Eastmond, Clifford John, BSc, MD, FRCP, FRCPE, OStJ. Retired Consultant Rheumatologist; previous appointments: Associate Medical Director and Consultant Rheumatologist, NHS Grampian (Clinical Director of Medicine, 1995-99); Clinical Senior Lecturer, Aberdeen University; private practice, Albyn Hospital, Aberdeen; b. 19.1.45, Ashton-under-Lyne; m., Margaret Wadsworth; 2 s.; 1 d. Educ. Audenshaw Grammar School; Edinburgh University. House Officer posts, Edinburgh, one year; moved to Liverpool for further training, subsequently to Rheumatism Unit, Leeds. Elder, Church of Scotland; Past President, Westhill and District Rotary Club; Paul Harris Fellow; Director, Seabank House, Aberdeen, since 2007, Vice Chairman, since 2019; Member, Aberdeen and North East Committee of Order of St John. Clubs: Royal Northern and University Club, Aberdeen; The Cairngorm Club. Publications: scientific papers and book chapters on rheumatology topics. Recreations: skiing; hill-walking; music; shooting; curling. Address: (h.) The Rowans, Skene, Aberdeenshire AB32 6YP; T.-01224 790370.

Easton, Rev. Dr David. Interim Moderator, Glasgow Cathedral, since 2017. Address: Glasgow Cathedral, Castle Street, Glasgow G4 0QZ; T.-0141 552 8198.

Easton, Robin Gardner, OBE, MA, DUniv, DipEd. Rector, The High School of Glasgow, 1983-2004; b. 6.10.43, Glasgow; m., Eleanor Mary McIlroy; 1 s.; 1 d. Educ. Kelvinside Academy; Sedbergh School; Christ's College, Cambridge; Wadham College, Oxford. Teacher of French and German, Melville College, Edinburgh, 1966-72; Housemaster and Deputy Head, French Department, Daniel Stewart's and Melville College, 1972-78; Head, Modern Languages, George Watson's College, 1979-83. Elder, Church of Scotland; former Member, Glasgow Children's Panel, Glasgow University Court, Scripture Union Scotland Board; Glasgow Street Pastor. Recreations: preaching; politics (Scottish Independence); history; hill walking. Address: (h.) 21 Stirling Drive, Bearsden, Glasgow G61 4NU; T.-0141-943 0368.

Eddie, Rev. Duncan Campbell, MA (Hons), BD (Hons). Minister, Holburn West, Aberdeen, since 1999; Moderator, Presbytery of Aberdeen, 2015-16; b. 17.2.63, Fraserburgh; m., Dr. Carol Buchanan; 2 s. Educ. Mackie Academy, Stonehaven; Aberdeen University; Edinburgh University. Assistant Minister, Edinburgh, 1990-91; Minister, Old Cumnock: Crichton West linked with St. Ninian's, 1992-99. Recreations: music; reading. Address: 9 Ashley Park Drive, Aberdeen AB10 6RY; T.-01224 571120.
E-mail: minister@holburnwestchurch.org.uk

Edie, Paul. Chair, Care Inspectorate, since 2013; Director, Edie Associates, 2016-2021; Councillor, City of Edinburgh Council, Lothian Regional Council, 1994-2017; b. 9.64. Educ. St Augustine's; Napier University. Career: Non Executive Director, NHS Lothian, 2007-2012; Convenor of Health, Social Care and Housing, City of Edinburgh Council, 2007-2012; Local Community Planning Engagement Officer, East Lothian Council, 2012-2013. Member of the Board, Edinburgh International Film Festival, 2001-2010; Audit Officer, Intellectual Property and Licensing Associate, Assay Technician, Scottish National Blood Transfusion Service, 1988-2007; Health Care Improvement Scotland Board, since 2013; Scottish Social Services Council Member, since 2013. Address: Care Inspectorate, Compass House, 11 Riverside Drive, Dundee DD1 4NY; T.-0845 600 9527.
E-mail: enquiries@careinspectorate.com

Edward, Rt. Hon. Sir David Alexander Ogilvy, KCMG, QC, LLD, FRSE; b. 14.11.34, Perth; m., Elizabeth Young McSherry; 2 s.; 2 d. Educ. Sedbergh School; University College, Oxford; University of Edinburgh. National Service, RNVR, 1955-57 (Sub-Lt.); Advocate, 1962; Clerk, Faculty of Advocates, 1967-70, Treasurer, 1970-77; Queen's Counsel, 1974; President, Consultative Committee, Bars and Law Societies of the European Community, 1978-80; Salvesen Professor of European Institutions, University of Edinburgh, 1985-89; Professor Emeritus, 2008; Judge of the Court of First Instance of EC, 1989-92; Judge of the Court of Justice of EC, 1992-2004; Temporary Judge of the Court of Session, 2004-09. Member, Panel of Arbitrators, International Centre for Settlement of Investment Disputes, 1981-89, 2004-; Chairman, Continental Assets Trust plc, 1986-89; Director, Adam & Company plc, 1984-89; Director, Harris Tweed Association Ltd., 1985-89; Specialist Adviser to House of Lords Select Committee on the European Communities, 1985-88; Member: British Council Law Advisory Committee, 1974-88, Scotland Advisory Committee, 2008-2014; Trustee: National Library of Scotland, 1966-95, Industry and Parliament Trust, 1995-2013 (Vice President, since 2013), Carnegie Trust for the Universities of Scotland, 1995-2015 (Chairman, 2003-2015), Hopetoun Foundation, 1992-2010 (Chairman, Hopetoun Preservation Trust, 1988-92); Chairman, Scottish Council of Independent Schools 2005-2010; President, Franco-Scottish Society, 1996-2015 (Hon. President, since 2015); President, Johnson Society, 1995-96; President, Edinburgh Sir Walter Scott Club, 2001-02; Patron, Scottish European Educational Trust, since 2014; Hon. Bencher,

Gray's Inn, 1992; Hon. LLD: Edinburgh University, 1993, Aberdeen University, 1997, Napier University, 1998, Glasgow University, 2003, St Andrews University, 2015; Dr. h.c.: Universität des Saarlandes, 2001, Westfälische Wilhelms-Universität Munster, 2001; Doctor of the University (D Univ) honoris causa Surrey, 2003; Knight Commander of the Order of St Michael & St George, 2004 (CMG. 1981); Privy Counsellor, 2005; Officier de l'Ordre de la Légion d'Honneur and Chevalier de l'Ordre des Arts et des Lettres (France) 2012; Fellow of the Royal Society of Edinburgh, 1990 (Royal Medallist, 2005); Convener, International Committee, 2008-2013. Vice-President: British Institute of International and Comparative Law; Member: the Calman Commission on Scottish Devolution, 2008-09, the Commission on a Bill of Rights, 2011-12; Hon. President, Scottish Arbitration Centre, since 2011; Member, First Minister's Standing Council on Europe, since 2016. Address: (h.) 32 Heriot Row, Edinburgh EH3 6ES; T.-0131-225 7153; e-mail: david.edward@dileas.net

Edward, Ian, MA, LLB. Solicitor (retired); b. 3.9.35, Aberdeen; m., 1, Marguerite Anne Leiper (deceased); m., 2, Gudrun Clapier; 2 s.; 1 d. Educ. Robert Gordon's College, Aberdeen; University of Aberdeen; Fitzwilliam College, University of Cambridge. HM Colonial Service (District Officer, Northern Rhodesia), 1959-63; C. & P. H. Chalmers, Solicitors, Aberdeen (now Ledingham Chalmers): Legal Assistant, Partner, Senior Partner, Consultant, 1963-2000. Part-time Chairman of Employment Tribunals, 1997-2004; sometime historian, Royal Aberdeen Golf Club. Recreations: hill-walking; golfing; gardening. Address: (h.) 23 St. Fillan's Terrace, Edinburgh EH10 5PJ; T.-0131-447 8353.

Edward, John David, MA (Hons) St Andrews, MPhil (Glasgow). Director/Chief Executive of Scottish Council of Independent Schools, since 2010; b. 22.09.68, Edinburgh; m., Alexandra Angulo Noriega; 1 s.; 1 d. Educ. The Edinburgh Academy; University of St Andrews; University of Glasgow; Università per Stranieri, Siena. European Community Humanitarian Office (ECHO), 1994-95; The European Policy Centre, Brussels, 1995-96; EU Policy Manager, Scotland Europa, Brussels, 1996-2001; Parliamentary Manager, Scottish Enterprise, 2002-03; Head of European Parliament Office in Scotland, Edinburgh, 2003-09; Senior Campaign Spokesman, Scotland Stronger in Europe, 2016; Scotland Advisor, Open Britain, 2016-18. Member: The Steel Commission, 2003-06; Campbell Commission on Home and Community Rule, 2011-2012; Member, Commission on Parliamentary Reform, 2017; Trustee, Scottish European Educational Trust, since 2011; Member of Business Committee, General Council, University of St Andrews, since 2021. Recreations: rugby; matters European and Colombian. Address: (b.) The Scottish Council of Independent Schools (SCIS), 1 St Colme Street, Edinburgh EH3 6AA; T.-0131 556 2316. E-mail: john@scis.org.uk; web: johnedward.com

Edwards, Professor Kevin John, MA, PhD, DSc, FRGS, FRSGS, FSA, FSAScot, FRSE, MAE. Emeritus Professor in Physical Geography, University of Aberdeen (appointed Professor in 2000); Adjunct Chair in Archaeology, since 2007; Adjunct Professor, Graduate School in Anthropology, City University of New York, since 2002; Life Member, Clare Hall, University of Cambridge, since 2012, Fellow Commoner, since 2020; Institute Associate of the Scott Polar Research Institute, since 2018; Senior Fellow, McDonald Institute for Archaeological Research, since 2019, University of Cambridge; Coppock Research Medal and Honorary Fellowship, Royal Scottish Geographical Society, 2018; b. 18.9.49, Dartford; 2 s. Educ. Northfleet Boys' School; Gravesend Grammar School; St. Andrews University;

Aberdeen University. Tutorial Fellow in Geography, University of Aberdeen, 1972-75; Lecturer in Environmental Reconstruction and Research Member, Palaeoecology Centre, Queen's University of Belfast, 1975-80; University of Birmingham: Lecturer in Biogeography, 1980-90, Senior Lecturer in Geography, 1990-92, Reader in Palaeoecology, 1992-94; Honorary Research Fellow, Limnological Research Center, University of Minnesota, 1983; Professor of Palaeoecology, Department of Archaeology and Prehistory, University of Sheffield, 1994-2000 (Head of Department, 1996-99); Visiting Researcher, Department of Geography and Geology, University of Copenhagen, 2007-09; Visiting Fellow, Clare Hall and Visiting Scholar, McDonald Institute for Archaeological Research, University of Cambridge, 2011-2012; Christensen Fellow, St Catherine's College, University of Oxford, 2012; 133rd Rhind Lecturer, Society of Antiquaries of Scotland/Royal Society of Edinburgh, 2012. Member, NERC Radiocarbon Dating Laboratory Committees, 1995-2000; Chairman, Oxford University Radiocarbon Accelerator Unit Users' Committee, 1995-2000; Deputy Chairman, SCAPE Trust, 2001-04; Panel Member for Geography and Environmental Studies, UK Research Assessment Exercise (RAE2008) and for Geography, Environmental Studies and Archaeology, UK Research Excellence Framework (REF2014). Publications: Quaternary History of Ireland (Co-Editor), 1985; Scotland: Environment and Archaeology 8000BC-AD1000 (Co-Editor), 1997; Holocene Environments of Prehistoric Britain (Co-Editor), 1999; Historical Human Ecology of the Faroe Islands (Editor), 2005; The Vikings (Co-Author), 2019; James Croll – from janitor to genius (Editor) 2021; numerous articles in geography, archaeology, botany and quaternary science of the British Isles and the North Atlantic area. Recreations: reading; family history.
E-mail: kevin.edwards@abdn.ac.uk

Edwards, Rob (Robert Philip), MA. Freelance Journalist, since 1980; Founder Member and Director, The Ferret (www.theferret.scot), since 2015; b. 13.10.53, Liverpool; m., Fiona Grant Riddoch; 2 d. Educ. Watford Boys Grammar School; Jesus College, University of Cambridge. Organiser, Scottish Campaign to Resist the Atomic Menace, 1977-78; Campaigns Organiser, Shelter (Scotland), 1978-80; Research Assistant to Robin Cook, 1980-83; Freelance Journalist, writing for Social Work Today, The Scotsman, New Statesman, 1980-89; Environment Editor, Scotland on Sunday, 1989-94; Correspondent, The Guardian and Columnist, Edinburgh Evening News, 1989-94; Consultant, New Scientist, 1994-2015; Environment Editor, Sunday Herald, 1999-2018; Journalist with The Ferret from 2015; various media awards. Publications: Co-author of three books, including Still Fighting for Gemma, 1995. Recreations: music; opera; mountains. Address: 53 Nile Grove, Edinburgh EH10 4RE; T.-0131-447 2796; e-mail: rob.edwards@blueyonder.co.uk
Website: www.robedwards.com

Eglinton and Winton, Earl of (Hugh Archibald William Montgomerie), MBA; b. 24.7.66; m., Carol Anne Robinson; 3 c. Educ. University of Edinburgh. Shipping operations manager, Royal Navy (retired from the military in 1993); succeeded as the 20th Lord Montgomerie on 14 June 2018; succeeded as the 7th Earl of Winton on 14 June 2018; succeeded as the 8th Baron Ardrossan, of Ardrossan, on 14 June 2018; succeeded as the 19th Earl of Eglinton on 14 June 2018.

Eilbeck, Professor John Christopher, BA, PhD, FRSE. Professor Emeritus, Department of Mathematics, Heriot-Watt University, since 2010 (Head of Department, 1984-89,

Dean of Science, 1998-2001); b. 8.4.45, Whitehaven; 3 s. Educ. Whitehaven Grammar School; Queen's College, Oxford; Lancaster University. Royal Society European Fellow, ICTP, Trieste, 1969-70; Research Assistant, Department of Mathematics, UMIST, Manchester, 1970-73; Heriot-Watt University: Lecturer, Department of Mathematics, 1973-80, Senior Lecturer, 1980-85, Reader, 1985-86; Long-term Visiting Fellow, Center for Nonlinear Studies, Los Alamos National Laboratory, New Mexico, 1983-84; Visiting Fellow, Corpus Christi College, Cambridge, 2001. Publications: Rock Climbing in the Lake District (Co-author), 1975; Solitons and Nonlinear Wave Equations (Co-author), 1982. Recreation: mountaineering. Address: (b.) Department of Mathematics, Heriot-Watt University, Riccarton, Edinburgh EH14 4AS; T.-0131-451 3220.

Elder, Professor Andrew, FRCPE, FRCPSG, FRCP, FACP, FICP(Hon), FAMM, BSc, MBCHB, Medicine. President, Royal College of Physicians of Edinburgh, 2020 and since 2021. Educ. The University of Edinburgh. Career history: Consultant Physician, NHS Scotland, since 1992; Clinician Adviser, Scottish Public Services Ombudsman, 2008-2018; Medical Director, MRCP (UK), 2014-18; Visiting Professor, The Stanford Program in Bedside Medicine, Stanford University of Medicine, since 2013; Honorary Professor, The University of Edinburgh, since 2015; Presence CASBS Fellow and Scholar, Center for Advanced Study in the Behavioral Sciences, Stanford University, since 2018. Address: Royal College of Physicians of Edinburgh, 9 Queen Street, Edinburgh EH2 1JQ; T.-0131 225 7324; e-mail: president@rcpe.ac.uk

Elder, Dorothy-Grace. MSP, Glasgow, 1999-2003 (Independent, formerly SNP MSP); newspaper columnist; television scriptwriter and producer (documentaries); Hon. Professor, The Robert Gordon University, Aberdeen, since 2006; m., George Welsh; 1 s.; 2 d. D.C. Thomson newspapers; Glasgow Herald as reporter, investigations writer, news feature writer, leader writer; TV and radio news, BBC Scotland; feature writer and columnist, Scottish Daily News Co-operative; campaigns feature writer and columnist, Sunday Mail; Columnist "Rattling the Cages", Scotland on Sunday; productions for Scotland and the network, BBC and Scottish TV. Honorary President, Glasgow NE Multiple Sclerosis Society; Oliver Award winning columnist, 1995-96; British Reporter of the Year (Investigations), UK Press Awards, 1996-97; citation, Humanitarian Aid Work, City of Pushkin, Russia, 1998, 1999; Medical Journalists' Association UK award for campaigns for pain patients 2014; Founder, Scottish Parliament Cross Party Group on Chronic Pain (Hon. Secretary, since 2001); Lifetime Achievement Award, Scottish Press Awards, 2019.
E-mail: dg.elder@ntlworld.com

Elgin, 11th Earl of, and Kincardine, 15th Earl of, (Andrew Douglas Alexander Thomas Bruce), KT (1981), Chevalier de la Légion d'honneur (2016), CD (1979), DL, JP; 37th Chief of the Name of Bruce; Captain, Queen's Bodyguard for Scotland (Royal Company of Archers); b. 17.2.24; m., Victoria Usher; 3 s.; 2 d. Educ. Eton; Balliol College, Oxford. Lord Lieutenant of Fife, 1987-99; President, Scottish Amicable Life Assurance Society, 1975-94; Chairman: National Savings Committee for Scotland, 1972-78, Lloyds TSB Foundation, 1986-99; Member, Scottish Postal Board, 1980-96; Lord High Commissioner, General Assembly, Church of Scotland, 1980-81; Grand Master Mason of Scotland, 1961-65; President, Royal Caledonian Curling Club, 1968-69; President, Boys Brigade (UK), 1963-85; Hon. LLD, Dundee, 1977, Glasgow, 1983. Address: (h.) Broomhall, Dunfermline KY11 3DU; T.-01383 872222; e-mail: elginkincardine@gmail.com

Eliott of Redheugh, Margaret Frances Boswell. Chief of Clan Elliot; Chairman, Elliot Clan Society and Sir Arthur Eliott Memorial Trust; Deputy Lieutenant of Roxburgh, Ettrick & Lauderdale; Member, Standing Council of Scottish Chiefs; Trustee, Boswell Museum & Mausoleum Trust, Boswell Book Festival and the Roxburgh Landward Benevolent Trust; b. 13.11.48; m., 1, Anthony Vaughan-Arbuckle (deceased); 1 s.; 1 d.; 2, Christopher Powell Wilkins. Educ. Hatherop Castle School. Address: Redheugh, Newcastleton, Roxburghshire.

Elliot, Dr Alison Janet, CBE, MA, MSc, PhD, LLD, DD, DUniv, FRCPEdin, FRSE; b. 27.11.48, Edinburgh; m., John Christian Elliot; 1 s.; 1 d. Educ. Bathgate Academy; Edinburgh University; Sussex University. Research Associate, Department of Linguistics, Edinburgh University, 1973-74; Lecturer in Psychology, Lancaster University, 1974-76, Edinburgh University, 1977-85; Convener, Church and Nation Committee, Church of Scotland, 1996-2000; Moderator of the General Assembly of the Church of Scotland, 2004-05; Honorary Fellow, New College, University of Edinburgh, 2001-2020; Associate Director, Centre for Theology and Public Issues, University of Edinburgh, 2001-2017; Convener, Scottish Council for Voluntary Organisations (SCVO), 2007-2013; Chair, Land Reform Review Group, 2012-14; Chair: Scottish Fundraising Standards Panel, 2016-18, International Futures Forum, 2017-19; General Secretary, Royal Society of Edinburgh, 2018-2021. Publications: Child Language, 1981; The Miraculous Everyday, 2005. Recreations: music; cookery. E-mail: alison.j.elliot@gmail.com

Elliot, Bob. Director, OneKind, since October 2018. Career history: Head, Warden Farne Islands, National Trust; Senior Ranger and Countryside Manager, The National Trust for Scotland, 1992-93; Senior Operations Manager, Loch Lomond & The Trossachs National Park, 1993-2004; Head of Investigations, Scotland, RSPB, 2004-2007; Head of Investigations and Head of Conservation Programmes, RSPB, 2007-2012; Animal Welfare Campaigner and Conservationist, 2012-18. Address: OneKind, 50 Montrose Terrace, Edinburgh EH7 5DL; T.-0131 661 9734.

Elliott, Professor Robert F., BA (Oxon), MA (Leeds), FRSE. Emeritus Professor of Economics, Aberdeen University (Director, Health Economics Research Unit, 2001-2012); b. Thurlow, Suffolk; m., Susan Elliott Gutteridge; 1 s. Educ. Haverhill Secondary Modern School, Suffolk; Ruskin College and Balliol College, Oxford; Leeds University. Joined Aberdeen University, 1973, as Research Fellow, then Lecturer; Director, Scottish Doctoral Programme in Economics, 1989-99; Member, Training Board, ESRC, 1995-99; Chair of Reviews for, and Consultant to, many public and private sector organisations, including Megaw Committee of Inquiry into Civil Service Pay, the EEC Commission, HM Treasury OECD, HIDB, DETR, Police Federation of England and Wales, Scottish Police Federation, McCrone Committee and WHO; President, Scottish Economic Society, 2002-05; Commissioner, Low Pay Commission, 2007-2015. Publications: books on Pay in the Public Sector, 1981; Incomes Policies, Inflation and Relative Pay, 1981; Incomes Policy, 1981; Unemployment and Labour Market Efficiency, 1989; Labour Economics: a comparative test, 1991; Public Sector Pay Determination in the EU, 1999; Advances in Health Economics, 2003; Decentralised Pay Setting, 2003. Recreations: music; reading; hill-walking; golf. Address: (h.) 11 Richmondhill Place, Aberdeen AB15 5EN.

Ellis, Tim. Deputy Director, Performance and Outcomes, Scottish Government, since 2018. Career: Head of FOI

Unit, Scottish Executive, 2003-06; Senior Manager, Communities Scotland, 2006-08; Deputy Director, Housing Investment, The Scottish Government, 2008-2010; Head of Cabinet and Corporate Secretariat, The Scottish Government, 2011-13; Chief Executive, Keeper and Registrar General, National Records of Scotland, 2013-18. Address: St Andrew's House, Regent Road, Edinburgh EH1 3DG; T.-0131 244 9094.

Elphinstone, 19th Lord (Alexander Mountstuart Elphinstone); b. 15.4.80; m., Nicola Hall; 3 c. Educ. Belhaven Hill School; Eton College; Newcastle University; SOAS, University of London. Succeeded to title, 1994.

Elvidge, Sir John William, KCB, FRSE, BA. Chairman, Edinburgh Airport Limited, since 2012; Permanent Secretary, Scottish Government, 2003-2010; b. 9.2.51, London; m., Maureen Margaret Ann McGinn. Educ. Sir George Monoux School; St Catherine's College, Oxford. Scottish Office, 1973-88; Director of Implementation, Scottish Homes, 1988-89; Scottish Office, 1989-98, latterly as Head of Economic Infrastructure Group, Scottish Office Development Department; Cabinet Office, 1998-99 (Deputy Head of Economic and Domestic Secretariat); Head, Scottish Executive Education Department, 1999-2002; Head, Scottish Executive Finance and Central Services Department, 2002-03. Recreations: reading; theatre; music; film; painting; food; wine; sport; walking. Address: Edinburgh Airport Limited, Edinburgh EH12 9DN.

Emslie, Rt. Hon. Lord; Hon. (George) Nigel (Hannington) Emslie, PC (2011). Senator of the College of Justice in Scotland, 2001-2012 (retired); b. 17.4.47. Admitted, Faculty of Advocates, 1972; QC (Scotland), 1986; Dean, Faculty of Advocates, 1997-2001.

Emslie, Donald Gordon. Executive Chairman, Castle Hotel Management Company; Director, The Edinburgh Tourism Action Group, since 2019; Chairman, Thorpe Hall Leisure Ltd; Chief Executive, SMG plc, July 2006-March 2007; Chief Executive, SMG Television, 1999-July 2006; Managing Director, Broadcasting, Scottish TV, 1997-99; b. 8.5.57; m., Sarah; 2 d. Appointed to SMG plc Board, 1999; Ex Chairman, ITV Council; Ex Chairman, The Royal Lyceum Theatre Company; Ex Chairman, Royal Zoological Society Scotland; Chair of Edinburgh Tourism Action Group (ETAG); Non Executive Director: Scottish Rugby plc, 2008-2012, Scottish Water, 2008-2016; former Director, joint board, Scottish Arts Council and Scottish Screen Skillset UK; Fellow, Royal Television Society; Fellow, Royal Society of Arts; awarded Honorary Doctorate, DBA, Robert Gordon University Aberdeen, 2010. Address: (b.) 32 Drumsheugh Gardens, Edinburgh EH3 7RN.

Engstrand, Nigel, BA Hons (Eng), PGCE. Rector, Inverness Royal Academy, since 2016. Educ. Penlan Comprehensive School, Swansea; The Marine Society; Coleg Harlech, Gwynedd; University of Wales Trinity Saint David; University of Wales, Bangor; University of Edinburgh; Education Scotland. Career history: Soldier, British Army, 1980-82; Seaman, Merchant Navy, 1982-90; Principal Teacher of English, Fife Council, 2002-05; Depute Rector, Buckie High School, 2005-2011; Rector, Speyside High School, 2011-15. Address: Inverness Royal Academy, Culduthel Road, Inverness IV2 6RE; T.-01463 222884.

Entwistle, Raymond Marvin, OBE, FCIB, FCIBS. Former Chairman, Scoban plc (now Hampden & Co. plc), 2010-18; former Chairman, Adam & Company Group (2005-10); Managing Director, Adam & Company Group plc, 1993-2004; b. 12.6.44, Croydon; m., Barbara Joan Hennessy; 2 s.; 1 d. Educ. John Ruskin Grammar School. Several

managerial appointments with Lloyds Bank. Governor, Edinburgh College of Art, 1989-99; Chairman, Fruit Market Gallery, Edinburgh, 1988-2000; Non-executive Director: John Davidson (Holdings) Ltd, 1992-96, JW International Plc., 1995-96, Dunedin Smaller Companies Investment Trust PLC, 1998-2014, I & H Brown Ltd, since 2003; Chairman, Scottish Civic Trust, 2003-2012; Trustee, Victim Support Scotland Campaign Board, 2008-2014; Chairman: Bonhams Scotland, 2016-2020, Revverbank Advisory Board, 2019; Trustee, RHS Preservation Trust, since 2015. Recreations: golf; shooting; fishing; antiques.

Erdal, David Edward, MA, MBA, PhD. Trustee, Russell Trust (Chairman, 1985-96); b. 29.3.48, Umtali, Zimbabwe; m. (1), Susie; 1 s.; 1 d.; m. (2), Jennie (deceased); 3 stepchildren: 2 d.; 1 s. Educ. Glenalmond; Brasenose College, Oxford; Harvard Business School; University of St. Andrews. English Language Teacher, London, 1972-74; Tianjin Foreign Language Institute, People's Republic of China, 1974-76; Tullis Russell Group, 1977-2004 (Director, 1981-2004; Chairman, 1985-96); Baxi Partnership Ltd, 1987-2012 (Director, 1994-2012, Chairman, 1994-99); Childbase CASP Trust, 2007-2013 (Chairman, 2007-2013); Chancellor's Assessor, University of St Andrews, 2010-14. Fellow, Royal Society of Arts. Publication: 'Local Heroes: how Loch Fyne Oysters embraced employee ownership and business success', 2008; 'Beyond the Corporation: Humanity Working', 2011. Recreations: sailing; reading; coastal rowing. Address: (h.) 11 High Street West, Anstruther KY10 3DJ; e-mail: david@erdal.org.uk

Erroch, Bruce, QC, LLB (Hons). Sheriff, North Strathclyde at Paisley, since 2021. Educ. University of Glasgow. Career history: solicitor until 1997; admitted to the Faculty of Advocates in 1998; civil practice before entering the Crown Office as an advocate depute in 2009; appointed senior advocate depute in 2013. Convener of the Mental Health Tribunal; legal chair of the Scottish Social Services Council; a legal member of the Parole Board for Scotland; took silk in 2018. Address: Paisley Sheriff Court, St James Street, Paisley PA3 2HW; T.-0141 887 5291.

Erroll, 24th Earl of (Merlin Sereld Victor Gilbert Hay). Hereditary Lord High Constable of Scotland; Chief of Scottish Clan Hay; b. 20.4.48; m.; 2 s.; 2 d. Educ. Eton; Trinity College, Cambridge. Succeeded to title, 1978.

Erskine, Professor Andrew William, MA, DPhil (Oxon). Professor of Ancient History, University of Edinburgh, since 2007; m., Michelle; 1 s. Educ. Southend High School, Southend-on-Sea; New College, Oxford. Lecturer, University of Birmingham, 1986-89; University of Wales Fellow, 1989-90; Lecturer, University College Dublin, 1990-2002; Alexander Von Humboldt Fellow, University of Munich, 1997-98; Professor of Classics, National University of Ireland Galway, 2002-04; Reader, University of Edinburgh, 2005-07; Leverhulme Research Fellow, 2008-09, 2021-22. Publications: The Hellenistic Stoa: Political Thought and Action, 1990; Troy Between Greece and Rome, 2001; A Companion to the Hellenistic World, 2003; A Companion to Ancient History, 2009; Roman Imperialism, 2010; Form and Function in Roman Oratory, 2010 (Co-Author); The Gods of Greece, 2010 (Co-Author); Creating a Hellenistic World, 2011 (Co-Author); Encyclopedia of Ancient History, 2013 (General Editor); Plutarch: The Hellenistic Lives, 2016 (Co-Author); Hellenistic Court, 2017 (Co-Author). Recreation: Lego. Address: (b.) School of History, Classics and Archaeology, Teviot Place, University of Edinburgh EH8 9AG; e-mail: andrew.erskine@ed.ac.uk

Erskine, Colonel James Malcolm Kenneth, MBE. Educ. Wellington College; RMAS. Career: Black Watch, 1976-2006; Commandant, Black Watch Battalion Army Cadet Force, 2012-2017; Regimental Secretary, The Royal Scots Dragoon Guards; Governor, Cargilfield School, 1998-2003;

Chairman: The Baird Trust, Scotland's Churches Trust; Trustee, Housing and Loan Fund, Church of Scotland; Member of the Royal Company of Archers. Recreations: golf; shooting; curling. Clubs: Cavalry and Guards, Royal Scots Club. Address: Hilton of Duncrievie, Glenfarg, Perthshire PH2 9PD.

Evans, Professor Brian Mark, BSc (Hons), PG Dip (Dist), MSc, PhD, FRTPI, FLI, FCSD, FAcSS, FRGS, AoU. City Urbanist, Glasgow, since 2019; Professor of Urbanism and Landscape, The Glasgow School of Art, since 2015; Strategic Adviser, United Nations Economic Commission for Europe, Geneva, Switzerland, since 2015; Head of Urbanism, Mackintosh School of Architecture, The Glasgow School of Art, since 2010; Partner, Gillespies LLP, Landscape Architects and Urban Designers, 1989-2015; Honorary Professor, University of Glasgow/The Glasgow School of Art, 2008-2012; Deputy Chair, Architecture and Design Scotland, 2004-2010; Founding Board Member, The Academy of Urbanism, 2005-2010; Joint Chair, Sheffield Sustainable Development & Design Panel, 2009-2015; Enabler, Commission for Architecture and the Built Environment, 2003-2008; Artistic Professor, Stadsbyggnad (City Building), School of Architecture, Chalmers University, Gothenburg, Sweden, 1998-2004; Deputy Design Coordinator, the Glasgow Garden Festival, 1985-1988; early career – William Gillespie and Partners and Scottish Planning Authorities, 1975-1985. Educ. Linlithgow Academy; University of Edinburgh; University of Strathclyde; University of Glasgow. Principal Publications: Growing Awareness – How green consciousness can change perceptions & places (author & editor), 2016; Towards a City-focussed, People-centred and Integrated Approach to the New Urban Agenda, Regional Report on the UNECE to Habitat III, UN-Habitat, Geneva, 2017; Urban Identity – Learning from Place II (editor), 2011; Space, Place, Life – Learning from Place I (editor), 2011; Tomorrow's Architectural Heritage – Landscape and Buildings in the Countryside, 1991; monographs and articles in English, Swedish, Russian, German, Italian and Dutch on urbanism, urban design and landscape planning. Address: (b.) The Glasgow School of Art, 167 Renfrew Street, Glasgow G3 6RQ; T.-0141 353 4447.
E-mail: b.evans@gsa.ac.uk

Evans, Professor George William, BA (Oxon), BA, MA, PhD (Berkeley). Professor, School of Economics and Finance, University of St Andrews, since 2007; Professor, Economics Department, University of Oregon, USA, since 1994; b. 3.4.49, New York; m., Pauline Andrews; 2 s. Educ. University of California, Berkeley; Balliol College, Oxford University. Lecturer, Economics, University of Stirling, 1978-81; Assistant Professor, Stanford University, 1981-87; Lecturer, Senior Lecturer, Reader, Economics, London School of Economics, 1987-92; Professor, Economics, University of Edinburgh, 1993-94. Publications: over 75 papers published in refereed journals; book: Learning and Expectations in Macroeconomics (Co-Author), 2001. Address: (b.) School of Economics and Finance, Castlecliffe, The Scores, University of St Andrews, St Andrews KY16 9AL; T.-01334 462425; e-mail: ge21@st-andrews.ac.uk

Evans, Leslie Elizabeth, BA (Hons) Music. Permanent Secretary to the Scottish Government, 2015-2021, Director-General, Learning and Justice, 2010-15, Director-General, Education, 2009-2010, Director, Europe, External Affairs and Culture, DG Economy, 2007-09; Head of Tourism, Culture and Sport, Scottish Executive Education Department, 2006-07; b. 11.12.58; m., Derek George McVay; 1 s. Educ. Liverpool University. Assistant to Director, Greenwich Festival, 1981; Entertainments Officer, London Borough of Greenwich, 1981-83; Arts Co-ordinator, Sheffield CC, 1983-85; Senior Arts Officer, Edinburgh DC, 1985-87; Principal Officer, Stirling CC, 1987-89; City of Edinburgh Council: Assistant Director of Recreation, 1989-99, Strategic Projects Manager, 1999-2000; Scottish Executive: Head: Local Government, Constitution and Governance, 2000-03, Public Service Reform, 2003-05. Member, Scotch Malt Whisky Society. Recreations: the arts; baking; yoga and visiting her home on the Isle of Skye.

Evans, Martyn, BA (Hons), MA (Econ). Chair, Scottish Police Authority, since 2021. Educ. City of Birmingham Polytechnic; University of Manchester. Career history: Director (Scotland), Shelter UK, 1987-92; Chief Executive, Citizens Advice Scotland, 1992-97; Visiting Professor of Law, University of Strathclyde, 1996-2002; Director, Scottish Consumer Council, 1998-2008; Director (Scotland), Consumer Focus, 2008-09; Vice-Chair, NHS Quality Improvement Scotland, 2004-2011; Chair, Expert Working Group on Welfare, Scotland, 2013-14; Co-Chair, Northern Ireland Roundtable on Wellbeing, Belfast, 2013-15; Chair, Public Libraries National Strategy Group (Scotland), Edinburgh, 2014-15; Chair, Fairer Fife Commission, 2015; Trustee, Peter Gibson Memorial Fund, 2007-2017; Independent Co-Chair, Review of Scottish Health Council, Edinburgh, 2016-17; Chair, Independent Review of Legal Aid, Scotland, 2017-18; Co-Chair, Civic participation and economic wellbeing in Ireland, 2016-18, measuring job quality group, 2018; Advisory Board Member, Institute for Social Renewal, University of Newcastle, 2015-19; Chief Executive, Carnegie UK Trust, Dunfermline, 2009-2019; Executive Chair, Alex Ferry Foundation, London (part-time), 2018-2020; Member, Advisory Board, IPPR Scotland, since 2016; Board Member, Scottish Police Authority, since 2018. Address: Scottish Police Authority, 1 Pacific Quay, Glasgow G51 1DZ; T.-01786 896630.

Everett, Peter, BSc (Hons), SPMB; b. 24.9.31, London; m., Annette Patricia Hyde; 3 s.; 1 d. Educ. George Watson's College; Edinburgh University. Royal Engineers, 1953-55 (2nd Lt.); joined Shell International Petroleum Company, 1955; Managing Director: Brunei Shell Petroleum Co. Ltd., 1979-84, Shell UK Exploration and Production, 1985-89; retired, 1989. Honorary Professor, Heriot Watt University, 1989. Recreation: golf. Address: (h.) Cluain, Castleton Road, Auchterarder, Perthshire PH3 1JW.

Ewart, Michael, BA, DPhil. Trustee, Scottish International Education Trust, since 2021; Director, Scottish International Education Trust, 2009-2021; Lay Member, Judicial Appointments Board for Scotland, 2009-18; b. 9.9.52, Anthorn; m., Dr. Sally Anderson; 1 s.; 1 d. Educ. St Peter's, Southbourne; Jesus College, Cambridge; York University. 1977: joined Scottish Office: Scottish Education Department, Scottish Home and Health Department, Royal Commission on Legal Services in Scotland; Assistant Private Secretary to Secretary of State for Scotland, 1981-82; Civil Service Fellow in Politics, Glasgow University, 1982-83; Scottish Home and Health Department, Scottish Education Department, 1983-91; Chief Executive, Scottish Court Service, 1991-99; Head of Schools Group, Scottish Executive Education Department, 1999-2002, Head of Department, 2002-07; Chief Executive, Scottish Prison Service, 2007-09. Board Member: Scottish Ballet, 2007-13, Phoenix Futures, Education Scotland, 2012-19; Chair, Phoenix Scotland. Recreations: music; books; climbing; skiing; running; geocaching. Address: 33/35 Water Street, Edinburgh EH6 6SZ; e-mail: m.ewart@outlook.com

Ewing, Annabelle, LLB (Hons). MSP (SNP), Cowdenbeath, since 2016 (Mid Scotland and Fife region, 2011-16); SNP MP, Perth, 2001-05; Minister for Community Safety and Legal Affairs, Scottish

Government, 2016-18, Minister for Youth and Women's Employment, 2014-16; b. 20.8.60, Glasgow. Educ. Craigholme School; Glasgow University; Johns Hopkins University; Europa Institute, Amsterdam University. Admitted Solicitor, 1986; Legal Service, EC, 1987; worked for law firms in Brussels, 1987-96; lawyer, EC, 1997; Ewing & Co., Solicitors: Associate, 1998-99, Partner, 1999-2001; Consultant, Leslie Wolfson & Co., Glasgow, 2001-03. Honorary President, SNP Brussels Branch. Recreations: walking; swimming; travel; reading. Address: Scottish Parliament, Edinburgh EH99 1SP.

Ewing, Fergus. MSP (SNP), Inverness and Nairn, since 2011, Inverness East, Nairn and Lochaber, 1999-2011; Cabinet Secretary for Rural Economy and Tourism, 2016-2021; Minister for Business, Energy and Tourism, 2011-16; Minister for Community Safety, 2007-2011; b. 20.9.57; m., Margaret Ewing (deceased). Educ. Loretto School, Edinburgh; Glasgow University. Solicitor. Recreations: piano; reading; running; hill-walking; former member of local mountain rescue team. Address: Scottish Parliament, Edinburgh EH99 1SP; T.-01463 713004.

F

WHO'S WHO IN SCOTLAND 151

Fabiani, Linda. MSP (SNP), East Kilbride, 2011-2021, Central Scotland, 1999-2011; Minister for Europe, External Affairs and Culture, 2007-09; Deputy Presiding Officer, 2016-2021; b. 14.12.56, Glasgow. Educ. Hyndland School, Glasgow; Napier College, Edinburgh; Glasgow University. Various Housing Association posts, 1982-99. Recreations: music; literature; friends.

Fair, Rev Dr W. Martin. Moderator of the General Assembly of the Church of Scotland, 2020-21; Minister, St Andrew's Parish Church, Arbroath, since 1992; b. 1964; m., Elaine; 3 s. Ordained as a minister in 1992; served on the Mission & Discipleship Council of the denomination, becoming a vice-convener; chaired the Church Without Walls committee. Address: St Andrew's Parish Church, 21 Hamilton Green, Arbroath, Angus DD11 1JG; T.-01241 431135.
E-mail: office@arbroathstandrews.org.uk

Fairbairn, The Hon. Mrs Elizabeth, MBE. Trustee, Scottish National War Memorial; Hon. President, Clan Mackay Society; b. 21.6.38; 3 d. Address: 38 Moray Place, Edinburgh EH3 6BT; T.-0131-225 2724.

Fairbairn, Martin MacLean, BCom, CA. Non Executive Board Member, NHS Forth Valley (Part-time), since 2021; public, college and university sector governance expert, since 2021; Non Executive Director and Treasurer, The Glasgow Barons (Part-time), since 2021; b. 20.9.63, Dunfermline; m., Anne Fairbairn (nee Marshall); 2 s.; 1 d. Educ. Queen Anne High, Dunfermline; University of Edinburgh. Auditor, Touche Ross & Co., 1984-93; Director of Finance, Stevenson College Edinburgh, 1993-2000; Deputy Director, FE Funding, Scottish Funding Councils for Further and Higher Education, 2000-04; Scottish Further and Higher Education Funding Council: Director of Governance & Management: Appraisal & policy, 2004-09, Senior Director, 2009-15, Chief Operating Officer and Deputy Chief Executive, 2015-2021. Recreations: church organist; youth work; badminton; golf; cycling.

Fairgrieve, James Hanratty, DA, RSA, RSW. Painter; b. 17.6.44, Prestonpans; m., Margaret D. Ross; 2 s.; 1 d. Educ. Preston Lodge Senior Secondary School; Edinburgh College of Art. Postgraduate study, 1966-67; Travelling Scholarship, Italy, 1968; Senior Lecturer in Drawing and Painting, Edinburgh College of Art, 1968-98; President, SSA, 1978-82; exhibited in Britain and Europe, since 1966. Recreation: angling. Address: (h.) Burnbrae, Gordon, Berwickshire.

Fairlamb, Professor Alan Hutchinson, CBE, MB, ChB, PhD, FLS, FRSE, FMedSci, FRSB. University of Dundee, since 1996, Emeritus Professor, since 2021, Professor of Biochemistry, 1996-2021, Head of Division of Biological Chemistry & Drug Discovery, 1996-2012, Wellcome Principal Research Fellow, 1996-2016, Co-Director of Drug Discovery Unit, 2006-2016; b. 30.4.47, Newcastle-upon-Tyne; m., Carolyn Strobos; 1 s.; 2 d. Educ. Hymers College, Hull; Edinburgh University. Surgical and Medical House Officer, Longmore and Western General Hospitals, Edinburgh, 1971-72; Faculty of Medicine Research Scholar, University of Edinburgh, 1972-75; MRC Travelling Fellow, University of Amsterdam, 1975-76; Research Fellow: University of Edinburgh, 1976-80, London School of Hygiene and Tropical Medicine, 1980-81; Assistant Professor, The Rockefeller University, New York, 1981-87; Senior Clinical Lecturer, London School of Hygiene & Tropical Medicine, 1987-90; Professor of Molecular Parasitology and Head, Biochemistry and Chemotherapy Unit, LSHTM, 1990-96. Current committee memberships: Governing Board, Tres Cantos Open Lab Foundation. Publications: author of more than 300 scientific articles and reviews on biochemistry and chemotherapy of neglected tropical diseases. Recreations: gardening; fishing; photography; dancing. Address: (b.) Division of Biological Chemistry & Drug Discovery, School of Life Sciences, Wellcome Trust Building, University of Dundee, Dundee DD1 5EH; T.-01382 385542; Fax: 01382 385764.
E-mail: a.h.fairlamb@dundee.ac.uk

Fairley, The Hon Lord (Douglas Fairley), LLB (Hons). Senator of the College of Justice, since 2020; Queen's Counsel, since 2012; b. 20.2.68, Glasgow; m., Una Doherty. Educ. Hutchesons' Grammar School; University of Glasgow. Solicitor, Maclay Murray and Spens, 1992-98; Admitted to the Faculty of Advocates, 1999; Employment Judge, 2010-2011; Advocate Depute, 2011-15. Publication: Contempt of Court in Scotland (Co-Author). Recreations: music; tennis; skiing; curling. Address: Parliament House, 11 Parliament Square, Edinburgh EH1 1RQ.

Fairlie, Jim. MSP (SNP), Perthshire South and Kinross-shire, since 2021; b. 3.67. Former farmer (5500 acre hill farm in Perthshire hills, running blackface sheep and native bred cattle); founder of Perth Farmer's Market in 1999; Co-founder of Scottish association of farmers markets; former partner of an outside catering business The Kitchen Farmer; worked with Perth and Kinross Council and the Scottish Government to promote food education and sustainable procurement; Director of Perthshire Farmers and Producers. Address: The Scottish Parliament, Edinburgh EH99 1SP; T.-01738 620540.
E-mail: Jim.Fairlie.msp@parliament.scot

Fairweather, Cllr David. Leader, Angus Council, since 2017; represents Arbroath West and Letham (Independent); b. 1956. Committees: Civic Licensing; Policy and Resources; Member: Angus Council Charitable Trust, Arbroath Golf Links Limited. Address: Angus Council, Municipal Buildings, Castle Street, Forfar DD8 3AF; T.-01307 494245.

Falconer, Professor Kenneth John, MA, PhD (Cantab), FRSE. Regius Professor of Mathematics, St Andrews University, since 2017, and Professor in Pure Mathematics, St Andrews University, since 1993; b. 25.1.52, Middlesex; m., Isobel Jessie Nye; 1 s.; 1 d. Educ. Kingston Grammar School; Corpus Christi College, Cambridge. Research Fellow, Corpus Christi College, Cambridge, 1977-80; Lecturer, then Reader, Bristol University, 1980-93; Visiting Professor: Oregon State University, 1985-86; Isaac Newton Institute, Cambridge, 1999, 2011 & 2015, IHES, Paris, 2005-06, Australian National University, Canberra, 2009, East China Normal University, Shanghai, 2010, Mittag-Leffler Institute, Sweden, 2017. London Mathematical Society Shephard Prize, 2020. Publications Secretary, London Mathematical Society, 2006-09. Publications: The Geometry of Fractal Sets; Fractal Geometry - Mathematical Foundations and Applications; Techniques in Fractal Geometry; Fractals: A Very Short Introduction; Unsolved Problems in Geometry (Co-Author); 115 papers. Recreations: hill-walking and long distance walking (Long Distance Walkers Association: Vice President, since 2021, Chair, 2000-03, Editor of its journal Strider, 1987-92 and 2007-2012). Address: (h.) Lumbo Farmhouse, St. Andrews, Fife; T.-01334 478507.
E-mail: kjf@st-andrews.ac.uk

Falkland, 15th Viscount (Lord Lucius Edward William Plantagenet Cary). Premier Viscount of Scotland on the

Roll; b. 8.5.35, London; 2 s.; 3 d. (1 deceased). Educ. Wellington College; Alliance Francaise, Paris. Formerly journalist, theatrical agent, chief executive of international trading company; entered Parliament, 1984 (SDP), 1987 (Liberal Democrats); Deputy Chief Whip, House of Lords, for Liberal Democrats, 1987-2001; Culture, Media, Sport and Tourism Spokesman, 1994-2007; Chairman, House of Lords Works of Art Committee, 2008-2010; joined independent crossbenches, House of Lords, 2012; elected Member, House of Lords, since 1999. Recreations: racing; cinema. Club: Brooks's. Address: (b.) House of Lords, London SW1; e-mail: lordfalkland@aol.com

Fallick, Professor Anthony Edward, BSc, PhD, FRSE, FRSA. Emeritus Professor, University of Glasgow; Professor of Isotope Geosciences, University of Glasgow, 1996-2012; b. 21.4.50, Chatham. Educ. St. Columba's High School, Greenock; University of Glasgow. Research Fellow: McMaster University, Canada, 1975-78; University of Cambridge, 1978-80; Research Fellow, Lecturer, Reader, Professor, Scottish Universities Research and Reactor Centre, East Kilbride, 1980-98; Head of Isotope Geosciences Unit, Scottish Universities Research and Reactor Centre, East Kilbride, 1986-99; Director, Scottish Universities Environmental Research Centre, 1998-2007; 1997 Schlumberger Medallist, Mineralogical Society of Great Britain and Ireland; 2001 Richard A. Glenn Award, American Chemical Society; 2004 Coke Medal of the Geological Society of London; 2009/10 Distinguished Lecturer of the Mineralogical Society; 2013 Clough Medallist, Edinburgh Geological Society; Honorary Professor in the Universities of Glasgow, Edinburgh and St. Andrews. Address: (b.) S.U.E.R.C., Rankine Avenue, East Kilbride, Glasgow G75 0QF; T.-013552 23332.
E-mail: anthony.fallick@glasgow.ac.uk

Fannin, A. Lorraine, OBE, BA (Hons), DipEd. Board Member, StAnza, Scotland's International Poetry Festival, 2016-18; Director, BookSource, 1995-2015; Trustee, National Library of Scotland, 2001-2014; Trustee, Edinburgh UNESCO City of Literature Trust, 2005-2014; Chief Executive, Publishing Scotland, 1987-2008; b. 8.44. Educ. Victoria College, Belfast; Queen's University, Belfast; Reading University. Previously teacher; broadcaster; journalist; children's book supplier, 1979-89. Recreations: galleries; books and friends.

Farley-Sutton, Captain Colin David, RN, DL; b. 20.12.31, Rugby; m., Sheila Wilson Baldwin; 2 s.; 2 d. Educ. Rugby College of Technology and Arts; RN Engineering College, Plymouth; RN College, Greenwich. Royal Navy, 1950-82. President, Caithness Branch, Red Cross, 1991-97. Address: (h.) Shepherd's Cottage, Lynegar, Watten, Caithness KW1 5UP; T.-01955 621697.

Farmer, Professor John Gregory, BSc, PhD, CChem, FRSC, FGS. Professor Emeritus, Edinburgh University, since 2009; b. 18.02.47, Market Bosworth; m., Margaret Ann McClimont; 2 s.; 1 d. Educ. Kilmarnock Academy; Glasgow University. Post-Doctoral Investigator, Woods Hole Oceanographic Institution, Mass., USA, 1972-74; Research Assistant and Fellow, Department of Forensic Medicine and Science, Glasgow University, 1974-86; Lecturer, Senior Lecturer and Reader in Environmental Chemistry, Edinburgh University, 1987-2003; Professor of Environmental Geochemistry, Edinburgh University, 2004-08; Chairman, 8th International Conference on Heavy Metals in the Environment, Edinburgh, 1991; Chairman, 6th International Symposium on Environmental Geochemistry, Edinburgh, 2003; President, Society for Environmental Geochemistry and Health, 2002-05; Executive Editor, Science of the Total Environment, 2002-11. Recreations:

cricket; Kilmarnock FC; history; hill walking; wine. Address: (b.) School of Geosciences, Edinburgh University; Crew Building, Alexander Crum Brown Road, Edinburgh EH9 3FF.

Farmer, Sir Tom, CVO, CBE, KCSG, FRSE. Founder and former Chairman and Chief Executive, Kwik-Fit Holdings PLC (1984-2002); former Chancellor, Queen Margaret University (2007-2016); b. 10.7.40, Edinburgh; m., Anne Drury Scott; 1 s.; 1 d. Educ. Holy Cross Academy. Founding Chancellor of Queen Margaret University. Address: (b.) Maidencraig House, 192 Queensferry Road, Edinburgh EH4 2BN; T.-0131 315 2830.
E-mail: info@maidencraig.com

Farquharson, Sheriff Jane, QC, LLB (Hons). Sheriff, Lothian and Borders, since 2021. Educ. University of Newcastle Upon Tyne; Inns of Court School of Law, London. Career history: called to the Bar of England and Wales in 1993; common law and criminal pupillages at 1 Essex Court, 1 Middle Temple Lane and 5 Paper Buildings, all London, 1994-97; Barrister: Chambers of Sir Ivan Lawrence QC, London, 1997-2000, Chambers of Desmond Da Silva QC, London, 2000-01; Research Assistant, HBOS plc, Edinburgh, 2001-02; practising Counsel at the Scottish Bar, since 2002; became an Advocate Depute in 2010, latterly the Assistant Principal Crown Counsel; appointed Queen's Counsel in 2019. Address: Livingston Sheriff Court, West Lothian Civic Centre, Howden Road South, Livingston EH54 6FF; T.-01506 402400.

Farquharson, Kenny (Kenneth James), MA (Hons), DipJour. Columnist and senior writer, The Times, since 2015; b. 8.5.62, Dundee; m., Caron Stoker; 2 s. Educ. Lawside R.C. Academy, Dundee; University of Aberdeen; University College, Cardiff. Industry Reporter, Coventry Evening Telegraph, 1985-88; Scotland on Sunday: Investigative Reporter, 1989-93, Political Editor, 1993-97; Political Editor, Daily Record, 1997-98; Scottish Political Editor, The Sunday Times, 1998-2002; Assistant Editor: The Sunday Times (Scotland), 2002-07, Scotland on Sunday, 2007-09; Deputy Editor, Scotland on Sunday, 2009-2015; Deputy Editor, The Scotsman, 2013-2015. Director, Scottish European Aid, 1993-94; Convenor, Scottish Parliamentary Journalists' Association, 1997-2000. Political Journalist of the Year, 2001, Scottish Press Awards. Publication: Restless Nation (Co-author), 1996. Recreations: cooking; architecture; art; photography.

Farrell, Sheriff James Aloysius, QC, MA, LLB. Sheriff of Lothian and Borders, 1986-2009; b. 14.5.43, Glasgow; m., 1, Jacqueline Allen (divorced); 2 d.; m., 2, Patricia McLaren. Educ. St. Aloysius College; Glasgow University; Dundee University. Admitted to Faculty of Advocates, 1974; Advocate-Depute, 1979-83; Sheriff: Glasgow and Strathkelvin, 1984-85, South Strathclyde, Dumfries and Galloway, 1985-86; 2010 Temporary Sheriff Principal, Glasgow and Strathkelvin; 2010, 2011 Temporary Sheriff Principal, Central, Tayside and Fife; 2012, 2013 Temporary Sheriff Principal, South Strathclyde, Dumfries and Galloway, 2012, 2013 Temporary High Court Judge. Recreations: sailing; cycling; hill-walking. Address: (b.) Merchiston Park, Edinburgh EH10 4PN.

Farrer, Peter William. Chief Operating Officer, Scottish Water, since 2013; b. 1962, Balerno, Midlothian; m., Caroline; 1 s.; 1 d. Educ. Currie High School, Midlothian; Heriot-Watt University, Edinburgh. Thirty-four years in water industry in Scotland since graduating in 1984 for Scottish Water and predecessor organisations; Engineering Design & Construction, 1984-96; various operational senior management roles, 1996-2002; General Manager Operations, 2002-2006; General Manager (Tactical Planning & Performance), 2006-08. Chartered Civil Engineer, 1990; MBA, 2001. Recreations: rugby; cycling. Address: (b.) 6 Castle Drive, Carnegie Campus, Dunfermline KY11 8GG; T.-01383 848466; e-mail: peter.farrer@scottishwater.co.uk

Faulds, Ann, BA. Lay Governor, The Glasgow School of Art, since 2019; Non Executive Director, Nevis Technology, 2018-2021; Non Executive Director, Scottish Futures Trust, 2017-2021; Partner, CMS Cameron McKenna LLP, 2014-19; former Chairman, Lothian Buses. Appointed Member, Strathclyde Partnership for Transport (SPT), since 2012; former Board Member, Fife NHS Board. Member, Accounts Commission for Scotland, 2003-09; Chair, Edinburgh Chamber of Commerce transport policy group, 2009-2014; Member, Lothian Buses Board, 2010-2014. Publications: Scottish Roads Law; annotated the Transport (Scotland) Act 2001. Address: The Glasgow School of Art, 167 Renfrew Street, Glasgow G3 6RQ.

Fawcett, Richard, OBE, BA, PhD, FRSE, FSA, Hon FSA Scot. Emeritus Professor, School of Art History, University of St Andrews; b. 31.12.46, Hoyland, Yorkshire; m., Susan; 1 s.; 1 d. Educ. Ecclesfield Grammar School; University of East Anglia. Ancient Monuments Inspectorate, Historic Scotland (and its predecessor bodies), 1974-2010. Publications: books include: "Scottish Architecture 1371-1560", 1994; Scottish Medieval Churches, 2002; "The Architecture of The Scottish Medieval Church", 2011. Recreations: architectural history; music; reading. Address: (h.) Flat 12, Station Court, Kirkcaldy KY1 1AH; T.-01592 643918; e-mail: richard.fawcett@hotmail.co.uk

Fearn, Professor David Ross, BSc, PhD, FIMA, FRSE. Dean for North America, University of the West of Scotland, since 2019; Emeritus Professor of Applied Mathematics, University of Glasgow (appointed Professor in 1993), International Dean for North America, 2010-2019, Vice Principal and Acting Head of the College of Science and Engineering, 2014, Dean, Learning and Teaching, College of Science and Engineering, 2010-2014, Dean, Faculty of Information and Mathematical Sciences, 2004-2010, Head, Department of Mathematics, 1997-2003; b. 11.2.54, Dundee; m., Elvira D'Annunzio; 1 s.; 1 d. Educ. Grove Academy, Dundee; University of St. Andrews; University of Newcastle upon Tyne. Research Associate: Florida State University, 1979-80, University of Cambridge, 1980-85; University of Glasgow: Lecturer, 1985-90, Senior Lecturer, 1990-92, Reader, 1992-93. Recreations: walking; gardening; DIY. E-mail: davidrfearn@gmail.com

Fee, Mary. MSP (Labour), West Scotland, 2011-2021; Shadow Cabinet Secretary for Infrastructure, Investments and Cities, 2014-16; b. 23.3.54, Edinburgh. Educ. Leith Walk Primary, Edinburgh; Broughton Secondary, Edinburgh. Employment with the Bank of Scotland, 1972-1974; British Telecom, 1974-1984, transferred within British Telecom to their Glasgow offices; joined Tesco in 1990 in Renfrew; Renfrewshire Councillor, 2007-2012. Member, Usdaw (trade union); became a shop steward in 1990; elected onto the Usdaw Executive in 2000 and later became a member of the STUC General Council; served as a member of the Employment Tribunals until 2011.

Fellows, Marion. MP (SNP), Motherwell and Wishaw, since 2015; SNP Spokesperson for Disabilities, since 2020; SNP Whip, since 2015; SNP Spokesperson for Small Business, Enterprise and Innovation, 2017-2020; b. 5.5.49.

Educ. Heriot Watt University. Early career in a variety of related roles in both the public and private sectors; subsequently taught in further education, spending 19 years teaching business studies at West Lothian College, where she was an active and senior member of the EIS Trade Union; has lived with her family in Wishaw and Bellshill for 40 years; represented Wishaw as a local SNP councillor (2012-15). Senior figure in the Yes Motherwell and Wishaw campaign, which won a majority locally in the 2014 Independence Referendum. Address: House of Commons, London SW1A 0AA.

Ferguson, Professor Allister Ian, CBE, BSc, MA, PhD, FInstP, FRSE, CPhys, FFCS, MSc. Emeritus Professor (appointed Professor of Photonics, Strathclyde University in 1989); Technical Director, Institute of Photonics, University of Strathclyde, since 1996, Deputy Principal, 2004-2011, Adviser to Principal, since 2012; b. 10.12.51, Aberdeen; m., Kathleen Ann Challenger. Educ. Aberdeen Academy; St. Andrews University. Lindemann Fellow, Stanford University, 1977-79; SERC Research Fellow, St. Andrews, 1979-81; SERC Advanced Fellow, Oxford, 1981-83; Junior Research Fellow, Merton College, Oxford, 1981-83; Lecturer, then Senior Lecturer, Southampton University, 1983-89. Fellow: Royal Society of Edinburgh, since 1993, Institute of Physics, Optical Society of America, Institution of Electrical and Electronics Engineers. Address: (b.) McCance Building, University of Strathclyde, Glasgow G1 1XQ; T.-0141 548 3264.

Ferguson, Iain William Findlay, QC, LLB (Hons), DipLP. Queen's Counsel, since 2000; b. 31.7.61, Edinburgh; m., Valerie Laplanche; 2 s. Educ. Firrhill High School, Edinburgh; Dundee University. Advocate, 1987; Standing Junior Counsel to Ministry of Defence (Army), 1991-98, and to Scottish Development Department (Planning matters), 1998-2000. Recreations: cooking; rugby; cycling. Address: (h.) 16 McLaren Road, Edinburgh EH9 2BN; T.-0131-667 1751.

Ferguson, Sir Michael Anthony John, BSc, PhD, Kt, CBE, FRS, FRSE, FMedSci, FRSB. Regius Professor of Life Sciences, since 2013, Academic Lead for Research Strategy, School of Life Sciences, University of Dundee, since 2007, Professor of Molecular Parasitology, since 1994; b. 6.2.57, Bishop Auckland; m., Dr Lucia Güther; 1 s. Educ. St. Peter's School, York; University of Manchester. Post-doctoral fellow: Rockefeller University, New York, 1982-85, Oxford University, 1985-88; Lecturer, University of Dundee, 1988-91, Reader, 1991-94. Colworth Medal (Biochemical Society), 1991; Member, European Molecular Biology Organisation, 1999; Wright Medal (British Society for Parasitology), 2006; Royal Society of Edinburgh Royal Medal, 2013; American Society of Biochemistry and Molecular Biology Wang Award in Molecular Parasitology, 2016. Honorary degree (DSc), University of St Andrews, 2017; Outstanding Alumnus Award, University of Manchester, 2018. Recreations: travel; astronomy. Address: (b.) School of Life Sciences, University of Dundee, Dundee DD1 5EH; T.-01382 386672; e-mail: m.a.j.ferguson@dundee.ac.uk

Ferguson, Professor Pamela Ruth, LLB (Hons), Dip LP, PhD. Professor of Scots Law, University of Dundee, since 2000; b. 7.4.63, Glasgow; m., Dr. Euan W. Macdonald; 1 s. Educ. Bearsden Academy; Glasgow University; Dundee University. Procurator Fiscal Depute/Trainee Solicitor, Crown Office, Edinburgh and Procurator Fiscal's Office, Kirkcaldy, 1986-89; Lecturer, 1989-95; Senior Lecturer, 1995-99. Winner, Dr. John McCormick Prize (jointly); Most Distinguished Law Graduate, 1985; awarded Royal

154 WHO'S WHO IN SCOTLAND

Society of Edinburgh Research Fellowship, 1997. Publications: Co-author of Draft Criminal Code for Scotland; Scots Criminal Law: A Critical Analysis; Breach of the Peace. Address: (b.) School of Law, University of Dundee, Dundee DD1 4HN; T.-01382 385189; e-mail: p.r.ferguson@dundee.ac.uk

Ferguson, Patricia. MSP (Labour), Glasgow Maryhill and Springburn, 2011-16, Glasgow Maryhill, 1999-2011; former Minister for Tourism, Culture and Sport; former Deputy Presiding Officer and Minister for Parliamentary Business; b. 1958, Glasgow; m., William G. Butler. Educ. Gartnethill Convent Secondary School, Glasgow.

Ferguson, Ron, MA, BD, ThM. Freelance journalist and author; Minister, St. Magnus Cathedral, Orkney, 1990-2001; former Columnist, The Herald; b. 27.10.39, Dunfermline; m., Cristine Jane Walker; 2 s.; 1 d. Educ. Beath High School, Cowdenbeath; St Andrews University; Edinburgh University; Duke University. Journalist, Fife and Edinburgh, 1956-63; University, 1963-71; ordained Minister, Church of Scotland, 1972; Minister, Easterhouse, Glasgow, 1971-79; exchange year with United Church of Canada, 1979-80; Deputy Warden, Iona Abbey, 1980-81; Leader, Iona Community, 1981-88. Publications: Geoff: A Life of Geoffrey M. Shaw, 1979; Grace and Dysentery, 1986; Chasing the Wild Goose, 1988; The Whole Earth Shall Cry Glory (Co-Editor), 1985; George MacLeod, 1990; Daily Readings by George MacLeod (Editor), 1991; Black Diamonds and the Blue Brazil, 1993; Technology at the Crossroads, 1994; Love Your Crooked Neighbour, 1998; Donald Dewar Ate My Hamster, 1999; Hitler Was A Vegetarian, 2001; The Reluctant Reformation of Clarence McGonigall, 2003; Fear and Loathing in Lochgelly, 2003; Blue Rinse Dreams and Banoffee Pie, 2005; Mole Under The Fence: Conversations with Roland Walls, 2006; Helicopter Dreams: The Quest for the Holy Grail, 2006; George Mackay Brown: The Wound and the Gift, 2011; plays: Every Blessed Thing, 1993, Orkneyinga, 1997; Ending It All, 2006; new, updated edition of Black Diamonds and the Blue Brazil, 2014; librettist, The Story of Magnus Erlendsson, 2017; poetry: Pushing the Boat Out (Contributor), 1997. Honorary D.Litt., Glasgow Caledonian University, 2010. Recreation: supporting Cowdenbeath Football Club. Address: (h.) Vinbrek, Orphir, Orkney KW17 2RE; T.-01856 811378.
E-mail: ronbluebrazil@aol.com

Ferguson, Professor Ronald Gillies, MA, BPhil, CertSecEd. Emeritus Professor of Italian, University of St Andrews, since 2014, Professor of Italian, 2004-14, Head of The School of Modern Languages, 2005-09; b. 21.7.49, Birkenshaw, Lanarkshire; m., Annie Ferguson (nee Ballouard); 1 s.; 1 d. Educ. Uddingston Grammar School; University of Glasgow; University of St. Andrews; Jordanhill College of Education. University of Lancaster: Lecturer in Italian, 1979-96, Senior Lecturer in Italian, 1996-97; University of St. Andrews: Senior Lecturer in Italian, 1997-2004, first ever Chair of Italian. Made Cavaliere della Stella della Solidarietà Italiana (one of Italy's highest honours) by the President of Italy for distinction in the fields of Italian Renaissance theatre, Italian identity studies, and Venetian language linguistics and culture, and for making St. Andrews a centre for the study of Italian, 2005; made Fellow of the Ateneo Veneto di Scienze, Lettere ed Arti (one of Italy's foremost learned societies) for distinguished contributions to Venetian language and culture, 2006; made Research Professor, St Andrews, 2010; made Fellow of the Academia Galileiana of Padna in 2020. Publications: Italian False Friends, 1994; The Theatre of Angelo Beolco (Ruzante): Text, Context and Performance, 2000; Italian Identities (ed.), 2002; A Linguistic History of Venice, 2007; Saggi di Lingua e

Cultura Veneta, 2013; Venetian Inscriptions. Vernacular Writing for Public Display in Medieval and Renaissance Venice, 2021. Recreations: birdwatching; reading. Address: (h.) 3 Muir Gardens, St. Andrews, Fife KY16 9NH; T.-01334 472 383; e-mail: rgf@st-and.ac.uk

Ferguson, Professor Sinclair Buchanan, MA, BA, PhD. Scottish theologian; Chancellor's Professor of Systematic Theology, Reformed Theological Seminary, since 2017; Assistant Minister, St. Peter's Free Church of Scotland, Dundee, since 2013; b. 21.2.48. Educ. University of Aberdeen. Ordained as a minister in the Church of Scotland in 1971, becoming the minister of St. John's, Baltasound on the island of Unst, Shetland (pastor for 10 years); became part-time Professor of Systematic Theology, Westminster Theological Seminary, Philadelphia; moved back to Scotland in 1997 to George's-Tron Church, Glasgow; transferred back to the US in the mid-2000s to the Associate Reformed Presbyterian Church, serving as the senior pastor of historic First Presbyterian Church of Columbia, South Carolina. Publications include: Reformed Confessions Harmonized, 1999; In Christ Alone: Living the Gospel Centered Life, 2007; The Christian Life: A Doctrinal Introduction, 2013. Speaks at numerous conferences worldwide. Address: St. Peter's Free Church, St. Peter's Street, Dundee DD1 4JJ; T.-01382 807004.

Ferguson, William James, OBE, FRAgS. Farmer, since 1954; Director, Hannah Research Institute, since 1995; Vice Lord Lieutenant, Aberdeenshire; Honorary Fellow, SAC, since 1999; Trustee, Aberdeen Endowments Trust, 2002-2012; Chair, Land and Finance Committee, since 2005; b. 3.4.33, Aberdeen; m., Carroll Isobella Milne; 1 s.; 3 d. Educ. Turriff Academy; North of Scotland College of Agriculture. National Service, 1st Bn., Gordon Highlanders, 1952-54, serving in Malaya during the emergency. Former Director, Rowett Research Institute, Aberdeen; former Chairman, Aberdeen Milk Company; former Chairman, North of Scotland College of Agriculture; former Member, Scottish Country Life Museums Trust Ltd.; former Vice Chairman, SAC. Recreations: golf; field sports. Address: (h.) Nether Darley, Fyvie, Turriff, Aberdeenshire AB53 8LH.

Fergusson of Kilkerran, Sir Adam, 10th Baronet; b. 29.12.62; m., Jenifer.

Fergusson, Professor David Alexander Syme, OBE, MA, BD, DPhil, DD, FBA, FRSE. Regius Professor of Divinity, Cambridge University, since 2021; b. 3.8.56, Glasgow; m., Margot McIndoe; 2 s. Educ. Kelvinside Academy; Glasgow University; Edinburgh University; Oxford University. Assistant Minister, St. Nicholas Church, Lanark, 1983-84; Associate Minister, St. Mungo's Church, Cumbernauld, 1984-86; Lecturer, Edinburgh University, 1986-90; Professor of Systematic Theology, Aberdeen University, 1990-2000; Professor of Divinity, University of Edinburgh, 2000-2021; Chaplain to Moderator of the General Assembly, 1989-90; President, Society for the Study of Theology, 2000-02. President, Association of University Departments of Theology and Religious Studies, 2005-08; Principal of New College, 2008-18; Vice-Principal, University of Edinburgh, 2009-11; Chaplain-in-Ordinary to HM The Queen in Scotland, 2015; Dean of the Chapel Royal in Scotland; Dean of the Order of the Thistle, 2019. Publications: Bultmann, 1992; Christ, Church and Society, 1993; The Cosmos and the Creator, 1998; Community, Liberalism and Christian Ethics, 1998; John Macmurray: Critical Perspectives, 2002; Church, State and Civil Society, 2004; Scottish Philosophical Theology, 2007; Faith and Its Critics, 2009; Blackwell

Companion to 19th Century Theology, 2010; Cambridge Dictionary of Christian Theology, 2011; Creation, 2014; Christian Theology: 21st Century Challenges, 2015; Cambridge Companion to Reformed Theology, 2016; The Providence of God, 2018; History of Scottish Theology, 3 vols., 2019. Recreations: football; golf. Address: 19 The Eights Marina, Mariners Way, Cambridge CB4 1ZA; 14/3 Howden Hall Road, Edinburgh EH16 6PQ; T.-07888037381.
E-mail: daf52@cam.ac.uk

Fernie, Professor John, MA, MBA, PhD. Honorary Professor, University of St Andrews; Emeritus Professor of Retail Marketing, Heriot-Watt University, Head of School of Management and Languages, 2002-07 (Head of School of Management, 1999-2002); Director of Institute of Retail Studies, University of Stirling, 1996-98; b. 4.3.48, East Wemyss, Fife; m., Suzanne Ishbel; 1 s.; 1 d. Educ. Buckhaven High School; Dundee University; Edinburgh University; Bradford University. Lecturer/Senior Lecturer, Huddersfield Polytechnic, 1973-88; Senior Lecturer, University of Abertay Dundee, 1988-96; Senior Lecturer/Professor, University of Stirling, 1996-98. Recent books include: Principles of Retailing (co-author) and Logistics and Retail Management (co-author). Recreations: golf; travelling; 5 a side football. Address: (b.) Heriot-Watt University, Edinburgh EH14 4AS; T.-0131-451-3880; e-mail: j.fernie@hw.ac.uk

Ferrell, Professor William Russell, MB, ChB, PhD, FRCP(Glas). Honorary Senior Research Fellow, Institute of Infection Immunity and Inflammation, University of Glasgow; b. 8.3.49, St. Louis, USA; m., Anne Mary Scobie; 3 s. Educ. St. Aloysius College; University of Glasgow. University of Glasgow: Lecturer, Senior Lecturer, Reader in Physiology; Visiting Professor, University of West of Scotland. Recreations: skiing; computing; tennis. Address: (b.) Room 407, Level 4, McGregor Building, University of Glasgow, Glasgow G12 8QQ.

Ferrier, Margaret. MP (Independent), Rutherglen and Hamilton West, since 2020, SNP, 2019-2020 and 2015-17; Shadow SNP Spokesperson, Scotland Office, 2015-17; b. 1960, Glasgow; 1 d. Former commercial sales manager for a manufacturing construction company in Motherwell. Joined the Rutherglen branch of the SNP in Cambuslang in 2011. Address: House of Commons, Westminster, London SW1A 0AA.

Ferris, Tom. Chief Dental Officer, The Scottish Government, since 2019, previously Deputy Chief Dental Officer, 2010-18. Career history: qualified from Glasgow in 1982 and has worked in general practice, the public dental service in Scotland and in the hospital service in Malta; posts with NHS Forth Valley and NHS Education for Scotland. Closely involved in the development of the Oral Health Improvement Strategy for Priority Groups (2012) and the Oral Health Improvement Plan (2018). Address: Scottish Government, Room 1W06, St Andrew's House, Edinburgh EH1 3DG; T.-0131 244 2302.
E-mail: ceu@gov.scot

Fife, 4th Duke of (David Charles Carnegie); MA (Cantab), MBA. Chairman, Elsick Development Company; Estate Management (the Southesk Estate); b. 3.3.61; m., Caroline Anne Bunting; 3 s. Educ. Eton; Cambridge; Royal Agricultural College, Cirencester; Edinburgh University. Career history: Stockbroker: Cazenove & Co., London, 1982-85, Bell Lawrie, Edinburgh, 1988-89; Chartered Accountant, Reeves & Neylan, Forfar, 1992-96. Honorary President, Angus Show; Vice-Chairman, Historic Houses Association for Scotland; Honorary Patron, The Edinburgh Angus Club; Vice-Patron, The Braemar Royal Highland Society. Address: Kinnaird Castle, Brechin, Angus DD9 6TZ.

Findlay, David J., BSc (Hons), MB, ChB, FRCPsych. Retired Consultant Psychiatrist, Tayside Primary Care (1991-2014); part-time Policy Adviser, Care of the Elderly, Scottish Executive Health Department, 1998-2001, Departmental Specialty Adviser in Psychiatry (Old Age), 2001-07; Honorary Senior Lecturer, Department of Psychiatry, Dundee University, since 1991; b. 2.6.54, Duns; m., Patricia; 1 s.; 3 d. Educ. Ayr Academy; Glasgow University. Junior House Officer, 1979-80; Gartnavel Royal Hospital Training Scheme, 1980-83; Lecturer in Psychiatry, Dundee University, 1984-87; Consultant Psychiatrist and Clinical Tutor, Gartnavel Royal Hospital, 1987-91; Royal Dundee Liff Hospital: Service Manager, Old Age Psychiatry, 1993-1996, Clinical Director, Elderly Services, 1996-99; Chair, RCPsych Philosophy Special Interest Group (Scotland), 2002-07; Chair, RCPsych in Scotland Old Age Faculty, 2008-2012. Recreations: chess; reading; films.

Findlay, Donald Russell, QC, LLB (Hons), MPhil, FRSA. Advocate, since 1975; Chairman, Cowdenbeath Football Club; former Lord Rector, St. Andrews University; b. 17.3.51, Cowdenbeath; m., Jennifer E. Borrowman. Educ. Harris Academy, Dundee; Dundee University; Glasgow University. Sometime Lecturer in Commercial Law, Heriot-Watt University. Elected Chairman, Faculty of Advocates Criminal Bar Association, 2010. Recreations: Glasgow Rangers FC; Egyptology; archaeology; wine; ethics; travelling first class; Cowdenbeath FC. Address: (b.) Optimum Advocates, Glasgow High Court, 1 Mart Street, Saltmarket, Glasgow G1 5JT; e-mail: donaldrfin@aol.com

Findlay, Laurence. Director of Education and Children's Services, Aberdeenshire Council, since 2018. Educ. Aberdeenshire. Career history: Teacher in Edinburgh area, Aberdeenshire and Moray Councils (worked as Teacher of French and German, Head Teacher, Head of Schools and then Director). Address: Aberdeenshire Council, Education and Children's Services, Woodhill House, Westburn Road, Aberdeen AB16 5GB; T.-03456 08 12 02.

Findlay, Neil, BA. MSP (Labour), Lothian, 2011-2021; Shadow Cabinet Secretary for Fair Work, 2015-16; Shadow Cabinet Secretary of State for Health, 2013-15; b. 6.3.69; m.; 1 d. Educ. St. Kentigern's Academy, Blackburn; University of Strathclyde. Apprentice bricklayer; worked in the social housing sector; PGCE in secondary education; formerly Company secretary, Fauldhouse Community Development Trust; formerly West Lothian councillor, and part-time support for learning teacher with Falkirk Council, until 2012. Member, EIS and Unite Trade Union.

Findlay, Russell, MSP (Scottish Conservative and Unionist Party), West Scotland (Region), since 2021; 1 d. Career history: Trinity Mirror plc: News and Sports Reporter, The Glaswegian, 1993-95; News Reporter, Sunday Mail, 1995-98; News Reporter, The News of the World, 1998-99; Deputy News Editor and News Reporter, The Sunday Mail, Trinity Mirror plc, 1999-2014; Investigations Editor, Scottish Sun, 2014-17; freelance journalist, 2017-18; Assistant Producer, Special Investigations, STV Group plc, 2018-2020; Director of Communications, Scottish Conservatives, 2020-21. Publications: Fitted Up: A True Story of Police Betrayal, Conspiracy and Cover Up; Acid Attack: A Journalist's War With Organised Crime; Caught in the Crossfire: Scotland's Deadliest Drugs War; The Iceman: The Rise and Fall of a Drug Lord. Address: The Scottish Parliament, Edinburgh EH99 1SP; T.-0131 348 6975; e-mail: Russell.Findlay.msp@parliament.scot

Finlay, Robert Derek, BA, MA, FInstD, FRSA, MCIM; b. 16.5.32, London; m., Una Ann Grant; 2 s.; 1 d. Educ. Kingston Grammar School; Emmanuel College, Cambridge. Lt., Gordon Highlanders, Malaya, 1950-52; Captain, Gordon Highlanders TA, 1952-61; Mobil Oil Co. UK, 1953-61; Associate, Principal, Director, McKinsey &

Co., 1961-79; Managing Director, H.J. Heinz Co. Ltd., 1979-81; Senior Vice-President, Corporate Development, 1981-93, Chief Financial Officer, 1989-92, Area Vice President, 1992-93, World HQ; H.J. Heinz Co., 1981-93; Chair, Dawson International PLC, 1995-98 (non executive Chair, 1998). Member, London Committee, Scottish Council Development and Industry, 1975-2003; Member: Board, US China Business Council, 1983-93, Board, Pittsburgh Public Theatre, 1986-93, US Korea Business Council, 1986-92, Board, Pittsburgh Symphony Society, 1989-93; Vice Chairman, World Affairs Council of Pittsburgh, 1986-93; Chairman, Board of Visitors Center for International Studies, University of Pittsburgh, 1989-93. Publication: 2006 Autobiograpy "Time To Take Her Home - The Life and Times of RDF". Recreations: rowing; music; theatre. Address: (h.) Mains of Grantully, by Aberfeldy, PH15 2EG.

Finlayson, Niall Diarmid Campbell, OBE, MBChB, PhD, PPRCPE, FRCPL, FRCPSG, FRCSE. Consultant Physician, Royal Infirmary of Edinburgh, 1973-2003; President, Royal College of Physicians of Edinburgh, 2001-04; Director of Communications, Royal College of Physicians of Edinburgh, 2004-09; Chief Medical Officer, Royal London Insurance, since 2003; Chairman, Life Care (Edinburgh) Ltd, 2005-2015; b. 21.4.39, Georgetown, Guyana; m., Dale Kristin Anderson; 1 s.; 1 d. Educ. Loretto School, Musselburgh; Edinburgh University. Lecturer in Therapeutics, Edinburgh University, 1966-69; Assistant Professor of Medicine, Cornell University Medical College, New York Hospital, USA, 1970-72. Recreations: history; music. Address: (h.) 10 Queens Crescent, Edinburgh EH9 2AZ; e-mail: niall.finlayson@icloud.com

Finn, Anthony, CBE (2014), MA (Hons), FRSA, FEIS (1997), Special FEIS (2010). Retired Chief Executive, General Teaching Council for Scotland (2008-2013); Honorary Professor of Teacher Education, University of Glasgow; Chair, Scottish College for Educational Leadership, 2013-18; former Member, Management Board, Curriculum for Excellence, until 2013; Rector, St. Andrew's High School, Kirkcaldy, 1988-2006; formerly Senior Manager, Fife Council Education Service, 2006-08; b. 4.6.51, Irvine; m., Margaret Caldwell. Educ. St. Joseph's Academy, Kilmarnock; Glasgow University. Teacher, Principal Teacher, Assistant Head Teacher, Depute Head Teacher, Acting Head Teacher, St. Andrew's Academy, Saltcoats, 1975-88. Member, SEED Teachers' Agreement Communication Team, 2001-08; Elected Member, General Teaching Council, 1991-2001; Convener, General Teaching Council Education Committee, 1993-2001; Chair, SEED Memorandum Committee, 1991-2001; Member, Executive, Catholic Headteachers' Association Scotland, 2001-06; Member, Catholic Education Commission for Scotland, until 2008; formerly Teachers' Representative, National Committee for the Staff Development of Teachers; Member, Advisory Committee, Scottish Qualification for Headship; Governor, Moray House Institute of Education; Assessor, Teacher Education, Scottish Higher Education Funding Council; Chair, Fife Secondary Head Teachers Association. Recreations: sport; travel; literature; current affairs. Address: (h.) 89 Bowfield Road, West Kilbride, Ayrshire KA23 8JZ; T.-01294 421368.

Finnie, James Ross, CA. Chair, Food Standards Scotland; Non-executive member, Joint Management Board of Secretary of State for Scotland and Advocate General for Scotland; Non-executive member, the Water Industry Commission Scotland, 2012-2020; Vice-Chair, NHS Greater Glasgow and Clyde Board, 2016-2020; Honorary President, Scottish Environment LINK, 2011-15; Member, The Poverty Truth Commission, 2014-15; b. 11.2.47, Greenock; m., Phyllis Sinclair; 1 s.; 1 d. Educ. Greenock Academy. Member, Executive Committee, Scottish Council (Development and Industry), 1976-87; Chairman, Scottish Liberal Party, 1982-86; Member: Inverclyde District Council, 1977-97, Inverclyde Council, 1995-99; MSP (Liberal Democrat), West of Scotland, 1999-2011; Minister for Rural Affairs, 1999-2000; Minister for Environment and Rural Development, Scottish Executive, 2000-07; Liberal Democrat Shadow Secretary for Health and Well being, 2007-2011; Vice Convener, Health and Sport Committee, 2007-2011. Address: (h.) 91 Octavia Terrace, Greenock PA16 7PY; T.-01475 631495.

Finnie, John. MSP (Green), Highlands and Islands, 2016-2021 (SNP, 2011-12, Independent, 2012-16); b. 31.12.56, Clunes, Lochaber. Educ. Achnacarry Primary; Lochaber High School. Served for 30 years in the police. Formerly SNP group leader on Highland Council. Member of the Scottish Green Party, since 2014.

Firth, Dr Howie, MBE. Director, Orkney International Science Festival, since 1991. Educ. University of Edinburgh. Career history: postgraduate research at Durham University; took a break from physics to become a travelling teacher in the smaller island schools of his native Orkney; broadcaster, BBC Radio Orkney. Awards include an honorary degree from the Open University, an award from the Institute of Physics, and an MBE for services to popular science in the UK; has lectured in 11 countries and written widely, and has a particular interest in the history and philosophy of science. Recreation: playing traditional music.

Fisher, Archie, MBE. Folk singer, guitarist, composer, broadcaster; b. 1939, Glasgow. First solo album, 1966; formerly presenter, Travelling Folk, BBC Radio; Artistic Director, Edinburgh International Folk Festival, 1988-92.

Fisher, Barry, BTechnol (Hons) Mgmt. Chief Executive Officer, Keep Scotland Beautiful, since 2020. Educ. Arran High School; University of Glasgow; Scottish Agricultural College. Career history: Area Manager, Ocean Youth Trust, 1996-99; General Manager, Ocean Youth Trust Scotland, 1999-2002; Charity Foundation Officer, Rangers Football Club, 2003-04; The Duke of Edinburgh's Award: Assistant Award Director, 2003-08, Director - Scotland, 2008-2020. Board Member: Ocean Youth Trust Scotland, Remembering Srebrenica Scotland. Address: Keep Scotland Beautiful, Glendevon House, The Castle Business Park, Stirling FK9 4TZ; T.-01786 464611. E-mail: ceo@keepscotlandbeautiful.org

Fisher, Gregor. Actor (television, theatre, film). Credits include (BBC TV): Rab C. Nesbitt series (leading role), Naked Video series, Scotch and Wry, Para Handy, Oliver Twist, Empty. Best Actor award, Toronto Festival, for One, Two, Three.

Fitton, Professor John Godfrey, BSc, PhD, FGS, FRSE. Professor of Igneous Petrology, Edinburgh University, since, 1999; b. 1.10.46, Rochdale; m., Dr Christine Ann Fitton; 2 s.; 1 d. Educ. Bury Grammar School; Durham University. Turner and Newall Research Fellow, Manchester University, 1971-72; Edinburgh University: Lecturer, 1972-89; Senior Lecturer, 1989-94; Reader, 1994-99; served on NERC Research Grants and ODP Committees; Co-Chief Scientist, Ocean Drilling Programme Leg 192, 2000. Publications: Section Editor, Encyclopedia of Geology (2nd edition); Alkaline Igneous Rocks (ed.); Origin and Evolution of the Ontong Java Plateau (ed.); more than 130 refereed papers. Recreations: house restoration; walking; wine; old maps; antiques; gemmology; lapidary work; collecting mineral specimens. Address: (b.)

School of GeoSciences, Edinburgh University, Grant Institute, James Hutton Road, Edinburgh EH9 3FE; T.-0131-650 8529; e-mail: godfrey.fitton@ed.ac.uk

Fitzgerald, Professor Alexander Grant, BSc, PhD, DSc, FRMS, CPhys, FInstP, FRSE. Emeritus Harris Professor of Physics, Dundee University, since 2005; b. 12.10.39, Dundee; m., June; 1 s.; 2 d. Educ. Perth Academy; Harris Academy; St. Andrews University; Cambridge University. Research Fellow, Cambridge University and Lawrence Berkeley Laboratory, University of California; Lecturer, Senior Lecturer, Reader, Professor, Dundee University. Publications: 231 conference and journal papers; book: Quantitative Microbeam Analysis (Co-editor). Recreations: swimming; golf. Address: (b.) Department of Physics, Dundee University, Dundee DD1 4HN; T.-01382 384553. E-mail: a.g.fitzgerald@dundee.ac.uk

Fitzhenry, Daren, LLB, LLM, DipLP. Scottish Information Commissioner, since 2017. Educ. University of Glasgow. Career history: solicitor until 2018; joined the RAF in 2000; a former Group Captain in the Royal Air Force Legal Branch, heading up its legal advisory team, with wide-ranging experience in the development, implementation and enforcement of regulatory systems. Address: Scottish Information Commissioner, Kinburn Castle, Doubledykes Road, St Andrews, Fife KY16 9DS; T.-01334 464610.

FitzPatrick, Joe. MSP (SNP), Dundee City West, since 2007; Minister for Public Health, Sport and Wellbeing, 2018-2020; Minister for Parliamentary Business, 2012-18; b. 1.4.67. Educ. Whitfield High School; Inverness College; Abertay University; Dundee University. Career: worked as an assistant to Shona Robison MSP and Stewart Hosie MP in their Dundee Constituency Office and was a Dundee City Councillor from 1999 serving as SNP group Whip and Finance Spokesperson on Dundee Council; member of all the main Committees during term of office as a Dundee Councillor, 1999-2007, and a member of the Licensing Board, 2003-07; also represented the Council on a number of outside bodies. After election to the Scottish Parliament, became Parliamentary Liaison Officer for Cabinet Secretary for Finance, John Swinney; helped to set up a Cross Party Group on Life Sciences. Address: (b.) Scottish Parliament, Edinburgh EH99 1SP; Constituency Office: 37 Dock Street, Dundee DD1 3DR; T.-01382 843244.

Fitzpatrick, Professor Julie Lydia, OBE, BVMS (Hons), MSc, PhD, DSc, DipECBHM, DipECSRHM, DLSHTM, FIBiol, MRCVS, FRAgs, FRSE. Chief Scientific Adviser, The Scottish Government, since 2021; Scientific Director of The Moredun Research Institute and Chief Executive of The Moredun Group, since 2004; b. 1.3.60, Glasgow; m., Dr. Andrew Fitzpatrick; 2 s. Educ. Wellington School, Ayr; University of Glasgow; University of Bristol; University of London. Veterinary Practitioner, Northumberland, 1982-87; Research Assistant, University of Bristol, 1987-88; PhD student, University of Bristol, 1988-92; Lecturer, University of Glasgow Veterinary School, 1993-98; Head of Division of Farm Animal Medicine and Production, 1998; Personal Chair in Farm Animal Medicine, 1999. Awarded the G. Norman Hall medal for research in animal diseases, 2003; President of the Association of Veterinary Readers and Research Workers, 2003-04; Member: Royal College of Veterinary Surgeons Research Committee, 2002-2012, Scottish Science Advisory Committee, 2004-2010, Advisory Committee on Animal Feedstuffs, 2002-07; Director: Edinburgh Centre for Rural Research, since 2004, Moredun Scientific Limited, since 2005; Member: Agricultural Strategy Group for Scotland, 2005-07, Scottish Animal Health and Welfare Advisory Group, since 2005, Veterinary Fellowships Committee, The Wellcome Trust, 2007-2012, International Panel, The Royal Society of Edinburgh, 2007-2010, Sustainable Agriculture Strategy Panel, Biotechnology and Biological Sciences Research Council, 2008-2011; Chairman, Veterinary Policy Group of the British Veterinary Association, 2004-07; Trustee, Global Alliance for Livestock Veterinary Medicines, 2007-2012; Fellow of The Royal Agricultural Societies, 2010; Member, BBSRC Food Security Advisory Panel, 2012-15; Chair of the Southern African Centre for Infectious Disease Surveillance, 2011-15. DSc (Heriot-Watt), 2012; OBE (2014) for services to Animal Medicine and Science; British Veterinary Association Chiron Award, 2014; Board member, Quality Meat Scotland, since 2014; Vice-Chair, Scottish Food Commission, since 2015, Co-Chair, 2016-18; Chair, UK Science Partnership for Animal and Plant Health, since 2016; Chair, Independent Scientific Advisory Board of the Southern African Centre for Infectious Disease Surveillance; Chair, Science Advisory Board and non-executive Director of the Animal and Plant Health Agency Board, since 2017; Vice-President, Royal Highland and Agricultural Society of Scotland, 2017-2018; Chair, Scottish Aquaculture Innovation Centre's Independent Scientific Panel, since 2018. Recreations: walking; golf; reading. Address: (b.) Moredun Research Institute, Pentlands Science Park, Bush Loan, Penicuik, nr. Edinburgh EH26 0PZ; T.-0131 445 5111. E-mail: julie.fitzpatrick@moredun.ac.uk

Fitzpatrick, Cllr Lawrence. Chartered Secretary. Leader of West Lothian Council, since 2017; represents Livingston South ward (Labour); b. Whitburn; m., Margaret; 1 d. First elected to West Lothian Council in 1999; previously worked in the construction, legal and housing sector for over 25 years. Publication: 'A self build - A Practitioners Critique' commissioned by the Planning Exchange (Author). Recreations: bird watching; rambling; literature and bridge. Address: West Lothian Civic Centre, Howden South Road, Livingston, West Lothian EH54 6FF; T.-01506 281731; e-mail: Lawrence.Fitzpatrick@westlothian.gov.uk

Flanagan, Caroline Jane, LLB, DipLP, NP. Partner/Member, Ross & Connel LLP, Solicitors, Dunfermline, 1990-2019 (retired); Member, Council, Law Society of Scotland, 1998-2007; President, Law Society of Scotland, 2005/06; b. 12.1.61, Bridge of Allan; m., Roy Flanagan; 1 s.; 1 d. Educ. Dollar Academy; Edinburgh University. Trainee, then Assistant Solicitor, Edinburgh, 1982-87; Assistant, then Partner, Ross and Connel, since 1988; accredited as specialist in family law, since 1996; family law arbitrator; Dean, local Faculty of Solicitors, 1998-2000.

Flanagan, Larry. General Secretary, Educational Institute of Scotland (EIS), 2012-2022; b. 1955. Educ. University of Stirling. Career: Teacher, Blantyre High School; Senior Teacher, Penilee High School; Principal Teacher of English, Hillhead High School, Glasgow, 1996-2013. Career long association with the EIS: as an activist, school representative, local office bearer, Council and Executive Committee member and Convener of the EIS Education Committee. Member of the STUC General Council, the TUC General Council and the ETUCE Executive Committee.

Flanagan, Paul, MA (Hons), PG Dip. Stategy Director for Dairy and Scotland Director, AHDB - Agriculture and Horticulture Development Board, Stoneleigh and Edinburgh, since 2018, Strategy Director for Dairy (interim), Warwickshire, since 2018. Educ. University of Aberdeen; University of Strathclyde. Career history:

Diageo, London: Graduate Trainee, 1993-95, various employee communication roles, 1995-2002, PR Manager, 2002-05; First Milk Ltd, Glasgow: Communications Director, 2006-2010, External Relations Director, 2010-14, External Relations and Membership Director, 2014-17. Lead contact for the Scottish Government and NFU Scotland; sits on the Partnership Board for Scotland Food and Drink. E-mail: paul.flanagan@ahdb.org.uk

Flavell, Professor Andy, BSc, PhD. Professor in Plant Genomics, University of Dundee, since 2010; b. 27.03.51, Brentwood; m., Julie; 1 s.; 1 d. Educ. King Edward VIII Grammar, King's Lynn; University of Sheffield. Postdoctoral research: Imperial Cancer Research Fund Laboratories, London, 1975-79, Dana Farber Cancer Centre, Boston, USA, 1979-80, Imperial Cancer Research Fund, Mill Hill Laboratory, London, 1980-83; University of Dundee: Lecturer in Biochemistry, 1983-93, Senior Lecturer in Biochemistry, 1993-2002, Reader in Plant Genetics, 2002-2010. Recreations: cycling; hill walking; slot racing. Address: (b.) Division of Plant Sciences, University of Dundee at SCRI, Invergowrie, Dundee DD2 5DA; e-mail: a.j.flavell@dundee.ac.uk

Fleck, Professor James, MA, BSc, MSc. Honorary Professor, University of Edinburgh Business School (2015); Deputy Director of *Optima*, ESRC and MRC Integrated PhD studies in optical medical imaging with innovation and entrepreneurship, University of Edinburgh and University of Strathclyde (2014-2018); Editor-in-Chief of the international journal, *Technology Analysis & Strategic Management* (2013); Freeman of The Worshipful Company of Information Technologists; b. 18.7.51, Kano, Nigeria; m., Heather Anne Morrison; 2 s.; 3 d. Educ. Perth Academy; University of Edinburgh; Manchester University. Engineer, MK-Shand, Invergordon, 1974-75; Computer Programmer, CAP Limited, London, 1976; Research Fellow and Lecturer, Technology Policy Unit, University of Aston, 1980-85; Lecturer in Operations Management, Heriot-Watt University, 1985-86; Lecturer, then Senior Lecturer, Department of Business Studies, University of Edinburgh, 1986-96, Chair of Organisation of Industry and Commerce, 1996-2004 (Director, University of Edinburgh Management School, 1996-99); Professor of Innovation Dynamics, Open University, 2005-2013; Dean, The Open University Faculty of Business and Law (2005-2011). Joseph Lister Lecturer for the Social Sciences, British Association for the Advancement of Science, 1995-96. Publications: Expertise and Innovation – Information Technology Strategies in the Financial Services Sector (Joint Author), 1994; Exploring Expertise (Joint Editor), 1998. Recreations: park running; reading; DIY; windsurfing; eating out. Address: (h.) Grange Park House, 38 Dick Place, Edinburgh EH9 2JB; T.-07753600055.

Fletcher, James Macmillan. Provost, East Renfrewshire Council, since 2017 (Leader, 2004-2017); Director, Scottish Futures Trust, 2008-2017; b. 27.04.54, Glasgow; m., Alison; 2 d. Educ. Penilee Secondary School; Stow College of Education. Local Government: Councillor, Eastwood District Council, 1988-95; Convener of Education, East Renfrewshire Council, 1995-2004; Professional: Contracts Officer with Ministry of Defence until 1994; Head of Army Pensions Office, 1994-97; Head of Army Pensions Agency, 1997-2001; Head of Tri-Service Pensions Agency with EDS Ltd., 2001-05. Non Executive Director of Scottish Enterprise Renfrewshire, 2000-08. Recreations: watching sport and travel. Address: (h.) 35 Fowlis Drive, Newton Mearns, East Renfrewshire G77 6JL; T.-0141 639 6201. E-mail: jim.fletcher@eastrenfrewshire.gov.uk

Fletcher, Sheriff Michael John, LLB. Sheriff of Tayside Central and Fife at Perth, 2000-2014 (retired); b. 5.12.45, Dundee; m., Kathryn Mary; 2 s. Educ. High School of Dundee; St. Andrews University. Partner, Ross Strachan &

Co., 1970-88; Partner, Miller Hendry (Hendry and Fenton), 1988-94; Part-time Lecturer in Civil and Criminal Procedure, University of Dundee, 1974-94; Legal Aid Reporter, 1978-94; Temporary Sheriff, 1991-94; Sheriff of South Strathclyde Dumfries & Galloway at Dumfries, 1994-99; Sheriff of Lothian and Borders at Edinburgh, 1999-2000; Editor, Scottish Civil Law Reports, since 1999; Member, Sheriff Court Rules Council, 2001-2010; President, Sheriffs' Association, 2009-2011, formerly Vice President; Member, Judicial Studies Committee, 2006-2012; Council Member, Commonwealth Magistrates and Judges Association, 2009-2012, Regional Vice President, 2012-2018. Publication: Delictual Damages (Co-Author). Recreations: golf; gardening; travel; fine wines; learning Japanese language.

Flint, Sir Douglas Jardine, CBE. Chairman, abrdn (formerly Standard Life Aberdeen), since 2019; b. 8.7.55. Educ. University of Glasgow; Harvard Business School. Career history: Peat Marwick Mitchell & Co. (now KPMG), appointed a partner in 1988; Group Finance Director, HSBC, 1995-2010; Chairman, HSBC Holdings plc, 2010-2017; appointed Director and Chairman Designate, Standard Life Aberdeen in November 2018. Chairman, IP Group plc; Non-Executive Director, Centre for Policy Studies; Member, Global Advisory Council of Motive Partners; Board Member, the Institute of International Finance; Chairman: Just Finance Foundation, Corporate Board of Cancer Research UK; Trustee of the Royal Marsden Cancer Charity; Special Envoy to China's Belt and Road Initiative, since 2017. Chairman of the Financial Reporting Council's review of the Turnbull Guidance on Internal Control, 2004-05; member of The Accounting Standards Board and the Standards Advisory Council of the International Accounting Standards Committee Foundation, 2001-04. Address: abrdn, 30 Lothian Road, Edinburgh EH1 2DH; T.-0131 245 2151.

Flint, Professor Harry James, BSc, PhD. Emeritus Professor, University of Aberdeen; b. 5.1.51, London; m. Irene; 1 s. Christopher; 2 d. Kathryn, Rowan. Educ. Abingdon School, Abingdon, Oxfordshire; Edinburgh University. PhD in Genetics, University of Edinburgh, 1972-76; Lecturer in Genetics, University of Nottingham, 1976-80; Lecturer in Biology, University of The West Indies (Barbados), 1980-82; Research Fellow, University of Edinburgh (Dept. of Genetics), 1982-85; Research Scientist (1985-2017) and Head of Gut Health Division (1999-2016), Rowett Institute, Aberdeen (merged with University of Aberdeen, 2008); Emeritus since 2017. Publications: Author of 198 primary research papers, 65 reviews and book chapters, most focussed on the contributions of gut micro-organisms to nutrition and health in humans and animals. Author of the book 'Why Gut Microbes Matter' (Springer, Fascinating Life Sciences, 2020). Editorial Boards/Editorial duties: Environmental Microbiology, FEMS Microbiology Ecology, Applied and Environmental Microbiology, Microbiology, Gut Microbes, Gut Microbiome, Eur J Nutrition. Member, UK Advisory Committee on Novel Foods and Processes (2006-12); Scientific Governor of British Nutrition Foundation (2014-16). Recreations: music; countryside; natural history; art; history. Address: Rowett Institute, University of Aberdeen, Foresterhill, Ashgrove Road West, Aberdeen AB25 2ZD; e-mail: harry.flint@abdn.ac.uk

Flowerdew, Stuart Alan, LLB (Hons), DipLP, NP. Solicitor; Partner: Gray and Gray Solictors, since 2020, Adam and Flowerdew Solicitors, 2016-2020, AFJ Solicitors, 2014-16; Secretary and Treasurer, Faculty of Solicitors in Peterhead and Fraserburgh, 1993-2010;

Chairman, Victim Support, Aberdeenshire, 2000-04; b. 5.2.67, Kings Lynn; m., Natalie Anne Lamb; 1 d. Educ. Forres Academy; University of Dundee. Trainee/Assistant, Miller Hendry, Perth, 1989-92; Assistant: Stewart and Watson, Peterhead, 1992-94, Masson & Glennie, Peterhead, 1994-96; Associate, John MacRitchie & Co., SSC, Peterhead, 1997-1999; Partner: Flowerdew Allan, Solicitors, Peterhead, 1999-2010, Flowerdew Solicitors Ltd, 2010-2014. Recreation: cricket. Address: (b.) 2 Kirk Street, Peterhead; T.-01779 481717; (h.) Braemount, 27 Balmoor Terrace, Peterhead; T.-01779 473117.
E-mail: stuart@adamandflowerdew.com

Flyn, Derek, LLB, WS, FSAScot. Solicitor (retired), former partner, Macleod and MacCallum, Inverness (1978-2008); b. 22.8.45, Edinburgh; m., Fiona Mairi Macmillan; 2 s.; 1 d. Educ. Broughton School, Edinburgh; Dundee University. Scottish Court Service, 1962-72 (Sheriff Clerk Depute at Portree, 1967-70); First specialist in crofting law accredited by Law Society of Scotland, 1993; President, Scottish Law Agents Society, 1999-2000; Vice-Chairman, Crofting Law Group, 1994-2004; Chairman, Riding for the Disabled (Highland Group), 2007-2012; Chairman, Scottish Crofting Federation, 2012-2014. Publications: Crofting Law (Co-author), 1990 and 2017; Green's Annotated Crofters Act (Co-author), 1993 and 2010; Countryside Law in Scotland (Contributor), 2000; Stair Encyclopaedia (Contributor), 2009; Scottish Life and Society (Contributor), 2012. Recreations: music; walking; Ross County FC. Address: (h.) Croyardhill, Beauly IV4 7EX; e-mail: derekflyn@yahoo.co.uk

Flynn, Stephen Mark. MP (SNP) Aberdeen South, since 2019; SNP Shadow Secretary of State for Business, Energy and Industrial Strategy, since 2021; b. 13.10.88. Former SNP councillor on Aberdeen City Council and became group leader in 2016. Address: Houses of Parliament, Westminster, London SW1A 0AA; e-mail: stephen.flynn.mp@parliament.uk

Foggie, Rev Dr Janet Patricia, MA, BD, PhD. Chief Executive Officer, Community Energy Scotland, 2021-22; Pioneer Minister, University of Stirling, 2016-2021; Minister, St Andrew's Parish Church, 2009-2016; b. 9.4.71, Greenock; m., Dr Alan R. Macdonald; 2 s.; 1 d. Educ. Greenock Academy; Universities of Edinburgh and St Andrews. Post-doctoral research post: Browne Downie Research Fellowship, St Mary's College, University of St Andrews, 2000-01; Assistant Minister, Hope Park Church, St Andrews, Fife, 2001-03; Hospital Chaplain to the Royal Victoria Hospital, Dundee (Part time), 2003-04; Mental Health Care Chaplain/Spiritual Care Provider, Dundee, NHS Tayside, 2004-09; Seconded to NHS Education for Scotland, 2007-2008; Joint Editor, Scottish Journal of Healthcare Chaplaincy, 2006-2011. Publications: Academic: Urban Religion in Renaissance Scotland: The Dominican Order 1450-1560, 2003; Capabilities and Competences for Healthcare Chaplains (Joint Author), 2008; various articles; Fiction: 'The News Steps' in Doris Lumsden's Heart Shaped Bed and Other Stories, 2004. Recreations: reading; sewing; gardening; cooking and eating.

Forbes, Very Rev. Dr. Graham John Thomson, CBE (2004). Former Provost, St Mary's Cathedral, Edinburgh (1990-2017); b. 10.6.51; m., Jane; 3 s. Educ. George Heriot's School, Edinburgh; University of Aberdeen; University of Edinburgh; Edinburgh Theological College. Curate, Old St Paul's Edinburgh, 1976-82; Provost: St. Ninian's Cathedral, Perth, 1982-90; Non-Executive Director, Radio Tay, 1986-90; Founder, Canongate Youth Project, Edinburgh; President, Lothian Association of Youth Clubs, since 1986; HM (lay) Inspector of Constabulary for Scotland, 1995-98; Chairman: Scottish Executive MMR Expert Group, 2001-02, Scottish Criminal Cases Review Commission, 2002; Director, Theological Institute of the Scottish Episcopal Church, 2002-04; Member: Scottish Community Education Council, 1981-87, Children's Panel Advisory Committee, Tayside, 1986-90, Parole Board for Scotland, 1990-95, Scottish Consumer Council, 1995-98, GMC, since 1996, Clinical Standards Board for Scotland, 1999-2005, Historic Buildings Council for Scotland, 2000-02, Scottish Council, Royal College of Anaesthetists, 2001-04; former Chairman, Scottish Criminal Cases Review Commission. Chair, Mental Welfare Commission for Scotland; Chair, OSCR (Office of the Scottish Charity Regulator); Chair of Court, Edinburgh Napier University; also serves on the Armed Forces Pay Review Body and the Security Vetting Appeals Panel. Recreations: fly fishing; running.

Forbes, Kate, BA. MSP (SNP), Skye, Lochaber and Badenoch, since 2016; Cabinet Secretary for Finance and Economy, since 2021; Cabinet Secretary for Finance, 2020-21; b. 6.4.90, Dingwall; m., Alasdair MacLennan. Educ. Dingwall Academy; University of Edinburgh; University of Cambridge. Minister for Public Finance and Digital Economy, 2018-2020. Address: Scottish Parliament, Edinburgh EH99 1SP.

Forbes, 23rd Lord (Malcolm Nigel Forbes); b. 1946. Succeeded to title, 2013.

Forbes, Ronald Douglas, RSA, RGI. Artist; Leverhulme Artist in Residence, Scottish Crop Research Institute, Dundee, 2006-09; Visiting Professor, University of Abertay Dundee, since 2003; Head of Painting, Duncan of Jordanstone College of Art, 1995-2001; b. 22.3.47, Braco; m., Sheena Henderson Bell; 1 s.; 2 d. Educ. Morrison's Academy, Crieff; Edinburgh College of Art. Leverhulme Senior Art Fellow, Strathclyde University, 1973-74; Head of Painting, Crawford School of Art, Cork, Ireland, 1974-78; Artist in Residence, Livingston, 1978-80; Scottish Arts Council Studio Residence Bursary, Amsterdam, 1980; Lecturer, Glasgow School of Art, 1979-83; Director, Master Fine Art postgraduate studies, Duncan of Jordanstone College of Art, University of Dundee, 1983-95; Artist in Residence, University of Tasmania Hobart Centre for the Arts. First Prize, first Scottish Young Contemporary Exhibition, 1967; BBC Scope Film Prize, 1975; RSA Guthrie Award, 1979; Scottish Arts Council Award for Film-making, 1979; RSA Highland Society of London Award, 1996; elected to Royal Scottish Academy (Associate, 1996, Academician, 2005); elected RGI (Royal Glasgow Institute of the Fine Arts), 2013. Recreations: cinema; theatre; gardening. Address: (h.) 15 Fort Street, Dundee DD2 1BS; T.-07400 219135.
E-mail: ronnieforbes@blueyonder.co.uk
Website: www.ronald-forbes.com

Ford, Andy, BSc (Hons), MSc. Director of Nature and Climate Change, Cairngorms National Park Authority, since 2021. Educ. University of Sunderland; University of the West of Scotland. Career history: Assistant Reserve Manager, VSO/Ministry of Environment, Nigeria, 1995-98; Countryside ranger, Loch Lomond and the Trossachs National Park Authority, 1998-2000; Operations Manager, Protected Areas Development Programme, Ghana, 2000-01; Senior Countryside Ranger, Wigan Leisure and Culture Trust, 2001-05; Cairngorms National Park Authority: Visitor Services Officer, 2005-2012, Cairngorms Nature Manager, 2012-18, Head of Conservation, since 2018. Address: Cairngorms National Park Authority, Grantown on Spey PH26 3HG; T.-01479 870558.
E-mail: andyford@cairngorms.co.uk

Ford, Professor Ian, BSc, PhD, FRCP (Glas), FRCP (Edin), FISI, FSCT, FRSE. Professor of Biostatistics, University of Glasgow; Senior Research Fellow and Director, Robertson Centre for Biostatistics; Director, Glasgow Clinical Trials Unit, 2007-2016; Dean, Faculty of

Information and Mathematical Sciences, 2000-04; b. 4.2.51, Glasgow; m., Carole Louise Ford; 1 s. Educ. Hamilton Academy; Glasgow University. Visiting Lecturer, University of Wisconsin, Madison, 1976-77; Lecturer, then Senior Lecturer, Reader, Personal Professor and Professor, Glasgow University, since 1977. Publications: 440 papers. Recreations: gardening; travel. Address: (b.) Robertson Centre for Biostatistics, Boyd Orr Building, Glasgow University, Glasgow; T.-0141-330 4744.

Ford, John Noel Patrick, KStJ, FInstD. Retired (1992) as Chairman, Scotland and Northern Ireland, and Marketing Director, OCS Group Ltd; Director/Administrator, Scottish Civic Trust, 1993-2004; b. 18.12.35, Surbiton; m., Roslyn Madeleine Penfold; 2 s.; 2 d. Educ. Tiffin School, Kingston on Thames. Chancellor, The Priory of Scotland of the Order of St. John, 2002-2011. Deacon, Incorporation of Masons of Glasgow, 1985-86; Deacon Convener, Trades House of Glasgow, 1991-92; Regional Chairman, Glasgow, Princes Scottish Youth Business Trust, 1993-2001; Chairman, Glasgow Committee, Order of St. John, 1993-2002; Trustee, New Lanark Conservation Trust, 1994-2009; Governor, Hutchesons' Educational Trust, 1986-2001; Member, Council, Europa Nostra, 1999-2005; General Commissioner of Inland Revenue, Glasgow North, 1993-2009. Recreations: golf and sport in general; gardening. Address: (h.) Ballindalloch South Lodge, Balfron G63 0RQ; T.-01360 440347.

Forrest, Archie, RGI. Artist; b. 1950, Glasgow. Educ. Glasgow School of Art. Taught at Glasgow School of Art, 1978-85; works in the Glasgow School/Scottish Colourist tradition with still life, figure and landscape subjects (often France or Italy) of brilliant colour and bravura handling underpinned by fine drawing and sense of form; also a sculptor of considerable merit. Shows with great success in London and in Edinburgh. Member of the Royal Glasgow Institute of Fine Arts, since 1988 and regular exhibitor there and at the Royal Scottish Academy, since 1975; won numerous awards for both his paintings and sculpture. Example of his work can be found in private and corporate collections worldwide. Address: 2 Cleveden Crescent, Glasgow G12 0PD.

Forrest, Robert John, BSc. Chief Executive, GreenPower, since 2000; Chair of Board, Scottish Renewables, 2018-2021, Director, 2016-2021; b. 1964. Educ. Alleyn's School; Kingston University. Career history: Postgraduate Researcher, The Open University, 1985-89; Research Fellow, University of Strathclyde, 1989-91; Partner, Energy Unlimited, 1991-2000; Director, Scottish Renewables, 1999-2010. Recreations: keen follower of cycle racing; cyling; family; travelling; hill walking. Address: Scottish Renewables, 46 Bath Street, Glasgow G2 1HG; T.-0141 353 4980.

Forrester, Ian Stewart, QC, MA, LLB, LLD, MCL. Honorary Professor, Glasgow University; b. 13.1.45, Glasgow; m., Sandra Anne Therese Keegan; 2 s. Educ. Kelvinside Academy, Glasgow; Glasgow University; Tulane University of Louisiana. Admitted to Faculty of Advocates, 1972; admitted to Bar of State of NY, 1977; Queen's Counsel (Scotland), 1988; called to Bar, Middle Temple, 1996; Bencher, 2012; Maclay, Murray & Spens, 1968-69; Davis Polk & Wardwell, 1969-72; Cleary Gottlieb Steen & Hamilton, 1972-81; established independent chambers, Brussels, 1981; Co-Founder, Forrester & Norall, 1981 (Forrester Norall & Sutton, 1989; White & Case/Forrester Norall & Sutton, 1998), practising before European Commission and Courts. Chairman, British Conservative Association, Belgium, 1982-86; Arbitrator, Court of Arbitration for Sport, since 2012; author of numerous papers on European law; Elder, St. Andrew's Church of Scotland, Brussels. Recreations: politics; wine; cooking; restoring old houses.

Forrester, Professor John V., MD (Hons), FRCS(Ed), FRCOphth, FRCS(G), FRCP(Ed), FMedSci, FRSE, FIBiol, FARVO. Emeritus Professor; Professor of Ocular Immunology, University of Western Australia, since 2012; Cockburn Professor of Ophthalmology, since 1984; Raine Visiting Professor, University of Western Australia; b. 11.9.46, Glasgow; m., Anne Gray; 2 s.; 2 d. Educ. St. Aloysius College, Glasgow; Glasgow University. Various hospital appointments, Glasgow, 1971-78; MRC Travelling Fellow, Columbia University, New York, 1976-77; Consultant Ophthalmologist, Southern General Hospital, 1979-83. Editor, British Journal of Ophthalmology, 1992-2000; Spinoza Professor, University of Amsterdam, 1997; Master, Oxford Ophthalmological Congress, 2000-02; President, European Association for Vision and Eye Research, 2002. Awards: McKenzie Medal 2006; Doyne Medal, 2007; Adjunct Professor, Ophthalmology, University of Western Australia, 2009; Recipient, Alcon Award, 2011; Mildred Weisenfeld Award, 2012; Donders Medal, 2012; Bowman Lectures and Medal, 2012. Address: (b.) Immunology and Infection, Institute of Medical Sciences, Aberdeen University, Aberdeen AB25 2ZD; T.-01224 553782.

Forrester, Rev Margaret Rae, MA, BD, DD; b. 23.11.37, Edinburgh; m., Duncan B. Forrester; 1 s.; 1 d. Educ. George Watson's Ladies' College; Edinburgh University and New College. Assistant Pastor, Tambaram, Madras; Minister, Telscombe Cliffs URC, Sussex; Assistant Minister, St. George's West, Edinburgh; Chaplain, Napier College, Edinburgh; Minister, St. Michael's, Edinburgh, 1980-2003; Convener, Board of World Mission and Unity, Church of Scotland, 1992-96; Moderator, Presbytery of Edinburgh, 2000-01. Publications: Touch and Go, 2002; The Cat Who Decided, 2007; My Cat Mac, 2010; Mac's Christmas Star, 2012. Recreations: gardening; bridge; reading. Address: 25 Kingsburgh Road, Edinburgh EH12 6DZ; T.-0131-337 5646; e-mail: margaret@rosskeen.org.uk

Forsyth of Drumlean, Rt. Hon. Lord (Michael Bruce Forsyth), PC, Kt, MA. Life Peer; MP (Conservative), Stirling, 1983-97; Non-Executive Director: J & J Denholm Ltd; Chairman: Secure Trust Bank, Safor Ltd, House of Lords Economic Affairs Select Committee; Deputy Chairman, J.P. Morgan UK, 2002-05; Secretary of State for Scotland, 1995-97; b. 16.10.54, Montrose; m., Susan Jane; 1 s.; 2 d. Educ. Arbroath High School; St. Andrews University. National Chairman, Federation of Conservative Students, 1976; Member, Westminster City Council, 1978-83; Member, Select Committee on Scottish Affairs; Parliamentary Private Secretary to the Foreign Secretary, 1986-87; Chairman, Scottish Conservative Party, 1989-90; Parliamentary Under Secretary of State and Minister of State, Scottish Office, 1987-92; Minister of State, Department of Employment, 1992-94; Minister of State, Home Office, 1994-95; Parliamentarian of Year, 1996; Member, Select Committee on Monetary Policy, House of Lords; Member, Joint Committee of both Houses of Parliament on future of House of Lords; Director, Robert Fleming International Ltd., 1997-2000; Vice Chairman, Investment Europe, J P Morgan Chase, 2001-2002; Member, Development Board, National Portrait Gallery, 1999-2003; Barnett Formula Select Committee. Recreations: fly fishing; mountaineering; astronomy; gardening; art; steam engines; skiing. Address: House of Lords, London SW1A 0PW.

Forsyth of that Ilk, Alistair Charles William, JP, KHS, FSCA, FSA Scot, FInstPet, CStJ. Baron of Ethie; Chief of the Name and Clan of Forsyth; b. 7.12.29; m., Ann Hughes; 4 s. Educ. St. Paul's School; Queen Mary College, London. Company Director; CStJ, 1982; KHS, 1992; Freeman of the

City of London; Liveryman of the Scriveners Company. Recreations: Scottish antiquities.

Forsyth of that Ilk Younger, Alistair James Menteith, OStJ, MTheol, LLB, DipLP, ACII, FSAScot. Advocate, since 1995; b. 21.12.60, Calcutta; m., Isabelle Richer. Educ. Fettes College; St. Andrews University; Buckingham University; Edinburgh University; Inns of Court School of Law. Executive, publishing and insurance, 1983-86; called to English Bar, Inner Temple, 1990, Member, Lincolns Inn, 1991; employed Lindsays WS, 1992-94; qualified as Solicitor and Notary Public, 1993. Lt., Ayrshire (Earl of Carrick's Own) Yeomanry Sqn., Queen's Own Yeomanry, 1983-88, Inns of Court and City Yeomanry, 1988-90; Member, Committee, Heraldry Society of Scotland, 1983-86; Secretary, Angus Branch, Order of St. John, 1983-86; Liveryman of the Worshipful Company of Scriveners, 2009; Freeman of the City of London, 2009; Member, Company of Merchants of the City of Edinburgh, 2010. Recreations: heraldry; genealogy; history; wine. Address: Dundrennan, Horsemarket, Falkland, Fife KY15 7BG; T.-01337 858735.

Forsyth, Bill. Film Director and Script Writer; b. 1946, Glasgow. Films include: Gregory's Girl, 1981, Local Hero, 1983, Comfort and Joy, 1984, Housekeeping, 1988, Breaking In, 1990, Being Human, 1993; Gregory's Two Girls, 1999. BAFTA Awards: Best Screenplay, 1982, Best Director, 1983.

Forsyth, Janice, MA (Hons). Broadcaster; b. Glasgow. Educ. Glasgow High School for Girls; Glasgow University. Presenter, The Culture Studio; TV includes: Filmnight (C4), Don't Look Down, NB and Festival Cinema (all Scottish); writes a weekly blog for HeraldScotland. Board Member, Giant Productions. Recreations: cinema; travel; theatre.

Forsyth, Roderick Hugh (Roddy). Journalist; Director, SPFL Trust, since 2013; b. 22.9.53, Lennoxtown; m., Marian Charlotte Reilly; 2 d. Educ. Allan Glen's School, Glasgow. Journalist, D.C. Thomson & Co., 1972-74; Scottish Daily News, 1975; Editor, Carnoustie Times, 1976-77; Editor, What's On in Glasgow, 1978-79; Editor, Clyde Guide, 1979-80; Journalist, Glasgow Herald, 1980-81; Sunday Standard, 1982-83; freelance, since 1983; Scottish Football Correspondent: The Times, 1988-93, Daily and Sunday Telegraph, since 1993, BBC Radio Sport, since 1983, RTE Ireland, since 1988, Ireland on Sunday, since 1996. President, Scottish Football Writers' Association, 2010-13; Director, SPL Trust, 2012-13. Publications: The Only Game, 1990; Fields of Green, 1996; Blue and True, 1996.

Forsythe, Professor John L.R., MD, FRCSEd, FRCSEng, MBBS, FEBS, FRCP (Ed). Consultant transplant surgeon, since 1995; Honorary Professor, University of Edinburgh; b. 27.2.58, Co. Antrim; m., Lorna; 1 s.; 2 d. Educ. Belfast Royal Academy; University of Newcastle upon Tyne. Consultant in General Surgery, Newcastle upon Tyne, 1992-95; Consultant Transplant Surgeon, Royal Infirmary of Edinburgh, since 1995; Chairman, Scottish Transplant Group, 1999-2016; President, British Transplantation Society, 2005-07; Non-Executive Board Member, NHS Blood and Transplant, 2005-2013; Lead Clinician for Organ Donation and Transplantation (Scotland), 1999-2016; Chairman, Advisory Committee on Safety of Blood, Tissues and Organs (UK Advisory Group), 2008-2015; Secretary, European Society of Organ Transplantation, 2009-2013; Past President, European Society of Organ Transplantation. Honorary degree

awarded, 2013; Medical Director, Organ Donation and Transplant section of NHS Blood and Transplant. Address: (b.) Transplant Unit, Royal Infirmary of Edinburgh, 51 Little France Crescent, Old Dalkeith Road, Edinburgh EH16 4SU; T.-0131 242 1715. E-mail: john.forsythe@nhslothian.scot.nhs.uk

Forteviot, 4th Baron (Sir John James Evelyn Dewar Bart). Member, Queen's Bodyguard for Scotland (Royal Company of Archers); b. 5.4.38. Educ. Eton. Black Watch (RHR), 1956-58.

Foster, Professor John Odell, MA, PhD. Emeritus Professor of Social Sciences, University of the West of Scotland; b. 21.10.40, Hertford; m., Renee Prendergast; 1 d. Educ. Guildford Grammar School; St. Catherine's College, Cambridge. Postdoctoral Research Fellow, St. Catherine's College, Cambridge, 1965-68; Lecturer in Politics, Strathclyde University, 1966-81. International Secretary, Communist Party of Britain 2000-2021 (Scottish Secretary, 1988-2000). Publications: Class Struggle and the Industrial Revolution, 1974; Politics of the UCS Work-In, 1986; Track Record: the Caterpillar Occupation, 1988; Paying for the Piper (Co-Author), 1996; History of the TGWU Vol I, 1922-1931 (Co-Author) and Vol IV, 1960-1972 (2021-22). Recreation: walking. Address: (h.) 845 Govan Road, Glasgow G51.

Foster-Fulton, Rev. Sally. Head of Christian Aid Scotland, since 2016; b. 1964. Previously Associate Minister, Dunblane Cathedral. Convener, Church and Society Council, 2012-16. Address: Christian Aid Scotland, First Floor, Sycamore House, 290 Bath Street, Glasgow G2 4JR; T.-0141 221 7475; e-mail: sfoster-fulton@christian-aid.org

Foulis, Alan Keith, BSc, MD, FRCPath, FRCP(Ed). Former Consultant Pathologist, Royal Infirmary, Glasgow (retired, 2015); Honorary Clinical Professor, Glasgow University, since 2010; b. 25.5.50, Glasgow; m., (1) Anne Don Martin (deceased); 1 s.; 1 d.; m., (2) Doreen P. Dobson. Educ. Glasgow Academy; Glasgow University. Trained in pathology, Western Infirmary, Glasgow, following brief flirtation with surgery at Aberdeen Royal Infirmary; C.L. Oakley Lecturer, Pathological Society, Oxford, 1987; Bellahouston Medal, Glasgow University, 1987; R.D. Lawrence Lecturer, British Diabetic Association, Manchester, 1989. Publications: research papers on diseases of the pancreas and colon. Recreations: singing; walking; cycling; reading; natural history. Address: (h.) 7 Heathfield Drive, Milngavie, Glasgow; T.-07879660309.

Foulis, Sheriff Lindsay David Robertson, LLB (Hons). Sheriff at Perth, 2001-2021 (retired); Honorary Professor in Scots Law, Dundee University, since 2001; b. 20.4.56, Dundee; m., Ellenore; 2 s.; 1 d. Educ. High School of Dundee; Edinburgh University. Legal apprenticeship, Balfour and Manson, Edinburgh, 1978-80; Legal Assistant, Fred Tyler; Assistant, Reid Johnston Bell and Henderson, 1981; became Partner, 1984; appointed an all-Scotland Floating Sheriff, 2000. Part-time Lecturer, Dundee University, 1994-2000; Member, Sheriff Court Rules Council, 1996-2000; Temporary Sheriff, 1998-99. Publication: Civil Court Practice materials (Co-author). Recreations: sport; now mainly golf (badly); music.

Foulis, Michael Bruce, BSc (Hons), FRGS. Visiting Professor, Humanities and Social Sciences, Strathclyde University, since 2015; b. 23.8.56, Kilmarnock; m., Gillian Tyson; 1 s.; 1 d. Educ. Kilmarnock Academy; Edinburgh University. Joined Scottish Office, 1978; Private Secretary to Parliamentary Under Secretary of State, 1987-89; seconded to Scottish Financial Enterprise as Assistant Director, 1989-92; Private Secretary to Secretary of State for Scotland, 1993-95; seconded to Cabinet Office as Deputy Head, Devolution Team,

Constitution Secretariat, 1997-98; Head of Group, Scottish Education and Industry Department, 1998-99; Head of Economic Development, Enterprise and Lifelong Learning Department, 1999-2001; Head of Environment Group, Environment and Rural Affairs Department, 2001-05; on secondment to Scottish Resources Group working on Corporate Strategy, 2006-07; Director for Housing and Regeneration, Scottish Government, 2007-2010; Director for Strategy and Performance, 2011; Director for Children and Families, 2011-2015. Board Memberships: Children 1st, 2002-08; WASPS (Workshop and Artists Studio Provision (Scotland) Limited), 2008-2011; Morvern Community Development Company, since 2016. Recreations: appreciating lithographs; chopping wood; walking. Address: (b.) University of Strathclyde, Lord Hope Building, 141 St James Road, Glasgow G4 0LT; T.-0141 444 8513.

Foulkes of Cumnock, Rt. Hon. Lord (George Foulkes), PC, JP, BSc. MSP (Labour), Lothians, 2007-2011; MP (Labour and Co-operative), Carrick, Cumnock and Doon Valley, 1979-2005; b. 21.1.42, Oswestry; m., Elizabeth Anna; 2 s.; 1 d. Educ. Keith Grammar School; Haberdashers' Aske's School; Edinburgh University. Opposition Spokesman on Foreign Affairs, 1984-92, Defence, 1992-93, Overseas Development, 1994-97; Parliamentary Under-Secretary of State, Department for International Development; 1997-2001; Minister of State for Scotland, 2001-02. President, Scottish Union of Students, 1964-66; Director: European League for Economic Co-operation, 1967-68, Enterprise Youth, 1968-73, Age Concern Scotland, 1973-79; Chairman: Lothian Region Education Committee, 1974-79, Education Committee, COSLA, 1975-79; Rector's Assessor, Edinburgh University, 1968-71; Treasurer, Parliamentarians for Global Action; Chair, Labour Movement for Europe in Scotland; Member: Joint Committee on National Security Strategy, 2010-2013, Lords EU Select Committee, 2011-2015, Lords EU Sub Committee on Foreign Policy, Defence and International Development and Trade, 2011-2015; President, Caribbean Council, 2011-2016; Member, Board of Directors of Westminster Foundation for Democracy, 2007-2013; Trustee (Vice-Chair), Age Scotland, 2014-2016, Chair, 2016-2020; Treasurer, The Climate Parliament, 2014-2016; Member: Lords Liaison Committee, 2015-19, Lords Procedure Committee, 2018-2020; Delegate to Parliamentary Assembly of Council of Europe (PACE), since 2015; Member: Common Framework Scrutiny Committee, since 2020, European Affairs Select Committee, since 2021. Recreations: boating; watching football (Heart of Midlothian and Ayr United). Address: (h.) 18 Barony Terrace, Edinburgh EH12 8RE.

Fourman, Professor Michael Paul, BSc, MSc, DPhil, FBCS, CITP. Professor, Computer Systems, The University of Edinburgh, since 1988; b. 12.09.50, Oxford; divorced; 2 s.; 1 d. Educ. Allerton Grange, Leeds; Bristol University; Linacre, Oxford. Assistant Professor, Clark University, Worcester, Mass., 1976-77; J.F. Ritt Assistant Professor, Columbia University, NYC, 1977-82; Fellow, University of Cambridge, 1979-80; Reader, Brunel University, London, 1986-87, Professor, Formal Systems, 1987-88; Technical Director, Abstract Hardware Ltd., Uxbridge, 1986-96. Recreations: cooking; sailing. Address: (b.) University of Edinburgh, School of Informatics, Appleton Tower, Crichton Street, Edinburgh EH8 9LE; T.-0131 650 2690.
E-mail: michael.fourman@ed.ac.uk

Fowkes, Professor Francis Gerald Reid, MB, ChB, PhD, FRCPE, FFPH. Emeritus Professor of Epidemiology, Edinburgh University, since 2011; Director, Wolfson Unit for Prevention of Peripheral Vascular Diseases, 1989-2011; Hon. Consultant, Public Health Medicine, 1985-2011; b. 9.5.46, Falkirk; 1 s.; 1 d. Educ. George Watson's College,

Edinburgh; Edinburgh University. Senior Lecturer, University of Wales, 1980-85; Reader/Professor, Edinburgh University, since 1985. Address: (b.) Usher Institute of Population Health Sciences and Informatics, Edinburgh University, Teviot Place, Edinburgh EH8 9AG; T.-0131-650 3220.

Fowlie, Anna. Chief Executive, The Scottish Council for Voluntary Organisations (SCVO), since 2018; Chief Executive, Scottish Social Services Council, 2009-2018. Educ. Edinburgh University and Napier Polytechnic. Career history: worked for 18 years in HR in local authorities; worked within the Employers' Organisation in COSLA, across all local government negotiating bodies; became Team Leader for Children and Young People in COSLA, lobbying on behalf of local government on all policy issues relating to education and children's services with a lead role on the social services workforce; headed up the Scottish Government team improving outcomes for Looked After Children; worked closely with local authorities and other services to raise awareness and aspiration for children and young people in public care. Chartered Member of the Chartered Institute of Personnel and Development; Fellow of the RSA. Address: (b.) Brunswick House, 51 Wilson Street, Glasgow G1 1UZ; T.-0141 552 7111.

Fox, Colin Anthony. MSP (Scottish Socialist Party), Lothians, 2003-07; Joint National Spokesperson, Scottish Socialist Party, since 2008, National Convener, 2005-08; b. 17.6.59, Motherwell; 1 s.; 1 d. Educ. Our Lady's High School, Motherwell; Bell College, Hamilton. Spent 20 years as a (socialist) political organiser; SSP Lothians Convenor, 1998-2003. Publication: Motherwell is Won for Moscow. Recreations: reading; walking; golf; sports. Address: 24/3 Ivanhoe Crescent, Edinburgh EH16 6AN; T.-0131-348 6389.

Foxley, Michael Ewen, MRCS, LRCP, DA. GP in Fort William, 1980-2010; b. 22.09.48, London; m., Mairead MacRae; 2 s. Educ. Harrow County Boys Grammar School; Middlesex Hospital Medical School, London University. Anaesthetics, then Training for General Practice; Highland Regional Councillor, 1986-96 (Vice-Chair of Planning); Highland Councillor, 1995-2012 (Fort William and Ardnamurchan); Chair of Land and Environment, 1995-2003; Vice Convener, 2003-07; Leader, 2008-12. Chair of the UHI Rural and Islands Colleges Merger Board. Board Member, Crown Estate Scotland; Director, community owned land trust. Recreations: hill walking; fishing; crofting. Address: (h.) Dun Famh, 2, Achaphubil, by Fort William PH33 7AL; T.-01397 772 775.
E-mail: michael.foxley@uhi.ac.uk

Foyer, Rozanne. General Secretary, The Scottish Trades Union Congress (STUC), since 2020. Career history: twenty-five years' experience in the trade union movement; began as a workplace activist in the Benefits Agency; led a successful campaign against support services privatisation; recruited by the printer workers union as a trainee organiser, before gaining prominence in the Scottish movement as an Assistant Secretary at the STUC; became a National Officer with the Transport and General Workers Union, later moving into Unite's National Organising Department; excelled as a strategist who delivered a series of successful membership campaigns; former Chair of the STUC Youth Committee, member of the STUC General Council; became an established voice in Scottish politics and the media. First woman to hold the position of the most senior representative of Scotland's 540,000 trade union members, in The STUC's 123 year history. Address:

STUC, 333 Woodlands Road, Glasgow G3 6NG; T.-0141 337 8100.

France, Professor (Emeritus) Peter, MA, PhD, FBA, FRSE. Professor of French, Edinburgh University, 1980-90, Endowment Fellow, 1990-2000; b. 19.10.35, Londonderry; m., Siân Reynolds; 3 d. Educ. Bradford Grammar School; Magdalen College, Oxford. Fellow, Magdalen College, Oxford, 1960-63; Lecturer, then Reader in French, Sussex University, 1963-80; French Editor, Modern Language Review, 1979-85; President: British Comparative Literature Association, 1992-98, International Society for the History of Rhetoric, 1993-95. Chevalier de la Légion d' Honneur, 2001. Publications: Racine's Rhetoric, 1965; Rhetoric and Truth in France, 1972; Poets of Modern Russia, 1982; Diderot, 1982; Rousseau: Confessions, 1987; Politeness and its Discontents, 1992; New Oxford Companion to Literature in French, 1995; Translator: An Anthology of Chuvash Poetry, 1991, Gennady Aygi: Selected Poems, 1997; Poems of Osip Mandelstam, 2014; Yevgeny Baratynsky: Half-Light, 2015; Konstantin Batyushkov: Writings from the Golden Age of Russian Poetry; Oxford Guide to Literature in English Translation, 2000; Mapping Lives: the uses of biography, 2002; General Editor, Oxford History of Literary Translation in English, since 2005; After Lermontov: Translations for the Bicentenary, 2014. Address: (b.) 10 Dryden Place, Edinburgh EH9 1RP; T.-0131-667 1177.

Franceschild, Donna, BA. TV Scriptwriter, since 1990; playwight, since 1979; b. 22.11.53, Illinois; partner, Richard Golding; 1 s. Educ. University of California, Los Angeles. TV credits include: The Key, Eureka Street, A Mug's Game, Takin' Over the Asylum, And the Cow Jumped Over the Moon, Bobbin' and Weavin', The Necklace; theatre credits include: And the Cow Jumped Over the Moon, The Sunshine Cafe, Rebel!, Songs for Stray Cats and Other Living Creatures; Tap Dance on a Telephone Line; Mutiny on the M1, Diaries, The Soap Opera, The Cleaning Lady; film credit: Donovan Quick. Creative Writing Fellow, Universities of Glasgow and Strathclyde. Recreation: hill-walking.

Franchi, Leandro, MA, LLB. Partner, Franchi Law LLP, since 2009; formerly Partner with Franchi Finnieston, Solicitors; formerly Honorary Consul for Italy (1991-2016); b. 5.6.60, Paisley; m., Gillian Elaine. Educ. St. Aloysius College, Glasgow; Dundee University; Glasgow University; Strathclyde University. Address: Queens House, 19 St. Vincent Place, Glasgow G1 2DT; T.-0141 225-3811.
E-mail: leandro@franchilaw.co.uk

Franchi, (Sarah) Jane. Reporter/Presenter, BBC Scotland, 1979-2003; b. 15.10.50, Calcutta; m., Alan Franchi. Educ. Benenden School; Edinburgh College of Commerce. Reporter, Aberdeen Journals, 1970; Press and Publicity Officer, Grampian TV, 1971-79. Recreations: swimming; football (spectating!); embroidery; theatre. Address: (h.) 9 Osborne Place, Aberdeen AB25 2BX; T.-01224 645883.

Francis, Alphonse. Founder and Trustee, Hope-Human Development & Welfare Association. Address: (b.) 9 Catacol Grove, Lindseyfield, East Kilbride, Glasgow G75 9FD; T.-44 7850645602; e-mail: afrancis@hope-hdwa.co.uk

Francis, Eileen, MPhil, MRCSLT, FRSA; b. 2.3.40, Tynemouth; m., John Francis; 2 d. Educ. Church High School, Newcastle upon Tyne; Kingdon Ward School of Speech Therapy, London. Speech and language therapist, Cardiff Hospitals, 1962; Lecturer, Moray House Institute of Education, 1971; Senior Lecturer, 1988; Vector, consultancy and training, 1992; Chair, Scottish Institute of Human Relations, 2005-2011. Recreations: community networks; Virginia Woolf Society. Address: (h.) 49 Gilmour Road, Edinburgh EH16 5HU; T.-0131 667 3996.

Francis, John Michael, BSc, ARCS, PhD, DIC, Hon FRSGS, Hon FRZSS, FRSE. UK National Commission for UNESCO; Deputy Chair, UNESCO Scotland; former Convener, United Nations Association/Edinburgh; Trustee, The RSE Scotland Foundation, 2004-07; Steering Group Scottish Sustainable Development Forum, 2004-12; Consultant & Advisor to UNESCO, since 1999; Chair, UK National Commission for UNESCO, 2000-03; Honorary Fellow, University of Edinburgh, 2000-10; Fellow, Royal Society of Edinburgh, since 1991; b. 1.5.39, London; m., Eileen; 2 d. Educ. Gowerton Grammar School, Glamorgan, South Wales; Royal College of Science/Imperial College of Science and Technology, University of London. CEGB R & D Department, Berkeley Nuclear Laboratories, 1963-70; First Director, Society, Religion and Technology Project, Church of Scotland, 1970-74; Senior Research Fellow in Energy Studies, Heriot-Watt University, 1974-76; Principal, Scottish Office (SDD & SHHD) 1976-81; Assistant Secretary, Scottish Office, 1981-84 & 1992-95; Director Scotland, Nature Conservancy Council, 1984-92; then Chief Executive Officer, Nature Conservancy Council for Scotland; Senior Policy Adviser, Home Department, Scottish Office, 1995-99. Consultant, World Council of Churches, 1971-83; Chairman, SRT Project, Church of Scotland, 1979-94; Founder Member: Oil Development Council for Scotland, 1973-76, Advisory Committee for Scotland, Nature Conservancy Council, 1973-76, Council, National Trust for Scotland, 1984-92; Chair, Edinburgh Forum, 1986-92; Professional Member, World Future Society, Washington DC, 1992-2002; Member: John Muir Trust, 1994-2009, British Association for the Advancement of Science; UK Representative, Millennium Project, United Nations University; Trustee, Society, Religion and Technology Project Trust, 1998-2007; Chair, UK National Commission for UNESCO, Sector Committee on 'Sustainable Development, Peace and Human Rights', 1999-2003; Founding Chair, UK National Commission for UNESCO, 1999-2003; Member, Church & Nation Committee, then Church & Society Council, Church of Scotland, 2002-2012; Emeritus Member, SRT Committee, since 2013. Publications: Scotland in Turmoil, 1972; Scotland's Pipe-Dream, 1973; Scottish Oil Shakedown, 1974; Changing Directions (UK Independent Commission on Transport), 1973; Facing Up to Nuclear Power, 1976; The Future as an Academic Discipline, 1975; The Future of Scotland, 1977; North Sea Oil and the Environment (Jointly), 1992; 'Conserving Nature: Scotland and the Wider World' (jointly), 2005; contributions to scientific/environmental journals, including Resurgence & Ecologist. Recreations: theatre; poetry, hill-walking and annual travels in France.

Francis, Michelle Ruth, BSc (Hons), MSc, CEnv, FIEMA. Director: Sustainability Catalyst Ltd, since 2012, Eracura Consulting Ltd, since 2016; Sustainability and Environmental Consultant, since 2005; Board Member, The Scottish Environment Protection Agency Board, 2014-2021 (Deputy Chair, 2020-21); Main Board Member, Scottish Natural Heritage, 2005-2011; b. 19.1.71, Braintree; m., James Francis; 2 s. Educ. Wallace Hall Academy, Thornhill; Marr College, Troon; University of Aberdeen; Napier University. Environmental Scientist, RSK Environment, Aberdeen, 1993-95; Environment Manager, Railtrack Scotland, Glasgow, 1995-98; Head of

Environment, Railtrack/Network Rail, London, 1998-2004. Member, The Wild Fisheries Review Panel, 2014. Address: (h./b.) Glenhead Cottage, Dunblane FK15 9PD; T.-01786 822581; e-mail: michelle@francis-hq.co.uk

Francis, Neil, BSc (Hons), MBA. Interim Managing Director, Scottish Development International, since 2020. Educ. Pentrehafod Comprehensive, Swansea; Loughborough University; University of Strathclyde. Career history: Scottish Enterprise: Director of Operations and Project Manager, The Alba Centre, Livingston, 1998-2000, Chief Executive (Temp), Executive Director, and Network Director for Micro and Opto Electronics Cluster, 2000-08, Director, Industries, Innovation and Commercialisation, 2008-2010, Senior Director, Technology and Engineering and Project Delivery, 2010-2013; Scottish Development International: Director, International Trade and Investment, Scotland, 2013-19, Director, Global Trade, Glasgow, 2019-2020. Address: Scottish Development International, 5 Atlantic Quay, 150 Broomielaw, Glasgow G2 8LU; T.-0300 013 2734.

Franks, Peter, AGSM. Principal Trumpet, Scottish Chamber Orchestra, since 1984; Trumpet Teacher, Royal Conservatoire of Scotland, since 1989; b. 22.4.58, Aylesbury; m., Maureen Hilary Rutter; 1 s.; 1 d. Educ. Aylesbury Grammar School; Guildhall School of Music and Drama. Sub-principal Trumpet, Scottish Chamber Orchestra, 1981-84. Address: Croft House, Kilncroft, Selkirk TD7 5AQ; T.-07774 866177.
E-mail: peterfrankstpt.gmail.com

Fraser, Alan William, MA (Hons); b. 1951; m., Joan; 1 d.; 2 s. Educ. Daniel Stewart's College; Banff Academy; Aberdeen University. Entered Scottish Office, 1973; Assistant Secretary to Inquiry into UK Prison Services, 1978-79; Private Secretary to Minister of State, 1979-81; Manager, Scottish Office Efficiency Unit, 1985-88; Head, Industrial Policy and Technology Division, SOID, 1988-91; Principal Private Secretary to Secretary of State for Scotland, 1991-93; Head, Enterprise and Tourism Division, Scottish Office Education and Industry Department, 1993-99; Director of Personnel, Scottish Executive, 1999-2000; Director for Civil Service Reform, 2000-01; Head of 21st Century Government Unit, Scottish Executive, 2001-05. Board Member, Cruse Bereavement Care Scotland, from 2006, Chairman, 2008-13; Secretary, Lothian Sea Kayak Club, 2008-2020. Recreations: skiing; sea kayaking. Address: Edinburgh.
E-mail: alanwilliamfraser@blueyonder.co.uk

Fraser, Andrew Kerr, OBE (2018), MB, ChB, MPH, FRCP, FFPH. Senior Adviser, Public Health Scotland, since 2020; b. 10.12.58, Edinburgh; m.; 3 s.; 1 d. Educ. George Watson's College; Aberdeen University; Glasgow University. Medical Director, National Services Division, NHS in Scotland; Director of Public Health, Highland Health Board; Deputy Chief Medical Officer, Scottish Executive; Director of Health and Care, Scottish Prison Service; Director of Public Health Science, NHS Health Scotland, 2012-2020. Recreations: music; mountain walking. Address: (b.) Meridian Court, 5 Cadogan Street, Glasgow G2 6QE; e-mail: andrewkfraser@gmail.com

Fraser, Sir Charles Annand, KCVO, WS, DL. Partner, W. & J. Burness, 1956-92 (retired); former Chairman, Adam and Company PLC; former Director: British Assets Trust PLC, Scottish Television PLC, Scottish Business in the Community, Stakis PLC; b. 16.10.28, Humbie, East Lothian; m., Ann Scott-Kerr; 4 s. (1 s. deceased). Educ. Hamilton Academy; Edinburgh University. Purse Bearer to

Lord High Commissioner to General Assembly of Church of Scotland, 1969-88; served on Court, Heriot-Watt University, 1972-78; Council Member, Law Society of Scotland, 1966-72; Chairman, Lothian & Edinburgh Enterprise, 1991-94. Publications: Pipe music; The Shepherd House Garden. Recreations: gardening; skiing; piping. Address: (h.) Shepherd House, Inveresk, Midlothian; T.-0131-665 2570.

Fraser, Eddie. Chief Executive, East Ayrshire Council, since 2020. Career history: over 34 years of local government experience; worked at Strathclyde Regional Council and Glasgow City Council; joined East Ayrshire Council in 1998; Head of Community Care, South Ayrshire Council, 2007; East Ayrshire Council: Head of Community Care/Chief Social Work Officer, 2008-2014, appointed Director of Health and Social Care in 2014. Address: Council Headquarters, London Road, Kilmarnock KA3 7BU; T.-01563 554400.

Fraser, James Edward, CB, MA (Aberdeen), BA (Cantab), FSA Scot. Assistant Local Government Boundary Commissioner for Scotland, 1997-2011; Secretary of Commissions for Scotland, 1992-94; b. 16.12.31, Aberdeen; m., Patricia Louise Stewart; 2 s. Educ. Aberdeen Grammar School; Aberdeen University; Christ's College, Cambridge. Royal Artillery, 1953-55 (Staff Captain, "Q", Tel-El-Kebir, 1954-55); Assistant Principal, Scottish Home Department, 1957-60; Private Secretary to Permanent Under-Secretary of State, Scottish Office, 1960-62; Private Secretary to Parliamentary Under-Secretary of State, Scottish Office, 1962; Principal, 1962-69: SHHD, 1962-64, Cabinet Office, 1964-66, HM Treasury, 1966-68, SHHD, 1968-69; Assistant Secretary: SHHD, 1970-76, Scottish Office Finance Division, 1976; Under Secretary, Local Government Finance Group, Scottish Office, 1976-81, Scottish Home and Health Department, 1981-91. President: Scottish Hellenic Society, Edinburgh and Eastern Scotland, 1987-93, Aberdeen Grammar School Former Pupils' Club, 1997-98 (Hon. Vice-President, since 1998). Recreations: reading; music; walking; Greece, ancient and modern. Address: (h.) 59 Murrayfield Gardens, Edinburgh EH12 6DH; T.-0131-337 2274.

Fraser, Professor James Mackenzie, CBE, MA, MEd. Former Principal & Vice-Chancellor, University of the Highlands and Islands (2011-13); Principal, UHI Millennium Institute (UHI), 2009-2011, Deputy Principal, 2007-09, Secretary, 2002-09; b. 29.07.48, Poolewe; m., Janet Sinclair (deceased); 1 d.; m., Sheila; 1 s.; 1 d. Educ. Plockton High School; University of Edinburgh; University of Stirling. Lecturer, Inverness Technical College, 1971-77; Assistant Registrar, University of Stirling, 1977-87; College Secretary, Queen Margaret College, Edinburgh, 1987-89; Secretary, University of Paisley, 1989-2002. Chair, The Solas Centre for Public Christianity; Chair, Highland Community Care Forum; Member, New Club, Edinburgh.

Fraser, Lindsey M., BA (Hons), PGCE. Partner, Fraser Ross Associates, literary agency; b. 15.8.61, Edinburgh. Educ. George Watson's College; York University; Froebel Institute, London. Manager, Heffers Children's Bookshop, Cambridge, 1986-91; Executive Director, Scottish Book Trust, 1991-2002. Sir Stanley Unwin Travelling Fellowship, 1989. Address: (b.) 6 Wellington Place, Edinburgh EH6 7EQ; T.-0131-553 2759.
E-mail: agentlmfraser@gmail.com
web: www.fraserross.co.uk

Fraser, Murdo Mackenzie, LLB, DipLP. MSP (Conservative), Mid-Scotland and Fife, since 2001; Shadow Cabinet Secretary for Covid Recovery since 2021; Deputy Convener, Scottish Parliament Covid-19 Recovery Committee, since 2021; Deputy Leader, Scottish Conservatives, 2005-2011; b. 5.9.65, Inverness; m., Emma

Jarvis; 1 s.; 1 d. Educ. Inverness Royal Academy; University of Aberdeen. Solicitor, Ross Harper and Murphy and Ketchen and Stevens, WS, Edinburgh, 1989-2001. Chairman, Scottish Young Conservatives, 1989-91, National Young Conservatives, 1991-92; Parliamentary Candidate: East Lothian, 1997, North Tayside, 1999, 2001, 2003, 2007, Perthshire North, 2011, 2016 and 2021. Publications: The Blue Book (2007); The Rivals: Montrose and Argyll and the Struggle for Scotland (2015). Recreations: climbing; classic cars; travel; Scottish history. Address: Scottish Parliament, Edinburgh EH99 1SP; T.-0131-348 5293; e-mail: murdo.fraser.msp@parliament.scot

Fraser, Patricia. Chair, The Hugh Fraser Foundation. Address: c/o Turcan Connell, 180 St Vincent Street, Glasgow G2 5SG; T.-0141 441 2111.

Fraser, Sheriff Simon William Hetherington, LLB. Sheriff of North Strathclyde at Dumbarton, 1989-2014; b. 2.4.51, Carlisle; m., Sheena Janet (marr. diss.); m. (2), Fiona; 1 d. Educ. Glasgow Academy; Glasgow University. Solicitor, 1973; Partner, Flowers & Co., Solicitors, Glasgow, 1976-89; Temporary Sheriff, 1987-89. Glasgow Bar Association: Secretary, 1977-79, President, 1981-82; Council member, Sheriffs' Association, 2007-2010. Recreations: watching cricket, and Partick Thistle.

Fraser, Professor William Hamish, MA, DPhil, FRHistS. Honorary Doctor of Southern Federal University, Russia; Professor Emeritus, Strathclyde University; b. 30.6.41, Keith; m., Helen Tuach; 1 d. Educ. Keith Grammar School; Aberdeen University; Sussex University. Formerly Professor of History and Dean of Arts and Social Studies, Strathclyde University. Associate Editor, Dictionary of Nineteenth Century Journalism. Publications: Trade Unions and Society 1850-1880, 1973; Workers and Employers, 1981; The Coming of the Mass Market, 1982 (new edition 2017); Conflict and Class: Scottish Workers 1700-1838, 1988; People and Society in Scotland 1830-1914, 1990; Glasgow 1830-1914 (Co-Editor), 1996; Alexander Campbell and the Search for Socialism, 1996; A History of British Trade Unionism, 1700-1998, 1999; Scottish Popular Politics, 2000; Aberdeen: A New History (Co-Editor), 2000; Dr John Taylor, Chartist, 2006; British Trade Unions 1707-1918, 2007; Britain since 1707 (Co-Author), 2010; Chartism in Scotland, 2010; The Wars of Archibald Forbes, 2015. Recreations: travel; golf. Address: (h.) Braehead, Culvardie, Nethy Bridge PH25 3DH; T.-01479 821291. E-mail: hamishf@btinternet.com

Frater, John W.B., MA. Honorary Fellow, Keep Scotland Beautiful; b. 12.5.58, Irvine; m., Caroline E. Mackenzie. Educ. Loudoun Academy; Dundee University. Recreations: reading; gardening; wine; pottering around locomotive sheds. Address: (b.) Glendevon House, Castle Business Park, Stirling FK9 4TZ; T.-01786 471333.

Frazer, Rev Dr Richard Ernest, BA, BD, DMin(Prin). Minister, Greyfriars Kirk, Edinburgh, since 2003; Convener of Church and Society Council, the Church of Scotland, 2016-2020; Minister, St. Machar's Cathedral, Old Aberdeen, 1993-2003; b. 20.11.57, Stirling; m., Katherine Tullis Sinclair; 2 s.; 1 d. Educ. Doncaster Grammar School; University of Newcastle upon Tyne; University of Edinburgh; Princeton Theological Seminary. Assistant Minister, St. Giles Cathedral, Edinburgh, 1985-87; Minister, Schoharie, Breakabeen, N. Bleheim, New York, USA, 1987-88; Minister, Cargill-Burrelton with Collace, 1988-93. Publications: A Collace Miscellany: a History of the Parish of Collace (Co-Editor and Contributor), 1992;

Travels with a Stick: A Pilgrim's Journey to Santiago de Compostela, 2019. Recreations: family; walking; slow food. Address: (b.) Greyfriars Kirk, Greyfriars Place, Edinburgh EH1 2QQ; T.-0131 225 1900.

Freeman, Jeane, OBE. MSP (SNP), Carrick, Cumnock and Doon Valley, 2016-2021; Cabinet Secretary for Health and Sport, 2018-2021; Minister for Social Security, 2016-18; Director, Freeman Associates, 2005-2016; b. 28.09.53, Ayr. Educ. Ayr Academy; Caledonian and Glasgow Universities. Saatchi & Saatchi; BBC, 1983-87; Director, Apex Scotland, 1987-2000; Senior Civil Servant, 2000-01; Principal Policy Adviser, First Minister, 2001-05. Board Chair, Golden Jubilee National Hospital, 2011-16; Board Member: Scottish Police Authority, 2013-16, Judicial Appointments Board for Scotland, 2011-16; Member, Parole Board for Scotland, 2006-2011.

French, William Allan, DL, BSc, MSc, CEng, FIMMM, FIET. Depute Lieutenant, Stirling and Falkirk Districts, since 1994; b. 30.12.41, Falkirk; m., Joyce; 2 d. Educ. George Watson's College, Edinburgh; Strathclyde University. Scientific Officer, UKAEA, Dounreay; Production Manager, British Aluminium Co. Ltd., Falkirk; Lecturer, Napier College, Edinburgh; Head, Department of Industrial Engineering, Falkirk College of Technology; Associate Principal, Falkirk College of Further and Higher Education, 1986-99. Director, Careers Central Ltd., 1995-99; Secretary, Forth Valley Area Scout Council, 1990-2008; District Scout Commissioner, 1980-1990; Board member, Lochgoilhead Scout Centre; founder Area Chairman, Central Scotland Round Table; Past President, Larbert Rotary Club; Secretary, Golf House Club, Elie Seniors Section, since 2010. Recreations: golf; bridge; scouting; rotary; music. Address: (h.) 26 Broomhill Avenue, Larbert FK5 3EH; T.-07711815653. E-mail: allanfrench69@gmail.com

Frew, Rev. Rosemary, MA, BD (Hons). Minister, Bowden and Melrose Parish Church, since 2017; b. 2.10.61, Glasgow; m., David J A Frew; 1 s.; 1 d. Educ. Linlithgow Academy; Edinburgh University. Assistant Minister, Markinch Parish Church, 1986-87; Minister, Largo and Newburn Parish Church linked with Largo, St. David's Parish Church, 1988-2005; Minister, Abbotshall Parish Church, Kirkcaldy, 2005-2017. Vice-Convener, Mission and Discipleship Council, Church of Scotland, 2005-07; Clerk to the Presbytery of Kirkcaldy, 2007-2017; Convener, Faith Nurture Forum, Church of Scotland, since 2020. Recreations: ski-ing; cycling; walking; reading. Address: (work and home) The Manse, Tweedmount Road, Melrose, Scottish Borders TD6 9ST; T.-01896 822217; e-mail: revrosiefrew@gmail.com

Frew, Tim, MA (Hons), PGCCE, MBA. Chief Executive, YouthLink Scotland, the National Agency for Youth Work, since 2018. Educ. University of Glasgow; University of Edinburgh; University of Strathclyde. Career: Project Co-ordinator, Penicuik Churches Youth Project, 1997-99; Community Education Worker, Clackmannanshire Council, 2000-02; Workforce Development Manager, 2002-2018. Address: YouthLink Scotland, Caledonian Exchange, 19A Canning Street, Edinburgh EH3 8EG; T.-0131 313 2488. E-mail: ceo@youthlinkscotland.org; twitter @timfrew

Friedrich, Karin, MA, PhD, FRHistS. Professor of Early Modern European History, School of Divinity, History and Philosophy, University of Aberdeen, since 2004; School of Slavonic and East European Studies, University College London, 1995-2004; b. 12.06.63, Munich, Germany; m., Prof. Robert I. Frost; 1 s.; 1 d. Educ. University of Munich;

Georgetown University, Washington DC. Fellow, Royal Historical Society; Chair, German History Society, UK. Publications: The Other Prussia. Poland, Prussia and Liberty, 1569-1772, 2000, Polish trans. 2006 (Orbis Prize in 2001 by American Association for the Advancement of Slavic Studies); ed., Festivals in Germany and Europe: New Approaches to European Festival Culture, 2000; ed., Citizenship and Identity in a Multinational Commonwealth. Poland-Lithuania in Context, 1500-1750, 2008; The Cultivation of Monarchy and the Rise of Berlin. Brandenburg-Prussia 1700 (Co-Author), 2010; Brandenburg-Prussia, 1450-1806. The Rise of a Composite State, 2011; Die Erschließung des Raumes: Konstruktion, Imagination und Darstellung von Räumen und Grenzen im Barockzeitalter, 2014; Duncan Liddel (1561-1613). Networks of Polymathy and the Northern European Renaissance, 2016 (Co-Editor). Recreations: flute; skiing; tennis; reading; mountaineering. Address: (b.) Crombie Annexe, Meston Walk, Aberdeen AB24 3FX; T.-01224 272451.

Frier, Professor Brian Murray, BSc (Hons), MD, FRCP (Edin), FRCP (Glas). Consultant Physician, Royal Infirmary, Edinburgh, 1987-2012; Honorary Professor of Diabetes, The Queen's Medical Research Institute, Edinburgh University, since 2001; b. Edinburgh; m., Dr. Isobel M. Wilson; 1 d. Educ. George Heriot's School, Edinburgh; Edinburgh University. Research Fellow in Diabetes and Metabolism, Cornell University Medical Centre, The New York Hospital, 1976-77; Senior Medical Registrar, Royal Infirmary, Edinburgh, 1978-82; Consultant Physician, Western Infirmary and Gartnavel General Hospital, Glasgow, 1982-87. Chairman, Honorary Advisory Panel for Driving and Diabetes to Secretary of State for Transport, 2001-2012; Chairman, Chief Scientist Office Committee for Diabetes Research in Scotland, 2003-06; International Hypoglycaemia Study Group, since 2013; R.D. Lawrence Lecturer, 1986, Banting Memorial Lecturer, 2009, Diabetes UK; Somogyi Award, Hungarian Diabetes Association, 2004; EASD Camillo Golgi Prize and lecture, 2017; Governor, George Heriot's Trust, Edinburgh, 1987-94; Vice-President, Royal College of Physicians of Edinburgh, 2008-2012. Publications: Hypoglycaemia and Diabetes: clinical and physiological aspects, 1993; Hypoglycaemia in Clinical Diabetes, 1999, 2nd Edition, 2007, 3rd Edition, 2014; Insulin Therapy: A Pocket Guide, 2013; 500+ papers and reviews on diabetes, and on hypoglycaemia. Recreations: appreciation of the arts; ancient and modern history. Address: (h.) 100 Morningside Drive, Edinburgh EH10 5NT; T.-0131-447 1653. E-mail: brian.frier@ed.ac.uk

Frost, Professor Robert Ian, MA (Hons) St. Andrews, PhD (London), FBA, FRSE, FRHistS. Knight's Cross of the Order for Merits to Lithuania (2020); Knight's Cross of the Order of Merit of the Republic of Poland (2021). Burnett Fletcher Chair in History, University of Aberdeen, since 2013, Professor of Early Modern History, 2004-2013, Head of The School of Divinity, History and Philosophy, 2004-09; Director, Centre for Polish-Lithuanian Studies, University of Aberdeen; b. 20.06.58, Edinburgh; m., Professor Karin Friedrich; 1 s.; 1 d. Educ. Edinburgh Academy, George Watson's College, Edinburgh; University of St. Andrews; School of Slavonic and East European Studies, University of London; Jagiellonian University, Cracow, Poland. School Teacher, Charterhouse, 1984-87; University Teacher, King's College London, 1987-2004, Reader in Early Modern History, History Department, 2001-04. Council of the Royal Historical Society, 2004-08; British Academy Wolfson Foundation Research Professor, 2009-2012; Leverhulme Major Research Fellow (2016-2019); Elected Fellow of the British Academy, 2016; Elected Fellow of the Royal Society of Edinburgh, 2020; Elected Fellow of the Polish Academy of Arts and Sciences,

2020. Publications: Author of: After The Deluge: Poland-Lithuania and the Second Northern War, 1655-1660, 1993; The Northern Wars: War, State and Society in North Eastern Europe, 1558-1721, 2000; The Oxford History of Poland-Lithuania, Vol. I: The Making of the Polish-Lithuanian Union, 1385-1569, 2015. Winner of the Pro Historia Polonorum Prize (2017), awarded by the Society of Polish Historians. Recreations: skiing; golf; opera; guitar. Address: (h.) 50 Forest Road, Aberdeen AB15 4BP; T.-01224 322824.

Frutin, Bernard Derek, MBE, FRSA. Inventor; Executive Chairman, Rocep Group of Companies; Director, Gizmo Packaging Ltd; b. 7.2.44, Glasgow; m., 1, Victoria Dykes (divorced); m., 2, Karen Smith; 1 s.; 4 d. Educ. Kelvinside Academy, Glasgow. Winner of nine international innovator awards since 1989, including John Logie Baird and British Institute of Packaging Environmental Awards; Innovator of the Year, 1989 (Institute of Packaging); Finalist, 1992 Prince of Wales Award; Institute of Packaging Starpack Award for TEC Innovation, 2001. Recreations: sailing; fine food; listening to music. Address: (b.) Rocep Lusol Holdings Ltd., Suite 2, Floor 1, Merlin House, Mossland Road, Hillington, Glasgow GS2 4XZ; T.-0141-885 2222.

Fry, Professor Stephen C., BSc, PhD, FRSE. Professor of Plant Biochemistry, Edinburgh University, since 1995; b. 26.11.53, Sheffield; m., Verena Ryffel; 3 d. Educ. Thornbridge School, Sheffield; Leicester University. Postdoctoral Research Fellow, Cambridge University, 1978-79; Royal Society Rosenheim Research Fellow, Cambridge University, 1979-82; Senior Research Associate, University of Colorado, 1982-83; Lecturer in Botany, then Reader in Plant Biochemistry, Edinburgh University, 1983-95. President's Medal, Society for Experimental Biology, 1988. Publications: The Growing Plant Cell Wall: Chemical and Metabolic Analysis, 1988; 80 review articles; 231 research papers. Recreations: hillwalking; paper electrophoresis. Address: (b.) The Edinburgh Cell Wall Group, Institute of Molecular Plant Sciences, School of Biological Sciences, Edinburgh University, King's Buildings, Max Born Crescent, Edinburgh EH9 3BF; T.-0131-650 5320. E-mail: S.Fry@ed.ac.uk

Fulton, Rev. John Oswald, BSc, BD. General Secretary, United Free Church of Scotland, since 1994; Moderator, General Assembly, United Free Church, since 2019 and 2000-01; b. 9.7.53, Glasgow; m., Margaret P.; 1 d. Educ. Clydebank High School; Glasgow University. Ordained as minister, 1977; Minister, Croftfoot U.F. Church, Glasgow, 1977-94. Recreations: reading; gardening; photography. Address: (b.) 11 Newton Place, Glasgow G3 7PR; T.-0141-332 3435; e-mail: office@ufcos.org.uk

Furnell, Professor James R.G., MA (Hons), DCP, PhD, LLB, DipLP, FBPsS. Advocate (called to Scottish Bar, 1993); Chartered Clinical and Forensic Psychologist; b. 20.2.46, London; m., Lesley Anne Ross; 1 s.; 1 d. Educ. Leighton Park Society of Friends School, Reading; Aberdeen University; Glasgow University; Stirling University; Dundee University. Clinical Psychologist, Royal Hospital for Sick Children, Glasgow, 1970-72; Forth Valley Health Board: Senior Clinical Psychologist, 1972-80, Consultant Clinical Psychologist (Child Health), 1980-98. Member: National Consultative Committee of Scientists in Professions Allied to Medicine, 1984-87 (Secretary, Clinical Psychology Sub-Committee), Forth Valley Health Board, 1984-87; Chairman, Division of Clinical Psychology, British Psychological Society, 1988-89; Visiting Professor, Caledonian University, since 1996. Club: Royal Northern and University, Aberdeen.

Recreations: flying; cross-country skiing. Address: (h.) Glensherup House, Glendevon, by Dollar, Perthshire FK14 7JY.

Furness, Col. Simon John, MBE (2012), OstJ, DL. Landowner; Vice Lord Lieutenant, Berwickshire, 1990-2009; b. 18.8.36, Ayton. Educ. Charterhouse; RMA, Sandhurst. Commissioned Durham Light Infantry, 1956, 2nd Lt.; served Far East, UK, Germany; active service, Borneo, MID Northern Ireland, 1972; retired, 1978; Deputy Colonel (Durham) The Light Infantry, 1989-93. Member, Executive, National Trust for Scotland, 1986-96; Chairman: Berwickshire Civic Society, 1996-2005, Eyemouth Museum Trust, 1981-2005, Eyemouth Harbour Trust, 2003-06; Trustee, Gunsgreen House Trust, since 2003, Chairman, 2011-2015. Recreations: field sports; gardening. Address: The Garden House, Netherbyres, Eyemouth, Berwickshire TD14 5SE; T.-01890 750337.

Fyfe, Professor Nicholas Robert, MA, PhD (Cantab), FAcSS, FRSA. Vice Principal for Research and Community Engagement, Robert Gordon University, since 2021; b. 17.10.62, London; m., Gillian Fyfe; 2 s. Educ. Haberdashers' Aske's Hatcham Boys' School; Sidney Sussex College, University of Cambridge. Junior Research Fellow, Sidney Sussex College, Cambridge, 1989-90; Lecturer, Senior Lecturer, University of Strathclyde, 1990-2000; Senior Lecturer, then Reader, University of Dundee, from 2000; Professor of Human Geography, 2006-2021, Dean of Social Sciences, 2018-2021. Fellow of the Academy of Social Sciences; Fellow of Royal Society of Arts; Visiting Professor, Norwegian Police University College, 2016-2022. Publications: Crime, Policing and Place: essays in Environmental Criminology (Co-Editor), 1992; Images of the Street: planning, identity and control in public space, 1998; Protecting intimidated witnesses, 2001; The Urban Geography Reader (Co-Author), 2005; Centralizing forces? Comparative perspectives on police reform in northern and western Europe (Co-Editor), 2013; Moral Issues in Intelligence-Led Policing (Co-Editor), 2017; The Abstract Police (Co-Editor), 2022. Recreations: golf; gardening; travel. Address: (b.) Robert Gordon University, Aberdeen AB10 7QB; T.-07823 374610. E-mail: n.fyfe3@rgu.ac.uk

G

Gaffney, Cllr Hugh. MP (Labour), Coatbridge, Chryston and Bellshill, 2017-19; b. 10.8.63, Uddingston; m.; 3 s. Career: Royal Mail and Parcelforce; elected to North Lanarkshire Council (2017-19). One of the founding members of the Keir Hardie Society in 2010.

Galán, Ignacio. Chairman, ScottishPower, since 2007; b. 1950, Salamanca, Spain; 4 c. Educ. ICAI (Madrid); ICADE (Madrid); Escuela de Organización Industrial (Madrid). Career: various positions in Grupo Tudor, 1972-1991; Director, Industria de Turbo Propulsores, 1991-1995; Managing Director, Airtel Movil (today Vodafone Spain), 1995-2001; joined Iberdrola as Executive Vice-Chairman and Managing Director, 2001. Visiting Professor, University of Strathclyde, since 2011. Address: ScottishPower Ltd, 1 Atlantic Quay, Glasgow G2 8SP.

Galbraith, Rev. David. Locum Minister, Maryculter Trinity Church of Scotland. Address: Kirkton of Maryculter, Aberdeenshire AB12 5FS; T.-01561 320779.

Galbraith, Rev. Douglas. MA, BD, BMus, MPhil, ARSCM, PhD. Editor, The Church of Scotland Yearbook, since 2011; former Convener, Action of Churches Together in Scotland (2011-13); b. 1940.

Galbraith, Jackie, BSc, PGDip. Principal and Chief Executive, West Lothian College, since 2018. Educ. Glasgow Polytechnic; The University of Stirling. Career history: Assistant Chief Executive, Learning and Teaching Scotland, 2000-02; The Scottish Government: Policy Manager, 2003-08, Head of Economic Recovery Unit, 2009; Head of Home Affairs, Social Policy and Elections Unit in the Scotland Office, 2009-2011; The Scottish Government: Policy Manager, 2011-12, Senior Policy Adviser to the Minister for Youth Employment, 2012-13; Vice Chair, Developing the Young Workforce - Ayrshire, 2015-17; Scottish Apprenticeship Advisory Board Frameworks and Standards Group, Skills Development Scotland, 2016-18; Vice Principal, Ayrshire College, 2013-18. Gender Governance Group, Scottish Funding Council, since 2014; Member of Skilled Workforce Forum, Colleges Scotland, since 2018. Address: West Lothian College, Almondvale Crescent, Livingston, West Lothian EH54 7EP; T.-01506 418181.

Galbraith, Professor Roderick Allister McDonald, BSc, PhD (Cantab), CEng, MRAeS, FRSE. Honorary Senior Research Fellow, School of Engineering, Glasgow University; b. 4.8.47, Lowmoor, England; m., Lynn Margaret Fraser. Educ. Greenock High School; James Watt Memorial College; Paisley College of Technology; Cambridge University. Apprentice Draughtsman/Engineer, Scott's Shipbuilding & Engineering Co. Ltd., 1964-72; Department of Aerospace Engineering, Glasgow University: joined 1975; Reader, 1989, Professor, 1992. Publications: over 100 reports and publications on aerodynamics. Recreations: sailing; walking. Address: (b.) School of Engineering, Glasgow University, Glasgow G12 8QQ; T.-0141-330 5295.

Galea, Paul, MD (Malta), DCH, FRCP (Glas), FRCPCH. Formerly Consultant Paediatrician, Royal Hospital for Sick Children, Yorkhill, Glasgow (retired, 2012); previously Consultant Neonatologist, Royal Maternity Hospital, Glasgow; b. 8.10.50, Rabat, Malta; m., Irene. Educ. Royal University of Malta. Recreations: gardening; DIY, classical music. Address: (h.) 30 Garngaber Avenue, Lenzie, Glasgow G66 4LL; T.-0141-776 6031.
Home e-mail: paul.galea31@btinternet.com

Gallacher, Meghan, MSP (Scottish Conservative and Unionist Party), Central Scotland (Region), since 2021; b. 1992, Bellshill. Educ. University of the West of Scotland. Elected to North Lanarkshire Council for the Motherwell West ward in 2017, subsequently became the party's group leader. Address: The Scottish Parliament, Edinburgh EH99 1SP; T.-0131 348 5633.
E-mail: Meghan.Gallacher.msp@parliament.scot

Gallagher, Sister Maire T., CBE, MA (Hons), MEd, FScotVec, DCE, FSQA. Retired Headteacher; Sister of Notre Dame Religious Congregation, since 1959; b. 27.5.33, Glasgow. Educ. Notre Dame High School, Glasgow; Glasgow University; Notre Dame College of Education. Principal Teacher of History, Notre Dame High School, Glasgow; Lecturer in Secondary Education, Notre Dame College of Education; Headteacher, Notre Dame High School, Dumbarton, 1974-87; Chairman, Scottish Consultative Council on the Curriculum, 1987-91 (Member, Consultative Committee on the Curriculum, since 1976). Member, Executive, Secondary Heads Association (Scottish Branch), 1976-83; Coordinator, Christian Life Movement Groups, West of Scotland; Convener, Action of Churches Together in Scotland, 1999-2002 (Member, Central Council, 1990-99); Fellow, Scottish Qualifications Authority, 1997; Member, Glasgow Churches Together, since 2004. Recreations: reading; dress-making; bird-watching. Address: (h.) Sisters of Notre Dame, 2/2 90 Beith Street, Glasgow G11 6DQ; T.-0141 357 4576.

Gallagher, Susan. Acting Chief Executive, Victim Support Scotland, 2014-17. Career history: Victim Support Scotland: support after murder project leader, 1998-2004 (implemented the first Victim Support Scotland responses to supporting people in the aftermath of murder to the development of services to help people affected by crimes committed by young people), special projects to Head of Youth Justice, 2004-08, Director of Development, 2008-10, Deputy Chief Executive, 2010-14. Member, Criminal Justice Rules Council, 2015-17. Many years spent working at pan-European level on a variety of joint projects with sister victim agencies across Europe; qualified social worker.

Galley, Professor Helen Frances, ONC, HNC, FIMLS, PhD, FBS, FRCA. Professor of Anaesthesia and Intensive Care, University of Aberdeen, since 2010; Director and Trustee, British Journal of Anaesthesia (Editor, 2008-18); Chair, North East Scotland Research Ethics Service; b. 13.01.62, Nottingham; m.; 1 s.; 1 d. Educ. King James' School, Knaresborough; University of Leeds. Research Fellow, University of Leeds, 1989-95; University of Aberdeen: Lecturer, 1995-2002, Senior Lecturer, 2002-09. Sir Humphrey Davy Award, 2002; Grants Officer, Anaesthetic Research Society, since 2007; Member of Senate, University of Aberdeen, since 2010. Recreations: horse riding; playing flute; jewellery making. Address: (h.) Overton of Auchnagatt, Ellon AB41 8TJ; T.-01224 437363.
E-mail: h.f.galley@abdn.ac.uk

Galloway, 14th Earl of (Andrew Stewart); b. 13.3.49; succeeded to title, 2020; m. (1), Sara Pollock (divorced); m. (2), Christine Merrick. Educ. Eton College, Windsor. Succeeded as the 8th Baron Stewart of Garlies, in the

Stewartry of Kirkcudbright, 2020; succeeded as the 14th Lord of Garlies, 2020; succeeded as the 12th Baronet Stewart, of Burray, 2020; succeeded as the 13th Baronet Stewart, of Corsewell, 2020.

Galloway, George. Politician, broadcaster and writer; Leader of the Workers Party of Britain, since 2019; b. 16.8.54, Dundee; m.; 6 c. Educ. Harris Academy, Glasgow. Production Worker, Michelin Tyres, 1974; Dundee Labour Party Organiser, 1977; General Secretary, War on Want, 1983; Member of Parliament for four constituencies, 1987-2015 (except 2010-2012), first for the Labour Party and later the Respect Party, the latter of which was founded in 2004 and led until its dissolution in 2016; former presenter, The Mother of All Talk Shows on Radio Sputnik and Sputnik on RT UK; Founder and Lead Spokesman of All for Unity Party; Chairman, Scottish Labour Party, 1981-82; Member, Scottish Labour Party Executive Committee, 1974-84; Founder and first General Secretary, Trade Union Friends of Palestine, 1979. Recreations: football; music; films.

Galloway, Janice. Writer; b. 2.12.55, Saltcoats. Educ. Ardrossan Academy; Glasgow University. Variety of paid and unpaid work, including 10 years' teaching English in Ayrshire; music criticism for Glasgow Herald, The Observer, Scotland on Sunday; fiction writing, including collections of short stories and novels; Co-Editor, New Writing Scotland, 1990-92; Editor, The Scotsman and Orange Short Story Collection, 2005; Times Literary Supplement Research Fellow to the British Library, 1999. Publications: The Trick Is To Keep Breathing, 1990; Blood, 1991; Foreign Parts, 1994; Where You Find It, 1996; Pipelines, 2000; Clara, 2002; Boy Book See, 2002; Rosengarten, 2004; This is Not About Me, 2008 (Autobiography) (winner of the Scottish Mortgage Trust Book of the Year (non-fiction) 2009); All Made Up, 2011 (won Best Scottish Book of the Year 2012, Mortgage Trust); Jellyfish, 2015. Staged work: The Trick is to Keep Breathing; Fall. Song cycle: Clara; Monster, for orchestra and voices. Opera: Monster (Co-Writer).

Galloway, Rev. Kathy, DD, BD, DPS. Former Leader, The Iona Community (2018-2020); former Head of Christian Aid Scotland (2009-2016); b. 6.8.52, Dumfries. Educ. Boroughmuir High School, Edinburgh; Glasgow University. Assistant Minister, Muirhouse Parish Church, Edinburgh, 1976-79; Co-ordinator, Edinburgh Peace and Justice Centre, 1980-83; Warden, Iona Abbey, 1983-88; freelance theological consultant, editor and writer, 1989-99; Linkworker for Scotland, Church Action on Poverty, 2000-02; Leader, The Iona Community, 2002-09. Publications include: Talking to the Bones; A Story to Live By; Walking in Darkness and Light; Sharing the Blessing; Living by the Rule. Address: (h.) 20 Hamilton Park Avenue, Glasgow G12 8DU.

Gamble, Alan James, LLB (Hons), LLM, Advocate. Judge, Upper Tribunal (Administrative Appeals Chamber), Edinburgh (fee-paid), since 2016 (salaried, 2008-16); Convenor, Mental Health Tribunal for Scotland, since 2005; b. 29.4.51, Glasgow; m., Elizabeth Waugh; 2 s.; 1 d. Educ. High School of Glasgow; University of Glasgow; Harvard Law School, USA. Law Apprentice, 1974-76; admitted to Faculty of Advocates, 1978; Lecturer, then Senior Lecturer in Law, University of Glasgow, 1976-93; District Chairman, Tribunals Service, Glasgow, 1993-2008; Deputy Social Security and Child Support Commissioner, Edinburgh, 1994-2008; Social Security and Child Support Commissioner, Edinburgh, 2008; Deputy Social Security and Child Support Commissioner for Northern Ireland, 2011-2021. Bible Teacher, Christian Brethren Assemblies;

Trustee of Christian charitable trusts; Dr J. McCormick Prize, 1972; Harkness Fellow, 1972-74. Publications: Contributor, Stair Memorial Encyclopedia; articles in legal journals and Christian periodicals. Recreations: reading; hill-walking. Address: (b.) George House, 126 George Street, Edinburgh EH2 4HH; T.-0131-271-4310.

Gambles, Colin, BSc, PGCE. Rector, Hutchesons' Grammar School, Glasgow, since 2016; b. 1.9.71, Dorchester; m., Catriona; 3 s. 1 d. Educ. Wootton Bassett Comprehensive School, Wiltshire; University of Edinburgh; University of Cambridge. Biology Teacher, Newcastle-under-Lyme School, 1995-98; Head of Biology and Head of Psychology, West Buckland School, 1998-2005; Head of Biology, George Watson's College, 2005-2011; Deputy Head, Robert Gordon's College, 2011-2016. Recreations: hockey; jungle expeditions; the outdoors. Address: (b.) Beaton Road, Glasgow G41 4NW; T.-0141 423 2933. E-mail: rector@hutchesons.org

Gammell, Geraldine, MA, CA. Former Director, The Prince's Trust - Scotland; Trustee, Reform Scotland. Educ. Stirling University; Glasgow University. Co-founder and Director, Dundas Commercial Property Funds I and II, 2002-2006; Partner, Springfords Chartered Accountants, 1993-2002; Manager, Business Services, KPMG, 1990-93; Lecturer in Business Finance and Accounting, Napier University and Edinburgh University, 1986-90; Financial Controller/Company Secretary, Ash Gupta Advertising, 1984-86; CA Apprentice, Audit Senior, Management Consultant, Thomson McLintock, 1978-83. Other non-executive Director Appointments: Lothian University Hospitals NHS Trust, 1999-2004; Sick Children's NHS Trust, 1995-99; Traverse Theatre Ltd., 1997-2001. Institute of Chartered Accountants, 1978-81; Chartered Accountant, 1981.

Gammie, Professor Elizabeth, DipM, BA, CA, PhD. Professor of Accountancy, Robert Gordon University, since 2000; b. 20.12.61, Dundee; 1 s.; 1 d. Educ. High School of Dundee; Robert Gordon University. Qualified as CA, 1986, with Ernst and Whinney; became a Lecturer, 1989 and Head of Aberdeen Business School, 2016. Trustee, ICAS Foundation; Trustee, RDA Aberdeen; Trustee, St Margaret's School for Girls; Member, ICAS Members Board; Chair, ICAS Grampian Area Committee and VP - Education IAAER. Recreation: equestrianism. Address: (h.) Bogfon Cottage, Maryculter, Aberdeen AB12 5GR; T.-01224 735403.

Garbutt, David, QPM, LLD, CFCIPD. Chair, NHS Education for Scotland, since 2018; Chair, NHS Chairs Group, since 2019; b. 16.8.45, Harthill; m., Moira Murdoch; 1 s.; 1 d. Educ. Edinburgh Napier University. Career history: Assistant Chief Constable, Lothian and Borders Police, 1964-92; Deputy Chief Constable, Grampian Police, 1992-96; HM Assistant Inspector of Constabulary, Scottish Government, 1996-98; Director, Scottish Police College, 1998-2006; UK Governing Board Member and President, European Police College, 1998-2006; Law Enforcement and Training Consultant, David Garbutt Consulting, 2006-09; Chairman, Scottish Ambulance Service, 2009-2018. Recreations: hill walking; cycling. Address: NHS Education for Scotland, 102 West Port, Edinburgh EH3 9DN.

Garden, Michael, MA. Director, Scottish International Education Trust (Part-time), since 2021; former Unit

Head - National Healthcare Priorities, The Scottish Government (2017-18); former Chief Executive, Judicial Appointments Board for Scotland (2012-17). Educ. Perth High School; University of Edinburgh. Career: The Scottish Government: Policy Manager (Health, Agriculture, Job Dispersal), 2000-07, SEARS Frontline Delivery Project Manager, 2007-2011.

Garden, Professor Olivier James, CBE, BSc, MBChB, MD, DSc (Hon), FRCS (RCPSG), FRCS (Ed), FRCP (Ed), FRACS (Hon), FRCPSCan (Hon), FRSE, FACS (Hon), FRCS (Hon), FCSHK (Hon), FRCSI (Hon). Professor Emeritus; Past Regius Professor of Clinical Surgery, Edinburgh University (2000-2018); Dean International, 2015-2021; Head, School of Clinical Sciences and Community Health, 2002-06; Director of Edinburgh Surgery Online, since 2007; b. 13.11.53, Carluke; m., Amanda; 1 s.; 1 d. Educ. Lanark Grammar School; Edinburgh University. Lecturer, Glasgow University, 1985-88; Chef de Clinique, Unite de Chirurgie Hepatobiliaire et Digestif, Villejuif, France, 1986-87; Senior Lecturer, Edinburgh University, 1988-97; Professor of Hepatobiliary Surgery, Edinburgh University, 1997-2000; Honorary Consultant Surgeon, Royal Infirmary of Edinburgh, since 1988; Director, Scottish Liver Transplant Unit, 1992-2005; President, Association of Upper G1 Surgeons of Great Britain and Ireland, 2002-04; Honorary Company Secretary, British Journal of Surgery Society Ltd., 2003-2012; Surgeon to the Queen in Scotland, 2004-2018; President, International Hepato-Pancreato-Biliary Association, 2012-2014; Chairman: British Journal of Surgery Society Ltd., 2012-19, Edinburgh World Heritage Trust, since 2019, Melville Trust for the Care and Cure for Cancer, since 2019. Recreations: golf; ski-ing. Address: (b.) Clinical Surgery, Royal Infirmary of Edinburgh, 51 Little France Crescent, Edinburgh; T.-0131 242 3614. E-mail: ojgarden@ed.ac.uk

Gardham, Magnus. Special Adviser to the Secretary of State for Scotland. Former Political Editor, The Herald Scotland; previously worked for the Daily Record, Daily Mail and the Edinburgh Evening News. Address: Scotland Office, 1 Melville Crescent, Edinburgh EH3 7HW; T.-0131 2449089.
E-mail: Magnus.Gardham@scotlandoffice.gsi.gov.uk

Gardiner, Iain Derek, FRICS. Chartered Surveyor, since 1957; Senior Partner, Souter & Jaffrey, Chartered Surveyors, 1986-95; b. 22.12.33, Glasgow; m., Kathleen Elizabeth Johnson; 2 s.; 1 d. Educ. Hutcheson's Grammar School, Glasgow; Royal Technical College, Glasgow. Trainee and Assistant Quantity Surveyor, John H. Allan & Sons, Glasgow, 1950-57; National Service, Royal Engineers, 1957-59; Souter & Jaffrey, Inverness: Quantity Surveyor, 1959-63, Partner, 1963-86. Past Chairman, Royal Institution of Chartered Surveyors in Scotland; Chairman: Inverness Area, RICS in Scotland, 1969-70, Quantity Surveyors Committee, RICS in Scotland, 1989-90, Friends of Eden Court Theatre, 1981-82; Chairman, Inverness Area Scout Council, 1993-2009. Recreations: swimming; travel; cookery; Scouting. Address: (h.) 77 Stratherrick Road, Inverness IV2 4LL; T.-01463 235607.

Gardiner, John Ronald, BL, WS. Consultant, Brodies WS, Solicitors, 2001-04 (Senior Partner, 1992-2001, Partner, 1964-2001); b. 25.10.38, Rangoon; m., Aileen Mary Montgomery; 1 s.; 1 s. (deceased); 1 d. Educ. Fettes College; University of Edinburgh. Admitted Solicitor, 1963; admitted Writer to the Signet, 1964; Partner, Brodie Cuthbertson & Watson W.S. (thereafter Brodies W.S.), 1964; Notary Public, 1966-2007. Governor, Fettes Trust,

1986-96; Member, Rent Assessment Panel for Scotland, 1973-97; River Tweed Commissioner, since 2007; Hon. Secretary: Standing Council of Scottish Chiefs, 1970-72, Salmon and Trout Association (Scottish Branch), 1971-84. Recreations: fishing; golf; gardening; birdwatching. Address: (h.) 24 Mortonhall Road, Edinburgh EH9 2HN; T.-0131-667 5604.

Gardiner, Lindsay. UK Audit Executive - Regional Markets Leader, PwC in Scotland, 2019-2021, Regional Leader, 2012-2019; m.; 2 c. Over 20 years experience of auditing and advising retail financial services and major listed companies, working in a number of locations including San Francisco in the US; joined Pwc in 1989: admitted to partnership in 1999, Head of Financial Services in Scotland, 2005-2010, Head, Audit and Assurance practice, Scotland, 2010-2012. Chair of the Trustees of Sick Kids Friends Foundation, since 2015. Recreations: golfing; walking; gardening.

Gardner, Angela Joy, BSc (Hons). Public Affairs Consultant, AJ Enterprises, since 1994; b. 16.9.62, Wolverhampton; m., Andrew Ronald Gardner; 2 d. Educ. Codsall High School; UMIST. BP Chemicals Ltd., South Wales and Grangemouth, 1984-90; BP Schools Link Officer, 1985-90; Senior Public Affairs Officer, BP, 1990-94. Member, General Teaching Council for Scotland, 1990-98; Member, Scottish Examination Board, 1991-94; Member, Scottish Qualifications Authority Engineering Advisory Group, 1999-2003; Associate, Centre for Studies in Enterprise, Career Development and Work, Strathclyde University, 2003-07; Member, Goodison Group in Scotland; Advanced Professional Member, Chartered Institute of Editing and Proofreading; publish Informed Scotland - learning and skills digest. Address: (b.) Evergreen Studio, 3 Tweeddale Court, 14 High Street, Edinburgh EH1 1TE; T.-0131-336 5164.
E-mail: angela.gardner@ajenterprises.co.uk
Web: www.ajenterprises.co.uk

Gardner, Jann, BSc (Hons), MSc, MBA. Chief Executive, NHS Golden Jubilee – GJ National Hospital, Centre for Sustainable Delivery (CfSD), NHS Scotland Academy (joint initiative with NES) and GJ Hotel and Conference Centre, since 2019; Visiting Professor, Strathclyde Business School, since 2021; Director of Scottish Health Innovations Ltd (SHIL), since 2019; b. 9.66. Educ. University of Strathclyde; Robert Gordon University; University of Warwick; Rotterdam Business School; ESADE Business and Law School. Career history: Clinical and Medicines Information Pharmacist, North Yorkshire NHS Trust, 1994-95; Chief Pharmacist/Senior Clinical Pharmacist, Health Care International, 1995-97; Principal/Chief Pharmacist, NHS Stirling, Falkirk and Forth Valley, 1997-2009; NHS Forth Valley: Hospital Improvement Lead and Acute Chief Pharmacist, Forth Valley Royal Hospital, Larbert, 2009-2015; Head of EPQ and Innovation (Executive Team Member), 2012-15; Chief Operating Officer and Deputy Chief Executive Officer/Director of Planning and Strategic Partnerships, NHS Fife, 2015-19. Keen interest in entrepreneurship, robotics, innovation and harnessing transformational solutions to accelerate outcomes and resilience in health. Address: NHS Golden Jubilee, Beardmore Street, Clydebank G81 4HX; T.-0141 951 5000.
E-mail: commsenquiries@gjnh.scot.nhs.uk

Gardner, Rev'd Neil, MA, BD. Minister of Canongate Kirk, Edinburgh. Career history: served with the Royal Army Chaplains' Department in Germany, Hong Kong, Northern Ireland, Surrey, and Hampshire; seven years as minister of Alyth Parish Church in rural Perthshire; Minister of Canongate Kirk (The Kirk of Holyroodhouse and Edinburgh Castle), since 2006. Director, Richmond's Hope; Domestic Chaplain to HM The Queen; Dean of the Order of St John in Scotland; Trustee of the Scottish National War Memorial at Edinburgh Castle. Address: Manse of Canongate, Edinburgh EH8 8BR; T.-0131 5563515.

Garland, Charles, BA (Classics), LLB, DipLP. Interim Chief Executive, Scottish Law Commission, since 2021. Educ. University of Oxford; The University of Edinburgh; Paris-Sud University (Paris XI). Career history: Trainee Solicitor, Shepherd and Wedderburn, 1994-97; Project Manager, Scottish Law Commission, 2007-2016; Solicitor: The Scottish Parliament, 2016-17, The Scottish Government, since 1997; Session Clerk (Elder and Trustee), Mayfield Salisbury Parish Church, Edinburgh, since 2018; Project Manager, Scottish Law Commission, 2018-2021. Address: Scottish Law Commission, 140 Causewayside, Edinburgh EH9 1PR; T.-0131 668 2131.

Garland, Harry Mitchell, MBE, CQSW, FBIM. Retired Chairman, Secretary of State's Advisory Committee on Scotland's Travelling People (1987-95); b. 7.7.28, Aberdeen; m., Phyllis Sandison; 1 s.; 1 d. Educ. Rockwell Academy, Dundee; Robert Gordon's College, Aberdeen; Moray House College, Edinburgh. Probation Officer/Senior Probation Officer/Principal Probation Officer, 1958-69; Depute Director of Social Work, Aberdeen and Kincardine Counties, 1969-73; Director of Social Work: Paisley Burgh, 1973-74, Western Isles, 1974-78, Central Region, 1978-86. Chairman, National Association of Probation Officers in Scotland, 1968-69; President, Association of Directors of Social Work, 1983; Member, Forth Valley Health Board, 1986-90. Recreations: voluntary work; church; golf; walking. Address: (h.) 7 Cromarty View, Nairn IV12 4HX; T.-01667 453684; e-mail: harryandphyllis@btinternet.com

Garner, John Angus McVicar, MB, ChB, DRCOG, DCH, FRCGP, FRCPEdin. Principal in general practice, since 1980; British Medical Association: former Chairman, Scottish Council; former Vice Chairman, Medical and Dental Defence Union of Scotland; BMA Pension Fund Trustee; Tribunal Member, Medical Practitioners Tribunal Service; b. 4.9.50, London; m., Catherine Lizbeth; 1 s.; 1 d. Educ. Eltham College; Edinburgh University. Lothian Local Medical Committee: Secretary, 1986-89, Chairman, 1991-92; Member: General Medical Services Committee, 1989-2001, National Medical Advisory Committee, 1989-95; Past Chairman, Scottish General Medical Services Committee; former Treasurer, General Medical Services Defence Fund Ltd. Recreations: amphibians and photographing fungi. Address: (h.)1, Drylaw Avenue, Edinburgh EH4 2DD; T.-07702269515.
E-mail: johngarne@aol.com

Garrod, Professor Simon Christopher, MA, PhD, FRSE. Professor Emeritus, Glasgow University; b. 19.11.47, London; 1 s.; 1 d. Educ. Bradfield College, Berks; Oxford University; Princeton University. Lecturer, Senior Lecturer, Reader in Psychology, Glasgow University, 1975-90, Professor 1990-2019; Visiting Research Fellow, Max Plank Institute, 1980; Residential Fellow, Netherlands Institute for Advanced Study, 1988. Publications: Understanding Written Language; Language Processing; Saying, Seeing and Acting; Understanding Dialogue, language use and social interaction. Recreations: fishing; hill-walking; sailing. Address: (b.) Institute of Neuroscience and Psychology, Glasgow University, 58 Hillhead Street, Glasgow G12 8QT; T.-0141-330 5033.
E-mail: simon@psy.gla.ac.uk

Garry, James, BSc (Hons), MSc, MRTPI, MCIEEM, CEnv. Assistant Director, The Cockburn Association. Educ. Glasgow and Edinburgh Universities. Chartered Environmentalist and Chartered Planner; currently engaged in a part-time Classics degree programme with the Open University; professional career with several Scottish local authorities and Public Bodies specialising in sustainability, carbon and climate issues. Address: The Cockburn Association, Trunk's Close, 55 High Street, Edinburgh EH1 1SR; T.-0131 557 8686.

Garside, Professor Paul. Dean of Global Engagement (Middle East & Africa), University of Glasgow; Chair in Basic Immunology; Associate, School of Life Sciences. Address: University of Glasgow, RB526 Level B5, University Place, Glasgow G12 8TA; T.-0141 330 7251. E-mail: Paul.Garside@glasgow.ac.uk

Gebbie, George C., LLB (Hons). Advocate, since 1987; b. 27.1.58, Motherwell; m., Anne Gebbie-Oiben; 1 s.; 1 d. Educ. Dalziel High School, Motherwell; Aberdeen University. Legal apprentice to Crown Agent, 1979-81; Procurator Fiscal Depute, Glasgow, 1981-83; Solicitor in private practice, Glasgow, 1983-87. SNP candidate, East Kilbride, 1997 General Election. Recreation: socialising with friends. Address: (b.) Advocates' Library, Edinburgh EH1 1RF; T.-0131-226 5071.

Geddes, Keith, CBE. Policy Director, Pagoda PR, since 1999; b. 8.8.52, Selkirk. Educ. Galashiels Academy; Edinburgh University; Heriot Watt University. Housing Rights Worker, Shelter, 1977-84; Chair, Lothian Region Education Committee, 1987-90; Leader, Lothian Regional Council, 1990-96; Past President, Convention of Scottish Local Authorities; Leader, City of Edinburgh Council, 1996-99. Board Member: Scottish Natural Heritage, 2000-09, Accounts Commission, 2002-08, Greenspace Scotland, 2002-2010; Chair, Central Scotland Green Network, 2014-2020. Recreations: golf; cricket; hill-walking. Address: (h.) 12 Woodmill Terrace, Dunfermline, Fife KY11 4SR; T.-01383 623947.

Geddes, Marion Rhona. Chairperson, Cairn Mhor Childcare Partnership, since 2019; b. 6.51. Career history: worked within the children and families social work service of a local authority for many years; managed a Family Placement team for over 20 years; moved to an independent fostering agency in 2010 to set up and manage their Permanence Service, before retiring in 2017. Volunteers for Scottish Adoption Register and English for speakers of other languages. Address: Cairn Mhor Childcare Partnership, Airlie House, Pentland Park, Saltire Centre, Glenrothes KY6 2AG; T.-01592 631031.

Geekie, Rhondda. Former Leader, East Dunbartonshire Council (2007-2017); former Councillor (1995-2017); b. 18.7.49, Dundee; m., Allan; 2 s.; 1 d. Educ. St. Michael's Secondary. Dental Surgery Assistant; Optical Assistant. Chair, Silver Birch Scotland (Ltd); Director, EDCAB; Chair, EDVA. Recreations: reading; walking. Address: 59 Iona Way, Kirkintilloch, Glasgow G66 3QB; e-mail: rhonddageekie@hotmail.com

Geissler, Martin. Journalist; b. 1971; m.; 2 c. Scotland-based reporter, 1990-92; Reporter/Presenter, ITV Regional News, 1992-98; Scotland Correspondent, ITV News, ITN, 2002-06, Africa Correspondent, 2006-2010, Europe Correspondent, 2010-19; co-anchor of the new BBC Scotland channel's News service, since 2019. Recreation: keen supporter of Heart of Midlothian. Address: BBC Scotland, Pacific Quay, Pacific Drive, Glasgow G51 1DA.

Gemmell, Professor Curtis Glen, BSc, PhD, MIBiol, FRCPath. Honorary Senior Research Fellow, School of Medicine, College of Medical, Veterinary and Life Sciences, Glasgow University; Research Professor, University of Strathclyde; formerly Director, In Vivo

Simulations Ltd; formerly Director, Scottish MRSA Reference Laboratory and Honorary Bacteriologist, Greater Glasgow Health Board; formerly Professor of Microbial Infection, Medical School, University of St Andrews (2006-2010); b. 26.8.41, Beith, Ayrshire; m., Anne Margaret; 2 d. Educ. Spier's School, Beith; Glasgow University. Glasgow University: Assistant Lecturer, 1966-68, Lecturer, 1968-69; Paisley College of Technology: Lecturer, 1969-71, Senior Lecturer, 1971-76; Glasgow University: Senior Lecturer, 1976-90, Reader, 1990-2000; Professor of Bacterial Infection and Epidemiology, Medical School, 2000-06. Visiting Associate Professor, University of Minnesota, Minneapolis, 1979-80. Recreations: gardening; golf. Address: (h.) Southfield, 18 Milton Road, Pittenweem, Anstruther, Fife KY10 2LN.

Gemmell, Rev. David Rankin, MA, BD. Minister, Ayr Auld Kirk, since 1999; b. 27.2.63, Girvan; m., Helen; 1 s.; 1 d. Educ. Carrick Academy; University of Glasgow. Assistant Minister, Girvan North Church, 1990-91; Minister, Fenwick Parish Church, 1991-99. Chaplain to Ayr Academy, Kyle Academy, Holmston Primary, Southcraig Special Needs School, Ayr College: Parent Council, Ayr Academy; Trustee, McLaurin Gallery; Church Rep on south Ayrshire Council Leadership Panel. Recreations: ex SRU rugby referee; single figure handicap golfer. Address: (h.) 58 Monument Road, Ayr KA7 2UB; T.-01292 262580; e-mail: drgemmell@hotmail.com

Gemmell, Gavin John Norman, CBE, DUniv, CA; b. 7.9.41, Edinburgh; m., Kathleen Fiona Drysdale; 1 s.; 2 d. (1 d. deceased). Educ. George Watson's College. Qualified CA, 1964; joined Baillie, Gifford & Co., 1964; retired as Joint Senior Partner, 2001; Chairman: Scottish Widows Group, 2001-07, Standing Committee, Scottish Episcopal Church, 1997-2002; Director: Lloyds TSB Group, 2001-07, Archangel Informal Investments, 2001-2016, St. Mary's Music School, 2010-18; Trustee, National Galleries of Scotland, 1999-2007; Chairman, Court, Heriot Watt University, 2002-08; Honorary doctorate, Heriot-Watt University, 2009. Recreations: golf; foreign travel. Address: (h.) 79/7 Braid Avenue, Edinburgh EH10 6ED.
E-mail: gavingemmell@blueyonder.co.uk

Gemmell, William Ruthven, LLB, WS. Partner, Murray Beith Murray; Solicitor in Scotland and England and Wales; Chief Executive, Murray Asset Management UK Limited; Director, Personal Investment Management and Financial Advice Association (PIMFA) and other companies; b. 4.4.57; m. Fiona Elizabeth Watson; 1 s.; 1 d. Educ. Loretto; Edinburgh University (Law); Aberdeen University (Accountancy). Murray Beith Murray, since 1985; Law Society of Scotland: President, 2006-07; Council Member of the Institute of Chartered Accountants of Scotland, 2007-11; Financial Services Tribunal, 1993-2002; Financial Services Authority Small Businesses Practitioner Panel, 1999-2007 (Chairman, 2004-06); Financial Services and Markets Tribunal, 2001-2010; VAT and Duties Tribunal, 2002-09; Judge, First-tier Tribunal (Tax Chamber), since 2009; Member, Upper Tribunal (Tax and Chancery Chamber), since 2010; Legal Member of The Mental Health Tribunal for Scotland, since 2016; President, Tax Tribunals for Scotland, 2016-2017; Legal Member, Upper Tribunal for Scotland, since 2017; Head of the UK Delegation to the Council of European Bars and Law Societies, 2010-13; President of the Council of European Bars and Law Societies, 2017. Address: (b.) 3 Glenfinlas Street, Edinburgh EH3 6AQ; T.-0131 225 1200.
E-mail: ruthven.gemmell@murraybeith.co.uk

Gerstenberg, Frank Eric, MA (Cantab), PGCE. Principal, George Watson's College, Edinburgh, 1985-2001; b.

23.2.41, Balfron; m., Valerie MacLellan; 1 s.; 2 d. Educ. Trinity College, Glenalmond; Clare College, Cambridge; London University. Assistant Master, Kelly College, Tavistock, 1963-67; Housemaster and Head of History, Millfield School, 1967-74; Headmaster, Oswestry School, 1974-85. Chairman of Governing Council, Glenalmond College, 2005-2011. Recreations: skiing; sailing; travelling; music; journalism; golf. Address: (h.) 6, Park Drive, Dornoch IV25 3TE; T.-01862 810210.
E-mail: frankandval@gmail.com

Gethins, Stephen. MP (SNP), North East Fife, 2015-19; SNP Spokesperson on International Affairs and Europe at Westminster, 2017-19; b. 28.3.76, Perth. Educ. Perth Academy; University of Dundee; University of Antwerp; University of Kent. Career in the political and international NGO sector; has worked in peace-building, arms control and democratisation in the Caucasus and Balkans; worked with the NGO Links, based in Tbilisi, with a focus on the conflicts surrounding the breakaway entities in the South Caucasus such as South Ossetia, Abkhazia and Nagorno-Karabakh; worked for Saferworld on arms control and peace-building in the former Soviet Union and Balkans; involved in a range of democratisation projects across the former Soviet Union and Western Balkans. Former Special Adviser to Scotland's First Minister, advising on European and International Affairs as well as Rural Affairs, Energy and Climate Change; also a Political Advisor with the Committee of the Regions in the European Union, worked with local authorities from across Europe; helped Scottish organisations gain influence and funding in the EU at Scotland Europa; involved in the US Government's International Visitor Leadership Programme which analysed 'US Foreign Policy Challenges' in 2011.

Gibb, George Frederick Cullen, MA, LLB. Formerly Consultant to Messrs Marshall Wilson, Solicitors, Falkirk (1997-2009); Honorary Sheriff at Falkirk, since 1987; b. 19.3.33, Edinburgh; m., Inga Mary Grieve; 1 s.; 2 d. Educ. George Heriot's School, Edinburgh; Edinburgh University. Messrs Marshall Wilson, Solicitors: Partner, 1964, Senior Partner, 1990. Recreations: golf; music; bowls; reading. Address: (h.) Noustigar, Holm Road, St. Ola, Orkney KW15 1SX; T.-01856 872369.
E-mail: gibbfamily48@gmail.com

Gibbons, Gwilym, MSc, FRSA, FCMI, CMgr. Chief Executive, The Crichton Trust, since 2018. Educ. Queen Margaret University. Career: Chair of the Board of Trustees, MADCAP Trust Ltd, 1987-98; Events Ranger, The Parks Trust, Milton Keynes, 1992-99; Entertainment Operations Manager, University of Warwick Students' Union, 1999-2001; Development Manager (Leisure and Arts), Argyll and Bute Council, 2002-03; Partnership Manager, Kintyre Healthy Living Partnership, NHS Argyll and Clyde, 2003-04; Stronger Safer Communities Manager, West Wiltshire District Council, 2004-06; Local Advisor, Scottish Natural Heritage, 2009-2010; Board Member, Creative Scotland, 2010-12; Trustee, Highlands and Islands Promoters Arts Network, 2006-13; Advisory Group Member, Highlands and Islands Structural Funds Partnership Ltd (HIPP), 2008-13; Director, Shetland Arts Development Agency, 2006-2014; Chief Executive, Horsecross Arts - Perth Concert Hall & Theatre, 2015-18; Board Member, Perth City Development Board, 2016-18; Capital Project Advisory Board Member, Friends of Britannia Panopticon Music Hall Trust, since 2018; Board Member, Regional Screen Scotland, since 2015; Chair of the Board, Future Economy Company Ltd, since 2014; Chair of the Board Tourbook CIC, since 2018; Founder, Creative Help Ltd, since 2013. Address: The Crichton Trust, Grierson House, Bankend Road, Dumfries DG1 4ZE; T.-01387 247544.

Gibbs, Professor Robert, BA. Emeritus Professor of Pre-Humanist Art History, University of Glasgow, since 2011 (Professor, 2006-2011); b. 02.07.46, London. Educ. Ealing Grammar School for Boys; Courtauld Institute, University of London. Research Assistant to Sir Nicolas Pevsner for The Buildings of England: Dorset, Birkbeck College, University of London, 1968-69; University of Glasgow: Lecturer, then Senior Lecturer, from 1991, then Reader, 2001-06, Department of History of Art. Publications: Boggi, Flavio and Gibbs, Robert: Lippo di Dalmasio. Assai valente pittore, 2013; Illuminating the Law: Medieval Legal Manuscripts in Cambridge Collections (Co-Author), 2001; The Development of the Illustration of Legal Manuscripts by Bolognese Illuminators between 1250 and 1298, Juristische Buchproduktion im Mittelalter, 1998; Landscape as Property: Bolognese Law Manuscripts and the Development of Landscape Painting, Atti del Congresso della Societa di Storia della Miniatura, 1992; L'Occhio di Tomaso, Treviso, 1981; Tomaso da Modena: Painting in Emilia and the March of Treviso, 1340-80, 1989; In search of Ambrogio Lorenzetti's Allegory of Justice in the Good Commune, 1999; also written on 19th century design. Recreations: music of all genres except 'Light Music'; popular science and evolution. Address: (b.) Department of History of Art, University of Glasgow, Glasgow G12 8QQ; T.-0141 649 1575.
E-mail: robert.gibbs@glasgow.ac.uk

Gibson, David Bisset, LLB (Hons), DipLP. Chairman, BTO Solicitors, since 2019, Partner, since 2011. Educ. The University of Edinburgh. Trainee/Assistant/Associate, W & J Burness WS, 1984-90; Partner, Burness, 1990-2011. Recreations: golf; tinkering with classic cars. Address: BTO Solicitors, 48 St. Vincent Street, Glasgow G2 5HS; T.-0141 221 8012; e-mail: dbg@bto.co.uk

Gibson, Edgar Matheson, MBE, TD, DL, DA. Vice Lord Lieutenant, Orkney, 2007-2011; Deputy Lieutenant, Orkney, 1976-2007; Honorary Sheriff, Grampian, Highlands and Islands, since 1992; full-time professional artist, since 1990; b. 1.11.34, Kirkwall; m., Jean McCarrick; 2 s.; 2 d. Educ. Kirkwall Grammar School; Gray's College of Art, Aberdeen. National Service, 1958-60; TA and TAVR service to 1985 with Lovat Scouts, reaching Lt. Col.; Battalion Second in Command, 2/51 Highland Volunteers, 1973-76; Head of Art Department, then Assistant Headmaster, Kirkwall Grammar School, until 1990; Assessor in Higher Art & Design, Scottish Certificate of Education Examination Board, Dalkeith, 1978-93; Joint Services Liaison Officer for Orkney, 1980-85; Cadet Commandant, Orkney Lovat Scouts ACF, 1979-86, Honorary Colonel, 1986-2004; Member, Orkney Health Board, 1991-99; Chairman, Italian Chapel Preservation Committee, 2006-2015, Honorary President, since 2015 (Member, since 1976); Trustee, T.A. Military Museum, Weyland, since 1983; Hon. President: Society of Friends of St. Magnus Cathedral, since 1994, Orkney Craftsmen's Guild, 1997-2002 (Chairman, 1962-82); President, Orkney Branch, SSFA and FHS, 1997-2013 (Chairman, 1990-97); Chairman: St. Magnus Cathedral Fair Committee, 1982-2004, Northern Area, Highland TA&VR Association, 1987-93; Member of Selection Committee of Operation Raleigh, then County Coordinator, 1991-93. Recreation: whisky tasting. Address: (h.) Transcona, New Scapa Road, Kirkwall, Orkney; T.-0185687 2849.

Gibson, J.N. Alastair, DSc, MD, FRCS (Edin), FRCS (Tr & Orth), MFSTEd; b. 21.10.54, Bellshill; m., Laurie-Ann; 2 s.; 1 d. Honorary Treasurer and Council Member, The Royal College of Surgeons of Edinburgh; Consultant to joimax GmbH, Karlsruhe, Germany. Formerly King James IV Professorship (RCSEd); Consultant Spinal Surgeon, Lothian University Hospitals, 1993-2017; Honorary Senior Lecturer, University of Edinburgh; Visiting Surgeon, Spire Murrayfield Hospital, 1998-2019. Educ. King Edward VII Grammar School, Sheffield; Royal London Hospital Medical College, London. House Surgeon, London Hospital, 1978-79; Surgical Registrar, Ninewells Hospital, Dundee, 1981-83; Clinical Research Fellow, University of Dundee, 1984-86; University of Edinburgh: Lecturer, 1986-91, Senior Lecturer, 1993-97; Spinal Fellow, Royal North Shore Hospital, Sydney, 1992; Visiting Scholar, University of Sydney, 1992; Burgess, The City of Edinburgh; Member: The Edinburgh Merchant Company, British Association of Spine Surgeons, European Spine Society, International Society for the Study of the Lumbar Spine. Author: books, chapters and contributions to professional journals; Patents: cervical disc replacement prosthesis, neural retraction device. Recreations: Member of Mortonhall GC and Lamlash GC; Past President, Thistle LTC. Address: Royal College of Surgeons of Edinburgh, Nicolson Street, Edinburgh EH8 9DW; T.-0131-4455586.
E-mail: j.n.a.gibson@gmail.com

Gibson, Kenneth. MSP (SNP), Cunninghame North, since 2007; b. 8.9.61, Paisley. Career: SNP councillor in Glasgow for Mosspark, 1992-99; Leader of the Opposition, Glasgow City Council, 1998-99; MSP, Scottish Parliament, 1999-2003; Shadow Cabinet front bencher, 1997-2003; SNP Local Government Convenor, 1997-99 (responsible for writing and producing the SNP manifesto and co-ordinating the campaign for the 1999 local government elections); Convener, Scottish Parliament's Finance Committee, 2011-16, Convener: Finance and Public Administration Committee, since 2021, Culture, Tourism, Europe and External Affairs Committee. Address: Scottish Parliament, Edinburgh EH99 1SP.

Gibson, Leigh. Director, British Council Scotland, since 2020. Career history: British Council: Director for Content and Programme, Shanghai World Expo, 2007-2010; Director, UK Now Festival, China 2012, 2011-2013; Executive Director, UK-Russia Year of Culture, 2013-2014; Director, Festivals and Season, 2014-16; Director, USA, 2016-2020. Former Cultural Counsellor for the British Embassy in Washington. Address: British Council Scotland, 2-4 Waterloo Place, Edinburgh EH1 3EG; T.-0131 524 5700.

Gibson, Patricia, MA (Hons). MP (SNP), North Ayrshire and Arran, since 2015; SNP Shadow Secretary of State for Housing, Communities and Local Government, since 2021; Spokesperson for Consumer Affairs, since 2016; b. 12.5.68, Glasgow; m., Kenneth Gibson. Educ. University of Glasgow. Career: Teacher of English for over 23 years in Glasgow, Lanarkshire and East Renfrewshire; served as SNP Education Spokesperson on Glasgow City Council for 5 years, representing Glasgow Pollok Ward as a councillor (2007-2012). Address: House of Commons, London SW1A 0AA.

Gibson, Robert McKay, MA (Hons). MSP (SNP), Caithness, Sutherland and Ross, 2011-2016, Highlands and Islands, 2003-2011; b. 16.10.45, Glasgow; divorced. Educ. High School of Glasgow; University of Dundee. Executive Officer, Civil Service, 1965-68; Teacher (geography and modern studies), 1973-74; Assistant Principal Teacher, Guidance, 1974-77; Principal Teacher, Guidance, 1977-95; writer and musician, since 1995. Recreations: organic gardening; hill-walking; traditional music. Address: (h.) Tir nan Oran, 8 Culcairn Road, Evanton, Ross-shire IV16 9YT; T.-01349 830388.

Gilbert, George, DA, RSW. Painter; Partner, Courtyard Gallery, 1994-2001; many solo and group shows in Glasgow and Edinburgh; b. 12.9.39, Glasgow; m., Lesley Johnston; 3 s. Educ. Victoria Drive Secondary School, Glasgow; Glasgow School of Art. Teacher of Art,

Aberdeenshire, Glasgow, Fife, 1963-89; painter (exhibited widely), since 1963. Elected: RSW, 1973 (Council Member, 1994-98); SAAC, 1991, PAI, 1992. Artstore Award, 1992; Gillies Award (RSW), 1993; RSPSG Award (RGI), 2006; Strathearn Award (RGI), 2007; RSW Council Award, 2007; Scottish Drawing Competition, 2009 (Art Store Award); Scottish Arts Club Award (RSW), 2011; Armour Memorial Award, Paisley Art Institute, 2013; shortlisted for Sunday Times Watercolour Competition, 2018; Busby Award (RSW), 2019. Recreations: walking; reading; music; the arts. Address: 4 Station Place, Aberdour, Burntisland, Fife KY3 0SN.

Gill, Professor Evelyn Margaret, OBE, FRSE, FRSB, FRSGS, BSc, PhD, BA. Emeritus Professor, School of Biology, University of Aberdeen; b. 1.1.51, Edinburgh. Educ. Mary Erskine School for Girls; Edinburgh University; Massey University, New Zealand; Open University. Researcher, Forage Intake, AFRC Grassland Research Institute, 1976-89; Overseas Development Administration, 1979-81; Natural Resources Institute, Kent, 1989-96; Chief Executive, Natural Resources International Ltd., 1996-2000; Chief Executive and Director of Research, Macaulay Land Use Research Institute, Aberdeen, 2000-06. Chief Scientific Adviser, Scottish Government Environment and Rural Affairs, 2006-2011; Senior Research Fellow (10%), DFID, 2009-2016; Professor (part-time) of Integrated Land Use, University of Aberdeen, 2006-2019; Chair of the International Science and Partnership Council of the CGIAR, 2014-19; Chair of Scottish Science Advisory Council, since 2019. Recreations: hill walking; reading. Address: 14B/10 Riverside Crescent, Edinburgh EH12 5QT; T.-07703131373; e-mail: e.m.gill@care4free.net

Gill, Kerry James Graham. Journalist; retired Scottish Daily Express Political Editor; b. 29.4.47, Newcastle; m., Andrea Kevan; 2 d. Educ. Durham School; Warwick University. Westminster Press, 1969-71; Evening Post, 1971-72; The Journal, 1972-77; The Scotsman, 1977-87 (Reporter and Glasgow Editor); The Observer, 1979-87; The Times, 1987-93; Daily Record, 1994; joined Scottish Daily Express in 1996 (Assistant Editor, Executive Editor, Editor, Political Editor). Recreations: modern French history; gardening; reading. Address: (h.) Spout Burn, Main Street, Fintry, Stirlingshire; T.-01360 860427.

Gillan, Rev David Stewart, BSc, MDiv, PhD. Former Minister, St. Michael's Parish Church, Linlithgow; Moderator, West Lothian Presbytery, 2014-15; Vice-Convener, World Mission Council, Church of Scotland, 2009-2011; b. 1.10.58, Newfoundland, Canada; m., Sarah Ormerod; 1 d.; 1 s. Educ. Sydney Mines High School, Nova, Scotia; Universities of Edinburgh, Toronto and Mount Allison. Interim Minister, Morija, Lesotho, 1986-87; Minister, Gauteng, South Africa, 1987-98 (including Alexandra, Tembisa, Katlehong and Atteridgeville); Researcher, Commission on the Restitution of Land Rights, South Africa, 1997-98; Executive Director, Churches Council on Theological Education in Canada, 1999-2004. Publication: Book edited, "Church, Land and Poverty", Johannesburg, 1998. Chairperson, Commission on Faith and Witness, Canadian Council of Churches; Lieutenant Governor's Medal, NS, 75. Recreations: writing; Celtic music; guitar (with Sarah, fiddle).

Gillespie, Adrian, BAcc, MBA. Chief Executive, Scottish Enterprise, since 2021; Chief Commercial Officer, University of Strathclyde, 2018-2021; Managing Director of Operations (Growth Companies, Innovation and Infrastructure), Scottish Enterprise, 2013-17. Educ.

Glasgow University; University of Strathclyde. Career: ten years in commercial and financial management positions within Marks and Spencer plc; Senior Director of Energy and Low Carbon Technologies for Scottish Enterprise with responsibility for working with industry to establish and deliver clear priorities for investment and growth, with a particular focus on offshore energy. Trustee, Glasgow Science Centre. Address: Scottish Enterprise, Floor 4, Atrium Court, 50 Waterloo Street, Glasgow G2 6HQ.

Gillespie, Fiona. Head of Charities (Scotland), Rathbone Investment Management, since 2019. Educ. The British School Al Khubairat, Abu Dhabi; St George's School for Girls, Edinburgh; Edinburgh Napier University; University of Stirling. Career history: Investment Manager, Edinburgh Fund Managers, 1993-2003; Senior Investment Manager, Multi Asset Solutions, Aberdeen Asset Management, Edinburgh, 2003-2017; Senior Investment Manager, Anderson Strathern Asset Management, Edinburgh, 2017-19; Children's Hospice Association Scotland (CHAS): Non-Executive Director, 2015-2021, Member of Finance and Investment Board, since 2015; Board Trustee (Voluntary), The Stafford Trust, since 2017; Trustee (Voluntary), SCVO (Scottish Council for Voluntary Organisations), since 2018; Steering Committee Member, Future Asset, since 2020; Board Trustee, Medical Research Scotland, Edinburgh, since 2021. Address: Rathbone Investment Management, 28 St Andrew Square, Edinburgh EH2 1AF; T.-0131 550 1350. E-mail: Fiona.Gillespie@rathbones.com

Gillespie, Dr. Gary. Chief Economist, Scottish Government, since 2011. Joined the Scottish Government in 2000 from the Fraser of Allander Institute at the University of Strathclyde; appointed to the Senior Civil Services in 2006 and has provided economic advice in a range of policy areas over this time including Economy, Health, Enterprise and Finance. Honorary Professor, Glasgow Caledonian University, since 2011; Visiting Professor, University of Strathclyde since 2015; Fellow of the Academy of Social Sciences, since 2017. Address: Room 4N-01, St. Andrew's House, Edinburgh EH1 3DG.

Gillespie, Professor Iain, BSc, PhD, MA, MBA. Principal and Vice Chancellor, University of Dundee, since 2021. Career history: Lecturer in Microbiology and Biology, American University of Beirut, Lebanon, 1986-89; Research Project Manager, Agricultural Genetics Company Ltd, Cambridge, 1989-90; Branch Head, Biotechnology Unit, UK Department of the Environment, London, 1991-94; Team Leader, Office of Science and Technology, UK Cabinet Office, London, 1994-95; Assistant Director, Science in Government Division, Office of Science and Technology, UK Department of Trade and Industry, London, 1995-98; Section Head, Industry & International Branch, UK Department of Health, Richmond House, London, 1998-2001; OECD: Head of Biotechnology Unit, 2001-04; Head of Biotechnology Division, Directorate for Science, Technology and Industry, 2005-09; Head of Science and Technology Policy Division, 2009-2011; University of Edinburgh: Visiting Professor, Institute for Innovation Generation in the Life Sciences, since 2011; Bright Ideas Fellow, 2011; Director of Science and Innovation, Natural Environment Research Council, Swindon, 2013-15; Pro-Vice-Chancellor (Research and Enterprise), University of Leicester, 2016-2021. Address: University of Dundee, Nethergate, Dundee DD1 4HN; T.-01382 385561; e-mail: v.a.dorward@dundee.ac.uk

Gillespie, Ken, FRICS. Chair, Homes for Scotland, since 2017. Previously Chief Operating Officer, Galliford Try, 1996-2017. Address: Homes for Scotland Ltd, 5 New Mart Place, Edinburgh EH14 1RW; T.-0131 455 8350.

Gillespie, Professor Thomas Alastair, BA, PhD, Hon DSc (Heriot Watt), FRSE. Emeritus Professor of Mathematics, University of Edinburgh (Professor, since 1997); b. 15.2.45, Torrance; m., Judith Anne Nelmes; 2 s.; 1 d. Educ. Glasgow Academy; University of Cambridge; University of Edinburgh. Lecturer, 1968-87, Senior Lecturer, 1987-92, Reader in Mathematics, 1992-97, University of Edinburgh; Visiting Professor, Indiana University, 1973-74, 1983-84. Recreations: gardening; making music; hill walking. Address: (b.) School of Mathematics, James Clerk Maxwell Building, Edinburgh EH9 3FD; T.-0131 667 8792.

Gillies, Anne Lorne, MA, PhD, PGCE, LRAM, Dr honoris causa. Singer, Writer, Educationalist; b. 21.10.44, Stirling; 1 s.; 2 d. Educ. Oban High School; University of Edinburgh; University of London; Jordanhill College of Education; University of Glasgow. Singer: TV, radio, concert, recital, theatre, recording. Writer: scripts, film and TV; songs; children's books (Acair Earranta, National Gaelic Resource Centre, Brìgh); short stories (as Anne Bree, Polygon, 2000, 2001); autobiography ('Song of Myself' – Mainstream Publishing, 1992). Ethnomusicology ('Songs of Gaelic Scotland', Birlinn Ltd, 2005: awarded Ratcliff Prize (2006), for major contribution to the study of folklore in UK and Ireland). Gaelic development National Education officer: Comann na Gàidhlig (1988-90); community development: Arts Development Office, Govan Initiative Ltd (1991-93); TV production: Gaelic Producer, Scottish Television Ltd (1993-95); lecturer in Gaelic, Faculty of Education, University of Strathclyde (1995-98); politics: SNP: member of National Executive (1996-2000: Spokesperson, Transport; Arts, Culture and Gaelic); candidate for Western Isles, General Election, 1997, and European Parliament Election, 1999. Co-director, with husband Kevin Bree, in Brìgh Productions (Ayrshire-based multi-media publishing partnership, 2000-2015). Honours include Rotary Paul Harris Fellowship, 2003; Speaker of Year, elected by Assoc. Speakers' Clubs of Great Britain, 2005; Honorary Fellowships: University of Highlands and Islands, Royal Incorporation of Architects in Scotland, Association for Scottish Literary Studies; Scottish Government's Ambassador for Gaelic, 2009-2010; Inducted into Scottish Traditional Music Hall of Fame, 2012. Appointed Board of Governors, Royal Conservatoire of Scotland, 2017. Work in progress: novel set in 17th century Scotland, Ireland, France. Address: (h.) 49 Aytoun Road, Pollokshields, Glasgow G41 5HW; e-mail: anne@annelornegillies.co.uk

Gillies, Crawford Scott, LLB, ACA, MBA. Chair, Pitlochry Festival Theatre, since 2020; Chairman, Control Risks Group Ltd., 2006-2017; Director, Standard Life plc, 2007-2016; Director, Barclays plc, since 2014; Director, SSE plc, since 2015; b. 5.56, Scotland; m., Alison; 3 s. Educ. Perth Academy; Edinburgh University; Harvard University. Bain and Company, 1983-2008; Touch EMAS Ltd, 2006-2011; Hammonds, 2005-09; Scottish Enterprise plc, 2009-2015; Mitie PLC, 2012-2015. Recreation: trees. Address: 101 George Street, Edinburgh EH2 3ES.

Gillies, Hugh, BEng (Hons). Interim Chief Executive Officer, Transport Scotland, since 2021. Educ. Stewarton High School; Edinburgh Napier University. Career history: Transport Scotland: Head of Network Operations, 2010-2013, Head of Transport Scotland 2014 Team, 2013-15, Head of Network Operations, 2015-16, Director of Trunk Road and Bus Operations, 2016-2021, Director of Roads, 2018-2021. Chartered Civil Engineer; Transport Planning Professional; member of the Chartered Institution of Highways and Transportation. Address: Transport Scotland, Buchanan House, 58 Port Dundas Road, Glasgow G4 0HF; T.-0141 272 7100.

Gillies, Norman Neil Nicolson, OBE, BA, Dr.hc (Aberdeen), DUniv (Open University), FRSA; Fellowship of the Royal Conservatoire of Scotland; b. 1.3.47, Flodigarry, Isle of Skye; m., Jean Brown Nixon; 1 s.; 2 d.

Educ. Portree High School; Strathclyde University; Open University. College Secretary, Sabhal Mor Ostaig, 1983-88; Director, Sabhal Mor Ostaig, 1988-2008; Director of Development, Clan Donald Lands Trust, 2009-2012; Director: Skye and Lochalsh Enterprise Ltd., 1990-99; Chief, Gaelic Society of Inverness, 2000; Honorary Professor in Contemporary Highland Studies, Aberdeen University, 2002; Professor Emeritus, UHI Millennium Institute, 2009; Chair of the Board of Governors of West Highland College, 2009-2011; Member of the Board of Governors of the Royal Conservatoire of Scotland, 2009-2019; Chair, Atlas Arts, 2009-2019; Chair, Sabhal Mòr Ostaig Development Trust; Board Member, Urras Fhlòdaigearraidh. Recreations: reading; broadcasting; family. Address: (h.) Innis Ard, Ardvasar, Isle of Skye IV45 8RU; T.-01471 844 281.
E-mail: tormod281@btinternet.com

Gillies, Professor Pamela, CBE, BSc, PGCE, MEd, MMedSci, PhD, FRSA, FFPH, FAcSS, Hon FRCPS (Glas), FRSE, DSc (Hons). Principal and Vice-Chancellor, Glasgow Caledonian University, since 2006; b. 13.02.53, Dundee. Educ. University of Aberdeen; University of Nottingham. Member, Global Advisory Council of African Leadership University; Member, Grameen Caledonian College of Nursing Board, Dhaka; Member, National University of Science and Technology Board, Oman; Founding Member: RFK UK Human Rights Board, 2018-2020; Member, Scottish Institute for Enterprise Board; Board Member, Scottish Institute for Excellence in Social Work (SIESWE), 2006-08; Founding Trustee, Grameen Scotland Foundation, 2012-18; Member, Board of Trustees of the British Council, 2008-2014; Member, Scottish Poverty and Truth Commission, 2009-2010; Elected Fellow of the Royal Society of Edinburgh (2015) and of the Faculty of Public Health, Royal College of Physicians of London in 2002; Academician of the Academy for Social Sciences in 2005; Honorary Fellow, Royal College of Physicians of Glasgow, 2007; Fellow of RSA, 1996; Harkness Fellow, Commonwealth Fund of New York at Harvard School of Public Health, 1992-93; Visiting Scholar in Residence, Cabot House, Radcliffe College, Harvard. Publications: over 100 academic journals and government reports on health promotion; cross cultural perspectives on HIV/AIDS, sexuality and health; partnership responses to health improvement and community development responses to inequalities in health, focusing on the potential of social action for health. Recreations: tennis; gardening; Glamis Castle Musicale; Member of Glyndebourne Opera. Address: Glasgow Caledonian University, Cowcaddens Road, Glasgow G4 0BA; T.-0141 3313113.
E-mail: pamela.gillies@gcu.ac.uk

Gillies, Rt. Rev. Robert Arthur, BD, PhD. Bishop of Aberdeen and Orkney, 2007-2016 (retired); b. 21.10.51, Cleethorpes; m., Elizabeth; 3 s. Educ. Barton-upon-Humber Grammar School; Edinburgh University; St. Andrews University. Medical Laboratory Technician, 1968-72; Curate: Christ Church, Falkirk, 1977-80, Christ Church Morningside, and Chaplain, Napier College, 1980-84; Chaplain, Dundee University, 1984-90. Hon. Lecturer, Department of Philosophy, Dundee University, 1985-95; Rector, St. Andrew's Episcopal Church, St. Andrews, 1991-2007; Honorary Canon, Diocese of Mzimvubu, South Africa, since 2015. Publications: A Way for Healing, 1995; Informing Faith, 1996; Healing: Broader and Deeper, 1998; New Language of Faith, 2001; Where Earth and Heaven Meet, 2005; Sounds Before The Cross, 2007; Three Days in Holy Week, 2014; Approaching the Cross, 2018; Guilt and Forgiveness: A Study in the Thought and Personality of Paul Ricoeur, 2019; The Approaching Word, 2020. Recreation: family. Address: 4 Kilrymont Place, St Andrews, Fife KY16 8DH.

Gillies, Valerie, MA, MLitt, FSAScot. Poet; b. 4.6.48, Edmonton, Canada; m., William Gillies; 1 s.; 2 d. Educ.

Edinburgh University; University of Mysore, S. India. Writer in Residence, Duncan of Jordanstone College of Art and Dundee District Libraries; Writer in Residence, East Lothian and Midlothian District Libraries; Writer in Residence, Edinburgh University; Royal Literary Fellow, Queen Margaret University, 2010-2012; Senior Arts Worker (Hospital Arts), Artlink; Trainer for Lapidus Scotland; Facilitator for Maggie's Cancer Care Centre, Edinburgh. Creative Scotland Award, 2005; The Edinburgh Makar; Associate of Harvard University. Creative Scotland Open Fund Award, 2021-22, with Rebecca Marr, photographer; research and development for website and Kist o Wild Grasses: www.whenthegrassdances.art. Publications: Each Bright Eye; Bed of Stone; Tweed Journey; The Chanter's Tune; The Ringing Rock; St. Kilda Song; Men and Beasts; The Lightning Tree; The Spring Teller; The Cream of the Well: New and Selected Poems. Recreations: whippet-racing; field-walking; Qigong; swimming. Address: (h.) 67 Braid Avenue, Edinburgh EH10 6ED; T.-0131-447 2876.
E-mail: valeriegillies@hotmail.com
Website: www.valeriegillies.com

Gillies, Professor William, MA (Edin), MA (Oxon), Hon. D.Litt. (Ulster). Professor of Celtic, Edinburgh University, 1979-2009; Visiting Professor, Harvard University, 2009-10, 2013-15; b. 15.9.42, Stirling; m., Valerie; 1 s.; 2 d. Educ. Oban High School; Edinburgh University; Corpus Christi College, Oxford; Dublin University. Dublin Institute for Advanced Studies, 1969-70; Lecturer, Edinburgh University, 1970-79; Director, Pittencrieff International, Ltd.; Fellow, Royal Society of Edinburgh, 1990; Fellow, Royal Historical Society, 2002. Recreations: walking; gardening; music; Tai chi. Address: (h.) 67 Braid Avenue, Edinburgh EH10 6ED.

Gillis, Richard, OStJ. Solicitor, since 1975; Managing Director, family investment companies, since 2001; b. 22.4.50, Dundee; m., Ruth J. P. Garden. Educ. High School of Dundee. Solicitor, Greater London Council, 1975-77; Archer & Wilcock, Nairobi, Kenya, 1977-80; Shoosmiths, 1980-81; Assistant to the Secretary, TI Group plc, 1981-85; Secretary, ABB Transportation Holdings Ltd (British Rail Engineering Ltd until privatisation, now Alstom) & Trustee, Company Pension Schemes, 1985-95; Clerk to the Council and Company Secretary, University of Derby, 1995-2002; University Court, 2003-17. Secretary, Justice report on perjury; Director, then Vice-Chairman, Crewe Development Agency, 1992-95; CBI East Midlands Regional Council, 1993-95; Chairman, Property Committee, Derbyshire Council of the Order of St. John, 1994-2003; Trustee, Priory of England and the Islands of the Order of St. John and Trustee, St. John Ambulance, 1999-2003; Chairman, Audit Committee and Priory Regulations Committee, Regional Member of Priory Chapter, 1999-2005; Court of Assistants, Worshipful Company of Basketmakers, 2004-13, Upper Warden, 2012-13. Recreations: Freemasonry; historical films; music; Clubs: Athenæum, New (Edinburgh); Blairgowrie Golf. Address: (h.) Nether Kinfauns, Church Road, Kinfauns, Perth PH2 7LD; T.-01738-860886.

Gillon, Karen Macdonald. General Secretary, Church of Scotland Guild, since 2022; MSP (Labour), Clydesdale, 1999-2011; formerly Shadow Minister for Rural Development; b. 18.8.67, Edinburgh; m., James Gillon; 2 s.; 1 d. Educ. Jedburgh Grammar School; Birmingham University. Youth Worker, Terminal One Youth Centre, Blantyre, 1991-94; Community Education Worker, North Lanarkshire Council, 1994-97; PA to Rt. Hon. Helen Liddell, MP, 1997-99. Recreations: sport; music; flower arranging; reading; cooking. Address: Church of Scotland Guild, 121 George Street, Edinburgh

EH2 4YN; T.-0131 240 2217.
E-mail: kgillon@churchofscotland.org.uk

Gilloran, Professor Alan James, MA PhD. Former Deputy Principal, Queen Margaret University, Edinburgh (1996-2016); Sociologist; b. 7.6.56, Edinburgh; m., Barbara; 1 s.; 1 d. Educ. Daniel Stewart's College, Edinburgh; University of Edinburgh. Researcher, Wester Hailes Representative Council; Research Assistant, Moray House; Research Fellow, University of Edinburgh; Lecturer in Sociology and Social Policy, University of Stirling. Member, Care Development Group on Free Personal Care for Elderly People; Vice Chair, East Lothian Partnership. Publications: academic articles; book chapters; five funded research reports into dementia and mental health. Recreations: badminton; wine; travel. Address: (b.) Queen Margaret University, Craighall, Edinburgh EH21 6UU; T.-0131-474 0000; e-mail: rhorne@qmu.ac.uk

Gilmore, Sheila. MP (Labour), Edinburgh East, 2010-15; Parliamentary Private Secretary to: Michael Dugher, 2013-15, Angela Eagle, 2013-15, Jon Trickett, 2011-13; b. 1.10.49, Aberdeen; m., Brian Gilmore; 3 s.; 1 d. Educ. George Watson's College, Edinburgh; University of Kent at Canterbury; Edinburgh University. Career history: Legal Advisory Officer, Scottish Consumer Council; private law practice in Edinburgh focusing on family law; elected in an Edinburgh District Council by-election for Moredun ward in 1991; Election agent to Nigel Griffiths MP, 1992-2005; Convenor for Housing, 1999-2007; candidate, Scottish Parliament constituency of Edinburgh Pentlands, 2007 Scottish Parliament elections. Member, Select Committee on Political and Constitutional Reform, 2010-15; Chair PLP Departmental Group for Work and Pensions, 2011-15; Member, DWP Select Committee, 2011-15. Recreations: cycling; reading.

Gilmore, Professor William C., Medal of Honour (Council of Europe, 2017), LLB, LLM, MA, PhD. Emeritus Professor, International Criminal Law, Edinburgh University, since 2012, Professor, 1996-2012, Dean and Head of the School of Law, 2004-07; External Commissioner, Financial Services Commission, British Virgin Islands since 2021; Director, CIMA, Cayman Islands, 2006-2018; Scientific Expert (Legal), MONEYVAL, Strasbourg, 1997-2017; b. 31.3.51, Nassau, Bahamas; m., Dr Patricia Shepherd; 1 s.; 1 d. Educ. St Joseph's College, Dumfries; Edinburgh University; University of London; Carlton University. Lecturer, Law, University of West Indies, Barbados, 1973-75; Commonwealth Projects Officer, IILED, Washington D.C., 1977-79; Lecturer/Senior Lecturer/Reader, Faculty of Law, Edinburgh University, 1979-96; Assistant Director, Legal Division/Head, Commercial Crime Unit, Commonwealth Secretariat, Marlborough House, London, 1991-93. Publications include: The Confederate Jurist, 2021; Dirty Money, 4th ed. 2011; Newfoundland and Dominion Status, 1988; The Grenada Intervention, 1984. Recreations: travel; fishing. Address: (b.) Old College, South Bridge, Edinburgh EH8 9YL.

Gilmour, Simon, MA (Hons), PhD, FSAScot, MCIfA. Director of The Society of Antiquaries of Scotland, since 2007; b. 12.06.70, Dundee; m. Dr. Rebecca Jones; 1 d.; 1 s. Educ. Alford Academy; University of Edinburgh. Department of Archaeology Tutor, University of Edinburgh, 1999-2001; numerous excavations and other archaeological projects in Scotland and abroad, since 1996; Aerial Survey Liaison Officer, Royal Commission on The Ancient and Historical Monuments of Scotland, 2001-05;

Project Manager in the construction industry, 2005-07. Elected Vice President of The Council for Scottish Archaeology, 2004-2010; elected Hon. Secretary of The Council for Scottish Archaeology, 2001-04; Honorary Fellow of The University of Edinburgh, 2001-04, and 2008-2011; Visiting Fellow of the University Campus Suffolk School of Business, Leadership and Enterprise, 2013-16; elected Vice Chair, Built Environment Forum Scotland, 2010-2015. Recreations: skiing; eating out; cinema; archaeology. Address: (b.) Society of Antiquaries of Scotland, c/o National Museums Scotland, Chambers Street, Edinburgh EH1 1JF; T.-0131 247 4115.
E-mail: director@socantscot.org

Gilroy, Elizabeth Patricia. Lord-Lieutenant of the Stewartry of Kirkcudbright, since 2018; b. East Kirkcarswell; 1 d. Educ. Dundrennan Primary School; Mount School, York. Career: Dumfries and Galloway Council: fomer councillor (19 years), Dee and Glenkens; convener, 2007-2012. Served as a director of the Wickerman Festival; district commissioner of The Stewartry Pony Club; chairman of the Three Counties Horse Show and committee member of the Malcolm Sargent Cancer Fund for Children; founder member of the Galloway Trust for the Head Injured.

Gilruth, Jenny. MSP (SNP), Mid Fife and Glenrothes, elected in 2016, re-elected in 2021; Minister for Transport, since 2022; Minister for Culture, Europe and International Development, since 2021; Minister for Europe and International Development, since 2020; b. 1984. Educ. Madras College, St Andrews; University of Glasgow; University of Strathclyde. Former high school head of department and Modern Studies teacher. Address: Scottish Parliament, Edinburgh EH99 1SP.

Gimblett, Sheriff Margaret, MA. Sheriff at Dunoon, 1999-2005, part-time Sheriff, 2005-09 (retired); b. 24.9.39, Perth; m., Iain; 1 s.; 1 d. Educ. St. Leonards, St. Andrews; University of Edinburgh; University of Glasgow. Retail Management, John Lewis Partnership, London, until 1970; Partner, Russel and Aitken, Solicitors, 1972-95; Temporary Sheriff, 1994-95; Sheriff, Glasgow and Strathkelvin, 1995-99; Sheriff, Dunoon, 1999-2005; part-time Sheriff, 2005-09; Churchill Fellow. Recreation: gardening. Address: (h.) Fehmarn, Bridge of Earn PH2 9AH.

Girdwood, David Greenshields, DL, BSc, MEd, SQH. Rector, St. Columba's School, Kilmacolm, 2002-2017 (retired); b. 14.10.57, Tillicoultry; m., Lisa; 2 d. Educ. Alva Academy; St. Andrews University; Jordanhill College; Stirling University; Edinburgh University. Lornshill Academy: Teacher of Chemistry, 1979-85, Assistant Principal of Science, 1985-87; Daniel Stewart's and Melville College: Principal Teacher of Chemistry and Head of Science, 1987-96, Head of Upper School, 1996-2002. Associate Assessor, HMI, 1999-2002; Deputy Lord Lieutenant of Renfrewshire, since 2009. Recreations: rugby; walking.

Girvin, Professor Brian, BA, MA, PhD, FRHS. Professor of Comparative Politics, University of Glasgow (Emeritus); Honorary Professor of Politics, University of Glasgow; Visiting Research Fellow, Trinity College Dublin; Editorial Board, Irish Political Studies; Contributing Editor to H-Nationalism (https://networks.h-net.org/h-nationalism); b. 16.7.50, Cork; partner, Rona Fitzgerald; 1 s. Educ. Sullivan's Quay CBS, Cork; University College, Cork. Temporary Lecturer, National Institute for Higher Education, Limerick, 1978-82; University College, Cork: Temporary Teaching Assistant, 1983-86, Director of European Studies, 1986-88, Lecturer in Modern History, 1986-95; Senior Lecturer in Politics, University of Glasgow, 1995-2000. Member of PEN Scotland. Publications: Politics and Society in Contemporary Ireland (Co-Editor), 1986; The Transformation of Contemporary

Conservatism (Editor), 1988; Between Two Worlds: Politics and Economy in Independent Ireland, 1989; The Right in the Twentieth Century: Conservatism and Democracy, 1994; The Green Pool Negotiations and the Origins of the Common Agricultural Policy (Co-Editor), 1995; Ireland and the Second World War: Politics, Society and Remembrance (Co-Editor), 2000; From Union to Union: Nationalism, Democracy and Religion in Ireland since 1800, 2002; The Lemass Era (Co-Editor), 2005; The Emergency: Neutral Ireland, 1939-45, 2006; Continuity, Change and Crisis in Ireland, since the 1960s (Co-Editor), 2008; Continuity and Change in Contemporary Ireland (Co-Editor), 2010; multiple contributor to The Cambridge History of Ireland: Volume IV 1880 to the Present (2018). Recreations: mountaineering; cooking; archaeology and photography; film; music; books. Address: School of Political and Social Sciences, University of Glasgow G12 8RT; T.-0141-330 5353.
E-mail: brian.girvin@glasgow.ac.uk

Glasby, Michael Arthur, BM, BCh, MA, MSc (Oxon), MA (Cantab), MTh, PhD, MD, DSc (Edin), BD (Lond), FRCP (Edin), FRCS (Edin), FRCS (Eng); b. 29.10.48, Nottingham; m., Celia M.E. Robinson. Educ. High Pavement Grammar School, Nottingham; Christ Church, Oxford; Oxford Medical School. Senior Scholar and Assistant Tutor in Physiology, Christ Church, Oxford, 1971-76; Cardiac Surgeon, Harefield Hospital Transplant Trust, 1981-83; Fellow and Lecturer in Anatomy, New Hall, Cambridge, 1983-87; Lecturer in Anatomy, Royal College of Surgeons of England, 1984-87; joined Edinburgh University as Lecturer, 1987; Reader in Anatomy, 1992-97; Reader in Experimental Neurology, 1997-2004; retired Honorary Fellow, University of Edinburgh, since 2004; Consultant Neurophysiologist, Scottish National Spinal Deformity Centre, Royal Hospital for Sick Children, Edinburgh, 2004-2015. Editor, anatomy textbook for surgeons and physiology textbook for surgeons; numerous scientific articles; author, works on medicine in Old Testament times. Recreations: Classical and Semitic languages; The Ancient Near East; music; beekeeping; wine; bookbinding; golf. Address: (h.) 3 Cluny Drive, Morningside, Edinburgh EH10 6DN; T.-0131 447 3836.
E-mail: maglasby@ed-alumni.net

Glasgow, Mary. Chief Executive Officer, Children 1st, since 2018. Educ. Moray House, Edinburgh; University of Dundee. Career history: qualified as a social worker in 1991; Senior Training Officer, Child Protection (seconded to Strathclyde Police), Glasgow City Council, 1996-97; Senior Social Worker, Renfrewshire Council, 1997-2000; Quarriers: Project Manager, 2000-04, Service Manager, 2004-2010; Assistant Director, Children's Services, Barnardo's, 2010-14; Director of Children's Services and External Affairs, Children 1st, 2014-17, Interim Chief Executive, 2017-18. Address: Children 1st, 83 Whitehouse Loan, Edinburgh EH9 1AT; T.-0131 446 2300.

Glasgow, 10th Earl of (Patrick Robin Archibald Boyle), DL. Television Director/Producer; b. 30.7.39; m., Isabel Mary James; 1 s.; 1 d. Educ. Eton; Paris University. Sub.-Lt., RNR, 1959-60; Producer/Director, Yorkshire TV, 1968-70; freelance Film Producer, since 1971; created Kelburn Country Centre (leisure park), 1977, and now oversees this and Kelburn Estate; Deputy Lieutenant, Ayrshire; Lib Dem Peer, House of Lords. Address (b.) Kelburn Castle, Fairlie, Ayrshire KA29 0BE; T.-01475 568685; T.-020 7219 5419.
E-mail: admin@kelburncountrycentre.com

Glasier, Anna, OBE, MB, ChB, BSc, FRCOG, MD, DSc, FFPRHC. Director, Lothian Primary Care NHS Trust Family Planning and Well Woman Services, 1990-2010; Emeritus Professor, Edinburgh University; Honorary Professor, University of London; b. 16.4.50, Salisbury; m., Dr. David T. Baird. Educ. Lord Digby's School, Sherborne.

Clinical Research Scientist, Medical Research Council Centre for Reproductive Biology, Edinburgh, 1989-90. Recreation: ski mountaineering.

Glass, Douglas James Allan, LVO, MB, ChB. Apothecary to the Queen at Balmoral, since 2006; Apothecary to Her Majesty's Household at Balmoral, since 1988; b. 8.10.53, Dinnet, Aboyne; m., Alison; 1 s.; 4 d. Educ. Aboyne Academy; Banchory Academy; Aberdeen University. Junior House Officer in Penzance (Medicine), then Kirkwall (Surgery), 1977-78; Senior House Officer in Bangor (Anaesthetics), 1978-79; General Practitioner trainee in Aboyne, Aberdeenshire, 1979-80; General Practice in Australia and New Zealand, 1980-81; General Practice Principal, Peterhead, 1981-87; General Practice Principal, Ballater, 1987-2013, including 3 months at Ekwendeni Mission Hospital, Malawi, in 1995; General Practice Associate in Braemar, since 2013; tenant farmer at Deecastle, since 1982. Board member of Cairngorms National Park, 2004-08; Elder at Glenmuick Church, since 1988. Recreations: dry stane dyking; golf; snooker; football. Address: Deecastle, Dinnet, Aboyne, Aberdeenshire AB34 5NU; T.-01339 755958.

Glen, Eric Stanger, MB, ChB, FRCSGlas, FRCSEdin. Professore Visitatore, Università degli Studi di Pavia; Consultant Urological Surgeon, Walton Urological Teaching and Research Centre, Southern General Hospital, Glasgow, 1972-99; b. 20.10.34, Glasgow; m., Dr. Patricia. Educ. Airdrie Academy; Glasgow University. Pre-Consultant posts, Western and Victoria Infirmaries, Glasgow; Ship Surgeon, Royal Fleet Auxiliary. Formerly Medical Director, Continence Resource Centre and Helpline for Scotland; Past Chairman, Greater Glasgow Area Medical Committee; Founder and Honorary Member, International Continence Society; former Honorary Clinical Senior Lecturer, Glasgow University; former Member, Surgical Examination Panel, Royal College of Physicians and Surgeons of Glasgow; Founder, Urological Computing Society; Honorary Co-Chairman, 41st Annual Meeting of the International Continence Society (ICS), 29 August - 2 September, 2011; Lifetime Achievement Award, International Continence Society, Beijing, October 2012. Publications: Co-Editor, ICS History Book "The First 40 Years 1971-2010, 2011; chapters in books; papers on urodynamics, urology and computing. Memberships: Senior Member of British Association of Urological Surgeons, Societe Internationale d'Urologie, and European Association of Urology. Recreations: travel; writing; computer applications. Address: (h.) 9 St. John's Road, Pollokshields, Glasgow G41 5RJ; T.-0141-423 0759. E-mail: ericnetherlee@btinternet.com

Glen, Marlyn. MSP (Lab), North East Scotland, 2003-2011; b. 30.9.51, Dundee; widowed; 1 s.; 1 d. Educ. Kirkton High School, Dundee; St. Andrews University; Dundee University; Open University. Former teacher.

Glen, Thomas. Chief Executive, Perth and Kinross Council, since 2021. Career history: community worker in the late 1980s; worked across local/central government, the voluntary sector and consultancy; appointed to East Dunbartonshire Council in 2009, Depute Chief Executive, 2016-2021. Address: Perth and Kinross Council, Pullar House, 35 Kinnoull Street, Perth PH1 5GD; T.-01738 475000; e-mail: chiefexec@pkc.gov.uk

Glenarthur, 4th Baron (Simon Mark Arthur), Bt, DL. DL, Aberdeenshire, since 1987; Director: Millennium Chemicals Inc., 1996-2004, Medical Defence Union, 2002-06, Audax Global Sàrl, since 2005; a Governor, Nuffield Health, 2000-09; b. 7.10.44; m.; 1 s.; 1 d. Educ. Eton. Retired Major, 10th Royal Hussars (PWO); Helicopter Captain, British Airways, 1976-82; a Lord in Waiting, 1982-83; Parliamentary Under Secretary of State: Department of Health and Social Security, 1983-85, Home Office, 1985-86; Minister of State: Scottish Office, 1986-87, Foreign and Commonwealth Office, 1987-89; Consultant: British Aerospace PLC, 1989-99, Hanson PLC, 1989-99, Imperial Tobacco Ltd., 1996-98; Deputy Chairman, Hanson Pacific Ltd., 1994-97; Chairman, St. Mary's Hospital, Paddington, NHS Trust, 1991-98, British Helicopter Advisory Board, 1992-2004, European Helicopter Association, 1996-2003; President: National Council for Civil Protection, 1991-2003, British Helicopter Association, since 2004; Member, Queen's Bodyguard for Scotland (Royal Company of Archers); Scottish Patron, The Butler Trust, 1994-2014; Trustee, Royal College of Organists, 2014-2022 (Chairman, Trustee Council, 2017-2021); Non-executive Director, Audax Global S.a.r.l, since 2005; a Commissioner, Royal Hospital Chelsea, 2001-07; Honorary Colonel, 306 Hospital Support Medical Regiment (Volunteers), 2001-2011; Honorary Air Commodore, 612 (County of Aberdeen) Squadron, Royal Auxiliary Air Force, 2004-2014; Chairman, National Employer Advisory Board for the Reserves of the Armed Forces, 2002-09; Governor: King Edward VII Hospital (Sister Agnes), 2010-2013 (Chairman of Council, 2012-2013), Sutton's Hospital in Charterhouse, 2011-19; Chairman, British European Aviation Group Ltd, 2015-20. Address: (b.) Northbrae Farmhouse, Crathes, Banchory AB31 6JQ; T.-01330 844467; e-mail: glenarthur@northbrae.co.uk

Glennie, Lord (Angus James Scott), MA (Hons). Chair of the Scottish Arbitration Centre, since 2021; Senator of the College of Justice, 2005-2020 (retired); m., Patricia Jean Phelan. Educ. Sherborne School, Dorset; Trinity Hall, University of Cambridge. Called to the Bar at Lincoln's Inn, 1974; appointed a Bencher, 2007; worked mainly in commercial and international arbitration whilst at the English Bar, before the Commercial Court and Court of Appeal; took silk there in 1991, and the following year was admitted to the Faculty of Advocates; practised mostly in commercial law, but also worked in other areas, such as judicial review and reparation; appointed Queen's Counsel in Scotland in 1998; variously Intellectual Property Judge, Commercial Judge and Arbitration judge before appointment to Inner House, 2016; appointed to Privy Council, 2016; Hon FCIArb, 2019; elected Honorary Fellow of Trinity Hall, 2019.

Glennie, Dame Evelyn Elizabeth Ann, CH, DBE. Chancellor, Robert Gordon University, since 2021; Solo Percussionist, since 1985; b. 19.7.56, Methlick, Aberdeenshire. Numerous awards achieved and 28 honorary doctorates awarded. Address: Office of Evelyn Glennie, 6 Ramsay Court, Hinchingbrooke Business Park, Kingfisher Way, Huntingdon, Cambridgeshire PE29 6FY; T.-01480 459 279; e-mail: admin@evelyn.co.uk

Glennie, John, OBE. Non Executive member, Healthcare Improvement Scotland (Interim Chief Executive, 2013-14); b. 1949. Career history: joined local health board as a trainee accountant in 1966, and worked in the NHS ever since; became a Director of Finance and Deputy Chief Executive with Central Manchester Healthcare Trust before moving to the Borders to take charge of Borders General Hospital NHS Trust in 1995; Chief Executive, NHS Borders, 2003-09. Chair, NHS 24's Remuneration Committee. Address: Healthcare Improvement Scotland, Gyle Square, 1 South Gyle Crescent, Edinburgh EH12 9EB; T.-0131 623 4300.

Gloag, Dame Ann, DBE, OBE. Stagecoach Group plc: Managing Director, 1986-94, Executive Director, 1986-2000, Non-Executive Director, 2000-2019; b. 10.12.42. Educ. Perth High School. Nursing, 1960-80; Founding

Partner, Stagecoach, 1980. Address: (b.) Stagecoach Group, 10 Dunkeld Road, Perth PH1 5TW.

Glover, Dame Anne, DBE, FRS, FRSE, FASM. Scottish molecular biologist and academic; President, Royal Society of Edinburgh, since 2018; Special Adviser to the Principal and Vice-Chancellor of the University of Strathclyde; former Vice Principal, External Affairs and Dean for Europe, University of Aberdeen (Personal Chair of Molecular and Cell Biology); b. 19.4.56. Educ. High School of Dundee; University of Edinburgh; King's College, Cambridge. Career history: first ever Chief Scientific Adviser for Scotland, 2006-2011; former Joint Chair of the Scottish Science Advisory Committee and served on the Scottish Council of Economic Advisers; first ever Chief Scientific Adviser to the President of the European Commission, 2012-14. Council member of the Natural Environment Research Council, 2001-11. Recognised in 2008 as a Woman of Outstanding Achievement by the UK Resource Centre for Women in Science, Engineering and Technology. Assessed as the 19th most powerful woman in the United Kingdom by Woman's Hour on BBC Radio 4 (February 2013). Chair of the Carnegie Trust for the Universities of Scotland, since 2015; Board Member, Scottish Enterprise, since 2015; Fourteen Honorary Doctorates from UK and International Universities. Honorary Fellow of Royal Society of Chemistry; Honorary Fellow of Academia Europaea; Honorary Fellow of the Royal Scottish Geographical Society; Honorary Fellow, Royal Scottish Society of Arts.

Glover, Rev. Robert Lindsay, BMus, BD, MTh, ARCO. C of S Minister (retired) & Organist; b. 21.7.45, Watford; m., Elizabeth Mary Brown; 2 s.; 2 d. Educ. Langholm Academy; Dumfries Academy; Glasgow University. Minister: Newton Parish, near Dalkeith, 1971-76, St. Vigeans Parish, Arbroath, 1976-85, Knox's, Arbroath, 1982-85, St. George's West, Edinburgh, 1985-97, Cockenzie and Port Seton: Chalmers Memorial, 1997-2010. Recreations: music (organ, piano accompaniment, listening); supporting Heart of Midlothian F.C.; reading; travel. Address: 12 Seton Wynd, Port Seton, Prestonpans, East Lothian EH32 0TY; e-mail: rlglover@btinternet.com

Glover, Sue, MA. Writer; b. 1.3.43, Edinburgh; divorced; 2 s. Educ. St. George's School, Edinburgh; Montpellier University; Edinburgh University. Original drama and other scriptwriting for radio, television and theatre; theatre productions include: The Seal Wife, Edinburgh Festival, 1980; An Island in Largo, Byre Theatre, 1981; The Bubble Boy, Glasgow Tron, 1981; The Straw Chair, Traverse Theatre, 1988; Bondagers, Traverse Theatre, 1991 (winner, 1990 LWT Plays on Stage Award); Sacred Hearts, 1994; Artist Unknown, 1996; Shetland Saga, Traverse Theatre, 2000; Blow-outs, Wrecks and Almanacs, 2002; Marilyn en Chantée, 2007; Bear on a Chain, 2010; Marilyn, 2011, Citizens Theatre and Royal Lyceum Theatre; Lion, Lion, 2019; television work includes: The Spaver Connection; Mme Montand and Mrs Miller; Dear Life; televised version of The Bubble Boy won a silver medal, New York Film and Television Festival, and a merit, Chicago International Film Festival, 1983. Publications: The Bubble Boy: You Don't Know You're Born, 1991; Bondagers (Made in Scotland), 1995; Bondagers and The Straw Chair, 1997; Shetland Saga, 2000; The Seal Wife, 2008; Artist Unknown, 2008; Sacred Hearts, 2009; The Bubble Boy, 2009. Recreations: house and garden. Address: (b.) Charles Walker, United Agents, 12-26 Lexington Street, London W1F 0LE.

Gold, Lex, CBE; b. 14.12.40, Rigside; m., Eleanor; 1 s.; 1 d. Educ. Lanark Grammar School. Sub-Editor, Daily Record; professional footballer; joined Civil Service, Glasgow, 1960; Inland Revenue, two years, Civil Service Department, four years, Home Office, 21 years, Training Agency, three years; former Managing Director, Scottish Enterprise; former Director, CBI Scotland; former Director,

Scottish Chambers of Commerce; former Chairman, Hibernian Football Club Ltd.; former Chairman, Lanarkshire NHS Board; former Director, Caledonian MacBrayne; former Chairman, Scottish Premier League.

Golden, Maurice, BA, MPhil, LLM. MSP (Scottish Conservative), North East region, since 2016; Shadow Cabinet Secretary for Economy, Fair Work and Culture, since 2020; Chief Whip, 2017-2020; b. 12.1.80. Educ. High School of Dundee; Routt High School; University of Dundee. Career history: Internship, Murray Darling River Basin Commission, 2004; Guest Lecturer, University of Dundee, 2005-07; Director, Golden's Limited, 1998-2007; Campaign Manager, Waste Aware Scotland, 2005-09; Transmission Policy Analyst, Ofgem, 2009-11; appointed Circular Economy Programme Manager, Zero Waste Scotland in 2011. Address: Scottish Parliament, Edinburgh EH99 1SP.

Goldie, Baroness Annabel MacNicoll, DL, LLB. MSP (Conservative), West of Scotland, 1999-2016; Leader, Scottish Conservative Party, 2005-2011; former Convener, Justice 2 Committee; Deputy Lord Lieutenant, Renfrewshire, since 1993; Partner, Donaldson, Alexander, Russell and Haddow (formerly Dickson Haddow and Co.), 1978-2006; b. 27.2.50, Glasgow. Educ. Greenock Academy; Strathclyde University. Admitted Solicitor, 1974; Scottish Conservative Party: Deputy Chairman, 1995-97, Chairman, March-July 1997, Deputy Chairman, 1997-98, Deputy Leader, 1998-2005. Elder, Church of Scotland; Member, West of Scotland Advisory Board, Salvation Army; Honorary Fellow, Strathclyde University; became a Life Peeress in the House of Lords, 2013; Government Whip in the House of Lords, 2016-19; Minister of State at the Department for Defence, since 2019. Recreations: bird watching; cycling; listening to music.

Gondzio, Professor Jacek. Professor of Optimization, Edinburgh University, since 2005; b. 01.01.60, Skrzynki, Poland; m., Joanna Karpinska-Gondzio; 1 s. Educ. Warsaw University of Technology. Polish Academy of Sciences, Poland: Research Assistant, 1983-89, Assistant Professor, 1989-98; Research Fellow: Universite Paris Dauphine, France, 1990-91, University of Geneva, Switzerland, 1993-98; Lecturer, Edinburgh University, 1998-2000, Reader, 2000-05. Address: (b.) School of Mathematics, Edinburgh University, King's Buildings, Edinburgh EH9 3FD; T.-0131 650 8574; e-mail: j.gondzio@ed.ac.uk

Good, Professor Anthony, BSc, PhD (Edin), PhD (Dunelm). Head, School of Social and Political Science, University of Edinburgh, 2006-09, Professor Emeritus in Social Anthropology, since 2009; b. 15.12.41, Congleton, Cheshire; m., Alison; 2 d. Educ. Kings School, Macclesfield; University of Edinburgh; University of Durham. Postdoctoral Research Fellow in Chemistry, University of Alberta, Canada, 1967-69; SRC Postdoctoral Fellow in Chemistry, University of Cambridge, 1969-70; Commonwealth Educational Co-operation Scheme Senior Lecturer in Chemistry, University of Peradeniya, Sri Lanka, 1970-72; Research Fellow in Chemistry, City University, London, 1973-74; SSRC Conversion Fellow in Anthropology, University of Durham, 1974-77; Lecturer in Sociology, University of East Anglia, 1978-79; Lecturer in Social Anthropology: University of Manchester, 1979-80, University of Edinburgh, 1980-91, Senior Lecturer, 1991-2004; Senior Social Development Adviser to the Joint Funding Scheme, Department for International Development, 1987-99. Member, Scottish Advisory Council, Immigration Advisory Service, 2002-08. Publications: Research Practices in the Study of Kinship (Co-Author), 1984; The Female Bridegroom: A Comparative Study of Life-Crisis Rituals in South India and Sri Lanka, 1991; Worship and the Ceremonial Economy of a Royal South Indian Temple, 2004;

Anthropology and Expertise in the Asylum Courts, 2007. Address: (b.) School of Social and Political Science, University of Edinburgh, Edinburgh EH8 9LD; T.-0131-650-3941; e-mail: a.good@ed.ac.uk

Goodwin, Frederick Anderson, DUniv, LLB, CA, FCIBS, FCIB, LLD, FRSE. Former Group Chief Executive, Royal Bank of Scotland Group plc (2000-09); former Senior Adviser, RMJM (2010); b. 17.8.58, Paisley; m.; 2 c. Educ. Glasgow University. Touche Ross: joined, 1979; Partner, 1988; Chief Operating Officer, BCCI Worldwide Liquidation, 1992-95; Deputy Chief Executive, Clydesdale Bank Plc, 1995; Chief Executive/Director, Clydesdale Bank, 1996; Chief Executive/Director, Clydesdale Bank and Yorkshire Bank Plc, 1997-98; Deputy Chief Executive, Royal Bank of Scotland, Plc, 1998-2000. Recreations: golf; cars.

Gordon, Charlie. MSP (Labour), Glasgow Cathcart, 2005-2011; b. 28.10.51, Glasgow; m.; 3 s. Councillor, Strathclyde Regional Council, 1987-96; Vice Convenor, Roads and Transport (SRC), 1990-94; Convenor, Roads and Transport (SRC), 1994-96; Councillor, Glasgow City Council, 1995-2005; Convenor, Roads (GCC), 1995-96; Chair, Strathclyde Passenger Transport, 1996-99; Deputy Leader, Glasgow City Council, 1997-99, Leader, 1999-2005.

Gordon, Donald Neil, MA, LLB, WS, NP. Partner, Blackadders (formerly Carltons) Solicitors, 1979-2013 (retired); Senior Tutor, Diploma in Legal Practice, University of Dundee, 1994-2014; Dean, Faculty of Procurators and Solicitors in Dundee, 1999-2001; b. 30.3.51, Aberdeen; m., Alison Mary Whyte; 1 s.; 1 d. Educ. Robert Gordon's College, Aberdeen; University of Aberdeen; University of Edinburgh. Law Apprenticeship, Edinburgh, 1973-75; Assistant Solicitor, Carlton & Reid, Dundee, 1975-79. WS, 1975; Notary Public, 1975; Chairman, Dundee Citizens Advice Bureau, 1996-2001; Honorary French Consul, Dundee, 1996-2016; President, Broughty Ferry (formerly Abertay) Rotary Club, 2001-02 and Secretary, 2015-2021; President, Dundee Orchestral Society, 2003-08; Past Chairman, High School of Dundee Parents Association; Director, High School of Dundee, 2008-2020; joint Editor, Green's Practical Styles (Wills), 2005; Scottish Tutor, STEP, until 2015; former Chairman, Dundee Chamber Music; Chairman: Dundee Civic Trust, since 2019, Dundee Botanic Garden Endowment Trust, since 2016. Recreations: music; cycling; gardening; Rotary.

Gordon, Emeritus Professor George, MA (Hons), PhD, FRSGS, FBAASc, FRSA, FFCS, FRGS. Director of Academic Practice, Strathclyde University, 1987-2005, Professor of Academic Practice, 1991-2005; b. 14.11.39, Edinburgh; m., Jane Taylor Collins; 2 d. Educ. George Heriot's School; Edinburgh University. Edinburgh University: Vans Dunlop Scholar, 1962-64, Demonstrator, 1964-65; Strathclyde University: Assistant Lecturer, 1965-66, Lecturer, 1966-80, Dean, Faculty of Arts and Social Studies, 1984-87; served on SUCE and SCE Geography Panels, SCOVACT, and General Teaching Council for Scotland; Chairman, Council, Royal Scottish Geographical Society, 1999-2005; Hon. Treasurer, Society for Research into Higher Education, 2002-06, Chair of Council, 2007-09; Board of Directors, The Higher Education Academy, 2004-05; Honorary Auditor, Australian Universities Quality Agency, 2002-05; Vice President, British Association for the Advancement of Science, 1991-97; former Member, General Assembly of Open University; Strathclyde University: Member, Senate, 1984-2002, Member, Court, 1984-87, 2000-02; Governor, Jordanhill College of Education, 1982-93 (Chairman, 1987-93). Publications: Regional Cities of the UK 1890-1980 (Editor), 1986; Perspectives of the Scottish City (Editor), 1985; The Making of Scottish Geography (Co-Author), 1988; Urban Geography (Co-Author), 1981; Scottish Urban History (Co-Editor), 1983; Settlement Geography (Co-Author), 1983;

Academic and Professional Identities (Co-Editor), 2009; Enhancing Quality in Higher Education (Co-Editor), 2013; Reconstructing Relationships in Higher Education (Co-Author), 2017. Recreations: theatre-going; watching sport. Address: (b.) Learning Enhancement, Strathclyde University, 50 George Street, Glasgow.

Gordon, Sir Gerald Henry, CBE, QC, MA, LLB, PhD, LLD, HonFRSE. Sheriff of Glasgow and Strathkelvin, 1978-99; Temporary Judge, Court of Session and High Court of Justiciary, 1992-2004; b. 17.6.29, Glasgow; m., Marjorie Joseph; 1 s.; 2 d. Educ. Queen's Park Senior Secondary School; Glasgow University. Advocate, 1953; Procurator Fiscal Depute, Edinburgh, 1960-65; Edinburgh University: Head, Department of Criminal Law and Criminology, 1965-72, Personal Professor of Criminal Law, 1969-72, Dean, Faculty of Law, 1970-73, Professor of Scots Law, 1972-76; Sheriff of South Strathclyde, Dumfries and Galloway, at Hamilton, 1976-77; Member: Interdepartmental Committee on Scottish Criminal Procedure, 1970-77, Committee on Criminal Appeals and Miscarriages of Justice, 1995-96, Scottish Criminal Cases Review Commission, 1999-2008. Publications: Criminal Law of Scotland, 1967, 1978; Renton & Brown's Criminal Procedure (Editor), 1972, 1983, 1996. Recreations: Jewish studies; coffee conversation; crosswords.

Gordon, Nicola, BSc, MEng. Member of Board and Audit Committee, Scottish Environment Protection Agency, since 2018. Educ. Newcastle University (Chemical Engineering); FT NED Diploma (Non-Executive Director Post-Graduate Diploma); Heriot-Watt University (Petroleum Engineering). Career history: Shell, 2010-16; Member, Board of Directors and Audit Committee, Arts & Business Scotland, Edinburgh, 2017-2020; Chair of Strategy Advisory Board, Heriot-Watt University, Institute of Petroleum Engineering, Edinburgh, 2015-2020; Lay Chairing Member, Judicial Appointments Board for Scotland, Edinburgh, 2017-2021; Edinburgh Printmakers: Interim Chair, Board of Directors, 2018; Trustee and Member, Board of Directors, since 2017; Member of Board and Chair of Risk Committee, OKEA AS, Trondheim, Norway, since 2019; Scottish Energy Forum, Edinburgh: Member of Board of Directors, 2015-2019; Executive Vice President, 2017-2019; President, since 2019; Member of Strategy Advisory Board, Institute of GeoEnergy Engineering, Heriot-Watt University, since 2020. Address: Scottish Environment Protection Agency, Edinburgh Office, Silvan House, 3rd Floor, 232 Corstorphine Road, Edinburgh EH12 7AT; T.-0131 449 7296.

Gordon, Tom, MA. Scottish Political Editor, The Herald, since 2016. Educ. University of Edinburgh. Career history: General Reporter: the Glaswegian, 1998-2000, The Scotsman, 2000-01; The Herald: Local Government Correspondent, 2002-04, Scottish Political Correspondent, 2004-07; Scottish Political Editor: Sunday Times, 2007-08, Sunday Herald, 2008-16. Address: HeraldScotland, 200 Renfield Street, Glasgow G2 3QB.

Gorman, Gayle, BEd, AdvDip. Her Majesty's Chief Inspector for Scotland/Chief Executive, Education Scotland, since 2017. Educ. Glasgow University; Jordanhill College; Homerton College, Cambridge University. Career: Curriculum Adviser, Suffolk County Council, 1997-98; Lead Senior Adviser, Essex County Council, 1998-2001; National Strategies: Director, Intensifying Support Programme, 2001-03, Regional Adviser, 2003-06, Senior Regional Adviser, 2006-08, Senior Director, 2008-2010; Director of Learning, Cambridgeshire County Council, 2010-13; Aberdeen City Council: Director of Education, Culture and Sport, 2013-14, Director of Education and Children's Services, 2014-17; appointed Northern Alliance Regional Improvement Lead in 2017. Address: Education Scotland, The Optima, 58 Robertson Street, Glasgow G2 8DU; T.-0131 244 300.

Gosal, Pam. MSP (Scottish Conservative and Unionist Party), West Scotland (Region), since 2021; b. 25.4.72, Glasgow. Helped run family business, then worked in Local Government. The first Sikh in the Scottish Parliament and the first Indian female. Address: The Scottish Parliament, Edinburgh EH99 1SP; T.-0131 348 5950.
E-mail: Pam.Gosal.msp@parliament.scot

Goudie, Professor Andrew William, CB, FRSE, PhD, MA, BA (Econ), BA (Maths). Special Adviser to the Principal and Vice Chancellor, and Professor of Practice, Chair of the Fraser of Allander Advisory Board, and Co-Director of the Strathclyde Centre for Sustainable Development, University of Strathclyde, since 2011; Director-General Economy and Chief Economic Adviser, Scottish Government, 2003-2011, Chief Economic Adviser, 1999-2011, and Head of Finance and Central Services Department, 2003-07; b. 3.3.55, London. Educ. Haberdashers' Aske's School, Elstree; Queens' College, University of Cambridge. University of Cambridge, 1978-85: Research Officer, Department of Applied Economics, Research Fellow, Queens' College, Fellow and Director of Studies, Robinson College; Senior Economist, The World Bank, Washington DC, 1985-90; Senior Economic Adviser, Scottish Office, 1990-95; Principal Economist, OECD, Paris, 1995-96; Chief Economist, DFID (formerly ODA), London, 1996-99; Doctor of Letters, University of Strathclyde, 2003. Publications: articles in learned journals. Address: (b.) University of Strathclyde, 16 Richmond Street, Glasgow G1 1XQ; T.-0141 552 4400; e-mail: goudie_a@hotmail.com

Gougeon, Mairi, MA. MSP (SNP), Angus North and Mearns, since 2016; Cabinet Secretary for Rural Affairs and Islands, since 2021; Minister for Public Health and Sport, 2020-21; Minister for Rural Affairs and the Natural Environment, 2018-2020; m., Baptiste Gougeon. Educ. University of Aberdeen. Senior Assistant, National Trust for Scotland, 2002-2010; Councillor, Angus Council, 2007-2017 (spokesperson on economic development), became convener of infrastructure services, then later the development and enterprise convener. Former Chairwoman of the East of Scotland European Consortium; represented Convention of Scottish Local Authorities (COSLA) on the executive of the Council of European Municipalities and Regions. Address: Scottish Parliament, Edinburgh EH99 1SP.

Gow, Alan, BSc (Hons), MSc, PhD. Professor, Heriot-Watt University, since 2019; Deputy Director, Centre for Applied Behavioural Sciences, since 2020. Educ. University of Edinburgh. Career history: University of Edinburgh: Research Fellow, 2005-09, Senior Research Fellow, 2009-2012; University of Copenhagen: Guest Researcher, 2011-15; RSE Young Academy of Scotland: Co-Chair, 2011-13, Member, 2011-16, Emeritus Member, since 2016; Heriot-Watt University: Assistant Professor/Lecturer, 2013-15, Associate Professor, 2015-19. Address: Heriot-Watt University, Edinburgh Campus, Mary Burton Building, The Avenue, Currie EH14 4AS; T.-0131 451 8239.
E-mail: a.j.gow@hw.ac.uk

Grace, Professor John, BSc, PhD, FIBiol, FRSE. Emeritus Professor of Environmental Biology, Edinburgh University, Professor, since 1992; Head, School of Geosciences, 2002-03; Head, Institute of Ecology and Resource Management, 2000-02; Head, Institute of Atmospheric and Environmental Sciences, 2003-08; b. 19.9.45, Northampton; m., Elizabeth Ashworth; 2 s.; 1 d. Educ. Bletchley Grammar School; Sheffield University. Lecturer, then Reader in Ecology, Edinburgh University, 1970-92. Co-Editor, Functional Ecology, 1986-99; Technical Editor, International Society for Biometeorology, 1983-98; Member, Terrestrial Life Sciences Committee, Natural Environment Research Council, 1986-89; President, British Ecological Society, 2002-03; Chairman, Botanical Society of Scotland, 2012-

2017; Member, Scottish Forestry Trust, since 2013; BES Award, 2007; Scientific Advisory Committee, Royal Botanic Gardens, Edinburgh, since 2016; Researcher, Czech Academy of Sciences, since 2018; Marsh Award, 2009. Publications: Plant Response to Wind, 1977; Plants and their Atmospheric Environment (Co-Editor), 1981; Plant-atmosphere Relationships, 1983. Recreations: hill-walking; cycling; fishing; bridge; allotments. Address: (h.) 25 Craiglea Drive, Edinburgh EH10 5PB; T.-0131-447 3030; e-mail: jgrace@ed.ac.uk

Grace, Paul Henry, BSc, FFA. Director, Scottish Equitable Policyholders Trust Ltd., 1998-2012; Director and Honorary Treasurer, Victim Support Scotland Ltd., 1998-2004; Chairman, National Provident Life Fund Supervisory Board, 2000-2010; Member, Scottish Life Fund Supervisory Committee, 2001-2012; b. 25.9.38, Bletchley; m., Aileen Anderson; 1 d. Educ. Bedford Modern School; St. Andrews University. Joined Scottish Equitable as Actuarial Trainee, 1960; joined Zurich Life Assurance Co. as Actuary and Life Manager, 1965; rejoined Scottish Equitable as Actuary, 1980-93; Deputy Chief Executive, 1985-93, Director, 1987-93; Managing Director and Actuary, Scottish Equitable Policyholders Trust Ltd., 1994-98. President, Faculty of Actuaries, 1996-98; Director, Student Loans Company Ltd., 1999-2002; Chairman, Groupe Consultatif Actuariel Europeen (now called "European Actuarial Association"), 2004-05. Publication: Introduction to Life Assurance, 1988. Recreation: gardening. Address: 8 March Pines, Edinburgh EH4 3PF; T.-0131 312 6357.

Grady, Patrick. MP (SNP), Glasgow North, since 2015; SNP Chief Whip, 2017-2021; Spokesperson on International Development, 2015-17; b. 5.2.80, Edinburgh. Educ. Inverness Royal Academy; University of Strathclyde. Advocacy Manager, Scottish Catholic International Aid Fund, 2011-15; lived and worked in London and Malawi. Joined the SNP in 1997, aged 17 and headed the "Yes" campaign in the Kelvin area of Glasgow during the 2014 referendum on Scottish independence. Address: House of Commons, London SW1A 0AA.

Graham, Professor David I., MB, ChB, PhD, FRCPath, FRCPS, FMedSci, FRSE. Emeritus Professor; b. 20.7.39, Glasgow; m., Joyce; 1 s.; 1 d. Educ. Penarth County Grammar School; Welsh National School of Medicine, Cardiff. Registrar, Western Infirmary, Glasgow, 1965-68; Lecturer, Department of Neuropathology, Glasgow, 1968-72; Fogarty Fellow, Laboratory of Neuropathology, Philadelphia, 1972-74; Senior Lecturer, Glasgow, 1974-83; Professor of Neuropathology, Glasgow University, 1983-2005; retired. Publications: several books; 300 papers. Recreations: hill-walking; music. Address: (b.) 44 Sycamore Avenue, Lenzie, Kirkintilloch, East Dunbartonshire G66 4NY.
E-mail: neuropathology44@yahoo.co.uk

Graham, (Lord) Donald, FCIBS, BSc, MBA. Director: Children's Music Foundation, since 1995, LCDK Limited, since 2008, Property Developers, 1992-2010; b. 28.10.56, Salisbury, Southern Rhodesia; m., Bridie; 1 s.; 3 d. Educ. St. Andrews College, South Africa; St. Andrews University; INSEAD. Recreations: piping; music; golf. Address: (b.) Children's Music Foundation, 46A Fortrose Street, Glasgow G11 5LP.

Graham, Elspeth Forbes, MA, PhD, FRGS. Emeritus Professor of Geography, University of St Andrews, since 2019; Professor of Geography, University of St Andrews, 2012-2018; Co-director, ESRC Centre for Population Change, 2010-18; Head of School of Geography and Geosciences, 2004-08; Member, Local Boundary Commission for Scotland, 1994-2004; Member, Boundary Commission for Scotland, 1999-2010; b. 7.2.50, Edinburgh; 1 s.; 1 d. Educ. George Watson's Ladies College,

Edinburgh; St Andrews University; Durham University. Visiting Lecturer, University of Minnesota, 1979-1980; Visiting Senior Research Fellow, National University of Singapore, 2004, 2008, 2012 and 2018. Publications: Postmodernism and the Social Sciences (Co-editor), 1992; The Geography of Health Inequalities in the Developed World (Co-editor), 2004; research papers on population policies and population change, including fertility change in Europe and Singapore, and on health and well-being, including child health and migrant parents in Southeast Asia. Recreations: Celtic music and literature; Gaelic language; local history. Address: (b.) School of Geography and Sustainable Development, University of St Andrews, KY16 9AL; T.-01334 462894.

Graham, George, QPM. Board Member, Scottish Police Authority, 2015-17; Her Majesty's Inspector of Constabulary (HMIC) for Scotland, 2013-14; Chief Constable, Northern Constabulary, 2011-13; b. Dumfries. Joined Dumfries and Galloway Constabulary in 1982; stationed at Dumfries and Locharbriggs; held the position of Chief Superintendent, Head of Operations, until promotion to Deputy Chief Constable, 2006. Represented the Force on the Association of Chief Police Officers Scotland (ACPOS) General Policing Business Area, Crime Business Area, Professional Standards Business Area and Information Management Business Area, gaining a specific portfolio responsibility for Public Interface.

Graham, Gill, BSc, MSc, MBA. Board Member, Healthcare Improvement Scotland, since 2019. Educ. University of Dundee; Strathclyde University; Heriot-Watt University. Career history: Mathematics Lecturer, Glasgow Caledonian University, 1987-90; several positions, Scottish Power, 1990-2002; Director, Risk Management, Nuon, Amsterdam Area, Netherlands, 2002-2010; Vattenfall, Amsterdam Area, Netherlands: Head of Market Risk and Deputy CRO, 2010-2012; Head of Financial Risk and Deputy CRO, 2013; Vice President Operations, Business Area Markets, 2014-2018. Address: Healthcare Improvement Scotland, Delta House, 50 West Nile Street, Glasgow G1 2NP; T.-0141 225 6999.

Graham, Luke, BA (Econ/SocPol). MP (Conservative), Ochil and South Perthshire, 2017-19; Member, Finance Committee, 2018-19; b. 1985. Educ. University of Sheffield. Member of the Chartered Institute of Management Accountants. Career: worked for Tesco plc, Marks and Spencer plc and Tough Mudder Inc; contested the 2014 General Election in Ochil and South Perthshire; Finance Director, Britain Stronger in Europe; Member, Public Accounts Committee, 2017-2018; Parliamentary Private Secretary to the Cabinet Office, 2018-2019; Parliamentary Private Secretary to the Ministry of Housing, Communities and Local Government, January 2018-July 2018.

Graham, Norma, QPM, DipAppCrim & PolMgmt (Cantab). Chief Constable, Fife Constabulary, 2008-2012; b. 19.08.62, Musselburgh; m., Malcolm Graham. Educ. Musselburgh Grammar School. Extensive policing experience in broad range of operational and corporate roles in Edinburgh and the Lothians between 1981 and 2002; noteable posts include: Head of Force Drugs Squad; National role with HMIC - inspection of all Scottish forces and services; Divisional Commander for North East Edinburgh; Detective Chief Superintendent, Head of Crime Investigations; Assistant Chief Constable, Central Scotland Police, 2002-05; Deputy Chief Constable, Fife Constabulary, 2005-08. Chair, ACPOS Operational Policing Business Area; first woman Chief Constable in Scotland.

Graham, Lieutenant General Sir Peter, KCB, CBE, HonDLitt. Vice Patron, Gordon Highlanders Museum; Chairman, Regimental Trust Fund, The Gordon Highlanders, 1986-2004; Chairman, The Gordon Highlanders Museum Management Committee, 1994-2003; Chairman, Gordon Highlanders Museum Appeal, 1993-98 and 2002-06; b. 14.3.37; m., Dr Alison Mary Morren, MB, ChB, MRCGP; 3 s. Educ. Fyvie Village School, Aberdeenshire; Hall School, Hampstead; St. Paul's School, London, 1955-56; RMA Sandhurst. Commissioned The Gordon Highlanders, 1956; regimental appointments, Dover, Germany, Scotland, Kenya, 1957-62; HQ Highland Brigade, 1962-63; Adjutant 1 Gordons, Kenya, Edinburgh, Borneo (Despatches), 1963-66; Staff Captain, HQ 1 Br Corps, 1966-67; Australian Staff College, 1968; Company Commander, 1 Gordons, Germany, 1969-70; Brigade Maj., HQ 39 Brigade, Northern Ireland, 1970-72 (MBE); 2nd i/c, 1 Gordons, Scotland, Ulster, Singapore, 1972-74; Military Assistant to Adjutant General MoD, 1974-75; CO, 1 Gordons, Scotland, Ulster, Chester, 1976-78 (OBE); COS, HQ 3 Armoured Division, Germany, 1978-82 (CBE); Comd UDR, Ulster (Despatches), 1982-84; Canadian National Defence College, Kingston, 1984-85; Deputy Military Secretary, MoD, 1985-87; GOC Eastern District, 1987-89; Commandant RMA, Sandhurst, 1989-91; GOC Army in Scotland and Governor, Edinburgh Castle, 1991-93. Colonel, The Gordon Highlanders, 1986-94; Chairman, Gordon Highlanders Museum, 1994-2003; Member, Royal Company of Archers, since 1985. Burgess of Guild, City of Aberdeen, since 1994; HonDLitt, Robert Gordon University, 1996; Hon. Firemaster, Grampian Fire and Rescue Services, 2010-13; Member, NE Scotland Coord Committee, Better Together, 2013-14; Vice President, Old Pauline Club, since 2016. Publication: The Gordon Highlanders Pipe Music Collection (Co-author) Volume 1, 1983 and Volume 2, 1985. Recreations: walking; reading; pipe music; gardening under my wife's directions; amusing grandchildren; military history. Address: (b.) c/o The Gordon Highlanders Musuem, Viewfield Road, Aberdeen AB15 7XH; T.-01224 311200.

Graham, Riddell, BSc. Former Director of Industry and Destination Development, VisitScotland (retired); Chief Executive, Scottish Borders Tourist Board, 1996-2005, Director, 1990-96; b. 13.2.54, Galashiels; 1 s. Educ. Galashiels Academy; Edinburgh University. Borders Regional Council, 1976-83, latterly as Assistant Tourist Officer; joined Scottish Borders Tourist Board, 1983, as Assistant Director of Tourism. Recreations: good food and wine; watching rugby. T.-07387700833.
E-mail: riddellgraham46@gmail.com

Graham, Rev. William Peter, MA, BD; b. 24.11.43, Edinburgh; m., Isabel Arnot Brown; 2 s. Educ. George Watson's College, Edinburgh; Edinburgh University. Assistant Minister, Dundee (St. Mary's) Parish Church, 1966-68; Minister, Chirnside Parish Church, 1968-93, Bonkyl & Preston, 1973-93, Edrom-Allanton, 1978-93; Clerk, Edinburgh Presbytery, 1993-2008; Ministerial Assistant, Greenbank Parish Church, Edinburgh, 2009-2018; Clerk, Duns Presbytery, 1982-93; Convener, General Assembly's Nomination Committee, 1990-93, Board of Communication, 2003-05; Vice-Convener: Committee on Education for Ministry, 1996-98, Board of Ministry, 1998-99, Board of Communication, 1999-2002; Governor, George Watson's College, 1998-2008; Secretary, Old Edinburgh Club, 2013-19; President, Old Edinburgh Club, since 2019; President, Braid Bowling Club, 2015, Secretary, since 2018. Recreations: golf; bowls; theatre; reading. Address: (h.) 23/6 East Comiston, Edinburgh EH10 6RZ.

Grahame, Christine, MA, LLB, DipEd, DipLLP. MSP (SNP), Midlothian South, Tweeddale and Lauderdale, since 2011, South of Scotland, 1999-2011 (former Convener: Justice Committee, Justice sub-committee on policing); Deputy Presiding Officer of the Scottish Parliament, 2016-2021; b. 9.9.44, Burton-on-Trent; 2 s. Educ. Boroughmuir School; Edinburgh University.

Secondary teacher, 1966-82; solicitor, 1987-99. Convener, Cross-Party Group on Animal Welfare. Recreations: gardening; drinking malt whisky; cats; black and white movies. Address: Scottish Parliament, Edinburgh EH99 1SP; T.-0131-348 5729.
E-mail: christine.grahame.msp@scottish.parliament.uk

Grahame, David Currie, OBE, MA (Hons). Chief Executive, LINC Scotland, since 1993; b. 10.12.53, Hawick. Educ. Langholm Academy; Lockerbie Academy; St. Andrews University. Founding Director, LINC Scotland; Founding Board Member of European Business Angels Network, Brussels; Past Chairman, The Western Club. Recreations: music; classic cinema; food and wine. Address: (b.) Queens House, 19 St. Vincent Place, Glasgow G1 2DT; e-mail: david_grahame@lincscot.co.uk

Grahame, Rev Dr Roderick. Interim Moderator, Broughty Ferry New Kirk Church. Address: 370 Queen Street, Broughty Ferry, Dundee DD5 2HQ; T.-01382 738264.
E-mail: RGrahame@churchofscotland.org.uk

Grainger, Dame Katherine Jane, DBE, LLB, MPhil, PhD. Chancellor, University of Glasgow, since 2020; Chair, UK Sport, since 2017; former rower; b. 12.11.75, Glasgow. Educ. Bearsden Academy; University of Edinburgh; University of Glasgow; King's College London. Great Britain's joint most decorated female Olympian with five Olympic medals; 2012 Summer Olympics gold medallist; four-time Olympic silver medallist and six-time World Champion. Chancellor, Oxford Brookes University, 2015-2020.

Grant, Bill. MP (Conservative), Ayr, Carrick and Cumnock, 2017-2019; b. 26.8.51, Irvine; m., Agnes; 2 c. Educ. Littlemill Primary School, Rankinston; Glaisnock House Rural School, Cumnock; BTEC HND Fire Command and Management Studies (Lancaster University). Career: served in Strathclyde Fire and Rescue Service for 31 years, retiring as a Deputy Commander in 2005; served as a Justice of the Peace for ten years on Ayr District Court; elected as a Conservative Councillor on South Ayrshire Council at the 2007 Council elections; re-elected in the 2012 Council elections; Conservative Party candidate in Ayr, Carrick and Cumnock at the 2010 UK General Election. Member: Kyle and Carrick Civic Society, the Alloway Rotary, the Ayr Classic Motorcycle Club. Recreations: keen DIY; gardening; loves to travel; motorcycling enthusiast.

Grant, Sir Ian David, CBE, DL, FRAgS; b. 28.7.43, Dundee; m., Eileen May Louisa Yule; 3 d. Educ. Strathallan School; East of Scotland College of Agriculture. Chairman, EEC Cereals Working Party, 1982-88 and International Federation of Agricultural Producers, Grains Committee, 1984-90; Board Member, Scottish Hydro-Electric, 1992-98, Scottish and Southern Energy PLC, 1998-2003 (Deputy Chairman, 2000-03); President, NFU of Scotland, 1984-90; Director: East of Scotland Farmers Ltd., 1978-2002, NFU Mutual Insurance Society Ltd., 1990-2008 (Deputy Chairman, 2003-08), Clydesdale Bank PLC, 1989-97; Member: Scottish Council, CBI, 1984-96, Board, British Tourist Authority, 1990-98, Scottish Economic Council, 1993-97; Chairman: Scottish Tourist Board, 1990-98 (Member, 1988-90), Cairngorms Partnership, 1998-2003, Crown Estate, 2002-09 (Commissioner, 1996-2009); Scottish Exhibition Centre, 2002-2013; Vice President, Royal Smithfield Club; Honorary Doctorate, Business Administration, Napier University; Trustee: NFU Mutual Charitable Trust, 2009-2016, Castle Mey Trust, 2010-2018; Honorary Director, RHASS, 2014-19. Recreations: travel; gardening; music. Address: (h.) 42 Castleton Park, Auchterarder PH3 1QA.

Grant, Major James Macalpine Gregor, TD, NDA, MRAC. Landowner and Farmer, since 1961; b. 18.2.38,

Nakuru, Kenya; m., Sara Marjory, DL; 3 d. Educ. Eton; Royal Agricultural College, Cirencester. National Service, Queen's Own Cameron Highlanders, 1957-58; TA with 4/5th Queen's Own Cameron Highlanders; Volunteers with 51st Highland Volunteers. Retired Member, Royal Company of Archers, Queen's Bodyguard for Scotland. Address: Roskill House, Munlochy, Ross-shire IV8 8AB; T.-01463 811207.

Grant, Jane. Chief Executive, NHS Greater Glasgow and Clyde, since 2017 (Chief Executive, NHS Forth Valley, 2013-2017). Joined the NHS in 1983 as a Management Services Officer within Highland Health Board; worked in Stobhill Hospital as Deputy Administrator; moved to Lanarkshire Health Board as Hospital Administrator within Hairmyres Hospital in the early 1990's; undertook a variety of posts associated with planning, information and contracting within Lanarkshire, culminating in appointment as General Manager of Hairmyres Hospital in 1999; moved back to Glasgow in 2000 to become the General Manager for Surgery in North Glasgow and from April 2005 acted as Chief Executive within the North Glasgow Division; appointed as Director of Surgery and Anaesthetics for NHS Greater Glasgow and Clyde in early 2006 and became the Board's Chief Operating Officer in 2009. Address: NHS Greater Glasgow and Clyde Corporate HQ, J B Russell House, Gartnavel Royal Hospital Campus, 1055 Great Western Road, Glasgow G12 0XH; T.-0141 201 4444.

Grant, Nicky. Executive Chief Officer, Education and Learning, The Highland Council, since 2020; Headteacher, Alness Academy, 2018-2020; b. 1976, Aberdeen. Career history: professional footballer, Cove Rangers captain (won 4 in a row Scottish Women's Cup finals); won a domestic treble with Cumbernauld United, 1997-98; first professional contract in Miami in 1999; won 2000 Scottish Women's Cup final with Stenhousemuir; joined ÍBV in Iceland in the 2001 summer season to play professional; collected an FA Women's Premier League winners medal with Arsenal Ladies in 2002 and player of the year; joined Frauen Bundesliga champions Frankfurt as a full-time professional in 2003 playing in the champions league; returned to Scotland due to career threatening injuries to work as a teacher while playing for Kilmarnock; joined Doncaster Rovers on loan to prevent them being relegated; joined Swedish Damallsvenskan club QBIK in 2007; joined Hamilton Academical, then Celtic in 2011; joined Forfar Farmington ahead of the 2012 season helping them to their best overall premier league position (2nd) and a Scottish cup final, top goal scorer; made senior debut for Scotland against Italy in October 1993 as left back, playing a total of 99 times as a central midfielder. Graduated with first class honours; Physical Education Teacher; Depute Head, Kemnay Academy, Aberdeenshire; Depute Headteacher, Elgin High School, Moray, 2016-18. Address: Council Headquarters, Glenurquhart Road, Inverness IV3 5NX.

Grant, Peter. MP (SNP), Glenrothes, since 2015; b. 12.10.60, Coatbridge, Lanarkshire; m., Fiona. Professional qualification in public sector finance. Career history: Councillor in Glenrothes (elected in 1992); served for 5 years as leader of Fife Council; leader of the SNP group. Keen amateur musician and a past president of Leslie Bowling Club. Ambassador for the charity Breast Cancer Now. Address: House of Commons, London SW1A 0AA.

Grant, Professor Peter Mitchell, OBE, PhD, FIEEE, FRSE, FREng. Emeritus Professor; Regius Professor of Engineering, Edinburgh University, 2007-09 (Professor of Electronic Signal Processing, 1987-2007, Head, School of Engineering and Electronics, 2002-08, Head, Department of Electronics and Electrical Engineering, 1999-2002); b. 20.6.44, St. Andrews; m., Marjory Renz; 2 d. Educ. Strathallan School; Heriot-Watt University; Edinburgh University. Three Honorary DEng degrees from Heriot-Watt, Napier and Edinburgh Universities, 2007 and 2016.

Publications: Digital Communications (Co-author, 3rd edition) 2009; Digital Signal Processing (Co-author, 2nd edition), 2002. Winner, the Institution of Electrical Engineers Faraday Medal, 2004. Address: (b.) School of Engineering, Edinburgh University, Edinburgh EH9 3FG.

Grant, Philip, MBA. Chairman, Scottish Financial Enterprise, since 2019; Chief Operating Officer - Insurance & Wealth, Lloyds Banking Group, since 2020; b. 1.66. Educ. The Chartered Banker Institute; Strathclyde Business School. Career history: Bank of Scotland: Branch Banking Roles, 1983-93, Associate Director of Structured Finance, 1993-97, Director of Structured Finance, 1997-2001; HBOS plc: Head of Infrastructure Finance, 2001-04, MD Intermediary Distribution - Retail Banking, 2005-08, Chief Operating Officer - Corporate Banking, 2008-09; President, The Chartered Banker Institute (Part-time), 2009-2011; Chair, Bank of Scotland Foundation (Part-time), since 2015; Advisory Council Member, TheCityUK (Part-time), since 2019; Scotland Council Member (Part-time), CBI (Confederation of British Industry), since 2017; Co Chair, First Minister's Advisory Board on Financial Services (Part-time), since 2019; Lloyds Banking Group: Chief Operating Officer - Wholesale Division, 2009-2010, Managing Director, UK Wealth, 2010-2012, Managing Director - Risk & Ops - Wealth, Asset Finance & International Division. 2012-13, Managing Director, Customer & Risk - Consumer Finance Division, 2013-16, Managing Director - Customer & Business Risk - Insurance & Wealth Division, 2016-2020, Chair, Scottish Executive Committee, since 2011. Address: Scottish Financial Enterprise, 24 Melville Street, Edinburgh EH3 7NS; T.- 0131 247 7700.

Grant, Rhoda, BSc (SocSci). MSP (Labour), Highlands and Islands, 1999-2003 and since 2007; b. 26.6.63, Stornoway; m., Christopher Mark. Educ. Plockton High School; Open University. Address: Scottish Parliament, Edinburgh EH99 1SP; Constituency Office: Regional Office, PO Box 5717, Inverness IV1 1YT; T.-01463 716299; e-mail: Rhoda.Grant.msp@parliament.scot

Grant, Dr Robert, MBChB, MD, FRCP(Glas), FRCP(Edin). Consultant Neurologist, since 1991; Department of Clinical Neurosciences, Western General Hospital, Edinburgh; b. 19.4.57, Greenock; m., L. Joy C. Grant; 2 s.; 3 d. Educ. Greenock Academy; Glasgow University. Lead Clinician, Scottish Adult Neuro-Oncology Network; Past President, European Association for Neuro-Oncology. Recreations: rugby; karate; golf. Address: Western General Hospital, Crewe Road South, Edinburgh EH4 2XU.

Grant Peterkin, Major General Anthony Peter, CB, OBE, BA. Army Officer, 1967-2004; Serjeant at Arms, House of Commons, 2004-07; Landowner; b. 6.7.47, London; m., Joanna Young; 1 s.; 1 d. Educ. Ampleforth College; University of Durham; University of Madras. Commissioned into Queen's Own Highlanders, 1967: service in Middle East, Germany, Northern Ireland, Belize, Hong Kong and India; ADC to CGS; Command of 1st Bn. Queen's Own Highlanders, Belize and Germany, 1987-89; Higher Command and Staff Course, Camberley, 1991; Military Adviser to UN Mission, Iraq and Kuwait, 1991; Commander, 24 Airmobile Brigade, 1993-94; Royal College of Defence Studies, 1995; Army Director of Manning and Career Management, 1996-98; Managing Director, OSCE Mission in Kosovo, 1999; GOC, 5 Division, 2000; Military Secretary and Chief Executive, Army Personnel Centre, Glasgow, 2000-04. Recreation: travelling off the beaten track in Indochina. Address: (h.) Grange Hall, Forres, Morayshire; T.-01309 672742.

Gray, Alistair B., BA, CA. Chairman, Hammars Hill Energy Limited, since 2006; Managing Director, Climate Tech Capital Partners Ltd, since 2020; Director, The Pier Arts Centre, since 2016; Managing Director, North Wind Associates Ltd, since 2007; Founder, Alistair Gray Chartered Accountant, since 1984; Managing Director, Ortak Jewellery Limited, 1990-2014; Board Member, Highlands and Islands Enterprise, 1997-2004; b. 14.6.58, Kirkwall, Orkney; m., Linda; 3 s.; 1 d. Educ. Kirkwall Grammar School; Heriot-Watt University. Chartered Accountant, Arthur Young, Edinburgh, 1979-84. Address: Hatston, Kirkwall, Orkney KW15 1RW; T.-01856 872224.

Gray, Lord (Andrew Godfrey Diarmid Stuart Campbell-Gray); b. 3.9.64. Address: (h.) Airds Bay, Taynuilt, Argyll.

Gray, Henry Withers, MD, FRCP (Lond), FRCP (Glas), FRCR. Retired Consultant Physician in Medicine and Nuclear Medicine; b. 25.3.43, Glasgow; m., Mary Elizabeth Shaw MBE; 1 s.; 2 d. Educ. Rutherglen Academy; University of Glasgow. Lecturer in Medicine, Glasgow Royal Infirmary, 1969-77; Research Fellow, Johns Hopkins Medical Institutions, USA, 1974-76; retired Medical Adviser to University of Strathclyde. Publications: chapters in 10 books; 103 articles. Recreations: guitar; photography; Scottish small pipes. Address: (h.) 26 Strathwhillan Court, East Kilbride, Glasgow G75 8FH; T.-01355 229525. E-mail: harry.gray4@icloud.com

Gray, Iain Cumming, BSc Hons (Physics), CertEd. MSP (Labour), East Lothian, 2007-2021; Education, Skills and Science spokesperson, 2016-2021; Shadow Cabinet Spokesperson for Opportunity, 2015-16; Shadow Cabinet Secretary for Education and Lifelong Learning, 2014-15; Shadow Cabinet Secretary for Finance, 2013-14; Leader of Labour in The Scottish Parliament, 2008-2011; Shadow First Minister, 2008-2011; b. 7.6.57, Edinburgh; m., Gillianne; 1 d.; 2 step d. Educ. George Watson's; Inverness Royal Academy; Edinburgh University; Moray House College. Teacher: Gracemount High; Escola Basica Chokwe, Mozambique; Inveralmond High; Campaigns Manager, Oxfam in Scotland; MSP, Edinburgh Pentlands, 1999-2003; Scottish Labour: Deputy Minister for: Community Care 1999-2000, Justice, 2000-01; Minister for: Social Justice, 2001-02, Enterprise, Transport and Lifelong Learning, 2002-03; Special Adviser to Alistair Darling (Secretary of State for Scotland), 2003-06; Shadow Minister for Enterprise, Energy and Tourism, 2007; Shadow Cabinet Secretary for Finance and Sustainable Growth 2007-08.

Gray, Professor James Robertson, OBE, BSc, FRSGS, DipActMaths, FFA, FIMA, CMath, FSS, FFCS. Professor and Head, Department of Actuarial Mathematics and Statistics, Heriot-Watt University, 1971-89 (now Emeritus); b. 21.2.26, Dundee; m., Catherine McAulay Towner. Educ. High School of Dundee; Edinburgh University. Actuarial Trainee, Scottish Life Assurance Company, 1947-49; St. Andrews University: Lecturer in Mathematics, 1949-50, Lecturer in Statistics, 1950-62, Senior Lecturer in Statistics (also Head of Department), 1962-71, Member of University Court and Finance Committee; Heriot-Watt University: established first Department of Actuarial Science in UK; Dean, Faculty of Science, 1978-81, Member of University Court and Finance Committee; Council Member, Faculty of Actuaries, 1969-87 (Vice President, 1983-87); Vice-Chairman, Scottish Examination Board, 1984-90 (Convener of Examinations Committee, 1982-90); former Council Member, Royal Scottish Geographical Society and former Convener, Lecture Committee; former Vice-Chairman, Scottish Universities Council on Entrance; Past Chairman: Scottish Branch, Institute of Mathematics and Its

Applications, Edinburgh Branch, Royal Statistical Society; Past President, Murrayfield-Cramond Rotary Club; Past President, Murrayfield-Cramond Probus Club; Past Captain, Senior Section of Royal Burgess Golfing Society; Statistical Consultant to Law Society of Scotland, 1978-89; Member: Royal Burgess Golfing Society. Publication: "Probability", University Mathematical Texts, 1967. Recreations: golf; bridge; music; Probus. Address: (h.) Green Gables, 9 Cammo Gardens, Edinburgh EH4 8EJ; T.-0131-339 3330.

Gray, Lorraine. Chief Executive, Scottish Social Services Council (SSSC), since 2018. Career: background is in welfare rights, social change campaigns and community work; worked at Children 1st for six years as a policy officer and then the communications manager; joined the SSSC in 2001 as the Communication Manager and has held a number of roles in policy, performance and communications and was most recently Director of Strategic Performance and Engagement. Address: (b.) Compass House, 11 Riverside Drive, Dundee DD1 4NY; T.-0345 603 0891.

Gray, Muriel, BA (Hons). Author, broadcaster and journalist; b. 30.8.58, East Kilbride. Educ. Glasgow School of Art. Worked as an illustrator; then as a designer with National Museum of Antiquities; was member of rock band, The Family Von Trapp; had own show with Radio Forth; was frequent presenter on Radio 1; co-presented The Tube, Channel 4; had own arts programme, The Works, Tyne Tees; own music programme, Studio 1, Border TV; presented Casebook Scotland, BBC Scotland; Frocks on the Box, Thames TV; Acropolis Now, ITV; presented The Media Show, Channel 4; Co-Producer and Presenter, Walkie Talkie, Channel 4; currently the first female chair of the board of governors, Glasgow School of Art; first woman Rector, Edinburgh University; Producer/ Presenter/Director, The Munro Show, Scottish TV; Producer/Presenter, Art is Dead...Long Live TV!, Channel Four; The Golden Cagoule, BBC; Ride On. Publications: The First Fifty, 1991; The Trickster (novel), 1994; Furnace (novel), 1997; The Ancient, 2001; Kelvingrove: portal to the world, 2006. Recreation: being in the Scottish Highlands — gets grumpy and miserable if can't be up a mountain every few weeks.

Gray, Neil Charles, BA. MSP (SNP), Airdrie & Shotts, since 2021; MP (SNP), Airdrie & Shotts, 2015-2021; Minister for Culture, Europe and International Development, since 2022; SNP Spokesperson for Work and Pensions, 2018-2021; Spokesperson for Social Justice, 2017-18; Spokesperson for Fair Work & Employment, 2015-17; b. 1986, Orkney; m.; 3 d.; 1 s. Educ. Kirkwall Grammar School; University of Stirling. Employed as a producer and reporter with BBC Radio Orkney, 2003-08; press and research intern for the SNP parliamentary group at the Scottish Parliament for several months before being appointed as constituency office manager for Alex Neil MSP until election to Parliament. Address: The Scottish Parliament, Edinburgh EH99 1SP.

Gray, Paul. Consulting Partner, Charlotte Street Partners, since 2019; Honorary Professor, University of Glasgow, since 2019; Director General, Health and Social Care, Scottish Government, 2013-19; Chief Executive, NHS Scotland, 2013-19; Director General, Governance & Communities, Scottish Government, 2010-2013. Joined the Scottish Government in 1979; appointed to the post of Director General Rural Affairs, Environment and Services at the Scottish Government in July 2009; previous post, up to July 2009, was as the Scottish Government's Director of Change and Corporate Services; previously Director of Primary and Community Care - having joined Health in October 2005; held the role of Director of eHealth simultaneously; prior to that he was the Scottish Executive Director for Social Justice, covering Social Inclusion, Equalities and Voluntary Issues, from October 2003, and before that, he was the Scottish Executive Director of Information and Communications Technology. Career has covered such diverse areas as Criminal Injuries Compensation, fisheries quota management and licensing, and work with Her Majesty's Inspectorate of Education. Address: Charlotte Street Partners, 16 Alva Street, Edinburgh EH2 4QQ.

Gray, Peter, LLB (Hons). Queen's Counsel, since 2002; b. 7.11.59, Inverness; m., Bridget; 1 s.; 2 d. Educ. Fettes College, Edinburgh; Southampton University. Called to Bar of England and Wales, 1983; Admitted to Faculty of Advocates, 1992; Advocate Depute, 1998-2000. Address: (b.) Compass Chambers, Advocates Library, Parliament House, Edinburgh EH1 1RF; T.-0131-2265071.
E-mail: peter.gray@compasschambers.com

Gray, Professor Peter Michael David, MA, DPhil, FBCS. Professor Emeritus (formerly Professor, Department of Computing Science, Aberdeen University, 1989-2005); b. 1940, Abingdon; m., Doreen F. Ross; 1 s.; 1 d. Educ. Abingdon School; Queens' College, Cambridge; Jesus College, Oxford. Systems Analyst, Plessey Co., Poole, 1966-68; Research Fellow, Aberdeen University, 1968-72; Lecturer in Computing Science, Aberdeen University, 1972-84; Visiting Associate Professor, University of Western Ontario, 1985; Senior Lecturer, 1985-89. Reader, Church of Scotland. Publication: Logic, Algebra and Databases. Recreations: gardening; croquet. Address: 165 Countesswells Road, Aberdeen AB15 7RA; T.-01224 318172.

Green, Alexander M. S., MTheol (Hons), LLB, LLM, MLitt, FSA (Scot). Procurator Fiscal to The Court of the Lord Lyon, since 2010; Director, The Law Agency (Scotland) Ltd., 2006-2018; Solicitor; President, First Tier Tribunal (General Regulatory Chamber) Scotland; Employment Judge (England & Wales); Judge, First Tier Tribunal (Immigration and Asylum Chamber); b. 31.12.63, Worcester; m., Sophy M Green or Thomson; 1 d.; 2 gs.; 1 gd. Educ. Dyson Perrins CE High School; St. Andrews University; University of Aberdeen. Article Clerk, Cameron Markby Hewitt, 1991-93; CMS Cameron McKenna LLP: Assistant Solicitor, 1993-2000, Partner, 2000-06. Clubs: The New Club. Societies: The Heraldry Society of Scotland, The White Lion Society. Board of Management, The Instant Neighbour Charity; Free Burgess and Guild Member, The Burgh of Aberdeen; Liveryman of the Worshipful Company of Scriveners of the City of London; Freeman of the City of London. Recreations: history; literature; heraldry; fly fishing; shooting; cycling. Address: (b.) 43 Cairnfield Place, Aberdeen AB15 5LX; T.-01224 639712; e-mail: alex@the-lawagency.com

Green, David Russell, OBE, MA (Hons). Member, Scottish Land Fund Committee, since 2016; Scottish Council for Development and Industry (SCDI) Board Director, since 2019; Partner, Stac Pollaidh Self Catering, since 1990; b. 13.6.51, Aberdeen; m., Sheila; 1 s; 3 d. Educ. Glasgow University. Career: Convener, Highland Council, 1999-2003; Chairman, Crofters Commission, 2002-06; Scotland Committee Member, Big Lottery Fund, 2006-2014; Chairman, Cairngorms National Park Authority, 2006-2012; Chairman, Scottish Government – Instrumental Music Group (IMG) (2012/13); Chairman, Scottish Government – Instrumental Music Implementation Group (IMIG) (2014), Chairman (2015), Scottish Government Music Education Strategy Group (MESG); Director, Scottish

Agricultural College Commercial (SACC) Ltd (2008-2016). Marketing consultant; trainee chartered accountant; hotelier; snowplough driver; fully diversified crofter. Address: (h. & b.) Stac Pollaidh Self Catering, Achnahaird, Achiltibuie, Ullapool IV26 2YT; T.-01854 622340; (mobile) 07747007144.
E-mail: dgachiltibuie@hotmail.co.uk

Green, Jo, BSc. Acting Chief Executive, Scottish Environment Protection Agency, since 2022; Chair, AAI (Adopt an Intern), since 2012. Educ. University of Strathclyde. Career history: Senior Consultant, Scottish Enterprise, 1995-96; Senior Consultant (URS, Dames & Moore), URS Corporation, An AECOM Company, 1993-99; Scottish Environment Protection Agency: Corporate Support Manager, 2010-2013, Head of Change, 2013-16, Chief Officer, Performance and Innovation, 2016-2022. Board Member, Construction Scotland Innovation Centre, since 2019. Address: SEPA, Angus Smith Building, 6 Parklands Avenue, Eurocentral, Holytown, North Lanarkshire ML1 4WQ.

Greene, Jamie Gillan. MSP (Scottish Conservative), West Scotland region, since 2016; Shadow Cabinet Secretary for Justice, since 2021; Shadow Cabinet Secretary for Education and Skills, 2020-21; Shadow Cabinet Secretary for Transport, Infrastructure and Connectivity, 2019-20; b. 19.3.80, Greenock. Educ. St John's Primary, Port Glasgow; St Stephen's High School, Port Glasgow; James Watt College, Greenock. Career history: worked for a spell at IBM in Greenock as a call centre analyst before moving to a career in radio - working in advertising sales; moved to London and trained as a TV producer working for many years on a number of productions for TV channels including the BBC and other commercial broadcasters, often using French and Spanish language skills to work and live overseas including stints in Spain, France and Australia; became a commercial manager with a private media company which launched dozens of new television channels, both in the UK and overseas; also helped set up the foundations of the UK's local TV network; became an executive at Viacom - the owners of MTV, Paramount and Nickelodeon as Director of Business Development; former Head of UK Sales at a US television software company. Conservative candidate for North Ayrshire and Arran, United Kingdom general election in 2015; Conservative candidate for the Cunninghame North constituency in the 2016 Scottish Parliament election. Qualified TESOL/TEFL English language teacher; holds a PADI Scuba diving qualification and a sailing skipper licence. Recreations: amateur silversmith; garden; golf; sailing; travel. Address: Scottish Parliament, Edinburgh EH99 1SP.

Greening, Professor Andrew Peter, BSc, MBChB, FRCPE. Professor of Pulmonary Disease, University of Edinburgh; Consultant Physician, Western General Hospital, Edinburgh, 1984-2013; b. 10.10.48, London; m., Rosemary Jean Renwick; 2 s. Educ. George Watson's College, Edinburgh; University of Edinburgh. House Officer and Senior House Officer posts, Edinburgh, 1973-75; Registrar, Senior Registrar, MRC Training Fellow posts, St. Bartholomew's and Hammersmith Hospitals and Royal Postgraduate Medical School, London, 1975-82. Director, Scottish Adult Cystic Fibrosis Service, Western General Hospital, Edinburgh, 1992-2005; Lead Clinician, Respiratory Medicine, Lothian Health, 2005-09; Associate Editor, Thorax and Respiratory Medicine; Member, Grants Committees: Chest, Heart and Stroke Association, British Lung Foundation (Chair), Cystic Fibrosis Trust. International Lecturer on asthma and cystic fibrosis; Member, Scottish, British, European and American Thoracic Societies; President, Scottish Thoracic Society, 2008-2010; President, British Thoracic Society, 2011-2012.

Greenshields, Rev Dr Iain M. Minister, Dunfermline St Margaret's Parish Church of Scotland, since 2007; Moderator of the General Assembly of the Church of Scotland, since 2022; b. 1954, Drumchapel, Glasgow; m., Linda; 6 c. First full-time position as a Minister of Word and Sacrament was in Cranhill near Easterhouse (9 years); second charge was St Machan Parish Church in Larkhall, South Lanarkshire; Minister of Snizort Church, Isle of Skye, 2002-07 (served as a hospital chaplain and the Moderator of Lochcarron and Skye Presbytery in 2003-2004 as a well as its finance convener). Set up a charity called Hope4China's Children which provides education, support, medical care and foster care. Recreations: lifelong fan of Partick Thistle Football Club; enjoys reading, cycling, badminton and the very occasional game of golf. Address: 38 Garvock Hill, Dunfermline KY12 7UU; T.-01383 723955; e-mail revimaclg@hotmail.co.uk

Greenwood, Professor Justin, BA (Hons), PhD. Emeritus Professor of European Public Policy, Robert Gordon University, Aberdeen (appointed Professor in 1996); b. 17.5.60, Windlesham. Educ. Newton Abbot Grammar School; Nottingham University; College of Expert Reviewers, European Science Foundation, 2018-2021; EU Horizon research programme expert reviewer; Editorial Advisory Board, Journal of Public Affairs, Interest Groups & Advocacy; Chair, Economic and Social Research Advanced Quantitative Methods Stipend Panel, 2009-10; Principal Investigator, ESRC grant 'Democratic legitimacy in the EU: Inside the black box of trilogues', 2016-2019; Trainer, Diplomatic Training Path, European Commission, and International Labour Organisation International Training Centre; Trade Association Forum, Final Judging Awards panel, 2003-2020. Publications: Book: Interest Representation in the EU, 2017 (4th edtn.); The Challenge of Change in EU Business Associations (Editor), 2003; Inside the EU Business Associations, 2002; The Effectiveness of EU Business Associations (Editor), 2001; Social Partnership in the European Union (Co-Editor), 2001; Representing Interests in the European Union, 1997; Organised Interests in the New Global Order (Co-Editor) 1999; Collective Action in the European Union: Interest and the New Politics of Associability (Co-Editor) 1997; European Casebook on Business Alliances (Editor) 1995; Organised Interests and the European Community, (jointly), 1992. Address: (b.) Robert Gordon University, Garthdee Road, Aberdeen, AB10 7QE; T.-01224 263406.

Greer, Ross. MSP (Green Party), West of Scotland region, since 2016; b. 1.6.94. Educ. Bearsden Academy; University of Strathclyde. Communities Coordinator, Yes Scotland, Scottish independence referendum, 2014. Scottish Green candidate in the East Dunbartonshire constituency in the United Kingdom general election, 2015. Youngest ever MSP, elected at the age of 21. Address: Scottish Parliament, Edinburgh EH99 1SP.

Gregor, Dr. Anna, CBE, FRCR, FRCP. Retired Medical Practitioner, since 2008; b. 13.8.48, Prague, Czechoslovakia; m., Neil P. Magee; 2 s. Educ. Royal Free Hospital School of Medicine. Postgraduate Training, Royal Marsden and Brompton Hospitals London, 1973-80; Imperial Cancer Research Fellow, University of Edinburgh, 1980-83; Consultant Clinical Oncologist, Glasgow, 1983-87; Senior Lecturer, Oncology, University of Edinburgh, 1987-97; Consultant Clinical Oncologist, Edinburgh, 1997-2008; Clinical Director SCAN, Macmillan Lead Cancer Clinician, NHS Lothian, Lead Cancer Clinician, Scottish Government, 2001-06; Associate Medical Director, NHS Lothian. Trustee, National Museums of Scotland; Member of Court, Queen Margaret University, Edinburgh. Recreations: cooking; music; travel. Address: (h.) 26/2

Drumsheugh Gardens, Edinburgh EH3 7RN; e-mail: annagregor@doctors.net.uk

Gregory, Rear Admiral Michael, OBE. Lord Lieutenant, Dunbartonshire, 2008-2020; b. 15.12.45. Wide ranging career in the Royal Navy spanning 36 years (most of this time spent in the Submarine Service with three Submarine Commands followed by Command of a Frigate), then Assistant Director Naval Staff Duties in the MOD Whitehall and Naval and Defence Attaché (Policy) in Washington DC; finished career as Flag Officer, Scotland, Northern England and Northern Ireland; on retirement from the Royal Navy, became CEO of two Industry Support Organisations. Brigadier in the Royal Company of Archers, Queen's Body Guard for Scotland.

Greig, Rev. Alan, BSc, BD. Retired Church of Scotland Minister; b. 19.11.51, Helensburgh; m., Ruth D. Evans; 2 s. Educ. Coatbridge High School; University of Strathclyde; University of Edinburgh. Probationer Minister, Northfield Parish, Aberdeen, 1976-77; Minister, Hurlford Reid Memorial Church, Ayrshire, 1977-83; Church of Scotland Missionary working with United Church of Zambia, 1983-92; Minister, Kintore Parish Church, 1992-2013; Convener, Church of Scotland World Mission Council, 2002-06; Convener, Church of Scotland Council of Assembly, 2008-2012; Member of Interim Ministry Team, 2013-2017. Recreations: swimming; cycling and walking. Address: 1 Dunnydeer Place, Insch, Aberdeenshire AB52 6HP; e-mail: greig@kincarr.free-online.co.uk

Greig, David. Scottish playwright; Artistic Director, Edinburgh's Royal Lyceum Theatre, since 2016; b. 1969; m.; 2 c. Educ. Bristol University. Work has been performed at all of the major theatres in Britain, including the Traverse Theatre, Royal Court Theatre, Royal National Theatre and the Royal Shakespeare Company, and been produced around the world. After university, in 1990, co-founded Suspect Culture Theatre Company with Graham Eatough and Nick Powell in Glasgow; wrote texts for almost all of their shows until 2004, including Timeless (1997), Mainstream (1999), Candide 2000 (2000), Casanova (2001), Lament (2002), and 8000m (2004); stand-alone plays, from Stalinland (1992) performed at the major theatres; the Traverse produced Europe (1995), The Architect (1996, made into a film of the same title in 2006), Outlying Islands (2002), Damascus (2007) and Midsummer (a play with songs by Gordon McIntyre, 2008); Dunsinane (2010); The Monster in the Hall (2010); The Strange Undoing of Prudencia Hart (2011); The Letter of Last Resort (2012); The Events (2013); Adventures With The Painted People (2020); produced around 50 plays, texts, adaptations, translations and libretti in the first two decades of his career. Address: Royal Lyceum Theatre, 30B Grindlay Street, Edinburgh EH3 9AX; T.-0131 248 4800.

Greig, G. Andrew, MA. Author; b. 23.9.51, Bannockburn; m., Lesley Glaister. Educ. Waid Academy, Anstruther; Edinburgh University. Full-time writer, since 1979; Writer-in-Residence, Glasgow University, 1979-81; Scottish-Canadian Exchange Fellow, 1981-82; Writer-in-Residence, Edinburgh University, 1993-94; climbed on Himalayan expeditions. Publications include (poetry): This Life, This Life: New and Selected Poems; Found At Sea; four mountaineering books; novels: Electric Brae, Return of John Macnab; When They Lay Bare; That Summer; In Another Light; Romanno Bridge; Fair Helen; non-fiction: Preferred Lies; At the Loch of the Green Corrie. Recreations: music; hills; golf.
Website: andrew-greig.weebly.com

Grice, Sir Paul Edward, FRSE, FAcSS. Principal and Vice Chancellor, Queen Margaret University, since 2019; b. 13.10.61; m.; 2 d. Department of Transport, 1985-87; Department of Environment, 1987-92; Scottish Office,

1992-99 (latterly Head of Division, Constitution Group, then Director of Implementation); Clerk and Chief Executive, Scottish Parliament, 1999-2019; Member, Stirling University Court, 2005-2013; Hon. Fellow, Royal Incorporation of Architects in Scotland, since 2006; Member, Economic and Social Research Council, 2009-2015; Trustee, Bank of Scotland Foundation, 2011-2020; Member, Edinburgh International Festival Board, 2013-19; Board Member, Policy Scotland (Glasgow University), 2013-2019; Scientific Advisory Board Member, Behaviour Change by Design research project, since 2017; Fellow, Royal Society of Edinburgh, since 2017; Advisory Board Member, Scottish Centre of Social Research, 2017-2020; Chair and Trustee, Queen's Nursing Institute Scotland, since 2021; Convener, Universities Scotland Learning and Teaching Committee, since 2020; Board Member of the British University in Egypt, since 2020; Member of Place2Be Development Advisory Group for Scotland, since 2021; Member of Board of James Hutton Institute, since 2021. Recreations: performing arts; sports; travel. Address: Queen Margaret University, Edinburgh EH21 6UU.

Grier, Scott, OBE, MA, CA, FCIT. President, Loganair Limited; Director, Morrison Glasgow Distillers Ltd; Ninesquare Design Ltd; b. 7.3.41, Kilmacolm; m., Frieda Gardiner; 2 s. Educ. Greenock High School; Glasgow University. Apprenticed, Grahams Rintoul & Co., 1962-66; Accountant, Ardrossan Harbour Company Ltd./Clydeport, from 1967; various posts, Loganair, since 1976; Director: Glasgow Chamber of Commerce, 1990-98, Caledonian MacBrayne Limited, 1996-2006; Chairman, Scottish Tanning Industries Ltd., 1997-2003; Governor, Scottish Sports Aid, 1993-2004; Member, Scottish Tourist Board, 1992-98. Publication: Loganair, A Scottish Survivor, 1962-2012. Recreations: golf; gardening. Address: (h.) Lagavulin, 23c Summerlea Road, West Kilbride KA23 9HP; T.-01294 823138.

Grieve, Professor Andrew Robert, OBE, DDS, BDS, FDS, RCSEd. Professor of Conservative Dentistry, 1980-99, Dean of Dentistry, 1993-97, Dundee University; Consultant in Restorative Dentistry, Tayside Health Board, 1980-99; b. 23.5.39, Stirling; m., Frances M. Ritchie; 2 d. Educ. Perth Academy; St. Andrews University. Junior hospital appointments and general dental practice, 1961-63; Lecturer in Operative Dental Surgery and Dental Therapeutics, St. Andrews University, 1963-65; Lecturer in Conservative Dentistry, Birmingham University, 1965; appointed Senior Lecturer and Consultant in Restorative Dentistry, Birmingham Area Health Authority (Teaching), 1975. Member, Dental Council, Royal College of Surgeons of Edinburgh, 1983-88; President: British Society for Restorative Dentistry, 1986-87 (Honorary Fellow, 2000); President: Royal Odonto-Chirurgical Society of Scotland, 1994-95 (Council Member, 1985-88); Chairman, Tayside Area Dental Advisory Committee, 1987-90; Member, General Dental Council, 1989-99 (Chairman, Legislation Committee, 1994-99); Trustee, Armitstead Lecture Trust, 2003-2011; Member and Trustee, Tayside Pre-Retirement Council, 2003-2014 (Chairman, 2010-2014); Chair, Dundee RSNO Circle, since 2016. Recreations: furniture making; music; hill-walking; travel. Address: (h.) 23c Summerlea Road, West Kilbride KA23 9HP.

Grieve, Elaine. Lord-Lieutenant of Orkney, since 2020; b. Aberdeen. Career history: worked for 34 years at Orkney Islands Council, initially as a primary school teacher, followed by a period as Assistant Head, then Head Teacher; became Assistant Director of Education and finally Assistant Chief Executive and Director of Corporate Services; retired in 2011; supported many local organisations and served on many local boards; appointments include: Chair of Orkney Folk Festival, Director of the Pier Arts Centre, Director of the Orkney Housing Association, Vice-Chair of Voluntary Action Orkney. Recreations: music; enjoys listening to, and participating in music-making and writing. Address: Orkney Islands Council, School Place, Kirkwall, Orkney KW15 1NY; T.-01856 873535.

Griffin, Professor Julian, DPhil (Oxon). Director, The Rowett Institute of Nutrition and Health, University of Aberdeen, since 2021. Educ. University of Oxford. Career: worked as a Harvard Medical School/Massachusetts General Hospital Fellow in Radiology, then as a postdoctoral researcher in the lab of Prof. Jeremy Nicholson at Imperial College London; awarded a Royal Society University Research Fellowship, before setting up a research group at the Department of Biochemistry, University of Cambridge in 2002; became a programme leader in human nutrition research at MRC Human Nutrition Research in 2011; appointed Chair of Biological Chemistry at Imperial College London in 2019. Address: The Rowett Insitute, University of Aberdeen, Ashgrove Road West, Foresterhill, Aberdeen AB25 2ZD; T.-01224 438642; e-mail: j.ingram@abdn.ac.uk

Griffin, Mark. MSP (Labour), Central Scotland, since 2011; Shadow Minister for Transport and Veterans, 2013-14; Scottish Labour Spokesman for Sport, 2012-2013; North Lanarkshire Councillor, 2008-2012; b. 19.10.85; m., Stephanie. Educ. University of Strathclyde. Worked in the engineering industry; formerly a serving soldier in the British Territorial Army (TA). Member, Social Security Committee, Scottish Parliament. Became not only the youngest MSP of the current Parliament, but the youngest in the history of the Parliament upon his election at the age of 25. Address: Scottish Parliament, Edinburgh EH99 1SP.

Griffiths, Professor Anne Marjorie Ord, LLB (Edin), PhD. Emeritus Professor of Anthropology of Law, Edinburgh University; first female professor of law at Edinburgh University in 297 years; b. 30.12.53, Edinburgh; m., Edwin N. Wilmsen. Educ. St George's School for Girls, Edinburgh; University of Edinburgh; University of London. Apprentice with Messrs Dundas & Wilson, Edinburgh, 1978-1980; Admitted as solicitor in Scotland, 1980; appointed to the University of Edinburgh as a Lecturer in 1980; Lecturer in Law, 1980-1992; Senior Lecturer in Law, 1992-1999; Reader in Law, 1999-2004; Professor, Personal Chair in Anthropology of Law 2004; Distinguished Visiting Professor, Faculty of Law, University of Toronto, 2008; International Institute for the Sociology of Law, Oñati - Gipuzkoa, Spain, 2008 and 2007; Max Planck Institute for Social Anthropology, Halle/Saale, Germany, Visiting Fellow 2005, 2006, 2007, 2008; Centre for Socio-Legal Studies, University of Oxford; Visiting Fellow at International Law & Society Summer Institute, 2005, The University of Texas at Austin; Visiting Professor of Law, 1996, 1998, 2000, 2002, 2004, University of Zimbabwe; Visiting Professor, Southern and Eastern African Regional Centre for Women's Law (SEARCWL-UZ) 2003, 2005, 2007, University of Malaya; Edinburgh University Gender Studies Link Coordinator, 2001; University of Witwatersrand, South African Human Sciences Research Council Research Fellow, 1993, Kenyatta University; Edinburgh University Gender Studies Link Coordinator, 1993; Cornell University, Visiting Associate Professor of Law, 1988; Wolfson College, Oxford, Visiting Scholar, Center for Socio-Legal Studies, 1985; American Bar Foundation, Chicago, and Northwestern University, African Studies Dept., Research Scholar, 1990-1991; ESRC Research Fellowship, Botswana, 1982. Consultant to UN study on Informal Justice, 2008/9; Special Advisor to International Council on Human Rights Policy, Geneva. Publications include: In the Shadow of Marriage: Gender and Justice in an African Community, 1997; Family Law (Scotland) (Co-Author), 1997, revised second edition in 2006; Mobile People, Mobile Law: Expanding Legal Relations in a Contracting World (Co-Editor), 2005; 'Using Ethnography as a Tool in Legal Research: An Anthropological Perspective', in Theory and Method in Socio-Legal Research in 2005; and 'Localising the Global: Rights of Participation in the Scottish Children's Hearings System and Hearing Children in Children's Hearings', (Co-Author), 2000 and 2005. President, Commission on Legal Pluralism, 2003-2009, Board Member, since 1989; Assistant Editor, Journal of Legal Pluralism and Unofficial Law, (since 1996); Editorial Board, Social Justice, Anthropology, Peace and Human Rights (since 2004); Advisory Board, International Journal of Human Development (since 2001); Editorial Board, Critical African Studies, newly established (2008); e-journal at Edin.Univ.; African Studies Association, UK Executive Member; Centre of African Studies Committee, Edin. Univ. Recreations: theatre; music, especially opera; yoga; cooking. Address: (b.) School of Law, Edinburgh University, Old College, South Bridge, Edinburgh EH8 9YL; T.-0131 650 2057; e-mail: Anne.Griffiths@ed.ac.uk

Griffiths, Martin, LLB (Hons), CA. Chief Executive, Stagecoach Group PLC, since 2013, previously Finance Director (2000-2013). Career: former Chairman of the Group of Scottish Finance Directors and a former Director of Troy Income & Growth Trust plc, Trainline Holdings Limited, RoadKing Infrastructure (HK) Limited and Citybus (HK) Limited. Former Senior Independent Non-Executive Director of Robert Walters plc; Young Scottish Finance Director of the year in 2004. Co-Chairman, Virgin Rail Group Holdings Limited; Non-Executive Director, AG Barr plc; Chairman, Rail Delivery Group Limited. Address: Stagecoach Group Head Office, 10 Dunkeld Road, Perth PH1 5TW; T.-01738 442111.

Griffiths, Mike, BA, MBA. Co-Chief Executive Director, The Royal Lyceum Theatre Company, since 2019; b. 12.60. Educ. The University of Stirling; Royal Scottish Academy of Music and Drama; The Open University. Career history: Company Stage Manager, Northern Stage, 1992-93; Traverse Theatre: Production Manager, 1993-2001, Administrative Director, 2001-09; Sponsorship Manager, National Performing Companies, The Scottish Government, 2009-2012; Venue Producer, Paterson's Land, 2013-14; Relationship Manager, Big Big Sing, 2014-15; Producer, Our Land Productions, 2015-17; Producer, Janis Claxton Dance, 2015-17; Development Producer, Eden Court Theatre, 2015-17; Interim CEO: Eden Court Theatre, 2017-18, Horsecross Arts - Perth Concert Hall & Theatre, 2018-19; Director of Productions, KT Wong Foundation, 2012-19; Member, Board of Trustees, Leith Theatre, 2015-19; Executive Producer: Leith Theatre Trust, 2016-19, Brunstane Productions Ltd (appointed in 2015). Fellow of the Royal Society of Arts (FRSA); currently Board Member, Pachamama; Graduate, Common Purpose Matrix Programme, 2009; recently member of International Assessment Panel (Abbey Theatre) for Arts Council of Ireland and member of Creative Scotland's Peer Review Panel; Board Member and Executive Producer, Pearlfisher Theatre; Project Producer, Freedom on the Tyne, 2016-17. Address: The Royal Lyceum Theatre, 30b Grindlay Street, Edinburgh EH3 9AX; T.-0131 248 4848.

Griffiths, Professor Peter Denham, CBE, BSc, MD, LRCP, MRCS, FRCPath, FRCP(Edin), FCMI. Emeritus Professor of Biochemical Medicine, Dundee University (Vice-Principal, 1979-85, Dean of Medicine and Dentistry, 1985-89); Director and Trustee, Scottish Hospitals Endowment Research Trust, 1994-98; b. 16.6.27, Southampton; m., Joy Burgess; 3 s.; 1 d. Educ. King Edward VI School, Southampton; Guy's Hospital, London University. House appointments, Guy's Hospital, 1956-57; Junior Lecturer in Physiology, Guy's Hospital, 1957-58; Registrar and Senior Registrar, Guy's and Lewisham Hospitals, 1958-64; Consultant Pathologist, Harlow

Hospitals Group, 1964-66; Senior Lecturer in Clinical Chemistry/Honorary Consultant, St. Andrews University, then Dundee University, 1966-68. Member, General Medical Council, 1986-93; President, 1987-89, and sometime Chairman of Council, Association of Clinical Biochemists; Tayside Health Board: Honorary Consultant, 1966-89, Member, 1977-85; former Director, Dundee Repertory Theatre Board. Recreations: music; domestic activities. Address: (h.) 52 Albany Road, West Ferry, Dundee DD5 1NW; T.-01382 776772.

Griggs, Professor Russel, OBE. Chair, South of Scotland Economic Partnership; b. Edinburgh. Educ. Heriot Watt University. Non executive positions in the private, public and third sector; former Chair of the Audit Committee of VisitScotland; former Board member of Scottish Enterprise; currently chairs the Scottish Government's independent Regulatory Review Group who advise and work on better regulation in Scotland; former Non Executive Director of the Scottish Government; appointed as the independent external reviewer to the five clearing banks in the UK in 2011. Honorary Professor of the University of Glasgow; awarded an honorary doctorate by the university in 2002 for services to the industry and to the university; former Associate Professor of Boston University, and former member of the board of the Business School at Georgia Southern University.

Grimes Douglas, Linda. Head of News and Current Affairs, STV, since 2020. Career history: joined STV as a journalist over 20 years ago and holds an extensive range of editorial and production experience, having been Output editor for the station and Deputy Head of News. Sits on STV's Diversity and Inclusion Group. Address: STV Central Limited, STV, Pacific Quay, Glasgow G51 1PQ.

Grimmond, Iain William, BAcc (Hons), CA. Former General Treasurer, Church of Scotland (2005-2016); former Director of Finance, Erskine Hospital for Disabled Ex-Servicemen and Women (1981-2004); b. 8.8.55, Girvan; m., Marjory Anne Gordon Chisholm; 1 s.; 2 d. Educ. Hutchesons' Boys Grammar School; Glasgow University. Trainee CA, Ernst & Whinney, Glasgow, 1976-79; Assistant Treasurer, Erskine Hospital, 1979-81. Elder, Giffnock South Parish Church. Recreations: golf; football; reading. Address: (h.) 9 Wemyss Avenue, Crookfur, Newton Mearns, Glasgow G77 6AR; T.-0141-639 4894.

Grimmond, Steve, MA, MBA, FRSA. Chief Executive, Fife Council, since 2013; b. 12.6.63, Dundee; m., Audrey Krawec; 1 s.; 1 d. Educ. Craigie High School, Dundee; Dundee University. Dundee District Council: Principal Officer, Area Renewal; Policy Planning Manager, Chief Executive's Department, Dundee City Council; Area Manager, Aberdeenshire Council; Director, Arts and Heritage, Dundee City Council; Director, Leisure and Arts, Dundee City Council; Director, Creative Scotland; Executive Director, Environment, Enterprise and Communities, Fife Council. Recreations: football; painting; boating. Address: (b.) Fife House, Glenrothes KY7 5LT; T.-03451 555555 ext. 444143; e-mail: steven.grimmond@fife.gov.uk

Groeneveld, Eva, MA (Hons), MPhil. Policy and Stakeholder Manager, Competition and Markets Authority, since 2020. Career history: Account Executive, Ranelagh International Ltd, 2006-07; WWF-UK: Senior Public Affairs Officer, 2007-2010, Public Affairs Manager (Scotland), 2010-2015; Head of Public Affairs (Scotland), Which?, 2015-18; Freedom of Information Officer, Scottish Information Commissioner, 2018-2020. Short term observer, Democracy Volunteers, since 2021; Member, Board of Trustees, David Hume Institute, since 2021. Address: (b.) CA House, 21 Haymarket Yards, Edinburgh EH12 5BH.

Grover, Hugh, MBA, FCMgt, FRSA. Former Chief Executive, The Scottish Police Authority (2018-19). Educ. Imperial College London. Career history: Deputy Director, Department for Communities and Local Government, 2004-09; London Councils: Policy Director, 2009-2014, Programme Director, London LGPS CIV, 2014-15; Chief Executive Officer: London LGPS CIV Limited, 2015-17.

Gruer, Professor Laurence David, OBE, BSc (Hons), MB, ChB, MD, MPH, FFPH, MRCP (UK). Honorary Professor of Public Health, University of Edinburgh; b. 6.7.53, Aberdeen; m., Nana (deceased); 1 s.; 2 d. Educ. Robert Gordon's College; George Watson's College; Hamilton College, New York, USA; University of Edinburgh; University of Glasgow. Medical laboratory research, Lyon, France, 1983-85; Consultant, Public Health Medicine, Greater Glasgow Health Board, 1989-2001; Director, HIV and Addictions Resource Centre, Glasgow, 1990-97 (establishing Glasgow needle exchange and methadone programmes and health services for people with HIV/AIDS, drug users and other marginalised groups); Consultant in Public Health Medicine, Public Health Institute of Scotland, 2001-03; Director, Scottish Public Health Specialist Training Programme, 2002-04; Director, Public Health Science, NHS Health Scotland, 2003-2012; Member, UK Advisory Council on the Misuse of Drugs, 1996-2006; OBE, Services to Public Health, 2000; Member, Scottish Committees for AIDS, Drug Misuse, Alcohol, Tobacco; Chair, Scottish Committees on Smoking Prevention, Tobacco Control Research; Co-founder, Glasgow Psychosis Clinical Information System, 2002; Founder, Scottish Suicide Information Database, 2008; Charity Founder and CEO, Dr Nana Gruer Health Initiative, Ghana, 2015-21; Secretary and Trustee, Global Society on Migration, Ethnicity, Race and Health, since 2020. Publications: over 150 reports, chapters in books and papers in journals on HIV and AIDS, drug misuse, tobacco control, health inequalities, ethnicity and health, obesity and infections. Recreations: cooking; cycling; free-style swimming; music; French and Spanish; photography. E-mail: gruer.health@gmail.com

Gulhane, Dr Sandesh, MBBS. MSP (Scottish Conservative and Unionist Party), Glasgow (Region), since 2021; b. 1982, London; 2 c. Educ. Imperial College London. Career history: Doctor by profession; worked in Birmingham and Sunderland; worked as an orthopaedic registrar in hospitals in Glasgow and East Kilbride after moving to Scotland around 2011; latterly operated as a general practitioner. Club Doctor as part of the medical staff of SPFL football club Queen's Park F.C., since 2017. Address: The Scottish Parliament, Edinburgh EH99 1SP T.-0131 348 6162. E-mail: Sandesh.Gulhane.msp@parliament.scot

Gulland, Iain. Chief Executive, Zero Waste Scotland, since 2014; b. 5.64. Educ. University of St Andrews. Career history: worked with initiating recycling systems in the public, private and third sectors and led the Community Recycling Network, Scotland until 2008; currently President of the Association of Cities and Regions for Resource Management (ACR+); member of several Scottish Government Programme Boards including those covering low carbon and manufacturing. Named the 'most influential person in the UK waste and resource efficiency sector' by Resource Magazine

(2014); Fellow of the Chartered Institution of Waste Management, since 2016. Address: Zero Waste Scotland, Moray House, 2a Forthside Way, Stirling FK8 1QZ; T.-01786 433 930.

Gunn, Alexander MacLean, MA, BD; b. 1943, Inverness; m., Ruth T.S.; 1 s.; 1 d. Educ. Edinburgh Academy; Beauly; Dingwall Academy; Edinburgh University and New College. Parish Minister: Wick St. Andrews and Thrumster, 1967-73; Member, Caithness Education Committee, 1968-73; Parish Minister, Glasgow St. David's Knightswood, 1973-86; Minister, Aberfeldy with Amulree and Strathbraan with Dull and Weem, 1986-2006; Convener: Church of Scotland Rural Working Group, 1988-90, General Assembly's Presbytery Development Committee, 1990-92, General Assembly's Mission and Evangelism Resource Committee, 1992-95; Interim Convener, Board of National Mission, 1996; Convener, Regional Committee, Scripture Union Scotland, 1998-2005. Chairman, Breadalbane Academy School Board, 1989-92 and 1996-2002; Lay Member, Education Scotland; Street Pastor; Vice-Chairman, Ascension Trust Scotland; National Chaplain to Workplace Chaplaincy Scotland. Address: "Navarone", 12 Cornhill Road, Perth PH1 1LR; T.-01738-443216; e-mail: sandygunn@btinternet.com

Gusterson, Professor Barry Austin, PhD, FRCPath. Emeritus Professor of Pathology, Glasgow University (Professor, since 2000); b. 24.10.46, Colchester; m., Ann Josephine Davies; 1 s.; 2 d. Educ. St Bartholomew's Hospital, London. Senior Clinical Scientist and Consultant, Ludwig Institute of Cancer Research, London, 1983-86; Consultant in Histopathology, Royal Marsden Hospital, 1984; Professor of Histopathology and Chairman, Section on Cell Biology and Experimental Pathology, Institute of Cancer Research, London University, 1986-2000; Founding Director, Toby Robins Breast Cancer Research Centre, London, 1998. Director, Pathology, International Breast Cancer Study Group, Berne, 1995; Oakley Lecturer, Pathological Society of Great Britain and Ireland, 1986; Chairman, Pathology Group, Organisation of European Cancer Institutes, Geneva, 1992-96. Recreations: antique English glass and furniture; gardening; walking; reading. Address: (b.) Department of Pathology, Western Infirmary, Glasgow, G11 6NT; T.-0141-211 2233.

Gwilt, George David, MA, FFA, FBCS, CITP; b. 11.11.27, Edinburgh; m., Ann Sylvester (deceased); 3 s. Educ. Sedbergh; St. John's College, Cambridge. Standard Life, 1949-88, latterly as Managing Director; Director: European Assets Trust NV, 1979-2000, Scottish Mortgage & Trust plc, 1983-98, Hodgson Martin Ltd., 1989-2000, Edinburgh Festival Society Ltd., 1989-95; President, Faculty of Actuaries, 1981-83; Trustee, South of Scotland TSB, 1966-83; Member: Younger Committee on Privacy, 1970-72, Monopolies and Mergers Commission, 1983-87; Convener, Scottish Poetry Library, 1988-2000. Recreations: flute playing; squash. Address: (h.) 39 Oxgangs Road, Edinburgh EH10 7BE; T.-0131-445 1266.

H

Haas, Professor Harald, FRSE, PhD. Professor (Chair of Mobile Communications), University of Edinburgh, since 2010; b. 15.03.68, Neustadt/Aisch, Germany; m., Sybille Haas; 1 s.; 1 d. Educ. University of Applied Sciences, Nürnberg; University of Edinburgh, College of Science and Engineering. Engineer (Heinz-Nixdorf scholar), Siemens AG, Bombay, India, 1995; Engineer, Siemens AG/Semiconductor Division (now Infineon), Munich, Germany, 1997; Consultant, Nokia Networks, Nokia/Oulu, 1999-2000; Research Associate, Dept. of Electronics & Electrical Engineering/Signals and Systems Group, University of Edinburgh, 1999-2001; Project Manager, Siemens AG/Information & Communication Mobile Networks, Munich, Germany, 2001-02; Associate Professor of Electrical Engineering, School of Engineering and Science, Jacobs University Bremen, 2002-07; Lecturer, School of Engineering, Institute of Digital Communications (IDCOM), University of Edinburgh, 2007-08, Reader, 2008-2010; Chief Scientific Officer, pureLiFi Ltd, since 2012. Publications: Next Generation Mobile Access Technologies: Implementing TDD (Co-Author), 2008; Principles of Impaired and Visible Light Communications (Co-Author), 2015. Address: (b.) The King's Buildings, The University of Edinburgh, Mayfield Road, Edinburgh EH9 3JL; T.-0131 650 5591; e-mail: h.haas@ed.ac.uk

Hadden, William A., BSc, BAO, BCh, MB, FRCSEd and Orth. Consultant Orthopaedic Surgeon, since 1984; b. 23.5.46, Northern Ireland; 3 s. Educ. Methodist College, Belfast; Portadown College, Co. Armagh; Queen's University, Belfast. Surgical training, Northern Ireland, Edinburgh, Dundee, Christchurch (New Zealand). Recreations: golf; squash. Address: (b.) Perth Royal Infirmary, Perth PH1 1NX; T.-01738 473698.

Haddington, 14th Earl of (George Edmund Baldred Baillie Hamilton); b. 27.12.85. Educ. Eton; Glasgow University. Address: Mellerstain, Gordon, Berwickshire TD3 6LG.

Haddock, Graham, MBChB, MD, FRCS (Glas), FRCS (Edin), FRCS (Paed). Consultant Paediatric Surgeon, since 1995; Clinical Director of Surgery, 2000-03; b. 7.8.60, Greenock. Educ. Notre Dame High School, Greenock; Glasgow University. Trained in adult general surgery, Glasgow and Edinburgh, in paediatric surgery, Royal Hospital for Sick Children, Yorkhill, Royal Hospital for Sick Children, Edinburgh, and Hospital for Sick Children, Toronto. Chair, JCST Quality Assurance Committee; Honorary Clinical Associate Professor, University of Glasgow; Deputy Head of Admissions, University of Glasgow Medical School. Former Chairman, Specialist Advisory Committee for Paediatric Surgery of The Joint Committee for Surgical Training (JCST), 2009-2012. Formerly National (UK) Commissioner for Explorer Scouts (The Scout Association), 2001-06; Depute Chief Commissioner for Scotland (Programme), 2008-2010; Chief Commissioner for Scotland; former UK Trustee (The Scout Association), 2007-2013. Address: (b.) Department of Paediatric Surgery, Royal Hospital for Sick Children, Yorkhill, Glasgow G3 8SJ; T.-0141-201 0289.

Haddow, Christopher, QC, LLB (Hons); b. 15.5.47, Edinburgh; m., Kathleen; 3 s. Educ. George Watson's College; Edinburgh University. Admitted to Faculty of Advocates, 1971; Queen's Counsel, 1985. Former Member, Secretary of State's Valuation Advisory Council and of Scottish Valuation and Rating Council; Joint Editor, Armour on Valuation for Rating, since 1990. Recreations: hockey; walking; classic cars. Address: (h.) Abbot's Croft House, North Berwick EH39 5NG.

Haggerty, Lara. Library Manager and Keeper, Innerpeffray Library (Scotland's oldest free Public Lending Library, founded 1680), since 2009. Address: (b.) Crieff, Perthshire PH7 3RF; T.-01764 652819.

Hair, Professor Graham Barry, MMus, PhD. Composer; Emeritus Professor of Music, Honorary Research Fellow, School of Engineering, Glasgow University; Director, Scottish Voices ensemble, since 1991; b. 27.2.43, Geelong, Australia; m., Dr Greta Mary Hair. Educ. Geelong College, Australia; Melbourne University; Sheffield University. Senior Lecturer, Latrobe University, 1975-80; Head, School of Composition, Sydney Conservatorium of Music, 1980-90; has had many commissions, performances, CD recordings, broadcasts and musical works published. Address: (h.) 45 St. Vincent Crescent, Glasgow G3 8NG; T.-0141-221 4933; e-mail: sv@n-ism.org

Hair, Kirstene. MP (Conservative), Angus, 2017-19; b. 1989, Brechin, Angus. Educ. University of Aberdeen. Career: worked for publishers DC Thomson. Conservative candidate for Angus South in the 2016 Scottish Parliament election.

Haites, Emeritus Professor Neva, OBE, MB, ChB, PhD, FRCP, FRCPath, FMedSci. Retired Professor in Medical Genetics, formerly Vice-Principal for Development, Honorary Consultant in Clinical Genetics, University of Aberdeen; b. 4.6.47, Brisbane, Australia; m., Roy; 2 d. Educ. Somerville House, Brisbane; Queensland University; University of Aberdeen. Formerly: Human Fertilisation and Embryology Authority Member, Vice Chair, Royal Society of Edinburgh, Lead Clinician, North of Scotland Cancer Network, Member, National Screening Committee, Head of Service in Medical Genetics. Address: University of Aberdeen, King's College, Aberdeen; T.-01224 437082. E-mail: n.haites@abdn.ac.uk

Hajivassiliou, Constantinos, BSc (Hons), MBChB, MD, FRCS (Edin), FRCS (Glas), FRCS (Paed), MD, FEBPS, FRCPCH, FRSA. Paediatric/Neonatal Surgeon (Consultant), Royal Hospital for Sick Children, Glasgow, since 1998; Wellcome Trust Senior Lecturer, Glasgow University, since 1999; b. 27.4.61, Nicosia; m., Eva; 2 d. Educ. Edinburgh University. House Officer, then Senior House Officer, 1986-89; Registrar, West of Scotland Rotation, 1989-92; Senior Registrar/Lecturer, Yorkhill and Glasgow University, 1992-98. Lord Moynihan Prize, Association of Surgeons of Great Britain and Ireland, 1995; many other prizes. Recreations: radio amateur; diving; flying; fishing; cooking. Address: (b.) Department of Paediatric Surgery, Royal Hospital for Sick Children, Govan Road, Glasgow G51 4TF; T.-0141 4516525.

Halcro Johnston, Jamie, MSP (Scottish Conservative and Unionist Party), Highlands and Islands (Region), since 2017; Shadow Minister for Business, Trade, Tourism and Enterprise, since 2021; p. 10.75, Oxford. Educ. Radley College; University of Exeter. Career history: Senior Sales, Financial Times, 2000-01; Special Advisor, Scottish

Parliament, 2003-07; Freelance Senior Account Manager, Holyrood Communications, 2007-2017; Director, Campaignhouse, Edinburgh, 2012-17. Address: The Scottish Parliament, Edinburgh EH99 1SP; T.-0131 348 6140; e-mail: Jamie.HalcroJohnston.msp@parliament.scot

Haldane of Gleneagles, James Martin, MA, BA, DUniv (Stirling), CA, FRSA. 28th Laird of Gleneagles; Director: Investors Capital Trust PLC, 1995-2010 (Chairman, since 2004); (Stace Barr Angerstein PLC, 1997-2004), Shires Income plc, 1996-2008 (Chairman, 2003-08); former Chairman, Chiene & Tait, CA (Partner, 1989-2001); former Deputy Chairman, Scottish Life Assurance Co. (Director, 1990-2001); Chairman, Queen's Hall (Edinburgh) Ltd., 1987-2001; Chairman, Scottish Opera Endowment Trust, 2010-2016; b. 18.9.41, Edinburgh; m., Petronella Victoria Scarlett; 1 s.; 2 d. Educ. Winchester College; Magdalen College, Oxford. Partner, Arthur Young, 1970-89. Chairman, Scottish Chamber Orchestra, 1978-85; Chairman, Craighead Investments PLC, 1982-90; Trustee, D'Oyly Carte Opera Trust, 1985-92 and since 2012; Treasurer, Queen's Bodyguard for Scotland (Royal Company of Archers), 1992-2001; Member: Council, Edinburgh Festival Society, 1985-89, Northern and Scottish Board, Legal and General Assurance Co., 1984-87, Council, National Trust for Scotland, 1992-97, Court, Stirling University, 1997-2005; Chairman of Governors, Innerpeffray Library, 1994-2006. Recreations: music; golf. Address: (h.) Gleneagles, Auchterarder PH3 1PJ; T.-01764 682 388; (b.) 01764 682535.
E-mail: haldane@gleneagles.org

Haldane, Professor John Joseph, BA, PGCE, BA, PhD, Hon LLD, Hon DLitt, FRSA, FRSE, KCHS. J. Newton Rayzor Sr Distinguished Professor of Philosophy, Baylor University, Texas, USA, since 2015; Emeritus Professor of Philosophy, St. Andrews University (appointed Professor in 1994); Senior Fellow, Centre for Ethics, Philosophy and Public Affairs; b. 19.2.54, London; m., Hilda Marie Budas; 2 s.; 2 d. Educ. St. Aloysius College, Glasgow; Wimbledon School of Art; London University. Art Master, St. Joseph's Grammar School, Abbey Wood, 1976-79; Lecturer in Moral Philosophy, St. Andrews University, 1983-90, Reader, 1990-94; Stanton Lecturer, University of Cambridge, 1999-2002; Royden Davis Professor of Humanities, Georgetown University, 2001-02; Gifford Lecturer, University of Aberdeen, 2004; Joseph Lecturer, Gregorian University, Rome, 2004; Visiting Professor, Institute for the Psychological Sciences, Virginia, USA, 2005-08; Consultor to Pontifical Council for Culture, Vatican, since 2005; Senior Fellow, Witherspoon Institute Princeton, since 2007; McDonald Lecturer, University of Oxford, 2011; Renwick Fellow, University of Notre Dame, 2013-14; Permanent Fellow, Center for Ethics and Culture, University of Notre Dame, since 2014; Chairman, Royal Institute of Philosophy; Vice President (Scotland), Catholic Union; Member, Editorial Board: American Journal of Jurisprudence, Cambridge Studies in Philosophy, Ethical Perspectives, Journal of Philosophy of Education, Philosophical Explorations, Philosophical Quarterly; Contributor: The Scotsman, The Tablet, Modern Painters etc; and to BBC radio and television, and National Public Radio, USA. Address: (b.) Department of Philosophy, University of St Andrews, St Andrews KY16 9AL; T.-01334 462488; e-mail: jjh1@st-and.ac.uk

Haldane, The Hon Lady (Shona Haldane). Senator of the College of Justice, since 2021. Educ. University of Edinburgh. Career history: admitted to the Faculty of Advocates in 1996, and took silk in 2010; appointed by the Advocate General for Scotland as Standing Junior Counsel (firstly to the Forestry Commission in 2001, and then to the Home Office, 2008-2011); served as an ad hoc Advocate Depute with the Crown Office, 2010-2016. Address: Court of Session, Parliament House, Parliament Square, Edinburgh EH1 1RQ.

Halden, Derek, BSc (Hons), MEng, CEng, FCILT, FRSA, FICE. Director, DHC and Loop Connections Ltd., Transport Planning and Technology Services, since 1996; Editor, Scottish Transport Review, since 2004; b. 3.10.60, Irvine; m., Deborah; 1 s.; 1 d. Educ. Glasgow High School; Merchiston Castle School; University of Aberdeen; University of Glasgow. Jamieson, Mackay and Partners, Transport Planning Consultants, Glasgow and Sir William Halcrow and Partners, 1982-86; Civil Service - Scottish Office Road and Bridge Projects, Transport Policy, Research, and Transport Research Laboratory, 1987-96. Honorary Research Fellow: University of Aberdeen, 2003-2015, University of Strathclyde, since 2017; Committee Member: European Transport Conference, 2003-2019, Scottish Transport Studies Group, since 1995 (Chair, 2007-2017, Secretary, since 2017); Chair, Chartered Institute of Logistics and Transport Scotland (2011-2013). Recreations: tennis; squash; hill walking; guitar. Address: Longview, Kames, Tighnabruaich PA21 2AB.
E-mail: derek@dhc1.co.uk

Halfpenny, Lynne, BA, DRLP. Freelance Consultant; Chair/Director of Imaginate, since 2021; Director, WCCF LTD, since 2021; Director of Culture, City of Edinburgh Council, 2015-2021 (retired), Head of Culture and Sport, 2006-2015, Head of Museums and Arts, Culture and Leisure Department, 2002-2006, Principal Arts Officer, 1992-1998, Arts Manager, 1992-1998, Senior Arts Officer, 1989-1992; various arts and cultural roles with Local Authorities as well as Commonwealth Arts Festival, 1985-89; Board Member, Museums Galleries Scotland, 2006-2016; Common Purpose Advisory Group Member, 2008-2016; Board Member, Eastgate Theatre, Peebles, 2010-2012; Visiting Professor, Edinburgh Napier University, since 2011; Advisor to the School of Arts, Social Sciences and Management, Queen Margaret University, since 2012; b. 18.12.63, Aberdeen; m., Robert Orr; 1 s.; 1 d. Educ. Waid Academy; Queen Margaret University; Dunfermline College of Physical Education. Address: (h.) 14 Swanston Gardens, Fairmilehead, Edinburgh EH10 7DL; e-mail: lynne.halfpenny@me.com
Twitter: @HalfpennyMe

Hall, Professor Christopher, MA, DPhil, DSc, CEng, FRSC, FIMMM, FREng, FRSE. Emeritus Professor and Professorial Fellow, University of Edinburgh, since 2010, Professor of Materials, 1999-2010, Director, Centre for Materials Science and Engineering, 1999-2010, Director of Research, School of Engineering and Electronics, 2002-08; b. 31.12.44, Henley-on-Thames; m., Sheila McKelvey (deceased); 1 d.; 1 s. Educ. Royal Belfast Academical Institution; Trinity College, Oxford. Lecturer, Building Engineering, UMIST, 1972-83; Head, Rock and Fluid Physics, Schlumberger Cambridge Research, 1983-88; Head, Chemical Technology, Dowell Schlumberger, St Etienne, France, 1988-89; Scientific Advisor, Schlumberger Cambridge Research, 1990-99; Visiting Fellow, Princeton Materials Institute, Princeton University, USA, 1998; Visiting Professor, University of Manchester, 1994-2016; Senior Member, Robinson College, Cambridge, since 1989; Royal Society Mercer Senior Award for Innovation, 2001; Fellow and Curator, Royal Academy of Engineering; Fellow, Royal Society of Edinburgh (Curator, 2017-2021). Address: (h.) 36 Mayfield Terrace, Edinburgh EH9 1RZ.
E-mail: Christopher.Hall@ed.ac.uk

Hall, Professor Graham Stanley, BSc, PhD, FRSE, FRAS. Professor Emeritus, University of Aberdeen, since 2011 (Professor of Mathematics, 1996-2011); b. 5.9.46, Warrington; 1 s.; 1 d. Educ. Boteler Grammar School,

Warrington; University of Newcastle upon Tyne (Earl Grey Memorial Fellow, 1971-73); Lecturer in Mathematics, University of Aberdeen, since 1973 (Senior Lecturer, 1982, Reader, 1990, Head of Department, 1992-95). Over 200 invited lectures worldwide. Publications: over 180 articles in research journals; General Relativity (Co-Editor), 1996; Recent Developments in Mathematical Relativity (Co-Editor), 2012; book: Symmetries and Curvature; Structure in General Relativity (Author), 2004. Recreations: music (piano); reading; astronomy; history; sport. Address: (b.) Institute of Mathematics, University of Aberdeen, Aberdeen AB24 3UE; T.-01224 272748; e-mail: g.hall@abdn.ac.uk

Hall, Hugh. Principal, Fife College, since 2017; Chair, Historic Environment Scotland, since 2022; b. 5.58, Glasgow. Career history: began working life straight from school in the local Benefits Agency office in Easterhouse; chartered accountant with expertise in transformational change, governance and major project development and delivery; has held a number of senior appointments in a wide range of public service organisations; formerly Chief Operating Officer, University of Strathclyde. Awarded the Public Sector Finance Director of the Year award in recognition of leadership role in the transformation of Scotland's enterprise network (2009). Non-executive roles past and present include: eight years as a member of Court at Edinburgh Napier University; Chairman of the Chartered Institute of Public Finance and Accountancy in Scotland; Chair of Forth Valley College; Chair of Colleges Scotland and Chair of the Scottish Children's Lottery. Address: Fife College, Pittsburgh Road, Dunfermline KY11 8DY.

Hall, Stewart Martin, FRICS, FAAV, ACIArb, FRAgS. Chartered Surveyor & Arbiter; Senior Director, Davidson & Robertson, since 2005; b. 6.11.70, Cumbria; m., Isla; 2d ; 1s. Educ. Harper Adams University. Davidson & Robertson, since 1991; Chairman, RICS matrics Scotland, 2004-05; Hon. Treasurer, RICS Scotland, 2005-08; President of Scottish Agricultural Arbiters & Valuers Association, 2012-14; Hon. Vice President, Royal Highland and Agricultural Society for Scotland; Director, Central Association of Agricultural Valuers. Director, Kirknewton Community Development Trust. Recreation: curling. Address: (b.) Riccarton Mains, Currie, Midlothian EH14 4AR; T.-0131 449 6212.

Halliday, David James Finlay, LLB (Hons), DipLP, NP, WS. Partner, Halliday Campbell WS, since 2009; b. 25.7.62, Dunfermline; m., Rona Dougall; 2 d. Educ. High School of Dundee; University of Edinburgh. Qualified as Solicitor, 1988; Assistant Solicitor, Edinburgh, 1989-92; Partner, Orr MacQueen, Solicitors, 1992-99; Partner and Head of Litigation, Boyds Solicitors LLP, 1999-2007; Partner, HBJ Gateley Wareing (Scotland) LLP, 2007-09. Recreations: music; current affairs; cycling; family. Address: (b.) 7 Crawfurd Road, Edinburgh EH16 5PQ; T.-0131 668 3000.
E-mail: david.halliday@hallidaycampbell.com

Halliday, Dr John Dixon, BA (Hons), PhD. Former Rector, High School of Dundee (2008-2020); b. 24.6.55, Wantage, Berkshire; m., Anna Salvesen; 2 s.; 1 d. Educ. Abingdon School; Exeter University; Robinson College, Cambridge. Lecturer in English, Universitat Passau, Germany; freelance translator; Head of German, Merchiston Castle School; Head of Modern Languages, Housemaster and Director of Middle School, Sedbergh School; Headmaster, Rannoch School; Teacher of Modern Languages, Dollar Academy; Headmaster, Albyn School, 2002-08. Recreations: music – singing, viola; sport; reading.

Halliday, Rt. Rev. Robert Taylor, MA, BD. Bishop of Brechin, 1990-96; b. 7.5.32, Glasgow; m., Dr. Gena M. Chadwin (deceased 2013); 1 d. Educ. High School of Glasgow; Glasgow University; Trinity College, Glasgow; Episcopal Theological College, Edinburgh. Deacon, 1957; Priest, 1958; Assistant Curate, St. Andrew's, St. Andrews, 1957-60, St. Margaret's, Newlands, Glasgow, 1960-63; Rector, Holy Cross, Davidson's Mains, Edinburgh, 1963-83; External Lecturer in New Testament, Episcopal Theological College, Edinburgh, 1963-74; Canon, St. Mary's Cathedral, Edinburgh, 1973-83; Rector, St. Andrew's, St. Andrews, 1983-90; Tutor in Biblical Studies, St. Andrews University, 1984-90; Post-retiral ministry, Christ Church, Morningside, Edinburgh, 1997-2009; St Peter's, Lutton Place, Edinburgh, 2009-2018; St Cuthbert's, Colinton, since 2019. Recreations: reading; visiting gardens and art exhibitions. Address: 28 Forbes Road, Edinburgh EH10 4ED; T.-0131-221 1490.

Halliday, Roger. Chief Executive Officer, Research Data Scotland, since 2020; Chief Statistician, Scottish Government, 2011-2022. Educ. St. Andrews University. Career: joined the Government fast stream as an assistant statistician; worked for various UK Government Departments and at the Scottish Government in a number of statistical and policy making roles; served as Scottish Government's Chief Data Officer role, 2017-2020; jointly led a Covid Modelling and Analysis Division in Scottish Government, since March 2020; Honorary Professor, University of Glasgow, since 2019.

Halling, Professor Peter James, BA, PhD, FRSE. Honorary Research Professor, Department of Pure & Applied Chemistry, University of Strathclyde (appointed Professor in 1996); b. 30.3.51, London. Educ. Calday Grammar School; Churchill College, Cambridge; Bristol University. Postdoctoral Fellow, University College, London, 1975-78; Research Scientist, Unilever Research, Bedford, 1978-83; Professor of Biocatalyst Science, Strathclyde University, 1990-96. Recreation: orienteering. Address: (h.) 34 Montague Street, Glasgow G4 9HX; T.-0141-552 4400.

Halliwell, Professor Francis Stephen, MA, DPhil (Oxon), FBA, FRSE. Professor of Greek, University of St. Andrews, 1995-2020 (now Emeritus); b. 18.10.53, Wigan; m., Helen Ruth Gainford (divorced); 2 s. Educ. St. Francis Xavier's, Liverpool; Worcester College, University of Oxford. Lecturer in Classics and Drama, Westfield College, London, 1980-82; Fellow in Classics, Corpus Christi College, University of Cambridge, 1982-84; Lecturer, Senior Lecturer, Reader in Classics, University of Birmingham, 1984-95; Visiting Professor in Classics, University of Chicago, 1990; Visiting Faculty Fellow, University of California at Riverside, 1993; Visiting Professor in Aesthetics, University of Rome, 1998; H. L. Hooker Distinguished Visiting Professor, McMaster University, 2009; Chaire Cardinal Mercier, Catholic University of Louvain, 2010; Townsend Visiting Professor, Cornell University, 2012. Winner of Premio Europeo d'Estetica 2008, Criticos Prize 2008. Publications: twelve books and more than 100 articles on Greek literature and philosophy, including Aristophanes, Plato, Aristotle, and Longinus. Recreation: music. Address: (b.) School of Classics, Swallowgate, University of St. Andrews, St. Andrews KY16 9AL; e-mail: fsh@st-andrews.ac.uk

Hallsworth, Fred, BAcc, CA. Founder and Principal, The Hallsworth Partnership, since 2005; NED, Offshore Renewable Energy Catapult, since 2015; NED and Chair of Audit Committee, Scottish Enterprise, 2004-2010; Chairman, Forth Dimension Displays Limited, 2007-

2011; NED and Chair of Audit Committee, Central Marketing Agency (Scotland) Limited, since 2007; NED, Point 35 Microstructures Limited, since 2006; NED, Elonics Limited, 2006-2010; NED and Vice-Chairman, Microvisk Technologies Limited, since 2006; NED Golden Charter Limited, 2009-2011; NED, Metaforic Limited, 2009-2014; Advisory Board Member, Lane Clarke & Peacock LLP, since 2009; b. 03.05.53, Paisley; m., Nicola; 2 s.; 3 d. Educ. St. Mirins Academy; University of Glasgow. Audit Manager: Andersen Brussels, 1981, Andersen Scotland, 1982-88; Head of Audit, Andersen Cambridge, 1994-98; Head of Corporate Finance, Andersen Cambridge, 1988-95; Managing Partner, Andersen Cambridge, 1995-98; Membership of Partnership Council, Andersen UK, 1999-2002; Managing Partner, Andersen Scotland, 1998-2002; Senior Client Service Partner and Head of TMC Deloitte Scotland, 2002-05. Board Member, Scottish Institute for Enterprise, 1999-2008; Chairman, The Kelvin Institute, 2005-08; Council Member: CBI Scotland, 1999-2004, CBI Eastern Region, 1994-98; Co-founder and Board Member, The Cambridge Network, 1996-2002; Board Member, University of Cambridge Finance Committee, 1996-98. Recreations: golf; tennis; gym. Address: (h./b.) The Garden Wing, Houston House, Kirk Road, Houston, Renfrewshire PA6 7AR; T.-07889 721321; e-mail: fred@fredhallsworth.com

Hally, Paul William. Partner, Shepherd and Wedderburn LLP, since 1987 (Chairman, 2014-2020). Convenor, ICAS Business Policy Panel. Address: (b.) 1 Exchange Crescent, Conference Square, Edinburgh EH3 8UL; T.-0131 473 5183.
E-mail: paul.hally@shepwedd.com

Hamblen, Professor David Lawrence, CBE, MB, BS, PhD, DSc (Hon), FRCS, FRCSEdin, FRCSGlas. Chairman, Greater Glasgow NHS Board, 1997-2002; Emeritus Professor of Orthopaedic Surgery, Glasgow University; Hon. Consultant Orthopaedic Surgeon to Army in Scotland, 1976-99; b. 31.8.34, London; m., Gillian; 1 s.; 2 d. Educ. Roan School, Greenwich; London University. The London Hospital, 1963-66; Teaching Fellow in Orthopaedics, Harvard Medical School/Massachusetts General Hospital, 1966-67; Lecturer in Orthopaedics, Nuffield Orthopaedic Centre, Oxford, 1967-68; Senior Lecturer in Orthopaedics/Honorary Consultant, Edinburgh University/South East Regional Hospital Board, 1968-72; Professor of Orthopaedic Surgery, Glasgow University; 1972-99. Honorary Consultant in Orthopaedic Surgery, Greater Glasgow Health Board, 1972-99; Visiting Professor to National Centre for Training and Education in Prosthetics and Orthotics, Strathclyde University, 1981-2008; Member, Chief Scientist Committee and Chairman, Committee for Research on Equipment for Disabled, 1983-90; Chairman, Journal of Bone and Joint Surgery, 1995-2002 (Member, Editorial Board, 1978-82 and 1985-89); Secretary and Treasurer, JBJS Council of Management, 1992-95; Member, Physiological Systems Board, Medical Research Council, 1983-88; President, British Orthopaedic Association, 1990-91 (Chairman, Education Sub-Committee, 1986-89); Non-Executive Director, West Glasgow Hospitals University NHS Trust, 1994-97; Interim Board Member, Medical Devices in Scotland, 2001-02; Council Member, St. Andrews Ambulance Association, 1998-2013; Consulting Medical Editor, Orthopaedics Today International, 2002-2010; Member, Strathclyde Committee, Tenovus Scotland, since 2018. Publications: Outline of Fractures (Co-Author), (12th edition, 2007); Outline of Orthopaedics (Co-Author), (14th edition, 2010). Recreations: golf; curling. Address: (h.) 3 Russell Drive, Bearsden, Glasgow G61 3BB.

Hamblin, Janet, BSc (Maths), CA (ICAS), ICAEW. Non Executive Director, Royal Lyceum Theatre, since 2020; Non Executive Director and Chair of Audit and Risk Committee, Scottish Government, 2014-2020; Charities, Housing Associations and Education Audit Partner, RSM UK, 1997-2020. Educ. St Hilary's School; Edinburgh University; Heriot Watt University. Career history: Senior Manager, PwC, 1980-96; Director, Scottish Business in the Community, 2000-14. Recreations: golf; curling; theatre; foreign travel; dance.

Hamilton, Rev. Dr Alan James, LLB, BD, DipLP, PhD. Minister, Killermont Parish Church, Bearsden, since 2003; b. 14.8.63, Glasgow; m., Hazel; 3 s. Educ. Williamwood High School; Eastwood High School; Glasgow University; Edinburgh University. Solicitor, 1987; Advocate, 1990. Address: 8 Clathic Avenue, Bearsden, Glasgow G61 2HF; T.-0141 942 0021.
E-mail: ahamilton@churchofscotland.org.uk

Hamilton, 16th Duke of (Alexander Douglas-Hamilton). Hereditary Keeper of the Palace of Holyroodhouse; b. 31.3.78; m., Sophie Ann Rutherford; 3 s. Educ. Keil School, Dumbarton; Gordonstoun. Styled Marquess of Douglas and Clydesdale from birth until the 5th of June 2010; currently styled His Grace The Duke of Hamilton and Brandon.

Hamilton, Rt. Hon. Lord (Arthur Campbell Hamilton), BA (Oxon), LLB (Edin). Lord Justice General of Scotland and Lord President of the Court of Session, 2005-2012; b. 10.6.42, Glasgow; m., Christine Ann; 1 d. Educ. High School of Glasgow; Glasgow University; Worcester College, Oxford; Edinburgh University. Advocate, 1968; Standing Junior Counsel to Scottish Development Department, 1975-78, Inland Revenue (Scotland), 1978-82; Queen's Counsel, 1982; Advocate Depute, 1982-85; Judge of the Courts of Appeal of Jersey and of Guernsey, 1988-95; President, Pensions Appeal Tribunals for Scotland, 1992-95; Senator of the College of Justice, 1995-2005. Hon. Fellow, Worcester College, Oxford, 2003; Hon. Bencher, Inner Temple, 2006; Member, supplementary panel of the Supreme Court of the United Kingdom, 2012-17; Judge of the Court of Appeal of Botswana (part time, from 2012); Judge of the Qatar International Court (part time, since June 2015). Recreations: music; history. Address: 8 Heriot Row, Edinburgh EH3 HU; T.-0131-556-4663.

Hamilton, Sir David. Labour MP, Midlothian, 2001-2015; b. 24.10.50, Dalkeith; m., Jean; 2 d. Educ. Dalkeith High School. Former coal miner, landscape gardener, training officer, training manager, chief executive, and local councillor. Recreations: films; five grandchildren.

Hamilton, Gillian, BEd, MSc. Strategic Director, Education Scotland, since 2018. Educ. Craigie College of Education; University of Glasgow. Career history: East Ayrshire Council: Head Teacher, Stewarton, 2000-04, CPD Co-ordinator, 2004-07, Quality Improvement Officer, East Ayrshire, 2007-2011; Head of Educational Services, GTC Scotland, 2011-2014; Chief Executive, Scottish College for Educational Leadership, 2014-18. Address: Education Scotland, Denholm House, Almondvale Business Park, Almondvale Way, Livingston EH54 6GA; T.-0131 244 4330.

Hamilton, Ian Robertson, QC (Scot), BL, LLD (Hon); b. 13.9.25, Paisley; m., Jeannette Patricia Mairi Stewart; 1 s.; 1 s., 2 d. by pr. m. Educ. John Neilson School, Paisley; Allan Glen's School, Glasgow; Glasgow University; Edinburgh University. RAFVR, 1944-48; called to Scottish Bar, 1954, and to Albertan Bar, 1982; Founder, Castle Wynd Printers, Edinburgh, 1955; Advocate Depute, 1962; Director of Civil Litigation, Republic of Zambia, 1964-66; Hon. Sheriff of Lanarkshire, 1967; retired from practice to work for National Trust for Scotland and later to farm in Argyll, 1969; returned to practice, 1974; Sheriff of Glasgow and Strathkelvin, May-December, 1984; returned to practice. Chief Pilot, Scottish Parachute Club, 1979-90; Student President, Heriot-Watt University, 1990-96; Rector, Aberdeen University, 1994-96; Honorary Member, Sir William Wallace Free Colliers of Scotland, 1997. University of Aberdeen, 1997: LLD (Hon), Hon Research Fellow; Sorley Lifetime Achievement Award, 2008; Law Awards, Scotland 2009 Lifetime Achievement. Publications: No Stone Unturned, 1952; The Tinkers of the World, 1957 (Foyle award-winning play); A Touch of Treason, 1990; The Taking of the Stone of Destiny, 1991, reprinted as Stone of Destiny, 2008 (film of same name released in Scotland, 2008 and worldwide, 2009); A Touch More Treason, 1993; From Amento Boothill (e-book), 2011. Recreation: being grumpy. Address: (h.) Lochnaheithe, North Connel, Argyll PA37 1QX; T.-01631 710 427.

Hamilton, Rev. Ian William Finlay, BD, LTH, ALCM, AVCM. Minister Emeritus, Nairn Old Parish Church, 1986-2012; b. 29.11.46, Glasgow; m., Margaret McLaren Moss; 1 s.; 2 d. Educ. Victoria Drive Senior Secondary School, Glasgow; University of Glasgow and Trinity College. Employed in banking, then music publishing; ordained, Alloa North Parish Church, 1978. Moderator, Presbytery of Inverness, 1990-91; Member: General Assembly Parish Re-appraisal Committee, 1994-97; former Member, General Assembly Maintenance of the Ministry Committee; Chaplain to the Moderator of the General Assembly of the Church of Scotland, 2005/06; has participated in several pulpit exchanges to Churches in the USA; Presenter, Reflections (Grampian TV), Crossfire (Moray Firth Radio). Publications: Reflections from the Manse Window; Second Thoughts; They're Playing My Song; Take Four!; I'm Trying to Connect You!; From Pen to Parish; A Preacher's Dozen; A Century of Christian Witness; several children's talks published in The Expository Times; regular contributor to Manse Window page in People's Friend. Recreations: music (piano and organ); writing; broadcasting on radio and television. Address: (h.) "Mossneuk", 5 Windsor Gardens, St Andrews, Fife KY16 8XL; T.-(h.) 01334 477745; e-mail: reviwfh@btinternet.com

Hamilton, Dr Mark Patrick Rogers, MBChB, MD, FRCOG. Consultant Gynaecologist, Aberdeen Maternity Hospital, 1990-2018 (retired); Honorary Clinical Senior Lecturer, Aberdeen University; b. 24.4.55, Glasgow; m., Susan Elizabeth Duckworth; 1 s.; 1 d. Educ. High School of Glasgow; Glasgow University. Lecturer, National University of Singapore, 1985-87; Senior Registrar, Glasgow Royal Infirmary, 1987-90. Chair, British Fertility Society Executive Committee (2006-08); Chair, of Board of Trustees, British Fertility Society Charity, since 2019; International Federation of Fertility Societies Board Member, since 2015.
E-mail: m.hamilton@abdn.ac.uk

Hamilton, Rachael Georgina. MSP (Scottish Conservative), Ettrick, Roxburgh & Berwickshire, since 2017; Shadow Cabinet Secretary for Rural Affairs and Islands; b. 9.70; m.; 3 c. Formerly MSP for South Scotland region, 2016-17, before winning by-election in 2017 and subsequent Scottish Parliament Election in 2021. Director of Borders Hotels Ltd. Address: Scottish Parliament, Edinburgh EH99 1SP.

Hamilton, Trisha. Communications Officer Scotland, UNISON Scotland. Address: (b.) UNISON House, 14 West Campbell Street, Glagow G2 6RX; T.-0141 342 2877; e-mail: t.hamilton@unison.co.uk

Hammond, Charles, OBE. Chief Executive Officer, Forth Ports Limited, since 2001; Non Executive Director, Ports of Jersey Ltd, since 2019; Non Executive Chairman, Space and People, 2014-18. Educ. Airdrie Academy; University of Glasgow; University of Toronto; Fellow of Chartered Institute of Logistics and Transport. Career history: served at McGrigor Donald; joined Forth Ports as Company Secretary in 1989, appointed Commercial Director in 1992; appointed Managing Director, Port of Tilbury London Limited in 1995; former Chairman of Scottish Enterprise Edinburgh. Currently a member of The Scottish Energy Advisory Board and a member of the Cabinet Secretary's 2020 Vision for Health & Social Care. Address: Forth Ports Limited, Registered Office: 1 Prince of Wales Dock, Edinburgh EH6 7DX; T.-0131 555 8700.

Hampshire, Cllr Norman. Leader of East Lothian Council, since 2021; represents Dunbar and East Linton (Scottish Labour Party); Proprietor, The Eden Hotel, Dunbar; Director, Dunbar Community Development and Heritage Trust, since 1998; b. 9.59, Dunbar. Address: East Lothian Council, John Muir House, Brewery Park, Haddington, East Lothian EH41 3HA; T.-01620 827009; e-mail: nhampshire@eastlothian.gov.uk

Hampson, Christopher. Chief Executive/Artistic Director, Scottish Ballet, since 2015, Artistic Director, since 2012; b. 31.3.73. Educ. Royal Ballet School. English National Ballet (ENB), until 1999, created numerous award-winning works, including Double Concerto (Critics' Circle National Dance Award and TMA Theatre Award), Perpetuum Mobile, Country Garden, Concerto Grosso, Trapèze and The Nutcracker. Romeo and Juliet, created for the Royal New Zealand Ballet (RNZB), was nominated for a Laurence Olivier Award (Best New Production). Created Sinfonietta Giocosa for the Atlanta Ballet (USA) in 2006 and after a New York tour it received its UK premiere with ENB in 2007; created Cinderella for RNZB in 2007, which was subsequently hailed as Best New Production by the New Zealand Herald and televised by TVNZ in 2009. Work has toured Australia, China, the USA and throughout Europe; most recent commissions are Dear Norman (Royal Ballet, 2009); Sextet (Ballet Black/ROH2, 2010); Silhouette (RNZB, 2010), Rite of Spring (Atlanta Ballet, 2011) and Storyville (Ballet Black/ROH2, 2012 and National Dance Award nominated). Co-founder of the International Ballet Masterclasses in Prague and has been a guest teacher for English National Ballet, Royal Swedish Ballet, Royal New Zealand Ballet, Hong Kong Ballet, Atlanta Ballet, Bonachela Dance Company, Matthew Bourne's New Adventures and the Genée International Ballet Competition; work now forms part of the Solo Seal Award for the Royal Academy of Dance; participated in TEDx Glasgow, giving a talk on 'Creative Thinking'; also developed and led the inaugural Young Rural Retreat for Aspiring Leaders, in association with Dance East. Address: Scottish Ballet, Tramway, 25 Albert Drive, Glasgow G41 2PE; T.-0141 331 2931.

Hancock, Professor Peter J. B., PhD, MSc, MA. Professor of Psychology, University of Stirling, since 2007; b. 1958, UK; m., Clare Allan; 2 s. Educ. Leighton Park School, Reading; Trinity College, Oxford. Synthetic chemist, computer programmer, systems manager, Amersham International plc, 1980-87; University of Stirling: Research Fellow, 1987-95, Lecturer, Psychology, 1995, Senior Lecturer, 2002. Recreation: photography. Address: (b.) Psychology, Faculty of Natural Sciences, University of Stirling, Stirling FK9 4LA; T.-01786 467675.
E-mail: p.j.b.hancock@stir.ac.uk

Hanlon, Professor Philip, BSc, MD, MRCGP, FRCP, FFPHM, MPH. Honorary Senior Research Fellow (Institute of Health & Wellbeing), University of Glasgow (appointed Professor of Public Health in 1999);

b. 24.6.54, British North Borneo; m., Lesley; 1 s.; 1 d. Educ. Uddingston Grammar School; Glasgow University. Research Scientist, Medical Research Council, The Gamba, 1984-87; Consultant in Public Health Medicine and Director of Health Promotion, Greater Glasgow Health Board, 1988-93; Medical Director, Royal Alexandra Hospital, Paisley, 1993-94; Senior Lecturer in Public Health, Glasgow University, since 1999; Director, Public Health Institute of Scotland, 2001-03. Recreations: cycling; walking; reading; spending time with family. Address: (b.) Public Health, University of Glasgow, 1 Lilybank Garden G12 8RZ. T.-0141 330 5641; e-mail: phil.hanlon@glasgow.ac.uk

Hanna, Linda. Board Chair, SRUC - Scotland's Rural College, Edinburgh, since 2022; Estates Committee Member, University of Glasgow (Part-time), since 2021; Interim Chief Executive, Scottish Enterprise, 2020-September 2021 (Managing Director, Scottish Economic Development, 2018-2020; Strategy & Economics Director, 2013-2018). Joined Scottish Enterprise in 1991; previous roles have included leading the Scottish Enterprise approach to support growth businesses in Scotland, identifying how to help businesses achieve and accelerate sustainable growth and sector-specific work such as aerospace and food and drink; works closely with some of Scotland's key partners in public sector agencies.

Hannaford, Professor Philip Christopher, FRSE, MD, MBChB, FRCGP, FFPH, FFRSH, DRCOG, DCH. NHS Grampian Emeritus Professor of Primary Care, University of Aberdeen, since 2020; Professor of Primary Care, 1997-2020; Vice Principal (Digital Strategy), 2014-18; Guardian, RCGP Oral Contraception Study, since 2001; Head, College of Life Sciences and Medicine, 2014-17; Vice Principal, Research and Knowledge Exchange, 2011-14; Director, Institute of Applied Health Sciences, 2002-2011; b. 1.7.58, London; m., Dr. Anne Carol Gilchrist; 1 s.; 1 d. Educ. Aberdeen Grammar School; Aberdeen University. GP training, Sheffield, 1982-85; research training posts, RCGP Manchester Research Unit, 1986-94; Principal, general practice, Manchester, 1986-92; Director, RCGP Manchester Research Unit, 1994-97. Publications: Evidence Guided Prescribing of the Pill (Co-Editor); over 220 contributions on contraception, cardiovascular disease, primary care epidemiology, HRT in scientific journals. Recreations: family; walking; music; cycling. Address: (b.) Academic Primary Care, Polwarth Building, Foresterhill, Aberdeen AB25 2ZD; T.-01224 437211.

Hanvey, James Neale, RGN, DipHE, MSc. MP: Alba (Kirkcaldy and Cowdenbeath), since 2021; SNP, 2020-21; Independent, 2019-20; b. 12.64. Educ. Napier University; London South Bank University; City University. Career history: University College London Hospitals NHS Foundation Trust: Teenage Cancer Trust Unit Charge Nurse, 1998-2002, Senior Nurse Oncology, 2002-05; Divisional Nurse Director, The Royal Marsden NHS Foundation Trust, 2005-2010; Councillor, Fife Council, 2012-17; Freelance Videographer, 2017-19. Address: Houses of Parliament, Westminster, London SW1A 0AA.

Hardacre, Jacky. Chief Executive, Scottish Youth Theatre, since 2016. Career history: Artistic Director, Burnley Youth Theatre, 1997-2005; Cultural Coordinator (Museums, Galleries & Heritage), Aberdeen City Council, 2008-2012, Creative Learning Manager, 2012-16. Address: Scottish Youth Theatre, The Old Sheriff Court, 105 Brunswick Street, Glasgow G1 1TF; T.-0141 552 3988.
E-mail: info@scottishyouththeatre.org

Hardcastle, Professor Emeritus William John, BA, MA, PhD, Hon DSc, FBA, FRSE, Hon FRCSLT.

Director, Speech Science Research Centre, 2004-09; Dean of Research, Queen Margaret University, 1999-2004; Professor of Speech Sciences, since 1993; Dean of Health Sciences, 1999-2002; b. 28.9.43, Brisbane; m., Francesca; 2 s.; 1 d. Educ. Brisbane Grammar School; University of Queensland; Edinburgh University. Lecturer, Institut für Phonetik, Universität Kiel, 1973-74; Lecturer, then Reader, then Professor, Department of Linguistic Science, Reading University, 1974-93; Director, Scottish Centre for Research into Speech Disability, 1997-2003. President, International Clinical Phonetics and Linguistics Association, 1991-2000; Convenor, Scottish Universities Research Policy Consortium, 2001. Publications include: Physiology of Speech Production; Disorders of Fluency and their Effects on Communication (Co-Author); Speech Production and Speech Modelling (Co-Editor); Handbook of Phonetic Sciences (Co-Editor); Co-articulation: Theory, Data and Techniques (Co-Editor). Recreations: hill-walking; badminton; gardening; golf. Address: (b.) Queen Margaret University, Queen Margaret University Drive, Musselburgh, East Lothian EH21 6UU; T.-0131-4740000.

Hardie, Rt. Hon The Lord (Andrew Rutherford Hardie), PC, QC (Scot); b. 8.1.46, Stirling; m., Catherine Storrar Elgin; 2 s.; 1 d. Educ. St. Modan's High School, Stirling; Edinburgh University. Enrolled Solicitor, 1971; Member, Faculty of Advocates, 1973; Advocate Depute, 1979-83; Dean, Faculty of Advocates, 1994-97; Lord Advocate, 1997-2000; created Life Peer and Privy Counsellor, 1997; Senator of the College of Justice, 2000-2012. Address: (b.) House of Lords, Westminster, London SW1A 0PW.

Hardie, David, LLB Hons, WS. Interim Chair, Murray International Trust PLC, since 2021; Non-Executive Director, Murray International Trust PLC, since 2014; Non-Executive Chairman, WNL Investments Limited (formerly WN Lindsay Ltd), since 2014; b. 17.9.54, Glasgow; m., Fiona Mairi Willox; 3 s. Educ. Greenock High School; University of Dundee. Dundas & Wilson CS (now CMS), 1976-2014: Apprentice Solicitor, 1976-78; Solicitor, 1978-83; Partner, 1983-2014; Head of former Corporate Department and latterly Head of Corporate Finance, 1987-97; Interim Managing Partner and Head of Corporate Finance, 1997-98; Head of Corporate, 1998-2004; Head of Knowledge & Learning, 2005-06; Chairman, 2009-12. Notary Public, 1982-2014. Head of Venture Philanthropy, Inspiring Scotland (charity), 2008-2016; Non-Executive Chairman, Keppie Design Ltd, 2015-2017 (fixed 2 year appointment). E-mail: david_hardie@icloud.com

Hardie, Donald Graeme, CVO, KStJ, TD, JP, FIMMM. Director, Hardie Polymers Ltd., 1976-2001; b. 23.1.36, Glasgow; m. (1961) 1, Rosalind Allan Ker (divorced 1995); 2 s.; m. (1999) 2, Sheena McQueen. Educ. Blairmore and Merchiston Castle. Commissioned 41st Field Regiment RA, 1955; Battery Commander 277 (Argyll & Sutherland Highlanders) Regiment RA (TA), 1966; Commanding Officer GSVOTC, 1973; TA Col. Lowlands, 1976; TA Col. DES, 1980; TA Col. Scotland, 1985; ACF Brigadier Scotland, 1987; Hon. Colonel Commandant, Royal Regiment of Artillery, 2003-07 (retired); Vice President, NAA, 2003-2018. UTR Management Trainee, 1956-59; F.W. Allan & Ker, Shipbrokers, 1960-61; J. & G. Hardie & Co. Ltd., 1961-2001 (former Chairman); Director, Gilbert Plastics Ltd., 1973-76; Director, Ronaash Ltd., 1988-99; Director, Preston Associates (Europe) Ltd., 2002-04; Managing Director, Preston Stretchform Ltd., 2004-2011. Lord Lieutenant, Dunbartonshire, 1990-2007; Hon. Col. 105 Regiment RA(V), 1992-99; Hon. Col. Glasgow & Lanarkshire ACF, 1991-2000; Keeper, Dumbarton Castle, since 1996; Chairman, RA Council of Scotland, 1993-2000; former Chieftain, Loch Lomond Games (retired, 2009); former Trustee, Tullochan Trust (retired, 2011). Recreations: skiing; sailing; shooting; fishing. Address: (h.) East Lodge, Arden, Dunbartonshire G83 8RD; e-mail: donalddghardie@gmail.com

Hardie, Fraser. Partner, Blackadders Solicitors, since 2015; Consultant, Lindsays, 2013-2015; b. 4.4.59. Educ. Aberdeen University. Address: (b.) 5 Rutland Square, Edinburgh, Midlothian EH1 2AX; T.-0131 222 8000.

Hardie, Katharine, LLB (Hons), DLP. Chair, Scotland and Northern Ireland, Pinsent Masons, since 2019; b. 10.67. Educ. Harlaw Academy, Aberdeen; Aberdeen University. Career history: joined Pinsent Masons as a trainee lawyer in 1990; Partner: McGrigors, 2001-2012, Pinsent Masons, since 2012; specialises in commercial and residential property development and recently acted for Barclays Bank in its acquisition of a new office campus at Buchanan Wharf in Glasgow. Address: Pinsent Masons, 141 Bothwell Street, Glasgow G2 7EQ; T.-0141 567 8400.

Harding, Professor Dennis William, MA, DPhil, FRSE. Abercromby Professor of Archaeology, University of Edinburgh, 1977-2007; b. 11.4.40; m., Carole J.A. Forbes. Educ. Keble College, University of Oxford. Assistant Keeper, Department of Antiquities, Ashmolean Museum, University of Oxford, 1965; Lecturer in Celtic Archaeology, University of Durham, 1966 (Senior Lecturer, 1975); Dean, Faculty of Arts, 1983-86, Vice-Principal, 1988-91, University of Edinburgh. Member, S.A.A.S. Studentships Committee, 1982-2001 (Chairman, 1997-2001). Address: (h.) Hilltop Cottage, Hill Road, Gullane, East Lothian EH31 2BE.

Hardy, Richard John. Just Transition Commissioner, Scottish Government's Just Transition Commission, 2018-2021; National Secretary, Scotland, Prospect (formerly IPMS), since 2017; b. 7.6.68, Hemsworth; m., Carley Louise Wood. Educ. Lytham St Annes County High School; University of London (Queen Mary College); Leading Change Graduate, TUC/Harvard Law School. Civil Service (Department for Social Security), 1990-2000; Prospect (formerly IPMS), since 2000. Member: Scottish Government Tourism Taskforce, since 2020, Scottish Government Sustainable Renewal Advisory Group, since 2020. Address: Ground Floor, Cairncross House, 25 Union Street, Edinburgh EH1 3LR; T.-0131 558 2660.

Hargreave, Timothy Bruce, MB, MS, FRCSEdin, FRCS, FEB (Urol), FRCP(Ed). Senior Fellow, Department of Surgery, University of Edinburgh, Medical School, Little France, Edinburgh; b. 23.3.44, Lytham; m., Molly; 2 d. Educ. Harrow; University College Hospital, London University. Senior Registrar: Western Infirmary, Glasgow, University College Hospital, London; Co-Chair, Technical Advisory Group on Devices and Innovations for Male Circumcision, Department of HIV, WHO Geneva; former Consultant Urologist and Renal Transplant Surgeon, Western General Hospital, Edinburgh; Medical Officer, Paray Mission Hospital, Lesotho; former Chair, Science and Ethics Review Group, Human Reproduction Programme, WHO Geneva. Publications: Diagnosis and Management of Renal and Urinary Disease; Male Infertility (Editor); Practical Urological Endoscopy; The Management of Male Infertility; Andrology for the Clinician (Joint Editor), English Edition, 2006, French Edition, 2008, Russian Edition, 2011; WHO Manual for Male Circumcision under Local Anaesthesia and HIV Prevention Services for Adolescent Boys and Men, 2018. Recreation: skiing. Address: (h.) 20 Cumin Place, Edinburgh.

Harkess, Janette, MA (Hons). Director of External Relations, Royal Conservatoire of Scotland, since 2015. Educ. University of Edinburgh (English Language &

Linguisitics). Career history: Deputy Editor: The Evening Times, 2000-06, The Herald, 2006-09; Director of Policy and Research, Scottish Council for Development and Industry, Glasgow, 2009-2011; Head of Media, Glasgow 2014, 2011-2014; Strategic Consultant, Commonwealth Games Federation, 2014-15. Appointed in 2014 to the UK press regulator, the Independent Press Standards Organisation (IPSO), sat on the Complaints Committee, 2014-2021; an Honorary Vice President of the Journalists' Charity; served as a Commissioner to the Poverty Truth Commission in Scotland; Board Member, National Theatre of Scotland; British Council Scotland, Advisory Committee. Address: Royal Conservatoire of Scotland, 100 Renfrew Street, Glasgow G2 3DB; T.-0141 332 4101. E-mail: j.harkess@rcs.ac.uk

Harkess, Ronald Dobson, OBE, BSc, MS, PhD, NDA, CBiol, MRSB, FRAgS, FRSA, FFCS. Emeritus Fellow, Scottish Rural University College; Agricultural Scientist and Consultant; b. 11.7.33, Edinburgh; m., Jean Cuthbert Drennan (deceased); 2 d. Educ. Royal High School, Edinburgh; Edinburgh University; Cornell University. Senior Fison Research Fellow, Nottingham University, 1959-62; Assistant Grassland Adviser, West of Scotland Agricultural College, Ayr, 1962-72; Senior Agronomist, 1972-86; Technical Secretary, Council, Scottish Agricultural Colleges, 1986-90, Company Secretary, 1987-90; Company Secretary, Scottish Agricultural College, 1990-91; Assistant Principal, Scottish Agricultural College, 1991-93. Past President, Scotia Agricultural Club; Secretary, Perth Amateur Radio Group, since 1993; Past President, Tay Probus. Recreations: amateur radio; philately; gardening. Address: (h.) Friarton Bank, Rhynd Road, Perth PH2 8PT; T.-01738 643435.

Harkness, Very Rev. James, KCVO, CB, OBE, KStJ (2012), MA, DD, FRSA. Extra Chaplain to the Queen, since 2006; Dean of the Chapel Royal in Scotland, 1996-2006; Moderator, General Assembly of the Church of Scotland, 1995-96; Dean of the Order of St. John in Scotland, 2005-2011; President: Royal British Legion, Scotland, 2001-06, Earl Haig Fund Scotland, 2001-06, The Officers' Association, Scotland, 2001-06; Member, Board, Mercy Corps Scotland, 2001-09; b. 20.10.35, Thornhill; m., Elizabeth Anne; 1 s.; 1 d. Educ. Dumfries Academy; Edinburgh University. Assistant Minister, North Morningside Parish Church, 1959-61; Chaplain: KOSB, 1961-65, Queen's Own Highlanders, 1965-69; Singapore, 1969-70; Deputy Warden, RAChD, 1970-74; Senior Chaplain, Northern Ireland, 1974-75; 4th Division, 1975-78; Staff Chaplain, HQ BAOR, 1978-80; Assistant Chaplain General, Scotland, 1980-81; Senior Chaplain, 1st British Corps, 1981-82; BAOR, 1982-84; Deputy Chaplain General, 1985-86; Chaplain General to the Forces, 1987-95. QHC, 1982-95; General Trustee, Church of Scotland, 1996-2011; Chairman, Carberry Board, 1997-2000; Member, Committee on Chaplains to HM Forces, 1997-2005; Member, Board of World Mission, 1997-2000; President, Army Cadet Force Association Scotland, 1996-2004; President, Society of Friends of St. Andrew's, Jerusalem, 1998-2005. Hon. Chaplain to BLESMA, 1995-2002; Governor, Fettes College, 1999-2009; Trustee, Scottish National War Memorial, 2003-2015. Recreations: walking; reading; watching sport. Address: (h.) Lang Glen, Durisdeer, Thornhill, Dumfriesshire DG3 5BJ; T.-01848 500 225.

Harlen, Professor Wynne, OBE, MA (Oxon), MA (Bristol), PhD. Director, Scottish Council for Research in Education, 1990-99; Visiting Professor, University of Bristol, since 1999; Project Director, University of Cambridge, 2003-06; b. 12.1.37, Swindon; 1 s.; 1 d. Educ. Pate's Grammar School for Girls, Cheltenham; St.

Hilda's College, Oxford; Bristol University. Teacher/Lecturer, 1958-66; Research Associate, Bristol University School of Education, 1966-73; Research Fellow, Project Director, Reading University, 1973-77; Research Fellow, Centre for Science Education, King's College, London, 1977-84; Sidney Jones Professor of Science Education, Liverpool University, 1985-90; Director, Scottish Council for Research in Education, 1990-99. Chair, Children in Scotland Early Years Forum, 1991-95; Member, Secretary of State's Working Party on the Development of the National Curriculum in Science, 1987-88; President, British Educational Research Association, 1993-94; Chair, OECD Science Expert Group, 1997-2003; Fellow, Educational Institute of Scotland, 2000; Fellow, Scottish Council for Research in Education, 2002; Member, Interacademies Working Group on IBSE, 2005-2012; Member, International Advisory Board of the global IAP Science Education Programme; President, Association for Science Education, 2009; Chair, Working Group of the Royal Society for SRN report on Science and mathematics Education 5-13. Awarded the OBE for services to education in 1991 and given a special award for distinguished service to science education by the (ASE) in 2001. In 2008 she was a winner of the international Purkwa prize for science education; honoured by the Mexican Ministry of Education in 2011. Publications: 43 books, and contributions to 54 others; 180 papers. Recreations: concerts; opera; piano playing. Address: Haymount Coach House, Bridgend, Duns, Berwickshire TD11 3DJ; T.-01361 884710.

Harley, Professor Simon Leigh, BSc (Hons), MA (Oxon), PhD, FRSE. Professor of Lower Crustal Processes, Edinburgh University, since 1997; b. 2.7.56, Sydney, Australia; m., Anne Elizabeth; 3 s.; 1 d. Educ. Punchbowl Boys' High School; University of New South Wales; University of Tasmania. Post-doctoral Research Assistant, ETH-Zentrum, Zurich, 1981-83; Lecturer: Oxford University/Fellow St Edmund Hall, 1983-88; Edinburgh University, 1988-92; Reader, Edinburgh University, 1992-97. Member: Sciennes School Board, 1992-96, Australian National Antarctic Research Expeditions (ANARE), 1979-80, 1982-83, 1987-88, 1992-93 and 2006-07; Polar Medal, 2002; Member, CoRWM, 2007-2016; Mineralogical Society Schlumberger Medal, 2015. Recreations: hill walking; skiing; cycling. Address: (h.) 15 Moston Terrace, Newington, Edinburgh EH9 2DE; T.-0131-650 4839; e-mail: Simon.Harley@ed.ac.uk

Harper, Emma. MSP (SNP), South Scotland region, since 2016; b. Stranraer. Former Clinical Nurse Educator, NHS Dumfries and Galloway. SNP candidate for Dumfriesshire, Clydesdale & Tweeddale in the 2015 UK Parliament election. Address: (b.) Unit 7, Loreburne Shopping Centre, High Street, Dumfries DG1 2BD.

Harper, Professor John, PhD, FRSC. Former Principal, Robert Gordon University (2018-2020); b. Wick; m; 4 c. Educ. University of Aberdeen. Career history: Lecturer in Chemistry at the former Robert Gordon Institute of Technology and subsequently progressed to Senior-Lectureship and then Head of School of Applied Sciences; Robert Gordon University: Assistant Principal; Dean of the Faculty of Health and Social Care; Deputy Principal and Chief Academic Officer; Deputy Principal and Vice Chancellor. Member of a number of national committees associated with institutional quality assurance, quality enhancement and widening participation; former member of the Health Professions Council; current member of the Board of Management of North East Scotland College and School Council for St Margaret's School for Girls,

Aberdeen. Recreations: enjoys following a range of sports with active participation now being restricted to playing golf!

Harper, Robin C. M., OBE (2018), MA, DipGC, Hon. FRIAS, FRSA. FEIS, FRSSA. MSP, Lothians, 1999-2011; Co-Convener, Scottish Green Party, 2004-08; Chairman, Scottish Wildlife Trust, 2014-2017; Hon.Vice President, Arboriculture Association, since 2010; b. 4.8.40, Thurso; m., Jenny Helen Carter Brown. Educ. St. Marylebone Grammar School; Elgin Academy; Aberdeen University. Teacher, Braehead School, Fife, 1964-68; Education Officer, Kenya, 1968-70; Assistant Principal Teacher, Boroughmuir High School, 1972-99; Musical Director, Theatre Workshop, Edinburgh, 1972-75, member of board 2002-5; President, Edinburgh Classical Guitar Society, 1980-90; Member, Lothian Children's Panel, 1985-88; Member, Lothian Health Council, 1993-97; President, EIS Edinburgh Local Association, 1990-91; elected Rector: University of Edinburgh, 2000-03, Aberdeen University, 2005-08; Parliament responsibilities included Convener, CPG's (Cross Party Groups): Children and Young People, Architecture and the Built Environment, Renewable Energy and Energy Efficiency; Member, Environment and Transport Committee, Petitions Committee; Elected Trustee, National Trust for Scotland, 2011-2018; Trustee, Scottish Wildlife Trust, 2011-2017; Ambassador, Play Scotland, since 2011; Ambassador, Edinburgh & Lothians Greenspace Trust, 2011; Patron, Scottish Ecological Design Association, since 2011; Trustee, Dundee Students Association, 2012-14; Chair of Board of Trustees, Communicado Theatre Company, 2011-13; Patron: South Edinburgh Older People's Arts Festival, since 2012, E.U. Savoy Opera Group, 2001-2014, Forth Children's Theatre Company, since 1999; Board of Trustees: ESU English Speaking Union, 2011-15, Scottish Lime Centre, 2008-2011; Interim Convener, Astley Ainslie Community Trust, since 2018. Recreations: music; walking; travel; theatre; growing oak trees. Address: 11 Greenbank Terrace, Edinburgh EH10 6ER.

Harries, Professor Jill Diana, MA, DPhil, FRSE (2010), FRHistS. Emeritus Professor of Ancient History, St Andrews University (Professor, 1997-2014, Head of School, Greek, Latin and Ancient History, 2000-03); b. 20.5.50, London. Educ. Bromley High School GPDST; Somerville College, Oxford. Kennedy Scholar, 1973-74; Lecturer in Ancient History, St Andrews University, 1976-95; Senior Lecturer, 1995-97; Visiting Fellow, All Souls College, Oxford, 1996-97; Leverhulme Fellow, 1996-97; Bird Exchange Fellow, Emory, Atlanta, 2003; Member of Council, St Leonard's School, St Andrews, 1998-2000. Publications: Religious Conflict in Fourth Century Rome, 1983; The Theodusian Code (Editor), 1993; Sidonius Apollinaris and the Fall of Rome, 1994; Law and Empire in Late Antiquity, 1998; Cicero and the Jurists, 2006; Law and Crime in the Roman World, 2007; Imperial Rome AD 284-363: The New Empire (2012). Recreations: travel; hill-walking. Address: (b.) School of Classics, St Salvator's College, St Andrews KY16 9AL; T.-01334 462600.

Harris, Alison. MSP (Scottish Conservative), Central Scotland region, 2016-2021; former Scottish Conservative spokesperson for taxation and financial sustainability; former Deputy Convener of the Public Audit Committee; b. 23.7.65. Chartered accountant. Conservative candidate (Falkirk constituency) for the 2015 United Kingdom general election; Falkirk West constituency candidate for the 2016 Scottish Parliament election.

Harris, Rev. John William Forsyth, MA; b. 10.3.42, Hampshire; m., Ellen Lesley Kirkpatrick Lamont; 1 s.; 2 d.

Educ. Merchant Taylors' School, London; St. Andrews University; New College, Edinburgh. Ordained Assistant, St. Mary's, Haddington, 1967-70; Minister: St. Andrew's, Irvine, 1970-77, St. Mary's, Motherwell, 1977-87, Bearsden South, 1987-2006, Bearsden Cross, 2006-2012. Convener: Scottish Churches' Christian Aid Committee, 1986-90, Scottish Christian Aid Committee, 1990-98, Scottish Television's Religious Advisory Committee, 1990-98, Jubilee Scotland, 2001-06, Scottish Palestinian Forum West of Scotland Committee, 2005-07; Vice-Convener, Board of World Mission, 1996-99; Member: Jubilee 2000 Scottish Coalition Steering Group, 1997-2000, Board of Christian Aid, 1990-98, Executive, Church and Nation Committee, 1985-91, Executive, Scottish Churches Council, 1986-90, Make Poverty History Scottish Coalition Steering Group, 2005. Moderator, Dumbarton Presbytery, 1994-95. Fencing Blue, St. Andrews and Edinburgh; Scottish Fencing Team, 1963-66; Scottish Sabre Champion, 1965. Recreations: enjoying grandchildren; holiday home in Kintyre. Address: Flat 21, Strathmore Court, 20 Abbey Drive, Jordanhill, Glasgow G14 9JX; T.-0141 321 1061.
E-mail: jwfh@sky.com

Harris, Julie Elizabeth, LLB (Hons), DipLP, NP. Solicitor Advocate; b. 10.12.71, Farnborough, Kent. Educ. John Paul Academy, Glasgow; Strathclyde University. Joined Allan McDougall & Co, SSC, as trainee Solicitor, 1994; Qualified Solicitor, since 1996. Address: (b.) 3 Coates Crescent, Edinburgh EH3 7AL; T.-0131-225 2121.

Harris, Stewart. Chief Executive, sportscotland, since 2005. Previously held positions at sportscotland of Acting Chief Executive and Director of Widening Opportunities (responsible for developing the School Sport Co-ordinator Programme and Active Schools Network, which is playing a key part in increasing physical activity levels of children in schools across Scotland); 12 years as a PE teacher. Lifelong involvement with basketball in Scotland as a board member, club and international coach for 25 years at both Scottish and Great Britain students level, as well as extensive experience of working with local authorities. Address: (b.) Doges, Templeton on the Green, 62 Templeton Street, Glasgow G40 1DA; T.-0141 534 6500.

Harris, Tom. Director, Third Avenue Public Affairs, since 2015; Non-Executive Director, HS2 Ltd, since 2020; Labour MP, Glasgow South, 2005-2015; Glasgow Cathcart, 2001-05; Shadow Minister for the Environment, Food and Rural Affairs, 2012-13; b. 20.2.64, Irvine; m., Carolyn Moffat; 3 s. Educ. Garnock Academy; Napier College. Reporter, East Kilbride News/Paisley Daily Express, 1986-90; Press Officer, Labour Party in Scotland, 1990-92; Press Officer, Strathclyde Regional Council, 1993-96; Senior Media Officer, Glasgow City Council, 1996; Public Relations Manager, East Ayrshire Council, 1996-98; Chief Public Relations Officer, SPTE, 1998-2001; Parliamentary Private Secretary to Rt. Hon. John Spellar MP, 2004-05; Parliamentary Private Secretary to Rt. Hon. Patricia Hewitt MP, 2005-06; Parliamentary Under Secretary of State for Transport, 2006-08. Recreations: tennis; astronomy; cinema; hill-walking.
E-mail: info@thirdavenue.org.uk

Harrison, Professor Andrew, OBE, BA, MA, DPhil (Oxon), CChem, FRSC, FRSE. Honorary Professor, University of Edinburgh (appointed Professor of Solid State Chemistry in 1999); Chief Executive Officer, Diamond Light Source Ltd, since 2014; b. 3.10.59, Oxford; m., Alison Ironside-Smith; 3 d. Educ. Newcastle-under-Lyme High School; St John's College, Oxford. Fereday Fellow, St John's College, Oxford, 1985-88; Research Fellow, McMaster University, Canada, 1988-89; Royal Society University Research Fellow, 1990-92; Reader, Department of Chemistry, Edinburgh University, 1996; Nuffield Research Fellow, 1997-98; Eminent Visiting Professor, Riken, Japan, 2000-2003; appointed Director, Institut Laue-Langevin, Grenoble in 2006 (on secondment from Edinburgh University); Honorary Fellow, St. John's College, Oxford, since 2015; Honorary Doctorate, Bath University, 2019. Recreations: cycling on and off-road; skiing; music of almost every variety; eating and drinking.

Harrison, Professor Bryan Desmond, CBE, BSc, PhD, Hon. DAgricFor, FRS, FRSE. Emeritus Professor of Plant Virology, Dundee University, since 1997 (Professor of Plant Virology, 1991-96); b. 16.6.31, Purley, Surrey; m., Elizabeth Ann Latham-Warde; 2 s.; 1 d. Educ. Whitgift School, Croydon; Reading University. Agricultural Research Council Postgraduate Research Student, 1952-54; Scientific Officer, Scottish Horticultural Research Institute, 1954-57; Senior and Principal Scientific Officer, Rothamsted Experimental Station, 1957-66; Scottish Horticultural Research Institute/Scottish Crop Research Institute: Principal Scientific Officer, 1966, Senior Principal Scientific Officer (Individual Merit), 1969, Deputy Chief Scientific Officer (Individual Merit), 1981; Head, Virology Department, 1966-91; Foreign Associate, US National Academy of Sciences; Honorary Professor, Department of Biochemistry and Microbiology, St. Andrews University, 1987-99; Honorary Research Fellow, The James Hutton Institute, since 1991; Honorary Visiting Professor, Dundee University, 1987-91; Honorary Visiting Professor, Zhejiang University, China, since 2001; Past President, Association of Applied Biologists; Honorary Member: Association of Applied Biologists, Phytopathological Society of Japan, Society for General Microbiology; Honorary Fellow, Indian Virological Society. Recreation: gardening. Address: (b.) The James Hutton Institute, Invergowrie, Dundee DD2 5DA; e-mail: BryanHarrison@Hutton.ac.uk

Harrison, Professor David James, BSc, MBChB, MD, FRCPath, FRCPE, FRCSE. Director of Laboratory Medicine, NHS Lothian, since 2009; John Reid Chair of Pathology, University of St Andrews, since 2012; Director, Edinburgh Breakthrough Breast Cancer Research Unit, 2007-2012; Director, University of Edinburgh Cancer Research Centre and Cancer Research UK Clinical Cancer Centre, 2005-08; Adjunct Professor of Medicinal Chemistry, University of Florida, Gainesville, 2003; Adjunct Professor of Pathology and Forensic Education, University of Canberra, 2004; b. 24.3.59, Belfast; m., Jane; 2 d. Educ. Campbell College, Belfast; Edinburgh University. House Surgeon to Professor Sir Patrick Forrest, Royal Infirmary of Edinburgh, 1983-84, and House Physician to Professor J S Robson, 1984; University Department of Pathology, Edinburgh: Registrar and Senior House Officer, 1984-86, Lecturer, Honorary Registrar, 1986-87; Lecturer, Honorary Senior Lecturer, 1987-91, Senior Lecturer, 1991-97 and Honorary Consultant, Lothian University Hospitals Division, since 1991. Chairman of 1 healthcare charity. Address: (b.) Director's Office, Laboratory Medicine, Royal Infirmary of Edinburgh, 51 Little France Crescent, Edinburgh EH16 4SA.
E-mail: david.harrison@st-andrews.ac.uk

Harrower, The Hon Lord (Sean Smith Harrower), QC. Senator of the College of Justice, since 2020. Educ. Flora Stevenson's; Broughton High School, Edinburgh; Glasgow University. Career history: admitted to the Faculty of Advocates in 1999, and became a Queen's Counsel in 2012, specialising in building law; at various times, standing junior to the Scottish Government, HM Revenue and Customs and to the Office of the Advocate General; served as advocate depute, 2017-19. Address: Parliament House, 11 Parliament Square, Edinburgh EH1 1RQ.

Hart, Rt. Rev. Monsignor Daniel J., PhL, STL, MA(Hons), Dip Ed. Retired Parish Priest, St. Helen's Langside, Glasgow (1984-2007); Domestic Prelate to His Holiness The Pope; b. 29.5.32, Shenfield. Educ. St. Patrick's High School, Dumbarton; Blairs College, Aberdeen; Pontifical Gregorian University, Rome; University of Glasgow. Principal Teacher of History, Blairs College, Aberdeen, 1961-69; Notre Dame College of Education, 1969-81: Lecturer in Religious Education, Lecturer, In-Service Department, Director, Postgraduate Secondary Course; Director, Papal Visit to Scotland, 1981-82; Director, Religious Education Centre, Archdiocese of Glasgow, 1981-83; Catholic Church Representative, Strathclyde Regional Education Committee, 1983-84; Chairman, Children's Panel Advisory Committee for Strathclyde, 1977-84 (Vice-Chairman, National Advisory Committee, 1977-84); Judge, Scottish Catholic Interdiocesan Tribunal, since 1989; Member, Archdiocese of Glasgow Finance Council, 1986-90; Vice-Chairman, Archdiocesan Council of Priests, 1982-84 and 1998-2005; Member, Board of Governors, St. Andrew's College of Education, 1991-99; Member, Merger Committee, St. Andrew's College of Education and University of Glasgow, 1997-99; Chairman, Glasgow Archdiocesan Pilgrimage Committee, 2003-2010. Recreations: golf; photography; swimming; travel. Address: 33 Sanderling View, 1 Barassie Street, Troon KA10 6LU.

Hart, John Francis, MA, LLB. Solicitor; b. 18.10.38, Clydebank; m., Winefride; 3 s. Educ. St Aloysius College; Glasgow University. Solicitor, since 1962; former Lecturer, Glasgow University. Recreations: golf; reading; opera. Address: (h.) 9A Crosbie Road, Troon KA10 6HE; T.-01292 311987.

Hart, Morag Mary, MBE, JP, DL, RGN, RSCN. Deputy Lieutenant, Dunbartonshire, since 1989; Director, Scotsell Ltd., 1982-2007; b. 19.4.39, Glasgow; m., Tom Hart; 1 d.; 1 s. Educ. Westbourne School for Girls, Glasgow. Sick Children's Hospital, Glasgow, 1956-59; Western General Hospital, Edinburgh, 1960-62. County Commissioner, Girlguiding Dunbartonshire, 1982-90; Chairman, Dunbartonshire Area Scout Council, 1994-2004; Member, The Guide Association Council for Scotland, 1982-2000. Justice of the Peace for East Dunbartonshire Commission Area, 1992-2009; President of Girlguiding Dunbartonshire, 2009-2020. Recreations: reading; gardening; walking. Address: (h.) 18 Campbell Drive, Bearsden, Glasgow G61 4NE; T.-0141-942 1216.

Hart, Professor Robert Albert, BA (Hons), MA, FRSE. Emeritus Professor, Stirling University, since 2014 (Professor of Economics, 1986-2014); b. 7.1.46, Hartlepool; widower; 3 d. Educ. Hartlepool Grammar School; Liverpool University. Economics Lecturer, Aberdeen University, 1969-73, Leeds University, 1974-75; Senior Lecturer, Strathclyde University, 1976-80; Senior Research Fellow, Science Centre, Berlin, 1980-86; Head, School of Management, Stirling University, 1991-94. Recreations: walking; reading; drinking beer. Address: (b.) Department of Economics, Stirling University, Stirling FK9 4LA; T.-01786 467471; e-mail: r.a.hart@stir.ac.uk

Hart, Thomas, MA, LLB. Editor, Scottish Transport Review, 1998-2004; President, Scottish Association for Public Transport, 2013-15; Lecturer, Department of Economic and Social History, Glasgow University, 1965-98; b. 15.11.39, Kilmarnock; m., Ellen Elizabeth Jones; 2 s. Educ. Spiers School, Beith; Glasgow University. Writer and Consultant on transport and environmental issues; Founder Member of Scottish Transport Studies Group (Secretary, 1984-94, Chair, 1994-2004); Founder Member, Scottish Railway Development Association (Secretary, 1962-67, Vice Chairman, 1967-72); Chairman, Scottish Association for Public Transport, 1972-76; Member, Board, TRANS*form* Scotland, 1997-2011; Member, SPT (Strathclyde Partnership for Transport), 2006-2016. Publication: Chapters on 'Surface Transport for the 20th Century in Transport and Communications' in K. Veitch (Editor), Vol. 8, Scottish Life and Society, December, 2009; 50 Years of Scottish Transport Campaigns - From Beeching to High Speed Rail, 1962-2012, 2012 (Co-Author). Recreations: walking; travel; gardening. Address: (h.) Birchfield, 81A Kings Road, Beith, Ayrshire KA15 2BN; T.-01505 502164; e-mail: thstsg@btinternet.com

Harte, Professor Ben, BA, MA, PhD (Cantab), FRSE. Professor Emeritus and Senior Honorary Professorial Fellow, University of Edinburgh; b. 30.5.41, Blackpool; m., Angela Elizabeth; 1 s.; 2 d. Educ. Salford Grammar School; Trinity College, Cambridge University. Lecturer/Reader, Edinburgh University, 1965-91; Professor, University of Edinburgh, 1992-2007; Guest Research Investigator, Carnegie Institution of Washington, 1974-75; Visiting Associate Professor, Yale University, 1982; Visiting Research Fellow, University of Cape Town, 1990; JSPS Research Fellow, Ehime University, Japan, 1999; President of the Mineralogical Society of Great Britain and Ireland, 2006-08. Address: (b.) School of GeoSciences, CSEC, Erskine Williamson Building, University of Edinburgh, Edinburgh EH9 3FD; T.-0131-651 7220.
E-mail: ben.harte@ed.ac.uk

Harte, Chris. Chief Executive, Morton Fraser, since 2013 (Partner, since 1999). Member of Morton Fraser's managing board, since 2005, joined as a trainee in 1994. Member of CBI Scotland Council, since 2014. Address: Morton Fraser, Quartermile Two, 2 Lister Square, Edinburgh EH3 9GL; T.-0131 247 1000.

Hartley, Keith Scott, BA, MA. Deputy Director, Scottish National Gallery of Modern Art; b. 27.1.49, Evesham. Educ. Prince Henry's Grammar School, Evesham; St. Catherine's College, University of Oxford; Courtauld Institute, University of London; Freie Universität, W. Berlin. Curator of numerous exhibitions, and author of corresponding catalogues, including: Scottish Art Since 1900, 1989; Otto Dix, Tate Gallery, 1992; The Romantic Spirit in German Art 1790-1990, 1994; Andy Warhol, 2007; Douglas Gordon; Gerhard Richter, 2008; Peter Doig, 2013. Recreations: travel; reading. Address: (b.) Scottish National Gallery of Modern Art, Belford Road, Edinburgh EH4 3DR; T.-0131-624 6251.

Harvey, Liam. Headmaster, St. Mary's School, Melrose. Address: (b.) St. Mary's School, Abbey Park, Melrose TD6 9LN; T.-01896 822517.
E-mail: office@stmarysmelrose.org.uk

Harvey, Ruth. Leader, The Iona Community, since 2020; Mediator/Facilitator, Place for Hope, since 2012; m., Nick; 3 d. Educ. Wallace High School, Stirling; Bellahouston Academy, Glasgow; Aberdeen University; New College, Edinburgh. Career history: Church of Scotland minister; member of the Society of Friends (Quakers); member of the Iona Community for 27 years (served on several of its committees, member of its staff and edited Coracle, its magazine); experienced writer, preacher and trainer/mediator; Ecumenical Development Officer, Churches Together in Cumbria, 2010-2014. Address: The Iona Community, Suite 9, Fairfield, 1048 Govan Road, Glasgow G51 4XS.

Harvey, Rev. William John, BA (Hons), BD (Hons). Moderator, Glasgow Presbytery, 1998-99; b. 17.5.37, Glasgow; m., Isabel Mary Douglas; 2 s.; 2 d. Educ. Fettes

College, Edinburgh; Oxford University; Glasgow University. National Service, Argyll & Sutherland Highlanders, 1956-58; Ordained Assistant, Govan Old Parish Church, 1964-66; Member, Gorbals Group Ministry, 1963-71; Minister, Laurieston-Renwick Parish Church, Glasgow, 1968-71; Warden, Iona Abbey, 1971-76; Minister: Raploch Parish Church, Stirling, 1976-81, Govan Old Parish Church, 1981-88; Leader, The Iona Community, 1988-95. Member, Church of Scotland Committee on Church and Nation, 1978-86; Kerr Lecturer, Glasgow University, 1987; Team Member, The Craighead Institute of Life and Faith, Glasgow, 1995-2000; Interim Minister, Board of Ministry, The Church of Scotland, 2000-03. Honorary Doctorate of Divinity, Glasgow University, 2012. Publications: Bridging the Gap: Has the Church failed the poor? (Author), 1987, reprinted 2008; Journeys in Community: Father-daughter conversations about faith, love, doubt and hope (Joint Author), 2020. Recreations: reading; history; bread and wine-making; sea-bird watching. Address: (h.) 501 Shields Road, Glasgow G41 2RF; T.-0141-429 3774.
E-mail: jonmol@phonecoop.coop

Harvie, Professor Christopher Thomas, MA Hons (Edin), PhD (Edin). MSP (SNP), Mid Scotland and Fife, 2007-2011; Professor (Hon.) of History, Strathclyde, since 1995; b. 21.9.44, Motherwell; m., Virginia Roundell (deceased); 1 d. Educ. St. Boswells Primary School; Kelso High School; Royal High School, Edinburgh; Edinburgh University. Tutor, Edinburgh University, 1966-69; Lecturer/Senior Lecturer in History, Open University, 1969-80; appointed Professor of British Studies, Eberhard-Karls Universitaet, Tuebingen in 1980; Visiting Fellow, Merton and Nuffield Colleges, Oxford, Strathclyde and Edinburgh; Hon. Professor: Strathclyde University, since 1996, Aberystwyth, since 1996. Founder, Freudenstadt Colloquium, 1991; Co-Chair, Baden-Wuerttemberg Colloquium, 1996; Hon. President, Scottish Association for Public Transport, since 2002. Candidate (SNP) for Kirkcaldy (Scottish Parliament), 2007. 'Free Spirit of the Year' in Herald's Scottish Political Awards, 2008. Publications: The Lights of Liberalism, 1860-86, 1976; Scotland and Nationalism, 1976, 4 eds by 2004; No Gods and Precious Few Heroes, 4 eds by 2000; The Centre of Things: British Political Fiction, 1991; Cultural Weapons: Scotland and Europe, 1992; The Rise of Regional Europe, 1993, 2nd ed. 2006; The Road to Home Rule (Co-Author), 1999; Travelling Scot, 1999; Scotland: a Short History, 2002; Scotland's Transport, 2001; Mending Scotland, 2004; A Floating Commonwealth: Politics, Technology and Culture on the West Coast, 1860-1930, 2008; Broonland, 2010; Scotland the Brief, 2010; International Men: Liberals in European Politics, 2010; essays; articles; reviews. Recreations: any human activity except sport (but principally painting, music, travel).
Websites: www.uni-tuebingen.de/intelligent-mr-toad/ and www.chrisharvie.co.uk

Harvie, David B. Chief Executive, Crown Office & Procurator Fiscal Service (COPFS), since 2016. Solicitor Advocate; joined the Crown Office and Procurator Fiscal Service, following a spell in private practice, in 1996; has held various senior posts including Procurator Fiscal, North of Scotland; interim Procurator Fiscal, East of Scotland; Director of Serious Casework and Procurator Fiscal, West of Scotland. Address: (b.) Crown Office, 25 Chambers Street, Edinburgh EH1 1LA.

Harvie, Patrick. MSP (Green), Glasgow, since 2003; Minister for Zero Carbon Buildings, Active Travel and Tenants' Rights, Scottish Government, since 2021; Co-

Leader, Scottish Green Party; b. 18.3.73. Educ. Dumbarton Academy; Manchester Metropolitan University. Address: Scottish Parliament, Edinburgh EH99 1SP; T.-0131 348 6363.

Haslam, Cllr Shona, MA (PolStud). Leader, Scottish Borders Council, since 2017; Programme Manager, Peeblesshire Youth Trust, since 2015; National Director, Asthma UK Scotland, 2007-2015; b. 6.9.74, Kirkcaldy, Fife; m., Marc Haslam; 2 s. Educ. Peebles High School; Aberdeen University. Parliamentary Officer, Evangelical Alliance, 1996-2003; Public Affairs Manager, Asthma UK Scotland, 2003-07. Recreations: walking; family; church; cooking. T.-07957 383 663.

Hassan, Professor Gerry, MA (Hons), PhD, Professor of Social Change, Glasgow Caledonian University; writer, commentator, academic; b. 21.3.64, Dundee; m. Rosemary Catherine Ilett. Educ. Rockwell High School, Dundee; Glasgow University; University of the West of Scotland. Previously worked at the University of the West of Scotland; Dundee University; Institute for Public Policy Research; Demos; Centre for Scottish Public Policy. Author and editor of over 30 books on Scotland, the UK and social change including: A Better Nation: The Challenges of Scottish Independence (2022); Scotland After the Virus (2020); The People's Flag and the Union Jack: An Alternative History of Britain and the Labour Party (2019); Scotland the Bold (2016); Independence of the Scottish Mind (2014); Caledonian Dreaming (2014); The Strange Death of Labour Scotland (2012). Recreations: listening to and collecting music; Frank Sinatra albums; watching non-senior football.
Email: gerry@gerryhassan.com
Website: www.gerryhassan.com

Hastings, Gavin, OBE, DUniv (Paisley). Chairman, Hastings Investment Management, since 2021; Business Development Consultant, Ceannas, since 2020; former rugby player; b. 1962, Edinburgh. Educ. George Watson's College, Edinburgh; Paisley University; Cambridge University. 61 Scotland Caps, 1986-95 (20 as Captain); 3 World Cups, 1987, 1991, 1995; 2 British Lions Tours: 1989, Australia, 3 Tests, 1993, New Zealand (Captain), 3 Tests.

Hatfield, Dr Emma. Secretary, North Atlantic Salmon Conservation Organization (NASCO), since 2017. Career: Research Scientist, British Antarctic Survey, 1987-97; NRC Research Associate, NEAFSC Woods Hole, MA, 1997-99; Senior Fishery Scientist: Fisheries Research Services, Marine Laboratory, Aberdeen, 2000-09, Marine Scotland Science, 2009-2014; Scientific/Technical Project Officer, DG MARE, European Commission, 2014-17. Address: (b.) 11 Rutland Square, Edinburgh EH1 2AS; T.-0131 228 2551.

Hatton, Amanda. Executive Director, Education and Children's Services, City of Edinburgh Council, since 2021; previously Director, Children, Education and Communities, then Corporate Director of People, York Council. Address: City of Edinburgh Council, City Chambers, High Street, Edinburgh EH1 1YJ.

Hatton, Craig. Chief Executive, North Ayrshire Council, since 2018. Career history: building surveyor by profession and managed a wide range of local government services; developed a commercial approach in response to the deregulation and self-financing requirements of the

Building Control market in England; moved into Environmental Services and led the introduction of new waste management services enabling his former Council to become the first in the UK to achieve a 60% Household Waste recycling rate; joined North Ayrshire Council in 2009 as Executive Director of Place and led a strong team delivering significant transformation across a broad range of services securing many national awards along the way, notably a Municipal Journal Award for Workforce Transformation in the creation of a fully integrated Streetscene service. Address: North Ayrshire Council, Cunninghame House, Irvine KA12 8EE; T.-01294 324124.

Haughey, Clare. MSP (SNP), Rutherglen, since 2016; Minister for Children and Young People, since 2021; Minister for Mental Health, 2018-2021; b. 4.67, Glasgow. Former Clinical Nurse Manager with the Perinatal Mental Health Service and specialised in working with mothers who are pregnant or have a baby under one; active trade unionist and a divisional convenor in UNISON; former Trustee of Maternal Mental Health Scotland, a mental health charity. Joined the SNP in 2014 and acted as a team leader during the General Election. Address: Scottish Parliament, Edinburgh EH99 1SP.
E-mail: clare.haughey.msp@parliament.scot

Haughey, Lady Susan, CBE. Lord Lieutenant, Lanarkshire, since 2017; m., Baron William Haughey. Educ. Holyrood Secondary School. Career history: owner and director, City Refrigeration Ltd, since 1985; set up the City Charitable Trust in 2002, donated to registered charities, local charities and deserving causes every year; Director, Kilbryde Hospice in Lanarkshire. Deputy Lord Lieutenant, Lanarkshire, 2012-18. Awarded the Loving Cup in October 2015 by the Lord Provost of Glasgow; winner of the Women of Influence Award, 2016. Awarded a CBE for services to business and philanthropy in 2016. Address: North Lanarkshire Council, Civic Centre, Windmillhill Street, Motherwell ML1 1AB.

Haughey of Hutchesontown, Baron (William Haughey), OBE (2003). Chairman, City Facilities Management Holdings Ltd, since 1985; b. 2.7.56, Glasgow; m., Susan née Moore; 1 s. Educ. Holyrood Senior Secondary School, Glasgow; Springburn College, Glasgow. Engineering Supervisor, Turner Refrigeration Ltd, 1973-83; Head of Engineering, UAE UTS Carrier, 1983-85; Charter Member, Duke of Edinburgh Awards Scheme; Member, Growth Fund Panel, Prince's Scottish Youth Business Trust; Patron, CSV; Entrepreneur of the Year, Entrepreneurial Exchange, 2000 (finalist 1999); Business to Business section and Masterclass winner, Ernst & Young Awards, 2000; Refrigeration Industry Business of the Year, 2000; Lanarkshire Business of the Year, 2002; Business Man of the Year, Award Insider Publications, 2003; Bighearted Business Person of the Year, 2004; Excellence in Public Service Award, 2004; Business Award, Great Scot 2005 Awards, Sunday Mail, 2005; Loving Cup from Lord Provost of Glasgow for charity work, 2001; Hon DTech, Glasgow Caledonian University. 2005; St Mungo Medal (awarded to the citizen of Glasgow who has worked tirelessly to promote and enhance the wellbeing of its less fortunate citizens, and at the same time adding to the reputation of Glasgow as the Caring City), December 2006. Recreations: golf; reading; football. Address: (b.) City Refrigeration Holdings (UK) Ltd, 17 Lawmoor Street, Glasgow G5 0US; T.-0141-418 9117.
E-mail: willie.haughey@city-holdings.co.uk

Hawkins, Anthony Donald, CBE, BSc, PhD, FSA Scot, FRSE. Currently the Director of Loughine Ltd, a private company dealing with marine biology; formerly the Director, Fisheries Research for Scotland and an Honorary Professor, Aberdeen University; b. 25.3.42, Poole, Dorset; m., Susan Mary; 1 s. Educ. Poole Grammar School; Bristol University. Entered Scottish Office as Scientific Officer, Marine Laboratory, Aberdeen, 1965; Senior Scientific Officer, 1969, Principal Scientific Officer, 1972, Senior Principal Scientific Officer, 1978, Deputy Chief Scientific Officer, 1983; Deputy Director of Fisheries Research for Scotland, 1983. Appointed Director of Fisheries Research for Scotland in 1987 and served in that post until 2002, when he had to retire from the UK Civil Service at the age of 60. In the 1970s he also worked for the Food and Agriculture Organization of the United Nations in Peru, at the Peruvian Marine Institute (IMARPE) examining the anchovy and sardine fishery. Later, he worked in Guayaquil, Ecuador, on the adverse effects of the prawn farms upon aquatic environments there; and later in North Dakota on the fish within Lake Sakakawea. He has been conducting research since 1963 on the behaviour and physiology of fish; and was awarded the A.B. Wood Medal by the Institute of Acoustics in 1978. In the 1980s he also studied the migrations of salmon, in the North Sea, within the Aberdeenshire River Dee, and in Spanish rivers, writing a book on The Atlantic Salmon in Spain in 1987. In 1991, he set up and became Chairman of the North Sea Commission Fisheries Partnership. He later set up and became the Rapporteur of the North Sea Regional Advisory Committee (NSRAC), providing advice from fishers and scientists to the European Commission on the management of North Sea fisheries. He left this when the UK began to leave the EU in 2019. Principal of the North Atlantic Marine Centre, Scalloway, Shetland, 2008-09. He is currently an organiser of the Aquatic Noise Conferences; held in Nyborg, Denmark (2007), Cork (2010), Budapest (2013), Dublin (2016), and Den Haag (2019). The next one will be in Berlin in 2022. His publications include: books and papers on fish sounds, fish physiology, effects of underwater sound on aquatic life, aquarium systems, the biology of Atlantic salmon, and fisheries management. Recreations: reading; soccer; walking whippets. Address: Kincraig, Blairs, Aberdeen; T.-01224 868984.
E-mail: a.hawkins@btconnect.com

Hawkins, Nigel. Co-Founder and former Chief Executive, John Muir Trust; b. 12.9.46, Dundee. Educ. Madras College, St Andrews. Co-Founder, John Muir Trust, 1982 (Trustee, 1984-96, Director (CEO), 1996-2009); Creator, Dundee City of Discovery Campaign, 1985; Chairman, Prospect PR Ltd., 1985-2006; Co-Founder, The Knoydart Foundation, 1983 (Director, 1998-2003); Director, North Harris Trust, 2003-08; Director, Assynt Foundation, 2005-08; Deputy Chairman and Director, Dundee Science Centre Trust, 1998-2004; Director, Sensation Ltd., 1999-2004; Trustee, Dundee Science Centre Endowment Fund, since 2005; Univ. of Abertay Dundee: Fellow, 1998, Member, Court, 1999-2012, Deputy Chairman, Court, 2006-09, Chairman of Court, 2009-2012; President, Dundee and Tayside Chamber of Commerce and Industry, 1997-98; Board Member, North of Scotland Water Authority, 1998-2002. Recreations: mountaineering; cycling; running; good food; Italy. Address: (b.) 1 Auchterhouse Park, Auchterhouse, by Dundee DD3 0QU; T.-01382 320252; e-mail: nigelrobinhawkins@btinternet.com

Hawley, Dr Graham. Headmaster, Loretto School, since 2014; m., Rachel; 2 c. Educ. Mill Hill School; Durham University. Worked for the National Rivers Authority in Exeter; moved to Scotland and investigated the water quality of the major lochs along the west coast; returned to Devon to complete a Postgraduate Certificate in Education; Assistant Master, Ardingly College, West Sussex, 1996-2000, Housemaster, 2000-04; Deputy Headmaster, Warwick School, 2004-08; Headmaster, Kelly College, Devon, 2008-2014. Recreations: golf; walking; occasional fly-fishing. Address: Loretto School, Linkfield Road, Musselburgh, East Lothian EH21 7RE; T.-0131 653 4441.

Hawthorn, Patricia. Consultant, Shepherd and Wedderburn LLP (appointed Partner in 2007); Chairman, Scottish Renewables, 2015-18. Working on consenting wind farms both on and offshore in Scotland and offshore in UK waters. Member of RenewableUK's consents and licensing group. Address: Shepherd and Wedderburn LLP, 1 West Regent Street, Glasgow G2 1RW.

Hawthorne, Eddie. Chief Executive and Group Managing Director, Arnold Clark; Chairman, Cash for Kids, since 2018; b. 1966. Career history: began career in the Audit Department of Arthur Young in Glasgow and became a qualified Chartered Accountant in 1989; joined Arnold Clark Automobiles Limited as Group Financial Controller in 1989 working closely with Sir Arnold Clark; promoted to Group Managing Director in 1998. Won a Glassdoor Employee's Choice award in 2018 (honours the top CEOs throughout North America and Europe). Address: Arnold Clark Automobiles Ltd, Head office, 454 Hillington Road, Glasgow G52 4FH; T.-0141 648 1115.
E-mail: eddie.hawthorne@arnoldclark.com

Hay, Alasdair George, CBE, QFSM. Chief Officer, Scottish Fire and Rescue Service, 2013-19 (retired); b. 24.12.61, Edinburgh. Educ. University of Abertay Dundee; Dundee College. Firefighter with Essex County Fire and Rescue Service, 1983-92; senior instructor at the Scottish Fire Services College, 1992-94; joined Tayside Fire and Rescue in 1994, achieved the rank of Deputy Chief Fire Officer by 2009; seconded to the Scottish Fire and Rescue Services Advisory Unit, 2011-12; Acting Chief Fire Officer, Tayside Fire and Rescue, 2012-13. Recipient of the Queen Elizabeth II Golden Jubilee Medal, the Queen Elizabeth II Diamond Jubilee Medal and the Fire Brigade Long Service and Good Conduct Medal.

Hay, Ken. Chief Executive: Centre for the Moving Image, since 2011, Edinburgh International Film Festival, EM Media, Nottingham, 2001-05, Scottish Screen, 2005-2011. Address: (b.) Centre for the Moving Image, 88 Lothian Road, Edinburgh EH3 9BZ; T.-0131 228 6382.

Hay, Neil, MA (Hons), LLB, DipLP. Solicitor-Advocate/Director, MTM Defence Lawyers, since 2001; b. 8.70. Educ. University of Dundee; University of Glasgow; University of Edinburgh. Member: The Fraud Lawyers Association (UK), since 2020; Health & Safety Lawyers Association (UK), since 2019; The Professional Practice Committee, Centre for Law, Edinburgh Napier University, since 2013; Part-time Lecturer in Court & Tribunal Advocacy, University of Glasgow, since 2010; Member: The Law Society of Scotland; The Society of Solicitor-Advocates. Address: MTM Defence Lawyers, 5 Semple Street, Edinburgh EH3 8BL; T.-07866 734524.
E-mail: nhay@mtmdefence.co.uk

Hay, Robert King Miller, BSc, MSc, PhD, FRSB, FSA Scot. Writer and Editor; Archivist, Lismore Museum; Visiting Professor, Swedish University of Agricultural Sciences, Uppsala, 2005-07; Director, Scottish Agricultural Science Agency, 1990-2004; Honorary Fellow of SAC (Scottish Agricultural College), since 2004; b. 19.8.46, Edinburgh; m., Dorothea Harden Vinycomb; 2 s.; 1 d. Educ. Forres Academy, Moray; Aberdeen University; University of East Anglia. AFRC Research Fellow, Edinburgh University, 1971-74; Lecturer in Crop Production: University of Malawi, 1974-76, Edinburgh University, 1976-77; Lecturer in Environmental Sciences, Lancaster University, 1977-82; Leverhulme European Fellow, Agricultural University of Norway, 1981; Head of Plant Sciences, Scottish Agricultural College, Ayr, 1982-90; British Council Research Fellow, University of Western Australia, 1989; Visiting Scientist, McGill University, Montreal, 1997. Publications: Environmental Physiology of Plants, 1981, 1987, 2002; Chemistry for Agriculture and Ecology; The Physiology of Crop Yield, 1989, 2006; Volatile Oil Crops (Ed); Science Policies in Europe: Unity and Diversity (Ed); Lochnavando No More: The Life and Death of a Moray Farming Community, 1750-1850; Lismore: The Great Garden; How an Island Lost its People; The Story of Lismore in 50 Objects; contributions to the Compendium of Scottish Ethnology, the Review of Scottish Culture, History Scotland and Sources in Local History; Annals of Botany (Editor), 1995-2006; 60 scientific papers. Recreations: walking; museum curating; community singing. Address: (h.) Park Steading, Isle of Lismore, Oban PA34 5UN; T.-01631 760 393; e-mail: dot.bob@btopenworld.com

Haydon, Professor Daniel Thomas, BSc, PhD. Professor of Population Ecology and Epidemiology, University of Glasgow, since 2007; b. 10.06.65, Cambridge; m., Dr. Barbara Mable (common-law). Educ. Perse School, Cambridge; University of Southampton; University of Texas at Austin. Post-doctoral research assistant at University of Oxford, 1992-96, University of British Columbia, 1996-98, University of Edinburgh, 1998-2001, University of Guelph, 2001-04; Lecturer, University of Glasgow, 2004-07. Scientific Medal (Zoological Society of London, 2005); British Lichen Society. Recreations: mountaineering; hill-walking; photography. Address: (b.) Graham Kerr Building, University of Glasgow, Glasgow G12 8QQ; T.-0141 330 6637.
E-mail: d.haydon@bio.gla.ac.uk

Hayes, Lyndsey. Secretary, Scottish Consortium for Rural Research. Address: 18 Hoghill Court, East Calder, Livingston EH53 0QA; T.-01506 880929.
E-mail: lyndsey.hayes@ed.ac.uk

Haywood, Brent William, LLB, BA, Dip Forensic Medicine, LLM (Mediation and Conflict Resolution). Solicitor Advocate and Mediator, Partner in Lindsays Solicitors; b. 14.8.65, Riverton, New Zealand; m., Heather; 2 sons, Gregor and Jonty. Educ. Southland Boys' High School, New Zealand; Otago University, Dunedin, New Zealand; Glasgow University; Strathclyde University. Writer to Her Majesty's Signet (W.S.); Practitioner with Place For Hope; Director of Logos Scotland Limited. Recreations: ultra distance running; straplining; cycling; kayaking; ukulele; member of Jelly Appreciation Society. Address: (b.) Caledonian Exchange, 19A Canning Street, Edinburgh EH3 8HE.
E-mail: brenthaywood@lindsays.co.uk

Hazel, Dr George McLean, OBE, BSc, MSc, PhD, FCIT, FIHT. Director, George Hazel Consultancy Ltd; Chairman, MRC McLean Hazel, 2005-2012, McLean Hazel Ltd., 2001-05; b. 27.1.49, Dunfermline; m., Fiona Isabella Gault; 1 s.; 2 d. Educ. Dunfermline High School; Heriot-Watt University; Cranfield Institute of Technology.

Transportation Engineer: City of Edinburgh Corporation, 5 years, Lothian Regional Council, 4 years; Lecturer, Senior Lecturer, Head of Dept., and first Professor of Transport in Scotland, Napier College/Polytechnic/University, 11 years; Director, Oscar Faber TPA, three years; Director of Transportation, Lothian Regional Council, three years; Director of City Development, City of Edinburgh Council, 1996-99. Member, Secretary of State for Scotland's Advisory Group on Sustainable Development; Chair, Urban Design Alliance, 2004/06; Member, Secretary of State's Steering (2004) Group on National Road User Charging; Advisor to the Commission for Integrated Transport, Lorry Road User Charging Committee of Transport, 2000; Chairman, Edinburgh and East of Scotland Association, Institution of Civil Engineers; President, Chartered Institution of Highways and Transportation, 2003-04; International Advisor to the Queensland State Government, Australia; Chair, Advisory Board, Transport Research Institute, Edinburgh Napier University, 2011-19; Board Member: Strathclyde Partnership for Transport, since 2020, Transport for Edinburgh, since 2020. Awarded Officer of the British Empire (OBE) for services to transport, 2006. Publication: "Making Cities Work" (Author), 2004. Recreations: golf; gardening; travel; music; vintage cars. Address: (h.) Rufaro, 332 Lanark Road, Edinburgh EH14 2LH; e-mail: george@georgehazel.com

Hearne, John Michael, BMus, MMus, DMus, FISM. Publisher (Longship Music); Freelance Composer; Conductor and Copyist; b. 19.9.37, Reading; m., Margaret Gillespie Jarvie. Educ. Torquay Grammar School, 1948-55; St. Luke's College, Exeter, 1957-59; University College of Wales, Aberystwyth, 1964-68. Teaching, Rugeley, Staffordshire, 1959-60; Warehouseman/Driver, Torquay, 1961-64; Teaching: Tónlistarskóli Borgarfjarðar, Iceland, 1968-69, UCW Aberystwyth, 1969-70; Lecturer, Aberdeen College of Education, 1970-87. Composer, vocal, instrumental and incidental music: BBC commission for BBCSSO, 1990 (trumpet concerto); McEwen Commission, Glasgow University, 1979 (Channel Firing); A Legend of Margaret, commissioned to celebrate 150th anniversary of St. Margaret's School, Aberdeen, 1996; Into Uncharted Seas, commissioned to commemorate centenary of launch of RRS Discovery on Antarctic expedition; The Ben – a Cantata for Bennachie, commissioned by Gordon Forum for the Arts, 2001; Member, John Currie Singers, 1973-2003; Awarded Radio Forth Trophy, 1985, for most outstanding work on Edinburgh Festival Fringe (The Four Horsemen); joint winner, Gregynog Composers' Award for Wales, 1992. Chorus Manager, Aberdeen International Youth Festival, 1978-2012; Chairman: Scottish Music Advisory Committee, BBC, 1986-90, Gordon Forum for the Arts, 1991-94; Conductor, Stonehaven and District Choral Society (The Stonehaven Chorus), 1989-2014; now Conductor Emeritus; Past Chairman, Scottish Society of Composers; former Member, Board, National Youth Choir of Scotland; Winner, Gregynog Composers' Award for Wales, 1998 (Solemn and Strange Music); Conductor, Inverurie Choral Society, 1998-2003; Warden, Performers and Composers Section, Incorporated Society of Musicians, 1999; Member, Board, Enterprise Music Scotland, until 2011; Member, Management Committee, Aberdeen "Sound" Festival, since 2018; Winner, Caledonian Hilton Audience Prize, Waverley Care carol competition, 2010. Recreations: revisiting the past: re-reading long-forgotten books; old diaries; photos; maps and programmes. Address: (h.) Smidskot, Fawells, Keith-Hall, Inverurie AB51 OLN; T.-01651 882 274.
Website: www.impulse-music.co.uk/johnhearne

Hedderwick, Mairi Crawford, DA (Edin). Illustrator, Writer and Public Speaker; b. 2.5.39, Gourock; 1 s.; 1 d. Educ. St. Columba's School, Kilmacolm; Edinburgh College of Art; Jordanhill College of Education.

Publications: for children: Katie Morag series, A Walk with Grannie; The Utterly Otterleys; for adults: An Eye on the Hebrides, Highland Journey; Sea Change; Shetland Rambles; The Last Laird of Coll. Hon. Doctorate, Stirling University. Recreations: a day outside ending round a table with friends, food and wine.

Heddle, Dr Steven, BSc, PhD. Environment and Economy Spokesperson, COSLA, since 2017; Territorial Development Spokesperson, CEMR; former Convener, Orkney Islands Council (2012-17); represents Kirkwall East ward; b. Kirkwall; m.; 1 s. Educ. Aberdeen and Edinburgh Universities. Career: worked in R&D and engineering; former IT specialist with Highlands and Islands Enterprise (HIE); previously chair of the authority's education committee; runs a business and technical consultancy, often working with HIE Orkney. Recreations: listening to music; keen football supporter; cycling. Address: (b.) Newington, Holm Road, Kirkwall KW15 1PY; T.-01856 877119.

Heggie, Dr Douglas Cameron, MA, PhD, FRAS, FRSE; b. 7.2.47, Edinburgh; m., Linda Jane Tennent; 2 d. Educ. George Heriot's School, Edinburgh; Trinity College, Cambridge. Research Fellow, Trinity College, Cambridge, 1972-76; Lecturer in Mathematics, Edinburgh University, 1975-85, Reader, 1985-94, Professor of Mathematical Astronomy, 1994-2012, Professor Emeritus, since 2012. Council Member, Royal Astronomical Society, 1982-85; President, Commission 37, International Astronomical Union, 1985-88; Member, Board of Editors, Monthly Notices of the RAS, 1994-2017. Publications: Megalithic Science; The Gravitational Million-Body Problem; scientific papers on dynamical astronomy. Recreations: family life; walking; music. Address: (b.) Edinburgh University, School of Mathematics, King's Buildings, Edinburgh EH9 3FD; T.-0131 650 5904.
E-mail: d.c.heggie@ed.ac.uk

Heller, Martin Fuller Vernon, FRSAMD. Actor, since 1947; b. 20.2.27, Manchester; m., Joyce Allan; 2 s.; 4 d. Educ. Rondebosch Boys High School, Cape Town; Central School of Speech Training and Dramatic Art, London. Compass Players, 1948-52; repertory seasons and/or individual productions at following Scottish theatres: St. Andrews Byre, Edinburgh Gateway, Glasgow Citizens' (eight seasons), Edinburgh Royal Lyceum, Edinburgh Traverse, Dundee Repertory, Perth Repertory, Pitlochry Festival; Founder/Artistic Director, Prime Productions, 1985-2014; extensive television and radio work; Member: Scottish Arts Council, 1975-82 (latterly Chairman, Drama Committee); Governor, Pitlochry Festival Theatre (retired 2005); Governor, Royal Scottish Academy of Music and Drama, 1982-94. Recreations: politics; history; listening to music. Address: (h.) 54 Hermiston Village, Currie, Midlothian EH14 4AQ; T.-0131-449 4055.

Hemphill, Greg. Actor, comedian and movie producer (best known for appearances in Still Game and Chewin' the Fat); b. 14.12.69, Glasgow; m., Julie Wilson Nimmo; 2 s. Educ. University of Glasgow. Rector, University of Glasgow, 2001-04.

Hems, Alexandra. Head Teacher, St George's School for Girls, Edinburgh, since 2017. Educ. St Helen's School, Northwood; Somerville College, Oxford; Sidney Sussex College, Cambridge. Career: Teacher of English and Latin, Alleyn's School, 1993-96; Teacher and Assistant Head of Senior School, St Paul's Girls' School, London, 1996-2003; Head of Sixth Form, North London Collegiate School, 2003-2006; Head of Senior School, St Paul's Girls' School, London, 2007-2010; Deputy Head, Francis Holland School,

Sloane Square, London, 2011-2012; Deputy Head, Wycombe Abbey School, 2013-16. Address: St George's School for Girls, Garscube Terrace, Edinburgh EH12 6BG; T.-0131 311 8000.

Henderson, Dr. Callum. Honorary Consul of Rwanda to Scotland, since 2013; Director, Comfort International, since 1999. Educ. High School of Dundee; University of Edinburgh. Pastor, Elim Pentecostal Church, 1990-98; Leader, Free for Life, 2002-03; Manager of youth homeless units, Bethany Christian Trust, 2003-2006; Chair, Rwanda Scotland Alliance, 2009-2013. Publication: Beauty From Ashes, 2007; Unforgotten: Cherishing the Story of Rwanda's Abasesero People, 2020. Address: Lochty House, 23 Lochty Street, Carnoustie, Angus DD7 6EE; T.-07542 731983; e-mail: chenderson@minaffet.gov.rw

Henderson, Donald Cameron. Head of Scottish Government Redress and Survivor Relations Division, since 2019; b. 1961, Shropshire; m., Catherine Louise Fox; 1 s.; 1 d. Educ. Lenzie Academy. Scottish Office, 1981-1999; seconded to FCO, 1984-85; MAFF, 1992-93; UK Cabinet Office, 1999-2002; Scottish Executive/Government, since 2002; Head of Teachers Division, 2002-07; Interim Chief Executive of Skills Development Scotland, 2007-08; EU Director and Head of Scottish Government Office in Brussels, 2008-11; Head of Public Health Division, 2011-15; Head of Scottish Government Care, Protection and Justice Division, 2015-19. Recreations: family; cycling; walking. Address: Scottish Government, Victoria Quay, Edinburgh EH6 6QQ.

Henderson, Jennifer, BA (Hons) Oxon, FCMI. Keeper of the Registers of Scotland, since 2018. Educ. Oxford University. Career history: Researcher, Defence Evaluation and Research Agency, 1994-1998; Research customer, MOD, 1998-2001; Defence Science and Technology Laboratory (Dstl): Programme manager, 2001-2004, Business manager, 2004-2010, Operations Director, 2010-2015; Non-Executive Director, Ploughshare Innovations Limited, 2012-2017; Transformation Director, Defence Science and Technology Laboratory (Dstl), 2015-2017; Deputy Director, Ministry of Housing, Communities and Local Government, 2017-2018. Address: (b.) Meadowbank House, 153 London Road, Edinburgh EH8 7AU; e-mail: jennifer.henderson@ros.gov.uk

Henderson, John Gunn, BA, FRSA. Interim Regional Chair, North East of Scotland College (Member, Board of Management, since 2014); former Chief Executive, Colleges Scotland (2011-2014); Deputy Director, Scotland Office, 2007-2011; Head, International Division, Scottish Executive, 2003-07; Euro 2008 Bid Director, Scottish Football Association (on secondment from the Scottish Executive), 2001-03; b. 29.5.53, Edinburgh; m., Karen; 1 s.; 2 d. Educ. Broughton Secondary, Edinburgh; Open University. Scottish Development Department, 1970-78; Department of Agriculture and Fisheries for Scotland, 1978-85; Scottish Development Department, Trunk Roads Division, 1985-88; Scottish Office Education and Industry Department, 1988-97 (Head, Further Education Funding Unit, 1992-97); Assistant Director of Finance and Head, Private Finance Unit, 1997-2001. Recreations: reading; gardening; beachcombing.

Henderson, Meg. Author, Journalist and Scriptwriter; b. 1948, Glasgow; m., Rab; 1 s.; 2 d. Educ. Garnethill Convent Secondary School (reluctantly). Chief Cardiology Technician, Western Infirmary and Royal Infirmary, Glasgow; VSO, India; spent years fostering children; has worked for the broadsheets, Daily Mail, BBC, Channel 4.

Publications: Finding Peggy, 1994; The Holy City, 1997; Bloody Mary, 1998; Chasing Angels, 2000; The Last Wanderer, 2002; Second Sight, 2004; Daisy's Wars, 2005; A Scent of Bluebells, 2006; Ruby, 2010. Recreations: reading, history, walking, radio, peace and quiet, golf, tennis, F1 racing (without having the slightest aptitude for any of them); shouting at politicians on television (or wherever encountered).

Henderson, Cllr Peter. Leader, South Ayrshire Council, 2020-2022; Councillor, Ward 8 - Girvan and South Carrick (SNP), since 2017. Address: South Ayrshire Council, Wellington Square, Ayr KA7 1DR; T.-0300 123 0900. E-mail: peter.henderson@south-ayrshire.gov.uk

Henderson, Major Sir Richard Yates, KCVO, TD, JP, BA (Oxon), LLB. Lord Lieutenant, Ayrshire and Arran, 1991-2006; b. 7.7.31, Nitshill; m., Frances Elizabeth Chrystal; 3 s. (inc. 1 s. dec.); 1 d. Educ. Rugby; Hertford College, Oxford; Glasgow University. Royal Scots Greys, 1950-52; TA Ayrshire (ECO) Yeomanry, 1953-69 (Major); Deputy Lieutenant, Ayrshire and Arran, 1970-90; Partner, Mitchells Roberton, Solicitors, 1958-90, Consultant, 1991-92. Ensign, Queen's Bodyguard for Scotland (Royal Company of Archers); President, Lowland TAVRA, 1996-2000; Hon. Colonel, Ayrshire Yeomanry Sqn., Scottish Yeomanry, 1992-97; Honorary Sheriff, South Strathclyde Dumfries and Galloway at Ayr, since 1997. Recreations: country pursuits; tennis; golf. Address: (h.) 5 Cambusdoon Drive, Ayr KA7 4PL; T.-01292 441601. E-mail: henderson@blairston.co.uk

Henderson-Howat, David Barclay, BSc, MA, MBA, FICFor. Convenor, National Access Forum, Scottish Natural Heritage, 2017-2020; b. 23.1.54, Trinidad; m., Jean Buchanan-Smith; 1 s.; 3 d. Educ. Abingdon School; University of Edinburgh; Magdalene College, University of Cambridge; University of Strathclyde. Scottish Office, 1976-79; Personal Assistant to Chief Executive, Scottish Development Agency, 1979-80; Harvesting and Marketing Manager, Thetford Forest, 1980-84; Forest Manager, Shiselweni Forest, Swaziland, 1984-86; Forest District Manager, Aberfoyle, Perthshire, 1986-90; Forestry Commission Headquarters, 1990-96; Chief Conservator, Forestry Commission Scotland, 1996-2003; United Nations Forum on Forests, New York, 2003-05; Head of Agriculture Division, Rural Directorate, Scottish Government, 2005-08; Acting Director, Forestry Commission England, 2010-11; Deputy Director, Forestry Commission Scotland, 2012-13; President, Institute of Chartered Foresters, 2015-17; consultancy work for UN Forum on Forests and FAO, since 2013; Elder and Treasurer, Kirkurd and Newlands Church. Publications: The State of the World's Forests, 2016 (Contributor) and 2018 (Editor). Recreations: walking; sailing. Address: (h.) Stoneyknowe, West Linton, Peeblesshire EH46 7BY; T.-01968 660677.

Hendry, Drew. MP (SNP), Inverness, Nairn, Badenoch and Strathspey, since 2015; SNP Shadow Secretary of State for International Trade, since 2021; SNP Spokesperson for Business, Energy and Industrial Strategy, 2017-2021; Transport Spokesperson, 2015-17; Leader, Highland Council, 2012-15; SNP Group Leader, 2011-15; represented Aird and Loch Ness ward (SNP), 2007-2015; b. 21.5.64, Edinburgh; m.; 4 c. Former Director with a multinational appliance manufacturer and has long experience in Retail, including online, from the shop floor to senior management; founded a company, Teclan, in Inverness, which offers services for company websites. Former Board Member of the Cairngorms National Park; Member: COHI, H & I Convener's Group, Scottish Cities Alliance - Leadership Group, Inverness Campus - Partnership Forum; Chair:

Advisory Board, Caithness and North Sutherland Regeneration Partnership (CNSRP), Highland Public Services Partnership Board (HPSP), since 2012. SNP Group Leader, COSLA. Chair, Highlands & Islands of Scotland European Partnership (HIEP), since 2012; Vice-President and Sole UK representative to the European Union Political Bureau of the Committee of the Regions (CPMR); COSLA European Representative; Honorary Consul to Romania for the Highlands and Islands, since 2012. Director, Teclan Ltd, Inverness; Member, Institute of Directors. Recreations: enjoys walking the dogs in the Highland countryside; reading; films; football. Address: House of Commons, London SW1A 0AA.

Hendry, Duncan, BSc. Freelance Arts Consultant, Hendry Consultants, since 2019; b. 11.51. Educ. University of St Andrews. Career history: Director, Aberdeen Alternative Festival, 1988-98; Chief Executive, Aberdeen Performing Arts, 1999-2012; Chief Executive, Capital Theatres, Edinburgh, 2012-19. Chairperson, Lung Ha's Theatre Company Limited, since 2020; Board Member: Eden Court Theatre, since 2019, Edinburgh International Jazz and Blues Festival Limited, since 2019, Creative Scotland, since 2021. Address: Lung Ha's Theatre Company Limited, 7 Restalrig Terrace, Edinburgh EH6 8EA.

Hendry, Dr. Joy McLaggan, MA (Hons), DipEd, DLitt (Hon) (Edin). Writer; Editor, Chapman Magazine, 1972-2005; b. 3.2.53, Perth; m., Ian Montgomery. Educ. Perth Academy; Edinburgh University. Former teacher; Co-Editor, Chapman, 1972-76, Sole Editor, since 1976; Deputy Convener, Scottish Poetry Library Association, 1983-88; Convener, Committee for the Advancement of Scottish Literature in Schools; Member AdCas; Scottish National Theatre Steering Committee; Campaign for a Scottish Assembly; Member, Drama Committee, Scottish Arts Council; Chair, Scottish Actors Studio, 1993-2000; Member, Literature Forum for Scotland; Member, Scottish Parliament Scots Language Cross-Party Group; Lecturer in drama, Queen Margaret University College, 2000-04; Lecturer in periodical journalism, Napier University, 2000-04; poet and playwright; gives lectures and talks and performances of poetry and song; radio critic, The Scotsman, 1988-97; theatre reviewer; Writer-in-Residence, Stirling District Council, 1991-93. Hon DLitt, University of Edinburgh, 2005. Publications: Scots: The Way Forward; Poems and Pictures by Wendy Wood (Editor); The Land for the People (Co-Editor); Critical Essays on Sorley MacLean (Co-Editor); Critical Essays on Norman MacCaig (Co-Editor); autobiographical essay in Spirits of the Age: Scottish Self Portraits (Saltire Society); Gang Doun wi a Sang (play); radio: The Wa' at the World's End, Radio 3 (play); A Many-Faceted Thing (Memory), Radio 4 (major 4-part series). Recreations: going to theatre; cinema; reading; dogs and animal welfare. Address: 4 Broughton Place, Edinburgh EH1 3RX; T.-0131-557 2207.
E-mail: joyhendry@blueyonder.co.uk

Hendry, Stephen, MBE. Professional snooker player; b. 13.1.69; 2 s. Youngest-ever Scottish Amateur Champion (aged 15); has won 75 tournaments worldwide; youngest player to attain No. 1 ranking; youngest player to win World Championship, 1990; World Champion seven times; UK Champion, five times; Masters Champion, six times.

Hendry, Stuart, LLB (Hons), LLM, NP. Partner, MBM Commercial LLP, since 2005; b. 12.1.73, Aberdeen. Murray Beith Murray WS: Solicitor, 1999-2003, Associate Partner, 2003-05. Address: (b.) 5th Floor, 7 Castle Street, Edinburgh EH2 3AH; T.-0131 226 8203; e-mail: stuart.hendry@mbmcommercial.co.uk

Henley, Professor John Sebastian, BSc (Eng), PhD. Emeritus Professor of International Management, University of Edinburgh Business School; b. 5.4.43, Malvern; m., Sarah J. Sieley; 2 d. Educ. King Edward's School, Birmingham; University College, London; London School of Economics. Personnel Officer, Glaxo Laboratories, 1966-68; Lecturer, Industrial Relations Department, London School of Economics, 1968-72; Lecturer, Faculty of Commerce, University of Nairobi, 1972-75; joined Department of Business Studies, University of Edinburgh, 1975. Publications: co-author of three books; editor of two books; author of over 50 academic papers. Recreations: gardening; theatre; opera; sailing. Address: (b.) University of Edinburgh Business School, 29 Buccleuch Place, Edinburgh EH8 9JY; T.-07812154772; e-mail: J.Henley@ed.ac.uk

Henry, Hugh. MSP (Labour), Renfrewshire South, 2011-16, Paisley South, 1999-2011; former Shadow Cabinet Secretary for Justice; b. 1952, Glasgow; m.; 1 s.; 2 d. Educ. St Mirin's Academy, Paisley; University of Glasgow; Jordanhill College of Education, Glasgow. Career history: worked as an accountant with IBM UK Ltd; teacher and welfare rights officer with Strathclyde Regional Council; local councillor, 1984-99, including 4 years as leader of Renfrewshire Council (1995-99); was appointed Deputy Minister for Health and Community Care in the Scottish Executive in 2001, and moved to become Deputy Minister for Social Justice in 2002; was appointed Deputy Minister for Justice after the Scottish Parliamentary Election, 2003, and became Minister for Education in 2006; retained the education brief in opposition after the 2007 election. Former Convener, European Committee. Scottish Politician of the Year in 2010, for his performance as Convenor of the Public Affairs Committee.

Henry, Roddy. Principal and Chief Executive, Newbattle Abbey College, since 2021. Career history: Glasgow College of Nautical Studies: Lecturer, Faculty of Maritime Studies, 1998-2003, Senior Lecturer and Course Leader, 2003-05, Academic Registrar, 2005-07; Associate Director/Head of Centre for Learning Effectiveness, Scotland's Colleges/SFEU, 2007-2010; Her Majesty's Inspector of Education, Education Scotland, 2010-2013; Deputy Principal, Inverness College, University of the Highlands and Islands, 2013-2021. Address: Newbattle Road, Newbattle, Dalkeith EH22 3LL.

Henton, Margaret Patricia, MBE, BSc, CGeol, FGS, FCIWEM, FCIWM, FRSE. Non Executive Director, Board Member, The Coal Authority, 2010-2017; Board Member, Royal Botanic Garden Edinburgh, 2011-18; b. Edinburgh; m., Richard Henton; 1 s.; 1 d. Educ. George Watson's College; University of Manchester. Clyde River Purification Board, 1972-75; National Coal Board, 1975; Hydrogeologist, Forth River Purification Board, 1975-78, Inspector, 1978-83; Manager, Scotland, Aspinwall & Co., 1983-89; Director, Scotland and Northern Ireland, Aspinwall & Co., 1989-95; Director, Environmental Strategy, Scottish Environment Protection Agency, 1995-2000; Chief Executive, SEPA, 2000-02; Director of Business and Environment, Environment Agency, 2005-2010. Past President, Chartered Institution of Water and Environmental Management, 1996/7; Chair, Independent Regulatory Challenge Panel, HSE; Trustee, Institute for European Environmental Policy, since 2011; former Council Member, Geological Society of London (2011-18); former Council Member, RSPB (2003-09); former Board Member, UK Carbon Capture and Storage Research Centre (2012-16); Member: RSPB Scotland Committee, since 2018; Board Member, International Centre for Mathematical Sciences. Recreations: travel; hill walking; birdwatching; gardens. E-mail: t.henton@btopenworld.com

Hepburn, Jacqui, MEd, PhD. Director of Workforce, NHS 24, since 2021; UK Head of Organisation Effectiveness (secondment), Abellio Group, 2017-2021. Educ. University of Aberdeen; Ashridge Business School; University of Stirling. Career history: Area Manager, Training and Guidance Unit, Highland Communities NHS Trust, 1991-99; Inverness College UHI: Support Staff Representative, College Board, 1999-2005, Senior College Manager, 1999-2005; SSDA Manager Scotland, Sector Skills Development Agency, 2005-08; Director Scotland, Alliance of Sector Skills Councils, 2008-2010; Director UK, Alliance of Sector Skills Councils UK, 2010-2012; Director Training Academy, Flybe, 2012-14; Member, Strategic Advisory Board for Engineering, Maths and Physical Science, University of Exeter, 2013-14; Governor, Whipton Barton Nursery and Infant School, 2013-14; Director, Ted Wragg Trust, 2013-14; Consultant, The Scottish Government, 2014; Chair, Scottish Passenger Transport Advisory Board, People 1st, 2013-14; Consultant, Scottish Prison Service, 2014-15; Consultant, Police Scotland, 2015-16; Deputy Chief Executive, The Wise Group, 2016-17; Interim Human Resources Director, Abellio ScotRail Ltd, 2017-19.

Hepburn, James Douglas, MSP (SNP), Cumbernauld and Kilsyth, since 2011, Central Scotland, 2007-2011; Minister for Higher Education and Further Education, Youth Employment and Training, since 2021; Minister for Business, Fair Work and Skills, 2018-2021; Minister for Employability and Training, 2016-18; Minister for Sport, Health Improvement and Mental Health, 2014-16; b. 21.5.79, Glasgow; m., Julie Shackleton. Educ. Hyndland Secondary, Glasgow; University of Glasgow. Recreations: football; reading; cinema. Address: Scottish Parliament, Edinburgh EH99 1SP; T.-0131 3486573.
E-mail: jamie.hepburn.msp@scottish.parliament.uk

Herald, Sheriff John Pearson, LLB, SSC. Sheriff of North Strathclyde at Greenock and Rothesay, 1992-2012 (retired); b. 12.7.46, Glasgow; m., Catriona; 1 d. Educ. Hillhead High School, Glasgow; Glasgow University. Partner, Carlton Gilruth, Solicitors, Dundee, 1970-91; Depute Town Clerk, Newport-on-Tay, 1970-75; Member, Angus Legal Aid Committee, 1970-79, Secretary, 1979-87; Member, Legal Aid Central Committee, 1981-87; Temporary Sheriff, 1984-91; part-time Chairman, Industrial Tribunals, 1984-91. Chairman, Dundee Citizens Advice Bureau, 1972-79 and 1982-91; President, Rotary Club of North Fife, 1989. Recreations: football; reading.
E-mail: j.p.herald@talk21.com

Herdman, John Macmillan, MA (Hons), PhD (Cantab), DipTh. Writer, since 1963; b. 20.7.41, Edinburgh; m., Mary Ellen Watson. Educ. Merchiston Castle School, Edinburgh; Magdalene College, Cambridge. Creative Writing Fellow, Edinburgh University, 1977-79; Scottish Arts Council bursaries, 1976, 1982, 1998, 2004; Scottish Arts Council Book Awards, 1978 and 1993; Hawthornden Writer's Fellowship, 1998 and 1995; William Soutar Fellowship, 1990-91. Publications: Descent, 1968; A Truth Lover, 1973; Memoirs of My Aunt Minnie/ Clapperton, 1974; Pagan's Pilgrimage, 1978; Stories Short and Tall, 1979; Voice Without Restraint: Bob Dylan's Lyrics and Their Background, 1982; Three Novellas, 1987; The Double in Nineteenth Century Fiction, 1990; Imelda and Other Stories, 1993; Ghostwriting, 1996; Cruising (play), 1997; Poets, Pubs, Polls and Pillar Boxes, 1999; Four Tales, 2000; The Sinister Cabaret, 2001; Triptych, 2004; My Wife's Lovers, 2007; Some Renaissance Culture Wars, 2010; Another Country, 2013. Recreations: reading; walking; listening to music. Address: (h.) 2/14 Chalmers Crescent, Edinburgh EH9 1TP; T.-0131 667 9554.

Herries, Amanda J. D, MA. Decorative Arts Writer and Lecturer; b. 1.2.55, Belfast, Northern Ireland; formerly

married to William Young-Herries; 3 s. Educ. Christ's Hospital; Newnham College, Cambridge. Curator at The Museum of London (10 years); Residence in Japan (7 years), Lecturing, Advising Arts Companies and Museums; NADFAS Lecturer (range of approximately 12 subjects); Board of Trustees, National Trust for Scotland; Catalogue Co-ordinator, Southern Scotland, Public Catalogue Foundation. Chairman of former arts and fundraising committees in Tokyo and London; Committee Member, Kirkudbright 2000 supporting provision of Art Exhibitions in Kirkcudbright. Recreations: gardening; opera; theatre; exhibitions. Address: (h./b) Herriesdale House, Haugh of Urr, Stewartry of Kirkcudbright DG7 3JZ; T.-07801 537018; e-mail: amandaherries@gmail.com

Hesford, Joanne. Head Teacher, Oldmachar Academy, since 2022. Address: Jesmond Drive, Bridge of Don, Aberdeen AB22 8UR; T.-01224 820887.

Hewitt, Professor David S., MA, PhD, FRSE, FEA, FASLS, Professor Emeritus, formerly Regius Chalmers Professor of English Literature, Aberdeen University; b. 22.4.42, Hawick; m., Angela Catherine Williams; 1 s.; 1 d. Educ. Melrose Grammar School; George Watson's College, Edinburgh; Edinburgh University; Aberdeen University. Aberdeen University: Assistant Lecturer in English, 1964, Lecturer, 1968, Senior Lecturer, 1982, Professor in Scottish Literature, 1994; Treasurer, Association for Scottish Literary Studies, 1973-96; Editor-in-Chief, Edinburgh Edition of the Waverley Novels, complete in 30 vols, 1993-2012; President, Edinburgh Sir Walter Scott Club, 1988-89; Honorary Member, Association for Scottish Literary Studies, 1996; Managing Editor, New Writing Scotland, 1983-86; General Editor, The Oxford Edition of Charles Dickens, since 2014. Publications: Scott on Himself (Editor), 1982; Literature of the North (contributor), 1983; Scott and His Influence, 1984; Longer Scottish Poems, Vol. 2 1650-1830, 1987; Scott in Carnival, 1993; The Antiquary, 1995; Northern Visions, 1996; The Edinburgh Edition of the Waverley Novels: A Guide for Editors, 1996; Redgauntlet, 1997; The Heart of Mid-Lothian, 2003; Rob Roy, 2008; The Betrothed (2009); The Talisman (2009); Woodstock (2009); Sketches by Boz (2020). Address: 21 Ferryhill Place, Aberdeen AB11 7SE; T.-01224 580834; e-mail: david.hewitt@abdn.ac.uk

Hewitt, Gavin Wallace, CMG, MA. Non-Executive Director, Artisanal Spirits Company plc; Non-Executive Chairman, Findr Ltd; Chairman, Friends of Abbotsford; formerly Chief Executive, The Scotch Whisky Association (2003-2013); President, European Spirits Organisation, 2010-2013; Member, Convocation of Heriot Watt University, 2005-2011; Member, Executive Group of Scotland Food & Drink, 2008-2013; Member, Executive of SCDI, 2003-2013; Member of CBI Trade Association Council, 2003-2013; b. 19.10.44, Hawick; 2 s.; 2 d. Educ. George Watson's College, Edinburgh; University of Edinburgh. Ministry of Transport, 1967; seconded to HM Diplomatic Service, and posted to serve overseas at Brussels for negotiation of EC entry, 1970; HM Diplomatic Service with service at home and overseas, 1972, culminating in HM Ambassador to Croatia, 1994-97; HM Ambassador to Finland, 1997-2000; HM Ambassador to Belgium, 2001-2003; Member, International Advisory Board, Scotland Asia Institute, 2013-17; Global Scot, since 2001; Keeper of the Quaich, 2009; Liveryman, Worshipful Company of Distillers, since 2014. Address: (h.) Birchgrove, Eildon, Melrose TD6 0RT; T.-07720842722.
E-mail: gavinhewitt2@googlemail.com

Hewitt, Simon, BSc, PGCert. Principal and Chief Executive Officer, Dundee and Angus College, since 2020. Educ. Abertay University; University of Dundee; Saïd Business School, University of Oxford. Career history: Dundee College, 2008-2014; Digital Schools Awards Validator, Digital Schools Awards, 2017-18; Board Member: Dundee Science Centre, 2017-2021, Digital Skills Partnership Scotland, since 2017; Associate Assessor, Education Scotland, since 2013; Board Member, Workers' Education Association Scotland, since 2019; Non Executive Board Member, Student Awards Agency Scotland (SAAS), since 2020; SQA Advisory Council Member, SQA - Scottish Qualifications Authority, since 2020; Skills Advisory Board Member, DataLab Scotland, since 2021; Chairperson, Energy Skills Partnership (ESP) Scotland, since 2020; Skills Advisory Board Member, ScotlandIS, since 2020; Dundee and Angus College: Academic Head, Creative and Digital Industries, 2014-16; Vice Principal (Curriculum and Attainment), 2016-2020. Address: Dundee and Angus College, Kingsway Campus, Old Glamis Road, Dundee DD5 1NY; T.-0300 123 1010.

Hewitt, Very Rev. William Currie, BD, DipPS. Retired Minister; b. 6.4.51, Kilmarnock; m., Moira Elizabeth MacLeod; 2 s.; 1 d. Educ. Kilmarnock Academy; Glasgow University. Minister: Elderslie Kirk, 1978-2012, Westburn Church, Greenock, 1994-2012; Clerk to the Presbytery of Glasgow, 2012-2017. Moderator, Greenock Presbytery, 1996-97; Moderator, Greenock and Paisley Presbytery, 2003-04; Business Convener, Moderator, General Assembly of the Church of Scotland, 2009-2010. Past President: Innerkip Society, Johnstone Rotary; Paul Harris Award (Greenock Rotary). Recreations: golf; Burns.

Heycock, Professor Caroline Bridget, MA, PhD, FBA. Professor of Syntax, University of Edinburgh, since 2007; b. 22.11.60, Folkestone; m., Robert Sandler. Educ. St. Columba's School; King's College, Cambridge University; University of Pennsylvania. Assistant Professor: Oakland University, USA, 1991-92, Yale University, USA, 1992-94; University of Edinburgh: Lecturer, 1994-99, Reader, 1999-2007. President, Linguistic Association of Great Britain and Northern Ireland (LAGB). Former Editor, Journal of Linguistics. Recreations: walking; cycling. Address: (b.) Room 2.10A, Dugald Stewart Building, 3 Charles Street, Edinburgh EH8 9AD; T.-0131 651 1999.

Heymans, Professor Catherine, MPhys, DPhil, FRSE. Astronomer Royal for Scotland, since 2021; Professor, Astrophysics, University of Edinburgh; Director, German Centre for Cosmological Lensing, Ruhr-University Bochum, Germany. Educ. University of Edinburgh; University of Oxford. Won a series of prestigious fellowships at Max Planck Institute for Astronomy, Canadian Institute of Theoretical Astrophysics, Institut d'astrophysique de Paris and University of Edinburgh; awarded a starting grant and a consolidator grant from the European Research Council (ERC) in 2009 and 2015; appointed a lecturer at the University of Edinburgh; awarded the George Darwin Lectureship by the Royal Astronomical Society in 2017; awarded the Max Planck-Humboldt Research Award in 2018; elected a Fellow of the Royal Society of Edinburgh in 2018. Numerous publications including The Dark Universe (short e-book). Address: Royal Observatory, Room R7, Blackford Hill, Edinburgh EH9 3HJ; T.-0131 668 8301; e-mail: heymans@roe.ac.uk

Heys, Professor Steven Darryll, BMedBiol, MB, ChB, MD, PhD, FRCS(Glas), FRCS(Ed), FRCS(Eng), FHEA. Formerly Head of School of Medicine, Medical Sciences & Nutrition, University of Aberdeen (Emeritus Professor of Surgical Oncology); Consultant Surgeon, Aberdeen Royal Infirmary, since 1992; Honorary Research Fellow, Rowett Research Institute, since 1992; b. 5.7.56, Accrington; m., Margaret Susan Proctor; 2 s.; 1 d. Educ. St. Mary's College, Blackburn; Aberdeen University Medical School. House Officer/SHO, Surgery, Aberdeen Royal Infirmary, 1981-84; Registrar, Grampian Health Board, 1984-87; Wellcome Research Training Fellow, Rowett Research Institute, 1987-89; Lecturer in Surgery, Aberdeen University, 1989-92; Senior Lecturer, 1992-96; Reader, 1996-99; appointed Professor in 1999. Examiner in Surgery, Royal College of Surgeons of Glasgow; External Examiner in Surgery, Royal College of Surgeons of England; External Examiner, Universities of London, Dundee, Belfast; Quality Assurance Team Leader, Postgraduate Medical Education Training Board; Quality Assurance Basic Medical Education and Quality Assurance of Postgraduate Education, General Medical Council; Member, NHS Grampian Board, since 2017. Publications: numerous scientific papers on aspects of breast cancer, oncology, nutrition and metabolism; book chapters on nutrition, metabolism, oncology; author of 3 books focusing on the history of medicine related to the Great War, 1914-18. Recreations: history; piping; flying; cycling. Address: (b.) University of Aberdeen, School of Medicine, Medical Sciences and Nutrition, Polwarth Building, Foresterhill, Aberdeen AB25 2ZD.

Heywood, Karen. Interim Chief Reporter, The Scottish Government. Address: Planning and Environmental Appeals, The Scottish Government, Unit 4, The Courtyard, Callendar Business Park, Falkirk FK1 1XR.

Heywood, Peter. Director, The Living Tradition Ltd., publisher, since 1993; b. 4.10.49, Manchester; m., Heather; 3 d. Educ. Heywood Grammar School. Long involvement with traditional music; founded The Tradition Bearers, recording traditional musicians, 1999; founded Common Ground on the Hill, Scotland, 2001. Recreations: traditional music; hill-walking. Address: (b.) The Living Tradition Ltd, 16 Annandale Gardens, Crosshouse, Kilmarnock, Ayrshire KA2 0LE. E-mail: pete@thetraditionbearers.com

Hibbert, Professor Paul, MBA, PhD, FHEA. Professor of Management, University of St Andrews. Career history: came to academia after a career in industry and management consulting; began academic career as a Research Fellow at the University of Strathclyde, completed an MBA and a PhD (entitled The Past in Play: Tradition and Collaboration); Lecturer and subsequently Reader; appointed to University of St Andrews in 2011, former Head of the School of Management. Contributed to leading journals such as Academy of Management Learning and Education, Journal of Management Studies, Leadership Quarterly, Management Learning, Organizational Research Methods, and Organization Studies; also contributed to a range of scholarly edited collections, such as the Oxford Handbook of Inter-Organizational Relations. Received awards from the Academy of Management, the Australia and New Zealand Academy of Management, and the British Academy of Management. Associate Editor of both Management Learning and the journal Management Teaching Review; elected to the leadership team of the Academy of Management's Management Education and Development Division, and has previously led the British Academy of Management's Inter-Organizational Collaboration group; Fellow of the Higher Education Academy. Address: School of Management, University of St Andrews, The Gateway, North Haugh, St Andrews KY16 9RJ; e-mail: ph24@st-andrews.ac.uk

Hicks, Clare, MA. Director for Education Reform, Scottish Government, since 2021; Deputy Director, Police Division, 2019-2021; Deputy Director, People and Infrastructure, 2015-19. Educ. Sullivan Upper School, Holywood, Co Down; University of Edinburgh.

Career history: Private Secretary to the DFM, Scottish Government, 2007-09; Head of Pay and Reward, Scottish Government Health Directorates, 2009-2013; Deputy Director, Head of the Office of the Chief Scientific Adviser, Scottish Government, 2013-15.

Higgins, Benny, BSc, FFA, FCIBS, DUniv, FRSE. Chairman, National Galleries of Scotland, since 2017; Executive Chairman, Forster Chase Advisory Group, since 2019; Chairman, Buccleuch Group, since 2019 (previously Non-Executive Director, 2012-2019); Chairman of Sistema Scotland, since 2019; Non-Executive Chairman, Markerstudy, since 2021; Non-Executive Chairman, AAB Wealth (Anderson Anderson & Brown Wealth), since 2020; Chairman, The Fine Art Society (London & Edinburgh), since 2021; Chairman, Edinburgh Fringe Society, since 2021; Trustee of Burrell Renaissance, since 2017; Non Executive Director of Arabian Centres, since 2018; Trustee, Edinburgh International Cultural Summit, since 2014; Visiting Professor, University of Strathclyde; Honorary Professor, Edinburgh Business School, Heriot-Watt University; Honorary Professor, University of Edinburgh; Honorary Professor, University of Glasgow; Chairman: N4 Partners, since 2021, Lavanya Plus, since 2021; b. 12.12.60, Paisley; m., Sharon; 2 s.; 4 d. Educ. Holyrood Secondary School; University of Glasgow. Career history: General Manager (Sales), Standard Life, 1995-97; Chief Executive (Retailing Banking), Royal Bank of Scotland (RBS), 1997-2006; Chief Executive Officer (Retail), HBOS plc, 2006-07; Chief Executive, Tesco Bank, 2008-18. Member of the Tesco Executive Committee; Fellow of the Faculty of Actuaries (1986); Fellow of the Chartered Institute of Bankers in Scotland; Fellow of the Royal Society of Edinburgh; Non-Executive Director, Glasgow Life; Trustee, the Edinburgh International Culture Summit; Doctor of University, Glasgow University; Prince's Trust Ambassador. Recreations: reading; poetry; art; football; travel; Italy. Clubs: New Club; Groucho; Two Brydges; Soho House; The Ivy Club; The Academy; 5 Hertford Street. Address: (h.) 7 Doune Terrace, Edinburgh EH3 6DY.

Higgins, John, MBE. Professional snooker player; b. 18.5.75, Wishaw, North Lanarkshire; m., Denise; 2 s.; 1 d. Four time World Champion winning in 1998, 2007, 2009 and 2011. Has won 54 tournaments worldwide. Lives in Bothwell, Lanarkshire.

Higgins, Sheriff Michael. Sheriff at North Strathclyde, since 2021. Educ. Strathclyde University. Career history: completed traineeship with Pacitti Jones, Solicitors, Glasgow in 1990; a Solicitor, and latterly a Partner, with T G Bradshaw & Co, Bellshill; joined Lanarkshire Law Practice Limited in 2013; became a Summary Sheriff in 2019. Former Dean of the Society of Solicitors of Hamilton and Districts; former Tutor in the Diploma in Legal Practice, Glasgow University. Address: Greenock Sheriff Court, 1 Nelson Street, Greenock PA15 1TR; T.-01475 787073.

Higgs, Professor Peter Ware, CH, FRS, FRSE, HonFInstP, DSc (Hon). Professor of Theoretical Physics, Edinburgh University, 1980-96; b. 29.5.29, Newcastle-upon-Tyne; m., Jo Ann Williamson; 2 s. Educ. Cotham Grammar School, Bristol; King's College, London. Postdoctoral Fellow, Edinburgh University, 1954-56, and London University, 1956-58; Lecturer in Mathematics, University College, London, 1958-60; Lecturer in Mathematical Physics, then Reader, Edinburgh University, 1960-80. Hughes Medal, Royal Society, 1981; Rutherford

Medal, Institute of Physics, 1984; James Scott Prize, Royal Society of Edinburgh, 1993; Paul Dirac Medal and Prize, Institute of Physics, 1997; High Energy and Particle Physics Prize, European Physical Society, 1997; Royal Medal, Royal Society of Edinburgh, 2000; Wolf Prize, 2004; Oskar Klein Medal, Royal Swedish Academy of Sciences, 2009; Sakurai Prize, American Physical Society, 2010; Nonino Prize, 2013; Prince of Asturias Prize, 2013; Nobel Prize, 2013; Galileo Galilei Award, 2014; Copley Medal, Royal Society, 2015; Royal Commission for the Exhibition of 1851 Medal. Recreations: music; walking. Address: (h.) 2 Darnaway Street, Edinburgh EH3 6BG; T.-0131-225 7060.

Hill, Professor Malcolm, PhD. Emeritus Professor, University of Strathclyde; formerly Professor for the Child and Society and Professor of Social Work, University of Glasgow; b. 18.9.46, London; m., Dr. Wan Ying Hill; 1 s.; 1 d. Educ. Latymer Upper School, Hammersmith; St. Edmund Hall, Oxford; University of London; University of Edinburgh. Social Worker, 1968-79; Researcher, 1979-84; Lecturer, 1985-93; Senior Lecturer, 1993-96. Publications: books on adoption, child care, youth crime, foster care, middle childhood, children and society. Recreations: bridge; gardening; swimming. Address: 66 Oakfield Avenue, Glasgow G12 8LS.

Hill, Martin, PG Cert, BSc. Chair, Lanarkshire NHS Board, since 2022. Educ. Royal High School, Edinburgh; Institute of Health Service Administrators (Diploma); University of Aberdeen; The Open University. Career history: NHS Trust Chief Executive, NHS Argyll and Clyde, 1993-99; NHS Lanarkshire: NHS Trust Chief Executive, 1999-2004, Depute Chief Executive and Director of Strategic Planning and Performance, Hamilton, 2004-07; Non Executive Board Member, NHS24, 2007-2015; Director, Hill Consulting, 2008-2017; Scottish Institute of Health Management (SIHM): Secretary, 2010-16, Company Secretary, 2016-17; Non Executive Board Member/Vice Chair, NHS Lothian, 2015-2021; Non Executive Board Member, Scottish Environmental Protection Agency (SEPA), since 2016. Address: NHS Lanarkshire Headquarters, Kirklands, Fallside Road, Bothwell G71 8BB.

Hillhouse, Sir (Robert) Russell, KCB, FRSE; b. 23.4.38, Glasgow; m., Alison Fraser (deceased 2015); 2 d. Educ. Hutchesons' Grammar School, Glasgow; Glasgow University. Entered Home Civil Service as Assistant Principal, Scottish Education Department, 1962; Principal, 1966; HM Treasury, 1971; Assistant Secretary, Scottish Office, 1974; Scottish Home and Health Department, 1977; Principal Finance Officer, Scottish Office, 1980; Under-Secretary, Scottish Education Department, 1985; Secretary, 1987; Permanent Under-Secretary of State, Scottish Office, 1988-98. Director: Bank of Scotland, 1998-2001, Scottish Provident Institution, 1999-2001; Governor, Royal Scottish Academy of Music and Drama, 2000-08; Chairman, Edinburgh Competition Festival Association, 2010-14. Recreations: making music. Address: 12 Russell Place, Edinburgh EH5 3HH; e-mail: rhillhouse@blueyonder.co.uk

Hillier, Professor Stephen Gilbert, OBE, BSc, MSc, PhD, DSc, FRCPath, FRCOG. Professor (Emeritus), Edinburgh University, since 2014, Vice Principal - International, 2008-14; Honorary Consultant Clinical Scientist, NHS Lothian; Professor, MRC Centre for Reproductive Health, Edinburgh University, 1994-2014; Governor, George Watson's College, since 2015; Member: Edinburgh University General Council Business Committee, since 2016; Curator of Patronage, University of Edinburgh, 2016-19; Editor-in-Chief, Journal of Endocrinology, 2000-05; Editor-in-Chief, Molecular Human Reproduction, 2007-2012; b. 16.1.49, Hillingdon; m., Haideh; 2 d. Educ. Hayes County Grammar School; Leeds University; Welsh National School of Medicine. Postdoctoral Research Fellow, National Institutes of Health, USA, 1976-78; Research Scientist, University of

Leiden, 1978-82; Senior Lecturer: Reproductive Biochemistry, RPMS, London University, 1982-85, Department of Obstetrics and Gynaecology, Edinburgh University, 1985-94. Member: Interim Licensing Authority for Human Fertilisation and Embryology, 1987-91, Human Fertilisation and Embryology Authority, 1990-96; 1991 Society for Endocrinology Medal; 2004 British Fertility Society Patrick Steptoe Medal; 2006 Society for Endocrinology Jubilee Medal. Appointed OBE in the 2015 New Year's Honours list for services to international higher education. Publications: Ovarian Endocrinology, 1991; Scientific Essentials of Reproductive Medicine, 1996. Recreation: fly-fishing. Address: (b.) MRC University of Edinburgh Centre for Reproductive Health, Queen's Medical Research Institute, Edinburgh BioQuarter, 47 Little France Crescent, Edinburgh EH16 4TJ.
E-mail: s.hillier@ed.ac.uk

Hillmeyer, Jack. Consul General at U.S. Consulate General Edinburgh, since 2021. Career history: Public Affairs, U.S. Consulate General Milan, 2008-2011; Spokesperson, U.S. Embassy Pretoria, South Africa, 2012-15; U.S. Mission to NATO: Public Affairs Advisor, 2015-18, Political Advisor, 2018-19; Deputy Consul General, U.S. Consulate General Karachi, Pakistan, 2019-2021. Address: U.S Consulate General in Edinburgh, 3 Regent Terrace, Edinburgh EH7 5BW; T.-0131 556 8315.

Hillston, Jane, FRSE, PhD, MSc, BA, FBCS, MAE. Chair, Quantitative Modelling, University of Edinburgh, since 2006; Deputy Vice Principal, Research, since 2020; Head of School of Informatics, since 2018; Deputy Head of School and Director of Research, School of Informatics, 2016-18; Director of the Laboratory for Foundations of Computer Science (2011-2014); b. 14.11.63, Manchester. Educ. Fallowfield High School for Girls, Manchester; University of York; Lehigh University, USA; University of Edinburgh. Business Analyst, Logical Financial Software Ltd, 1987-88; Research Assistant: Kingston Business School, Kingston University, 1988-89, Department of Computer Science, University of Edinburgh, 1989-91; PhD in Computer Science, 1994; EPSRC Postdoctoral fellowship, 1994-95; Distinguished Dissertation Award from the British Computer Society and the Council of Professors and Heads of Computing, 1995; Lecturer, Department of Computer Science, University of Edinburgh, 1995-2001, Reader, School of Informatics, 2001-06; Roger Needham Award, 2005; Elected Fellow of the British Computer Society; Elected Fellow, RSE, 2007; EPSRC Advanced Research Fellow, 2005-2010. Member, Learned Society and Knowledge Services Board and the Learned Society Awards Committee of the British Computer Society, 2006-09; Chair of the judging panel of the BCS/CPHC Distinguished Dissertation competition (2007-09); Member: Board of Informatics Europe, 2014-2017, UK Computing Research Committee, EPSRC College of Peers, B4 Sectional Committee of the RSE, 2008-2012 and 2019-2022; Executive Committee of UK Computing Research Committee, 2016-2022 (Chair, 2018-21); member of the Strategic Advisory Board of the DataLab Innovation Centre, since 2021. Address: (b.) School of Informatics, University of Edinburgh, The Informatics Forum, 10 Crichton Street, Edinburgh EH8 9AB; T.-0131 650 5199; e-mail: jane.hillston@ed.ac.uk

Hilton, Cara. MSP (Labour), Dunfermline, 2013-16; Chair, Scottish Labour, since 2020; m., Simon; 3 c. Daughter of former Labour MSP Cathy Peattie.

Hinds, Lesley. Lord Lieutenant and Lord Provost, City of Edinburgh, 2003-07; former Councillor, Inverleith Ward of the City of Edinburgh Council (2012-17); former Convener of Transport and Environment Committee (2012-17); former Chair, Transport for Edinburgh Board; b. 3.8.56, Dundee; m., Martin; 1s.; 2d. Educ. Kirkton High School, Dundee; Dundee College of Education. Teacher, Deans Primary School, 1977-80; Chair, Health Scotland, 2001-07; Labour Councillor, Edinburgh DC, 1984-96 (Leader, 1993-96); City of Edinburgh Council, since 1996; Past Chair: Edinburgh International Festival Society; Edinburgh Military Tattoo Ltd; N Edinburgh Area Renewal (NEAR); Director: N Edinburgh Arts; former Chair, Edinburgh International Conference Centre. Recreations: theatre; dance; swimming; travel.

Hinds, Ronnie. Chair, Local Government Boundary Commission for Scotland, since 2013. Career history: qualified accountant with over 30 years' experience in local government in Scotland and the UK; Director of Finance, North Lanarkshire Council, 1999-2000; Controller of Audit, Audit Scotland, 2000-03; Head of Financial Services, City of Edinburgh Council, 2003-06; Chief Executive, Fife Council, 2006-2013; Deputy Chair, Accounts Commission, until 2019. Address: Local Government Boundary Commission, Thistle House, 91 Clifton Terrace, Edinburgh EH12 5HD.

Hine, Professor Harry Morrison, MA, DPhil (Oxon). Scotstarvit Professor of Humanity, St. Andrews University, 1985-2008 (Emeritus); b. 19.6.48, Portsmouth; m., Rosalind Mary Ford; 1 d.; 1 s. Educ. King Edward's School, Birmingham; Corpus Christi College, Oxford. P.S. Allen Junior Research Fellow, Corpus Christi College, 1972-75; Lecturer in Humanity, Edinburgh University, 1975-85. Editor (Joint), The Classical Review, 1987-93. Publications: An Edition with Commentary of Seneca, Natural Questions, Book Two, 1981; Studies in the Text of Seneca's Naturales Quaestiones, 1996; L. Annaei Senecae Naturales Quaestiones (Editor), 1996; Seneca, Medea, Translation and commentary, 2000; Seneca, Natural Questions, Translation, 2010. Recreations: walking; reading. Address: (h.) 33 Drumcarrow Road, St. Andrews, Fife KY16 8SE; e-mail: hmh@st-and.ac.uk

Hirst, Sir Michael William, LLB, CA, FRSA, MCIPR, DLitt (2004), FRCP (Edin), 2012. Chairman, Scottish Conservative and Unionist Party, 1993-97; b. 2.1.46, Glasgow; m., Naomi Ferguson Wilson; 1 s.; 2 d. Educ. Glasgow Academy; Glasgow University. Partner, Peat Marwick Mitchell & Co., Chartered Accountants, until 1983; Chairman: Pagoda Public Relations Ltd. (2000-2016), Millstream Associates Ltd. (2001-2016); Director of and Consultant to various companies; contested: Central Dunbartonshire, February and October, 1974, East Dunbartonshire, 1979; MP (Conservative), Strathkelvin and Bearsden, 1983-87; Member, Select Committee on Scottish Affairs, 1983-87; Parliamentary Private Secretary, Department of Energy, 1985-87; Vice-Chairman, Scottish Conservative Party, 1987-89; Chairman, Scottish Conservative Candidates Association, 1978-81; Chairman, Stirling and Clackmannanshire Conservative and Unionist Association, since 2017, and President (2001-2017); Member, Court, Glasgow Caledonian University, 1992-98; Member, Council of the Imperial Society of Knights Bachelor and Chairman, Scottish Division, since 2002 and Registrar, since 2017; President, Scottish Conservative and Unionist Association, 1989-1992; Chairman, Diabetes UK, 2001-06, Vice President, 2006-2019; Vice-President, International Diabetes Federation, 2006-09, President-Elect, 2009-2012, Global President, 2012-15, Hon. President, since 2015; Chairman, Global Network of Parliamentary Champions for Diabetes (PDGN Limited), since 2015; Chairman, The Park School Educational Trust, 1993-2010; Chairman, Friends of Kippen Kirk Trust, since 2003; Director, Children's Hospice Association Scotland, 1995-2005; Director, Erskine Hospital, Erskine, 1980-2011;

Elder, Kippen Parish Church. Recreations: golf; hill-walking; skiing. Address: (h.) Thistle Cottage, Fore Road, Kippen, Stirlingshire FK8 3DT.
E-mail: smh@glentirran.co.uk

Hiscox, Professor Caroline. Chief Executive, NHS Grampian, since 2020. Career history: Executive Nurse Director, NHS Grampian, 2018-2020; awarded a PhD in 2019 following extensive research into the behavioural aspects of professional accountability in the nursing workforce; Honorary Chair, University of Stirling; Visiting Chair, Robert Gordon University. Address: NHS Grampian, Summerfield House, 2 Eday Road, Aberdeen AB15 6RE; T.-01224 558642.
E-mail: gram.grampianchiefexecutive@nhs.scot

Hitchman, Professor Michael L., BSc, DPhil, CSci, CChem, FRSC, FRSA, FRSE. Emeritus Professor, University of Strathclyde, since 2004; Young Professor of Chemistry, Strathclyde University, 1984-2004; b. 17.8.41, Woburn, Bedfordshire; 1 s.; 2 d; m., Dr. Migeun Park; 2 step d. Educ. Stratton Grammar School, Biggleswade; Queen Mary College and King's College, London University; University College, Oxford. Assistant Lecturer in Chemistry, Leicester Regional College of Technology, 1963-65; Junior Research Fellow, Wolfson College, Oxford, 1968-70; ICI Postdoctoral Research Fellow, Physical Chemistry Laboratory, Oxford University, 1968-70; Chief Scientist, Orbisphere Corporation, Geneva, 1970-73; Staff Scientist, Laboratories RCA Ltd., Zurich, 1973-79; Lecturer, then Senior Lecturer, Salford University, 1979-84; Strathclyde University: Chairman, Department of Pure and Applied Chemistry, 1986-89, Vice-Dean, Faculty of Science, 1989-92; Honorary Professor, Taiyuan University of Technology, China, since 1994; Visiting Professor, University of West of Scotland, since 2006. Royal Society of Chemistry: Chairman, Electro-analytical Group, 1985-88, Treasurer, Electrochemistry Group, 1984-90; Member, Chemistry and Semiconductor Committees, Science and Engineering Research Council; Member, 1985-92, Chairman, 1989-92, International Advisory Board, EUROCVD; Director, Thin Film Innovations Ltd., 2000-2012; Director, Innovative Coating Technologies Ltd., 2010-2017; Director, Jinju Consultancies Ltd., 2004-2019; Director, Campsie Initiatives Ltd., since 2019; Medal and Prize, British Vacuum Council, 1993. Editor, Chemical Vapor Deposition (CVD), 1995-2015. Publications: Ring-disk Electrodes (Co-Author), 1971; Measurement of Dissolved Oxygen, 1978; Proceedings 8th European Conference on CVD (Co-Editor), 1991; Chemical Vapor Deposition (Co-Editor), 1993; Proceedings 15th International Symposium on CVD (Co-Editor), 2000; Proceedings 15th European Conference on CVD (Co-Editor), 2005; Chemical Vapour Deposition: Precursors, Processes and Applications (Co-Editor), 2008. Recreations: humour; eating; rambling; losing weight.

Hockley, Rear Admiral Chris, CBE, DL. Chief Executive, The MacRobert Trust, since 2014; Deputy Lieutenant of Aberdeenshire, since 2018; b. 24.8.59. Educ. Dulwich College; Royal Naval Engineering Coll. Manadon. Defence Logistics Organisation/Director Supportability & Logistics, MoD/Royal navy, 2005-07; Naval Base Commander Clyde, UK Ministry of Defence, 2007-2011; Deputy Director, Defence Support Review, Ministry of Defence of UK, 2011; Rear Admiral - FOSNNI, FORF, FORes, Ministry of Defence, 2011-14; Chairman, Marine Engineering Advisory Panel, Royal Navy, 2012-14; Rear Admiral, Royal Navy, 1977-2014. Address: The MacRobert Trust, Cromar, Tarland, Aberdeenshire AB34 4UD; T.-013398 81444.

Hodge, The Rt. Hon. Lord (Patrick Stewart Hodge), QC, BA, LLB. Deputy President of the Supreme Court of the United Kingdom, since 2020; b. 19.5.53; m. Penelope Jane Wigin; 2 s.; 1 d. Educ. Croftinloan School, Pitlochry; Trinity College, Glenalmond; Corpus Christi College, Cambridge; University of Edinburgh, School of Law. Career history: worked as a civil servant at the Scottish Office, 1975-78; admitted to the Faculty of Advocates in 1983; Standing Junior Counsel to the Department of Energy, 1989-1991; Inland Revenue, 1991-96; took silk in 1996; served as a part-time Commissioner, Scottish Law Commission, 1997-2003; a Judge of the Courts of Appeal of Jersey and Guernsey, and Procurator to the General Assembly of the Church of Scotland, 2000-2005; appointed a Senator of the College of Justice in 2005 (particular responsibility as the Exchequer judge in the Court of Session); became a Justice of the Supreme Court of the United Kingdom in 2013. Governor, Merchiston Castle School, Edinburgh, since 1998. Recreations: opera; skiing; member of Bruntsfield Links Golfing Society.

Hodge, Robin Mackenzie, OBE, BA (Hons). Publisher, The List magazine, since 1985; b. Edinburgh. Educ. Edinburgh Academy; Clifton College, Bristol; Durham University. Certificat Europeen en Administration de Projects Culturels (Bruxelles). Production Director, Canongate Publishing Ltd., 1981-84; restoration of 16th-century buildings around Tweeddale Court, Edinburgh Old Town, 1981-88; founded The List, 1985; Chairman, PPA Scotland, 2002-04. OBE (New Year Honours 2012). Address: (b.) 14 High Street, Edinburgh EH1 1TE; T.-0131-550 3050.

Hodgson, Fiona, BAcc (Hons). Chief Executive, Scottish & Northern Ireland Plumbing Employers' Federation (SNIPEF), since 2016. Educ. Monifieth High School; University of Dundee. Career history: Manager, Deloitte, 1990-95; SNIPEF: Finance Manager, 1995-2014, Head of Finance and Membership Services, 2014-16. Address: Scottish & Northern Ireland Plumbing Employers' Federation, Bellevue House, 22 Hopetoun Street, Edinburgh EH7 4GH; T.-0131 556 0600; e-mail: info@snipef.org

Hodson, Celia. Founder, Hey Girls, since 2017. Educ. University of Suffolk. Career history: Deputy Chief Executive, Social Enterprise UK (Social Enterprise Coalition), 2005-08; Chief Executive, Suffolk Development Agency, 2008-2011; Founding Chief Executive, Eastern Enterprise Hub, East of England, 2010-2012; Chief Executive Officer, School for Social Entrepreneurs Australia, 2012-15; Chief Executive, Journeys for Change, UK, India, Brazil, Australia, 2016-17; Non Executive Director, Social Enterprise Academy International Ltd, 2017-2020; Board Member, The Asda Social Enterprise Supplier Development Academy, 2016-20. Multi Award-winning CEO: Great British Entrepreneur National Winner, 2019; STV Social Entrepreneur of the year, 2018; Virgin Start-Up of the Year and Women in Business Social Impact and Start-Up, 2018. Address: Hey Girls, Unit 2 Newhailes Business Park, Newhailes Road, Musselburgh EH21 6RH; T.-0131 665 6483; e-mail: contact@heygirls.co.uk

Hodson, Rev Martin. General Director, The Baptist Union of Scotland, since 2019; m., Rebekah; 3 s. Educ. Oxford University. Career history: initial career in production management with Kangol Ltd; served as a minister in churches in Cumbria and Aberdeen and then as senior minister at St Peter's Baptist Church, Worcester; spent four years serving as Ministry Development Coordinator, The Baptist Union of Scotland (2015-19). Currently working on a doctorate in Practical Theology, Glasgow University. Address: The Baptist Union of Scotland, 48 Speirs Wharf, Glasgow G4 9TH; T.-0141 4334559.
E-mail: martin@scottishbaptist.org.uk

Hogg, Lt. Col. Colin Grant Ogilvie, OBE, DL. King's Own Scottish Borderers (KOSB), 1962-2008; Regimental Secretary, 1991-2008; b. 6.12.43, Glasgow; m., Cynthia Rose Mackenzie; 2 d. Educ. St. Mary's Preparatory School;

Merchiston Castle School. Commissioned into KOSB, 1965; service with 1st Battalion in Aden, Hong Kong, Borneo, BAOR, Berlin, Northern Ireland; Deputy Assistant Adjutant General, HQ of 1st Armoured Division, Germany, 1981-83; on directing staff, Royal Military Academy, Sandhurst, 1983-84; Commanding Officer, 2nd Battalion, 52 Lowland Volunteers, 1985-88; SOI, Foot Guards and Infantry Manning and Records Office, 1988-91; retired from active list, 1991; Honorary Colonel of the Lothian and Border Army Cadet Force, 1997-2006. Member, Queen's Bodyguard for Scotland, since 1986; Member, Ancient Order of Mosstroopers; Chairman, Borders Branch, SSAFA Forces Help, 1993-2010, National Vice President, since 2010, Member, National Council, 2000-06; Board Member, South of Scotland Youth Awards Trust, since 1994, Trustee and Chairman, since 2010; Chairman, Roxburgh and Berwickshire Conservative and Unionist Association, 1995-98; Governor: Oxenfoord Castle School, 1986-93, St. Mary's School, Melrose, 1994-98; President, Jedburgh Branch, Royal British Legion Scotland, 2005-2012; Member, National Council, Royal British Legion Scotland, 1998-2004; Trustee, Poppyscotland (Earl Haig Fund Scotland), 2000-2011; Member, Poppyscotland Scottish Advisory Committee to the Royal British Legion, 2011-16; Honorary Director, Lord Roberts Workshops; Chairman, South of Scotland Youth Awards Trust, since 2012; Deputy Lieutenant, Roxburgh, Ettrick and Lauderdale, 1995-2018; appointed to the Church of Scotland Committee on Chaplains to HM Forces, 2015. Recreations: field sports and equestrian events. Address: (h.) Viewfield, Bowden, Melrose TD6 0ST.

Hogg, Kenneth. Scottish Government Director, 2018-2020; Interim Chief Officer, Scottish Police Authority, 2017-18; m.; 2 c. Educ. University of Edinburgh; IoD. Career history: Private Secretary, UK Government Cabinet Office, 1993-94; Health policy adviser, US Government Department of Health & Human Services, 1995-96; Business Development, ScottishPower plc, 2000-01; Scottish Government: Head of Public Transport & Aviation, 2001-02, Head of Rail, 2002-05, Head of Public Health & Substance Misuse, 2005-08, Head of Health Delivery, 2008-09, Director for Safer Communities, 2009-2012, Director for Local Government and Communties, 2013-17.

Holden, Catherine Ann, MA (Oxon). Director of independent consultancy providing strategy, facilitation and coaching across the arts, heritage and creative industries (www.CatherineHoldenConsulting.com); b. 26.9.64, Blackburn, Lancs. Educ. Oxford University; Droitwich High School. Career history: Brand Manager, Rank Hovis McDougall, 1987-90; Marketing Manager, National Theatre, 1990-94; Head of Marketing, Tate, 1994-2001; Head of Communications, Natural History Museum, 2001-04; National Museums Scotland: Director of Marketing & Development, 2004-2012, Director of External Relations, 2012-2016. Non-executive roles include Chair, Craft Scotland, since 2016; Board Member: Clore Leadership, since 2022, Fruitmarket Gallery, since 2009, Craft Scotland, since 2015, Edinburgh Art Festival, 2014-15, Arts Marketing Association, 1998-2001. Recreations: visual and performing arts; reading; writing; horse riding.

Holdsworth, Professor Lesley, PhD, MPhil, FCSP, MSCP, DipPT, SRP. Clinical Lead for Digital Health and Care, Scottish Government, since 2015; Professor, Glasgow Caledonian University, since 2021; Associate Director, NHS Education Scotland (Part-time), since 2021. Educ. Sheffield University; Glasgow University. Career history: various clinical positions in Sheffield and Nottingham, NHS in England, 1980-83; Senior Physiotherapist, NHS Tayside, 1983-86; Superintendent Physiotherapist, NHS Greater Glasgow and Clyde, 1985-86; NHS Tayside: Superintendent Physiotherapist, 1986-89, Research and Audit Lead, 1989-99; Head of

Governance and Effectiveness, NHS Forth Valley, 1999-2007; Winston Churchill Fellow, Winston Churchill Memorial Trust, 2011-12; Lecturer/Senior Lecturer/Honorary Lecturer, Glasgow Caledonian University, 1997-2012; AHP Director, NHS 24, 2010-2013; Chair, Scottish NMAHP ehealth network, 2013-15; Healthcare Improvement Scotland: Head of Health Services Research and Effectiveness, 2007-2013, Special Programmes and Internal Improvement Lead, 2013-15. Vice Chair, Board of Management, Bield Housing and Care, since 2014. Scottish Digital Impact of the Year Award 2018 at the 1st Annual Scottish Digital Health and Care Awards. Address: (h.) 84 West Road, Newport on Tay, Fife DD6 8HP.
E-mail: lkholdsworth@gmail.com

Holliday-Williams, Mike, BA (Hons), DMS, MBA. Chief Executive Officer, Aegon UK, since 2019; b. 6.70. Educ. Bangor University; Oxford Brookes University; Ashridge Executive Education, Hult International Business School. Career history: Store Manager, WHSmith, 1991-97; P&L MD, Marketing, Strategy and Business Development - Energy and Telecoms, Centrica, 1997-2006; RSA: Managing Director, MORE TH>N and Personal Lines, 2006-2011, CEO Scandinavia, 2011-14; Managing Director, UK Personal Lines, Direct Line Group, 2014-19. Member, Aegon's Management Board, since March 2020. Address: Aegon UK, 1 Lochside Crescent, Edinburgh EH12 9SE; T.-0370 600 0337.

Holloway, James Essex, BA (Hons), CBE. Director, Scottish National Portrait Gallery, 1997-2012; b. 24.11.48, London. Educ. Marlborough College; Courtauld Institute, London University. Assistant Keeper, National Gallery of Scotland; Assistant Keeper, National Museum of Wales; Deputy Keeper, Scottish National Portrait Gallery. Trustee, Abbotsford House (Chairman of the Trustees), Fleming Collection, Historic Scotland Foundation. Recreations: India; motorbikes; French Horn. Address: (h.) 20 India Street, Edinburgh EH3 6HB.

Holloway, Rt. Rev. Richard Frederick, BD, STM, DUniv (Strathclyde), DD (Aberdeen), DLitt (Napier), DD (Glasgow), FRSE, DUniv (OU), LLD (Dundee), 2009, DUniv (Stirling), 2010, DLitt (St Andrews), 2017. Gresham Professor of Divinity, 1997-2001; Bishop of Edinburgh, 1986-2000; Primus of the Scottish Episcopal Church, 1992-2000; Chair, SAC, since 2005; Chair, Scottish Screen, since 2007; Chair, Creative Scotland Joint Board, 2007-2010; Chair, Sistema Scotland, 2007-2018; b. 26.11.33; m., Jean Elizabeth Kennedy; 1 s.; 2 d. Educ. Kelham Theological College; Edinburgh Theological College; Union Theological Seminary, New York. Curate, St. Ninian's, Glasgow, 1959-63; Priest-in-charge, St. Margaret and St. Mungo's, Glasgow, 1963-68; Rector, Old St. Paul's, Edinburgh, 1968-80; Rector, Church of the Advent, Boston, Mass, 1980-84; Vicar, St. Mary Magdalen's, Oxford, 1984-86. Doctor of The Royal Conservatoire of Scotland, 2012. Recreations: long-distance walking; reading; going to the cinema; listening to music. Address: (h.) 6 Blantyre Terrace, Edinburgh EH10 5AE.
E-mail: richard@docholloway.org.uk

Holmes, Professor Megan Christine, BSc, PhD. Professor of Molecular Neuroendocrinology, University of Edinburgh; m., Dr Ferenc A. Antoni; 3 s. Educ. Stourbridge Girls' High School; London University. Exchange Fellow, Royal Society, London, and Hungarian Academy of Sciences, Budapest, at Institute of Experimental Medicine, Budapest, 1982-83; Fogarty Visiting Fellow, Endocrinology and Reproduction Research Branch, National Institute of Child Health, Bethesda, 1983-85; Department of Medicine, Western General Hospital, Edinburgh: Wellcome Postdoctoral Fellowship, 1992-94, Wellcome Career Development

Fellowship, 1995-98. Recreation: hill-walking. Address: (b.) Endocrine Unit, Centre for Cardiovascular Sciences, Queen's Medical Research Institute, Little France, Edinburgh EH16 4TJ; T.-0131 242 6737.

Holmes, Professor Peter Henry, OBE, BVMS, PhD, DUniv (hc), DSc (hc), FRCVS, FRSE. Emeritus Professor of Veterinary Physiology, University of Glasgow, Professor, 1982-2008 (retired); formerly Pro Vice-Principal, Vice-Principal, 1997-2005; b. 6.6.42, Cottingham, Yorkshire; m., Ruth Helen; 2 d. Educ. Beverley Grammar School, Yorkshire; University of Glasgow. Joined staff of University of Glasgow Veterinary School, Department of Veterinary Physiology, 1966. Member, Court, University of Glasgow, 1991-95; served on committees of ODA (DfID), BVA, UFAW, RSE; former chair, WHO Strategic & Technical Advisory Group (STAG) for Neglected Tropical Diseases. Recreations: hillwalking; golf; cycling. Address: (b.) 2, Barclay Drive, Helensburgh G84 9RD.

Holmes, Stephen Ralph, MA (Cantab), MTh, PhD. Head of School of Divinity, University of St Andrews, since 2016, Senior Lecturer in Theology, since 2009; b. 8.9.69, Belper; m., Heather Clare (nee Taylor); 3 d. Educ. Dover Grammar School for Boys; Peterhouse, Cambridge; Spurgeon's College, London; King's College London. Minister, West Wickham & Shirley Baptist Church, 1996-98; Research Fellow, Spurgeon's College, 1996-99; Lecturer in Christian Doctrine, King's College London, 1998-2004; Lecturer in Theology, University of St Andrews, 2005-09. Accredited minister, Baptist Union of Scotland; Council member: Evangelical Alliance UK, Scottish Bible Society; published numerous books on topics in Christian theology at academic and popular level; numerous articles in learned journals. Address: (b.) St. Mary's College, St Andrews KY16 9JU; T.-01334 462838; e-mail: sh80@st-andrews.ac.uk

Holroyd, Nicholas Weddall, BCL (Oxon), LLB, TEP, FSA Scot. Advocate, since 1992. Educ. Christ Church, Oxford University; University of Edinburgh, Thow Scholarship in Jurisprudence. Trainee, Dundas and Wilson, CS, 1989-91; "devilling" for the Bar, 1991-92; part-time Tutor, Edinburgh University, 1993-2001; Part-time Tutor, University of Glasgow, 2013-2015; Clerk to Faculty of Advocates Law Reform Committee, 1996; Member of Faculty Council, 2004-07; Contributor, Greens' Litigation Styles, since 1996; Contributor, Tolley's Pension Dispute Procedures and Remedies; Committee Member, Society of Trust and Estate Practitioners (Scotland), 2007-2013; Member, Society of Trust and Estate Practitioners EU Committee, 2012-2018; Chairman, Trust Bar, 2015-2018. Recreation: golf. Address: Advocates Library, Old Parliament House, Edinburgh EH1 1RF; T.-0131-226 5071.

Holt, Rebecca Louise. Chief Executive, Eden Court Theatre, Inverness, since 2022; b. 1.88. Career history: Battersea Arts Centre: Assistant to the Directors, 2011-13, Executive Manager, 2013-15, Chief Operating Officer, 2015-15, Executive Director and Deputy Chief Executive Officer, 2017-2022. Former Trustee of Polka children's theatre and a former Director of the London Theatre Consortium. Address: Eden Court Theatre, Bishop's Road, Inverness, IV3 5SA; T.-01463 239841. E-mail: lalexander@eden-court.co.uk

Holton, Yvonne, BA (Hons), FRSA, SHA. Islay Herald, since 2021; b. 2.7.59, Aberdeen; m. Derek Holton. Educ. St. Margaret's School for Girls, Aberdeen; Edinburgh College of Art. Career history: freelance jeweller designer and book illustrator; Heraldic Artist appointed to the Court of the Lord Lyon in 1990; appointed Dingwall Pursuivant in 2011; Herald Painter to the Court of the Lord Lyon, 2005-2021. Recreations: gemmology; gardening. Address: 11 Mayburn Terrace, Loanhead, Midlothian EH20 9EH. E-mail: yholton@freeuk.com

Home, Earl of (David Alexander Cospatrick Douglas-Home), KT, CVO, CBE. Chairman, Grosvenor Group Ltd., 2007-2010; Chairman, Coutts & Co. Ltd. 2000-2017; Chairman, Coutts & Co., 1999-2013; b. 20.11.43, Coldstream; m., Jane Margaret Williams-Wynne; 1 s.; 2 d. Educ. Eton; Christ Church, Oxford. Joined Morgan Grenfell & Co. Limited, 1966; appointed Director, 1974 (retired, 1999); Chairman, Morgan Grenfell (Scotland) Ltd., 1986 (resigned 1999); ECGD: Member, Export Advisory Council, 1988-93, Member, Projects Committee, 1989-93; Member, Advisory Board, National Forest, 1991-94; Chairman, CEGELEC Controls Ltd., 1991-94; Council Member, Glenalmond School, since 1995; Conservative Front-Bench Spokesman on Trade, Industry and Finance, 1997-98; appointed Director, Coutts & Co., 1999; Trustee, The Grosvenor Estate, 1993-2010; Chairman, MAN Ltd., 2000-09; Director, Dubai Financial Services Authority, 2005-2012. Recreations: outdoor sports. Address: (b.) Coutts & Co., 440 Strand, London WC2R 0QS; T.-020 7753 1000.

Home Robertson, John David. MSP (Labour), East Lothian, 1999-2007 (Convenor, Holyrood Progress Group, 2000-04, Scottish Executive Depute Minister for Rural Affairs, 1999-2000, former Member, Communities Committee, Scottish Parliament); MP (Labour), East Lothian, 1983-2001 (Berwick & East Lothian, 1978-83); b. 5.12.48, Edinburgh; m., Catherine Brewster; 2 s. Educ. Ampleforth College; West of Scotland Agricultural College. Farmer; Member: Berwickshire District Council, 1974-78, Borders Health Board, 1975-78; Chairman, Eastern Borders Citizens' Advice Bureau, 1976-78; Member, Select Committee on Scottish Affairs, 1979-83; Chairman, Scottish Group of Labour MPs, 1983; Scottish Labour Whip, 1983-84; Opposition Front Bench Spokesman on Agriculture, 1984-87, on Scotland, 1987-88, on Agriculture, 1988-90; Member, Select Committee on Defence, 1990-97; Member, British-Irish Parliamentary Body, 1993-99; Parliamentary Private Secretary to Dr Jack Cunningham, 1997-99; established Paxton Trust, 1988; Edinburgh Direct Aid convoys to Bosnia, 1994 and 1995 (HGV driver); Observer, elections in Sarajevo, 1996.

Honeyman, Greig, LLB (Hons), NP, WS. Consultant, Shepherd and Wedderburn LLP, since 2014; b. 1.10.55, Kirkcaldy; m., Alison; 1 s.; 1 d. Educ. Dunfermline High School; University of Edinburgh. Apprenticeship, W. & J. Burness, WS, 1977-79; enrolled as a Solicitor, 1979; Solicitor, Scottish Special Housing Association, 1979-81; Admitted as Notary Public, 1983; Admitted to the WS Society, 1984; Partner: McNiven & Co., 1981-85, Honeyman & Mackie, 1985-90, Bird Semple Fyfe Ireland - (de-merger 1994), later Fyfe Ireland WS, 1990-2005, later Fyfe Ireland LLP merged with Tods Murray, 2012, merged with Shepherd and Wedderburn, 2014. Recreation: rugby spectating. Address: (b.) 1 Exchange Crescent, Edinburgh EH3 8UL; e-mail: greig.honeyman@shepwedd.com

Hood, Very Rev. Dr. E. Lorna, OBE, MA, BD, DD. Minister, Renfrew North Parish Church, 1979-2016; Honorary Chaplain to the Queen in Scotland, since 2008; Moderator of the General Assembly of the Church of Scotland, 2013-14; b. Irvine, 1953; m., Peter; 2 c. Educ. Kilmarnock Academy; University of Glasgow. Ordained by the Church of Scotland's Presbytery of Edinburgh in 1978 whilst serving as Assistant Minister at St Ninian's Church in Corstorphine, Edinburgh. Assessed as one of the 100 most powerful women in the United Kingdom by Woman's Hour on BBC Radio 4 in February 2013. Honorary Degree of Doctor of Divinity awarded by Glasgow University, December 2014; General Trustee, Church of Scotland, since 2001. Awarded Point of Light by Prime Minister, July 2015; Chair of Remembering Srebrenica Scotland, 2015-2020; Chair of Youthlink Scotland, since November 2016. Awarded OBE in Queen's Birthday Honours list, 2017.

Hook, Professor Andrew Dunnet, MA, PhD, FRSE, FBA. Bradley Professor of English Literature, Glasgow University, 1979-98; b. 21.12.32, Wick; m., Judith Ann (deceased); 2 s.; (1 deceased); 1 d. (deceased). Educ. Wick High School; Daniel Stewart's College, Edinburgh; Edinburgh University; Manchester University; Princeton University. Edinburgh University: Assistant Lecturer in English Literature, 1961-63, Lecturer in American Literature, 1963-70; Senior Lecturer in English, Aberdeen University, 1970-79; Chairman, Committee for Humanities and Member, Committee for Academic Affairs, CNAA, 1987-92; Chairman: Scottish Universities Council on Entrance English Panel, 1986-92, Universities and Colleges Admissions Service English Panel, since 1995; Member: Scottish Examination Board, 1984-92, Scottish Qualifications Authority English Panel, 1996-99; President, Eighteenth-Century Scottish Studies Society, 1990-92. Publications: Scotland and America 1750-1835, 1975, second edition, 2008; American Literature in Context 1865-1900, 1983, reprint, 2016; Scott's Waverley (Editor), 1971; Charlotte Brontë's Shirley (Editor, with Judith Hook), 1974; Dos Passos: A Collection of Critical Essays (Editor), 1974; The History of Scottish Literature II, 1660-1800 (Editor), 1987; Scott Fitzgerald, 1992; The Glasgow Enlightenment (Co-Editor), 1995, second edition, 2021; From Goosecreek to Gandercleugh, 1999; Scott's The Fair Maid of Perth (Co-Editor), 1999; F. Scott Fitzgerald: A Literary Life, 2002; Francis Jeffrey's American Journal: New York to Washington 1813 (Co-editor), 2011; Eliza Oddy, A Mississippi Diary: From St Paul, Minnesota to Alton, Illinois, October 1894 to May 1895 (Editor), 2013; From Mount Hooly to Princeton: A Scottish-American Medley, 2020. Recreations: theatre; opera; catching up on reading. Address: 5 Rosslyn Terrace, Glasgow G12 9NB; e-mail: nassau@palio2.vianw.co.uk

Hooper, Ian Ross, BA; b. 26.5.49, Edinburgh; m., Julie Ellen Vaughan; 1 d.; 1 s. Educ. Hornchurch Grammar School, Essex; Faculty of Fine Arts, University of East Anglia. Department of the Environment, 1973-89; English Heritage, 1984-85; Depute Director and Museum of Scotland Project Director, National Museums of Scotland, 1989-99; Head of Economy and Industry Division, Scotland Office, 1999-2003; Head of Natural Resources Division, Scottish Government, 2003-2011. Recreations: art, music, mountains. Address: 3 Inverleith Row, Edinburgh EH3 5LP.

Hope of Craighead, Rt. Hon. Lord (James Arthur David Hope), KT, PC, FRSE. HM Lord High Commissioner to the General Assembly of the Church of Scotland, 2015-2016; Convener, Crossbench Peers, 2015-19; Chief Justice, Abu Dhabi Global Market Courts, since 2015; Deputy President of the Supreme Court of the United Kingdom, 2009-2013; Chancellor, Strathclyde University, 1998-2013; b. 27.6.38, Edinburgh; m., Katharine Mary Kerr; 1 d. Educ. Edinburgh Academy; Rugby School; St. John's College, Cambridge (BA); Edinburgh University (LLB); Hon. LLD, Aberdeen (1991), Strathclyde (1993), Edinburgh (1995), Glasgow (2013); DUniv, Strathclyde (2014), BPP University (London), Abertay; Fellow, Strathclyde, 2000. National Service, Seaforth Highlanders, 1957-59; admitted Faculty of Advocates, 1965; Standing Junior Counsel to Inland Revenue, 1974-78; QC, 1978; Advocate Depute,

1978-82; Chairman, Medical Appeal Tribunal, 1985-86; Legal Chairman, Pensions Appeal Tribunal, 1985-86; Dean, Faculty of Advocates, 1986-89; A Senator of the College of Justice, Lord Justice General of Scotland, and Lord President of the Court of Session, 1989-96; A Lord of Appeal in Ordinary, 1996-2009. President, The Stair Society, 1993-2013; President, Commonwealth Magistrates' and Judges' Association, 2003-06; Hon. Professor of Law, Aberdeen, 1994; David Kelbie Award, 2007; Fellow, WS Society, 2011; Baron (Life Peer), 1995. Publications: Gloag and Henderson's Introduction to Scots Law (Joint Editor, 7th edition, Assistant Editor, 8th and 9th editions, Contributor, 11th edition); Armour on Valuation for Rating (Joint Editor, 4th and 5th editions); (Contributor) Stair Memorial Encyclopaedia of Scots Law and Court of Session Practice; Lord Hope's Diaries, 1996-2015 (5 volumes). Address: (h.) 34 India Street, Edinburgh EH3 6HB; T.-0131-225 8245.
E-mail: hopejad@parliament.uk

Hope, Graham, MA, CPFA. Chief Executive, West Lothian Council, since 2010; b. 1966; m.; 2 c. Educ. University of St Andrews. West Lothian Council: Corporate Finance Manager, 2001-06, Head of Corporate Services, 2006-08, Depute Chief Executive, 2008-2010. Address: (b.) West Lothian Council, West Lothian Civic Centre, Howden South Road, Livingston, West Lothian, EH54 6FF.

Hopkins, Professor David James, PhD, MA (Dist), PGCE (Dist), BA (Hons). Professor of Art History, University of Glasgow; b. 29.08.55, Derby; 1 s. Formerly Lecturer at Universities of Edinburgh, St. Andrews and Edinburgh College of Art; from 2000 has been Senior Lecturer, Reader and now Professor, Glasgow University. Publications: books include: 'Marcel Duchamp and Max Ernst', 1998; After Modern Art: 1945-2000, 2000; Dada and Surrealism, 2003; Neo-Avant-Garde, 2006; Dada's Boys: Masculinity after Duchamp, 2007; Virgin Microbe: Essays on Dada, 2014; A Companion to Dada and Surrealism, 2016; Dark Toys: Surrealism and the Culture of Childhood, 2021. Exhibition Curation: includes: Dada's Boys, Fruitmarket Gallery, Edinburgh, 2006; Childish Things, Fruitmarket Gallery, Edinburgh, 2010-2011. Address: (b.) Department of Art History, University of Glasgow G12 8QH.

Horner, Professor Robert Malcolm Wigglesworth, CEng, BSc, PhD, FRSE, FICE, Hon. FRIAS. Professor Emeritus, Dundee University, since 2006, Professor of Engineering Management, 1986-2006, Vice Principal, 2012, Deputy Principal, 2002-06, and Director, Enterprise Management, 2000-06 (Chair, School of Engineering and Physical Sciences, 1997-99); b. 27.7.42, Bury; m., Beverley Anne Wesley; 1 s.; 1 d. Educ. The Bolton School; University College, London. Civil Engineer, Taylor Woodrow Construction Ltd., 1966-77; Lecturer, Senior Lecturer, Head, Department of Civil Engineering, Dundee University, 1977-91; Managing Director, International Maintenance Management, 1996-97. Founder Chairman, Dundee Branch, Opening Windows on Engineering; Winner, CIOB Ian Murray Leslie Award, 1980 and 1984; Atlantic Power and Gas Ltd.: Non-executive Director, 1991-97, Director, Research and Development, 1993-97; Chairman, Winton Caledonian Ltd., 1995-97; Chairman, Whole Life Consultants Ltd., since 2004; Director, Dundee Rep., 1991-2003; Director, Scottish Institute for Enterprise, 1999-2005; Director, Objective 3 Partnership, 2000-03 (Vice Chairman, 2002-03); Member, Council, National Conference of University Professors, 1989-93; Director, Scottish International Resource Project, 1994-95; Member: Technology Foresight Construction Sector Panel, 1994-98,

British Council Advisory Committee on Science, Engineering and the Environment, 1994-2005; Member, Construction Futures Technical Reference Group, since 2005 (Chair, 2011-2014); Director, Scottish Enterprise Tayside, 2003-08, Chair, 2005-08; Member, Tayside and Central Scotland Transport Planning Partnership Executive, 2006-2010; Director, Citizens Advice Bureau, Dundee, 1993-2003; Chairman, Friends of St. Paul's Cathedral, 1993-95; Non-Executive Director, CXR Bioscience, 2008-2015; Member, Construction Industry Training Board Council, 2015-17. Recreations: rotary; gardening. Address: (h.) Westfield Cottage, 11 Westfield Place, Dundee DD1 4JU; T.-01382 225933.

Horsman, Stefan, MA (Oxon), PGCE, FRGS. Headmaster, Albyn School, Aberdeen, since 2021; b. 5.77; m., Shona; 2 c. Educ. Bolton School; University of Oxford, Magdalen College; University of Cambridge, Queens' College. Career history: Alumni Relations - Telephone Fundraising, Bolton School, 1998; Teacher of Geography, St John's Secondary School, Lilongwe, Malawi, 1998; Alumni Relations, Organiser of Centenary Reunion, Bolton School, 1999; Teacher of Geography, The Portsmouth Grammar School, 2000-03; Assistant Head of Geography, Latymer Upper School, 2003-05; Head of Geography, Cheadle Hulme School, 2006-2011; Robert Gordon's College: Deputy Head, Director of Digital Strategy (Whole School), 2013-15, Deputy Head (Senior School), 2012-2021. Fellow of the Royal Geographical Society. Address: Albyn School, 17-23 Queen's Road, Aberdeen AB15 4PB; T.-01224 322408.

Hosie, Stewart. MP (SNP), Dundee East, since 2005; Shadow Chancellor of the Duchy of Lancaster and Shadow Minister for the Cabinet Office, since 2021; Deputy Leader, SNP, 2014-16; Shadow SNP Westminster Group Leader (Economy), 2015-17; b. 1963, Dundee; m. (1), Shona Robison; 1 d. (marr. diss.); m. (2), Serena Cowdy. Educ. Carnoustie High School; University of Abertay. Career history: IT systems; SNP Youth Convener, 1986-89; SNP National Secretary, 1999-2003; Organisation Convener, 2003-05; UK Parliament: contested 1992 and 1997 general elections in Kirkcaldy; SNP Spokesperson for Women, 2005-07, Home Affairs, 2005-07, Economy 2005-2010, Shadow Chief Whip (Commons), 2007-2010; Shadow SNP Spokesperson (Treasury), 2010-2015; SNP Deputy Westminster Leader, 2010-17; SNP Chief Whip, 2010-2015. Member, Select Committees on: Members Estimate, since 2015, House of Commons Commission, since 2015, Treasury, 2010-2015. Recreations: football; hill-walking; rugby. Address: House of Commons, London SW1A 0AA. E-mail: stewart.hosie.mp@parliament.uk

Hossack, Dr. William Strachan, MB, ChB, DObstRCOG, Cert. Aviation Medicine; b. 10.9.29, Macduff; m., Catherine Sellar (widower); 1 s.; 1 d. Educ. Banff Academy; Aberdeen University. House Officer, Aberdeen Maternity Hospital and City Hospital, Aberdeen; Junior Specialist Obstetrics, RAF Hospital, St. Athan; GP, Banff, Visiting M.O., Chalmers Hospital and Ladysbridge Hospital, Banff; authorised Medical Examiner (PPL), Civil Aviation Authority. Hon. Medical Adviser, RNLI Macduff; Chairman, Banffshire Hospitals Board; Honorary Sheriff, Grampian Region; General Comissioner, Inland Revenue; Chairman, Martin Trust. Recreations: music; choral singing; watercolour painting; amateur radio. Address: (h.) Kincraig, 39 Skene Street, Macduff, Aberdeenshire AB44 1RP; T.-01261 832099.

Hough, Professor Sir James, OBE, BSc, PhD, DSc (Hon Glasgow), DSc (Hon Edinburgh), FRS, FRSE, FAPS, FInstP, FIoP (Hon), FISGRG, FRAS, CPhys. Professor of Experimental Physics, Glasgow University, since 1986; emeritus holder of the Kelvin Chair of Natural Philosophy; Associate Director, Institute for Gravitational Research, 2000-09; Member, PPARC Council, 2005-07; Chair, PPARC (now STFC) Education and Training Committee,

2006-2010; Member, ESF Physical and Engineering Science Committee, 2010-2014; Member, Scottish Science Advisory Council, 2010-2015; Chief Executive, Scottish Universities Physics Alliance, 2011-15; Member, Council, Institute of Physics, 2011-15; Chair, Education Committee, Institute of Physics in Scotland, 2011-17; Member, Executive Committee, European Physical Society, 2012-15; Member, Institute of Physics Audit and Risk Committee, since 2015; Chair, Partnership Grants Committee, Royal Society of London, since 2017; b. 6.8.45, Glasgow; m., Anne Park McNab (deceased); 1 s.; 1 d. Educ. High School of Glasgow; Glasgow University. Glasgow University: Lecturer in Natural Philosophy, 1972, Senior Lecturer, 1983; Visiting Fellow, JILA, University of Colorado, 1983; Max Planck Research Prize, 1991; Duddell Prize, IOP, 2004; Phillips Award, Institute of Physics, 2016; Special Breakthrough Prize in Fundamental Physics, 2016 and 11 other prizes/awards including the President's medal of the Royal Society of Edinburgh, 2016, the Royal Medal of the Royal Society of the Edinburgh, 2016; Gold Medal of the Royal Astronomical Society, 2017; Edison Volta Medal of the European Physical 2018; OBE, 2013; Kt, 2018; 390 refereed publications in learned journals. Address: (b.) School of Physics and Astronomy, University of Glasgow, Glasgow G12 8QQ; T.-0141-330 4706.
E-mail: james.hough@glasgow.ac.uk

Houghton, Victoria, BA. Chief Executive Officer, Hamilton & Inches, Edinburgh, since 2019; b. 1.76. Educ. Combe Bank School; Tonbridge Grammar School; University of Brighton; The Gemmological Association of Great Britain. Career history: Assistant Buyer, Marks and Spencer, London, 1998-2000; Junior Buyer, River Island, London, 2000-01; Senior Product Developer, Next Sourcing Limited, Bangkok, Thailand, 2001-04; Buyer, Next Group Plc, 2004-07; Consultant Associate, Q5, 2010-2018; Owner, Chief Executive Officer, Ixy Retail (Next PLC Franchise), Bucharest, Romania, since 2007; Board Director, Hamilton & Inches, Edinburgh, since 2018. Named as one of the 50 most influential people in British luxury in Walpole's 2022 Power List. Address: Hamilton & Inches, 87 George Street, Edinburgh EH2 3EY; T.-0131 225 4898.

Housden, Stuart David, OBE, BSc (Hons) (Zoology). Chair, Scottish Seabird Centre, since 2021; Member, Scottish Committee of the National Lottery Heritage Fund, since 2017; Trustee, Brazilian Atlantic Rainforest Trust, since 2017; Fellow, Scottish Environment Link, since 2018; Trustee of the Gillman Trusts; Leader, Speyside Wildlife, since 2017; Director, RSPB Scotland and Board Member, RSPB, 1994-2017 (retired); b. 24.6.53, Croydon; m., Catherine Juliet Wilkin; 3 d. Educ. Selhurst Grammar School; Royal Holloway College, London University. Freshwater biologist, Thames Water, 1976; RSPB: Species Investigation Officer, 1977-79, Parliamentary Officer, 1979-82, Manager, Government Unit, 1982-85, Head, Conservation Planning Department, 1985-90, Head, Conservation Planning, 1990-93. Member, Cairngorms Partnership Board, 1995-97; Member, Scottish Power Environment Forum, 1999-2016; Chaired, Scottish Government's Rural Development Council; former member, Scottish Biodiversity Group; Churchill Fellow, 1992. Public speaker. Publications: Important Bird Areas in the UK (Co-Editor); RSPB Handbook of Scottish Birds (Joint Author); numerous articles. Recreations: ornithology; travel; rugby football; public service.

Houslay, Professor Miles Douglas, BSc, PhD, FRSE, FRSB, FRSA, FIBiol, CBiol, FMedSci. Principal Scientific Advisor and Co-Founder (Part-time), Mironid Ltd, since 2019 (Chief Scientific Officer, since 2014); Director and Chief Scientific Officer, Managing Director, BioGryffe Consulting Ltd.; Professor of Pharmacology (part time), University of Strathclyde, 2011-2015; Professor of Pharmacological Innovation, King's College London (part time), since 2012; Emeritus Professor, Glasgow University, since 2011; Gardiner Professor of Biochemistry, Glasgow University, 1984-2011; b. 25.6.50, Wolverhampton; m., Rhian Mair; 2 s.; 1 d. Educ. Grammar School, Brewood, Stafford; University College, Cardiff; King's College, Cambridge; Cambridge University. ICI Research Fellow and Fellow, Queens' College, Cambridge, 1974-76; Lecturer, then Reader in Biochemistry, UMIST, 1976-82; Selby Fellow, Australian Academy of Science, 1984; Colworth Medal, Biochemical Society of Great Britain, 1984; Honorary Research Fellow, California Metabolic Research Foundation, since 1981; Editor in Chief, Cellular Signalling, 1984-2014; Deputy Chairman, Biochemical Journal, 1984-89; Editorial Board, Biochimica Biophysica Acta; Member: Committee, Biochemical Society, 1982-85, Research Committee, British Diabetic Association, 1986-91; Chairman, Grant Committee A, Cell and Disorders Board, Medical Research Council, 1989-92; Member: Scientific and Medical Grant Committee, Scottish Home and Health Department, 1991-94, Advisory Board for External Appointments, London University, 1990-92, HEFC RAE Basic Medical and Dental Sciences Panel, since 1996, Wellcome Trust BMB Grant Panel, 1996-2000; Chairman, British Heart Foundation Project Grant Panel; Member, British Heart Foundation Chairs and Programme Grant Panel, 1997-2000; Trustee, British Heart Foundation, 1997-2001; 1998 Founder Fellow, Academy of Medical Sciences; Burroughs-Wellcome Visiting Professor, USA, 2001; Joshua Lederberg Society Prize, Celgene Corp, USA, 2012; Consultant, various pharmaceutical companies in UK, Europe, Asia and USA; co-founder, Biotheryx, inc. Publications: Dynamics of Biological Membranes; over 440 scientific papers. Address: (b.) Mironid Ltd (Biology Laboratories), Strathclyde Institute of Pharmacy and Biomedical Sciences, Strathclyde University, 161 Cathedral Street, Glasgow G4 0RE; e-mail: miles.houslay@kcl.ac.uk

Houston, Alexander Stewart, BSc (Hons), PhD, FIPEM. Honorary Professor, University of Stirling, since 2007; Medical Imaging Consultant, Hermes Medical Solutions, since 2004; b. 16.06.44, Glasgow; m., Roberta Ann; 1 s.; 2 d. Educ. Woodside Senior Secondary School, Glasgow; University of Glasgow; University of Edinburgh. Research Assistant, University of Dundee, 1971-75; Clinical Scientist: Royal Naval Hospital Haslar, 1975-2001, Portsmouth Hospitals NHS Trust, 2001-04; Visiting Professor, University of Portsmouth, 2004-07. Norman Veall Medal, 2001. Recreations: astronomy; audio-visual; bridge; photography; songwriting; watching Partick Thistle. Address: (b.) Department of Psychology, University of Stirling FK9 4LA; T.-01786-467640.
E-mail: alex.houston@stir.ac.uk

Houston, Anne C., OBE, DUniv, CQSW, FRSA. Independent Chair, North Ayrshire Child Protection Committee, 2014-2020; former Chief Executive, Children 1st (2007-2014); Director, ChildLine Scotland, 1994-2007 and Deputy Chief Executive, Childline UK, 2003-07; b. 28.8.54, Glasgow. Educ. Bishopbriggs High School; Strathclyde University. Social Worker, Intermediate Treatment Officer, Team Leader, Southampton Social Services Department, 1980-86; Project Manager/Tutor, Richmond Fellowship, Glasgow, 1986-90; Counselling Manager, Childline Scotland, 1990-94. Trustee of Cattanach Charitable Trust; Board Member and Vice Chair, Care Inspectorate, 2014-2022; Chair, Child Protection Committees Scotland, 2015-2019; Panel Member, Redress Scotland, since 2021. Received Honorary Doctorate from University of West of Scotland, June 2015. Recreations: music; gardening; walking; animals; designing and making silver jewellery; food and wine with friends; travel. Address: 20 Bellshaugh Lane, Glasgow G12 0PE; T.-07809609571; e-mail: anne@achouston.plus.com

Houston, Cllr Graham. Vice President, COLSA, since 2017; former Chairman, Scottish Qualifications Authority (2009-2017). Experienced, qualified management coach

throughout the private and public sectors. Formerly Scottish Director of the Work Foundation (formerly the Industrial Society), then established own consultancy. Elected Councillor, Stirling Council, since 2007; Board Member, Scottish Police Authority, 2012-18.

Houston, Professor Robert Allan, MA, PhD, FRHS, MAE, FRSE. Emeritus Professor of Modern History, University of St Andrews (appointed Professor in 1995); b. 27.9.54, Hamilton; m., Dr Veronica Anne O'Halloran. Educ. Edinburgh Academy; University of St Andrews; University of Cambridge. Research Fellow, Clare College, Cambridge, 1981-83; University of St Andrews: Lecturer in Modern History, 1983-93, Reader in Modern History, 1993-95. Visiting Professor, Faculteit der Historische en Kunstwetenschappen, Erasmus University Rotterdam, 1994; Leverhulme Research Fellowship, 1996-97; "Distinguished Visiting Scholar", Department of History, University of Adelaide, 1996. Publications include: Conflict and identity in the history of Scotland and Ireland from the seventeenth to the twentieth century (Co-Editor), 1995; Social change in the age of Enlightenment: Edinburgh, 1660-1760, 1994; Madness and society in eighteenth-century Scotland, 2000; Autism in history. The case of Hugh Blair of Borgue (Co-Author), 2000; The New Penguin History of Scotland (Co-Editor), 2001; Scotland: a very short introduction, 2008; Punishing the dead? Suicide, lordship and community in Britain, 1500-1830, 2010; Bride ales and penny weddings: recreations, reciprocity, and regions in Britain from the sixteenth to the nineteenth century, 2014. Recreations: scuba diving; yoga; tai chi; cooking; travel. Address: University of St Andrews, St Katherine's Lodge, The Scores, St Andrews KY16 9AR.

Howard, Dr Grahame Charles William, BSc (Hons), MBBS, MD, FRCP(Ed), FRCR. Consultant Clinical Oncologist and Honorary Senior Lecturer, Edinburgh University, 1987-2011; Clinical Director, Edinburgh Cancer Centre, 1999-2005; Clinical Director, Cancer Services, 2005-07; b. 15.5.53, London; 3 s. Educ. King Edward VI School, Norwich; St Thomas' Hospital Medical School, London University. Registrar in Oncology, Royal Free Hospital, London; Senior Registrar, Addenbrookes Hospital, Cambridge; appointed Consultant Oncologist, Edinburgh Cancer Centre, 1987; Head of Radiotherapy then Clinical Director, 1999-2005; Chair, Lothian Cancer Planning and Implementation Group, since 2006; several commitments to Royal College of Radiologists; previously Vice-Chair, Scottish Intercollegiate Guideline Network and Chair, Cancer subgroup, until 2007; Chair, Oncology Section, S.E. Scotland Urological Oncology Group, until 2007; Scottish Government Health Department Speciality Adviser for Clinical Oncology. Assistant Editor, Clinical Oncology. Publications: author of scientific papers and the novels, "The Tales of Dod", 2010, "Spoz and Friends, Tales of a London Medical Student", 2013; "The Euthanasia Protocol", 2015; "The Marble Corridor", 2017; "The Norris Sanction", 2019; "Coda, Fantaisie and Intermezzo". Recreations: music; sailing; reading. Address: (h.) 4 Ormelie Terrace, Joppa, Edinburgh EH15.
E-mail: spoz.howard@gmail.com

Howat, Eileen. Chief Executive, South Ayrshire Council, since 2013. Formerly Executive Director - Resources, Governance and Organisation, South Ayrshire Council. Address: South Ayrshire Council, County Buildings, Wellington Square, Ayr KA7 1DR.

Howat, Richard. Chief Executive: Churches Action for the Homeless, since 2021, Scottish Churches Housing Action,

2019-2020. Career history: many years of experience in the care and homelessness sector; worked with Transform Community Development (formerly Dundee Cyrenians); Operations Manager, Positive Steps, Dundee, 2011-19. Address: Churches Action for the Homeless, 188-190 High Street, Perth PH1 5PA; T.-01738 580188.

Howatson, William, MA (Hons). Freelance journalist and columnist, since 1996; b. 22.1.53, Dumfries; m., Hazel Symington Paton; 2 d. Educ. Lockerbie Academy; Edinburgh University. Press and Journal: Agricultural Editor, 1984-96, Leader Writer, 1990-96. Chairman, Guild of Agricultural Journalists, 1995; Member, Scottish Water and Sewerage Customers Council, 1995-99; Member, Angus College Board of Management, since 1996 (Chairman, 2003-06, Vice Chairman, since 2006); Member, Health Education Board for Scotland, 1997-2003; Vice Chair, NHS Health Scotland, 2003-05; Member, East Areas Board, Scottish Natural Heritage, 1997-2003 (Deputy Chairman, 2000-03); Non Executive Director, Angus NHS Trust, 1998; Governor, Macaulay Land Use Research Institute, 1998-2003; Member, Aberdeenshire Council, since 1999; Chairman, North of Scotland Agriculture Advisory Committee, since 2003; Director, Ash Scotland, 2006-08; Board Member, Scottish Environment Protection Agency, 1999-2005 (Chairman, East Regional Board, 2003-05); Member, East Regional Board, 2006-08; Member, Rail Passenger Committee for Scotland, 2001-03; Member, Esk District Salmon Fishery Board, 2003-07; Provost, Aberdeenshire Council, 2007-12; Chairman, North East of Scotland Fisheries Development Partnership, 2007-12; Member, Grampian Health Board, 2007-11, Chairman, 2011-14; Chairman, Aberdeen City Community Health Partnership, 2009-2012; Provost, Aberdeenshire Council, since 2017; Chairman, North East of Scotland Agricultural Advisory Group, since 2017. Columnist of the Year, Bank of Scotland Press Awards, 1992; Fellow of the Royal Agricultural Societies. Publication: Farm Servants and Labour in Lowland Scotland, 1770-1914 (Contributor). Recreations: gardening; hillwalking; reading; Scottish history. Address: (h.) Stone of Morphie, Hillside, Montrose; T.-01674 830746; e-mail: billhowatson@btinternet.com

Howells, Laurence. Co-Director, theSitarProject, since 2005; former Chief Executive, Scottish Funding Council (2014-16); previously a Senior Director responsible for skills, research and knowledge exchange. Educ. Southampton University. Career: worked for the British Library both in Yorkshire and in London, in a number of administrative and policy roles; worked for the London Borough of Waltham Forest as Assistant Education Officer responsible for the Borough's education budget; joined the Scottish Higher Education Funding Council (a predecessor body to SFC) in 1994.

Howes, Major General Francis Hedley Roberton "Buster", CB, OBE, BSc, MA. Chief Executive of the Royal Edinburgh Military Tattoo, since 2020; b. 22.3.60, Newcastle upon Tyne. Educ. Christ's Hospital, West Sussex; University of York; University of London. Career history: commissioned into the Royal Marines in 1982; became a troop commander in 42 Commando and had his first posting to Northern Ireland; after training as a Mountain Leader, he transferred to 45 Commando; served in the Gulf War while on secondment to the USMC; served as a planner in the Rapid Reaction Force Operations Staff of UNPROFOR during the Bosnian War in 1995; became Commanding Officer of 42 Commando (during the Iraq War) in 2003; Chief Joint Coordination and Effects in Headquarters ISAF in Afghanistan in 2007 and Director of Naval Staff later that year; went on to be Commander of 3 Commando Brigade in April 2008, Head of Overseas Operations in the Ministry of Defence in 2009 and Commandant General Royal Marines in February 2010; Head of the British Defence Staff – US and Defence Attaché in Washington, D.C., 2011-2015; appointed non-executive director of the Royal Edinburgh Military Tattoo organisation in 2015 whilst CEO of Here Be Dragons on the Island of Principe. Address: The Tattoo Office, 1-3 Cockburn Street, Edinburgh EH1 1QB.

Howie, Andrew Law, CBE, FRAgrS. Chairman: Howie Animal Feed Ltd., 2001-04, Robert Howie & Sons, 1982-2001, Scottish Milk Ltd., 1994-95; b. 14.4.24, Dunlop; m., Joan Duncan; 2 s.; 2 d. Educ. Glasgow Academy. Joined Robert Howie & Sons, 1941; War Service, RN; became Director, 1965; President, Scottish Compound Feed Manufacturers, 1968-70 and 1983-85; President, Compound Animal Feed Manufacturers National Association, 1971-72; Director, Scottish Corn Trade, 1976-78; Vice-President/Feed, UK Agricultural Supply Trade Association, 1980-81; Chairman, Scottish Council, UKASTA, 1985-87; Director, Scottish Milk Marketing Board, 1980-94 (Chairman, 1982-94); Member, CBI Scottish Council, 1989-95; Fellow of Royal Agricultural Society (FRAGS), elected 1987; Chairman, Scottish Council of Council of Awards of Royal Agricultural Societies (CARAS), 2001/03; Chairman, National Council of CARAS, 2003/05. Recreations: golf; gardening; wood-turning. Address: (h.) Newmill House, Dunlop, Kilmarnock KA3 4BQ; T.-01560 484936.

Howie, Professor John Garvie Robertson, CBE, MD, PhD, Hon DSc, FRCPE, FRCGP, FMedSci. Professor of General Practice, Edinburgh University, 1980-2000; b. 23.1.37, Glasgow; m., Elizabeth Margaret Donald; 2 s.; 1 d. Educ. High School of Glasgow; Glasgow University. Registrar, Laboratory Medicine, Western Infirmary, Glasgow, 1962-66; General Practitioner, Glasgow, 1966-70; Lecturer/Senior Lecturer in General Practice, Aberdeen University, 1970-80; Member: Biomedical Research Committee, SHHD, 1977-81, Health Services Research Committee, SHHD, 1982-86, Chief Scientist Committeee, SHHD, 1987-97, Committee on the Review of Medicines, 1986-91. Publications: Research in General Practice; A Day in the Life of Academic General Practice; Academic General Practice in the UK Medical Schools, 1948-2000. Recreations: golf; gardening; music. Address: (h.) 4 Ravelrig Park, Balerno, Midlothian EH14 7DL; T.-0131-449 6305; e-mail: john.howie23@btinternet.com

Howie, Pauline, OBE. Chief Executive, Scottish Ambulance Service Board, since 2009. Career history: CSL Group in London, working mainly with the Health and Local Government Sectors; qualified as an accountant in 1990, winning the Richard Emmott Memorial Prize for Best Performance in the Case Study Paper; returned to Scotland and joined the NHS in Glasgow as Project Accountant with the Glasgow Royal Infirmary Unit, joined the South Glasgow Unit in 1992 as Deputy Director of Finance and helped in its NHS Trust formation; seconded to the Scottish Executive Health Department as Head of Trust Finance in 1996, and later that year joined the State Hospitals Board for Scotland as Finance and Planning Director; joined the Scottish Ambulance Service as Finance Director in March 2000, also taking responsibility for Information and Communications Technology, Fleet Services, Procurement, Planning and Performance management and Risk Management; took on the role of Chief Operating Officer in 2006, becoming Acting Chief Executive in May 2008. Awarded an OBE in the 2015 New Year's honours for services to Scottish Ambulance Service and NHS Scotland. Address: Scottish Ambulance Service Board, National Headquarters, Tipperlinn Road, Edinburgh EH10 5UU.

Howitt, Janice, LLB, DipLP. Head of Human Resources, Abellio ScotRail Ltd, 2018-19. Educ. Hutchesons' Grammar; Strathclyde University. Career history: TM Solicitors, Glasgow Solicitors, 1990-1992; Personnel

Manager, Yarrow Shipbuilders, BAE Systems, 1993-96; Senior HR Business Partner, Stirling Council, 1996-1999; Senior HR Leader, RBS, 2000-2016; Human Resources Transformation Lead, Police Scotland, 2016-17.

Howson, Peter, OBE. Painter; b. 1958, London; m., 1 d. Moved to Glasgow, 1962; attended Glasgow School of Art, 1975-77; spent a short period in the Scottish infantry, travelling in Europe; returned to Glasgow School of Art, 1979-81, studying under Sandy Moffat; Artist in Residence, St Andrews and part-time Tutor, Glasgow School of Art, 1985; commissioned by Imperial War Museum to visit Bosnia as war artist, 1993. Address: c/o Flowers East, 82 Kingsland Road, London E2 8DP.

Hoy, Sir Chris, kt (2009), MBE (2005), BSc (Hons). Former Scottish track cyclist; b. 23.3.76; m., Sarra; 1 s.; 1 d. Educ. George Watson's College; University of St. Andrews; Moray House, University of Edinburgh. Eleven-times world champion and Olympic Games gold and silver medal winner (3 gold medals in 2008 and 2 gold medals in 2012). Second most decorated Olympic cyclist of all time. Awarded honorary doctorates from Edinburgh University (2005); Heriot-Watt University (2005) and University of St Andrews (2009).

Hoy, Craig William, BA (Hons). MSP (Scottish Conservative and Unionist Party), South Scotland (Region), since 2021; Shadow Health Minister for Mental Health and Social Care, since 2021. Educ. Lasswade High School Centre; University of Edinburgh; City University, London. Career history: Reporter, Investment Week, 1995-96; Freelance Researcher and Assistant to Production Teams, BBC, 1995-97; Reporter, then Editor and Lobby Correspondent, Parliamentary Communications Ltd., London and Edinburgh, 1997-2000; co-launched Holyrood Magazine in 1999; Dods: Editorial Director and Editor-in-Chief, 2000-05, Managing Director, 2005-08; Executive Director and Shareholders, PublicAffairsAsia, 2008-2018; Parliamentary Candidate, East Lothian Councillor, Journalist, Entrepreneur, 2019-2021. Address: The Scottish Parliament, Edinburgh EH99 1SP; T.-0131 348 6976; e-mail: Craig.Hoy.msp@parliament.scot

Hubbuck, Professor John Reginald, BA (Cantab), MA, DPhil (Oxon), FRSE, FRSA, CMath, FIMA. Emeritus Professor of Mathematics, Aberdeen University; b. 3.5.41, Girvan; m., Anne Neilson; 1 s.; 1 d. Educ. Manchester Grammar School; Queens' College, Cambridge; Pembroke College, Oxford. Fellow: Gonville and Caius College, Cambridge, 1970-72, Magdalen College, Oxford, 1972-78; President, Edinburgh Mathematical Society, 1985-86. Recreation: hill-walking. Address: (h.) 8 Fonthill Terrace, Aberdeen AB11 7UR; T.-01224 588738.
E-mail: johnhubbuck@btinternet.com

Hudghton, Ian. Member of the European Parliament (SNP), 1998-2019; m., Lily; 1 s.; 1 d. Ran family home decorating business, 20 years; former Member, EU's Committee of the Regions; elected to Angus District Council, 1986 (Housing Convener, eight years); Depute SNP Group Leader and Property Convener, Tayside Regional Council, 1994-96; elected to Angus Council, 1995 (Leader, 1996-98); President, Scottish National Party, 2005-2020; President, European Free Alliance, 2004-09.

Hudson, Professor John Geoffrey Henry, MA (Oxon), MA (Toronto), DPhil, FRHistS, FRSE, FBA, MAE. Professor of Legal History, University of St Andrews, since 2003; b. 7.5.62, Romford; m., Lise Alexandra McAslan Hudson; 2 d. Educ. Brentwood School; Worcester College, Oxford. Career history: Junior Research Fellow, Worcester College, Oxford; Scouloudi Research Fellow, Institute of Historical Research, University of London; Lecturer in Mediaeval History, University of St Andrews, Reader in Mediaeval History, Professor of Legal History; R. Bates Lea Global Law Professor, University of Michigan Law School; Council Member, Selden Society. Publication: Oxford History of The Laws of England, II: 871-1216, 2012. Recreations: running; music; literature. Address: Department of Mediaeval History, 71 South Street, St Andrews, Fife KY16 9QW; T.-01334 462888; e-mail: jghh@st-andrews.ac.uk

Hudson, Lise, MA (Hons), PGCE. Rector, High School of Dundee, since 2020. Educ. St Andrews University; University of Cambridge. Career history: High School of Dundee: appointed History Teacher in 1990; became Principal Teacher of Guidance (played a key part in the major development of the pastoral life of the school); appointed Head of Guidance in 2008, then Deputy Rector (2016-2020). First female Rector of High School of Dundee. Address: High School of Dundee, Euclid Crescent, Dundee DD1 1HU; T.-01382 202921.

Huggins, Geoff, LLB, MSSc. Director of Digital, The Scottish Government, since 2021; b. 9.65. Educ. Queen's University Belfast; The University of Edinburgh. Career history: Policy Lead, Northern Ireland Office, 1991-98; Director and Member, Board of Trustees, Life Changes Trust, 2013-14; The Scottish Government: Head of School Standards, 1998-2000, Deputy Director of Housing, 2000-04, Head of Mental Health, 2004-2014, Director of Digital Health and Social Care, 2017-18, Director for Health and Social Care Integration, 2014-18; Director, NDS Scotland, Edinburgh, 2018-2021; Non Executive Director: International Initiative for Mental Health Leadership, Global, since 2019, Cornerstone, since 2019, Penumbra, since 2020; Director, Digital Third Sector Transformation, The Scottish Government, 2021. Address: The Scottish Government, Victoria Quay, Edinburgh EH5 6QQ.

Hughes, Dale William Alexander, LLB (Hons), DipLP. Advocate, since 1993; b. 21.1.67, Glasgow; m., Sally Jane Henderson (deceased); 2 s.; 1 d. Educ. Kirkcaldy High School; George Watson's College, Edinburgh; Aberdeen University; Edinburgh University. Solicitor, 1990-93. Tutor, University of Edinburgh. Recreations: travel; arts; sport. Address: Advocates Library, Edinburgh.

Hughes, Rev Derek Walter, BSc, BD (Hons), DipEd. Minister, Easterhouse Parish Church, Glasgow, since 2018; b. 27.4.60, Motherwell; m., Elizabeth Haddow Hill McGhie (03.04.82); 2 d. (Diahann and Claire); 1 s. (David); 4 grandchildren (Callum, Emma, Amelia, Jacob). Educ. Law Primary School; Garrion Academy, Wishaw; Stirling University; Edinburgh University. Teacher of Chemistry, The Berwickshire High School, Duns, 1981-86; Minister, Townhead Parish Church, Coatbridge, 1990-96; Minister, Dalziel St. Andrew's Parish Church, Motherwell, 1996-2018. Recreations: running; reading; cinema; theatre; travel; photography. Address: 3 Barony Gardens, Springhill, Glasgow G69 6TS.
E-mail: DHughes@churchofscotland.org.uk
E-mail: derekthecleric@gmx.co.uk

Hughes, Sheriff Joseph. Sheriff, North Strathclyde, since 2019; Solicitor Advocate; Managing Partner of J C Hughes Solicitors, Glasgow, since 1986. Educ. The University of Edinburgh. Appointments from 2004: The Mental Health

Tribunal for Scotland, Health and Education Chamber, Pension Appeals Tribunals for Scotland, Scottish Solicitors Discipline Tribunal, NHS Tribunal for Scotland, Police Appeals Tribunal, Housing and Property Chamber, General Regulatory Chamber (Charity), Institute and Faculty of Actuaries Disciplinary Panel, Scottish Housing Regulator Appeals and SFA Disciplinary Judicial Panel; held a number of non-executive, public and charitable positions. Address: Greenock Sheriff Court, 1 Nelson Street, Greenock PA15 1TR; T.-01475 787073.

Hughes, Professor Michael David. Emeritus Professor of Management, University of Aberdeen Business School; b. 8.2.47, London; m., Ewa Maria Helinska-Hughes; 1 s.; 2 d. Educ. Farnborough Grammar School; Brunel University. Address: (b.) University of Aberdeen Business School, Edward Wright Building, Aberdeen AB24 3QY; T.-01224 272167.

Hughes, Dr. Peter Travers, OBE (1993), FREng, FIMMM. Former President, Robert Burns World Federation (2015-16); b. 24.12.46; m. (1) 2 s.; m. (2) 1 s.; m. (3). Educ. Wishaw High School; Technical College, Coatbridge; Strathclyde University; Dundee University. Trainee Metallurgist, Clyde Alloy (latterly British Steel), Foundry Metallurgist rising to Foundry Manager, North British Steel Group, 1968-76; General Manager, Lake and Elliot Essex, 1976-80 (Director, 1977-80); Managing Director, National Steel Foundry (1914) Ltd. (subsidiary of Lake and Elliot), 1980-83; initiated MBO forming Glencast Ltd., 1983 (company sold to NACO Inc Illinois USA, 1994); Chairman and Managing Director, Glencast Ltd, 1983-98 (winners Queen's Award for Technological Achievement 1990); Chief Executive, Scottish Engineering, 1998-2012 (President, 1993); Chairman: Steel Castings Research and Trade Association, 1988-92 (Chairman, Research Committee, 1985-88), DTI Steering Committee on UK Development of Solidification Simulation Programmes for Castings, 1988-89; guest lecturer at various conferences UK and abroad; UK President, Institute of British Foundrymen, 1994-95 (President, Scottish Branch, 1984-85); former Chairman, Scottish Steel Founders' Association; former Governor and Member, Court, University of Abertay (formerly Dundee Institute of Technology; Member, Court, University of Strathclyde, 2003-2012; Chairman, Board, New Park Preparatory School, 1998-2001; former Chairman, Advisory Board of Primary Engineer (2012-2017); Elder, Church of Scotland, 1976; Hon Dr: University of Paisley, 2001; University of Strathclyde, 2006, Napier University, 2006; Fellow, University of Abertay, 2001; FIMgt 1986; FIBF 1988; FIM 1993; CEng 1994; FREng 1995; DMS, University of Strathclyde, 1976; MBA, University of Dundee, 1991; elected Fellow of The Royal Society of Edinburgh (FRSE), 2013. Recreations: soccer; golf; tennis; curling; music; church; after dinner speaking. E-mail: peterthughes@btinternet.com

Hughes, Rhona Grace, MD, FRCOG, FRCPE. Consultant Obstetrician, since 1996; Honorary Senior Lecturer, since 1996; b. 29.1.58, Portsmouth; m., Tommy Hepburn; 2 s.; 1 d. Educ. Craigmount High School, Edinburgh; Edinburgh University. House Officer in Medicine and Surgery, 1983-84; Senior House Officer in Obstetrics and Gynaecology, 1984-85; Research Fellow in Virology and Gynaecology, 1985-87; Registrar in Obstetrics and Gynaecology, 1987-90; Senior Registrar, 1990-96 (job share). Recreations: hill-walking; travel; literature; family. Address: (b.) New Royal Infirmary, Little France, Edinburgh; T.-0131 242 2524; e-mail: rhona.hughes@luht.scot.nhs.uk

Hughes, Thomas George, LLB. Sheriff, since 2004; b. 2.1.55, Glasgow; m., Janice; 1 s.; 1 d. Educ. St. Mirin's Academy, Paisley; Strathclyde University. Solicitor, 1979-2004. Recreations: sport; reading. Address: (b.) Sheriff Court House, 6 West Bell Street, Dundee; T.-01382 229961; e-mail: sheriffthughes@scotcourts.gov.uk

Hughes Hallett, David John. Formerly FRICS and Consultant (now retired); Main Board Member, Scottish Environment Protection Agency, 1995-2002; Board Member, Loch Lomond and the Trossachs National Park Authority, 2002-2010 (Deputy Convener, 2006-2009); Member, East Areas Board of Scottish Natural Heritage, 2005-2008, Local Adviser for SNH, 2008-2012; Panel Member, Waterwatch Scotland, 2006-2009; Board Member, OSCR (Office of the Scottish Charity Regulator), 2008-2016; Lay Member, Audit Registration Committee, Institute of Chartered Accountants in Scotland, 2008-2014; Member, Registration and Conduct Committee, Scottish Social Services Council, 2010-2017; Independent Board Member, Public Prosecution Service, Northern Ireland, 2011-18; Member of Adjudicating Panels, General Teaching Council for Scotland, 2012-19; Member of the Private Rented Housing Panel and Homeowner Housing Panel (now 1st tier tribunals), 2012-19; b. 19.6.47, Dunfermline; m., Anne Mary Wright; 2 s.; 1 d. Educ. Fettes College; Reading University. Chartered Surveyor, rural practice, 1966-76; Land Use Adviser, then Director, Scottish Landowners' Federation, 1976-89. Chairman, Royal Institution of Chartered Surveyors in Scotland, 1988-89; Director, Scottish Wildlife Trust, 1989-98; Member, Policy Committee, Scottish Council for Voluntary Organisations, 1997-2002. Recreations: sailing; golf; cycling; singing. Address: (h.) The Old School, Back Latch, Ceres, Fife KY15 5NT.
E-mail: david@hugheshallett.co.uk

Hulbert, Dr. John Kenneth Macdonald, MB, ChB, MD. FRSGS, OStJ. Provost of Perth and Kinross, 2007-2012; Councillor, Perth and Kinross, 1995-2012; b. 24.03.39, Madras, S. India; m., Sara née Dobie; 1 s.; 2 d. Educ. Madras College, St. Andrews; Edinburgh University. Knight's Cross of the Order of Merit of the Republic of Poland. Honorary Fellow of the Royal Scottish Geographical Society, University Lecturer, 1965-72; General Practitioner, 1972-2003. Publication: Perth: A Comprehensive Guide for Locals and Visitors (Author); Scotland's Oldest and Newest City (Author). Recreations: managing a National Heritage Collection of Scottish pear trees; gardening; beekeeping. Address: (h.) "Wayside", 6 Castle Road, Longforgan, Perthshire DD2 5HA; T.-01382 360294.

Hume, James (Jim) Robert, DipAg, MBA. MSP (Liberal Democrat), South of Scotland, 2007-2016; b. 4.11.62; m., Lynne; 2 s.; 1 d. Educ. Yarrow Primary; Selkirk High School; East of Scotland College of Agriculture; University of Edinburgh. Farming, Partner in "John Hume and Son", since 1988; elected Councillor, Galashiels and District Ward, Scottish Borders in 2007; Director, NFUS (National Farmers Union of Scotland), 2004-06 and 2007; Chair of Borders Foundation for Rural Sustainability, 2000-06; Director, Scottish Enterprise Borders, 2002-07. Trustee, Borders Forest Trust, 2000-06. Publication: Co-Author, "Shepherds" by Walter Elliot. Recreations: amateur radio; gardening. Address: (h.) Sundhope Burn, Yarrow, Selkirk TD7 5NF; T.-0131 348 6702.

Hume, John Robert, OBE, BSc, ARCST, FSA Scot, Hon FRIAS, Hon FRSGS, FIESIS. Honorary Professor: Faculty of Arts, University of Glasgow, since 1998, School of History, University of St. Andrews, since 1999; Honorary Life President, Seagull Trust, since 1994 (Chairman, 1978-93); Honorary Vice-President, Association for Industrial Archaeology; Honorary Vice-President, Scottish Railway Preservation Society, since 2000 (Chairman, 1967-76); b.

26.2.39, Glasgow; m., Catherine Hope Macnab; 4 s. Educ. Hutchesons' Boys' Grammar School; Glasgow University; Royal College of Science and Technology. Assistant Lecturer, Lecturer, Senior Lecturer in Economic History, Strathclyde University, 1964-91; Chief Inspector of Historic Buildings, Historic Scotland, 1993-99. Member, Inland Waterways Amenity Advisory Council, 1974-2001; Director, Scottish Industrial Archaeology Survey, 1978-84; Member, Ancient Monuments Board for Scotland, 1981-84; Member, Committee on Artistic Matters, Church of Scotland, 1999-2008 (Convener, 2003-08); Member, Mission and Discipleship Council, Church of Scotland, 2006-08; Member, Emerging Ministries Task Group, Church of Scotland, 2006-2010; Advisory Member, General Trustees, Church of Scotland, 1999-2016; Chairman, Scottish Stained Glass Symposium; Trustee: Scottish Maritime Museum, 1983-98 and since 2009, The Waterways Trust, 2000-2012, Scotland's Churches Scheme, 2000-2012, Scotland's Churches Trust, 2012-19; Member, Industrial Archaeology Sub-Committee, English Heritage, 1985-2002; Chair, Royal Commission on the Ancient and Historical Monuments of Scotland, 2005-2015; Chairman, Govan Heritage Trust, since 2015; Patron, Glasgow City Heritage Trust, since 2015; Patron, Scottish Redundant Churches Trust, 2016-19. Publications: The Industrial Archaeology of Glasgow; The Industrial Archaeology of Scotland; Dumfries and Galloway, an illustrated architectural guide; Vernacular Buildings of Ayrshire; Wigtownshire Vernacular Buildings; Scotland's Best Churches; West Lothian Churches: an Introduction; The Church Buildings of Ayrshire; Glorious Gloucester; Church Buildings in Wigtownshire; Scotland's Lighthouses; as Co-Author: Workshop of the British Empire: Engineering and Shipbuilding in the West of Scotland; Beardmore: the History of a Scottish Industrial Giant; The Making of Scotch Whisky; A Bed of Nails: a History of P. MacCallum & Sons Ltd.; Shipbuilders to the World: a History of Harland and Wolff; Steam Entertainment; Historic Industrial Scenes: Scotland; Industrial History in Pictures: Scotland; Glasgow's Railway Stations; Industry and Transport in Scottish Museums. Recreations: photography; reading; drawing. Address: (h.) 28 Partickhill Road, Glasgow G11 5BP.

Hume, Professor Robert, BSc, MBChB, PhD, FRCP(Edin), FRCPCH. Professor of Developmental Medicine, Dundee University; Consultant Paediatrician, Tayside Universities NHS Trust; b. 5.4.47, Edinburgh; m., Shaena Finlayson Blair; 2 d. Educ. Dalkeith High School; Edinburgh University. MRC Fellow, Department of Biochemistry, Edinburgh University, 1975-78; Lecturer, Department of Child Life and Health, Edinburgh University, 1978-80; Senior Lecturer, Department of Child Life and Health, Edinburgh University. Address: (b.) Maternal and Child Health Sciences, Ninewells Hospital and Medical School, Dundee DD1 9SY; T.-01382 660111.

Humphrey, James Malcolm Marcus, CBE, DL, OStJ, MA. Member, Aberdeenshire Council, 1995-2012 (Member, Grampian Regional Council, 1974-94); Leader, Conservative Group, 1999-2012; Deputy Lieutenant, Aberdeenshire, since 1989; Chairman, North East Scotland Preservation Trust, since 2005; Sovereign Grand Commander, The Supreme Council for Scotland, since 1995; b. 1.5.38, Montreal, Canada; m., Sabrina Margaret Pooley; 2 s.; 2 d. Educ. Eton College; Oxford University. Conservative Parliamentary candidate, North Aberdeen, 1966, Kincardine and Deeside, 1991; Council Member, National Farmers Union of Scotland, 1968-73; Member, Aberdeen County Council, 1970-75 (Chairman of Finance, 1973-75); Grampian Regional Council, 1974-94 (Chairman of Finance, 1974-78, Leader, Conservative Group); Member, Aberdeenshire Council, 1995-2012; Deputy Provost, 2007-2012; Member, Cairngorms National Park Authority Board, 2004-2012; Grand Master Mason of Scotland, 1983-88; former Chairman, Clinterty Agricultural

College Council; Member, Queen's Bodyguard for Scotland (Royal Company of Archers); Chairman, North of Scotland Board, Eagle Star Group, 1973-91; Non-Executive Director, Grampian Healthcare NHS Trust, 1993-99; Alternate Member, European Committee of the Regions, 1994-2002; Chairman of the Court of the Convention of The Baronage of Scotland, since 2007; Director: Cairngorms Outdoor Access Trust, 2007-2013, Upper Deeside Access Trust, 2003-07. Recreations: shooting; fishing; photography. Address: (h.) Rhu-Na-Haven, Aboyne, Aberdeenshire.

Humphris, Gerald Michael, BSc (Hons), MClinPsychol, PhD, FRCP (Edin). Emeritus Chair, Medical School, University of St Andrews, since 2003; retired Honorary Consultant Clinical Psychologist, NHS Lothian, since 2005; b. 18.9.54, Kingston, Surrey; 2 d. Educ. Rutlish Grammar, Merton, London; University of Reading. BSc (Hons), University of Reading, 1973-76; PhD, University of London, 1984; University of Liverpool: MClin in Psychology, 1985, Lecturer/Senior Lecturer, 1991-2001; Reader, University of Manchester, 2001-03. Member: The European Association for Communication in Healthcare, British Psychological Society (Divisions: Health and Clinical). Recreation: gardening. Address: (b.) Medical School, University of St Andrews, Medical and Biological Sciences Building, North Haugh, St Andrews KY16 9TF; T.-01334 463565; e-mail: gmh4@st-andrews.ac.uk

Hunter, Andrew Reid, BA (Hons), PGCE; b. 28.9.58, Nairobi, Kenya; m., Barbara G.; 2 s.; 1 d. Educ. Kenton College, Nairobi; Aldenham School, Elstree; University of Manchester; St. Luke's College, Exeter. Career: Westbrook Hay Preparatory School, 1978-79; Worksop College, 1983-91 (Housemaster, 1987-91); Bradfield College, 1991-98 (Housemaster, 1992-98); Headmaster, Merchiston Castle School, Edinburgh, 1998-2018. Former Chairman, Public Schools Hockey Festival, Oxford; former Committee Member, Public Schools Lawn Tennis Association; Member, Headmasters' and Headmistresses' Conference, 1998-2018; Governor: Ardvreck Prep School, Crieff, 2008-18; Trustee, Laidlaw Schools Trust, Newcastle-upon-Tyne, 2009-21; Advisory Board, Royal National Children's SpringBoard Foundation, 2012-19; played a leading role in the development of Merchiston International, (MIS), Shenzhen, China, since 2013; Educational Consultant & Deputy Chair of Governors, Merchiston International, Shenzhen (MIS), since 2018; Interim Head, Merchiston International School (MIS), April 2020-April 2021; Headmasters' and Headmistresses' Conference Appraisal and Mentoring Schemes for Heads, since 2018; Saxton Bampfylde, Executive Search & Leadership Advisors, Partner, Consultant, Schools' Adviser, since April 2019; Governor, Aldenham School, Elstree, Herts, since August 2021. Recreations: reading; attending theatre; tennis; squash; hockey (spectator these days); international cuisine and culture. Address: 10A, Redhall House Drive, Graysmill Dell, Edinburgh EH14 1JE.
E-mail: andrewhunter4@icloud.com

Hunter, Bobby. Lord-Lieutenant, Shetland, since 2011; b. 1949; m., Mabel; 3 c; 5 grandchildren. Educ. Lerwick; Strathclyde University. Career history: early employment in shipbuilding and marine electrical equipment supply; after periods with Shetland Islands Council and the fish processing industry, returned to marine engineering and supplies until taking early retirement in 2006. Director appointments on behalf of Shetland council's economic development unit, and is a prominent member in the Althing debating society and the Windfarm Supporters Group.

Hunter, Colin M., OBE, MB, ChB, FRCP(Ed), FRCGP, FIHM(Hon). Vice Chair, Leonard Cheshire Disability; Chair, Board of Governors, Robert Gordon University; Trustee, Drinkaware; Trustee, St Margaret's Arts Trust, Braemar; b. 28.4.58, Stirling. Educ. High School of Stirling;

Aberdeen University. Principal in general practice, Skene Medical Group, 1986-2018; Honorary Senior Lecturer, Aberdeen University, 1988-2018; Hon. Secretary, N.E. Scotland Faculty, RCGP, 1989-96; first member, RCGP in Scotland, to attain Fellowship of Royal College by Assessment, 1993; Sally Irvine Lecture, Glasgow, 1996; Ian Murray - Scott Lecture, 2003; Chairman, Scottish Council, Royal College of General Practitioners, 1996-2000; National Co-ordinator Primary Care, NHS Education for Scotland, 1999-2005; Hon. Treasurer, Royal College of General Practitioners, 2003-2012; Chair, Board of Trustees, Royal College of General Practitioners, 2012-18. Recreations: hill-walking; singing. Address: Inver Cottage, Auchendryne Square, Braemar, Aberdeenshire AB35 5WS; T.-07778 996018; e-mail: colin_m_hunter@yahoo.co.uk

Hunter, David Ian, FRICS. Honorary Swedish Consul to Glasgow, since 2003; Managing Director, Hunter Advisers, since 2005; b. 01.10.53, Glasgow; m., Anna; 2 d. Educ. Eastwood High School, Glasgow. Appentice Surveyor, James Barr & Son, 1972-78; Assistant Surveyor, ultimately Property Director, Scottish Amicable, 1978-96; Managing Director: Argyll Property Asset Manager, 1996-2001, Aberdeen Property Investors, 2001-04. Had a number of honorary property industry roles, including Board membership of the British Property Federation, membership of the Property Advisory Group of the National Association of Pension Funds, and membership of the Bank of England Property Forum. Recreations: field sports; golf; walking. Address: (b.) 185 St. Vincent Street, Glasgow G2 5QD; T.-0141 204 4041; e-mail: david@hunteradvisers.co.uk

Hunter, George Alexander, OBE (1980), KStJ, KLJ. Founder Governor, Scottish Sports Aid Foundation (1980-2014); Member, Edinburgh City Council, 1992-2006; b. 24.2.26, Edinburgh; m., Eileen Elizabeth. Educ. George Watson's College, Edinburgh. Served with Cameronians, seconded to 17th Dogara Regiment, Indian Army, 1944-47 (Captain); Lawson Donaldson Seeds Ltd., 1942-82 (Director, 15 years); Honorary Consul for Malta; Secretary, Scottish Amateur Rowing Association, 1948-78 (President, 1978-84); Commonwealth Games Council for Scotland: Treasurer, 1962-78, Secretary, 1978-99; Adviser, Sports Aid Foundation, since 1979; Member, Scottish Sports Council, 1976-84 (Chairman, Games and Sports Committee, 1976-84); Chairman, Scottish Standing Conference for Sport, 1977-84; Secretary, Order of St. John Edinburgh and South East Branch, 1987-2011; Edinburgh Citizen of the Year, 2011. Address: (h.) 1 Craiglockhart Crescent, Edinburgh EH14 1EZ; T.-0131-443 2533.

Hunter, Graham Cran, MA, LLB, MUniv (Hon.). Solicitor and part-time University Lecturer (retired); b. 4.10.36, Huntly; m. Janet Catherine Matheson; 3 s. Educ. Gordon Schools, Huntly; Fettes College, Edinburgh; University of Aberdeen, 1955-60. Legal Assistant, Edmonds and Ledingham, Aberdeen 1958-61; Anderson MacArthur & Co., Stornoway, 1961-62; Anderson, Shaw & Gilbert, Inverness, 1962-63; Legal Assistant, Partner, Consultant, Edmonds and Ledingham (later Ledingham Chalmers), Aberdeen, 1963-2001. Territorial Army, 1959-72, Captain, RA, TA; Part-time Lecturer in School of Law, University of Aberdeen, 1980-2002; Secretary and Treasurer of the Financial Board of Christ's College, Aberdeen, 1972-2001 and Board Member, 2001-2015. Clerk and Assessor to the Seven Incorporated Trades of Aberdeen, 1976-2002; Business Manager of Scotland the What? 1969-96; Hon. Vice-President, Lonach Highland and Friendly Society, since 1996; Trustee, Aberdeen International Youth Festival, 1996-2008; Member of the Board of the National Youth Orchestras of Scotland, 2006-2011. Treasurer, and thereafter Chair, of the Friends of Aberdeen University Library, 1998-2013; Rector's

Assessor, University of Aberdeen: Stephen Robertson, 2008-2011, Dr Maitland Mackie, 2011-2014; Member of Court, University of Aberdeen, 2008-2014; Member of the Business Committee of the General Council of the University of Aberdeen, since 2015. Honorary Archival Assistant, University of Aberdeen, until 2017. Recreations: supports Aberdeen Football Club fervently; plays golf inadequately; escapes to the Western Isles frequently. Address: (h.) 62 North Deeside Road, Bieldside, Aberdeen AB15 9DT.

Hunter, James, CBE, FRSE, MA (Hons), PhD. Writer and Historian; Emeritus Professor of History, University of the Highlands and Islands; former Chairman, Highlands and Islands Enterprise; b. 22.5.48, Duror, Argyll; m., Evelyn; 1 s.; 1 d. Educ. Duror Primary School; Oban High School; Aberdeen University; Edinburgh University. Former Director, Scottish Crofters Union; former Chairman, Skye and Lochalsh Enterprise; former Member, Broadcasting Council for Scotland; former Member, Board of Scottish Natural Heritage; former Member, Board of Community Land Scotland. Publications: The Making of the Crofting Community, 1976; Skye: The Island, 1986; The Claim of Crofting, 1991; Scottish Highlanders: A People and their Place, 1992; A Dance Called America: The Scottish Highlands, the United States and Canada, 1994; On the Other Side of Sorrow: Nature and People in the Scottish Highlands, 1995; Glencoe and the Indians, 1996; Last of the Free: A History of the Highlands and Islands of Scotland, 1999; Culloden and the Last Clansman, 2001; Scottish Exodus: Travels Among a Worldwide Clan, 2005; From the Low Tide of the Sea to the Highest Mountain Tops: Community Ownership in the Highlands and Islands, 2012; Set Adrift Upon The World: The Sutherland Clearances, 2015; Insurrection: Scotland's Famine Winter, 2019. Address: (b.) 19 Mansefield Park, Kirkhill, Inverness IV5 7ND; T.-01463 831228.
E-mail: jameshunter22548@btinternet.com

Hunter, Professor John Angus Alexander, OBE, BA, MD, FRCPEdin. Professor Emeritus of Dermatology, University of Edinburgh, since 2000; Grant Professor of Dermatology, Edinburgh University, 1981-99; b. 16.6.39, Edinburgh; m., Ruth Mary Farrow; 1 s.; 2 d. Educ. Loretto School; Pembroke College, Cambridge; Edinburgh University. Research Fellow, Institute of Dermatology, London, 1967; Registrar, Department of Dermatology, Edinburgh Royal Infirmary, 1968-70; Exchange Research Fellow, Department of Dermatology, Minnesota University, 1968; Lecturer, Department of Dermatology, Edinburgh University, 1970-74; Consultant Dermatologist, Lothian Health Board, 1974-80; Member: Executive Committee of Investigative Group, British Association of Dermatologists, 1974-76; Executive Committee, British Association of Dermatologists, 1977-79; Secretary, Scottish Dermatological Society, 1980-82; Specialist Advisory Committee, (Dermatology), Joint Committee on Higher Medical Training, 1980-87 (Chairman, 1986-90); Medical Appeal Tribunal, 1981-99; Scottish Committee for Hospital Medical Services, 1983-85; President: Section of Dermatology, Royal Society of Medicine, 1993-94, Scottish Dermatological Society, 1994-97, British Association of Detmatologists, 1998-99. Publications: Common Diseases of the Skin (Co-author); Clinical Dermatology, 1st, 2nd, 3rd and 4th edition (Co-author); Skin Signs in Clinical Medicine (Co-author); Davidson's Principles and Practice of Medicine, 18th, 19th and 20th edition (Co-editor); Davidson's Clinical Cases, 1st and 2nd edition (Co-editor). Recreations: music; gardening; golf. Address: (h.) Sandy Lodge, Nisbet Road, Gullane EH31 2BQ; T.-01620-842-220.

Hunter, Sir Laurence Colvin, Kt, MA, DPhil, FRSE, FRSA, DUniv (Paisley). Professor of Applied Economics, Glasgow University, 1970-2003, Emeritus Professor, since 2003; b. 8.8.34, Glasgow; m., Evelyn Margaret Green; 3 s.;

1 d. Educ. Hillhead High School, Glasgow; Glasgow University; University College, Oxford. Assistant Lecturer, Manchester University, 1958-59; 2nd Lt., RAEC, 1959-61; Walgreen Postdoctoral Fellow, University of Chicago, 1961-62; joined Glasgow University as Lecturer, 1962; Vice-Principal, 1982-86; Director: External Relations, 1987-90, Business School 1996-99. Council Member, ACAS, 1974-86; Chairman, Police Negotiating Board, 1986-2000; Council Member, Economic and Social Research Council, 1989-92; Editor, Scottish Journal of Political Economy, 1966-97; President, Scottish Economic Society, 1993-96; Treasurer, Royal Society of Edinburgh, 1999-2004. Recreations: golf; painting. Address: (h.) 7 Boclair Crescent, Bearsden, Glasgow G61 2AG; T.-0141-563 7135.

Hunter, Neil. Principal Reporter/Chief Executive Officer, Scottish Children's Reporter Administration, since 2011. Educ. University of Glasgow; Glasgow Caledonian University; Strathclyde University; 1 d. Career: involved in the management of support services for young homeless people in Glasgow and later established one of Scotland's first substance misuse services for children and young people in Springburn, North Glasgow; led the Addictions Partnership for the City of Glasgow; Director of West Glasgow Community Health and Care Partnership (CHCP), until 2010. Address: Scottish Children's Reporter Administration, Ochil House, Springkerse Business Park Stirling FK7 7XE; T.-0300 200 1555.

Hunter, Peter Matheson, BSc, MPhil, LLB. Regional Manager, UNISON Scotland; Lay Member, Employment Appeal Tribunal, since 2000; STUC General Council; Chair, Scottish Union Learning; b. Aberdeen. Educ. Cults Academy; Edinburgh University; Glasgow University; Strathclyde University. Scottish Low Pay Unit, 1992, Director, 1999-2001. Lay Member, Employment Tribunal, 1995-2000. Voluntary work in recovery communities. Recreation: Aberdeen FC. Address: (b.) 14 West Campbell Street, Glasgow G2 6RX; T.-0845 355 0845.

Hunter, Russell. Lyon Clerk and Keeper of the Records, since 2018. Educ. University of Glasgow; University of Edinburgh. Admitted as a solicitor in 1997. Address: (b.) Court of the Lord Lyon, HM New Register House, Edinburgh EH1 3YT; T.-0131 556 7255.

Hunter, Sir Thomas Blane, Kt (2005), BA. Entrepreneur; Chairman: West Coast Capital, since 1998, Hunter Foundation, since 1998; Chief Executive Officer, Sports Division, 1984-98; b. 6.5.61, Irvine; m., Marion McKillop; 2 s.; 1 d. Educ. Cumnock Academy; University of Strathclyde. Carnegie Medal of Philanthropy. Address: Marathon House, Olympic Business Park, Drybridge Road, Dundonald KA2 9AE.

Hunter Blair, Sir Patrick, Bt, FICFor, BScFor; b. 12.5.58, Dumfries; m., Marguerite; 3 s.; 2 d. Educ. The Edinburgh Academy; The University of Aberdeen. Former Director of Policy and Standards for the Forest Service in Northern Ireland; returned to Scotland in 2005 and owns and manages a small estate in south Ayrshire. Fellow of the Institute of Chartered Foresters; Director, Scotland's Finest Woodlands; Chair, South Scotland Forestry Forum; Chairman, River Girvan District Salmon Fishery Board; Chairman, Straiton Village Co-operative; Trustee, Ayrshire Rivers Trust; Immediate Past-President, Royal Scottish Forestry Society, 2015-17; Board Member, Scottish Natural Heritage, 2013-17. Recreations: family; food; forestry and fishing.

Huntly, Marquess of (Granville Charles Gomer Gordon). Chief, House of Gordon, since 1989; b. 4.2.44, Aberdeen; m., 1, Jane Gibb; m., 2, Catheryn Kindersley; 1 s.; 3 d. Educ. Gordonstoun School; Institute of Commercial Management; PhD, University of Buckingham, 2018. President, Institute of Financial Accountants, 1989-2000; Chief, Aboyne Highland Games. Recreations: British domestic architecture. Address: Aboyne Castle, Aberdeenshire AB34 5JP; T.-01339 887 778.

Hutcheon, William Robbie. Editor, Courier and Advertiser, Dundee, 2002-2011; b. 19.1.52, Aberdeen; m., Margo; 1 s.; 2 d. Educ. Aberdeen Academy. Reporter (D.C. Thomson Office in Aberdeen), 1969-70; Sports Sub-Editor, Sports Editor, Chief Sub-Editor, Night News Editor, Deputy Editor, Editor, since 1970, with Courier and Advertiser. Chairman, Editors' Committee, Scottish Daily Newspaper Society, 2007-08. Recreations: sport; travel; music; computing. Address: (h.) 42 Ferndale Drive, Broughty Ferry, Dundee DD5 3DF; T.-01382 774552; e-mail: hutcheonbill@gmail.com

Hutchinson, Peter, PhD, FIFM. Secretary of the inter-governmental North Atlantic Salmon Conservation Organization (NASCO), 2012-17; b. 26.5.56, Glasgow; m., Jane MacKellaig; 1 s.; 1 d. Educ. Queen Elizabeth's Grammar School, Blackburn; Edinburgh University. Assistant Secretary (1986-2012), North Atlantic Salmon Conservation Organization (Chairman, Scientific Committee, 1992-2013); Project Co-ordinator, Surface Water Acidification; Research Biologist, Institute of Terrestrial Ecology, Edinburgh University; Member, Consular Corps in Edinburgh and Leith, since 1991. Recreations: most sports, particularly rugby union, travel and walking. Address: Edinburgh.
E-mail: peter@phutchinson.net

Hutchison, David, MA, MLitt. Academic and writer; Honorary Professor in Media Policy, Glasgow Caledonian University; Acting Director, Scottish Centre of Journalism Studies, 2003-04; Visiting Professor, Brock University, Canada, 2004; b. 24.9.44, West Kilbride; m., Pauleen Frew; 2 d. Educ. Ardrossan Academy; Glasgow University. Tutor/Organiser, WEA (West of Scotland), 1966-69; Teacher, Reid Kerr College, Paisley, 1969-71; various posts, Glasgow College of Technology/Glasgow Caledonian University, since 1971; Member, West Kilbride District Council, 1970-75 (Chairman, 1972-75); Governor, Scottish Film Council, 1987-95; Member, General Advisory Council, BBC, 1988-96; Board Member, Regional Screen Scotland, 2008-14 (Chair, 2010-14); author of plays, Deadline, Pitlochry Festival Theatre, 1980; Too Long the Heart, Siege Perilous, Edinburgh, 2013; The Blood is Strong, Finborough Theatre, London, 2013. Publications: The Modern Scottish Theatre, 1977; Headlines (Editor), 1978; Media Policy, 1998; The Media in Scotland (Co-Editor), 2008; Centres and Peripheries: Metropolitan and Non-Metropolitan Journalism (Co-Editor), 2011; Scotland's Referendum and The Media (Co-Editor), 2016; Stuart Hood: Twentieth-Century Partisan (Co-Editor), 2020; various articles/chapters. Recreations: walking; the arts; golf. T.-01294 823321.
E-mail: dbhutchison@btinternet.com

Hutchison, Professor James D., PhD, FRCSEd, FRCSEng, FRCSGlas, FFSTEd. Emeritus Professor, Regius Chair of Surgery and Sir Harry Platt Chair of Orthopaedics, University of Aberdeen; Honorary Consultant Orthopaedic Surgeon, NHS Grampian, since 1991; b. 8.10.55, Dundee; m., Kate Douglas; 2 s.; 1 d. Educ. High School of Dundee; University of Dundee. Lecturer in Orthopaedics, Edinburgh and Aberdeen, 1986-91; Senior Lecturer, Aberdeen, 1991-95. President, Moynihan Chirurgical Club, 2016-17; Chairman, Scottish Orthopaedic Services Development Group for Scottish Government Health Department; Past Chairman, Scottish Committee for Orthopaedics and Trauma; previously Specialty Advisor in Orthopaedics to CMO and SGHD; Past Vice-President (2012-15); Fellow of the Faculty of Surgical Trainers of Royal College of Surgeons of Edinburgh; Past President, Aberdeen Medico Chirurgical Society (2005-06); Chair, Board of Governors, Robert Gordon's College, Aberdeen, since 2013; Chairman, Royal Northern & University Club, Aberdeen, 2017-18. Clubs: Royal Northern & University Club, Aesculapian Club, Harveian Society, Moynihan Chirurgical Club. Recreations: family; dogs; curling; shooting; art. Address: Department of Orthopaedics, Woodend Hospital, Eday Road, Aberdeen AB15 8XS; T.-01224 556462; e-mail: j.d.hutchison@abdn.ac.uk

Hutchison, John Charles, MBE, JP, BSc (Hons), CEng, FICE, FIES; b. 23.7.47, Edinburgh; m., Christine Laidlaw; 1 s.; 2 d. Educ. Leith Academy; Heriot-Watt University. Early career in steel structures and bridges with Redpath Dorman Long; road construction on Skye and maintenance of roads, bridges, ferries, piers and jetties for Highland Regional Council, Lochaber, as Divisional Engineer; Highland Council, Lochaber Area Manager. Honorary Sheriff and Justice of the Peace. Past Chair, Isle of Eigg Heritage Trust, Scottish Rural Action, John Muir Trust, West Highland Museum Trust, West Highland College UHI. Past Director of Nevis Partnership and Community Land Scotland. Vice Convener, Mòd Lochabair, 2007. Trustee, Constitution for Scotland, Castle Tioram Trust; Chair, East Lochaber Community Trust and Kilmallie Community Council. Recreations: singing; mountaineering and reading. Address: Taigh na Coille, Badabrie, Fort William PH33 7LX; T.-01397 772252.
E-mail: jch@abrach.scot

Hutt, Stephen M. Chief Financial Officer, Forsa Energy since 2021; Managing Director, SIMEC Green Highland Renewables Ltd, 2018-2020. Educ. George Heriot's School; University of Edinburgh. Career history: Managing Director, Smith, Anderson & Company Ltd, 1999-2006; Business Finance Director, Kerry Ingredients & Flavours, 2007-2011; Chief Executive, Royal Highland and Agricultural Society of Scotland, 2011-2016; Non Executive Director: Paper Industry Technical Association (PITA), since 2008, Institute of Occupational Medicine (IOM), since 2014. Address: Clyde View (Suite F3), Riverside Business Park, 22 Pottery Street, Greenock PA15 2UZ; T.-01475 749941.

Hutton, Alasdair Henry, OBE, TD, OStJ. Writer and Narrator, Royal Edinburgh Military Tattoo and other public events, concerts, videos and audio guides, since 1992; b, 19.5.40, London; 2 s. Educ. Dollar Academy; Brisbane State High School. Journalist, The Age, Melbourne, 1959-61; Aberdeen Journals, 1962-64; Broadcaster, BBC, 1964-79; Member, European Parliament, 1979-89; Convener, Scottish Borders Council, 2003-12 (Councillor, Kelso, 2002-12); Member, Queen's Bodyguard for Scotland (Royal Company of Archers); former 2iC, 15th (Scottish Volunteer) Bn., The Parachute Regiment; Elder, Kelso North Church of Scotland; President, Kelso Branch, Royal British Legion Scotland; President, Edinburgh, Lothians and Border Area, Royal British Legion Scotland; Member and former Chairman & Vice President, John Buchan Society; Life Member, Edinburgh Sir Walter Scott Club, since 1994 (Chairman, 2013-2016); Patron, Kelso Laddies' Association; Reader, Borders Talking Newspaper, since 1997, Patron, 2008, Convener 2020; Patron, Borders Independent Advocacy Service, since 2001; Chairman, Disease Prevention Organisation, 1990-2013; River Tweed Commissioner, 2004-2013; Founder Member, The Robert Burns Guild of Speakers, 2012; Honorary Colonel, Lothian and Borders Battalion, Army Cadet Force, 2006-09; Friend of Abbotsford, since 2010, Honorary Patron, 2017; President, Kelso Farmers Market, 2006-12; Chairman, Kelso Carers Initiative Trust, 2006-12; Chairman, Order of St John, SE Scotland Area, since 2012; Fellow, Industry and Parliament Trust. Author: "15 Para 1947-1993", 1997; "The Tattoo Fox", 2013; "The Tattoo Fox Makes New Friends", 2014; "The Greatest Show On Earth", 2016; Treasury of Scottish Nursery Rhymes, 2016; "Mustard and Pepper", 2019; Scotland's Greatest Storyteller – The Life of Sir Walter Scott, 2021; The Castle Cat, 2021. Address: 4 Broomlands Court, Kelso TD5 7SR; T.-01573 224369; Mobile: 07753 625734.
E-mail: alasdairhutton@yahoo.co.uk

Hutton, Graeme, BSc (Hons), DipArch, RSA, RIBA, FRIAS. Professor of Architecture, University of Dundee, since 2002; Practising Architect, since 1990; b. 2.6.64, Shrewsbury; m., Julie; 1 s.; 2 d. Educ. Carnoustie High School; Robert Gordon University. Partner, Hutton Rattray Architects, 1992-96; Design Architect, RMJM Scotland Ltd., 1996-99; University of Dundee, since 1999; Design Consultant, LJRH Architects Dundee, since 2000. Recreations: photography; music. Address: University of Dundee, Dundee DD1 4HN; T.-01382 385270.
E-mail: g.hutton@dundee.ac.uk

Hutton, Professor Neil, MA, PhD. Professor of Criminal Justice, University of Strathclyde, b. 20.12.53, Dundee; m., Michele Burman; 2 d. Educ. High School of Dundee; Edinburgh University. Research Fellow: University of Dundee, 1981-83, University of Edinburgh, 1984-87, Victoria University of Wellington, NZ, 1987-90; joined University of Strathclyde in 1990 as Lecturer, then became Senior Lecturer. Member: Sentencing Commission for Scotland, 2003-06. Recreations: cooking; golf. Address: (b.) McCance Building, Richmond Street, Glasgow G1 1XQ; T.-0141-552 4400; e-mail: n.hutton@strath.ac.uk

Hutton, William Riddell, BDS. Dentist, 1961-2001; Honorary Sheriff, since 1996; b. 22.10.38, Glasgow; m., Patricia Margaret Burns; 1 s.; 1 d. Educ. Hamilton Academy; Glasgow University Dental School. International Grenfell Association, Newfoundland and Labrador, 1961-64; General Practice, Lanark, 1964-2001; Member, Secretary and Chairman, Lanarkshire Local Dental Committee, 1964-94; Member and Chairman, Lanarkshire Area Dental Committee, 1975-94; Lord Cornet, Lanark, 1984. Recreations: music; golf; hillwalking; travel. Address: (h.) St. Anthony, 9 Braedale Road, Lanark ML11 7AW; T.-01555 662927; e-mail: wrh.brae@gmail.com

Hvide, Professor Hans Krogh, MSc, PhD. Professor of Economics and Finance, University of Aberdeen, since 2006, SIRE Professor, since 2007; b. 26.09.68, Bergen, Norway; m., Siri Brekke; 2 s.; 1 d. Educ. Norwegian School of Economics and Business; London School of Economics. Associate Professor, Department of Finance and Management Science, NHH, 2002-06; Visiting Associate Professor, MIT/Sloan School, 2005; Professor, Norwegian School of Economics and Business (NHH), 2007. Post-doc at Tel-Aviv University, Research Affiliate, CEPR and IZA. Recreations: tennis; hiking; skiing; reading. Address: (b.) Edward Wright Building, Dunbar Street, Old Aberdeen AB24 3QY; T.-01224 273 411; e-mail: hans.hvide@gmail.com

Hynes, Alex, BA (Hons). Managing Director, Scotland's Railway, since 2019; Managing Director, ScotRail Alliance, since 2017. Educ. Altrincham Grammar School for Boys; University of Leeds. Career history: Halcrow Group Ltd: Consultant, 1998-2000, Senior Consulant, 2000-02; Office of Rail Regulation: Senior Economist, 2002-04, Manager, Policy Unit, 2004-05; Strategic Planning Manager - Rail, The Go-Ahead Group plc, 2005-07; Commercial Director, London Midland, 2007-

2011; Managing Director - Rail Development, The Go-Ahead Group plc, 2012-13; Managing Director: Northern Rail, 2013-16, Arriva Rail North Ltd, 2016-17; Adviser, Arriva Rail North (Northern), 2017. Address: ScotRail Alliance, Atrium Court, 50 Waterloo Street, Glasgow G2 6HQ; T.-020 7430 8270.

Hyslop, Fiona J., MA (Hons). MSP (SNP), Linlithgow, since 2011, Lothians, 1999-2011; Cabinet Secretary for Culture, Tourism and External Affairs, 2016-2020; Cabinet Secretary for Culture and External Affairs, 2011-16; Minister for Culture, 2009-2011; Cabinet Secretary for Education and Lifelong Learning, 2007-2009; b. 1.8.64, Irvine; m.; 2 s.; 1 d. Educ. Ayr Academy; Glasgow University. Standard Life, 1986-99, various sales and marketing positions, latterly Marketing Manager. Recreations: swimming; cinema. Address: (b.) Scottish Parliament, Edinburgh EH99 1SP; T.-0131-348 5921.

I

Ibbotson, Sally Helen, BSc (Hons), MD, MBChB (Hons), FRCP (Edin). Professor of Photodermatology, University of Dundee, since 2016; Clinical Senior Lecturer in Photobiology, Honorary Consultant Dermatologist, University of Dundee, Ninewells Hospital and Medical School, 1998-2016; b. Newcastle upon Tyne. Educ. Central Newcastle High School for Girls; University of Leeds. House Physician and House Surgeon, Leeds General Infirmary and St. James' University Hospital, 1986-87; Teaching Fellow in Medicine, Leeds General Infirmary, 1987-89; Research Fellow, University of Leeds, 1989-92; Royal Victoria Infirmary, Newcastle upon Tyne: Registrar in Dermatology, 1992-94, Senior Registrar in Dermatology, 1994-98; Research Fellow, Harvard University, Boston, USA, 1996-97. Address: (b.) Photobiology Unit, Dermatology Department, University of Dundee, Ninewells Hospital and Medical School, Dundee DD1 9SY; T.-01382 383499; e-mail: s.h.ibbotson@dundee.ac.uk

Illingworth, Blair. Chief Executive Officer, Aggreko, since 2021; b. 3.63. Previous executive and board experience: Director of Marshalls plc; Chief Executive of Polypipe plc; Chief Executive of Tarmac Building Products and Chief Executive of Brush Group (owned by Melrose plc); military service as a commissioned officer in the Royal Marines. Address: Aggreko, Lomondgate, Stirling Road, Dumbarton G82 3RG; T.-01389 767821; e-mail: blair@aggreko.com

Imery, Gill, QPM. HM Chief Inspector of Constabulary in Scotland, 2018-2022. Career history: joined Lothian and Borders Police in 1986 and served in a variety of uniform and detective officer posts in both city and county divisions; promoted to Detective Superintendent and took up post as National Drugs Co-ordinator with the Scottish Crime and Drug Enforcement Agency in 2004; became Head of Complaints and Conduct for Lothian & Borders Police in 2007; promoted to Chief Superintendent in 2008, taking on the role of Head of Safer Communities Division; became the first female commander of the city of Edinburgh in 2010; moved to Detective Chief Superintendent and Head of CID for Lothian and Borders Police before the transition to Police Scotland in 2013; served the new national force as Detective Chief Superintendent for local crime across the country and all public protection areas of business; appointed Divisional commander for J division, in charge of over 900 officers, and covering the areas of West, Mid and East Lothian, and the Scottish Borders in 2014; Assistant Inspector of Constabulary, HM Inspectorate of Constabulary in Scotland (HMICS), 2016-18. Awarded the Queens Police Medal (QPM) in the 2017 Queen's Birthday Honours.

Ingle, Professor Stephen James, BA, MA (Econ), DipEd, PhD. Emeritus Professor of Politics, Stirling University; b. 6.11.40, Ripon; m., Margaret Anne; 2 s.; 1 d. Educ. The Roan School, London; Sheffield University; Wellington University, NZ. Commonwealth Scholar, 1964-67; Lecturer in Politics, Hull University, 1967-80; Senior Lecturer, 1980-91; Head of Department, 1985-90. Secretary, Political Studies Association, 1988-89; Member, East Yorkshire Health Authority, 1985-90; Visiting Research Fellow, Victoria University of Wellington, 1993; Academic Fellow of the Open Society Institute, 2006-08; panel member and assessor, Arts and Humanities Research Council, 2009-14; research assessor for the Carnegie Trust, 2014-2021. Publications: Socialist Thought in Imaginative Literature, 1979; Parliament and Health Policy, 1981; British Party System, 1987, 1989, 1999, 2008; George Orwell: a political life, 1993; Narratives of British Socialism, 2002; The Social and Political Thought of George Orwell: A Reappraisal, 2006; Orwell Reconsidered, 2020. Recreations: theatre; reading; music; travel. Address: (b.) Department of Politics, Stirling University, Stirling FK9 4LA; T.-01786 467568; e-mail: s.j.ingle@stir.ac.uk

Inglis, John, PPRSW, RGI, HAWI, DA. Painter and Lecturer; b. 27.7.53, Glasgow; m., Heather; 2 s.; 2 d. Educ. Hillhead High School; Gray's School of Art. Travelling scholarships to Italy, 1976; Member, Dundee Group, 1979-84; Recent solo exhibitions: Compass Gallery, Glasgow 2020; Lillie Art Gallery, Milngavie 2021; Scottish Arts Council Award, 1981; RSA Keith Prize, 1975; SAC Bursary, 1982; RSA Meyer Oppenheim Prize, 1982; RSW EIS Award, 1987; SAC Grant, 1988; May Marshall Brown Award, 1994, 2000; Paisley Art Institute Bessie Scott Award, 2007; Bet Low Trust Award, 2013; AAS Prize, 2020; Elected Honorary Member, Australian Watercolour Institute, 2010; e-mail: j.inglis@hotmail.co.uk

Inglis, Morag. Chairman, Mitchells Roberton Solicitors, since 2021; b. 9.63. Educ. University of Aberdeen. Commenced traineeship with Mitchells Roberton in 1985, became Partner in 1993; Director: Ross Harper Nominees Limited, since 2012, Chelton Trustees Limited, since 2014, Legesgain Investments Limited, since 2019, Craigend Moor Investments Limited, since 2019. Recreations: walking; travelling; music; spending time with family and friends. Address: Mitchells Roberton Solicitors, George House, 36 North Hanover Street, Glasgow G1 2AD; T.-0141 548 1701; e-mail: mmi@mitchells-roberton.co.uk

Ingold, Professor Timothy, PhD, FBA, FRSE. Professor of Social Anthropology, University of Aberdeen, 1999-2018, Professor Emeritus, since 2018; b. 1.11.48, Sevenoaks; m., Anna Kaarina; 3 s.; 1 d. Educ. Leighton Park School; Churchill College, Cambridge University. University of Manchester: Lecturer, Department of Social Anthropology, 1974-85, Senior Lecturer, 1985-90, Professor, 1990-95, Max Gluckman Professor of Social Anthropology, 1995-99; Visiting Professor: University of Helsinki, 1986, University of Tromsø, 1996-2000. Royal Anthropological Institute Rivers Memorial Medal, 1989; Award of Jean-Marie Delwart Foundation, Belgian Academy of Sciences, 1994; Retzius Medal, Swedish Society for Anthropology and Geography, 2004; Royal Anthropological Institute Huxley Memorial Medal, 2014; Knight, First Class, of the Order of the White Rose of Finland, 2014; Honorary Doctorate in Philosophy, Leuphana University, Lüneburg, 2015; Honorary Doctorate in Social Sciences and Art, University of Lapland, Rovaniemi, 2019. Publications: The Skolt Lapps Today, 1976; Hunters, Pastoralists and Ranchers, 1980; Evolution and Social Life, 1986; The Appropriation of Nature, 1986; What Is An Animal? (Editor), 1988; Tools, Language and Cognition in Human Evolution (Co-Editor), 1993; Companion Encyclopedia of Anthropology: humanity, culture and social life (Editor), 1994; Key Debates in Anthropology (Editor), 1996; The Perception of the Environment, 2000; Creativity and Cultural Improvisation (Co-Editor), 2007; Lines: a brief history, 2007; Ways of Walking (Co-Editor), 2008; Being Alive, 2011; Redrawing Anthropology (Editor), 2011; Imagining Landscapes (Co-Editor), 2012; Biosocial Becomings (Co-Editor), 2013; Making, 2013; Making and Growing (Co-Editor), 2014; The Life of Lines, 2015; Anthropology and/as Education, 2017; Anthropology: Why it Matters, 2018; Correspondences, 2020; Imagining for Real, 2021. Recreation: music. Address: 18 Osborne Place, Aberdeen AB25 2DA; T.-01224 646826. E-mail: tim.ingold@abdn.ac.uk

Ingram, Rt. Hon. Adam. MP (Labour), East Kilbride, 1987-2010; Minister of State for the Armed Forces, 2001-07; b. 1.2.47, Glasgow; m., Maureen McMahon. Educ.

Cranhill Senior Secondary School. Programmer/analyst, 1965-1970; systems analyst, 1970-77; trade union official, 1977-87; Councillor, East Kilbride District Council, 1980-87 (Leader of the Council, 1984-87); PPS to Neil Kinnock, Leader of the Opposition, 1988-92; Labour Opposition Spokesperson on Social Security, 1993-95, Science and Technology, 1995-97; Minister of State for Northern Ireland, 1997-2001; Head of Study Team on Defence Role in Counter-Terrorism and Resiliance, 2007-08. Recreations: fishing; cooking; reading.

Ingram, Adam Hamilton, BA (Hons). MSP (SNP), Carrick, Cumnock and Doon Valley, 2011-16, South of Scotland, 1999-2011; Minister for Children and Early Years, 2007-2011; b. 1.5.51, Kilmarnock; m., Gerry; 3 s.; 1 d. Educ. Kilmarnock Academy; Paisley College. Manager, A.H. Ingram & Son, Bakers, 1971-76; Senior Economic Assistant, Manpower Services Commission, 1985-86; Researcher and Lecturer, Paisley College, 1987-88; economic development consultant, 1989-99. Recreation: golf.

Ingram, Professor David Stanley, OBE, VMH, BSc, PhD (Hull), MA, ScD (Cantab), HonDUniv (Open, Scotland), FRSB, FCIHort, FRSGS (Hon), FRCPEd, FRSE. Honorary Professor, Science, Technology and Innovation Studies, University of Edinburgh, since 1991; Honorary Fellow, Royal Botanic Garden Edinburgh, since 1998; Honorary Professorial Fellow, Science, Technology & Innovation Studies, Social and Political Science, University of Edinburgh, since 2012, Honorary Professor, from 2021; Honorary Professor, Lancaster Environment Centre, Lancaster University, since 2007. Formerly, Regius Keeper (Director), Royal Botanic Garden, Edinburgh, 1990-1998, then Master, St Catharine's College, Cambridge, 2000-2006. Honorary Professor in Botany, University of Glasgow, 1991-2010; Honorary Professor, Napier University, 1998-2003; Royal Society of Edinburgh Programme Convenor, 2005-2010 and Secretary of the Dining Club, 2010-2013; Senior Visiting Fellow and Advisory Board Member, ESRC Genomics Forum, University of Edinburgh, 2006-2013; Chairman, Advisory Committee to the Darwin Initiative for the Survival of the Species, 1999-2005; Main Board Member, Scottish Natural Heritage, 1999-2000; Independent Member and Deputy Chairman, Joint Nature Conservation Committee, 2001-08. Fellow: Royal Society of Edinburgh, Royal Society of Biology, Chartered Institute of Horticulture and Royal College of Physicians, Edinburgh; Honorary Fellow: Royal Scottish Geographical Society, since 1998, Downing College, Cambridge, since 2001, Myerscough College, Preston, since 2001, Worcester College, Oxford, since 2003, St. Catherine's College, Cambridge, since 2006, Ruskin Foundation, since 2014; Honorary Member, British Society for Plant Pathology, since 2008; Companion, Guild of St George, since 2015; b. 10.10.41, Birmingham; m., Alison; 2 s. Educ. Yardley Grammar School, Birmingham; University of Hull; University of Cambridge. Research Fellow, University of Glasgow, 1966-68, University of Cambridge, 1968-69; Senior Scientific Officer, Unit of Development Botany, Cambridge, 1969-74; Lecturer, then Reader in Plant Pathology, Botany School, University of Cambridge, 1974-90; Fellow (also Tutor, Dean and Director of Studies in Biology), Downing College, Cambridge, 1974-90; Honorary Professor of Horticulture, Royal Horticultural Society, 1995-2000; President, International Congress of Plant Pathology, 1998; President, British Society for Plant Pathology, 1998; Appointed Officer of the Order of the British Empire, 1998; Awarded Victoria Medal of Honour, Royal Horticultural Society, 2004; author of several books and many papers in learned journals on botany, plant pathology, horticulture, conservation and the synergy between 19th century European art, botany and horticulture. Recreations: gardening; music; ceramics;

poetry. Address: Royal Society of Edinburgh, 22-26 George Street, Edinburgh EH2 2PQ.

Ingram, Professor Malcolm David, BSc, PhD, DSc. Emeritus Professor of Chemistry, Aberdeen University; m., Lorna Hardman; 1 s.; 1 d. Educ. Oldershaw Grammar School; Liverpool University. Career at Aberdeen University. Chairman, Aberdeen and North of Scotland Section, Royal Society of Chemistry, 1990-93; Humboldt Research Award Winner, 2002; Editor, Physics and Chemistry of Glasses, 1998-2008; Honorary Fellow of the Society of Glass Technology. Publications: 200 in scientific journals. Recreations: gardening; foreign travel. Address: (b.) Department of Chemistry, Aberdeen University, Aberdeen AB24 2UE; T.-01224 272943.

Innes, Callum. Scottish abstract painter; b. 1962. Educ. Gray's School of Art; Edinburgh College of Art. Began exhibiting in the mid-to-late 1980s and in 1992 had two major exhibitions in public galleries, at the ICA, London, and the Scottish National Gallery of Modern Art, Edinburgh; numerous solo exhibitions throughout Britain, Europe, North America, New Zealand and Asia; short-listed for the Turner and Jerwood Prizes in 1995, won the prestigious NatWest Prize for Painting in 1998, and in 2002 was awarded the Jerwood Prize for Painting; exhibited widely both nationally and internationally; work is held in public collections worldwide including the Guggenheim, New York; National Gallery of Australia; Tate, London; Musée national d'art moderne, Paris, and Scottish National Gallery of Modern Art. Lives and works in Edinburgh. Represented by Frith Street Gallery, London.

Innes, Norman Lindsay, OBE, BSc, PhD, DSc, FRSE; b. 3.5.34, Kirriemuir; m., Marjory Niven Farquhar, MA; 1 s.; 1 d. Educ. Websters Seminary, Kirriemuir; Aberdeen University; Cambridge University. Senior Cotton Breeder: Sudan, 1958-66, Uganda, 1966-71; Head, Cotton Research Unit, Uganda, 1972; National Vegetable Research Station, Wellesbourne: Head, Plant Breeding Section, 1973-84, Deputy Director, 1977-84; Scottish Crop Research Institute: Deputy Director, 1986-94, Head, Plant Breeding Division, 1984-89; Honorary Lecturer, then Honorary Professor, Birmingham University, 1973-84; Member, Board of European Association of Plant Breeders, 1981-86; Chairman, British Association of Plant Breeders, 1982-84; Governing Board Member, International Crops Research Institute for Semi-Arid Tropics, India, 1982-88; Honorary Professor, Dundee University, 1988-95; Honorary Research Professor: Scottish Crop Research Institute, 1994-2011, James Hutton Institute (appointed in 2011); Governing Board Member, International Potato Centre, Peru, 1988-95, Chairman, 1991-95; Vice-President, Association of Applied Biologists, 1990-92, President, 1993-94; Governing Council Member, 1996-2001, Chairman, 1997-2000, International Centre of Insect Physiology and Ecology, Kenya; Member, Board of Trustees, West Africa Rice Development Association, Côte d' Ivoire, 1998-2004, Chairman, 2000-03; Member, Oxfam Council of Trustees, 1982-85; Book Review Editor, Experimental Agriculture, 1996-2012. Recreations: photography; travel.

Innes, Steven G., BArch (Hons), DipArch (Glas), RIBA, RIAS. Director, The McLennan Partnership, since 2008. Educ. Mackintosh School of Architecture. Career history: work in the private and public sectors before joining the McLennan Partnership in 2006. ARB registered chartered architect and a member of both the RIBA and the RIA; council member and Practice/CPD Convenor of the Glasgow Institute of Architects (GIA); employment mentor to staff members. Address: The McLennan Partnership, Suite 12, Second Floor, Burgh Business Centre, 75 King

Street, Rutherglen G73 1JS T.-0141 647 9162.
E-mail: admin@mclarchitects.co.uk

Inverarity, James Alexander (Sandy), CBE, FRSA, FRAgS, CA. Farmer and Landowner; Chairman: Scottish Agricultural College, 1990-98, Scottish Agricultural Securities Corporation, plc, 1987-2016; President, Scottish Farm and Countryside Educational Trust, 1990-98; b. 17.9.35; m., Jean (deceased); 1 s.; 2 d; m. (2), Frances. Educ. Loretto School. President, National Farmers Union of Scotland, 1970-71; Member: Eggs Authority, 1971-74, Farm Animal Welfare Council, 1978-88, Panel of Agricultural Arbiters, 1983-2007, Governing Body, Scottish Crop Research Institute, 1984-97, Dairy Produce Quota Tribunal for Scotland, 1984-85; Director, United Oilseed Producers Ltd., 1985-97 (Chairman, 1987-97). Recreations: shooting; curling. Address: Cransley, Fowlis, Dundee DD2 5NP; T.-01382 580327.

Ireland, Professor Elizabeth. Chair, NHS National Services Scotland, 2013-19 (Non-Executive on the board, since 2007 and Vice-Chair in 2012). Career history: University of Stirling: developed partnerships across healthcare and academia to promote learning and the transfer of knowledge - especially regarding qualitative approaches to learning from and improving people's experiences of care; leadership roles at board, regional and national levels, culminating in 4 years (2008-12) as national clinical lead for Palliative and End of Life Care for the Scottish Government; national clinical leadership support to the Better Together programme. Honorary Chair, School of Management, University of Stirling; active within the NHS chairs' group.

Ireland, Helen. Director of External Relations, National Museums Scotland, since 2015. Educ. University of Oxford. Career history: Publishing Director, Nursing Times, Emap Business Communications, 1997-2002; Director of Marketing and Communications, Scottish Opera, 2007-2015. Address: National Museums Scotland, Chambers Street, Edinburgh EH1 1JF; T.-0131 247 4332. E-mail: h.ireland@nms.ac.uk

Ireland, W. Seith S., LLB (Hons). Retired Sheriff in North Strathclyde, South Strathclyde and Glasgow, since 2021; Sheriff, Paisley Sheriff Court, 2014-2021; formerly Sheriff at Kilmarnock Sheriff Court, 2003-2014; b. 5.4.56, Glasgow; m., Elizabeth. Educ. The High School of Glasgow; University of Glasgow. President: Student Representative Council, University of Glasgow, 1977-78, Glasgow Bar Association, 1993-94; Member, Council of Law Society of Scotland, 1995-98; Convener, Law Society Devolution Committee, 1997-98; Admitted Solicitor, 1982; Assistant: Ross Harper and Murphy, 1982-85, Jim Friel & Co, 1985-86; Principal, Ireland & Co Solicitors, Glasgow, 1986-2003. Member, Council of the Sheriffs' Association, 2009-2013, Honorary Secretary and Treasurer, 2010-2012; Board Member, Phoenix Futures Scotland, since 2013; Member, Council of Scottish Association for the Study of Offending (SASO), since 2013; Member, Business Committee, General Council of University of Glasgow, 2005-09 and since 2016. Recreations: golf; theatre; cooking. Address: (b.) Sheriffs' Chambers, Sheriff Court House, St James Street, Paisley PA3 2HW.
E-mail: sheriffwsireland@scotcourts.gov.uk

Irons, Professor Alastair, MA, MSc, MEd, PhD. Deputy Vice-Chancellor, University of Abertay, since 2022. Educ. The University of Edinburgh; Heriot-Watt University; Northumbria University; Durham University. Career history: Systems Analyst, ICI, 1985-91; Associate Dean, Northumbria University, 1992-2008; Regional Skills Senior Specialist, One NorthEast, 2008; Visiting Scholar, University of Cape Town, 2013-15; University of Sunderland: Head of Department, Computing, Engineering and Technology, 2008-2015, Academic Dean for Faculty of Technology, St Peter's Campus, 2018-2021, appointed Professor of Computing Science in 2015, Academic Director for Digital Education, 2021-22. National Teaching Fellow, since 2010; Senior Research Associate, University of Johannesburg. Address: Abertay University, Bell Street, Dundee DD1 1HG.

Irons, Norman MacFarlane, CBE, DL, DLitt, DUniv, Hon. FRCS Ed, CEng, MIMechE, MCIBSE, Knight of The Order of the Dannebrog, Denmark, 2008. Lord Provost and Lord Lieutenant of the City of Edinburgh, 1992-96; Partner, Building Services Consulting Engineers, since 1993; Royal Danish Consul, Edinburgh and Leith, 2000-2011; Consul of Hungary in Scotland, 2013-2018; b. 4.1.41, Glasgow; m., Anne Buckley; 1 s.; 1 d. Held various posts as Consulting Engineer; founded own practice, 1983. SNP Member, City of Edinburgh District Council, 1976-96; President, Edinburgh Leith and District Battalion, Boys' Brigade, 1998-2003; Dean of Consular Corps, Edinburgh and Leith, 2010-11; Commander with Star Royal Norwegian Order of Merit, 1994; Knight's Cross of The Order of Merit of Hungary, 2018. Recreation: rugby football. Address: (h.) 141 Saughtonhall Drive, Edinburgh EH12 5TS; T.-0131-337 6154; e-mail: norman.irons@hotmail.co.uk

Ironside, Leonard, CBE, JP, FRSA. Member: Grampian Regional Council, 1982-1996, Aberdeen City Council, 1995-2017 (elected Councillor, 1982-2017; Convener of Social Care and Wellbeing Committee, 2012-14; Council Leader, 1999-2003; Convener, Social Work Committee); Chairman, Horizon Rehabilitation Centre, 1997-2004; former Director, Grampian Food Resource Centre Ltd; Patron, Grampian Special Olympics for Handicapped; Commonwealth Professional Wrestling Champion, since 1981; Athletics Coach, Bon Accord (Special Needs); former Member, Board, Robert Gordon University, 1999-2008; Feature Writer - Freelance, Aberdeen Independent and Press & Journal Newspapers; Member, Board, NHS Grampian, 2001-03; Board Member: North East Sensory Services, since 2013, Alcohol Support Board, 2014-16; Chairman, Aberdeen Health & Social Care Partnership, since 2014; b. Aberdeen; m., Wendy; 2 d. Educ. Hilton Academy, Aberdeen. Member, Grampian Regional Council, 1982-96; Inspector, contributions agency, DHSS, since 1990; formerly Chairman and Founder Member, Grampian Initiative; won Commonwealth Professional Wrestling Championship at Middleweight, 1979; lost Championship, 1981; regained title, 1981; gained European Lightweight title, 1985, relinquished title, 1989; Grampian Ambassador for services to industry, 1996; awarded Scottish Sports Council Rosebowl for services to disabled sports; former Director: Grampian Enterprise Ltd., Scottish Sub-Sea Technology Group; Chair, Aberdeen International Youth Festival, since 2014; former Member, Grampian Racial Equality Commission; Member, Aberdeen Sports Council; former Director, Voluntary Service, Aberdeen; Audio Describer for Visually Impaired, since 2014; former Area Manager, Parkinson's Disease Society (retired 2015); Board Member, Aberdeen Exhibition and Conference Centre, 1999-2003 and 2007-2010; Member, Granite City Chorus; Childline Counsellor, since 2016; Chairman, Befriend A Child Charity, since 2018; wrestling coach, since 2016. Publication: When You're Ready Boys - Take Hold: My Grappling Story. Recreations: yoga teacher; also plays tennis, squash, badminton; cycling; after-dinner speaking. Address: 42 Hillside Terrace, Portlethen, Kincardineshire; T.-07802332656; e-mail: lenironside@outlook.com

Irvine of Drum, (Alexander Irvine). 27th Laird of Drum and Chief of the name Irvine of Drum, since 2019.

Irvine of Lairg, Baron (Alexander Andrew Mackay Irvine), PC. Lord High Chancellor of Great Britain, 1997-2003; b. 23.6.40; m. Alison Mary; 2 s. Educ. Inverness Royal Academy; Hutchesons' Boys' Grammar School, Glasgow; Glasgow University; Christ's College,

Cambridge. Called to the Bar, Inner Temple, 1967; Bencher, 1985; QC, 1978; a Recorder, 1985-88; Deputy High Court Judge, 1987-97; Lecturer, LSE, 1965-69; Contested (Labour), Hendon North, 1970; elevated to the Peerage, 1987; Opposition Spokesman on Legal and Home Affairs, 1987-92; Shadow Lord Chancellor, House of Lords, 1992-97; Joint President: Industry and Parliamentary Trust, since 1997, British American Parliamentary Group, since 1997, IPU, since 1997, CPA, since 1997; President, Magistrates' Association; Church Commissioner; Trustee: John Smith Memorial Trust, 1992-97, and since 2003, Whitechapel Art Gallery, since 1990, Hunterian Collection, since 1997; Member, Committee, Friends of the Slade, since 1990; Honorary Bencher, Inn of Court of NI, 1998; Fellow, US College of Trial Lawyers, 1998; Honorary Fellow, Society for Advanced Legal Studies, 1997; Honorary Member, Polish Bar, 2000; Knight Commander of the Order of Merit of the Republic of Poland (with Star); Hon. LLD, Glasgow, 1997; Honorary Fellow, London School of Economics, 2001; Dr hc, Siena, 2000; Honorary Fellow, Christ's College, Cambridge, 1996; Visiting Professor, University College London, 2004. Recreations: cinema; theatre; collecting paintings; travel. Address: House of Lords SW1A 0PW.

Irvine, Fiona, BA (BusEcon). Director, Rainbow HR Ltd; formerly Director of Business Change, Phones 4u; HR Director, First ScotRail, 2006-09; b. 24.9.69, Johnstone; m., Brian; 2 d. Educ. Paisley Grammar School; Paisley University. Training and Development Assistant, Keyline Business Merchants, 1989-92; Staff Manager, Sainsbury Homebase, 1992; HR Business Partner, Royal Bank of Scotland, 1993-2002; Senior Human Capital Consultant, PWC, 2002; Lloyds TSB: Head of HR, 2003-04, Head of Reward, 2004-05. HR Director of the Year, HR Network Scotland. Address: (b.) Rainbow HR Ltd, 14 Marchbank Gardens, Paisley PA1 3JD; T.-07739 447 369.

Irvine, Nicola. Managing Partner, Russells Gibson McCaffrey, Glasgow (Partner, since 2008; joined the company in 2002); Dean, Royal Faculty of Procurators in Glasgow, 2017-19. Educ. University of Strathclyde. Address: Russells Gibson McCaffrey, 3 Bath Street, Glasgow G2 1HY; T.-0141 271 1000.

Irvine, Professor Stewart. Former Chair of Project Board and former Executive Director of Medicine, NHS Education for Scotland (retired); Acting Chief Executive, 2019-2021. Educ. The University of Edinburgh. Career history: held posts as RCOG College Tutor and Regional College Advisor, before assuming the responsibility of Associate Postgraduate Dean in South-East Scotland Deanery, responsible for training in the 'surgical' specialties; Deputy Director of Medicine for NHS Education for Scotland, from 2008; particular responsibility for quality management of PGME across Scotland, and for the performance management of the Medical ACT funding used to support undergraduate medical students in clinical placements. General Medical Council (GMC) Associate, sits on the GMC Quality Scrutiny Group; extensively involved as a GMC Visitor to medical schools and postgraduate deaneries elsewhere in the UK; appointed Director of Medicine for National Education Scotland, from April 2012, then Deputy Chief Executive. Awarded Honorary Professorship by the University of Edinburgh in August 2013.

Ivory, Sir Brian Gammell, Kt 2006, CVO 2018, CBE 1999, MA (Cantab), CA, FRSA, FRSE. Chairman, Marathon Asset Management Ltd, since 2011; Chairman, Arcus European Infrastructure Fund Advisory Council, since 2010; Chairman, IPSX (International Property Securities Exchange Ltd), since 2020; Director, Insight Investment Management Ltd, since 2003; b. 10.4.49, Edinburgh; m., Oona Mairi MacPhie Bell-Macdonald (see Oona Mairi MacPhie Ivory); 1 s.; 1 d. Educ. Eton College; Magdalene College, Cambridge. CA apprentice, Thomson McLintock, 1971-75; Highland Distillers, 1976-99, Director, 1978, Managing Director, 1988, Group Chief Executive, 1994, Chairman, 1997; Chairman, Macallan Distillers Ltd., 1997-99; Chairman, The Scottish American Investment Company PLC, 2000-2016; Deputy Chairman, Shawbrook Bank Ltd, 2011-15; Director, Bank of Scotland, 1988-2007; HBOS plc, 2001-07; Remy Cointreau SA, 1991-2014; Chairman, The National Piping Centre, since 1996; Trustee, The Royal Collection Trust, since 2021; Vice Chairman, Scottish Art Council, 1988-92; Member, Arts Council of GB, 1988-92; Chairman, National Galleries of Scotland, 2000-09; Governance & Nominations Committee, St Andrews University, 2007-2016; Great Steward of Scotland's Dumfries House Trust, 2011-2017; Member, Queen's Bodyguard for Scotland (Royal Company of Archers); Freeman, City of London, 1996. FRSA 1993; CIMgt 1997; FRSE 2001. Paolozzi Gold Medal 2009. Clubs: Beefsteak, New (Edinburgh). Recreations: the arts; travel and wild places.

Ivory, Lady Oona Mairi MacPhie, DL (1998), MA (Cantab), ARCM, FRSA (1993). Joint Chairman, The National Piping Centre, since 2017; Director, The Glasgow International Piping Festival, since 2004; b. 21.7.54, Ayr; m., Sir Brian Gammell Ivory (qv); 1 s.; 1 d. Educ. King's College, Cambridge; Royal Scottish Academy of Music and Drama; Royal Academy of Music. Former Chairman, Scottish Ballet (1995-97), former Director (1988-97); former Director, RSAMD (1989-2002). Trustee, Sri Lanka Reconcilliation Music Trust, 2010-15. Recreations: the arts; wild places; sailing. E-mail: judy@enitar.co.uk

Izod, Professor (Kenneth) John, BA (Hons), PhD, FRSA, FFCS. Retired Professor of Screen Analysis, Stirling University (Dean, Faculty of Arts, 1995-98; Senior Lecturer, Department of Film and Media Studies, 1978-98); Head, Department of Film and Media Studies, 2005-07; b. 4.3.40, Shepperton; m., Irene Chew Geok Keng (divorced 1994); 1 s.; 1 d.; m., Kathleen Morison. Educ. Prince Edward School, Harare City, Zimbabwe; Leeds University. Clerk articled to Chartered Accountant, 1958-63; Projectionist, mobile cinema unit, 1963; Lecturer in English, New University of Ulster, 1969-78; former Governor, Scottish Film Council; Chairman, Stirling Film Theatre, 1982-89 and 1991-92; Principal Investigator, Arts and Humanities Research Council funded project 'The Cinema Authorship of Lindsay Anderson', 2007-10; Co-Investigator, Arts and Humanities Research Council funded project 'British Silent Cinema and the Transition to Sound', 2014-2017. Publications: Reading the Screen, 1984; Hollywood and the Box Office, 1895-1986, 1988; The Films of Nicolas Roeg, 1991; Introduction to Television Documentary (Co-Author), 1997; Myth, Mind and the Screen, 2001; Screen, Culture, Psyche, 2006; Lindsay Anderson: Cinema Authorship (Co-Author), 2012; Cinema as Therapy: Grief and Transformational Film (Co-Author), 2015. Address: 13 Easter Cornton Road, Stirling FK9 5ER; T.-01786 450532 and T.-07940 362394. E-mail: k.j.izod@stir.ac.uk

J

Jack, The Right Hon. Alister William, DL. MP (Conservative), Dumfries & Galloway, since 2017; Secretary of State for Scotland, since July 2019; Lord Commissioner of HM Treasury, April-July 2019; Assistant Government Whip, February-April 2019; PPS to the Leader of the House of Lords, 2018-19; Member of Treasury Select Committee, 2017-18; Chairman, Edinburgh Self Storage Ltd, 2006-2017; Chairman, Galloway Woodlands Ltd, 2012-19; Partner, Courance Farms & Dairy; Chairman, Alligator Self Storage Ltd., 2007-2014; Managing Director, Armadillo Self Storage Ltd., 2003-07; b. 7.7.63, Dumfries; m., Ann Hodgson; 1 s.; 2 d. Educ. Trinity College, Glenalmond. Knight Frank, 1983-86; Managing Director, Aardvark Self Storage Limited, 1995-2002; Director, Field and Lawn (Marquees) Ltd., 1986-2019; Non-Executive Director, James Gordon (Engineers) Ltd., 2003-08; Chairman, Fulling Mill Limited, 2013-19; Member, Executive Board, Scottish Conservative Party, 1997-2001; Parliamentary Candidate, Tweeddale, Ettrick and Lauderdale, 1997 General Election; Vice Chairman, Scottish Conservative and Unionist Party, 1997-2001 (Scottish Conservative Party Spokesman on Industry and Economic Affairs, 1996-99); Chairman, River Annan Trust, 2014-18; Chairman, River Annan District Salmon Fishery Board, 2014-18; Chairman, Fisheries Management Scotland, 2016-18; Member, Queen's Body Guard for Scotland, Royal Company of Archers; Member, Board of Trade; Winner, Leith Enterprise Award, 1989; Finalist, The New Venturers 1990. Recreations: fishing; shooting. Address: House of Commons, London SW1A 0AA; T.-0207 2192994.

Jack, James Alexander Penrice, BSc (Hons), BArch, BD, DMin, RIBA, ARIAS. Minister of Duddingston, since 2001; b. 10.12.60, Bellshill; m., Rev. Elizabeth Margaret Henderson. Educ. Dalziel High School; University of Strathclyde; University of Glasgow; Princeton Theological Seminary. Pentland & Baker (Architects) Toronto, Canada, 1981-82; Estates & Buildings Division, University of Strathclyde, 1983-85; Student Placement at parish of Rogart, Sutherland, 1986-87; Probationary Assistant, Dundee Parish (St. Mary's), 1988-89; Minister of Abernyte *linked with* Inchture & Kinnaird *linked with* Longforgan, 1989-2001. Senior Chaplain at HM Prison Castle Huntly, 1989-2001; Trustee of Prison Fellowship Scotland, 1992-2001; General Trustee of the Church of Scotland, since 1995 (appointed Chairman, 2010-2014); Member of Board of Practice and Procedure, 1999-2006; Trustee of Richmond's Hope, since 2008. Publications: author of "Summer in a Highland Parish", article, 1986; co-author, "And You Visited Me", 1993; "Understanding a ministry to Prison Officers" in "Theology Scotland", 2003; "The Reverend John Thomson of Duddingston", 2005. Recreations: genealogy; painting and visiting Edinburgh. Address: (b.) The Manse of Duddingston, 5 Old Church Lane, Edinburgh EH15 3PX; T.-0131 661 4240.

Jack, Lorna, CA, MA. Chief Executive, Law Society of Scotland, 2009-2021; Chair and Director of Highlands & Islands Airports Limited; Vice Chair and Board Member, Scottish Funding Council. Educ. Aberdeen University; Harvard Business School; Institute of Chartered Accountants of Scotland. Former: President Americas, Scottish Development International, CEO/chief operating officer for Scottish Enterprise Forth Valley, Head of Global Companies Research Project, Scottish Enterprise, Head of National Food Industry Team, Scottish Enterprise; Trustee and Treasurer of the McConnell International Foundation;

former Member of Court, Aberdeen University; Trustee of Aberdeen University Charity, 2017-2020. Recreations: skiing; travel; reading; music. Address: (b.) HIAL Head Office, Inverness Airport, Inverness IV2 7JB.

Jackson, Gordon, QC, LLB. Dean of the Faculty of Advocates, 2016-2020; b. 5.8.48; m., Anne Stevely; 1 s.; 2 d. Educ. Ardrossan Academy; University of St Andrews. Career history: admitted to the Faculty of Advocates in 1979; served as an Advocate Depute, 1987-90; called to the Bar of England and Wales (Lincoln's Inn), 1989; appointed QC in 1990; Labour MSP for Glasgow Govan, 1999-2007. Honorary Vice-President of English-Speaking Union Scotland; Board Member, Glasgow Rep - Bard in the Botanics, since 2002; Director, Kilmarnock Football Club, since 2004. Address: The Faculty of Advocates, Parliament Square, Edinburgh EH1 1RF; T.-0131 226 5071.

Jackson, Ian, MBE, MA. Former Director, General Dental Council (2009-2019); b. 30.3.54, Perth; m., Susan (Arthur); 2 s.; 1 d. Educ. Perth Academy; Edinburgh University. Northern Foods, Hull, 1976-78; John Bartholomew & Son, Edinburgh, 1978-80; Lloyds and Scottish Finance, Edinburgh; Self Employed, 1981-82; BT PLC, 1982-2008 (range of roles in sales, business management, recruitment and consultancy). Member, Perth and Kinross Council Lifelong Learning Committee, 2002-2017; Council Member, General Teaching Council Scotland, 2005-2020; Chair of Finance Committee, GTCS, 2012-2020; Lay Member, Education Scotland, since 1986; Member, Perth College UHI Board, 2012-2017; Member, Society of High Constables of the City of Perth, since 2011; Member, Investigating Committee, Institute of Chartered Accountants Scotland, since 2016; Member, Education Panels GTCS, since 2020; MBE for services to Education, 2005. Recreations: rugby; walking; industrial archaeology. Address: (h.) 9 Muirend Road, Perth PHI IJS; T.-01738 639393; e-mail: i.jackson@btinternet.com

Jackson, Jack, OBE, BSc (Hons), PhD, CBiol, FRSB, FRSE; b. 31.5.44, Ayr; m., Sheilah Margaret Fulton; 1 s.; 3 d. Educ. Ayr Academy; Glasgow University; Jordanhill College of Education. Demonstrator, Zoology Department, Glasgow University, 1966-69; Lecturer in Zoology, West of Scotland Agricultural College, 1969-72; Assistant Teacher of Biology, Cathkin High School, 1972-73; Principal Teacher of Biology, Ayr Academy, 1973-83. Senior Examiner and Setter, Scottish Examination Board, 1978-83; Director, Board, Scottish Youth Theatre, 1979-82; Member: Scottish Council, Institute of Biology, 1980-83, School Board, Balerno High School, 1989-99; former Assistant Chief Inspector of Schools with responsibility for science subjects. Visiting Professor, Department of Curricular Studies, University of Strathclyde, since 2007. Lay Examiner, Royal College of Surgeons of Edinburgh, since 2008. Recreations: family life; gardening; hill-walking; conservation. Address: (h.) 9 Newlands, Kirknewton, West Lothian EH27 8LR.
E-mail: profjackjackson@btinternet.com

Jackson, Sheriff Matthew, QC, LLB (Hons), LLP. Sheriff, Glasgow & Strathkelvin, since 2021. Educ. University of Edinburgh. Joined the Crown Office and Procurator Fiscal Service in 1992, working as a Depute Procurator Fiscal before becoming an Assistant Solicitor at Sinclairs SSC in 1993; became a Sole Partner in 1996; appointed Queen's Counsel in 2019. Address: Glasgow Sheriff Court, 1 Carlton Place, Glasgow G5 9DA; T.-0141 429 8888.

Jameson, Sir Melville Stewart, KCVO, CBE, CStJ; b. 17.07.44, Clunie; m., Sarah Amy Walker-Munro; 2 s.

(Harry and Michael); 4 grandsons. Educ. Glenalmond College; RMA Sandhurst. Commissioned, The Royal Scots Greys, 1965; served in Germany, Northern Ireland, Cyprus and The Middle East and Edinburgh, where in 1971 the Regiment was amalgamated to form The Royal Scots Dragoon Guards. He was appointed to Command The Royal Scots Dragoon Guards, 1986-88 and after service at MOD London, Commanded 51 Highland Brigade, 1994-97. On leaving the Army he was Producer and Chief Executive, The Royal Edinburgh Military Tattoo, 1995-2007. Other appointments he held: Colonel of The Royal Scots Dragoon Guards, 2004-2009; Her Majesties Lord-Lieutenant for Perth and Kinross, 2006-2019; Chairman, The Regional Committee of Scottish Lord-Lieutenants, 2014-2019; President of The Order of St John, Perth and Kinross; President of SSAFA, Perth and Kinross; President of The Black Watch Association; Senior Adviser, The Royal Edinburgh Military Tattoo; The Basel Tattoo; The Queen's 90th Birthday Celebrations, Windsor; Chairman of The Royal Scots Dragoon Guards Museum; Officer in The Royal Company of Archers, The Queen's Body Guard for Scotland. Patron of: PKAVS, Perth; The Crieff Highland Gathering and The Pitlochry Festival Theatre; appointed Knight Commander of The Victorian Order in 2018; granted The Freedom of The City of Perth in 2019; member of The Royal Caledonian Hunt and The Cavalry and Guards Club. Recreations: shooting; trees; music; wine. Address: c/o HHQ Scots DG, The Castle, Edinburgh EH1 2YT.

Jamie, Professor Kathleen, MA. Writer; Scots Makar, since 2021; University of Stirling's first appointed Professor of Creative Writing; formerly part-time Lecturer in Creative Writing, School of English, University of St. Andrews; b. 13.5.62, Johnstone. Educ. Currie High School; Edinburgh University. Publications: The Way We Live; The Autonomous Region; The Queen of Sheba; The Golden Peak; The Tree House (won the 2004 Forward Poetry Prize and Scottish Arts Council Book of Year award, 2005); Findings, 2005; Waterlight: selected poems, 2007; Sightlines, 2012 (won the 2014 John Burroughs Medal and the 2014 Orion Book Award); The Overhaul, 2012 (won the 2012 Costa poetry award); The Bonniest Companie, 2015.

Jamieson, Cathy, BA (Hons), CQSW. Chief Executive Officer, Children's Services, Care Visions Residential, since 2017, Managing Director, 2015-17; MP (Labour), Kilmarnock and Loudoun, 2010-2015; former Shadow Economic Secretary to the Treasury, UK Government; MSP (Labour and Co-operative), Carrick, Cumnock and Doon Valley, 1999-2011; Minister for Education and Young People, Scottish Executive, 2001-03; former Minister for Justice; b. 3.11.56, Kilmarnock; m., Ian Sharpe; 1 s. Educ. James Hamilton Academy, Kilmarnock; Glasgow Art School; Glasgow University; Goldsmiths College, London; Caledonian University. Professional qualification in art therapy; later trained in social work; Senior IT Worker, Strathclyde Region; Principal Officer, Who Cares? Scotland, developing policy and legislation for young people in care; Member, inquiry team which investigated child abuse in Edinburgh children's homes; Director: Scotwest Credit Union, since 2017, Killie Trust, since 2017, Kilmarnock Football Club, since 2018. Address: Care Visions Residential, Stirling Office, Bremner House, Castle Business Park, Stirling FK9 4TF; T.-01576 204 939.

Jamieson, Charles Reginald Wingate, DA (Glasgow), MFA, PAI, PPAI. Artist, since 1976; Actor, since 1976; b. 12.03.52, Rutherglen; m., Sally Ann Muir. Educ. Hutcheson's Boys Grammar School, Glasgow; Glasgow School of Art; Texas Christian University, Fort Worth, Texas. Borderline Theatre, 1977-79; acted in many TV and Film Productions - Blake's Seven, Goodnight and

Godbless, Wheels, Bad Boys; Repertory Theatre with Swansea Grand Theatre; acted in Take The High Road (five years in the 1980's), Scottish Television; also appeared in '2000 Acres of Sky', 'Taggart', 'Still Game', The Angels' Share (Director, Ken Loach), 'River City', BBC Scotland, 2012; 'Outlander', 2016. Exhibited paintings widely across the country with solo shows: The Dryden Street Gallery, 1984; Gallerie Marie, London, 1990, Duncan Miller Fine Arts, Hampstead, 2000, Panter & Hall, Mayfair, 2001, Duncan R Miller Fine Arts, St. James's, 2003, The Richmond Hill Gallery, Richmond, Surrey, 2004, Duncan R Miller Fine Arts, St. James's, 2006, Mansfield Park Gallery, Glasgow, 2007, The Richmond Hill Gallery, Richmond Hill, Surrey, 2007, Panter & Hall in The Lennox Gallery, Fulham, 2009; The Richmond Hill Gallery, 2009, 2010; The Brownston Gallery, Modbury, Devon, 2012; solo show with The Stafford Gallery in conjunction with Wimbledon Fine Art, 2013; solo show with The Doubtfire Gallery, 2013; solo show with The Brownston Gallery, Modbury, Devon, 2015; 3 person exhibitions: The Doubtfire Gallery and The Stafford Gallery with Wimbledon Fine Art, 2016; Thompson's Gallery, London, 2018; 2 person exhibition: Red Rag Gallery, Bath, 2018; Scottish Exhibition, 2019: Wimbledon Fine Art; 2 person exhibition, 2019: Brownston Gallery, Modbury, South Devon; Summer Exhibition, 2019: Jerram Gallery, Sherborne, Dorset; two person show at Nadia Waterfield Fine Art, Bruton, Somerset, October 2021; paintings in collections across the world. Member of the organising committee and Chair of Judging of The Aspect Prize from its conception in 2002 until 2010. Awards: Sculpture Prize, Scottish Young Contemporaries, 1972; Norden Scholarship, 1974; GSA Travelling Scholarship, 1974; William Bowie Award, 1999; Richmond Hill Gallery Award, 2004; Diploma of the Paisley Art Institute, 2005; Richmond Hill Gallery Award, 2007. Paisley Art Institute: President, 2004-07, Member of Committee, 2000-07; Committee Member, Dunlop and Lugton Regeneration Group, 1999-2002. Publication: 'Glasgow', 2009 (book of photographs). Recreations: gardening; travel; cooking; reading; films. Address: (h.) The Steading, 41 Lugton Road, Dunlop, Ayrshire KA3 4DL; T.-01560 482419.
E-mail: jamieson.charles@btinternet.com

Jamieson, Sheriff George, LLB (Hons), DipLP. Sheriff of North Strathclyde at Kilmarnock, since 2019; Solicitor (Scotland, since 1985, England and Wales, since 2002); b. 21.8.61, Paisley. Educ. Paisley Grammar School; Strathclyde University. Trainee Solicitor, Hart, Abercrombie, Caldwell and Co., Paisley, 1984-86; Walker Laird, Paisley: Assistant Solicitor, 1986-89, Partner, 1990-2001; Consultant, Pattison and Sim, Paisley, 2001-08. Part-time Immigration Adjudicator, 2002-05; Immigration Judge, 2005-09; Part Time Sheriff, 2006-09; Council Member, Paisley Sheriff Court District, Law Society of Scotland, 1997-2005; Sheriff of South Strathclyde, Dumfries and Galloway at Dumfries, 2009-2019. Publications: Parental Responsibilities and Rights, 1995; Summary Applications and Suspensions, 2000; Scottish Family Law Legislation (Editor), 2002; Family Law Agreements, 2005.

Jamieson, Gordon. Chief Executive, NHS Western Isles, since 2008; b. Castle Douglas. First came to the Western Isles in September 2006 as part of a Ministerial Support Team; former Nurse Director/Director of Patient Safety, NHS Dumfries and Galloway; joined NHS Western Isles in February 2008 as Nurse Director/Chief Operating Officer. Significant experience of working in the NHS, including almost 20 years at Executive Board level. Address: (b.) 37 South Beach Street, Stornoway, Isle of Lewis HS1 2BB; T.- 01851 702997; e-mail: gordon.jamieson@nhs.net

Jamieson, Rev. Gordon David, MA, BD. Retired Church of Scotland Minister; b. 1.3.49, Glasgow; m., Annette; 1 s.; 1 d. Educ. Hamilton Academy; Edinburgh University.

Assistant Minister, Tron Moredun, Edinburgh, 1973-74; Minister: Schaw Kirk, Drongan, 1974-79, Elie Parish Church, linked with Kilconquhar and Colinsburgh Parish Church, 1979-86, Barnhill St. Margaret's Parish Church, Dundee, 1986-2000, Head of Stewardship, 2000-2012; Depute Clerk of the Presbytery of West Lothian, 2019-2021. Address: (h.) 41 Goldpark Place, Livingston EH54 6LW; T.-01506 412020.

E-mail: gordonjamieson182@gmail.com

Jardine, Professor Alan George. Emeritus Professor of Renal Medicine; Professor of Renal Medicine, University of Glasgow, 2006-2018, Head of the School of Medicine, 2013-16, Head of the Undergraduate Medical School, 2011-14; President, Royal Medico-Chirurgical Society of Glasgow, 2015-16; Consultant Physician, Western Infirmary, Glasgow, 1996-2015; Consultant Physician, Queen Elizabeth University Hospital, Glasgow, since 2015; b. 27.08.60, Thurso; m., Catherine Pickering; 1 s.; 2 d. Educ. Bearsden Academy; University of Glasgow. MRC Clinical Scientist, 1987-90; MRC Blood Pressure Unit, Registrar in Nephrology, 1990-92, then Lecturer in Medicine and Senior Registrar in Medicine, Inverness and Aberdeen, 1992-93, joined University of Glasgow in 1994 as Lecturer, became Senior Lecturer, then Reader in Renal Medicine. Articles on renal, transplant and cardiovascular medicine. Recreations: golf and the outdoors. Address: (h.) "Dornoch", Shore Street, Bowmore, Islay PA43 7LB.

E-mail: alan.jardine@glasgow.ac.uk

Jardine, Christine Anne, MA (Hons). MP (Liberal Democrat), Edinburgh West, since 2017; Liberal Democrat Treasury spokesperson, since 2020; Liberal Democrat Spokesman for Europe, Exiting the European Union and Trade; b. 1960; m., Calum Macdonald (deceased); 1 d. Educ. Braidfield High School; University of Glasgow. Senior Production Journalist, BBC, 1991-97; Journalism tutor/lecturer, University of Strathclyde, 1997-2002; Editor (Scotland), Press Association, 2002-04; Project Manager, International Programme, TRC Media, 2009-2011; Scotland Media Adviser, HM Government, 2011-12; Media consultant and political commentator, since 2012. Former Liberal Democrats Spokesperson on work and pensions and former member of the Scottish Affairs Committee at Westminster; Board Member, Westminster Foundation for Democracy. Address: House of Commons, London SW1A 0AA.

Jardine, Ian William, BSc, PhD. National Adviser (Scotland) on Environmental Policy, 2017-19; Member, Board of Trustees: Royal Botanic Garden Edinburgh (RBGE), since 2019, Scottish Wildlife Trust, since 2021; b. 22.5.59, Edinburgh; m., Anne Daniel; 3 s. Educ. Royal High School, Edinburgh; Durham University; Leeds University. Joined Scottish Office, 1984; worked in various departments, including Scottish Development and Industry Department; Private Secretary to Ian Lang MP; involved in setting-up of urban partnership initiatives and management of Castlemilk Partnership; Scottish Natural Heritage: joined 1992, former Director of Strategy and Operations (East), 1997-2002; Chief Executive, 2002-2017; President, Eurosite, 2007-2010; Seconded to European Commission, DG Environment, 2015-16. Recreations: acting; gardening; natural history.

Jardine, Stephen. Journalist and broadcaster; Founder, Taste Communications (2011); presenter on BBC Radio Scotland, since 2014 and Debate Night, BBC Scotland, since 2019; co-presenter, STV's The Hour, 2009-2011; regular Columnist for The Scotsman and Daily Record; former Scottish Television presenter; b. 1963, Dumfries. Joined Radio Tay as a reporter before joining Scottish Television (now STV Central) to work on Scotland Today; former presenter, Scotland Today's East news opt-out, and anchored the main bulletin on Friday night, until December 2007; left STV to become GMTV's Scotland Correspondent, 1993-99; moved to Paris as Europe Correspondent, and also presented on GMTV; rejoined STV in 1999 as host of the station's Millennium Hogmanay Show live from the centre of Edinburgh, then moved onto presenting the afternoon talk show Room at the Top and his own evening chat show Tonight at the Top; also presented a number of current affairs programmes for the station, such as Seven Days, Wheel Nuts, Sunday Live and the channel's coverage of The State Opening of the Scottish Parliament; also fronted feature programmes for STV including Drivetime, Summer Discovery, Rich, Gifted & Scots and The Talent; presented a Saturday morning show on Talk 107 until February 2007; presented STV's daily magazine programme, The Five Thirty Show and its successor The Hour, 2008-10; Columnist for Edinburgh Evening News, 2006-09. Address: (b.) Taste Communications, 20 Hill Street, Edinburgh EH2 3JZ.

Jarvie, Professor Grant, BEd, MA, PhD, PhD (Hon). Professor of Sport, Director of Academy of Sport, University of Edinburgh, since 2012; Senior Management Group and Visiting Professor, University of Toronto, Canada, since 2012; Vice-Principal, University of Stirling, 2005-2012; Head of School, Arts and Humanities, University of Stirling, 2010-11, Chair of Sport and Vice Principal responsible for Sport, 1997-2012; Honorary Professor, University of Warsaw; Honorary Doctorate, National University Taiwan, 2009; Ministerial Adviser to Scottish Government on both Education and Sport; adviser to a number of governments (United Kingdom, Montenegro, Romania, Portugal, Monaco, Malaysia, and Kenya) on key matters of policy and development; past and present Board Membership includes Sportscotland, Quality Assurance Agency, UNESCO, Prince Albert Foundation; b. 7.11.55, Motherwell. Educ. School, Edinburgh; University of Exeter; Queen's University (Canada); University of Leicester. Recreations: squash; hillwalking. Address: University of Edinburgh, Academy of Sport, St Leonard's Land, Holyrood Road, Edinburgh EH8 8AQ; T.-07729500769; grantjarvie1@gmail.com

Jasper, Professor David, MA (Cantab), MA (Oxon), PhD (Dunelm), BD (Oxon), DD (Oxon), TEOL.DR (Uppsala-HC), FRSA, FRSE. Canon Theologian in the Diocese of Glasgow and Galloway, since June 2017; Clergyman; Professor of Literature and Theology, University of Glasgow, since 1998; Changjiang Chair Professor, Renmin University of China, Beijing, 2009-2011, Distinguished Overseas Professor, 2013-15; b. 1.8.51, Stockton-on-Tees, since 2009; m., Dr. Alison E. Jasper; 3 d. Educ. Dulwich College; Cambridge (Jesus); Oxford (Keble); Durham. Curate, Buckingham Parish Church, England, 1976-79; Chaplain, Fellow, Hatfield College, Durham University, 1979-87; Principal, St. Chad's College, Durham University, 1988-91; Senior Lecturer, Reader, Professor, University of Glasgow, 1991-2012. Elected Fellow of Royal Society of Edinburgh, since 2006. Publications include: The Sacred Desert, 2004; The Sacred Body, 2009; The Sacred Community, 2012; The Study of Literature and Theology as a Grammar of Assent, 2016. Recreations: reading; music. Address: (h.) 32 Crompton Avenue, Cathcart, Glasgow G44 5TH; T.-0141 588 3468.

E-mail: davidjasper124@gmail.com

Jeeves, Professor Malcolm Alexander, CBE, MA, PhD (Cantab), Hon. DSc (Edin), Hon. DSc (St. And.), Hon.

DUniv (Stir.), FBPsS, FMedSci, FRSE, PPRSE. Professor of Psychology, St. Andrews University, 1969-93, Emeritus Professor, since 1993; President, Royal Society of Edinburgh, 1996-99 (Vice-President, 1990-93); b. 16.11.26, Stamford, England; m., Ruth Elisabeth Hartridge; 2 d. Educ. Stamford School; St. John's College, Cambridge University. Lt., 1st Bn., Sherwood Foresters, BAOR, 1945-48; Exhibitioner, St. John's College, Cambridge, 1948-52; research and teaching, Cambridge and Harvard Universities, 1952-56; Lecturer, Leeds University, 1956-59; Professor and Head, Department of Psychology, Adelaide University, 1959-69 (Dean, Faculty of Arts, 1963-64); Member: Council, SERC, 1985-89, Neuroscience and Mental Health Board, MRC, 1985-89, Council, Royal Society of Edinburgh, 1985-88 (Vice President, 1990-93); Director, Medical Research Council Cognitive Neuroscience Research Group, 1983-88; Vice-Principal, St. Andrews University, 1981-85; Chairman, Executive Committee, International Neuropsychological Symposium, 1986-91; Editor-in-Chief, Neuropsychologia, 1990-93; Cairns Memorial Lecturer, Australia, 1986; New College Lecturer, University of NSW, 1987; Drummond Lectures, Stirling University, 2001. Honorary Sheriff, Fife, since 1986. Publications: Analysis of Structural Learning (Co-Author); Psychology Survey No. 3 (Editor); Experimental Psychology: An introduction for biologists; The Effects of Structural Relations upon Transfer (Co-Author); Thinking in Structures (Co-Author); Behavioural Science and Christianity (Editor); Free to be Different (Co-Author); Psychology and Christianity: The View Both Ways; The Scientific Enterprise and Christian Faith; Psychology: Through the eyes of faith (Co-Author); Mind Fields; Human Nature at the Millennium; Science, Life and Christian Belief (Co-Author); From Cells to Souls – and Beyond (Editor and Contributor); Human Nature (Editor and Contributor); Neuroscience, Psychology and Religion (Co-Author); Rethinking Human Nature (Editor and Contributor); Minds, Brains, Souls and Gods (Author); The Emergence of Human Personhood: A Quantum Leap? (Editor and Contributor); Psychological Science and Christian Faith: Insights and Enrichments from Constructive Dialogue, 2018 (Co-Author); Why Science and Faith Belong Together: Stories of Mathematical Enrichment. Recreations: walking; music; fishing. Address: (b.) School of Psychology and Neuroscience, St. Andrews University, St. Andrews KY16 9JU; T.-01334 462072.

Jeffrey, Rev. Kenneth Samuel, BA, BD, PhD, DMin. Senior Lecturer, Church History, University of Aberdeen; b. 30.09.69, Dundonald, Northern Ireland; m., Linda; 3 s.; 1 d. Educ. Sullivan Upper School, Holywood, Co. Down; Stirling University; Aberdeen University; Pittsburgh Theological Seminary. Teacher, Livingstonia Secondary School, Malawi, 1992-94; Assistant Minister, Rubislaw Parish Church, Aberdeen, 2000-02; Minister, The Parish Church of Cupar Old and St Michael of Tarvit, 2002-2014. Padre of 7 SCOTS. Publications: 'When The Lord Walks The Land - The 1858-62 Revival in the North East of Scotland', 2002; written other articles and contributed to several books. Recreations: walking; reading; supporting Manchester United. Address: (h.) The North Steading, Dalgairn, Cupar, Fife KY15 4PH; T.-01334 653196; e-mail: ksjeffrey@btopenworld.com

Jeffreys-Jones, Professor Rhodri, BA (Wales), PhD (Cantab). Emeritus Professor of American History and Senior Honorary Professorial Fellow, Edinburgh University (Chair of History 2001-03); b. 28.7.42, Carmarthen; m., Mary Fenton; 2 d. by pr. m. Educ. Ysgol Ardudwy; University of Aberystwyth; Cambridge University; Michigan University; Harvard University. Tutor: Harvard, 1965-66, Fitzwilliam College, Cambridge, 1966-67; Assistant Lecturer, Lecturer, Senior Lecturer, Reader, Professor, Edinburgh University, 1967-2008; Fellow,

Charles Warren Center for the Study of American History, Harvard, 1971-72; Canadian Commonwealth Visiting Fellow and Visiting Professor, University of Toronto, 1993; Hon. President, Scottish Association for the Study of America. Publications: Violence and Reform in American History; American Espionage: From Secret Service to CIA; Eagle Against Empire: American Opposition to European Imperalism 1914-82 (Editor); The Growth of Federal Power in American History (Joint Editor); The CIA and American Democracy; North American Spies (Joint Editor); Changing Differences: Women and the Shaping of American Foreign Policy, 1917-1994; Eternal Vigilance? – 50 years of the CIA (Joint Editor); Peace Now! American Society and the Ending of the Vietnam War; American-British-Canadian Intelligence Relations 1939-2000 (Joint Editor); Cloak and Dollar – A History of American Secret Intelligence; The FBI: A History; In Spies We Trust: The Story of Western Intelligence; The American Left: Its Impact on Politics and Society since 1900 (Neustadt Prize, 2013); We Know All About You: The Story of Surveillance in Britain and America; Ring of Spies: How MI5 and the FBI Brought Down The Nazis in America. Recreations: snooker; vegetable gardening. E-mail: R. Jeffreys-Jones@ed.ac.uk

Jenkins, Blair, OBE (2010), MA (Hons). Chief Executive, Yes Scotland campaign, 2012-2014; Chairman, Scottish Broadcasting Commission, 2007-08; Chairman, Scottish Digital Network Panel, 2010-11; Visiting Professor in Journalism, Strathclyde University, 2010-2012; Governor, Glasgow School of Art, 2008-2012; former Head of News and Current Affairs, BBC Scotland (2000-06); b. 8.1.57, Elgin; m., Carol Sinclair; 3 d. Educ. Elgin Academy; Edinburgh University. Reporter, Aberdeen Evening Express, 1974-76; student, 1976-80; Producer, BBC Television News, London, 1981-84; Producer, Reporting Scotland, BBC Scotland, 1984-86; Scottish Television: Producer, Scotland Today, 1986-90, Head of News, 1990-93, Head of Regional Broadcasting, 1993-94, Director of Broadcasting, 1994-97; Media Consultant, 1998-2000. Young Journalist of the Year, Scottish Press Awards, 1977; Chairman, BAFTA Scotland, 1998-2004; Fellow, Carnegie UK Trust, 2011-13. E-mail: blairjenkins@btinternet.com

Jessamine, Rev. Alistair Lindsay, MA, BD. Minister of Dunfermline Abbey, 1991-2011; b. 17.6.49, Hill of Beath; m., Eleanor Moore. Educ. Beath High School, Cowdenbeath; University of Edinburgh. Assistant Minister, Newlands South Parish Church, Glasgow, 1978-79; Minister, Rankin Parish Church, Strathaven linked with Chapelton, 1979-91; Chaplain: HM Prison, Dungavel, 1979-91, RAF Pitreavie Castle, 1991-95; Moderator, Presbytery of Dunfermline, 1993-94. Recreations: travel; cooking; golf. Address: 11 Gallowhill Farm Cottages, Strathaven ML10 6BZ; T.-01357 520934.

Jiwa, Shainool, PhD. Head, Constituency Studies Research at The Institute of Ismaili Studies, London; Court Member, Edinburgh Napier University, since 2012; Commissioner, Mental Welfare Commission for Scotland, 1998-2002; Chief Examiner, International Baccalaureate Organization, 2002-09; Associate Assessor with Her Majesty's Inspectorate for Education, Scotland, since 2003; m., Shahnavaz Jiwa; 1 s. (Adil); 1 d. (Nabila). Educ. McGill University, Montreal (MA); Edinburgh University (PhD). Began career as Lecturer in Islamic History, Edinburgh University, 1989-91; embarked on career in community development, training and practising as a counsellor; leading role in setting up a range of community-based services for minority ethnic women in Edinburgh at Saheliya, 1991-99; volunteer counsellor, Edinburgh Association for Mental Health, 1996-98; voluntary involvement with Ismaili Muslim community in UK, since 1979. Publications: Towards a Shi'i Mediterranean Empire,

2009; Founder of Cairo, 2013; The Shi'i World: Pathways in Tradition and Modernity (Co-Editor and Contributor), 2015; The Fatimid Caliphate: Diversity of Traditions (Co-Editor and Contributor), 2017; The Fatimids: The Rise of a Muslim Empire, 2018, translated and published in Portuguese (2019), Russian (2019), Persian (2020) and Gujarati (2021). Recreations: swimming; reading; walks.

Johnson, Daniel. MSP (Labour), Edinburgh Southern, since 2016; Scottish Labour Spokesperson for Finance, since 2021; Justice Spokesperson, 2017-19; b. 3.9.77; m.; 2 d. Educ. Bonaly Primary School; Daniel Stewart's and Melville College; University of St Andrews; University of Strathclyde. Ran a group of five shops in Edinburgh's City Centre, bringing a strong business experience; the first independent retailer in Edinburgh to become an accredited Living Wage employer. Address: Scottish Parliament, Edinburgh EH99 1SP.
E-mail: daniel.johnson.msp@scottish.parliament.uk

Johnston, Geoffrey Edward Forshaw, LLB, CA. Past Chairman, Hebridean Pursuits Outdoor Learning; Vice Chairman, Scottish Friendly Assurance Society Ltd., 2006-2010 (retired); Director, Lamellar Therapeutics, 2000-05; Managing Director, Arbuckle, Smith and Company, 1972-99; Chairman, Scottish Chambers of Commerce, 1996-2000; b. 20.6.40, Burton-Wirral, England; m., Elizabeth Anne Lockhart; 2 d. Educ. Loretto School, Musselburgh; University of St. Andrews. Wilson Stirling & Co. CA, 1959-65; Arbuckle Smith Group, since 1965: Director, 1968, management buy-out, 1984. Honorary Consul for Belgium, Scotland West and Northern Islands, 1989-95; National Chairman, British International Freight Association, 1990-91; President, Glasgow Chamber of Commerce, 1994-95; Member, Scottish Valuation and Rating Council, 1981-2001; Chairman, Central College of Commerce, 1999-2005. Recreations: sailing; skiing; hillwalking; golf. Address: (h.) Flat 20, 14 Ravelston Terrace, Edinburgh EH4 3TP; T.-0131 315 4495.

Johnston, George Bonar, DA, RSW. Artist; b. 14.6.33, Edinburgh; m., Margaret (deceased); 1 s.; 1 d. Educ. Bathgate Academy; Edinburgh College of Art. Teacher, 1955-56; Army Officer, 1956-58; Teacher, 1958-59; Lecturer, 1959-66; Art Adviser, Tayside Region, 1966-91. Paintings in private and public collections in Scotland, England, France, North America, Canada. Recreations: fly fishing; reading. Address: 10 Collingwood Crescent, Barnhill, Dundee DD5 2SX; T.-01382 779857.

Johnston, Grenville Shaw, CVO, OBE, OStJ, TD, KCSG, CA. Chartered Accountant, since 1968; President, Institute of Chartered Accountants of Scotland, 2000-01; Vice Lord Lieutenant of Moray, 1996-2005, Lord Lieutenant, 2005-2020 (retired); Territorial Army Officer, 1964-89 (Lt. Col.); b. 28.1.45, Nairn; m., Marylyn Jean Picken; 2 d. Educ. Blairmore School; Fettes College. Qualified in Edinburgh with Scott Moncrieff Thomson & Sheills; Thomson McLintock & Co., Glasgow, 1968-70; joined family firm, W.D. Johnston & Carmichael, Elgin, 1970, Senior Partner, 1975-2001, Consultant, 2001-05 (retired). Commanding Officer, 2nd 51st Highland Volunteers, 1983-86; Hon. Col., 3rd Highland Volunteers, 1997-99; Knight Commander, Order of St. Gregory, 1982, for work for Pluscarden Abbey; OBE for services to Territorial Army, 1986; appointed an Officer of the Order of St John, 2011; Chairman, Grampian Committee, Royal Jubilee Trusts, 1982-91; Member, Cairngorm Mountain Trust Ltd.; Trustee and Council Member: Queens Own Highlanders, The Highlanders, 1996-2013; Trustee, National Museums of Scotland, 1998-2006; Director: Cairngorm Mountain Ltd. (Chairman, 1999-2014), Highlands and Islands Airports Ltd, 2001-08,

(Chairman, 2009-2016); Caledonian Maritime Assets Ltd, Chairman, 2006-2014; President, Highland Reserve Forces and Cadets Association, 2007-2012; Honorary Member, Elgin Rotary Club, since 2008; Hon President, Moray Scouts, 2005-2020 (retired); Patron, Morayvia Aerospace Project, since 2017; Farmer, Spynie Kirk Farms, since 2006; Regt Sec, The Lovat Scouts, 1986-2017; Chair, Grant Lodge Trust, since 2015; Hon President, The Moray Society (Elgin Museum), since 2010; Trustee, Holy Trinity Church, Elgin, since 2013; Chair, Calmac Pension Fund, 2015-2020; Commander of the Royal Victorian Order (CVO), June 2018; made a "Freeman of Moray" by Moray Council, 2020; appointed a Companion of The Memorial of Merit of King Charles the Martyr, 2021. Recreations: tennis; dog walking; shooting; fishing; skiing; singing (tenor). Address: (h.) Spynie Kirk House, Spynie, by Elgin, Moray IV30 8XJ.

Johnston, Cllr Harvey. Convener, Orkney Islands Council, since 2017; represents West Mainland Ward; m., Helen; 5 c. Educ. Harray Public School; Stromness Academy; studied Agriculture in Aberdeen. Born and bought up on a small farm in Harray. Career: construction industry; civil servant with the Department of Agriculture before embarking on a career of over 30 years at Orkney College; retired as Depute Principal in 2014; runs farm above Dounby. Recreations: giving talks on Orkney dialect, culture or history; speaking at Harvest Homes, Burns Suppers etc; performing at concerts and festivals; writing poetry. Address: (h.) Brettovale, Knarston, Dounby KW17 2HZ; T.-01856 771443.

Johnston, Professor Ian Alistair, BSc, PhD, FRSE. CEO and Co-founder, Xelect Ltd., since 2013; Emeritus Professor, School of Biology, St Andrews University, since 2019; Chandos Professor of Physiology, 1997-2016; Director, the Scottish Oceans Institute, University of St Andrews, 2012-16; appointed Professor of Biology, 2016-2019; Director, Gatty Marine Laboratory, 1985-2008; b. 13.4.49, Barking, Essex. Educ. Addey and Stanhope Grammar School, London; Hull University. NERC Postdoctoral Research Fellow, Bristol University, 1973-75; Lecturer in Physiology, St. Andrews University, 1976-84; Reader, 1984-85; Visiting Senior Lecturer, Department of Veterinary Physiology, Nairobi University, 1981; Visiting Scientist, British Antarctic Survey base, Signy Island, South Orkneys, 1983-84; Council Member, NERC, 1995-2000; Chairman, NERC Marine Science and Technology Board; awarded Scientific Medal, Zoological Society of London; President, Society for Experimental Biology, 2007-09. Recreations: photography; walking; reading. Address: (b.) Xelect Ltd, Horizon House, Abbey Walk, St Andrews, Fife KY16 9LB.

Johnston, Professor Marie, BSc, PhD, DipClinPsych, DipSpan, CPsychol, HonFBPsS, FRSE, FMedSci, FASS, FRCPE, FEHPS, FSBM. Emeritus Professor in Psychology, Aberdeen University; b. 6.7.44, Aberdeen; m., Derek Johnston. Educ. High School for Girls, Aberdeen; Aberdeen University; Hull University. Research Officer, Oxford University, 1971-77; Lecturer, Senior Lecturer, Reader, Royal Free Hospital School of Medicine, 1977-90; Reader, Professor of Psychology, St. Andrews University, 1990-2003; first Chair, Section of Health Psychology, British Psychological Society; Past President, European Health Psychology Society. Recreation: gardening. Address: (b.) Aberdeen Health Psychology Group, Health Sciences Building, University of Aberdeen, Aberdeen AB25 2ZD.

Johnston, Paul. Director General for Communities, Scottish Government, since 2021; Director General for Education, Communities and Justice, 2017-2021; Director General for Learning & Justice, 2015-17. Qualified lawyer and joined the Scottish Government Legal Directorate in May 2000; appointed to the Senior Civil Service in October 2007, carrying out a number of roles before being appointed to Director level as Head of the Advocate General's Office in April 2011; Director for Safer Communities, Scottish Government (responsibility for Police, Fire, Resilience, Defence, Security, Drugs Policy and Community Safety), 2013-15. Address: Scottish Government, St. Andrew's House, Regent Road, Edinburgh EH1 3DG.

Johnston, Peter William, MA, LLB. Convener, Risk Management Authority, 2008-2016; Adviser, accounting and auditing regulation and related legislation, 2003-2019; b. 08.02.43, Peebles; m., Patricia S. Johnston (Macdonald); 1 s.; 1 d. Educ. Larbert High School; University of Glasgow. Career History: Partner, MacArthur & Co Solicitors, Inverness; Procurator Fiscal Service, Assistant Solicitor, Crown Office; Chief Executive: The Institute of Chartered Accountants of Scotland, International Federation of Accountants. Recreations: grandchildren; music; languages; walking. Address: 18 Fraserburgh Way, Orton Southgate, Peterborough PE2 6SS; T.-01733 232918. E-mail: peter@13scotstoun.co.uk

Johnstone, Alison. MSP (no party affiliation), Lothian (Region) since 2021; MSP (Green), 2011-2021; Presiding Officer of The Scottish Parliament, since 2021; Co-Leader, Scottish Greens in the Scottish Parliament, 2019-2021; b. 11.10.65, Edinburgh; m.; 1 d. Educ. St. Augustine's High School, Edinburgh. Assistant to Robin Harper, 1999-2011; Councillor for the Meadows/Morningside ward for the City of Edinburgh Council, 2007-2012; joint convenor of the Scottish Green Party, 2007-08. Board of Directors, Scottish Athletics. A former East of Scotland athletics champion. Address: Scottish Parliament, Edinburgh EH99 1SP.

Johnstone, Professor Eve Cordelia, CBE, MB, ChB, MD (Glas) 1976, FRCP, FRCPsych, FMedSci, FRSE, DPM, Hon MD (Edin) 2014. Emeritus Professor of Psychiatry and Honorary Assistant Principal, University of Edinburgh for Mental Health Research and Development; formerly Professor of Psychiatry and Head, Department of Psychiatry; b. 1.9.44, Glasgow. Educ. Park School, Glasgow; University of Glasgow. Junior posts in Glasgow hospitals; Lecturer in Psychological Medicine, University of Glasgow, 1972-74; Member of Scientific Staff, Medical Research Council, Clinical Research Centre, Northwick Park, 1974-89. Member of Council, Medical Research Council, 1997-2002; Chairman, MRC Neurosciences Board, 1999-2002. Publications: eight books on psychiatric illness; over 400 papers on biological psychiatry. Address: (b.) Royal Edinburgh Hospital, Morningside Park, Edinburgh.

Johnstone, Rev. Mark Edward, DL, MA, BD. Minister, Glasgow Cathedral, since 2019; Minister of Religion, St. Mary's Manse, Kirkintilloch, 2000-19; Deputy Lieutenant of Dunbartonshire; b. 28.5.68, Glasgow; m., Audrey Gail Cameron; 2 s.; 1 d. Educ. Kingsridge Secondary, Drumchapel; University of Glasgow; Trinity College. Parish Minister, Denny, Falkirk; Chaplain to Strathcarron Hospice, Bellsdyke Psychiatric Hospital; Minister In Charge, Northminster United Church, Toronto, Canada; Parish Minister, St. Mary's, Kirkintilloch; Convener, Eldership Working Party/Membership. Convener, Education and Nurture task group; Convener, Mission and Discipleship; Chairman, Board of Directors of Lodging House Mission. Recreations: gym; conjouring; dog walking; fishing. Address: Glasgow Cathedral, Castle Street, Glasgow G4 0QZ; T.-0141 552 8198. E-mail: mark.johnstone2@ntlworld.com

Johnstone, Sir Raymond, CBE, BA, CA; b. 27.10.29, London; m., Susan Sara; 5 step s.; 2 step d. Educ. Eton; Trinity College, Cambridge. Investment Analyst, Robert Fleming & Co. Ltd., London, 1955-60; Partner (CA),

Brown, Fleming & Murray (later Whinney Murray & Co.), 1960-68; Director, Shipping Industrial Holdings Ltd., 1964-73; Chairman, Murray Johnstone Ltd., 1984-91 (Managing Director, 1968-88); Director: Scottish Amicable Life Assurance Society, 1971-97 (Chairman, 1983-85); Dominion Insurance Co. Ltd., 1973-95 (Chairman, 1978-95); Scottish Financial Enterprise, 1986-91 (Chairman, 1989-91); Summit Group PLC (Chairman, 1989-98); Murray Income PLC, 1989-99; Murray International PLC, 1989-2005; Murray Global Markets PLC, 1989-2000; Murray Ventures PLC, 1984-99; Murray Enterprise PLC, 1989-00; Chairman, Forestry Commission, 1989-94; Chairman, 1982-86, Hon. President, 1986-97, Scottish Opera; Chairman, Patrons of the National Galleries of Scotland, 1995-2003, Chairman, 1995-99; Chairman, Historic Buildings Council for Scotland, 1995-2002; Chairman, The Nuclear Trust, 1996-2003; Director, The Nuclear Trust, 1996-2007; Director, The Nuclear Liabilities Fund Ltd., 1996-2007; Director, RJ KILN PLC, 1995-2002; Chairman, Atrium Underwriting PLC (formerly Lomond Underwriting plc), 1993-2003. Recreations: fishing; shooting; opera; farming. Address: (h.) 32 Ann Street, Edinburgh EH4 1PJ.

Johnstone, Professor William, BD, MA (Hons), DLitt. Professor of Hebrew and Semitic Languages, Aberdeen University, 1980-2001, Emeritus Professor, since 2001; Minister, Church of Scotland, since 1963; b. 6.5.36, Glasgow; m., Elizabeth M. Ward; 1 s.; 1 d. Educ. Hamilton Academy; Glasgow University; Marburg University. Lecturer in Hebrew and Semitic Languages, Aberdeen University, 1962-72, Senior Lecturer, 1972-80, Dean, Faculty of Divinity, 1983-87; President, Society for Old Testament Study, 1990. Recreation: alternative work. Address: (h.) 9/5 Mount Alvernia, Edinburgh EH16 6AW.

Jones, Alan, BEd, MEd. Leisure consultant, since 2002; Director of Cultural and Leisure Services, Highland Council, 1987-2002; Member, Board, Sportscotland; b. 14.7.56, Bathgate; m., Lesley; 2 d. Educ. St Mary's Academy, Bathgate; Jordanhill College, Glasgow; Glasgow University; Stirling University. Lecturer, Physical Recreation, Stirling University, 1978-81; Sports Officer, Stirling District Council, 1981-86; Community and Leisure Manager, Clackmannan District Council, 1986-87; Director of Leisure and Recreation, Inverness District Council, 1987-95. Set up project to "Green" Inverness; winner, Queen Mother's Birthday Award. Recreations: Member, Physical Activity Task Force; golf; ski-ing. Address: 62 Boswell Road, Inverness IV2 3EJ; T.-01463 718715; e-mail: alanjonesassociates@btopenworld.com

Jones, Bernadette. Headteacher, St. Joseph's College, Dumfries, since 2008. Address: (b.) Craigs Road, Dumfries DG1 4UU.

Jones, Professor Colin Anthony, BA (Hons), MA. Professor of Estate Management, Heriot-Watt University, since 1998; b. 13.1.49, Wallasey; m., Fiona Jones; 2 d. Educ. Price's School, Fareham, Hants; Wallasey Grammar School; York University; Manchester University. Research associate, Manchester University; Lecturer, Applied Economics, Glasgow University, 1975-80; Department of Land Economics, Paisley University, 1980-98; Member, UK Board, Shelter, 1978-84, and 1990-2007. Publication: The Right to Buy. Address: (b.) School of Energy, Geoscience, Infrastructure and Society, Heriot-Watt University, Riccarton, Edinburgh, EH14 4AS; T.-0131-451 4628; e-mail: c.a.jones@hw.ac.uk

Jones, Graeme, MA. Chief Executive Officer, Scottish Financial Enterprise, 2016-2020 (retired). Educ. Dingwall Academy; University of Aberdeen; The Chartered Insurance Institute (CII). Career history: Sales Process and

Operations Manager, Standard Life, 1989-2000; Head of Regulated Sales, Royal Bank of Scotland, 2000-04; Head of Distribution, Aviva Life, 2004-06; Experian: Director of Banking and Financial Services, 2006-2015, Senior Partner, 2015.

Jones, Professor Hamlyn Gordon, MA (Cantab), PhD, FCIHort. Emeritus Professor, University of Dundee, since 2009, Professor of Plant Ecology, 1997-2009; Adjunct Professor in School of Agriculture and Environment, University of Western Australia, since 2013; Honorary Research Professor, Scottish Crop Research Institute, Dundee, 1998-2011; m., Amanda Jane Corry; 2 d. Educ. St. Lawrence College, Ramsgate; St. John's College, University of Cambridge; Australian National University, Canberra. Research Fellow, St. John's College, Cambridge, 1973-76; Researcher, Plant Breeding Institute, Cambridge, 1972-76; Lecturer in Ecology, University of Glasgow, 1977-78; Leader of Stress Physiology Group, East Malling Research Station, Kent, 1978-88; Director, Crop Science Research and Head of Station, Horticulture Research International, Wellesbourne, Warwick, 1988-97; Special Professor, University of Nottingham, 1991-97; Honorary Professor, University of Birmingham, 1995-98. Member, Scientific Advisory Committee, Scottish Natural Heritage, 2005-2011. Publications: Plants and Microclimate, 1983/1992/2013; Remote Sensing of Vegetation (Co-Author), 2010; joint editor of five other books. Recreations: squash; tennis; mountains; lounging. Address: (b.) Plant Sciences Division, School of Life Sciences, University of Dundee at JHI, Invergowrie, Dundee DD2 5DA; T.-0844 928528.

Jones, Heather A., MA, MBA. Chief Executive Officer, Scottish Aquaculture Innovation Centre, since 2014; b. 23.11.66, Irvine. Educ. Withington Girls' School, Manchester; University of Edinburgh. Policy Officer (Fast Stream), Housing, Rural Affairs and Constitutional Issues, 1989-92; Private Secretary to Lord James Douglas-Hamilton, Under Secretary of State, Scottish Office, 1992-94; Principal, Scottish Office, Sea Fisheries Division, 1994-97; Manager, Locate in Scotland, Houston, Texas, USA, 1997-2000; Cabinet Secretariat, Scottish Executive, 2000-01, Deputy Director, Lifelong Learning, 2001-04, Deputy Director, Education, 2004-05; Secondment, University of Glasgow, 2006; Deputy Director, Food Policy, Scottish Government, 2007; Deputy Director, Marine Scotland, 2008-2010; Deputy Director, International Division, Scottish Government, 2010-2014. Recreations: canicross; oenophilia. Address: (b.) Scion House, Stirling University Innovation Park, Stirling FK9 4NF; T.-01786 278320.

Jones, Emeritus Professor Huw, BA, MA. Emeritus Professor of Geography, Dundee University; b. Llanidloes; 2 s. Educ. Newtown Boys Grammar School, Powys; University College of Wales, Aberystwyth. Address: (b.) 73 Portree Avenue, Broughty Ferry, Dundee DD5 3EG; T.-01382-738513; e-mail: huwrjones@yahoo.co.uk

Jones, Right Revd. Idris, BA, DMin. Episcopal Bishop of Glasgow and Galloway, 1998-2009; Primus, Scottish Episcopal Church, 2006-09 (retired); National Spiritual Director, Cursillo UK, 2011-14; b. 1943. Educ. University College St. David, Lampeter; New College, Edinburgh; Edinburgh Theological College. Deacon, 1967; Priest, 1968; Curate, St. Mary's, Stafford, 1967-70; Precentor, St. Paul's Cathedral, Dundee, 1970-73; Priest-in-Charge, St. Hugh's, Gosforth, Newcastle, 1973-80; Chaplain, St. Nicholas Hospital, 1975-80; Rector, St. Mary's and St. Peter's, Montrose with St. David's, Inverbervie, 1980-89; Anglican Chaplain, Dundee University and Priest-in-Charge, All Souls, Invergowrie, 1989-92; Canon, St. Paul's Cathedral, Dundee, 1984-92; Rector, Holy Trinity, Ayr,

1992-98; Director, Pastoral Studies, TISEC, 1995-99; President, Rotary Club of Queens Park, 2003; Deacon, Incorporation of Skinners and Glovers, 2007; Hon. Fellow, University of Wales, 2007; President, Glasgow XIII, 2005, Member; Collector, Trades House of Glasgow, 2012-13; Director, Merchant House of Glasgow, 2011; Hon. Fellow, University of Wales, 2006; Deacon Convenor of The Trades of Glasgow, 2014-15. Address: 10 Swan Mews, Eglinton, Kilwinning KA13 7QE.

Jones, John Owain Ab Ifor, OSrJ, MA, BD, FSAScot. Minister, United Church of Bute (C. of S.), since 2011; b. 16.5.57, St. Asaph, Flintshire; m., Carolyn; 1 s.; 1 d. Educ. Ysgol Syr Hugh Owen, Caernarfon; University of St Andrews. Minister, Tywyn and District Congregational Churches, Tywyn, Merionethshire, 1981-87; Lecturer (Part Time), Hebrew and Old Testament, United Theological College, Aberystwyth, and Aberystwyth-Lampeter School of Theology, University of Wales, 1983-87; Assistant, then Associate Minister, Mearns Parish Church, 1987-90; Minister, Arnsheen Barrhill linked with Colmonell Parish Church, 1990-98; Minister, Langside Parish Church, 1998-2002; Minister, Kilbarchan East Church, 2002-2011. Contributor: "Thought for the Day", Radio Scotland (and Radio Cymru equivalent), Radio 4 Daily Service; Convener, Zimbabwe Twinning Committee, Presbytery of Greenock and Paisley, 2005-10. Recreations: reading; music (especially post romantic and twentieth century); astronomy. Address: (h.) UCB Manse, 10 Bishop Terrace, Rothesay PA20 9HF; T.-01700 504502; e-mail: johnowainjones@hotmail.com

Jones, Sir Mark, MA, Hon DLitt (Lond), Hon DArts (Abertay), Hon LLD (Dund), Hon DLitt (East Ang), FRSE, FSA. Chairman, National Trust for Scotland, since 2019. Career history: Curator of Medals at the British Museum, 1974-1990; Keeper of Coins and Media, 1990-92; Director of the National Museums of Scotland, 1992-2001, oversaw the project to create and open the 'Museum of Scotland'; Director of the Victoria & Albert Museum, London, 2001-2011; Master of St Cross College, 2011-2016. Chair of the Pilgrim Trust, the Grimsthorpe and Drummond Trust, The Sarikhani Art Foundation and the Patrick Allan-Fraser of Hospitalfield Trust; owns the Golden Hare bookshop in Stockbridge, Edinburgh. Written on the history of the medal, fakes and forgeries, collecting and museums, and restitution. Visitor of the Ashmolean Museum and a trustee of Tullie House; Member of the Council of the Royal Society of Edinburgh. Address: National Trust for Scotland, Hermiston Quay, 5 Cultins Road, Edinburgh EH11 4Df; T.-0131 458 0200.

Jones, Professor Peter (Howard), MA, FRSE, FRSA, FSA Scot. Director, Foundation for Advanced Studies in the Humanities, 1997-2002; Professor of Philosophy, University of Edinburgh, 1984-98, Professor Emeritus, since 1998; Director, Institute for Advanced Studies in the Humanities, 1986-2000; b. 1935, London; m., Elizabeth Jean Roberton (deceased); 2 d. Educ. Highgate School; Queens' College, Cambridge. Regional Officer, The British Council, London, 1960-61; Research Scholar, University of Cambridge, 1961-63; Assistant Lecturer in Philosophy, Nottingham University, 1963-64; University of Edinburgh: Lecturer in Philosophy, 1964-77, Reader, 1977-84; Visiting Professor of Philosophy: University of Rochester, New York, 1969-70, Dartmouth College, New Hampshire, 1973, 1983, Carleton College, Minnesota, 1974, Oklahoma University, 1978, Baylor University, 1978, University of Malta, 1993, Belarusian State University, 1997, Jagiellonian University, Cracow, since 2001; Distinguished Foreign Scholar, Mid-America State Universities, 1978; Visiting Fellow, Humanities Research Centre, Australian National University, 1984, 2002; Calgary Institute for the

Humanities, 1992; Lothian Lecturer, 1993; Gifford Lecturer, University of Aberdeen, 1994-95; Loemker Lecturer, Emory University, 1996; Trustee: National Museums of Scotland, 1987-99 (Chairman, Museum of Scotland Client Committee, 1991-99), University of Edinburgh Development Trust, 1990-98, Morrison's Academy, Crieff, 1984-98, Fettes College, 1995-2005, Scots at War Trust, Policy Institute, 1999-2008, MBI; Member: Court, University of Edinburgh, 1987-90, Council, Royal Society of Edinburgh, 1992-95, UNESCO forum on Tolerance, Tblisi, 1995, UNESCO dialogue on Europe and Islam, since 1997; Founder Member, The Hume Society, 1974. Publications: Philosophy and the Novel, 1975; Hume's Sentiments, 1982; A Hotbed of Genius, 1986; Philosophy and Science in the Scottish Enlightenment, 1988; The Science of Man in the Scottish Enlightenment, 1989; Adam Smith Reviewed, 1992; James Hutton, Investigation of the Principles of Knowledge, 1999; The Enlightenment World, 2004; Lord Kames: Elements of Criticism, 2005; The Reception of David Hume in Europe, 2005; Ove Arup - Masterbuilder of the Twentieth Century, 2006. Recreations: opera; chamber music; the arts; architecture.

Jones, Rev. William Gerald, MA, BD, ThM. Minister, Kirkmichael with Straiton St. Cuthbert's, since 1985; b. 2.11.56, Irvine; m., Janet Blackstock. Educ. Dalry High School; Garnock Academy, Kilbirnie; Glasgow University; St. Andrews University; Princeton Theological Seminary, Princeton, New Jersey. Assistant Minister, Glasgow Cathedral, 1983-85. Freeman Citizen of Glasgow, 1984; Member, Incorporation of Gardeners of Glasgow, 1984; Moderator, Presbytery of Ayr, 1997-98; Member: General Assembly Panel on Worship, 1987-91, Council, Church Service Society, 1986-98, Committee to Nominate the Moderator of the General Assembly, 1988-92 and 1998-2003, Committee on Artistic Matters, 2000-01; Societas Liturgica, since 1989; Officer and Assistant Chaplain, Order of St. Lazarus of Jerusalem (international Christian order of chivalry), since 1995; Ayr Presbytery Representative, Ayrshire Regional Council of the Scottish Episcopal Church, since 2002; Convener, Administration Committee, Presbytery of Ayr, 1988-91, 2005-08, 2008-09, 2013-14, 2015-16, 2016-17, 2017-18, 2018-19, 2019-20 and 2020-21; various times Member, Ayr Presbytery Business Committee; Member: Society for Liturgical Study, since 1995; Society for the Study of Theology, since 2000; Council, Scottish Church Society, 2000-06 (Secretary, since 2004, and Editorial Committee member, since 2006); Ayr Presbytery Vacancy Procedure Committee, since 2012 (Acting Convener, 2015-16; Vice-Convener, since 2016); Member, Ayr Presbytery Sub-Committee on the Troon Churches, 2018, and Convener, Review Committee on the Troon Churches, 2018-19 and 2019-21; Volunteer Worker, Kirkmichael Community Shop, 2010-13; Honorary Chaplain, York Minster, since 2001; Member, The Priory of Scotland of The Order of St. John of Jerusalem, 2006 (now St. John Scotland); Life Member, St. John Ayrshire and Arran; Life Member, Ayrshire Archaeological and Natural History Society; broadcaster, West Sound Radio, 1998-2012; Convener, Selection Committee to appoint Associate Presbytery Clerk, 2008-09; Member, Dalmellington Parish Church Support Group, 2007-12; Member, Planning Group, and Co-organiser, Ayr Presbytery Rural Church Conference, 2015, 2016, 2017, 2018, 2019, 2020 (cancelled); Convener, Ayr Presbytery Discretionary Allowance Committee, since 2017; Trustee, McCandlish Hall, Straiton; Adviser to the (Church of Scotland) Committee on Church Art and Architecture; Chairman, Straiton McCandlish Hall Committee, since 2009; Honorary Patron, Kirkmichael and Water of Girvan Curling Club, since 2013; appointed line manager by Ayr Presbytery in 2017 for the new pioneer ministry, based in Ayr, for farming community outreach. Represented the Dean of the Chapel Royal in Scotland at the ecumenical service held at

Crossraguel Abbey in June 1987 to mark the 800th anniversary of Carrick becoming an independent part of Scotland. Publications: Prayers for the Chapel Royal in Scotland, 1989; Worshipping Together (Contributor), 1991; Common Order (Contributor), 1994; The Times Book of Prayers (Contributor), 1997; A Lenten Meditation (Scottish Church Society), 2005; Sharing the Past: Shaping the Future (Co-editor), 2009; Reflections for Holy Week 2017: Action of Churches Together in Scotland (ACTS Website), 2017; Holy Common Sense: David H.C. Read Remembered (private study); articles on learned and other subjects. Recreations: music; books; writing; liturgies; country life. Address: The Manse, Kirkmichael, Maybole, Ayrshire KA19 7PJ; T.-01655 750286.

Jordan, Eoin, EdD, SFHEA. Director of the International Education Institute, University of St Andrews, since 2018. Educ. Reading School; University of Nottingham; RSA/Cambridge; University of Liverpool. Career history: English Instructor: Yokkaichi High School, UK JET Programme, Oita, Japan, 2001-04; International House Budapest, Hungary, 2004-05; Keio Academy, Oita, Japan, 2005-06; Short-term Language Programme Coordinator, Ritsumeikan Asia Pacific University, 2006-2010; Xi'an Jiaotong-Liverpool University, China, 2010-2018. Address: International Education Institute, University of St Andrews, 4 Kennedy Gardens, St Andrews KY16 9DJ; T.-01334 46 2261; e-mail: ie@st-andrews.ac.uk

Joseph, Robert William, CBE, MUniv, BSc (Hons). Administrator/Chief Executive, The MacRobert Trust, 2004-2014; b. 6.10.49, Perth; m., Janet Joseph (nee Keighley); 1 s.; 1 d. Educ. Archbishop Holgate's Grammar School, York; Enfield College of Technology; Middlesex University. Entered Civil Service from University, 1972; commissioned into The Royal Air Force as a General Duties/Navigator, 1973; General Duties Aerosystems Course, Royal Air Force College, Cranwell, 1980; Royal Naval Staff College, Greenwich, 1987; Command of Two Front-Line Nimrod MR2 Squadrons, 1992-94; Officer Commanding Royal Air Force Kinloss, Moray, 1994-96; Joint Services Command and Staff College Higher Command and Staff Course, 2000; senior appointment in Nato Supreme Allied Command Headquarters, Virginia, USA, 2000-02; Nato Senior Officers' Course, Rome, 2002. UK staff appointments, 2002-04; retired in Rank of Air Commodore, 2004. Recreations: golf; walking; gardening.

Jowitt, Professor Paul William, CBE, PhD, DIC, BSc(Eng), FCGI, CEng, FREng, FICE, FIPENZ, FRSE. Professor of Civil Engineering Systems, Heriot-Watt University, since 1987; Editor, Civil Engineering and Environmental Systems, since 1985; b. 3.8.50, Doncaster. Educ. Maltby Grammar School; Imperial College. Lecturer in Civil Engineering, Imperial College 1974-86 (Warden, Falmouth Hall, 1980-86); Director, Tynemarch Systems Engineering Ltd., 1984-91 (Chairman, 1984-86); Head, Civil Engineering Department, Heriot-Watt University, 1989-91, Head, Civil and Offshore Engineering, 1991-99. Director, Scottish Institute of Sustainable Technology, 1999-2013; Member, East of Scotland Water Authority, 1999-2002; Member, Scottish Water, 2002-08; Board Member, United Utilities Water, 2009-2011; President, Institution of Civil Engineers, 2009-2010; President, Commonwealth Engineers Council, since 2011. Recreations: painting; Morgan 3-wheelers; Jowett cars; Canal narrow boats; digging an allotment. Address: (h.) 14 Belford Mews, Edinburgh EH4 3BT; T.-0131-225 7583; e-mail: p.w.jowitt@hw.ac.uk

Joyce, Eric. BA, MA, MBA, PGCE. MP (Independent), Falkirk, 2012-2015; Labour MP (Falkirk), 2005-2012,

Falkirk West, 2000-05; b. 13.10.60, Perth; m.; 2 c. Soldier, Black Watch, 1978-81; Officer, Adjutant General's Corps, 1987-99; Public Affairs Officer, Commission for Racial Equality, 1999-2000. Executive Member, Fabian Society, 1998-2006, Chair, 2004-05; Member, Camelon Labour Club; former Scottish judo champion.

Judge, Professor David, BA, PhD, FRSA. Emeritus Professor of Politics, University of Strathclyde, since 2013; b. 22.5.50, Sheffield; m., Lorraine; 1 s.; 1 d. Educ. Westfield School; Exeter University; Sheffield University. Lecturer, Paisley College, 1974-88; University of Strathclyde: Lecturer, 1988-90, Senior Lecturer, 1990-91, Reader, 1991-94, Professor, 1994-2013, Head of Department, 1994-97, 2004-2010, Head of School, 2011; Fulbright Fellow and Visiting Professor, University of Houston, USA, 1993-94; Visiting Professor, College of Europe, Bruges, 2004-07. Publications: Backbench Specialisation in the House of Commons, 1981; The Politics of Parliamentary Reform (Editor), 1983; The Politics of Industrial Closure (Joint Editor), 1987; Parliament and Industry, 1990; A Green Dimension for the European Community (Editor), 1993; The Parliamentary State, 1993; Theories of Urban Politics (Co-Editor), 1995; Representation: Theory and Practice in Britain, 1999; The European Parliament (Co-Author), 2003, 2nd edn. 2008; Political Institutions in the UK, 2005; Democratic Incongruities: Representative Democracy in Britain, 2014. Recreation: breathing. Address: (b.) School of Government and Public Policy, University of Strathclyde, Glasgow G1 1XQ; T.-0141-548 2365; e-mail: d.judge@strath.ac.uk

Judson, Jane-Claire, MA (Hons), MBA, PGDip. Chief Executive, Chest Heart & Stroke Scotland (CHSS), since 2017; Director, Diabetes UK Scotland, 2009-2017; Commissioner, Scottish Human Rights Commission, since 2017. Educ. University of Dundee; The Open University; Ashridge Business School. Career history: Public Affairs Manager, NUS Scotland, 2002-04; The Scottish Parliament: Corporate Policy Manager, 2003-08, Senior Clerk, Local Government & Communities Committee, 2007-08; Member of the Board, Association of Chief Officers of Scottish Voluntary Organisations, 2013-16; Board Member (2010), Vice Chair, Volunteer Development Scotland, since 2012; Member of the Board: NHS Health Scotland, 2016-2020, Public Health Scotland, since 2020. Address: Chest Heart and Stroke Scotland, Head Office, Third Floor, Rosebery House, 8 Haymarket Terrace, Edinburgh EH12 5EZ; T.-0131 225 6963.

Jukes, Paul, MSc. Executive Advisor, Amey, since 2018; Chair, The Board of Directors, ENABLE Scotland, since 2021; Chief Executive, North Lanarkshire Council, 2015-18. Educ. University of Strathclyde; Newcastle Polytechnic; Heriot-Watt University. Career history: Technical Advisor, British Seed Houses Limited, 1985-87; Assistant Director, Motherwell District Council, 1987-96; North Lanarkshire Council: Director, 1996-2007, appointed Executive Director, Regeneration & Environment in 2007. Address: (b.) International House, Stanley Boulevard, Blantyre, Glasgow G72 0BN; T.-01698 207222.

Jung, Roland Tadeusz, BA, MA, MB, BChir, MD, MRCS, LRCP, MRCP, FRCPEdin, FRCPLond. Consultant Physician (Specialist in Endocrinology and Diabetes), 1982-2008 (retired); Chief Scientist, Scottish Executive Health Department, 2001-07; Honorary Professor, Dundee University, since 1998; Chairman, Scottish Hospital Endowments Research Trust, 2000-01; Senior Distinction Advisor (Eastern Region) for Scottish Advisory Committee on Distinction Awards, 2003-08; Member and Chair, Programme Management Group, Rowett Institute of Nutrition and Health, Aberdeen University, 2006-12; Visiting Professor, University of Southampton, since 2009. Educ. St. Anselm's College, Wirral; Pembroke College, Cambridge; St. Thomas Hospital and Medical School, London. MRC Clinical Scientific Officer, Dunn Nutrition Unit, Cambridge, and Honorary Senior Registrar, Addenbrooke's Hospital, Cambridge, 1977-79; Senior Registrar in Endocrinology and Diabetes, Royal Postgraduate Medical School, Hammersmith Hospital, London, 1980-82; Card Medal and Lecture on Obesity research, Western Infirmary, Edinburgh University, 1987; Clinical Director of General Medicine, Dundee Teaching Hospitals Trust, 1991-94; Director of R and D, Tayside NHS Consortium, 1997-2001; Edinburgh Lecture, Royal Society of Edinburgh, 2005. Named lecture honour by University of Dundee and NHS Tayside: The Jung-Newton Diabetes Lecture, 2012, 2013, 2014, 2015, 2017. Publication: Endocrine Problems in Oncology (Co-Editor), 1984; Colour Atlas of Obesity, 1990. Recreations: gardens; walking; volunteer with National Trust.

Junor, Gordon James, LLB (Hons). Retired Advocate; b. 18.1.56, Stannington, Northumberland. Educ. King Edward VI Grammar School, Morpeth; Edinburgh University. Solicitor, local government, 1982-92; Advocate in 1993. Publication: Scottish Older Client Law Service (Housing and Residential Care). Recreation: hillwalking. Address: Freelands, 9 Taits Hill, Selkirk TD7 4LZ; T.-01750 22121.

K

Kane, Patrick Mark, MA (Hons). Writer and Broadcaster; b. 10.3.64, Glasgow; m., Joan McAlpine (divorced); 2 d. Educ. St. Ambrose RC Secondary, Coatbridge; Glasgow University. Worked in London as a freelance writer; returned to Scotland to start professional music career with brother Gregory; achieved Top 10 and Top 20 singles and albums successes with Hue and Cry, 1987-89; TV arts presenter; former Rector, Glasgow University. Publication: The Play Ethic: A Manifesto for a Different Way of Living, 2004.

Kay, Jackie, CBE, FRSE, FRSL. Scottish poet and novelist; Scots Makar - the National Poet for Scotland, 2016-2021; Professor of Creative Writing, Newcastle University; Cultural Fellow, Glasgow Caledonian University; b. 9.11.61, Edinburgh; 1 s.; 1 d. Educ. Stirling University. First book of poetry, The Adoption Papers, published in 1991, won the Saltire Scottish First Book Award; appointed Member of the Order of the British Empire (MBE) in the 2006 Birthday Honours for services to literature, and Commander of the Order of the British Empire (CBE) in the 2020 New Year Honours, for services to literature.

Kay, William (Billy), MA. Freelance Broadcaster/Writer/ Producer; Director, Odyssey Productions; b. 24.9.51, Galston, Ayrshire; m., Maria João de Almeida da Cruz Dinis; 1 s.; 2 d. Educ. Galston High School; Kilmarnock Academy; Edinburgh University. Producer, Odyssey series, Radio Scotland; produced about 240 documentaries on diverse aspects of working-class oral history; Writer/Presenter, TV documentaries, including Miners, BBC Scotland; Presenter, Kay's Originals, Scottish TV. Commandeur d'Honneur, Commanderie du Bontemps de Médoc et des Graves; won Australasian Academy of Broadcast Arts and Sciences Pater award, 1987, 1988; Medallist, International Radio Festival of New York, 1990-92; Sloan Prize for writing in Scots, 1992; Wine Guild of UK 1994 Houghton Award, for Fresche Fragrant Clairettis; Winner: Heritage Society Award, 1995, Wines of France Award, 1996. Awarded Honorary Degree: Doctor of The University of The West of Scotland (DUniv), 2009. Received the Oliver Award from the Scots Independent newspaper in 2010 and made Honorary Preses of the Scots Language Society; Honorary Fellow of The Association for Scottish Literary Studies, since 2015; inducted into the Scottish Traditional Music Hall of Fame and given their very first Services to Scots Award in 2016; 2019 Winner of The Scots Media Person of the Year Award at the first Scots Language Awards Event; Winner of The Mark Twain Award given by The St Andrew's Society of the State of New York. Publications: Odyssey: Voices from Scotland's Recent Past (Editor); Odyssey: The Second Collection (Editor); Knee Deep in Claret: A Celebration of Wine and Scotland (Co-author); Made in Scotland (poetry); Jute (play for radio); Scots — The Mither Tongue; They Fairly Mak Ye Work (for Dundee Repertory Theatre); Lucky's Strike (play for radio); The Dundee Book; The Scottish World. Narrated the audiobook version of Scots The Mither Tongue for Audible, 2021. Recreations: wine; novels; languages; films; fitba, both Scotland and Dundee United. Address: (h.) 72 Tay Street, Newport on Tay, Fife DD6 8AP; e-mail: billy@billykay.scot; web: www.billykay.scot

Kayembe, Debora. Scottish human rights lawyer and political activist; Rector, University of Edinburgh, since 2021; b. 4.75. Educ. University of Edinburgh; University Libre de Kinshasa, Democratic Republic of the Congo;

University of Strathclyde; Heriot-Watt University. Career history: Humanitarian Internship, Office of the Coordination of Humanitarian affairs (OCHA), 1999-2000; Community Outreach Coordinator, The National Health Services (part-time), Blackburn, 2007-09; Board Member, The Scottish Refugee Council (part-time), Glasgow, 2012-16; Barrister At Law, self employed (Kinshasa, since 2000); Blackburn, 2007-09; Board Member, The Scottish Refugee Council (part-time), Glasgow, 2012-16; Founder of Full Options Scio, since 2018; Young Academy of Scotland, 2016-2021; Royal Society of Edinburgh; working group for Africa, 2019; Owner of Diversity Translation Service; sole trader, 2000-2019. Visionary Leader of the freedom Walk campaign, 2020; Member of the office of the prosecutor at the International Criminal Court and the International Criminal Court, since 2011 and the International Criminal Court Bar Association, since 2016. Address: University of Edinburgh, Old College, South Bridge, Edinburgh EH8 9YL; T.-0131 650 9561.
E-mail: rector@ed.ac.uk

Kayne, Steven Barry, BSc, PhD, MBA, LLM, MSc (Med Sci), FRPharmS, FCPP, FIPMI, DAgVetPharm, FFHom, MPS(NZ), FNZCP. Consultant Veterinary Homeopathic Pharmacist; book publisher; b. 8.6.44, Cheltenham Spa; m., Sorelle; 2 s. Educ. Westcliff High School; Aston University; Strathclyde University; Glasgow University; University of Wales. Professional Director & Visiting Lecturer in Veterinary Pharmacy, Harper Adams University, since 2009; Lecturer; Honorary Lecturer, University of Strathclyde School of Pharmacy (1989-2011); Honorary Consultant Pharmacist, Glasgow Homeopathic Hospital; Pharmacy (1991-2014); Dean to UK Faculty of Homoeopathy, 1998-2003; Member: Scottish Executive, Royal Pharmaceutical Society of Great Britain, 2000-07, Academic Board, UK Faculty of Homoeopathy, 1999-2003, UK Government Advisory Board on Homoeopathic Registration, 1993-2008, UK Government Herbal Medicines Advisory Committee, 2007-2011, Veterinary Products Committee of Veterinary Medicines Directorate, 2005-13; Governor and Hon. Treasurer, College of Pharmacy Practice, 2002-2010. Publication: Homoeopathic Pharmacy, 1997 (2nd edn 2005); People are Pets (Co-author), 1998; Complementary Therapies for Pharmacists, 2001; Veterinary Pharmacy (Co-editor), 2003; Pharmacy Business Management (Editor), 2004; Sports Medicine for Pharmacists (Editor), 2005; Pocket Companion Homeopathic Prescribing (Joint Author), 2007 (2nd Edn 2017); Homeopathic Practice (Editor), 2008; Complementary and Alternative Medicine (Editor), 2008; Traditional Medicine - A global perspective (2010); An Introduction to Veterinary Medicine (Editor), 2011; 450 papers and articles. Recreations: relaxing in Spey Valley; watching rugby; photography. Address: (b.) 18-20 Main Street, Busby, Glasgow G76 8DU; T.-0141 644 4344.

Kearns, Professor Ade J., BA (Hons). Professor of Urban Studies, University of Glasgow, since 2000; b. 11.10.59, Luton; 1 s.; 1 d. Educ. Cardinal Newman RC Secondary, Luton; Sidney Sussex College, Cambridge University. Research, Shelter; Senior Housing Investment Analyst, Housing Corporation; University of Glasgow: Research Fellow, Lecturer, Senior Lecturer; Deputy Director, ESRC Centre for Housing Research and Urban Studies; Acting Director, ESRC Cities Research Programme; Co-Director, ESRC Centre for Neighbourhood Research, 2001-05; Director, ESRC/ODPM Postgraduate Research Programme, 2003-06; Principal Investigator, The Gowell Programme, 2005-2020; Director of Research, School of Social and Political Sciences, University of Glasgow. Editor, two special issues, Urban Studies journal. Recreations: reading contemporary fiction; listening to music, especially pop and jazz; city and country walking. Address: Department of Urban Studies, R210 Level 2, 26 Bute Gardens, University of Glasgow G12 8QQ; T.-0141-330 5049.
E-mail: a.j.kearns@socsci.gla.ac.uk

Keating, Professor Michael James, MA, PhD, FRSE, AcSS, FBA, MAE. Professor of Politics, Aberdeen University, since 1999; General Secretary, The Royal Society of Edinburgh; b. 2.2.50, Hartlepool; m., Patricia Ann; 1 s. Educ. St Aidan's Grammar School, Sunderland; Oxford University; Glasgow College of Technology. Part-time Lecturer, Glasgow College of Technology, 1972-75; Senior Research Officer, Essex University, 1975-76; Lecturer, North Staffs Polytechnic, 1976-79; Lecturer/Senior Lecturer, Strathclyde University, 1979-88; Professor of Political Science, University of Western Ontario, 1988-99; Professor, European University Institute, Florence, 2000-10. Publications include: The Politics of Modern Europe; Nations against the State, the new politics of nationalism in Quebec, Catalonia and Scotland; The Government of Scotland; The Independence of Scotland; Rescaling the European State. Recreations: sailing; hill-walking; traditional music; reading. Address: (h.) 27 Dundas Street, Edinburgh EH3 6QQ.

Keeble, Professor Neil Howard, BA, DPhil, DLitt, FRSE, FRHistS, FEA. Professor Emeritus of English, Stirling University, since 2011; b. 7.8.44, London; m., Jenny Bowers; 2 s.; 1 d. Educ. Bancroft's School, Woodford Green; St. David's College, Lampeter; Pembroke College, Oxford. Foreign Lektor, Department of English, University of Aarhus, Denmark, 1969-72; Lecturer in English, Aarhus, 1972-74; Stirling University: Lecturer in English, 1974-88, Reader in English, 1988-95, Professor of English, 1995-2001, Head, Department of English Studies, 1997-2000, Deputy Principal, 2001-03 and Senior Deputy Principal, 2003-2010; Honorary Fellow, University of Wales, Lampeter, 2000. Publications: Richard Baxter: Puritan Man of Letters, 1982; The Literary Culture of Nonconformity in later seventeenth-century England, 1987; The Autobiography of Richard Baxter (Editor), 1974; The Pilgrim's Progress (Editor), 1984; John Bunyan: Conventicle and Parnassus (Editor), 1988; A Handbook of English and Celtic Studies in the United Kingdom and the Republic of Ireland (Editor), 1988; The Cultural Identity of Seventeenth-Century Woman (Editor), 1994; Lucy Hutchinson, Memoirs of the Life of Colonel Hutchinson (Editor), 1995; Cambridge Companion to Writing of the English Revolution (Editor), 2001; John Bunyan: Reading Dissenting Writing (Editor), 2002; Calendar of the Correspondence of Richard Baxter (Co-Compiler), 1991; Daniel Defoe, Memoirs of the Church of Scotland (Editor), 2002; The Restoration: England in the 1660s, 2002; Andrew Marvell, Remarks upon a Late Disingenuous Discourse (Editor), 2003; Daniel Defoe, Memoirs of a Cavalier (Editor), 2008; John Milton, Vernacular Regicide and Republican Writings (Co-Editor), 2013; 'Settling the Peace of the Church': 1662 Revisited (Editor), 2014; Textual Transformations: Purposing and Repurposing Books from Richard Baxter to Samuel Taylor Coleridge (Co-Editor), 2019; Richard Baxter, Reliquiae Baxterianae (Co-Editor), 2020. Recreations: books and book-collecting; films; gardening; walking. Address: (h.) 21 Alexander Drive, Bridge of Allan FK9 4QB.
E-mail: n.h.keeble@stir.ac.uk

Keel, Professor Aileen, CBE, MB, ChB, FRCP(G), FRCP(E), FRCPath, MFPH, FRCS(E), FRCGP. Director, Innovative Healthcare Delivery Programme, Usher Institute, University of Edinburgh; Honorary Professor, University of Edinburgh; b. 23.8.52, Glasgow; m., Paul Dwyer (deceased); 1 s. Educ. Glasgow University. Postgraduate training in general medicine and haematology, 1976-87; practised haematology at consultant level in both NHS and private sector in London, 1987-92, including period as Director of Pathology, Cromwell Hospital; Senior Medical Officer, Scottish Office Department of Health, 1992-98;

Principal Medical Officer, 1999; Deputy Chief Medical Officer, 1999-2015. Member of a number of medical advisory committees in Scotland and UK. Chair of the National Cancer Recovery Group; Friend of the Royal Scottish Academy; Member of Cockburn Association and Architectural Heritage Society of Scotland. Recreations: arts in general; music in particular, especially opera; keeping fit; current affairs; Member of Art in Healthcare; Member of Alexander Gibson Circle, Scottish Opera. Address: 23 Danube Street, Edinburgh EH4 1NN.

Keeling, Dr Jean Winifred, FRCPath, FRCPEd, FRCPCH. Retired; formerly Consultant Paediatric Pathologist, Royal Hospital for Sick Children, Edinburgh (1989-2005); Honorary Senior Lecturer, Pathology, Edinburgh University, since 1990; b. 13.3.40, Doncaster; m., 1, Anthony Millier; 1 s.; 1 d.; 2, Frederick Walker. Educ. Pontefract and District Girls' School; Royal Free Hospital School, London University. Lecturer in Morbid Anatomy, Institute of Child Health, London University; Consultant Paediatric Pathologist, John Radcliffe Hospital, Oxford; Hon. Clinical Lecturer, Oxford University; Member, Royal Liverpool Children's Inquiry; Past President, Paediatric Pathology Society; Past President, International Paediatric Pathology Association. Publications: Fetal Pathology; Fetal and Neonatal Pathology (Editor); Paediatric Forensic Medicine and Pathology (Joint Editor); papers on fetal and paediatric pathology. Recreations: walking; cooking. Address: (h.) 9 Forres Street, Edinburgh EH3 6BJ; T.- 0131 225 9673; e-mail: jeanwkeeling@aol.com

Keen of Elie, Baron (Richard Sanderson Keen), LLB (Hons). Advocate General for Scotland, 2015-2020; Queen's Counsel, 1993; Chairman, Scottish Conservative and Unionist Party, 2014-2015; Dean of The Faculty of Advocates, 2007-2014; Lords Minister for Ministry of Justice, 2016-2020; b. 29.03.54, Rustington, Sussex; m., Jane; 1 s.; 1 d. Educ. Dollar Academy; University of Edinburgh. Admitted to the Faculty of Advocates, 1980; Standing Counsel to the DTI, 1986-93; Elected Treasurer of the Faculty of Advocates, 2006. Member of the Bar of England and Wales, 2009. Bencher of the Honourable Society of the Middle Temple, 2010. Recreations: golf; skiing; shooting. Clubs: Hon. Co. Edinburgh Golfers; Golf House Elie; New Club (Edin).

Keiller, Bob. Former Chairman, Scottish Enterprise (2016-18); b. 29.1.64; m.; 3 c. Educ. Heriot-Watt University. Career history: CEO, Wood Group PSN, 2011-12; CEO, Wood Group, 2012-15; Business Advisor, AB15, since 2015; former Chairman of the Offshore Contracting Association (OCA) and the cross-industry trade body Oil and Gas UK; sat on 'Pilot' – the industry-government steering group; former member of the UK cross-industry Step Change in Safety Leadership Team; led the UK Helicopter Task Group formed in 2009 to accelerate safety improvements in air safety; former Chairman of the Entrepreneurial Exchange. Awarded Entrepreneur of the Year in 2006 and 2008; Scottish Businessman of the Year in 2007 and Grampian Industrialist of the Year in 2008; recognised for outstanding contribution to the oil and gas industry at the Scottish Offshore Achievement Awards in 2009; awarded the International Regulators Forum's "Carolita Kallaur" Award in 2010 (first individual to receive global recognition in safety leadership); "Scottish Male Business Leader of the Year" at the Scottish Leadership awards, 2011.

Keir, Colin. MSP (SNP), Edinburgh Western, 2011-16; b. 9.12.59, Edinburgh. Elected Member of City of Edinburgh

Council (Drum Brae/Gyle Ward), 2007-2012. Spent 16 years in the office equipment trade and 13 years working with Lothian Buses. Former convener of the regulatory committee of the City of Edinburgh Council. Former Scottish Schools 5000m Champion; former Scottish schools cross-country international.

Kelly, Dame Barbara Mary, CBE, FRSE, LLD, DipEd. Partner in farming enterprise; Chairman, Crichton Campus Leadership Group; President, Galloway National Park Association; President, Crichton Foundation; President, Southern Upland Partnership. Past Chairman, The Robertson Trust; Past Chairman, Peter Pan Moat Brae Trust; Past Convener, Millennium Forest for Scotland Trust; Past Trustee, Royal Botanic Garden Edinburgh; Deputy Lieutenant, Dumfriesshire (retired); former Chairman, Dumfries and Galloway Arts Festival; b. 27.2.40, Dalbeattie; m., Kenneth A. Kelly; 2 s.; 2 d. Educ. Dalbeattie High School; Kirkcudbright Academy; Moray House College. Past Member, Scottish Bank BP plc; Past Director, Scottish Post Office Board; Past Chairman, Scottish Consumer Council; former Member: Scottish Economic Council, National Consumer Council, Scottish Enterprise Board, Scottish Tourist Board, Priorities Board MAFF, Board, Scottish Natural Heritage (and former Chair, West Areas Board), Broadcasting Council for Scotland; former national Vice-Chairman, SWRI; Duke of Edinburgh's Award, former Chairman, Scottish Advisory Committee and former Member, UK Advisory Panel; former EOC Commissioner for Scotland; Past Chairman, Dumfries and Galloway Area Manpower Board, Manpower Services Commission; former Director, Clydesdale Bank plc; Past President, Rural Forum; former Chairman, UK Architects' Registration Board. Hon Degrees: University of Strathclyde, 1995; Aberdeen, 1997; Glasgow, 2002; Bell College, 2005; Queen Margaret University, 2005; University of the West of Scotland, 2010; Freeman City of London, 2002; Hon Fellow, RIAS; FRSGS; FRSE. Recreations: painting; music. Address: (h.) Barncleugh, Irongray, Dumfries DG2 9SE; T.-01387 730210.

Kelly, Sheriff Daniel, QC, LLB (Hons), CertAdvEurStud. Sheriff at Edinburgh, since 2021; Sheriff of South Strathclyde, Dumfries and Galloway, 2011-2021; b. 22.1.58, Dunfermline; m., Christine Marie MacLeod; 3 s.; 1 d. Educ. Edinburgh University; College of Europe, Bruges. Apprenticeship, Dundas and Wilson CS, 1979-81; Solicitor, Brodies WS, and Tutor in European Institutions, Edinburgh University, 1982-83; Solicitor, Community Law Office, Brussels, 1983-84; Procurator Fiscal Depute, 1984-90; Advocate, since 1991; Temporary Sheriff, 1997-99; Part-time Sheriff, 2005-2011. Sheriffs' Association: President, since 2019, Vice President, 2017-19. Editor: Scots Law Times, Sheriff Court Reports, since 1992. Queen's Counsel, since 2007. Publication: Criminal Sentences, 1993. Recreations: swimming; cycling; golf. Address: (b.) Sheriff Court House, 27 Chambers Street, Edinburgh EH1 1LB.

Kelly, David, MA, FRSA. Director for Scotland, Community Transport Association, since 2021. Educ. Dunblane High School; The University of Edinburgh. Career history: Constituency and Parliamentary Intern, Keith Brown MSP, 2011; Cushion Hire Assistant, The Royal Edinburgh Military Tattoo, 2013 and 2014; Delegate, National Union of Students (UK), Dundee, 2013-14; Youth Football Scotland, Edinburgh: Journalism and Media Intern, 2015, Content and Media Assistant, 2015-16; Political Affairs Intern, United Nations, New York City, USA, 2016; Writer, Politik und Gesellschaft, Hamburg, Germany, 2014-17; Business Management and Improvement Officer, Stirling Council, 2016-17; Scottish Council for

Development and Industry (SCDI): Policy Analyst, 2018-19, Policy Manager, 2019-2021. Address: 83 Princes Street, Edinburgh EH2 2ER; T.-0131 220 0052.
E-mail: david.kelly@ctauk.org

Kelly, James. General Secretary of the Scottish Labour Party, since 2021; MSP (Labour), Glasgow region, 2016-2021, Rutherglen, 2011-2016, Glasgow Rutherglen, 2007-2011; Shadow Cabinet Secretary for Justice, 2019-2020; Shadow Cabinet Secretary for Finance and the Constitution, 2017-19; General Election Campaign Manager, 2017; Scottish Election Campaign Manager, 2016; Parliamentary Business Manager, 2014-17; Spokesperson for Infrastructure, Investment and Cities Strategy, 2013-14; Chief Whip, 2012-13; Shadow Minister for Community Safety, 2008-2011; Whip, 2007-08; b. 23.10.63; m., Alexa; 2 d. Served as the election agent for the former Rutherglen and Hamilton West MP Tommy McAvoy at the 1997, 2001, and 2005 general elections; also Chair of the Rutherglen and Hamilton West Constituency Labour Party; background in computing and finance; chartered accountant; worked as a Business Analyst in East Kilbride prior to election in 2007.

Kelly, Col. John L., MBE. Soldier, organiser, geographer and noted public speaker. Retired in 2011 after a distinguished 40 year career with the British Army; formerly Joint Regional Liaison Officer for Scotland, in which capacity he was the Military enabling Officer when the Civilian Community required Military Assistance, be it for fire, floods, foot and mouth, severe weather and counter terrorism related matters; commissioned into the Royal Highland Fusiliers (Princess Margaret's own Glasgow and Ayrshire Regiment) and has served across the world principally in the UK, Northern Ireland, Canada, Germany, Belize, Brunei and Berlin; has held a variety of appointments including Chief of Staff of the Ulster Defence Regiment, Commanding Officer of 2nd Battalion 51st Highland Volunteers and Deputy Project Manager in the Procurement Executive. Formerly Deacon Convener of the Trades House in Glasgow. Grand Baillie of the Scottish Jurisdiction of the Order of St Lazurus, the international Christian order of chivalry, since 2011. Address: The Bent, Gartocharn, Dunbartonshire G83 8SB.

Kelly, Professor John Shearer, BSc, MB, ChB, PhD, MA, FRSE, FRCPE, FMedSci, FBPS (Hon). Emeritus Professor of Pharmacology, University of Edinburgh, since 2002; Director, Fujisawa Institute of Neuroscience, 1992-2002; Deputy Editor, Journal of the Royal College of Physicians, Edinburgh, 2002-09; b. 3.3.37, Edinburgh; m., E. Anne Wilkin; 1 s.; 1 d. Educ. George Heriot's School, Edinburgh; University of Edinburgh. House Physician, Western General Hospital, Edinburgh, 1962; House Surgeon, Royal Hospital for Sick Children, Edinburgh, 1963; University of Edinburgh, Department of Pharmacology: Assistant Lecturer, 1963-65, Lecturer, 1965-68; McGill University, Canada: Wellcome Post-doctoral Fellow, Department of Research in Anaesthesia, 1967-68, Canadian Medical Research Council Scholar and Assistant Professor, Departments of Research in Anaesthesia and Physiology, 1968-71; IBRO Research Fellow, University of Geneva, 1970; MRC Scientific Staff, Department of Pharmacology, Cambridge, 1971-79; Fellow of King's College, Cambridge and Lecturer in Pharmacology and Neurobiology, 1976-79; Professor and Chairman, Pharmacology, St. George's Hospital Medical School, London, 1979-85; Professor of Pharmacology, Edinburgh University, 1985-2002; Founding Editor, 1978 and Editor in Chief of the Journal of Neuroscience Methods, 1978-99; Editor of the Journal of the Royal College of Physicians Edinburgh, 2001-09. Publications: The Enduring Legacy of 250 Years of Pharmacology in Edinburgh, Annual Review of

Pharmacology and Toxicology, 2018; 132 papers on neuroscience; 59 book chapters; 216 abstracts. Recreations: classical music; Scottish Malt Whisky Society; Scottish restaurants; Scottish outdoors. Address: (b.) Tamarack, 11 Redhall Bank Road, Edinburgh EH14 2LY; e-mail: j.s.kelly@ed.ac.uk

Kelly, Michael, CBE (1983), OStJ, JP, BSc(Econ), PhD, LLD, DL, FCIM, Knight's Star Order of Merit Poland. Public Relations Consultant, since 1984; Honorary Vice-President, Children 1st, since 1996 (Chairman, Royal Scottish Society for the Prevention of Cruelty to Children, 1987-96); Columnist: Scotsman, Evening Times; Broadcaster, Radio Clyde; b. 1.11.40, Glasgow; m., Zita Harkins; 1 s.; 2 d. Educ. St. Joseph's College, Dumfries. Assistant Lecturer in Economics, Aberdeen University, 1965-67; Lecturer in Economics, Strathclyde University, 1967-80; Lord Provost of Glasgow, 1980-84; Rector, Glasgow University, 1984-87; Member, National Arts Collection Fund, 1990-96; Secretary, Scottish Industry Forum, 1995-2000; Scottish Convener, Socialist Civil Liberties Association, since 2002; Chairman, ILI Group, since 2018; British Tourist Authority Medal for services to tourism, 1984; Robert Burns Award from University of Old Dominion, Virginia, for services to Scottish culture, 1984; Scot of the Year, 1983; Radio Scotland News Quiz Champion, 1986, 1987; Radio Scotland Christmas Quiz Champion, 1987; Honorary Mayor of Tombstone, Arizona; Kentucky Colonel, 1983; Pollok Golf Club: Committee Member, 2009-2012, Seniors Vice Captain, since 2018, Seniors Captain, since 2020. Publications: Paradise Lost: the struggle for Celtic's soul, 1994; London Lines: the capital by underground, 1996. Recreations: golf; skiing. Address: (b.) 6/5 Mains Avenue, Giffnock G46 6QY. E-mail: kellymkelly1@aol.com

Kelly, Neil Joseph, LLB (Distinction), DipLP, NP, WS, HonRICS, HonFRIAS, ACIArb. Solicitor, since 1984; Partner, MacRoberts, Solicitors, since 1991, Head of Construction, since 2003, Chairman, 2011-2014; b. 28.6.61, Bellshill; m., Alison Jane (Whyte); 2 s.; 1 d. Educ. St. Patrick's High School; Aberdeen University. Qualified in all forms of dispute resolution mechanisms with particular focus on construction industry. Editor, Scottish Construction Law Review, 2003-08; Contributor, MacRoberts on Scottish Construction Contracts; Convener, Adjudication Society (Scottish Region); Past Chairman of Chartered Institute of Arbitrators (Scottish Branch). Recreations: travel; opera; classical music. Address: (b.) 10 George Street, Edinburgh EH2 2PF; T.-0131 248 2124. E-mail: neil.kelly@macroberts.com

Kelly, Owen Dennis, OBE, MA (Hons) Chinese, DipSocPol (Edin). Director of Engagement, University of Edinburgh Business School, since 2016; Deputy Director, Edinburgh Futures Institute, University of Edinburgh, since 2018; Lecturer, Edinburgh Napier University Business School, 2016-17; Chief Executive, Scottish Financial Enterprise, 2008-2015; b. 17.7.63, Redhill, Surrey; m., Michelle Anderson; 1 s. 2 d. Educ. John Fisher School, Purley, Surrey; University of Edinburgh. HM Customs and Excise, 1987; Scottish Office, 1988-99; Private Secretary to Minister for Home Affairs and Environment, 1990-92; Locate in Scotland, Director, Japan (Tokyo), 1994-96; Scottish Government, 1999-2008; Principal Private Secretary to First Minister of Scotland, 2003-05; Director of Communications and International, Scottish Government, 2005-07. Made Officer of the British Empire (OBE) in New Year's Honours List, 2014; Charity Trusteeships: Historic Scotland Foundation (Chair); McConnell International Foundation. Honorary Fellow, Chartered Banker

Institute. Recreations: reading; cooking; walking the dog; guitar.

Kelly, Patrick Joseph, BSc. Author of 'Scotland's Radical Exports'; Chair of editorial board of Scottish Left Review; Non-Executive Director, Scottish Water, 2003-2013; Non-Executive Director, NHS 24, 2001-07; b. 26.10.50, Glasgow; 1 s.; 3 d. Educ. St. Mungo's Academy, Glasgow; Glasgow University. Civil Engineer, Central Regional Council, 1973-86; became active in local government union Nalgo and was elected to National Executive, 1979-86; Scottish Secretary, Society of Civil and Public Servants, 1986-99; former Member and President (1998), General Council, STUC; since 1999, working on various Boards in the public sector, including Civil Service Appeal Board; Board Member, Scottish Enterprise, Edinburgh and Lothian, 1991-2000; Management Committee, War on Want (charity); Anti-apartheid Scottish Committee. Publication: Scotland's Radical Exports, 2011. Recreations: golf; watching football; reading; walking. E-mail: pat1950@btinternet.com

Kelly, Fr. Peter. Parish Priest of Banchory, since 2020. Address: Corsee Cottage, 5 High Street, Banchory AB31 5RP; T.-01330 822835; e-mail: deeside@rcda.scot

Kelly, Sally Ann. Chief Executive, Aberlour Child Care Trust, since 2014. Qualified as a Social Worker in 1990; promoted to management post in 1996; has worked in a number of Scottish Local Authorities in middle and senior management positions; moved to the Third Sector to take up position as Head of Operations with Barnardo's Scotland in 2008, then temporary role of Acting Director; Senior Manager for the National 3rd Sector GIRFEC Project, 2013-14. Former Member, Scottish Government Early Years Taskforce; involved in supporting the implementation of the Early Years Collaborative through role as the National Champion for 1-3 year olds; sits on the National Child Protection Leadership Group and has a deep interest in the impact of poverty on families and campaigns against poverty alongside colleagues in Aberlour. Address: Aberlour Child Care Trust, Kintail House, Forthside Way, Stirling FK8 1QZ; T.-01786 450335.

Kelly, Sheriff Tony. Sheriff, Glasgow & Strathkelvin, since 2019. Educ. University of Strathclyde. Career history: started traineeship in 1990 with Messrs. Hannay, Fraser & Co, Solicitors; became associate, then partner; worked with Taylor & Kelly, Court Solicitors in Coatbridge, 1997-2016; granted Rights of Audience as a Solicitor Advocate in both the Court of Session and High Court of Justiciary in 2012; former First-Tier tribunal judge in the Social Entitlement and Immigration and Asylum Chambers; appointed Summary Sheriff of Glasgow and Strathkelvin in 2016. Visiting Professor in human rights in the University of Strathclyde; legal member of the Parole Board for Scotland. Address: Glasgow Sheriff Court, 1 Carlton Place, Glasgow G5 9TW.

Kelman, James. Novelist; b. 1946, Glasgow. Works include: The Busconductor Hines; A Chancer; Greyhound for Breakfast; A Disaffection; How Late It Was How Late (Booker Prize, 1994); The Good Times (Scotland on Sunday/Glenfiddich Spirit of Scotland Award and the Stakis Prize for Scottish Writer of the Year, 1998); Translated Accounts, 2001; And the Judges Said... (essays), 2002; You have to be careful in the Land of the Free, 2004; Kieron Smith, Boy, 2008 (won

Scotland's most prestigious literary award the Saltire Society's Book of the Year award, 2008); If It is Your Life, 2010; Mo Said She Was Quirky, 2012; A Lean Third, 2014; Dirt Road, 2016; That Was a Shiver, 2017; Tales of Here & Then, 2020. Address: c/o Rogers, Coleridge and White, 20 Powis Mews, London W11 1JN.

Kelsey, Rachael Joy Christina, LLB, DipLP, NP. Founding Partner, SKO Family Law Specialists. Educ. Culloden Academy, Inverness; Edinburgh University. Accredited as Specialist in Family Law and Family Mediator by Law Society of Scotland; FLAGS Family Law Arbitrator; President-Elect, International Academy of Family Lawyers, since 2021; appointed by Lord President to Scottish Civil Justice Council, Family Law Committee, since 2016; Scottish Law Commission Arbitration Advisory Group for the Review of Contract Law: Third Party Rights, 2016; Chair, Director and Trustee, Family Mediation Lothian, 2009-2017; Chair, Family Law Association, 2005-06. Recreations: wine; gardening; children; boxing. Address: (b.) 18 George Street, Edinburgh EH2 2PF; T.-0131 322 6669; e-mail: rachael.kelsey@sko-family.co.uk

Kemp, Kenny. Journalist and Writer; Director and Owner, Kemp Communications (UK) Ltd, since 2003; Editor, Business Insider magazine, 2021-22; b. 4.57. Educ. University of Strathclyde. Career history: The Scotsman, 1988-98; Business Editor, Sunday Herald, 1999-2004; Media consultant/adviser, Scottish Widows, 2004-05; worked with Richard Orr on the book Be A Winner, Winning Scotland Foundation, 2007-08; Co-writer/ghost-writer with Random House/Sir Richard Branson, 2008; Sunday Herald, 2007-2010; Co-Author, Be Silent or Be Killed, 2009-2010; Associate, The VeryPeople, 2007-2012; Editor, BQ Scotland, 2010-2015; Co-Writer, Cruzach Inc, Beverley Hills, CA, 2015; Ghost-Writer of Navigating the Digital Age, Palo Alto Networks, Edinburgh, 2016-17; Director, Intrinsic QC, Edinburgh and London, 2016-17; Corporate Communications Associate, The City Partnership (UK) Limited, Edinburgh, 2015-17; Editor At Large, Panmure House Perspectives, Edinburgh, 2017-2020; Bylined Writer and Ghost Writer, Kemp Communications (UK), Edinburgh, 2003-2021; Special Communications Adviser, John Swift QC on Lessons Learned inquiry into IRHPs, 2019-2022; Freelance Writer, since 2007; Associate, University of Edinburgh Business School, Edinburgh, since 2015. Address: Kemp Communications (UK) Limited, 81a Mayfield Road, Edinburgh EH9 3AE.

Kennedy, Alison Louise, BA (Hons). Writer; b. 22.10.65, Dundee. Educ. High School of Dundee; Warwick University. Community Arts Worker, 1988-89; Writer in Residence, Project Ability, 1989-94; Writer in Residence, Hamilton/East Kilbride Social Work Department, 1990-92; fiction critic for Scotsman, etc.; Booker Prize Judge, 1996; five S.A.C. book awards; Saltire Best First Book Award; 2 Saltire Best Book Awards; John Llewellyn Rees/Mail on Sunday Prize; listed, Granta/Sunday Times Best of Young British Novelists; Encore Award; Festival Fringe First; Social Work Today Award; Premio Napoli; Lannan Award for Literature; Austrian State Prize for European Literature; Costa Prize. Honorary Degree, Glasgow University. Publications: Night Geometry and the Garscadden Trains; Looking for the Possible Dance; Now That You're Back; So I Am Glad; Original Bliss; The Life and Death of Colonel Blimp (essay); Everything you Need; On Bull Fighting (non-fiction); Indelible Acts; Paradise; Day; What Becomes; The Blue Book (novel); All The Rage (short stories); The Audition (play); Stella Does Tricks (film); Permanent Sunshine (short film); Delicate (performance piece); True (performance piece); Like an Angel (radio play); Confessions of a Medium (radio play); Love Love

Love Like The Beatles (radio play); That I should Rise (radio play); Subterranean Homesick Blues (radio play); On writing (essays); All The Rage (short stories); Serious Sweet (novel); Uncle Shawn and Bill and the Almost Entirely Unplanned Adventure (children's fiction); Uncle Shawn and Bill and the Pajimminy Crimminy Adventure (children's fiction); The Little Snake (fiction); We Are Attempting to Survive Our Time (short stories); Uncle Shawn and Bill and the Not One Tiny Bit Lovey-Dovey Moon Adventure (children's fiction). Recreations: cinema; banjo; Tai Chi. E-mail: alkenn@talktalk.net

Kennedy, Rev. Gordon, BSc, BD, MTh. Minister, Craiglockhart Parish Church, Edinburgh, since 2012; Church of Scotland Minister, Portpatrick linked with Stranraer St. Ninian's, 2000-2012; b. 15.9.63, England. Educ. Crookston Castle Secondary; University of Strathclyde; University of Glasgow. Graduate Civil Engineer, Strathclyde Regional Council, 1985-89; Probationer Assistant, Bearsden North Parish Church, 1992-93; Minister, New Cumnock Parish Church, Ayrshire, 1993-2000. 2005 Master of Theology, University of Glasgow. Address: 20 Craiglockhart Quadrant, Edinburgh, Midlothian EH14 1HD.
E-mail: gordonkennedy@craiglockhartchurch.org

Kennedy, Gordon Philip, MA (Hons), MPhil, MBA, MRTPI, MIED. Director, Clearbluewater 2.0 Ltd., economic development consultants; Board Member, Refuweegee; Board Member, Four Acres Charitable Trust; Deputy Chief Executive, Scottish Enterprise Glasgow, 2001-08; b. 30.5.57, Glasgow. Educ. St. Mungo's Academy; Glasgow University; Strathclyde University. Planning Assistant, Clydebank District Council, 1982-85; Industrial Economist, Scottish Development Agency, 1985-91; Glasgow Development Agency: Head of Strategic Projects, 1991, Head of Corporate Strategy, 1991-93; Director, Corporate Development, Glasgow Development Agency, 1993-99; Deputy Chief Executive, Scottish Enterprise Glasgow, 1999-2001. Strategic Adviser to Glasgow Chamber of Commerce, since 2001. Recreations: cinema; theatre; eating out. Address: (b.) 35 Caird Drive, Glasgow G11 5DX; T.-0141-334-7075.
E-mail: g.kennedy174@btinternet.com

Kennedy, Professor Malcolm William, BSc, PhD. Professor Emeritus of Natural History, and Honorary Senior Research Fellow, University of Glasgow since 2020. Educ. Hutchesons Grammar School, Glasgow; University of Glasgow. Scientific Staff, Division of Immunology, National Institute for Medical Research, London, 1979-83; Wellcome Trust University Award Lecturer, University of Glasgow, 1983-90; Senior Lecturer, 1990-91; Reader, 1991-96; Professor of Infection Biology, 1996; Professor of Natural History, 2007. Pfizer Academic Award, 1995; Wright Medal of the British Society for Parasitology, 2000. Address: (b.) Graham Kerr Building, University of Glasgow, Glasgow G12 8QQ.
E-mail: malcolm.kennedy@glasgow.ac.uk

Kennedy, Martin. President, NFU Scotland, since 2021; b. 11.65; m., Jane; 3 d. Tenant farmer in Highland Perthshire. Served two years as Highland Perthshire Branch Chairman, before representing East Central region on the LFA committee in 2009; became Vice Chairman, then chaired the committee for three years; elected Vice President in 2017. Address: NFU Scotland, The Rural Centre, West Mains, Ingliston, Newbridge EH28 8LT; T.-0131 472 4000.

Kennedy, Neil, LLB (Hons). Managing Partner, MacRoberts LLP, since 2018. Educ. The Glasgow

Academy; University of Strathclyde; University of Aberdeen. Career: former Head of Corporate Finance, MacRoberts LLP (joined MacRoberts in 1999). Scottish Business Insider's SME of the Year 2017. Address: MacRoberts LLP, Capella, 60 York Street, Glasgow G2 8JX; T.-0141 303 1270.
E-mail: neil.kennedy@macroberts.com

Kennedy, Professor Peter Graham Edward, CBE (2010), MB, BS, MPhil, MLitt, PhD, MD, DSc, FRCPath, FRCPLond, FRCPGlas, FRSE, FMedSci. Honorary Professor and Senior Research Fellow, University of Glasgow, since 2016; Burton Professor of Neurology and Head of Department, Glasgow University, 1987-2016; Consultant Neurologist, Institute of Neurological Sciences, Southern General Hospital, Glasgow, 1986-2016; b. 28.3.51, London; m., Catherine Ann; 1 s.; 1 d. Educ. University College School, London; University College, London; University College Medical School. Medical Registrar, University College Hospital, 1977-78; Hon. Research Assistant, MRC Neuroimmunology Project, University College, London, 1978-80; Research Fellow, Institute of Virology, Glasgow University, 1981; Registrar and Senior Registrar, National Hospital for Nervous Diseases, London, 1981-84; Assistant Professor of Neurology, Johns Hopkins University School of Medicine, 1985; "New Blood" Senior Lecturer in Neurology and Virology, Glasgow University, 1986-87. BUPA Medical Foundation "Doctor of the Year" Research Award, 1990; Linacre Medal and Lectureship, Royal College of Physicians of London, 1991; T.S. Srinivasan Endowment Lecturer and Gold Medal, 1993; Fogarty International Scholar, NIH, USA, 1993-94 (Fogarty Medal); Distinguished Service Award (2010), International Society for Neurovirology; Senior Associate Editor, Journal of Neurovirology; Member: Medical Research Advisory Committee, Multiple Sclerosis Society, 1987-98, Association of Physicians Great Britain and Ireland, Association of British Neurologists; Fellow of the Academy of Medical Sciences; President, International Society for Neurovirology, 2004-2010; Sir James Black Medal (Senior Prize Life Sciences), Royal Society of Edinburgh, 2014; Royal Medal (2020), Royal Society of Edinburgh; 2018 Pioneer in Neurovirology Award, International Society for Neurovirology. Publications: Infectious Diseases of the Nervous System (Co-Editor), 2000; numerous papers on neurology, neurovirology, neurobiology and sleeping sickness; The Fatal Sleep (popular science), 2007; Reversal of David (novel), 2014; Brothers in Retribution (novel), 2015; Return of the Circle (novel), 2017; Catapult in Time (novel), 2018; Twelve Months of Freedom (novel), 2019; Arcadian Memories and other poems, 2020; The Image in my mind (novel), 2020, Two Centuries of Doubt (novel), 2021. Recreations: reading and writing; music; astronomy; tennis; walking in the country; philosophy. Address: (b.) Institute of Neuroscience and Psychology, Garscube Campus, University of Glasgow G61 1QH.

Kennedy, Professor Robert Alan, BA, PhD, FBPsS, FRSE. Emeritus Professor of Psychology, University of Dundee (Professor, since 1972); b. 1.10.39, Stourbridge; m., Elizabeth Wanda; 1 d. Educ. King Edward VI Grammar School, Stourbridge. Senior Tutor then Lecturer in Psychology, University of Melbourne, 1963-65; Lecturer in Psychology; Queen's College, University of St. Andrews, University of Dundee, 1965-72; Senior Lecturer in Psychology, University of Dundee, 1972. Member, Psychology Committee, Social Science Research Council (UK), 1980-82; Committee Member, Experimental Psychology Society, 1984-88; Member, Scientific Affairs Board, British Psychological Society, 1986-88; Member, MRC Neuropsychology Sub-committee, 1982-89; Editorial Board: Acta Psychologica, 1980-88, Psychological Research, 1978-88; Founder Member, European Conference on Eye Movements, since 1980; Convener, Scottish Group of Professors of Psychology, 1985-91; Governor, Dundee College of Education, 1974-78; Member of Court, University of Dundee, 1976-80 and 1990-99; Convener, University Research Committee, 1994-97; Member, Council, Royal Society of Edinburgh, 1999-2001; Honorary Member, Experimental Psychology Society, 2009. Publications: Studies in Long-Term Memory (Co-author); The Psychology of Reading; Reading as a Perceptual Process (Editor); Eye Movements and Information Processing During Reading (Co-editor). Recreations: hill-walking; playing the piano. Address: (b.) Psychology Department, University of Dundee, Dundee DD1 4HN; T.-01382 344622.

Kent, Mark, MA (Oxon). Chief Executive, Scotch Whisky Association, since 2022. Educ. King Prajadhiphok's Institute; Queen Elizabeth's Grammar School, Horncastle; University of Oxford; Universite Libre de Bruxelles; The Open University; Khon Kaen University; Chiang Mai University. Career history: Second Secretary (Press, Political and Development), British Embassy, Brasilia, 1989-93; First Secretary, External Relations, UK Permanent Representation to the European Union, Brussels, 1993-98; Spokesperson, Foreign and Commonwealth Office, London, 1998-2000; Consul General and Director of Trade and Investment, British Embassy, Mexico City, 2000-04; Special Adviser to SACEUR, Supreme Headquarters Allied Powers Europe, Mons, Belgium, 2004-05; Deputy Director, Migration, Foreign and Commonwealth Office, London, 2005-07; Ambassador, British Embassy Hanoi, Vietnam, 2007-2010; Thai language and other training, Foreign and Commonweath Office, 2010-2022; Ambassador: British Embassy, Bangkok, 2012-16, British Embassy, Buenos Aires, 2016-2021; Diplomat, 2021-22. Address: The Scotch Whisky Association, Edinburgh HQ: Quartermile Two, 2 Lister Square, Edinburgh EH3 9GL; T.-0131 222 9200.

Kenway, Professor Richard Donovan, OBE, FRSE, BSc, DPhil, CPhys, FInstP, FLSW. Emeritus Professor of Mathematical Physics, Edinburgh University, since 2021; b. 8.5.54, Cardiff; m., Anna Kenway; 1 s.; 2 d. Educ. Stanwell School, Penarth; Exeter University; Oxford University. Research Associate, Brown University, 1978-80; Post-doctoral Fellow, Los Alamos National Laboratory, 1980-82; Edinburgh University: Post-doctoral Fellow, 1982-83; Lecturer, 1983-90; Reader, 1990-94; Director of Edinburgh Parallel Computing Centre, 1993-97; Tait Professor of Mathematical Physics, 1994-2021; Head, Department of Physics and Astronomy, 1997-2000; Chairman, Edinburgh Parallel Computing Centre, 1997-2016; Chairman, UK National e-Science Centre, 2001-2011; PPARC Senior Research Fellow, 2001-04; Assistant Principal, 2002-05; Vice Principal, 2005-2021; Head, School of Physics and Astronomy, 2008-2011; Trustee, The Alan Turing Institute, since 2015; Member, National and International Peer Review and Research Strategy Committees. Publications: co-authored one book; co-edited two books; 145 papers on theoretical particle physics and high performance computing. Recreations: munroing; running; gardening. Address: (b.) School of Physics and Astronomy, Edinburgh University, James Clerk Maxwell Building, Peter Guthrie Tait Road, Edinburgh EH9 3FD; T.-0131-650 5245.
E-mail: r.d.kenway@ed.ac.uk

Kerevan, George, MA (Hons). MP (SNP), East Lothian, 2015-17; Journalist; co-organiser of the Prestwick World Festival of Flight; former Chief Executive, What If Productions (Television) Ltd.; Associate Editor, The Scotsman, 2000-09; b. 28.9.49, Glasgow. Educ. Kingsridge Secondary School, Drumchapel; Glasgow

University. Academic posts, Napier University, 1975-2000; freelance journalist and broadcaster, since 1980; Creative Director, Alba Communications Ltd., 2005-06; TV director, producer and script writer, Lamancha Productions Ltd., 1989-2000; Chair, Edinburgh Technology Transfer Centre, 1985-92; Board, Edinburgh Co-operative Development Agency, 1987-92; Chair, EDI Ltd., 1988-95; Board, Edinburgh Venture Trust, 1988-93; Board, Capital Enterprise Trust, 1993-94; Chairman, New Edinburgh Ltd., 1989-95; Board, Lothian and Edinburgh Enterprise Trust, 1989-96; Chair, Edinburgh and Lothians Tourist Board, 1992-95; Board, Traverse Theatre, 1980-84; Council, Edinburgh International Festival, 1984-92; Board, Assembly Productions, 1984-88; Board, Royal Lyceum Theatre, 1984-88; Board, Edinburgh Old Town Trust, 1984-90; Board, 7:84 Theatre Company, 1986-88; Board, Edinburgh International Film Festival, 1988-94; Chair, Edinburgh International Science Festival, 1989-95; Chair, Edinburgh Film House, 1989-94; Board, Boxcar Films, 1993; Chair, Manifesto International Festival of Architecture, 1995; elected Member, Edinburgh District Council, 1984-96 (Convenor, Economic Development Committee, 1986-95); Vice-Convenor, Economic Affairs Committee, COSLA, 1988-90; Board, John Wheatley Centre for Public Policy Research, 1988-93; SNP National Council, 1996-98; SNP environment spokesperson, 1996-98; SNP Parliamentary Candidate for Edinburgh East, 2010 General Election. Recreations: cooking; cats; cinema. Address: (h.) Brunstane House (South Wing), Brunstane Road South, Edinburgh EH15 2NQ; T.-0131-669 8234.

Kernahan, Gary William, BA (Hons). Director of Fundraising and Business Development, Children 1st, since 2020; b. 12.82. Educ. Glasgow Caledonian University. Career history: Cancer Research UK: Area Volunteer Manager, Glasgow and Manchester, 2004-08, Interim Regional Manager, Scotland and Northern Ireland, 2008-09; Interim Regional Fundraising Manager, Scotland and Northern Ireland, National Autistic Society, 2009; Muscular Dystrophy UK: Volunteer Fundraising Manager - Scotland, 2009, Head of Regional Development and Supporter Care, Glasgow/London, 2010-17; Senior Consultant, THINK Consulting Solutions, 2017-2019; Institute of Fundraising: Chair, Professional Development Committee, 2012-14, Vice Chair, Executive Committee, 2011-17, Chair, Scottish Fundraising Conference, since 2014; Trustee, Thistle Foundation, since 2018. Address: Children 1st, 83 Whitehouse Loan, Edinburgh EH9 1AT; T.-0131 446 2300.
E-mail: Gary.Kernahan@children1st.org.uk

Kernohan, Robert Deans, OBE, MA, FFCS. Journalist, writer and sometime broadcaster, including 520 BBC Thoughts for the Day, 1975-2019 and Scottish team on Round Britain Quiz; b. 9.1.31, Mount Vernon, Lanarkshire; m., Margaret Buchanan Bannerman; 4 s. Educ. Whitehill School, Glasgow; Glasgow University; Balliol College, Oxford. RAF, 1955-57; Editorial Staff, Glasgow Herald, 1957-67 (Chief Leader Writer, 1962-65, Assistant Editor, 1965-66, London Editor, 1966-67); Director-General, Scottish Conservative Central Office, 1967-71; Freelance Journalist and Broadcaster, 1972; Editor, Life and Work, The Record of the Church of Scotland, 1972-90. Chairman, Federation of Conservative Students, 1954-55; Conservative Parliamentary candidate, 1955, 1959, 1964; Member: Newspaper Panel, Monopolies and Mergers Commission (subsequently Competition Commission), 1987-99, Ancient Monuments Board for Scotland, 1990-97, Broadcasting Standards Council, 1994-97, Broadcasting Standards Commission, 1997-99; Chairman, Scottish Christian Conservative Forum, 1991-97; HM Inspector of

Constabulary for Scotland (Lay Inspector), 1992-95; Director, Handsel Press Ltd, 1996-2003; Institute of Contemporary Scotland Magnus Magnusson Medal, 2011; Elder, Cramond Kirk, Edinburgh; Honorary President, Scottish Church Theology Society, 1994. Publications: Scotland's Life and Work, 1979; William Barclay, The Plain Uncommon Man, 1980; Thoughts through the Year, 1985; Our Church, 1985; The Protestant Future, 1991; The Road to Zion, 1995; The Realm of Reform (Editor), 1999; John Buchan in a Nutshell, 2000; An Alliance across the Alps, 2005; numerous contributions to collective works, reviews (notably Scottish Review and Contemporary Review) and reference books, including New Dictionary of National Biography. Recreations: rugby-watching; reminiscence; painting; pontification; conservatism. Address: (h.) 5/1 Rocheid Park, Edinburgh EH4 1RP; T.-0131-332 7851.

Kerr, Andrew, CertEd, ILAM, MBA. Chief Executive, City of Edinburgh Council, since 2015. Educ. Borough Road College; Loughborough University; Cardiff Business School; Harvard, MIT, Stanford and Berkeley Haas - British Telecom. Area Leisure Officer, Falkirk District Council, 1982-87; Principal Officer, Cardiff City Council, 1987-90; Head of Participation, Sports Council for Wales, 1990-96; Head of Lifelong Learning and Leisure, Caerphilly County Borough Council, 1996-2000; Lead Inspector, Audit Commission, 2000-02; Director, Leisure and Culture, Birmingham City Council, 2002-04; President, ILAM, 2004-05; Director, Performance Improvement, Birmingham City Council, 2004-05; Chief Executive: North Tyneside Council, 2005-2010, Wiltshire Council, 2010-11; Board Member and Trustee, Wiltshire and Swindon Community Foundation, 2010-13; Chief Operating Officer, Cardiff Council, 2012-13; Owner, Kerr Strategic Consultancy Ltd, 2011-15; Chief Executive, Cornwall Council, 2013-15. Former bronze medal-winning 400m sprinter, and represented Great Britain in international athletics. Address: City of Edinburgh Council, Waverley Court, 4 East Market Street, Edinburgh EH8 8BG; T.-0131 200 2300; e-mail: chief.executive@edinburgh.gov.uk

Kerr, Andrew Palmer. Chief Operating Officer, The Piper Group, since 2019; Chair, Quality Scotland, since 2016; Chief Executive Officer, Sense Scotland, 2011-2019; former MSP (Labour), East Kilbride (1999-2011); Shadow Cabinet Secretary for Finance and Sustainable Growth, 2007-2011; Minister for Health and Community Care, 2004-07; Minister for Finance and Public Services, Scottish Executive, 2001-04; b. 17.3.62, East Kilbride; m., Susan; 3 d. Educ. Claremont High School; Glasgow College. Research Officer, Strathkelvin District Council, 1987-90; Achieving Quality Consultancy, 1990-93; Glasgow City Council, 1993-99. Address: (b.) The Piper Group, INSPIRE House, 3 Renshaw Place, Eurocentral, North Lanarkshire ML1 4UF; T.-01698 737000.

Kerr, Calum. MP (SNP), Berwickshire, Roxburgh and Selkirk, 2015-17; SNP Environment and Rural Affairs and Digital spokesperson in the House of Commons, 2015-17; b. 5.4.72; m.; 3 c. Educ. St Andrews University. Worked in sales for IT companies including Avaya. Chair of Yes Scottish Borders in the run-up to the referendum. Recreations: rugby; family; malt whisky.

Kerr, Sheriff Joan, MA (Hons), LLB. Sheriff, Glasgow and Strathkelvin, since 2015. Admitted as a solicitor in 1991; solicitor, then partner, HBM Sayers, 1994-2008; appointed as a Stipendiary Magistrate in 2008 and Part Time Sheriff in 2011. Address: Glasgow Sheriff Court,

Sheriff Clerk's Office, Sheriff Court House, 1 Carlton Place, Glasgow G5 9DA; T.-0141 429 8888.

Kerr, Liam, MA. MSP (Scottish Conservative), North East Scotland region, since 2016; Shadow Cabinet Secretary, Net Zero, Energy and Transport, since 2021; Scottish Conservatives Shadow Cabinet Secretary for Justice, 2017-2021; Deputy Leader of the Scottish Conservative Party, 2019-2020; b. 23.1.75. Educ. George Watson's College; University of St Andrews; University of Edinburgh; University of Law; Open University. Career history: Trainee Solicitor, Coffin Mew & Clover, 2001-04; Solicitor, Ledingham Chalmers, 2004-06; Senior Associate Employment Lawyer, McGrigors, 2006-2011; In-House Employment Law Adviser (Secondment), KPMG UK, 2010-11; Lecturer/tutor, Robert Gordon University, 2006-2012; Senior Associate Employer Lawyer, CMS Cameron McKenna, 2011-15; Contractor, Allen & Overy, 2015-16; appointed Managing Director, Employment Lawyer, Notary Public, Trinity Kerr Limited in 2015. Non-Executive Director, Family Mediation (Grampian), 2004-07; Non-Executive Director, Aberdeen Foyer, 2007-13. Address: Scottish Parliament, Edinburgh EH99 1SP.

Kerr, Lisa, BA Hons (Music). Principal, Gordonstoun School, since 2017; Deputy Lieutenant, Moray, since 2019. Educ. City of Edinburgh Music School; University of York. Career history: Presenter and Producer, Radio Forth, 1993; Producer, Classic FM, 1993-95; Managing Director, Radio Services Ltd (part of Radio Investments), 1995-2001; Director, Salisbury International Arts Festival, 2002-05; External Affairs Manager, Commercial Radio Companies Association, 2001-06; Director of External Affairs, RadioCentre, 2006-2010; Director, Broadcast Training & Skills Regulator, 2009-2011; Director of Strategy, RadioCentre, 2010-2011; Vice Chairman, Scottish Opera, 2006-2014; Governor, Gordonstoun Schools, 2006-2016; Owner, Lisa Kerr Media & Communications Consultancy, 2012-17; Member, UK & Ireland Regulatory Sub-Board, Royal Institution of Chartered Surveyors, 2012-2018; appointed Principal Designate, Gordonstoun School in 2016. Conductor, The Lantern Singers. Address: Gordonstoun School, Elgin, Moray IV30 5RF; T.-01343 837837; e-mail: principalpa@gordonstoun.org.uk

Kerr, Michelle, MBE. Scottish football manager; Head Coach, Scotland women's team, 2017-2020; b. 15.10.69, Broxburn. Senior career: Edinburgh Dynamo; Inveralmond Thistle; Heart of Midlothian; Giuliano's, 2001-02; Kilmarnock, 2002-05; Doncaster Rovers Belles, 2005-07; Hibernian, 2007-08; Spartans, 2008-2010; Scotland National team, 1989-2008. Teams managed: Kilmarnock, 2004; Hibernian, 2007-08; Spartans, 2008-2010; Scotland U19, 2009-13; Arsenal, 2013-14, Stirling University FC, 2014-17. Honours include: Honorary degree, University of Stirling; Scottish Women's Premier League, 2017 (player); Scottish Cup, 2007, 2008 (player); FA Women's Cup, Arsenal, 2013, 2014 (manager); FA WSL Cup, 2013, Arsenal (manager); Queen's Park Shield, 2016-17, Stirling University (manager).

Kerr, Norman, OBE. Director and Company Secretary, Energy Action Scotland, 2005-2020 (retired). Car Industry, Engineer, 1971-81; Heatwise Glasgow (now The Wise Group), Insulation Supervisor then Production Unit Manager, 1984-96; Development Manager and Deputy Director, Energy Action Scotland, 1996-2005. Trustee: National Energy Action, Scottish Power's Energy People Trust, Aberdeen Heat and Power Company, the Claremount Trust. Awarded an OBE in the Queen's Birthday Honours list 2016 for services to the Children's Hearing System in Scotland and for voluntary and charitable work in Glasgow.

Served 32 years in the Children's Hearing system as a volunteer holding a number of posts at local and national levels before stepping down in June 2016.

Kerr, Rev. Mgr. Philip John, PhB, STL. Minister of Religion, St Paul's Parish RC Church, Glenrothes; former Parish Priest, St Patrick's, Edinburgh; Vicar General, Archdiocese of St. Andrews and Edinburgh, 2000-2016; b. 23.4.56, Edinburgh. Educ. Holy Cross Academy; St. Augustine's High School, Edinburgh; Scots College and Gregorian University, Rome. Assistant Priest, St. Francis Xavier's, Falkirk, 1980-82; Lecturer in Systematic Theology, St. Andrew's College, Drygrange, 1982-86; Vice-Rector and Lecturer in Systematic Theology, Gillis College, Edinburgh, 1986-93; Lecturer in Systematic Theology, Scotus College, Bearsden, 1993-96; R.C. Chaplain, Stirling University, 1993-99; Parish Priest: Sacred Heart, Cowie, 1993-99, Our Lady and St. Ninian, Bannockburn, 1996-99, St. Francis Xavier, Falkirk, 1999-2014. Recreations: classical music; theatre; walking. Address: St Paul's RC Church, Warout Road, Glenrothes KY7 4ER.

Kerr, Stephen Charles. MSP (Scottish Conservative and Unionist Party), Central Scotland (Region), since 2021; Chief Whip of the Scottish Conservative Party, since 2021; MP (Conservative), Stirling, 2017-19; b. 26.9.60, Dundee; m., Yvonne; 4 c. Educ. University of Stirling. Worked for Kimberly Clark before election to Parliament. Conservative Party candidate in Stirling at both the 2005 and 2015 general elections. Member of The Church of Jesus Christ of Latter-day Saints (Mormons); has served in a number of positions in the LDS Church, including as an area seventy (2006-2013). Address: The Scottish Parliament, Edinburgh EH99 1SP; T.-0131 348 5616.
E-mail: Stephen.Kerr.msp@parliament.scot

Kerr, Cllr Tom, ChEng, FIMarE. Provost of West Lothian, since 2007; Councillor, Linlithgow, since 1992; b. 22.07.46, Linlithgow; m., Marion; 1 s.; 1 d. Educ. Linlithgow Academy; Glasgow College of Nautical Studies. Engineer Cadet - Chief Engineer (BP Tanker Co. Ltd), 1962-76; Senior Lecturer: Glasgow College of Nautical Studies, 1976-84, Jeddah, Saudi Arabia (Gray MacKenzie) Inchcape Group; self employed marine consultant, 1988-2009; elected councillor - Linlithgow, 1992-2009. Royal Society of Arts and Institute of Marine Engineers Silver Medal Winner, 1976; various local government committees and local voluntary groups. Recreations: cricket; reading and travel. Address: (b.) West Lothian Council, West Lothian Civic Centre, Howden South Road, Livingston EH54 6FF; T.-01506 281728.

Kerr, William Revill, LLB, LLM, MSc, MBA, PhD, FCG, FCIM, FIH. General Manager, The Glasgow Academy, 2003-2018; Director, Blackhill Consultancy, since 2018; b. 26.4.48, East Kilbride; m. Educ. Duncanrig Senior Secondary School, East Kilbride; Glasgow University; Strathclyde University; Glasgow Caledonian University; Robert Gordon University. Former Secretary, Malin Housing Association, 1988-2003; Chair, Scottish Enterprise Ayrshire, 2000-03; Advisory Board Member, Scottish Enterprise, 2001-02; Ambassador, Princes Scottish Youth Business Trust, 2000-07. Local Enterprise Company Chairs Group, 2000-03; Director, Scottish Enterprise Ayrshire, 1998-2003; Director, Investors in People, Scotland, 2000-02; Director, Ayrshire Development Loan Fund, 2000-02; Director, Business Excellence Ayrshire, 1998-2000; Director, Springboard, 1998-2000; Member, Scottish Disability Consulting Group, 1999-2000; Member, Scottish Qualifications Authority SVQ Advisory Board, 1998-2000; Chairman, Ayrshire and Arran Tourism Industries Forum,

1993-2000; Vice-Chairman, Scotland Committee, British Hospitality Association, 2001; Panel Member, Investors in People, 1997-2001. Publication: Tourism, Public Policy and the Strategic Management of Failure, 2003. Recreations: sport; writing; old books; gardening. Address: (h.) 2 Uist Way, Doonfoot, Ayr KA7 4GF; (m.) 07711 798 756; e-mail: williamrevillkerr@gmail.com

Kesting, Very. Rev. Dr. Sheilagh Margaret. Moderator of The General Assembly of The Church of Scotland, 2007-08; Secretary, Ecumenical Relations, Church of Scotland, 1993-2016 (retired); b. 10.6.53, Stornoway. Educ. Nicolson Institute; Edinburgh University. Parish Minister: Overtown, Lanarkshire, 1980-86, St. Andrews High, Musselburgh, 1986-93. Recreations: gardening; photography; embroidery.

Kettle, Ann Julia, OBE, MA, FSA, FRHistS, FRSA; b. 2.8.39, Orpington. Educ. Lewes Grammar School; St. Hugh's College, Oxford. University of St. Andrews: Hebdomadar, 1991-94, Dean of Arts, 1998-2002; President, Association of University Teachers (Scotland), 1994-96; Member, Scottish (Garrick) Committee of National (Dearing) Committee of Inquiry into Higher Education, 1996-97; Member, Scottish Higher Education Funding Council, 1997-2000; Trustee, Arts and Humanities Research Board, 2001-05; Trustee, Newbattle Abbey College, since 2012; Chair, Board of Governors, Newbattle Abbey College, 2004-2010. Address: Sunset View, Ellice Place, St. Andrews KY16 9HU; T.-01334 473057; e-mail: ajk@st-andrews.ac.uk

Khan, Asif. Director, Scottish Poetry Library, since 2016. Educ. University of Stirling. Career history: business development, marketing and engagement roles covering public libraries and literature to the visual and performing arts in Bristol and London; led on national cultural policy for the Bicentenary of the Abolition of the Slave Trade commemorative programme in 2007; wrote the international visual arts strategy for Barbados in 2009 as an associate of the Cultural Leadership Programme; invited by the Government of Jamaica to produce a showcase event with their new Poet Laureate, Mervyn Morris and emerging Jamaican writers in 2014 following the success of the Yardstick Festival in Bristol and Bath showcasing contemporary poets and writers from the African Diaspora; also produced a poetry festival on the theme of Climate Change for Bristol and Bath Festival of Nature. Address: Scottish Poetry Library, 5 Crichton's Close, Canongate, Edinburgh EH8 8DT; T.-0131 557 2876.
E-mail: asif.khan@spl.org.uk

Khan, Uzma, MA (Hons) Econ, MSc (BusEcon). Director of Planning and Deputy Secretary, University of Glasgow, since 2020; Executive Director for Research and Innovation; b. 1.77. Educ. University of Glasgow; University of Strathclyde. Career history: Economic Adviser roles, The Scottish Government, 1999-2013; Rail Policy Infrastructure, Transport Scotland, 2013-15; The Scottish Government: Head of Economic Policy and Strategy, 2015-16; Deputy Director for Economic Strategy, 2016-19; Deputy Director for Economic Policy, 2019-2020; Economy Covid-19 Response Hub, Programme Director (Strategy), 2020. Trustee: Poverty Alliance, David Hume Institute. Address: University of Glasgow, University Avenue, Glasgow G12 8QQ; T.-0141 330 3839.
E-mail: Uzma.Khan@glasgow.ac.uk

Kidd, Bill. MSP (SNP), Glasgow Anniesland, since 2011, Glasgow, 2007-2011; SNP Chief Whip in the Scottish Parliament, 2012-18; SPPA Committee Convener, since 2018; b. 24.7.56, Glasgow. Address: Scottish Parliament, Edinburgh EH99 1SP.

Kidd, Professor Colin Craig, MA, DPhil, FBA, FRHistS, FSA (Scot), FRSE. Professor of History, University of St Andrews; b. 5.5.64. Educ. Gonville and Caius College,

Cambridge University; All Souls, Oxford University. Career history: University of Glasgow until 2010, then Professor of Intellectual History and the History of Political Thought, Queen's University Belfast. Fellow of All Souls College, Oxford (1987-94 and 2005-2019) and a regular contributor to the London Review of Books, The New Statesman and The Guardian; held fellowships at Oxford and Harvard Universities. Publications include: "Subverting Scotland's Past: Scottish Whig Historians and the Creation of an Anglo-British Identity 1689-1830" (1993); "British Identities Before Nationalism: Ethnicity and Nationhood in the Atlantic World, 1600-1800" (1999); "The Forging of Races: Race and Scripture in the Protestant Atlantic World, 1600-2000" (2006) and "Union and Unionisms: Political Thought in Scotland, 1500-2000" (2008); "The World of Mr Casaubon" (2016). Recreations: Watergate; Galloway. Address: School of History, Modern History, St Katharine's Lodge, The Scores, St Andrews KY16 9BA.

Kidd, Mary Helen (May), JP, MA. World President, Associated Country Women of The World, 2010-2013; Deputy World President, Associated Country Women of The World, 2007-2010; Area President (Europe and the Mediterranean), Associated Country Women and the Council, 2001-07; former Member, Advisory Board and Council, Scottish Agricultural College; m., Neil M.L. Kidd; 2 s. Educ. Brechin High School; Edinburgh University. Retired farmer; former Member: MAFF Consumer Panel, Scottish Consumer Council, Women's National Commission; National Chairman, Scottish Women's Rural Institutes, 1993-96. Recreations: playing piano and organ; creative writing. Address: (h.) 'Holemill', 5 Bon Scott Place, Kirriemuir, Angus DD8 4LD.

Kidd, Steven, BA (Hons). Professional Adviser (Scotland), UNICEF UK, since 2017. Educ. The Open University (Social Sciences with Politics and Economics; Diploma, Politcs and Government). Career history: Development Officer, Learning and Teaching Scotland, Glasgow, 2011; Development Manager, Scottish Youth Parliament, Edinburgh, 2004-2014; Education Programme Manager, Glasgow 2014 Limited, 2013-14; Project Manager, UK Programmes, Scotland, 2014-17, UNICEF UK. Currently working in child rights education for UNICEF UK; non-executive director of YouthBank Scotland. Member, Scotland Advisory Council, British Council, since 2018. Address: British Council Scotland, Waverley Gate (Fourth Floor), 2-4 Waterloo Place, Edinburgh EH1 3EG.

Kilbride, Professor Lynn, BA, MSc, PGCertEd, PhD. Vice Principal for Academic Development and Student Experience, Robert Gordon University, Aberdeen; former Dean of the School of Health Sciences, University of Dundee. Educ. Glasgow Caledonian University; The University of Edinburgh; Edinburgh Napier University. Career history: Research Nurse, NHS Lothian, 1997-99; Lecturer/Practitioner, Queen Margaret University, 2004-07; Professor/International Business Development, Edinburgh Napier University, 2010-2014; External Assessor and Workshop Facilitator, British Council, SCVC, Saudi Arabia, Lithuania, Malaysia, China, since 2010; Head of Department, Nursing and Community, Glasgow Caledonian University, 2014-17. Co-Convenor of the Council of Deans, Health Scotland; works closely with Scottish Government and NHS Education for Scotland. Address: Robert Gordon University, Garthdee House, Garthdee Road, Garthdee, Aberdeen AB10 7AQ.

Kilgour, Robert Dow. Property developer, investor, philanthropist and entreprenuer; Co-Founder and Chairman, British Civic Institute, Edinburgh, since 2022; Co-Founder and Ambassador, Better Local Ltd, Scotland, since 2022;

Founder and Chief Executive Officer, Dow Investments Plc, London, since 1990; b. 5.57, Edinburgh; m. (1); 4 c; m. (2), Jacqueline. Educ. Craigflower School; Loretto School; University of Stirling. Career history: Founder and Managing Director: Linden Hotel Ltd, Edinburgh, 1982-87, Four Seasons Health Care (Services) Ltd, Fife, 1990-94; Non Executive Director, Cochrane McGregor, Edinburgh and London, 1992-94; Founder and Managing Director/Chairman/Joint Chief Executive/Group Commercial Director, Four Seasons Health Care, 1987-2000; Co-Founder and Chairman/CEO/Deputy Chairman, CamVista Ltd, Fife, 1999-2002; Founder Shareholder and Non Executive Chairman, Kingdom FM, Fife, 2007-2019; Non Executive Director, Hamilton Kilgour Ltd, London, 2009-2021; Founder and Director, My Care Staff Ltd, Kirkcaldy, Fife, since 2017; Founder and Chairman, Scottish Business UK, since 2017; Director, Robert Kilgour Ltd, London, since 2015; Non Executive Director: StoriiCare, London and US, since 2017, Borland Insurance, London, since 2018, Morphose Capital Partners, London and Hong Kong, since 2015; Co-Founder and Non Executive Director, NW Security Group, Hoylake and London, since 2004; Advisory Board Director, E2E, London, since 2020; Founder and Executive Chairman, Renaissance Care (Scotland), since 2004; Advisory Council Member, The TaxPayers' Alliance, London, since 2021; appointed as the first Macmillan Cancer Support Ambassador in December 2018. Recreations: travel; tennis; skiing; politics. Address: Robert Kilgour Ltd, Archibald Hope House, Straiton Road, Musselburgh EH21 7PQ.

Killeen, Jackie. Director of Regulation, Equality and Human Rights Commission, since 2021, Director of Compliance, 2020-21. Educ. University of Glasgow; University College Dublin. Career history: Head of Policy & External Relations, New Opportunities Fund, 2002-05; Big Lottery Fund: Head of Policy & Public Affairs, 2004-2010, Director, Scotland, 2010-16; Director, Scotland, British Council, 2016-2020; Acting Director, UK Region, British Council, 2018-19. Board Trustee: Evaluation Support Scotland, since 2018, Shelter UK, since 2019. Address: Equality and Human Rights Commission, 151 West George Street, Glasgow G2 2JJ; T.-0141 228 5910.

Killen, Gerard. MP (Labour), Rutherglen and Hamilton West, 2017-19; b. 1.5.86; m., Peter. Educ. Trinity High School, Rutherglen. Joined the Labour Party in 2007 and was elected as a Councillor for the Rutherglen South ward of South Lanarkshire Council at a 2013 by-election; retained council seat at the 2017 UK local elections (Rutherglen Central and North ward).

Kilshaw, David Andrew George, OBE. Solicitor, since 1979; Chairman, Borders Health Board, 1993-2001; b. 18.3.53, Glencoe; 3 s. Educ. Keil School, Dumbarton. Traineeship, Brunton Miller, Solicitors, Glasgow, 1975-80; Solicitor, Borders Regional Council, 1980-83; Partner, Cullen Kilshaw Solicitors and Estate Agents, Galashiels, Hawick, Jedburgh, Melrose, Peebles, Kelso and Selkirk, since 1983; Chair: Borders Solicitors Property Centre, since 2000, Border Reivers Professional Rugby Team Board, 2006. Recreation: golf. Address: (b.) Waverley Chambers, Ladhope Vale, Galashiels TD1 1BW.

Kinclaven, Lord (Alexander Featherstonhaugh Wylie), OBE, QC, LLB, FCIArb. Lawyer; Member of the Scottish Bar, since 1978; b. 2.6.51, Perth; m., Gail Elizabeth Watson Duncan; 2 d. Educ. Edinburgh University. Qualified Solicitor in Scotland, 1976; called to Scottish Bar, 1978; Standing Junior Counsel to Accountant of Court, 1986-89; Advocate Depute, 1989-92; called to English Bar, 1990; QC (Scot), 1991. Part-time Joint Chairman, Discipline Committee, Institute of Chartered Accountants of Scotland, 1994-2005; Member, Scottish Legal Aid Board, 1994-2002; part-time Sheriff, 2000-05; part-time Chairman, Police Appeals Tribunal, 2001-05; Member, Scottish Criminal Cases Review Commission, 2004-05; Senator of the College of Justice, 2005-2020; Convener, Children in Scotland, 2012-17; Bencher, Lincoln's Inn, 2018. Address: (b.) Parliament House, Edinburgh EH1 1RQ.

King, Emeritus Professor Bernard, CBE, MSc, PhD, CCMI, CBiol, FRSB. Principal and Vice-Chancellor, University of Abertay, Dundee, 1992-2011; b. 4.5.46, Dublin; m., Maura Antoinette Collinge; 2 d. Educ. Synge St. Christian Brothers School, Dublin; College of Technology, Dublin; University of Aston in Birmingham. Research Fellow, University of Aston, 1972-76; Dundee Institute of Technology, 1976-91: Lecturer, Senior Lecturer, Head, Department of Molecular and Life Sciences, Dean, Faculty of Science; Assistant Principal, Robert Gordon Institute of Technology/Robert Gordon University, 1991-92. Governor, Board, Unicorn Preservation Society; Board of Higher Education Academy, 2007-2010; Vice-Chair, Universities Scotland, 2006-2010; Convenor, Universities Scotland and Vice-President, Universities UK, 2010-2011. Recreations: reading; music; sailing. Address: (h.) 11 Dalhousie Place, Arbroath, DD11 2BT; T.-01382 308012.

King, Professor David Neden, MA, DPhil, CertEd. Emeritus Professor of Economics, Stirling University, since 2009; b. 10.04.45, Birmingham; m., Victoria Susan Robinson; 2 s. Educ. Gresham's School, Norfolk; Magdalen College, Oxford; York University. Consultant Economist, Royal Commission on the Constitution, 1971-72; Economics Master and Head of Economics, Winchester College, 1972-78; Lecturer, Stirling University, 1978-87; Economic Adviser, Department of the Environment, 1987-88; Senior Lecturer, Stirling University, 1987-2002, Professor of Public Economics, 2002-09. Conductor, Stirling University Choir, 1990-2009. Consultant to OECD and the World Bank. Publications: Financial and Economic Aspects of Regionalism and Separatism, 1973; Taxes on Immovable Property, 1983; Fiscal Tiers: the Economics of Multi-level Government, 1984 and 2016; An Introduction to National Income Accounting, 1984; Banking and Money, 1987; The Complete Works of Robert and James Adam, 1991 and 2001; Local Government Economics in Theory and Practice (Editor), 1992 and 2022; Financial Claims and Derivatives, 1999; Unbuilt Adam, 2001; Economics, 2012; Adam Ceilings: a Geometric Study, 2020. Recreations: architecture; music. Address: (b.) Division of Economics, Stirling University, Stirling FK9 4LA; T.-01786 473171. E-mail: d.n.king@stir.ac.uk

King, Dr Elspeth Russell, MA, FMA, DUniv. Curator, writer and social historian. Former Director, Smith Art Gallery and Museum, Stirling (1994-2018); b. 29.3.49, Lochore, Fife. Educ. Beath High School; St. Andrews University; Leicester University. Curator, People's Palace, Glasgow, 1974-91, with responsibility for building up the social history collections for the city of Glasgow; Director, Dunfermline Heritage Trust, 1991-94; responsible for restoration of, and new displays in, Abbot House. Honorary Doctorate, Stirling University, 2005; Fletcher Award, Saltire Society, 2006. Publications include: The Thenew Factor: the hidden history of women in Glasgow, 1993; Blind Harry's Wallace by Hamilton of Gilbertfield (Editor), 1998; Stirling Girls, 2003; The Face of Wallace, 2005; A History of Stirling in 100 Objects, 2011.

King, Dr. Steve, MBE. Composer/Music Educationalist; Director of Music, Heriot-Watt University, since 1998; Viola Player, Scottish Chamber Orchestra, since 1984; b. 4.12.56, Waltham Cross; 2 s. Educ. Queen Eleanor Grammar School; Royal Northern College of Music. E-mail: s.king@hw.ac.uk

Kingarth, Rt. Hon. Lord (Hon. Derek Emslie), QC. Senator of the College of Justice, 1997-2010; b. 21.6.49. Educ. Cambridge University; Edinburgh University. Advocate, 1974; Advocate Depute 1985-1988.

Kinloch, Professor Maggie. Professor Emerita of The Royal Conservatoire of Scotland (Deputy Principal, 2006-2016); Director, Scottish Funding Council, since 2012; former Board Member, Creative Scotland; b. 7.54. Career history: worked at a senior level, nationally and internationally, as a theatre director and teacher; currently a freelance theatre director and international arts education consultant; deep practical experience of, and commitment to, Equality, Diversity and Inclusion in the Arts and Arts Education; experienced strategic thinker and currently serves as Chair of the Scottish Drama Training Network and as a Director of the the European League of Institutes of the Arts; a founding director of the Board of the National Theatre of Scotland; former Chair of Glasgay and has wide experience on a range of other boards.

Kinnaird, Alison, MBE, MA, FGE. Glass Engraver and Artist; Clarsach Player; b. 30.4.49, Edinburgh; m., Robin Morton; 1 s.; 1 d. Educ. George Watson's Ladies College; Edinburgh University. Freelance glass artist, since 1971; exhibitions in Edinburgh, 1978, 1981, 1985, in London, 1988, 1995; work in many public and private collections; professional musician, since 1970; has produced three LPs as well as film and TV music; served on Council, Scottish Craft Centre, 1974-76; Council, SSWA, 1975-76; Member: BBC Scottish Music Advisory Committee, 1981-84, BBC Broadcasting Council for Scotland, 1984-88, SAC Crafts Commitee, 1993-96; awarded: SDA/CCC Craft Fellowship, 1980, Glass-Sellers of London Award, 1987, Creative Scotland Award, 2002. Recreations: children; cooking; garden. Address: (h.) Shillinghill, Temple, Midlothian EH23 4SH; T.-01875 830328.

Kinniburgh, Cllr David. Provost, Argyll and Bute Council; Councillor (Conservative), Helensburgh and Lomond South; b. 1959; m., Linda; 2 s. Educ. Hermitage Academy. Career history: served apprenticeship as a motor vehicle technician at a local garage in Helensburgh; left the motor trade in 1983 and, for over six years, worked in the insurance industry; employed by Helensburgh Toyota, since 1990; played various roles within the company, including technician, workshop controller, sales executive, and service advisor; Argyll and Bute Council: served on the Council's Audit Committee, 2007-2012; served on Planning, Protective Services, and Licensing Committee (PPSL); member of the administration which ran the council, 2010-2012; appointed a Senior Councillor as the Policy Lead for Planning and Regulatory Services in 2013. Member of several Burns Clubs; Past President of Helensburgh Burns Club; currently Treasurer of the Club. Recreations: enjoys playing golf; cooking. Address: 15 Fraser Avenue, Dumbarton G82 3LS; T.-01389 768412. E-mail: david.kinniburgh@argyll-bute.gov.uk

Kinnoull, 16th Earl of (Charles William Harley Hay); b. 20.12.62; m., Clare; 3 d.; 1 s. Educ. Eton College; Christ Church, Oxford. Qualified barrister; worked for insurance provider Hiscox for 25 years; also farms in Perthshire. Succeeded to title, 2013.

Kinross, Lord (Christopher Patrick Balfour), LLB, WS. Solicitor, 1975-2009 (retired); b. 1.10.49, Edinburgh; m., Susan Jane Pitman (divorced); m. (2), Catherine Taylor LLB; 2 s. Educ. Eton College; Edinburgh University. Member, Royal Company of Archers, Queen's Bodyguard for Scotland. Recreations: off-road motorsport; shooting.

Kinsman, Stewart Hayes, OBE, BSc, FRICS. Chief Executive, Hanover (Scotland) Housing Association Ltd., 1979-2007; Chairman, Edinburgh Flood Prevention Group, 2000-06; b. 18.9.43, Burntisland, Fife; 1 s.; 1 d. Educ.

Kirkcaldy High School; Heriot-Watt University. Chartered Surveyor, 1966-71; Estates and Buildings Officer, Stirling University, 1971-76; Regional Manager, Hanover Housing Association (GB), 1976-79. Chairman, Scottish Federation of Housing Associations, 1998-2001. Recreations: sailing; wines; digital photography; natural history. Address: (h.) 14 Dryburn Brae, West Linton EH46 7JG; T.-01968 660 198.

Kintore, 14th Earl of (James William Falconer Keith); b. 1976. Succeeded to title, 2004.

Kirby, Mike. Scottish Secretary, UNISON Scotland. Address: (b.) UNISON House, 14 West Campbell Street, Glasgow G2 6RX; T.-0845 355 0845. E-mail: m.kirby@unison.co.uk

Kirchin, David, LLB (Hons). Head of Scotland and Corporate Partner, Addleshaw Goddard LLP, since 2017; b. 9.72. Educ. Rijksuniversiteit, Leiden, The Netherlands; University of Edinburgh. Career history: Legal Adviser, BP Exploration, Aberdeen, 2000-2002; Partner, HBJ Gateley, Edinburgh, 2002-2017. Member, Law Society of Scotland. Address: Addleshaw Goddard LLP, Exchange Tower, 19 Canning Street, Edinburgh EH3 8EH; T.-0131 222 9813. E-mail: david.kirchin@addleshawgoddard.com

Kirk, David, MA, BM, BCh, DM, FRCS (Eng), FRCS-RCPS (Glas), FRCS (Edin); b. 26.5.43, Bradford; m., Gillian Mary Wroot; 1 s.; 2 d. Educ. King Edwards School, Birmingham; Balliol College, Oxford; Oxford University Clinical Medical School. Resident House Physician and House Surgeon, Radcliffe Infirmary, Oxford; University Demonstrator, Oxford; clinical surgical posts, Oxford and Bristol; Arris and Gale Lecturer, Royal College of Surgeons (England), 1980-81; rotating surgical Registrar appointment, Sheffield; academic surgical research, Sheffield University; Senior Registrar in General Surgery, then in Urology, Bristol; Honorary Clinical Lecturer, Glasgow University, 1984-95; Consultant Urological Surgeon, NHS Greater Glasgow, 1982-2005; Honorary Professor, Glasgow University, 1995-2005; Examiner in Surgery, Royal College of Physicians and Surgeons of Glasgow, 1983-2011; Assessor for IMRCS (Intercollegiate Membership of Royal College of Surgeons) Examinations, 2011-14; Lead Assessor, 2012-14; College representative on IMRCS Quality Assurance Committee, 2008-2014. Secretary/Treasurer, 1983-85, Chairman, 1985-88, Scottish Urological Oncology Group; Council Member: Urology Section, Royal Society of Medicine, 1984-87, British Association of Urological Surgeons, 1988-91; Chairman: Prostate Forum, 1991-94, Intercollegiate Board in Urology, 1994-97; Specialist Adviser in Urology, National Medical Advisory Committee (Scottish Executive), 1996-2004; Member, Specialist Advisory Committee in Urology, Joint Committee on Higher Surgical Training, 1999-2004; President, Scottish Urology Society, 2004-06; Chair, Forth Valley Branch, Cruse Bereavement Care Scotland, 2004-07; Performance Assessor, General Medical Council, 2006-2010; Clinical Adviser, Healthcare Commission, 2007-09; Elder, Dunblane Cathedral; Trustee, Dunblane Cathedral Trust, 2004-2010; Convener, Pastoral Care Committee, 2014; Society of Friends, Dunblane Cathedral: Council Member, 2006-09 and 2011-14, Executive Comm. member and Trustee, since 2014, Convener of Projects Comm., 2014. Publications: Understanding Prostate Disorders (author); Managing Prostate Disease (author); International Handbook of Prostate Cancer (editor); book chapters and original papers on urological cancer and other topics; annual articles on the history of The Society of Friends of Dunblane Cathedral and related topics: Journal of Society of Friends, 2011-17. Recreations: skiing; hill-walking/rambling; classical music; gardening; cooking.

Address: (h.) 4 Young Road, Dunblane FK15 0FT; T.-01786 439799; e-mail: kirkdavid71@gmail.com

Kirk, Professor James, MA, PhD, DLitt, FRHistS, FRSE. Professor of Scottish History, Glasgow University, 1999-2005; Hon. Professorial Research Fellow in Ecclesiastical History, School of Divinity, University of Glasgow, 2006-09; b. 18.10.44, Falkirk; m., Dr. Daphne Waters. Educ. Stirling High School; Edinburgh University. Lecturer in Scottish History, Glasgow University, 1972-89, Senior Lecturer, 1989-90, Reader, 1990-99. David Berry Prize, Royal Historical Society, 1973; Wolfson Award, 1977; Hume Brown Senior Prize in Scottish History, 1977; British Academy Major Research Awards, 1989-96; ESRC Research Award, 1993-95. President, Scottish Church History Society, 1989-92; Hon. Secretary: Scottish Record Society, since 1973, Scottish Society for Reformation History, 1980-90; Scottish Section Editor, Royal Historical Society, Annual Bibliography of British and Irish History; an Associate Editor, The New Dictionary of National Biography, 1998. Publications: The University of Glasgow 1451-1577, 1977; Records of the Synod of Lothian and Tweeddale, 1977; The Second Book of Discipline, 1980; Stirling Presbytery Records, 1981; Visitation of the Diocese of Dunblane, 1984; Patterns of Reform, 1989; Humanism and Reform, 1991; The Books of Assumption of the Thirds of Benefices: Scottish Ecclesiastical Rentals at the Reformation, 1995; Scotland's History (Editor), 1995; The Medieval Church in Scotland (Editor), 1995; Her Majesty's Historiographer, 1996; Calendar of Scottish Supplications to Rome 1447-1471, vol. 5 (Editor), 1997; The Church in the Highlands (Editor), 1998; The Scottish Churches, Politics and the Union Parliament (Editor), 2001; Contributor to: The Renaissance and Reformation in Scotland, 1983; Voluntary Religion, 1986; The Seventeenth Century in the Highlands, 1986; Scotland Revisited, 1991; Encyclopedia of the Reformed Faith, 1992, Dictionary of Scottish Church History and Theology, 1993, The Oxford Encyclopedia of the Reformation, 1996; John Knox and the British Reformations, 1999; The New Dictionary of National Biography, 2004; Caindel Alban: Fèill-sgriobhainn do Dhòmhnall E. Meek, 2008. Recreations: living in Wester Ross; viticulture. Address: (h.) Woodlea, Dunmore, Stirlingshire FK2 8LY; T.-01324 831240.
E-mail: jameskirk1810@gmail.com

Kirkhill, Baron (John Farquharson Smith); b. 7.5.30; m.; 1 step d. Lord Provost of Aberdeen, 1971-75; Minister of State, Scottish Office, 1975-78; Chairman, North of Scotland Hydro-Electric Board, 1979-82; Delegate, Parliamentary Assembly, Council of Europe, and W.E.U., 1987-2000 (Chairman, Committee on Legal Affairs and Human Rights, 1991-95); Hon LLD, Aberdeen University, 1974.

Kirkwood of Kirkhope, Lord (Archy Kirkwood), Kt, BSc; b. 22.4.46, Glasgow; m., Rosemary Chester (deceased); 1 s.; 1 d. Educ. Cranhill School; Heriot-Watt University. Solicitor; Aide to Sir David Steel, 1971-75, 1977-78; MP (Liberal Democrat), Roxburgh and Berwickshire, 1983-2005; Liberal Spokesman on Health and Social Services, and on Social Security, 1985-87; Alliance Spokesman on Overseas Development, 1987; Liberal Scottish Whip, 1987-88; Social and Liberal Democrat Convener on Welfare, Health and Education, 1988-89; Liberal Democrat Deputy Chief Whip, and Spokesman on Welfare and Social Security, 1989-92; Community Care, 1994-97; Chief Whip, 1993-97; Chairman, Work and Pensions Select Committee (formerly Social Security Select Committee), 1997-2005. Former Trustee, Joseph Rowntree Reform Trust; former Governor, Westminster Foundation for Democracy. Recreations: music; photography. Address: (b.) House of Lords, London SW1A 0PW.

Kirkwood, Robert. Head of the Office of the Chief Executive, NHS Scotland. Address: Scottish Government, St. Andrew's House, Regent Road, Edinburgh EH1 3DG.

Kitchen, John Philip, MBE, MA, BMus, PhD (Cantab), FRCO, LRAM. Senior Lecturer in Music, Edinburgh University, 1987-2014; Honorary Fellow, Reid School of Music, 2015-2018; Tutor, St Mary's Music School Edinburgh. Concert Organist, Harpsichordist, Pianist; Edinburgh City Organist, since 2002; b. 27.10.50, Airdrie. Educ. Coatbridge High School; Glasgow University; Cambridge University. Lecturer in Music, St. Andrews University, 1976-87; Harpsichordist/Organist, Scottish Early Music Consort, 1977-98; BBC and commercial recordings; music reviewer; Director of Music, Old Saint Paul's Episcopal Church, Edinburgh. Recreations: more music; restaurants.

Knops, Professor Robin John, BSc, PhD, Hon.DSc, FRSE. Emeritus Professor of Mathematics, Heriot-Watt University; b. 30.12.32, London; m., Margaret; 4 s.; 2 d. Educ. Nottingham University. Nottingham University: Assistant Lecturer in Mathematics, 1956-59, Lecturer in Mathematics, 1959-62; Newcastle-upon-Tyne University: Lecturer in Applied Mathematics, 1962-68, Reader in Continuum Mechanics, 1968-71; Professor of Mathematics, Heriot-Watt University, Edinburgh, 1971-98 (Head, Department of Mathematics, 1971-83; Dean of Science, 1984-87, Vice Principal, 1988-95; Special Adviser to the Principal, 1995-97). Visiting Professor: Cornell University, 1967 and 1968; University of California, Berkeley, 1968; Pisa University, 1974; Ecole Polytechnique Federale Lausanne, Switzerland, 1980; Royal Society of Edinburgh: Council Member, 1982-92, Executive Committee Member, 1982-92, Meetings Secretary, 1982-87, Chief Executive Editor, Proceedings A, 1982-87, Curator, 1987-92; President: Edinburgh Mathematical Society, 1974-75, International Society for the Interaction of Mechanics and Mathematics, President, 1991-95 (Vice-President, 1995-99, Senior Medal, 2020); Editor, Applied Mathematics and Mathematical Computation, 1990-2002; Convener, Executive Committee, International Centre for Mathematical Sciences, Edinburgh, 1996-99; Leverhulme Emeritus Fellowship, 2000-02. Publications: Uniqueness Theories in Linear Elasticity (Co-author), 1971; Theory of Elastic Stability (Co-author), 1973. Recreations: reading; speculation. Address: (b.) School of Mathematical and Computer Sciences, Colin Maclaurin Building, Heriot-Watt University, Edinburgh EH14 4AS; T.-0131-451 3363; e-mail: r.j.knops@hw.ac.uk

Knottenbelt, Dr Clare Margaret, BVSc, MSc, DSAM, MRCUS. Director and Oncology Consultant, Hawk and Dove Ltd; Director, Equine Medical Solutions Ltd; Professor of Small Animal Medicine and Oncology, University of Glasgow, since 2010; b. 5.2.70, Edinburgh; m., David Henderson; 2 d. Educ. Arundel School, Harare, Zimbabwe; Bristol University; Masters by Research, University of Edinburgh. Veterinary Surgeon, Yorkshire, 1994-95; Petsavers Resident in Small Animal Medicine, University of Edinburgh, 1995-99; Lecturer in Small Animal Medicine, Glasgow University, 2000-06, Senior Clinician in Small Animal Medicine and Oncology, 2006-2010. Address: 26 Lampson Road, Killearn, Stirlingshire G63 9PD; T.-0141 628 0666.
E-mail: clarek@hawkanddovevets.co.uk

Knox, James Richard Dunsmuir, MA, MBA, FSA (Scot). Director, Fleming-Wyfold Art Foundation, since 2015; Author; b. 18.10.52, Kilwinning; m., Caroline Angela Owen; 1 s.; 1 d. Educ. Eton College; Trinity College, Cambridge; INSEAD, Fountainbleau; Institute of Business

Administration. Feature Writer, The Antique Collector; Associate Publisher, Ebury Press, 1975-78; Associate Publisher, Illustrated News Group, 1980-82; Publisher, The Spectator, 1982-92; Founder, Art for Work, 1992-2005; Managing Director, The Art Newspaper, 2005-2015. Chairman, The Boswell Trust. Publications: Trinity Foot Beagles, 1978; Robert Byron, 2004; The Genius of Osbert Lancaster, 2008; Curator, The Genius of Osbert Lancaster, 2008; The Wallace Collection; Scottish Country Houses, 2012; The Scottish Colourists, 2019; The Glasgow Girls and Boys, 2020. Recreations: visual arts; architecture. Address: (h.) Martnaham Lodge, Ayr KA6 6ES.

Knox, Lesley Mary, MA (Cantab). NED and Chair, Remuneration Committee, Legal & General Plc, since 2016; Chair, L&G Investment Management, since 2019; Genus plc, NED and SID, since 2018; b. 19.9.53, Johannesburg, South Africa; m., Brian Knox; 1 d. Educ. St. Denis, Edinburgh; Cheltenham Ladies College; Cambridge University. Slaughter and May (qualified as Solicitor), 1976-79; Shearman and Sterling New York (qualified as Attorney), 1979-80; Kleinwort Benson, Corporate Finance Division, 1981-91 (became Director in 1986); Head of Institutional Asset Management, Kleinwort Investment, 1991-96; NED, Bank of Scotland, 1993-2001; NED, Scottish Provident, 1995-2001; British Linen Bank, 1997-99 (became Governor in 1998); Chair, V&A Dundee, 2010-2019; wholly Non Executive of a number of companies. Recreations: family; textile artist; opera. Address: (h.) 10A Circus Lane, Edinburgh EH3 6SU; T.-07768 046 422.

Knox, Liz, DA (Edin), PAI, PPAI. Painter, since 1971; President, Paisley Art Institute, 2007-2010; b. 20.01.45, Glasgow; m., Peter Whittle; 2 s. Educ. Hillhead High School, Glasgow and John Neilson, Paisley; Edinburgh College of Art. Art Teacher, Secondary Education, 1971-73; bringing up sons and lecturing part time, 1973-83; Lecturing in Fine Art for Further Education, 1983-2003 (part of this period, member of Advisory Panel, Gray's School of Art, Aberdeen and wrote entire HND Environmental Art validated by SQA, 2001); painting part time, from 1971; full time painter, since 2003 (exhibiting Britain including Edinburgh, Glasgow and London, also France and Netherlands, since 2003). Member, committee of Paisley Art Institute, 1997-2004; Member of Council, The Glasgow Art Club, 2006-07; Vice President, Paisley Art Institute, 2004-07; Member of Council, The Royal Glasgow Institute of the Arts, 2010-17; Assessor, Scottish Drawing Competition, 2007, 2009; Assessor, Aspect Prize, 2010, 2011; Retrospective, "Singular", Maclaurin Galleries, Ayr, 2012; "Emphatic Interpretations", in collaboration with musician Ben Whittle (First Family Riot) in MacGyver, Westermarkt, Amsterdam, 2015; work held in many private and corporate collections internationally. Selected solo Exhibitions include Calton Gallery, Edinburgh, Duncan Campbell Fine Art, London, Catto Gallery, Hampstead and St. Mary's Episcopal Cathedral, Glasgow. Work selected for book cover by Bloodaxe Books. Awards include: Winner of The Aspect prize, 2003; The Bessie Scott Award at PAI, 2004; The Diploma of Paisley Art Institute, "PAI", 2005; The University of Paisley (now University of The West of Scotland) Award, 2006; The Blythswood Square Quaich at Glasgow Society of Women Artists, 2007; the Arnold Clark Award, 2010; The Concept Gallery Fine Art Award, 2013. Recreations: music; photography; books; travel. Address: (h.) Jesmond, High Street, Neilston, Glasgow G78 3HJ; T.-0141 587 5559.
E-mail: lizknox1@ntlworld.com; web: www.lizknox.com

Kuenssberg, Nicholas Christopher, OBE, FRSE, DUniv, BA (Hons) (Oxon), FCIS, FIoD, CCMI, FRSA. Chairman: Royal Conservatoire of Scotland, since 2016, Klik2learn Ltd, since 2013, Frog Systems Ltd, since 2015; b. 28.10.42, Edinburgh; m., Sally Robertson; 1 s.; 2 d. Educ. Edinburgh Academy; Wadham College, Oxford; Manchester Business School. Director, J. & P. Coats Ltd., 1978-91; Chairman, Dynacast International Ltd, 1978-91; Director, Coats Patons plc, 1985-91; Director, Coats Viyella plc, 1986-91; Managing Director, Dawson International plc, 1991-95; Non-executive Director: Bank of Scotland West of Scotland Board, 1984-88, ScottishPower plc, 1984-97, Standard Life Assurance Company, 1988-99, Baxi Partnership Ltd., 1996-99, Chamberlin and Hill plc, 1999-2006, Amino Technologies plc, 2004-07; Chairman: GAP Group Ltd., 1996-2005, Stoddard International PLC, 1997-2000, David A. Hall Ltd., 1996-98, Canmore Partnership Ltd., 1999-2016, iomart Group plc, 2000-08, Keronite plc, 2004-07, eTourism Ltd., 2007-08, Scott & Fyfe Ltd, 2009-2017; mLED Ltd., 2010-16, Scotland the Brand, 2002-04, ScotlandIS, 2001-03, Institute of Directors, Scotland, 1997-99, Association for Management Education and Training in Scotland, 1996-98; Governor, Queen's College, 1988-91; Visiting Professor, Strathclyde Business School, 1988-91; Trustee, David Hume Institute, 1994-2008; Member, Advisory Group to Secretary of State on Sustainable Development, 1996-99; Member, Scottish Legal Aid Board, 1996-2004; Member, Scottish Environment Protection Agency, 1997-2007 (Deputy Chairman, 2003-07); Member, British Council, Scottish Committee, 1999-2008; Board Member, Citizens Theatre, Glasgow, 2000-03; Honorary Professor, University of Glasgow, 2008-2017; Chairman: Glasgow School of Art, 2003-2010, QAA Scotland, 2007-2010, Social Investment Scotland, 2013-18; Public Interest Member, Council of Institute of Chartered Accountants of Scotland, 2008-2011; Trustee, Pitlochry Festival Theatre, 2010-16. Editor, Argument amongst Friends: twenty five years of sceptical enquiry and The David Hume Institute: The first decade. Recreations: languages; opera; travel; sport. Address: 9 Hillside Gardens Lane, Glasgow G11 5BX; e-mail: horizon@sol.co.uk

Kuenssberg, Sally, CBE, BA (Oxon), PhD, DipAdEd, FRSA; b. 30.7.43, Edinburgh; m., Nicholas; 1 s.; 2 d. Educ. St Leonard's School; University of Oxford. Teacher of English, British Council, Lima, Peru, 1968-74; Tutor, Glasgow Adult Literacy Programme, 1978-83; Partner, Heatherbank Press, Milngavie, 1981-90; Member, Strathclyde Children's Panel, 1983-90; Lecturer, University of Glasgow Department of Adult and Continuing Education, 1990-95; Chair, Scottish Children's Reporter Administration, 1995-2002; Chair, Yorkhill NHS Trust, 2001-04; Member, NHS Greater Glasgow and Clyde Health Board, 2001-07; Hon. Fellow, Royal College of Paediatrics and Child Health, 2008; Trustee, Save The Children UK, 2003-2011; Trustee, Includem, since 2015; Trustee, EIL (UK), since 2020.

Kunkler, Professor Ian Hubert, MA, MB, BChir, DMRT, FRCR, FRCPE, FRSA. Consultant and Honorary Professor in Clinical Oncology, Western General Hospital, University of Edinburgh; b. Wilmslow; m., Alison Jane; 1 s. Educ. Clifton College, Bristol; Magdalene College, Cambridge; St Bartholomew's Hospital, London. President, London Medical Group, 1976-77; House Officer, 1978-79; Senior House Officer, Nottingham City Hospital, 1979-81; Registrar and Senior Registrar, Clinical Oncology, Western General Hospital, Edinburgh; French Government and EEC Research Fellow, Institut Gustave Roussy, Paris, 1986-87; Consultant and Hon. Lecturer in Clinical Oncology, Weston Park Hospital, Sheffield, 1988-92; Honorary Reader, University of Edinburgh, 2006. President, British Oncological Association, 2000-02; Founder and Trustee, Clerk Maxwell Cancer Research Fund, 1998-2004; Member, IAEA international quality assurance group for radiotherapy, since 2005;

International adviser in radiotherapy, Institut National du Cancer, France; 2006 British Oncological Association, Excellence in Oncology Team of The Year; Chief Investigator, MRC SUPREMO breast cancer trial. Publications: Walter and Miller's Textbook of Radiotherapy, 1993, 2002; various papers on breast cancer, radiotherapy and telemedicine. Address: (b.) Institute of Genetic and Molecular Medicine, Western General Hospital, Edinburgh EH4 2XU; T.-0131-651-8606; Fax: 0131-777-3520; e-mail: i.kunkler@ed.ac.uk

Kyle, James, CBE, DSc, MCh, FRCS. Chairman, Raigmore Hospital NHS Trust, Inverness, 1993-97; b. 26.3.25, Ballymena, Northern Ireland; m., Dorothy Elizabeth Galbraith; 2 d. Educ. Ballymena Academy; Queen's University, Belfast. Scholarship to Mayo Clinic, USA, 1950; Tutor in Surgery, Royal Victoria Hospital, Belfast, 1952; Lecturer in Surgery, Liverpool University, 1957; Senior Lecturer in Surgery, Aberdeen University, 1959-60, and Consultant Surgeon, Aberdeen Royal Infirmary, 1959-89. Member, Grampian Health Board, 1973-77, Chairman, 1989-93; Chairman, Raigmore Hospital NHS Trust, Inverness, 1993-97; Chairman, Scottish Committee for Hospital Medical Services, 1976-79; elected Member, General Medical Council, 1979-94; Chairman: Scottish Joint Consultants Committee, 1984-89, Representative Body, British Medical Association, 1984-87; President, Aberdeen Medico-Chirurgical Society, 1989-90; British Council Lecturer, SE Asia and South America, 1963-85; Examiner: Belfast, Dublin, Dundee, Edinburgh, Sydney, University of West Indies; Burgess of Aberdeen. Patron: Royal Scottish National Orchestra, Scottish Opera. Publications: Peptic Ulcer; Pye's Surgical Handicraft; Crohn's Disease; Scientific Foundations of Surgery. Recreations: Fellow, Royal Philatelic Society, London; Fellow, Royal Astronomical Society, London; licensed radio amateur, GM4 CHX. Address: (h.) 7 Fasaich, Strath, Gairloch IV21 2DH; T.-01445 712398.

Kyle, Peter McLeod, MBChB, FRCS(Edin), FRCS(Glas), FRCOphth. Consultant Ophthalmologist, Southern General Hospital NHS Trust, 1982-2010 (Clinical Director of Ophthalmology, 1995-2000); Honorary Clinical Senior Lecturer, Glasgow University, 1985-2010; Member, Medical Appeal Tribunals, Scotland, since 1986; Member, Criminal Injuries Compensation Tribunal, since 2009; Member, General Medical Council Fitness to Practice Panel, since 2010; Member, General Optical Council, 1998-2009; Member, General Optical Council Education Committee and Working Group, since 1998; b. 19.8.51, Rutherglen; m., Valerie Anne Steele; 1 s.; 2 d. Educ. High School of Glasgow; Glasgow University. Lecturer in Ophthalmology, Glasgow University, 1980-84. Convener, Ophthalmology Sub-committee, Royal College of Physicians and Surgeons of Glasgow; Member, Opthalmology Specialist Advisory Board, Royal College of Surgeons of Edinburgh; Deacon, Incorporation of Barbers of Glasgow, 1998-99. Recreations: walking; skiing. Address: (h.) The Stables, Earlsferry, Fife; T.-01333 330647.

Kynoch, George Alexander Bryson, OBE, BSc. Non-Executive Chairman: Red Squirrel Wine Ltd, 2014-19, Muir Matheson Ltd., 1998-2007, London Marine Group Ltd., 1997-2004, Benson Group Ltd., 1998-2005, The TEP Exchange Group PLC, 2006-09, RDF Group PLC, 2003-06, TOLUNA PLC, 2005-2011; Non-Executive Director: Talent Group PLC, 2003-2014, TECC-IS PLC, 2003-05; Non Executive Chairman: OCZ Technology Group Inc., 2006-09, Mercury Group PLC, 2007-08, ITWP Acquisitions Ltd, since 2011; Deputy Chairman, The Scottish Conservative and Unionist Party, 2008-2012; MP (Conservative), Kincardine and Deeside, 1992-97; b.

7.10.46, Keith; m. (1), Dr. Rosslyn Margaret McDevitt (deceased); 1 s.; 1 d.; m. (2), Dorothy Anne Stiven. Educ. Cargilfield School, Edinburgh; Glenalmond College, Perth; Bristol University. Plant Engineer, ICI Ltd., Nobel Division, 1968-71; G. and G. Kynoch PLC, 1971-92, latterly as Group Executive Director; Parliamentary Under Secretary of State for Scotland – Minister for Industry and Local Government, 1995-97; Non-Executive Director: Kynoch Group PLC, Aardvark Clear Mine Ltd., 1992-95, PSL Holdings Ltd., 1998, Silvertech International plc, 1997-2000, Midmar Energy Ltd., 1998-99, Premisys Technologies PLC, 1998-2001, Jetcam International Holdings Ltd., 1998-2003; Member, Aberdeen and District Milk Marketing Board, 1988-92; Director, Moray Badenoch and Strathspey Local Enterprise Co. Ltd., 1991-92; Chairman, Scottish Woollen Publicity Council, 1983-90; President, Scottish Woollen Industry, 1990-91; Vice Chairman, Northern Area, Scottish Conservative and Unionist Association, 1991-92; Deputy Chairman, Carlton Club, 2012-18. Recreations: golf; travel.

L

Lacy, Very Rev. Dr. David William, DL, BA, BD, DLitt. Retired Minister, Kay Park Parish Church, Kilmarnock (1989-2017); Moderator of the General Assembly of the Church of Scotland, 2005-06; b. 26.4.52, Inverness; m., Joan Stewart Roberston; 1 s.; 1 d. Educ. Aberdeen Grammar School; High School of Glasgow; University of Strathclyde; University of Glasgow and Trinity College. Assistant Minister, St. George's West, Edinburgh, 1975-77; Minister, Knightswood: St. Margaret's, Glasgow, 1977-89. Depute Lieutenant of Ayrshire and Arran, since 2013. Recreations: sailing; snooker; choral singing. Address: 4, Cairns Terrace, Kilmarnock, Ayrshire KA1 2JG; T.-01563 624034.

Lafferty, Austin. Dean, Royal Faculty of Procurators in Glasgow; Owner, Austin Lafferty Solicitors, since 1987; b. 6.59. Educ. St. Aloysius College. Occasional night lawyer, Scottish Daily Record and Sunday Mail Ltd, 1999-2016; Law Society of Scotland: President, 2012-13, Past President, since 2013. Address: Royal Faculty of Procurators in Glasgow, 12 Nelson Mandela Place, Glasgow G2 1BT; T.-0141 363 3203.

Laidlaw, Alan, MRICS, FRAgS. Chief Executive Officer, Royal Highland and Agricultural Society of Scotland, since 2016. Educ. Harper Adams University College. Career history: The Crown Estate: Head of New Business Development, 2005-2012, Portfolio Manager - Scotland and Northern Ireland, 2012-16, Head of Property - Scotland Portfolio, 2016; Past Director, Oxford Farming Conference. Address: The Royal Highland and Agricultural Society of Scotland, Ingliston House, Royal Highland Centre, Ingliston, Edinburgh EH28 8NB; T.-0131 335 6200. E-mail: alaidlaw@rhass.org.uk

Laing, Alasdair North Grant, OBE, DL, FRAgS. Director, Fisheries Management Scotland; b. 30.12.49, Forres; m., Lucy Ann Anthea Low; 2 s.; 1 d. Educ. Belhaven Hill; Eton College; Royal Agricultural Collge, Cirencester. Trustee, Macaulay Development Trust, 2009-2018; President, Royal Highland and Agricultural Society of Scotland, 2004/05; Director, PDG Helicopters Ltd, 1975-2015; Director, Scottish Agricultural College, 1995-2003; Vice Convenor, Scottish Landowners Federation, 2000-04. Recreations: walking; fishing; stalking. Address: (b.) Logie Estate Office, Forres, Moray IV36 2QN; T.-01309 611300. E-mail: alaing@logie.co.uk

Laing, The Hon. Mark Hector, MA. Chairman, Nairn's Oatcakes Ltd., since 1996; b. 22.2.51, London; m., Susanna Crawford; 1 s.; 2 d. Educ. Eton College; Cambridge University. United Biscuits p.l.c., 1972-96: Factory Director, Glasgow, 1985; Production Director, McVities, 1988; Managing Director, Simmers Biscuits, 1990; Chairman, Findhorn, Nairn and Lossie Rivers Trust. Recreations: walking; gardening; fishing; photography. Address: (b.) Nairn's Oatcakes Ltd., 90 Peffermill Road, Edinburgh EH16 5UU; T.-0131-620 7000. E-mail: mark@nairns-oatcakes.com

Laird, Lesley. Director, Equate Scotland, since 2020; MP (Labour), Kirkcaldy and Cowdenbeath, 2017-19; Deputy Leader of the Scottish Labour Party, 2018-19; Shadow Secretary of State for Scotland, 2017-19; b. 15.11.58, Greenock. Educ. James Watt College; Glasgow Caledonian University; Edinburgh Napier University. Career: worked for various organisations: IBM, NHBC, NEC, Burr-Brown, Damon BioTech, Melville Craig, BBN, Digital, Motorola, Intelligent Finance; latterly until 2011, Royal Bank of Scotland as Senior Talent Manager before forming Lesley Laird & Associates; Fife Council: elected Councillor for Ward 6 - Inverkeithing, Aberdour, Dalgety Bay & Hillend, 2012-18; Deputy Leader of Council, 2014-17; Spokesperson for Economy & Planning, 2013-17. Recreations: enjoys most sports but especially running, football and yoga; musical theatre; reading. Address: Equate Scotland, Edinburgh Napier University, Craiglockhart Campus, 219 Colinton Road, Edinburgh EH14 1DJ; T.-0131 455 5108.

Lake, Jonathan, QC. Senator of the College of Justice, since 2022. Career history: completed traineeship, then an assistant solicitor at Maclay Murray and Spens; practice at the Bar, since 1994; took Silk in 2008; part of the team in the Lockerbie prosecution while junior counsel; senior counsel to Lord Hardie's Inquiry into the Edinburgh Tram Project. Instructed in many cases in the fields of commercial law, construction law and intellectual property law. Address: Parliament House, Parliament Square, Edinburgh EH1 1RQ.

Lamb, Caroline. Chief Executive, NHS Scotland, and Director-General Health and Social Care, Scottish Government, since 2021; Director of Digital Reform and Service Engagement, 2019-2021; led the establishment of the SG Test and Protect Programme, and the Covid Vaccination Programme in 2020; Chief Executive, NHS Education for Scotland, 2015-19. Educ. King's College London. Trained as a Chartered Accountant with KPMG, working with clients including Castle Cement, Citibank, Nestle and the International Committee of the Red Cross in Geneva. Qualified as a Chartered Accountant, then moved to Scotland and became Director of Finance, Edinvar Housing Association; Director of Finance, then University Secretary and Director of Operations, University of Abertay Dundee; joined NHS Education for Scotland in 2004 as Director of Finance and Corporate Resources and Deputy Chief Executive. Address: Scottish Government, St. Andrew's House, Regent Road, Edinburgh EH1 3DG.

Lambe, Ronan, LLB, LLM. Partner, Pinsent Masons, Edinburgh, since 2021. Educ. Nottingham Trent University; Trinity College Dublin; University of Cambridge. Associate, White & Case LLP, 2004-2010; Pinsent Masons: Senior Associate, 2010-18, Legal Director, 2018-2021. Address: Pinsent Masons, Princes Exchange, 1 Earl Grey Street, Edinburgh EH3 9AQ; T.-0131 777 7077. E-mail: ronan.lambe@pinsentmasons.com

Lambert, Marc, MA (Hons). Chief Executive, Scottish Book Trust, since 2002. Educ. Uppingham School, Leicestershire; University of Edinburgh. Sales Representative, Penguin Books, 1990-95; Interpretation Officer, The Fruitmarket Gallery, 1995-2000; Assistant Director, Edinburgh International Book Festival, 2000-02. Address: (b.) Sandeman House, Trunk's Close, 55 High Street, Edinburgh EH1 1SR; T.-0131 524 0160.

Lamont, D. Murray, BA, MHCIMA (Dip), MSIM, ACIM. Honorary Sheriff, Wick; Hotelier; Company Director; Proprietor: Mackays Hotel Wick, Bin Ends, The Fine Wine Shops, since 1995; b. 1.9.57, Wick, Caithness; 1 d. Educ. Wick High School; Abertay University. Purchased and developed Mackays Hotel; started and developed Bin Ends, The Fine Wine Shops; started and developing, Ebenezer Leisure Ltd.

Chairman, Wick Branch RNLI; Director: The Highland Tourism Operators Group, The Scottish Licensed Trade Benevolent Society. T.-01955 602678; e-mail: murray@mackayshotel.co.uk

Lamont, Johann, MA (Hons). MSP (Labour), Glasgow region, 2016-2021 (Glasgow Pollok, 1999-2016); Leader, Scottish Labour Party, 2011-14; Deputy Leader of The Labour Party in The Scottish Parliament, 2008-2011; Deputy Minister for Justice, 2006-07; Deputy Minister for Communities, 2004-06; Convener, Communities Committee, 2001-04 (former Deputy Convener, Local Government Committee); b. 1957, Glasgow; m.; 1 s.; 1 d. Educ. Woodside Secondary School; Glasgow University; Jordanhill College of Education; Strathclyde University. Former teacher.

Lamont, John. MP (Conservative), Berwickshire, Roxburgh and Selkirk, since 2017; MSP (Conservative), Ettrick, Roxburgh and Berwickshire, 2011-17, Roxburgh and Berwickshire, 2007-2011; Shadow Cabinet Secretary for Justice, 2010-2011; Chief Whip and Business Manager, 2011-17; b. 15.4.76, Irvine. Educ. Kilwinning Academy, Ayrshire; Glasgow University. Solicitor: Brodies, 2005-07, Freshfields, London, 2000-04, Bristows, London, 2004-05. Recreations: running; swimming; cycling; cooking; ironman triathlons. Address: (h.) 63 High Street, Coldstream TD12 4DL; (b.) 25 High Street, Hawick TD9 9BU.

Lamont-Brown, Raymond, JP, MA, FSA Scot. Author and Broadcaster; Lecturer, Centre for External Services, St. Andrews University, 1978-98, Centre for Continuing Education, Dundee University, 1988-98; Founder, Japan Research Projects, since 1965; b. 20.9.39, Horsforth, Leeds; m., Dr. Elizabeth Moira McGregor. Educ. Wheelwright Grammar School, Dewsbury; Bradford Technical College; SOAS; Nihon Daigaku, Japan. Honorary Secretary/Treasurer, Society of Authors in Scotland, 1982-89; Past President, St. Andrews Rotary Club; Vice-Chairman, St. Andrews Community Council, 1988-91; Chairman, Arthritis Care Liaison Committee (Central, Fife and Tayside), 1991-97; Member, Council, Arthritis Care, 1991-97. Publications: 60 published books, including Discovering Fife; Phantoms of the Sea; The Life and Times of Berwick-upon-Tweed; The Life and Times of St. Andrews; Royal Murder Mysteries; Scottish Epitaphs; Scottish Superstitions; Scottish Traditions and Festivals; Famous Scots; Scottish Witchcraft; Around St. Andrews; Scottish Folklore; Kamikaze: Japan's Suicide Samurai; Scotland of 100 Years Ago; Kempeitai: Japan's Dreaded Military Police; Edward VII's Last Loves; Tutor to the Dragon Emperor; John Brown; Royal Poxes and Potions; Ships from Hell; Fife in History and Legend; Villages of Fife; Humphry Davy; Andrew Carnegie; St Andrews: City by the Northern Sea; How Fat Was Henry VIII? Address: (h.) 76T Strathern Road, Broughty Ferry, Dundee DD5 1PH; T.-01382 732032.

Lancaster, Colin, LLB, MSc, PhD. Chief Executive, Scottish Legal Aid Board, since 2015. Educ. University of Edinburgh. Director of Policy and Development, Scottish Legal Aid Board, 2007-2015. Address: The Scottish Legal Aid Board, Thistle House, 91 Haymarket Terrace, Edinburgh EH12 5HE; T.-0131 226 7061.

Landels, Ann, MA (Hons), PGCert, MEd. Chair, Apex Scotland, since 2021; b. 1.53; 3 s. Educ. University of Edinburgh; Aberdeen College of Education; University of Aberdeen; Robert Gordon University (Diploma in Change Management). Worked as a community education worker;

became a head of service for Culture and Learning at Aberdeen City Council; moved from the statutory sector to the voluntary sector and started work with Crisis, the national charity for homeless people in 2011; Director of Crisis Skylight Edinburgh for 7 years (established and developed the charity's outreach services, delivering education, training and one-to-one support to homeless people in Edinburgh). Vice Chair, Board of Edinburgh College; a trustee of the Edinburgh Development Trust; Secretary of Southside Community Choir. Address: Apex Scotland, 9 Great Stuart Street, Edinburgh EH3 7TP; T.-0131 220 0130.

Lander, Ronald, OBE, BSc, FIET, FSQA. Chairman, Extra Mile Studios Ltd, since April 2013; Chairman and Managing Director, Scotlander Ltd (formerly plc), 1985-2018; Director: Logical Innovations Ltd., 2001-2010, Pyramid Research and Development Ltd., 2000-06, Young Enterprise Scotland, 1998-2001; Director and Chairman, Armadale Tech. Ltd., 2007-2010; b. 5.8.42, Glasgow; m., Elizabeth Stirling; 2 s. Educ. Allan Glen's School; Glasgow University. Chairman and Managing Director, Lander Grayburn & Co. Limited, 1970-83; Deputy Managing Director, Lander Alarm Company (Scotland) Limited, 1975-79; Managing Director, Lander Alarms Limited and Lander Alarms (Scotland) Limited, 1979-85; Chairman, Lander & Jess Limited, 1983-87; Director, Centre for Entrepreneurial Development, Glasgow University, 1985-88; Chairman, Newstel Information Ltd., 1998-99; Member, CBI Scottish Council, 1977-83, 1984-90 and 1992-98; (founding) Chairman, CBI Scotland's Smaller Firms' Working Group, 1977-80; founding Chairman, Entrepreneurial Exchange, 1995-96; founder Member, CBI Industrial Policy Committee, London, 1978-86; Chairman, CBI Scotland Smaller Firms' Committee, 1993-95; Chairman, Scottish Fire Prevention Council, 1979-80; Member, Glasgow University Appointments Committee, 1979; CBI Representative, Home Office/CBI/TUC Joint Committee on Prison Industries, 1980-87; Industrial Member, Understanding British Industry, Scotland, 1981-89; Member, Council, Scottish Business School, 1982-87; Director, British Security Industry Association Council, 1984-85; Governor, Scottish Sports Aid Foundation, 1985-88; Member: Kincraig Committee (review of parole system and related matters), 1987-89, Manpower Services Committee for Scotland (later the Training Agency), 1987-88; founder Chairman, Local Employer Network (LENS) Scottish Co-ordinating Committee, 1987; Chairman, CBI Scotland Education and Training Committee, 1987-89; Director, SCOTVEC, 1987-93; Member, CBI Business/Education Task Force (the Cadbury Report), 1988; Member, Scottish Consultative Council on the Curriculum, 1988-91; Vice-Convener, Scottish Education/Industry Committee, 1988-91; Founder Member, Glasgow Action, 1985-91; Member, Secretary of State for Scotland's Crime Prevention Committee, 1984-87; Companion IEE, 1986; Board Member, Glasgow Development Agency, 1991-99; Visiting/Honorary Professor, Glasgow University, 1991-2007; National Judge, National Training Awards, 1989-92; Board Member, Glasgow Science Centre, 1999-2007; Director, Picardy Media Group Plc, 1998-2001.

Lang, Adam, MA Hons (Hist). Head of Nesta Scotland, since 2019; m.; 3 c. Educ. University of Glasgow. Career history: Production Assistant, STV Group plc, Glasgow, 2006-2007; Press and Media Officer (Scotland), Liberal Democrats, Scottish Parliament, 2007-2010; Account Manager, Stripe Communications, Edinburgh, 2010-2012; Senior Public Affairs and Communications Officer, YouthLink Scotland, Edinburgh, 2011-2012; Account Director, Public Affairs, Weber Shandwick, Edinburgh, 2012-14; Head of Policy and Communications, Shelter Scotland, Edinburgh, 2014-2019; Steering Committee,

Scotland's AI Strategy, Edinburgh, 2019-2021; National Digital Ethics Advisory Group, The Scottish Government, since 2020; Board Trustee, SCVO (Scottish Council for Voluntary Organisations), since 2018; Programme Delivery Board, Data-Driven Innovation Initiative, Edinburgh, since 2020. Recreations: enjoys cooking; reading; cinema; single malt Islay whisky. Address: Nesta, The Bayes Centre, 47 Potterow, Edinburgh EH8 9BT.
E-mail: scotland@nesta.org.uk

Lang, Alison. Director, Gaelic Books Council, since 2019. Established Gaelic writer and editor. Worked as an official reporter at the Scottish Parliament, as corporate affairs officer for the Gaelic media service MG ALBA and as literary assistant (Gaelic) at the National Theatre of Scotland. Published Cainnt na Caileige Caillte (collection of short stories shortlisted for the Saltire Society's First Book of the Year Award in 2009); awarded Playwrights' Studio Scotland's New Playwrights' Award in 2013; novel Am Balach Beag a dh'Èisteadh aig Dorsan won the Adult Book of the Year award, Royal National Mod, 2018. Address: Gaelic Books Council, 32 Mansfield Street, Glasgow G11 5QP; T.-0141 337 6211.

Lang of Monkton, Baron (Ian Bruce Lang), DL, PC, OStJ, BA. Life Peer; Deputy Lieutenant, Ayrshire and Arran, since 1998; President of the Board of Trade, 1995-97; Company Directorships including: Chairman, Marsh & McLennan Companies Inc., 2011-2016 (Director, 1997-2016); Chairman, Lovat Parks Ltd., since 2019; Chairman, Patrons of the National Galleries of Scotland, 1999-2006; b. 27.6.40, Glasgow; m., Sandra Caroline Montgomerie; 2 d. Educ. Lathallan School; Rugby School; Sidney Sussex College, Cambridge. MP (Conservative), Galloway and Upper Nithsdale, 1983-97 (Galloway, 1979-83); Member, Select Committee on Scottish Affairs, 1979-81; Trustee, Glasgow Savings Bank and West of Scotland TSB, 1969-82; Scottish Whip, 1981-83; Lord Commissioner of HM Treasury, 1983-86; Vice-Chairman, Scottish Conservative Party, 1983-87; Parliamentary Under Secretary of State, Scottish Office, 1986-87, and at Department of Employment, 1986; Minister of State, Scottish Office, 1987-90; Secretary of State for Scotland, 1990-95. Chairman, The Prime Minister's Advisory Committee on Business Appointments, 2009-2014; Member, House of Lords Select Committee on the Constitution, 2000-05 and 2012-17, Chairman, 2014-17; Member, House of Lords Liaison Committee, since 2017; Member, Special Committee on the Barnett Formula, 2009; Member, Queen's Bodyguard for Scotland (Royal Company of Archers), since 1974; Governor, Rugby School, 1997-2007; President, Association for the Protection of Rural Scotland, 1998-2001; Hon. President, St. Columba's School, Kilmacolm, 1999-2008. Publication: Blue Remembered Years, 2002. Address (b.) House of Lords, Westminster, London SW1A 0PW.

Lang, Dr Brian Andrew, CBE, MA, PhD, FRSE. Chairman, Edinburgh World Heritage Trust, 2015-19; Chair, Dovecot Tapestry Studio, since 2017; Chairman, RSNO, 2008-2015; Principal and Vice-Chancellor, St Andrews University, 2001-08; b. 2.12.45; 2 s.; 1 d.; m., Tari. Educ. Royal High School, Edinburgh; Edinburgh University. Social anthropology research, Kenya, 1969-70; Lecturer, Social Anthropology, Aarhus University, 1971-75; Scientific Staff, SSRC, 1976-79; Secretary, Historic Buildings Council for Scotland, 1979-80; Secretary, National Heritage Memorial Fund, 1980-87; Director, Public Affairs, National Trust, 1987-91; Chief Executive and Deputy Chairman, British Library, 1991-2000; Chairman, European National Libraries Forum, 1993-2000; Chair, Heritage Image Partnership, 2000-02; Board Member, Scottish Enterprise Fife, 2003-08; Dr hc,

University of Edinburgh, 2008; Hon LLD, University of St. Andrews, 2008; Member: Library and Information Services Council (England), 1991-94, Library and Information Commission, 1995-2000, Council, St. Leonards School, St Andrews, 2001-08; FRSE, 2006; Visiting Professor, Napier University, Edinburgh, since 1999; Visiting Scholar, Getty Institute, Los Angeles, California, 2000; Pforzheimer Lecture, University of Texas, 1998; Trustee: 21st Century Learning Initiative, 1995-99, Hopetoun House Preservation Trust, 2001-05; Deputy Chair, National Heritage Memorial Fund, 2005-2011; Member, Council, National Trust for Scotland, 2001-04; President, Institute of Information Scientists, 1993-94 (Hon. Fellow, 1994); Hon. FLA, 1997; Chairman of Trustees, Newbattle Abbey College, 2004-08; Member: Committee for Scotland, Heritage Lottery Fund, 2004-2011 (South-2011), Cultural Commission, 2004-05; Trustee, National Museums of Scotland, since 2014. Publications: numerous articles and contributions to professional journals. Recreations: music; museums and galleries; pottering. Address: (b.) 4 Manor Place, Edinburgh EH3 7DD; T.-0131 260 9617; e-mail: brian@lang-uk.com

Lang, Professor Chim, MD, FRCP, FRCPE, FACC, FESC. Professor of Cardiology, University of Dundee, since 2004; Head, Division of Molecular and Clinical Medicine, University of Dundee, since 2018; Consultant Cardiologist, Ninewells Hospital and Medical School, Dundee, since 2004; b. 12.10.60, Kuala Lumpur, Malaysia; m., Anna-Maria Choy; 2 s.; 1 d. Educ. Kingswood School, Bath; University of Dundee. Lecturer, University of Dundee, 1990-93; Merck International Fellow in Clinical Pharmacology, Vanderbilt University, USA, 1993-96; Professor of Medicine and Deputy Dean, University of Malaya, 1996-2004. Fulbright Scholar, Columbia University, USA, 2001-02; Editor-in-Chief, Cardiovascular Therapeutics; Associate-Editor, Heart, 2010-14; Associate Editor, Clinical Science, 2002-2014; Chair, Scottish Medical Academic Staff Committee, BMA Scotland, 2009-2015; Member, Executive Committee, Association of Physicians of Great Britain and Ireland, 2012-15. Recreations: travel; reading. Address: (b.) Division of Molecular and Clinical Medicine, Ninewells Hospital and Medical School, Dundee DD1 9SY; T.-01382 383283.
E-mail: c.c.lang@dundee.ac.uk

Lang, Stephen, MBChB, FRCPath. Consultant Histopathologist, Ninewells Hospital, Dundee since 1990; Clinical Leader, Pathology, NHS Tayside, 2013-15; Honorary Senior Lecturer in Histopathology, University of Dundee, since 1990; Associate, General Medical Council; b. 19.9.58, Glasgow; m., Dorothy; 2 s.; 1 d. Educ. Holy Cross High School, Hamilton; Glasgow University. RAF Medical Officer, 1982-87 (RAF Leuchars, 1982-83, RAF Halton, 1983-87); Lecturer/Honorary Senior Registrar in Histopathology, St. Bartholomew's Hospital and The Hospital for Sick Children, Great Ormond Street, London, 1987-90. Recreations: football; golf; cinema; theatre. Address: 56 Wyvis Road, Broughty Ferry, Dundee DD5 3SU; T.-01382 800886; e-mail: stephen.lang@nhs.net

Lang, Tari. Corporate, Reputation and Leadership Adviser, The Lang Consultancy, since 2008; b. 18.06.51, Prague, Czech; 1 s.; 1 d.; m., Dr. Brian Lang. Educ. St. Theresa, Jakarta, Indonesia; Roehampton Institute (London University). Managing Director, The Rowland Company, 1988-95; UK CEO, Edelman Public Relations Worldwide, 1995-2002; Founder Partner, ReputationInc, 2002-08. Board of Trustees, National Galleries of Scotland; Board, Edinburgh Festival Fringe Society; Chair, Royal Lyceum Theatre, Edinburgh. Recreations: cinema; theatre; music; travelling. Address: 4 Manor

Place, Edinburgh EH3 7DD; T.-0131 260 9617; e-mail: tari@lang-uk.com

Langley, Anne, BA, PG Cert. Executive Director of Operations, Creative Scotland, since 2022. Educ. University of Bedfordshire; The Open University; Ashridge Executive Education, International Business School. Career history: Buyer, Jaguar Land Rover, Warwickshire, 2001-05; Sub Contract Manager, GE Aviation, Gloucester, 2005-07; Procurement Manager, The National Trust, Swindon, 2007-2010; Global Commodity Manager, Dell, 2010-2013; Department for International Development (DFID): Head of Programme Sourcing, 2013-17, Head of Group Operations, Glasgow, 2017-2020; Portfolio Director, Places for Growth, Cabinet Office, since 2020. Address: Creative Scotland, Waverley Gate, 2-4 Waterloo Place, Edinburgh EH1 3EG.

Langley, Crawford James, LLB (Hons), BD, DPA, ACIS, NP. Freelance Electoral Consultant; Senior Depute Returning Officer, Aberdeen Constituencies, 1996-2017; Corporate Director for Legal and Democratic Services, Aberdeen City Council, 2002-06 (Director of Legal and Corporate Services, 1995-2002); Advocate in Aberdeen; b. 21.11.51, Glasgow; m., Janette Law Hamilton (deceased); m. (2), Judith Ann Cripps. Educ. Bellahouston Academy, Glasgow; Glasgow University. Legal apprentice, Corporation of Glasgow, 1973-75; various legal posts, Strathclyde Regional Council, 1975-89, Principal Solicitor, 1984-89; Depute Director of Law and Administration, Tayside Regional Council, 1989-91; Director of Law and Administration, Tayside Regional Council, 1991-95. Recreation: travel. Address: (h.) "Canouan", Eassie, Angus DD8 1SG; e-mail: c.j.langley@btinternet.com

Lascarides, Professor Alex, BSc, PhD. Professor, University of Edinburgh, since 2010; b. 2.9.63, London. Educ. NHEHS; University of Durham; University of Edinburgh. Address: (b.) School of Informatics, University of Edinburgh, 10 Crichton Street, Edinburgh EH8 9AB.

Lauder, David Mark, MA (Hons). Headmaster, Strathallan School, Forgandenny, since 2017; b. 21.01.68, Elderslie; m., Caroline; 2 s. Educ. Hermitage Academy, Helensburgh; Aberdeen University; St. Edmund Hall, Oxford. Assistant Master, History, Shiplake College, 1994-97, Head of History, 1997-99; Head of History, St Edward's School, Oxford, 1999-2003, Housemaster, 2003-07; Deputy Headmaster: Felsted School, 2007-2010, Ashville College, Harrogate, 2010-17. Graduate Scholarship, St Edmund Hall, Oxford, 1990; Master i/c Rowing, Shiplake College, 1996-99, Hall Blues, 1993 & 1994, Oxford, for Lightweight Rowing; Head Coach, OULRC, 1998-2000; Member: Vincent's Club, Oxford, Leander Club; Chair, Boarding Schools' Association (BSA), 2020. Address: Coventrees, Strathallan School, Forgandenny PH2 9EG; T.-01738 815000; e-mail: headmaster@strathallan.co.uk

Lavery, Anne, OBE, BA (Econ). Deputy Chief Executive Officer, Citizens Advice Scotland, since 2017, Acting Chief Executive Officer, 2015-17, Chief Operating Officer, 2014-15. Educ. Thurso High School; University of Strathclyde. Career history: Customer Service Analyst, Royal Bank of Scotland, 1997-1999; Researcher, Training and Employment Research Unit, Glasgow University, 1998-2000; Economic Regulation Analyst, Scottish Water, 2000-02; Deputy Principal Analyst, Strathclyde Police, 2006-2008; Principal Analyst, ACPOS, 2006-2013; Project Lead Strategic Planning and Analysis, National Police Reform Team, 2011-13; Strategy and policy performance principal analyst, Scottish Police Services Authority, 2013; Interim Principal Analyst (secondment), National Crime Agency, 2013-14. Address: Citizens Advice Scotland, Broadside, 2 Powderhall Road, Edinburgh EH7 4GB; T.-0131 550 1000.

Law, Chris. MP (SNP), Dundee West, since 2015; b. 21.10.69. Trained as a French Chef and then went on to the University of St Andrews where he received a degree in Cultural and Social Anthropology; operated a tourism business providing tours of the Himalayas on 1950s motorcycles; operated a business as a financial advisor in Dundee for 10 years. Address: House of Commons, London SW1A 0AA.

Law, Professor Derek, MA, DUniv, FLA, FIInfSc, FKC, FRSE, FCLIP. Emeritus Professor, University of Strathclyde; b. 19.6.47, Arbroath; m., Jacqueline Anne; 2 d. Educ. Arbroath High School, George Watson's College, Edinburgh; University of Glasgow. Assistant Librarian, St. Andrews University, 1970-77; Sub Librarian, Edinburgh University, 1977-81; Librarian, Erskine Medical Library, 1981-83; Director of Automation, Edinburgh University Library, 1983-84; King's College, London: Librarian, 1984-93, Director of Information Services, 1993-98; Librarian and Head of Information Resource Directorate, University of Strathclyde, 1998-2008; former Chair, JISC Advance. Barnard Prize for Informatics, 1993; IFLA Medal, 2003. Hon. Doctorate, University of Paris. Publications: Royal Navy in World War Two; The Battle of the Atlantic; Networking and the Future of Libraries; Digital Libraries. Address: (b.) Alexander Turnbull Building, 155 George Street, Glasgow G1 1RD; T.-0141-548 4997; e-mail: d.law@strath.ac.uk

Law, Professor Robin C. C., BA, PhD, FRHS, FBA, FRSE. Emeritus Professor of African History, University of Stirling; b. 7.8.44, Chester. Educ. Southend-on-Sea High School; Balliol College, University of Oxford; Centre of West African Studies, Birmingham. Research Assistant in African History, University of Lagos, Nigeria, 1966-69; Research Fellow in West African History, University of Birmingham, 1970-72; University of Stirling: Lecturer in History, 1972-78, Senior Lecturer, 1978-83, Reader, 1983-93, Professor, 1993-2009. Editor, Journal of African History, 1974-82, 1991-95; Series Editor, Hakluyt Society, 1998-2003. Publications: The Oyo Empire c.1600-c.1836, 1977; The Horse in West African History, 1980; The Slave Coast of West Africa, 1550-1750, 1991; The Kingdom of Allada, 1997; The Biography of Mahommah Gardo Baquaqua (Co-author), 2001; Ouidah: The social history of a West African slaving 'port', 1727-1892, 2004. Address: (b.) History and Politics Division, School of Arts and Humanities, University of Stirling, Stirling FK9 4LA; e-mail: r.c.c.law@stir.ac.uk

Lawrence, Professor Andrew, BSc, PhD, FRAS, FRSE. Regius Professor of Astronomy, Edinburgh University, since 1994, Head of Physics, 2004-08; b. 23.4.54, Margate; partner, Debbie Ann Capel; 3 s.; 1 d. Educ. Chatham House Grammar School, Ramsgate; Edinburgh University; Leicester University. Exchange Scientist, Massachusetts Institute of Technology, 1980-81; Senior Research Fellow, Royal Greenwich Observatory, 1981-84; Research Assistant, then SERC Advanced Fellow, School of Mathematical Sciences, Queen Mary College, London, 1984-89; Lecturer, Physics Department, Queen Mary and Westfield College, London, 1989-94. Visiting Physicist, Stanford, 2008-09. Publications: over 100 in learned journals. Recreations: painting electrons and teasing publishers; acting. Address: (b.) Institute for Astronomy, Edinburgh University, Royal Observatory, Blackford Hill, Edinburgh.

Lawrence, Rhona. President: The Lawrence Dance Academy, UKA Dance, since 2019. Career history: started teaching highland dance at a young age; taught a class of 20 pupils once a week in the home village of New Pitsligo; teaches at least five times a week to well over 100 pupils in Aberdeen and Aberdeenshire and her school has reached championship status; teaching, judging and lecturing, always representing Scotland, the Lawrence Dance Academy and the UKA. Member: BATD, SDTA; SOBHD delegate; Vice President of UKA for 11 years; President of the international body of UKA; Chairperson of the UKA Highland Division (runs and organises events including the Annual Conference in Aberdeen, which has become the biggest gathering of Teachers of Highland Dance in Scotland); heavily involved in the achievement of SQA and QCF Credits for the UKA; organiser of the City of Aberdeen Championship, United Kingdom Championship, and Secretary of the Commonwealth Championship; Chairperson of Grampian Festivals and promotes many other events throughout the season, including involvement in many Highland Games; a key driving force is the setting up and organising of the International Gathering of Scottish Highland Dance annual event in Disneyland Paris; organiser of the Paris International Highland Gathering Championship. Address: Lawrence Dance Academy, 67 Broad Street, Peterhead, Aberdeenshire AB42 1JL; T.-01358 789492.
E-mail: rhona@lawrencedanceacademy.co.uk

Lawrie, Kenneth, MBA, MA (Econ). Chief Executive, Falkirk Council, since 2018. Educ. St Andrews University; Strathclyde University. Held senior positions with Dartford Borough Council and Scottish Borders Council; Chief Executive, Midlothian Council, 2009-2018. Address: (b.) The Foundry, 4 Central Boulevard, Central Park, Larbert FK5 4RU; T.-01324 506070.

Lawrie, Paul, MBE, OBE. Professional golfer; b.1.1.69, Aberdeen; m., Marian; 2 s. Assistant, Banchory; turned professional, 1986; Winner, UAP Under 25s Championship, 1992; Winner, Open Golf Championship, 1999. Honorary law doctorate, Robert Gordon University; Honorary Life Member, European Tour. Recreations: snooker; Aberdeen Football Club; cars.

Lawson, Isobel, FFCS. Director/Company Secretary, Stepping Stones for Families, since 1988; Board Member, Childcare First Paisley Partnership; Member, Scottish Government's Early Years Task Force subgroup; b. Paisley; 2 d. Training and consultancy, voluntary sector childcare/education development. Address: (b.) Studio 3003A, Mile End Mill, Paisley PA1 1JS.

Lawson, John Philip, MBE, BSc, FEIS. Honorary Member, Scottish Youth Hostels Association, since 2001 (Chairman, 1980-2001); Headteacher, St. Joseph's School, Linlithgow, 1974-94; b. 19.8.37, Bathgate; m., Diana Mary Neal. Educ. St. Mary's Academy, Bathgate; Edinburgh University; Moray House College of Education. Teacher, West Lothian, 1962-94; held various offices in the Educational Institute of Scotland, including President, West Lothian Local Association and Chairman, Lothian Regional Executive; Member, West Lothian Children's Panel, 1972-81; Member, SYHA National Executive, 1966-2001; Vice-Chairman, SYHA, 1975-80; awarded: Richard Schirrmann Medal by German Youth Hostels Association, 1988, Gezel van de Rugzak, Flemish Youth Hostels Association, 1993; a Director, Scottish Rights of Way Society Ltd (Scotways), 1979-2016; a Director, Gatliff Hebridean Hostels Trust, 1988-2019, Hon. Treasurer, 2006-2016; President, West Lothian Headteachers Association, 1986-88; President, Federation of Youth Hostels Associations in the European Community, 1990-2001; Vice-President and Board Member, International Youth Hostel Federation, 1994-2002; Member, The Gatliff Trust, since 2003. Recreations: hill-walking; travel; music; reading. Address: (h.) Ledmore, Carnbee, Anstruther KY10 2RU; T.-01333 720312.

Lawson, Lilian Keddie, OBE, BSc (Hons), MBA. Formerly Director, Scottish Council on Deafness (2000-2014); b. 23.2.49, Pittenweem; m., John McDonald Young (deceased); 2 d. Educ. Donaldson's School, Edinburgh; Mary Hare Grammar School, Newbury; Edinburgh University; Strathclyde University. Administrative Assistant, progressing to Head of Administration, British Deaf Association, 1981-92; Manager, Sign Language Interpreting Services, Strathclyde Regional Council, 1992-93; Director, RNID Scotland, 1993-2000. Publication: Words in Hand (Co-Author), 1984. Recreations: gardening; genealogy; travel; her children.

Lawson, Peter A., LLB (Hons), DipLP. Chairman, Burness Paull, since 2018, Partner, since 2001; b. 20.7.70, Edinburgh; m., Andrea; 2 d.; 1 s. Educ. Dunfermline High School; Edinburgh University. Trainee, Burness LLP, 1994-96, Assistant, 1996-98; Associate, Freshfields Bruckhaus Deringer, 1998-2001. Recreation: sport. Address: (b.) Lothian Road, Edinburgh EH3 9WJ; T.-0131 473 6108; e-mail: peter.lawson@burnesspaull.com

Lawson, Peter John, LLB, NP. Chairman, Scottish Opera; Solicitor; Partner, Miller Samuel Hill Brown, Glasgow, since 1990; b. 25.3.58, Visakapatnam, India. Educ. Glasgow University. Director, Raindog TV Ltd; Director, NVA Europe; Chairman, St Peter's Kilmahew Ltd (arts organisation spearheading the restoration and development of the former St Peter's Seminary and grounds in Cardross); former Committee Member, BAFTA Scotland. Recreations: theatre; travel. Address: (b.) Miller Samuel Hill Brown Solicitors, The Forsyth Building, 5 Renfield Street, Glasgow G2 5EZ; T.-07768 244 844.
E-mail: pjl@mshblegal.com

Laybourn, Professor Peter John Robert, MA (Cantab), PhD, FIET, FRSE. Professor of Electronic Engineering, Glasgow University, since 1985, now Emeritus; b. 30.7.42, London; m., Ann Elizabeth Chandler; 2 d. Educ. William Hulme's Grammar School; Bristol Grammar School; Clare College, Cambridge. Research Assistant, Leeds University, 1963-66; Research Fellow, Southampton University, 1966-71; Lecturer, then Senior Lecturer, then Reader, Glasgow University, 1971-85. Recreations: sailing; boat-building; choral singing. Address: (h.) 33 Woodlands Street, Milngavie, Glasgow G62 8NS; T.-0141 956 4969.

Layden, Patrick John, QC, TD, LLB (Hons). Commissioner, Scottish Law Commission, 2008-2014; Deputy Solicitor, Scottish Government Legal Directorate, 2003-08; Legal Secretary to the Lord Advocate, 1999-2003; b. 27.6.49, Edinburgh; m., Patricia Mary Bonnar; 3 s.; 1 d. Educ. Holy Cross Academy, Edinburgh; University of Edinburgh. Scottish Bar, 1973-77; Junior Legal Secretary/Assistant Parliamentary Counsel, Lord Advocate's Department, 1977-83; Assistant Legal Secretary and Scottish Parliamentary Counsel, 1983-99. Appointed Queen's Counsel, 2000. University of Edinburgh OTC, 1967-71; 2/52 Lowland Vol., 1971-77; 1/51 Highland Vol., 1977-81 (O.C., London Scottish, 1978-81); O.C., 73 Ord. Co. (V), 1981-84; Territorial Decoration, 1984. Recreations: walking; reading; woodworking.

Lazarowicz, Mark, MA, LLB, DipLP. MP, Edinburgh North and Leith, 2001-2015 (Member, Environmental Audit Committee, 2005-2015; previously Member of Scottish Affairs; Environmental, Food and Rural Affairs; Modernisation; Regulatory Reform Committees); Shadow Minister for International Development, 2010-2011; Advocate; b. 8.8.53. Educ. St. Andrews University;

Edinburgh University. Member, Edinburgh District Council, 1980-96: Leader of the Council, 1986-93, Chairperson, Labour Group, 1993-94; Member, City of Edinburgh Council, 1999-2001 (Executive Member for Transport, 2000-01, Convenor, Transportation Committee, 1999-2000); Deputy Leader, COSLA Labour Group, 1990-93; Vice-Chairperson, 1988-89, Chairperson, 1989-90, Scottish Labour Party; Founder Member and Board Member, Centre for Scottish Public Policy, 1990-2009; Chairperson, Edinburgh International Conference Centre Ltd., 1992-93; Chairperson, Edinburgh Tourist Board, 1993-94.

Learoyd, Dr Simon, PhD. Former Chair, National Library of Scotland; recently retired after a 35-year career in financial services, most of which was with Clydesdale Bank; b. 11.59. Member of the National Library of Scotland Board, since 2014 (former Chair, Audit Committee); Trustee: National Library of Scotland Foundation, Community Integrated Care, Pittenweem Arts Festival. Address: National Library of Scotland, George IV Bridge, Edinburgh EH1 1EW.

Leckie, (Gordon Kenneth) Stephen, BA, CDir. Chairman and Chief Executive Officer of the Crieff Hydro Family of Hotels, since 1994; Lord-Lieutenant of Perth and Kinross, since 2019; b. 4.65 (s. of William Gordon John Leckie, MBE and Janet Ida Leckie (nee Kincaid); m. (1990), Fiona Barbara Willins; 2 s.; 2 d. Educ. Morrison's Acad.; Strathallan School; Edinburgh Napier University (BA Hospitality and Tourism, 1986). Career history: Hotel General Manager, Queens Moat House Hotel, 1986-1994; Chairman, Scottish Tourism Alliance (STA), since 2011; Chair and Board Member, Scottish Chambers of Commerce, since 2021; Past President and Director, Perthshire Chamber of Commerce (2011-2021); Deputy Lieutenant for Perth and Kinross, 2012-19; Past Chair and Member of Scotland Committee, UK Hospitality (formerly British Hospitality Association), since 1995; Board Member, Meikle Paton Trust, since 1997; Director and joint owner, Strathearn Engineering Ltd, since 2005; Member of Young Presidents' Organisation, since 1997. Chairman, Tourism Leadership Group (TLG), 2010-2021; Chairman, Crieff Community Council, 2011-2016; Board Member, BID Scotland, Crieff (2014-2021); Scottish School Piping Champion, 1982; Scottish Espoir Wrestling Champion, 1984; Silver Thistle Award, Scottish Tourism, 2013. Recreations: classic cars; member of clubs (20-Ghost; Alvis Owners; Armstrong Siddeley Owners; Aston Martin Owners; Daimler and Lanchester Owners; Jaguar Drivers; Jaguar E-type; Lagonda; Lagonda Rapier Register; Rolls Royce Enthusiasts; Strathearn Classic Car; Sunbeam Talbot Alpine Register and Vintage Sports Car; Land Rovers; piping; skiing; trials biking; sailing. Address: Crieff Hydro, Strathearn House, Ferntower Road, Crieff, Perthshire PH7 3LQ; T.-01764 651 620. Clubs: Royal Highland Yacht; Border Vintage Automobile; Vintage Motorcycle.

Lederer, Peter J., CBE. Chairman, Royal Edinburgh Military Tattoo, since 2017; Chairman, Gleneagles Hotels Limited, 2007-2014, Managing Director and General Manager, 1984-2007; Director, Diageo Scotland, 2008-2014; Chairman: VisitScotland, 2001-2010, One and All Foundation, Hamilton & Inches Ltd, Taste Communications; Non-Executive Director: Baxters Food Group Ltd; Director, The Hotel Management Company; b. 30.11.50; m., Marilyn Ruth MacPhail. Four Seasons Hotels, Canada, 1972-79; Vice President, Wood Wilkings Ltd., Toronto, 1979-81; General Manager, Plaza Group of Hotels, Toronto, 1981-83. Patron, Hospitality Industry Trust Scotland; Freeman, City of London; FHCIMA; Master Innholder; Liveryman, Worshipful Company of Innholders. Address: (b.) 18, Great Stuart Street, Edinburgh EH3 7TN.

Ledingham, Professor Iain McAllan, MSc (Hons), MD (Hons), FRCS (Ed), FRCP (Ed, Glas), FInstBiol, FCCM, DMI (RCSEd), FFICM, FRSE. Professor Emeritus of Medical Education, University of Dundee; formerly Consultant, Middle East Affairs, Royal College of Surgeons of Edinburgh; Special Adviser, University of Durham; b. 26.2.35, Glasgow; m., Eileen; 3 s. Educ. King's Park Senior Secondary, Glasgow; Central School, Aberdeen; University of Glasgow. Early training in surgery/trauma/intensive care; MRC Senior Research Fellow in hyperbaric medicine; first UK Professor of Intensive Care Medicine, University of Glasgow, 1980; Chair, Intensive Therapy Unit, Western Infirmary, Glasgow, 1985; Foundation Chair, Department of Emergency and Critical Care Medicine, Faculty of Medicine and Health Sciences, United Arab Emirates University, 1988 (Dean, FMHS, 1989). First President, Intensive Care Society, UK; President: European Shock Society, European Society of Intensive Care Medicine; Bellahouston Medal, University of Glasgow; La Médaille de la Ville de Paris; The College Medal (RCSEd). Recreations: jogging; hill-walking; music; reading; tree propagation; woodworking; occasional bad golf. Address: Kir Royale, Westown, by Errol, Perthshire PH2 7SU; T.-01821 670210; e-mail: iml@scotpad.co.uk

Lee, John Richard, MA, PhD. Professor of Digital Media, University of Edinburgh; b. 10.01.58, St. Alban's; m., Rosemary Fawcett; 2 s.; 4 d. Educ. Lochaber High School; University of Edinburgh. Research Associate/Part-time Lecturer, University of Edinburgh, 1985; Lecturer, 1993; Senior Lecturer, 1997; Personal Chair in Digital Media, 2010. Joint appointment in Architecture (now Edinburgh College of Art) and Informatics; Director, Edinburgh Computer-Aided Architectural Design Research Unit (EdCAAD), from 1991; Deputy Director, Human Communication Research Centre, since 1993. Recreations: music; running. Address: (b.) School of Informatics, Informatics Forum, 10 Crichton Street, Edinburgh EH8 9AB; T.-0131 650 4420; e-mail J.Lee@ed.ac.uk

Lee, Dame Laura Elizabeth, RGN, MSC, DipN. Chief Executive, Maggie's Cancer Caring Centres, since 1996; b. 15.10.66, Whitbank, South Africa; m., Hani Gabra; 2 s.; 1 d. Educ. Peterhead Academy; Birmingham University. Qualified RGN, 1987; various posts in nursing in cancer care in Edinburgh and London, 1987-91; clinical nurse specialist, Edinburgh Breast Unit, 1991-96. Recreations: reading; running; swimming. Address: (b.) The Stables, Western General Hospital, Crewe Road, Edinburgh, EH4 2XG; T.-0131-537 2456.

Leigh, Professor Irene May, CBE (2012), OBE (2006), FRSE, DSc, FRCP, FMedSci. Emeritus Professor, University of Dundee; b. 25.4.47, Liverpool; m. (1), P N Leigh; m. (2), JE Kernthaler; 1 s.; 3 d. Educ. Merchant Taylors' School for Girls, Great Crosby; London Hospital Medical College. Consultant Dermatologist, London Hospital, 1983-2006; Professor of Dermatology, 1989-99, Professor of Cellular and Molecular Medicine, 1999-2006, Research Dean, Barts and London School of Medicine and Dentistry, 1997-2002; Director, CRUK Skin Tumour Laboratory, since 1989; Vice Principal and Head of College of Medicine, Dentistry and Nursing, University of Dundee, 2006-2011. Recreations: grandchildren; music. E-mail: i.m.leigh@dundee.ac.uk

Leighton, Sir John, MA (Hons) Edin, MA, FRSE. Director-General, National Galleries of Scotland, since 2006; b. 22.2.59, Belfast; m., Gillian Keay; 1 s.; 1 d. Educ. Portora Royal School, Enniskillen; University of Edinburgh; Edinburgh College of Art; Courtauld Institute. Lecturer and Tutor, Department of

Humanities, Edinburgh College of Art, 1983-86; Curator, 19th-Century Paintings, National Gallery, London, 1986-96; Director, Van Gogh Museum, Amsterdam, 1997-2006. Board Member, De Pont Museum for Contemporary Art, Tilburg, since 1998; Trustee, Rijksmuseum, Amsterdam. Appointed Chevalier in the French Ordre des Arts et des Lettres; numerous exhibitions organised. Publications include (Books and Exhibition Catalogues): Co-Author, Signac 1863-1935, 2001; The Van Gogh Museum: A portrait, 2003; Co-Author, Manet and the Sea, 2003; 100 Masterpieces from the National Galleries of Scotland, 2015. Address: (b.) National Galleries of Scotland, 73 Belford Road, Edinburgh EH4 3DS.

Leighton-Beck, Dr Linda Bryce, BEd (Hons), MSc, PhD, DRM, FHEA. Head of Social Inclusion, NHS Grampian, 2003-2020; Honorary Senior Lecturer, Centre of Academic Primary Care, University of Aberdeen, 2001-2014; b. 23.5.53, Greenock; m., David; 2 d. Educ. Greenock Academy; Aberdeen University; Purdue University; Dunfermline College of Physical Education (now University of Edinburgh). Teacher of Physical Education, Strathclyde Regional Council, 1975; Lecturer, Dunfermline College of Physical Education; Assistant Director of Leisure Services, East Lothian District Council; Researcher, Scottish Council for Research in Education; Executive Manager, North of Scotland Health Services Research Network, Aberdeen University; Education Manager (North East), Scottish Council for Postgraduate Medical and Dental Education (now NHS Education Scotland); Health Improvement Programme Manager, NHS Grampian. Non-Executive Director, Sportscotland, 2000-08; Board of Directors, Aberdeen Foyer, 2001-09. Faculty of Public Health (Scottish Committee) Elizabeth Russell Prize 2016, with NHS Grampian and Third Sector colleagues. Recreations: walking; indoor rowing; music.
E-mail: lindaleightonbeck@icloud.com

Leiper, Joseph, OBE, DL, MA, DipEd, ACII. Rector, Oldmachar Academy, 1984-2004; b. 13.8.41, Aberdeen; m., Moira Taylor; 2 d. Educ. Aberdeen Grammar School; Aberdeen University. English Teacher: Robert Gordon's College, 1972-73; Bankhead Academy, 1973-75; Principal Teacher, English, Bankhead Academy, 1975-80; Assistant Rector, 1980-82; Depute Rector, Ellon Academy, 1982-84; Chairman, Aberdeen University Business Committee, General Council, 2000-06; appointed to Court, Aberdeen University, General Council Court Assessor, 2000-08; awarded OBE in July 2004 for services to education; appointed as Deputy Lieutenant of Aberdeen City, 2005; appointed as part-time Associate Teaching Fellow in the School of Education, University of Aberdeen, 2005-07; appointed Burgess of Guild of Aberdeen City, 2005. Recreations: sailing; reading; walking. Address: (h.) 5 Fairview Place, Bridge of Don, Aberdeen AB22 8ZJ.

Leishman, Brian Archibald Scott, MBE; b. 16.9.36; 1 s.; 1 d. Educ. Fettes College. Retired Regular Army Officer; commissioned The Cameronians (Scottish Rifles); re-badged on disbandment in 1968 The King's Own Scottish Borderers, service in the Arabian Gulf, East Africa and Europe; Italian Staff College, 1971-73; Assistant Defence Attache, British Embassy, Rome, 1974-76; Edinburgh Military Tattoo, 1977, Business Manager, 1978-98. Scottish Tourist Board Silver Thistle Award, 1996; Box Office Management International (New York) Lifetime Achievement Award, 1997; variously, Event Consultancy and Organisation, Editor, Regimental Journal, The Cameronians (Scottish Rifles), 1983-2004; European co-ordinator, International Ticketing Association (New York),

1998-2003; Board Member, Edinburgh Military Tattoo Ltd/Edinburgh Military Tattoo (Charities) Ltd; Founder Member, Edinburgh Capital Group (Edinburgh Entertains), Ticketing Consultant XIII Commonwealth Games Edinburgh, 1986; Chairman, Edinburgh International Jazz and Blues Festival; Board Member, Edinburgh Tourist Board and Edinburgh and Lothians Tourist Board; Member, Advisory Board, International Festival and Events Association (Europe). Recreations: music; photography. Address: (h.) Flat 5, Ramsay Grange, 29 Barnton Grove, Edinburgh EH4 6EQ; T.-0131 339 1048.

Leitch, Angela. Chief Executive, Public Health Scotland, since 2019. Educ. Glasgow Caledonian University; Edinburgh Napier University. Career history: Head of Service: West Lothian Council, 1996-2006, The City of Edinburgh Council, 2006-09; Chief Executive: Clackmannanshire Council, 2009-2011, East Lothian Council, 2011-19. Address: (b.) Gyle Square, 1 South Gyle Crescent, Edinburgh EH12 9EB.

Leitch, Jason Andrew, CBE, BDS (Dentistry), MPH (Public Health). National Clinical Director, The Scottish Government, since 2012; b. 25.10.68; m., Lynn. Educ. Airdrie Academy; University of Glasgow; Harvard T.H. Chan School of Public Health. Career history: qualified as a dentist in 1991, Consultant Oral Surgeon in Glasgow; Health Foundation/IHI Fellow, Institute for Healthcare Improvement, Boston, 2005-06; Honorary Consultant, Dental School, University of Glasgow, since 2005; National Clinical Lead for Quality, The Scottish Government, 2007-12. Non-executive Board member of the Medical and Dental Defence Union of Scotland; Director of the Nazareth Trust; Trustee of the UK wing of the Indian Rural Evangelical Fellowship which runs orphanages in south east India. Honorary Professor, University of Dundee; Fellow: The Royal College of Surgeons of England, The Royal College of Physicians and Surgeons of Glasgow, The Royal College of Surgeons of Edinburgh, The Higher Education Academy. HFMA UK Clinician of the Year, 2011. Numerous presentations, books and articles. Address: The Scottish Government, St. Andrew's House, Regent Road, Edinburgh EH1 3DG.

Leith, Professor Murray Stewart, BA, MA, PhD, FRSA. Professor, School of Education and Social Sciences, University of the West of Scotland, since 2020. Educ. Aurora University; Eastern Illinois University; Miami (Ohio) University; University of Glasgow. Career history: University of the West of Scotland: Lecturer in Politics, 2007-2012; Senior Lecturer, 2012-17; Reader in Politics, 2017-18; Assistant Dean, School of Media, Culture and Society, 2018-19; (Acting) Head of Division, 2019-2020. Member, Editorial Board for the journal 'National Identities'. Research interests include nationalism, national identity; Scottish and US politics; leading expert on the contemporary Scottish diaspora. Address: University of the West of Scotland, Paisley Campus, Paisley PA1 2BE.
E-mail: Murray.Leith@uws.ac.uk

Lennon, Professor Justin John, BSc (Hons), MPhil, PhD. Dean, Glasgow School for Business and Society; Director of the Moffat Centre for Travel and Tourism Business Development, Glasgow Caledonian University (Professor of Travel and Tourism Business Development, since 1999); Dean, Glasgow School for Business and Society; Head of Department, Business Management; Specialist Policy Advisor, Visit Scotland, 2005-2015; Non-Executive Director: Historic Scotland (Historic Environment Scotland), 2007-2015, Glasgow Chamber of Commerce; b. 19.6.61, Birmingham; m., Joanne Lesley; 2 s.; 1 d. Educ. Central Grammar School, Birmingham; Glasgow

Caledonian University, Strathclyde University; Oxford Brookes University. Hotel Management, 1983-94; Hotel and Tourism Consultancy, 1992-97; University of Strathclyde, 1995-98. Director, Scottish Tourism Forum, 2005-08; Board Member, Canadian Tourism Commission European Marketing Group, 2005-2014. Author of 9 books (Dark Tourism, Tourism Statistics, Benchmarking National Tourism Organisations); over 100 journal articles. Address: (b.) Moffat Centre, Travel and Tourism, Glasgow Caledonian University, Glasgow G4 0BA; T.-0141 331 8400; e-mail: j.j.lennon@gcu.ac.uk

Lennon, Monica, BA (Hons). MSP (Labour), Central region, since 2016; Shadow Cabinet Secretary for Economy, Jobs and Fair Work, since 2021; Shadow Cabinet Secretary for Health and Sport, 2018-2021; b. 7.1.81, Bellshill; m.; 1 d. Educ. John Ogilvie High School; University of Strathclyde. Career history: Operator, Motorola, 1999-2001; Graduate Planner, Keppie Design, 2001; Planning Officer, South Lanarkshire Council, 2001-07; Senior Planner, Atkins, 2007; Project Manager, Kier Homes Limited, 2008; Senior Planner, The Scottish Government, 2008-09; Planning Consultant, MLA Planning and Development, 2008-2011; Chair, Lanarkshire Business Group, 2011-12; Planning Consultant, Knight Frank, 2011-12; External Engagement and Fundraiser, Scottish Labour Party, 2015; elected to represent Hamilton North and East, South Lanarkshire Council election, 2012. Finalist, UK Young Planner of the Year, Royal Town Planning Institute, 2012. Address: Scottish Parliament, Edinburgh EH99 1SP.

Leonard, Richard. MSP (Labour), Central Scotland region, since 2016; Leader of the Scottish Labour Party, 2017-2021; b. 1.62, Yorkshire; m., Karen; 1 s.; 1 stepdaughter. Educ. Pocklington School, East Riding of Yorkshire; University of Stirling. Former Organiser for the GMB trade union (represented workers in manufacturing industry and public services across Central Scotland); former Scottish TUC economist; written extensively on the Scottish economy and served on the Boards of several economic regeneration companies. Founder of the Keir Hardie Society; Member of the Scottish Labour History Society; Convener, RMT Scottish Parliamentary Group; Convener, Scottish Parliament Public Audit Committee; Labour candidate in the Carrick, Cumnock and Doon Valley constituency for the Scottish Parliament election in 2011 and for Airdrie and Shotts in 2016 and 2021. Address: Scottish Parliament, Edinburgh EH99 1SP.
E-mail: richard.leonard.msp@parliament.scot

Leslie, Sheriff Desmond. Sheriff at Ayr. Served Legal apprenticeship with JNO Shaughnessy Quigley and McColl, Glasgow, 1980-1982; qualified as a solicitor in 1982 working with Lambie & Co, Glasgow as assistant and partner until 2005; appointed Part-time Sheriff in 2005 and appointed full-time as All-Scotland Floating Sheriff in 2006; Resident Sheriff in Ayr, since 2010. Address: Sheriff Court House, Wellington Square, Ayr KA7 1EE; T.-01292 292200.

Leslie Melville, The Hon. Mrs Ruth Jacquelyn, MBE, OSTJ. Provost of Angus, 2007-2012 (retired); Independent Councillor, 1989-92 and 1995-2012; b. 7.4.41, Aberdeen; m., The Hon Ronald Jocelyn Leslie Melville (widowed); 1 d.; 4 s. (1 son deceased). Educ. Stoneywood Primary School; Inverurie Academy; School for the Blind, Edinburgh. Founder and Vice Chair, Brechin Youth Project (The Attic); District Organiser for Angus, WRVS; Member, then Chair of Tayside Health Council; Founder/Chair, Bel-

Aid (Scotland working for The Belarussian Victims of Chernobyl); Founder of The Friends of Stracathro Hospital; Founder/Chair, Brechin Arts Festival; Campaigner for the Saving of Stracathro Hospital; former Non Executive Director, Tayside Health Board (retired); Minister, Esk Congregational Church. Address: 34 Park Road, Brechin, Angus DD9 7AP; T.-01356 625259; m.-07745662213.
E-mail: ruthlm1941@gmail.com

Lessels, Norman, CBE, CA; b. 2.9.38, Edinburgh; m., Christine Stevenson Hitchman; 1 s. Educ. Edinburgh Academy. Partner, Ernst & Whinney, until 1980; Partner, Chiene & Tait, CA, until 1998. President, Institute of Chartered Accountants of Scotland, 1987-88; former Director: Standard Life Assurance Company (Chairman, 1988-98), Bank of Scotland, Cairn Energy, Robert Wiseman Dairies PLC; Partner, Sheehan Tate (Senior Partner, 1993-98). Recreations: golf; music; bridge. Address: (h.) 15 India Street, Edinburgh EH3 6HA; T.-0131-225 5596.

Levein, Craig William. National Coach, Scottish Football Association, 2009-2012; Manager, Heart of Midlothian FC, 2017-19, Director of Football, 2014-19; b. 22.10.64, Dunfermline. Senior Clubs played: Cowdenbeath, 1981-83, Heart of Midlothian, 1983-95. Sixteen appearances for National Team, 1990-94. Teams managed: Cowdenbeath, 1997-2000, Heart of Midlothian, 2000-04, Leicester City, 2004-06, Raith Rovers, 2006, Dundee United, 2006-09.

Leven, Marian Forbes, RSA, RSW. Artist; b. 25.3.44, Edinburgh; m., Will Maclean; 2 s.; 1 d. Educ. Bell-Baxter School, Cupar; Gray's School of Art, Aberdeen. Exhibited RSA, RSW, RGI, SSA, AAS; work in private and public collections; Winner, Noble Grossart Painting Prize, 1997; 2013 Winner, Saltire Society Award, Art in Architecture, with Will Maclean. Address: (h.) Bellevue, 18 Dougall Street, Tayport, Fife DD6 9JD.

Leven and Melville, Earl of (Alexander Ian Leslie-Melville); b. 29.11.84. Succeeded to title, 2012. Educ. Gordonstoun. Address: Glenferness House, Nairn IV12 5UP.

Levick, Jemima. Artistic Director, A Play, A Pie and A Pint, since 2021; Artistic Director and Chief Executive, Stellar Quines Theatre Company, 2016-2021. Educ. Queen Margaret University. Artistic Director, Dundee Rep Theatre, 2015-2016, Joint Artistic Director, 2013-2015, Associate Director, 2009-2013. Nominated for a number of theatre awards and won a best director Critics' Award for Theatre in Scotland (CATS) for work on the 2009 Rep production of The Elephant Man. Address: A Play, A Pie and A Pint, Òran Mór, Byres Road, Glasgow G12 8QX; T.-0141 357 6200.

Levinthal, Terrence Scott, BES, DipUD, FSAScot. Executive Director, The Cockburn Association, since 2017; Director of Conservation Services and Projects, National Trust for Scotland, 2010-2016; Director, Scottish Civic Trust, 1999-2010 (Technical Director, 1999-2002); Board Member, Loch Lomond and the Trossachs National Park Authority, 2002-2010; b. 9.12.61, Winnipeg. Educ. University of Waterloo; Heriot-Watt/Edinburgh College of Art. Investigator, Royal Fine Art Commission for Scotland, 1988-92; Secretary, The Cockburn Association (Edinburgh Civic Trust), 1992-99. Recreations: hill-walking; skiing; cycling and other outdoor pursuits; the arts; woodworking.

Lewis, Bryan David, MBE, BA (Hons) Classics, HDipEd (Hons). Director of Development, Erskine Stewart's Melville Schools, since 2016; formerly Headmaster, ESMS Junior School (1989-2016); formerly Vice Principal, ESMS (1995-2016); b. 16.2.50, Dublin, Ireland; m., Susan; 3 d. Educ. Dublin High School; Trinity College, Dublin. Taught Classics in Dublin High School, 1973-74; Classics Teacher,

Stewart's Melville College, 1974-77, Housemaster, 1977-80, Head of Classics, 1980-89, Assistant Head, 1987-89. Publication: 'Stewart's Melville: The First 10 Years' (Co-Author), 1984. Recreations: sport of all kinds, especially rugby and golf; walking; musical theatre. Address: (b.) Queensferry Road, Edinburgh EH4 3EZ; T.-07776140417; e-mail: bryan.d.lewis@btinternet.com

Lewis, Sheriff Marysia, LLB. Sheriff Principal, Tayside, Central and Fife, since 2015. Educ. University of Strathclyde. Apprenticeship at Dunlop Gordon & Smythe, 1979-81; Solicitor: Monklands District Council, 1981-83, City of Aberdeen District Council, 1983-87; Solicitor, then partner, Ledingham Chalmers LLP (formerly Edmonds & Ledingham), 1987-2008. Appointed part-time sheriff in 2006, then sheriff in 2008. Address: Perth Sheriff Court, Tay Street, Perth PH2 8NL; T.-01738 620546.

Lewis, Paul, BSc (Hons), MBA. Senior Inward Investment Specialist, Investment Policy & Promotion Global Practice, World Bank Group, since 2020; Managing Director, Scottish Development International, 2015-2019. Educ. University of Edinburgh; University of Strathclyde. Career history: Senior Director (Business Infrastructure), Scottish Enterprise, 2005-07; Chief Executive, ITI Scotland, 2009-2010; Managing Director (Operations, Sectors & Commercialisation), Scottish Enterprise, 2007-2015.

Lewis, Sian, MA, DPhil (Oxon). Senior Lecturer in Ancient History, University of St. Andrews, since 2004; b. 30.06.66, Bridgend, Mid Glamorgan. Educ. St. Clare's Convent Grammar School, Porthcawl; University College, Oxford. Teaching Fellow, Trinity College, Dublin, 1991-92; College Tutor, University of Oxford, 1992-94; Tutorial Fellow, University of Wales Swansea, 1994-96; Lecturer in Ancient History, University of Wales Cardiff, 1996-2004. Publications: News and Society in the Greek Polis, 1996; The Athenian Woman: an iconographic handbook, 2002; Ancient Tyranny (ed), 2006; Greek Tyranny, 2009. Recreations: magic: The Gathering; science fiction; running. Address: (b.) School of Classics, University of St. Andrews, St. Andrews, Fife KY16 9AL; T.-01334 462600; e-mail: sl50@st-andrews.ac.uk

Liddell, Colin, OBE. Director, Friarbank Management Services; b. 28.8.47, Falkirk; m, Sheena Wood Mackay. Educ. Denny High School. Journalist, Johnston Newspaper Group, 1964-69; Editor, Linlithgow Journal & Gazette, 1968-69; Journalist, Scotsman Publications, 1969-1977; Senior Press Officer, Scottish Development Agency, 1977-82; PR Director, then Chief Executive, Charles Barker Scotland, 1982-86; Corporate Affairs Director, United Distillers, 1986-93; Corporate Communications Director, ScottishPower plc, 1993-95; Director, Liddell Thomson Consultancy, 1995-2011; Director, Billcliffe Gallery, 1996; Director, The HALO Kilmarnock Ltd., 2016-18; Director, Spreng & Co, 2008-16; Director, Falkirk FC, 2014-16; Vice Chairman, Falkirk FC 1998-2004; Member, CBI Scotland Council, 2002-09 and 2012-14; Board Member, Scottish Enterprise Glasgow, 1999-2002, Scottish Ballet, 1990-95, Royal Scottish National Orchestra, 1995-98, Quality Scotland Foundation, 1991-94. Recreations: golf; gardening; football.

Liddell, David, OBE, BSc (Hons), CQSW. Director, Scottish Drugs Forum, since 1993; b. 1957; 3 s.; 1 d. Educ. Riddlesdown High School; Sheffield University; Edinburgh University. Bristol Cyrenians, 1978; Dublin Simon Community, 1979; Biochemist: Queen Charlotte's Hospital, London, 1980, Temple Street Children's Hospital, Dublin, 1980; Dublin Committee for Travelling People, 1981-82;

Fieldworker, Standing Conference on Drug Abuse, 1985-86; Co-ordinator, Scottish Drugs Forum, 1986-93. Member: Ministerial Drug Task Force, 1994, Scottish Advisory Committee on Drug Misuse, 2008-2017. Publications: Drug Problems in Edinburgh (Co-author), 1987; Understanding Drug Problems in Scotland (Co-author), 1998; Understanding Drug Issues in Scotland (Co-author), 2000. Recreations: landscape gardening; camping; hostelling; allotment; chauffeur. Address: (b.) 5 Waterloo Street, Glasgow G2 6AY; T.-0141-221 1175. E-mail: dave@sdf.org.uk

Liddell of Coatdyke, Baroness (Helen Lawrie Liddell). Chairman, Annington Ltd; Member, Advisory Council, PWC, since 2014; Chairman, G3 (Good Governance Group), 2014-18; Member, Advisory Committee on Business Appointments, 2013-19; b. 6.12.50; m., Alistair; 1 s.; 1 d. Educ. St. Patrick's High School, Coatbridge; University of Strathclyde. Career: contested East Fife in October 1974; former BBC Scotland economics journalist, 1976-77; General Secretary of Labour Party in Scotland, 1977-86; public affairs director of Scottish Daily Record, 1986-93; Chief Executive, Business Ventures, 1993-94; MP (Labour), Monklands East, 1994-97, Airdrie and Shotts, 1997-2005; Cabinet Minister as Secretary of State for Scotland, 2001-03; British High Commissioner to Australia, 2005-2009; Honorary Patron, St Andrew's Society of Western Australia, since 2021. Address: House of Lords, London SW8 0AA.

Lilley, Professor David Malcolm James, FRS, FRSE, FRSC. Professor of Molecular Biology, Dundee University, since 1989; b. 28.5.48, Colchester; m., Patricia Mary; 2 d. Educ. Gilberd School, Colchester; Durham University. Joined Biochemistry Department, Dundee University, 1981; awarded: Colworth Medal by Biochemical Society, 1982, Gold Medal of G. Mendel, Czech Academy of Sciences, 1994, Gold Medal of V. Prelog in Stereochemistry, ETH, Zurich; Royal Society of Chemistry Award in RNA and Ribozyme Chemistry; Royal Society of Chemistry Interdisciplinary Award; Khorana Prize, 2016. Publications: 360 scientific papers. Recreations: foreign languages; running; skiing. Address: (b.) School of Life Sciences, Dundee University, Dundee DD1 5EH; T.-01382 344243. E-mail: d.m.j.lilley@dundee.ac.uk

Linden, David. MP (SNP), Glasgow East, since 2017; Shadow Secretary of State for Work and Pensions, since 2021; Spokesperson for Housing, Communities and Local Government, 2020-2021; b. 14.5.90; m., Roslyn; 1 s.; 1 d. Educ. Milncroft Primary School; Garrowhill Primary School; Bannerman High School, Baillieston. Apprenticeship in Business Administration with Glasgow City Council; Parliamentary Assistant for Alison Thewliss MP, 2015-17. Recreation: fan of Airdrieonians Football Club. Address: House of Commons, London SW1A 0AA.

Lindhurst, Gordon John S., LLB (Hons), DipLP, LLM. MSP (Scottish Conservative), Lothian region, 2016-2021; Advocate, since 1995; Barrister at law, of the Middle Temple, since 2008. Educ. University of Edinburgh; University of Glasgow; Universität Heidelberg. Admitted as Solicitor, 1991; Notary Public, 1992. Legal Reporter: Scots Law Times, 1995-2000, Session Cases, 2000-2018. Recreations: hillwalking; cabinet making; music.

Lindley-Highfield of Ballumbie Castle, Mark Paul, BA (Hons), BSc (Hons), MA (Hons), MA Ed, MEd, MRes, MPhil, FRAI, FRGS, FHEA, FCIEA, FRSA, FSA Scot. University Lecturer, Community Councillor, Anthropologist, and Chartered Educational Assessor; b.

1.2.75; m., Bethan Frances Marion Lindley-Highfield of Ballumbie Castle.; 1 s.; 1 d. Educ. Barr Beacon School; Walsall College of Arts and Technology; Westminster College, Oxford; University of Oxford; Open University; University of Aberdeen; University of Edinburgh. Career history: 14th Baron of Cartsburn, 2008-2010, remains Lord of Wilmington and Baron of Middle Ards; elected councillor (unopposed) on Turriff & District Community Council in 2016; co-opted onto Croy and Culloden Moor Community Council in 2018; elected councillor (unopposed) on Slackbuie Community Council in 2019 and Chairman, 2020; Plenipotentiary and Special Adviser of the Association of the Representatives of Bunyoro-Kitara and the Kingdom of Bunyoro-Kitara for Scotland, 2016-2019; given an award by the Omukama of Bunyoro-Kitara for charitable work done for the benefit of the Banyoro people in 2016; founder of the newly created Centre for the Study of the Kingdoms and Chiefdoms of Africa; Assistant Chancellor and Private Secretary to the Mwami of Rwanda, since 2019; Companion of the Order of Malta, since 2013; Burgess of the City of Glasgow, since 2016; Freeman of the City of London and Liveryman of the Worshipful Company of Arts Scholars; Associate Lecturer with the Open University, since 2004; Lecturer in Teacher Education at the University of the Highlands and Islands, Inverness College, since 2017. Address: Ballumbie Castle, Elm Rise, Broughty Ferry, Dundee DD5 3UY; c/o Royal Scots Club.

Lindsay, Carrie. Executive Director of Education and Children's Services, Fife Council, since 2017. Educ. Bell Baxter High School, Cupar. Career history: Teacher, Donibristle Primary School, from 1987, promoted to Acting Head Teacher; became Headteacher, Cowdenbeath Primary School; became a Quality Improvement Officer in Angus Council; returned to Fife in 2003 and developed role in Children's Services working with schools and community planning partners; appointed Head of Education and Children's Services, Fife Council in 2015. Address: Fife Council, Fife House, North Street, Glenrothes, Fife KY7 5LT.

Lindsay, 16th Earl of (James Randolph Lindesay-Bethune), MA, PhD. President, National Trust for Scotland, 2012-17; Non-Executive Director, Brockwell Energy, since 2017; Chairman, Frelish Energy, 2011-13; Chairman, Greenfield Holdings, 2009-2011; Chairman, Scottish Quality Salmon, 1998-2006; Chairman, United Kingdom Accreditation Service, since 2002; Managing Director, Marine Stewardship Council International, 2001-05; Chairman, RSPB Scotland, 1998-2003; Council Member, RSPB UK, 1998-2003; Vice President, RSPB, since 2004; Board Member, Cairngorms Partnership, 1998-2002; Non-Executive Director, UA (Scotland) plc, 1998-2005; Member, Scottish Power Environment Forum, 1998-2002; President, International Tree Foundation, 1995-2005, Vice President, since 2005; Chairman, Genesis Quality Assurance, 2001-02; Chairman, Elmwood College, 2001-09; Chairman, BPI Pension Scheme Trustees, since 2009; Non-Executive Director, Scottish Resources Group Ltd., 2001-2013; Non-Executive Director, SAC Ltd. (now SRUC), 2005-2015, Chairman, 2007-2015; Non-Executive Director, BPI plc, 2006-2015; Non-Executive Director, Hargreaves Energy Projects Ltd., 2015-2017; Member, Select Committee on the EU: Financial Affairs Sub-Committee, 2015-19; Member, Better Regulation Commission and Risk & Regulation Advisory Council, 2006-10, Deputy Chairman, from 2007; President, Royal Scottish Geographical Society, 2005-2012, currently Vice President; Chairman, Moorland Forum, 2007-2018; Associate Director, National Non-Food Crops Centre, 2007-2012; b. 19.11.55; m., Diana Mary Chamberlayne-Macdonald. Educ. Eton; Edinburgh University; University of California, Davis. Lord in Waiting (Government Whip), 1995; Parliamentary Under Secretary of State, Scottish

Office, 1995-97; Member, Secretary of State's Advisory Group on Sustainable Development, 1998-99; Member, Select Committee on European Community Affairs: Environment, Public Health and Consumer Protection Sub-Committee, 1997-99; Member, UK Round Table on Sustainable Development Sub-Group, 1998-2000; Chairman, Assured British Meat Ltd., 1997-2001; President, Royal Highland Agricultural Society of Scotland (RHASS), 2005-06; Member, Commission on Scottish Devolution, 2008-09; Member, Secondary Legislation Scrutiny Committee, since 2019; Chairman, Clearbank Tide Business Banking Grant Implementation Steering Committee, since 2019; Green Ribbon political award, 1995. Address: (h.) Lahill, Upper Largo, Fife KY8 6JE.

Lindsay, Gerald, BAcc, CA. Managing Director, Hansel Foundation; b. 12.2.64, Glasgow; 2 d. Educ. Marr College, Troon; University of Glasgow; ICAS (Institute of Chartered Accountants of Scotland). Auditor, to management level, Downie Wilson CA, Glasgow, 1985-97; Finance Manager, St Andrew's Ambulance Association, 1997-2000; Finance Director, Hansel, 2000-2011. Recreations: fitness; sports; travel. Address: Broadmeadows, Symington, Ayrshire KA1 5PU; T.-01563 830340.
E-mail: gerry.lindsay@hansel.org.uk

Lindsay, Jenny. Spoken word poet and writer; Director of Flint & Pitch Productions. Performed across the UK and further afield at a variety of festivals and events including Latitude, the Edinburgh International Book Festival, the 'Where I'm Calling From' Literary Festival in Montenegro, and the Ubud Writers and Readers Festival in Bali. Author of two full collections and two pamphlet collections of poetry; was longlisted for the inaugural Jerwood Compton Poetry Fellowship in 2017; winner of a John Byrne Award for Critical Thinking, 2020. Author, This Script, 2019, second edition, 2022. E-mail: jennylindsay@gmail.com

Lindsay, Mark Stanley Hunter, QC, LLB (Hons), DipLP. Advocate, since 1995; Owner, Axiom Advocates, since 1996; Standing Counsel to Home Secretary, 2000-2012; b. 17.5.69, Maybole; m., Rosemary; 2 s.; 1 d. Educ. Carrick Academy, Maybole; University of Glasgow. Energy Consultant, Jacek Mawkowski Associates, Boston, Mass., USA; Congressional Intern, Capitol Hill, Washington DC; Articled Clerk, Macallister Mazengarb, Wellington, NZ; Trainee Solicitor, Tods Murray, WS, Edinburgh; Solicitor, Scottish Office. Recreations: hillwalking; squash; classic cars; American history. Address: Advocates' Library, Parliament House, Edinburgh EH1 1RF; T.-0131-226 5071; (h.) 0131-467 1451; e-mail: MshLindsay@aol.com

Lindsay, Ranald Bruce, LLB(Hons), DipLP, NP. Solicitor-Advocate, since 1993; Solicitor, since 1986; b. 18.3.62, Bellshill; m.; 3 s.; 1 d. Educ. Wishaw High; University of Glasgow. Trained with Bishop & Co., Glasgow, 1984-86; qualified as first Solicitor Advocate in both civil and criminal law, 1993; established own practice, 1994; elected Law Society of Scotland Council Member for Dumfries, 2005-09; Convenor, Law Society of Scotland Access to Justice Committee, 2006-09; Dean, Faculty of Procurators of Dumfriesshire, 2009-2014; qualified light aircraft pilot, 2012. Recreations: reading; films; history; flying; getting away from it all. Address: (b.) Lindsay Solicitors, 75 Buccleuch Street, Dumfries DG1 2AB; T.-01387 259236.

Lingard, Joan Amelia, MBE. Author; b. 23.4.32, Edinburgh; 3 d. Educ. Bloomfield Collegiate School, Belfast; Moray House College of Education, Edinburgh. Member, Scottish Arts Council, 1980-85; Chair, Society of

Authors in Scotland, 1980-84; a Director, Edinburgh Book Festival, 1994-98; Hon. Vice-President, Scottish PEN, since 2001; first novel published, 1963; has also written plays for TV, including 18-part series, Maggie, adapted from quartet of teenage books; novels: Liam's Daughter, 1963; The Prevailing Wind, 1964; The Tide Comes In, 1966; The Headmaster, 1967; A Sort of Freedom, 1968; The Lord on our Side, 1970; The Second Flowering of Emily Mountjoy, 1979; Greenyards, 1981; Sisters By Rite, 1984; Reasonable Doubts, 1986; The Women's House, 1989; After Colette, 1993; Dreams of Love and Modest Glory, 1995; The Kiss, 2002; Encarnita's Journey, 2005; After You've Gone, 2007; 40 children's books; Awards: ZDF Preis der Leseratten, W. Germany, for The Twelfth Day of July, 1986; Buxtehuder Bulle, W. Germany for Across the Barricades, 1987; Scottish Arts Council awards for After Colette, 1994, Tom and the Tree House, 1998; Tug of War shortlisted for 1989 Carnegie Medal, 1989 Federation of Children's Book Groups Award, 1989 Sheffield Book Award, runner-up for 1990 Lancashire Children's Book Club of the Year; MBE for Services to Children's Literature, 1999; shortlisted, Scottish Royal Mail Awards for The Sign of The Black Dagger, 2006; nominated for the Astrid Lingren Award, 2006; shortlisted for the Scottish Royal Mail Award, West Sussex Children's Book Award and The Lancashire School Librarian Award 2009 for 'The Eleventh Orphan'; The Chancery Lane Conspiracy, 2010. Recreations: reading; walking; travelling. Address: (b.) David Higham Associates, 5-8 Lower John Street, Golden Square, London W1R 4HA.

Lingard, Robin Anthony, MA, MLitt, FTS; b. 19.7.41, Enfield; m., Margaret; 2 d. Educ. Felsted School; Emmanuel College, Cambridge. Joined Ministry of Aviation, 1963; Private Secretary to Joint Parliamentary Secretary, Ministry of Technology, 1966-68; appointments, Department of Industry, DTI, etc., to 1984; Head, Enterprise Unit, Cabinet Office, 1984-85; Head, Small Firms and Tourism Division, Department of Employment, 1985-87; full-time Board Member, Highlands and Islands Development Board, 1988-91; Director of Training and Social Development, Highlands and Islands Enterprise, 1991-93; Project Director, University of the Highlands and Islands Project, 1993-97. Member, Scottish Tourist Board, 1988-92; Chairman, Prince's Trust Committee for Highlands, Western Isles and Orkney; Member, Management Board, Prince's Trust and Royal Jubilee Trusts, 1989-95; Chairman, Youth Link Scotland, 1997-2000; Chairman, BBC Scotland Children in Need and Appeals Advisory Committee, 1999-2004; Chairman, Fusion Scotland, 2002-05; Chairman, Sustainable Development Research Centre, 2004-09; Chairman, Highland Community Care Forum, 2007-09; DUniv (Open), 1999; Hon. Fellow, UHI Millennium Institute, 2006. Recreations: watching birds; walking; reading; aviation history. Address: (h.) Kinnairdie House, Dingwall IV15 9LL; T.-01349 861044.

Linklater of Butterstone, Baroness (Veronica Linklater). Life Peer, since 1997; Founder and President, The New School, Butterstone, since 1991; President, Society of Friends of Dunkeld Cathedral, 1989-2013; Trustee, Esmée Fairbairn Foundation, 1991-2014; b. 15.4.43, Meikleour, Perthshire; m., Magnus Duncan Linklater (qv); 2 s.; 1 d. Educ. Cranborne Chase; Sorbonne; University of Sussex; University of London. Child Care Officer, London Borough of Tower Hamlets, 1967-68; Co-Founder, Visitors Centre, Pentonville Prison, 1971-77; Governor, three Islington schools, 1970-85; Prison Reform Trust Winchester Prison Project, 1981-82; Butler Trust: Founder, Administrator, Consultant, 1983-87, Trustee, 1987-2001, Vice President, 2001-2016; JP, Inner London, 1985-88; Co-ordinator, Trustee, Vice Chairman, Pushkin Prizes (Scotland), 1989-2020; Member, Children's Panel, Edinburgh South, 1989-

97; Committee Member, Gulliver Award for the Performing Arts in Scotland, 1990-96; Patron, Sutherland Trust, 1993-2003; Trustee, Young Musicians Trust, 1993-97; Candidate (Liberal Democrat), Perth & Kinross By-Election, 1995; Director, Maggie Keswick Jencks Cancer Caring Centres Trust, 1997-2004; Foundation Patron, Queen Margaret University College, since 1998; Member, Beattie Committee on Post School Provision for Young People with Special Needs, 1998-99; Patron, The Airborne Initiative, 1998-2004; Trustee, Development Trust, University of the Highlands and Islands, 1999-2001; Secretary, Scottish Peers Association, 2000-07; Chancellor's Assessor, Napier University Court, 2001-04; Patron, Family and Parenting Institute, since 2002; Patron, Support in Mind, Scotland (formerly National Schizophrenia Fellowship, Scotland), since 2000; Patron, The Probation Boards Association; Appeal Patron, Hopetoun House Preservation Trust, 2001; Member, Advisory Board, The Beacon Fellowship Charitable Trust, 2003-2018; Member, Scottish Committee, Barnardo's, 2001-04; Patron, Research Autism, since 2004; Patron, The Calyx, Scotland's Garden Trust, 2004-08; Advisor, Koestler Awards Trust, 2004-2010; Chairman, House of Lords All Party Parliamentary Group on Offender Learning & Skills, 2005-06; Patron, Action for Prisoners' Families, since 2005; Council Member, The Winston Churchill Memorial Trust; Patron, Home Start Perth, since 2006; Patron, Push, since 2007; President, Crime Reduction Initiative, 2007-2010; Patron, University of St Andrews Medical Campaign Committee, since 2007; President, SOVA, 2009-2017; Patron, Tacade, 2009-2012; Patron, Epilepsy Scotland, since 2009; Patron, Contact a Family, 2011. Hon. Degree, Queen Margaret University College, Edinburgh. Recreations: music; theatre; gardening. Address: (h.) Riemore Lodge, Dunkeld, Perthshire PH8 0HP; T.-01350 724205; e-mail: magnus.linklater1@gmail.com

Linklater, Emeritus Professor Karl Alexander, BVM&S, PhD, CBiol, FIBiol, FRAgS, FRCVS, FRSE. Principal, Scottish Agricultural College, 1999-2002, Emeritus Professor, since 2002; Professor of Agriculture, University of Glasgow, 1999-2002; a Director, The Moredun Foundation, 1991-2009; Director, Vet CPD, 1992-98; Director, the British Veterinary Association, 2003-06; Honorary Fellow, University of Edinburgh, 1998-2010; b. 1.9.39, Stromness, Orkney; m., Margaret; 1 s.; 1 d. Educ. Robert Gordon's College, Aberdeen; Edinburgh University. General veterinary practice, Tarland, Aberdeenshire, 1962-66; North of Scotland College of Agriculture, Aberdeen, 1966-67; Royal (Dick) School of Veterinary Studies, Edinburgh University, 1967-73; East of Scotland College of Agriculture, St. Boswells, 1973-86; Director, SAC Veterinary Services, 1986-97; Vice Principal, SAC, 1997-99; Member, Veterinary Products Committee, 1990-2001; President: Sheep Veterinary Society, 1983-85, British Veterinary Association, 1996-97, Association of Veterinary Teachers and Research Workers (Scotland), 1988-90, Scottish Branch, British Veterinary Association, 1992-94, Scottish Metropolitan Division, BVA, 1979-80; Alan Baldry Award, 1982; Lifetime Service Award by the International Sheep Veterinary Association, 2013. Recreations: sport; gardening; sheep breeding. Address: (h.) Bridge Park, Old Bridge Road, Selkirk TD7 4LG; T.-01750 20571; e-mail: k.linklater@btopenworld.com

Linklater, Magnus Duncan, CBE. Journalist; Columnist for The Times; President, The Saltire Society, 2011-2017; Chairman, The Little Sparta Trust, since 2000; Chairman, Horsecross Arts Company (Perth Theatre and Concert Hall), 2013-2020; b. 21.2.42, Harray, Orkney; m., Veronica Lyle; 2 s.; 1 d. Educ. Eton College; Cambridge University. Reporter, Daily Express, Manchester, 1965-66; London Evening Standard: Diary Reporter, 1966-67, Editor, Londoner's Diary, 1967-69; Sunday Times: Editor,

Spectrum, 1969-72, Editor, Colour Magazine, 1972-75; News Editor/Features Editor, 1975-83; Managing Editor, The Observer, 1983-86; Editor, London Daily News, 1986-87; Editor, The Scotsman, 1988-94; Chairman, Edinburgh Book Festival, 1994-96; Chairman, Scottish Arts Council, 1996-2001; Presenter, Eye to Eye, Radio Scotland, 1994-97; Columnist, The Times and Scotland on Sunday; Member, National Cultural Strategy Review Group, 1999-2000. Publications: Hoax: the Howard Hughes-Clifford Irving Affair (Co-Author); Jeremy Thorpe: A Secret Life (Co-Author); The Falklands War (with Sunday Times Insight team); Massacre — the story of Glencoe; The Fourth Reich — Klaus Barbie and the Neo-Fascist Connection (Co-Author); Not With Honour — the inside story of the Westland Affair (Co-Author); For King and Conscience — John Graham of Claverhouse, Viscount Dundee (Co-Author); Anatomy of Scotland (Co-Editor); Highland Wilderness: People in a Landscape; Edinburgh (Co-Author); Great Scottish Lives (Ed.), 2017. Fellow, Royal Society of Edinburgh; Honorary Doctor of Arts, Napier University; Honorary Doctor of Law, Aberdeen University; Honorary Doctor of Letters: Glasgow University, Queen Margaret University; Dr *honoris causa*, University of Edinburgh; Hon Fellow, University of the Highlands and Islands. Recreations: walking, fishing, shooting. Address: (h.) Riemore Lodge, Dunkeld, Perthshire PH8 0HP; T.-01350 724205.
E-mail: magnus.linklater1@gmail.com

Linkston, Alex, CBE. Former Chair, Forth Valley NHS Board (2012-2020); former Chief Executive of West Lothian Council. Awarded Quality Scotland's Leadership Award in 2007; Prince's Trust Scottish Volunteer of the Year in 2009; currently Chair of West Lothian College; member of the Scottish Council of the Prince's Trust.

Linlithgow, 4th Marquess of (Adrian John Charles Hope); b. 1.7.46; divorced; 1 s.; 1 d.; 2 s. by pr. m.; succeeded to title, 1987. Educ. Eton. Stockbroker. Address: Hopetoun House, Queensferry, South Queensferry EH30 9RW.

Lister-Kaye, Sir John, 8th Bt. of Grange, OBE, DUniv, DSc, FRGS. Naturalist, Author, Lecturer; Member, International Committee, World Wilderness Foundation, since 1984; Vice President, Association for the Preservation of Rural Scotland, since 1998; President, Scottish Wildlife Trust, 1996-2001; Vice President, RSPB, since 2006; b. 8.5.46; m., 1, Lady Sorrel Deirdre Bentinck; 1 s.; 2 d.; 2, Lucinda Anne Law; 1 d. Educ. Allhallows School. Founded Field Studies Centre, Highlands, 1970; founder Director, Aigas Trust, 1979; Chairman, Scottish Committee, RSPB, 1985-92; Member, Committee for Scotland, NCC, 1989-90; NW Regional Chairman, Scottish Natural Heritage, 1992-96; Honorary Doctorate, University of Stirling, 1995; Honorary Doctorate, St. Andrews University, 2005. Honorary Member and awarded the Geddes Medal for Environmental Education by The Royal Scottish Geographical Society, 2016. Awarded OBE, 2003. Publications: The White Island, 1972; Seal Cull, 1979; The Seeing Eye, 1980; One for Sorrow, 1994; Ill Fares the Land, 1995; Song of the Rolling Earth, 2003; Nature's Child, 2004; At The Water's Edge, 2010; Gods of the Morning, 2015 (Winner, The Richard Jefferies Award for Nature Writing); The Dun Cow Rib, 2017. Address: (h.) House of Aigas, Beauly, Inverness-shire IV4 7AD; e-mail: jlk@aigas.co.uk

Little, Dr Paul G. K. Founding Principal and Chief Executive, City of Glasgow College (Scotland's Super College and WorldSkills ranked number 1); 42 years Public Service; published author and Global Thought Leader; Wallace Award holder for transatlantic relations; 133rd President, Glasgow Chamber of Commerce; Chairman of European Foundation for Quality Management (Brussels); Member of Scottish Funding Council; Member of WorldSkills UK Board; Member of Merchant Navy Training Board. Career history: over 34 years' experience in Higher and Further Education; Fellow of Royal Society Edinburgh; Fellow of the Royal Society of Arts; Fellow of Nautical Institute; Fellow of Institute of Directors; Fellow of University College London; Fellow of Institute of Innovation & Knowledge Exchange; Member of the Chartered Institute of Public Relations; decorated 30 year veteran HM Coastguard Officer; Honorary US Coastguard; Honorary Captain in Royal Navy. Address: (b.) City of Glasgow College, 190 Cathedral Street, Glasgow G4 0RF.

Littlejohn, Professor David, BSc, PhD, CChem, FRSC, FRSE. Professor of Analytical Chemistry, Strathclyde University, since 1988; b. 1.5.53, Glasgow; m., Lesley Shaw MacDonald; 1 d. Educ. Duncanrig Secondary School, East Kilbride; Strathclyde University. Technical Officer, ICI Petrochemicals Division, Wilton, Middlesborough, 1978-80; Lecturer/Senior Lecturer in Chemistry, Strathclyde University, 1981-88; Head of Department, 2005-2010; Associate Deputy Principal (Research and Knowledge Exchange), 2010-2014; Executive Dean of Science, 2014-18; Associate Principal, 2016-18; Special Adviser to the Principal of University of Strathclyde, since 2018. Co-founder of the Centre for Process Analytics and Control Technology (www.cpact.com) in 1997 and Operations Director of CPACT since 2018. Awarded 15th SAC Silver Medal by Royal Society of Chemistry, 1987; Theophilus Redwood Lectureship, 2001; Royal Society of Chemistry Award in Chemical Analysis and Instrumentation, 2005; joint Editor in Chief, Talanta, International Journal of Pure and Applied Analytical Chemistry, 1989-91. Publications: 217 research papers; 10 reviews; 1 book; 6 book chapters. Address: (b.) Department of Pure and Applied Chemistry, Strathclyde University, 295 Cathedral Street, Glasgow G1 1XL; T.-0141 548 2067.
E-mail: d.littlejohn@strath.ac.uk

Littlejohn, Doris, BL, DUniv, CBE. Former President, Employment Tribunals (Scotland); b. 19.3.35, Glasgow; m., Robert (deceased); 3 d. Educ. Queen's Park School, Glasgow; University of Glasgow. Solicitor in private practice in Stirling until 1977. Former Chairman of Court, University of Stirling; former Member: Lord Chancellor's Panel on Review of Tribunals, Review Panel on Retention of Organs after Post Mortems, Human Genetics Advisory Commission, Broadcasting Council for Scotland, General Advisory Committee, BBC. Address: Suilven, 125 Henderson Street, Bridge of Allan FK9 4RQ; T.-01786 832032.

Livingston, Professor Kay, BEd, MEd, PhD, FRSA. Professor of Educational Research, Policy and Practice, University of Glasgow, since 2007, Research in Teacher Education; b. Girvan; m.; 1 s. Educ. University of Glasgow. Teacher, 1978-87; Lecturer, Craigie College of Education, Ayr, 1987-92; Secondment to Socrates Technical Assistance in European Commission, Brussels, 1997; Senior Lecturer, Coordinator of International Education, University of Paisley, 1993-2001; Director of the Quality in Education Centre (QIE) and Reader in Education, University of Strathclyde, 2001-05; Professor of Education and Director of Scottish Teachers for a New Era, University of Aberdeen, 2005-07; Secondment to Learning and Teaching Scotland (LTS) as Director of International, Research and Innovation and Member of the Corporate Management Team, 2007-2011; Secondment to Education Scotland as Director of International, Research and

Innovation and Member of the Corporate Management Group, 2011-12. Editor, European Journal of Teacher Education and Curriculum Journal; Member of UK National Commission UNESCO Scotland Committee; Member of European Union Group on Professional Development of Teachers; Chair of the Commonwealth Games Legacy for Learning Group. Recreations: running; skiing; hill walking; reading.

Livingstone, Bill (William). Former Editorial Director, Forth Weekly Press, a division of Clyde & Forth Press; Trustee, Carnegie Dunfermline and Hero Fund Trusts, 1992-2014 (Chairman, 2010-2012); Trustee, Carnegie United Kingdom Trust, 2002-2014; b. 23.7.44, Dunfermline; m., Margaret Stark; 2 s.; 2 d. Educ. Dunfermline High School. Entire career with Dunfermline Press Group: Editor, Dunfermline Press, 1984-96. Chairman, Guild of Editors (Scotland), 1994-96. Address: 11 St. Margaret Wynd, Dunfermline KY12 0UT; T.-01383 726182.

Livingstone, Iain, QPM 2015. Chief Constable, Police Service of Scotland, since 2018; b. 6.10.66, Dunfermline; m., Jane Cairney; 3 d. Educ. Aberdeen University (LLB Hons 1988); Strathclyde University (DipLP 1989); John Jay College, City University of New York (MA Criminal Justice 1998). Career: Solicitor, Maclay Murray and Spens, 1989-92; Police Officer, Lothian and Borders Police, 1992-2013; Deputy Chief Constable, Police Service of Scotland, 2013-18. Recreations: sport; running; dog walking; family. Address: Police Scotland Headquarters, Tulliallan Castle, Kincardine, Fife FK10 4BE; T.-01786 893111.
E-mail: cc.office@Scotland.pnn.police.uk

Livingstone, Ian Lang, CBE, BL, NP. Chairman: Lanarkshire Health Board, 1993-2002, Lanarkshire Development Agency, 1991-2000, New Lanarkshire Ltd., until 2015; Consultant Solicitor, since 1989; Chairman, Kingdom FM Ltd., 2008-2018; Chairman, Scottish Local Authorities Remuneration Committee, 2004-2013; Deputy Lord Lieutenant for Lanarkshire, 2008-2013; b. 23.2.38, Hamilton; m., Diane; 2 s. Educ. Hamilton Academy; Glasgow University. Qualified as Solicitor, 1960; Partner, Senior Partner, Ballantyne & Copland, Solicitors, Motherwell, 1962-86, Consultant, until 2014; Chairman and Director, family property investment and development company, since 1987. Former Chairman, Motherwell Football Club; Chairman, Board, Motherwell College, 1989-97; Member, Dalziel High School Board; Chairman, David Livingstone Memorial Trust; Elder, St. Mary's Parish Church, Motherwell; Honorary President, Lanarkshire Chamber of Commerce, since 2006; awarded Doctorate, The University of the West of Scotland, 2008. Recreations: walking; football; music. Address: (h.) 223 Manse Road, Motherwell ML1 2PY; T.-01698 253750.

Livingstone, Jamie. Head of Oxfam Scotland, since 2013. Former print and broadcast journalist, including Political Correspondent on STV News; joined Oxfam in 2011 as Campaigns and Communications Manager, overseeing Oxfam's campaigns, media output and supporter communications in Scotland. Director of Stop Climate Chaos Scotland and plays a leading role within the Disasters Emergency Committee in Scotland. Address: Oxfam Scotland, 10 Bothwell Street, Glasgow G2 6LU; T.-0141 285 8850; e-mail: jlivingstone@oxfam.org.uk

Livingstone, Marilyn. MSP (Labour), Kirkcaldy, 1999-2011; b. 1952, Kirkcaldy. Educ. Viewforth Secondary School; Fife College. Fife College of Further and Higher Education: Head of Section – Administration and Consumer Studies, Youth Training Manager, Head of Business School. Member, Kirkcaldy District Council, four years; Member, Fife Council, five years (Chair, Vocational Education and Training Committee, Chair, Fife Vocational and Training Strategy, Member, New Deal Steering Group).

Llewellin, Magnus. Editor (Scotland), The Times, since 2016; Editor-in-Chief, Herald & Times, 2015-16 (formerly Editor, The Herald); b. 1965; 2 c. Career: joined Edinburgh Evening News in 1990, then the Daily Record, then The Scotsman and Business AM. Committee member of the Journalists' Charity in Scotland. Recreations: hillwalking; running; travel. Address: (b.) The Times, Guildhall, 87 Queen Street, Glasgow G1 3EN; T.-0141 420 5151.

Llewellyn, Howard Neil, BA (Hons) Law, Barrister. Diocesan Secretary and Chief Executive, Diocese of St Davids, since 2018; Immigration Judge, 2006-13; Chair, MAPPA SOG Practice Group, Tayside MAPPA, 2014-15; Chief Officer of the Tayside Community Justice Authority, since 2010; Member of the Adoption Panel, Action for Children, since 2016; Member, Parole Board For Scotland, 2003-2010; Independent Chair of Significant Case Reviews (Child Protection), since 2008; b. 29.12.54, London; m., Rosemary; 1 s.; 1 d. Educ. Chingford County High School; The Inns of Court School of Law. Career History: Called to the Bar, 1982; Pupillage; Assistant Justices Clerk; County and Crown Prosecutor; Director of Legal Services, Cambridgeshire Constabulary. The Standards Commission for Scotland; Member, The Highland Children's Panel, 2002-08. Recreation: family life. Address: (h.) Inchstelly House, Alves, Elgin, Morayshire IV80 8UY; T.-07787 525903; e-mail: howardllewellyn@hotmail.co.uk

Lloyd-Jones, Glyn Robin, MA, BA. Author and Novelist; President, Scottish PEN International, 1997-2000; b. 5.10.34, London; m., Sallie Hollocombe; 1 s.; 2 d. Educ. Blundell's School, Tiverton; Selwyn College, Cambridge University; Jordanhill College of Education. Teaching in Scottish secondary schools; Director, Curriculum Development Centre, Clydebank; English-Speaking Union Thyne Travel Scholarship to America, 1974; President, Scottish Association of Writers, 1981-86; Adviser, Education Department, Dunbartonshire, 1972-89; Co-ordinator, Scottish Forum for Development Education in Schools, 1996-99; radio drama: Ice in Wonderland, 1992 (winner, Radio Times new drama script award); Rainmaker, 1995. Publications: children's: Where the Forest and the Garden Meet, 1980; Red Fox Running, 2007; novels: Lord of the Dance (Winner, BBC/Arrow First Novel Competition, 1983); The Dreamhouse, 1985; Fallen Angels, 1992; education books: Assessment: From Principles to Action, 1985; How to Produce Better Worksheets, 1985; non-fiction: Argonauts of the Western Isles, 1989; Fallen Pieces of the Moon, 2006; The Sunlit Summit, 2013; The Sweet Especial Scene, 2014; Autumn Voices: Scottish writers over 70 talk about creativity in later life, 2018; The New Frontier: making a difference in later life, 2019. Recreations: mountaineering; sea-kayaking; photography; chess. Address: (h.) 26 East Clyde Street, Helensburgh G84 7PG; T.-01436 672010.
E-mail: robinlj34@gmail.com
Web: www.robinlloydjones.com; www.autumnvoices.co.uk

Loasby, Professor Brian John, MA, MLitt, DUniv, FBA, FRSE. Emeritus and Honorary Professor of Economics, University of Stirling, since 1984; b. 02.08.30, Kettering; m., Judith Ann (Robinson); 2 d. Educ. Kettering Grammar School; Emmanuel College, Cambridge. Assistant in Political Economy, University of Aberdeen, 1955-58; Bournville Research Fellow, University of Birmingham, 1958-61; Tutor in Management Studies, University of

Bristol, 1961-67; Lecturer in Economics, University of Stirling, 1967-68, Senior Lecturer in Economics, 1968-71, Professor of Management Economics, 1971-84. Publications: The Swindon Project, 1973; Choice, Complexity and Ignorance, 1976; The Mind and Method of The Economist, 1989; Equilibrium and Evolution, 1991; Knowledge, Institutions and Evolution in Economics, 1999 - Schumpeter Prize, 2000; articles and book chapters. Address: (b.) Division of Economics, University of Stirling, Stirling FK9 4LA; T.-01786 472124.
E-mail: b.j.loasby@stir.ac.uk

Lochhead, Liz. Poet and Playwright; Scots Makar, 2011-2016; b. 1947, Motherwell. Educ. Glasgow School of Art. Combined teaching art and writing for eight years; became full-time writer after selection as first holder, Scottish/Canadian Writers' Exchange Fellowship, 1978; former Writer in Residence, Tattenhall Centre, Chester. Publications include: Memo for Spring, Islands, Grimm Sisters, Dreaming of Frankenstein, True Confessions; plays include: Blood and Ice, Dracula, Same Difference, Sweet Nothings, Now and Then, True Confessions, Mary Queen of Scots Got Her Head Chopped Off, The Big Picture, Perfect Days, Good Things, Educating Agnes, Liz Lochhead: Five Plays; poetry includes: The Colour of Black and White: Poems 1984-2003, 2003.

Lochhead, Richard Neilson, BA (Hons). MSP (SNP), Moray, since 2006, North East of Scotland, 1999-2006; Minister for Just Transition, Employment and Fair Work, since 2021; Minister for Further Education, Higher Education and Science, 2018-2021; Cabinet Secretary for Rural Affairs, Food and the Environment, 2007-2016; b. 24.5.69, Paisley; m.; 2 s. Educ. Williamwood High School, Clarkston; Stirling University. Financial trainee, South of Scotland Electricity Board, 1987-89; Economic Development Officer, Dundee City Council, 1998-99; Office Manager for Alex Salmond, 1994-98. Recreations: cinema; travel; reading fiction and history non-fiction; watching Elgin City, Aberdeen and Scotland football teams; listening to music, cycling & the countryside. Address: (b.) Office 2, Gairland Business Centre, 8 West Street, Fochabers, Moray IV32 7DJ; T.-01343 545077.
E-mail: richard.lochhead.msp@parliament.scot

Locke, Alasdair James Dougall, MA. Chairman, First Property Group plc, since 2000; b. 29.8.53, Aldershot; m., Kathleen Anne; 2 s. Educ. Uppingham School, Rutland; Wadham College, Oxford University. Assistant Vice President: Citibank N. A., 1974-78, Oceanic Finance Corporation, 1978-81; Vice President, American Express Leasing Corporation, 1981-83; Director, Henry Ansbacher and Co., Ltd., 1983-87; Deputy Chairman, Kelt Energy PLC, 1987-91; Executive Chairman, Abbot Group PLC, 2000-09. Former Member, OSO Advisory Board. Recreations: shooting; golf; skiing. Address: (b.) Minto Drive, Altens, Aberdeen AB12 3LW; T.-01224 299600.

Lockhart of the Lee, Ranald. Twenty-eighth hereditary Chief of the Lockharts of Lee and thirteenth of Carnwath. Chief of the Clan Lockhart, since 2015.

Lockhart, Brian Alexander, BL. Formerly Sheriff Principal, South Strathclyde, Dumfries and Galloway (2005-2015); b. 1.10.42, Ayr; m., Christine Ross Clark; 2 s.; 2 d. Educ. Glasgow Academy; Glasgow University. Partner, Robertson Chalmers and Auld, Solicitors, 1967-79; Sheriff, North Strathclyde, at Paisley, 1979-81; Sheriff, Glasgow and Strathkelvin, 1981-2005; President, Sheriffs' Association, 2003-05; Member, Parole Board for Scotland,

1997-2003; Temporary High Court Judge, 2008-2015; Appeal Sheriff, 2015-2017. Recreations: fishing; family. Address: (h.) 18 Hamilton Avenue, Glasgow G41; T.-0141-427 1921.

Lockhart, Brian Robert Watson. MA (Hons), DipEd. Headmaster, Robert Gordon's College, Aberdeen, 1996-2004; b. 19.7.44, Edinburgh; m., Fiona Anne Sheddon; 1 s.; 2 d. Educ. George Heriot's School, Edinburgh; Aberdeen University; Moray House; University of Edinburgh. Teacher of History and Economic History, George Heriot's School, 1968-72; Principal Teacher of History, 1972-81; Deputy Rector, High School of Glasgow, 1981-96. Headteachers' Association of Scotland: Member, Council, 1988-2003, Member, Executive, 1989-94; Chair, Universities and Colleges Admissions Service Scottish Standing Committee, 1998-2000 and 2002-03; Member, Higher Still Implementation Group, 1998-2001; Member, Headmasters Conference Universities Committee, 1998-2003; Secretary, HMC (Scottish Division), 2003; Chairman, HMC (Scottish Division), 2004; Member, Business Committee, Aberdeen University, 1999-2011, Vice-Convener, 2006-2010; Member, Council, St. Margaret's School for Girls, Aberdeen, 2004-13; Member, Board of Voluntary Service Aberdeen (VSA), 2004-2011; Member, Board of Hutchesons' Educational Trust, Glasgow, 2005-12, Convenor, Education Committee, 2012-13; Trustee, Robert Nicol Trust, 2006-2017, Convener, 2013-2017; Member, Audit Committee, Aberdeen University, 2007-13; Member, Court of University of Aberdeen, 2008-12; Member, University Learning and Teaching Committee, 2010-12; Member, University Remuneration Committee, 2010-12; Convenor, University Student Affairs Committee, 2010-12; Member, University Staff Promotion Committee, 2012; Member, Friends of Aberdeen University Library (FAUL), 2013-2018; Member, Board of Governors, Lathallan School, 2013-2018. Publications: Jinglin' Geordie's Legacy, 2003; Robert Gordon's Legacy, 2007; "The Town School": A History of the High School of Glasgow, 2010; "Bon Record": A History of Aberdeen Grammar School, 2012; 'A Great Educational Tradition': A History of Hutchesons' Grammar School, 2015. Recreations: education history research; reading biographies; sport; films; politics. Address: (h.) 80 Gray Street, Aberdeen AB10 6JE; T.-01224 315776.
E-mail: brian.lockhart1@btinternet.com

Lockhart, Dean. MSP (Scottish Conservative), Mid Scotland and Fife region, since 2016; Shadow Cabinet Secretary for Constitution, Europe and External Affairs, 2020-21. Asia-based international lawyer and business adviser for 20 years: Linklaters, London/Singapore, 1992-96, Linklaters, Tokyo, 1997-98, First Secretary (Commercial), Diplomat, British Embassy, Manila, 1999-2000, Partner, Linklaters: Singapore, 2001-02, Hong Kong, 2002-06, Singapore, 2007-2015. Scottish Parliament Chair, Cross Party Groups on the United States, China and Japan. Address: Scottish Parliament, Edinburgh EH99 1SP.
E-mail: dean.lockhart@scottishconservatives.com

Lockhead, Sir Moir, OBE, DHC. Chairman, The National Trust for Scotland, 2015-19; Chairman, Scottish Rugby Union, 2011-16; Sen Gov., University of Aberdeen Court, 2009-2016 (joined Court as a member in 2002); Patron, Society of Operations Engineers, 2013-2016; Deputy Chairman and Chief Executive, FirstGroup plc, 1995-2010; b 25.4.45, County Durham; m. (1964), Audrey Johnson; 3 s.; 1 d. Educ. West Cornforth Secondary Modern School. Apprentice mechanic in a bus garage in Darlington, then management trainee with Tarmac; Chief Engineer, Strathclyde Passenger Transport Executive, 1979-85; General Manager, Grampian Transport, 1985-89; led employee/management buyout, 1989; Executive Chairman,

Grampian Transport, subsequently GRT Bus plc, FirstBus plc, then FirstGroup plc, 1989-94. Past President of the Confederation of Passenger Transport; awarded an OBE in 1996 and knighted in the 2008 Birthday Honours; awarded a Doctorate honoris causa in 2009 by University of Aberdeen; awarded the VisitScotland Silver Thistle Award in 2010 for outstanding services to the tourism industry in Scotland; Degree of Doctor of Laws awarded by University of Aberdeen, 2017.

Logan, Brian James, BCom (Hons), CPFA, FRSA. Chief Executive: Capability Scotland, since 2019, Bield Housing & Care, 2010-19; b. 5.7.71, Edinburgh. Educ. Ross High School, Tranent; University of Edinburgh. Career history: Trainee Accountant, Edinburgh District Council, 1993-96; Accountant, City of Edinburgh Council, 1996-2001; Senior Finance Manager, Hanover (Scotland) Housing Association, 2001-05; Director of Financial Services, Bield Housing & Care, 2005-2010. Board Member (since 1995) and Vice Chair (since 2017), East Lothian Housing Association Ltd; Board Member, Reside Housing Association, since 2017; Trustee, Community Integrated Care, 2017-2020. Address: Capability Scotland, Osborne House, 1 Osborne Terrace, Edinburgh EH12 5HG; T.-0131 337 9876.

Logan, Elaine, MA (Edin), PGCE. Headteacher, Glenalmond College, 2015-19. Educ. Edinburgh University. Career: began teaching career at Viewforth High School in Kirkcaldy where she taught English for 3 years before taking up the position of English and Drama teacher at Dollar Academy; successfully completed Post Graduate Certificates in Counselling (Moray House, University of Edinburgh) and in Pupil Support and Guidance (Northern College, University of Dundee); became Housemistress of Holm House, Loretto School in September 2001 and continued in this post for 5 years, became Assistant Head - Day Pupils and Pastoral Coordinator, then Acting Head; became the first member of staff in a Scottish school to take up the Senior Management post of 'Director of Compliance, Inspections and Child Protection' in 2009. Teaches English, Drama and Theatre Studies.

Logan, Fiona. Chief Executive Officer, Insights Learning & Development Ltd, since 2018 (previously Chief Operating Officer); former Vice President for Europe, Insights; Chief Executive, Loch Lomond and The Trossachs National Park Authority, 2008-2015. Educ. Strathclyde University Business School. Career history: blue chip companies including IBM and Unilever in UK, Europe and Asia Pacific, in marketing, sales and management roles where she continued her professional development at both Macquarie University in Sydney and Harvard Business School. Address: Insights Learning and Development Ltd, Terra Nova, 3 Explorer Road, Dundee DD2 1EG; T.-01382 908050.

Logan, Graeme. Director of Learning, Scottish Government, since 2019. Career history: Headteacher in a West Lothian school; joined Education Scotland in 2008; seconded to be professional advisor to the National Review of Teacher Education, resulting in the publication of Teaching Scotland's Future, 2010-11; Assistant Director of Community Learning and Development (CLD), Education Scotland; Interim HM Chief Inspector of Education and Chief Education Advisor to Scottish Ministers, until 2017; Deputy Director of Learning, Scottish Government, 2017-19. Address: Scottish Government, Victoria Quay, Edinburgh EH6 6QQ; T.-0131 244 0859.

Logan, Stephen Douglas, BSc, PhD, LLD (Hon). Chairman of Board, Aberdeen Science Centre, since 2020; Chairman, NHS Grampian, 2015-18; b. 16.10.50, Glasgow; m., Anne; 2 s. Educ. Annan Academy, Dumfriesshire; University of St. Andrews. Medical Research Council Fellow, Senior Lecturer and Professor of Neuroscience,

University of Birmingham; Professor of Neuroscience, University of Aberdeen, 1994-96, Head of Department of Biomedical Sciences, 1996-98, became Vice-Principal and Dean of The Faculty of Medicine and Medical Sciences in 1998. Chairman, Grampian University Hospitals NHS Trust, 2002-04, Vice-Chairman, 1998-2002; Member, NHS Grampian Board, 2002-04; Member, SHEFC, 2003; Head of College of Life Sciences and Medicine, 2003; Senior Vice-Principal, University of Aberdeen, 2004-2015. Board Member: Opportunity North East (ONE), TauRx Pharmaceuticals Ltd; Chair, ONE Life Sciences Board. Over 100 research publications. Recreations: rugby; golf; reading.

Logie, Professor Robert Howie, BSc, PhD, CPyschol, FBPsS, FRSE, FPsyS. Professor of Human Cognitive Neuroscience, Edinburgh University, since 2004; Anderson Professor of Psychology, Aberdeen University, 1998-2003 (Head, Department of Psychology, 1997-2002); b. 23.3.54, Ajmer, India; m., Elizabeth; 2 s. Educ. Aberdeen Academy; Aberdeen University; University College, London. Researcher, MRC Applied Psychology Unit, Cambridge, 1980-86; Aberdeen University: Lecturer in Psychology, 1987, Senior Lecturer, 1992, Personal Professor, 1995. Publications: over 300 including 19 authored or edited books, notably Visuo Spatial Working Memory, 1995; Cognitive Neuroscience of Working Memory, 2007; Working Memory and Ageing, 2015; Working Memory: State of the Science, 2021; Dorothy Hodgkin Lecturer, British Association for the Advancement of Science, 1995. Editor, Quarterly Journal of Experimental Psychology, 2002-05; Associate Editor, Journal of Experimental Psychology: General; Chair, Psychonomic Society, 2015; Chair, European Research Council Advanced Grants Panel SH4, 2015-16; Member, REF subpanel for Psychology, Psychiatry and Neuroscience, 2021-22; Bartlett lifetime achievement prize from Experimental Psychology Society, 2022.

Logue, Cllr James. Leader of North Lanarkshire Council, since 2016; representing Airdrie Central (Scottish Labour Party), since 1996. Address: c/o Civic Centre, Motherwell ML1 1AB; T.-01698 302416.
E-mail: loguej@northlan.gov.uk

Long, Louise. Chief Executive, Inverclyde Council, since 2021. Educ. Robert Gordon University. Career history: social worker with Glasgow City Council; held social work management roles with East Renfrewshire Council; Head of Service at South Ayrshire Council; worked with children's charity Aberlour for five years; joined Argyll and Bute Council as Head of Children's Services in 2012; became Chief Social Work Officer and Head of Children and Families and Justice, 2015-17. Chief Officer for the Inverclyde Integration Joint Board, since 2017; Corporate Director of the Inverclyde Health and Social Care Partnership, since 2017. Address: Municipal Buildings, Clyde Square, Greenock PA15 1LY; T.-01475 717171.

Long, Philip, OBE, FRSE. Chief Executive, National Trust for Scotland, since 2020. Career history: Senior Curator at the National Galleries of Scotland; Founding Director, V&A Dundee, 2011-2020; international work has included the curation of Scotland's presentation at the Venice Biennale (2007), responsibility for the UK presentation at the Milan Design Triennale (2016) and advising museums and government agencies on the development of new cultural and heritage organisations. Honorary Professor of the University of Dundee; Honorary Research Fellow of St Andrews University; member of the British Council's Arts and Creative Economy Committee; Board member of Creative Scotland; recipient of a unique award for

Transforming Scotland from the Institute of Directors in 2019. Address: National Trust for Scotland, Hermiston Quay, 5 Cultins Road, Edinburgh EH11 4DF; T.-0131 458 0200.

Lord, Jonathan Christopher, MA. Director, RSAC Motorsport Ltd and consultant; Secretary, The Glasgow Art Club; b. 29.4.53, Alverstoke; 1 s. Educ. Dollar Academy; St. Andrews University. Ministry of Defence (Naval), 1975-76; Royal Scottish Automobile Club, 1976-2006; Member, British Motor Sports Council, 1991-2006; MSA Rallies Committee, 1982-2003; Administrator, The McGlashan Charitable Trust, 2008-15; FIA Observer for International Rallies; Motorsport UK Steward and Safety Delegate; Clerk of the Course, RSAC International Scottish Rally, since 1982 and other international rallies; Secretary to the Vestry, St. Bride's Episcopal Church, Glasgow, since 1991. SMMC Jim Clark Marshalling Award, 1999; Motorsport UK Lifetime Achievement Award, 2021. Recreations: music (especially choral singing); cricket; motor sport; following Dunfermline Athletic FC. Address: (h.) 11 Melrose Gardens, Glasgow G20 6RB; T.-0141-946 5045; e-mail: jcl30@btinternet.com

Lorenzo, Antonio. Chief Executive Officer, Scottish Widows plc, since 2015; Group Director, Insurance, Lloyds Banking Group, since 2015; b. 1966. Career history: over nine years at Arthur Andersen; worked in a number of different leadership roles and jurisdictions, Santander, from 1998; part of the management team that completed the take-overs of Abbey National in 2004, then Bradford & Bingley and Alliance & Leicester in 2008; Chief Financial Officer, Santander UK; Lloyds Banking Group: Head of the Wealth and International division and Group Corporate Development, 2011-13; Group Director, Consumer Finance & Group Corporate Development, leading the division's growth strategy whilst completing the sale of TSB, 2013-15. Address: Scottish Widows plc, 69 Morrison Street, Edinburgh EH3 8YF; T.-0845 7678910.

Lorimer, A. Ross, CBE, MD, DUniv (Glasgow), FMedSci, FRCP. Retired. Previously President, Royal College of Physicians and Surgeons of Glasgow (2000-03); Honorary Professor, Glasgow University; Consultant Physician and Cardiologist, Glasgow Royal Infirmary; b. 5.5.37, Bellshill; m., Fiona Marshall; 3 s. Educ. Uddingston Grammar School; High School of Glasgow; Glasgow University. Recreations: reading; walking. Address: 12, Uddingston Road, Bothwell G71 8PH.

Lorimer, Elaine. Chief Executive, Revenue Scotland, since 2016. Career history: Head of Legal and Administrative Services, Strathclyde Passenger Transport, 1996-2001; Deputy Director, Office of the Rail Regulator, 2001-03; Director of Corporate Services, National School of Government, 2006-2012; Chief Executive, Law Commission of England and Wales, 2012-2016. Member of the Board, ACE Association of Chief Executives, 2013-16. CEO of the Year at the Scottish Women's Awards 2019. Address: Revenue Scotland, PO Box 24068, Victoria Quay, Edinburgh EH6 9BR; T.-03000 200 310.

Lothian, Marquis of (Rt. Hon. Michael Andrew Foster Jude Kerr Ancram), PC, DL, QC. Advocate; MP (Conservative), Devizes, 1992-2010; Deputy Leader of the Opposition and Shadow Foreign Secretary, 2001-05; Shadow Defence Secretary, 2005; former Chairman, Conservative Party; Member, Intelligence and Security Committee, 2006-2019; b. 7.7.45; m.; 2 d. Educ. Ampleforth; Christ Church, Oxford; Edinburgh University. MP: Berwickshire and East Lothian, 1974, Edinburgh

South, 1979-87; Parliamentary Under Secretary of State, Scottish Office, 1983-87; Northern Ireland Office: Parliamentary Under Secretary, 1993-94, Minister of State, 1994-97; Chairman, Conservative Party in Scotland, 1980-83. Created Life Peer, 2010; DL, Roxburgh District; Freeman of the City of Gibraltar, 2011; Freedom of Devizes, 2011; Chairman, Global Strategy Forum, 2006-2019; Chairman, MEC, 2013-2021. Address: (b.) House of Lords, London SW1A 0PW.

Loudon, Alasdair John, LLB, NP, WS. Consultant, Gilson Gray LLP, Solicitors, Edinburgh, since 2019; Consultant, Cape Renewables Energy Group, since 2019; b. 7.4.56, Edinburgh; 2 s.; 1 d. Educ. Edinburgh Academy; Dundee University. Apprentice, Tods, Murray and Jamieson, WS, 1978-80; Qualified Assistant, Warner & Co., 1980-82, Partner, 1982-92; founded Loudons WS, 1992, Senior Partner, until 2001; Partner, Turcan Connell Solicitors, 2001-2019. Accredited FLAGS arbitrator; formerly Member, Sheriff Court Rules Council for Scotland; President, Edinburgh Bar Association, 1996-98. Fellow of International Academy of Matrimonial Lawyers; Chair, Family Law Arbitration Group Scotland. Recreations: golf (Honourable Company of Edinburgh Golfers; Bruntsfield Links, Luffness New and Royal Wimbledon); football (Heart of Midlothian supporter). Address: (b.) 29 Rutland Square, Edinburgh EH19 2BW.
E-mail: alasdair@ajloudonconsulting.com

Loudon, Colonel Angus J., MBE, OStJ, MPhil, MA, BA. Chief Executive Officer, St John Scotland, since 2019 (Executive Director, 2015-19). Educ. The Edinburgh Academy; University of Edinburgh; King's College London; University of Cambridge. Army Officer, Ministry of Defence, 1981-2015; Chief of Staff, UN Forces in Cyprus, 2012-2015. President and Chairman of the Trustees, The King's Own Scottish Borderers Association; Member: Queen's Body Guard for Scotland, Royal Company of Archers, New Club, Edinburgh, The Golf House Club, Elie; Trustee: The Royal Regiment of Scotland, The Edinburgh Academy Foundation Trust. Address: St John Scotland, 21 St John Street, Edinburgh EH8 8DG.

Loudon, John Alexander, LLB, SSC. Retired accredited specialist in Liquor Licensing (Betting and Gaming) Law; former Convenor of the City of Edinburgh Licensing Forum; Chairman of the Edinburgh Croquet Club; Chairman of the Cramond and Barnton Community Council; b. 5.12.49, Edinburgh; m., Alison Jane Bruce Laird; 2 s. Educ. Edinburgh Academy; Dundee University. Apprenticeship, Tindal, Oatts and Roger, Solicitors, Glasgow. Former Member, Council, Law Society of Scotland; Past President, SSC Society. Recreations: croquet; golf; gardening; skiing. Address: (b.) The Laurels, 6c Essex Road, Edinburgh EH4 6LG.

Loudon, William Euan Buchanan (Euan), CBE, FCMI. Chief Executive, St Andrews Links Trust, 2011-2021; b. 12.3.56, Lanarkshire; m., Penny. Educ. Uddingston Grammar School and RMA Sandhurst. Commissioned into The Royal Highland Fusiliers, 1975; served at regimental duty and with the Commando Training Centre in Devon, before attending the Army Staff College in 1988; Chief of Staff 7 Armoured Brigade, 1988-91; appointed OBE after Operation GRANBY, 1991; Military Assistant to Chief of the General Staff, 1993-94; Chief Operations Officer of the UN Military Observer Mission to Croatia, Bosnia, Montenegro, Macedonia and the remainder of the former Yugoslavia; Commanding Officer, 1st Battalion, The Royal Highland Fusiliers, 1995-97; Colonel, Army Personnel Centre, Glasgow, 1997-99; commanded 39 Infantry

Brigade, 1999-2001; Chief of Staff and Commander Force Troops, HQNI, 2001-03; General Officer Commanding 2nd Division and Governor of Edinburgh Castle, 2004-07. Appointed CBE, 2004; Graduate of Higher Command and Staff Course and attended the Royal College of Defence Studies, January-March 2004; Chief Executive, Royal Edinburgh Military Tattoo, 2007-2011; Chair, Royal Highland Fusiliers Trust. Recreations: golf; shooting and conservation; farming; fishing; Scottish Contemporary Art.

Louw, Rev Dewald, Bth, MDiv, BA. Minister, Kinloss and Findhorn Parish Church, since 2021. Address: Kinloss and Findhorn Parish Church, 4 Manse Road, Kinloss, Forres IV36 3GH; T.-01309 690359.

Lovat, 16th Lord (Simon Fraser); b. 13.2.77. Educ. Harrow; Edinburgh University. Succeeded to title, 1995.

Love, Professor James, BA, MSc, PhD. Professor of Economics, Adam Smith Business School, University of Glasgow, 2013-2016 (former Head of School); Emeritus Professor of Economics, formerly Deputy Principal, University of Strathclyde, Vice Principal, 2006-08, Pro Vice-Principal, 2004-06; b. 31.7.48, Dunfermline; m., Jane Lindores Scott; 2 d. Educ. Beath High School; Strathclyde University. Lecturer, Haile Sellassie 1 University, 1971-74; Lecturer, Strathclyde University, 1974-79; Lecturer, Ghana University, 1979-80; Senior Lecturer, University of Lund, 1980-81; Senior Research Fellow, Fraser of Allander Institute, 1984-86; Lecturer, Senior Lecturer, Reader, Strathclyde University, 1986-95; Head, Department of Economics, and Vice-Dean (Research), Strathclyde Business School, 1994-99, Dean, 1999-2004. Chairman, Board of Trustees, SOLAS. Recreations: sport; particularly the (mis)fortunes of Aberdeen FC and Cowdenbeath FC.

Love, Robert Malcolm, MA (Hons), FRSAMD. Independent Producer; Head of Drama, Scottish Television, 1979-2000; b. 9.1.36, Paisley. Educ. Paisley Grammar School; Glasgow University; Washington University, St. Louis, USA. Actor and Director, various repertory companies, including Nottingham Playhouse, 1962-65; Producer, Thames TV, 1966-75, including Public Eye, The Rivals of Sherlock Holmes, Van Der Valk; freelance Producer, 1976-79, including Thames TV, LWT, Seacastle Film Productions, Scottish TV. Awards including: Commonwealth Festival, New York TV and Film Festival, Chicago Film Festival, BAFTA Scotland, nominated for International Emmy, New York, 1982; productions for Scottish include Taggart, Take the High Road, Doctor Finlay, McCallum, The Steamie, Machair. Governor, RSAMD, 1994-2002; Drama Chair, Scottish Arts Council, 1994-99; Chair, Beckett Time Festival, 2000; opera productions include Tosca, Susanna's Secret, Scott at the Opera; Director, Scottish International Piano Competition, 2001-2010. Recreations: literature; music; theatre; travel.

Love, Professor Sandy, BVMS, PhD. Chair, Equine Clinical Studies, University of Glasgow, since 1997; b. 14.3.60, Paisley. Educ. Kelvinside Academy; University of Glasgow. Private practice, Wetherby, Yorkshire 1982-84; Junior Fellow in Veterinary Surgery, University of Bristol, 1984-86; Horserace Betting Levy Board Research Scholar, 1986-87; Lecturer, Equine Medicine, University of Glasgow, 1987-97. Past President, British Equine Veterinary Association; Aberdeen Angus cattle breeder; British Horseracing Authority Racecourse Steward at Ayr, Hamilton Park and Perth. Recreation: racehorse owner. Address: Meikle Burntshields, Kilbarchan PA10 2PD; T.-01505 702642; e-mail: s.love69@btinternet.com

Lovell, Deborah Anne, LLB (Hons), DipLP. Partner, Anderson Strathern, Solicitors, since 2004; b. 28.12.72, Kirkcaldy. Educ. Balwearie High School, Kirkcaldy; Aberdeen University; Edinburgh University. Trainee, Campbell Smith WS, 1995-97; Assistant, McKay & Norwell, Solicitors, 1997-98; Assistant Solicitor, Shepherd and Wedderburn, Solicitors, 1998-2002; Anderson Strathern, Solicitors, since 2002. Notary Public; Member, Law Society of Scotland Conveyancing Committee; Member, BCSC; Member, SPF Property Tax Group; Member, The WS Society Knowledge Services Committee; Tutor in Property on The University of Edinburgh Diploma in Legal Practice; Tutor on WS Society/Glasgow School of Law Professional Competence Course; voted a "Rising Star" in the World of Commercial Real Estate by Property Executive Magazine; Member, The Anderson Strathern Team which won The Scott & Co. Specialist Client Team of The Year Award at The Scottish Legal Awards, 2006 for Property Work on The Stirling-Alloa Kincardine Railway Act. Recreations: horse riding; reading; ski-ing. Address: Anderson Strathern, 1 Rutland Court, Edinburgh EH3 8EY; T.-0131 270 7700.
E-mail: deborah.lovell@andersonstrathern.co.uk

Lovie, Robert Gordon. Musician and entertainer. Director, Dumfries House Home Farm Limited, 2017-2021; b. 1969. Formerly Director: Braemar Royal Highland Charity, 2017-18, Dumfries House Trust Trading Limited, 2015-17, The Prince's Foundation, 2015-17. Lifelong user of the Doric tongue. Address: (h.) Auld Cummerton, Strathdon, Aberdeenshire AB36.

Lowden, Jack Andrew, BA. Actor; b. 2.6.90, Chelmsford, Essex. Training: Manor School of Ballet, Edinburgh; English National Ballet School; Royal Ballet School, London; Scottish Youth Theatre; Royal Scottish Academy of Music and Drama. Credits include: (film) '71; Ghosts; Tommy's Honour; A United Kingdom; Denial; Dunkirk; England is Mine; Calibre; Mary Queen of Scots; Fighting with My Family; Capone; Kindred; Benediction (television) Being Victor; Mrs Biggs; The Tunnel; The Passing Bells; War & Peace; The Long Song; Small Axe; Slow Horses (theatre) Black Watch; Chariots of Fire; Ghosts; Electra; Measure for Measure. Awards: Ian Charleson Awards, 2014; Laurence Olivier Award, 2014; Young Scot Awards, 2016; British Academy Scotland Awards, 2016, 2018, 2019; British Academy Film Awards, 2020; British Academy Scotland Awards, 2021.

Lowder, George, MBE, LLB, MA, QCVS. Chief Executive, Transport for Edinburgh, since 2015; Chair, UK Tram, since 2019; Chairman, Scottish Veterans' Residencies and Housing Association, since 2016; b. Edinburgh. Educ. Cranfield University; University of Aberdeen; University of Strathclyde. Commander and Operations Director, Defence/Army, 1981-2016; Commanding Officer, Army/Defence, 2004-2006; Head of Strategic Planning, United States Department of Defense, 2006; Deputy Director, Strategy, Plans and Policy, UK Ministry of Defence - Defence Intelligence, 2006-09; Head, Security Sector Reform, US Department of State, 2009-2010; Commander of The Army in Scotland, 2010-12; Head of Defence Intelligence Operations, UK Ministry of Defence, 2012-15; Senior Executive, Ministry of Defence, 2012-15. Trustee, The Royal Regiment of Scotland, since 2010; Trustee, The Royal Scots (The Royal Regiment), since 2004, Chairman of Trustees, since 2017. Commendation, Operation Granby, May 1991; Bronze Star, USA, 2006. Recreations: keen skier; sailor and golfer. Address: (b.) City Chambers, Edinburgh EH1 1YJ; T.-0131 469 5401.

Lowe, Euan. Chief Executive Officer, Scottish Swimming, since 2019. Career history: Falkirk College: Lifestyle Coordinator, 1995-98, Senior Health and Fitness Officer - Project Officer (secondment), 1998-2000; National Coach -

Canoe Slalom, Scottish Canoe Association, 2001-07; Programme Manager, SportTayside and Fife, 2007-2010; Lead Manager - Central and Tayside and Fife Regional Sporting Partnerships, sportscotland, 2010-2014; Chief Executive Officer, Scottish Gymnastics, 2014-19. Address: Scottish Swimming, Airthrey Castle, Hermitage Road, University of Stirling, Stirling FK9 4LA; T.-01786 466520.

Lowe, Professor Gordon Douglas Ogilvie, DSc, MB, ChB, MD, FRCPEdin, FRCPGlas, FRCPLond, FFPH. Emeritus Professor, Glasgow University; b. 2.1.49, London; m., Ann Harvie; 1 s.; 1 d. Educ. Dundee High School; St. Andrews University. House Officer, Royal Infirmary and Maryfield Hospital, Dundee, 1972-73; Senior House Officer, City Hospital, Nottingham, 1973-74; Registrar, Royal Infirmary, Glasgow, 1974-77; Lecturer, Glasgow University, 1978-85, Senior Lecturer, 1985-92, Reader, 1992-93, Professor of Vascular Medicine, 1993-2009. Former Assessor, RCPEdin.; Chairman, SIGN, 2002-07; Past President, British Society for Haemostasis and Thrombosis. Publications: editor of books and author of publications on thrombosis and bleeding disorders. Recreations: travel; railways; gardening.

Lowe, Dr. Janet, CBE, BA (Hons), MBA, EdD, DEd, FRSE. Member, Scottish Further and Higher Education Funding Council, 2005-2013; b. 27.9.50, South Normanton; m., Donald Thomas Stewart. Educ. Swanwick Hall Grammar School; Hull University; Dundee University; Stirling University. Immigration Officer, Home Office, 1973-76; Personnel Assistant, Hull University, 1976-80; Administrator, Lothian Region Social Work Department, 1980-82; Napier University: Examinations Officer, Personnel Officer, Assistant Academic Registrar, 1982-88; Secretary and Registrar, Duncan of Jordanstone College of Art, 1988-93; Lauder College: Depute Principal, 1993-96, Principal, 1996-2005. Member: Local Government Finance Review Committee, 2004-06, Board of Management, Scottish Further Education Unit, 1993-2001, Court, Heriot-Watt University, 1999-2005, Court, Dundee University, 2005-2013, Board, Scottish Enterprise, 1998-2004, Board, Skills Development Scotland, 2008-2013; President, Rotary Club of Dunfermline Carnegie, 2008-09; US-UK Fulbright Commissioner, 2009-2012; Honorary Professor, Stirling University, 2010-2015; Elected Fellow of The Royal Society of Edinburgh, 2010; Trustee, Carnegie Trust for the Universities of Scotland, 2006-2015; Trustee, Dundee Botanic Garden Endowment Trust, 2015-18. Awarded an Honorary Doctor of Education by Queen Margaret University, Edinburgh in 2007. Recreations: travel; photography; gardening. Address: 42 Gamekeepers Road, Kinnesswood, Kinross KY13 9JR; T.-01592 840277. E-mail: janetlowe@aol.com

Lowe, Paul, BSc, BDS. Chief Executive, National Records of Scotland, since 2018. Educ. University of Glasgow. Career history: The Crown Office and Procurator Fiscal Service (COPFS): Programme Director, 2015-16, Head of Business Management, 2012-15; Chief Executive Officer, Student Award Agency Scotland, 2016-18. Address: HM General Register House, 2 Princes Street, Edinburgh EH1 3YY.

Ludlam, Professor Christopher A., BSc (Hons), MB, ChB, PhD, FRCP, FRCPath. Emeritus Professor of Haematology and Coagulation Medicine, University of Edinburgh; formerly Consultant Haematologist, Edinburgh Royal Infirmary, 1980-2011; Director, Edinburgh Haemophilia and Thrombosis Centre, 1980-2011; b. 6.6.46, Edinburgh. Educ. Edinburgh University. MRC Research Fellow, 1972-75; Senior Registrar in Haematalogy, University Hospital of Wales, Cardiff, 1975-78; Lecturer in Haematology, University of Wales, 1979. Address: (b.) School of Clinical Sciences and Community Health, University of Edinburgh, 47 Little France Crescent, Edinburgh. E-mail: Christopher.Ludlam@ed.ac.uk

Lugton, (Charles) Michael Arber, MA. Chief Executive, Scottish Law Commission, 2005-08; b. 5.4.51, South Africa; m. Joyce Graham; 2 s (Sheriff Charles Lugton and James). Educ. St. John's College, Johannesburg; the Edinburgh Academy; University of Edinburgh. Joined Scottish Office in 1973; Private Secretary to Permanent Under Secretary of State, 1976-78; Principal Private Secretary to successive Secretaries of State, 1995-97; Head of Constitution and Legal Services Group, Scottish Executive, 2004-05. Convener, Administration Board, Scottish Episcopal Church, 2010-15; Member, Business Committee, General Council, University of Edinburgh, 2010-15; a Governor, Merchiston Castle School, 1998-2014. Recreation: South Africa.

Luke, Garry Alec, PhD (Aberdeen), MBA (Heriot-Watt), MSc (Aberdeen), BSc (Aberdeen), MA (St Andrews), FRSB, FIBMS. Research Scientist; b. 19.2.54, Aberdeen; m., Jane Knowles Murray. Educ. Mackie Academy, Stonehaven; University of St Andrews. Research Scientist, Department of Obstetrics and Gynaecology, University of Aberdeen, 1983-89; Research Fellow, Glasgow Dental Hospital and School, University of Glasgow, 1989-90, University of St Andrews, since 1990. Listed in Who's Who in the World, since 2003; Who's Who in Science and Engineering, since 2007 and biographical dictionaries (Dictionary of International Biography, 2004, Cambridge Blue Book, 2005/06). Over 60 Peer reviewed publications in numerous scientific journals/books. Recreations: natural history; walking; mediaeval history. Address: (h.) 5 Carr Crescent, Crail, Anstruther, Fife KY10 3XR; (b.) Centre for Biomolecular Sciences, University of St Andrews, Fife KY16 9ST; T.-01334 463415. E-mail: gal@st-andrews.ac.uk

Lumsden, Douglas Aaron, BEng. MSP (Scottish Conservative and Unionist Party), North East Scotland (Region), since 2021; Councillor for Airyhall, Broomhill and Garthdee, Aberdeen City Council, since 2017; b. 1971. Educ. Robert Gordon University. Career history: Technip: Senior Network Engineer, 2004-06, IT Infrastructure Manager, 2006-11, Global Hosting and Operations Manager, 2011-12, Global Vessel IT Infrastructure Manager, 2012-14; Vessel IT Manager/Regional IT Operations Manager, Harkand group, Aberdeen, 2014-15; IT Project Manager, Plan b Professional Services, 2015-16; IT Consultant, 2016-17. Address: The Scottish Parliament, Edinburgh EH99 1SP; T.-0131 348 5967. E-mail: Douglas.Lumsden.msp@parliament.scot

Lumsden, Vivien Dale Victoria, DSD, CDS. Journalist and Television and Radio Presenter, since 1984; b. 22.11.52, Edinburgh; m., Alan Douglas (qv); 1 s.; 1 d. Educ. James Gillespie's High School for Girls, Edinburgh; RSAMD. Full-time mother, 1975-82; AA Traffic News Reporter, 1982-84; BBC Scotland: Breakfast Newsreader, 1984-85, Reporting Scotland Presenter, 1985-89, Garden Party, 1988; joined Scottish TV as Presenter, Scotland Today, 1989; also presented chat show, Telethon, BAFTA Awards, Business Game, Home Show; Member of the fundraising committee for Cancer Support Scotland. Recreations: acting; cooking; writing; wine; food; travel; grandchildren! E-mail: viv.lumsden@ntlworld.com

Lunan, Charles Burnett, MD, FRCOG, FRCS. Consultant Obstetrician, Princess Royal Maternity, Glasgow, 1977-

2005; Consultant Gynaecologist, Royal Infirmary, Glasgow, 1977-2005; b. London; m., Helen Russell Ferrie; 2 s.; 1 d. Educ. High School of Glasgow; Glasgow University. Lecturer, Obstetrics and Gynaecology, Aberdeen University, 1973-75; Senior Lecturer, University of Nairobi, 1975-77; WHO Consultant, Family Planning Programme, Bangladesh, 1984-85. Treasurer, 1982-90, Vice-President, 1990-91, President, Royal Medico-Chirurgical Society of Glasgow, 1991-92; Secretary, Glasgow Obstetrical and Gynaecological Society, 1978-82, Vice President, 1998-2002, President, 2002-04. Recreations: gardening; photography; hill-walking. Address: (h.) Little Newhall, Kinrossie, Perthshire PH2 6HP.

Lunn, John Alexander, LLB (Hons), DipLP, NP. Partner, Morton Fraser LLP, since 2002, Solicitor, since 1988; b. 23.2.64, Haddington; m., Joan; 2 s. Educ. Knox Academy, Haddington; Edinburgh University. Recreations: karate; golf; skiing. Address: (b.) Quartermile Two, 2 Lister Square, Edinburgh EH3 9GL; T.-0131 247 1066. E-mail: john.lunn@morton-fraser.com

Luscombe, Rt. Rev. Lawrence Edward, ChStJ, MA, MPhil, PhD, LLD, DLitt, CA, FRSA, FSA Scot. Primus of the Scottish Episcopal Church, 1985-90, and Bishop of Brechin, 1975-90; a Trustee of the Scottish Episcopal Church, since 1985; b. 10.11.24; m., Dr. Doris Morgan (deceased); 1 d. Educ. Kelham College; King's College, London; Dundee University. Indian Army, 1942-47; Major; Chartered Accountant, 1952; Partner, Galbraith Dunlop & Co. (later Watson and Galbraith), CA, 1953-63; Curate, St. Margaret's, Glasgow, 1963-66; Rector, St. Barnabas', Paisley, 1966-71; Provost, St. Paul's Cathedral, Dundee, 1971-75. Honorary Canon, Trinity Cathedral, Davenport, Iowa, since 1983; Member, Education Committee, Renfrew County Council, 1967-71; Chairman, Governing Body: Glenalmond College, 1986-94; President, Old Glenalmond Club, 1998-2007; Chairman, Governing Body, Edinburgh Theological College, 1985-90; Governor: Lathallan School, 1982-2000, Dundee College of Education, 1982-87; Chairman, Inter-Anglican Finance Committee, 1989-93; Member, Tayside Health Board, 1989-93; Honorary Research Fellow, Dundee University, 1993; Member, Court of Corporation of the Sons of the Clergy, 1985-99. Address: (h.) Woodville, Kirkton of Tealing, by Dundee DD4 0RD; T.-01382 380331.

Lusk, Dr. Christine (Chris), MBE, PhD (St. Andrews), BSc (Edin), CQSW, DipSW, PTA. Head of Covid Rapid Response Team, Head of Special Projects, University of St. Andrews; Executive Director of CATRiS (Coalition of Anti-Trafficking Research in Scotland); b. 04.06.59, Glasgow; m., Andy Neil; 2 s.; 2 d. Educ. Madras College; Universities of Edinburgh, Dundee and St. Andrews. Social Worker in Childcare, NAI Investigations and Homefinding work, 1981-92; University of St. Andrews: Welfare Adviser, Students' Association, 1992-97, Assistant Hebdomadar, 1997-2001, Director of Student Support, 2001-06, Director of Student Services, 2006-2017, Director of Student Wellbeing, 2017-18. Research Interests and publications on the cultural interaction between the diverse student and ancient higher education. Recreations: hill-walking; music; cinema; wild water swimming; family. Address: (b.) College Gate, North Street, St Andrews, Fife KY16 9AL; T.-01334-462020. E-mail: clusk@st-andrews.ac.uk

Lyall, Professor Fiona, BSc, PhD, MBA, MRCPath. Professor of Maternal and Fetal Health, Yorkhill Hospital, Glasgow, 2003-2018; b. Johnstone. Educ. Uddingston Grammar Secondary School; University of Glasgow.

British Heart Foundation Fellow, MRC Blood Pressure Unit, Glasgow, 1990-92; Obstetrics and Gynaecology, University of Glasgow: Lecturer, 1992-97, Senior Lecturer, 1997-2001, Reader, 2001-02. Member of Medical Advisory Committee for "Tommys The Baby Charity". Publicaton: Pre-Eclampsia: Etiology and Clinical Practice, 2007. Recreations: aerobics instructor; ski instructor; own horse and dogs.

Lyall, Ian James Graeme, MA, LLB, NP. Partner (Property Finance), Pinsent Masons, 2012-19 (McGrigors, Solicitors, Edinburgh, 1987-2012); b. 25.4.55, Glasgow; m., Pamela Lyall (nee Coats); 2 s.; 2 d. Educ. Greenock Academy; Aberdeen University. McGrigors, Glasgow Office, Trainee/Apprentice, 1978-80; Assistant Solicitor: McGrigors, Glasgow Office, 1980-84, Baker & McKenzie, London, 1984-86; Head of Real Estate, McGrigors, 1997-2000. A Director and latterly Chairman, EMMS Nazareth (Scottish Charity owning and operating a hospital and school of nursing in Nazareth, Israel), 1987-2013. Currently Director of Belville Community Garden Trust; Director/ Trustee of Bethany Christian Trust; Member of the Board of Management of the Braid Estate Recreation Grounds and an Adviser to the Board of Trustees of The Free Church of Scotland. Recreations: skiing; church; motorcycling; family. Address: (h.) 16 Nile Grove, Morningside, Edinburgh EH10 4RF; T.-0131 447 6248. E-mail: ian.j.g.lyall@gmail.com

Lyall, Michael Hodge, MB, ChB, ChM, FRCSEdin. Consultant Surgeon, Tayside University Hospitals NHS Trust, 1975-2006, Medical Director, 2001-06; Honorary Senior Lecturer, Dundee University, since 1975; b. 5.12.41, Methilhill, Fife; m., Catherine B. Jarvie; 3 s. Educ. Buckhaven High School; St. Andrews University. Past President, North Fife Rotary Club; Paul Harris Fellow. Recreation: digital photography. Address: 436 Riverside Drive, Dundee DD1 4XB; e-mail: mhlyall@aol.com

Lyle, David Angus, MA, LLB, SSC, FLSS. Consultant, Solicitor, and Chartered Company Secretary, in private practice, 1993-2010 (retired 2010); b. 7.9.40; m. (1) (1969), Dorothy Ann Clark (marr. diss. 2004); 1 s.; 3 d.; m. (2) (2007), Joyce Simpson (nee Walton). Educ. George Watson's College, Edinburgh; Edinburgh University. Account Executive, Advertising Agencies, London; Indentured, Edinburgh Corporation; Solicitor, Lloyds and Scottish Finance Ltd., Edinburgh; Depute County Clerk, East Lothian County Council; Director of Administration and Law, Dumfries and Galloway Regional Council; Agency Secretary, Scottish Development Agency; Director/Company Secretary, Scottish Enterprise. Recreations: travel; golf; rambling; munro-bagging. Address: (h.) 56 Strathspey Drive, Grantown-on-Spey, Morayshire PH26 3EY; T.-01479 873814.

Lyle, Cllr Murray. Leader, Perth and Kinross Council, since 2018; representing Strathallan Ward (Conservative), since 2007. Address: c/o Perth & Kinross Council, 2 High Street, Perth PH1 5PH; T.-01738 475037. E-mail: mlyle@pkc.gov.uk

Lyle, Richard. MSP (SNP), Uddingston and Bellshill, 2016-2021 (Central Scotland region, 2011-16); b. 12.6.50, Bothwellhaugh, Lanarkshire. Educ. Lawmuir School; Bellshill Academy. Joined the SNP at the age of 16; served as local councillor in Motherwell and North Lanarkshire Council, since 1976; SNP group leader, 1976-95 and North Lanarkshire Council Leader, 1995-2011; COSLA, 2007-2009.

Lynch, Professor Lynda, BSc (Hons), PhD. Chairman, NHS Grampian, 2019-2021; Visiting Professor, Robert Gordon University, since 2019. Educ. Queen Mary, University of London; Institute of Psychiatry, University of London. Career history: Neuroimaging Researcher, Institute

WHO'S WHO IN SCOTLAND 271

of Psychiatry, 1994-98; Brand Manager, Eli Lilly, 1998-2003; Director, CNS Business Unit, Datamonitor, 2003-06; Director, Shire Pharmaceuticals, 2006-09; Independent Investor and Writer, 2010-2013; Chair, Aberdeenshire Health and Social Care Partnership, 2018-19.

Lynch, Margaret, MA (Hons). Consultant, Communitas Scotland, since 2016; former Chief Executive, Citizens Advice Scotland (2012-2016). Educ. Glasgow University. Career: Development Officer, Technical Services Agency, 1983-87; Director, Labour Communications Ltd, 1987-90; Development Officer, Greater Easterhouse Initiative, 1990-91; Researcher, Scottish Low Pay Unit, 1991-92; Corporate Policy Officer, Central Regional Council, 1991-92; Chief Executive, War on Want, 1995-98; Head of Overseas Programmes, Scottish Catholic International Aid Fund (SCIAF), 2000-07; Quality Matters Co-ordinator, Scottish Council for Voluntary Organisations (SCVO), 2009-10; Director, Scottish Mediation Network, 2010-12. Board Member, Conforti Institute.

Lynch, Professor Michael, MA, PhD, FRHistS, FSAScot. Sir William Fraser Professor of Scottish History, University of Edinburgh, 1992-2005; Chairman, Ancient Monuments Board for Scotland, 1996-2002; President, Society of Antiquaries of Scotland, 1996-99; Trustee, National Museums of Scotland, 2002-05; b. 15.6.46, Aberdeen. Educ. Aberdeen Grammar School; University of Aberdeen; University of London. Lecturer, Department of History, University College, Bangor, 1971-79; Department of Scottish History, University of Edinburgh: Lecturer, 1979-88, Senior Lecturer, 1988-92. Chairman, Historical Association Committee for Scotland, since 1992; Editor, The Innes Review, 1984-92. Publications: Edinburgh and the Reformation, 1981 (SAC Literary Award); The Early Modern Town in Scotland, 1986; The Scottish Medieval Town, 1987; Mary Stewart: Queen in Three Kingdoms, 1988; Scotland: A New History, 1991 (SAC Literary Award); The Reign of James VI, 2000; The Oxford Companion to Scottish History, 2001; Aberdeen before 1800: A New History, 2002; The University of Edinburgh: An Illustrated History, 2003.

Lynes, Stewart Alan, BSc. Chief Executive, Miller Homes, since 2022, previously Chief Operating Officer; Director, Walker Timber Limited, since 2021; Director, Castle UK Finco PLC, since 2022; b. 7.78. Educ. Craigmount High; Edinburgh Napier University. Address: Miller House, 2 Lochside View, Edinburgh Park, Edinburgh EH12 9DH.

Lyon, Rev Deirdre. Minister, United Free Church of Scotland. Address: 169 Glen Moriston Road, Glasgow G53 7HT; T.-0141 390 1099.

Lyon, George. Former Member, European Parliament (Liberal Democrat, 2009-2014); b. 16.7.56; m. (divorced); 3 d. Educ. Rothesay Academy; Nuffield Scholar. Founder and owner of farming business, 1994-2009; Director, Scottish Quality Beef and Lamb Association, 1996-97; MSP (Lib Dem), Argyll & Bute, 1999-2007. Member, National Farmers Union of Scotland (held every office including President); Past Chairman, Port Bannatyne School Board; FRAgS. Recreations: swimming; football; skiing; reading.

Lyon, Inglis E., BSc (Hons), LLB (RGU). Chief Executive, Highlands and Islands Airports Ltd, since 2005; b. Aberdeen. Educ. Inverness High School; University of Ulster in Belfast. Career history: completed an apprenticeship with a local garage before gaining an honours degree in Transport Technology; joined Stagecoach; held a variety of management positions, initially in depot management in Chorley, Bolton and Carlisle, before moving into senior management; held the posts of Operations Director in Cumbria and Managing Director of Stagecoach divisions throughout England and also in Africa; formerly Managing Director of Stagecoach East. Address: (b.) Head Office, Inverness Airport, Inverness IV2 7JB.

Mac/Mc

McAllan, Màiri Louise, LLB, DipPLP. MSP (SNP), Clydesdale, since 2021; Minister for Environment, Biodiversity and Land Reform, since 2021; b. 1993, Glasgow. Educ. University of Glasgow; Ghent University. Career history: Information Officer, Scottish National Party (SNP), Edinburgh, 2014-16; Trainee Solicitor, Maclay Murray & Spens LLP, Glasgow, 2016-17; Director, East Ayrshire Women's Aid, Kilmarnock, 2017-18; Trainee Solicitor, Pollock & McLean Solicitors & Estate Agents, 2017-18; Solicitor, Harper Macleod LLP, Glasgow, 2018-2020; Special Adviser to First Minister of Scotland, The Scottish Government, 2020-21. Address: The Scottish Parliament, Edinburgh EH99 1SP; T.-0131 348 5501. E-mail: Mairi.McAllan.msp@parliament.scot

McAllan, Mary. Director of Economic Development, Scottish Government, since 2016; m.; 3 d. Career history: first joined the Civil Service in 1993, joining the former Scottish Office; also worked in health and was involved in the creation of the Food Standards Agency; worked in rural affairs (including the 2001 Foot and Mouth Outbreak), business and economic development, public service reform, fisheries management, HR and organisational development since the 1998 Scotland Act and Devolution; former Principal Private Secretary to the First Minister of Scotland, then Director for Energy and Climate Change, Scottish Government (2013-16). Address: Scottish Government, St. Andrews House, Regent Road, Edinburgh EH1 3DG.

McAllion, John, MA (Hons). MSP, Dundee East, 1999-2003 (Labour); b. 13.2.48, Glasgow; m., Susan Jean; 2 s. Educ. St. Augustine's Secondary, Glasgow; St. Andrews University. Teacher: St Saviours Secondary, Dundee, 1973-78, Social Studies, Balgowan List D School, Dundee, 1978-82; Research Assistant to Bob McTaggart, MP, 1982-86; Regional Councillor, 1986-87; Convener, Tayside Regional Council, 1986-87; Member, Scottish Executive, Labour Party, 1986-88; Senior Vice Chairperson, Dundee Labour Party, 1986, 1987; MP (Labour), Dundee East, 1987-2001. Member, Scottish Socialist Party. Recreations: football; reading; music. Address: (h.) 3 Haldane Street, Dundee DD3 0HP; e-mail: johnmcallion@yahoo.co.uk

McAllister, Eleanor, OBE, HonFRIAS, FRSA, MA, MSc. Consultant in Regeneration; Managing Director, Clydebank Re-built, 2002-2012; b. 08.12.53, Glasgow; 2 d. Educ. Notre Dame High School; Glasgow and Strathclyde. Director, Glasgow Building Preservation Trust, 1984-91; Depute Head, Strathclyde Partnership Office, SRC, 1992-96; Depute Director, Glasgow 1999 Festival Company, 1996-99; Head of Economic and Social Initiatives, Glasgow City Council, 1999-2002. Governor, Glasgow School of Art; Member, Heritage Lottery Fund Scotland Committee. Address: (b.) 10 Vancouver Road, Glasgow G14 9HJ; T.-0141 533 2589; e-mail: ellie53@ntlworld.com

McAlpine, Alastair. Chief Statistician, The Scottish Government, since 2022. Educ. University of Stirling. Career history: Economic Researcher, BiGGAR Economics, 2008-09; Police Scotland: Performance Manager, 2012-13, Progress and Delivery Officer, 2013; The Scottish Government: Statistician (responsibility for the Scottish Index of Multiple Deprivation), 2013-17, Senior Statistician, since 2017. Address: Scottish Government, St. Andrew's House, Regent Road, Edinburgh EH1 3DG.

McAlpine, Joan, MA (Hons). MSP (SNP), South Scotland, 2011-2021; Columnist, Daily Record, since 2012; b. 28.1.64, Gourock; m., Pat Kane (qv) (divorced); 2 d. Educ. St. Columba's RC Comprehensive, Greenock; James Watt College, Greenock; Glasgow University; City University, London. Reporter, Greenock Telegraph, The Scotsman; Reporter, Feature Writer, Columnist, The Scotsman, 1992-95; Feature Writer and Columnist, Daily Record, 1995; Columnist and Feature Writer, then Deputy Editor (News), Sunday Times, 1996-2000; Editor, Sunday Times Scotland, 2000-01; Deputy Editor, The Herald, 2001-06; formerly Columnist, The Scotsman. Journalist of the Year, Scottish Press Awards, 1999; Feature Writer of the Year, Scottish Press Awards, 1999. Publication: A Time to Rage (Co-author with Tommy Sheridan), 1994. Recreations: family; listening to R&B; visiting Islay; Scotland.

McAndrew, Nicolas, CA. Chairman: Martin Currie Enhanced Income Investment Trust PLC, 1998-2005, Beauly District Fishery Board, 2003-2012; Director, Liverpool Victoria Friendly Society, 1996-2005; b. 9.12.34, London; 2 s.; 1 d. Educ. Winchester College. National Service (The Black Watch) commission, 1953-55; articled clerk, Peat Marwick Mitchell, 1955-61; qualified CA, 1961; S.G. Warburg & Co. Ltd., Merchant Bankers, 1962-78; became Chairman, Warburg Investment Management Ltd., and Director, Mercury Securities Ltd.; Managing Director, N.M. Rothschild & Sons Ltd., Merchant Bankers, 1979-88; Chairman: Murray Johnstone Ltd., 1992-99, Derby Trust PLC, 1999-2003. Master, Worshipful Company of Grocers, 1978-79; Board Member: Highlands and Islands Enterprise, 1993-97, North of Scotland Water Authority, 1995-2002. Recreations: fishing; gardening. Address: (h.) Ard-na-Coille, Ruisaurie, by Beauly, Inverness-shire IV4 7AJ; T.-01463 782524.

McAra-McWilliam, Professor Irene, OBE, MA, FRSA. Professor of Design; Director, The Glasgow School of Art, since 2018; Consultant to industry and government, since 2001; b. 4.2.54, Dufftown; m., Angus McAra. Educ. Mortlach Senior Secondary School; University of Aberdeen. Director of Design Research, Philips Electronics, The Netherlands, 1992-2001; Advisor to European Commission, 1995-2001; Professor of Design Research, University of Technology, Eindhoven, The Netherlands, 2003-05; Professor of Interaction Design and Head of Department, Royal College of Art, London, 2001-04; appointed Head of School of Design, The Glasgow School of Art in 2005. FRSA; FRCA. Address: (b.) The Glasgow School of Art, 167 Renfrew Street, Glasgow G3 6RQ; T.-0141-353-4589. E-mail: i.mcara-mcwilliam@gsa.ac.uk

McArdle, David Anthony, LLB, PhD. Head of the Law School and the Law REF Co-ordinator, University of Stirling (Senior Lecturer, since 2005); b. 03.09.67, Chesterfield; m., Charity McArdle (artist); 2 s.; 1 d. Educ. Chesterfield School; University of Wales Aberystwyth; Manchester Metropolitan University. Research Assistant, Manchester Metropolitan University, 1993-97; Research Fellow, De Montfort, Middlesex University, 1997-2001; Lecturer, Robert Gordon University, 2002-05. Several books and numerous articles on legal issues in sport; advice work for various national and international sports bodies and local authorities. Recreations: running; cycling; hillwalking. Address: (b.) School of Law, University of Stirling, Stirling FK9 4LA; T.-01786 467285; e-mail: d.a.mcardle@stir.ac.uk

McArdle, Professor Harry John, BSc (Hons), PhD. Emeritus Professor, University of Aberdeen (appointed Professor of Biomedical Sciences in 2000); Honorary Professor in Biological Sciences, University of Nottingham, since 2006; Fellow of Royal Society of Medicine, since 2011; Fellow of Royal Society of Biology, since 2016; b. 4.1.53, Glasgow; m., Karen Ann. Educ. St. Augustine School, Edinburgh; St. Andrews University. Raines

Research Fellow, University of Western Australia; Senior Scientist, Murdoch Institute for Research into Birth Defects, Melbourne, Australia, 1985-90; Lecturer/Senior Lecturer, Department of Child Health, University of Dundee, 1990-96. Recreations: hillwalking; horse riding; skiing. Address: (h.) Castle Cottage, 52, West Road, Newport on Tay, Fife DD6 8HP; T.-01224 716628.
E-mail: h.mcardle@abdn.ac.uk

McArdle, Professor Karen Ann, MA (Hons), MEd, DPhil, FRSA. Professor in Education (emerita); b. 16.03.58, Leeds; m., Harry John McArdle. Educ. Harrogate Grammar School; St. Andrews University; La Trobe University; University of West of England. Training and Development Officer, RYMC Training and Development Service, 1981-84; University of Western Australia: Graduate Research Assistant, 1984-85, Extension Officer, 1985-86; Manager, Special Projects, Melbourne College of Textiles, 1986-89; Senior Research Consultant, State Training Board, Australia, 1989-90; Executive Officer, Fife Regional Council, 1990-94; Northern College of Education: Lecturer, 1994-96, Programme Director, 1996-2003; appointed Director of Research and Knowledge Exchange, School of Education, University of Aberdeen in 2003; Vice Convenor, WEA Scotland. Recreations: horse riding; reading. Address: (b.) University of Aberdeen, King's College Campus, Aberdeen AB24 5UA.
E-mail: k.a.mcardle@abdn.ac.uk

McArthur, Elspeth, OBE, MA. Director, Stellar Quines, since 2018; former Director, Scottish Community Development Centre; former Board member, John Wheatley College; member, Judicial Appointments Board for Scotland (2007-2013); b. 4.2.51, St. Andrews; m., Prof. Michael Anderson. Educ. Madras College; University of Aberdeen; University of Strathclyde. Personnel Assistant, Remploy Ltd, 1975-81; Senior Personnel Officer and Deputy Head of Personnel, British Standards Institution, 1981-91; Assistant/Deputy Director of Personnel, University of Edinburgh, 1991-98, Director of Human Resources, 1998-2007. Scottish HR Director of the Year (not for profit), 2003; Chair, Universities Personnel Association (UK), 2005-07. Address: (b.) Stellar Quines Ltd, 30b Grindlay Street, Edinburgh EH3 9AX.
E-mail: elspethmacarthur@btinternet.com

McArthur, Liam, MA (Hons). MSP (Liberal Democrat), Orkney, since 2007; b. 8.8.67; m.; 2 s. Educ. Kirkwall Grammar School, Orkney; Edinburgh University. Researcher, Jim Wallace MP, House of Commons, 1990-92; Trainee, European Commission (External Affairs directorate), 1992-93; Account Executive, various EU public affairs consultancies, 1993-96; Associate Director, APCO and APCO Europe, 1996-2002; Special Adviser to Deputy First Minister, Jim Wallace MSP, 2002-05; Director, Greenhaus communications, 2005-06; self employed political consultant, 2006-07. Member: Scottish Parliament Corporate Body, Justice Committee, Justice Sub-Committee on Policing, Education and Skills Committee (Substitute Member). Address: (b.) Scottish Parliament, Edinburgh EH99 1SP; T.-0131 348 5815; Constituency Office: 14 Palace Road, Kirkwall, Orkney KW15 1PA; T.-01856 876541.
E-mail: liam.mcarthur.msp@parliament.scot

MacAskill, Kenny, LLB (Hons). MP: Alba (East Lothian), since 2021; SNP, 2019-2021; MSP (SNP), Edinburgh Eastern, 2011-2016, Edinburgh East and Musselburgh, 2007-2011, Lothians, 1999-2007; Cabinet Secretary for Justice, 2007-2014; Shadow Justice Minister, 2004-07; b. 1958, Edinburgh; m.; 2 s. Educ. Linlithgow Academy; Edinburgh University. Former Solicitor. Former member of

the SNP's National Executive Committee and has served as National Treasurer and Vice Convener of Policy. Address: House of Commons, Westminster SW1A 0AA.

McAteer, Dympna, MB, BCh, BAO, FRCP, MRad, FRCR. Consultant Radiologist, since 1999; b. 7.11.65, Letterkenny. Educ. Loreto College, Milford; Trinity College Dublin. Junior House Officer, Altnagelvin Hospital, Derry, 1989-90; Medical Senior House Officer, Royal Victoria Hospital, Belfast, 1990-92; Medical Registrar, Belfast City and Whiteabbey Hospitals, 1992-94; Radiology Registrar, Aberdeen Royal Infirmary, 1994-99. Recreations: squash; running; skiing. Address: Department of Radiology, Aberdeen Royal Infirmary, Foresterhill, Aberdeen AB25 2ZN; T.-01224 681818, Ext. 52178; e-mail: d.mcateer@abdn.ac.uk

McAteer, Ian. Group Chairman of The Union, one of the UK's leading regional marketing agencies; former Chair of the Board, Project Scotland. Career: Barrister-at-law; former Director, Saatchi & Saatchi London; No.2 at Faulds Advertising for three years before setting up The Union in 1996 with three partners; Fellow, IPA and the Marketing Society; Governor, Merchiston Castle School; Mentor, The Kilfinan Group.

MacAulay, Fred. Comedian; Television and Radio Presenter; b. 29.12.56, Perth; m., Aileen; 3 c. Educ. University of Dundee (MA in Accountancy and Jurisprudence); Honorary Doctorate (LLD), University of Dundee. Rector, University of Dundee, 2001-04; Presenter, MacAulay & Co, BBC Radio Scotland, 2006-2014; Television includes: Presenter, Life According to Fred; Co-host, New Year Live; Co-host, series and World Cup special, McCoist and MacAulay; Co-host, The 11 O'Clock Show; Team Captain, The Best Show in the World...Probably; Team Captain, Bring Me the Head of Light Entertainment; Team Captain, A Game of Two Halves; Presenter, Comedy Rules; Presenter, Now You See It; theatre: Bad and Crazy in a Jam. Guest appearances on I'm Sorry I Haven't a Clue, Just A Minute, The Unbelievable Truth and The News Quiz. Regular panellist on Mock the Week, QI and Have I Got News For You. 2003 BBC Television - Comic Relief Does Fame Academy; scaled Mount Kilimanjaro for Sport Relief, 2011; STV Fred MacAulay's West Highland Way-Hey, 2012; Clyde Radio Presenter, since 2021.

McAveety, Frank (Francis), BA (Hons). Member, Glasgow City Council (elected to represent Ward 19 (Shettleston), since 2012; MSP (Labour and Co-Op.), Glasgow Shettleston, 1999-2011; Minister of Tourism, Culture and Sport, 2003-04; Deputy Minister of Health and Community Care, 2002-03; Deputy Minister for Local Government, 1999-2000; b. 27.7.62, Glasgow; m., Anita Mitchell; 1 s.; 1 d. Educ. All Saints Secondary School, Glasgow; Strathclyde University; St. Andrew's College, Bearsden. Councillor, Glasgow District Council, 1988-96; Leader, Glasgow City Council, 1997-99 and 2015-17; Councillor, 1995-99. Board Member, Scottish Youth Theatre. Recreations: labour history; record collecting; football. Address: (h.) 156 Glenbuck Avenue, Robroyston, Glasgow G33 1LW.

McAvoy of Rutherglen, Baron (Thomas McLaughlin), PC. Opposition Chief Whip, 2018-2021; former Government Whip; MP (Labour and Co-operative), Glasgow Rutherglen, 1987-2005, Rutherglen and Hamilton West, 2005-2010; b. 14.12.43, Rutherglen; m., Eleanor Kerr; 4 s. Comptroller of Her Majesty's Household, 1997-2008; Treasurer of Her Majesty's Household and

Government's Deputy Chief Whip, 2008-2010. Member, Strathclyde Regional Council, 1982-87; Opposition Whip, 1990-93.

McBain, Fiona. Chair, Scottish Mortgage Investment Trust, since 2017. Educ. University of Glasgow. Career history: chartered accountant; employed by Prudential plc and Arthur Young (now Ernst & Young); worked across a number of industry sectors, both in the UK and in the United States; joined Scottish Friendly Assurance in 1998, appointed to the Board in April 2005, Chief Executive, 2006-2016. Trustee of Save the Children UK; non-executive director of the Humanitarian Leadership Academy and Dixons Carphone plc. Address: Scottish Mortgage Investment Trust, Calton Square, 1 Greenside Row, Edinburgh EH1 3AN.

McBryde, Professor William Wilson, LLB, PhD, LLD, FRSE. Professor of Commercial Law, Edinburgh University, 1999-2005, Emeritus Professor, since 2005; b. 6.7.45, Perth; 1 s; 2 d. Educ. Perth Academy; Edinburgh University. Apprentice and Assistant, Morton, Smart, Macdonald & Milligan, WS, Edinburgh, 1967-70; Court Procurator, Biggart, Lumsden & Co., Glasgow, 1970-72; Lecturer in Private Law, Glasgow University, 1972-76; Member, Scottish Law Commission Working Party on Contract Law, 1975-2000; Senior Lecturer in Private Law, Aberdeen University, 1976-87; Professor of Scots Law, Dundee University, 1987-99 (Deputy and Vice Principal, 1991-94); Visiting Professor, L'Université de Paris V, 2000-05; Van der Grinten Professor of Commercial Law, University of Nijmegen, 2002-07. Specialist Parliamentary Adviser to House of Lords Select Committee on the European Communities, 1980-83; Member, Scottish Consumer Council, 1984-87; Director, Scottish Universities' Law Institute, 1989-95; Honorary Sheriff, Tayside, Central and Fife, at Dundee, since 1991; Preacher, Nairn United Reformed Church, 2015-21. Recreations: walking; photography; theology.

McCabe, Jackie. Chief Executive, The Royal Environmental Health Institute of Scotland, since 2020; Director of Training, since 2014. Educ. Queen Margaret College, Edinburgh; Adam Smith College, Fife. Training Manager, C J Lang & Son Limited, 1999-2014. Address: The Royal Environmental Health Institute of Scotland, 19 Torphichen Street, Edinburgh EH3 8HX; T.-0131 229 2968; e-mail: jm@rehis.com

McCabe, Cllr Stephen, BA (Hons). Leader of Inverclyde Council, since 2007; Assistant Chief Executive of Govan Housing Association Ltd., 1997-2014; b. 25.04.64, Port Glasgow; 3 s.; 1 d. Educ. St. Stephen's High School, Port Glasgow; University of Strathclyde. Trainee Accountant, Inverclyde District Council, 1986-91; Finance Officer, Paisley South Housing Association, 1991-97; Elected Member: Inverclyde District Council, 1992-96, Inverclyde Council, since 1999. Chair, Inverclyde Alliance, since 2007. Recreation: Celtic supporter. Address: (h.) 10 Victoria Gardens, Kilmacolm PA13 4HL.
E-mail: stephen.mccabe@inverclyde.gov.uk

McCafferty, Rev. Allan, BSc, BD (Hons). Minister, St Andrews: Hope Park and Martyrs linked with Strathkinness, since 2011; b. 19.1.67, Motherwell. Educ. Garrion Academy, Wishaw; Glasgow University; Edinburgh University. Probationer Minister, Holy Trinity Church, Bridge of Allan, 1991-93; Minister, Kirkwall East Church, 1993-2011. Recreations: choral singing; hill-walking; bowling. Address: 20 Priory Gardens, St Andrews, Fife KY16 8XX; T.-01334 478287.

McCaig, Callum, MA (Hons). MP (SNP), Aberdeen South, 2015-17; SNP Energy and Climate Change spokesperson in the House of Commons, 2015-17; b. 6.1.85, Aberdeen.

Educ. Edinburgh University. Former Parliamentary Assistant to SNP MSP Maureen Watt; first elected to Aberdeen City Council in 2007; became Leader of the SNP group on the council in 2011, then Deputy Council Leader, then Leader of the Council (2011-12); re-elected as a councillor in 2012.

McCaig, Professor Colin Darnley, BSc, PhD, FRSE. Regius Professor of Physiology, University of Aberdeen, since 2002; b. 26.6.53, Galashiels; 1 s.; 2 d. Educ. The High School of Glasgow; University of Edinburgh; Glasgow University. Beit Memorial Fellow, University of Edinburgh, 1983-86; Wellcome University Award Lecturer, University of Aberdeen, 1988-2002, Head of School of Medical Sciences, 2003-2015. Address: (b.) Institute of Medical Sciences, University of Aberdeen, Aberdeen AB25 2ZD; e-mail: c.mccaig@abdn.ac.uk

McCall, Anne, MSC. Director, RSPB Scotland, since 2017. Educ. University of Edinburgh; Heriot-Watt University. Career: Internship, State of Maine Planning Office, Augusta, Maine, USA, 1992; Co-ordinator of 1994 International Youth Conservation Exchange (Scotland-Slovakia), Scottish Environment Education Council, 1993-94; Planning Advisor, New Lives New Landscapes, 1995; Scottish Wildlife Trust: Peatland Officer, 1996, Greenspace Planning Researcher, 1996; Planning Assistant, North Lanarkshire Council, 1996-98; Conservation Planning Officer, RSPB, 1998-2000; Head of Planning and Development, RSPB Scotland, 2000-08; Regional Director, RSPB, 2008-2017. Address: Scotland Headquarters, 2 Lochside View, Edinburgh Park, Edinburgh EH12 9DH; T.-0131 317 4100.

McCall Smith, Professor Alexander, CBE, LLB, PhD, FRSE, FRCP(E) (Hon), DIuris (hc), DLitt (hc), LLD (hc), DSc (hc), LittD (hc). Advocate; Professor Emeritus, Faculty of Law, Edinburgh University; Author; Member, International Bioethics Commission, UNESCO, 1998-2004; Vice Chairman, Human Genetics Commission, 2000-04; b. 24.8.48, Zimbabwe; m., Dr. Elizabeth Parry; 2 d. Publications: (non-fiction): Law and Medical Ethics (Co-Author); Butterworth's Medico-Legal Encyclopaedia (Co-Author); Scots Criminal Law (Co-Author); The Duty to Rescue (Co-Author); The Criminal Law of Botswana; Forensic Aspects of Sleep (Co-Author); Errors, Medicine and the Law (Co-Author); Justice and the Prosecution of Old Crimes (Co-Author); fiction: Children of Wax; The Girl who Married a Lion; Heavenly Date; Dream Angus; La's Orchestra Saves The World; Trains and Lovers; The No. 1 Ladies' Detective Agency; Tears of the Giraffe; Morality for Beautiful Girls; The Kalahari Typing School for Men; The Full Cupboard of Life; In The Company of Cheerful Ladies (Saga Prize for wit, 2003); The Miracle at Speedy Motors; The Good Husband of Zebra Drive; Blue Shoes and Happiness; Portuguese Irregular Verbs; The Finer Points of Sausage Dogs; At the Villa of Reduced Circumstances; Unusual Uses for Olive Oil; The Sunday Philosophy Club; Friends, Lovers, Chocolate; The Right Attitude to Rain; The Comfort of Saturdays; The Lost Art of Gratitude; The Charming Quirks of Others; The Forgotten Affairs of Youth; 44 Scotland Street; Espresso Tales; The World According to Bertie; The Unbearable Lightness of Scones; The Importance of Being Seven; Bertie Plays the Blues; Corduroy Mansions; The Dog Who Came in from the Cold; A Conspiracy of Friends; The Saturday Big Tent Wedding Party; The Uncommon Appeal of Clouds; Sunshine on Scotland Street; Bertie's Guide to Life and Mothers; The Handsome Man's Deluxe Café, 2014; Fatty O'Leary's Dinner Party, 2014; What W H Auden can do for you, 2013; The Forever Girl, 2014; A Work of Beauty: Alexander McCall Smith's Edinburgh, 2014; Emma: A Modern Retelling, 2014; The Woman Who

Walked in Sunshine, 2015; The Novel Habits of Happiness, 2015; The Revolving Door of Life, 2015; Precious and Grace, 2016; The House of Unexpected Sisters, 2017; A Time of Love and Tartan, 2017; The Good Pilot Peter Woodhouse, 2017; A Distant View of Everything, 2017; My Italian Bulldozer, 2017; The Colours of All the Cattle, 2018; The Quiet Side of Passion, 2018; To The Land of Long Lost Friends, 2019 (No.1 Ladies' Detective Agency series); The Peppermint Tea Chronicles, 2019 (44 Scotland Street series); Pianos & Flowers, 2019; numerous books for children. Author of The Year, 2004, British Book Awards Booksellers' Association Waterstones; Walpole Award for Excellence, 2005; Guiseppe Acerbi Literary Prize, Italy, 2010; Duke LEAF Award for Environmental Achievement, 2013; Burke Medal, Trinity College, Dublin, 2012; Presidential Award of Botswana, 2011; Bollinger Everyman Wodehouse Prize for Comic Fiction, 2015; National Arts Club of America Medal of Honor for Achievement in Literature, 2017; Fellow of Royal Society of Literature. Recreation: sailing and boats. Address: (b.) c/o David Higham Associates Ltd, 6th Floor, Waverley House, 7-12 Noel Street, London W1F 8GQ.

McCallum, Kevin, QC, LLB (Hons), Dip LP. Sheriff, Dumfries & Galloway, since 2022. Educ. Strathclyde University; Aberdeen University (Master's Degree in International Commercial Law). Career history: traineeship in Barrhead, 1990-1999; worked as a Procurator Fiscal Depute and a defence solicitor in Glasgow; called to the Bar in June 2000; served as an Advocate Depute and Senior Advocate Depute, 2004-09; returned to defence practice in January 2010; appointed Queen's Counsel in 2020; Member of the Bar of England & Wales; appointed Solicitor, 3PB Barristers in 2021. Address: Dumfries Sheriff Court, Buccleuch Street, Dumfries DG1 2AN.

McCallum, Richard. Director, Health Finance and Governance, The Scottish Government, since 2019. Career history: Assistant Manager, KPMG UK, Edinburgh, 2006-2010; Governance and Financial Accountant, The Scottish Government, 2010-2011; Senior Financial Accountant, NHS Fife, Kirkcaldy, 2011-13; The Scottish Government: Finance and Policy Manager, 2013-14, Head of Financial Accounting and Planning, 2014-16, Deputy Director, Health Finance and Infrastructure, 2016-19. Member: Chartered Institute of Public Finance and Accountancy (CIPFA), Healthcare Financial Management Association (HFMA); Chair, NHS Directors of Finance Group. Address: The Scottish Government, Victoria Quay, Edinburgh EH6 6QQ; e-mail: Richard.McCallum@gov.scot

McCann, James Aloysius, MA, LLB. Solicitor and Notary Public; a founding Director, Legal Defence Union in Scotland, 1987, Honorary President; b. 14.8.39, Glasgow; m., Jane Marlow; 3 s.; 1 d. Educ. St. Mungo's Academy, Glasgow; Glasgow University. Former Member, Legal Aid Central Committee; Dean, Faculty of Dunbartonshire Solicitors, 1986-88; Convenor for Law Society PQLE Advocacy Training Courses, 1983-91; Senior Tutor (Professional Legal Practice), Glasgow University, 1981-91; Member, Law Society of Scotland Legal Aid Committee, 1987-97; Reporter, Scottish Legal Aid Board (Co-opted Member, Criminal Applications Committee, 1987-93); appointed Honorary Sheriff at Dumbarton, 1990; Temporary Sheriff, 1991-99. Recreations: sailing; chess; music; golf. Address: (b.) 499 Kilbowie Road, Clydebank G81 2AX.

McCann, Michael. MP (Labour), East Kilbride, Strathaven and Lesmahagow, 2010-2015; b. 2.1.64, Glasgow; m., Tracy Thomson; 1 s.; 1 d. Educ. St Brides High School; St Andrews High School. Secretary, East

Kilbride, Strathaven and Lesmahagow CLP, 2004-2010; elected member, Civil and Public Services Association, 1982-92; Scottish Officer, Civil and Public Services Association (CPSA), 1992-98; Deputy Scottish Secretary, Public and Commercial Services Union (PCS), 1998-2008. Member, Labour Party, since 1987; Member, GMB, since 1992. Recreations: golf; music.

McCarter, Keith Ian, DA (Edin) 1961. Sculptor; b. 15.3.36; m., Brenda Maude Edith; 1 s. (deceased); 1 d. Educ. The Royal High School of Edinburgh; Edinburgh College of Art. National Service, RA, 1954-56; sculptor: primarily involved in architectural and landscaped situations; numerous commissions including: Ordnance Survey HQ Southampton, 1967, Lagos Nigeria, 1974, Wingate Centre City of London, 1980, Goodmans Yard City of London, 1982, 1020 19th Street Washington DC, 1983, American Express Bank City of London, 1984, Guy's Hospital NCC London, 1986, Royal Executive Park NY, 1986, Evelyn Gardens London, 1987, London Docklands 1988, Midland Bank London, 1989, Vogans Mill London, 1989, Moody Gardens Galveston Texas USA (with Sir Geoffrey Jellicoe), Abbey Road London 1991, Monks Cross York, 1992, John Menzies HQ Edinburgh, 1995, Aldermanbury Bradford, 1998, F I Group Edinburgh, 1999; Monks Cross Technology Park, York, 2001; Norfolk & Norwich University Hospital, 2002; Riverside Greenock, 2008; Marchmont House, Greenlaw, 2019; works in private collections world-wide. Sir Otto Beit medal RBS, 1993; FRSA 1970; ARBS 1991. Appointed Art Strategy Consultant by NGP for their Edinburgh waterfront development masterplanned by Foster and Partners; exhibits at Cyril Gerber Fine Art Gallery, Glasgow and Open Eye Gallery, Edinburgh. Recreations: music; literature; beachcombing. Clubs: Farmers', Melrose RFC. Address: (h.) 13 Scottsdale, Melrose TD6 9QE; T.-01896 822535.
E-mail: keith@keith-mccarter.com
web: keith-mccarter.com

McCarthy, James, BSc, FRZSS (Hon). Lecturer and writer; b. 6.5.36, Dundee; m.; 2 s.; 1 d. Educ. Harris Academy, Dundee; Aberdeen University; University of East Africa, Kampala. Military Service, 1954-56 (Royal Marines, commissioned Black Watch, seconded King's African Rifles); Leverhulme Scholar, Makerere College, Kampala, 1959-61; Assistant Conservator of Forests, Tanzania, and Lecturer in Forest Ecology, Forest Training School, 1961-63; Deputy Regional Officer (North England), Nature Conservancy, 1963-69; Deputy Director (Scotland), Nature Conservancy Council, 1975-91; Churchill Fellow, USA, 1976; Nuffield/Leverhulme Fellow, 1988. Recreation: cross-country skiing. Address: (h.) 36 Spylaw Road, Edinburgh EH10 5BL; T.-0131-229 1916.
E-mail: mccarthy-james4@sky.com

McCarthy, Shona. Chief Executive, Edinburgh Festival Fringe Society, since 2016; Director, Shona McCarthy Consulting, since 2014. Educ. University of Ulster Coleraine. Director, Foyle Film Festival, 1995-98; Chief Executive, Cinemagic, 1991-2001; Chief Executive, Imagine Belfast 2008, 2001-02; Executive Director, Rubyblue Ltd, 2002-09; Director, British Council Northern Ireland, 2009-2011; Chief Executive, Culture Company 2013, 2011-2014. Chair, Walk the Plank, since 2015; Chair, Oh Yeah Music Centre, since 2015. Recreations: film and film-making; hill-walking; badminton; music and literature; travel. Address: Edinburgh Festival Fringe Society, 180 High Street, Edinburgh EH1 1QS; T.-0131 226 0021.
E-mail: admin@edfringe.com

McCarthy, Colonel Peter Thomas. Lord-Lieutenant, East Renfrewshire, since 2019; b. 1954; m., Jean (née

Drummond); 3 s. Educ. John Fisher School; Welbeck College. Career history: commissioned into the Royal Electrical & Mechanical Engineers (REME) in 1973; completed a 30 year military career, which included service in Germany and Northern Ireland, attaining the rank of Colonel; became Operations Director with the British Red Cross in Glasgow, after leaving the Army in 2004; managed a large team which delivered services in West Central and South West Scotland for several years before taking on a part-time role in 2011 to support operations in the UK and abroad, before retiring in 2015; appointed Deputy Lieutenant for Renfrewshire in 2011; promoted to Vice Lord-Lieutenant in 2016. Elected to the Master Court of the Incorporation of Hammermen of Glasgow in 2010, and became Deacon in 2015; also served as a trustee of the Trades House of Glasgow (chairs an external consultative group which provides advice on the Trades House support programme for children in kinship care). Actively supports local veterans and is the Vice President of the Royal Electrical & Mechanical Engineers Association in Scotland, as well as being Patron of a local Army Cadet detachment. Address: East Renfrewshire Council HQ, Eastwood Park, Rouken Glen Road, Giffnock, East Renfrewshire G46 6UG.

Macaulay, Iain, CQSW. Lord Lieutenant for the Western Isles, since 2022; b. 5.58, Sollas, North Uist. Educ. Inverness Royal Academy; Robert Gordon Institute of Technology (now Robert Gordon University). Career history: Social Worker in Strathclyde, then moved to Lewis and appointed Depute Director of Social Work with Comhairle nan Eilean Siar in 1997; Director of Social and Community Services, until retirement in 2016. Involved with a number of community voluntary organisations including Vice-Chair of Western Isles Cancer Care Initiative, Chair of Comunn na Gàidhlig and a Trustee of Neuro Hebrides; Deputy Lieutenant, 2003-2022.

McCausland, Professor W. David, BSc (Econ), MSc (Econ), PhD, SFHEA. Director of Education, University of Aberdeen Business School, since 2020; Professor of Economics, University of Aberdeen, since 1995; b. Sheffield. Educ. Universities of Hull, Warwick, Keele. Associate of Higher Education Academy's Economics Network. Address: (b.) University of Aberdeen Business School, MacRobert Building, Old Aberdeen AB24 5UA; T.-01224 272180; e-mail: d.mccausland@abdn.ac.uk

McClatchie, Colin James Stewart, CBE, FRSE. Chairman, Prescient, since 2007; Public Interest Member, Council, Institute of Chartered Accountants Scotland, since 2017; Member, Global Irish Network, since 2010; b. 1.1.49, Belfast; m., Claire McConaghy; 2 d. Educ. Coleraine Academical Institution; Queen's University, Belfast. Senior mgmt., Thomson Regional Newspapers, Belfast, Newcastle, Reading, Edinburgh, 1971-84; Circulation/Marketing Director, Scottish Daily Record and Sunday Mail Ltd., 1984-94 (and Managing Director, Maxwell Free Newspapers Ltd., 1990-93); Marketing Consultant, 1995. General Manager, News International Newspapers (Scotland) Ltd., 1995-2004; Managing Director, Scotland & Ireland, News International Newspapers, 2004-07; Trustee, RSE Foundation, 2017-19; Chairman, St Columba's School, Kilmacolm, 2011-15; Chairman, Scottish Opera, 2008-2014 (Vice-Chairman, 2004-07, Director, 2003-2014, Vice President, 2015-2020); Chairman, Saints & Sinners, 2009-2011; Chairman, Glasgow UNESCO City of Music, 2008-12; Non-Executive Director, Scottish Enterprise, 2004-09 (Chairman, Nomination and Remuneration Committees), Beattie Communications, 2007-08; Dunfermline Press Group, 2007-08; Chairman, The Kemsley Agency, 2008-10. Life Vice President, Newspaper Press Fund (Chairman, West of Scotland District, 1998-2000); Chairman, Institute of Directors,

Scotland, 2002-04 (Chairman, West of Scotland Branch, 2001-02); Director, Scottish Networks International, 2001-03; Director, Scottish Enterprise Glasgow, 2002-04; Chairman, Scottish Society of Epicureans, 2002-04; President, Queens University Association Scotland, 2003-05. Publication: A Musing (autobiography), 2018. Clubs: Saints & Sinners, since 2001; Founder Member, Edinburgh Oyster, 2003. Recreations: family; golf; cooking; opera; theatre. E-mail: colin@mcclatchie.co.uk

McClelland, John Ferguson, CBE, FRSE; b. 27.3.45, Glasgow; m., Alice; 1 d. Educ. North Kelvinside School; Glasgow College. South of Scotland Electricity Board, 1963-68; IBM Corporation, 1968-95: European Director of Operations, 1980, European Manufacturing Controller, 1983, Managing Director of Manufacturing, Greenock, 1987, Director of UK Manufacturing and Product Development, 1992, Vice President, Worldwide Manufacturing, IBM PC Co., 1994; Digital Corporation, 1995-98, V.P. Worldwide Manufacturing; Global Chief Industrial Officer, and Board Member, Philips B.V., 1998-99; 3 Com Corporation, 1999-2003: Senior Vice President, Worldwide Operations, 1999-2001, President, Business Networks Company, 2001-03; Rangers FC PLC, 2000-2011; Executive Chairman, 2002-04; Vice Chairman, 2004-2011; Vice-President, European Club Association and Member of the UEFA Club Competitions Committee, 2002-2011; former Chairman: Judging Panel, Quality Scotland Excellence Award, Renfrewshire Enterprise Company, CBI UK Technology and Innovation Committee, Hub South West Limited, Scottish Further and Higher Education Council, Skills Development Scotland; IOD Non-Executive Director of the Year, 2007. Conducted Review of Public Procurement in Scotland, 2006; Public Sector ICT in Scotland, 2011; Public Procurement in Wales, 2012. Recreations: golf; football.

McClements, David Elliott, LLB (Hons), DipLP. Partner and Member, Russel and Aitken Denny LLP, Solicitors, Denny, since 1998; b. 25.6.67, Kilmarnock; m., Louise; 2 d. Educ. Falkirk High School; University of Edinburgh. Russel and Aitken, Denny, 1990-92, and since 1995; Sandeman and Co., Falkirk, 1992-93; John G. Gray and Co., Edinburgh, 1993-95. Member, Council, Law Society of Scotland, 2001-12, Treasurer, 2009-12; former Chair, Falkirk District Association for Mental Health (2010-18); Convenor, Board, Alzheimer Scotland – Action on Dementia; Elder, Church of Scotland, Lenzie Old; Member, Master Court, Cordiners of Glasgow. Recreations: golf; Boys' Brigade. Address: (h.) 41 Kirkintilloch Road, Lenzie, Glasgow G66 4LB.
E-mail: davidmcclements1967@gmail.com

McClure, Heather, LLB, DipLP, LLM. Senior Solicitor, Head of Private and Family Law, Records and Charities, The Scottish Government, since 2021; Senior Solicitor, Head of Access to Justice, Courts, Tribunals and Inquiries, 2019-2021. Educ. Dunblane High School; Tilburg University; University of Glasgow; Glasgow Graduate School of Law; Kaplan Law School. Career history: Caseworker, The AIRE Centre, London, 2009-2010; Paralegal, Loch Lomond & The Trossachs National Park, Balloch, 2010; The City of Edinburgh Council: Trainee Solicitor, 2010-12; Solicitor (Employment Law), 2012-15; Solicitor, Ministry of Justice UK, 2015-2016; Office of the Advocate General, Dover House, Whitehall: Assistant Legal Secretary to the Advocate General, 2016-17, Senior Assistant Legal Secretary to the Advocate General, 2017-19. Address: Scottish Government, Victoria Quay, Edinburgh EH6 6QQ.

McClure, J. Derrick, MBE, MA, MLitt. Retired Senior Lecturer, Aberdeen University (rtd. 2009); b. 20.7.44, Ayr; m., Ann Celeste nee Bolinger; 3 s. Educ. Ayr Academy; Glasgow University; Edinburgh University. Lektor in Englische Phonetik, University of Tübingen, Germany,

1968-69; Chargé de Cours en Linguistique, University of Ottawa, Canada, 1970-72; English Department, Aberdeen University: Lecturer, 1972-90, Senior Lecturer, 1990-2009 (part-time, 2007-09). Chairman, Forum for Research in the Languages of Scotland and Ulster, 1991-2009; Chairman, Scottish Government's Ministerial Advisory Group on the Scots Language, 2009-2010; Member: Scottish Dictionaries Joint Council, Association for Scottish Literary Studies International Committee, Bibliography of Scottish Literature in Translation Committee. Publications: A Kist o Skinklan Things: an anthology of Scots poetry from the first and second waves of the Scottish Renaissance; numerous articles on Scottish language and literature; Why Scots Matters (Author); Language, Poetry and Nationhood (Author); Doric: The Dialect of North-East Scotland (Author); translations including Sangs tae Eimhir, Ailice's Anters in Ferlielann, Throwe the Keekin-Gless an Fit Ailice Funn There, The Prince-Bairnie and poems and selections from Gaelic and other languages. Recreations: native American history; Japanese language and literature; amateur musical theatre. Address: (b.) School of Language and Literature, University of Aberdeen, Old Aberdeen AB24 2UB; T.-01224-272625.
E-mail: derrickmcclure2@gmail.com

McClure, Judith, CBE, MA (Oxon), DPhil, Honorary DUniv, Heriot-Watt University, June 2014, FSAScot. Head, St. George's School, Edinburgh, 1994-2009; Chairman, Scottish Region, 1995-98, and Member, Council, Girls' Schools Association; b. 22.12.45, Stockton; m., Dr. Roger Collins. Educ. Newlands Grammar School, Middlesbrough; Somerville College, Oxford. Sir Maurice Powicke Research Fellow, Lady Margaret Hall, Oxford, 1976-77; Lecturer in Medieval Latin and Medieval History, Liverpool University, 1977-79; Lecturer in History, Oxford University (Jesus, Somerville and Worcester Colleges), 1979-81; Teacher and Head of Department in History and Politics, School of St. Helen & St. Katherine, Abingdon, 1981-84; Assistant Head, Kingswood School, Bath, 1984-87; Head, Royal School, Bath, 1987-93. Member: Court, University of Bath, 1989-92, General Convocation, Heriot Watt University, 1994-2011, Court, Heriot Watt University, 2003-2013, Board of Governors, Clifton Hall School, 1994-99, Governing Body, Scottish Council of Independent Schools, 1995-2007, Management Committee, 1998-2007 (Chairman, Management Committee, 2001-07), Board, Scottish Qualifications Authority, 1999-2000, Board, Merchiston Castle School, 1999-2005, Ministerial Strategy Committee on Continuing Professional Development, 2000-03 (Chairman, Leadership and Management Sub-group, 2001-03); Trustee, Hopetoun House, 1997-2002; Convener, Scottish Educational Leadership Management and Administration Society, 2003-09; Member, Judicial Studies Committee, 2006-2013; Chair, Advisory Board of the Scottish Council for Studies in School Administration (SCSSA), Moray House School of Education, 2012-17; Member, China Planning Group, Scottish Government, since 2006; Convener, Scotland-China Educational Network, 2006-2018; Member, Advisory Board, Confucius Institute for Scotland, University of Edinburgh, since 2007 and Confucius Institute Ambassador for the teaching of Chinese in Scottish Schools, since 2010; Member of the Education Committee of the Royal Society of Edinburgh, 2009-2013; Member, Commission on School Reform, 2012; Judicial Institute Advisory Council, 2013-2016; Scottish International Education Trust, 2013-2016; Secretary of the Cross Party Group on China at the Scottish Parliament, 2013-16; Member of the UK Committee of The 48 Group Club (The Icebreakers), 2014-16; Acting Chair of the 48 Group Ltd, August-December 2016; Member of the Management Committee of The Scottish Churches' China Group, 2014-15; Chair of the Scotland-China Education Network (SCEN), SCIO, 2015-2018; Convener of the Asia Connections Network Scotland, 2015-2018; Chair of the Languages Think Tank, 2015-2018; Member of the

Committee of Managers and of the Property Committee, The New Club, Edinburgh, since 2018; Chairman of The New Club, Edinburgh, 2020-2022; Fellow, One-Edinburgh, since 2021. Publications: Bede: The Ecclesiastical History (Co-Author), 1994; Thinking About Snow, 2018; articles in historical and educational journals. Recreations: reading; using a computer; travelling. Address: 12A Ravelston Park, Edinburgh EH4 3DX.

McCluskey, Karyn. Forensic psychologist; Chief Executive, Community Justice Scotland, since 2017; b. Falkirk. Trained as a nurse; worked in Accident and Emergency; continued to work in nursing while studying for a BSc in psychology, then a masters in offender profiling; worked for the West Mercia Police, then Strathclyde Police in 2002 as Head of Intelligence Analysis; put together a report on how to reduce rates of violence in Glasgow which led to the Violence Reduction Unit (VRU) being created in 2005. Member of the WHO Violence Prevention Alliance; helped set up the Medics Against Violence charity in Scotland; developed a plan to tackle violence for the Metropolitan Police and has published work on Armed Robbery teams, Alcohol and Violence Interventions in a clinical setting and Violence Reduction. Appointed to the board of the Scottish Professional Football League (SPFL) as a non-executive director in 2016. Received an honorary degree from the Open University in 2015; received an honorary doctorate from University of Glasgow in 2014 and The President's medal from Royal College of Physicians and Surgeons of Glasgow in 2018. Address: Community Justice Scotland, Broomhouse Drive, Edinburgh EH11 3XD; T.-0300 244 8420.

McCluskey, Mary, DCE. Former Artistic Director, Scottish Youth Theatre (1992-2018); freelance Theatre Director/Drama Tutor, since 1985; b. 16.9.54, Glasgow. Educ. West Senior High School, Garden City, Michigan, USA; Hamilton College of Education; Royal Scottish Academy of Music and Drama. President, Hamilton College of Education SRC, 1975-76; Teacher, Glenlee Primary, Hamilton, 1976-79; Assistant Stage Manager, Dundee Repertory Theatre, 1980-81; YOP Supervisor, Community Projects Agency (East End), 1981-83; YTS Training Officer, Community Projects Agency (South East), 1983-85; Associate Director, Scottish Youth Theatre, 1989-91, Chief Executive, 1992-2016; Education Officer, Royal Shakespeare Company, 1991-92. Member, BAFTA. Adapted: Wee MacGreegor, Wee MacGreegor Enlists, Medea, Hamlet, Macbeth, The Glory; Jury's Prize for Direction and Pedagogy, Rainbow Festival, St. Petersburg (for Born Bad). Recreations: theatre; films; books; visiting historic sites.

McClymont, Gregg. Executive Director, IFM Investors, since 2020; Director of Policy and External Affairs, B&CE, 2018-2020; Head of Retirement, Aberdeen Asset Management, 2015-18; MP (Labour), Cumbernauld, Kilsyth and Kirkintilloch East, 2010-2015; b. 3.6.76, Cumbernauld. Tutorial Fellow, St Hugh's College, Oxford, 2007-10. Visiting Fellow, Nuffield College, Oxford, since 2014.

McCoist, Alistair (Ally) Murdoch, MBE. Manager, Glasgow Rangers, 2011-14, Assistant Manager, 2007-2011; former footballer: Glasgow Rangers F.C., Kilmarnock F.C.; b. 24.9.62, Bellshill; m.; 5 s. Educ. Hunter High School. Debut for St. Johnstone aged 16; signed for Sunderland, 1981; joined Rangers, 1983; became club's leading goal-scorer, August 1997 (421 goals); 61 caps for Scotland, since 1986; Member, Scotland squad, 1990 World Cup Finals, 1992 and 1996 European Championships; former contributor to

Question of Sport, BBC TV; ITV football pundit. Scottish Sports Personality of the Year, 1992; Scottish Sports Writers' Player of the Year, 1992. Recreations: reading autobiographies; listening to music. Address: (b.) 16 Royal Terrace, Glasgow G3 7NY.

McColgan-Nuttall, Elizabeth, MBE. Former middle-distance and long-distance track and road-running athlete; b. 24.5.64, Dundee; m. (1), Peter Conor McColgan (divorced); 3 s.; 2 d.; m. (2), John Nuttall. Educ. University of Alabama. Commonwealth Games Gold medallist (10,000 metres), 1986; Silver medallist, World Cross-Country Championships, 1987; Olympic Games Silver medallist (10,000 metres), 1988; Silver medallist, World Indoor Championships, 1989; Gold medallist (10,000 metres) and Bronze medallist (3,000 metres), Commonwealth Games, 1990; World 10,000 Meters Champion (Track), 1991; New York Marathon Winner, 1991; Tokyo Marathon Winner, 1992; London Marathon Winner, 1996; world records: 5,000, 10,000, half marathon on roads.

MacColl, Anne, MA Hons (Glas). Owner and Founder, Saint Amans French Gin, since 2019; Managing Director: Anne MacColl Consulting Ltd, since 2016, Syntaq Global (UK/Europe), 2016-18; Non Executive Board Member, James Hutton Limited, since 2017; Member of the Board of Trustees, Parkinson's UK, 2016-19; Non Executive Director: Social Enterprise Academy, 2016-18, CEFAS, 2018-20, Glasgow Caledonian University School for Business and Society, 2014-18; Associate Director, University of Stirling, 2015-16; Chief Executive, Scottish Development International (SDI), 2011-15; former Chair, Scottish Salmon Producers Organisation. Educ. Glasgow University; Strathclyde Graduate Business School (MBA). Career history: lived and worked for two years in Madrid and for 3 years near Toulouse, France, as a management consultant to the French Chambers of Commerce network, and as part of a national private Spanish consultancy, Soluziona; Regional Head for Southern Europe for SDI; Operations Director for the EMEA (Europe, Middle East and Africa) region of SDI (managed SDI's overseas sales & marketing efforts and worked with teams directly to both attract inward investors and support Scottish companies to successfully trade internationally). Strong interest in developing international education links for Scotland. Address: (b.) 57/59 High Street, Dunblane, Perthshire FK15 0EE.

McColl, James Hamilton, MBE, NDH, SDH, SHM. Freelance Horticulturalist; b. 19.9.35, Kilmarnock; m., Billie; 1 s.; 1 d. Educ. Kilmarnock Academy; West of Scotland Agricultural College. Staff Member, WSAC, Auchincruive, Ayr, 1956-59; Assistant Head Gardener, Reading University Botanic Garden, 1959-61; Horticultural Adviser/Lecturer, Shropshire Education Authority, 1961-67; Horticultural Adviser: MAFF, Leicestershire, Northants and Rutland, 1967-73, North of Scotland College of Agriculture, 1973-78; Manager of Morrison Bowmore Distillers Ltd (formerly Stanley P Morrison) Innovative Waste Energy Re-Cycling Project at Glengarioch Distillery, Oldmeldrum, 1978-88; featured in the British Pavilion at World Fair, Knoxville, USA (1982) and at the Glasgow Garden Festival (1988); former PRO, Morrison Bowmore Distillers Ltd.; Co-Presenter, The Beechgrove Garden, 1978-2018; Chairman, Gardening Scotland, 2005-09; Board Member, The Calyx. Honorary Fellowship of RIAS; Lifetime Achievement Award by Garden Media Guild; 2016 RTS Scotland Award for Beechgrove Garden; awarded for 1000th programme; awarded the Royal Horticultural Society Victoria Medal of Honour (VMH), 2020; regular weekly column in The Press & Journal. Recreations: music; rugby. Address: (h.) Ayrshire Cottage, 45 King Street, Oldmeldrum AB51 0EQ; T.-01651 873955.

McComb, Professor (William) David, BSc, MSc, PhD. Emeritus Professor of Physics, Edinburgh University, since 2006; b. 31.10.40, Belfast; m., Doyleen M. McLeod; 3 d. Educ. Methodist College, Belfast; Queens University, Belfast; Manchester University. Senior Scientific Officer, Theoretical Physics Division, AERE, Harwell; Edinburgh University: Lecturer in Engineering Science, Lecturer in Physics, Reader in Physics, Professor of Statistical Physics. Guest Professor, The Technical University of Delft, 1997; Visiting Fellow, Wolfson College, Cambridge, 1999; Senior Honorary Professorial Fellow, Edinburgh University, 2008; Leverhulme Emeritus Fellow, 2007-09. Publications: The Physics of Fluid Turbulence, 1990; Dynamics and Relativity, 1999; Renormalization Methods: a guide for beginners, 2003; Homogeneous isotropic turbulence: phenomenology, renormalization and statistical closures, 2014. Recreations: reading; gardening; listening to music. Address: (b.) School of Physics, King's Buildings, Edinburgh University, Edinburgh.

McConnell of Glenscorrodale, Lady (Bridget Mary McConnell), CBE, EdD, MA (Hons), DIA, MEd, FRSA, FFCS, FRSE. Chief Executive, Glasgow Life, 2007-2022; Executive Director, Culture and Sport, Glasgow City Council, 2005-07, Director, Cultural and Leisure Services, 1998-2005; b. 28.5.58, Lennoxtown; m., Jack Wilson McConnell (qv); 1 s.; 1 d. Educ. St. Patrick's High School, Kilsyth; Our Lady's High School, Cumbernauld; St. Andrews University; Dundee College of Commerce; Stirling University. Curator, Doorstep Gallery, Fife Regional Council, 1983-84; Arts Officer, Stirling District Council, 1984-88; Principal Arts Officer, The Arts in Fife, Fife Regional Council, 1988-96; Service Manager, Community Services, Fife Council, 1996-98. Conference Co-ordinator, Fourth International Conference in Adult Education and the Arts, St. Andrews, 1995; External Verifier, SCOTVEC Arts and Leisure Management Courses, 1990-97; Member, Board, Workshop and Artists Studio Provision Scotland (WASPS) Ltd, 1985-90; Chair, Scottish Youth Dance Festival, 1993-96 (Founder Member, 1988); Chair, Scottish Local Authority Arts Officers Group, 1993-96 (Founder Member, 1991); Vice Chair, Scottish Arts Lobby (SALVO), 1995-97; Member, Scottish Arts Council Combined Arts Committee, 1988-94; Arts Adviser to COSLA, 1997-2001; Member, Scottish Executive, National Culture Strategy Focus Group, 1999-2000; Member, Scottish Executive, Social Inclusion Task Group, 1999-2000; Board Member, RSAMD, 2001-07, Vice Chair, 2007-13; Member, Heritage Lottery Fund Committee, 2004-2010; Chair of Ceremonies, Celebration and Shared Experiences Working Group of European Championships Board, 2018, 2016-2018; Member of Board of Arts and Business Scotland, since 2016; Member of European Championships 2018 Board, 2015-2018; Chair of European Championships 2018 (Scotland) Board, 2015-2018; Member of Public Catalogue Foundation, since 2015; Member of Board of Trustees, Public Catalogue Foundation, 2015-2017; Trustee, John Mather Trust, 2011-2016; Member (representing RCOS), Committee of Scottish Chairmen (Higher Education Institutions, 2009-2014); Member of Board of UNESCO City of Music, 2008-2012; Member of the 2014 Commonwealth Games Organising Committee for Glasgow, April 2008-October 2014; Member of National Arts Advisory Group for the Advisory Group on Economic Recovery, April-June 2020; Member of Scottish Events Industry Advisory Group, since May 2020; Board Member of The Carnegie Trust for the Universities of Scotland, since May 2020; Chair of Health and Well-Being Economy working group of the Events Industry Advisory Group, since June 2020; Member of RSE Post-Covid Futures Commission Inclusive Public Services Group, since August 2020; Director of Festival UK 2022 Limited, since November 2020. Awards: British/American Arts Association/University of Minnesota Fellowship, 1987. Awarded Doctor Honoris Causa in July 2008 from

Aberdeen University; Doctor of Literature Honoris Causa (DLit), St Andrews University, 2008; Honorary Doctorate: Royal Conservatoire of Scotland, 2013, University of Glasgow, 2014. Awarded CBE for services to Culture in the 2015 New Years Honours List. Publications: Modernising Britain: Creative Futures (Co-Author), 1997; conference papers on arts and adult education. Fabian pamphlet on cultural policy and celebrating 50 years since Jennie Lee's White Paper, November 2015; Fabian Article: From 'First Steps' to 'Structural pivot'. Where next for cultural policy and practice in Scotland's local authorities. Recreations: walking; playing piano; swimming; reading.

McConnell of Glenscorrodale, Rt. Hon. Lord (Jack Wilson McConnell), BSc, DipEd, DUniv. Chancellor, University of Stirling, since 2018; MSP (Labour), Motherwell and Wishaw, 1999-2011; First Minister of Scotland, 2001-07 (Minister for Education, Europe and External Affairs, 2000-2001, Minister for Finance, 1999-2000); b. 30.6.60, Irvine; m., Bridget (qv); 1 s.; 1 d. Educ. Arran High School; Stirling University. Mathematics Teacher, Lornshill Academy, 1983-92; General Secretary, Scottish Labour Party, 1992-98; Chief Executive, Public Affairs Europe Limited, 1998. Member, Stirling District Council, 1984-93, Council Leader, 1990-92, Treasurer, 1988-92, Chair, Leisure and Recreation Committee, 1986-87, Equal Opportunities Committee, 1986-90; Member, European Committee of the Regions, 2001-07; President, 1980-82, Hon. President, 1984-85 and 1991-93, Stirling University Students Association; Executive Member, Scottish Constitutional Convention, 1990-98; Deputy President, NUS Scotland, 1982-83; Chair, Board of Directors, Stirling Windows Ltd., 1988-92; Member, Labour Party Scottish Executive Committee, 1989-92; Parliamentary candidate, Perth and Kinross, 1987. President, European Legislative Regions, 2004; Prime Minister's Special Representative for Peacebuilding, 2008-2010; Chair, Clyde Cash for Kids, 2011; Advisory Board, Institute for Cultural Diplomacy, since 2009; UK/Japan 21st Century Group Board, since 2010; Fellow, UK/China Icebreakers, 2007; Patron, Diana Awards, 2011; Patron, Positive Women, 2011; Chair: APPG on the Sustainable Development Goals; SSE Sustainable Development Fund; Advisory Board, PricewaterhouseCoopers (PwC); Ambassador, Action for Children UK; Professorial Fellow, Stirling University (2014); Vice President, UNICEF UK (2014); Chairperson, McConnell International Foundation (2013). Publication: Proposals for Scottish Democracy, 1989. Recreations: golf; gardening; cinema; music. Address: House of Lords, London SW1A 0PW.

McCorkindale, Rev. Donald George Bruce, BD, DipMin. Church of Scotland Minister at Strontian linked with Morvern linked with Ardgour and Kingairloch, since 2011; Clerk to the Presbytery of Lochaber, since 2016; Convener, Assembly Business Committee, since 2019; Chaplain to the Moderator of the General Assembly, 2011-2012; b. 27.12.63, Glasgow; m., Lesley Rona (Page); 2 s.; 1 d. Educ. Kelvinside Academy, Glasgow; St. Andrews University. Minister, Bonnybridge St. Helens Church, 1992-2000; Dalgety Parish Church, 2000-2011. Publication: The Millennium Challenge, 2000. Address: (h.) The Manse, 2 The Meadows, Strontian PH36 4HZ; T.-01967 402234. E-mail: donald.mccorkindale@live.com

McCormac, Professor Gerry, FRSE, FSA, FRSA, FHEA. Principal and Vice Chancellor, University of Stirling, since 2010; b. 1.8.58. Career: University of Michigan: worked on the NASA Dynamics Explorer satellite programme and subsequently became Director of the high-precision carbon dating facility at Queen's University Belfast; Pro-Vice Chancellor, Queen's University Belfast, 2001-2010 (responsibility for Academic and Financial Planning,

Economic Development and External Affairs). Served on the Northern Ireland (NI) Committee of the Institute of Directors, the NI Economic Development Forum, the NI Science and Industry Panel (MATRIX) and the boards of both the NI Science Park and Business in the Community; formerly a Director and Chair of the Management Board of Queen's University's commercialisation company, QUBIS. Currently a member of Universities Scotland, Universities UK, the Carnegie Trust for the Universities of Scotland Executive Committee, the Universities and Colleges Employers' Association (UCEA) Scottish Committee, the United States/Northern Ireland Economic Development Working Group and a board member of Invest Northern Ireland; Fellow of the Society of Antiquaries, the Higher Education Academy and the Royal Society of Arts, Commerce and Manufacturers. Address: (b.) University of Stirling FK9 4LA; T.-01786 473171.

McCormack (Darroch), Angela Janet; b. 13.09.71, Busby. Educ. Mearns Castle High School; University of the West of Scotland. Career history: The Royal Bank of Scotland plc., 1990-2003; Voluntary Action/Disabled Persons Housing Service, 2003-05; Stepping Stones for Families, 2005-09. Postwatch Scotland Committee, 2004-08; Consumer Focus Scotland Board, 2008-13; Trustee/Company Secretary, Voluntary Action TSI East Renfrewshire, 2007-15; MS Society Scotland Council, 2011-17; MSSS current committee & panel member, since 2017; Independent Advocate, since 2017; Lieutenant Girls Brigade; Sergeant Instructor, West Lowland Army Cadet Force; Glasgow Youth Choir; Paisley Philharmonic Choir; involved with SDS Collective, since 2021. Address: (h.) 49 Langcraigs Drive, Paisley PA2 8JP. E-mail: angela.mccormack13@yahoo.com

McCormick, John, FRSE, MA, MEd. Former Electoral Commissioner (2008-2016); m., Jean Frances Gibbons; 1 s.; 1 d. Educ. St. Michael's Academy, Irvine; University of Glasgow. Teacher, St. Gregory's Secondary School, Glasgow, 1968-70; Education Officer, BBC School Broadcasting Council, 1970-75; Senior Education Officer, Scotland, 1975-82; Sec., and Head of Information, BBC Scotland, 1982-87; The Sec. of the BBC, 1987-92; Controller of BBC Scotland, 1992-2004. Chairman, Edinburgh International Film Festival, 1996-2008; Chairman, Scottish Qualifications Authority, 2004-2008; Member, Lay Advisory Committee, Royal College of Physicians, Edinburgh, 2010-2014; Member, Board, Scottish Screen, 1997-2005 (Vice-Chairman, 2004-05); Member, Board, Skillset, 2002-04; Member, Glasgow Science Centre Charitable Trust, 1999-2005; Member, Board, Scottish Opera, since 2005 (Vice-Chair, since 2008); Member, Board, Glasgow School of Art, 2004-07; Member, Board, Royal Scottish Academy of Music and Dance, 2003-08; Non-executive Director, Lloyds TSB Scotland, 2007-09; Director, Irvine Bay Urban Regeneration Company, 2007-2013; Member, Court, University of Strathclyde, 1996-2002; Independent Director, Glasgow Life, since 2013. FRTS 1998; FRSE 2003. Hon. DLitt (Robert Gordon University, Aberdeen), 1997; Hon. LLD (Strathclyde), 1999; DUniv: Glasgow, 1999; Paisley, 2003. Recreation: newspapers.

McCormick, John William Penfold, BSc, PhD. Chairman, Scottish Association for Public Transport, since 1988; Information Technology Manager, Weir Pumps Ltd., 1979-2003; I.T. and transport consultant; Strategy Officer, Friends of West Highland Lines; President, Rotary Club of Helensburgh, 2012/2013; Director, Transform Scotland, since 2011; b. 9.6.46, Renfrew; m., Linda M.L.; 1 d. Educ. Paisley Grammar School; Glasgow University. Research Fellow, Glasgow University, 1971-74; computer management, since 1975. Recreations: hill-walking;

transport; music. Address: (b.) 11 Queens Crescent, Glasgow G4 9BL; T.-07760 381 729.
E-mail: mail@sapt.org.uk

McCourt, Arthur David, CBE, BSc (Hons). Chief Executive, Highland Council, 1995-2007; b. 11.7.47, Newburgh, Fife; m., Jan; 1 d. Educ. Bell-Baxter High School, Cupar; Edinburgh College of Art; Heriot-Watt University. Various posts with Northumberland County Council, Central Regional Council, Stirling District Council; Assistant Chief Executive, Tayside Regional Council, 1990-93. Recreation: mountaineering. Address: Westcroft, Lentran, Inverness IV3 8RN; T.-01463 831762; e-mail: arthurm@lentran.net

McCowan, Cllr David James, BAcc (Hons), FPC. Director of James Cargill Ltd (Financial Services), since 2002; Councillor, West Loch Lomond and Balloch, since 2018; Board Member (Elected), Loch Lomond and Trossachs National Park Authority, since 2010; b. 2.6.75, Glasgow; divorced. Educ. Loretto School, Musselburgh; University of Abertay, Dundee. Pensions and Investment Consultant, Norwich Union, 1997-2001; Director of Rochester International Ltd, since 2010. President, Helensburgh Tennis Club, 2011; Director, Balloch Community Interest Council. Recreations: tennis; golf; waterskiing; skiing. Address: Auchendennan Farm, Arden, Alexandria, Dunbartonshire G83 8RB; T.-01389 710 000.
E-mail: davidjcmccowan@gmail.com

McCowan, Ray. Chair, Borders College, since 2022. Educ. Heriot-Watt University; Institute of Directors; Scotland Colleges Leadership Programme. Career history: personal training and lifestyle consultant, 1995-2002; Learning Manager, Jewel and Esk Valley College, 2002-06; Assistant Principal, Curriculum and Strategic Planning, Perth College UHI, 2006-2010; Assistant Principal, Adam Smith College, 2010-2011; Vice Principal, Edinburgh College, 2011-2022. Member, Education Scotland. Address: Borders College, Nether Road, Galashiels TD1 3HE; T.-01896 662600.

McCracken, Gordon Angus, BD, CertMin, DMin (Prin). Clerk to the Presbytery of Hamilton, since 2015; Church of Scotland Interim Minister, 2005-2015; b. 8.7.56, Glasgow; m., Jessie Malcolm. Educ. Woodside Senior Secondary, Glasgow; University of Glasgow; Princeton Theological Seminary, N. J. Church of Scotland - Parish Minister, Whitburn South, 1988-2002; Parish Minister, Kilwinning Abbey, 2002-05. Served on West Lothian Council Education Committee, 1996-2002. Publications: Bygone Days of Yore, 1990; Whitburne - A Historie O' Its Auld Parioch Kirk, 2000; Boyne Water: Commemorating the Twelfth in Scotland, 1821-1919, 2021. Address: (h.) 1 Kenilworth Road, Lanark ML11 7BL; T.-0791 8600 720.
E-mail: GMcCracken@churchofscotland.org.uk

McCreadie, Robert Anderson, QC, LLB, PhD, Advocate; b. 17.8.48, St. Andrews. Educ. Madras College, St. Andrews; Edinburgh University; Christ's College, Cambridge. Lecturer, Dundee University, 1974-78, Edinburgh University, 1978-93; called to Scottish Bar, 1992; Standing Junior Counsel, Department of Transport, 1994-95, Scottish Home and Health Department, 1995-99, Home Affairs and Justice Department, 1999-2000, Advocate Depute, 2000-02; Standing Junior Counsel to Advocate General for Scotland, 2002-03; Queen's Counsel, 2003; part-time Sheriff, 2003-04; Sheriff of Tayside Central and Fife at Perth, 2004-2013. Recreations: music; Scottish history; walking; book collecting. Address: (h.) 18 Merchiston Park, Edinburgh EH10 4PN; T.-0131-667 1383.

McCrone, Iain Alistair, CBE (1987), SDA, NSch, ARAgS. Farmer and Company Director; b. 29.3.34, Glasgow; m., Yvonne Findlay (div.); 4 d. Educ. Glasgow Academy; Trinity College, Glenalmond; West of Scotland Agricultural College. Farming on own account, since 1956;

Managing Director, McCrone Farmers Ltd., since 1958; began fish farming, 1968; Director: Highland Trout Co. (later Marine Harvest McConnell), 1968-97, Otter Ferry Salmon Ltd. (now Otter Ferry Seafish Ltd.), since 1974; Member: Fife Regional Council, 1978-82; Parliamentary candidate (Conservative), Central Fife, 1979, Council, National Farmers Union of Scotland, 1977-82, Board, Glenrothes Development Corporation, 1980-96, Fife Health Board, 1983-91; Chairman, Oxford Farming Conference, 1988; Chairman, The Farmers Club, 2001; Nuffield Farming Scholar, 1966; President, Scottish Conservative and Unionist Association, 1985-87. Recreations: golf; rugby (spectator). Address: (h.) Cardsknolls, Markinch, Fife KY7 6LP; T.-01337 830267.
E-mail: iain.mccrone@outlook.com

McCrone, Professor Robert Gavin Loudon, CB, MA, MSc, PhD, Hon.LLD, FRSE, Hon FRSGS. General Secretary, Royal Society of Edinburgh, 2005-07 (Vice President, 2002-05); Hon. Fellow of the Europa Institute, since 1992, Edinburgh University; b. 2.2.33, Ayr; m., 1, Alexandra Bruce Waddell (deceased); 2 s.; 1 d.; m., 2, Olive Pettigrew Moon (née McNaught); 2 step-d. Educ. St. Catharine's College, Cambridge; University of Wales; Glasgow University. National Service with RASC, 1952-54; Fisons Ltd., 1959-60; Lecturer in Economics, Glasgow University, 1960-65; Fellow, Brasenose College, Oxford, 1965-70; Consultant, UNESCO, 1964; Member, NEDC Working Party on Agricultural Policy, 1967-68; Adviser, House of Commons Select Committee on Scottish Affairs, 1969-70; Chief Economic Adviser, Scottish Office, 1970-92; Secretary, Industry Department for Scotland, 1980-87; Secretary, Scottish Office Environment Department, 1987-92; Professor, Centre for Housing Research, University of Glasgow, 1992-94; Visiting Professor, Edinburgh University Management School, 1994-2005. Member: Economic and Social Research Council, 1986-89, Council, Royal Economic Society, 1977-82, Council, Scottish Economic Society, 1982-91; Board, Scottish Opera, 1992-98, Trustee, Scottish Opera Endowment Trust, 1998-2011; Member, Advisory Committee, Inquiry into Implementation of Constitutional Reform, 1995-97; Deputy Chairman: Royal Infirmary of Edinburgh NHS Trust, 1994-99, Lothian University Hospitals' Trust, 1999-2001; Member, National Review of Resources Allocation in the NHS in Scotland 1998-2000; Commissioner, Parliamentary Boundary Commission for Scotland, 1999-2005; Chairman, Committee of Inquiry into Professional Conditions of Service for Teachers, 1999-2000; Vice Chairman: Royal Society of Edinburgh Inquiry into Foot and Mouth Disease in Scotland, 2001-02, Royal Society of Edinburgh Inquiry into the Crisis in the Scottish Fishing Industry, 2003; Chairman, Royal Society of Edinburgh's Inquiry into the Future of Scotland's Hill & Island Areas, 2007-08. Publications: The Economics of Subsidising Agriculture, 1962; Scotland's Economic Progress 1951-60, 1963; Regional Policy in Britain, 1969; Scotland's Future, 1969; Housing Policy in Britain and Europe (Co-Author), 1995; European Monetary Union and Regional Development, 1997; Scottish Independence: Weighing Up the Economics, 2013, second enlarged edition, 2014; After Brexit: The Economics of Scottish Independence, 2022. Recreations: music; walking. Address: (b.) 11A Lauder Road, Edinburgh EH9 2EN; T.-0131 667 4766.

McCrorie, Professor James Roderick, BSc, MA, PhD. Professor of Economics and Finance, St. Andrews University, since 2007, Head of School of Economics and Finance, 2010-14; b. 15.08.68, Greenock. Educ. Greenock Academy; St. Andrews University; Essex University. Lecturer in Economics: Essex University, 1995-97 and 1999-2000, London School of Economics, 1997-99, Queen Mary University of London, 2000-03; Lecturer in Econometrics, Essex University, 2003-05; Reader in

Economics, Leicester University, 2005-07; Visiting Fellow, CentER, Tilburg University, 2004; Associate Fellow, CORE, Université catholique de Louvain, 2007-08; Research Affiliate, Scottish Institute for Research in Economics, since 2007; External Fellow, Essex Centre for Financial Econometrics, Essex University, since 2014; Director, Centre for Dynamic Macroeconomic Analysis, St Andrews University, since 2015; Part-Time Lecturer, New York University in London, 2002-06; Teaching Fellow, University College London, 2006-07; Guest Teacher, London School of Economics, 2011; Academic Assessor, Civil Service Selection Board, since 2003. Recreations: mountaineering; Clyde and West Highland Steamers; music and choral singing; Scotch Malt Whisky. Address: (b.) School of Economics and Finance, University of St. Andrews, St. Salvator's College, St. Andrews KY16 9AR; T.-01334 462482; e-mail: mccrorie@st-andrews.ac.uk

McCuaig, Margot. Director, purpleTV, since 2012; b. 2.68. Address: Film City, 4 Summertown Road, Glasgow G51 2LY.

McCue, Isabel, MBE. Co-Founder, Theatre Nemo, since 1998. Educ. Shawlands Academy; Coatbridge College; common purpose graduate. Career history: Managing Director, Carnwadric Sub post office, 1965-93; Theatre Nemo: The living history of Barlinnie, 2013-14. Inducted into the Saltire Society 'Outstanding Women of Scotland' in 2018. Address: Theatre Nemo, 141 Bridgegate, Unit 235, Glasgow G1 5HZ.

McCue, Mark. Director, McCue Wealth Management Ltd, since 2015; Partner Practice of St. James's Place Wealth Management; b. 6.6.73; m., Zoey (nee Keenan); 2 c. Educ. Westhill Academy; Aberdeen University. Career history: began career as a Stockbroker with Abtrust Bell Lawrie, before moving into Investment Management with Brewin Dolphin; appointed a Director in 2003 and served on the Investment Committee; joined Barclays Wealth as a Director and Private Banker in 2011 before establishing McCue Wealth Management Ltd as a Partner Practice of St. James's Place in 2015. Free Burgess and Guild Member of the Burgh of Aberdeen; Member of Aberdeen Shoemakers Incorporation, since 2015; Treasurer for the Confraternity of the Knights of the Most Holy Trinity (Priory of Scotland). Recreations: family and sports enjoyed, and an active member at Trump International Golf Links. Address: McCue Wealth Management Ltd, 58 Queen's Road, Aberdeen AB15 4YE; T.-01224 745200. E-mail: mark.mccue@sjpp.co.uk

McCulloch, Andrew Grant, LLB, BSc (Soc Sci). Retired Sheriff at Kirkcaldy; b. 10.2.52, Edinburgh; m.; 1 s.; 1 d. Educ. Glasgow Academy; Edinburgh University. Trained, then Assistant, Drummond Miller WS, 1974-79; Partner, 1979-2004; Member, Council, Law Society of Scotland, 1987-98, President, 1996-97; Solicitor Advocate, since 1992; Temporary Sheriff, 1992-99; part-time Sheriff, 2003-04. President, Grange Sports Club, 1990-92. Recreations: golf; cricket; wine.

McCulloch, Ian, DA, RSA. Painter and Printmaker; b. 4.3.35, Glasgow; m., Margery Palmer; 2 s. Educ. Eastbank Academy; Glasgow School of Art. Elected Member, Society of Scottish Artists, 1964; elected Associate, Royal Scottish Academy, 1989; elected Academician, Royal Scottish Academy, 2005; paintings in many private and public collections; numerous one-man and group exhibitions; 1st prize, Stirling Smith Biennial, 1985; winner, Glasgow International Concert Hall Mural Competition, 1989-90; most recent solo exhibition, RSA Edinburgh, 2007; Collins Gallery, Glasgow, 2009. E-mail: mpm@waitrose.com

McCulloch, Revd. James Donald, BD, MIOP, MIP3, FSA Scot (PTC). Emeritus Minister of Hurlford Church; b. 11.4.51, Coatbridge; m., Ann Johnston; 2 d. Educ. Coatbridge High School (Senior Secondary); University of Glasgow, Trinity College. Winner, Marcus Dods Prize in Advanced Ordinary New Testament Studies, 1995. Newspaper and Commercial Hot Metal Compositor, Baird & Hamilton, then Scottish & Universal Newspapers Hamilton, 1969-91; Glasgow College of Building and Printing: Printing Technician's Certificate, 1974, Winner of Andrew Holmes Memorial Scholarship, 1975; Assistant Minister, Bothwell Parish Church; Past Moderator, Presbytery of Irvine and Kilmarnock (2004-05); Editor of Scottish Church Society Report. Recreations: walking; reading (non-fiction). Address: (h.) 18 Edradour Place, Dunsmuir Park, Kilmarnock KA3 1US; T.-01563 535833.

McCulloch, James Macdonald, BA. Formerly Principal, James McCulloch Consulting; formerly Member, Law Society of Scotland Planning Law Specialist Accreditation Panel; Director for Planning and Environmental Appeals and Chief Reporter, Scottish Government Legal Directorate (aka Scottish Executive and Scottish Office), 2002-2008; b. 1948, Dorchester; m., Jennifer Anne Hay; 3 s.; 3 grandsons; 1 granddaughter. Educ. Hardye's School, Dorchester; Lanchester Polytechnic, Coventry. Planning Assistant, Coventry Corporation, 1971-73; Senior Planner and Principal Planner, Scottish Development Department, 1973-84; Reporter, then Principal Reporter, then Deputy Chief Reporter, 1984-2002. Recreations: mountain walking; eating; the people, landscapes and language of Spain; motorcycling; dry-stone walling; electronics; mending stuff - sometimes effectively and contemplation - mostly futile. E-mail: james.mcculloch100@gmail.com

McCulloch, Jane, MA. Consul General of Ireland to Scotland, since 2019. Educ. University of St Andrews. Career history: Commercial Co-ordinator, RAF Leuchars Airshow, 2002-05; City Events Officer, Bristol City Council, 2005-07; Protocol Officer, Department of Foreign Affairs, 2007-08; Deputy Head of Mission, Embassy of Ireland in Denmark, 2008-2012; Embassy of Ireland in Poland: Deputy Head of Mission, 2012-13, Second Secretary & Consul, 2013-15; Department of Foreign Affairs and Trade, Ireland: Desk Officer, Humanitarian Unit, Irish Aid, 2015-16, Head of Integrity, Passport Service, 2016-19. Address: Consulate General of Ireland, 16 Randolph Crescent, Edinburgh EH3 7TT; T.-0131 2267711.

McCulloch, John David, DL. Deputy Lieutenant, Midlothian, since 1992; Clerk to Church of Scotland Presbytery of Lothian, since 1994; b. 5.4.37, Edinburgh; m., Cicely Blackett; 2 s.; 2 d. Educ. Belhaven Hill, Dunbar; Marlborough College. Address: (h.) 20 Tipperwell Way, Penicuik EH26 8QP; T.-01968 672943.

McCulloch, Margaret. MSP (Labour), Central Scotland, 2011-16; b. 9.5.52, Glasgow; m., Ian. Educ. Glasgow Caledonian University. Formerly an independent training consultant; own business based in East Kilbride; formerly an External Verifier with the Scottish Qualifications Authority; worked at the University of Strathclyde for 17 years as a training executive.

McCulloch, Stewart, OBE. Chairman, Crimestoppers Scotland (2001-07); Chairman, Inverclyde Globetrotters

(inaugural year 2010) (remaining active patron); b.
30.12.40, Strathaven, Lanarkshire; m., Janice Ruth
(radiographer); 1 s.; 1 d. Educ. Allan Glen's School,
Glasgow. Junior reporter, Glasgow Eastern Standard, 1958-
60; Reporter, Head of Bureau, Scottish Daily Express,
1960-74; Writer/Deputy News Editor, Scottish Sunday
Express, 1974-80; Director/purchasing and promotions,
McCulloch Associates (restaurants), 1980-82; Diarist, 'Mr
Glasgow', Glasgow Evening Times, 1982-83; Associate,
Scottish Television's weekly 'What's Your Problem?'
consumer slot, 1983-86; Planning Editor, News, Sport and
Current Affairs, STV, 1986-97; Head of Media Relations,
Rosyth, 2000; Lecturer, Media Studies, since 2001.
Recreations: keep fit; modern history; travel. Address: (h.)
15, Levan Point, Cloch Road, Gourock PA19 1BL; T.-
01475 630629 or 07768911895 (m).
E-mail: mccullochmedia@btinternet.com

McCulloch, Stuart James, BSc, MEd, DipEd, MLitt.
Former Headmaster, Belmont House School (1999-2005);
b. 26.12.50, Melfort; m., (1) Anne Elizabeth (deceased); (2)
Maureen Collison; 2 s.; 1 d. Educ. Queen Mary College,
London; Stirling University; Glasgow University. Head of
Geography, Stewart's Melville, Edinburgh, 1973-92;
Deputy Head, Beaconhurst School, 1992-98. Local
Historian. Publications: A Scion of Heroes (Biography);
The Edge of Everywhere (Local History). Recreations:
cycling; historical research. Address: (h.) 11 Golf Court,
Cleghorn, Lanark ML11 8TE; T.-01555 780055.
E-mail: maculafailte@yahoo.co.uk

McCullough, Luke, LLB (Law). Chair, Corra Foundation,
since 2020; b. 9.72. Educ. University of Aberdeen. Career
history: Commercial Scriptwriter, Moray Firth Radio, 1998-
2001; broadcaster, journalist, presenter, actor and
voiceover, Aberdeen, 1995-2003; Lecturer and Project
Leader, Radio Broadcasting, Aberdeen College, 2001-03;
Programme Director, Northsound Radio, Aberdeen, 2003-
05; Programme Director, Radio Forth, Edinburgh, 2005-08;
Managing Director, Northsound Radio, Aberdeen, 2008-09;
BBC: National Manager Scotland/Outreach Manager
UK/Portfolio Manager, 2009-2015; Senior Policy
Adviser/Parliamentary and Corporate Affairs Manager,
Scotland, since 2015. Address: Corra Foundation, Riverside
House, 502 Gorgie Road, Edinburgh EH11 3AF; T.-0131
444 4020.

McCusker, Janie, MA. Chair, NHS Forth Valley, since
2020. Educ. University of Bradford. Extensive career with
the Royal Air Force and has also worked with international
organisations including the United Nations and the
Organization for Security and Cooperation in Europe;
experience of establishing, directing and managing security
departments and was a member of the United Nations
governance body responsible for the development of UN
security policies and procedures; also represented UNICEF
on a high level strategic task for addressing the duty of care
of personnel in high risk locations; Chair of the Glasgow
Colleges Regional Board and is experienced in strategic
leadership, governance, financial accountability, planning
and delivery; strong track record in influencing and
managing change as well as building sustainable
relationships across the public and private sectors. Address:
NHS Forth Valley, Forth Valley Royal Hospital, Stirling
Road, Larbert FK5 4WR; T.-01324 566000.

McDaid, Professor Seamus, CBE, CA, MBA. Non-
executive Board Member, Scotland's Rural College;
formerly Principal and Vice-Chancellor, University of the
West of Scotland (formerly Paisley University) (2005-
2013); Convener, Universities Scotland, 2011-2012; Vice
President, UUK, 2011-2012; b. 23.7.52, Glasgow; m.,

Alice; 2 d. Educ. St. Mungo's Academy; Glasgow
University; Strathclyde University. Qualified as CA, 1974;
trained with Wylie & Bisset, CA; worked for Coopers &
Lybrand; joined Glasgow College as Lecturer, 1976; Senior
Lecturer, 1980, Head, Department of Finance and
Accounting, 1987; Dean, Faculty of Business, Glasgow
Caledonian University, 1992; Vice Principal, University of
Paisley, 1997-2005. Recreations: football; badminton.

McDermid, Val, FRSE, FRSL, HFRIAS. Scottish crime
writer; b. 4.6.55, Kirkcaldy; m., Jo Sharp. Educ. Kirkcaldy
High School; St Hilda's College, Oxford. Began career as a
journalist and worked briefly as a dramatist; first success as
a novelist in 1987 with Report for Murder: The First
Lindsay Gordon Mystery; works fall into five series:
Lindsay Gordon, Kate Brannigan, Tony Hill and Carol
Jordan, Inspector Karen Pirie and Allie Burns. One book for
children, My Granny is a Pirate, and one graphic novel as
co-author, Resistance. Also non fiction works including My
Scotland and Imagine a Country, co-authored with her
partner. Co-founder of the Harrogate Crime Writing
Festival and the Theakston's Old Peculier Crime Novel of
the Year Award, part of the Harrogate International
Festivals. Captained a team of St Hilda's alumnæ to win the
Christmas University Challenge, 2016. Contributes to
several British newspapers and often broadcasts on BBC
Radio 4 and BBC Radio Scotland. Holds six honorary
doctorates and is a fellow of St Hilda's College, Oxford.
Address: Little, Brown Book Group, 100 Victoria
Embankment, London EC4Y 0DY; T.-020 3122 7000.
E-mail: info@littlebrown.co.uk; web: Valmcdermid.com

MacDermid, Yvonne Jean, OBE, DPA, DCA, DTM.
Chief Executive, Money Advice Scotland, 1997-2021; b.
Glasgow. Educ. Woodside Senior Secondary School;
Glasgow Caledonian University; Stow College; Central
College of Commerce. Local government service, 1975-97;
police and trading standards; former Member, Scottish
Consumer Council; past Member, Financial Services
Authority Independent Consumer Panel; Member, UK
Money Advice Trust Partnership; Member, Cross Party
Working Group on Poinding and Warrant Sales; Member,
Scottish Government Debt Action Forum and
Repossessions Sub Group; Member, Protected Trust Deeds
Working Group (chaired by the Accountant in Bankruptcy);
Non-Executive Board Member, Accountant in Bankruptcy.
Publications: A Guide to Money Advice in Scotland (Co-
Author), 2nd and 3rd editions; Managing Debt. Regular
speaker and contributor/broadcaster in respect of consumer
issues relating to credit and debt; Winner of the Martin
Williams Award (Credit Today Awards 2013). Recreations:
opera; swimming; entertaining; gardening; reading.

McDevitt, Emeritus Professor Denis Gordon, DSc, MD,
FRCP, FRCPI, FRCPEd, FFPM, FRSE. Professor of
Clinical Pharmacology, Dundee University Medical School,
1984-2002, now Emeritus Professor (Dean, Faculty of
Medicine, Dentistry and Nursing, 1994-97); Honorary
Consultant Physician, Tayside Universities Hospitals Trust,
1984-2002; Civil Consultant in Clinical Pharmacology,
RAF, 1987-2002; Member, General Medical Council, 1996-
2003 (Treasurer, 2001-03); b. 17.11.37, Belfast; m., Anne
McKee; 2 s.; 1 d. Educ. Campbell College, Belfast; Queen's
University, Belfast. Assistant Professor of Medicine and
Consultant Physician, Christian Medical College, Ludhiana,
North India, 1968-71; Senior Lecturer in Clinical
Pharmacology and Consultant Physician, Queen's
University Medical School, 1971-76; Merck International
Fellow in Clinical Pharmacology, Vanderbilt University,
Nashville, Tennessee, 1974-75; Reader in Clinical
Pharmacology, Queen's University Medical School, 1976-
78; Professor of Clinical Pharmacology, Queen's University
of Belfast and Consultant Physician, Belfast Teaching

Hospitals, 1978-83. Chairman, Clinical Section, British Pharmacological Society, 1985-88 (Secretary, 1978-82); Member, Medicines Commission, 1986-95; President, Association of Physicians of Great Britain and Ireland, 1987-88; Member, Council, Royal College of Physicians of Edinburgh, 2003-08; Member, Board, Faculty of Pharmaceutical Physicians, 2003-08. Recreations: golf; classical music. Address: (h.) 10 Ogilvie Road, Broughty Ferry, Dundee DD5 1LU.

MacDonald, Alastair, BA (Hons). Former Chair, Victim Support Scotland. Educ. Edinburgh Academy; University of Reading. The Home Office: Director of Enforcement & Removals, 2006-07, Deputy Director, Immigration Enforcement & Compliance, 2007-08; Jobcentre Plus: Director Scotland, 2008-2010, Director of Jobcentres (Great Britain), 2010-11; Associate Inspector, Her Majesty's Inspectorate of Constabulary for Scotand, 2012-14 (included an attachment to Police Scotland as programme adviser and risk manager for safety and security for the Glasgow 2014 Commonwealth Games); Director, Stirling MacDonald Ltd, 2013-16; Trustee, Victim Support Scotland, since 2015.

Macdonald, 8th Baron, (Godfrey James Macdonald of Macdonald). Chief of the Name and Arms of Macdonald; b. 28.11.47; m., Claire Catlow; 1 s.; 3 d. Address: (h.) Kinloch Lodge, Isle of Skye.

Macdonald of Tradeston, Rt. Hon. Lord (Gus Macdonald), CBE. Prime Minister's Advisory Committee on Business Appointments, 2009-13; House of Lords Select Committees on Economic Affairs, 2004-2008; Communications, 2008-2012; Digital Skills, 2014-15; Chairman, All Party Parliamentary Humanist Group, 2005-2010; Court Member, Sussex University, 2009-2011; Chancellor, Glasgow Caledonian University, 2007-2012; Senior Advisor, Macquarie Group Ltd., 2004-2016; Non Executive Director, Scottish Power, 2009-2015; Advisory Board, OECD International Transport Forum, 2009-13; Patron, Dystonia Society, 2006-2016; Minister for the Cabinet Office and Chancellor of Duchy of Lancaster, 2001-03; Minister for Transport, Department of Environment, Transport and the Regions, 1999-2001; Minister for Business and Industry, Scottish Office, 1998-99; b. 20.8.40, Larkhall; m., Teen; 2 d. Educ. Allan Glen's School, Glasgow. Marine engineer, Stephens, Linthouse, 1955-62; Circulation Manager, Tribune, 1964-65; Journalist, The Scotsman, 1965-67; Television producer/presenter, Granada, 1967-85; C4, Right to Reply, 1982-88; Scottish Television: Director of Programmes, 1986-90, Managing Director, 1990-96; Chairman, Scottish Television, subsequently Scottish Media Group plc, 1996-98; Scottish Business Elite Awards: Business Leader of the Year, Chairman of the Year, 1997; founder Chairman, Edinburgh International Telvision Festival, 1976; Chairman, Edinburgh International Film Festival, 1993-96; Governor, National Film and Television School, 1986-97; Visiting Professor, Film and Media, Stirling University, 1986-98; Member, Boards: Scottish Enterprise, 1998, Bank of Scotland, 1998, Scottish Screen, 1997, British Film Institute, 1997-98; Chairman, Cairngorms Partnership, 1997-98; Chairman, Taylor and Francis Group plc, 1997-98. Recreations: words; music; pictures; sports. Address: (b.) House of Lords, London SW1A 0PW.

McDonald, The Very Reverend Alan Douglas, LLB, BD, MTH, DLitt (honoris causa), DD (honoris causa). Parish Minister, St, Leonard's and Cameron, St. Andrews, 1998, (retired, 30.06.16); b. 06.03.51, Glasgow; m., Dr Judith McDonald (nee Allen); 1 s.; 1 d. Educ. Glasgow Academy; Strathclyde University; Edinburgh University. Legal Apprentice, Biggart Baillie & Gifford, 1972-74; Solicitor, Farquharson Craig, 1974-75; Community Minister, Pilton, Edinburgh, 1979-83; Minister, Holburn Central, Aberdeen, 1983-98; Convener, Church and Nation Committee, 2000-04; Moderator of the General Assembly of the Church of Scotland, 2006-07. Honorary Degree, St Andrews University. Recreations: walking; golf; music; poetry; travel; football. Address: (h.) 7 Duke Street, Cromarty IV11 8YH; T.- 01381 600954.
E-mail: alan.d.mcdonald@talk21.com

Macdonald, Alison. Executive Director of Nursing, Midwifery and Allied Health Professionals, NHS Lothian, since 2022; previously joint Director of East Lothian Health and Social Care Partnership (ELHSCP) and Chief Officer, East Lothian Joint Integration Board. Over 40 years of nursing experience. Address: NHS Lothian, Waverley Gate, 2-4 Waterloo Place, Edinburgh EH1 3EG.

MacDonald, Allan, MA. Chair, MG Alba, since 2019; Director, purpleTV, 2012-18; Chief Executive, mneTV, 1989-2017; Chairman, Producers Alliance for Cinema and Television (PACT), Scotland, 2002-07; b. 11.6.53, Eriskay; m., Marion Margaret; 1 d. Educ. St. Vincent's College, Langbank; Blairs College, Aberdeen; Glasgow University. Senior Producer, BBC Highland, Inverness; Senior Producer/Manager, BBC Radio Nan Eilean, Stornoway; Manager, BBC Highland, Inverness; Television Producer, BBC Scotland, Glasgow; Head of Gaelic Television, Grampian TV, 1992-94. Member, Board of Management, Lews Castle College, 1992-95; Skillset National Board for Scotland, 2006-12; Founding Fellow of Institute of Contemporary Scotland. Address: (h.) 39 Hughenden Gardens, Hyndland, Glasgow G12 9YH.

MacDonald, Angus. MSP (SNP), Falkirk East, 2011-2021; b. 11.10.63, Stornoway. Educ. Grangemouth High School; Keil School; the College of Estate Management and the Centre for Industrial Studies. Falkirk councillor, 1992-2012.

Macdonald, Professor Angus David, MA (Hons) (Cantab), DipEd. Professor; retired Headmaster, Lomond School, Helensburgh (1986-2009); b. 9.10.50, Edinburgh; m., Isabelle Marjory Ross; 2 d. Educ. Portsmouth Grammar School; Cambridge University; Edinburgh University. Assistant Teacher, Alloa Academy, 1972-73; Assistant Teacher, Edinburgh Academy, 1973-82 (Exchange Teacher, King's School, Parramatta, NSW, 1978-79); George Watson's College, Edinburgh: Principal Teacher of Geography, 1982, Deputy Principal, 1982-86. Recreations: outdoor recreation; gardening. Address: Shenavail Farm, Camserney, nr. Aberfeldy, Perthshire PH15 2JF; T.-01887 820728.

Macdonald, Professor Angus John, BSc (Hons), PhD, FSA (Scot), HonFRSGS, AMICE. Professor Emeritus, Edinburgh College of Art; Writer on architecture; Head, School of Arts, Culture and Environment, University of Edinburgh, 2002-07 (Senior Lecturer, Department of Architecture, 1988-2002, Head of Department of Architecture, 1996-99, Head of Environmental Studies Planning Unit, 1998-2002); b. 17.1.45, Edinburgh; m., Patricia Clare Mazoura Morrow Scott. Educ. George Heriot's School, Edinburgh; University of Edinburgh. Partner, Aerographica, since 1986 (www.aerographica.org); Commissioner, Royal Commission on the Ancient and Historical Monuments of Scotland, 1999-2009; Member, Board of Governors, Edinburgh College of Art, 2003-08. Publications: Wind Loading on Buildings, 1975; Above Edinburgh, 1989; The Highlands and Islands of Scotland,

1989; Granite and Green, 1992; Structure and Architecture, 2019; Structural Design for Architecture, 1997; Anthony Hunt, 2000; Hebrides: an aerial view of a cultural landscape, 2010 (Co-Author); Routledge Companion of Architectural Design and Practice, 2015 (Contributor); High Tech Architecture, 2019; Steel Architecture, 2021. Recreations: hillwalking; music. Address: Department of Architecture, University of Edinburgh, 20 Chambers Street, Edinburgh EH1 1JZ; T.-0131-650 2309.
E-mail: angus.macdonald@ed.ac.uk

MacDonald, Calum Sutherland, Corporate member of the Chartered Institution of Wastes Management. Executive Director, Scottish Environment Protection Agency, since 2004; b. 18.7.54, Glasgow; m., Nancy; 1 s.; 2 d. Educ. Allan Glen's School, Glasgow; Glasgow College of Food Technology. Glasgow City Council; Environmental Health Department Student Sanitary Inspector; Environmental Health Officer; Senior Environmental Health Officer; Pollution Control Manager; Principal Environmental Health Officer, 1973-96; Scottish Environment Protection Agency, Divisional Manager West; Environmental Regulation and Improvement Manager, Highlands, Islands and Grampian; Environmental Development Manager; Acting Director of Strategic Planning, 1996-2004. Honorary Vice President, Environmental Protection UK; Member, Zero Waste Scotland Programme Board, Board of Metropolitan Glasgow Strategic Drainage Partnership and Executive Committee of Scottish Council Development and Industry. Founder member and Chairman of Helping Hands Associates, a charitable association helping good causes in Scotland and beyond. Address: (b.) Scottish Environment Protection Agency, Strathallan House, Castle Business Park, Stirling FK9 4TR; T.-01786 452 438; e-mail: calum.macdonald@sepa.org.uk

Macdonald, Professor David Iain Macpherson, BSc, PhD, CGeol, FGS, FRGS, Polar Medal 1987. Honorary Professor, Perm National Polytechnic Research University, Russia, 2016; Professor of Petroleum Geology, University of Aberdeen, since 1999 (Emeritus, since 2018); Head of School of Geosciences, 2005-2010; b. 31.5.53, Bridge of Allan; m., Dr. Christine Mousley; 2 d. Educ. High School of Stirling; University of Glasgow; University of Cambridge. Geologist, British Antarctic Survey, Cambridge, 1975-80; Post Doctoral Fellow, University of Keele, 1980-82; Geologist, BP Petroleum Development, London, 1982-84; Senior Sedimentologist, British Antarctic Survey, 1984-93; Director, Cambridge Arctic Shelf Programme, 1993-99. Publications: Sedimentation, Tectonics and Eustasy, 1991; more than 60 scientific papers. Recreations: hillwalking; reading; Scottish Country Dancing (Board Member, RSCDS, 2017-18). Address: (b.) University of Aberdeen, School of Geosciences, Meston Building, Aberdeen AB24 3UE; T.-01224 273451; e-mail: d.macdonald@abdn.ac.uk

MacDonald, Donald. Managing Director, Aros, since 1992; b. 1.3.61, Uig, Isle-of-Skye; m., Sine Ghilleasbuig; 1 s.; 1 d. Educ. Napier University, Edinburgh. Management, Mount Royal Hotel, Edinburgh; returned to his native Skye to manage Co Chomunn Stafainn (community co-operative); Managerial role on the estate of Sir Iain Noble in south Skye in 1986 where he served on the board of Fearann Eilean Iarmain, managing Hotel Eilean Iarmain as well as a whisky company, Praban na Linne; in 1988, invested in the partnership of Tulloch Castle in Dingwall to create hotel and conference centre; Managing Director, Tulloch Castle until 1991, when he relocated to Skye; Co-founder, Aros Centre in Portree (opened in 1993 as a Visitor and Heritage Centre; the Centre was further developed to include a purpose built theatre/cinema with conference facilities in 1998). Former Board Member, Skye

and Lochlash Enterprise, acting as Chair of the Audit Committee; became Chairman, Comunn na Gàidhlig (Gaelic Development Agency), 2008-2011; became Chairman, National Gaelic Arts Agency, 2010; served on the board of Highlands and Islands Enterprise, since 2010 and sat on their Risk and Assurance Committee (until 2018); Co-founder, Urras an Taobh Sear (Staffin Community Trust), 1994. Recreations: keen crofter; raising sheep; growing vegetables and soft fruits; keeping bees; an elder of the Church of Scotland and a precentor of Gaelic psalms. Address: (h.) Glaic a' Lochain, 3 Glasphein, Staffin, Skye IV51 9JZ; T.-01470 562 325.
E-mail: donaldsine@aol.com

Macdonald, Elspeth, BSc, MSc. Chief Executive Officer, Scottish Fishermen's Federation, since 2019. Educ. Tobermory High School; Oban High School; University of Stirling; University of Aberdeen. Career history: Food Standards Agency: Head of Policy and Operations, 2011-14, Head of Regulatory and International Unit, 2014-15; Deputy Chief Executive, Food Standards Scotland, 2015-19. Address: Scottish Fishermen's Federation, 24 Rubislaw Terrace, Aberdeen AB10 1XE; T.-01224 646944.

MacDonald, Finlay. Director of Piping, The National Piping Centre, since 2020; Artistic Director of the Piping Live! Glasgow International Festival of Piping, since 2020; b.10.77. Career history: former Head of Piping Studies: National Piping Centre (2002-2020), BA Music (Piping) program, Royal Conservatoire of Scotland; performer and composer, working with the likes of Fred Morrison, La Banda Europa, Old Blind Dogs, Chris Stout and the Unusual Suspects; compositions and arrangements are played throughout the piping and Celtic folk worlds. Address: The National Piping Centre, 30-34 McPhater Street, Glasgow G4 0HW; T.-0141 353 0220.

Macdonald, Very Rev. Finlay Angus John, MA, BD, PhD, DD. Former Principal Clerk, General Assembly of the Church of Scotland (retired, 2010); Moderator, General Assembly, Church of Scotland, 2002-03; Extra Chaplain to HM the Queen; b. 1.7.45, Watford; m., Elizabeth Mary Stuart; 2 s. Educ. The High School of Dundee; St. Andrews University. Assistant Minister, Bo'ness Old Kirk, 1970-71; Minister, Menstrie Parish Church, 1971-77; Junior Clerk and Treasurer, Stirling and Dunblane Presbytery, 1973-77; Minister, Jordanhill Parish Church, Glasgow, 1977-96; Convener, General Assembly Board of Practice and Procedure, 1988-92; Convener, General Assembly Business Committee, 1989-92; Depute Clerk, General Assembly, 1993-96. Fellow of University of Strathclyde; Member, Scottish Inter Faith Council, 2005-08; Co-Leader, Scottish Inter Faith Pilgrimage to Israel/Palestine, 2008. Publications: Confidence in a Changing Church, 2004; Luke Paul, 2012; Luke Paul and the Mosque, 2013; From Reform to Renewal: Scotland's Kirk Century by Century, 2017. Recreations: music; hill-walking; reading; gardening. Address: (h.) 8 St Ronan's Way, Innerleithen, Peeblesshire EH44 6RG; T.-01896 831631.
E-mail: finlaymacdonald5@gmail.com

MacDonald, Gordon. MSP (SNP), Edinburgh Pentlands, since 2011; b. 2.1.60, Glasgow. Educ. Cumbernauld High School; Central College of Commerce; Glasgow College of Technology. Management accountant for Lothian Buses, 1989-2011. Address: (b.) Scottish Parliament, Edinburgh EH99 1SP.

McDonald, Horse. Scottish female singer-songwriter, since 1976; b. 22.11.58, Newport on Tay, Fife. Educ. Lanark Grammar School; Stevenson College, Edinburgh;

Cardonald, Glasgow. Publishing EMI, 1984-2012; Artist: Capitol Records, 1987-92, MCA Records, 1993-95, Randan (owner), since 1999. Wide following in the UK and worldwide and has toured with Tina Turner, BB King and secured several record chart hits in Europe. Nordoff Robbins Ambassador; Patron for 'Switchboard'; Awards and Honours: World Pride Power List top 100: 2013, 2014, 2015, 2016, 2017, 2018, 2019 #46; Inducted into Saltire Society Outstanding Women of Scotland, 2017; Nordoff Robbins/SSEC/REO STAKIS Award for Services to Music, 2017; DIVA Lifetime Achievement Award, 2018; DIVA Power List, 2019 #19; Portrait by Roxana Halls acquired for the nation by Scottish National Portrait gallery, 2020.

McDonald, Sheriff Iona Sara, OBE, MA, LLB, NP. Solicitor, since 1980; Sheriff of North Strathclyde at Kilmarnock and Paisley, since 2002; Lord-Lieutenant of Ayrshire and Arran, since 2017 (Deputy Lieutenant, 2013-17); All Scotland Sheriff (floating), 2000-02; former Partner, Mathie Morton Black and Buchanan, Ayr; former Temporary Sheriff (all Scotland jurisdiction); b. 18.11.54; m., Colin Neale McDonald; 1 s.; 1 d. Educ. Cumnock Academy; Glasgow University. Apprentice Solicitor, Cannon Orpin and Co., Glasgow, 1978-80; joined Mathie Morton Black and Buchanan, Ayr, 1980. Safeguarder; Reporter to the Court and Curator Ad Litem in adoption hearings; facilitator for judicial studies training and a mentor to newly appointed Sheriffs; appointed a member of the Scottish Courts Service Board in 2010 (Chair of the Estates Committee; also involved in the training of Justices of the Peace and Children's Panel members); involved in charity fundraising, in particular for the British Heart Foundation. Address: Kilmarnock Sheriff Court, Sheriff Court House, St Marnock Street, Kilmarnock KA1 1ED; T.- 01563 550024.

McDonald, Professor Sir James, BSc, MSc, PhD, DSc, FREng, FRSE, FIET, FInstP, FEI. Principal and Vice Chancellor, University of Strathclyde, since 2009; Rolls-Royce Chair in Electrical Systems; President, Royal Academy of Engineering, since 2019. Educ. University of Strathclyde. Actively involved in energy research and advising government, industry and commerce and holds a number of public posts including: Co-Chair with First Minister, Scottish Energy Advisory Board; Chairman, Scottish Research Partnership in Engineering; Chairman, Energy Technology Partnership; Chairman, Glasgow Economic Leadership Board; Chairman, Glasgow Science Centre; Chairman, Glasgow Sustainable City Initiative; Chairman, Royal Academy of Engineering Research Committee; Honorary Chair, IET Scotland. Non-Executive Director roles: Weir Group PLC, Scottish Power PLC, UK National Physical Laboratory, UK Offshore Renewable Energy Catapult. Member: Scottish Technology Advisory Board, Innovate UK Energy Catalyst Advisory Board, Innovate UK Emerging Technologies and Industries Steering Group. Address: (b.) 16 Richmond Street, Glasgow G1 1XQ; T-0141 548 2485.

McDonald, Emeritus Professor Janet B.I., MA, FRSE, FRSAMD. Hon Fellow, University of Glasgow; Professor of Drama, 1979-2005 (Head, Department of Theatre, Film and Television Studies, 2001-04); b. 28.7.41, Netherlee, Renfrewshire; m., Ian James McDonald; 1 d. Educ. Hutchesons' Girls' Grammar School; Glasgow University. Member: Governing Body, Royal Scottish Academy of Music and Drama, 1979-94, Academic Council, 1994-2002, Board, Citizens' Theatre, 1979-82 (Chair, 1991-2005); Member, Glasgow University Court, 1991-94; Council Member, Royal Society of Edinburgh, 1994-97, Vice-President, 2005-08; Chairman: Drama and Theatre Board, Council for National Academic Awards, 1981-85, Standing Committee of University Departments of Drama, 1982-85,

Drama Committee, Scottish Arts Council, 1985-88; Chair, Creative and Performing Arts Committee, CNAA, 1989-91; Member, RAE Drama Panel, 1988, 1992; Member, Performing Arts Advisory Group, Scottish Qualifications Authority, 1999-2002; Member, Music and Performing Arts Research Committee, Arts and Humanities Research Board, 2000 (Chair, 2001-04); Board Member, 2002-04; Director, Merchants House, Glasgow, 2002-08; Dean of Faculties, Glasgow University, 2007-2018; Council Member, Royal Philosophical Society, since 2010, President, 2016-18; Royal Glasgow Institute, 2013-14. Address: (h.) 4/1 88 Victoria Crescent Road, Glasgow G12 9JL; T.-0141 339 3193; e-mail: chaika61@outlook.com.

McDonald, Janis. Associate Director (Sensory), The Alliance, since 2021. Educ. St Mungo's, Alloa; University of Aberdeen. CEO: Deafscotland, Voluntary Action Lochaber, Renfrewshire CVS, AACS in Aberdeen. Address: Scottish Sensory Hub, c/o Alliance, 349 Bath Street, Venlaw Building, Glasgow G2 4AA.

MacDonald, Jim, MPhil (Town Planning), DipMgmt. Chief Executive, Architecture and Design Scotland, since 2010. Educ. Edinburgh University; UCL, London. Career: worked with Glasgow City Council, North Lanarkshire Council and the City of Westminster Council; joined A+DS from Historic Scotland. Address: (b.) Architecture and Design Scotland, Bakehouse Close, 146 Canongate, Edinburgh EH8 8DD; T.-0131 556 6699.

MacDonald, John Neil, BA. Director for Scotland, Community Transport Association, 2006-2019; Chief Executive, Royal Scottish Agricultural Benevolent Institution, 2002-06; b. 8.1.60, Daliburgh, South Uist. Educ. St. Vincent's College, Langbank; Blairs College, Aberdeen; Nicolson Institute, Stornoway, Napier College; Strathclyde University. Contracts Supervisor, SGB plc, 1984-86; Sales Executive: Mannesmann Kienzle, 1986-88; Decision Data Computer (GB) Ltd., 1988-89; Sales and Marketing Consultant, Sequel UK Ltd., 1989-91; Development Officer, Scottish Council for Voluntary Organisations, 1991-2002. Recreations: football; literature; cinema.

Macdonald, Louise, OBE, FRSE. Director-General Economy, Scottish Government, since 2022; National Director, IoD Scotland, The Institute of Directors, 2021-2022; b. 2.68. Educ. Journalism at Edinburgh Napier College (Hon Doctorate from Napier University awarded in 2017). Career history: professional journalist on daily print titles across the UK, before moving to the voluntary sector, with a focus on youth engagement and communications; Young Scot: Communications Director and Depute CEO, 2001-08, Chief Executive, 2008-2021. Winner of the Institute of Directors (IoD) Scotland Director of the Year Awards Female Director of the Year, 2016; awarded IoD UK Third Sector Director of the Year, 2016 and inducted as Saltire Society Outstanding Women of Scotland, 2019; Board Trustee of the 5Rights Foundation and of the Scottish Parliament's "think tank" Scotland's Futures Forum; Co-Chair of the First Minister's National Advisory Council on Women and Girls and Honorary Fellow of the Royal Scottish Geographical Society; former NXD of the UK Money Advice Service, and previous Board member of the Scottish Children's Reporters Administration (SCRA). CABx Chair; Community Councillor; Trustee of the RSA. President of the European Youth Card Association and founder of the Natural Change Foundation and the 2050 Climate Group. Address: The Scottish Government, Director-General Economy, St Andrew's House, Regent Road, Edinburgh EH1 3DG; e-mail: ceu@gov.scot

McDonald, Mark, MA, MLitt. MSP (Independent), Aberdeen Donside, 2018-2021; b. 7.6.80, Inverurie; 1 s.; 1 d. Educ. Dyce Primary School; Dyce Academy; University of Dundee; University of Aberdeen. Parliamentary Researcher to MSPs Richard Lochhead, Maureen Watt, and

Nigel Don, 2003-2011; elected to Aberdeen City Council in 2007 at the age of 26 (Dyce/Bucksburn/Danestone ward); SNP candidate, Aberdeen by-election, 2004; SNP candidate for Aberdeen South in the 2010 UK general election; SNP MSP: North East Scotland, 2011-2013, Aberdeen Donside, 2013-18; Minister for Childcare and Early Years in the Scottish Parliament, 2016-17.

Macdonald, Rev. Mhorag, MA (Hons), BD (Hons). Minister of Cambusnethan Parish Church, 1989-2021; Moderator, Hamilton Presbytery, 2006-07; b. 6.4.53, Lagos, Nigeria. Educ. Dumbarton Academy; Glasgow University. Secondary Teacher (Modern Languages), Boclair Academy, Bearsden, 1978-83 (Exchange Teacher, Soultz, Haut Rhin, France, 1981-82); Principal Teacher (Modern Languages), Grovepark, Greenock, 1983-85; Probationer Minister, Bishopton Erskine Church, 1988-89; Ordained and Inducted to Cambusnethan North Parish Church as Parish Minister in 1989. Part-Time Chaplain, Wishaw General; Chaplain, Cambusnethan Primary and Coltness High; Advisor to Board of MADE4U in ML2. Recreations: gardening; walking dog; sudoku, music; photography.

McDonald, Rev. Moira, MA, BD. Minister of Corstorphine Old Parish Church, Edinburgh, since 2005; b. 6.1.69, Elderslie; m., Ian Gates; 1 s.; 1 d. Educ. Renfrew High School; University of Dundee; University of Edinburgh. Minister of Musselburgh: St. Clement's and St. Ninian's Parish Church, 1997-2005. Recreations: gardening; cycling; reading; keeping chickens; playing the piano. Address: (h.) 23 Manse Road, Edinburgh EH12 7SW.
E-mail: moira-mc@live.co.uk

Macdonald, Professor Murdo, MA, PhD, LCAD, FRSA, FSA Scot, HRSA, FASLS. Emeritus Professor of History of Scottish Art, University of Dundee; b. 25.1.55, Edinburgh. Educ. Hammersmith College of Art, Edinburgh University. Commissioning editor, Polygon Books, 1982-94; art school and university lecturing, 1986-90; art critic (mainly for The Scotsman) 1987-1992; Editor, Edinburgh Review, 1990-1994; Lecturer and Adviser in Scottish Studies, Centre for Continuing Education, University of Edinburgh, 1990-97; Professor of History of Scottish Art, University of Dundee, 1997-2017. Trustee, Sir Patrick Geddes Memorial Trust, 1996-2011; Trustee, Scottish Centre of Tagore Studies. Publications: papers and chapters on visual thinking in Scotland, in particular re: Patrick Geddes, Highland/Gàidhealtachd Art, Ossian, Burns, Celtic Revival; Scottish Art, 2000, 2021; Patrick Geddes's Intellectual Origins, 2020. Recreation: hill-walking. Address: 2 Sail Loft, North Beach, Stornoway, Isle of Lewis HS1 2XN.
E-mail: mjsmacdonald@dundee.ac.uk

McDonald, Sheriff Robert. Sheriff, Grampian, Highland and Islands, since 2018. Educ. University of Glasgow. Career history: appointed to Anderson Fyfe Stewart & Young, Glasgow in 1976; moved to Inverness in 1980 joining MacArthur & Co as Legal Assistant and becoming partner; joined Munro and Noble as litigation Partner in 1986 before moving to Stronachs in 2002, became Head of the Dispute Resolution Department and Client Relations Partner; Solicitor Advocate, since 2003. Address: Sheriff Court House, Low Street, Banff AB45 1AU; T.-01261 812140.

Macdonald, (Roderick) Lewis, MA, PhD. MSP (Labour), North East Scotland, 2011-2021, Aberdeen Central, 1999-2011; Convener, Health & Sport Committee (Scottish Parliament), 2017-2021; Shadow Labour Spokesperson for Culture, Sport, Tourism and External Affairs, 2016-17; Shadow Minister for Energy, 2015-16; Opposition Chief Whip, 2013-2015; Shadow Cabinet Secretary for Justice, 2011-2013; Shadow Cabinet Secretary for Infrastructure and Capital Investment, 2011; Shadow Minister for Energy, Enterprise and Tourism, 2007-2011; Deputy Minister for Health and Community Care, 2005-07; for Environment and Rural Development, 2004-05; Deputy Minister for Enterprise and Lifelong Learning, 2003-04; for Enterprise, Transport and Lifelong Learning, 2001-03; for Transport and Planning, 2001; Convener, Holyrood Progress Group, 2000-01; b. 1.1.57, Stornoway; m., Sandra Inkster; 2 d. Educ. Inverurie Academy; Aberdeen University. Research and teaching posts outwith politics, 1983-87, 1992-93; Parliamentary Researcher, office of Frank Doran MP, 1987-92; Shadow Cabinet Adviser to Tom Clarke MP, 1993-97; Member, Labour Party Scottish Executive Committee, 1997-99; Parliamentary candidate, Moray, 1997; Parliamentary Researcher, office of Frank Doran MP, 1997-99. Member, Management Committee, Aberdeen Citizens' Advice Bureau, 1997-99; Member, Grampian Regional Equality Council. Recreations: history; sports and games; the countryside.

MacDonald, Professor Ronald, BA (Hons), MA (Econ), PhD, OBE. Research Professor of Macroeconomics and International Finance, Glasgow University, since 2016; b. 23.4.55, Glasgow; m., Catriona Smith. Educ. Falkirk High School; Heriot Watt University; Manchester University. Midland Bank Fellow in Monetary Economics, Loughborough University, 1982-84; Lecturer in Economics, Aberdeen University, 1984-88; Senior Lecturer, 1988-89; Robert Fleming Professor of Finance and Investment, Dundee University, 1989-93; Professor of International Finance, Strathclyde University, 1993-2004; Bonar MacFie Professor of Economics, Glasgow University, 2005-06, Adam Smith Professor of Political Economy, 2006-2015. Elected Member, Highland Council, Eilean a' Cheò Ward, May 2017-December 2019. Visiting Professor: Queen's University, Canada, 1988, University of New South Wales, Australia, 1989, European University Institute, Florence, 1998 and 2000, University Cergy-Pontoise, 1999, Centre for Economic Studies, 1999, Reserve Bank of New Zealand, 2000; Visiting Scholar, Monetary Authority of Singapore, 2003; Visiting Economist, African Department, International Monetary Fund, Washington DC, 2003; Visiting Scholar, Central Bank of Norway, 2003; Member, European Monetary Forum, since 1994; Visiting Scholar, International Monetary Fund, Washington DC, since 1991; Advisor to World Bank; Advisor to UK Audit Office; Advisor to the Planning Authority of Qatar; Research Fellow, CESIFO, Munich, since 2000; International Fellow of Kiel Institute for World Economics; Consultant to the European Commission and European Central Bank; Monetary Adviser, IMF, 2012; Founding Director of The Scottish Institute for Research in Economics; Academic Advisor to The Commonwealth Scholarship Commission; served as Committee Member of Scottish Economic Society and The Scottish Doctoral Programmes; Member, Scottish Future Growth Council; Co-Founder of The HIAlba-IDEA Think Tank; expert witness to various committees of the Scottish Parliament, the House of Commons Scottish Affairs Committee and the House of Lords Economic Affairs Committee; FRSE, 2002-2014. Publications: Floating Exchange Rates; Exchange Rate Modelling; Exchange Rate Economics: Theories and Evidence; International Money: theory evidence and institutions (Co-Author); The Political Economy of Financing Scottish Government: Considering a New Constitutional Settlement; nine co-edited books; over 170 refereed journal articles; 37 articles in edited books; over 18,000 citations recorded on Google Scholar; Top 1% of Economists in the RePEc/Ideas World Ranking; fine art landscape photography; Certificate in Christian Theology, Edinburgh Theological College. Co-owner, An t-Eilean Photographic Gallery, Portree. Released music album titled 'Time Stands Still', March 2022. Recreations: music; abstract art; boating; cycling; reading; photography. Address: (b.) Department of Economics, Adam Smith Business School, Gilbert Scott Building, Glasgow University, Glasgow G12 8QQ; T.-0141-330-1988; e-mail: ronald.macdonald@glasgow.ac.uk

McDonald, Sheena Elizabeth, MA, HC, DLitt. Journalist and broadcaster. Address: (b.) Curtis Brown, 28/9 Haymarket, London SW1Y 4SP.
E-mail: se.mcdonald@virgin.net

MacDonald, Professor Simon Gavin George, MA, PhD, FInstP, FRSE; b. 5.9.23, Beauly, Inverness-shire; m., Eva Leonie Austerlitz; 1 s.; 1 d. Educ. George Heriot's, Edinburgh; Edinburgh University. Junior Scientific Officer, Royal Aircraft Establishment, Farnborough, 1943-46; Lecturer in Physics, St. Andrews University, 1948-57; Senior Lecturer in Physics: University College of the West Indies, 1957-62, St. Andrews University, 1962-67; Dundee University: Senior Lecturer in Physics, 1967-73, Professor of Physics, 1973-88, Dean of Science, 1970-73, Vice-Principal, 1974-79, Head, Department of Physics, 1979-85; Chairman, Statistics Committee, Universities Central Council on Admissions, 1989-93; Member, Scottish Universities Council on Entrance, 1969-82 (Vice-Convener, 1973-77, Convener, 1977-82); Chairman, Technical Committee, UCCA, 1979-83; Deputy Chairman, UCCA, 1983-89; Chairman, Board of Directors, Dundee Repertory Theatre, 1975-89. Publications: Problems and Solutions in General Physics; Physics for Biology and Premedical Students; Physics for the Life and Health Sciences; Death is my Mistress; The Crime Committee; My Frail Blood; Publish and be Dead; Swallow Them Up; Dishing The Dirt; A Family Affair; Playing Away; Bloody and Invisible Hand; The Truth In Masquerade; I Spy, I Die; Bow At A Venture; Passport to Perdition; The Plaintive Numbers; The Root of all Evil; Pay the Price; The Forsyth Saga; Murder at the Museum; The Second Forsyth Saga; Mysteries of Space and Time; Murder of an Unknown; The Long Arm; A Further Forsyth Saga, Amorphous; Double Jeopardy; Rendezvous with Death: A Forsyth Duo; Forsyth Triumphant; Encore Forsyth; Green Pastures. Recreations: bridge; golf; fiction writing. Address: (h.) 7A Windmill Road, St Andrews KY16 9JJ; T.-01334 478014; e-mail: simon.macdonald1@virgin.net

McDonald, Stewart. MP (SNP), Glasgow South, since 2015; b. 24.8.86, Castlemilk, Glasgow. Educ. Govan High School. Career in retail management; holiday rep in Tenerife; parliamentary case worker for Anne McLaughlin MSP, then case worker for James Dornan MSP in 2011. Address: House of Commons, London SW1A 0AA.

McDonald, Stuart. MP (SNP), Cumbernauld, Kilsyth and Kirkintilloch East, since 2015; SNP Home Affairs Spokesperson, since 2021; SNP Spokesperson on Immigration, Asylum and Border Control, 2015-2021; b. 1978. Educ. Kilsyth Academy; University of Edinburgh. Legal Trainee, Simpson and Marwick Solicitors, 2001-03; Solicitor, NHS Scotland's Central Legal Office, 2003-05; Human Rights Solicitor, Immigration Advisory Service (IAS), 2005-09; Senior Researcher, Scottish Parliament, 2009-2013; Senior Researcher for the pro-independence Scottish independence referendum campaign Yes Scotland, 2013-14; Parliamentary and Public Affairs Officer for the Coalition for Racial Equality and Rights, a Glasgow-based charity, 2015. Member of the House of Commons Home Affairs Select Committee. Address: House of Commons, London SW1A 0AA.

Macdonald, Very Rev. Susan. Rector of Christ Church Morningside, Edinburgh, since 2007; former Dean, Diocese of Edinburgh (2012-17); b. 1951. Career: Thelogical Institute of the Scottish Episcopal Church, 1993-96; Deaconed, 1996; Priested, 1997; Assistant Curate, St John's, Jedburgh, 1996-98; Priest, St Peter, Galashiels, 1998-2001; Priest-in-Charge, Gordon Chapel, Fochabers, 2001-04; Mission 21 Co-ordinator Diocese of Moray, Ross & Caithness, 2001-04; Canon, St Andrew's Cathedral, Inverness, 2003-04; Mission & Ministry Officer, Aberdeen & Orkney, 2005-2007. Address: Christ Church Morningside, 6a Morningside Road, Edinburgh EH10 4DD.

Macdonell, Hamish Alasdair, BA (Hons). Director of Strategic Engagement, Salmon Scotland, since 2018; Scottish Political Editor, The Times, 2017-18; Company Director, Holyrood News, 2009-2017; b. 5.1.68, Inverness; m., Louisa Mary Buller; 2 s. Educ. Fettes College, Edinburgh; University of York. Reporter, Yorkshire Evening Press, 1990-94; freelance journalist, Africa and Australia, 1994-95; Press Association: Parliamentary Reporter, 1995-97, Scottish Political Editor, 1997-98; Political Editor, Scottish Daily Mail, 1998-2001; Scottish Political Editor, The Scotsman, 2001-09; Founding Member, Caledonian Mercury, 2009-2013; Co Founder, Scottish Speakers, 2013-2015. Recreations: golf; rugby; jazz. E-mail: hamishmacdonell@fsmail.net

McDonnell, Michael Anthony, BD, DipTheol, DipCE, Hon MAIRSO. Director, Road Safety Scotland, since 2004; b. 13.5.55, Bellshill; m., Rosemary Boyle; 1 s. Educ. St. Patrick's High School, Coatbridge; Hamilton College of Education; St. Andrew's College Drygrange; Chesters College, Glasgow. Strathclyde Regional Council, 1976-81, 1982-83, 1988-90, latterly as Road Safety Training Officer; Royal Society for the Protection of Accidents (ROSPA), 1990-2004. Recreations: football; cinema. Address: (b.) Transport Scotland, Buchanan House, 58 Port Dundas Road, Glasgow G4 0HF.
E-mail: michael.mcdonnell@transport.gov.scot

Macdougall, Rev. Malcolm McAllister (Calum), BD, DChrEd, MTh. Minister, Eddleston linked with Peebles Old Parish Church, 2001-2019; Minister, St James' Parish Church, Portobello, 1981-2001; served as Probationary Assistant Minister, Greenbank Parish Church, Edinburgh, 1980-81; b. 20.3.52, Greenock; m., Janet F. MacVicar; 1 s.; 1 d. Educ. Greenock Academy; Kelvinside Academy; University of Edinburgh. Worked in Rope and Canvas Industry and in Banking before entering The Church of Scotland Ministry. Trustee, Peeblesshire Charitable Trust; former Chair, Peeblesshire Foodbank; former member, various Church of Scotland General Assembly committees; former Chair, Edinburgh and District Churches Council on Local Broadcasting. Recreations: walking; music; reading; conversation. Address: 2 Woodilee, Broughton, Biggar ML12 6GB; T.-01899 830615.
E-mail: calum.macdougall@btopenworld.com

McDougall, Margaret. MSP (Labour), West Scotland, 2011-16; b. 23.1.49. Previously represented the Kilwinning South Ward on North Ayrshire Council.

McDougall, Peter. Screenwriter; b. 1947, Greenock. Television and film work includes: Just Another Saturday, 1974 (Prix Italia); Elephant's Graveyard, 1976; Just A Boy's Game, 1979; Shoot for the Sun, 1985; Down Where The Buffalo Go, 1988; Down Among The Big Boys, 1993.

MacDougall, Professor Robert Hugh, MB, ChB, DMRT, FRCS, FRCPEdin. Formerly Visiting Professor, University of Edinburgh; HM Inspector of Anatomy for Scotland; Bute Professor and Dean of Medicine, School of Medicine, University of St. Andrews; Honorary Consultant Clinical Oncologist, Edinburgh Cancer Centre, Western General Hospital, Edinburgh; b. 9.8.49, Dundee; m., Moira Jean

Gray; 1 s.; 2 d. Educ. High School of Dundee; St. Andrews University; Edinburgh University. Demonstrator in Anatomy, St. Andrews University; Registrar in Surgery, Aberdeen Royal Infirmary; Lecturer in Clinical Oncology, Edinburgh University; Consultant Radiotherapist and Oncologist, Tayside Health Board; Clinical Director, Department of Clinical Oncology, Western General Hospitals, Edinburgh. Recreation: reading. Address: (b.) 21 Belgrave Crescent, Edinburgh EH4 3AJ.

McDougall, Sandra, LLB (Hons). Deputy Director of Quality Assurance, Healthcare Improvement Scotland, since 2021, Interim Director of Quality Assurance, 2019-2021. Educ. University of Glasgow. Career history: Solicitor, Rennie & Company Solicitors, Irvine, 1998-2000; SAMH: Legal Officer, 2000-05, Influence and Change Manager, 2005-07; Scottish Health Council: Corporate Projects Manager, 2007-2010, Head of Policy, 2010-2017, Acting Director, 2017-19. Address: (b.) 1 South Gyle Crescent, Edinburgh EH12 9EB.
E-mail: sandra.mcdougall1@nhs.net

McDowall, Stuart, CBE, MA. Local Government Boundary Commissioner for Scotland, 1982-99; b. 19.4.26, Liverpool; m., Margaret B.W. Gyle (deceased); 3 s. Educ. Liverpool Institute; St. Andrews University. Royal Air Force, 1944-47; Lecturer then Senior Lecturer in Economics, St. Andrews University, 1961-91; Deputy Chairman, Central Arbitration Committee, 1976-96; Master, United College of St. Salvator and St. Leonard, St. Andrews University, 1976-80; Member: Monopolies and Mergers Commission, 1985-90, Restrictive Practices Court, 1993-96; Chairman, Fife Healthcare NHS Trust, 1994-96; Secretary, Scottish Economic Society, 1970-76. Recreations: golf; gardening; music. Address: (h.) 10 Woodburn Terrace, St. Andrews, Fife KY16 8BA; T.-01334 473247.

McEachran, Colin Neil, MBE, QC, MA, LLB, JD. QC, since 1981; b. 14.1.40, Glasgow; m., Katherine Charlotte; 2 d. Educ. Glenalmond College; Merton College, Oxford; Glasgow University; University of Chicago. Advocate, since 1968; Advocate Depute, 1974-77; QC, 1981; Member, Scottish Legal Aid Board, 1990-98; President, Pension Appeal Tribunal Scotland, 1994-2013; Chairman, Commonwealth Games Council for Scotland, 1995-99. Recreations: target shooting; golf; hill-walking. Address: 13 Saxe Coburg Place, Edinburgh; T.-0131-332 6820.
E-mail: colinneilmce@gmail.com

McEwan, Hon. Lord (Robin Gilmour McEwan), QC, LLB, PhD. Senator of the College of Justice, 2000-08; b. 12.12.43, Glasgow; m., Sheena McIntyre; 2 d. Educ. Paisley Grammar School; Glasgow University. Faulds Fellow in Law, Glasgow University, 1965-68; admitted to Faculty of Advocates, 1967; Standing Junior Counsel, Department of Energy, 1974-76; Advocate Depute, 1976-79; Chairman, Industrial Tribunals, 1981; Sheriff of Lanark, 1982-88, of Ayr, 1988-2000; Member, Scottish Legal Aid Board, 1989-96; Temporary Judge, Court of Session and High Court of Justiciary, 1991-99; appointed Deputy Chairman, Boundaries Commission for Scotland in 2007. Publications: Pleading in Court, 1980; A Casebook on Damages (Co-author), 1983; Contributor to Stair Memorial Encyclopaedia of the Laws of Scotland, 1986.

McEwan, Angus Maywood, BA (Hons), RSW, RWS, RGI (elected 2016). Artist; Lecturer (part-time) in Art and Design, Dundee College, 1997-2021; b. 19.7.63, Dundee; m., Wendy Ann Bell McEwan; 3 s. Educ. Carnoustie High School; Duncan of Jordanstone College of Art. Elizabeth Greenshields Foundation Award, Canada, 1987, 1990; RSA Latimer Award, 1995; scholarship to China, 1996; RSW Prize, 1999; Alexander Graham Munro Award; RSW Prize, 2001; Glasgow Arts Club Fellowship; RSA Diana King/ Scottish Gallery Prize, 2002; John Gray Award; RSW Prize, 2004; John Blockley Prize, Royal Institute of Painters in Watercolours (RI), 2005; 2nd Prize, Kaupthing Singer and Friedlander Watercolour Competition; Bronze Award, Shenzhen International Watercolor Biennial, 2013; May Marshall Brown Award, RSW, 2015; awarded Honorary Citizen of Fabriano, Italy, 2016; awarded "Watercolour Enthusiasts" prize, SDWS, San Diego, USA; Master World Watercolour Artist 2016 award, Thailand; elected Member of International Guild of Realism, USA; solo exhibitions: Riverside Gallery, Stonehaven, 1990, Tolquhon Gallery, Aberdeenshire, 1992, Gallery 41, Edinburgh, 1994, Royal Scottish Academy, 1996, Leith Gallery, 1997, Le Mur Vivant Fine Art, London, 1997, Leith Gallery, 2000, Open Eye Gallery, Edinburgh, 2002; Glasgow Arts Club, 2002; solo shows: Open Eye Gallery, 2004, 2006, 2008, 2010; Queens Gallery, 2005; Art of the Real Exhibitions, USA, England, Scotland, China, 2012; many mixed and group exhibitions; work in public and private collections. Recreations: art; photography; reading; playing with children; enjoying life. Address: (h.) 7 Glenleven Drive, Wormit, Newport on Tay, Fife DD6 8NA; T.-01382 542314; e-mail: art@angusmcewan.com
Website: www.angusmcewan.com
Blogsite: www.artmcewan.blogspot.com

MacEwan, Rev. Donald. Chaplain, St Andrews University, since 2011; m., Maya. Educ. Aberdeen University; Edinburgh University. Career: taught English in Japan for two years; later appointed to an assistantship in Elgin, then obtained PhD in Dublin; Church of Scotland Minister in Largoward and St Monans, 2001-2011. Address: The Chaplaincy Centre, Mansefield, University of St Andrews, 3 St Mary's Place, St Andrews, Fife KY16 9UY; T.-01334 46 2866.

McEwan-Brown, Roy James, OBE, BSc (Econ), DAARL, DMus (Hon), FRSA; Knight (First Class) Order of the Lion of Finland. Former Chief Executive, Scottish Chamber Orchestra (1993-2016); Member, Scottish Arts Council, 2003-07; Chairman, Glasgow Grows Audiences, 2004-2010; b. 12.5.51, Dumfries. Educ. Dumfries High School; Carlisle Grammar School; London School of Economics; Polytechnic of Central London. House Manager, St. George's Theatre, London, 1977-78; Manager, Whitechapel Art Gallery, 1978-79; Administrator, then Director, MacRobert Arts Centre, Stirling, 1979-91; Director of Arts Development, North West Arts Board, Manchester, 1991-93. Chairman, Federation of Scottish Theatres, 1988-91; Scottish Arts Council: Member, Drama Committee, 1991, Member, Combined Arts Committee, 1993-99; Member, Board, Association of British Orchestras, 1993-2003 and 2014-16; Member, Board, Scottish Music Information Centre, 1994-2000; Member, Board, Traverse Theatre, since 2012; Vice Chair, Board, Sage Gateshead, since 2016; Trustee, Dewar Arts Awards, since 2017; Culture Division Assessor, Scottish Government; Adviser, DCMS, UK City of Culture 2021, since 2018. Address: Weirgate House, Weirgate Brae, St Boswells, Scottish Borders TD6 0BD.

McEwen, Professor James, MB, ChB, FRCP (Glasgow, Edinburgh, London), FFPH, FFOM, FDSRCS, DIH, FMedSci, HonDSc. Emeritus Professor, Glasgow University, since 2001; Chair, UK Register for Public Health Specialists, 2003-09; Chair, Advisory Group, Health Protection Scotland, 2005-2013; Professor of Public Health, Glasgow University, 1999-2001; Henry Mechan Professor of Public Health, 1989-99; Consultant in Public Health Medicine, Greater Glasgow Health Board; b. 6.2.40,

Stirling; m., Elizabeth May Archibald; 1 s.; 1 d. Educ. Dollar Academy; St. Andrews University. Lecturer in Industrial Medicine, Dundee University; Senior Lecturer in Community Medicine, Nottingham University; Chief Medical Officer, The Health Education Council; Professor of Community Medicine, King's College, University of London. President, Faculty of Public Health Medicine, Royal Colleges of Physicians UK, 1998-2001; Chair, Governors of Dollar Academy, since 2014; Chairman, Dunhill Medical Trust, 2016-20. Recreations: church; gardening. Address: (b.) Auchanachie, Ruthven, Huntly, Aberdeenshire AB54 4SS; T.-01466 760742; e-mail: j.mcewen@tiscali.co.uk

McFadden, Jean Alexandra, CBE, JP, DL, MA, LLB. Member, Garscadden/Scotstounhill Ward, Glasgow City Council, 2007-2012, Chair, Finance, Policy Development and Scrutiny Committee, 2007-09, Executive Member for Corporate Governance, 2009-2010, Executive Member for Education, 2010-2012, Convener, Labour Group, 1995-2012, Convener, Strathclyde Joint Police Board, 2003-07; Senior Lecturer in Law, Strathclyde University, 1992-2006; b. 26.11.41, Glasgow; m., John (deceased). Educ. Hyndland Secondary School; Glasgow University; Strathclyde University. Principal Teacher of Classics, Glasgow and Strathclyde schools, 1967-86; entered local government as Member, Cowcaddens Ward, Glasgow Corporation, 1971; Glasgow District Council: Member, Scotstoun Ward, 1984, Chairman, Manpower Committee, 1974-77, Leader, Labour Group, 1979-86, and 1992-94, Leader, Council, 1979-86, and 1992-94, Treasurer, 1986-92, Convener, 1995-96, Convener, Social Strategy Committee, 1996-99; Vice Lord Lieutenant, City of Glasgow, 1980-92, Deputy Lord Lieutenant, since 1992; President, COSLA, 1990-92; Convener, Scottish Local Government Information Unit, 1984-2003; Member, Board, Scottish Development Agency, 1989-91, GDA, 1992-2000; Chairman, Mayfest, 1983-97; Member, Secretary of State's Health Appointments Advisory Committee, 1994-2000; Convener, West of Scotland Archaeological Joint Committee, 1996-2012; Chair, Charity Law Review Commission in Scotland, 2000-01; Member, Ancient Monuments Board for Scotland, 2000-03; Executive Board Member, Royal Glasgow Institute of the Fine Arts, 2007, President, 2014-15, Company Secretary, 2012-14. Recreations: theatre; walking; golf; West Highland terriers; Yorkshire terriers. Address: (h.) 16 Lansdowne Crescent, Glasgow G20 6NG; T.-0141-334 3522.

MacFadyen, Alasdair Lorne, LLB. Sheriff, South Strathclyde, Dumfries and Galloway, since 2012; Sheriff, Grampian Highland and Islands at Dingwall, Inverness and Portree, 2002-2012; Appeal Sheriff, since 2015; b. 18.9.55, Glasgow; m., Lynne Ballantyne; 2 d. Educ. High School of Glasgow; Glasgow University. Qualified as Scottish Solicitor, 1978; practised as Solicitor in Private Practice, Edinburgh, Glasgow and Inverness, 1978-2001; Temporary Sheriff, 1995-2000; Part-Time Chairman, Employment Tribunals (Scotland), 2000-01; Part-Time Sheriff, 2000-01; All Scotland Floating Sheriff, based in Aberdeen, 2001-02. Recreations: sailing in Tall Ships; music; cycling. Address: (b.) 4 Beckford Street, Hamilton ML3 0BT; T.-01698 282957.

McFadyen, Jock, RA. Contemporary British painter; b. 1950, Paisley; m. (1), Carol Hambleton; 1 s; m. (2), Susie Honeyman; 1 d.; 1 s. Educ. Chelsea School of Art (BA, MA). Taught one day a week at the Slade School of Art, 1980-2005; created The Grey Gallery in 2005. Appointed Artist in Residence at the National Gallery, London in 1981, designed sets and costumes for Sir Kenneth MacMillan's last ballet The Judas Tree at the Royal Opera House 1992. Over 40 solo exhibitions including the Imperial War Museum 1991; Manchester Art Gallery 1991; Kelvingrove Art Gallery, Glasgow 1992; Festival Exhibition, Talbot Rice Art Gallery, 1998; St Magnus Festival, Pier Art Centre, Orkney 1999; City Art Centre, Edinburgh 2020; Dovecot Studios, Edinburgh 2020; The Lowry, Salford 2021; Royal Academy, London 2022. McFadyen's work is held in 40 public museum collections including Tate, the National Gallery, the V&A, the British Museum and the Scottish National Gallery of Modern Art, as well as many corporate and private collections in the UK and abroad. Elected a Royal Academician in 2012. https://www.instagram.com/thegreygallerylondon; www.jockmcfadyen.com

McFadyen, Norman, CBE, FSA Scot, LLB. Sheriff of Lothian & Borders at Edinburgh, since 2015; Appeal Sheriff, since 2017; Temporary Judge, High Court of Justiciary, since 2019; b. 24.06.55, Glasgow; m., Pauline Brown; 1 s. Educ. High School of Glasgow; University of Glasgow. Procurator Fiscal Depute, Airdrie, Glasgow and Crown Office, 1978-88; Head of Fraud and Specialist Services, Crown Office, 1988-94; Deputy Crown Agent, 1994-98; Regional Procurator Fiscal for Lothian and Borders, 1999-2002; Crown Agent Designate, 2002-03; Crown Agent and Chief Executive, 2004-2010; Sheriff of South Strathclyde, Dumfries and Galloway, 2010-2015. Co-Chair, High Court Reform Programme Board, 2004-07; Director, International Society for the Reform of Criminal Law, since 2008; Member: Sentencing Council for Scotland, since 2015, Criminal Courts Rules Council, since 2017. Recreations: walking; swimming. Address: (b.) Sheriff's Chambers, Sheriff Court House, 27 Chambers Street, Edinburgh EH1 1LB; T.-0131 225 2525.

McFall of Alcluith, Baron (John McFall), BSc (Hons), BA, MBA. Life Peer. Lord Speaker, House of Lords, since 2021 (Senior Deputy Speaker, 2016-2021); MP (Labour), Dumbarton, 1987-2010; Chairman, Treasury Committee, 2001-10; Parliamentary Under Secretary of State, Northern Ireland Office, 1998-99; served on: Information Committee, Parliamentary and Scientific Committee, Executive Committee – Parliamentary Group for Energy Studies, British/Italian Group, British/Peru Group, Retail Industry Group, Roads Study Group, Scotch Whisky Group, Parliamentary and Scientific Committee; formerly Opposition Whip with responsibility for Foreign Affairs, Defence and Trade and Industry (resigned post at time of Gulf War); former Deputy Shadow Secretary of State for Scotland; Scottish Whip, 1997-98. Honorary Doctorates from the universities of Glasgow, Strathclyde, Stirling and the West of Scotland; Doctor of Business Administration, BPP Business School (London). Recreations: jogging; reading; golf. Address: House of Lords, Westminster, London SW1A 0PW.

McFarlane, Jim, DipTP. Chairman, Lothian Buses, since 2016. Educ. Glasgow School of Art. Scottish Enterprise: Senior Director, Business Transformation, 2001-03, Chief Executive of SE, Edinburgh and Lothian, 2003-07 (led the project teams that established the Edinburgh International Conference Centre and Exchange Financial District, Our Dynamic Earth and the Edinburgh Festival Theatre), Managing Director, Operations, 2007-2015. Significant involvement in the development and implementation of numerous landmark projects including the Edinburgh BioQuarter and The Scottish Centre for Regenerative Medicine. Degree of Doctor Honoris Causa for Leadership to Scottish Enterprise. Address: Lothian Buses, Annandale Street, Edinburgh EH7 4AZ.

Macfarlane of Bearsden, Lord, (Norman Somerville Macfarlane), KT (1996), Kt (1983), DL, FRSE. Life Peer;

Honorary Life President, Macfarlane Group PLC (Chairman, 1973-98, Managing Director, 1973-90, Honorary Life President, 1999, Macfarlane Group (Clansman PLC); Honorary Life President, United Distillers (Chairman, 1987-96); Honorary Life President, Diageo (Scotland) Ltd.; Lord High Commissioner, General Assembly of Church of Scotland, 1992, 1993, 1997; b. 5.3.26; m., Marguerite Mary Campbell; 1 s.; 4 d. Educ. High School of Glasgow. Commissioned, Royal Artillery, 1945, served Palestine, 1945-47; founded N.S. Macfarlane & Co. Ltd., 1949 (became Macfarlane Group (Clansman) PLC, 1973); Underwriting Member of Lloyd's, 1978-97; Chairman: The Fine Art Society PLC, 1976-98 (Honorary Life President, 1998), American Trust PLC, 1984-97 (Director, since 1980), Guinness PLC, 1987-89 (Joint Deputy Chairman, 1989-92); Director: Clydesdale Bank PLC, 1980-96 (Deputy Chairman, 1993-96), General Accident Fire and Life Assurance Corporation plc, 1984-96, Edinburgh Fund Managers plc, 1980-98, Glasgow Chamber of Commerce, 1976-79; Member: Council, CBI Scotland, 1975-81, Board, Scottish Development Agency, 1979-87; Chairman, Glasgow Development Agency, 1985-92; Vice Chairman, Scottish Ballet, 1983-87 (Director, 1975-87), Hon. President, since 2001; Director, Scottish National Orchestra, 1977-82; President, Royal Glasgow Institute of the Fine Arts, 1976-87; Member, Royal Fine Art Commission for Scotland, 1980-82; Scottish Patron, National Art Collection Fund, since 1978; Governor, Glasgow School of Art, 1976-87, Hon. President, since 2001; Trustee: National Heritage Memorial Fund, 1984-97, National Galleries of Scotland, 1986-97; Director, Third Eye Centre, 1978-81; Hon. President, Charles Rennie Mackintosh Society, since 1988; Hon. President, High School of Glasgow, since 1992 (Chairman of Governors, 1979-92); Member, Court, Glasgow University, 1979-87; Regent, RCSE, since 1997; President: Stationers' Association of GB and Ireland, 1965, Company of Stationers of Glasgow, 1968-70, Glasgow High School Club, 1970-72; Patron, Scottish Licensed Trade Association, since 1992; Honorary Patron, Queen's Park FC; Vice President, Professional Golfers Association; KT, 1996; DL, Dunbartonshire, 1993, CIMgt, 1996, HRSA, 1987, HRGI, 1987, Hon. FRIAS, 1984, FRSE, 1991, Hon.FScotvec, 1991, Hon. FRCPS Glas., 1992, Hon. Fellow, Glasgow School of Art, 1993; Hon. LLD: Strathclyde, 1986, Glasgow, 1988, Glasgow Caledonian, 1993, Aberdeen, 1995; DUniv., Stirling, 1992; Dr (hc), Edinburgh, 1992; Glasgow St. Mungo Award, 2005; Hon. President, Tenovus Scotland, 2006; Hon. Life Member, Scottish Football League, 2006; Director, Culture and Sport Glasgow, since 2007; Freeman of Dumfries and Galloway, 2006; Freeman of the City of Glasgow, 2007. Recreations: golf; cricket; theatre; art. Address: (b.) Macfarlane Group PLC, Clansman House, 3 Park Gardens, Glasgow G3 7YE; (h.) 50 Manse Road, Bearsden, Glasgow G61 3PN.

Macfarlane, Professor Peter Wilson, CBE, DSc, FBCS, FRCP (Glasg), eFESC, FRSE. Emeritus Professor; Prof. of Electrocardiology, Glasgow University, 1995-2010; Chairman, 40th International Congress on Electrocardiology, Glasgow, 2013; b. 8.11.42, Glasgow; m., Irene Grace Muir; 2 s. Educ. Hyndland Senior Secondary School, Glasgow; Glasgow University. Glasgow University: Assistant Lecturer in Medical Cardiology, 1967, Lecturer, 1970, Senior Lecturer, 1974, Reader, 1980, Professor, 1991, Hon. Senior Research Fellow, since 2010; President, 5th and 40th International Congresses on Electrocardiology, Glasgow, 1978, 2013; Chairman, 15th and 18th Annual Conferences, International Society of Computerized Electrocardiology, 1990, 1993 (President, 2017-20); President: International Society of Electrocardiology, 2007-09, Computing in Cardiology, 2008-14. Author/Editor, 15 books. Recreations: supporting Ayr United; running half-marathons. Address: (h.) 12 Barrcraig Road, Bridge of Weir PA11 3HG; T.-01505 614443.

MacFarlane, Emeritus Professor Thomas Wallace, DDS, DSc, FRSE, FDSRCSEdin, FRCPath, FDSRCPSGlas. Professor of Oral Microbiology, Glasgow University, 1991-2001; Honorary Consultant in Oral Microbiology; Dean of the Dental School, 1995-2000; b. 12.12.42, Glasgow; m., Nancy McEwan Fyfe; 1 s. Educ. Hyndland Senior Secondary School; Glasgow University. Assistant Lecturer, Dental Histology and Pathology, 1966-69; trained in Medical Microbiology and Histopathology, Glasgow Royal Infirmary; Lecturer in Oral Medicine and Pathology, 1969-77; organised and ran the diagnostic service in Oral Microbiology, Glasgow Dental Hospital and School; Senior Lecturer in Oral Medicine and Pathology and Consultant in Oral Microbiology, 1977; Reader in Oral Medicine and Pathology, 1984-91; Head, Department of Oral Sciences, 1992-95. Recreations: music; reading; walking. Address: 29 Cherrylea, Castleton Park, Auchterarder, Perthshire PH3 1QG; T.-01764 664 356.

McGarry, Gerald William. MBChB, MD, FRCS(ORLHNS), FFSTEd. Consultant Otolaryngologist, Head and Neck Surgeon, since 1995; Honorary Senior Lecturer, University of Glasgow; former Professor of Surgical Studies, RCSEd (2014-2017); b. 30.1.62, Glasgow; m., Carol; 3 s. Educ. St. Augustine Secondary School, Glasgow; Glasgow University. Senior Registrar in Otolaryngology: Glasgow Rotational Scheme, 1992, Royal Brisbane Hospital, Australia, 1993; Locum Consultant Otolaryngologist, Glasgow Royal Infirmary, 1994. Former Vice President, Royal Society of Medicine Section of Laryngology; former Member, Medical Appeals Tribunal; Founder, Scottish Sinus Surgery Group. Publications: Picture Tests in ENT, 1999; Endoscopic Dissection of the Nose and Paranasal Sinuses; papers on rhinology and head and neck cancer; textbook editor and contributor. Recreation: mountaineering. Address: Department of Otolaryngology, Royal Infirmary, Glasgow G31 2ER; T.-0141-211 1660.

McGarry, Natalie. MP (Glasgow East): Independent, 2015-17, SNP, 2015; b. 1981, Inverkeithing. Educ. University of Aberdeen. Former convener of the SNP's Glasgow Region Association; co-founder of the Women for Independence group in 2012.

McGarva, Andrew. Head, Morrison's Academy, Crieff, since 2021. Career history: taught both in the UK and internationally; former Deputy Head of Prep School and Director of Music, Kilgraston School; former Head of Music, the British School in Tokyo; former Director of Music, Wellington School, then Assistant Headteacher, Jersey College for Girls. Address: Morrison's Academy, Ferntower Road, Crieff, Perthshire PH7 3AN; T.-01764 915 683; e-mail: enquiries@morrisonsacademy.org

McGarvey, Darren. Scottish rapper, hip hop recording artist, and social commentator; b. 1984. Educ. Glasgow Clyde College. Wrote and presented eight programmes about the causes of anti-social behaviour and social deprivation for BBC Radio Scotland, 2004-06; worked with youth organisation Volition, teaching young people to rap; led a workshop as part of a PowerRap competition for schools, encouraging young people to explore important issues through music and language in 2012; part of the Poverty Truth Commission hosted in Glasgow in 2009; six months as rapper-in-residence with the Violence Reduction Unit in 2015; appeared in a documentary The Divide which discussed alcoholism and its impact on his life in 2016. Orwell Prize winning author of Poverty Safari: Understanding the Anger of Britain's Underclass, 2018. Address: Luath Press, 543/2 Castlehill, The Royal Mile, Edinburgh EH1 2ND; T.-0131 225 4326.

McGee, Right Reverend Brian. Bishop of Argyll and Isles, since 2016; b. 8.10.65, Greenock. Educ. St Joseph's Primary School, Greenock; Holy Cross Primary School, Greenock; St. Vincent's College, Langbank; St. Mary's College, Blairs; studied for the priesthood at St Patrick's College, Thurles, County Tipperary, 1983-89; Sarum College, Salisbury (Master of Arts degree in Christian Spirituality). Ordained in 1989 as a priest for the Diocese of Paisley by Bishop John Mone; Assistant Priest, St Charles Borromeo Parish, Paisley, 1989-1995; Assistant Priest, Holy Family Parish, Port Glasgow, 1995-1997; Parish Priest, St Joseph's Parish, Clarkston, 1997-2007; Spiritual Director, Scotus College, National Seminary, 2007-2009; Parish Priest, Holy Family Parish, Port Glasgow, 2009-2015. Vicar General of the Diocese of Paisley, since 2014. Address: Diocesan Office, Bishop's House, Esplanade, Oban, Argyll PA34 5AB; T.-01631 567436.

McGee, John. Entreprenuer - Redevelopment and Regeneration, Dumfries and Galloway, since 2012; Lifetime Ambassador, West Lothian College, since 2019; Strategic Planning, JL Com Group, since 2019; Industry Executive, Coleman Research, since 2000; b. Edinburgh. Educ. St Catherine's Primary; Holyrood High School, Edinburgh. Sales & Marketing Manager, Wallace Brown Limited, 1983-92; Managing Director, Georgeson Group, 1992-2000; Sales & Marketing Director, Morris Furniture Group, 2000-04; Managing Director, Georgeson Group (Constructive Workspace), formally Axis Interiors, 2004-09; SC Collective UK, 2009-2015. Awarded for 'Outstanding achievements to innovation and workplace performance' in 2005; received prestigious awards and recognitions by the British Council for Offices (BOC) for the innovation, sustainability and creativity elements of project delivery for eight corporate organisations and public sector clients in the UK; awarded Outstanding Entrepreneur Award and Lifetime Ambassador Award in November 2020.

McGeorge, James, BSc, PhD, CBiol, FRSB. University Secretary and Chief Operating Officer, University of Dundee, since 2009; b. 16.10.68, Derby; m., Dr. Helen Ruth McGeorge; 1 d. Educ. Bemrose School, Derby; University of Liverpool; University of Stirling. Research Fellow, University of Stirling, 1994-96; University of Abertay Dundee: Executive Assistant, then Assistant Secretary, then Deputy Secretary, then Academic Secretary and Registrar, 1996.-2005; Director of Strategic Planning and Governance, then Deputy Secretary, University of Stirling, 2005-09. Convener, Universities Scotland Secretaries' Group; Chairman, Advanced Procurement for Universities & Colleges; Member, Audit Committee, Universities & Colleges Admissions Service (UCAS); Member, Universities and Colleges Employers' Association Scottish Committee; Member, Executive Committee, Association of Heads of University Administration (AHUA). Recreations: sport; distance running; food and drink. Address: (b.) University Executive Office, University of Dundee, Dundee DD1 4HN; T.-01382 384006.
E-mail: j.mcgeorge@dundee.ac.uk

McGeough, Professor Joseph Anthony, FRSE, FREng, BSc, PhD, DSc, CEng, FIMechE. Regius Professor of Engineering, Edinburgh University, 1983-2005; Emeritus Professor, since 2005; Honorary Professorial Fellow, 2007-2023; Honorary Professor, Nanjing Aeronautical and Astronautical University, China, since 1991; Visiting Professor: University Federico II of Naples, 1994, Glasgow Caledonian University, 1997-2003, Tokyo University of Agriculture and Technology, 2004, Monash University, 2005, University of Manchester, 2019-2020; b. 29.5.40, Kilwinning; m., Brenda Nicholson; 2 s.; 1 d. Educ. St. Michael's College; Glasgow University. Research

Demonstrator, Leicester University, 1966; Senior Research Fellow, Queensland University, Australia, 1967; Research Metallurgist, International Research and Development Co. Ltd., Newcastle-upon-Tyne, 1968-69; Senior Research Fellow, Strathclyde University, 1969-72; Lecturer in Engineering, Aberdeen University, 1972-77 (Senior Lecturer, 1977-80, Reader, 1980-83). Member, Council, IMechE, 2000-03, Trustee, Board, 2004-2010, Vice-President, 2006-2010, President, 2019-2020; Member of Council, CIRP, 2006-08, Fellow, since 1987, Emeritus, since 2018; Chairman, CIRP UK, 2000-03; Editor, Journal of Processing of Advanced Materials, 1991-94; CIRP Editor, Journal of Materials Processing Technology, 1991-2006; Editor, Proceedings of International Conference on Computer-Aided Production Engineering, since 1986; Fellow, International Society for Nanomanufacturing, since 2017; President, Colinton Parish Church Literary Society, 2009-2012. Publications: Principles of Electrochemical Machining, 1974; Advanced Methods of Machining, 1988; Micromachining of Engineering Materials (Editor), 2001; Engineering of Human Joint Replacements, 2013. Recreations: gardening; golf.
E-mail: j.a.mcgeough@ed.ac.uk

McGettrick, Emeritus Professor Andrew David, BSc, PhD, FRSE, FIEE, FBCS, CEng. Emeritus Professor, Strathclyde University (formerly Professor of Computer Science, formerly Head, Computer and Information Sciences Department, Head, Computer Science Department, 1996-2001); b. 15.5.44, Glasgow; m., Sheila Margaret Girot; 5 s.; 1 d. Educ. St. Aloysius College, Glasgow; Glasgow University; Cambridge University. Lecturer, then Reader, then Professor, Strathclyde University, since 1969; Editor, Addison Wesley's International Computer Science series; Chairman, IEE Safety Critical Systems Committee; Chairman, UK Computer Science Professors Conference, 1991-93; Vice-President, British Computer Society, since 2004; Chair, Education Board and Education Council of US Association for Computing Machinery (ACM). Publications: four books as author, three books edited. Recreations: running; golf; squash. Address: (b.) Strathclyde University, Glasgow G1 1XH; T.-0141-548 3589.

McGhie, Hon. Lord (James Marshall), QC, LLB (Hons). Chairman, Scottish Land Court, 1996-2014; President, Lands Tribunal for Scotland, 1996-2014; Court of Session (part-time), 2012-18; appointed a Judge at Abu Dhabi Global Market Courts in 2016; b. 15.10.44, Perth; m., Ann M. Cockburn; 1 s.; 1 d. Educ. Perth Academy; Edinburgh University. Scots Bar, 1969; QC, 1983; Advocate-Depute, 1983-86; part-time Chairman, Medical Appeal Tribunals, 1987-92; Member, Criminal Injuries Compensation Board, 1992-96. Address: (b.) c/o Parliament House, High Street, Edinburgh; T.-0131 226 5071.

McGhie, Duncan Clark, CA. Chairman, Scottish Ballet and Scottish Opera, 1999-2004; b. 6.12.44, Newton Mearns, Renfrewshire; m., Una G. Carmichael; 1 s.; 1 d. Educ. George Watson's College; Institute of Chartered Accountants. CA apprenticeship, 1962-67; Financial Controller, Scottish Division, British Steel Corporation, 1967-78; Group Finance Director, Wm. Collins Publishers, 1978-84; Partner, Coopers and Lybrand (latterly Pricewaterhouse Coopers), 1984-2000. Elder, Church of Scotland; Member, Inland Waterways Advisory Council, 2006-2012. Recreations: golf; music; walking. Address: (b.) 65 Corrour Road, Newlands, Glasgow, G43 2ED; T.-0141-632 4502; e-mail: dcmcghie@outlook.com

McGibbon, David Campbell, FIOD, FCMA, CCMA, DipMS. Chairman, David MacBrayne Group Limited, 2012-2021 (Deputy Chairman, since 2008); Non-Executive Director and Chair, The Audit Committee; Chair, The Scottish Group, The Pensions and Lifetime Savings

Association (PLSA), 2011-2020; Vice-Chair, PLSA Regions Board and Member of Defined Benefits Council; Non-Executive Director and Chair, The Audit Committee, Historic Scotland, 2005-2011, Independent Chair, The Audit Committee, 2012-2020; Independent Chair, The Audit Committee, Historic Environment Scotland (HES), 2015-17; b. 03.12.47, Airdrie; m., Anne Gillon Ferguson; 2 d. Educ. Coatbridge High School. Various Accountancy posts with Spillers Ltd., 1968-72 and Scottish & Newcastle Breweries, 1972-77; joined Grampian Holdings plc, 1978, Group Financial Controller, 1978-83, Group Finance Director, 1983-97, Group Finance Director and Company Secretary, 1997-2002; Non-Executive Director, Paladin Resources plc, 1993-2001. Chairman, Group of Scottish Finance Directors, 1993-95; Chairman, London Stock Exchange, Scottish Council, 1998-2001; Chairman of Trustees, Caledonian MacBrayne Pension Fund, 2006-2018. Recreations: golf (Glasgow Golf Club); reading and travel. Address: (b.) David MacBrayne Ltd, Ferry Terminal, Gourock PA19 1QP.
E-mail: davidmcgibbon@btopenworld.com

McGill, David. Chief Executive, Scottish Parliament, since 2019. Educ. Glasgow Caledonian University. Career history: worked as a civil servant, firstly as executive officer at Registers of Scotland and then as deputy clerk to the Lands Tribunal for Scotland; worked at the Scottish Parliament since 1999; performed a variety of roles including clerking parliamentary committees and Principal Private Secretary to the Presiding Officer; served as Assistant Chief Executive, working directly with political parties and advising the Presiding Officer on procedural and parliamentary matters. Chairs meetings of the leadership group and attends meetings of the Scottish Parliamentary Corporate Body and the Parliamentary Bureau in an advisory capacity. Address: Scottish Parliament, Edinburgh EH99 1SP.

McGill, Grace, LLB, PG DipLP, LLM. Partner, Burness Paull LLP (Immigration Division), since 2021; Principal, McGill & Co Solicitors, Edinburgh and Glasgow, 2008-2021. Educ. St Andrews Academy; Edinburgh Napier University; University of Strathclyde; University of Edinburgh. Career history: Court Assistant, Scottish Legal Aid Board, Edinburgh, 1986-93; Assistant Solicitor, Skene Edwards, 1993-2003; Partner, Wilson Terris & Co, Edinburgh and Glasgow, 2003-08; Council Member, The WS Society, Edinburgh, since 2018; Professional conduct committee member, The Law Society of Scotland, since 2018; Board of Trustees, ILPA Immigration Law Practitioners' Association Ltd, London, since 2015; Global Scot, Scottish Development International, since 2021. Address: Burness Paull LLP, 50 Lothian Road, Edinburgh EH3 9WJ.

MacGillivray, Alan, MA, DipEd. Writer, since 1987; Ex-President and Honorary Fellow, Association for Scottish Literary Studies; b. 5.6.35, Kirkcaldy; m., Isobel McCorkindale; 2 s.; 1 d. (deceased). Educ. Dumfries Academy; Edinburgh University. Teacher of English, 1958-67: Ardrossan Academy, Annan Academy, Inverness Royal Academy; Principal Teacher of English, Anderson High School, Lerwick, 1967-72; Lecturer/Senior Lecturer in English, Jordanhill College of Education, Glasgow, 1973-87; Honorary Lecturer in Scottish Literature, University of Strathclyde, 1987-2003. Director, Jordanhill Scottish Literature and Language Project, 1980-82. Publications: The Ring of Words (Joint Editor), 1970; Teaching Scottish Literature (Editor), 1997; Scottish Literature in English and Scots (Joint Editor), 2002; study guides on George Mackay Brown and Iain Banks; Kindly Clouds (Poems), 2005; The Bountiful Loch (Poems), 2007; the saga of fnc gull (Poem), 2009; An Altitude Within (Poems), 2010; RB Cunninghame Graham - Collected Stories and Sketches (Joint Editor), 2011-12; Redomones, and Eye to the Future (Poems), 2016; Riding to Trapalanda (Poems), 2018; Walking to the Island (Poems), 2018; Sonnets to Hugh MacDiarmid, and Other Scots Poems, 2020; articles, teaching materials, short stories, etc. Recreations: reading; verse writing; family history. Address: (h.) 23 Beechlands Avenue, Netherlee, Glasgow G44 3YT.

McGillivray, Rev. (Alexander) Gordon, MA, BD, STM; b. 22.9.23, Edinburgh; m., Winifred Jean Porter; 2 s.; 2 d. Educ. George Watson's College, Edinburgh; Edinburgh University; Union Theological Seminary, New York. Royal Artillery, 1942-45; Assistant Minister, St. Cuthbert's Parish Church, Edinburgh; Minister: Waterbeck Church, 1951-58, Nairn High Church, 1958-73; Clerk, Presbytery of Edinburgh, 1973-93; Clerk, General Assembly of Church of Scotland, 1971-94, retired. Editor, Church of Scotland Yearbook, 1996-99. Recreation: theatre. Address: 36 Larchfield Neuk, Balerno EH14 7NL; T.-0131-449 3901.

McGillivray, Professor David. Professor of Event and Digital Cultures, University of The West of Scotland, since 2013. Educ. Glasgow Caledonian University. Career history: Senior Lecturer, Glasgow Caledonian University, 2006-2010; Reader in Events and Culture, University of The West of Scotland, 2010-2013. Co-investigator on a major UK/Canadian collaborative project exploring the role of sport events for persons with a disability in influencing community accessibility and community perceptions of disability. Address: School of Business and Creative Industries, University of the West of Scotland, Paisley Campus, Paisley PA1 2BE.
E-mail: David.McGillivray@uws.ac.uk

McGlinchey, Scott, BA, DipM, FRSA, FIoD, FCIM. Director, Exception Holdings and CEO Exception Limited; b. 1961, Edinburgh; m.; 3 s. Educ. Royal High School; Napier University; Chartered Institute of Marketing; Ashridge Business School. ICL/Fujitsu Services, 1988-2002; positions include General Manager, Managing Director; Newell & Budge, Chief Operating Officer, 2002-04. Non-Executive Directorships: Young Scot Enterprise, Waracle Ltd; Past Directorships: ScotlandIS, Edinburgh Chamber of Commerce. Founding Member of Generation Science. Past Member: Scottish Executive Digital Task Force, Modernising Government Reference Group, CBI Council. Recreations: rugby; music; film.
E-mail: scott.mcglinchey@exceptionuk.com

McGorum, Professor Bruce Campbell, BSc, BVMS, PhD, CEIM, DECEIM, MRCVS. Professor of Equine Medicine, University of Edinburgh since 2002; b. 9.3.61, Dunfermline; m., Isabel Maria McGorum; 3 d. Educ. Queen Anne High School; University of Edinburgh. Veterinary Practitioner, Buckinghamshire, 1985-87; University of Edinburgh: Horserace Betting Levy Board Resident in Equine Studies, 1987-90, Lecturer, then Senior Lecturer, Easter Bush Veterinary Centre, 1990-98, RSE/SOEID Support Research Fellow, 1998-99, Senior Lecturer, 1999-2002. 2004 Animal Health Trust Veterinary Achievement Award. Recreations: outdoor sports. Address: (b.) Easter Bush Veterinary Centre, Easter Bush, Roslin, Midlothian EH25 9RG; T.-0131-650-6230.
E-mail: bruce.mcgorum@ed.ac.uk

McGovern, James. MP (Labour), Dundee West, 2005-2015; b. 17.11.56; m., Norma Ward; 1 s.; 1 d. Educ. Lawside Roman Catholic Academy, Dundee; Telford College, Edinburgh. Trade union official; PPS to Pat McFadden as Minister of State, Department for Business, Enterprise and Regulatory Reform, 2007-08. Member, Select Committee on Scottish Affairs, 2005-2015. Recreations: reading; gym; watching football.

McGowan, Professor David Alexander, MDS, PhD, FDSRCS, FFDRCSI, FDSRCPSG, FDSRCS (Edin). Professor of Oral Surgery, Glasgow University, 1977-99,

Emeritus Professor, since 1999 (Dean of Dental Education, 1990-95); Consultant Oral Surgeon, Greater Glasgow Health Board, 1977-99; b. 18.6.39, Portadown, Co. Armagh; m., Vera Margaret Macauley; 1 s.; 2 d. Educ. Portadown College; Queen's University, Belfast. Oral surgery training, Belfast and Aberdeen, 1961-67; Lecturer in Dental Surgery, Queen's University, Belfast, 1968; Lecturer, then Senior Lecturer and Deputy Head, Oral and Maxillofacial Surgery, London Hospital Medical College, 1968-77. Postgraduate Adviser in Dentistry, Glasgow University, 1977-90; Chairman, Dental Committee, Scottish Council for Postgraduate Medical Education, 1980-90; Dean, Dental Faculty, and Member of College Council, Royal College of Physicians and Surgeons of Glasgow, 1989-92; Member and Vice-Chairman of Executive, General Dental Council, 1989-99; Member, Court, Glasgow University, 1995-99; Chairman, National Dental Advisory Committee, 1996-99; Member, EC Advisory Committee on Training of Dental Practitioners, 1993-2001; former Council Member, British Association of Oral and Maxillofacial Surgeons; Founder Editor, 'Dental History Magazine', 2007-12; President, Lindsay Society, 2016-19. Recreations: photography; painting; music. Address: Glenderry, 114 West King Street, Helensburgh G84 8DQ.
E-mail: dmmcgowan@btinternet.com

McGowan, Sheriff John, LLB. Sheriff of South Strathclyde, Dumfries and Galloway at Ayr, 2000-2012; b. 15.1.44, Kilmarnock; m., Elise Smith; 2 s. Educ. St. Joseph's Academy, Kilmarnock; Glasgow University. Admitted Solicitor, 1967; partner in Black Hay & Co, Solicitors, Ayr, 1970-93; Temporary Sheriff, 1986-93; Sheriff of Glasgow and Strathkelvin, 1993-2000. Council Member, Law Society of Scotland, 1982-85; Chairman, Social Security Appeal Tribunal, 1980-86. Recreations: golf; choral singing; listening to music. Address: (h.) 20 Auchendoun Crescent, Ayr KA7 4AS; T.-01292 260139.

McGowan, Mhairi, BSc (Hons). Violence Against Women Consultant, since 2019; Head of Service, ASSIST & Domestic Abuse Services, Community Safety Glasgow, 2005-19. Educ. Vale of Leven Academy; The Open University. Career: various, DWP, 1973-95; Support and Development Worker, Glasgow East Women's Aid, 1995-2005.

McGrath, Professor John Christie (Ian), BSc, PhD. Regius Professor of Physiology, Glasgow University, 1991-2012; Professor Emeritus and Senior Honorary Research Fellow, Glasgow University, since 2012; Senior Principal Research Fellow, Neuroscience Australia, Sydney NSW, since 2009; Chairman, The Physiological Society, 2006-08, Hon. Member, 2017; b. 8.3.49, Johnstone; m., Wilma Nicol (deceased); 1 s.; 1 d. Educ. John Neilson Institution, Paisley; Glasgow University. Glasgow University: Research Fellow in Pharmacology and Anaesthesia, 1973-75, Lecturer, 1975-83, Senior Lecturer, 1983-88, Reader, 1988-89, Titular Professor, 1989-91; Co-Director, Clinical Research Initiative in Heart Failure, 1994-2000; Head of Division, Department of Neuroscience and Biomedical Systems, Institute of Biomedical and Life Sciences, 1991-93, 1997-2004; Head of Division of Integrated Biology, 2008-2010. Sandoz Prizewinner, British Pharmacological Society, 1980; JR Vane Medal Winner, British Pharmacological Society, 2011; Pfizer Award for Biology, 1983; British Journal of Pharmacology: Editor, 1985-91 and since 2018; Editor Senior, 2001-07; Editor in Chief, 2009-2015. Fellow of British Pharmacological Society, 2004-2017, Honorary Fellow, 2017; Fellow of Society of Biology, since 2013; Honorary Member of Australian Society for Clinical and Experimental Pharmacology and Therapeutics, since 2013; Honorary Senior Research Fellow, Neuroscience Australia, Sydney, since 2009; Honorary Professor, University of Sydney Medical School, 2013-2020. Recreations: running; swimming; cycling; politics (Member, Scottish Labour Party, since 1983); travel

(residing in Scotland and Australia, since 2012). Address: 7 Horselethill Road, Glasgow G12 9LX.
E-mail: i.mcgrath@bio.gla.ac.uk

McGregor, Bill, MA, MEd. General Secretary, School Leaders Scotland, 2004-08; b. 14.2.44, Kilmarnock; m., Elspeth Barbara Greene; 1 s.; 1 d. Educ. Kilmarnock Academy; Glasgow University. Teacher, Assistant Rector, Depute Rector, Mainholm Academy, Ayr, 1968-89; Rector, James Hamilton Academy, Kilmarnock, 1989-2004. Member, National Executive, Headteachers' Association of Scotland (Convener, Public and Parliamentary Committee); President, Irvine Burns Club, 2010-11; Director, Irvine Burns Club, since 2012; Member, Rotary Club of Kilmarnock, since 1994; President, Rotary Club of Kilmarnock, 2006-07; Rotary Paul Harris Fellowship, 2014. Publications: bus histories. Recreations: photography (transport); writing. Address: (h.) 25 Blackburn Drive, Ayr KA7 2XW; T.-01292 282043.
E-mail: valayrmac@btinternet.com

MacGregor, Professor Bryan Duncan, BSc (Hons), MSc, PhD, DipSurv, CertHE, MRTPI, MRICS. MacRobert Professor of Land Economy, Aberdeen University, since 1990, Dean of Social Science and Law, 2002-03, Vice-Principal and Head, College of Arts and Social Sciences, 2003-08, Vice-Principal for Curriculum Reform, then for Special Projects, 2008-11, Vice-Principal and Head of College of Physical Sciences, 2011-16, Vice-Principal for Research, 2015-17, Vice-Principal and Executive Dean of the Business School, 2016-18; b. 16.10.53, Inverness; m., Nicola; 2 twin d. Educ. Inverness Royal Academy; Edinburgh University; Heriot Watt University; Cambridge University; College of Estate Management; Sabhal Mòr Ostaig (Gaelic College). Lecturer, Department of Land Management, Reading University, 1981-84; Lecturer, Department of Town and Regional Planning, Glasgow University, 1984-87; Deputy, then Property Research Manager, Prudential Portfolio Managers, 1987-90. Recreations: Gaelic; hill-walking; football; literature; music; thinking. Address: (b.) Edward Wright Building, Dunbar Street, King's College, University of Aberdeen, Aberdeen AB24 3QY; T.-01224 273831.

Macgregor, Dr Donald Finlay, BSc, MBChB, FRCP(Edin), FRCPCH. Consultant Paediatrician (Hon. Senior Lecturer), Tayside University Hospitals, Dundee, since 1996; b. 22.9.56, Bridge of Allan; m., Elspeth Mary McLeod; 1 s.; 3 d. Educ. Falkirk High School; St Andrews University; Manchester University. Senior House Officer, 1984; Registrar, 1984-88; Provincial Paediatrician, Eastern Highlands, Papua New Guinea, 1986-88; Fellow, University of British Columbia, Vancouver, 1988-90; Clinical Fellow, BC Children's Hospital, Vancouver, 1988-90; Senior Registrar, Royal Hospital for Sick Children, Edinburgh, 1990-92; Consultant Paediatrician, Lancaster and Kendal Hospitals, 1992-96. Secretary, Scottish Paediatric Society; Regional Advisor, Royal College of Paediatrics and Child Health. Recreations: family; outdoor pursuits; Third World issues. Address: (h.) Bon Accord, 2 Viewlands Road, Perth PH1 1BH; T.-01738 625796.

MacGregor, Fulton. MSP (SNP), Coatbridge and Chryston, since 2016. Educ. Coatbridge High School; University of Strathclyde; University of Edinburgh. Elected to North Lanarkshire Council, Coatbridge North and Glenboig ward in 2012. Address: Scottish Parliament, Edinburgh EH99 1SP.

McGregor, Gillian, CBE. Director, Office of the Secretary of State for Scotland, 2017-2020. Educ. Montrose Academy; Aberdeen University. Career history: majority of career in immigration and counter-terrorism roles in the Home Office in London; also spent 3 years on secondment to the Cabinet Office in the

1990s; spent 8 years working in counter-terrorism roles including VIP and Royal Security, Critical Infrastructure Protection and Crisis Management from 2001 onwards; in 2007 had a central role in creating the Office for Security & Counter Terrorism (OSCT), forming it into a successful cross-government hub for work on terrorism and serious crime; Principal Private Secretary to the Home Secretary, Home Office, 2009-11; Director, Operational Intelligence, UK Border Agency, 2011-13; Director, Immigration Enforcement (Scotland and Northern Ireland), Home Office, 2013-17.

McGregor, Professor Heather Jane, CBE, PhD, MBA, BSc (Hons), PFHEA, FRSE. British executive, journalist, and academic; Executive Dean, Edinburgh Business School, Heriot-Watt University, since 2016; b. 27.3.62. Educ. Newcastle University; London Business School; University of Hong Kong. Career history: experienced writer and broadcaster, including writing for the Financial Times for 17 years; Chief Executive of Taylor Bennett, 2000-2016; established the Taylor Bennett Foundation, a charity that encourages black, Asian and minority ethnic people to consider a career in communications and PR in 2008; founding member of the 30% Club, which campaigns for more women on the boards of FTSE 100 companies; wrote a column for the Financial Times from 1999 to 2016 as "Mrs Moneypenny"; columnist for The Sunday Times, 2019-2021. Address: Heriot-Watt University, Edinburgh EH14 4AS.

McGregor, Iain. Honorary Secretary, SABRE (Scotland Against Being Ruled By Europe); b. 19.3.37, Stirling. Educ. Selkirk High School; Kelso High School. Army Service, REME; International Trade Exhibitions Publicist, London; Editor, BIPS International Photo-Feature Agency; Journalist, Fleet Street and provinces; Writer and Lecturer in Journalism, Asia, Europe, North America; Founding Director, Institute for Christian Media (Canada); Editor, The Patriot for Scotland; Editor and Publisher, Social Credit International. Recreations: local history; travel; music; theatre; film; books. Address: (h.) 16 Inch Gardens, Kelso, Roxburghshire TD5 7JS; T.-01573 224404.

Macgregor, Jimmie, MBE, DA, FRZSS. Scottish folksinger and broadcaster; b. 10.3.30, Glasgow. Educ. Springburn Academy; Glasgow School of Art. Forefront of British folk revival for more than 20 years; countless radio and TV appearances, tours in Britain and abroad; more than 20 albums recorded; own daily radio programme, Macgregor's Gathering, for more than 10 years; regular TV series on long-distance walks; various books on folk song and the outdoors; has written theme music for TV and radio, illustrated books; gives regular lectures and slide shows; Life Member: RSPB, Scottish Wildlife Trust, Friends of Loch Lomond, John Muir Trust; President, Friends of River Kelvin; Vice-President, Scottish Conservation Projects and Scottish Youth Hostels Association; twice Scot of the Year. Recreations: collecting paintings, pottery, glass, furniture; the outdoors; wildlife; hill-walking; theatre; art; music; antiques; old cars; anything and everything Scottish.

MacGregor of MacGregor, Sir Malcolm, FRGS, FRPS, MBA, ABIPP. Photographer and author, since 2001. Author of 4 Books: Wilderness Oman; The Outer Hebrides; Mull, Iona and Staffa; Oman, Eloquence and Eternity. Major Scots Guards (retired): served UK, Rhine Army, Oman, Brunei, Hong Kong with 6th Gurkha Rifles; b. 23.3.59; m., Fiona Armstrong. Educ. Eton College; Cranfield School of Management. Convener, Standing Council of Scottish Chiefs.

Chairman, Scots Guards Association. 24th Chief of Clan Gregor, since 2003. Recreations: fly-fishing; travel; culture; history. Address: c/o Knight Ayton Management, Cobham House, 9 Warwick Court, London WC1R 5DJ.

McGregor, Margaret Morrice, MA, JP, DL. Director, McGregor Connexions, since 1998; Co-ordinator, British Thyroid Foundation, since 2004; b. 22.10.42, Aberdeen; m., Michael McGregor; 2 s.; 2 step d. Educ. Aberdeen Academy; Aberdeen University. Member, Edinburgh District Council, 1987-96 (Chair, Women's Committee, 1988-96, Licensing Board, 1992-96); Chair, Equal Opportunities Committee, COSLA, 1992-96; Member, City of Edinburgh Council, 1996-99 (Chair, Women's Committee, 1996-99); Depute Lord Provost, 1996-99; Chair, Zero Tolerance Charitable Trust, 1999-2008; Chair, Scottish Refugee Council, 1995-2000; Vice-President, Darfur Training Committee (UNA Edinburgh), 2008-2010. Recreations: campaigning (human rights, prison reform, animal welfare); reading; sailing. Address: (h.) 17 Greenpark, Liberton, Edinburgh EH17 7TA; T.-0131-664 7223.
E-mail: m2mcgregor@aol.com

McGrigor, Sir James Angus Roderick Neil, Bt. MSP (Conservative), Highlands and Islands, 1999-2016; Elected Councillor for Argyll and Bute Ward 4, Oban South and the Isles, May 2017; b. 19.10.49, London; m.; 1 s.; 5 d. Educ. Eton; Neuchatel University, Switzerland. Traveller, shipping agent, stockbroker, fish farmer, hill farmer; Conservative candidate, Western Isles, 1997; Euro candidate, Scottish list, 1999; Chairman, Loch Awe Improvement Association; Member, Atlantic Salmon Trust Council; Created Kentucky Colonel, 2010; Member, Royal Company of Archers. Hon President: Clyde Fishermen's Association, Highland Disabled Ramblers Association; Vice President, English Speaking Union; President, Western Isles Conservative Association. Recreations: music; films; fishing; literature. Address: (h.) Ardchonnel, by Dalmally, Argyll PA33 1BW; T.-0183 8200678; mobile: 07788900998.
E-mail: jamiemcgrigor@outlook.com
E-mail: jamie.mcgrigor@argyll-bute.co.uk

McGrory, Euan, BA (Hons). Editor, Edinburgh Evening News - edinburghnews.com, since 2021; Editor (Print) Scotland, The Scotsman, Scotland on Sunday, Falkirk Herald and Fife Free Press, 2020-2021. Educ. University of Leeds. Career history: Staff Reporter, Wiltshire Times, 1994-95; Northern Echo: Staff Reporter, 1995-97, Deputy Chief Regional Reporter, 1997-99, Deputy News Editor, 1999-2000; Edinburgh Evening News: Assistant News Editor, 2000-02, Deputy News Editor, 2002-04, News Editor, 2004-07, Head of Content, 2007-2010; Deputy Editor, Edinburgh Evening News, 2010-2015; Editor, Midlothian Advertiser, East Lothian News, Musselburgh News, 2015-16; Deputy Editor, The Scotsman, Scotland on Sunday and Edinburgh Evening News, 2015-2020; Editor, Edinburgh Evening News, 2018-2020.

McGuire, Rt. Hon. Dame Anne, PC, MA (Hons). Former MP (Labour), Stirling (1997-2015); b. 26.5.49, Glasgow; m., Len McGuire, CA; 1 s.; 1 d. Educ. Our Lady and St. Francis School, Glasgow; University of Glasgow; Notre Dame College of Education. Development Officer, Community Service Volunteers, 1984-88; National Officer, CSV, 1988-93; Depute Director, Scottish Council for Voluntary Organisations, 1993-97. Assistant Government Whip (Scotland), 1998-2001; Lord Commissioner, HM Treasury (Government Whip), 2001-02; Parliamentary

Under Secretary of State (Scotland Office), 2002-05; Parliamentary Under Secretary of State (Minister for Disabled People), Department of Work and Pensions, 2005-08; Advisor to Cabinet Office on Voluntary Sector, 2008-09. Member of Public Accounts Committee, 2010-2015; PPS to Rt Hon Ed Milliband MP, 2010-11; Shadow Minister for Disabled People, 2011-13; former Chair, All Party Disability Group; former Chair, All Party Group on Wood Panel Industry.

McGuire, Edward, ARCM, ARAM. Composer; b. 15.2.48, Glasgow. Educ. St. Cuthbert's Primary and St. Augustine's Secondary School, Glasgow; Junior Department, RSAMD; Royal Academy of Music, London; State Academy of Music, Stockholm. Won National Young Composers Competition, 1969; Rant selected as test piece for 1978 Carl Flesch International Violin Competition; Proms debut, 1982, when Source performed by BBC SSO; String Quartet chosen for 40th Anniversary Concert, SPNM, Barbican, 1983; featured composer, Park Lane Group series, Purcell Room, 1993, Bath International Guitar Festival, 1996, International Viola Congress, 1998; Edinburgh International Harp Festival, 2004; frequent commissions and broadcasts including Euphoria (EIF/Fires of London), Songs of New Beginnings (Paragon Ensemble), Quintet II (Lontano), Peter Pan (Scottish Ballet), A Glasgow Symphony (NYOS), The Loving of Etain to a libretto by Marianne Carey (Paragon Opera), Trombone Concerto (Aix-en-Provence Festival), Encores en Suite (BBC SSO, 2010), Symphonies of Galaxies (University of St Andrews, 2016), Cello Concerto (Robert Irvine, Broen Ensemble, 2022), plays flute with and writes for Whistlebinkies folk group, CDs include Albannach (Greentrax), 2006. In 2022 the group's performance of his 'Riverside' with Glasgow Barons Orchestra was broadcast on You Tube. His CDs on Delphian Recordings, 'Entangled Fortunes' (2015) and 'Music for Flute, Guitar and Piano' (2006), have both received 'Editor's Choice' in Gramophone Magazine. His 'Three Donne Lyrics', recorded on CD in 2020 by Paisley Abbey Choir, received several plays on BBC Radio 3. Recipient of British Composer Award, 2003 and Creative Scotland Award, 2004; Chair, Scottish Region Musicians' Union, 2001-2016; writes for Workers magazine. Address: c/o Scottish Music Centre, City Hall, Candleriggs, Glasgow G1 1NQ.

McHarg, Jim, FIMechE, FCIPD. Head of Human Resources, College of Social Sciences, University of Glasgow, since 2020; Immediate Past President, Glasgow Chamber of Commerce; Divisional HR Director, Flow Control, The Weir Group PLC, 2018-19. Educ. University of Strathclyde; University of the West of Scotland. Career history: Production Manager, Weir Pumps Ltd, 1994-97; Operations Manager, Clyde Blowers, 1997-2002; Work Optimisation Manager, Network Rail, 2002-04; Head of HR, BAE Systems, 2004-2010; The Weir Group PLC: Group Head of Learning and Organisational Development, 2010-14, appointed Group Head of Learning and HR Business Partner in 2014, then HR Director - Organisational Development in 2016; Deputy President, Glasgow Chamber of Commerce, 2016-18.
E-mail: Jim.McHarg@glasgow.ac.uk

McHugh, Jack. Interim Moderator, St Margaret's Church, Greenock. Address: St Margaret's Church, Greenock, 67 Finch Road, Greenock PA16 7DE.

McInnes, Alison, OBE. MSP (Scottish Liberal Democrat), North East Scotland, 2007-2016; former spokesperson for Justice and former Business Manager in the Scottish Parliament; b. 17.7.57; m.; 2 c. Educ. Irvine Royal Academy; McLaren High School, Callendar; University of Glasgow. Career history: 1992-1995: Councillor, Gordon District Council; 1995-2007: Councillor, Aberdeenshire Council; Chair, Infrastructure Services Committee; Chair, Nestrans - the Regional Transport Partnership for North East Scotland; Scottish Liberal Democrat spokesperson on Transport, Local Government and Climate Change, 2007-2011; spokesperson on Health and Justice, 2011-2012. Formerly non-executive director with Scottish Enterprise; formerly Chair, Sustainable Development Group, North Sea Commission; formerly member, Area Board for Scottish National Heritage. Fellow of the Royal Society of Arts; made an OBE in June 2013.

Macinnes, Professor Allan Iain, MA, PhD, FRHistS, FRSE, FFCS. Emeritus Professor of History, University of Strathclyde; b. 26.11.49, Inverness; m., Tine Wanning. Educ. Oban High School; University of St. Andrews; University of Glasgow. University of Glasgow: Lecturer in Scottish History, 1973-89, Senior Lecturer in Scottish History, 1989-93, Director, Postgraduate School of Scottish Studies, 1992-93; Burnett-Fletcher Professor of History, University of Aberdeen, 1993-2007; Professor of Early Modern History, University of Strathclyde, 2007-2014. Visiting Professor in British History, University of Chicago, 2003; Chair, Scottish Land Commission, 1996-99; Joint Founder (Chair, Steering Committee), Northern European Historical Research Network, 1997-2002. Research Fellow of the Huntington Library, San Marino, California, 1993, 2002, 2005 and 2012; Ecole des Hautes Etudes en Sciences Sociales, Paris, 2005; Frank Watson Prize in Scottish History, University of Guelph, 1997. Publications: Charles I and the Making of the Covenanting Movement, 1625-41, 1991; Clanship, Commerce and the House of Stuart, 1603-1788, 1996; The British Revolution, 1629-1660, 2004; Union & Empire: The Making of the United Kingdom in 1707, 2007; The British Confederate: Archibald Campbell, Marquess of Argyll, c.1607-1661, 2011; A History of Scotland, 2019. Recreations: supporting Hibernian; gardening with a touch of zen; hillwalking; listening to music – especially jazz; drinking malt whisky. Address: Laingseat Farmhouse, Potterton, Aberdeenshire AB23 8UE; e-mail: allan.macinnes@strath.ac.uk

McInnes, Professor Colin Robert, MBE, DSc, CEng, FInstP, FREng, FRSE. James Watt Chair, Professor of Engineering Science, James Watt School of Engineering, University of Glasgow, since 2014; Royal Academy of Engineering Chair in Emerging Technologies: Space. Educ. University of Glasgow. Career history: Department of Aerospace Engineering, University of Glasgow: Lecturer, 1991-96, Reader, 1996-99, Professor of Space Systems Engineering, 1999-2004; University of Strathclyde, Professor of Engineering Science, 2004-2014. Royal Society of Edinburgh Bruce Preller Prize Lecture, 1998; Royal Society of Edinburgh Makdougall-Brisbane Prize, 2006; Royal Aeronautical Society Pardoe Space Award, 2000; Philip Leverhulme Prize, 2001; Royal Aeronautical Society Ackroyd Stuart Prize, 2004; Association of Space Explorers Leonov Medal, 2007; Royal Society of Edinburgh Kelvin Prize, 2012; Royal Society Wolfson Research Merit Award, 2015. Publications: Solar Sailing, 1999; around 200 journal papers. Recreations: photography; hillwalking; history of science. Address: James Watt School of Engineering, University of Glasgow, Glasgow G12 8QQ; T.-0141-330 8511; e-mail: colin.mcinnes@glasgow.ac.uk

McInnes, Emeritus Professor William McKenzie, MSc, PhD, CA. Professor of Accounting, Stirling University, 1994-2007; (Head, Department of Accounting, Finance and Law, 1995-98, Vice-Dean, Faculty of Management, 1996-97); b. 24.5.42, Hawick; m., Christine Mary; 1 s.; 1 d. Educ. George Watsons College, Edinburgh; Durham University; Glasgow University. Management Accountant, IBM (UK)

Ltd., 1966-68; Lecturer, Kirkcaldy Technical College, 1968-70; Audit Senior, Coopers and Lybrand, Bermuda, 1970-72; Senior Lecturer, Newcastle upon Tyne Polytechnic, 1974-76; Lecturer, then Senior Lecturer, Strathclyde University, 1976-91; Director of Research, Institute of Chartered Accountants of Scotland, 1992-93; SHEFC Team Leader for Quality Assessment of Finance and Accounting, 1995-96; Elder, Cadder Parish Church, since 1984. General Trustee of the Church of Scotland, 2012-17. Chairman, Cadder Men's Club, since 2015. Publications: author or co-author of a number of research papers and reports on accounting and related topics. Recreations: golf; music. Address: (h.) 14 Gleneagles Gardens, Bishopbriggs, Glasgow G64 3EF; T.-0141 772 2639; e-mail: mcinnesbill@hotmail.com

Macintosh, Rt Hon. Kenneth Donald, MA. MSP (no party affiliation), West Scotland region, 2016-2021 (Eastwood, 1999-2016); Presiding Officer of the Scottish Parliament, 2016-2021; b. 15.1.62, Inverness; m., Claire Kinloch Anderson; 2 s.; 4 d. Educ. Royal High School, Edinburgh; Edinburgh University. Joined BBC, 1987; worked in News and Current Affairs, including Breakfast News, Breakfast with Frost, Nine O'Clock News; left as Senior Broadcast Journalist, 1999. Recreations: reading; music; sport – football, golf, tennis.

McIntosh, Sir Neil, CBE, FIPD, ACIS ;New Zealand Honorary Consul for Scotland, 2013-2020; Trustee, Vice-Chair National Library of Scotland 2013 - 2020; UK Civil Service Commissioner, 2008-2013; Member, BBC Audience Council for Scotland 2007-2012; Chairman, Audit Committee of Scottish Public Service Ombudsman Service 2007-2011; Member S. Gov't Independent Budget Review Panel, 2010; Member, UK Electoral Commission, 2001-08; Trustee, National Museums of Scotland, 2000-08; Returning Officer, Greater Manchester Transport Referendum, 2008; Chairman, Judicial Appointments Board for Scotland, 2001-08; Independent Expert Adviser to N. Ireland Executive Review of Public Administration, 2002-06; Convener, Scottish Council for Voluntary Organisations, 1995-2001; b. 30.1.40, Glasgow; m., Marie; 1 s.; 2 d. Educ. King's Park School, Glasgow; Gold Award, Outward Bound Moray Sea School; Industry and local government, 1957-69; Director of Personnel, Inverness County/Highland Region, 1969-85; Chief Executive: Dumfries and Galloway Region, 1985-92, Strathclyde Region, 1992-96; various public service duties, since 1996, including: Counting Officer, Scottish Devolution Referendum 1997, Deputy Lieutenant Dumfriesshire 1998-2015; Chairman, Commission on Local Government and the Scottish Parliament, Crown Agent's Adviser, Shanghai Municipal Government; Hon. Doctorate, Syracuse University, and Hon. Doctorate, Glasgow Caledonian University. Recreations: collecting; curling; drystane dyking.

McIntosh, Neil. Editor, The Scotsman, since 2021. Educ. Edinburgh Napier University; The Open University; IESE Business School. Career history: Sub Editor, Edinburgh Evening News, 1997-98; freelance journalist, 1995-99; Duty Editor, Teletext, Daily Mail General Trust, 1998-99; Guardian Unlimited, London: Deputy Editor, Online, 1999-2004; Assistant Editor, 2004-06; Head of Editorial Development, guardian.co.uk, Guardian News & Media, 2006-08; The Wall Street Journal: Editor, WSJ.com Europe, 2009-2011; Deputy Editor, Europe, 2011-13; Managing Editor, BBC Online, 2013-2021. Trustee of the Palace for Life Foundation. Address: The Scotsman, Room 8 & 9, 100 Brand Street, Glasgow G51 1DG; T.-0131 311 7311.

Macintyre, Iain Melfort Campbell, MB, ChB, MD, FRCSE, FRCPE, FSA (Scot). President, British Society for the History of Medicine, 2015-17; Apothecaries' Lecturer in History of Medicine, University of Edinburgh. Formerly Consultant Surgeon, Edinburgh; Surgeon to the Queen in Scotland, 1997-2004; Vice President, Royal College of Surgeons of Edinburgh, 2003-2006; Chairman, Edinburgh Postgraduate Board for Medicine, 1995-2000; b. 23.6.44, Glasgow; m., Tessa Lorna Mary Millar; 3 d. Educ. Daniel Stewart's College, Edinburgh; Edinburgh University. Lecturer in Surgery, Edinburgh University, 1974-78; Visiting Professor, University of Natal, 1978-79; Council of Europe Travelling Fellow, 1986; Honorary Secretary, Royal College of Surgeons of Edinburgh, 2001-03; Member National Medical Advisory Committee, 1992-95.

McIntyre, Rev. Mgr. John Canon, MA (Hons), STL, PhL, DipEd. Retired Parish Priest, St. Bridget's, Baillieston (1995-2015); b. 12.11.37, Airdrie. Educ. St. Aloysius College, Glasgow; Gregorian University, Rome; Glasgow University; Jordanhill College of Education. Ordained to priesthood, Rome, 1961; Assistant, St. Monica's, Coatbridge, 1962-63; student, 1963-68; staff, St. Vincent's College, Langbank, 1968-69, St. Mary's College, Blairs, Aberdeen, 1969-86 (Rector, 1985-86); Parish Priest, St. Bride's, East Kilbride, 1986-89; Rector, Scots College, Rome, 1989-95. Bradley Medal, Glasgow University, 1967. Publications: Scotland and the Holy See (Editor), 1982; The Scots College, Rome 1600–2000 (Co-Author), 2000. Recreations: English literature; bird-watching; history.

Macintyre, Lorn, BA (Hons), PhD. Freelance Writer; b. 7.9.42, Taynuilt, Argyll; m., Mary. Educ. Stirling University; Glasgow University. Poet, novelist, short story writer. Publications include: (poetry), A Snowball in Summer. Novels: Cruel in the Shadow, The Blind Bend, Empty Footsteps and The Broken Lyre in Chronicles of Invernevis Series. Adoring Venus; The Madonna at Montecassino; The Leaper; The Summer Stance. Short stories: Tobermory Days; Tobermory Tales; Maclay Days; Miss Esther Scott's Fancy; Heavenly Pursuits. Recreation: the paranormal. Address: (h.) Tobermory, Priormuir, St. Andrews, Fife; T.-01334 476428.
E-mail: lorn.macintyre@btinternet.com

Macintyre, Professor Dame Sally, DBE, FRSE, BA, MSc, PhD, HonDSc. Emeritus Professor, University of Glasgow; b. 27.2.49, Edinburgh; m., Dr Guy Muhlemann. Educ. Durham, London and Aberdeen Universities. Research Fellow, Aberdeen University, 1971-75; Researcher, MRC Medical Sociology Unit, Aberdeen, 1975-83; Director, MRC Medical Sociology Unit, Glasgow, 1983-98; Director, MRC Social and Public Health Sciences Unit, Glasgow, 1998-2008; Hon Director, MRC/CSO Social and Public Health Sciences Unit, Glasgow, 2008-2013; Director, Institute of Health and Wellbeing, Glasgow University, 2011-14. Foundation Fellow, Academy of Medical Sciences. Recreations: skiing; hill-walking; climbing.

Maciver, Rev. James, MA, BD, DipTh. Minister, Stornoway Free Church, Isle of Lewis, since 2016; Minister, East Kilbride Free Church, 1987-97; Minister, Knock Free Church, Isle of Lewis, 1997-2016. Principal Clerk of Assembly, Free Church of Scotland, 2000-2017; Moderator of 2011 General Assembly. Educ. Nicolson Institute, Stornoway; Glasgow University; Free Church College, Edinburgh; London University. Visiting Lecturer, Glasgow Bible College, 1989-95. Recreations: reading; music; golf. Address: (b.) 46 Francis Street, Stornoway, Isle of Lewis HS1 2NF; T.-01851 702279.

Maciver, John Angus, LLB (Hons) (First Class), DipLP. Partner, Pinsent Masons LLP (formerly McGrigors LLP), since 2008; b. 17.1.73, Inverness. Educ. Currie High School, Edinburgh; University of Edinburgh. McGrigor

Donald, Glasgow and Edinburgh, 1997-2002; Clifford Chance, London, 2002-04; DLA Piper, 2004-08. Recreations: golf; skiing; travel. Address: (b.) Princes Exchange, 1 Earl Grey Street, Edinburgh EH3 9AQ; e-mail: john.maciver@pinsentmasons.com

MacIver, Professor Matthew M., CBE, MA, MEd, Dhc (Abdn), DEd (Edin), FEIS, FRSA. UK representative on Committee of Experts of the European Charter for Regional or Minority Languages, 2013-19; Chairman, Court, University of Highlands and Islands, 2009-2014; Chief Executive/Registrar, General Teaching Council for Scotland, 2001-08; Chair, Bòrd na Gàidhlig, 2008-08; Chairman, Highlands and Islands Educational Trust, since 1994; Honorary Professor of Gaelic Education, University of the Highlands and Islands (Hon. Fellowship, since 2014); Governor, George Watson's College, Edinburgh, 2009-2017; Committee member, Scottish Association of Churchill Fellows, 2009-2014; Member, BBC's Audience Council for Scotland, 2011-2017; member, Gaelic Language Promotion Trust, since 2017; b. 5.7.46, Isle of Lewis; m., Katrina; 1 s.; 1 d. Educ. Nicolson Institute, Stornoway; Edinburgh University; Moray House College. History Teacher, 1969-72; Principal Teacher of History, Craigmount High School, 1972-80; Assistant Rector, Royal High School, 1980-83; Depute Head Teacher, Balerno High School, 1983-86; Rector, Fortrose Academy, 1986-89; Rector, Royal High School, Edinburgh, 1989-98; Depute Registrar (Education), General Teaching Council for Scotland, 1998-2001. Chairman, Comataidh Craolaidh Gaidhlig (Gaelic Broadcasting Committee), 1996-2001; Member for Scotland on the Ofcom Content Board, 2003-06; Winston Churchill Travelling Fellowship, 1998. Address: (h.) 21 Durham Road, Edinburgh EH15 1NY; T.-0131-669 5029.

MacIver, Netta, OBE. Chief Executive, Scottish Children's Reporter Administration, 2008-2011. Over 30 years' experience of working in Scotland's social care sector, including working with families and children affected by serious physical or sexual abuse; previously Chief Executive, Turning Point Scotland; also a qualified social worker, and spent her earlier career in Strathclyde in a specialist unit providing services to families where children had been seriously physically or sexually abused; Assistant Director of Social Work for Comhairle nan Eilean in the 1980s before returning to Strathclyde to work with drug and alcohol services and developing the region's strategic response to HIV/AIDS in collaboration with local health boards; joined Turning Point in 1995 as Development Director. Awarded an OBE in 2001 for her work with women offenders and drug misusers.

Mackay, Alan. Deputy Vice-Principal (International) and Director, Edinburgh Global, University of Edinburgh, since 2012. Previously worked for the University of St Andrews. Member, Scotland Advisory Committee, British Council Scotland, since 2020. Address: Edinburgh Global, University of Edinburgh, 33 Buccleuch Place, Edinburgh EH8 9JS; T.-0131 650 4315; e-mail: dvp@ed.ac.uk

Mackay, Angus Victor Peck, OBE, MA, BSc (Pharm), PhD (Cantab), MB, ChB, FRCPsych, FRCP (Ed), TPsych. Physician Superintendent and Clinical Director, Lomond and Argyll Mental Health Service, 1980-2004; Honorary Professor in Psychological Medicine, Glasgow University, since 1980; Member, Faculty of Neuroscience, University of Edinburgh; Chairman, Health Technology Board for Scotland, 2000-2014; Member, Panel of Experts for the European Medicines Evaluation Agency; Psychiatric Representative, Committee on Safety of Medicines, DHSS; Chairman of the Secretary of State's Independent Scrutiny Panel on Health Services along the Clyde, 2005-06; Member, Commission on Human Medicines, 2004-06; Board Member (Department of Health, London), 2004-2014; Chairman, Advisory Board on the Registration of Homeopathic Products, since 2014; Member of the Mental Health Tribunal for Scotland, since 2015; b. 4.3.43, Edinburgh; m., Elspeth M.W. Norris; 2 s.; 2 d. Educ. George Heriot's School, Edinburgh; Edinburgh University; Churchill and Trinity Colleges, Cambridge. MRC Research Fellow, Cambridge; Member, senior clinical staff, MRC Neurochemical Pharmacology Unit, Cambridge, with appointment as Lector in Pharmacology, Trinity College (latterly, Deputy Director of Unit). Deputy Chairman, Health Services Research Committee of the Chief Scientist for Scotland; Chairman: Scottish Working Group on Mental Illness, Research and Clinical Section of Royal College of Psychiatrists (Scotland), National Mental Health Reference Group; Member: Research Committee, Mental Health Foundation, Scottish Executive, Royal College of Psychiatrists, NHS Policy Board for Scotland; Honorary Senior Lecturer, Department of Psychology, University of St. Andrews; Medical Director, Argyll and Bute NHS Trust. Recreations: rowing; sailing; rhododendrons. Address: (h.) Tigh an Rudha, Ardrishaig, Argyll; T.-01546 603272.

McKay, Professor Brad, BA (Hons), MLitt (Distinction), PhD, FRSA. Vice Principal (International, Strategy and External Relations) and Senior Vice-Principal, University of St Andrews, since 2017, Professor of Strategy, since 2016. Educ. Dalhousie University; University of St Andrews. Career history: Lecturer in Strategy, University of St Andrews, 2004-08; University of Edinburgh: Associate Professor/Senior Lecturer in Strategy, 2008-2013, MBA Director, 2009-2011, Head, Strategy and International Business Development, 2011-14, Professor of Strategic Management and Director of Engagement, 2013-16. A Senior Fellow for the Scotland Analysis, investigating the impact of the independence debate in Scotland and the United Kingdom on business decision-making (appointed by the Economic Social Research Council). Sits on the Executive Council for the Chartered Institute of Bankers. Published in a range of scholarly journals including the Academy of Management Journal, Organization Studies, Human Relations, the European Management Review, Futures, International Studies of Management and Organization, Management and Organization History, and Technological Forecasting and Social Change; co-editor of the Edward Elgar Handbook of Research on Strategy and Foresight (2009). Address: School of Management, University of St Andrews, The Gateway, North Haugh, St Andrews, Fife KY16 9RJ; T.-01334 462810.
E-mail: Brad.Mackay@st-andrews.ac.uk

Mackay, Colin. Political Editor, STV news. Worked for Bauer Radio for 16 years as their Scottish Political Editor; joined STV in 2015. Won "News Reporter of the Year award" at the Independent Radio News Awards, 2007. Address: (b.) Pacific Quay, Glasgow G51 1PQ; T.-0141 300 3000.

MacKay, Colin Hinshelwood, MA (Hons), FSA Scot. Broadcaster and Writer; b. 27.8.44, Glasgow; m., Olive E.B. Brownlie; 2 s. Educ. Kelvinside Academy, Glasgow; Glasgow University; Jordanhill College of Education. Reporter/Presenter: Border Television Ltd., 1967-70, Grampian Television Ltd., 1970-73; Political Editor, Scottish Television PLC, 1973-92 (Presenter, Ways and Means, 1973-86), Parliamentary Lobby Correspondent, 1985-95; recent programmes include: A Life in Question, People and Power, Politics Tonight, Scotland at Ten, and Sunday Morning with Colin MacKay (BBC Radio Scotland); Talk-In Sunday (Radio Clyde); Westminster File (Border TV); Eikon (Scottish TV); General Assembly (BBC TV/Radio); contributions to BBC World Service,

Radio 4, Radio 5 Live; ITV Commentator: Papal Visit to Scotland, 1982, CBI Conference, Glasgow, 1983. Winner, Observer Mace, 1967 (British Universities Debating Championship); Member, two-man British Universities Canadian Debating Tour, 1967; Commonwealth Relations Trust Bursary to Canada, 1981; Member, Scottish Arts Council, 1988-94; BT Scottish Radio News Broadcaster of the Year, 1997. Publications: Kelvinside Academy: 1878-1978, 1978; The Scottish Dimension in Central and Eastern Canada, 1981. Recreations: music (especially opera); reading; writing. E-mail: colin.mackay@hotmail.co.uk

McKay, Professor Colin Ian, LLB (Hons), DipLP, MPhil. Chair, JustRight Scotland, since 2021; Professor, Napier University, since 2020; Chief Executive, Mental Welfare Commission, 2014-2020; b. Scotland; m., Allison Brisbane; 2 s.; 1 d. Educ. North Berwick High School; Edinburgh University; Glasgow University. Solicitor in Private Practice, 1984-86; Solicitor, Lothian Regional Council, 1986-88; Legal and Policy Adviser, Enable (Scottish Society for the Mentally Handicapped), 1989-98; Civil Servant, 1999-2014 (Secretary, Millan Committee on Mental Health Law and Maclean Committee on Violent and Sexual Offenders, 1999-2001, Head of Mental Health Bill Team, 2003-04, Member, latterly Acting Head, Strategy and Delivery Unit, 2003-2004, Head of Efficient Government Unit/Public Service Reform Development Division, 2005-07, Head of Legal System Division, 2007-13, Head of Strategy Unit, 2013-2014). Commissioner, Mental Welfare Commission for Scotland, 1996-98.

Mackay, David James, FCILT. Former Chairman, Lothian Buses plc (resigned, 2010); Chairman, tie Ltd. (Transport Initiatives Edinburgh), 2008-2010 (resigned); Chairman, TEL Ltd., 2006-2010 (resigned); Chairman, Malcolm Group, 2003-05; Chairman, Executive Board, Scottish Rugby Union, 2003-05; Hon. Colonel, Scottish Transport Regiment, 2004-2011 (retired); Chief Executive, John Menzies PLC, 1997-2003; Deputy Chairman, Portland Media Group UK Ltd., 2007-09; Chairman, Glasgow Hawks Sports Trust, 2009-2012; b. 20.5.43, St. Andrews; m., Jane; 1 s.; 1 d. Educ. Kirkcaldy High School; Bradford University; Edinburgh University; Companion, Institute of Management, 1998; FCIT, 1993. Recreations: golf; walking; vintage cars. Address: (h.) 4 East Harbour Road, Charlestown, Fife KY11 3EA.

Mackay, Derek, MSP (SNP), Renfrewshire North and West, 2011-2021; Cabinet Secretary for Finance, Economy and Fair Work, 2018-2020 (Finance and the Constitution, 2016-18); Minister for Transport and Islands, 2014-16; b. 30.7.77; 2 s. Leader of Renfrewshire Council, 2007-2011; Minister for Local Government and Planning, Scottish Government, 2011-14.

Mackay, Donald George, MA, PhD; b. 25.11.29; m. (1), Elizabeth Ailsa Barr (deceased); 2 s.; 1 d.; m. (2), Catherine Anne McDonald (deceased). Educ. Morgan Academy, Dundee; St. Andrews University; Aberdeen University. Assistant Principal, Scottish Home Department, 1953; Secretary, Royal Commission on Local Government in Scotland, 1966-69; Assistant Secretary, Scottish Development and Agriculture Departments, 1969-83; Under Secretary, Scottish Agriculture and Environment Departments, 1983-88. Member, Scottish Agricultural Wages Board, 1991-97. Publications: Forestry as a Land Use in Scotland, in Rural Land Use: Scotland and Ireland, 1994; Scotland's Rural Land Use Agencies, 1995. Recreations: writing; photography; music. Address: (h.) 25 Melville Street, Perth PH1 5PY; T.-01738 621274.

Mackay, Gillian Audrey. MSP (Scottish Green Party), Central Scotland (Region), since 2021; b. 1991, Falkirk. Educ. Heriot-Watt University. Career history: Postgraduate Student (marine biodiversity and biotechnology), Heriot-Watt University, 2013-14; Regional Campaign Support Officer, Scottish Green Party, Edinburgh, 2016; Parliamentary Assistant to Andy Wightman MSP, Scottish Parliament, 2016-2021. Address: The Scottish Parliament, Edinburgh EH99 1SP; T.-0131 348 6341. E-mail: Gillian.Mackay.msp@parliament.scot

Mackay of Clashfern, Lord (James Peter Hymers), Baron (1979), PC (1979), KT (1999), FRSE, Hon. FRICE, FRCOG, FRCPE, FRCSE. Lord Clerk Register, since 2007; Lord High Commissioner to the General Assembly of the Church of Scotland, 2005 and 2006; Lord High Chancellor of Great Britain, 1987-97; Chancellor, Heriot Watt University, 1991-2005; b. 2.7.27, Edinburgh; m., Elizabeth Gunn Hymers; 1 s.; 2 d. Educ. George Heriot's School, Edinburgh; Edinburgh University (MA Hons). Lecturer in Mathematics, St. Andrews University, 1948-50; Major Scholar, Trinity College, Cambridge, in Mathematics, 1947, taken up, 1950; Senior Scholar, 1951; BA (Cantab), 1952; MA (Cantab), 2016; LLB Edinburgh (with distinction), 1955; admitted, Faculty of Advocates, 1955; QC (Scot), 1965; Standing Junior Counsel to: Queen's and Lord Treasurer's Remembrancer, Scottish Home and Health Department, Commissioners of Inland Revenue in Scotland; Sheriff Principal, Renfrew and Argyll, 1972-74; Vice-Dean, Faculty of Advocates, 1973-76; Dean, 1976-79; Lord Advocate of Scotland, 1979-84; a Senator of the College of Justice in Scotland, 1984-85; a Lord of Appeal in Ordinary, 1985-87. Part-time Member, Scottish Law Commission, 1976-79; Hon. Master of the Bench, Inner Temple, 1979; Fellow, International Academy of Trial Lawyers, 1979; Fellow, Institute of Taxation, 1981; Director, Stenhouse Holdings Ltd., 1976-77; Member, Insurance Brokers' Registration Council, 1977-79; a Commissioner of Northern Lighthouses, 1975-84; Hon. LLD: Edinburgh, 1983, Dundee, 1983, Strathclyde, 1985, Aberdeen, 1987, Cambridge, 1989, Birmingham, 1990, University of India Law School, 1994, Glasgow 1994, Bath, 1996, Leicester University, 1996, De Montfort, 1999; Hon. DCL: Newcastle, 1990, Oxford, 1998, Robert Gordon, 2000, Northumbria, 2017; Hon. Doctor of Laws, College of William and Mary, 1989; Hon. Fellow, Institution of Civil Engineers, 1988; Hon. Fellow, Trinity College, Cambridge, 1989; Hon. Fellow, Girton College, Cambridge, 1989; Hon. Fellow, Royal College of Surgeons, Edinburgh, 1989; Hon. Fellow, Royal College of Physicians of Edinburgh, 1990; Hon. Fellow, Royal College of Obstetricians and Gynaecologists, 1996; Fellow, American College of Trial Lawyers, 1990; Royal Medal, RSE, 2003; Commissary, University of Cambridge, 2003-2016. Recreations: walking; travel. Address: House of Lords, London, SW1A 0PW.

MacKay, John. Broadcast journalist, television presenter and producer; presenter, STV News at Six and Scotland Tonight; b. 1965. Educ. Penilee Secondary School; University of Glasgow. Began journalism career with The Sunday Post before joining BBC Scotland in 1987 as a reporter, presenter and producer; joined Scottish Television in 1994 as a reporter and presenter for Scotland Today. Publications: The Road Dance, 2002; Heartland, 2004; The Last of the Line, 2006; Notes of a Newsman, 2015. Address: STV, Pacific Quay, Glasgow G51 1PQ.

Mackay, John, TD, MA, FRSGS, FInstD; b. 14.9.36, St. Andrews; m., Barbara Wallace; 1 s.; 2 d. Educ. Madras College; Dunfermline High School; Kirkcaldy High School; Edinburgh University. Lieutenant, 1st East Anglian Regiment, 1959-63; Territorial Army, 1964-86: Colonel, Royal Engineers (Postal and Courier); Royal Mail, 1963-96: Director, Philately, 1979-84, Chairman, Scottish Post Office Board, 1988, Operations Director, UK, 1991-92, Director and General Manager, Scotland and Northern Ireland, 1986-96; Chairman, Earl Haig Fund Scotland, 1999-2004. President, Lord's Taverners Scotland, 1994-98; Chairman: Scottish Premier Rugby Limited, 1996-97, Scottish Business in the Community Executive Council, 1995-98, Scotland the Brand Judging Panel, 1998-2002, Edinburgh

Common Purpose, 1995-96; Member: Committee, Army Benevolent Fund Scotland, 1988-98, Board, Quality Scotland, 1991-98, Board, Scottish Business in the Community, 1993-98, Quality Assessment Committee, Scottish Higher Education Funding Council, 1994-96; Chairman, Lowland Employers Liaison Committee, 2001-03; Founder Member, The Breakaways Golf Club; Elder, Dean Parish Church. Recreations: golf; watching cricket and rugby; military and European history; Battlefields 19th Century German Art. Address: (h.) Kinrymont, 8 Damside, Dean Village, Edinburgh EH4 3BB; T.-0131-226 2512; e-mail: johnandbarbaramackay@btinternet.com

Mackay, John Angus, OBE, MA, MSc. Former Chief Executive, Bòrd na Gàidhlig; former Director, Gaelic Media Service; former Member: Bòrd na Gàidhlig, An Lanntair, Scottish Arts Council, Highlands and Islands Enterprise; former Chair: NHS Western Isles Board, An Lanntair, Sabhal Mòr Ostaig, The Columba Initiative, BBC Gaelic Advisory Committee; b. 24.6.48, Shader, Isle of Lewis; m., Maria. Educ. Nicolson Institute; University of Aberdeen; University of Stirling; Jordanhill College. Sales Rep, D.C. Thomson, Aberdeen, 1971-72; English teacher, Glasgow, 1973-77; Co-operative Development Officer, Highlands and Islands Development Board, 1977-80; Investigating Officer and Senior Development Manager, Highland and Islands Development Board, 1980-84; Chief Executive, Communn na Gaidhlig, 1985-91. 2016 Saltire Society Fletcher of Saltoun Award for contribution to Scottish public life. Recreations: books; skiing; swimming. Address: (h.) Druimard Arnol, Isle of Lewis H52 9DB; T.-01851 710479.

McKay, Rev. Johnston Reid, MA (Glasgow), BA (Cantab), PhD (Edin). Barony St. John's Church, Ardrossan, 2002-08; Clerk to the Presbytery of Ardrossan, 2003-2010; Kilwinning Old Parish Church, 2008-2010; b. 2.5.42, Glasgow. Educ. High School of Glasgow; Glasgow University; Cambridge University. Assistant Minister, St. Giles' Cathedral, 1967-71; Church Correspondent, Glasgow Herald, 1968-70; Minister, Bellahouston Steven Parish Church, 1971-78; Governor, Paisley College; Minister, Paisley Abbey: Ardrossan, Barony St John's; Kilwinning Old; Gourock St John's, 1978-87; Saltcoats St Cuthbert's Parish Church, 2011-2012; Senior Producer, Religious Programmes, BBC Scotland, 1987-99; Editor, Religious Programmes, BBC Scotland, 1999-2002. Editor, The Bush (newspaper of Glasgow Presbytery), 1975-78; Chairman, Scottish Religious Advisory Committee, BBC, 1981-86; Stanley Mair Lecturer on Preaching, Glasgow University, 1995; Trustee, Baird Trust, since 1999; Wallace Lecturer, 2000; Chalmers Lecturer, 2010-12; Visiting Fellow of New College, University of Edinburgh, 2010-2011; Theological Forum of the General Assembly, 2015-17; Member of Scottish PEN. Publications: From Sleep and From Damnation (with James Miller), 1970; Essays in Honour of William Barclay (Joint Editor), 1976; Through Wood and Nails, 1982; This Small Pool, 1996; The Very Thing, 2001; Glimpses of Hope – God Beyond Ground Zero, 2002; Netting Citizens (ed), 2004; A Touch Personal, 2005; Christian Faith and the Welfare of the City - Essays for Alison Elliot (Ed), 2008; The Kirk and the Kingdom - A century of tension in Scottish Social Theology, 2011; Scots Worship, Lent, Holy Week, Easter, 2013 (Ed); Scots Worship, Advent, Christmas, Epiphany, 2014 (Ed). Recreations: walking; gardening. Address: 40 Sinton Park, Dunbar EH42 1ZP.
E-mail: johnston.mckay@btopenworld.com

Mackay, Kenneth James, MA, BD. Minister of St Nicholas Sighthill Church, 1976-2007; b. 14.9.41, Inverness; m., Janet; 1 s.; 1 d. Educ. Fortrose Academy; Aberdeen University. Minister of Church of Scotland, Maryfield - Victoria St., Dundee, 1971-76. Member, Botanical Society of Scotland. Recreations: hill-walking;

golf. Address: (h.) 46 Chuckethall Road, Livingston EH54 8FB; T.-01506 410 884.

McKay, Linda, MBE. Non-Executive Director, The Scottish Government; b. 27.5.51, Dunfermline. Educ. Aberdeen High School for Girls; Aberdeen University; Universite de Haute-Bretagne; Scottish School of Further Education, Jordanhill. Assistant Principal, Dundee College of Further Education, 1990-93; Deputy Principal, Glenrothes College, 1993-99; Principal and Chief Executive, Falkirk College of Further and Higher Education, 1999-2005; Principal, Forth Valley College, 2005-2013 (led an innovative and highly successful institution through merger, regionalisation and the delivery of an award winning £60 million estates development). Served as a Board Member of the Enterprise Network, Scottish Enterprise Forth Valley and subsequently on the Regional Advisory Board for Edinburgh; former Member of the Leadership Group of Chemical Sciences Scotland; former Member of the Scottish Funding Council Skills Committee (led a national project on workforce development); appointed to the Board of the Scottish Qualifications Committee in 2000 (charged with restoring public confidence in the Scottish examination system and in this role chaired the SQA Advisory Committee and the SQA Qualifications Committee); worked closely with the Police Service as a member of the Police Advisory Board for Scotland, a Governor of the Scottish Police College and Chair of the Police Scotland Examination Board; former Convener of the Loch Lomond and Trossachs National Park Authority. Address: Scottish Government, St. Andrew's House, Regent Road, Edinburgh EH1 3DG; T.-0131 244 2636.

Mackay, Peter, CB; b. 6.7.40, Arbroath; m., Sarah Holdich; 1 s.; 2 d. Educ. Glasgow High School; St. Andrews University. Scottish Office civil servant, 1963-1995, retiring as Secretary and Chief Executive, Scottish Office Industry Department, 1990-95; former Member, Board, Business Banking Division, Bank of Scotland; Member, Competition Commission (formerly Monopolies and Mergers Commission), 1996-2002; Member, Board, Scottish Natural Heritage, 1997-2003; Commissioner, Northern Lighthouse Board, 1999-2008 (Chairman, 2005-07); Chairman, Pacific Horizon Investment Trust, 2004-2010; Chairman, Northern Lighthouse Heritage Trust, 2013-2017. Recreations: Scotland; hill walking; sea canoeing; sculling. Address: (h.) Silverwood, Dunachton Road, Kincraig, Kingussie PH21 1QE.
E-mail: strathbogie@btinternet.com

Mackay, Rona. MSP (SNP), Strathkelvin and Bearsden, since 2016; m., Ian Mackay. Career: journalist and author; worked as a Parliamentary assistant to Gil Paterson, the SNP MSP for Milngavie and Clydebank. Address: Scottish Parliament, Edinburgh EH99 1SP.

Mackay, Tim, BSc. Deputy Chair of the Accounts Commission, since 2020. Educ. St Aloysuis College, Glasgow; University of St Andrews. Career history: Senior Lecturer, Edinburgh Napier University, 1997-2007; City of Edinburgh Council: Councillor, 2007-2012, Vice Convener (Economic Development), 2007-2012; Chair, Pension Trustees, Lothian Pension Fund, 2007-2012; Chair, NHS Pension Board, 2015-2017; Consultant, AllenbridgeEpic Investment Advisers Limited, since 2012. Board Member, Accounts Commission, since 2014; Member and Chair of Audit Committee, Scottish Legal Aid Board, since 2016. Address: Audit Scotland, Head office, 4th Floor, 102 West Port, Edinburgh EH3 9DN; T.-0131 625 1500.

Mackay, Rev. William Morton, MA (Hons), DipEd, DipTh, FCS, FRSGS, FRGS, AFAPC, MACE. Moderator, General Assembly of Free Church of Scotland, 2001; Part-time Lecturer in Church History, Free Church of Scotland

College, Edinburgh, 1998-2005; Free Church of Scotland: Clerk of Public Questions, Religion and Morals Committee, 1999-2002, Chairman, International Missions Board, 2002-07; b. 26.3.34, Dundee; m., Catherine; 2 s.; 1 d. Educ. Morgan Academy, Dundee; Queen's College, Dundee; University of St. Andrews; Dundee College of Education; Free Church of Scotland College, Edinburgh. Teacher, Buckhaven High School, Fife, 1959-61; ordained, 1961; Teacher, Colegio San Andres, Lima, Peru, 1961-65, Headmaster, 1966-78; Teacher, Lothian Regional Council, 1978-85; Principal, Presbyterian Ladies' College, Burwood, Victoria, Australia, 1986-97. Diploma of Honour, Government of Peru, for services to education. Royal Scottish Geographical Society: Member of Council, 2003-06 and 2007-2010; Vice Chairman of the Edinburgh Centre; Clan Mackay Society: Member of Council and a Vice-President. Publication: Thomas Chalmers: A Short Appreciation, 1980. Recreations: music; photography; cricket; rugby; reading. Address: 53 Lauderdale Street, Edinburgh EH9 1DE.

McKechin, Ann, LLB, DipLP. Vice Chair, Public Health Scotland (Part-time), since 2021; Hearings Panel Lay Member, General Optical Council, since 2019; Hearings Panel Lay Member, General Chiropractic Council, since 2021; Board Member, Smart Energy GB, since 2021; Head of Corporate Social Responsibility, ScottishPower, 2017-19; Trustee, UN Women National Committee UK, since 2016; Member of University of West of Scotland Court, since 2016; Solicitor; Labour MP, Glasgow North, 2005-2015, Glasgow Maryhill, 2001-05; Member, Business, Innovation and Skills Select Committee, 2011-15; Shadow Secretary of State for Scotland, 2010-11; Parliamentary Under Secretary of State, Scotland Office, 2008-10; Partner, Pacitti Jones, Solicitors, 1990-2000; b. 22.4.61, Johnstone. Educ. Paisley Grammar School; Strathclyde University. Hearings Panel Lay Member, General Optical Council, since 2019; Board Member, Public Health Scotland, since 2020. Recreations: films; art history; reading. E-mail: mckechina@gmail.com

McKechnie, Aileen, MA (Hons), MBA. Principal and Chief Executive, South Lanarkshire College, since 2020. Educ. University of Glasgow; University of Freiburg. Career history: Senior Development Manager, Glasgow City Council, 1990-94; Senior Development Manager: Scottish Homes, 1994-96, Thistle Housing Association, 1996-98; The Scottish Government: Head of Local Economic Development, 1999-2002, Head of Higher Education Strategy and Funding, 2002-04, Head of Further and Adult Education Division, 2004-09, Head of Innovation, Investment and Industries Division, 2009-2012, Director, Culture, External Affairs & Consulting (Acting), 2012; Director, The Scottish Arbitration Centre, 2011-13; Scottish Government: Director of Culture & Heritage, 2012-15, Director of Advanced Learning & Science, 2015-2020. Address: South Lanarkshire College, Scottish Enterprise Technology Park, College Way, East Kilbride, Glasgow G75 0NE; T.-01355 807780.

McKechnie, Anne Elizabeth, MA, MSc, CPsychol. Consultant Forensic Clinical Psychologist: Scottish Child Abuse Inquiry, since 2018, Fcpsyservices, since 2013, Good Shepherd Secure Care Centre, 2012-2020, NHS Greater Glasgow and Clyde, 2014-18; b. 21.06.62, Aberdeen; m., Henry Robert John Parsons; 1 s.; 1 d. Educ. Linlithgow Academy; Aberdeen University. Clinical Psychologist: East Berkshire Health Authority, 1986-89, Parkhead Hospital, Glasgow Health Trust, 1989-91, Douglas Inch Centre, 1991-99. Member: Victim Support Scotland Training Advisory Group, 1991-93 and 1993-95, Mental Health Act Scotland Implementation Group, 2004. Commissioner on Time

To Be Heard Pilot Forum, 2010. Recreations: drawing; gardening; cooking; walking. Address: (b.) 16 Bruce Road, Pollokshields G41 5EJ. E-mail: fcpsyservices@gmail.com

McKee, Ian, MBE, MBChB, DObst, RCOG, FSOMM. MSP (SNP), Lothians, 2007-2011; Minister for Trade, Investment and Innovation, 2018-2020; b. 2.4.40, South Shields; m., Penelope Ann; 1 s. and 1 stepson; 2 d. and 1 stepdaughter. Educ. Fettes College; Edinburgh University. House Officer: Ingham Infirmary, South Shields, 1965-66, Royal Infirmary Edinburgh, 1966; Medical Officer, Royal Air Force, 1966-71; General Practitioner, Sighthill and Wester Hailes Health Centres, Edinburgh, 1971-2006; Managing Director, Hermiston Publications, 1980-2000. Recreations: hill walking; music.

McKee, Ivan, BSc, BEng. MSP (SNP), Glasgow Provan, since 2016; Minister for Business, Trade, Tourism and Enterprise, since 2021; Minister for Trade, Innovation and Public Finance, 2020-21; b. 9.63, Helensburgh, Dunbartonshire. Educ. University of Strathclyde; Newcastle University. Career history: worked for a variety of manufacturing companies following 2 years of voluntary service in Bangladesh with VSO; set up an international manufacturing consultancy business in 2005; invested in, and successfully turned around, a number of manufacturing businesses including the rescue of Dunfermline based Simclar from Administration, 2009-2015; significant international experience having managed businesses in Scotland, England, Poland, Finland, Croatia and Bosnia. Director of Business for Scotland during the Scottish Independence Referendum; formerly Trustee of the charity CEI which supports educational and health projects in rural Bangladesh; formerly Director of The Common Weal. Address: Scottish Parliament, Edinburgh EH99 1SP.

McKee, Professor (James Clark St. Clair) Sean, BSc, MA, PhD, DSc, FIMA, CMath, FRSE. Research Professor, Strathclyde University, since 2010; b. 1.7.45, Belfast. Educ. George Watson's College, Edinburgh; St. Andrews University; Dundee University; Oxford University. NCR Research Fellow, 1970-72; Lecturer in Numerical Analysis, Southampton University, 1972-75; Fellow, Hertford College, Oxford, 1975-86; Professor of Industrial Mathematics, Strathclyde University, and Consultant Mathematician, Unilever Research, 1986-88; Professor of Mathematics, Strathclyde University, 1988-2010, Research Professor, since 2010. Homenagem (University of São Paulo), 2003; ICMC Medal of Honour (University of São Paulo), 2009; Homenagem (State University of São Paulo), 2014; Member, Council, ECMI, 1986-2006; Convener of the Informatics, Mathematics and Statistics Sector Committee of the Royal Society of Edinburgh, 2002-06. Founding Fellow, Institute of Contemporary Scotland; Elected Associate of the Institute for Non-Newtonian Fluid Mechanics, 2016. Publications: 220 papers; Industrial Numerical Analysis (Co-Editor), 1986; Vector and Parallel Computing (Co-Editor), 1989; Artificial Intelligence in Mathematics (Co-Editor), 1994. Recreations: climbing Munros; golf; theatre; gardening. Address: (b.) Department of Mathematics and Statistics, Strathclyde University, Glasgow G1 1XH; T.-0141-548-3671.

McKellar, Keith Alexander James. Chief Executive, Royal College of Physicians of Edinburgh, since 2019; Chair, Belmont House School, since 2021 (Board member, since 2014); Trustee, Church of Scotland; Acting Treasurer, Presbytery of Ayr, since 2017; Chief Executive Officer, Hannah Dairy Research Foundation/Journal of Dairy Research; b. 29.6.68, Ayrshire; m. Catriona (nee Geddes); 2 s. 1 d. Educ. Universities of Strathclyde, Glasgow and

Oxford. Career history: Chief Executive Officer, Pharmalmaging Group Ltd, 2000-05; Chaired/Authored Review of the Scottish Venison Industry, Deer Commission Scotland, 2009; Non-executive Director, Blackford Analysis Ltd, 2009-12; Chairman, Stow College, 2012-13, Vice-Chairman, 2012; Chief Executive Officer, Hannah Research Institute, 2005-2013; Chief Executive Officer, Scottish Health Innovations Ltd and NHS Research Scotland Central Management, 2013-16; Regional Chair, West College Scotland, 2014-2020; Non-executive Director, Colleges Scotland, 2014-2020; Chairman, Ardgowan University Teaching Hospice, Greenock, 2014-2021. Recreations: history; painting.
E-mail: kajmckellar@aol.com

McKellar, Peter Archibald, LLB (Hons). Global Head of Private Markets, Aberdeen Standard Investments, 2017-2020; b. 28.5.65, Glasgow; m., Karen Emery; 2 s. Educ. Daniel Stewart's and Melville College, Edinburgh; Edinburgh University. J.P. Morgan, Investment Bank, New York and London, 1986-88; EFT Group PLC, Corporate Finance Division, 1988-89; London and Edinburgh Trust plc, 1989-90; Co-Founder, Barry McKellar Ltd., 1990-95; Group Finance Director, Clydeport plc, 1995-98; Group Finance Director, Donside Paper Company Limited, 1998-99; Non-Executive Chairman, Red Lemon Studios Ltd, 1998-99; Governor, Cargilfield School, 2002-2011; Board Member, Scottish Enterprise, since 2021; Non Executive Director, AssetCo plc, since 2021. Recreations: golf; shooting; swimming.

McKellar-Young, Rev Cheryl, BA (Hons), BD, MSc. Minister, Fairmilehead Parish Church, Edinburgh, since 2018. Educ. Université Paris-Sorbonne; Open University; University of Edinburgh; University of Glasgow. Minister, Church of Scotland, since 2013. Address: Fairmilehead Parish Church, 1a Frogston Road West, Edinburgh EH10 7AA; T.-0131 445 2374.

McKelvie, Christina. MSP (SNP), Hamilton, Larkhall and Stonehouse, since 2011, Central Scotland, 2007-2011; Minister for Equalities and Older People, since 2018; b. 4.3.68, Glasgow; 2 s. Educ. St. Leonards Secondary; Nautical College; Anniesland College, Cardonald; St. Andrews University. Eastern College of Nursing, 1986-87; Glasgow City Council Social Work Department, 1988-2007: Day Service Officer, Depute Manager, Learning and Development Officer. Unison Steward; Community Council; Garrowhill Action Partnership. Recreations: hillwalking; painting; reading; politics. Address: (b.) Scottish Parliament, Holyrood Road, Edinburgh EH99 1SP; T.-0131 348 6680.
E-mail: christina.mckelvie.msp@parliament.scot

McKenna, Moira, DL, BSc (Hons), MB, ChB (Edin), FRCGP. Scottish Chief Commissioner, Girlguiding Scotland, since 2017; b. 1966, Stirling. Educ. Balfron High School; Edinburgh University. General Practitioner, Dingwall Medical Group, since 1994, Group Leader, since 2006; Ross-shire County Commissioner, 2011-16; Scottish Executive member, Girlguiding Scotland, since 2014. Address: Girlguiding Scotland HQ, 16 Coates Crescent, Edinburgh EH3 7AU.

McKenna, Rosemary, CBE, DCE. MP (Labour), Cumbernauld and Kilsyth, 1997-2010; b. 8.5.41, Kilmacolm; m., James Stephen McKenna; 3 s.; 1 d. Educ. St. Augustine's Secondary School, Glasgow; St. Andrew's College, Bearsden. Taught in various primary schools, 1974-93; Leader of Council, Cumbernauld and Kilsyth, 1984-88, Provost 1988-92, Leader of Council, 1992-94;

former Member, North Lanarkshire Council; former Policy Board Member: Local Government Management Board, Local Government International Bureau; former Member, Board, Scottish Enterprise; former Member, Executive, Scottish Constitutional Convention; Chair, Scottish Libraries and Information Council, 1999-2002; PPS to John Battle, MP, 1998-2000, to Brian Wilson, MP, 2000-01; President, Convention of Scottish Local Authorities, 1994-96. Recreations: reading; cooking.

McKenna, Revd. Scott S., BA, BD (Hons), MTh, MPhil, PhD. Minister, Ayr: St Columba, since 2019; b. 3.2.66, Dunfermline; m., Shelagh M. Laird; 1 s. Educ. Kirkton High School, Dundee; St. Mary's College, University of St. Andrews. Accountant; Probationer Minister, Wellington Church, Glasgow, 1992-93; Minister: Viewpark Parish Church, Uddingston, 1994-2000, Edinburgh: Mayfield Salisbury Church, 2000-2019. Member, Panel on Worship, General Assembly, 1994-98; Member, World Mission Council, General Assembly, 2005-08. Address: (b.) 3 Upper Crofts, Alloway, Ayr KA7 4QX; T.-01292 226 075.
E-mail: scottsmckenna@aol.com

McKenna, Professor Stephen James, BSc (Hons), MSc, PhD. Professor (Personal Chair of Computer Vision), University of Dundee, since 2008; b. 03.01.69; m., Collette; 3 s.; 1 d. Educ. University of Edinburgh; University of Dundee. Research Fellow, Technopolis Csata, Italy, 1994-95; Post-Doctoral Researcher, Queen Mary College, University of London, 1995-98; Visiting Researcher, George Mason University, USA, 1999; Lecturer, Applied Computing, University of Dundee, 1998-2004, Senior Lecturer, Computing, 2004-07. Publications: Co-Author, Dynamic Vision, 2000; Associate Editor for Journal "Machine Vision & Applications". Recreation: guitar. Address: (b.) School of Computing, University of Dundee DD1 4HN; T.-01382 384732.
E-mail: stephen@computing.dundee.ac.uk

Mackenzie, Professor Ann Logan, MA. E. Allison Peers Professorial Research Fellow, The Bulletin of Spanish Studies Trust, since 2020; Honorary Professorial Research Fellow, Glasgow University, since 2006; Ivy McClelland Research Professor of Spanish, Glasgow University, since 1995; General Editor, Bulletin of Spanish Studies (1923-), since 1992; General Editor, Bulletin of Spanish Visual Studies, since 2017; b. Greenock. Educ. Greenock Academy; Glasgow University. Lecturer, Senior Lecturer, Reader, Liverpool University, 1968-95. Publications: books and articles on the theatre and literature of 17th-century Spain (especially Calderón and his school of dramatists) and on the development of British Hispanism (especially the career and writings of E. Allison Peers/Bruce Truscot and the history of the Bulletin of Spanish Studies since he founded it in 1923). Recreations: theatre; walking the dogs; house improvements. Address: (b.) The Bulletin of Spanish Studies Trust, 38 Fairacres Road, Bebington, Wirral, Merseyside CH63 3HB; T.-0151 644 6377.
E-mail: Ann.Mackenzie@glasgow.ac.uk

Mackenzie, Colin, BA, DipSW, CQSW. Retired Chief Executive, Aberdeenshire Council (2008-2015). Educ. Forfar Academy; Strathclyde University; Glasgow University. Trainee Social Worker, Dundee City Corp, 1973-75; Child Care Specialist, 1975-77, Area Team Leader, 1977-82, Tayside Regional Council; Social Work Manager, 1982-85, Divisional Officer, 1985-96, Grampian Regional Council; Head of Service, 1996-2000, Director of Housing and Social Work, 2000-08, Aberdeenshire Council. Member, 21st Century Review of Social Work, 2004-05, Pres., ADSW, 2005-06. Non Executive Member,

Scottish Prison Service Board, 2007-08. Joint Improvement Partnership Board, 2013. Joint Chair, Health and Social Care Delivery Group, 2012-15; Non Executive Director, North East Scotland Preservation Trust; Chair, Healthcare Improvement (Scotland) Governance Working Group.

Mackenzie, Sheriff Colin Scott, OBE, DL, BL, FSA Scot. Sheriff of Grampian Highland and Islands, at Lerwick and Kirkwall, 1992-2003; part-time Sheriff, 2004-08; Sheriff, 2009-2015 (retired); Hon. Sheriff of Grampian, Highland and Islands, since 2009; b. 7.7.38, Stornoway; m. (1966), Christeen E.D. MacLauchlan. Educ. Nicolson Institute; Fettes College; Edinburgh University. Procurator Fiscal, Stornoway, 1969-92; Burgh Prosecutor, Stornoway, 1971-75; JP Fiscal, 1971-75; Deputy Lieutenant, 1975-2013 and Clerk to Lieutenancy of the Western Isles, 1975-92; Vice Lord Lieutenant of Islands Area, Western Isles, 1984-92; Founder President, Stornoway Flying Club, 1970; Founding Dean, Western Isles Faculty of Solicitors; elected Council Member, Law Society of Scotland, 1985-92; Convener, Criminal Law Committee, 1991-92; Council Member, Sheriffs' Association, 2002-03; Elder, Church of Scotland, since 1985; Member, Board of Social Responsibility, Church of Scotland, 1990-96; Convener, Assembly Study Group on Young People and the Media, 1991-93; Judicial Commission of General Assembly, Church of Scotland, since 2011; Member, Committee to nominate Moderator of General Assembly, 2021; President, Stornoway Rotary Club, 1977; President, Isle of Lewis Probus Club, 2010; Patron, Lewis Pipe Band; Chairman, Queen's Own Highlanders Association (Lewis Branch), 2009-2014; Chairman, Urras Eaglais Na H-Aoidhe, 2014-2018, Honorary President, since 2018; Trustee, Founder, Dileab An T-Siorraidh (Scottish Charity), since 2017. Publications: author of article on Lieutenancy, Stair Memorial Encyclopaedia of Law of Scotland, 1987; The Last Warrior Band, 2000; Shetland, Orkney and Western Isles, Personal Reflections, 2010; St Columba's Ui Church otherwise Eaglais Na h-Aoidhe, 2012; Gael Force on Gallipoli, 2016; In Search of Colin Gill, 2021; The Overlooked Jewel in our Crown, 2021. Recreation: fishing. Address: (h.) Park House, Matheson Road, Stornoway, Lewis.
E-mail: colinsmackenzie@btinternet.com

MacKenzie, Professor Donald, BSc, PhD, FRSE, FBA. Professor of Sociology, University of Edinburgh, since 1992; b. 3.5.50, Inverness; m., Caroline Bamford; 1s.; 1 d. Educ. Golspie High School; University of Edinburgh. University of Edinburgh: Lecturer in Sociology, 1975-88, Reader in Sociology, 1988-92. Visiting Professor of the History of Science, Harvard University, 1997. Co-winner, U.S. Navy Prize in Naval History, 1989; American Sociological Association Merton Award, 1993 and 2003, Zelizer Prize, 2005 and 2008 and Granovetter Award, 2012; Society for Social Studies of Science Fleck Prize, 1993 and 2003. Publication: Trading at the Speed of Light, 2021. Recreations: cycling; walking; chess. Address: (b.) School of Social and Political Science, George Square, Edinburgh EH8 9LD; T.-0131-650 3980.

Mackenzie, Elizabeth Alice, MA (Post-Grad), CertEd., AMBDA; b. 10.9.41, Glasgow; m., Ian Mackenzie (deceased); 1 s.; 1 d. Educ. St Columba's, Kilmacolm; Laurel Bank, Glasgow; St George's, Edinburgh; Froebel Educational Institute, Roehampton; Kingston University. Primary teacher in London and Scottish schools, 1963-68; Adviser on Children's Religious Programmes, ABC TV, 1965-68; research into children's books for ABC TV, 1968-70; Senior Teacher, Dyslexia Institute, Glasgow, 1989-92; Principal, Dyslexia Institute Scotland, 1992-2004. Management Team, "Dyslexia At Transition", Parents Transition Support Materials and DVD-Rom for Secondary Schools, 2004-07; Member, Scottish Dyslexia Forum, 1996-2004; Project Team, "Count Me In: Responding to Dyslexia", pack of materials for Scottish Primary Schools, 2002-04; Course Director, Dyslexia Institute Teacher Training Course, 1994-98; Course Tutor, Post Graduate Course in Dyslexia and Literacy, York University, 2003-04; Self Esteem Research Project (Glasgow/Paisley Universities), 2003-04. Publications: Dimensions of Dyslexia, Volume I (Contributor); Dyslexia and the Young Offender (paper). Recreations: cooking; design. Address: (h.) The Glebe, Southwick, by Dumfries, Dumfries and Galloway DG2 8AR; T.-01387 780276.

Mackenzie, Fiona I., MA (Hons), MBA, CIHM (Dip). Self Employed Consultant and crofter; formerly Chief Executive, NHS Board Forth Valley (2001-2013); b. 19.7.58, Edinburgh. Educ. Eastwood High School, Glasgow; University of St. Andrews; Hull University. NHS Graduate Trainee, 1980-82; Hospital Administrator, West Lothian, 1982-84; Operational Manager, Royal Edinburgh Hospital, 1986-89; Assistant Unit General Manager, Mental Health Unit, Lothian Health Board, 1989-91; Acute Services Manager, Monklands Hospital, Lanarkshire Health Board; Director of Planning, Monklands and Bellshill NHS Trust, 1993-96; Chief Executive, Highland Communities NHS Trust, 1996-99; Chief Executive, Highland Primary Care NHS Trust, 1999-2001. Awarded Companionship of the Institute of Health Management, 2009; Board Member, Scottish Futures Trust; Chairperson, Applecross Historical Society; Honorary Professor, Stirling University. Recreations: sport; cooking. Address: Toscaig, Applecross, Ross-shire IV54 8LY; e-mail: fionatoscaig@btinternet.com

McKenzie, Iain. MP (Labour), Inverclyde, 2011-15; b. 4.4.59, Greenock. Former employee of IBM; elected to Inverclyde Council (Leader of the Council, 2011).

McKenzie, John Murchison, LLB, MCLIP. Chief Executive, Royal Faculty of Procurators in Glasgow, since 2008, Faculty Librarian, 2002-08; b. 7.8.71, Lakhnadon, M. P., India; m., Eleanor; 1 s.; 1 d. Educ. Hebron School, TN, India; High School of Glasgow; Dundee University; Strathclyde University. Legal Librarian, Glasgow City Council, 2000-02. Recreations: football; reading; crafts. Address: (b.) Royal Faculty of Procurators in Glasgow, 12 Nelson Mandela Place, Glasgow G2 1BT; T.-0141 332 3593; e-mail: jmckenzie@rfpg.org

MacKenzie, Kenneth John, CB, MA, AM. Chairman, Historic Scotland Foundation, 2001-2011; Chairman, Edinburgh City Centre Churches Together, 2010-2012; Honorary Professor, Department of Politics and International Relations, University of Aberdeen, 2001-04; Member, National Board of Christian Aid, 2005-08; Member, British Waterways Scotland Group, 2002-07; Associate Consultant, Public Administration International, 2002-08; b. 1.5.43, Glasgow; m., Irene Mary Hogarth; 1 s.; 1 d. Educ. Birkenhead School, Cheshire; Pembroke College, Oxford; Stanford University, California. Assistant Principal, Scottish Home and Health Department, 1965-70; Private Secretary to Joint Parliamentary Under Secretary of State, Scottish Office, 1969-70; Principal: General Register Office, 1970, Regional Development Division, Scottish Office, 1970-73, Scottish Education Department, 1973-77; Civil Service Fellow: Downing College, Cambridge, 1972, Department of Politics, University of Glasgow, 1974-75; Principal Private Secretary to Secretary of State for Scotland, 1977-79; Assistant Secretary: Scottish Economic Planning Department, 1979-83, Scottish Office Finance Division, 1983-85; Principal Finance Officer, Scottish Office, 1985-88; Under Secretary, Scottish Home and Health Department, 1988-91; Scottish Office, Agriculture and Fisheries Department: Under Secretary, 1991-92, Secretary, 1992-95; Head Economic and Domestic Secretariat, Cabinet Office, 1995-97; Head, Constitution

Secretariat, Cabinet Office, 1997-98; Secretary and Head of Department, Scottish Executive Development Department, 1998-2001. Member, Agriculture and Food Research Council, 1992-94; Member, Biotechnology and Biological Sciences Research Council, 1994-95; Quinquennial Reviewer for Court Service, Lord Chancellor's Department, 2001-02. Recreations: amateur dramatics (Member, Edinburgh Makars); church activities (Elder, St Cuthbert's Parish Church, Edinburgh). Address: (h.) 23C/1 Ravelston Park, Edinburgh EH4 3DX; T.-0131 315 2113; e-mail: kenneth@voltaire.plus.com

MacKenzie, Madeleine, LLB (Hons), DipLP. Parliamentary Counsel, since 2002; b. 27.8.63, Inverness; d. of William Gordon MacKenzie and the late Veronica Dorothy Rachel MacKenzie. Educ. Inverness High School; Aberdeen University. Solicitor in private practice, 1986-90; Assistant, then Depute Scottish Parliamentary Counsel, 1990-2002. Recreations: reading; bridge; music. Clubs: Athenaeum, New. Address: (b.) Parliamentary Counsel Office, Victoria Quay, Edinburgh EH6 6QQ; T.-0131-244 1667; e-mail: madeleine.mackenzie@gov.scot

MacKenzie, Mike. MSP (SNP), Highlands and Islands, 2011-16; b. 18.11.58, Oban; m., Lynn. Brought up in Glasgow and lived in Argyll from 1980. Ran a building business on Easdale until 2011. Founding director of Eilean Eisdeal, a community development company in Argyll.

Mackenzie, Dr Monique, PhD. Assistant Vice-Principal (Provost), Head of St Leonard's College, University of St Andrews, since 2018; previously Director of the Graduate School for Interdisciplinary Studies. Educ. The University of Auckland. Career: University of St Andrews: Senior Lecturer, since 2002; statistician developing methods and software for data collected over space and time; previously served as the Director of Teaching in the School of Mathematics and Statistics and Deputy Director of the Graduate School. Actively involved in several conservation projects in Africa as a statistician; also volunteers on the Children's Panel in Scotland. Address: University of St Andrews, College Gate, St Andrews KA16 9AJ; T.-01334 461836; e-mail: provost@st-andrews.ac.uk

Mackenzie, Professor Robin Kenneth; BSc, MSc, PhD, CEng, FIOA, FRSA. Emeritus Professor; Vice Principal, Edinburgh Napier University, 2007-12; b. 28.8.44, Edinburgh; m., Georgina Fiona; 3 s. Educ. Trinity Academy; Heriot-Watt University, Edinburgh University; MIT (USA). Research Fellow, Massachusetts Institute of Technology, 1970-72; Lecturer/Senior Lecturer, Heriot-Watt University, 1973-85; Reader in Acoustics, Heriot-Watt University, 1985-90; Royal Society Industrial Fellow, 1990-93; Professor of Acoustics, Sheffield Hallam University, 1993-95; Cruden Fellowship, National Science Foundation Fellowship (USA); Tyndall Medal, Institute of Acoustics, 1980; Queen's Anniversary Prize, 2009; Chairman of various ISO and BSI committees on sound insulation. Publication: Auditorium Acoustics, 1974. Recreations: tennis; chess; skiing. Address: (b.) Edinburgh Napier University, Unit 1, 7 Hills Business Park, Bankhead Crossway South, Edinburgh EH11 4EP; T.-0131-455 5140.
E-mail: r.mackenzie@napier.ac.uk

McKenzie Smith, Ian, CBE, OBE, PPRSA, PPRSW, RGI, FMA, FRSA, FRSE, FSAScot, FSS, HRA, HRHA, HRUA, HRWA, LLD, DArt, DA, PG Dip (Grays School of Art). Artist (painter); b. 3.8.35; m., Mary Rodger Fotheringham; 2 s.; 1 d. Educ. Robert Gordon's College, Aberdeen; Gray's School of Art, Aberdeen; Hospitalfield College of Art, Arbroath; Aberdeen College of Education. Teacher of Art, 1960-63; Education Officer, Council of Industrial Design,

Scottish Committee, 1963-68; Director, Aberdeen Art Gallery and Museums, 1968-89; City Arts and Recreation Officer, City of Aberdeen, 1989-96. Awards: SED Travelling Scholarship (France/Italy); Institute of Contemporary Prints Award, 1969; RSA Guthrie Award, 1971; RSA Sir William Gillies Award, 1980; EUS Thyne Scholarship, 1980; RSW May Marshall Brown Award, 1980; RSW Sir William Gillies Award, 2008; Arts and Business Scotland Award, 2011. Work in permanent collections: Scottish National Gallery of Modern Art, Scottish Arts Council, Arts Council of Northern Ireland, Contemporary Art Society, Aberdeen Art Gallery and Museums, Glasgow Art Gallery and Museums, Abbot Hall Art Gallery, Kendal, Hunterian Museum, Glasgow, Nuffield Foundation, Carnegie Trust, Strathclyde Education Authority, Lothian Education Authority, Royal Scottish Academy, Department of the Environment, City Art Centre, Edinburgh, Perth Art Gallery, IBM, Robert Fleming Holdings, Deutsche Bank, Grampian Hospital Art Trust, The Robert Gordon University, Stirling University, Angus Council; Member, Scottish Arts Council, 1970-77; Member, Scottish Museums Council, 1980-87; Member, Committee of Enquiry into the Economic Situation of the Visual Artist, Gulbenkian Foundation, 1978; Arts Advisor, COSLA, 1977-84; Member, Aberdeen University Museums Committee, 1970-96, and Music Committee, 1970-96; Honorary Member, Friends of Aberdeen Art Gallery and Museums, since 2000; Honorary Member, Peacock Printmakers, since 1993; Trustee: Third Eye Centre, 1966-70, Glasgow Arts Centre, 1966-68, Alba Magazine, 1977-80, WASPS (Scotland), 1973-77, Painters Workshop (Scotland), 1975-89, John Kinross Fund, 1990-2007, Alexander Naysmith Fund, 1990-2007, Spalding Fund, 1990-2007, Sir William Gillies Fund, 1990-2007, Hospitalfield Trust, 1990-2007 (Chair, 2003-07), RSA Enterprise, 1972-2007; Member, ICOM International Exhibitions Committee, 1986-96; Member, Advisory Council on the Export of Works of Art, 1991-2018; Member, Re:Source AIL Panel, 2000-01; External Assessor, Glasgow School of Art, 1982-86, Duncan of Jordanstone College of Art, Dundee, 1986-90, SAC Gifting Scheme, 1997; Assessor: Ruth Davidson Memorial Trust, Morrison Portrait Award, Salvesen Art Trust, Noble Grossart Award, RGU Collections Forum, since 2000; President, RSW, 1988-98; President, Royal Scottish Academy, 1998-2007; Deputy President, RSA, 1990-91, Treasurer, 1990, Secretary, 1991-98; Governor, Edinburgh College of Art, 1976-88 (Chair, Anderw Grant Committee, 1977-88); Governor, The Robert Gordon University, 1989-95; Member, Advisory Board, Robert Gordon University Heritage Unit, 1993-95; Member, Board, Scottish Sculpture Workshop, 1976-2000; Aberdeen Maritime Museum Appeal, 1981-98; Member, National Heritage Scottish Group, 1977-99; National Trust for Scotland: Member, Curatorial Committee, 1991-2001, Member of Council, 1995-99, Member, Buildings Committee, 1998-2000; Commissioner, Museums and Galleries Commission, 1997-2000; Trustee, National Galleries of Scotland, 1999-2007; Vice President, NADFAS, 2000-07; Chairman, Marguerite McBey Trust, since 2000; Member, Aberdeen Art Gallery Alexander Macdonald Committee, since 2000; Trustee, Royal Scottish Academy Foundation, since 2015. Clubs: Royal Northern and University, Scottish Arts, Royal Overseas League. Address: (h.) Heron House, Angus DD10 9TJ; T.-01674 675898.
E-mail: i.mckenziesmith@btinternet.com

McKerrell of Hillhouse, Charles James Mure, OStJ, FSA Scot. Matriculated Arms 1973, Court of the Lord Lyon, and recognised by interlocutor of the Lord Lyon as Head of the Name and Family. Tartans:- McKerrell of Hillhouse recorded Court of the Lord Lyon, 25 June 1982; McKerrell of Hillhouse (Dress) recorded Court of the Lord Lyon, 2002. Recognised by the Chief Herald of Ireland as 15th Head of the Name, 1975; b. 23.1.51; m., May Weston

Cochrane, née White. Educ. Cranleigh. Guardian of the Nobiliary Fraternity of the Nia Naisc, Knight of St Micheil of the Wing (Granted by HRH The Duke of Braganza), Hereditary Companion of the Royal House of O'Conor; GCLJ, Knight Grand Cross of St. Antioche; Kentucky Colonel; Hon. ADC to the Governor of Kentucky; Board Member, EU Commissioner Society of Scottish Armigers; Honorary Captain, Canadian Bush Pilots; Freeman, City of London; Trustee Member, Royal Celtic Society; Life Member, Royal Stuart Society; representative on Scottish Clans and Families Forum; Member of the Community Council of the Royal Burgh of Lochmaben. Address: (h.) Magdalene House, Lochmaben, Dumfries DG11 1PD; T.- 01387 810439.

E-mail: mckerrellofhillhouse@btinternet.com

MacKessack-Leitch, Hilda Jane Marshall. Deputy Lieutenant, Moray, since 1993; Chairman, Moray and Banff Support Group of NOS (National Osteoporosis Society); b. 4.9.40, Rothes; m., 1, Dr. Ernest V. C. Dawson (deceased); 2, David C. MacKessack-Leitch (deceased); 2 s. Educ. Elgin Academy. Past County Commissioner, The Guide Association, Moray; Past Chairman, Cancer Research Campaign Committee, Elgin and District; Elgin Local Organiser, WRVS, 1976-2000; County President, Girl Guiding Moray, Girl Guiding Scotland, 2014. Recreations: cooking; walking; reading; music. Address: (h.) Sillerton, 61 Mayne Road, Elgin, Moray IV30 1PD; T.-01343 544711.

McKie, Alastair John. Partner, Head of Planning and Environment, Anderson Strathern, since 1998; b. 15.6.62, Ipswich, Suffolk; m., Dr. Margaret Mitchell; 1 d. Educ. Lornshill Academy, Alloa; Dundee University. Qualified as a Solicitor, 1987; elected Legal Associate, Royal Town Planning Institute; Accredited as Specialist in Planning Law, Law Society of Scotland; Writer to Her Majesty's Signet. Recreations: hill walking; fishing; tennis; dogs. Address: (b.) 1 Rutland Court, Edinburgh EH3 8EY; T.- 0131 625 7257.

E-mail: alastair.mckie@andersonstrathern.co.uk

McKiernan, Professor Peter, BA, MA, PhD, CABS, FBAM, FEURAM, FAcSS, FGIA, FCIS, FRSA, FCMI. Professor of Management, University of Strathclyde; b. 28.12.53, Accrington; 1 s.; 1 d. Educ. Preston Catholic College; Lanchester Polytechnic; Lancaster University; Surrey University; Professor of Management (including Global MBA Director, Interim Head of Department, PGR Director, Strategy Head), University of Strathclyde, since 2011; Distinguished Professor of Management Adjunct, Vesalius College, Vrje University of Brussels, since 2016; APS Chair of Strategy at the University of Malta, since 2015; Professor of Management, Adjunct University of Notre Dame, Australia, since 2017; former FD of mechanical engineering company; Lecturer in Management, University of St Andrews, 1982-1988; Senior Lecturer in Strategic Management, Warwick University, 1988-1992; Professor of Management including Chair of Department of Management, University of St Andrews, 1992-1994; 1997-2000; Inaugural Head of School of Management, University of St Andrews, 2004-2010; Dean, School of Management and Governance, Murdoch University, Perth, Australia, 2012-2015; Chairman and President of British Academy of Management, 2001-2006; Vice President and President of European Academy of Management, 2001-2010; Chair, Board of Governors, Madras College, 1999-2008; Chair, Board of Governors, West Lothian College, 2009-2012; appointed Chair of West Lothian Region College, 2012; Executive Board of the Association of Business Schools, 2009-2011; Executive Board Member, Scotland's Colleges, 2011-2012; received CEEMAN Institutional Champion Award, 2012; honoured with Lifetime Achievement Award

by British Academy of Management, 2015; Dean of the Fellows College of the British Academy of Management, 2006-2008; 2018-2019; Foundational Dean of the Fellows College of the European Academy of Management, 2021. Publications include books on Sharpbenders, Strategies of Growth, Inside Fortress Europe, Historical Evolution of Strategic Management, Management Culture in Oman, Strategy, Leadership and Governance. Strategic Foresight Director of many corporate, regional and national scenario planning projects, including the 'Scenarios for Scotland'. Recreations: sailing; cycling; swimming; poetry. Address: Strathclyde Business School, University of Strathclyde, 99 Cathedral Street, Glasgow G1 6XQ.

McKillop, Professor James Hugh, BSc, MB, ChB, PhD, FRCP, FRCR, FMedSci, Hon FAcadMEd, Hon. Doctorate (Orebro); Hon. MD (International Medical University, Kuala Lumpur). Muirhead Professor of Medicine, Glasgow University, 1989-2011 (Associate Dean for Medical Education, 2000-03 and Head of Undergraduate Medical School, 2003-06, Deputy Dean of Medicine, 2007-2010, Deputy Head of School of Medicine 2010-11); Honorary Consultant Physician, NHS Greater Glasgow, 1982-2011; b. 20.6.48, Glasgow; m., Caroline A. Oakley; 2 d. Educ. St. Aloysius' College, Glasgow; Glasgow University. Hall Fellow in Medicine, then Lecturer in Medicine, Glasgow University, 1974-82; Harkness Fellow, Stanford University Medical Center, California, 1979 and 1980; Senior Lecturer in Medicine, Glasgow University, 1982-89. Robert Reid Newall Award, Stanford University, 1980; Honorary Treasurer, Scottish Society of Experimental Medicine, 1982-87; Council Member, British Nuclear Medicine Society, 1985-94 (Hon. Secretary, 1988-90, President, 1990-92); Editor, Nuclear Medicine Communications, 1989-98; Congress President, European Association of Nuclear Medicine, 1997, Member, Executive Committee, 1995-98, Chairman, Education Committee, 1998-2001, Member, Strategy Committee, 1999-2008; Chairman, Administration of Radioactive Substances Advisory Committee, Department of Health, 1996-2004 (Vice Chairman, 1989-95); Member, National Medical Advisory Committee, 1995-98; Vice-President, Nuclear Medicine Section, Union Europeene Medecines Specialistes; Member, Scottish Medical and Scientific Advisory Committee, 1999-2001, Chairman, 2001-07; Team Leader for GMC Quality Assurance of Basic Medical Education, 2003-2008; Member, GMC, 2009-2016, Chair, Undergraduate Board, 2009-2012, Chair, Audit and Risk Committee, 2015-16, Chair, Pension Trustees, 2017-2021; Chairman, Medical Advisory Group, NHS Education for Scotland, 2004-2011; Chairman, Scottish Deans' Medical Curriculum Group, 2005-09; Chair, Expert Advisory Panel, British Polio Fellowship, 2008-2012; Member, Caribbean Accreditation Authority for Medicine, 2010-2014 and 2017-2020; Vestry Secretary, St Mary's Episcopal Cathedral, Glasgow, 2011-2020, Warden, since 2016. Recreations: music (especially opera); history; football. Address: (h.) Flat 1, 6 Kirklee Gate, Glasgow G12 0SZ. E-mail: jim.mckillop@glasgow.ac.uk

McKirdy, Mike. President, Royal College of Physicians and Surgeons of Glasgow, since 2021. Educ. University of Glasgow. Career history: surgical training in the west of Scotland, London and Manchester, then appointed a consultant surgeon at the Royal Alexandra Hospital Paisley in 1997; led and developed breast cancer services in the Clyde area of the West of Scotland forming a three hospital service; sat on the Councils of the Association of Breast Surgery and the Association of Surgeons of Great Britain and Ireland; trained reviewer for the Royal College of Surgeons of England Invited Review Mechanism, having conducted reviews across England, and in Scotland; Board Trustee, THET (Tropical Health and Education Trust), London, since 2019; Consultant

Surgeon, NHS, Glasgow, since 1997; Director of Global Health, Royal College of Physicians and Surgeons of Glasgow, 2016-2022. Address: 232-242 St Vincent Street, Glasgow G2 5RJ; T.-0141 221 6072.

MacKinnon, Donalda. Director, BBC Scotland, 2016-2020, responsible for the strategic direction and for the programmes and services produced by Scotland.

Mackinnon, John Duncan, BVetMed, CertPM, FRCVS. Chairman, Moredun Scientific Ltd, since 2016. Educ. Royal Veterinary College, University of London. Career history: Assistant Veterinary Surgeon: JA Abraham, Veterinary Surgeons, 1972-73, Bowditch, Grime & Partners, 1973-74; Elanco Products: Veterinary Adviser, 1974-77, Manager, Technical Services, 1977-82; European Projects Team Leader, Lilly Research Laboratories, 1982-87; Partner: Douglas & Mackinnon, Veterinary Surgeons, 1987-96, Stowe Veterinary Group, 1996-2003; Principal, Pig Health & Production Consultancy, 2003-2017. Fellow of Royal College of Veterinary Surgeons; Past President, Pig Veterinary Society; inaugural Past President, European Association for Porcine Health and Management. Recreations: horticulture; beekeeping; shooting; woodwork; acoustic and electric guitar. Address: The Moredun Group, Pentlands Scientific Science Park, Bush Loan, Penicuik, Midlothian EH26 0PZ; T.-0131 445 5111.

MacLachlan, Alison, MA (Hons). UK Director, The Wood Foundation, since 2018; Chair, Scottish Grantmakers, since 2021. Educ. University of Aberdeen. Career history: Head of Marketing & Volunteer Recruitment, Project Trust, Isle of Coll, 2004-2010; External Examiner, MSc CSR, Robert Gordon University, Aberdeen, since 2016; Trustee, University of Aberdeen Development Trust, since 2019; UK Manager, The Wood Foundation, 2010-2018. Board Member, Xchange Scotland, 2013-17; National Advisory Group, MCR Pathways, since 2018. Address: The Wood Foundation, Blenheim House, Fountainhall Road, Aberdeen AB15 4DT; T.-01224 619862.
E-mail: alison.maclachlan@thewoodfoundation.org.uk

McLachlan, Gavin, BSc, MBA. Vice-Principal, Chief Information Officer and Librarian, University of Edinburgh, since 2015. Educ. Crescent School; Dalhousie University; Loyola Marymount University, College of Business Administration. Career history: Director of Operations, Robert L. DeYoung Companies, 1986-90; Vice President, Product Development and Operations, CCC Information Services, 1991-2001; Product Development Director, Capita Education Services, 2001-03; Information Services Director, Computacenter, 2004-09; Director, Research IT and Technology Services, University College London, 2009-2015. Address: University of Edinburgh, Information Services, Argyle House, 3 Lady Lawson Street, Edinburgh EH3 9DR; T.-0131 650 4959.
E-mail: Gavin.McLachlan@ed.ac.uk

McLaren, Carol. Chief Executive, RSABI, since 2022. Educ. Morrison's Academy, Crieff; Aberdeen University. Career history: PR Manager, The Famous Grouse, The Edrington Group, 2002-06; Scottish Correspondent, Farmers Weekly, 2006-08; PR Manager, Diageo Scotland, 2008-09; Quality Meat Scotland: Director of Marketing and Communications, 2009-2019, Head of Communications, 2009-2019, Director of Marketing and Communications, 2018-19; Director of Marketing and Communications, Glenalmond College, 2019-2022; Partner, Strathearn Cider Company, since 2017; Supporter, RSABI, since 2018. Address: RSABI, The Rural Centre, West Mains of Ingliston, Newbridge EH28 8LT; T.-0131 364 4205.

MacLaren of MacLaren, Donald. Chief of Clan Labhran of Balquhidder and Strathearn; b. 1954; m., Maida Jane

Aitchison; 3 s. 2 d. Educ. Dragon School, Oxford; Trinity College, Glenalmond; Edinburgh University. Joined the Foreign and Commonwealth Office in 1978; after postings in Berlin, Moscow, Havana, Caracas and Kiev, served in Tbilisi, Georgia as Her Majesty's Ambassador; left the FCO in 2008 and now runs a partnership teaching people to speak persuasively called Perfect Pitch. Succeeded his father as Chief in 1966; twenty-fifth head of the Clan since Labhran, name-forefather of the Clan eight hundred years ago; descended from King Lorn Mor of the fifth century. Address: Kirkton Farm, Balquhidder, Lochearnhead, Perthshire.

McLaren, Dr Duncan Bruce, MB, BS, BSc, FRCR, FRCP (Edin). Consultant Clinical Oncologist, Western General Hospital, Edinburgh, since 1998; b. 20.3.65, Redditch; m., Dr. Pamela McLaren; 2 d. Educ. Finham Park School; St. Mary's Hospital Medical School, London. Specialist in urological cancer; Member, National Cancer Studies Groups in Prostate and Bladder Cancer; Lead, Scottish Cancer Trials Network, SE Scotland GU Trials Group. Recreations: avid sportsman – former rugby player, now keen squash player and golfer. Address: (b.) Edinburgh Cancer Centre, Western General Hospital, Edinburgh EH4 2XU; T.-0131-537 2215.
E-mail: duncan.mclaren@luht.scot.nhs.uk

McLaren, Jim, MBE. Farmer; owner, J.C. McLaren & Partners; Chairman, NFU Mutual, since 2019, Non Executive Director, since 2012. Educ. Morrison's Academy; East of Scotland Agricultural College. Career history: President, NFU Scotland, 2007-11; Non Executive Director, SRUC, 2011-13; Chairman, Quality Meat Scotland, 2011-18. Address: J.C. McLaren & Partners, Coldwells Road, Crieff PH7 4BB; T.-01764 652564.

McLaren, Ross. Head Teacher, Harlaw Academy, since 2020; previously Deputy Head, Galashiels Academy. Address: Harlaw Academy, 18-20 Albyn Place, Aberdeen AB10 1RG; T.-01224 589251.

McLatchie, Cameron, CBE, LLB. Chairman, British Polythene Industries, since 2003, formerly Scott & Robertson PLC, 1988-2003; b. 18.2.47, Paisley; m., Helen Leslie Mackie; 2 s.; 1 d. Educ. Boroughmuir School, Edinburgh; Largs High School; Ardrossan Academy; Glasgow University. Whinney Murray & Co., Glasgow, 1968-70; Thomas Boag & Co. Ltd., Greenock, 1970-75; Chairman and Managing Director, Anaplast Ltd., Irvine, 1975-83; this company purchased by Scott & Robertson. Deputy Chairman, Scottish Enterprise, 1997-2000; Non-Executive Director, Royal Bank of Scotland Group PLC, 1998-2002. Recreations: bridge; golf. Address: (b.) 96 Port Glasgow Road, Greenock; T.-01475 501000.

McLaughlin, Anne. MP (SNP), Glasgow North East, 2015-17 and since 2019; SNP Shadow Minister for Women and Equalities, 2019-2021; SNP Shadow Minister for Justice and Immigration, since February 2021; b. 8.3.66. Educ. Port Glasgow High School; Royal Scottish Academy of Music and Drama; University of Glasgow. Professional background in charity fundraising, communications, event management, political campaigning; trained political activists and elected members in public speaking across Africa and Asia, 2017-2019; political interests include supporting refugees, campaigning for recognition of drug addiction as a public health crisis, fighting racism, empowering communities, Sri Lanka, The Gambia. Member of SNP Socialists; Board Member, The Scottish Pantry Network; Board Member, Flag up Scotland Jamaica. SNP campaign co-ordinator when John Mason won the

Glasgow East by-election, 2008; former member of the Public Audit and Public Petitions parliamentary committees of the Scottish Parliament, 2009-2011; MSP, Scottish Parliament (Glasgow), 2009-2011; former member of the Committee on Standards and Select Committee on Women and Equalities at Westminster. Address: Houses of Parliament, Westminster, London SW1A 0AA.

McLaughlin, Christine. Director for Scottish Covid-19 Test and Protect Programme, The Scottish Government, since 2020; Director of Planning, NHS Scotland, The Scottish Government, 2020-2021 (Director of Health Finance, 2016-18, Chief Finance Officer, NHS Scotland and Director of Health Finance, Corporate Governance and Value, 2018-2020). Educ. St Ninian's High School, Kirkintilloch; University of Strathclyde. Career history: Financial Management, NHS Greater Glasgow & Clyde, 1992-2000; Executive Consultant: Atos Origin Consulting, 2000-04, Capgemini, 2004-05; Senior Consultant, PricewaterhouseCoopers, 2005-06; NHS National Services Scotland: Head of Financial Services, 2006-08, Interim Director of Finance, 2008-09; Deputy Director, The Scottish Government, 2010-2015. Address: Scottish Government, St. Andrews House, Regent Road, Edinburgh EH1 3DG; T.-0131 244 4000.

McLaughlin, Gerald. Chief Executive, NHS Health Scotland, 2010-2020 (retired). Career: worked for 20 years as a local authority social work manager, then Glasgow's principal child protection officer; Assistant Director, Royal National Institute for the Blind, Scotland, 1998-2000; Director, British Red Cross, 2000-2010. Formerly non executive member, Board of NHS Greater Glasgow and Clyde, 2004-2010.

McLaughlin, Sheriff Morag. Sheriff, Grampian, Highland and Islands, since 2018. Educ. University of Glasgow. Admitted as a solicitor in 1988; held a number of roles in the Crown Office between 1990 and 2011, including Area Procurator Fiscal for Grampian, 2005-2008 and Area Procurator Fiscal for Lothian and Borders, 2008-2011; Member of the Scotland committee of the Equality and Human Rights Commission, 2011-16; a Board Member of the Scottish Police Authority, 2012-16; a legal member of the Parole Board for Scotland, 2011-16; Summary Sheriff, Grampian, Highland and Islands, 2016-18. Address: Aberdeen Sheriff Court, 53 Castle Street, Aberdeen AB11 5BB; T.-01224 657200.

MacLaverty, Bernard. Writer; b. 14.9.42, Belfast; m., Madeline McGuckin; 1 s.; 3 d. Educ. St Malachy's College, Belfast; Queen's University, Belfast. Moved from Belfast to Scotland, 1975; has been a medical laboratory technician, a mature student, a teacher of English and, for two years in the mid-1980s, Writer-in-Residence at Aberdeen University; has been a Guest Writer for short periods at Liverpool John Moore's University, the University of Augsburg and Iowa State University; Member, Aosdana in Ireland; has published six collections of short stories and five novels; has witten versions of his fiction for other media, including radio plays, television plays, screenplays and libretti. Publications: Secrets and Other Stories, 1977; Lamb, 1980; A Time to Dance and other Stories, 1982; Cal, 1983; The Great Profundo and Other Stories, 1987; Walking the Dog and Other Stories, 1994; Grace Notes, 1997; The Anatomy School, 2001; Matters of Life & Death and other stories, 2006; Collected Stories, 2013; Midwinter Break, 2017; Blank Pages and Other Stories, 2021.

MacLaverty, Jude. Director, BAFTA Scotland, since 2011. Educ. Edinburgh College of Art. Career: Event Manager, The List Ltd, 2001; Event Co-ordinator, BAFTA Scotland, 2004; Celtic Media Festival: Festival Producer, 2001-07, Festival Director, 2007-2010.

Address: BAFTA Scotland, 103 Trongate, Glasgow G1 5HD; T.-0141 553 5402; e-mail: JudeM@bafta.org

Maclay, Baron (Joseph Paton Maclay), 3rd Baron; Bt. Deputy Lieutenant, Renfrewshire, 1986-2008; Director, Altnamara Shipping Plc, 1994-2002; Chairman, Northern Lighthouse Board, 2001-03 (Commissioner, 1996-2003, Vice Chairman, 2000-01); Chairman, Scottish Maritime Museum, 1998-2005; Chairman, Scottish Nautical Welfare Society, 2002-04; b. 11.4.42; m., Elizabeth Anne Buchanan; 2 s.; 1 d. Educ. Winchester; Sorbonne. Managing Director: Denholm Maclay Co. Ltd., 1970-83, Denholm Maclay (Offshore) Ltd., Triport Ferries (Management) Ltd., 1975-83; Deputy Managing Director, Denholm Ship Management Ltd., 1982-83; Director: Milton Shipping Co. Ltd., 1970-83, Marine Shipping Mutual Insurance Company, 1982-83; President, Hanover Shipping Inc., 1982-83; Director: British Steamship Short Trades Association, 1970-83, North of England Protection and Indemnity Association, 1976-83; Chairman, Scottish Branch, British Sailors Society, 1979-81; Vice-President, Glasgow Shipowners & Shipbrokers Benevolent Association, 1982-83 and 1997-98; President, Glasgow Shipowners and Shipbrokers Benevolent Association, 1998-99; Director, Denholm Ship Management (Holdings) Ltd., 1991-93; Group Marketing Executive, Acomarit Group, 1993-99; Trustee: Cattanach Charitable Trust, 1991-2011 (Chairman, 2009-2011), Western Isles Fisheries Trust, 2004-06, Western Isles Salmon Fisheries Board, 2004-06, Younger Benmore Trust, 2018-2021 (retired); President, The Garden Society of Scotland, 2019-2021 (retired). Address: (h.) Milton House, Kilmacolm, Renfrewshire PA13 4RP.

MacLean, Rt. Hon. Lord (Ranald Norman Munro MacLean), BA, LLB, LLM, PC, LLD, FSA(Scot), FRSE. Senator of the College of Justice, 1990-2005; Queen's Counsel, since 1977; b. 18.12.38, Aberdeen; m., Pamela Ross (m. dissolved); 3 s. (1 son deceased); 1 d. Educ. Inverness Royal Academy; Fettes College, Edinburgh; Cambridge University; Edinburgh University; Yale University. Advocate, 1964; Advocate Depute, 1972-75; Advocate Depute (Home), 1979-82; Chairman, The Cockburn Association (Edinburgh Civic Trust), 1988-96; Member, Secretary of State for Scotland's Criminal Justice Forum, 1996-2000; Member, Parole Board for Scotland, 1998-2000; Chairman, Committee on Serious Violent and Sexual Offenders, 1999-2000; Member, Scottish Judicial Appointments Board, 2002-05; Chairman: Sentencing Commission for Scotland, 2003-05, The Billy Wright Inquiry (Banbridge, Northern Ireland), 2004-2010, The Vale of Leven Hospital Inquiry, 2009-2014; Surveillance Commissioner, 2010-2016; Chairman of Governors, Fettes College, 1996-2006.

MacLean, A. Duncan, LLB, DipLP, NP, WS. Partner, Brodies LLP, since 2004 (specialist in shipping, transport and insurance); b. 19.2.66, Inverness; m., Esther; 2 d. Educ. Achtercairn Secondary; Dingwall Academy; Edinburgh University. Admitted as Solicitor, 1988; Trained, Guild & Guild, WS, Edinburgh; Solicitor, Brodies, WS, 1989-94; Associate, Henderson Boyd Jackson (now Addleshaw Goddard), Edinburgh, 1994, then Partner, 1996-2004. Member: Law Society of Scotland, UK Chamber of Shipping, British Ports Association, Scottish Maritime Cluster, British Maritime Law Association, Forum of Insurance Lawyers. Recreations: family; social action; sport; the outdoors; charity trustee. Address: (b.) 15 Atholl Crescent, Edinburgh EH3 8HA.

McLean, Catriona Mary, MB, BS, MRCP, FRCR. Consultant Clinical Oncologist, Western General Hospital,

Edinburgh, since 1996; b. 30.3.62, Kampala, Uganda; m., Cliff Culley; 1 s.; 1 d. Educ. Sutton High School GPDST; St. Bartholomew's Medical College, London. Address: (b.) Department of Clinical Oncology, Western General Hospital, Edinburgh; T.-0131-537 1000.

Maclean of Dunconnel, Sir Charles (Edward), Bt; b. 31.10.46; m.; 4 d. Educ. Eton; New College, Oxford. Publications: The Wolf Children; The Watcher; Island on the Edge of the World; Scottish Country; Romantic Scotland; The Silence. Address: (h.) Strachur House, Cairndow, Argyll PA27 8BX.

McLean, Colin William, MA, MBA, FIA, FSIP, FCSI. Managing Director, SVM Asset Management, since 1990; Non Executive Director, Public Health Scotland, since 2020; b. 1.10.52. Educ. Jordanhill College School, Glasgow; Glasgow University; Deputy General Manager, FS Assurance, 1974-86; Chief Investment Officer, Scottish Provident, 1986-88; Managing Director, Templeton International, 1988-90; Honorary Professor, Heriot-Watt University Edinburgh. Address: (b.) SVM Asset Management Ltd, 7 Castle Street, Edinburgh EH2 3AH; T.-0131-226 6699.

MacLean, Elizabeth Anne, OBE, MA. Former Convener, Mobility and Access Committee, Transport Scotland (2009-2017); b. 3.9.41, Falkirk; m., Alan Shute; 1 s. Educ. Beacon School, Bridge of Allan; University of London. Civil Servant, MOD and DHSS, 1964-73; Trade Union Officer, National Union of Civil and Public Servants, 1973-90; Assessor, Commissioner for Public Appointments Scotland, 2001-07; Board Member, Cairngorms National Park Authority, 2003-2010; Board Member and Chair, Albyn Housing Society, 1997-2007; Trustee, RNIB Scotland, 2002-2012; Committee Member, Sight Action Highlands & Islands, 1996-2012; Board Member and Vice Chair, Grantown Museum Heritage Trust, 1991-2001; Honorary Life Vice President, Grantown Museum and Heritage Trust, since 2017; Member of executive of the Scottish Labour Party, 1995-2005 and Chair, 2001-02; Member, Sensory Impairment Project Advisory Group of the Scottish Government. Recreations: reading; cooking; music (listening). Address: 8 Strathspey Gardens, Grantown on Spey PH26 3GZ; T.-01479 872812.

MacLean, Eoghainn Charles McEwen, LLB (Private Law Hons), DipLP. Advocate, since 1995; b. 17.4.66, Port of Aden; 2 s. Educ. High School of Glasgow; Glasgow University. Solicitor, McClure Naismith, 1991-93; Solicitor, McGrigor Donald, 1993-94; devil, 1994-95; called to Scots Bar, 1995; Member, Ampersand Stable of Advocates (see ampersandstable.com). Address: (h.) 4 Athole Gardens, Glasgow G12 9AY; T.-0141 560 2003.
E-mail: eoghainn.maclean@advocates.org.uk

MacLean, Gavin. Rector, Fortrose Academy, since 2018. Career history: started teaching at Dingwall Academy; moved to Fortrose Academy, promoted to senior teacher and became involved with pupil support; Principal Teacher of Physical Education and Acting Assistant Head, Crieff High School with curriculum, pupil support and guidance responsibilities; Depute Head Teacher (pupil support), Inverness High School; Acting Head Teacher at Kilchuimen Academy, Fort Augustus; Head Teacher, Glen Urquhart High School; Headteacher, Millburn Academy, 2011-18. Address: Academy Street, Fortrose IV10 8TW; T.-01381 620310.

Maclean, Iain Farquhar, LLB (Hons), LLM, MSc, DipLP. Advocate. Educ. Portree High School; University of Aberdeen; Emmanuel College, Cambridge; University of Edinburgh. Trainee Solicitor, Brodies WS, 1990-92; Legal Assistant to the Lord President, Court of Session, 1992-93;

admitted, Faculty of Advocates, 1994. Member, Scottish Government EU Agricultural Subsidies Appeals Procedure External Advisory Panel, 2005-2013; Member and Deputy Chairman, Scottish Land Court, since 2015. Address: George House, 126 George Street, Edinburgh EH2 4HH; T.-0131 271 4360.

McLean, Jack, DA, MSIAD. Freelance Writer and Broadcaster; b. 10.8.46, Irvine. Educ. Allan Glen's School; Edinburgh College of Art; Jordanhill College. Art Teacher in Glasgow for many years; The Scotsman, 1977-81; Glasgow Herald, 1981-97; The Scotsman, 1997-98; Scotland on Sunday, 1997-99; Sports Columnist, Scottish Daily Mail, 1999-2000; Columnist: The Herald, 2000-06, The Scottish Review, since 2006, other publicatons; Radio Clyde, 1982-85; BBC Scotland Art Critic and Adviser, 1991-95; Presenter, The Jack McLean Talk Show, Scottish Television. Columnist of the Year, British Press Awards, 1985; Recipient of several Scottish Press Awards. Publications: The Bedside Urban Voltaire; More Bedside Urban Voltaire; The Sporting Urban Voltaire; City of Glasgow; Hopeless But Not Serious; Earthquake; The Compendium of Nosh, 2006. Recreations: smoking; poverty; dressing; cooking.

MacLean, James Gordon Bruce, MBChB, FRCS. Consultant Orthopaedic Surgeon, Perth Royal Infirmary and Ninewells Hospital, Dundee, since 1994; Honorary Lecturer, Dundee University, since 1994; b. 17.5.58, Carlisle; m., Susan Jane Roberts; 2 s.; 2 d. Educ. Merchiston Castle School, Edinburgh; Dundee University Medical School. Basic surgical training, Norfolk and Norwich Hospitals; specialist orthopaedic training, St Bartholomew's Hospital, Great Ormond Street, Stanmore; Research Fellow/Junior Consultant, University of Capetown; Regional Children's Orthopaedic Surgeon, Tayside. Recreations: hill-walking; rugby; racquet sports; boating. Address: (b.) Orthopaedic Department, Perth Royal Infirmary, Perth PH1 1NX; T.-01738 623311.

Maclean of Duart, Major The Hon. Sir Lachlan, DL. Major, Scots Guards (retired); 28th Chief of Clan Maclean; b. 25.8.42.

MacLean, Rev. Marjory Anne, LLB, BD, PhD. Minister, Burray and South Ronaldsay Parish Church, Orkney, and Presbytery Development Officer, Presbytery of Orkney, since 2020; b. 11.6.62, Forfar. Educ. Forfar Academy; Edinburgh University. Trainee Solicitor, T.P. & J.L. Low, Kirkwall, 1985-87; Probationer, then Assistant Minister, Fairmilehead Parish Church, Edinburgh, 1990-92; Minister, Stromness Parish Church, 1992-98; Depute Secretary, Legal Questions Committee, and Depute Clerk, General Assembly of Church of Scotland, 1996-2010; Acting Principal Clerk, 2002-03 and 2009; Royal Naval Reserve Chaplain, 2004-2017; Minister, Abernyte linked with Inchture and Kinnaird linked with Longforgan Parish Churches, 2011-2020. Vice-Convener, Church of Scotland Ministries Council, 2014-2017; Convener, Church of Scotland Committee on Chaplains to Her Majesty's Forces, since 2018; Trustee, St Andrews Voices Festival, since 2019. Recreation: choral music. Address: The Manse, Church Road, St Margaret's Hope, Orkney KW17 2SR.

McLean, Miller Roy, MA, LLB, WS, NP, FCIBS, FIB. Group General Counsel, and Group Secretary, The Royal Bank of Scotland Group PLC, 2003-2010; former Chairman of the Industry and Parliament Trust and the Whitehall & Industry Group; b. 4.12.49, Scotland; m., Anne Charlotte Gourlay; 1 s.; 1 d. Educ. Vale of Leven Academy; Glasgow

University; Edinburgh University. The Royal Bank of Scotland Group plc: Assistant Secretary, 1982-83, Secretary, 1983-88; The Royal Bank of Scotland plc: Secretary, 1985-88, Group Secretary, 1988-90, Assistant Director, Legal and Administration, 1990-91, Director, Legal and Regulatory Affairs, 1991-94, Director, Group Legal and Regulatory Affairs and Group Secretary, 1994-2003; Director: Adam & Company Group Ltd, 1998-2017, The Royal Bank of Scotland, 2009-2017. Member of Court of Queen Margaret University, Edinburgh and the Executive Committee of the David Livingston Trust; Trustee of the Academy of Medical Royal Colleges. Recreations: golf; gardening; reading; music.

Maclean, Rob. Television presenter, sports commentator and sports writer; b. 26.11.58, Inverness; m., Pauline; 1 s.; 1 d. Educ. Invergordon Academy. Began career with the Highland News Group in Inverness; worked for an Aberdeen news agency, 1979-81; Northsound Radio for 6 years; BBC Scotland's flagship evening news programme Reporting Scotland, 1986-88; Scotland Today on STV, 1988-90; reporter for both Reporting Scotland and Sportscene, BBC Scotland, 1990-2004; main anchorman for live coverage of Scottish Premier League matches, Setanta Sports, 2004-09; main anchor of STV's UEFA Champions League coverage, 2010; commentator and reporter for BBC Radio Scotland; former Presenter, Sportscene, BBC. Recreations: playing football; golf; skiing; music; movies. Address: BBC Scotland, 40 Pacific Quay, Glasgow G51 1DA.

McLean, Una, MBE. Actress; b. 1930, Strathaven. Trained, Royal Scottish Academy of Music and Drama; professional debut, Byre, St. Andrews, 1955; pantomime debut, Mother Goose, 1958; joined Citizens' Theatre, Glasgow, 1959; appeared in Five Past Eight revue, 1960s; many television appearances.

Maclean, Emeritus Professor William James, MBE (2006), DA, RSA, FRSE, RGI, RSW. Emeritus Professor of Visual Arts, University of Dundee, since 2002, formerly Professor of Fine Art, Duncan of Jordanstone College, University of Dundee; b. 12.10.41, Inverness; m., Marian Forbes Leven; 2 s.; 1 d. Educ. Inverness Royal Academy; HMS Conway; Grays School of Art, Aberdeen. Postgraduate and Travel Scholarship, Scottish Education Trust Award, Visual Arts Bursary, Scottish Arts Council; Benno Schotz Prize; one-man exhibitions in Rome, Glasgow, Edinburgh and London; group exhibitions in Britain, Europe and North America; represented in private and public collections including Arts Council, British Museum, Scottish National Gallery of Modern Art, Fitzwilliam Museum, Cambridge, and Scottish museum collections. Hon. DLitt, St. Andrews University; Hon. Fellowship UHI (Univ. of Highlands), 2008; Hon. DLitt, University of Aberdeen, 2009; Fellow of Royal Society of Edinburgh (RSE). Address: (h.) Bellevue, 18 Dougall Street, Tayport, Fife.

MacLeary, Alistair Ronald, MSc, DipTP, FRICS, FRTPI. Honorary Fellow, Commonwealth Association of Surveying and Land Economy; Honorary Professor, Heriot-Watt University, 2003-09; Member, Administrative Justice and Tribunals Council and Chairman of its Scottish Committee, 2005-09; Member, Lands Tribunal for Scotland, 1989-2005; MacRobert Professor of Land Economy, Aberdeen University, 1976-89 (Dean, Faculty of Law, 1982-85); b. 12.1.40, Glasgow; m., Claire Leonard; 1 s.; 1 d. Educ. Inverness Royal Academy; College of Estate Management; Heriot-Watt University; Strathclyde University. Assistant Surveyor, Gerald Eve & Co., Chartered Surveyors, 1962-65; Assistant to Director, Murrayfield Real Estate Co. Ltd.,

1965-67; Assistant Surveyor and Town Planner/Partner, Wright & Partners, 1967-76; seconded to Department of the Environment, London, 1971-73; Member: Committee of Inquiry into the Acquisition and Occupancy of Agricultural Land, 1977-79, Home Grown Timber Advisory Committee, Forestry Commission, 1981-87; Chairman, Board of Education, Commonwealth Association of Surveying and Land Economy, 1981-90; President, Planning and Development Division, Royal Institution of Chartered Surveyors, 1984-85; Editor, Land Development Studies, 1986-90; Member, Natural Environment Research Council, 1988-91. Recreation: golf. Address: (h.) 1/A Greenhill Court, Edinburgh EH9 1BF; T.-0131 452 8775.

McLeish, Alex. National Coach, Scottish Football Association, 2018-19; b. 21.1.59, Glasgow. Educ. Barrhead High School; John Neilson High School. Began professional career playing for Aberdeen Football Club, 1976; won with Aberdeen: European Cup Winners Cup medal, Super Cup medal, five Scottish Cup medals, two League Cup medals, three Championship medals; Player of the Year, Aberdeen, 1990; 77 caps for Scotland, 1980-83; Manager: Motherwell, 1994-98, Hibernian, 1998-2001, Rangers, 2001-06, Scotland, 2007, Birmingham City, 2007-2011 (League Cup winners, 2011), Aston Villa, 2011-12, Nottingham Forest, 2012-13, Genk, 2014-15, Zamalek, 2016.

McLeish, Chris, LLB (Hons). Partner, Morton Fraser LLP, since 2021; b. 2.77. Educ. University of Glasgow. Career history: Trainee Solicitor, Davidson Chalmers LLP, 1999-2001; Partner, DWF, Glasgow, 2001-2021. Address: Morton Fraser LLP, 5th Floor, Quartermile Two, 2 Lister Square, Edinburgh EH3 9GL; T.-0141 375 0792. E-mail: chris.mcleish@morton-fraser.com

McLeish, Rt. Hon. Henry Baird, PC. MP (Labour), Fife Central, 1987-2001; MSP (Labour), Central Fife, 1999-2003; First Minister of Scotland, 2000-01, Minister for Enterprise and Learning, 1999-2000; b. 15.6.48; m.; 1 s.; 1 step-s.; 1 d.; 1 step-d. Educ. Buckhaven High School, Methil; Heriot-Watt University. Former Research Officer and Planning Officer in local government; former Member, Kirkcaldy District Council and Fife Regional Council (Leader, 1982-87); Scottish Front Bench Spokesman for Education and Employment, 1988-89, for Employment and Training, 1989-92; Shadow Scottish Minister of State, 1992-94; Shadow Minister of Transport, 1994-95; Shadow Minister for Health, 1995-97; Minister of State, Scottish Office (Minister for Home Affairs, Local Government and Devolution), 1997-99. Visiting Professor: University of Arkansas, University of Denver; Visiting Lecturer, US Airforce Academy, Colarado. Honorary Fellow: Edinburgh University; Cambridge Land Institute at Fitzwilliam College, Cambridge. Publications: Scotland First: truth and consequences, 2004; Global Scots: Making It in the Modern World (Co-Author), 2006; Wherever the Saltire Flies (Co-Author), 2006; Scotland: The Road Divides (Co-Author), 2007. Recreations: reading; history; life and work of Robert Burns; malt whisky; Highlands and Islands.

McLeish, John F., BCom, PGDip, FSA (Scot), FCIBS, Chartered FCIPD, FCMI. Chief Executive, The Gordon Highlanders Museum, since 2019; Chair, The Scottish Tartans Authority, since 2012; Trustee, Museums Galleries Scotland, 2017-18 and since February 2019; Director, Braemar Highland Games Visitor Centre, since 2018. Educ. Perth Grammar School; The University of Edinburgh; Napier University; Harvard Business School. Career: Head of HR, TSB Scotland and Lloyds TSB Scotland, 1997-2001; HR Director, Andersen, 2001-02; HR Director, UK Bus Division, FirstGroup, 2003-05; Group HR Director, RBG Limited, 2006-2011; Integration Director, Stork, 2011-12; Vice President, Human Resources, Stork, 2012-15; HR Consultancy, Museums Galleries Scotland, 2016; HR Business Consultant, Amec Foster Wheeler, 2016-17;

Interim CEO, Museums Galleries Scotland, 2018-19. Awards Judge and Advisor, Family Friendly Working Scotland, since 2015. Advisor to Scottish Register of Tartans, since 2015. Address: Museums Galleries Scotland, Waverley Gate, 2-4 Waterloo Place, Edinburgh EH1 3EG.

McLellan, Very Rev. Andrew Rankin Cowie, CBE, MA, BD, STM, DD. HM Chief Inspector of Prisons for Scotland, 2002-09; Minister, St. Andrew's at St. George's, Edinburgh, 1986-2002; Moderator, General Assembly, Church of Scotland, 2000; b. 16.6.44, Glasgow; m., Irene L. Meek; 2 s. Educ. Kilmarnock Academy; Madras College, St. Andrews; St. Andrews University; Glasgow University; Union Theological Seminary, New York. Assistant Minister, St. George's West, Edinburgh, 1969-71; Minister: Cartsburn Augustine, Greenock, 1971-80, Viewfield, Stirling, 1980-86; Member, Inverclyde District Council, 1977-80; Tutor, Glasgow University, 1978-82; Chaplain, HM Prison, Stirling, 1982-85; Convener, Church and Nation Committee, General Assembly, 1992-96; Chairman, Scottish Religious Advisory Committee, BBC, 1996-2001; Moderator, Church and Society Forum, Churches Together in Britain and Ireland, 1999-2002; Convener, Parish Development Fund, General Assembly, 2002-06; Director, Scottish Television, 2003-07. Warrack Lecturer on Preaching, 2000; Unitas Award, Union Seminary, 2008; Convener, World Mission Council, General Assembly, 2010-2014; Boys' Brigade Chaplain, UK and Ireland, 2013-2016; Convener, McLellan Commission on Safeguarding in the Catholic Church in Scotland, 2015; Chair, National Prison Visitors Centre Steering Group, 2017-2020. Publications: Preaching for these People, 1997; Gentle and Passionate, 2001. Recreations: sport; travel; books; gardening. Address: (h.) 4 Liggars Place, Dunfermline KY12 7XZ.

McLellan, Douglas Richard, MD, FRCPath, FRCP (Glas). DipFM. Consultant, Victoria Infirmary/Southern General Hospital, Glasgow, since 1989; Honorary Senior Lecturer, Glasgow University, since 1989; b. 13.6.55, Glasgow; m., Caitriona; 3 s. Educ. High School of Glasgow; Glasgow University. Registrar in Pathology, Southern General Hospital, Glasgow, 1978-81; Honorary Senior Registrar in Neuropathology (MRC Head Injury Project), Institute of Neurological Sciences, Glasgow, 1981-84; Senior Registrar in Pathology, Western Infirmary, Glasgow, 1984-89. Recreations: bibliomania; Celtology. Address: (h.) 8 Calderwood Road, Newlands, Glasgow G43 2RP.

MacIellan, Professor Euphemia (Effie), BA (Hons), PhD, CPsychol, FHEA, AFBPsS. Emeritus Professor of University of Strathclyde; Research Professor of Education, School of Education, 2010-2014; Professor of Education and Vice Dean (Research), 2005-09; b. Glasgow; m., Alasdair Graham. Taught and researched at the psychological/educational interface, 1988-2005; Associate Lecturer, Open University, 1992-99. Working in higher education followed 21 years of professional practice in mainstream primary and special education. Member of the European Association for Research on Learning and Instruction, of the British Psychological Society, of the General Teaching Council (Scotland); Member of the Editorial Boards of Educational Research Review and of Instructional Science. Executive Editor of Teaching and Teacher Education (TATE). Recreation: keen Scottish country dancer. Address: (b.) School of Education, University of Strathclyde, Lord Hope Building, Glasgow G4 0LT; e-mail: e.maclellan@strath.ac.uk

McLellan, John Crawford, BA. Director, The Scottish Newspaper Society, since 2013; Honorary Professor, Communications, Media and Culture Department, University of Stirling, since 2012; b. 8.2.62, Glasgow; m., Patricia; 2 s.; 1 d. Educ. Hutchesons' Grammar School; Stirling University; Preston Polytechnic. Chester Observer, 1984-86; NW Evening Mail, 1987-90; The Journal, Newcastle, 1990-93; Edinburgh Evening News, 1993-2001 (Editor, 1997-2001 and 2004-09); Editor, Scotland on Sunday, 2002-04; Editor, The Scotsman, 2009-2012; Director of Communications, Scottish Conservative Party, 2012-2013. Former Commissioner, Press Complaints Commission; Member, Defence and Security Media Advisory Committee. Recreations: rugby; football; music. Address: (b.) 17 Polwarth Grove, Edinburgh, EH11 1LY.

McLennan, Paul Stewart. MSP (SNP) East Lothian, since 2021. Educ. Dunbar Grammar School. Career history: Bank of Scotland, Edinburgh: Financial Adviser, 2000-06; Business Banking Client Manager, 2006-2010; East Lothian Council: Senior Councillor, Haddington, 2007-2012; Council Leader, Haddington, 2010-2012; Senior Researcher, The Scottish Parliament, 2012-16; Consultant, Newgate Communications, Edinburgh, 2016-2017; Consultant (Account Manager), PPS Group, Edinburgh, 2016-2021; Associate Director, Playfair Scotland, Edinburgh, 2017-2021. Former Board Member: NHS Lothian, the regional offices of Scottish Enterprise and the Commission on School Reform. Address: The Scottish Parliament, Edinburgh EH99 1SP; T.-0131 348 5083. E-mail: Paul.McLennan.msp@parliament.scot

MacLennan, Shona C., MA. Chief Executive, Bòrd na Gàidhlig, since 2016. Educ. University of Edinburgh. Career history: Owner, Solas Business Services Ltd, 1999-2013; Director of Business and Organisational Development, Sabhal Mòr Ostaig, 2013-16. Address: Bòrd na Gàidhlig, Great Glen House, Leachkin Road, Inverness IV3 8NW; T.-01463 225454.

McLeod, Dr Aileen. Member of the European Parliament for Scotland (SNP), 2019-2020; MSP (SNP), South Scotland, 2011-16; Minister for Environment, Climate Change and Land Reform, 2014-16; b. 24.8.71, East Kilbride. Educ. Edinburgh University; University of Central Lancashire. Joined the SNP in 2004 on leaving post in the Scottish Parliament; spent 5 years living in Brussels and working as Head of Policy for Alyn Smith MEP; returned home in 2009 to fight the European Parliamentary elections for the SNP; Parliamentary Assistant to Michael Russell MSP, 2009-2011.

MacLeod, Alasdair Fraser, MA (Hons). Head of Editorial Standards and Compliance, BBC Scotland, since 2009; b. 11.1.64, Inverness; m., Catriona Murray; 1 s.; 2 d. Educ. Millburn Academy, Inverness; Glasgow University. BBC Scotland: trainee journalist, Radio Nan Gaidheal, 1986; Researcher, Gaelic television, 1987; Producer, Radio Nan Gaidheal, 1988; Producer, Radio Scotland, 1990; Senior Producer, Radio Scotland, 1993; Editor, weekly programmes, News and Current Affairs, 1994; Editor, Scottish Parliamentary Unit, 1999; Executive Editor, Political Programmes, 2004; Executive Editor, News Programmes, 2007. Address: (b.) BBC Scotland, Pacific Quay, Glasgow G51 1DA.

Macleod, Rev. Callum. Minister, Shawbost Free Church of Scotland; Principal Clerk of the General Assembly, Free Church of Scotland, 2016-18. Address: Shawbost Free Church of Scotland, Free Church Manse, Shawbost, Isle of Lewis HS2 9BD; T.-01851 710216. E-mail: cmacleod@freechurch.org

MacLeod, Rev. Calum I., BA (Econ), BD (Divinity). Minister, St Giles' Cathedral, The High Kirk of Edinburgh, since 2014; b. 1968; m., Missy; 1 d. Educ. University of

Strathclyde; University of Glasgow. Probationer Assistant, then Assistant Minister, St Columba's Church of Scotland, London, 1994-97; Ordained in March 1996; appointed to the staff of Fourth Presbyterian Church, Chicago in September 1997; served the congregation in a number of capacities concluding as Executive Associate Pastor and Head of Staff. Address: St Giles' Cathedral, High Street, Edinburgh EH1 1RE; T.-0131 226 0674.
E-mail: calum.macleod@churchofscotland.org.uk

McLeod, Fiona. MSP (SNP), Strathkelvin and Bearsden, 2011-16; Acting Minister for Children and Young People, 2014-15; b. 3.12.57; m.; 1 s. Graduated in medieval and modern history at Glasgow University. A chartered librarian, has worked in education and the health service. SNP regional list member of the Scottish Parliament, 1999-2003.

MacLeod of MacLeod, Hugh. 30th Chief of Clan MacLeod; b. 24.07.73, London; 1 d.; 1 s. Succeeded to title, 2007. Address: (h.) Dunvegan Castle, Isle of Skye IV55 8WF.

MacLeod, Professor Iain Alasdair, BSc, PhD, CEng, FIES, FICE, FIStructE. Professor Emeritus; Professor of Structural Engineering, Strathclyde University, 1981-2004; b. 4.5.39, Glasgow; m., Barbara Jean Booth; 1 s.; 1 d. Educ. Lenzie Academy; Glasgow University. Design Engineer, Crouch and Hogg, Glasgow, 1960-62; Assistant Lecturer in Civil Engineering, Glasgow University, 1962-66; Design Engineer, H.A. Simons Ltd., Vancouver, 1966-67; Structural Engineer, Portland Cement Association, Illinois, 1968-69; Lecturer in Civil Engineering, Glasgow University, 1969-73; Professor and Head, Department of Civil Engineering, Paisley College of Technology, 1973-81; Chairman, Scottish Branch, Institution of Structural Engineers, 1985-86; Vice-President, Institution of Structural Engineers, 1989-90; Member, Standing Committee on Structural Safety, 1989-97; President, Institution of Engineers and Shipbuilders in Scotland, 2012-14. Recreations: hill walking; sailing. Address: (b.) Department of Civil Engineering, Strathclyde University, 75 Montrose Street, Glasgow G1 1XJ.

MacLeod, Professor James Summers, BA, LLM, CA, CTA. Honorary Professor, Department of Accountancy, Edinburgh University, since 1984; Visiting Professor, Faculty of Law, Edinburgh University, 1998-2002; b. 3.8.41, Dumfries; m., (1.) Sheila Stromier (deceased); (2.) Rosemary Hoy; 2 s.; 1 d. Educ. Dumfries Academy; Glasgow University. Lecturer, Edinburgh University, 1965-68; Lecturer, Heriot Watt University, 1968-71; joined Arthur Young (now Ernst & Young), 1971; Partner, Ernst & Young, Edinburgh, 1973-98; former Director, British Assets Trust PLC, Scottish Investment Trust PLC and other companies (1998-2015). Publications: Taxation of Insurance Business (Co-author), 4th edition, 1998; 250 papers. Recreations: bridge; music; reading. Address: (h.) 50 New Swanston, Edinburgh; T.-0131-445 4748.

MacLeod, Jane Margaret. Lord-Lieutenant for Argyll and Bute, since 2020; previously Vice Lord-Lieutenant; leading member of the local business community.

Macleod, John Francis Matheson, MA, LLB, NP. Solicitor in Inverness, 1959-94; b. 24.1.32, Inverness; m., Alexandra Catherine (deceased); 1 s. Educ. Inverness Royal Academy; George Watson's College; Edinburgh University. Solicitor, Fife County Council, 1957-59; in private practice, 1959-94; Parliamentary candidate (Liberal): Moray and

Nairn, 1964, Western Isles, 1966; Chairman, Highland Region, Scottish Liberal Party, until 1978; former Vice-Chairman, Broadcasting Council for Scotland; Dean, Faculty of Solicitors of the Highlands, 1988-91; Chairman, Crofters Commission, 1978-86; Member, Council, Law Society of Scotland, 1988-92; Chairman of Council, Gaelic Society of Inverness, 1996-97, Chief for 2005; Chairman, National Trust for Scotland's Culloden Advisory Panel, 2006-2011. Address: (h.) Bona Lodge, Aldourie, Inverness; T.-01463 751327.

MacLeod, John Murray, MA (Hons). Journalist; Writer at Large: Columnist, The Scotsman, 1990-92; Columnist, The Herald, 1991-2002; Columnist, Scottish Daily Mail, since 2002; b. 15.4.66, Kilmallie, Inverness-shire. Educ. Jordanhill College School, Glasgow; James Gillespie's High School, Edinburgh; Edinburgh University. Freelance journalist and writer, since 1988; Scottish Journalist of the Year, 1991; Young Scottish Journalist of the Year, 1991, 1992; Runner-up, Columnist of the Year, 1992, 2008; Runner-up, Feature Writer of the Year, 1996; nominations for Columnist of the Year, 1999, 2001 and 2003; Columnist of the Year, UK Press Gazette Regional Newspaper Awards, 1996. Publications: No Great Mischief If You Fall – The Highland Experience, 1993; Highlanders – A History of the Gaels, 1996; Dynasty – The Stuarts 1560-1807, 1999; Banner in the West - A Spiritual History of Lewis and Harris, 2008; When I Heard The Bell - The Loss of the Iolaire, 2009; Banner in the West, 2010; River of Fire, 2010; None Dare Oppose, 2011. Recreations: walking; cooking; gawking at car ferries. Address: (h.) Drover's Rest, Marybank, Isle of Lewis HS2 0DG; T.-mobile 07776-236-337; 01851-700-275.
E-mail: jm.macleod@btinternet.com

MacLeod, Lorne Buchanan, BA, CA. Commissioner, Scottish Land Commission, since 2017; Commercial Director, Jans (Isle of Skye), since 2001; Chartered Accountant; b. 13.4.63, Oban. Educ. Oban High School; University of Strathclyde. Ernst and Whinney, Inverness, 1983-87; Highlands and Islands Development Board, 1987-92; Chief Executive, Skye and Lochalsh Enterprise, 1992-98; Director of Strengthening Communities, Highlands and Islands Enterprise, 1998-2000. Director, Comunn na Gaidhlig, 1998-2000; Director, Highlands and Islands Screen Services Ltd., 1998-2000; Board Member, Community Fund, 2001-03. Council Member, Scottish Further Education Funding Council, 2001-05; Director: Isle of Gigha Heritage Trust, 2002-08, Oban War and Peace Museum, 2003-07; Chairman, Highlands & Islands Community Energy Company, 2004-08; Director: Gigha Renewable Energy Ltd., 2004-08, Canan Limited, 2006-11, Cal Mac Ferries Limited, 2006-2012, David MacBrayne Limited, 2006-2012, Stòras Uibhist, South Uist Estate, 2007-2016, Northlink Ferries Ltd., 2009-11, Community Land Scotland, 2010-2016, latterly as Chairman; Winston Churchill Travelling Fellowship, 1997. Recreations: cycling, hillwalking; gardening. Address: (h.) 4/6 Lismore House, Station Road, Oban, Argyll PA34 4NU.
E-mail: lorne.macleod@btconnect.com

McLeod, Professor Malcolm Donald, CBE, DLitt (Hon), MA, BLitt (Oxon), FRSE, FSA Scot. Vice-Principal, Advancement, University of Glasgow, 1999-2005, Pro Vice-Principal, 2005-06; Trustee, The Hunterian Museum, London, since 1998; b. 19.5.41, Edinburgh; 2 s.; 1 d. Educ. Birkenhead School; Hertford and Exeter Colleges, Oxford. Research Assistant, Institute of Social Anthropology, Oxford, 1964-65; Lecturer, Sociology Department, University of Ghana, 1967-69; Assistant Curator, Museum of Archaeology and Ethnology, Cambridge, 1969-74; College Lecturer and Director of Studies, Magdalene and Girton Colleges, Cambridge, 1969-74; Fellow, Magdalene

College, 1972-74; Keeper of Ethnography, British Museum, 1974-90; Director, Hunterian Museum and Art Gallery, Glasgow University, 1990-99; Honorary Lecturer, Department of Anthropology, UCL, 1976-81; Honorary Lecturer, Department of Archaeology, University of Glasgow, 1992-2006; Chairman, Scottish Museums Council, 1996-2001; Curator, The Royal Society of Edinburgh, 1999-2002; Chairman, Caledonian Foundation Inc., USA, 2003-07; Trustee, National Museum of Scotland, 2005-2013; Trustee, Borders Sculpture Park, since 2013. Publications: The Asante, 1981; Treasures of African Art, 1981; Ethnic Sculpture (Co-author), 1985; Jacob Epstein Collector (Co-author), 1989; Peter Manuel, Serial Killer (Co-author), 2009. Address: (h.) The Schoolhouse, Oxnam, Jedburgh TD8 6NB.

Macleod, Mary Elizabeth, LLB (Hons), DipLP, NP. Solicitor of the Church of Scotland and Law Agent to the General Assembly, since 2016; b. 23.12.63, Stornoway. Educ. Nicolson Institute, Stornoway; Edinburgh University. Trainee Solicitor, Anderson, Shaw and Gilbert, Inverness, 1986-88; Assistant: Morton, Fraser and Milligan, WS, Edinburgh, 1988-90, Skene, Edwards and Garson, W. S., Edinburgh, 1990-92, Campbell Smith, Edinburgh, 1992-95; Depute Solicitor, Church of Scotland, 1995-2016. Recreations: travel; music; reading. Address: (b.) 121 George Street, Edinburgh EH2 4YN; T.-0131-225 5722.

Macleod, Michelle. Police Investigations & Review Commissioner, since 2019; previously Her Majesty's Chief Inspector of Prosecution, 2013-19. Career history: joined the Fiscal Service in 1992 as a trainee and has held various roles across Scotland, including Area Procurator Fiscal for Central, Head of Policy at Crown Office and Procurator Fiscal, High Court East (responsible for the investigation, prosecution and management of all High Court cases in the East of Scotland). Address: Hamilton House, Hamilton Business Park, Caird Park, Hamilton ML3 0QA; T.-01698 542900.

Macleod, Peter. Chief Executive, Care Inspectorate, 2018-2022 (retired). Educ. Robert Gordon University. Career history: began career as a social worker in Glasgow in 1987; worked in a range of front line social work services, with a particular interest in working with children and young people; joined Renfrewshire council in 1996 as an area manager, responsible for adult, children's and criminal justice social work in a busy locality team; appointed head of children's services and criminal justice for social work and the community health partnership in 2007; appointed director of social work in 2007; appointed president of the Association of Directors of Social Work in 2012; Renfrewshire's first director of a new children's services directorate, bringing together children's social work, education and criminal justice services, 2015-18. Chair of the Institute for Research and Innovation in Social Services; co-chaired national groups looking at outcomes and commissioning in relation to health and care integration; sit on the boards of MacMillan Cancer Support TCAT Programme and Scottish Government's Re-aligning Children's Services programme. Volunteered in social care services abroad, including in Tanzania. Recreations: enjoy mountains; outdoor swimming and cycling; my family; climbed Mount Kilimanjaro in 2017.

MacLeod, Rev. Dr Roderick Alexander Randle, MA, MBA, BD, DMin. Minister, Strath & Sleat, Isle of Skye, since 2015; formerly Minister, Parish Church of The Holy Trinity, St. Andrews (2004-2015); b. 16.2.65, Edinburgh; m., Annice (nee MacDonald); 1 s.; 2 d. Educ. Fettes College; Universities of Cambridge, Edinburgh, St. Andrews, Aberdeen and Pittsburgh Theological Seminary.

Army: Short Service Limited Commission (SSLC), Queens Own Highlanders; Teaching: Schoolmaster, Loretto School, Musselburgh; Church: Assistant Minister, Portree, Isle of Skye; Parish Minister, Bracadale, Isle of Skye; Navy Chaplain, 40 Commando; Commando Training Centre; Royal Marines, Poole; Parish Minister, Holy Trinity, St. Andrews. Recreations: traditional Scottish music; outdoor pursuits; travel; Gaelic language and culture. Address: Church of Scotland Manse, 6 Upper Breakish, Isle of Skye IV42 8PY; e-mail: rorymofg@gmail.com

MacLeod, Roderick John, MBE, BSc. Former Principal, The National Piping Centre (1996-2020); b. 26.8.62, Johnstone; m., Margaret. Educ. Eastwood High School; University of Strathclyde. Mathematics Teacher, Cleveden Secondary School, Glasgow, 1983-93; Assistant Principal, Mathematics, Dalziel High School, Motherwell, 1993-96. Winner, Highland Society of London gold medals; winner, piping, National Mod; Editor, Piping Today. Publication: The Highland Bagpipe Tutor Book (Editor). Address: (h.) 12 Medrox Gardens, Condorrat, Cumbernauld; T.-0141 353 0220.

MacLeod, Veronika. Honorary Consul of the Czech Republic in Scotland, since 2021. Educ. Technical University of Liberec. Czech language Tutor, The Univesity of Edinburgh, 2014-2022; Director, Czech School Scotland CIC, Edinburgh, since 2018. Address: Consulate General of the Czech Republic, 14 Eskside West, Musselburgh EH21 6PL; T.-0773 296 1720.
E-mail: edinburgh@honorary.mzv.cz

MacLeod, Rev. William, BSc, ThM. Minister, Knightswood Free Church (Continuing), 2006-2021; Principal, Free Church Seminary, 2002-2014; Lecturer in Systematic Theology, Free Church Seminary, 2017-2021; Editor, Free Church Witness, 2000-2017; b. 2.11.51, Stornoway; m., Marion; 2 s.; 1 d. Educ. Aberdeen University; Free Church College; Westminster Seminary. Minister: Partick Free Church, Glasgow, 1976-93, Portree Free Church, 1993-2006. Editor, Free Church Foundations, 1997-2000; former Chairman, Portree High School Board. Recreations: gardening; fishing; reading. Address: (h.) 25 Branklyn Crescent, Academy Park, Glasgow G13 1GJ; T.-0141 959 0292; e-mail: william@themacleods.org.uk

McLusky, Donald S., BSc, PhD. Senior Lecturer in Marine Biology, Stirling University, 1977-2003; Editor, Estuarine Coastal and Shelf Science, 2000-2010; b. 27.6.45, Harrogate; m., Ruth Alicia Donald; 1 s.; 2 d. Educ. Latymer Upper School, London; Aberdeen University; Stirling University. Stirling University: Assistant Lecturer, 1968-70, Lecturer, 1970-77, Head of Department of Biological Sciences, 1985 and 1992-98. Member, Council, Scottish Marine Biological Association, 1976-82, and 1985-91; Member, Scientific Advisory Committee, Scottish Natural Heritage, 1999-2005; Trustee, Estuarine and Coastal Sciences Association; Chair, Central Scotland Valuation Appeal Committee. Publications: Ecology of Estuaries, 1971; The Estuarine Ecosystem, 2004; The Natural Environment of the Estuary and Firth of Forth, 1987; The Estuaries of Central Scotland, 1997; Central Scotland, Land, Wildlife, People, 1993; The Freshwaters of Scotland, 1994; Treatise on Estuarine and Coastal Science, 2011. Recreations: nature; walking; swimming; travel. Address: (h.) Ardoch Cottage, Strathyre, Callander FK18 8NF; T.-01877 384309; e-mail: d.mclusky@btinternet.com

McMahon, Professor Alex. Chief Nursing Officer, The Scottish Government, since 2021; Executive Director of Nursing, Midwifery and AHPs, NHS Lothian, 2008-2021.

Career history: started career as an NHS student nurse in 1983; trained in psychiatric nursing and then later general nursing training; worked as a staff nurse, then a charge nurse and manager for many years until leaving the NHS in 1994; took up the post as Head of Policy at the Royal College of Nursing before leaving that post in 2002; moved to AstraZeneca, a global pharmaceutical company, as their Head of Government Affairs for Scotland and Ireland; worked for the Scottish Government for five and a half years until 2008; Honorary Chair of the University of Stirling, Professor of Applied Social Sciences. Address: The Scottish Government, St Andrew's House, Edinburgh EH1 3DG.

McMahon, Hugh Robertson, MA (Hons), FEIS. Member (Labour), European Parliament, Strathclyde West, 1984-99; Scottish Political Editor, World-Parliamentarian Magazine, since 1999; Lecturer/Consultant, James Watt College, 1999-2011 (retired); Lecturer, Politics, University of Edinburgh, 2003-2010; Visiting Professor, Brookdale CC, New Jersey, 2001; b. 17.6.38, Saltcoats; m., Helen Paterson Grant; 1 s.; 1 d. Educ. Stevenston High School; Ardrossan Academy; Glasgow University. Schoolteacher in Ayrshire (Largs High, Stevenston High, Irvine Royal Academy, Mainholm Academy); Assistant Head, Ravenspark Academy, 1971-84. Vice-Chair, EP Social Affairs, Employment and Working Environment Committee, 1992-94; Member, Social Affairs, Fisheries and Transport Committees; Chair, EP Delegation with Norway, 1989-92; Member: Delegation with Czechoslovakia, EIS, NUJ, GMB; Delegation with Hungary, 1994-96. Scottish Parliament Cross Party Group, Poland, since 2013; Chair, Paisley First Steering Group, 2011-15. Recreation: golf. Address: 47 Roffey Park Road, Paisley PA1 3JL.

McMahon, Professor Malcolm Iain, BSc, PhD, DSc, FInstP. Professor of High Pressure Physics, The University of Edinburgh, since 2007; b. 13.01.65, Dundee. Educ. Carnoustie High School; The University of Edinburgh. Postdoctoral Research Associate, University of Edinburgh, 1990-96; Royal Society University Research Fellow: University of Liverpool, 1996-98, University of Edinburgh, 1998-2003; Reader in Physics, University of Edinburgh, 2002-07. Recreations: hillwalking; whisky appreciation. Address: (b.) School of Physics, The University of Edinburgh, Mayfield Road, Edinburgh EH9 3JZ; T.-0131 650 5956; e-mail: m.i.mcmahon@ed.ac.uk

McMahon, Michael, BA (Hons). MSP (Labour), Uddingston and Bellshill, 2011-16, Hamilton North and Bellshill, 1999-2011; Shadow Cabinet Secretary for Local Government & Planning, 2009-2016; Convener, Public Petitions Committee, Scottish Parliament, 2003-07; Shadow Deputy Minister for Parliament and Labour Chief Whip, since 2007; Shadow Cabinet Secretary for Parliamentary Business, 2007-09; b. 18.9.61; m.; 1 s.; 2 d. Educ. Our Lady's High School, Motherwell. Worked as a welder before leaving to go to university; then pursued a career in social and political research.

MacMahon, Professor Michael Kenneth Cowan, BA, PhD, DipLing, FBAAP, FRSA. Honorary Professorial Research Fellow; Professor Emeritus of Phonetics, Glasgow University; b. 7.8.43, Winchester; m., Janet (deceased); 1 s.; 1 d. Educ. Hymers College, Hull; Durham University; Göttingen University; Glasgow University; Reading University. Lecturer in Phonetics and Linguistics, Jordanhill College, Glasgow, 1966-72; Lecturer in Linguistics and Phonetics, 1972-83, Lecturer in English Language, 1983-87, Senior Lecturer in English Language, 1987-97, Professor of Phonetics, 1997-2008, Glasgow University. Senate Assessor to the University Court, 1995-99.

Governor, Hutchesons' Educational Trust, 2003-08; Consultant to the Oxford English Dictionary; Treasurer, International Phonetic Association, 2003-08; President, Henry Sweet Society for the History of Linguistic Ideas, 2008-2016; Archivist and Secretary, British Association of Academic Phoneticians, 1978-2012. Publications: numerous. Recreations: researching and playing the flute; singing. Address: (h.) 44 Norwood Park, Bearsden, Glasgow G61 2RZ.
E-mail: mike.macmahon@glasgow.ac.uk

McMahon, Siobhan. MSP (Labour), Central Scotland, 2011-16; b. 4.7.84. Graduated from Glasgow Caledonian University with a degree in politics. Worked for the Labour group in the Scottish Parliament and was a research assistant to Jim Murphy MP and Ken Macintosh MSP.

McManus, Janie. Strategic Director (Scrutiny), Education Scotland. Responsible for leading and directing inspection programmes across Education Scotland, ensuring they provide assurance on quality and improvement in education and ensuring inspection makes significant contribution to Education Scotland's suite of improvement approaches; responsibility for the future direction of all Education Scotland's scrutiny work. Previously worked jointly with Scottish Government developing the Scottish Attainment Challenge programme; seconded to work with The Standing International Conference of Inspectorates to develop their strategic plan; also led Education Scotland's work with local authorities. Address: Education Scotland, The Optima, 58 Robertson Street, Glasgow G2 8DU; T.-0131 244 3000.

McManus, Professor John, DSc, PhD, ARCS, DIC, FRSE, FRSGS, CGeol. Professor of Geology, St. Andrews University, 1993-2001, now Emeritus Professor (Reader, 1988-93); Honorary Director, Tay Estuary Research Centre, 1979-92; b. 5.6.38, Harwich; m. (1), J. Barbara Beveridge (deceased 2007); 2 s.; 1 d.; m. (2), Winifred Harley, 2020. Educ. Harwich County High School; Imperial College, London University. Assistant, then Lecturer, St. Andrews University, 1964-67; Lecturer, Senior Lecturer, Reader, Dundee University, 1967-88; UNESCO Representative, International Commission on Continental Erosion, 1980-84 and 1986; Member: Scottish Natural Heritage East Areas Board and Scientific Advisory Committee, 1992-99, Secretary of State's Committee on Waste Discharges into the Marine Environment; President, Estuarine and Brackish Water Sciences Association, 1995-98; Member, Executive, European Union for Coastal Conservation, 1997-2000; Member, Scottish Environment Protection Agency East Region Board, 2000-07; Member, Eden Estuary Nature Reserve Management Committee; former Treasurer, British Sedimentological Research Group; Consultant on Coastal Erosion and Protection to four Regional Councils; Honorary Fellow, Royal Scottish Geographical Society, since 2001; Trustee, Fife Folk Museum, 2011. Publications: Mining between Ceres and St Andrews, 2010; History of Coal Mining in the East Neuk of Fife, 2017; The Centurion's Daughter, 2020; Executive Editor, Transactions of the Royal Society of Edinburgh, Earth Sciences, 1988-95; Associate Editor, Continental Shelf Research. President: Cupar Choral Association, 1968-78, Cupar Amateur Opera, 1979-91. Recreations: music; East Fife Male Voice Choir; Fife Folk Museum. Address: (b.) School of Geography and Geology, Irvine Building, St. Andrews University, St. Andrews, Fife KY16 9AL; e-mail: jm@st-andrews.ac.uk

McManus, Very Rev. Matthew Francis. Retired Parish Priest, St. Peter-in-Chains, Ardrossan (2004-2017); b. 22.9.40, Rutherglen. Educ. Sacred Heart High School, Girvan; St. Andrew's College, Drygrange, Melrose. Assistant Priest, St. Margaret's, Ayr, 1965-76; Chaplain:

Ayr County Hospital, 1967-76, Queen Margaret Academy, Ayr, 1968-79; Member, Strathclyde Children's Panel Advisory Committee, 1970-75; Parish Priest: New Cumnock, Kirkconnel and Sanquhar, 1976-81, Kirkcudbright, 1981-88, St. Winin's, Kilwinning, 1988-2004; Chairman, Dumfries and Galloway Local Health Council, 1983-87; Chair, Castle Douglas Dumfries District CAB, 1984-87; Member: Stewartry Council of Volunary Service, 1985-88, Stewartry School Council, 1985-87, Scottish Consumer Council, 1983-90; Convenor, Association of Scottish Local Health Councils, 1983-92; Complaints Reporter, Law Society of Scotland, 1985-87; Secretary, Association of Vocations Directors of Scotland, 1987-96; Member, Ayrshire and Arran Health Council, 1988-97; Non-Executive Director, Ayrshire and Arran Health Board, 1997-2001; Member, Ayrshire and Arran Health Council, 2001-07; Chair, Ayrshire and Arran Research Ethics Committee, 2001-2010; Member: Scotland Research Ethics Committee, 2005-2010, North Ayrshire Council Education Committee, 1998-2017; Founding Member, Chair, Minerva Housing Association, 1990-2008; Member, National Appeals Panel (Pharmacy), 1997-2005; Lay Partner, Health Professions Council, 2001-04; Custody Visitor, Police Service Scotland, since 2001; Chair, Interim School Board; new Denominational school for North Ayrshire; Member, CHI Group of Scottish Health Service, 2008-2015; appointed Canon of the Galloway Diocese, 2009; Member: St. Matthew's Academy Parent Council, 2005-2017, West of Scotland Research Ethics Service (Member and Vice-Chair), 2010-2021. Address: 41a Gladstone Road, Saltcoats KA21 5LF; T.-01294 287339; mob: 07711 888244.
E-mail: mattmcmanus@btconnect.com

McManus, Stella, MA. Depute Principal, South Lanarkshire College, since 2020. Educ. Glasgow Caledonian University; Langside College; King's College London. Career history: Southgate College, London: Curriculum Leader, ESOL, 2008-09, Head of ESOL/EFL, 2009-2012; Barnet and Southgate College: Head of Languages and International Curriculum, 2012-14, Deputy Director, Lifelong Learning, 2014-16; Director of Curriculum Operations, North Hertfordshire College, 2016-18; Deputy Principal, Waltham Forest College, 2018-2020. Address: South Lanarkshire College, Scottish Enterprise Technology Park, College Way, East Kilbride, Glasgow G75 0NE; T.-01355 807780.

McMenamin, Frances Jane, QC, BA, LLB, DUniv. Queen's Counsel, since 1998; b. 21.5.51, Glasgow; m., Ian McCarry. Educ. Notre Dame High School, Glasgow; Strathclyde University. Legal apprenticeship, Hughes, Dowdall & Co., Solicitors, Glasgow, 1974-76; Procurator Fiscal Depute, 1976-84; devilling at Scottish Bar, 1984-85; admitted, Faculty of Advocates, 1985; Junior Counsel practising in criminal law, 1985-98; Temporary Sheriff, 1991-97; Advocate Depute, 1997-2000; criminal defence work, since 2000; Visiting Lecturer, Scottish Police College, Tulliallan, 1991-2013. Member, Strathclyde University Law School Advisory Panel, since 2000; Director of Faculty Services Ltd., 2003-07; Member of Management Committee of Faculty of Advocates Free Legal Advice Unit, 2005-09; Member of Court, Strathclyde University, 2005-09; Vice Chairperson, Faculty of Advocates Criminal Bar Association, 2007-08; Member, Scottish Criminal Cases Review Commission, 2010-2019. Awarded Honorary Doctorate, University of Strathclyde, May 2009; appointed Member of Lord Bonomy's Post-Corroboration Review Group, 2014; Director, The Merchants House of Glasgow, since 2016; Joint Investigative Interviews Governance Group (Scottish Government), 2018-2020; Lord Justice Clerk's Review Group on Management of Sexual Abuse Cases, 2019-2021; Member of Audit and Accountability Committee of Police

Investigations and Review Commission, 2018-2020; Legal Consultant to Scottish Criminal Cases Review Commission, since 2020; Trustee, Bellahouston Trust, 2020. Recreations: learning Spanish; reading; spending time with family. Address: (h.) 59 Hamilton Drive, Glasgow G12 8DP; T.-0141-339 0519; (b.) Advocates Library, Parliament House, Edinburgh EH1 1RF; T.-0131-226 5071.

McMicking, Major David John, LVO, MSc. Consultant, Human Resources/Sporting, since 1986; b. 29.4.39, Jerusalem; m., Janetta; 1 s.; 1 d. Educ. Eton; RMA, Sandhurst; Strathclyde University. Career soldier, Black Watch, rising to rank of Major; left Army, 1973; executive positions, John Menzies Holdings Ltd., 1973-86; family farming interests, since 1996. Formerly Extra Equerry, Queen Elizabeth The Queen Mother; Chairman, Officers Association Scotland; Director, Earl Haig Fund Scotland, 1997-2000; Secretary, Friends of St. Andrew's, Jerusalem, 1994-2007. Recreation: field sports. Address: (b.) Drumknock, Kilry, Blairgowrie PH11 8HR; T.-01575 560731.

McMillan, Alan Charles, MA (Hons), LLB, DipLP, LLM (Distinction), FCIArb, NP. Partner, Commercial Dispute Resolution, Burness Paull LLP, since 2005; b. 5.12.64, Hamilton; m., Isla; 2 s.; 1 d. Educ. Garrion Academy; University of Edinburgh. Teacher of English as a Foreign Language for Business Purposes in Spain, Thailand and Scotland, 1987-91; Trainee Solicitor, MacRoberts, 1995-96; Solicitor, Dundas & Wilson, 1996-2005. Co-Editor, "Dilapidations in Scotland" (2nd ed.); Chair, Property Litigation Association (Scotland) for 6 years to 2015; CEDR-accredited Mediator (Burness Paull); Director of Youth Theatre Arts Scotland, since 2014. Recreations: reading; walking; cycling; music; languages. Address: (h.) 28 Inverleith Row, Edinburgh EH3 5QH; T.-0131-473-6141 (day); e-mail: alan.mcmillan@burnesspaull.com

MacMillan of MacMillan and Knap, George Gordon, MA (Cantab). Chief of Clan MacMillan; b. 20.6.30, London; m., (Cecilia) Jane Spurgin (deceased 2005); 2 s. Educ. Aysgarth School; Eton; Trinity College, Cambridge. Schoolmaster, Wellington College, 1953-63; Lecturer, Trinity College, Toronto, 1963-64; Lecturer, Bede College, Durham, 1965-74. Resides in small historic house with gardens and woods open to the public. Address: (h.) Applehouse, Finlaystone, Langbank, Renfrewshire PA14 6TJ; T.-01475 540285; e-mail: chief@clanmacmillan.org

Macmillan, Very Rev. Gilleasbuig Iain, MA, BD. Minister, St. Giles', The High Kirk of Edinburgh, 1973-2013; Chaplain to the Queen in Scotland, since 1979; Dean of the Order of the Thistle, 1989-2014.

McMillan, Sir Iain (Macleod), Kt, CBE, FRSE, FCIB, FCIBS, FAIA, FSQA, DL. Chairman, Skill Force Development Ltd, 2016-2022; Member, Competition Appeal Tribunal; Member, Competition Service Audit and Risk Assurance Committee; Director, CBI Scotland, 1995-2014; Chairman, Scottish Business Education Coalition, 2002-2007; Vice Chairman, Scottish Qualifications Authority, 2004-2006, Member, Board, 1997-2006; Non-Executive Director, Scottish Ambulance Service, 2000-2008 (Chairman, Audit Committee, 2000-2008); Chairman, Scottish North American Business Council, 2009-2015, Member, Board, 1999-2015; Member, Board, British American Business Council, 2010-2016; Member, Executive Committee, British American Business Council, 2010-2017; Member, Advisory Committee, Scottish Economic Policy Network (scotecon), 2002-2007; Chairman, Advisory Board, University of Strathclyde

Business School; Member, Advisory Board, Scottish Co-investment Fund, 2003-2008; Member, Advisory Board, Scottish Enterprise Investments, 2008-2010; Chairman, The Industrial Mission Trust, 2008-2013, Trustee, 2000-2013; Trustee, The Teaching Awards Trust, 2007-2013; Member, Commission on Scottish Devolution, 2008-2009; Selected Air Member, Lowland Reserve Forces' and Cadets' Association, 2010-2020; Member, Literacy Commission, 2008-2010; Member, Standing Literacy Commission, 2011-2015; Freeman, City of Glasgow, 2011; Trustee, The Carnegie Trust for the Universities of Scotland, 2010-2019; Honorary Air Commodore, 602 (City of Glasgow) Squadron, Royal Auxiliary Air Force, 2009-2020; Member, Scottish Advisory Committee SkillForce, 2015-2019; Chairman, Independent Commission for Competitive and Fair Taxation in Scotland, 2015-2016; Chairman, Work Place Chaplaincy Scotland, 2014-2016; b. 25.4.51, Glasgow; m., Giuseppina; 3 s. Educ. Bearsden Academy. Trainee Banker, 1970-1976; Management and Senior Management, TSB Group plc, 1976-1993; Liaison Officer for Scotland and Northern England, The Royal Jubilee and Prince's Trusts (secondment), 1984-1985; Assistant Director, CBI Scotland, 1993-1995. Member, Scottish Advisory Board, Equal Opportunities Commission, 1995-2001; Chairman, Higher Still Employment and Training Group, 1997-2000; Member, Scottish Executive's Committee of Review into the Careers Service, 1999-2000; Member, Board, Young Enterprise Scotland, 1999-2003; Deputy Lieutenant of Stirling and Falkirk, since 2018; FRSE 2020. Publications: Manufacturing Matters (Co-Author), 1994; The Challenge for Government in Scotland (Principal Author), 1996; Scottish Manufacturing: a Shared Vision (Co-Author), 1997; Business and Parliaments – Partners for Prosperity (Co-Author), 1998; Towards a Prosperous Scotland (Co-Author), 1999; Scotland's Economy: an Agenda for Growth (Co-Author), 2003; The Scottish Economy: The Priority of Priorities (Co-Author), 2006; Energising the Scottish Economy: a Business Agenda for Reform and Recovery (Co-Author), 2010; A Dynamic Scotland: the Role of Competitive and Fair Taxes (Co-Author), 2016. Recreations: reading; walking.

Macmillan, Ian, MA, BD, PhD. Chair of the Board, The Crichton Trust, since 2016. Educ. Universities of Glasgow, St Andrews and Edinburgh. Former Managing Director at J.P. Morgan (a large investment bank with over 260,000 employees and operations in over 100 countries); has over 28 years financial services experience, and has performed a number of management roles in the asset management, investment banking and securities broking, and spent five years in the Far East. Address: The Crichton Trust, Grierson House, The Crichton, Bankend Road, Dumfries DG1 4ZE; T.-01387 247 544.

MacMillan, Sir James Loy, CBE, BMus, PhD. Composer and Conductor; Professor of Theology, Imagination and the Arts, University of St Andrews; Founder and Artistic Director, The Cumnock Tryst; b. 16.7.59, Kilwinning; m., Lynne; 2 d.; 1 s. Educ. Cumnock Academy; Edinburgh University; Durham University. Principal compositions: The Confession of Isobel Gowdie, London Proms, 1990; Busqueda, Edinburgh International Festival, with Diana Rigg, 1990; featured composer, Musica Nova, 1990, Huddersfield Contemporary Music Festival, 1991; Veni, Veni, Emmanuel, percussion concerto for Evelyn Glennie, London Proms, 1992; Visitatio Sepulchri, one act opera, Mayfest, 1993; Ines de Castro, for Scottish Opera, Edinburgh International Festival, 1996; The World's Ransoming, for orchestra and cor anglaise, 1996; Cello Concerto, 1996; Symphony: Vigil, 1997; featured composer, Edinburgh International Festival, 1993; recording of Tryst and The Confession of Isobel Gowdie by BBC SSO won Gramophone Award, contemporary music

category, 1993; Seven Last Words, BBC TV, 1994; Raising Sparks, 1997, for chamber ensemble; String Quartet: Why Is This Night Different?, 1988; featured composer, Raising Sparks Festival, South Bank Centre, London, 1997 (South Bank Show Award for Classical Music, 1997); Evening Standard Classical Music Award, 1997 for Outstanding Artistic Achievement for Symphony: Vigil and Raising Sparks Festival; Quickening, 1998; Mass, 2000; Cello Sonata No.2 dedicated to Julian Lloyd Webber; The Birds of Rhiannon, 2001; O Bone Jesu, 2001; Piano concerto No.2, 2003; A Scotch Bestiary, 2004; Sundogs, 2006; The Sacrifice, 2007; St John Passion, 2008; Violin Concerto, 2010; Oboe Concerto, 2010; Clemency, for Scottish Opera, the Royal Opera House, London, and Boston Lyric Opera, 2009-2010; Trombone Concerto, 2016; Stabat Mater, 2015; All the Hills and Vales Along, 2017; Symphony No. 5, Le Grand Inconnu (The Great Unknown), 2018. Honorary Fellow, Blackfriars Hall, University of Oxford; Patron: St Mary's Music School, Edinburgh; Patron: Schola Cantorum. DUniv (Paisley); DLitt (University of Strathclyde); FRASMD; HonFRIAS (University of St Andrews; University of Edinburgh; University of Durham; University of Glasgow; Newman College); DMus (University of Glasgow); Hon LTC, Trinity College, London. Royal Medal, Royal Society of Edinburgh, 2010; Sigillo della Città di Malano (seal of the city of Milan), 2019.

Macmillan, Emeritus Professor (John) Duncan, MA, PhD, LID, FRSA, FRSE, HRSA. Emeritus Professor of the History of Scottish Art, Edinburgh University; Curator, Talbot Rice Gallery, Edinburgh University, 1979-2004; Hon. Curator, Royal Society of Edinburgh, 2008-2012; Art Critic, The Scotsman; b. 7.3.39, Beaconsfield; m., Vivien Rosemary Hinkley; 2 d. Educ. Gordonstoun School; St. Andrews University; London University; Edinburgh University. Lecturer, then Senior Lecturer, then Reader, then Professor, Department of Fine Art, Edinburgh University. Recreation: walking. Address: (h.) 20 Nelson Street, Edinburgh; T.-0131-556 7100.

Macmillan, John Ernest Newall, LLB, NP. Employment Consultant, MacRoberts Dundee; Managing Partner, MacRoberts Glasgow, 1998-2005 and 2014-2018; b. 27.9.56, Kilmarnock; m., Caroline Elizabeth; 2 s.; 2 d. Educ. Merchiston Castle School, Edinburgh; Dundee University. Apprenticeship, Bird Semple and Crawford Herron, Glasgow, 1978-80; Solicitor, J. and J. Sturrock & Co., Kilmarnock, 1980-82; Solicitor, MacRoberts Glasgow, 1982-86, Partner (Litigation and Employment), 1986-2020 (moved to Dundee in 2013); Board Member, EELA, 2007-2017; IOD Tayside Committee, 2013-2020; Chairman, Cumnock Tryst, since 2018. Former Captain, Kilmarnock (Barassie) Golf Club. Recreations: golf; skiing; bridge; travel. Address: (b.) 5 West Victoria Dock Street, Dundee DD1 3JT; e-mail: john.macmillan@macroberts.com and john.macmillan28@gmail.com

McMillan, Joyce Margaret, MA (Hons), DipEd, DLitt. h.c. (Queen Margaret Univ. College). Journalist and Arts Critic; Theatre Critic and Columnist, The Scotsman, since 1998; b. 29.8.52, Paisley. Educ. Paisley Grammar School; St. Andrews University; Edinburgh University. Theatre Reviewer, BBC Radio Scotland and The Scotsman, 1979-81; Theatre Critic, Sunday Standard, 1981-83; Radio Critic, The Herald, 1983-95; Scottish Theatre Critic, The Guardian, 1984-93; Scotland on Sunday: Social/Political Columnist, 1989-97, Theatre Critic, 1993-97; Arts/Political Columnist, The Herald, 1997-98. Chair, NUJ Freelance Branch, Edinburgh; Member, National Executive Committee, NUJ, London; Member, Consultative Steering Group on the Scottish Parliament, 1998-99; Member, Scottish National Theatre Working Group, 2000-01; Chair,

Hansard Society Working Group, Scotland; Visiting Professor, Drama and Creative Industries, Queen Margaret University, Edinburgh, since 2006. Publications: The Traverse Story, 1963-88, 1988; Charter for the Arts in Scotland, 1992. Recreations: food; drink; films; music; talking politics. Address: 8 East London Street, Edinburgh, EH7 4BH; T.-0131-557 1726.

McMillan, Malcolm. Chief Executive, Scottish Law Commission, 2008-2021 (retired); b. 27.3.55, Ayr; m., Mary Clare Campbell; 3 d. Educ. Royal High School, Edinburgh; University of Edinburgh. Admitted as Solicitor in 1979; Legal Assistant, Argyll and Bute District Council, 1979-80; Legal Adviser in the Office of Solicitor to the Secretary of State for Scotland, 1982-99; Deputy Legal Secretary to the Lord Advocate, 1999-2003; Divisional Solicitor for the Rural Affairs Division in the Scottish Government Legal Directorate, 2003-08. Recreations: walking; swimming.

McMillan, Michael Dale, KSG, BSc, LLB, FFICS. Retired Solicitor; formerly Managing Partner of Burnett & Reid LLP, Solicitors, Aberdeen; Senior Tutor, The University of Aberdeen Law School, 2000-2019; b. 15.2.44, Edinburgh; m., Isobel Ross Mackie; 2 s.; 1 d. Educ. Edinburgh Academy; Edinburgh University. Partner, Macdonalds Sergeants, Solicitors, East Kilbride and Glasgow, 1971-92; Secretary: East Kilbride Chamber of Commerce, 1971-86, East Kilbride Chamber of Trade, 1971-92; Board Member, East Kilbride Development Corporation, 1979-84; Secretary, Pilgrim Legal Users' Group, 1985-92; Captain, East Kilbride Golf Club, 1979; Chairman, Strathaven Academy School Board, 1991-92; President, East Kilbride Burns Club, 1989-91; Captain, Inchmarlo Golf Club (Banchory), 1997-99; President, Deeside Musical Society, 1998-2000 and 2007-08 and Treasurer, 2004-17; Burgess of Guild, City of Aberdeen. Recreations: golf; sailing; gardening. Address: (h.) Belnies, Strachan, Banchory, Aberdeenshire AB31 6LU; T.-01330 850249; e-mail: mike.mcmillan@me.com

McMillan, Stuart, MBA, BA (Hons). MSP (SNP), Greenock and Inverclyde, since 2016 (West of Scotland region, 2007-2016); b. 6.5.72, Barrow-in-Furness; m., Alexandra; 2 d. Educ. Port Glasgow High School; University of Abertay, Dundee. Supply Analyst, IBM UK Ltd., Greenock, 1998-2000; Parliamentary Researcher, SNP Whips Office, Westminster, London, 2000-03; Office Manager, Bruce McFee MSP, Scottish Parliament, 2003-07. Recreations: play bagpipes; sport; travel. Address: Scottish Parliament, Edinburgh EH99 1SP; Constituency Office: 26 Grey Place, Greenock PA15 1YF; T.-01475 720930. E-mail: stuart.mcmillan.msp@parliament.scot

McMillan, Professor Thomas Murray, BSc, MAppSci, PhD, FBPsS. Professor of Clinical Neuropsychology, Glasgow University, since 1999; Adviser to NHS Greater Glasgow & Clyde, since 1999; b. 7.3.54, Prestwick; m., Sarah Louise Wilson; 1 d. Educ. Prestwick High School; Ayr Academy; Aberdeen University; London University; Glasgow University. Lecturer in Clinical Psychology, Institute of Psychiatry, London; Head of Clinical Neuropsychology, St George's Healthcare, London; Professor of Clinical Psychology, Surrey University. Publications include: Handbook of Neurological Rehabilitation; Neurobehavioural Disability and Social Handicap. Recreations: cross-country running. Address: (b.) Mental Health and Wellbeing, University of Glasgow, Gartnavel Royal Hospital, Glasgow G12 0XH; T.-0141-211 0354.

McMillan, William Alister, BL. Retired Solicitor; b. 19.1.34, Ayr; m., Elizabeth Anne; 3 d. Educ. Strathallan; Glasgow University. Clerk of the Peace, County of Ayr, 1974-75; Honorary Sheriff, Ayr; Hon. Governor, Strathallan School; Hon. President, Ayr RFC. Recreation:

golf. Address: (h.) 101 Fairfield Park, Ayr KA7 2AU; T.-01292 520 710.

Macmillan Douglas, Angus William, OBE, BA. Elected Member of Angus Council (Kirriemuir and Dean Ward), since 2017 (Depute Leader of Council, since 2017). Former Director, National Support Services, NHS Scotland; National Director, Scottish Blood Transfusion Service, 1997-2004. B. 18.11.46, Edinburgh; m. Rosie Jane Meynell, 86, divorced 2019; 2 d. Educ. Douglastown Primary; Blairmore School; Wellington College; Ealing Business School; INSEAD. Graduate Apprentice and various appointments with British Petroleum plc, 1965-1981; Assistant UK Co-ordinator BP, 1981-84; Business Manager, BP Information Systems, 1984-85; European Developments Manager, BP Gas, 1985-88; Managing Director, BP East Africa Trading and Director, BP Africa, 1988-91; Director of International Political Affairs and Advisor to BP Board, 1991-96; Relationship Director, BP – Mobil Corporation European Partnership, 1996-97. Director, Brigton Consultancy Ltd, 2004-8; Director, Douglas Gorham Consultancy Ltd, 2008-16. Representative, East African Trade Organisation, 1988-91; Member, Governing Council and Energy Policy Committee, CBI, 1992-96; Member, Management Committee, Industry and Parliament Trust, 1992-96; Director, European Blood Alliance, 1998-2007; Member, Executive of Scottish Conservative Party, 2006-10; Member, Candidate Selection Board of Scottish Conservative Party, 2006-7; Chair, Angus Conservative and Unionist Association, 2004-9; Chair, UK Forum of Blood and Tissue Services, 2001-4; Member, Royal Company of Archers (Queen's Bodyguard for Scotland); Governor, Butterstone School, 1999-2002; Governor, Kilgraston School, 2002-2005; Member, Scottish Conservative Party Policy Advisory Group, 2006; Member of Court, Abertay University, 2004-16 (Chair of Court's Finance, HR and General Purposes Committee, 2008-15); Honorary Fellow, Abertay University, 2017; Chair, New Club, 2014-16; Member, Better Together Funding Board and Advisor to Better Together Campaign, 2014. Recreations: family; gentle tennis; walking. Address: (h. and b.) Brigton, Douglastown, by Forfar DD8 1TP; T.-01307-820-215.

McMurray, Professor John J.V., OBE, BSc (Hons), MBChB (Hons), MD, FRCP (Edin and Glas), FESC, FACC, FAHA, FRSE, FMedSci. Professor of Medical Cardiology, Glasgow University, since 1999; Honorary Consultant Cardiologist; Western Infirmary, Glasgow, 1995-2015; Queen Elizabeth University Hospital, Glasgow, since 2015; Deputy Director (Clinical), Institute of Cardiovascular and Medical Sciences, University of Glasgow, since 2015; Professorial Fellow, Mary MacKillop Institute for Health Research, Australian Catholic University, since 2017; b. 17.12.58, Enniskillen, Co. Fermanagh; m., Christine; 5 s.; 1 d. Educ. St Patrick's College, Knock, Belfast; Manchester University. Consultant Cardiologist, Western General Hospital, Edinburgh, 1993-95. Publications: over 900 medical and scientific papers; 15 books. Recreations: reading; travelling; Celtic FC. Address: (b.) British Heart Foundation Cardiovascular Research Centre, University of Glasgow G12 8TA; T.-0141 330 3479; Fax: 0141 330 6955; e-mail: john.mcmurray@glasgow.ac.uk

McMurray, Karyn (Millar), MA (Hons), MA, MSc. Editor, Floris Books, since 2017. Educ. University of Glasgow; University of York; Napier University. Career: PA to MD, Neil Wilson Publishing, 2002; Temporary Administrative Roles, Bruce Murray Recruitment, 2003-04; Office Administrator, The Prince's Scottish Youth Business Trust, 2004; Wiley-Blackwell: Production

Assistant, 2006-07, Production Editor, 2007-08; Freelance reviewer and researcher, The List Eating & Drinking Guide, 2008-12; Editor, Mainstream Publishing, 2008-2013; Copy-editor and proofreader, Freelance, 2013-15; Editor, Black & White Publishing, 2013-17. Address: Floris Books, 2A Robertson Avenue, Edinburgh EH11 1PZ; T.-0131 337 2372.

Macnab of Macnab, James William Archibald. 24th Chief, Clan Macnab; b. 1963. Succeeded to title, 2013.

Macnair, Sheriff Charles Neville, QC, LLB. Queen's Counsel, since 2002; Sheriff of Tayside, Central and Fife at Cupar, since 2009; Sheriff (floating), Tayside Central and Fife at Dunfermline, 2006-2009; b. 18.3.55, London; m., Patricia Anne Dinning; 2 d. Educ. Bryanston School; Aberdeen University. Commissioned, Queen's Own Highlanders, 1977-80; Solicitor, 1982-87; admitted, Faculty of Advocates, 1988; Part time Sheriff, 2005-06. Recreations: sailing; reading. Address: Sheriff Court House, County Buildings, St Catherine Street, Cupar KY15 4LX.

McNair, Marie, MSP (SNP), Clydebank and Milngavie, since 2021; previously a councillor in Clydebank. Address: The Scottish Parliament, Edinburgh EH99 1SP; T.-0131 348 5068.
E-mail: Marie.McNair.msp@parliament.scot

McNairney, John, CBE. Chief Planner for the Scottish Government, 2012-2021 (retired). Career: practiced as a chartered town planner in local government, planning consultancy and, most recently, in central government over the last 30 years; joined the Scottish Office at devolution initially leading a range of planning and transport policy developments and subsequently implementation of the Scottish Executive's Freedom of Information legislation; appointed Assistant Chief Planner (2005) supporting modernising planning, digital transformation and Place-making.
E-mail: j.mcnairney@btinternet.com

McNally, John. MP (SNP), Falkirk, since 2015; b. 1.2.51, Denny; m., Sandra; 2 c. Elected to Falkirk council in 2005, after winning the Herbertshire by-election. Member of the Environmental Audit Select Committee, House of Commons. Address: House of Commons, London SW1A 0AA.

McNamara, Lauren. Director of Strategy and Operations and Interim Chief Executive Officer, Student Awards Agency Scotland. Career history: Registers of Scotland, 1999-2017; joined Student Awards Agency Scotland as Director of Policy and Engagement in 2017. Address: Student Awards Agency, Broomhouse Drive, Edinburgh EH11 3UT; T.-0300 555 0505.

McNamara, Sean. Head of Chartered Institute of Library and Information Professionals in Scotland (CILIPS), since 2018. Educ. University of Strathclyde. Career history: Library Assistant, Glasgow Libraries, 2007-08; freelance journalist, 2005-08; Learning Services Librarian, Inverclyde Council, 2008-2013; Policy and Digital Officer, CILIP in Scotland, 2013-18. Event support, C-Change, 2012-13. Address: Chartered Institute of Library and Information Professionals in Scotland (CILIPS), 152 Bath Street, Glasgow G2 4TB; T.-0141 353 5637.

Macnaughton, Rev. (Gordon) Fraser (Hay), MA, BD, DipCPC. Minister, St. Magnus Cathedral, Kirkwall, Orkney, since 2002; b. 27.3.58, Glasgow; m., Carole; 2 d. Educ. Glasgow Academy; Glasgow University; Edinburgh University. Assistant, Newlands South Church, Glasgow, 1981-85; Parish Minister, Fenwick Parish Church, 1985-91; Chaplain, Dundee University, 1991-97; Parish Minister, Killermont Parish Church,

Bearsden, 1997-2002. Coach to Scottish Universities Rugby XV, 1995-97. Recreations: rugby; bird-watching; conservation issues; history; cycling. Address: (h.) Cathedral Manse, Berstane Road, Kirkwall, Orkney KW15 1NA; T.-01856 873312.
E-mail: fmacnaughton@churchofscotland.org.uk

McNaughton, John Ewen, OBE, FRAgS. Retired Justice of the Peace. Past Member, Scottish Beef Council; Chairman, Forth Valley Countryside Initiative, 1999-2003; b. 28.5.33, Edinburgh; m., Jananne Ogilvie Honeyman; 2 s.; 2 d. Educ. Cargilfield; Loretto. Born and bred a hill sheep farmer; after a short spell in America, began farming at Inverlochlarig with father; served on Council, NFU of Scotland; Chairman, Scotch Quality Beef & Lamb Association, 1981-97; Vice President, Royal Highland and Agricultural Society of Scotland, 1997-98; Member: British Wool Marketing Board, 1975-2000, Panel of Agricultural Arbiters, 1973-98, Red Deer Commission, 1975-92; Elder, Church of Scotland. Recreations: woodworking; gardening. Address: Inverlochlarig, Balquhidder, Lochearnhead, Perthshire FK19 8PH; T.-01877 384 232; e-mail: john@inverlochlarig.com

MacNeacail, Aonghas. Writer (poetry, journalism, scriptwriting for TV, film and radio, librettoes); b. 7.6.42, Uig, Isle of Skye; m., Gerda Stevenson (qv); 1 s. Educ. Portree High School; Glasgow University. Writing fellowships: Sabhal Mor Ostaig, 1977-79, An Comunn Gaidhealach, 1979-81, Ross and Cromarty District Council, 1988-90, Glasgow and Strathclyde Universities, 1993-95, Sabhal Mor Ostaig, 1995-98; tours to Ireland, Germany, North America, Japan, Israel, etc.; opera librettoes for Alasdair Nicolson and William Sweeney; songs for Capercaillie, Phil Cunningham; art with Simon Fraser, Kenny Munro, Diane MacLean; short-listed, Paul Hamlyn Foundation Award for Poets, 1997; Stakis Award, Scottish Writer of the Year, 1997. Publications: books: An Seachnadh, 1986; Rock-Water, 1990; Oideachadh Ceart, 1996; Laoidh an Donais òig ('hymn to a young demon'), 2007; poems widely anthologised. Recreations: newsprint; red wine; thinking about walking.

MacNee, Professor William, MB, ChB (1975), MD (Hons 1985), FRCP (Glas1989), FRCP (Edin 1990), FERS (2014). Emeritus Professor of Respiratory Medicine, Edinburgh University; Visiting Professor, School of Life Sciences, Napier University; Honorary Consultant Physician, Lothian Health Board, 1987-2018; Professor of Respiratory and Environmental Medicine, University of Edinburgh, 1997-2016; Clinical Director, Respiratory Medicine Unit, 1992-98; Clinical Director, Respiratory Medicine, Lothian University Hospitals NHS Trust, 1998-2005; b. 18.12.50, Glasgow; m., Edna Marina Kingsley; 1 s.; 1 d. Educ. Coatbridge High School; Glasgow University. House Physician/House Surgeon, Glasgow and Paisley, 1975-76; SHO/Registrar in Medicine, Western Infirmary/Gartnavel Hospitals, Glasgow, 1976-79; Registrar in Respiratory Medicine, City Hospital, Edinburgh, 1979-80; MRC Research Fellow/Honorary Registrar, Department of Respiratory Medicine, Royal Infirmary, Edinburgh, 1980-82; Lecturer, Department of Respiratory Medicine, City Hospital, Edinburgh, 1982-83; Senior Registrar, Respiratory Medicine/Medicine, Lothian Health Board, 1983-87; MRC Research Fellow, University of British Columbia, Vancouver, 1985-86; Senior Lecturer in Respiratory Medicine, 1987-93; Reader in Medicine, Edinburgh University, 1993-97; Head, Cardiovascular-Thoracic Service, Royal Infirmary of Edinburgh, 1998-99. Council Member, Scottish Thoracic Society, 1990-93; Hon. Secretary, British Lung Foundation (Scotland); Chairman, British Lung Foundation Scientific Committee, 1997-2000; Chairman, European Respiratory Society Scientific

Programme Committee, 1999-2003; Congress Chair, European Respiratory Society, 2003-04; President, European Respiratory Society, 2006-07; Council Member, Royal College of Physicians of Edinburgh, 2001-04; Vice President, British Lung Foundation, since 2005. Publications: scientific papers, reviews and books on respiratory medicine topics. Recreations: music; walking; reading. Address: (h.) 4 Alnwickhill Road, Edinburgh EH16 6LF; e-mail: w.macnee@ed.ac.uk

MacNeil, Angus, BEng, PGCE. MP (SNP), Na h-Eileanan An Iar, since 2005; Spokesperson on Environment, Food & Rural Affairs, SNP, 2017-18, Deputy Foreign Affairs Spokesperson, 2015-17, Spokesperson for Transport, 2005-2015; 3 d.; b. 21.7.70. Educ. Castlebay Secondary School, Isle of Barra; Nicolson Institute, Stornoway, Isle of Lewis; Strathclyde University; Jordanhill College. Career history: Teacher; Convener, Lochaber branch SNP, 1999; SNP Spokesperson for: Environment, 2005-07; Fishing, 2005-10, Food and Rural Affairs, 2005-10, Work and Pensions, 2007-08; contested Inverness East, Nairn and Lochaber, 2001 general election. Chair, International Trade Committee, since 2016; Chair, Energy and Climate Change Select Committee, 2015-16; Member, Scottish Affairs Committee, 2005-09. Recreations: football; sailing; crofting; fishing. Address: (b.) House of Commons, London SW1A 0AA.

McNeil, Duncan. MSP (Labour), Greenock and Inverclyde, 1999-2016; b. 7.9.50, Greenock. Career history: worked as a boilermaker at Scott Lithgow, initially as an apprentice, 1965-79; after working as a co-ordinator for the Unemployed Workers Centres in Glasgow, became a full-time official in the GMB Union in 1981 and later a Regional Organiser; for six years prior to his election from his current constituency, in May 1999, he was on the Labour Party's Scottish Executive Committee. Served on the Enterprise and Lifelong Learning Committee for 15 months and went on to became Labour's Chief Whip; elected to the Scottish Parliamentary Corporate Body in December 2001. Following re-election in May 2003, became Chair of the Scottish Parliamentary Labour Party.

McNeil, Lynne. Editor, Life and Work, since 2002; b. 19.12.67, Dunfermline; m., Charles Craig Robin McNeil; 1 d. Educ. Inverkeithing High School; Napier College, Edinburgh. East Lothian Courier, 1986-89; United News Service, Edinburgh, 1989-94; Telegraph and Argus, Bradford, 1994; Railtrack North East, 1994; Greenock Telegraph, 1994-95; The Herald, 1995-2002. Recreations: reading; swimming. Address: (b.) 121 George Street, Edinburgh EH2 4YN; T.-0131 225 5722.
E-mail: lrobertson@lifeandwork.org

Macneil of Bara, Roderick 'Rory' Wilson. Chief of Clan Niall and 27th of Barra; b. 22.10.54; m., Sau Ming. Succeeded to title, 2010.

McNeill, Avril. Head Teacher, Glenrothes High School, 2014-2020 and since 2021; Rector, Madras College, St Andrews, 2020-21; b. 1973; m., Alasdair; 2 c. Educ. Jordanhill College; University of Edinburgh (Scottish Qualification for Headship). Career history: Lecturer in Economics (part-time), University of Glasgow, 1996; Teacher of Modern Studies, St. Stephen's High School, 1996-98; Teacher of Modern Studies/History, Madras College, St Andrews, 1998-2005; PTC International Relations & Citizenship, Kirkland High School & Community College, 2005-2010; Depute Head Teacher, Perth Academy, 2011-14. Address: Glenrothes High School, Napier Road, Glenrothes KY6 1HJ; T.-01592 583476.

McNeill, James Walker, QC. Advocate, 1978-2018; a Judge of the Courts of Appeal of Jersey and Guernsey, 2006-2022; b. 16.2.52, Dunoon; m., Katherine Lawrence McDowall; 2 s.; 1 d. Educ. Dunoon Grammar School; Sidney Sussex College, Cambridge; Edinburgh University; Open University. QC, 1991; Standing Junior Counsel, Department of Transport in Scotland, 1984-88, Inland Revenue, 1988-91. Member of Council, Commonwealth Law Association, 2005-2011; Session Clerk, St. Andrew's and St. George's Parish Church, Edinburgh, 1999-2003; Chair of Music Committee, Scottish International Piano Competition, 2004-2011; Member, Judicial Appointments Board for Scotland, 2012-2018; Trustee and Secretary, Edinburgh City Centre Churches Together, 2012-2018; Chair, Disciplinary Appointments Committee of the Institute and Faculty of Actuaries, 2013-2019; Administrative Trustee, Assembly Trustees of The Church of Scotland, 2019-2022; General Editor: A Practical Guide to Charity Law in Scotland, 2016. Recreations: music; cycle touring; travel.

McNeill, Patricia Anne. Vice Chair, A Heart for Duns; formerly Project Manager, Blend2Learn (2006-09); b. 03.08.48, Duns, Berwickshire; 2 s. Educ. Berwickshire High School. Career History: Head of Student Services, Queen Margaret College; Training and Media Manager, Integrated Micro Applications Ltd. (INMAP); Commercial Manager, Centre for Software Engineering, Stirling Univ.; Managing Dir., Talkback Training Ltd., 1987-2005. Expert Advisor/Evaluator, European Learning Programmes (Leonardo & Erasmus). Address: Cheeklaw Brae House, Station Road, Duns, Berwickshire TD11 3HS; T.-07939 023211.
E-mail: annemcneill38@gmail.com

McNeill, Pauline, LLB. MSP (Lab), Glasgow, since 2016 and 1999-2011 (Glasgow Kelvin); b. 12.9.62, Paisley; m., William Joseph Cahill. Educ. Our Lady's High School, Cumbernauld; Strathclyde University. President, National Union of Students (Scotland), 1986-88; Regional Organiser, GMB, 1988-99. Recreations: music; films; guitar; singing. Address: Scottish Parliament, Edinburgh EH99 1SP.

McNeilly, Professor Alan S., BSc, PhD, DSc (Ed), DSc (hon causa RVC), FSB, FRSE. Honorary Professor, University of Edinburgh, since 1994; b. 10.2.47, Birmingham; m., Judy; 1 s.; 3 d. Educ. Handsworth Grammar School, Birmingham; Nottingham University; Reading University; Edinburgh University. Research Lecturer, Department of Reproductive Medicine, St. Bartholomew's Hospital, London, 1971-75; Visiting Professor, University of Manitoba, Canada, 1975-76; Research Scientist, MRC Reproductive Biology Unit, Edinburgh, 1976-2011, Deputy Director, 1986-2008. Editor-in-Chief, Journal of Endocrinology, 1995-2000; Member, Home Office APC, 1998-2006; Chairman: Society for Reproduction and Fertility, 1999-2005, Science Committee Society for Endocrinology, 2008-2012. Fellow of Royal Society of Edinburgh, 1995; Fellow of Society of Biology, 2010; Member, Faculty of 1000, 2010-2015; Society for Endocrinology Dale Medallist, 2008; Society for Reproduction and Fertility Marshall Medallist, 2008. Recreations: walking; golf; gardening. E-mail: a.mcneilly@ed.ac.uk

McNeish, Cameron, FRSGS. Scottish mountaineer. Best known as an author and broadcaster; a lecturer and after dinner speaker as well as being an adviser to various outdoor organisations. Patron of Mountain Aid; Patron of Orienteering Scotland; Patron of Perth & Kinross Countryside Trust: Honorary Fellow of the Royal Scottish Geographical Society. Lifetime Achievement Award by PPA (Professional Publishers Association) Scotland for services to magazine publishing in 2010; Lifetime Achievement Award by the National Adventure Awards in 2015; Oliver Brown Award by the Scots Independent newspaper for work in showcasing Scotland, 2016; recipient of the annual Scottish Award for Excellence in Mountain Culture, 2018. E-mail: mcneishcameron@gmail.com

Macniven, Ruaraidh, LLB (Hons). Director of the Scottish Government Legal Directorate, since 2019. Educ. University of Aberdeen. Career history: joined the Civil Service in 1998; worked in the Government Legal Service for Scotland (GLSS), since April 1999; previous roles include: Head of the Civil Recovery Unit within COPFS; Acting Head of the Constitutional and Civil Law Division, SGLD; Legal Secretary to the Lord President; worked in the Scottish Parliament and the Office to the Solicitor to the Secretary of State for Scotland; Legal Secretary to the Advocate General, 2013-2016; Head of Advisory and Legislation Division of the Office of the Advocate General, 2016-19. Address: Scottish Government Legal Directorate, Victoria Quay, The Shore, Edinburgh EH6 6QQ.

McNulty, Des, BA (Hons). Honorary Fellow, Civic Partnership and Place Leadership, University of Glasgow; Vice Chair of the Glasgow Commission for Economic Growth; MSP (Labour), Clydebank and Milngavie, 1999-2011; former Minister for Social Justice; b. 28.7.52, Stockport; m.; 2 s. Educ. St. Bede's College, Manchester; University of York; University of Glasgow. Formerly Assistant Vice-Principal (Economic Development and Civic Engagement), University of Glasgow; Head of Sociology, Glasgow Caledonian University; Director of Strategic Planning, Glasgow Caledonian University; Member, Strathclyde Regional Council, 1990-96; Member, Glasgow City Council, 1995-99; Member of Court, University of Glasgow, 1994-99; Board, Scottish Opera, 1996-99; Chair, Glasgow Healthy City Partnership, 1995-99; Chair, Glasgow 1999 Festival of Architecture and Design; Non-Executive Director, Greater Glasgow Health Board, 1998-99; Board Member, The Wise Group, 1995-2021.

McPhee, George, MBE, BMus, FRCO, DipMusEd, RSAM, Hon. FRSCM, Hon. FGCM. Visiting Professor of Organ, St. Andrews University; Chairman, Paisley International Organ Festival; Organist and Master of the Choristers, Paisley Abbey, since 1963; b. 10.11.37, Glasgow; m., Margaret Ann Scotland; 1 s.; 2 d. Educ. Woodside Senior Secondary School, Glasgow; Royal Scottish Academy of Music and Drama; Edinburgh University. Studied organ with Herrick Bunney and Fernando Germani; Assistant Organist, St. Giles' Cathedral, 1959-63; joined staff, RSAMD, 1963; Conductor, Scottish Chamber Choir, 1971-75; Conductor, Kilmarnock and District Choral Union, 1975-84; since 1971, has completed 12 recital tours of the United States and Canada; has been both Soloist and Conductor with Scottish National Orchestra; numerous recordings and broadcasts; has taken part in numerous music festivals as Soloist; Adjudicator; Examiner, Associated Board, Royal Schools of Music; Special Commissioner, Royal School of Church Music; Visiting Professor of Music, St Andrews University, 1994-2014; President, Incorporated Society of Musicians, 1999-2000; Silver Medal, Worshipful Company of Musicians; Honorary Doctorate, University of Paisley; Vice President, Royal College of Organists. Recreations: golf; walking. Address: (h.) 17 Main Road, Castlehead, Paisley PA2 6AJ; T.-0141-889 3528; e-mail: profmcphee@aol.com

Macpherson, Archie. Sports broadcaster and journalist. Former headmaster; football commentator, BBC Scotland, until 1990; reported Olympic Games, 1984 and 1988, for BBC network; commentator, Scottish Television, since 1988; author of: Action Replays, 1991; Blue and Green, 1989; Jock Stein: The Definitive Biography, 2004; Flower of Scotland?, 2005; A Game of Two Halves, 2009; Undefeated: The Life and Times of Jimmy Johnstone, 2010; Silent Thunder, 2014 (novel); Adventures in the Golden Age: Scotland in the World Cups, 1974-98; More Than A Game: Living with the Old Firm, 2020. Inducted into Scottish Football's Hall of Fame, 15th October 2017; Scottish BAFTA Award for Services to Broadcasting, 2005. E-mail: archie613@btinternet.com

Macpherson, Ben, BA, LLB, DipLP. MSP (SNP), Edinburgh Northern and Leith, since 2016; Minister for Social Security and Local Government, since 2021; Minister for Rural Affairs and the Natural Environment, 2020-21; Minister for Public Finance and Migration, 2020-21; Minister for Europe, Migration and International Development, 2018-2020. Educ. University of York; University of Edinburgh; The Open University. Career history: Data Processor, Standard Life, 2002-03; Volunteer English Teacher, Projects Abroad, 2003; Peace One Day: Campaigner, 2004, Intern, 2005; Intern, Citigate Public Affairs (now Grayling), 2006; Clerical Assistant, James Gillespie's High School, 2008-09; Intern, Scottish Parliament, 2009-2010; Marketing/Public Affairs Assistant, Aquamarine Power, 2010; Voluntary Public Affairs Advisor, Campaign for Fair Access to the Legal Profession, 2012-13; Brodies LLP: Trainee Solicitor, 2013-15, Solicitor, 2015-16. Member of British delegation, Jung Königswinter Conference, July 2013. Recreations: current affairs; economics; political philosophy; political activism; running; football; playing guitar; travel. Address: Scottish Parliament, Edinburgh EH99 1SP.

Macpherson of Cluny (and Blairgowrie), James, BSc. 28th Hereditary Chief of the Clan Macpherson (Cluny-Macpherson); b. 5.6.72; m., Annie; 3 c. Educ. Summer Fields, Oxford; Fettes College, Edinburgh; Guildford College, Greensboro, North Carolina. Career history: Whitbread plc in London, then joined Ben Sayers Golf Company as a Commercial Manager, before going into property and thereafter set up his own property business in Melrose. Recreations: golf; rugby; fishing. Address: Newton Castle, Blairgowrie, Perthshire PH10 6SU.

McPherson, Malcolm Henry, LLB, WS. Solicitor; Senior Partner, Addleshaw Goddard LLP; b. 22.5.54, Edinburgh; 1 s.; 3 d. Educ. George Watson's College, Edinburgh; Edinburgh University. Apprentice, Henderson & Jackson, WS, 1975-77. Non-executive director of many successful Scottish companies with a particular focus on fundraising and corporate affairs advice; former Vice Chairman of the Scottish Solicitors' Discipline Tribunal; currently a Judicial Panel Chairman for the Scottish Football Association; principal fundraiser for the Edinburgh-based Headway charity group. Recreations: field sports; sailing; golf; Hibernian FC. Address: (b.) Exchange Tower, 19 Canning Street, Edinburgh EH3 8EH; T.-0131-228 2400. E-mail: Malcolm.mcpherson@addleshawgoddard.com

MacPherson, Robin. Head of College, Robert Gordon's College, since 2020; previously Assistant Rector, Dollar Academy. Educ. Gordon Primary School, Huntly; Merchiston Castle School, Edinburgh; Oxford University; University of Edinburgh. Career history: has held teaching and senior leadership roles throughout the UK and overseas with experience of day and boarding schools, as well as having worked as an examiner for the Scottish Qualifications Authority, Edexcel and the International Baccalaureate Organisation. Fellow of the Royal Society of Arts and a keen advocate and public speaker in international education. Board Member for the educational charity Remembering Srebrenica Scotland. Publication: What Does This Look Like In The Classroom? (Co-Author), 2017. Address: Robert Gordon's College, Schoolhill, Aberdeen AB10 1FE; T.-01224 646346.

Macpherson, Professor Robin David, BA (Hons), MLitt, FRSA. Former Chair, Creative Industries, University of Highlands and Islands (2015-18); Director, Screen Academy Scotland, 2006-2015; Director, Institute for Creative Industries, Edinburgh Napier University, 2010-15; b. 24.12.59, Glasgow; 1 d. Educ. Garthamlock Secondary, Glasgow; Stirling University. Freelance Photographer, Writer and Bookseller, 1980-89; Producer/Director of Documentary, Current Affairs and Drama for Edinburgh Film Workshop Trust, 1989-97; Independent Television Producer/Managing Director, Asylum Pictures Ltd., Edinburgh, since 1997; Development Executive, Scottish Screen, 1999-2002; Napier University, since 2002 (Lecturer, then Senior Lecturer, then Professor). BAFTA (UK) Nomination 1996, for Channel 4 Drama 'The Butterfly Man'; Vice Chair, Producers Association for Cinema and Television in Scotland, 1997-99; Trustee, Edinburgh Television Trust, 1993-99; Board Member, Creative Scotland, 2010-15; Board Member, Creative Edinburgh, 2011-15. Recreation: hillwalking.

Macpherson, Roderick Alexander. Unicorn Pursuivant of Arms in Ordinary, since 2021; Lyon Macer, 2012-18, then Falkland Pursuivant Extraordinary; A messenger-at-arms and sheriff officer; Fellow of the Society of Antiquaries of Scotland and sometime Secretary of the Oxford University Heraldry Society; Past President of the Society of Messengers-at-Arms and Sheriff Officers; Preses of the Grand Antiquity Society of Glasgow; past President of the Glasgow Highland Club. Address: The Court of Lord Lyon, HM New Register House, Edinburgh EH1 3YT.

Macpherson, Shonaig, CBE, LLB (Hons), BA (Hons), FRSE. Solicitor, DUniv (Gla), DUniv (Heriot-Watt). Chairman, National Trust for Scotland, 2005-2010; Chairman, ITI Scotland Limited, 2003-09; Chairman, SCDI, 2004-09; Senior Partner, McGrigors, 2002-04; b. 29.9.58. Educ. University of Sheffield; College of Law, Chester; Strathclyde University; Open University. Articled Clerk, Norton Rose, London, 1982-85; qualified as Solicitor (England), 1984; Solicitor in Corporate/Commercial Department, Knapp Fisher, London, 1985-87; Assistant Company Secretary, Storehouse PLC, 1987; in-house lawyer, Harrods Ltd., and associated companies, 1987-89; Partner, Calow Easton, London 1989-91; Partner, McGrigor Donald, London and Edinburgh, 1991-2004; qualified as Solicitor (Scotland), 1992; Managing Partner, McGrigor Donald, Edinburgh, 1996; appointed Senior Partner (Scotland), McGrigor, 2002-04. Non-executive Member, Scottish Executive Management Group, 2001-07; President, Edinburgh Chamber of Commerce and Enterprise, 2002-04; Visiting Professor, Department of Mechanical Engineering, Heriot Watt University; Chairman, Scottish Council for Development and Industry, 2004-09; Chairman, Scottish Council Foundation, 2004-09; Director and Secretary, Edinburgh International Film Festival, 2001-09; Director, Young Enterprise Scotland, 2001-04; Deputy President, British Chambers of Commerce, 2004-06; Director, Edinburgh International Conference Centre Limited, 2004-2014 (retired); Chairman, Princes Scottish Youth Business Trust Limited, 2005-2012 (retired); Director, Braveheart Investment Group plc, 2006-08; Trustee, The Prince's Trust Council, 2007-2010; Chairman, The Robertson Trust, 2017-2021; Governor, Edinburgh College of Art, 2000-2011; Vice Chairman, The Royal Edinburgh Military Tattoo Ltd., 2007-2015; Council Member, The Open University, 2008-2016; Member of Court, Heriot Watt University, 2009-

2015; Chairman, Royal Lyceum Theatre, Edinburgh, 2012-2021; Member, Commission on Scottish Devolution (Calman Commission), 2009-2010; Trustee, Dunedin Consort, 2012-18 (retired); Chairman, Macpherson Coaches Ltd, 2012-13 (retired); Member, Joint Managerial Board of Scotland Office and Office of Advocate General, 2015-2020; Trustee, Euan's Guide Limited, 2015-18 (retired); former Governor, Royal Conservatoire of Scotland; Chair, Edinburgh Business School, 2015-16; Director, FutureLearn Ltd, 2016-19; President, Scottish Council of Development and Industry, since 2020. Recreations: film; music; reading; theatre. Address: (b.) Lochcote, Linlithgow EH49 6QE; e-mail: shonaigm@btconnect.com

Macpherson, Professor Stuart Gowans, OBE, MB, ChB, FRCS (Glas), FRCP (Edin), FRCS (Edin), FRCS (England), FRCGP, FAcadMEd (Hon). Professor Emeritus, Postgraduate Medical Education, University of Edinburgh; b. 11.7.45, Glasgow; m., Norma Elizabeth Carslaw; 2 s.; 1 d. Educ. Alan Glen's School, Glasgow; University of Glasgow. Formerly Senior Lecturer in Surgery, University of Glasgow and Consultant General Surgeon. Sat on Scottish and UK national committees on postgraduate medical education; formerly Chair, Postgraduate Medical Education and Training Board. Recreations: travelling; family; golf. Address: 33/4 Blackford Road, Edinburgh EH9 2DT; T.-0131 668 4574.
E-mail: macphersonsg@gmail.com

Macphie, Alastair. Lord-Lieutenant for Kincardineshire, since 2020; b. 6.61, Kilmacolm. Educ. school in Edinburgh and Perth. Career history: joined Macphie Limited, the family business, in 1987; appointed Managing Director in 1995 and Executive Chairman in 2007; owns Glenbervie Management Limited, a farming and estate business (farm spans over 1800 acres and is known for breeding Aberdeen Angus cattle). Awarded an honorary degree at Abertay University for contribution to the Food Industry; Fellow of the Royal Agricultural Society. Chair of Drumlithie Village Hall, since 1992; Regional Director of Scotland Land and Estates, since 2004; undertakes a variety of community projects; worked to set up internships for various universities across Scotland. Address: Glenbervie House, Glenbervie, Stonehaven, Kincardineshire AB39 3YA.

MacQuarrie, John Kenneth (Ken), MA (Eng/Hist), DipEd. Director, BBC Nations and Regions, 2016-2020 (retired); b. 5.6.52, Tobermory; m., Angela Sparks; 1 s.; 2 d. Educ. Oban High School; Edinburgh University; Moray House College of Education. Joined BBC Scotland as Researcher, 1975; Radio Producer, BBC Highland, 1976; Producer, Television, 1979; Head of Gaelic, 1988; Head of Gaelic and Features, 1992; Head of Broadcast, 1997; Head of Programmes and Scottish Services, 2000. Board Member, Gaelic Media Service, 2004-08; Vice Chair, Celtic Film and Television Association, 1986-93; Founder Member, Scottish Screen Forum; Former Governor, Scottish Film Council. Recreations: sailing; reading; walking.

McQueen, Bill, CBE, BA, MBA. Non Executive Director, NHS Lothian, since 2018. Educ. Queen Mary, University of London; University of California, Los Angeles; University of Strathclyde. Career history: Scottish Government: Deputy Director, Head of Management and Organisation Division, 1992-1995, Deputy Director, Head of Transport Division, 1995-2001; Deputy Chief Executive, Crown Office and Procurator Fiscal Service, 2001-08; Non Executive Director, Disclosure Scotland, 2010-13; Commission Member, Accounts Commission for Scotland, 2008-2014; Non Executive Board Member, Scottish Legal Aid Board, 2010-2018; Lay Member, Employment

Tribunals for Scotland, 2009-2018; Non Executive Director and Deputy Chair of the Board, Scottish Fire and Rescue Service, since 2013. Address: Lothian NHS Board, Waverley Gate, 2-4 Waterloo Place, Edinburgh EH1 3EG.

McQueen, Eric. Chief Executive, Scottish Courts and Tribunals Service, since 2013. Address: (b.) Parliament House, Edinburgh EH1 1RQ; T.-0131 444 3300.

McQueen, Professor Fiona Catherine, CBE. Chief Nursing Officer for Scotland, 2015-2021; b. 1962. Nursing career began in 1982; promoted to be an executive director of nursing for Lanarkshire in 1993; moved to lead nursing at NHS Ayrshire and Arran in 1999; became Scotland's Interim Chief Nursing Officer in 2014. Honorary Professor, University of the West of Scotland; appointed Commander of the Order of the British Empire (CBE) in the 2021 Birthday Honours for services to the NHS in Scotland.

MacQueen, Professor Hector Lewis, CBE (2019), LLB (Hons), PhD, FRSE, FBA. Emeritus Professor of Private Law, Edinburgh University, since 2021; Dean of Law, 1999-2003; Dean of Research, College of Humanities and Social Science, 2004-08; Scottish Law Commissioner, 2009-2018; b. 13.6.56, Ely; m., Frances Mary Young; 2 s.; 1 d. Educ. George Heriot's School, Edinburgh; Edinburgh University. Lecturer, Senior Lecturer, Reader, all in Law, Edinburgh University, 1979-94; Professor of Private Law, 1994-2021; Director, David Hume Institute, Edinburgh, 1991-99; Visiting Professor, Cornell University, 1991; Visiting Professor, Utrecht University, 1997; Distinguished International Professor, Stetson University College of Law, Florida, USA, 2007-09; Secretary, Scottish Historical Review, 1986-99; Editor, Hume Papers on Public Policy, 1993-99; Editor, Edinburgh Law Review, 1996-2001; Scottish Representative, European Contract Commission, 1995-2001; Member, Co-ordinating Committee, Study Group towards a European Civil Code, 1999-2008; Literary Director, Stair Society, 1999-2016; Chair, Scottish Records Advisory Council, 2001-08; Member, DTI Intellectual Property Advisory Committee, 2003-05; Ministry of Justice (UK) Advisory Panel on Public Sector Information, 2004-11; Director, AHRC Research Centre for Studies in Intellectual Property and Information Technology Law, Edinburgh University, 2002-07; Vice-President (Humanities), Royal Society of Edinburgh, 2008-2011; Chair, Scottish Medievalists Conference, 2007-2011; Chair of Trustees, The David Hume Institute, 2012-2015; President, Society of Legal Scholars, 2012-13. Publications: Common Law and Feudal Society in Medieval Scotland; Studying Scots Law; Copyright, Competition and Industrial Design; Contract Law in Scotland (Co-Author); Unjustified Enrichment Law Basics; Contemporary Intellectual Property: Law and Policy (Co-Author). Recreations: Scotland; cricket; walking – sometimes with golf clubs, sometimes with a camera; reading. Address: (b.) School of Law, University of Edinburgh, Edinburgh EH8 9YL; T.-0131 650 4596.

E-mail: hector.macqueen@ed.ac.uk

McQueen, James Donaldson Wright, MA, PhD, ARSGS; b. 14.2.37, Dumfries; m., Jean Evelyn Brown; 2 s.; 1 d. Educ. King's Park School, Glasgow; Glasgow University. Assistant Lecturer, Department of Geography, Glasgow University, 1960-61; Management Trainee, Milk Marketing Board (England and Wales), 1961-63; Marketing Economist, The Scottish Milk Marketing Board, 1963-67, subsequently Marketing Director (1967-85) and Deputy Managing Director (1985-89); Chief Executive, Scottish Dairy Trade Federation (latterly Scottish Dairy Association), 1989-95; UK representative on the Board of the European Dairy Association (EDA), Brussels, 1990-95;

CBI National Council Member, 1990-95; Adviser on Milk Industry Matters to the States of Jersey, 2003-07; Chairman, Milk Price Review Panel, States of Guernsey, 2007; Honorary Research Fellow, School of Geographical and Earth Sciences, University of Glasgow, 1999-2011; Royal Scottish Geographical Society Council Member, 1997-2012; food industry map publisher and analyst, 1995-2020 (t/a Agri-Food Market Analysis). Address: Ormlie, 53 Kingston Road, Bishopton, Renfrewshire PA7 5BA. E-mail: mcqueen@agri-food.co.uk

MacQueen, Norrie, BA, MSc (Econ), DPhil. Honorary Research Fellow, School of International Relations, University of St Andrews; Volunteer Adviser (employment), Citizens Advice Scotland; b. 11.4.50, Glasgow; m., Betsy (nee King); 1 d. Educ. Shawlands Academy; University of Ulster; London School of Economics. Ministry of Education, Mozambique, 1977-79; Research Officer, Glasgow University, 1980-83; Senior Lecturer, University of Papua New Guinea, 1986-90; Research Fellow, Australian National University, 1990; Reader, University of Sunderland, 1990-96; Dundee University, 1996-2012 (Senior Lecturer, Head of Department of Politics, 1998-2005); United Nations Electoral Officer, Timor-Leste, 2012. Publications: The Decolonization of Portuguese Africa, 1997; United Nations Peacekeeping in Africa, 2002; Peacekeeping and the International System, 2006; European Security after Iraq, 2006 (Joint Editor); Colonialism, 2007; The United Nations: a Beginner's Guide, 2010; The United Nations, Peace Operations and the Cold War, 2011; Humanitarian Intervention and the United Nations, 2011; The Oxford Handbook of United Nation Peacekeeping Operations, 2015 (Joint Editor). Recreations: hillwalking; cycling; music. Address: 6 Glenalmond Terrace, Perth PH2 0AU; e-mail: norriemacqueen@yahoo.co.uk

McQuillan, Kathleen T., OBE, BA, LLB. Solicitor; Vice-Chair, Parole Board for Scotland, 2009-2011; Legal Convenor, Mental Health Tribunal for Scotland, 2007-2017; b. Glasgow; m., James McQuillan; 1 s. Educ. Bellarmine Secondary School; University of Strathclyde. Admitted as Solicitor in 1981; Solicitor in practice specialising in criminal law, 1981-89; Authority's Advocate, Criminal Injuries Compensation Authority, 1989-2002; Solicitor to the Board, Strathclyde Joint Police Board, 2003-04; Member, Parole Board for Scotland, 2004-2011 and 2014-17. Recreations: cinema; reading; music; current affairs.

MacRae, Alan. President, Scottish Football Association, 2015-19. Joined Cove Rangers as a player in 1979, became Chairman (1984-1999), leading the Aberdeenshire club from the amateurs, to the ranks of the Juniors and eventually to the Highland League; appointed President, Cove Rangers (1999), then Honorary President until 2007; appointed Council Member, Scottish Football Association in 1993 before becoming 1st Vice President, served as 2nd Vice-President.

McRae, Andrew, MA (Hons). Retail Entrepreneur; Business Owner: Museum Context, Edinburgh and Hong Kong, since 2007, John Kay's Shop Ltd, since 2017, The Earl Grange Cafe, since 2019; Scottish Policy Convener, Federation of Small Business Scotland, since 2018; b. 12.77. Educ. Edinburgh College of Art. Vice Chair, Original Edinburgh, since 2020; Member, GlobalScot, since 2020. Address: Museum Context, 40 Victoria Street, Edinburgh EH1 2JW; T.-01407 4715026.

MacRae, Professor Donald J. R., OBE, BSc (Hons), MBA, FCIBS, FRSE, FRAgS. Chair, Water Industry

Commission for Scotland; Board Member, Highlands and Islands Enterprise; former Chief Economist, Lloyds Banking Group Scotland (retired in 2015); former Director, Lloyds TSB Scotland plc; Past Board Member, Scottish Enterprise; b. 12.8.54, Inverness; m., Anne de Diesbach; 1 s.; 1 d. Educ. Fortrose Academy; Edinburgh University. Economist/Analyst, Imperial Chemical Industries, 1979-82; Project Manager, Farmplan Computer Systems, 1982-84; Lecturer, University of Newcastle upon Tyne, 1984-86; TSB Bank Scotland plc: Manager, 1986-90, Senior Manager, 1990-98, Chief Manager, Strategy and Development, 1998-2001. Member, Advisory Board, Interface; Past Member, Rural Development Council; Past Member, Scottish Government: Purchasers Information Advisory Group; Member: Economic Statistics Advisory Group, Committee of Inquiry on Crofting; former Trustee, David Hume Institute; former Honorary Professor, University of Edinburgh; Visiting Professor, University of Abertay Dundee; former Member of Court, University of Highlands and Islands; Member of Court, Royal Conservatoire of Scotland; Past Member, Skills Committee of Skills Development Scotland and Scottish Funding Council. Recreations: music; film; theatre; vintage tractors.

McSherry, Sheriff John Craig Cunningham, LLB (Hons). Advocate; part-time Sheriff, 2000-03; All-Scotland Floating Sheriff, 2003-06; resident Sheriff at Dunfermline, 2006-2019; b. 21.10.49, Irvine; m., Elaine Beattie; 2 s. Educ. Ardrossan Academy; Glasgow University. Senior Partner, McSherry Halliday, Solicitors, 1983-92. Chairman, Largs and Saltcoats Citizens Advice Bureaux, 1976-83; Council Member, Law Society of Scotland, 1982-85; part-time Immigration Appeals Adjudicator, 2001-03. Recreations: country pursuits; skiing; music; bridge; golf. Address: (h.) 2 Heriot Row, Edinburgh EH3 6HU; T.-0131-556 8289; e-mail: jccmcs@hotmail.com

McSherry, Mark. Chief Executive, Risk Management Authority, since 2019. Educ. University of Glasgow. Career history: worked in residential care and alternative to custody programmes; worked in youth justice and with care organisations such as Alzheimer Scotland before joining SACRO in 1997; studied social work which included placements with Glasgow Women's Reproductive Health Services, children and families social work and a counselling service for survivors of childhood sexual abuse; provided programmes on Domestic Abuse and support services to woman and children across the Forth Valley as well as programmes for those convicted of sexual offending and for young people on Probation; held posts at Glasgow Community Safety Services providing restorative programmes with young people and Renfrewshire Council prior to becoming Head of the Scottish Government's Effective Practice Unit in 2007; joined Risk Management Authority in 2010 as Head of Development; led development and research programmes, as well as delivery functions relating to OLRs, including approval of Risk Management Plans, review of Annual Implementation Reports and the accreditation of assessors. Panel Member for the Scottish Advisory Panel for Offender Rehabilitation to providing assistance to the accreditation of programmes. Address: Risk Management Authority, 7 Thread Street, Paisley PA1 1JR; T.-0141 278 4478.

McTaggart, Bailie Anne. SNP Councillor in the Drumchapel/Anniesland ward of Glasgow City Council, since 2019 and 2009-2012 (Labour); MSP (Labour), Glasgow, 2011-16; former Shadow Minister for Democracy; b. 30.1.70, Coatbridge; m.; 3 c. Educ. Chryston High School, North Lanarkshire; University of Strathclyde. Previously social worker and local chair of the local primary school's parents council. Former member of the Glasgow Labour Women's Forum and the Co-operative

Party; member of Community Union.
E-mail: anne.mctaggart@glasgow.gov.uk

MacTaggart, Kenneth Dugald, BA (Hons), PhD; b. 15.4.53, Glasgow; m., Caroline McNicholas; 2 d. Educ. Allan Glen's School, Glasgow; Glasgow University; Paisley College (Univ. West of Scotland); Aston University. Economic Research, Aston University, 1976-80; Editor, Export Times, London 1980-84; Editor, Property International, London and Bahrain, 1984-87; Director, Inc. Publications, London, 1987-88; Senior Economist, HIDB, 1988-91; Chief Economist, then Director of Strategy, then Head of Knowledge, Highlands & Islands Enterprise, 1991-2001; Managing Director, Alba Consult, economic development, 2001-2020; Development Economics Consultant, Upper Quartile, 2009-2016; Fellow, British Interplanetary Society; Committee, Neil Munro Society. Co-editor, NASA Apollo 11 Flight Journal; Author, Haynes Astronaut Manual. Civilian Service Medal (Afghanistan), 2012. Recreations: hill-walking; piano; astronomy. Address: (h.) The Sutors, 28 Broadstone Park, Inverness IV2 3LA; T.-01463 233717.

Mactaggart, Sheriff Mhairi. Sheriff, South Strathclyde, Dumfries and Galloway, since 2020. Trained with Robert Carty & Co; became a Partner in 1985; joined Milligan Mactaggart & Perkins Solicitors as a Partner before becoming a Senior Partner with Mhari S Mactaggart Family Law Practice in 1996; appointed Part-Time Sheriff in 2005; joined Hamilton Burns WS in 2008 as a consultant and Head of Family Law Team; appointed a Summary Sheriff in Ayr in 2016.

McVey, Cllr Adam. Leader, Edinburgh Council, since 2017; representing Leith ward (SNP), since 2012. Educ. University of Dundee; University of Edinburgh. Appointed Vice-Convener of Transport and Environment, Edinburgh Council in 2014. Address: City of Edinburgh Council, City Chambers, High Street, Edinburgh EH1 1YJ; T.-0131 529 3279; e-mail: adam.mcvey@edinburgh.gov.uk

McVicar, Fr. Duncan. Minister, Church of St. Peter-in-Chains, Ardrossan, since 2017; previously Administrator, St. John Ogilvie's, Irvine. Address: 1 South Crescent Road, Ardrossan, Ayrshire KA22 8DU.

McVicar, William, RD*, CA. Past Chairman of Trustees, Church of Scotland Housing and Loan Fund for Retired Ministers and Widows and Widowers of Ministers, 1983-2008 (Trustee, 1976-2008); Retired Chartered Accountant; b. 29.6.32, Rutherglen; m., Doreen Ann; 1 s.; 1 d. Educ. George Heriot's School, Edinburgh. Royal Navy, 1950-52; RNVR/RNR, 1955-86 (retired list, Commander RNR); Admitted ICAS, 1958 (T.C. Garden & Co., CA, Edinburgh); Partner, T.C. Garden & Co., CA, Edinburgh, 1962-79; Partner, Coopers and Lybrand, 1979-91. Recreations: travel; food and wine; gardening; grand-children. Address: (h.) The Kirn, Kerfield, Innerleithen Road, Peebles EH45 8LY; T.-01721 927197.
E-mail: williammcvicar@btinternet.com

MacWalter, Dr Ronald Siller, BMSc (Hons), MB, ChB (Hons), MD, MRCP (UK), FRCP (Edin), FRCP (Glas). Retired Consultant Physician in Stroke Medicine and General Medicine, Ninewells Hospital, Dundee; Consultant Physician in Medicine for the Elderly, Royal Victoria Hospital, Dundee, 1986-97; Honorary Associate Professor of Medicine, Kigezi International School of Medicine, Cambridge, 2001-04; b. 14.12.53, Broughty Ferry; m., Sheila Margaret Nicoll; 2 s. Educ. Harris Academy,

Dundee; Dundee University; University of Florida. Registrar in Medicine and Haematology, Department of Clinical Pharmacology, Ninewells Hospital, Dundee; Senior Registrar in General Medicine and Geriatric Medicine, Nuffield Department of Medicine, John Radcliffe Hospital, Oxford. Publication: Secondary Prevention of Stroke; Managing Stroke and TIAs in Practice; Aids to Clinical Examination; papers on stroke.

Macwhirter, Iain. Scottish political commentator; Rector, Edinburgh University, 2009-2012. Educ. University of Edinburgh; b. London; 3 c. Career: worked for the BBC for almost 20 years, becoming Scottish political correspondent in 1987, then from 1989 as a member of the Westminster press contingent; worked at both the UK Parliament and Scottish Parliament, presenting the BBC2 programmes "Westminster Live" and "Scrutiny"; writes weekly columns for The Herald, The Scotsman and Scotland on Sunday; helped launch the Sunday Herald in 1999; presented the Scottish Parliament magazine programme "Holyrood Live". Published Road to Referendum in 2013. Recreation: hill walking. Address: (b.) The Herald, 200 Renfield Street, Glasgow G2 3PR.

McWilliam, Rev. Thomas Mathieson, MA, BD. Retired Minister; Clerk, Presbytery of Ross, 2000-09; b. 12.11.39, Glasgow; m., Patricia Jane Godfrey; 1 s.; 1 d. Educ. Eastwood Secondary School; Glasgow University; New College, Edinburgh. Assistant Minister, Auld Kirk of Ayr, 1964-66; Minister: Dundee St. David's North, 1966-72, East Kilbride Greenhills, 1972-80, Lylesland Parish Church, Paisley, 1980-97, Contin Parish, 1997-2003. Convener, Youth Education Committee, General Assembly, 1980-84; Moderator, Paisley Presbytery, 1985-86; Convener, Board of Practice and Procedure, General Assembly, 1992-96. Recreations: walking; reading; gardening; bowling. Address: (h.) Flat 3, 13 Culduthel Road, Inverness IV2 4AG; T.-01463 718981.

M

Mackie, Dr. Willie. Deputy Chair, Scottish Enterprise; Chair, hub South West Scotland Ltd, since 2020; Regional Chair, Ayrshire College, since 2013; b. 7.59. Educ. University of the West of Scotland. Career history: Project Manager Credit Re-engineering, National Australia Bank, Melbourne, 1996; Senior Project Manager, Clydesdale Bank, Glasgow, 1996-99; Programme Director, Business Transformation Programme, National Australia Group, Glasgow, 1999-2001; Managing Partner, Ayr, Clydesdale Bank, 2001-2012; Director, Willie Mackie (Consulting) Limited, Troon, since 2013. Fellow of the Institute of Bankers in Scotland; Board member: College Scotland, College Development Network (Chair of the Audit Committee), Skills Development Scotland, since 2014 (Chair of the Finance and Operational Committee). Address: Scottish Enterprise HQ, Atrium Court, 50 Waterloo Street, Glasgow G2 6HQ.

Mackison, Duncan. Chief Executive Officer, David MacBrayne Ltd, since 2019; Chairman of Governors, The Glasgow Academy. Educ. The Glasgow Academy; Henley and Aston Business Schools. Career history: Royal Marine Officer; Director of Operations and Business Development, G4S, 1998-2005; Serco: Director of Business Development, Civil Government, 2005-08, Chief Executive Officer, ACCESS LLP, 2008-2012, Managing Director, Defence, 2012-14; Chief Operating Officer, Buccleuch, 2014-17; Chief Executive Officer, Jahama Highland Estates, 2017-19. Address: David MacBrayne Ltd, Ferry Terminal, Gourock PA19 1QP.

Magee, Jane Deborah, MA (St Andrews), MA (London), PGCE (Dundee). Senior Consultant, University of St Andrews (former Director, English Language Teaching); b. 26.07.51, Glasgow; m., Stephen Magee; 2 s.; 1 d. Educ. Park School, Glasgow; St. Andrews; Institute of Education, University of London. Legal Executive, London, 1977-79; Librarian, University of London, 1974-75; Teacher: Scotland, 1975-77, Markopoulo, Greece, 1979-80; Management Accountant: Schlumberger, London, 1982-84, Schlumberger, China, 1985-86; Administrator, Beijing Normal University, 1987-89; Programme Director, ELT, St Andrews, 1996-2006. Recreations: photography; (slow) walking; swimming; gardening; running; travelling. Address: (b.) University of St Andrews, ELT, Kinnessburn, Kennedy Gardens, St Andrews, Fife KY16 9DJ; T.-01334-462255; e-mail: jane.magee@st-andrews.ac.uk

Magnusson, Sally Anne, MA (Hons). Presenter, Reporting Scotland, BBC, since 1998; Presenter, Hard Cash, BBC, 2000-02; Reporter, 4 X 4 Reports, 2001-03; Presenter, Britain's Secret Shame, 2003-04; Presenter, Songs of Praise, BBC, 1984-2018; Presenter, Daily Politics, BBC; Reporter, Panorama, BBC1; Presenter, Tracing Your Roots, Radio 4; Presenter, Sally on Sunday, Radio Scotland; Presenter, Sunday Morning, Radio Scotland; b. 11.10.55, Glasgow; m., Norman Stone; 4 s.; 1 d. Educ. Laurel Bank School; Edinburgh University. Reporter, The Scotsman, 1979-81; News/Feature Writer, Sunday Standard, 1981-83; Reporter, Current Account, BBC Scotland, 1983, Presenter, Sixty Minutes, BBC, 1983-84; Presenter, London Plus, BBC, 1984-85; Presenter, Breakfast News (formerly Breakfast Time), BBC, 1985-99. Awards: Feature Writer of the Year, 1982; Royal Television Society, 2004; Institute of Contemporary Scotland, 2007; Glenfiddich Spirit of Scotland Award for Writing, 2014. Publications: The Flying Scotsman, 1981; Clemo - A Love Story, 1984; A Shout in the Street, 1990; Family Life, 1999; Dreaming of Iceland, 2004; Glorious Things, 2004; Life of Pee, 2010; Horace and the Haggis Hunter, 2012; Horace and the Ghost Dog, 2013; Horace and the Christmas Mystery, 2014; Where Memories Go: Why Dementia Changes Everything, 2014; The Sealwoman's Gift, 2018; The Ninth Child, 2020. Honorary Degrees: Edinburgh University, Stirling University, Glasgow Caledonian University, Open University. Honorary Fellow of Royal College of Physicians and Surgeons Glasgow; Hon FRIAS. Founder of charity Playlist for Life.

Maguire, Joanne, BA (Hons) Econ, Spanish. Chief Operating Officer, ScotRail Trains Ltd, since 2022; b. 6.79. Educ. Turnbull; University of Strathclyde. Career history: Regional HR Generalist, ROC ExxonMobil, 2007; HR Consultant, Avis Rent a Car, 2007-08; HR Manager, Guala Closures Group, 2008-2014; Bakkavor: Business HR Manager, Caledonian Produce, 2014-15, Head of HR, 2015-16; University of the West of Scotland: Executive Director of HR, 2018-2020, Vice Principal - Resources, 2020-22. Address: ScotRail Trains Ltd, Atrium Court, 50 Waterloo Street, Glasgow G2 6HQ.

Maguire, Ruth. MSP (SNP), Cunninghame South, since 2016. Educ. Millburn Academy; Sabhal Mòr Ostaig. Career history: Sales and Marketing Manager, Praban Na Linne, 1994-96; Account Manager/Customer Service Team Leader, Compaq, 1997-2001; Sales (Acquisition SME), Integral Arm, 2005-06; Mentor - New Deal Clients, Glasgow Mentoring Network, 2010-11; Ùlpan Gaelic Tutor, 2011; Therapist - Reflexology and Hypnotherapy, Ruth Maguire Reflexology, 2004-2012; SNP Councillor, North Ayrshire Council, 2012-16; Cabinet Member for Finance and Corporate Support, North Ayrshire Council, 2013-16; Cunninghame South Women's Officer, SNP, 2014-15; Cunninghame South Political Education Officer, SNP, 2014. Daughter of John Finnie, Scottish Green MSP. Address: Scottish Parliament, Edinburgh EH99 1SP.

Mahal, Neena, MBE. Chair, NHS Lanarkshire, 2013-2021. Educ. Glasgow University. Career history: qualified Careers Guidance Adviser and has previously worked in the Equalities field within Education and as a Training Consultant; served on the Boards of various Public Bodies, charitable and voluntary sector organisations including the Broadcasting Council for Scotland, National Museums Scotland, BBC Children in Need and The Glasgow Academy (formerly Chair of the Education Committee). Lay Governor of the Court of Glasgow Caledonian University (Chair of the People Committee and a Member of the Audit Committee). Depute Lieutenant for Lanarkshire, since 2014 (Vice Chair of the Lieutenancy's Community and Voluntary Organisations Committee). Address: Glasgow Caledonian University, Cowcaddens Road, Glasgow G4 0BA; T.-0141 331 3000.

Mahoney, Professor Craig, BEd, MA, PhD, TTC, CPsychol. Principal and Vice-Chancellor, University of the West of Scotland, since 2013; b. Tasmania. Educ. Tasmanian College of Advanced Education (now the University of Tasmania); Birmingham University; The Queen's University of Belfast. Career: founding Dean of the School of Sport, Performing Arts and Leisure, Wolverhampton University; Deputy Vice-Chancellor, Northumbria University; Chief Executive, Higher Education Academy, 2010-2013. Served as a reviewer for the Quality Assurance Agency in England and since 1995 has been on numerous committees and validation panels in UK Higher Education; part of a panel to produce a new quality benchmark for Hospitality, Leisure, Sport and Tourism in 2008; has held a variety of external examination engagements (at subject, programme and PhD level) to confirm standards and oversee the assurance of quality in UK Higher Education; past Chair of the British Association of Sport and Exercise Sciences (BASES); won a number of awards including Distinguished Professor, Changchun Institute of Technology, China (2019); Guardian Outstanding Leader in UK Higher Education finalist (2018); Outstanding Business Leader from Renfrewshire Chamber (2015); Outstanding Service to Higher Education Award from the International Higher Education Teaching and Learning Association, USA (2014); Honorary Doctor of Arts from University of Abertay Dundee, UK (2011); Distinguished Scholar from Olabisi Onabanjo University, Nigeria (2011). Chair of British Universities and Colleges Sport; Board member on the UK Quality Assurance Agency; Board member for Glasgow City of Sciences; Trustee on the Carnegie Trust for Universities of Scotland; Convener of Universities Scotland Efficiency and Effectiveness Committee; Board member for SportScotland; Board member of Converge Challenge; an industry adviser to VerfiyEd. Recreations: travel; music; sport; spending time with family. Address: (b.) Paisley Campus, Paisley PA1 2BE; T.-0141 8483000.

Main, Very Rev. Professor Alan, TD, MA, BD, STM, PhD, DD. Professor of Practical Theology, Christ's College, Aberdeen, 1980-2001; Moderator, General Assembly, Church of Scotland, 1998-99; b. 31.3.36, Aberdeen; m., Anne Louise Swanson; 2 d. Educ. Robert Gordon's College, Aberdeen; University of Aberdeen; Union Theological Seminary, New York. Minister, Chapel of Garioch Parish, Aberdeenshire, 1963-70; Chaplain, University of Aberdeen 1970-80; Chaplain, 153(H) Artillery Support Regiment, RCT(V), 1970-92; Provost, Faculty of Divinity, Aberdeen University, 1990-93; Master, Christ's College, Aberdeen, 1992-2001. Moderator: Garioch Presbytery, 1969-70, Aberdeen Presbytery, 1984-85; Convener, Board of World Mission, 2000-02; Adviser in Religious Broadcasting, Grampian Television, 1976-86; Chairman: Grampian Marriage Guidance, 1977-80, Cruse, 1981-84; Patron, Seven Incorporated Trades of Aberdeen, 2000-2013; Minister, St. Andrews Scots Kirk, Colombo, 2002-03; Convener, Israel Centres, 2003-04; President, The Boys' Brigade, 2005-07. Recreations: music; golf. Address: (h.) Kirkfield, Barthol Chapel, Inverurie AB51 8TD.

Main, Professor Brian G.M., BSc, MBA, MA, PhD, FRSE. Professor of Business Economics, Edinburgh University, since 1991; Director, David Hume Institute, 1995-2005; b. 24.8.47, St. Andrews; m., June Lambert; 2 s.; 1 d. Educ. Buckhaven High School; St. Andrews University; University of California, Berkeley. Lecturer, then Reader in Economics, Edinburgh University, 1976-87; Professor of Economics and Chairman, Department of Economics, St. Andrews University, 1987-91. Recreation: fishing. Address: (b.) University of Edinburgh Business School, 29 Buccleuch Place, Edinburgh EH8 9JS; T.-0131-650 8360; e-mail: Brian.Main@ed.ac.uk

Main, Carol, BLD, MBE, BA. Director, Live Music Now Scotland and International Development, since 1984; Founding Director, National Association of Youth Orchestras, 1979-2003; Classical Music Editor, The List, since 1985; 1 d. Educ. Kirkcaldy High School; Edinburgh University. Freelance music critic; radio broadcaster. Board Member: Creative Scotland; Board Director: The Night With... (Chair); Traditional Music Forum (former Vice-Chair); Governor: Royal Conservatoire of Scotland. Previous Board Directorships include: Association of British Orchestras (2011-17); Voluntary Arts Scotland (Vice-Chair); Hebrides Ensemble (Chair, 2004-2011); Enterprise Music Scotland (Chair, 1999-2001); St Mary's Music School, Edinburgh Festival Fringe Society (1986-2005). Address: (b.) 14 Lennox Street, Edinburgh EH4

1QA; T.-0131 332 2110. E-mail: carol.main@gmail.com

Main, Professor Ian Graham, BSc, MSc, PhD, FRSE. Professor of Seismology and Rock Physics, University of Edinburgh, since 2000; Member: the Research Advisory Forum of the Scottish Energy Technology Partnership (ETP); the Scottish Regional Advisory Group for Enhanced Learning and Research for Humanitarian Assistance (ELRHA); b. 8.9.57, Aberdeen; m., 1. Anthea Stephen (divorced); 1 d.; m., 2. Melanie Miller; 1 d. Educ. Ross High School, Tranent, East Lothian; University of St. Andrews; University of Durham; University of Edinburgh. Lecturer in Geophysics, University of Reading, 1985-89; Lecturer, then Reader in Seismology and Rock Physics, University of Edinburgh, 1989-2000; Visiting Professor: École Normale Supérieure, Paris, 1999, University of Bologna, 2000, Autonomous University of Barcelona, 2021, University of Stanford, 2022; Head of the Earth Sciences research group, School of Geosciences, 2003-07; Director, Joint Research Institute in Subsurface Science and Engineering (Ecosse), 2007-09; Director of Research, School of Geosciences, 2015-2020; Member: International Seismological Centre Governing Council, 1988-89; Moderator: Nature debate on earthquake prediction, 1999; Member: Royal Society of Edinburgh Sectional Committee on Chemistry and Earth Sciences, 2009-2012, International Commission on Earthquake Forecasting for civil protection, 2010-2011, The HEFCE Research Excellence Framework (REF) Panel on Earth Systems and Environmental Sciences, 2013-14; Awards: Bullerwell Lecturer in Geophysics, 1997, Elected Fellow, Royal Society of Edinburgh, 2009, Royal Society of Edinburgh Research Fellowship, 2010, Louis Néel medal of the European Geosciences Union, 2014; Ed Lorenz Lecture, American Geophysical Union, 2019. Recreations: writing and performing folk music; running (very slowly). Address: (b.) School of Geosciences, University of Edinburgh, James Hutton Road, Edinburgh EH9 3FE; T.-0131-650 4911; e-mail: ian.main@ed.ac.uk

Mair, Alistair S.F., MBE, DL, LLD, BSc, BA, FRSA. Managing Director, Caithness Glass Ltd., 1977-98, Chairman, 1991-98; b. 20.7.35, Drumblade; m., 1, Anne Garrow (deceased); 2, Mary Bolton; 4 s.; 1 d. Educ. New Machar School; Robert Gordon's College, Aberdeen; Aberdeen University; Open University. Rolls Royce, Glasgow, 1957-71: graduate apprentice, PA to General Manager, Production Control Manager, Product Centre Manager; RAF, 1960-62 (short-service commission, Technical Branch); Managing Director, Caithness Glass Ltd., 1971-75; Marketing Director, Worcester Royal Porcelain Co., 1975-76. Non-Executive Director: Grampian Television, 1986-2001, Crieff Hydro Ltd., 1994-2003 (Chairman, 1996-2003), Murray VCT 3 PLC, 1997-2005; Governor, Morrison's Academy, Crieff, 1985-2006 (Chairman, 1996-2006); Commissioner, Queen Victoria School, Dunblane, 1992-97; Member, Aberdeen University Court, 1993-2010, Convener, Finance and Estates Committee, 1998-2003, Chancellor's Assessor, Senior Lay Member, and Vice Chairman, 2000-2010; Member, UHI Board, 2008-2013; Chairman, Scottish Committee of University Chairmen, 2001-07; Chairman, CBI Scotland, 1989-91, and Member, CBI Scottish Council, 1985-97; President, British Glass Manufacturers Confederation 1997, 1998; Chairman, Crieff Auxiliary Association (Richmond House), 1993-99; Honorary President, Duke of Edinburgh Award, Perth and Kinross, since 1993; Chairman, Perth, Ochil and South Perthshire Conservative and Unionist Associations, 1999-2009 (Deputy Chairman, since 2014). Recreations: reading; history; gardening; walking; current affairs. Address: (h.) Woodend, Madderty, Crieff PH7 3PA; T.-01764 683210.

Mair, Christopher John Montgomerie Alpine, FICS. Honorary Consul for Norway, since 1963; C. A. Mair (Shipping) Ltd., since 1987; Shipping Agent and Broker, since 1956; b. 10.06.39, The Hague, Netherlands; m., Janette Louise; 2 d. Educ. Cranleigh. R. L. Alpine & Co. Ltd., 1956-87. Honorary Vice Consul for Denmark, since 1966. Recreations: swimming; golf. Address: (h.) 32 Caldwell Road, West Kilbride KA23 9LF. Address: (b.) Winton Buildings, Ardrossan KA22 8BY; T.-01294 605284; e-mail: chris@mairshipping.co.uk

Mair, Colin David Robertson, MA, CertEd. Rector, The High School of Glasgow, 2004-2015; b. 4.8.53, Edinburgh. Educ. Kelvinside Academy; St. Andrews University; Glasgow University; Jordanhill College. The High School of Glasgow: Teacher of Latin, 1976-79, Head of Rugby, 1977-88, Head of Latin, 1979-85, Bannerman Housemaster, 1982-85, Assistant Rector, 1985-96, Deputy Rector, 1996-2004; General Convocation of the University of Strathclyde, 2009-2010. Commonweal Committee, Trades House of Glasgow, 2004-06; awarded the SQA Fellowship Award 2014; Member, UCAS Scottish Standing Group, 2003-2015; Member, School Leaders Scotland Council, 1997-2013; Member, Merchants House of Glasgow; Chair of Board, West of Scotland Cricket Club; Trustee, Cricket Development Trust Scotland; Trustee, High School of Glasgow Educational Trust; received Scottish Cricket Writers Award, 1993 "for services to cricket". Recreations: cricket; golf; rugby; walking; Partick Thistle. Address: (h.) 17 Ladywood, Milngavie, Glasgow G62 8BE; T.-0141 956 5792.

Mair, Rory, CBE. Chair, Citizens Advice Scotland, since 2017; b. 1.57. Career history: worked in a number of senior Local Government roles, including as Strategic Director for Social Strategy with Fife Council, and Chief Executive of Ross & Cromarty District Council; spent five years as Director of Aviemore Projects for Highlands & Islands Enterprise; Chief Executive of COSLA, 2002-2015. Address: Citizens Advice Scotland, 1st Floor, Broadside, Powderhall Road, Edinburgh EH7 4GB; T.-0131 550 1000.

Maitland, Peter Salisbury, BSc, PhD, FRSE. Independent Consultant in Freshwater Ecology, since 1986; Visiting Professor, Glasgow University, since 1997; Founder, Scottish Freshwater Group; b. 8.12.37, Glasgow; m., Kathleen Ramsay; 1 s.; 2 d. Educ. Bearsden Academy; Glasgow University. Lecturer in Zoology, Glasgow University, 1959-67; Senior Scientific Officer, Nature Conservancy, 1967-70; Principal Scientific Officer, Institute of Terrestrial Ecology, 1970-86; Senior Lecturer in Ecology, St. Andrews University, 1978-82. Royal Society of Edinburgh Fellowship, 1980; Neill Medal, 1993; Freshwater Biological Association Fellowship, 1996; Zoological Society of London's Marsh Wildlife Award for Conservation, 1999; Fishery Society of the British Isles: Beverton Medal, 2009. Publications: 12 books; 260 scientific papers. Recreations: wildlife conservation; fish-keeping; gardening; walking; music. Address: (h.) Nether Sunnyside, Gladshot, Haddington EH41 4NR; T.-01620 823691.

Maitland-Carew, The Hon. Gerald Edward Ian, CVO, DL. Lord Lieutenant, Roxburgh, Ettrick and Lauderdale, 2007-2016 (retired); b. 28.12.41, Dublin; m., Rosalind Averil Speke (1972); 2 s. (Edward, 1976 and Peter, 1978); 1 d. (Emma, 1974). Educ. Harrow School. Army Officer, 15/19 The Kings Royal Hussars, 1960-72; looked after family estates, 1972-2013; Lieutenant, Royal Company of Archers; Chairman, Lauderdale Hunt, 1980-2000; Chairman, Lauderdale and Galawater Branch, Royal British Legion Scotland; Deputy Lieutenant, Ettrick and Lauderdale and Roxburgh, 1989; elected Member, Jockey Club, 1987; Steward at Newmarket, Cheltenham, Newcastle, Ayr, Kelso and Musselburgh Racecourses,

1976-2012; Member, Border Area, TA Committee 1979-2000; Chairman, International League for the Protection of Horses, 1999-2007; Chairman, Musselburgh Racecourse, 2000-2012; Vice President, World Horse Welfare, since 2007-2017; President, Gurkha Welfare Trust of Scotland, since 2003; President, Border Rifle League, 1994; Chairman, Gurkha Welfare Trust of Scotland, 1996-2003; Elder, Church of Scotland, since 1977; Trustee: Thirlestane Castle Trust, 1983-2013, Mellerstain Trust, 1984-2019; Patron, Trimontium Trust, since 2011; President of the Scottish Borders Branch of the Scouts, since 2021. Invested with 'Commander Of The Victorian Order' in 2016 on retiring as Lord Lieutenant. Recreations: shooting; horse riding; horse racing. Address: (h.) The Garden House, Thirlestane Castle, Lauder, Berwickshire TD2 6PD; T.-07971196351.
E-mail: maitland-carew@thirlestanecastle.co.uk

Maizels, Professor Rick, BSc, PhD, FRSE, FMedSci. Professor of Parasitology, University of Glasgow, since 2016; b. 14.5.53, London. Educ. University College London. MRC Scientific Staff, NIMR, Mill Hill, 1979-83; Lecturer, Reader and Professor, Department of Biology, Imperial College, London, 1983-95; Professor of Zoology, University of Edinburgh, 1995-2015. Address: (b.) Glasgow Biomedical Research Centre, 120 University Avenue, Glasgow G12 8TA; T.-0141 330 3745.

Majcher, Rev Iain, BD (Hons). Minister, Bothwell Parish Church, since 2021; m., Celeste; 5 c. Educ. Cargilfield School; Gordonstoun School; The University of Edinburgh. Project Leader for the Amsterdam (Diaconal) Volunteer Year, Protestantse Kerk Amsterdam, 2009-2014; Trainer for Togetthere, Protestantse Kerk in Nederland, 2009-2014; De Regenboog Groep, Amsterdam: Coordinator, De Kloof, 2008-2013, Senior Coordinator - De Kloof, 2013-14; Child and Youth Worker, Gorgie Dalry Steenhouse Church, 2014-16; Church of Scotland: Minister in training, Edinburgh, 2015-2020. Recreation: long walks with family and dog. Address: Bothwell Parish Church, Main Street, Bothwell, Glasgow G71 8EX; T.-01698 854933.
E-mail: minister@bothwellparishchurch.org.uk

Malcolm, Chris. Partner, Ryder Architecture, since 2020. Design Studio Tutor, Strathclyde University, 1998-2012; Associate, GMA/Ryder, 2012-2020. Elected a Fellow of the RIAS in 2020. Recreations: hill walking; keen student of history. Address: Ryder Architecture, 221 West George Street, Glasgow G2 2ND; T.-0141 285 0230.

Malcolm, Hon. Lord (Colin Campbell), LLB (Hons); b. 1.10.53; m., Fiona Anderson. Senator of the College of Justice, since 2007. Educ. Grove Academy, Broughty Ferry; School of Law, University of Dundee. Admitted to the Faculty of Advocates in 1977; Lecturer, School of Law, University of Edinburgh, 1977-79; Standing Junior Counsel to the Scottish Development Department, 1984-1990, appointed Queen's Counsel in 1990; elected Vice-Dean of the Faculty of Advocates in 1997, Dean of the Faculty, 2001-04; part-time member of the Mental Welfare Commission for Scotland, 1997-2001; one of the first members of the Judicial Appointments Board for Scotland on its establishment in 2002, serving until 2005; appointed to the Bench of the Supreme Courts of Scotland in 2007, succeeding Lord Wheatley in the Outer House of the Court of Session; took the judicial title, Lord Malcolm; served as a judge of the Commercial Court of the Court of Session; appointed to the Second Division of the Inner House in 2014; appointed a member of the Privy Council of the United Kingdom in 2015; sworn a member of the Council on 19 March 2015. Address: (b.) Parliament House, 11 Parliament Square, Edinburgh EH1 1RQ.

Malden, Reginald John, FMA, MPhil; b. 5.12.44. Educ. Durham School; University of York. FSA Scot, 1963; FMA, 1982. Linlithgow Pursuivant Extraordinary, 1994 & 2010; Unicorn Pursuivant, 2012-15; Slains Pursuivant to the Earl of Errol, Lord High Constable of Scotland, since 2016; Editor (1979-87), Chairman (1987-1991), Vice President (1991-2015), President (2015-2021) and Fellow of the Heraldry Society of Scotland. Fellow of the Heraldry Society (England), 2017. Worked in Local Government Museums & Galleries, 1963-2001, before becoming Director of the Paxton Trust, 2002-09. Secretary, York Philosophical Society (1970-76), York Archaeological and Yorkshire Architectural Society (1970-76); Secretary, British Association for the Advancement of Science (Section H Anthropology & Archaeology) (1978-81). Chairman, Dalrymple Donaldson Fund (1995-2005). Published prize winning books of photographic history; written and lectured widely on local history and heraldry. Articles in The Double Tressure; The York Historian; Archaeologia Aeliana &c. Publications: Let Paisley Flourish (1991); Let Durham Flourish (1996); The Monastery & Abbey of Paisley (2000); The Dunvegan Armorial (2006); Floreat Dunelmia - 600 years of Durham School (2014); We Shall Go Not Forth Again (2015); The World of James Howe (2016); Borland's Fowler: an annotated copy of Fowler's Paisley Directory, 1841-42 (2019); Paisley Abbey Rental 1460-1550 (2020); The Voyage of the Blonde, a biography of Charles Robert Malden 1797-1855 (2021). Collaborated with his wife Eilean in the pre-1672 Armorial, Ordinary and Gazetteer Scottish coats of arms (2016). Lives in Berwickshire.

Malik, Cllr Hanzala, BSc. MSP (Labour), Glasgow, 2011-16; Councillor, Hillhead, Glasgow City Council, since 2017 and 1995-2012; b. 26.11.56, Glasgow; m., Haleema Sadia; 1 s.; 1 d. Educ. University of the West of Scotland. Manager, Dhool Farms Ltd, 1982-87; Financial Consultant, 1987-88; Director, Azad Video, 1988-92. Chair, Board, West of Scotland Regional Equality Council. Recreations: badminton; charity work; community work; cooking; philately; swimming.

Malik, Dr Poonam, MBA, PhD, FRSB. Scottish Enterprise: Board Member, Non Executive Director, Member, Nominations & Governance and Remuneration Committees, since 2018; b. 10.70. Educ. Dayalbagh Educational Institute, Agra; Indian Veterinary Research Institute, Izatnagar; University of Glasgow; University of Edinburgh Business School. Career history: Research Assistant, NII - National Institute of Immunology, 1994-96; Scientist, Indian Veterinary Research Institute, Izatnagar, 1996-99; Medical Research Council, Postdoctoral Research Associate, The University of Glasgow, 2002-06; International Project Manager, Royal College of Physicians of Edinburgh, 2013; The University of Edinburgh: Principal Investigator (PI), Group Leader & Royal Society UK Research Fellow, 2006-2010, Wellcome Trust - University of Edinburgh VIP Award, 2010-11, Academic Lecturer, 2009-2013, Research Fellow Visiting, 2011-16; University of Cumbria: Consultant Advisor - MBA Capstone Consultancy, Sunergos Innovations, 2016, Research Innovation LEAD/Coordinator, Health & Sciences Faculty; External Partnerships, Research Office & Graduate School, Carlisle, Lancaster, 2014-15, Associate Professor of Biomedical Sciences & Research Innovation LEAD, Health & Science Strategic Partnerships, 2015-17; Futurize Research & Innovation Lead, Future Leaders Club, 2017-18; Lancaster Medical School - Visiting Lecturer, Clinical Research Teaching, Lancaster University, 2016-19; Global Respiratory Health Partnerships Management - Governance & Stakeholder Engagement, The University of Edinburgh, 2018-2020; Fellow of Royal Society of Biology (FRSB), since 2017; Director, Strategy, Innovation & Impact - STEM, Data & Digital Technology in Health, World Health Innovation Summit, since 2017; Investing Women: Consultant, Mentor, Trainer & Business Angel Coach, since 2017, Investor - Business Angel Syndicate, since 2018; Advisory Board Member, Wallet Services, since 2018; Governor, University Court, Board NXD Finance & General Purposes and Equality-Diversity Committees, University of the Highlands and Islands, since 2018; Non-Executive Director (NED), Trustee - Social Enterprise National Social Enterprise Development Organisation, Firstport, since 2018; Member, Economy and Enterprise Committee (EEC), Royal Society of Edinburgh, since 2019; Board Member, Director of Board of Directors, Life Sciences & Health, BioTech & MedTech, Skills Development Scotland, since 2020. Address: Scottish Enterprise HQ, Atrium Court, 50 Waterloo Street, Glasgow G2 6HQ; T.-0300 013 3385.

Mallinson, Edward John Harold, LLM, MPharm, FRPharmS. Chairman, Social Secretary, Heraldry Society of Scotland; Honorary Photographer to the Court of the Lord Lyon; Secretary & Treasurer, Pharmacy Law & Ethics Association; b. 15.03.50, Bingley, West Yorkshire; m., Diana Gray; 2 d. Educ. Bradford Grammar School; Bradford University; Cardiff Law School. Staff Pharmacist (Ward Pharmacy Services), Bradford Royal Infirmary, 1973-78; District Pharmaceutical Officer, Perth and Kinross District, 1978-83; Chief Administrative Pharmaceutical Officer (Consultant in Pharmaceutical Public Health), Lanarkshire Health Board, 1984-2010; Secretary, Scottish Specialists in Pharmaceutical Public Health (formerly Scottish Chief Administrative Pharmaceutical Officers' Group), 1988-90, 1996 and 1999-2001 (Chairman, 1990-92 and 1997-98); Member, Scottish Executive, Royal Pharmaceutical Society of Great Britain, 2000-02 (Hon. Secretary, Bradford & District Branch, 1978; Hon. Secretary, Dundee & Eastern Scottish Branch, 1979-83; Hon. Secretary & Treasurer, Lanarkshire Branch, 1984-2004; Vice-Chairman, Lanarkshire Branch, 2004-06 and Chairman 2006-08); Charter Silver Medallist, 2001; Member, Royal Pharmaceutical Society of Great Britain Disciplinary Committee, 2007-2010; Member, General Pharmaceutical Council Fitness to Practise Committee, 2010-2016; Member of Council, Royal Society of Health, 1992-96 and 2004-2011, Honorary Treasurer, 1996; Vice-Chairman & Secretary, Pharmaceutical Group, Royal Society of Health, 1986-89; Chairman, Strathclyde Police/Lanarkshire Heath Board Drug Liaison Committee, 1985-91; Member, General Synod, Scottish Episcopal Church, 1986-95; Honorary Treasurer, Comunn Gaidhlig na h-Eaglaish Easbaigich, 1986-2017; Honorary Treasurer, Affirming Apostolic Order, 1993-98; Secretary, Lanarkshire Branch, British Institute of Management, 1989-91 (Chairman, 1991-94); Hon. Treasurer, Scottish Medico Legal Society, 2012-2021. Recreations: genealogy; heraldry; photography; Gaelic language and culture; cooking. Address: (h.) Malden, North Dean Park Avenue, Bothwell, Glasgow G71 8HH.
E-mail: e.mallinson@talktalk.net

Mallon, Gerry, MBA, MA (Econ). Chief Executive Officer, Tesco Bank, since 2018; b. 1969; m., Una; 4 c. Educ. Ulster University; University of Cambridge. Career history: Engagement Manager, McKinsey & Company, 1998-2002; Director, Business and Retail Banking, Bank of Ireland, 2002-06; Deputy Chief Executive Officer and Head of Business Development, Northern Bank, 2006-08; Chairman of Council, University of Ulster, 2009-2015; Chief Executive Officer, Danske Bank UK (Northern Bank Ltd), 2008-16; Chief Executive Officer, Ulster Bank, 2016-18. Chairman, Irish Football Association, 2014-2020. Address: Tesco Bank, 2 South Gyle Crescent, Edinburgh EH12 9FQ; T.-0131 203 5000.

Mallon, Maureen, MBA. Chief Executive Officer, Scottish Charity Regulator (OSCR), since 2019; m., Malcolm. Educ. Jordanhill College; Edinburgh University. Career history:

Head of Development, YouthLink Scotland, 1994-2005; The Scottish Government: HM Inspector of Education, 2005-2014, Assistant Director in Education, 2014-19. Recreations: learning about vegetable gardening; walking. Address: Scottish Charity Regulator, Quadrant House, 9 Riverside Drive, Dundee DD1 4NY; T.-01382 220446.

Mann, Professor David George, BSc, BA, PhD, DSc. Senior Principal Research Scientist, Royal Botanic Garden, Edinburgh, since 1996; b. 25.2.53, Romford, Essex; m. (1), Lynn Barbara (divorced); 1 s.; 1 d. (2) Rosa Trobajo. Educ. Brentwood School; Bristol University; Edinburgh College of Art. Edinburgh University: Demonstrator, 1978-81, Lecturer, 1981-90, Director of Studies, 1989-90; Deputy Regius Keeper (Deputy Director), Royal Botanic Garden, Edinburgh, 1990-96. G.W. Prescott Award, 1991, 1997. Publications: editor/author of 200 papers and books. Recreations: classical piano; printmaking and painting. Address: (b.) Royal Botanic Garden, Inverleith Row, Edinburgh EH3 5LR; T.-0131-552 7171; e-mail: d.mann@rbge.org.uk

Mansfield and Mansfield, 9th Earl of (Alexander David Mungo Murray); b. 17.10.56; m., Sophia Mary Veronica Ashbrooke; 1 s.; 3 d. Succeeded to title, 2015. Address: Estate Office, Scone Palace, Perth PH2 6BD.

Manson, Alexander Philip, BCom. Lord-Lieutenant of Aberdeenshire, since 2020; b. 12.61. Educ. University of Edinburgh (graduated in 1982). Trained and qualified as a Chartered Accountant with Arthur Andersen in 1985; Johnston Carmichael LLP, Chair, since 2019, Chief Executive, 2007-2019 and Partner, since 1993; Partner in farming partnership of A Manson & Son, since 2003; Chair and Trustee of Salvesen Mindroom Centre, since 2020; University of Aberdeen Development Trust, Trustee, 2012-19, Chair of Trust, 2013-17; Member of the Council of the Institute of Chartered Accountants of Scotland, 2011-19 and President, 2018-19; Honorary Consul for the North of Scotland for the Kingdom of the Netherlands, since 2012.

Manson, Donna. Chief Executive, The Highland Council, since 2018; previously Service Director for Children and Young People in the Scottish Borders. Started career teaching in areas of deprivation; worked in Education in Edinburgh and Fife. Address: The Highland Council Headquarters, Glenurquhart Road, Inverness IV3 5NX.

Mapstone, Sally Louise. Principal and Vice-Chancellor, University of St Andrews, since 1 September 2016; Emeritus Fellow, St Hilda's College, Oxford, since October 2016; Honorary Fellow, Wadham College, Oxford and St Cross College, Oxford, since June 2017; Honorary President, Scottish Text Society, since 2012; President, Saltire Society, since 2018; FRSE, 2019; Hon. DLitt, University of Aberdeen, 2019; b. Hillingdon, Middlesex; m., Martin Griffiths. Educ. Vyners Grammar School, Ickenham, Middlesex; Wadham College, Oxford University. Editor, Weidenfeld & Nicolson Publishers, London, 1978-81; Junior Research Fellow, St Hilda's College, Oxford, 1984-86; Lecturer and Supernumerary Fellow, St Hilda's College, Oxford, 1986-89; Junior Proctor, Oxford University, 2006-07; Fellow and Tutor in English, St Hilda's College, Oxford, 1989-2016; Pro-Vice Chancellor (Personnel and Equality), University of Oxford, 2009-11, Pro-Vice Chancellor (Education), 2011-16. Trustee, Carnegie Trust for Universities of Scotland, since 2016, Vice-Chair, since 2019; Board member, Universities UK and UCAS; Member, Higher Education Policy Institute advisory board, since 2017; Chair of Trustees, Higher Education Policy Institute, since 2021; Trustee, Europaeum,

since 2018; Vice-Convener, Universities Scotland, since 2020. Publications: author and editor of 7 books on Older Scots literature, and numerous articles on the same subject. Recreations: reading and running. Address: Office of the Principal, University of St Andrews, College Gate, North Street, St Andrews, Fife KY16 9AJ; T.-01334 462545. E-mail: principal@st-andrews.ac.uk

Mar and Kellie, Earl of (James Thorne Erskine). Estate Worker; Member, House of Lords Select Committee on the Constitution, 2001-04; Liberal Democrat Spokesman on Scotland, 2001-04; Liberal Democrat Assistant Whip, 2002-07 and 2009-2010; Assistant Transport Spokesman, 2004-2013; b. 10.3.49, Edinburgh; m., Mary Irene; 1 step s.; 3 step d.; 1 step d. deceased. Educ. Eton; Moray House College of Education; Inverness College. Community Service Volunteer, York, 1967-68; Youth and Community Worker, Craigmillar, 1971-73; Social Worker, Sheffield, 1973-76, Grampian Region, 1976-78; Social Worker, Prison Social Worker, Community Service Supervisor, Highland Region, 1979-87; Builder, Kincardine, 1990-92; Project Worker, SACRO, Falkirk, 1992-93; Royal Auxiliary Air Force Regiment, 1979-85; Royal Naval Auxiliary Service, 1985-88; hereditary peer, 1994-1999; Chairman, Strathclyde Tram Inquiry, 1996; Parliamentary Commissioner, Burrell Collection (Lending) Inquiry, 1997; returned to the Lords in 2000 as a life peer - Lord Erskine of Alloa Tower; Member, House of Lords Select Committee on Religious Offences, 2002-03; Member, House of Lords administration and works committee, 2004-08; campaigning for a Dominion with UN, NATO and EU Member status, since 2004; Member, Independence Convention, since 2005; Member, House of Lords ad hoc Committee for the Barnett Formula, 2008-09; Member, Joint Committee on Statutory Instruments, 2008-2013; retired from the House of Lords in 2017. Recreations: canoeing; hill-walking; boat building; Alloa Tower. Address: Hilton Farm, Alloa FK10 3PS.

Marcella, Professor Rita Christina, MA (Hons), DipLib, DipEd, PhD, FCMI, FCILIP. Professor of Information Management, Aberdeen Business School, Robert Gordon University (previously Dean); b. 10.7.56, Fraserburgh; m., Philip Marcella; 1 s.; 1 d. Educ. Peterhead Academy; Aberdeen University; Robert Gordon University. Librarian, RGIT, 1983-86; Lecturer, Robert Gordon University, 1986-94; Senior Lecturer, 1994-97; Depute Head of School, Robert Gordon University, 1998-2001; Head of School, Northumbria University, 2001-02. Committee Member: Scottish Council for Development and Industry (SCDI) North East, Grampian Racial Equality Council; Arts and Humanities Research Council. Research into fake news and the use of the internet in election campaigns. Recreations: reading; visiting Italy. Address: (b.) Aberdeen Business School, Robert Gordon University, Garthdee Road, Aberdeen AB10 7QE; T.-01224 263904. E-mail: r.c.marcella@rgu.ac.uk

Markland, John A., CBE, MA, PhD, Hon. Dr.h.c, ACG. Member of Court, University of Edinburgh, 2001-2011, Convener of Audit Committee, 2003-06, Vice Convener of Court, 2006-2011; Trustee, Gannochy Trust, 2009-2017; Member, Scotland Advisory Group, The Woodland Trust; Chairman, Scottish Leadership Foundation, 2001-08; Board Member, Horsecross Arts Ltd., 2007-2013; President, Old Boltonians Association, 2006-07; b. 17.5.48, Bolton; m., Muriel Harris; 4 d. Educ. Bolton School; Dundee University. Demographer, Somerset County Council, 1974-76; Senior Professional Assistant, Tayside Regional Council, 1976-79; Personal Assistant to Chief Executive, then Assistant Chief Executive, then Chief Executive, Fife Regional Council, 1979-95; Chief Executive, Fife Council, 1995-99; Chairman, Scottish Natural Heritage, 1999-2006.

Vice Chairman, then Chairman, Environmental Campaigns, 2000-06; Chairman: Forward Scotland, 1996-2000, Society of Local Authority Chief Executives (Scotland), 1993-95, Secretary of State for Scotland's Advisory Group on Sustainable Development, 1998-99; Trustee, Kincarrathie Trust, since 2012, Chairman, since 2021. Recreation: trying to keep fit. Address: 3, St. Leonard's Bank, Perth PH2 8EB; T.-01738 441798.

Marnoch, The Rt. Hon. Lord (Michael Stewart Rae Bruce), MA, LLB, LLD (Aberdeen). Senator of the College of Justice, 1990-2005 (retired); b. 26.7.38; m., Alison Stewart; 2 d. Educ.; Loretto; Aberdeen University. Advocate, 1963; QC, 1975; Sworn of the Privy Council, 2001; Standing Counsel to Department of Agriculture and Fisheries for Scotland, 1973; to Highlands and Islands Development Board, 1973; Advocate-Depute, 1983-86; Member, Criminal Injuries Compensation Board, 1986-89. Chairman for Scotland, Salmon and Trout Association, 1989-94. Recreations: golf; fishing.

Marquis, Alistair Forbes, MBE, BA, MEd, DipCE, FCollP. Appointed a Member of the British Empire by HM The Queen, Jan. 2011 for services to education, young people and the community. International Education Consultant, working for The World Bank (mainly in Sri Lanka, 2012-2020), the Government of Dubai, 2012-2020 and the Government of The Cayman Islands (2021). Board Member of Council of Management of Bright Light (relationship counselling - Lothians), 2011-21; HM Inspector/Assistant Chief Inspector/Chief Inspector, 1989-2011; b. 13.01.50, Glasgow; m.; 1 d. Educ. Queen's Park Senior Secondary School; Jordanhill College, Glasgow; Open University; Edinburgh University. Assistant Teacher, Leithland Primary School, Glasgow, 1971-77; Depute Head Teacher, Dedridge Primary School, West Lothian, 1977-79; Head Teacher, Bankton Primary School, West Lothian, 1979-89. Member, Scottish Committee for Special Educational Needs, 1985-88; Scottish Government representative on the European Evaluation in Education Network, 2006-11; Chairman, Lanthorn Community Complex Management Committee, Livingston, 1979-82; SFA Football Referee, 1972-2020; Church of Scotland Elder, 1985-2021 and National Safeguarding Committee, 2005-08, elected Vice-Chairman, Livingston United Parish Church Council, 2006-2018 and Chairman, 2018-21; Captain, 5th Livingston Company of The Boys' Brigade, 1979-89, Chairman of the Scotland Committee of The Boys' Brigade, 1991-2000; Elected Representative, UK Brigade Executive for East Lowland Area, 1989-2000; Scottish Member, UK Management Committee, 1991-99; President, West Lothian Battalion, 2000-04 and 2007-11, Hon Vice-President, 2011-21; Hon Vice-President, The Scout Association, The Scottish Council, 1996-2000. Member, Rotary International; President of the RC of Whitburn, 2002-03 and 2020-21; Assistant District Governor (D1020), 2010-12, District Governor Nominee, 2012-13, District Governor Elect, 2013-14, District Governor, 2014-15 and Past District Governor, 2015-20. Member, Great Britain & Ireland Rotary Leadership, Training & Development Committee, 2015-18. Recreations: gardening; reading; walking; foreign holidays.
E-mail: afmarquis@blueyonder.co.uk

Marr, Colin. Theatre Director: Edinburgh Playhouse, since 2017, Eden Court Theatre, 1997-2017; b. 3.4.66, Glasgow; m., Nicky; 2 d. Educ. Hutcheson's Grammar School; University of Edinburgh; Open University. Hall Manager, Queen's Hall, Edinburgh, 1988-92; Theatre and Commercial Manager, Traverse Theatre, Edinburgh, 1992-97. Address: Edinburgh Playhouse, 18-22 Greenside Lane, Edinburgh EH1 3AA.

Marr, Douglas, CBE, MA, MEd. Columnist, The Herald, Glasgow; Writer and Educationalist; Her Majesty's Inspector of Education (HMIE) (part-time), 2004-2011;

Principal Consultant, Acorn Consulting (Scotland), since 2004; School Management and Curriculum Co-ordinator, Aberdeenshire Education and Recreation, 2002-04; Senior Teaching Fellow, University of Aberdeen, School of Education, 2004-06; b. 7.2.47, Aberdeen; m., Alison; 1 d. Educ. Aberdeen Grammar School; University of Aberdeen. Teacher of History, Hilton Academy, Aberdeen, 1970-71; Assistant Principal Teacher of History, Aberdeen Grammar School, 1971-76; Principal Teacher of History, Hilton Academy, Aberdeen, 1976-81; Assistant Rector, Kemnay Academy, 1981-84; Depute Rector, The Gordon Schools, Huntly, 1984-87; Headteacher: Hilton Academy, 1987-88, St. Machar Academy, Aberdeen, 1988-95; Rector, Banchory Academy, 1995-2002. Member, Business Management Committee, University of Aberdeen, 2001-06; Member, Aberdeen University Court, 2002-06. Publication: Leisure Education and Young People's Leisure (Co-Author), 1988. Recreations: squash; suffering at the hands (and feet) of Aberdeen F. C.; Member, Leicestershire County Cricket Club; walking; gardening. Address: (h.) Derbeth Grange, Aberdeen AB15 8UD.
E-mail: douglas.marr@alford.co.uk

Marra, Jenny. MSP (Labour), North East Scotland, 2011-2021; former Shadow Cabinet Secretary for Health, Wellbeing and Sport; former Shadow Minister for Youth Employment; b. 6.11.77, Dundee; m., John Thomson.

Marra, Michael, MA, MSc. MSP (Scottish Labour), North East Scotland (Region), since 2021; Shadow Cabinet Secretary for Education and Skills, since 2021. Educ. University of Glasgow; London School of Economics and Political Science. Career history: Head of Policy and Public Affairs, Oxfam Scotland, 2008-2010; Senior Political Adviser, Scottish Parliament, 2010-12; Director of Five Million Questions, University of Dundee, 2012-14; Head of Strategic Planning and Creatives, Better Together Ltd, Glasgow, 2014; Deputy Director, Design in Action, Dundee, 2012-16; Research Strategist, Leverhulme Research Centre for Forensic Science, University of Dundee, 2016-18; Member of the Science and Justice Forum, UK Home Office, 2018-19; Deputy Director, Leverhulme Research Centre for Forensic Science, University of Dundee, 2018-2021; Member, Board of Trustees, Leisure and Culture Dundee, since 2019; elected Councillor for the Lochee Ward, Dundee City Council in 2017. Address: The Scottish Parliament, Edinburgh EH99 1SP; T.-0131 348 5943.
E-mail: Michael.Marra.msp@parliament.scot

Marrian, Ian Frederic Young, MA, CA. Accountancy Education Advisor; b. 15.11.43, Kilwinning; m., Moira Selina McSwan; 1 s.; 2 d. Educ. Royal Belfast Academical Institution; Queens University, Belfast; Edinburgh University. Qualified as CA, 1969; Deloitte Haskins & Sells: audit practice, Rome, 1969-72, London, 1972-73, Audit Partner, Edinburgh, 1973-78, Technical Partner, London, 1978-81; Chief Executive and Secretary, Institute of Chartered Accountants of Scotland, 2003-04. Chairman, Paxton Trust. Recreations: gardening; developing an arboretum; wines. Address: (h.) Walled Garden, Bowerhouse, Dunbar EH42 1RE; T.-01368-862293.
E-mail: ian@ianmarrian.co.uk

Marsack, Robyn Louise, BA, BPhil, DPhil, FRSE; b. 30.1.53, Wellington, New Zealand; m., Stuart Airlie; 1 d. Educ. Wellington Girls' College; Victoria University, Wellington; Oxford University. Junior Research Fellow, Wolfson College, Oxford, 1979-82; Editor, Carcanet Press, 1982-86; freelance editor, translator and writer, 1987-99; Director, Scottish Poetry Library, 2000-2016; Royal Literary Fund Writing Fellow, University of Glasgow,

2016-18. Member, Board of Directors, Carcanet Press, since 2005; Trustee, Edwin Morgan Trust; Chair, StAnza Board of Trustees, 2017-2022. Recent publications: edited the Selected Poems of Edmund Blunden, 2018; translations include The Way of the World by Nicolas Bouvier, 1992, 2007; So It Goes by Nicolas Bouvier, 2019. Recreations: reading, reading, reading. Address: (h.) 10 Roxburgh Street, Glasgow G12 9AP.

Marsh, Professor John Haig, BA, MEng, PhD, CEng, FREng, FIET, FOSA, FInstP, FRSA, FIEEE, FRSE, FFCS. Director of James Watt Nanofabrication Centre, since 2019; Dean of Transnational Education for University of Glasgow-UESTC, 2016-19; Head of School of Engineering, University of Glasgow, 2010-2016; Professor of Optoelectronic Systems, University of Glasgow, since 1996; Visiting Professor at Queen's University Belfast and Northwest University, Xi'an, China; Founder and Chief Technical Officer, Intense Ltd, 2000-2011; b. 15.4.56, Edinburgh; m., Anabel Christine Mitchell. Educ. Glasgow Academy; Cambridge University; Liverpool University; Sheffield University. University of Sheffield: Research Fellow, 1980-83, Research Scientist, 1983-86; University of Glasgow: Lecturer, 1986-90, Senior Lecturer, 1990-94, Reader, 1994-96. Director, NATO Advanced Study Institute, Glasgow, 1990; Founding Chair, Scottish Chapter, IEEE/LEOS, 1996-98; Vice President, LEOS, 1999-2001 and 2003-05; President, 2008-09 of IEEE Photonics Society (IEEE LEOS, prior to February 2009); elected Member, Board of Governors, 2001-03. Member, Board of Governors, IEEE Technology Management Council, 2012-13. Awards: Red Herring 100 Europe Award, 2005 (for Intense Ltd); LEOS Engineering Achievement, 2006 (jointly with A.C. Bryce); LEOS Distinguished Service Award, 2006; Insider & Scott-Moncrieff E250 'Best newcomer' Award, 2008 (for Intense Ltd); Chengdu Jinsha Friendship Award, 2017. Publications: Waveguide Optoelectronics (Co-editor); more than 500 papers, book chapters and patents. Recreations: cycling; walking; cooking; music; malt whisky. Address: (b.) James Watt School of Engineering, James Watt Building South, University of Glasgow, Glasgow G12 8QQ. E-mail: john.marsh@glasgow.ac.uk

Marshall, Leon McGregor, CA. Senior Partner, Stevenson & Kyles, CA, Glasgow, since 1995; Member, Church of Scotland Trust, since 2017; Moderator, Presbytery of Greenock, 2002-03; Session Clerk, Kilmacolm Old Kirk, since 1997; b. 10.6.50, Glasgow; m., 1, Barbara Anne McLean (deceased); 2 s.; 1 d.; 2, Judith Margaret Miller (deceased); 3, Barbara Anne Orr. Educ. High School of Glasgow; Glasgow University (as part of CA training). Joined Stevenson & Kyles as a student, 1967; qualified CA, 1972 (joint winner, ICAS Gold Medal); made Partner, 1974. Treasurer, St Enoch's Hogganfield Church, Glasgow, 1973-80; Treasurer, Kilmacolm Old Kirk, 1984-97; Member, Church of Scotland World Mission Council, 2005-2013 (Vice-Convener, 2006-09); Convener, Church of Scotland Central Services Committee, 2001-05; Member, Board of Stewardship and Finance, General Assembly, Church of Scotland, 1990-2001 (Convener, 1997-2001; Convener, Budget and Allocation Committee, 1993-97); Reader, Church of Scotland, since 1987. Recreations: reading; travel; watching football. Address: (b.) 25 Sandyford Place, Glasgow G3 7NG; T.-0141-248 3856; e-mail: lm@stevenson-kyles.co.uk

Marshall, Professor Mary Tara, OBE, MA, DSA, DASS, FRSE. Emeritus Professor, University of Stirling; former Director, Dementia Services Development Centre; Director, HammondCare UK and Europe Ltd, since 2020; b. 13.6.45, Darjeeling, India. Educ. Mary Erskine School for Girls;

Edinburgh University; London School of Economics; Liverpool University. Child Care Officer, London Borough of Lambeth, 1967-69; Social Worker, Personal Service Society, Liverpool, 1970-74; Research Organiser, Age Concern, Liverpool, 1974-75; Lecturer in Social Studies, Liverpool University, 1975-83; Director, Age Concern Scotland, 1983-89. Former Member, Royal Commission on Long-term Care of the Elderly; Hon. DEd, Queen Margaret University College; Hon. Degree of Doctor of Science in Social Science, University of Edinburgh, 2004; Hon DUniv, University of Stirling, 2006; Fellow of the Royal Society of Edinburgh; Fellow of the British Society of Gerontology; 2008 British Geriatrics Society medal for the relief of suffering of older people; 2010 RC of Psych, Faculty of Old Age Psych: Lifetime achievement award. Sessional Inspector with Care Inspectorate, 2007-2015; Senior Consultant, Dementia Centre, HammondCare, 2015-19; Hon. Professor, University of Edinburgh, since 2016. Publications: The State of Art in Dementia Care, 1997; Food Glorious Food, perspectives on food and dementia, 2003; Perspectives on Rehabilitation and Dementia, 2005 (Ed); Walking not Wandering, 2006 (Ed) (Co-Author); Social Work and people with dementia (Co-author), 2006; Time for dementia (Co-Ed), 2010; Designing balconies, roof terraces and roof gardens for people with dementia, 2010; Transforming the quality of life for people with dementia through contact with the natural world (Co-Editor), 2011; Designing outdoor spaces for people with dementia, University of Stirling/Hammond Care (Co-Editor), 2012; Designing mental health units for older people, 2014; Creating culturally appropriate outside spaces and experiences for people with dementia (Co-Author), 2014; Toilet talk: Accessible design for people with dementia, 2017; Talking Murals, 2019. Recreations: photography; bird-watching. Address: (h.) 24 Buckingham Terrace, Edinburgh EH4 3AE; T.-0131 343 1732.

Martin, Dr Catherine, MA, PhD, CA, FRSA. Vice-Principal, Corporate Services, University of Edinburgh, since 2020; b. 6.74; m.; 3 c. Career history: taught French, University of St Andrews, then trained as a chartered accountant, working in audit and corporate finance for global accountancy firms, Arthur Andersen, Deloitte and Mazars LLP; College Secretary in the College of Arts, University of Glasgow, 2010-15; moved to the University of Edinburgh in 2015, as Registrar, College of Arts, Humanities & Social Sciences. Fellow of the Royal Society of Arts; former member of the Arts & Humanities Research Council audit committee; has held a variety of non-executive director and trustee roles in the public and voluntary sectors; member of the Scotland Advisory Group for Parkinson's UK. Address: University of Edinburgh, Charles Stewart House, 9-16 Chambers Street, Edinburgh EH1 1HT; T.-0131 650 9844.
E-mail: Catherine.Martin@ed.ac.uk

Martin, David Weir, BA (Econ), MA. Vice-President, European Parliament, 1989-2004, Member (Labour) for Lothians, 1984-99, Senior Member for Scotland, 1999-2019; Co-Convener of the Citizens' Assembly of Scotland; b. 26.8.54, Edinburgh; 1 s.; 1 d. Educ. Liberton High School; Heriot-Watt University; Leicester University. Worked as stockbroker's assistant and animal rights campaigner; became Lothian Regional Councillor, 1982; Rapporteur; Intergovernmental Conferences; The EU's Aid for Trade; Economic Relations with Korea. Publications: Bringing Common Sense to the Common Market — A Left Agenda for Europe; European Union and the Democratic Deficit; Europe — An Ever Closer Union; Towards a Wider, Deeper, Federal Europe; Maastricht in a Minute; 1996 and all that; A Partnership Democracy for Europe. Recreations: soccer; reading.

Martin, Donald. Editor-in-Chief, Newsquest Scotland, since 2017; Editor, The Herald, since 2018, and The Herald on Sunday, since 2018; formerly Editor, The Evening

Times (2017-2020); Head of Publishing, D.C. Thomson & Co. Ltd., 2015-16. Formerly Editor: The Sunday Post and The Weekly News, and Editor-in-Chief of newspapers, D.C. Thomson & Co. Ltd and Aberdeen Journals Ltd (2010–2015), The Herald (2008-2010), The Evening Times, Aberdeen Evening Express and North West Evening Mail. Past President of the UK Society of Editors and former Chairman of the Scottish Newspaper Society. Address: (b.) 125 Fullarton Drive, Glasgow East Investment Park, Glasgow G32 8FG; T.-0141 302 6017; mobile: 07711 451330; e-mail: Donald.martin@newsquest.co.uk

Martin, Donald, CVO, OBE. Lord-Lieutenant for Western Isles, 2016-2022 (previously Vice Lord-Lieutenant). Career history: appointed Clerk to the Lieutenancy in 1997; appointed Deputy Lieutenant in 2002; worked in a variety of posts within the Civil Service, Highlands and Islands Development Board and Western Isles Islands Council; Interim Chief Executive, Bord na Gaidhlig, 2010-11; Chairman, Harris Tweed Authority, 2007-13; Chairman, Acair Ltd, a publicly funded Gaelic bilingual publishing company, since 2008; Trustee, Scottish Hydro Electric Community Trust, since 2008. Participated in local, national and European seminars on minority languages, especially during period as Secretary of the UK and Scottish Committees of the European Bureau of Lesser Used Languages; fluent Gaelic speaker and regular contributor to Gaelic radio and TV programmes. Lives in Stornoway, Isle of Lewis.

Martin, Gillian. MSP (SNP), Aberdeenshire East, since 2016; m.; 2 c. Educ. Ellon Academy. Career history: worked as a lecturer for 15 years in TV production; lecturer at North East Scotland College; became politically active during the Scottish independence referendum; helped found Women for Independence (WFI), on the WFI executive, as the member for North East. Address: Scottish Parliament, Edinburgh EH99 1SP.

Martin, Graham Dunstan, MA, BLitt, GradCertEd. Writer; Senior Lecturer, Edinburgh University, 1982-2000; b. 21.10.32, Leeds; m., 1, Ryllis Daniel; 2 s.; 1 d.; 2, Anne Crombie; 2 s. Educ. Leeds Grammar School; Oriel College and Linacre College, Oxford. Schoolteacher, 1956-65; Assistant Lecturer, then Lecturer, in French, Edinburgh University, 1965-82. Publications: (philosophy) Language, Truth and Poetry, 1975; The Architecture of Experience 1981, Shadows in the Cave, 1990; Inquiry into Speculative Fiction, 2003; Does it Matter?, 2005; Living on Purpose, 2008; (novels) Giftwish, 1980; Catchfire, 1981; The Soul Master, 1984; Time-Slip, 1986; The Dream Wall, 1987; Half a Glass of Moonshine, 1988; (pamphlets) Invention of Whisky; Little Richard and the Snake-Charmers; poems and poetry translations including Jules Laforgue, 1998; Blog: Soul Reasons. Recreations: music; jazz; walking; good food; the Celtic past. Address: 21 Mayfield Terrace, Edinburgh EH9 1RY; T.-0131-667 8160; e-mail: gdunstanmartin@btinternet.com

Martin, Rev. Iver, BSc, MTh. Principal, Edinburgh Theological Seminary; b. 29.6.57, Grantown on Spey; m., Mairi Isabel Macdonald; 2 s.; 4 d. Educ. Camphill High School, Paisley; Robert Gordon's Institute of Technology; Free Church College. National Semiconductor (UK) Ltd.: Graduate Process Engineer, 1980, Senior Engineer, 1983; European Process Engineer, Lam Research Corporation Ltd., 1985; European Product and Sales Engineer, Silicon Glen Technology, 1987-90; own company, Solus (UK) Ltd., 1990-92; Assistant Minister, Stornoway Free Church, 1995-97; Minister, Bon Accord Free Church, Aberdeen, 1997-2003; Minister, Stornoway Free Church of Scotland, 2003-2015. Recreations: reading; music. Address: ETS, 15

North Bank Street, Edinburgh EH1 2LS; T.-0131 376 3148. E-mail: imartin@ets.ac.uk

Martin, Jaclyn. Head Teacher, Dalziel High School, since 2021; previously Depute Head Teacher. Address: Crawford Street, Motherwell ML1 3AG; T.-01698 274900.

Martin, Jim, CBE. Chair of the Scottish Legal Complaints Commission, since 2018; b. Larbert. Career history: Economics and Modern Studies Teacher at Falkirk High School; Chair of Educational Institute of Scotland, 1987-1995; worked for the life assurance society Scottish Amicable; appointed as Scotland's first independent police complaints commissioner in 2007; Scottish Public Services Ombudsman, 2009-2017. Address: Scottish Legal Complaints Commission, 10-14 Waterloo Place, Edinburgh EH1 3EG; T.-0131 201 2130.

Martin, Linda, BA, MSc, MCIPR. Chief Media Officer, Scotland Office, since 2016. Educ. Glasgow Caledonian University; Oxford Brooks University; University of Stirling. Career: Deputy Head of News, The Home Office, 2000-06; Head of News and Communications, Department of Culture, Media and Sport, 2006-2013. Address: Scotland Office, 1 Melville Crescent, Edinburgh EH3 7HW; T.-0131 244 9010.

Martin, Dame Louise, DBE, CBE. President, The Commonwealth Games Federation; Immediate Past-Chair, sportscotland (previously served two terms on the Board, 1997-2005); b. 1946. Past Chair of the Commonwealth Games Scotland (CGS) and has a long and ongoing association with the Games as a competitor, team manager and administrator. First elected as a board member of CGS in 1995 (Chair, 1999-2007); Commonwealth Games Federation Honorary Secretary, since 2011 (the first woman to hold a position on their Executive Board); Chair of the Commonwealth Advisory Board on Sport; responsible for the introduction of the Commonwealth Youth Games to the international sporting calendar, the Commonwealth Sports Development Conference and the development of the Commonwealth Sports Awards; led the successful bid for the 2014 Commonwealth Games which resulted in Glasgow being awarded the Games in November 2007 and was appointed as Vice Chair of the Organising Committee. Board Member, UK Sport and Chair of the Scottish Sports Hall of Fame Committee.

Martin, Paul. MSP (Labour), Glasgow Provan, 2011-16, Glasgow Springburn, 1999-2011; b. 1967, Glasgow; m., Marie; 2 d. Educ. All Saints RC Secondary. Career: served an apprenticeship in the construction industry, then became a construction manager; at the age of 26, became a Glasgow District Councillor following a Council By-Election in December 1993; formerly Vice-Convenor of the Glasgow District Council Economic and Development Committee, Convenor of the North Area Committee and Convenor of the Youth Committee; served as the Parliamentary aide to the Lord Advocate, 2001-07; Labour's shadow minister for Justice, 2007-09; promoted to the shadow cabinet in November 2009 as Labour's business manager; appointed Labour's shadow spokesman on community safety in 2007; appointed Business Manager for Labour in the Scottish Parliament in 2009, sitting on the Business Bureau of the Scottish Parliament. Recreations: golf; football (in goals); playing keyboard.

Martin, Ross, BSc (Hons), PGCE. Adviser on Regional Economies, The Scottish Government, since 2018; Chair of the Board: Link Group Ltd, since 2017, Forth Valley College, since 2017; Chair, Board of Trustees, Scottish Waterways Trust, since 2014; Founding Partner, Adopt an Intern Ltd, since 2010. Educ. Moray House College; Heriot-Watt University. Elected Member, Lothian Regional Council, 1990-96; Chair, Lothian & Borders

Police Authority, 1991-96; Convener of Education Authority, West Lothian Council, 1995-1999; Deputy Leader, West Lothian Council, 1995-1999; Director, Networks Central Ltd, 1999-2003; Director, Scottish Forum for Modern Government, RGU, 2003-2006; Director, TPS, 2005-2013. Policy Director, Centre for Scottish Public Policy, 2006-2013; Adviser, Scotland's Towns Partnership, 2012-13; former Chief Executive, Scottish Council for Development and Industry (2014-17); Adviser at Commission on School Reform, 2012-13; Adviser at Business Improvement Districts Scotland, 2011-13. Member, Heriot Watt University Court, 1986-96; Board Member, Scottish Police College, 1992-95; High School Teacher, Fife Council, 1989-93; Board Member, West Lothian College, 1990-1992; Student President, Heriot-Watt University, 1986-88. Address: Scottish Waterways Trust, New Port Downie, Lime Road, Falkirk FK1 4RS.

Martin, Professor William, BSc, PhD. Professor of Cardiovascular Pharmacology, University of Glasgow, since 1995; Head of Division of Neuroscience and Biomedical Systems, 2004-08; Senate Assessor on University Court, 2010-2013; b. 12.7.55, Glasgow; m., Anne Marie McCartney; 1 s.; 1 d. Educ. Glenwood Secondary; University of Glasgow. Post-doctoral Research Fellow, Babraham, Cambridge, 1980-83; Post-doctoral Research Fellow, State University of New York, 1983-85; Lecturer, Department of Cardiology, University of Wales College of Medicine, 1985-87; External Examiner: National University of Ireland, 2009-14, University College Dublin, 2002-07, University of Nottingham, 2002-07, King's College London, 2006-2010. Institute for Scientific Information Highly Cited Researcher Award in Pharmacology, 2002; Elected Fellow of the British Pharmacological Society, 2012. Recreations: hill-walking; ballroom dancing; keeping fit. Address: (b.) School of Life Sciences, College of Medical, Veterinary & Life Sciences, University of Glasgow, Glasgow G12 8QQ; T.-0141-330 4489; e-mail: William.Martin@glasgow.ac.uk

Martin-Brown, Sheriff Jillian, LLB (Hons), DipLP. Sheriff, Tayside, Central and Fife, since 2019; appointed as a commercial sheriff in 2020. Educ. University of Aberdeen; University of Edinburgh. Career history: Solicitor in private practice, representing the Scottish Prison Service at fatal accident inquiries throughout Scotland; appointed as a Summary Sheriff in Tayside, Central and Fife in 2016; particular responsibility for the Problem Solving Court in Forfar; worked as an advocate, developing particular expertise in the fields of personal injury and medical negligence; appointed as Standing Junior Counsel to the Scottish Government and served as an ad-hoc advocate depute for the prosecution service. Address: Dundee Sheriff Court, 6 West Bell Street, Dundee DD1 9AD; T.-01382 229961.

Martindale, Dr Linda. Dean, School of Health Sciences, Associate Dean, Learning and Teaching, University of Dundee. Teaches across pre-registration and post-qualifying programmes, and is also a Masters dissertation supervisor and PhD supervisor; University QAA Enhancement Theme Lead for the Resilient Learning Communities work, 2020-2023; workforce lead and member of Council of Deans Scotland. Recreations: hill walking; skiing. Address: School of Health Sciences, 11 Airlie Place, Dundee DD1 4HJ; T.-01382 381969; e-mail: L.Martindale@dundee.ac.uk

Marwick, George Robert, SDA, CVO. Lord Lieutenant for Orkney, 1997-2007 (Vice Lieutenant, 1995, Deputy Lieutenant, 1976); Chairman, Swannay Farms Ltd., 1972-2010; Chairman, Campbeltown Creamery (Holdings) Ltd., 1974-90; Honorary Sheriff, Grampian Highlands and Islands, since 2000; b. 27.2.32, Edinburgh; m., 1, Hanne Jensen; 3 d.; 2, Norma Gerrard. Educ. Port Regis;

Bryanston; Edinburgh School of Agriculture. Councillor, local government, 1968-78; Vice-Convener, Orkney County Council, 1970-74, Convener, Orkney Islands Council, 1974-78; Chairman, North of Scotland Water Board, 1970-73; Member, Scottish Agricultural Consultative Panel, 1972-98 (formerly Winter Keep Panel, 1964-72); Director, North Eastern Farmers Ltd., 1968-98;. Member: Countryside Commission for Scotland, 1978-86, Council, National Trust for Scotland, 1979-84. Recreations: shooting; motor sport. Address: (h.) Whitewisp, Orchil Road, Auchterarder, Perthshire; T.-01764 662381.

Marwick, Rt. Hon. Tricia. MSP, Mid Fife and Glenrothes, 2011-16, Central Fife, 2007-2011, Mid-Scotland and Fife, 1999-2007; Presiding Officer, Scottish Parliament, 2011-16 (resigned membership of the Scottish National Party to be independent of any party); b. 5.11.53, Cowdenbeath; m., Frank; 1 s.; 1 d. Public Affairs Office, Shelter Scotland, 1992-99; Chair, NHS Fife Board, 2016-2020. Recreations: reading; watching sport.

Mason, John. MSP (SNP), Glasgow Shettleston, since 2011; MP (SNP), Glasgow East, 2008-10; b. 15.5.57. Trained as an accountant in Glasgow, then worked for housing associations, nursing homes, and with a charity in London; spent 3 years in Nepal with an NGO representing churches from all over the world. Elected as the Councillor for the Garrowhill ward in 1998 at a by-election and held the seat in 1999 and 2003. Former SNP Council Group Leader (1999-2008). Recreations: supporter of Clyde FC; hill walking; camping; reading Scottish history. Address: 1335 Gallowgate, Glasgow G31 4DN.

Mason, Professor Roger A., MA, PhD, FRHistS. Emeritus Professor of Scottish History, University of St Andrews (appointed Professor in 2005); Director, St Andrews Institute of Scottish Historical Research, since 2007; b. 29.07.54, Aberdeen; m., Ellen Colingsworth. Educ. Rannoch School; Edinburgh University. Lecturer, then Reader, St Andrews University, from 1983. Extensive publications in Scottish History; former Editor 'Scottish Historical Review'; President, Scottish History Society, 2013-16. Recreations: reading; walking the dog. Address: (b.) School of History, University of St Andrews, St Andrews, Fife KY16 9AL; T.-01334 462882; e-mail: ram@st-andrews.ac.uk

Massie, Alex. Journalist; Scotland Editor of The Spectator; columnist for the Scottish edition of The Times; regular contributor to Border Television as well as BBC Television and radio; b. 1.7.74. Educ. Glenalmond College; Trinity College, Dublin. Career history: Washington correspondent for The Scotsman and Assistant Editor of Scotland on Sunday; also written for The Washington Post, Politico, The Daily Telegraph, The New Republic, Foreign Policy, The Sunday Times, The Daily Beast, The Los Angeles Times, The Scottish Daily Mail, National Review Online, The Sunday Telegraph, The New York Times, The American Conservative, TIME magazine, Bloomberg Businessweek, The Observer, the New Statesman, The Big Issue, Slate, CapX, the Irish Independent, Newsweek and The Sunday Business Post; edited a political blog, 'The Debatable Land'. Writes a blog that is published by The Spectator; short-listed in the blog section for the Orwell Prize for political writing in 2012. Won the John Smith Memorial Mace debating competition in 1997 (represented the University Philosophical Society). Recreations: plays for Selkirk Cricket Club; supports Scottish football side Heart of Midlothian.

Massie, Allan Johnstone, CBE, BA, FRSL. Author and Journalist; b. 16.10.38, Singapore; m., Alison Langlands; 2 s.; 1 d. Educ. Drumtochty Castle; Trinity College, Glenalmond; Trinity College, Cambridge. Schoolmaster, Drumtochty Castle, 1960-71; taught EFL, 1972-75;

Creative Writing Fellow, Edinburgh University, 1982-84, Glasgow and Strathclyde Universities, 1985-86; Editor, New Edinburgh Review, 1982-84; Fiction Reviewer, The Scotsman, since 1975; Television Critic, Sunday Standard, 1981-83 (Fraser of Allander Award, Critic of the Year, 1982); Sports Columnist, Glasgow Herald, 1985-88; Columnist: Daily Mail, The Scotsman, Sunday Times; contributor to The Spectator, the Literary Review and The Independent. Publications: (novels): Change and Decay in all around I see; The Last Peacock; The Death of Men (Scottish Arts Council Book Award); One Night in Winter; Augustus; A Question of Loyalties; The Sins of the Father; Tiberius; The Hanging Tree; Shadows of Empire; Caesar; These Enchanted Woods; The Ragged Lion; King David; Antony; Nero's Heirs; The Evening of the World; Arthur the King; Caligula; Charlemagne and Roland; Surviving; Death in Bordeaux (non-fiction): Colette; How Should Health Services be Financed?: A Patient's View; Muriel Spark; Ill Met by Gaslight; Five Edinburgh Murders; The Caesars; A Portrait of Scottish Rugby; The Royal Stuarts: A History of the Family That Shaped Britain; 101 Great Scots; Byron's Travels; Glasgow: Portraits of a City; Edinburgh; The Novel Today: A Critical Guide to the British Novel, 1970-89; The Thistle and the Rose: Six Centuries of Love and Hate Between the Scots and the English (as Editor): Edinburgh and the Borders in Verse (radio play): Quintet in October (plays): The Minstrel and the Shirra; First-Class Passengers. Recreations: reading; watching rugby; cricket, racing; walking the dogs. Address: (h.) Thirladean House, Selkirk TD7 5LU; T.-Selkirk 20393.

Masters, Christopher, CBE, BSc (Hons), PhD, AKC, FRSE; b. 2.5.47, Northallerton; m., Gillian Mary Hodson; 2 d. Educ. Richmond School; King's College, London; Leeds University. Shell Research BV/Shell Chemicals UK Ltd., 1971-77; joined Christian Salvesen as Business Development Manager, 1979; transferred to Christian Salvesen Inc., USA, 1982, as Director of Planning; Managing Director, Christian Salvesen Seafoods, 1983-85; Managing Director, Industrial Services Division, 1985-89; a Director, Christian Salvesen PLC, 1987-97; Chief Executive, Christian Salvesen PLC, 1989-97; Executive Chairman, Aggreko plc, 1997-2002; Chairman: Babtie Group Ltd., 2002-04, Voxar Ltd., 2002-04, SMG plc, 2004-07, Sagentia Group plc, 2006-2010, Energy Assets Group plc, 2012-16, Young Enterprise Scotland, 1994-97, Quality Assessment Committee of Higher Education Funding Council, 1991-95; Vice Chairman, Scottish Opera, 1996-99; Member, Scottish Higher Education Funding Council, 1995-2005, Chairman, 1998-2005; Chairman, Festival City Theatres Trust, 2002-2013; Independent Co-Chairman, Scottish Science Advisory Council, 2011-16; Non-Executive Director: British Assets Trust, 1989-2009, Scottish Widows, 1991-2000, Scottish Chamber Orchestra Trust, 1993-2012, John Wood Group PLC, 2002-2012, The Alliance Trust PLC, 2002-2012, The Crown Agents, 2005-2016, Speedy Hire plc, 2011-15, Murgitroyd Group PLC, 2015-2017; Master, The Merchant Company of Edinburgh, 2007-09; Lord Dean of Guild of the City of Edinburgh, 2009-2011; Member of Court of Edinburgh University, 2011-2017; Honorary Degrees: Strathclyde University and St. Andrews University, 2006, University of Abertay Dundee and Edinburgh University, 2007. Recreations: wines; opera and classical music. Address: (h.) 12 Braid Avenue, Edinburgh EH10 6EE; T.-0131-447 0812. E-mail: cm@chrismasters.co.uk

Masters, Richard, LLB, DipLP, Law. Chief Executive, Faculty of Advocates, since 2021; Non Executive Director, iomart Group, since 2017. Educ. University of Strathclyde; Harvard Business School. Career: McGrigors: Partner, 1995-2008, Managing Partner, 2008-12; Head of Client Operations, Pinsent Masons, 2012-15; Director, Complete Electronic Risk Compliance Limited, 2013-18; Chair,

Scotland and Northern Ireland, Pinsent Masons, 2017-19; Partner, Pinsent Masons, 2012-19. Address: iomart Group plc, Kelvin Campus, West of Scotland Science Park, Lister Pavillion, Glasgow G20 0SP.

Masterton, Professor Gordon Grier Thomson, OBE, DL, DTech, DEng, BSc, BA, MSc, DIC, FREng, FRSE, FICE, FIStructE, FIES. Chair of Future Infrastructure, Edinburgh University, since 2015; Vice President, Jacobs Engineering Inc, 2004-2014; President, The Institution of Civil Engineers, 2005-06; President, Institution of Engineers and Shipbuilders in Scotland, 2010-12; Founder of Scottish Engineering Hall of Fame, 2011; b. 9.6.54, Charlestown, Fife; m., Lynda Christine Jeffries; 1 s.; 1 d. Educ. Dunfermline High School; University of Edinburgh; Imperial College London; Open University. Babtie Shaw & Morton, 1976; Director, Babtie Group Ltd., 1993; Director, Babtie International Ltd., 1993; Director, Babtie Malaysia, 1995 (based in Kuala Lumpur); Managing Director, Facilities Business, 2002, Environment Business, 2004; UK Government Project Representative for Crossrail Project, London, 2009-2013; Independent Assurance Panel for HS2, since 2015. Visiting Professor: University of Paisley, 2001-05, Glasgow Caledonian University, since 2011, Edinburgh University, 2012-15; Member, Smeatonian Society, since 2004; Chairman, Construction Industry Council, Scotland, 2002-04, Chairman, Construction Industry Council UK, 2010-12; Royal Commissioner on the Ancient and Historical Monuments of Scotland, 2003-2015, Vice-Chairman, 2010-15; Member, Historic Scotland/RCAHMS Transition Advisory Board, 2013-15; Court Assistant, Worshipful Company of Engineers, since 2012, Master, 2020-21; Founder of City of London Engineering Hall of Fame, 2020; Member of Master Court, Incorporation of Hammermen of Glasgow, since 2015, Collector 2016-17; Deacon, 2018-19; Chairman, Scottish Lime Centre Trust, 2007-09; President, Glasgow Grand Opera Society, 1991-94; Trustee: Royal Society of Edinburgh Foundation, since 2016 (Chairman, since 2019), MacRobert Trust, since 2018; Society of Friends of Paisley Abbey, since 2018; appointed a Deputy Lieutenant of Renfrewshire in 2018; Honorary Doctorate: Caledonian University, 2007, Heriot-Watt University, 2012; TV appearances as presenter in 'Life After People', The History Channel, 2008, and two subsequent series and as himself in Unbuilt Britain, BBC, 2014; Thomas Telford: The Man who Built Britain, BBC, 2007; Canals: The Making of a Nation, BBC, 2015; The World's Greatest Bridges, Channel 4, 2018; When Buildings Collapse, Channel 5, 2019. 'Supreme Sacrifice: A Small Village and the Great War', 2016 (Co-Author). Recreations: opera; engineering history; sailing; genealogy. T.-01505 613503; e-mail: themastertons@btinternet.com

Masterton, Paul, LLB (Hons). MP (Conservative), East Renfrewshire, 2017-19; b. 2.11.85; m.; 2 c. Educ. George Watson's College; University of Dundee. McGrigors: Trainee Solicitor, 2008-2010, Solicitor, 2010-12; Pinsent Masons: Solicitor, 2012-14, Associate, 2014-17.

Matchett, Conor, MA. Deputy Political Editor, The Scotsman, since 2022. Educ. All Saints RC School; The University of Edinburgh. Career history: Intern, Youth Football Scotland, Edinburgh, 2015; work experience: BBC, 2016, Sky, 2016, Guardian News & Media, 2016; Student Caller, The University of Edinburgh, 2014-17; Sports Editor and Writer, The Student (newspaper), Edinburgh, 2014-17; FreshAir.org.uk, 2013-17; work experience, The Scotsman, 2015-17; Trainee, Press Association, 2017; Freelance Journalist, 2017-19; Junior Reporter, Archant, Norwich, 2018-19; Student Publication Association, 2018-19; JPIMedia: Digital Journalist, 2019, Multimedia Reporter, Edinburgh Evening News, 2019-2020, Political Reporter, The Scotsman, 2020-22. Winner,

Young Journalist of the Year at the Regional Press Awards in 2021; runner-up in the Scottish Press Awards for Young Journalist of the Year in 2020 and 2021. Address: The Scotsman, Barclay House, 108 Holyrood Road, Edinburgh EH8 8AS; T.-0131 225 3361.
E-mail: conor.matchett@jpimedia.co.uk

Mather, Jim. Chairman, Homes for Scotland, 2015-17; Visiting Professor at Heriot-Watt and Strathclyde Universities; MSP (SNP), Argyll & Bute, 2007-11, Highlands and Islands, 2003-07; Minister for Enterprise, Energy and Tourism, 2007-11; b. 6.3.47; m.; 1 s.; 1 d. Educ. Paisley Grammar School; Greenock High School; Glasgow University. Chartered Accountant.

Mathers, Neil, BA, PGCert. Chief Executive, Curiosity Collective, since 2017. Educ. Northern College of Education; Heriot-Watt University; Robert Gordon University. Career history: Youth Worker, Tayside Regional Council, 1994-95; Counselling and Community Support Worker, Barnardos Scotland, 1995-98; Coordinator, West Hailes Youth Agency, 1998-2002; Programme Coordinator (Volunteer), Voluntary Service Overseas, 2002-04; Board Director, Befriending Network Scotland, 2005-2012; Service Manager, Children 1st: Edinburgh, 2004-2010, East Lothian, 2010-2012; Voluntary Services Overseas, 2007-2013; Save the Children UK: Head of Programmes Scotland, 2012-13, Acting Director of UK Programmes, 2014-15, Head of Scotland, 2013-17. Children of Songea Trust: Chief Executive, 2008-2015, Chairperson, since 2015; Board Member, One Parent Families Scotland, 2014-19. Address: (b.) 44 King Street, Stirling FK8 1AY; T.-0330 175 5740.

Matheson, Alexander (Sandy), CVO, OBE, FRPharmS, JP. Lord Lieutenant, Western Isles Area, 2001-2016 (retired); Chairman, Highlands and Islands Airports Ltd., 2001-07; Chairman, Harris Tweed Authority, 2001-07; b. 16.11.41, Stornoway; m., Irene Mary Davidson, BSc, MSc; 2 s.; 2 d. Educ. Nicolson Institute, Stornoway; Robert Gordon's Institute of Technology, Aberdeen. Chairman, Stornoway Pier and Harbour Commission, 1991-2001 (Member, 1968-2010); Member, Stornoway Trust Estate, 1967-2009 (Chairman, 1971-81); Chairman: Stornoway Branch, RNLI (1974-81 and 1994-2004), Western Isles Development Fund, 1972-98, Western Isles Health Board, 1993-2001 (Member, 1973-2001); Member, Stornoway Town Council, 1967-75; Provost of Stornoway, 1971-75; Member: Ross and Cromarty County Council, 1967-75, Western Isles Islands Council, 1974-94 (Chairman, Development Services, 1974-80, Vice-Convener, 1980-82, Convener, 1982-90); President, Islands Commission of the Conference of Peripheral Maritime Regions of Europe, 1987-91 and 1993-94; Honorary Sheriff, since 1972; Chairman, Roderick Smith Ltd., Stornoway; Founding Chairman, Hebridean Men's Cancer Support Group, 2007-2012. Address: (h.) 33 Newton Street, Stornoway, Isle of Lewis.

Matheson, Ann, OBE, MA, MLitt, PhD, Hon. DLitt (St And), Drhc (Edin); b. 5.7.40, Wester Ross; m., T. Russell Walker. Educ. Dingwall Academy; St Andrews University; Edinburgh University. Ferranti Ltd., 1962-64; Teaching in Finland, 1964-67; National Library of Scotland: Assistant Keeper, 1972-83, Keeper, 1983-2000. Chairman, Literature Committee, Scottish Arts Council, 1997-2003; Chairman, Consortium of European Research Libraries; Chairman, NEWSPLAN 2000; Chairman, Literature Alliance Scotland; Chairman, Sabhal Mòr Ostaig Library Advisory Committee; Secretary, General Council, University of Edinburgh; Saltire Society Literary Panel; Secretary General, Ligue

des Bibliothèques Européennes de Recherche; Trustee and Secretary, Scottish Poetry Library. Fletcher of Saltoun Award (Arts and Humanities), 2014; Professor h.c., Sofia, 2015. Publications: Theories of Rhetoric, 1995; Gaelic Union Catalogue (Co-Editor) 1984; For the Encouragement of Learning, (Co-Editor), 1989. Recreations: literature; travel. Address: Yewbank, 52 Liberton Brae, Edinburgh, EH16 6AF; T.-0131-629 9109; e-mail: a.matheson@tinyworld.co.uk

Matheson, Gordon, CBE, MA, FCIPD. Head of Scottish Affairs, General Dental Council, since 2020; Member, Scottish Water Independent Customer Group, since 2021; Visiting Professor, University of Strathclyde, 2016-19; Honorary Professor, Glasgow Caledonian University, 2016-2019; Trustee, Interfaith Glasgow, 2018-2020; former Leader, Glasgow City Council (2010-2015), Councillor, 1999-2016, including terms as City Treasurer, Chair of Education, Bailie, and Justice of the Peace; Scottish Local Politician of the Year, 2012 and 2014, Herald Awards; former Member, Scottish Labour Party wider Shadow Cabinet; b. 1.11.66, Glasgow; m., Stephen Wallace. Educ. University of Glasgow; University of Strathclyde. Former Member, Board: UK Core Cities, Royal Scottish National Orchestra, Scottish Low Pay Unit, Strathclyde University Court, Glasgow City Marketing Bureau (Chair), 2010-2015, Glasgow 2014 Commonwealth Games Strategic Group, Strathclyde Pension Fund, Strathclyde Police. Awarded CBE in HM The Queen's New Year Honours for Services to Local Government and the Community. Has run Great Scottish Run and New York Marathon.

Matheson, John Alexander, CBE, BA, MBA, CPFA. President, Chartered Institute of Public Finance and Accountancy, 2015-16; Board Member, Doctors and Dentists Review Board, since 2017; Chair, Audit and Risk Committee, Transport Scotland, since 2017; Director of Health Finance, eHealth and Analytics in the Health and Social Care Directorate of Scottish Government, 2008-2016; Past Chairman, Scottish Branch and Past President, Chartered Institute of Public Finance and Accountancy (2015); Member, Board of Management, Edinburgh's Telford College, 1998-2007; b. 23.6.55, Dingwall; m., Judi; 1 s.; 1 d. Educ. Invergordon Academy; Heriot-Watt University; Edinburgh University. Finance Director of, Edinburgh Healthcare NHS Trust, 1994-99; Finance Director, NHS Lothian, 2000-08. Finance Director of the Year, 2004 (non profit sector). Recreation: hill-walking; golf. T.-0131-244 3464.

Matheson, Michael, BSc, BA, Dip. Applied Soc Sci. MSP (SNP), Falkirk West, since 2007, Central Scotland, 1999-2007; Cabinet Secretary for Net Zero, Energy and Transport, since 2021; Cabinet Secretary for Transport, Infrastructure and Connectivity, 2018-2021; Cabinet Secretary for Justice, 2014-18; Minister for Public Health, 2011-14; Member: Health and Sport Committee, 2007-2011, Justice and Home Affairs Committee, 2000-01, Justice 1 Committee, 2001-2004, Enterprise and Culture Committee, since 2004; Vice Convener: Cross Party Group on Sport, 2007-2011, European and External Relations Committee, 2009-2010, Cross Party Group on Cuba; Co-Convenor, Cross Party Group on Malawi; End of Life Assistance Committee, June 2010 - December 2010; b. 8.9.70, Glasgow. Educ. John Bosco Secondary School; Queen Margaret College, Edinburgh; Open University. Community Occupational Therapist: Highland Regional Council, Social Work Department, 1991-93, Stirling Council, Social Work Department, 1993-99. Member, Ochils Mountain Rescue Team. Recreation: mountaineering. Address: (b.) 15A East Bridge Street, Falkirk FK1 1YD; T.-01324 629271.

Matheson, Sheriff Sara. Sheriff, Grampian, Highland and Islands, since 2019; b. 11.70; 2 d. Educ. Aberdeen University. Career history: accredited as a specialist in child law in 2005 and in family law in 2008; appointed as a Convenor of the Additional Support Needs Tribunal in 2008; Owner, HBJ Gateley, 2008-2012; Family Law Solicitor, MTM Family Law LLP, 2012-2016; President of the Glasgow Bar Association in 2008; LLP Member, Matheson Property LLP, since 2014; appointed as a Summary Sheriff at Airdrie in 2016. Address: The Inverness Justice Centre, Longman Road, Inverness IV1 1AH; T.-01463 230782.

Mathewson, Sir George Ross, CBE, BSc, PhD, MBA, LLD (Dundee), LLD (St. Andrews), DUniv (Glasgow), Dr.hc (Edinburgh), FCIBS, CEng, MIEE, CCMI. Chairman, Royal Bank of Scotland Group plc, 2001-06; President, International Monetary Conference, 2005-06; Director, Scottish Investment Trust Ltd., 1981-2009; b. 14.5.40, Dunfermline; m., Sheila Alexandra Graham Bennett; 2 s. Educ. Perth Academy; St. Andrews University; Canisius College, Buffalo, New York. Assistant Lecturer, St. Andrews University, 1964-67; Systems Engineer (various positions), Bell Aerospace, Buffalo, New York, 1967-72; ICFC: Executive in Edinburgh Area Office, 1972-81, Area Manager, 1974-79, Director and Assistant General Manager, 1979-81; Chief Executive, Scottish Development Agency, 1981-87; Royal Bank of Scotland Group plc: joined as Director, Strategic Planning and Development, 1987, Group Chief Executive, 1992-2000, Executive Deputy Chairman, 2000-2001; National Business Lifetime Achievement Award, 2003. Appointed Non-Executive Director, Stagecoach Group in 2006; appointed Chairman, Royal Botanic Garden Edinburgh Campaign Board, Wood Mackenzie Ltd. in 2007; appointed Chairman, Council of Economic Advisers to the Scottish Government in 2007. Recreations: tennis; skiing; gardening; rugby; golf; business; shooting.

Mathieson, Rev Fiona McDougall, BEd, BD, PGCommEd, MTh. Minister, Carrick Knowe Parish, Edinburgh, since 2001; b. 28.12.62, Lennoxtown; m., Angus Mathieson. Educ. Mearns Castle High; Williamwood Secondary; Jordanhill College; Glasgow University; Edinburgh University; Heriot Watt University. Career History: Assistant Minister, Greenbank Edinburgh; Church of Scotland National Youth Adviser; Chaplain to The University of Glasgow. Recreations: food; wine and friends. Address: 21 Traquair Park West, Corstorphine, Edinburgh EH12 7AN; T.-0131-334-9774.
E-mail: fiona.mathieson@ukgateway.net

Mathieson, Professor Peter William. Vice-Chancellor and Principal, University of Edinburgh, since 2018; b. 18.4.59. Educ. London Hospital Medical College; University of Cambridge. Career: appointed Foundation Professor of Renal Medicine, University of Bristol (1995) and Honorary Consultant Nephrologist, North Bristol NHS Trust; became Head of the University Department of Clinical Science, North Bristol; Director of Research & Development, North Bristol NHS Trust; appointed Dean, Faculty of Medicine and Dentistry, University of Bristol in 2008; Vice Chancellor and President, University of Hong Kong, 2014-18. Elected as the youngest ever President of the Renal Association in 2007; Chair, Research Grants Committee of Kidney Research UK, 2003-07; Member, Renal Association Clinical Trials Committee, 1996-2007 (Chairman, 2000-2003); lead member for security issues in higher education, since 2021 (appointed by Universities UK and the Russell Group Board). Address: Old College, South Bridge, Edinburgh EH8 9YL.

Matthews, Baird, BL. Solicitor in private practice, 1950-2003; b. 19.1.25, Newton Stewart; m., Mary Thomson Hope; 2 s.; 1 d. Educ. Douglas Ewart High School; Edinburgh University. Commissioned, Royal Scots Fusiliers, 1944; demobilised as Captain, 1st Bn., 1947; Partner, A. B. & A. Matthews, Solicitors, Newton Stewart; Clerk to General Commissioners of Income Tax, Stranraer and Newton Stewart Districts, 1952; Burgh Prosecutor, Newton Stewart, 1968; Depute Procurator Fiscal for Wigtownshire, 1970; Chairman, Board of Local Directors, General Accident Fire and Life Assurance Corporation, 1988; Director, Newcastle Building Society (Scottish Board), 1991; Dean of Faculty of Stewartry of Kirkcudbright Solicitors, 1979; Dean of Faculty of Solicitors of the District of Wigtown, 1983. Recreations: travel; conversation; gliding. Address: (h.) Marchbank, Newton Stewart; T.-01671 403143.
E-mail: baird.matthews@gmail.com

Matthews, Bill. Chairman, Scottish Criminal Cases Review Commission, since 2020. Career history: engineer, then business and operations management roles with Motorola; five years running technology start-ups before building a portfolio of non-executive roles spanning media, health and criminal justice, including the BBC and the NHS. Currently a member of the board of the Independent Office for Police Conduct in England and Wales; Non-Executive Director, the Scottish Futures Trust; the Scottish Member of the British Transport Police Authority. Chartered Engineer; holds an MBA and Bachelor's degrees in Humanities and Psychology. Address: Portland House, 17 Renfield Street, Glasgow G2 5AH; T.-0141 270 7030.

Matthews, Graham George. President, Law Society of Scotland, 2017/18; Partner, Peterkins, 2002-2021 (retired); b. 1956. Represented city of Aberdeen and Aberdeenshire solicitors on the Law Society's Council until 2017 and served on a number of committees, including the Client Protection (formerly Guarantee Fund), Professional Practice, Remuneration and Regulation Committees.

Matthews, the Hon. Lord (Hugh Matthews). Senator of the College of Justice, since 2007; b. 4.12.53, Port Glasgow; m., Lindsay Mary Auld Wilson. Educ. St Joseph's Academy, Kilmarnock; Glasgow University. Admitted to Faculty of Advocates, 1979; Standing Junior Counsel, Department of Employment, 1984-88; Advocate Depute, 1988-93; QC, 1992; Temporary Sheriff, 1992-97; Sheriff of Glasgow and Strathkelvin, 1997-2007; Temporary Judge, 2004-07. Recreations: sport; music; looking after animals; ancient history; science fiction and astronomy.
E-mail: lordmatthews@scotcourts.gov.uk

Mauger-Thompson, Annie, BA (Hons), DipLib, CMS, MBA. Chief Executive Officer, Sacro, since 2020. Educ. Jersey College for Girls; University of Exeter; Aberystwyth University; Edinburgh Napier University; Leeds Beckett University. Career history: Head of Libraries and Heritage, City of York Council, 2000-03; Chief Executive, MLA Yorkshire, 2003-08; Executive Consultant, 2009-2010; Chief Executive, CLIP, 2010-15; Executive Director, Devolved Nations, Chartered Institute of Housing, 2015-18; Interim Chief Executive, CVS Inverclyde, 2019; Board Member, Home Group Scotland, since 2018; Director and Lead, Mauger-Thompson-Solo Ltd, Edinburgh, since 2018. Address: Sacro, National Office, 29 Albany Street, Edinburgh EH1 3QN; T.-0131 624 7270.

Maver, Professor Thomas Watt, BSc (Hons), PhD, DSc, HonFRIAS. Former Research Professor, Mackintosh School of Architecture, Glasgow School of Art; Emeritus Professor of Computer Aided Design, Department of Architecture and Director of the Graduate School,

Strathclyde University, 1982-2003 (Head of Department, 1983-85, 1988-91, Vice-Dean, Faculty of Engineering, 1993-2002); b. 10.3.38, Glasgow; m., Avril Elizabeth Cuthbertson; 2 d. Educ. Eastwood Secondary School; Glasgow University. Special Research Fellow, Engineering Faculty, Glasgow University, 1961-67; Strathclyde University: Research Fellow, School of Architecture, 1967-70, Director, Architecture and Building Aids Computer Unit, Strathclyde, since 1970; Visiting Professor: Technical University Eindhoven, Universiti Sains Malaysia, University of Rome (La Sapienza); Past Chairman and first Honorary Fellow of the Design Research Society; CIBSE Bronze Medal, 1966; Royal Society Esso Gold Medal, 1989; Distinguished Service Awards: BEPAC, eCAADe, SIGRADIA, IBPSA and ACADIA; Founder, CAAD Futures and eCAADe. Recreation: sailing a Drascombe Lugger out of Maidens, Ayrshire. Address: (h.) 8 Kew Terrace, Glasgow G12 0TD; T.-0141-339 7185; e-mail: t.w.maver@strath.ac.uk

Mavor, Prof. John, BSc, MPhil, PhD, DSc (Eng), FREng, FRSE, FIEEE. Vice-President (Physical Science and Engineering), Royal Society of Edinburgh, 2004-Sept. 2007; Principal and Vice-Chancellor, Napier University, 1994-2002; b. 18.7.42; m., Susan Christina Colton; 2 d. Educ. City University, London; London University; Edinburgh University. AEI Research Labs, London, 1964-65; Texas Instruments Ltd, Bedford, 1968-70; Emihus Microcomponents, Glenrothes, 1970-71; University of Edinburgh: Lecturer, 1971, Reader, 1979, Lothian Chair of Microelectronics, 1980, Head of Department of Electrical Engineering, 1984-89, Professor of Electrical Engineering, 1986-94, Dean, 1988-94, and Provost, 1992-94, Faculty of Science and Engineering. Hon. DSc, Greenwich, 1998, City, 1998. Publications: MOST Integrated Circuit Engineering, 1973; Introduction to MOS LSI Design, 1983; over 150 technical papers in professional electronics journals. Recreations: gardening; walking; steam railways. Address: 1/11 Succoth Avenue, Edinburgh EH12 6BE.

Maxwell, Donald, MA, DMus (Hon), FRWCMD, FLeedsCM. Professional Singer; b. 12.12.48, Perth; 1 d. Educ. Perth Academy; Edinburgh University. Since 1976, professional Singer with British opera companies and orchestras; Principal Baritone, Scottish Opera, 1978-82; Principal Baritone, Welsh National Opera, 1982-85; guest appearances, BBC Proms, Edinburgh Festival, Royal Opera House, London, Vienna, Paris, Milan, Tokyo, New York, Chicago, Amsterdam, Salzburg, Buenos Aires – notably as Falstaff; Director, National Opera Studio, 2001-08; Head of Opera, RWCMD, 2004-09; comedy – The Music Box with Linda Ormiston. Recreation: railways. Address: (b.) Music International, 13 Ardilaun Road, Highbury, London N5 2QR; T.-020 7359 5183.
E-mail: donmaxpen@hotmail.com

Maxwell, Ian. Chief Executive, Scottish Football Association, since 2018; former Scottish football player; b. 2.5.75. Senior Career: Queen's Park, 1993-98; Ross County, 1998-2002; St Johnstone, 2002-05; St Mirren, 2005-08; Partick Thistle, 2008-2010. Managing Director, Partick Thistle, 2014-18. Address: Hampden Park, Glasgow G42 9AY; T.-0141 6166000.

Maxwell, Ingval, OBE, DA (Dun), FRIBA, FRIAS, FSA Scot. International Consultant in Architectural Conservation and Education, since 2008; Director, Technical Conservation Research and Education, Historic Scotland, 1993-2008; b. 28.5.44, Penpont; m., Susan Isabel Maclean; 1 s.; 1 d. Educ. Dumfries Academy; Duncan of Jordanstone College of Art, Dundee. Joined Ministry of Public Buildings and Works as Architect, 1969; Area Architect,

then Principal Architect, Ancient Monuments Branch, 1972-85; Assistant Director of Works, Historic Scotland, 1985-93; Architectural Advisor, Ancient Monuments Board for Scotland, 1993-2003; Architectural Advisor, Historic Buildings Council for Scotland, 1993-2003; RIBA Research Award, 1970-71; RIAS Thomas Ross Award, 1988; Chairman, Scottish Vernacular Buildings Working Group, 1990-94; Chairman, Scottish Conservation Forum in Training and Education, 1994-2008; Convenor, Scottish Stone Liaison Group, 1997-2007; Member, RIAS Conservation Committee; Member, European Commission COST Action C5, 1996-2000; Chairman, European Science Foundation COST Action C17, 2002-06; Member, European Construction Technology Platform - Focus Area Cultural Heritage, 2006-2008; Member, Architects Accredited in Building Conservation, 1999-2020; Member, ICOMOS UK Executive Committee, 1995-2006; Member, ICOMOS International Scientific Committee on Stone, since 2000; Member, UCL Centre for Historic Buildings, Collections and Sites Academic Advisory Committee, 2001-08; Member, UK and Ireland Blue Shield Organisation, 2001; Member, AHRC EPSRC Science and Heritage Advisory Committee, 2008-2014; Trustee, Charles Wallace India Trust, 2003-2013; Trustee, Council on Training in Architectural Conservation, 2008-2022; Chairman, COTAC, since 2013; UNESCO/ICOMOS World Heritage Official, 2008-2013; RIBA Conservation Accreditation Steering Group Member, since 2009; Adviser, EC FP7 Cultural Heritage Identity Card, 2009-2013; Member, Advisory Board, Learn Direct and Build, 2010-17; External Examiner, Faculty of Arts, University of Plymouth, 2010-2013; RIBA Conservation Training Course Leader, 2011-2013; Director, CyArk Europe, 2013-16; Member, Historic Environment Forum, Heritage Skills Task Group, 2013-2017; Member, European Commission study on Safeguarding Cultural Heritage from Natural and Man-Made Disasters, 2016-18; Member, RIBA Conservation Group, since 2018. Publications: Building Materials of the Scottish Farmstead, 1996; Conservation of Historic Graveyards Guide for Practitioners (Co-Author), 2001; Stone in Scotland (Co-Author), 2006; INFORM - Masonry Decay, 2005, Fire Safety, 2005, Repairing Scottish State Roofs, 2006, Repointing Rubble Stonework, 2007, Cleaning Sandstone, 2007; COST Action C17 "Fire Loss to Historic Buildings" Final Report (3 vols) (Editor), 2007; COST Action C17 "Fire Loss to Historic Buildings" Conference Proceedings (4 vols) (Editor), 2007; Stone in Context Conference Proceedings (Editor), 2008; Integrating Digital Technologies in Support of Historic Building Information Modelling: BIM4C (Author), 2014; Fire and Flood in the Built Environment: Keeping the threat at Bay (2 vols) (Author), 2015; Integrating HBIM Framework Report Part 1: Conservation Parameters; Part 2: Conservation Influences (Author), 2016; BIM4Heritage Where We Are and Where We are Going (Author), 2017; The Potteries and Surrounding Areas. Part 1: Understanding The Region; Part 2: Appreciating The Region (Co-Author), 2019. Recreations: photography; astronomy; aircraft; buildings. Address: (h.) 135 Mayfield Road, Edinburgh EH9 3AN.

Maxwell, Professor Simon, BSc, MBChB, MD, PhD, FRCP, FRCPE, FBPhS, FHEA. Consultant Physician, Western General Hospital, Edinburgh, since 1998; Professor of Student Learning (Clinical Pharmacology and Prescribing), University of Edinburgh, since 1998; b. 14.2.62, Edinburgh; m.; 1 s. Educ. Nottingham High School; University of Birmingham. Lecturer in Medicine, Birmingham Medical School, 1990-96; Senior Lecturer in Medicine, Leicester Medical School, 1996-98. Chairman, Scottish Medical Academic Staff Committee, BMA (2002-04); Vice-President, British Pharmacological Society (2002-04); Medical Director, Centre for Adverse Reactions to Drugs Scotland, since 2008; Medical Director, UK Prescribing Safety Assessment, since 2010; Chairman, Lothian NHS Area Drug and Therapeutics Committee,

2014-20; Scottish Medicines Consortium, 2008-18; MHRA Pharmacovigilance Expert Advisory Group, 2010-20. Address: (b.) Internal Medicine, Medical Education Centre, University of Edinburgh, Western General Hospital, Edinburgh EH4 2XU; e-mail: s.maxwell@ed.ac.uk

Maxwell, Stewart, MSP, BA (Hons). MSP (SNP), West of Scotland, 2003-2016; Minister for Communities and Sport, 2007-09; SNP Parliamentary Group Secretary, 2003-07; b. 24.12.63, Glasgow; m., Mary; 1 d. Educ. King's Park Secondary School; Glasgow College of Technology. Strathclyde Fire Brigade: Industrial Training Manager, 1993-94; Senior Admin Officer, 1994-2000; Management Information System Project Manager, 2000-03. SNP Deputy Health Spokesperson, 2004-06; SNP Spokesperson on Sport, Culture and Media, 2006-07; Honorary Vice President, Royal Environmental Health Institute of Scotland, since 2006. Recreations: reading; swimming; golf; scuba diving; photography; watching rugby; eating out.

Maxwell, Dr. William (Bill), MA (Hons), MAppSci, PhD, CPsychol, FRSA. Former Chief Executive, Education Scotland (retired, 2017); b. 14.11.57, Edinburgh; m., Margaret; 2 d. Educ. High School of Dundee; University College Oxford; Glasgow University; Edinburgh University. Area Principal Psychologist, Grampian Council, 1992-94; HM Inspector of Schools, 1994-2002; HM Chief Inspector of Education, 2002-06; Head of Education, Information and Analytical Services, Scottish Government, 2006-08; HM Chief Inspector of Education and Training in Wales, 2008-2010; HM Senior Chief Inspector of Education (Scotland), 2010-11; Transitional Chief Inspector, Education Scotland, July 2011 to December 2011. Recreations: climbing and mountaineering; cycling and the arts.

Maxwell-Irving, Alastair Michael Tivey, BSc, CEng, MIEE, MIMgt, PhD, FSA, FSAScot, Antiquarian and Archaeologist; b. 1.10.35, Witham, Essex; m., Esther Mary Hamilton, MA, LLB. Educ. Lancing College; London University; Oxford University (1975); Stirling University (1992); Glasgow Caledonian University (2019-20). General Electric Company, 1957; English Electric Company, 1960-64; Assistant Factor, Annandale Estates, 1966-9; Weir Pumps Ltd., 1970-91; co-founder, Member and Secretary, 1975-78, Central Scotland Branch, British Institute of Management. Contributor, Burke's Landed Gentry, 1968-2001; Nigel Tranter Memorial Award, 2003; Trustee, Bonshaw Preservation Trust, 2007; Matriculated Arms, 1961. Publications: Genealogy of the Irvings of Dumfries, 1965; The Irvings of Bonshaw, 1968; The Irvings of Dumfries, 1968; Lochwood Castle, 1968; Early Firearms and their Influence on the Military and Domestic Architecture of the Borders, 1974; Cramalt Tower: Historical Survey and Excavations, 1977-79, 1982; Borthwick Castle: Excavations 1979, 1982; Andrew Dunlop (Clockmakers' Company 1701-32), 1984; Hoddom Castle: A Reappraisal of its Architecture and Place in History, 1989; Lochwood Castle, 1990; The Castles of Buittle, 1991; Lockerbie Tower, 1992; Torthorwald Castle, 1993; Scottish Yetts and Window Grilles, 1994; Blairgowrie, 1994 (in Scottish World); The Tower-Houses of Kirtleside, 1997; Kenmure Castle, 1997; The Border Towers of Scotland: their history and architecture – The West March, 2000; The Maxwells of Caerlaverock (in Lordship and Architecture in Medieval and Renaissance Scotland), 2005; Family Memoirs, 2007 and 2008; Reginald Tivey: A Celebration of his Art, 2011; The Border Towers of Scotland 2, 2014; How many towers were in the Scottish Borders?, 2012; Towers and Timber - Superstructures, 2017. Recreations: architecture and history of the Border towers of Scotland; archaeology; family history and genealogy; Florence and the architecture of Tuscany; horology; heraldry; photography; gardening. Address: (h.) Telford House, Blairlogie, Stirling FK9 5PX.
E-mail: a.maxwellirving@gmail.com

Maxwell Stuart of Traquair (Catherine Margaret Mary Maxwell Stuart). 21st Lady of Traquair; Scottish landowner, politician, hotelier, brewer and writer; b. 16.11.64, Peebles. Educ. Peebles High School; London School of Economics; m. (1), John Grey (deceased); (2), Mark Muller; 3 c. Succeeded to title in 1990.

May, Douglas James, LLB. Queen's Counsel, since 1989; b. 7.5.46, Edinburgh. Educ. George Heriot's; Edinburgh University. Advocate, 1971; Temporary Sheriff, 1990-99; Social Security Commissioner, Child Support Commissioner, 1993-2008; Judge of the Upper Tribunal, Administrative Appeals Chamber, since 2008; fee-paid, 2015-2021; Member of Tribunal Procedure Committee, 2008-2015; Parliamentary candidate (Conservative), Edinburgh East, 1974, Glasgow Cathcart, 1983. Recreations: golf (Captain: Scotland Universities Golfing Society, 1990-91, Merchants of Edinburgh Golf Club, 1997-99); photography (ARPS, 1997, FRPS, 2002, President, Edinburgh Photographic Society, 1996-99); Chairman, Conceptual Contemporary Panel of Royal Photographic Society distinction awards, 2010-2017.

Mayhew, Dr. Peter Watts, BSc, PhD. Director, Nature and Climate Change, Cairngorms National Park Authority, 2017-2021; b. 30.6.59, Glasgow; m., Alison Fleming; 2 d. Educ. Hutchesons' Grammar, Glasgow; Glasgow University. Research Ornithologist, 1980-83; Head of Conservation, British Association for Shooting and Conservation, 1984-89; Senior Conservation Manager, RSPB Scotland, 1990-2017. Board Member, Deer Commission for Scotland, 2005-10; Member, Scottish Natural Heritage Deer Panel, 2010-2013; Chair, Scottish Capercaillie Group; Chair, Cairngorms, Speyside, Deer Management Group. Recreations: mountaineering; sailing; bird watching. Address: (h.) 13, Seafield Court, Grantown on Spey PH26 3LE.
E-mail: petemayhew2@gmail.com

Mays, Deborah Clare, MA (Hons), PhD, IHBC, FRSA, FSA (Scot), Hon FRIAS. CEO, The Heritage Place, since 2014; Head of Listing, Historic England, since 2019, Head of Listing Advice, 2016-19; Director, Berwickshire Housing Association Enterprise, 2014-16; Director and Assistant Secretary, Royal Incorporation of Architects in Scotland, 2012-14, and Chief Executive Officer, Scottish Building Contract Committee, 2012-14; b. 10.8.62, Redhill, Surrey; m., Dr Sean O'Reilly; 2 d. Educ. Lavant House School; University of St Andrews. Historic Scotland: Inspector of Historic Buildings, listing and casework, also Assessor to the Historic Buildings Council, then Project Manager, Modernisation, then Deputy Chief Inspector, latterly Director of Policy and Outreach. Secretary, Society of Architectural Historians of Great Britain; Editor of 3 books; full list of published articles; lectures. Recreations: culture; architecture. Address: (b.) The Heritage Place, 115 Henderson Row, Edinburgh EH3 5BB; T.-07794 705163.

Meadows, Netta. Chief Executive, Scottish Borders Council, since 2021. Career history: held director roles at Bristol City Council, working across strategic commissioning, commercial relations, social care and neighbourhood services; joined South Somerset District Council in 2017 as the director for strategy and support services; previously director for service delivery.

Address: Council Headquarters, Newtown St. Boswells, Melrose TD6 0SA.

Mealor, Professor Paul, OStJ, BA, PhD, DMus, FUniv, FRSA. Composer and Professor of Music, The University of Aberdeen, since 2003; b. 25.11.75, St Asaph, North Wales. Composer of music for the wedding of TRH The Duke and Duchess of Cambridge (2011) and other Royal events including HM The Queen's Diamond Jubilee and the 65th and 70th Birthdays of HRH The Prince Charles, Duke of Rothesay. Member of The Queen's Medal for Music Committee (Buckingham Palace); Patron of the Welsh Music Guild; President of Ty Cerdd; Patron of the North East of Scotland Music School; Burgess of Guild of the City of Aberdeen; Vice-President of the Llangollen International Eisteddfod; President of the JAM on the Marsh Festival (Kent). Recreations: narrowboating; hill walking. Address: Department of Music, University of Aberdeen, MacRobert Building, King Street, Aberdeen AB24 5UD; T.-01224 274603.
E-mail: p.mealor@abdn.ac.uk

Medhurst, Teresa. Chief Executive, Scottish Prison Service, since 2020; previously Director of Strategy and Innovation; Senior Sponsor of the Scottish Prison Service Women's Development Network. Address: Scottish Prison Service Headquarters, Communications Branch, Room G20, Calton House, 5 Redheughs Rigg, Edinburgh EH12 9HW; T.-0131 330 3500.
E-mail: teresa.medurst@sps.pnn.gov.uk

Meek, Professor Donald Eachann MacDonald, MA, LittD (Cantab), MA, PhD, DLitt (Glas), FRHistS. Hon. Fellow of the Association for Scottish Literary Studies; FRSE, 2003-2013; Professor of Scottish and Gaelic Studies, Edinburgh University, 2002-08; Chairman, Gaelic Books Council, 2002-04; b. 16.5.49, Glasgow, brought up in Tiree; m., Rachel Jane Rogers; 2 d. Educ. Oban High School; Glasgow University; Emmanuel College, Cambridge. Lecturer, Senior Lecturer and Reader in Celtic, Edinburgh University, 1979-92; Professor of Celtic, Aberdeen University, 1993-2001. Assistant Editor, Historical Dictionary of Scottish Gaelic, Glasgow University, 1973-79; Honorary Secretary, Gaelic Society of Glasgow, 1974-79; Member, Gaelic Advisory Committee to Broadcasting Council for Scotland, 1976-78 and of Gaelic Panel, National Bible Society of Scotland, 1978-2008; President, Edinburgh and Lothians Baptist Association, 1992-93; Clerk and Treasurer, Board of Celtic Studies (Scotland), 1994-2009; Chief, Gaelic Society of Inverness, 1998, 1999; Chairman, Ministerial Advisory Group on Gaelic, Scottish Executive, 2001-02; Editor, Gaelic Bible, 1992 edition and later revisions; a General Editor, Dictionary of Scottish Church History and Theology, 1993; President, Scottish Church History Society, 2001-04; President, Scottish Gaelic Texts Society, 2011-15. Publications: books include Mairi Mhor nan Oran, 1977, second edition 1998; The Campbell Collection of Gaelic Proverbs and Proverbial Sayings, 1978; Island Harvest: A History of Tiree Baptist Church, 1988; Sunshine and Shadow: the story of the Baptists of Mull, 1991; A Mind for Mission: essays (Editor), 1992; Tuath is Tighearna: Poetry of the Clearances and the Land Agitation (Editor), 1995; The Quest for Celtic Christianity, 2000; Caran an t-Saoghail: Anthology of Nineteenth-century Gaelic Poetry, 2003; The Kingdom of MacBrayne (Co-Author), 2006, second edition, 2008; Gaelic Prose Writings of the Rev. T. M. Murchison (Editor), 2010; Steamships to St Kilda, 2010; Mo Là Gu Seo, Gaelic autobiography of T. M. Murchison (Editor), 2011; From Comet to CalMac: Two Hundred Years of Hebridean and Clyde Shipping (Co-Author), 2011; Laoidhean Spioradail Dhùghaill Bhochanain (Editor), 2015; Sreathan anns a' Ghainmhich, collection of original Gaelic verse, 2017; Iasad Rann, Gaelic poems by John Maclean (Co-Editor), 2018; Shore Lines, original English verse (2019); Seòl Mo Bheatha, Gaelic autobiography (2019); Dugald Buchanan, Canna Lecture 2016 (2019); From the Clyde to St Kilda: The Ships and Services of Martin Orme and John McCallum, 2020; Scottish Gaelic Studies, vols. 18, 19, 20, 21 (Editor); Gath, Vol. I - 4 (Co-Editor); A Croft in Caolas: A Tiree Holding and its People 1770-2020, 2021; endless articles on Gaelic and Highland themes. Recreations: boat-building; art; photography; getting to know the Highlands; watching CalMac; filling the wastepaper basket. Address: (h.) 18 Cricket Place, Brightons, Falkirk FK2 0HZ.

Meldrum, Angus Alexander, BSc, DIA in Mathematics, Physics and Industry; Trustee and Co-Founder of the Tennent's Archives Trust and "The Tennent's Story" visitor centre, Tennent's Wellpark Brewery, Glasgow; Fellow of the UK Marketing Society. Director, Crerar Hotel Group Ltd., 1999-2017; The Patron, Benevolent Society of The Licensed Trade of Scotland, 2005-2017; Chairman, Thistle Pub Company 3 plc, 2006-2013; Director, An Lochran (Glasgow Gaelic Arts Agency) Ltd., 2006-2013; Group Chairman, Belhaven Brewery Group plc, 2004-05 (Director, 2002-05); Managing Director, Tennent Caledonian Breweries Ltd., 1992-2001 (Director, since 1981); Chairman, Chrysalis Radio/Arrow Glasgow Ltd., 2003-04; b. 7.11.45, Stornoway; m., Anne-Marie; 1 s. Educ. Bayble School, Lewis; Kingussie High School; Edinburgh University; Bath University Management School. Joined Bass plc, London, 1971; Market Analyst and Group Product Manager, Bass Brewers Ltd., 1971-78; Marketing Manager, Tennent Caledonian Breweries Ltd., 1978-81; Marketing Director, Tennent Caledonian Breweries Ltd., 1981-90; Marketing Director, Bass Brewers (Scotland and Ireland), 1981-90; Brands Marketing Director (UK and International), Bass Brewers Ltd., Burton-on-Trent, 1990-92; Director, Bass Ireland Ltd., 1981-95; Director, Tennents Ireland Ltd. (Dublin), 1981-95; Director, Bass Export Ltd., 1990-94; Director, Maclay's Brewery & Co. plc, Alloa, 1992-2002; Managing Director, J.G. Thomson Ltd. (Wines and Spirits Merchants), 1992-2001; President, Brewers Association of Scotland, 1992-94; Council Member, UK Brewers Society, 1992-94; Millennium Chairman, Scottish Licensed Trade Association, 1999-2000; Freeman, City of Glasgow, since 1982; Glasgow Incorporation of Maltmen, since 1982; Keeper of the Quaich, since 1992; Baron d'Honneur de Confrerie des Compagnons Goustevin de Normandie, since 2001; Scottish Licensed Trade Lifetime Achievement Award, 2001; Scottish Advertising Industry Awards 2007 Special 21st Anniversary Award of Scotland's Best Marketeer Ever. Recreations: fishing; history; rugby; football; shinty; Scottish music; Gaelic culture. Address: (b.) Lochgreen Consultants, Lochgreen, Gryffe Road, Kilmacolm, Renfrewshire PA13 4BA; T.-01505 872609.

Meldrum, James, MA (Hons), FRSA; b. 9.8.52, Kirkintilloch. Educ. Lenzie Academy; Glasgow University. Administration Trainee/HEO (Admin), Scottish Office, 1973-79; Principal grade posts, Scottish Economic Planning Department, Scottish Development Department, Scottish Office Personnel Division, 1979-86; Deputy Director, Scottish Courts Administration, 1986-91; Head, Investment Assistance Division, Scottish Office Industry Department, 1991-94; Registrar General for Scotland, 1994-99; Director of Administrative Services, Scottish Executive, 1999-2002; Director of Business Management and Area Business Manager, Glasgow, Crown Office and Procurator Fiscal Service, 2002-03; Keeper of the Registers of Scotland, 2003-2009. Address: (h.) 5 Roman Road, Kirkintilloch, Glasgow G66 1EE; T.-0141 776 7071.
E-mail: jim.meldrum1@btinternet.com

Melloy, Cllr Dennis. Provost, Perth and Kinross Council, since 2017; representing the Strathmore Ward

(Conservative), since 2007; m., Libby. Qualified ballroom dancing teacher; runs Solutions based in Alyth. Recreation: keen golfer. Address: c/o Perth and Kinross Council, 2 High Street, Perth PH1 5PH; T.-01738 475034.
E-mail: dmelloy@pkc.gov.uk

Mennie, William Patrick, BL, IAC, MCSI. Partner, Grigor & Young, Solicitors, Elgin and Forres, 1964-2004 (Senior Partner, from 1984); Consultant, 2004-08; b. 11.10.37, Elgin; m., Patricia Leslie Bogie; 2 s.; 1 d. Educ. Elgin Academy; Edinburgh University. Solicitor and Notary Public, 1960-2018; Honorary Sheriff at Elgin, since 1993; accredited by Law Society of Scotland as a specialist in agricultural law, 1993-2013; Secretary, Malt Distillers Association of Scotland, 1980-2003. Recreations: game shooting and fishing. Address: (h.) Innesmill, Urquhart, Elgin; T.-01343 842643.

Menzies, Rt. Hon. Lord (Duncan A.Y. Menzies). Senator of the College of Justice, 2001-2021; appointed to the Inner House, 2012; sworn of the Privy Council, 2012; b. 28.8.53, Edinburgh; m., Hilary Weston; 2 s. Educ. Edinburgh Academy; Cargilfield; Glenalmond (scholar); Wadham College, Oxford (scholar); Edinburgh University. Advocate, 1978; Standing Junior Counsel to The Admiralty, 1984-91; Queen's Counsel, 1991; accredited mediator, 1992; Temporary Sheriff, 1996-97; Advocate Depute, 1998-2000; Home Advocate Depute, 1998-2000; Chairman, Scottish Planning, Local Government and Environmental Bar Group, 1997-2001; Member, Faculty Council, 1997-2001; Parliamentary Candidate, Midlothian, 1983, Edinburgh Leith, 1987; founder, Scottish Wine Society; 2012: Maître de la Commanderie de Bordeaux à Edimbourg; Deputy Chairman, Scottish Civil Justice Council, 2013-19; Honorary Bencher of the Inner Temple, 2013; Chairman of Council, Glenalmond College, 2014-2017. Recreations: shooting; golf; wines; planting trees.

Meredith, Dr Lucy, MSc, PhD. Interim Principal and Vice-Chancellor, University of the West of Scotland, since 2020. Educ. University of Salford; University of Leeds; University of the West of England. Career history: appointed Lecturer in Environmental Health, Bristol Polytechnic in 1991; worked in a number of Higher Education Institutions including Bath Spa University, University of Bristol and University of the West of England; Dean of Computing Engineering and Science, University of South Wales, 2016-18; Deputy Vice Chancellor, Royal Agricultural University, 2018-19; Higher Education Specialist, 2019-2020. Chartered Fellow of the Institute of Environmental Health; Senior Fellow of the Higher Education Academy; Fellow of the Leadership Foundation. Recreations: sailing; kayaking; mountaineering; skiing. Address: University of the West of Scotland, Technology Avenue, Blantyre, Glasgow G72 0LH; T.-01698 283100; e-mail: lucy.meredith@uws.ac.uk

Merrill, Alastair, FCIPS (Chtd), FRSA. Vice Principal, Governance, University of St Andrews, since 2015. Educ. Pembroke College, University of Cambridge; Said Business School, University of Oxford. Career history: joined the civil service fast stream in 1986, served in a variety of posts in Ministry of Defence and the Foreign Office, including secondments to the private sector and the UN peacekeeping force in the former Yugoslavia; Deputy Director, Private Office, HQ NATO, 1996-2001; The Scottish Government: Head of Education Analytical Services, 2001-03; Deputy Director, Changing to Deliver, 2003-05, Deputy Director, Police Performance and Resources, 2005-08, Director, Corporate Services, Scottish Prison Service, 2008-09; Director, Procurement and Commercial, The Scottish Government, 2009-2015; Assessor, College of Policing,

since 2008. Address: University of St Andrews, College Gate, St Andrews KA16 9AJ; T.-01334 462553; e-mail: vpgov@st-andrews.ac.uk

Merrylees, Andrew, RSA, BArch, DipTP, RIBA, FRIAS, FCSD, FRSA. Honorary Professor of Architecture, University of Dundee; b. 13.10.33, Newmains; m., Maie Crawford; 2 s.; 1 d. Educ. Wishaw High School; University of Strathclyde. Sir Basil Spence, Glover and Ferguson: joined 1957, Associate, 1968, Partner, 1972; set up Andrew Merrylees Associates, 1985 (now retired). Member: Advisory Council for the Arts in Scotland. RIBA Bronze Medal; Saltire Award; Civic Trust Award; Art in Architecture Award; RSA Gold Medal; SCONUL Award; RIAS Lifetime Achievement Award. Recreations: architecture; painting; cooking. Address: (b.) 32 Ravelston Garden, Edinburgh EH4 3LE; T.-0131 337 9019; e-mail: amerrylees32@gmail.com
web: www.royalscottishacademy.org/members

Michie, Deirdre, OBE, LLB (Hons). Chief Executive Officer, Offshore Energies UK, since 2015; b. 12.64. Career history: Business Manager, Shell U.K. Downstream, London, 1991-94; Senior Commercial Negotiator, Shell U.K., Aberdeen/London, 1994-2000; External Affairs Business Advisor, Shell U.K., Aberdeen, 2000-03; Shell Exploration and Production Europe: Communications Manager, 2003-07, Contracting & Procurement Manager for Europe, Aberdeen, 2003-07; Sabbatical, 2011; General Manager, Strategic Sourcing, Shell International, Aberdeen, 2011-14; Project Manager, Shell U.K. Limited, Aberdeen, 2014-15; Non Executive Director, Scottish Water, since 2017. Burgess of Aberdeen. Address: Offshore Energies, 4th Floor, Annan House, 33-35 Palmerston Road, Aberdeen AB11 5QP; 01224 577250.

Michie, Gerald. Governor, HMYOI Polmont, since 2021; previously Deputy Governor, HMP Edinburgh. Address: 13 Blairlodge Avenue, Falkirk, Polmont FK2 0AD; T.-01324 722299.

Middleton, David Fraser, CBE, MA. Chair, Scottish Qualifications Authority Board, since 2017; former Chief Executive, Historic Environment Scotland (2015-16); b. 23.6.56, Paisley; m., Diane Lamberton; 1 d. Educ. Paisley Grammar School; Glasgow University. Joined Scottish Office as Administration Trainee, 1978; Private Secretary to Minister of State, Scottish Office, 1982-84; seconded to Cabinet Office, 1984; Principal, Scottish Office Finance Group, 1984-89; Director of Strategy, Whitfield Urban Partnership, 1989-91; Assistant Secretary, Housing, 1991-96; Assistant Secretary, 1996-97, Roads; Head of Personnel, 1997-99; Head of Local Government, Europe and External Relations Group, Department of Finance and Central Services, Scottish Executive, 1999-2002; Head of Food and Agriculture Group, Environment and Rural Affairs Department, Scottish Executive, 2002-06; Special Projects Officer, UHI (Millennium Institute), 2006-07 (on loan from Scottish Executive); Head of Scotland Office, Ministry of Justice, 2007-09; Chief Executive, Transport Scotland, Scottish Government, 2009-2015. Recreation: golf (Royal Musselburgh Golf Club). Address: Scottish Qualifications Authority, The Optima Building, 58 Robertson Street, Glasgow G2 8DQ.

Middleton, Jeremy Richard Hunter, LLB, BD. Minister, Gilcomston Church, Aberdeen; b. 19.3.53, Kilbarchan; m., Susan (nee Hay); 3 s. Educ. Craigflower Preparatory School, Charterhouse; Old College, New College, Edinburgh. Address: 5 Earlspark Road, Bieldside, Aberdeen AB15 9BZ.

Miell, Professor Dorothy, OBE, CPsychol, FBPS, FRSE. Vice Principal, Chair of the IASH Advisory Board, Head of the College of Arts, Humanities and

Social Sciences, The University of Edinburgh. Career history: former Dean, Social Sciences, the Open University; joined the University of Edinburgh in 2010; a Social Psychologist working on relationships and communication and especially how these are involved in the process of collaborative working across disciplines. Fellow of the Royal Society of Edinburgh, since 2015, Grants Committee Member; Member: Council of the Edinburgh International Festival, Board of Directors of Scottish Opera, Academic Board, Royal Conservatoire of Scotland. Recently served as President of the British Psychological Society (2014-15), currently Fellow of the Society, former Chair of its Psychology Education Board and Trustee. Address: The Institute for Advanced Studies in the Humanities, The University of Edinburgh, Hope Park Square, Edinburgh EH8 9NW; T.-0131 650 4671; e-mail: d.e.miell@ed.ac.uk

Millar, Professor Alan, MA, PhD, FRSE. Emeritus Professor of Philosophy, Stirling University; b. 14.12.47, Edinburgh; m., Rose-Mary Marchand; 1 s. Educ. Edinburgh University; Cambridge University. Stirling University: Lecturer in Philosophy, 1971, Senior Lecturer, 1991, Head, Department of Philosophy, 1988-94, 2003-06. Awarded Mind Association Research Fellowship, 1996-97; Visiting Fellow, Clare Hall, Cambridge, 1997; elected Fellow of the Royal Society of Edinburgh, 2005; Member, Editorial Board, Philosophical Quarterly, 2002-2017; Member, the Executive and Council of the Royal Institute of Philosophy, 2009-2017; Vice-President, Mind Association, 2013-14; President, Mind Association, 2014-15. Publications: Reasons and Experience, 1991; Reason and Nature (Co-Editor), 2002; Understanding People, 2004; Epistemic Value (Co-Editor), 2009; Social Epistemology (Co-Editor), 2010; The Nature and Value of Knowledge (Co-Author), 2010; Knowing By Perceiving, 2019; articles in the philosophy of mind, epistemology, philosophy of religion, history of ethics. Recreations: reading; walking; films; cooking. Address: (b.) Stirling University, Stirling FK9 4LA; T.-01786 467555; e-mail: alan.millar@stir.ac.uk

Millar, Amanda, LLB (Hons), DipLP, Cert Social Welfare Law. Chair of Court, University of Dundee, since 2022; Chair, Samaritans Scotland Committee & Samaritans UK & Ireland Trustee, Samaritans, since 2022; President, The Law Society of Scotland, 2020-21, Vice President, 2019-2020; b. 8.71. Educ. University of Strathclyde. Career history: Tutor in Law, University of Strathclyde, 1994-95; Lecturer/Tutor, Glasgow Caledonian University, 1994-96; Litigation solicitor, Blackadders, Dundee, 2000-02; Tutor, University of Dundee, 2001-03; Associate, Miller Hendry, Perth, 2002-06; Policy Committee Member, SCVO (Scottish Council for Voluntary Organisations), Edinburgh, 2013-15; Director/Trustee/Chair, Mindspace Ltd, Perth, 2006-2017; Chair of the Board of Directors, Changing the Chemistry (SCIO), 2016-19; McCash and Hunter LLP, Perth: Associate, 2006-2015, Partner, 2015-2019; Centre for Mental Health & Incapacity, Edinburgh Napier University, since 2014; Independent Chair, Diversity & Inclusion Advisory Group, Institute of Directors Scotland, since 2020; The Law Society of Scotland: Council Member, since 2010, Rules Waivers and Guidance Regulatory Sub Committee Convener, 2016-2020, Board Member, since 2017, LawScot Tech Advisory Board Member, since 2018. Address: University of Dundee, Nethergate, Dundee DD1 4HN.

Miller, Professor Alan, BSc, PhD, CPhys, FInstP, FRSE, FIEEE (USA), FOSA (USA). Chief Executive Officer, Scottish Universities Physics Alliance (SUPA), University of Glasgow, since May 2015, and Emeritus Professor of Physics, Heriot-Watt University, since January 2015; Trustee and Board Member, Royal Zoological Society of Scotland (RZSS), since May 2015; Deputy Principal (Research and Knowledge Transfer) and Professor of Physics, Heriot-Watt University, 2009-14; Fellowship Secretary and Council Member, 2011-14, and Research Awards Convenor, 2008-11, Royal Society of Edinburgh (RSE); Vice-Principal (Research), 2003-09, Head of School of Physics and Astronomy, 1997-2003, Professor of Semiconductor Physics, 1993-2009, University of St Andrews; Professor of Physics and Electrical Engineering, University of Central Florida, USA, 1989-93; Senior Principal Scientific Officer, Royal Signals and Radar Establishment, Malvern, 1981-89; Visiting Assistant Professor of Physics, North Texas University, 1979-81; Research Fellow, Heriot-Watt University, 1974-79; b. 5.6.49, Dunfermline; m. Susan Linklater; 3 d. Educ. Woodmill High School; Gibraltar Grammar School; University of Edinburgh; University of Bath. Past Editor, Optical & Quantum Electronics (Chapman & Hall); Past Editor, Cambridge Studies in Modern Optics (series of monographs, CUP); Past Chair, Institute of Physics Semiconductor Group; Past Chair; Committee of Scottish Professors of Physics; Past Chair, Scottish Chapter, IEEE Lasers and Electro-Optics Society; Past Chair, Royal Society of Edinburgh Physics Committee. Publications: Nonlinear Optics in Signal Processing (Editor); Nonlinear Optical Materials and Devices for Applications in Information Technology (Editor); Laser Sources and Applications (Editor); Semiconductor Quantum Optoelectronics: From Quantum Physics to Smart Devices (Editor); Ultrafast Photonics (Editor); 200 journal research papers. Recreations: music and grandchildren. Address: Kelvin Building, University of Glasgow, Glasgow G12 8QQ; T.-0141-330-8790.
E-mail: Alan.Miller@supa.ac.uk

Miller, Alexandra, MA, MSc. Director, Clearview Strategy & Coaching, since 2018; former Head of External Relations and Governance, National Library of Scotland (appointed Head of Communications & Enterprise in 2012, Director of Customer Services, Development & External Relations, 2011-12); b. Scotland; m., Colin Balfour. Educ. University of St. Andrews; Napier University. Communications posts with Spider Systems, Glasgow City Council, KPMG, the Scottish Arts Council, the Scottish Health Service and the Civil Service, 1975-91; Director of Corporate Affairs, Telewest plc, 1991-97; Director of Consultancy, Clearview Strategy, 1997-2004. Member, Chartered Institute of Marketing and the Chartered Institute of Public Relations; Member, BBC Broadcasting Council for Scotland, 2002-06; Member, BBC Audience Council Scotland, 2006-07.

Miller, Professor Andrew, CBE, MA, BSc, PhD, DUniv (Stirling, Open University), FRSE. Principal and Vice-Chancellor, University of Stirling, 1994-2001; Emeritus Professor, since 2001; General Secretary, Royal Society of Edinburgh, 2001-05; Secretary and Treasurer, Carnegie Trust for the Universities of Scotland, 2004-2013; b. 15.2.36, Kelty, Fife; m., Rosemary S.H. Fyvie; 1 s.; 1 d. Educ. Beath High School; Edinburgh University. Assistant Lecturer in Chemistry, Edinburgh University, 1960-62; Postdoctoral Fellow, CSIRO, Melbourne, and Tutor in Chemistry, Ormond College, Melbourne University, 1962-65; Staff Scientist, MRC Laboratory of Molecular Biology, Cambridge, 1965-66; Lecturer in Molecular Biophysics, Oxford University and (from 1967) Fellow, Wolfson College, 1966-83 (Honorary Fellow, since 1995); on secondment as first Head, European Molecular Biology Laboratory, Grenoble Antenne, France, 1975-80; Professor of Biochemistry, Edinburgh University, 1984-94; Vice-Dean of Medicine, Edinburgh University, 1991-93; Vice-Principal, Edinburgh University, 1993-94; co-opted on to Business Committee of General Council, 2017-2021, Edinburgh University: Committee Member: British

Biophysical Society, 1972-74, Honorary Member, British Biophysical Society, 2017: SERC Synchrotron Radiation Facility Committee, 1979-82, Biological Sciences Committee, 1982-85, Neutron Beam Research Committee, 1982-85; Council Member, Institut Laue-Langevin, 1981-85; Member: MRC Joint Dental Committee, 1984-86, UGC Biological Sciences Committee, 1985-89; (part-time) Director of Research, European Synchrotron Radiation Facility, Grenoble, 1986-91; Member: Advisory Board, AFRC Food Research Institute, 1985, UFC Advisory Groups on Biological Sciences and Pre-clinical Medicine, 1989, Scientific Council, Grenoble University, 1989; Director, Scottish Knowledge plc, 1997-2002; Member, Minister of Education's Action Group on Standards in Scottish Schools, 1997-99; Member, Council, Royal Society of Edinburgh, since 1997 (Convener, International Committee, 1999-2001, Chairman, RSE Scotland Foundation, 2005-09, Bicentennial Medal, 2008); Member, UNESCO UK Science Committee, 2002-03; Adviser to Wellcome Trust on UK–French Synchrotron, 1999-2000; Member, Scottish Executive Science Strategy Group, 1999-2000; Interim Chief Executive, Cancer Research UK, 2001-02; Chairman, International Centre for Mathematical Sciences, Edinburgh, 2001-05; Member, Council, Open University, 2001-05; Deputy Chairman, Scottish Food Advisory Committee, 2003-05; Board Member, Food Standards Agency, 2003-05. Publications: Minerals in Biology (Co-Editor), 1986; over 180 research papers. Address: 5 Blackford Hill Grove, Edinburgh EH9 3HA.

Miller, Sheriff Colin Brown, LLB. Honorary Sheriff, since 2017; Sheriff for South Strathclyde, Dumfries and Galloway, 1991-2010, retired and then re-employed Sheriff, 2010-2016; b. 4.10.46, Paisley; m., Joan Elizabeth Blyth; 3 s. Educ. Paisley Grammar School; Glasgow University. Partner, McFadyen & Semple, Solicitors, Paisley, 1971-91; Council Member, Law Society of Scotland, 1983-91 (Convener, Conveyancing Committee, 1986-89; Convener, Judicial Procedure Committee, 1989-91; Chairman, Working Party on Rights of Audience in Supreme Courts, 1990-91); Dean, Faculty of Procurators in Paisley, 1991. Recreations: walking; photography; travel; railways; ships. Address: (b.) c/o Ayr Sheriff Court, Wellington Square, Ayr; T.-01292 268474.

Miller, Sir Donald John, FREng, FRSE, BSc(Eng), DSc, DUniv, FIMechE, FIEE; b. 9.2.27, London; m., Fay G. Herriot; 1 s.; 2 d. Educ. Banchory Academy; Aberdeen University. Metropolitan-Vickers, 1947-53; British Electricity Authority, 1953-55; Preece Cardew & Rider (Consulting Engineers), 1955-66; Chief Engineer, North of Scotland Hydro-Electric Board, 1966-74; South of Scotland Electricity Board: Director of Engineering, 1974, appointed Deputy Chairman, 1979; Chairman, Scottish Power, 1982-92. Chairman, Power Division, IEE, 1977. Recreations: reading; gardening; golf. Address: (h.) Puldohran, Gryffe Road, Kilmacolm, Renfrewshire; T.-01505 873988.

Miller, Sheriff Ian Harper Lawson, MA (Hons), LLB. Sheriff of Grampian, Highland and Islands at Aberdeen, 1998-2001 and since 2021; b. 16.1.54, Aberdeen; m., Sheila Matthews Howie; 1 s.; 3 d. Educ. Robert Gordon's College, Aberdeen; Aberdeen University. Admitted as a Solicitor, 1980; Partner, Burnett & Reid, Solicitors, Aberdeen, 1986-91; Advocate, 1992; Sheriff of Glasgow and Strathkelvin at Glasgow, 2001-2021. Recreations: family activities; reading; music; golf. Address: (h.) "Ataraxia", 114 Anderson Drive, Aberdeen AB15 6BW.

Miller, Rev. Ian Hunter, BA, BD. Retired Minister at Bonhill (1975-2012); b. 30.5.44, Johnstone; m., Joan Elizabeth Parr; 2 s. Educ. Johnstone High School; Glasgow University; Open University. Travel agent, latterly Branch Manager, A.T. Mays, 1962-69; Assistant Minister, Renfrew Old Kirk, 1974-75. Freeman of Dumbarton. Moderator, Dumbarton Presbytery, 1985-87; Past Chairman, Lomond and Argyll Division, NHS Argyll and Clyde; Past Chairman, West Dunbartonshire Health and Social Justice Committee. Ambassador for Beatson Charity. Publications: "Habbie to Jeely-Eater" (Author); Children's book "The Knights of Pegasus" (Author). Currently locum at Lomond Parish Church, Balloch linked with Gartocharn and participant in over 4000 marriages. Recreations: golf; badminton; music; drama and public speaking. Address: Derand, Queen Street, Alexandria G83 0AS; T.-01389 753039; e-mail: revianmiller@btinternet.com

Miller, Ian James, OBE, MA, LLB. Chairman, Mental Welfare Commission for Scotland, 2000-08; Member, National Appeal Panel for Entry to Health Boards' Pharmaceutical Lists, 1997-2008; Governor, Morrison's Academy, Crieff, 1998-2002; Member, Business Committee, University of Edinburgh General Council, 2001-05; Director, Edinburgh Healthcare NHS Trust, 1995-99; Trustee, Lothian Primary Care NHS Trust, 1999-2000; Member: Police Complaints Commissioner for Scotland Advisory Panel, 2008-2010, Executive Committee, Edinburgh Headway Group, 2008-2010; Trustee, Edinburgh Napier University Development Trust; b. 21.10.38, Fraserburgh; m., Sheila Mary Hourston; 1 s.; 2 d. Educ. Fraserburgh Academy; Aberdeen University; Edinburgh University. Private legal practice, 1963-68; Senior Legal Assistant, Inverness County Council, 1968-70; Depute County Clerk, then County Clerk, Ross and Cromarty County Council, 1970-75; Chief Executive, Inverness District Council, 1975-77; Director of Law and Administration, Grampian Regional Council, 1977-84; Director, Kildonnan Investments Ltd., Aberdeen, 1984-87; Secretary and Academic Registrar, Napier University, Edinburgh, 1987-99. Recreations: golf; curling; bridge. Address: (h.) 80 Craiglockhart Road, Edinburgh EH14 1EP.

Miller, James, CBE (1986), MA, CBIM. Chairman, 1970-99, Managing Director, 1970-91, The Miller Group Ltd. (formerly James Miller & Partners); Chairman, Royal Scottish National Orchestra, 1997-2002; b. 1.9.34, Edinburgh; m., 1, Kathleen Dewar (deceased); 2, Iris Lloyd-Webb (deceased); 1 s.; 3 d. Educ. Edinburgh Academy; Harrow School; Balliol College, Oxford. National Service, Royal Engineers. James Miller & Partners Ltd.: joined, 1958, appointed Director, 1960; Scottish Representative, Advisory Committee to the Meteorological Services, 1980-92; Chairman, Federation of Civil Engineering Contractors, 1985-86, President, 1990-93; Director, British Linen Bank Ltd., 1983-99 (Chairman, 1997-99); Member, Scottish Advisory Board, British Petroleum, 1990-2001; Director, Bank of Scotland, 1993-2000; Deacon Convener, Incorporated Trades of Edinburgh, 1974-77; President, Edinburgh Chamber of Commerce, 1981-83; Assistant, 1982-85, Treasurer, 1990-92, Master, 1992-94, Merchant Company of Edinburgh; Chairman, Court, Heriot-Watt University, 1990-96. Recreation: shooting. Address: (h.) Flat 71, 1 Donaldson Drive, Edinburgh EH12 5FA; T.-0131-337 2289.

Miller, Professor James Alexander, PhD, MBA, BSc (Hons), RN, FRSM. Deputy Vice-Chancellor, Glasgow Caledonian University, since 2015; Director, The Open University in Scotland, 2010-2015; Chief Executive, Royal College of Physicians and Surgeons of Glasgow, 2005-August 2010; b. 11.3.64, Bridge of Allan; m., Winnie Miller (nee Dekonski); 1 s.; 1 d. Educ. Alloa Academy; University of Edinburgh; Napier University; Abertay University. Student Nurse, North Lothian College of Nursing and Midwifery, 1983-86; various clinical and senior nurse roles in Edinburgh, 1986-92; West Lothian NHS Trust: Deputy Director of Nursing, 1992-94, Nurse Manager, 1994-98, General Manager, 1998-2001; General Manager, NHS Greater Glasgow, 2001-05. Non-executive roles: Lay Governor, Glasgow Caledonian University, 2006-2014; British Geriatric Society, 2012-15; British Council Digital Advisory Board, since 2012; Amity University International Advisory Board, India, 2020; Board Secretary, Glasgow Caledonian New York College, USA, since 2017. Publications: a number of peer reviewed manuscripts in journals. Recreations: golf; reading; music. Address: (h.) Tweeniehills, 33 Sandholes Road, Brookfield, Renfrewshire PA5 8UY; T.-01505 336057; e-mail: jamesm31@aol.com

Miller, Jim. Chief Executive, NHS 24, since 2021. Career history: over 30 years of experience across the private and public sectors in commercial, service delivery and senior leadership roles; worked at a senior level in areas including aviation, constriction and public organisations; joined the NHS in 2006 as Director of Strategic resourcing; served as a Non-Executive Shadow Board Member during the creation of Scotland's regional colleges before becoming the Director of Procurement Commissioning and Facilities for NHS Scotland in 2015; central role to many areas of the NHS response to COVID-19 including the provision of PPE and other equipment, infection prevention and control guidance and infrastructure capacity. Address: NHS24, Caledonia House, Fifty Pitches Road, Cardonald Park, Glasgow G51 4EB.
E-mail: chairandchiefexecutivesoffice@nhs24.scot.nhs.uk

Miller, Keith Manson, CBE, D (Eng), BSc (Hons), DipMS, FCIOB, FRICS. Retired Chief Executive, Miller Group (1994-2015); b. 19.3.49, Edinburgh. Educ. Loretto; Heriot-Watt University; Glasgow University. Recreations: sailing; skiing.

Miller, Professor Kenneth, LLB, LLM, PhD. Professor Emeritus, Strathclyde University (former Vice Principal); b. 11.12.51, Paisley; m., Margaret Macleod. Educ. Paisley Grammar School; Strathclyde University; Queen's University, Canada. Lecturer in Law, then Senior Lecturer, Strathclyde University, 1975-91; Deputy General Editor, Stair Memorial Encyclopaedia of the Laws of Scotland, 1990-96; Editor, Juridical Review, 2000-08; Deputy Chair, Central Arbitration Committee. Publications: Employment Law in Scotland (Co-Author); Law of Health and Safety at Work in Scotland; Employment Law – A Student Guide. Recreations: reading; golf; walking. Address: (b.) Royal College, Strathclyde University, 204 George Street, Glasgow G1 1XW; T.-0141-552 4400.
E-mail: kenneth.miller@strath.ac.uk

Miller, Laura, LLB, MA. Presenter/Correspondent, BBC Scotland, since 2018; b. 28.11.80; m.; 1 d. Educ. Kilsyth Academy; The University of Glasgow; University College Falmouth. Journalist, STV Group, 2007-2018; Presenter, Reporting Scotland, BBC Scotland, since 2019. Address: BBC Scotland, 40 Pacific Quay, Glasgow G51 1DA.

Miller, May, MA. Board Member, City of Glasgow College; Board Member, Creative Scotland, 2012-16; Deputy Chair, BAFTA Scotland, 2011-16; Executive Producer, Kirsty Wark: the Menopause and Me; Executive Producer of The Insiders' Guide to the Menopause (documentary); b. Dumbarton; m., Alan Mitchinson; 1 s.; 1 d. Educ. Clydebank High School; Glasgow University; Strathclyde University. Creative Director, Arts and Factual, BBC Scotland; Creative Director, Mentorn (Scotland); Head of Talkback Thames (Scotland). Board Member,

Glasgow City Heritage Trust; RTS Member. Recreations: film; tv; music; art. E-mail: may.miller@hotmail.com

Miller, Michelle, BA (Hons). Chair of the Board, Scottish Children's Reporter Administration, since 2018. Educ. University of Southampton; University of York. Career: Depute Chief Inspector of Social Work, Social Work Services Inspectorate, 2002-04; Head of Children and Criminal Justice, Fife Council, 2004-07; City of Edinburgh Council: Chief Social Work Officer, 2007-2015, Head of Safer and Stronger Communities, 2015-18. Board Member, Scottish Police Authority, since 2018. Address: Scottish Children's Reporter Administration, Ochil House, Stirling FK7 7XE; T.-0131 244 4111.

Miller, Nigel. Chairman, Livestock Health Scotland, since 2015; Chair, Ruminant Health and Welfare Group (RHWG), since 2020; President, NFU Scotland, 2011-2015, formerly Vice-President (2007-2011). Member, Board: Scotland's Rural College (SRUC), SAC Commercial Ltd, Moredun Research Institute, Pentland Science Park.

Miller, Sir Ronald Andrew Baird, CBE (1985), BSc, CA, DSc, DUniv; b. 13.5.37, Edinburgh. Former Chairman, Dawson International PLC; former Chairman, Court, Edinburgh Napier University.

Millican, Douglas, BCom, CA, AMCT. Chief Executive, Scottish Water, since 2013, Finance and Regulation Director, 2007-2013, Finance Director, 2002-07; Trustee, World Vision UK, since 2017; b. 13.9.64, Edinburgh; m., Jane; 2 s.; 1 d. Educ. Edinburgh Academy; Edinburgh University. Price Waterhouse, 1986-91, 1993-96; East of Scotland Water: Financial Controller, 1996-2002; Commercial Director, 2000-02. Recreations: Church; skiing; cycling. Address: (b.) Scottish Water, Castle House, 6 Castle Drive, Dunfermline, Fife KY11 8GG; T.-01383 848465; e-mail: douglas.millican@scottishwater.co.uk

Milligan, Eric. Former Lord Provost and Lord Lieutenant, City of Edinburgh (1996-2003); former Convener, Lothian and Borders Police Board (2003-07); b. 27.1.51, Edinburgh; m., Janis. Educ. Tynecastle High School; Napier College of Commerce and Technology. Former printer; Member (Labour), Edinburgh District Council, 1974-78; Lothian Regional Councillor, 1978-96 (Chairman, Finance Committee, 1980-82, 1986-90, Convener, 1990-96); President, COSLA, 1988-90; City of Edinburgh Councillor, 1995-2017 (Convener, 1995-96); JP, Edinburgh, 1996; awarded Chevalier, Ordre National du Mérite, 1996; Honorary Degree: Doctor of Business Administration, Napier University, 1999; Honorary Fellow, Royal College of Surgeons of Edinburgh, 2000; Honorary Degree: Doctor of the University, Heriot-Watt University, 2004.

Milligan, Janey Louise, LLM, FRICS, FCIArb. Managing Director, Construction Dispute Resolution, since 1997; Chairman, Royal Institution of Chartered Surveyors, 2007-08; b. 27.05.60, Glasgow; m., Andrew Milligan; 2 d. Educ. Kilsyth Academy; Glasgow College of Building & Printing; University of Strathclyde. Director of Quantity Surveying, UNICK Architects, 1986-93; Lecturer, Glasgow Caledonian University, 1993-97. Non Executive Member, RICS UK and Ireland World Regional Board (UK & I WRB), 2010-2014; Director, Scottish Arbitration Centre, since 2011; Treasurer, Airdrie Clarkston Parish Church of Scotland, 2008-2017. Recreations: swimming; photography; golf; reading. Address: (b.) 1 George Square, Glasgow G2 1AL; T.-0141 773 3377; e-mail: jlm@cdr.uk.com

Mills, Ian Thomas, BSc, MPhil. Arts/Education Consultant; b. 20.5.48, Hamilton; m., Margaret; 2 d. Educ. Dalziel High School, Motherwell; Glasgow University; Strathclyde University. Chemistry Teacher, Dalziel High School, Motherwell, 1970-75; Senior Housemaster, Lanark Grammar School, 1975-78; Assistant Head Teacher, then

Depute Head Teacher, Carluke High School, 1978-85; Area Education Officer, Perth and Kinross, 1985-91; Assistant Director of Education, Tayside Regional Council, 1991-95; Director of Education and Leisure Services, East Dunbartonshire Council, 1995-2000; General Manager, National Youth Choir of Scotland, 2001-07; Head of Principal's Office, Royal Conservatoire of Scotland (formerly RSAMD), 2007-2014. Administrator, Scottish International Piano Competition, 2003-2020; Chairman, Drake Music Scotland Board, 2008-2018; Member, Children's Classic Concerts Board; Member Wallace Collection Board; Chairman, Music Education Partnership Group. Recreations: music; travel; family-based activities; Rotary International (District Governor, 2010-11). Address: 28 Kirkhouse Road, Blanefield G63 9BX; T.-07814989155; e-mail: ian@ian-mills.co.uk

Mills, Peter Rodney, BSc, MD, FRCP, FACP. Consultant Physician and Gastroenterologist, Western Infirmary, Glasgow, 1988-2018 (retired); b. 27.12.48, St. Albans; m., Hazel; 1 s.; 1 d. Educ. St. George's School, Harpenden; University of St. Andrews. Senior Registrar in Medicine/ Gastroenterology, Royal Infirmary, Glasgow, 1979; Visiting Assistant Professor, Yale University School of Medicine, 1983; Associate Professor, Division of Gastroenterology, Medical College of Virginia, 1985; Honorary Professor, University of Glasgow, 2010; Director of Medical Examinations, Royal College of Physicians and Surgeons of Glasgow, 2000-06; Chairman, Board for SCE in Gastroenterology, 2007-2012; President, Scottish Society of Gastroenterology, 2007-2010. Publications: 165 papers in gastroenterology and liver journals. Recreations: golf; hillwalking. Address: (h.) 2 Seaview Row, Pittenweem KY10 2PQ; T.-01333 278578.
E-mail: peter.mills@glasgow.ac.uk

Milne, James S., CBE, DL, DHC, Hon DBA, Hon FRIAS. Chairman and Managing Director, Balmoral Group Holdings Ltd., since 1980; b. 26.12.40, Aberdeen; m., Gillian; 2 s.; 2 d. Burgess of Guild, City of Aberdeen; Fellow of the Scottish Council for Development and Industry; Chairman of Friends of ANCHOR ARI.

Milne, Professor Lorna Catherine, MA, PhD, Chevalier dans l'Ordre des Palmes Académiques. Master of the United College and Deputy Principal, University of St Andrews, since 2019 (Professor of French, since 2006, Dean of Arts, 2006-09, Vice-Principal, 2011-18); b. 19.08.59, Stirling. Educ. Dollar Academy; St. Andrews; Auckland (New Zealand). HM Diplomatic Service, London and East Berlin, 1983-87; Doctoral Studies, 1987-91; Lecturer: Aston University, 1991-96, St. Andrews University, 1996-2001, Senior Lecturer, 2001-06. Publications: Author: L'Evangile Selon Michel, 1994, Patrick Chamoiseau: Espaces d'une écriture antillaise, 2006; numerous scholarly articles and edited volumes. Address: (b.) University of St Andrews, St Andrews, Fife KY16 9AH; T.-01334 46 2552.
E-mail: master@st-andrews.ac.uk

Milne, Nanette Lilian Margaret, OBE, MBChB, FFARCS. MSP (Conservative), North East region, 2003-2016; former Conservative Spokesman on Public Health; Spokesman on Environment, 2007-2010; Spokesman on Health and Community Care, 2005-07; b. 27.4.42, Aberdeen; m., Dr. Alan D. Milne; 1 s.; 1 d. Educ. Aberdeen High School for Girls; University of Aberdeen. Various hospital posts (to registrar grade), 1965-73; career break, 1973-78; part-time medical research, 1978-92. Vice-chairman, Scottish Conservative Party, 1988-92; Aberdeen City Councillor, 1988-99; Director, Grampian Enterprise Ltd., 1992-98; Trustee, Aberdeen International Youth

Festival; Member, Aberdeen University Court, 1996-2005. Recreations: the countryside (hill-walking, etc); skiing; golf; gardening.

Milne, Pamela, MA, MBA, FCIPD. Director of Human Resources and Organisational Development, University of Dundee, since 2002. Educ. University of Glasgow; University of Dundee. Director, University of Dundee Nursery; Board Member, Dundee and Angus College; Governor, Strathallan School. Address: University of Dundee, Nethergate, Dundee DD1 4HN; T.-01382 384014. E-mail: p.a.milne@dundee.ac.uk

Milne, Pippa, LLB, Law. Chief Executive, Argyll and Bute Council, since 2019. Educ. Cults Academy, Aberdeen; University of Aberdeen. Career history: Trading Standards Officer, Telford & Wrekin Council, 1996-98; Team Manager, Borough of Poole, 1998-2002; Recycling and Waster Manager, Leeds City Council, 2002-08; Waste Services Manager, City of Edinburgh Council, 2008-2014; Executive Director, Development and Infrastructure, Argyll and Bute Council, 2014-19. Address: Argyll and Bute Council, Kilmory, Lochgilphead, Argyll PA31 8RT; T.-01546 605522.

Milne, Simon Stephen, MBE, BSc, FRGS. Regius Keeper, Royal Botanic Garden Edinburgh, since 2014; b. 30.1.59, Dundee; m., Françoise (né Sevaux); 1 s.; 2 d. Educ. University of St Andrews; Royal Naval College, Greenwich. Commissioned into Royal Marines, 1976; retired from Royal Marines in Rank of Lieutenant Colonel, 2000; Director, Sir Harold Hillier Gardens and Arboretum, 2000-04; Chief Executive, Scottish Wildlife Trust, 2004-2014. Member: National Reintroductions Forum, International Dendrology Society; Honorary Professor, University of Edinburgh (2016); Member, Her Majesty's Body Guard of the Honourable Corps of Gentlemen at Arms (appointed 2011); Trustee: Sibbald Trust, Younger Benmore Trust, MacIntyre Begonia Trust, Botanics Foundation; Hon. Vice President, The Royal Caledonian Horticultural Society. Address: Royal Botanic Garden Edinburgh, 20A Inverleith Row, Edinburgh EH3 5LR.

Milne, Stewart, CBE. Chairman of Aberdeen F.C., 1998-2019; b. 1950. Founded the Aberdeen-based Stewart Milne Group in 1975, a housebuilding contractor; started off his business renovating bathrooms. Scottish Entrepreneur of the Year award, 2005; Commander of the Order of the British Empire (CBE) in 1998 for services to the house building industry in Scotland. Honorary Chairman, Cornton Football Club, since 2009.

Milner, Edward, MA, BMus (Hons). Chief Executive Officer, National Youth Choir of Scotland, since 2019. Educ. Queen Elizabeth High School, Hexham; University of Newcastle-upon-Tyne; Sheffield University. Career history: self employed, 2000-02; Vocal Coordinator, Northumberland County Music Service, 2002-07; Director of Workforce Development, Sing Up, 2007-2011; Sage Gateshead: Head of Learning, 2013-17, Head of Music Education, 2017-18; Interim Chief Executive, The Voices Foundation, 2018-19. Address: National Youth Choir of Scotland, The Mitchell, North Street, Glasgow G3 7DN; T.-0141 287 2856.

Milton, Ian Murray. Chairman, Milton Hotels Ltd.; b. 25.7.45, Glasgow; m., Ann; 1 s.; 3 d. Educ. Lochaber High School; Scottish Hotel School, Glasgow. Began Milton Hotels with brother, 1965. Recreations: golf; skiing; computing. Address: (b.) Milton Hotels Ltd., Best Western

Palace Hotel, 8 Ness Walk, Inverness IV3 5NG; T.-01463 223243; e-mail: ian.milton@miltonhotels.com

Minginish, Lord (Roderick John MacLeod), QC, LLB (Hons). Advocate; Chairman, Scottish Land Court, since 2014; President, Lands Tribunal for Scotland, since 2014; b. 1953, Skye; m., Lorna. Educ. Portree High School; University of Edinburgh. Career history: two-year legal apprenticeship in Edinburgh, 1977-78; Gaelic-language broadcasting, BBC Scotland, 1977-79 (presented current affairs programmes on television); qualified as a solicitor in Motherwell, 1980; practised as a solicitor in Edinburgh until 1993; admitted to the Faculty of Advocates in 1994; appointed as a Sheriff to Edinburgh Sheriff Court in 2000; "took silk", becoming a Queen's Counsel in 2013; became Deputy Chair of the Scottish Land Court in 2006; Director of Sabhal Mòr Ostaig, since 2006 (Chair, Board of Directors, since 2007). Member of the council of the Royal Celtic Society. Address: Scottish Land Court, 126 George Street, Edinburgh EH2 4HH; T.-0131 271 4360.

Minto, Jenni, MA (Acc). MSP (SNP), Argyll and Bute, since 2021; b. 1968, Elgin. Educ. Madras College, St Andrews; University of Aberdeen. Career history: Business Executive, BBC, 2006-2011; self-employed accountant (accounts preparation for small charities), from 2013; became Museum Manager, Museum of Islay Life in 2018, worked in the Museum part time from 2013. Address: The Scottish Parliament, Edinburgh EH99 1SP; T.-0131 348 5106; e-mail: Jenni.Minto.msp@parliament.scot

Miskin, Rebecca. Chief Executive Officer, DC Thomson, since 2021. Educ. University of London; Cranfield School of Management. Career history: Business Development Director, International, Reed Elsevier, London, Prague and Lisbon, 1992-95; Commercial Director, Time Inc. UK, Munich, London, 1995-2001; Managing Director, Excite@Home, London, 2001-02; Director of Operations, LTA, 2003-06; GM, NBC Universal, Greater New York City and London, 2007-2010; Digital Strategy Director/Change Agent, Hearst, London, 2010-15; Advisory Board Member, meltygroup, Paris, 2015-16; Chief Executive Officer, Gloo Networks plc, London, 2015-18; Non Executive Director, Centaur Media Plc, 2011-2020; Non Executive Director and Chair, The Stylist Group, 2018-2021; Chair, DC Thomson Media, 2020-21. Address: DC Thomson, 2 Albert Square, Dundee DD1 1DD; T.-01382 223131.

Mitchell, Alan, BA (Hons). Chief Executive, Fife Chamber of Commerce, since 2016. Educ. Dundee College of Commerce; University of Strathclyde. Career history: Business Development Manager, The Industrial Society/Capita Learning and Development, 1997-2001; Assistant Director, CBI Scotland, 2001-07; Chief Executive, Dundee & Angus Chamber of Commerce, 2007-2013; Membership Advisor, CBI Scotland, 2013-14; Employment Adviser, Claverhouse Group, 2014-15; Consultant, DH Recruitment, 2015-16; Consultant and Secretary, Dundee & Angus Visitor Accommodation Association, 2016. Address: Fife Chamber of Commerce and Enterprise Ltd, John Smith Business Centre, 1 Begg Road, John Smith Business Park, Kirkcaldy, Fife KY2 6HD; T.-01592 647740.

Mitchell, Rev. Alexander Bell, DipTechEd, BD. Retired Minister, St. Blane's Church, Dunblane (2003-2014); b. 28.6.49, Baillieston; m., Elizabeth Brodie; 1 s.; 2 d. Educ. Uddingston Grammar School; New College, Edinburgh. Assistant Minister, Dunblane Cathedral, 1979-81; Minister, St Leonard's Church, Dunfermline, 1981-2003. Recreations:

golf; hill-walking. Address: 24 Hebridean Gardens, Crieff PH7 3BP; T.-01764 652241.
E-mail: alex.mitchell6@btopenworld.com

Mitchell, Alison. Headteacher, Rosshall Academy. Address: 131 Crookston Road, Crookston, Glasgow G52 3PD; T.-0141 582 0200.

Mitchell, Angela, BA (Hons), PgDip, FRSA. National Director Scotland, Diabetes UK, since 2018. Educ. University of Stirling; University of California San Diego; Amex Leadership Academy; Queen Margaret University. Career: Researcher/Assistant Producer/Director, Wark Clements Ltd, 1995-2000; Producer/Director, BBC, 2000-04; Multimedia Consultant, sole trader, 2005-08; Assistant Manager/Manager, A Scottish Government/Big Lottery funded exemplar pilot; Soil Association Scotland: Food for Life Scotland Programme Manager, 2012-14, Acting Director, 2015, Deputy Director, 2016-17, Acting Director, 2017-18. Address: Diabetes Scotland, 349 Bath Street, Glasgow G2 4AA; T.-0141 245 6380.

Mitchell, Dr. David Scott, MSc, IHBC. Director of Conservation, Historic Environment Scotland, since 2010 (Acting Chief Executive, April - September, 2016, Director of Technical Conservation Group, 2008-2016); b. 28.1.70; m., Lesley; 2 s.; 1 d. Educ. High School of Stirling; Strathclyde University; Edinburgh University. Career History: Director, Heritage Engineering, Industrial Heritage Co. Ltd, Head of Conservation Resources. Director, The Centre for Digital Documentation and Visualisation, The Scottish Ironwork Foundation; Scouts Scotland Trustee. Recreations: scouting; photography. Address: (b.) Historic Environment Scotland, Longmore House, Salisbury Place, Edinburgh EH9 1SH; T.-0131 668 8929.
E-mail: david.mitchell@hes.scot

Mitchell, David William, CBE. Hon. President, Scottish Conservative and Unionist Party, 2004-2010; Chairman, Scottish Conservative and Unionist Party, 2001-04; b. 4.1.33, Glasgow; m., Lynda Katherine Marion Guy; 1 d. Educ. Merchiston Castle School. Cmmnd (NS), RSF, 1950; Western Regional Hospital Board Member, 1965-72; President, Timber Trades Benevolent Society of UK, 1974; Member, Scottish Council, CBI, 1979-85; Director, Mallinson-Denny (Scotland), 1977-90; Hunter Timber Scotland, 1990-92; Joint Managing Director, M. & N. Norman (Timber) Ltd., 1992-96 (Non-Executive, 1996-98); President: Scottish Timber Trade Association, 1980-82, Scottish Conservative and Unionist Association, 1981-83; Member: Scottish Council (Development and Industry), 1984-95, Board of Cumbernauld New Town, 1985-97 (Chairman, 1987-97), Board of Management, Craighalbert Centre for Children with Motor Impairment, 1992-96; Treasurer, Scottish Conservative Party, 1990-93 and 1998-2001. Clubs: Royal & Ancient Golf; Prestwick Golf; Queens Park FC. Recreations: fishing; shooting; golf. Address: Old Mill House, Symington, Ayrshire KA1 5QL; T.-01563 830851; e-mail: david.mitchell33@outlook.com

Mitchell, Derek. Chief Executive, Citizens Advice Scotland, since 2017. Career history: worked for the Scottish Government as a Policy Advisor in the Homelessness Team; joined COSLA in 2005. Address: Citizens Advice Scotland, 1st Floor, Broadside, 2 Powderhall Road, Edinburgh EH7 4GB; T.-0131 550 1000.

Mitchell, Rev. Duncan Ross, BA (Hons), BD (Hons). Retired Minister, St. Andrews Church, West Kilbride; b. 5.5.42, Boddam, Aberdeenshire; m., Sandra Brown; 2 s.; 1 d. Educ. Hyndland Senior Secondary School, Glasgow; Strathclyde University; Glasgow University. Worked in insurance industry, four years; Minister, Craigmailen UF Church, Bo'ness, 1972-80; Convener, Assembly Youth

Committee, UF Church, 1974-79; Member: Scottish Joint Committee on Religious Education, 1974-79, Multilateral Conversation in Scotland; Minister, St Andrew's Church, West Kilbride, 1980-2007, 1976-79, Board of Social Responsibility, Church of Scotland, 1983-86; Ardrossan Presbytery: Convener, World Mission and Unity, 1984-88, Convener, Stewardship and Finance, 1988-91, Convener, Superintendence Committee, 1994-97; Convener, Vacancy Procedure Committee, 2015-2021; Convener, General Assembly Board of World Mission and Unity's Local Involvements Committee, and Executive Member of the Board, 1987-92; Church of Scotland Delegate to Council of Churches for Britain and Ireland Assembly; Moderator, Ardrossan Presbytery, 1992-93. Recreations: supporting Partick Thistle and writing. Address: 11 Dunbar Gardens, Saltcoats; T.-01294 474375.
E-mail: revrossmitchell@gmail.com

Mitchell, Elinor, BN, CIPD, CIMA. Director-General Economy, Scottish Government, 2021-2022; Director of Community Health and Social Care Directorate, 2019-2020; Director of Agriculture and Rural Economy Directorate, 2016-19; b. Glasgow. Educ. Cleveden Secondary School; University of Glasgow. Career history: joined the civil service in 1988, starting career in Whitehall and then moving to Scotland; Head of HR, Scottish Government, 2010-12; Director, HR and OD, Scottish Ambulance Service, 2012-14; Deputy Director, public bodies and public service reform, Scottish Government, 2014-16. Chartered Fellow of the Chartered Institute of Personnel and Development (CIPD), and Chartered Institute of Management Accounts (CIMA) qualified.

Mitchell, Frank. Chair, Skills Development Scotland, since 2018; Chief Executive Officer, SP Energy Networks; m.; 3 c. Co-Chair, Scottish Apprenticeship Advisory Board (SAAB); Chair, Energy Skills Action Group for Scotland. Recreations: enjoys football; golf; rugby; mentoring business start-ups. Address: Skills Development Scotland, Monteith House, 11 George Square, Glasgow G2 1DY; T.-0141 285 6000.

Mitchell, George Edward, CBE. Former Governor, Bank of Scotland; b. 7.4.50, Edinburgh; m., Agnes; 3 d. Educ. Forrester High School, Edinburgh. Joined the Bank of Scotland in 1966. Recreations: football; tennis; family.

Mitchell, Gordon K., DA, RSA, RSW, RGI. Artist; b. 16.11.52, Edinburgh; m., Deirdre; 1 s.; 3 d. Educ. Royal High School; Edinburgh College of Art. Former Art Teacher (Deputy Headmaster, St. Serf's School, 1986-89); elected: SSA, 1977, SAAC, 1990 (President, 1993-96), RSW, 1996, ARSA, 1998, RGI, 1998, RSA, 2005. Served on council of SSA, SAAC, RSW, SABA, RSA; Vice President of the RSA, 2006-2009; President of The Scottish Artists Benevolent Association (SABA), since 2014; Director, Art in Healthcare, since 2017; Inverarity One to One Travel Award, RGI; Artist Convener, RGI, 2001-06; President of The Scottish Arts Club, 2008-2010; Director of The Scottish Portrait Awards, 2016; exhibited widely at home and abroad; work in public and private collections. Prizes and awards include: RSA Student Prize; Borders Biennial Competition; Scottish Drawing Competition; Mayfest Award; William Gillies Award; Scottish Amicable Prize; Scottish Provident Award; Whyte and Mackay Award; Dunfermline Building Society Award; RSA J. Murray Thompson Award; RSA Maude Gemmel Hutchison Award x3; Royal Bank of Scotland Award, RGI. Recreations: current affairs; golf. Address: (h.) 6 Learmonth Terrace, Edinburgh EH4 1PQ; T.-0131 332 3588; e-mail: gordon@gordonmitchell.co.uk
website: www.gordonmitchell.co.uk

Mitchell, Iain Grant, QC, LLB (Hons), FSA Scot, FRSA, FFCS. Queen's Counsel, since 1992; Barrister (Middle Temple), since 2012; Vice-Chairman, Surveillance Working Party, CCBE, since 2020 (Vice-Chairman, 2015-20); United Kingdom Expert, IT Committee, CCBE, since 2011; member UK Delegation to CCBE, since 2017; Temporary Sheriff, 1992-97; Joint Editor, Journal of Open Law, Technology and Society; Honorary Lecturer, Institut für Informations, Telekommunikations und Medienrecht, Westfälische Wilhelms-Universität, Münster; b. 15.11.51, Edinburgh. Educ. Perth Academy; Edinburgh University. Called to Scottish Bar, 1976; Conservative candidate, Falkirk West, General Election, 1983, Kirkcaldy, General Election, 1987, Cumbernauld and Kilsyth, General Election, 1992, Dunfermline East, General Election, 1997, Edinburgh North and Leith, General Election, 2001, Dundee East, Scottish Parliament Election, 1999, Scotland, European Election, 1999, Falkirk West, Scottish Parliament Election, 2002; Honorary Secretary, Scottish Conservative and Unionist Association, 1993-98, Scottish Conservative and Unionist Party, 1998-2001; Chairman, North Queensferry Community Council; Chairman, North Queensferry Community Trust; Reader, Church of Scotland; Member, Church of Scotland Church & Society Council; Chairman, Trust for an International Opera Theatre of Scotland; Chairman, Scottish Baroque Ensemble Ltd., 1999-2001; Member: Executive Committee of European Movement (Scottish Council); Chairman, Perthshire Public Arts Trust; Trustee, Forth Bridge Memorial Public Arts Trust; Board Member, Capella Nova; Board Member, Animotion Art (London) Ltd; Chairman, Scottish Society for Computers and Law; Member, IT Panel of the Bar Council of England and Wales; Chair of Legal Panel, Whistleblowers UK. Publications: contributor to "Electronic Evidence", 3rd edition, 2012; "Open Source Software - Law Policy and Practice", 2013. Burgess of the City of Edinburgh; Freeman, City of London; Liveryman, Worshipful Company of Information Technologists. Recreations: music and the arts; photography; cinema; walking; history; travel; writing; finding enough hours in the day. Address: (b.) Advocates Library, Parliament House, High Street, Edinburgh; T.-0131-226 5071.

Mitchell, Ian, BSc (Hons), MSc (Distinction). Interim Director, The Scottish Government, since 2021, Deputy Director, 2021; Chief Executive Officer, Community Enterprise in Scotland, 2019-2021; Chief Executive, CEIS Group, 2019-2021; Head of EU Strategy and Migration, Scottish Government, 2016-19, Deputy Director, Learning and Schools, 2011-16, Deputy Director, Environmental Quality, 2010, Deputy Director, Public Bodies Policy, 2007-2010; Director of Regeneration, Communities Scotland, 2003-07; b. 11.10.63, Dumfries; spouse, Elizabeth Riach; 1 s. Educ. Dumfries Academy; Heriot Watt University; Napier University. Senior Economic Policy Officer, Corporate Policy, Fife Council, 1990-99; Senior Civil Servant, Scottish Government (Enterprise Networks; Local Government Constitution and Governance; Public Service Reform; Environment; Education; Health and Social Care), 1999-2015; Board Member, Community Enterprise in Scotland. Former Member, Community Planning Task Force/Implementation Group. Recreations: cycling; hill walking; travel writing. Address: The Scottish Government, Victoria Quay, Edinburgh EH6 6QQ.

Mitchell, (Janet) Margaret. Member (C), Central Scotland, Scottish Parliament, 2003-2021; former Deputy Convenor, Committee on the Scottish Government Handling of Harrassment Complaints; Convener, Scottish Parliament Justice Committee, 2016-20; former Deputy Convener, Scottish Parliament Justice Sub-Committee on Policing; b. 15.11.52, d. of late John Aitken Fleming and of Margaret McRae Fleming (nee Anderson); m. (1978), Henry Thomson Mitchell. Educ. Coatbridge High School;

Hamilton Teacher Training College (DipEd); Open University (BA); Strathclyde University (LLB: DipLLP); Jordanhill College (Dip Media Studies). Primary School Teacher, Airdrie and Bothwell, 1974-93; Mem. and Cons. Gp. Leader, Hamilton DC, 1988-96; Non-Exec. Dir., Stonehouse and Hairmyres NHS Trust, 1993-97; Special Adviser to David McLetchie, MSP and James Douglas-Hamilton, MSP, 1999-2002; Scottish Cons. Justice Spokesman, 2003-07, 2013-2016; Convener, Scottish Parliamentary Equal Opportunities Committee, 2007-2011; Scottish Cons. Local Government and Planning Spokesman, 2011-13; Mem., Scottish Cons. Party Exec., 2002-03. Clubs: The New Club, Edinburgh. Recreations: music; cycling; photography.

Mitchell, Joan, MA (Edin), MA (Manitoba), PhD (Glasgow). Scottish Natural Heritage Board, 2007-2013; b. 17.12.42, Carsluith; m., Steve; 2 s. Educ. Douglas Ewart High School; University of Edinburgh; University of Manitoba; University of Glasgow. Lecturer in Geography, University of Glasgow, 1966-71; self employed Farmer, since 1972; elected Member, Dumfries and Galloway (Regional) Council, 1994-2007; EU Committee of The Regions, 1997-2001; Trustee of Galloway and Southern Ayrshire Biosphere. Recreations: hill walking (Chair, Newton Stewart Walking Festival). Address: (h./b.) Bagbie, Newton Stewart, Carsluith, Dumfries and Galloway DG8 7DU; e-mail: joan@bagbie.co.uk

Mitchell, John, BSc. Head Teacher, Kilsyth Academy, 1985-2005; Non-Executive Trustee of Lanarkshire Acute Hospitals Trust, 2001-04; Board Member, Learning Teaching Scotland, 2002-06; Board Member, SQA, 2006-2010; b. 4.1.45, Kirkintilloch; m., Irene; 1 s.; 1 d. Educ. Lenzie Academy; Glasgow University; Jordanhill College. Teacher, North Kelvinside Secondary, Glasgow, 1968-70; Physics Teacher, Balfron High School, 1970-72; Bishopbriggs High School, 1972-79; Assistant Head Teacher, Kilsyth Academy, 1979-84; Depute Head Teacher, Knightswood Secondary, 1984-85. President, HAS, 1996. Address: (h.) 10 Blair Drive, Milton of Campsie; T.- 01360 310477; john@jamitchell.co.uk

Mitchison, Neil, MA, MBCS, CITP, CEng. Research Manager, Risk Analyst and Broadcaster; b. 02.05.51; m., Aideen O'Malley; 3 s.; 2 d. Educ. Edinburgh Academy; Trinity College, Cambridge; Edinburgh University. Research Fellow, University of Sussex, 1978-79; Radio Producer, Presenter, and Journalist, BBC Highland, 1980-84; Computer Analyst and Research Project Manager, European Commission, 1985-93; Consultant Editor, Europe, BBC TV, 1993-94; Program Manager, Major Accident Hazards Bureau, European Commission, 1994-2002, Research Action Leader in Cyber Security, 2005-06, European Commission Representative in Scotland, 2006-2012, Research Manager, 2012-14. Vice President, Commission Scientifique "Risques Accidentels", INERIS (F), 1999-2006; President, Association for Go in Italy, 1999-2005; Parliamentary Candidate (Lib Dem), 1989, 1992, 1997 and 1999. Publications: Identity Theft - a discussion paper, 2004; Accident Scenarios and Emergency Response, 1999; Guidelines on a Major Accident Prevention Policy and Safety Management System, 1998; Safety and Runaway Reactions, 1997; Safety Management Systems in the Process Industry, 1994.

Mobarik of Mearns, Rt. Hon. (Baroness Nosheena Shaheen Mobarik), CBE, BA (Hons). Member of the European Parliament for Scotland (Conservative), 2017-2020; created life peer in 2014; b. 16.10.57; m., Dr Iqbal Mobarik. Educ. University of Strathclyde. Career: Chairman, CBI Scotland, 2011-13, Vice-Chairman, 2013-

14, member of Council, since 2001; Director and Trustee of Craigholme School; Board member of Glasgow Film Theatre; founder and Convener of the Scotland Pakistan Network; Chairman, Pakistan Britain Trade & Investment Forum, since 2012. Awarded the degree of Doctor honoris causa by the University of Edinburgh in 2013; awarded a national award, the Tamgha-i-Imtiaz (Medal for Excellence) in August 2012 by the State of Pakistan; appointed to join the Commission on future devolution in Scotland chaired by Lord Strathclyde on behalf of the Scottish Conservative Party in June 2013; former Board member of the Better Together Campaign, 2014 Referendum on Scottish Independence.

Mochan, Carol. MSP (Scottish Labour), South Scotland (Region), since 2021; Shadow Minister for Mental Wellbeing, Women's Health and Sport, since 2021. Educ. Girvan Primary School; Auchinleck Academy; m.; 2 c. Career history: worked in the NHS as a dietician for 17 years; lifelong trade union member; runs a small family business; active in many roles within the community: former member of the community council and community association; former Chair of a parent led toddler group; served as Chair of the Carrick, Cumnock and Doon Valley Constituency Labour Party; candidate in the council elections for East Ayrshire Council, 2017; stood in 2017 for the UK Parliamentary seat of Ayr, Carrick and Cumnock; stood twice in Carrick, Cumnock and Doon Valley. Address: The Scottish Parliament, Edinburgh EH99 1SP; T.-0131 348 6993.
E-mail: Carol.Mochan.msp@parliament.scot

Moffat, Alistair Murray, MA (Hons), MPhil, FRSA. Rector, University of St Andrews, 2011-2014; Journalist; Writer; b. 16.6.50, Kelso; m., Lindsay Thomas; 1 s.; 2 d. Educ. Kelso High School; St. Andrews University; Edinburgh University; London University. Ran Edinburgh Festival Fringe, 1976-81; Arts Correspondent/Producer/Controller of Features/Director of Programmes, Scottish Television; Managing Director, Scottish Television Enterprises. Publications: The Edinburgh Fringe, 1978; Kelsae — A History of Kelso from Earliest Times, 1985; Remembering Charles Rennie Mackintosh, 1989; Arthur and the Lost Kingdoms, 1999; The Sea Kingdoms, 2001; The Borders, 2002; Homing, 2003; Heartland Images of the Scottish Borders, 2004; Before Scotland, 2005; Tyneside, 2005; East Lothian, 2006; "The Reivers", 2007; "Fife", 2007; "The Wall", 2008; "Edinburgh", 2008; "Tuscany. A History", 2009; The Faded Map, 2010; The Scots: A Genetic Journey, 2011; The British: A Genetic Journey, 2013; The Great Tapestry of Scotland, 2013; The Great Tapestry of Scotland: The Making of a Masterpiece, 2013; Hawick, A History From Earliest Times, 2014; Britain's Last Frontier, 2014; Bannockburn, 2014; Scotland: A History from Earliest Times, 2015; The Hidden Ways, 2017; To the Island of Tides, 2019; Fife: A History (Co-Author), 2019; In Search of Angels, 2020; The Secret History of Here, 2021; The Night Before Morning, 2021. Recreations: sleeping; supporting Kelso RFC. Address: (h.) The Henhouse, Selkirk TD7 5EY.

Moffat, Anne, RMN. Labour MP, East Lothian, 2001-10; b. 30.3.58, Dunfermline; m.; 1 s. Educ. Woodmill High School. Nursing sister; NEC, Cohse and Unison; former National President, Unison; former Ashford Borough Councillor; former Chair of Organisation, Labour Party; formerly on Labour Party NEC.

Moffett, Ian Weatherston, LLB (Hons), WS, NP. Retired Solicitor; b. Edinburgh; m., Jinty; 3 s. Educ. George Watson's Boys College, Edinburgh; Edinburgh University. Partner, Dundas & Wilson, 1977-2005; Partner, Anderson

Strathern, 2005-2010; Consultant, Anderson Strathern, 2010-2013; Non Executive Director, Registers of Scotland, 2007-2012; Chair, LawWorks Scotland, the pro bono legal charity, 2011-2015; Chair, Outdoor Access Trust for Scotland (formerly Cairngorms Outdoor Access Trust (COAT)); Chair, Kingussie Community Development Company; Chair, Badenoch Heritage. Recreations: family; walking and country pursuits; collecting books relating to Scottish History (particularly Badenoch); cricket and India. Address: St Giles, Acres Road, Kingussie, Inverness-shire PH21 1LA; T.-01540 661 414.
E-mail: ianwmoffett@hotmail.com

Mohamed, Judith. Head Teacher, Arbroath Academy, since 2022. Educ. Rainey Endowed School, Magherafelt; University of Stirling. Aberdeen City Council: Strategic Officer - seconded, 2013; Deputy Head Teacher, 2008-2014; Head Teacher, Oldmachar Academy, 2014-2022. Address: Arbroath Academy, Glenisla Drive, Arbroath DD11 5JD; T.-01241 465200.

Moignard, Professor Elizabeth Ann, MA, DPhil, FSA, FRSE. Professor of Classical Art and Archaeology, University of Glasgow, 2000-2011, now Professor Emerita; Director, Institute for Art History, University of Glasgow, 1998-2004; Dean, Faculty of Arts, 2005-09; b. 3.1.51, Poole; m., A.E. Yearling; 1 step-s.; 1 step-d. Educ. King's High School for Girls, Warwick; St. Hugh's College, Hertford College, Oxford University. Temporary Lecturer in Classics, University of Newcastle-upon-Tyne, 1977-78; University of Glasgow: Lecturer in Greek, 1978-92, Senior Lecturer in Classics, 1992-2000. Publications: Corpus Vasorum Antiquorum; Great Britain Fascicles 16 (National Museum of Scotland), 1989; 18 Glasgow Collections, 1997; 22 (Aberdeen University), 2006; Greek Vases, an Introduction, 2006; Knossos, The North Cemetery, 1996; Master of Attic Black-figure Painting - the Art and Legacy of Exekias, 2015. Recreations: music; collecting contemporary decorative art; crime fiction. Address: Classics, School of Humanities, University of Glasgow, Glasgow G12 8QQ; T.-0141 330 7361.
E-mail: elizabeth.moignard@glasgow.ac.uk

Moir, Grant. Chief Executive Officer, Cairngorms National Park Authority, since 2013. Educ. Aberdeen University. Career: Rural Affairs Department of the Scottish Executive; formerly Director of Conservation and Visitor Experience, Loch Lomond and the Trossachs National Park Authority. Address: (b.) 14 The Square, Grantown on Spey PH26 3HG; T.-01479 873535.

Moir, Mark Duncan, LLB, DipLP. Advocate, since 2000; b. 11.9.64, Edinburgh. Educ. Boroughmuir High School; Edinburgh University. Royal Air Force Police, 1983-92; Strathclyde Police, 1992-93. Address: Optimum Advocates, Glasgow High Court, 1 Mart Street, Saltmarket, Glasgow G1 5JT; T.-0141 370 8667.

Mollison, Professor Denis, ScD. Professor of Applied Probability, Heriot-Watt University, 1986-2003, Professor Emeritus, since 2003; Chairman, Hebridean Whale and Dolphin Trust, 2013-18; Co-Founder of John Muir Trust, 1983, Trustee, 1986-2007 and 2008-13; Chair, Liberal Democrats for Electoral Reform, 2018-21; b. 28.6.45, Carshalton; m., Jennifer Hutton; 1 s.; 3 d. Educ. Westminster School; Trinity College, Cambridge. Research Fellow, King's College, Cambridge, 1969; Lecturer in Statistics, Heriot-Watt University, 1973. Elected Member of Council, National Trust for Scotland, 1979-84, 1999-2004 and 2005-2010; Chairman, Mountain Bothies Association, 1978-94; Convener, Scottish Green Liberal Democrats,

2001-17. Publications: research papers on epidemics, ecology and wave energy. Address: (h.) The Laigh House, Inveresk, Musselburgh EH21 7TD; T.-0131-665 2055.
E-mail: denis.mollison@gmail.com
Web: www.macs.hw.ac.uk/~denis/

Monaghan, Carol, BSc (Hons). MP (SNP), Glasgow North West, since 2015; SNP Education, Armed Forces and Veterans spokesperson in the House of Commons, since 2017; b. 2.8.72, Glasgow; m., Feargal Dalton; 1 s.; 2 d. Educ. Strathclyde University. Trained as a teacher, gaining a PGCE in Physics and Mathematics; worked in many Glasgow schools, including 14 years at Hyndland Secondary (Head of Physics and Head of Science); spent two years as a Glasgow University lecturer training future teachers; SQA consultant (involved in developing physics qualifications at a national level). Address: House of Commons, London SW1A 0AA.

Monaghan, Professor Pat, FRSE. Professor of Animal Ecology, University of Glasgow, since 1997. Address: Environmental and Evolutionary Biology, Graham Kerr Building, University of Glasgow, Glasgow G12 8QQ; T.-0141 330 6640.
E-mail: Pat.Monaghan@glasgow.ac.uk

Monaghan, Dr Paul. MP (SNP), Caithness, Sutherland and Easter Ross, 2015-17; b. 1965, Montrose; m.; 1 d. Educ. Inverness Royal Academy; University of Stirling. Joined the Scottish National Party in 1994 and has held various roles within their Wester Ross branch.

Monckton, Professor Darren George, BSc, PhD. Professor of Human Genetics, University of Glasgow, since 2005; b. 28.8.66, Eastleigh. Educ. Wyvern Comprehensive, Fair Oak; University of Bath; University of Leicester. Postdoctoral Research Assistant, University of Leicester, 1992-93; Postdoctoral Research Fellow: Baylor College of Medicine, Houston, Texas, USA, 1993-95, UTMD Anderson Cancer Center, Houston, Texas, USA, 1995-96; University of Glasgow: Lecturer in Genetics, 1996-2000, Reader in Genetics, 2000-05. Muscular Dystrophy Association Neuromuscular Disease Research Fellow, 1993; Muscular Dystrophy Association Sammy Davis Jr. Neuromuscular Disease Named Research Fellow, 1994-96; Lister Institute Research Fellow, 1998-2003; Genetical Society Balfour Lecturer, 1999; Member of the Lister Institute of Preventive Medicine, since 2005; Leverhulme Research Fellow, 2007-08; Tenovus (Scotland) Medal Lecturer, 2008; Scientific Meetings Officer for the UK Genetics Society, 2002-06; Chairman of the 4th International Myotonic Dystrophy Consortium Meeting, 2003. More than 50 journal articles, and book chapters published; more than 100 invited seminars and conference presentations. Recreations: fishing; football; wildlife and photography. Address: (b.) Institute of Molecular, Cell and Systems Biology, University of Glasgow, Glasgow G12 8QQ; T.-0141 330 6213.
E-mail: Darren.Monckton@glasgow.ac.uk

Mone of Mayfair, Baroness (Michelle Mone), OBE. Founder, MJM International Ltd., inventor of the Ultimo bra; b. 8.10.71, Glasgow; m., Michael (divorced 2013); 3 c. Career: modelling in Glasgow, then Labatts Brewers; started MJM International Ltd in 1996. World Young Business Achiever, 2000; winner of 'Business Woman of the Year' at the Corporate Elite Awards, 2000.

Monro, Major General The Honourable Seymour, CBE, LVO. Lord-Lieutenant for Moray, since 2020; b. 7.5.50,

Edinburgh. Educ. Glenalmond College. Career history: commissioned into the Queen's Own Highlanders in 1970 from RMA Sandhurst; awarded the Sword of Honour; commanded the 1st Battalion Queens Own Highlanders in Belfast and in the First Gulf War; commanded the 39 Infantry Brigade in Belfast and later was the United Kingdom's Director of Infantry; last military appointment was as Deputy Commander of the NATO Rapid Deployable Corps, in Italy; became Executive Director of the Atlantic Salmon Trust and Adjutant of The Queen's Body Guard for Scotland and later Chairman of the Highlanders' Museum at Fort George, responsible for its £2.75 million upgrade project; former Chairman of the Prince's Trust in the Highlands and of the Findhorn, Nairn and Lossie Fisheries' trust; served on the board of Cairngorm Mountain Ltd; instrumental in establishing The Highland Military Tattoo at Fort George in 2014 and was its Executive Chairman and Tattoo Director until it ceased in 2017; Honorary Air Commodore of 2622 (Highland) Squadron The Royal Auxiliary Air Force at RAF Lossiemouth, 2008-2019. Currently Chairman of the Northern Meeting Piping Trust; Honorary President of Forres and District Pipe Band, of the Forres Branch of the Royal British Legion Scotland, of Forres in Bloom and of the Brisbane Observatory Trust in Largs; President of the Leanchoil Trust which will turn the former cottage hospital in Forres into a Veterans' Activity Centre and a local community health and wellbeing hub; Director of the Moray Emergency Relief Fund set up to help those in need during the coronavirus pandemic. Eldest son of Lord Monro of Langholm. Address: The Moray Council, High Street, Elgin IV30 1BX; T.-01343 563002.

Monro, Stuart Kinnaird, OBE, BSc, PhD, DUniv, DSc, CGeol, FGS, FHEA, FRSSA, FSAScot, FRSGS, FRSE. Scientific Director, Scottish Consortium for Rural Research, 2008-2018; Honorary Professor in the School of Geosciences, University of Edinburgh, since 2008; Scientific Director, Our Dynamic Earth, 1996-2014; b. 3.3.47, Aberdeen; m., Shiela Monro, nee Wallace; 3 s.; 1 d. Educ. Aberdeen Academy; University of Aberdeen; University of Edinburgh. Appointed as Geologist to British Geological Survey (then, Institute of Geological Sciences), 1970; retired as Principal Geologist, 2004. President: Edinburgh Geological Society, 2005-07 and 2016-18, Westmorland Geological Society, 1994-2005, Royal Scottish Society of Arts, 2002-05 and 2014-17; Honorary Fellow, College of Science and Engineering, Edinburgh University, 2005-08, Edinburgh University Court: co-opted member, 2007-2014, Vice Convener, 2011-2014; Member of St Andrews University Court, 2014, Deputy Chair, since 2018, Convener, Governance and Nominations Committee, since 2018; Independent Co-Chair, Scottish Science Advisory Council, 2007-09; Trustee, National Museums of Scotland, 2005-2012; Non-executive Director of the Edinburgh International Science Festival, 2004-2019; Trustee, Brisbane Observatory Trust, 2015; Honorary Geological Advisor to the John Muir Trust; Open University Tutor in Earth Sciences, 1982-2009; Convener, Young People's Committee, Royal Society of Edinburgh, 2015-2020; Member of Nominations Committee and Council, Royal Society of Edinburgh, 2020; OBE for Services to Science, 2006; Distinguished Service Award, Geological Society of London, 2009; Silver medal of Royal Scottish Society of Arts, 2017; Honorary doctorates: Open University, Heriot-Watt University, Edinburgh University; Honorary Fellowship, Royal Scottish Geographical Society. Recreations: reading; travel; hill walking. Address: (h.) 34 Swanston Grove, Edinburgh EH10 7BW; T.-0131 477 1124; e-mail: stuart.monro@blueyonder.co.uk

Monteith, Brian. Editor, ThinkScotland.org; Director of Communications, Global Britain (think tank); Columnist, The Scotsman, City AM & Edinburgh Evening News; Member of the European Parliament (MEP) for North East

England (Brexit Party), 2019-2020; MSP Mid-Scotland and Fife, 1999-2007; Conservative spokesman on Education, Culture & Sport (1999-2003), spokesman on Finance, Local Government & Public Services (2003-05), then independent 2005-07; divorced; 2 s.; m., Jacqueline Anderson. International Public relations consultant; former Chairman, English Speaking Union Scotland, 2009-14; National Chairman, Scottish Young Conservatives (1988) and Federation of Conservative Students (1982); National Co-ordinator, No, No Campaign, Scottish devolution referendum 1997.

Montgomerie, Colin, OBE (2005), MBE (1998); Professional golfer; b. 23.6.63; m. (1), Eimear, née Wilson (m dis 2006); 2 d.; 1 s.; m. (2), Gaynor Knowles (divorced 2016). Amateur victories: Scottish Amateur Stroke-play Championship 1985, Scottish Amateur Championship 1987; tournament victories since turning professional in 1987: Portuguese Open 1989, Scandinavian Masters 1991, 1999 and 2001, Dutch Open 1993, Volvo Masters 1993 and 2002, Spanish Open 1994, English Open 1994, German Open 1994 and 1995, Trophee Lancome 1995, Alfred Dunhill Cup 1995, Dubai Desert Classic 1996, Irish Open 1996, 1997 and 2001, European Masters 1996, Sun City Million Dollar Challenge 1996, European Grand Prix 1997, King Hassan II Trophy 1997, World Cup (Individual) 1997, Andersen Consulting World Champion 1997, PGA Championship 1998, 1999 and 2000, German Masters 1998, British Masters 1998, Benson and Hedges International Open 1999, Standard Life Loch Lomond Invitational 1999, Int Open Munich 1999, World Matchplay Championships Wentworth 1999, French Open Paris 2000, Skins Game USA 2000, Ericsson Australian Masters 2001, TCL Classic 2002, Macau Open 2003, Caltex Masters presented by Carlsberg, Singapore 2004, Dunhill Links Championship 2005, UBS Hong Kong Open 2006, European Open Ireland 2007; US Open: third 1992, second 1994, 1997 and 2006; second, The Open, 2005; US PGA 1995 (second); Tournament Players Championship 1996 (second); team memb: Eisenhower Trophy (amateur) 1984 and 1986, Walker Cup (amateur) 1985 and 1987, Alfred Dunhill Cup 1988, 1991, 1992, 1993, 1994, 1995 (winners), 1996, 1997, 1998, 1999 and 2000, World Cup 1988, 1991, 1992, 1993, 1997, 1998, 1999 and 2007 (winners), Ryder Cup 1991, 1993, 1995 (winners), 1997 (winners), 1999, 2002 (winners), 2004 (winners) and 2006 (winners), UBS Cup 2003 and 2004; Henry Cotton Rookie of the Year 1988, winner European Order of Merit 1993, 1994, 1995, 1996, 1997, 1998, 1999 and 2005. Non playing Captain, European Ryder Cup Team, 2010 (winners). Publication: The Real Monty: The Thinking Man's Guide To Golf. Recreations: motor cars; music; DIY.

Montgomery, Sir (Basil Henry) David, 9th Bt, JP, DL. Lord Lieutenant, Perth and Kinross, 1995-2006; Chairman, Forestry Commission, 1979-89; b. 20.3.31.

Montgomery, Iona Allison Eleanor, BA (Hons), RSW. Artist; Lecturer (part-time): Edinburgh College of Art, since 1997, Grays School of Art, since 1994; b. 14.4.65, Glasgow. Educ. Boclair Academy; Glasgow School of Art; Tamarind Institute, University of New Mexico. Exhibited widely in UK, Europe, USA and Japan, since 1989; solo exhibitions in UK, Europe, USA; work in numerous public collections; Alexander Graham Munro Award, RSW, 1990; Lauder Award, 1991, Lady Artists Club Trust Award, 1992, Cross Trust Bursary, 1994, Glasgow District Council Bursary, 1995; elected, RSW, 1991. Recreations: walking; music; film; travel. Address: (h.) 13 Avon Avenue, Bearsden, Glasgow G61 2PS.

Montgomery, John, LLB (Hons). Sheriff at Ayr, since 2005; Solicitor, since 1976; b. 17.9.51, Kilwinning; m., Susan Wilson Templeton; 1 s.; 3 d. Educ. Ardrossan Academy; Glasgow University. Partner in Carruthers Curdie Sturrock & Co. Solicitors, Kilmarnock, 1980-2003;

Temporary Sheriff, 1995-2000; Part-time Sheriff, 2000-03; Floating Sheriff, 2003-05. Recreations: gardening; walking; travel. Address: (b.) Sheriff Court, Wellington Square, Ayr KA7 1DR.

Montgomery, Steve. Managing Director of First Rail at Firstgroup plc, since 2015. Former Passenger Service Manager for the Glasgow Queen Street, Edinburgh and North of Scotland areas in 1997; held various senior posts before becoming Operations and Safety Director when FirstGroup took over the franchise in 2004. Address: (b.) 395 King Street, Aberdeen AB24 5RP.

Montrose, 8th Duke of (James Graham), OStJ. Captain, Queen's Bodyguard for Scotland, 2006-2015, Member, since 1965; Member, House of Lords, since 1996, elected Hereditary Peer, 1999, Conservative Opposition Whip, 2001-2010; Opposition Spokesman for Scottish Affairs, 2001-2010; b. 6.4.35, Salisbury, Rhodesia; m., Catherine Elizabeth MacDonell Young (deceased); 2 s.; 1 d. Educ. Loretto. Farmer/Landowner; Member of Council, National Farmers Union of Scotland, 1981-86; Vice Chairman, Loch Lomond and Trossachs Working Party, 1991-93; President, Royal Highland and Agricultural Society, 1997-98; Chairman, Buchanan Community Council, 1982-93; President, National Sheep Association, 2011-17. Address: (b.) Montrose Estates Ltd., Buchanan Castle, Drymen, Glasgow G63 0AG; T.-01360 870382.

Moody, Sue. Chair, Stellar Quines Theatre Company. Career history: involved in art-based organisations for over twenty years, primarily as a Board member of Dundee Rep for 12 years with particular responsibility for Creative Learning matters; also a long-standing member of Loadsa Weeminsingin, a Dundee based all-women singing group, and of Engender; worked with and for survivors of crime for more than thirty years, as a researcher, University teacher, service provider, policy analyst and senior manager in the Scottish prosecution service; currently chairs the PPT for a Lottery funded heritage project celebrating over 130 years of change making and change makers linked to Abertay University and its predecessors; sits on the Scottish Sentencing Council as an expert on victims; previously chaired the Scottish Refugee Council Board, 2015-18. Address: 30 Grindlay Street, Edinburgh EH3 9AP; T.-0131 229 3851.

Moody, Cllr Vaughan. Joint Leader, East Dunbartonshire Council, since 2018; representing Bearsden South Ward (Liberal Democrats), since 1999. Address: East Dunbartonshire Council, 12 Strathkelvin Place, Kirkintilloch G66 1TJ; T.-0300 123 4510.
E-mail: vaughan.moody@eastdunbarton.gov.uk

Moonie, Helen. Provost, South Ayrshire, since 2012; represents Ward 2, Prestwick (Labour). Address: South Ayrshire Council, Council Headquarters, County Buildings, Wellington Square, Ayr KA7 1DR; T.-01292 612289.
E-mail: helen.moonie@south-ayrshire.gov.uk

Moore, George, QC, LLB (Hons). Solicitor and Solicitor Advocate; formerly Senior Partner, HBM Sayers (currently consultant); b. 7.11.47, Kilmarnock; m., Ann Beattie; 2 s.; 1 d. Educ. High School of Glasgow; Glasgow University. Former Member, Glasgow and North Argyll Legal Aid Committee; former Reporter to Scottish Legal Aid Board; former part-time Chairman, Industrial Tribunals in Scotland; former Member, Sheriff Court Rules Council, 1987. Recreations: tennis; golf; boating. Address: (b.) 13 Bath Street, Glasgow G2 1HY; T.-0141-353 2121.

Moore, Professor Johanna D., BS, MS, PhD, FRSE, FBCS, CITP. Professor, School of Informatics, Edinburgh University, since 1998, Head of School of Informatics, 2014-18; b. 16.7.57, USA; m., Dr N. Goddard; 2 s. Educ. University of California at Los Angeles (UCLA). Graduate Research Assistant, then Teaching Assistant/Teaching Fellow, UCLA; University of Pittsburgh: Research Scientist, Learning Research and Development Centre, 1990-98, Assistant Professor of Computer Science and Intelligent Systems, 1990-96, Associate Professor of Linguistics, 1996-98, Associate Professor of Computer Science and Intelligent Systems, 1996-98, Director, Intelligent Systems Program, 1996-98. President, Association for Computational Linguistics, 2004; Chair, Cognitive Science Society, 2007-08; Associate Editor, Speech Communication; Associate Editor, Cognitive Science. Publication: Participating in Explanatory Dialogues: Interpreting and Responding to Questions in Context, 1995. Address: (b.) School of Informatics, Edinburgh University, 10 Crichton Street, Edinburgh EH8 9AB; T.-0131-651 1336.

Moore, Michael, MA, CA. Director General, British Private Equity and Venture Capital Association, since 2019; Senior Adviser on Devolution and Brexit, PwC, 2016-17; Visiting Professor, International Public Policy Institute, University of Strathclyde, 2016-19; Chairman, Borders Book Festival, since 2015; Trustee/Director, The Tweed Foundation, 2015-18; MP (Liberal Democrat), Berwickshire, Roxburgh and Selkirk, 2005-2015; Tweeddale, Ettrick and Lauderdale, 1997-2005; Representative on the Smith Commission on Devolution, 2014; European Business Adviser to the Deputy Prime Minister, 2013-15; Secretary of State for Scotland, 2010-2013; UK Spokesman on Transport, 1999-2001, Spokesman on Scotland, 2001, Deputy Foreign Affairs Spokesman, 2001-05, Defence Spokesman, 2005-06, Foreign Affairs Spokesman, 2006-07; Deputy Leader, Scottish Liberal Democrats, 2002-2010; International Development Spokesman, 2007-2010; Scotland and Northern Ireland Spokesman, 2008-2009; b. 3.6.65; m., Alison Louise Hughes; 1 d.; 1 s. Educ. Strathallan School; Jedburgh Grammar School; Edinburgh University. Manager, Corporate Finance practice, Coopers and Lybrand. Member, House of Commons Scottish Select Committee, 1997-99; Governor and Vice Chairman, Westminster Foundation for Democracy, 2002-05; Council Member, Royal Institute of International Affairs, 2004-2010; Parliamentary Visiting Fellow, St. Antony's College, Oxford, 2003-04; Governor, The Ditchley Foundation, since 2010. Recreations: jazz; films; walking; rugby. Address: 15 Coatburn Green, Darnick, Melrose TD6 9FD.

Moos, Khursheed Francis, OBE, MB, BS, BDS, FRCSEdin, FDS RCS (Eng, Edin), FDS RCPS (Glas). Consultant Oral and Maxillofacial Surgeon (retired); Honorary Professor, Glasgow University; b. 1.11.34, London; m., Katharine Addison; 2 s.; 1 d. Educ. Dulwich College; Guy's Hospital, London; Westminster Hospital. National Service, RADC, Lt., 1959, Capt., 1960; Registrar in Oral Surgery, Mount Vernon Hospital, Middlesex, 1966-67; Senior Registrar, Oral Surgery, University of Wales, Cardiff, 1967-69; Consultant Oral Surgeon, S. Warwicks and Coventry Hospitals, 1969-74; Consultant Oral and Maxillofacial Surgeon, Canniesburn Hospital, Glasgow, 1974-99; Dean, Dental Faculty, Royal College of Physicians and Surgeons of Glasgow, 1992-95; Chairman, Intercollegiate Examination Board in oral and maxillofacial surgery, 1995-98; Civilian Consultant to Royal Navy, 1976-2010; President: Cranio-facial Society of Great Britain, 1994-95, British Association of Oral and Maxillofacial Surgeons, 1991-92; Down Surgical Prize, 1988; Colyer Medal, Royal College of Surgeons of England, 1997; Indian

Medical Association (UK): Chairman, Board of Directors, 1999-2000, President, 1998-99; Honorary Senior Research Fellow, Glasgow University, since 1999. Publications include contributions to books and various papers. Recreations: music; natural history; philately; Eastern philosophy; gardening. Address: (h.) 120 West King Street, Helensburgh G84 8DQ; T.-01436 673232.
E-mail: khursheed.moos@gla.ac.uk

Moray, Earl of (John Douglas Stuart); b. 29.8.66. Succeeded to the title, 21st Earl of Moray, 2011. Address: (h.) Darnaway Castle, Forres, Moray.

Morgan, Alasdair, MA, BA. Electoral Commissioner, since 2014; MSP (SNP), South of Scotland, 2003-2011; MSP (SNP), Galloway and Upper Nithsdale, 1999-2003; MP (SNP), Galloway and Upper Nithsdale, 1997-2001; Deputy Presiding Officer, Scottish Parliament, 2007-2011; b. 21.4.45, Aberfeldy; m., Anne Gilfillan; 2 d. Educ. Breadalbane Academy, Aberfeldy; Glasgow University. SNP: National Treasurer, 1983-90, Senior Vice-Convener, 1990-91, Depute Leader, 1990-91, National Secretary, 1992-97, Vice President, 1997-2004. Recreation: hillwalking.

Morgan, Diane, MA, BA, MUniv. Writer, historian. Educ. Aberdeen High School for Girls; Aberdeen University; Cambridge University. Law Lecturer, RGIT; Founding Editor/Publisher, Leopard, 1974-88. Aberdeen Civic Society Award, 1982 and 2000. Publications: The Aberdeen Series: Footdee, 1993, Round About Mounthooly, 1995, The Spital, 1996, The Spital Lands: From Sunnyside to Pittodrie, 1997, Old Aberdeen, Vol. 1, 2000; A Monumental Business, 2001; The Woodside Story, 2003; Lost Aberdeen, 2004; Lost Aberdeen: The Outskirts, 2007; The Granite Mile, 2008; Lost Aberdeen: The Freedom Lands, 2009; Aberdeen's Union Terrace Gardens: War and Peace in the Denburn Valley, 2015. Recreations: book collecting; travel; local history. Address: (b.) 'The Braes' 36 Ferryhill Place, Aberdeen AB11 7SE.

Morgan, Mary, BSc, MSc. Chief Executive, NHS National Services Scotland, since 2021; Senior Programme Director, NHS Lothian, 2019-2021; Director of Strategy, Performance and Service Transformation, NHS National Services Scotland, 2018-19; Director/Trustee of the Board, The Scottish Centre For Children With Motor Impairments, since 2014. Educ. Boclair Academy; Western College of Nursing and Midwifery, Glasgow; Stow College, Glasgow; Glasgow Caledonian University; Kings College London. Career: Nursing Manager, Medical Directorate, NHS Argyll & Clyde, November 1996-April 2000; Directorate Manager, Medicine, NHS Argyll & Clyde, April 2000-March 2003; Acting Hospital Manager, Royal Alexandra Hospital, March 2003-March 2004; Service General Manager, NHS Argyll and Clyde, April 2004-May 2006; General Manager, Emergency Care & Medicine, NHS Greater Glasgow and Clyde, April 2006-August 2008; Director, Health Protection Scotland, NHS National Services Scotland, September 2008-January 2012; Director of the Scottish National Blood Transfusion Service (SNBTS), 2012-18. Address: NHS National Services Scotland, 2, Meridian Court, 5 Cadogan Street, Glasgow G2 6QE.

Morgan, Professor Peter John, BSc, PhD, FRSE. Chair in Nutrition, University of Aberdeen; Director, Rowett Institute, University of Aberdeen, 2008-2021, formerly Vice Principal (2008-2014); b. 23.2.56, Armthorpe, Yorkshire; m., Professor Denise Kelly; 1s.; 1d. Educ. Aylesbury Grammar School; Queen Mary College, London; University of Aberdeen; Imperial College,

London. Recreations: music (classical and jazz); swimming. Address: (b.) Rowett Institute, University of Aberdeen, Foresterhill AB25 2ZD; T.-01224 438660.

Morison, Hugh, CBE, MA, DipEd. Chief Executive, Scotch Whisky Association, 1994-2003; b. 22.11.43, Bognor Regis; m.; 2 d. Educ. Chichester High School for Boys; St. Catherine's College, Oxford. Assistant Principal, Scottish Home and Health Department, 1966-69; Private Secretary to Minister of State, Scottish Office, 1969-70; Principal: Scottish Education Department, 1971-73, Scottish Economic Planning Department, 1973-79 (seconded to Offshore Supplies Office, Department of Energy, 1974-75); Assistant Secretary, Scottish Economic Planning Department, 1979-82; Gwilym Gibbon Research Fellow, Nuffield College, Oxford, 1982-83; Assistant Secretary, Scottish Development Department, 1983-84; Under Secretary, Scottish Home and Health Department, 1984-88, Scottish Office Industry Department, 1988-93; Non-Executive Director, Weir Group PLC, 1988-93; Member, Health Appointments Advisory Committee (Scotland), 1995-2000; Member, Executive Committee, Barony Housing Association, 1996-2010, Convenor, 2005-09; Chairman, Scottish Business and Biodiversity Group, 1999-2003; President, Confédération Européenne des Producteurs de Spiritueux, 2001-03; Chairman, Letterfearn Moorings Association, since 2001; Governor, UHI Millennium Institute, subsequently University of the Highlands and Islands, 2004-2013; Non-Executive Director, Praban na Linne Ltd., 2005-06; Lay Member, General Synod, Scottish Episcopal Church, since 2020. Publications: The Regeneration of Local Economies, 1987; Dauphine (Co-Author), 1991; The Feelgood Fallacy, 2008. Recreations: sailing; archaeology; literature; playing the euphonium.

Morrice, Graeme. MP (Labour), Livingston, 2010-2015; b. 23.2.59, Edinburgh. Educ. Broxburn Academy; Napier University. Parliamentary Private Secretary to Harriet Harman MP (Shadow Deputy Prime Minister); Councillor, West Lothian, 1987-2012; Council Leader, West Lothian, 1995-2007. Recreations: music; art; literature.

Morris of Balgonie & Eddergoll, Stuart Gordon Cathal, OStJ, DHM, FRSA, FSA Scot. Director, Balgonie Castle Enterprises, since 1985; Historian, Armorist and writer; b. 17.04.65, Aberfeldy, Perthshire; m., Kelly Hollie-Whittaker. Educ. Bell Baxter High School; Elmwood College; Napier College; University of Birmingham. Director, Theobald-Hicks, Morris & Gifford, 2001-06. Matriculated Arms (Morris of Balgonie & Eddergoll, quartered with Stuart, formerly of Langlees), Court of the Lord Lyon, Tartan, Morris of Balgonie, 1987; Member, Officer (2011) of the Venerable Order of St John of Jerusalem, 2003; Commander of the Order of Polonia Restituta, 1990; Companion of the Order of Malta, 2007; 2010 Grand Cross of The Order of The Eagle of Georgia; Rector for Scotland for the Order of the Eagle of Georgia, 2011-15; Cross of Merit 2nd Class, Red Cross of the Republic of San Marino, 2012; Member, Military Order of the Stars and Bars, 2012; Freeman of the City of London, 2001; Liveryman, Worshipful Company of Meadmakers, 1982; Grand Officer, Order of St Agatha, Republic of San Marino, 2012; FSA Scot, 1983; FRSA, 1990; MInstLM, 2021; Hon. Colonel, Commonwealth of Kentucky, 1999; Hon. Lieutenant Colonel and ADC to the Governor of the State of Georgia, 1991; Founder Member: Heraldry Society of Scotland, Scottish Castles Association (Membership Secretary, 1996-2010, Secretary, 1998-2003, Chairman, 2003-05, Vice-Chairman, since 2005); Member of the Stewart Society (Council, 1998-2006 and since 2010); Chairman, Central Fife Group of the Order of St John, 2007-08, Chairman, since 2008, Fife Area Chairman, since

2015; Royal Celtic Society (Member of Council, 2009); HRFCA, since 2015; Member, Sons of Confederate Veterans, 2012; Vice-Chairman, Markinch Heritage Group, 2007-2011; Diploma of Honour, St. Andrew Association, Austria, 1994; Advance the Colors Award, Sons of Confederate Veterans, 2001; awarded 10th Anniversary Medal of the Albert Schweitzer Society of Austria, 1994; Founder, Tay Rail Bridge Disaster Memorial Trust, 2010. Club: Royal Scots Club, Edinburgh. Recreations: heraldry; genealogy; history; history of highland dress; castles; portrait painting; archery. Address: Balgonie Castle, by Markinch, Fife KY7 6HQ; T.-01592 750 119.
E-mail: sbalgonie@yahoo.co.uk

Morris, Professor Andrew David, CBE, MBChB, MSc, MD, FRCPEdin, FRCPGlas, FRSE, FMedSci. Director of Health Data Research UK; Professor of Medicine and Vice Principal, Data Science, University of Edinburgh, since 2014; Honorary Professor, University of Dundee; Dean of Medicine, University of Dundee, 2012-14; Chief Scientist, Scottish Government Health Department, 2012-2017; Chair, Scottish Diabetes Group (lead clinician for diabetes in Scotland), 2002-06; b. 7.10.64; m., Elspeth Claire; 2 d.; 1 s. Educ. Robert Gordon's College, Aberdeen; Glasgow University. Undergraduate and research training, Glasgow University; Governor, Health Foundation, 2008-2017; Co-founder, Aridhia Informatics, 2007-2015; Saltire Society Scottish Science Award, 2005; Royal Society of Edinburgh Royal Medal, 2021. Recreations: golf; squash; family life. Address: (b.) University of Edinburgh, No. 9 Edinburgh Bioquarter, 9 Little France Road, Edinburgh EH16 4UX.

Morris, Professor Christopher David, BA, DipEd, MIFA, FSA, FSA Scot, FRHistS, FRSA, FRSE. Professor of Archaeology, Glasgow University, 1990-2006, Vice-Principal, 2000-06; Chair in Archaeology, UHI Millennium Institute, 2007-09; Interim Director, Conservation Services, Projects and Policy, National Trust for Scotland, 2009-2010; b. 14.4.46, Preston. Educ. Queen Elizabeth's Grammar School, Blackburn; Durham University; Oxford University. Assistant Lecturer, Hockerill College of Education, Bishops Stortford, 1968-72; Lecturer, then Senior Lecturer in Archaeology, 1972-88, Reader in Viking Archaeology, 1989-90, Durham University. Member, Ancient Monuments Board for Scotland, 1990-2001; Royal Commissioner, Ancient and Historical Monuments of Scotland, 2000-09, Vice-Chair, 2006-09. Recreations: classical music and opera; singing and choirs; jazz; theatre; dog walking; ski-ing; fun runs. Address: 2 Pinel Lodge, Druid's Park, Murthly PH1 4ES.
E-mail: chris@cdmorris.co.uk

Morris, Professor Eleanor Smith, AB Arch Sci Cum Laude (Harvard/Radcliffe), MCP (U Penn), PhD (Edinburgh) AICP, RTPI. Town Planning Consultant, Director, Governing Board, Commonwealth Human Ecology Council, London, 1997-2014; Chair, CHEC Executive Committee (2008-2010); Visiting Professor, Urban Planning and Sustainable Development, Clemson University, South Carolina, USA, 2003; NGO Delegate, 2009, UN Commission Human Settlements (Habitat), Nairobi, Kenya; NGO Delegate, UN World Urban Forum, Barcelona, Spain, 2004; 8th, 11th and 12th Commission on Sustainable Development, UN, New York, 1999, 2003 and 2004; Habitat (+5) UN General Assembly (UNGASS), 2001; Pre-Commonwealth Heads of Government Meeting, Edinburgh, 1997, Durban, S.A. 1999; Abuja, Nigeria, 2003, Trinidad, 2009; Rapporteur, 16th Session UN Commission Human Settlements (Habitat), Nairobi, Kenya, 1997; b. 14.11.35, Washington, D.C.,; dau of Hon. Lawrence M C Smith and Eleanor Houston Smith; m. James Shepherd Morris, RSA, FRIBA, FRIAS, ALI (deceased); 2 s.; 1 d. Educ. National Cathedral School for Girls, Washington, D.C.; Germantown Friends School, (Cum laude) Philadelphia, Pa. Academic Director Emerita, Centre for the Study of Environmental Change and Sustainability, Institute of Ecology and Resource Management, Edinburgh University, 1996-99; Faculty Lecturer, Centre for Human Ecology, 1990-1995; Lecturer/Course Director, Department of Urban Design and Regional Planning, 1967-90; Lecturer/Course Administrator, Department of Architecture, 1960-67. Planning Practice in Philadelphia City Planning Commission, New Jersey State Planning Board, London County Council; Past Chairman, Royal Town Planning Institute, Scotland, 1986-1987; Member, Council, Royal Town Planning Institute, London, 1982, 1986-87; Member, Executive Committee, RTPI Scottish Branch, 1977-94; Member, Board, Environment Show, Glasgow Garden Festival, 1988-92; Member, Board Link Housing Association, 1987-1995; Member, Council, Executive, Building and American Liaison Committees, National Trust for Scotland, 1992-2004; Trustee, Schuylkill Center for Environmental Education, Philadelphia, 1995-2001; 2003-2009; Co-Chair, Friends of the Schuylkill Nature Center, since 2009; Member, National Advisory Board, National Museum for Women in Arts, Washington DC, since 1989; Member, Lothian Committee, National Art Collections Fund, 1993-2001; President, Harvard Club of Scotland, 1965-1970. Publications of numerous reports including "Down with Eco-Towns! Up with ECO Communities. A Review of the 2009-2010 Eco Town Proposals in Britain", 2011; James Morris Architect and Landscape Architect, 1931-2006, 2007; British Town Planning and Urban Design: Principles and Policies, 1997; "Berlin, London or Paris - A New Capital for Europe", 1994; Focus on the Habitat Agenda of the Commonwealth, 2019; Cosmopolitan Club Philadelphia, 1958-2020; Acorn Club Philadelphia, 1959-2021. Recreation: piano; sailing; 15th Laird, Woodcote Estate, since 1970. Address: Woodcote Park, Fala and Soutra, Midlothian EH37 5TG; T.-01875-833-684.
E-mail: emorrischec@yahoo.co.uk

Morris, Jason. Regional Market Leader, PwC Scotland, since 2022; b. 6.70. Educ. University of Strathclyde. Partner, Pricewaterhouse/PwC, since 1991: leads UK Transaction Services Renewables team; senior member of the Power & Utilities deal team; over 15 years' experience of working on international transactions with both corporate clients and private equity and infrastructure investors. Address: PwC in Scotland, 141 Bothwell Street, Glasgow G2 7EQ; T.-07710 120 544.

Morris, Sheriff John C., QC, LLB. All Scotland Floating Sheriff, attached to Edinburgh, 2014-17 (retired); Board Member, Scottish Legal Aid Board, since 2018; b. 11.4.52. Educ. Allan Glen's School, Glasgow; Strathclyde University. Solicitor, 1975-85; called to Scottish Bar, 1985; Advocate Depute, 1989-92; called to English Bar, 1990; Temporary Sheriff, 1993-98; took silk, Scottish Bar, 1996. Chairman, Advocates Criminal Law Group, 1996-98; Member, Temporary Sheriffs Association Committee, 1994-98; appointed Temporary Judge, 2008; appointed Sheriff's Appeal Court, 2015. Recreations: golf; bird-watching; walking; wine.

Morris, Professor Richard Graham Michael, MA, DPhil, FRSE, FMedSci, CBE, FRS. Neuroscience, Edinburgh University (Professor of Neuroscience, since 1993, Reader, 1989-93); b. 27.6.48, Worthing; divorced; m., Dr. Monica Muñoz; 2 d. 1 s. Educ. St. Albans, Washington DC; Marlborough College; Cambridge University; Sussex University. Addison Wheeler Fellow, Durham University, 1973-75; SSO, British Museum (Natural History), 1975-77;

Researcher, BBC Television, 1977; Lecturer, St. Andrews University, 1977-86; MRC University Research Fellow, 1983-86. Member, MRC Neurosciences Grants Committee, 1981-85, MRC Neurosciences Board, 1993-98, Innovation Panel, 1997-2001, Strategy Development Group, 2000-04; Hon. Secretary, Experimental Psychological Society, 1985-89; Chairman: Brain Research Association, 1990-94, Sectional Committee for Medicine and Biomedical Sciences, Royal Society of Edinburgh, 1995-97; Member, Council, European Neuroscience Association, 1994-98; Member, Council, Royal Society of Edinburgh, Scottish Science Advisory Committee; President, Federation of European Neuroscience Societies, 2006-08; Member, Council, Royal Society (London); Chair, Brain Prize Selection Committee (2019-2022); Fellow, Royal Society, Royal Society of Edinburgh, Academy of Medical Sciences, American Academy of Arts and Sciences, American Association for Advancement of Science, Norwegian Academy of Science and Letters, and the US National Academy of Sciences; Prizes: Zotterman Medal (Sweden), 1999; Outstanding Contribution to British Neuroscience, 2002; EJN Award, 2004; Santiago Grisolia Award, 2007; Fondation IPSEN Prize, 2013; Royal Medal, Royal Society of Edinburgh, 2014; Brain Prize (Denmark), 2016; Chancellor's Medal, The University of Edinburgh, 2019; Fyssen Prize for Neuroscience, 2020; Chairman, Department of Neuroscience, Edinburgh University, 1998-2002; Co-Director, Edinburgh Neuroscience, 2005-09; Head of Neurosciences and Mental Health, The Wellcome Trust, 2007-2010; Royal Society/Wolfson Professor of Neuroscience, 2006-2017; Member: Centre for Discovery Brain Sciences, since 2017, Simons Institute for the Developing Brain (Edinburgh), since 2018, Scientific Affiliate, Edinburgh Futures Institute. Publications: over 200 academic papers and 4 books. Recreation: sailing. Address: (b.) Centre for Discovery Brain Science, Edinburgh Neuroscience, Edinburgh University, 1 George Square, Edinburgh EH8 9JZ; T.-0131-650 3518/3520. E-mail: r.g.m.morris@ed.ac.uk

Morris, Professor Robert John, BA, DPhil. Emeritus Professor of Economic and Social History, Edinburgh University (appointed Professor in 1993); b. 12.10.43, Sheffield; m., Barbara; 1 s.; 1 d. Educ. Acklam Hall, Middlesbrough; Keble and Nuffield Colleges, Oxford. Lecturer, Senior Lecturer, then Professor, Economic and Social History, Edinburgh University, from 1968. Editor, Book of the Old Edinburgh Club; Founding Editor, History and Computing; Patron, Thoresby Society, Leeds; President, Scottish Economic and Social History Society; President, European Urban History Association, 2000-02; Editor Emeritus, Book of the Old Edinburgh Club. Recreation: planting apple trees. Address: (b.) William Robertson Wing, Teviot Place, Edinburgh EH8 9AG.

Morris, Professor Russell Edward, FRS, FRSE, FRSC, FLSW. Bishop Wardlaw Professor of Chemistry, University of St Andrews; b. 8.6.67, St Asaph, Flintshire, Wales. Educ. Ysgol Dyffryn Conwy; Oriel College, Oxford. Recognized as a pioneer in the use of porous materials for the storage and delivery of biologically active gases for medical applications. Address: University of St Andrews, School of Chemistry, Purdie Building, North Haugh, St Andrews; T.-01334 463804; e-mail: rem1@st-andrews.ac.uk

Morrison, Sir Alexander Fraser, CBE, FRSA, BSc, CEng, FICE, MIHT. Director, Morrison Construction Group Plc, 1970-2001 (Chairman, 1984-2000); Deputy Chairman, Clydesdale Bank Plc, 1999-2004 (Director, 1994-99); b. 20.3.48, Dingwall; m., Patricia Janice Murphy; 1 s.; 2 d. Educ. Tain Royal Academy; Edinburgh University. National Federation of Civil Engineering Contractors: Chairman, 1993-94, Vice President, 1994-96;

Chairman, Highlands and Islands Enterprise, 1992-98; Vice President, Royal Highland and Agricultural Society of Scotland, 1995-96; Chairman, University of the Highlands and Islands Project, 1997-2000; Director, Aberforth Split Level Trust plc, 1991-2003; Director, Chief Executives Organisation, 2003-2013 and International President, 2009/10; Chairman, Teasses Capital Ltd., since 2003; Chairman, Ramco Holdings Ltd., 2005-2013; Chairman, American Patrons of the National Library and Galleries of Scotland, 2011-2017; RMJM Ltd, 2007-2013; Duthus Group Investments Ltd, 2013-2018; Vermilion Holding, 2007-2016; winner, 1991 Scottish Business Achievement Award; Hon. Doctor of Technology: Napier University, 1995, Glasgow Caledonian University, 1997; Honorary Doctor, Open University, 2000; Chairman, Council, St. Leonard's School, St Andrews, 1999-2007. Recreations: rugby; golf; skiing; opera; the countryside; theatre; art.

Morrison, Very Rev. Angus, MA, BD, PhD, DD. Moderator of the General Assembly of the Church of Scotland, 2015-16; Chaplain to the Queen in Scotland, since 2006; b. 30.8.53, Oban; m., Marion Jane Matheson; 3 s.; 1 d. Educ. Oban High School; Glasgow University; London University; Edinburgh University. Minister, Free Presbyterian Church of Scotland Oban Congregation, 1979-86, Edinburgh Congregation, 1986-89; Moderator, Southern Presbytery, Free Presbyterian Church, 1987-88; Minister, Associated Presbyterian Churches, Edinburgh, 1989-2000; Moderator, APC General Assembly, 1998-99; Minister, St. Columba's Old Parish Church, Stornoway, 2000-2011; Minister, Parish of Orwell and Portmoak, Kinross-shire, 2011-2021; Convener, Church of Scotland Mission and Discipleship Council, 2005-2009; Church of Scotland Ecumenical Representative on Church of England General Synod, 2016-19; Convener, Gaelic Group, Church of Scotland, 2016-19; President, Scottish Churches Disabilities Group, 2016-19; National Chaplain, Girls' Brigade, Scotland, 2016-19; Trustee, National Prayer Breakfast for Scotland, since 2018; Chair, Novum Trust, since 2014. Contributor, Dictionary of Scottish Church History and Theology, 1993; Contributor, New Dictionary of National Biography; Contributor, Dizionario di Teologia Evangelica, 2007; Editor, Tolerance and Truth. The Spirit of the Age or the Spirit of God?, 2007; Moderator, Presbytery of Lewis, 2003-04; Chaplain to the Lord High Commissioner to the General Assembly of the Church of Scotland, 2005, 2006; Visiting Scholar, Princeton Theological Seminary, July-October 2009. Recreations: reading; walking; music; cycling. Address: (h.) 170 The Murrays, Liberton, Edinburgh, EH17 8UP.
E-mail: angusmorrison3@gmail.com

Morrison, Beth. Founder and Chief Executive Officer, Positive and Active Behaviour Support Scotland (PABSS), since 2016. Educ. Auchterderran High School; University of Abertay Dundee. Career history: Assistant Manager, Blenheim Travel, 1987-97; Personal Travel Advisor, The Co-operative Travel, since 1997; Author and Campaigner, since 2006. Inducted into Outstanding Women of Scotland 2018, The Saltire Society. Address: Birnie Development Centre, Raigmore Hospital, Inverness IV2 3UJ; T.-01463 711180.

Morrison, Colin Andrew, BA, MEd, DipM, FCIM, CertEd, FCIBS. Deputy Chief Executive and Director of Education, Chartered Banker Institute; b. 14.10.61, Ellon; m., Stella Ross Ingram. Educ. Peterhead Academy; Robert Gordon's Institute of Technology; Aberdeen College of Education; Edinburgh University. Former Outdoor Pursuits Instructor and F.E. Lecturer/Senior Lecturer; Head of Business Studies, Stevenson College, 1990-91. Recreation: skiing. Address: (b.) 38b Drumsheugh Gardens, Edinburgh EH3 7SW; T.-0131-473 7777.

Morrison, Professor Jill, MBChB, MSc, PhD, FRCGP, FAcadMed, FRCP, FHEA, DCH, DRCOG. Clerk of Senate and Vice Principal (Academic Services), University of Glasgow, since 2018, Associate (Institute of Health & Wellbeing). Educ. Glasgow University; vocational training in Paisley. Career history: became a GP principal in Bathgate in 1987, then lecturer in Glasgow in 1990, promoted to a personal chair in 2001, Head of the Undergraduate Medical School, 2007-2010, then Dean for Learning and Teaching in the College of Medical, Veterinary and Life Sciences. Chair, West of Scotland Regional ACT Priorities Group, College Honorary Status Committee. Research interests include: primary care management of depression; learning disabilities; medical education and RCTs. Address: University of Glasgow, Senate Office, Level 5, Main Building, Glasgow G12 8QQ; T.-0141 3308744; e-mail: Jill.Morrison@glasgow.ac.uk

Morrison, John Lowrie, OBE. Scottish contemporary artist; b. 1948, Maryhill, Glasgow; m., Maureen; 3 s. Educ. Dowanhill Primary School; Glasgow; Hyndland Prep School, Glasgow; Hyndland Secondary School, Glasgow; Glasgow School of Art. Founded the Jolomo Award in 2007 - the prestigious annual award for Scottish Landscape Painting (the largest arts award in Scotland and the UK's largest privately funded arts award with a prize currently of £25,000 for the winner, and £35,000 for all the prizes). Appointed Officer of the Order of the British Empire (OBE) in the 2011 New Year Honours for services to art and charity in Scotland. Address: Jolomo Ltd, The Jolomo Studio, Tigh-na-Barnashalg, Tayvallich, by Lochgilphead, Argyll PA31 8PN; T.-01546 870303.
E-mail: jolomo@thejolomostudio.com

Morrison, Katrina Croft, MA (Hons), MBA. Marketing and Tourism Consultant; Director, Morrison Glasgow Distillers Ltd; Senior International Manager and other roles, Scottish Enterprise, 1993-2018; Trustee, Royal Botanic Garden Edinburgh, 2005-2013; b. 18.12.59, Aberdeen; m., Colin McLean; 1 s.; 1 d. Educ. Dollar Academy; Aberdeen University. Manager, Blackwell Retail Ltd., 1983-93. Recreations: traditional music and dance; gardening; silversmithing.

Morrison, Dr Lewis, MBChB (Hons) Edin, FRPC (Ed). Chair, BMA Scotland, since 2018. Consultant Physician in Geriatric Medicine, since 2000, current post at Edinburgh Royal Infirmary. Specific interests in Parkinsonian disorders and end of life care. Address: BMA Scotland, 14 Queen Street, Edinburgh EH2 1LL; T-0131 247 3030.

Morrison, Sheriff Nigel Murray Paton, QC. Sheriff of Lothian and Borders at Edinburgh, 1996-2017 (part-time, since 2017); Appeal Sheriff, 2015-17 (part-time, since 2017); Temporary judge of the Court of Session and High Court, 2013-2019; b. 18.3.48, Paisley. Educ. Rannoch School. Called to the Bar of England and Wales, Inner Temple, 1972; admitted to Scottish Bar, 1975; Assistant Editor, Session Cases, 1976-82; Assistant Clerk, Rules Council, 1978-84; Clerk of Faculty, Faculty of Advocates, 1979-86; Standing Junior Counsel to Scottish Development Department (Planning), 1982-86; Temporary Sheriff, 1982-96; Chairman, Social Security Appeal Tribunals, 1982-91; Second (formerly Junior) Counsel to the Lord President of the Court of Session, 1984-89; First Counsel to the Lord President, 1989-96; Counsel to Secretary of State under Private Legislation Procedure (Scotland) Act 1936, 1986-96; QC, 1988; Chairman, Medical Appeal Tribunals, 1991-96; Trustee, National Library of Scotland, 1989-98; Director of Judicial Studies, 2000-04; Vice-President, Sheriffs' Association, 2009-2011, President, 2011-13. Publications: Green's Annotated Rules of the Court of

Session (Principal Editor); Stair Memorial Encyclopaedia of the Laws of Scotland (Contributor); Sentencing Practice (Editor). Recreations: music; riding; Scottish country dancing; being taken by his dogs for walks. Address: 27 Chambers Street, Edinburgh EH1 1LB; T.-0131-225 2525.

Morrison, Peter, MA, LLB. Singer (Baritone) entertainer and former solicitor; b. 14.8.40, Greenock; m., Irene McGrow; 1 s.; 1 d. Educ. Greenock Academy; Glasgow University. Local Authority (Paisley and Clydebank) legal departments, 1965-68; Private legal practice with Torrance Baird and Allan, Solicitors, Glasgow, 1968-77; own legal practice, 1977-96; consultant with Paton Farrell Solicitors, 1996-2000; now an associate with Adie Hunter, Solicitors, Glasgow; 1958 - singing pupil of Cecil Cope and then Marjorie Blakeston; Choral Scholar with Glasgow University Chapel Choir for 5 years; toured English Cathedrals, 1964/65 with choir; principal singer with University Cecilian Society for 6 years and also the University Choral society; started broadcasting with BBC in 1961 as a group singer and later as soloist; auditioned as soloist for BBC in 1967 and solo broadcasts and recitals thereafter; founder member of the John Currie Singers in 1968; first television series for BBC Scotland, 1971, continuing until 1979 and including Show of the North, Castles in the Air, Songs of Scotland, Something to Sing About (for BBC 2), This is Peter Morrison, 1977; other work includes Hogmanay shows, Friday Night is Music Night (radio), 1976-97, concerts in Royal Festival Hall, Albert Hall, Fairfield Halls, The Barbican Centre; television series for Channel 4 (Top Cs and Tiaras), STV and Grampian; innumerable theatre and concert performances in UK and abroad; continues to promote and perform in concert and theatre shows around the country; entertained the Royal Family at public occasions and private parties; many commercial CD recordings; immediate past President, Scottish Showbusiness Benevolent Fund; past Honorary President, Glasgow Phoenix Choir; Honorary President, Arran Music and Drama Club. Recreations: golf; watching rugby, cricket and football; loves working with his children on stage whenever possible; along with wife Irene in thrall to his four grandchildren Peter, Robin, Henrietta and Bertie. E-mail: peterdmorrison@talktalk.net
web: www.petermorrison.net

Morrison, Steve. Scottish television producer; former Rector, University of Edinburgh (2015-18); b. 3.3.47, Glasgow. Educ. University of Edinburgh; National Film and Television School. Career: radio producer with BBC Scotland; joined Granada Television in 1974; formed Granada Film before becoming Director of Programmes, then Chief Executive (2001); co-founded independent TV production and distribution company all3media in 2003, becoming non-executive chairman in 2013. Advisory board of the Edinburgh College of Art. Production credits include My Left Foot, The Field and Jack and Sarah. Instrumental in the formation of the campaign group Third World First, which went on to become the anti-poverty organisation People and Planet. First student to run for Rector of the University of Edinburgh in 1969.

Morrow, Dr Joseph John, CBE, QC, LLD, FRSE. Lord Lyon King of Arms, since 2014. Labour councillor for the Maryfield ward, until 2009 (held the positions of Convenor of the Economic Development Committee, Convenor of the Dundee Waterfront Development Board, and was Depute Lord Provost); Her Majesty's Commissioner for the Mental Welfare Commission for Scotland (1999-2006); President of the Mental Health Tribunal for Scotland (2008-2019); appointed as Vice Lord Lieutenant of the City of Dundee in 2009; President of the Additional Support Needs Tribunals for Scotland (2010-2014); Member, Faculty of Advocates and took silk, 2015; the 108th Grand Master of the Grand Lodge of Scotland, 2004-05; Honorary Squadron Colonel of 32nd Signal Regiment, 2nd (City of Dundee) Signal Squadron. Recreations: ecclesiastical history; rearing rare breed sheep; study of Robert Burns. Address: Court of The Lord Lyon, HM New Register House, Edinburgh EH1 3YT; T.-0131 556 7255.

Morrow, Martin Thomas, LLB (Hons), DipLP, NP. Solicitor Advocate; b. 2.7.64, Glasgow; m., Amanda Catherine; 1 s.; 2 d. Educ. St. Aloysius College, Glasgow; University of Strathclyde. Ian McCarry Solicitors, Glasgow, 1986-88; Levy, McRae, Solicitors, Glasgow, 1988-89; Blackadder, McMonagle, Solicitors, Falkirk, 1990-92; Principal, Milligan Telford and Morrow, Solicitors, since 1992. Member, Council, Law Society of Scotland, 1997-2001. Recreations: golf; tennis. Address: MTM Defence Lawyers Ltd, Campfield House, Falkirk FK1 5RL; T.-01324 633221; e-mail: mmorrow@mtmdefence.co.uk

Morton, Aileen, MA (Eng), MSc (IT). Councillor (Liberal Democrat), Helensburgh Central, 2012-2022; Leader, Argyll and Bute Council, 2017-2020. Educ. Notre Dame High School, Dumbarton; University of Glasgow; Paisley University. Career history: Argyll and Bute Council: Policy Lead - Education, Lifelong Learning & Strategic IT Services, 2013-15.

Morton, Alan. Chief Executive, SecuriGroup, since 2021 (founded the organisation in 1994, Manging Director, since 2008); b. 10.68. Director: Group Contractor Services Limited, since 2008, Group Employment Services Limited, since 2008. Address: SecuriGroup, Glasgow Head Office, 349 Bath Street, Glasgow G2 4AA.

Morton, Rev. Alasdair J., MA, BD, DipEd, DipRE, FEIS. Minister, Bowden linked with Newtown St. Boswells, 1991-2000; b. 8.6.34, Inverness; m., Gillian M. Richards; 2 s.; 2 d. Educ. Bell-Baxter School, Cupar; St. Andrews University; Hartford Theological Seminary. District Missionary/Minister, Zambia (Northern Rhodesia), 1960-65; Chaplain and Religious Education Lecturer, Malcolm Moffat Teachers' College, Serenje, Zambia, 1966-67; Principal, David Livingstone Teachers' College, Livingstone, Zambia, 1968-72; Minister, Greyfriars Parish Church, Dumfries, 1973-77; General Secretary, Department of Education, Church of Scotland, 1977-91. Recreations: choral singing; gardening. Address: 16 St Leonard's Road, Forres IV36 1DW; e-mail: alasgilmor@hotmail.co.uk

Morton, Fiona. Chair, Gillespie Macandrew LLP, since 2017. Educ. University of Edinburgh; Royal Institution of Chartered Surveyors. Career history: Chartered Surveyor, Montagu Evans, Glasgow, 1985-87; Principal Surveyor, Drivers Jonas, Aberdeen, 1987-89; Secondee, Property Finance Group, Royal Bank of Scotland, Edinburgh, 1998-99; Ryden LLP: Associate, Investment, 1989-95, Partner, 1995-2005, Managing Partner, 2005-2011, Chairman, 2011-13; Managing Director, Millar & Bryce Ltd, Edinburgh, 2014-16; Chair of Judging Panel, Scottish Property Awards, 2014-2020. Made regular appearances in the Scottish Business Insider Top 100 Business Leaders, including Business Woman of the Year; frequently chaired major property industry events in Scotland for organisations such as Investment Property Forum, Investment Property Databank, Price Waterhouse Coopers and Urban Land Institute. Address: Gillespie Macandrew, 5 Atholl Crescent, Edinburgh EH3 8EJ; T.-0131 221 6671.

E-mail: fiona.morton@gillespiemacandrew.co.uk

Morton, J. Gavin, CA, CTA. Consultant, Chiene & Tait CA (formerly Chairman, Senior Private Client Partner and Partner). Address: (b.) 61 Dublin Street, Edinburgh EH3 6NL; T.-0131 558 5800.
Web: www.chiene.co.uk

Morton, Earl of (John Stewart Sholto Douglas). Scottish peer and landowner; Partner of Dalmahoy Farms Ltd; President of the Convention of the Baronage of Scotland; b. 17.1.52; m., Amanda Kirsten Mitchell; 3 c. Educ. Dunrobin Castle; North of Scotland Agricultural College. Farming at Backbridge, Malmesbury, 1974-77; Director of Dalmahoy Country Club, 1978. Address: Old Mansion House, Dalmahoy, Kirknewton, Midlothian EH27 8EB.

Morton, 'Uel (Samuel). Non Executive Director: Moredun Research Institute, since 2017, Fane Valley Group, since 2020, Fane Valley Stores Ltd, 2017-2020; Development Director, Scotbeef Ltd, 2017-19; former Chief Executive, Quality Meat Scotland (2006-17); formerly with United Farmers. Address: (b.) Moredun Research Institute, Pentlands Science Park, Bush Loan, Penicuik, Midlothian EH26 0PZ.

Mosson, Alexander Francis, KHS. Lord Provost of the City of Glasgow, 1999-2003; b. 27.8.40, Glasgow; m., Maureen; 4 s.; 3 d. Educ. St Patrick's Primary School; St Patrick's Junior Secondary School; St Mungo's Academy. Served apprenticeship, Barclay Curles boiler shop and Alexander Stephen shipyard, Linthouse, as a plater; worked in insulating industry; then employed as an Industrial Appeals Organiser with British Red Cross Society, Scottish Branch; elected Councillor, 1984; former Deputy Lord Provost; former Vice Convener and Convener, Protective Services Committee; former Vice Convener of Personnel. Officer, Order of St. John, since 2000; Hon. Fellow of the Royal College of Physicians and Surgeons, 2003; Order of St. Christopher of Barga, 2004; Knight of the Holy Sepulchre of Jerusalem, September 2005; Freeman of the City of Bethlehem, 2004; Deputy Lord Lieutenant, 2004. Hon. LLD, Glasgow; Hon. LLD, Glasgow Caledonian; Hon. LLD, Strathclyde. Recreations: reading Scottish and Irish history; painting; watching football. Address: (h.) 1 Danes Drive, Glasgow G14 9HZ; T.-0141954 3360.

Moule, Linda, A. Principal, Erskine Stewart's Melville Schools, Edinburgh, 2018-2022; b. 10.11.58; m.; 2 s. Educ. Leeds, Manchester and Liverpool. Career history: taught Religious Studies in a comprehensive school, Sixth Form Colleges and the independent sector; worked in senior roles in independent schools in the South and South East of England; nine years at the helm of The Mary Erskine School; the first female Principal of the three schools which make up the Erskine Stewart's Melville family of schools known as ESMS.

Mounfield, J. Hilary, OBE, MA (Hons), FRSA. Ambassador, Scottish Epilepsy Centre; Vice-President, Scottish Arts Club; Trustee, Scottish Arts Trust; Chair, Art in Healthcare, 2014-18; Convenor, Dementia Services Development Trust, 2008-2014; Non-Executive Director, National Waiting Times Centre NHS Board, 2003-11; Chief Executive, Epilepsy Scotland, 1995-2005; Chair, European Committee of the International Bureau for Epilepsy, 2001-05; International Ambassador for Epilepsy; b. 19.7.41, Edinburgh; 2 s.; 1 d. Educ. Boroughmuir School; Edinburgh University. Research, Scottish Development Department and Ministry of Housing, 1963-66; teaching, London, 1973-84; fund-raising for charities, 1984-91; Appeals Director,

Penumbra, 1991-95. Chair: ICFM, Scotland, 1993-95, Bighearted Scotland, 1993-96, Joint Epilepsy Council, 1998-2001; Convenor, ACOSVO, 1997-2000; Chair, Voluntary Health Scotland, 2000-03; Founding Fellow, Institute of Contemporary Scotland. Recreations: reading; art; travel. E-mail: hilary.mounfield@blueyonder.co.uk

Mountain, Sir Edward Brian Stanford (4th Baronet). MSP (Scottish Conservative), Highlands and Islands region, since 2016; Deputy Chief Whip; b. 19.3.61. Joined the Blues and Royals regiment of the British Army from Royal Military Academy Sandhurst in October 1981. Caithness, Sutherland and Ross constituency candidate in the 2011 Scottish Parliament election; Inverness, Nairn, Badenoch and Strathspey constituency candidate in the 2015 United Kingdom general election; Inverness and Nairn constituency candidate in the 2016 Scottish Parliament election. Address: Scottish Parliament, Edinburgh EH99 1SP; Regional Office: 10 Drummond Street, Inverness IV1 1QD; T.-01463 230 777/0131 348 6143. E-mail: edward.mountain.msp@scottish.parliament.uk

Muir, Eunice Elizabeth, MBA, FCMI. (Other qualifications RN, RM, ADM.) Executive Coach, since 2019; Chairman, St. Vincent's Hospice Howwood, since 2013; Chairman, Ranfurly Castle Golf Club, since 2021; b. 24.1.57, Greenock; widow. Educ. Greenock High School; Glasgow Caledonian University. Career history: Apprentice Tracer/Draughtsman, John G Kincaid & Co. Ltd, Greenock/Springburn College of Engineering, Glasgow, 1973-1976; Student Nurse, Inverclyde College of Nursing, 1976-1979; Student Midwife, University Hospital of Wales, Cardiff, 1979-1980; Staff Midwife, Paisley Maternity Hospital, 1980-1981; Labour Suite Midwifery Sister, Paisley Maternity Hospital, 1981-1990; Clinical Manager, Royal Alexandra Hospital, 1991-1994; Head of Midwifery/Service Manager, Royal Alexandra Hospital, 1994-1998; Deputy Director of Nursing, Quality & Planning, Falkirk & District Royal Infirmary, 1998-1999; Deputy Director of Nursing & Planning, Forth Valley Acute Hospitals NHS Trust, 1999-2000; Clinical Lead/Risk Management Executive, CNORIS, SEHD/Willis, 2000-2002; Deputy Director of Nursing & Operations, NHS 24, 2002-2004; Executive Nurse Director, NHS 24, 2004-2006; Professional Adviser, NHS Scotland Maternity Telehealth Project (secondment), SEHD/NES, 2006-2007; Interim Nurse Director (secondment), Acute Division, NHSGGC, 2007-2008; Executive Nurse Director, NHS 24, 2008-2012; Clinical eHealth Lead (NMAHP's), The Scottish Government, 2012-16. Director and Vice Chair, Cruse Bereavement Care Scotland, 2003-09; Director, Ranfurly Castle Golf Club, 2003-2010; Director, St. Vincent's Hospice, Renfrewshire, since 2009. Recreations: golf; gym; reading; music. Address: (h.) Nithsdale, Bridge of Weir, Renfrewshire PA11 3AN; T.-07803 609492; e-mail: eemuir@icloud.com

Muir Wood, Professor David, MA, PhD, FREng, FRSE, FICE. Professor of Geotechnical Engineering, University of Dundee, 2009-2014, Emeritus Professor, since 2014; Emeritus Professor of Civil Engineering, University of Bristol, since 2009; Professor affilierad i geoteknik, Chalmers tekniska högskola, Gothenburg, Sweden, since 2014; b. 17.3.49, Folkestone; m., Helen Rosamond Piddington; 2 s. Educ. Royal Grammar School, High Wycombe; Peterhouse, Cambridge. 1973-75: William Stone Research Fellow, Peterhouse, Cambridge; 1975: Royal Society Research Fellow, Norwegian Geotechnical Institute, Oslo; 1975-87: Fellow, Emmanuel College, Cambridge; 1975-78: University Demonstrator, Soil mechanics, Cambridge University Engineering Department; 1978: Geotechnical engineer, Scott, Wilson, Kirkpatrick

and Partners, Hong Kong; 1978-87: University Lecturer, Soil mechanics, Cambridge University Engineering Department; since 1983: Associate, Geotechnical Consulting Group; 1986: Visiting Research Associate, University of Colorado, Boulder; 1987-95: Cormack Prof. of Civil Engineering, Univ. of Glasgow; 1995-96: Royal Society Industry Fellow, Babtie Group, Glasgow; 1995-2009: Prof. of Civil Engineering, Univ. of Bristol; 1997-2002: Head, Department of Civil Engineering, Univ. of Bristol; 2000: MTS Visiting Prof. of Geomechanics, Univ. of Minnesota; 2003: Foundation for Industrial Science Visiting Prof., Institute for Industrial Science, University of Tokyo; 2003-07: Dean, Faculty of Engineering, University of Bristol; 2008: Japan Society for Promotion of Science Visiting Professor, Nagoya Institute of Technology; 2013: Martin Fahey Visiting Professor, Centre for Offshore Foundation Systems, University of Western Australia, Perth; 2014: Visiting Professor, Politecnico di Milano; 2015 Senior Fellow, Technical University, Dresden; 2016 Visiting Professor, University of Innsbruck; 2016 Visiting Professor, University of Western Australia, Perth; JSPS Visiting Professor, Yokohama National University, 2017. Elder, Cairns Church of Scotland, Milngavie, 1993-98; Elder, Church of Scotland, Monikie & Newbigging, Murroes & Tealing, since 2011; Rex Moir Prize (1969); Archibald Denny Prize (1970); British Geotechnical Society Prize (1978); 20th Bjerrum Lecturer, Oslo (2005); Poulos Lecturer, Sydney (2010); 19th Prague Geotechnical Lecturer (2011); 4th Bishop Lecturer, Seoul (2017); Associate Editor, Canadian Geotechnical Journal, since 2002; Member, Smeatonian Society of Civil Engineers, 2011-16. Publications: Books: 'Pressuremeter testing' (Co-Author), 1987; 'Soil behaviour and critical state soil mechanics', 1990; 'Piled foundations in weak rock' (Co-Author), 1999; 'Geotechnical modelling', 2004; 'Soil mechanics: a one-dimensional introduction', 2009; 'Civil engineering: a very short introduction', 2012. Recreations: music; opera; singing; travel; photography. Address: (h.) Kirklands, Kirkton of Monikie, Broughty Ferry, Angus DD5 3QN; T.-01382 370685. E-mail: muirwood@talk21.com

Muldoon, Cllr Cathy. Provost, West Lothian Council, since 2022; representative of Fauldhouse and the Breich Valley (Scottish Labour Party), since 1999; b. 3.63. Director, W L Ventures Group Limited, 2012-2017. Address: West Lothian Civic Centre, Howden South Road, Livingston EH54 6FF; T.-01506 281738. E-mail: Cathy.Muldoon@westlothian.gov.uk

Mulholland, Lord Francis, PC, CBE, QC, LLB (Hons), MBA, DipLP, NP, LLD (Hon). Senator of the College of Justice, since 2016; Member of the Parole Board of Scotland, since 2019; Member of the Upper Tribunal for Asylum and Immigration, since 2018; Lord Advocate, 2011-16; Solicitor General for Scotland, 2007-2011; b. 18.4.59, Coatbridge; m., Lady Marie Elizabeth. Educ. Columba High School, Coatbridge; Aberdeen University; Edinburgh University. Trainee, Bird Semple & Crawford Herron, Solicitors, Glasgow, 1982-84; Procurator Fiscal Depute: Greenock, 1984-87; Glasgow, 1987-91; Solicitor, Crown Office, Edinburgh, 1991-96; Procurator Fiscal Depute, Edinburgh, 1996; Advocate Depute, 1997-99; Assistant Procurator Fiscal, Edinburgh, 1999-2002; Procurator Fiscal, Edinburgh, 2002-03; Senior Advocate Depute, 2003-06; Area Procurator Fiscal, Lothian and Borders, 2006-07. Member of the Privy Council, since 2011; LLD (Honorary), University of Aberdeen, June 2013. Recreations: football; golf; military history.

Mulholland, John. Solicitor and Past President, Law Society of Scotland (2019-20); former Vice President (2017-19). Educ. Strathclyde University. Career history:

criminal defence solicitor and partner based in Glasgow and Falkirk; private practice work included running own firm for almost ten years; joined Marshall Wilson in 2011 as criminal law consultant at Falkirk-based Marshall Wilson Law Group; joined Law Society of Scotland Council in 2012, Chair of the Board; former convener of both the Nominations committee and the Finance Committee and a former member of the Appeals and Reviews Subcommittee.

Mullen, Ian M., OBE, BSc, MRPharmS, DL. Chairman, Hub East Central Scotland, since 2012; Consultant on healthcare and pharmaceutical issues; accredited executive coach; self-employed community pharmacist, since 1971; Chair, Forth Valley NHS Board, 2002-2012; Deputy Lieutenant, Stirling and Falkirk; b. 11.5.46, Stirling; m., Veronica Drummond; 2 s.; 1 d. Educ. St. Modan's High School, Stirling; Heriot-Watt University. Registered MPS, 1970; Chairman, Pharmaceutical General Council (Scotland), 1986-88; Vice-Chairman, National Pharmaceutical Consultative Committee, 1987-89; Member, UK Advisory Committee on Borderline Substances, 1986-89; Vice-Chairman, Forth Valley Health Board, 1989-91; Director, Common Services Agency of the NHS in Scotland, 1991-94, Vice-Chairman, 1993; Director, Central Scotland Chamber of Commerce, 1990-93; Chairman: St. Andrew's School Board, 1990-93, Falkirk and District Royal Infirmary NHS Trust, 1993-99, Scottish NHS Trust Chairmen's Group, 1998-2000, Forth Valley Acute Hospitals NHS Trust, 1999-2002, Scottish NHS Chairmen's Group, 2000-02, Scottish Health Matters (Communications Group), Urban Life Properties Ltd, Serco Health Advisory Board UK & Europe, 2012-13; Serco Non-Executive (Scotland); Director, Scottish Parliament and Business Exchange, 2013-2016. Recreations: walking; golf; watching football. Address: (b.) Robertson House, Castle Business Park, Stirling FK9 4TZ; T.-01786 431627.

Mullen, Professor Thomas John, LLB (Hons), Glasgow, LLM (Harvard). Professor of Law, School of Law, University of Glasgow, since 2004; b. 26.01.59, Glasgow; m., Christine Hamilton; 1 s.; 1 d. Educ. St. Aloysius College, Glasgow; University of Glasgow; Harvard Law School. Legal Apprentice, Hughes Dowdall & Co, Glasgow, 1981-83; Solicitor (Scotland), since 1984; University of Glasgow: Lecturer in Public Law, 1983-92, Senior Lecturer in Public Law, 1992-2003. Special Adviser to House of Commons Select Committee on Scottish Affairs, 1996-97. Publications: Judicial Review in Scotland (Co-Author), 1996; Public Law in Scotland, eds (Co-Author), 2006. Recreations: reading; running; tennis; cooking. Address: (b.) School of Law, University of Glasgow G12 8QQ; T.-0141 330 4179; e-mail: tom.mullen@glasgow.ac.uk

Mulligan, Margaret Mary, BA (Hons). MSP (Labour), Linlithgow, 1999-2011; Shadow Minister for Housing and Communities, 2008-2011; Deputy Minister for Communities, 2003-04; Convenor, Education, Culture and Sport Committee, 1999-2001; b. 12.2.60, Liverpool; m., John; 2 s.; 1 d. Educ. Notre Dame High School; Manchester University. Retail and personnel management, 1981-86; Councillor, Edinburgh District Council, 1988-95 (Chair of Housing, 1992-97); Councillor, City of Edinburgh Council, 1995-99. Recreations: music; theatre; reading.

Mullin, Roger, MA (Hons). MP (SNP), Kirkcaldy and Cowdenbeath, 2015-17; Founding Director, Momentous Change Ltd; appointed Special Envoy for the All Party Parliamentary Group on Explosive Threats in 2017; b. 12.3.48; m., Barbara. Educ. University of Edinburgh. Honorary Professor, University of Stirling (teaches postgraduates Applied Decision Theory, The Political Environment, and Organisation Change); undertaken many international assignments for the United Nations and governments in many parts of the world; former columnist for The Times Educational Supplement Scotland; freelanced as an education consultant; wide range of publications in the fields of Decision Making, Education, Leadership and Politics; former SNP Vice Convener. Address: Momentous Change Ltd, Unit G6 Granary Business Centre, Coal Road, Cupar KY15 5YQ.

Mumford, Colin John, BMedSci, DM, FRCP(E), DIMCRCS(Ed). Consultant Neurologist, Royal Infirmary of Edinburgh, since 1996; b. 24.11.59, Liverpool. Educ. St. Margaret's High School, Liverpool; Nottingham University Medical School. Senior House Officer in Medicine, Newcastle upon Tyne teaching hospitals; Registrar in Neurology, Queen's Medical Centre, Nottingham and National Hospital for Neurology, London; Research Fellow, University of Cambridge; Senior Registrar in Neurology, Edinburgh teaching hospitals. Recreations: hillwalking; motorcycling. Address: (b.) Department of Clinical Neurosciences, 50 Little France Crescent, Edinburgh BioQuarter, Edinburgh EH16 4TJ; T.-0131 312 0695.

Mundell, Rt. Hon. David Gordon, LLB (Hons), MBA. MP (Conservative), Dumfriesshire, Clydesdale and Tweeddale, since 2005; UK Trade Envoy to New Zealand, since 2021; Secretary of State for Scotland, 2015-19; Parliamentary Under-Secretary of State for Scotland, 2010-2015; Chairman, Scottish Conservative and Unionist Party, 2007-08 and 2011-13; Shadow Secretary of State for Scotland, 2005-10; MSP (C), South of Scotland, 1999-2005; b. 27.5.62, Dumfries; m., Lynda Carmichael (divorced); 2 s.; 1 d. Educ. Lockerbie Academy; Edinburgh University; Strathclyde University. Trainee Solicitor, Tindal Oatts, Glasgow, 1987-87; Solicitor, Maxwell Waddell, Glasgow, 1987-89; Commercial Lawyer, Biggart Baillie, Glasgow, 1989-91; Group Legal Adviser Scotland, BT, 1991-98; Head of National Affairs, BT Scotland, 1998-99. Recreations: family pursuits; travel. Address: House of Commons, London SW1A 0AA; T.-020 7219 4895.
E-mail: david@davidmundell.com

Mundell, John Weir, OBE. Interim Chief Executive, Orkney Islands Council, since 2019; Local Government and Business Consultant; Solace in Business Associate, APSE Solutions Associate, since 2016; former Chief Executive, Inverclyde Council (2006-2016); formerly Corporate Director – Environment, East Dunbartonshire Council; b. Edinburgh; m., Karen; 3 s. Educ. Currie High School; Heriot-Watt University. Entered local government, 1974 (City of Edinburgh Corporation, then Commercial Manager, Lothian Regional Council); Head of Central Contracts, Central Regional Council, 1994-95. Recreations: karate; farming.

Mundell, Oliver Gordon Watson. MSP (Scottish Conservative), Dumfriesshire, since 2016; Shadow Cabinet Secretary for Education and Skills, since 2021; b. 1.12.89, Irvine; m., Catherine. Educ. Moffat Academy; University of Edinburgh. Career history: worked for multinational oil and gas firm Royal Dutch Shell; senior parliamentary aide to Geoffrey Cox QC MP in the UK Parliament; co-ordinated the local Better Together campaign across Dumfries and Galloway on behalf of the Conservative Party in the run up to the Independence Referendum; played a key role in a number of local election campaigns. Recreations: keen swimmer and enjoys relaxing in front of a good film. Address: Scottish Parliament, Edinburgh EH99 1SP.

Munn, Professor Pamela, OBE, AcSS, MA, MLitt, CertEd. Emeritus Professor of Curriculum Research, University of Edinburgh, since 2010; formerly Dean, Moray House School of Education; b. 31.3.49, Glasgow; m., Graham Hamilton Munn. Educ. Hermitage School, Helensburgh; Aberdeen University. Teacher of History, 1972-78; Research Fellow, Stirling University, 1979-84; Lecturer in Applied Research in Education, York University, 1984-86; Senior Research Officer, then Depute Director, Scottish Council for Research in Education, 1986-94; Professor of Curriculum Research, Moray House Institute of Education, 1994-98. Member, Scottish Consultative Council on the Curriculum; Fellowship, CIDREE, 1996; SCRE Silver Medal, 1984; Fellowship, SCRE, 2002; Fellow, Society for Educational Studies, 2012; Chair, Education for Citizenship Review Group; Member, Discipline Task Group, Review of Initial Teacher Education Group; President, British Educational Research Association, 2007-09; Honorary Member, SERA, 2012; Convenor, Appeal Board, GTCS, 2012-2017. Publications: The Changing Face of Education 14-16; Education in Scotland: policy and practice from pre-school to secondary, 1997; Parents and Schools: customers, managers or partners?, 1993; Alternatives to Exclusion from School, 2000. Recreations: hill-walking; gardening; reading, especially crime fiction. Address: (b.) Simon Laurie House, School of Education, University of Edinburgh, Holyrood Road, Edinburgh EH8 8AQ.

Munro of Foulis, Hector William, MRICS. 31st Chief of Clan Munro; b. 20.2.50; m., Sarah Duckworth; 1 s.; 2 d. Educ. Oratory School; Royal Agricultural College, Cirencester. Farmer and Chartered Surveyor. Address: (h.) Foulis Mains, Evanton, Ross-shire.

Munro, Professor Colin Roy, BA, LLB. Emeritus Professor, scholar and teacher; Visiting Professor: Institute of Law (Jersey), University of London (International Programmes); Professor of Constitutional Law, Edinburgh University, 1990-2009 (Dean, Faculty of Law, 1992-94); b. 17.5.49, Aberdeen; m., Ruth Elizabeth Pratt; 1 s.; 1 d. Educ. Aberdeen Grammar School; Aberdeen University. Lecturer in Law, Birmingham University, 1971-72, Durham University, 1972-80; Senior Lecturer in Law, then Reader in Law, Essex University, 1980-85; Professor of Law, Manchester University, 1985-90; Chief Examiner, London University LLB (External) Degree, 1991-97; Member, Consultative Council, British Board of Film Classification, 2000-2011; Member, Advertising Advisory Committee, 2005-09. Publications: Television, Censorship and the Law; Studies in Constitutional Law; Devolution and the Scotland Bill (Co-author); The Scotland Act 1998 (Co-author). Recreations: sport; cinema and theatre; real ale. Address: (b.) School of Law, Old College, South Bridge, Edinburgh EH8 9YL.

Munro, Professor David Mackenzie, MBE, BSc, PhD, FRGS, FRSA, FSAScot. Geographical Consultant; Member, Scientific and Technical Committee, Prince Albert II of Monaco Foundation, since 2009; Patron, Wild Camel Protection Foundation, since 2008; Honorary President, Kinross-shire Civic Trust, since 2007; Director and Secretary, Royal Scottish Geographical Society, 1996-2008; Honorary Professor, Dundee University, since 2007; Member, Council, National Trust for Scotland, 1995-2008; Chairman, Permanent Committee on Geographical Names for British Official Use, 1999-2009; Chairman, UK Division of United Nations Group of Experts on Geographical Names, 1999-2009; b. 28.5.50, Glasgow.

Educ. Daniel Stewart's College; Edinburgh Academy; Edinburgh University. Research Associate, then Research Fellow, Edinburgh University, 1979-96; Leader/Co Leader, Edinburgh University expeditions to Central America, 1981, 1986, 1988, 1991. Chairman, Michael Bruce Trust; Honorary President, Jules Verne Film Festival, Paris, 2001; Vice-President, 8th UN Conference on the Standardization of Geographical Names, 2002; Scotia Centenary Medal, 2005; Chairman, South Georgia Heritage Trust, 2006; Business Committee, General Council, University of Edinburgh, 2012-20. MBE, 2008; Knight Officer of the Order of St Charles of Monaco, 2015; Patron, Haywards Heath Sinfonietta, since 2015. Publications: Chambers World Gazetteer (Editor); Oxford Dictionary of the World (Editor); Gazetteer of the Baltic States; A World Record of Major Conflict Areas; Loch Leven and the River Leven – a Landscape Transformed; Consultant, Times Atlas of the World; Scotland: an Encyclopedia of Places and Landscapes; numerous articles and reports on land use in Central America. Recreations: walking; travel; exploring landscapes. Address: (h.) Rose Cottage, The Cobbles, Kinnesswood, Kinross KY13 9HL; T.-01592-840-203; e-mail: davidmunro@kinaskit.co.uk

Munro, Dr Donnie, DA (Hons), PGCSE, Hon FRIAS. Director of Development, Fundraising and the Arts, Sabhal Mòr Ostaig UHI-The National Centre for the Gaelic Language, Culture and the Arts; Chairman of Tobar an Dualchais - Kist o Riches - National Cultural Heritage Conservation and Digitisation Programme; Director of Sabhal Mòr Ostaig Developments Ltd; Director of Canan Alba Ltd; Patron of the Scottish Child Psychotherapy Trust; Patron of Skye Dance, Visual Artist; Singer-songwriter and former Lead Singer of Scottish Rock Band, Runrig; b. 2.8.53, Uig, Skye; m.; 4 children, 4 grandchildren. Former Teacher of Art and Design, Inverness Royal Academy, Leith Academy and Tynecastle High School, Edinburgh; Rector of Edinburgh University and Chair of the University Court and General Council, 1991-94; First Rector of the University of the Highlands and Islands (UHI) and Chairman of UHI Foundation, 1997-2000; Member of the Board of the St Columba Centre, Islay; Former Chair of CLP and Scottish Labour Party Spokesperson on Highlands and Islands and Gaelic; Member of the Ministerial Advisory Committee on The National Cultural Strategy, 1999; contested (Labour) Ross, Skye and Inverness West, 1997 & 1999. Dr. Honoris Causa, Edinburgh, 1994. Former Guest Columnist with: The Scotsman, Glasgow Herald, Glasgow Evening Times, The Press and Journal, The Guardian, and the West Highland Free Press. Delivered the Sabhal Mor Ostaig Annual Televised Lecture-'Dreams from Hard Places' 1996. Won Album of the Year in the Scottish TradMusic Awards, 2006 (solo studio album, 'Heart of America'); and inducted into Scottish Trads Music Hall of Fame.

Munro, Iain. Chief Executive, Creative Scotland, since 2019 (appointed Deputy Chief Executive in 2013). Career history: music study before diversifying into Economics and Surveying, becoming a specialist in Cultural Development and working internationally before returning to the UK to help establish the National Lottery for the arts; formerly Co-Director of Arts, Scottish Arts Council before joining Creative Scotland in 2010 as Director of Creative Development, appointed Acting Chief Executive for 6 months in 2013. Member, Management Board of the National Lottery; National Lottery Awards Judge. Address: Creative Scotland, Waverley Gate, 2-4 Waterloo Place, Edinburgh EH1 3EG; T.-0131 523 0027. E-mail: Iain.Munro@creativescotland.com

Munro, Ian, BA (Hons) Zoology, PGCE (Biol), FSB. Rector, Dollar Academy, since 2019; b. 1981. Educ. George

Heriot's School; Royal Zoological Society of Scotland; University of Edinburgh; University of Cambridge. Teacher of Biology: George Heriot's School, 2005, Gordonstoun School, 2006; George Heriot's School: Director of Rowing & Teacher of Biology, 2006-2010, Head of Extracurricular Activities, Head of Year & International Service Coordinator, 2007-2010; Head of Biology, Gordonstoun School, 2010-2013; Deputy Headmaster, Shiplake College, 2013-16; Headmaster, Kelvinside Academy, 2016-19. Address: (b.) Dollar Academy, Dollar FK14 7DU.

Munro, Jean Mary, BA (Hons), PhD. Vice President, Society of Antiquaries of Scotland, 2002-05; Chairman, Council, Scottish History Society, 1989-93; b. 2.12.23; m., Robert William Munro. Educ. London University; Edinburgh University. WRNS, 1944-47; freelance historical researcher; Member, Council, National Trust for Scotland, 1964-69 and 1987-92 (Executive, 1968-80); Chairman, Council, Scottish Genealogy Society, 1983-86 (Vice-President, since 1987); Chairman, Council, Scottish Local History Forum, 1984-88. Publications (as Jean Dunlop): the British Fisheries Society; the Clan Chisholm; the Clan Mackenzie; the Clan Gordon; the Scotts; the Clan Mackintosh; (as Jean Munro): ed texts for the Scottish Record Society; (with R.W. Munro): Tain through the Centuries; The Scrimgeours; The Acts of the Lords of the Isles. Recreations: reading; walking. Address: Grianach, Nethy Bridge, Highland PH25 3DR.

Munro, Nicola Susan, CB, BA; b. 11.01.48, Hitchin; m., Graeme Munro; 1 s.; 1 d. Educ. Harrogate Grammar School; Warwick University. Scottish Office posts dealing with health, civil and criminal justice, museums, special needs and human resources, 1970-85; Head of Specialist Hospital Services and Food Division, Scottish Office, 1985-89; Head of Urban Regeneration and Local Economic Development, 1989-92; Head of Curriculum, Testing and Careers Division, 1992-95; Head of Public Health Policy Unit, Scottish Executive, 1995-2000; Head of Environment Group, Scottish Executive, 2000-01; Head of Scottish Development Department, Scottish Government, 2001-07. Consumer Advisory Panel, Office of Rail Regulator, Member; Board Member: Consumer Futures Scotland, 2008-2014, Scottish Refugee Council, 2008-2015, Scottish Wildlife Trust, 2015-2021. Recreations: travel; family; theatre and art. T.-0131 556 3201.
E-mail: gandnmunro@hotmail.com

Muqit, Professor Miratul Mohamid Khan, FRSE, FRCP. Professor of Experimental Neurology and Wellcome Trust Senior Clinical Fellow, University of Dundee, since 2013; Hon. Consultant Neurologist, Ninewells Hospital, since 2011; b. 12.10.73, Glasgow. m. (2006), Panna Maieda Hussain; 2 s.; 1 d. Educ. Glasgow Academy (War Memorial Scholar); Univ. of Edinburgh (BSc Hons 1995, MB, ChB Hons 1997); Harvard Univ., 2000-2001 (Kennedy Scholar); University College London (PhD 2007); MRCP 2000, FRCP 2016. House Officer, Royal Inf. of Edinburgh, 1997-98; Sen. House Officer, 1998-2000 (Brompton Hosp., Charing Cross Hosp., Hammersmith Hosp., Whittington Hosp.); Visiting Res. Fellow, Brigham & Women's Hospital, Boston, 2000-2001; MRC Training Fellow, UCL Inst. of Neurology, 2001-2004; Specialist Registrar (Neurol.), 2004-2008, Royal London & Barts. Hosp., Natl. Hosp. for Neurol. and Neurosurgery, King's Coll. Hosp., Hurstwood Park Neurol. Hosp.; Wellcome Intermediate Fellow & Sen. Lecturer in Neurology, 2008-2013, MRC Protein Phosphorylation Unit, University of Dundee. Awards: Queen Square Prize in Neurol., 2006; Linacre Prize Lecture of Royal College of Physicians (RCP), 2013; EMBO Young Investigator Award, 2017; Graham Bull Prize and Goulstonian Lecture of RCP, 2018; Royal Society Francis Crick Medal and Lecture, 2018; Elected Fellow of Royal Society of Edinburgh (FRSE), 2020. Address: Medical Research Council Protein Phosphorylation and Ubiquitylation Unit, University of Dundee, Sir James Black Centre, School of Life Sciences, University of Dundee, Dundee DD1 5EH; T.-01382 388377.
E-mail: m.muqit@dundee.ac.uk

Murdoch, Professor Brian Oliver, BA, PhD, LittD, FRHistS, AMusTCL. Professor of German, Stirling University, since 1991; Emeritus, 2007; b. 26.6.44, London; m., Ursula Irene Riffer; 1 s.; 1 d. Educ. Sir George Monoux Grammar School, London; Exeter University; Jesus College, Cambridge. Lecturer in German, Glasgow University; Assistant/Associate Professor of German, University of Illinois; Lecturer/Senior Lecturer in German, Stirling University; Visiting Fellow, Trinity Hall, Cambridge, 1989; Visiting Fellow and Waynflete Lecturer, Magdalen College, Oxford, 1994; Hulsean Lecturer in Divinity, University of Cambridge, 1997-98; Speaker's Lecturer in Biblical Studies, and Visiting Fellow of Oriel College, University of Oxford, 2000-02; author of a number of books and articles on medieval German and Celtic literature, also on literature of the World Wars. Recreations: jazz; numismatics; books. Address: 4 St James Orchard, Stirling FK9 5NQ.

Murdoch, Helen Elliot, MBA, FCIH, MRICS, ACIPD. Chief Executive, Hanover (Scotland) Housing Association Ltd., 2007-2021 (retired), Director, Housing & Care Services, 1995-2007; m., John Murdoch; 1 s. Professional Housing Management Trainee and other senior posts with SSHA (Scottish Special Housing Association), 1974-85; Area Housing Manager, Dunfermline District Council, 1985-95. Chartered Surveyor; Member, various Scottish Government Working Parties; particular interest and experience in Strategic Management, Management of Change and Organisational Culture. Recreations: running; hill-walking; art.

Murdoch, Rev Iain Campbell, MA, LLB, DipEd, BD. Retired Minister, Cambusnethan Old and Morningside Parish Church, Wishaw (1995-2017); Locum Minister, Shotts Calderhead Erskine, since 2017, Interim Moderator; b. 16.10.50, Glasgow; m., Elizabeth Gibson (deceased); 1 s.; 1 d. Educ. Larchfield School, Helensburgh; Haileybury College, Hertford; Trinity College, Oxford; University of Edinburgh. Legal Apprentice, Simpson & Marwick WS, 1973-74; Economics Teacher, Brighton College, 1976-77; PT History, Keil School, 1977-79; Principal Teacher, General Studies, Rossall School, Fleetwood, 1979-89; Assistant Minister, Duddingston Kirk, Edinburgh, 1992-94; Founder Member and Present Advisor, MADE4U in ML2 (a charitable company making a difference in Wishaw), Chair of Board of Trustees, since 2018; Parliamentary Candidate, SDP/Liberal Alliance, Wyre, 1983 and 1987; successful petitioner to Scottish Parliament, 2001-03; Member, Church of Scotland Church and Society Council, 2010-14. Recreations: hill walking; being a grandad.

Murdoch, Professor Jim, CBE, MA, LLM. Professor of Public Law, Glasgow University, since 1998; b. 26.6.55, Hamilton. Educ. Strathaven Academy; Hutcheson's Grammar School; Glasgow University; University of California at Berkeley; Open University. Solicitor; Glasgow University: Lecturer; Senior Lecturer; Visiting Professor: University of Mainz; University of Hamburg; University of Freiburg; University of Paris Ouest; Council of Europe, Strasbourg: Professor Stagiere; long term consultant; Pro Merito medal, Council of Europe, 2012; European Award for Excellence in Teaching in the Social Sciences and Humanities, 2016. Publications: Reed and Murdoch, Human Rights Law in Scotland (4th Edition), 2017; The Protection of Liberty and Security of Person (2nd Edition), 2002; The Treatment of Prisoners:

European Standards, 2006. Recreations; hill walking; foreign travel. Address: (b.) School of Law, Glasgow University, Glasgow G12; T.-0141-330 4178.

Murison, Alison. Head Teacher, Aberdeen Grammar School, since 2015. First female Head Teacher in the school's 759 year history. Former Head Teacher, Hazelhead Academy (2009-2015). Address: Aberdeen Grammar School, Skene Street, Aberdeen AB10 1HT; T.-01224 642299.

Murning, Lt. Col. Ian Henry, TD, LLB (Hons), LLM, DPA, FRICS, MInstRE. Principal, Murning Associates, Chartered Surveyors and Property Consultants, since 1994; Visiting Professor, Edinburgh Napier University, School of Engineering and the Built Environment, 2012-2017; Honorary Secretary, Royal Institution of Chartered Surveyors in Scotland, 2006-2012; Member, Investigation and Professional Conduct Enforcement Committee, Institute of Chartered Accountants of Scotland, 2007-2013; Board Member, Scottish Funding Council for Further and Higher Education, 2005-2011; Board Member, Scottish Further Education Funding Council, 2003-05; Member, Homeowners Housing Panel, 2012-16; Member, Private Rented Housing Panel, 2012-16; Chairman, Capital Investment Committee, Scottish Funding Council, 2003-09; Programme Director, Napier University, 1994-2007; b. 24.12.43, Chapelhall; m., Seona Jean Meiklejon; 1 s.; 2 d. Educ. Dalziel High School; Glasgow University; College of Estate Management; London University; Edinburgh University. Valuer, Stirling Valuation Office, Highlands and Islands; Office of Chief Valuer (Scotland); District Valuer, Dumfries and Galloway, 1988-94. Chairman, Royal Institution of Chartered Surveyors in Scotland, 1995-96; Member, General Council, Royal Institution of Chartered Surveyors, 1994-96; Commander, Royal Engineers (National Defence), Army HQ Scotland, 1991-95; Commander, District Specialist Training Team, Army HQ Scotland, 1996-97; served with 52(L) Div/Dist Engrs (TA), 1963-67, Royal Monmouthshire Royal Engineers (Militia), 1967-68, 71 (Scottish) Engineer Regt (V), 1968-74; 12 Engr Bde, 1984-86, Member: Society of High Constables of Edinburgh, 1993-2012, Merchant Company of Edinburgh, 1995; Freeman, Honourable Company of Air Pilots, 2014; Military Member, The Reserve Forces and Cadets Association for the Lowlands of Scotland, 1997; Governor, George Watson's College, 2000-09; Chairman, UNIFI Scotland, 2009-2012. Chairman, Scottish Civil Service Flying Club, 2009-2017; Director and Secretary, RAF Leuchars Flying Club, 2011-2014; Non-Trustee Member, Air Pilots Benevolent Fund, since 2016; Liveryman, Honourable Company of Air Pilots, 2018. Admitted to the Freedom, City of London, 18 June 2018. Address: (b.) 21 Redhall House Avenue, Edinburgh EH14 1JJ; T.-0131-443 8839; e-mail: ianmurning@hotmail.com

Murphy, Jim. MP (Labour), East Renfrewshire (formerly Eastwood), 1997-2015; Leader of the Scottish Labour Party, 2014-15; Shadow Secretary of State for International Development, 2013-14; Shadow Defence Secretary, 2010-13; Secretary of State for Scotland, 2008-10; Minister for Europe, 2007-08; b. 23.8.67, Glasgow; m.; 3 c. Educ. Bellarmine Secondary School, Glasgow; Milnerton High School, Cape Town. National President, National Union of Students, 1994-96; Special Projects Manager, Scottish Labour Party, 1996-97; PPS to Helen Liddell (Secretary of State for Scotland), 2001-02; Assistant Government Whip, 2002-05; Parliamentary Secretary, Cabinet Office, 2005-06; Minister of State for Employment and Welfare Reform, 2006-07. Recreations: football; cinema; reading.

Murphy, Peter Alexander, MA, MEd. Rector, Whitfield High School, Dundee, 1976-93; b. 5.10.32, Aberdeen; m., Margaret Christie; 3 s.; 1 d. Educ. Aberdeen Grammar School; Aberdeen University. Assistant Principal Teacher of English, Aberdeen Grammar School, 1963-65; Principal

Teacher of English, Summerhill Academy, Aberdeen, 1965-71; Head Teacher, Logie Secondary School, Dundee, 1971-76; Labour Councillor (Carnoustie & District), Angus Council, 1999-2012 and Depute Provost of Angus, 2007-2012. Publications: Life and Times of Logie School (Co-Author); The Life of R.F. MacKenzie (A Prophet without Honour), 1999. Address: Ashlea, 44 Burnside Street, Carnoustie, Angus DD7 7HL.

Murphy, Sheriff Sean Francis, QC, MA (Hons), LLB, DipLP, PGCE. Sheriff of Glasgow and Strathkelvin, since 2007; b. 17.07.58, Glasgow; m., Honor; 1 s.; 2 d. Educ. St Aloysius College, Glasgow; University of St Andrews; Strathclyde University; Christ's and Notre Dame College of Education, Liverpool. Assistant Master of History, St Edmund Campion Upper School, Oxford, 1981-83 and St. Augustine's Upper School, Oxford, 1983-86; Messrs Ross Harper and Murphy, Glasgow: Trainee Solicitor, 1989-91, Court Assistant Solicitor, 1991; Visiting Lecturer in Law, Glasgow College of Technology, 1988-90; Advocate, 1992; Advocate Depute, 1991-2001; Standing Junior Counsel to the Scottish Executive, 2001-03; QC, 2003; Senior Advocate Depute, 2003-07. Secretary, Faculty of Advocates Criminal Lawyers Group, 1997-99; Committee Member, Scottish Medico-Legal Council, since 2006; Chairman, Glenmarnock Wheelers CC, 1994-2004. Recreations: cycling; reading; listening to radio drama and sitting patiently at Firhill. Address: (b.) Sheriff Court of Glasgow and Strathkelvin, 1 Carlton Place, Glasgow G5 9DA; T.-0141 429 8888. E-mail: sheriffsmurphy@scotcourts.gov.uk

Murray, (Bridget) Jane, BA (Oxon), MA, PhD. Commissioner, Royal Commission on the Ancient and Historical Monuments of Scotland, 1999-2009; Chair, The Whithorn Trust, 2005-08; b. 25.7.37, Tunbridge Wells; m., John Murray, QC (Lord Dervaird); 3 s. Educ. Royal Tunbridge Wells County Grammar School for Girls; St Hugh's College, Oxford; Edinburgh University. Involved in various archaeological projects and organisations. Recreations: gardening; walking; architecture. Address: (h.) 18/2 Coates Crescent, Edinburgh EH3 7AF; Auchenmalg House, Auchenmalg, Glenluce, Newton Stewart DG8 0JS.

Murray, Des. Chief Executive, North Lanarkshire Council, since 2018. Career history: Principal Advisor, APSE, 1998-2006; Business Development Manager, South Lanarkshire Council, 2006-2011; Property Services Manager, NLC, 2011-14; North Lanarkshire Council: Head of Housing Property, 2014-16, Assistant Chief Executive (Enterprise and Housing), 2016-18. Address: North Lanarkshire Council, PO Box 14, Civic Centre, Motherwell ML1 1TW; T.-01698 403200.

Murray, Sir David Edward (Kt 2007). Chairman, Murray Capital Limited; Founder, The Murray Foundation, 1996; Queen's Award for Voluntary Service, November 2006; b. 14.10.51, Ayr; 2 s. Educ. Fettes College; Broughton High School. Young Scottish Businessman of the Year, 1984; Hon. Doctorate, Heriot-Watt University, 1986; Hon. Doctorate, University of Edinburgh, 2008; Chairman, UK 2000 (Scotland), 1987; Governor, Clifton Hall School, 1987. Recreations: sports sponsorship; collecting and producing wine, Chevaliers du Tastevin - Clos de Vougeot, November 2006. Address: (b.) 26 Charlotte Square, Edinburgh EH2 4ET.

Murray, Diana Mary, CBE, MA (Cantab), FRSE, FRSGS, FSA, HonFSAScot, MCIFA, MIoD. Chief Executive, Royal

Commission on the Ancient and Historical Monuments of Scotland (RCAHMS) (2004-2015) and Historic Scotland (2013-2015); Honorary Fellow of the School of History, Classics and Archaeology, Edinburgh University; b. 14.9.52, Birmingham; m., Robin F. Murray; 2 d. Educ. King Edward VI Camp Hill School for Girls, Birmingham; New Hall, Cambridge. RCAHMS: Research Assistant, 1976-83, Head of Recording Section, 1983-90, Curator, Archaeology Record, 1990-95, Curator Depute, National Monuments Record of Scotland (NMRS), 1995-2004. Chairman, Institute of Field Archaeologists, 1995-96; Board Member: National Trust for Scotland, 2008-2014, Scottish Waterways Trust, 2012-18, Scottish Seabird Centre, Royal Botanic Gardens of Edinburgh, 2013-21, Scottish International Education Trust; Chair, Arts and Business Scotland; Chair, Scottish Association for Marine Science (SAMS). Recreations: choral singing; gardening. Address: (b) The Rowans, 15 Manse Road, Dirleton EH39 5EL. E-mail: diana.murray@rowanberry.co.uk

Murray, Duncan Law, LLB (Hons). Sheriff Principal, North Strathclyde, since 2014; part time Sheriff, 2006-2014; b. 5.5.59; m., Ianthe Elizabeth Lee Craig; 2 s.; 1 d. Educ. Aberdeen Grammar School; Aberdeen University. Robson McLean Paterson: apprentice, 1980-82; Assistant, 1982-85; Partner, Robson McLean, 1985-2002; Partner, Morton Fraser, 2002-2014. President, Law Society of Scotland, 2004-05. Recreations: golf; ski-ing; hill-walking; family. Club: Luffness New Golf.

Murray, Cllr Elaine Kildare, BSc (Hons), PhD. Leader, Dumfries and Galloway Council, since 2017; (elected to the Nith ward in 2017 and was elected the Group Leader of Labour in the council); former MSP (Labour), Dumfriesshire (2011-16), Dumfries (1999-2011); former Shadow Minister, Community Safety & Legal Affairs; former Vice Convenor, Justice Committee; Shadow Minister for Housing and Transport, 2011-13; Shadow Minister for Environment, 2008-2011; Shadow Minister for Enterprise, 2007-08; Vice Convener, Finance Committee, 2007-08; Deputy Minister for Tourism, Culture and Sport, 2001-03; b. 22.12.54, Hitchin, Herts; m., Jeff Leaver; 2 s.; 1 d. Educ. Mary Erskine School, Edinburgh; Edinburgh University; Cambridge University. Postdoctoral Research Fellow: Cavendish Laboratory, Cambridge, Royal Free Hospital, London; Senior Scientific Officer, Institute of Food Research, Reading; Associate Lecturer, Open University in Scotland. Recreations: family activities; reading; cooking; music. Address: Dumfries & Galloway Council, English Street, Dumfries DG1 2DD; T.-030 33 33 3000.

Murray, Elma, OBE. Interim Chair of the Accounts Commission, since 2020. Career history: Chief Executive, North Ayrshire Council, 2009-2018; Chair, SOLACE, 2014; Deputy Chair of the Accounts Commission, 2019-2020. Chair of Young Scot; Board member, SRUC. Address: Audit Scotland, Head office, 4th Floor, 102 West Port, Edinburgh EH3 9DN; T.-0131 625 1500.

Murray, Euan, LLB (Hons). Partner, Shepherd and Wedderburn, since 2021. Educ. University of Aberdeen. Career history: Brodies LLP: Trainee, 2003-05, Solicitor, 2005-07; Secondment, Wind Energy (Services) Limited, 2009-2010; Solicitor (on secondment), SP Energy Networks, 2016-17; Shepherd and Wedderburn: Solicitor, 2007-2011, Associate, 2011-15, Senior Associate, 2015-2020, Director, 2019-2020; Energy Construction and Procurement Solicitor, SP Energy Networks, 2020-21. Address: Shepherd and

Wedderburn, Edinburgh Office, 1 Exchange Crescent, Conference Square, Edinburgh EH3 8UL; T.-0131 228 9900.

Murray, Professor Gordon Cameron, BSc, BArch, MCIArb, RIBA, RTPI, PPRIAS. Partner, Ryder Architecture, 2012-2021 (retired); Founding Principal, Gordon Murray Architects, 2010-12; Professor of Architecture, University of Strathclyde, 2007-2015; Visiting Professor, since 2016; b. 26.7.52; m., Sharon Boyle; 2 d. Educ. University of Strathclyde. Assistant Architect: Richard Moira, Betty Moira & James Wann, 1974; Department of Architecture and Related Services, 1975-76; Project Architect, Sinclair and Watt Architects, 1977-79; Senior Architect/Partner, Cunningham Glass Murray Architects, 1979-84; Partner, Glass Murray Architects, 1984-99; Founding Principal, gm and ad architects, 1999-2010. External Examiner: University of Ulster, 2004-09, University of Bath, 2012-15, University of Manchester since 2015, University of Dundee, since 2016. President: Glasgow Inst. of Architects, 1998-2000; RIAS, 2003-05. Member, Board, Lighthouse Trust, 2003-09; Chair, Technologies Excellence Group - Curriculum for Excellence, 2009-10; Chair, Standing Council of Heads of UK Schools of Architecture, 2010-12.

Murray, Gordon Lindsay Kevan. Consultant, Murray Snell WS, Solicitors; former Partner; Secretary, Royal Scottish National Orchestra Society Ltd.; Director, 1990-93, Secretary and Treasurer, The RSNO Foundation; b. 23.5.53, Glasgow; m., Susan Patricia; 1 s.; 3 d. Educ. Lenzie Academy; Edinburgh University. Address: (b.) 40 Castle Street, Edinburgh EH2 3BN; T.-0131-625 6625; e-mail: mail@murraysnell.com

Murray, Sheriff Gregor Kenneth, LLP, DipLP. Sheriff: Dundee Sheriff Court, since 2021, Forfar Sheriff Court, 2011-2021; b. 8.9.64, Dundee; m., Jane; 1 d. Educ. Morgan Academy, Dundee; University of Dundee. Partner: Carltons, Dundee, 1990-99, Blackadders, Dundee, 1999-2004, RSB Macdonald, Dundee, 2004-2011; Lecturer and Course Leader, Civil Procedure Course, University of Dundee, 2000-2011. Recreations: golf; Dundee United; reading; cookery. Address: Dundee Sheriff Court and Justice of the Peace Court, 6 West Bell Street, Dundee DD1 9AD; T.-01382 229961.

Murray, Ian. MP (Labour), Edinburgh South, since 2010; Shadow Secretary of State for Scotland, since 2020; b. 10.8.76. Educ. Dumbryden Primary School; Wester Hailes Education Centre; University of Edinburgh. Worked at the Royal Blind, then pensions management; joined Edinburgh-based internet television station (Worldart.com) helping to build a new online TV station; set-up 100 mph Events Ltd (event management business); elected to Edinburgh City Council in 2003, represented Alnwickhill ward, 2003-07, then the larger Liberton/Gilmerton ward, 2007-2010; Shadow Minister for Employment Relations, Consumer and Postal Affairs, 2011-2013; Shadow Minister for Trade & Investment (including Employment Relations and Postal Affairs), 2013-15; Shadow Secretary of State for Scotland, 2015-16. Address: House of Commons, London SW1A 0AA.

Murray, Rev. Ian. Interim Minister, The Kirk of St Nicholas Uniting, since 2020. Address: New Vestry, Back Wynd, Aberdeen AB10 1JZ; T.-01224 643494.

Murray, Professor Isobel (Mary), MA, PhD. Writer and Critic; Honorary Research Professor in Modern Scottish Literature, Aberdeen University; Fellow, Association of Scottish Literary Studies; Associate Editor, Oxford Dictionary of National Biography; b. 14.2.39, Alloa; m., Bob Tait. Educ. Dollar Academy; Edinburgh University. Assistant Lecturer, Lecturer, Senior Lecturer, Reader,

Professor, Department of English, Aberdeen University; books include several editions of Oscar Wilde (most recently Oscar Wilde: The Major Works, 2000), introductions to new editions of J. MacDougall Hay's Gillespie, Ian MacPherson's Shepherds' Calendar, Robin Jenkins' Guests of War, Iain Crichton Smith's Consider the Lilies, George MacKay Brown's Magnus, and Jessie Kesson's Where the Apple Ripens; edited, Beyond This Limit: Selected Shorter Fiction of Naomi Mitchison; A Girl Must Live: stories and poems by Naomi Mitchison; Ten Modern Scottish Novels (with Bob Tait), 1984; Scottish Writers Talking, 1996; Somewhere Beyond: A Jessie Kesson Companion; published Jessie Kesson: Writing Her Life, 2000 (National Library of Scotland/Saltire Society Research Book of the Year); Scottish Writers Talking 2, 2002; Scottish Writers Talking 3, 2006; Scottish Writers Talking 4, 2008; Jessie Kesson: A Country Dweller's Years, from 2008; Series Editor, Naomi Mitchison Library: Introductions to: When We Become Men, Travel Light, The Conquered, Anna Comnena, Cleopatra's People, The Bull Calves, We Have Been Warned, The Delicate Fire, 2012; Scottish Novels of the Second World War. Address: 3A Old Mill Lane, Edinburgh EH16 5TZ.

Murray, Len, JP(Retd), BL, KCJSJ. Retired Solicitor, formerly Senior Partner of Levy & McRae, Glasgow; after-dinner speaker; Scottish Wit of the Year 2012, 2015 and 2017; Dean of the Guild of Robert Burns Speakers; Ambassador to Glasgow Caledonian University; Honorary President, Greenock Burns Club; Author "The Pleader"; member of the Committee of Justice for Megrahi; former member of the Executive of the Robert Burns World Wide Federation. Address 43 Riverwood, Milngavie G62 7AD; T.-07836 707031; e-mail: len.murray100@gmail.com Web: lenmurray.co.uk

Murray, Peter, LLB (Hons), DipLP. Partner, Ledingham Chalmers LLP, since 2002, Board Member, since 2012; b. 10.71, Edinburgh; m., Alison; 2 d.; 1 s. Educ. Easthampstead Park; Dunfermline High; Aberdeen University. Trainee Solicitor, Clark & Wallace, Solicitors, 1994-97; Solicitor/Associate, Ledingham Chalmers, Solicitors, 1997-2002. Chairman, Ledingham Chalmers Financial Limited; Director, VSA (Aberdeen Association of Social Service); Governor/Deputy Chairman, Albyn School, Aberdeen, 2005-16; Burgess of Guild of The City of Aberdeen; Burgess of Trade of the City of Aberdeen; Notary Public; Registrar to the Episcopal Diocese of Aberdeen and Orkney; Advocate in Aberdeen; Member, Weavers Incorporation of Aberdeen. Recreation: family. Club: The Royal Northern and University Club. Address: (h.) 4 Springdale Road, Bieldside, Aberdeen AB15 9FA. E-mail: peter.murray@bieldside.org

Murray, Robert John, MSc, MCIBS. Angus Council, 1995-2017; Vice President, COSLA, 2007-2012; Leader, Angus Council, 1998-2007 (Deputy Leader, 1995-98); b. 3.2.51, Montrose; 1 s.; 1 d. Educ. Montrose Academy; University of Abertay, Dundee. Member, Tayside Regional Council, 1994-96; Board Member, NOSWA, 1996-99; Non Executive Director, Improvement Service, 2008-2017; Board Member, Fields in Trust Scotland, since 2008. Recreations: photography; walking. Address: (h.) 8 Beechgrove, Monifieth DD5 4TE. E-mail: beechgrove58@gmail.com

Murray, Roderick Macpherson, BA (Hons). Head of Visual Arts & Literature, An Lanntair (1985); Writer, Bleak: the mundane comedy, 2020; b. 31.3.56, Coll, Isle of Lewis. Educ. Back Junior Secondary School; Nicolson Institute, Stornoway; Glasgow School of Art. Recreations: cycling; chess; arts.

Murray, Susan, BSc (Hons), PGCE, MSc, MCIPR. Director, The David Hume Institute, since 2019. Educ. The University of Edinburgh; Goldsmiths College, University of London; Robert Gordon University. Career history: Macmillan Cancer Support, various roles, 2000-05; Campaign Development Officer, See Me, 2005-07; Communications Manager, Sustainable Development Commission Scotland, 2007-08; Assistant Director for Public Affairs, SCVO (Scottish Council for Voluntary Organisations), 2008-2015; Trustee (Lay Public Interest Board Member), ICAS Foundation (formerly known as the Scottish Accountancy Trust for Education and Research), 2011-17; Secondment to Standard Life Sustainability team (part of Clore Social Fellowship), Standard Life, 2013; Interim Co-Director, Zero Tolerance, 2018; Interim Head of External Relations, Corra Foundation, 2018-19; Director, Agent M Consulting, 2016-2020; Clore Social Fellow, Clore Social Leadership Programme, since 2011; Board Member (public appointment), Scottish Natural Heritage now known as NatureScot, 2016-2021. Conservation Volunteer and Project Leader, National Trust for Scotland, 2000-08; Community Councillor (volunteer), 2016-19. Address: The David Hume Institute, CodeBase, Argyle House, 3 Lady Lawson Street, Edinburgh EH3 9DR. E-mail: director@davidhumeinstitute.com

Murray, Professor T. Stuart, MD, PhD, FRCGP, FRCPGlas. West of Scotland Director of Postgraduate General Practice Education, 1985-2011; Professor of General Practice, University of Glasgow, 1992-2011 (retired); b. 22.7.43, Muirkirk, Ayrshire; m., Anne Smith; 1 s.; 2 d. Educ. Muirkirk Junior Secondary School; Cumnock Academy; University of Glasgow. Early training in cardiology; entered general practice, 1971; Senior Lecturer in General Practice, 1977. Publication: Modified Essay Questions for the MRCGP Examination; Guide to Postgraduate Medical Education (Co-author). Recreations: travel; reading; sport. Address: (h.) 46 Ellangowan Court, Milngavie G62 8PP; T.-0141-956-1981. E-mail: t.smurray@btinternet.com

Murray, Thomas Kenneth, WS. Founder, Charityflow; Partner, Gillespie MacAndrew LLP Solicitors, 1983-2017; b. 25.6.58, Edinburgh; m., Sophie Mackenzie; 3 d. Educ. Sedbergh School; Dundee University. Purse Bearer to Lord High Commissioner to Church of Scotland, since 2003; Deacon, Incorporation of Goldsmiths of the City of Edinburgh; Director of Reasort Estates Ltd; Trustee, The Scottish National War Memorial. Recreations: fishing; golf. Address: Charityflow, Adams Loan, Kemback, Cupar, Fife KY15 5TJ: T.-0131 247 6884. E-mail: tom.murray@charityflow.co.uk

Murray-Smith, Professor David James, MSc, PhD, DSc, CEng, FIET. Emeritus Professor and Honorary Senior Research Fellow, Glasgow University; b. 20.10.41, Aberdeen; m., Effie Smith; 2 s. Educ. Aberdeen Grammar School; Aberdeen University; Glasgow University. Engineer, Inertial Systems Department, Ferranti Ltd., Edinburgh, 1964-65; Glasgow University: Assistant, Department of Electrical Engineering, 1965-67, Lecturer, 1967-77, Senior Lecturer, 1977-83, Reader, 1983-85, Professor of Engineering Systems and Control, 1985-2005, Dean, Faculty of Engineering, 1997-2001. Past Chairman, United Kingdom Simulation Council. Recreations: hill-walking; photography; strong interest in railways. Address: (b.) School of Engineering, Rankine Building, University of Glasgow, Glasgow G12 8QQ; T.-077-4884-5876; e-mail: david.murray-smith@glasgow.ac.uk

Murray-Smith, Professor Roderick, BEng, PhD. Professor of Computing Science, University of Glasgow, since 1999; b. 03.04.69, Glasgow; m., Sophie; 2 s. Educ. Bearsden Academy; University of Strathclyde. Research Engineer, Daimler Benz Research, Berlin, Germany, 1990-97; Visiting Researcher, MIT, 1994-5; Research Fellow, Technical University of Denmark, 1997-99; Senior Researcher, Hamilton Institute, NUIM Ireland, 2002-2008; Seconded to Nokia Denmark, 2008-2009; Director of SICSA (The Scottish Informatics and Computer Science Alliance), 2012-2014. Publications: 3 edited books and a wide range of scientific papers. Address: School of Computing Science, University of Glasgow; T.-0141 330 4984; e-mail: Roderick.Murray-Smith@glasgow.ac.uk

Murrell, Peter T. Chief Executive, Scottish National Party, since 2001; b. 8.12.64, Edinburgh; m., Nicola Sturgeon. Educ. Craigmount High School, Edinburgh. Publicity Officer, Church of Scotland, 1984-87; Parliamentary Assistant to: Alex Salmond, MP, 1987-94, Allan Macartney, MEP, 1994-98; Head of Office, Ian Hudghton, MEP, 1998-99; Parliamentary Co-ordinator, SNP Westminster Group, 2000-01. Recreations: golf; cooking; gardening. Address: (b.) 3 Jackson's Entry, Edinburgh EH8 8PJ; T.-0131-525 8907.
E-mail: peter.murrell@snp.org
twitter.com/PeterMurrell; facebook.com/PeterMurrellSNP

Muscatelli, Professor Sir Vito Antonio, MA (Hons) (Logan Prize), PhD, FRSE, AcSS, FRSA, Hon LLD (McGill). Principal and Vice-Chancellor, University of Glasgow, since 2009, Daniel Jack Professor of Political Economy, Department of Economics, 1992-2007, Vice Principal (Strategy and Advancement), 2004-07; Principal and Vice-Chancellor, Heriot-Watt University, 2007-09; b. 1.1.62, Bari, Italy; m., Elaine Flood; 1 s.; 1 d. Educ. High School of Glasgow; Glasgow University. Lecturer, Senior Lecturer, Glasgow University, 1984-92, Dean, Faculty of Social Sciences, 2000-04; Visiting Professor: University of Parma (Italy), 1989, Catholic University, Milan, 1991, 1997, University of Bari (Italy), 1995-2004; Editor, Scottish Journal of Political Economy, 1989-2003; Member, Editorial Advisory Board, International Review of Economics and Business, 1995-2001; Member, Advisory Panel of Economic Consultants to the Secretary of State for Scotland, 1998-2000; Research Fellow, CESifo Research Institute, Munich, since 1999; Special Adviser, House of Commons Treasury Select Committee, 2007-10; HEFCE RAE Panel, 2001, 2008; Member, Council, Royal Economic Society, 2002-06; Member, ESRC Research Grants Board, 2002-07; Convener, Universities Scotland and Vice-President, Universities UK, 2008-2010; Member, Financial Services Advisory Board for Scotland, 2009-2011; Member of Board, Scottish Funding Council, 2012-19; Director, UK National Centre for Universities and Business, 2013-17; Hon. Fellow, Societa Italiana Degli Economisti, 1996; Fellow, Royal Society of Edinburgh, 2003; Academician, Learned Societies in the Social Sciences, 2004; Knight Commander (Commendatore), Republic of Italy, 2009; Kt 2017. Director: High School of Glasgow Board, 2000-2019, Russell Group of Universities, since 2009, Universitas 21 Group of Universities, 2009-2016; Board, Glasgow City Marketing Bureau, 2009-2016; Chair, Council for the Advancement and Support of Education (CASE) Europe, 2017-19; Chair, Commission on Economic Growth for the Glasgow City Region, since 2015; Honorary President, David Hume Institute, 2014-2018; Director, Beatson Institute, 2014-2019; Member, Scottish Government's Council of Economic Advisers, 2015-2021; Director, Universities Superannuation Scheme Board, since 2015; Director, Glasgow Life, since 2016; Chair, Scottish Government's Standing Council on Europe, 2016-2021; Chair, Russell Group of Universities, 2017-2020; Governor, National Institute of Economic and Social Research, since 2020; Member, Scottish Government's Advisory Council for Economic Transformation, since 2021; Adviser, Nurse Review of the Research and Innovation Landscape, since 2021; Chair, High School of Glasgow Educational Trust, since 2021; Commissioner, Productivity Commission, since 2021; Board Member, University Grants Committee (Hong Kong), since 2022. Publications: Macroeconomic Theory and Stabilisation Policy (Co-Author), 1988; Economic and Political Institutions in Economic Policy (Editor of volume), 1996; Monetary Policy, Fiscal Policies and Labour Markets: Macroeconomic Policymaking in the EMU, 2004; articles in journals. Recreations: music; literature; football; strategic games. Address: University of Glasgow, Glasgow G12 8QQ; T.-0141 330 5995; e-mail: principal@glasgow.ac.uk

Myles, Bob. Former Leader, Angus Council (2017-18 and 2007-2012); Councillor for Brechin and Edzell (Independent), since 1999; b. 9.2.54; m., Agnes; 3 d. Educ. Brechin High School; Edinburgh University. Livestock Farmer. Board and Committee member of SNFU, 1998-2009, and past Angus Branch President; President, Edzell Curling Club; past President of North and South Esk Province, 1999-2000; Committee Member, Angus and Fettercairn shows; Member: Edzell Drama Club, Edzell Burns Club; past Chairman and Member, Brechin Round Table. Address: (h.) Dalbog, Edzell, Brechin DD9 7UU; T.-01356 648265; e-mail: cllrmyles@angus.gov.uk

Myskow, Lyndsey Morag, BSc, MB, ChB, DCH, DFFP. Principal in General Practice, 1984-2020 (retired); appointed Honorary Senior Lecturer, Department of General Practice, University of Edinburgh in 1999; appointed Associate Specialist in Psychosexual Medicine, Royal Infirmary in 2005; b. 28.10.55, Ilford, Essex; m., Derrick Wrenn. Educ. Linlithgow Academy; Edinburgh University Medical School. Recreations: cooking; exercise; cats. Address: (h.) 8 Magdala Crescent, Edinburgh EH12 5BE; T.-0131-337 1043.
E-mail: lyndsey.myskow@lothian.scot.nhs.uk

N

Nagl, Hazel Anna, RSW, RGI, PAI. Artist/Painter (still life and landscape painter with a special interest in the Scottish garden); b. 2.11.53, Glasgow; 1 d. Educ. Glasgow School of Art. Exhibits on a regular basis throughout Scotland; RSW, 1988; PAI, 1995; SAAC 1994; RGI Stone Prize, 1987 and 1990; RGI Mackinlay Award, 1994; RGI Eastwood Publications Award, 1994; SAAC Prize, 1994; PAI Prize 1996 and 1998; 1st Prize, Laing Competition, 1999; RGI, 2000; Alexander Graham Award; RSW, 2010; Convener, RGI, 2012-19. Address: (h.) 10 Low Barholm, Kilbarchan, Renfrewshire PA10 2ET.

Nairn, Nicholas Cameron Abel. Known as Nick Nairn. Current occupation: Chef; Food Consultant; TV chef; TV presenter; writer of cook books; proprietor and teacher at both Nick Nairn Cook Schools (one in Port of Menteith, one in Aberdeen) (www.nicknairn.com); proprietor and consultant at Nick Nairn Consulting (www.nicknairn.com) which operates Kailyard restaurant by Nick Nairn at Doubletree Hilton Dunblane Hydro. He has Nick Nairn food range, including shortbread biscuits, oatcakes, breakfast cereals and bread products sold in Scottish supermarkets, including Morrisons. Honours: 2007 Honorary Doctorate from Stirling University for outstanding contribution to Scottish cuisine and promoting healthy eating, plus multiple food awards including 2003 Fellowship to the Master Chefs of Great Britain; Glenfiddich Spirit of Scotland Awards 2000 for contribution to Food & Drink; 1996 Scottish Chef of the Year; 1991 Michelin star at Braeval Restaurant; 1986 Scottish Field/Bollinger Newcomer of the Year. Books: Nick has published 10 cook books of his own and collaborated on many others. These include: Nick Nairn Cook School Book, 2008; Fish 'n' Tips, 2006; Nick Nairn's Top 100 Chicken Recipes, 2004; Great British Menu, 2006; New Scottish Cookery, 2002; Nick Nairn's Top 100 Salmon Recipes, 2002; Island Harvest, 1998; Wild Harvest I and II, 1996/7. Television: Nick appears regularly on Saturday Kitchen, Landward, The One Show, This Morning. Other television: Paul & Nick's Big Food Trip, 2 series, 2012/13; series 3, 2015; 2010 Channel 4, co-presenter, Iron Chef UK; 2009 ITV, presenter, Taste The Nation; 2009 BBC2, presenter, Eating In The Sun; 2009 BBC2, Put Your Menu Where Your Mouth Is; 2009 onwards: BBC1, The One Show, presenter of one-off specials; 2007 BBC2, represented Scotland, Great British Menu; 2007-present, BBC2 Scotland co-presenter, Landward; 2007-present, BBC1 presenter and contributor, Saturday Kitchen; 2006 BBC2, finalist for Scotland, Great British Menu; 2003 BBC Scotland presenter, Nick Nairn And The Dinner Ladies; 2003 Actor, Scottish Executive Healthy Eating advertising campaign; 2002 BBC1, presenter So You Think You're A Good Driver?; Foodfest 2001, TV advertising campaign; 2001 BBC2, presenter Kitchen Invaders; 2000 BBC radio Scotland, presenter Cooking With History; 2000 Carlton TV presenter, Back To Basics with Nick Nairn; 1998 ITV presenter, GMTV Christmas Cooking with Nick Nairn; 1998-present, BBC1 presenter, Celebrity Ready Steady Cook; 1997 BBC1, Island Harvest; 1996 BBC2, Wild Harvest 2 with Nick Nairn; 1996-98 BBC2 Presenter, Who'll Do The Pudding; Weakest Link, Chefs TV Blunders, Beechgrove Garden, This Morning and Good Food Live; Masterchef, Light lunch and Carlton Daily, appearances on Friends Like These, Celebrity; regular contributor to Food and Drink, Masterchef, Junior, from 1996; BBC2 presenter, Ready Steady Cook, 1996-2010; BBC2, Wild Harvest with Nick Nairn, 1996. B. 12.1.59, Stirling. Educ. Mclaren High School, Callander; Merchant Navy 1976-83. Became chef, self-taught. Previous restaurants: Braeval, Aberfoyle, 1986; Nairns, Glasgow 1997. Recreations: cycling; hill-walking; eating out; travel. Nick is married with 2 children. Address:

(b.) Nick Nairn Enterprise, Nick Nairn Cook School, Port of Menteith, Stirling FK8 3JZ; T.-01877 389 900.
E-mail: info@nicknairncookschool.com

Nanjiani, Shereen, MBE, MA (Hons). Presenter, BBC Radio Scotland, since 2006; Journalist, Scottish Television, 1983-2006; b. 4.10.61, Elderslie. Educ. John Neilson High School, Paisley; Glasgow University. Joined STV as a trainee journalist, 1983; moved to reporting two years later; became presenter of Scotland Today, 1985; presented election programmes; presented, Secret Scotland documentary series; presented Scottish Politician of the Year Awards.

Napier, Brian William, MA, LLB, PhD, QC. Advocate (and barrister at the English bar), since 1996; Queen's Counsel, since 2002; b. 09.01.49, Dublin, Republic of Ireland; m., Elizabeth. Educ. George Watson's College, Edinburgh; University of Edinburgh; University of Cambridge. Lecturer and Teacher of Law, Queens' College, Cambridge, 1974-89; Professor of Law, Queen Mary College, University of London, 1989-96. Recreations: walking; music. Address: (b.) c/o Faculty of Advocates, Edinburgh EH1 1RF.

Napier, 15th Lord, 6th Baron Ettrick (Francis David Charles Napier); b. 3.11.62; m., Zara Jane McCalmon; 2 c. Clan Chief of Clan Napier; 12th Baronet of Nova Scotia. Succeeded to the title, 2012.

Nash, Professor Anthony Aubrey, BSc, MSc, PhD, FMedSci, FRSE. Emeritus Professor in Infectious Diseases, University of Edinburgh (appointed Professor in 1994); b. 6.3.49, Coalville; m., Marion Ellen Bazeley; 4 d. Educ. Nenbridge Secondary Modern School; Queen Elizabeth College, London University. Lecturer, Department of Pathology, Cambridge University, 1984; Visiting Investigator, Scripps Research Institute, La Jolla, USA, 1989; appointed Head, Department of Veterinary Pathology, Edinburgh University in 1994; Eleanor Roosevelt Cancer Fellowship, 1989-90. Recreations: family; gardening; football. Address: (b.) The Roslin Institute, University of Edinburgh, Easter Bush, Edinburgh EH25 9RG; T.-0131 651 9177; e-mail: tony.nash@ed.ac.uk

Nash, Derek Andrew, LLB, DipLegPrac, NP, WS. Partner and Head of Commercial Property, Lindsays WS, Solicitors, since 2003; b. 18.12.64, Glasgow; m., Anne; 1 s.; 1 d. Educ. Daniel Stewart's and Melville College, Edinburgh; University of Edinburgh. Training, Balfour and Manson, Solicitors, 1987-89; Orr MacQueen WS: Assistant, 1990-92, Associate, 1992-95, Partner, 1995-99; Partner, Skene Edwards WS, 1999-2003. Trustee, Heralds Trust. Recreations: golf; family; church; books; film. Address: (b.) Caledonian Exchange, 19A Canning Street, Edinburgh EH3 8HE; T.-0131 656 5734.
E-mail: dereknash@lindsays.co.uk

Nash, Pamela. MP (Labour), Airdrie and Shotts, 2010-2015; Chief Executive, Scotland in Union, since 2017; b. 24.6.84, Airdrie. Educ. St Margaret's School, Airdrie; Glasgow University. Formerly constituency assistant for John Reid and subsequently his parliamentary assistant for 3 years.

Naylor, (Charles) John, OBE, MA, CCMI, FRSA. Chair, Office of the Scottish Charity Regulator, 2006-2011; b. Newcastle upon Tyne; m., Margery Thomson; 2 s. Educ.

Royal Grammar School, Newcastle upon Tyne; Haberdashers' Aske's School, Elstree; Clare College, Cambridge University. Chair, Strange Town Youth Theatre Company, 2011-2020, Life President, since 2020, Board Member, since 2008; Foundation Scotland Trustee, 2011-2020, Investment Committee, since 2020; Chair, Cambridge Society of Edinburgh, since 2018; various World YMCA Committees, since 2018; Elder, Cramond Kirk, since 1998; District Scout Executive Trustee, since 2016. Employment: Director, YMCA National Centre, Lakeside, Cumbria, 1975-80; National Council of YMCAs: Deputy Secretary, 1980-82, National Secretary, 1982-93; Chief Executive, Carnegie United Kingdom Trust, 1993-2003. Previous voluntary roles: Member and Chairman, YMCA European and World Committees, 1976-92; Chair, Association of Heads of Outdoor Education Centres, 1979-80; Chair, MSC and DES Working Party on Residential Experience and Unemployment, 1980-81; Joint Founder, Y Care International, 1984; Member, National Advisory Council for Youth Service, 1985-88; Vice-Chairman, National Council for Voluntary Youth Services, 1985-88; Founding Convener, Scottish Grant-making Trusts' Group, 1994-97; Chairman, Brathay Exploration Group, 1995-2000, Trustee, 2000-06; Group Scout Leader, 82nd Inverleith (Cramond) Scouts, 1996-2003; Member, Development Grants Board, Scout Association (UK), since 2002, Chairman, 2005-2010; Member of UK Scout Council, 2005-2010; Member, Scottish Charity Law Review Commission, 2000-01; Big Lottery Fund (BLF) UK Board Member, 2004-06; Medical Research Scotland Board Member, 2005-2014; Chair, BLF Community Fund Scotland Committee; Chairman, BLF Scotland Young Peoples Fund; Treasurer and Trustee, The Tomorrow Project, 2002-2013; Chair, RSA Scotland, 2012-2014; National Trust for Scotland, Audit and Risk Management Committee, 2011-18. President, YMCA Scotland, 2012-2021. Publications: Guide to Scottish Grant-making Trusts; Writing Better Fund Raising Applications (Contributor); Charity Law and Change: British and German Perspectives (Contributor); contributions to other books and periodicals. Address: Orchard House, 25B Cramond Glebe Road, Edinburgh EH4 6NT; e-mail: cjohn.naylor@outlook.com

Naylor, Craig. HM Chief Inspector of Constabulary in Scotland, since 2022. Educ. University of Strathclyde (Bachelor's Degree); Edinburgh Business School, Heriot-Watt University (MBA). Career history: National academy programme, Federal Bureau of Investigation (FBI), Quantico, Virginia, 2002; Police Scotland: Superintendent, 2013-14, Divisional Commander, 2015, Head of Organisational Development and Performance, 2015-16; Lincolnshire Police: Assistant Chief Constable, 2017, Deputy Chief Constable, 2017-19; Deputy Director Investigations, National Crime Agency (NCA), 2019-2022. Address: HM Inspectorate of Constabulary in Scotland, Hamilton House, Hamilton Business Park, Caird Park, Hamilton ML3 0QA; T.-0808 178 5577.

Neil, Alex., MA (Hons). MSP (SNP), Airdrie and Shotts, 2011-2021, Central Scotland, 1999-2011; Cabinet Secretary for Social Justice, Communities and Pensioners' Rights, 2014-16; Cabinet Secretary for Health and Wellbeing, 2012-14; Cabinet Secretary for Infrastructure and Capital Investment, 2011-12; Minister for Housing and Communities, 2009-2011; (former Deputy Convener, European and External Relations Committee; former Member, Finance Committee; former Member, Regional Congress of the Council of Europe; former Convener, Enterprise and Culture Committee, 2004-07, former Chairman, Enterprise and Lifelong Learning Committee, 2000-03); Economic Consultant; b. 22.8.51, Irvine; m., Isabella Kerr; 1 s. Educ. Dalmellington High School; Ayr Academy; Dundee University. Scottish Research Officer, Labour Party, 1975; General Secretary, Scottish Labour Party (SLP), 1976; Marketing Manager, 1979-83; Director: Cumnock and Doon Enterprise Trust, 1983-87, Prince's

Scottish Youth Business Trust, 1987-89; Chairman, Network Scotland Ltd., 1987-93; Policy Vice-Convener, Scottish National Party, 1994-2000. Recreations: family; reading; gardening; travel. Address: (h.) 26 Overmills Road, Ayr KA7 3LQ; T.-01292 286675.

Neil, Andrew Ferguson, MA (Hons). Presenter, The Andrew Neil Show, Channel 4, since 2022; Chairman and prime time presenter, GB News, 2021; Publisher, The Scotsman, Scotland on Sunday, Edinburgh Evening News, Scotsman.com, 1996-2006; Chief Executive: The Business, 1999-2008; Chairman: The Spectator, since 2004, Apollo, since 2004, handbag.com, 2004-06; Presenter: Politics Live and The Andrew Neil Show, BBC2, 2019-20, This Week with Andrew Neil, BBC1, 2003-2019, The Sunday Politics, BBC1, 2011-2017, The Daily Politics, BBC2, Straight Talk, BBC News Channel, 2006-2010; Chairman: Sky TV (1988-1990), ITP Dubai, since 2006; Lord Rector, University of St. Andrews, 1999-2002; b. 21.5.49. Educ. Paisley Grammar School; Glasgow University. Conservative Research Department, 1971-72; Correspondent in Belfast, London, Washington, New York, for The Economist, 1973-82, UK Editor, London, 1982-83; Editor, Sunday Times, 1983-94; Executive Chairman, Sky TV, 1988-90; Executive Editor, Fox News, New York, 1994; author of Full Disclosure (autobiography). Address: (b.) 22 Old Queen Street, London SW1H 9HP; T.-020 7961 0000.
E-mail: afneil@icloud.com

Neil, John, OBE. Honorary President, The Boys' Brigade UK & Republic of Ireland, since 2005; b. 19.04.35, Coatbridge; m., Nancy McCreadie Henry (deceased); 1 s.; 1 d. Educ. Airdrie Academy; Coatbridge Albert Secondary. Structural Engineering Industry, Wm. Bain & Co. Ltd., Coatbridge, 1951-61; Military Service, RAF Regiment, Egypt & Iraq, 1953-55; various professional positions, The Boys' Brigade: Secretary for Leadership Training (Scotland and Ireland), 1961-79; Chief Executive, Glasgow Battalion, 1979-2000; Brigade President, United Kingdom & Republic of Ireland, 2003-05; Ambassadorial BB Tours to New Zealand, Hong Kong, Ghana, South Africa, Thailand, China and Australia. National Youth Agency for Scotland (YouthLink Scotland): Representative Member, 1997-98, Vice-Chairman, 1998-2001, Chairman to Board of Directors, 2001-05; various positions in The Church of Scotland including Elder, Hamilton Old Parish Church, since 1975, Treasurer and Finance Convener, 1988-98; Chairman, National Audit Committee and Vice-Convener, General Assembly Central Coordinating Committee, 2001-05. Fundraiser & Financial Adviser to major Youth Development Projects, since 1967; Fundraising Advisor to The Boys' Brigade Hong Kong, since 2011; Musical Director & Organist, Lanarkshire Churches, since 1970; led a major two-way youth exchange visit to Bavaria, Southern Germany, involving 18 year old members of The Boys' and Girls' Brigade in Scotland and the Bavarian Red Cross in Germany, 1981; Member, The Duke of Edinburgh's Award Committee for Scotland, 1984-88; Founding Trustee (& Secretary), The Sir James Robertson Charitable Trust, 1994-2012; Trustee, Netherton Amateur Athletic Association Sports Trust, 1994-2000; Honorary Life Member, St Andrews Ambulance Association Scotland, since 1994; Holder of The Lord Provost of Glasgow Gold Medal "for Public Service" 2000; Tax Commissioner for Lanark Division, 2001-05; Chairman, Parliamentary Cross Party Conference on Anti-Social Behaviour Bill, 2002; Member, The Merchants House of Glasgow, since 2002; Founding Chairman to Board of Trustees, Search for Truth Charitable Trust, 2007-09; Initiator and Patron, Glasgow Stedfast Association, 2008-2015; National President and Chairman, Federation of Stedfast Associations United Kingdom and Republic of Ireland, 2013-2015. Publications: series of educational work books for young people, on Overseas Mission; Brigade Song Book; Text Books on specialised B.B. subjects; Historic Millennium Directory of The Old Parish Church of Hamilton, 2000. Recreations: golf; music; reading; spectator sports; overseas travel. Address: (h.) 150 Silvertonhill Avenue, Hamilton, South Lanarkshire ML3 7PP; T.-01698 335462; e-mail: jneilbb@blueyonder.co.uk

Nelson, Donald Bruce, BSc, MBA, PhD, FCMI. Registrar, College of Science and Engineering, University of Edinburgh, since 2009; b. 9.8.58, Stranraer; m., Christine Diane Thorburn; 1 s.; 1 d. Educ. Stranraer Academy; University of Glasgow; University of Edinburgh. HM Inspector of Taxes, 1983-84; University of Edinburgh: various administrative posts, 1984-98, Director of Planning, 1998-2003, Director of Planning and Deputy Secretary, 2003-04, Academic Registrar and Deputy Secretary, 2004-09; Director, Edinburgh University Press, 2001-03. Director, FloWave TT Ltd; Director, SSTRIC Ltd; Director, UoE Accommodation Services Ltd; Chairman, Edinburgh South Liberal Association, 1986-88; Treasurer, Edinburgh South Liberal Democrats, 1988-91; Member, The Association of University Teachers Administrative Staff Committee, 1991-97/Chairperson, 1994-97; Member, Association of University Administrators Board of Trustees, 2003-12; Vice-Chair and Chair-Elect, 2005-06/Chair, 2006-08, Treasurer, 2010-12; Member, Higher Education Senior Managers Forum, 2006-08; Non-Executive Board Member, Student Awards Agency Scotland, 2007-13; Member of Court, University of the Highlands and Islands, 2011-14. Awarded Robbie Ewen Fellowship for University Administrators, 1997 and AUA Lifetime Achievement Award, 2021. Recreations: reading; listening to classical music; Stranraer Football Club; wilfing. Address: (h.) 47 Beauchamp Road, Edinburgh EH16 6LU; T.-0131-664 3020.
E-mail: dbnelson99@gmail.com

Nelson, (Peter) Frederick, BSc, CEng, MIEE. Senior Consultant, Electrical Engineering, Atkins Power Generation; b. 2.9.52, Glasgow; m., (Caroline) Ann; 3 s. Educ. John Neilson; Strathclyde University. President, Scottish Canoe Association, 1980-90; Member, Commonwealth Games Council for Scotland, since 1982; Chairman, Scottish Sports Association, 1990-96; Member, Scottish Sports Council, 1990-98; Chairman, Scottish Outdoor Recreation Network, 2000-06; Elder, Davidson's Mains Parish Church. Recreations: kayaking; cycling; DIY. Address: (h.) 11 Barnton Park Place, Edinburgh EH4 6ET.

Neville, Richard. Head of Newspapers, DC Thomson, since January 2019. Career history: Edinburgh Evening News; Daily Record and The Press, York, then The Scotsman as News Editor and Deputy Editor, then Editor, Business AM, 2000-2002, then Deputy Editor of The Press and Journal, Aberdeen, 2003-2011, then Editor, The Courier, Dundee, 2011-2017, then Editor in Chief of DC Thomson morning newspapers covering The Courier and The Press and Journal, August 2017-December 2018. Address: DC Thomson, 2 Albert Square, Dundee DD1 1DD; T.-07557746886; e-mail: rneville@dctmedia.co.uk

Newell, Emeritus Professor Alan F., MBE, BSc, PhD, FIEE, CEng, FBCS, FRSE, ILTM, HonFCSLT. NCR Emeritus Professor of Electronics and Microcomputer Systems, Dundee University (appointed Professor in 1980); appointed Director, Dundee University Microcomputer Centre in 1980; (Head, Department of Applied Computing, 1997-2002, Deputy Principal, 1993-95); Academic Leader, Queen Mother Research Centre for Information Technology to support older people, 2003-06; b. 1.3.41, Birmingham; m., Margaret; 1 s.; 2 d. Educ. St. Philip's Grammar School; Birmingham University. Research Engineer, Standard Telecommunication Laboratories; Lecturer, Department of Electronics, Southampton University. Recreations: family life; walking; bicycling. Address: (b.) School of Computing, Dundee University, Dundee, DD1 4HN; T.-01382 388085.

Newlands, Gavin. MP (SNP), Paisley and Renfrewshire North, since 2015; Shadow Secretary of State for Transport, since 2020; b. 2.2.80, Paisley; m., Lynn; 2 d. Educ. St James' Primary School; Trinity High School; James Watt College. Member of the SNP for 25 years, joining the youth wing of the party in 1992, getting involved during the campaigns against the poll tax; became a local community council councillor for Renfrew in 2011 and has supported many local causes, including a West of Scotland-based foodbank. Member of Paisley Rugby Club for 16 years, serving as club captain for 3 years. Address: House of Commons, London SW1A 0AA.

Newman, Elizabeth. Artistic Director, Pitlochry Festival Theatre, since 2018. Career history: Artistic Director of Shared Property Theatre Company and Acting Artistic Director of Southwark Playhouse; Artistic Director, the Octagon Theatre Bolton, 2015-18, Associate Director, 2010-18. Received awards for Women of Social Leadership, Young Entrepreneur of the Year, and Bolton Woman of the Year; won the award for Best Director (for direction of Brian Friel's Faith Healer), Critics'Awards for Theatre in Scotland (CATS), 2020; work was recognised by The Stage amongst the Best Shows of 2017 across the UK. Address: Pitlochry Festival Theatre, Port Na Craig, Pitlochry PH16 5DR; T.-01796 484 626.

Newman, Professor Simon Peter, BA, MA, MA, PhD, FRSA, FRHistS. Honorary Professorial Research Fellow, University of Glasgow (appointed Professor of American Studies in 2002); b. 8.7.60, Basildon; m., Marina Moskowitz. Educ. St. Joseph's College, Ipswich; University of Nottingham; University of Wisconsin; Princeton University. Assistant Professor of History, Northern Illinois University, 1991-97; Mellon Postdoctoral Fellow in the Humanities, University of Pennsylvania, 1994-95; Senior Lecturer in History, University of Glasgow, 1997-2002; Director, Andrew Hook Centre for American Studies, University of Glasgow, 1997-2002; Chairman, British Association for American Studies, since 2004. Philip A. Rollins Fellowship in History, Princeton University, 1989-90; Mellon Postdoctoral Fellowship in the Humanities, University of Pennsylvania, 1994-95; Resident Fellowship, Rockefeller Study and Conference Center, Bellagio, Italy, 1998; Coca Cola Fellowship, International Center for Jefferson Studies, Monticello, Virginia, 2000; Member, Executive Committee, British Association for American Studies, 1999-2006; Chair, Scottish Association for the Study of America, 2001-03; former Chairman, British Association for American Studies. Publications: Vue D'Amérique: La Révolution Française Jugée Par Les Américains (Co-editor), 1989; Parades and the Politics of the Street: Festive Culture in the Early American Republic, 1997; Embodied History: The Lives of the Poor in Early Philadelphia, 2003. Clubs: Reform Club. Recreations: long distance and cross country running; cooking. Address: (b.) History, School of Humanities, 1 University Gardens, University of Glasgow, Glasgow G12 8QQ.
E-mail: Simon.Newman@glasgow.ac.uk

Ni, Professor Xiongwei, BSc, PhD, CEng, FIChemE, Professor of Process and Reaction Engineering, Heriot-Watt University, since 1999; b. 22.2.60, Beijing, China; m., Wendy Margaret Hogg; 1s.; 1d. Educ. Yan-Ting Primary and High School, Sichuan China; Chong-Qing University, Sichuan; Leeds University. Research Fellow, Edinburgh University, 1986-89; Research Associate, Cambridge University, 1989-91; Lecturer, Teeside University, 1991-94; Strathclyde University: Lecturer, 1994-96; Senior Lecturer, 1996-97; Senior Lecturer, Heriot-Watt University, 1997-99; Foxwell Memorial Award, Institute of Energy, 1985. Recreations: tennis; badminton; golf; bridge. Address: (b.) School of Engineering and Physical Sciences, Heriot-Watt University, Edinburgh, EH14 4AS; T.-0131-451 3781.
E-mail: X.Ni@hw.ac.uk

Nicholson, Professor Keith, BSc (Hons), MSc, PhD, CISA, CISM, MIoD. Cyber Security Compliance and Risk Management Consultant, IT and Digital Strategy Advisor, since 2000; b. Lochiver; m. Angela. Educ. Kelvin; Univ. Manchester; Univ. Strathclyde. Founder and Executive Chair, Cyber Security Scotland, since 2016; Founder and Principal, Cyber Security Institute, since 2019; Member, National Cyber Resilience Leaders Board Chair, since 2017; Joint-Chair, Public Sector Steering Group, NCRLB, since 2017; Chair, Revenue Scotland, 2015-2021; Non-executive Board Member, Visit Scotland, since 2019; Member, Audit Committee, Visit Scotland, since 2019; Non-executive Board Member, Scottish Environmental Protection Agency, 2011-2019; Member, Audit Committee, SEPA, 2011-2019; Non-executive Board Member, Scottish Higher and Further Education Funding Council, 2012-2019; Member, Audit Committee, Scottish Higher and Further Education Funding Council, 2012-2019; Member, Research & Knowledge Exchange Committee, Scottish Higher and Further Education Funding Council, 2012-19; Managing Director, 55 North Network Ltd, since 2008; Non-executive Board Member, Scottish Natural Heritage, 2010-16; Chair, Audit & Risk Committee, Scottish Natural Heritage, 2012-16; Member, Cross Public Sector Cyber group, 2015-2017; Technology Advisor, Scottish Government, 2008-15; Member, Scottish Government Cyber Security Strategy Board, 2011-15; Hon. Fellow, Univ. Paisley, 2002-07; CEO, TP Group, 1991-2000; Professor of Energy & Environmental Engineering, University of Aalborg, Denmark, 1999-2000; Professor of Energy & The Environment, Robert Gordon University, Aberdeen, 1991-99; A. Professor, Geochemistry, Geothermal Energy Institute, University of Auckland, New Zealand, 1987-1991; CEO, Envirosurveys, Auckland, New Zealand, 1987-1990. Publications: Doing Business on the Internet, 1993; Geothermal Fluids: Chemistry & Exploration Techniques, 1993, 2011; Skye: The Complete Visitors Guide (Co-author), 1994; Geothermal Energy, 1987 (Ed); Geothermal Energy, 1989 (Ed); Manganese Mineralisation (Ed), 1997; Energy & the Environment (Ed), 1999; over 150 scientific papers and reports. Best Business Award, 1993; winning medallist, IoD IT Director, 2002. Recreations: wildlife; hill-walking; photography; golf; archaeology; antiquarian books; malt whisky. Address: (b.) Cyber Security Scotland, Naver Business Centre, Thurso KW14 7QA; T.-01847 500 101; e-mail: knicholson@knicholson.co.uk

Nicholson, Peter Alexander, LLB (Hons). Editor, Journal of the Law Society of Scotland, since 2004; Deputy Editor, 2003-04; Managing Editor, W. Green, The Scottish Law Publisher, 1989-2003; General Editor, Scots Law Times, 1985-2003; Scottish Editor, Current Law, 1985-96; General Editor, Greens Weekly Digest, 1986-2003; b. 22.5.58, Stirling; m., Morag Ann Fraser; 1 s.; 3 d. Educ. St. David's RC High School, Dalkeith; Edinburgh University. Admitted as Solicitor, 1981. Reporter, Client Relations Office, Law Society of Scotland, 2005-2012. Lay Minister of the Eucharist. Recreations: choral singing; gardening; keeping fit; President, Kevock Choir, since 2018. Address: (h.) 32 Buckstone Loan, Edinburgh EH10 6UD; T.-0131-445 1570.

Nickson of Renagour, Lord (David Wigley Nickson), KBE (1987), CBE (1981), DL, CBIM, FRSE. Life Peer (1994); Chancellor, Glasgow Caledonian University, 1993-2002; Vice Lieutenant, Stirling and Falkirk, 1997-2004 (Deputy Lieutenant, 1982-97); b. 27.11.29, Eton; m., Helen Louise Cockcraft (deceased 2012); 3 d.; m. (2), Eira Drysdale, 2013. Educ. Eton College; Royal Military Academy, Sandhurst. Commissioned, Coldstream Guards, 1949-54; William Collins: joined, 1954, Director, 1961-85, Joint Managing Director, 1967, Vice-Chairman, 1976-83, Group Managing Director, 1979-82; Director: Scottish United Investors plc, 1970-83, General Accident plc, 1971-98 (Deputy Chairman, 1993-98), Scottish & Newcastle Breweries plc, 1981-95 (Chairman, 1983-89), Radio Clyde Ltd., 1982-85, National Australia Bank Ltd., 1991-96,

National Australian Group (UK) Ltd., 1993-98, Hambros PLC, 1989-98; Chairman, Clydesdale Bank, 1991-98 (Director, 1981-98); Chairman, Pan Books, 1982-83; Chairman, Scottish Enterprise, 1990-93 (SDA, 1988-90); President, CBI, 1986-88; Chairman, CBI in Scotland, 1979-81; Chairman, Countryside Commission for Scotland, 1983-86; Member: Scottish Industrial Development Advisory Board, 1975-80, Scottish Committee, Design Council, 1978-81, Scottish Economic Council, 1980-95, National Economic Development Council, 1985-88; Chairman, Atlantic Salmon Trust, 1988-95; Chairman, Senior Salaries Review Body, 1989-95; President, Association of District Salmon Fisheries Board, 1996-2012; Chairman, Secretary of State for Scotland's Scottish Salmon Strategy Task Force, 1995-97; Chairman, Scottish Advisory Committee, Imperial Cancer Research Fund, 1994-2001; Trustee: Princes Youth Business Trust, 1987-90, Princess Royal's Trust for Carers, 1990-94; Director, Countryside Alliance, 1998-2000; Captain of Queen's Bodyguard for Scotland (Royal Company of Archers); D.Univ, Stirling, 1986; Hon. DBA Napier Polytechnic, 1990; Honorary Fellow, Paisley College, 1992; Honorary Freeman, Fishmongers Company, 1999, Honorary Freeman, City of London, 1999. Recreations: fishing; bird-watching; the countryside. Address: (h.) The River House, Doune, Perthshire FK16 6DA; T.-01786 841614.

Nicol, Rev. Douglas Alexander Oag, MA, BD (Hons); b. 5.4.48, Dunfermline; m., the late Anne Wilson Gillespie; 2 s.; 1 d. Educ. Kirkcaldy High School; Edinburgh University; Glasgow University. Assistant Warden, St. Ninian's Centre, Crieff, 1972-76; Minister, Lochside, Dumfries, 1976-82; Minister, St. Columba, Kilmacolm, 1982-91. Chairman, Board of Directors, National Bible Society of Scotland, 1984-87; Convener, Board of National Mission, Church of Scotland, 1990-91; General Secretary, Church of Scotland Board of National Mission, 1991-2005; Secretary, Church of Scotland Mission and Discipleship Council, 2005-2009; Minister, Hobkirk and Southdean linked with Ruberslaw, 2009-2018. Recreations: family life and family history; travel; athletics. Address: 1/2 North Werber Park, Edinburgh EH4 1SY; T.-07811 437075. E-mail: daon@lineone.net

Nicoll, Alan John, LLB, NP. Business Development Manager (part-time), Laurie and Company Solicitors LLP (former Senior Partner, 2002-16); b. 28.7.55, Aberdeen; m., Carole Jane Burtt; 2 s.; 2 d. Educ. Robert Gordon's College; University of Aberdeen. Served Apprenticeship at AC Morrison & Richards, 1976-78; Employed as Solicitor, Edmonds & Ledingham, 1978-80; Employed by John Laurie & Co, 1980-81, became a Partner in 1981. Recreations: tennis; golf; skiing; hillwalking; cycling. Address: (b.) 17 Victoria Street, Aberdeen AB10 1UU; T.-01224 645085; e-mail: alan@laurieandco.co.uk

Nicoll, Andrew Ramsay, MA (Hons), MPhil, GradDipARM, RMARA. Deputy Head of Archives, Historic Environment Scotland, since 2017, Development Manager, Scran, 2015-16 (RCAHMS, 2014-15); Archivist, Society of Helpers of the Holy Souls, British Province, 2013-19; Outreach Officer, ScotlandsPlaces, Royal Commission on the Ancient and Historical Monuments of Scotland, 2013-2014; Keeper of The Scottish Catholic Archives, 2003-2012; b. 2.5.78, Dundee. Educ. Forfar Academy; University of Dundee; University College London. Treasurer and Trustee, Scottish Catholic Historical Association, since 2010; Director and Trustee, Archives and Records Association, United Kingdom and Ireland, 2009-2012 and since 2019, Vice Chair, since 2020. Address: (b.) HES, John Sinclair House, 16 Bernard Terrace, Edinburgh EH8 9NX; T.-0131 662 1456.

Nicoll, Audrey. MSP (SNP), Aberdeen South and North Kincardine, since 2021; b. 1961, Aberdeen; m., Alex Nicoll. Worked as a detective sergeant police officer in both uniformed and specialist roles, retiring in 2015; gave lectures in the School of Nursing, Midwifery and Paramedic Practice, Robert Gordon University; elected to Aberdeen City Council in the by-election for the Torry/Ferryhill ward in 2019. Address: The Scottish Parliament, Edinburgh EH99 1SP; T.-0131 348 5490. E-mail: Audrey.Nicoll.msp@parliament.scot

Nicolson, Alastair. Area Manager for Lochaber, Skye and Wester Ross, Highlands and Islands Enterprise, since 2020. Educ. Heriot Watt University. More than 20 years' experience in economic and community development in the Highlands and Islands. Address: Highlands and Islands Enterprise, An Lòchran, 10 Inverness Campus, Inverness IV2 5NA; T.-01463 245 245.

Nicolson, Cllr Iain. Leader, Renfrewshire Council, since 2017; representing Erskine and Inchinnan Ward (SNP), since 1995. Address: 54 Allands Avenue, Inchinnan PA4 9LG; T.-0300 300 1252. E-mail: cllr.iain.nicolson@renfrewshire.gov.uk

Nicolson, John, MA (Hons). MP (SNP): Ochil and South Perthshire, since 2019, East Dunbartonshire, 2015-17; SNP Shadow Secretary of State for Digital, Culture, Media and Sport, since 2020; former spokesperson on Culture, Media and Sport; b. 1961, Glasgow. Educ. University of Glasgow; Harvard University. Joined the BBC in 1987; reported for a variety of heavyweight BBC programmes including On the Record, Panorama, Assignment, The Late Show, and numerous live general election, European election, and budget programmes; reporter on Newsnight for three years, presented Watchdog Healthcheck on BBC1 and the BBC's Breakfast News; studio presenter for the BBC on 11 September 2001 as the Twin Towers collapsed, anchoring live on BBC News 24 and BBC1 - a broadcast which won the BBC a Foreign Press Association award for best breaking news coverage; moved to ITV and presented Live with John Nicolson, a three-hour morning news magazine on the ITV News Channel; guest reported on Holiday; presented radio show on LBC and has been a panellist on Radio 4's long running comedy show The News Quiz; regular contributor to the Cumulus Media Networks radio programme The John Batchelor Show. Writes extensively about architecture and design, as well as politics and travel. Address: Houses of Parliament, Westminster, London SW1A 0AA.

Nicolson, Sheriff Linda. Sheriff, South Strathclyde, Dumfries and Galloway, since 2020. Educ. University of Strathclyde; gained Diploma in Legal Practice in 1987. Career history: practised as a solicitor, starting career in 1987 as a trainee and then assistant with Livingstone Brown before becoming a principal in private practice with Nicolson & Co. in 1993; worked part time for some years before returning to full time practice in 2013; became a summary sheriff in 2017. Address: Hamilton Sheriff Court, Sheriff Court House, 4 Beckford Street, Hamilton ML3 0BT.

Nimmo, The Very Rev. Dr. Alexander Emsley, BD, MPhil, PhD, FSA (Scot), RNR, ChLJ. Dean Emeritus of Aberdeen and Orkney, since 2019; Dean of Aberdeen & Orkney, 2008-2017; Rector of St Margaret's, Aberdeen, since 1990; Honorary Canon of Christ Church Cathedral, Hartford, Connecticut, USA, 2016-2019; b. 28.02.53, Glasgow. Educ. University of Aberdeen; University of Edinburgh. Precentor, Inverness Cathedral, 1978-81; Priest-in-Charge, St. Peter's Stornoway, 1981-83, Rector, 1984; Rector, All Saints' Edinburgh, 1984-90. Chairman, 1745 Association, 2011-2014; President, 1745 Association, 2019; Member of The Royal Celtic Society. Publications: contributor to Dictionary of Scottish Church History and Theology, 1993; After Columba, After Calvin, 1999 (contributor); A Life Less Ordinary: The Life of Fr John Comper, 2003; contributor to Sir Thomas Urquhart of

Cromarty, 2011; contributor to Scottish Liturgical Tradition; occasional papers; The Aberdeen Doctors (Friends of St Machar's Cathedral), 2011; contributor to Living with Jacobitism, 1690-1788, 2014; Liturgy: The Sacramental Soul of Jacobitism; contributor to Scottish Church History Society, 2018 Vol XLVII, Archibald Campbell: Aberdeen's Absentee Bishop?; Religious Politics: Reformers to Jacobites 1560-1764 (forthcoming). Recreations: gardening; walking; music. Address: St. Margaret of Scotland, Gallowgate, Aberdeen AB25 1EA; T.-01224-644969.

Nimmo, John, LLB, LLM. Partner, MBM Commercial, Edinburgh, since 2022; solicitor admitted in Scotland and attorney admitted in New York; b. 8.76. Educ. Stewart's Melville College; University of Hamburg; The University of Edinburgh; Cornell Law School; Glasgow Graduate School of Law. Career history: Lawyer: Dickson Minto WS, 2000-09, Nimmo WS, 2009-2016; Rooney Nimmo, Edinburgh, 2016-2022. Recreations: musical instruments; pottering in the garden to relax. Address: MBM Commercial, Suite 2, Ground Floor, Orchard Brae House, 30 Queensferry Road, Edinburgh EH4 2HS; T.-0131 226 8202; e-mail: john.nimmo@mbmcommercial.co.uk

Nimmo, Rev. Peter William, BD, ThM. Minister of Cambuslang Parish Church, since 2020; Minister of Old High St. Stephen's Church of Scotland, Inverness, 2004-2020; b. 19.1.66, Dumbarton; m., Katharina; 1 s.; 1 d. Educ. Vale of Leven Academy, Alexandria; Glasgow University; Princeton Theological Seminary, NJ, USA (Fulbright Scholar). Associate Minister, Currie Kirk, Edinburgh, 1996-98; Minister of High Carntyne Parish Church, Glasgow, 1998-2004. Member: General Assembly's Parish Development Fund Committee, 2005-07, Iona Community Board, 1999-2003, Church and Society Council, 2013-2019, Faith Impact Forum, since 2020; Chair, Waverley Care Highland and Argyll and Bute Advisory Group, 2010-12. Creator of Church of Scotland Voices Twitter account (@churchscovoices). Address: Cambuslang Parish Church, 1 Arnott Way, Cambuslang, Glasgow G72 7SQ; T.-0141 586 2126.

Nimmo Smith, Rt. Hon. Lord (William Austin Nimmo Smith), BA, LLB. Senator of the College of Justice, 1996-2009 (retired); b. 6.11.42, Edinburgh; m., Dr. Jennifer Nimmo Smith; 1 s.; 1 d. Educ. Eton (King's Scholar); Balliol College, Oxford; Edinburgh University. Advocate, 1969; Standing Junior Counsel, Department of Employment, 1977-82; QC, 1982; Advocate Depute, 1983-86; Chairman, Medical Appeal Tribunals and Vaccine Damage Tribunals, 1986-91; part-time Member, Scottish Law Commission, 1988-96; Temporary Judge, Court of Session, 1995-96; Outer House, Court of Session, 1996-2005; Insolvency Judge, 1997-2005; Intellectual Property Judge, 1998-2005; Judge in the Lands Valuation Appeal Court, 2002-09; Inner House, First Division, Court of Session, 2005-09; Judge in the Registration Appeal Court, 2005-09; Privy Counsellor, 2005; Chairman of Council, Cockburn Association (Edinburgh Civic Trust), 1996-2001. Recreations: mountaineering; music. Address: (b.) Parliament House, Edinburgh EH1 1RQ.

Nisbet, James Barry Consitt, LLB. Stipendiary Magistrate, Glasgow, 1984-2007 (retired); b. 26.7.42, Forfar; m., Elizabeth McKenzie; 2 d. Educ. Forfar Academy; Edinburgh University. Legal Assistant, Warden Bruce & Co., WS, Edinburgh, 1967-68; Legal Assistant, then Junior Depute Town Clerk, then Depute Town Clerk, Perth City Council, 1968-75; Senior Depute Director of Administration, Perth and Kinross District Council, 1975-84; Past Head Server, St. Ninian's Episcopal Cathedral,

Perth; Membership Secretary, Past Secretary-General, Scottish Guild of Servers. Recreations: transport, especially railways and tramways; archaeology; music; foreign travel; genealogy. Address: (b.) 35 Hutchison Drive, Scone, Perth PH2 6GB.

Nish, David. Former Chief Executive, Standard Life plc (2010-2015); b. 5.5.60, Glasgow; m., Caroline; 1 s.; 1 d. Educ. Paisley Grammar School; Glasgow University. Price Waterhouse: Graduate Trainee to Senior Manager, 1981-93, Partner, 1993-97; Deputy Finance Director, Scottish Power, 1997-99, Finance Director, 1999-2005, Executive Director, Infrastructure Division, 2005; Finance Director, Standard Life plc, 2006-2010. Recreations: cycling; travel; family; watching sport.

Noakes, Rab. Director, Neon Productions Limited, since 1995; b. 13.5.47, St. Andrews; m., Stephanie Pordage. Educ. Bell Baxter Senior High School, Cupar, Fife. Minor Civil Service career in the MPNI working in Glasgow, Alloa and London, 1963-67; various labouring jobs including Flying Carpet Servicer, Guardbridge Paper Mill, 1967-69; in 1969 a summer of music residency in Denmark kick-started the ability to make a living from performing, writing, production and recording which continues to this day (many albums and songs recorded); in 1987 a contract with BBC culminated in the position of Head of Entertainment at BBC Radio Scotland; since setting up Neon Productions in 1995 thousands of hours have been provided for broadcast on radio and TV including a weekly show, Brand New Country, for BBC Radio Scotland; the company is also a record company and engages in music publishing. Council Member, SAC; Executive Committee, MU. Address: (b.) Studio Two, 19 Marine Crescent, Glasgow G51 1HD; T.-0141 429 6366.
E-mail: mail@go2neon.com

Noble, R. Ross, MBE, MA, FSA (Scot). Museum Curator, 1973-2003 (retired); Member, Scottish Committee of Heritage Lottery Fund, 2009-2015; Member, Historic Environment Advisory Council for Scotland, 2003-09; b. 9.6.42, Ayr; m., Jean; 1 s.; 1 d. Educ. Ardrossan Academy; Aberdeen University. Travelling Curator, Scottish Country Life Museums Trust, 1973-76; Curator, Highland Folk Museum and Regional (later Highland) Curator for the local authority's Museum Service, 1976-2003. Elected Fellow, Society of Antiquaries of Scotland, since 1982; Convenor, Scottish Country Life Museums Trust, 2000-07; Elected Director, Newtonmore Community Woodland and Development Trust, 2003-09; Member: Museums Association, Scottish Vernacular Buildings Working Group, British Regional Furniture Society, Scottish History Society; Member and Past President, Society for Folk Life Studies; Member, United Nations Association UK (UNA-UK), since 2012. Publications include: The Cultural Impact of the Highland Clearances, BBC History On-Line, 2001; Earth Buildings in the Central Highlands: Research and Reconstruction. Medieval or Later Rural Settlements: 10 Years On, 2003; "Highland Vernacular Furniture and Context" in Furniture and Fittings in the Traditional Scottish Home, Scottish Vernacular Buildings Working Group, 2007. Recreations: walking; swimming; sailing; painting. Address: (h.) "Creageiro", Church Terrace, Newtonmore PH20 1DT; T.-01540 673392.

Noble, Sir Timothy Peter, Bt, MA, MBA; b. 21.12.43; m., Elizabeth Mary Aitken; 2 s.; 1 d. Educ. University College, Oxford; Gray's Inn, London; INSEAD, Fontainebleau. Publications: Noble Blood; The First Shadows of Morning; The Singer With No Song. Recreations: skiing; tennis; golf; music; bridge; wine; astronomy; poetry. Clubs: Bruntsfield, Summit. Address: (h.) Ardnahane, Barnton Avenue, Edinburgh; T.-0131-336 3565.

Nolan, Andrea, OBE, FRSE. Principal, Edinburgh Napier University, since 2013. Educ. Trinity College Dublin.

Career: veterinary practice; Researcher, Universities of Cambridge, Bristol and the Technical University, Munich; joined the University of Glasgow in 1989 as Lecturer and was appointed Professor of Veterinary Pharmacology in 1998 and Dean of the Faculty of Veterinary Medicine in 1999; joined the Senior Management Group as Vice Principal for Learning & Teaching in 2004; Senior Vice-Principal & Deputy Vice Chancellor, 2009-2013. Address: (b.) Sighthill Campus, Sighthill Court, Edinburgh EH11 4BN.

Nolan, Rev William. Archbishop of Glasgow, since 2022; Bishop of Galloway, 2015-2022; b. 26.1.54. Educ. Cathedral Primary School, Motherwell; St Patrick's Primary School, Craigneuk; St Vincent's College, Langbank; St Mary's College, Blairs. Completed studies for ordination at the Pontifical Scots College, Rome, 1971-78, earning a Licence in Sacred Theology from the Gregorian University in June 1978; ordained priest for the Diocese of Motherwell on 30 June 1977 in St Bernadette's Church, Motherwell; subsequently held the following pastoral assignments: Assistant Priest, Our Lady of Lourdes, East Kilbride, 1978-1980; Assistant Priest, St. David's, Plains, 1980-1983; Assistant Priest, St Bridget's, Baillieston, 1990-1994; Parish Priest, Our Lady of Lourdes, East Kilbride, 1994-2015. Served as Vice-Rector of the Scots College in Rome, 1983-90; appointed Administrator of St John Ogilvie parish, Blantyre in November 2013 and Vicar General of the Motherwell Diocese in June 2014. Address: Archdiocese of Glasgow, 196 Clyde Street, Glasgow, Scotland G1 4JY; T.-0141 226 5898.

Normand, Andrew Campbell, LLB (Hons), DipLP. Partner, DAC Beachcroft Scotland LLP; b. 4.12.62, Perth; m., Sheila; 3 s.; 1 d. Educ. Perth High School; Edinburgh University. Traineeship, Nightingale and Bell SSC, 1985-87; Assistant Solicitor, Gray Muirhead WS, 1991-96; Partner, HBJ Gateley Wareing (formerly Henderson Boyd Jackson), 1996-2008. WS Society; Director, Scottish National Jazz Orchestra. Recreations: jazz; piano. Address: (b.) 24 Dublin Street, Edinburgh EH1 3PP; T.-0131 524 7797.
E-mail: cnormand@dacbeachcroft.com

Normand, Andrew Christie, CB, MA, LLB, LLM, SSC, FSAScot. Former Sheriff at Glasgow (2003-2016); Crown Agent for Scotland, 1996-2003; b. 7.2.48, Edinburgh; m., Barbara Jean Smith; 2 d. Educ. George Watson's College, Edinburgh; Edinburgh University; Queen's University, Kingston, Ontario.

Norrie, Professor Kenneth McKenzie, LLB, DLP, PhD, FRSE. Professor, University of Strathclyde; b. 23.6.59, Dundee. Educ. Kirkton High School, Dundee; University of Dundee; University of Aberdeen. Lecturer in Law: University of Dundee, 1982-83, University of Aberdeen, 1983-90; Gastprofessor, Universität Regensburg, Germany, 1990; Senior Lecturer in Law, University of Strathclyde, 1990-95; Visiting Professor, University of Sydney, Australia, 1997; Visiting Professor, Victoria University of Wellington, 2008. Publications: Parent and Child; Defamation; Trusts; Children's Hearings. Recreations: gardening; travel. Address: (b.) Law School, Lord Hope Building, University of Strathclyde, 141 St James Road, Glasgow G4 0LT.

Norris, Richard, BA (Hons). Director, Scottish Health Council, 2005-2019; b. 01.04.59, Luton; m., Morag; 2 d. Educ. Branston School, Lincolnshire; City of London Polytechnic. Chief Executive, Centre for Scottish Public Policy, 1993-97; Director of Policy, Scottish Association for Mental Health, 1997-2005. Visiting Fellow, Academy of Government, University of Edinburgh, 2017-18, Academic Visitor, 2019-2020.

Northesk, 15th Earl of (Patrick Charles Carnegy); b. 23.9.40. Music and theatre critic. Educ. Trinity Hall, Cambridge. Written a number of books on Richard Wagner, including one on the subject of his operas that took 40 years to write; also written about stage and theatre, both as an author and critic, and has appeared on radio programmes such as Radio 3's CD Review. Succeeded to title, 2010.

Northrop, Alasdair, BA (Hons). Tourist guide and professional writer; Owner, Caledonia Tours, since 2016; Editor, Scottish Business Insider, 2000-2016; b. 23.5.57, Chalfont-St-Giles; 1 s. Educ. Leamington College for Boys; Middlesex Polytechnic. Reporter, Heart of England Newspapers, 1978-83; Sub Editor, Southern Evening Echo, Southampton, 1983-85; Deputy Editor, North Western Evening Mail, Barrow-in-Furness, 1985-89; Business Editor, Western Daily Press, Bristol, 1989-94; Business Editor, Manchester Evening News, 1994-2000. BT Business Journalist of the Year, 1996; BT North West Business Journalist of the Year, 1996. Recreations: theatre; music; walking; swimming; badminton; travelling.

Nutton, Richard William, MB, BS, MD, FRCS. Consultant Orthopaedic Surgeon, since 1987; Honorary Senior Lecturer, since 1989; b. 16.11.51, Halifax; m., Theresa Mary Turney; 2 s.; 1 d. Educ. Sedbergh School; Newcastle upon Tyne University. Special interest in knee and shoulder surgery; Honorary Medical Adviser to the Scottish Rugby Union; Governor, Merchiston Castle School, Edinburgh. Recreations: fishing; shooting; golf; skiing; cycling. Address: Spire Murrayfield Hospital, 122 Corstorphine Road, Edinburgh EH12 6UD; T.- 07738260764; e-mail: info@richardnutton.co.uk

O

Ó Baoill, Professor Colm, MA, PhD. Professor of Celtic, Aberdeen University, since 1996; b. 22.9.38, Armagh, Ireland; 3 d. Educ. St. Patrick's College, Armagh; Queen's University of Belfast. Assistant Lecturer, Queen's University of Belfast, 1962; Aberdeen University: Lecturer, 1966, Senior Lecturer, 1980, retired 2003. Chief, Gaelic Society, Inverness, 1993. Address: (h.) 19 King's Crescent, Old Aberdeen AB24 3HJ; T.-01224 637064; e-mail: c.oboyle@abdn.ac.uk

O'Brien, Gerry. Non-Executive Director; supporting growth and development with strategic, financial, risk management and government expertise; Chief Executive, NHS Orkney, 2018-2020. Educ. St Ambrose High School; University of Stirling. Career history: Deputy Finance Director, NHS Borders, 1998-2009; Director of Finance: NHS Orkney, 2009-2015, Scottish Ambulance Service, 2015-18.

O'Brien, Susan, BA (Hons), BPhil, LLB. Chair of the Scottish Child Abuse Inquiry, 2015-2016; Queen's Counsel, since 1998; Fellow of the Chartered Institute of Arbitrators, since 2018; Advocate, since 1987; b. 13.8.52, Edinburgh; m., Professor Peter Ross; 2 d. Educ. St George's School for Girls, Edinburgh; York University; Edinburgh University. Admitted Solicitor, 1980; Assistant Solicitor, Shepherd and Wedderburn, WS, 1980-86; Standing Junior Counsel to Registrar General, 1991, and to Home Office, 1992-97, and to Keeper of the Registers, 1998; Temporary Sheriff, 1995-99; fee paid Employment Judge, Employment Tribunals, 2000-2015; Member of Investigatory Powers Tribunal, 2009-2020; fee paid Chairman of Pensions Appeal Tribunals for Scotland, 2012-2015; Reporter to Scottish Legal Aid Board, 1999-2005; Chair, Caleb Ness Inquiry for Edinburgh and The Lothians Child Protection Committee, 2003; Chairman, Faculty Services Ltd., (and office bearer in the Faculty of Advocates), 2005-07. Address: (b.) Advocates' Library, Parliament Square, Edinburgh EH1 1RQ; T.-0131-226 5071.

O'Carroll, Aidan. Chair, Institute of Directors in Scotland, since 2018; Chair, Revenue Scotland, since 2021; appointed Global & EMEIA Compliance and Reporting Leader, EY in 2013, appointed Tax Partner in 2017; appointed Global Tax Markets Leader, Ernst & Young Global in 2006. Address: Institute of Directors Scotland, 10 Charlotte Square, Edinburgh EH2 4DR; T.-0131 557 5488.

O'Carroll, Derek, LLB (Hons), DipLP. Appointed Sheriff in 2010, based at Airdrie; called to Bar, 2000; part-time Chairman, Social Security Appeals Tribunal, 1999-2007; part-time Chairman, Private Rented Housing Panel for Scotland, 2007-2010; part-time Chairman, Rent Assessment Panel for Scotland, 2002-07; part-time Chairman, Mental Health Tribunal for Scotland, 2005-2010; part-time Sheriff, 2006-2010; b. 20.1.60, St Albans. Educ. Cults Academy, Aberdeen; Edinburgh University. Citizens Rights Office, Edinburgh, 1982-85; Castlemilk Law Centre, Glasgow, 1985; Uludag University, Turkey, 1985-88; Transfert, Paris, 1988-90; Legal Services Agency, Glasgow, 1990-94; Govan Law Centre, Glasgow, 1995-99. Member, Scottish Legal Aid Board, 1998-2002; Convener, Scottish Legal Action Group, 2001-04; Director, Faculty Services Ltd., 2003-07; Member, Council of Faculty of Advocates, 2005-08;

Member, Council of the Sheriffs' Association, 2011-2014; Honorary Secretary and Treasurer, Sheriffs' Association, 2015-2020; Director, Thistle Foundation, 2005-07. Recreations: good food and wine; swimming; pool; keep-fit; travel; hill walking.
E-mail: sheriffdocarroll@scotcourts.gov.uk

O'Connor, Dr Susan. Director, Scottish Civic Trust, since 2018; previously Senior Projects Advisor for Scotland with the Prince's Regeneration Trust. Educ. Trinity College Dublin; University College Dublin; University of the West of England; Glasgow School of Art; University of Bath. Address: Scottish Civic Trust, 42 Miller Street, Glasgow G1 1DT; T.-0141 221 1466.

O'Donnell, Annemarie. Chief Executive, Glasgow City Council, since 2014; m.; 2 c. Joined Glasgow District Council from a legal practice in the east end of Glasgow in 1991; worked as a solicitor and then senior solicitor in a team focusing on construction, housing and planning; promoted to Chief Solicitor - leading the council's work on commercial contracts, procurement, planning and environmental law (1996-2003); appointed Assistant Head of Legal and Administrative Services, a new post with responsibility for the running of elections - along with committee services, registrars, litigation, licensing and corporate law; two-year secondment as Depute Director of Social Work Services (played a key role in steering the service through a significant programme of service reform); returned to Corporate Services in 2007, serving as Assistant Director and Head of External Governance; Executive Director of Corporate Services, 2011-2014. Member of the Law Society of Scotland. Address: City Chambers, Glasgow G2 1DU; T.-0141 287 4552.
E-mail: annemarie.o'donnell@glasgow.gov.uk

O'Donnell, Cllr Fiona. Councillor (Labour), East Lothian Council, since 2017; MP (Labour), East Lothian, 2010-15; b. 27.1.60, Nanaimo, Vancouver Island, Canada; 3 s.; 1 d. Educ. Lochaber High School; University of Glasgow. Member, Select Committee on Scottish Affairs, 2010-2011; Shadow Minister for Fisheries and the Natural Environment, 2011-2012; Member, Select Committee on International Development, 2012-15; Member, GMB. Address: East Lothian Council, John Muir House, Brewery Park, Haddington, East Lothian EH41 3HA; T.-01620 827022.

O'Donnell, Frank, MA (Hons). Editor-in-Chief: The Press and Journal, since 2020, The Scotsman, Edinburgh Evening News and Scotland on Sunday, 2017-2020. Educ. George Heriot's School, Edinburgh; University of Edinburgh. Career history: Reporter, Carrick Gazette, 1997-98; Bureau Chief, Scottish News Agency/Dundee Press Agency, 1998-2000; The Scotsman: General Reporter, 2000-01, Edinburgh Correspondent, 2001-02, Consumer Affairs Correspondent, 2003-04, Forward Planning Editor, 2004, Deputy News Editor, 2005-07, News Editor, 2007-09, Assistant Editor (Group Head of News), 2009-2012; Editor, Edinburgh Evening News, 2012-15; Managing Editor, The Scotsman, Edinburgh Evening News, Scotland on Sunday, 2015-16; Director of Digital Content, Johnston Press, 2016-17. Address: Aberdeen Journals Ltd, 5th Floor, 1 Marischal Square, Broad Street, Aberdeen AB10 1BL.

O'Donnell, Mark, MA (Hons), MSc. Strategy Director, Philanthropy & Fundraising Europe, since 2022. Educ. Portobello High School; University of Edinburgh; Open University. Development Officer, Drugs and Alcohol, West Lothian Council, 2000-02; Director of Projects & Service Development, ASH Scotland, 2002-06; Head of Planning,

Performance & Estates (General Manager), Scottish Ambulance Service, 2006-09; Director of Planning & Equalities (maternity cover secondment), NHS Health Scotland, 2009; Scottish Government: National Smoking Cessation Co-ordinator (Secondment), 2010-11, Acting Policy Director Health & Social Care (Secondment), 2013-14, Deputy Director Health & Social Care (Secondment), 2011-14; Director, MS Society Scotland, 2014-15; Chief Executive, Chest Heart & Stroke Scotland, 2015-17; Chief Executive, Sight Scotland and Sight Scotland Veterans, 2017-2021; Senior Manager, Infrastructure, Government & Healthcare Consulting, KPMG UK, 2021-2022. Board Member/Vice Chair, Scottish Drugs Forum, 2000-04; Scottish Advisory Board Member, Marie Curie UK, 2009-12; Board Member, Health and Social Care Alliance Scotland, 2015; Trustee, SCVO (Scottish Council for Voluntary Organisations), since 2014; Chair, Liberton Primary School Association, 2012-14. Address: (b.) The Inch, Fort Augustus PH32 4BL.

O'Donovan, Professor Oliver Michael Timothy, MA, DPhil, FBA, FRSE. Emeritus Professor, University of Edinburgh, since 2012 (Professor, Christian Ethics and Practical Theology, 2006-2012); Honorary Professor, University of St Andrews, since 2013; b. 28.06.45, Edgware, Middlesex; m., Joan Elizabeth Lockwood; 2 s. Educ. University College School, Hampstead; Balliol College, Oxford. Lecturer, Wycliffe Hall, Oxford, 1972-77; Assistant Professor, Wycliffe College, Toronto, 1977-82; Regius Professor of Moral and Pastoral Theology and Canon of Christ Church, Oxford, 1982-2006. Publications: Author: Resurrection and Moral Order, The Desire of The Nations, The Ways of Judgment, The Church in Crisis, The Word in Small Boats, Self, World and Time; Finding and Seeking; Entering into Rest. Address: 6a Comely Park, Dunfermline KY12 7HU.
E-mail: oliver.odonovan@ed.ac.uk

Ogilvie, Campbell. Former President, Scottish Football Association (2011-2015). Career history: appointed General Secretary, Rangers F.C. in 1978 and later became a director until 2005; Operations Director, Heart of Midlothian, 2005-08, appointed Managing Director in 2008; second vice-president of the Scottish Football Association, 2003-2007, first vice-president, 2007-2011.

Ogilvy, Sir Francis (Gilbert Arthur), 14th Bt, MRICS. Chartered Surveyor; b. 32.4.69; m., Dorothy Margaret Stein; 3 s.; 1 d. Educ. Edinburgh Academy; Glenalmond College; Royal Agricultural College, Cirencester; BSc (Hons) (Reading). Address: (h.) Winton Castle, Pencaitland, East Lothian EH34 5AT.

Ogle, Geoff. Chief Executive Officer, Food Standards Scotland (FSS), since 2015; Interim Director, Food Standards Agency in Scotland (FSA), June 2014 - March 2015. Civil servant, since 1984 and during this time has undertaken a variety of posts including Private Secretary to the Child Support Agency (CSA), Chief Executive and both Head of External Relations and Head of Internal Communications in the CSA; moved in 2002 to the Department for Work and Pensions (DWP) as a pension Centre Manager and then Head of the International Pension Centre; joined the Food Standards Agency in 2008, posts included Senior Investigating officer during the horsemeat incident and FSA's Acting Director in Wales.

O'Hagan, Professor David, BSc, PhD, DSc, CChem, FRSC, FRSE. Professor, School of Chemistry, University of St Andrews, since 2000; b. 29.9.61, Glasgow; m., Anne; 3 d. Educ. Holyrood Secondary School, Glasgow; Glasgow University; Southampton University. Postdoctoral research, Ohio State University, 1985-86; University of Durham: Demonstrator, 1986-88, Lecturer in Chemistry, 1988-99, Professor of Organic Chemistry, 1999-2000. Chairman, Editorial Board, Natural Product Reports, and Journal of Fluorine Chemistry; Chairman, RSC Fluorine Subject Group. Publication: The Polyketide Metabolites, 1991. Recreations: golf; walking; gardening. Address: Millbank Park, 51 Millbank, Cupar, Fife KY15 5EA; T.-01334 650708; e-mail: dol@st-andrews.ac.uk

O'Hara, Brendan. MP (SNP), Argyll and Bute, since 2015; Culture and Media spokesperson, 2017-18; spokesperson on Defence, 2015-17; b. 27.4.63, Glasgow. Educ. St. Andrew's Secondary, Carntyne. Educ. Strathclyde University. Successful career as a TV producer; wrote, produced and directed the "Road To Referendum" documentary series which was broadcast on STV in 2013 and was subsequently nominated for a BAFTA Scotland award in the Current Affairs category; worked for STV, Sky Sports and the BBC. Credits include Comedy Connections and Movie Connections (BBC1), The Football Years (STV) and Scotland's Greatest Album (STV). Currently working on the second series of David Hayman's very successful series following in the footsteps of Tom Weir. Address: House of Commons, London SW1A 0AA.

O'Hare, Raymond. Chair of Technology and Change Board (part-time), ENABLE Scotland, since 2020; Chair, Project Scotland, 2016-2021; m., Elizabeth; 1 s.; 1 d. Career history: Sales Executive, Nixdorf Computer, 1981-87; Senior Sales Executive, ICL/Fujitsu, 1987-89; Account Director, Digital Equipment Corporation, 1989-97; Director, Microsoft Scotland, 1997-2010; Chairman, Institute of Directors Scotland, 2007-2011; Founder and Director, OCSolutions (O'Hare Consulting Solutions), since 2010; Member of the Board of Management, Scottish Qualifications Authority, 2010-18; Non Executive Advisor: SnapDragon Monitoring Ltd, 2015-17, Loxley Colour, since 2012; Non Executive Board Member: Exception Ltd, since 2010, Castle Computer Services, 2012-18; Business Development Director, Level10, 2012-16; Independent Non Executive Director: Xedo Software Ltd, 2010-17, ACS Group Board, 2014-17. Regular contributor to press and media over the last 15 years and speaks regularly at conferences and events on the topics of practical leadership, technology trends and the importance of innovation in business and government. Recreations: music; football; golf; travel.

O'Kane, Paul, MA (Hons). MSP (Scottish Labour), West Scotland (Region), since 2021; Shadow Minister for Public Health and Social Care, since 2021. Educ. University of Glasgow. Career history: Parliamentary Researcher, Office of Rt Hon Jim Murphy MP, House of Commons, 2007-2010; Development Officer (Volunteers and Organisations), Volunteer Centre, Kirkintilloch, 2010-2012; Parliamentary Researcher, Office of Gemma Doyle MP, House of Commons, 2012-13; Volunteer Development Officer, The Beardmore Trust, Dalmuir, 2013-14; ENABLE Scotland: National Volunteer Co-ordinator, 2014-15, Campaigns and Parliamentary Officer, 2015-2018, Public Affairs Officer, 2018-2021, Policy and Participation Manager, 2019-2021; appointed Depute Convener, Renfrewshire Valuation Joint Board, Paisley in 2012; APSE Scotland: Chair, Roads and Street Lighting, Hamilton, 2012-17, appointd Chair, Transport and Mechanical Advisory Group, Hamilton in 2017; elected Councillor, East Renfrewshire Council in 2012, became Deputy Leader and Convenor for Education and Equalities. Address: The Scottish Parliament, Edinburgh EH99 1SP; T.-0131

348 5942.
E-mail: Paul.O'Kane.msp@parliament.scot

Oldfather, Irene, BA (Hons), MSc. Director, Health and Social Care Alliance, since 2011; MSP (Lab), Cunninghame South, 1999-2011; former Chair, Scottish Parliament European Committee, 2002-2011; Member, European Committee of Regions, 1997-2011; Vice President, Socialist Group, 2002-2011; former Chair, Cross Party Group on Alzheimers; former Member, Cross Party Group on Tobacco Control; b. Glasgow. Educ. Strathclyde University; University of Arizona. Researcher, Dumbarton Council on Alcohol, 1976-77; Lecturer, University of Arizona, 1977-78; Research Officer, Strathclyde Regional Council, 1978-79; various posts, Glasgow District Council Housing Department, 1979-90; Political Researcher, 1990-98; writer and broadcaster on European affairs, 1994-98; part-time Lecturer, University of the West of Scotland, 1996-98; Councillor, North Ayrshire, 1995-99 and since 2012; UK Member, European Economic and Social Committee (EESC), 2015-2020; Director Engagement, Strategic Partnership Health and Social Care Alliance, since 2011; Vice Chair, Scottish Ambulance Board, since 2019; Flu/Covid Vaccination Board, since 2020; Chair, EUPATI Scotland, since 2020.

Oliver, Professor Christopher William, BSc, MBBS, FRCS (Eng), FRCS (Tr&Orth), FRCP (Ed), FRCS (Ed), DMI RCSEd, MD, FFSTEd, FRSA. Associate Research Fellow, Transport Research Institute, Edinburgh Napier University, since 2019; King James IV Professor, Royal College of Surgeons Edinburgh (RCSEd), 2018-2020; retired Consultant Trauma and Orthopaedic Surgeon, Royal Infirmary of Edinburgh, 1997-2018; Honorary Professor, Physical Activity for Health, University of Edinburgh, 2015-2018; Patron, Ambassador Mobile International Surgical Teams, 2015-2020 and since 2021. Board Member: Edinburgh and Lothians Greenspace Trust, 2015-2020, Drug and Alcohol, Psychotherapies Ltd (DAPL) Fife, 2015-2020; b. 5.1.60, Stratford, London; m., Josephine Hilton; 2 d. Educ. Romford Technical High School, London; University College Hospital, London. Basic surgical training, London and Harrow, 1985-89; Orthopaedic Registrar, York, Leeds, Harrogate, 1989-92; Research Fellow, Spinal Science, Middlesbrough, 1992-94; Senior Registrar, Oswestry and Stoke-on-Trent, 1994-96; Trauma Fellow, Harborview Hospital, Seattle, USA, 1996; Consultant Trauma Surgeon, John Radcliffe Hospital, Oxford, 1996-97. Member, Council, RCSEd, 2002-12; Convener of Examinations, RCSEd, 2006-08; Chairman, Intercollegiate Committee for Basic Surgical Examinations, 2008-2011. Senior Editor of trauma surgery section of Oxford Textbook "Fundamentals of Surgery, Oxford Textbooks in Surgery", 2016. Listed by The Sunday Herald as a leader of innovation in "NHS at 70: Celebrating a Revolution in Scotland's Healthcare", 2018. Lifetime career was profiled by the British Medical Journal, "From orthopaedic surgeon to fitness professor", 2018. Gold Medal Lecture, Old Oswestrian's, Robert Jones & Agnes Hunt Orthopaedic Hospital, Oswestry, Shropshire, 2021. Recreations: data visualisation; cycling; whitewater and sea kayaking; boat restoration; computers. Address: 21 George Street, Anstruther, Cellardyke, Fife KY10 3AS.
E-mail: cwoliver@btopenworld.com
Web: https://cyclingsurgeon.bike
Orcid: https://orcid.org/0000-0003-1331-6429
Twitter: @CyclingSurgeon

Oliver, Neil, MA, HonDLitt. Television presenter, freelance archaeologist and author; b. 21.2.67, Renfrewshire; m., Trudi; 3 c. Educ. Dumfries Academy; University of Glasgow. Worked as a freelance archaeologist, before training as a journalist; best known as a presenter of several BBC historical and archaeological documentary series, including A History of Scotland, Vikings, and Coast. Received honorary degrees from Abertay University in 2011 and the University of Glasgow in 2015. Patron of the Association of Lighthouse Keepers. Publications: Castles and Forts (Co-Author), 2006; Not Forgotten, 2006; Coast from the Air, 2007; Amazing Tales for Making Men Out of Boys, 2008; A History of Scotland, 2009; A History of Ancient Britain, 2011; Vikings, 2012; Master of Shadows, 2015; The Story of the British Isles in 100 Places, 2018; Wisdom of the Ancients: Life lessons from our distant past, 2020.

Olivier, Professor Steve, PhD. Principal and Vice-Chancellor, Robert Gordon University, since 2020; b. 11.3.60, Pretoria, South Africa; m., Jennifer; 2 s; 2 step d. Educ. Northlands Boys High School, 1974-77; Rhodes University. Career history: Senior Sports Officer, Rhodes University, 1989-93; Senior Lecturer: University of Zululand, 1994-98, Staffordshire University, 1999; Head of Department, Sports Science, Edge Hill University, 2000; Head of Department, Northumbria University, 2001-05; Abertay University: Head of School, Social and Health Sciences, 2005-08, Deputy Principal, 2008-09, Pro-Vice-Chancellor, 2010-12, University Vice-Principal and Deputy Vice-Chancellor, 2012-2020; Provost, Deputy Principal and Deputy Vice-Chancellor, University of the West of Scotland, 2018-2020. Governor, Fife College, 2015-18; Trustee, Rhodes University UK Trust, since 2005. Publications: book chapters; contributions to journals. Recreations: surfing; swimming; surfski paddling; multisport endurance events; former Rugby player and coach; former triathlete; former RNLI lifeboat crew member; reading; family. Address: Robert Gordon University, Garthdee House, Garthdee Road, Garthdee, Aberdeen AB10 7AQ; T.-01224 262001.
E-mail: steve.olivier@rgu.ac.uk

Olumide, Eunice, MBE, BA, PG Degree, MA. Scottish supermodel, actress and curator; b. 6.10.87, Edinburgh. Educ. Balerno Community High School; Glasgow Caledonian University; Queen Mary, University of London; University of Pennsylvania. Career history: Presenter, BBC Television, 2013-14; Broadcaster, Sky, 2014; Television Presenter, BBC, 2015-16; Radio Presenter, BBC Radio, 2015-16; Broadcaster Television Presenter, Film and Television, since 2013; Actress, since 2014; Patron, AAI (Adopt an Intern), since 2014. Appeared in world wide campaigns, fashion weeks and editorials including WAD Paris, ID Magazine, Dazed & Confused, Oyster, Paper Cut NY, New York Magazine, Pride, Vogue.com, Vogue.it, Bahrain Confidential and many more. Walking for designer's including Mulberry, JJ Noki, Christopher Kane, Henry Holland and Harris Tweed. Fundraiser for charities including Children's Hospice Scotland, The Well Foundation and The Columbus Hospice. Nominated for the "Model of the Year" in the Scottish Fashion Awards, sponsored by Vogue in 2007, 2011 and 2013; awarded Best Contribution to Fashion and Media in Scotland at the Scottish Fashion Awards, 2013.

O'Mahony, Sheriff Keith Peter. Sheriff, Tayside, Central and Fife, since 2020. Educ. Glasgow University; Haarlem Business School, Netherlands (Diploma in European Law). Career history: Jackson Hetherington Solicitors in 1997; solicitor with Scottish Borders Council, East Lothian Council and McKay and Norwell Solicitors; joined the COPFS in 2001, became Senior Procurator Fiscal Depute; appointed a Solicitor Advocate and Advocate Depute in 2015; appointed a summary sheriff in 2018. Address: Falkirk Sheriff Court, Main Street, Falkirk FK1 4AR.

Ó Maolalaigh (Mullally), Professor Roibeard, BA Hons, MA, PhD. Professor of Gaelic, University of Glasgow, since 2005, Vice-Principal and Head of the College of Arts, since 2015, Head of Department, Department of Celtic,

2007-2011, Head of School of Humanities, 2012-14, Holder of the first ever established Chair of Gaelic, since 2010; b. 05.07.66, Dublin, Ireland; m., Margaret MacLeod; 4 s. Educ. Drimnagh Castle, CBS; University College, Dublin; University of Edinburgh. Career: Lecturer, Department of Celtic, University of Edinburgh; Assistant Professor and Bibliographer, School of Celtic Studies, Dublin Institute for Advanced Studies. Chairman, Gaelic Books Council, 2005-2010. Address: (b.) Celtic and Gaelic, School of Humanities, University of Glasgow G12 8QQ; T.-0141-330-4222; e-mail: roibeard.omaolalaigh@glasgow.ac.uk

O'Neill, Dr Eamonn, BA Hons (Modern History), PhD. Associate Professor and School Leader in Journalism, Edinburgh Napier University, since 2016; Course Director, MSc in Investigative Journalism and Lecturer in Journalism and English, University of Strathclyde, since 2002. Educ. University of Strathclyde. Career history: Senior Producer, Scottish Television, 1990-96; Contributing Editor, GQ magazine, London, 1995-98; Special Contributor, The Scotsman, 1999-2003; Lecturer in Journalism and Programme Director of MSc in Investigative Journalism, University of Strathclyde, 2002-16; Special Correspondent, The Herald, 2003-09; Writer At Large, Esquire magazine, 1998-2011; researched, produced, directed and presented investigative productions for STV, Channel 4, BBC, Discovery, National Geographic and The Crime & Investigation Network. National and international awards including: The Paul Foot Award; The British Press Awards; The Scottish BT Media Awards and The British Film & Television Academy; awarded an American IRE (Investigative Reporters and Editors) honour in the Special Award category for lifetime's investigative work on miscarriages of justice; joined the Council of JUSTICE Scotland in 2012; gave expert evidence to The Scottish Parliament and The House of Lords on Investigative Journalism in 2013; chaired international conferences regularly for the International Network of Street Papers (INSP); regularly review the media on BBC Radio Scotland and contribute to various productions. Address: School of Arts and Creative Industries, Edinburgh Napier University, Merchiston Campus, Colinton Road, Edinburgh EH10 5DT; T.-0845 260 6040; e-mail: e.o'neill@napier.ac.uk

O'Neill, John, MA (Hons), PGCE (Distinction). Rector, The High School of Glasgow, since 2015. Educ. The University of Glasgow. Teacher of History, Politics and Religion, St Thomas More School, 1988-89; Teacher of History & Modern Studies, Glasgow City Council, 1989-92; Teacher of History & Politics & House Tutor (Rogerson West), Merchiston Castle School, 1992-97; Teacher of History/Modern Studies and Assistant Housemaster, The Glasgow Academy, 1997-2000; House Master, Rogerson West House, Merchiston Castle School, 2000-02; Head of Sixth Form and Housemaster, Merchiston Castle School, 2002-04; Senior Deputy Rector, The High School of Glasgow, 2004-15; Member of Glasgow Medieval Trust; Member of Board of Governors, Morrison's Academy, Crieff. Address: (b.) 637 Crow Road, Glasgow G13 1PL; T.-0141 954 9628.

O'Neill, Dr Mark William Robert, BA Hons, HDipEd, FMA, PhD. Honorary Research Fellow, School of Culture & Creative Arts, University of Glasgow; Museum Consultant, since 2016; Director of Policy and Research, Glasgow Life (formerly Culture and Sport Glasgow), 2009-2016; b. 10.11.56. Educ. University College, Cork; Leicester University; Getty Leadership Inst. Curator, Springburn Museum, 1985-90; Glasgow Museums, since 1990; Keeper of Social History, 1990-92; Senior Curator of History, 1992-97; Head, Curatorial Services, 1997-98; Head, Glasgow Museums, 1998-2005, appointed Head of Arts and Museums in 2005. Publications: numerous articles on philosophy and practice of museums. Recreations: classical music; fiction; psychology.

O'Neill, Professor Shane, BA, MA, PhD. Senior Vice-Principal, University of Dundee, since 2021. Educ. Belvedere College, Dublin; University College Dublin; University of Glasgow. Career history: Queen's University Belfast: Professor of Political Theory, 2002-2016, Dean of Arts, Humanities and Social Sciences, 2009-2015; University Envoy to the Americas, 2010-2015; Keele University: Pro Vice-Chancellor for Planning and Advancement, 2016-2021, Executive Dean of the Faculty of Humanities and Social Sciences, 2016-2021, Executive Lead for Race Equality Charter Self-Assessment (Part-time), 2016-2021. Fulbright Senior Scholar, University of Pennsylvania in 2004/5; also held Visiting Professorships at Hong Kong University, Macquarie University in Sydney, Australia and Queen's University in Ontario, Canada. Address: University of Dundee, Nethergate, Dundee DD1 4HN; e-mail: soneill001@dundee.ac.uk

Ord, Peter John, CVO, BSc (Hon Ag), FBA, FRICS, FRAgS. Chartered Surveyor; b. 18.5.47, Edinburgh University; London University (Wye College). Hamilton and Kinneil Estates, 1971-74; Factor of Strathmore Estates and Strathmore English Estates, 1974-95; Arthur Young McLelland Moors/Ernst and Young, 1974-90; Partner, Youngs Chartered Surveyors, 1990-95; Resident Factor of Balmoral Estate, 1995-2009; Consultant with Bell Ingram; Trustee, Invercauld Estate, Braemar; Director and Trustee, The Outdoor Access Trust for Scotland; Director, Shielbridge Ltd; Elder, Glamis Parish Church. Recreations: skiing; sailing; fishing; shooting; curling; Scottish Country Dancing. Address: (h.) The Mill, Milton of Ogilvie, Glamis, Forfar, Angus DD8 1UN; T.-01307 840719. E-mail: pordbnc@aol.com

O'Regan, Noel, BMus, MSc, DPhil. Retired Reader in Music, University of Edinburgh; b. 27.12.49, Roscommon, Ireland. Educ. Gormanston College; University College Galway; University College Cork; Oxford University. Research Chemist, Pfizer Corporation, 1974-78; Teacher, Christian Brothers College, Cork, 1978-80; Lecturer in Music, University of Lancaster, 1984-85, University of Edinburgh, 1985-96; Senior Lecturer, University of Edinburgh, 1996-2015; Reader in Music, 2015-17. Chairman, Georgian Concert Society; Editor, Music & Letters, since 2018. Recreations: music; films; hillwalking; travelling. Address: (h.) 14 Rankeillor Street, Edinburgh EH8 9HY; T.-0131 667 7853; e-mail: n.o.regan@ed.ac.uk

Ormiston, Linda, OBE (2001), MA, DRSAMD, Hon. DMus (St. Andrews). Singer — Mezzo Soprano; b. 15.1.48, Motherwell. Educ. Dalziel High School, Motherwell; Glasgow University; Royal Scottish Academy of Music and Drama; London Opera Centre. Has sung all over Britain, France, Belgium, Italy, Germany, Austria, Holland and Yugoslavia; has sung regularly at Scottish Opera, Opera North, and Glyndebourne; also well-known in lighter vein and as a member of The Music Box; recordings include Noyes Fludde, HMS Pinafore and Ruddigore with New Sadlers Wells Opera and Tell Me Pretty Maiden; has appeared at New York, Vancouver, Monte Carlo, Brussels and Tokyo; debut, Frankfurt Opera, 1993; debut, Salzburg Festival, 1994; debut, English National Opera, 1995. Recreations: playing the piano; skating; golf.

Ormond, Rupert Frank Guy, BA, MA, PhD. Director, Marine Conservation International; Hon. Professor, Heriot-Watt University, Edinburgh; b. 1.6.46, Bristol; m., Mauvis ne Gore; 2 s.; 1 d. Educ. Clifton College, Bristol; Peterhouse, Cambridge. Career history: Research Chair, King Abdulaziz University, Jeddah, Saudi Arabia, 2015-2019; Secretary, International Coral Reef Society, 2011-18; Director, University Marine Biological Station Millport, 1999-2006; Senior Lecturer, London University, 1999-

2006; Visiting Professor, Glasgow University, 2000-07; Chief Scientist, Save Our Seas Foundation, 2007-2011; Lecturer/Senior Lecturer, Biology Department, 1974-99, Director, Tropical Marine Research Unit, 1982-99, York University. District Councillor, Ryedale District Council, 1987-96; Council, WWF Scotland, 2000-06, Scottish Natural Heritage Scientific Advisory Committee, 2000-04. Publications include: Red Sea Coral Reefs (Co-Author); Marine Biodiversity (Co-Author). Recreations: natural history; travel; classical music. Address: (h.) Komani, Aros Mains, Aros, Isle of Mull, Argyll & Bute PA72 6JP.

O'Rourke, Daniel (Donny), MA, MPhil. Poet, journalist, film-maker, broadcaster, and teacher; b. 5.7.59, Port Glasgow. Educ. St. Mirin's Academy, Paisley; Glasgow University; Pembroke College, Cambridge. Vice President, European Youth Council, 1983-85; Chairman, Scottish Youth Council, 1982-84; Producer, BBC TV and Radio Scotland, 1984-86; Reporter, Scottish Television, 1986-87, Producer, 1987-92, Head of Arts, 1992-93, Head of Arts and Documentaries, 1993-94; Executive Producer, BBC Scotland, 1994-95; folk music reviewer, The Herald and New Statesman, 1985-90; Creative Writing Fellow, Glasgow University and Strathclyde University, 1995-97; Head of English and Media Studies, Department of Adult and Continuing Education, Glasgow University, 1996-98; Poet in Residence, Edinburgh International Book Festival, 1999; Columnist, Sunday Herald, 1999; Member, Manpower Services Commission Youth Training Board, 1982-84; Member, Scottish Community Education Council, 1981-84; Chairman of Judges, Scottish Writer of the Year Award, 1996, 1997; Director, Tron Theatre Company, 1993-95; Member, Editorial Board, "11/9"; Artistic Director, Reacquaintance Robert Burns in Glasgow (year-long celebration), 2000; theatre: The Kerrera Saga (with George Wyllie), 1998, On Your Nerve, A Wake for Frank O'Hara, 1996. Major 'special recognition' Scottish Arts Council Award, 2008, 2009; Swiss Scots exchange fellow, Bern. 2008; shortlisted for National Library of Scotland pamphlet prize for 'One Light Burning'; Dave Whyte CD of his setting of these songs launched, March 2009. Publications: Second City, 1991; Rooming Houses of America, 1993; Dream State, the new Scottish poets, 1994; chapter in Burns Now, 1994; Eftirs/Afters, 1996; The Waist Band and Other Poems, 1997; Modern Music, 1997; Ae Fond Kiss, 1999; Across the Water, 2000 (Co-Editor); New Writing Scotland anthologies – Some Kind of Embrace, 1997; The Glory Signs, 1998; Friends and Kangaroos, 1999; The Cleft in My Heart, 2008; Blame Yesterday, 2008; Still Waiting To Be Wise (CD, with Dave Whyte), 1999; On A Roll, 2001; poems in various anthologies and textbooks. Recreations: Italian food; playing guitar; Irish literature; Americana. Address: (h.) 63 Barrington Drive, Glasgow G4 9ES.
E-mail: donny.orourke@btinternet.com

Orr, John Douglas, CBE, MB, ChB, MBA, FRCSEd, FRCP (Edin). Consultant Paediatric Surgeon, Royal Hospital for Sick Children, Edinburgh, 1984-2009; b. 11.7.45, Edinburgh; m., Elizabeth Erica Yvonne Miklinska; 2 s.; 1 d. Educ. George Heriot's School, Edinburgh; High School, Dundee; University of St. Andrews; Stirling University. Formerly Medical Director, The Royal Hospital for Sick Children, Edinburgh and Associate Medical Director, University Hospitals Division - NHS Lothian. President, Royal College of Surgeons of Edinburgh, 2006-09. Recreations: golf; gardening. Address: (b.) Royal College of Surgeons of Edinburgh, Nicolson Street, Edinburgh EH8 9DW; T.-0131-527 1600; e-mail: PastPresident@rcsed.ac.uk

Orr-Ewing, Duncan Charles, BA, MRICS. Head of Species and Land Management, RSPB Scotland, since 1999; b. 19.01.64, Redhill; m., Caroline Louise; 1 d. Educ. Dr Challoner's Grammar School, Amersham, Bucks; Durham University. Chartered Surveyor, Humberts, Hatfield, Herts, 1986-91; Project Officer for Red Kite Reintroduction, RSPB Scotland, Inverness, 1991-94; Conservation Officer, Central Scotland, RSPB Scotland, Glasgow, 1994-99; Head of Species and Land Management and member of Scottish Leadership Team, RSPB Scotland, Edinburgh, since 1999. Member of Scotland's Moorland Forum; Chair, Advisory Board, Scottish Land and Estates Wildlife Estates, Board of South of Scotland Golden Eagle Project, Link Deer Task Force; Chair, Central Scotland and member of Tayside Raptor Study Groups and Scottish Ornithologist's Club. Recreations: birdwatching; bird ringing; foreign travel. Address: (b.) RSPB Scotland, 2 Lochside View, Edinburgh EH12 9DH; T.-0131 317 4100; e-mail: duncan.orr-ewing@rspb.org.uk

Orr Ewing, Major Edward Stuart, DL, JP, CVO. Lord Lieutenant, Wigtown, 1989-2006; b. 28.9.31, London; m. (1), F.A.B. Farquhar (m. dissolved); 1 s.; 2 d.; m. (2), Diana Mary Waters. Educ. Sherborne; RMCS, Shrivenham. Black Watch RHR, 1950-69 (Major); Farmer and Landowner, since 1964. Recreations: country sports; sailing; painting.

Osborne, Rt. Hon. Lord (Kenneth Hilton Osborne), QC (Scot). Senator of the College of Justice, 1990-2011; b. 9.7.37. Advocate, 1962; QC, 1976; Chairman, Local Government Boundary Commission, 1990-2000.

Osborne, Sandra, MSc. MP (Labour), Ayr, Carrick and Cumnock, 2005-2015, Ayr, 1997-2005; b. 23.2.56; m., Alastair; 2 d. Educ. Camphill Senior Secondary School, Paisley; Anniesland College; Jordanhill College; Strathclyde University. Former community worker.

Osborne, Stephen Peter, BA, MSc, MSocSci, PhD. Professor of Public Management, University of Edinburgh, since 2006; b. 25.9.53, Birmingham; divorced; 3 s.; 2 d. Educ. Solihull School; Universities of Sussex, Bath, Birmingham and Aston. Social Worker, 1976-85; Social Work Manager, 1985-90; Lecturer/Professor, University of Aston, 1990-2006; University of Edinburgh, since 2006; Associate Dean for Quality, University of Edinburgh, 2012-2013; Deputy Dean of University of Edinburgh Business School, 2013-16, Director of Centre for Service Excellence, since 2016. Fellow of the Edinburgh Futures Institute and of the Academy of Social Sciences. Recreations: gardening; hill-walking; music; reading. Address: (b.) University of Edinburgh Business School, 29 Buccleuch Place, Edinburgh; T.-07848979975.
E-mail: stephen.osborne@ed.ac.uk

O'Shea, Professor Sir Timothy Michael Martin, FAcSS, FRSE, FREng, PhD, BSc. Professor Emeritus, University of Edinburgh; former Principal and Vice-Chancellor (2002-2018); appointed Professor of Informatics and Education in 2002; b. 28.3.49; m., Professor Eileen Scanlon; 2 s.; 2 d. Educ. Royal Liberty School, Havering; Sussex University; Leeds University. Open University: Founder, Computer Assisted Learning Research Group, 1978, Lecturer, 1980-82, Senior Lecturer, 1983-87, Institute of Educational Technology, Professor of IT and Education, 1987-97, Pro-Vice-Chancellor for QA and Research, 1994-97; Master, Birkbeck College and Professor of Information and Communication Technologies, 1998-2002; Provost, Gresham College, 2000-02; Pro-Vice-Chancellor, 2001-02, University of London. Address: University of Edinburgh, Old College, South Bridge, Edinburgh EH8 9YL.

Osler, Douglas Alexander, CB, KSG, MA (Hons). HM Senior Chief Inspector and Chief Executive, HM Inspectorate of Education, Scottish Executive, 1996-2002; b. 11.10.42, Edinburgh; m., Wendy I. Cochrane; 1 s.; 1 d. Educ. Royal High School, Edinburgh; Edinburgh University; Moray House College of Education. Teacher of

History/Careers Master, Liberton Secondary School, Edinburgh, 1965-68; Principal Teacher of History, Dunfermline High School, 1968-74. English Speaking Union Fellowship to USA, 1966; International Leadership Visitor Program to USA, 1989; President, Standing International Conference of Inspectorates, 1999-2002; Visiting Professor, University of Strathclyde, 2003-05; Interim Scottish Prisons Complaints Commissioner, 2003; Chair, Statutory Inquiry, Northern Ireland, 2004; led inquiry into Scottish Court Service, 2005; Chairman of Commissioners, South Eastern Education and Library Board, Northern Ireland, 2006-2010; Chairman, Royal Blind Asylum and School, 2008-2014; Member, Scottish Committee of SkillForce; Trustee, Scottish Schools Pipes and Drums Trust; Past President, Rotary Club of Edinburgh. Book reviewer, Scotsman newspaper. Publications: Queen Margaret of Scotland; Sources for Modern Studies, Volumes 1 and 2.

Osowska, Francesca, OBE, MA (Econ), MA (EuroEcon), FRSE. Chief Executive Officer, NatureScot, since 2017. Educ. Cumbria; Cambridge University; College of Europe in Bruges. Career history: joined the civil service as an economist in 1993 (Employment Department in Sheffield); after brief stints in London and Brussels, moved to Edinburgh in 1997 as a government economist with the then Scottish Office; joined the Scottish Office education department in 1998 before going on to hold posts in the education and justice departments of the Scottish Executive and was appointed Head of Sport at the Scottish Executive/Government; Principal Private Secretary to the First Minister, 2007-09; Director for Culture, External Affairs and Tourism, Scottish Government, 2009-2010, Director for Housing, Regeneration and the Commonwealth Games, 2010-2013, Director for the Commonwealth Games and Sport, 2013-14; Director for the Scotland Office, The UK Government, 2015-17. Recreations: former competitive triathlete competing for GB at standard and long distance. Completed four "Ironman" triathlons. Address: NatureScot, Silvan House, 231 Corstorphine Road, Edinburgh EH12 7AT; T.-01463 725001; e-mail: ceo@nature.scot

Østergaard, Erik Jorgen. Non Executive Chairman, David MacBrayne Limited, since 2022; b. 3.59. Originally trained in shipping, then studied international economics and management at IMD in Lausanne, Stanford Graduate School of Business, California, and Boot School of Business, University of Chicago (Master of Business Administration degree). More than 35 years of experience in senior management positions in the shipping, ferry and transportation industry; held and holds office as a Non-Executive Board Member or Chairman of several companies in the shipping and transportation industry, numerous government committees and boards of trade associations. Address: David MacBrayne Limited, Ferry Terminal, Gourock PA19 1QP.

O'Sullivan, Very Reverend Monsignor Canon Basil, JCL. Parish Priest, Holy Family, Dunblane, since 1988; appointed Chaplain to His Holiness Benedict XVI, October 2008; b. 1932, Fishguard. Educ. St. Finbarr's College, Cork; All Hallow's College, Dublin; Pontifical University of St. Gregory, Rome. Assistant Priest: St. Joseph's, Dundee, 1959-63, St. Andrew's Cathedral, Dundee, 1963-70; R.C. Chaplain, Dundee University, 1964-70; Parish Priest: St. John Vianney's, Alva, 1970-74, St. Columba's, Dundee, 1974-88. Canon of Dunkeld Chapter, since 1992. Judge of The Scottish Catholic Tribunal; formerly Administrator, Diocese of Dunkeld. Recreations: reading; gardening; walking. Address: (h.) St. Clare's, Claredon Place, Dunblane FK15 9HB; T.-01786 822146.

Oswald, Kirsten Frances. MP (SNP), East Renfrewshire, since 2019 and 2015-17; Deputy Leader of the SNP in the House of Commons, since 2020; Chairman and Business Convener, SNP, since 2018; b. 21.12.72, Dundee; m.; 2 s.

Educ. Carnoustie High School; Glasgow University. Senior Human Resources professional; became active in the Scottish National Party during the 2014 Scottish independence referendum, serving on the committee of the local Women for Independence group with responsibility for local food bank collections. Ran community social media sites. Recreation: keen Dundee United fan. Address: Houses of Parliament, Westminster, London SW1A 0AA.

O'Toole, Ray. Chairman, Stagecoach Group plc, since 2020; b. 7.55. Career history: Group Chief Operating Officer and UK Chief Executive, National Express plc, 2000-2010; responsible for the National Express Group's bus and coach businesses and rail franchises, with operations in Spain, the USA, Canada and the UK; Non Executive Director: ORR - Office of Rail and Road, 2011-15, British Transport Police Authority, 2015-16; Chief Executive, Essential Fleet Services Ltd, Lincoln, 2015-17; Senior Independent Director, Yorkshire Water, since 2014; appointed Non Executive Chairman, Stagecoach Group plc in 2016. Address: Stagecoach Group Head Office, 10 Dunkeld Road, Perth PH1 5TW; T.-01738 442111.

Ouston, Hugh Anfield, MA (Hons), DipEd, DPhil (Oxon). Educational Consultant, since 2020; Warden, Glenalmond College, 2019-2020; b. 4.4.52, Dundee; m., Yvonne; 2 s.; 2 d. Educ. Glenalmond College; Christ Church, University of Oxford. Teacher of History, North Berwick High School, 1977-84; Head of History, Beeslack High School, 1984-92; Assistant Head, Dunbar Grammar School, 1992-97; Deputy Principal, George Watson's College, 1997-2004; Head of College, Robert Gordon's College, Aberdeen, 2004-2014. Recreations: birdwatching; gardening; hill walking; sailing; poetry. Address: (h.) Pitscaff House, Newburgh, Aberdeenshire AB41 6AQ; e-mail: hughouston@gmail.com

Owens, Professor Nicholas J. P., CBiol, MBiol, BSc (Hons), PhD, FRSB, FRGS, FMBA. Executive Director, The Scottish Association for Marine Science (SAMS), since 2015. Educ. University of Liverpool; University of Dundee. Career history: Research Scientist. Plymouth Marine Laboratory, 1979-93; Chair of Marine Science, University of Newcastle, 1993-2000 (also Head of Department for Marine Sciences and Coastal Management, 1994-99); Chief Executive, Plymouth Marine Laboratory, 2000-07; Director, British Antarctic Survey, 2007-12; Director, Sir Alister Hardy Foundation for Ocean Science, 2012-2015. Board directorships: SAMS (non-executive), 2003-05; UK Marine Information Council (non-executive), 2002-05; Plymouth Marine Applications Ltd (executive), 2002-07; National Marine Aquarium (non-executive), 2000-08; Centre for Environment, Fisheries and Aquaculture Science - Defra agency (non-executive and Chair of Science Committee), 2008-2012; SAMS Research Services Ltd, now SAMS Enterprise (executive), since 2015. Chair, Partnership for the Observation of the Global Ocean, since 2019. Past and current membership and chairmanship of numerous national and international environmental scientific committees and advisory boards, including NATO, EU, ICSU, Royal Society; past and present national governmental delegate for a range of marine, polar, earth science and environmental organisations; specialist advisor for national and international environmental and Earth sciences research reviews. Numerous publications; Co-Editor of many journals. Recreations: angling; mountaineering; sailing. Address: SAMS, Scottish Marine Institute, Oban, Argyll PA37 1QA; T.-01631 559000.

P

Address: (h.) Westlands, Westfield Road, Cupar, Fife KY15 5DR.

Pacione, Professor Michael, MA, PhD, DSc, FRSGS. Emeritus Professor, University of Strathclyde; appointed Professor of Geography in 1990; b. 14.10.47, Dundee; m., Christine Hopper; 1 s.; 1 d. Educ. Lawside Academy, Dundee; Dundee University. Lecturer in Geography, Queens University, Belfast, 1973-75; Lecturer, Senior Lecturer, Reader, Strathclyde University, Glasgow, 1975-89; Visiting Professor, University of Guelph, 1984, and University of Vienna, 1995. Publications: 25 books and more than 150 academic research papers. Recreations: travel; photography; scuba diving. Address: (b.) Faculty of Humanities and Social Sciences, Lord Hope Building, St. James Road, Glasgow G4 0LT.
E-mail: m.pacione@strath.ac.uk

Padgett, Professor Miles J., OBE, FRS, FRSE, BSc, MSc, PhD. Kelvin Chair of Natural Philosophy, University of Glasgow, since 2011; Professor of Optics; Vice Principal for Research, 2014-2020; b. 1.6.63; m., Heather Reid; 1 d. Educ. University of Manchester; University of York; University of St Andrews; University of Cambridge. Research has been published in leading peer reviewed scientific journals including Science, Nature, Physical Review Letters, Optics Express and Progress in Optics. Awarded the Institute of Physics Young Medal in 2009 for conducting pioneering work on optical angular momentum; won the Royal Society of Edinburgh's Kelvin Medal in 2014; won the Science of Light Prize from the European Physical Society in 2015. Recreation: keen cyclist. Address: University of Glasgow, R157B Level 1, Physics & Astronomy, Kelvin Building, Glasgow G12 8QQ; T.-0141 330 5389; e-mail: Miles.Padgett@glasgow.ac.uk

Pagan, Graeme Henry, MBE, BL, WS. Solicitor, Hosack & Sutherland, Oban, 1960-2007; Member, Solicitors Discipline Tribunal, 1995-2006; Honorary Sheriff of North Strathclyde at Oban, since 1988; b. 20.3.36, Cupar; m., Heather; 1 s.; 2 d. Educ. New Park, St. Andrews; Bedford School; Edinburgh University. Part-time Procurator Fiscal, Oban, 1970-79; Regional Organiser, Shelter Campaign for the Homeless, 1968-75; Chairman, Oban Housing Association, 1971-98; Founder Member, Oban Abbeyfield Society; Founder of Solicitors charitable ventures Will Aid and Will Relief Scotland; Convener, Argyll & Bute Scottish Liberal Democrats, 1991-2000; Joint Convenor, Oban Concern for Palestine; Director of Charitable Companies, Mary's Meals and Will Relief Scotland; Director, Oban Hospice, 2000-2010; Trustee, The Oban Charitable Trust; Local Treasurer, Yes Lorn and The Isles for the 2014 referendum; Lifetime Achievement Award, Law Awards of Scotland, 2006. Publication: Memoirs: Once Bitten Twice Fined, 2004; bereavement book "Don't Mention The Coal Scuttle" (Co-Author). Recreations: family; jazz; malt whisky; wandering in the Highlands on foot and bike. Address: (h.) Neaveton, Oban, Argyll; T.-01631 563737.

Page, Professor Alan Chisholm, LLB, PhD. Emeritus Professor of Public Law, Dundee University; b. 7.4.52, Broughty Ferry; m., Sheila Duffus; 1 s.; 1 d. Educ. Grove Academy; Edinburgh University. Lecturer in Law, University College, Cardiff, 1975-80; Senior Lecturer in Law, Dundee University, 1980-85; Professor of Public Law, Dundee University, 1985-2020; Head, Department of Law, 1980-95, 2005-06; Dean, School of Law, 2006-2015; Dean, Faculty of Law, 1986-89; Deputy Principal, Research Governance, 2011-15. Publications: Constitutional Law of Scotland; The Executive in the Constitution; Investor Protection; Legislation. Recreation: mountaineering.

Paisley of Westerlea, The Much Hon. Duncan Wilson, FRSA, FSA Scot. Succeeded as 16th Head of the Name; 5th Laird of the Barony of Westerlea (15th May 1993); Ambassador (Overseas), Capability Scotland, 1993-2006; Patron: Westerlea School, Edinburgh, 1993-2006, Kagyu Samye Ling Monastery and Tibetan Centre, Eskdalemuir, Paisley Museum Reimagined; b. 30.8.48, Woodcote; m., Jane Crichton Rankin; 3 d; Sarah (The Maid of Westerlea); Claire; Olivia. Educ. Cannock House School; Westwood. Regular Army, 1966-90 (Gordon Highlanders, RAOC) General List; King's Own Scottish Borderers, 1990-95; attended Barony College of Agriculture, 1991-92; Regional Liaison Officer, Scottish Landowners' Federation, 1992-93; The Guild of Master Craftsmen: Assessment Officer (S.W. Scotland), 1993-96; Regional Manager and Trainer (W), 1996-2000; Chief Assessor (Scotland), since 2000; Director, Westerlea Trading; PPC, The Referendum Party, 1996-97; President, Scottish Tartans Society, 1997-2001; Director, Register of All Publicly known Tartans, 1997-2001; Hon. Col. Legion of Frontiersmen, 2001-04; Freeman of Glasgow; Member, Incorporation of Weavers, Glasgow; Member, Incorporation of Weavers, Edinburgh; Member, Heraldry Society of Scotland; Member, Royal Celtic Society and Royal Scots Club. Recreations: hill-walking; Scottish domestic architecture; family history; gardening. Address: (h.) Ardtalla, Kirkburn, Slamannan, Stirlingshire FK1 3AE; T./Fax: 01324 851535; Mob: 07739 749038; e-mail: paisleyofwesterlee@aol.co.uk

Palfreyman, Professor John, BSc, DPhil, FIWSc. Former Head of the School of Contemporary Sciences, University of Abertay Dundee (now retired); BioScientist; b. 30.7.51, Potters Bar; 2 d. Educ. Stationers' Company's School; London and Sussex Universities. Research Biochemist, Royal Infirmary Glasgow; Research Fellow, MRC Institute of Virology, Glasgow; University of Abertay Dundee. Member, Coupar Angus Community Council; Board Member: Forward Coupar Angus, Windfall Community Development Trust. Recreations: theatre; photography; hill walking (Munro bagging); cycling. Address: The Neuk, Caddam Road, Coupar, Angus, Perthshire PH13 9EF.
E-mail: palfreyman85@gmail.com

Palmer, Sir Godfrey Henry Oliver (Geoff), OBE. Chancellor, Heriot-Watt University, since 2021; Professor Emeritus in the School of Life Sciences; human rights activist; b. 9.4.40, St Elizabeth, Jamaica; m., Margaret. Educ. Kingston Senior School; North Street Congregational School, Jamaica; Highbury County School, London; University of Leicester; University of Edinburgh; Heriot-Watt University. Career history: junior lab technician, Queen Elizabeth College, London University, 1958-61; University of Leicester degree, 1961-64; doctorate, Heriot-Watt College and the University of Edinburgh, 1965-67; Brewing Research Foundation, Surrey, 1968-77; appointed to Heriot-Watt University in 1977; received a Doctorate of Science in 1985. Honoured with the American Society of Brewing Chemists (ASBC) Award for distinction in scientific research and good citizenship, 2008; awarded Honorary Doctorates by Abertay University in 2009, the Open University in 2010, the University of the West Indies in 2015, and Heriot-Watt University in 2015. Knighted in the 2014 New Year Honours for services to human rights, science, and charity. Honorary President, Edinburgh and Lothians Regional Equality Council (ELREC). Address: Heriot-Watt University, Edinburgh Campus, Edinburgh EH14 4AS.

Park, John William. MSP (Labour), Mid Scotland and Fife, 2007-2012; b. 14.9.73; 2 d. Educ. Woodmill High School; Blacklaw Primary (both Dunfermline); Adam Smith College, Kirkcaldy; Carnegie College, Dunfermline. Rosyth Dockyard: Electrical Fitter, 1989-98, Trade Union

376 WHO'S WHO IN SCOTLAND

Convenor, 1998-2001; AEEU, formerly AMICUS, now UNITE: Research Officer, 2001-02, National Industrial Campaigns Officer, 2002-03; Head of Employee Relations, Babcock Naval Services, 2003-04; Assistant Secretary, STUC, 2004-07.

Park, Neil Ferguson, BSc, MBA. Secretary, Scottish Pentathlon Ltd, since 2021, Executive Director, since 2016; Secretary/Treasurer, Lothians Golf Association, 2013-17; b. 26.9.62, Gosport; m., Judith Frances; 1 s.; 1 d. Educ. Daniel Stewart's and Melville College, Edinburgh; Aberdeen University; Edinburgh University. Recreations: golf; triathlons; road-running; writing. Address: (b.) Scottish Pentathlon Limited, Caledonia House, 1 Redheughs Rigg, South Gyle, Edinburgh EH12 0DQ.

Parker, Cameron Holdsworth, CVO, OBE, DL, BSc. Lord Lieutenant of Renfrewshire, 1998-2007; b. 14.4.32, Dundee; m., Marlyne Honeyman; 3 s. Educ. Morrison's Academy, Crieff; Glasgow University. Managing Director, latterly also Chairman, John G. Kincaid & Co. Ltd., Greenock, 1967-80; Chairman and Chief Executive, Scott Lithgow Ltd., Port Glasgow, 1980-83; Board Member, British Shipbuilders, 1977-80, 1981-83; Chief Executive, Prosper Enginering Ltd., Irvine, 1983-84; Managing Director, Lithgows Limited, 1984-92, Vice-Chairman, 1992-97. Freeman, City of London; Liveryman, Worshipful Company of Shipwrights; Member, Council, CBI Scotland, 1986-92; Member, Argyll and Clyde Health Board, 1991-95; Board Member, Scottish Homes, 1992-96; Director, Clyde Shaw Ltd., 1992-94; Honorary President, Accord Hospice, 1998-2007; President, SSAFA Forces Help, Renfrewshire, 1998-2007; DUniv University of Paisley, 2003. Recreation: golf; gardening. Address: (h.) 8 Ardleighton Court, Dunblane FK15 0NE.

Parker, Rosemary, BA (Hons), Dip Arch, RIBA, RIAS. Partner, BPA Architecture, since 2012. Career history: joined BPA in 2010 as an Associate; previous experience of working on multi-million pound hospital and school projects throughout the UK; particularly interested in sustainable building, Passive House design and designing for dementia. Associate of the University of Stirling's Dementia Services Development Centre, 2012-2015. Address: BPA Architecture, 4 Sandport Place, Edinburgh EH6 6EU; T.-0131 555 3338.

Parkinson, Frederick Alexander Ian. Honorary Consul for Netherlands, 1998-2012; Chairman, Grampian Valuation Panel, 1997-2020; b. 12.10.41, Royston; m., Ann Delyth; 1 s.; 2 d. Educ. Sutton Valence, Kent; Hatfield Polytechnic. Articled Clerk, Chartered Accountants, 1958-62; Officer, Royal Navy, 1963-79; Projects Manager, Software Company, 1980-83; MD, Profit Through Partnership Ltd., 1983-98. Chairman, Aberdeen CAB, 1993-2004; Member, Grampian Valuation Committee and Panel, 1983-2020; Deputy Lieutenant, Kincardineshire, 2009-2016; Ridder van Oranje-Nassau, 2012. Recreation: sailing. Address: Inverary Cottage, 106 High Street, Bonnyrigg, Midlothian EH19 2AQ.

Parks, Rowan Wesley, MB, BCh, BAO, MD, FRCSI, FRCS(Edin). Professor of Surgical Sciences, University of Edinburgh, since 2010; Honorary Consultant Surgeon, Royal Infirmary of Edinburgh, since 1999; b. 5.3.66, Belfast; m., Janet Margaret; 2 s.; 2 d. Educ. Royal Belfast Academical Institution; Queen's University, Belfast. Research Fellow, Queen's University, Belfast, 1994-96; Higher Surgical Trainee, Northern Ireland, 1996-98; Clinical Fellow, Edinburgh, 1998-99. Moynihan Medal, Association of Surgeons of Great Britain and Ireland; Millin

Lecturer and Medal, Royal College of Surgeons of Ireland. Recreation: boating. Address: Department of Clinical Surgery, Royal Infirmary of Edinburgh, Edinburgh EH16 4SA; T.-0131 242 3616; e-mail: R.W.Parks@ed.ac.uk

Parr, Rose Marie, BSc (Hons), FRPharmS, PhD. Chief Pharmaceutical Officer for Scotland, 2015-2020. Educ. University of Strathclyde; University of Glasgow. Career history: registration in 1982, then hospital pharmacist with Lanarkshire Health Board; became Director of Pharmacy in 1993 at the Scottish Centre for Pharmacy Postgraduate Education (SCPPE) which would later become the Scottish Centre for Post Qualification Education; became the Director of Pharmacy of NHS Education for Scotland (NES) in 2002, when several healthcare education organisations joined to form a single national body. Appointed as an Honorary Professor, Robert Gordon University in Aberdeen in 2004; Visiting Professor, University of Strathclyde in Glasgow. Elected the first Chair of the Scottish Pharmacy Board of the Royal Pharmaceutical Society of Great Britain (RPSGB) in 2007.

Parratt, David Richmond, QC, LLB (Hons), PhD, DipLP, DipICArb, FCIArb, FRHistS, FSALS, FSA Scot, FCS, FRSA. Advocate, since 1999; Barrister of Lincoln's Inn, since 2009; Honorary Professor of Law (International Arbitration), University of Aberdeen, since 2017; Mediator and Arbitrator; Director of Training and Education at the Faculty of Advocates, 2012-17; b. 13.2.70, Dundee; m., Margaret Sarah Thomson. Educ. Glasgow Academy; High School of Dundee; Aberdeen University; Edinburgh University. Solicitor, 1995-99; Tutor, Faculty of Law, Edinburgh University, 1996-98; Honorary Lecturer, Centre for Energy, Petroleum and Mineral Law and Policy (CEPMLP), University of Dundee; Honorary Research Fellow, School of Law, University of Dundee; CEDR Accredited Mediator; Called to the Scottish Bar, 1999; Called to the Bar of Dubai International Finance Centre, 2007; Called to the English Bar, 2009; Supporting Member, London Maritime Arbitration Association; Member: LCIA, BIICL; Freeman, The Worshipful Company of Arbitrators, London; Clerksroom, London; Terra Firma Chambers, Edinburgh. Publications: "The Development and Use of Written Pleadings in Scots Civil Procedure" (Stair Society); various articles on Scottish Legal History, Civil Procedure and International Arbitration. Recreations: golf; skiing; antiquarian books. Address: (b.) Advocates' Library, Parliament House, Edinburgh EH1 1RF; T.-0131 226 5071; e-mail: dparratt@hotmail.com

Parratt, Emeritus Professor James Roy, MSc, PhD, DSc, MD (h.c.), DSc (med), FRCPath, DipRelStudies (Cantab), FRPharmS, FESC, FISHR, FIBiol, FRSE. Professor Emeritus, Strathclyde University, since 1998; b. 19.8.33, London; m., Pamela Joan Lyndon Marels; 2 s.; 1 d. Educ. St. Clement Danes Holborn Estate Grammar School; London University. Spent nine years in Nigeria as Head of Pharmacology, Nigerian School of Pharmacy, then in Physiology, University Medical School, Ibadan; joined Strathclyde University, 1967; appointed Reader, 1970; Personal Professor, Department of Physiology and Pharmacology, 1975-83; Professor of Cardiovascular Pharmacology, 1983-98; Research Professor, 2001-06, Head, Department of Physiology and Pharmacology, 1986-90; Honorary Research Professor, Albert Szent-Gyorgy: Medical Faculty, University of Szeged, Hungary, since 1998; Chairman, Cardiac Muscle Research Group (now British Society for Cardiovascular Research), 1980-83; Vice President, European Shock Society, 1995-98; Gold Medal, Szeged University, 1975; Honorary Member, Hungarian Pharmacological Society, 1983; Fellow, Royal Society of Edinburgh, 1986; Honorary Doctorate, Albert Szent-Gyorgi Medical University, Hungary, 1989;

Founding Fellow, International Society for Heart Research, 2001; Gold J.E. Purkyne Honorary Medal, Academy of Sciences of Czech Republic, 1995; Honorary Fellow, British Pharmacological Society, 2015; Fellow, International Academy of Cardiovascular Sciences (Lifetime Achievement Award, 2014); Sodalem honoris causa, Slovak Medical and Cardiological Societies, 1997; Honorary Member, Czech Cardiological Society, 1998; Chairman, Universities and Colleges Christian Fellowship, 1984-90; Chairman, Interserve Scotland, 2000-03; Leverhulme Trust Emeritus Fellow, 2001-03; Szent-Gyorgyi Fellow, Hungarian State Government, 2002-03; former Vice-Chairman, Scripture Union; Past Chairman, SUM Fellowship; Lay Preacher, Baptist Unions of Scotland and Great Britain; Honorary President, Baptist Lay Preachers Association of Scotland, 1985-90; former Member, Board of Ministry, Baptist Union of Scotland. Author: Marvellously Made, 2017 (reprinted 2019), Highways of the Heart, 2019; A sense of water - adventures in faith and science, 2021. Recreations: music; piano playing; making jam; Scottish islands. Address: (h.) 10 St. Germains, Bearsden, Glasgow G61 2RS; T.-0141-942 7164; e-mail: pimjam.parratt@btinternet.com

Parsons, Ruth. Former Chief Executive, Historic Scotland (2010-12); previously Director of Local Government, the Third Sector and Public Service reform in Scottish Government (2005-09); b. Fife; 1 s. Director of Large Business Group, HM Customs & Excise, 2001-05; HM Customs & Excise, 1983-2005; worked with Cabinet Office supporting Public Service Reform Agenda, Improving Leadership Capacity of Leading Change in the Senior Civil Service. Recreations: enjoying historic sites across Scotland; football; travelling; reading.

Patel of Dunkeld, Baron (Narendra Babubhai Patel). Former Chancellor, University of Dundee (2006-2017); b. 1938, Tanzania; m., Dr. Helen Dally; 2 s.; 1 d. Educ. Harrow High School; St. Andrews University. Previously President, Royal College of Obstetrics and Gynaecologists; previously Chairman: Academy of Medicine, Royal College; Clinical Standards Board, Scotland, Quality Improvement Scotland; currently Chairman: National Patient Safety Agency, Stem Cell Oversight Committee, UK National Stem Cell Network; Member, Science and Technology Committee, since 1999; Patron of several charities; Fellow, Academy of Medical Science, Royal Society of Edinburgh; Hon. Dr. and Hon. Fellow, Universities and Colleges. Author of numerous publications on maternal/foetal medicine, epidemiology, obstetrics and gynaecology. E-mail: patel_naren@hotmail.com

Paterson, Professor Alan Alexander, OBE, LLB (Hons), DPhil (Oxon), FRSA, FRSE. Solicitor. Professor of Law, Strathclyde University, since 1984; international and expert adviser to the Independent Review of Legal Aid in Scotland, since 2017; b. 5.6.47, Edinburgh; m., Alison Jane Ross Lowdon; 2 s.; 1 d. Educ. Edinburgh Academy; Edinburgh University; Pembroke College, Oxford. Research Associate, Oxford Centre for Socio-Legal Studies, 1972-73; Lecturer, Law Faculty, Edinburgh University, 1973-84; Visiting Professor, University of New Mexico Law School, 1982, 1986. Former Chairman: Committee of Heads of University Law Schools of the UK, Scottish Legal Action Group and British and Irish Legal Education and Technology Association; Chairman, Legal Services Group, Citizens Advice Scotland; Vice-Chair, Joint Standing Conference on Legal Education in Scotland; former Member, Council, Law Society of Scotland; past President, Society of Legal Scholars; Member, Judicial Appointments Board, 2002-08; Member, Scottish Legal Complaints Commission, 2008-2011. Publications: Lawyers and the Public Good, 2012; The Law Lords, 1982; The Legal System of Scotland (Co-Author), 1993; Law, Practice and Conduct for Solicitors (Co-Author), 2006; Paths to Justice Scotland (Co-Author), 2001. Address: (b.) Centre for Professional Legal Studies, Strathclyde University Law School, Graham Hills Building, Level 7, 50 George Street, Glasgow G1 1BA.
E-mail: prof.alan.paterson@strath.ac.uk

Paterson, Alex. Chief Executive: Historic Environment Scotland, since 2016, Highlands and Islands Enterprise, 2010-16. Educ. University of Strathclyde; University of Bath. Career History: Industrial marketing with Esso Chemicals and Volvo; joined the Scottish Development Agency, and on the formation of Scottish Enterprise, became Head of Small Business Development in Renfrewshire Enterprise; Managing Director of a consultancy and training organisation based in Glasgow and operating throughout the UK; joined HIE, 2001 as Director of Developing Skills, became Director of Regional Competitiveness, 2008. Address: (b.) Historic Environment Scotland, Longmore House, Salisbury Place, Edinburgh EH9 1SH; T.-0131 668 8600.

Paterson, Calum, BA, MBA, CA, FRSE. Managing Partner, Scottish Equity Partners, since 2000; b. 13.4.63, Edinburgh; m., Amanda McLean. Educ. Linlithgow Academy; University of Strathclyde. Ernst and Young, 1985-88; Scottish Development Agency, 1988-91; Scottish Enterprise, 1991-2000. Chair of the British Private Equity and Venture Capital Association, 2018/19; serving member of the BVCA Council. Alumnus of the Year, University of Strathclyde, 2017. Recreation: various sports. Address: (b.) 17 Blythswood Square, Glasgow G2 4AD; T.-0141-273 4000.

Paterson, Collette Patricia. Chief Executive, The Judicial Appointments Board for Scotland, since 2021; previously at The Judicial Institute for Scotland and Law Society of Scotland. Career history: solicitor qualified in Scotland and legal educator; experience in legal services regulation and specifically professional standards and competencies for qualification/appointment, education and training. Address: Judicial Appointments Board for Scotland, Thistle House, 91 Haymarket Terrace, Edinburgh EH12 5HE.

Paterson, Craig. Head Teacher, Alness Academy, since 2021; previously Depute Head, Inverurie Academy in Aberdeenshire; most recent role was working as a lead officer for secondary curriculum for the Northern Alliance. Address: Dalmore Road, Alness IV17 0UY; T.-01349 883341.

Paterson, Professor David Maxwell, BSc, PhD. Executive Director of the Marine Alliance for Science and Technology for Scotland (MASTS), University of St Andrews, since 2011; Champion for the Sustainable Management of UK Marine Resources (SMMR) Programme, UKRI, since 2020; Royal Society University Research Fellow; Professor, Coastal Ecology, since 2000; b. 16.6.58, Dalry; m., Marie; 2 d. Educ. Royal High School, Edinburgh; University of Glasgow; University of Bath. Royal Society Research Fellow, University of Bristol, 1988; University of St. Andrews: Lecturer, 1993, Reader in Environmental Biology, 1996; Council of the Scottish Association for Marine Science (SAMS). Publications: 130 peer reviewed publications; Editor, Marine Biodiversity; 4 edited books including "Marine Biodiversity and Ecosystem Functioning". Recreations: natural history; music; squash; family. Address: (h.) 22 Pinkerton Road, Crail, Fife KY10 3UB; T.-01333 450047; e-mail: d.paterson@st-and.ac.uk

Paterson, Dianne Elizabeth, LLB, NP. Managing Partner, Russel + Aitken Edinburgh, Solicitors, Edinburgh, since 2006, Partner, since 1985; Non Executive Director of ESPC, 2001-07; b. 8.1.58, Dundee; m., Dr. John W. Paterson. Educ. High School of Dundee; University of

Aberdeen. Apprenticeship (Legal) with Robson McLean and Paterson, Solicitors, 1979-81; Solicitor with Russel + Aitken, since 1981. Credited for opening a property shop in The Royal Infirmary of Edinburgh (1988-2000); responsible for the launch of the 'Russel + Aitken Design Award'. Recreations: appreciation of art; sculpture; opera; classical music. Address: (b.) 27 Rutland Square, Edinburgh EH1 2BU; T.-0131 228 5500.

E-mail: dianne.paterson@russelaitken-edinburgh.com

Paterson, Gil. MSP (SNP), Clydebank and Milngavie, 2011-2021, West of Scotland, 2007-2011; b. 11.11.42, Glasgow. Educ. Possilpark Secondary School. Career history: Gil's Motor Factors (own business); served as a Scottish National Party (SNP) councillor in Strathclyde Regional Council and sat on the SNP's National Executive Committee; MSP, Central Scotland, Scottish Parliament, 1999-2003 (sat on Local Government and Procedures committees in the Parliament); returned to running his business but stayed active in the SNP, becoming the party's Vice-Convenor in charge of Fundraising. Elected as the SNP Group Convener.

Paterson, Rev. John Love, MA, BD, STM. Minister Emeritus, St. Michael's Parish Church, Linlithgow, since 2003 (Minister, 1977-2003); Chaplain to The Queen, since 1996; b. 6.5.38, Ayr; m., Lorna Begg. Educ. Ayr Academy; Glasgow University; Edinburgh University; Union Theological Seminary, New York. Minister: Presbyterian Church of East Africa, 1964-72, St. Andrew's, Nairobi, 1968-72; Chaplain, Stirling University, 1973-77. Moderator, West Lothian Presbytery, 1985. Recreations: gardening; Rotary. Address: 9 The Pines, Murdoch's Lone, Ayr KA7 4WD; T.-01292 443615.

Paterson, Julie. Chief Executive, Mental Welfare Commission for Scotland, since 2020. Career history: qualified as a social worker/mental health officer; two year secondment to the Mental Welfare Commission in 2007, before returning to Fife Council; Divisional General Manager (Fifewide division) at Fife Health and Social Care Partnership (career in social work in the region), 2015-2020. Address: Mental Welfare Commission for Scotland, Thistle House, 91 Haymarket Terrace, Edinburgh EH12 5HE; T.-0131 313 8777.

Paterson, Laura. Scotland Editor, PA Media, since 2020. Began career at The Digger in Glasgow in 2009 and went on to hold senior reporting positions at The Press and Journal (Inverness), Central Scotland News Agency (Stirling), the Dumbarton and Vale of Leven Reporter (Clydebank) and Sunday Mail (Glasgow); joined PA as a reporter in 2016, later assuming the role of Political Reporter before taking on News Editor duties. Address: PA Scotland, 1 Central Quay, Glasgow G3 8DA.

Paterson, Lewis, BSc, SQH. Insight Advisor, The Scottish Government, since 2018; Acting Principal, Wester Hailes Education Centre, 2015-16. Educ. Kilmarnock Academy; Glasgow Caledonian University; University of Paisley; Glasgow University; University of Edinburgh. Curriculum Leader of Numeracy and ICT, McLaren High School, 2002-06; Deputy Head Teacher, Currie Community High School, 2006-12; Acting Head Teacher, Gracemount High School, 2012; Depute Rector, Trinity Academy, Edinburgh, 2012-14, Acting Rector, 2014, Depute Rector, 2014-15; Deputy Head Teacher, Leith Academy, 2017-18.

Paterson, Ross, CB, OBE, ADC, DL. Air Officer Scotland, Royal Air Force (RAF), since 2015; Chief Executive,

Scottish Public Pensions Agency, 2015-17. Educ. University of Portsmouth; University of Surrey.

Paterson, Steven. MP (SNP), Stirling, 2015-17; b. 1975, Stirling. Educ. Cambusbarron Primary School; Stirling High School; Robert Gordon University; Stirling University. Appointed as media and communications manager to the SNP MSP Bruce Crawford in 2006; elected to Stirling Council in 2007 for the Stirling East ward, re-elected (2012-15), deputy SNP group leader, 2013-15.

Paterson, Stuart. Chairman, Macfarlane Group, since 2017; Chief Financial Officer, Forth Ports Limited, 2011-18. Career history: Chartered Accountant; worked in senior financial management roles at the electronics group Motorola Corporation, and then as Group Finance Director and then Managing Director, Europe for Aggreko PLC, the global power hire group; Chief Financial Officer, Johnston Press PLC, 2001-2010; served as a non-executive director with Devro plc, 2006-2012 (chaired the Audit Committee); joined the Board of Macfarlane Group in 2013 as a non-executive director. Trustee of the Royal Yacht Britannia and a member of their Audit, Risk and Remuneration Committee; Member of the Remuneration and Nominations Committees, Macfarlane Group. Address: (b.) 21 Newton Place, Glasgow G3 7PY; T.-0141 333 9666.

Paterson, Dr Sue, BSc, PhD. Board Member, Scottish Enterprise, since 2018. Educ. Imperial College London; University of Cambridge; The Open University. Career history: experience with oil & gas multinational operator, Shell, 1981-2010; Director, IPKA consultancy, 2012-2020; Member, Expert Advisory Group, IERC - International Energy Research Centre, 2015-2020; Board experience, various (Shell, British Geological Survey, CLAN, Woodend Arts), since 2004; Director, Arbeadie Consultants, since 2010; Associate, Pale Blue Dot Energy Ltd, since 2015; Governor, Heriot-Watt University, since 2018; Board Member, Company of Wolves Ltd, since 2019. Publication: The Fear Free Organisation: Vital Insights from Neuroscience to Transform Your Business Culture (Co-Author), 2015. Address: Scottish Enterprise HQ, Atrium Court, 50 Waterloo Street, Glasgow G2 6HQ; T.-0300 013 3385.

Paterson, Wilma, DRSAM. Freelance Composer/Music Critic/Travel Writer; b. 23.4.44, Dundee; 1 s.; 1 d. Educ. Harris Academy; Royal Scottish Academy of Music. Composition study with Luigi Dallapiccola in Florence; writes chamber and incidental music; contributes to: Odyssey, Heritage, The Scotsman, The Herald, The Sunday Times, Essentially America, Sunday Herald, etc. Publications: A Country Cup; Was Byron Anorexic?; Shoestring Gourmet; A Fountain of Gardens: Flowers and Herbs of the Bible; Lord Byron's Relish; Salmon & Women: The Feminine Angle; Songs of Scotland (Illustrated by Alasdair Gray). Address: 88 Ashburton Road, Glasgow G12 0LZ.

E-mail: williepaterson9@icloud.com

Paton, Alasdair Chalmers, BSc, CEng. Chief Executive, Scottish Environment Protection Agency, 1995-2000; Retired Company Director; b. 28.11.44, Paisley; m., Zona G. Gill; 1 s.; 1 d. Educ. John Neilson Institution, Paisley; Glasgow University. Assistant Engineer, Clyde Port Authority, 1967-71; Assistant Engineer, DAFS, 1971-72; Senior Engineer, SDD, 1972-77; Engineer, Public Works Department, Hong Kong Government, 1977-80; Senior Engineer, then Principal Engineer, SDD, 1980-87; Deputy Chief Engineer, 1987-91; Director and Chief Engineer, Engineering, Water and Waste Directorate, Scottish Office

Environment Department, 1991-95. Recreations: Rotary; sailing; golf. Address: (h.) Oriel House, Academy Square, Limekilns, Fife KY11 3HN; T.-01383 872218.

Paton, Hon. Lady (Ann Paton). Senator of the College of Justice, since 2000; Chair, Scottish Law Commission, since 2019; b. 1952, Glasgow; m., Dr James Y. Paton. Educ. Laurel Bank School, Glasgow; Glasgow University (MA, LLB). Advocate, 1977; Standing Junior Counsel: Queen's and Lord Treasurer's Remembrancer, 1979, Office of Fair Trading in Scotland, 1981; QC (Scot), 1990; Advocate Depute, 1992-94. Director, Scottish Council of Law Reporting, 1995-2000; Member, Criminal Injuries Compensation Board, 1995-2000. Recreations: sailing; music; art. Address: Parliament House, Edinburgh EH1 1RQ.

Paton, Rev. Anne Shaw, BA, BD. Minister, East Kilbride Old Parish Church, since 2001; b. 10.11.63, Glasgow; m., Thomas Moan; 2 s. Educ. Vale of Leven Academy; Jordanhill College of Education; Glasgow University. Primary School Teacher, West Dunbartonshire. Address: 40 Maxwell Drive, The Village, East Kilbride G74 4HJ; T.-01355 220732; e-mail: annepaton@fsmail.net

Paton, Dr. James Y., BSc, MBChB, MD, DCH, FRCPH, FRCP. Hon. Consultant Respiratory Paediatrician, Royal Hospital for Children, Glasgow, since 1989; Reader, Paediatric Respiratory Medicine, University of Glasgow, since 2001; b. 8.12.51, Glasgow; m., Ann Paton. Educ. Jordanhill College School; Glasgow University. Publications: chapters and articles on Paediatric Respiratory Disease. Recreations: cycling; sailing; hill walking; music. Address: (b.) Office Block, Ground Floor, Zone 1 (Paediatrics), South Glasgow University Hospital, 1345 Govan Road, Glasgow G51 4TF; T.-0141-451 5841.
E-mail: james.paton@glasgow.ac.uk

Paton, Laura, LLB, LLM. HM Chief Inspector of Prosecution in Scotland, since 2019; Lead Inspector, HM Inspectorate of Constabulary for Scotland (HMICS), 2013-19. Educ. University of Glasgow; Glasgow Graduate School of Law. Policy Officer, Children 1st, 2004-05; Policy Development, Scotland's Commissioner for Children and Young People, 2005-09; Senior Policy Officer & National Preventive Mechanism Co-ordinator, HM Inspectorate of Prisons, 2009-13. Address: Inspectorate of Prosecution in Scotland, Legal House 2nd Floor, 101 Gorbals Street, Glasgow G5 9DW; T.-0141 420 0378.

Patterson, Monica, MBA. Chief Executive, East Lothian Council, since 2020. Educ. Strathclyde Graduate Business School. Career history: East Lothian Council: Executive Director of Community Services, 2010-2013, Deputy Chief Executive (Partnerships and Services for Communities), 2013-2020. Address: East Lothian Council, John Muir House, Brewery Park, Haddington, East Lothian EH41 3HA; T.-01620 827 827.

Pattison, Rev. Kenneth John, MA, BD, STM. Retired Minister; b. 22.4.41, Glasgow; m., Susan Jennifer Brierley Jenkins; 1 s.; 2 d. Educ. Lenzie Academy; Glasgow University; Union Theological Seminary, New York. Minister, Church of Central Africa Presbyterian, Malawi, 1967-77; Minister, Park Parish Church, Ardrossan, 1977-84; Chaplain, Glasgow Royal Infirmary, 1984-90; Associate Minister, St. Andrew's and St. George's, Edinburgh, 1990-96; Minister, Kilmuir and Logie Easter Parish Church, Ross-shire, 1996-2004. Convener, Chaplaincies Committee,

Church of Scotland, 1993-96. Recreations: gardening; family history. Address: (h.) 27/303 Mayfield Court, West Savile Terrace, Edinburgh EH9 3DT; T.-01738 860340.

Patton, John. National Development Officer, Scottish League of Credit Unions, 2000-07; National President, Educational Institute of Scotland, 1999-2000; b. Derry, 1942; m., Elizabeth Scott; 3 c. Educ. St Columb's College; St Mary's University College, Belfast; University of Delaware. Taught English in Northern Ireland, 1964-71; Press Officer, civil rights movement in Derry, 1968-70; taught in West Lothian, 1971-73, Zambia, 1973-76, Central Region, since 1976; Headteacher, Banchory Primary School, Tullibody, 1985-90, Craigbank Primary School, Sauchie, 1990-2000. Occasional contributor to BBC, Herald and Scotsman on micro-finance and educational issues; fluent Irish Gaelic speaker. Recreations: Scottish and Irish traditional music; photography. Blogs at phototilly.eu
E-mail: john.patton@phototilly.eu

Pattullo, Sir (David) Bruce, Kt, CBE, BA, Hon. LLD (Aberdeen), DUniv (Stirling), Hon. DBA (Strathclyde), FRSE, FCIB (Scot). Governor, Bank of Scotland, 1991-98; Director (Non-Executive): British Linen Bank, 1977-98, Bank of Wales PLC, 1986-98, NWS Bank, 1986-98; b. 2.1.38, Edinburgh; m., Fiona Jane Nicholson; 3 s.; 1 d. Educ. Belhaven Hill School; Rugby; Hertford College, Oxford. National Service commission, Royal Scots (seconded to West Africa); joined Bank of Scotland, 1961; winner, first prize, Institute of Bankers in Scotland, 1964; Bank of Scotland: Manager, Investment Services Department, 1967-71, Deputy Manager, Bank of Scotland Finance Co. Ltd., 1971-73, Chief Executive, Group Merchant Banking Activities, 1973-78, Deputy Treasurer, 1978, Treasurer and General Manager, 1979-88, Director, 1980-98, Group Chief Executive and a Deputy Governor, Bank of Scotland, 1988-91. Chairman, Committee of Scottish Clearing Bankers, 1981-83 and 1987-89; Director, Standard Life Assurance Co., 1985-96; President, Institute of Bankers in Scotland, 1990-92. Recreations: tennis; hill-walking. Address: (h.) 6 Cammo Road, Edinburgh EH4 8EB.

Paul, Professor Jeanette McIntosh, BSc, BArch (Hons), RIBA, ARIAS. Emeritus Professor, Duncan of Jordanstone College of Art & Design, University of Dundee, since 2020; appointed Deputy Dean in 2017; appointed Associate Dean of Learning and Teaching in 2014 (Head of Learning and Teaching, 2010-2014, Head of Postgraduate Studies, 2007-2010, Head of School of Design, 2004-07); b. 27.10.56, Giffnock; m., Roderick. Educ. St. Denis School, Edinburgh; Duncan of Jordanstone College, University of Dundee. Assistant Architect, Sir Basil Spence Glover of Ferguson, Edinburgh, 1982-85; Project Architect, Andrew Merrylees Associates, Edinburgh, 1985-87; Senior Architect, Wilson of Wolmersley, Perth, 1987-88; University of Dundee: Lecturer in Interior and Environmental Design, 1988-2002, Senior Lecturer and Deputy Head, School of Design, 2002-04. President, Dundee Institute of Architects, 1999-2001; Board of Directors for WASPS (Workshop of Artists' Studio Provision Scotland Ltd.), since 1999; Joint Winner of The Scottish Design Award 2000 for best commercial/product design. Recreations: travelling; reading; dancing. Address: (b.) Duncan of Jordanstone College, Perth Road, Dundee DD1 4HT; T.-01382 345290.
E-mail: j.m.paul@dundee.ac.uk

Paxton, Professor Roland Arthur, MBE, MSc, PhD, HonDEng, CEng, FICE, FRSE, AMCST. Chairman,

Institution of Civil Engineers Panel for Historical Engineering Works, 1990-2003, Member Scotland, since 1975, Emeritus 2015; Chairman, Historic Bridge and Infrastructure Awards Panel, England and Wales, 1998-2007; ICE Scotland Museum: Founder Member, 1971, Chairman, 1987-2017, Curator Emeritus, since 2017; Commissioner, Royal Commission on the Ancient and Historical Monuments of Scotland, 1992-2002; Hon. Professor, School of the Built Environment, Heriot-Watt University, since 1994; b. 29.6.32, Altrincham; m., Ann; 2 d. Educ. Altrincham Grammar School; Manchester College of Science and Technology; Heriot-Watt University. Cartographical surveyor, Ordnance Survey, 1949-55; National Service Royal Artillery, 1951-53; Civil Engineer, Corporations of Sale, Manchester, Leicester, Edinburgh, and Lothian Regional Council, retiring as Senior Principal Engineer, 1959-90; Hon. Senior Research Fellow, Heriot Watt University, 1990-94. Chairman, Forth Bridges Visitor Centre Trust, 1997-2012; Secretary and Director, Laigh Milton Viaduct Conservation Project, 1992-99; Trustee, James Clerk Maxwell Foundation, 1999-2021, Fellow, since 2021; President, Edinburgh Bibliographical Society, 1992-95, Member, since 1966; Co-Patron, Friends of the Union Chain Bridge, since 2016; Winner, Institution of Civil Engineers' Garth Watson Medal, 1999 and Carr Prize, 2001; Lecturer Award, Philadelphia, Association for Preservation Technology International, 2000; American Society of Civil Engineers' History and Heritage Award, 2003; Appreciation Award, 2013; author of publications on technical innovation, use of radar to locate hidden structural details, bridge conservation, Telford, Rennie, the Stevensons and historical engineering; organiser, historical engineering plaques; contributor to BBC radio and TV news and documentaries. Address: (b.) School of Energy, Geoscience, Infrastructure and Society, Heriot-Watt University, Edinburgh EH14 4AS; T.-0131-449 5111.

Peacock, Andrew John, BSc, MPhil, MD, FRCP. Honorary Professor, Glasgow University, since 2003; Research and Medical Director, British Lung Foundation, 2017-18; Consultant Physician (Respiratory), West Glasgow Hospitals, since 1990; Director, Scottish Pulmonary Vascular Unit, 1995-2017; b. 13.11.49, Montreal; m., Jila Pezeshgi; 1 s.; 2 d. Educ. Westminster School; St. Bartholomew's Hospital Medical College, London University; Caius College, Cambridge University. Senior House Officer, St. Bartholomew's, Addenbrookes and Queen Square Hospitals; Registrar, Brompton Hospital; Senior Registrar, Southampton Hospitals; Research Fellow, University of Colorado; Visiting Scientist, National Heart and Lung Institute, London. Physiologist, 1993 British Expedition to Everest. Publication: Pulmonary Circulation: a handbook for clinicians. Recreations: anything to do with mountains; wine; tennis; golf. Address: (b.) Scottish Pulmonary Vascular Unit, Regional Heart and Lung Centre, Golden Jubilee National Hospital, Glasgow G81 4HX; T.-0141-951-5497.

Peacock, Professor John Andrew, MA, PhD, FRS, FRSE. Professor of Cosmology, Edinburgh University, since 1998; b. 27.3.56, Shaftesbury; m., Heather; 1 s.; 2 d. Educ. Cedars School, Leighton Buzzard; Jesus College, Cambridge. Research Astronomer, Royal Observatory, Edinburgh, 1981-92; Head of Research, Royal Observatory, Edinburgh, 1992-98; UK representative, Anglo-Australian Telescope Board, 1995-2000; Head of Institute for Astronomy, 2007-13. Winner of Shaw Prize in Astronomy, 2014. Publications: Cosmological Physics, 1999. Recreations: playing classical clarinet; hill walking. Address: (b.) Institute for Astronomy, Edinburgh University, Royal Observatory, Edinburgh, EH9 3HJ; T.-0131-668 8100; e-mail: jap@roe.ac.uk

Peacock, Peter James, CBE. Former MSP (Labour), Highlands and Islands (1999-2011); former Member: Rural Affairs and Environment Committee, Scotland Bill Committee; formerly Minister for Education and Young People and variously, Minister with responsibility for: Finance, EU Structure Funds, Public Service Reform, Local Government, Gaelic, Children and Education, 1999-2006; b. 27.2.52, Edinburgh; 2 s. Educ. Hawick High School; Jordanhill College of Education, Glasgow. Community Worker, Orkney Islands, 1973-75; former Area Officer, Highlands, Islands, Grampian, Scottish Association of Citizens Advice Bureaux; Member, Highland Regional Council, 1982-96; former Leader and Convener, Highland Council (1995-99); formerly: Member, Highlands and Islands Convention, Honorary President, Scottish Library Association, Board Member, Centre for Highlands and Islands Policy Studies, Member, Scottish Natural Heritage, Non-Executive Director, Scottish Post Office Board, Member, Highland Area Committee, SCDI, Chairman, Scottish Library and Information Council, Vice-President, COSLA; Member, European Committee of the Regions, 1993-99; Chair, Commonwealth Education Ministers Conference, 2003; former Training, Organisation and Policy Consultant; former Member, RSPB Committee for Scotland; former Chair, Customer Forum for Water; former Policy Director, Community Land Scotland; Co-author, Vice-Chairman, subsequently Chairman of successful applicant group for Independent Local Radio franchise, Moray Firth. Recreations: ornithology; golf; watching rugby union. Address: (h.) 'Birchwood', IV2 7QR; T.-01667 460190.

Peaker, Professor Malcolm, FRS, DSc, HonDSc, PhD, FZS, FIBiol, FRSE. Director, Hannah Research Institute, Ayr, 1981-2003; Hannah Professor, Glasgow University, 1981-2003; b. 21.8.43, Stapleford, Nottingham; m., Stephanie Jane Large; 3 s. Educ. Henry Mellish Grammar School, Nottingham; Sheffield University, BSc Zoology; DSc; University of Hong Kong, SRC NATO Scholar; PhD. ARC Institute of Animal Physiology, 1968-78; Head, Department of Physiology, Hannah Research Institute, 1978-81. Chairman, London Zoo Board, 1992-93; Vice-President, Zoological Society of London, 1992-94; Member, Editorial Board: Journal of Dairy Science, 1975-78, International Zoo Yearbook, 1978-82, Journal of Endocrinology, 1981-91; Editor, British Journal of Herpetology, 1977-81; Munro Kerr Lecture, 1997; Raine Distinguished Visitor, University of Western Australia, 1998; 10th Edinburgh Centre for Rural Research/Royal Society of Edinburgh/Institute of Biology Annual Lecture, 2000; Distinguished Lecturer, University of Hong Kong 2002; Chairman, British Nutrition Foundation, 2002-04, Governor, 1997-2018; Member, Rank Prize Funds Advisory Committee on Nutrition, 1997-2018. Publications: Salt Glands in Birds and Reptiles, 1975; Avian Physiology (Editor), 1975; Comparative Aspects of Lactation (Editor), 1977; Physiological Strategies in Lactation (Co-Editor), 1984; Intercellular Signalling in the Mammary Gland (Editor), 1995; Biological Signalling and the Mammary Gland (Editor), 1997; papers. Recreations: vertebrate zoology; natural history; golf; grumbling about bureaucrats. Address: (b.) 13 Upper Crofts, Alloway, Ayr KA7 4QX.

Pearce, Professor Chris, BA, PhD. Vice Principal (Research), University of Glasgow, since 2019; Professor of Computational Mechanics, since 2010; Royal Academy of Engineering/EDF Energy Research Chair, since 2015. Educ. Kingston Grammar School; Swansea University. Career history: University of Glasgow: Lecturer, 1997-2004; Senior Lecturer, 2004-08; Reader, 2008-2010; Deputy Head, College of Science and Engineering, 2016-2020; Dean of Research, College of Science and Engineering, 2016-2020. Address: R703 (level 7), School of Engineering, Rankine Building, University of Glasgow, Glasgow G12 8LT; T.-0141 3305207. E-mail: Chris.Pearce@glasgow.ac.uk

Pearce, Matthew, BA Eng (Hons) Dunelm, PGCE (Strathclyde). Rector, The Glasgow Academy, since 2019; b. 23.12.77, Wolverhampton. Educ. The King's School, Worcester; Grey College, Durham. Career history: English Teacher and Principal Teacher (Enterprise), St Luke's High School, Barrhead, 2001-08; Bishopbriggs Academy: Head of English, 2008-2010, Deputy Head, 2010-15; Deputy Rector, The Glasgow Academy, 2015-19. Recreations: family; sport; fitness; reading. Address: (b.) Colebrook Street, Glasgow G12 8HE; T.-0141 342 5485.
E-mail: rector@tga.org.uk

Pearce, Professor Nicholas. Sir John Richmond Chair of Fine Arts, University of Glasgow; Head of the School of Culture and Creative Arts, since 2010. Career history: held curatorial positions at the Victoria & Albert Museum in London, The Burrell Collection in Glasgow and the Oriental Museum, University of Durham; joined University of Glasgow in 1998; held the position of Head of History of Art and latterly Head of the School of Culture & Creative Arts within the College of Arts. Inducted to The Senate, University of Glasgow in 2006; appointed to The National Galleries of Scotland Board in 2014. Publications: Asian Art: The Formation of Collections (Journal for Art Market Studies), Vol. 4, No. 2, 2020 (Guest Editor); Collecting and Provenance: A Multidisciplinary Approach (Co-Editor). Address: University of Glasgow, R201 Level 2, School of Culture & Creative Arts, 8 University Gardens, Glasgow G12 8QH; T.-0141 3303826.
e-mail: Nick.Pearce@glasgow.ac.uk

Pearson of Rannoch, Lord (Malcolm Everard MacLaren Pearson). Life Peer; Leader, United Kingdom Independence Party (UKIP), 2009-2010; b. 20.7.42; m.; 3 d. Founded Rannoch Trust, 1984. Hon. President, RESCARE (National Society for Mentally Handicapped People in Residential Care), since 1994; Hon. President, The Register of Chinese Herbal Medicine, since 1998. Hon. LLD, CNAA.

Pearson, Graeme. Honorary Professor, University of Glasgow, since 2008; former Chief Executive, Scotland In Union (2017); MSP (Labour), South Scotland, 2011-16; Shadow Cabinet Secretary for Justice, 2013-16; b. 1.4.50. Educ. University of Glasgow. A police officer for 38 years, ending his career as director-general of the Scottish Crime and Drug Enforcement Agency. Was responsible for the introduction of the first Scottish CCTV system in Airdrie in the 1980s.

Pearson, The Right Reverend Kevin. Bishop to Diocese of Glasgow & Galloway, since 2020; b. 27.8.54, Sunderland; m., Dr Elspeth Atkinson (1992). Educ. Leeds University; Edinburgh University; Edinburgh Theological College. Made Deacon at Petertide, 1979 and Ordained Priest, the next Petertide, 1980 — both times by John Habgood, Bishop of Durham at Durham Cathedral; began career as Curate at St Mary, Horden; Rector at St Salvador Edinburgh, 1987-93; Associate Rector, Old Saint Paul's, Edinburgh, 1993-94; Priest in charge at Linlithgow, 1994-95, became Rector of St Michael and All Saints Church, Edinburgh, then Dean of the Diocese, 2004-2010; elected Bishop of Argyll and The Isles in late 2010; consecrated and installed as Bishop on Oban at Candlemas in 2011; enthroned in the Cathedral of The Isles, 2011-2020. Convenor of Scottish Episcopal Institute Church, 2013-2020. Address: Diocese of Glasgow & Galloway, 49 Cochrane Street, Glasgow G1 1HL; T.-0141 221 6911.

Pearson, Robbie. Chief Executive, Healthcare Improvement Scotland, since 2016 (previously Acting Chief Executive); m., Fiona; 1 d.; 1 s. Educ. University of St Andrews. Director of Planning and Performance, NHS Borders, 2003-2010; Acting Deputy Director/Head of Healthcare Planning, Scottish Government, 2010-2012; Deputy Chief Executive/Director of Scrutiny and Assurance, Healthcare Improvement Scotland, 2012-16. Lay Member, General Teaching Council for Scotland, 2016-18; Vice Chair, NHS Scotland Board Chief Executives Group, since 2021; Chair, NHS Scotland National Planning Board, since 2021. Address: Edinburgh Office, Gyle Square, 1 South Gyle Crescent, Edinburgh EH12 9EB; T.-0131 623 4300.

Peat, Jeremy Alastair, OBE, BA, MSc, FRSE, FRSA, Fellow of the Royal Zoological Society of Scotland (FRZSS). Vice President (Business), RSE, since 2021; Member, Economics Committee, South of Scotland Enterprise, since 2021; Director, David Hume Institute, 2005-2014; monthly columnist, The Herald, since 2005; Board Member, Scottish Enterprise, 2011-17; Chair, Economic Policy Committee; Board of Governors, BBC, 2005-06; Panel member: Competition Commission, 2005-2014, Competition and Markets Authority, 2014-2016; National Trustee for Scotland and Board Member, BBC Trust, 2007-2010; Chair, BBC Pension Trust, 2005-2011; Visiting Professor, University of Strathclyde's International Public Policy Institute; Trustee, Royal Zoological Society of Scotland, 2010-2020, Chair of Trustees, 2012-2020; Co-chair of Carnegie UK Working Group on Sources of Affordable Credit, 2014-2016; formerly Member, Church of Scotland Commission on the Purposes of Economic Activity; Group Chief Economist, Royal Bank of Scotland, 1993-2005; formerly Vice Chair, Scottish Higher Education Funding Council; Honorary Professor, Heriot-Watt University; Honorary Doctor of Law, Aberdeen University; Honorary Doctor of Letters, Heriot Watt University; Fellow, Industry and Parliament Trust; Fellow, Chartered Institute of Bankers for Scotland; b. 20.3.45, Haywards Heath; m., Philippa Ann; 2 d. Educ. St. Paul's School, London; Bristol University; University College London. Economic Assistant/Economic Adviser, Ministry of Overseas Development, 1969-77; Economic Adviser, Manpower Services Commission, 1978-80; Head, Employment Policy Unit, Ministry of Finance and Development Planning, Government of Botswana, 1980-84; Economic Adviser, HM Treasury, 1984-85; Senior Economic Adviser, Scottish Office, 1985-93. Fellow of the Royal College of Physicians in Edinburgh (2015). Recreations: walking; reading; listening to music; golf; bridge.

Peattie, Cathy. MSP (Labour), Falkirk East, 1999-2011; Chair, Scottish Labour Party, 2019-2020; b. 24.11.51; m. Ian Peattie; 2 d. Former Deputy Convener, Transport Infrastructure and Climate Change Committee; former Convener, cross-party groups on: Carers; Culture and Media; Men's Violence against Women and Children. Former Convenor, Council of Voluntary Service Scotland; former Chair, Scottish Labour Women's Committee.

Peddie, Professor Clare, BSc, PhD. Vice Principal Education (Proctor), University of St Andrews, since 2019. Educ. University of St Andrews. Career history: Pro Dean Undergraduate (Science), University of St Andrews, 2006-2010; Chairman, British Sub-Aqua Club, 2008-2014; University of St Andrews: Director of Teaching, 2011-13, Pro Dean Postgraduate, 2013-17, Head of School, 2017-19. Address: University of St Andrews, St Katharine's West, The Scores, St Andrews KY16 9AX; T.-01334 463548.
E-mail: cmp@st-andrews.ac.uk

Peden, Professor George Cameron, MA, DPhil, FRHistS, FRSE. Emeritus Professor of History, Stirling University, since 2008; b. 16.2.43, Dundee; m., Alison Mary White; 3 s. Educ. Grove Academy, Broughty Ferry; Dundee University; Brasenose College, Oxford. Sub-Editor, Dundee

Evening Telegraph, 1960-68; mature student, 1968-75; Tutorial Assistant, Department of Modern History, Dundee University, 1975-76; Temporary Lecturer, School of History, Leeds University, 1976-77; Lecturer in Economic and Social History, then Reader in Economic History, Bristol University, 1977-90; Professor of History, Stirling University, 1990-2008; Visiting Fellow: All Souls College, Oxford, 1988-89, St. Catherine's College, Oxford, 2002. Publications: British Rearmament and the Treasury 1932-39, 1979; British Economic and Social Policy: Lloyd George to Margaret Thatcher, 1985; Keynes, The Treasury and British Economic Policy, 1988; The Treasury and British Public Policy, 1906-1959, 2000; Keynes and his Critics: Treasury Responses to the Keynesian Revolution, 1925-46 (Editor), 2004; The Transformation of Scotland: The Economy, since 1700 (Co-Editor), 2005; Arms, Economics and British Strategy: From Dreadnoughts to Hydrogen Bombs, 2007. Recreation: hill-walking. Address: (h.) Ardvurich, Leny Feus, Callander FK17 8AS; T.-01877 30488; e-mail: george.peden@stir.ac.uk

Pedersen, Dr Line Clausen. Director of Collections and Research, National Galleries of Scotland, since 2020. Educ. Copenhagen University; The Courtauld Institute of Art; University of London; Università degli Studi di Firenze. Employed in various curatorial roles at the Ny Carlsberg Glyptothek (NCG) in Copenhagen, from 2003; Head of the Modern Collection, 2010-2020. Address: National Galleries of Scotland, 73 Belford Road, Edinburgh EH4 3DS.

Peebles, Don. Head of CIPFA (Chartered Institute of Public Finance and Accountancy) Policy & Technical UK, since 2018; previously Head of CIPFA Scotland, 2013-18. Qualified accountant; background in local authority finance, Audit Scotland; joined CIPFA in 2002, led on CIPFA's work on local taxation, 2002-04, Policy & Technical Manager, 2004-2013, became CIPFA's Head of Devolved Government in 2014; led on the Institute's work on the Scottish referendum; appointed as the budget adviser to the Welsh Assembly's Finance Committee for the 2015/16 budget process. Member of the Commission on Local Taxation, 2016 and Scottish Parliament Budget Review Group, 2017. Address: CIPFA Scotland, 160 Dundee Street, Edinburgh EH11 1DQ; T.-0131 221 8640. E-mail: don.peebles@cipfa.org

Peggie, Robert Galloway Emslie, CBE, DUniv, FCCA. Chairman, Board, Edinburgh College of Art, 1998-99; Chairman, Local Government Staff Commission for Scotland, 1994-97; b. 5.1.29, Bo'ness; 1 s.; 1 d. Educ. Lasswade High School. Trainee Accountant, 1946-52; Accountant in industry, 1952-57; Edinburgh Corporation, 1957-72: O. and M. Officer, Assistant City Chamberlain, Deputy City Chamberlain, Reorganisation Steering Committee; Chief Executive, Lothian Regional Council, 1974-86; Commissioner (Ombudsman) for Local Administration in Scotland, 1986-94. Former Member, Court, Heriot-Watt University (Convener, Finance Committee); Governor, Edinburgh College of Art; former Trustee, Lloyds TSB Foundation. Recreation: reading. Address: 9A Napier Road, Edinburgh EH10 5AZ; T.-0131-229 6775.

Pelan, John David Augustine, BA (Hons). Director: Scottish Council on Archives, since 2017, Scottish Civic Trust, 2010-17; b. 18.5.64, Belfast; m., Jane Ogden-Smith. Educ. St. Mary's CBS Belfast; Trinity College Dublin. Formerly Director of Communications and Depute Secretary, Royal Incorporation of Architects in Scotland, 1993-2006; Director John Pelan Associates, since 2006. Editor, Prospect Magazine, 1999-2001. Recreations: literature; photography.

Pelham Burn, Angus Maitland, MBE, LLD, JP, DL. Director, Bank of Scotland, 1977-2000, Chairman, North of Scotland Board, 1973-2000; Chairman, Aberdeen Airport Consultative Committee, 1986-2006; Director, Dana Petroleum plc, 1999-2008; b. 13.12.31, London; m., Anne (deceased, 2021); 4 d. Educ. Harrow; North of Scotland College of Agriculture. Hudson's Bay Company, 1951-58; Wolf Bounty Officer (Ontario), 1956-59; Company Director, since 1958; Chairman, Scottish Provident, 1995-98; Chairman, Aberdeen Asset Management PLC (formerly, Aberdeen Trust PLC), 1992-2000; Director, Abtrust Scotland Investment Company, 1989-96; Member, Kincardine County Council, 1967-75 (Vice Convener, 1973-75); Member, Grampian Regional Council, 1974-94; Member, Accounts Commission for Scotland, 1980-94 (Deputy Chairman, 1987-94); Member, Gordon Highlander Museum Committee, 1994-2009; Director, Aberdeen Association for Prevention of Cruelty to Animals, 1975-95 (Chairman, 1984-89); former Chairman, Order of St. John (Aberdeen) Ltd.; Council Member, Winston Churchill Memorial Trust, 1984-94; Member, Queen's Bodyguard for Scotland (Royal Company of Archers), 1968-2009; Vice Lord Lieutenant, Kincardineshire, 1978-99, Deputy Lieutenant, since 1999; Governor, Lathallan School, 2001-04; Honorary Degree of Doctor of Law, (Robert Gordon University), 1996; Patron, Knockando Woolmill Trust, since 2012. Recreations: gardening; wildlife photography. Address: The Kennels Cottage, Dess, Aboyne, Aberdeenshire AB34 5AY. E-mail: snow.bunting2@gmail.com

Pelly, Frances, RSA. Sculptor; b. 21.7.47, Edinburgh. Educ. Morrison's Academy, Crieff; Duncan of Jordanstone College of Art, Dundee. Part-time lecturing, Dundee, 1974-78; full-time lecturing, Grays School of Art, Aberdeen, 1979-83. Recreations: riding; wildlife; gardening.

Pender, Sheriff David James, LLB (Hons). Sheriff of North Strathclyde, 1995-2021; b. 7.9.49, Glasgow; m., Elizabeth; 2 s.; 2 d. Educ. Queen's Park Senior Secondary School, Glasgow; Edinburgh University. Partner, MacArthur Stewart, Solicitors, Oban, 1977. Recreations: reading; travel; bridge.

Pender, Professor Gareth, BSc, PhD, CEng, FREng, FRSE, FICE, FCIWEM. Professor of Civil Engineering, Heriot-Watt University, since 2016, Deputy Principal for Research and Innovation; b. 24.1.60, Helensburgh; m., Isobel McNaught Connell; 2 s. Educ. Vale of Leven Academy; University of Strathclyde. Civil Engineer, Crouch and Hogg, Consulting Engineers, 1984-89; Lecturer, University of Glasgow, 1989-2000. Recreations: golf; skiing. Address: (b.) Heriot-Watt University, Edinburgh EH14 4AS; T.-0131-451 3312. E-mail: g.pender@hw.ac.uk

Penman, Derek, QPM, LLB (Hons). Honorary Professor, University of Dundee, since 2017; Police Advisor on Ministry of Defence Police Committee, UK Ministry of Defence, since 2020; Non Executive Director, Peoplematters (Europe) Ltd, since 2019; Director, Learntech Scotland Ltd, since 2018. Educ. Glasgow University. Career: joined Central Scotland Police in 1982 as a cadet before becoming a Constable in 1984; had a varied career, rising through the ranks before being appointed as Temporary Assistant Chief Constable in 2007. Following completion of the UK Strategic Command Course in 2008, was appointed as Assistant Chief Constable with Grampian Police; Deputy Chief Constable, Central Scotland Police, 2011, temporary Chief Constable, 2011-13; Assistant Chief Constable, Local Policing North, 2013-14; HM Chief Inspector of Constabulary for Scotland,

2014-18. Awarded QPM in the 2014 Queen's Birthday Honours; Honorary Professor with the University of Dundee; Honorary Colonel with Angus and Dundee Battalion of Army Cadet Force.

Penman, Ian Douglas, BSc (Hons), MD, FRCP(Edin). Consultant Gastroenterologist, Western General Hospital, Edinburgh, since 1997; part-time Senior Lecturer, University of Edinburgh, since 1997; b. 2.2.64, Ayr; m., Jacqueline Patricia Kellaway; 1 s.; 1 d. Educ. Ayr Academy; University of Glasgow. Advanced Fellow, Medical University, South Carolina, USA, 1997-98. T.-0131-537 1758; e-mail: ian.penman@luht.scot.nhs.uk

Pennington, Professor (Thomas) Hugh, CBE, MB BS, PhD, Hon. DSc (Lancaster, Strathclyde, Aberdeen, Hull, Harper Adams), FRCPath, FRCPEdin, FRSA, FMedSci, FRSE. Professor of Bacteriology Emeritus, University of Aberdeen; b. 19.4.38, Edgware, Middlesex; m., Carolyn Ingram Beattie; 2 d. Educ. Lancaster Royal Grammar School; St. Thomas's Hospital Medical School, London University. House appointments, St. Thomas's Hospital, 1962-63; Assistant Lecturer in Medical Microbiology, St. Thomas's Hospital Medical School, 1963-67; Postdoctoral Fellow, University of Wisconsin (Madison), 1967-68; Lecturer then Senior Lecturer in Virology, University of Glasgow, 1969-79; Dean of Medicine University of Aberdeen, 1987-92; Professor of Bacteriology, Aberdeen University, 1979-2003; Governor, Rowett Research Institute, 1980-88, and 1996-2003; Member, Board of Directors, Moredun Research Institute, 2002-06; Chair, Expert Group on 1996 E.coli Outbreak in Central Scotland; Member: BBC Broadcasting Council for Scotland, 2000-05 (Vice Chair, 2003-05); Member, Scottish Food Advisory Committee of the Food Standards Agency, 2000-05; Member, Advisory Council of Campaign for Science and Engineering in the UK; Member, Technical Advisory Group, World Food Program, 2002-07; President, Society for General Microbiology, 2003-06; Chair, Public Inquiry into 2005 South Wales E. coli Outbreak; Chair, Aberdeen Science Centre Board, 2016-17; Caroline Walker Trust Consumer Advocate Award, 1997; Royal Institute of Public Health John Kershaw Memorial Prize, 1998; Thomas Graham Medal, Royal Glasgow Philosophical Society, 2001; Observer Food Monthly Hall of Fame Winner, 2005; Royal Scottish Society of Arts, Silver Medal, 2001, Keith Prize, 2006; Burgess of Guild, City of Aberdeen, 2002; Joseph Lister Medal, Society of Chemical Industry, 2009; Royal Environmental Health Institute of Scotland, Award for Meritorious Endeavours in Environmental Health, 2010. Publications: When Food Kills, 2003; Have Bacteria Won?, 2016; papers, articles and book chapters on viruses and bacteria, particularly their molecular epidemiology, and on food safety; contributor, London Review of Books; Editorial Consultant, The Lancet. Recreations: collecting books; dipterology. Address: (b.) 13 Carlton Place, Aberdeen AB15 4BR; e-mail: mmb036@abdn.ac.uk

Penrose, Rt. Hon. Lord (George William Penrose), PC, MA, LLB, LLD, DUniv, CA, FRSE. Senator of the College of Justice, 1990-2005; b. 2.6.38, Port Glasgow; m., Wendy Margaret Ralph Cooper; 1 s.; 2 d. Educ. Port Glasgow High School; Greenock High School; University of Glasgow. Advocate, 1964; QC, 1978; Procurator to General Assembly of the Church of Scotland, 1984-90; Advocate Depute, 1987-88; Home Advocate Depute, 1989-90; Judge (1990), First Division, Inner House, Court of Session, 2001-05; PC, 2001; Equitable Life Inquiry Reporter, 2004; Chairman of Court, Heriot-Watt University, since 2008; Reporter, The Penrose Inquiry into blood infection. Recreation: walking.

Pentland, John. MSP (Labour), Motherwell and Wishaw, 2011-16. Born in Motherwell, worked as a welder and spent 28 years with the British Steel Corporation. Elected to Motherwell Council in 1992. PA to Frank Roy MP from 1997 and chair of North Lanarkshire Municipal Bank for 14 years.

Pentland, The Rt. Hon. Lord (Paul B. Cullen), LLB (Hons), QC. Chairman, Scottish Law Commission, 2014-18; Senator of the College of Justice, since 2008; Inner House of Court of Session, July 2020; Queen's Counsel, since 1995; b. 11.3.57, Gosforth; m., Joyce Nicol; 2 s.; 1 d. Educ. St Augustine's High School, Edinburgh; Edinburgh University. Clerk, Faculty of Advocates, 1986-91; Standing Junior Counsel, Department of the Environment in Scotland, 1988-91; Advocate Depute, 1992-95; Solicitor General for Scotland, 1995-97; Consultative Steering Group on the Scottish Parliament, 1998-99. Recreations: tennis; bridge. Address: (b.) Supreme Courts, Parliament House, Edinburgh EH1 1RQ; T.-0131 225 2595.

Peppé, William Lawrence Tosco, OBE, JP, DL; b. 25.11.37, India; m., Deirdre Eva Preston Wakefield; 3 s. Educ. Wellington College; King's College, Cambridge. Naval Officer, 1955-91 – Commander. Vice Lord Lieutenant, Ross and Cromarty, Skye and Lochalsh, 2005-2012; Hon. Sheriff, Portree and Lochmaddy Courts, 2007; Chairman, Skye and Lochalsh Access Forum, 2007-2010. Recreation: country. Address: Glendrynoch Lodge, Carbost, Isle of Skye IV47 8SX; T.-01478 640218; e-mail: peppe@glendrynoch.co.uk

Percy, Professor John Pitkeathly (Ian), CBE, LLD, CA, FRSA. Chairman, John Menzies Pensions, 2007-2021, Trustee; former Senior Partner, Grant Thornton, London and Scotland; Chairman: Queen Margaret University, 2004-2010, CALA Group Ltd, 2000-2011; Deputy Chairman, The Weir Group PLC, 1996-2010; Scottish Provident, 1993-2001; Director and Deputy Chairman of Ricardo plc, 2000-08; President of the Foundation for Governance Research and Education; former Chairman: The Accounts Commission, Audit Scotland, Kiln PLC (retired 2005), Companies House (retired 2006); former Deputy Chairman: UK Auditing Practices Board (1991-2002), International Auditing Standards Board (1995-2000); b. 16.1.42, Southport; m., Sheila; 2 d. Educ. Edinburgh Academy; Edinburgh University. Managing Partner, Grant Thornton, London, 1981-88; Honorary Professor of Accounting, Aberdeen University, 1988. Freeman, City of London; Member, British Academy of Experts; Elder, St. Cuthbert's Church of Scotland; President, Institute of Chartered Accountants of Scotland, 1990-91; Deputy Chairman and Trustee, National Trust for Scotland, 2000-2014; Member, Court of Directors of The Edinburgh Academy, 1993-2000 (Chairman, 1995-2000); Member, Scottish Legal Aid Board, 2000-05. Recreations: golf; fishing. Address: (h.) 4 Westbank, Easter Park Drive, Edinburgh EH4 6SL.

Perman, Ray, BA Hons (Mod Hist), MBA, FRSE. Author of The Rise and Fall of the City of Money (2019); Hubris: How HBOS wrecked the best bank in Britain (2012); The Man Who Gave Away His Island, A Life of John Lorne Campbell of Canna, 2010; Director, David Hume Institute, 2014-17; Chairman, The James Hutton Institute, 2011-17; Chairman, Access to Finance Expert Group, Department Business, Innovation & Skills, 2005-2013; b. 1947, London; m., Fay Young; 3 s. Educ. University of St. Andrews; Open University; University of Edinburgh. Journalist: The Times, the Financial Times; Deputy Editor, the Sunday Standard, 1969-83; Insider Publications Ltd: Managing Director, 1983-94, Chairman, 1994-96, Director, 1996-99; Development Director, Caledonian Publishing plc, 1994-96; Director, GJWS Ltd, 1997-99; Chief Executive, Scottish Financial Enterprise, 1999-2003. Chairman, Inner Ear Ltd, since 2000; Member of the Court, Heriot-Watt University, 2003-09; Board Member, Scottish Enterprise, 2004-09; Chairman, Social Investment Scotland, 2001-09; Chairman, Good Practice Ltd, 2005-2013. Trustee, Botanics Foundation, 2008-2011; Trustee, Poorboy Theatre

Company; Chairman of Worldwide Fund for Nature (WWF) Scottish Advisory Council, 1998-2004; Member of the UK Board of Trustees of the WWF, 2001-04; Trustee of the Stewart Ivory Foundation, 2001-08. Recreations: painting; playing the blues; planting trees. Address: 14 East Claremont Street, Edinburgh EH7 4JP; T.-0131 556 4646; mobile: 07971 164315; e-mail: ray@rayperman.com

Perrie, Walter, MA, MPhil. Poet; b. 5.6.49, Lanarkshire. Educ. Hamilton Academy; Edinburgh and Stirling Universities. Publications: Books: Poem on a Winter Night, 1976; A Lamentation for the Children (SAC book award 1978), 1978; By Moon and Sun, 1980; Out of Conflict: Essays on Literature and Ideas, 1982; Concerning the Dragon (Poems), 1984; Roads that Move: a Journey through eastern Europe, 1991; From Milady's Wood and Other Poems, 1997; Caravanserai (poems), 2004; Decagon: Selected Poems, 1995-2005 (selected and edited with an introduction by John Herdman), 2005; Rhapsody of the Red Cliff (Poems), 2005; As Far as Thales: Beginning Philosophy, 2006; The King of France is Bald: Philosophy and Meaning, 2007; Twelve Fables of La Fontaine Made Owre intil Scots, 2007; Lyrics & Tales in Twa Tongues, 2010; First Fragments for an Unknown Lover (poem), 2012; Vigils (poems), 2015; A Minding for Merrill, 2017; Sorceries (poems), 2018; The Ages of Water: Poems by Walter Perrie, 2020; Nietzsche, Dostoievsky & MacDiarmid's Drunk Man, 2021; Walter Perrie in Conversation with Scottish Writers, 2021; Editing: Co Founding editor of Chapman, 1969-75; Guest editor, double issue of Lines Review on Canadian Literature, 1986; Managing editor, Margin, an international quarterly of the arts, 1986-91; presently Editor of Fras Scottish literary journal, since 2004. Fellowships: Scottish-Canadian exchange fellowship, 1984-85 (based at UBC Vancouver); University of Stirling writer-in-residence, 1991; Strathkelvin District creative writing fellow, 1992-93; Merrill House fellowship (2017), USA. Address: (h.) 10 Croft Place, Dunning, Perthshire PH2 0SB.

Perry, John Scott (Jack), CBE, DL, BSc, CA. Chairman: European Assets Trust PLC, since 2014, ICG-Longbow Senior Secured UK Property Debt Investments Limited, since 2012; Non-Executive Director: Witan Investment Trust plc, since 2017; Chairman, Board of Directors, Hospice Developments Limited, 2012-19; b. 23.11.54; m., Lydia; 1 s.; 2 d. Educ. Glasgow University; Strathclyde University. CA (ICAS), 1979; Certified Public Accountant (USA), 1985; Ernst & Young, 1976-2003: Managing Partner, Glasgow, 1995-2003; Regional Industry Leader, Technol. Communications and Entertainment, Scotland and NI, 1999-2003; Chairman, CBI Scotland, 2001-03 (Member, Council, since 1996); Chief Executive, Scottish Enterprise, 2004-09; Non-Executive Director, Robert Wiseman Dairies, 2010-2012. Treasurer and Member of Court, University of Strathclyde, 2010-17; Chairman: Craigholme School, 2000-07, TMRI Limited, 2007-09; Member, Barclays Wealth Advisory Committee, 2010-2014. Former Member, Ministerial Task Force on Economic Forums. Honorary Doctorate in Business Administration, Edinburgh Napier University, 2010, University of Abertay Dundee, 2011; Doctor of the University, Strathclyde, 2018. Deputy Lieutenant, Renfrewshire, 2011-2019 and Fife, since 2019. Recreations: golf; skiing; reading; current affairs. Clubs: Glasgow Academical; Royal and Ancient Golf; Western Gailes Golf. Address: European Assets Trust PLC, c/o BMO Global Asset Management (EMEA), 6th Floor, Quartermile 4, 7a Nightingale Way, Edinburgh EH3 9EG.

Perth, 9th Earl of (John Eric Drummond), BA, MBA; b. 7.7.35. Educ. Downside School; Trinity College, Cambridge; Harvard University. Succeeded to title, 2002.

Pertwee, Professor Roger Guy, MA, DPhil, DSc. Emeritus Professor, University of Aberdeen, since 2015, Professor of Neuropharmacology, 1999-2015; Director of Pharmacology/Research and Development Director, GW Pharmaceuticals, 2002-2021; b. 21.9.42, Wembley; m., Teresa Bronagh; 1 s. Educ. Eastbourne College; Christ Church, Oxford. International Cannabinoid Research Society: International Secretary, since 1992, President, 1997-98 and 2007-08; First Chairman, International Association for Cannabinoid Medicines, 2005-07; Honorary Senior Research Fellow, Rowett Research Institute, since 1992; Visiting Professor, University of Hertfordshire, 2000-2018; Co-chairman of the Subcommittee on Cannabinoid Receptors of the International Union of Basic and Clinical Pharmacology (IUPHAR), since 2001; Mechoulam Award for Outstanding Contributions to Cannabinoid Research, 2002. Numerous papers on cannabinoids, and a 2020 Highly Cited Researcher Award from Clarivate Analytics in recognition of the production of Pharmacology papers ranking in the top 1% worldwide by citations. British Pharmacological Society's Wellcome Gold Medal for Outstanding Contributions to Pharmacology (based mainly on research achievements, 2011). Honorary Fellowship of the British Pharmacological Society, 2012; International Association for Cannabinoid Medicines' Special Award for Major Contributions to the Re-introduction of Cannabis as a Medicine, 2013. The 2018 Lifetime Achievement Award from the International Cannabinoid Research Society (ICRS) for Outstanding Contributions to Cannabinoid Research and to the ICRS. Recognized by The Cannabinoid Scientist as an R&D trailblazer in its 2020 Power List of top scientists in cannabis research. Address: School of Medicine, Medical Sciences and Nutrition, Institute of Medical Sciences, University of Aberdeen, Foresterhill, Aberdeen AB25 2ZD; e-mail: rgp@abdn.ac.uk

Peterkin, Tom, MA Hons (Econ). Special Adviser to the Secretary of State for Scotland, Scotland Office, UK Government, since 2021; Political Editor: The Press and Journal, 2018-2021, Scotsman/Scotland on Sunday, 2014-18. Educ. Clifton Hall, Midlothian; Glenalmond College, Perthshire; University of Edinburgh. Daily Telegraph: Scottish Political Correspondent, 2001-05, Ireland Correspondent, 2005-08, Correspndent based in London, 2008; Scottish Political Editor, Scotland on Sunday/Scotsman, 2008-2014. Recreations: golf; piping; skiing. Address: Scotland Office, 1 Melville Crescent, Edinburgh EH3 7HW.

Peterson, Eric Spence, LLB, DipLP, NP. Solicitor, since 1983; Honorary Sheriff, since 2010; b. 20.06.60, Lerwick; m., Moira Anne Stewart; 1 s.; 1 d. Educ. Anderson High School, Lerwick; Aberdeen University; Dundee University. Partner, Tait & Peterson, Solicitors & Estate Agents, Lerwick, since 1984; Accredited as a Specialist in Crofting Law by Law Society of Scotland, 2006-2011. Member, Law Society of Scotland Crofting Law Accreditation Panel, since 2009; Deacon, Lerwick Baptist Church; Member, Good News for Everyone (formerly Gideons UK). Recreations: cycling; reading; occasional trout fishing. Address: (b.) Bank of Scotland Buildings, Lerwick, Shetland; T.-01595 693010.
E-mail: eric.peterson@tait-peterson.co.uk

Petrie, Murray, FRICS; b. 8.6.46, Keith; m., Jennifer; 3 s. Educ. High School of Dundee. Consultant Chartered Surveyor. Former Vice Chair, NHS Tayside; former Director, Maggie Centre (Dundee). Former Chairman, Tayside Primary Care NHS Trust, 1999-2004; former Chair, Perth and Kinross Health and Social Care Co-operative. Recreations: rugby; golf; travelling. Address: (h.) Craigard, 6 Guthrie Terrace, Barnhill, Dundee DD5 2QX; T.-01382 776180.

Petrie, Roderick McKenzie. President, Scottish Football Association, since 2019; b. 22.4.56. Career history:

qualified chartered accountant and trained with Ernst & Young, became audit partner in 13 years with the firm; Managing Director of investment bank Quayle Munro for over 6 years; joined Hibernian FC's board of directors in 1996 and was appointed Managing Director in 1997, Chairman and Chief Executive for over 20 years; served on the committees of the Scottish Football Association (SFA) since 1998, elected second Vice-President in 2011, then became first Vice-President; served on the board of the Scottish Premier League. Address: The Scottish Football Association, Hampden Park, Glasgow G42 9AY; T.-0141 616 6000.

Pettegree, Professor Andrew David Mark, FRHS. Professor of Modern History, St Andrews University, since 1998, former Head of School of History; b. 16.9.57, Rhyl; m., Jane Ryan; 2 d. Educ. Oundle School; Oxford University (BA Hons). Schmidt Scholarship, 1980 (MA, DPhil, 1983); research scholarship, University of Hamburg, 1982-84; Research Fellow, Peterhouse, Cambridge; became Lecturer, St Andrews University, 1986; Reader, 1994; Director, St Andrews Reformation Studies Institute, 1993; Literary Director, Royal Historical Society, 1998. Publications include: Foreign Protestant Communities in Sixteenth Century London; Emden and the Dutch Revolt. Exile and the Development of Reformed Protestantism, 1992; The Early Reformation in Europe, 1992; Calvinism in Europe, 1540-1610 (Co-Editor); The Reformation of the Parishes. The Ministry and the Reformation in Town and Country, 1993; Calvinism in Europe, 1540-1620 (Co-Editor); Marian Protestantism. Six Studies, 1996; The Reformation World, 2000; Europe in the Sixteenth Century, 2001. Recreations: golf; tennis. Address: (b.) Reformation Institute, 69 South Street, St Andrews KY16 9AL; T.-01334 462903.

Pettigrew, Colin William, LLB (Hons). Retired Sheriff of North Strathclyde at South Strathclyde, Dumfries and Galloway, 2002-2021; President, The Sheriffs Association, 2015-17; b. 19.6.57, Glasgow; m., Linda; 1 s.; 1 d. Educ. The High School of Glasgow; The University of Glasgow. Assistant Court Solicitor, McClure, Naismith, Brodie and Co., Glasgow, 1980-82; Litigation Partner, Borland Johnston and Orr, Glasgow, then Borland Montgomerie Keyden, Glasgow, also TJ & WA Dykes, Hamilton, 1982-2002; Temporary Sheriff, 1999; Part Time Sheriff, 2001-02. Church of Scotland Elder, since 1983. Recreations: golf; travel; gardening and watching sport.

Pettigrew, James Neilson, LLB, DipAcc. Chairman, Scottish Ballet; former Chairman, CYBG PLC (the owners of Clydesdale Bank, Yorkshire Bank and the digital app based current account provider, B); Chairman, Scottish Financial Enterprise, 2016-19; b. 28.7.58, Dundee. Educ. High School of Dundee; University of Aberdeen; University of Glasgow. Career history: qualified as a CA with Ernst and Young before moving into the corporate sector; Sedgwick Group plc: Group Treasurer, then Deputy Group CFO, 1988-99; Group Finance Director, ICAP plc, 1999-2006; Chief Operating and Financial Officer, Ashmore Group plc, 2006-07; Chief Executive Officer, CMC Markets plc, 2007-09; joined CYBG PLC as a non-executive director in 2014. Co-Chair, the Financial Services Advisory Board (FiSAB); on the advisory board of TheCityUK; Chairman of Miton Group PLC; Senior Independent Non-Executive Director of Rathbone Brothers Plc and Rathbone Investment Management Limited (part of the Rathbone Brothers Plc group); Chairman: RBC Europe Limited, BlueBay Asset Management (Services) Ltd, BlueBay Asset Management LLP (members of the RBC Group); City UK Advisory Board; former President of ICAS.

Phelps, Professor Alan David Reginald, MA, DPhil, CPhys, MIEEE, FInstP, Fellow APS, FRSE. Professor, Physics, Strathclyde University, since 1993 (Head of Department, 1998-2001); b. 2.6.44, Basingstoke; m., Susan Helen Marshall; 1 d. Educ. Haverfordwest Grammar School; King's College, Cambridge; University College, Oxford. Research Associate, National Academy of Sciences (USA), 1972-73; Research Officer, Oxford University, 1973-78; Lecturer, then Senior Lecturer, then Reader in Physics, Strathclyde University, 1978-93, Deputy Head of Department, 1993-98 and 2004-09. Chairman, Plasma Physics Group, Institute of Physics, 1995-97. IEEE Plasma Science and Applications Award, 2017; HPEM Fellow of SUMMA Foundation, 2018. Publications: 650 research papers and reports. Recreations: hill-walking; country pursuits. Address: (b.) Department of Physics, John Anderson Building, Strathclyde University, Glasgow G4 0NG; T.-0141-548 3166; e-mail: a.d.r.phelps@strath.ac.uk

Philip, Rt. Hon. Lord (Alexander Morrison). Senator of the College of Justice, 1996-2007; b. 3.8.42, Aberdeen; m., Shona Mary Macrae (m. diss. 2013); 3 s. Educ. Glasgow High School; St. Andrews University; Glasgow University. Solicitor, 1967-72; Advocate, 1973; Advocate Depute, 1982-85; QC, 1984; Chairman, Medical Appeal Tribunals, 1988-92; Chairman, Scottish Land Court, 1993-96; President, Lands Tribunal for Scotland, 1993-96; Privy Counsellor, 2005. Recreations: piping; golf.

Philip, Andy. Political Editor, The Press & Journal, since 2021; former reporter in 2008 before moving on to other roles, including the Press Association and the Daily Record as Live Politics Editor. Address: Aberdeen Journals Ltd, 5th Floor, 1 Marischal Square, Broad Street Aberdeen AB10 1BL; e-mail: andy.philip@pressandjournal.co.uk

Philip, Rev Dr William, MB, ChB, MRCP, BD. Minister, The Tron Church, Glasgow, since 2004; b. 1967, Edinburgh; m., Rebecca; 2 d. Educ. Aberdeen University. Career history: trained as a medical doctor at the University of Aberdeen, specialising in cardiology, before entering ministry in the Church of Scotland; Assistant Minister in a parish in Aberdeen, before moving to London in 1999 to be Director of Ministry at The Proclamation Trust until 2004; started Cornhill Scotland (training for ministry) in 2006, currently Chairman. Publications: Teaching John (Co-Author); Teaching Matthew (Co-Author); The Law of Promise; Why We Pray; Songs for a Saviour's Birth. Address: The Tron Church, 25 Bath Street, Glasgow G2 1HW; T.-0141 332 2795.
E-mail: william.philip@tron.church

Phillips-Davies, Alistair. Chief Executive, SSE plc (formerly Scottish and Southern Energy plc), since 2013; b. 1967, Wiltshire. Career: joined Southern Electric in 1997; joined the SSE Board as Energy Supply Director in 2002, Deputy Chief Executive, 2012-13 (Board-level responsibility for Generation, Energy Trading, Electricity and Gas Supply, Energy Efficiency, Customer Service, Sales, Marketing and Energy Services). Address: (b.) Inveralmond House, 200 Dunkeld Road, Perth PH1 3AQ.

Pia, Paul Dominic, LL.B. (Hons), WS, NP. Director of PaulPia Ltd: providing directorships, trusteeships and board advisorships, since 2010; b. 29.3.47, Edinburgh; m. Dr Anne Christine Argent; 3 d. Educ. Holy Cross Academy, Edinburgh; Universities of Edinburgh and Perugia; law apprentice, Lindsays WS, 1968-70; admitted as solicitor and member of Society of Writers to HM Signet, 1971; Solicitor, Burness LLP (formerly W & J Burness), 1970 and Partner, latterly Senior Corporate Partner, 1974-2010; Associate Member, American Bar Association; Fellow of Institute of Directors and member of Corporate Governance Unit, 2003-04; Director of Scottish North American

Business Council, 2000-04 and Trustee of Dewar Arts Awards, 2002-07; Chairman of Japan Society of Scotland, 1996-2000 and of Big Issue Foundation Scotland, 2000-08; Chairman of various pensions schemes including Baxters Food Group Pension Scheme and Royal Zoo of Scotland Pension Scheme. Publications: Care Diligence and Skill (handbook for directors). Recreations: hill-walking; travel; foreign languages and oriental culture. Address: (b. & h.) 34/8 Rattray Grove, Edinburgh EH10 5TZ; T.-0131 447 5122; e-mail: paul@paulpia.com

Pickard, Willis Ritchie Sturrock, MA, LLD, DEd, FSA Scot; b. 21.5.41, Dunfermline; m., Ann Marie nee MacNeil; 2 d. Educ. Daniel Stewart's College; St. Andrews University. The Scotsman: Sub-editor, 1963-72, Leader writer, 1967-72, Features Editor, 1972-77; Editor, Times Educational Supplement Scotland, 1977-2001. Liberal Candidate, East Fife, 1970, 1974. Member, Scottish Arts Council; Chairman, Book Trust Scotland; Rector, Aberdeen University, 1988-90; former Chairman, Scottish Liberal Club; Trustee, National Library of Scotland, 2006-14; former Chairman, Theatre Objektiv; committee member of European Movement in Scotland; Chairman, Liberal International in Scotland; Fellow, Scottish Vocational Education Council. Publication: 'The Member for Scotland: a life of Duncan McLaren' (2011). Recreations: reading; history research. Address: (h.) 13 Lockharton Gardens, Edinburgh EH14 1AU; T.-0131 443 7755.

Pickering, Professor Martin John, BA, PhD, FRSE. Professor of The Psychology of Language and Communication, University of Edinburgh, since 2003; b. 02.06.66, London; m., Elizabeth; 1 s.; 2 d. Educ. City of London School; University of Durham; University of Edinburgh. Science and Engineering Research Council Postdoctoral Fellow, 1990-92; British Academy Postdoctoral Fellow, 1992-95; Glasgow University: Lecturer, 1995-99, Reader, 1999; Reader, Edinburgh University, 2000-03; British Academy Research Readership, 2005-07. Broadbent Lecturer, British Psychological Society, 2006. Publications: Associate Editor, Psychological Science, since 2007; over 70 journal papers. Recreation: entertaining my children. Address: (b.) Department of Psychology, University of Edinburgh, 7 George Square, Edinburgh EH8 9JZ; T.-0131 650 3447; e-mail: martin.pickering@ed.ac.uk

Pieri, Frank, LLB. Sheriff of South Strathclyde, Dumfries and Galloway, 2005-2019 (retired); b. 10.8.54, Glasgow; m., Dorothy Telfer; 2 d. Educ. St. Aloysius College, Glasgow; Glasgow University. Solicitor, 1976-93; Advocate at Scottish Bar, since 1994; Full Time Immigration Adjudicator, 2000-04; Part Time Sheriff, 2004. Council Member: Scottish Law Agents Society, 1991-93, Council of Immigration Judges, 2003. Recreations: ambling; American crime fiction; Partick Thistle; opera.

Pighills, (Christopher) David, MA. Former Chairman, Pitlochry Festival Theatre; Board Member, New Park Educational Trust, since 2007; former Chairman, Board of Governors, Strathallan School; b. 27.11.37, Bradford. Educ. Rydal School; Cambridge University. Fettes College, 1960-75; Headmaster, Strathallan School, 1975-93. Recreations: shooting; gardening; golf. Address: 3 John Coupar Court, St Andrews KY16 9EB; T.-01334-477264.
E-mail: cpighills@gmail.com

Pignatelli, Frank, CBE, MA, MEd, DEd, DUniv, CCMI, FSQA, FICPD, FScotvec, FRSA, FCIPD, FSC. Pro bono adviser/mentor to individuals and charitable/voluntary/not-for-profit organisations, since 2007; b. 22.12.46, Glasgow;

m., Rosetta Anne; 1 s.; 1 d. Educ. St. Mungo's Academy, Glasgow; University of Glasgow. Teacher, head of modern languages, assistant head teacher, 1970-1978; member of directorate Strathclyde education department, 1978-1988; Executive Director of Education, Strathclyde Regional Council, 1988-96; Group Director, Human Resources, Associated Newspapers, London, 1996-97; Chairman and Managing Director, Executive Support and Development Consultancy, 1997-99; Chief Executive Officer, SUfI Ltd., 1999-2006; Visiting Professor, University of Glasgow: School of Education, 1993, Business School, 1997; Independent Adviser to Secretary of State for Scotland on appointments to public bodies, 1996-1999; Chairman: Scottish Management and Enterprise Council, 1999-2002, Strategic Review group on e-learning, 2004-2005, Scottish Parliament Futures Forum Project Board, 2007-08. E-mail frank@pignatelli.co.uk

Pike, Jo, BA, PGCertEd. Chief Executive, Scottish Wildlife Trust, since 2019. Educ. University of Cambridge; Homerton College, Cambridge. Career history: Teacher of English as a Foreign Language, various including Bell School and London School, Prague, 1992-94; Director of Studies, 3D Language Services, Prague, 1994-95; Fundraiser, Children of the Earth, Prague, 1995-96; Temporary Donor Development Officer, CancerBACUP (now part of Macmillan), 1997; Teacher Support Network: Fundraising Officer, 1997-98, Head of Fundraising, 1998-2000; Fundraising Manager Scotland, Leonard Cheshire Disability, 2000-2010; Director of Public Affairs and Deputy Chief Executive, Scottish Wildlife Trust, 2010-2019. Board Member, Turning Point Scotland, since 2011. Address: Scottish Wildlife Trust, Harbourside House, 110 Commercial Street, Edinburgh EH6 6NF; T.-0131 312 7765.

Pike, (Kathryn) Lorna, MA (Hons). Director of Lexicography, Faclair na Gàidhlig, since 2003; b. 8.8.56, Fort William. Educ. Lochaber High School, Fort William; Edinburgh University. Editor, Concise Scots Dictionary, 1979-83; Dictionary of the Older Scottish Tongue: Assistant Editor, 1984-86, Editor, 1986-2001; Editor, Scottish National Dictionary Association, 2001-02; Research Officer, Feasibility Study, Institute for the Languages of Scotland, 2001-02; Senior Editor, Scottish Language Dictionaries, 2002-04. Recreations: horses; music; reading. Address: (b.) Faclair na Gàidhlig, Fàs, Sabhal Mòr Ostaig, Sleat, Isle of Skye IV44 8RQ; T.-01471 888 273.

Pippard, Professor Martin John, BSc, MB, ChB. Emeritus Professor of Haematology, Dundee University; b. 1948, London; m., Grace Elizabeth; 2 s.; 1 d. Educ. Buckhurst Hill County High School; Birmingham University. House Physician and House Surgeon, 1972-73; Senior Medical House Officer, 1973-75; Research Fellow, Nuffield Department of Clinical Medicine, Oxford, 1975-78; MRC Travelling Research Fellow, University of Washington, Seattle, 1978-80; Wellcome Trust Research Fellow and Clinical Lecturer, Nuffield Department of Clinical Medicine, 1980-83; Consultant Haematologist, MRC Clinical Research Centre and Northwick Park Hospital, 1983-88; Professor of Haematology and Honorary Consultant Haematologist, Ninewells Hospital and Medical School, Dundee, 1989-2009, Dean of Medical School, 2006-2009. Recreations: gardening; hill-walking.
E-mail: mjpippard@doctors.org.uk

Pittock, Professor Murray, MAE, FRSE, MA, DPhil, DLitt, FRSA, FEA, FRHistS, FHEA, FASLS, FSAScot. Bradley Professor of English Literature, Pro Vice-Principal, University of Glasgow (formerly Dean and Vice-Principal,

2009-2015); formerly Professor of Scottish and Romantic Literature, Manchester University, 2003-07; Professor in Literature, Strathclyde University, 1996-2003; b. 5.1.62; m., Anne Grace Thornton Martin; 2 d. Educ. Aberdeen Grammar School; Glasgow University; Balliol College, Oxford (Snell Exhibitioner). Lecturer, then Reader, Edinburgh University, 1989-96. Associate Editor, New Dictionary of National Biography; Convener, International Association for the Study of Scottish Literatures, 2014-17 and Chair of Trustees; Treasurer, Jacobite Studies Trust; Trustee and Adviser in Scottish History, National Trust for Scotland; Co-Chair, Scottish Arts and Humanities Alliance; Royal Society of Edinburgh BP Humanities Research Prize, 1992-94; British Academy Chatterton Lecturer in Poetry, 2002; Visiting appointments: Auburn, Charles University, Prague, NYU, Notre Dame, Trinity College Dublin, Yale. General Editor, Collected Works of Allan Ramsay, since 2015. Publications: The Invention of Scotland, 1991, 2014, 2016; Spectrum of Decadence, 1993, 2014, 2016; Poetry and Jacobite Politics in Eighteenth-Century Britain and Ireland, 1994, 2006; Inventing and Resisting Britain, 1997; Jacobitism, 1998; Celtic Identity and the British Image, 1999; Scottish Nationality, 2001; A New History of Scotland, 2003; The Edinburgh History of Scottish Literature (Co-Editor), 2006; The Reception of Sir Walter Scott in Europe, 2007; James Boswell, 2007; Scottish and Irish Romanticism, 2008, 2011; The Myth of The Jacobite Clans: The Jacobite Army in 1745, 2009; The Edinburgh Companion to Scottish Romanticism, 2011; Robert Burns in Global Culture, 2011; Material Culture and Sedition, 2013; The Road to Independence? Scotland in the Balance, 2014; The Reception of Robert Burns in Europe, 2014; Culloden, 2016, 2021; Scots Musical Museum, 2018; Enlightenment in a Smart City, 2018. Address: (b.) 7 University Gardens, Glasgow G12 8QH; e-mail: Murray.pittock@glasgow.ac.uk

Pitts, Simon, BA, MA. Chief Executive, STV Group plc, since 2018. Educ. University of Bath; College of Europe. Career history: Parliamentary Advisor, European Parliament, 1998-2000; ITV: European Affairs Manager, 2000-02, Head of Public Affairs, 2002-04, Controller of Regulatory Affairs, 2004-06, Controller of Digital Platforms, 2006-08, Managing Director, SDN, 2006-2011, Controller of Strategy, 2008-2011, Director of Strategy & Transformation, 2011-13, Director of Strategy & Technology, 2013-14, Managing Director - Online, Pay TV, Interactive & Technology, 2014-17. Vice Chairman, Royal Television Society, 2012. Address: STV plc, 10 George Street, Edinburgh EH2 2DU; T.-0131 200 8000.

Placido, Professor Francis, BSc, PhD, FInstP, FSAS. Professor Emeritus, University of the West of Scotland (appointed Professor in 1999); b. 29.9.46, Dalkeith; m., Dorothy Charlotte Torrance; 2 d. Educ. Dalkeith High School; University of Edinburgh. Demonstrator, University of Edinburgh, 1972-77; Paisley College of Technology: Lecturer, 1977-89, Reader in Physics, 1989-99. John Logie Baird Award for Innovation, 1998. Founder and Director of the Thin Film Centre, 2000-2014. Recreations: food and wine; painting. Address: (b.) Institute of Thin Films, Sensors and Imaging, University of the West of Scotland, High Street, Paisley PA1 2BE; e-mail: frank.placido@uws.ac.uk

Pollard, Professor Jeffrey W., PhD, FRSE, FRSB, FMedSci, FAAAS. Director of the MRC Centre for Reproductive Health, University of Edinburgh, since 2013. Educ. Sheffield University; Imperial Cancer Research Fund (now CRUK), London; Ontario Cancer Institute, Toronto. Career history: Faculty position at King's College, University of London; joined the Albert Einstein College of Medicine in New York in 1988 and became Louis Goldstein Swann Chair in Women's Health, 1989-2013, Deputy Director of the NCI funded Cancer Center and Director of the NIH funded Center for the Study of Reproductive Biology and Women's Health. Scientific Advisory Boards: Campbell Breast Cancer Center, Toronto,

since 2006, Knight Cancer Institute, Oregon Health & Science University, since 2013, Sun Yat-sen Medical School, Guangzhou, China, since 2016. Received several awards most notably the American Cancer Society "Medal of Honour for Basic Science Research" for studies in tumour immunology (2010), the Royal Society Wolfson Research Merit Award (2013-2018), the Welcome Trust Senior Investigator Award (2013-2021), Rothschild Yvette-Meynet Curie award (2009). Address: MRC Centre for Reproductive Health, The Queen's Medical Research Institute, Edinburgh BioQuarter, 47 Little France Crescent, Edinburgh EH16 4TJ; T.-0131 242 6231. E-mail: Jeff.Pollard@ed.ac.uk

Pollock, Sheriff Alexander, MA (Oxon), LLB. Sheriff of Grampian, Highland and Islands, at Inverness, 2005-09; b. 21.7.44, Glasgow; m., Verena Francesca Gertraud Alice Ursula Critchley; 1 s.; 1 d. Educ. Rutherglen Academy; Glasgow Academy; Brasenose College, Oxford; Edinburgh University; University for Foreigners, Perugia. Partner, Bonar Mackenzie & Kermack, WS, 1971-73; called to Scottish Bar, 1973; Conservative candidate: West Lothian, General Election, February 1974, Moray and Nairn, General Election, October 1974; MP, Moray and Nairn, 1979-83; Moray, 1983-87; Parliamentary Private Secretary to Secretary of State for Scotland, 1982-86; PPS to Secretary of State for Defence, 1986-87; Advocate Depute, 1990-91; Sheriff (Floating) of Tayside, Central and Fife, at Stirling, 1991-93; Sheriff of Grampian, Highland and Islands, at Aberdeen and Stonehaven, 1993-2001; Sheriff of Grampian, Highland and Islands, at Inverness and Portree, 2001-05. Member, Queen's Bodyguard for Scotland (Royal Company of Archers), since 1984. Recreations: walking; music. Address: (h.) Drumdarrach, Forres, Moray.

Pollock, Linda Catherine, BSc, PhD, MBA, RGN, District Nursing Cert, RMN. Associate with Dementia Development Centre, University of Stirling, 2012-2015; Scottish Legal Complaints Commissioner, 2008-2011; Accounts Commission Board Member, 2009-2015; ENABLE Scotland Board Member, 2012-16; Board Non-Executive Director, Care Inspectorate for Scotland, 2014-20; b. 26.11.53, Ayr. Educ. Boroughmuir Senior Secondary; Alloway Primary; Edinburgh University; Aberdeen University; Robert Gordons University. General District and Psychiatric Nursing; teaching and research roles before opting from a management career in NHS; Director of Nursing from 1989; Mental Welfare Commissioner (1997-2005), and specialised in Community and Primary Care before retiring; worked as Nurse Adviser in Nurse Prescribing, to the Chief Nurse in Scotland; worked with Nursing Regulator (NMC) until 2012, and is Chair of an Advisory Board in a charity, Pain Concern; Trustee and Vice Chair of The Queen's Nursing Institute of Scotland (Trustee, since 2014); independent prison monitor with HMIPS. Publications: numerous articles in professional journals and chapters in nursing books; author, "Community Psychiatric Nursing: Myth and Reality", 1989. Recreations: bridge; Scottish Country Dancing; skiing; jogging. E-mail: linda.pollock5@btinternet.com

Polson, Cllr Andrew. Joint Leader, East Dunbartonshire Council, since 2018; representing Bearsden South Ward (Scottish Conservatives), since 2017; Revival FM's Station Manager; Founder Director, Revival Radio Ltd. Leads The Gospel Heirs, the well known and respected gospel singing group; released several CDs over the years including the 25 Anniversary Special Edition CD. Producer of recording artists. Address: East Dunbartonshire Council, 12 Strathkelvin Place, Kirkintilloch G66 1TJ; T.-0300 123 4510.

Ponsonby, Bernard Joseph. Special Correspondent, STV News; Political Editor, 2000-2019; Reporter/Presenter, since 1990; b. 3.3.63, Glasgow. Educ. Trinity High School, Rutherglen; Strathclyde University. Researcher to Rt. Hon.

Dr Dickson Mabon, 1987; Press Officer, Scottish Liberal Democrats, 1988-89; party's first Parliamentary candidate, Glasgow Govan, 1988; PR and Media Consultant, freelance Reporter for BBC Radio Scotland, 1989-90; Principal Presenter of political, election, referendum and election results programmes, STV, since 1994; Presenter: Scottish Questions, Trial by Night, Scottish Voices, Platform, Seven Days and Politics Now. Commentator for Papal Visit coverage 2010. Producer of political documentaries: The Salmond Years (2000), The Dewar Years (2001), The Road to Holyrood (2004), Gordon Brown: Made in Scotland (2007). Presenter of live broadcast from a Scottish Court, The Carmichael Trial (2015). Royal Television Society (Scotland) TV journalist of the year 2014 and 2015. Publication: Donald Dewar: Scotland's first First Minister (contributor); The Scottish Parliament at 20 (contributor). Recreations: golf; Celtic Football Club. Address: (b.) STV, Pacific Quay, Glasgow G51 1PQ.
E-mail: bernard.ponsonby@stv.tv

Poole, Lady Anna I., MA, MSt, QC, FCIArb. Senator of the College of Justice, since 2020; b. 11.8.70, Craigtoun; m.; 1 d.; 1 s. Educ. Madras College, St Andrews; Oxford University. Qualified as a Solicitor of the Supreme Court of England and Wales with Linklaters, 1996; then as a Scottish Solicitor with Brodies, 1997; called to Scottish Bar, 1998; First Standing Junior Counsel to the Scottish Government, 2010-2012; QC, 2012; part-time Judge of the First-tier Tribunal, 2014-2018; Upper Tribunal Judge (Administrative Appeals Chamber), 2018-19. Chancellor of the Diocese of Edinburgh. Recreations: music; walking; travel; reading.

Poole, Eve, BA (Theology), MBA (Business), PhD (Theology and Capitalism). Writer; Interim Chief Executive Officer, The Royal Society of Edinburgh, since 2022; b. 5.2.72, St Andrews; m. Nathan Percival; 2 c. Educ. schools in Scotland and the US; University of Durham; University of Edinburgh; University of Cambridge. Career history: Ecclesiastical Civil Servant, Church Commissioners for England, 1993-97; Administrator, Scottish Redundant Churches Trust, 1997-98; Management Consultant, Deloitte Consulting, 1998-2002; Book Author, 2010-2015; Director, Ashridge Executive Education, Hult International Business School, 2002-2018; Chairman of the Board of Governors, Gordonstoun School, Elgin, 2015-2021; Third Church Estates Commissioner, Church Commissioners for England, Westminster, 2018-2021; Ashridge Adjunct Faculty, Hull International Business School, Ashridge, since 2022. Publications: Ethical Leadership (Co-Author), 2010; The Church on Capitalism, 2010; Capitalism's Toxic Assumptions, 2015; Leadersmithing, 2017; Buying God, 2018; Leadersmithing (Chinese language edition), 2019. Life Fellow of the Royal Society of Arts; Visiting Scholar, Sarum College. Address: The Royal Society of Edinburgh, 22-26 George Street, Edinburgh EH2 2PQ.

Poon, Professor Wilson, MA (Cantab), PhD (Cantab), FInstP, CPhys, FRSE. Chair of Natural Philosophy, since 2016, Professor of Condensed Matter Physics, Edinburgh University, 1999-2016, Director of Research, School of Physics & Astronomy, since 2006; Engineering and Physical Sciences Research Council (EPSRC) Senior Research Fellow, 2007-2012; b. 1962, Hong Kong; m., Heidi Lau; 1 s.; 1 d. Educ. St Paul's Co-educational College, Hong Kong; Rugby School; Peterhouse and St. John's College, Cambridge. Research Fellow, St Edmund's College, Cambridge, 1986-88; Lecturer, Department of Applied Physics, Portsmouth Polytechnic, 1989; Edinburgh University: Lecturer, 1990-97; Senior Lecturer, 1997-99. Founder, Edinburgh Complex Fluids Partnership (ECFP). Member, Scottish Episcopal Church, Doctrine Committee (2003-2011) and Liturgy Committee (2011-2015). IOP Sam Edwards Award, 2019; RSC/SCI Thomas Graham Lectureship, 2019; ECIS Solvay Prize, 2020. Recreation: piano. Address: (b.) School of Physics & Astronomy, Edinburgh University, Mayfield Road, Edinburgh EH9 3JZ; T.-0131-650 5297; e-mail: w.poon@ed.ac.uk

Porteous, Rev Brian William, BSc (Hons), DipCS. Ordained Local Minister, Church of Scotland, since 2018; b. 6.2.51, Falkirk; m., Shena; 4 s. Educ. Falkirk High School; St. Andrews University; Moray House College of Education; Loughborough University; Aberdeen University. Joined Scottish Sports Council as Development Officer, 1979, appointed Director of Operations, 1989; Depute Director, Cultural and Leisure Services and Parks and Recreation, Glasgow City Council, 1994-2001; Director of Culture, Sport and Lifestyle, Genesis Consulting, 2001-09. Honorary Secretary, British Orienteering Federation, 1974-76; President, Scottish Orienteering Association, 1996-2000; Board Member, SportsCoach UK, 2002-06; Vice President, International Orienteering Federation, 2004-2012, President, 2012-2016, Hon. Life President, since 2016. Publication: Orienteering, 1979. Recreations: golf; orienteering; singing; caravanning. Address: (h.) Kildene, Westfield Road, Cupar KY15 5DS.

Postecoglou, Angelos "Ange". Manager, Celtic FC, since 2021; b. 27.8.65, Nea Filadelfeia, Athens, Greece; m., Georgia; 3 s. Youth career: South Melbourne, 1978-83; Senior Career: South Melbourne, 1984-93; Western Suburbs, 1994; National team: Australia U20, 1985; Australia, 1986. Teams managed: South Melbourne, 1996-2000; Australia U17, 2000-05; Australia U20; Panachaiki, 2008; Brisbane Roar, 2009-2012; Melbourne Victory, 2012-13; Australia, 2013-17; Yokohama F. Marinos, 2018-2021. Playing honours: South Melbourne: National Soccer League Championship: 1984, 1990-91; National Soccer League Premiership: 1992-93; National Soccer League Southern Conference: 1984, 1985; NSL Cup, 1989-90; Dockerty Cup, 1989, 1991. Management honours include three premierships, four championships and a continental title. Address: Celtic Football Club, Celtic Park, Glasgow G40 3RE.

Potter, Carol, BA (Hons), CIPFA. Chief Executive, NHS Fife, since 2020. Educ. Abertay University. Career history: Graduate Finance Trainee, NHS Scotland, 1993-96; NHS Forth Valley: Senior Management Accountant, 1996-2000, Assistant Director of Finance, 2000-03; Finance Training & Development Consultant, Scottish Executive Health Department, 2003-04; Deputy Director of Finance, NHS Lanarkshire, 2004-09; Associate Director of Finance, NHS Lothian, 2009-2013; Finance Director, SRUC, 2013-14; Trustee, HFMA, since 2018; NHS Fife: Assistant Director of Finance, 2014-16, Director of Finance, 2016-2020, Deputy Chief Executive, 2019-2020, Board Trustee, since 2016. Address: NHS Fife, Hayfield Road, Kirkcaldy KY2 5AH; T.-01592 643355.

Powell, Professor Wayne, PGCert, MSc, PhD, DSc. Principal and Chief Executive, Scotland's Rural College (SRUC), since 2016; b. Abercraf, Swansea. Educ. University College of Wales, Aberystwyth; University of Birmingham. Career: Director of Institute of Biological, Environmental & Rural Sciences, Aberystwyth University; Chief Science Officer, CGIAR Consortium in Montpellier, France. Elected Fellow of the Learned Society of Wales; winner of the Broeckhuizen Prize in 1990 for outstanding contribution to cereal science research in Europe by a scientist under the age of 40; involved at Board Level for a number of companies and institutes and on International Scientific Advisory Committees. Personal research interests are in the domestication and evolution of crops and the production of global public goods; published over 280 refereed papers, more than 120 book chapters and an H index of 78. Address: Scotland's Rural College (SRUC), Peter Wilson Building, Kings Buildings, West Mains Road, Edinburgh EH9 3JG; T.-0131 535 4129.

Prag, Thomas Gregory Andrew, MA, FCMI. Liberal Democrat Highland Councillor, 2007-2017 (retired); b. 2.1.47, London; m., Angela; 3 s. Educ. Westminster School; Brasenose College, Oxford. Joined BBC, 1968, as Studio Manager; Producer, BBC Radio Oxford; Programme Organiser, BBC Radio Highland; first Chief Executive, Moray Firth Radio, 1981, then Managing Director, then Chairman until 2001. Past President, Inverness and District Chamber of Commerce; Fellow, Radio Academy; Chairman, Inshes Park Community Association; Non Executive Director, iMedia Associates Ltd; Chairman of an NGO - Media Support Partnership; Hon Fellowship, University of the Highlands and Islands; Convener, Highland Liberal Democrats. Recreations: good intentions towards restoration of 1950 Daimler; keeping clock collection wound; family; growing vegetables; chasing deer off vegetables; Inverness Choral ('cracking' tenor) Truly Terrible Orchestra (scraping fiddler). Address: Windrush, Easter Muckovie, Inverness IV2 5BN.
E-mail: thomas@prags.co.uk

Prentice, Alex, QC. Principal Crown Counsel, since 2011. Career: qualified as a solicitor in 1983 and as a Solicitor Advocate in 1994; practised as a defence solicitor for 21 years; became the first Solicitor Advocate from outwith the Crown Office and Procurator Fiscal Service to be appointed as an Advocate Depute in 2004; appointed as a Senior Advocate Depute in 2006 and became a QC in 2007. Prosecuted a number of significant cases including the shotgun murder at the "Marmion" public house in Edinburgh, the murder of Jolanta Bledaite and HM Advocate v Sheridan and Sheridan. In 2012 he twice secured a murder conviction without a body in the murder of Suzanne Pilley and the retrial in the murder of Arlene Fraser. Address: Crown Office, 25 Chambers Street, Edinburgh EH1 1LA; T.-0131 226 2626.

Prentice-Hyers, Rev. David, BA, MDiv. Minister, Troon Old Parish Church, since 2013. Address: Ayr Street, Troon KA10 6EB; T.-01292 313520.

Preston, Glenn, BA Hons (EngLit). Director, Scotland at Ofcom, since 2016. Educ. University of Stirling. Career history: Head, Constitutional Policy, Scotland Office, 2005-07; UK Ministry of Justice: Head, Education and Outreach Team, 2007-2011, Bill Manager, Justice Policy Group, 2011, Deputy Director, Information and Devolution, 2011-13; Deputy Director, Policy, Scotland Office, 2013-16. Address: Ofcom, 4th Floor, 125 Princes Street, Edinburgh EH2 4AD; T.-0131 220 7300.

Price, Professor David Brendan, BA (Hons), MBBChir, MA, DRCOG, FPCert, MRCGP. General Practice Airways Group Professor of Primary Care Respiratory Medicine, since 2000; b. 28.10.60, Slough; m., Dr Daryl Freeman; 2 s.; 2 d. Educ. Slough Grammar School; University of Cambridge. Paediatric Registrar, Australia, 1988-89; GP, 1999-2000; Chairman, Norwich Vocational Training Scheme, 1990-95; Director, Thorpe Respiratory Research, since 1998; Research Director, General Practice Airways Group, since 2000. Recreations: skiing; scuba diving; horse riding. Address: Department of General Practice and Primary Care, University of Aberdeen, Westburn Road, Aberdeen AB25 2AY; e-mail: d.price@abdn.ac.uk

Priest, Professor Eric Ronald, BSc, MSc, PhD, DSc, FRSE, FRS. Emeritus Professor, St Andrews University, since 2010 (appointed Gregory Professor of Mathematics, St Andrews University in 1997, then Wardlaw Professor in 2002, then Professor of Theoretical Solar Physics in 1983); b. 7.11.43, Birmingham; m., Clare Wilson; 3 s.; 1 d. Educ. King Edward VI School, Birmingham; Nottingham University; Leeds University. St. Andrews University: Lecturer in Applied Mathematics, 1968, Reader, 1977; SERC Senior Fellow, 1992-97. Elected Member, Norwegian Academy of Sciences and Letters, 1994; Chair, PPARC Astronomy Committee, 1998-2001; Chair, RSE Mathematics Committee, 1996-1998; Member, HEFC Research Assessment Exercise Committee, 1992, 1996, 2007; Chair, RSE Physics Committee, 2007-2010; Hale Prize, American Astronomical Society, 2002; Gold Medal of Royal Astronomical Society, 2009; Payne-Gaposchkin medal and prize, Institute of Physics, 2009; Honorary DSc (St Andrews), 2014; Alfvén medal of European Geophysical Union, 2017. Recreations: bridge; walking; singing; children. Address: (b.) Mathematics and Statistics Department, St Andrews University, St Andrews KY16 9SS; T.-01334 463709.

Pringle, Alastair. Chief Executive Officer, Venture Trust, since 2021; Executive Director - Legal, Compliance and Scotland, Equality and Human Rights Commission, 2015-2021, National Director (Scotland), 2012-2015. Career: former Head of Patient Focus and Equalities in the Scottish Government Health and Social Care Directorate. Member of the Scotland Committee of the EHRC; has worked extensively in the field of equalities and in tackling discrimination, predominantly in the health sector, and in the design, development and delivery of public services; led on the implementation of health policy on a range of issues including patients' rights, patient information and equalities strategy and policy for both the Health & Wellbeing portfolio of the Scottish Government and for NHS Scotland. Address: Venture Trust, Argyle House, 3 Lady Lawson Street, Edinburgh EH3 9DR; T.-0131 2287700.

Pringle, Dame Anne Fyfe, DCMG. British diplomat; Senior Governor, University of St Andrews, since 2016; b. 13.1.55. Educ. University of St Andrews. Career history: Foreign and Commonwealth Office: Ambassador to the Czech Republic, 2001-2004; Director for Strategy and FCO Board member, 2004-2007; Ambassador to Russia, 2008-2011; consultancy and non-executive director roles. Address: University of St Andrews, College Gate, St Andrews KY16 9AJ.

Prior, Professor Alan, BSc (Hons), MLitt, MRTPI. Acting Head, School of Life Sciences, Heriot-Watt University, 2009-11; Dean, Arts, Humanities and Social Sciences, Heriot-Watt University, 2004-07, Deputy Head, School of the Built Environment, Heriot-Watt University, 2002-09; b. 21.12.51, Edinburgh; m., Brenda; 2 d. Educ. Portobello High School, Edinburgh; Heriot-Watt University; Glasgow University. Assistant Planning Officer, Perth and Kinross District Council, 1975-77; Senior/Principal Planning Officer, East Kilbride District Council, 1977-85; Lecturer/Senior Lecturer, Edinburgh College of Art, 1985-95; Head, School of Planning and Housing, Edinburgh College of Art, 1996-2002. Publication: joint editor, "Introduction to Planning Practice", 2000. Recreation: hill walking. Address: (b.) Heriot-Watt University, Edinburgh EH14 4AS; e-mail: a.prior@hw.ac.uk

Prior, Colin. Landscape Photographer: b. Glasgow 1958; m., Geraldine; 2 c. Shoots internationally; clients include, British Airways, Bowmore Whisky, Calmac, Visit Scotland; personal projects include a four-year exploration of Pakistan's Karakoram Mountains and a study of wild bird habitats; runs exclusive photographic workshops in Scotland and overseas; Fellow of the Royal Photographic Society. Publications: Highland Wilderness, Constable; Scotland – The Wild Places, Constable, Living Tribes, Constable, The World's Wild Places, Constable, Scotland's Finest Landscapes, Constable. Exhibitions: The Scottish Visual Experience, Linhof Gallery, London; Land's End, Museum of Education, Glasgow; The World's Wild Places, OXO Tower Gallery, London. Address: Colin Prior Limited, 4 Princes Gate, Bothwell, Glasgow G71 8SP; T. 01698 816333; e-mail: colin@colinprior.co.uk

Pritchard, Kenneth William, OBE, BL, WS. Secretary, Law Society of Scotland, 1976-97; Temporary Sheriff, 1995-99, Part-time Sheriff, 2000-03; b. 14.11.33, London; Honorary Sheriff, Dundee; m., Gretta Murray; 2 s.; 1 d. Educ. Dundee High School; Fettes College; St. Andrews University. National Service, Argyll and Sutherland Highlanders, 1955-57; 2nd Lt., 1956; TA, 1957-62 (Captain); joined J. & J. Scrimgeour, Solicitors, Dundee, 1957; Captain, DHSFPRFC, 1959-62; Senior Partner, 1970-76; Member: Sheriff Court Rules Council, 1973-76, Lord Dunpark's Committee considering Reparation upon Criminal Conviction, 1973-77; Hon. Visiting Professor, Law School, Strathclyde University; Hon. Member, Law Institute of Victoria, 1985; Hon. Member, Law Society of New Zealand, 1987; Hon. Member, Faculty of Procurators and Solicitors in Dundee; Member, University Court of Dundee, 1989-93; President, Dundee High School Old Boys Club, 1975-76. Recreation: golf. Address: (h.) 22/4 Kinellan Road, Edinburgh EH12 6ES; T.-0131-337 4294; e-mail: kw.pritchard@btinternet.com

Proctor, Cllr Ronnie, MBE (1992), FSA (Scot), OStJ. Provost, Angus Council, since 2017. Educ. Webster's Seminary. Secretary, The Black Watch Association, since 2008; The Black Watch Association/Museum, since 1999; Councillor, Angus Council, since 2012. Chair, SSAFA Dundee and Angus; Director, Houses for Heroes Scotland; Director, Perth Forces Trust, since 1999. Address: Angus Council, Members' Services, Municipal Buildings, Castle Street, Forfar DD8 3AF; T.- 01307 492570. E-mail: CllrProctor@angus.gov.uk

Prokopyszyn, Carol, LLB. Director of Finance, University of Dundee; b. 1966. Educ. Hills Road Sixth Form College, Cambridge; University of Nottingham. Career history: Trainee to Audit Manager, PwC, 1987-91; various roles, Boots, 1991-97; Business Development General Manager, Boots Retail International, 1997-99; Boots: Project Manager (Investor Relations), 2000-01, Financial Planning Manager, 2001-03; University of Leciester: Head of Financial Reporting/Management Accounting, 2008-2011, Deputy Director of Finance, 2012-15; Deputy Director of Finance, Loughborough University, 2015-18. Address: University of Dundee, Nethergate, Dundee DD1 4HN; T.- 01382 384043.

Provan, Derek, MSc, BSc, MIFirE, GIFireE. Chief Executive Officer, AGS Airports, since 2018; b. Glasgow. Educ. Glasgow Caledonian University; Henley Business School. Career: Head of Airport Security, BAA, 2005-07; Customer Services Director, BAA Glasgow Airport, 2007-2010; Interim Operations Director, BAA Stanstead Airport, 2010; Managing Director, Aberdeen Airport, 2010-17; Heathrow Airport Ltd: appointed Director of Airside Operations in 2013, appointed Airside and Expansions Operations Director in 2015, then Chief Operating Officer in 2017. Address: Glasgow Airport, Paisley PA3 2SW; T.- 0344 481 5555.

Provan, James Lyal Clark. Member, South East Region, European Parliament, 1999-2004, Member, South Downs West, 1994-99, Member (Conservative), European Parliament, NE Scotland, 1979-89; Vice President, European Parliament, 1999-2004; Chairman, EP Tourism Group, 1997-2004; Chairman, EP Conciliation Committee with Council of Ministers, 1999-2003; Founder Chairman, EP internal Audit group, 2002-04; Chairman, Rowett Research Institute, Aberdeen, 1991-99 (Board Member, 1990-2005); Non-Executive Director, CNH Global N.V. and New Holland (Holdings), N.V., 1993-2007; Farmer; b. 19.12.36, Glenfarg, Perthshire; m., Roweena Adele Lewis; 2 s.; 1 d. Educ. Ardvreck School, Crieff; Oundle School, Northants; Royal Agricultural College, Cirencester. National Farmers Union of Scotland: Area President, Kinross, 1965, Fife and Kinross, 1971; Tayside Regional Councillor, 1978-81; Member, Tay River Purification Board, 1978-81; European Democratic (Conservative) Spokesman on Agriculture and Fisheries, 1981-87; Questor of European Parliament, 1987-89; former Executive Director, Scottish Financial Enterprise (1990-93); Chairman, McIntosh of Dyce Ltd., McIntosh Donald Ltd., 1989-94; Member, Agriculture and Food Research Council, 1990-94; Member, Lloyds of London, since 1984. Recreations: country pursuits; sailing; flying; politics; agriculture. Address: Summerfield, Glenfarg, Perthshire PH2 9QD; e-mail: jameslcprovan@gmail.com

Pugh, Alistair. Chair of College, Edinburgh Steiner School. Address: (b.) 60-64 Spylaw Road, Edinburgh EH10 5BR; T.-0131 337 3410.

Pupillo, Thirza, BA (Hons), PGCE. Headteacher, Perth High School, 2016-2021. Educ. Knox Academy; Edinburgh College of Art; Exeter University. Career history: Teacher: Matravers School, 1986-89, Wheatley Park School, 1989-90, Tarbert Academy, 1997-2004; Depute Head, Oban High School, 2004-2013; Head Teacher, Pitlochry High School, 2013-16.

Purcell, Steven John, JP. Leader, Glasgow City Council, 2005-2010; Director, Twenty Ten Consultancy, 2010-16; b. 19.9.72, Glasgow. Educ. St Thomas Aquinas Secondary School. Glasgow City Council, 1995-2010; Convener, Property Services, 1997-99; Convener, Development and Regeneration Services, 1999-2003; Convener, Education Services Committee, 2003-2005. Recreations: history; music; football.

Purdie, Allister. Governor, HMP & YOI Cornton Vale, 2013-19. Joined the Scottish Prison Service in November 1988 starting at Shotts Prison in Lanarkshire, having worked ten years in a family business; moved to Perth Prison in April 1999 as a Unit Manager; HM Prison Edinburgh, 2001-04; HM Prison Barlinnie, 2004-09, Head of Operations and Residential, then Deputy Governor; Scottish Prison Service Headquarters, Senior Operational Advisor leading in the design and build of the new prisons at HM Prison Low Moss and HM Prison Grampian, 2009-2011; Deputy Governor, HM Prison and Young Offenders, Cornton Vale, Stirling, 2011-13.

Purser, John Whitley, MA, PhD, DHC (Aberdeen). Composer and Lecturer; Poet, Playwright, Musicologist, and Broadcaster; b. 10.2.42, Glasgow; 1 s.; 1 d. Educ. Fettes College; Glasgow University; Royal Scottish

Academy of Music and Drama. Manager, Scottish Music Information Centre, 1985-87; Researcher, Sabhal Mòr Ostaig, since 2006; compositions include two operas, numerous orchestral and chamber works; 4 CDs of his compositions, Dreaming of Islands, Circus Suite, Bannockburn and Consider the Story; five books of poetry, The Counting Stick, A Share of the Wind, Amoretti, There Is No Night and This Much Endures; six radio plays and two radio series, A Change of Tune and Scotland's Music; music history: Is the Red Light On?, Scotland's Music; Erik Chisholm, Scottish Modernist, 1904-1965; Other: Window to the West (Co-Author); The Literary Works of Jack B. Yeats; awards: McVitie Scottish Writer of the Year, 1992; Glenfiddich Living Scotland Award, 1991; Giles Cooper Award, 1992; New York International Radio Festival Gold Medal, 1992; Sony Gold Medal, 1993; Oliver Brown Award, 1993; Scottish Heritage Award, 1993; Hon. Life Member, Saltire Society, 1993; Scottish Traditional Music Awards, 2007; Services to Industry. Recreations: numerous. Address: (b.) 3 Drinan, Elgol, Isle of Skye IV49 9BG; T.-01471 866262. Web: www.johnpurser.net

Purvis of Tweed (Baron Jeremy Purvis). MSP (Liberal Democrat), Tweeddale, Ettrick and Lauderdale, 2003-2011; b. 15.1.74, Berwick-upon-Tweed. Educ. Berwick-upon-Tweed High School; Brunel University. Research Assistant to Sir David Steel, 1993; Parliamentary Assistant: Liberal International, 1994, ELDR Group, European Parliament, 1995; Personal Assistant to Sir David Steel, subsequently Lord Steel of Aikwood, 1996-1998; GJW Scotland, 1998-2001; Company Director, McEwan Purvis, 2001-03. Member, Finance Committee, Scottish Parliament, 2003-05, Justice 2 Committee, 2005-07, Education, Lifelong Learning and Culture Committee, 2007-08, Finance Committee, 2008-2011. Director, Keep Scotland Beautiful, 2013. Member: Lords International Relations Committee, since 2016, IPU UK Executive Committee, 2016-17, CPA UK Executive Committee, 2015-17.

Purvis, John Robert, CBE, MA (Hons). Member for Scotland, European Parliament, 1999-2009 (Member, Industry, Research and Energy Committee; Vice-Chairman, Economic and Monetary Affairs Committee); International Business Consultant (Managing Partner, Purvis & Co.), 1973-2008; Director, European Utilities Trust PLC, 1994-2007; Chairman, Kingdom FM Radio Ltd., 1997-2008, Director, 1997-2013; Chairman, Belgrave Capital Management Ltd., since 1999; Chairman, Financial Future, Brussels, 2009-2020; b. 6.7.38, St. Andrews; m., Louise Spears Durham; 1 s.; 2 d. Educ. Glenalmond; St. Andrews University. 2nd Lt., Scots Guards, 1956-58; First National City Bank (Citibank NA), London, New York City, Milan, 1962-69; Treasurer, Noble Grossart Ltd., Edinburgh, 1969-73; Director and Secretary, Brigton Farms Ltd., 1969-86; Managing Director, Founder, Owner, Edinburgh Management Services Ltd., 1973-92; Director: James River UK Holdings Ltd., 1984-95, Jamont NV, 1994-95; Member, European Parliament, Mid Scotland and Fife, 1979-84 (Deputy Chief Whip, Group Spokesman on Monetary Affairs, Energy, Research and Technology; Vice Chairman, European Parliament Delegation to the Gulf States); Chairman, IBA Scottish Advisory Committee, 1985-89; Member for Scotland, IBA, 1985-89; Member of Council, St. Leonards School, St. Andrews, 1981-89; Chairman, Economic Affairs Committee, Scottish Conservative and Unionist Association, 1986-97, Vice-President of Association, 1987-89; Member, Scottish Advisory Committee on Telecommunications, 1990-97; Director: Curtis Fine Papers Ltd., 1995-2001, Crown Vantage Ltd., 1995-2001. Recreations: Italy and Scotland.

Pusey, Professor Peter Nicholas, MA, PhD, FRS, FRSE. Emeritus Professor of Physics, Edinburgh University, Senior Honorary Research Fellow; b. 30.12.42, Oxford; m., Elizabeth Nind; 2 d. Educ. St Edward's School, Oxford; Cambridge University; University of Pittsburgh, USA. Post-doctoral Fellow, IBM, New York, 1969-72; Royal Signals and Radar Establishment (now QinetiQ), Malvern, 1972-91 (Grade 6 from 1980); Head, Department of Physics and Astronomy, Edinburgh University, 1994-97 and 2000-03. Publications: numerous in scientific literature. Address: (b.) School of Physics, Edinburgh University, Mayfield Road, Edinburgh, EH9 3JZ, T.-0131-650 5255; e-mail: pusey@ed.ac.uk

Pyle, Sheriff Derek Colin Wilson, LLB (Hons), NP, WS. Sheriff Principal of Grampian, Highland and Islands, since 2012; Sheriff of Dundee, 2008-2012; Sheriff of Grampian, Highland and Islands at Inverness, 2005-08; Sheriff of Tayside Central and Fife, 2000-05; b. 15.10.52, Cambridge; m., Jean Blackwood Baillie; 5 s.; 1 d. Educ. Royal High School, Edinburgh; Edinburgh University. Solicitor, since 1976; Partner, Wilson Pyle & Co., WS, 1980-89; Partner, Henderson Boyd Jackson, WS, 1989-99; Solicitor Advocate, since 1994. Formerly Fiscal to Law Society of Scotland; former Council Member, WS Society. Recreations: golf; hill-walking; painting house. Address: (b.) Scottish Courts and Tribunals Service, The Inverness Justice Centre, Longman Road, Inverness IV1 1AH.

Q

Qaisar-Javed, Anum. MP (SNP), Airdrie and Shotts, since 2021; b. 11.9.92, Scotland. Educ. University of Stirling; University of Strathclyde. Career history: Modern Studies teacher; parliamentary researcher for Carol Monaghan MP; case-worker for Humza Yousaf MSP. Address: House of Commons, London SW1A 0AA.

Quartson-Mochrie, Judith Alice Araba Siripiwa, BA (Hons), BArch (Hons), ARB. Architect; m., Neil A. Mochrie; 1 s. Educ. King James' School, Knaresborough; Newcastle University. Christian Hauvette Architecte, Paris 1988; Baasner Möller of Langwald, Berlin, 1992; Troughton McAslan, 1994; Foster & Partners, London, 1996; Architect, Associate, Communications Director, Gareth Hoskins Architects, Glasgow, 1998; Jens Bergmark Architects, Edinburgh, 2011. Royal Commissioner for the Royal Commission on the Ancient and Historical Monuments of Scotland, 2010-2015. Recreations: photography; illustration; yoga.
E-mail: jude.qm@googlemail.com

Queen, Neil, DipLP. Partner, Ross & Connell LLP. Educ. Dundee University. Career history: 5 years at a prominent local firm; joined Ross & Connel in November 2015; deals predominantly with residential conveyancing, as well as all aspects of private client work. Recreations: enjoys playing golf and following Dunfermline Athletic. Address: (b.) 18 Viewfield Terrace, Dunfermline, Fife KY12 7JH; T.-01383 721156.

Queensberry, 12th Marquess of (David Harrington Angus Douglas); b. 19.12.29. Educ. Eton. Professor of Ceramics, Royal College of Art, 1959-83; succeeded to title, 1954.

Quigley, Elizabeth, MA (Hons). Correspondent, BBC Scotland, since 1999; b. 30.10.71, Glasgow; m., John Swinney MSP; 1 s (Matthew). Educ. Lenzie Academy; St Andrews University. Reporter, The Scotsman, 1995-96;

Reporter, Scotland on Sunday, 1996-97; Scottish Daily Mail, from 1997: Political Reporter/Features Editor/Feature Writer; Patron, Perth and Kinross Branch, MS Society Scotland; Presenter of a variety of documentaries including Scotland's Hidden Epidemic: The Truth About MS; The woman who can smell Parkinson's; The Duchess and the Fuhrer... The story of Scotland's first female MP, the Duchess of Atholl. Address: (b.) BBC Scotland, The Tun, Holyrood Road, Edinburgh EH8 8PJ; T.-0131-248 4215.

Quinault, Francis Charles, BSc, PhD, FRSAMD, DCon. Retired Director of Learning and Teaching Quality, St Andrews University (formerly Hebdomadar, Assistant Principal for External Affairs and Senior Lecturer in Psychology); formerly Chairman, Byre Theatre; b. 8.5.43, London; m., Wendy Ann Horton; 1 s.; 2 d. Educ. Dulwich College; St. Catharine's College, Cambridge; Bristol University. Ford Foundation Scholar, Oslo University, 1969-70. Member, National Committee for the Training of University Teachers, 1981-87; Academic Board, RSAMD, 2004-07; Hon. Treasurer, The Kate Kennedy Trust; Past President, St Andrews Business Club; former Chairman, University of St Andrews Students' Association; Director, The Canadian Robert T. Jones Jr Scholarship Foundation; former Member, Quality Board for Higher Education in Iceland; Director, Fife Cultural Trust; Trustee, New Park Educational Trust; Member, Rotary Club of St Andrews; President, St Andrews Burns Club. Recreations: acting; singing; hill-walking; learning languages. Address: 5 Hope Street, St Andrews KY16 9HJ; T.-01334 474560; e-mail: fcq@st-and.ac.uk

Quinlan, Kevin, BA, MBA. Director of Environment and Forestry, The Scottish Government, since 2021. Educ. Waterford Institute of Technology; University of Warwick. Career history: Audit Supervisor/Chartered Accountant, PwC, 1987-91; Lecturer, Business Studies, Government of Ireland, Lusaka, Zambia, 1991-92; Oxfam: Management Systems Trainer, Oxford, 1992-94, Programme Manager, Turkana, Kenya, 1994-95, Country Director, Malawi, 1995-99; Management and Organisational Development Consultant, Malawi, 1999-2000; Department for International Development, 2001-17; Director of International Trade and Investment, The Scottish Government, 2017-2021. Member, CIPFA, 2013-14; Fellow, Chartered Accountants Ireland, 1988-92. Address: The Scottish Government, St Andrew's House, Regent Road, Edinburgh EH1 3DG.

Quinn, Andrea, BEng (Hons). Managing Director, Geelox Ltd; Chief Executive Officer, Scottish Police Services Authority (SPSA), 2010-13; Head of Environment, City of Edinburgh Council, 2006-2010; b. 27.4.70, Widnes, Cheshire. Educ. St. Josephs RC High School; Bolton Institute of Higher Education (now the University of Bolton). Career: Trainee Technician, Halton Borough Council (1989); United Utilities (1998). Member, Wastewater Board (2004); as a member of Water UK, represented the company nationally on matters of policy and internationally on a variety of sustainability and research projects.
T.-07545 197693; e-mail: andrea@geelox.co.uk

Quirk, Norman Linton, CA, CLJ. Deputy Chair, Mull Theatre, 2010-2011; Executive Director, Mull Theatre, 2008-2010; Chairman, Scottish Chambers of Commerce, 2007-2009; Managing Director, SAGA 105.2 fm, 2004-07; Executive Director, Scottish Ballet, 2000-2004, Vice Chairman and Managing Director, 1998-2000; Partner, Quirk & Co., business and management consultancy, 1991-2011; President, Glasgow Chamber of Commerce, 2006-08; Director: David MacBrayne Ltd., Caledonian MacBrayne Ltd., NorthLink Ferries Ltd, 2008-2013; b. 28.7.47, Glasgow; m., Lesley Helen Quirk (qv); 2 s.; 2 step-s. Educ. Dulwich College. Apprentice CA, 1965-71; Accountant/Office Manager, Thom Decorators, Coatbridge, 1971-74; Chief Accountant, Radio Clyde, Glasgow, 1974-84; Assistant Director, Institute of CAs of Scotland, 1985-87; Regional Controller, Joint Monitoring Unit, 1988-91; Managing Director, Scot FM, 1996. Chairman, Independent Radio Group of Scotland, 1996-2000; President, Glasgow Chamber of Commerce, 2006-08; Director, Scottish Chamber of Commerce, 2006; Community Councillor, Strathard Ward, 2000-06; Member, Incorporation of Hammermen; Director and Treasurer, Scottish Society for Autism; Director, Mull Theatre; Lord's Taverner; Commander, Order of St Lazarus of Jerusalem. Recreations: scuba diving; working with arts organisations. Address: (h.) Ardsorn, Raeric Road, Tobermory, Isle of Mull PA75 6PU; T.-01688-301223; e-mail: norman@quirk.co.uk

R

Radcliffe, Nicholas John, BSc (Double Hons), PhD. Director, Stochastic Solutions Limited, since 2007; Visiting Professor, Maths and Statistics, Edinburgh University, since 1995; b. 31.07.65, London; m., Morag Radcliffe; 1 s. Educ. Sir Frederic Osborn School; Univ. of Sussex; Edinburgh Univ. Manager, Information Systems Group, Edinburgh Parallel Computing Centre, University of Edinburgh, 1990-95; Technical Director, Quadstone Limited, 1995-2007; Advisor: Scottish Equity Partners, 2000-2010, Fluidinfo Limited, since 2006. Publications: Sustainability: A Systems Approach (Co-Author), 1996; Getting Started with Fluidinfo (CoAuthor), O'Reilly Media, 2012. Blogs: The Scientific Marketer (http://scientificmarketer.com); The Test Driven Data Analysis Blog (http://www.tdda.info). Recreations: guitar/music; literature; film; golf.
E-mail: njr@stochasticsolutions.com

Rae, Barbara Davis, CBE, RA, RSA, HRWS, RGI, RE, FRCA, FRSE, HFRIAS, Hon. D.Art, Hon. D.Litt. Painter and Master Printmaker; b. Falkirk; 1 s. Educ. Morrisons Academy, Crieff; Edinburgh College of Art. Elected Royal Etcher, 2016; President, SSA, 1983; works purchased by international private and commercial collectors; elected RSA, 1992; elected RA, 1996; study visit, Arizona Desert, 1998; doctorate, St Andrews University and Napier University; various solo exhibitions in Royal Academy, London, Edinburgh International Arts Festival and internationally including Norway, USA and Mexico; work in many public collections. Hon. Fellowship, Royal College of Art, London; Hon. DLitt, Aberdeen University, 2003; Hon. DLitt, University of St. Andrews, 2008; Fellow, Royal Society of Edinburgh, 2011. Recreation: travel. Contact: Royal Academy of Arts, London.

Rae, The Honourable Lady Rae (Rita Emilia Anna Rae), QC, LLB (Hons). Rector, University of Glasgow, since 2021; Senator of the College of Justice, 2014-2020; appointed Upper Tribunal Judge in Immigration and Asylum; Sheriff of Glasgow and Strathkelvin, 1997-2013. Educ. St. Patrick's High School, Coatbridge; Edinburgh University. Apprentice, Biggart, Lumsden & Co., Glasgow, 1972-74; Assistant Solicitor: Balfour & Manson, Edinburgh, 1974, Biggart, Baillie & Gifford, Glasgow, 1974-76; Solicitor and Partner, Ross Harper & Murphy, Glasgow, 1976-81; Former Tutor, Advocacy and Pleading, Strathclyde University; Advocate, 1982; Queen's Counsel, 1992. Temporary High Court Judge, 2004-2013; Member, Sentencing Commission for Scotland, 2003-06; Vice Chair, Parole Board for Scotland, 2005-07, Member, since 2001; 2010 Member of Legal 40, University of Glasgow Law School; Member, National Strategic Advisory Group on Violence Reduction, 2011-17; 2010 Director, Conforti Institute, Coatbridge; Member, Sacro; Life Member, Scottish Association for the Study of Offending, Chair, Glasgow Branch, 2002-2014. Awarded Honorary Doctor of Laws, University of Glasgow, 27 June 2019. Recreations: piano; theatre; driving; walking; opera; music; Italy; gardening.

Rae, Simon Scott, LLB (Hons), DipLP, NP. Managing Partner and Head of Corporate, DLA Piper Scotland (Partner), since 2004; b. 28.12.72, Edinburgh. Educ. George Watson's College, Edinburgh; Strathclyde University, Glasgow. Dundas & Wilson CS, Edinburgh, 1995-98; Clifford Chance, London, 1998-2004. Address: (b.) Rutland Square, Edinburgh (c/o DLA Piper); T.-0131-242-5085; e-mail: simon.rae@dlapiper.com

Raeburn, James B., OBE, FCG. Director, Scottish Print Employers Federation and Scottish Newspaper Publishers' Association, 1984-2007; Director, Scottish Daily Newspaper Society, 1996-2010; Director, Scottish Newspaper Society, 2010-12; b. 18.3.47, Jedburgh; m., Rosemary Bisset; 2 d. Educ. Hawick High School. Edinburgh Corporation, 1964-69; Roxburgh County Council, 1969-71; Electrical Contractors' Association of Scotland, 1972-83 (Secretary, 1975-83). Director: Press Standards Board of Finance Ltd., 1990-2013 (Secretary and Treasurer, 2003-2013), Advertising Standards Board of Finance Ltd., 1990-2013, National Council for the Training of Journalists, 1993-2006, Publishing National Training Organisation Ltd., 2000-03; Moderator, The Society of High Constables of Edinburgh, 2015-17. Recreation: golf. Address: (h.) 44 Duddingston Road West, Edinburgh EH15 3PS.

Raeburn, Sheriff Susan Adiel Ogilvie, LLB, QC. Sheriff of Grampian, Highland and Islands at Elgin, 2011-2015; b. 23.4.54, Ellon. Educ. St. Margaret's School for Girls, Aberdeen; Edinburgh University. Admitted, Faculty of Advocates, 1977; took silk, 1991; part-time Chairman, Social Security Appeal Tribunals, 1986-91; Temporary Sheriff, 1988-92; part-time Chairman, Medical Appeal Tribunals, 1992-93; Reporter to Scottish Legal Aid Board, 1990-93; Sheriff of Glasgow and Strathkelvin, 1993-2011.

Rafferty, Andrew Gordon, BVMS, MRCVS, CertSHP, CertCHP. Principal, Mixed Veterinary Practice, since 1990; b. 18.02.55, Grantown-on-Spey; m., Carol; 4 s. Educ. Edinburgh Academy; Edinburgh University. Grantown Mixed Practice, 1977-81; Castle Douglas Mixed Practice, 1981-89; Grantown-on-Spey Mixed Practice, since 1989. Farmer. Recreations: outdoor sports. Address: Strathspey Veterinary Centre, Forest Road, Grantown-On-Spey, Morayshire PH26 3JJ; T.-01479 872252.

Raistrick, Evlyn, MA. Chairman, Scottish Hockey Union, 1992-96; Tournament Director: Atlanta Olympics, 1996, Commonwealth Games, Manchester, 2002; b. 13.8.42, Edinburgh; m., David William; 3 s. Educ. Boroughmuir School; Edinburgh University. Maths Teacher, Liberton High, 1964-72. Member, Scottish Sports Council, 1993-2001; Vice-Chairman, Executive, Scottish Sports Association, 1993-2001. Captain, Craigielaw Golf Club, 2019-2021. Recreations: hockey; squash; golf. Address; (h.) Orchard House, Longniddry, East Lothian EH32 0PG.

Ralston, Professor Ian Beith McLaren, OBE, MA, PhD, DLitt, FRSE, MAE, FSA, FSA Scot, MCIfA. Abercromby Emeritus Professor of Archaeology, University of Edinburgh; Head of School of History, Classics and Archaeology, 2013-16; Abercromby Professor of Prehistoric Archaeology, 2012-19; Chair, CFA Archaeology Ltd., 2000-18; President, since 2020; formerly Vice-President, Society of Antiquaries of Scotland, 2007-2010; Chair, Standing Committee for Archaeology in the Universities, 2007-2010; b. 11.11.50, Edinburgh; m., Sandra Webb; 1 s.; 1 d. Educ. Edinburgh Academy; Edinburgh University. Career history: Aberdeen University: Research Fellow in Archaeology, 1974-77, Lecturer in Geography/Archaeology, 1977-85; University of Edinburgh: Lecturer in Archaeology, 1985-90, Senior Lecturer, 1990-98, Personal Chair, 1998-2012. Honorary Chair, Institute of Field Archaeologists, 1991-92; Chair, Scottish Archaeological Finds Allocation Panel, 2004-2011; President, Council for Scottish Archaeology, 1996-2000. Publications: Archaeological Resource Management in the United Kingdom – an introduction (Co-Editor), 2 edn., 2006; The Archaeology of Britain – an Introduction from the Upper Palaeolithic to the Industrial Revolution (Co-Editor), 2 edn., 2009; Scotland after the Ice Age (Co-Editor), 2003; Celtic Fortifications (revised edition), 2013;

Angus: archaeology and early history (Co-Author), 2008; Scotland in later prehistoric Europe (Co-Editor), 2015; The Neolithic of mainland Scotland (Co-Editor), 2016; Atlas of Hillforts of Britain and Ireland (online), 2017; Papers from the Atlas of Hillforts of Britain and Ireland conference 2019; Atlas of Hillforts of Britain and Ireland, 2022 (Co-Author); books on French archaeology; exhibition catalogues; papers. Recreations: walking; watching St. Johnstone. Address: (b.) William Robertson Wing, Old Medical School, Teviot Place, Edinburgh EH8 9AG.
E-mail: ian.ralston@ed.ac.uk
Web: www.ianralston.co.uk

Ralston, Professor Stuart Hamilton, MBChB, MRCP (UK), MD, FRCP (Glas), FRCP (Edin), FMedSci, FRSE, FFPM (Hon). Professor of Rheumatology, University of Edinburgh; Chair of the Commission on Human Medicines (CHM), 2013-2021; b. 24.10.55, Glasgow; m., Janet Thomson; 2 s.; 2 d. Educ. Allan Glen's School, Glasgow; Glasgow University. Junior House Officer, Glasgow Royal Infirmary, 1978-79; Senior House Officer, Falkirk and District Royal Infirmary and Aberdeen Teaching Hospitals, 1979-81; Registrar, General Medicine, Glasgow Royal Infirmary, 1981-84; Senior Registrar, Glasgow Royal Infirmary and Southern General Hospital, Glasgow, 1984-87; Locum Consultant Physician, Stobhill Hospital, Glasgow, 1989; Wellcome Senior Research Fellow and Honorary Consultant Physician, Northern General Hospital, Edinburgh, 1989-91; Senior Lecturer, Medicine and Therapeutics, Aberdeen University and Honorary Consultant Physician, Aberdeen Royal Hospitals NHS Trust, 1991-94, Reader, 1994-99; Director, Institute of Medical Science, University of Aberdeen; Professor of Medicine and Bone Metabolism, University of Aberdeen, 1999-2005. President, European Calcified Tissues Society, 1997-2005; Joint Editor-in Chief, Calcified Tissue International, since 2000; Board Member, International Bone and Mineral Society, 2001-2008; Examiner, Royal College of Physicians of Edinburgh, since 1996; Council Member, American Society of Bone and Mineral Research 2007-2010; NHS Research Scotland Musculoskeletal Research Champion, 2015-2021; Chairman of the Board of Trustees: Paget's Association, since 2018; Chair, Causes subgroup of the Royal Osteoporosis Society; Osteoporosis and Bone Research Academy, since 2019. Recreations: mountaineering; snowboarding, cycling. Address: (b.) Centre for Genomic and Experimental Medicine, Western General Hospital, Edinburgh EH4 2XU.
E-mail: stuart.ralston@ed.ac.uk

Ramage, Alan W., CBE. Formerly Keeper of the Registers of Scotland; b. 4.12.43, Edinburgh; m., Fiona Lesslie. Educ. Boroughmuir School, Edinburgh; Edinburgh University. Recreations: keeping fit; reading; dog walking. Address: (h.) 12 St Fillan's Terrace, Edinburgh EH10 4NH; T.-0131 447 8463.

Rampling, Professor Roy, PhD, MSc, BSc, DIC, ARCS, MBBS, FRCR, FRCP. Honorary Senior Research Fellow (Institute of Cancer Sciences), University of Glasgow (appointed Professor in 2000); b. 13.9.46, Malta; m., Susan Bonham-Carter; 2 s.; 1 d. Educ. Clacton County High School; Imperial College, London; University College, London. University of Glasgow: Senior Lecturer, Radiation Oncology, 1987-97, Reader, 1997-2000. Address: Beatson Oncology Centre, Western Infirmary, Glasgow G11 6NT; T.-0141-211 2627; e-mail: r.rampling@udcf.gla.ac.uk

Ramsay, Rev. (Alexander) Malcolm, BA, LLB, DipMin. Transition Minister of Willowbrae, Edinburgh; b. 4.3.57, Livingstone, N. Rhodesia (now Zambia); m. Cati Balfour Paul; 1 d.; 1 s. Educ. Merchiston Castle School, Edinburgh; St. John's College, Cambridge; Edinburgh University. Solicitor, 1982-83; ordained Minister of Church of Scotland, 1986; Parish Minister of Bargrennan linked with Monigaff, Wigtownshire, 1987-93; Mission Partner of Church of Scotland teaching Theology in Presbyterian Church of Guatemala, 1994-98; Parish Minister of Pitlochry, Perthshire, 1998-2011; Mission Partner of Church of Scotland serving in Pastoral Care and Support to United Mission to Nepal, 2012-2016; Transition Minister of Willowbrae, Edinburgh, since 2017. Recreations: family life; cycling; poetry. Address: 19 Abercorn Road, Edinburgh EH8 7DP.

Ramsay, Dr Lorna. Medical Director, NHS National Services Scotland, since 2018; previously Interim Director. Held a number of senior medical positions across NSS, including Medical Director of IT; experience in a range of clinical practice settings, public health medicine and medical management; longstanding interest in data and technology, in particular the digital enablement of health and care, which aligns with a strong focus on enabling clinical service change across Scotland; strives to optimise the value delivered through NSS services to care professionals and the people of Scotland. Address: NHS National Services Scotland, Gyle Square, 1 South Gyle Crescent, Edinburgh EH12 9EB.

Ramsay, Peter John, MCIBS, PMA. Non-Executive Director, National Waiting Times Centre, Golden Jubilee National Hospital, 2003-2011; Stakeholder Director, ABC Schools Ltd, since 2005; b. 13.01.55, Edinburgh; divorced; 1 s.; 2 d. Educ. Gordonstoun School. Former Chair, Gordonstoun Association (retired, 2015). Recreations: rugby (watching); swimming; walking; dogs. Address: (h.) 27 Kildonan Drive, Helensburgh G84 9SB; T.-01436 675414; e-mail: peter.ramsay6@btinternet.com

Ramsey, Nicola, BA (Hons), MPhil. Chief Executive Officer, Edinburgh University Press, since 2021. Educ. Longfield Academy; King Edward VII Upper School; University of Reading; University of Stirling. Career history: Edinburgh University Press: Commissioning Editor, 1996-2000, Senior Commissioning Editor, 2000-2013, Head of Editorial (Books), 2013-2021. Address: Edinburgh University Press, The Tun - Holyrood Road, 12 (2f) Jackson's Entry, Edinburgh EH8 8PJ; T.-0131 650 4218.

Randall, Rev. David James, MA, BD, ThM. Minister, Church of Scotland, Macduff, 1971-2010; retired May 2010; b. 5.6.45, Edinburgh; m., Nan Wardlaw; 3 s.; 1 d.; 6 grandchildren. Educ. George Heriot's School; Edinburgh University; Princeton Theological Seminary. Recreations: jogging; reading; swimming. Address: 3 Mallard Way, Forfar DD8 3FN; T.-01307 479442.
E-mail: djrandall479@btinternet.com

Randall, Rev. David Steven, BA, BD. Minister, Falkirk Free Church, since 2014; Minister, Loudoun Parish Church, Newmilns, 2009-2014; Minister, Bo'ness Old Kirk (Church of Scotland), 2003-09; b. 28.1.71, Edinburgh; m., Linnea; 2 s.; 2 d. Educ. Banff Academy; Robert Gordon University; University of Aberdeen. Provision of Accounting Services to North Sea Oil Industry, Andersen Consulting (now known as Accenture), 1993-99; Parish Minister, The Church of Scotland, since 2002. Recreations: golf; running; current affairs; reading. Address: Falkirk Free Church, Beaumont Drive, Carron, Falkirk FK2 8SN; e-mail: dsrandall71@icloud.com

Randall, John Norman, BA, MPhil. Trustee, The Islands Book Trust, 2002-2015; b. 1.8.45, Bromley, Kent; 1 s.; 1 d. Educ. Bromley Grammar School; Bristol University; Glasgow University. Department of Economic Affairs; Scottish Office - Assistant Secretary, 1985-99; Registrar General for Scotland, 1999-2003. Recreations: hill-walking;

island history. Address: (h.) 31 Lemreway, South Lochs, Isle of Lewis; T.-01851 880365.

Randle, Jacqui. Head of Corporate Communications, Scottish Government, since 2019. Educ. University of Glasgow; London Metropolitan University; Chartered Institute of Public Relations. Career history: Senior Communication Manager, Home Office, 2007-2010; Scottish Government: Senior Communications Manager, 2010-2015, Business and Behaviour Change Manager, Digital Communications Programme, 2015-17, Head of Intranet and Organisational Behaviour Change, 2017-19. Address: The Scottish Government, St Andrew's House, Regent Road, Edinburgh EH1 3DG.

Rankin, Professor Andrew C., BSc, MBChB, MD, MRCP, FRCP. Professor, Medical Cardiology, University of Glasgow, since 2006; Reader, Glasgow Royal Infirmary, 2002-06; b. 15.6.52, Larkhall; m., Clare Fitzsimons; 3 s. Educ. Hamilton Academy; Glasgow University. Registrar, Medical Cardiology, 1980; Lecturer, 1984, then Senior Lecturer, 1993, Medical Cardiology. Hon. Consultant Cardiologist, Glasgow Royal Infirmary, since 1993. Address; (b.) Department of Medical Cardiology, Glasgow Royal Infirmary, Glasgow; T.-0141-211 4833.

Rankin, Professor David W.H., MA, PhD, FRSC, FRSE. Horticultural Consultant; Director, Kevock Garden Plants, 2010-2016; Emeritus Professor of Chemistry, Edinburgh University, since 2010; Professor of Structural Chemistry, Edinburgh University, 1989-2010; b. 8.6.45, Birkenhead; m., Stella M. Thomas; 3 s.; 1 d. Educ. Birkenhead School; King's College, Cambridge. Edinburgh University: ICI Research Fellow, 1969, Demonstrator, 1971, Lecturer, 1973, Reader, 1980, Professor, 1989. Publication: Structural Methods in Molecular Inorganic Chemistry. Address: (b.) 16 Kevock Road, Lasswade EH18 1HT.

Rankin, Sir Ian James, OBE, FRSE. Novelist; b. 1960, Fife; m.; 2 s. Educ. Edinburgh University. Has been employed as grape-picker, swine-herd, taxman, alcohol researcher, hi-fi journalist and punk musician; creator of the Inspector Rebus novels; first Rebus novel, Knots and Crosses, 1987; this series now translated into 25 languages; elected Hawthornden Fellow; former winner, Chandler-Fulbright Award; two CWA "Daggers"; 1997 CWA Macallan Gold Dagger for fiction for Black and Blue; Mystery Writers of America Edgar Award for best novel: Resurrection Men, 2005; ITV3 Crime Thriller Award for Author of the Year, for Exit Music, 2008; awarded the CWA Cartier Diamond Dagger for lifetime's achievement in crime writing; UNESCO City of Literature Visiting Professor at University of East Anglia, 2016; RBA Prize for Crime Writing for Even Dogs in the Wild, the world's most lucrative crime fiction prize at €125,000, 2016; elected a Fellow of the Royal Society of Literature, 2016; award wins at the Capital Crime/Amazon Publishing Readers' Awards, 2019: Best Mystery and Best Crime Novel for In A House of Lies; Alumnus of the Year, Edinburgh University, 1999; Honorary Doctorate: University of Abertay Dundee, University of St. Andrews, University of Edinburgh; University of Hull.

Rapport, Professor Nigel Julian, BA, MA, PhD, FRSA, FRSE, FLSW. Emeritus Professor of Anthropological and Philosophical Studies, St Andrews University (appointed Professor in 1996), Head of School of Philosophy, Anthropology, Film & Music, 2014-2017; b. 8.11.56, Cardiff; m., Elizabeth J.A. Munro; 1 s.; 1 d. Educ. Clifton College, Bristol; Cambridge University; Manchester University. Research Fellow and Associate, Institute of Social and Economic Research, Memorial University of Newfoundland, 1983-87; Lecturer, Blaustein Institute for Desert Research, Ben-Gurion University of the Negev, Israel, 1988; Lecturer, Department of Social Anthropology, Manchester University, 1989; joined St. Andrews University as Lecturer, 1993. Hon. Secretary, Association of Social Anthropologists of the UK and Commonwealth, 1994-98; President, Anthropology and Archaeology Section, British Association for the Advancement of Science, 2000-01; Canada Research Chair in Globalization, Citizenship and Justice, 2004-07; 1996 Royal Society of Edinburgh prize lectureship in the humanities, 1996; Royal Anthropological Institute, Curl Essay Prize, 1996; Royal Anthropological Institute, Rivers Memorial Medal, 2012; Chair, Association of Social Anthropologists of the UK and Commonwealth, 2017-21; elected Fellow, Learned Society of Wales (FLSW), 2019. Publications: Talking Violence: an anthropological interpretation of conversation in the city, 1987; Diverse World-Views in an English Village, 1993; The Prose and the Passion: anthropology, literature and the writing of E.M. Forster, 1994; Questions of Consciousness (Co-editor), 1995; Transcendent Individual, towards a literary and liberal anthropology, 1997; Migrants of Identity: Perceptions of Home in a World of Movement (Co-editor), 1998; Social and Cultural Anthropology: The Key Concepts, 2000; British Subjects: An Anthropology of Britain (Editor), 2002; The Trouble With Community: Anthropological Reflections on Movement, Identity and Collectivity, 2002; I am Dynamite: an alternative anthropology of power, 2003; Science, Democracy and The Open Society (Editor), 2006; Of Orderlies and Men: Hospital Porters Achieving Wellness at Work, 2009; Human Nature as Capacity - Beyond Discourse and Classification (Editor), 2010; Reveries of Home: Nostalgia, Authenticity and the Performance of Place (Co-Editor), 2010; Community, Cosmopolitanism and the Problem of Human Commonality, 2012; Anyone, the Cosmopolitan Subject of Anthropology, 2012; Distortion and Love: An anthropological reading of the art and life of Stanley Spencer, 2016; Distortion: Social Processes Beyond the Structured and Systemic (Editor), 2017; The Composition of Anthropology: How Anthropological Texts are Written (Editor), 2018; Cosmopolitan Love and Individuality: Ethical Engagement Beyond Culture, 2019. Recreations: travel; sport; literature. Address: (b.) Department of Social Anthropology, St Andrews University, St Andrews KY16 9AL; T.-01334 462977.

Rattray, Dr Liz, BSc (Hons), PhD. Director, Research and Innovation, University of Aberdeen, since 2016. Educ. University of Aberdeen. Career: joined Research and Innovation, University of Aberdeen in 1997; appointed Deputy Director in 2005 to lead the business development and commercialisation teams; extensive experience of research administration, project and contract management together with commercialisation of research (from collaborating with industry, knowledge exchange, licensing to new company formation); held board positions with a number of companies, and previously been a member of the Scottish Funding Council's research committee. Address: King's College, Aberdeen AB24 3FX.

Raven, Hugh J. E. Managing Director, Ardtornish Estate Company; Chair, Environmental Funders Network (the umbrella organisation of philanthropists giving to environmental causes); Chair, John Ellerman Foundation; Chair, Highlands and Islands Environment Foundation; Chair, the Open Seas Trust; Chair, Scotland's Moorland Forum; b. 20.4.61, London; m., Jane Stuart-Smith; 2 d. Educ. various schools; Harper Adams Agricultural College; University of Kent at Canterbury. Policy Strategist for the British Overseas Aid Group (a coalition of Oxfam, Christian Aid, Save the Children (UK), CAFOD and

ActionAid), 1996; Convenor of the UK Government Green Globe Task Force, 1997-99; Advisor on Rural Policy to Environment Minister Michael Meacher MP, 1999-2000. Director of Ardtornish Estate, Morvern, Argyll, since 1996. Councillor, Royal Borough of Kensington and Chelsea, 1990-94; Member of the BBC Rural and Agricultural Affairs Advisory Committee, 1994-97; Member of the UK Executive Committee of the British American Project, 1996-98; Trustee of the Soil Association, 1992-99; Chair of SERA, the environmental affiliate of the Labour Party, 1997-99; Chair, Lochaber and District Fisheries Trust, 1995-2002; Chair, Marine Conservation Society, 2015-2019; Trustee of the Royal Society for the Protection of Birds, 1997-2002; 1999, 2001 and 2003: Parliamentary Candidate, Scottish Labour Party, Argyll and Bute; Member, UK Sustainable Development Commission, 2004-10; Member of Board, Scottish Natural Heritage, 2004-07; Environment Adviser, Esmee Fairbairn Foundation, 2000-2010; Director, Soil Association Scotland, 2006-2011; Board Member, Crown Estate Scotland, 2017-2020. Recreations: walking; fishing; sailing; reading. Address: (h.) Kinlochaline, Morvern, Oban, Argyll PA80 5UZ; e-mail: hugh@ardtornish.co.uk

Reay, Professor David Sean, BSc, PhD. Professor of Carbon Management, University of Edinburgh, since 2008; Climate Change Scientist, Author and Advisor, since 1994; b. 02.12.72, Fleet; m., Sarah Louise; 2 d. Educ. Alun School, Mold, N. Wales; University of Liverpool; University of Essex. Senior Research Officer, University of Essex, 1998-2001; Post-Doctoral Research Fellow, University of Edinburgh, 2001-04 and 2004-05, Natural Environment Research Council Fellow, 2005-08, Lecturer in Carbon Management, 2008-09. Natural Environment Research Council Fellowship; British Council Scotland Advisory Committee, since 2009. Publication: Author of: 'Climate Change Begins at Home, 'Your Planet Needs You', 'Methane and Climate Change'. Recreations: writing stories; running; gardening. Address: (b.) School of Geosciences, University of Edinburgh, Edinburgh EH8 9XP; T.-0131 6507723; e-mail: david.reay@ed.ac.uk

Reay, 15th Lord (Aeneas Simon Mackay); b. 1965. Succeeded to title, 2013.

Redpath, Keith. Chair, NHS National Services Scotland, since 2019. Career history: spent a total of 42 years working in both local government and the NHS in Scotland; Chief Officer, West Dunbartonshire Health and Social Care Partnership, 2010-17; Chief Officer of the West Dunbartonshire Integrated Joint Board, 2015-17; non-executive positions with the Care Inspectorate and the Scottish Social Services Council, since retiring in 2017; former Chair of the National Chief Officers Group representing the views of chief officers across the health and care system in Scotland; spent 20 years promoting and advocating for the integration of health and social care services. Address: NHS National Services Scotland, 5 Cadogan Street, Glasgow G2 6QE.

Reed of Allermuir, The Rt. Hon. Lord (Robert John Reed), PC 2008. President of the Supreme Court of the United Kingdom, since 2020; Deputy President, 2018-2020; b. 7.9.56, Edinburgh; m., Jane Mylne; 2 d. Educ. George Watson's College, Edinburgh; Edinburgh University (LLB, 1st class Hons); Balliol College, Oxford (DPhil). Admitted to Scottish Bar, 1983; Standing Junior Counsel: Scottish Education Department, 1988-89, Scottish Office Home and Health Department, 1989-95; called to English Bar, 1991; QC, 1995; Advocate Depute, 1996-98; Judge of the Outer House of the Court of Session, 1998-2008; Principal Commercial Judge, 2006-08; Judge of the Inner House, 2008-2012; Justice of the Supreme Court, since 2012; ad hoc Judge of the European Court of Human Rights, since 1999; non-permanent Judge of the Hong Kong Court of

Final Appeal, since 2017; Expert Adviser, EU/Council of Europe Joint Initiative with Turkey, 2002-04; Member, Advisory Board, British Institute of International and Comparative Law, 2001-05, Trustee, since 2015; Chairman, Franco-British Judicial Co-operation Committee, 2005-2012; President, EU Forum of Judges for the Environment, 2006-07, Vice-President, 2008-09; Member, UN Task Force on Access to Justice, 2006-08; Convener, Children in Scotland, 2006-2012; Member, Advisory Board, Oxford Institute of European and Comparative Law, since 2014; Bencher of Inner Temple, since 2012; Hon. Professor, University of Glasgow, since 2006; High Steward, Oxford University, since 2018; Visitor: Balliol College, Oxford, since 2011, Linacre College, St Cross College and Wolfson College, Oxford, since 2018; Hon LLD, Glasgow University, 2013; FRSE, 2015. Recreation: music. Address: (b.) Supreme Court of the United Kingdom, Parliament Square, London SW1P 3BD.

Reed, Professor Peter, BA, RIBA, FRIAS, FSAScot. Emeritus Professor, Strathclyde University; b. 31.1.33, Hayes, Middlesex; m., Keow Chim Lim; 2 d. Educ. Southall Grammar School; Manchester University (State Scholar); Open University. Commissioned Officer, RAF, 1960-61; Assistant Lecturer, University of Hong Kong, 1961-64; Architect in practice, Malaysia, 1964-70; joined Strathclyde University Department of Architecture and Building Science as Lecturer, 1970; Professor of Architecture, 1986; Dean, Faculty of Engineering, 1988-90; Vice-Principal Elect, 1990-92; Vice-Principal, 1992-94. Secretary, Kilsyth Civic Trust, 1975-80; Chairman, Kilsyth Community Council, 1975-78; GIA Council, 1982-84; ARCUK Board of Education, 1985-95; Governor, Glasgow School of Art, 1982-94; Glasgow West Conservation Trust, 1990-2000, Convener, 1996-2000; Chairman, Council, Charles Rennie Mackintosh Society, 1991-94. Publications include Glasgow: The Forming of the City (Editor); Church Architecture in Early Medieval Spain. Recreations: trees; classical music. Address: 67 Dowanside Road, Glasgow G12 9DL; T.-0141-334 1356.

Reedijk, Alex. General Director, Scottish Opera, since 2006; Vice Chair, Citizens Theatre; Chair, The Beacon Arts Centre, Greenock; Foundation Board, Royal Botanic Gardens of Edinburgh. Educ. Victoria University of Wellington. Career history: extensive experience in festivals and opera; worked in the UK for several major arts festivals and opera companies, including Scottish Opera, Wexford Festival Opera, Opera Ireland and Garsington Opera in the 1980s and 1990s; New Zealand Festival: Deputy Executive Director, 1998-2000, Executive Director, 2000-02; Producer, Edinburgh Military Tattoo in New Zealand; General Director, NBR New Zealand Opera, 2002-06. Awarded a Fellowship of the Royal Conservatoire of Scotland in 2011. Address: Scottish Opera, 39 Elmbank Crescent, Glasgow G2 4PT; T.-0141 248 4567.

Reekie, Peter, MEng, FICE. Chief Executive Officer, Scottish Futures Trust, since 2018; Deputy Chief Executive & Director of Investments, 2009-2018; b. 14.09.71, Manchester; m., Nikki Temple; 2 d. Educ. Stockport Grammar School; University of Oxford, Hertford College. Allot and Lomax (now Jacobs) Consulting Engineers, 1994-2000; PricewaterhouseCoopers (Consulting and Corporate Finance at The Public Private Interface), 2000-09. Emeritus Member, RSE Young Academy of Scotland. Recreations: family and the great Scottish outdoors. Address: Scottish Futures Trust, 11-15 Thistle Street, Edinburgh EH2 1DF; T.-0131 510 0802.
E-mail: peter.reekie@scottishfuturestrust.org.uk

Reeks, David Robin, MBE, TD, DL, BSc (Eng). Vice Lord Lieutenant of Lanarkshire, 2002-2010; b. 15.6.35, Parkstone; m., Kathleen Veronica Stephens; 1 s.; 1 d. Educ. Canford School; London University. Rig Engineer, UKAEA Dounreay, 1962-67; Senior Engineer, SSEB,

1967-90; Reactor Thermal Performance Engineer, Scottish Nuclear Ltd., 1990-94. Committee Member and Volunteer Convoy Leader, Edinburgh Direct Aid to Bosnia; TA Royal Engineers/Royal Corps of Transport, 1962-90. Recreations: hill-walking; Scottish country dancing. Address: 3 Cedar Place, Strathaven, Lanarkshire ML10 6DW; T.-01357 521695; e-mail: d.reeks@talktalk.net

Rees, Professor Jonathan, BMedSci, MBBS, FRCP, FRCPE, FMedSci. Grant Chair of Dermatology, University of Edinburgh, since 2000; b. 10.10.57, Cardiff; 2 d. Educ. St. Illtyd's College, Cardiff. Trained in internal medicine, Newcastle upon Tyne; trained in dermatology, Vienna and Newcastle-upon-Tyne; trained in molecular genetics, Newcastle-upon-Tyne and Strasbourg; Professor of Dermatology, University of Newcastle, 1992-2000. President, European Society for Dermatology Research. Recreation: rugby. Address: (b.) Department of Dermatology, University of Edinburgh, Lauriston Building, Lauriston Place, Edinburgh EH3 9HA; T.-0131-536 2041; e-mail: jonathan.rees@ed.ac.uk

Reeve, Bill, BSc (Hons) Dunelm, MBA, CEng, FIMechE. Director of Rail, Transport Scotland, since 2005; b. 22.08.64, Redruth; m., Helen Redican; 2 s. Educ. Hove County Grammar; Brighton, Hove and Sussex VIth Form College; St. Chad's College, Durham; Strathclyde Graduate Business School. Career History: Rolling Stock Maintenance Engineer, British Rail, then Rail Freight Investment Manager; Rail Freight Business Development Manager, EWS Ltd.; Director, Project Sponsorship, Strategic Rail Authority. Past Chairman, Railway Division of Institution of Mechanical Engineers. Recreations: time with family; sailing; international rail travel; lepidoptery. Address: (b.) Buchanan House, 58 Port Dundas Road, Glasgow G4 0HF; T.-0141 272 7420.
E-mail: Bill.Reeve@transport.gov.scot

Regan, Ashten, MSc. MSP (Scottish National Party), Edinburgh Eastern, since 2016; Minister for Community Safety, since 2018; b. 8.3.74. Educ. Keele University; Open University. Career history: PR and Marketing Officer, ScottClem, 1998-2001; Senior Account Executive, Spreckley Partners, 2001-02; Events Executive, Zinc Management, 2002; Account Manager, Rocket PR, 2002-03; Digital Marketing, Tearfund, 2012-13; Head of Campaigns and Advocacy, Common Weal Scotland, 2013-15. Address: Scottish Parliament, Edinburgh EH99 1SP.

Rehman, Satwat. Director, One Parent Families Scotland, since 2011. Career history: set up and ran the employability charity Skillnet, bringing together employers and job-seekers from ethnic minorities; ten years at Camden London Borough Council, latterly as Deputy Head of Integrated Early Years Services. Address: (b.) Headquarters, 13 Gayfield Square, Edinburgh EH1 3NX; T.-0131 556 3899; e-mail: info@opfs.org.uk

Reicher, Professor Stephen David, FBA, FRSE, PhD. Bishop Wardlaw Professor of Social Psychology, University of St Andrews. Vice-President of the Royal Society of Edinburgh; Fellow of the British Academy; Fellow of the Academy of Social Sciences; Fellow of the British Psychological Society; Fellow of the Canadian Institute for Advanced Research. Educ. University of Bristol. Career history: held positions at the University of Dundee and University of Exeter before moving to St Andrews in 1997; formerly Head of the School of Psychology at St Andrews; former Associate Editor of the Journal of Community and Applied Social Psychology and Chief Editor of the British Journal of Social Psychology; Editor for a number of journals including Scientific American Mind. Collaborated with Alex Haslam of the University of Exeter on the BBC television programme The Experiment, which became known as the BBC Prison Study. Advisor to the UK Government and the Scottish Government on Covid-19. Member of Independent SAGE. Address: School of Psychology & Neuroscience, Westburn Lane, St Andrews; T.-01334 463057.
E-mail: sdr@st-andrews.ac.uk

Reid, Alan, MP. Liberal Democrat MP, Argyll and Bute, 2001-2015; b. 7.8.54. Educ. Prestwick Academy; Ayr Academy; Strathclyde University. Maths Teacher, 1976-77; Computer Programmer, 1977-85; Computer Project Manager, Glasgow University, 1985-2001.

Reid, Claire. Regional Leader for Scotland at PwC, since 2019. Educ. University of Strathclyde; EDHEC Business School. Career history: PwC: Senior Associate - Senior Manager, 1998-2006, Senior Manager - Director, 2006-2012, Partner, since 2012. Address: PwC in Scotland, 141 Bothwell Street, Glasgow G2 7EQ; T.-0141 355 4000.

Reid, Professor Colin Turriff, MA, LLB, FRSA. Professor of Environmental Law, Dundee University, since 1995 and Dean of the Faculty of Law and Accountancy, 2004-06; b. 10.6.58, Aberdeen; m., M. Anne Palin; 2 d. Educ. Robert Gordon's College, Aberdeen; University College, Oxford; Gonville and Caius College, Cambridge. Lecturer in Public Law, Aberdeen University, 1980-90; Senior Lecturer in Law, Dundee University, 1991-95; Patron, UK Environmental Law Association. Publications: Nature Conservation Law; Environmental Law in Scotland (Editor); A Guide to the Scotland Act 1998 (Co-Author); The Privatisation of Biodiversity? (Co-Author). Recreations: cricket; hockey. Address: (b.) Dundee Law School, Dundee University, Dundee DD1 4HN; T.-01382 384637.

Reid, Gavin. Chief Executive, Scottish Chamber Orchestra, since 2016; Co-Chair, IMPACT Scotland, since 2020, Trustee, since 2017; Director of the BBC Scottish Symphony Orchestra, 2006-2016; Chair of the Association of British Orchestras, 2017-2020, previously a Director of the Board, 2007-2013; Fellow of the Royal Conservatoire of Scotland, previously on Board of Governors, 2013-2018; General Manager, Manchester Camerata, 2002-2006; Fellow on the Clore Leadership Programme, 2004-2006; Freelance trumpet player, teacher, administrator, 1989-2002. Educ. Napier College Edinburgh; Royal Northern College of Music Manchester; Guildhall School of Music and Drama London. Address: Scottish Chamber Orchestra, 4 Royal Terrace, Edinburgh EH7 5AB; T-0131 557 6800.

Reid, Professor Gavin Clydesdale, MA, MSc, PhD, FRSA, FFCS, Hon. DBA (Abertay, 2010), DLitt (Aberdeen, 2012). Professor of Economics, St. Andrews University, 1991-2013; Founder/Director, Centre for Research into Industry, Enterprise, Finance and the Firm (CRIEFF), 1991-2013; Visiting Professor in Accounting and Finance, University of Strathclyde, 2007-2015; Member, Competition Appeal Tribunal, 2011-18; Honorary Professor of Economics, University of St Andrews, since 2013; Senior Research Associate, Centre for Business Research, Judge Business School, University of Cambridge, since 2019; b. 25.8.46, Glasgow; m., Dr. Julia A. Smith; 2 s.; 4 d. Educ. Lyndhurst Prep School; Frimley and

Camberley Grammar School (Head Boy); Aberdeen University MA (1st Class Hons) (Stephen Scholar), 1969; Southampton University MSc (SSRC Scholar), 1971; Edinburgh University PhD, 1975. Lecturer, Senior Lecturer, Reader in Economics, Acting Head of Department, Edinburgh University, 1971-91; Visiting Associate Professor: Queen's University, Ontario, 1981-82, Denver University, Colorado, 1984; Visiting Scholar, Darwin College, Cambridge, 1987-88; Visiting Professor, University of Nice, 1998; Leverhulme Trust Research Fellowship, 1989-90; Nuffield Foundation Social Science Research Fellowship, 1997-98; Professor of Enterprise and Innovation, University of the West of Scotland Business School, 2013-14; Professor of Business Management and Strategy, Head of School, Dundee Business School, University of Abertay, 2014-18. Editorial Board: Scottish Journal of Political Economy, 1986-98, Small Business Economics, 1997-2016, Venture Capital, 1998-2008; Member, Council, Scottish Economic Society, 1990-2002, President, 1999-2002, Medal of Honour, 2017; Research Fellow, EIM Business and Policy Research, Rotterdam, 2002; Chairman, ESRC Network of Industrial Economists, 1997-2001; Member, Economic Council, Britain in Europe, 2002-04; Chair, Scottish Institute for Enterprise Research Forum, 2002-03; National Conference of University Professors, President, 2003-06, Vice-President, 2002-03, Member, Council, since 1999; President, Institute of Contemporary Scotland, 2005-06; Chairman, ESRC Seminars in Accounting, Finance and Economics, 2006-08. Publications: The Kinked Demand Curve Analysis of Oligopoly, 1981; Theories of Industrial Organization, 1987; The Small Entrepreneurial Firm (Co-author), 1988; Classical Economic Growth, 1989; Small Business Enterprise, 1993; Profiles in Small Business (Co-author), 1993; Venture Capital Investment, 1998; Information System Development in the Small Firm (Co-author), 2000; The Foundations of Small Business Enterprise, 2007; Risk Appraisal and Venture Capital in High Technology New Ventures (Co-Author), 2008. Past External Examiner: Universities of Aberdeen, Cambridge, Cork, Durham, Glasgow, Malawi, West Indies. Advisor: Centre for Business Research, University of Cambridge, 2009-2020, The Keynes Centre, University College Cork, 2015-2019. Recreations: music; reading; running; poetry. Address: (h.) 23 South Street, St. Andrews KY16 9QS; T.-01334 472932.

Reid, The Rt Hon. Sir George, MA, PC (2004), kt (2012), FRSE (2015). Lord-Lieutenant of Clackmannanshire, 2011-2014; Lord High Commissioner, 2008 and 2009; UK Electoral Commissioner, 2010-2014; Chair, Independent Remuneration Board of National Assembly for Wales, 2010-2014; Director of Strategic Review of Northern Ireland Assembly, 2007-09 and of National Trust for Scotland, 2009-2010; Visiting Professor at Universities of Glasgow and Stirling, 2007-2014; MSP (Elected SNP, but no political allegiance as Presiding Officer), Ochil, 2003-07; Presiding Officer and Convener of Parliamentary Bureau and Corporate Body, Scottish Parliament, 2003-07; MSP (SNP), Mid-Scotland and Fife, and Deputy Presiding Officer, 1999-2003; b. 4.6.39, Tullibody; m., Daphne Ann MacColl; 2 d. Educ. Dollar Academy; St Andrews University. Reporter, Daily Express; Reporter, Scottish Television; Producer, Granada Television; Head of News and Current Affairs, Scottish Television; Presenter, BBC; Director of Public Affairs, International Red Cross and Red Crescent, 1984-1995. MP, Clackmannan and East Stirlingshire, 1974-79; Member, Parliamentary Assembly of the Council of Europe, 1975-79; Trustee, Glasgow Life and Edinburgh International Tattoo, 2007-2014; Independent Adviser, Scottish Ministerial Code, 2008-2011; Professorial Fellow in Humanitarian Studies, University of Stirling, since 2014. Member, Scottish Government's Standing Council on Europe, since 2016; Honorary

doctorates, Universities of St. Andrews, Queen Margaret, Edinburgh, Stirling and Glasgow.

Reid, Harry William, BA (Hons), Dr hc (Edinburgh), DUniv (Glasgow), FRSA. Writer; former Editor, The Herald; b. 23.9.47, Glasgow; m., Julie Davidson (qv); 1 d. Educ. Aberdeen Grammar School; Fettes College; Oxford University. The Scotsman: Education Correspondent, 1973-77, Features Editor, 1977-81; Sports Editor, Sunday Standard, 1981-82; Executive Editor, Glasgow Herald, 1982-83, Deputy Editor, 1983-97; Chairman, Scottish Editors' Committee, 1999-2001. Visiting Fellow, Faculty of Divinity, Edinburgh University, 2001-02; Governor, Fettes College, 2002-2012; Columnist, The Herald, 2004-2014; Oliver Brown Award, 2007. Publications: Dear Country: a quest for England, 1992; Outside Verdict: An Old Kirk in a New Scotland, 2002; The Final Whistle? Scottish Football: The Best and Worst of Times, 2005; Deadline: The Story of the Scottish Press, 2006; The Independence Book (Co-Ed), 2008; Reformation: The Dangerous Birth of the Modern World, 2009. Recreations: reading; walking; supporting Aberdeen Football Club. Address: 12 Comely Bank, Edinburgh EH4 1AN; T.-0131-332 6690; e-mail: harry.reid@virgin.net

Reid, Heather M.M., OBE, BSc (Hons), MSc, CPhys, MInstP, FRMS. Science Education Consultant; former Weather Forecaster, Met Office; BBC Scotland Weather Forecaster, 1994-2009; b. 6.7.69, Paisley; m., Miles Padgett; 1 d. Educ. Camphill High School, Paisley; Edinburgh University. Joined Met Office to work in satellite image research; became forecaster at Glasgow Weather Centre; known as "Heather the Weather" to viewers. Past-Chair, Institute of Physics in Scotland, 1999-2001; active involvement in Edinburgh Science Festival, Techfest, and promoting the public understanding of science; member of the science and engineering education advisory group set up by the Scottish Government. Recreations: apart from lecturing and giving talks in spare time – watch cricket; hill-walking.

Reid, Iain, LLB. Non-Executive Director: The James Hutton Institute, since 2017, Lothian Buses, since 2018; Chief Executive Officer, The Faculty of Advocates, 2017-2021; Finance Director, Sunergos Innovations, 2016-17; former Interim Chief Executive, The National Trust for Scotland (2015) (Finance Director, 2010-2015). Educ. University of Edinburgh. Company Secretary, Scottish Widows, 1995-2001; Finance Director, Sopra Group, 2001-07; Global CFO, Axway Software, 2007-08; Finance Director, Grant Management, 2008-09; Director, Reid & Co, 2009-2010.

Reid of Cardowan, Rt. Hon. Lord (John Reid), PC, PhD. MP (Labour), Airdrie and Shotts, 2005-10, Hamilton North and Bellshill, 1997-2005, Motherwell North, 1987-97; Secretary of State for the Home Department, 2006-07; b. 8.5.47, Bellshill; m., 1, Catherine McGowan (deceased), 2, Carine Adler; 2 s. Educ. St. Patrick's Senior Secondary School, Coatbridge; Stirling University. Scottish Research Officer, Labour Party, 1979-83; Political Adviser to Rt. Hon. Neil Kinnock, 1983-85; Scottish Organiser, Trade Unionists for Labour, 1986-87; Armed Forces Minister, 1997-98; Minister of Transport, 1998-99; Secretary of State for Scotland, 1999-2001; Secretary of State for Northern Ireland, 2001-02; Party Chair and Minister without Portfolio, 2001-02; Leader of the Commons and President of the Council, 2002-03; Secretary of State for Health, 2003-05; Secretary of State for Defence, 2005-06. Member, National Preparedness Commission, since 2021; Member, International Relations Committee, House of Lords, 2015-21; Member, Joint National Security Strategy Committee,

Commons and Lords, since 2021. Hon. Prof., University College London; Chair, Institute for Strategy, Security and Resilience Studies at UCL, since 2010; Chairman, Advisory Board, The Shearwater Group, since 2017; Senior Advisor, The Chertoff Group; Chairman, Celtic Football Club, 2007-2011. Publication: Cyber Doctrine: Towards a framework for learning resilience (Co-Author), 2011. Recreations: football; crossword puzzles. Special interests: defence; security; cyber; foreign affairs. Address: House of Lords, London SW1A 0PW.

Reid, Karen. Chief Executive, NHS Education for Scotland, since 2021. Career history: Head of Corporate Services, IRISS - Institute for Research and Innovation in Social Services, 2006-09; SCSWIS: Director of Operations, 2009-2012; Director of Strategic Development/Depute CE, SCSWIS/Care Inspectorate, 2012-15; Chief Executive, Care Inspectorate, 2015-18; Chair, Audit Committee, University of Dundee (part-time), 2015-2020; Chief Executive Officer, Perth and Kinross Council, 2018-2021. Address: NHS Education for Scotland, 102 West Port, Edinburgh EH3 9DN; e-mail: CEO.nes@nes.scot.nhs.uk

Reid, Professor Kenneth Gilbert Cameron, CBE (2005), MA, LLB, LLD, WS, FRSE, FBA (2008). Professor Emeritus of Scots Law, Edinburgh University, since 2019, Professor of Scots Law, 2008-2019, Professor of Property Law, 1994-2008; Director, Edinburgh Centre for Private Law, 2009-2012; Law Commissioner for Scotland, 1995-2005; b. 25.3.54, Glasgow; m., Elspeth Christie; 2 s.; 1 d. Educ. Loretto; St. John's College, Cambridge; Edinburgh University. Admitted as a Solicitor, 1980; Lecturer in Law, Edinburgh University, 1980. Author of numerous books and papers on the law of property. Recreation: classical music. Address: (b.) School of Law, Old College, South Bridge, Edinburgh EH8 9YL.

Reid, Melanie Frances, MA (Hons) MBE. Writer and Columnist, The Times, since 2007; Writer, Spinal Column in The Times Magazine, since 2010; Senior Assistant Editor and Columnist, The Herald, 2001-07; b. 13.4.57, Barnet; m., Clifford Martin; 1 s.; divorced; m., David McNeil. Educ. Ormskirk Grammar School; Edinburgh University. The Scotsman: Graduate Trainee, 1980-82, Woman's Editor, 1983-87; Sunday Mail: Woman's Editor, 1987-2000, Associate Editor, 2000; Columnist, The Express, 2000. Member, Carnegie Commission for Rural Community Development, 2004-07. Journalist and Columnist of the Year 2010, Scottish Press Awards; Columnist of the Year, 2011 and 2020, UK Press Awards; Chair's Choice, the Comment Awards 2014; Edgar Wallace Award 2014; UK Magazine Editors Awards 2017 Columnist of the Year; Co-writer (with Sally Beamish) of musical piece Spinal Chords 2012 for the orchestra of the Age of Enlightenment; Honorary Degree from Stirling University, 2014. Co-authored (with Gregor Fisher) The Boy From Nowhere, 2015; The World I Fell Out Of (memoir), 2019; awarded the Saltire prize for non-fiction, 2019. Recreation: staying cheerful. Address: (b.) The Times, 1 London Bridge Street, London SE1 9GF; e-mail: melanie.reid@thetimes.co.uk

Reid, Sheriff Paul, LLB. Sheriff, Glasgow & Strathkelvin, since 2019; Advocate, since 2011. Educ. The University of Edinburgh; Lund University. Career history: Assistant, Shepherd and Wedderburn, 2005-08; Associate, CMS Cameron McKenna, 2008-2010; Tutor and part-time lecturer in Public Law, The University of Edinburgh, since 2004; Founding partner of Fleming and Reid (Glasgow); appointed a part time sheriff in 2009; appointed as Standing Junior Counsel to the Scottish Government in 2015; appointed an ad hoc Advocate Depute in 2017. Previously held membership of the Scottish Civil Justice Council;

presently a member of the Scottish Legal Aid Board. Address: Glasgow Sheriff Court, 1 Carlton Place, Glasgow G5 9TW.

Reid, Dame Seona Elizabeth, DBE, BA, HonDArt, HonDLitt, FRSA. Chair of the National Theatre of Scotland; Chair, British Council Scotland's Advisory Committee, since 2019; Director, Glasgow School of Art, 1999-2013; Honorary Professor; b. 21.1.50, Paisley. Educ. Park School, Glasgow; Strathclyde University; Liverpool University. Business Manager, Theatre Royal, Lincoln, 1972-73; Press Officer, Northern Dance Theatre, Manchester, 1973-76; PRO, Ballet Rambert, London, 1976-79; freelance arts consultant, 1979-81; Director, Shape, London, 1981-87; Assistant Director, Greater London Arts, 1987-90; Director, Scottish Arts Council, 1990-99; April 2011: Deputy Chair, National Heritage Memorial Fund and Chair of Scottish Committee of Heritage Lottery Fund; Scottish Commissioner, US-UK Fulbright Commission. Board Member, Cove Park; Universities Scotland Executive Committee; Member, Board of the Edinburgh International Cultural Summit. Recreations: walking; travel; the arts.

Reid, Sir William Kennedy, KCB, MA, LLD (Aberdeen and Reading), FRCPEd, FRSE; b. 15.2.31, Aberdeen; m., Ann Campbell; 2 s.; 1 d. Educ. Robert Gordon's College; George Watson's College; Edinburgh University; Trinity College, Cambridge. Civil Servant, 1956-89, Department of Education and Science, Cabinet Office, Scottish Office; Member, Council on Tribunals and Its Scottish Committee, 1990-96; Member, Commission for Local Administration in England, 1990-96; Member, Commission for Local Administration in Wales, 1990-96. A Director, International Ombudsman Institute, 1992-96; Parliamentary Commissioner for Administration (Ombudsman), 1990-97; Health Service Commissioner for England, Scotland, Wales, 1990-97; Chairman, Mental Welfare Commission for Scotland, 1997-2000; Chairman, Advisory Committee on Distinction Awards, 1997-2000; Queen Elizabeth the Queen Mother Fellow, Nuffield Trust, 1998; Chairman of Council, St. George's School for Girls, 1997-2003; Chairman, Edinburgh Competition Festival Association, 2007-2010; Chairman, Scottish Churches Architectural Heritage Trust, 2011-2012; Vice-President, Scotland's Churches Trust, 2017-2021; Hon. D.Litt (Napier), 1998; Hon. FRCSEd, 2002. Recreations: verse; biography. Address: (h.) Darroch House, 9/1 East Suffolk Park, Edinburgh EH16 5PL.

Reilly, Kerry. National General Secretary/Chief Executive, YMCA Scotland, since 2015. Educ. The Open University; Northern College of Education; Edinburgh Napier University; University of Leeds. Programme Secretary, Dumfries YMCA, 1992-93; Youth Worker, Bellshill & Mossend YMCA, 1995-98; Youth Work Development Officer, YMCA Scotland, 1998-2006; Chair, YMCA Europe Festival 2013, 2010-13; YMCA Manager, YMCA Edinburgh, 2007-2014; Event Director, YMCA175, YMCA Europe, 2017-19; Elder, Longniddry Parish Church; Director, Youthlink Scotland and Y Care International. Address: YMCA Scotland, 1 Chesser Avenue, Edinburgh EH14 1TB; T.-0131 228 1464.

Reilly, Victoria, MA (Hons) French and Spanish, PGCE. Rector, St Columba's School, Kilmacolm, since 2020. Educ. Wakefield Girls' High School; University of Edinburgh. Career history: worked in business; studied for postgraduate certificate in education at the University of Sheffield; joined St Columba's School in 1992, appointed Depute Rector in 2012 and Senior Depute Rector in 2016. Associate Assessor with Her Majesty's

Inspectors of Schools, since 2015. Address: St Columba's School, Duchal Road, Kilmacolm PA13 4AU; T.-01505 872238.

Reith, Sheriff Fiona Lennox, LLB, QC, FSA Scot. Sheriff of Lothian and Borders at Edinburgh, 2007-2019 (part-time, since 2020); Specialist Sheriff, All-Scotland Sheriff Personal Injury Court, 2015-2019; Lead Sheriff, Guardianship Court, Edinburgh Sheriff Court, 2015-19. Educ. Perth Academy; Aberdeen University. Solicitor, Edinburgh, 1979-82; devilled, 1982-83; admitted to Faculty of Advocates, 1983; Standing Junior Counsel in Scotland to Home Office, 1989-92; Advocate-Depute, 1992-95; Standing Junior Counsel, Scottish Office Environment Department, 1995-96; QC, 1996; Sheriff of Tayside, Central and Fife, at Perth, 1999-2000; Sheriff of Glasgow and Strathkelvin, 2000-07. Member, Scottish Legal Aid Board Civil Legal Aid Sub-Committee and Supreme Court Reporter, 1989-92; Member, Sheriff Court Rules Council, 1989-93; External Examiner in Professional Conduct, Faculty of Advocates, 2000-06; Member, Council of Sheriffs' Association, 2003-06 and 2009-2011; Member, Criminal Courts' Rules Council, 2004-2011; Member, Parole Board for Scotland, 2005-07, Vice-Chairman, 2008-09; Member, Lord Coulsfield's Civil Justice Advisory Group, 2004-05 (Report in relation to the Civil Justice System in Scotland, published November 2005). Recreations: walking; music; theatre; good food and wine; travel.

Reith, Professor Gerda, MA (Hons), PhD. Professor of Social Science, University of Glasgow, since 2010; b. 24.5.69, Aberdeen; m., Andy Furlong; 2 s.; 1 d. Educ. Lossiemouth High School; Glasgow University. Glasgow University: Research Fellow, 1996-98, Lecturer and Senior Lecturer, 1998-2010. Chair, Research Panel - Responsible Gambling Strategy Board, since 2008. Publications: The Age of Chance: Gambling in Western Culture, 1999 (winner of The Philip Abrams Prize); Gambling - Who Wins? Who Loses? (2002). Address: School of Social and Political Sciences, Adam Smith Building, University of Glasgow, Glasgow G12 8RT; T.-0141 330 3849.
E-mail: gerda.reith@glasgow.ac.uk

Rennick, Neil. Director of Justice, The Scottish Government, since 2014. Educ. University of Glasgow. Career history: worked in a variety of roles within the Civil Service, including as private secretary to the Permanent Secretary and Head of Public Bodies Division; Executive Director of Strategy and Infrastructure for the Scottish Court Service (SCS); Deputy Director of Criminal Law and Licensing Division. Address: Director of Justice, The Scottish Government, St. Andrew's House, Regent Road, Edinburgh EH1 3DG.

Rennie, Colin. Former Manager for Scotland, Fields in Trust (FIT), formerly National Playing Fields Association (NPFA); b. 1956, Montrose, Angus; m., Alyson; 2 s. Educ. Dundee College; Kingsway Technical College. Career history: Westminster Parliamentary Adviser; Chairman: North of Scotland Water Authority, Dundee Partnership; Convenor, Economic Development, Dundee City Council; Journalist; Architectural Draughtsman. Former SET Board Member; former Dundee and Angus Tourist Board Member. Recreations: hill walking; fly fishing; visiting historic buildings; sport. Address: (b.) The Circle, Staffa Place, Dundee DD2 3SX; T.-01382 817427.
E-mail: colinprennie@hotmail.co.uk

Rennie, Rev. Scott, MA (Hons), BD (Hons), FRSA. Parish Minister, Queen's Cross Church, Aberdeen, since 2009; b. 31.3.72, Bucksburn, Aberdeen; m. (1), Ruth (divorced); 1 d.; m. (2), David Smith. Educ. University of Aberdeen; Union Theological Seminary in the City of New

York. Assistant Minister, Queen's Cross Parish Church, Aberdeen, 1996-98; Distribution Assistant, Aberdeen Independent Newspaper, March 1998-July 1998, July 1999-October 1999; Cathedral Minister, Brechin Cathedral, 1999-2009. Board Member, Instant Neighbour, since 2015; Member of the Liberal Democrats (candidate for the Angus constituency in the 2005 UK general election); well-known supporter of Aberdeen Football Club, aka 'The Dons'. Address: Queen's Cross Church, Albyn Place, Aberdeen AB10 1YN; T.-01224 644742.

Rennie, Willie. MSP (Liberal Democrat), North East Fife, since 2016 (Mid Scotland and Fife region, 2011-16); Education, Economy and Social Security Spokesperson; Leader, Scottish Liberal Democrats, 2011-2021; MP (Liberal Democrat), Dunfermline and Fife West, 2006-10; b. 27.9.67; m., Janet; 2 s. Educ. Paisley College. Chief Executive, Scottish Liberal Democrats and the Party's Chief of Staff, Scottish Parliament, 1997-2001; formerly adviser to Fife's Lib Dem Council Group; self-employed consultant, 2001-03; Account Director, McEwan Purvis, 2003-06. Recreations: road running; hill running. Address: (b.) Scottish Parliament, Edinburgh EH99 1SP.

Renshaw, Professor Eric, BSc, ARCS, DipStats, MPhil, PhD, CStat, FRSE. Emeritus Professor of Statistics, Strathclyde University (Professor, since 1991); b. 25.7.45, Preston; m., Anne Renshaw. Educ. Arnold School, Blackpool; Imperial College, London; Manchester University; Sussex University; Edinburgh University. Lecturer, then Senior Lecturer in Statistics, Edinburgh University, 1969-91. Publication: Modelling Biological Populations in Space and Time; Stochastic Population Processes. Recreations: skiing; golf; hill-walking; mandolin; photography. Address (h.) 42 Leadervale Road, Edinburgh EH16 6PA; T.-0131 664 2370; e-mail: e.renshaw@strath.ac.uk

Renwick, Professor John Peter, MA, PhD, DLitt, FRHistS, FRSE, Commandeur des Palmes Académiques. Emeritus Professor, University of Edinburgh; John Orr Professor of French, 1980-2006; Director, Centre de Recherches Francophones Belges, 1995-2010; appointed Research Fellow, The Voltaire Foundation, University of Oxford in 2008; b. 25.5.39, Gillingham; m., Claudette Gorse; 1 s.; 1 d. Educ. Gillingham Grammar School; St. Bartholomew's Grammar School, Newbury; St. Catherine's College, Oxford; Sorbonne; British Institute in Paris (Leverhulme Research Scholar). Assistant Lecturer, then Lecturer, Glasgow University, 1964-66; Fellow, Churchill College, Cambridge, 1966-72; Maître de Conférences Associé, Départment de Français, Université de Clermont-Ferrand, 1970-71, 1972-74; Professor of French, New University of Ulster, 1974-80 (Pro-Vice-Chancellor, 1978-80); Member, Editorial Committee, The Complete Works of Voltaire; Member, Executive Committee, Voltaire Foundation; Member, Editorial Committee, Moralia (Paris); General Secretary, Society of the Friends of the Institut Français d'Ecosse, since 2000; President, Comité Consultatif, Institut Français d'Ecosse, 1996-2010; Médaille de la Ville de Bort. Publications: La destinée posthume de Jean-Francois Marmontel, 1972; Marmontel, Mémoires, 1972; Marmontel, Voltaire and the Belisaire affair, 1974; Marmontel, Correspondence, 1974; Catalogue de la bibliotheque de Jean-Baptiste Massillon, 1977; Voltaire et Morangies, ou les Lumieres l'ont échappé belle, 1982; Chamfort devant la posterité, 1986; Catalogue de la Bibliotheque du Comte D'Espinchal, 1988; Language and Rhetoric of the French Revolution, 1990; Voltaire, La Guerre Civile de Genève, 1990; Catalogue de la Bibliotheque du College de l'Oratoire de Riom 1619-1792, 1997; Voltaire, Brutus, 1998; Voltaire, Les Guèbres, 1999; Voltaire, Traité sur la Tolérance, 1999 and 2000;

L'Invitation au Voyage (Studies in Honour of Peter France), 2000; Jean-Francois Marmontel (1723-1799): Dix études, 2001; Voltaire, Histoire du parlement de Paris, 2005; Voltaire, Essai sur les Probabilités en fait de Justice; Nouvelles Probabilités, 2006; 60@ifecosse, 2006; Marmontel, Mémoires, new edition, revised and considerably expanded, 2008; General editor (and contributor: twelve critical editions), vols. 75A-75B, Oeuvres complètes de Voltaire, 2009; General editor (and contributor), Voltaire, la tolérance et la justice, 2010; Co-Director of and contributor to the critical edition of the Essai sur les moeurs (Oeuvres complètes de Voltaire, vols. 21-27 (vol. 22, 2009: vol. 23, 2010: vol. 24, 2011: vol. 25, 2012: vol. 26A, 2013: vol. 26B, 2014: vol. 26C, 2015): vol. 27 (2016); numerous editions of single texts in vols. 60B, 78C and 144A-B (2018); in vol. 145 (2019); in vols. 29B and 84 (2020), and in vol. 147 (2021). Editor, with G. Laudin, of the Annales de l'Empire (Œuvres complètes de Voltaire), vols. 44A-44C (2019). Awarded the Prix littéraire Auvergne-Rhône-Alpes de la Francophonie 2021 for the 'pioneering rehabilitation' of Jean-François Marmontel (March 2021). Awarded the Royal Society of Edinburgh's Senior Career Medal (the 'Sir Walter Scott Medal') in the Arts, Humanities and Social Sciences (July 2021) for the 'monumental and ground-breaking' contribution to the critical edition of the Œuvres complètes de Voltaire' (Oxford, 1970-2021, 203 volumes), and the 'scholarly resurrection' of Marmontel. Address: (b.) 50 George Square, Edinburgh EH8 5LH.

Reoch, Torquil, MA. Retired Broadcasting Journalist; Producer, BBC Newsnight Scotland, 1999-2014; b. 17.6.54, Glasgow; m., Christine; 1 s.; 2 d.; 2 g-s.; 1 g-d. Educ. George Watson's College, Edinburgh; Edinburgh University; Glasgow University. News Trainee, BBC London, 1979; Reporter, BBC Radio Scotland, 1980; Scotland Correspondent, TV-am, 1983; News Producer, BBC Scotland, 1985; Producer, European Business Channel, Zurich, 1989; Editor, Good Morning Scotland, 1991; News Operations Editor, BBC Scotland, 1997. Recreation: family. T.-07850 715100.
E-mail: torquil@reoch.eu

Reynolds, Paul, BA, PhD. Chairman, STV Group plc, since 2021; b. 3.57. Educ. University of Strathclyde; University of London; London Business School. Career history: BT: senior roles in Corporate Strategy, Operations Technology, Product Management and Marketing, 1983-97, Managing Director, Networks and Information Services, 1997-2000; Chief Executive Officer, BT Wholesale, London, 2000-07: Chairman, AAPT, 2007-2012; Chief Executive Officer, Telecom New Zealand, Auckland, 2007-2012; Chairman: FibreNation, London and Manchester, 2018-2020, 9 Spokes, Auckland, since 2014. Member of the Board: BT, 2001-07, eAccess, Tokyo, 2004-09; Member of the Board, Chair of Audit and Regulatory Committees, eir Ireland, Dublin, 2016-2018; Member of the Board, XConnect, London, 2012-2019; Member of the Board and Audit Committee, Computershare, Melbourne, since 2018; Member of the Board, TalkTalk, London and Manchester, since 2020. Address: STV, Pacific Quay, Glasgow G51 1PQ; T.-0141 300 3000.

Reynolds, Professor Siân, BA, MA, PhD, Officier dans l'Ordre des Palmes académiques, Fellow of the Learned Society of Wales. Professor (now emerita) of French, Stirling University, since 1990; Honorary Visiting Professor, University of Nottingham, 2015-18; Translator; b. 28.7.40, Cardiff; m., Peter France; 3 d. Educ. Howell's School, Llandaff; St. Anne's College, Oxford; University of Paris VII. Lecturer and Senior Lecturer, Sussex University, 1974-89; Lecturer, Edinburgh University, 1989-90; President, UK Association for the Study of Modern and

Contemporary France, 1993-99; Chair, Scottish Working People's History Trust, 2009-2021. Publications: Women, State and Revolution (Editor); Britannica's Typesetters; France Between the Wars, gender and politics; Contemporary French Cultural Studies (Joint Editor), 2000; co-editor, The Biographical Dictionary of Scottish Women, 2006 (new edition, 2018); Paris-Edinburgh, 2007; Marriage and Revolution, 2012 (winner, R.H. Gapper Book Prize 2013); translations include F. Braudel, The Mediterranean and novels by crime writers, Fred Vargas and Georges Simenon. Four times co-winner of CWA International Dagger, 2006, 2007, 2009, 2013. Recreation: going to the pictures. Address: (h.) 10 Dryden Place, Edinburgh EH9 1RP; e-mail: sian.reynolds@stir.ac.uk

Rhodes, Professor Neil Patrick Pawson, MA, DPhil. Professor of English Literature and Cultural History, University of St. Andrews; b. 30.05.53, Carlisle; m., Shirley McKay; 1 s.; 1 d. Educ. Uppingham School; St. Catherine's College, Oxford. Visiting Professor, University of Granada; General Editor, MHRA Tudor and Stuart Translations. Publications include: Common: The Development of Literary Culture in Sixteenth-Century England, 2018; English Renaissance Translation Theory, 2013; Shakespeare and the Origins of English, 2007; The Renaissance Computer, 2000. Address: (h.) 36 Marketgate, Crail, Fife; E-mail: nppr@st-andrews.ac.uk

Riach, Alan, BA (Cambridge), PhD (Glasgow). Professor and Chair, Department of Scottish Literature, University of Glasgow, since 2006; Head of Department, 2001-07; President, Association for Scottish Literary Studies, 2006-2010; b. 1.8.57, Airdrie; m., Rae; 2 s. Educ. Gravesend School for Boys, Gravesend, Kent; Churchill College, University of Cambridge, 1976-79: BA; Department of Scottish Literature, University of Glasgow, 1979-85: PhD. Freelance writing and teaching, Scotland, 1985-86; Post-Doctoral Research Fellow, Lecturer, Senior Lecturer, Associate Professor of English, University of Waikato, Hamilton, New Zealand, 1986-2000; Pro-Dean, Faculty of Arts and Social Sciences, University of Waikato, Hamilton, New Zealand, 2000. Many appearances on radio and television in New Zealand, Australia and Scotland. Publications: Representing Scotland in Literature, Popular Culture and Iconography, 2005; Hugh MacDiarmid's Epic Poetry, 1991; The Poetry of Hugh MacDiarmid, 1999; Hugh MacDiarmid: The Collected Works (General Editor), since 1992 (15 volumes published to 2020); The Radical Imagination: Lectures and Talks by Wilson Harris (Co-Editor); Scotlands: Poets and the Nation (Co-Editor); Arts of Resistance: Poets, Portraits and Landscapes of Modern Scotland (Co-Author); Arts of Independence: The Cultural Argument and Why It Matters Most (Co-Author): J.D. Fergusson: Modern Scottish Painting (Co-Editor); Arts and the Nation (Co-Author); contributions to over 20 books and numerous contributions to journals; books of poetry: For What It Is (Co-Author), 1988; This Folding Map (Poems 1978-1988), 1990; An Open Return, 1991; First and Last Songs, 1995; From the Vision of Hell: An Extract of Dante, 1998, Clearances, 2001; Homecoming: New Poems 2001-09, 2009; The Hunterian Poems (Editor), 2015; The Hunterian Museum Poems (Editor), 2017; The Winter Book: New Poems, 2017; contributor to other books of poetry. Address: (b.) Department of Scottish Literature, University of Glasgow, 7 University Gardens, Glasgow G12 8QH; T.-0141-330 6144.
E-mail: Alan.Riach@glasgow.ac.uk

Rice, Dame Susan, DBE, CBE, BA, MLitt, DBA (Hon), DHC (Hon), DLitt (Hon), DUniv (Hon), LLD (Hon), Chartered Banker, FCIBS, CCMI, FRSA, RRCSE, FRSE. Chair, Scottish Water, since 2015; Chair, Business Stream, since 2015; Chair, Scottish Fiscal Commission, since 2014; Chair, Financial Services Culture Board (previously Banking Standards Board), since 2020; Managing Director,

Lloyds Banking Group Scotland, 2009-2014; Chairman, Chief Executive, Lloyds TSB Scotland plc, 2000-09; Managing Director, Bank of Scotland, 1997-2000; b. 7.3.46, Rhode Island, USA; m., Professor Sir C. Duncan Rice (qv); 2 s.; 1 d. Educ. Wellesley College, Mass., USA; Aberdeen University. Hon. Degrees: Robert Gordon University, Edinburgh University, Heriot-Watt University, Paisley University, Glasgow University, Queen Margaret University, Aberdeen University, Glasgow Caledonian University. Dean, Yale University, 1973-79; Staff Aide to President, Hamilton College, 1980-81; Dean of Students, Colgate University, 1981-86; Senior Vice President and Division Head, Natwest Bancorp, 1986-96; Head, Branch Banking, then Managing Director, Personal Banking, Bank of Scotland, 1997-2000. Chair: Edinburgh International Book Festival, Edinburgh Festivals Forum, Governor's Patrons of the National Galleries of Scotland, 2020 Climate Group, Committee of Scottish Clearing Banks, Centre for Social Justice Research in Scotland, Senior Independent Director: SSE plc, J Sainsbury's plc, North American Income Trust: Chair-elect; Non-Executive Director: Court of the Bank of England, C. Hoare & Co, Big Society Capital plc, Charity Bank, National Centre for University and Business (NCUB). President: Scottish Council for Development and Industry; Advisor: First Minister's Council of Economic Advisors, Fraser of Allander Institute Advisory Board. Regent, Royal College of Surgeons, Edinburgh; Freeman of the City of London. Recreations: opera; modern art; hill-walking; fly fishing. Address: (b.) Scottish Water, Castle House, 6 Castle Drive, Dunfermline KY11 8GG; e-mail: susan.rice@scottishwater.co.uk

Richards, Professor David, MA (Cantab), MA (Lond), PhD (Cantab). Emeritus Professor of English Studies, University of Stirling; Visiting Professor, Division of English, NTU, Singapore; b. 15.09.53, Oldham; m., Susan; 1 s.; 1 d. Educ. Manchester Grammar School; Churchill College, Cambridge University. Lecturer, University of Birmingham, 1981-83; Senior Lecturer, University of Leeds, 1983-2002; Founding Director, The Ferguson Centre, Open University, 2002-06. Publication: Masks of Difference: Cultural Representations in Literature, Anthropology and Art, 1995. Recreations: art; sailing; travel. Address: (b.) Department of English Studies, University of Stirling, Stirling; T.-01786 467502; e-mail: david.richards@stir.ac.uk

Richards, Professor Randolph Harvey, CBE, MA, VetMB, PhD, DipECAAH, MRCVS, FRSM, CBiol, FSB, FRAgS, FRSE. Vice-Chairman, Moredun Foundation, since 2014; awarded RCVS Queen's Medal, 2016; Director, Institute of Aquaculture, University of Stirling, 1996-2009; Roberts Morris Bray Professor of Aquatic Veterinary Studies, since 1991; Veterinary Adviser, Scottish Salmon Producers' Organisation, since 2006; Veterinary Adviser, Scottish Quality Salmon, 1999-2006 (Veterinary Adviser, Scottish Salmon Growers' Association, 1986-99); b. 4.3.48, London; m., Jennifer Halley; 1 d. Educ. Grove Park Grammar School, Wrexham; Jesus College, Cambridge University; University of Stirling. University of Stirling: Deputy Director, Unit of Aquatic Pathobiology, 1976-79, Deputy Director, Institute of Aquaculture, 1979-96. Member, Veterinary Products Committee, Medicines Commission, 1992-2000. Publications: numerous papers on fish pathology in learned journals. Recreations: fine wine and food; shooting. Address: University of Stirling, Stirling FK9 4LA; T.-01786 467904; e-mail: r.h.richards@stir.ac.uk

Richardson, Emeritus Professor John Stuart, MA, DPhil, FRSE. Professor of Classics, Edinburgh University, 1987-2002, Emeritus Professor, since 2002; Dean, Faculty of Arts, and Provost, Faculty Group of Arts, Divinity and Music, 1992-97; Hon. Professor, Durham University, since 2003; Hon. Vice-President, Society for the Promotion of Roman Studies, since 2012, President, 1998-2001; b. 4.2.46, Ilkley; m., (1) Patricia Helen Robotham (deceased); (2) Joan McArthur Taylor; 2 s. Educ. Berkhamsted School; Trinity College, Oxford. Lecturer in Ancient History, Exeter College, Oxford, 1969-72, St. Andrews University, 1972-87; Priest, Scottish Episcopal Church, since 1980; Anglican Chaplain, St. Andrews University, 1980-87; Team Priest, St. Columba's, Edinburgh, 1987-2018; Honorary Canon, St. Mary's Cathedral, Edinburgh, since 2000. Publications: Roman Provincial Administration, 1976; Hispaniae, 1986; The Romans in Spain, 1996; Appian: The Wars of the Romans in Iberia, 2000; The Language of Empire, 2008; Augustan Rome 44 BC to AD 14, 2012; papers on ancient history. Recreation: choral singing. Address: (h.) Marketgate Farmhouse, Main Street, Ormiston, Tranent EH35 5HT; T.-01875 613850. E-mail: richardsonjohn4246@gmail.com

Richardson, The Hon Lord (Martin Richardson), QC, LLB, LLM. Senator of the College of Justice, since 2021. Educ. Edinburgh University; Universiteit Leiden. Career history: practised as a solicitor from 2000; following a stage at the European Commission, became an advocate in 2003; specialised in commercial law and was standing junior to the Scottish Government and to the Office of the Advocate General; appointed Queen's Counsel in 2017; Advocate Depute, 2016-18. Address: Court of Session, Parliament House, Parliament Square, Edinburgh EH1 1RQ.

Richardson, Neil, OBE, QPM. Chief Executive, Turning Point Scotland, since 2017; Deputy Chief Constable, Police Scotland, 2012-2016. Career: joined Lothian and Borders Police in 1985: served in operational posts such as Community Safety, Firearms, Divisional Operations, and CID, including a secondment to the Scottish Crime and Drug Enforcement Agency (SCDEA), promoted to Assistant Chief Constable for Territorial Policing (2006-08); joined Strathclyde Police as Deputy Chief Constable in 2008 with responsibility for matters including professional standards, complaints and discipline, organisational development, health and safety, change management and overseeing Force programmes and projects; appointed Transformation Director of the National Police Reform Programme in 2011, with responsibility for driving the reform of Scottish Policing through to Day One of the new service to its ultimate end state. Awarded the Queen's Police Medal in 2011. Address: Turning Point Scotland, Head office, 54 Govan Road, Glasgow G51 1JL; T.-0141 427 8200.

Richardson, Professor Neville Vincent, BA, DPhil, FRSC, FInstP, FRSE. Emeritus Professor, University of St Andrews; former Master of the United College (appointed Professor of Physical Chemistry, University of St Andrews in 1998); b. 25.2.50, Tadcaster; m., Jennifer Margaret; 2 step-s.; 2 step-d. Educ. Oglethorpe Grammar School, Tadcaster; Jesus College University of Oxford. SRC Research Fellow, Chemistry Department, University of Birmingham, 1974-77; Research Assistant, Fritz-Haber Institute, Max Planck Society, 1974-77; University of Liverpool: Lecturer, Chemistry Department, 1979, Senior Lecturer, 1984, Professor, 1988, Director, Surface Science, IRC. Marlow Medal, Royal Society of Chemistry, 1984; British Vacuum Society Medal, 1996; Surface and Colloid Chemistry Prize, RSC, 2003. Recreations: hillwalking; rock and ice climbing; skiing; squash. Address: School of Chemistry, North Haugh, University of St Andrews, St Andrews, Fife KY16 9ST; T.-01334 462395. E-mail: neville.richardson@st-andrews.ac.uk

Riches, Christopher Gabriel, BSc. Publishing Consultant, Riches Editorial Services, since 2006; Project Editor, The

Times Good University Guide, 2006-2017; b. 25.3.52, Oxford; m., Catherine Mary Gaunt; 3 s. Educ. Marlborough College; Manchester University. Copy Editor, Penguin Books, 1973-74; Oxford University Press: Science Education Editor, 1974-76, Publishing Manager, Hong Kong, 1976-81, Reference Editor, 1981-88; Publishing Manager, Collins Reference, Glasgow, 1989-94, Editorial Director, 1994-2006. Council Member, Scottish Publishers' Association, 1995-2003; Hon. Secretary, St. Mary's Episcopal Church, Aberfoyle, 1994-98; Chair, School Board, Killearn Primary School, 1997-99; Member, Killearn Community Council, 2008-09; Director, Gavin's Mill Ltd, since 2020. Publications: Britain the Facts (5 vols), 2008; The History of The Beano (Editor), 2008; The Broons Days Oot, 2009; Oxford Dictionary of Political Biography, 2009, 2013; The Broons Gairdenin' Wisdoms, 2009; Oor Wullie's Dungarees Book for Boys, 2010; The Times Atlas of Britain, 2010; The Times Atlas of London, 2011; The Art and History of The Dandy (editor), 2012; Royal Canadian Geographical Society Atlas of Canada, 2014; Oxford Guide to Countries of the World, 2016, 2018, 2020; Oxford Dictionary of Contemporary World History, 2016, 2018, 2020; Great Expeditions (Contributor), 2016. Recreations: book collecting; gardening; walking. Address: (h.) Achadhu House, Main Street, Killearn G63 9RJ; T.- 01360 550544; e-mail: christopher@riches-edit.co.uk

Richmond, John Kennedy, JP, DL. Chairman, Glasgow Airport Consultative Committee, 1979-2017; b. 23.4.37, Glasgow; m., Elizabeth Margaret; 1 s.; 1 d. Educ. King's Park Secondary School. Conservative Member, Glasgow Corporation, 1963-75; Member, Glasgow District Council, 1975-84; Deputy Lord Provost, 1977-80; Conservative Group Leader, 1975-77. Recreations: tennis; music; travel. Address: (h.) 32 Lochhead Avenue, Lochwinnoch, Renfrewshire PA12 4AW; T.-01505 843 193. E-mail: richmond32@tiscali.co.uk

Richmond, Lynn, LLB (Hons). Partner, BTO Solicitors LLP, since 2017; b. 1.81. Educ. University of Glasgow; University of Dundee. Career history: Associate, Turcan Connell Group, 2003-2017; Director, Scottish Society for Computers and Law, Edinburgh, 2008-2020; Trustee, National Galleries of Scotland, since 2020. Advises and supports not for profit arts organisations. Address: BTO Solicitors, One Edinburgh Quay, Edinburgh EH3 9QG; T.- 0131 222 2939; e-mail: lyr@bto.co.uk

Rickman, David Edwin, BCom (Hons). Executive Director - Governance and Chief of Staff, The R & A, since 2016; b. 9.10.64, St. Andrews; m., Jennifer Mary Cameron; 3 d. Educ. Madras College, St. Andrews; Edinburgh University. Joined R. & A. staff, 1987; appointed Assistant Secretary (Rules), 1990. Recreations: sport, especially golf and cycling. Address: (b.) c/o The R & A, St. Andrews, Fife KY16 9JD; T.-01334 460000.

Riddell-Webster, Major General Michael Lawrence, CBE, DSO, MSc. Governor of Edinburgh Castle, 2015-19; b. 6.12.60; m., Sarah Maria Clotilde Findlay; 2 s. Educ. Harrow School; Heriot-Watt University; RMA Sandhurst. Commissioned into The Black Watch, 1983. Served in Northern Ireland (awarded the Queen's Commendation for Valuable Service in 2007), Germany, Hong Kong, former Republic of Yugoslavia (awarded the Queen's Commendation for Valuable Service in 2001), Iraq (awarded the Distinguished Service Order in 2003). Commanding Officer, 1st Battalion The Black Watch, 2000-2003; Deputy Director Equipment Capability Ground Manoeuvre, 2003-2005; Commander 39 Infantry Brigade, 2005-2007; Director Army Division, Joint Services Command and Staff College, 2007-08; Head of Capability

(Ground Manoeuvre), 2008-2011; Member at Royal College of Defence Studies, 2011-12; Director, College of Management and Technology, Defence Academy, 2012-14; Student Energy MSc, Heriot Watt University, 2014-15. Member, Queen's Bodyguard of Scotland (Royal Company of Archers).

Riddle, Gordon Stewart, MA. Principal and Chief Ranger, Culzean Country Park, 1976-2001 (Property Manager, Culzean Country Park, 2001-05, Country Park and Conservation Manager, 2004-05); retired; b. 2.10.47, Kelso; m., Rosemary Robb; 1 s.; 1 d. Educ. Kelso High School; Edinburgh University; Moray House College of Education. Biology and History Teacher, Lasswade High School, 1970-71; National Ranger Training Course, 1971-72; Ranger and Depute Principal, Culzean Country Park, 1972-75; National Park Service (USA) Training Course, 1978; Winston Churchill Travelling Fellowship, USA, 1981. Member, Royal Society for the Protection of Birds, Scottish Committee, 1995-99; Chairman, South Strathclyde Raptor Study Group, since 1994. 2005 George Waterstone Memorial Award for services to the National Trust for Scotland; Member, the Scottish Raptor Monitoring Group representing the Scottish Ornithologists' Club; 2010 Donald & Jeff Watson Raptor Award; 2010-2012 Chairman, Ayrshire Branch, Scottish Ornithologists Club. Publications: The Kestrel; Seasons with the Kestrel; Kestrels for Company. Recreations: sport; gardening; birds of prey; photography; hill-walking; music; writing. Address: (h.) Roselea, 5 Maybole Road, Kirkmichael, Ayrshire KA19 7PQ; T.-01655 750335; e-mail: gordon@riddle-kestrel.com; web: www.riddle-kestrel.com

Riddoch, Lesley, BA (Hons). Award-winning broadcaster, journalist and author; columnist for The Scotsman; b. 21.2.60, Wolverhampton; m., Chris Smith May. Educ. High School of Glasgow; Wadham College, Oxford; University College, Cardiff. Sabbatical President, Oxford University Students Union, 1980; Reporter, BBC Radio Scotland, 1985-88; Co-Presenter, Head On, 1988-90; Presenter, Speaking Out, 1990-94; The Scotsman: Assistant Editor, 1994-96, Associate Editor, 1996-97; Speaker, The People's Parliament, Channel 4, 1994-98; Presenter, You and Yours, BBC Radio 4, 1996-98; Presenter, Midnight Hour, BBC2, 1996-98; Presenter, Channel 4's Powerhouse, 1997-98; Presenter, Lesley Riddoch Programme, BBC Radio Scotland, 1999-2005. Founder and Director, Harpies and Quines (feminist magazine); Trustee, Isle of Eigg Trust, since 1993; Founder and Director, Worldwoman. Norman McEwen Award, 1992; Cosmopolitan Woman of the Year (Communications), 1992; Plain English Award, 1993; Sony Broadcaster of the Year, Silver Award, 2000, 2001. Recreations: playing pool; walking.

Ridge, Jacqueline, BSc (Chem). Director of Conservation and Collection Management, National Galleries of Scotland, since 2006. Educ. Northumbria University; Harvard University; King's College London. Career history: Paintings Conservator - Advanced level intern, Harvard University, 1985-86; Paintings Conservator, Worcester Art Museum, USA, 1986-88; Head of Paintings and Frames Conservation: National Museums Liverpool, 1988-96; Tate, London, 1996-2006. Fellow of the International Institute for Conservation; Advisory Council member, Hamilton Kerr Institute, Cambridge University. Address: National Galleries of Scotland, 73 Belford Road, Edinburgh EH4 3DS.

Rifkind, Rt. Hon Sir Malcolm Leslie, KCMG, QC, LLB, MSc. Secretary of State for Foreign and Commonwealth Affairs, 1995-97; Secretary of State for Defence, 1992-95; Secretary of State for Transport, 1990-92; Secretary of State for Scotland, 1986-90; MP (Conservative), Edinburgh Pentlands, 1974-97, Kensington and Chelsea, 2005-2010, Kensington, 2010-2015; director of several companies; b. 21.6.46, Edinburgh; m., Edith Amalia Steinberg (deceased); 1 s.; 1 d. Educ. George Watson's College, Edinburgh; Edinburgh University. Assistant Lecturer, University of Rhodesia, 1967-68; called to Scottish Bar, 1970; Opposition Front-Bench Spokesman on Scottish Affairs, 1975-76; Member, Select Committee on European Secondary Legislation, 1975-76; Chairman, Scottish Conservatives' Devolution Committee, 1976; Chairman, Intelligence and Security Committee, since 2010; Joint Secretary, Conservative Parliamentary Foreign and Commonwealth Affairs Committee, 1977-79; Member, Select Committee on Overseas Development, 1978-79; Parliamentary Under-Secretary of State, Scottish Office, 1979-82; Parliamentary Under-Secretary of State, Foreign and Commonwealth Office, 1982-83; Minister of State, Foreign and Commonwealth Office, 1983-86; Member, Queen's Bodyguard for Scotland (Royal Company of Archers); Member, Commonwealth Eminent Person Group, 2010.

Rintoul, Gordon, CBE, FRSE, BSc, MSc, PhD, AMA. Director, National Museums Scotland, 2002-2020; b. 29.5.55, Glasgow; m., Stephanie; 1 s. Educ. Allan Glen's School, Glasgow; University of Edinburgh; University of Manchester. Curator, Colour Museum, Bradford, 1984-87; Director, Catalyst, The Museum of the Chemical Industry, Widnes, 1987-98; Chief Executive, Sheffield Galleries and Museums Trust, 1998-2002. Member, National Museum Directors Council; Honorary Degree, Doctor of the University (HonDUniv), Napier University; Doctor "honoris causa", University of Edinburgh. Recreations: running; reading; travelling.

Ritchie, Anna, OBE, BA, PhD, FSA, Hon FSA Scot. Freelance archaeologist; b. 28.9.43, London; m., Graham Ritchie; 1 s.; 1 d. Educ. Woking Grammar School for Girls; University of Wales; Edinburgh University. Excavations on Neolithic, Pictish and Viking sites in Orkney; archaeological research and writing; Vice-President, Society of Antiquaries of London, 1988-92; President, Society of Antiquaries of Scotland, 1990-93; Trustee: National Museums of Scotland, 1993-2003, British Museum, 1999-2004. Address: (h.) 11/13 Powderhall Rigg, Edinburgh EH7 4GG; T.-0131 556 1128.

Ritchie, Cameron, LLB. Past President, Law Society of Scotland (2012-2013), Vice President, 2010-2011; Area Procurator Fiscal, Fife, 2002-2010; Procurator Fiscal, Stirling and Alloa, 1996-2002; Solicitor Advocate; b. 25.9.52, Paisley; m., Hazel; 2 s. Educ. John Neilson Institution, Paisley; Glasgow University. Apprentice Solicitor, Wright and Crawford, Paisley, 1972-74; Procurator Fiscal Depute, Ayr, 1974-75, Glasgow, 1975-88; Senior Procurator Fiscal Depute, Hamilton, 1988-93; Assistant Procurator Fiscal, Dundee, 1993-96. Recreations: golf; rugby; watching cricket; military history.

Ritchie, Gordon James Nixon, MVO, DL, LLB. Deputy Lord Lieutenant of Kincardineshire; Honorary Sheriff of Grampian Highland and Islands at Stonehaven, since 2004; Partner, Connons of Stonehaven, Solicitors, 1980-2019 (retired); Clerk to the Lieutenancy of Kincardineshire, since 1996; b. 2.5.52, Aberdeen; m., Isobel; 2 s.; 2 d. Educ. Mackie Academy; Aberdeen University. Founder, Stonehaven Heritage Society; Editor, Stonehaven of Old, Vols. 1 & 2. Trustee, Stonehaven Tolbooth Association; Secretary, Grampian Forest Rally. Recreations: rallying; Hillman Imps; local history; The Beatles. Address: (h.) Brewlaw, Catterline, Stonehaven, Kincardineshire AB39 2TY.

Ritchie, Ian Cleland, CBE, FREng, FRSE, FBCS, CEng, BSc. Chairman: iomart plc, 2008-2018, Tern plc, since 2017, Caspian Learning, 2007-2011, Our Dynamic Earth,

2010-2018; Independent Co-Chair, Scottish Science Advisory Council, 2009-11. Board Director: Scottish Council for Development & Industry (SCDI), since 2018, Digital Bridges Ltd., 2000-07; Director: Scottish Enterprise, 2000-05, Scottish Funding Council, 2002-07; b. 29.6.50, Edinburgh; m., Barbara Allan Cowie (deceased); 1 s.; 1 d. Educ. West Calder High School; Heriot-Watt University. Development Manager, ICL, 1973-82; Founder and CEO, Office Workstations Ltd., Edinburgh and Seattle, 1984-92; Chair: Voxar, 1995-2002, VIS, 1995-2000, Orbital Software PLC, 1995-2001, Active Navigation Ltd., 1997-2003, Interactive University, 2001-2005, Sonaptic Ltd., 2002-06, Connect, 2006-2008, Scapa Ltd., 2006-10; Director: Particle Physics and Astronomy Research Council, 1999-2002, Epic Group PLC, 1999-2005, Sonaptic Ltd., 2003-06, Channel Four Television Corp, 2000-05, Our Dynamic Earth, 2004-2018, GO Group, 2008-2012, Edinburgh International Film Festival, 2002-10, Edinburgh International Science Festival, 2003-18, ShotScope Ltd, since 2017; Chair, Scottish Software Federation, 1988-89; President: British Computer Society, 1998-99; Trustee: Bletchley Park, 2000-2009, SCRAN, 1996-2005, National Museums of Scotland, 2002-10, National Theatre of Scotland, 2014-21, Saltire Foundation, 2009-2017, Nominet Trust, 2008-2014; Member, Scottish Funding Council, 2002-07; Chairman: Red Fox Media Ltd, 2012-15, Blipfoto Ltd, 2012-15, Cogbooks Ltd, 2012-16, Krotos Ltd, since 2015; Vice President (Business), Royal Society of Edinburgh, 2012-16; Honorary Treasurer, Royal Academy of Engineering, 2012-16; Chairman: Computer Application Services, since 2005, Interactive Design Institute, 2007-2016. Recreations: travel; theatre; arts; web browsing. Address: Coppertop, Green Lane, Lasswade EH18 1HE; T.-0131 663 9486; M.-07973 214024.
E-mail: IRitchie@coppertop.co.uk

Ritchie, Ian Kristensen, MB, ChB, FRCPE, FRCS (Ed), FRCS (Glasg), FRACS (Hon), FCSHK (Hon), FAMS (Hon), FCSSL (Hon), FCSI (Hon). Vice Chair, NHS Greater Glasgow & Clyde (part-time), since 2020; retired Consultant Orthopaedic Surgeon, Forth Valley Acute Hospitals Trust (1992-2015); President, The Royal College of Surgeons of Edinburgh, 2012-2015; b. 2.1.53, Annebk, Syria; m., Alyson; 3 d. Educ. Gordon Schools, Huntly; University of Aberdeen. Medical Officer, Royal Navy, 1978-83; surgical and orthopaedic training, Aberdeen Royal Infirmary, 1983-91; Postgraduate Tutor, Stirling Royal Infirmary, 1999-2003. Member, Council, Royal College of Surgeons of Edinburgh, 2000-05, 2006-2010; Lead Clinician, Orthopaedic Dept., Forth Valley, 2007; Vice President, RCSEd, 2009-2012; Her Majesty's Commissioner, The Queen Victoria School, Dunblane, since 2012; Non Executive Member, NHS GG&C, 2016-2020. Recreations: hillwalking; reading. Address: 13 Abercromby Place, Stirling FK8 2QP; T.-07872 585635.
E-mail: ian.ritchie4@btinternet.com

Ritchie, John Douglas, CA. Consultant, Jeffrey Crawford incorporating Barstow and Millar, since 2014; Principal, Barstow and Millar, CA, 2002-2014; b. 9.10.52, Edinburgh; m., Joan Moira. Educ. George Watson's College. Barstow & Millar, CA, 1971-85 (Partner, 1978-85); Partner, Pannell Kerr Forster, 1985-98 (Chairman, Edinburgh office, 1993-97). Member, National Board for Nursing, Midwifery and Health Visiting for Scotland, 1988-93, Hon. Consultant, 1993-97; Partner, Whitelaw Wells, 1998-2002; Member, Board, Viewpoint Housing Association, 1991-2000, and 2002-09; Trustee, Viewpoint Trust, 1991-2008; Trustee, New Lanark Trust, 2008-2018; Director: New Lanark Mill Hotel Ltd, 2008-2018, New Lanark Trading Ltd., 2008-2013; President, Rotary Club of Braids, 1991-92; Member, Morningside Christian Council, 1985-92; Member, Church of Scotland Board of Parish Education, 1994-99; Treasurer, Scottish Churches Open College, 1995-99; Member, Merchant Company of the City of Edinburgh, since 1985, Assistant, Master's Court, 1998-2001; Trustee, Merchant

Company Widows' Fund, 1997-2002; Member, Board of Management, Edinburgh's Telford College, 1998-2001; Trustee, Bequest Fund for Ministers in Outlying Districts of the Church of Scotland, 1994-2017; Director, Association of Independent Accountants in Scotland, 1999-2002 (Chairman, 2001-02); Director, Scottish Love in Action, 2001-2011; Secretary and Treasurer, Douglas Hay Trust, since 2000; Governor, Melville College Trust, 2001-2012; Trustee, The Merchant Company Retirement Benefits Scheme, 2005-2012; Director, Jamaica Education Support, 2005-2012; Treasurer, Challenger Children's Fund, 2006-09; Member, New College Financial Board, since 2007; Trustee, The Nurses Memorial to King Edward VII in Scotland Scottish Committee, since 2012, Chairman, since 2018; Treasurer, Greenbank Parish Church, 2016-2020. Address: (b.) Midlothian Innovation Centre, Pentlandfield, Roslin, Midlothian EH25 9RE.

Ritchie, Karen Joy, BSc. Chief Executive, Midlothian & East Lothian Chamber of Commerce, since 2021; b. 12.79. Educ. Monifieth High School; University of Dundee. Career history: Education Officer, Dundee Science Centre, 2002-04; Operations Manager, Deep See World, North Queensferry, Fife, 2004-09; Bright Green Business: Operations Manager, 2020-21, Chief Executive, since 2021; Bright Green Hydrogen Ltd: Demonstration Centre Manager, 2009-2020, Operations Manager, 2020-21, Chief Executive, since 2021. Address: Midlothian & East Lothian Chamber of Commerce, 24D Milton Road East, Edinburgh EH15 2PP; T.-0131 603 5040.
E-mail: karen@thebusinesspartnership.org.uk

Ritchie, Professor Sir Lewis Duthie, kt (2011), OBE (2001), FRSE, BSc, MSc, MBChB, MD, FRCSE, FRCPEdin, FRCPSGlas, FRCGP, FFPH, FBCS, CEng (Computer Science), CITP, DRCOG, FRSA, MREHIS. James Mackenzie Professor of General Practice, University of Aberdeen, since 1992; Honorary/Visiting Professor of Primary Care and Public Health, University of the Highlands and Islands (UHI), since 2014; Honorary Professor of General Practice, University of Edinburgh, since 2015; b. 26.6.52, Fraserburgh. Educ. Fraserburgh Academy; University of Aberdeen; University of Edinburgh. General practitioner vocational training, 1979-82; public health medicine vocational training, 1982-87; Lecturer in General Practice, University of Aberdeen, 1984-92; Consultant/Honorary Consultant in Public Health Medicine, NHS Grampian, 1987-2012 and since 2014; Principal General Practitioner, Peterhead Health Centre and Community Hospital, 1984-2012; Director of Public Health, NHS Grampian, 2012-14. Chair/member of a number of national governmental advisory committees; former chair, Scottish Medical and Scientific Advisory Committee (SMASAC) and Biomedical and Therapeutics Research Committee (BTRC), Scottish Government; Chair, Independent Review of Primary Care Out of Hours Services in Scotland, 2015; Chair, Queen's Nursing Institute Scotland (QNIS), 2015-2021; Chair, Scottish Health Protection Network Oversight Group, since 2016; Chair, Advisory Board: Advanced Care Research Centre, University of Edinburgh, since 2021; Co-investigator, EAVE II Study examining the safety, effectiveness of the Covid-19 vaccination programme, the potential impacts and remedies of Covid-19 treatments, since 2020. Scottish Government advisor on primary care and public health responses to the Covid-19 Pandemic. Publications: 200 cumulative total. Book: Computers in Primary Care; Reports: Community Hospitals in Scotland: Promoting Progress; Developing Primary Care in Scotland; Meningococcal C Immunisation Programme in Scotland; Promoting Professionalism and Excellence in Scottish Medicine; Securing the Future of GP Academic Careers in Scotland; Improving the Seasonal Influenza Vaccination Programme in Scotland; Community Pharmacy:

Establishing Effective Therapeutic Partnerships; Pulling Together: Transforming Urgent Care for the People of Scotland; Independent Review, Staging Report and sequalae updates on the Finances of NHS Tayside; Promoting the National Resilience of NHS and Social Care Services over Public Holiday Periods; Independent Review and Report of Primary Care Out-of-Hours Services in Skye, Lochalsh and South West Ross; Independent Review and Report of Primary Care Out of Hours Services in NHS Greater Glasgow and Clyde; Shaping the Future Together - Report of the National Remote and Rural General Practice Working Group. Chair: Rapid External Review and Report - NHS Ayrshire and Arran Redesign of Urgent Care Pathfinder Programme; Co-Chair (with Professor Derek Bell OBE), Staging Reports Evaluation of Redesign of Urgent Care in Scotland; Chair, Scottish Inter-Collegiate Guidelines Network (SIGN) Guidelines on the Prevention, Management and Rehabilitation of Cardiovascular Disease (SIGN 40, SIGN 93-98, SIGN 148-152). Papers on computers, cardiovascular disease, cancer, community hospitals, community pharmacy and immunisation. Awards: John Perry Prize, British Computer Society, 1991; Ian Stokoe Award, Royal College of General Practitioners UK, 1992; Blackwell Prize, University of Aberdeen, 1995; Richard Scott Lecture, 2007, University of Edinburgh; Eric Elder Medal, Royal New Zealand College of General Practitioners, 2007; Provost Medal, Royal College of General Practitioners North East Scotland Faculty, 2010; James Mackenzie Lecture and Medal, Royal College of General Practitioners UK, 2010; Stock Memorial Lecture, Association of Port Health Authorities, 2012; Fulton Lecture, Royal College of General Practitioners, West of Scotland Faculty, 2012; DARE Lecture, Faculty of Public Health UK, 2014; Hon Fellowship, Royal College and Physicians and Surgeons of Glasgow, 2015; Fellowship of the Royal Society of Edinburgh, 2016; Fellowship of the Royal College of Surgeons of Edinburgh ad hominem, 2016. President: Harveian Society of Edinburgh, 2018-19. Recreations: church; dog walking; jogging; classical music; art appreciation; military/naval history; RNLI/civilian gallantry. Address: (h.) 33 Queen Street, Edinburgh EH2 1JX; T.-0131 2261992; e-mail: l.d.ritchie@abdn.ac.uk

Ritchie, Murray. Scottish Political Editor, The Herald, 1997-2004; b. 5.9.41, Dumfries; m.; 1 s.; 2 d. Educ. High School of Glasgow. Scottish Farmer, 1958-60; Dumfries and Galloway Standard, 1960-65; Scottish Daily Record, 1965-67; East African Standard, 1967-71; joined Glasgow Herald, 1971. Journalist of the Year, Fraser Press Awards, 1980. Publication: Scotland Reclaimed, 2000.

Ritchie, Sheila. Member of the European Parliament for Scotland (Scottish Liberal Democrat), 2019-2020; consultant (formerly partner) at an Aberdeen law firm; formerly the leader of Gordon District Council. Spent over 20 years supporting small start-up businesses and entrepreneurs in the Aberdeen area through her work with the Enterprise Trust, Business Gateway and Elevator; also served as a Scottish Government appointee (2000-03) on the European Economic and Social Committee, which involved bi-monthly trips to Brussels for consultation.

Roads, Elizabeth Ann, LVO, OStJ, FSA, FSA Scot, FHSS, FRHSC, FHSNZ, FHS, AIH, LLB. Lyon Clerk and Keeper of the Records, 1986-2018; Snawdoun Herald of Arms, 2010-2021; Carrick Pursuivant of Arms, 1992-2010; Secretary of the Order of the Thistle, since 2014; b. 5.7.51; m., Christopher George William Roads TD; 1 d. Educ. Lansdowne House School, Edinburgh; Cambridge College of Technology; Study Centre for Fine Art, London; Edinburgh Napier University. Christie's, Art Auctioneers, 1971-74; Court of the Lord Lyon, since 1975; temporarily Linlithgow Pursuivant Extraordinary, 1987; Vice President,

Heraldry Society of Scotland; Trustee and Vice Chair, Scottish Council on Archives; President, Bureau Permanent des Congrès International de Généalogique et d'Héraldique; Dean of Guild, Merchant Guildry of Stirling. Recreations: history; heraldry; genealogy; reading; countryside activities. Address: Duchray, Aberfoyle, Stirlingshire FK8 3XL.

Robb, David, MA Hons (Oxon). Chief Executive Officer, The Scottish Public Pensions Agency (SPPA), since 2021; Chief Executive Officer, Student Awards Agency for Scotland (SAAS), 2019-2021. Educ. Speyside High School; University of Oxford. Career history: The Scottish Government: Head of Public Service Reform and Efficiency, 2010-11, Deputy Director, Digital Public Services and Business Transformation, 2016-17; Chief Executive, Office of the Scottish Charity Regulator, 2011-19. Address: (b.) The Scottish Public Pensions Agency, 7 Tweedside Park, Tweedbank, Galashiels TD1 3TE.

Roberton, Esther A., BA. Non Executive Director, Scotland's Futures Forum, since 2021; Chair, Fife Cultural Trust (OnFife), since 2021; Interim Chair, NHS Lothian, 2020-21; Chair, NHS 24, 2015-19; Senior Governor, University of Aberdeen, 2019-2020; Non Executive Director: Scottish Government, 2014-17, Scottish Ambulance Service, 2014-18; b. 24.6.56, Kirkcaldy; m., William J. Roberton; 2 s. Educ. Buckhaven High School; Edinburgh University. Played a leading role in the campaign to secure and shape Scotland's Parliament, 1994-99; Chair, NHS Fife, 2000-04; Chair, Scottish Further Education Funding Council, 1999-2005; Member, Press Complaints Commission, 2007-2014; Chair, Sacro, 2010-2014. E-mail: esther@roberton.uk.com

Roberts, Professor Bernard, BSc, PhD, FRAS, FRSE. Professor of Solar Magnetohydrodynamics, since 1994; Emeritus Professor, since 2010; b. 19.2.46, Cork; m., Margaret Patricia Cartlidge; 4 s. Educ. Bletchley Secondary Modern and Bletchley Grammar Schools; Hull University; Sheffield University. Lecturer in Applied Mathematics, St. Andrews University, 1971-87, Reader, 1987-94. Chairman, UK Solar Physics Community, 1992-98; Member, Theory Research Assessment Panel, UK Particle Physics and Astronomy Research Council, 1998-2001, Member, Solar System Science Advisory Panel, 2001-03. Saltire Science Award (Saltire Society), 1997; Chapman Medal of the Royal Astronomical Society, 2010. Recreation: hill-walking. Address: (b.) Mathematical Institute, St. Andrews University, St. Andrews KY16 9SS; T.-01334 871494.

Roberts, Dawn. Chief Executive, Dumfries and Galloway Council, since 2022. Career history: various research and policy management roles, Rotherham Metropolitan Borough Council, 1996-2005; Head of Strategy and Partnerships, Hull City Council, 2005-09; Cumbria County Council: Assistant Director, Policy and Performance, 2009-2013, Assistant Director, Corporate Governance (Monitoring Officer), 2013-16, Corporate Director, Resources and Transformation, 2016-18, Executive Director of Corporate, Customer and Community Services, 2018-2022. Address: Council HQ, English Street, Dumfries DG1 2DD; T.-030 33 33 3000.

Roberts, James Graeme, MA Hons (1964), PhD (1971), FRSA: b. 7.11.42, Glasgow; m. Elizabeth Watson Milo Tucker; 2 s. 3 d. Educ. Hutchesons' Boys' Grammar School, Glasgow, St. Andrews University and Aberdeen University. Aberdeen University: Assistant Lecturer in English, 1965; Lecturer in English, 1968; Senior Lecturer, 1985; Head, Department of English, 1993-1996; Dean of Arts and Divinity and Vice Principal, 1996-2001; Vice Principal

(Teaching and Learning), 2001-05; Professor Emeritus (2005). University Senate, 1978-89, 1993-2005 and University Court, 1981-89, 1995-2005. Senior Associate, Higher Education Academy, 2006-2010; Bologna Promoter/Expert, 2005-11. Chair, Aberdeen Performing Arts, 2002-2014; Chair, Scottish Museums Council, 2001-07; Convener, Church of Scotland Committee on Church Art and Architecture (2012-16); Convener, Aberdeen Presbytery Business and Finance Committee, 2017-20; Assembly Business Committee, since 2018; Elder, Ferryhill Parish Church, Aberdeen, 1976. Recreations: reading; gardening; music. Address: (h.) 17 Devanha Gardens, Aberdeen AB11 7UU; T.-01224 582217. E-mail: j.g.roberts@abdn.ac.uk

Roberts, Rev. Maurice Jonathon, BA, BD. Minister: Ayr Free Church of Scotland, 1974-94, Inverness Greyfriars Free Church of Scotland, 1994-99, Inverness (Westhill) Free Church of Scotland (Continuing), 2000-2010 (retired since 2011); Editor, The Banner of Truth, 1988-2003; Lecturer in Greek and New Testament, Free Church Seminary, Inverness, 2003-2012; b. 8.3.38, Timperley; m., Alexandra Macleod; 1 d. Educ. Lymm Grammar School; Durham University; London University; Free Church College, Edinburgh. Schoolteacher. Publications: The Thought of God; Sanctification and Glorification; In Deep Valley of Truth (Korean language); The Christian's High Calling; Great God of Wonders; Can We Know God?; Union and Communion with Christ; The Happiness of Heaven; The Mysteries of God; Finding Peace with God; What Does it Mean to Love God?; Heavenly Mindedness and Spiritual Conversation; Simplified Confession of Faith (free e-book available on mauriceroberts.org); Simplified Shorter Catechism (also available as a free e-book on mauriceroberts.org); The Larger Catechism Simplified (3rd free e-book, available on mauriceroberts.org); The Great Transformation. Recreations: reading; walking. Address: 5 Muirfield Park, Inverness IV2 4HA.

Roberts, Ralph M. H., BSc. Chief Executive: NHS Borders, since 2019, NHS Shetland, 2011-19; b. 1.9.64, Canterbury; m., Mhairi Mackinnon; 3 d. Educ. The King's School, Canterbury; Oxford Polytechnic. Volunteer Teacher, Kenya, 1982-83; Local Government Officer, 1987-89; NHS Management Trainee, 1989-91; NHS Manager, NHS Lothian and NHS Borders, 1991-2000; NHS Director, NHS Borders, 2000-2010. Recreations: theatre; music; golf; football; rugby. Address: (b.) NHS Borders, Headquarters, Borders General Hospital, Melrose, Roxburghshire TD6 9BS; T.-01896 826000.

Robertson of Port Ellen, Rt. Hon. Lord (George Islay MacNeill Robertson), KT, GCMG, HonFRSE, FRSA, MA, PC. Deputy Chairman, TNK-BP, 2006-2013; Secretary-General, NATO, 1999-2003; b. 12.4.46, Port Ellen, Islay; m., Sandra Wallace; 2 s.; 1 d. Educ. Dunoon Grammar School; Dundee University. Tayside Study Economics Group, 1968-69; Scottish Organiser, General, Municipal, Boilermakers Union, 1969-78; Chairman, Scottish Labour Party, 1977-78; Member, Scottish Executive, Labour Party, 1973-79, 1993-97; MP, Hamilton, 1978-97, Hamilton South, 1997-99; PPS to Secretary of State for Social Services, 1979; Opposition Spokesman on Scottish Affairs, 1979-80, on Defence, 1980-81, on Foreign and Commonwealth Affairs, 1981-93, on Scottish Affairs, 1993-97; Principal Spokesman on Europe, 1984-93; Member, Shadow Cabinet, 1993-97; Shadow Scottish Secretary, 1993-97; Secretary of State for Defence, 1997-99. Member of Board, Scottish Development Agency, 1976-78; Board of Governors, Scottish Police College, 1975-78; Vice Chairman, British Council, 1985-93; President, Royal Institute of International Affairs, 2001-2011; Elder Brother, Trinity House, since 2002. Chairman,

John Smith Memorial Trust, 2004-08; Chancellor, Order of St Michael and St George, since 2011; Board, Western Ferries (Clyde), since 2006, Chairman, since 2019; Board, Weir Group plc, 2004-2015; Adviser, The Cohen Group (USA), since 2004; Chairman, Ditchley Foundation, 2009-2017; Chairman, FIA Foundation, since 2015. Hon LLD (Dundee), 2000; Hon DSc (Cranfield), 2000; Hon LLD (Bradford), 2000; Hon LLD (St Andrews); DUniv (Paisley), 2006; Hon Doct (Baku State University, Azerbaijan), 2001; Hon. Regt. Colonel, London Scottish Regiment, 2000-2017; Hon. FRSE, 2003; GCMG (2004); KT (2004); LRPS (2009); US Presidential Medal of Freedom, 2003; Patron, Glasgow Islay Association, since 2003; Honorary Professor, Stirling University, since 2006; Visiting Professor, King's College, London, since 2018. Publication: 'Islay and Jura - Photographs', Birlinn, 2006. Recreations: family; photography; golf. Address: (b.) House of Lords, London SW1A 0PW.

Robertson, Professor A. G. Boyd, MA, Hon DEd, FRSE, FASLS. Chair, NHS Highland Board, since 2019; former Principal of Sabhal Mòr Ostaig, Isle of Skye (2009-2018); b. 14.06.49, Lennoxtown; m., Sheila Finlayson; 3 s. Educ. Paible Secondary, North Uist; Portree High, Skye; Aberdeen University; Aberdeen College of Education. Career History: Teacher of Gaelic, then Principal Teacher of Gaelic, Oban High School; Lecturer, Jordanhill College of Education; University of Strathclyde: Senior Lecturer in Gaelic, Reader in Gaelic and Head of Language Education. Honorary Doctor of Education, University of Edinburgh, 2014; Fellow of the Association of Scottish Literary Studies (ASLS), 2012. Publications: Ty Complete Gaelic (Co-Author); Ty Essential Gaelic Dictionary (Co-Author); Ty Speak Gaelic with Confidence (Co-Author). Recreations: photography; fishing; reading; walking. Address: Ashtree House, Ferindonald, Sleat, Isle of Skye IV44 8RF; T.-01471 844394.
E-mail: boydrobertson@hotmail.co.uk

Robertson, Professor Alastair Harry Forbes, BS, MA, PhD, FRSE. Professor of Geology, Edinburgh University, since 1996; b. 6.12.49, Edinburgh; m., Gillian Mary Robertson; 1 s.; 1 d. Educ. Edinburgh Academy; Edinburgh University; Leicester University. Demonstrator, Cambridge University, 1974-76; Lecturer in Oceanography, Edinburgh University. 1977-85; Academic Visitor, Stanford University. USA, 1985- 86; Reader, Geology and the International Ocean Discovery Program, Edinburgh University, 1986-96. Publications: numerous scientific papers and edited volumes mainly concerning the geology of the Eastern Mediterranean region. Recreations: outdoor activities; mountain walking; travel; music. Address: (b.) Grant Institute, James Hutton Road, Edinburgh EH9 3FL.
E-mail: alastair.robertson@ed.ac.uk

Robertson, Andrew Ogilvie, OBE, LLB. Glasgow's Carers' Champion, since 2015; former Chairman, Greater Glasgow and Clyde NHS Board; Partner, T.C. Young, Solicitors, 1968-2006; Secretary, Erskine Hospital, 1976-2002, Vice Chairman, 2006-2011, Chairman, 2011; Secretary, Princess Royal Trust for Carers, 1990-2006, Trustee, 2006-2012; Carers Trust, Vice Chairman, 2012; Chairman, Lintel Trust (formerly Scottish Housing Association Charitable Trust), 1991-2007; Director, Scottish Building Society, 1994-2008, Chairman, 2003-06; Chairman, Greater Glasgow Primary Care NHS Trust, 1999-2004; Vice Chairman, Greater Glasgow and Clyde NHS Board, 2004-07; Governor, Sedbergh School, 2000-08; Trustee, Music in Hospitals, since 2007; Trustee, Scotcash, 2007-2011 (Chairman, 2009); Director, Special Olympics, National Summer Games Glasgow 2005 Ltd.; b.

30.6.43, Glasgow; m., Sheila Sturton; 2 s. Educ. Glasgow Academy; Sedbergh School; Edinburgh University. Director, Merchants House of Glasgow, 1978-2006; Secretary, Clydeside Federation of Community Based Housing Associations, 1978-93; Secretary, The Briggait Company Ltd., 1982-88; Director, Glasgow Chamber of Commerce, 1982-93; Chairman, Post Office Users Council for Scotland, 1988-99; Chairman, Greater Glasgow Community and Mental Health Services NHS Trust, 1994-97; Chairman, Glasgow Royal Infirmary University NHS Trust, 1997-99. Recreations: climbing; swimming; sailing; fishing.

Robertson, Angus Struan Carolus, MSP (SNP), Edinburgh Central, since 2021; Cabinet Secretary for the Constitution, External Affairs and Culture, since 2021; MP (SNP), Moray, 2001-2017; former SNP Group Leader in Westminster; b. 28.9.69, London; m.; 2 c. Educ. Broughton High School; University of Aberdeen. News Editor, Austrian Broadcasting Corporation, 1991-99; Reporter, BBC Austria, 1992-99; Contributor: National Public Radio, USA, Radio Telefis Eireann, Ireland, Deutsche Welle, Germany; Consultant, Communication Skills International, 1994-2001. Member, Privy Council. Recreations: sport (football, rugby, skiing, playing golf badly); films; travel; music; books; history; socialising. Address: The Scottish Parliament, Edinburgh EH99 1SP; T.-0131 348 5125.
E-mail: Angus.Robertson.msp@parliament.scot

Robertson, Bruce. Rector, Berwickshire High School, since 2020. Career history: Scottish Borders Council: Deputy Headteacher (Teaching & Learning), Eyemouth High School, 2012-19; Quality Improvement Officer, 2019-2020. Author of The Teaching Delusion trilogy; contributor, Times Educational Supplement. Address: Berwickshire High School, Langtongate, Duns, Berwickshire TD11 3QG; T.-01361 883710.

Robertson, Bryan, BSc, MRICS, MBA. Chief Operating Officer, National Galleries of Scotland, since 2018; b. 4.64. Educ. University of Abertay Dundee; University of Edinburgh Business School. Career history: Associate Director, various private consultancies, 1986-94; Head of the Programme Office, Motorola, 1994-2001; Head of Global Programme Management Office, Damovo, 2001-03; Head of Business Transformation, RBS, 2003-06; Direct Line Group: Director, Business Transformation, 2006-09, Director, Lean Transformation, 2009-2012; Chief Operating Officer, Lomond Capital, 2013-15; Chief Executive, Lomond Mortgage Services, 2014-16; Chief Operating Officer, Lomond Investment Management, 2015-18; Strategy Consultant, NHS Tayside, 2018-2020; Director, Business Transformation, Dakota Transformation, 2018-2021; Trustee, National Galleries of Scotland Foundation, since 2019. Address: Princes Exchange, 1 Earl Grey Street, Edinburgh EH3 9EE.

Robertson, Professor David, BSc, PhD. Head of College of Science and Engineering, The University of Edinburgh, since 2017, Professor, since 2008, Dean, 2014-17, Chair of Applied Logic. Educ. The University of Edinburgh; Universitat Autònoma de Barcelona. Career: Director of the Centre for Intelligent Systems and their Applications, University of Edinburgh, 2002-2009, Head of School of Informatics, 2009-2014. Fellow of the British Computing Society and chaired the executive of the UK Computing Research Committee (the expert panel of BCS and IET). Member: EIT Digital Supervisory Board, EPSRC Strategic Advisory Team for ICT, MRC Population Health Sciences advisory group, management board for the Scottish Innovation Centre in

Data Science; on the Industry Advisory Board for Innovate UK's Complex Systems programme; co-director of the Edinburgh node of Health Data Research UK. Address: University of Edinburgh, College of Science and Engineering, Murchison House, The King's Buildings, Max Born Crescent, Edinburgh EH9 3BF; T.-0131 650 5754; e-mail: D.Robertson@ed.ac.uk

Robertson, Cllr Dennis. MSP (SNP), Aberdeenshire West, 2011-16; Councillor, Aberdeenshire Council (Stonehaven and lower Deeside ward), since 2017; b. 14.8.56, Aberdeen; m., Anne. Educ. Royal Blind School, Edinburgh; Langside College. Registered blind at the age of 11. Qualified in social work and has worked in both the statutory and voluntary sectors. Address: c/o Woodhill House, Westburn Road, Aberdeen AB16 5GB; T.-07919 557152; e-mail: cllr.d.robertson@aberdeenshire.gov.uk

Robertson, Rev Douglas, BA (Christian Studies). Minister, Crown Church of Scotland, since 2020. Educ. University of Aberdeen. Parish Minister, Church of Scotland, Appin, North Argyll, 1995-2001; Senior Minister, The Scots' Church, Melbourne, Australia, 2001-2020. Address: Kingsmills Road, Inverness, Highland IV2 3JT; T.-01463 231140; e-mail: drobertson@churchofscotland.org.uk

Robertson, Professor Edmund Frederick, BSc, MSc, PhD, FRSE. Professor Emeritus of Mathematics, St. Andrews University, since 2008; b. 1.6.43, St. Andrews; m., Helena Francesca; 2 s. Educ. Madras College, St. Andrews; St. Andrews University; Warwick University. Lecturer in Pure Mathematics, Senior Lecturer, then Professor of Mathematics, 1968-2008, St. Andrews University. Vice Chairman, Chairman, then Vice Chairman, since 1986, Madras College Endowment Trust; Member, Scottish Mathematical Council, 1997-2004; EPSRC Peer Review College, 1997-2010; Governor, Morrison's Academy, 1999-2006; Chairman, GAP Council, 2003-2009; Chairman, British Mathematical Colloquium Scientific Committee, 2005-2008. Partnership Award, 1992; European Academic Software Award, 1994; American Computational Engineering and Science Award, 1995; Scientific American web site award, 2002; MERLOT award, 2002; "Signum Pro Scientia Absoluta Vera" award, 2008; Comenius Medal, Societas Comeniana Hungarica, 2012; London Mathematical Society Hirst Prize and Lectureship, 2015. Publications: 26 books; 150 papers. Recreations: history of mathematics; computers; family. Address: (b.) Mathematical Institute, North Haugh, St. Andrews KY16 9SS; T.-01334 463702.

Robertson, Fiona. Chief Executive, Scottish Qualifications Authority, since 2019; previously Director of Learning, Scottish Government, 2013-19; led the work within the Scottish Government on school education which included a wide range of issues, from the development and delivery of Curriculum for Excellence, the Scottish Attainment Challenge, to the National Improvement Framework for Education and Education Reform. Address: Scottish Qualifications Authority, The Optima Building, 58 Robertson Street, Glasgow G2 8DQ; T.-0345 279 1000.

Robertson, Iain Alasdair, CBE, LLB; b. 30.10.49, Perth; m., Judith Helen Stevenson; 2 s.; 1 d. Educ. Perth Academy; Aberdeen University. Qualified as a Solicitor, 1973; service at home and abroad with British Petroleum, 1975-90, latterly as BP America's Director of Acquisitions; Chief Executive, Highlands and Islands Enterprise, 1990-2000. Board Member, Scottish Tourist Board, 1993-95; Board Member, Locate in Scotland Supervisory Board, 1992-2000; Board Member, Cairngorm Partnership, 1998-2000; Director, Quality Scotland, 1999-2000; Director, Development and Strategy, AWG plc, 2000-03; Member, Accounts Commission, 2003-2010; Independent Member, BIS Legal Services Group Board, 2004-2011; Independent Member, HMRC Solicitor's Office Strategic Management Group, 2009-2013; Chairman: Keep Scotland Beautiful, 2012-16, Scottish Legal Aid Board, 2006-2016, Coal Liabilities Strategy Board, 2006-2018. Recreations: skiing; music.

Robertson, Ian. Director of Ceremonies, the Most Venerable Order of the Hospital of St John of Jerusalem in Scotland, since 2022. Fellow of the Chartered Institute of Personnel and Development; volunteer in many St John Scotland roles, including area secretary, fundraising chair and area chair; currently serves at a national level as a Board member of St John Scotland supporting the life saving work of the charity. Address: St John Scotland, 21 St John Street, Edinburgh EH8 8DG.

Robertson, James, PhD. Writer; runs an independent publishing company, Kettillonia, and is a co-founder and general editor of the Scots language imprint Itchy Coo, which produces books in Scots for children and young people; b. 1958. Educ. Glenalmond College; Edinburgh University; University of Pennsylvania in Philadelphia. Worked in a variety of jobs after leaving university, mainly in the book trade; a publisher's sales rep and later worked for Waterstone's Booksellers, first as a bookseller in Edinburgh and later as assistant manager of the Glasgow branch; first writer in residence at Hugh MacDiarmid's house outside Biggar, Lanarkshire, 1993-95. Author of several short story and poetry collections, and has published seven novels: The Fanatic, 2000; Joseph Knight, 2003; The Testament of Gideon Mack, 2006; And the Land Lay Still, 2010; The Professor of Truth, 2013; To Be Continued, 2016; and News of the Dead, 2021. Address: (b.) c/o Rogers, Coleridge & White Ltd, 20 Powis Mews, London W11 1JN.

Robertson, James Roy, LVO, MBE, BSc, MBChB, FRCGP, FRCP, FRSE, MFPH (Hon). Principal, General Practice, Muirhouse Medical Group, since 1980; Professor, School of Clinical Sciences, University of Edinburgh; Apothecary to the Queen at the Palace of Holyroodhouse; b. 15.3.51, Edinburgh; m., Elizabeth; 3 s. Educ. Merchiston Castle School, Edinburgh; University of Edinburgh. Chairman and Member, various national governmental committees and working parties on drug abuse issues, HIV and AIDS and alcohol problems; author of papers on these subjects. Publication: Management of Drug Users in the Community (Editor), 1998. Recreations: outdoor activities; travel; family. Address: Molecular, Genetic and Population Health Sciences, University of Edinburgh, Medical School, Teviot Place, Edinburgh EH8 9AG.
E-mail: roy.robertson@ed.ac.uk

Robertson, John. MP (Labour), Glasgow North West, 2005-2015, Glasgow Anniesland, 2000-05; PPS to Secretary of State for Work and Pensions, Yvette Cooper, 2009-2010; PPS to Treasury Secretary, Yvette Cooper, 2008-09; b. 17.4.52, Glasgow; m.; 3 c. Educ. Stow College, Glasgow. Before entering Parliament, worked for 31 years with BT as telephone engineer and local customer manager.

Robertson, John Graeme, CBiol, FRSB, FCMI, FLS, FRGS, FRSA. Director, Global Islands Network, since 2002; b. 15.8.54, Edinburgh; m., Anne Christie; 1 s.; 1 d. Educ. Scotus Academy, Edinburgh. Career History: Co-ordinator, Edinburgh Environment Centre; Director, Friends of the Earth Scotland; Director, Habitat Scotland; Manager, Scottish Islands Network; Editor, Islander Magazine; Chief Executive, Island Web Consortium. Secretary, International Small Islands Studies Association; Editorial Board Member, Island Studies Journal; Chairman, Small Islands Film Trust. Churchill Fellow, 1996; English Speaking

Union William Thyne Scholar, 1999; Honorary Research Fellow, Scottish Centre for Island Studies, University of the West of Scotland, 2009-2012; Research Associate, Institute of Island Studies, University of Prince Edward Island, Canada, 2015-2025. Recreations: birding; exercising dogs; fishing; philately of the Falkland Islands & Tristan da Cunha; travel to islands worldwide. Address: Struan House, Knockintorran, North Uist, Western Isles HS6 5ED; e-mail: graeme@globalislands.net

Robertson, Judith. Chair, Scottish Human Rights Commission, 2016-2022. Long-standing involvement in social justice campaigning and advocating for the rights of many disadvantaged groups; 17 year career with Oxfam as both Programme Manager for Oxfam's Poverty Programme in Scotland (8 years) and as Head of Oxfam Scotland (9 years); previously Programme Director of See Me.

Robertson, Malcolm George Wallace. Founding Partner, Charlotte Street Partners, since 2013; b. 12.72. Educ. Dunblane High School. Career history: HR, Diageo, 1990-96; Account Manager, Beattie Media, 1996-99; BAA: Head of Public Affairs, 1999-2005, Director of Communications, 2005-07, Deputy Communications Director, 2007-2010, Director of Communications, 2010-2011; Non Executive Director, Scottish Golf, 2015-2018; Managing Director, Ramoyle Investments Limited, 2011-2019; Chair, Street Soccer Scotland, since 2021. Address: Charlotte Street Partners, 13 Rutland Street, Edinburgh EH1 2AE. E-mail: Malcolm@charlottestpartners.co.uk

Robertson, Professor Pamela, BA (Hons), FRSA, FRSE. Professor Emerita of Mackintosh Studies and Honorary Professorial Research Fellow, Glasgow University. Educ. St George's School for Girls, Edinburgh; University College, London. Member, Historic Buildings Council for Scotland, 1998-2002; Chair, C.R. Mackintosh Society, 2003-06; Member, Reviewing Committee for the Export of Works of Art, 2003-2010; Governor, Glasgow School of Art, 2006-2010; Advisory Panel, Willow Tea Rooms Trust, 2015-18; Honorary Vice President, C.R. Mackintosh Society, since 2018; winner, Iris Foundation Award for outstanding contributions to the decorative arts, Bard University, New York, 1997. Publications include: C.R. Mackintosh: the architectural papers, 1990; C.R. Mackintosh: Art is the Flower, 1994; The Chronycle, 2001; Doves and Dreams: The Art of Frances Macdonald and J. Herbert McNair, 2006; Mackintosh Architecture: Context, Making and Meaning (www.mackintosh-architecture.gla.ac.uk), 2014. Recreations: good food; good wine; good company; tennis. Address: (b.) Hunterian Art Gallery, Glasgow University, Glasgow G12 8QQ. E-mail: pamela.robertson@glasgow.ac.uk

Robertson, Raymond Scott, MA. Director of Public Affairs, Halogen Communications, since 2002; Chairman, Scottish Conservative and Unionist Party, 1997-2001; b. 11.12.59, Hamilton. Educ. Garrion Academy, Wishaw; University of Glasgow; Jordanhill College of Education. Teacher of History and Modern Studies; MP, Aberdeen South, 1992-97; PPS, Northern Ireland Office, 1993-95; Minister for Education, Housing, Fisheries and Sport, Scottish Office, 1995-97. Recreations: watching football; reading; travelling.

Robertson, William, DipLP, LLB (Hons). Head of Corporate and Commercial, Burnett & Reid LLP, since 2008; b. 7.81. Educ. University of Aberdeen; CLT Scotland. Career history: Trainee Solicitor, Alexander George & Co, Aberdeenshire, 2004-06; Associate Solicitor, MacRae Stephen & Co, Aberdeenshire, 2006-08; Legal Director, SparkOut Sports Limited, 2015-17. Trustee/Senior Pastor, Grace Church Family, since 2019. Address: Burnett & Reid, Suite A, Ground Floor, 9 Queens Road, Aberdeen AB15 4YL; T.-01224 655016.
E-mail: william.robertson@burnett-reid.co.uk

Robertson, William Nelson, CBE, MA, FCII. Member, Advisory Board, Scottish Amicable, 1997-2003; b. 14.12.33, Berwick upon Tweed; m., Sheila Catherine; 2 d. Educ. Berwick Grammar School; Edinburgh University. Joined General Accident, 1958: Deputy Chief General Manager, 1989-90, Group Chief Executive, 1990-95, Director, 1984-95. Board Member, Association of British Insurers, 1991-95; Director: Morrison Construction, 1995-2001, Scottish Community Foundation, 1996-99, Edinburgh New Tiger Investment Trust, 1996-2001, Alliance Trust, 1996-2002, Second Alliance Trust, 1996-2002. Member, Court, University of Abertay, Dundee, 1996-99. Recreations: hill-walking; gardening.

Robins, John F. Secretary and Campaigns Consultant, Animal Concern, 1988-2021; Managing Director, Ethical Promotions Ltd., since 1988; Secretary, Save Our Seals Fund, 1996-2019; Secretary, Animal Concern Advice Line, since 2001; b. 2.1.57, Glasgow; m., Mary E.; 1 s.; 1 d. (deceased). Educ. St. Ninian's High School. Co-ordinator, Glasgow Energy Group, 1978-80; Company Secretary, Scottish Anti-Vivisection Society, since 1981; Ecology Party activist and candidate, 1978-81; Delegate, Anti-Nuclear Campaign, 1978-81; Vice-Chair, Friends of the Earth (Scotland) Ltd., 1981-82; Co-ordinator, Scottish Animal Rights Network, 1983-91; Founder and Co-ordinator, Save Scotland's Seals Fund, 1988-96. Recreation: catching up on lost sleep. Address: (b.) P.O. Box 5178, Dumbarton G82 5YJ; T.-01389 841111; e-mail: animals@jfrobins.force9.co.uk

Robinson, Claire. Manager/Director, Cairn Mhor Childcare Partnership, since 2009. Educ. Northern College Dundee. Career history: Generic Social Worker, Buckinghamshire County Council, 1989-90; Social Worker, 1990-94; Starley Hall School Limited: Senior Social Worker, 1994-97, Deputy Principal, 1997-2002; Inspection Officer, Care Inspectorate, 2002-03; External Manager, Forth Craig Residential Child Care, since 2016; Chief Executive Director, Cairn Mhor Childcare Partnership, 2003-2015. Address: Cairn Mhor Childcare Partnership, Airlie House, Pentland Park, Saltire Centre, Glenrothes KY6 2AG; T.-01592 631031.

Robinson, Gary. Chairman, NHS Shetland, since 2018. Educ. Scalloway Junior High School; Anderson High School. Career history: Financial Consultant, Pearl, 1992-96; Service Manager, Shetland Office Supplies, 1996-2002; Advisory Board Member, Shetland Oil Terminal Environmental Advisory, 2007-2012; Trustee, Shetland Charitable Trust, 2005-2012; Chairman of the Board of Directors, Shetland Heat Energy and Power Ltd, 2007-2013; Duty Officer, Shetland Recreational Trust, 2002-2014; Commissioner, Shetland Tackling Inequalities Commission, 2015-16; Council Leader, Shetland Islands Council, 2012-17; Director, Sullom Voe Association Ltd, 2012-17; Committee Member, European Committee of the Regions, 2015-17; Member of the Board, Lerwick Port Authority, since 2013. Local Politician of the Year 2013. Address: NHS Shetland Board Headquarters, Upper Floor Montfield, Burgh Road, Lerwick, Shetland ZE1 0LA; T.-01595 743060.

Robinson, Mike, BA (Hons). Chief Executive, Royal Scottish Geographical Society (RSGS), since 2008; m.; 3 s. Educ. University of Stirling. Co-Chair, Farming for 1.5C Independent Inquiry, since 2019; Board Member, Stop Climate Chaos Scotland, 2006-2020. Recreations:

squash; mountaineering; environment; cutting carbon footprint. Address: (b.) RSGS, 15-19 North Port, Perth PH1 5LU.

Robinson, Professor Olivia F., MA, PhD, FRSE, FRHistS. Professor Emeritus, University of Glasgow, since 2004; b. 22.11.38, Dublin, Ireland. Educ. Newton Manor, Swanage, Dorset; Lady Margaret Hall, Oxford University; Westfield, London University. Successively Lecturer, Senior Lecturer, Reader and Professor in Roman Law in The Law School of Glasgow University; Rice Visiting Professor in the University of Kansas, 1995. Publications: Ancient Rome: City Planning and Administration, 1992; The Criminal Law of Ancient Rome, 1995; Penal Practice and Penal Policy in Ancient Rome, 2007; Sir George Mackenzie's The Laws and Customs of Scotland in Matters Criminal, 2012. Recreations: fishing; wine. Address: (b.) School of Law, University of Glasgow, Glasgow G12 8QQ; T.-(h.) 0141 339 4115; e-mail: olivia.robinson1938@gmail.com

Robison, Shona. MSP (SNP), Dundee City East, since 2011; MSP (SNP), North East Scotland, 1999-2011; Cabinet Secretary for Social Justice, Housing and Local Government, since 2021; Cabinet Secretary for Health and Sport, 2014-2018; Cabinet Secretary for Commonwealth Games, Sport, Equalities and Pensioners' Rights, 2014; Minister for Commonwealth Games and Sport, 2011-2014; Minister for Public Health and Sport, 2007-2011; formerly Shadow Minister for Health; b. 26.5.66, Redcar; m., Stewart Hosie (divorced); 1 d. Educ. Alva Academy; Glasgow University; Jordanhill College. Admin Officer, 1989-90; Community Worker, 1990-93; Home Care Organiser, 1993-97. Recreation: hill-walking. Address: (b.) The Factory Skatepark, 15 Balunie Drive, Dundee DD4 8PS; T.-01382 903218.
E-mail: shona.robison.msp@scottish.parliament.uk
Web: www.shonarobison.com

Robson, Cllr Euan Macfarlane, BA, MSc. Councillor, Scottish Borders Council, since May 2017; Convener, Borders Citizens Advice Consortium, 2012-17; Associate, Caledonia Public Affairs Ltd, since 2008; Scottish Manager, Gas Consumers' Council, 1986-1999; b. 17.2.54, Northumberland; m., Valerie; 2 d. Educ. Trinity College, Glenalmond; Newcastle-upon-Tyne University; Strathclyde University. Teacher, 1976-79; Deputy Secretary, Gas Consumers' Northern Council, 1981-86. Member, Northumberland County Council, 1981-89; Honorary Alderman, Northumberland CC, since 1989; Liberal/SDP Alliance candidate, Hexham, 1983, 1987; Liberal Democrat Scottish Parliamentary spokesman on: Rural Affairs, 1998-99, Justice and Home Affairs, 1999-2001; MSP for Roxburgh and Berwickshire, 1999-2007; Deputy Minister for Parliamentary Business, 2001-03; Deputy Minister for Education and Young People, 2003-05; Convener, Scottish Liberal Democrat Parliamentary Party, 2005-07. River Tweed Commissioner, 1995-2001; author.

Robson, Godfrey, CB (2002), MA. Secretary to the (Anglican) Diocese of Edinburgh, since 2017; Director, TSB Banking Group plc, 2013-2015; Director, Lloyds TSB Scotland, 2001-2013; Chairman, Frontline Consultants, 2003-2013; b. 5.11.46; m. Agnes Robson nee Wight (marr. diss.); 1 s. Educ. St. Joseph's College, Dumfries; Edinburgh University. Scottish Office Civil Servant, 1970-2002, Under Secretary, Economic and Industrial Affairs, 1993-2000, Director of Health Policy, 2000-02; Founding Chairman, National Jubilee Hospital, Clydebank, 2002-03; Director and Trustee, Caledonia Youth, 2003-12; Senior Policy Advisor, ICAP, Washington DC, 2004-14.

Recreations: walking; travel by other means; reading history. Address: 50 East Trinity Road, Edinburgh EH5 3EN; T.-0131 552 9519; Chemin sous Baye, 84110 Vaison la Romaine, France; T.-04 90 37 18 32.
E-mail: godfreyrobson@aol.com

Rochester, Alison, LLB (Hons), DipLP. Partner, Trade and Commerce, Shepherd and Wedderburn LLP, since 2022. Educ. Banchory Academy; University of Aberdeen. Career history: In House Lawyer (Secondee), Sainsbury's Bank, Edinburgh, 2012-13; Legal Counsel (Secondee), Baillie Gifford, Edinburgh, 2016; Shepherd and Wedderburn LLP, Edinburgh: Trainee Solicitor, 2008-2010, Solicitor, Finance and Restructuring, 2010-2013, Solicitor, Trade and Commerce, 2013-2022, Legal Director, Trade and Commerce, 2020-22. Address: Shepherd and Wedderburn, 1 Exchange Crescent, Conference Square, Edinburgh EH3 8UL; T.-0131 473 5350.
E-mail: Alison.Rochester@shepwedd.com

Roddick, Emma, CertHE. MSP (SNP), Highlands and Islands (Region), since 2021; b. 30.7.97. Educ. Alness Academy; Edinburgh College; University of Edinburgh; Open University. Career history: Sales Assistant, Next Retail Ltd, Inverness, 2013-15; Project Coordinator for Drew Hendry MP, Inverness, 2015; College Support Administrator and Receptionist, University of the Highlands and Islands, 2016; Parliamentary Assistant, Scottish Parliament, 2014-17; Deliveroo rider, Inverness, 2018-19; Scheduled Care Coordinator, Scottish Ambulance Service, Inverness, 2016-19; Election Agent, SNP, 2017-19; Project Consultant, Social Justice & Fairness Commission, 2020-21; elected Councillor, Highland Council, Inverness in 2019. Recreation: plays the fiddle. Address: The Scottish Parliament, Edinburgh EH99 1SP; T.-0131 348 6328.
E-mail: Emma.Roddick.msp@parliament.scot

Roddick, Jeanne Nixon, BD (Hons). Minister of Greenbank Parish Church, Glasgow, since 2003; b. 16.05.55, Lennoxtown; m., Graham; 1 s.; 2 d. Educ. Bellahouston Academy; Glasgow University. Address: Greenbank Manse, 38 Eaglesham Road, Clarkston, Glasgow G76 7DJ; T.-0141 644 1395.
E-mail: jeanne.roddick@ntlworld.com

Rodger, Professor Albert Alexander, FREng, FRSE, DSc (Hon), BSc (Eng), PhD, CEng, FICE, FGS. Emeritus Professor of Civil Engineering, University of Aberdeen; Vice Principal (External Affairs), University of Aberdeen, 2011-14; Visiting Professor, University of Strathclyde, 2015-17; Vice Principal and Head of College of Physical Sciences, University of Aberdeen, 2003-2011; Board Member, Scottish Further and Higher Education Funding Council, since 2009; Chair of Research and Knowledge Exchange Committee, Scottish Further and Higher Education Funding Council, 2010-2017 (Board Member, 2009-2017); Director of the National Subsea Research Institute, 2009; Established Professor of Civil Engineering, Aberdeen University, since 1997 (Dean, Faculty of Science and Engineering, 2001-03); b. 12.5.51, Greenock; m., Jane Helen; 2 d. Educ. Aberdeen University. Project Engineer, Cementation Research Ltd., London, 1977-79; Aberdeen University: Lecturer in Engineering, 1979-89, Senior Lecturer, 1989-95, Personal Professor, 1995-97. Winner: Award for Excellence, Aberdeen University, 1994; 1997 National John Logie Baird Award for Innovation; Halcrow Premium, Institution of Civil Engineers, 1997; Design Council Millennium Product Award, 1999; Silver Medal, Royal Academy of Engineering, 2000; Fellow of The Royal Academy of Engineering, 2010; Fellow of the Royal Society of Edinburgh, 2016. Recreations: photography & travel. Address: 7 Mill Lade Wynd, Aberdeen AB22 8QN.
E-mail: a.a.rodger@abdn.ac.uk

Rodger, Professor Richard, MA, PhD, AcSS. Professor Emeritus of Economic and Social History, University of

Edinburgh (appointed Professor in 2007); b. 01.10.47, Norfolk. Educ. University of Edinburgh. Lecturer in Economic History, University of Liverpool, 1972-79; Lecturer and Senior Lecturer in Economic and Social History, University of Leicester, 1979-99; Associate Professor of History, University of Kansas, 1982-83, 1987; Visiting Research Fellow, Center for the Humanities, University of Kanas, 1986-87; Director, Centre for Urban History, 1999-2006; Project Director, East Midlands Oral History Archive, 2000-07; Professor of Urban History, University of Leicester, 1999-2007. Awards: Elected Member, Academy of Social Sciences, 2004, Frank Watson Prize for Best Book in Scottish History, 2001-02, Plain English Society Crystal Mark for Software Made Simple series of books. Publications: 16 books including The Transformation of Edinburgh: Land, Property and Trust in the Nineteenth Century, 2001; pbk 2004; Housing the People: the 'Colonies' of Edinburgh, 1860-1950, 1999; Testimonies of the City: Identity, Community and Change in a Contemporary Urban World (Co-Author), 2007; Housing in Urban Britain, 1780-1914, 1995; Cities of Ideas: Civil Society and Urban Governance in Britain 1800-2000 (Co-Author), 2004. Recreations: cricket; long-distance paths; landscapes. Address: (b.) School of History, Classics and Archaeology, University of Edinburgh, Edinburgh EH8 9JY.

Rodney, Philip Emanuel, LLB. Governor, Royal Conservatoire of Scotland, since 2019; Founder, Rimalower Consulting, since 2018; Chairman, Burness Paull LLP, 2012-18; b. 21.08.53, Glasgow; m., Cherie Lindy Rodney; 3 s. Educ. High School of Glasgow; University of Strathclyde. Career: Law Apprentice, McGrigor Donald; Assistant Solicitor, then Partner, Alexander Stone & Co; Partner, then Chairman, Burness LLP. Board, LAR Housing Trust, since 2019; Business Consultant, The Times, since 2019; Board of Directors, Dunedin Consort (Part-time), since 2019. Recreations: family; travel; photography; fast cars and loud music. Address: (b.) c/o Consilium Chartered Accountants, 169 West George Street, Glasgow G2 2LB.

Roe, Professor Nicholas Hugh, MA (Oxon), DPhil (Oxon), FBA, FRSE, FEA. Bishop Wardlaw Professor of English Literature, St. Andrews University, since 2017; b. 14.12.55, Fareham; m., Prof. Susan Jane Stabler (divorced 2021); 1 s. Educ. Royal Grammar School, High Wycombe; Trinity College, Oxford. Lecturer in English, Queen's University of Belfast, 1982-85; St. Andrews University: Lecturer in English, 1985-94, Reader in English, 1994-96; Professor of English Literature 1996-2017; Bishop Wardlaw Professor of English Literature, since 2017; Visiting Professor, University of Sao Paulo, 1989; Leverhulme Research Fellow, 1994-95; Visiting Professor, University of Malta, since 2014; Keats-Shelley Association of America Distinguished Scholar, 2014; Director, Coleridge Conference, 1994-2010; Trustee, Keats-Shelley Memorial Association, 1997-2015; Chair, Wordsworth Conference Foundation, 2008-2012 and since 2019; Chair, Keats House Foundation, London, since 2010; Editor, Romanticism (journal), since 1995; Keats-Shelley Review (journal), 2008-2015; Founder and Director, St. Andrews Poetry Festival ('StAnza'), 1986-92; elected to the Athenaeum Club, London, 2022; Visiting Fellow, University of Tokyo, 2022. Publications: Coleridge's Imagination, 1985; Wordsworth and Coleridge, The Radical Years, 1988; The Politics of Nature, 1992; Selected Poetry of William Wordsworth, 1992; Keats and History, 1995; Selected Poems of John Keats, 1995; John Keats and the Culture of Dissent, 1997; Samuel Taylor Coleridge and the Sciences of Life, 2001; Leigh Hunt: Life, Poetics, Politics, 2003; Fiery Heart: The First Life of Leigh Hunt, 2005; English Romantic Writers and the West Country, 2010; John Keats. A New Life, 2012; John Keats and the Medical Imagination, 2017; Wordsworth and Coleridge, The Radical

Years, Second Edition, 2018. Address: (b.) School of English, St. Andrews University, St. Andrews KY16 9AL; T.-01334 462666.

Roe, William Deas, CBE, DUniv (Open), BSc, FRSA, FRI. Trustee, British Council, 2017-19; Chair, British Council Scotland, 2015-19; Chair, Edinburgh World Heritage, 2012-2015; Non-Executive Board Member, Department for Work and Pensions, 2011-2015; Chair, Pension, Disability and Carers Service, DWP, 2008-2011; Principal, William Roe Associates, since 1992; b. 9.7.47, Perth. Educ. St Modan's High School, Stirling; University of Edinburgh. Assistant Director, Scottish Council for Voluntary Organisations; Councillor, Edinburgh City and Lothian Region, 1978-84; Board Member, Training and Development Corporation, Maine, USA; National Champion, National Endowment for Science, Technology and Arts (NESTA), 2005-2010; Chair, Highlands and Islands Enterprise, 2004-2012; Leader, Independent Review of Social Work Services in Scotland, 2005-2007; Leader, Independent Review of Post-16 Education and Vocational Training in Scotland, 2010-2011. Interests: sustainable development; organic gardening; renewable energy; community ownership of assets; creativity and design. Recreations: hill-walking; cycling; visual arts; music. Address: (h.) Duirinish Oaks, Duirinish, Kyle of Lochalsh IV40 8BE; T.-07771 930880. E-mail: willyroe@gmail.com

Roffe, Melvyn Westley, BA, FRSA, FCOpt (Hon). Principal, George Watson's College, Edinburgh, since 2014; Director: Scottish Council of Independent Schools, 2015-18, Connect (formerly Scottish Parent Teacher Council), since 2017; b. 15.6.64, Derby; m., Catherine Stratford; 1 s.; 1 d. Educ. The Noel-Baker School, Derby; University of York; University of Durham. Assistant Master, Oundle School, Northants, 1986-93; Monmouth School: Head of English, 1993-97, Director of Studies, 1997-2001; Headmaster, Old Swinford Hospital, Stourbridge, 2001-07; Principal, Wymondham College, Norfolk, 2007-2014. Parliamentary Candidate (Lib Dem), Corby, 1992; Mayor of Oundle, 1993; Lay Member of the Council of the College of Optometrists, 2001-04; Chairman: State Boarding Schools' Association, 2004-06; Chairman: Boarding Schools' Association, 2008-09; Governor and Trustee, The Thetford Academy, 2010-2013; Member, Corporation, City College Norwich, 2009-2013; Honorary Fellow, College of Optometrists, 2009. Recreations: historic transport; cultural pursuits. Address: Colinton Road, Edinburgh EH10 5EG; T.-0131 446 6000; e-mail: principal@gwc.org.uk

Rogers, David A., MA, PhD. Director (Constitution and Cabinet), Scottish Government, since 2012. Educ. University of Oxford; University of Cambridge. Address: (b.) Scottish Government, St Andrew's House, Regent Road, Edinburgh EH1 3DG; T.-0131-244 5210. E-mail: david.rogers@gov.scot

Rogers, Ian Hart. Chairman, Scottish Decorators Federation, since 2019, Chief Executive, since 1999; b. 11.6.52, Glasgow; m., Helen; 2 s. Educ. Bearsden Academy; Clydebank College. Began career with Daily Record and Sunday Mail Ltd.; became Sales Manager/Director of roofing and housebuilding company; joined Scottish Building Employers Federation as HQ Secretary. Director, SCORE; Member, Scottish Advisory Committee, ConstructionSkills; Trustee, Scottish Painting and Decorating Apprenticeship Council (SPADAC). Recreations: golf; walking; reading. Address: (b.) Castlecraig Business Park, Players Road, Stirling FK7 7SH; T.-01786 448838. E-mail: info@scottishdecorators.co.uk

Rolfe, William David Ian, PhD, FRSE, FGS, FMA. Keeper of Geology, National Museums of Scotland, 1986-

96; b. 24.1.36; m., Julia Mary Margaret Rayer; 2 d. Educ. Royal Liberty Grammar School, Romford; Birmingham University. Geology Curator, University Lecturer, then Senior Lecturer in Geology, Hunterian Museum, Glasgow University, 1962-81; Deputy Director, 1981-86; Keeper of Geology, National Museums of Scotland, 1986-96. President, Geological Society of Glasgow, 1973-76; Editor, Scottish Journal of Geology, 1967-72; President, Edinburgh Geological Society, 1989-91; President, Palaeontological Association, 1992-94; President, Society for the History of Natural History, 1996-99. Recreations: visual arts; music. Address: 4A Randolph Crescent, Edinburgh, EH3 7TH; T.- 0131-226 2094.

Rolland, Dr. Lawrence Anderson Lyon, DA, PPRIBA, PPRIAS, FRSE, FRSA. President, Royal Incorporation of Architects in Scotland, 1979-81; President, Royal Institute of British Architects, 1985-87; retired Senior Partner, Hurd Rolland Partnership; General Trustee, Church of Scotland, 1979-2013; Chairman, Court, University of Dundee, 1998-2004, Chancellor's Assessor, 2005-2010; former Member, Architects Registration Board, London, and Chairman, Education and Practise Advisory Group; Member, Board, NTS, 2005-2011; b. 6.11.37, Leven; m., Mairi Melville; 2 s.; 2 d. Educ. George Watson's Boys College; Duncan of Jordanstone College of Art. Entered father's practice, 1959; joined partnership with Ian Begg bringing L. A. Rolland and Partners and Robert Hurd and Partners together as one partnership; Architect for: The Queen's Hall, Edinburgh; restoration and redesign of Bank of Scotland Head Office (original architect: Sibbald, Reid and Creighton, 1805 and later Bryce, 1870); much housing in Fife's royal burghs; British Golf Museum, St Andrews; General Accident Life Assurance, York; Minshull Street Crown Courts, Manchester; redesign of council chamber GMC; winner of more than 20 awards and commendations from Saltire Society, Stone Federation, Concrete Society, Civic Trust, Europa Nostra, R.I.B.A. and Times Conservation Award. Founder Chairman, Scottish Construction Industry Group, 1979-81; Member, Building EDC NEDC, 1982-88; Chairman, Board of Governors, Duncan of Jordanstone College of Art, 1993-94. Recreations: music; fishing. Address: (h.) Blinkbonny Cottage, Newburn, Fife KY8 6JF; e-mail: rolland@newburn.org.uk

Rollo, 14th Lord (David Eric Howard Rollo); b. 1943. Succeeded to title, 1997.

Rosborough, Dr Linda, BSc, PhD. Chair of Council, Scottish Wildlife Trust, since 2017; former Director, Marine Scotland, Scottish Government; Head, Common Agricultural Policy Management Division, Scottish Government, 2002-08. Former Lecturer in planning and environmental studies; former advisor to Environment Committee, House of Commons. Address: Scottish Wildlife Trust, 110 Commercial Street, Edinburgh EH6 6NF.

Rose, Alison. Chair, Scotland Leadership Board, Business in the Community Scotland; Chief Executive Officer, NatWest Group, London, since 2019; b. 11.69; m.; 2 c. Educ. Durham University. Career history: joined the NatWest graduate scheme in 1992; senior leadership roles include: Deputy CEO of NatWest Holdings; Chief Executive of Commercial & Private Banking; Head of Europe, Middle East and Africa, Markets & International Banking; and Global Head of International Banking Capital and Balance Sheet. Commissioned by the UK Government to report on the barriers to women starting businesses; sits on the Rose Review Board; Board Member of the Institute of International Finance; Member of the International Business Council for the World Economic Forum; Trustee of Business in the Community (BITC); Non-executive director of Great Portland Estates plc; Director of the Coutts Charitable Foundation; Member of the UK Government's Help to Grow Advisory Council. Publication: The Alison Rose Review of Female Entrepreneurship, 2019. Address: Business in the Community Scotland, Discovery Terrace, 43a Heriot-Watt Research Park, Edinburgh EH14 4AP.

Rose, Dilys Lindsay, BA. Writer of fiction, poetry, drama, librettos, since 1980; Teacher, Creative Writing, University of Edinburgh, 2001-2017; b. 7.2.54, Glasgow; 2 d. Educ. University of Edinburgh. Publications include: fiction: Our Lady of the Pickpockets, Red Tides, War Dolls, Pest Maiden, Lord of Illusions, Pelmanism, Unspeakable; poetry: Beauty is a Dangerous Thing, Madame Doubtfire's Dilemma, Lure, When I Wear My Leopard Hat, Bodywork, Twinset; Stone the Crows, 2020. Winner, first Macallan/Scotland on Sunday short story competition, 1991; Hawthornden Fellow; RLS Memorial Award recipient, 1997; Society of Authors Travel Award; Canongate Prizewinner, 2000; UNESCO/World City of Literature Exchange Fellow, 2006; McCash poetry winner, 2006; Leverhulme Research Fellow, 2009. Website: dilysrose.com

Rose, Professor Richard, BA, DPhil, FBA, FRSE. Director and Professor of Public Policy, Centre for the Study of Public Policy, University of Strathclyde, since 2012; b. 9.4.33; m., Rosemary J. (deceased); 2 s.; 1 d. Educ. Clayton High School, Missouri, USA; Johns Hopkins University; London School of Economics; Lincoln and Nuffield Colleges, Oxford University. Political public relations, Mississippi Valley, 1954-55; Reporter, St. Louis Post-Dispatch, 1955-57; Lecturer in Government, Manchester University, 1961-66; Professor of Politics and Director, Centre for the Study of Public Policy, University of Strathclyde, 1966-2006, and since 2012; Sixth Century Professor, University of Aberdeen, 2005-2011; Consultant Psephologist, The Times, Independent Television, Daily Telegraph, STV, UTV, etc., since 1964; Scientific Adviser, Paul Lazarsfeld Society, Vienna, since 1991; American SSRC Fellow, Stanford University, 1967; Visiting Lecturer in Political Sociology, Cambridge University, 1967; Director, ISSC European Summer School, 1973; Secretary, Committee on Political Sociology, International Sociological Association, 1970-85; Founding Member, European Consortium for Political Research, 1970; Member: US/UK Fulbright Commission, 1971-75, Eisenhower Fellowship Programme, 1971; Guggenheim Foundation Fellow, 1974; Visiting Scholar: Woodrow Wilson International Centre, Washington DC, 1974, Brookings Institution, Washington DC, 1976, American Enterprise Institute, Washington, 1980, Fiscal Affairs Department, IMF, Washington, 1984; Visiting Professor, European University Institute, Florence, 1977, 1978 and Visiting Fellow, since 2010; Visitor, Japan Foundation, 1984; Hinkley Professor, Johns Hopkins University, 1987; Guest Professor, Wissenschaftzentrum, Berlin, 1988-90, 2005-09 and since 2015, Central European University, Prague, 1992-95, Max Planck Institute, Berlin, 1996; Ransome Lecturer, University of Alabama, 1990; Consultant Chairman, NI Constitutional Convention, 1976; Home Office Working Party on Electoral Register, 1975-77; Co-Founder, British Politics Group, 1974; Convenor, Work Group on UK Politics, Political Studies Association, 1976-88; Member, Council, International Political Science Association, 1976-82; Keynote Speaker, Australian Institute of Political Science, Canberra, 1978; Technical Consultant: OECD, World Bank, Council of Europe, International IDEA UN agencies; Member, National Endowment for Democracy International Forum, since 1997; Member, Transparency International Research Advisory Panel, since 1998; Advisor, House of Commons Public Administration Committee, 2003; Director, ESRC Research Programme,

Growth of Government, 1982-86; Honorary Vice President, Political Studies Association, UK, 1986; Editor, Journal of Public Policy, 1985-2011; Foreign Member, Finnish Academy of Science and Letters, 1985; Fellow of the British Academy, 1992; Fellow, American Academy of Arts and Sciences, 1994; Robert Marjolin AMEX Prize in International Economics, 1992; Lasswell Award for Lifetime Achievement in Public Policy, USA, 1999; Political Studies Association Award for Lifetime Achievement, 2000; Lifetime Achievement Award, Comparative Study of Electoral Systems, 2008; Dogan Foundation for European Political Sociology, 2009; Sir Isaiah Berlin Award for Lifetime Achievement, 2009; International Public Policy Association, 2019; Fellow, Royal Society of Edinburgh, 2019; Honorary doctorate, Orebru University, Sweden, 2005; European University Institute, 2010. Publications: The British General Election of 1959 (Co-author), 1960; Must Labour Lose? (Co-author), 1960; Politics in England, 1964; Politics in Britain, 2018; Studies in British Politics (Editor), 1966; Influencing Voters, 1967; Policy Making in Britain (Editor), 1969; People in Politics, 1970; European Politics (Joint Editor), 1971; Governing Without Consensus — An Irish Perspective, 1971; International Almanack of Electoral History (Co-author), 1974; Electoral Behaviour — A Comparative Handbook (Editor), 1974; Lessons From America (Editor), 1974; The Problem of Party Government, 1974; The Management of Urban Change in Britain and Germany (Editor), 1974; Northern Ireland — A Time of Choice, 1976; Managing Presidential Objectives, 1976; The Dynamics of Public Policy (Editor), 1976; New Trends in British Politics (Joint Editor), 1977; Comparing Public Policies (Joint Editor), 1977; What is Governing? — Purpose and Policy in Washington, 1978; Elections Without Choice (Joint Editor), 1978; Can Government Go Bankrupt? (Co-author), 1978; Britain — Progress and Decline (Joint Editor), 1980; Do Parties Make a Difference?, 1980; Challenge to Governance (Editor), 1980; Electoral Participation (Editor), 1980; Presidents and Prime Ministers (Joint Editor), 1980; Understanding the United Kingdom, 1982; United Kingdom Facts (Co-author), 1982; The Territorial Dimension in United Kingdom Politics (Joint Editor), 1982; Fiscal Stress in Cities (Joint Editor), 1982; Understanding Big Government, 1984; The Nationwide Competition for Votes (Co-author), 1984; Public Employment in Western Nations, 1985; Voters Begin to Choose (Co-author), 1986; Patterns of Parliamentary Legislation (Co-author), 1986; The Welfare State East and West (Joint Editor), 1986; Ministers and Ministries, 1987; Taxation By Political Inertia (Co-author), 1987; The Post-Modern President — The White House Meets the World, 1988; Ordinary People in Public Policy, 1989; Training Without Trainers? (Co-author), 1990; The Loyalty of Voters (Co-author), 1990; Lesson-Drawing in Public Policy, 1993; Inheritance before Choice, 1994; What Is Europe?, 1996; How Russia Votes (Co-author), 1997; Democracy and its Alternatives (Co-author), 1998; A Society Transformed: Hungary in Time-Space Perspective, (Co-author), 1999; The International Encyclopedia of Elections (Editor), 2000; Prime Minister in a Shrinking World, 2001; Elections Without Order: Russia's Challenge to Vladimir Putin (Co-author), 2002); Elections and Parties in New European Democracies (Co-author), 2003 (translations in 17 languages), 2nd edition, 2009; Learning from Comparative Public Policy, 2005; Russia Transformed (Co-author), 2006; Parties and Elections in New European Democracies (Co-author), 2009; Understanding Post-Communist Transformation, 2009; Popular Support for an Undemocratic Regime (Co-Author), 2011; Representing Europeans: a Pragmatic Approach, 2013, 2015 (updated edition); Learning about Politics in Time and Space, 2014 (translations in 17 languages); Paying Bribes for Public Services (Co-Author), 2015; Bad Governance and Corruption (Co-Author), 2018; How Referendums Challenge European Democracy: Brexit and Beyond, 2020; How Sick is British Democracy? A Clinical Analysis, 2021.

Recreations: architecture (historical, Europe; modern, America); music; writing; philanthropy. Address: (h.) 1 East Abercromby Street, Helensburgh G84 7SP; (b.) CSPP, McCance Building, University of Strathclyde, Glasgow G1 1XQ.

Rosebery, 7th Earl of (Neil Archibald Primrose), DL; b. 11.2.29; m., Alison Mary Deirdre Reid; 1 s.; 4 d. Educ. Stowe; New College, Oxford. Succeeded to title, 1974. Address: (h.) Dalmeny House, South Queensferry, West Lothian.

Rosie, Elaine, BA, MIoH. Business Manager, Blackwood Housing & Care, since 2014; Director, Elaine Rosie Associates Ltd., 2008-2014; Associate, SOLACE Enterprises, 2010-2014; Scottish Legal Aid Board Member, 2005-2012; b. 6.9.62; m., Paul Grice; 2 d. Educ. James Gillespie's High School; Stirling University. Management Trainee, City of Edinburgh Council Housing Dept., 1984-86; London and Quadrant Housing Trust: Housing Officer, 1986-87, Special Projects Officer, 1987-88, Senior Development Officer, 1989-91; Senior Development Officer, Whiteinch and Scotstoun Housing Association, 1991-92; Depute Director, Shelter Scotland, 1992-2000; Scottish Homelessness Advisory Service Manager, 2000-04; Homepoint National Advisory Committee, 1993-2006; Training and Development Manager, Shelter Scotland, 2004-06; Inspector, The Scottish Housing Regulator, 2006-08. Recreations: hill walking; reading; swimming; dancing. E-mail: rosie_elaine@yahoo.co.uk

Rosie, George. Freelance Writer and Broadcaster; b. 27.2.41, Edinburgh; m., Elizabeth Ann Burness; 2 s.; 1 d. Educ. Trinity Academy, Edinburgh; Edinburgh School of Architecture. Editor, Interior Design magazine, 1966-68; freelance magazine writer, 1968-76; Scottish Affairs Correspondent, Sunday Times, 1976-86; Reporter, Channel 4 TV series Down the Line, 1986-87, Scottish Eye, 1988; Reporter/Writer, The Englishing of Scotland, 1988, Selling Scotland, 1989; Scotching the Myth, 1990; Losing the Heid, 1991; Independence Day, 1996; Secret Scotland, 1997-98, Our Friends in the South, 1998; After Lockerbie (BAFTA Best Documentary winner, 1999); Our Friends in the South, 2000; Chief Braveheart, 2005; Editor, Observer Scotland, 1988-89; award winner, RSPB birds and countryside awards, 1988. Publications: British in Vietnam, 1970; Cromarty, 1975; The Ludwig Initiative, 1978; Hugh Miller, 1982; The Directory of International Terrorism, 1986; as contributor: Headlines, the Media in Scotland, 1978; Death's Enemy, the Pilgrimage of Victor Frankenstein, 2001 (fiction); Curious Scotland, 2004; Tyneside, 2005; Flight of the Titan, 2010; Scottish Government Yearbook, 1982; Scotland, Multinationals and the Third World, 1982; World Offshore Oil and Gas Industry Report, 1987; stage plays: The Blasphemer, 1990; Carlucco and the Queen of Hearts, 1991 (winner, Fringe First, The Independent Theatre Award); It Had To Be You, 1994; radio plays: The Parsi, 1992; Postcards from Shannon, 2000. Recreation: hill-walking. Address: (h.) 70 Comiston Drive, Edinburgh EH10 5QS; T.-0131-447 9660.

Ross, Rt. Hon. Lord (Donald MacArthur Ross), PC, MA, LLB. Lord Justice Clerk and President of the Second Division of the Court of Session, 1985-97; a Senator of the College of Justice, 1977-97; Chairman, Judicial Studies Committee, Scotland, 1997-2001; Lord High Commissioner to the General Assembly of the Church of Scotland, 1990 and 1991; b. 29.3.27, Dundee; m., Dorothy Margaret Annand (d. 2004); 2 d. Educ. High School of Dundee; Edinburgh University. Advocate, 1952; QC, 1964; Vice-Dean, Faculty of Advocates, 1967-73; Dean of Faculty, 1973-76; Sheriff Principal of Ayr and Bute, 1972-73;

Member, Scottish Committee, Council of Tribunals, 1970-76; Member, Committee on Privacy, 1970; Deputy Chairman, Boundary Commission for Scotland, 1977-85; Member, Court, Heriot-Watt University, 1978-90, Chairman, 1984-90; Member, Parole Board for Scotland, 1997-2002; Vice President, Royal Society of Edinburgh, 1999-2002 (Member, Council, 1997-99). Hon. LLD, Edinburgh, Dundee, Abertay Dundee, Aberdeen; Hon. DUniv, Heriot-Watt; FRSE. Recreation: gardening; walking; travel. Address: (h.) 7/1 Tipperlinn Road, Edinburgh EH10 5ET; T.-0131 447 6771.
E-mail: RosD33@aol.com

Ross, Dr. Alastair Robertson, CStJ, DA, PGDip, RSA, RGI, FRBS, FSA Scot, FRSA, MBIM, Hon. FRIAS, DArts, PAI. Baron-Bailie of Easter Moncrieffe, since 1974; Artist; Lecturer in Fine Art, Duncan of Jordanstone College, University of Dundee, 1994-2003; b. 8.8.41, Perth; m., Kathryn Margaret Greig Wilson; 1 d. Educ. St. Mary's Episcopal School, Dunblane; McLaren High School, Callander; Duncan of Jordanstone College of Art, Dundee; Greek National Academy of Fine Art, Athens. SED Postgraduate Scholarship, 1965-66; Dickson Prize for Sculpture, 1962; Holokrome (Dundee) Sculpture Prize and Commission, 1962; SED Travelling Scholarship to Amsterdam, 1963; Royal Scottish Academy Chalmers Bursary, 1964; Royal Scottish Academy Carnegie Travelling Scholarship, 1965; Duncan of Drumfork Scholarship to Italy and Greece, 1965; Member, Society of Portrait Sculptors, 1966; award winner, Paris Salon, 1967; Medaille de Bronze, Societe des Artistes Francais, 1968; Elected Associate of the Royal Society of British Sculptors, 1968; Professional Member, Society of Scottish Artists, 1969; Visiting Lecturer, Glasgow School of Art, 1974; Lecturer in Fine Art, Duncan of Jordanstone College of Art, Dundee, 1966-94; Honorary Lecturer, Dundee University, 1969-94; Visiting Lecturer, University of Texas, Arlington, USA, 1996; Medaille D'Argent and elected Membre Associe, Societe des Artistes Francais, 1970; Scottish Representative and Member, Council, Royal Society of British Sculptors, 1972-92; Elected Fellow of the Royal Society of British Sculptors, 1975; Member, Fife St John Executive Committee, 1979-2010 (SBStJ 1979, OStJ 1984, CStJ 1997); Member, Priory Council, Priory of Scotland 1996-2004; Elected Associate of Royal Scottish Academy, 1980; Sir Otto Beit Medal, Royal Society of British Sculptors, 1988; Member, RSA Alexander Naysmith Fund Committee, 1986-89; Member, RSA Spalding Fund Committee, 1986-89; Member, RSA Kinross Fund Committee, 1994-97 and 2005-09; Freeman, City of London, 1989; Sir William Gillies Bequest Award, Royal Scottish Academy for Art History research in Vienna, 1989; Council Member, Society of Scottish Artists, 1972-75; Comm. Bronze relief panel for Royal Calcutta Golf Club; Vice President, Royal Society of British Sculptors, 1988-90; RIAS Dundee Institute of Architects Architectural Awards Panel, 1988-2000; Council Member, British School at Rome, 1990-96; Invited Tutor, School of Scottish Artists in Malta, 1991-93; Hon. Fellow, Royal Incorporation of Architects in Scotland, 1992; Member, Board of Directors, Workshop and Artists' Studio Provision Scotland Ltd., 1997-2004; Council Member, Royal Scottish Academy, 1998-2001; commissioned to design and sculpt Spirit of Scotland Awards, since 1998; exhibited work widely in UK and abroad; work in: Scottish Arts Council Collection; Perth Art Gallery and Museum; Dundee Education Authority Collection; Dundee Art Gallery and Museum; Collection of Royal Scottish Academy; Collection of the Lamp of Lothian Collegiate Centre, Haddington, East Lothian; University of Abertay Dundee; University of St Andrews; University of Dundee; University of Stirling; Glasgow Caledonian University; Royal Incorporation of Architects in Scotland Headquarters Collection, Edinburgh; Royal Burgh of St Andrews; City Chambers Dundee; Blackness Primary School, Dundee (Dundee Public Arts Scheme); Collection of Paisley Art Institute; Paisley Museum & Art Galleries; P & O Steam Navigation Company; Superliner "Aurora"; St Leonard's School, St Andrews, Fife; Court of the Lord Lyon HM New Register House, Edinburgh; Rank Xerox HQ, Bucks; RC Diocese of Dunkeld; St Vincent's Church, Edinburgh; The Royal College of Ophthalmologists, London; private collections in France, Germany, Austria, Switzerland, Egypt, USA, Norway, Bahamas, Canada, Portugal, India, UK; awarded Personal Civic Reception by City of Dundee, 1999; Publication Award, Carnegie Trust for the Universities of Scotland, 1999-2000; Member, Saltire Society Arts and Crafts in Architecture Awards Adjudication Panel, 2001-05; Member, Board of Trustees, St Andrews Fund for Scots Heraldry, since 2001; Royal Scottish Academy representative, Trust for St. John's Kirk of Perth, 2001-05; Hon. Doctorate of Arts, University of Abertay Dundee, 2003; Elected RGI, 2004; Hon. Life Member, Perthshire Art Association, 2005; External Assessor to the JD Fergusson Arts Awards Trust for the Trust's 2006 Travel Award, 2005; Member, Montrose Heritage Trust Sculpture Commission Adjudication Panel, 2005; Royal Scottish Academician, 2005; Member, RSA General Purposes Committee, 2005-09; Elected Librarian of the Royal Scottish Academy, 2003-2010; Awarded Reid Kerr College Sculpture Prize of Paisley Art Institute, 2006; Invited Distinguished Guest Artist, Brechin Arts Festival, 2006; Member, Board of Patrons, University of Abertay Dundee Foundation, since 2006; Hon. Life Member, Paisley Art Institute, 2007; Awarded Reid Kerr College Sculpture Prize of Paisley Art Institute, 2008; Assessor, 2009 Scottish Drawing Competition; Paisley Art Institute Glasgow Art Club Fellowship Award, 2010; Awarded Diploma of Paisley Art Institute (PAI), 2010; Appointed Hon. Vice President, Paisley Art Institute, 2010-2018; Admitted Burgess of the City of Dundee, 2011; presented Masterclass at Glasgow Caledonian University, 2012; Elected Member of Council, Scottish Artists' Benevolent Association, 2012; Guest Lecturer, University of Stirling, 2013; Guest Lecturer to the Burgesses of the City of Dundee, 2013; Elected Vice President, Scottish Artists' Benevolent Association, 2015; Elected to Board of Trustees, City of Dundee Burgess Charity, 2015-18. Recreations: genealogy; heraldry; travel. Address: (h.) Ravenscourt, 28 Albany Terrace, Dundee DD3 6HS; T.-01382 224235; e-mail: a.r.ross@arross.co.uk; web: www.arross.co.uk or www.arross.com

Ross, Alexander (Sandy), LLB, CYCW. Rector's Assessor, Edinburgh University, 2015-2018; former Chief Executive, Murrayfield Media (2007-2014); Managing Director, International Development, STV, 2004-07; Managing Director, Scottish Television, 2000-04; b. 17.4.48, Grangemouth; m., Alison Fraser; 2 s.; 1 d. Educ. Grangemouth High School; Edinburgh University; Moray House College. Apprentice lawyer, 1971-73; Lecturer, Paisley College, 1974-75; Producer, Granada TV, 1978-86; Controller, Arts and Entertainment, Scottish Television, 1986-95; Deputy Chief Executive, Scottish Television Enterprises, 1995-97; Controller Regional Production, Scottish Media Group, 1997-2000. Member, Edinburgh Town Council, 1971-74; Member, Edinburgh District Council, 1974-78; President, Moray House Students Union, 1976; Member, BAFTA; Director, Assembly Theatre. Recreations: golf; music; reading; watching football; curling; member: Glen Golf Club, Haunted Major Golf Society, Prestonfield Golf Club, Edinburgh Corporation Golf Club, East Linton Curling Club (President, 2016-18), Veterans Curling Club; Oyster Club Edinburgh; North Berwick Rugby Club. Address: (h.) 64 Glasgow Road, Edinburgh EH12 8LN; T.-0131-539 1192; mobile: 07803 970 107; e-mail: sandy.ross@murrayfieldmedia.com

Ross, Commodore Angus, BA, MSc, FCILT. Chairman, Scottish Association for Marine Science, 2014-17; b. 1956; m., Irene; 2 d. Career history: Programme Management experience in the Ministry of Defence, both strategic (the Navy's long term capability programme) and tactical (delivering information systems); served at sea as the Logistics Officer in HMS Illustrious, HMS London and HMS Galatea, and also served aboard HMS Fearless during the Falklands campaign; served in the Royal Navy for 36 years; Director, Royal Navy Logistics in the Fleet Headquarters, then Operations Director in the service personnel and veteran's agency responsible for human resources, payroll and pensions to all Armed Forces personnel; retired form the Royal Navy in 2010. Consultant in the defence and maritime industries; set up a not for profit business to assist small to medium businesses to work with the Government. Joined the Council of the Scottish Association for Marine Science as Non-Executive Chairman of the audit committee in 2011; Elder in the Church of Scotland; member of the Merchants House of Glasgow; member, committee of the Highland Reserve Forces' and Cadets' Association. Recreations: yacht skipper; shoots target rifle; climbs mountains; coastal shipping.

Ross, David Craib Hinshaw, LLB (Hons). Chair of the Chancellor's Fund Advisory Board, University of Glasgow, since 2020, Chair of the Investment Advisory Committee, 2012-2021; Member, then Chair of Panels for the Prince's Trust, since 1990s; Convener, Court of University of Glasgow, 2010-16; Chair of the Committee of Scottish University Chairs, 2013-16; Partner, Biggart Baillie, Solicitors, 1977-2009, Chairman and Senior Partner, 2001-2008; Director, Glasgow Chamber of Commerce, 1996-2008, President, 2002; Chairman, Scottish Chambers of Commerce, 2003-07; Director, APUC Ltd., 2007-2015; Member, Advisory (then Strategy) Board of Interface Knowledge Connection Business, 2009-2016; b. 14.1.48, Glasgow; m., Elizabeth Clark; 2 s.; 1 d. Educ. Kelvinside Academy, Glasgow; Trinity College, Glenalmond; University of Glasgow. Maclay Murray and Spens: Apprenticeship, 1970-72, Assistant, 1972-75; Assistant, Biggart Baillie and Gifford, 1975-77, Head of Corporate, 1997-2001. Director, Scottish Council Development and Industry, 2003-07; Director, British Chambers of Commerce, 2003-07; Chairman, Euro-American Lawyers Group, 1997-2002; Director, Loganair Ltd., 2009-2012, Secretary, 1997-2012. Recreations: rhododendrons; windsurfing (formerly). Address: (h.) Harwood, 9 Upper Glenburn Road, Bearsden, Glasgow G61 4BW; T.-0141-942 2569.

Ross, Douglas Gordon. Leader of the Scottish Conservative Party, since 2020; MSP (Scottish Conservative and Unionist Party), Highlands and Islands (Region), since 2021; MP, Moray, since 2017; MSP, Highlands and Islands region, 2016-17; Under Secretary of State for Scotland, 2019-2020; Shadow Cabinet Secretary for Justice, 2016-17; b. 27.01.83; m., Krystle; 2 c. Educ. Forres Academy; Scottish Agricultural College. Career history: elected to Moray council, 2007-2017, representing the Fochabers-Lhanbryde ward; Conservative candidate in the Moray constituency in the 2010 and 2015 elections. Football referee, who has officiated as an assistant in the Scottish Premiership and in international play; one of the referees chosen for the 2015 and 2018 Scottish Cup Finals. Address: The Scottish Parliament, Edinburgh EH99 1SP; T.-0131 348 6161.
Email: Douglas.Ross.msp@parliament.scot

Ross, Cllr Frank, BA, CIMA. Lord Provost, City of Edinburgh Council, since 2017; representing Corstorphine and Murrayfield Ward (SNP), since 2012; b. 1959, London; m., Hanna; 2 c. Educ. Leith Academy; George Watson's College; Edinburgh Napier University. Career: Senior Management Accountant, Guardall Ltd, 1980-99; Finance Director, Sunvic Controls Ltd, 1999-2002; Managing Director: Sunvic Controls Ltd, 2002-04, MB Inspection Ltd, 2005-09; General Manager, Storage Tanks, Motherwell Bridge Ltd, 2009-2010; Group Finance Director (Interim), Edinburgh Chamber of Commerce, 2011; Interim Managing Director, Moorbrook Textiles Ltd, 2010-2011; Group Operations Officer (Interim), Edinburgh Chamber of Commerce, 2011; CEO, Crostorfin Associates, 2010-12; Director/Chairman, The EDI Group Ltd, 2013-16; Director, Essential Edinburgh, 2013-16; Director/Vice Chair, Marketing Edinburgh Ltd, 2013-19. Recreations: bowling; curling; rugby; football. Address: Council Headquarters, City Chambers, High Street, Edinburgh EH1 1YJ; T.-0131 529 4987; e-mail: frank.ross@edinburgh.gov.uk

Ross, Gail Elizabeth. MSP (SNP), Caithness, Sutherland and Ross, 2016-2021; SNP Councillor, Highland Council, 2011-16; m.; 1 s. Educ. Wick High School. Confectioner, MacDonald's Bakery, 1988-2000; Marketing Manager, Grey Coast Theatre Company, 2001-03; Advertising Field Sales, The Scotsman, 2003-05; Sales Co-ordinator, Football Aid, 2005-06; Dispenser, Boots, 2006-07; appointed Office Manager, The Scottish Parliament in 2007. Board Member, North Highland College.

Ross, Helen Elizabeth, BA, MA (Oxon), PhD (Cantab), FBPsS, CPsychol, FRSE. Honorary Professor, Stirling University, since 2017; b. 2.12.35, London. Educ. South Hampstead High School; Somerville College, Oxford; Newnham College, Cambridge. Assistant Mistress, schools in London and Oxfordshire, 1959-61; Research Assistant and student, Psychological Laboratory, Cambridge University, 1961-65; Lecturer in Psychology: Hull University, 1965-68, Stirling University, 1969-72; Senior Lecturer in Psychology, Stirling University, 1972-83; Research Fellow, DFVLR Institute for Aerospace Medicine, Bonn, 1980-81; Leverhulme Fellowship, 1983-84; Reader in Psychology, Stirling University, 1983-94; Honorary Reader, Stirling University, 1994-2016. Member, S.E. Regional Board, Nature Conservancy Council for Scotland, 1991-92; Fellowship Secretary, Royal Society of Edinburgh, 1994-97. Publications: Behaviour and Perception in Strange Environments, 1974; E.H. Weber: The Sense of Touch (Co-translator), 1978; E.H. Weber on the Tactile Senses (Co-translator), 1996; The Mystery of the Moon Illusion (Co-author), 2002. Recreations: Gaelic (Diploma, UHI, 2013); hill-walking; compleat Munroist, 1998; traditional music; concertina; smallpipes. Address: (b.) Department of Psychology, Stirling University, Stirling FK9 4LA; T.-01786 467647; e-mail: h.e.ross@stir.ac.uk

Ross, Ian, OBE, FICFor, FRSA. Chair, Caithness and North Sutherland Regeneration Partnership; Chair, High Life Highland, since 2019; Past Chair, Community Woodlands Association, 2018-20; Chairman, Scottish Natural Heritage, 2014-17. Educ. Aberdeen University. Formerly Highland Councillor for 13 years; past chair of the Highland Council's Planning, Environment and Development Committee; led on a number of significant strategic developments, including the Council's Highland-wide Local Development Plan and the Onshore Wind Farm Strategy; has been active on sustainability and community engagement issues within both the Highland Council and Scottish forestry; over 30 years of experience of working within the wider Scottish land use sector; extensive experience of working with public sector bodies in best value reviews and the development of improved governance processes. Recreation: attempts to be an enthusiastic cyclist.

Ross, Dr John Alexander, CBE, DVMS, FRAgS, LL. Lord Lieutenant of Wigtown, 2015-2020 (retired); Chairman, Dumfries and Galloway NHS Board, 2001-08; Chairman, Moredun Research Institute, 2002-04; Chairman, Moredun Foundation, 2004-2012; Commissioner, The Northern Lighthouse Board, 2008-2017; Chairman, Programme Board for Prison Healthcare, 2009-2012; Chairman, Care Farming Scotland, 2011-16; Vice-President, Royal Highland Agricultural Society, 2012; b. 19.2.45, Stranraer; m., Alison Jean Darling; 2 s.; 1 d. Educ. George Watson's College, Edinburgh. NFU of Scotland: Convener, Hill Farming Sub-Committee, 1984-90,

Wigtown Area President, 1985-86, Convener, Livestock Committee, 1987-90, Vice-President, 1986-90, President, 1990-96. Chairman, Stranraer School Council, 1980-89; Session Clerk, Portpatrick Parish Church, 1975-80; Director, Animal Diseases Research Association; Commissioner, Meat and Livestock Commission, 1996-2002; Chairman, Dumfries and Galloway Health Board, 1997-2000; Chairman, Dumfries and Galloway Primary Care NHS Trust, 2000-01; Director, NFU Mutual Insurance Society, 1996-2012. Fellow of Scottish Agricultural College, 2011; Hon. Doctor of Veterinary Medicine and Surgery (DVMS), University of Glasgow, 2013. Recreations: golf; curling. Address: Low Auchenree, Portpatrick, Stranraer DG9 8TN.
E-mail: auchenree@outlook.com

Ross, Kenneth Alexander, LLB (Hons). Sheriff of South Strathclyde, Dumfries and Galloway at Dumfries, 2000-2014; President, Law Society of Scotland, 1994-95 (Vice-President, 1993-94); b. 21.4.49; m., Morag Laidlaw; 1 s.; 1 d. Educ. Hutchesons' Grammar School, Glasgow; Edinburgh University. President, Edinburgh University Union, 1970-71. Partner, Gillespie, Gifford & Brown (formerly McGowans), Solicitors, Dumfries, 1975-97; Temporary Sheriff, 1987-97; Sheriff of Lothian and Borders at Linlithgow, 1997-2000. Member, Scottish Legal Aid Board, 2004-09; Member, Judicial Appointments Board for Scotland, 2008-12; Member, Council, Law Society of Scotland, 1987-96. Contested General Elections (C): Kilmarnock, Feb. 1974, Galloway, Oct. 1974. Recreations: gardening; golf; curling; violin. Address: Slate Row, Auchencairn, Castle Douglas, Kirkcudbrightshire DG7 1QL; Orchard Brae Avenue, Edinburgh EH4 2GA.

Ross, Marcus. Vice Principal (Planning and Recruitment), University of the West of Scotland, since 2021. Educ. University of Paisley. University of the West of Scotland: Director of Facilities, Marketing and Internationalisation, 2012-2021, Executive Director, Strategic Planning and Development/Marketing, Recruitment and Engagement, 2018-2021. Address: University of the West of Scotland, Technology Avenue, Blantyre, Glasgow G72 0LH; T.-01698 283100; e-mail: Marcus.Ross@uws.ac.uk

Ross, Thomas Leonard, QC (2017), LLB, DipLP. Advocate, since 2000; b. 25.10.63, Glasgow; m., Alison Mary Laurie; 2 d. Educ. Penilee Secondary, Glasgow; Strathclyde University; Glasgow University. Admitted as Solicitor, 1985; Solicitor Advocate, 1998; admitted to Bar, 2000. President, Glasgow Bar Association, 1995; Vice Chair, Faculty of Advocates Criminal Bar Association, 2012-14; President, Scottish Criminal Bar Association, 2015-17; Member, Glasgow Art Club. Address: (h.) 7 Buchlyvie Road, Ralston, Renfrewshire PA1 3AD; T.-0141-810 4161.
E-mail: TLRQC@benchmarkadvocates.co.uk

Rothach, Dr Gillian, PhD. Principal, Sabhal Mòr Ostaig, since 2018; previously Deputy Director of Studies and Head of Research. Address: Sabhal Mòr Ostaig, Isle of Skye, Sleat IV44 8RQ; T.-01471 888200.
E-mail: runaire@smo.uhi.ac.uk

Rothes, 22nd Earl of (James Malcolm David Leslie); b. 1958. Succeeded to title, 2005.

Roughead, Malcolm, OBE. Chief Executive, VisitScotland, since 2010. Educ. Glasgow University. Previously held a number of senior marketing positions with Guinness in Africa, Europe, the Middle East and North America; also worked in marketing with Nestlé and Beechams in London; joined VisitScotland from Diageo in 2001. Awarded the title of Scottish Marketeer of the Year, Scottish Marketing Awards, 2004; Fellow, Institute of Direct Marketing; Fellow and former Chair, Marketing Society in Scotland; OBE for services to tourism, 2005. Address: (b.) VisitScotland, Ocean Point One, 94 Ocean Drive, Edinburgh EH6 6JH.

Roughead, Sarah. Acting Chief Executive Officer, Scottish National Investment Bank, since 2022, appointed Chief Financial Officer in 2021; b. 2.83. Career history: former Head of Private Equity, KPMG LLP; former Director of Fund Reporting, Scottish Equity Partners Ltd, then Head of Fund Reporting, 2016-2021. Address: Scottish National Investment Bank, Waverley Gate, 2-4 Waterloo Place, Edinburgh EH1 3EG.

Rowallan, Lord (John Polson Cameron), ARICS. Chairman, Lochgoin Covenanters Trust; b. 8.3.47, Glasgow; m., Claire; 2 s.; 2 d; 1 steps.; 1 stepd. Educ. Eton College; Royal Agricultural College. Estate Agent, since 1969; Company Director, since 1989; Commentator, since 1986. Recreations: equestrianism and auctions. Address: (h.) Ladeside House, Skeldon, Hollybush, Ayr KA6 7EB.
E-mail: john.rowallan@gmail.com

Rowan, Professor John. Vice Principal (Research), University of Dundee, Professor of Physical Geography, since 2012. Educ. Exeter University; Miami University; Glasgow University. Career history: PhD, University of Exeter, Devon, 1987-90; Lecturer in Environmental Management, Lancaster University, 1990-98; University of Dundee: Lecturer and Senior Lecturer in Physical Geography, 1998-2006, Reader in Physical Geography, 2006-2012, Head of the Environmental Systems Research Group (ESRG), in the School of the Environment, 2008-2011, Founding Director, Centre for Environmental Change and Human Resilience (CECHR), 2009; appointed Director, MSc Sustainability Programme in 2014; appointed Dean, School of Social Sciences in 2015. Serves in an advisory capacity to the Scottish Government's Centres of Expertise in Climate Change (CXC) and Centre for Research on Water (CREW). Address: University of Dundee, Nethergate, Dundee DD1 4HN; T.-01382 384194; e-mail: j.s.rowan@dundee.ac.uk

Rowell, Katherine. Chair, Quality Meat Scotland Limited, since 2018; Partner, J & W Brown, since 2002. Educ. Peebles High School. Member, Quality Meat Scotland Board, since 2015; Convener, Peebles March Riding and Beltane Queen Festival; Guide Leader, Girlguiding Scotland, since 2005. Address: Quality Meat Scotland, The Rural Centre, West Mains, Ingliston, Newbridge EH28 8NZ; T.-0131 510 7920.

Rowley, Alex, MA (Hons), MSc. MSP (Labour), Mid Scotland and Fife region, since 2016 (Cowdenbeath, 2014-16); Shadow Cabinet Secretary for Transport, Infrastructure and Connectivity; Deputy Leader, Scottish Labour Party, 2015-17, Acting Leader, August-November 2017; b. 30.11.63, Dunfermline; 3 c. Educ. St Columba's High School, Dunfermline; Newbattle Abbey College, Dalkeith; Edinburgh University. General Secretary of the Scottish Labour Party, 1998-99; worked as an education official with the TUC and worked for five years as an assistant, election agent and constituency manager to Gordon Brown; first elected to Fife Regional Council in 1990, became Chairman of Finance, later became the first leader of the new Fife Council and Labour Council Group Leader; Labour candidate, 2011 Scottish Parliament election. Address: Scottish Parliament, Edinburgh EH99 1SP.

Rowley, Danielle, BA. MP (Labour), Midlothian, 2017-19; b. 25.2.90. Educ. Dalkeith High School; Edinburgh Telford College; Edinburgh Napier University. Career: Producer and Presenter, 107.8 Black Diamond FM, 2008-2011; Social Media Officer, Scottish Youth Parliament, 2011; Page Editor, Edinburgh Now, Scottish Daily Record and Sunday Mail Ltd, 2013; Local Digital Content, STV Group plc, 2013; Campaigns Coordinator, Local Campaign Group, 2013-15; Constituency Media Manager, Gordon Brown MP, 2014-15; E-Communications Officer, The Scottish Parliament, 2015; Communications and Marketing Officer, ACOSVO, 2015-16; Campaigns and Public Affairs Officer, Shelter Scotland, 2016-17.

Rowling, Joanne Kathleen (J.K.), CH (Companion of Honour), OBE, BA. Writer; b. 31.7.65; m. (1); 1 d.; m. (2); 1 s.; 1 d. Educ. Exeter University. Publications: Harry Potter and the Philosopher's Stone, 1997; Harry Potter and the Chamber of Secrets, 1998; Harry Potter and the Prisoner of Azkaban, 1999; Harry Potter and the Goblet of Fire, 2000; Fantastic Beasts and Where to Find Them, 2001; Quidditch Through The Ages, 2001; Harry Potter and the Order of the Phoenix, 2003; Harry Potter and the Half-Blood Prince, 2005; Harry Potter and the Deathly Hallows, 2007; The Tales of Beedle the Bard, 2008; The Casual Vacancy, 2012; The Cuckoo's Calling (pseudonym: Robert Galbraith), 2013; The Silkworm (pseudonym: Robert Galbraith), 2014; Very Good Lives, 2015; Career of Evil (pseudonym: Robert Galbraith), 2015; Lethal White (pseudonym: Robert Galbraith), 2018; Troubled Blood (pseudonym: Robert Galbraith), 2020; The Ickabog, 2020; The Christmas Pig, 2021. Address: The Blair Partnership, PO Box 7828, London W1A 4GE.

Rowlinson, Professor Peter, MA, DPhil. Emeritus Professor of Mathematics, University of Stirling, since 2006; b. 23.10.44, Cambridge; m., Carolyn. Educ. Cambridgeshire High School; New College, Oxford. University of Stirling: Lecturer in Mathematics, 1969-92, Senior Lecturer in Mathematics, 1992-94, Reader in Mathematics, 1994-96, Professor of Mathematics, 1996-2006. Visiting Associate Professor of Mathematics, California Institute of Technology, 1975-76; President, Edinburgh Mathematical Society, 2003-05. Publications: Eigenspaces of Graphs (Co-author), 1997; Spectral Generalizations of Line Graphs (Co-author), 2004; An Introduction to the Theory of Graph Spectra (Co-author), 2010; journal articles. Address: Division of Computing Science and Mathematics, University of Stirling, Stirling FK9 4LA; T.-01786 467468.
E-mail: p.rowlinson@stirling.ac.uk

Roxburghe, 11th Duke of (Charles Innes-Ker); b. 18.2.81; m., Hon. Charlotte Aitken (divorced). Educ. The Royal Military Academy Sandhurst. Formerly styled Marquess of Bowmont & Cessford (1981-2019). Address: Floors Castle, Kelso TD5 7RW.

Roy, Frank, BA. MP (Labour), Motherwell and Wishaw, 1997-2015; b. 29.8.58, Motherwell; m., Ellen Foy; 1 s.; 1 d. Educ. St Joseph's High School, Motherwell; Our Lady's High School, Motherwell; Motherwell College; Glasgow Caledonian University. Ravenscraig steelworker, 1977-91; PPS to Helen Liddell, Deputy Secretary of State for Scotland, 1998-99; PPS to Dr John Reid, MP, Secretary of State for Scotland, 1999-2001; PPS to Helen Liddell, Secretary of State for Scotland, 2001; Government Whip, 2005-2010; Campaign Director: Scotland Stronger in Europe Campaign, 2015-16, Arden Strategies Ltd, 2018-19.

Roy, Professor Graeme, MA (Econ), MS (Econ), PhD (Econ). Dean of External Engagement, College of Social Science, University of Glasgow, since 2021. Educ.

University of Glasgow; University of Edinburgh. Career history: The Scottish Government: Economist/Senior Economist, 2007-2011; Senior Economic Adviser and Head of the Office of the Chief Economic Adviser (OCEA), 2011-14; Head of First Minister's Policy Unit, 2014-16; Director, Fraser of Allander Institute, University of Strathclyde, 2016-2021; Head of Department of Economics, 2018-2021. Address: University of Glasgow, College of Social Science, Florentine House, 53 Hillhead Street, Glasgow G12 8QF.
E-mail: Graeme.Roy@glasgow.ac.uk

Roy, Lindsay Allan, CBE, BSc, FRSA. Former MP (Labour), Glenrothes and Central Fife (2008-2015); Headteacher, Kirkcaldy High School, February-November 2008; Rector, Inverkeithing High School, 1989-2008; b. 19.1.49, Perth; m., Irene Elizabeth Patterson; 2 s.; 1 d. Educ. Perth Academy; Edinburgh University. Assistant Rector, Kirkcaldy High School, 1983-86; Depute Rector, Glenwood High School, Glenrothes, 1986-89; Chairman, Modern Studies Association, 1976-79; Chairman, Modern Studies Panel, Scottish Examination Board, 1980-83; Member, Consultative Committee on the Curriculum Central Committee for Social Subjects, 1978-85; Chairman, Higher Still Group Awards Steering Committee, 1996-98; Member, Board of Management, Lauder College, 1998-2006; past President, Headteachers' Association of Scotland; Member, National Qualifications Steering Group, 2003-08.

Royan, Professor Bruce, BA (Hons), MBA, MBCS, FCLIP, FCMI, FRSA, FSA (Scot). Chief Executive, Concurrent Computing Ltd., since 2002; b. 22.1.47, Luton; m., Ann Elizabeth Wilkins; 1 s.; 1 d. Educ. Dunstable Grammar School; North West Polytechnic; Glasgow University. Systems Development Manager, British Library, 1975-77; Head of Systems, National Library of Scotland, 1977-85; Director, Singapore Integrated Library Automation Service, 1985-88; Principal Consultant, Infologistix Ltd., 1988-98; Director of Information Services and University Librarian, Stirling University, 1989-96; Chief Executive, Scottish Cultural Resources Access Network, 1996-2002; Visiting Professor, School of Creative Industries, Napier University, 1997-2011; Interim Director of Knowledge and Information, The Robert Gordon University, 2004-05. Secretary, Working Party on Access to the National Database, 1980-83; Member, Council, Library Association of Singapore, 1987-88; Convenor, Higher Education IT Directors in Scotland, 1991-93; Executive Chairman, Bath Information and Data Services, 1991-96; Councillor, The Library Association, 1994-99; Chair, National Datasets Steering Group, 1994-96; Board Member, Croydon Libraries Internet Project, 1995-96; Chair, Scottish Collaborative On-demand Publishing Enterprise (SCOPE), 1996-98; Councillor, Institute of Information Scientists, 1997-99; Member, Content Creation Task Group, New Opportunities Fund, 1998; Member, National Grid for Learning Scottish Steering Group, 1998-2003; Chair, UK Metadata for Education Group, 2000-04; Chair, British Council Library and Information Advisory Committee, 2001-03; Member, Culture Online Steering Committee, 2001-03; Director, Virtual Hamilton Palace Trust, 2003-11; Councillor, Chartered Institute of Library and Information Professionals, 2006-11; Chair, Coordinating Council of Audiovisual Archives Associations, 2009; Trustee, The Edinburgh Singers, since 2013; Chair, The Edinburgh Singers, 2014-16. Recreations: choral singing, antique maps; travel. Address: (h.) Bowmont Tower, Greenhill Gardens, Edinburgh EH10 4BL.

Royle, Trevor Bridge, MA, FRSE. Author and Journalist; Honorary Fellow, School of History, Classics and

418 WHO'S WHO IN SCOTLAND

Archaeology, University of Edinburgh; Honorary Fellow, Association for Scottish Literary Studies; b. 26.1.45, Mysore, India; m., Dr. Hannah Mary Rathbone; 3 s. Educ. Madras College, St. Andrews; Aberdeen University. Editor, William Blackwood & Sons Ltd.; Literature Director, Scottish Arts Council, 1971-79; Presenter for BBC Radio Scotland and BBC World Service, 1980-88; Literary Editor, Scotland on Sunday, 1988-90; Associate Editor, Scotland on Sunday, 1991-97; Associate Editor, Sunday Herald, 1999-2015; Member, Scottish Government's Commemoration Panel for First World War, 2013-19. Publications: We'll Support You Evermore: the Impertinent Saga of Scottish Fitba' (Co-Editor), 1976; Jock Tamson's Bairns (Editor), 1977; Precipitous City: The Story of Literary Edinburgh, 1980; A Diary of Edinburgh, 1981; Edinburgh, 1982; Death Before Dishonour: The True Story of Fighting Mac, 1982; The Macmillan Companion to Scottish Literature, 1983; James and Jim: The Biography of James Kennaway, 1983; The Kitchener Enigma, 1985; The Best Years of their Lives: The Post-War National Service Experience, 1986; War Report: The War Correspondents' View of Battle from the Crimea to the Falklands, 1987; The Last Days of the Raj, 1989; A Dictionary of Military Quotations, 1989; Anatomy of a Regiment, 1990; In Flanders Fields: Scottish poetry and prose of the First World War, 1990; Glubb Pasha, 1992; Mainstream Companion to Scottish Literature, 1993; Orde Wingate: Irregular Soldier, 1995; Winds of Change, 1996; Scottish War Stories (Editor), 1999; Crimea: The Great Crimean War, 1854-56, 1999; Civil War: the wars of the three kingdoms 1638-1660, 2004; Patton: Old Blood and Guts, 2005; The Flowers Of The Forest: Scotland And The First World War, 2006; The Royal Scots: A Concise History, 2006; The Black Watch: A Concise History, 2006; The Gordon Highlanders: A Concise History, 2007; The Royal Highland Fusiliers: A Concise History, 2007; Queen's Own Highlanders: A Concise History, 2007; The King's Own Scottish Borderers: A Concise History, 2008; The Argyll and Sutherland Highlanders: A Concise History, 2008; The Cameronians: A Concise History (2008); The Road to Bosworth Field: A New History of the Wars of the Roses (2009); Montgomery: Lessons in Leadership from the Soldier's General, 2010; A Time of Tyrants: Scotland and the Second World War, 2011; ed, Isn't All This Bloody? Scottish Writing From The First World War, 2014; Britain's Lost Regiments: The Illustrious Band of Brothers Time Has Forgotten, 2014; Bearskins, Bayonets and Body Armour: Welsh Guards 1915-2015, 2015; Culloden: Scotland's Last Battle and the Forging of The British Empire, 2016; Facing The Bear: Scotland and the Cold War, 2019; radio plays: Magnificat, 1984; Old Alliances, 1985; Foreigners, 1987; Huntingtower, 1988; A Man Flourishing, 1988; The Pavilion on the Links, 1991; The Suicide Club, 1992; Tunes of Glory, 1995; stage play: Buchan of Tweedsmuir, 1991. Recreations: watching rugby football; hill-walking; investigating battlefields. Address: (h.) 6 James Street, Edinburgh EH15 2DS; T.-0131 669 2116.

Ruckley, Professor Charles Vaughan, CBE, MB, ChM, FRCSEdin, FRCPEdin. Emeritus Professor of Vascular Surgery, Edinburgh University; former Consultant Surgeon, Royal Infirmary, Edinburgh; b. 14.5.34, Wallasey; m., Valerie Anne Brooks; 1 s.; 1 d. Educ. Wallasey Grammar School; Edinburgh University. Research Fellow, University of Colorado, 1967-68. Vascular Surgical Society, Great Britain and Ireland: President, 1993-94, Secretary/ Treasurer; Chairman, Venous Forum, Royal Society of Medicine, 1997-99; Member, Association of Surgeons of Great Britain and Ireland. Recreations: angling; music; tennis; gardening. Address: 3 Blackbarony Road, Edinburgh EH16 5QP.

Rudman, Dr Hannah, PhD, FBCS, FRSA. Digital transformation expert practitioner, entrepreneur and academic; Senior Challenge Research Fellow and Data Policy Lead, Scotland's Rural College (SRUC), since 2020; b. 2.75. Educ. Royal Holloway, University of London; Edinburgh Napier University. Career history: Research Consultant, AEA Consulting, London, 1999; New Media Producer, Royal Shakespeare Company, Stratford-upon-Avon and London, 1999-2001; Business Development, Immersive Education, International, 2001-03; Chair of the Board, Digital North, North of England, 2005-08; Specialist Advisor: Scottish Arts Council, Edinburgh, 2008-09, Innovative Craft, 2008-2011; Non Executive Director, New Media Scotland, Edinburgh, 2006-2012; Board Trustee, Macrobert, Stirling, 2012-14; Associate (Digital and Environmental), Missions Models Money, 2008-2014; Associate Researcher and Lecturer, School of Computing, Edinburgh Napier University, 2009-2015; Specialist Advisor, Digital, Cultural Enterprise Office, Scotland, 2010-15; Board Member, Dynamo NE, North East England, 2014-15; Director, Envirodigital, 2008-2016; Member, Scotland's 2020 Climate Group, 2012-16; Director, Rudman Consulting Ltd, 2003-2018; Strategic Transformation Director, Wallet Services, SICCAR, Edinburgh, 2018-2020; Expert Evaluator, European Commission, since 2015; Member, Board of Trustees, National Galleries of Scotland, since 2018; Executive Management Team Member, Agrimetrics, since 2020. Address: Scotland's Rural College (SRUC), Peter Wilson Building, The King's Buildings, West Mains Road, Edinburgh EH9 3JG; T.-0131 535 4000.

Rumbles, Michael John, MSc (Econ), BEd. MSP, North East Scotland region (Liberal Democrat), 2016-2021, West Aberdeenshire and Kincardine, 1999-2011; b. 10.6.56, South Shields; m., Pauline; 2 s. Educ. St James' School, Hebburn; Durham University; University of Wales. Army Officer, 1979-94; Team Leader, Business Management, Aberdeen College, 1995-99. Convener, Standards Committee, Scottish Parliament, 1999-2003; Liberal Democrat Chief Whip and Business Manager, 2008-2011.

Rummery, Professor Kirstein, LLB (Hons), MA, PhD, FASS, FRSA. Professor of Social Policy, University of Stirling, since 2007; b. 12.06.70, London; m., Simon Lippmann; 2 s.; 1 d. Educ. Vienna International School; University of Kent; University of Birmingham. Research Fellow in Social Policy, University of Birmingham, 1992-95; Research Fellow, NPCRDC, University of Manchester, 1995-2002, Lecturer in Social Policy, 2002-05, Senior Lecturer, 2005-07. Member, The Social Policy Association; Member of Board of Directors of Inclusion Scotland; Founder member, Women's Equality Party. Publications: Author of 'Disability, Citizenship and Community Care', 2002; What Works in Improving Gender Equality: International Best Practice in Childcare and Long-term Care Policy; Co-editor, 'Partnerships, New Labour and the Governance of Welfare', 2002; Co-editor, 'Women And New Labour', 2007; Co-editor, Local Policy Review. Recreations: choral singing; cycling; cooking. Address: (b.) Faculty of Social Sciences, Colin Bell Building, University of Stirling FK9 4LA; T.-01786-467693; e-mail: kirstein.rummery@stir.ac.uk; Twitter@KirsteinRummery

Rush, Dr. Christopher, MA (Hons). Writer; b. 23.11.44, St. Monans; m., Patricia Irene Boyd (deceased); 1 s.; 1 d.; re-married Anna Kurkina; 1 d. Educ. Waid Academy; Aberdeen University. Former Teacher, George Watson's College, Edinburgh. Has won six Scottish Arts Council bursaries, two SAC book awards, twice been short-listed for Scottish Book of the Year Award; shortlisted for McVitie Scottish Writer of the Year, 1988; Screenwriter, Venus Peter (based on own book). Publications include: Peace Comes Dropping Slow; A Resurrection of a Kind; A Twelvemonth and A Day; Two Christmas Stories; Into the

Ebb; With Sharp Compassion; Venus Peter Saves the Whale; Last Lesson of the Afternoon; To Travel Hopefully: Journal of a Death Not Foretold; Hellfire and Herring; Will; Sex, Lies and Shakespeare; Aunt Epp's Guide For Life; New Words in Classic Guise: An Introduction to the Poetry of Felix Dennis; Collected Poems of Alastair Mackie 1954-1994 ed.; Penelope's Web. Recreation: staying alive. Address: (h.) 107 Dalkeith Road, Edinburgh EH16 5AJ; T.-01333 451229; e-mail: anna.rush59@gmail.com

Ruskell, Mark Christopher, BSc (Hons), MSc. MSP (Scottish Green), Mid Scotland and Fife, since 2016; b. 14.5.72. Educ. University of Stirling; SAC - University of Aberdeen. Career history: LETS Project Development Worker, Falkirk Voluntary Action Resource Centre, 1997-2001; Community Economic Development Officer, Midlothian Council, 2001-02; Policy and Campaigns Consultant, Organic Targets Bill Steering Group, 2000-03; Project Development Worker, Soil Association Scotland, 2002-03; Member of the Scottish Parliament (Mid-Scotland and Fife region), 2003-07; Marine & Coastal Policy Officer, RSPB Scotland, 2007-08; Director of Communications, Scottish Renewables, 2008-2010; Business Development Manager, GreenEnergyNet.com, 2011; Consultant, Realise Renewables, 2011. Address: Scottish Parliament, Edinburgh EH99 1SP.

Russell, Sir (Alastair) Muir, KCB (2001), FRSE, FInstP. Chairman, Board of Trustees, Moredun Research Institute, since 2020 and Trustee, 2009-2018; Chair of Trustees, Lammermuir Festival, since 2021; Chairman, Board of Trustees, Royal Botanic Garden Edinburgh, 2011-19; Board Member, National House Building Council, and Chair of Scottish Committee, 2012-2020; Chairman, Dunedin Concert Trust, 2009-2021; Trustee, Glasgow School of Art, 2009-2018; Chairing Member, Judicial Appointments Board for Scotland, 2008-16; b. 9.1.49; m., Eileen Alison Mackay. Educ. High School of Glasgow; Glasgow University (BSc NatPhil). Joined Scottish Office, 1970; seconded as Secretary to Scottish Development Agency, 1975-76; Assistant Secretary, 1981; Principal Private Secretary to Secretary of State for Scotland, 1981-83; Under Secretary, 1990; seconded to Cabinet Office, 1990-92; Under Secretary (Housing), Scottish Office Environment Department, 1992-95; Deputy Secretary, 1995, Secretary and Head of Department, Scottish Office Agriculture, Environment and Fisheries Department, 1995-98; Permanent Under-Secretary of State, Scottish Office, 1998-99; Permanent Secretary, Scottish Executive, 1999-2003; Principal and Vice-Chancellor, University of Glasgow, 2003-09. Non-Executive Director, Stagecoach Holdings, 1992-95. Council Member, Edinburgh Festival Society, 2004-09. Director, UCAS, 2005-09; Convener, Universities Scotland, 2006-08; Board Member, USS, 2007-09; FRSE, 2000; FInstP, 2003; Hon. LLD, Strathclyde, 2000; DUniv, Glasgow, 2001; Dr HC, Edinburgh, 2009; Hon FRCPS (Glasg), 2005. Freeman, City of London, 2006. Recreations: music; food; wine. Club: New (Edinburgh).
E-mail: muir.russell@btinternet.com

Russell, Clare Nancy, CVO. Scottish Landowner; Lady Laird of Ballindalloch Castle; Lord Lieutenant of Banffshire, 2002-2019; b. 4.8.44; m., Oliver Henry Russell; 2 s.; 1 d. Chair, Queen Mary's Clothing Guild (Scotland), since 1986; served on the main board of the Children's Hospice Association Scotland (CHAS) for six years; involved with the Moray Health Council, the National Trust for Scotland, and the Scotland Garden Scheme. Appointed Deputy Lieutenant for Banffshire in 1991, becoming Vice Lord Lieutenant in 1998; led a campaign to have road signs marking the historic county's boundaries reinstated in 2008. Publications: three cookery books: I Love Food, I Love

Food 2 and I Love Food 3. Address: Ballindalloch Highland Estate, Ballindalloch, Banffshire AB37 9AX; T.-01807 500 205.

Russell, Emeritus Professor Elizabeth Mary, CBE, MD, DSc, DipSocMed, DObstRCOG, FFCM, FRCPGlas, FRCPEdin, MRCGP, FRSE. Emeritus Professor of Social Medicine, Aberdeen University; Hon. Consultant in Public Health Medicine, 1972-2001; b. 27.1.36, Preston; m., Roy Weir (2007). Educ. Marr College, Troon; Glasgow University. General practice until 1964; public health management and social medicine, 1964-72; academic public health and health services research, since 1972. Recreations: gardening; music; voluntary work. Address: (b.) Kilburn, Inchgarth Road, Pitfodels, Aberdeen AB15 9NX; T.-01224 861216; e-mail: e.m.russell@abdn.ac.uk

Russell, Professor Ian Gordon, MBE, BEd, PhD. Emeritus Professor, since 2014; Director, Elphinstone Institute, Aberdeen University (1999-2014); b. 17.2.47, Aberdeen; m., Norma; 1 s. Educ. King's School, Ely; Nottingham High School; Sheffield City College of Education; Leeds University. Headteacher, Anston Greenlands School, Rotherham, 1986-99; fieldwork in folklore and ethnology, since 1969; broadcast, made films, lectured, in UK and USA; created archive of Village Carols; published widely on traditional singing, humour, and Christmas carols; Director, Village Carols; Director, Festival of Village Carols; Editor, Folk Music Journal, 1980-93; President, North Atlantic Fiddle Convention. Recreations: singing and playing folk music; walking; Morris dancing; travel. Address: (b.) Elphinstone Institute, Aberdeen University, MacRobert Building, King's College, Aberdeen AB24 5UA; T.-01224 272386.

Russell, Rev. John, MA. Minister, Tillicoultry Parish Church, 1978-2000; b. 29.5.33, Glasgow; m., Sheila Spence; 2 s. Educ. Cathedral School, Bombay; High School of Glasgow; Glasgow University. Licensed by Glasgow Presbytery, 1957; ordained by United Church of Canada, 1959; Assistant Minister: Trinity United Church, Kitchener, Ontario, 1958-60, South Dalziel Church, Motherwell, 1960-62; Minister: Scots Church, Rotterdam, 1963-72, Southend Parish Church, Kintyre, 1972-78; Member of various General Assembly Committees, since 1972; Convener, General Assembly's Committee on Unions and Readjustments, 1987-90; Convener, Parish Reappraisal Committee, 1990-94; Vice Convener, Board of National Mission, 1994-95; Convener, Board of National Mission, 1995-96; Moderator, Presbytery of Stirling, 1993-94; Clerk, Presbytery of Northern Europe, 1967-71; Clerk, Presbytery of Dunkeld and Meigle, 2001. Recreations: travel; reading. Address: Kilblaan, Gladstone Terrace, Birnam, Dunkeld PH8 0DP; T.-01350 728896.

Russell, John Graham, FCIT. Chairman: John G. Russell (Transport) Ltd., since 1969, Fife Warehousing Ltd., since 1988, Carntyne Transport Co. Ltd., since 1970; Director: Alloa Warehousing, since 1988, Impact Holdings UK plc, since 2009; b. 1937, Edinburgh; m., Isobel Margaret Hogg; 2 s.; 2 d. Educ. Merchiston Castle School, Edinburgh. Address: (b.) Deanside Road, Hillington, Glasgow G52 4XB; T.-0141 810 8200.
E-mail: john.russell@johngrussell.co.uk

Russell, Jonathan. Business Consultant, Jonathan Russell Consulting Limited, since 2020; Publishing Director (Regionals), Media Scotland, 2013-2020; former Editor, The Herald (2010-2012); previously Assistant Editor of the Daily Record and Sunday Mail; b.

11.69. Began career as a reporter on the Evening Express in Aberdeen and also worked on weekly newspaper, the Inverurie Advertiser; held several senior editorial roles, including Scottish Editor of the Daily Mirror and Editor of the Paisley Daily Express. Address: (b.) 172 Kelvinhaugh Street, Glasgow G3 8PR.

Russell, Keith, BA. Chief Executive Officer, Badminton Scotland, since 2018. Educ. Northumbria University. Career history; Head of Sport, Glasgow Life, 2006-2015; Director of Domestic Rugby, Scottish Rugby Union, 2015-17; Interim Chief Executive Officer, Snowsport Scotland, 2017-18; Director, Keith Russell Consulting, since 2017; Interim Chief Executive Officer, Badminton Scotland, July 2018-October 2018. Address: Badminton Scotland, 40 Bogmoor Place, Glasgow G51 4TQ; T.- 0141 445 1218.

Russell, Laurie James, BSc, MPhil. Former Chief Executive, The Wise Group (2006-2017); b. 8.8.51, Glasgow; m., Pam; 2 s. Educ. Glasgow University. Researcher, Planning Department, Strathclyde Regional Council, 1976-78; Area Co-ordinator, Faifley Initiative, Clydebank, 1978-84; Executive, Chief Executive's Department, Strathclyde Regional Council, 1984-87; PA to Chief Executive, Strathclyde Regional Council, 1987-89; Chief Executive, Strathclyde European Partnership, 1989-2006. Recreations: politics; European issues; music; golf.

Russell, Professor Michael, MA, FRSA. President, Scottish National Party, since 2020; Professor in Scottish Culture and Governance, The University of Glasgow, 2015-16 and since 2021; Hon. President, The European Movement in Scotland, since 2021; Hon. Patron, The Burgh Hall, Dunoon, since 2021; Patron, National Adult Learners Forum, since 2021; MSP (SNP), Argyll and Bute, 2011-2021, South of Scotland, 2007-2011 (previously 1999-2003); Cabinet Secretary for the Constitution, Europe and External Affairs, 2020-21; Cabinet Secretary for Government Business and Constitutional Relations, 2018-2020; Minister for UK Negotiations on Scotland's Place in Europe, 2016-18; Cabinet Secretary for Education and Lifelong Learning, 2009-2014; Minister for Culture, External Affairs and the Constitution, February-December, 2009; Minister for Environment, 2007-09; Professor of Scottish Culture and Governance, University of Glasgow, since 2015 (on leave of absence, since 2016); Hon. Professor in the School of Humanities, Glasgow University, 2017-2021; b. 9.8.53, Bromley; m. Cathleen Macaskill; 1 s. Educ. Marr College, Troon; Edinburgh University. Creative Producer, Church of Scotland, 1974-77; Director: Cinema Sgire, Comhairle Nan Eilean, 1977-81, Celtic Film and TV Festival, 1981-83; Executive Director, Network Scotland Ltd., 1983-91; Director, Eala Bhan Ltd., 1991-2009; Chief Executive, SNP, 1994-99. Active in various voluntary and arts bodies. Publications: author of 7 books, including a novel, 'The Next Big Thing', 2007. Address: (h.) Feorlean, Glendaruel, Argyll PA22 3AH.

Russell, Professor Ric William Lockerby, OBE, DA, ARSA, ARIBA, FRIAS. Architect, since 1970; Director, Nicoll Russell Studios Ltd, since 2016; Senior Partner, Nicoll Russell Studios, 1982-2016; b. 12.8.47, Stockton-on-Tees; m., Irene Hill (divorced); 1 s.; 3 d.; m., Helen Keir (2007). Educ. Dundee High School; Duncan of Jordanstone College of Art; University of Dundee. Robbie and Wellwood Architects (Partner, 1977); co-founded Nicoll Russell, 1982; architect and designer responsible for major civic buildings and civil engineering structures throughout Britain; has lectured and tutored at many universities throughout career. Commissioner, Royal Fine Arts

Commission for Scotland, 1998-2004; Advisory Board Member, Architecture and Design Scotland, 2004-07; Board Member, 2007-2011; Member, Student Awards Committee, Royal Incorporation of Architects in Scotland, 1993-2005; Member, Housing Awards Panel, Saltire Society, 2000-04; has received seven Royal Institute of British Architects awards and six Civic Trust awards. Recreations: drawing; music; DIY. Address: (b.) Nicoll Russell Studios, 111 King Street, Broughty Ferry, Dundee; T.-01382 778966; e-mail: ric.russell@nrsarchitects.com

Russell, Sophie, LLB (Hons), DipLP. Solicitor, MTM Defence Lawyers, Glasgow, since 2019. Educ. Loretto; Earlston High School; University of Dundee. Career history: Helpline volunteer, Abused Men in Scotland, 2013-14; Showroom Assistant, Alba Kitchens, Musselburgh, 2010-15; Trainee Solicitor, Wardlaw Stephenson Allan, Galashiels, 2015-17; Criminal Defence Solicitor, Robert More & Company, Hawick, 2017-19. Address: MTM Defence Lawyers, 2 West Regent Street, Glasgow G2 1RW; T.-07710 347241; e-mail: srussell@mtmdefence.co.uk

Russon-Taylor, Imogen. Director, Kingdom Scotland - Scotland's First Luxury Fragrance House, since 2016; b. 11.70; 3 c. Educ. University of Edinburgh. Career history: Brand Manager Back Catalogue (Secondment), United International Pictures, London, 1997-99; Communications Consultant, Porter Novelli, London, 1995-99; Board Director and Creative Director, Phipps, London, 2000-04; freelance PR, BIG Partnership, 2004-05; PR Director, Fashion and Beauty, Ketchum, London, 2004-06; Head of Global Brand Communications - The Glenmorangie Company, LVMH, 2006-2011; Director, Mr Taylor's Brand Emporium, Edinburgh and London, since 2011; Scotland's Fragrance House, Founder and Creative Director, RBS, since 2018. Address: Kingdom Scotland Limited, 15 Young Street, Edinburgh EH2 4HU; T.-0784 344 1427.

Rutter, John, FRGS, CGeog, MEd. Head Teacher, Inverness High School, since 2014. Educ. Newcastle University; Moray House of Edinburgh. Formerly Year Head and Deputy Head, North Berwick High School and Ross High School, Tranent. Publications: Higher Geography; Mining, Minerals and Metals; Geography for CSEC; AQA Geography B; IGCSE Geography. Address: Montague Row, Inverness, Inverness-Shire IV3 5DZ; T.-01463 233586.

Ryan, Eleanor Avril, BSc, PhD. Founder and Director, Glen Shuraig Consulting Ltd, since 2019; Non-Executive Adviser, Scottish Forestry, since 2019; Director of Budget and Sustainability, The Scottish Government, 2017-19; Director of Financial Strategy, Scottish Government, 2012-14; Chief Executive, Scottish Court Service, 2004-2012; Head of New Educational Developments Division, Scottish Executive Education Department, 2001-04. Educ. Arran High School; St Andrews University. Senior Assistant Statistician, Retail Prices Index, Central Statistical Office, 1993-95; Head, GES Data Unit, HM Treasury, 1995-98; Finance Co-ordinaton Team Leader, Scottish Executive Finance, 1998-99; Head of Curriculum, International and Information Technology Division, Scottish Executive Education Department, 1999-2001.

Ryan, Professor Kevin Martin, BSc (Hons), PhD, FRSE. Professor, Faculty of Medicine, University of Glasgow, since 2007; Senior Group Leader, Beatson Institute for Cancer Research, Glasgow, since 2007; b. 14.06.70, Stoke-on-Trent; m., Justine Nicola Parrott; 2 s. Educ. Biddulph High School, Staffordshire; University of Liverpool;

University of Glasgow. Pre-Doctoral Fellow, Beatson
Institute for Cancer Research, 1995-96; Post-Doctoral
Fellow, United States National Cancer Institute, Maryland,
USA, 1996-2001; Group Leader and Head, Tumour Cell
Death Laboratory, Beatson Institute for Cancer Research,
2001-07. Fellowships and Awards: Cancer Research UK
Senior Fellow, 2002-08; European Association for Cancer
Research - Certificate of Merit, 2002; Elected Fellow of
The Institute of Biology (FIBiol), 2009; Conferred Fellow
of The Society of Biology (FSB), 2009; Recipient of the
2010 European Association for Cancer Research 'Cancer
Researcher Award'. Awarded the 2012 Tenovus Medal;
Fellow of the Royal Society of Edinburgh (FRSE), 2016.
Recreations: swimming; hill-walking and travel. Address:
(b.) Beatson Institute for Cancer Research, Garscube Estate,
Switchback Road, Glasgow G61 1BD; T.-0141 330 3655.

Ryder, Jane, MA, WS, FSA Scot. Consultant; Chair,
Historic Environment Scotland, 2015-2022; Board Member:
Scottish Police Authority, since 2018, Revenue Scotland,
2015-2020; Deputy Chair, Seafish Industry Authority,
2012-15; Chair, Arts & Business Scotland, 2011-15; Chief
Executive, Office of the Scottish Charity Regulator
(OSCR), 2006-2011. Educ. St Andrews University.
Qualified as a solicitor in both England and Scotland and
for 11 years was a partner in a commercial firm in
Edinburgh; became Director of the Scottish Museums
Council, 1995; appointed by Scottish Ministers in 2003 to
establish the Office of the Scottish Charity Regulator
(OSCR). Author of various articles and the textbook
Professional Conduct for Scottish Solicitors. Appointed by
English Ministers as Non Executive Director of Marine
Management Organisation (2010). Formerly Chair, Scottish
Refugee Council; formerly Vice Chair, Stevenson College
of Further Education.
E-mail: jane@janeryder.co.uk

S

Salmond, Alexander Elliot Anderson, MA (Hons). Economist; Leader of the Alba Party, since 2021; MP (SNP), Gordon, 2015-17, MSP Aberdeenshire East, 2011-16, Gordon, 2007-2011; First Minister of Scotland, 2007-2014; MP, Banff and Buchan, 1987-2010; Leader, Scottish National Party, 1990-2000 and 2004-2014; MSP, Banff and Buchan, 1999-2001; SNP International Affairs and Europe spokesperson in the House of Commons, 2015-17; b. 31.12.54, Linlithgow; m., Moira McGlashan. Educ. Linlithgow Academy; St. Andrews University. Vice-President: Federation of Student Nationalists, 1974-77, St. Andrews University SRC, 1977-78; Founder Member, SNP 79 Group, 1979; Assistant Agricultural and Fisheries Economist, DAFS, 1978-80; Economist, Royal Bank of Scotland, 1980-87. Hon. Vice-President, Scottish Centre for Economic and Social Research; former Member, Select Committee on Energy.

Salmond, Catherine, MA (Hons). Editor, Scotland on Sunday, since 2021. Educ. University of Glasgow. Career history: Trainee Reporter, Dumfriesshire Newspaper Group, Annan, 2005-06; Senior Reporter, The Fife Free Press, Kirkcaldy, 2006-08; Edinburgh Evening News: Senior Reporter, 2008-2010, Acting Features Editor, 2010-2011; Assistant News Editor, Edinburgh Evening News/The Scotsman, 2011-2020; Live News Editor, The Scotsman, 2020-2021. Address: Scotland on Sunday, Barclay House, 108 Holyrood Road, Edinburgh EH8 8AS; T.-0131 620 8620; e-mail: catherine.salmond@jpimedia.co.uk

Salter, Professor Donald McGovern, BSc, MBChB, MD, FRCPath, FRCP (Edin). Professor of Osteoarticular Pathology, University of Edinburgh, since 2005; Consultant Histopathologist, Lothian University Hospital Trust; b. 28.02.57, Edinburgh; m., Marleen; 2 s.; 1 d. Educ. Ross High School, Tranent; University of Edinburgh. Lecturer, Pathology, University of Edinburgh, then Senior Lecturer, then Reader. Recreations: golf; gardening; dodging. Address: (b.) Molecular Medicine Centre, Western General Hospital, Crewe Road, Edinburgh.
E-mail: donald.salter@ed.ac.uk

Saltoun, Lady (Flora Marjory). Elected Member, House of Lords, 1999-2014; Chief of the Name of Fraser, since 1979; b. 18.10.30, Edinburgh; 3 d. Educ. St. Mary's School, Wantage.

Salvesen, Alastair Eric Hotson, CBE, DSc (Cranfield), MBA, CA, HRSA, FCIM, FCMI, FRSA, FSAS, FRAgS, FRIAS. Chairman, Dawnfresh Seafoods Ltd., since 1983 (Managing Director, 1981-93); Chairman, Edinburgh New Town Cookery School, since 2009; b. 28.7.41; m., Elizabeth Evelyn; 1 s.; 1 d. Educ. Fettes; Cranfield. Chairman: Starfish Ltd., since 1986, Mull of Kintyre Seafoods, since 1988, Silvertrout Ltd, 2004, Dovecot Foundation, since 2001; Director: Dovecot Studios Ltd., since 2001 (Chairman, 2001-17), Salvesen Mindroom Centre, since 2017, Archangels Investment Ltd, until 2019, Praha Investment Holdings Ltd., since 1985, Richmond Foods plc, 1994-2003, New Ingliston Ltd., since 1995, Luing Cattle Society, 1966-99; President, Royal Highland and Agricultural Society of Scotland, 2001-02; Member, Council, Shellfish Association of GB, since 2003; Governor: Fettes College Trust, 1994-2016 (Deputy Chairman, since 2010), Donaldson Trust, 1997-2009, Compass School, 1994-2009 (Chairman, 1996-2009);

Member, Queen's Bodyguard for Scotland (The Royal Company of Archers); Liveryman, Worshipful Company of Fishmongers. Awarded Honorary Doctorate of Science, Cranfield University in 2017. Recreations: shooting; archery; farming; forestry; contemporary Scottish art. Address: Whitburgh, Pathhead, Midlothian EH37 5SR; T.-01875 320304; (b.) Dawnfresh Seafoods Ltd., Bothwell Park Industrial Estate, Uddingston, Lanarkshire G71 6LS; T.-01698 810008.

Salvesen, Robin Somervell, FBIM, Chevalier de Dannebrog 1st Class; b. 4.5.35, Edinburgh; m., Sari; 3 s.; 4 d. Educ. Fettes College; Oxford University. The Royal Scots, Queen's Own Nigeria Regiment; TA, 7/9 Bn., The Royal Scots, 8/9 Bn., The Royal Scots 52 Lowland Volunteers; retired Major; Director, shipping companies, A.F. Henry & Macgregor, Christian Salvesen plc; Lloyds Register of Shipping, 1974-87; Chamber of Shipping, 1974-88; British Shipowners Association, 1984-99; Member, Lights Advisory Committee, 1987-2003; Member, East Lothian Council, 1965-68; Royal Danish Consul, 1972-87; Vice Convenor, Daniel Stewarts and Melville College, 1978-80; Governor, Fettes College, 1975-85; Chairman, Leith Nautical College, 1979-88; former Chairman, Association for the Protection of Rural Scotland; President, Edinburgh Area Scouts, 1991-2008; Member, Merchant Company of the City of Edinburgh (Assistant, 1977-80); Elder, Church of Scotland, St Mary's, Haddington; President, South East Region Scotland Scouts, 2008-2015 (retired). Address: Eaglescairnie House, Haddington EH41 4HN.

Sanders, John, BA (Hons), DipCons. Architectural Conservator, since 1988; Simpson & Brown Architects, Edinburgh, since 1989; Buildings Conservation Partner, since 2000; b. 9.3.61; m., Susan. Educ. Central School of Art, London; Heriot Watt University. Assistant on Conservation Projects, Charlewood Curry Partnership, Newcastle-upon-Tyne, 1985-87. Interests in Scottish fortified and church architecture. Address: Simpson & Brown, The Old Printworks, 77a Brunswick Street, Edinburgh EH7 5HS; T.-0131 555 4678.
E-mail: jsanders@simpsonandbrown.co.uk

Sanderson of Bowden, Lord (Charles Russell Sanderson), KB, DL. Life Peer; Chairman, Scottish Mortgage and Trust, 1993-2003; Chairman, Hawick Cashmere Co., 1991-2013, Director, since 2013; Chairman, Clydesdale Bank, 1999-2004; President, Royal Highland Agricultural Society, 2002-03; Vice Lord Lieutenant, Roxburgh and Selkirk, 2003-08; Director, Develica Deutschland plc, 2006-08; Director, Accsys plc, 2007-2013; b. 30.4.33, Melrose; m., Frances Elizabeth Macaulay; 1 s.; 1 s. deceased; 2 d. Educ. St. Mary's School, Melrose; Glenalmond College; Bradford University; Scottish College of Textiles. Commissioned, Royal Signals; Partner, Charles P. Sanderson, 1958-87; former Director, Johnston of Elgin, Illingworth Morris, Edinburgh Woollen Mills; former Chairman, Shires Investment PLC, Edinburgh Financial Trust, Scottish Pride Holdings; President, Scottish Conservative and Unionist Association, 1977-79; Chairman, National Union of Conservative and Unionist Associations Executive Committee, 1981-86; Minister of State, Scottish Office, 1987-90; Chairman, Scottish Conservative Party, 1990-93; Chairman, Scottish Peers Association, 1998-2000; Director: United Auctions Ltd., 1993-99, Watson and Philip PLC, 1993-99, Morrison Construction PLC, 1995-2001; Member, Board, Yorkshire Bank and National Australia Bank Europe, 1999-2004; Chairman, Eildon Housing Association, 1976-83; Member, Court, Napier University, 1994-2001; Chairman, Glenalmond Council, 1994-2000; Chairman, St Mary's School, Melrose, 1998-2004; Member, Court, Frameworker

Knitters Company, since 2000; Under Warden, 2003-04; Upper Warden, since 2004; Master, 2005-06; Chairman, The Abbotsford Trust, 2008-2015, Board Member, 2015-2017; DL. Recreations: golf; amateur dramatics; photography; fishing. Address: (h.) Becketts Field, Bowden, Melrose, Roxburgh, TD6 0ST.

Sanderson, William. Farmer; Honorary Treasurer, Royal Highland and Agricultural Society of Scotland, 2005-09, Honorary Vice President, 2009-2010, Chairman, 2002-04; Vice President, Dalkeith Agricultural Society; b. 9.3.38, Lanark; m., Netta; 4 d. Educ. Dalkeith High School. Past Chairman, South Midlothian and Lothians and Peeblesshire Young Farmers Clubs; Past Chairman, Dalkeith Agricultural Society; President, Royal Caledonian Curling Club, 1984-85; Honorary Life Member, Oxenfoord and Edinburgh Curling Clubs; Past President, Oxenfoord and Edinburgh Curling Clubs; Scottish Curling Champion, 1971 and 1978 (2nd, World Championship, 1971); won 5 Championships at the Highland Show and received the great honour of judging the overall champion sheep (Highland Show, 2017). Recreations: curling; exhibiting livestock. Address: (h.) Blackshiels Farm, Blackshiels, Pathhead, Midlothian; T.-01875 833288.

Sandison, The Hon Lord (Craig Sandison), QC, LLB (Hons), PhD. Senator of the College of Justice, since 2021. Educ. University of Aberdeen; Edinburgh University; Glasgow University. Career history: gained Masters in 1991 and PhD in 1994 at the University of Cambridge; joined Brodies as a Bar trainee; admitted to the Faculty of Advocates in 1996, and took silk in 2009. Address: Court of Session, Parliament House, Parliament Square, Edinburgh EH1 1RQ.
E-mail: craig.sandison@advocates.org.uk

Sandison, Rachel, MA, PDip, PGDip, MBA. Deputy Vice-Chancellor, External Engagement, University of Glasgow, since 2021, Vice Principal (External Relations), since 2019. Educ. University of Aberdeen; Chartered Institute of Marketing; Harvard Business School. Career history: University of Aberdeen: Marketing Officer, 2001-05, Head of Marketing, 2005-07, Head of Student Recruitment and Admissions, 2007-2010, Director of Marketing, Student Recruitment and Alumni Relations, 2011-13; University of Glasgow: Director, Recruitment and International, 2013-15, Director, Marketing, Recruitment & International, 2015-17, Executive Director, External Relations, 2017-19. Chair, CASE Marketing Institute; represent the University on the Universities Scotland International Committee and a number of sector advisory boards; school governor for the last five years. Regular conference speaker, delivered presentations at EAIE, CASE Europe Annual Conference, American Marketing Association, Going Global and the World 100 Forum. Leadership Foundation for Higher Education Aurora mentor. Address: University of Glasgow, External Relations, 1 The Square, Glasgow G12 8QQ; T.-0141 330 3999.
E-mail: Rachel.Sandison@glasgow.ac.uk
Twitter: @RachelSandison

Sanguinetti, Bob, MA. Chief Executive Officer, Aberdeen Harbour Board, since 2021; b. 7.65. Educ. Gibraltar; Oxford University; King's College London. Career history: Her Majesty's Ship: Commanding Officer, 1992-94, Operations Officer, 1995-97, Commanding Officer, 1998-2000; Senior Financial Planner, Capability, Ministry of Defence, London, 2000-02; Senior Human Resources Manager, Navy Command HQ, Portsmouth, 2003-04; Assistant Director,

Commitments, Ministry of Defence, London, 2004-06; Maritime Coalition Commander, Coalition Forces, North Arabian Gulf, 2007; Senior Manager, Navy Command HQ, Portsmouth, 2007-2010; Deputy Strategic Finance and Programme Director, Ministry of Defence London, 2010-2011; Head of Intelligence, National Operational Headquarters, Northwood, 2012-2014; Chief Executive Officer: Gibraltar Port Authority, 2014-18, UK Chamber of Shipping, London, 2018-2021. Address: Aberdeen Harbour Board, Harbour Office, 16 Regent Quay, Aberdeen AB11 5SS; T.-01224 597000.
E-mail: b-sanguinetti@portofaberdeen.co.uk

Sannella, Professor Donald Theodore, BS, MS, PhD, FRSE. Professor of Computer Science, Edinburgh University, since 1998; b. 7.12.56, Boston USA; m., Monika Maria Deiters; 1 s.; 1 d. Educ. Yale University; University of California at Berkeley; Edinburgh University. Editor-in-Chief, Theoretical Computer Science, since 2000; Director, Contemplate Ltd, since 2009. Address: (b.) Laboratory for Foundations of Computer Science, School of Informatics, Edinburgh University, EH8 9AB; T.-0131-650 5184.
E-mail: dts@inf.ed.ac.uk

Sansom, Professor Owen, FRSE, FMedSci. Director, Cancer Research UK Beatson Institute. Address: Cancer Research UK Beatson Institute, Garscube Estate, Switchback Road, Bearsden, Glasgow G61 1BD.
E-mail: Owen.Sansom@glasgow.ac.uk

Sarwar, Anas. Leader of the Scottish Labour Party, since 2021; MSP (Labour), Glasgow region, since 2016; MP (Labour), Glasgow Central, 2010-2015; Shadow Minister of State for International Development, 2014-15; Deputy Leader of the Scottish Labour Party, 2011-14; b. 14.3.83; m., Furheen; 3 c. Educ. Hutchesons' Grammar School; Glasgow University. Formerly NHS General Dental Practitioner. Former Member of Select Committees on: International Development, Arms Export Controls; former Vice-chair, PLP Departmental Group for International Development; Member, Labour Party, since 1999. Awards: The Sun's "Best New Politician" award, 2009; Politician of the Year award at the British Muslim Awards, 2014; Spirit of Britain award, British Muslum Awards, 2015. Address: Scottish Parliament, Edinburgh EH99 1SP.

Satsangi, Jack (Jyoti), BSc, MBBS, DPhil, FRCP (Edin), FRCP (UK), FMedSci, FRSE. Honorary Professor of Gastroenterology, University of Edinburgh, since 2018; Professor of Gastro-intestinal Medicine, Green Templeton College Oxford and Honorary Consultant Physician, John Radcliffe Hospital, since 2018; Professor of Gastroenterology, University of Edinburgh; Consultant Physician, Western General Hospital, Edinburgh, 2000-2018; b. 8.5.63, Batley. Educ. Brentwood School, Essex; St. Thomas's Hospital, London; Worcester College, University of Oxford. University of Oxford: MRC Training Fellow, 1992-96, MRC Clinician Scientist, 1997-2000; Honorary Consultant Physician, John Radcliffe Hospital, Oxford, 1999-2000. Fellow, Association of Physicians of Great Britain and Ireland, Royal Colleges of Physicians of Edinburgh and London; Fellow, Royal Society of Edinburgh; Fellow, Academy of Medical Sciences; RCP Director, UK IBD Registry. Recreations: cycling; running; tennis; reading. E-mail: j.satsangi@ed.ac.uk; e-mail: jack.satsangi@ndm.ox.ac.uk

Saunders, Professor Alison Marilyn, BA, PhD. Emeritus Professor of French, Aberdeen University; b. 23.12.44, Darlington. Educ. Wimbledon High School GPDST;

Durham University. Lectrice, the Sorbonne, 1968-69; Lecturer in French, Aberdeen University, 1970-85; Senior Lecturer in French, 1985-90; Professor of French, 1990-2003; Carnegie Professor of French, 2003-2010. Recreations: swimming; gardening; DIY; cooking; antiquarian book-collecting; endurance riding. Address: (h.) 75 Dunbar Street, Old Aberdeen, Aberdeen AB24 3UA; T.-01224 494806.

Saunders, Donald Goodbrand. Poet and Writer, since 1968; b. 16.7.49, Glasgow; m., Anne; 1 s. Educ. McLaren High School, Callander. Writer, mainly of poetry, for 45+ years; published four books, as well as contributing to various Scottish and UK periodicals and anthologies; has received three Scottish Arts Council writers' bursaries. Publications include: The Glasgow Diary, 1984; Findrinny, 1990; Sour Gas and Crude, 1999; 13 Poems frae Heine, 2015. Libretto of "Knotgrass Elegy", 2001 and book and lyrics of musical "Shenachie", 2006. Work in progress: 'Sanders and McLearie in the West End'; Collected Poems of R. Crombie Saunders (Ed.). Address: (h.) 17 Jellicoe Avenue, Gartmore FK8 3RQ; T.-01877 3989451. E-mail: dongosa@hotmail.co.uk

Saunders, Professor William Philip, BDS, DSc (hc), PhD, FRCSEd (Hon), FDSRCS (Edin), FDSRCPS (Glas), FDSRCS (Eng), MRD, FHEA, FDTFEd, FHKCDS. Emeritus Professor, University of Dundee (Professor of Endodontology, 2000-2013); Dean of Dentistry, 2000-2011; Consultant in Restorative Dentistry, 1988-2013; b. 12.10.48, Carlisle; m., Jennifer Anne; 1 s.; 1 d. Educ. Maidstone Grammar School; Royal Dental Hospital of London. Dental Officer, RAF, 1970-75; general dental practice, 1975-81; Lecturer, Department of Conservative Dentistry, Dundee University, 1981-88; Senior Lecturer in Clinical Practice, Glasgow Dental Hospital and School, 1988-93; Professor of Clinical Dental Practice, Glasgow University, 1993-95, Professor of Endodontology, 1995-2000. Postgraduate Dental Hospital Tutor, Glasgow Dental Hospital, 1992-95; Editor, International Endodontic Journal, 1992-98; President, British Endodontic Society, 1997-98; Chairman, Association of Consultants and Specialists in Restorative Dentistry, 1999-2002; Dental Council, Royal College of Surgeons of Edinburgh, 2000-09 and 2011-17, Dean, Dental Faculty, 2014-17; Chairman, Speciality Advisory Board in Restorative Dentistry RCSEd, 2006-2012; President, European Society of Endodontology, 2009; Chair, Dental Schools Council, UK, 2008-2011; Recipient, Inaugural Scottish Dental Lifetime Achievement Award, 2012; Honorary Diplomate, Indian Board of Endodontics, 2017; Faculty Medal, Royal College of Surgeons of Edinburgh, 2018. Publications: papers and chapters in books on endodontology and applied dental materials science. Clubs: Royal Air Force, New (Edinburgh). Recreations: ornithology; natural history; Scottish art; yoga. Address: (h.) 139 Glasgow Road, Perth PH2 0LU.

Savege, Jim, BA, PhD. Chief Executive, Aberdeenshire Council, since 2015. Educ. St. Columba's College; Liverpool Polytechnic; University of Sheffield. Director, @Ichemy, 1996-2000; Director & Senior Consultant, International Consulting Group Ltd, 2000-02; HR Shared Service Project Leader, Staffordshire County Council, 2002-03; HR Director, Staffordshire County Council, 2004-07; Cumbria County Council: Corporate Director, Human Resources, 2007-08, Corporate Director, Organisational Development, 2008-2012, Corporate Director, Environment, 2012-13, Corporate Director, Environment and Community Services, 2013-15. Member, Fair Work Convention, since 2021; Chair, Scottish Resilience Partnership, since 2020; Board Member, Opportunity North East Limited Digital & Entrepreneurship Board, since 2018; Board Member, Electoral Management Board, since 2016. Publications: Proposed Development of Otterburn Military Training Area in Northumberland National Park: A National Perspective, Journal of Environmental Planning and Management, 1995; The future for the defence estate - Changing demands for army training, Brassey's for the Centre for Defence Studies, 1995; Soldiers, Stone Curlews, and SSSI's: Maintaining the Balance, ECOS 18, 68-74, 1997. Address: Woodhill House, Westburn Road, Aberdeen AB16 5GB; T.-08456 081207.

Savidge, Malcolm Kemp, MA (Hons), FRGU. Former UK Vice-President, United Nations Association; MP (Labour), Aberdeen North, 1997-2005; b. 9.5.46, Redhill. Educ. Wallington County Grammar School, Surrey; University of Aberdeen; Aberdeen College of Education. Production/Stock Control and Computer Assistant, Bryans' Electronics Ltd., 1970-71; Mathematics Teacher, Greenwood Dale Secondary School, Nottingham, 1971; Mathematics and Religious and Social Education Teacher, Peterhead Academy, 1972-73; Mathematics Teacher, Kincorth Academy, Aberdeen, 1973-97. Member, Aberdeen City Council, 1980-96: Vice-Chair, Labour Group, 1980-88, Finance Convener, Policy Vice-Convener, Deputy Leader, 1994-96; Governor, Robert Gordon's Institute of Technology, 1980-88; Governor, Aberdeen College of Education, 1980-87; JP, 1984-96; Fellow, Robert Gordon University, 1997. Recreations: exploring life; puzzles; reading; real ale; spectator sport.

Savill, Professor Sir John Stewart, BA, MBChB, PhD, FRCP, FRCPE, FRCSEd (Hon), FRCPCH (Hon), FASN, FAHMS, FMedSci, FRSE, FRS. Regius Professor of Medical Science, University of Edinburgh, since 2018; b. 25.4.57, London; m., Barbara; 2 s. Educ. Thames Valley Grammar School; University of Oxford; University of Sheffield; University of London. House Surgeon, House Physician and House Officer, Sheffield, 1981-83; Senior House Officer, General Medicine, University Hospital, Nottingham, 1983-84; Rotating Registrar in Renal and General Medicine, Ealing and Hammersmith, 1984-86; MRC Training Fellow and Honorary Senior Registrar, Royal Postgraduate Medical School, 1986-89; Senior Registrar, Renal and General Medicine, Hammersmith Hospital, 1989-90; Wellcome Trust Senior Research Fellow in Clinical Science, and Senior Lecturer, University of London, 1990-93; Professor in Medicine, Head, Division of Renal and Inflammatory Disease, University of Nottingham and Honorary Consultant Physician, University Hospital, Nottingham, 1993-98; Professor of Medicine, 1998-2006, Professor of Experimental Medicine, 2006-2018, Director, MRC/University of Edinburgh Centre for Inflammation Research, 1998-2002, Vice Principal and Head, College of Medicine and Veterinary Medicine, 2002-2018, University of Edinburgh; Honorary Consultant Physician, Royal Infirmary of Edinburgh, 1998-2010. Chief Executive, Medical Research Council, 2010-2018; Chief Scientist for the Scottish Government Health Directorates, 2008-2010; Governor, Health Foundation, 2001-2010. Recreations: hockey; rugby; cricket; football; literature. Address: University of Edinburgh, Queen's Medical Research Institute, 47 Little France Crescent, Edinburgh EH16 4TJ; T.-0131 242 9313; e-mail: john.savill@ed.ac.uk

Sawers, Professor Lesley, MA, PhD. Commissioner for Scotland, Equalities and Human Rights Commission, since 2016; Executive Chair, GenAnalytics Ltd, since 2015; Honorary Professor, Glasgow Caledonian University; formerly Vice Principal and Pro Vice Chancellor, Business and Innovation, Glasgow Caledonian University (2013-

2015); Chief Executive, Scottish Council for Development and Industry, 2008-2013. Educ. Glasgow University; Stirling University. Previously held a number of senior posts in the public and private sectors; joined SCDI from Glasgow Chamber of Commerce, where she was Chief Executive; formerly Strategic Communications Advisor to the Board of VisitScotland; formerly Royal Mail Group Director of Scottish Affairs and Chairman of the Royal Mail Group Advisory Board (Scotland); nine years at ScottishPower in a number of senior management roles, and has worked in strategic management consultancy in both London, Europe and North America. Non Executive Director, Scottish Environment Protection Agency; Trustee, Glasgow Life; Trustee, Commonwealth Youth Trust; Ambassador for Edinburgh Royal Military Tattoo; Member of Secretary of State's Business Board. Awarded an Honorary Doctorate from Strathclyde Business School in 2009 and Glasgow Caledonian University in 2012. Address: (b.) Cowcaddens Road, Glasgow G4 0BA; T.-0141 331 8728.

Sawkins, Professor John William, MA (Hons), MSc (Econ), PhD, FHEA. Deputy Principal (Education and Student Life), Pro-Vice-Chancellor and Professor of Economics, Heriot-Watt University; b. 27.10.65, Croydon; m., Morag Easson; 2 s. Educ. Wolfreton School; Edinburgh University; Glasgow University. Lecturer, Department of Economics, University of Aberdeen, 1992-95, Heriot-Watt University, 1995-2001; Senior Lecturer, Heriot-Watt University, 2001-05, Reader, 2005-08, Professor, since 2008, Dean of The University (Arts, Humanities and Social Sciences), 2007-2012, Head of Accountancy, Economics and Finance, 2009-2012, Deputy Principal, since 2012. Member, South East Scotland Water Customer Consultation Panel (Waterwatch Scotland), 2003-2011; Board Member: Consumer Focus Scotland, 2008-2013, QAA, since 2019. Recreations: gardening; music. Address: (b.) George Heriot Wing, Heriot-Watt University, Edinburgh EH14 4AS; T.-0131 4513611; e-mail: j.w.sawkins@hw.ac.uk

Scally, Dr John, BA (Hons). Chief Executive, The National Library of Scotland, 2014-October 2021. Educ. University of Strathclyde; University of Cambridge; Aberystwyth University. Curator in the British Antiquarian Division, National Library of Scotland, 1993-2002, Deputy Head of Rare Books, 2002-03; Director of University Collections, University of Edinburgh, 2003-2012, Director of Library & University Collections, 2012-14.

Scanlon, Mary, CBE. MSP (Conservative), Highlands and Islands region, 1999-2006 and 2007-2016; former Scottish Conservative and Unionist Party's spokesperson for Education and Lifelong Learning; b. 25.5.47, Dundee.

Schaper, Professor Joachim Ludwig Wilhelm, PhD (Cantab), Habilitation (Tübingen). Professor and Chair in Hebrew, Old Testament and Early Jewish Studies, University of Aberdeen, since 2006; b. 19.03.65, Hanover, Germany; m., Dr. Marie-Luise Ehrenschwendtner; 1 d. Educ. Schiller Schule (Hanover, Germany); Universität Tübingen; University of Cambridge, Trinity College. PhD Cambridge, 1993; Habilitation Tübingen, 1999; Universität Tübingen, 1999-2005; Heisenberg-Fellow of The Deutsche Forschungsgemeinschaft, 2002-05; Reader in Old Testament, University of Aberdeen, 2005-06. Recreations: books; travel. Address: (b.) University of Aberdeen, School of Divinity, History and Philosophy, Aberdeen AB24 3UB; T.-01224-272840; e-mail: j.schaper@abdn.ac.uk

Schlesinger, Professor Philip Ronald, BA, PhD, DrHC, DrHC, FRSE, FAcSS, FRSA, Socio de Honor, Asociación Española de Investigación de la Comunicación. Professor in Cultural Policy, University of Glasgow, 2007-2019, Professor in Cultural Theory, since 2019; Deputy Director, CREATe, UK Centre for Copyright and the Creative Economy, since 2012; b. 31.8.48, Manchester; m., Sharon Joy Rose; 2 d. Educ. North Manchester Grammar School; Queen's College, Oxford; London School of Economics. University of Greenwich: Lecturer, 1974, Senior Lecturer, 1977, Principal Lecturer, 1981, Head, Division of Sociology, 1981-88, Professor of Sociology, 1987-89; Professor of Film and Media Studies, University of Stirling, 1989-2006; Social Science Research Fellow, Nuffield Foundation, 1982-83; Jean Monnet Fellow, European University Institute, Florence, 1985-86; British-Hispanic Chair of Doctoral Studies, Complutense University of Madrid, 2000-01; Chair, Research Assessment Panel for Communication, Cultural and Media Studies, 1995-96 and 1999-2001; Visiting Professor of Media and Communication, University of Oslo, 1993-2004; Visiting Fellow, Maison des Sciences de l'Homme, Paris, 2002, 2005; Visiting Professor: University of Lugano, 2006-07; Institut d'Etudes Politiques, Toulouse, 2009, CELSA, Université de Paris-Sorbonne (Paris IV) 2010, London School of Economics, 2010-2022, LUISS University, Rome, 2011; Wenceslas Roces/UNAM Visiting Chair of Communication, University of Salamanca, 2012; Robert Schuman Fellow, European University Institute, Florence, 2018; Co-Editor, Media, Culture and Society, since 1982; Media Adviser, UK Government's Know How Fund, 1994-98; Board Member, Scottish Screen, 1997-2004; Board Member, TRC Media, Glasgow, 1998-2008; Member, Film Education Working Group reporting to Department of Culture, Media and Sport, 1998-99; Member, Scottish Advisory Committee of Ofcom, 2004-18, Chairman, 2009-2014; Member, Ofcom Content Board, 2014-18; Expert Adviser on broadcasting, Scotland Bill Committee, Scottish Parliament, 2012. Publications: Putting "Reality" Together, 1978, 1987; Televising "Terrorism", 1983; Communicating Politics, 1986; Media, Culture and Society, 1986; Los Intelectuales en la Sociedad de la Informacion, 1987; Media, State and Nation, 1991; Women Viewing Violence, 1992; Culture and Power, 1992; Reporting Crime, 1994; European Transformations, 1994; International Media Research, 1997; European Communication Council Report, 1997; Men Viewing Violence, 1998; Consenting Adults?, 2000; Open Scotland?, 2001; Mediated Access, 2003; The SAGE Handbook of Media Research, 2004; The European Union and the Public Sphere, 2007; Curators of Cultural Enterprise, 2015; The Rise and Fall of the UK Film Council, 2015. Recreations: the arts; walking; travel. Address: Centre for Cultural Policy Research, University of Glasgow, Glasgow G12 8QQ; T.-0141 330 5036; e-mail: philip.schlesinger@glasgow.ac.uk

Scholten, Steph. Director, Hunterian Museum and Art Gallery, since 2017; previously Director of Heritage Collections, University of Amsterdam. Experienced museum director and academic with over 25 years experience in the cultural sector; art historian by background with an international reputation and extensive knowledge of museum collections; worked for the Ministry of Education, Science and Culture, for the National Institute for Conservation, at the National Museum of Antiquities in The Netherlands and was in charge of the extensive and important collections and museums of the University of Amsterdam. Former member and chair of several national committees, amongst them the one that designed the new deaccessioning guidelines for Dutch museums and that have been implemented in the Dutch law on cultural heritage in 2016; currently member of EthCom, the standing committee on professional ethics of the International Council of Museums. Address: The Hunterian, University of Glasgow, University Avenue, Glasgow G12 8QQ; T.-0141 330 4221. E-mail: Steph.Scholten@glasgow.ac.uk

Scobie, William Galbraith, MB, ChB, FRCSEdin, FRCSGlas. Former Consultant Paediatric Surgeon, Lothian Health Board, now retired; part-time Senior Lecturer, Department of Clinical Surgery, Edinburgh University,

1971-92; Assistant Director, Edinburgh Postgraduate Board for Medicine, 1986-92; b. 13.10.36, Maybole; m., Elizabeth Caldwell Steel; 1 s.; 1 d. Educ. Carrick Academy, Maybole; Glasgow University. Registrar, General Surgery, Kilmarnock Infirmary; Senior Registrar, Royal Hospital for Sick Children, Glasgow; Senior Registrar, Hospital for Sick Children, London; Senior Paediatric Surgeon, Abu Dhabi, 1980-81. Recreations: fishing; golf; gardening; music. Address: (h.) 133 Caiyside, Fairmilehead, Edinburgh EH10 7HR; T.-0131-445 7404.

Scothorne, Richard Mark, MA, MPhil. Co-founder and Director, Rocket Science UK Ltd.; b. 17.7.53, Glasgow; m., Dr. Sarah Gledhill; 1 s.; 1 d. Educ. Royal Grammar School, Newcastle upon Tyne; St. Catharine's College, Cambridge; Edinburgh University. Various posts in local government, 1977-86; Scottish Director, British Shipbuilders Enterprise Ltd., 1986-87; Economic Development Manager (Depute Director of Planning), Lothian Regional Council, 1987-92; Director, Partners in Economic Development Ltd., 1992-99; Director, Workforce One Ltd., 1999-2001. Specialist Adviser to House of Commons Select Committee on Education and Employment, 1997-2000; Council Member, The Cockburn Association, since 2014; Trustee, The Fruitmarket Gallery, since 2017, Vice Chair, since 2018; Trustee, The Mental Health Foundation, since 2021. Publication: The Vital Economy: integrating training and enterprise (Co-Author), 1990. Recreations: hill-walking; mountain biking and bikepacking; Scottish and Italian art and architecture. Address: 7 Alfred Place, Edinburgh EH9 1RX.

Scott, Alastair, BA. Travel writer and author, freelance photographer, broadcaster and Yachtmaster Ocean skipper; b. 19.3.54, Edinburgh; m., Sheena. Educ. Blairmore; Sedbergh; Stirling University. Travelled around the world, 1978-83; wrote three travel books, 1984-87 – Scot Free, A Scot Goes South, A Scot Returns; cycled 5,000 miles in E. Europe, 1987-88; wrote Tracks Across Alaska (800-mile sled dog journey), 1988-90; travelled Scotland, 1993-94, wrote Native Stranger; presented BBC film version of Native Stranger, 1995; worked on fiction, took up sailing, 1996-2007; solo voyages round Ireland, Faroes & Shetland and became yacht charter skipper. Publications: Stuffed Lives (novel), 2004; Salt and Emerald - A Hesitant Solo Voyage Round Ireland and the Irish, 2008; Degrees of Illusion (novel), 2009; Eccentric Wealth - The Bulloughs of Rum, 2011. Currently cycling from North Cape (Norway) to Cape Town in stages over several years. Recreations: reading; running; sailing; playing concertina. Address: Mill of Kincraigie, Coull, Tarland, Aberdeenshire AB34 4TT; e-mail: frog@alastair-scott.com; web: www.alastair-scott.com

Scott, Andrew, MA (Hons), MA, DPhil (Soc). Scottish Government Director: Taxes & Revenues, since 2022, Sustainable Land Use, 2019-2022, EU Exit & Transition, 2019, Population Health Improvement, 2015-19. Educ. University of Edinburgh; University of Warwick; Nuffield College, University of Oxford. Member of the University Court, Queen Margaret University, since 2017. Address: (b.) St Andrew's House, Regent Road, Edinburgh EH1 3DG.

Scott, Professor Andrew George, BA. Professor Emeritus of European Union Studies, University of Edinburgh (appointed Professor in 2002); b. 3.10.53, Lanark. Educ. Lanark Grammar School; Heriot-Watt University. Economist, Scottish Office, 1978-79; Lecturer, Department of Economics, Heriot-Watt University, 1979-92; Senior Lecturer, Faculty of Law, University of Edinburgh, 1992-2002. Published widely on economic and political aspects

of European integration. Recreations: hillwalking; running; reading; music. Address: (b.) School of Law, University of Edinburgh, Old College, Edinburgh.

Scott, Craig Alexander Leslie, QC. Retired Sheriff Principal, Glasgow and Strathkelvin (2011-2016). Career: solicitor in 1984, then admitted to the Faculty of Advocates in 1986; from then until 1999 practised as an Advocate, working principally in the areas of reparation, (including medical and professional negligence), defamation, commercial law, property law and administrative law; served as an Advocate Depute, 1994-97; Standing Junior Counsel to the Scottish Office Environment Department, 1994-97, and to the Scottish Office Development Department, 1997-1999; Sheriff of Glasgow and Strathkelvin, 1999-2011; served as a specialist Sheriff in the Commercial Court in Glasgow.

Scott, Eleanor, R., MB, ChB. MSP (Green), Highlands and Islands, 2003-07; b. 23.7.51, Inverness; divorced; 1 s.; 1 d.; partner: Rob Gibson. Educ. Bearsden Academy; University of Glasgow. Junior hospital doctor posts, Inverness, Stirling, Elgin, 1974-78; Trainee, general practice, Nairn, 1979; Community Paediatrician, Highlands, 1980-2003. Has stood for election at all levels, 1990-2001. Recreations: traditional music; gardening. Address: Tir nan Oran, 8 Culcairn Road, Evanton, Ross-shire IV16 9YT; T.-01349 830388; e-mail: eleanorsco@googlemail.com

Scott, Frazer, BSc, MSc, FRSA. Chief Executive Officer, Energy Action Scotland, since 2020. Educ. University of Glasgow; University of Aberdeen; The Institute of Leadership & Management; Chartered Institute of Wastes Management (CIWM). Career history: Zero Waste Scotland: Head of Business Development and Planning, 2012-2017, Head of Litter Prevention, 2014-15, Head of Organisational Development, 2017-19; JFScott Consulting: Business and Organisational Development Adviser, 2019-2020, Interim Manager - Changeworks, 2020; CEO, Forward Scotland; Board Member, Aberdeen Heat & Power, since 2020; Trustee, National Energy Action, since 2020; Commissioner, Scottish Government Energy Consumers Commission, since 2020. Authored and edited innovative work on employability in a greener economy and wellbeing as a measure of social progress. Recreations: cycling; helping out at swimming competitions. Address: Energy Action Scotland, Ingram House, 227 Ingram Street, Glasgow G1 1DA; T.-0141 226 3064.
E-mail: frazer.scott@eas.org.uk

Scott, Hugh Johnstone, DA, CertEd. Writer; Art tutor, Pitlochry Festival Theatre, 2004-2014; Drawing tutor, Argyll College, 2008-2012; b. Paisley; m., Mary (Margo) Smith Craig Hamilton; 1 s.; 1 d. Educ. Paisley Grammar School; Glasgow School of Art. Various jobs, then art school; art teacher, until 1984; full-time writing since 1984, including Writing Fellow, City of Aberdeen, 1991; Lecturer in Creative Writing, Glasgow University Adult and Continuing Education Department, since 1988, Art Tutor, since 1998; Tutor in Creative Writing; winner, Woman's Realm children's short story competition, 1982; winner, children's category, Whitbread Book of the Year, 1989, for Why Weeps the Brogan?; short-listed, Mcvitie's Prize, 1990; Tutor, Arvon Foundation Ltd., 1994; Writing guru for Writers' Forum magazine, since 2007. Publication: Likely Stories, 2011. Recreations: weight training; exploring England; day-dreaming; reading, of course; painting.

Scott, Ian Edward. Deputy Chief Executive and Director of Change, Scottish Court Service, 1995-2004; m., Maureen Ferrie; 1 s.; 1 d. Educ. Bellahouston Academy. Regional

Sheriff Clerk, Lothian and Borders, 1992-95; Sheriff Clerk, Edinburgh, 1992-95; Sheriff Clerk of Chancery, 1992-95; Regional Sheriff Clerk, Glasgow and Strathkelvin, 1996-98; Regional Sheriff Clerk, North Strathclyde, 1997-98; Area Director West, 1998-2001. Hon. Member, Royal Faculty of Procurators, Glasgow. Recreations: amateur astronomy; rugby; making changes. Address: (h.) Meadowbank, Annandale Avenue, Lockerbie; T.-01576 203132.

Scott, James Niall, OBE, LLB; b. 5.4.52, Glasgow; m., Judith; 3 s.; 2 d. Educ. Jordanhill College School; Aberdeen University. External Examiner, Glasgow University Law School, 1990-92; Managing Partner, McGrigor Donald, 1994-97; Chairman, KLegal and McGrigors, 2002-04; Executive Chairman, UK Fisheries Offshore Oil and Gas Legacy Trust Fund Limited, 2007-2017; Chairman, Mark Scott Foundation; Managing Director, The Offshore Pollution Liability Association Limited, 2011-2016; Director, JW Galloway Limited, 2006-2013; Director, Save and Invest Group Limited, 2008-2011; Public Interest Member of Council of The Institute of Chartered Accountants of Scotland, 2007-2013; Non Executive Director, Board of The Treasury Solicitor, 2007-2013; Director, Scottish Ballet, 2009-2015; Director, Barcapel Foundation Limited, 2002-2020. Recreations: swimming; golf; hill-walking. Address: 66 Langside Drive, Glasgow G43 2ST; T.-0141-637 8759; e-mail: nscottnsbs.org.uk

Scott, James Orrock, FCCA. Board Member, Angus, East of Scotland Housing Association, 1988-2012 (retired); Chairman and Board Member, Northern Housing Company Limited, 2000-2010 (retired); Treasurer, SHARP (Scottish Heart and Arterial Disease Risk Prevention), 1992-2005; b. 13.12.40, Dundee; m., Alva; 1 s. Educ. Grove Academy. Former Senior Partner, Henderson Loggie, Chartered Accountants. Past President, Scottish Branch Executive, Society of Certified Accountants; first President, Scottish Athletics Federation. Recreations: athletics; bowling. Address: (h.) 99 Monifieth Road, Broughty Ferry, Dundee DD5 2SL; T.-01382 731822.

Scott, Janys Margaret, QC, MA (Cantab). Called to bar, 1992, took silk, 2007; b. 28.8.53, Radcliffe; m., Rev'd Dr Kevin F. Scott; 2 s.; 1 d. Educ. Queen Elizabeth's Girls Grammar School, Barnet; Newnham College, Cambridge. Lecturer in Iraq, 1976-78; Solicitor, Oxford, 1978-86; Solicitor, Edinburgh, 1987-91; Honorary Lecturer, Dundee University, 1989-94. Convener, Scottish Child Law Centre, 1992-97; Chairman, Stepfamily Scotland, 1998-2002; Visiting Bye-Fellow, Newnham College, Cambridge, 2002; Chairman, BAAF Scottish Legal Group, 2004-2010; UK delegate to CCBE Family Law Committee, since 2012; Chairman, Advocates' Family Law Association, 2013-2018; appointed Part-time Sheriff, 2005; Chairman, Board of Trustees, Adoption and Fostering Alliance Scotland, since 2016; President, Part-Time Sheriffs' Association, since 2018; Trustee, Lawyers Christian Fellowship, since 2018. Recreations: gardening; cooking; reading. Publication: Education Law in Scotland, 2016. Address: (b.) Parliament House, Edinburgh EH1 1RF; T.-0131-226 5071.

Scott, John. MSP (Conservative), Ayr, 2000-2021; Deputy Presiding Officer of the Scottish Parliament, 2011-16; m., Charity (deceased); 1 s.; 1 d. Farming at Balkissock, Ayrshire, since 1973; Founder Director, Ayrshire Country Lamb Ltd., 1988-93; partner in family catering enterprises, 1986-2000; established Ayrshire Farmers' Markets, 1999; Convener, Hill Farming Committee, National Farmers' Union of Scotland, 1993-99; Chairman, Ayrshire and Arran Farming and Wildlife Advisory Group, 1993-99; Chairman,

South of Scotland Regional Wool Committee, 1996-2000; JP; Elder, Ballantrae Church; Chairman, Scottish Area Committee, UK Conservative Countryside Forum, 1998-2000; Chairman, Ayrshire Farmers' Market, since 2000; Chairman, Scottish Association of Farmers' Markets, 2001-04; Council Member, Scottish Agricultural Society, 2004; Coopted Regional Adviser on South of Scotland Board, Moredun Foundation, 2004. Recreations: geology; curling; bridge; rugby.

Scott, John Andrew Ross. Orkney Islands Council Member, since 2017; Vice Chair, Planning; Vice Chair, Education, Leisure and Housing, 2017-19; Chair, Orkney College/UHI, 2017-19; Chairman, NHS Orkney, 2007-2015; Editor, Living Orkney Magazine, 2008-2018 (Winner of Chairman's Prize at Scottish Magazine Award, 2011); Editor, Orkney Today, 2003-08; Leader, Scottish Borders Council, 2002-03; Member, since 1995 (Liberal Democrat Scottish Transport Spokesman, 1998-99); Honorary Provost of Hawick, 1999-2002; News Editor, Hawick News, 2001-02; b. 6.5.51, Hawick; 2 s.; 2 d. Educ. Hawick High School. Worked on father's farm, 1966-74; Journalist, Hawick News, 1977-78, Tweeddale Press Group, 1978-2002, Chief Reporter, Southern Reporter, 1986-2000; first SDP Member, Roxburgh District Council (1980-85) and Borders Regional Council; Chairman, Roxburgh District Licensing Board, 1984-85; first Chairman, Borders Area Party, SDP, 1981-84; Secretary, Roxburgh and Berwickshire Liberal Democrats, 1988-89, Vice Chairman, 1993-94; Chairman, Scottish Association of Direct Labour Organisations Highways Division, 1994-96; Chairman, South East Scotland Transport Partnership, 1998-2003; Chairman, COSLA Road Safety Task Group, 1999-2001; Chairman, South of Scotland Rural Partnership, 2003; Liberal Democrat Candidate, Dumfries, 2001; South of Scotland Liberal Democrat List Candidate, 1999 and 2003. Performed in the first Scottish Amateur Dramatic productions of both 'Cats' (2014) and 'Les Miserables' (2015) with Kirkwall Amateur Operatic Society. Rejoined SNP (2014-16); served on Ministerial Task Group on Health and Social Care Integration (2013-15) and Ministerial Task group on Health Promoting Health Service (2013-15); member of the Scottish Public Health Review Group (2015). Publication: Beyond Tweedbank: The case for extending the Borders Rail Link to Hawick, 2004; Being Heard: Helping To Create The Next Generation of Civic Leaders in Scotland (Co-Author), 2018; Being Heard: One Year On (Co-Author), 2020. Recreations: writing; singing; amateur dramatics; walking. Address: (h.) 19, Torness, Papdale, Kirkwall, Orkney KW15 1UU; T.-01856 988161; m.-07720630337; e-mail: johnross.scott@orkney.gov.uk

Scott, John Dominic, QC, Solicitor Advocate, LLB, DipLP. Senator of the College of Justice, since 2022; Partner, Capital Defence Lawyers, 1991-2018; Solicitor-Advocate, since 2001; b. 20.7.64, Glasgow. Educ. Holyrood Secondary School, Glasgow; Glasgow University. Trainee and Assistant, Hughes, Dowdall & Company, Glasgow, 1985-88 (qualified Solicitor, since 1987); joined Capital Defence Lawyers, Edinburgh (formerly Gilfedder & McInnes), 1988; Member, Executive Committee, Howard League for Penal Reform in Scotland, Convenor, 2006-2018; Past President, Edinburgh Bar Association; Chair, Scottish Human Rights Centre, 1997-2005; appointed President of Society of Solicitor Advocates in 2016; Vice-President (Crime) of Society of Solicitor Advocates, 2008-2016; Chair, Scottish Mental Health Law Review, since May 2019. Address: (b.) 34 Leith Walk, Edinburgh EH6 5AA; T.-0131-553 4333.
E-mail: johndscott@talk21.com

Scott, Sir John Hamilton, KCVO. Farmer; Lord-Lieutenant, Shetland, 1994-2011; Chairman, Woolgrowers

of Shetland Ltd., 1981-2016; b. 30.11.36; m., Wendy Ronald; 1 s.; 1 d. President, Shetland NFU, 1976; Nature Conservancy Council Committee for Scotland, 1984-91; N.E. Scotland Board, Scottish Natural Heritage, 1992-97; Chairman, Shetland Crofting, Farming and Wildlife Advisory Group, 1984-94; Chairman: Shetland Arts Trust, 1994-98, Sail Shetland Ltd., 1996-2000, The Belmont Trust, 1996-2011; Trustee, Shetland Charitable Trust, 1994-2011. Club: The Alpine Club. Recreations: hills; music; pruning. Address: (h.) Keldabister Banks, Bressay, Shetland, ZE2 9EL; T.-01595 820281.
E-mail: scott.gardie@virgin.net

Scott, The Hon. Lady (Margaret E. Scott), QC, LLB, DipLP. Senator of the College of Justice, since 2012; b. 1960, Nairobi, Kenya; partner, Sheriff Frank Crowe; 1 s. Educ. University of Edinburgh; University of Strathclyde. Admitted as a solicitor in 1989 and to the Faculty of Advocates in 1991; became a QC in 2002; has been involved mainly in criminal defence work, specialising in appeals, since 1991; regularly acted as senior counsel from 1995 and from 1996 for a period as an ad hoc Advocate Depute; has been lead counsel in some of the most difficult and serious cases including numerous full bench cases and cases before the Judicial Committee of the Privy Council and United Kingdom Supreme Court, since 2002; appointed as a part-time sheriff in 2002; lead counsel on the Lockerbie appeal, 2007-2009. Address: (b.) Parliament House, Edinburgh EH1 1RQ.

Scott, Primrose Smith, CA. Head of Quality Review, Institute of Chartered Accountants of Scotland, 1999-2002; Senior Partner, The McCabe Partnership, 1987-99; b. 21.9.40, Gorebridge. Educ. Ayr Academy. Trained with Stewart Gilmour, Ayr; qualified as CA 1963; joined Romanes & Munro, Edinburgh, 1964; progressed through manager ranks to Partner, Deloitte Haskins & Sells, 1981-87; set up own practice, Linlithgow, 1987; moved practice to Edinburgh, 1997. Member, Accounts Commission, 1988-92; Non-Executive Director: Dunfermline Building Society, 1990-2005, Northern Venture Trust plc, 1995-2010; Director, Ecosse Unique, since 2004; Institute of Chartered Accountants of Scotland: Member, Council, 1988-95, first Convener, GP Committee, 1990, Vice President, 1992-94, President, 1994-95; Honorary Treasurer, Hospitality Industry Trust Scotland, 1994-2002; Trustee, New Lanark Conservation Trust, 2002-06; Commissioner, Queen Victoria School, Dunblane, 1998-2006; Treasurer: Age Concern Scotland/Age Scotland, 2003-2014, Borders Youth Theatre, 2007-2014; Fellow, SCOTVEC, 1994. Recreation: walking her dogs. Address: (h.) The Cleugh, Redpath, Earlston TD4 6AD.

Scott, Robert. Chief Inspector, HM Chief Inspector, Scottish Fire and Rescue Service, since 2021. Career history; held various strategic roles within the Scottish Fire and Rescue Service including Director of Strategic Planning, Performance and Communication and also Director of Service Delivery for the North of Scotland; served as a Fire Officer for almost 30 years and retired from the post of Assistant Chief Fire Officer at the Scottish Fire and Rescue Service in 2017. Awarded the Queen's Fire Service Medal for distinguished service in 2015. Address: Westburn Drive, Cambuslang G72 7NA; T.-0141 646 4500.

Scott, Professor Roger Davidson, BSc, PhD, FInstP, FRSE. Personal Professorship, University of Glasgow, 1994; Non-Executive Director, Nuclear Decommissioning Authority, 2004-08; b. 17.12.41, Lerwick; m., Marion McCluckie; 2 s.; 1 d. Educ. Anderson Institute, Lerwick; Edinburgh University. Demonstrator, Edinburgh University, 1965-68; Lecturer, then Depute Director, then Director,

SURRC, 1968-98. Recreations: watching football; walking dogs; home maintenance. Address: (h.) 6 Downfield Gardens, Bothwell G71 8UW; T.-01698 854121.

Scott, Roy, DL, JP, OStJ, VMSM, GCLJ, CMLJ, MD, FRCS (Glas), FRCS (Edin), FSA (Scot). Hon. Sheriff, South Strathclyde/Dumfries/Galloway; retired Urologist; b. 17.7.35, Waterloo, Wishaw; m., Janette J.C.; 1 s.; 2 d. Educ. Wishaw High School; University of Glasgow. House Physician, Strathclyde Infectious Diseases Hospital; House Surgeon, Orthopaedic and Casualty Law Hospital; Captain (Temp. Major), RAMC - Kenya, Aden; Surgical Junior posts, Stobhill/Royal Infirmary Glasgow; Consultant Urologist, Glasgow Royal; Hon. Clinical Senior Lecturer, University of Glasgow; Hon. Lecturer, Strathclyde University; Hon. Member, South Central Section, American Urological Society; Ext. Referee, University of Amman; Past Council Member, British Association Urological Surgeons. Author/Co-Author, several books including The Trades House of Glasgow; Co-Author, 6th/7th Edition, 1st Aid Manual; various articles, Burns Chronicle; Member, Millennium and New Millennium Masters; (Livery Companies) London; Past Chairman, Glassford Trust; Arkansas Traveller. Ex Deacon Inc Tailors; Ex Deacon Convener, Trades House Glasgow; Grand Bailliwick of the Military and Hospitaller, Order of St. Lazarus (Scotland) (holding positions of Grand Baillie; Hospitaller and Chancellor); Hon. Member, Sandyford Burns Club; President, Sandyford Burns Club; former Secretary, Sandyford Burns Club; Chairman and Founder Member, Clan Scott Scotland; Past President, Greenock Medical Faculty; Chairman, Luggiebank Fly Dresser Club. Formerly Co-Editor, Justices of the Peace Handbook. Recreations: fishing; Burns; gardening; music. Address: (h.) Garrion, 27 Forest View, Kildrum, Cumbernauld G67 2DB.
E-mail: roy-janette@blueyonder.co.uk

Scott, Stephen R., LLB, WS. Consultant, Burness Paull LLP, since 2015; Owner, McClure Naismith, 2000-2015; Solicitor, since 1988; b. 16.10.64, Elgin; m., Jane; 1 s. Educ. Elgin Academy; Edinburgh University. McClure Naismith: Assistant, 1993-96, Associate, 1996-2000. Recreation: marathon running.

Scott, Tavish Hamilton, BA (Hons). MSP (Liberal Democrat), Shetland, 1999-2019; Leader, Scottish Liberal Democrats, 2008-2011; Deputy Minister for Finance, Public Services and Parliamentary Business, Scottish Executive, 2003-05; Minister for Transport, 2005-07; b. 6.5.66, Inverness; 3 s.; 1 d. Educ. Anderson High School, Lerwick; Napier College, Edinburgh (which became Napier University). Research Assistant to Jim Wallace, MP, 1989-90; Press Officer, Scottish Liberal Democrats, 1990-92; Owner/Manager, Keldabister Farm, Bressay, 1992-99; Shetland Islands Councillor, 1994-99; Chairman, Lerwick Harbour Trust, 1997-99. Recreations: football; golf; cinema; reading.

Scott-Dempster, Robert Andrew, LLB (Hons), WS. Partner, Gillespie Macandrew LLP, since 2003 (Head of Land and Rural Business); b. 30.4.67, Reading; m., Camilla; 2 s. Educ. Marlborough College; Edinburgh University. Captain, 1st Battalion The Black Watch, 1990-95; Associate, Murray Beith Murray WS, 1997-2002. Chairman, Scottish Land & Estates Legal and Taxation Committee; Director, Atlantic Salmon Trust. Recreations: fishing; golf; climbing/hill walking; biography. Address: (b.) 5 Atholl Crescent, Edinburgh EH3 8EJ; T.-0131 225 1677.
E-mail: robert.scott-dempster@gillespiemacandrew.co.uk

Scott Moncrieff, John Kenneth, LLB, WS. Partner, Murray Beith Murray, WS, 1978-2015; Director, Murray Asset Management; b. 9.2.51, Edinburgh; m., Pilla; 1 s.; 2 d. Educ. Marlborough College; Edinburgh University. Bailie of Holyroodhouse and Honorary Consul of Monaco;

Convener, The Saltire Society; Trustee, various charitable trusts and companies. Recreations: football; theatre; horse-racing; hillwalking and writing light verse. Address: 23 Cluny Drive, Edinburgh EH10 6DW; T.-0131-447-1791.
E-mail: john.scottmoncrieff@outlook.com

Scouller, Glen, DA, RGI, RSW. Artist; b. 24.4.50, Glasgow; m., Carol Alison Marsh; 2 d. Educ. Eastbank Academy; Garthamlock Secondary; Glasgow School of Art; Hospitalfield College of Art, Arbroath. RSA Painting Award, 1972; W. O. Hutcheson Prize for Drawing, 1973; travelling scholarship, Greece, 1973; started teaching, Glasgow schools, 1974; part-time tutoring, Glasgow School of Art, 1986-89; Lauder Award, Glasgow Art Club, 1987; Scottish Amicable Award, RGI, 1987; David Cargill Award, RGI, 2006; Residency, L'Association Charles Rennie Mackintosh, Collioure, 2008; Crinan Residency Award, RGI, 2013; elected, RGI, 1989; painting full-time since 1989; elected, RSW, 1997; solo exhibitions: John D. Kelly Gallery, Glasgow, 1977; The Scottish Gallery, Edinburgh, 1980; Fine Art Society, Glasgow, 1985, 1988; Harbour Arts Centre, Irvine, 1986; Fine Art Society, Edinburgh, 1989; Portland Gallery, London, 1989, 1992, 1994, 1998, 2011; Macauley Gallery, Stenton, 1990, 1993, 1996; French Institute, Edinburgh, 1990; Open Eye Gallery, Edinburgh, 1992, 1994, 1997, 2000, 2002, 2007, 2012, 2014, 2016, 2018, 2020; Roger Billcliffe Gallery, Glasgow, 1992, 1995, 1998, 2003, 2007, 2010, 2015, 2018; Everard Read Gallery, Johannesburg, 1997, 2000 (CT), 2001, 2006, 2007, 2008 (CT); Corrymella Scott Gallery, Newcastle-upon-Tyne, 1999; Lemon Street Gallery, Truro, 2002; John Davies Gallery, Moreton-in-Marsh, 2004, 2008; Red Box Gallery, Newcastle upon Tyne, 2005; Henshelwood Gallery, Newcastle upon Tyne, 2005; Thompson's Marylebone, London, 2006; Lemond Gallery, 2011; Inverarity, Glasgow, 2010; Rowallan Castle, Ayrshire, 2012; Gallery 1 at Crinan Hotel, 2014; Maclaurin Art Gallery, Ayr, 2019; The Table, Hay-on-Wye, 2021; works in public, corporate and private collections worldwide. Recreations: travel; music; gardening.
Web: www.glenscouller.com
E-mail: glen.scouller@btinternet.com

Seafield, Earl of; b. 20.3.39, London; m., Leila Refaat (2nd m.); 2 s. Educ. Eton; Cirencester Agricultural College. Recreation: countryside activities. Address: Old Cullen, Cullen, Buckie AB56 4XW; T.-01542 840221.

Searle, Rev. David Charles, MA, DipTh, FSA (Scot). Retired; Minister of the Church of Scotland, since 1965; Warden, Rutherford House, Edinburgh, 1993-2003; b. 14.11.37, Swansea; m., Lorna Christine Wilson; 2 s.; 1 d. Educ. Arbroath High School; St. Andrews University; London University; Aberdeen University. Teacher, 1961-64; Assistant Minister, St. Nicholas Church, Aberdeen, 1964-65; Minister: Newhills Parish Church, 1965-75, Larbert Old, 1975-85, Hamilton Road Presbyterian Church, Bangor, Co. Down, 1985-93; Contributor, Presbyterian Herald; Editor, Rutherford Journal of Church and Ministry, 1993-2003. Publications: Be Strong in the Lord; Truth and Love in a Sexually Disordered World; The Ten Commandments; Through the Year with William Still; abridged version of Calvin's 'Commentary on Psalms'; Joseph: His Arms Were Made Strong; Translation of Robert Bruce's six sermons on Isaiah 38, preached in 1588 in St Giles, Edinburgh; Translation of Robert Bruce's twenty-eight sermons on Hebrews 11, preached 1590-92 in St Giles, Edinburgh. Recreations: gardening; hill-walking; stick-making. Address: (h.) 30 Abbey Lane, Grange, Errol PH2 7GB; e-mail: dcs@davidsearle.plus.com

Seaton, Professor Anthony, CBE, BA, MD (Cantab), DSc(hc) Aberdeen, FRCPLond, FRCPEdin, FFOM, FMedSci. Emeritus Professor, Aberdeen University; Hon. Consultant, Institute of Occupational Medicine, Edinburgh, since 2003; b. 20.8.38, London; m., Jillian Margaret Duke;

2 s. Educ. Rossall School, Fleetwood; King's College, Cambridge; Liverpool University. Assistant Professor of Medicine, West Virginia University, 1969-71; Consultant Chest Physician, Cardiff, 1971-77; Director, Institute of Occupational Medicine, Edinburgh, 1978-90; Professor of Environmental and Occupational Medicine, Aberdeen University, 1988-2003; Editor, Thorax, 1977-82; Chairman, Department of Environment Expert Panel on Air Quality Standards, 1991-2002; President, British Thoracic Society, 1999; Member, Department of Health Committee on Medical Aspects of Air Pollution, 1991-2003; Member, Royal Society Working Group on nanoscience, 2003/04; Chairman, Natural Environment Research Council's Research Advisory Committee on Human Health and the Environment, 2006/07; Member, Industrial Injuries Advisory Council, 2013-19; Member, EU Scientific Committee on Occupational Exposure Limits, 2015-17. Publications: Farewell, King Coal, 2018; books and papers on occupational and respiratory medicine; essays in Scottish Review. Recreations: keeping fit; opera; painting; sculpture. Address: (h.) 8 Avon Grove, Cramond, Edinburgh, EH4 6RF; T.-031-336 5113.

Seaton, Professor Nigel, BSc (Hons), MSE, PhD. Emeritus Professor, Abertay University, since 2022, Principal and Vice-Chancellor, 2012-2022; Governor, Robert Gordon University, since 2022; b. 1960, Falkirk; m.; 3 c. Educ. University of Edinburgh; University of Pennsylvania. Career: worked as a research engineer with Atkins Research and Development and BP, 1986-89; lecturer in chemical engineering at the University of Cambridge and fellow, tutor and Director of Studies in Chemical Engineering and Natural Sciences at Clare College, 1989-97; Visiting Professor, School of Chemical Engineering at Cornell University, 1996-97; Head of the School of Chemical Engineering, becoming Head of the Division of Engineering and then Head of the Institute for Materials and Processes, University of Edinburgh, 1998-2003, Dean of Undergraduate Studies, College of Science and Engineering, then Assistant Principal (Taught Programme Development) and later Vice-Principal (Academic), 2003-08; Deputy Vice-Chancellor (Academic Development), University of Surrey, then Senior Deputy Vice-Chancellor, 2008-2012.

Seckl, Professor Jonathan Robert, OBE, BSc, MB, BS, MRCP(UK), PhD, MAE, FRCPE, FMedSci, FRSE. Moncrieff-Arnott Professor of Molecular Medicine, Edinburgh University, since 1997; Professor of Endocrinology, 1996-97; Head, School of Molecular and Clinical Medicine, 2002-05; Director of Research, College of Medicine and Veterinary Medicine, 2005-2012; Executive Dean (Medicine), since 2010; Vice-Principal (Planning, Resources and Research Policy), 2012-19; Senior Vice-Principal, since 2020; Chairman, Molecular Medicine Centre, 1996-2001; Member: Scottish Science Advisory Committee, 2004-08, Council of Academy of Medical Sciences, 2009-2011, Council, Society for Endocrinology, 2011-16; Co-Chair, Innovate UK-MRC Biomedical Catalyst Major Awards Committee, 2013-18; Chair, Developmental Pathway Funding Scheme, MRC, since 2018; Member, Research Knowledge Exchange Committee, Scottish Funding Council, since 2017; b. 15.8.56, London; m., Molly; 1 s.; 1 d. Educ. William Ellis School, London; University College Hospital Medical School, London. Sir Jules Thorn Research Fellow in Neuroendocrinology, Charing Cross and Westminster Medical School, 1984-87; Honorary Clinical Assistant, National Hospital for Nervous Diseases, London, 1984-87; Lecturer in Medicine, Edinburgh University, 1987-89; Wellcome Trust/Royal Society of Edinburgh Senior Clinical Research Fellow, 1989-97. Publications: 400 papers on glucocorticoids and their metabolism in stress, cognitive aging and metabolic disorders, as well as developmental programming of disease. Address: (b.) Charles Stewart House, 9-16 Chambers Street, Edinburgh EH1 1HT; T.-0131 650 6443; e-mail: j.seckl@ed.ac.uk

Secombes, Professor Christopher John, BSc, PhD, DSc (hc), DSc (Aberdeen), FRSB, FRSE. Regius Chair of Natural History, University of Aberdeen, 2014-2019 (retired); former Head, Scottish Fish Immunology Research Centre, University of Aberdeen, 2001-19; b. 1.4.56, London; m., Karen Ruth; 2 s.; 1 d. Educ. Longdean School, Hemel Hempstead; University of Leeds; University of Hull. Department of Zoology, University of Aberdeen: Lecturer, 1984-91, Senior Lecturer, 1991-97, Professor, 1997, Head of Zoology, 2001-02, Head of Biological Sciences, 2002-2011. President, International Society for Developmental and Comparative Immunology, 2003-06; Adjunct Professor, University of Tromso, 2003-06; Established Chair of Zoology, School of Biological Sciences, University of Aberdeen, 2004-2014. Editor, Fish and Shellfish Immunology. Address: 22 Old Mill Crescent, Balmedie, Aberdeenshire AB23 8WA.
E-mail: christopher.secombes@abdn.ac.uk

Selkirk of Douglas, Rt. Hon. Lord (James Alexander Douglas-Hamilton), PC, QC, MA, LLB. Appointed Life Peer, 1997; MSP (Conservative), Lothians, 1999-2007; MP (Conservative), Edinburgh West, 1974-97; b. 31.7.42, Dungavel House, Strathaven; m., (Priscilla) Susan (Susie) Buchan; 4 s. Educ. Eton; Balliol College, Oxford; Edinburgh University. Officer, TA 6/7 Bn. Cameronians Scottish Rifles, 1961-66, TAVR, 1971-74, Captain in the Cameronian Company of the 2nd Battalion of Lowland Volunteers, 1973-74; Advocate, 1968-74; Councillor, Murrayfield-Cramond, 1972-74; Scottish Conservative Whip, 1977; a Lord Cmnr., HM Treasury, 1979-81, PPS to Malcolm Rifkind MP, at Foreign Office, later as Secretary of State for Scotland, 1983-87; Parliamentary Under Secretary of State: at the Scottish Office for Home Affairs and Environment, 1987-89; for Home Affairs and Environment, 1989-92 (with additional responsibility for local government finance 1989-90, and with additional responsibility for the arts in Scotland, 1990-92); for Education and Housing, Scottish Office, 1992-95; Minister of State for Home Affairs and Health, Scottish Office, 1995-97. Member, Scottish Select Committee, Scottish Affairs, 1981-83; Honorary Secretary: Conservative Parliamentary Constitutional Committee, Conservative Parliamentary Aviation Committee, 1983-87; Chairman, Scottish Parliamentary All-Party Penal Affairs Committee, 1983; Honorary President, Scottish Amateur Boxing Association, 1975-98; President: Royal Commonwealth Society (Scotland), 1979-87, Scottish National Council of UN Association, 1981-87; Member, Council, National Trust for Scotland, 1977-82; Honorary Air Commodore No. 2 (City of Edinburgh) Maritime Headquarters Unit, 1995-2015 and President International Rescue Corps, 1995; an Honorary Air Commodore No. 603 (City of Edinburgh) Squadron; President, International Rescue Corps, since 1995; Patron, Hope and Homes for Children (Chairman, Edinburgh Support Group, 2002-07); President, Veterans Housing Scotland, since 2020 (President, Scottish Veterans Garden City Association Incorporated, 2003-2020); President, Trefoil House Charity, 2007; Chairman, Scottish Advisory Committee of Skill Force, 2009-2019; Lord High Commissioner to the General Assembly of the Church of Scotland, 2012 and 2013; Chair, Scottish Peers Association, 2016-2019. Oxford Boxing Blue, 1962; President, Oxford University Conservative Association, 1963; President, Oxford Union, 1964. Publications: Motive For A Mission: The Story Behind Hess's Flight to Britain, 1971; The Air Battle for Malta: The Diaries of a Spitfire Pilot, 1981 (new edition, 2006); Roof of the World: Man's First Flight over Everest, 1983; The Truth about Rudolf Hess, 1993, 2016 (new paperback edition, 2018); "After You, Prime

Minister", 2009. Recreations: debating; history. Address: House of Lords, London SW1A 0PW.

Sellers, Shona. Head Teacher, Peterhead Academy, since 2014. Previously Depute Head Teacher. Address: (b.) Prince Street, Peterhead, Aberdeenshire AB42 1SY; T.-01779 472231.

Sellers, Professor Susan Catherine, MA, DEA, PhD. Professor of English and Related Literature, St Andrews University, since 1998; b. 7.5.57, Lymington; m., Jeremy Thurlow; 1 s. Educ. British School, Brussels; Sorbonne, Paris. Senior Researcher, Ecole Normale Superieure, Paris, 1989-95; Reader, St Andrews University, 1995-98; Visiting Fellow, New Hall, Cambridge, 1994-95; Invited Fellow, St John's College, Oxford, Summer 1994; Leverhulme Research Fellow and Senior Visiting Scholar, Trinity College, Cambridge, 2001-02. Publications: Writing Differences; Delighting the Heart; Taking Reality by Surprise; Feminist Criticism: Theory and Practice; Language and Sexual Difference; Coming To Writing (translation); Three Steps on the Ladder of Writing (translation); The Semi-Transparent Envelope: Women Writing (Co-author); The Hélène Cixous Reader; Instead of Full Stops; Hélène Cixous: Authorship, Autobiography and Love; The Cambridge Companion to Virginia Woolf (Co-editor); Myth and Fairy Tale in Contemporary Women's Fiction; The Writing Notebooks of Hélène Cixons (Editor). Address: (b.) School of English, University of St. Andrews, Fife, KY16 9AL; T.-01334 462666.

Sempill, 21st Baron (James William Stuart Whitemore Sempill); b. 25.2.49; m.; 1 s.; 1 d. Educ. St Clare's Hall, Oxford. Succeeded to title, 1995; Company Director; contested (Conservative) Edinburgh North and Leith, Scottish Parliamentary election, 1999.

Semple, Professor Colin, PhD. Professor of Computational Biology, University of Edinburgh, since 2015; Head of the IGC Bioinformatics Analysis Core, MRC Human Genetics Unit, since 2001. Career history: Postdoctoral Research Fellow: University of Michigan, 1994-96, Trinity College Dublin, 1996-98, University of Edinburgh, 1998-2001; Principal Investigator, Institute of Genetics and Molecular Medicine, University of Edinburgh, since 2007; appointed Reader in 2014. Member of the MRC Research Training Referee Panel for Special Training Fellowships in Computational Biology, since 2003; Associate Editor of BMC Bioinformatics, since 2005. Address: Institute of Genetics and Cancer, Western General Hospital, Crewe Road, Edinburgh EH4 2XU; T.-0131 651 8614.
E-mail: colin.semple@ed.ac.uk

Semple, David, LLB. Mediator, business adviser; Chairman, Non Intrusive Crossover System Ltd; Past Chair, Cancer Support Scotland (Tak Tent); formerly Partner and Chairman, Semple Fraser WS; b. 29.12.43, Glasgow; m., Jet; 2 s.; 1 d. Educ. Loretto School; Glasgow University. Partner, Bird Son & Semple, 1968-73; Bird Semple and Crawford Herron, 1973-88; Bird Semple Fyfe Ireland, 1988-90. President, Glasgow Chamber of Commerce, 1996-97; Chairman, Interactive Media Alliance Scotland, 1998-99. Recreations: golf; hill-walking; bagpipes. Address: (b.) Flat P, Regent Court, 15 Hughenden Lane, Glasgow G12 9XU; T.-0141-3340744.
E-mail: david.semple@btinternet.com

Semple, Peter d'Almaine, DL, MD, FRCPGlas, FRCPEdin, FRCPLond. B. 30.10.45, Glasgow; m., Judith

Mairi Abercromby; 2 d. Educ. Belmont House; Loretto; Glasgow University. Consultant Physician, Inverclyde Royal Hospital, 1979-2009 (retired); former Postgraduate Medical Tutor, Inverclyde District; Honorary Clinical Senior Lecturer, Glasgow University (retired). Past Chairman, Medical Audit Sub-Committee, Scottish Office; Past President, Greenock and District Faculty of Medicine; Past Chairman, West of Scotland Branch, British Deer Society; Past Director, Medical Audit, and Property Convenor, Royal College of Physicians and Surgeons of Glasgow; Deputy Lieutenant, Renfrewshire; Past Chairman, Ardgowan Hospice; industrial lung disease medico-legal expert; licenced venison dealer. Recreations: field sports; gardening. Address: (h.) Woodside Cottage, Inverkip PA16 0AX; T.-01475 520743.

Semple, Walter George, BL, DUniv. Solicitor, 1963-2012; b. 7.5.42, Glasgow; m., Dr. Lena Ohrstrom; 3 d. Educ. Belmont House, Glasgow; Loretto School; Glasgow University. President, Glasgow Juridical Society, 1968; Tutor and Lecturer (part-time), Glasgow University, 1970-79; Council Member, Law Society of Scotland, 1976-80 and 2003-2011; Chairman, Scottish Lawyers European Group, 1978-81; Member, Commission Consultative des Barreaux Europeens, 1978-80, 1984-87; President, Association Internationale des Jeunes Avocats, 1983-84; Chairman, Scottish Branch, Institute of Arbitrators, 1989-91; Board Member, Union Internationale des Avocats, 1997-2001; Dean, Royal Faculty of Procurators in Glasgow, 1998-2001; President, Franco Scottish Business Club, 2000-01; Trustee and Treasurer, John Muir Trust, 2007-2013; Chairman, Campbell Lee plc, 2002-07; Chairman, Fossil Grove Trust; Honorary Secretary, Geological Society of Glasgow; Hon Treasurer, Scottish Geology Trust. Recreations: walking; music; geology.

Senior, Nora. Chair, Enterprise and Skills Strategic Board, Scottish Government, since 2017; Chair, Scottish Chambers of Commerce, 2013-17; President, British Chambers of Commerce, 2013-16; b. St. Andrews. Educ. University of Glasgow. Career: established The PR Centre in 1990; Managing Director at Hall Associates, Saatchi & Saatchi's Scottish-based PR consultancy; became Executive Chair, UK Regions and Ireland of global public relations and public affairs consultancy, Weber Shandwick in 2009. Recognised by a number of industry awards including Scottish Businesswoman of the Year (2003); a global 'Stevie' award for Best Woman in Business in Europe, Middle East and Asia; a Scottish Woman of Achievement Award and a Fellow of the Chartered Institute of Public Relations for outstanding contribution to the PR industry in Scotland; non-executive Board member of the National Trust for Scotland; Vice Chair of the Scottish Chamber of Commerce (SCC); a Regional Adviser to the London Stock Exchange; Chair of the Women in Business Group (Edinburgh Chamber of Commerce). Address: Scottish Government, Third Floor, 5 Atlantic Quay, 150 Broomielaw, Glasgow G2 8LU; T.-0300 244 6701.

Serafini, Nigel Murray. Interim Managing Director, Lothian Buses, since 2020; b. 2.60. Address: Lothian Buses, 55 Annandale Street, Edinburgh, Midlothian EH7 4AZ; T.-0131 554 4494.

Sewel, Baron (John Buttifant Sewel), CBE, LLD. Senior Vice-Principal, University of Aberdeen, 2001-04; Parliamentary Under-Secretary of State, Scottish Office, 1997-99; b. 1946; m., Jennifer; 1 s.; 1 d.; 2 step-d. Educ. Hanson Boys' Grammar School, Bradford; Durham University; University College Swansea; Aberdeen University. Councillor, Aberdeen City Council, 1974-84 (Leader of the Council, 1977-80); President, COSLA, 1982-

84; Member, Accounts Commission for Scotland, 1987-96; Member, Scottish Constitutional Convention, 1994-95. Research Assistant, Department of Sociology and Anthropology, University College of Wales, Swansea, 1967-69; Aberdeen University, 1969-2004; successively Research Fellow, Lecturer, Senior Lecturer, Professor, Dean, Faculty of Economic and Social Sciences, 1989-94; Vice Principal and Dean, Faculty of Social Sciences and Law, 1995-97, Professor and Vice-Principal, 1999-2001, Senior Vice-Principal, 2001-04; Member of the House of Lords, 1996-2015; Opposition Spokesperson for Scotland, 1996-97; Parliamentary Under-Secretary of State, Scottish Office (Minister for Agriculture, the Environment and Fisheries), 1997-99. Recreations: hill-walking; skiing; watching cricket.

Sewell, Professor John Isaac, PhD, DSc, CEng, FIEE, FIEEE. Emeritus Professor of Electronic Systems, since 2005; Professor of Electronic Systems, Glasgow University, 1985-2005 (Dean, Faculty of Engineering, 1990-93, Member, Court, 2000-04); b. 13.5.42, Kirkby Stephen; m., Ruth Alexandra Baxter; 2 d. Educ. Kirkby Stephen Grammar School; Durham University; Newcastle-upon-Tyne University. Lecturer, Senior Lecturer, Reader, Department of Electronic Engineering, Hull University, 1968-85. Publications: 163 papers. Recreations: swimming; climbing. Member, Council, Baptist Union of Scotland, 2008-2013. Address: (h.) 16 Paterson Place, Bearsden, Glasgow G61 4RU; T.-0141-586 5336.
E-mail: Sewellmac@aol.com

Sha, Amina, MA (Hons), PGDip. National Librarian and Chief Executive, National Library of Scotland, since 2021. Educ. University of Dundee; University of Strathclyde. Career history: Deputy Head, Leisure and Culture Dundee, Dundee Libraries, 2001-2015; Chief Executive Officer, Scottish Library and Information Council, 2014-16; Director of Programme, Scottish Book Trust, 2016-18; Assistant Director, University of St Andrews, 2018-2021. Trustee, Scottish Library and Information Council, since 2021; Chair, Legal Deposit Implementation Group, since 2022; Chair, Edinburgh Advisory Group, Common Purpose, since 2022; Advisory Board Member, The British Library, since 2021; Trustee, Friends of the National Libraries, since 2021; President, CILIPS, since 2021; Board Member, StAnza, Scotland's International Poetry Festival, since 2020; Visiting Professor, Robert Gordon University, since 2015; Board Trustee, Chair of Governance Committee, National Library of Scotland, 2015-2021. Address: National Library of Scotland, 312.320 Lawnmarket, Edinburgh EH1 2PH; T.-0131 623 3700.
E-mail: a.shah@nls.uk

Shanks, Duncan Faichney, RSA, RGI, RSW. Artist; b. 30.8.37, Airdrie; m., Una Brown Gordon. Educ. Uddingston Grammar School; Glasgow School of Art. Part-time Lecturer, Glasgow School of Art, until 1979; now full-time painter; one-man shows: Stirling University, Scottish Gallery, Fine Art Society, Talbot Rice Art Gallery, Edinburgh University, Crawford Centre, Maclaurin Art Gallery, Glasgow Art Gallery, Fine Art Society, touring exhibition (Wales); taken part in shows of Scottish painting, London, 1986, Toulouse, Rio de Janeiro, 1985, Wales, 1988; Scottish Arts Council Award; Latimer and MacAulay Prizes, RSA; Torrance Award, Cargill Award, MacFarlane Charitable Trust Award, RGI; May Marshall Brown Award, RSW; The Lord Provost's Prize for painting (GOMA), 1996; tapestry commissioned by Coats Viyella, woven by Edinburgh Tapestry Company, presented to Glasgow Royal Concert Hall, 1991. Gifted 106 sketchbooks to Hunterian Art Gallery, Glasgow University with Exhibition and Publication, 2015. Recreations: music; gardening.

Shanks, Melvyn D., BSc, DipEd, MInstP, CPhys, SQH. Principal, Belmont House School, since 2006; b. 15.7.62, Glasgow; m., Lynn; 2 s. Educ. The High School of

Glasgow; University of Glasgow; University of Strathclyde. Teacher of Physics and Maths, The High School of Glasgow, 1985-90; Belmont House School: Head of Physics, 1990-97, Depute Head, 1997-2005. Recreation: member of the Salvation Army; music; golf; reading. Address: (b.) Belmont House School, Newton Mearns, Glasgow G77 5DU; T.-0141-639-2922.
E-mail: admin@belmontschool.co.uk

Shanks, Rev. Norman James, MA, BD, DD; b. 15.7.42, Edinburgh; m., Ruth Osborne Douglas; 2 s.; 1 d. Educ. Stirling High School; St. Andrews University; Edinburgh University. Civil Servant, Scottish Office, 1964-79; Chaplain, Edinburgh University, 1985-88; Lecturer in Practical Theology, Glasgow University, 1988-95; Leader, Iona Community, 1995-2002; Minister, Govan Old Parish Church, Glasgow, 2003-07. Convener, Acts Commission on Justice, Peace, Social and Moral Issues, 1991-95; Chairman, Edinburgh Council of Social Service, 1985-88; Chairman, Secretary of State's Advisory Committee on Travelling People, 1985-88; Convener, Church and Nation Committee, Church of Scotland, 1988-92; Moderator, Glasgow Presbytery, 2002-03; President, Scottish Churches Open College, 2001-03; Member, Broadcasting Council for Scotland, 1988-93; Member, Scottish Constitutional Convention, 1989-97; Central Committee of World Council of Churches, 1998-2006 (Moderator of WCC 9th Assembly Planning Committee, 2003-06); Member of Board of Christian Aid, 2000-05; Member of Greater Glasgow and Clyde Health Board, 2010-2016; HonDD, Glasgow University, 2005. Recreations: armchair cricket; occasional golf. Address: (h.) 1 Marchmont Terrace, Glasgow G12 9LT; T.-0141-339 4421.

Sharkey, Professor Jeffrey. Principal, Royal Conservatoire of Scotland, since 2014. Educ. Manhattan School of Music; Yale University; University of Cambridge. Director of Music, The Purcell School and Head of Academic Music, Wells Cathedral School, 1996-2001; Dean, Cleveland Institute of Music, 2001-06; Director, Peabody Institute, 2006-2014. Founding member of the Pirasti Piano Trio, which recorded with ASV Records in the United Kingdom and toured throughout Europe and the United States; coached chamber music as a faculty member and in master classes and summer festivals; performed with the Baltimore Symphony and collaborated with members of the Cleveland, Orion, and Cavani Quartets. Address: Royal Conservatoire of Scotland, 100 Renfrew Street, Glasgow G2 3DB; T.-0141 332 4101.

Sharp, Kerry. Director, Entrepreneurship & Investment, Scottish Enterprise, since 2022, Interim Managing Director, Scottish Economic Development, 2020-2021. Educ. Newton Stewart; Glasgow Caledonian University. Career history: Structured Finance Analyst, Bank of Scotland, 1995-2001; Portfolio Manger, 3i Group plc, 2001-05; Property Specialist, Anglo Irish Bank Corporation Ltd, 2005-2006; Director of Portfolio Management, The Scottish Investment Bank, 2006-2013, Director (Full-time), 2013-2020. Address: Scottish Enterprise HQ, Atrium Court, 50 Waterloo Street, Glasgow G2 6HQ.
E-mail: kerrysharp@scotent.co.uk

Sharp, Paul M., BSc, PhD, MRIA, FRSE, FRS. Alan Robertson Chair of Genetics, University of Edinburgh, since 2007; b. 12.09.57, Heanor. Educ. University of Edinburgh. Lecturer, Associate Professor, Trinity College, University of Dublin, 1982-93; Professor of Genetics, University of Nottingham, 1993-2007. President, Society for Molecular Biology and Evolution, 2008. Address: (b.) Institute of Evolutionary Biology, University of Edinburgh, Kings Buildings, Edinburgh EH9 3FL; T.-0131-651-3684; e-mail: paul.sharp@ed.ac.uk

Sharp, Professor Peter Frederick, OBE, BSc, PhD, CPhys, CSci, FInstP, ARCP, FIPEM, FRSE. Emeritus

Professor of Medical Physics, University of Aberdeen; b. 13.8.47, Spalding; 2 s. Educ. Spalding Grammar School; Durham University; Aberdeen University. University of Aberdeen: Lecturer in Medical Physics, 1974-83, Senior Lecturer in Medical Physics, 1983-90, Professor of Medical Physics, 1990-2012. Publication: Practical Nuclear Medicine (Editor). E-mail: p.sharp@abdn.ac.uk

Sharwood Smith, Professor Michael Anthony, PhD, MA, DipAppLing. Professor Emeritus, Heriot-Watt University; b. 22.5.42, Cape Town, South Africa; m., Ewa Maria Wróblewska; 2 d. Educ. King's School, Canterbury; St Andrews University; Edinburgh University. English Teacher: Centre Pédagogique Regionale, Montpellier, France; British Centre, Sweden; British Council Senior Lecturer, Adam Mickiewicz University, Poznan, Poland; Senior Lecturer, Utrecht University, Netherlands. Founding Vice-President, European Second Language Association; Honorary Professorial Fellow, Edinburgh University. Publications on language acquistion, billingualism and cognitive science. Books include Second Language Acquisition: Theoretical Foundations, 1994 and Introducing Language and Cognition, 2017. Founding Editor, Second Language Research. Recreations: painting and drawing; music, trumpet and guitar; flight simulation. Address: (b.) Room 4.03 Charteris Land, University of Edinburgh, Old Moray House, Holyrood Road, Edinburgh EH8 8AQ.

Shaw, Rev. Dr. Alistair Neil, MA (Hons), BD (Hons), MTh, PhD. Minister, Howwood Parish Church linked with St. Paul's Parish Church, Johnstone, since 2003; b. 6.7.53, Kilbarchan; m., Brenda Bruce; 2 d. Educ. Paisley Grammar School; University of Glasgow. Minister: Relief Parish Church, Bourtreehill, Irvine, 1982-88, Laigh Kirk, Kilmarnock, 1988-99, Greenbank Parish Church, Clarkston, Glasgow, 1999-2002. Moderator of Presbytery of Irvine and Kilmarnock, 1995-96; Moderator of Presbytery of Greenock and Paisley, 2009-10; Clerk to Presbytery of Greenock and Paisley, 2019-20. Publication: Oral Transmission and the Dream Narratives of Matthew 1-2. Recreations: foreign travel; ancient history; swimming; cycling; walking. Address: 9 Stanley Drive, Brookfield, Johnstone, Renfrewshire PA5 8UF; T.-01505 320060.
E-mail: ans2006@talktalk.net

Shaw, Major General David, CBE, MDA, DipM. Director, David Shaw Ltd; CEO, AF&V Launchpad (charity); CEO, The Veterans' Foundation (charity); Artist, www.davidshawart.co.uk; Visiting Professor, Aberdeen Business School, since 2010; b. Ceylon (Sri Lanka). Career history: commissioned into the Royal Artillery in 1976; commanded 40 Regiment Royal Artillery (The Lowland Gunners); commanded 15 (North East) Brigade, 2002-2004; Director of Media and Communication for the Army, Headquarters Land Forces, 2007-2009; General Officer Commanding 2nd Division, 2009-2012; Governor, Edinburgh Castle, 2009-2012. Royal Scots Club; Bembridge Sailing Club; former Commodore, Royal Artillery Yacht Club. Instagram@davidshawinedinburgh
E-mail: dahshaw@gmail.com

Shaw, Donald. Head, Queen Victoria School, Dunblane, since 2016. Career history: began teaching career at Inveralmond Community High School, Livingston, West Lothian (promoted to Principal Teacher of Mathematics with whole-school responsibility for raising attainment); appointed Head of Mathematics, Queen Victoria School, Dunblane in 2006, Senior and Academic Deputy Head, 2012-16. Recreations: keen runner; cyclist; hill walking.

Shaw, Rev. Duncan, BD (Hons), MTh. Minister, St. John's, Bathgate, since 1978; b. 10.4.47, Blantyre; m., Margaret S. Moore; 2 s.; 1 d. Educ. St. John's Grammar School, Hamilton; Hamilton Academy; Trinity College,

Glasgow University. Assistant Minister, Netherlee Parish Church, Glasgow, 1974-77. Clerk, West Lothian Presbytery, since 1982 (Moderator, 1989-90). Recreations: gardening; travel (in Scotland). Address: St. John's Parish Church Manse, Mid Street, Bathgate EH48 1QD; T.-Bathgate 653146.
E-mail: westlothian@churchofscotland.org.uk

Shaw, Jo, BA (Cantab), LenDr (Brussels), LLD (Edin), FRSE, AcSS. Salvesen Chair, European Institutions, University of Edinburgh, since 2005; Dean of Research, College of Humanities and Social Science, 2009-2013; Director, Institute for Advanced Studies in the Humanities, 2014-2017; Senior Research Fellow, Federal Trust, London, since 2001; b. 17.09.61, Shipley; 1 s. Educ. Bradford Girls' Grammar School; Trinity College, Cambridge. Lecturer in Law, University of Exeter, 1984-90; Senior Lecturer in Law, Keele University, 1990-95; Professor of European Law and Director of The Centre for The Study of Law in Europe, University of Leeds, 1995-2001; Professor of European Law, University of Manchester, 2001-04. Author of many books and papers on European Union Law and citizenship. Recreations: photography; swimming; walking. Address: (b.) School of Law, University of Edinburgh, Old College, South Bridge, Edinburgh EH8 9YL; T.-0131 650 9587.
E-mail: jo.shaw@ed.ac.uk

Shaw, Martin. Headteacher, Perth High School, since 2021. Address: Perth High School, Oakbank Road, Perth PH1 1HB; T.-01738 628271; e-mail: mshaw@pkc.gov.uk

Shaw, Neil, BSc, BA (Hons). Field Officer, School Leaders Scotland; Past President, School Leaders Scotland; b. 30.12.53, Airdrie; m., Nan; 1 s.; 1 d. Educ. Airdrie Academy; University of Glasgow. Mathematics Teacher, Caldervale High School, Airdrie, 1977-87; Principal Teacher of Mathematics: Crookston Castle Secondary School, Glasgow, 1987-90, Carluke High School, 1990-93; Assistant Head Teacher, Boclair Academy, Bearsden, 1993-98; Head Teacher: Broxburn Academy, 1998-2002, Boclair Academy, 2002-2013. Recreation: golf (Airdrie Golf Club, New Club St Andrews). E-mail: nshaw@ascl.org.uk

Shaw, Richard Wright, CBE, MA. Principal and Vice Chancellor, University of Paisley, 1992-2001; b. 22.9.41, Preston; m., Susan Angela; 2 s. Educ. Lancaster Royal Grammar School; Sidney Sussex College, Cambridge. Assistant Lecturer in Management, then Lecturer in Economics, Leeds University, 1964-69; Lecturer in Economics, then Senior Lecturer, Stirling University, 1969-84; part-time Lecturer, Glasgow University, 1978-79; Visiting Lecturer, Newcastle University, NSW, 1982; Head, Department of Economics, Stirling University, 1982-84; Professor and Head, Department of Economics and Management, Paisley College, 1984-86, Vice Principal, 1986, Principal, 1987-92. Director, Renfrewshire Enterprise, 1992-2000; Member, Scottish Economic Council, 1995-98; Director, Higher Education Careers Service Unit, 1996-2001; Member, Board of Management, Reid Kerr College, 1993-2001; Member, Scottish Business Forum, 1998-99; Convener, Committee of Scottish Higher Education Principals, 1996-98; Member, Independent Review of Higher Education Pay and Conditions, 1998-99; Chairperson, Lead Scotland, 2001-07. Fellow, Scottish Vocational Education Council, since 1995; DUniv (Glasgow), 2001; DUniv (University of the West of Scotland), 2008. Recreations: sketching and painting. Address: (b.) Drumbarns, 18 Old Doune Road, Dunblane FK15 9AG.

Shearer, David James Buchanan, BAcc, CA, FRSA. Partner, Buchanan Shearer Associates LLP, since 2011; Chairman: Esken Limited, since 2019 (Executive Chairman, since 2021), Socium Group, since 2019,

Speedy Hire plc, since 2018, Liberty Living Group, 2015-18 (Executive Chairman, 2016-18), Scottish Edge Fund, since 2014, Aberdeen New Dawn Investment Trust plc, 2012-2019, Mouchel Group, 2012-14, Crest Nicholson plc, 2007-09; Co-Chairman, Martin Currie (Holdings) Limited, 2012-14; Non-Executive Director: Speedy Hire plc, 2016-18; Mithras Investment Trust plc, 2007-2018; Senior Independent Director: STV Group plc, 2007-2017; Renold plc; Superglass Holdings plc, 2007-2012; Scottish Financial Enterprise, 2005-2010; Governor, The Glasgow School of Art, 2004-2010; Chief Strategic Adviser and Non-Executive Director, City Inn Limited, 2010-2011; Non-Executive Director, HBOS plc, 2004-07; b. 24.3.59, Dumfries; partner, Virginia Braid. Educ. Eastwood High School, Glasgow; Glasgow University; Columbia Business School (Leadership Development Programme). Joined Deloitte & Touche (formerly Touche Ross & Co.), 1979; qualified CA, 1982; Partner, 1988; Partner in charge, Corporate Finance, 1992-99; National Corporate Finance Executive Member, 1992-99; Global Director of Corporate Finance, Deloitte Touche Tohmatsu, 1996-99; Senior Partner, Scotland & Northern Ireland, 1999-2003; UK Board Member, 1999-2003; UK Executive Group Member, 1999-2003. Recreations: heli-skiing; yachting; rugby; golf; art; wine. Address: (b.) Buchanan Shearer & Co Limited, 32 Great Western Terrace Lane, Glasgow G12 9XA; T.-07785 701889.
E-mail: djbshearer@btopenworld.com

Shearer, Theresa, BA (Hons). Group Chief Executive Officer, ENABLE Group, since 2019. Educ. University of Strathclyde (Human Resources Management); The Institute of Directors (Diploma in Corporate Direction); Harvard Business School (Certificate: Strategic Perspectives in Non-Profit Management). Career history: Executive Director, Kinetic plc, Manchester, 1996-2004; Chief Operating Officer, ENABLE Scotland, 2008-2014; Board/Strategic Advisor to Charity Sector, 2014-15; Chief Executive Officer, ENABLE Scotland, 2015-19. First Minister's 'First Mentor' scheme: Mentor, The Scottish Government, since 2018; IoD Director of the Year: Judging panel member, The Institute of Directors Scotland, since 2020; Advisory Council Member, Young Scot, since 2019; Board Director, Inclusion Europe, since 2018; Board Director/Vice Convenor, SCVO (Scottish Council for Voluntary Organisations), since 2015; Member of the Post-Covid-19 Futures Commission Inclusive Public Service Working Group, Royal Society of Edinburgh, since 2020; Commissioner of the Law Family Commission on Civil Society, Pro Bono Economics, since 2020. Member, The Institute of Directors, since 2003; Chartered Fellow, CIPD, since 2003; FRSA, since 2017. Address: ENABLE Scotland, INSPIRE House, 3 Renshaw Place, Eurocentral, North Lanarkshire ML1 4UF; T.-01698 737 000.
E-mail: theresa@enable.org.uk

Shedden, Fred, MA, LLB. Chair, The Centre for Confidence and Well-being, since 2007; Non Executive Director: iomart Group plc, 2000-2011, Murray International Trust plc, since 2000; b. 30.6.44, Edinburgh; m., Irene; 1 s.; 1 d. Educ. Arbroath High School; Aberdeen University. McGrigor Donald: Partner, 1971, Managing Partner, 1985-92, Senior Partner, 1993-2000. Director, Scottish Financial Enterprise, 1989-99; Director, Standard Life Assurance Society, 1992-99; Director, Scottish Metropolitan Property PLC, 1998-2000; Non executive director, Glasgow School of Art, 2002-2010. Address: The Centre for Confidence and Well-being, Suite 403, 111 West George Street, Glasgow G2 1QX; T.-07516 961 800.
E-mail: shedden@madasafish.com

Sheehan, Wendy Anne, LLB, DipLP, NP. Sheriff, Scottish Court Service, since 2005; Partner, Sheehan Kelsey Oswald Family Law Specialists, 2008-2011; b. 26.12.68,

Glasgow. Educ. St. George's School for Girls; University of Aberdeen. Trainee, Assistant, Associate Solicitor, Russel and Aitken, Solicitors, 1990-96; Associate, Balfour and Manson, Solicitors, 1996-2000; Partner, MHD Solicitors, 2000-06. Former Chair, Couple Counselling Lothian; former Convener, CALM. Author for Butterworths Family Law Service; various published articles on family law. Listed as leading family lawyer in both Chambers and Partners guide to the legal profession and The Legal 500.

Sheldon, David Henry, QC, LLB (Hons), DipLP; b. 22.4.65, Dundee. Educ. High School of Dundee; Aberdeen University. Admitted as Solicitor, 1990; Lecturer in Private Law, Edinburgh University, 1990-98; Associate Dean, Faculty of Law, Edinburgh University, 1994-97; admitted to Faculty of Advocates, 1998; took silk, 2013. Publications: Evidence: Cases and Materials, 1996; Scots Criminal Law, 2nd edition, 1997; The Laws of Scotland: Stair Memorial Encyclopaedia (Contributor); Court of Session Practice (Contributor). Recreations: rock climbing; cycling; music; song; laughter and the love of friends. Address: (b.) Advocates' Library, Parliament House, Edinburgh EH1 1RF; T.-0131-667 2043.

Shepherd, Professor James, BSc, MB, ChB, PhD, FRCPath, FRCP (Glas), FMedSci, FRSE. Emeritus Professor in Vascular Biochemistry, University of Glasgow, since 2006; b. 8.4.44, Motherwell; m., Janet Bulloch Kelly; 1 s.; 1 d. Educ. Hamilton Academy; Glasgow University. Lecturer, Glasgow University: Biochemistry, 1968-72, Pathological Biochemistry, 1972-77; Assistant Professor of Medicine, Baylor College of Medicine, Houston, Texas, 1976-77; University of Glasgow: Senior Lecturer in Pathological Biochemistry, 1977-84, Professor in Pathological Biochemistry, 1984-2006; Visiting Professor of Medicine, Geneva University, 1984; Director, West of Scotland Coronary Prevention Study; Director, Prospective Study of Pravastatin in the Elderly at Risk; Executive Member, Treating to New Targets Study, 1998-2005; Principal Investigator, Jupiter UK, 2005-08; Chairman, European Atherosclerosis Society, 1993-96; Visiting Professor, The Cleveland Clinic, 1998; author of textbooks and papers on lipoprotein metabolism and heart disease prevention. Address: 17 Barriedale Avenue, Hamilton ML3 9DB.

Shepherd, Dr Robbie (Robert Horne), MBE, MUniv (Aberdeen), Doctor of Music (honoris causa), The Royal Conservatoire of Scotland, 2017. Freelance Broadcaster, since 1976, including presenter of BBC Radio Scotland's Take The Floor (1981-2016); Journalist and Author, specialising in the Doric language; b. 30.4.36, Dunecht, Aberdeen; m., Agnes Margaret (Esma) (1961); 1 s. Educ. Robert Gordon's College, Aberdeen. Left school at 15 to work in accountant's office, eventually becoming ACCA; management accountant, fish firm, 13 years; self-employed accountant. Hon. President, Friends of Elphinstone Institute, University of Aberdeen; Hon. President, Buchan Heritage Society. Received the Hamish Henderson Award for services to Traditional Music and inducted into the Hall of Fame - Scots Trad Music Awards, 2006. Hands up for Trad Landmark Award (2016) and Honoured Member of Braemar Royal Highland Society (2010). Recreations: gardening; traditional arts of Scotland, especially the use of the Doric tongue.

Sheppard, Tommy. MP (SNP), Edinburgh East, since 2015; former SNP Shadow Leader of the House; b. 1959, Coleraine, County Londonderry. Educ. local grammar school in Coleraine; Aberdeen University. Elected Vice President of the NUS (1982-84); worked in the East End of London and in 1986 was elected as a Labour member on Hackney London Borough Council; became Deputy Leader of the Council in 1990; employed by Edinburgh District Council in 1994; Assistant General Secretary, Labour Party, 1994-97. Founded The Stand Comedy Club in Edinburgh in 1995; (expanded to include branches in Glasgow and Newcastle upon Tyne and is now one of the largest venues at the Edinburgh Fringe Festival). Edinburgh South organiser of the Yes Scotland campaign in 2012; Member, SNP, since 2014. Member: National Council of the Scottish Independence Convention, Common Weal. Address: House of Commons, London SW1A 0AA.

Sheridan, James. Councillor (Labour), Houston, Crosslee and Linwood, 2017-2022; Labour MP, Paisley and Renfrewshire North, 2005-2015, West Renfrewshire, 2001-05; b. 24.11.52, Glasgow; m., Jean; 1 s.; 1 d. Educ. St Pius Secondary School. Trade union official, TGWU, 1999-2000; material handler, 1984-99; TGWU Convenor, Pilkington Optronics, 1985-99. Recreation: keep-fit activities. Address: (h.) 31 Park Glade, Erskine, Renfrewshire PA8 7HH.

Sheridan, Michael. Principal Solicitor, Sheridans, Glasgow, since 1974; Secretary, Scottish Law Agents Society, since 2004; b. 28.3.48, Glasgow; m., Carole; 3 s. Educ. St. Aloysius College, Glasgow; St. Mungo's Academy; University of Glasgow. Solicitor at Dundee and Glasgow, since 1972; College and University Lecturer, 1974-2001; Joint Standing Committee on Legal Education, 1998-2001; First Tier Tribunal Judge, Her Majesty's Courts and Tribunal Service, 2000-2019. Recreations: hill walking; cycling; travel. Address: (b.) 166 Buchanan Street, Glasgow G1 2LW; T.-0141 332 3536.
E-mail: michael@sheridansolicitors.co.uk

Sheridan, Tommy. Convenor, Solidarity, 2019-2021 (Joint Convenor, 2006-2016). Educ. University of Stirling; b. 7.3.64, Glasgow; m., Gail. MSP (Solidarity), Glasgow, 2006-07 (Scottish Socialist, 1999-2006). Member, Glasgow City Council, 1992-2003; President, Anti Poll Tax Federation, 1989-92; Member, The Alba Party, since 2021.

Shiach, Allan G., BA. Chairman, Macallan-Glenlivet PLC, 1979-96; Chairman, Scottish Film Council, 1991-97; Chairman, Scottish Film Production Fund, 1991-96; Chairman, Scottish Screen, 1996-98; b. 16.9.40, Elgin; m., Kathleen Breck; 2 s.; 1 d. Educ. Gordonstoun School; McGill University, Montreal. Writer/Producer, since 1970; Writer/Co-Writer: Don't Look Now, The Girl from Petrovia, Daryl, Joseph Andrews, Castaway, The Witches, Cold Heaven, Regeneration, In Love and War, and other films; Member: Broadcasting Council for Scotland, 1988-91; Member, Council, Scotch Whisky Association, 1984-96; Chairman, Writers' Guild of G.B., 1989-91; Director, Rafford Films, since 1982; Director, Scottish Media Group plc, 1993-2006; Governor, British Film Institute, 1992-98. Hon. Doctorate of Arts, Napier University (June, 2007); Hon. Doctorate Honoris Causa, Aberdeen University (November 2007). Co-author, co-producer, "Priscilla, The Musical", Palace Theatre, London, March 2009-January 2012; also productions in New York, Brazil, Italy etc; co-writer and script consultant on the Norwegian film Kon-Tiki (2012), which was nominated for an Oscar in 2013 in the foreign language category; co-creator and Executive Producer, The Queen's Gambit for Netflix, 2020; winner of Golden Globe, PGA and WGA awards; Emmy Award, 2021 as Co-creator and Producer, The Queen's Gambit; Honorary Fellowship, The Marketing Society; Visiting Professor, Edinburgh Napier University, since 2015; Freeman, City of London, 1988.
E-mail: algscott@gmail.com

Shields, Tom, BA. Journalist; b. 9.2.48, Glasgow; 1 s.; 1 d. Educ. Bellarmine Comprehensive; Lourdes Secondary

School (no miracle); Strathclyde University. Journalist, Sunday Post; Diary Writer, The Herald, 1979-2002; Columnist, Herald Scotland. Publications: Tom Shields' Diary; Tom Shields Too; Tom Shields Free at Last; Tom Shields Goes Forth; Just the Three Weeks in Provence (Co-author); 111 Places in Glasgow That You Shouldn't Miss, 2018. Recreation: Celtic studies.

Shinwell, Sir (Maurice) Adrian, Kt, DL, LLB, NP. (Retired) Solicitor; Senior Partner, Kerr Barrie, Glasgow, 1991-2016; Deputy Lieutenant, Renfrewshire, 1999-2011; b. 27.2.51; m., Lesley McLean; 2 s.; 1 d. (1 s. deceased). Educ. Hutchesons' Boys' Grammar School; Glasgow University. Admitted Solicitor, 1975; joined Kerr, Barrie & Duncan, 1976; Notary Public, since 1976; Tutor (part-time), Law Faculty, Glasgow University, 1980-84; Solicitor-Mediator, 1994-2004; Director: National Theatre of Scotland, 2007-15, Digital Animations Group plc, 2002-07, St. Leonards School, 2001-2004, Kerr Barrie Nominees Ltd., 1991-2017. Scottish Conservative and Unionist Association: Member, Scottish Council, 1982-98; Chairman, Eastwood Association, 1982-85; Chairman, Cumbernauld and Kilsyth Association, 1989-91; Vice-President, 1989-92; President, 1992-94; Scottish Conservative and Unionist Party: Chairman, Candidates' Board, Member, Scottish Executive and Scottish Council, 1998-2000; Member, Central Advisory Committee on Justices of the Peace, 1996-99; Vice Chairman, Justices of the Peace Advisory Committee, East Renfrewshire, 2000-06.

Shirreffs, Jennifer Anne, MBE (2009), DL, CStJ, M.Univ, BSc. Director, Aberdeen and NE Deaf Society, 1984-2009, Chairman, Board of Directors, 1992-2003 and 2008-09; Deputy Lieutenant, City of Aberdeen, since 2005; Burgess of the City of Aberdeen, since 2000; b. 20.1.49, Aberdeen; m., Dr Murdoch J. Shirreffs. Educ. Aberdeen High School for Girls; University of Aberdeen. PA to Rt. Hon. Jo Grimond MP while Rector of Aberdeen University, 1971-72; Co-ordinator, Community Arts Projects, Rowntree Trust, 1972-73. Chairman, Aberdeen Centenary Committee, Royal Scottish Society for Prevention of Cruelty to Children (now Children First), 1983-85; Trustee, Aberdeen Gomel Trust (Aberdeen City Council), since 1990; Vice-Chairman, St. John's Association (Aberdeen) and Order Committee, since 1994 and Chairman, 2011-2016; Elected Commander of the Order of St John, 2004; Chairman, Friends of Scottish Ballet (Grampian), 1989-2007; Chairman, Trading Company of Scottish Ballet, 2000-07; Director and Chairman, Friends of Aberdeen and NE Scotland Music School, 1998-2016 (now Patron); Director, Aberdeen Performing Arts running His Majesty's Theatre Music Hall, Lemon Tree and Aberdeen Box Office, 2001-2014; Chairman: HMT Centenary Committee, Music Hall 150th Anniversary Committee; University of Aberdeen: Member, General Council Business Committee, since 1994, Member of University Court, since 2012, Convener, Student Experience Committee, since 2012, Chairman, Friends of the Elphinstone Institute, since 2006; Member and past president (2005-06) of Rotary Club of Aberdeen St. Machar; Member and past president (2006-07) of the Inner Wheel of Aberdeen St. Machar; Vice President, Bon Accord Ladies' Probus Club (Aberdeen), 2009 and President, 2010. Member of the Torry Trust, 2010-13. Recreations: piano playing (pianist for 66th Aberdeen Company Boys Brigade, since 1963); Boys' Brigade 50 year service medal awarded, 2013; philately; travel and languages; crosswords & sudoku; cooking and entertaining; visual and performing arts and music of all types. Address: (h.) 72 Gray Street, Aberdeen AB10 6JE; T.-01224-321998. E-mail: jennys72@hotmail.co.uk

Shirreffs, Murdoch John, MB, ChB, DObstRCOG, FRCGP, MFHom. General Medical Practitioner, Gilbert Road Medical Group, Bucksburn, Aberdeen, 1974-2015; retired Medical Hypnotherapist and Homoeopathic Specialist and Specialist in Charge, NHS Grampian Homeopathy Service; b. 25.5.1947, Aberdeen; m., Jennifer McLeod. Educ. Aberdeen Grammar School; Aberdeen University. General Practice Trainer, 1977-99; Secretary, Grampian Division, British Medical Association, 1978-2005; former Member, BMA Scottish Council. Awarded Provost Medal, NE Scotland Faculty, Royal College of General Practitioners, 2012. Past President, North of Scotland Veterans' Hockey Club; Member, Scottish LX (over 70s) Masters Hockey Team; Burgess, Guild of City of Aberdeen, since 2001. Recreations: hockey; opera and classical music; big band jazz; DIY; gardening; food and wine; travel. Address: (h.) 72 Gray Street, Aberdeen AB10 6JE; e-mail: murdoch_and_jenny_shirreffs@msn.com

Sibbett, Professor Wilson, CBE, FRS, FRSE, BSc, PhD. Emeritus Professor; Wardlaw Professor of Natural Philosophy, St. Andrews University (Director of Research, 1994-2003, Chairman, Department of Physics and Astronomy, 1985-94); Chair, Scottish Science Advisory Committee, 2002-06; b. 15.3.48, Portglenone, N. Ireland; m., Barbara Anne Brown; 3 d. Educ. Ballymena Technical College; Queen's University, Belfast. Postdoctoral Research Fellow, Blackett Laboratory, Imperial College, London, 1973-76; Lecturer in Physics, then Reader, Imperial College, 1976-85. Fellow: Institute of Physics, Royal Society of Edinburgh, Royal Society (of London). Honorary Degrees: LLD (Dundee), DSc (Trinity College Dublin), DSc (Glasgow), DU (Strathclyde), DSc (London City). Recreation: golf. Address: (b.) School of Physics and Astronomy, St. Andrews University, North Haugh, St. Andrews KY16 9SS; T.-01334 463100.

Siddiqui, Professor Mona, OBE (2011), MA, MIL, PhD, DLitt (Hons), FRSE, FRSA, Hon FRIAS. Professor of Islamic and Interreligious Studies, Assistant Principal for Religion and Society, Divinity School, University of Edinburgh, since 2011; Professor of Islamic Studies and Public Understanding, Glasgow University, 2006-2011; Director, Centre for the Study of Islam, Glasgow University, 1998-2011; Commissioner on the Calman Commission, 2008-09; b. 3.5.63, Karachi, Pakistan; m., Farhaj; 3 s. Educ. Salendine-Nook High School, Huddersfield; Leeds University; Manchester University. Lecturer in Arabic and Islamic Studies: Manchester Metropolitan University, 1989-90, Glasgow Caledonian University, 1993, Glasgow University, 1995. Chair, BBC Scottish Religious Advisory Council, 2005; Member, BBC Central Religious Advisory Council, 2003; Member, World Economic Forum Council on Faith, 2007-09; Contributor, Thought for the Day, BBC Scotland and Radio 4. Three Hon. Degrees: HDLitt (Leics), HD Civil Laws (Huddersfield), DLitt (Wolverhampton); Hon. Doctorate, University of Roehampton, 2014; Debretts 500 Most Influential, January 2014. Awarded OBE for services to interfaith relations, 2011. Recreations: interior decorating; cooking; reading. Address: (b.) Divinity School, University of Edinburgh, New College, Mound Place, Edinburgh EH1 2LX; e-mail: Mona.Siddiqui@ed.ac.uk

Sillars, James; b. 4.10.37, Ayr; m., Margo MacDonald (qv) (deceased); 1 s.; 3 d. Educ. Ayr Academy. Member, Ayr Town Council and Ayr County Council Education Committee, 1960s; Member, Western Regional Hospital Board, 1965-70; Head, Organisation Department, Scottish TUC, 1968-70; MP, South Ayrshire, 1970-79; Co-Founder, Scottish Labour Party, 1976; MP, Glasgow Govan, 1988-92; Assistant Secretary-General, Arab-British Chamber of Commerce, 1993-2002.

Sim, Alastair Elliot, BA (Hons), MA, MPhil, FRSA. Director, Universities Scotland, since 2009; b. 24.8.67,

Edinburgh; m., Fiona Parker; 2 s. Educ. Oxford University; University of Delaware; Glasgow University; Queen Margaret University. Civil Servant, Scottish Office/Scottish Government, 1989-2009; Private Secretary to Minister for Agriculture and the Environment, 1992-93; developed policy and legislation on constitutional reform and protection of the natural heritage, 1993-2000 (seconded to European Commission DG - Environment, 1994-95); Senior Civil Service, since 2000; Head of Division, Environment and Rural Affairs, 2000-04; Director of Planning, University of Glasgow (secondment), 2004-06; Director of Policy and Strategy, Scottish Court Service, 2006-09. Publications: Author: Rosslyn Blood, 2004, The Unbelievers, 2009. Recreations: family; writing; cycling; the outdoors. Address: (b.) Universities Scotland, Holyrood Park House, 106 Holyrood Road, Edinburgh EH8 8AS; T.-0131 226 1111.
E-mail: alastair@universities-scotland.ac.uk

Sime, Martin, MA. Director and Chief Executive, Scottish Council for Voluntary Organisations, 1991-2017 (retired); b. 23.9.53, Edinburgh. Educ. George Heriot's; St. Andrews University; Edinburgh University. Social and Economic History Researcher, 1976-78; Sheep Farmer, 1978-81; Freelance Researcher, 1982; Project Manager, Sprout Market Garden, 1983-85; Development/Principal Officer (Day Services), Scottish Association for Mental Health, then Director, 1985-91. Recreations: cinema; food; bridge.

Simmers, Graeme Maxwell, CBE, CA; b. 2.5.35, Glasgow; m., Jennifer M.H. Roxburgh; 2 s.; 2 d. Educ. Glasgow Academy; Loretto School. Qualified CA, 1959; commissioned Royal Marines, 1959-61, Hon. Colonel, Royal Marines Reserve, 2000-06. Former Partner, Kidsons Simmers CA; Chairman, Scottish Highland Hotels Group Ltd., 1972-92; Member, Scottish Tourist Board, 1979-86; Chairman, HCBA (Scotland), 1984-86; Past Chairman, Board of Management, Member of National Executive, BHA; Elder and Treasurer, Killearn Kirk; Governor, Queen's College, Glasgow, 1989-93; Chairman, Scottish Sports Council, 1992-99; Non-Executive Director: Forth Valley Acute Hospitals Trust, 1993-2001, Forth Valley Health Board, 2002-2010; Past Chairman of Governors, Loretto School; Member, Stirling University Court, 2000-2010; 2012 Honorary Degree of Doctor of The University of Stirling; Captain, Royal and Ancient Golf Club of St. Andrews, 2001-02 (Past Chairman, Championship Committee). OBE, 1982; Chairman, British Golf Museum, since 2011. Recreations: rugby; golf; skiing. Address: (h.) 11 Crawford Gardens, St Andrews, Fife KY16 8XG; T.-01334 475519; e-mail: graeme.simmers@btinternet.com

Simon, Shona M. W., MA, LLB, DipCG, DipLP. President, Employment Tribunals (Scotland), since 2009, Vice President, 2004-09; Visiting Professor of Law, University of Strathclyde, since 2015; b. 9.5.60, Greenock; m., Dr. E. J. Simon; 2 s. Educ. Greenock Academy; University of Edinburgh. Careers Adviser, 1984-88; Partner, Mackay Simon, Employment Lawyers, 1993-2002; Equal Opportunities Development Adviser, Scottish Parliament, 2001-02. Publications: joint author, Employment Law (textbook); joint Update Editor, Employment Tribunal Practice in Scotland. Recreations: cooking; reading; gardening. Address: (b.) Central Office of Employment Tribunals, Glasgow Tribunals Centre, 20 York Street, Glasgow G2 8GT.
E-mail: glasgow.president@justice.gov.uk

Simpson, Alan Gordon, OBE, DL, MA (Oxon), DUniv, CEng, MICE. Lord-Lieutenant, Stirling and Falkirk, since 2017; Chairman, Macrobert Arts Centre, since 2015; Technical Advisor, Summit Power, 2011-18;

Partner, W. A. Fairhurst and Partners, 1989-2009; Chairman, University of Stirling Court, 2007-2015; Chairman, Lake of Menteith Fisheries Ltd, since 2009; Chairman, National Youth Orchestras of Scotland, 1998-2011; b. 15.2.50, Edinburgh; m., Jan; 1 s.; 1 d. Educ. Rugby School; Magdalen College, Oxford; Honorary Doctorate, University of Stirling. Brian Colquhoun and Partners, 1972-78; W.A. Fairhurst and Partners, 1979-2009; Deputy Lieutenant, Stirling and Falkirk, 2004-2017; Chairman, Institution of Civil Engineers Scotland, 2011-2012; Chairman, Glasgow and West of Scotland Branch of the Institution of Civil Engineers, 2006-07; Member, Council, Institution of Civil Engineers, 2000-03. Recreations: music; skiing; archery. Address: (h.) Arntomie, Port of Menteith, by Stirling.

Simpson, Andrew, BD, PGCertEd. Lord-Lieutenant of Banffshire, since 2019; m., Louise. Educ. University College School, Hampstead; University of Aberdeen. Career history: Teacher of Religious and Moral Education, Turriff Academy; became Head of the Department, then Staff Tutor in Grampian Region; later promoted to Assistant Head Teacher and Deputy Head posts in Aberdeenshire and Moray; Head Teacher of Elgin High School, 2003-2016. Held various national responsibilities including with the Scottish Examination Board, Higher Still developments and as an Associate Assessor with Her Majesty's Inspectors of school. Currently works part-time as a Visiting Tutor in the School of Education, University of Aberdeen. Held numerous roles within the local community, including Session Clerk at Macduff Parish Church; Past President of the Banff Rotary Club; served on Presbytery and national committees of the Church of Scotland; Deputy Lieutenant of Banffshire, 2017-2019. Recreations: swimming; hill walking; genealogy; local history; reading; international affairs; golf. Address: Chief Executive's Office, The Moray Council, Council Offices, High Street, Elgin, Moray IV30 1BX; T.-01343 563520; e-mail: lieutenancy@moray.gov.uk

Simpson, Christine. Provost, Stirling Council, 2017-2022; Stirling West Ward Labour Councillor, 2012-2022. Educ. Edinburgh and Stirling Universities. Career: broad experience of working in the public sector, both in local government and with the Police and the NHS in role as Inter-agency Child Protection Training Co-ordinator for Forth Valley; Convener of the Social Care & Health Committee, 2012-17. Served in a voluntary capacity on the Stirling Children's Panel and on the Executive Committee of Family Mediation Central Scotland.

Simpson, Evelyn, BSc, PhD. Chief Planner, The Scottish Government, since 2021. Educ. Heriot-Watt University. Associate Environmental Planner, Land Use Consultants, 1999-2006; Head of Environmental Assessment Team, 2006-2013; Address: Scottish Government, St. Andrew's House, Regent Road, Edinburgh EH1 3DG.
E-mail: chief.planner@gov.scot

Simpson, Graham. MSP (Scottish Conservative and Unionist), Central Scotland region, since 2016; Shadow Cabinet Secretary for Transport, Infrastructure and Connectivity, 2020-21; South Lanarkshire Councillor, 2007-2017. Worked as a journalist for 26 years at News Corporation. Address: Scottish Parliament, Edinburgh EH99 1SP.

Simpson, James, OBE, DSc, BArch, FRIAS, RIBA FSAScot. Architect & Conservator; Working Consultant, Simpson & Brown; b. 27.07.44, Edinburgh; m. Ann Bunney (1968). Educ. Belhaven Hill; Trinity College Glenalmond; Edinburgh College of Art. Ian G. Lindsay & Ptrs, Edinburgh, 1962-71; Feilden+Mawson, Norwich &

Edinburgh, 1972-77; Simpson & Brown, from 1977; Surveyor of the Fabric of York Minster (1993-4); Vice-President, ICOMOS-UK; past Commissioner, RCAHMS; past chairman, Scottish Society for Conservation & Restoration (SSCR); past member: Ancient Monuments Board for Scotland (AMBS), Scottish Conservation Bureau Advisory Panel (SCBAP), Cockburn Association Council, Historic Environment Advisory Council for Scotland (HEACS), Edinburgh World Heritage Trust (EWHT) & Scottish Lime Centre Trust; Building Preservation Trusts: Cockburn Conservation Trust, Scottish Historic Buildings Trust, Mavisbank Trust, Penicuik House Preservation Trust, Scottish Redundant Churches Trust, St Stephen's Playfair Trust, Perth City Market Trust & Asia Scotland Trust. Work in India, from 2004: Golden Temple & Gobindgarh Fort, Amritsar; Victoria Memorial Hall, Indian Botanic Garden & St Andrew's Church, Calcutta; Secretariat, Rangoon. Address: (b.) The Old Printworks, 77a Brunswick Street, Edinburgh EH7 5HS; T.-0131 555 4678.

Simpson, Very Rev. James Alexander, BSc (Hons), BD, STM, DD. Chaplain to the Queen in Scotland; Moderator, General Assembly of the Church of Scotland, 1994; b. 9.3.34, Glasgow; m., Helen Gray McCorquodale; 3 s.; 2 d. Educ. Eastwood Secondary School; Glasgow University; Union Seminary, New York. Minister: Grahamston Church, Falkirk, 1960-66, St. John's Renfield, Glasgow, 1966-76; Minister, Dornoch Cathedral, 1976-97; Captain of Royal Dornoch Golf Club, 1993-94. Publications: There is a time to ....; Marriage Questions Today; Doubts are not Enough; Holy Wit; Laughter Lines; The Master Mind; More Holy Wit; Keywords of Faith; All About Christmas; The Laugh Shall Be First; Life, Love and Laughter; A Funny Way of Being Serious; At Our Age; The Magic of Words, 2013; Uncommon Sense and Comic Nonsense, 2016. Recreations: golf; photography; writing. Address: Dornoch, Perth Road, Bankfoot, Perthshire PH1 4ED; T.-01738 787710.

Simpson, Rev. James Hamilton, BD, LLB. Minister, The Mount Kirk, 1965-2004; Chairman, Church of Scotland General Trustees, 2003-07; b. 29.6.36, Overtown; m., Moira W. Sellar; 2 s. Educ. Buckhaven High School; Edinburgh University; Glasgow University. Prison Chaplain, Greenock, 1971-81; Hospital Chaplain, Ravenscraig, 1983-2006. Recreations: sea fishing; boating; gardening; touring (especially Iberia). Address: (h.) 82, Harbourside, Kip Village, Inverkip PA16 0BF; T.-01475 520 582; e-mail: jameshsimpson@yahoo.co.uk

Simpson, John. Chief Executive, Our Dynamic Earth, since 1998. Address: Dynamic Earth, Holyrood Road, Edinburgh EH8 8AS; T.-0131 550 7800.

Simpson, Kenneth James, BMSc, MBChB (Hons), MSc, MD, PhD, FRCP(Edin). Senior Lecturer in Hepatology, University of Edinburgh, since 2000; Consultant Physician, Royal Infirmary, Edinburgh, since 1996; b. 11.8.60, Edinburgh; m., Rona; 2 s.; 1 d. Educ. Craigmount High School, Edinburgh; University of Dundee, University of London; University of Edinburgh. House Physician and Surgeon, Ninewells Hospital, Dundee, 1983-84; Senior House Officer, Western Infirmary/Gartnavel General, Glasgow, 1984-86; MRC Clinical Scientist, Clinical Research Centre, Northwick Park, London, 1986-89; Medical Registrar, Guildford and Kings College Liver Unit, 1989-91; Lecturer in Medicine/Senior Registrar, University of Edinburgh, Royal Infirmary, 1991-95; MRC Travelling Fellow, University of Michigan, USA, 1995-96. Publications: contributor, textbooks on hepatology; scientific papers. Recreations: reading crime novels; running. Address: (b) Royal Infirmary of Edinburgh, Old Dalkeith Road, Edinburgh EH16 4SA; T.-0131-536 2248; e-mail: k.simpson@ed.ac.uk

Simpson, Professor Mary, MA, PhD. Professor Emeritus, University of Edinburgh, since 2006; b. 4.12.42, Inverurie; m., Thomas Hardy Simpson; 1 s.; 1 d. Educ. Aberdeen Academy; Aberdeen University. Assistant Experimental Officer, Torry Research Station, Aberdeen, 1959-65; Researcher in Education, then Professor of Educational Research, Northern College, 1976-99; Professor of Classroom Learning, Edinburgh University, 1999-2005. Independent Member, National Educational Development Groups for: Standard Grade, 1983-87, 5-14 Assessment, 1989-92, Higher Still, 1994-97, 5-14 Evaluation Programme, 1991-97. Member, Scottish Consultative Council on the Curriculum, 1991-2000; Director and Chairman, Cornerstone Community Care Ltd., 1979-2000. Address: (h.) 6 Osborne Terrace, Edinburgh EH12 5HG.

Simpson, Myrtle Lillias, DL. Author and Lecturer; former Member, Scottish Sports Council; Past Chairman, Scottish National Ski Council; b. 5.7.31, Aldershot; m., Professor Hugh Simpson (qv); 3 s.; 1 d. Educ. 19 schools (father in Army). Writer/Explorer; author of 12 books, including travel, biography, historical and children's; first woman to ski across Greenland; attempted to ski to North Pole (most northerly point reached by a woman unsupported); numerous journeys in polar regions on ski or canoe; exploration in China and Peru; Mungo Park Medal, Royal Scottish Geographical Society; Perrie Medal, Ski Club of Great Britain; received the Scottish Award for Excellence in Mountain Culture, 2013; awarded the Polar Medal for outstanding achievement in the field of exploration in Arctic regions, 2017; former Editor, Avenue (University of Glasgow magazine). Recreations: climbing; skiing; canoeing; beekeeping. Address: (h.) Farletter, Kincraig, Inverness-shire PH21 1NU; T.-01540 651288. E-mail: h.simpson257@btinternet.com

Simpson, Philip James Dalrymple, QC, LLB (Hons), LLM, DipLP, CIOT. Advocate, since 2001; Barrister (England and Wales), since 2001; b. 23.2.73, Glasgow; m., Joya van Hout; 2 d.; 1 s. Educ. Bearsden Academy; University of Aberdeen; University of Regensburg; University of Edinburgh. Legal Assistant to the Lord President, 1999-2000; freelance legal translator, 2001-08; called to English Bar (Inner Temple), 2001. Member: Terra Firma Chambers, Edinburgh, Old Square Tax Chambers, Lincoln's Inn, London. Publications: articles on Scots law and legal history. Recreations: opera; chess; European literature. Address: (b.) Advocates Library, Parliament House, Edinburgh EH1 1RF; T.-0131-226 5071. E-mail: philip.simpson@advocates.org.uk

Simpson, Dr. Richard John, OBE, MB ChB, FRCGP, FRCPsych, DSHEC. MSP (Labour), Mid Scotland and Fife, 2007-2016; Shadow Minister for Public Services and Wealth Creation, 2015-16; Shadow Minister for Public Health, 2007-2015; b. 22.10.42, Edinburgh; m., Christine Margaret MacGregor; 2 s. Educ. Perth Academy; Trinity College, Glenalmond; Edinburgh University. Career history: President of Scottish Union of Students; Principal in General Practice; Psychiatrist and Honorary Professor, Stirling University; MSP, Ochil Constituency and Deputy Justice Minister; Consultant Psychiatrist in Addictions. Chair, Council of Management, Strathcarron Hospice; Chair, Medical Group of Scottish BAAF. Publications: 40 peer reviewed medical papers; 3 chapters of books on psychiatry in general practice; benzodiazepines psychology in general practice. Recreations: golf; gardening; classical music.

Sinclair, 18th Lord (Matthew Murray Kennedy St Clair). Lord-Lieutenant of the Stewartry of Kirkcudbright, since 2021; Succeeded to title, 2004; b. 9.12.68; m., Laura Cicely Coode; 2 s. Hon Harry (Murray Kennedy) St Clair.

Master of Sinclair; b. 6.10.07; Hon James (Jonathan Kennedy) St Clair; b. 24.5.09. Director, Saint Property Limited; Director, Knocknalling Farms; Board of Governors, Cargilfield Prep School, Edinburgh; Trustee, Dalry Town Hall; Board Member, Dee (Kirkcudbright) District Salmon Fishery Board; Past Chairman, Game Conservancy Scottish Auction; Past Chairman, Scottish Land and Estates South West Region; Member, Royal Company of Archers. Address: Knocknalling, St. Johns Town of Dalry, Castle Douglas DG7 3JT.
E-mail: ms@knocknalling.com

Sinclair, Celia Margaret Lloyd, RGN, DMS, MBA, FCMI, FRIAS (Hon). Chief Executive, Coralyn Ltd; Founder and Chairman of the Willow Tea Rooms Charitable Trust Mackintosh at the Willow, established to safeguard and restore Charles Rennie Macintosh's iconic original Willow Tearooms in Sauchiehall Street. Past Chairman of Court, Glasgow Caledonian University; formerly Board Member: Scottish Enterprise; Glasgow Chamber of Commerce; National Board for Nursing, Midwifery and Health Visiting for Scotland; Cumbernauld Development Corporation, Glasgow Development Agency; Member: Merchants House, Glasgow; The Western Club, Glasgow; The Glasgow Art Club (Trustee and Vice Chairman of the Building Steering Group for the Club's renovations). E-mail: celia.acharn@gmail.com

Sinclair, Colin, MA (Hons). Former Delivery Director of Scotland's Covid Vaccination Programme (2021); Chief Executive, NHS National Services Scotland, 2016-2021. Educ. Douglas Academy, Milngavie; University of Glasgow. Career history: Director of National Procurement, NHS National Procurement, 2008-2013; NHS National Services Scotland: Director of Procurement, Commissioning and Facilities, 2013-2015, Interim Chief Operating Officer, 2015-2021.

Sinclair, Very Rev. Colin Andrew Macalister, BA (Hons), BD (Hons). Minister, Palmerston Place Church of Scotland, since 1996; b. 16.9.53, Glasgow; m., Ruth Mary Murray; 1 s.; 3 d.; 4 grandsons; 1 granddaughter; 2 granddaughters. Educ. Glasgow Academy; Stirling University; Edinburgh University. Training Officer, Scripture Union, Zambia, 1974-77; Assistant Minister, Palmerston Place Church of Scotland, Edinburgh, 1980-82; Church of Scotland Minister, Newton on Ayr, 1982-88; General Director, Scripture Union Scotland, 1988-96. Chair, Scripture Union International Council, 2004-2017; Convener, Mission and Discipleship Council, 2012-2016; Moderator of Presbytery of Edinburgh, 2017-2018; Moderator of the General Assembly of the Church of Scotland, 2019-2020. Publications: A Hitch-Hiker's Guide to the Bible; Follow me - the adventure of faith. Recreations: family; reading; sport. Address: (b.) Annan House, 10 Palmerston Place, Edinburgh EH12 5AA.

Sinclair, Eric T.A., MA, DipEd. Former non-executive member, NHS Grampian Board; b. 20.9.48, Edinburgh; m., Johanna Beckley; 3 c. Educ. Bell Baxter High School, Cupar; St. Andrews University; Edinburgh University; Moray House College. Taught, Teacher Training Colleges, Cameroon, Nigeria; Head of English, English High School, Istanbul; Head of English, St Joseph's College, Dumfries; Assistant Rector, Forres Academy; Depute Rector, Bridge of Don Academy; Rector, Kirkwall Grammar School; Rector, Aboyne Academy and Deeside Community Centre, Aberdeenshire. Publication: Man, Dog, Stroke: Musings of a Deeside Whippet and his Master, 2011. Recreations: reading; music; voluntary work for The Stroke Association. Address: 38 Barclay Park, Aboyne; T.-07442 502574.
E-mail: ericsinclair@btconnect.com

Sinclair, Liam. Executive Director/Joint Chief Executive, Dundee Repertory Theatre and Scottish Dance Theatre, since 2019; previously Artistic Director, Byre Theatre, St Andrews (2016-18). Address: Scottish Dance Theatre, 9 Tay Square, Dundee DD1 1PB; T.-01382 342600.

Sinclair, Marion, MA (Hons), MPhil (Publishing), MBA. Chief Executive, Publishing Scotland, since 2008. Educ. University of Glasgow; University of Stirling; University of Edinburgh. Editorial and Marketing Assistant, Polygon, 1988-90; Editorial Director, Polygon, 1990-97; Lecturer, Publishing Studies, Edinburgh Napier University, 1997-2003; Business Development, Publishing Scotland, 2003-08. Worked in the book publishing sector for 33 years, running a literary press, awarded Sunday Times UK Small Publisher of the Year, and published books appearing on the Booker shortlist and winners of the Saltire Society Book of the Year, McVitie's Prize, The John Llewellyn Rhys prize and the Betty Trask Award. Board Member: MG Alba, The Gaelic Books Council, BookSource Ltd. Address: Publishing Scotland, Scott House, 10 South St Andrew Street, Edinburgh EH2 2AZ; T.-0131 228 6866.

Sinclair-Gieben, Wendy. HM Chief Inspector of Prisons, since 2018. Educ. University of the West of England; Cambridge University. Background in justice in the UK and Australia, including terms as a prison governor in England, a prison director at HMP Kilmarnock and Justice Director (prisoners and court escorts) in Perth, Western Australia. Non-executive Director of the Charity NOFASD in Australia. Address: HM Inspectorate of Prisons for Scotland, Saughton House, Broomhouse Drive, Edinburgh EH11 3XD; T.-0131 244 8482.

Skene, Charles Pirie, CBE, DBA, FBIPP, ARPS, FRSA. Chairman, Skene Group of companies; Visiting Professor of Entrepreneurship, Robert Gordon University; Holder of the Queen's Award for Enterprise Promotion, 2005; b. 30.4.35, Aberdeen; m., Alison; 1 s.; 2 d. Educ. Loretto. Past President of numerous organisations, including Aberdeen Chamber of Commerce and Association of Scottish Chambers of Commerce; Past Chairman: Industry Year 1986, Industry Matters 1987; Donor of the Annual Skene Aberdeen Festival Award, 1976-99; Past Chairman, CBI Education and Training Committee; Chairman, CBI (Scotland) Enterprise Group, 1994-96; Member, Task Force to investigate under-achievement in schools, 1996-97; organised Skene Young Entrepreneur's Award, Scotland, 1986-2002; Member, Scottish Executive's Review of Education for Work and Enterprise Group, 2001-02; endowed Chair of Entrepreneurship, The Robert Gordon University Centre for Entrepreneurship, 2001. Developer and owner of the first Continuing Care Retirement Community in Scotland. Recipient of Global Healthcare Award 2012 and UK Healthcare Award 2015 for his contribution to the care of the elderly. Address: (b.) 23 Rubislaw Den North, Aberdeen, AB15 4AL; T.-01224 326221.

Skeoch, Norman (Keith), BA, MA. Chief Executive, Abrdn plc (formerly Standard Life Aberdeen), 2017-2020; b. 11.56; m.; 2 s. Educ. University of Sussex; University of Warwick. Career history: Government Economic Service, 1979-80; James Capel & Co Limited (HSBC Securities from 1996), 1980-99: International Economist (1980), Chief Economist (1984), Director of Economics and Strategy (1993), Managing Director of International Equities (1998); joined Standard Life Investments in 1999 as Chief Investment Officer and then became Chief Executive, Standard Life Investments in 2004. Joined the Board of Standard Life plc in 2006 and became Chief Executive, Standard Life plc in 2015. Trustee, Edinburgh International

Festival, since 2019; Chair, Board of Directors, Investment Association Board, since 2019; doctorates from the University of Sussex and Teesside University; worked with government and trade bodies in establishing best practice in stewardship and governance in the wake of the global financial crisis. Fellow of the Society of Business Economists; European Personality of the Year by Funds Europe, 2013.

Skinner, Caitlin. Artistic Director and Chief Executive, Stellar Quines Theatre Company, since 2021; Director: Jordan & Skinner, since 2020, Pearlfisher Theatre Ltd, since 2018; b. 5.85. Formerly Artistic Director of the Village Pub Theatre and Associate Director at Pitlochry Festival Theatre. Recent directing credits include: Distance Remaining by Stewart Melton (Helen Milne Productions); Alone by Janey Godley (National Theatre of Scotland); Five from Inside by Rona Munro (Traverse Theatre); formerly Associate Director on Lament for Sheku Bayoh by Hannah Lavery (National Theatre of Scotland). Address: Stellar Quines Theatre Company, 30b Grindlay Street, Edinburgh EH3 9AX; T.-0131 229 3851.

Skinner, Denzil, MBA. Chair, Essential Edinburgh, since 2011; Partner, Denzil Skinner & Partners LLP, since 2012. Educ. Heriot Watt University. HM Forces, 1977-1988, Commissioned into 16/5 The Queen's Royal Lancers; Director & Company Secretary, Hamilton & Inches, 1989-2010. Address: Essential Edinburgh, 139 George Street, Edinburgh EH2 4JY; T.-0131 220 8580.

Skinner, Simon, MBA. Chief Executive, The National Trust for Scotland, 2015-2020. Educ. Stirling University. Career history: Director, Marketing and Client Services, Scottish Widows, 1996-2002; Director, Sales and Service, The AA, 2003-2004; Director, Corporate Services, Equitable Life, 2005-09; AEGON Scottish Equitable: Director, Customer Services, 2009-11, Chief Operating Officer, 2011; Chief Executive, AEGON Ireland, 2011-15.

Slater, Lorna. MSP (Scottish Green Party), Lothian (Region), since 2021; Co-Leader, Scottish Green Party, since 2019; Minister for Green Skills, Circular Economy and Biodiversity, since 2021; b. 1975, Calgary, Alberta, Canada. Educ. Western Canada High School; University of British Columbia. Career history: Software Engineer, Telescope Technologies Ltd, 2000-01; Design Engineer and Project Manager, GB Innomech, 2001-04; Senior Design Engineer, Memsstar Ltd, Edinburgh, 2004-2013; Lead Controls and Instrumentation Engineer and Project Engineer, Aquamarine Power Ltd, Edinburgh, 2014-15; Project and Systems Manager, Atlantis Resources Limited, Edinburgh, 2015-16; Engineering Project Manager, Orbital Marine Power Ltd, Edinburgh, 2016-2021. Recreation: aerialist. Address: The Scottish Parliament, Edinburgh EH99 1SP; T.-0131 348 6997.
E-mail: Lorna.Slater.msp@parliament.scot

Slater, Professor Peter James Bramwell, BSc, PhD, DSc, FRSB, FRSE. Kennedy Professor of Natural History, St. Andrews University, 1984-2008, Emeritus, since 2008 (Head, School of Biological and Medical Sciences, 1992-97; Dean, Faculty of Science, 1998-2002); b. 26.12.42, Edinburgh; m., Elisabeth Vernon Smith; 2 s. Educ. Edinburgh Academy; Glenalmond; Edinburgh University. Demonstrator in Zoology, Edinburgh University, 1966-68; Lecturer in Biology, Sussex University, 1968-84. Secretary, Association for the Study of Animal Behaviour, 1973-78, President, 1986-89, Medallist, 2000; European Editor, Animal Behaviour, 1979-82; Editor, Advances in the Study of Behavior, 1990-2005. Recreations: walking; ornithology;

music. Address: (b.) Vagaland, Stromness, Orkney KW16 3AW; T.-01856 850148.

Slaven, Tracey, BA (Hons) Econ, MBA. University Secretary & Chief Operating Officer, University of Aberdeen, since 2021; b. 23.04.67, Jarrow; m., Mark Slaven; 3 d. Educ. Hedworthfield Comprehensive, Jarrow; Strathclyde University; Durham University. Economic Assistant, Industry Department for Scotland, 1989-92; Economist and Head of Corporate Planning, Highlands and Islands Enterprise, 1992-2001; Corporate Planning, AWG PLC, 2001-03; Executive Director, Countryside Agency, 2003-05; Deputy Director, Scottish Government, 2005-09; Chief Executive, Student Awards Agency Scotland, 2009-2012; Deputy Director for Higher Education and Learner Support, Scottish Government, 2012-2013; Deputy Secretary, Strategic Planning, University of Edinburgh, 2013-2020. Recreations: reading; explore Aberdeen City and the Shire; learning Spanish; Director/Trustee on HESA's board, since October 2018. Address: (b.) University of Aberdeen, King's Office, Aberdeen AB24 3FX; T.-01224 272000.
E-mail: tracey.slaven@abdn.ac.uk

Sleeman, Professor Derek Henry, BSc, PhD, FBCS, FRSE. Fellow of European Artificial Intelligence Societies (2004); Emeritus Professor of Computing Science, Aberdeen University; b. 11.1.41, Penzance; m., Margaret G. Rankine; 1 d. Educ. Penzance Grammar School; King's College, London. Secretary, SS AISB, 1979-82; Academic Co-ordinator, European Network of Excellence in Machine Learning, 1992-95. Publications: 200 technical papers. Recreations: hill and coastal path-walking; photography. Address: (b.) Computing Science Department, King's College, Aberdeen University, Aberdeen AB24 3FX; T.-01224 272288.

Sloan, Brian. Chief Executive, Age Scotland, since 2012; b. 28.12.61, Glasgow; m., Katie; 2 s.; 2 d. Educ. Keil School (Dumbarton); Liverpool Hope University. Bank Officer, Clydesdale Bank, 1980-84; Sales Director, Capital Bank, 1984-2000; Senior Executive, Bank of Scotland, 2000-09; Managing Director, Hotel Connections Ltd, 2009-2010; Business Development: Capital Credit Union, 2010-2011, Young Enterprise Scotland, 2011-2012; Chairman, Age Scotland Enterprises, 2011-2013. Volunteer Panel Member, Children's Hearing System. Recreations: golf (8 handicap); competitive squash player. Address: (b.) Causewayside House, 160 Causewayside, Edinburgh EH9 1PR; T.-07961 083203.
E-mail: brian.sloan@agescotland.org.uk

Slumbers, Martin, BSc, ACA. Chief Executive of The R&A and Secretary, The Royal and Ancient Golf Club of St Andrews, since 2015; b. 1960, Brighton. Educ. University of Birmingham; Price Waterhouse. Accounting Trainee, PwC, 1981-85; Finance, Salomon Brothers, London, 1985-94; CFO, Salomon Brothers Hong Kong Limited, 1994-97; Finance, Salomon Brothers AG, 1984-98; CFO, Salomon Brothers, UK, 1997-98; Deutsche Bank, London: CFO Global Markets, 1998-2001, COO, 2001-03; Head, Global Business Services, Deutsche Bank, 2003-2013; own business, since 2013. Address: Royal and Ancient Golf Club of St Andrews, Fife KY16 9JD.

Smaill, Cllr Peter, LLB (Hons). Provost, Midlothian Council, since 2018; representing Midlothian East (Conservative), since 2017. Educ. University of Edinburgh. Holds qualifications in law, business studies and accountancy. Career: Director, County NatWest Ventures, 1989-97; Chairman, Pension Fund Trustees, Portman

Holdings Limited, since 2007; Chairman of Trustees (charity), Bach Network UK, 2010-17; Trustee, Handel Institute (charity), since 2018; Chair of Midlothian Council's Audit Committee, 2012-17. Address: Midlothian Council, 40-46 Buccleuch Street, Dalkeith EH22 1DN.

Small, Emeritus Professor John Rankin, CBE, DLitt, BSc (Econ), FCCA, FCMA. Emeritus Professor, Department of Accountancy and Finance, Heriot-Watt University; b. 28.2.33, Dundee; m., Catherine Wood; 1 s.; 2 d. Educ. Harris Academy; Dundee School of Economics. Industry and commerce; Lecturer, Edinburgh University; Senior Lecturer, Glasgow University. Director of and Consultant to various organisations; President, Association of Chartered Certified Accountants, 1982-83; Vice-Principal, Heriot-Watt University, 1974-78, 1987-90, Deputy Principal, 1990-94. Chairman, Commission for Local Authority Accounts in Scotland, 1983-92; Chairman, National Appeal Panel for Entry to Pharmaceutical Lists (Scotland), 1987-95; Board Member, Scottish Homes, 1993-2002. Recreation: golf. Address: (h.) 39 Caiystane Terrace, Edinburgh EH10 6ST; T.-0131-445 2638.

Small, Stephen J., CQSW. Director, St Andrew's Children's Society Ltd., since 1996; b. 3.11.61, Edinburgh; m., Kay L. Anderson; 1 s.; 2 d. Educ. Holyrood RC High School, Edinburgh; Moray House College of Education. Social Worker, Humberside County Council, 1986-88; Social Worker, Lothian Regional Council (Midlothian District), 1988-95; Senior Social Worker, Director, St Andrew's Children's Society Ltd., since 1995. Address: (b.) 7 John's Place, Leith, Edinburgh EH6 7EL; T.-0131 454 3370; e-mail: ssmall@standrews–children.org.uk

Smart, Ian Stewart, LLB, NP. Past President, Law Society of Scotland; Solicitor; Legal Consultant, The Cumbernauld Law Practice (former Senior Partner); Partner, Ian S. Smart & Co., 1991-2017; b. 10.9.58, Paisley. Educ. Paisley Grammar School; Glasgow University. Solicitor and then Partner, Ross Harper & Murphy, 1980-91; Council Member, Law Society of Scotland, since 1997. Recreation: St Mirren; Labour Party politics. Address: (b.) 30 Ettrick Walk, Cumbernauld G67 1NE; T.-01236 731911.

Smillie, Anne. Former Chief Executive, Badminton Scotland (1989-2018); Executive Board Member, Badminton World Federation, 2002-08; Chair, BWF Events Committee, 2007-08; b. 17.8.56, Glasgow. Educ. Victoria Drive Secondary School; Anniesland College. Joined Scottish Badminton Union, 1980; Director of major badminton events, including 1992 European Championships, 1994 World Team Championships, 1997 World Team and Individual Championships, 2007 World Team Badminton Championships and 2017 BWF World Championships. Recreations: music; reading. Address: (h.) 55 Westerton Avenue, Westerton, Glasgow; T.-0141-942 9804.

Smillie, Carol. Television Presenter. Credits include: Wheel of Fortune; The Travel Show; Holiday; The National Lottery Live; Hearts of Gold; Smillie's People; Changing Rooms; Midweek National Lottery Live; Summer Holiday; Star Secrets; Holiday Swaps; Dream Holiday Homes; Postcode Challenge; Strictly Come Dancing; A Brush with Fame; Duke of Edinburgh 80th Birthday. Web: www.carolsmillie.tv

Smith, Aedán. Head of Policy and Advocacy, RSPB Scotland, since 2019. Educ. University of Edinburgh; Heriot-Watt University. Career history: Environment Planning Consultant, Halcrow, 2001-04; Planning Officer, Loch Lomond and the Trossachs National Park Authority, 2004-07; Head of Planning and Development, Scotland, RSPB, 2008-2019. Recreations: St. Johnstone fan; mountain biker. Address: Scotland Headquarters, 2 Lochside View, Edinburgh Park, Edinburgh EH12 9DH; T.-0131 317 4100.

Smith of Gilmorehill, Baroness (Elizabeth Margaret Smith), MA. Peer, House of Lords, since 1995; Deputy Lieutenant, City of Edinburgh; former Chairman, Edinburgh Festival Fringe Society (1995-2012); Council Member, Russo-British Chamber of Commerce; Governor, English Speaking Union; Trustee, John Smith Memorial Trust; Patron, University of Glasgow 2001 Campaign; b. 4.6.40, Ayr; m., Rt. Hon. John Smith, MP (deceased); 3 d. Educ. Hutchesons Girls Grammar School; Glasgow University. LLD, Glasgow University, 1998. Recreations: family; garden; the arts. Address: (b.) House of Lords, London SW1A 0PW.

Smith, Alyn. MP (SNP), Stirling, since 2019; SNP Foreign Affairs Spokesperson, since 2020; Member of the European Parliament for Scotland (SNP), 2004-2019; b. 1973, Glasgow. Educ. Leeds University; University of Heidelberg; Nottingham Law University; College of Europe in Natolin. Taught English in India and worked with Scotland Europa in Brussels; later moved to London and qualified as a lawyer with commercial law firm Clifford Chance. SNP staff worker in Holyrood prior to election in 2004; Contested Edinburgh West for the SNP at the 2001 general election and the 2003 Scottish Parliament election; Honorary President of the Young Scots for Independence; member of the SNP's National Executive Committee; member of the SNP's Standing Council on Europe; Candidate in the 2016 SNP Depute Leadership election. Full member of the European Parliament Foreign Affairs Committee; full member of the Delegation for relations with the Arab Peninsula; full member of the Delegation for relations with Iraq. Honorary Vice President of the Scottish Society for the Prevention of Cruelty to Animals, Scotland's animal welfare charity (voluntary and unpaid post). Alyn lives in Stirling. Address: Houses of Parliament, Westminster, London SW1A 0AA.

Smith, The Rt. Hon. Lady (Anne Smith), QC. Senator of the College of Justice in Scotland; b. 1955; m.; 1 s.; 1 d. Educ. Edinburgh University. Admitted, Faculty of Advocates, 1980. Honorary Fellow of The Academy of Experts, since 2019. Recreations: music; gardening; walking. Address: Parliament House, Parliament Square, Edinburgh EH1 1RQ.

Smith, Rt. Rev. Dr Brian Arthur. Episcopal Bishop of Edinburgh, 2001-2011; b. 1943; m., Elizabeth Hutchinson; 2 d. Educ. George Heriot's School, Edinburgh; Edinburgh University; Fitzwilliam College, Cambridge; Jesus College, Cambridge; Westcott House, Cambridge. Curate, Cuddesdon, 1972-79; Tutor, Cuddesdon College, Oxford, 1972-75; Ripon College, Cuddesdon: Director of Studies, 1975-78, Senior Tutor, 1978-79; Director of Training, Diocese of Wakefield, 1979-87; Priest-in-Charge, St. John, Cragg Vale, Halifax, 1979-85; Honorary Canon, Wakefield Cathedral, 1981-87; Archdeacon of Craven, 1987-93; Bishop Suffragan, Tonbridge, later 1993-2001. Member, Scotland UNESCO Committee, 2008-2014; Vice-President, Modern Church, since 2009; Director, St Mary's Music School, 2010-2017; Governor, Loretto School, 2012-2017; President Emeritus, RMCU, since 2012; Hon. Lecturer, St Augustine Theological School, Botswana, 2013, 2015; Business Committee of General Council of University of

Edinburgh, since 2017; HonDD, University of Edinburgh, 2018. Recreations: reading; music; walking; browsing in junk shops. Address: Flat E, 2A Dean Path, Edinburgh EH4 3BA; T.-0131 220 6097.
E-mail: bishopsmith@btinternet.com

Smith, David Bruce Boyter, OBE, Drhc, MA, LLB, FRSA, FInstD. Director and Chief Executive, Dunfermline Building Society, 1987-2001; Vice Chairman, Scottish Opera, 2000-04; Past Chairman, Building Societies Association; b. 11.3.42, St. Andrews; m., Christine Anne; 1 s.; 1 d. Educ. High School, Dunfermline; Edinburgh University. Legal training, Balfour & Manson, Edinburgh; admitted Solicitor, 1968; Solicitor, Standard Life Assurance Co., 1969-73; Dunfermline Building Society: Secretary, 1974-81, General Manager (Admin.), 1981-86, Deputy Chief Executive, 1986. Past Chairman, Northern Association of Building Societies; Vice President, European Mortgage Federation; Chairman, NHBC (Scotland) and Board Member, NHBC (UK), 2004-12; Member, Scottish Conveyancing and Executry Services Board, 1996-2003; Deputy Chairman, Glenrothes Development Corporation, 1990-96; Chairman, Institute of Directors, Scottish Division, 1994-97; Vice Chairman, Scottish Fisheries Museum, 1993-2007; former Vice Chairman of Court and Finance Convener, Edinburgh University; Chairman, University of Edinburgh Investment Committee, 2004-2011; Chairman, Carnegie Dunfermline & Hero Fund Trusts, 2008-2010; Board Member, Carnegie UK Trust, 2002-14; Executive Committee, Carnegie Trust for Universities of Scotland, 2005-2015. Recreations: golf; sailing; the arts.

Smith, Donald Alexander, MA, PhD. Director, Netherbow Arts Centre, 1983-2001; Curator, John Knox House, 1989-2013; Director, Scottish Storytelling Centre, 1995-2013; Director, Scottish International Storytelling Festival, since 1989; Director/CEO, Tracs (Traditional Arts and Culture Scotland), since 2014; b. 15.2.56, Glasgow; m., Alison; 3 s.; 2 d. Educ. Stirling High School; Edinburgh University. Researcher, School of Scottish Studies, 1979-82. Chairperson, Scotland 97 (anniversaries of St. Ninian and St. Columba); Organiser, Scottish Churches Millennium Programme; Chair, Scottish National Theatre Working Party (SAC/Scottish Executive), 2000-01; Chair, Literature Forum for Scotland, 2002-06; Board Member, National Theatre of Scotland, 2004-07; Vice-Chair, Literature Alliance Scotland, since 2016. Publications: The Scottish Stage, 1994; Edinburgh Old Town Pilgrims' Way, 1995; John Knox House: Gateway to Edinburgh's Old Town, 1996; Celtic Travellers: Scotland in the Age of the Saints, 1997; History of Scottish Theatre, 1998; Storytelling Scotland: A Nation in Narrative, 2001; A Long Stride Shortens the Road: Poems 1979-2004, 2004; The English Spy, 2007; Between Ourselves, 2008; God, the Poet and the Devil: Robert Burns and Religion, 2008; Arthur's Seat: Journeys and Evocations, 2009; Ballad of the Five Marys, 2013; Freedom and Faith, 2013; Edinburgh's Old Town: Journeys and Evocations, 2014; Scotland's Democracy Trail, 2014; Pilgrim Guide to Scotland, 2015; Flora McIvor, 2017; Travelling the Tweed Dales, 2017; Wee Folk Tales, 2018; Year of Sham, 2018; Why Gardens Matter, 2020; Folk Tales from the Garden, 2021. Address: (b.) Scottish Storytelling Centre, The Netherbow, 43-45 High Street, Edinburgh EH1 1SR; T.-0131-652 3271.

Smith, Drew. Former MSP (Labour), Glasgow (2011-16). Formerly Spokesperson on Social Justice; formerly Deputy Equalities Spokesperson; formerly Shadow Cabinet Secretary for the Constitution. Studied at the universities of Aberdeen and Glasgow. Worked for Labour at Holyrood and Westminster and as a policy and communications officer in health promotion. Active in the north Glasgow community. Previous Chair, Scottish TUC Young Workers Committee (2008) and Scottish Young Labour (2006); Member, STUC General Council, 2006-2010.

Smith, Elaine A., BA (Hons), DPSM. MSP (Labour), Central Scotland region, 2016-2021 (Coatbridge and Chryston, 1999-2016); Deputy Presiding Officer, 2011-16; b. 7.5.63, Coatbridge; m., James Vann Smith; 1 s. Educ. St Patrick's School, Coatbridge; Glasgow College; St Andrew's Teacher Training College. Teacher, 1986-87; supply teacher, 1987-88; local government officer, Monklands District Council, 1988-90, Highland Regional Council, 1990-97; Volunteer Development Scotland, 1997-98; supply teacher, 1999. Recreations: family; swimming; reading.

Smith, Elaine Constance, BA. Actress; b. 2.8.58, Baillieston; m., Robert Morton; 2 d. Educ. Braidhurst High School, Motherwell; Royal Scottish Academy of Music and Drama; Moray House College of Education. Career: Teacher of Speech and Drama, Firrhill High School, Edinburgh, 1979-82; joined 7:84 Theatre Company, 1982; moved to Wildcat Stage Productions, 1982; since 1986, worked with Borderline Theatre Co., Royal Lyceum, Dundee Rep., Tron Theatre, Traverse, Byre Theatre and Lead in Glasgow and Aberdeen panto; two national tours of Calendar Girls including West End run; co-written and starred in I Dreamed A Dream; TV work includes City Lights, Naked Video, Rab C Nesbitt and 2000 Acres of Sky; original cast member, The Steamie; Film work includes Women Talking Dirty, 16 Years of Alcohol and Nina's Heavenly Delights. Patron, Relationships Scotland, Zero Tolerance, Scottish Youth Theatre, Borderline Theatre and Byre Theatre; Hon. Doctorate, Dundee and Glasgow Universities; BA, Queen Margaret Univ., 2007; Agent: Independent Talent Group, London; Production company with husband (RPM Arts), since 1990. Recreations: swimming; tennis; reading.

Smith, Elizabeth Jane, MA (Hons), DipEd. MSP (Conservative), Mid Scotland and Fife, since 2007; Shadow Cabinet Secretary for Finance and the Economy, since 2021; Shadow Cabinet Secretary for the Environment, Climate Change and Land Reform, 2020-2021; Shadow Cabinet Secretary for Education and Skills, 2016-2020; b. 27.2.60, Edinburgh. Educ. George Watson's College; University of Edinburgh; Moray House College of Education. Teacher of Economics and Modern Studies, George Watson's College, 1983-98; Head of Chairman's Office, Conservative Central Office, Scotland, 1998-2003; Part Time Teacher and Political Consultant, 2003-07. Fellow Commoner, Corpus Christi College, Cambridge, 1992. Publications: History of George Watson's Ladies' College, 2006; Outdoor Adventures, 2003. Recreations: cricket; hill-walking; photography; travel. Address: Scottish Parliament, Holyrood Road, Edinburgh EH99 1SP; T.-0131 348 6762.
E-mail: elizabeth.smith.msp@scottish.parliament.uk

Smith, Rev Fiona. Principal Clerk to the General Assembly, since 2022; previously Minister, Ness Bank Church, Inverness. Former Vice-Convener of the Registration of Ministries Committee; former Convener of Assembly Business Committee and its predecessor the Assembly Arrangements Committee. Address: The Church of Scotland, 121 George Street, Edinburgh EH2 4YN; T.-0131 225 5722.

Smith, Gary. Head of News, BBC Scotland, since 2016. Educ. Kelvinside Academy; University of Glasgow; Cardiff

University. Career history: programme editor and senior political producer, Channel Four News; assistant editor on the BBC's Nine O'Clock news; editor, political news for the BBC; ran the home newsgathering team across the UK. Address: BBC Scotland, 40 Pacific Quay, Glasgow G51 1DA.

Smith, Gordon Duffield. Chief Executive, Scottish Football Association, 2007-10; b. 29.12.54, Kilwinning. Former football player; played for Rangers and Brighton & Hove Albion FC; later worked as a football agent and BBC football pundit.

Smith, Grahame. General Secretary, Scottish Trades Union Congress (STUC), 2006-2020 (retired). Partner, Liz Campbell; 2 s. Educ. Strathclyde University (Honours Degree in Economics and Industrial Relations). Joined STUC as an Assistant Secretary in 1986, Deputy General Secretary, 1996-2006 (heading up the STUC's policy and campaigns department); joined the Board of Scottish Enterprise, 2008; joined the Board of Skills Development Scotland, 2014; joined the Board of the Scottish Qualifications Authority, 2018. Recreations: enjoys reading and music and interested in most sports, but particularly football.

Smith, Sir Gregor Ian. Chief Medical Officer for Scotland, since 2020; b. 1971. Educ. Uddingston Grammar; University of Glasgow. Career history; GP, Larkhall; appointed Medical Director Primary Care, NHS Lanarkshire in 2008; Senior Medical Officer, The Scottish Government since 2012, appointed Deputy Chief Medical Officer in 2015. Honorary Clinical Associate Professor at the University of Glasgow and Fellow of both the Scottish Patient Safety Programme and Salzburg Global. Recreations: playing the guitar; cycling, cardiovascular and resistance training. Address: Scottish Government, St. Andrews House, Regent Road, Edinburgh, EH1 3DG.

Smith, Iain, BA (Hons). Scottish Public Policy Consultant; MSP (Scottish Liberal Democrat), North East Fife, 1999-2011; Deputy Minister for Parliament, Scottish Executive, 1999-2000; Convener, Procedures Committee, Scottish Parliament, 2003-05, Convener, Education Committee, 2005-07, Member, Europe and External Relations Committee, 2007-08; Convener, Economy, Energy and Tourism Committee, 2008-2011; b. 1.5.60, Gateside, Fife. Educ. Bell Baxter High School, Cupar; Newcastle upon Tyne University. Councillor, Fife Council, 1995-99 (Leader of Opposition and Lib Dem Group, 1995-99); Councillor, Fife Regional Council, 1982-95 (Leader of Opposition and Lib Dem Group, 1986-95). Chair, Scottish Liberal Democrat General Election Campaign, 2001 and 2005. Recreations: cinema; travel; reading.

Smith, Professor Ian K., MA, MEd, DipEd. Professor of Education, University of the West of Scotland (Emeritus, since October 2018); Dean of School of Education, University of the West of Scotland (formerly University of Paisley), 2003-09; Head of School of Education, University of Paisley, 2000-03; b. 28.7.53, Glasgow; m., Aileen; 1 s. Educ. Hutchesons' Boys' Grammar School, Glasgow; University of Glasgow. Teacher of History, Lanark Division, Strathclyde Region, 1976-82; Principal Teacher of History, Dunbarton Division, Strathclyde Region, 1982-89; Staff Development Trainer, Dunbarton Division, 1989; Secondary Assistant Headteacher Posts, including School Co-ordinator TVEI, Dunbarton Division, 1989-92; Senior Lecturer and PGCE (Secondary) Course Co-

ordinator, Craigie College of Education (subsequently Faculty of Education, University of Paisley), 1992-2000. Member: SOED National Steering Group on Training for Mentoring, 1994-95; GTCS Working Group on Partnership in Initial Teacher Education, 1996-97; National Working Group on Quality Assurance in Initial Teacher Education, 1999-2002; Scottish Teacher Education Committee, 2000-09 (Chair, 2005-08); Scottish Executive Induction Implementation Group, 2001-07; Scottish Executive National Chartered Teacher Review Group, 2007; General Teaching Council for Scotland, as Universities Scotland Representative, 2001-09; Convener, GTCS Education Committee, 2005-09. Expert consultant for The Teaching Council, Ireland, 2010, and The Council of Europe/European Union from 2010 (including work at Pan-European level, and in a range of countries, such as Albania, Armenia, Azerbaijan, Bosnia and Herzegovina, the Czech Republic, Greece, Kosovo, Montenegro, North Macedonia, Serbia and Ukraine). Editor, Scottish Educational Review, 2011-13. Publications: various books and book chapters, journal articles, conference papers and research reports, including 'Models of Partnership in Programmes of Initial Teacher Education. A Systematic Review Commissioned by the General Teaching Council Scotland' (Co-Author), 2005; Convergence or Divergence? Initial Teacher Education in Scotland and England (Co-Author), 2006 and a range of publications for the Council of Europe, since 2011, eg. "Underpinning Integrity in the Albanian Education System: Compilation of PACA (Project against Corruption in Albania) Outputs" (Co-Author), 2013. Recreations: reading; exercise; travel. Address: (b.) School of Education and Social Sciences, Univ. of the West of Scotland, Ayr Campus, University Avenue, Ayr KA8 0SX; T.-01292 886272.
E-mail: ian.smith@uws.ac.uk

Smith, Professor James, MA, MSc, PhD. Vice-Principal International and Professor of African and Developmental Studies, University of Edinburgh. Educ. Harris Academy; University of Dundee; University of the Witwatersrand. Career history: Research Fellow, University of the Witwatersrand, 2001-03; University of Edinburgh: Research Fellow, 2003-04, Lecturer/Senior Lecturer in African Studies, 2005-2010, appointed Assistant Principal and Professor in 2010; Honorary Researcher, University of Johannesburg, since 2012; Visiting Professor, The Open University, since 2010; Trustee, Practical Action, since 2011. Address: University of Edinburgh, International Strategy and Partnerships, Edinburgh Global, 33 Buccleuch Place, Edinburgh EH8 9JS; T.-0131 650 4315.
E-mail: James.Smith@ed.ac.uk

Smith, Professor Jeremy John, BA, MPhil, PhD, AKC, FEA, FRSE, HonFASLS, FRSA. Senior Research Fellow and Professor Emeritus, English Language & Linguistics, Glasgow University, and Honorary Professor, School of English, University of St Andrews, since 2021; b. 18.10.55, Hampton Court; m., Dr Elaine P. Higgleton; 1 d. Educ. Kingston Grammar School, Kingston-upon-Thames; King's College, London; Jesus College, Oxford; Glasgow University. College Lecturer, Keble College, Oxford. 1978-79; Glasgow University: Lecturer, English Language, 1979-90; Senior Lecturer, 1990-96; Reader, 1996-2000; Professor of English Philology, 2000-2021. Publications: Transforming Early English, 2020; Older Scots: A Linguistic Reader, 2012; Old English: A Linguistic Introduction, 2009; Sound Change and the History of English, 2007; Introduction to Middle English (Co-author), 2002; New Perspectives on Middle English Texts (ed. with S. Powell), 2000; Essentials of Early English, 1999; Historical Study of

English, 1996; English of Chaucer (with M. L. Samuels), 1988. Recreations: hill walking; opera. Address: (b.) English Language and Linguistics, Glasgow University, Glasgow, G12 8QQ.

Smith, John, Alexander, OND (Agri). Member, Scottish Land Court, since 2006; Partner, WW Smith and Son (Farmers), since 1978; b. 14.2.59, Cardenden; m., Susan Mary Watson; 3 d. Educ. Dundee High School; North of Scotland College of Agriculture, Craibstone. Member, Scottish Agricultural Wages Board, 1998-2006; Chairman, NFU Scotland Legal and Technical Committee, 2000-05; Director, NFU Scotland, 2000-05; Director, Royal Highland Educational Trust, 2001-06; Chairman, Lantranto Agricultural Crops Industry Group, 2001-06. School Speaker for Royal Highland Educational Trust; Trustee, Fowlis Easter Hall, 1986-2015; Member of Board of Governors, Angus College, 2009-2013; Member, Dundee and Angus Foundation, since 2014; Chairman, Kettins Parish Community Council, since 2017. Recreations: curling with Lundie and Auchterhouse Curling Club and Wengen Curling Club. Address: (h.) Bridgefield House, Kettins, Blairgowrie, Perthshire PH13 9JJ; T.-01828 628169.

Smith, Rev. John Raymond, MA, BD. Minister, Morningside United Church, Edinburgh, 1998-2013; b. 12.4.47, Dumfries; m., Isabel Jean McKemmie; 3 d. Educ. Dumfries Academy; University of Edinburgh; University of Geneva. Minister, School Wynd Church, Paisley, 1973-82; World Mission Secretary, Congregational Union of Scotland, 1978-86, President, 1988-89; Minister, Oakshaw Trinity Church, Paisley, 1991-98; Moderator, Presbytery of Edinburgh, 2007-08. Convenor, Education and Learning Committee, United Reformed Church, 2011-15; Examiner, Royal College of Surgeons, Edinburgh, 2008-16; Member, Intercollegiate Committee for Basic Surgical Examinations, 2013-16. Clubs: Royal Scots, Edinburgh. Recreations: walking; writing; travel; photography. Address: (h.) 25 Whitehaugh Park, Peebles EH45 9DB; T.-01721 724 464; e-mail: midmarjohn@gmail.com

Smith, Professor Leslie Samuel, BSc, PhD. Professor Emeritus of Computing Science, University of Stirling, since 2018; b. 3.10.52, Glasgow; m., Brigitte Beck-Woerner. Educ. Allan Glen's School; University of Glasgow. Started programming in 1974, and returned to University to study it properly in 1977; Lecturer, Glasgow University, 1980-83; joined Stirling University after a year as an independent consultant. Member, EPSRC College; Senior Life Member, IEEE; Member, Acoustical Society of America. Recreations: playing jazz piano. Address: (b.) Department of Computing Science and Mathematics, University of Stirling, Stirling FK9 4LA; T.-01786 467462; e-mail: lss@cs.stir.ac.uk

Smith, Professor Lorraine Nancy, BScN, MEd, PhD. Emeritus Professor, Glasgow University (Professor of Nursing, 1990-2011, Head of School, 1990-2001), Honorary Senior Research Fellow, since 2012; b. 29.6.49, Ottawa; m., Christopher Murray Smith; 1 s.; 1 d. Educ. University of Ottawa; Manchester University. Appointed, Clinical and Biomedical Research Committee (Scotland), 1992-94; co-opted to National Board of Scotland for Nursing, Midwifery and Health Visiting, 1997-2000; appointed, Clinical Standards Advisory Group (UK), 1994-99; Convenor, Royal College of Nursing Research Society (Scotland), 1999-2005; Chair, Work Group of European Nurse Researchers, 2004-08; Chair, SIGN 118 & 119; RCN Scotland Board Member, 2009-10; Director, St Andrew's Clinics for Children (STACC). Recreations: bridge; golf; sailing. Address: (b.) 5 Huntly Gardens, Glasgow G12 9AS; T.-0141-330 5498; e-mail: lorraine.smith@glasgow.ac.uk

Smith, Margaret, MA. Former MSP (Liberal Democrat), Edinburgh West (1999-2011); former Education Spokesperson; b. 18.2.61, Edinburgh; 1 s.; 1 d.; 3 step-sons. Civil partnership, 2006. Educ. Broughton High School; Edinburgh University. Political organiser; Member, City of Edinburgh Council, 1995-99. Recreations: reading; travel.

Smith, Matt, OBE, DL. Deputy Lieutenant, Ayrshire and Arran; Member, Employment Appeal Tribunal; Member, Central Arbitration Committee; Member ICAS Investigations Committee; Member, CIPFA Investigation Committee; Hon. Fellow, Scottish Council for Development and Industry. Former Scottish Secretary, UNISON, 1993-2010 (NALGO from 1973); STUC President (1999-2000); b. 4.2.52; m., Eileen; 1 s.; 1 d. Educ. Stevenston High School and Ardrossan Academy. Served on Commission for Scottish Devolution (Calman); Commission on Local Government and Scottish Parliament (McIntosh); served as JP (1986-2017) and Member of the North Strathclyde JP Advisory Committee. Former Non Executive Director, Scottish Water (2013-2021); Scottish Police Authority (2017-2021); ICAS Regulation Board; Scottish Human Rights Commission; Scottish Standards Commission; Broadcasting Council for Scotland; Irvine Bay Regeneration Company; Church of Scotland, Church and Nation Committee; Scottish Committee, Equal Opportunities Commission; Centre for Scottish Public Policy; Scottish Local Government Information Unit; Ayrshire Economic Forum; Scottish Government Economic Forum; Scotland Europa; Royal College of Physicians (Edinburgh) Lay Committee; UNITY Enterprise. Campaigner for Scottish Parliament including Scottish Constitutional Convention; Vice Chair, Labour for a Scottish Parliament. Councillor and Dean of Guild, Stevenston Town Council (1973-1975); Labour Parliamentary Candidate, Bute and North Ayrshire, 1979. Recreations: family; travel; music; golf. Email: mattsmith52@hotmail.co.uk

Smith, Ralph Andrew, QC, LLB, DipLP. Advocate, since 1985; QC, since 1999; b. 22.3.61, Scotland; m., Lucy Moore Inglis; 1 s.; 1 d. Educ. Edinburgh Academy; Kelvinside Academy; Aberdeen University. Junior Counsel to Lord President, 1989-90; Standing Junior Counsel to Department of Environment, 1992-99; Advocate Depute (ad hoc). Legal Member, Lands Tribunal for Scotland (Full Time), 2014. Address: (h.) Castlemains, Gifford, East Lothian EH41 4PL.

Smith of Kelvin, Baron (Sir Robert Haldane Smith), CA, FCIBS. Chairman, Scottish Enterprise, since 2019; Chancellor, University of Strathclyde, since 2013; Chair: Green Investment Bank, IMI plc, Alliance Trust PLC, Forth Ports Limited; appointed Chairman, Scotland Devolution Commission in 2014; Chancellor, University of The West of Scotland, 2003-2013; b. 8.8.44, Glasgow; m.; 2 d. Educ. Allan Glen's School. Robb Ferguson & Co., CA, 1963-68; qualified CA, 1968; ICFC (now 3i); Managing Director, National Commercial and Glyns Ltd., 1983-85; General Manager, Corporate Finance Division, Royal Bank of Scotland plc; Managing Director, Charterhouse Development Capital Ltd., and Executive Director, Charterhouse Bank Ltd., 1985-89; Morgan Grenfell Private Equity: CEO, 1989-96, Chairman, 1989-2001; Member, Group Executive Committee, Deutsche Bank, 1996-2000; Chief Executive, Morgan Grenfell Asset Management, 1996-99; Vice Chairman, Deutsche Asset Management, Deutsche Bank AG, 1999-2002; Chairman, The Weir Group plc, 2002-2013. Non-executive Director: Tip Europe plc, 1987-89, Stakis plc, 1997-99 (Chairman, 1998-99), Bank of Scotland plc, 1998-2000, MFI Furniture Group plc, 1987-2000. Member, Financial Services Authority, 1997-2000; Member, Board, Financial Reporting Council, 2001-04; Member, Board of Trustees, British Council, 2002-05; Chairman, FRC Group on Audit Committees Combined Code; Trustee, National Museums of Scotland, 1985-2002 (Chairman, Board of Trustees, 1993-2002); President, British Association of Friends of Museums, 1995-2005; President, Institute of Chartered Accountants of Scotland, 1996-97; Commissioner, Museums and Galleries Commission, 1988-98 (Vice Chairman, 1997-98). Hon. Doctorates, Edinburgh University, 1999, Glasgow University, 2001, Paisley University, 2003. Publication: Managing Your Company's Finances. Address: (b.) 39 Palmerston Place, Edinburgh EH12 5AU; T.-0131-527 6010.

Smith, Sir Robert Hill, Bt. MP (Liberal Democrat), West Aberdeenshire and Kincardine, 1997-2015; b. 15.4.58; m., Fiona Cormack; 3 d. Educ. Merchant Taylors' School, Northwood; University of Aberdeen. Managed family estate; Member, Aberdeenshire Council, 1995-97; Liberal Democrat Spokesman on Transport and the Environment, 1997-99, Scottish Affairs Spokesman, 1999-2001; Member, Scottish Affairs Select Committee, 1999-2001; Liberal Democrat Deputy Chief Whip, 2001-06, Scottish Whip, 1999-2001, Energy Spokesman, 2005-06, Trade and Industry Spokesman, 2005-06; Member: Trade and Industry Select Committee, 2001-05, European Standing Committee A, 2000-01, Procedures Committee, 2001-10, Unopposed Bills (Panel), 2001-10, Standing Orders, 2001-10, Accommodation and Works, 2003-05, International Development, 2007-09; Deputy Shadow Leader of the House, 2007-10. Honorary Vice President, Energy Action Scotland.

Smith, Sarah. Vice-Principal Strategic Change and Governance; and University Secretary, University of Edinburgh. Educ. Oxford University; Imperial College, London; Harvard Business School; Academy of Executive Coaching; Insead. Career: Civil Service, Whitehall and Scottish Government. Address: University of Edinburgh, Room 214, Old College, South Bridge, Edinburgh EH8 9YL; T.-0131 650 2144.

Smith, Shona Houston, LLB (Hons), DipLP, NP. Partner, Balfour and Manson; b. 17.11.66, Glasgow. Admitted, Solicitor, 1991; specialised in family law, since 1993; Board Member, Scottish Child Law Centre, 1996-99; former Chair and Treasurer of the Family Law Association; former Treasurer, Scottish Collaborative Family Law Group; Treasurer, Family Law Arbitration Group Scotland, since 2011. Address: (b.) 62 Frederick Street, Edinburgh EH2 1LS; T.-0131 200 1238; e-mail: shona.smith@balfour-manson.co.uk

Smith, Emeritus Professor Stanley Desmond, OBE, BSc, PhD, DSc, FRS, FRSE, FInstP. Emeritus Professor (Professor of Physics, Heriot-Watt University, 1970-96); Founder, Edinburgh Instruments Ltd., 1971, Chairman, 1971-2011; Founder, Chairman (1983-2019) and Chief Scientific Officer (CSO), Edinburgh Biosciences Ltd; b. 3.3.31, Bristol; m., Gillian Anne Parish; 1 s.; 1 d. Educ. Cotham Grammar School; Bristol University; Reading University. SSO, RAE, Farnborough, 1956-58; Research Assistant, Department of Meteorology, Imperial College, London, 1958-59; Lecturer, then Reader, Reading University, 1960-70; Head, Department of Physics, Heriot-Watt University, 1970-96. Member: Advisory Council for Applied Research and Development, 1985-87, Advisory Council on Science and Technology, 1987-88 (Advises PM), Defence Scientific Advisory Council, 1985-91, SERC Astronomy and Planetary Science and Engineering Boards, 1985-88, Council, Institute of Physics, 1984-87; Chairman, Scottish Optoelectronics Association, 1996-98. Royal

Medal, Royal Society of Edinburgh, 2011. Publications: Infrared Physics (Co-Author); Optoelectronic Devices, 1995; 230 scientific publications. Current R&D medical trials of non-invasive Diagnostics and treatment of cataract, including experiments with transgenic pigs at the Roslin Institute (human trials commenced in March 2021 with positive results). Recreations: skiing; mountaineering; golf. Address: (h.) Treetops, 29D Gillespie Road, Edinburgh EH13 0NW; desgillsmith@gmail.com; T.-0131 441 7225; (b.) Edinburgh Biosciences Ltd; T.-01506 429 274; e-mail: des@edinbio.com

Smith, Rev Stephen. Minister, St Andrew's Trinity Parish Church, Johnstone, since 2021; inducted to Kilbarchan Parish Church as Minister in 2013. Address: 82 Elm Drive, Johnstone, Renfrewshire PA5 9PW; T.-01505 702621; e-mail: stephenrevsteve@aol.com

Smith, Tommy, OBE, DUniv, DMus, DLitt, hon. FRIAS. Musician (tenor saxophone), Educator and Composer; b. 27.4.67, Edinburgh. Won best soloist and best group award, Edinburgh International Jazz Festival, aged 14; recorded his first albums as a leader, aged 15; joined Gary Burton Quintet, 1985-87; signed to Blue Note Records, 1989; won British Jazz Award, 1989; hosted Jazz Types, BBC TV; began recording for Linn Records, 1993; founded Scottish National Jazz Orchestra, 1995; won BT British Jazz Award for Best Ensemble, ScotRail Award for most outstanding group performance, Arts Foundation/Barclays Bank jazz composition fellowship prize, 1996; made youngest-ever Doctor of the University, Heriot-Watt University, 1999; has premiered four original saxophone concertos; Sound of Love album reached No. 20 in American Gavin Jazz Chart; started own record company, 2000; Honorary Fellow, Royal Incorporation of Architects of Scotland and Creative Scotland Award, 2000; Founder, The Tommy Smith Youth Jazz Orchestra, since 2002; Hamlet British Jazz Award for best tenor saxophonist, 2002; received second doctorate, Glasgow Caledonian University; won BBC 'Heart of Jazz' Award, 2008; winner of the Best Woodwind title at the inaugural Scottish Jazz Awards, 2009; Best Educator, Scottish Jazz Awards, 2011; Lord Provost Award for Music, 2009; 27 solo albums; 9 SNJO albums; 3 TSYJO albums; 17 other albums; appointed head of jazz, Scotland's first full time jazz course, Royal Conservatoire of Scotland; awarded Professorship, Royal Conservatoire of Scotland, 2010; Best Educator, Scottish Jazz Awards, 2012; Best Album of the year 'KARMA', Scottish Jazz Awards, 2012; received third doctorate, Edinburgh University, 2013; Best Big Band, Scottish Jazz Awards, 2009, 2011; Best Big Band, British Jazz Awards, Parliamentary Jazz Award, 2012; Best Educator, Parliamentary Jazz Award, 2015; British Jazz Award, 2017; OBE 2019; Scottish Jazz Award, 2019. Recreations: golf; cooking; poetry; cinema; art & design. Address: (b.) c/o Spartacus Records Ltd., PO Box 3743, Lanark ML11 9WD. E-mail: ts@tommysmith.scot

Smith, Victoria. Director of Education, Registration and Professional Learning (ERPL), The General Teaching Council for Scotland, since 2021. Career history: teacher at South Park Primary School in Fraserburgh, moving on to head teacher roles in several schools, as well as serving as a quality improvement officer; Service leader in Angus Council's education department. Address: The General Teaching Council for Scotland, Clerwood House, 96 Clermiston Road, Edinburgh EH12 6UT; T.-0131 314 6000.

Smith, Professor William Ewen, BSc, DIC, PhD, DSc, FRSC, FRSE. Emeritus Professor of Inorganic Chemistry (Professor from 1987); b. 21.2.41, Glasgow; m., Frances Helen Williamson; 1 s.; 1 d. Educ. Hutchesons' Boys Grammar School; Strathclyde University. Visiting Scientist,

Oak Ridge National Laboratory, 1965-67; SERC and ICI Fellow, University College, London, 1967-69; Lecturer, then Reader, then Professor, then Emeritus Professor, Strathclyde University, since 1969; Chief Scientific Officer, Reninshaw Diagnostics Ltd., 2010-2012 (Chief Executive Officer, 2007-2010). Publications: 300 papers and reviews. Recreations: golf; sailing. Address: Department of Pure and Applied Chemistry, Strathclyde University, Glasgow, G1 1XL; T.-0141-552 4400.

Smout, Professor Thomas Christopher, CBE, MA, PhD, FRSE, FSA (Scot), FBA. HM Historiographer in Scotland; b. 19.12.33. Address: Upper flat, Chesterhill, Shore Road, Anstruther, Fife KY10 3DZ.
E-mail: christopher@smout.org

Smyth, Colin. MSP (Labour), South Scotland region, since 2016; b. 11.72, Dumfries. Educ. University of Glasgow. Career history: worked as a teacher, becoming a Labour party organiser in 2003; General Secretary of the Scottish Labour Party, 2008-2012; elected to Dumfries and Galloway Council in 2007, representing the Nith Ward, re-elected in 2012. Address: Scottish Parliament, Edinburgh EH99 1SP.

Smyth, Professor John Fletcher, MD, FRCPE, FRCP, FRCSE, FRCR, FRSE, FACP (UK). Emeritus Professor of Medical Oncology; Honorary Assistant Principal, University of Edinburgh, since 2009, Director of Cancer Research Centre, 2002-05; Hon. Director, Cancer Research UK (formerly Imperial Cancer Research Fund) Medical Oncology Unit, now Clinical Cancer Research Centre, 1980-2005; b. 26.10.45; m., (1) Catherine Ellis; 2 d (marr. diss.); m., (2) Ann Cull; 2 step d. Educ. Bryanston School; Trinity College, Cambridge (BA, 1967, MA, 1971); St. Bartholomews Hospital (MB Chir 1970); MD Cantab, 1976; MSc London, 1975; MRCP, 1973. House Officer posts: St. Bartholomew's Hosp. and RPMS, London, 1970-72; Assistant Lecturer, Dept. of Med. Oncology, St. Bartholomew's Hospital, 1972-73; CRC Research Fellowship, Inst. Cancer Res., 1973-75; MRC Travelling Fellowship, Nat. Cancer Inst., USA, 1975-76; Senior Lecturer, Inst. Cancer Research, 1976-79. Honorary Consultant Physician, Royal Marsden Hospital and Brompton Hospital, 1977-79; Lothian Health Board, 1979-2008; Visiting Professor of Medicine and Associate Director for Medical Research, University of Chicago, 1979; Professor of Medical Oncology, University of Edinburgh, 1979-2008. Member of Council: EORTC, 1990-97; UICC, 1990-94; President, European Society for Medical Oncology, 1991-93; Federation of European Cancer Societies, Treasurer, 1992-97, President 2005-2007. Editor-in-Chief, European Journal of Cancer, 2000-2010; Member, Committee on Safety of Medicines, 1999-2005; Chair, Expert Advisory Group for Haematology & Oncology Commission on Human Medicines, 2006-13; Member, Board of Governors, Bryanston School, 1979-2014; Member, The Monteverdi Choir, 1964-2014; Member, Board of Directors of Monteverdi Choir and Orchestras Ltd, 2014-2020; Chair, Board of Directors, Ludus Baroque, 2017-19; Chair, The Cancer Drug Development Forum, since 2020. Publications: contributions to various medical and scientific journals on cancer medicine, pharmacology, clinical and experimental cancer therapeutics. Recreations: flying; singing; fishing. Club: Athenaeum. Address: 18 Inverleith Avenue South, Edinburgh EH3 5QA; T.-0131 552 3775.

Smyth, Professor Noel Frederick, BSc (Hons), PhD. Professor of Nonlinear Waves, University of Edinburgh, since 2009 (Lecturer, since 1990); Professor, University of Wollongong, since 2008; b. 16.5.58, Brisbane, Australia; m., Juliet Elizabeth Smyth; 1 s. Educ. Toowong State High School; University of Queensland; California Institute of Technology. Research Fellow: California Institute of Technology, 1984, University of Melbourne, 1984-86; Research Associate, University of New South Wales, 1986-87; Lecturer, University of Wollongong, 1987-90; University of Edinburgh: Lecturer, 1990-99, Senior Lecturer, 1999-2004, Reader, 2004-09. Librarian, Edinburgh Mathematical Society, 1992-97; Engineering and Physical Sciences Research Council Peer Review College, since 2006; Fellow of the Australian Mathematical Society (2015); Senior Member of the Optical Society of America (2011). Publications: 150 refereed scientific papers; 4 book chapters. Address: (b.) School of Mathematics, University of Edinburgh, Peter Guthrie Tait Road, Edinburgh EH9 3FD; T.-0131 650 5080; e-mail: n.smyth@ed.ac.uk

Sneddon, Cleland, BA, MBA, MSc. Chief Executive, South Lanarkshire Council, since 2019; b. 6.3.67. Educ. Wishaw High School; Robert Gordon's University; Glasgow University; Strathclyde University. Career history: Planning and Research Officer, Strathclyde Regional District, 1991-94; Housing Development Manager, Clydesdale District Council, 1994-96; Property Development Manager, Clydesdale District Council, 1996-98; Universal Connections Coordinator, South Lanarkshire Council, 1998-2001; Change & Development Manager, South Lanarkshire Council, 2001-08; Head of Performance & HR, Midlothian Council, 2009-10; Executive Director, Community Services, Argyll and Bute Council, 2010-2016, Chief Executive, 2016-19. Address: South Lanarkshire Council, Council Offices, Almada Street, Hamilton ML3 0AA; T.-0303 123 1015.

Somerville, Shirley-Anne, BA (Hons). MSP (SNP), Dunfermline, since 2016, Lothians, 2007-2011; Cabinet Secretary for Education and Skills, since 2021; Cabinet Secretary for Social Security and Older People, 2018-2021; Minister for Further Education, Higher Education and Science, 2016-18; Deputy Chief Executive, SNP, 2013-16; b. 2.9.74; m., Myles. Educ. Kirkcaldy High School; Strathclyde University; Stirling University. Scottish National Party: Member, since 1990. Contested Edinburgh Central constituency, 2007 Scottish Parliament election. Returned as replacement MSP for Lothians region on 5 September 2007. Trustee and Member of the Scotland Committee, Shelter UK, 2011-16; Director of Communities, Yes Scotland, 2012-13. Address: Scottish Parliament, Edinburgh EH99 1SP.

Sorensen, Alan Kenneth, DL, BD, MTh, DipMin, FSA (Scot). Minister, Wellpark Mid Kirk, Greenock, since 2000; previously in St. Christopher's, Pollok from 1983. Broadcaster, since 1979; b. 16.04.57, Clydebank. Educ. Hutchesons' Boys' Grammar; Glasgow University; Edinburgh University. Sometime gravedigger, musician and comedian; Retail Management prior to Parish Ministry. Appointed Deputy Lieutenant for Renfrewshire, 2014; Church of Scotland's National Advisor on local broadcasting for many years; has received 38 national and international broadcasting awards. Recreations: collecting 60's onwards pop music; family history; studying Scottish castles; enjoying fine wine. Address: (h./b.) 101 Brisbane Street, Greenock PA16 8PA.
E-mail: alan.sorensen@ntlworld.com

Soutar, David, MB, ChB, FRCS(Ed), FRCS(Glas), ChM. Consultant Plastic Surgeon, West of Scotland Regional Plastic Maxillofacial Surgery Unit, 1981-2008; Chairman, Division of Trauma and Related Services, North Glasgow Universities NHS Trust, 2000-06; b. 19.12.47, Arbroath; m., Myra; 2 s.; 1 d. Educ. Ayr Academy; University of

Aberdeen. General surgical training, Grampian Health Board; plastic surgery training, Aberdeen, Glasgow, Munich; Honorary Clinical Senior Lecturer, Glasgow University. Member, Council, British Association of Plastic Surgeons, 1988-92, 1994-2002 (President, 2001). Publications: four books; over 30 book chapters; over 70 articles. Recreations: music; gardening.

Soutar, Rucelle. Chief Financial Officer, Scottish Football Association, since 2021. Career history: Head of Finance, RZSS, Edinburgh Zoo, 2000-04; Finance and Operations Director, ProjectScotland, 2004-14; Board Member, Lothian Pension Fund, 2015-16; The Royal Edinburgh Military Tattoo: Head of Finance, 2014-18, Chief Operating Officer, 2018-2020; Board Trustee, National Galleries of Scotland, since 2020. Address: The Scottish Football Association, Hampden Park, Glasgow G42 9AY; T.-0141 616 6000.

Souter, Sir Brian, BA. Non-Executive Director, Stagecoach Group plc (Chief Executive, 2002-2013, Chairman, 1980-2002 and 2013-19); b. 1954; m., Elizabeth McGoldrick; 3 s.; 1 d. Educ. Dundee University; University of Strathclyde. UK Master Entrepreneur of the Year at the 2010 Ernst & Young Entrepreneur of the Year Awards and, in 2012, became the first public transport entrepreneur to be inducted into the British Travel and Hospitality Industry Hall of Fame. Address: (b.) 10 Dunkeld Road, Perth, PH1 5TW.

Souter, William Alexander, MBChB(Hons), FRCSEd. Consultant Orthopaedic Surgeon, Princess Margaret Rose Orthopaedic Hospital, Edinburgh, 1968-1997; b. 11.5.33, Cupar; m., Kathleen Bruce Georgeson Taylor; 1 s.; 2 d. Educ. Falkirk High School; George Watson's Boys' College, Edinburgh; Medical School, Edinburgh University. Registrar in Hand Surgery, Derbyshire Royal Infirmary, 1964; Senior Registrar, Orthopaedic Department, Edinburgh, 1965-68; Instructor in Orthopaedic Surgery, University of Washington, Seattle, 1967; Honorary Senior Lecturer in Orthopaedics, Edinburgh University, 1977-97; Visiting Professor, Bioengineering Department, Strathclyde University, 1985-88. Member, Council, British Orthopaedic Association, 1986-88 and 1993-95; Member, Council, Royal College of Surgeons of Edinburgh, 1988-98; Inaugural President, British Elbow and Shoulder Society, 1989-90; British Society for Surgery of the Hand: Member, Council, 1977-78, 1992-94, President, 1993; Chairman, Accreditation Committee, Federation of European Societies for Surgery of the Hand, 1992-96; European Rheumatoid Arthritis Surgical Society: Member, Executive Committee, 1979-81 and 1993-2001, President, 1995-99; President, Rheumatoid Arthritis Surgical Society, 1982 and 1998-2000; Honorary Member: British Society for Surgery of the Hand, 2001, Societe Francaise Chirurgie Orthopedique et Traumatologique, 1999, Netherlands Rheumatoid Arthritis Surgical Society, 2001, Spanish Society for Surgery of the Shoulder and Elbow, 1996, European Rheumatoid Arthritis Surgical Society, 2002, British Elbow and Shoulder Society, 2003; International Federation of Societies for Surgery of the Hand (IFSSH) Award: Pioneer of Hand Surgery, 2007. Recreations: gardening; music; hill-walking; photography; golf. Address: (h.) Old Mauricewood Mains, Penicuik, Midlothian EH26 0NJ; T.-01968 672609; e-mail: wsouter@btinternet.com

Spalding, Craig, BASc, MBA. Chief Executive, Sight Scotland and Sight Scotland Veterans, since 2022; b. 10.79. Educ. University of South Australia; Charles Sturt University. Career history: Technical Coordinator, Campbell Arnotts, 2005-07; Quality Manager, BTG, 2007-09; The Australian Red Cross Blood Service: Quality Manager, 2009-2010, Medical Services Manager, 2010-2012, National Quality Manager, Melbourne, Australia, 2012-2018; Director of Quality and Compliance, Irish Blood Transfusion Service, Dublin, Leinster, Ireland, 2018-19; Board Trustee: Be Healthy Together, Edinburgh, 2020, Health Opportunities Team, Edinburgh, 2020-21; Director, Scottish National Blood Transfusion Service, Edinburgh, 2019-2022. Address: Sight Scotland, 2a Robertson Avenue, Edinburgh EH11 1PZ; T.-0131 229 1456.

Sparks, Professor Leigh, MA, PhD. Professor of Retail Studies, Stirling University, since 1992, Deputy Principal, since 2016, Dean, Faculty of Management, 1995-2000, Head, Stirling Graduate School, 2011-2015; b. 15.2.57, Bridgend, Wales; m., Janice Lewis. Educ. Brynteg C.S.; Christ's College, Cambridge; St. David's University College, Wales. Researcher, Lecturer, Senior Lecturer, Professor, Institute for Retail Studies, Stirling University. Chair, Scotland's Towns Partnership. Recreation: watching sport, especially rugby. Address: (b.) Institute for Retail Studies, Stirling University, Stirling FK9 4LA; T.-01786 467014; e-mail: Leigh.Sparks@stir.ac.uk Web: www.stirlingretail.com

Spaven, David, MA (Hons) (Edin), MSc (Central London Poly), Honorary Fellow of the Royal Scottish Geographical Society; b. Edinburgh. Career history: rail freight marketing and contracts manager with Freightliner and British Rail in London and Glasgow, 1976-1993; Partner in The Spaven McCrossan Partnership rail consultancy, 1994-2002; Principal of sustainable transport consultancy, Deltix Transport Consulting, 2004-2021; Scottish Representative of the Rail Freight Group, 2011-2020. Campaigning and public service history: activist, candidate and spokesman for the Scottish Green Party, 1985-1992; Life Member of Campaign for Borders Rail, and campaigned for the re-opening of the Borders Railway, 1993-2015; founding Chair of Transform Scotland, the campaign for sustainable transport, 1997-2006; Member of the Rail Passengers Committee Scotland, 1998-2005; Member of the Climate Challenge Fund Panel, 2008-2011; Convenor of Living Streets Edinburgh Group, local arm of the national charity campaigning for improved conditions for 'everyday walking', 2014-2019. Selected publications: Co-Author of Mapping the Railways, 2011 (awarded '2013 Popular Transport Book of the Year' by the Railway & Canal Historical Society); Waverley Route: the battle for the Borders Railway, 2015; The Railway Atlas of Scotland, 2015; Highland Survivor: the story of the Far North Line, 2016 (awarded '2017 Railway Book of the Year' by the Railway & Canal Historical Society); Border Union Dream: the inside story of Britain's boldest railway preservation bid, 2018. Lifestyle: does not use air transport; non-car-owner; vegetarian. Address: 4 Church Hill Drive, Edinburgh EH10 4BT; T.-0131 447 7764. E-mail: david@deltix.co.uk

Speakman, Professor John Roger, FRS, FRSE, FRSB, FRSA, FMedSci, FRSS, BSc, PhD, DSc. Professor of Zoology, Aberdeen University, since 1997 (Director, Institute of Biological and Environmental Sciences, 2007-2011); b. 29.11.58, Leigh; m., Mary Magdelene; 1 s.; 1 d. Educ. Leigh Grammar School; Stirling University. Lecturer, 1989, Senior Lecturer, 1993, Reader, 1995, Aberdeen University; Chairman, Aberdeen Centre for Energy Regulation and Obesity, since 1998; Royal Society Leverhulme Senior Research Fellow, 2000. Publication: Body Composition Analysis: A Handbook of Non-Invasive Methods, 2001. Address: (b.) Department of Zoology, Aberdeen University, Aberdeen AB24 2TZ; T.-01224 272879.

Spence, Professor Alan, MA. Emeritus Professor in Creative Writing, University of Aberdeen; Artistic Director, WORD Festival, 1999-2011; Writer (poet, playwright, novelist, short-story writer); b. 5.12.47, Glasgow; m., Janani (Margaret). Educ. Allan Glen's School; Glasgow University. Writer in Residence, Glasgow University, 1975-77; Deans Community School, 1978; Traverse Theatre, 1983; City of Edinburgh, 1986-87; Edinburgh University, 1989-92; Aberdeen University, 1996-2001 (Professor in Creative Writing, 2001-2015; Professor Emeritus, from 2015); Edinburgh Makar, 2017-2021; winner, People's Prize, 1991; Macallan/Scotland on Sunday Short Story competition, 1993; TMA Drama Award, 1996; McVitie's Prize, 1996; Spirit of Scotland Award, 2006; Order of the Rising Sun (Government of Japan), 2018. Publications: poetry: ah!; Glasgow Zen; Seasons of the Heart; Clear Light; Morning Glory; short story collections: Its Colours They Are Fine; Stone Garden; novels: The Magic Flute; Way to Go; The Pure Land; Night Boat; plays: Sailmaker; Space Invaders; Changed Days; No Nothing. With wife, runs Sri Chinmoy Meditation Centre and Citadel Bookshop in Edinburgh. Address: 21/3 Waverley Park, Edinburgh EH8 8ER; T.-0131 661 8403; e-mail: a.spence@abdn.ac.uk

Spence, James William, KFO (Norway), RON (Netherlands), DL (Orkney), BSc, MNI, MICS. Lord-Lieutenant of Orkney, 2014-2020; Master Mariner, since 1971; Shipbroker, since 1975; Company Director, since 1977; Honorary Sheriff, Grampian Highland and Islands (Kirkwall), since 2000; Vice Lord-Lieutenant (Orkney), 2011-14; b. 19.1.45, St. Ola, Orkney; m., 1, Margaret Paplay Stevenson (deceased); 3 s. (one deceased); 2, Susan Mary Price. Educ. Leith Nautical College, Edinburgh; Robert Gordon's Institute of Technology, Aberdeen; University of Wales, Cardiff. Merchant Navy, 1961-74 (Member, Nautical Institute, 1972, Member, Royal Institute of Navigation, 1971); Micoperi SpA, 1974-75 (Temporary Assistant Site Co-ordinator on Scapa Flow Project); John Jolly (Shipbrokers, Stevedores, Shipping and Forwarding Agents), since 1975 (Manager, 1975, Junior Partner, 1976-77, Proprietor and Managing Director, since 1978, Chairman of the Board, since 2003). Vice-Consul for Norway, 1976, Consul, 1978-2015; Vice-Consul for the Netherlands, 1978-94; Member, Kirkwall Community Council, 1978-82; Member, Orkney Pilotage Committee, 1979-88; Chairman, Kirkwall Port Employers' Association, 1979-87 (Member, since 1975); Chairman, RNLI, Kirkwall Lifeboat Station Branch Committee, 1997-2004 (Station Hon. Secretary, 1987-96, Deputy Launching Authority, 1976-87); Chairman, Pier Arts Centre Trust, 1989-91 (Trustee, 1980-91); Chairman, Association of Honorary Norwegian Consuls in the UK and Ireland, 1993-95. Recreations: oenology; equestrian matters; Orcadian history; vintage motoring; apiculture. Address: (h.) Alton House, Kirkwall, Orkney KW15 1NA; T.-07885 200860. E-mail: bs3920@yahoo.com

Spence, Professor John, OBE, ARCST, BSc, MEng, PhD, DSc, FREng, FRSE, CEng, FIMechE. Professor Emeritus, Strathclyde University, since 2001, Trades House of Glasgow Professor of Mechanics of Materials, 1982-2001; b. 5.11.37, Chapelhall; m., Margaret Gray Hudson; 2 s. Educ. Airdrie Academy; Royal College of Science and Technology; Sheffield University. Engineering apprenticeship, Stewarts & Lloyds (now British Steel Corporation); Senior Engineer, then Head of Stress Analysis, Babcock & Wilcox Research Division; Strathclyde University: Lecturer, 1966, Senior Lecturer, Reader, Professor since 1979, Deputy Principal, Pro-Vice Principal and Vice Principal, 1994-2001; Acting Principal, Bell College, Hamilton, 2004/05. Served on many national committees: President, Institution of Mechanical Engineers, 1998/1999; EPSRC; British Standards Institution; Engineering Professors Council; Engineering Council

Senate and BER; Research Assessment Exercise Panel 30 in 1992, 1996 and Chair in 2001; Accreditation Board, Hong Kong Institution of Engineers; Scottish Higher Education Funding Council; Royal Academy of Engineering Council. Awarded OBE in Birthday Honours List in 2008; Chair, Search for Truth Charitable Trust, since 2009; Steering Board, Grasping the Nettle, since 2005. Address: Cairn O'Mount, 32 Commonhead Street, Airdrie ML6 6NS. E-mail: john.spence@strath.ac.uk

Spencer, Professor Alec P., BA (Hons), MA, MRes. Former Director, Rehabilitation and Care, Scottish Prison Service (2001-06); Honorary Professor, Faculty of Social Sciences, University of Stirling (2005); Non-Executive Director, Community Justice Scotland (2018); Trustee, Lucy Faithfull Foundation (2008); Public Appointments Adviser, Commission for Ethical Standards in Public Life in Scotland (2006); b. 12.3.46, London; m., Joan; 2 s.; 1 d. Educ. Dame Alice Owen's School; Keele University. Joined Scottish Prison Service, 1972; Governor, Dungavel, Peterhead, Edinburgh and Glenochil Prisons; Founder and Chair, Families Outside, 1990-2000; Chair, Scottish Accreditation Panel for Offender Programmes, 2006-10; Chief Officer, Tayside Community Justice Authority, 2010; Chair and Member of Board of Directors, INCLUDEM, 2001-10; Chair, Scottish Association for Study of Offending (SASO), 2006-2011; Adviser, Scottish Parliament, Justice 2 Committee Inquiry into sexual offenders against children, 2006; Convener, Scottish Consortium on Crime and Criminal Justice 2009-18; Chair, Dollar Community Council, 1990-93. Publications & Reports incl.: 'Working with Sex Offenders in Prisons and through Release to the Community', 1999; 'Balancing Risk and Need', 2009. Recreations: music; walking; early Penguin books (www.penguinfirsteditions.com). Address: Oakburn, 92 The Ness, Dollar, Clackmannanshire FK14 7EB; T.-01259 743044; e-mail: spencer@oakburn.co.uk

Spens, Michael Colin Barkley, MA. Educational Consultant, since 2017; Senior Advisor, RSAcademics Ltd, since 2018; former Headmaster, Fettes College, Edinburgh (1998-2017); b. 22.9.50, Weybridge; m., Deborah Susan; 1 s.; 2 d. Educ. Marlborough College; Selwyn College, Cambridge. United Biscuits Plc, 1972-74; Radley College, Oxon, 1974-93 (Assistant Master, 1974-93, i/c Careers, 1974-84, Housemaster, 1984-93); Headmaster, Caldicott, Farnham Common, 1993-98. Recreations: golf; running; wood-turning; bridge; geology; mountaineering; electronics.

Spowart, James McInally, FCIBS. Director, Business Stream, subsidiary of Scottish Water, 2017-2020; b. 19.11.50, Dunfermline; m., Janis Bell Spowart; 2 s. Educ. Beath High School, Cowdenbeath; Edinburgh College of Commerce; Napier University. Founder: Direct Line Financial Services, Standard Life Bank, Intelligent Finance; spent 25 years with Royal Bank of Scotland (prepared the blue print for telephone banking); led a campaign to save HBOS (2008-09). West Lothian Businessman of the Year, 2002; Business Insider Award, 2002. Honorary Doctor of Business, Napier University. Non-Executive Director of Scottish Water, 2009-2017; Commissioner to the Church of Scotland, 2011-12; Chairman of We-evolution (a Church of Scotland/Scottish Government run charity), 2011-2017. Recreations: golf; reading; swimming. Address: 59 West Cairn View, Livingston EH54 9FF; T.-01506 432193. E-mail: jimspowart@hotmail.com

Spray, Emeritus Professor Christopher James, MBE, FRSA, PhD, MA, FCIEEM. UNESCO Centre for Water Law, Policy & Science, Dundee University, 2009-2021; member of Board of Loch Lomond & Trossachs National

Park, 2018-22; NERC Knowledge Exchange Research Fellow, Welsh Government, 2015/16; b. 11.7.53, Marlborough; m., Deborah; 3 s. Educ. Marlborough College, Wiltshire; St. John's College, Cambridge; Aberdeen University. Research Fellow in Zoology, Aberdeen University, 1978-84; Anglian Water Authority, Cambridge, 1984-89; National Rivers Authority, Anglian Region, 1989-91; Conservation Manager, then Environment Director, Northumbrian Water Limited, 1991-2004; Director of Environmental Science, Scottish Environment Protection Agency, 2004-09; Chair of UK SPA RAMSAR Scientific Working Group, 2017-2021; President, Institute of Ecology and Environmental Management, 2004-06; Trustee, Wildfowl and Wetlands Trust, 2003-09; Trustee, Freshwater Biological Association, 2006-2013, Chair, 2010; Council Member, RSPB, 1999-2003; Trustee of British Trust for Ornithology, 2001-03; Director of River Restoration Project, 1995-99; past Chairman of Tweed Forum; past Board Member, Heritage Lottery Fund (NE) Committee, 2001-04; Member, Government's Advisory Committee on Releases to the Environment, 1999-2002; Member, England Biodiversity Group, 2002-04, Scotland Biodiversity Group, 2006-09. Recreations: birdwatching; running; conservation; hill walking. Address: (b.) UNESCO Centre for Water Law, Policy & Science, School of Social Sciences, University of Dundee, Dundee DD1 4HN; T.-01382 388362; e-mail: C.J.Spray@dundee.ac.uk

Spreng, Callum. Managing Director, Spreng Thomson Ltd; b. 28.7.61, St Andrews; m., Lorna Hunter. Educ. Dunfermline High School. Journalist, Dunfermline Press Newspaper Group, 1979-1984; Asst. Editor, SSEB News, SSEB, 1984-1986; various communications roles then Head of Communications, General Accident Fire & Life Assurance Corporation plc, 1986-1998; Communications Director, SMG plc, 1998-2007; Corporate Communications Director, ProStrakan Group plc, 2007-2008. Member, Council, CBI Scotland, 2007-2012. Recreations: golf; classic cars; motorsport. Address: (b.) 155 Albion Street, Glasgow G1 1RU.

Sproul-Cran, Robert Scott, MA (Cantab), PhD. Managing Director, Northlight Productions Ltd., since 1991; b. 14.8.50; m., Elizabeth Ann; 3 s.; 1 d. Educ. Daniel Stewart's College; Pembroke College, Cambridge; Edinburgh University. Trainee, Phillips & Drew, Stockbrokers, London, 1971-72; Announcer, then Head of Presentation, BBC Radio Scotland, 1979-85; Radio Manager, BBC Aberdeen, 1986-90; Scottish Correspondent, BBC Daytime Television, 1990-91; freelance Graphic Designer and Underwater Photographer, since 1976; Director, Scotland the Brand marketing organisation, 2003-04; Chief Executive, Tartan TV Ltd., 2000-07; Project Manager, Voice Of My Own (VOMO), 2013-2017. Winner, Scottish Corporate Communications Award, RTS Award for video graphics; directed "In Search of the Tartan Turban" which was nominated for an RTS award and won a BAFTA in the British Academy Children's Film and Television Awards, 2004; illustrated Maurice Lindsay's Glasgow; exhibited, Aberdeen Artists' annual exhibition; wrote and directed short film 'The Elemental' shown at Edinburgh International Film Festival, 2009 with completion funding from UK Film Council. Publication: Thicker than Water (novel and screenplay); Schrödinger's Caterpillar (novel); The Witching Ground (novel). Directed "Marrakech" and 'I Can't Remember Anything' for Treading The Borders theatre company. Created computer graphics for feature film 'The Happy Lands' (Dir: Robert Rae). Recreations: oil painting; sailing; playing bad rock guitar; Committee member, Hawick Rugby Club. Address: (b.) Northlight Productions Ltd., Hassendeanburn House, Hawick TD9 8RU; T.-01450 870106; web: www.northlight.tv

Spurway, Professor Neil Connell, MA, PhD. Emeritus Professor of Exercise Physiology, University of Glasgow; b. 22.8.36, Bradford; m., Alison Katherine Middleton; 3 s. Educ. The Grammar School, Falmouth, Cornwall; Jesus College, Cambridge University. Assistant, then Lecturer, then Senior Lecturer in Physiology, University of Glasgow, 1963-96, Professor of Exercise Physiology, 1996-2001. Chair, British Association of Sport and Exercise Sciences, 2000-02; Chair, Glasgow University Gifford Lectureships Committee, 1994-98; Member, Exercise Physiology Steering Group, BOA, 1991-2004; President, Royal Philosophical Society of Glasgow, 2003-05; Chair, Science and Religion Forum, 2006-09; Vice-President, European Society for Study of Science and Theology, 2008-2010; President, Scottish Church Theological Society, 2015-17; Fellow, International Society for Science and Religion, since 2017. Publications: Genetics and Molecular Biology of Muscle Adaptation (Co-Author); Creation and the Abrahamic Faiths; Theology, Evolution and the Mind; Laws of Nature, Laws of God?; Humanity, Environment and God; 40 years of Science and Religion: Looking back, looking forward (all as Editor); many papers and book chapters. Recreations: sailing; skiing; hill walking; philosophy; poetry; theatre; grandchildren. Address: 76 Fergus Drive, Glasgow G20 6AP; T.-07876 295979. E-mail: Neil.Spurway@glasgow.ac.uk

Sridhar, Professor Devi Lalita, BS, MPhil, DPhil. Professor of Global Public Health, The University of Edinburgh, since 2015; b. 7.84, Miami, Florida. Educ. Ransom Everglades School; University of Miami; University of Oxford. Career history: awarded a Rhodes Scholarship to study at All Souls College, Oxford University in 2008; became Associate Professor in Global Health Politics and Fellow, Wolfson College, Oxford University, 2011-14; appointed Reader and Senior Lecturer in Global Public Health, The University of Edinburgh in 2014. Member of the Scottish Government's COVID-19 advisory group; served on the Board of Save the Children UK; World Economic Forum Council on the Health Industry; Expert review group of the Wellcome Trust; Advisory Board of the Financial Flows Program at the Institute for Health Metrics and Evaluation (IHME; UW-Seattle); Co-Chair, Harvard School of Public Health/London School of Hygiene & Tropical Medicine Independent Panel on the Global Response to Ebola; Fellow, The Royal Society of Edinburgh, since 2021. Publications include: "The Battle against Hunger: Choice, Circumstance and the World Bank", 2007; "Governing Global Health: Who Runs the World and Why?", 2017; published work in Nature, Science, the New England Journal of Medicine, the Lancet and the British Medical Journal. Address: The University of Edinburgh, Usher Institute, College of Medicine and Veterinary Medicine, Old College, South Bridge, Edinburgh EH8 9YL; e-mail: Devi.Sridhar@ed.ac.uk

Stacey, Hon. Lady (Valerie Elizabeth), QC, LLB (Hons). Senator of the College of Justice, since 2009; Chairman, Employment Appeal Tribunal, 2013-15; Queen's Counsel, since 1999; Vice Dean, Faculty of Advocates, 2004-07; Member, Judicial Appointments Board for Scotland, 2005-07; Member, Sentencing Commission for Scotland, 2003-06; b. 25.5.54, Lanark; m., Andrew; 2 s. Educ. Elgin Academy; Edinburgh University. Solicitor, 1978; Advocate, 1987; Advocate Depute, 1993-96; Standing Junior Counsel, Home Office in Scotland, 1996-99; Temporary Sheriff, 1997-99. Recreation: listening to music. Address: (b.) Supreme Courts, Parliament House, Parliament Square, Edinburgh EH1 1RQ; T.-0131-225 2590.

Stachura, Professor Peter Desmond, MA, PhD, DLitt (Stirling), FRHistS. Professor of Modern European History and Director, Centre for Research in Polish History, Stirling University, 2000-2009, Director, Research Centre for Modern Polish History, since 2010; Member, Scottish

Parliamentary Cross Party Working Group on Poland, 2009-13; Member, Advisory Board of the Kresy-Siberia Foundation, 2010-13; Member of the Editorial Advisory Board of the academic history periodicals, Glaukopis (Warsaw) and Polish-Jewish Studies (Warsaw); Member, Academic Advisory Board, The Centre for Intermarium Studies, Institute of World Politics, Washington DC; Member, Academic Advisory Board, Leopolis Press (USA); b. 2.8.44, Galashiels; m., Kay Higgins; 1 s.; 1 d. Educ. St. Mirin's Academy, Paisley; Glasgow University; East Anglia University. Research Fellow, Institut für Europäische Geschichte, Mainz, Germany, 1970-71; Stirling University: Lecturer in History, 1971-83, Reader, 1983-2002. Chairman (and Founder), The Polish Society, 1996-2013; Editor, Occasional Papers Series, Centre for Research in Polish History, 2001-2010; Member, Academic Advisory Board, Leopolis Press (USA). Major publications: Nazi Youth in the Weimar Republic, 1975; The Weimar Era and Hitler: a critical bibliography, 1977; The Shaping of the Nazi State (Editor), 1978 (reprinted, 2014); The German Youth Movement, 1900-1945, 1981; Gregor Strasser and the Rise of Nazism, 1983 (reprinted, 2014); The Nazi Machtergreifung (Editor), 1983 (reprinted, 2014); Unemployment and the Great Depression in Weimar Germany (Editor), 1986; The Weimar Republic and the Younger Proletariat: an economic and social analysis, 1989; Political Leaders in Weimar Germany: a biographical study, 1992; Themes of Modern Polish History (Editor), 1992; Poland Between the Wars, 1918-1939 (Editor), 1998; Poland in the Twentieth Century, 1999; Perspectives on Polish History (Editor), 2001; The Poles in Britain 1940-2000 (Editor), 2004; Poland, 1918-1945: An Interpretive and Documentary History of the Second Republic, 2004; The Warsaw Rising, 1944 (Editor), 2007; numerous articles in scholarly journals and anthologies in English, German and Polish. Recreations: supporting Celtic FC; discovering Poland; vexillology. Address: (h.) Ashcroft House, Chalton Road, Bridge of Allan, FK9 4EF; T.-01786 832793.
E-mail: pdstachura@yahoo.com

Staff, Alan. Chief Executive, Apex Scotland, since 2010. Educ. Gilberd School, Colchester, Essex; University of East Anglia; Essex University. Career history: Director of Modernisation, Suffolk Mental Health Partnerships NHS Trust, 2002-06; CEO, CrossReach, 2006-09; President, Eurodiaconia, 2007-09. Recreations: performance art; rugby; politics; travel; walking; developing young musicians. Address: (b.) 9 Great Stuart Street, Edinburgh EH3 7TP; T.-0131 220 0130.
E-mail: admin@apexscotland.org.uk

Stafford, Alyson, CBE. Director-General Scottish Exchequer, Scottish Government, since 2017; Director-General Finance, 2010-17. Joined the Scottish Government as Director of Finance in June 2005. Qualified as a Chartered Accountant in 1992; services to the public sector were recognised in 2002 when received honorary membership of the Chartered Institute of Public Finance Accountants (nominated by CIPFA Scotland); career has spanned private, public and central government sectors; at the forefront of change leading strategic, operational and corporate services in the Health Service in England and Scotland as a Chief Executive as well as Director of Finance. Address: Scottish Government, St Andrew's House, Regent Road, Edinburgh EH1 3DG.

Stair, 14th Earl of (John David James Dalrymple); b. 4.9.61, Edinburgh. Army Officer, 1981-86; Land Owner/Manager, since 1989. Retired Board Member, Dumfries and Galloway Enterprise; Retired Board Member, Scottish Environment Protection Agency, West; House of Lords crossbench member, since 2008. Interests: farming; environmental matters. Recreations:

all outdoor activities; gardening; flying. Address: (b.) Stair Estates, Sheuchan, Castle Kennedy, Stranraer DG9 8SL; T.-01776 702024.

Stalley, Professor Richard Frank, MA, BPhil. Professorial Research Fellow in Philosophy, Glasgow University, since 2008, Professor of Ancient Philosophy, 1997-2008, Head of Philosophy Department, 1990-93, 2001-04; b. 26.11.42, Leamington; m., Ellen May Ladd; 1 s.; 1 d. Educ. De Aston School; Worcester College, Oxford; Harvard University. Lecturer in Moral Philosophy, Glasgow University, 1968-84; Senior Lecturer in Philosophy, 1984-97. Publications include: An Introduction to Plato's Laws, 1983; Aristotle's Politics, 1995; many articles on ancient philosophy and on Scottish philosophy. Recreations: walking; opera. Address: (h.) 73 Jordanhill Drive, Glasgow G13 1UW; T.-0141 959 2668.

Stanley, Kenneth Alan, LLB (Hons), NP, WS. Solicitor, since 1981; Partner, Aitken Nairn WS, Edinburgh, since 1981; b. 31.7.57, Edinburgh; 2 d. Educ. Boroughmuir High School; University of Edinburgh. Solicitor, 1981; Alston Nairn and Hogg, WS, later with W.G. Leechman, becoming Partner in both firms which amalgamated with Aitken Kinnear to become Aitken Nairn, then Lindsays. Recreation: golf. Address: (b.) Caledonian Exchange, 19a Canning Street, Edinburgh EH3 8HE; T.-0131 656 5537.
E-mail: kens@aitkennairn.co.uk

Stanley-Wall, Professor Nicola. Professor of Molecular Microbiology and Head of the Division of Molecular Microbiology, University of Dundee. Address: School of Life Sciences, University of Dundee, Dow Street, Dundee DD1 5EH; T.-01382 386335.
E-mail: n.r.stanleywall@dundee.ac.uk

Stannett, Alan Edward, JP, BSc (Hons), ACIArb, MIAgM, FBIAC. Farmer, since 1971; Business Consultant, since 2001; b. 25.9.49, Cambuslang; m., Sharon; 2 s.; 2 d. Educ. Coatbridge High School; University of Glasgow. Agricultural Consultant, Lugg and Gould Ltd, 1971-73; Farm Manager: Riverford Farms, Devon, 1973-76, Harviestoun Estate, Dollar, 1976-84, Buccleuch Estates, Thornhill, 1984-2001; Farmer, Dalgarnock Pigs, Thornhill, since 2001; Managing Director, Cara Consultants Ltd, since 2001. Court Serving Justice of the Peace, 1988-2019; Honorary Sheriff, 2019; Chair, Barony College, 2001-09; Council Member, Scottish Funding Council, 2007-2015; Board Member, Scotlean Ltd, 2006-2015; Council Member, SAAVA, 2014-2020; Board Member, Cample Line, since 2017. Recreations: family; rugby; photography. Address: Carronhill, Thornhill, Dumfriesshire DG3 5AZ; T.-01848 331510; e-mail: alan@cara.co.uk

Stanton, Jon. Chief Executive, The Weir Group, since 2016. Career history: graduate trainee, Ernst & Young (Birmingham office) in 1988, then joined The Weir Group PLC; significant corporate finance experience, including mergers and acquisitions and has been involved in a number of restructuring and business process improvement projects; served as a Partner in the London office of The Weir Group PLC from 2001 with lead responsibility for the audit of a number of FTSE 100 multinational clients, including Invensys, Hanson and InterContinental Hotels Group; extensive international experience including two years based in Ernst & Young's Detroit office; Group Finance Director, The Weir Group PLC, 2010-2016. Chartered Accountant; Member of the Institute of Chartered Accountants in England and Wales. Address: The Weir Group PLC, 1 West Regent Street, Glasgow G2 1RW.

Stark, Edi, MA (Hons), ALA. Broadcaster (BBC Radio Scotland), and journalist; b. Edinburgh; m., Gavin Stark; 1 s.; 1 d. Educ. Aberdeen University; RGIT. Community Librarian, Glasgow and Livingston; Northsound Radio, 1980-90. Awards: Two Sony Golds, two Silver and three Bronzes in categories for best speech programme, best speech broadcaster and best news special. President, Scottish Clinical Skills Network; Honorary Member Aberdeen Artists' Society; Honorary Degree of Master of Aberdeen University, 2009. Lives in Edinburgh. Recreations: conversation; food and drink; travel; reading; contemporary art. Address: (b.) c/o BBC Radio Scotland, The Tun, Holyrood Road, Edinburgh.

Stear, Professor Michael James, BSc, PhD. Professor of Immunogenetics, University of Glasgow, since 1999; b. 31.1.55, London; m., Lynne Carol Stear; 1 s.; 1 d. Educ. Queen Victoria School, Dunblane; University of Aberdeen. BSc (Hons), University of Aberdeen, 1976; PhD, University of Edinburgh, 1980; Research Fellow, Australian National University, 1980-85; Visiting Professor, University of Nebraska-Lincoln, USDA Meat Animal Research Center, 1985-88; Førsteamanuensis, National Veterinary Institute, Oslo, 1989; Senior Research Fellow, then Professor, Glasgow University Veterinary School, from 1990. Address: (b.) Institute of Biodiversity, Animal Health and Comparative Medicine, College of Medical, Veterinary & Life Sciences, Graham Kerr Building, University of Glasgow, Glasgow G12 8QQ; T.-0141-330-5762; e-mail: michael.stear@glasgow.ac.uk

Steedman, Professor Mark, FBA, FRSE, BSc (Hons), PhD. Professor of Cognitive Science, Edinburgh University, since 1998; b. 18.9.46, Middlesex; m., Professor Bonnie Webber. Educ. Watford Boys Grammar School; University of Sussex; Edinburgh University. Research Associate, School of Artificial Intelligence, Edinburgh University, 1969-72; Research Fellow: Edinburgh University, 1972-73, University of Sussex, 1973-76; Lecturer, University of Warwick, 1976-83; Edinburgh University: Lecturer, 1983-86, Reader, 1986-88; University of Pennsylvania: Associate Professor, Computational Linguistics, 1989-92, Professor in Computer and Information Science, 1992-98. Joint Founding Editor, Language Cognition and Neuroscience, 1984-92; Senior Editor, Cognitive Science, 1997-99; Advisory Editor: Cognition, 1980-2000; Linguistics, 1979-92; Journal of Semantics, since 1985; Language Cognition and Neuroscience, since 1993; Action Editor, Transactions of the Association for Computational Linguistics, since 2013. Publications: Surface Structure and Interpretation, Linguistic Inquiry Monograph 30, 1996; The Syntactic Process, 2000; Taking Scope, 2012. Recreations: jazz; hill-climbing. Address: (b.) Informatics, 10 Crichton Street, Edinburgh EH8 9AB; T.-0131-650 4631.

Steedman, Dr Nicola, MA, MBBS. Deputy Chief Medical Officer, The Scottish Government, since 2020. Educ. University of Cambridge; University of Oxford. Career history: Consultant in Sexual Health and HIV, Countess of Chester Hospital, 2008-2011; The Scottish Government: Senior Medical Officer, 2012-19, Acting Deputy Chief Medical Officer, 2015; Member, BASHH, since 2003; Consultant Physician in Sexual Health and HIV, since 2008; NHS National Services Scotland: CPHM and Clinical Lead for National Maternity and Sexual Health Data, 2017-2019, Medical Director, 2019-2020. Address: Scottish Government, St. Andrew's House, Regent Road, Edinburgh EH1 3DG.

Steedman, Robert Russell, OBE, RSA, RIBA, FRIAS, ALI, DA, MLA. Former Partner, Morris and Steedman, Architects and Landscape Architects (retired); b. 3.1.29, Batu Gajah, Malaysia; m., 1, Susan Scott (m. diss.); 1 s.; 2 d.; 2, Martha Hamilton. Educ. Loretto School; School of Architecture, Edinburgh College of Art; Pennsylvania University. Governor, Edinburgh College of Art, 1974-86; Commissioner, Countryside Commission for Scotland, 1980-88; Chairman, Central Scotland Woodlands Project, 1984-88; Association for the Protection of Rural Scotland Award Panel, 1995-99; elected Associate, Royal Scottish Academy, 1973, Academician, 1979; Council Member, RSA, 1981 (Deputy President, 1982-83, 1999-2000, Secretary, 1983-91); Commissioner, Royal Fine Art Commission for Scotland, 1983-96; Deputy Chairman, 1994-96, former Member, Council, RIAS; Member, Council, National Trust for Scotland, 1999-2006; Trustee, St. Andrews Preservation Trust, 2002-08; Trustee, Falkland Heritage Trust, 2002-2012; nine Civic Trust Awards, 1963-78; British Steel Award, 1971; RIBA Award for Scotland, 1974, 1989; European Heritage Medal, 1975; Association for the Protection of Rural Scotland, 1977, 1989; Borders Region Award, 1984; Honorary Degree, DLitt, University of St. Andrews, 2006; Royal Incorporation of Architects in Scotland (RIAS) Lifetime Achievement Medal, 2009; Scottish Design Awards 2009; Architecture Lifetime Achievement Award; Honorary Degree, DUniv, University of Stirling, 2011; "Architects Lives". Recording for British Library Archives, 2018. Address: (h.) Muir of Blebo, Blebocraigs, by Cupar, Fife KY15 5UG.

Steel, Professor Christopher Michael, BSc, MB, ChB, PhD, DSc, FRCPEdin, FRCPath, FRCSEdin, FRSE, FMedSci. Emeritus Professor in Medical Science, St Andrews University (Professor, 1994-2004); b. 25.1.40, Buckhaven; m., Dr. Judith Margaret Spratt; 2 s.; 1 d. Educ. Prince of Wales School, Nairobi; George Watson's College, Edinburgh; Edinburgh University. House Physician/House Surgeon/Resident/Senior House Officer, Edinburgh Teaching Hospitals; Graduate Research Fellow in Medicine, 1968; joined MRC staff, 1971; MRC Travelling Research Fellow, University of Nairobi, 1972-73; Assistant Director, MRC Human Genetics Unit, Edinburgh, 1979. Board Member: Scottish Cancer Foundation, Medical Research Scotland (2004-2010), Worldwide Cancer Research; published over 300 scientific papers and book chapters; Member, Government Gene Therapy Advisory Committee, 1994-99. Recreations: golf; skiing; music; theatre.

Steel of Aikwood, Rt. Hon. Baron (David Steel), KT, KBE, PC, DL. Non-Executive Director, General Mediterranean Holding S.A. (Luxembourg); Presiding Officer, Scottish Parliament, 1999-2003; MP, Tweeddale, Ettrick and Lauderdale, 1983-97 (Roxburgh, Selkirk and Peebles, 1965-83); Leader, Liberal Party, 1976-88; b. 31.3.38, Kirkcaldy; m., Judith MacGregor; 2 s.; 1 d. Educ. Prince of Wales School, Nairobi; George Watson's College, Edinburgh; Edinburgh University (MA, LLB). Assistant Secretary, Scottish Liberal Party, 1962-64; Interviewer, BBC TV Scotland, 1964-65; Presenter, weekly religious programme, STV, 1966-67, for Granada, 1969, for BBC, 1971-76; Liberal Chief Whip, 1970-75; Sponsor, Private Member's Bill to reform law on abortion, 1966-67; President, Anti-Apartheid Movement of Great Britain, 1966-69; Chairman, Shelter, Scotland, 1969-73; Member, British Council of Churches, 1971-75; Rector, Edinburgh University, 1982-85; Chubb Fellow, Yale, 1987; Hon. DUniv (Stirling), 1991; DLitt, University of Buckingham, 1994; Hon. Doctorate, Heriot Watt University, Edinburgh, 1996; HonLLD, Edinburgh, 1997; HonLLD, Strathclyde, 2000; HonLLD, Aberdeen 2001; HonDr, Open University, 2002; HonLLD, St Andrews, 2003; Hon LLD, Glasgow Caledonian, 2004; Hon LLD, Brunel, 2010; awarded Freedom of Tweeddale, 1988, and Ettrick and Lauderdale, 1990; The Commander's Cross of the Order of Merit (Germany), 1992; Chevalièr du Legion D'Honneur (France), 2003; Knight of the Order of the Thistle, 2004; DL, 1989-2013; contested Central Italy seat, European elections, 1989; President, Liberal International, 1994-96; former Vice President, Countryside Alliance; Visiting Fellow, St Antony's College, Oxford, 2013; Honorary Fellow, Royal College of Obstetricians and Gynaecologists, 2013; Lord High Commissioner, 2003/4; Honorary Fellow, Royal Zoological Society of Scotland, since 2016; Knight of St. George Habsburg; President: Jaguar Drivers' Club, 2007-2019, Federation of British Historic Vehicle Clubs, since 2017. Publications: Boost for the Borders, 1964; Out of Control, 1968; No Entry, 1969; The Liberal Way Forward, 1975; Militant for the Reasonable Man, 1977; High Ground of Politics, 1979; A House Divided, 1980; Border Country (with Judy Steel), 1985; The Time Has Come (with David Owen), 1987; Mary Stuart's Scotland (with Judy Steel), 1987; Against Goliath (autobiography), 1989. Recreations: angling; vintage motoring.

Steel, David Robert, OBE, MA, DPhil, FRCP (Edin). Senior Associate, Nuffield Trust, since 2016; b. 29.5.48, Oxford; m., Susan Elizabeth Easton; 1 s.; 1 d. Educ. Birkenhead School; Jesus and Nuffield Colleges, Oxford. Lecturer in Public Administration, Exeter University, 1972-84; Assistant Director, National Association of Health Authorities, 1984-86; Secretary, Health Board Chairmen's and General Managers' Groups and SCOTMEG, 1986-90; NHS in Scotland: Director of Corporate Affairs, 1990-95, Head of Health Gain, 1995-99; Chief Executive, Clinical Standards Board for Scotland, 1999-2002; Chief Executive, NHS Quality Improvement Scotland, 2003-09; Senior Research Fellow (Honorary), University of Aberdeen, 2009-2018. Address: (h.) 29 Park Road, Edinburgh EH6 4LA.

Steele, Professor Robert James Campbell, CBE, BSc, MB, ChB, MD, FRCSEd, FRCSEng, FCSHK, FRCPE, MFPH (Hon), FMedSci, FRSE. Professor of Surgery, Dundee University, since 1996; b. 5.3.52, Edinburgh; m., Annie Scott Anderson; 1 s.; 2 d. Educ. Daniel Stewart's College, Edinburgh; Edinburgh University. Surgical training, Edinburgh, 1977-85; Lecturer in Surgery, Chinese University of Hong Kong, 1985-86; Lecturer in Surgery, Aberdeen University, 1986-90; Senior Lecturer and Reader in Surgery, Nottingham University, 1990-96. President, Association of Coloproctology of Great Britain and Ireland, 2014-16; Independent Chair, UK National Screening Committee, since 2016. Publications in: breast cancer, gastrointestinal surgery, colorectal cancer and health screening. Recreations: music; Scottish country dancing; modern languages. Address: Mansefield, Dundee Road, Meigle PH12 8SF; T.-01828 640302.
E-mail: r.j.c.steele@dundee.ac.uk

Steele, Tom, BSc (Geog). Chair, Scottish Ambulance Service, since 2018; Non-Executive Director and Chair, Audit Committee, NHS Lanarkshire, 2014-18. Educ. The University of Edinburgh. Career history: Management Consultant, KPMG, 1983-87; Senior Executive, Fujitsu, 1987-2006; Census District Manager, National Records of Scotland, 2010-2011. Member, South Lanarkshire Health and Social Care Integration Joint Board. Address: Scottish Ambulance Service, National Headquarters, Gyle Square, 1 South Gyle Crescent, Edinburgh EH12 0EB; T.-0131 314 0000.

Steer, Christopher Richard, BSc (Hons), MB, ChB, DCH, FRCPE, FRCPCH. Retired Consultant Paediatrician; Special Adviser on Fetal Alcohol Spectrum Disorders to Scottish Government, 2015-2020; Lead Clinician; Hon. Senior Lecturer, Department of Child Life and Health, Edinburgh University; Hon. Senior Lecturer, Department of Biomedical Science, St. Andrews University; Hon. Senior Lecturer, Department of Child Life and Health, Dundee University; General Medical Council Examiner and Associate; Principal Regional Examiner, SE Scotland for Royal College of Paediatrics and Child Health; b. 30.5.47, Clearbrook, near Plymouth; m., Patricia Mary Lennox.

Educ. St. Olaves and St. Saviours Grammar School, London; Edinburgh University. Fellow, Royal Medical Society. Publications: Textbook of Paediatrics (Contributor); Treatment of Neurological Disorders (Contributor). Recreations: our garden; golf.

Steiner, Mark Rudie, LLB, NP. Legal Consultant; former part-time Chairman, Social Security Appeal Tribunal and Disability Appeal Tribunal; Scottish Representative, Consumers in the European Community Group; Member, Potato Marketing Board Consumer Liaison Committee; Member, National Pharmaceutical Consultative Committee Working Group on Quality Assurance; m., Dr. Eleanor Steiner (deceased); 1 s. Educ. Aberdeen University. Long-time international radio/TV commentator and Foreign Correspondent; Editor, Canadian Broadcasting Corporation, Toronto and Montreal; Editor, Swiss Broadcasting Corporation, Berne; Lecturer on Swiss affairs and advisor to Anglo-Swiss organisations and authorities; international war crimes investigator; Procurator Fiscal in Scotland; Partner and Director of various firms and companies; Past Chairman, Patients Association, Perth Community Relations Council; Delegate, Scottish Council for Racial Equality; neutral observer at various overseas political trials; contributor to various international journals; retired Principal, Goodman Steiner & Co., Defence Lawyers and Notaries in Central Scotland; former Member, Scottish Consumer Council. Publications: Alpine Legends of Switzerland; Nell of the Seas; Nell of The Islands; Boy on a Kite; The Wages of Pleasures and various travel and children's books; Literary Consultant and Editor with Nevis International Books. Visiting Lecturer and public speaker in UK and overseas. Recreations: sailing; developing international exchanges. Address: (h.) Atlantic House, Ellenabeich, Isle of Seil, by Oban, Argyll PA34 4RF; T.-Balvicar 300 593.

Stell, Geoffrey Percival, BA, FSA, FSA Scot. Visiting Lecturer, Edinburgh College of Art, University of Edinburgh; Head of Architecture, Royal Commission on the Ancient and Historical Monuments of Scotland, 1991-2004; b. 21.11.44, Keighley; m., Evelyn Florence Burns; 1 s.; 1 d. Educ. Keighley Boys' Grammar School; Leeds University; Glasgow University. Historic Buildings Investigator, RCAHMS, 1969-91; sometime Chairman, Scottish Vernacular Buildings Working Group; sometime Chairman, Scottish Urban Archaeological Trust; sometime Vice-President, Council for Scottish Archaeology. Publications include: Dumfries and Galloway; Orkney at War, volume 1 (World War I); Monuments of Industry (Co-author); Buildings of St Kilda (Co-author); Loads and Roads in Scotland (Co-editor); The Scottish Medieval Town (Co-editor); Galloway, Land and Lordship (Co-editor); Materials and Traditions in Scottish Building (Co-editor); Scotland's Buildings (Co-editor); Lordship and Architecture in Medieval and Renaissance Scotland (Co-editor). Recreations: gardening; music; travel, particularly in Scotland and France. Address: (h.) Beechmount, Borrowstoun, Bo'ness, West Lothian, EH51 9RS; T.-01506 510366; e-mail: gpstell@gmail.com

Stephen, Rev. Donald Murray, TD, MA, BD, ThM. Minister, Marchmont St. Giles' Parish Church, Edinburgh, 1974-2001; Secretary, Church of Scotland Chaplains' Association, 1991-2007; b. 1.6.36, Dundee; m., Hilda Swan Henriksen (deceased); 2 s.; 1 d; m., 2, Marjorie Roberta Bennet (deceased). Educ. Brechin High School; Richmond Grammar School, Yorkshire; Edinburgh University; Princeton Theological Seminary. Assistant Minister, Westover Hills Presbyterian Church, Arkansas, 1962-64; Minister, Kirkoswald, 1964-74; Chaplain, TA, 1965-85 (attached to 4/5 Bn., RSF, 205 Scottish General Hospital, 2nd Bn., 52nd Lowland Volunteers); Convener, Committee on Chaplains to Her Majesty's Forces, General Assembly, 1985-89. Interests: sport; reading; pottering in the garden. Address: 10 Hawkhead Crescent, Edinburgh EH16 6LR; T.- 0131 629 4523; e-mail: donaldmstephen@gmail.com

Stephen, Sheriff Principal Mhairi Margaret, BA, LLB, QC. President, Sheriff Appeal Court; Sheriff Principal of Lothian and Borders, since May 2011; Sheriff of Lothian & Borders at Edinburgh, 1997-2011; b. 22.1.54, Falkirk. Educ. George Watson's Ladies College; Edinburgh University. Allan McDougall and Co., SSC, 1976-97 (Partner, 1981-1997). Recreations: gardening; golf; walking; music. Address: Sheriff Principal's Chambers, Sheriff Court House, 27 Chambers Street, Edinburgh EH1 1LB; T.-0131 247 2561.

Stephen of Lower Deeside in the City of Aberdeen (Baron Nicol Stephen), LLB, DipLP. MSP (Liberal Democrat), Aberdeen South, 1999-2011; Deputy First Minister, and Minister for Enterprise and Lifelong Learning, 2005-07; Deputy Minister for Education and Young People, 2000-03 (Deputy Minister for Enterprise and Lifelong Learning, 1999-2000); Minister for Transport, 2003-05; b. 23.3.60, Aberdeen; m., Caris Doig; 2 s.; 2 d. Educ. Robert Gordon's College, Aberdeen; Aberdeen University; Edinburgh University. Trainee Solicitor, C. & P.H. Chalmers, 1981-83; Solicitor, Milne and Mackinnon, 1983-88; Senior Manager, Touche Ross Corporate Finance, 1988-91; Member, Grampian Regional Council, 1982-92 (Chair, Economic Development, 1986-91); MP, Kincardine and Deeside, 1991-92; Scottish Liberal Democrats: Parliamentary Spokesperson for Small Businesses, 1991-92, Treasurer, 1992-95, Health Spokesperson, 1995-97, Education Spokesperson, 1997-99, Scottish Party Leader, 2005-08; Director, Project Management, management consultancy company, 1992-99; Chairman of the Campaign for Rail Electrification Aberdeen to Edinburgh (CREATE), 1988-92; Director, Grampian Enterprise, 1989-92; Director, Grampian Youth Orchestra. Recreation: golf. Address: (b.) Room 103, Fielden House, House of Lords, London SW10 3SH. E-mail: stephenn@parliament.uk

Stephen, Dr Pauline Louise, MA (Hons), PGCE, MSc, DEdPsy. Chief Executive and Registrar, General Teaching Council for Scotland, since 2021; b. 22.3.74, Stonehaven. Educ. Mackie Academy; Aberdeen University; Moray House College of Education; Dundee University. Career history: Primary teacher, Educational Psychologist, Depute Principal Educational Psychologist, Principal Psychologist and Head of Inclusion and Integration, Aberdeenshire Council, 1997-2013; Head/Director of Schools and Learning, Angus Council, 2013-2019; Director of Education, Registration and Professional Learning, General Teaching Council for Scotland, 2019-2021. Recreations: reading; walking; yoga. Address: (b.) Clerwood House, 96 Clermiston Road, Edinburgh EH12 6UT; T.-0131 314 6000.

Stephens, Chris. MP (SNP), Glasgow South West, since 2015; b. 20.3.73, Glasgow. Educ. Trinity High School, Renfrew. Employed by Glasgow City Council, and is a Senior UNISON activist in the city, acting as a lead negotiator, and having represented trade union members on issues such as disability and racial discrimination, occupational pension protection, and on equal pay matters. Former Member of the SNP's National Executive Committee; former Convener of Glasgow Pollok Constituency Association; former Secretary of the SNP Trade Union Group. Recreation: proud Partick Thistle supporter and regularly attends matches. Address: House of Commons, London SW1A 0AA.

Stephens, Professor Jonathan Paul, MBE (2017), BA (Hons), MMus, PhD, PGCE. Emeritus Professor of Music and Music Education, University of Aberdeen; b. 12.7.51, Redruth, Cornwall; m., Rhona Lucas; 1 s.; 2 d. Educ. Redruth Grammar School; University of Wales, Aberystwyth. Secondary and private teaching, Wales, 1973-77; Lecturer in Music, Hertfordshire College of Higher Education, 1977-82; Lecturer in Music, 1982-84, Co-ordinator for Music Education, 1983-88, Principal Lecturer and Deputy Head of Music, 1984-88, Bretton Hall College of Higher Education; Director of Music (1988-2001) and Head of Aesthetic Education (1991-2001), Northern College, then Aberdeen University (2001-15), Professor in Music and Music Education (1993-2015). Chair, ISME Commission for Music in Schools and Teacher Training, 1988-92; Founder Member and British Representative, European Association for Music in Schools, 1990-2000; President, International Research Alliance of Institutions for Music Education, 1997-99; Board Member, ISME, 2000-04; Member, Music in Education Section Committee of Incorporated Society of Musicians (UK), 2002-05 and 2007-09, Warden, 2010-11, Member of Executive Committee and Council, ISM, 2009-2012; Executive Committee of National Association of Youth Orchestras, 2004-2010, Board Member, 2009-2010; Editorial Board of International Journal of Music Education, 2004-2012; compositions have been widely performed; frequent lecturer and consultant in music and music education, national and international. Recreations: reading; writing; composing; walking; gardening. Address: (h.) Chy Lowena, Auchattie, Banchory, Aberdeenshire AB31 6PT.

Stephenson, Professor Jill, MA, PhD. Professor Emeritus, Modern German History, University of Edinburgh; b. 17.01.44, Edinburgh; m., Dr. R. P. Stephenson (deceased). Educ. George Watson's Ladies' College; University of Edinburgh. Assistant Lecturer in Modern History, University of Glasgow, 1969-70; Lecturer in History, University of Edinburgh, 1970 (Senior Lecturer, 1984, Reader, 1991). Publications: Women in Nazi Society, 1975; The Nazi Organisation of Women, 1981; Women in Nazi Germany, 2001; Hitler's Home Front: Württemberg Under The Nazis, 2006. Recreations: gardening; food and wine; opera.

Stevely, Professor William Stewart, CBE, BSc, DPhil, DipEd, FRSB. Former Principal and Vice Chancellor, The Robert Gordon University (1997-2005); Professor Emeritus, The Robert Gordon University; Chairman, UCAS, 2001-05 (Member, Board, 2000-05); Convener, Universities Scotland, 2002-04; Board Member, Scottish University for Industry (SUFI), 2004-08; Board Member, Scottish Agricultural College, 2005-08, Vice Chair, 2008-2013; Board Member, Skills Development Scotland, 2008-2010; Chairman, Ayrshire and Arran Health Board, 2006-2011; Council Member, the Open University, 2008-2017, Vice Chair, 2010-2017; b. 6.4.43, West Kilbride; m., Sheila Anne Stalker; 3 s.; 2 d. Educ. Ardrossan Academy; Glasgow University; Oxford University. Lecturer and Senior Lecturer in Biochemistry, Glasgow University, 1968-88; Professor and Head, Department of Biology, Paisley College, 1988-92; Vice Principal, Paisley University, 1992-97. Member, Scottish Higher Education Funding Council, 1994-97; Member, National Board for Nursing, Midwifery and Health Visiting for Scotland, 1993-2000; Board Member, Quality Assurance Agency for Higher Education, 1998-2002. Address: (h.) Egerton, Bedwell Road, Cross Lanes, Wrexham LL13 0TR.

Steven, Professor Andrew John Maclean, LLB, PhD, DipLP, NP, WS. Professor of Property Law, University of Edinburgh, since 2020; Scottish Law Commissioner, 2011-19; b. 8.11.72, Banff. Educ. Banff Academy; University of

Edinburgh. Admitted as a Solicitor, 1999; Lecturer in Law, University of Edinburgh, 2000, then Senior Lecturer, 2010. Author of numerous publications on Property Law. Address: (b.) University of Edinburgh, Old College, South Bridge, Edinburgh EH8 9YL; T.-0131 650 2008.
E-mail: andrew.steven@ed.ac.uk

Stevenson, Alan, MSc. Chief Executive Officer, Volunteer Scotland, since 2021. Educ. University of Strathclyde. Career history: Corrosion Engineer, Motherwell Bridge, 1993-96; Quality Manager, Siemens Ltd/YDS Ltd, 1996-97; Strategy Executive, Catalyse International Ltd, 2000-01; Strategy Consultant, A Stevenson, 2001-02; Consultant, Parallel 56/Conkerhouse, 2002-07; Board Director, Eds Cycle Coop, 2014-16; Associate Director, Innovation Digital, 2007-2016; Associate Director, Digital Health and Care, Citrus Mind Ltd, 2009-2021; Visiting Lecturer/Project Supervisor, University of Strathclyde, since 2010; Visiting Lecturer, Glasgow Caledonian University, since 2012; Company Owner, AS Digital Business Ltd, since 2008; Digital Projects Manager, Volunteer Scotland, 2013-2021. Address: Volunteer Scotland, Jubilee House, Forthside Way, Stirling FK8 1QZ; T.-01786 479593.

Stevenson, Celia Margaret Stirton. Formerly Head of Inward Investment and Communications, Scottish Screen; b. Ballantrae; m., Charles William Forbes Judge; 2 s.; 1 d. Educ. Wellington School, Ayr; Edinburgh College of Art. Interior design business, 1970-80; Reporter/Presenter, West Sound, Ayr, 1981-84; Scottish Television: Reporter/Presenter, 1984-86, Promotions trailer-maker, 1987-89, Head of Programme Planning and Film Acquisition, 1990-95; Director, Scottish Screen Locations Ltd., 1995-97; Director of Locations, Scottish Screen, 1997-98. Board Member, British Film Commission, 1997-2000; Member, Steering Group, UK Film Commission Network, 1996-98. Recreations: cooking; reading; keeping fit; gardening.

Stevenson, Collette, BA (Acc). MSP (SNP), East Kilbride, since 2021; b. 1969, East Kilbride. Educ. University of the West of Scotland. Career history: Business and Administrative Support, South Lanarkshire Leisure and Culture Ltd, Hamilton, 2005-2021; elected Councillor, South Lanarkshire Council in 2017. Founding member of the East Kilbride branch of Women for Independence. Address: The Scottish Parliament, Edinburgh EH99 1SP; T.-0131 348 5502.
E-mail: Collette.Stevenson.msp@parliament.scot

Stevenson, Gerda. Actress, Singer, Writer, Book Illustrator, Director; b. 10.4.56, West Linton; m., Aonghas MacNeacail; 1 s. Educ. Peebles High School; Royal Academy of Dramatic Art, London (DDA, Vanbrugh Award). Has performed with 7:84 Theatre Co., Scottish Theatre Company, Royal Lyceum Theatre (Edinburgh), Traverse Theatre, Communicado, Monstrous Regiment, Victoria Theatre (Stoke on Trent), Contact Theatre (Manchester) and with Freefall at Lilian Baylis Theatre, London, and Birmingham Rep; directed Uncle Jesus for Edinburgh Festival Fringe; Assistant Director, Royal Lyceum, on Merchant of Venice and A Doll's House; Founder Member and Director, Stellar Quines Theatre Co.; TV work includes Clay, Smeddum and Greenden, Square Mile of Murder, Grey Granite, Horizon: Battered Baby, The Old Master, Taggart, Dr. Finlay, The Bill; films: The Stamp of Greatness, Tickets to the Zoo, Blue Black Permanent (BAFTA Scotland Best Film Actress Award, 1993), Braveheart; directed short film, An Iobairt, in Gaelic for BBC; extensive radio work includes title roles in Bride of Lammermoor and Catriona; adapted a number of works for

radio, including The Heart of Midlothian by Sir Walter Scott for BBC Radio 4 (nominated for a Sony Award in 2008); freelance producer for Radio Scotland; wrote and illustrated children's book, The Candlemaker.

Stevenson, (James Alexander) Stewart. MSP (SNP), Banffshire and Buchan Coast, 2011-2021 (Banff and Buchan, 2001-2011); Minister for Environment and Climate Change, 2011-2012; Minister for Transport, Infrastructure and Climate Change, 2007-2010; former Shadow Deputy Justice Minister; b. 15.10.46; m., Sandra Isabel Pirie. Educ. Bell Baxter School, Cupar; Aberdeen University. Director, Technology Innovation, Bank of Scotland, 1969-99.

Stevenson, Dr Katie, BA (Hons), PhD, FSA Scot, FSA, FRHistS, FRSA. Assistant Vice-Principal (Collections, Music and Digital Content), University of St Andrews, since 2018. Educ. University of Melbourne; University of Edinburgh. Career history: Director, Institute of Scottish Historical Research, 2013-2016; Co-founding Director and Chief Executive Officer, Smart History, 2015-16; Keeper of Scottish History and Archaeology, National Museums Scotland, 2016-18; Senior Lecturer in Late Medieval History, University of St Andrews, 2005-18. Publications (books): Chivalry and Knighthood in Scotland, 1424-1513, 2006; The Herald in Late Medieval Europe, 2009; Power and Propaganda: Scotland, 1306-1488, 2014; Chivalry and the Medieval Past, 2016; Medieval St Andrews: Church, Cult, City (Co-Author), 2017; numerous journal articles and chapters in books; Editor of the Journal of Scottish Historical Studies, 2010-2015. Secretary of the Scottish History Society, 2006-2014; served as a trustee on several boards of learned societies and charitable trusts; currently serving as Chair of the Recognised Collections of National Significance scheme for Museums Galleries Scotland. Address: University of St Andrews, College Gate, North Street, St Andrews; T.-01334 461616.
E-mail: avpcollections@st-andrews.ac.uk

Stevenson, Neil Alan, LLB, MSc. Chief Executive, Scottish Legal Complaints Commission, since 2015; Director of Representation and Professional Support, The Law Society of Scotland, 2009-2015. Educ. Dundee High School; University of Edinburgh; University of Birmingham. Training and Research Officer, NHS Education for Scotland, 2001-04; Deputy Director of Education and Training, The Law Society of Scotland, 2004-07, Head of Strategic Change, 2007-09; Director, Lawcare Ltd, 2006-2015, Trustee, 2006-2015; Trustee and Scottish National Council Member, ESU (Scotland), 2005-2013; Council Member (lay), General Dental Council, 2009-2017; Director, Scottish Arbitration Centre, 2011-2014; Council Member, Advertising Standards Authority, since 2017; Trustee, since 2016 and Vice Chair, since 2018, Changing the Chemistry. Address: The Stamp Office, 10-14 Waterloo Place, Edinburgh EH1 3EG; T.-0131 201 2130.

Stevenson, Paula. Chief Executive, The Judical Appointments Board for Scotland. Address: Thistle House, 91 Haymarket Terrace, Edinburgh EH12 5HE.

Stevenson, Professor Randall, MA, MLitt, FEA. Emeritus Professor of Twentieth-Century Literature, University of Edinburgh (appointed Professor in 2005); b. 25.6.53, Banff; m., Sarah Carpenter; 2 s.; 1 d. Educ. Hillhead High School, Glasgow; Edinburgh University; Linacre, Oxford. Assistant, then Principal Lecturer in English, Women Teachers' Training College, Birin-Kebbi, NW State Nigeria; Lecturer, then Senior Lecturer, then Reader in English, University of Edinburgh. Publications include: Scottish Theatre since the Seventies, ed (Co-Author), 1996; Modernist Fiction, 1998; Oxford English Literary History vol. 12, 1960-2000, 2004; Literature and the Great War, 2013; Reading the Times, 2018. Recreations: walking;

454 WHO'S WHO IN SCOTLAND

writing; photography; astronomy.
E-mail: randall.stevenson@ed.ac.uk

Stevenson, Struan John Stirton. Former MEP for
Scotland (1999-2014); b. 4.4.48, Ballantrae; m., Pat
Stevenson; 2 s. Educ. Strathallan School; West of
Scotland Agricultural College. Conservative Councillor,
Kyle and Carrick District Council, 1970-92 (Leader of
the Administration, 1986-88); Conservative Group
Leader, COSLA, 1986-88; European Parliament:
Chairman, Fisheries Committee, 2001-04; Conservative
Spokesman on Fisheries and Deputy Spokesman on
Agriculture; Vice President, EPP-ED (European
People's Party-European Democrats) Group in the
European Parliament, 2005-09. Hon. Doctor of Science,
State Medical Academy, Kazakhstan, 2000; Honorary
Citizen of Semipalatinsk, East Kazakhstan, 2004; Hon.
Professor, Sakharim University, Semey, 2007; Awarded
Order of 'Shapagat' (Mercy) by President of
Kazakhstan, 2007. Publication: 'Crying Forever'- A
Nuclear Diary, 2006, Russian Edition, 2007; Stalin's
Legacy - The Soviet War on Nature, 2012; "So Much
Wind - the Myth of Green Energy", 2013. Recreations:
contemporary art; music; theatre; opera; poetry; hill-
walking.

Stewart, A. J. (Ada F. Kay). Playwright and Author; b.
5.3.29, Tottington, Lancashire. Educ. Grammar School,
Fleetwood. ATS Scottish Command; first produced play,
1951; repertory actress, 1952-54; BBC TV Staff
Writer/Editor/Adaptor, Central Script Section, 1956-59;
returned to Scotland, 1959, as stage and TV writer; winner,
BBC New Radio Play competition, 1956; The Man from
Thermopylae, presented in Festival of Contemporary
Drama, Rheydt, West Germany, 1959, as part of Edinburgh
International Festival, 1965, and at Masquers' Theatre,
Hollywood, 1972; first recipient, Wendy Wood Memorial
Grant, 1982; Polish Gold Cross for achievements in literary
field. Publications: Falcon - The Autobiography of His
Grace, James the 4, King of Scots, 1970; Died 1513-Born
1929 - The Autobiography of A.J. Stewart, 1978; The Man
from Thermopylae, 1981. Recreation: work. Address: (h.)
33 Howe Street, Edinburgh EH3 6TF.

Stewart, Alan David, MA (Hons). Independent Board
Director, Falkirk Community Trust, 2019-22; Board
Trustee, Forth Environment Link, since 2019; Member,
General Teaching Council for Scotland's Appointments
Committee, since 2020; b. 27.7.58, Falkirk; m., Christine; 2
s. Educ. Graeme High School, Falkirk; Glasgow University;
Strathclyde University. Assistant Public Relations Officer,
Cumbernauld Development Corporation, 1983-86; Press
Officer, Strathclyde Regional Council, 1986-92; Principal
Officer (Corporate Communications and Marketing),
Lothian Regional Council, 1992-94; Head of Independent
Television Commission (Scotland), 2000-03; Office of
Communications, 2003-2018 (Head of Broadcasting and
Regulatory Affairs Manager, Scotland). Recreations: hill-
walking; cycling; supporting Falkirk FC. Address: (h.) 12
Heugh Street, Falkirk FK1 5QR.

Stewart, Alexander James. MSP (Scottish
Conservative), Mid Scotland and Fife region, since
2016; Conservative spokesperson and Shadow Minister
for Equalities and Older People in the Scottish
Parliament. Former Councillor, Perth City South;
Conservative candidate: Perth and North Perthshire
(General Election), 2015, Clackmannanshire and
Dunblane (Scottish Parliament election), 2016. Address:
Scottish Parliament, Edinburgh EH99 1SP.

Stewart, Andrew Fleming (Lord Ericht), LLB (Hons),
QC. Senator of the College of Justice, since 2016; b.
12.9.63, Dundee; m., Lesley Katherine Dawson; 2 d. Educ.
Perth High School; Edinburgh University. Solicitor:
Clifford Chance, London, 1988-90, Tods Murray WS,

Edinburgh, 1990-94; Legal Assistant to Lord President,
Court of Session, 1994-95; Advocate, since 1996; Tutor,
Law Faculty, University of Edinburgh, 1985-88 and since
1990; Lecturer (part-time), Université de Nancy 2, France,
since 1993; Standing Junior Counsel, Department of Trade
and Industry, 2000-09; Clerk to Examiners, Faculty of
Advocates, 2001-03; Clerk of Faculty of Advocates, 2003-
09; Advocate Depute, since 2009. Member, Board of
Practice and Procedure, Church of Scotland, 2001-05;
Chairman, Scottish Churches Committee, since 2007;
Treasurer, Scottish Committee, Franco-British Lawyers
Society, 1998-2001; Editor, Session Cases, since 2001.
Recreations: golf; music. Address: Advocates Library,
Parliament House, Edinburgh EH1 1RF; T.-0131-226 5071.

Stewart, The Hon. Lord (Angus Stewart), QC, BA,
LLB. Senator of the College of Justice, 2010-16
(retired); Queen's Counsel; b. 14.12.46; m., Jennifer
Margaret Stewart; 1 d. Educ. Edinburgh Academy;
Balliol College, Oxford University; Edinburgh
University. Called to the Scottish Bar, 1975; Trustee,
National Library of Scotland, 1994-2002; Treasurer, E
Boat International Offshore Class Association, since
1994; Keeper of the Advocates Library, 1994-2002;
President of the Stewart Society, 2001-04; Senior
Advocate Depute, 2005-08; Leading Counsel, Billy
Wright Inquiry, NI, 2008-10; Chair, Scottish Council of
Law Reporting, 1997-2001; Honorary Sheriff,
Campbeltown, 2014.

Stewart, David. MSP (Labour), Highlands and Islands,
2007-2021; MP, Inverness East, Nairn and Lochaber,
1997-2005; b. 5.5.56; m., Linda. Career history: member
of Labour's Executive; Assistant Director for Rural
Affairs, Scottish Council for Voluntary Organisations.
Formerly member of the Scottish and Work and
Pensions Select Committees; Parliamentary Private
Secretary to Alistair Darling, Secretary of State for
Scotland, 2003-05. Former Chief Whip of the Labour
Party in Holyrood.

Stewart, Douglas Fleming, MA, LLB, WS, FSA Scot,
FRSSA. Partner, J. & F. Anderson, WS, 1961-92;
Solicitor, Crown Estate Scotland, 1970-91; b. 22.5.27,
Sydney; m., Catherine Coleman; 2 d. Educ. George
Watson's College; Edinburgh University. RAF, 1945-48;
Chairman, Commercial Union, Edinburgh Board, 1979-
91, and its Scottish Advisory Committee, 1977-97.
Member, Edinburgh University General Council
Business Committee, 1961-69; Secretary/Treasurer,
Stewart Society, 1968-87 (also Hon. Vice-President);
Trustee, Church of Scotland Trust (former Chairman);
Session Clerk, Braid Church, Edinburgh, 1979-91;
President, Watsonian Club, 1989-90; Treasurer of
Friends of National Museums of Scotland, 1972-89;
Chairman, Comiston Probus Club, 1999; President,
Braid Bowling Club, 2003; Royal Overseas League,
Edinburgh Committee; Royal Scottish Society of Arts
(Science and Technology), Council. Recreation:
astronomy. Address: (h.) Greenhill Court, 98/5
Whitehouse Loan, Edinburgh EH9 1BD; T.-0131-447
4887.

Stewart, George Girdwood, CB, MC, TD, BSc, FICFor,
Hon. FLI; b. 12.12.19, Glasgow; m., Shelagh Jean Morven
Murray (deceased); 1 s.; 1 d. Educ. Kelvinside Academy,
Glasgow; Glasgow University; Edinburgh University.
Royal Artillery, 1940-46 (mentioned in Despatches);
Forestry Commission: District Officer, 1949-60, Assistant
Conservator, 1960-67, Conservator (West Scotland), 1967-
69, Commissioner, Forest and Estate Management, 1969-
79. Commanding Officer, 278 (Lowland) Field Regiment

RA (TA), 1957-60; President, Scottish Ski Club, 1971-75; Vice President, National Ski Federation of Great Britain and Chairman, Alpine Racing Committee, 1975-78; National Trust for Scotland: Member of Council, 1975-79, Representative, Branklyn Garden, 1980-84, Regional Representative, Central and Tayside, 1984-88; Chairman, Scottish Wildlife Trust, 1981-87; Member, Countryside Commission for Scotland, 1981-88; Member, Environment Panel, British Railways Board, 1980-90; Cairngorm Estate Adviser to Highlands and Islands Enterprise, 1988-98; Member, Cairngorm Recreation Trust, 1986-2014; President, Scottish National Ski Council, 1988-94, Hon. Vice-President, 1997-2014; Specialist Adviser to House of Lords Select Committee on EEC Forestry Policy, 1986; National Service to Sport Award (Scotland), 1995; Member, British Super Seniors Tennis Team, Seniors World Team Championships, 1999, 2001, 2002; International Tennis Federation Super Seniors World Individual Championships, 2006 and 2007, Winner Doubles; Fellow, Royal Society of Arts; London Olympics 2012 Torch Bearer; Hon Vice-President, Royal Scottish Forestry Society. Recreations: skiing; seniors tennis; studying Scottish painting; gardening. Address: (h.) Stormont House, 11 Mansfield Road, Scone, Perth PH2 6SA; T.-01738 551815.

Stewart, James Blythe, MA, LLB, LLB, Advocate; b. 22.4.43, Methil. Educ. Buckhaven High School; University of Edinburgh. Research Assistant, Faculty of Law, University of St. Andrews, 1966-67; Heriot-Watt University: Assistant Lecturer in Law, 1967-69, Lecturer in Law, 1969-76, Senior Lecturer in Law, 1976-98; retired 1998. Historian and Honorary Director, East Fife FC. Recreations: football spectating; bowls; golf. Address: (h.) 3 Comely Bank Terrace, Edinburgh EH4 1AT; T.-0131-332 8228.

Stewart, Rev. James Charles, MA, BD, STM, FSA Scot. Minister, Kirk of St. Nicholas, Aberdeen (The City Kirk), 1980-2000; b. 29.3.33, Glasgow. Educ. Glasgow Academy; St. Andrews University; Union Theological Seminary, New York. Assistant Minister, St. John's Kirk of Perth, 1959-64; Minister: St. Andrew's Church, Drumchapel, 1964-74, East Parish Church of St. Nicholas, Aberdeen, 1974-80. Chairman, Aberdeen Endowments Trust, 2002-2010; Honorary President, and former Editor (2004-2018) of 'The Record', of the Church Service Society; Hon. archivist, Kirk of St. Nicholas. Address: 54 Murray Terrace, Aberdeen AB11 7SB; T.-01224 587071.

Stewart, Lt Col (Retd). Johnny. Lord-Lieutenant for Clackmannanshire, since 2014; m., Katie; 3 c. Educ. Eton College. Served 22 years in the Scots Guards. Adjutant of the Royal Company of Archers (the Sovereign's Bodyguard in Scotland); Chairman of the Scots Guards Association; formerly Deputy Lord-Lieutenant for Clackmannanshire; runs family farm near Dollar comprising sheep and forestry. Recreations: shooting; tennis; golf.

Stewart, Kaukab. MSP (SNP), Glasgow Kelvin, since 2021. Educ. Northampton School for Girls; Bellahouston Academy, Glasgow; Moray House School of Education, Edinburgh; Napier Univerity, Edinburgh. Worked as a teacher. SNP candidate in the 1999 Scottish Parliament election; SNP candidate in the 2010 General Election. Address: The Scottish Parliament, Edinburgh EH99 1SP; T.-0131 348 5503.
E-mail: Kaukab.Stewart.msp@parliament.scot
Web: www.kaukabstewart.scot

Stewart of Dirleton, Baron (Keith Douglas Stewart), QC, LLB. Advocate General for Scotland, since 2020; m.; 2 c. Educ. Dirleton Primary School; George Heriot's School, Edinburgh; Keble College, Oxford; University of Edinburgh; University of Strathclyde. Called to the Bar in 1993 and took silk in 2011; specialises in criminal law, and has advised in other matters including defamation and intellectual property. Address: House of Lords, London SW1A 0PW.

Stewart, Kevin. MSP (SNP), Aberdeen Central, since 2011; Minister for Mental Wellbeing and Social Care, since 2021; Minister for Local Government, Housing and Planning, 2016-2021; b. 3.6.68, Aberdeen. Formerly local councillor (13 years); formerly depute leader of Aberdeen city council, having led the SNP group into coalition with the Lib Dems in 2007. Address: (b.) Third Floor, 27 John Street, Aberdeen AB25 1BT.

Stewart, Rev. Norma Drummond, MA, MEd, DipTh, BD, MTh, PhD. Minister, Strathbungo Queen's Park Church, Glasgow, 1979-2000; Locum Tenens, Dennistoun Blackfriars, Glasgow, 2000-06; Part-time Chaplain, Glasgow Royal Infirmary, 2001-06; b. 20.5.36, Glasgow. Educ. Hyndland Secondary School, Glasgow; University of Glasgow; Bible Training Institute, Glasgow; University of London (External); Trinity College, Glasgow; International Christian College, Glasgow; University of Aberdeen; University of Kent. Teacher, Garrioch Secondary School, Glasgow, 1958-62; Missionary, Overseas Missionary Fellowship, West Malaysia, 1965-74; ordained to ministry, Church of Scotland, 1977; occasional Lecturer and Tutor in Old Testament; Participant in Congress on World Evangelisation, Manila, 1989. Recreation: Old Testament research; PhD in Theology and Religious Studies, University of Kent (2017). Address: 127 Nether Auldhouse Road, Glasgow G43 2YS; T.-0141 637 6956.
E-mail: normadstewart@btinternet.com

Stewart, Norman MacLeod, BL, SSC. Consultant, Allan, Black & McCaskie, Solicitors, Elgin 1997-99, Senior Partner, 1984-97; Chairman, Elgin and Lossiemouth Harbour Board, 1993-2009; President, Law Society of Scotland, 1985-86; b. 2.12.34, Lossiemouth; m., Mary Slater Campbell; 4 d. Educ. Elgin Academy; Edinburgh University. Training and Legal Assistant, Alex. Morison & Co., WS, Edinburgh, 1954-58; Legal Assistant: McLeod, Solicitor, Portsoy, 1958-59, Allan, Black & McCaskie, Solicitors, Elgin, 1959-61 (Partner, 1961-97); Council Member, Law Society of Scotland, 1976-87 (Convener, Public Relations Committee, 1979-81, and Professional Practice Committee, 1981-84). Past President, Elgin Rotary Club; Past Chairman, Moray Crime Prevention Panel; President, Edinburgh University Club of Moray, 1987-89. Recreations: walking; golf; music; Spanish culture. Address: (h.) 25 Saltcoats Gardens, Bellsquarry South, Livingston, West Lothian EH54 9JD; T.-01506 419 439.

Stewart, Patrick Loudon McIain, CVO, MBE, LLB, WS, FSA (Scot). Lord Lieutenant, Argyll and Bute, 2011-2020; Stewart Balfour & Sutherland, Solicitors, Campbeltown, Senior Partner, 1982-2000; Secretary, Clyde Fishermen's Association, 1970-2009; Marine Environment Consultant, Scottish Fishermen's Federation, 2009-2014; Honorary Sheriff at Campbeltown; Secretary, South Kintyre Development Trust, 2017-19; Patron, Clyde Fishermen's Trust; Chairman, Argyll & Bute World War 1 Steering Group, 2014-19; b. 25.7.45, Campbeltown; m., Mary Anne McLellan; 1 s.; 1 d. Educ. Edinburgh Academy; Edinburgh University. Partner, Stewart Balfour & Sutherland, Campbeltown, 1970; former Executive Member, Scottish Fishermen's Federation; former Director, Scottish Fishermen's Organisation Ltd.; A Life Vice President of The Marine Society & Sea Cadets; An Honorary President of the Clyde Fishermen's Association; Cadet Forces Medal and two clasps. Recreations: walking; reading. Address: Craigadam, Campbeltown, Argyll PA28 6EP; T.-01586 552161.

Stewart, Robert. Headteacher, Biggar High School, since 2011. Formerly Deputy Head Teacher, Lower School, Uddingston Grammar School. Address: Biggar High School, Market Road, Biggar, South Lanarkshire ML12 6FX; T.-01899 222050.

Stewart, Susan, MA (Hons), MA, PGDip, FRSA, FCIPR. Director, The Open University in Scotland, since 2015. Educ. Renfrew High School; University of St Andrews; Smith College, Mass, USA; Strathclyde University; Caledonian University. Political Journalist, Scottish Television, 1991-93; Press and Parliamentary Liaison Officer, Strathclyde Regional Council, 1993-95; Head of Media Relations, Glasgow City Council, 1995-98; Depute Head, Press Office, Scottish Executive, 1998-2001; First Secretary, Scottish Affairs, British Embassy, Washington DC, The Scottish Government, 2001-05; Director of Corporate Communications, University of Glasgow, 2005-2012; Director of Communications, Yes Scotland, 2012-2013. Fulbright Commissioner, since 2018; founder member, Globalscot Network. Recreations: theatre; reading; walking. Address: The Open University in Scotland, Jennie Lee House, 10 Drumsheugh Gardens, Edinburgh EH3 7QJ.

Stewart-Clark, Sir Jack, Bt. Chairman, Dundas Castle Ltd, since 1999; Member of European Parliament for East Sussex and Kent South, 1979-99; Vice President, European Parliament, 1992-97; b. 17.9.29, West Lothian; m., Lydia Loudon; 1 s.; 4 d. Educ. Eton; Balliol College, Oxford; Harvard Business School. Coldstream Guards, 1948-49; J. & P. Coats, 1952-70 (Managing Director, J. & P. Coats Pakistan, 1961-66); Managing Director, J. A. Carp's Garenfabrieken, 1966-70; Philips Industries, 1970-79 (Managing Director, Philips Electrical Ltd., 1970-74, Pye of Cambridge Ltd., 1974-79). Member, Queen's Bodyguard for Scotland, Royal Company of Archers. Publications: European Competition Law; Drugs Education, It's My Problem as Well. Recreations: golf; photography; music; classic cars. Address: (h.) Dundas Castle, South Queensferry, near Edinburgh, EH30 9SP; T.-0131-331 1114.

Stimson, Professor William Howard, BSc, PhD, CBiol, FRSB, FIoN, FRSE. Emeritus Professor, Strathclyde University (former Professor of Immunology); Chairman: WH Stimson and Associates, Lanarkshire Laboratories Ltd.; CSO/Director, ILC Therapeutics Ltd.; b. 2.11.43, Liverpool; m., Jean Scott Baird; 1 s.; 1 d. Educ. Prince of Wales School, Nairobi; St. Andrews University. Research Fellow, Department of Obstetrics and Gynaecology, Dundee University, 1970-72; Lecturer, then Senior Lecturer, Biochemistry Department, Strathclyde University, 1973-80. Holder, Glasgow Loving Cup, 1982-83; Member, Editorial Boards, two scientific journals; 216 scientific publications; 66 patents. Recreations: mechanical engineering; walking; golf. Address: (b.) Immunology, Strathclyde Institute of Pharmacy and Biomedical Science, Strathclyde University, Hamnett Building, 161 Cathedral Street, Glasgow G4 0RE; T.-07776 215465.
E-mail: w.h.stimson@strath.ac.uk
E-mail: w.h.stimson@ilctherapeutics.com

Stirling of Garden, Sir James, KCVO, CBE, TD, BA, FRICS. Lord Lieutenant of Stirling and Falkirk, 1983-2005; Chartered Surveyor; b. 8.9.30; m., Fiona; 2 s.; 2 d. Educ. Rugby; Trinity College, Cambridge. Partner, Ryden and Partners, 1962-89; Director, Scottish Widows Life Assurance Society, 1974-96. Chairman, Highland TAVRA, 1981-86, President, 1990-96; Director, Woolwich Building Society, 1975-95; Honorary Sheriff, Stirling, 1996. Prior, Order of St. John, Scotland, 1997-2009; Hon. Doctor,

University of Stirling, 2004; Grand Cross of the Order of St. John, 2004. Address: (h.) Dambrae, Buchlyvie, Stirlingshire.

Stirling, John Boyd, WS. Clerk to HM Society of Writers to the Signet, 2002-08; Solicitor Advocate, since 2005; Partner, Gillespie MacAndrew, since 2005; b. 8.3.68, Glasgow; m., Julie; 2 s. Educ. Glasgow Academy; Edinburgh University. Trainee, W & J Burness WS; Solicitor, Scottish Office, Assistant, then Partner, Bennett and Robertson (which merged with Gillespie MacAndrew). Recreations: fly fishing; wine. Address: (b.) 5 Atholl Crescent, Edinburgh EH3 8EJ; T.-0131 225 1677; e-mail: john.stirling@gillespiemacandrew.co.uk

Stollery, Professor Peter John, BMus (Hons), MA, PhD, PGCE, FRSA. Professor of Electroacoustic Music and Composition, University of Aberdeen, since 2007; b. 24.07.60, Halifax; m., Catherine; 2 s.; 1 d. Educ. Heath Grammar School, Halifax; University of Birmingham. Assistant Teacher of Music, The Judd School, Tonbridge, 1984-89, Head of Music, 1989-91; Lecturer in Music, Northern College, Aberdeen, 1991-2001; University of Aberdeen: Lecturer in Music, 2001-02, Senior Lecturer in Music, 2002-05, Reader in Composition and Electroacoustic Music, 2005-07, Head of Music, 2006-2014, Head of School of Education, 2010-2011. Chair of Sound; former Chair, Sonic Arts Network, Aberdeenshire Music Forum; Vice-Chair, Culture Aberdeen; Board Member: invisiblEARts, Friendly Access. Recreation: listening. Address: (b.) School of Language, Literature, Music and Visual Culture, University of Aberdeen, MacRobert Building, Aberdeen AB25 5UA; T.-01224 274601; e-mail: p.stollery@abdn.ac.uk
Website: www.petestollery.com

Stone, James Hume Walter Miéville, MA, FRSA. MP (Liberal Democrat), Caithness, Sutherland and Easter Ross, since 2017; MSP (Liberal Democrat), Caithness, Sutherland and Easter Ross, 1999-2011; Councillor, The Highland Council (Tain and Easter Ross Ward), 2012-17; freelance newspaper columnist and broadcaster, since 1991; b. 16.6.54, Edinburgh; m., Flora Kathleen Margaret Armstrong; 1 s.; 2 d. Educ. Tain Royal Academy; Gordonstoun School; St Andrews University. Cleaner, fish-gutter, stores clerk, 1977-81; Assistant Site Administrator/Site Administrator, Bechtel G.B. Ltd., 1981-84; Administration Manager, Odfjell Drilling and Consulting Co. Ltd., 1984-86; Director, Highland Fine Cheeses Ltd., 1986-94; Member, Ross and Cromarty District Council, 1986-96; Member, The Highland Council, 1995-99 (Vice-Chair, Finance). Member, Cromarty Firth Port Authority, 1998-2001; Liberal Democrat Spokesman for: Education and Children, 1999-2000, Highlands and Fishing, 2000-01, Equal Opportunities, 2001-2011, Finance, 2002-2011; Trustee, Tain Museum Trust; Trustee, Tain Guildry Trust; Trustee, Highland Buildings Preservation Trust; Director, The Highland Festival, 1994-2000. Recreations: gardening; reading; music; butterflies and funghi.

Stone, Rodney, BA, DipRM. Leisure Manager, since 1976; Member, sportscotland Board, 2011-17; b. 11.10.51, Belfast; m., Alison; 1 s.; 1 d. Educ. Methodist College Belfast; University of Stirling. Local Authority Recreation Officer: Ayrshire, 1976-78, Cumbernauld, 1978-84, Glasgow, 1984-86; Leisure Centre Manager, Edinburgh, 1986-87; Leisure Services Manager, Midlothian District Council, 1987-95; Head of Leisure and Community Development, Moray Council, 1995-2000; Head of Lifelong Learning and Leisure,

Aberdeenshire Council, 2000-2011. Chair, Vocal (Chief Culture and Leisure Officers Association), 1998-2000 and 2007-2010; Secretary, 2001-06; former international athlete. Address: (h.) Tullynessle Steading, Tullynessle, Alford, Aberdeenshire AB33 8QR; T.-019755 62218; e-mail: jarstone@btinternet.com

Stone, Professor Trevor W., BPharm, PhD, DSc, FBPhS, Hon FRCP (Lond). Honorary Senior Research Fellow (Centre for Neuroscience), University of Glasgow (appointed Professor of Pharmacology in 1989); Honorary Senior Research Fellow, University of Oxford, since 2017; co-Director, PharmaLinks, since 2003; b. 7.10.47, Mexborough; m., (1) Anne Corina; divorced; m., (2) L. Gail Darlington. Educ. Mexborough Grammar School; London University; Aberdeen University. Lecturer in Physiology, Aberdeen University, 1970-77; Senior Lecturer/Reader in Neuroscience, then Professor of Neuroscience, London University, 1977-88. Editor-in-Chief, Journal of Receptor, Ligand and Channel Research, since 2008; Editor, British Journal of Pharmacology, 1980-86. Publications: 400 scientific papers and 13 books; Microiontophoresis and Pressure Ejection, 1985; Purines: Basic and Clinical Aspects, 1991; Neuropharmacology, 1995; Pills, Potions and Poisons – How Drugs Work, 2000. Recreations: photography; snooker; music; working. Address: (b.) Neuroscience and Psychology, West Medical Building, Glasgow University, Glasgow G12; T.-0141-330 4481.

Storey, Professor Kate Gillian, BSc (Hons), PhD. Head of Division of Cell and Developmental Biology, University of Dundee, since 2010, Chair of Neural Development, since 2007; b. 27.11.60, London; m., Jonathan Gordon; 1 s.; 1 d. Educ. Parliament Hill School, London; Sussex University; PhD Cambridge University; Harkness Fellowship, University of California at Berkeley, 1987. Lecturer, Department of Human Anatomy and Genetics, 1994-2000; College of Life Sciences, University of Dundee, since 2000. Major Science/Art Exhibition "Primitive Streak", since 1997. Fellow of Society of Biology; Fellow of the Royal Society of Arts; Fellow of the Royal Society of Edinburgh; Fellow of the Academy of Medical Sciences; Member, EMBO; BSDB Waddington Medal, 2019. Recreations: long distance running; beach combing. Address: (b.) School of Life Sciences, University of Dundee, Dow Street, Dundee DD1 5EH; T.-01382 385691.
E-mail: k.g.storey@dundee.ac.uk

Stove, Thomas William. Convener, Shetland Islands Council, 1999-2003; b. 17.7.35, Sandwick, Shetland; m., Alma; 2 d. Educ. Anderson Education Institute, Lerwick. Owner/Director, Televiradio (Shetland) Ltd., 1966-96; Member, Zetland County Council/Shetland Islands Council, 1970-78; Member, Lerwick Harbour Trust, 1980-96 (Chairman, 1983-96). Recreations: classic cars; DIY. Address: (h.) Nordaal, Sandwick, Shetland ZE2 9HP; T.-01950 431434.
E-mail: tandastove@btinternet.com

Strachan, Gordon, OBE. Scottish football manager; Manager, Scotland national team, 2013-17; b. 9.2.57; m., Lesley Scott; 2 s.; 1 d. Played for Dundee, Aberdeen, Manchester United, Leeds United and Coventry City, as well as the Scotland national team. Managed Coventry City, Southampton, Celtic and Middlesbrough. In club football, played 635 league games, scoring a total of 138 goals, playing 21 of 25 career seasons in either the English or Scottish top-flight. Earned 50 caps in international football, scoring five goals and playing in two FIFA World Cup final tournaments, Spain, 1982 and Mexico, 1986. Retired from playing in 1997 at age 40, setting a Premier League record for an outfield player.

FWA Footballer of the Year for the 1990-91 season while at Leeds; also named Manager of the Year in Scotland multiple times by writers and players while at Celtic; inducted into the Scottish Football Hall of Fame in 2007. Analysed football matches for the media, most notably on BBC Sport's Match of the Day 2; worked as a regular pundit for ITV and Sky Sports; official FIFA Ambassador for Scotland, 2006 FIFA World Cup.

Strachan, Professor Sir Hew Francis Anthony, MA, PhD, FBA, FRHistS, FRSE, HonDUniv (Paisley), 2005. Lord Lieutenant of Tweeddale, since 2014; Wardlaw Professor, International Relations, University of St Andrews, since 2015; Chichele Professor of the History of War and Fellow, All Souls College, University of Oxford, 2002-2015; Professor of Modern History, Glasgow University, 1992-2001; Director, Scottish Centre for War Studies, 1996-2001; Life Fellow, Corpus Christi College, Cambridge, since 1992; b. 1.9.49, Edinburgh; m., Pamela Dorothy Tennant (née Symes); 1 s.; 1 step s.; 2 d.; 1 step d. Educ. Rugby School; Corpus Christi College, Cambridge. Senior Lecturer, Department of War Studies and International Affairs, Royal Military Academy, Sandhurst, 1978-79; Research Fellow, Corpus Christi College, Cambridge, 1975-78; Fellow, Corpus Christi College, since 1979: Tutor for Admissions, 1981-88, Director of Studies in History, 1986-92, Senior Tutor, 1987 and 1989-92. Governor, Rugby School, 1985-2007, and Stowe School, 1990-2002; DL (Tweeddale), 2006-2014; Lord Lieutenant, Tweeddale, since 2014; Commonwealth War Graves Commission, 2006-2018; Member, Council, Society for Army Historical Research, 1980-95; President, Army Records Society, 2020; Council, National Army Museum, 1994-2003; Joint Editor, War in History, 1994-2013; Member, Queen's Bodyguard for Scotland (Royal Company of Archers); Brigadier, 2008; Ensign, 2019; Visiting Professor, Royal Norwegian Air Force Academy, since 2000; Trustee, Imperial War Museum, 2010-2018; Chair, Task Force on the Military Covenant for the Prime Minister, 2010; Lieutenant, Royal Company of Archers, since 2021. Publications: British Military Uniforms; History of the Cambridge University Officers Training Corps; European Armies and the Conduct of War; Wellington's Legacy: the Reform of the British Army 1830-54; From Waterloo to Balaclava: Tactics, Technology, and the British Army 1815-1854 (Templer Medal, 1986); The Politics of the British Army (Westminster Medal, 1998); Oxford Illustrated History of the First World War (Editor), 1998; The British Army, Manpower and Society into the 21st Century (Editor), 2000; The First World War Vol. I: To Arms, 2001; The First World War: a new illustrated history, 2003; Big Wars and Small Wars (Editor), 2006; Clausewitz's on War: A Biography, 2007; Clausewitz in the 21st Century (Editor), 2007; The Changing Character of War (Editor), 2011; How Wars End (Editor), 2012; British Generals and Blair's Wars (Editor), 2013; The Direction of War, 2013; numerous articles and reviews. Knighted in the 2013 New Year Honours for services to the Ministry of Defence. Pritzker Award for Lifetime Achievement in Military Writing, 2016. Recreations: shooting; rugby football. Address: (h.) Glenhighton, Broughton, Biggar ML12 6JF.

Strachan of Benholm, Baron (Roddy Strachan). Castle restorer; m., Fiona. Member, Clan Strachan Society; Trustee, Clan Strachan Charitable Trust. Address: Benholm Castle, Benholm, Kincardineshire.

Strang, Gavin Steel, BSc (Hons), DipAgriSci, PhD. MP (Labour), East Edinburgh, 1970-2010; b. 10.7.43, Dundee; m., Bettina Smith (deceased); 1 s. Educ. Morrison's Academy, Crieff; Edinburgh University. Parliamentary Under Secretary of State, Department of Energy, February to October, 1974; Parliamentary Secretary, Ministry of Agriculture, 1974-79; Principal Labour Agriculture Spokesman, 1992-97; Cabinet Minister with responsibility for Transport, 1997-98. Recreations: golf; swimming; the countryside.

Strang, Mike, BA, PG Cert. Chief Executive, Youth Scotland, since 2022. Educ. University of Strathclyde; University of Chester. Career history: Second Mate, Gordonstoun School, 2000; Duty Manager, Glasgow Climbing Centre, 1999-2001; Fairbridge: Team Leader, 2001-03, Skipper - Spirit of Fairbridge, 2003-08; career break, 2008-2010; Manager, Spirit of Fairbridge, 2010-2012; Fundraising Consultant, SD Consultants, 2014-16; The Prince's Trust: Head of Sail Training, National UK, 2012-14, Adventurous Activities Manager - Scotland, 2014-16; Chair - Scotland, Institute for Outdoor Learning, 2014-19; Venture Trust: Director of Operations, 2016-2021, Interim Chief Executive Officer, 2021, Chief Operating Officer, 2021-2022. Address: Youth Scotland, Balfour House, 19 Bonnington Grove, Edinburgh EH6 4BL; T.-0131 554 2561.
E-mail: mike.strang@youthscotland.org.uk

Strange, Most Revd. Mark. Bishop of Moray, Ross & Caithness, since 2007; Primus of Scottish Episcopal Church, since 2017; b. 2.11.61; m., Jane; 3 c. Educ. University of Aberdeen (currently a member of the University Business Committee); Lincoln Theological College. Ordained in the Anglican ministry a deacon in 1989 and priest in 1990; first pastoral appointment was as a curate at St Barnabas with Christ Church, Worcester (1989-92), then the Vicar of St Wulfstan's, Warndon, Worcester (1992-98); formerly canon of St Andrew's Cathedral, synod clerk of the diocese, and had a leading role in developing the church's youth network throughout Scotland and organising its annual youth week events; Rector of Holy Trinity Church, Elgin and priest in charge of St Margaret's, Lossiemouth, St Michael's, Dufftown and St Margaret's, Aberlour, 1998-2007. Honorary DD, University of The South, 2018. Address: The United Diocese of Moray, Ross and Caithness, 9-11 Kenneth Street, Inverness IV3 5NR; T.-01463 237503.

Strang Steel, Sir (Fiennes) Michael, 3rd Bt, CBE. Former Member, Deer Commission for Scotland (2000-2010); b. 22.2.43; m., Sally Russell; 2 s.; 1 d. Educ. Eton. Retired Major, 17th/21st Lancers, 1962-80. Former Forestry Commissioner. Address: (h.) Philiphaugh, Selkirk, TD7 5LX.

Strang Steel, Malcolm Graham, BA (Cantab), LLB. Partner, Turcan Connell, WS, 1997-2009; Partner, W. & J. Burness, WS, 1973-97; b. 24.11.46, Selkirk; m., Margaret Philippa Scott; 1 s.; 1 d. Educ. Eton; Trinity College, Cambridge; Edinburgh University. Sometime Chairman, Albyn Housing Society Ltd., Scottish Dyslexia Trust; Secretary: Standing Council of Scottish Chiefs, 1973-83, Scottish Agricultural Arbiters and Valuers Association, 1998-2009; Member, Council, Law Society of Scotland, 1984-90. Recreations: shooting; fishing; tennis; reading. Address: (h.) Greenhead of Arnot, Leslie, Glenrothes KY6 3JQ.

Strath, Alison. Chief Pharmaceutical Officer, The Scottish Government, since 2020. Educ. Robert Gordon University. Career history: Community Pharmacy Development Co-ordinator, National Pharmacy Association, 1995-99; Director, McPherson Pharmacy Ltd, 1996-2018; Professor of Community Pharmacy

Practice, Robert Gordon University, 2008-2018; Scottish Government: Principal Pharmaceutical Officer, 2002-2020. Address: Scottish Government, Pharmacy and Medicines Division, St Andrew's House, Regent Road, Edinburgh EH1 3DG; T.-0131 244 2823.
E-mail: alison.strath@gov.scot

Strathclyde, Lord (Thomas Strathclyde), PC. Leader of the House of Lords, 2010-2013; Chancellor of the Duchy of Lancaster, 2010-2013; Leader of the Opposition, House of Lords, 1998-2010; b. 22.2.60, Glasgow; m., Jane; 3 d. Educ. Wellington College; East Anglia University; University of Aix-en-Provence. Bain Clarkson, Insurance Brokers, 1982-88; Government Whip, 1988; Minister for Tourism, 1989; Minister for Agriculture and Fisheries, Scottish Office, 1990-92; Parliamentary Under Secretary of State, DoE, 1992-93; Minister of State, Department of Trade and Industry, 1993-94; Government Chief Whip, 1994-97; Opposition Chief Whip, 1997-98. Chairman, Strathclyde Commission on Restructuring the Scottish Conservative and Unionist Party, 1997-98. Directorships held: Trafalgar Capital Management Ltd., 2001-2010 (Chairman), Scottish Mortgage Investment Trust plc, 2004-2010, Galena Asset Management Ltd., 2004-2010, Marketform Group Ltd., 2004-2010, Hampden Agencies Ltd., 2008-2010, Trafigura Beheer BV; Adviser to various companies in the UK and internationally; Governor, Wellington College; Board Member, Centre for Policy Studies (CPS). Address: (b.) House of Lords, London SW1; T.-020 7219 3000.

Strathmore and Kinghorne, 19th Earl of (Simon Patrick Bowes Lyon); b. 18.6.86. Succeeded to title, 2016. First cousin twice removed of Queen Elizabeth II, and a great-great nephew of the late Queen Elizabeth, the Queen Mother. Address: Glamis Castle, Forfar DD8 1QJ.

Straton, Timothy Duncan, TD, CA, CTA. B. 1.10.42, Edinburgh; m., Gladys Margaret George (deceased); 1 s.; 1 d. Educ. Edinburgh Academy. Recreations: family; heritage railways; photography; curling; bowls. Address: (h.) 32 Wardie Road, Edinburgh EH5 3LG; T.-0131 552 4062.

Stringer, Professor Dame Joan Kathleen, DBE, CBE, BA, CertEd, PhD, CCMI, FRSA, FRSE, FIoD, HonDLitt (Keele). Principal and Vice-Chancellor, Edinburgh Napier University, 2003-2013; Board Member, Universities and Colleges Employers Association (UCEA), 2001-2010; Board Member, Leadership Foundation for Higher Education (LFHE), 2005-2010; Chair, Education UK Scotland Committee, 2005-2012; Board Member, Universities and Colleges Admissions Service (UCAS), 2009-2013; Board Member, National Theatre of Scotland, 2009-2016; Member: Executive Committee, Scottish Council Development and Industry, 1998-2013, Council, World Association for Co-operative Education, 1998-2003, Edinburgh International Festival Council, 1999-2005, Scottish Committee, British Council, 2000-2012, Judicial Appointments Board for Scotland, 2002-07; Convenor, Scottish Council for Voluntary Organisations, 2002-07; b. 12.5.48, Stoke on Trent; m., Roel Mali. Educ. Portland House High School, Stoke on Trent; Stoke on Trent College of Art; Keele University. Assistant Principal, Robert Gordon University, 1991-96, having joined as Lecturer, 1980; Principal, Queen Margaret University College, Edinburgh, 1996-2002; Visiting Lecturer, Aberdeen University, 1984-86. Member: Joint University Council for Social and Public Administration, 1982-91, Royal Institute of Public Administration, 1984-91, Management Board, North of Scotland Consortium on Wider Access, 1988-92, Board of Management, Aberdeen College, 1992-96,

Grampian Health Board, 1994-96, CVCP Commission on University Career Opportunities, 1995-2001, Scottish Committee, National Committee of Inquiry into Higher Education (The Dearing Committee), 1996-97, Human Fertilisation and Embryology Authority, 1996-99, Secretary of State's Consultative Steering Group and Financial Issues Advisory Group on the Scottish Parliament, 1998-99, Scottish Council for Postgraduate Medical and Dental Education, 1999-2002, Scottish Health Minister's Learning Together Strategy Implementation Group, 2000-01, Scottish European Structural Funds Forum, 2000-02, Department of Health's Working Group on the Modernisation of the SHO, 2000-02, Scottish Nursing and Midwifery Education Council Advisory Group, 2000-01; Auditor, Higher Education Quality Council, 1992-95; Commissioner (with responsibility for Scotland), Equal Opportunities Commission, 1995-2001; Chair, Northern Ireland Equality Commission Working Group, 1998-99; Vice Convener, Committee of Scottish Higher Education Principals, 1998-2002; Commissioner, Scottish Election Commission, 1999; Chair, Scottish Executive Strategic Group on Women, 2003; Member, Board: Higher Education Statistics Agency, 2003-2013, Quality Assurance Agency for Higher Education, 2002-06, Higher Education Careers Services Unit, 2000-05; Convenor, International Committee, Universities Scotland, 2006-2012; Honorary Doctorate 'honoris causa', University of Edinburgh, 2011; Council Member and Chair of Council, Institute of Directors, 2013-19, Senior Independent Council Member, 2016-19; Chair, Board of Trustees, Capital Theatres, since 2013; Non-Executive Director, City Refrigeration Holdings Ltd, since 2013; Non-Executive Director and Chair, Grant Property Ltd, 2013-17; Council Member, Royal Society of Edinburgh, 2013-17; Chair, Board of Directors, Community Integrated Care, 2014-19; Senior Education Adviser, British Council, 2013-16; Hon. Doctor of the University, Open University, 2014; Member and Chair of Remuneration and Nominations Committee, Entrepreneurial Scotland, since 2020. Publications: contributed articles in field of politics with particular reference to British Public Administration and employment and training policy. Recreations: music (especially opera); gardening; film; travel.

Struthers, Professor Allan, BSc, MD, FRCP, FESC, FRSE, FMedSci. Emeritus Professor of Cardiovascular Medicine, Dundee University (appointed Professor in 2000); b. 14.8.52, Glasgow; m., Julia Diggens; 1 s.; 1 d. Educ. Hutchesons' Boys' Grammar School; Glasgow University. Junior posts, Glasgow teaching hospitals, 1977-82; Senior Medical Registrar, Royal Postgraduate Medical School and Hammersmith Hospital, London, 1983-85; Wellcome Senior Lecturer, Department of Clinical Pharmacology, Ninewells Hospital, 1985-92; Professor of Clinical Pharmacology, 1992-2000. Recreations: cycling; walking; travel; opera.

Struthers, Shona. Chief Executive, Colleges Scotland, since 2014. Educ. University of Glasgow; Chartered Institute of Marketing; Chartered Institute of Management Accountants; Manchester Metropolitan University. Business/Product Development Management Accountant, Imperial Chemical Industries, 1988-95; Company Director, Webaspx Ltd, 1998-2001; Board Member, Falkirk Women's Technology Centre, 1995-2005; Finance and Communications Director, Zeneca/Avecia Ltd, 1995-2005; Board Member, Scottish Further Education Unit, 2005-08; Finance & Corporate Services Director/Company Secretary, Snowdon Consulting Ltd/Scottish Further Education, 2007-08; Business Merger Director, Snowdon Consulting Ltd/Scotland's Colleges, 2008-09; Executive Officer Adviser, Snowdon Consulting Ltd/City of Glasgow College, 2010-11; Merger Director, Snowdon Consulting Ltd/Scottish Agricultural College, 2011-12; Strategic Financial Advisor, Snowdon Consulting Ltd/DTZ

Consulting, 2006-2013; Director, Snowdon Consulting, 2006-2013; Board Support/CEO Advisor, Snowdon Consulting Ltd/Colleges Scotland, 2011-13; Director of Policy and Public Affairs, Colleges Scotland, 2013-14; Board Member, Forth Valley College, 2008-2014; Acting Chief Executive, Colleges Scotland, 2014; Strathcarron Hospice Board Member, since 2016. Address: Colleges Scotland, Argyll Court, The Castle Business Park, Stirling FK9 4TY; T.-01786 892100.

Stuart, John Forester, MA (Cantab). Secretary General, General Synod, Scottish Episcopal Church, since 1996; b. 26.5.59, Broughty Ferry; m., Sally Ann Bell; 2 s. Educ. Dundee High School; Daniel Stewart's and Melville College; Queens' College Cambridge, College of Law, Guildford.Articled Clerk and subsequently Solicitor, Macfarlanes, London, 1982-86; Solicitor and subsequently Partner, J. & F. Anderson, Solicitors, Edinburgh (merged, 1992, to become Anderson Strathern), 1986-96. Recreations: music; walking; astronomy. Address: (b.) 21 Grosvenor Crescent, Edinburgh EH12 5EE; T.-0131-225 6357.

Stuart, Mhairi Ross, MA (Hons). Presenter, Scotland Live, BBC Scotland, since 2006, Presenter, Good Morning Scotland, 1999-2006; b. 8.12.67, Glasgow; m., Roderick Stuart. Educ. Cleveden Secondary School, Glasgow; Glasgow University. BBC, since 1991 (News Trainee/Producer/Presenter). BT Scotland Radio News Broadcaster of the Year, 1999. Recreations: sailing; skiing. Address: (b.) News Room, BBC Scotland, 40 Pacific Quay, Glasgow G51 1DZ.

Stuart, Michael, QC. Senator of the College of Justice, since 2022. Educ. degrees in Economics and Law. Career history: called to the Scottish Bar in 2003 following a successful career in business; served as a full time Advocate Depute, 2009-2012; prosecuted many challenging trials, including those concerning murder and serious sexual offending; qualified as a mediator with Core Solutions Group in 2015; held offices as a Court Reporter in child related matters and as Standing Junior Counsel to the Scottish Government; appointed Queen's Counsel in 2017. Address: Parliament House, 11 Parliament Square, Edinburgh EH1 1RQ.

Sturgeon, Nicola, LLB (Hons), DipLP. MSP (SNP), Glasgow Southside, since 2011, Glasgow Govan, 2007-2011, Glasgow, 1999-2007; First Minister of Scotland, since 2014; b. 19.7.70, Irvine. Educ. Greenwood Academy, Irvine; University of Glasgow. Trainee Solicitor, Glasgow, 1993-95; Solicitor, Stirling, 1995-97; Solicitor, Drumchapel Law Centre, Glasgow, 1997-99; Deputy First Minister and Cabinet Secretary for Health and Wellbeing, 2007-2012; Deputy First Minister and Cabinet Secretary for Infrastructure, Investment and Cities (with responsibility for Government Strategy and the Constitution), 2012-14. Recreations: reading; theatre. Address: (b.) Govanhill Workspace, 69 Dixon Road, Govanhill, Glasgow G42 8AT.

Sturrock, John Garrow, QC, LLB (Hons), LLM, LLD, FRSA, MCIArb. Founder and Senior Mediator, Core Solutions Group Ltd., since 2004; Founder of Collaborative Scotland, since 2014; Queen's Counsel, since 1999; accredited Mediator, since 1996; Door Tenant, Brick Court Chambers, London, since 2013; Director of Training and Education, Faculty of Advocates, 1994-2002; Visiting Professor, University of Edinburgh, 2016-2019; Member of the Stewarding Group for Scotland's first Citizens' Assembly, 2019-21; Honorary Degree of Doctor of Laws, Edinburgh Napier

University, 2010; Distinguished Fellow, International Academy of Mediators, since 2009; b. 15.4.58, Stirling; m., Fiona Swanson; 2 s.; 1 d. Educ. Stirling High School; Waid Academy, Anstruther; Edinburgh University; University of Pennsylvania. Senior President, Edinburgh University Students' Association, 1980-81; apprentice Solicitor, 1981-83; qualified Solicitor, 1983-84; Harkness Fellow, US, 1984-85; Member, Faculty of Advocates, since 1986; Standing Junior Counsel to Department of Transport in Scotland, 1991-94; Member, Judicial Studies Committee in Scotland, 1997-2004; Member, Joint Standing Committee on Legal Education, 1988-2005. Recreations: family; golf; contemporary music; ships and the sea. Address: (h.) 6 Claverhouse Drive, Edinburgh EH16 6BS; T.-0131-667 8256; (b.) 10 York Place, Edinburgh EH1 3EP; T.-0131 524 8188; e-mail: John.Sturrock@core-solutions.com

Subramanya, Karthik, BEng, MBA. Board Member: Scottish Enterprise, since 2018, Creative Scotland, 2016-2020. Educ. Delhi University; Delhi College of Engineering; Indian Institute of Management Ahmedabad; London Business School. Career history: Summer Associate, ICICI Bank, 1998; Consultant, KPMG Consulting, 1999-2001; Associate, Mitchell Madison Group, 2001; Managing Consultant: EDS, HP Enterprise, 2001-04, RSM Robson Rhodes, 2004-05; HBOS Plc: Director, Group Strategy and M&A, 2005-07, Director, Integrated Finance Partnerships, 2007-09; Business Management, Specialised Industry Finance, Corporate Banking, Lloyds Banking Group, 2009-2011; SSE plc: Head of Corporate Planning, Glasgow, 2012-13, Corporate Projects Director, 2013-14, Director of Strategy and Performance, SSE Enterprise, Perth, 2004-2015; President, Scottish Indian Arts Forum, 2010-16; Non Executive Director, Our Power, 2017-19; Board Member, Changing the Chemistry (SCIO), since 2016; Managing Director, Carnatic Capital Limited, since 2015; Senior Advisor, The Boston Consulting Group, since 2015; Panel Member, Competition and Markets Authority, since 2019. Address: Scottish Enterprise HQ, Atrium Court, 50 Waterloo Street, Glasgow G2 6HQ; T.-0300 013 3385.

Suckling, Professor Colin James, OBE, BSc, PhD, DSc, CChem, FRSC, FRSA, FRCPS (Glasg), HonFRCS (Edin), FRSE. Freeland Professor of Chemistry, Strathclyde University, since 1984; b. 24.3.47, Birkenhead; m., Catherine Mary Faulkner; 2 s.; 1 d. Educ. Quarry Bank High School, Liverpool; Liverpool University. Lecturer, Department of Pure and Applied Chemistry, Strathclyde University, 1972; Royal Society Smith and Nephew Senior Research Fellow, 1980; Dean, Faculty of Science, 1992-96; Deputy Principal, 1996-98; Pro-Vice Principal, 1998-2000; Vice Principal, 2000-02; Convener, RSE Chemistry Committee, 1989-91; Member of Council, RSE, 1989-92; Member, General Teaching Council, 1993-95; Member, Board: Systems Level Integration Ltd., 1998-2000, Lanarkshire Technology and Innovation Centre, 1998-2000; Governor, Bell College of Technology, 1999-2007; Member of Court, University of Paisley (West of Scotland); Chairman, West of Scotland Schools Orchestra Trust, 1996-2016; Chairman, Scottish Advisory Committee on Distinction Awards, 2003-10; Chairman, Strathclyde Youth Jazz Orchestra Trust, 2000-2016; Member, Joint Committee on Higher Surgical Training, 2003-05; Member, Senate of Surgery, 2003-05; Public Partner, Scottish Medicines Consortium; Chairman, Patient and Public Involvement Group, Scottish Medicines Consortium, 2012-15. Royal Society of Chemistry Adrien Albert Prize Lecturer, 2009-10; Nexxus Lifetime Achievement Award, 2011; Indian Society of Chemists and Biologists Gold Medal, 2011; Honorary Life Fellow of Indian Society of Chemists and Biologists, 2015. Publications: Chemistry Through Models

(Co-author), 1978; Biological Chemistry (Co-author), 1980; Enzyme Chemistry, Impact and Applications (Co-author), 1984, 1989, 1998; 250 research publications. Recreations: music; horn playing. Address: (b.) Department of Pure and Applied Chemistry, Strathclyde University, 295 Cathedral Street, Glasgow G1 1XL; T.-0141-548 2271. E-mail: c.j.suckling@strath.ac.uk

Summers, Hon. Lord (Alan Andrew), QC, LLB, BCL. Advocate, since 1994; Senator of the College of Justice, since 2017; Treasurer, Faculty of Advocates, since 2012; Special Advocate to UK Government, since 2007; Standing Junior Counsel to Scottish Executive, 2000-05; b. 27.8.64, Bridge of Allan; m., Rosemary Helen Craig; 1 s.; 4 d. Educ. Grove Academy, Broughty Ferry; University of Dundee; St. Catherine's College, University of Oxford. Lecturer, Department of Scots Law, University of Edinburgh; Solicitor. Recreations: spending time with his family; reading.

Summers, John P., OBE, FREHIS, FCIWM. Chairman, Beautiful Perth; former Chief Executive, Keep Scotland Beautiful (1999-2009) (retired); b. 22.12.46, Rhynie; m., Alison; 1 s.; 1 d. Educ. Aberdeen Academy; Napier College, Edinburgh. Environmental Health Officer, Aberdeenshire, 1972-79; Depute Director of Environmental Health, Banff and Buchan District Council, 1979-90; Director of Environmental Health, Moray District Council, 1990-94, Chief Executive, 1994-96; Director of Technical Services, Moray Council, 1996-99. Director of Foundation for Environmental Education (FEE), 2001-2010. Recreations: reading; Scottish traditional music. Address: c/o Community Greenspace, 35 Kinnoull Street, Perth PH1 5GD; T.-01738 475000; e-mail: jpsumms@gmail.com

Summers, Sheriff William. Sheriff for Grampian, Highlands and Islands at Banff and Peterhead. Educ. University of Aberdeen. Career: admitted as a Solicitor in 1981 and as a Solicitor Advocate in 2003; accredited by the Law Society of Scotland as a commercial law mediator in 2004; a tutor in civil advocacy, and a civil reporter to the Scottish Legal Aid Board, 1997-2003.

Sussex, Paula, MSc. Chief Executive, Student Loans Company, since 2018. Educ. London Business School; King's College London; Inns of Court School of Law. Career history: originally trained as a barrister before working in the private sector; 25 year career has been primarily in consultancy, but also in the service delivery of large scale IT, latterly working as Senior Vice President with Logica; Chief Executive Officer, Charity Commission for England and Wales, 2014-18. Address: Student Loans Company, 100 Bothwell Street, Glasgow G2 7JD; T.-0141 306 2000.

Sutherland, Alan D.A., MA (Hons), MBA, MA. Chief Executive, Water Industry Commission for Scotland, since 2005; b. 8.4.62, Glasgow; m., Olga; 1 s.; 1 d. Educ. Eastwood High School; St Andrews University; University of Pennsylvania. Management trainee, Lloyds Bank PLC, 1984-85; Stockbroker, Savory Milln, 1985-86; Robert Fleming & Company, investment bank, 1986-91; Management Consultant, Bain & Company, 1992-97; Managing Director, Wolverine CIS Ltd., 1997-99; Water Industry Commissioner for Scotland, 1999-2005. Recreations: theatre; restaurants; history. Address: (b.) Water Industry Commission for Scotland, Moray House, Forthside Way, Stirling FK8 1QZ. E-mail: enquiries@watercommission.co.uk

Sutherland, 25th Earl of (Alistair Charles St. Clair Janson), BA; b. 7.1.47; m. (1) Eileen Elizabeth Baker (divorced); 2 d.; m. (2) Gillian Murray; 2 c. Educ. Eton College, Windsor, Berkshire; Christ Church, Oxford University. Styled as Master of Sutherland, 1947-63; name was legally changed to Alistair Charles St. Clair

Sutherland in 1963; styled as Lord Strathnaver, 1963-2019. Career history: The Metropolitan Police, 1969-74; IBM (UK) Ltd, 1976-79; Director: The Sutherland Dunrobin Trust, since 2004, Dunrobin Castle Limited, since 1988. Succeeded as the 25th Earl of Sutherland on 9 December 2019.

Sutherland, David I.M., CBE, MA, MEd, DLitt, DUniv, DPhil, FCCEAM. Chief Executive/Registrar, The General Teaching Council for Scotland, 1985-2001; b. 22.1.38, Wick; m., Janet H. Webster (deceased); 2 s. Educ. Aberdeen Grammar School; Aberdeen University; University of Zurich. Teacher of Modern Languages, Aberdeen Grammar School, 1962-66; Lecturer in Education, Stranmillis College of Education, Belfast, 1966-69; Lecturer in Educational Psychology, Craigie College of Education, Ayr, 1969-72; Assistant Director of Education, Sutherland County Council, 1972-75; Divisional Education Officer (Inverness), then Depute Director of Education, Highland Regional Council, 1975-85. Trustee, Gordon Cook Foundation. Recreations: golf; walking; theatre; reading. Address: Hazelwood, 5 Bonnington Road, Peebles EH45 9HF; T.-01721 722232.
E-mail: ivorsutherland@btinternet.com

Sutherland, Elizabeth (Elizabeth Margaret Marshall). Writer; b. 24.8.26, Kemback, Cupar; m., Rev. John D. Marshall; 2 s.; 1 d. Educ. St. Leonard's Girls' School, St. Andrews; Edinburgh University. Social Worker for Scottish Episcopal Church, 1974-80; Curator, Groam House Museum, Rosemarkie, 1982-93; author of: Lent Term (Constable Trophy), 1973, The Seer of Kintail, 1974, Hannah Hereafter (Scottish Arts Council Book Award), 1976, The Eye of God, 1977, The Weeping Tree, 1980, Ravens and Black Rain: The Story of Highland Second Sight, 1985, The Gold Key and The Green Life, 1986; In Search of the Picts, 1994; Guide to the Pictish Stones, 1997; Five Euphemias: Women in Medieval Scotland, 1999; Lydia, Wife of Hugh Miller of Cromarty, 2002; The Bird of Truth, 2006; Boniface, Bishops and Bonfires, 2010; Amendment of Life, 2010; One of the Good Guys, 2011; Spoiled Children, 2012; Of Sinks and Pulpits, 2013; The Great Triduum, 2015; Foretold: The Tale of a Highland Village, 2016; Church Street, 2018; Highland Cathedral, 2019. Saltire Society (Highland Branch) award for contribution to the understanding of Highland Culture, 2019. Recreations: Highland history; Gaelic folklore; the Picts. Address: (h.) 17 Mackenzie Terrace, Rosemarkie, Ross-shire IV10 8UH; T.-Fortrose 620924.

Sutherland, Graham. Chief Executive Officer, FirstGroup plc, since 2022; b. 11.63. Career history: former Chief Executive, NTL Ireland; held senior financial roles including at Bombardier; former Chief Executive, BT Ireland; held a number of senior executive roles within BT Group PLC over twelve years including Chief Executive Officer of the BT Business and Public Sector division; former Chief Executive Officer, KCOM Group plc (appointed in 2018). Non-executive Director, Savvi Credit Union. Address: FirstGroup plc, 395 King Street, Aberdeen AB24 5RP; T.-01224 650100.

Sutherland, Jonathan. Scottish television and radio presenter; Co-Presenter, Sportscene; b. 1977, Brae, Shetland Islands; m.; 1 s. Educ. Aberdeen University. Career history: BBC Radio Shetland; joined BBC Sport in 2003; left the BBC for Shetland Weekly, then rejoined the BBC as assistant producer of Sportscene; became the main presenter of the Sunday night SPFL highlights show Sportscene; formerly presented Keeping Loch Lomond. Address: BBC Scotland, Pacific Quay, Pacific Drive, Glasgow G51 1DA.

Suttie, Ian A. Chairman, First Tech Ltd. Career history: qualified as a Chartered Accountant with Deloitte's in Aberdeen; joined I.T.T Consumer Products at their UK headquarters in Hastings as Business Planning Manager; spent considerable periods in Brussels at their European headquarters; returned to Aberdeen in 1977 and held commercial positions with 3 drilling contractors before leaving Dan Smedvig as Operations Manager to join, as M.D., a subsidiary of the fully quoted Petrocon Group Plc; invited to join the Group Board in 1983 and completed a management buy-out of two of the subsidiaries in May 1988; over the next 13 years built the Orwell Group Plc to a turnover of £100M and employees in the excess of 600 operating in 14, fully staffed, international countries; established First Oil Plc, which was in 2014, the largest private, UK owned company producing oil and gas in the North Sea; purchased BSW based in Lancaster, now trading as First Subsea Ltd; also owns other mooring service businesses including Mooring Systems Ltd and First Marine Solutions Ltd. In 2012 Nautricity was acquired by a Strathclyde University spin out, which has patented 'CoRMaT' tidal turbine technology. Established the business of First Integrated Solutions in 2014 which provides Equipment Management and Maintenance to the Offshore Industry from offices in Aberdeen, Stavanger and Trinidad. Established in 2017, First Competence Ltd provides effective and efficient independent lifting products, bespoke training courses and assessments accredited and aligned with industry. Honoured with numerous awards including: Scottish Entrepreneur of the Year in 2001, by Ernst & Young; Grampian Industrialist of the Year in 2002; the Queens Award for Industry – International Trade in 2004; the Spotlight Award at the 2009 Offshore Technology Conference in Houston and the Scottish Business Awards Entrepreneur of the Year in 2011; awarded an Honorary Doctorate by Aberdeen University in 2012. Address: First Tech Ltd, 1 Queens Terrace, Aberdeen AB10 1XL; T.-01224 624666.

Sutton, Rev. Peter, BD, MTh, AKC, PGC Counselling. Minister, The Parish Church of St. Cuthbert, Edinburgh, since 2017. Educ. Fettes College; St Andrews University; King's College London; University of Edinburgh. Infantry Officer, The Black Watch, 1984-94; Chaplain, Loretto School, The Perse School and Gordonstoun School, 1994-2008; Headmaster, Ardvreck Prep School, 2008-2011. Address: 5 Lothian Road, Edinburgh EH1 2EP; T.-0131 229 1142; e-mail: PSutton@churchofscotland.org.uk

Swainson, Charles P., MBChB, FRCPE. Hon. Professor, University of Edinburgh, since 2007; Director, CSwainson Consulting, since 2011; Medical Director, E11 Ltd, since 2018; Convener, Business Committee, General Council, University of Edinburgh, 2012-16; Consultant Renal Physician, 1981-2010; Medical Director, NHS Lothian, 1998-2010; Medical Director and Vice Chair, Scottish Advisory Committee on Distinction Awards, 2009-2017; Treasurer, Royal College of Physicians of Edinburgh, 2011-2017; b. 18.5.48, Gloucester; m., Marie Irwin; 1 s. Educ. St. Edward's School, Cheltenham; Edinburgh University. Senior Lecturer, Christchurch, NZ, 1981-86; Consultant Physician, Royal Infirmary of Edinburgh, 1986-2010. Member, Lothian Children's Panel, 1987-95. Recreations: wine; hill walking; golf; skiing. Address: (h.) 33 Granby Road, Edinburgh EH16 5NP.

Swan, Iain Ruairidh Cameron, MD, FRCS (Edin). Senior Honorary Clinical Research Fellow (Medicine), University of Glasgow; appointed Lecturer in Otolaryngology in 1986; Consultant Otologist, MRC Institute of Hearing Research, since 1986; Honorary Consultant Otolaryngologist, Glasgow Royal Infirmary, since 1986; b. 19.5.52, Motherwell; m., Helen Buchanan; 1 s.; 1 d. Educ. Glasgow

Academy; Glasgow University. SHO/Registrar, Glasgow, 1978-81; Clinical Research Fellow, MRC Institute of Hearing Research, 1981; Senior Registrar in Otolaryngology, Glasgow, 1981-86; clinical attachment, University of Tubingen, 1984-85. Examiner, Final Fellowship, Royal College of Surgeons of Edinburgh and Royal College of Physicians and Surgeons, Glasgow. Recreations: bridge; opera; mountain biking. Address: (b.) Department of Otolaryngology, Royal Infirmary, Glasgow G31 2ER; T.-0141-211 4695; e-mail: iain@ihr.gla.ac.uk

Swan, Jeanna, LL. Lord-Lieutenant for Berwickshire, since 2014. Formerly a senior partner in a large veterinary practice in the Scottish eastern borders region; Trustee of the MacRobert Trust, 2001-2017; formerly Deputy Lord-Lieutenant for Berwickshire. District Commissioner of the Berwickshire Hunt Pony Club, 2016-2021; interested in farming and the local community. Address: c/o The Clerk, Democratic Services, Scottish Borders Council, Council Headquarters, Newtown St. Boswells, Melrose TD6 0SA; T.-01835 825005.

Swanson, Alexander James Grenville, MB, ChB, FRCS Edin. Consultant Orthopaedic Surgeon, 1980-2001; Honorary Senior Lecturer, University of Dundee, since 2001; b. 18.10.41, Ecclefechan; 2 s. Educ. Dingwall Academy; St. Andrews University. Postgraduate training: St. Andrews, 1967-68, Edinburgh, 1968-69, Glasgow, 1969-70, Edinburgh, 1970-74, Dunfermline, 1974-75; Lecturer, then Senior Lecturer and Honorary Consultant, Dundee University, 1975-83. Recreations: downhill skiing; travel. Address: (h.) 9 Roxburgh Terrace, Dundee DD2 1NX.

Sweeney, Jim, MBE, MSc, DipYCS. Former Chief Executive, YouthLink Scotland, 2006-2018 (retired); b. 5.6.53; m., Elizabeth; 2 s.; 2 grandchildren. Educ. Jordanhill (Diploma in Youth and Community Work); Strathclyde University (Masters Degree). Previously worked for 34 years in Local Government; presently Vice Chair of both Young Scot and Scotland's Learning Partnership. Trustee of Motherwell FC Community Trust; Interim Chair of Scottish CLD Standards Council, since 2019; MD of Education and Third Sector Consultancy RAAHP (Rock and a Hard Place Business Solutions); Ambassador and fundraiser for Mary's Meals; conference Chair and Keynote presenter and after dinner speaker. Recreations: football; golf; bowling; reading and writing; music; travel; whisky and wine appreciation; cooking; gardening.
E-mail: jimsweeney200@gmail.com

Sweeney, Paul, MA (Hons), FIES, VR. MSP (Scottish Labour & Co-op), Glasgow (Region), since 2021; MP, Glasgow North East, 2017-19; Shadow Minister for Employment and Public Finance, since May 2021; Shadow Minister for Trade, Investment and Innovation, March-May 2021; Shadow Under-Secretary of State for Scotland, 2017-19; b. 16.1.89, Glasgow. Educ. Turnbull High School; University of Stirling; University of Glasgow. Career: Business Development Intern, BAE Systems Surface Ships, 2010; Manufacturing & Production Operations Graduate, BAE Systems, 2011-13; Operations Strategy Coordinator, 2013-15; Senior Executive Account Manager, Scottish Enterprise, 2015-17; Army Reservist, Royal Corps of Signals and Regiment of Scotland, British Army, 2006-2018. Fellow and Council Member, Institution of Engineers and Shipbuilders in Scotland (IESIS), since 2016; Chairman, Springburn Winter Gardens Trust, since 2013, Trustee, Glasgow City Heritage Trust, since 2020, Trustee, Beatroute Arts, since 2020, Trustee, Egyptian Halls SCIO, since 2021. Recipient of The Herald Scottish Politician of the Year award for 'Best Scot at Westminster', 2018.

Address: The Scottish Parliament, Edinburgh EH99 1SP; T.-0131 348 6388.

Sweeney, Professor William John, DRSAM, ARAM. Composer, since 1974; Professor of Music, formerly Head of Department of Music, University of Glasgow; b. 05.01.50, Glasgow; m., Susannah Conway; 1 s.; 1 d. Educ. Knightswood Senior Secondary School; RSAMD; RAM. Teacher of Clarinet and Woodwind, Central Region, 1975-85; Performer, 1973-95, 2010; Lecturer, University of Glasgow, 1997-2020, now Emeritus Professor. National Executive Committee, Musicians Union, 1989-2004; Chair of EC, 2003; Board Member, Ivors Academy, 2017-2021. BAFTA (Scotland) Award for Best Music, 1997; Creative Scotland Award, 2005; British Composer Award (BASCA/Radio 3), 2011. Recreations: reading; walking; supporting Partick Thistle. Address: (h.) 4 Stonefield Avenue, Glasgow G12 0JF; T.-0141-579-4789.
E-mail: William.Sweeney@glasgow.ac.uk

Swinney, John Ramsay, MA (Hons). MSP (SNP), Perthshire North, since 2011, North Tayside, 1999-2011; Deputy First Minister of Scotland, since 2014; Cabinet Secretary for Covid Recovery, since 2021; Cabinet Secretary for Education and Skills, 2016-2021; Cabinet Secretary for Finance, Constitution and Economy, 2007-2016; Shadow Minister for Finance and Public Service Reform, 2005-07; Leader, Scottish National Party, 2000-04; Leader of the Opposition, Scottish Parliament, 2000-04; MP (SNP), North Tayside, 1997-2001; b. 13.4.64, Edinburgh; m., Elizabeth Quigley; 2 s.; 1 d. Educ. Forrester High School, Edinburgh; Edinburgh University. Research Officer, Scottish Coal Project, 1987-88; Senior Managing Consultant, Development Options Ltd., 1998-92; Strategic Planning Principal, Scottish Amicable, 1992-97. SNP Treasury Spokesman, 1995-99; Depute Leader, Scottish National Party, 1998-2000; Shadow Minister for Enterprise and Lifelong Learning, 1999-2000. Convener, Enterprise and Lifelong Learning Committee (Scottish Parliament), 1999-2000; Convener, European and External Relations Committee, 2004-05. Recreation: hill-walking. Address: (b.) 17-19 Leslie Street, Blairgowrie PH10 6AH; T.-01250 876576.

Swinson, Jo. Leader of the Liberal Democrats, July-December, 2019 (Deputy Leader, 2017-19); MP (Liberal Democrat), Dunbartonshire East, 2017-19 and 2005-2015; Liberal Democrat Spokesperson for Foreign and Commonwealth Affairs, 2017-19; Minister for Employment Relations, Consumer and Postal Affairs, Department for Business, Innovation and Skills, 2012-15; Minister for Women and Equalities, Department of Culture, Media and Sport, 2012-2015; b. 5.2.80; m., Duncan Hames; 2 s. Educ. Douglas Academy, Milngavie; London School of Economics. Formerly Marketing Manager; Chair, Liberal Democrats' Campaign for Gender Balance, 2006-08; Liberal Democrat Shadow Foreign Affairs Minister, 2008-2010; Deputy Leader, Scottish Liberal Democrats, 2011; Parliamentary Private Secretary to: Vince Cable, 2011-2012, Deputy Prime Minister Nick Clegg, 2012. Visiting Professor, Cranfield School of Management, Bedfordshire, since 2020. Publication: Equal Power, 2018. Recreations: running; reading; hiking; ceilidh dancing.

Swinton, Professor John, PhD, BD, RMN, RNMH. Professor in Practical Theology and Pastoral Care, Aberdeen University, since 1997; Honorary Professor, Centre for Advanced Nursing, Aberdeen University, since 1999; b. 20.10.57; m., Alison; 2 s.; 3 d. Educ. Summerhill Academy, Aberdeen; Aberdeen University. Registered nurse, 1976-90; Aberdeen University, 1990-97; Lecturer in

Practical Theology, Glasgow University, 1997. Address: (b.) School of Divinity, Religious Studies and Philosophy, King's College, Old Aberdeen, Aberdeen AB24 3UB; T.-01224 273224.

Swinton, Tilda. Award-winning British actress known for both arthouse and mainstream films; b. 5.11.60, London; partner, Sandro Kopp; 2 c. Educ. Queen's Gate School, London; West Heath Girls' School; Fettes College; New Hall (now known as Murray Edwards College), Cambridge University. Worked with the Traverse Theatre in Edinburgh, starring in Mann ist Mann by Manfred Karge, and the Royal Shakespeare Company, before embarking on a career in film in the mid-1980s; developed a performance/installation live art piece in the Serpentine Gallery, London in 1995 (on display to the public for a week, asleep or apparently so, in a glass case, as a piece of performance art); has appeared in a number of films, including Burn After Reading, The Beach, The Chronicles of Narnia, and was nominated for a Golden Globe for performances in The Deep End and We Need to Talk About Kevin. Won the Academy Award for Best Supporting Actress for her performance in Michael Clayton in 2007.

Sykes, Diana Antoinette, MA (Hons). Director, Fife Contemporary (formerly FCA&C and Crawford Arts Centre), since 1988; b. 12.9.59, Stirling. Educ. Stirling High School; University of St. Andrews; University of Manchester; Sweet Briar College, USA. Chair, Scottish Arts Council Exhibitions Panel, 1995-97; Member, St. Andrews Youth Theatre Board, 1991-2001; Chair, Management Committee, Mobile Projects Association Scotland, 1986-88; Trustee of the Barns-Graham Charitable Trust, 2005-2013; Trustee of Off the Rails Arthouse and of Lateral Lab. Recreations: travel; arts and museums and heritage. E-mail: das36fife@gmail.com
Web: www.fcac.co.uk

Symington, Rev. Alastair Henderson, MA, BD. Minister Emeritus, Troon Old Parish Church; Chaplain to The Queen in Scotland, 1996-2017; Extra Chaplain to The Queen in Scotland, since 2017; b. 15.4.47, Edinburgh; m., late Eileen Margaret Jenkins; 2 d. Educ. Daniel Stewart's College, Edinburgh; Edinburgh University; Tubingen University, West Germany. Assistant Minister, Wellington Church, Glasgow, 1971-72; Chaplain, RAF, 1972-76; Minister: Craiglockhart Parish Church, Edinburgh, 1976-85, New Kilpatrick Parish Church, Bearsden, 1985-98, Troon Old Parish Church, 1998-2012; Locum Minister: Galston Parish Church, 2013-2017, Dundonald Parish Church, 2017-19, Prestwick St Nicholas Parish Church, 2019-2020; Convener, Committee on Chaplains to HM Forces, 1989-93; Vice-Convener, Board of Practice and Procedure, 2002-05; Convener, Committee on Presbytery Boundaries, 1999-2004; Member, Church of Scotland Theological Forum, since 2017; Moderator, Presbytery of Dumbarton, 1992; Moderator, Presbytery of Ayr, 2012 and 2013. Contributor, Scottish Liturgical Review. Publications: Westminster Church Sermons, 1984; Reader's Digest Family Guide to the Bible (Co-author), 1985; For God's Sake, Ask!, 1993; The Memories and Musings of a Parish Minister, 2021. Recreations: golf; rugby; music; France; wines. Address: 70, The Walled Garden, Abbey Park Avenue, St Andrews KY16 9JW; e-mail: revdahs74@gmail.com

Symon, Ken. Editor, Scottish Business Insider, 2016-2021; Tai Chi Teacher, Rising Spring Tai Chi, since 2012; Founding Director, Symon Media Ltd, 2009-2016, Managing Director, 2009-2016. Educ. University of Strathclyde. Career history: Industrial Correspondent, Evening Times, 1988-95; Deputy Editor, The Sunday Times Scotland, 1995-98; Business Editor, The Scotsman,

1998-2000; Owner, Simple Communication, 2000-03; Business Editor, Sunday Herald, 2003-07; Business Development Director, McGarvie Morrison Media, 2007-09; Head of Business Engagement, Better Together Ltd, May 2014-September 2014; Associate Director, Hollicom, 2021. Fellow of the Royal Society for the encouragement of Arts, Manufactures and Commerce (RSA).

Szendrei, Tibor Csaba. Consul, Consulate General of Hungary in Edinburgh, since 2022; Envoy Extraordinary and Minister Plenipotentiary, Hungarian Embassy, 2018-2022. Educ. University of Pécs; Szent István University. Career history: several posts at Ministry of Foreign Affairs of Hungary, 1987-2014; Head of Secretariat for the Deputy State Secretary for Budget, Ministry of Justice of Hungary, 2014-16; Ministry of Foreign Affairs and Trade, since 2016; Honorary Associate Professor of Szent István University - Faculty of Economics and Social Sciences, since 2011. Address: Consulate of Hungary, 25 Union Street, Edinburgh EH1 3LR; T.-0131 556 3838.

T

Tait, A. Margaret, MBE, BSc. Former Vice-President, Graduate Women International, Geneva and member of the British Federation of Women Graduates; Flower Supervisor and member of Executive Committee of St. Margaret's Chapel Guild, Edinburgh Castle; Member, Egyptology Scotland, Royal Caledonian Horticultural Society and Royal Horticultural Society; Member, Lothian Pharmacy Practice Committee; b. 8.10.44, Edinburgh; m., J. Haldane Tait; 1 d. Educ. George Watson's Ladies' College, Edinburgh; Edinburgh University; Jordanhill College of Education. Former Teacher of Mathematics, Bellahouston Academy, Glasgow; former Member, Lothian Children's Panel; former Honorary Secretary, Scottish Association of Children's Panels; former Chairman, Dean House Children's Home, Edinburgh; former volunteer, Edinburgh Citizens' Advice Bureau; formerly Secretary of State's Nominee to General Teaching Council; former Member, Scottish Legal Aid Board; former Member, Lothian Health Council; former Vice Chairman, Lothian Healthy Volunteers and Student Research Modules Ethics Committee; former General Council Assessor, University of Edinburgh Court. Recreations: golf; horticulture; Spanish; playing bridge. Address: (h.) 6 Ravelston House Park, Edinburgh EH4 3LU; T.-0131-332 6795.
E-mail: margarettait@me.com

Tait, Cameron, LLB (Hons). Director, Capital Defence Lawyers, since 2007. Educ. University of Aberdeen. Career history: trained with Gilfedder and McInnes, qualified in 2003, Assistant, 2003-06; Associate with Capital Defence Lawyers, 2006-07; Partner/Director, since 2007; Solicitor-Advocate, since 2009; frequently appears in criminal cases at sheriff courts all over Scotland; recently been instructed as Junior Counsel in High Court Trials for offences including murder, serious drugs offences and rape; has been instructed in numerous appeals against both conviction and sentence in recent years. Member, Law Society of Scotland, Society of Solicitor-Advocates; President, Edinburgh Bar Association, 2012-13. Address: Capital Defence Lawyers, 9-10 St Andrew Square, Edinburgh EH2 2BH; T.-0131 553 4333.

Tait, Professor Elizabeth Joyce, CBE, FRSE, DUniv (Open), PhD, BSc, FSRA. University of Edinburgh joint appointments - Director/Co-Director, Innogen Institute, since 2007; Professor, Global Academy of Agriculture and Food Security, since 2017; Director, ESRC Innogen Centre, 2002-07; b. 19.02.38, Edinburgh; m., Dr. Alec Tait; 1 s.; 2 d. Educ. Glasgow High School for Girls; Glasgow University; Cambridge University. Career history: Lecturer, then Senior Lecturer, Technology Faculty, Open University; Professor, Environmental and Technology Management, University of Strathclyde; Deputy Director, Research and Advisory Services, Scottish Natural Heritage; Director, Scottish Universities Policy Research and Advice Centre (SUPRA), Edinburgh University. Member: Governing Council, Roslin Institute and Roslin Foundation Board (2006-19); UK Synthetic Biology Leadership Council (now Engineering Biology Leadership Council), since 2012; US National Academies of Sciences/National Research Council Committee on Re-programming Non-human Populations using "Gene Drives", 2015-16; Governing Board, Industrial Biotechnology Innovation Centre, 2017-20; Prime Minister's Council for Science and Technology, 2017-20; Regulatory Horizons Council, since 2020. Recreations: gardening; hill walking. Address: (b.) Innogen Institute, Old Surgeons Hall, High School Yards, Edinburgh EH1 1LZ; T.-0131 650 9174; e-mail: joyce.tait@ed.ac.uk

Tallach, Rev. James Ross, MB, ChB. Free Presbyterian Minister, Stornoway, since 2009; Assistant Clerk of Synod, since 2006; b. Tighnabruaich, Argyll; m., Mairi McCuish Martin; 2 d. Educ. Nicolson Institute, Stornoway; Aberdeen University. House jobs in surgery, medicine and obstetrics, Inverness, Aberdeen, and Bellshill, 1967-69; Medical Missionary, Mbuma, Zimbabwe, 1969-76; training for ministry, 1976-80; ordained medical missionery, Mbuma, 1980-83. Moderator of Synod, 1996; Clerk to Foreign Mission Committee of F.P. Church, since 1989; Convener, Church Home, Inverness, since 2001; Convener, Training of Ministry Committee, since 2004. Recreations: gardening; walking. Address: Free Presbyterian Manse, 2 Fleming Place, Stornoway, Isle of Lewis HS1 2NH; T.-01851 702501.
E-mail: jrtallach@btinternet.com

Tams, Professor Christian Jakob, State Exam (Law), LLM, PhD (Cantab). Professor of International Law, University of Glasgow, since 2008; b. 18.7.73, Hamburg, Germany. Educ. Martino Katharineum; University of Kiel; University of Lyon; University of Cambridge. Assistant Professor, University of Kiel (Germany), 2005-09. Various publications on International Law; Emeritus Member of the Royal Society of Edinburgh Young Academy and of the The German Court of Arbitration for Sport. Recreations: naval fiction; maritime history. Address: University of Glasgow, School of Law, Glasgow G12 8QQ; T.-0141 3305184; e-mail: christian.tams@glasgow.ac.uk

Tanner, Susanne Lesley Murning, LLB (Hons), DipLP, MCIArb, QC (took Silk 2016; called to the Bar 2000). Legal Member/Chair, First-tier Tribunal (Housing and Property Chamber and Health and Education Chamber). Executive Editor, Green's Scottish Education Manual; Advocate Depute, 2011-2014 and ad hoc, since 2014; Lecturer, Edinburgh Napier University, since 2006; Tutor, University of Edinburgh, since 2008; b. 29.10.74, Stirling; m., David Henderson Tanner; 1 s. Educ. George Watson's College, Edinburgh; University of Edinburgh. Assistant on Master's Court, Royal Company of Merchants of the City of Edinburgh, 2011-2014. Governor, Governing Council, George Watson's College, 2011-2014. Address: (b.) Ampersand, Parliament House, Parliament Square, Edinburgh EH1 1RF; T.-07739 639214.
E-mail: susanne.tanner@advocates.org.uk

Tasker, Moira, MA (Hons), MSc, FRSA. Chief Executive, Inclusion Scotland, since 2012; Managing Director, Euan's Guide, 2020-21; Membership & Support Services Review Lead, SCVO (Scottish Council for Voluntary Organisations), 2019-2020; Consultant, since 2016; former Director, The Cockburn Association (The Edinburgh Civic Trust), 2006-2009; Chief Executive, Citizens Advice Edinburgh, 2009-2015. Educ. Bell Baxter High School, Cupar, Fife; University of Edinburgh; Heriot-Watt University. Recreations: travel; horticulture.

Tate, Professor Austin, BA (Hons), MSc, PhD, CEng, FAAAI, FBCS, FBIS, FREng, FRSE. Emeritus Professor of Knowlege-Based Systems, University of Edinburgh; Director, AIAI (Artificial Intelligence Applications Institute), 1985-2019; b. 12.5.51, Knottingley, West Yorkshire; m., Margaret Mowbray. Educ. King's School, Pontefract; Lancaster University; Edinburgh University. Recreations: travel; walking; photography; graphic art; space. Address: (b.) AIAI, School of Informatics, University of Edinburgh, Informatics Forum, Crichton Street, Edinburgh EH8 9AB; e-mail: a.tate@ed.ac.uk

Tavener, Alan, BEM, MA, MSc, ARCO, ARCM, HonARSCM. Artistic Director, Cappella Nova, since 1982;

Director of Music, St Bride's Episcopal Church, Glasgow; freelance Musical Director and Consultant; Director of Music, University of Strathclyde, until 2012; b. 22.4.57, Weston-Super-Mare; m., Rebecca Jane Gibson. Educ. City of Bath Boys' School; Brasenose College, Oxford; University of Strathclyde. Conducted several world premieres of choral works and several CDs of early, romantic and contemporary music. Recreations: architecture; Italy; Scottish country dancing; food and drink. E-mail: alan.cappella-nova@strath.ac.uk

Tavener, Rebecca Jane. Soprano & writer; Creative Director, Cappella Nova; b. 3.5.58, Trowbridge; m., Alan Tavener BEM. Co-founded Cappella Nova, 1982; Concert Manager, Glasgow University, 1983-89; Founder and Director, Chorus International, 1990-94; founded Canty (medieval vocal ensemble), 1998; launched own recording label, ROTA, 1998; singing and public speaking coach; Early Music Editor, 'Choir & Organ' magazine, since 2001; Co-Director of Musica Sacra Scotland and the St Columbkille Schola Cantorum, since 2018. Commissioner of more than 100 contemporary choral works. Recreations: Italophilia; retail therapy; watching Coronation Street; reading history books; gardening. Address: (h.) 35 Crosbie Street, Glasgow G20 0BQ; T.-(b.) 07801 239596. E-mail: cappella.nova@strath.ac.uk

Taylor, Anita, BA (Hons), MA. Dean, Duncan of Jordanstone College of Art & Design, University of Dundee, since 2019. Educ. Gloucestershire College of Art & Technology; Royal College of Art. Career history: Deputy Head of Art, Media & Design; Head of School of Fine Art; Head of Painting, University of Gloucestershire, 1991-2003; Vice-Principal, Wimbledon School of Art, London, 2004-06; University of the Arts London: Dean of Wimbledon College of Art, 2006-09, Director, The Centre for Drawing (Research Centre), 2006-09; Council member, Royal West of England Academy, 2007-09; Director & Chief Executive Officer, National Art School, 2009-2013; Board member, International Association of Independent Art & Design Schools (AIAS), 2011-13; Bath Spa University: Executive Dean of Bath School of Art and Design, 2013-19, Professor Emeritus, 2019; Founding Director, Trinity Buoy Wharf Drawing Prize/Jerwood Drawing Prize/The Open Drawing Exhibition, since 1993; Director, Drawing Projects UK, since 2009; Chair, Council for Higher Education in Art and Design, since 2015; Trustee, Stroud Valley Arts, since 2014. Various panel memberships including the Art & Design Panel for the UK Higher Education Funding Councils Research Assessment Exercise, RAE 2008; honorary appointments include Academician of the Royal West of England Academy (2004), Adjunct Professor of the University of Sydney affiliated to Sydney College of the Arts, 2013-17 and membership of several trusts, boards, and selection panels. Award-winning artist, presenting work in solo and group exhibitions in national and international galleries and museums and with works held in public collections; curator of a number of exhibitions of drawing and contemporary art. Address: Duncan of Jordanstone College of Art & Design, University of Dundee, Matthew Building, 13 Perth Building, Dundee DD1 4HT; T.-01382 388828.

Taylor, Brian, MA (Hons). Political Commentator; Herald columnist; former Political Editor, BBC Scotland; b. 9.1.55, Dundee; m., Pamela Moira Niven; 2 s. Educ. High School of Dundee; St. Andrews University. Reporter, Press and Journal, Aberdeen, 1977-80; Lobby Correspondent, Thomson Regional Newspapers, Westminster, 1980-85; Reporter, BBC Scotland, Glasgow, 1985-86; Co-Presenter, Left, Right and Centre, BBC Scotland, 1986-88; Political Correspondent, BBC Scotland, 1988-90. DLitt, Napier University; DLitt, Abertay University; LLD, Dundee

University. Publications: The Scottish Parliament, 1999; Scotland's Parliament: Triumph and Disaster, 2002. Honorary Professor, Glasgow University. Recreations: golf; theatre.

Taylor, Rev. Ian, BSc, MA, LTh, DipEd. Lecturer on music and the arts, broadcaster, opera director; b. 12.10.32, Dundee; m., Joy Coupar, LRAM; 2 s.; 1 d. Educ. Dundee High School; St. Andrews University; Durham University; Sheffield University; Edinburgh University. Teacher, Mathematics Department, Dundee High School; Lecturer in Mathematics, Bretton Hall College of Education; Senior Lecturer in Education, College of Ripon and York St. John; Assistant Minister, St. Giles' Cathedral, Edinburgh; Minister, Abdie & Dunbog and Newburgh, 1983-97; Moderator, Presbytery of St. Andrews, 1995-96; Secretary, History of Education Society, 1968-73; extensive work in adult education (appreciation of music and the arts); Director, Summer Schools in Music, St. Andrews University; numerous courses for St. Andrews, Edinburgh, Cambridge and Hull Universities and WEA; has played principal roles in opera and operetta; Director, Gilbert and Sullivan Society of Edinburgh, 1979-87; Director, Tayside Opera, 1999; compiled Theatre Music Quiz series, Radio Tay; presented own operetta, My Dear Gilbert...My Dear Sullivan, BBC; Writer of revues and documentary plays with music, including Tragic Queen (Mary Queen of Scots), St. Giles' Cathedral, Edinburgh Festival Fringe, 1982, and John Knox (Church of Scotland Video); President, East Neuk of Fife Probus Club, 2007-08. Publications: How to Produce Concert Versions of Gilbert Sullivan; The Gilbert and Sullivan Quiz Book; The Opera Lover's Quiz Book; Maths for Mums and Dads. Address: Lundie Cottage, Arncroach, Fife KY10 2RN; T.-01333 720 222.

Taylor, Rev Ian, BD, ThM. Minister, St Mary's Parish Church, Kirkintilloch, since 2019; Minister, Springfield Cambridge Parish Church, Bishopbriggs, since 2006. Ministered in a city centre Parish in Stirling for 11 years. Member, Association of Pastoral Supervision and Education (APSE); Lead Trainer of Supervisors for the Church of Scotland. Address: St Mary's Parish Church, Cowgate, Kirkintilloch, Glasgow G66 1JT; T.-0141 775 1166.

Taylor, Dr Jackie, MB, ChB, FRCP. President, Royal College of Physicians and Surgeons of Glasgow (2018-2021); Consultant Physician, Glasgow Royal Infirmary, since 1997. Educ. University of Glasgow medical school (trained and dually accredited in General Internal Medicine and Geriatric Medicine). Career: full time clinician with a sub-specialty interest in heart failure; Clinical Director, Associate Medical Director and Clinical Quality Lead in Geriatric Medicine. Honorary Senior Clinical Lecturer; Chair, British Geriatrics Society Cardiovascular Section. Other main professional roles have been as Vice President and Honorary Secretary of the Royal College of Physicians and Surgeons of Glasgow.

Taylor, Kenneth. Headteacher, St Mary's Music School, Edinburgh. Address: Coates Hall, 25 Grosvenor Crescent, Edinburgh EH12 5EL; T.-0131 538 7766.

Taylor, Malcolm John, TD, DL, MA, FRICS. Chartered Surveyor/Land Agent; Partner, Bell Ingram LLP; b. 21.11.61, Glasgow; m., Helen McKay; 2 s. Educ. Dumfries Academy; Aberdeen University. Chairman, RICS in Scotland, 2004-05. Recreations: field sports; music; natural history. Address: (b.) Bell Ingram, Manor Street, Forfar; T.-01307 462516.

Taylor, Margie, CBE, MSc, MBA, FDSRCSEd, FDSRCPS(Glasg), FFPH, FFGDP (UK). Chief Dental Officer, Scottish Government, 2007-2018 (retired); Honorary Senior Lecturer, Glasgow University; Dundee University; b. Edinburgh. Educ. James Gillespie's High

School for Girls; Edinburgh University; Heriot-Watt University. Consultant in dental public health, NHS Lanarkshire, 1994-2007; formerly Chief Administrative Dental Officer, Fife Health Board, and Honorary Senior Lecturer, St. Andrews University. Board Member, Health Scotland; Past President, Royal Odonto-Chirurgical Society of Scotland; President, Council of European Chief Dental Officers, 2017-18.

Taylor, Martin, MBE, DUniv (Paisley). Guitarist/ Composer, since 1972; b. 20.10.56, Harlow, Essex; m., Elizabeth Kirk; 2 s. Educ. Passmores Comprehensive School, Harlow. Self-taught guitarist (began playing aged four); became professional musician at 15, touring UK, Europe and USA; solo recording debut, 1978 (for Wave Records); toured world with Stephane Grappelli, 1979-90; recorded eight solo albums for Linn Records, 1990s, becoming biggest selling British jazz recording artist in the UK; became first British jazz artist to sign recording contract with Sony Jazz (Columbia) in over 30 years; currently tours the world as solo artist and records and composes music for television and film. Founder, Kirkmichael International Guitar Festival; Founder, Guitars for Schools Programme. Best Guitarist, British Jazz Awards, eleven times; Grammy nomination, 1987; Gold Badge of Merit, British Academy of Composers and Songwriters, 1999; Freedom of the City of London, 1998; received the BBC Radio 2 "Heart of Jazz" Award in recognition of his career in music, 2007; presented with a Lifetime Achievement Award from the North Wales Jazz Guitar Festival for his "Contribution to Jazz Guitar Worldwide", 2007; 2010 BBC Folk Awards 'Best Original Composition' nomination; 2010 Doctor of Music (honoris causa), Royal Scottish Academy of Music and Drama (RSAMD). Publication: Kiss and Tell (autobiography), 1999. Recreations: horse racing; horse drawn gypsy wagons; collects vintage and rare American guitars and mandolins.

Taylor, Dr. Mary. Independent housing expert; former Chief Executive, Scottish Federation of Housing Associations (2010-17). Over thirty five years working in the Scottish housing sector; career ranges from a Housing Management Trainee at SSHA to Senior Teaching Fellow at the University of Stirling; worked with committees of various housing associations as well as previously sitting on the Board of the SFHA and Chartered Institute of Housing (CIH) Scotland. Fellow of the Chartered Institute of Housing (CIH). Honorary Fellow of RICS.

Taylor, Rt. Rev. Maurice, STD. Bishop Emeritus of Galloway, since 2004; Bishop of Galloway, 1981-2004; b. 5.5.26, Hamilton. Educ. St. Aloysius College, Glasgow; Our Lady's High School, Motherwell; Pontifical Gregorian University, Rome. Royal Army Medical Corps, UK, India, Egypt, 1944-47; Assistant Priest: St. Bartholomew's, Coatbridge, 1951-52, St. Bernadette's, Motherwell, 1954-55; Lecturer, St. Peter's College, Cardross, 1955-65; Rector, Royal Scots College, Spain, 1965-74; Parish Priest, Our Lady of Lourdes, East Kilbride, 1974-81. Publications: The Scots College in Spain, 1971; Guatemala, A Bishop's Journey, 1991; El Salvador: Portrait of a Parish, 1992; Opening Our Lives to the Saviour (Co-author), 1995; Listening at the Foot of the Cross (Co-author), 1996; Being a Bishop in Scotland, 2006; It's the Eucharist, Thank God, 2009; Life's Flavour, 2014; What Are They Talking About?, 2015; Weekday Thoughts on the Sunday Gospels, 2017. Address: 41 Overmills Road, Ayr KA7 3LH; T.-01292-285865.
Web: www.bishopmauricetaylor.org.uk

Taylor, Neil, MA, LLB, DipLP. Director at Office of the Advocate General, since 2017. Educ. University of Glasgow; University of Edinburgh Law School. Career history: Parliamentary Counsel, The Scottish Government, 2002-2013; Office of the Advocate General: Deputy

Director, Advisory and Legislation, 2013-16, Legal Secretary, 2016-17. Address: The Office of the Advocate General, Queen Elizabeth House, Edinburgh EH8 8FT.

Taylor, Peter Cranbourne, MA, CA. Chairman, Scottish National Blood Transfusion Association, 1995-2010; b. 11.8.38, Yeovil; m., Lois Mary; 1s.; 1d Educ. Edinburgh University. Chartered Accountant/Partner: Romanes and Munro, Edinburgh, 1964-74; Deloitte Haskins and Sells, 1974-90; Coopers and Lybrand, 1990-95. Member, Scottish Dental Practice Board, 1991-2001. Recreation: rural indolence. Address: (h.) Totleywells House, Winchburgh, West Lothian EH52 6QJ.

Taylor, Professor Samuel Sorby Brittain, BA, PhD, Officier dans l'Ordre des Palmes Academiques. Professor of French, St. Andrews University, 1977-95, now Professor Emeritus; b. 20.9.30, Dore and Totley, Derbyshire; m., Agnes McCreadie Ewan (deceased 2007); 2 d. Educ. High Storrs Grammar School, Sheffield; Birmingham University; Paris University. Royal Navy, 1956-58 (Sub Lt., RNVR); Personnel Research Officer, Dunlop Rubber Co. ("Sickness-Absence in Rubber Industry"), 1958-60; Research Fellow, Institut et Musee Voltaire, Geneva, 1960-63; St. Andrews University: Lecturer, 1963, Reader, 1972, Professor, 1977, retired, 1995; Chairman, National Council for Modern Languages, 1981-85; Member, Executive Committee, Complete Works of Voltaire, 1970-85; Project Leader, Inter-University French Language Teaching Research and Development Project ("Le Francais en Faculte""En fin de compte"), 1980-88; Director, Nuffield Foundation project ("Nuffield French for science students"), 1991-99; Chairman, Scottish Joint Working Party for Standard Grade in Modern Languages, 1982-84; Chairman, St Andrews Green Belt Forum, 2008-2015; Vice Chair, St Andrews Preservation Trust. Publications: definitive text of Voltaire's Works, 1974; definitive iconography of Voltaire, completed. Recreations: athletics timekeeping; photography; Liberal Democrats; Franco-Scottish Society. Address: (h.) 11 Irvine Crescent, St. Andrews KY16 8LG; T.-01334 472588; e-mail: ssbt423@btinternet.com

Taylor, Scott, BA (Hons) Marketing. Former Chief Executive, Advance City Marketing (2016-19); former Chief Executive, Glasgow City Marketing Bureau (2006-2016); b. 20.06.62, Manchester; m., Carol; 1 s.; 1 d. Educ. Clayton High School; University of Strathclyde. Former general manager of three Glasgow city centre hotels, as well as brand manager for two of Forte Hotels' brands; joined Greater Glasgow & Clyde Valley Tourist Board in 1998 as Director-Convention Bureau, later becoming Director of Marketing, encompassing both Leisure and Discretionary Business Tourism; took over as Chief Executive in July 2004, and then established Glasgow City Marketing Bureau (GCMB). Recreations: travelling; hill walking; mountain biking.

Taylor, William James, QC (Scotland), QC (England and Wales), MA, LLB, FRSA. Advocate, since 1971; Barrister, since 1990; Honorary Professor, University of St Andrews, since 2019; b. 13.9.44, Nairn. Educ. Robert Gordon's College, Aberdeen; Aberdeen University. Standing Junior Counsel to DHSS, 1978-79, to Foreign and Commonwealth Office, 1979-86; Temporary Sheriff, 1997-99; Member, Criminal Injuries Compensation Board, 1997-2000; Member, Scottish Criminal Cases Review Commission, 1999-2004. Parliamentary candidate (Labour), West Edinburgh, February and October, 1974; Lothian Regional Councillor, 1973-84 (Secretary, Labour Group); Chairman,

COSLA Protective Services Committee; Part-time Sheriff, since 1999; Chairman, Scottish Opera, 2004-07; Past Chairman, Traverse Theatre; previous Board Member, Royal Lyceum Theatre, Edinburgh; Past Chairman, Federation of Scottish Theatres; Honorary Professor, University of St Andrews, 2019. Recreations: the arts; sailing; Scottish mountains; restoring a garden. Address: (b.) Parliament House, Parliament Square, Edinburgh EH1 1RF; e-mail: Bill@durinish.com

Teasdale, Sir Graham Michael, Kt, MB, BS, FRCP, FRCSEdin, FRCSGlas, FRCSLond, FACSHon, FMedSci, FRSE. Professor and Head, Department of Neurosurgery, Glasgow University, 1981-2003; Consultant Neurosurgeon, Institute of Neurological Sciences, Glasgow, 1975-2003; President, Society of British Neurological Surgeons, 2000-02; b. 23.9.40, Spennymoor; m.; 3 s.; 3 d. Educ. Johnston Grammar School, Durham; Durham University. Postgraduate clinical training, Newcastle-upon-Tyne, London and Birmingham, 1963-69; Assistant Lecturer in Anatomy, Glasgow University, 1969-71; specialist training in surgery and neurosurgery, Southern General Hospital, Glasgow, 1971-75; Senior Lecturer, then Reader in Neurosurgery, Glasgow University, 1975-81. President, International Neurotrauma Society, 1993-2000; Chairman, European Brain Injury Consortium, 1995-2003; President, Section of Clinical Neurosciences, Royal Society of Medicine, 1998-99; former President, Royal College of Physicians and Surgeons of Glasgow, 2003-06; Chairman of Board, NHS Quality Improvement Scotland, 2006-10. Address: Duchal Road, Kilmacolm PA13 4AY.

Telfer, Andrew. Joint Senior Partner, Baillie Gifford, since 2012. Address: (b.) Calton Square, 1 Greenside Row, Edinburgh EH1 3AN.

Templeton, Professor Allan, CBE, MBChB, MD (Hons), FRCOG, FRCP, FRCPE, FACOG, FMedSci. Emeritus Professor of Obstetrics and Gynaecology, University of Aberdeen; President, Royal College of Obstetricians and Gynaecologists, 2004-07; Hon. Director, Office for Research and Clinical Audit, RCOG, 2008-2014; b. 28.6.46, Glasgow; m., Gillian Penney; 3 s.; 1 d. Educ. Aberdeen Grammar School; University of Aberdeen. Junior hospital posts, Aberdeen Royal Infirmary; Lecturer, then Senior Lecturer, University of Edinburgh. Former Member, Human Fertilisation and Embryology Authority. Publications: books and scientific papers on human reproduction. Recreation: Wester Ross. Address: (b.) Oak Tree Cottage, Leachnasaide, Gairloch IV21 2AP; e-mail: allan.templeton@abdn.ac.uk

Tennant, David. Actor; b. 18.4.71, Bathgate, Lothian; m., Georgia Moffett; 4 c. Educ. RSAMD. Acted with the 7:84 Theatre Company; Theatre includes: Touchstone in As You Like It (RSC), 1996, Romeo in Romeo and Juliet (RSC), 2000, Antipholus of Syracuse in Comedy of Errors (RSC), 2000, Jeff in The Lobby Hero (Donmar Warhouse and New Ambassadors), 2002 (nominated Best Actor Laurence Olivier Theatre Awards, 2003); Television includes: Casanova in Casanova 2005, The Doctor in Doctor Who, 2005-2010 and 2013 (tenth Doctor); Films include: Bright Young Things, 2003, Harry Potter and the Goblet of Fire, 2005. Address: (b.) c/o Independent Talent Group, Oxford House, 76 Oxford Street, London W1D 1BS.

Teusner, Carmel, MSc. Non-Executive Director, Scottish Enterprise, since 2016; b. 3.62. Educ. Edinburgh Napier University; Heriot-Watt University; Birkbeck, University of London; Centre for Coaching/University of Middlesex; Harvard Business School; Harvard Extension School; Australian Institute of Company Directors. Career history: Training and Development Consultant, Endeavour Scotland, 1994-97; Training and Development Manager, Scottish and Newcastle plc, 1997-99; Head of Learning and Organisational Development, BSkyB, 1999-2003; Interim Head of Organisational Development, Scottish Widows, 2005-06; HR Consulting, Penna, 2006-2010; Group Head of Leadership Development (interim), Westpac, Sydney, Australia, 2010; UGL Limited: General Manager, Human Resources, 2010-2011, Group Head of Organisational Development, 2010-14; Executive Vice President, Human Resources (acting), DTZ, Chicago, USA, 2013-14; Board Member, National Library of Scotland, 2015-19; Dir./Organisational Development Consultant, Akuiti, since 2006; Member: Ofcom Advisory Committee for Scotland, 2018-2021, Changing the Chemistry (SCIO), since 2015, Board of Trustees, Disability Snowsport UK (DSUK), since 2017. Address: Scottish Enterprise HQ, Atrium Court, 50 Waterloo Street, Glasgow G2 6HQ; T.-0300 013 3385.

Theodossiou, Professor Ioannis, BSc, MPhil, PhD. Professor, Economics, University of Aberdeen Business School, since 1998; b. 03.07.54, Athens, Greece; m., Eleni Mente-Theodossiou; 1 s.; 1 d. Educ. University of Piraeus (The Graduate School of Industrial Studies of Piraeus); The University of Glasgow. Bank Employee, 1976-81; Tutor in Economics, 1982-86; Teaching Assistant, 1987-88; Teaching Fellow, 1988-90; Lecturer in Economics, 1990-95; Senior Lecturer in Economics, 1995-98; Reader in Economics, 1998. Participated in and coordinated several European Commission funded projects on issues of health inequalities, low pay, well-being and job satisfaction. Fellow, Royal Statistical Society; Member, Council of the Scottish Economic Society (2008-2015). Publications: 'Wage Inflation and the Two Tier Labour Market' (book); edited volumes, chapters in books and research papers in many economic journals. Recreations: motorcycles; hill walking; sailing. Address: (b.) University of Aberdeen Business School, Edward Wright Building, Aberdeen AB24 3QY; T.-01224 272183; e-mail: theod@abdn.ac.uk

Thewliss, Alison. MP (SNP), Glasgow Central, since 2015; b. 13.9.82; m.; 1 s.; 1 d. Former Glasgow City councillor for the Calton ward (2007-2015). Address: House of Commons, London SW1A 0AA.

Thewliss, James, BSc (Hons). General Secretary, School Leaders Scotland; retired Head Teacher, Harris Academy, Dundee (1997-2015); b. 24.4.53, Motherwell; m., Ann White; 1 s.; 1 d. Educ. Dalziel High School, Motherwell; Glasgow University. Geography Teacher, Braidhurst High School, Motherwell, 1976 -85; Principal Teacher, Geography, Perth High School, 1986-89; Assistant Rector, Perth High School, 1989-91; Assistant Head Teacher, Carluke High School, 1991-93; Depute Rector, Wallace High School, Stirling, 1993-97. Vice Convener, General Teaching Council Scotland, 2005-09; President, School Leaders Scotland, 2010-2011. Recreations: supporting Motherwell Football Club; football purist.

Thiam, Sara, BA (Hons). Chief Executive, The Scottish Council for Development and Industry (SCDI), since 2019. Educ. Linlithgow Academy; University of Stirling. Career history: International Manager, Youthlink Scotland, 1992-2002; EU Projects Manager, City of Edinburgh Council, 2002-07; Projects Manager, City Centre Development Partnership (Edinburgh), 2007-2008; Trustee, Bridges Programme, 2009-2011;

Manager, Glasgow Edinburgh Collaboration Initiative, 2009-2011; Open Innovation Manager, City of Edinburgh Council, 2010-2011; Board Member, Construction Scotland Innovation Centre, since 2018; Commissioner, Infrastructure Commission for Scotland, 2019-2020; Regional Director, Institution of Civil Engineers (ICE), 2012-19. Recreations: family; food; jazz; exploring the world around me. Address: Scottish Council for Development and Industry, 1 Cadogan Square, Glasgow G2 7HF; T.-0141 243 2667.

Thin, Andrew, BSc (Hons), MBA, DipM. Chairman, Scottish Canals, since 2014; Chairman, Scottish Land Commission, since 2016; b. 21.1.59, Edinburgh; m., Frances Elizabeth; 1 s.; 1 d. Educ. Glenalmond College; Edinburgh University. Director, James Thin Booksellers, 1985-89; Team Leader, Highlands and Islands Development Board, 1989-91; Chief Executive, Caithness and Sutherland Enterprise, 1991-95. Chairman, John Muir Trust, 1997-2003; Board Member, Crofters Commission, 2001-06; Convener, Cairngorms National Park Authority, 2003-06; Chairman, Scottish Natural Heritage, 2006-2014. Recreations: long-distance running; canoeing; hill-walking. Address: (h.) Wester Auchterflow, by Munlochy, Ross-shire IV8 8PQ; T.-01463 811632.
E-mail: andrew.thin@hotmail.co.uk

Thin, David Ainslie, BSc. Chairman, James Thin Ltd., 1992-2002; b. 9.7.33, Edinburgh; m., Elspeth J.M. Scott; 1 s.; 2 d. Educ. Edinburgh Academy; Loretto School; Edinburgh University. James Thin Ltd., 1957-2002; President, Booksellers Association of GB and Ireland, 1976-78; Chairman, Book Tokens Ltd., 1987-95. Recreations: golf; travelling; reading. Address: (h.) Balfour House, 21/1 East Suffolk Park, Edinburgh EH16 5PN; T.-0131-667 2725.

Thomaneck, Emeritus Professor Jurgen Karl Albert, MEd, Drphil. Professor in German, Aberdeen University, 1992-2001; Aberdeen City Councillor, 1996-2003 (Convener, Education and Leisure Committee, 1999-2003); b. 12.6.41, Germany; m., Guinevere Ronald; 2 d. Educ. Universities of Kiel, Tubingen, Aberdeen. Lecturer in German, Aberdeen University, since 1968. Grampian Regional Councillor, 1984-96; President, Aberdeen Trades Council, 1982-2001; Convenor, Grampian Joint Police Board, 1995-98; Board Member, Grampian Enterprise Ltd., until 1995; President, KIMO UK, 1996-2003; author/editor of 10 books, 15 contributions to books, 30 articles in learned journals, all in German studies. Recreation: football. Address: (h.) 17 Elm Place, Aberdeen AB25 3SN.

Thomas, Sally, BA (Hons). Chief Executive, Scottish Federation of Housing Associations, since 2017. Educ. University of Leeds. Career: Finance Administrator, Circle 33 Housing Trust, 1980-83; Company Secretary, Solon Wandsworth, 1983-86; Senior Operations Officer, The Housing Corporation, 1986-88; Assistant Director, Tyne and Wear Development Corporation, 1988-94; Director, Social Regeneration Consultants, 1996-2017; Director of Communities, HACT, 2016-17; Head of Communities Investment, North Star Housing Group, 2012-17. Address: Sutherland House, 149 St Vincent Street, Glasgow G2 5NW; T.-0141 332 8113.

Thompson, Professor Alastair Mark, ALCM, MBChB, MD, FRSCEd. Honorary Professor, University of Dundee; b. 18.11.60. Educ. Boroughmuir High School, Edinburgh; Edinburgh University. Lecturer, University of Edinburgh, 1991-96; Senior Lecturer/Reader, University of Dundee, 1996-2002;

Visiting Professor of Surgical Oncology, MD Anderson Cancer Centre, Houston, 2010; Professor of Surgery, Department of Surgical Oncology, University of Texas. Address: (b.) Dundee Cancer Centre, Ninewells Hospital and Medical School, Dundee DD1 9SY; T.-01382 383223; e-mail: a.m.thompson@dundee.ac.uk

Thompson, David George, Dip in Consumer Affairs, FCTSI. Vice President, CTSI, since 2009; MSP (SNP), Skye, Lochaber and Badenoch, 2011-16, Highlands and Islands, 2007-2011; b. 20.9.49, Lossiemouth; m., Veronica; 1 s.; 3 d. Educ. Lossiemouth High Secondary. Trading Standards Officer (TSO), Banff Moray & Nairn CC, 1971-73; Assistant Chief TSO, Ross & Cromarty County Council, 1973-75; Chief TSO, Comhairle nan Eilean Siar, 1975-83; Depute Director of Trading Standards, Highland Regional Council, 1983-86; Director of Trading Standards, 1986-95; Director of Protective Services, Highland Council, 1995-2001. Church of Scotland Elder; Life member of GMB; Life member of An Comunn Gaidhealach; Vice Convenor, Scottish Independence Convention, 2018-19; Convenor of Christians for Independence, since 2009; Chair, Board of Voices for Scotland, January-August 2019; Member of SNP, 1965-2020; Founder Member and Leader of Action for Independence (AFI), 2020-2021; Member of Alba Party, 2021. Address: (h.) Balnafettack Farm House, Leachkin Road, Inverness IV3 8NL.

Thompson, Owen. MP (SNP), Midlothian, since 2019 and 2015-17; b. 17.3.78. Educ. Beeslack High School, Penicuik; Edinburgh Napier University. Career in Financial Services industry, then elected to Midlothian Council in November 2005 at the Loanhead by-election; re-elected in both 2007 and 2012; became Leader of Midlothian Council in 2013. Recreations: football; rugby; craft beer; films. Address: Houses of Parliament, Westminster, London SW1A 0AA.

Thompson, Simon, BA (Politics and Economics), MBA. Chief Executive, Chartered Institute of Bankers in Scotland, since 2007. Educ. University of Newcastle-upon-Tyne; University of Edinburgh. Lived and worked in Poland and the Czech Republic from 1994 to 2000, teaching and then managing a series of international education and training businesses; managed the International Accounting Education Standards Board (IAESB), an independent standards-setting board established by the International Federation of Accountants (IFAC), developing and promoting International Education Standards for Professional Accountants; previously worked for the Association of Chartered Certified Accountants (ACCA), establishing ACCA in 25 countries in Central & Eastern Europe, and leading a number of EU and other donor-funded accounting education and reform programmes. Address: (b.) The Chartered Institute of Bankers in Scotland, Drumsheugh House, 38b Drumsheugh Gardens, Edinburgh EH3 7SW; T.-0131 473 7777; e-mail: simon@charteredbanker.com

Thomson, Albert Adams, GCHT, KCSPP, ORLG, KOSMA, KEG, KG, CLJ, OMLJ, CStN, MMSN, OSS, BA, FSA Scot, MICPEM. Police Constable, Aberdeen City Police, 1969-75; Grampian Police, 1975-84; Police Sergeant, 1984-89; Police Inspector, 1989-99; Force Emergency Planning Officer, 1994-99; Delivery Team Leader, Rubicon Response Ltd, 1999-2005; Business Assurance Leader, Petrofac Training, 2004-10; Senior Project Manager, Altor Risk Group, 2010-14; Senior Project Manager, Stirling Group, 2014-16; retired in 2016; b. 24.6.50, Aberdeen; m., Linda Anne Hendry; 2 s

(Greg & Marc). Educ. Mile-End Primary and Rosemount Secondary Schools in Aberdeen; The Open University. Armiger; holder of Baton of Honour, Scottish Police College (1970); Founder and Past Chairman of the Grampian Police Diced Cap Charitable Trust; Honorary Firefighter, Grampian Fire & Rescue Service; Burgess of Guild and Burgess of Trade of the City of Aberdeen and Guardian of the March Stones marking the boundary of the Freedom Lands of the City of Aberdeen; Member of the Board of Directors of the Instant Neighbour Charity, Aberdeen (1999-2001); Member of the Aberdeen Shoemakers Incorporation; Fellow of the Society of Antiquaries of Scotland; Commander, Order of St Lazarus of Jerusalem & former Trustee of the Dame Bebe Barwiss-Holiday Memorial Trust (2014-19); Knight Grand Cross, member of the Grand Council and Grand Prior of Scotland of the Confraternity of the Knights of the Most Holy Trinity; Knight of the Portuguese Royal House and Honorary Member of the Portuguese Royal Honour Guard; Knight of the Dynastic Order of the Eagle of Georgia & the Seamless Tunic of our Lord Jesus Christ; Knight of the Royal Order of Saint Michael of the Wing; Knight Commander of Grace in the Confraternity of the Knights of St. Peter & St. Paul; Officer in the Royal Order of the Lion of Godenu; Nkyido (Knight) of the Royal Order of the Golden Fire Dog (Royal House of Sefwi Obeng-Mim); Taisho in the Order of the Scottish Samurai; Admitted into the Order of the Scottish Samurai Budo Martial Arts Hall of Fame with the rank of 5th Dan; Member of the Order of the Japanese Seal; Awarded Honorary Black Belt (1st Dan) by National Karate Institute, now 1st Dan in Shotokan Karate in his own right; Commissioned as Baron-Sergeant of Miltonhaven; Conferred with the hereditary title, Archon of the Primatial Throne of the Ukrainian Autocephalous Orthodox Church Abroad, by Metropolitan + Lorenzo, Archbishop of Palermo and All Italy; Cross of Merit of Saint Nicodemus of Palermo; Cruz De Merito Frei Sao Dom Nuno Alvares Pereira (The Cross of Merit of Saint Nuno); Kentucky Colonel; awarded Gold Cross D'Honneur by European Association of the Bodies and Public Organisations of Security and Defense at the Brigade of Gendarmerie, Port Vendres, France, 2018; Member of the Incorporation of Wrights in Glasgow; Burgess & Guild Brother & Freeman Citizen of Glasgow; Member of the Institute of Civil Protection & Emergency Management; Member of the Royal Celtic Society; Member, Merciful Society of Magi (Kentucky). Publications: Hungary to Holburn Street; Taranty Ha; Deacon Bards o Taranty Ha (Incorporated Trades of Aberdeen); contributor to 'Conquered by No One: A People's History of the Scots who made the Declaration of Arbroath in 1320'. Recreations: reading and history. Address: (h) 'Nanaimo', St Margarets Wells, Inverurie, Aberdeenshire AB51 0JN; T.-01467 620815. E-mail: albertthomson@btinternet.com

Thomson, Professor Ben, CBE (2017), MA Hons (Physics), Hon Doctorate. Chairman: Inverleith LLP, since 2009, Omnos, since 2019, Planet Organic, since 2019, Creative Scotland, 2017-18. Educ. Edinburgh University; INSEAD, 2008. Career: Researcher, H of C, 1981-82; Kleinwort Benson Ltd, 1985-90; Noble Group Ltd, 1990-2010: Dir., 1993; Chief Exec., 1997-2007; led mgt buy-out, 2000; Chm., 2007-10 (non-exec., 2008-10). Non-executive Director: Wellington Underwriting plc, 1993-97; Canmore Partnership, 1995-2003; CBS Private Capital SLP Ltd, 1996-2004; Roberts & Hiscox Gen. Partners Ltd, 1996-2011; PFI (NT) Ltd, 2001-05; Martin Currie Global Portfolio Trust (formerly Martin Currie Portfolio Investment Trust) plc (Sen. Ind. Dir.), 2001-13; Oval Insce, 2003-06; Fidelity Special Values plc (Sen. Ind. Dir.), 2008-15; Reform Scotland, 2008-15; Chm., Barrington Stoke, 2008-16; Chm., Urbicus Ltd, 2011-17; Castle Capital Ltd, 2013-17; Antonine Asset

Management LLP, since 2010; Artisanal Spirits Co. Ltd, 2016-2020; HotHouse Brands Ltd, since 2016; Aye Limited, since 2016. Non-executive Director: Scottish Financial Enterprise, 2001-08; Edinburgh Internat. Sci. Fest., 2008-15. Mem., Speculative Soc.; FRSE, 2014; Chairman, National Galleries of Scotland, 2009-2017. Recreations: enjoys opera and art; former Scottish international athlete and enjoys most sports, especially skiing and running. Address: (h.) 33 Inverleith Terrace, Edinburgh EH3 5NU.

Thomson, Callum, LLB, DipLP, MSc. Group Head, Research, Communications and Public Engagement, The Scottish Parliament, since 2014. Educ. University of Strathclyde; University of Edinburgh; Edinburgh Napier University. Career history: Strategy and Change Manager, Adam & Company Private Bank, Royal Bank of Scotland, Edinburgh, 2007-08; Member, Audience Council for Scotland, BBC, 2007-2012; Board Director, Ark Housing, Edinburgh, 2013-14; The Scottish Parliament: Parliamentary Clerk, 1999-2009, Head of Strategy and Change Management, 2009-2012, Head of Organisational Development, 2012-14. External Trustee, Citizens Advice Scotland; Member of the Association of Project Management and the Chartered Institute of Personnel and Development; former Member of the BBC Audience Council for Scotland. Address: The Scottish Parliament, Edinburgh EH99 1SP.

Thomson, David. Temporary Director, Scottish Police College; Head of Training Operations, 2007-2013; b. 6.4.56, Greenock; m., Denise; 1 s.; 1 d. Educ. Greenock Academy; Glasgow Caledonia University. Quantity Surveyor, 1974-82; Police Constable, Greenock, 1982-89; Police Sergeant, Paisley and Scottish Police College, 1989-94; Police Inspector, Glasgow Southside, 1994-2000; Chief Inspector, Emergencies Planning, 2000-04; Superintendent, Hamilton, Deputy Commander Glasgow City Centre, 2004-07. Home Office Research Award. Recreations: golf; running; music. Address: (b.) Tulliallan Castle, Kincardine, Fife FK10 4BE; T.-01259 73 2154; e-mail: davidbpthomson@hotmail.co.uk

Thomson, David, BA (Hons). Chief Operating Officer, DC Thomson; b. 11.73. Educ. Glenalmond College; University of Durham. Career history: Manager, PricewaterhouseCoopers, 1996-2003; Chairman (Tayside branch), Young Enterprise Scotland, 2006-09; DC Thomson: Commercial Executive, 2003-07, Head of Programme and Corporate Services, 2007-2010, Joint Managing Director of Newspapers, 2010-11, appointed Director in 2014. Non Executive Director: Design Dundee Ltd (VandA at Dundee), since 2011; British Ice Skating, Sheffield, since 2019; Non Executive Board Member, High School of Dundee, since 2020. Address: DC Thomson, Courier Buildings, 2 Albert Square, Dundee DD1 1DD; T.-01382 223 131. E-mail: david@dcthomson.co.uk

Thomson, Sheriff Fergus Cockburn Mackenzie, LLB (Hons), MSc. Sheriff, South Strathclyde, Dumfries and Galloway, since 2019. Educ. George Watson's College, Edinburgh; The University of Edinburgh; Heriot-Watt University. Career history: trained with Bell & Scott WS and qualified as a solicitor in 1996; worked initially as a banking solicitor with Dundas & Wilson and Maclay, Murray & Spens, and subsequently in litigation with DLA Piper; also worked in structured finance with Bank of Scotland; called to the Scottish bar in 2004; Member of The Society of Writers to Her Majesty's Signet; Member of The Royal Company of Merchants of The City of Edinburgh and Fellow of the Chartered Institute of Arbitrators; previously an Advocate in primarily civil practice, specialising in company and commercial work. Recreations: sports; gardening; the arts. Address: Airdrie Sheriff Court, Graham Street, Airdrie ML6 6EE; T.-01236 751121.

Thomson, Sir (Frederick Douglas) David, Bt, BA. Member, Royal Company of Archers (Queen's Bodyguard for Scotland); b. 14.2.40, Edinburgh; 2 s.; 1 d. Educ. Eton; University College, Oxford. Recreations: shooting; skiing. Address: (h.) Holylee, Walkerburn, Peeblesshire; T.-07831 355691; e-mail: sirdthomson@holyee.go-plus.net

Thomson, Rev. Iain Urquhart. Minister, Parish of Skene, 1972-2011 (retired); b. 13.12.45, Dundee; m., Christine Freeland; 1 s.; 2 d. Educ. Harris Academy, Dundee; Inverness Royal Academy; Aberdeen University; Christ's College, Aberdeen. Assistant Minister, Castlehill Church, Ayr, 1970-72. Clerk, Presbytery of Gordon, 1988-2000; Clerk and Treasurer, Synod of Grampian Trusts Committee, since 1993; Patron of the Seven Incorporated Trades of Aberdeen, since 2013. Recreations: golf; theatre; gardening. Address: 4 Keirhill Gardens, Westhill, Aberdeenshire AB32 6AZ; T.-01224 746743.
E-mail: iainuthomson@googlemail.com

Thomson, Professor James Alick, MA, PhD. Emeritus Professor of Psychology, Strathclyde University (Professor, since 2000); b. 9.12.51, Inverness; m., Dana O'Dwyer; 1 d. Educ. Inverness Royal Academy; Edinburgh University. Research Scholar, Uppsala University, Sweden, 1973; Post-doctoral Fellow, University of Paris, 1977-78; Strathclyde University: Lecturer, 1979-91, Senior Lecturer, 1992-94, Reader, 1995-99. Publications: The Facts About Child Pedestrian Accidents, 1991; Child Development and the Aims of Road Safety Education (Co-Author), 1996; Child Safety: Problem and Prevention from Pre-School to Adolescence (Co-Author), 1996; Kerbcraft: A Manual for Road Safety Professionals, 1997; Studies in Perception and Action V (Co-Editor), 1999; Crossroads: Smart Strategies for Novice Pedestrians, 2005; 80 scientific articles and government reports. Recreations: rock climbing; hillwalking; mountaineering; photography; travel; Gaelic language and literature. Address: (b.) Department of Psychology, Strathclyde University, 40 George Street, Glasgow G1 1QE; T.-0141-548 2572.
E-mail: j.a.thomson@strath.ac.uk

Thomson, Ken. Director-General for Constitution and External Affairs, Scottish Government, since 2017 (previously Director-General for Strategy & Operations). Career history: Private Secretary to Scottish Office Ministers in the early 1990s; involved in work to prepare for devolution in 1997; Principal Private Secretary to the Rt. Hon. Donald Dewar MP MSP, 1997-99; senior lead on constitutional policy, since 2005; other experience includes work in private offices, on public health, managing legislation, on secondment to the Scottish Prison Service and to the financial services sector, and on transport, natural heritage and economic development policy. Recreations: cycling; plays music; crosswords; makes bread. Address: Scottish Government, St. Andrew's House, Regent Road, Edinburgh EH1 3DG.

Thomson, Lesley, QC, LLB (Hons). Former Solicitor General for Scotland (2011-16). Twenty five years' experience as a prosecutor, including as District Procurator Fiscal for Selkirk, District Procurator Fiscal for Edinburgh, and interim Area Procurator Fiscal for Lothian & Borders, and led on trial advocacy and deaths investigation within COPFS; appointed Area Procurator Fiscal for Glasgow in May 2008. Acknowledged specialist in the prosecution of serious crime, including organised crime and financial crime, and an expert in the proceeds of crime legislation, having authored a textbook on criminal confiscation. Became the first woman to be appointed to Scottish Rugby's Board in 2013; awarded the honorary degree of Doctor of Laws from the University of Glasgow.

Thomson, Lesley Ann. Managing Director, Spreng Thomson Communications Consultants; b. 11.2.59,

Glasgow. Member, Entrepreneurial Scotland; Trustee, Dewar Arts Awards; Vice Chair, Glasgow School of Art; Member: Glasgow Life Tourism, Visitor Economy Leadership Group. Address: (b.) The Herald Building, 155 Albion Street, Glasgow G1 1RU; T.-0141 548 5191.
E-mail: info@sprengthomson.com

Thomson, Malcolm George, QC, LLB. Practice at Scottish Bar, since 1974; Temporary Judge, Court of Session, 2002-2017; b. 6.4.50, Edinburgh; m. (1), Susan Gordon Aitken (m. dissolved); 2 d.; m. (2), Maybel King. Educ. Edinburgh Academy; Edinburgh University. Standing Junior Counsel, Department of Agriculture and Fisheries and Forestry Commission, 1982-87; QC (Scotland), 1987; called to the Bar, Lincoln's Inn, 1991; Chairman, National Health Service Tribunal, Scotland, 1995-2005; Member, Scottish Legal Aid Board, 1998-2006; Editor, Scots Law Times Reports, 1989-99; Scottish Case Editor, Current Law, 1977-97. Recreations: sailing; skiing. Address: (h.)12 Succoth Avenue, Edinburgh EH12 6BT; T.-0131-337 4911.

Thomson, Michelle. MSP (SNP), Falkirk East, since 2021; MP, Edinburgh West, 2015-17 (SNP MP, 2015); Founding Director, Momentous Change Ltd; b. 11.3.65. Educ. Royal Scottish Academy of Music & Drama. Worked as a professional musician for a number of years; completed an MSc in IT and worked in Financial Services over 23 years in a variety of senior roles delivering IT and business change; set up small business in property in 2009 and spent 2 years as Managing Director of Business for Scotland; SNP Spokesperson for Business, Innovation & Skills, 2015. Ambassador for the All Party Parliamentary Group for Fair Business Banking, since 2017. Address: Scottish Parliament, Edinburgh EH99 1SP.

Thomson, Professor Neil Campbell, MBChB, MD, FRCPGlas, FRCPLond, FRS. Emeritus Professor, University of Glasgow, since 2011; Professor of Respiratory Medicine, Glasgow University, 2001-2011; b. 3.4.48, Kilmarnock; m., Lorna Jean; 2 s.; 1 d. Educ. Speir's School, Beith; Glasgow University. Junior hospital doctor, Glasgow teaching hospitals, 1972-80; Research Fellow, McMaster University, Hamilton, Ontario, 1980-81; Consultant Respiratory Physician, Western Infirmary & Gartnavel General Hospital, Glasgow, 1982-2011; Honorary Professor, Glasgow University, 1996-2001; Chair, British Lung Foundation Scientific Committee, 2001-2004; Member, Committee on Safety of Medicine, 1999-2001. Publications: Asthma and COPD: Basic Mechanisms and Clinical Management, 2009; Manual of Asthma Management (2nd edition), 2001. Recreations: reading; walking; gardening. Address: (b.) Department of Respiratory Medicine, Gartnavel General Hospital, Glasgow.

Thomson, Richard. MP (SNP), Gordon, since 2019; b. 16.6.76, Edinburgh. Educ. Tynecastle High School, Edinburgh; University of Stirling; Edinburgh Business School. Career history: worked for Scottish Widows in Edinburgh for six years, firstly as an Assistant Manager in their Customer Relations Department, and latterly as an Account Manager in Corporate Pensions; former journalist for the Ellon Times and the Inverurie Herald; Aberdeenshire Councillor, 2012-2019; Leader of Aberdeenshire Council, June 2015-May 2017. Recreations: involved in the Rotary Club of Oldmeldrum and is a traditional musician. Address: Houses of Parliament, Westminster, London SW1A 0AA.

Thomson, Professor Richard Ian, MA, DipHistArt (Oxon), MA, PhD, FRSE. Research Professor in the History of Art, University of Edinburgh (Watson Gordon Professor of Fine Art, 1996-2018); Director, Visual Arts Research Institute, Edinburgh, 1999-2004; Trustee, National Galleries of Scotland, 2002-2010; b. 1.3.53, Tenterden; m., Belinda Jane Greaves; 2 s. Educ. Dragon School, Oxford;

Shrewsbury School; St. Catherine's College, Oxford; Courtauld Institute of Art, London University. Lecturer/Senior Lecturer/Reader, Manchester University, 1977-96; Curator or Co-Curator of several exhibitions: The Private Degas, 1987, Camille Pissarro: Impressionist Landscape and Rural Labour, 1990, Monet to Matisse, 1994; Seurat and the Bathers, 1997; Theo van Gogh, 1999; Monet: the Seine and the Sea 1878-1883, 2003; Toulouse-Lautrec and Montmartre, 2005; Degas, Sickert, Toulouse-Lautrec, 2005; Monet, 1840-1926, 2010. Publications: Toulouse-Lautrec, 1977; Seurat, 1985; Degas: The Nudes, 1988; Edgar Degas: Waiting, 1995; Framing France (Editor), 1998; Soil and Stone (Co-Editor), 2003; The Troubled Republic. Visual Culture and Social Debate in France, 1889-1900, 2004. Van Gogh Visiting Fellow, University of Amsterdam (2007); Slade Professor of Fine Art, University of Oxford (2009); Conseil Scientifique, Institut National d'Histoire de l'Art, since 2008; Conseil Scientifique, Musée d'Orsay, since 2010. Recreations: jazz; gardening. Address: (b.) History of Art, Room 0.48, Higgitt Gallery, Hunter Building, University of Edinburgh EH3 9HQ; T.-0131-650 4124.

Thomson, Rosemarie, BA, PG. Head of Organisation Design and Development, Scotrail Limited, since 2020. Educ. Glasgow Caledonian University. Career history: Diaego: various HR specialist and Managerial roles, 1999-2009, OD Specialist, Glasgow, 2009-2011, HR Business Partner, Leven, 2011-12, Supply Chain OD & OE Manager, 2012-14, Supply Chain Business Transformation Manager, Glasgow, 2014-18, Change Manager, Edinburgh, 2018-2020. Address: Scotrail Railways Ltd, 50 Waterloo Street, Glasgow G2 6HQ; T.-0141 335 5050.

Thomson, Ross, MA (Hons). MP (Scottish Conservative), Aberdeen South, 2017-19; MSP (Scottish Conservative), North East Scotland region, 2016-17; b. 21.9.87, Aberdeen. Educ. University of Aberdeen. Career history: Gordon constituency candidate, United Kingdom general election, 2010; elected to Aberdeen City Council at the 2012 Aberdeen City Council election; contested the Aberdeen Donside by-election in 2013.

Thomson, S. Kenneth, BEM, MHSM, DipHSM. Chief Executive, Yorkhill NHS Trust, 1997-2000; Conductor, Glasgow Gaelic Musical Association, since 1983; Board Member, National Waiting Times Special Health Board, 2003-09; Lay Member, Employment Tribunals; Lay Member, General Pharmaceutical Council Investigating Committee, 2007-2016; Chair, Scottish Advisory Committee on Distinction Awards, since 2010; b. 20.8.49, Campbeltown; m., Valerie Ferguson (deceased 2009); 1 s.; 1 d. Educ. Keil School, Dumbarton. Administrative trainee, Scottish Health Service; various administrative and management posts, Glasgow and West of Scotland; Chief Executive, Law Hospital NHS Trust, 1997-2000. National Mod Gold Medallist, 1979. Publication: Slighe an Airgid - 20 Songs for Gaelic Choirs. Inducted into Traditional Music Hall of Fame, 2013; Lay Member, Scottish Social Services Council Committees. Awarded a BEM in the Queen's Birthday Awards for services to Gaelic choral music, 2021. Recreations: opera; Gaelic language and culture; theatre; The Archers; swimming; composing and arranging music. Address: (h.) 14 Cleveden Drive, Glasgow G12 0SE; T.-0141-334 7773.

Thorburn, David John, LLB, FCIBS. Former Chief Executive, Clydesdale Bank PLC (2011-2015); b. 9.1.58, Glasgow; m., Maureen. Educ. Hamilton Academy; Glasgow University. Harvard Business School. Clydesdale Bank PLC, 1978-83; TSB Group PLC, 1984-93; Clydesdale Bank PLC, 1993-2015.

Thornburrow, Alan, FRSA. Chief Executive, Scottish Mindroom Centre, since 2022. Educ. Linlithgow Academy; Chartered Insurance Institute; Common Purpose; Core Solutions; Society of NLP. Career history: Sales Consultant, Scottish Widows, 1996-2000; Business Development Manager, Franklin Templeton Investments, 2000-02; Product Manager, Brandes Investment Partners, 2002-03; Head of Product Development & Research, IA Clarington, 2003-05; Global Relocation and Transition, Franklin Templeton Investments, 2005-06; Vice Chairman (Scotland), Career Ready, 2009-2014; Chairman, Edinburgh & Lothians, Institute of Directors, 2014-16; Chief Executive, Scottish Investment Operations, 2006-2017; Scotland Director, Business in the Community, 2017-2022. Honorary Professor, Glasgow School for Business and Society, Glasgow Caledonian University, since 2015; Member of The Board of Advisors, National Suicide Prevention Leadership Group, since 2019. Address: Salvesen Mindroom Centre, Suite 4/3, Great Michael House, 14 Links Place, Edinburgh EH6 7EZ; T.-0131 370 6731.

Thornton, Philip John Roger, WS, MA, DipALP, NP. Consultant, Russel and Aitken, Solicitors, since 2012; b. 28.7.47, Prestbury; m., Alexandra Janet Taylor; 2 d. Educ. Manchester Grammar School; Edinburgh University. Solicitor, Russel and Aitken, WS, 1973-75; Partner, Russel and Aitken, 1975-2012. Tutor, Edinburgh University; Examiner, Society of Messengers at Arms and Sheriff Officers; Secretary, Edinburgh Family Planning Trust. Recreations: family holidays; art history; cinema; tennis. Address: (b.) 27 Rutland Square, Edinburgh EH1 2BU; T.-0131 228 5500.

Thurso, 3rd Viscount Rt. Hon. Sir (John Archibald Sinclair), BT, PC. HM Lord Lieutenant for Caithness, since 2017; MP (Liberal Democrat), Caithness, Sutherland and Easter Ross, 2001-2015; Spokesman for Business, Innovation and Skills, 2009-2010; b. 10.9.53; m.; 2 s.; 1 d. Educ. Eton. Chairman, Scrabster Harbour, 1997-2001; Non-Executive Director: Lochdhu Hotels, since 1975 (Chairman, since 1995), Sinclair Family Trust, since 1976 (Chairman, since 1995), Thurso Fisheries, since 1979 (Chairman, since 1995); Ulbster Holdings, since 1994 (Chairman, since 1994), Mossimans Ltd., 1998-2002; President, Academy of Food and Wine Service, since 1998; Chair, International Wine and Spirit Competition Ltd, since 1999; Member, Parliamentary Banking Standards Commission, 2012-2013; Chair, VisitScotland, since 2016; Director, Independent Parliamentary Standards Authority, 2015-16. Address: Thurso East Mains, Thurso.

Tiefenbrun, Ivor Sigmund, MBE. Founder, Linn Products Ltd., Glasgow (retired); Director, IST Marine Ltd; b. 18.3.46, Glasgow; m., Evelyn Stella Balarksy; 2 s.; 1 d. Educ. Strathbungo Senior Secondary School; Strathclyde University (Sixties dropout). Worked overseas, 1971-73; founded Linn Products, 1973. Chairman, Federation of British Audio, 1983-87; Council Member, Design Council, 1995-98; Founder Member, Entrepreneurial Exchange; Honorary Fellow, Glasgow School of Art, since 1999; Scottish Entrepreneur of the Year, 2001; established registered charity Cure Crohn's Colitis to raise funds for patient centric research into Inflammatory Bowel Disease, 2006. Appointed Visiting Professor at Strathclyde University by the Department of Design, Manufacture and Engineering Management, 2004; inducted to Entrepreneurial Exchange Hall of Fame, 2011; appointed Member of the William Robertson Society, The University of Edinburgh, 2011; appointed Founder Member, Strathclyde University's Academy of Distinguished Entrepreneurs, 2011. Recreations: thinking; music; reading; sailing.

Tierney, Professor Stephen (Joseph Anthony), FRSE, LLM (Toronto), LLM (Liverpool), LLB Hons (Glas), DipLP (Edin). Professor of Constitutional Theory, University of Edinburgh, since 2008; Vice Dean, Edinburgh Law School, 2017-2020; Visiting Professor and Distinguished Fellow, Notre Dame Law School, USA, since 2020; British Academy Senior Research Fellow, 2008-09; ESRC Senior Research Fellow, 2013-15; b. 11.03.67, Glasgow; m., Ailsa Barbara Henderson; 3 s. Educ. Our Lady of Lourdes Primary, East Kilbride; St. Bride's Secondary, East Kilbride; Universities of Glasgow, Liverpool, Toronto and Edinburgh. Lecturer in Law: University of Hull, 1995-97, Brunel University, 1997-99; University of Edinburgh: Lecturer in Law, 1999-2005, Reader in Law, 2005-08. Publications (books): The United Kingdom and the Federal Idea (Co-Author), 2018; Nationalism and Globalisation, 2015; Constitutional Referendums: The Theory and Practice of Republican Deliberation, 2012; Europe's Constitutional Mosaic (Co-Author), 2011; Public Law and Politics: The Scope and Limits of Constitutionalism (Co-Author), 2008; Multiculturalism and the Canadian Constitution, 2007; Accommodating Cultural Diversity: Contemporary Issues in Theory and Practice, 2007; Towards an International Legal Community? The Sovereignty of States and the Sovereignty of International Law (Co-Author), 2006; Constitutional Law and National Pluralism, 2004; Accommodating National Identity: New Approaches in International and Domestic Law, 2000. Legal Adviser to the House of Lords Constitution Committee, since 2015; Judicial Appointments Board for Scotland, since 2015; Executive Committee, UK Constitutional Law Association, since 2015; Co-Editor, UK Constitutional Law blog, 2015-2020; Constitutional Adviser to the Scottish Parliament Referendum Bill Committee, 2013-14; Constitutional Adviser to the Scottish Parliament Scotland Bill Committee, 2011; Editorial Board, European Public Law. Recreations: cycling; hill-walking; family recreation. Address: School of Law, University of Edinburgh, Old College, South Bridge, Edinburgh EH8 9YL; T.-0131 650 2070.
E-mail: s.tierney@ed.ac.uk

Tilley, Catrin, BSc (Econ). Associate Partner, More Partnership Fundraising Consultants, since 2012; b. 29.06.55, St. Neots; m., Prof. Rick Maizels; 2 s.; 1 d. Educ. Hinchingbrooke School, Huntingdon; University College London. Head, Fundraising, Membership, Publications, CND London, 1982-88; Assistant Director (Admin), Greenpeace UK, London, 1988-91; Deputy Director, Comic Relief, London, 1992-95; Director of Development and Alumni, University of Edinburgh, 1996-2003. Trustee, UK Institute of Fundraising, 2005-08; Executive Committee, Scottish Institute of Fundraising, 2005-08; Director of External Affairs, National Galleries of Scotland, 2003-2012. Address: (b.) More Partnership, 31 Exchange Street, Dundee DD1 3DJ; T.-0797 101 9226.
E-mail: ctilley@morepartnership.com

Timms, Peter, CBE. Chairman, Flexible Technology Ltd., since 1981; former Chairman: David MacBrayne Limited, Schroder UK Mid Fund Plc (2000-2014); Non Executive Director, Mount Stuart Trust. Address: (b.) Flexible Technology Ltd, Townhead, Rothesay, Isle of Bute PA20 9JH.

Tindall, Benjamin Hemsley, DipSocSci, FRIAS, RIBA, FSA (Scot). Principal, Benjamin Tindall Architects, since 1982; b. 21.12.53, Scotland; m., Jill Watson. Educ. University of Edinburgh; University of Pennsylvania. Notable architectural commissions in Edinburgh include, The Queen's Gallery Palace of Holyroodhouse, The Hub, Edinburgh's Festival Centre, Fringe Shop and Offices, Castle Rock Hostel, The Museum of Edinburgh, Bonnington House and Jupiter Artland. Elsewhere, housing on Barra, Melgund Castle, Forfar, An Camas Mòr, Rothiemurchus, Old Milton, Kingussie & Invercauld Estate, Braemar and projects on Orkney, Jersey, etc (see www.benjamintindallarchitects.co.uk). Former Trustee for National Trust for Scotland; Vice Chairman, Tim Stead Trust. Recreations: owner and harbourmaster, Cove, Berwickshire. Address: 17 Victoria Terrace, Edinburgh EH1 2JL; T.-0131 220 3366.

Tobin, Professor Alyson Kim, BSc (Hons), PhD, FRSB. Non Executive Director, James Hutton Institute, Scotland, since 2017; Honorary Professor, University of St Andrews, since 2013; Vice Principal for Learning & Teaching, Edinburgh Napier University, 2018-2021; Deputy Vice Chancellor, York St John University, 2013-2017; Dean of The Faculty of Science, University of St Andrews, 2007-2011, Acting Vice-Principal (Learning and Teaching), 2011, Professor in Biology, 2008-2013; b. 7.9.56, Coventry; m., Tim Tobin; 2 s. Educ. John Cleveland College, Hinckley, Leics; University of Newcastle upon Tyne. Royal Society Alfred Spinks Research Fellow, 1982-87; Royal Society University Research Fellow, 1987-97; Reader in Plant Sciences, University of St Andrews, 1997-2008. Fellow of the Royal Society of Biology, 2010; Council Member, Society of Biology (Scotland Branch), 2011-2013; Member, International Advisory Board Indus Foundation Indo-American Education Summit, 2013; Executive Committee, UK Deans of Science; Director, Dundee Science Centre Board, since 2010; Plant and Microbial Sciences Committee, Biotechnology and Biological Sciences Research Council, 2002-06; Executive Committee of The Federation of The European Societies of Plant Biology, 2007-09; Member (Scotland Representative), Biosciences Federation Education Committee, 2008-10; Spencer Industrial Arts Trust Scholar, 1978; Plant Science Scotland, Board Member, since 2005; Convener, Plant Metabolism Group, Society for Experimental Biology, 1995-2000; Honorary Research Fellow, Scottish Crops Research Institute, since 2005; Director, St Andrews Botanic Garden Education Trust, 2005-07. Publications: 'Plant Biochemistry' (Co-Author), 2008 and academic journal publications in plant physiology and biochemistry. Recreations: piano; hill walking. Address: (b.) University of St Andrews, School of Biology, Biomolecular Sciences Building, St Andrews, Fife KY16 9ST; T.-07979 787772; e-mail: a.tobin@st-andrews.ac.uk

Todd, Alison, BSc (Hons), DipAppSocSci, HND. Self-Employed Consultant, since 2018; Chief Executive, Children 1st, 2014-18, Director of Children and Family Services and External Affairs, 2009-2014; b. 21.3.66, Forfar. Educ. Brechin High School; Robert Gordon University; Open University. Various residential care positions, 1993-95; State Support Offficer, Ministry of Defence, 1995-98; Community Development Officer, Ormiston Housing Cooperative, 1998-2001; Centre Manager, Rathbone Charity, 2001; Services Manager, ChildLine Scotland and NorthWest, 2001-06; Assistant Director, NSPCC North of England, 2006-07; North of England Business Workstream Leader (Seconded), NSPCC, 2007-09. Voluntary Experience - Girl Guides Association Rainbow Leader, 1990-93; Homestart Volunteer, 1995-98; Children's Panel Member, 2000-01; Director, Scottish Alliance of Children's Rights, Angus Summer Playscheme. Recreations: reading; walking; overseas holidays.

Todd, Maree. MSP (SNP), Caithness, Sutherland and Ross, since 2021; Highlands and Islands region, 2016-2021; Minister for Public Health, Women's Health and Sport, since 2021; Minister for Children and Young People, 2017-2021. Educ. Ullapool primary school and high school; Robert Gordon University. Worked as a pharmacist for NHS Highland. Address: Scottish Parliament, Edinburgh EH99 1SP.

Toft, Anthony Douglas, CBE, LVO, BSc, MD, FRCPE, FRCPGlas, FRCPLond, FRCPI, FACP(Hon), FRACP(Hon), FRCSE, FRCPC(Hon), FRCGP(Hon), FFPM (Hon), FFAEM (Hon), FCPS Pakistan (Hon), FCPS Bangladesh (Hon), FAM Singapore (Hon), MAM Malaysia (Hon). Consultant Physician, Royal Infirmary, Edinburgh, 1978-2009; Physician to the Queen in Scotland, 1996-2009; Chief Medical Officer, Scottish Equitable Life Assurance (now Aegon UK), 1987-2015; b. 29.10.44, Perth; m., Maureen Darling; 1 s.; 1 d. Educ. Perth Academy; Edinburgh University. President, British Thyroid Association, 1996-99; Chairman, Professional and Linguistic Assessment Board, 1999-2006; President, Royal College of Physicians of Edinburgh, 1991-94; Chairman, Collegiate Members' Committee, Royal College of Physicians of Edinburgh, 1978; Vice-President, Royal College of Physicians, 1989-91; Chairman, Scottish Royal Colleges, 1992-94; Chairman, Joint Committee of Higher Medical Training, 1993-96; Member, Health Appointments Advisory Committee, 1994-2000. Recreations: gardening; collecting Scottish Art. Address: (h.) 41 Hermitage Gardens, Edinburgh EH10 6AZ; T.-0131-447 2221; e-mail: toft41@hotmail.com

Toley, Richard, BA (Hons), MPhil, PGCE. Headmaster, Lathallan School, Johnshaven, since 2009; b. 28.6.71, Kingston-Upon-Thames; m., Indrani; 1 s.; 1 d. Educ. Chatesmore; St David's University College, Lampeter; University of St Andrews; University of Strathclyde. Teacher of History/Classics/Rugby: Merchant Taylors School, Liverpool, 1996-99, Careers Co-ordinator, High School of Dundee, 1999-2004, Teacher of History, Director of Co-Curriculum, 2004-06; Head of Senior School, Lathallan School, 2006-09 (led development of only new Senior Independent School in country); while Headmaster, introduced 'Civilianship Programme from age 5-18 developing 'Confidence Without Arrogance'. Advanced Higher History Setter, 2007-09; made Fellow of Royal Society of Arts, 2012; Board member, SCIS (Scottish Council of Independent Schools), Chairman, Finance and General Purposes Committee, 2014. Recreations: Scottish Provincial Silver, 'Warhammer'; cricket. Address: Brotherton Castle, Johnshaven, Angus DD10 0HN; T.-01561 362220; e-mail: richardtoley@lathallan.org.uk

Tomkins, Professor Adam, LLB (UEA), LLM (Lond), FRSE. John Miller Professor of Public Law, University of Glasgow, since 2003; MSP (Scottish Conservative), Glasgow, 2016-2021; former Shadow Cabinet Secretary for Communities, Social Security, the Constitution and Equalities; former Legal Adviser to the House of Lords Select Committee on the Constitution (2009-2015); Adviser to Strathclyde Commission (2013-14); Member, Smith Commission on Scottish Devolution (2014); b. 28.06.69, Newbury. Educ. Gillingham School, Dorset; University of East Anglia; London School of Economics. Career History: Lecturer in Law, King's College London; Fellow and Tutor in Law, St. Catherine's College, Oxford. Publications: Author of: "The Constitution After Scott", 1998; "Public Law", 2003; "Our Republican Constitution", 2005; "European Union Law", 2006; "British Government and The Constitution", 2011. Address: University of Glasgow, R406 Level 4, Law, 6 The Square, Glasgow G12 8QQ; T.-0141 330 4180.
E-mail: Adam.Tomkins@glasgow.ac.uk

Tomlinson, Professor Alan, MSc, PhD, DSc, FCOptom, FAAO. Professor of Vision Science, Glasgow Caledonian University, since 1992; b. 18.3.44, Bolton; partner, Professor Daphne McCulloch; 1 s. Educ. Lampton Grammar School, North London; Bradford University; Manchester University Institute of Science and Technology. Fellowship, British Optical Association, 1966; Registration, General Optical Council, 1966; Lecturer, Opthalmic Optics: Bradford University, 1967-68; UMIST, 1968-77; Director, Clinical Research, Wesley Jesson Inc, Chicago, USA, 1977-79 and 1983-86; Professor of Optometry: Indiana University, 1980-83, Southern California College of Optometry, 1986-91; Council Member, General Optical Council, 1999-2009; Member, British Universities Committee of Optometry, 1992-2009, Chair, 1997-99; Council Member, College of Optometry (UK), 1994-98; Member, Advisory Committee, American Academy of Optometry, 1993-98. Publications: 140 papers in scientific journals; Complications of Contact Lens Wear, 1992. Recreations: tennis; running; theatre; music. Address: (b.) Vision Science, Department of Life Sciences, Glasgow Caledonian University, City Campus, Glasgow G4 0BA; T.-0141 331 3380.

Tomlinson, Anna, MTheol (Hons) (St Andrews), PGCE, SQH. Head of St Margaret's School for Girls, Aberdeen, since 2014; b. 1.12.74, Preston. Educ. St Aidan's C of E High School; University of St Andrews; Lancaster University; Edinburgh University. Head of Religion and Philosophy, St George's School for Girls, Edinburgh, 1999-2006, Deputy Head, 2006-2014. Recreations: cooking; singing; walking; travel. Address: St Margaret's School for Girls, 17 Albyn Place, Aberdeen AB10 1RU; T.-01224 584466.
E-mail: info@st-margaret.aberdeen.sch.uk

Tomlinson, John, PhD. Chair, NHS Grampian, since 2019. Educ. Universities of Manchester and Glasgow; Dundee College of Technology (now Abertay University); University of Aberdeen. Career history: Aberdeen City Council: Corporate Director of Neighbourhood Services, 2002-08, Interim General Manager, Rushmore Reviews, Aberdeen, 2012; Director, Footprints Connect, Aberdeen, 2011-15; Grampian Regional Equality Council Ltd, Aberdeen: Interim Chief Executive Officer, 2014-15, Research and Policy (part-time), 2015-17; Interim Director of Development (part-time), Inspire PTL, Aberdeen, 2017-19; Director and Owner, Sursum Consulting, Aberdeen, since 2010. Address: NHS Grampian, Summerfield House, 2 Eday Road, Aberdeen AB15 6RE.

Topping, Professor Barry H.V., BSc, PhD, DSc (hc), CEng, CMath, CITP, MBCS, MICE, MIStructE, MIMechE, FIMA. Emeritus Professor, Heriot-Watt University, Edinburgh; Director, Computational Technology Solutions, Stirlingshire; Honorary Professor, University of Pecs, Hungary; b. 14.2.52, Manchester. Educ. Bedford Modern School; City University, London. Lecturer in Civil Engineering, Edinburgh University, 1978-88; Von-Humboldt Research Fellow, Stuttgart University, 1986-87; Senior Lecturer, Heriot-Watt University, 1988-89, Reader, 1989-90, Professor of Structural Engineering, 1990-95, Professor of Computational Mechanics, 1995-2006. Co-Editor, Computers and Structures; Co-Editor, Advances in Engineering Software; Senior Editor, Civil-Comp Conference Series. Address: (b.) Dun Eaglais, Station Brae, Kippen, Stirlingshire FK8 3DY.

Topping, Professor Keith James, BA, MA, PhD, CPsychol, FBPsS. Emeritus Professor, Educational and Social Research, University of Dundee; b. 1.10.47, Stockport; m., Chen; 3 s. Educ. Marple Hall Grammar School; Universities of Sussex, Nottingham and Sheffield. After substantial practice as an educational psychologist for social services, health and education, moved to Dundee in 1992 to establish a training course for eucational psychologists; went on to establish a professional doctorate and become a professor specializing in research on peer learning, parental involvement and behaviour problems. Over 400 publications, including 28 books. Recreation: mountaineering. Address: Nethergate, Dundee DD1 4HN; e-mail: k.j.topping@dundee.ac.uk

Torphichen, 15th Lord (James Andrew Douglas Sandilands); b. 27.8.46; m.; 4 d. Address: Calder House, Mid Calder, West Lothian.

Torrance, David. MSP (SNP), Kirkcaldy, since 2011; b. 13.3.61, Kirkcaldy. Educ. Balwearie High School; Adam Smith College. Employed by British Gas and other companies before going into politics full-time in 2007, working for Chris Harvie MSP. Fife councillor. Assistant District Commissioner, Kirkcaldy Scouts. Address: (b.) Scottish Parliament, Edinburgh EH99 1SP.

Torrance, Very Rev. Professor Iain Richard, KCVO, Kt, TD, MA, BD, DPhil, Hon DD, Hon DTheol, Hon LHD, FRSE, Knight Commander of the Royal Victorian Order, 2019, Knight Bachelor, 2018. Pro-Chancellor, University of Aberdeen, since 2013; Hon Professor of Early Christian Doctrine and Ethics, University of Edinburgh, since 2013; formerly Dean of the Chapel Royal in Scotland, 2013-19; formerly Dean of the Order of the Thistle, 2014-19; formerly a Chaplain-in-Ordinary to HM The Queen in Scotland, 2001-19; an Extra Chaplain to The Queen, since 2019; President Emeritus and Professor of Patristics Emeritus, Princeton Theological Seminary, since 2013; Professor in Patristics and Christian Ethics (Emeritus), University of Aberdeen, since 2004; Master of Christ's College, Aberdeen, 2001-04; Moderator, General Assembly, Church of Scotland, 2003-04; Co-Editor, Scottish Journal of Theology, 1982-2015; b. 13.1.49, Aberdeen; m., Morag Ann MacHugh; 1 s.; 1 d. Educ. Edinburgh Academy; Monkton Combe School, Bath; Edinburgh University; St. Andrews University; Oriel College, Oxford University. Minister, Northmavine, Shetland, 1982-85; Lecturer in New Testament and Christian Ethics, Queen's College, Birmingham, 1985-89; Lecturer in New Testament and Patristics, Birmingham University, 1989-93; Aberdeen University: Lecturer, 1993-97, Senior Lecturer in Divinity, 1997-99, Professor in Patristics and Christian Ethics (Personal Chair), 1999-2004, Head, Department of Divinity with Religious Studies, 2000-01, Dean, Faculty of Arts and Divinity, 2001-03; President and Professor of Patristics, Princeton Theological Seminary, 2004-12. Chaplain to the Moderator of the General Assembly, 1976; Member, International Dialogue between the Orthodox and the Reformed Churches, 1992-2012, co-chair, since 2005; Member, General Assembly's Panel on Doctrine, 1993-2002; Member, Ethics Committee, Grampian Health Board, 1996-2000; Hon. Secretary, Aberdeen A.U.T., 1995-98, Hon. President, 1998-99; Secretary, Society for the Study of Christian Ethics, 1995-98; Judge, Templeton (UK) Awards, 1994-99; Templeton Advisory Board, 2008-11; TA Chaplain, 1982-97; ACF Chaplain, 1996-2000; Member, Academie Internationale des Sciences Religieuses, since 1997; Convener, General Assembly's Committee on Chaplains to HM Forces, 1998-2002; Senate Assessor to Aberdeen University Court, 1999-2003; Member, Committee of Highland TAVRA, 1999-2004; Member, QAA's Benchmarking Panel for Degrees in Theology and Religious Studies, 1999-2000; Member of the C-1 Religious Leader Commission, since 2010; Select Preacher, University of Oxford, 2004, 2016, University of Aberdeen, 2009, 2013, University of Cambridge, 2016; Convener of General Assembly of Church of Scotland's Theological Forum, 2013-17; Author of 'The Torrance Report' on the Diocese of Aberdeen & Orkney, 2021; Trustee, University of Aberdeen Development Trust, since 2013; Trustee, Scotland's Churches Trust, since 2017; Assembly Trustee (Church of Scotland), 2019-20; Trustee, Lord Lyon Society, since 2021; Patron, Elphinstone Institute, since 2015; Pluscarden Abbey South Range Appeal, since 2016; Chair, Edinburgh Sir Walter Scott Club, since 2019; Free Burgess of the Burgh of Aberdeen, 2004; Friend for Life Award 2004, Equality Network, Scotland; Honorary Doctor of Divinity (St Andrews, 2005; Aberdeen, 2005; Edinburgh, 2012); Honorary Doctor of Theology (Debrecen, 2006); Honorary Doctor of Humane Letters (King Coll, TN, 2007); Corresponding Fellow, Royal Society of Edinburgh, 2007 (converted to FRSE on return to Scotland, 2013); Fellow, Society of Antiquaries of Scotland, since 1971; Honorary Distinguished Alumnus, Princeton Theological Seminary, 2012; OStJ, 2015; Great Shogun Award (Order of Scottish Samurai), 2016; Honorary Black Belt (National Karate Association), 2016. Publications: Christology after Chalcedon, 1988, 1998, Arabic translation, 2016; Human Genetics: a Christian perspective (Co-Author), 1995; Ethics and the Military Community, 1998; To Glorify God: Essays on Modern Reformed Liturgy (Co-Author), 1999; Bioethics for the New Millennium (Editor), 2000; Oxford Handbook of Systematic Theology (Co-Editor), 2007; Cambridge Dictionary of Christian Theology (Co-Editor), 2011; The Correspondence of Severus and Sergius, 2011. Recreations: historical Scottish culture (buildings, literature, art); novels of Sir Walter Scott. Address: (h.) 25 The Causeway, Duddingston Village, Edinburgh EH15 3QA; T.-0131 661 3092; e-mail: irt@ptsem.edu

Tosh, Murray, MA. MSP (Conservative), West of Scotland, 2003-07, South of Scotland, 1999-2003 (Deputy Presiding Officer, Scottish Parliament, 2001-07); b. 1.9.50, Ayr; m., Christine (deceased); 2 s.; 1 d. Educ. Kilmarnock Academy; Glasgow University; Jordanhill College of Education. Principal Teacher of History, Kilwinning Academy, 1977, Belmont Academy, Ayr, 1984; Councillor, Kyle and Carrick District Council, 1987-96 (Convener of Housing, 1992-96); Chairman, Central Ayrshire Conservative and Unionist Association, 1980-83, Ayr Conservative and Unionist Association, 1985-90. Recreations: hill-walking; reading; watching football and cricket; family history; visiting mediaeval castles; foreign holidays.

Toth, Emeritus Professor Akos George, Dr. Jur., PhD. Professor of Law, Strathclyde University, 1984-2001; Jean Monnet Chair of European Law, 1991-2001; b. 9.2.36, Mezotur, Hungary. Educ. Budapest University; Szeged University; Exeter University. Strathclyde University: Lecturer in Law, 1971-76, Senior Lecturer, 1976-82, Reader, 1982-84; British Academy Research Readership, 1993-95. Publications: Legal Protection of Individuals in the European Communities, 1978; The Oxford Encyclopaedia of European Community Law: Vol. I: 1990, Vol. II: 2005, Vol. III: 2008. Recreations: travel; music; opera; theatre; swimming; walking. Address: (b.) Strathclyde University, Law School, Level 3, Lord Hope Building, 141 St. James Road, Glasgow G4 0LT; T.-0141 548 3738; e-mail: toth@strath.ac.uk

Townley, Professor Barbara, BA, MSc, PhD. Professor Emeritus of Management, Leverhulme Emeritus Professor Fellow, St Andrews University; b. 9.10.54, Manchester. Educ. Worsley Wardley Grammar School; Lancaster University; London School of Economics. Lecturer: Lancaster University, 1983-85, University of Warwick Business School, 1985-90; Professor, Faculty of Business, University of Alberta, Canada, 1990-2000; Chair of Management and Organization, Edinburgh University,

2000-05. Publications: author of four books and many articles on management, organisation, performance measurement. Currently researching the creative industries. Recreation: travel. Address: (b.) Management School, Gateway, North Haugh, University of St Andrews, St Andrews, Fife KY16 9RJ; T.-01334 462808.

Trainor, Professor Sir Richard Hughes, KBE (2010), BA, MA, DPhil, FRHistS, FAcSS, FRSA, FKC. Rector, Exeter College, Oxford, since 2014; Pro Vice Chancellor, University of Oxford, since 2016; Principal and Professor of Social History, King's College London, 2004-2014, Professor Emeritus, since 2014; b. 31.12.48, New Jersey; m., Dr. Marguerite Wright Dupree; 1 s.; 1 d. Educ. Calvert Hall High School, Maryland; Brown University; Princeton University; Merton and Nuffield Colleges, Oxford University. Junior Research Fellow, Wolfson College, Oxford, 1977-79; Lecturer, Balliol College, Oxford, 1978-79; Glasgow University: Lecturer in Economic History, 1979-89, Senior Lecturer in Economic and Social History, 1989-95, Director, Design and Implementation of Software in History Project, 1985-89, Professor of Social History, 1995-2000, Co-Director, Computers in Teaching Initiative Centre for History, 1989-2000, Dean of Social Sciences, 1992-96, Vice-Principal, 1996-2000, Senior Vice-Principal, 1999-2000; Vice-Chancellor and Professor of Social History, Greenwich University, 2000-04. Honorary Fellow, Trinity College of Music, since 2003; Honorary Fellow, Merton College, Oxford, since 2004; Honorary Fellow, Institute of Historical Research, since 2009; Rhodes Scholar; Chair, Advisory Council, Institute of Historical Research, 2004-09; Honorary Secretary, Economic History Society, 1998-2004 and President, 2013-16; President, Universities UK, 2007-09; Convener, Steering Group, Universities UK/DfES Review of Student Services, 2002; Member, US/UK Fulbright Commission, 2003-09 and Patron, since 2010; Council Member, Arts and Humanities Research Council, 2006-2011; Member, University of London Board of Trustees, 2009-2013; Joint Editor, Scottish Economic and Social History, 1989-94; Governor, St Paul's School, 2012-14; Governor, Royal Academy of Music, since 2013, Honorary Fellow, since 2017; Chair, Conference of Colleges, University of Oxford, 2017-19; Chair, Scholarship Committee, Jardine Foundation, since 2018; Honorary Degrees: University of Kent, 2009 (Doctor of Civil Law); Rosalind Franklin University of Medicine and Science, 2012 (Doctor of Humane Letters); University of Glasgow, 2014 (Doctor of the University); Member of Council, University of Oxford, 2015-19; Trustee, Museum of London, 2014-2021, Chair, Academic Panel, since 2016; Member, Council of Reference, Westminster Abbey Institute, since 2016. Publications: Black Country Elites: the exercise of authority in an industrialised area 1830-1900, 1993; University, City and State: the University of Glasgow since 1870 (Joint Author), 2000. Recreations: parenting; observing politics; tennis. Address: (h.) 45 Mitre Road, Glasgow G14 9LE; T.-01865 279605.

Trees, Professor the Lord Alexander (Sandy). Chairman, Moredun Research Institute, 2011-2020. Educ. Edinburgh University; Royal (Dick) School of Veterinary Studies (BVM&S 1969, PhD 1976). Has made an enormous contribution to research into livestock health and is internationally recognised for his knowledge of veterinary parasitology; appointed Lecturer in Veterinary Parasitology, University of Liverpool in 1980, then Senior Lecturer and, in 1994, Professor of Veterinary Parasitology; Dean of the University of Liverpool Faculty of Veterinary Science, 2001-08; Emeritus Professor, since 2011; President, Association of Veterinary Teachers and Research Workers, 1996-97; President, Royal College of Veterinary Surgeons, 2009; formerly Council member of the Royal Society of Tropical Medicine and Hygiene; a founding Diplomate of the European Veterinary Parasitology College; Executive Board member, World Association for Veterinary Parasitology. Chief Veterinary Adviser, Veterinary Record. Appointed Crossbench Peer in House of Lords, 2012; Member, EU Select Committee, 2015-2017 and EU Subcommittee for Energy and Environment, 2014-2017. FRCVS; FMedSci; Hon FRSE (2016). Over 150 scientific papers and numerous presentations at regional, national and international conferences. Address: House of Lords, London SW1 0PW.

Trew, Professor Arthur Stewart, BSc, PhD, FRSE, FRSA. Professor of Computational Science, University of Edinburgh, since 2006, Assistant Principal for Computational Science; b. Belfast, Northern Ireland; m., Lesley Margaret Trew (nee Smart); 1 s.; 1 d. Educ. Royal Belfast Academical Institution; University of Edinburgh. Computing Officer, University of Edinburgh, 1983-85; Lecturer, Department of Clinical Sciences, Glasgow, 1985-86; Research Fellow, Department of Physics, Edinburgh, 1986-90, Programme Manager, EPCC, 1990-94, Director, EPCC, 1994-2010, Deputy Director, Bayes Institute and Chairman, EPCC. Director, UoE HPCx Ltd. Recreations: running; cycling; hill walking. Address: (b.) School of Physics and Astronomy, University of Edinburgh, James Clerk Maxwell Building, Peter Guthrie Tait Road, King's Buildings, Edinburgh EH9 3JZ; T.-0131 650 5025; e-mail: a.s.trew@ed.ac.uk

Trewavas, Professor Anthony James, BSc, PhD, FRS, FRSE, FRSA, FWIF, Academia Europea. Professor, Institute of Plant Molecular Science, Edinburgh University, since 1990; b. 17.6.39, London; m., Valerie; 1 s.; 2 d. Educ. Roan Grammar School; University College, London. Lecturer/Reader, Edinburgh University; Visiting Professor, Universities of Michigan State, Calgary, California (Davis), Bonn, Illinois, North Carolina, National University of Mexico; University of Milan. Publications: 260 scientific papers; three books. Recreations: music (particularly choral); reading. Address: (h.) Old Schoolhouse, Croft Street, Penicuik EH26 9DH; e-mail: Trewavas@ed.ac.uk

Trotter, Alexander Richard, CVO (2013), OStJ, JP, FRSA. Lord Lieutenant of Berwickshire, 2000-2014; Chairman, Thirlestane Castle Trust, 1996-2007; b. 20.2.39, London; m., Julia Henrietta Greenwell; 3 s. Educ. Eton College; City of London Technical College. Royal Scots Greys, 1958-68; Member, Berwickshire County Council, 1969-75 (Chairman, Roads Committee, 1974-75); Manager, Charterhall Estate and Farm, since 1969; Chairman, Meadowhead Ltd. (formerly Mortonhall Park Ltd.), since 1974; Director, Timber Growers' GB Ltd., 1977-82; Vice Chairman, Border Grain Ltd., 1989-2003; Council Member, Scottish Landowners' Federation, 1975-2004 (President, 1996-2001, Chairman, Land Use Committee, 1975-78, Convener, 1982-85); Member, Department of Agriculture Working Party on the Agricultural Holding (Scotland) Legislation, 1981-82; Member, Nature Conservancy Council, and Chairman, Scottish Committee, 1985-90; Member, UK Committee for Euro Year of the Environment, 1986-88; Member, Scottish Tourist Board Graded Holiday Parks Overseeing Committee, 1993-2013; Ensign, Queen's Bodyguard for Scotland (Royal Company of Archers). Recreations: skiing; golf; shooting. Address: Whinkerstones Farm, Duns, Berwickshire TD11 3RE; T.-01890 840210. E-mail: alex@charterhall.net

Trotter, Christopher H. Food Writer/Food Consultant; b. 21.09.57, Aberdeen; m., Caroline; 2 s. Educ. Marlborough College; Oxford Polytechnic. Career: Manager, Chef, Portsonachan Hotel; Founder and Proprietor, "Scotland's Larder", Scottish Food Shop and Demonstration Facility; Founder, Momentum Food

Consultancy; Author. Commitee member, Pioneer Health Foundation; former member, Board of SFAC. Committee member of the Guild of Food writers. Publications: The Scottish Kitchen; Scottish Cooking; The Whole Hog; The Whole Cow; Cauliflower, 2017; Tomato, 2018; Broccoli, 2019; Coasts and Waters. The British seafood cook book, 2021. Founder of Christopher Trotter publishing; wrote and published Beetroot, Courgette, Kale and Carrot. Recreations: squash; tennis; food and drink; walking; cycling. Address: Buckthorns House, Upper Largo, Leven KY8 6EA; T.-01333 360 219; e-mail: ct@christophertrotter.co.uk

Troughton, Jamie Michael, DipArch, MA (Cantab), RIBA. Director, Ardchattan Hydro Ltd, since 2009; b. 8.11.50, Hambleden; m., Sarah Campbell-Preston; 1 s.; 2 d. Educ. Trinity College Cambridge. Qualified Architect, RIBA, 1977; Foster Associates, 1975-78; Richard Rogers and Partners, 1978-82; Founding Partner, Troughton McAslan Architects, 1983; Chairman, John McAslan and Partners, 1996-98; Award winning buildings for British Rail; London Underground; Apple Computers; Yapi Kredi Banksi, Istanbul; Canary Wharf FC3, London. Trustee, National Musuems of Scotland, 2011-19. Address: Atholl Estates Office, Blair Atholl, Pitlochry PH18 5TH; T.-01796 481355.

Truman, Donald Ernest Samuel, BA, PhD, FRSB. Higher Education Consultant; b. 23.10.36, Leicester; m., Kathleen Ramsay; 1 s.; 1 d. Educ. Wyggeston School, Leicester; Clare College, Cambridge. NATO Research Fellow, Wenner-Grenn Institute, Stockholm, 1962-63; MRC Epigenetics Research Group, Edinburgh, 1963-72; Lecturer, Department of Genetics, Edinburgh University, 1972-78; Senior Lecturer, 1978-89, Head of Department, 1984-89, Director of Biology Teaching Unit, 1985-89; Vice-Dean and Vice-Provost, Faculty of Science and Engineering, 1989-98; Assistant Principal, Edinburgh University, 1998-2002; Aneurin Bevan Memorial Fellow, Government of India, 1978; Chairman, Edinburgh Centre for Rural Research, 1993-2002; Member, Council, Scottish Agricultural College, 1995-2002; Director, Edinburgh Technopole Company Ltd., 1996-2002; Member, Board of Directors, Edin. Lifelong Learning Partnership, 1999-2002. Publications: The Biochemistry of Cytodifferentiation, 1974; Differentiation in Vitro (Joint Editor), 1982; Stability and Switching in Cellular Differentiation, 1982; Coordinated Regulation of Gene Expression, 1986. Recreations: gardening; books; birds. Address: (h.) 36 Ladysmith Road, Edinburgh EH9 3EU.

Truscott, Ian D., QC, LLB (Hons), LLM, PhD. Advocate; Visiting Professor of Law, Strathclyde University, 1998-2010; Fee-Paid Employment Judge, Employment Tribunal (England and Wales), since 2002; b. 7.11.49, Perth; m., Julia; 4 s. Educ. Perth Academy; Edinburgh University; Leeds University; Strathclyde University. Solicitor, 1973-87, and 2013-2017; Advocate, 1988-2013, and 2017-2019; Barrister, 1995-2013; QC, since 1997.

Tully, Marie Clare. Chief Executive, Columba 1400, since 2016. Educ. Loretto School; University of Aberdeen. Career history: Sales Account Manager, Antrim, 2004-05; Property Assistant, Menzies Dougal, 2005; Property Manager, Murray Beith Murray, 2005-07; Fundraising and Marketing Manager, Columba 1400, 2007-2009; Manager, Events and Online Communications, Social Ventures Australia, 2009-2011; Head of Development, Columba 1400, 2011-16. Address: Columba 1400, Staffin, Isle of Skye IV51 9JY; T.-01478 61400.

Tumilty, Mike, BA Hons (Econ). Global Chief Operating Officer, abrdn (formerly Standard Life Aberdeen), since 2019; b. 12.4.71, Hartlepool; m., Anne; 2 c. Educ. Heriot-Watt University. Career history: joined Standard Life as a graduate trainee in 1994; Standard Life Investments Ltd: former Board Member, Head, Mutual Funds Operations, 1998-2001, Head, Change Management, 2001-05, Director of Operations (appointed in 2010); Board Member: Aberdeen Standard Investments Ltd, Phoenix Group Holdings PLC, since 2019; appointed Member, Board of Trustees, Edinburgh Children's Hospital Charity in 2017; Non Executive Director: Heriot-Watt University, since 2018, Scottish Financial Enterprise, since 2021. Retired football referee, having taken charge of 60 Scottish Premier League games during 10 years operating at the top level of Scottish Football. Address: abrdn, 1 George Street, Edinburgh EH2 2LL.

Tunnock, Sir Boyd, CBE. Chairman and Managing Director, Thomas Tunnock Limited, since 1981; b. 25.1.33. Honorary Degree of Doctor of Business Administration, Glasgow Caledonian University, 2016. Address: Thomas Tunnock Limited, 34 Old Mill Road, Uddingston, Glasgow G71 7HH; T.-01698 813551.

Tunstall, Rev Lorna, MDiv (Hons). Minister, Clyne linked with Kildonan and Loth, Helmsdale, since 2020; b. 1967; m., Mark. Educ. New College, Edinburgh. Completed an 18 month probationary period at Barnhill St Margaret's Church in Broughty Ferry, Dundee; former telecommunications project manager. Recreation: long walks along the beach. Address: Clyne Church of Scotland, Victoria Road, Brora KW9 6QN; T.-01408 536 005.
E-mail: LTunstall@churchofscotland.org.uk

Turbyne, Dr Judith, BSc, PhD. Chief Executive Officer, Children in Scotland, since 2021. Educ. The University of Edinburgh; University of Bath. Career history: worked in Latin America and the Caribbean, in local frontline organisations and with multinational funders; Head of Religion, Christian Aid, 2006-2010; Chief Executive Officer, Progressio Ireland, 2010-2014; Head of Engagement, Scottish Charity Regulator (OSCR), 2013-2021. Address: Children in Scotland, Thorn House, 5 Rose Street, Edinburgh EH2 2PR; T.-0131 243 2781.

Turmeau, Professor William Arthur, CBE, FRSE, Dr. h.c. (Edinburgh University), Doctor of Education (Napier University), BSc, PhD, CEng, FIMechE. Chairman, Scottish Environment Protection Agency, 1995-99; Principal and Vice-Chancellor, Napier University, 1982-94; b. 19.9.29, London; m., Margaret Moar Burnett; 1 d. Educ. Stromness Academy, Orkney; Edinburgh University; Moray House College of Education; Heriot-Watt University. Royal Signals, 1947-49; Research Engineer, Northern Electric Co. Ltd., Montreal, 1952-54; Mechanical Engineer, USAF, Goose Bay, Labrador, 1954-56; Contracts Manager, Godfrey Engineering Co. Ltd., Montreal, 1956-61; Lecturer, Bristo Technical Institute, Edinburgh, 1962-64; Napier College: Lecturer and Senior Lecturer, 1964-68, Head, Department of Mechanical Engineering, 1968-75, Assistant Principal and Dean, Faculty of Technology, 1975-82. Member, IMechE Academic Standards Committee; Vice Chairman, ASH (Scotland). Recreations: modern jazz; Leonardo da Vinci. Address: (h.) 132 Victoria Street, Stromness, Orkney KW16 3BU; T.-01856 850500; e-mail: profwaturmeau@btinternet.com

Turnbull, The Hon. Lord (Alan), LLB. Senator of the College of Justice, since 2006. Educ. Dunfermline High School; University of Dundee. Career history: admitted to the Faculty of Advocates in 1982; worked initially in general practice at the Bar; developed specialities in criminal defence and fraud by 1988; appointed an Advocate Depute in 1995, taking silk in 1996, and returning to private practice in 1997; appointed one of two senior prosecuting counsel in the Lockerbie bombing trial in 1988; appointed Principal Advocate Depute in 2001; returned to private practice in 2006. Awarded Honorary Doctorate of Laws, University of Dundee, 2008. Address: (b.) Parliament House, 11 Parliament Square, Edinburgh EH1 1RQ.

Turnbull, Sheriff Craig. Sheriff Principal of Glasgow and Strathkelvin, since 2016. Educ. University of Strathclyde. Career history: admitted as a solicitor in 1988, working for A.C.White in Ayr and Levy & McRae in Glasgow before joining MacRoberts in 1993, became a partner in 1997 specialising in commercial and construction disputes and health and safety and environmental prosecutions, and served as the managing partner, 2011-14; appointed as a part-time sheriff in 2011 and became a full-time sheriff in 2014. Address: Glasgow Sheriff Court, 1 Carlton Place, Glasgow G5 9TW; T.-0141 429 8888.
E-mail: glasgow@scotcourts.gov.uk

Turner, John R., MA, HonMA, MusB, FRCO. Organist and Director of Music, Glasgow Cathedral, 1965-2010; Lecturer, Royal Scottish Academy of Music, 1965-2007; Organist, Strathclyde University, 1965-2010; b. Halifax. Educ. Rugby; Jesus College, Cambridge. Recreations: reading; travel. Address: (h.) Binchester, 1 Cathkin Road, Rutherglen, Glasgow G73 4SE; T.-0141-634 7775.

Turner, Jon. Chief Executive Officer, Link Group Ltd, since 2019; Trustee, Victim Support Scotland (Chair, 2019-2021). Educ. Oundle School; Birmingham City University. Career history: Associate Director, PwC, 2005-07; Clydesdale & Yorkshire Bank: Regional Credit Director, 2008-2011, Director - Growth Finance, Corporate & Structured Finance, 2011-12; Head of National Business Solutions/Specialist and Acquisition Finance, Clydesdale Bank, 2012-16; Director of Treasury, Wheatley Group, 2016-18. Address: Link Group Ltd - Head Office, Link House, 2C New Mart Road, Edinburgh EH14 1RL.

Turner, Professor Kenneth John, BSc, PhD. Emeritus Professor of Computing Science, Stirling University (Professor, 1987-2014); b. 21.2.49, Glasgow; m., Elizabeth Mary Christina; 2 s. Educ. Hutchesons' Boys Grammar School; Glasgow University; Edinburgh University. Data Communications Designer, International Computers Ltd., 1974-76; Senior Systems Analyst, Central Regional Council, 1976-77; Data Communications Consultant, International Computers Ltd., 1977-87. Recreations: choral singing; craft work; sailing. Address: (b.) Department of Computing Science and Mathematics, Stirling University, Stirling FK9 4LA; T.-01786 466000.

Turpie, Annabel. Director of Marine Scotland, The Scottish Government, since 2020; b. Glasgow. Educ. Edinburgh University. Career history: worked in both the UK and Brussels in both public and private sectors; held Deputy Director roles in the Prime Minister's Strategy Unit, the Office of Civil Society, Constitution Group and the Department for Communities and Local Government until 2015; The Scottish Government: Deputy Director, Resillience, 2015-16, Deputy Director, 2016-19, Director for Agriculture and Rural Delivery, 2019-2020. Address: Marine Scotland, The Scottish Government, 1A South, Victoria Quay, Edinburgh EH6 6QQ; T.-0300 244 4000.

Tweed, Evelyn. MSP (SNP), Stirling, since 2021; b. Ayr; m., Ahsan Khan; 2 c. Educ. West of Scotland University; Heriot-Watt University. Previously worked as a housing professional with Cube and Loreburn; elected Councillor in Stirling for Trossachs and Teith in 2017; held the portfolio for housing; became the council's public safety commission convener. Address: The Scottish Parliament, Edinburgh EH99 1SP; T.-0131 348 5088.
E-mail: Evelyn.Tweed.msp@parliament.scot

Tweeddale, 14th Marquis of (Charles David Montagu Hay); b. 6.8.47; succeeded to title, 2005.

Tweedie, Peter, LLB, DipLP. Chairman, Lindsays, since 2016 (Partner, since 1984). Educ. High School of Dundee; University of Dundee. Career history: Shield and Kyd: Partner, 1985-2009, Managing Partner, 1984-2012. Address: Lindsays, Caledonian Exchange, 19A Canning Street, Edinburgh EH3 8HE; T.-0131 656 5607.
E-mail: petertweedie@lindsays.co.uk

Twist, Dr Benjamin. Director, Creative Carbon Scotland; arts and climate change consultant; b. 17.4.62, London; m., Margaret Corr. Educ. Crown Woods Comprehensive School; University of Edinburgh; PhD - complexity theory and sustainable behaviours (Sociology), University of Edinburgh, 2018. Freelance Director of Theatre, Music Theatre and Opera throughout Scotland, UK, Europe, North America and New Zealand; Artistic Director of Contact Theatre, Manchester, 1994-98. Member, SAC Capital Committee, 1999-2003; Chair: SAC Capital Committee, 2003-07, SAC Lottery Committee, 2007-10; Member: SAC, 2003-07, Joint Board of SAC and Scottish Screen, 2007-2010; Trustee, The Theatres Trust, 2007-2013, Vice Chair, 2011-13; Chair, Hebrides Ensemble, 2010-2017. Address: (h.) 39 Rosslyn Crescent, Edinburgh EH6 5AT; e-mail: ben.twist@creativecarbonscotland.com

Tynte-Irvine, Claire, MA (Hons). Board Secretary, The Scottish Government, since 2021; b. 7.81. Educ. Clifton High School; Balliol College, University of Oxford. Career history: UK Government: EU Gibraltar Policy, 2003-04, EU Economic and Social Policy, 2004-06, EU and Economic Policy, British Embassy, Ankara, 2006-09, Corporate Change and Communications, 2009-2010, Private Secretary, EU Policy, Global Issues, Europe and Asia Pacific, 2010-2012; Economic and Trade Policy, British High Commission, New Delhi, 2012-2014; Head, Prosperity, British High Commission, New Delhi, 2014-17; The Scottish Government: Head of International Division, Edinburgh, 2017-2021. Address: Scottish Government, St. Andrew's House, Regent Road, Edinburgh EH1 3DG.

Tyre, The Hon. Lord (Colin Jack Tyre), CBE, LLB, DESU. Senator of the College of Justice, since 2010; b. 17.4.56, Dunoon; m., Elaine Patricia Carlin (deceased); 1 s.; 2 d. Educ. Dunoon Grammar School; Edinburgh University; Universite d'Aix Marseille. Lecturer in Scots Law, Edinburgh University, 1980-83; Tax Editor, CCH Editions Ltd., Bicester, 1983-86; Advocate, 1987-98; QC, 1998-2010; Standing Junior Counsel to Scottish Office Environment Department in planning matters, 1995-98; President, Council of Bars and Law Societies of Europe, 2007; Member, UK Delegation to CCBE, 1999-2004; Head of Delegation, 2004; Scottish Law Commissioner (part-time), 2003-09. Member of Board of Trustees of Academy of European Law, Trier, Germany, 2011-19; Chairman, Board of Governors, Fettes College, Edinburgh, 2012-18. Publications: CCH Inheritance Tax Reporter; contributor to Stair Memorial Encyclopaedia; Tax for Litigation Lawyers (Co-Author). Recreations: orienteering; golf; mountain walking; popular music. Address: (b.) Supreme Courts, 11 Parliament Square, Edinburgh EH1 1RQ; T.-0131 225 2595.

U

Uddin, Dr Wali Tasar, MBE, DBA, DLitt. President and Adviser of Bangladesh Private Medical College Association (BPMCA); Vice President of Voice 4 Global Bangladeshis; Hon Consul General of Bangladesh in Scotland, since 2002; b. 17.4.52, Moulvibazar, Bangladesh. Educ. Moulvibazar Govt. HS; Putney College (HNC); m., Syeda; 2 s.; 3 d. Chairman and Chief Executive, Universal Koba Corp Ltd and Britannia Spice Scot Ltd., 2000, also consultant, The Verandah and Lancers Brasserie; established Travel Link Worldwide Ltd.; Chairman and Chief Executive, Frontline International Air Services UK Ltd., 1997; consultant in restaurant and travel trade sectors; Hon Consul General of Bangladesh in Scotland, 1993-98; Chief Co-ordinator, Indian Earthquake Disaster Appeal Fund Scotland, 2001, Chief Co-ordinator, Bangladesh Flood Victim Appeal Fund Scot; Chairman, Bangladesh Br C of C; Founding Director, Edinburgh Mela (Asian Festival) Ltd.; Founder and Chairman, Bangladesh Samity (Association) Edinburgh; Co-ordinator, Expo Bangladesh, 2005; Chairman: Commonwealth Society Edinburgh; Bangladeshi Council in Scotland, Scotland Bangladeshi International Humanitarian Trust; Bangla Scot Foundation; Ethnic Enterprise Centre Edinburgh; Director, Edinburgh C of C, 2002; Patron: Bangladesh Cyclone Disaster Appeal Fund; Royal Hospital for Sick Children Edinburgh; Scotland School of Asian Cuisine, Fife College; Director, Sylhet Women's Medical College and Hospital, 2005; Adviser, Atish Dipankar, University of Science and Technology, 2004; Chairman, Advisory Board, University of East London Business School, 2004; former Chairman and Director-General, British Bangladesh Chamber of Commerce in UK; Patron, Lion Children's Hospital, Sylhet, 1997; Trustee: Bangladesh Female Academy, 2004, Shahajalal Mosque Edinburgh; Member, Edinburgh Merchant Co; Board Member, Council for Foreign C of C and Industries; Executive Member, Royal Commonwealth Society, Edinburgh; Young Scot Award, Int Jr C of C, 1992; Lifetime Achievement Award, Asian Jewel Awards, 2006; Outstanding Achievement in catering Award, The British Bangladeshi Who's Who; Curry King Award, Scottish Curry Awards; DBA (hc), Queen Margaret UC, 2000; Hon DLitt, Heriot Watt University, 2007; MInstD; MCMI; FInstSMM. Recreations: supporting Heart of Midlothian FC and the Bangladesh cricket team; football; family; working with the televisual media (ethnic, national and international). Clubs: Rotary International. Address: Universal Koba Corporation Ltd, Britannia Spice Restaurant, 150 Commercial Street, Ocean Drive, Leith, Edinburgh EH6 6LB; e-mail: waliuddin@aol.com
Web: www.britanniaspice.co.uk

Uist, The Hon. Lord (Roderick Macdonald), LLB. Senator of the College of Justice, 2006-2021 (retired); b. 1.2.51. Educ. St Mungo's Academy; University of Glasgow. Career history: admitted to the Faculty of Advocates in 1975; Advocate Depute, 1987-93 (Home Advocate Depute from 1990); appointed Queen's Counsel in 1989; called to the Bar of England and Wales in 1997 (Inner Temple); Legal Chairman of the Pension Appeal Tribunals for Scotland, 1995-2001; Member: Criminal Injuries Compensation Board, 1995-2000, Criminal Injuries Compensation Appeals Panel, 1997-99; Temporary Judge in 2001-06; took the judicial title Lord Uist and sits in the Outer House. Prominent cases presided over include the 2006 trial of three of the race hate murderers of Kriss Donald.

Ulph, Professor David Tregear, MA, BLitt, CBE, FRSA, FRSE. Professor of Economics, University of St. Andrews, since 2006; b. 26.10.46, Belshill; m., Elizabeth Margaret; 2 d. Educ. Hutchesons Boys Grammar School; University of Glasgow; University of Oxford. Lecturer in Economics: University of Stirling, 1971-77, University College London, 1977-82; Reader in Economics, University College London, 1982-84; Professor of Economics, University of Bristol, 1984-91, Head of Department of Economics, 1984-87; Professor of Economics, University College London, 1992-2001, Head of Department of Economics, 1992-97, Executive Director, ESRC Centre for Economic Learning and Social Evolution, 1997-2001; Chief Economist and Director of Analysis & Research, Inland Revenue, 2001-04; Chief Economist and Director of Analysis, HM Revenue & Customs, 2004-06; Director, Scottish Institute for Research in Economics (SIRE), 2009-2017. Member: Economic Affairs Committee, ESRC, 1986-88, Research Grants Board, ESRC, 1993-98, Council of European Economic Association, 1991-94, Council of Royal Economic Society, 1995-99, NHS Pay Review Body, 2015-2021, Competition Appeal Tribunal, since 2017; Commissioner, Scottish Fiscal Commission, since 2018; Member of Editorial Board: Review of Economic Studies, 1981-90, Journal of Industrial Economics, 1986-88, European Economic Review, 1991-95. Recreations: bridge; cinema; travel; cooking.
E-mail: david@ulph.me.uk

Upton, Emeritus Professor Brian Geoffrey Johnson, BA, MA, DPhil, FRSE, FGS. Emeritus Professor of Petrology, Edinburgh University, since 1999; b. 2.3.33, London; m., Bodil Aalbaek Upton; 2 s.; 1 d. Educ. Reading School; St John's College, Oxford University. Geological Survey of Greenland, 1958-60; Fulbright Fellow, California Institute of Technology, 1961-62; Lecturer, Geology, Edinburgh University, 1962-72; Carnegie Fellow, Geophysical Laboratory, Washington, 1970-71; Edinburgh University: Reader in Geology, 1972-82; Professor of Petrology, 1982-99; Executive Editor, Journal of Petrology, 1983-94; Clough Medallist, Geological Society, Edinburgh, 2001. Recreations: painting; gardening; travel. Address: (b.) Grant Institute, The King's Buildings, James Hutton Road, Edinburgh EH9 3FE; T.-0131 650 5110.

U'ren, William Graham, BSc (Hons), DipTP, FRTPI. Retired Town Planning Consultant; Trustee, Lanark Community Development Trust, since 2019, Secretary, Friends of New Lanark, since 2016; b. 28.12.46, Glasgow; m., Wendy; 2 d. Educ. Aberdeen Grammar School; Aberdeen University; Strathclyde University. Director of Planning and Technical Services, Clydesdale District Council, 1982-96; Director, Royal Town Planning Institute in Scotland, 1997-2007; Town Planning Consultant, Dundas and Wilson CS LLP, 2007-2012; Adviser to the Scottish Public Services Ombudsman, 2007-2016. Past Chairman, Scottish Society of Directors of Planning; former Member, Heritage Lottery Fund Committee for Scotland; former Member, Scottish Cricket Union Committee; Past President, Uddingston Cricket Club; formerly Founder Trustee, Built Environment Forum Scotland; formerly Trustee, Planning Aid for Scotland; formerly Trustee and Chair, Crichton Trust, Dumfries; formerly Trustee, New Lanark Trust, 2008-2018; formerly Chairman, New Lanark Trading Ltd, 2006-2018. Recreations: listening to music; travel; walking; heritage conservation; bird watching; philately. Address: (b.) 'Carseview', 125 Hyndford Road, Lanark ML11 9AU.

Urquhart, Jean. Former MSP (Independent), Highlands and Islands (2012-16) (SNP MSP, 2011-12); b. 17.5.49, West Lothian; m., Robert Urquhart (deceased). Educ. Lindsay High School, Bathgate. Former SNP councillor, Highland Council (2003-2011). Member, RISE - Scotland's Left Alliance, 2015-2020.

Urquhart, Canon John. Retired Parish Priest (St. Bernadette's, Larbert); Founder and Former Chairman, Diocesan Heritage and Arts Commission; b. 1.7.34,

Bowhill, Fife. Educ. St. Ninian's, Bowhill; St. Columba's Cowdenbeath; Blairs College, Aberdeen; Scots College, Spain; St. Andrew's College, Drygrange. Assistant: St. Joseph's, Sighthill, Edinburgh, Our Lady and St. Andrew's, Galashiels; Chaplain, St. Mary's Balnakiel; Parish Priest: St. Paul's, Muirhouse, Edinburgh, St. Margaret's, Dunfermline. Address: Christ The King, Bowhouse Road, Grangemouth, Falkirk FK3 0HB; T.-01324 472846.

Urquhart, Linda Hamilton, OBE, LLB, WS; b. 21.9.59, Edinburgh; m., Lord Burns (David S Burns); 2 d. Educ. James Gillespie's High School; University of Edinburgh. Trainee Solicitor, Steedman Ramage WS, 1981-83; Morton Fraser: Solicitor, 1983-85, Partner, 1985-2012, Chief Executive, 1999-2011, Chair, 2011-2017. Former Chairman, Remarkable (formerly Investors in People Scotland); Non-Executive Director: Edinburgh Airport, Coutts & Co; Trustee, Marie Curie; President, Girlguiding Scotland; former Chair, Scotland and Board Member, CBI; former Co-Chair, Fair Work Convention. Recreations: singing; sailing; walking; skiing; golf.

Usher, Professor John Richard, BSc (Hons), MSc, PhD, CMATH. Professor of Mathematics, Robert Gordon University, 1998-2001 (retired 2001); b. 12.5.44, London; m., Sheila Mary McKendrick; 1 d (Katherine Neva Margaret); 2 gd. Educ. St. Nicholas Grammar School, London; Hull University; St Andrews University. Lecturer, Mathematics, Teesside Polytechnic, 1970-74; Senior Lecturer, Mathematics, Glasgow College of Technology, 1974-82; Head of School of Mathematics (later School of Computing and Mathematical Sciences), Robert Gordon University, 1983-92; Senior Lecturer, Mathematics, 1992-98; Scottish Branch Committee, IMA: Vice-Chairman, 1983-85, Chairman, 1985-88, Hon. Member, 1988 -89; Member, IMA Council, 1987-90; External examiner for various Universities; Examiner for SCOTEC; Moderator for SCOTVEC; Member, UCAS Scottish Higher Education Mathematical Sciences and Computing Panel; Eucharistic Assistant, St. Ternans, Scottish Episcopal Church, Muchalls. Recreations: reading; walking; theatre-going; concert-going; bridge; croquet. Address: 20 St. Crispin's Road, Newtonhill, Stonehaven, Kincardineshire AB39 3PS. E-mail: j.s.usher44@gmail.com

V

van Bronckhorst, Giovanni Christiaan. Manager, Rangers FC, since 2021; b. 5.2.75, Rotterdam, Netherlands; m., Marieke; 2 c. Youth career: LMO Rotterdam, 1981-82, Feyenoord, 1982-93; Senior career: Fayenoord, 1993-98, RKC Waalwijk (loan), 1993-94; Rangers, 1998-2001; Arsenal, 2001-04; Barcelona (loan), 2003-04; Barcelona, 2004-07; Fayenoord, 2007-2010; Netherlands, 1996-2010; Management: Feyenoord, 2015-2019; Guangzhou R&F, 2020. Player Honours: Feyenoord, KNVB Cup: 1994-95, 2007-08; Rangers: Scottish Premier League: 1998-99, 1999-2000; Scottish Cup: 1998-99, 1999-2000; Scottish League Cup: 1998-99; Arsenal: Premier League: 2001-02, FA Cup: 2001-02, 2002-03; Barcelona: La Liga: 2004-05, 2005-06, Supercopa de España: 2005, 2006, UEFA Champions League, 2005-06; Netherlands: FIFA World Cup runner-up, 2010; Management Honours: Feyenoord: Eredivisie, 2016-17, KNVB Cup: 2015-16, 2017-18, Johan Cruyff Shield, 2017, 2018; Rangers: Scottish Cup: 2021-22, UEFA Europa League runner-up: 2021-22. Knight of the Order of Orange-Nassau, 2010. Address: Rangers Football Club, Ibrox Stadium, 1 Edmiston Drive, Glasgow G51 2XD.

Vance, Dr James. Acting Rector, Culloden Academy, since 2019; Rector, 2012-18. Educ. Belfast High School. Career history: PT History, PT Faculty, then Deputy Rector, Banff Academy, 2001-2010; Rector, Golspie High School, 2010-2012; Interim Head of Education, Highland Council, 2018-2019. Address: Culloden, Inverness IV2 7JZ; T.-01463 790851.

van der Kuyl, Professor Christiaan Richard David, CBE, BSc (Hons), FRSE, FRSA, Hon DBA, Hon LLD, Hon DSc, Hon DTech. Chairman, 4J Studios Limited, TVSquared Limited, Broker Insights Limited and Puny Astronaut Limited; b. 20.8.69, Dundee. Technology Entrepreneur; Director, Dundee Science Centre; Trustee, Dundee Museums Foundation (Fundraising for V&A) and Optimistic Sound (Charity to bring EI Sistema Orchestra to Dundee); Member: Scottish EDGE Advisory Board, University of Edinburgh Bayes Innovation Programme Advisory Board, University of Dundee Leverhulme Advisory Board, Informatics Ventures Advisory Board, Ace Aquatec Ltd Board, ADV Holdings Ltd Board; Chairman, Parsley Box Ltd. Recreations: playing computer games; music; cycling; skiing. Club: New Club. Address: (b.) 4J Studios Limited, Water's Edge, Camperdown Street, Dundee DD1 3HY.

Vannet, Sheriff Alfred Douglas, LLB, FRSA. Sheriff of South Strathclyde, Dumfries and Galloway at Airdrie, 2001-09, retired but part time until 2019; All-Scotland floating Sheriff, 2000-01; Honorary Professorial Teaching Fellow, since 2011 and Senior Tutor in criminal litigation, School of Law, University of Glasgow, since 2010; b. 31.7.49, Dundee; m., Pauline Margaret Renfrew; 1 s.; 1 d. Educ. High School of Dundee; Dundee University. Procurator Fiscal Depute, Dundee, 1976-77; Procurator Fiscal Depute, then Senior Procurator Fiscal Depute, Glasgow, 1977-84; Assistant Solicitor, Crown Office, 1984-90; Deputy Crown Agent, 1990-94; Regional Procurator Fiscal, Grampian, Highland and Islands at Aberdeen, 1994-97; Regional Procurator Fiscal, Glasgow and Strathkelvin, 1997-99. Honorary Member, Royal Faculty of Procurators in Glasgow, since 1997. Recreations: music; walking; curling.

Vardy, Professor Alan Edward, BSc, PhD, DSc, DEng, FREng, FRSE, EurIng, CEng, FICE, FASCE, FRSA. Emeritus Professor, University of Dundee, since 2006; Research Professor in Civil Engineering, University of Dundee, 1995-2016; Director, Dundee Tunnel Research, since 1995; b. 6.11.45, Sheffield; m., Susan Janet; 2 s.; 1 d. Educ. High Storrs Grammar School, Sheffield; University of Leeds. Lecturer in Civil Engineering, University of Leeds, 1972-75; Royal Society Warren Research Fellow, University of Cambridge, 1975-79; University of Dundee: Professor of Civil Engineering, 1979-95 (Deputy Principal, 1985-89, Vice-Principal, 1988-89); Director, Wolfson Bridge Research Unit, 1980-90; Royal Society/SERC Industrial Fellow, 1990-94; Director, Lightweight Structures Unit, 1998-2004; Technical Advisor, Sohatsu Systems Laboratory Inc., Japan, since 2000. Address: Kirkton of Abernyte, Perthshire PH14 9SS; T.-01828 686241.

Varty, Professor E. Kenneth C., BA (Hons), PhD, DLitt, Chevalier dans l' Ordre des Palmes Academiques, Chevalier dans l' Ordre des Arts et des Lettres. Professor Emeritus, Glasgow University, since 1990; Life Member, Clare Hall, Cambridge University, since 1984; b. 18.8.27, Derbyshire; m., Hedwig; 2 d. Educ. Bemrose School, Derby; Nottingham University. Assistant Lecturer, then Lecturer, French, University College of N.

Staffs, 1953-61; Lecturer/Senior Lecturer, French, Leicester University, 1961-68; Stevenson Professor of French, Glasgow University, 1968-90; Dean, Faculty of Arts, Glasgow University, 1978-81; President, Alliance Française de Glasgow, 1982-89. Publications: Reynard, Renart, Renaert, 1999; Reynard the Fox, 2000. Recreations: travel; art galleries; museums; historic sites etc. Address: (h.) 74 Tay Street, Newport on Tay, Fife DD6 8AP; T.-01283 760721.

Veal, Sheriff Kevin Anthony, KSG, KC*HS, LLB. Retired Sheriff (Tayside Central and Fife at Forfar, 1993-2014); b. 16.9.46, Chesterfield; m., Monica Flynn; 2 s.; 2 d. Educ. Lawside Academy, Dundee; St. Andrews University. Partner, Burns Veal and Gillan, Dundee, 1971-93; Legal Aid Reporter, 1978-93; Temporary Sheriff, 1984-93; Tutor, Department of Law, Dundee University, 1978-85; Dean, Faculty of Procurators and Solicitors in Dundee, 1991-93. Musical Director, Cecilian Choir, Dundee, since 1975; Member, University Court, Abertay Dundee, 1998-2009; Member, Council, Sheriffs' Association, 2000-03; Honorary President, Dundee Operatic Society, since 2003; Hon. Fellow, University of Abertay Dundee, 2010. Recreations: organ and classical music; hill-walking.

Vermeulen, Rev. Chris, BTh (Rhodes), MA (Sheffield). Independent Celebrant; Minister, St. Columba's Parish Church, Largs, 2014-17; Minister, Orchardhill Parish Church, Giffnock, 2005-14; b. 19.1.61, Vanderbijlpark, South Africa; m., Elaine; 1 s.; 1 d. Educ. Vaal High School, Vanderbijlpark, South Africa; Rhodes University; Sheffield University. Formerly Minister, St. David's Presbyterian Church (Nigel, South Africa); moved to Scotland to study at Glasgow University while still ministering part time in the Falkirk area; called to Barrhead Congregational Church (now part of the United Reformed Church) and served as their minister for 6 years until 2000; moved to Manchester to become Research Fellow, Woodlands Project on a 5 year contract. Publication: "The Church Facing the Future".

Vettese, Raymond John, DipEd, BA (Hons). Teacher and Writer; b. 1.11.50, Arbroath; m., Maureen Elizabeth. Educ. Montrose Academy; Dundee College of Education; Open University. Journalist, Montrose Review, 1968-72; student, 1972-75; barman, 1975-77; factory worker, 1977-78; clerical officer, 1978-85; teacher, since 1985 (supply teacher, 1997-2001); Library Assistant, 2001; Preses, Scots Language Society, 1991-94; William Soutar Fellowship, 1989-90; SAC Bursary, 1999. Publications: Four Scottish Poets, 1985; The Richt Noise, 1988 (Saltire Society Best First Book); A Keen New Air, 1995. Recreations: reading; music; cooking; chess. Address: (h.) 9 Tayock Avenue, Montrose DD10 9AP; T.-01674 678943.

Vettriano, Jack, OBE; b. 1951, Fife. Painter. Early career in Scottish coalfields; received no formal tuition in art; first submitted works to Royal Scottish Academy, 1988; sell-out solo exhibitions in Edinburgh, London, Hong Kong and New York.

Vickerman, Jill. National Director (Scotland), The British Medical Association (BMA), since 2013. Educ. Edinburgh University. Career: held a number of senior posts with the Scottish Government, including Head of Health Analytical and Policy Director in the quality unit of the Scottish Government's health and social care directorates and Deputy Chair of the Office of the Scottish Charity Regulator (OSCR). Address: BMA, 14 Queen Street, Edinburgh EH2 1LL; T.-0131 247 3000.

Vickers, Dr Grace, PhD, BMus. Chief Executive, Midlothian Council, since 2018. Educ. University of Edinburgh Business School. Career history: secondary school Head Teacher and Quality Improvement Manager with the City of Edinburgh Council; Head of Education and Chief Education Officer, Midlothian Council. Address:

Midlothian Council, Midlothian House, 40-46 Buccleuch Street, Dalkeith, Midlothian EH22 1DN; T.-0131 271 3002; e-mail: chiefexec@midlothian.gov.uk

Villalba, Mercedes. MSP (Scottish Labour), North East Scotland (Region), since 2021; Shadow Minister for Environment and Biodiversity, since 2021. Address: The Scottish Parliament, Edinburgh EH99 1SP; T.-0131 348 6390; e-mail: Mercedes.Villalba.msp@parliament.scot

Vincent, Jon, BA (Hons), PGDip. Principal and Chief Executive, Glasgow Clyde College, since 2017. Educ. University of Wales, Cardiff; Loughborough College; Notttingham Trent University. Career: Lecturer, Grantham College, 1993-95; various teaching and managerial roles, Lincoln College, 1995-2005; Deputy Principal, Burton College, 2005-09; Principal & Chief Executive, Tyne Metropolitan College, 2009-2016. Currently Chair of a large secondary school; Fellow of the Institute of Knowledge Exchange. Address: (b.) Anniesland Campus, 19 Hatfield Drive, Glasgow G12 0YE; T.-0141 272 9000.

Voas, Sheila, BVM&S, FRCVS. Chief Veterinary Officer, Scottish Government, since 2012; m.; 2 s. Career history: spent almost 20 years in private practice, in a variety of jobs in the Scottish Borders and the North of England, including 15 years in a mixed practice based between Biggar and Peebles; qualified from the 'Dick Vet' college at the University of Edinburgh in 1988; joined the Scottish Government in 2007 as a veterinary adviser, and then as deputy CVO, having previously worked for the State Veterinary Service as a field based veterinary officer. Address: Scottish Government, Saughton House, Broomhouse Drive, Edinburgh EH11 3XD.

von Prondzynski, Professor Ferdinand, BA, LLB, PhD, Law. Professor Emeritus, Robert Gordon University, Aberdeen, since 2018 (Principal and Vice-Chancellor, 2011-18); b. 30.6.54, Germany; m., Heather Ingman; 2 s. Educ. Headfort School, Kells, County Meath; Thomas-Morus Gymnasium, Oelde, Germany; Trinity College Dublin; University of Cambridge. Career: Lecturer (Fellow), Trinity College Dublin, 1980-90; Professor of Law, Dean, University of Hull, 1991-2000; Presdent, Dublin City University, 2000-2010. Board member: Aberdeen City and Shire Economic Future (ACSEF), Aberdeen City Council's City Centre Regeneration Board; active in leading projects on urban development in Aberdeen, and economic development in the North-East of Scotland. Member of the Church of Ireland; keen follower of Newcastle United football club; keen amateur photographer.

Voss, Jens-Peter. German Consul General in Scotland, since 2015; b. 5.9.53, Hamburg-Harburg; m., Barbara; 2 d. Final exams at school (Abitur), Alexander-von-Humboldt Gymnasium Hamburg-Harburg, 1972; Reserve Officer's Training Federal German Navy (Senior Commander Naval Reserve, rtd.), 1973-75; Studies in Economics and Business Administration, University of Hamburg, 1975-80; In Spierling & Voss Co., metal foundry and general machinery: trainee, assistant to the management, head of commercial department & partner, 1975-81; Preparatory courses for senior diplomatic service, Bonn, 1981-83; Secretary, press and cultural affairs, Embassy Kinshasa/Zaïre, 1983-86; Federal Ministry for Foreign Affairs, Bonn (international scientific and technological co-operation), 1986-89; Secretary (economics), Embassy Copenhagen/Denmark, 1989-92; Counsellor, Head of Trade Promotion Office, Embassy Peking/PR China, 1992-97; Federal Ministry for Foreign Affairs, Head of Special Unit "management modernisation", 1997-2000; Deputy Head of Economics Department, Embassy Rome/Italy, 2000-03; Deputy Head of Economics Department, Embassy Peking, 2003-06; Deputy Head of Mission, Embassy Pyongyang, DPR Korea, 2006-08; Ambassador Extraordinary and Plenipotentiary to the Republic of Haïti, Embassy Port-au-Prince, 2008-2012; Consul General, Shenyang/PR China, 2012-2015. Address: Consulate of the Federal Republic of Germany, 16 Eglinton Crescent, Edinburgh EH12 5DG; T.- 0131 337 2323.

W

Waddell, Bruce. Director: Postcode International Trust, 2014-2021, Bruce Waddell Communications, since 2013; b. 18.3.59, Bo'ness, West Lothian; m., Catherine; 1 s. Educ. Graeme High School, Falkirk; Napier University. Reporter, Journal and Gazette, Linlithgow, 1977-87; News Sub-editor, The Scottish Sun, 1987-90; Deputy Editor, Sunday Scot, 1991; Marketing Executive, Murray International, 1991-92; Features Sub-editor, The Sun, 1992-93; Deputy Editor, The Scottish Sun, 1993-98; Editor, The Scottish Sun, 1998-2003; formerly Director of Media, The Big Partnership; Editor-in-Chief, Scottish Daily Record and Sunday Mail Ltd, 2009-2011. Recreations: golf; football; classic cars.

Wade, Sheriff Gillian, QC. Floating Sheriff of Tayside, Central and Fife, since 2015; Head, National Sexual Crimes Unit (NSCU), 2011-13. Career: a solicitor qualified to practise both north and south of the border; specialised in media related matters including defamation, contempt of court and copyright; partner of firms in Glasgow and London; appointed Legal Convenor to the Mental Health Tribunal for Scotland in 2004; appointed an ad hoc Advocate Depute in 2007; assumed a full time post in Crown Office in 2008; joined the NSCU team at its inception in June 2009; appointed a Senior Advocate Depute and Deputy Head of the National Sexual Crimes Unit in 2010. Publications include: Associate Editor, Tolley's Journal of Media law and Practice, 1988-1996; Greens Weekly Digest "The Defamation Act 1996", 1997.

Wade, Professor Nicholas James, BSc, PhD, FRSE. Emeritus Professor of Psychology, Dundee University, since 2009; b. 27.3.42, Retford, Nottinghamshire; m., Christine Whetton; 2 d. Educ. Queen Elizabeth's Grammar School, Mansfield; Edinburgh University; Monash University. Postdoctoral Research Fellow, Max-Planck Institute for Behavioural Physiology, Germany, 1969-70; Lecturer in Psychology, Dundee University, 1970-78, Reader, 1978-91. Publications: The Art and Science of Visual Illusions, 1982; Brewster and Wheatstone on Vision, 1983; Visual Allusions: Pictures of Perception, 1990; Psychologists in Word and Image, 1995; A Natural History of Vision, 1998; Purkinje's Vision: The Dawning of Neuroscience, 2001; Destined for Distinguished Oblivion: The Scientific Vision of William Charles Wells (1757–1817), 2003; Perception and Illusion: Historical Perspectives, 2005; The Moving Tablet of the Eye. The Origins of Modern Eye Movement Research, 2005; Insegne Ambiguë. Percorsi Obliqui tra Storia, Scienza e Arte, da Galileo a Magritte, 2007; Circles: Science, Sense and Symbol, 2007; Giuseppe Moruzzi, Ritratti di uno scienziato, Portraits of a scientist, 2010; Visual Perception: an introduction, 3rd ed, 2013; Galileo's Visions: Piercing the Spheres of the Heavens by Eye and Mind, 2014; Art and Illusionists, 2016; Vision and Art with Two Eyes, 2022. Recreations: golf; cycling. Address: (h.) 36 Norwood, Newport-on-Tay, Fife DD6 8DW; T.-01382 543136. E-mail: n.j.wade@dundee.ac.uk

Walker, Audrey R., BA, MCLIP. Librarian, Turcan Connell, 2006-2016; b. 18.10.57, Glasgow. Educ. Clydebank High School; Robert Gordon University, Aberdeen. Library Assistant, 1975-80; Senior Library Assistant, Telford College, Edinburgh, 1980-84; Assistant Librarian: Scottish Office Library, 1987, Post-Graduate Medical Library, 1988-90, Advocates Library, 1990-94; Librarian, Signet Library, 1994-2006. Honorary Member, CILIP in Scotland (awarded in 2008); Honorary Treasurer, Chartered Institute of Library and Information Professionals in Scotland, 2011-2017. Recreations: cycling; reading; gardening; cinema.

Walker, Bill, BSc (Hons), MBA, FCMI, FIET, CEng. MSP (Independent), 2012-2013, (SNP), Dunfermline, 2011-12; Councillor, Fife Council, 2007-2012; m., June; adult children. Educ. Royal High School (Old), Edinburgh; University of Edinburgh; Illinois Institute of Technology, Chicago. Career: 1963-1990: various posts from design engineer to managing director in businesses specialising in medical scanning equipment (Scotland and overseas); 1990-2007: range of positions from sales manager to company director in energy supply and shipbuilding sectors (Scotland and overseas). Political interests: energy; environment; transportation; enterprise and regeneration; Scottish Independence. Recreations: gardening; reading; crosswords; travel; DIY as time permits.

Walker, Craig. Editor, Aberdeen Evening Express, since 2017. Educ. Ellon Academy. Joined Aberdeen Journals in 2004 as a reporter; formerly News Editor, Assistant Editor and Deputy Editor. Address: Aberdeen Journals Ltd, 1 Marischal Square, Broad Street, Aberdeen AB10 1BL.

Walker, Emeritus Professor David Morrison, OBE, DA, FSA, FSA Scot, FRSE, HFRIAS, Hon. LLD (Dundee), Hon. DLitt (St Andrews). Honorary Professor of Art History, University of St. Andrews, 1994-2001, Emeritus Professor, since 2001; Chief Inspector of Historic Buildings, Scottish Office Environment Department, 1988-93; Manager, Dictionary of Scottish Architects research and database project, 2002-07, Editor, 2007-2012, Consultant Editor, since 2012; b. 31.1.33, Dundee; m., Averil Mary Stewart McIlwraith (deceased); m. (2), Sheila Margaret Mould (2005), MA, MLitt, MCLIP; 1 s. Educ. Morgan Academy, Dundee; Dundee College of Art. Voluntary work for National Buildings Record, Edinburgh, 1952-56; National Service, Royal Engineers, 1956-58; Glasgow Education Authority, 1958-59; Dundee Education Authority, 1959-61; Historic Buildings Branch, Scottish Office: Senior Investigator of Historic Buildings, 1961-76, Principal Investigator of Historic Buildings, 1976-78; Principal Inspector of Historic Buildings, 1978-88. Alice Davis Hitchcock Medallion, 1970; Patron, Society of Architectural Historians of Great Britain, 2008; Europa Nostra Award for Dedicated Service, 2009. Publications: Dundee Nineteenth Century Mansions, 1958; Architecture of Glasgow (Co-author), 1968 (revised and enlarged edition, 1987); Buildings of Scotland: Edinburgh (Co-author), 1984; Dundee: An Illustrated Introduction (Co-author), 1984; St. Andrew's House: an Edinburgh Controversy 1912-1939, 1989; Central Glasgow: an illustrated architectural guide (Co-author), 1989; A Capital Investment, 2019. Address: (h.) 22 Inverleith Row, Edinburgh EH3 5QH.

Walker, Donald George, MA (Hons). Deputy Editor, The Scotsman and Scotland On Sunday, 2015-19; b. 1968, St. Andrews. Educ. Kirkcaldy High School; University of Edinburgh. Trainee journalist, DC Thomson, Dundee; Sub-Editor, Daily Mirror, London, 1993-97; Deputy Sports Editor, The Scotsman, 1997-98; Sports Editor, The Scotsman, 1998-2012; Assistant Editor, The Scotsman, 2012-2015. E-mail: donaldgwalker345@gmail.com

Walker, (Edward) Michael, CBE, FRICS. Chairman, Westerwood Ltd; Founder and former Chairman (1969-2019) - retired, Walker Group (Scotland) Ltd and associated companies; Chairman, Lothian and Edinburgh Ltd. (LEEL), 1996-2000 (Director, since 1991); b. 12.4.41, Aberdeen; m.,

Flora Margaret; 2 s.; 1 d. Educ. Aberdeen Grammar School. President, Edinburgh and District Master Builders Association, 1987 and 1996; Past President, Scottish House Builders Association; former Committee Member, NHBC (Scotland) Ltd., 1990-96; former Lord Dean of Guild, City of Edinburgh, 1992-96; Captain of Industry Award, Livingston Industrial and Commercial Association, 1987; Homes for Scotland Industry Achievement Award, 2009. Recreations: travel; pilates; walking; reading. Address: Westerwood Ltd, Atholl Exchange, Ground Floor, 6 Canning Street, Edinburgh EH3 8EG.

Walker, Flora Margaret, MBE (2016). Director (1969-2019) - retired, Walker Group (Scotland) Ltd; b. 24.11.41, Aberdeen; 2 s.; 1 d. Educ. Aberdeen Academy. British Red Cross Volunteer, since 1973; President, Lothian Branch of the British Red Cross, 2002-2019; Patron, British Red Cross East of Scotland; Volunteer skin camouflage practitioner for the British Red Cross and now the Changing Faces charity, since 2008. Recreations: family; reading; travel; walking.

Walker, Professor Greg Mapley, BA, PhD, FRHS, FEA, FSA, FRSE. Regius Professor of Rhetoric and English Literature, University of Edinburgh, since 2010, Masson Professor of English, 2007-10; b. 08.09.59, Coventry; m., Sharon; 2 s. Educ. Horndean School; Southampton University. Career history: British Academy Post-Doctoral Fellow, University of Southampton; Lecturer in English: University of Queensland, University of Buckingham, University of Leicester; Reader, and Professor of English, University of Leicester. Publications: author of books including, John Heywood: Comedy and Survival in Tudor England, 2020. Recreations: dog lover; fan of progressive rock music; Nottingham Forest FC. Address: (b.) Department of English Literature, University of Edinburgh, Edinburgh EH8 9LH; T.-0131 650 3049.
E-mail: greg.walker@ed.ac.uk

Walker, Rev. Dr James Bernard, MA, BD, DPhil. Chaplain, St. Andrews University, 1993-2011 (retired); Associate Director, Student Services (retired); b. 1946, Malawi; m., Sheila; 3 s. Educ. Hamilton Academy; Edinburgh University; Merton College, Oxford. Church of Scotland Minister: Mid Craigie linked with Wallacetown, Dundee, 1975-78, Old and St. Paul's, Galashiels, 1978-87; Principal, The Queen's College, Birmingham, 1987-93; joined St. Andrews University in 1993. Recreations: hill-walking; tennis; golf; swimming.

Walker, Michael, BSc (Hons), LLB, LLM, DipLP. Chief Executive, Scottish Criminal Cases Review Commission, from September 2021 (Head of Casework, 2013-2021, Senior Legal Officer, 2007-2013); b. 26.04.68, Cumbernauld. Educ. Ardrossan Academy; University of Strathclyde; University of Glasgow. Solicitor in Private Practice; Legal Officer, SCCRC, 2001-07 (Member of the team of Solicitors which reviewed the conviction of Abdelbaset Ali Mohmed Al Megrahi; Junior Legal Officer, SCCRC, 2007-2011. Address: (b.) Portland House, 17 Renfield Street, Glasgow G2 5AH; T.-0141 270 7030.
E-mail: mwalker@sccrc.org.uk

Walker, Scott. Chief Executive, NFU Scotland, since 2011. Progressed through a number of roles in NFUS, starting as Commodity Director in 1994; headed up the Union's Policy team as Policy Director, since 2004. Address: NFU Scotland, Head Office, Rural Centre - West Mains, Ingliston, Midlothian EH28 8LT; T.-0131 472 4000.

Walker, Dr Susan, OBE, PhD. Member, Boundary Commission for Scotland, since 2021. Educ. University of Durham; University of Manchester. Career history: worked in the rural and environment sector for over 30 years; former Professor of Geography and Environment, University of Aberdeen; appointed Member of the Local Government Boundary Commission for Scotland in 2013; Board Member of Food Standards Scotland, since 2015; Member of the Water Industry Customer Forum, since 2011. Address: Boundary Commission for Scotland, Thistle House, 91 Haymarket Terrace, Edinburgh EH12 5HD; T.-0131 244 2001.

Walker, Professor Todd, BAppSci, PhD, FIAC, GAICD, FRSA. Principal and Vice-Chancellor, University of the Highlands and Islands, since 2021; m., Jayne; 2 c. Educ. CQUniversity; Charles Sturt University; Australian Institute of Company Directors. Career history: Acting/Head of School of Biomedical Sciences, Charles Sturt University, Australia, 2005-07; University of Ballarat, Australia: Associate Professor of Biomedical Science, 2007-09, Pro Vice-Chancellor (Learning and Quality), 2009-2011, Chair, Academic Board, 2009-2012, Deputy Vice Chancellor (Learning and Quality), 2011-13; Deputy Vice Chancellor (Engagement), FedUni Australia, 2014-17; Provost and Deputy Vice-Chancellor, University of New England, 2018-2020. Address: University of the Highlands and Islands, 12b Ness Walk, Inverness IV3 5SQ; T.-01463 279246; e-mail: vice-chancellor@uhi.ac.uk

Walker, Professor William Barclay, BSc, MSc. Professor Emeritus of International Relations, University of St. Andrews, Head, School of International Relations, 2003-06; b. 7.12.46, Longforgan; m., Carolyn Scott; 1 s. Educ. Shrewsbury School; Edinburgh University. Design Engineer, Ferranti Ltd., 1970-72; Research Fellow, Science Policy Research Unit, Sussex University, 1974-78; Research Fellow, Royal Institute of International Affairs, 1978-80; Science Policy Research Unit, Sussex University: Senior Fellow, 1981-92, Professorial Fellow and Director of Research, 1993-96; Member, Strategic Research Board, Economic and Social Research Council, 2002-06; Recipient, Leverhulme Trust Research Fellowship, 2008-09; Nobel Institute (Oslo) Visiting Fellowship, 2009. Publications: Plutonium and Highly Enriched Uranium: World Inventories, Capabilities and Policies (Co-author), 1997; Unchartered Waters: The UK, Nuclear Weapons and the Scottish Question (Co-Author), 2001; Weapons of Mass Destruction and International Order, 2004; A Perpetual Menace: Nuclear Weapons and International Order, 2011. Recreations: piano-playing; literature; walking. Address: 41 Upper Gray Street, Edinburgh EH9 1SN; T.-0131 667 8664; e-mail: wbw@st-andrews.ac.uk

Wallace, Anne Maree, MBChB, MScComMed, FFPH, Diploma in Advanced Executive Coaching. Independent coach and mentor; Director of Public Health, NHS Forth Valley, 2008-2013; Non-Executive Director: NHS Health Scotland, 2009-2016, Food Standards Scotland, 2015-2021; b. 18.9.55, Edinburgh; m., David Wallace; 2 s.; 1 d. Educ. John Watson's School, Edinburgh; Aberdeen University. Graduated as a doctor in 1978 and completed initial training in Aberdeen and Falkirk; moved to Edinburgh to train in Public Health Medicine; worked as a Consultant, Public Health Medicine in NHS Lothian until 2000; Deputy Director of Public Health, 2001-04; Interim Director of Public Health, 2004-05; Director of Training in Public Health in Scotland and the lead consultant in the newly formed Scottish Public Health network, 2005-08. Honorary Senior Lecturer, Edinburgh University, until 2013; qualified advanced executive coach. Recreations: hill walking; cooking.

Address: (h.) 33 Malleny Millgate, Balerno, Edinburgh EH14 7AY; T.-0131 449 4310.
E-mail: annemareewallace@gmail.com

Wallace, Claire Denise, BA, PhD. Professor, Sociology, University of Aberdeen, since 2005; President, European Sociological Association, 2007-09; b. 04.12.56, London; m., Christian Haerpfer (President of the World Values Association). Educ. Walthamstow High School, London; University of Kent. Career History: Research Fellow, University of Kent; Lecturer, University of Plymouth; Visiting Professor, University of Derby; Senior Lecturer in Sociology, University of Lancaster; Head of Sociology, Central European University, Prague; Head of Sociology, Institute for Advanced Studies, Vienna. Vice Principal, Research and Knowledge Exchange, Aberdeen, 2011-2014. Recreations: hill walking; horse riding; music (classical and folk). Address: (b.) University of Aberdeen, Edward Wright Building, Aberdeen AB24 3QY; T.-01224 273137; e-mail: claire.wallace@abdn.ac.uk

Wallace, Colin Russell, FREHIS. Twice Past President, Royal Environmental Health Institute Scotland; former Environmental Health Manager, South Ayrshire Council (1996-2009). Commenced employment with Ayr County Council, 1970; Qualified as a Sanitary Inspector, 1974; Environmental Health Officer, Kyle & Carrick District Council, 1975, Senior Environmental Health Officer, 1985, Principal Environmental Health Officer, 1991. Recreations: music and hi-fi; mountain biking. Address: Royal Environmental Health Institute of Scotland (REHIS), 19 Torphicen Street, Edinburgh EH3 7DH; T.-0131-229-2968.

Wallace, David, BA. Deputy Chief Executive Officer and Director of Finance, Strategy and Corporate Services, Student Loans Company, since 2014, Interim Chief Executive, 2015-16. Educ. Hutchesons' Grammar School; Glasgow Caledonian University. Career history: Manager, Price Waterhouse, 1989-92; Abbey National plc: Finance & Admin Manager, Marketing & Sales, Special Projects Manager, 1992-97, Finance Director, Life Division, 1997-2002, Director, Transformation and Wealth Management & Long Term Savings, 2002-05; Chief Operating Officer for Santander's Insurance and Asset Management Division, 2005; CEO, Response Handling Limited, 2006-09; Director, MacDonald Wallace, 2009-2010; Student Loans Company: Interim Chief Operating Officer, 2010-2011, Deputy CEO and Executive Director for Strategic Development and Change Management, 2011-14, appointed Deputy Chief Executive and Executive Director for Finance, Strategy and Corporate Services in 2014. Governor of Court, Glasgow Caledonian University and Chair of its Finance and General Purpose Committee, 2007-2016. Founding member of the Scottish Government's Financial Services Advisory Board and its precursor, the Financial Services Strategy group. Recreations: sporting activities; cooking; the 'great outdoors'. Address: Student Loans Company, 100 Bothwell Street, Glasgow, Lanarkshire G2 7JD; T.-0141 306 2000.

Wallace, Professor Heather M., BSc, PhD, FRCPath, FBTS, FRSC, FRSB, FBPhS, ERT. Professor of Biochemical Pharmacology and Toxicology, School of Medicine, Medical Sciences and Nutrition, University of Aberdeen; b. Edinburgh; m., Professor R. John Wallace; 1 s.; 1 d. Educ. Hamilton Academy; University of Glasgow; University of Aberdeen. Career: University of Aberdeen: Postdoctoral Fellow, MRC, 1979-81; CRC, 1981-83; Wellcome Lecturer, 1983; New Blood Lecturer, 1983-91; University Research Fellow, 1991-92; Senior Lecturer, 1991-2013. Recreations: golf;

tennis; badminton. Address: (b.) University of Aberdeen, Room 6.21, Institute of Medical Science, Foresterhill, Aberdeen; T.-01224 437956.
E-mail: h.m.wallace@abdn.ac.uk

Wallace, Sheriff Ian. Sheriff at Grampian, Highland and Islands, since 2021. Educ. University of Glasgow; Free University of Berlin. Started traineeship with the Crown Office and Procurator Fiscal Service in 2003; worked as a Procurator Fiscal Depute in Dumfries, Edinburgh, and Crown Office; qualified as a Solicitor Advocate in 2014 and appointed an Advocate Depute; appointed as a Summary Sheriff in 2018. Address: Aberdeen Sheriff Court, 53 Castle Street, Aberdeen AB11 5BB; T.-01224 657200.

Wallace of Tankerness, Rt. Hon. Lord (James Robert Wallace), PC, QC, MA (Cantab), LLB (Edinburgh), Hon DLitt (Heriot-Watt), 2008, Hon. DUniv (Open), Doctor honoris causa (Edinburgh), 2009, FRSE, 2018. Moderator of the General Assembly of the Church of Scotland, 2021-22; Advocate General for Scotland, 2010-2015; Leader of Liberal Democrat Peers, 2013-2016; Deputy Leader of House of Lords, 2013-2015; Created Life Peer, 2007; Elected Honorary Bencher of Lincoln's Inn, 2012; Hon. Professor, Institute of Petroleum Engineering, Heriot-Watt University, 2007-2010; Chair, Relationships Scotland, 2008-2010; Board of St. Magnus International Festival, 2007-2014; MSP (Liberal Democrat), Orkney, 1999-2007; Deputy First Minister, 1999-2005; Minister for Justice, 1999-2003; Minister for Enterprise and Lifelong Learning, 2003-05; MP (Liberal Democrat, formerly Liberal), Orkney and Shetland, 1983-2001; Leader, Scottish Liberal Democrats, 1992-2005; Advocate, 1979; QC (Scot.), 1997; b. 25.8.54, Annan; m., Rosemary Janet Fraser; 2 d. Educ. Annan Academy; Downing College, Cambridge; Edinburgh University. Called to Scottish Bar, 1979; contested Dumfries, 1979, and South of Scotland Euro Constituency, 1979; Member, Scottish Liberal Party Executive, 1976-85 (Vice-Chairman, Policy, 1982-85); Honorary President, Scottish Young Liberals, 1984-85; Liberal Democrat Spokesman on Fisheries, 1988-97, and on Scotland, 1992-99; jointly awarded Andrew Fletcher Award for services to Scotland, 1998; Chair, Regulation Board of Institute of Chartered Accountants of Scotland, 2018-2021; Chair of Board of Trustees of Reprieve, 2017-2021; Honorary President, Greenock Burns Club (The Mother Club), 2020. Publication: New Deal for Rural Scotland (Co-Editor), 1983. Recreations: golf; reading; travelling. Address: (h.) Steinbrudd, Tankerness, Orkney KW17 2QS; T.-01856 861383; e-mail: wallacej@parliament.uk

Wallace, Professor John, CBE (2011), MA, FRSAMD, FRAM, HonRCM, HonLCM, DMus (Aberdeen), DCons (RCS), DLitt (Strathclyde). Principal, Royal Conservatoire of Scotland, 2002-2014; b. 1949, Methilhill. Educ. Buckhaven High School; King's College, Cambridge; York University; Royal Academy of Music. Principal Trumpet, Philharmonia Orchestra, 1976-95; Principal Trumpet, London Sinfonietta, 1987-2001; founded The Wallace Collection (brass ensemble), 1986; Artistic Director of Brass, Royal Academy of Music, 1993-2001; has premiered new works by Peter Maxwell Davies, Harrison Birtwistle, H K Gruber, Malcolm Arnold, James MacMillan, Stuart MacRae, Mark Anthony Turnage and Jonathan Dove. Publication: Companion to Brass Instruments (Co-Editor), 1997; The Trumpet (Co-Author), 2012. Address: 157B Camphill Avenue, Glasgow G41 3DR.

Wallace, Kate, MA (Eng), PgDip (SR), MBA (Public Service Mgmt). Chief Executive Officer, Victim Support Scotland, since 2017. Educ. University of Glasgow;

University of Strathclyde; Stirling University. Career history: Research Officer (Policy and Research) and (Children's Services), Scottish Children's Reporter Administration, 2000-04; Policy and Research Manager, Scottish Association for Mental Health, 2004-06; Senior Research and Evaluation Officer, Creative Scotland/Scottish Arts Council, 2006-2010; Barnardo's: Assistant Director - Research and Influencing (Maternity leave cover), 2010-11, Deputy Director - Policy and Research, 2011-12; Trustee, National Working Group tackling child sexual exploitation, 2011-14; UK Programme Director, Barnardo's, 2012-14; appointed CEO, Visualise in 2014. Address: Victim Support Scotland, 15-23 Hardwell Close, Edinburgh EH8 9RX; T.-0131 668 4486.

Wallace, Rev. Dr. William Fitch, BDS, BD. Minister, Pulteneytown and Thrumster Church, 1990-2008; Convener, Church of Scotland Board of Ministry, 2002-03; b. 6.10.39, Falkirk; m., Jean Wyness Hill; 1 s.; 3 d. Educ. Allan Glen's School; Glasgow University; Edinburgh University. Minister, International Church, Addis Ababa, 1971-73; Minister, Wick St. Andrew's and Thrumster Church, 1974-90; former missionary dentist. Convener, Church of Scotland Board of Social Responsibility, 1993-97. Recreations: family; golf; gardening. Address: Lachlan Cottage, 29 Station Road, Banchory, Aberdeenshire AB31 5XX; T.-01330-822-259.
E-mail: williamfwallace39@gmail.com

Walsh, Dr Garry Michael, MSc, PhD, FIMLS. Emeritus Reader in Inflammation & Immunity, University of Aberdeen (Reader, School of Medicine, since 2004); b. 4.8.57, London; m., Catherine. Educ. St. James' School, London; Brunel University; London University. Medical Laboratory Scientific Officer, Histocompatability Testing Laboratory, Royal Postgraduate Medical School, London; academic research, Cardiothoracic Institute, Brompton Hospital, London; Visiting Fellow, Allergy Division, National Children's Hospital, Tokyo, Japan; postdoctoral position, University of Oxford; Senior Research Fellow/Honorary Lecturer, later Honorary Senior Lecturer, Department of Medicine and Therapeutics, University of Leciester Medical School; joined Aberdeen University, 1997 as Senior Lecturer. Scientific Advisor, UCB Institute of Allergy, Brussels; Member, MRC Advisory Board; Founding Editor of Therapeutics and Clinical Risk Management; Member of Editorial Board of Clinical and Experimental Allergy. Publications: over 100 papers and review articles in international scientific and medical journals). Recreations: hillwalking; golf; gastronome; motorocycling. Address: Department of Medicine and Therapeutics, Institute of Medical Sciences, University of Aberdeen, Foresterhill, Aberdeen AB25 2ZD; T.-01224 552786; e-mail: g.m.walsh@abdn.ac.uk

Walsh, Professor Timothy Simon, BSc (Hons), MBChB (Hons), FRCP, FRCA, MD, MSc, FFICM. Head of Section/Lead of Edinburgh Critical Care Research Group, Edinburgh Royal Infirmary; Professor of Anaesthesia, Critical Care and Pain Medicine, University of Edinburgh, since 2006; b. 17.1.64, Redhill, Surrey; m., Claire Doldon; 3 s. Educ. Trinity School, Croydon; University of Edinburgh. Trained in general medicine, anaesthetics and intensive care in South East Scotland; medical officer, rural South Africa, 1989-90; research, Scottish Liver Transplant Unit. Publications: 100 publications in area of critical care, since 2000. Address: Royal Infirmary of Edinburgh, Edinburgh EH16 2SA; T.-0131-536 1000.

Walton, Professor John Christopher, BSc, PhD, DSc, CChem, FRSC, FRSE. Research Professor of Chemistry,

St. Andrews University, since 1997; b. 4.12.41, St. Albans; m., Jane Lehman; 1 s.; 1 d. Educ. Watford Grammar School for Boys; Sheffield University. Assistant Lecturer: Queen's College, St. Andrews, 1966-67, Dundee University, 1967-69; Lecturer in Chemistry, United College, St. Andrews, 1969-80; Senior Lecturer, 1980-86, Reader, 1986-96. Elder, Seventh-day Adventist Church. Recreations: music; philosophy. Address: (b.) School of Chemistry, St. Andrews University, St. Andrews, Fife, KY16 9ST; T.-01334 463864; e-mail: jcw@st-andrews.ac.uk

Wang, Professor Qi, BEng, MEng, PhD. Professor, School of Computing, Engineering and Physical Sciences, University of the West of Scotland, since 2008. Educ. Dalian Maritime University; University of Plymouth. Career history: Telecommunications Engineer, State Grid Corporation of China, 1998-2001; Research Fellow, University of Strathclyde, 2006-08; University of the West of Scotland: Technical Co-manager of EU 5G PPP Horizon 2020 Project SELFNET, 2015-2020. Best Paper Award Winner of IEEE Consumer Electronic Society's flagship conference, ICCE 2014 and IEEE ICCE 2012, SOFTNETWORKING 2017, and SIGMAP 2014; Best Paper Award Finalist of IEE 3G2003; Winner of UK Times Higher Education (THE) Awards 2020; Winner, Knowledge Exchange/Transfer Initiative of the Year Award and Winner of 2020 Scotland CeeD (Centre for Engineering Education & Development) Industry Awards - Innovation Award; served as Editor or Guest Editor for several international journals, and Chair or Invited Speaker for numerous international conferences and events; serves as an invited external PhD/research degree examiner for a number of other UK and European universities. Address: University of the West of Scotland, Technology Avenue, Blantyre, Glasgow G72 0LH; e-mail: Qi.Wang@uws.ac.uk

Wanless, Professor Sarah, FRSE, HonFBNA. Internationally recognised marine scientist; Natural Environment Research Council (NERC) individual merit scientist at the UK Centre for Ecology & Hydrology. Sought to understand the impact of global change on seabirds during 30 years of research; studies have concentrated on puffins, guillemots, kittiwakes, shags and gannets. Published over 200 papers. Elected Fellow of the Royal Society of Edinburgh in 2006; awarded Honorary professorships from the universities of Glasgow and Aberdeen; Lifetime Achievement awards from both the UK Seabird Group and the Pacific Seabird Group; received the Zoological Society Marsh Award for Conservation Biology in 2007, the British Ornithologists' Union Godwin-Salvin medal in 2014 and the Peter Scott Memorial Award and Honorary Fellowship of the British Naturalists' Association in 2019; retired in 2017 but remains closely involved with the Isle of May seabird studies as a UKCEH research fellow. Inducted into Outstanding Women of Scotland 2018, The Saltire Society.

Wannop, Professor Urlan Alistair, OBE, MA, MCD, MRTPI. Emeritus Professor of Urban and Regional Planning, Strathclyde University; b. 16.4.31, Newtown St. Boswells; 1 s.; 1 d. Educ. Aberdeen Grammar School; Edinburgh University; Liverpool University. Appointments in public and private practice, 1956-68; Team Leader, Coventry-Solihull-Warwickshire Sub-Regional Planning Study, 1968-71; Director, West Central Scotland Plan, 1972-74; Senior Deputy Director of Planning, Strathclyde Regional Council, 1975-81; Professor of Urban and Regional Planning, Strathclyde University, 1981-96. Member, Parliamentary Boundary Commission for Scotland, 1983-98. Address: (h.) 43 Lomond Street, Helensburgh G84 7ES; T.-01436 674622.

Ward, Professor Sir John MacQueen, CBE, CA, FRSE, FIET, FRSA. Former Resident Director, Scotland and North of England, IBM United Kingdom Ltd; Professor, Heriot Watt University; former Chairman, Scottish Homes;

former Chairman, Scottish Enterprise; former Chairman, Dunfermline Building Society; b. 1.8.40, Edinburgh; m., Barbara Macintosh; 1 s.; 3 d. Educ. Edinburgh Academy; Fettes College. Joined IBM UK Ltd. at Greenock plant, 1966; worked in France and UK; appointed European Director of Information Systems, 1975, and Havant Site Director, 1981. Past Chairman: SQA, Macfarlane Group, Queen Margaret University College, Governing Body, Scottish CBI, Scottish Post Office Board, Quality Scotland Foundation, Advisory Scottish Council for Education and Training Targets, Scottish Electronics Forum, Institute of Technology Management; European Assets Trust; former Director, Scottish Business in the Community; former Trustee, National Museums of Scotland; Honorary Doctorate, Napier University, Strathclyde University, Heriot-Watt University, Glasgow Caledonian University; Queen Margaret University College.

Ward, Maxwell Colin Bernard, MA. Managing Director, The Independent Investment Trust, since 2000; Chairman: Scottish Equitable Policyholders' Trust, 2004-2010; Director, Aegon UK, 1999-2010; Chairman, Dunedin Income Growth Investment Trust, 2002-06; Director, Foreign and Colonial Investment Trust, 2000-2011; Director, The Edinburgh Investment Trust, 2011-2021; b. 22.8.49, Sherborne; m., Sarah Marsham; 2 s.; 2 d. Educ. Harrow; St. Catharine's, Cambridge. Baillie Gifford & Co.: Trainee, 1971-75, Partner, 1975-2000. Director: Scottish Equitable Life Assurance Society, 1988-94, Scottish Equitable plc, 1995-99. Recreations: tennis; bridge; country pursuits. Address: (b.) 17 Dublin Street, Edinburgh EH1 3PG; T.-0131 558 9434.

Ward, Michael, MBE. Curator, Grampian Transport Museum, 1983-2021. Educ. Northampton Grammar School; Lincoln College of Art. Conservator, Bass Museum of Brewing, 1976-1983 (part of a three man team hired to establish the museum to celebrate Bass bi-centenary in 1977). Has collected and collated an extraordinary range of transport items, as well as the almost-complete restoration of a tramcar found buried in an Aberdeenshire field.

Ward, Rosemary, BEd (Primary), FRSA. Director of Programmes, Scottish Book Trust, since 2018; former Director, Comhairle nan Leabhraichean/The Gaelic Books Council - the lead organisation for Gaelic literature in Scotland (2010-18). Secretary, Gaelic Language Promotion Trust, since 2015. Treasurer, Literature Alliance Scotland, since 2015. Theatre Gu Leòr Board Member. Gaelic Education Manager, Bòrd na Gàidhlig, 2006-2010. Quality Improvement Officer, Argyll and Bute Council, 1996-2006; b. 16.1.62, Helensburgh; m. Gerard; 1 s.; 1 d. Educ. Nicolson Institute, Stornoway. Address: (b.) Scottish Book Trust, 55 High Street, Edinburgh EH1 1SR; T.-0131 524 0160.

Ward, Thomas, LLB (Hons). Retired Sheriff of North Strathclyde at Dunoon (2010-2021); b. 3.4.53, Glasgow; m., Ruth Zegleman; 3 s. Educ. St. Aloysius College, Glasgow; University of Dundee. Partner, Blair and Bryden Solicitors, Greenock, 1980; Part Time Sheriff, 1991-2000; Legal Member, CICAP, 2001; Legal Assessor, GMC, 2002; Part Time Immigration Judge, 2002; Legal Assessor, NMC; Legal Member, PMETB; Part Time Sheriff, 2005. Recreations: walking; watching cricket; visiting France.

Ward Thompson, Professor Catharine J., PhD, DipLA, BSc, FLI, FRSA. Professor of Landscape Architecture and Director of OPENspace Research Centre, University of Edinburgh, since 2011; b. 5.12.52; m., Henry Swift Thompson; 3 c. Educ. Holy Cross Convent, Chalfont St.

Peter; Southampton University; Edinburgh University. Landscape Assistant/Landscape Architect/Senior Landscape Architect, 1973-81; Lecturer and Studio Instructor, School of Landscape Architecture, Edinburgh College of Art, 1981-88; Head of School, 1989-2000; Director of Research, Environmental Studies, 2000-02; Research Professor of Landscape Architecture, Edinburgh College of Art, 2002-2011; Consultant, Landscape Design and Research Unit, Heriot-Watt University, 1989-2005; Honorary Professor: University of Edinburgh, 2007-2010, European Centre for Environment and Human Health, University of Exeter, 2016-19; Honorary Doctor, honoris causa, Swedish University of Agricultural Sciences, Uppsala, 2017. Recreations: dance; gardening. Address: (h.) 11 Douglas Crescent, Edinburgh EH12 5BB; T.-0131-6515827 (work).

Wark, Kirsty, BA, FRSE; b. 1955, Dumfries; m., Alan Clements; 1 s.; 1 d. Educ. Edinburgh University. Joined BBC as radio researcher, 1976; became radio producer, current affairs; produced and presented Seven Days, 1985; then concentrated on presenting (Reporting Scotland; Left, Right and Centre); General Election night coverage, 1987, 1992, 1997; BBC coverage, Scottish Parliamentary elections, 1999; Presenter, Breakfast Time, Edinburgh Nights; Presenter, The Late Show, 1990-93; Presenter, One Foot in the Past, 1993-99; joined Newsnight and Newsnight Review's team of presenters, 1993; Presenter, Restless Nation, Building a Nation; The Kirsty Wark Show; Lives Less Ordinary; Tales from Europe; The Book Quiz (BBC4), 2008; A Question of Genius (BBC2), 2009 and 2010; The Review Show (BBC2), since 2010; The Home Movie Roadshow (BBC2), 2010; Celebrity Masterchef (BBC1), 2010; cameo appearances in: Dr Who (BBC TV), 2007, Spooks (BBC TV), 2009, The I.T. Crowd (Channel 4), 2007, The Amazing Mrs Pritchard (BBC1), 2006; Beyond The Pole (Film), 2009; Party Animals (BBC TV), 2009; The Man Who Collected the World: William Burrell (BBC TV), 2013; Iain Banks: Raw Spirit (BBC TV), 2013; Blurred Lines: The New Battle of The Sexes (BBC TV), 2014; Would I Lie To You (BBC TV), 2014; Scotland's Art Revolution: The Maverick Generation (BBC TV), 2014; The Summer Exhibition: BBC Arts at the Royal Academy (BBC TV), 2014-19; Edinburgh Extra (BBC TV), 2014; General Election, 2015 (BBC TV); Our World: Kidnapped For A Decade (BBC TV), 2015; Manchester International Festival (BBC TV), 2015; BBC Proms (BBC TV), 2015; Edinburgh Nights, 2015 and 2016, BBC2; BBC TV Proms, 2015 and 2016; Absolutely Fabulous: The Movie, 2016; Only an Excuse (Cameo), BBC Scotland, 2015; The TV That Made Me, BBC1, 2016; Kirsty Wark: The Menopause and Me (BBC TV), 2017; Portrait Artist Of The Year (Sky Arts), 2017; National Theatre Live – Saint Joan Presentation, 2017; TV Proms: Zhang's Beethoven (BBC TV), 2017; Welcome to Edinburgh (BBC TV), 2017; Kirsty Wark's Edinburgh (BBC TV), 2017; The Many Primes of Muriel Spark (BBC Two), 2018; Royal Academy Summer Exhibition (BBC Two), 2018. Journalist of the Year, BAFTA Scotland, 1993; Best TV Presenter award, 1997; Scot of the Year, 1998; Scottish Insider Business Woman of the Year, 2002; Outstanding Contribution to Broadcasting - BAFTA Scotland, 2013; former Council Member, Prince's Trust; Patron, Maggie's Centre; formed production company with husband in 1990. Elected a Fellow of The Royal Society of Edinburgh, March 2017. Honorary Doctorate from University of the West of Scotland (UWS), 2018. Publications: The Legacy Of Elizabeth Pringle (Author), 2015; Building A Nation (Co-Author), 1997; The House by the Loch, 2019. Recreations: family; tennis; swimming; cooking; beach-combing; reading. Address: (b.) Black Pepper Media Ltd., PO Box 26323, Ayr KA7 9AY. E-mail: info@blackpeppermedia.com web: www.blackpeppermedia.com

Warner of Craigenmaddie, Gerald, OStJ, MA, FSAScot. Author; contributor to Reaction.life blog, since 2016; contributor to CapX blog (Centre for Policy Studies), 2014-

16; contributor to Breitbart London blog, 2014-15; occasional leader writer, The Sunday Telegraph, since 2009; columnist, Scotland on Sunday, 1997-2014; author, blog 'Is it just me?', The Daily Telegraph, 2008-2010; leader writer, Scottish Daily Mail, 1998-2014; b. 22.3.45. Educ. St. Aloysius' College, Glasgow; Glasgow University. Vice-Chairman, Una Voce (International Latin Mass Federation), Scotland, 1965-66; Administrative Assistant, Glasgow University, 1971-74; author and broadcaster, 1974-89; Diarist (under pseudonym Henry Cockburn), Sunday Times Scotland, 1989-95; columnist, 1992-95; Special Adviser to Secretary of State for Scotland, 1995-97. Council Member, 1745 Association, 1967-70; Member, Scottish Council of Monarchist League, 1969-71; Chairman, The Monday Club – Scotland, 1973-74; Secretary, Conservative Party's Scottish Policy Committee on Education, 1976-77; Parliamentary candidate, Hamilton, October 1974. Knight of Grace and Devotion, Sovereign Military Order of Malta, 1979; Knight, Jure Sanguinis, Sacred Military Constantinian Order of St. George, 1994; Knight of the Order of Merit of St. Joseph of Tuscany, 2005; Knight of the Order of St. Maurice and St. Lazarus, 2005. Publications: Homelands of the Clans, 1980; Being of Sound Mind, 1980; Tales of the Scottish Highlands, 1982; Conquering by Degrees, 1985; The Scottish Tory Party: A History, 1988; The Sacred Military Order of St. Stephen Pope and Martyr, 2005; Scotland's Ten Tomorrows (contributor), 2006; Secret Places, Hidden Sanctuaries (Co-Author), 2009. Recreations: literature; genealogy; Brummelliana. Address: 17 Huntly Gardens, Glasgow G12 9AT.

Warnock, Henry, BSc, CEng, MCIBSE, MIMechE. Director, Henderson Warnock, since 1993; formerly Chairman, Scottish Youth Theatre; b. 14.2.57, Glasgow; m., Felicity. Educ. Allan Glens School, Glasgow; University of Strathclyde. Design Engineer: IDC, Stratford-upon-Avon, DSSR, Glasgow; Senior Design Engineer: Building Design Partnership, Brian Ford Partnership. Director: Theatre Cryptic, Dancebase, Edinburgh. Recreations: travelling; rollerblading; music; film. Address: 38 New City Road, Glasgow G4 9JT; T.-0141-353 2444;
E-mail: hwarnock@hendersonwarnock.com

Warren, Gareth. Principal, George Heriot's School, Edinburgh, since 2021. Educ. Watford Grammar School for Boys. Taught chemistry at a number of schools in the UK and gained an international educational perspective on a three-year posting as head of science at an independent school in Bermuda; Deputy Head Teacher, George Watson's College, Edinburgh, 2009-2015; Principal, Morrison's Academy, Crieff, 2015-2021. Address: George Heriot's School, Lauriston Place, Edinburgh EH3 9EW; T.-0131 229 7263.

Waterhouse, Professor Lorraine Alice Margaret, BA (Maths/Psych), MSW. Professor of Social Work (Emeritus), University of Edinburgh; formerly Vice Principal, Equality and Diversity; b. 3.7.49, Toronto, Canada; m., J. D. Waterhouse; 1 s.; 1 d. Educ. St. Michaels, London, Ontario, Canada; University of Western Ontario, London, Canada. Social Worker, Royal Hospital for Sick Children, Edinburgh, 1972-76; Lecturer, Social Work (Half-Time), University of Edinburgh, 1976-80; Senior Social Worker (Half-Time), Royal Hospital for Sick Children, Edinburgh, 1976-80; University of Edinburgh: Lecturer, Social Work (Half-Time), 1980-92, Lecturer, Social Policy (Quarter-Time), 1988-94, Senior Lecturer, Social Work (Part-Time), 1992-94, formerly Head of School, Social and Political Studies. Member, Joint University Council (Social Work), 1994-2000; Convenor, Enquire, Children in Scotland, 2000-03. E-mail: Lorraine.Waterhouse@ed.ac.uk

Waters, Donald Henry, OBE, CA. Director, Scottish Media Group, 1997-2005; Chairman, Scottish and Grampian Television Retirement Benefits Scheme, 1999-2014; Chairman, Caledonian Publishing Pension Fund, (Herald and Evening Times), 1999-2014; Deputy Chairman and Chief Executive, Grampian Television PLC, 1993-97 (Chief Executive and Director, 1987-93); b. 17.12.37, Edinburgh; m., June Leslie Hutchison; 1 s.; 2 d. Educ. George Watson's, Edinburgh; Inverness Royal Academy. Director, John M. Henderson and Co. Ltd., 1971-76; Grampian Television PLC: Company Secretary, 1976, Director of Finance, 1979; Director: Scottish Television and Grampian Sales Ltd., 1980-97, Moray Firth Radio Ltd., 1982-89, Independent Television Publications Ltd. (TV Times), 1987-90, Cablevision Scotland PLC, 1987-91; Chairman, Celtic Film and Television Association, 1994-96; Vice-Chairman, BAFTA Scotland; Visiting Professor of Film and Media Studies, Stirling University, 1991-95; Chairman, Police Dependant Trust for Grampian, 1992-96; Chairman (1984), Royal Northern and University Club, Aberdeen (Member, since 1978); Chairman, Glenburnie Properties Ltd., 1993-97; Director: Central Scotland Radio Ltd. (Scot FM), 1994-96 (Chairman, 1995-96), GRT Bus Group PLC (now FirstGroup PLC), 1994-96, British Linen Bank Ltd., 1995-99, Bank of Scotland North of Scotland Local Board, 1999-2001, Scottish Post Office Board, 1996-2001, Consignia Advisory Board for Scotland, 2001-03, Johnstons of Elgin Ltd., 1999-2016, Aberdeen Asset Management PLC, 2000-2011; Member, ITV Council and ITV Broadcast Board, 1987-97; Fellow, Royal Society of Arts; Council Member, CBI Scotland, 1994-2001; Council Member, Cinema and Television Benevolent Fund, 1987-99; Member, Royal Television Society, since 1988; Director, Aberdeen Royal Hospital NHS Trust, 1996-99; Chairman, New Royal Aberdeen Children's Hospital Project Steering Group; Member of Council, Aberdeen Chamber of Commerce, 1996-2003; Governor, Aberdeen University, 1998; Member, Grampian and Islands Family Trust, 1988-2005; Joint Chairman, Grampian Cancer Macmillan Appeal, 1999-2004; Member of Council, SATRO; Burgess of Guild, since 1979 (Assessor, 1997-2002); Director, Blenheim Travel Ltd. Address: (h.) Balquhidder, 141 North Deeside Road, Milltimber, Aberdeen AB13 0JS; T.-Aberdeen 867131.
E-mail: donaldwaters@btinternet.com

Watkins, Laura. Chair, Victim Support Scotland, since 2021; Chief Executive Officer, Donaldson's, since 2014. Educ. University of Dundee; University of Strathclyde; Open University; University of Stirling; Institute of Directors. Career history: Lecturer, Glasgow College of Nautical Studies, 1998-2000; Depute Principal, National Autistic Society, Daldorch House School, 2000-09; Director of Autism Services, Spark of Genius, 2009-2012; Private Specialist Consultant, Dubai, United Arab Emirates, 2012-2013; Director of Parent and Familty Support, The Developing Child Centre (TDCC), United Arab Emirates, 2013-14; Non Executive Director, Scottish Council of Independent Schools, 2017-2021; Principal, Donaldson's, Linlithgow, 2014-15; The Institute of Directors: Member, since 2016, Fellow, since 2018; Victim Support Scotland: Board Trustee, since 2017, Vice Chair, 2019-2021. Address: Victim Support Scotland, 15-23 Hardwell Close, Edinburgh EH8 9RX; T.-0131 668 4486.

Watkins, Trevor, BA, PhD, FSA, FSAScot. Emeritus Professor of Near Eastern Prehistory, since 2004; Hon. Professorial Fellow, University of Edinburgh, since 2007; b. 20.2.38, Epsom; m., Antoinette (nee Loughran); 1 s.; 2 d. Educ. Kingston Grammar School; University of Birmingham. Career History: Research Fellow, University of Birmingham; Lecturer in Archaeology, University of Edinburgh, then Senior Lecturer, then Professor. Rhind Lecturer, 2009. Recreations: reading; theatre; classical music; walking. Address: (b.) School of History, Classics & Archaeology, University of Edinburgh EH8 9AG; T.-01383 412083; e-mail: t.watkins@ed.ac.uk

Watson, Alistair Gordon, LLB, DipLP, NP. Sheriff of North Strathclyde at Kilmarnock, since 2007; Temporary Judge of the Court of Session; b. 1.7.59, Dundee; m., Susan; 1 s.; 2 d. Educ. High School of Dundee; University of Dundee. Procurator Fiscal Depute (1984-89); Partner in Cameron Pinkerton & Co, Solicitors, then Watson & Mackay, Solicitors, 1989-98; appointed Scotland's First Public Defender in 1998; Director of Public Defence Solicitors' Office, 1998-2005; All Scotland Floating Sheriff, at North Strathclyde, 2005-07. Recreations: family; photography. Address: (b.) Sheriffs' Chambers, Kilmarnock Sheriff Court, St Marnoch Street, Kilmarnock KA1 1ED.

Watson, Andrew. Director of Budget and Public Spending, The Scottish Government, since 2019; m.; 2 d. Educ. Aberdeen University; The Open University. Career history: The Scottish Government: PS/Permanent Secretary, Head of Finance Policy and Infrastructure Investment, Deputy Director of Financial Strategy, Deputy Director for Agricultural Policy Implementation, 2017-19, Director for Sustainable Land Use and Rural Policy, 2019. Member: the Infrastructure Investment Board, Global Climate Emergency Programme Board, DGSE Transformation Programme Board, Fiscal Framework Review Programme Board, EU Exit Oversight Board, SNIB Programme Board, Scottish Government Remuneration Group, Economy Steering Group and Joint Exchequer Committee (Officials). Address: The Scottish Government, St Andrew's House, Regent Road, Edinburgh EH1 3DG.

Watson, Arthur James, RSA, DA. Senior Lecturer, Contemporary Art Practice, Duncan of Jordanstone College of Art & Design, University of Dundee (Senior Lecturer, since 1996); President, The Royal Scottish Academy, 2012-18 (Secretary, 2007-2012); b. 24.06.51, Aberdeen. Educ. Aberdeen Grammar School; Grays School of Art, Aberdeen. Founded Peacock Printmakers, an artists' print workshop, gallery and publisher, 1974; Board Member, Demarco Archive Trust. Recreation: traditional song. Address: (h.) 5B Melville Street, Perth PH1 5PY; T-07837 672337; e-mail: a.j.watson@dundee.ac.uk

Watson, Billy. Chief Executive, Scottish Association for Mental Health (SAMH), since 2008. Career history: Hospital Administrator, Stonehouse Hospital, 1992-94; Business Manager, Hairmyres and Stonehouse Hospitals NHS Trust, 1994-99; Regional Manager, RNIB, 1999-2000; Assistant Director, RNIB Scotland, 2000-03, Director, 2003-04; Group Director, RNIB, 2004-08. Address: Scottish Association for Mental Health, Brunswick House, 51 Wilson Street, Glasgow G1 1UZ; T.-0141 530 1000.

Watson, Dave, LLB. Head of Policy & Public Affairs, Unison Scotland, 1999-2018 (retired); b. 24.5.56, Liverpool. Educ. Nower Hill High School; Stanmore College; University of Strathclyde. Leisure Management, London Borough Harrow, 1974-79; Organising Assistant, South Wales NALGO; Branch Organiser, Dorset NALGO, 1980-90; Regional Officer, Unison Scotland, 1990-99; Scottish Executive Health Department HR Strategy Implementation Manager (Secondment), 1999-2001. Secretary, Socialist Health Association; Scottish Labour Party Executive; Vice-Chair, Scottish Labour Party, 2007; Secretary, Scottish Trade Union Labour Party (STULP); Chair, Scottish Labour Party, 2008/09; Jimmy Reid Foundation Board, 2015; Secretary, Keir Hardie Society, 2018. Recreations: military history; golf.

Watson, Derek A., FCCA. Quaestor and Factor, University of St Andrews; Chief Executive of St Andrews Applied Research Ltd (StAAR); lead employer nominated Trustee

of the St Andrews Superannuation and Life Assurance Scheme. Career history: Deputy Director of Finance and Property Development Manager of an NHS Trust, NHS Scotland; joined the University of St Andrews in December 2002 as Financial Controller. Address: University of St Andrews, College Gate, St Andrews KY16 9AJ; T.-01334 46 2016; e-mail: quaestor@st-andrews.ac.uk

Watson, Ellis. Executive Chairman, DC Thomson Media, 2018-2020. Career history: spent three years as the CEO of Celador, where he was largely responsible for the spread of the Who Wants to Be a Millionaire? format, spanning some 100 countries; Managing Director of Mirror Group Newspapers for 3 years (responsible for some five national and 240 regional newspapers); Board of Menzies Distribution, 2005-2009; appointed to the Board of First Group PLC in 2009; Managing Director of Newspapers for DC Thomson, 2011-12; former global CEO of Syco Entertainment; Chief Executive, DC Thomson Publishing, 2012-18.

Watson, Gordon. Chief Executive, Loch Lomond & The Trossachs National Park, since 2015; formerly Director of Operations; m.; 2 d. Instrumental in establishing Loch Lomond & The Trossachs National Park, including as a new planning authority; subsequently developed the planning function into a delivery focused operation using innovative approaches and partnership working to attract high quality and sustainable development to the National Park, 1999-2002. Address: (b.) Carrochan Road, Balloch G83 8EG; T.-01389 722600.

Watson, Graham, LLB, CA. Executive Chairman, Scottish Health Innovations Ltd, since 2015; Chair, Tennis Scotland, since 2020; Non Executive Director, Scottish Futures Trust, since 2017. Educ. George Heriot's School; The University of Edinburgh; Institute of Chartered Accountants of Scotland. Career history: Staff Accountant, KPMG, 1979-82; Director, Noble Grossart Limited, 1983-89; Chief Executive, Carnegie Sports International Limited, 1989-92; Partner, Deloitte, 1992-2003; Executive Director, Winning Scotland Foundation, 2004-09; Strategic Adviser: Macfarlane Gray Corporate Finance (now part of French Duncan), 2005-2013, Bioflow Sport, 2009-2013; Non Executive Director and Chair of Audit Committee, North Lanarkshire Leisure Ltd, 2007-2016; Founder, Positive Leadership Limited, since 2009; Member of the Council, Treasurer and Member of the Board, The Law Society of Scotland, since 2014; Member of Court and Chair of The Finance Committee of Court, Heriot-Watt University, since 2015; Associate, AGM Transitions, since 2016. Address: Scottish Health Innovations Ltd, The Golden Jubliee National Hospital, Fourth Floor East, Agamemnon Street, Clydebank G81 4DY.

Watson of Invergowrie, Lord (Michael Goodall Watson), BA (Hons). Labour Education spokesman in the House of Lords, since 2015; MSP (Labour), Glasgow Cathcart, 1999-2005; Minister for Tourism, Culture and Sport, Scottish Executive, 2001-03; MP (Labour), Glasgow Central, 1989-97; b. 1.5.49, Cambuslang. Address: House of Lords, Westminster, London SW1A 0PW; e-mail: watsonm@parliament.uk

Watson, Norma Anne, OBE, DCE, ACE, NFFC, FEIS, FRSA. Convener, General Teaching Council for Scotland, 1999-2007; Head Teacher, Kirkhill Nursery School, Broxburn, 1983-2007; b. Edinburgh; m., Christopher Simpson Watson. Educ. Broxburn Academy; Moray House College of Education. Vice-Convener, Educational Institute of Scotland Education Committee, 1992-2008; National

President of the Educational Institute of Scotland, 1994-95. Recreations: walking; reading. Address: (h.) 7, Queens Road, Broxburn, West Lothian EH52 5QZ.

Watson, Peter, BA, LLB, SSC. Solicitor, PBW Law; b. 22.1.54, Greenock; m., Claire Watson; 2 d. Educ. Eastwood High School, Glasgow; Strathclyde University; Edinburgh University; Scandinavian Maritime Law Institute, Norway; Dundee Petroleum Law Institute. Qualified, 1981; Solicitor to the Supreme Courts; Notary Public; former Temporary Sheriff; Visiting Professor, Law School, University of Strathclyde; Chairman, Glasgow Children's Hospital Charity; Past President, Society of Solicitor Advocates; Hon. Vice-President and former Chairman, Association of Mediators; Visiting Professor, Nova University, Fort Lauderdale, Florida; Member, Steering Committee, and Negotiator, Piper Alpha Disaster Group; Secretary, Braer Disaster Group; Secretary, Lockerbie Air Disaster Group; former Official Collaborator, International Labour Organisation, Geneva; Member, Criminal Rules Council; Member, Board, Sports Law Centre, Anglia University; Honorary Citizen of Nashville, Tennessee; large media practice based in Glasgow; elected to the Executive Committee of the British Academy of Forensic Science. Publications: Civil Justice System in Britain; Crimes of War – The Antony Gecas Story; The Truth Written in Blood; Dunblane – A Predictable Tragedy; DNA and the Criminal Trial; In Pursuit of Pan Am. Recreations: working out; drinking fine wine; golf. Address: (b.) PBW Law, 18 Woodside Place, Glasgow G3 7QF; T.-0141 439 1990.

Watson, Professor Roderick, MA, PhD, FRSE. Poet; Literary Critic and Writer; Professor Emeritus in English, Stirling University; b. 12.5.43, Aberdeen; m., Celia Hall Mackie; 1 s.; 1 d. Educ. Aberdeen Grammar School; Aberdeen University; Peterhouse, Cambridge. Lecturer in English, Victoria University, British Columbia, 1965-66; collections of poetry include Trio; True History on the Walls; Into the Blue Wavelengths. Other books include The Penguin Book of the Bicycle, MacDiarmid, The Poetry of Norman MacCaig, The Poetry of Scotland (Editor) and The Literature of Scotland (2 vols); From the Line: Scottish War Poetry 1914-1945 (Co-Editor). Recreations: cycling; motor cycling; alto saxophone. Address: (h.) 19 Millar Place, Stirling; T.-Stirling 475971.
E-mail: rbwatson19@gmail.com

Watson, Sharon. Headteacher, Holyrood Secondary School, Glasgow. Address: Holyrood Secondary School, 100 Dixon Road, Glasgow G42 8AU; T.-0141 582 0120.
E-mail: headteacher@holyrood-sec.glasgow.sch.uk

Watt, Alison, OBE, FRSE. Painter; b. 1965, Greenock. Educ. Glasgow School of Art. Won the John Player Portrait Award; became the youngest artist to be offered a solo exhibition at the Scottish National Gallery of Modern Art, in 2000, with an exhibition called Shift, with 12 huge paintings featuring fabric alone; shortlisted for The Jerwood Painting Prize in 2003; awarded the 2005 ACE (Art+Christianity Enquiry) award for 'a Commissioned Artwork in Ecclesiastical Space'; subsequent project Dark Light was supported by her Creative Scotland Award of 2004 from the Scottish Arts Council; took part in the prestigious Glenfiddich residency in 2005; served as the seventh artist in residence at the National Gallery, London, 2006-2008; youngest artist to present a solo exhibit at The National Gallery. Work is widely exhibited and is held in many prestigious private and public collections including, The Uffizi Gallery, Florence, The National Portrait Gallery, London and The British Council.

Watt, Allan. Senior Advisor, Global Ethical Finance Initiative (GEFI), since 2019; Director of Communication, Abellio Group, 2019-2020. Educ. University of Oxford. Consultant, Monitor Group, 1987-89; Project Manager and Executive Assistant, Scottish Enterprise, 1989-93; Director of Development, The Wise Group, 1993-2000; Head of Community Investment and Public Affairs, Royal Bank of Scotland, 2000-03; Interim Chief Executive, The Prince's Trust, 2003-04; Head of Group Brand Communication and Employee Communication, Royal Bank of Scotland, 2004-2010, Head of Communication and Marketing, Asia Pacific, 2010-2013; Director, Prince's Trust - Scotland, 2013-18; Interim Consulting, 2018-19.

Watt, David C., PhD (h.c.), Adv. DipEd, BA, DPE, CYS. Former Executive Director, Institute of Directors in Scotland; Honorary Colonel, RMR Scotland; Ambassador for Prince and Princess of Wales Hospice, Glasgow; author, commentator, contributor and consultant; m., Maggie. Chair, Board of Governors, Fife College; Director, Governance Express Ltd.; Non-Executive Director, BGR Fitness; Board Member, Goodison Group in Scotland; Honorary President, Scottish Gymnastics; Hon. Vice President, Basketball Scotland; formerly Scottish Partnership Manager, New Millennium Experience Company and Director, Organising Leisure and Leisure Training.com.

Watt, Jim, MBE (1980). Co-commentator and analyst, Sky Sports, 1996-2016; former boxer; b. 18.7.48, Glasgow. Turned professional, 1968; British Lightweight Champion, 1972-73, 1975-77; European Lightweight Champion, 1977-79; World Lightweight Champion, 1979-81; four successful defences of World title; Freedom of Glasgow, 1981.

Watt, John. Chairman of the Parole Board for Scotland, since 2013. Qualified solicitor; career in the Crown Office and Procurator Fiscal Service, latterly serving as area procurator fiscal in Grampian and then in Argyll & Clyde; extensive experience of managing a large caseload and making decisions in serious and high-profile cases, and of joint working with criminal justice partners such as the courts, police and social work departments. Address: Parole Board for Scotland, Saughton House, Broomhouse Drive, Edinburgh EH11 3XD; T.-0131 244 8373.

Watt, John Alexander, MA (Hons), MA, PhD, OBE. Director of High Life Highland, 2011-2013; Director of New Start Highland, 2012-16; Chair, Scottish Land Fund Committee, 2012-2021; Board Member, Community Land Scotland, since 2021; Member, Big Lottery Scotland Committee, 2013-18; Director, Kessock Books, 2014-16; Director of Strengthening Communities, Highlands and Islands Enterprise, 2003-2012; b. 16.9.51, Dunfermline; m., Hilary Lawson; 1 s.; 1 d. Educ. Inverness Royal Academy; University of Aberdeen; University of Waterloo, Ontario, Canada. Teacher, Chaminade Secondary School, Karonga, Malawi, 1973-74; Tutor, Open University, 1981-82; Highlands and Islands Development Board, 1981-91; Highlands and Islands Enterprise, 1991-2012. Recreations: hill walking; cycling; golf; land reform; social enterprise development. E-mail: johnawatt@btinternet.com

Watt, Karen, MA, MSc, ACIS. Chief Executive, Scottish Further and Higher Education Funding Council, since 2019; Director of External Affairs, Scottish Government, 2012-2015 and 2016-19, Director of Culture, Europe & External Affairs, 2015-16, Head of Enterprise and Tourism, 2012 (January-November); Principal Private Secretary to the First Minister of Scotland, 2009-2012; Director of Regulation and Inspection, Communities Scotland, 2003-08; Chief Executive, The Scottish Housing Regulator, 2008-09; b. 5.7.64, Antrim; m., Dr Stephen Watt; 3 s. Educ. Antrim Grammar School; St Andrews University. Department of Social Security, 1987-91; Scottish Homes: Senior Planning Analyst, 1991-96, Performance Auditor, 1996-98,

Performance Audit Manager, 1998-2001; Head of Regulatory Policy and Information, Communities Scotland, 2001-03. Address: (b.) Apex 2, 97 Haymarket Terrace, Edinburgh EH12 5HD.

Watt, Maureen. MSP (SNP), Aberdeen South and North Kincardine, 2011-2021, North East Scotland, 2006-2011; Minister for Mental Health, 2016-2018; Minister for Public Health, 2014-2016; Convener of the Infrastructure and Capital Investment Committee, 2011-14; Convener of the Rural Affairs and Environment Committee, 2009-2011; Minister for Schools and Skills, 2007-09; b. 23.6.51, Aberdeen; m.; 2 c. Educ. Keith Grammar School; University of Strathclyde; University of Birmingham. Comprehensive School Teacher, Social Studies, Reading, Berkshire, 1974-76; Personnel Assistant, then Personnel Manager, Deutag Drilling (now KCA Deutag). Daughter of the late Hamish Watt MP (Banffshire), 1974-79; mother of Stuart Donaldson MP (West Aberdeenshire & Kincardine), 2015-2017.

Watt, Professor Roger, BA (Cantab), PhD, FRSE. Professor of Psychology, Stirling University, since 1988; b. London; m., Helen; 2 s.; 1 d. Educ. St. Olaves School; Downing College, Cambridge. Formerly Scientist, MRC Applied Psychology Unit, Cambridge; expert witness, various including Cullen Inquiry and Ladbroke Grove Rail Crash. 2 books published. Recreation: trumpet player. Address: (b.) Department of Psychology, Stirling University, Stirling FK9 4LA; T.-01786 467640; e-mail: r.j.watt@stirling.ac.uk

Watt, Ronald Stewart "Ronnie", OBE. Scottish master of Shotokan karate; Founder, President and Chief Instructor for the National Karate Institute Scotland, a member of the International Karate Shotokan World Body; b. 16.4.47, Aberdeen. Started learning karate in 1965; has trained over 20,000 students. Awarded Order of the Rising Sun with Gold and Silver rays in 2010 on behalf of the Japanese government by the Japanese Consul General in Edinburgh (in recognition of an outstanding contribution to karate and commitment to strengthening the relationship between Scotland and Japan). Awarded a Commemorative Medal of the Trnava Self-Governing Region (TSGR) of Slovakia by the TSGR's president Tibor Mikuš in 2014. Knight of the Order of the Holy Trinity (2015); Knight Commander Cavaleiro da Casa Real Portuguesa (2015); Inducted into the European Martial Arts Hall of Fame (2015); Awarded 9th Dan (Hanshi) Master of Masters by the International Shotokan Karate DO, Shihankai (ISKS); Watt's OSS Awards world wide over 250 awards, Order of The Scottish Samurai, 2017; Japan tour awarded 11 OSS awards in Japan with Charles Lord Bruce, a founding member of the OSS (several of the OSS awards were given to members of the Japanses Diet); awarded an Honorary Degree of Master of the University; awarded Member of St John (MStJ) by the Queen; received OSS Letters Patent from the Lord Lyon King of Arms Dr Joseph Morrow at an award ceremony at Broomhall House, 2021.

Watt, Willie, MA (Hons). Chairman of The Board, Scottish National Investment Bank, since 2019; b. 5.59. Educ. Aberdeen Grammar School; Carnegie Trust for Universities of Scotland; INSEAD; University of Aberdeen. Career history: Managing Director, 3i Group plc, London, 1981-2000; Martin Currie: Chief Executive Officer, 2001-2019, Chairman, 2018-19; Board and Audit Committee Member, National Galleries of Scotland, since 2014; Advisory Board Member, Scottish Equity Partners (SEP), since 2016; Trustee of the National Galleries of Scotland Foundation, since 2020; member of the Advisory Board of Scottish Equity Partners. Address: Scottish National Investment Bank plc, Waverley Gate, 2-4 Waterloo Place, Edinburgh EH1 3EG.

Watterson, Professor Andrew, BA, PhD, CFIOSH, FCR. Emeritus Professor of Health, University of Stirling, since 2000; Public Health and Population Health Research Group, since 2000; b. 13.08.48. Lecturer in Health, Southampton University, 1980-92; Head of OSHU, NTU, 1992-94; Head of Department of Health, De Montfort University, Leicester and Professor of Occupational and Environmental Health, 1994-2000. Publications: author of 3 books, 1 edited book, 26 chapters in books, 33 published reports and over 100 publications in peer reviewed scientific and medical journals. On editorial boards and civil society organisations dealing with risks and hazards. Outputs on chemical, energy, agricultural, electronics and fish farming industries; acted as an advisor to the World Health Organization and project coordinator for UN FAO work. Main research interests relate to regulation and enforcement, health impact assessments, participatory action research and occupational cancer prevention and lately on worker and community hazards associated with covid, landfills and gas works. Address: (b.) Public Health and Population Health Research Group, Research Group, University of Stirling, Stirling FK9 4LA; e-mail: aew1@stir.ac.uk

Watts, Professor Colin, BSc, DPhil, FRS, FRSE, FMedSci. Emeritus Professor, University of Dundee, since 2017; b. 28.4.53, London; m., Susan Mary (nee Light); 1 s.; 2 d. Educ. Friend's School, Saffron Walden; Bristol University; Sussex University. EMBO Long Term Fellow, University of California, Los Angeles, 1980-82; Beit Memorial Fellow, MRC Lab of Molecular Biology, Cambridge, 1982-86; Lecturer, then Reader, Department of Biochemistry, University of Dundee, 1986-99; Professor of Immunobiology, University of Dundee, 1999-2017; Tenovus Scotland Margaret Maclellan Prize, 2000; Descartes Prize, European Union, 2002 (shared); Wellcome Trust Molecular and Cell Panel, 1993-96; MRC Training and Career Development Panel, 2005-09; Scientific Advisory Boards, Jenner Institute Vaccine Research, 2001-05; Lister Institute of Preventative Medicine, 2015-2018; Editorial Boards: Science, Eur. Journal of Immunology, Journal of Cell Biology, Journal of Cell Science. Recreations: music; cities; armchair sport. Address: (b.) Division of Cell Signalling and Immunology, College of Life Sciences, University of Dundee DD1 5EH; T.-01382 384233; e-mail: c.watts@dundee.ac.uk

Way of Plean, Sheriff George Alexander, OStJ, FSAScot, FRSA, Companion of the Order of Malta, Queen's Golden Jubilee Medal, California State Service Medal, The Much Hon. Baron of Plean in the County of Stirlingshire. Resident Sheriff at Dundee, since 2009; Chancellor, Diocese of Brechin (2020); Member, Scottish Civil Justice Council (2020); Solicitor Advocate and retired Senior Partner, Beveridge and Kellas SSC; Procurator Fiscal (2003-09), now Carrick Pursuivant, HM Court of the Lord Lyon; Lt. Colonel (Judge Advocate), California Military Reserve (retired 2009); b. 22.5.56, Edinburgh; 1 s. Educ. University of Edinburgh (LL.B Hons, 1978); Pembroke College, Oxford (Said Prize, 2015). Secretary, Standing Council of Scottish Chiefs, 1984-2003; Past President, Society of Solicitors in the Supreme Courts; Member, Council, Law Society of Scotland, 2001-09; Member, Sheriff Court Rules Council, 2007-09; Freeman, City of Glasgow, 1997; Guildsman of Dundee, 2018. Former Hon. Royal Consul of Portugal; enrolled in foreign orders of chivalry: St Maurice (Italy), Our Lady of Vila Vicosa and of St Michael de Ala (Portugal); Polonia Restituta (Poland); Order of St. Anna (Russia); Chancellor, Diocese of Brechin (2020); Companion of the Noble Crossbows of St Felipe y Santiago and of the Real Maestranza de Cabelleros Spain.

Publications: Clan and Family Encyclopaedia (3rd Edition, 2019); Homelands of the Clans; Scottish Clans and Tartans; Everyday Scots Law. Recreations: heraldry and chivalric studies.

Webb, Professor David John, CBE (2020), MD, DSc, FRCP, FRSE, FAHA, FESC, FFPM (Hon), FMedSci PFBPharmacolS (Hon), FBHS. Christison Professor of Therapeutics and Clinical Pharmacology, University of Edinburgh, since 1995 and Consultant Physician, Lothian University Hospitals NHS Trust, since 1990; b. 1.9.53; m.; 3 s. Educ. Dulwich College (Kent Scholarship), 1964-71; The Royal London Hospital, 1971-76; MB BS, University of London, 1977; MD, University of London, 1990; DSc, University of Edinburgh, 2000; MRCP UK (Royal College of Physicians, London), 1980; FRCP, Edinburgh, 1992; FFPM, UK, 1993; FFPM (Hon), 2016; FRCP, London, 1994; FAHA/International Fellowship, American Heart Association, 1998; FMedSci, UK, 1999; FESC, 2001; FRSE, 2004; FBPharmacolS, 2004; FBHS, 2014. House Officer Posts, The Royal London Hospital Scheme, 1977-78; Senior House Officer, Chelmsford Hospitals. 1978-79; Senior House Officer, medical rotational scheme, Stoke Mandeville Hospital, 1979-80; Registrar, medical rotational scheme, Royal London Hospital, 1980-82; Registrar in Medicine, Western Infirmary, Glasgow, 1982-85; MRC Clinical Scientist, MRC BP Unit, Western Infirmary, Glasgow, 1982-85; Lecturer in Clinical Pharmacology, St George's Medical School, London, 1985-89; Senior Registrar in Medicine, St George's Hospital, London, 1985-89; Consultant Physician, Lothian University Hospitals NHS Trust, since 1990; Senior Lecturer in Medicine, University of Edinburgh, 1990-95; Christison Professor of Therapeutics and Clinical Pharmacology, University of Edinburgh, since 1995; Director, Clinical Research Centre (CRC), University of Edinburgh, since 1990; Head, University Department of Medicine, University of Edinburgh, 1997-98; Head, Department of Medical Sciences, University of Edinburgh, 1998-2001; Wellcome Trust Research Leave Fellowship, and Leader, Wellcome Trust Cardiovascular Research Initiative (CVRI), University of Edinburgh, 1998-2001; Director of the Education Programme, Wellcome Trust Clinical Research Facility (WTCRF), Edinburgh, 1998-2015; Convenor, Cardiovascular Interdisciplinary Group, University of Edinburgh, 1999-2000; Head, Centre for Cardiovascular Science (CVS), University of Edinburgh, 2000-04; Chairman, New Drugs Committee (Scottish Medicines Consortium), 2001-05; Executive Committee, British Hypertension Society, 1991-94; British Pharmacological Society: Executive Committee, 1994-98, Clinical Vice-President, 1995-98, Director and Trustee, 1996-99, and 2004, Vice President (Meetings), 2012, President-Elect, 2014-15, President, 2016-17, Chairman, Committee of Professors and Heads of Clinical Pharmacology & Therapeutics, 2004-8; Section Committee I, Academy of Medical Sciences, 2000-02, Council, since 2020; Trustee, High Blood Pressure Foundation, since 1991; Research Director, High Blood Pressure Foundation, since 1993; Councillor, Clinical Division, International Union for Pharmacology (IUPHAR), since 2004; Chairman, Scottish Medicines Consortium, 2005-08; Vice-President, Royal College of Physicians of Edinburgh, 2006-09; Lead - Wellcome Trust Scottish Translational Medicine and Therapeutics Initiative (STMTI), 2008-2016; EACPT, President, 2009; President, Scottish Society of Physicians, 2010; Lead Clin Pharmacol, MRC Scottish Clin Pharmacol and Pathway Programme (SCP3), 2010-2014; Non-Executive Director, MHRA, 2013-21; Vice Chair, MHRA Board, 2018-21; Chair, Prescribing Skills Assessment (PSA) Executive Committee, 2014-19; Chair, NIBSC Scientific Advisory Committee, 2014-21; President, World Congress of Pharmacology, Glasgow SEC, 2023. Publications: The Molecular Biology & Pharmacology of the Endothelins (Molecular Biology Intelligence Unit Monograph Series), Co-Author, 1995; The Endothelium in Hypertension, ed, Co-Author, 1996; The Year in Therapeutics Vol 1, ed, Co-Author, 2005. Recreations: summer and winter mountaineering; ski-touring; scuba diving; reading late at night. Clubs: Scottish Mountaineering Club; Scottish Malt Whisky Society. Address: (h.) 75 Great King Street, Edinburgh EH3 6RN. E-mail: d.j.webb@ed.ac.uk

Webber, Sue, BSc (Hons). MSP (Scottish Conservative and Unionist Party), Lothian (Region), since 2021; Scottish Conservative Shadow Secretary for Public Health (including Drugs Policy), Women's Health and Sport; b. 8.72. Educ. Currie High School, Edinburgh; University of Edinburgh. Career history: Ethicon Endo-Surgery: Territory Manager, East Central Scotland, 1998-2002, UK Marketing Manager, Endoscopy, 2004, Regional Business Manager, North UK, 2004-2010; Commercial Business Manager, Johnson & Johnson, 2010-13; Northern UK Sales Manager, LocaMed, 2013-16; Account Manager, Purple Surgical, Scotland and NE England, 2017-18; Sales Agent, York Medical Technologies Ltd, Scotland, 2018-19; Northern UK Account Manager, CliniSupplies: Q CLOSE, 2016-2021; Sales Agent - Capital and Surgical Division, Pharmed UK - Medical and Scientific, Scotland, 2019-2021; elected Councillor (Pentland Hills), The City of Edinburgh Council in 2017; appointed Managing Director, MEDinburgh Ltd in 2013 (company ceased trading, July 2021). Address: The Scottish Parliament, Edinburgh EH99 1SP; T.-0131 348 6763; e-mail: Sue.Webber.msp@parliament.scot

Webster, Andrew George, QC, LLB (Hons), DipLP, FRSA. Advocate, since 1992; b. 20.7.67, Wick; m., Sheila Mairead; 2 d. Educ. Wick High School; University of Aberdeen. First Scottish Standing Junior Counsel; Part-time Sheriff; Part-time Chairman, Pension Appeal Tribunal for Scotland; Standing Junior Counsel to: Ministry of Defence (Air Force), 1997-2000, Ministry of Defence, 2000-2012; Legal Assessor: Medical Practitioners Tribunal Service (formerly General Medical Council), since 2010. Address: (b.) Advocates' Library, Parliament House, Edinburgh EH1 1RF; T.-0131-226 5071.

Webster, Professor Nigel Robert, BSc, MB, ChB, PhD, FRCA, FRCPEdin, FRCSEdin. Emeritus Professor of Anaesthesia and Intensive Care, Aberdeen University (appointed Professor in 1994); b. 14.6.53, Walsall; divorced; 1 s.; 2 d.; m. (2), Helen Frances Webster. Educ. Edward Shelley High School, Walsall; Leeds University. Member, scientific staff/Consultant, Clinical Research Centre, Northwick Park Hospital, Harrow; Consultant in Anaesthesia and Intensive Care, St. James's University Hospital, Leeds. Address: (b.) Institute of Medical Sciences, Foresterhill, Aberdeen AB25 2ZD; T.-01224 681818.

Webster, Professor Robin Gordon Maclennan, OBE, PPRIAS, RIBA, MA (Cantab), MA (Arch), FRSA. Emeritus Professor of Architecture, Scott Sutherland School of Architecture, The Robert Gordon University, Aberdeen; Partner, CameronWebster architects, since 2005; Partner, Spence & Webster, London, 1972-1984; Senior Partner, Robin Webster & Associates, Aberdeen, 1984-2004; b. 24.12.39, Glasgow; m., Katherine S. Crichton (deceased); 1 s.; 2 d.; m., Pauline Lawrence, 2012. Educ. Glasgow Academy; Rugby School; St. John's College, Cambridge; University College London. Commissioner, Royal Fine Art Commission for Scotland, 1992-98; Academician, Royal Scottish Academy, 1996. President, Royal Incorporation of Architects in Scotland, 2018-2020; Chairman, Alexander Thomson Association, 2011-2013; Secretary, Walmer Crescent Association; Trustee, Glasgow City Heritage Trust, 2007-2012; Trustee, Scottish Stained Glass

Symposium 2014; Chairman, Friends of Glenan Wood, 2017. Recreations: looking and drawing. Address: (h.) 7 Walmer Crescent, Glasgow G51 1AT; T.-0141 330 9898; Mobile: 07970 165 762; e-mail: robin.webster@mac.com

Webster, Sheila Mairead, LLB (Hons), MBA. President, Law Society of Scotland, since 2022; Partner and Head of Dispute Resolution, Davidson Chalmers Stewart LLP, Edinburgh, since 2009; b. 3.66. Educ. University of Aberdeen; Alliance Manchester Business School; Chartered Institute of Arbitrators. Career history: Associate, Commercial and Property Litigation, Dundas & Wilson, 1992-2002; Head of Property Litigation and Partner, Bell & Scott, 2003-09. Address: Davidson Chalmers Stewart, 12 Hope Street, Edinburgh EH2 4DB; T.-0131 625 9056. E-mail: sheila.webster@dcslegal.com

Weir, Viscount (William Kenneth James Weir), BA, Hon. DEng (Glasgow), Hon. FEng. Director, The Weir Group PLC, 1966-99 (Chairman, 1973-80, 1983-99); Director and former Vice-Chairman, St. James' Place Capital plc; Chairman, Balfour Beatty plc, 1996-2003 (Deputy Chairman, 1992-96, Director, since 1977); Chairman, CP Ships Ltd., 2001-04; Director, Canadian Pacific Railway Co., 1989-2004; Chairman, Major British Exporters; b. 9.11.33, Glasgow; m., 1, Diana MacDougall (m. diss.); 1 s.; 1 d.; 2, Jacqueline Mary Marr (m. diss.); 3, Marina Sevastopoulo; 1 s. Educ. Eton; Trinity College, Cambridge. Director, British Bank of the Middle East, 1974-80; Member, London Advisory Committee, Hongkong and Shanghai Banking Corporation, 1980-92; Deputy Chairman, Charterhouse J. Rothschild PLC, 1983-85; Member, Court, Bank of England, 1972-84; Co-Chairman, RIT and Northern PLC, 1982-83; Director, 1970, Chairman, 1975-82, Great Northern Investment Trust Ltd.; Member, Scottish Economic Council, 1972-85; Director, British Steel Corporation, 1972-76; Chairman, Patrons of National Galleries of Scotland, 1984-95; Member, Queen's Bodyguard for Scotland (Royal Company of Archers). Recreations: shooting; golf; fishing. Address: (h.) Rodinghead, Mauchline, Ayrshire.

Weir, Michael, LLB. MP (SNP), Angus, 2001-2017; SNP Chief Whip in the House of Commons, 2015-17; b. 24.3.57, Arbroath; m., Anne; 2 d. Educ. Arbroath High School; Aberdeen University. Myers and Wills, Montrose, 1979-81; Charles Wood and Son, Kirkcaldy, 1982-83; Myers and Wills, Montrose, 1983-84; J. & D.G. Shiell, Brechin, 1984-2001. Dean of Society of Procurators and Solicitors in Angus, 2001.

Weir, The Hon Lord (Robert Weir), QC, BA (Hist, Hons), LBE. Senator of the College of Justice, since 2020; Sheriff: Lothian and Borders at Edinburgh, 2018-2020, South Strathclyde, Dumfries and Galloway at Hamilton, 2016-2018. Educ. Durham University; Dundee University. Joined Maclay Murray & Spens as a trainee solicitor in 1992; admitted to the Faculty of Advocates in 1995, and practised principally in commercial dispute resolution, with a specialty in maritime law; Advocate Depute, 2005-08 and took silk in 2010. Address: Parliament House, Parliament Square, Edinburgh EH1 1RQ.

Weller, Professor David Paul, MBBS, MPH, PHD, FRACGP, MRCGP, FAFPHM. James Mackenzie Professor of General Practice, University of Edinburgh, since 2000, Head of School, Clinical Sciences and Community Health, 2005-2012; b. 21.7.59, Adelaide; m., Dr Belinda Weller; 1 s.; 2 d. Educ. Prince Alfred College, Adelaide; University of Adelaide. Training and working in family medicine, UK and Australia, 1984-90;

PhD studies, 1991-94; Senior Lecturer, Department of General Practice, Flinders University of South Australia, 1995-99. Board Member, Lothian Primary Care Trust, Scottish Cancer Foundation. Recreations: running; hill-walking; piano. Address: (h.) 42 Craiglea Drive, Edinburgh EH10 5PF.

Weller, Dr Richard, MD, FRCP (Ed). Reader, Dermatology, University of Edinburgh; Honorary Consultant Dermatologist, NHS Lothian; b. 21.7.62, Münster, Germany; m., Dr Julie Gallagher; 1 s.; 1 d. Educ. Malvern College; St. Thomas' Hospital, London University. General medical training, England and Australia, 1987-92; dermatology training: St. John's Institute of Dermatology, London, 1993, Aberdeen Royal Infirmary, 1994-96; Lecturer, Dermatology, Edinburgh Royal Infirmary, 1996-98; Visiting Research Fellow: Immunbiologie Abteilung, HHU, Düsseldorf, 1999, Department of Surgery, University of Pittsburgh, USA, 2000-01. Recreations: mountaineering; sailing. Address: (h.) 79 Dundas Street, Edinburgh EH3 6SD; e-mail: r.weller@ed.ac.uk

Wells, Carol Ann (Annie). MSP (Scottish Conservative), Glasgow region, since 2016; Shadow Cabinet Secretary for Communities and Local Government, 2020-21; former Deputy Leader of the Scottish Conservative Party (2020); b. 24.2.72. Worked as a retail manager for Marks & Spencer in various locations throughout Glasgow for 12 years. Sits on the Equality & Human Rights Committee of the Scottish Parliament. Address: Scottish Parliament, Edinburgh EH99 1SP.

Wells, Margaret Jeffrey, MA, CQSW. Non Executive Director, Fife NHS Board, since 2017; Independent Management and Care Consultant, since 2004; former Non Executive Board Member, Scottish Children's Reporter Administration; b. 22.7.55, Berwick-upon-Tweed; m., Tony Wells; 1 s.; 1 d. Educ. Berwickshire High School, Duns; University of Edinburgh; University of Glasgow. Director of Partnership Development and Child Health Commissioner, Lothian NHS Board, 2002-04; Director of Housing and Social Work, Aberdeenshire Council, 1995-2002; Depute Director of Social Work, Grampian Regional Council, 1993-95, Assistant Director of Social Work, 1992-93; District Manager (Dundee West), Tayside Regional Council, Area Fieldwork Manager (Hospitals), 1989-92, Senior Social Worker, Mental Health, Perth & Kinross. Governor, The Robert Gordon University, 2001/02; President, Association of Directors of Social Work, 2000; Social Work adviser to COSLA; Member: Ministerial Joint Futures Group, Mental Health References Group. Recreation: singing. Address: (h. & b.) 22 Comerton Place, Drumoig, Leuchors, St. Andrews, Fife KY10 0NQ; e-mail: margaretwells22@btinternet.com

Welsh, Barry, BSc, PGCE. Rector, Edinburgh Academy, since 2017. Educ. Loughborough University; Sheffield University. Career: Geography Teacher, Harrow School, London; Head of Geography, then Housemaster, Fettes College, Edinburgh; Deputy Head, Shawnigan Lake School, Vancouver Island, Canada, 2012-17. Address: 42 Henderson Row, Edinburgh EH3 5BL; T.-0131 624 4911; e-mail: rectorsoffice@edinburghacademy.org.uk

Welsh, Ian McWilliam, OBE, MA (Hons), MA, DPSE, FRSA. Former Chief Executive, Health and Social Care Alliance Scotland (2010-2022); b. 23.11.53, Prestwick; m., Elizabeth; 2 s. Educ. Prestwick Academy; Ayr Academy; University of Glasgow. Former professional footballer, Kilmarnock FC; Teacher (former Deputy Head Teacher, Auchinleck Academy); formerly Director, Human

Resources and Public Affairs, Prestwick International Airport; Chief Executive, Kilmarnock FC, 1997-2001. Former Member, Kyle and Carrick District Council, then South Ayrshire Council; former MSP; former Governor, Craigie College of Education; former Chair, North Ayrshire Partnership; former Chair, Scottish Advisory Committee of the Voluntary Sector National Training Organisation.

Wend, Prof. Petra, CBE, PhD, FRSA, FRSE. Professor Emeritus; Principal and Vice-Chancellor, Queen Margaret University, 2009-2019 (retired); Deputy Vice-Chancellor and Deputy Chief Executive, Oxford Brookes University, 2005-09; b. 21.01.59, Gütersloh, Germany; partner, Professor Philip James; 1 d. Educ. Münster University; University of Leeds. Middlesex Polytechnic, later Middlesex University: Lecturer, Senior Lecturer, then Principal Lecturer, 1989-97; Deputy Head, School of Languages, 1996-97 (Acting Head, 1995); Director of Curriculum, Learning and Quality, 1997-99; University of North London: Dean, Faculty of Humanities and Education, 1999-2002; Pro Vice-Chancellor (Learning and Teaching), 2000-02; Director of Learning, Teaching and Student Affairs, London Metropolitan University, 2002-05; Deputy Vice-Chancellor and Deputy Chief Executive, Oxford Brookes University, 2005-09. Member, Commission of Widening Access, 2015-16; Chair, National Implementation Board for Teaching Scotland's Future, 2012-2015; Vice-Convener, Universities Scotland, 2012-2014; Convenor, Universities Scotland Learning and Teaching Committee, 2010-12; Member: QAA Board, QAA Scotland, until 2016; SDS/SFC Skills Committee, until 2013; RSE Council Member, since 2017, RSE Education Committee, since 2016; British Council Scotland Advisory Committee, 2012-2018; Director of Goodison Board, since 2017; Member: Goodison Group Forum, since 2012; Convener of Common Purpose Edinburgh Advisory Group, 2017-19; Chair: University of Hamburg University Council. since 2020, Member, Global Universities Leaders Council, Universities UK; Universities Scotland, 2009-2019; Chair of Global University Leaders Council, 2019-2021. Publications: The Female Voice: Lyrical expression in the writings of five Italian Renaissance poets, 1994; German Interlanguage, 1996, 2nd edition, 1998; Geschäftsbriefe schnell und sicher formulieren, 2004; contributed articles to learned journals on linguistics and on institutional strategies. Recreations: painting; sport; Arsenal FC (season ticket holder). Address: (h.) 46 Royal Mile Mansions, 50 North Bridge, Edinburgh EH1 1QN.

Wernham, Allan, LLB. Managing Director, Scotland, CMS Cameron McKenna, since 2018, Partner, since 2014; b. 9.72. Educ. University of Aberdeen. Career history: Dundas & Wilson: Head of Operational Excellence, 2010-12, Practice Area Leader - Real Estate, 2010-12, Partner, 1996-2014, Managing Partner, 2012-14. Address: CMS Cameron Mckenna LLP, 191 West George Street, Glasgow G2 2LD; T.-0141 3046056.

Wersun, Ana, CSP. Honorary Consul, Republic of Slovenia in Scotland, since 2004; Consultant Physiotherapist, since 1976; b. 30.12.54, Brezice, Slovenia; m., Dr. Alec Wersun; 2 d. Educ. Brezice School; University of Ljubljana. Qualified as a Physiotherapist in Ljubljana, 1976; worked as a Physiotherapist in Slovenia, Switzerland and UK both in The National Health Services and in Private Practice, 1976-2008. Member, Consular Corps, Edinburgh and Leith, since 2004. Honorary Treasurer, Consular Corps of Edinburgh and Leith. Recreations: hill walking; classical music; painting; reading. Address: (h. & b.) 3 Coltbridge Terrace, Edinburgh EH12 6AB; T.-0131-337 5167; e-mail: sloveneconsulate@btinternet.com

West, Denise. Chief Commercial Officer, DC Thomson Media, since 2018 (appointed Head of Commercial in 2014). Commercial Director, Scottish Daily Record and

Sunday Mail Ltd, 2000-2013; Managing Director (Scotland and North East), Trinity Mirror, 2012-14. Address: (b.) Lang Stracht, Mastrick, Aberdeen AB15 6DF; T.-01224 690 222.

West, Professor Gary James, MA, PhD. Personal Chair in Scottish Ethnology; Director of the European Ethnological Research Centre, University of Edinburgh; Broadcaster, Presenter, BBC Radio Scotland, since 2003; b. 9.11.66, Aberfeldy. Educ. Pitlochry High School, Breadalbane Academy; University of Edinburgh. Lecturer, Celtic & Scottish Studies, University of Edinburgh, since 1994. Piper and Folk Musician; Member: Ceolbeg, Clan Alba, Hugh MacDiarmids Haircut, Vale of Atholl Pipe Band; toured widely in Europe and North America; regular recording artist; presenter of 'Pipeline', BBC Radio Scotland. Former Board Member, Creative Scotland; Board Member, Gordon Duncan Memorial Trust; Chair, Traditional Arts and Culture Scotland. Recreations: music; football; golf. Address: (b.) 50 George Square, Celtic and Scottish Studies, University of Edinburgh EH8 9LH; T.-0131 552 7087; e-mail: gary.west@ed.ac.uk

West, Peter William Alan, OBE, DL, MA, DUniv, DPhil; b. 16.3.49, Edinburgh; m. Margaret Clark; 1s; 1d. Educ. Edinburgh Academy; St Andrews University. Administrator, Edinburgh University, 1972-77; Assistant Secretary, Leeds University 1977-83; Deputy Registrar, Strathclyde University, 1983-89, Secretary to the University of Strathclyde, 1990-2010; Chief Operating Officer, Edinburgh College of Art, 2010-2011. Chair, Scotland/Malawi Partnership, 2005-2010; Doctor (honoris causa), University of Rostov-on-Don, Russia; Doctor (honoris causa), University of Malawi; Deputy Lieutenant of the City of Glasgow; Honorary Fellowships of University of Strathclyde and Bell College, Hamilton. Awarded the OBE for services to HE in Scotland and Malawi in the Queen's Birthday Honours, 2006. Scottish Honorary Consul of the Republic of Malawi from 2010. Recreations: reading, drinking wine; supporting the leading football teams of Scotland (Hibernian) and Africa (the Flames of Malawi) through thick and thin. Address: Wester Saltoun Hall, Pencaitland, East Lothian EH34 5DS; T.-07811946489.

Whaling, Rev. Professor Frank, BA, MA, PhD, ThD, FSAM, FRAS, FABI, FWLA, FIBA, FICS, FWIA. Emeritus Professor of the Study of Religion, Edinburgh University; Methodist Minister; b. 5.2.34, Pontefract; m., Margaret; 1 s.; 1 d. Educ. Kings School, Pontefract; Christ's College, Cambridge; Wesley House, Cambridge; Harvard University. Methodist Minister, Birmingham Central Hall, 1960-62, Faizabad and Banaras, North India, 1962-66, Eastbourne, 1966-69; Teaching Fellow, Harvard University, 1972-73 (Harvard Doctorate, 1969-73); appointed Lecturer, Study of Religion, Edinburgh University, 1973. Theyer Honor Award, Harvard; Maitland Award, Cambridge; various Reseach Awards; Chair, Scottish Churches China Group, 1985-93; Chair, Edinburgh Inter-Faith Association, 1985-99, President, since 1999; Director, Edinburgh Cancer Help Centre, 1987-91; Chair, Scottish Inter-Faith Symposium, 1987-94; Consultant, World Without Hunger (charity); BBC, Paulist Press, International Inter-Faith Council; Alistair Hardy Trust; Encyclopedia of World Spirituality (26 vols); Chair, Edinburgh International Centre for World Spiritualities, 1999-2004; Executive Director, Scottish Inter-Faith Council, 2002-05. Council Member, SHAP Working Party on Religion in Education, Religious Education Movement in Scotland. Visiting Lecturer and Professor, USA, China, South Africa, India, England; Hon. Life Fellow, British Association for the Study of Religion; ICS Scot of the Year, 2007. Publications: over 100 papers, over 250 reviews; books written and/or edited: An Approach to Dialogue: Hinduism and Christianity, 1966; The Rise of the Religious Significance of Rama, 1980; John and Charles Wesley, 1981; The World's Religious Traditions: Current Perspectives in Religious Studies, 1984; Contemporary Approaches to the Study of Religion: Vol. I, 1984, Vol. II, 1985; Christian Theology and World Religions, 1986; Religion in Today's World, 1987; Compassion Through Understanding, 1990; Dictionary of Beliefs and Religions, 1992; The World: How It Came Into Being and our Responsibility for It, 1994; Theory and Method in Religious Studies, 1995; Christian Prayer for Today, 2002; Understanding Hinduism, 2009; General Editor: (9 vol) Understanding Faith, since 2002; Understanding the Brahma Kumaris, 2012. Recreations: music; art; sport; inter-faith activities. Address: (h.) 21 Gillespie Road, Edinburgh EH13 0NW; T.-0131-441 2112.

Whatley, Professor Christopher Allan, OBE, BA, PhD, FRHistS, FRSE, FSA Scot. Emeritus Professor of Scottish History, Dundee University (Vice-Principal and Head, College of Arts and Social Sciences, 2006-2014, Dean, Faculty of Arts and Social Sciences, 2002-06, Head, Department of History, 1995-2002); b. 29.5.48, Birmingham; 1 s.; 1 d. Educ. Bearsden Academy; Strathclyde University. Lecturer, Ayr College, 1975-79, Dundee University, 1979-88, St. Andrews University, 1988-92, Dundee University, 1992-94; Senior Lecturer, 1994. Editor, Scottish Economic and Social History, 1995-99; Chairman, SCCC Review Group, Scottish History in the Curriculum; Consultant Editor, Scotland's Story; Chair, Scottish Historical Review Trust, 2002-06; Director, Dundee University Press, 2003-2014; Board member, Dundee Repertory Theatre, 2007-2015; Council member, Royal Society of Edinburgh, 2006-09; Council member, Royal Historical Society, 2009-11; Chairman, Board of Governance, Scottish Institute for Policing Research, 2009-2014; Hon President, Scottish Local History Forum, since 2015; Chairman, Scottish Records Association, since 2018. Publications: The Scottish Salt Industry, 1570-1850; Onwards from Osnaburgs: the rise and progress of a Scottish textile company; Bought and Sold for English Gold?: explaining the union of 1707; The Manufacture of Scottish History (Co-editor); The Life and Times of Dundee (Co-author); The Remaking of Juteopolis: Dundee 1891-1991 (Editor); John Galt (Editor); The Industrial Revolution in Scotland; Modern Scottish History, 1707 to the Present (Co-editor); Scottish Society 1707–1830: Beyond Jacobitism, Towards Industrialisation; Victorian Dundee: Image and Realities (Co-editor); The Scots and the Union; The Union of 1707: New Directions (Co-editor); A History of Everyday Life in Scotland, 1600-1800 (Co-editor); Jute No More: Transforming Dundee (Co-editor); The Scots and the Union: Then and Now; Immortal Memory: Burns and the Scottish People; Pabay: An Island Odyssey. Address: (h.) Tayfield Cottage, 51 Main Street, Longforgan, by Dundee DD2 5EW; T.-07972229750.
E-mail: c.a.whatley@dundee.ac.uk

Wheater, Professor Roger John, OBE, DUniv, CBiol, FRSB, FRSGS (Hon), FRZSS (Hon), FRSE. President, Scottish Wildlife Trust, 2006-08; Chairman, National Trust for Scotland, 2000-05; Director, Royal Zoological Society of Scotland, 1972-98; Honorary Professor, Edinburgh University, since 1993; b. 24.11.33, Brighton; m., Jean Ord Troup; 1 s.; 1 d. Educ. Brighton, Hove and Sussex Grammar School; Brighton Technical College. Commissioned, Royal Sussex Regiment, 1953; served Gold Coast Regiment, 1953-54; 4/5th Bn., Royal Sussex Regiment (TA), 1954-56; Colonial Police, Uganda, 1956-61; Chief Warden, Murchison Falls National Park, 1961-70; Director, Uganda National Parks, 1970-72; Member, Co-ordinating Committee, Nuffield Unit of Tropical Animal Ecology; Member, Board of Governors, Mweka College of

Wildlife Management, Tanzania; Director, National Park Lodges Ltd.; Member, Uganda National Research Council; Vice Chairman, Uganda Tourist Association; Council Member, 1980-91, and President, 1988-91, International Union of Directors of Zoological Gardens; Chairman, Federation of Zoological Gardens of Great Britain and Ireland, 1993-96; Chairman, Anthropoid Ape Advisory Panel, 1977-91; Member, International Zoo Year Book Editorial Board, 1987-99; President, Association of British Wild Animal Keepers, 1984-99; Chairman, Membership and Licensing Committee, 1984-91; Chairman, Working Party on Zoo Licensing Act, 1981-84; Council Member, Zoological Society of London, 1991-92, 1995-99, 2002-03, Vice President, 1999; Chairman, Whipsnade Wild Animal Park, 1999-2002; Vice-President, World Pheasant Association, since 1994; Trustee, Gorilla Organisation, 1995-2010, Chairman, 2008-2010; Chairman, European Association of Zoos and Aquaria, 1994-97; Member of Council, National Trust for Scotland, 1973-78, and 2000-05, Executive Committee, 1982-87, and 2000-05; Chairman, Cammo Estate Advisory Committee, 1980-95; ESU William Thyne Scholar, 1975; Assessor, Council, Scottish Wildlife Trust, 1973-92; Consultant, World Tourist Organisation (United Nations), 1980-2010; Member, Secretary of State for Scotland's Working Group on Environmental Education, 1990-94; Board Member, Scottish Natural Heritage, 1995-99 (Deputy Chairman, 1997-99); Chairman, Access Forum, 1996-2000; Founder Patron, Dynamic Earth, Trustee, 1999-2012; Patron, Friends of Kailzie Wildlife, since 2012; Member, Strategic Development Fund Panel - Royal Society of Wildlife Trust, 2007-2011; Vice-Chairman, Edinburgh Branch, English Speaking Union, 1977-81; President, Edinburgh Special Mobile Angling Club, 1982-86; President, Cockburn Trout Angling Club, 1997-2018; Trustee, Tweed Foundation, 2006-2018; Chairman, Tourism and Environment Forum, 1999-2003; Chairman, Heather Trust, 1999-2002; Deputy Chairman, Zoo Forum, 1999-2002; Vice-President, European Network of National Heritage Organisations, 2000-05; President, Tweeddale Society, 2007-2018; Chairman, Beaver-Salmonid Group, 2009-2015; President, Innerleithen Probus Club, 2010-2011, Vice President, 2009-2010; Member, Royal Zoological Society of Scotland Board, since 2011. Recreations: country pursuits; painting; gardening. Address: (h.) 17 Kirklands, Innerleithen, Borders EH44 6NA; T.-01896-830403.
E-mail: rogerwheater@gmail.com

Wheatley, Professor Denys N., BSc, PhD, DSc, MD (h.c.multi), CIBiol, FRSB, FRCPath. Chairman and Director, BioMedES UK (www.biomedes.biz); Past President, International Federation for Cell Biology; Director of the Chouden Research Foundation (HK); Visiting Professor of Physiology, Wayne State Medical School, Detroit; Professor, Semmelweis Medical University (Budapest, Hungary), Pécs Medical University (Pécs, Hungary) and National Medical University of Ukraine (Odessa); Foreign Member, Ukrainian Academy of Medical Sciences. Formerly at the Dept. of Pathology, University of Aberdeen; b. 18.03.40, Ascot; divorced; 2 d. Educ: Windsor Grammar School; King's College and the Institute of Cancer Research, University of London. Research Fellow Aberdeen University, 1964-67; MRC Travelling Fellow/USPHS Fellow, 1967-70; 1970 onwards: Lecturer, Senior Lecturer, Reader and Professor of Cell Pathology, Aberdeen University. Publications include: Cell Growth and Division; The Centriole - a Central Enigma of Cell Biology; About Life; Thinking About Life; Scientific Writing and Publishing - A Manual for Authors; formerly Editor-in-Chief: Cell Biology International; Cancer Cell International (founder); Theoretical Biology and Medical Modelling (founder); Oncology News. Recreations: art (book "BipolART: Art and Bipolar Disorder - a Personal Perspective", 2012); cello (Aberdeen City Orchestra, World Doctors Orchestra, European Doctors Orchestra, and others); piano; gardening; swimming. Address: (h.& b.) Leggat House, Keithhall, Inverurie AB51 0XL; T. -01467-670280.

Wheatley, The Right Hon. Lord (John Francis Wheatley), PC, QC, BL. Senator, College of Justice, 2000-2010 (retired); b. 9.5.41, Edinburgh; m., Bronwen Catherine Fraser; 2 s. Educ. Mount St. Mary's College, Derbyshire; Edinburgh University. Called to Scottish Bar, 1966; Standing Counsel to Scottish Development Department, 1968-74; Advocate Depute, 1974-78; Sheriff, Perthshire and Kinross-shire, at Perth, 1980-98; Temporary High Court Judge, 1992; Sheriff Principal of Tayside Central and Fife, 1998-2000. Member, Parole Board, 2000-03; Chairman, Judicial Studies Committee, 2000-06. Recreations: music; gardening. Address: Braefoot Farmhouse, Fossoway, Kinross-shire.

Wheeler, Professor Simon Jonathan, MA, DPhil, CEng, MICE. Cormack Professor of Civil Engineering, Glasgow University, since 1996; b. 30.4.58, Warlingham, Surrey; m., Noelle Patricia O'Rourke; 1 s.; 2 d. Educ. Whitehaven Grammar School; St. John's College, Cambridge; Balliol College, Oxford. University Lecturer in Soil Mechanics, Queen's University of Belfast, 1984-88; Lecturer in Soil Mechanics, Sheffield University, 1988-92; Lecturer in Civil Engineering, Oxford University, and Fellow of Keble College, Oxford, 1992-95. Recreation: mountaineering. Address: (b.) School of Engineering, Rankine Building, Glasgow G12 8LT; T.-0141-330 5202.

Wheelhouse, Paul. MSP (SNP), South Scotland, 2011-2021; Minister for Energy, Connectivity and the Islands, Scottish Government, 2018-2021, Minister for Business, Innovation and Energy, 2016-18, Minister for Community Safety and Legal Affairs, 2014-16, Minister for Environment and Climate Change, 2012-14; b. 22.6.70, Northern Ireland. Educ. Stewart's Melville College, Edinburgh; Aberdeen University (MA (Hons) Economic Science); Edinburgh University (MBA). Worked for 19 years as a professional economist with Pieda Consulting, DTZ and Biggar Economics; acted as a policy adviser to a wide range of public, private and voluntary organisations.

White, Iain, BSc (Hons), MEd. Director, Iain White Creative Leadership Ltd, since 2019; former Principal, Newlands Junior College (2014-19); b. 2.2.54, Greenock; m., Gail. Educ. Greenock High School; Glasgow University. Biology Teacher, then Principal Biology Teacher, Cowdenknowes High School, Greenock, 1977-87; Assistant Rector, Rothesay Academy, 1987-92; Depute Head Teacher, Port Glasgow High School, 1992-94; Head Teacher, Govan High School, Glasgow, 1994-2014. Past Captain, Greenock Golf Club. Recreations: golf; skiing; travel; watching football; Robert Burns; after-dinner speaking; playing the bagpipes. Address: (b.) 32 Duthie Road, Gourock PA19 1XS.

White, Sandra. MSP (SNP), Glasgow Kelvin, 2011-2021, Glasgow, 1999-2011; b. 17.8.51, Glasgow; m.; 3 c. Educ. Garthamlock Secondary School; Glasgow College; Cardonald College. Former SNP councillor in Renfrewshire; Press Officer, William Wallace Society. Served as an SNP Parliamentary group whip in the first parliamentary session and sat on the parliament's Public Petitions Committee, and Equal Opportunities Committee; Member of the SPCB and Health Committee. Forged a role as a crusading campaigner and working MSP while also holding her party's Deputy Social Justice portfolio. Campaigned against closures and downgrading (including a 1,600 signature petition) at the Royal Hospital for Sick Children, Yorkhill and the Queen Mother's Hospital; also campaigned extensively against racism and for better treatment of asylum seekers, including joining an occupation against so-called 'dawn raids'; other campaigns have included the successful attempts to save the 7:84 theatre group from threatened loss of funding by the Scottish Arts Council and involvement in Stop the War Coalition events. Recreations: reading; walking; meeting people.

White, Professor Stephen Leonard, MA, PhD, DPhil, LittD, FRSE, FBA. Emeritus Professor of Politics, Glasgow University, since 2017 (James Bryce Professor of Politics, 1991-2017); b. 1.7.45, Dublin; m., Ishbel MacPhie; 1 s. Educ. St. Andrew's College, Dublin; Trinity College, Dublin; Glasgow University; Wolfson College, Oxford. Lecturer in Politics, Glasgow University, 1971-85, Reader, 1985-91. President, British Association for Slavonic and East European Studies, 1994-97; Chief Editor, Journal of Communist Studies and Transition Politics, 1994-2011; Coeditor, Journal of Eurasian Studies, since 2010. Publications include: Political Culture and Soviet Politics, 1979; Britain and the Bolshevik Revolution, 1980; Origins of Detente, 1986; The Bolshevik Poster, 1988; After Gorbachev, 1993; Russia Goes Dry, 1996; How Russia Votes (with others), 1997; Values and Political Change in Postcommunist Europe (with others), 1998; Russia's New Politics, 2000; The Soviet Elite from Lenin to Gorbachev (Co-Author), 2000; Putin's Russia and the Enlarged Europe (with others), 2006; Understanding Russian Politics, 2011; Identities and Foreign Policies in Russia, Ukraine and Belarus, The Other Europes (Co-Author), 2014. Recreations: cinema; theatre; opera; foreign travel. Address: (h.) 11 Hamilton Drive, Glasgow G12 8DN; T.-0141-334 9541; e-mail: stephen.white@glasgow.ac.uk

White, Tess. MSP (Scottish Conservative and Unionist Party), North East Scotland (Region), since 2021. Worked in the oil and gas industry; former Board Director, Shell Renewables; former Vice President, Shell International; former HR Director, Centrica. Conservative candidate for Dundee West, 2019 United Kingdom general election. Address: The Scottish Parliament, Edinburgh EH99 1SP; T.-0131 348 6218. E-mail: Tess.White.msp@parliament.scot

Whitefield, Gavin, CBE, DL, CPFA, DPA. Chief Executive, North Lanarkshire Council, 2000-2015 (retired); Deputy Lieutenant for Lanarkshire, since 2016; b. 7.2.56; m., Grace; 2 d. Educ. Lanark Grammar School; Bell College, Hamilton. Audit Assistant, Exchequer and Audit Department, Civil Service, 1974-76; Clydesdale District Council: Assistant Auditor, 1976-84, Computer Development Officer, 1984-86, Principal Housing Officer (Finance and Administration), 1986-89; Assistant Director of Housing (Finance and Administration), Motherwell District Council, 1989-95; Director of Housing and Property Services, North Lanarkshire Council, 1995-2000. Past Chair, SOLACE Scotland, 2007/08. Recreations: hill-walking; football.

Whitefield, Karen. MSP (Labour), Airdrie and Shotts, 1999-2011; b. 8.1.70, Bellshill. Educ. Calderhead High School, Shotts; Glasgow Caledonian University. Civil servant, Benefits Agency, 1991-92; PA to Rachel Squire, MP, 1992-99. Congressional Intern on Capitol Hill, 1990. Recreations: swimming; reading; travel.

Whiteford, Eilidh, MA Hons, MA, PhD. MP (SNP), Banff and Buchan, 2010-2017; SNP Spokesperson for Work and Pensions, 2010-2017; b. 24.4.69, Aberdeen;

m., Stephen Smith. Educ. Banff Academy; Glasgow University; Guelph University, Ontario. Worked for Allan Macartney MEP, then Ian Hudghton MEP until the 1999 elections; later helped new MSP Irene McGugan establish a constituency office in the first term of the Scottish Parliament; returned to Glasgow University in 1999, lecturing in Scottish Literature and developing access routes into higher education for mature students (in Glasgow University's adult and continuing education department); campaigning role in the voluntary sector as Co-ordinator of the Scottish Carers' Alliance, from 2001; moved to Oxfam (2003), working as a policy adviser and campaigns manager for over six years. Very actively involved in the Make Poverty History campaign in 2005 and helped establish the Scottish Fair Trade Forum. Member, Select Committee on Scottish Affairs, 2010-2015. Recreation: reading.

Whiteford, Joanie Aileen. Lord-Lieutenant of Ross and Cromarty, Skye and Lochlash, since 2019; b. 1960; m., David; 3 c. Educ. Berwick-upon-Tweed Grammar School; Robert Gordon University; The Moray House School of Education. Career history: previously worked in Ernst & Young's Business Advisory Department; delivered Business Development courses for the Agricultural Training Board throughout Wester Ross, Lochaber, Orkney and Shetland; currently a self-employed computer trainer for Farmplan Computers; produces management accounts for a number of clients. Held numerous voluntary posts and is currently a Vestry member and treasurer of St Andrews Episcopal Church in Tain; treasurer of Tain Tennis Club, and is involved in junior tennis coaching; former committee member of Nigg & Shandwick Friendship and a member of Hilton and Cadboll School Board. Recreations: tennis; golf; cycling; skiing; gardening; walking her dogs; hill walking; farming and cooking. Address: Council Offices, High Street, Dingwall IV15 9QN.

Whitehorn, Will, MA Hons (Aberdeen). Chancellor, Edinburgh Napier University, since 2021; Chairman, Scottish Event Campus Limited, since 2013; Chairman, Clyde Space Ltd, 2016-18; Non Executive Chairman, The Scottish Gallery, since 2014; b. 2.60, Edinburgh. Educ. The Edinburgh Academy; University of Aberdeen. Career: Brand Development and Corporate Affairs Director, Virgin Management, 1987-2007, Virgin, 1987-2011; President, Virgin Galactic, 2004-2010; Chairman, next fifteen, 2004-2011. Chair, Transport Systems Catapult Ltd at Technology Strategy Board, since 2013; Chairman, Speed Communications, since 2011; Non Executive Director, Stagecoach Group plc, since 2011; Director, STFC Innovations Limited, since 2010; Director, ILN Media Group, since 2008; Trustee and Board Member, Internews Europe, 2011-2013; Non Executive Director, CA Coutts Holdings, 1999-2005; Fellow at The Royal Aeronautical Society. Address: Scottish Event Campus Limited, Glasgow G3 8YW; T.-0141 248 3000.

Whitelock, Emma. Chief Executive Officer, Lead Scotland, since 2015, Training and Development Officer, 2008-2013, Learning & Business Development Manager, 2013-15. Educ. Glasgow Caledonian University; Fife College; The University of Dundee. Address: Lead Scotland, 525 Ferry Road, Edinburgh EH5 2AW; T.-0131 228 9441; e-mail: ewhitelock@lead.org.uk

Whiten, Professor (David) Andrew, BSc, PhD, FBPS, FRSB, FRSE, FBA. Emeritus Wardlaw Professor of Evolutionary and Developmental Psychology, St. Andrews University; Wardlaw Professor of Psychology, since 2000; Royal Society Leverhulme Trust Senior Research Fellow, 2006-07; b. 20.4.48, Grimsby; m., Dr. Susie Challoner; 2 d.

Educ. Wintringham School, Grimsby; Sheffield University; Bristol University; Oxford University. Research Fellow, Oxford University, 1972-75; Lecturer, then Reader, St. Andrews University, 1975-97; Director, 'Living Links to Human Evolution' Research Centre (www.living-links.org.uk), 2008-2015; Visiting Professor, Zurich University, 1992, Emory University, 1996; Delwart International Scientific Prize, 2001; Rivers Memorial Medal, Royal Anthropological Institute of Great Britain and Ireland, 2007; Osman-Hill Medal, Primate Society of Great Britain, 2010; Sir James Black Medal, Royal Society of Edinburgh, 2013; Elected Fellow of the Cognitive Science Society, 2013; Senior Prize and Medal for Public Engagement, Royal Society of Edinburgh, 2014; Hon DSc, Heriot-Watt Univ., 2015; Hon DUniv, Univ. of Stirling, 2016; Hon DSc, Univ. of Edinburgh, 2017. Publications: see www.st-andrews.ac.uk/profile/aw2. Recreations: painting; walking; wildlife; good-lifing. Address: (b.) School of Psychology and Neuroscience, University of St Andrews, St. Andrews KY16 9JU; e-mail: a.whiten@st-and.ac.uk

Whitfield, Martin, BA (Hons), PGCPE. MSP (Scottish Labour), South Scotland (Region), since 2021; MP (Labour), East Lothian, 2017-19; b. 12.08.65, Gosforth, Newcastle-upon-Tyne; m., Rachel; 2 c. Educ. Huddersfield Polytechnic; University of Edinburgh. Career: law profession; retrained as a school teacher in 2002; worked at Prestonpans Primary School; Dirleton Primary School; served as a council member of the General Teaching Council of Scotland as well as a member of the EIS, Scotland's largest trade union. Address: The Scottish Parliament, Edinburgh EH99 1SP; T.-0131 348 5827. E-mail: Martin.Whitfield.msp@parliament.scot

Whitford, Dr Philippa. MP (SNP), Central Ayrshire, since 2015; SNP Health spokesperson in the House of Commons, since 2015; Spokesperson for Europe, since 2019; b. 24.12.58, Belfast, Northern Ireland; m., Hans Pieper; 1 s. Educ. Wood Green: St. Angela's Providence Convent Secondary School, London; Douglas Academy, Milngavie; University of Glasgow. Medical volunteer in a UN hospital in Gaza in 1991/92 just after the first Gulf War and during the Intifada; Consultant Breast Cancer Surgeon at Crosshouse Hospital, Kilmarnock for over 18 years; led the development of Scottish Breast Cancer standards to raise the quality of care across Scotland. Address: House of Commons, London SW1A 0AA.

Whitham, Elena, BA. MSP (SNP), Carrick, Cumnock and Doon Valley, since 2021; b. 1974, Kilmarnock; 2 c. Educ. Champlain Regional College Saint-Lambert, Canada; Concordia University, Canada (degree in Journalism). Career history: returned to Scotland from Canada in 1996; worked freelance in local media; worked in community support roles in Ayrshire; Scottish Women's Aid worker in Ayrshire for over 10 years (assisting victims of domestic abuse); Senior Caseworker for Alan Brown MP, 2015-2021; elected Councillor for the Irvine Valley, East Ayrshire Council in 2015, became Depute Leader of the Council. Address: The Scottish Parliament, Edinburgh EH99 1SP; T.-0131 348 5494.

E-mail: Elena.Whitham.msp@parliament.scot

Whittemore, Professor Colin Trengove, BSc, PhD, DSc, NDA, FRSE. Emeritus Professor; Professor of Agriculture and Rural Economy, Edinburgh University, 1990-2007; Head, Institute of Ecology and Resource Management, Edinburgh University, 1991-2001; Postgraduate Dean, College of Science and Engineering, 2002-07; b. 16.7.42, Chester; m., Chris; 1 s.; 3 d. Educ. Rydal School; Newcastle-upon-Tyne University. Lecturer in Agriculture, Edinburgh University and Head, Animal Production, Advisory and Development, Edinburgh School of Agriculture; Professor of Animal Production, Head, Animal Division, Edinburgh School of Agriculture; Head,

Department of Agriculture, Edinburgh University. Sir John Hammond Memorial Prize for scientific contribution to an understanding of nutrition and growth; President, British Society of Animal Science, 1998; Royal Agricultural Society of England Gold Medal for research; Mignini Oscar; David Black Award. Publications: author of over 200 research papers, five text books of animal sciences, animal farming and 'Farming Stories from the Scottish Borders'. Recreations: skiing; riding; writing local agricultural histories. Address: (h.) 17, Fergusson View, West Linton, Peeblesshire EH46 7DJ.

Whittle, Brian. MSP (Scottish Conservative), South Scotland region, since 2016; Chief Executive Officer, Demon Sport, 2013-2016; b. 26.4.64, Troon. Educ. Marr College; Glasgow University. Athlete, UK Athletics, 1985-96 (won the gold medal in the 4 x 400 metres relay at both the 1986 European Athletics Championships and 1994 European Athletics Championships); Manager, Spence Allan Associates Ltd/Corporate Events Scotland, 1996-98; Director: Catlayst Consulting/Events Ltd, 1998-2000, Ian McLauchlan Associates, 2000-03, PB Events Ltd, 2003-08; Director of Sport, Sports Social Media, 2008-2010; self-employed (special projects), since 2010; Global Head of Business Development, Uniquedoc, since 2013. Contested the 2015 UK general election in the constituency of Kilmarnock and Loudoun for the Conservatives. Address: Scottish Parliament, Edinburgh EH99 1SP.

Whittle, Pamela, CBE. Chair, Scottish Health Council, 2011-19; non-executive Board Member, Healthcare Improvement Scotland, 2011-19; b. 30.12.48, Bristol; m., Richard; 1 s. Educ. Monks Park School, Bristol; Sarum St Michael, Salisbury; Open University. Director, Health Improvement, Scottish Government, 2002-08. Former non-executive Board Member, NHS Quality Improvement Scotland. Former Chair, Greenspace Scotland; Board Member, Stevenson College, Edinburgh; President, Royal Caledonian Horticultural Society, 2011-2016.

Whitton, David Forbes. MSP (Labour), Strathkelvin and Bearsden, 2007-2011; b. 22.4.52, Forfar; m., Marilyn; 1 s.; 1 d. Educ. Morgan Academy, Dundee. Journalist, DC Thomson, Dundee, 1970-76; Fife Free Press, Kirkcaldy, 1976-78; Scotsman, Glasgow, 1978-81; Industrial Editor, Daily Record, Glasgow, 1981-86; Presenter, Producer, Head of Public Affairs, Scottish Television, Glasgow, 1986-96; Director, Media House Ltd, Glasgow, 1996-98; Special Adviser to Donald Dewar MSP, First Minister of Scotland, 1998-2000; Managing Director, Whitton PR Ltd, 2000-07. Recreations: golf; music; grandchildren.

Whitty, Professor Niall Richard, MA, LLB, FRSE. Honorary Professor, Edinburgh University School of Law, since 2014; b. 28.10.37, Malaya; m., Elke M.M. Gillis; 3 s.; 1 d. Educ. Morrison's Academy, Crieff; St Andrews University; Edinburgh University. Law apprenticeship, 1963-65; private practice, 1965-66; Member, legal staff, Scottish Office Solicitor's office, 1967-71; legal staff, Scottish Law Commission, 1971-94; Commissioner, Scottish Law Commission, 1995-2000. Visiting Professor, Edinburgh University School of Law, 2000-2014; General Editor, Stair Memorial Encyclopaedia, February 2000-June 2014. Recreations: gardening; piping; legal history. Address: (h.) St Martins, Victoria Road, Haddington EH41 4DJ; T.-0162 082 2234.

Whyte, Rev Dr George. Principal Clerk to the General Assembly, 2017-2022 (retired); Chaplain to the Queen, since 2019. Spent 27 years as a minister in parishes in Argyll, Glasgow and Edinburgh; Presbytery Clerk for Edinburgh, 2009-2017; Depute Principal Clerk to the General Assembly, 2011-17.

Whyte, Professor Iain Boyd, BA, MPhil, MA, PhD, FRSE, FRSA. Honorary Professor, Edinburgh College of Art, since 2015; appointed Professor of Architectural History, Department of Architecture, Edinburgh University in 1996; b. 6.3.47, Bexley; m., Deborah Smart; 1 s.; 1 d. Educ. St Dunstan's College; Nottingham University; Cornell University; Cambridge University; Leeds University. Lecturer, then Reader, then Professor of Architectural History, Edinburgh University; External Examiner: Courtauld Institute of Art, National University of Singapore, University College London. Getty Scholar, 1989-90; Getty Grant Program Senior Scholar, 1998-2000; Visiting Senior Program Officer, Getty Grant Program, 2002-04; Trustee, National Galleries of Scotland, 1998-2002; Member, Selection Committee, 23rd Council of Europe exhibition, 1995-96; Chair, RIHA (International Association of Research Institutes in the History of Art), 2010-2016; Samuel H. Kress Professor, Center for Advanced Study in the Visual Arts, National Gallery of Art, Washington, DC, 2015-2016; extensive publications on architectural and art history. Recreations: music; rowing. Address: (b.) Department of Architecture, 20 Chambers Street, Edinburgh EH1 1JZ; T.-0131-650 2322.

Whyte, Rev. James, BD, DipCE. Parish Minister, Fairlie, Ayrshire, 2006-2011 (retired); b. 26.4.46, Glasgow; m., Norma Isabella West; 1 s.; 2 d. Educ. Glasgow; Jordanhill College; Glasgow University. Trained as planning engineer; studied community education (Glasgow and Boston, Mass., USA); Community Organiser with Lamp of Lothian Collegiate Trust, Haddington; Organiser of Community Education, Dumbarton, 1971-73; Assistant Principal Community Education Officer, Renfrew Division, Strathclyde Region, 1973-77; entered ministry, Church of Scotland, 1977; Assistant Minister: Barrhead Arthurlie, 1977-78, St. Marks, Oldhall, Paisley, 1978-80; Minister: Coupar Angus Abbey, 1981-87, Broom, Newton Mearns, 1987-2006. Recreations: gardening; reading. Address: 32 Torburn Avenue, Giffnock, East Renfrewshire G46 7RB; T.-0141 620 3043.

Whyte, Moira Katherine Bridgid, OBE, FRCP, FMedSci, FRSE, FERS. Physician and medical researcher; Sir John Crofton Professor of Respiratory Medicine, University of Edinburgh, since 2014, Vice-Principal and Head of the College of Medicine and Veterinary Medicine, since 2018; b. 25.9.59. Educ. Convent of Notre Dame, Plymouth; Plymouth College; St Bartholomew's Hospital Medical College. Career history: worked and studied at Hammersmith Hospital, Royal Postgraduate Medical School and Imperial Cancer Research Fund; completed clinical fellowships funded by the Medical Research Council and Wellcome Trust; became Professor of Respiratory Medicine at the University of Sheffield in 1996, subsequently becoming Head of the Department of Infection and Immunity; honorary officer and Registrar of the Academy of Medical Sciences, 2012-16; appointed Director of the MRC University of Edinburgh Centre for Inflammation Research in 2014; appointed Head of the University of Edinburgh Medical School in 2016. Active in the Medical Research Council as the Chair of the their Clinical Training and Careers Panel; Honorary Consultant Physician. Address: The University of Edinburgh, Centre for Inflammation Research, The Queen's Medical Research Institute, Edinburgh BioQuarter, 47 Little France Crescent, Edinburgh EH16 4TJ; T.-0131 242 9312. E-mail: moira.whyte@ed.ac.uk

Whyte, Robert, MB, ChB, FRCPsych, DPM. Consultant Psychotherapist, Carswell House, Glasgow, 1979-2000; b. 1.6.41, Edinburgh; m., Susan Frances Milburn (deceased 2019); 1 s.; 1 d. Educ. George Heriot's, Edinburgh; St. Andrews University. House Officer in Surgery, Arbroath Infirmary, 1966; House Officer in Medicine, Falkirk and

District Royal Infirmary, 1967; Trainee in Psychiatry, Dundee Psychiatric Services, 1967-73; Consultant Psychiatrist, Duke Street Hospital, Glasgow, 1973. Past Chairman, Scottish Association of Psychoanalytical Psychotherapists. Address: (h.) Waverley, 70 East Kilbride Road, Busby, Glasgow G76 8HU; T.-0141-644 1659.

Wickham-Jones, Caroline R., MA, MSocSci, MIFA, FSA, Hon FSA Scot, FFCS. Archaeologist; b. 25.4.55, Middlesborough; 1 s. Educ. Teesside High School; Edinburgh University; University of Birmingham. Honorary Research Fellow, University of Aberdeen; author and communicator with research interests in early (postglacial) settlement of Scotland, submerged archaeology, landscape history, and the preservation of the cultural heritage; former Council Member, National Trust for Scotland; Council Member, Institute of Field Archaeologists, 1986-90; former Secretary, Society of Antiquaries of Scotland; former Trustee, John Muir Trust; Livery Woman of the City of London (Skinners Company); Vice Chair, Orkney Heritage Society. Publications: Scotland's First Settlers; Arthurs Seat and Holyrood Park, a Visitor's Guide; Orkney, an Historical Guide; The Landscape of Scotland, a hidden history; Between the Wind and the Water, World Heritage Orkney; Fear of Farming; Landscape Beneath The Waves. Recreations: cookery; travel; wilderness walking; socialising. Address: (h.) Cassie, St. Ola, Orkney KW15 1TP. E-mail: c.wickham-jones@mesolithic.co.uk Website: www.mesolithic.co.uk

Widdowfield, Dr Rebekah. Chief Executive, The Royal Society of Edinburgh, 2017-2022. Educ. University of Oxford; University of Newcastle. Career: worked for a number of years at the Universities of Bristol and Cardiff, researching homelessness, rural poverty and social exclusion; joined the Scottish Government in 2001, working in a number of roles before becoming a senior civil servant in 2008 (roles covering rural and environmental science and analysis, social research (as Chief Researcher), higher education and housing). Board Member: Scottish Book Trust, Centre for Homelessness Impact, City of Glasgow College. Recreations: reading; hill-walking; jazz.

Wiercigroch, Professor Marian, MEng, ScD, DSc, CEng, CMath, FIMechE, FIMA, FRSE. Sixth Century Chair in Applied Dynamics and Director, Centre for Applied Dynamics, Aberdeen University; b. 14.7.60, Poland. Educ. Silesian University of Technology, Poland; Aberdeen University. Research Fellow, Aberdeen University, 1990-91; Lecturer, Silesian University of Technology, 1992-93; Senior Fulbright Scholar, University of Delaware, USA, 1994; Lecturer, then Senior Lecturer, then Reader, Aberdeen University, 1994-2002, Professor of Engineering, 2002-06, Sixth Century Chair in Applied Dynamics, since 2006, Director for Internationalisation, 2009-2016; doctorate honoris causa from Lodz University of Technology, Poland, 2013; Editor in Chief of International Journal of Mechanical Sciences, since 2013; Honorary Professorship from Perm National Research Polytechnic University, Russia, 2017; Scottish Knowledge Exchange Champion, 2020; Honorary Professorship from Yashan University, China, 2021; REF 2014 and 2021 Panel member. Recreations: Alpine skiing; tennis; hill-walking; Munro bagging. Address: (b.) Centre for Applied Dynamics Research, School of Engineering, Aberdeen University AB24 3UE.

Wightman, Andy. Writer; MSP (Scottish Green), 2016-2021; b. Dundee. Educ. University of Aberdeen. Career history: scientist working on renewable energy at the University of Aberdeen; Projects Officer with Central Scotland Countryside Trust; became a self-employed writer and researcher in 1993; contributed to a wide range of debates on land use, land reform, the Crown estate, common good land, local democracy and fiscal reform, over the next 20 years; author of a number of reports on these topics; also served as a Specialist Adviser to the UK Parliament's Scottish Affairs Committee Inquiry on land reform, 2014-2015; coordinator of the Land Action Scotland campaign; member of the Commission on Local Tax Reform, 2015; Co-founder of Reforesting Scotland, a group dedicated to substantial reforestation. Publications: Who Owns Scotland, 1996; Scotland: land and power. An agenda for land reform, 1999; The Poor Had No Lawyers, 2015.

Wightman, Scott. Director of External Affairs, Scottish Government, since 2019. Educ. University of Edinburgh. Career history: Foreign and Commonwealth Office: Director, Global and Economic Issues, London, 2006-08, Director, Asia Pacific, 2008-2010, British Ambassador to the Republic of Korea, 2011-15; British High Commissioner to the Republic of Singapore, British High Commission, 2015-19. Address: Scottish Government, Victoria Quay, Edinburgh EH6 6QQ.

Wilcox, Christine Alison, BA (Hons), MCLIP. Librarian, S.S.C. Library, Edinburgh, since 1991; b. 18.7.63, New Zealand; m., Michael Wilcox; 2 s.; 1 d. Educ. South Wilts Grammar School, Salisbury; Manchester Polytechnic Library School. Assistant Librarian, Barlow Lyde and Barlow Gilbert, Solicitors, London, 1984-86; Librarian, Beaumont and Son, Solicitors, London, 1986-89; posting to Bahrain accompanying husband, 1989-91. Secretary, Scottish Law Librarians Group, 1993-95. Publications: Directory of Legal Libraries in Scotland; Union List of Periodical and Law Report Holdings in Scotland. Recreations: cycling; needlework; hill-walking. Address: (b.) S.S.C. Library, 11 Parliament Square, Edinburgh EH1 1RF; T.-0131-225 6268; e-mail: christine@ssclibrary.co.uk

Wild, John Robin, JP, BDS, DPD, FDSRCS(Edin), DGDP. Chief Dental Officer, Department of Health, 1996-2000; Consultant in Dental Public Health, NHS Dumfries and Galloway, 2005-07; b. 12.9.41, Scarborough; m., Eleanor Daphne Kerr; 1 s.; 2 d. Educ. Sedbergh School; Edinburgh University; Dundee University. General Dental Practitioner, Scarborough, 1965-71; Dental Officer, East Lothian, 1971-74; Chief Administrative Dental Officer, Borders Health Board, 1974-87; Regional Dental Postgraduate Adviser, S.E. Regional Committee for Postgraduate Medical Education, 1982-87; Deputy Chief Dental Officer, 1987-93, then Chief Dental Officer and Director of Dental Services for the NHS in Scotland, 1993-96, Scottish Office Department of Health; Hon. Senior Lecturer, Dundee Dental School, 1993-2003; JP for District of Ettrick and Lauderdale, 1982-2011; Chairman, Scottish Borders Justices Committee, 2000-05; Chairman, District Courts Association, 2002-04; Member, Judicial Council for Scotland, 2007-09; Past Chairman, Scottish Council, British Dental Association; Vice President, Commonwealth Dental Association, 1997-2003; President, Council of European Chief Dental Officers, 1999-2000; Member, Disciplinary Pool of Institute and Faculty of Actuaries, 2001-17. Recreations: vintage cars (restoration and driving); music; gardening. Address: (h.) Braehead Stables, St. Boswells, Roxburghshire; T.-01835 823203.

Wilkin, Andrew, BA, MA, MCIL. Senior Lecturer in Italian Studies, University of Strathclyde, 1986-2009; b. 30.5.44, Farnborough; m., Gaynor Carole Gray; 1 s.; 1 d. (also 1 s.; 1 d. by pr. m.). Educ. Royal Naval School, Malta; University of Manchester; Open University. Assistant Lecturer, then Lecturer in Italian Studies, University of

Strathclyde, 1967-86; Associate Dean, Faculty of Arts and Social Sciences, 1986-93; Course Director, BA European Studies, 1989-97. Governor, Craigie College of Education, 1985-91; Editor, Tuttitalia, 1992-97; Member, Modern Languages Panel, UCAS Scotland, 1993-2000. Publications: Harrap's Italian Verbs (Compiler), 1990, 2002, 2009; G. Verga, Little Novels of Sicily (Editor), 1973; 25 Years Emancipation? – Women in Switzerland 1971-96 (Co-Editor), 1997. Invested Cavaliere dell'Ordine al Merito della Repubblica Italiana, 1975; Elder, St. David's Memorial Park Church, Kirkintilloch; Member, Ministry Committee, Presbytery of Glasgow. Recreations: travel; reading; supporting Partick Thistle F.C. Address: (h.) 29 Forest Place, Lenzie, Glasgow G66 4UH; T.-0141-777-7607; e-mail: andrew.wilkin@hotmail.co.uk

Wilkinson, Sheriff Alexander Birrell, QC, MA, LLB. Sheriff of Lothian and Borders at Edinburgh, 1996-2001; Sheriff of Glasgow and Strathkelvin at Glasgow, 1991-96; Temporary Judge, Court of Session, 1993-2003; b. 2.2.32, Perth; m., Wendy Imogen Barrett; 1 s.; 1 d. Educ. Perth Academy; St. Andrews University; Edinburgh University. Advocate, 1959; practised at Scottish Bar, 1959-69; Lecturer in Scots Law, Edinburgh University, 1965-69; Sheriff of Stirling, Dunbarton and Clackmannan, at Stirling and Alloa, 1969-72; Professor of Private Law, Dundee University, 1972-86 (Dean, Faculty of Law, 1974-76 and 1986); Sheriff of Tayside, Central and Fife at Falkirk, 1986-91; a Chairman, Industrial Tribunals (Scotland), 1972-86; Chancellor, Dioceses of Brechin, 1982-98, and of Argyll and the Isles, 1985-98, Scottish Episcopal Church; a Director, Scottish Episcopal Church Nominees Ltd., 2004-2021, and a Trustee of the General Synod of the Scottish Episcopal Church, 2005-2021; Chairman, Scottish Marriage Guidance Council, 1974-77; Chairman, Legal Services Group, Scottish Association of CAB, 1979-83; President, The Sheriffs' Association, 1997-2000. Publications: Gloag and Henderson's Introduction to the Law of Scotland, 8th and 9th editions (Co-editor); The Scottish Law of Evidence; The Law of Parent and Child in Scotland (Co-author); Macphail's Sheriff Court Practice, 2nd Edition (Contributor); The Legal Systems of Scottish Churches (Contributor). Recreations: collecting books and pictures; reading; travel.

Wilkinson, Professor John Eric, BSc, MEd, PhD, CPsychol. Professor of Education, Glasgow University, 1998-2009; Deputy Dean, Faculty of Education, 2001-05; Emeritus Professor of Education, since 2009; b. 22.5.44, Lancashire; 2 s.; 1 d. Educ. Accrington Grammar School; St Andrews University; Dundee University; Glasgow University. Assistant Master, Brockenhurst Sixth Form College, 1968-70; Research Assistant, Nottingham University, 1970-72; Glasgow University: Lecturer, Education, 1973-91; Senior Lecturer, 1991-98; Head of Department, 1995-99; Professor, 1998-2009; Emeritus Professor, since 2009; Professor, University of Taipei, Taiwan, ROC, 2009. Publications: numerous journal articles, a book, and book chapters. Recreations: art collecting; ballet appreciation; swimming. Address: (b.) Department of Early Childhood Education, University of Taipei, West Aiguo Road, Taipei, Taiwan, Republic of China; (h.) Flat 4, 17 Crown Terrace, Glasgow G12 9ES. E-mail: jericwilkinson@hotmail.com

Will, James. Non-Executive Chairman, The Scottish Investment Trust PLC, since 2016, Non-Executive Director, 2013-16: Non-Executive Director, Herald Investment Trust PLC, since 2015, Asia Dragon Trust PLC, since 2018, Non-Executive Chairman, since 2019; formerly Chairman, Shepherd and Wedderburn (2010-2014).

Williams, Professor Brian Owen, CBE, MD, HonDSc, FRCP. Past President, Royal College of Physicians and Surgeons of Glasgow (2006-2009); retired Consultant Geriatrician; b. 27.02.47, Glasgow; m., Martha; 2 d. Educ. Kings Park Secondary, Glasgow; University of Glasgow. Trained in General Medicine and Geriatric Medicine; President: British Geriatrics Society, 1998-2000, European Union Geriatric Medicine Society, 1998-2000. Honorary Professor, University of Glasgow, since 2007; Trustee, Abbeyfield Society UK, since 2017. Publications: book chapters and original papers on medicine of old age. Recreations: gardening; theatre; literature. Address: (h.) 15 Thorn Drive, High Burnside, Glasgow G73 4RH; T.-0141 634 4480; e-mail: brianwilliams@gmx.com

Williams, Craig David, MA (Hons), PGDJ. Journalist, Producer/Director, BBC Scotland Current Affairs; b. 9.8.71, Edinburgh; m., Pauline McLean; 1 s. Educ. Royal High School, Edinburgh; University of Edinburgh; University of Strathclyde. Reporter: Border Telegraph, 1994-95; Radio Borders, 1995-96; Radio Forth, 1996-97; Journalist, BBC Scotland News and Current Affairs, 1997-2000; Media Correspondent, Business am, 2000-01; Editor, Newsnight Scotland, BBC, 2001-08; Executive Producer: 'Holyrood: What Went Wrong?', 'Did Your Vote Count?' (BAFTA Scotland winner, 2007); Producer-Director, documentaries and investigations, since 2008. Recreations: books; cinema; history; cats. Address: (b.) BBC Scotland, Zone 4.16, 40 Pacific Quay, Glasgow G51 1DA; T.-0141-422 6261; e-mail: craig.williams@bbc.co.uk

Williams, Professor Morgan Howard, BSc Hons, PhD, DSc, CEng, CITP, FBCS, FRSA. Professor Emeritus, Heriot-Watt University, since 2014 (Professor of Computer Science, 1980-2014, Head of Department, 1980-88 and 2002-03); b. 15.12.44, Durban; m., 1. Jean Doe (marr. diss.), 2 s.; m., 2. Pamela Mason (deceased); m., 3. Margaret Rae Wilson. Educ. Grey High School, Port Elizabeth; Rhodes University, Grahamstown. Physicist in Antarctic Expedition, 1968-69; Rhodes University: Lecturer in Computer Science, 1970-72, Senior Lecturer, 1972-77, Professor and Head of Department, 1977-80; British Council Visiting Researcher, Darwin College, Cambridge, 1974-75. Co-editor of Quaestiones Informaticae, 1978-80; Member, Standing Committee of IUCC, 1984-88; Member, Committee of Conference of Professors of Computer Science, 1986-88; Member of SERC Alvey LP, SIGKME and SIGPDS Committees, 1986-89; Member of EC Committee on Telemedicine, 1989-90; Member, SERC Systems Engineering Committee, 1992-94; Member, EPSRC IT College, 1995-2005. Over 250 peer reviewed publications. Recreations: family; gardening; swimming; photography. Address: (h.) 3 House O'Hill Brae, Edinburgh EH4 5DQ; T.-0131 3361215.

Williams, Professor Richard A., OBE, FREng, FRSE, FTSE, FIChemE, FIMMM, BSc (Eng), PhD. Principal and Vice Chancellor, Heriot-Watt University, since 2015; b. 1960, Worcester; m., Jane M. Taylor; 2 c. Educ. The King's School, Worcester; Imperial College London. Trainee graduate metallurgist, Anglo American Corporation in Johannesburg and Welkom, 1979-80; De Beers Industrial Diamonds Research Laboratory, South Africa and Imperial College London (Royal School of Mines), 1982-86; appointed Lecturer in Chemical Engineering, University of Manchester Institute of Science and Technology (now University of Manchester) in 1986; appointed Royal Academy of Engineering-Rio Tinto Professor of Minerals Engineering at the University of Exeter (based at the Camborne School of Mines) in 1993; University of Leeds: appointed as Anglo American plc Professor of Mineral and Process Engineering in 1999 (responsible for developing a new Institute of Particle Science and Engineering, a core development in re-development of chemical engineering at the University within the recently formed School of Process, Materials and Environmental Engineering); Head of the Department of Mining (2001-2003); Director of

British Nuclear Fuels Limited (BNFL) Research Alliance at the University, responsible for development of new activities in nuclear energy waste processing, 2000-2006; foundational Director of a regional Centre for Industrial Collaboration in Particle Science and Technology, 2003-2006, and of the Leeds Nanomanufacturing Institute, 2004-2010; appointed Pro-Vice-Chancellor in 2005, responsible for leadership of enterprise, knowledge transfer and international strategy; appointed Pro-Vice Chancellor and Head of the College of Engineering and Physical Sciences at the University of Birmingham in 2011. Involved in leading the development of major collaborative projects in establishing the Rolls-Royce Centre for High Temperature Research Centre (near Ansty, Coventry) the Midland Energy Accelerator and the Birmingham Centre for Cryogenic Energy Storage. Vice-President, Royal Academy of Engineering, 2005-08 and 2015-18; Visiting Professor: University of New South Wales (UNSW), 2002-2015, Southeast University Nanjing, since 2015, China Academy of Sciences, since 2015, Tianjin University of Finance and Economics, since 2017; Founder of: Industrial Tomography Systems plc; Structure Vision Ltd; former Council Member of the West Midlands CBI. Former Director of: Leeds, York and North Yorkshire Chamber of Commerce; Leeds Ventures Limited; Optomo plc (Founder); University of Leeds IP Limited; University of Leeds Consulting Limited; White Rose Technology Limited; University of Leeds Innovations Limited; Dispersia Ltd (Founder), Medilink (Yorkshire and Humber) Ltd, Alta Innovation Ltd, 2011-2015, Alta China Ltd, 2011-2015 and Manufacturing Technology Centre for CATAPULT High Value Manufacturing Centre, 2011-2015. Trustee of the Carnegie Trust (Scotland), 2015-19; Member of the Advisory Board of: the Lloyds Register Foundation, since 2016 and Lloyds Register 100A1 Ambassador, since 2017; PSB Academy, Singapore, since 2014; Board Member of Carnegie Trust for the Universities of Scotland (2015-2019); Director of the British Geological Survey, since 2018; member of Converge Challenge Strategic Advisory Board, since 2016; Chair and Director of the Scottish Institute for Enterprise, since 2017; Advisor to the UK Board of Trade, 2019-2020; UK Chair of UAE-UK Business Council for Education and Culture, since 2020. Editor of Minerals Engineering, Advanced Powder Technology, Chemical Engineering Reactional Design, Particle and Particle Systems Characterisation, Particuology. Graduate of the Higher Education Academy's Top Management Programme, 2007. Recipient of a number of awards and prizes including the Beilby Medal and Prize, 1997; Isambard Kingdom Brunel Lectureship, 1998; Noel E. Webster Medal, 2001; Royal Academy of Engineering Silver Medal, 2003; The Society of Chemical Industry Research and Development for Society Award, 2009; named as one of the UK's top 20 science innovators as a "RISE Fellow" by the Engineering and Physical Sciences Research Council, 2015; Royal Academy of Engineering President's Medal, 2019. Recreations: industrial history and art. Clubs: The Athaneum; The Glasgow Art Club. Address: Heriot-Watt University, Edinburgh Campus, Edinburgh EH14 4AS; T.-0131 451 3360.

Williams, Professor Richard John, BA (Hons), MA, PhD. Professor, Contemporary and Visual Cultures, University of Edinburgh; b. 01.06.67, Washington DC, USA; m., Stacy Boldrick; 1 s.; 1 d. Educ. Manchester Grammar School; Goldsmiths College, London; Manchester University. Lecturer in Art and Design, History and Theory, Liverpool John Moores University, 1997-2000; Lecturer/Senior Lecturer in History of Art, University of Edinburgh, since 2000. Publications: Author: 'After Modern Sculpture', 2000; 'The Anxious City', 2004; 'Brazil: Modern Architectures in History', 2009. Recreations: hillwalking; thinking about going hillwalking. Address: (b.) School of Arts, Culture and Environment, University of Edinburgh, Alison House, 12 Nicholson Square, Edinburgh EH8 9DF; T.-0131 650 4122; e-mail: r.j.williams@ed.ac.uk

Williams, Dr Roger Bevan, MBE, DMus, PhD, BMus, FRCO, FTCL, ARCM, PGCE, FGMS. Director of Music and Organist, St Machar Cathedral, Old Aberdeen; Music Adviser, NTS; Emeritus Organist, University of Aberdeen; formerly Conductor, Composer, Musician; formerly Master of Chapel and Ceremonial Music and Organist, University of Aberdeen; Head, Music Department, University of Aberdeen, 1988-2006; b. 30.8.43, Swansea; m., Ann Therese Brennan; 1 s.; m., Katherine Ellen Smith; 2 s.; 1 d. Educ. Mirfield Grammar School, Yorkshire; Huddersfield School of Music; University College, Cardiff; Goldsmiths' College, University of London; King's College, Cambridge. Assistant Organist, Holy Trinity Church, Brompton, 1971; Lecturer, 1971, Director, 1973-75, Chiswick Music Centre; Organist, St. Patrick's Church, Soho, 1973; Musical Director, Sacred Heart Church, Wimbledon, 1975; Lecturer, West London Institute, 1975-78; Organist, Our Lady of Victories, Kensington, 1978-97; Lecturer, University of Aberdeen, 1978-88; Chorus Master, SNO Chorus, 1984-88; Harpsichordist, Aberdeen Sinfonietta, since 1988; first recording of Arne's Six Organ Concertos, 1988; Music at Castle Fraser: catalogue, 1995, CDs, 1997; numerous compositions, editions, catalogues of music holdings in North East Scotland. Recreations: board games; cooking; gardening. Address: (h.) The Old Hall, Barthol Chapel, Oldmeldrum, Inverurie AB51 8TD; T.-01651 806634.

Williamson, (Andrew) Peter, MSc, HDip, MHCIMA. Managing Director, NMS Enterprises Ltd., since 2003; Director, Visitor Operations, National Museums Scotland; b. 23.9.63, Edinburgh; m., Jennifer; 2 s.; 1 d. Educ. George Watson's College; Napier University. Walt Disney Company, 1984-85; Sheraton International Hotel Company, 1986-93; Whitbread Hotel Company (Marriott Hotels UK), 1995-2002. Member: Edinburgh Tourism Action Group (ETAG), Unique Venues of Edinburgh (UVE), Institute of Directors (IOD). Recreations: golf; reading; travelling. Address: (b.) National Museums Scotland, Chambers Street, Edinburgh EH1 1JF; T.-0131 247 4365; e-mail: p.williamson@nms.ac.uk

Williamson, Raymond MacLeod, MA, LLB, FRSA, FRSAMD; b. 24.12.42, Glasgow; m., Brenda; 1 d.; 1 s. Educ. The High School of Glasgow; The University of Glasgow. Partner, MacRoberts, Solicitors, Glasgow and Edinburgh, 1971-2006 (Senior Partner, 2000-2006); Employment Judge, 2005-2014, Council Member, The Law Society of Scotland, 1990-1996, Convenor of The Law Society of Scotland Employment Law Committee, 1990-2006, Founding Committee Member of the European Employment Lawyers Association, 1997-2006 (Vice Chairman, 2003-2006); Dean, Royal Faculty of Procurators in Glasgow, 2001-2004; Director, Royal Scottish National Orchestra Society Ltd, 1970-1991 (Chairman, 1985-1991); Trustee, RSNO Pension Scheme, 1992-2019 (Chairman, 2009-2019); Chairman, RSNO Development Board; Chairman, RSNO Foundation; Governor, Royal Scottish Academy of Music and Drama (now Royal Conservatoire of Scotland), 1990-2002 (Vice Chairman, 1999-2002); Trustee, Royal Conservatoire of Scotland Trust and Endowment Trust; former Chairman, now Honorary President, National Youth Choir of Scotland; former Chairman, now Honorary President, Scottish International Piano Competition; Chairman, Children's Music Foundation in Scotland (Children's Classic Concerts), 1994-2000; Chairman, Westbourne Music; President, The Glasgow Art Club, 2009-2012; Governor, The High School of Glasgow, 1987-2015 (Vice Chairman, 2006-2015); President, Glasgow High School Club, 2003-04; Trustee, High School of Glasgow Educational Trust; founding Chairman, LAR Housing Trust (2015-2016); Trustee, Glasgow and Marshall Educational Trust; Trustee, Glasgow and West of Scotland Society for the Relief of Infirmity; Trustee, Royal Incorporation of Hutchesons' Hospital; Chairman of Trustees, Jennie S Gordon Memorial

Foundation; Chairman of Trustees, BeYonder INVOLVE; Lord Dean of Guild of Glasgow, 2013-2015; recipient, Lord Provost of Glasgow Award for Culture, 2010. Address: (h.) 11 Islay Drive, Newton Mearns, Glasgow G77 6UD; T.- 0141 639 4133.

Wills, Dr. Jonathan, MA, PhD; b. 1947. Shetland journalist, author, broadcaster, political activist, former Shetland Councillor (Lerwick South), mariner and wildlife expert; operates a wildlife tourism business around some of Shetland's finest seabird and seal colonies during the summer months. Educ. University of Edinburgh. Career history: first student to be Rector of the University of Edinburgh; Muckle Flugga Lighthouse boatman; Scotland correspondent for The Times; Senior Producer at BBC Radio Shetland, and editor of the Shetland Times, before pioneering the e-media Shetland News; also held a number of public posts and has written books for children. Honorary Warden of the Noss Island National Nature Reserve. Publications: Old Rock - Shetland in pictures; A Place in the Sun: Shetland and Oil, 1991; Innocent Passage: The Wreck of the Tanker Braer, 1993; The Travels of Magnus Pole, Chatto & Windus, 1984; Wilma Widdershins And The Muckle Tree: A Shetland Story, 1991; The Lands of Garth: A short history of Calback Ness, 1978.

Wilson of Tillyorn, Baron (David Clive Wilson), KT, GCMG, MA (Oxon), PhD, FRSE. Life Peer (1992). President, Royal Society of Edinburgh, 2008-2011; Master of Peterhouse, Cambridge, 2002-08; Chancellor, Aberdeen University, 1997-2013; Deputy Vice-Chancellor, Cambridge University, 2005-08; Member, Council, Glenalmond College, 1994-2005 (Chairman, 2000-05); President, Bhutan Society of the UK, 1998-2008; President, Hong Kong Association and Hong Kong Society, 1994-2012; Registrar, Order of St. Michael and St. George, 2001-2010; Vice-President, Royal Scottish Geographical Society, since 1998; Member, Board, Martin Currie Pacific Trust, 1993-2003; Trustee, Carnegie Trust for the Universities of Scotland, 2000-2016; Member, Prime Minister's Advisory Committee on Business Appointments, 2000-09 (Chairman, 2008-09); b. 14.2.35, Alloa; m., Natasha Helen Mary Alexander; 2 s (Peter and Andrew). Educ. Trinity College, Glenalmond; Keble College, Oxford. Entered Foreign Service, 1958; Third Secretary, Vientiane, 1959-60; language student, Hong Kong, 1960-62; Second, later First Secretary, Peking, 1963-65; FCO, 1965-68; resigned, 1968; Editor, China Quarterly, 1968-74; Visiting Scholar, Columbia University, New York, 1972; rejoined Diplomatic Service, 1974; Cabinet Office, 1974-77; Political Adviser, Hong Kong, 1977-81; Head, S. European Department, FCO, 1981-84; Assistant Under Secretary of State, FCO, 1984-87; Governor of Hong Kong, 1987-92. Member, Governing Body, School of Oriental and African Studies, 1992-97; Member, Council, CBI Scotland, 1993-2000; Chairman, Scottish and Southern Energy plc (formerly Scottish Hydro Electric), 1993-2000; Chairman, Scottish Committee, British Council, 1993-2002; Trustee, Scotland's Churches Scheme, 1999-2002 and 2008-2015, Vice President, since 2015; Chairman, Scottish Peers Association, 2000-02 (Vice-Chairman, 1998-2000); Chairman, Trustees, National Museums of Scotland, 2002-06 (Trustee since 1999); Chairman, Council of St. Paul's Cathedral, London, 2009-2015; Lord High Commissioner to the General Assembly of the Church of Scotland, 2010 and 2011; Burgess of Guild, City of Aberdeen, 1990; Hon Fellow, Keble College, Oxford, 1987; Hon Fellow, Peterhouse, Cambridge, 2008; Hon.LLD (Aberdeen); Hon.DLitt (Sydney); Hon.DLitt (Abertay, Dundee); Hon.LLD, Chinese University, Hong Kong; Hon.DLitt (Hong Kong); Hon.D*rhc* (Edin); KStJ. Recreations: hill walking; reading; theatre. Address: (h.) 2F, 7 Eildon Street, Edinburgh EH3 5JU; House of Lords, London SW1A 0PW.

Wilson, Alan, SNC, CIM, LLM. Managing Director, SELECT, since 2019. Educ. Portobello High School;

Telford College; Stevenson College; University of Strathclyde. Career history: Buyer, UBM, 1982-84, Administrator, SSHA, 1984-87; Head of Membership Services, SNIPEF, 1987-2014; National Executive Officer, SEC Group (Scotland), 2005-2020; Chairman, Scottish Energy Installers Alliance (SEIA), 2012-2020; Head of Membership and Communications, SELECT, 2014-2019; Director, The Scottish Building Contract Committee, 2016-2020; Chair, CICV Forum, since 2019. Recreations: keen golfer and walker. Address: SELECT, The Walled Garden, Bush Estate, Midlothian EH26 0SB; T.-0131 445 5577. E-mail: alan.wilson@select.org.uk

Wilson, Alan Oliver Arneil, MB, ChB, DPM, FRCPsych, FFCS. Former consultant in private practice, Murrayfield Hospital, Edinburgh (now retired); Member, Executive Group of Board of Directors, and First President, World Association for Psychosocial Rehabilitation; Consultant (in Scotland), Ex-Services Mental Welfare Society; b. 4.1.30, Douglas; m., Dr. Fiona Margaret Davidson; 3 s. Educ. Biggar High School; Edinburgh University. RAMC, 1953-55; psychiatric post, Stobhill General Hospital, Glasgow, and Garlands Hospital, Carlisle, 1955-63; Consultant Psychiatrist and Deputy Physician Superintendent, St. George's Hospital, Morpeth, 1963-77; Consultant Psychiatrist, Bangour Hospitals, 1977-89; former Member, Clinical Teaching Staff, Faculty of Medicine, Edinburgh University; Clinical Lecturer, University of Newcastle upon Tyne. Chairman, Group for Study of Rehabilitation and Community Care, Scottish Division, RCPsych. V.M. Bekhterev Medal awarded by Bekhterev Psychoneurological Research Institute, St. Petersburg; Gálfi Béla Award for services to Hungarian Psychosocial Rehabilitation; Member, Founding Group, Morpeth Northumbrian Gathering; former part-time Hibernian FC footballer. Recreations: golf; music; singer, guitarist, Radio Malaya etc; blethering; curling. Address: (h.) 1, Croft Wynd, Milnathort, Perth and Kinross KY13 9GH; T.-01577 864477; e-mail: olly_wilson@btinternet.com

Wilson, Andrew, BA Hons (Economics and Politics). Founding Partner, Charlotte Street Partners, since 2014; b. 12.70. Educ. Coltness High School, Wishaw; University of St Andrews; University of Strathclyde. Career history: Economist: Forestry Commission, Edinburgh, 1994-95; Economist, The Scottish Government, 1995-97; Researcher, Director, Business for Scotland, Scottish National Party, Edinburgh, 1995-97; MSP and Member of the Shadow Cabinet, The Scottish Parliament, 1999-2003; Columnist, The Sunday Mail, 1999-2003; Member of Board of Governors, SCRI (Scottish Crop Research Institute), Invergowrie, 2009-2011; Royal Bank of Scotland, 2003-2012 (latterly Head of Group Communications, 2010-2012); Group, WPP, London/Edinburgh, 2012-13; Director, Motherwell Football Club, 2010-2015; Member, Board of Trustees, John Smith Trust, 2005-2016; Columnist, Scotland on Sunday, 2012-16; Chairman, Sustainable Growth Commission, Edinburgh, 2016-18; Commission Member, Independent Commission on Referendums, Constitution Unit, University College London, 2017-18; Columnist, The National Newspaper Scotland, 2019-2020; Member, Board of Trustees, John Smith Centre for Public Service, University of Glasgow, since 2014; Director, Frame PR, Glasgow, since 2014; Member, Board of Trustees, Edinburgh International Culture Summit, since 2017; Non-Executive Director, Motherwell Football Club, since 2020; Non-Executive Board Director, National Galleries of Scotland (part-time), since 2020; Member, Board of Trustees, Sistema Scotland (part-time), since 2019. Address: Charlotte Street Partners Ltd, 16 Alva Street, Edinburgh EH2 4QG.
E-mail: info@charlottetestpartners.co.uk

Wilson, Brian, CBE, PC, MA (Hons). Director: Celtic plc, since 2005, AMEC Nuclear, 2005-2014, Shetland Space Centre, since 2019; Member of the Board of Trade, 2017-

2020; Chair: Harris Tweed Hebrides, since 2007, Havana Energy, since 2010, Britain's Energy Coast, 2009-2014; Prime Minister's Special Representative on Overseas Trade, 2003-05; MP (Labour), Cunninghame North, 1987-2005; former Minister for Energy and Industry, Department of Trade and Industry (2001-03); b. 13.12.48, Dunoon; m., Joni Buchanan; 2 s.; 1 d. Educ. Dunoon Grammar School; Dundee University; University College, Cardiff. Journalist; Publisher and Founding Editor, West Highland Free Press; Contributor to The Guardian, Scotsman, etc.; first winner, Nicholas Tomalin Memorial Award for Journalism; contested Ross and Cromarty, Oct., 1974, Inverness, 1979, Western Isles, 1983; front-bench spokesman on Scottish Home Affairs etc., 1988-92, Transport, 1992-94 and 1995-96, Trade and Industry, 1994-95; Minister of State, Scottish Office (Education, Industry and Highland and Islands), 1997-98; Minister for Trade, Department of Trade and Industry, 1998-99; Minister of State for Scotland, 1999-2001; Minister of State, Foreign and Commonwealth Office, 2001; Honorary Fellow, University of Highlands and Islands, 2010; Visiting Professor: Glasgow Caledonian University, 2008-14, University of Strathclyde, since 2016; UK Business Ambassador, since 2012; Institute of Directors UK Global Director of the Year, 2011. Address: Cnoc Na Meinn, 7A Mangersta, Isle of Lewis HS2 9EY.

Wilson, Brian, OBE, LLB. Deputy Chairman, Local Government Boundary Commission for Scotland, 1999-2008; b. 20.2.46, Perth; m., Isobel Esson; 3 d. Educ. Buckie High School; Aberdeen University. Various posts with Marks & Spencer, Banff County Council, Inverness County Council and Banff and Buchan District Council; Chief Executive, Inverness District Council, 1978-95; Depute Chief Executive, The Highland Council, 1995-98. Recreations: walking; painting; computing; cutting hedges. Address: (h.) 11 Lochardil Place, Inverness IV2 4LN; T.- 01463 237454.

Wilson, Colin Alexander Megaw, LLB (Hons). First Scottish Parliamentary Counsel, 2006-2012 (retired); b. 4.1.52, Aberdeen; m., Mandy Esca Clay (divorced); 1 s.; 1 d. Educ. High School of Glasgow; Edinburgh University. Admitted as a Solicitor, 1975; Assistant Solicitor, then Partner, Archibald Campbell & Harley, WS, Edinburgh, 1975-79; Assistant Legal Secretary to Lord Advocate, 1979-99, and until 1993 Assistant, then Depute, Parliamentary Draftsman for Scotland; Scottish Parliamentary Counsel, 1993-2006. Recreations: hill-walking; choral singing; family.

Wilson, Corri. MP (SNP), Ayr, Carrick and Cumnock, 2015-17; b. 11.4.65, Ayr. Educ. University of the West of Scotland. Elected to South Ayrshire council in the 2012 local elections for the ward of Ayr East.

Wilson, Donald, OStJ, Joint BA (Hons), MSc, TQ (Secondary). Lions International Award for humanitarian work (Melvin Jones Fellow); Fellow of the Scottish Ahlul Bayt Society; Burgess of the City of Edinburgh, since 2017; Convener of Culture and Communities at the City of Edinburgh Council, 2017-2022; b. 4.12.59, Selkirk; wife, Elaine; 1 step-s.; 1 step-d. Educ. Galashiels Academy; University of Stirling; The City University, London; Moray House College of Education, Edinburgh. Lord Provost and Lord Lieutenant of the City of Edinburgh, 2012-2017; Teacher of Computing, 1984-2012; Adult Education Tutor, 1984-2012; Acting Senior Teacher, ICT, 1997-99; Curriculum Development Officer, ICT, 1999-2001. Labour Councillor, City of Edinburgh Council, since 1999; Bailie of City of Edinburgh, 2007-2012; Member, Board: Edinburgh Technology Transfer Centre, 1999-2012, International Centre for the Mathematical Sciences, 1999-2017; Chair, Transnational Demos Project, 2001-2009; Board Member, Edinburgh International Science Festival, since 1999, Chair, 1999-2007, President, 2012-2017; Board Member, Edinburgh Science Foundation, 2007-2012; Chair,

Edinburgh Convention Bureaux, 2003-05; Chair, City of Edinburgh Council, Smart City & ICT Sounding Board, 2000-07; Executive Member for Smart City, 2000-07; Member, Edinburgh & Lothians Tourist Board, 1999-2005, Chair, 2003-05; Chair, Edinburgh & Lothians Area Tourism Partnership, 2005-06; Member, Board, Gorgie City Farm, 2008-2011; Member, Lothian and Borders Police Board, 2010-2011; Chair and Director, Edinburgh International Festival Society, 2012-2017; Chair, Edinburgh International Festival Board, 2012-2017; Director, Edinburgh International Festival Board, since 2012; Chair and Director, Edinburgh Royal Military Tattoo Ltd, 2012-2017; Director and Trustee, Our Dynamic Earth Charitable Trust, 2012-2017; Governor of the Incorporated Trades of Edinburgh, since 2014; Veterans and Armed Forces Champion, 2012-2017; Volunteering Ambassador, 2012-2017; Vice President, Shipwrecked Mariners' Society, 2014-2017; Member of the Incorporation of Baxters, since 2017; Deacon Convener, since 2019; Member of the Incorporation of Hammermen, since 2017; Patron, Scottish Indian Arts Forum, since 2017. Recreations: film; opera; sci-fi; computers; sudoku; antiques.

Wilson, Gerald R., CB, MA, FRSE, DUniv; b. 7.9.39, Edinburgh; m., Margaret (deceased); 1 s.; 1 d. Educ. Holy Cross Academy; Edinburgh University. Assistant Principal, Scottish Home and Health Department, 1961-65; Private Secretary, Minister of State for Scotland, 1965-66; Principal, Scottish Home and Health Department, 1966-72; Private Secretary to Lord Privy Seal, 1972-74, to Minister of State, Civil Service Department, 1974; Assistant Secretary, Scottish Economic Planning Department, 1974-77; Counsellor, Office of the UK Permanent Representative to the Economic Communities, Brussels, 1977-82; Assistant Secretary, Scottish Office, 1982-84; Under Secretary, Industry Department for Scotland, 1984-88; Secretary, Scottish Office Education and Industry Department, 1988-99, Scottish Executive Enterprise and Lifelong Learning Department, 1999; Special Adviser, Royal Bank of Scotland Group, 2000-09; Member, Court, Strathclyde University, 1999-2012, Vice Convener, 2008-2012; Member, Board: Royal Scottish National Orchestra, 2000-06 (Vice Chairman, since 2002), ICL (Scotland), 2000-02; Trustee, Royal Scottish National Orchestra Foundation, 2007-2017 (Chairman, since 2015); Chairman, Fairbridge in Scotland, 2006-2011; St Andrew's Children's Society, 2003-2010; Chairman, Scottish European Educational Trust, 2006-2012; Governor, George Watson's College, Edinburgh, 2000-09; Chairman, Scottish Biomedical Foundation Ltd., 1999-2004; Hon. Sec., Friends of the Royal Scottish Academy, 2009-2017; Treasurer, Royal Society of Edinburgh, 2012-2017. Recreation: music. Address: (b.) 17/5 Kinnear Road, Edinburgh EH3 5PG.

Wilson, Professor Gordon McAndrew, MA, PhD, FRSA; b. 4.12.39, Glasgow; m., Alison Rosemary Cook; 2 s.; 1 d. Educ. Eastwood Secondary School; Glasgow University; Jordanhill College of Education. Teacher of History and Modern Studies: Eastwood Secondary School, 1963-65, Eastwood High School, 1965-67; Lecturer in Social Studies, Hamilton College of Education, 1967-73 (Head of Department, 1973-81); Principal Lecturer in Inservice Education, then Assistant Principal, Jordanhill College of Education, 1981-88; Principal, Craigie College of Education, 1988-93; Assistant Principal and Director of University Campus Ayr, Paisley University, 1993-99, now Emeritus Professor. Chairman, South Ayrshire Hospitals NHS Trust, 1997-99; Chairman, Ayrshire and Arran Acute Hospitals NHS Trust, 1999-2004; Non-Executive Board Member, NHS Ayrshire and Arran, 1999-2007; President, Ayrshire Chamber of Commerce and Industry, 2002-04; Chair, East Ayrshire Community Health Partnership, 2005-08; President, Belleisle Conservatory Limited (2010-17). Recreations: reading; gardening; French and Italian language; music. Address: (h.) 51 Greenfield Avenue, Alloway, Ayr KA7 4NX; T.-01292 443889.

Wilson, Hamish Robert McHattie, CBE, MA (Aberd), MA, PhD (Cantab), FRCGP (Hon); b. 19.01.46, Aberdeen; m., Joyce Hossack; 3 d. Educ. Robert Gordon's College, Aberdeen; University of Aberdeen; Emmanuel College, Cambridge. Entered Health Service Administration in 1972; held range of posts with Grampian Health Board including Executive Board Member, 1991-99; Head of Primary Care Division, Scottish Executive Health Department, 1999-2006. Appointed to a number of Non-Executive Board posts from 2006 to 2020, including Scottish Commission for the Regulation of Care, General Medical Council, Scottish Dental Practice Board, Healthcare Improvement Scotland, Royal Pharmaceutical Society and Robert Gordon University. Recreations: music; theatre; cinema; hellenic studies; family history. Address: (h.) 9 Gordon Road, Aberdeen AB15 7RY; T.-01224 312226; e-mail: hamish.wilson60@btinternet.com

Wilson, Helen Frances, DA, RSW, RGI, PAI. Artist; b. 25.7.54, Paisley; 1 d. Educ. John Neilson High School, Paisley; Glasgow School of Art. Drawings and paintings in public and private collections; awards and prizes include: Cargill Travelling Scholarship (Colonsay and Italy), 1976; First Prize, Scottish Drawing Competition, 1997; elected: RGI, 1984, RSW, 1997 and PAI, 2005. Recreations: watching theatre, ballet, pantomime and people. Address: (h.) 1 Partickhill Road, Glasgow; T.-0141-339 5827. E-mail: helenfwilson@gmail.com

Wilson, Ian Matthew, CB, MA. b. 12.12.26, Edinburgh; m., 1, Anne Chalmers (deceased); 3 s.; 2, Joyce Town (deceased). Educ. George Watson's College; Edinburgh University. Assistant Principal, Scottish Home Department, 1950; Private Secretary to Permanent Under Secretary of State, Scottish Office, 1953-55; Principal, Scottish Home Department, 1955; Assistant Secretary: Scottish Education Department, 1963, Scottish Home and Health Department, 1971; Assistant Under Secretary of State, Scottish Office, 1974-77; Under Secretary, Scottish Education Department, 1977-86; Secretary of Commissions for Scotland, 1987-92. Member, RSAMD Governing Body, 1992-2000; President, University of Edinburgh Graduates' Association, 1995-97; Director, Scottish International Piano Competition, 1997-2004.

Wilson, James Wiseman, OBE, OStJ; b. 31.5.33, Glasgow; m., Valerie Grant; 1 s.; 3 d. Educ. Trinity College, Glenalmond; Harvard Business School. Marketing Director, Scottish Animal Products, 1959-63; Sales Director, then Managing Director, then Chairman, Robert Wilson & Sons (1849) Ltd., 1964-85; former Director, Barcapel Foundation. Trustee, Scottish Civic Trust, 1974-2004 and Chairman, Management Committee, 1984-2004; National Trust for Scotland: Member of Council, 1977-82 and 1984-89, President, Ayrshire Members' Centre; Honorary President, Skelmorlie Golf Club and Irvine Pipe Band; won Aims of Industry Free Enterprise Award (Scotland), 1980. Recreations: golf; backgammon; skiing; bridge; travelling. Address: (h.) The Turret House, Skelmorlie Castle, Skelmorlie, Ayrshire PA17 5EY; T.-01475 521127.

Wilson, Jim. Editor, Sunday Post. Address: (b.) D.C. Thomson & Co Ltd, 50 High Craighall Road, Glasgow G4 9UD; e-mail: jimwilson@sundaypost.com

Wilson, John. Chief Executive, NHS Fife, 2012-2014 (retired). Educ. degree in public administration, and a Postgraduate Diploma in Health Services Management. Thirty-five years operational experience of hospital management gained in Glasgow, Edinburgh and Fife; held a variety of management posts across Fife; formerly Chief Executive of NHS Fife Operational Division.

Wilson, John G., MA. Former MSP, Central Scotland (SNP, 2007-2014, Independent, 2014-16); Director, Scottish Low Pay Unit, 2001-07; b. 28.11.56, Falkirk; m., Frances M. McGlinchey; 1 d. Educ. Camelon High School; Coatbridge College; Glasgow University. Coachbuilder, 1972-82; Project Co-ordinator, Castlemilk Housing Involvement Project, 1987-94; Director, Glasgow Council of Tenants Associations, 1994-97; The Poverty Alliance: Senior Economic Development Officer, 1998-99, Fieldwork Manager, 1999-2001. Falkirk District Councillor, 1980-82; SNP Parliamentary candidate, Hamilton South, 2001, 2003; Westminster Candidate, 2005, Lanark and Hamilton East; Local Councillor, North Lanarkshire Council, 2007-09. Recreations: Tai Chi; archery; National Trust; Historic Scotland; RSPB; Woodlands Trust; Scottish CND.

Wilson, Dr. Lena, CBE, BA, MBA. Non-Executive Director, NatWest Group, since 2018; Chair, Chiene + Tait, since 2019; Chair, AGS Airports, since 2021; Visiting Professor, Strathclyde Business School, since 2018; Chief Executive, Scottish Enterprise, 2009-2017, Chief Operating Officer, 2005-09; Chief Executive Officer, Scottish Development International, 2006-2009; b. 13.2.64, Paisley. Educ. St Andrews High School, East Kilbride; Glasgow Caledonian University; Strathclyde University. Production and quality management, electronics industry, 1985-89; Manager, Locate in Scotland, 1989-94; Deputy Chief Executive, Scottish Enterprise Forth Valley, 1994-98; Senior Advisor, World Bank, Washington DC, 1998-2000; Senior Director, Customer Relations, Scottish Enterprise, 2000-05. Member, Financial Services Advisory Board; Board Member, Intertek Group PLC; member of UK Prime Minister Boris Johnson's Business Council, since 2022; Ambassador, Prince and Princess of Wales Hospice. Recreations: fitness; the arts; travel; family and friends.

Wilson, Les. Documentary Producer/Director, since 1980; Director, Caledonia TV Ltd., since 1992; b. 17.7.49, Glasgow; m., Adrienne Cochrane (marr. diss., 2006); 2 d.; m., Jenni Minto. Educ. Grove Academy, Broughty Ferry. Trainee Journalist, 1969-70; hippy trail, 1970-71; Reporter, Greenock Telegraph, 1972-73; Reporter, STV, 1973-78; Editor, STV political programme, Ways and Means, 1979-80; Producer/Director, STV, 1981-92. Winner, Celtic Film Festival Award, 1991; BAFTA Scotland and British Telecom Factual/Current Affairs awards, 1997; British Telecom Factual/Current Affairs award, 1998; Scots Independent, Oliver Brown Award, 2013; Saltire Society History Book of the Year, 2018. Publications: Scotland's War (Co-author), 1995; Fire in the Head (a novel), 2010; Islay Voices (Co-editor), 2016; The Drowned and the Saved, 2018; Putting the Tea in Britain: The Scots Who Made Our National Drink, 2021. Recreation: Islay – the island, its people, its malts. Address: (b.) 147 Bath Street, Glasgow G2 4SQ; T.-0141-564 9100. E-mail: lwilson@caledonia.tv

Wilson, Professor Lindsay, BA, DipEd, PhD, CPyschol. Emeritus Professor of Psychology, University of Stirling, since 2020; b. 24.6.51, Aberdeen; m., Jean; 2 s. Educ. Biggar High School; University of Stirling; University of Edinburgh. Research Fellow, Max Planck Institute for Psychiatry, Munich, 1979-80; University of Stirling: Medical Research Council Training Fellow, 1980-83, Lecturer then Senior Lecturer, 1983-98, Head, Department of Psychology, 1995-2001, Professor of Psychology, 1998-2020. Recreations: sailing; hillwalking. Address: (b.) Division of Psychology, University of Stirling, Stirling FK9 4LA; T.-01786 467640.

Wilson, Monica Anne, BA, DipPCT. Former Caledonian Professional Adviser, Effective Practice Unit, Community Justice Services Division, Scottish Government, 2009-2012; Counsellor in Primary Care, 1997-2013 (retired); b. 4.3.51,

Arundel; m., Keith Stewart; 1 step-d. Educ. Our Lady of Sion School, Worthing; Stirling University; Edinburgh University; Strathclyde University. Research Assistant, Stirling University, 1975-78; Research Officer, Scottish Consumer Council, 1978-80; Research Fellow, Edinburgh University, 1980-82; Research and Development Officer, Forth Valley Health Board, 1985-89; Joint Co-ordinator, CHANGE Project, 1989-96, Director, CHANGE, 1997-2009. Joint Developer, Caledonian System, accredited by the Scottish Accreditation Panel for Offender Programmes, 2004-2009; Member, Scottish Advisory Panel on Offender Rehabilitation, 2012-2018. Main publication: Men Who Are Violent to Women (Co-Author), 1997. Butler Trust Award, 2009. Trustee, Clackmannan Development Trust. Recreations: gardening; DIY; sailing; music. Address: (h.) 2 Kirk Brae, Clackmannan FK10 4JW; T.-01259 211 662. E-mail: monica.wilson78@yahoo.co.uk

Wilson, Rev Rachel, BA (Hons), MTh. Minister, Hobkirk and Southdean with Ruberslaw Church of Scotland, since 2018; m., Graeme; 2 c. Educ. Manchester University; Edinburgh University. Career history: sales consultancy; employee of the Berwick Citizens Advice Bureau; gained a Masters in Theology and Religious Studies at Edinburgh University in 2017 as part of ministry training; completed a probationary period as Assistant Minister at Maxton and Mertoun linked with Newtown linked with St Boswells. Recreations: keeps chickens; keen watercolourist. Address: Hobkirk and Southdean with Ruberslaw Manse, The Manse, Leydens Road, Denholm, Hawick TD9 8NB; T.-01450 870874.

Wilson, Robert. Chair, Creative Scotland, since 2018. Co-founder of Jupiter Artland Foundation, the award winning Sculpture Park near Edinburgh; served as Chair of Edinburgh Art Festival; Trustee of Little Sparta Trust; Trustee of the Royal Botanical Gardens Edinburgh; Trustee of the Dovecot Studios and Chair of the Arts Working Group at Inverleith House; Chairman, The Barcapel Foundation and Prostate Scotland; Chairman and co-owner of Nelsons, the UK's largest natural medicines producer. Address: Creative Scotland, The Lighthouse, 11, 56 Mitchell Street, Glasgow G1 3LX; T.-0330 333 2000.

Wilson-Cairns, Krysty. Scottish screenwriter; b. 26.5.87. Educ. Craigholme School; The Royal Conservatoire of Scotland; National Film and Television School. Feature film debut was the screenplay for the 2019 war film 1917 (co-written with Sam Mendes); received nominations for the Academy Award for Best Original Screenplay and the Writers Guild of America Award for Best Original Screenplay; first creative work at The Royal Conservatoire of Scotland was a short story about killer guinea pigs; spent a year working at the BBC Comedy Unit; moved to London and gained an MA in Screenwriting from the National Film and Television School (NFTS) in 2013.

Wilton, Brian, MBE. Managing Director, Tartan Ambassador Ltd, since 2014; Director, Scottish Tartans Authority, 1995-2015. Educ. English School, Nicosia, Cyprus. Address: Scottish Tartans Authority, Fraser House, Muthill Road, Crieff, Perthshire PH7 3AY.

Windsor, Malcolm L., PhD, FRSC, OBE. Secretary, North Atlantic Salmon Conservation Organization, 1984-2012; Buckland Foundation Professorship, 2014; Independent Reviewer of the EU-New Zealand Research Cooperation Agreement, 2013; b. Bristol; m., Sally (deceased); 2 d. Educ. Cotham Grammar School, Bristol; Bristol University. Researcher, University of California, 1965-67; fisheries research, Humber Laboratory, Hull, 1967-75; Fisheries

Adviser to Chief Scientist, Ministry of Agriculture and Fisheries, London, 1975-84. Ex-Chairman, Duddingston Village Conservation Society and Chair of Rutland Square and Street Association. Publication: "Roving Mad: Odd encounters", and a book on fishery products. Recreations: local conservation work; jazz; walking; Presenter of Jazz cabaret in Edinburgh Fringe Festival. Address: (h.) 1 Duddingston House Courtyard, Edinburgh EH15 1JG; T.-0131 661 7707; e-mail: mw@mwindsor.net

Winn, Professor Philip, BA, PhD. Emeritus Professor of Neuroscience, Strathclyde Institute of Pharmacy and Biomedical Sciences (SIPBS), University of Strathclyde; b. 31.10.54, Hull; m., Jane E. Burrows; 2 s.; 1 d. Educ. Isleworth Grammar School; University of Hull. Fellow: Royal Society of Biology, Association for Psychological Science (USA), Royal Society for the encouragement of Arts, Manufactures & Commerce; Chair, Medical Research Scotland; Member, Icelandic Quality Board for Higher Education. Address: SIPBS, 161 Cathedral Street, Glasgow G4 0RE.

Winney, Robin John, MB, ChB, FRCPEdin. Retired Consultant Renal Physician, Edinburgh Royal Infirmary; b. 8.5.44, Dunfermline. Educ. Dunfermline High School; Edinburgh University. Recreations: badminton; curling; bowls. Address: (h.) 74 Lanark Road West, Currie, Midlothian EH14 5JZ.
E-mail: robinwinney@btopenworld.com

Winstanley, Charles, TD, JP, MBA, DBA, DL. Chair of the Board, Academy of Medical Royal Colleges, since 2016; Chair of Sub-Committee, Cabinet Office, since 2018; Chairman, Contact Group, since 2018; Chair, Scottish Police Pension Board, 2015-18; Chairman: NHS Lothian, 2007-2013, Edinburgh Leisure, 2010-2015; Member, Asylum and Immigration Tribunal, since 2003; Non Executive Director: Ministry of Defence, 2010-2014, Scottish Government, 2010-2013; Independent Member of Audit and Risk Committee, UK Supreme Court, since 2011; b. 6.3.52, London; m., Columbine (divorced); 1 s.; 1 d.; m., Gillian (2018). Educ. Wellington College; RMA Sandhurst; Henley Management College. Served 16/5 Lancers and Royal Yeomanry, 1970-93; Justice of the Peace, since 1993; Member, National Consumer Council for Postal Services, 2002-08; Chairman, Norfolk Probation Board, 2001-06; Panel Chairman, General Medical Council, 2000-07; Non Executive Director, Norfolk and Norwich University Hospital Trust, 1999-2006. Deputy Lieutenant, Greater London, since 1997. Recreations: fly fishing; sailing; motorcycling.

Winter, Dr. Mike, FRCGP, FRCPsych, FSF, FMLM. Medical Director, Procurement Commissioning and Facilities SBU, NHS NSS, 2013-19 (retired); b. 17.06.56, Scotland; m., Margaret; 1 s.; 1 d. Educ. Bathgate Academy; Edinburgh University. General Practitioner, Whitburn, West Lothian, 1987-96; Medical Director: Lanarkshire Healthcare NHS Trust, 1996-99, NHS Lothian Primary Care, 1999-2008, National Services Division, 2008-2013. Ambassador, Girlguiding Edinburgh. Recreations: cooking; photography; skiing.

Winter, Robert, OBE. Lord-Lieutenant and Lord Provost of Glasgow, 2007-2012; b. 31.03.37, Glasgow; m., Sheena Morgan Duncan; 4 s.; 1 d. Educ. Allan Glen's High School; Strathclyde University; Glasgow University. Director of Social Work, Greenock and Port Glasgow, 1969-75; Strathclyde Regional Council Depute Director of Social Work, 1975-95, then Director of Social Work, 1995-96. Past President, Association of Directors of Social Work, 1980-81; Member, General Council, 1996-2005 (Chairman of Fitness to Practice Panel, until 2007). Member, Greater Glasgow Health Board PCT, 1996-2005; Convener, Risk Management Authority, 2004-08. Recreations: walking; swimming; reading; football.

Wise, Lady (The Right Hon. Morag B. Wise), QC, PC, LLB (Hons), DipLP, LLM. Senator of the College of Justice, since 2013. Educ. University of Aberdeen; McGill University. Became a solicitor in 1989 and joined Morton Fraser LLP; called to the bar in 1993, joining Westwater Advocates, and specialised in family law; Queen's Counsel, since 2005, and was appointed a Temporary Judge of the Court of Session in 2008; Member of the Disciplinary Committee of the Faculty of Advocates, since 2005; Chair of the Advocates' Family Law Association, since 2007, having served as Vice Chair, since 2000. Address: (b.) Parliament House, Edinburgh EH1 1RQ.

Wiseman, Alan William. Director and Chairman, Robert Wiseman Dairies, 1979-2010; National Dairy Council, Scottish Dairy Association; b. 20.8.50, Giffnock. Educ. Duncanrig Senior Secondary School, East Kilbride. Left school to be one of his father's milkmen, 1967; has been a milkman ever since. Scottish Businessman of the Year, 1992; Scottish Business Achievement Award, 1994; Fellow, Royal Agricultural Society. Recreation: golf.

Wishart, Beatrice. MSP (Scottish Liberal Democrats), Shetland Islands, since 2019; Education spokesperson; b. 1.1.55, Lerwick, Shetland. Educ. Anderson High School. Ran the offices of Alistair Carmichael MP and Tavish Scott MSP; elected Councillor (Independent) in the 2017 Scottish local elections for Shetland Islands Council, became Depute Convenor of the Council. Sits on Scottish Parliament committees for Education and Skills, for Culture, Tourism, Europe and External Affairs, and for COVID-19. Address: The Scottish Parliament, Edinburgh EH99 1SP; T.-0131 348 6296; e-mail: Beatrice.Wishart.msp@parliament.scot

Wishart, Colin Fraser, DA, RIBA, FRIAS, SSA. Chartered Architect; Principal, Freespace Architecture, since 2002; Visiting Teaching Fellow, Duncan of Jordanstone College, University of Dundee, 1997-2008; formerly Honorary Fellow, The School of Arts, Culture and Environment, The University of Edinburgh (appointed 2004); Professional Member, Society of Scottish Artists, since 1990; architectural photographer; b. 20.8.47, Dundee; divorced. Educ. Grove Academy; Duncan of Jordanstone College of Art. Architect, Thoms and Wilkie, Chartered Architects, Dundee, 1972-73; Senior Architect, City of Dundee Corporation, 1973-90; Principal Architect, City of Dundee Council, 1990-96; Partner, Battledown Studio, Natural Architecture, 1996-2002. Past President, Dundee Institute of Architects, since 1988; President, Dundee Institute of Architects, 1986-88; Vice President, Royal Incorporation of Architects in Scotland, 1986-88; RIBA Representative, Architects Registration Council, 1989-96; National Juror, RIBA Awards, 1988. Recreations: photography; fine art; music; poetry. Address: 12 Farm Road, Anstruther, Fife KY10 3ER; T.-01333 310 589. E-mail: colinform@hotmail.co.uk

Wishart, James, BD. Minister of Religion, 1985-2009 (retired); b. 26.12.44, South Ronaldsay, Orkney; m., Helen Donaldson; 1 s.; 1 d. Educ. Kirkwall Grammar School; Aberdeen University. Farming, 1960-80; University, 1980-85. Recreations: photography; European languages; walking. Address: (h.) Upper Westshore, Burray, Orkney KW17 2TE.

Wishart, Professor Jennifer Grant, MA, PhD, FRSE. Professor of Developmental Disabilities in Childhood, University of Edinburgh, since 1998; b. 9.5.48, Dundee; m., Thomas Arrol. Educ. Harris Academy, Dundee; University of Edinburgh. Research Psychologist, University of Edinburgh, 1970-95, Reader, 1995-96; first Scottish Chair in Special Education, Moray House Institute of Education, Heriot-Watt University, 1996-98. Research Advisor to Scottish and UK Down's Syndrome Associations, Down Syndrome International and National Down Syndrome Foundation (Canada); funding assessor for national/international research councils and charitable bodies. Peer reviewer for c40 academic journals; c100 papers/chapters in psychology/education/interdisciplinary publications. Recreations: wine/food; travel; English pointers. Address: 10/13 West Mill Road, Edinburgh EH13 0NX; e-mail: J.Wishart@ed.ac.uk

Wishart, Peter. MP (SNP), Perth and North Perthshire, since 2005, North Tayside, 2001-05; SNP Shadow Leader of the House of Commons, since 2015; Chair, Scottish Affairs Select Committee, since 2015; previously served as the SNP's Westminster Spokesperson for the Constitution, Home Affairs, Culture, Media and Sport, Transport, International Development and Chief Whip; b. 9.3.62; 1 s. Educ. Moray House College of Education. Community worker, 1984-85; musician with Runrig, 1985-2001. Address: (b.) 17-19 Leslie Street, Blairgowrie, Perthshire PH10 6AH; 63 Glasgow Road, Perth PH2 0PE. E-mail: pete.wishart.mp@parliament.uk

Wishart Ruth, BA (Hons), FRSA. Columnist and Broadcaster; b. Glasgow; m. Rod McLeod (died 2004). Educ. Eastwood Senior Secondary; Open University. Chair, Dewar Arts Awards. Contact: ghillie168@gmail.com

Wiszniewski, Adrian, BA (Hons). Artist/Designer; b. 31.3.58, Glasgow; m., Diane Foley; 2 s.; 1 d. Educ. Mackintosh School of Architecture, Glasgow School of Art. Around 40 solo exhibitions throughout the world, since 1983; commissions include: two large paintings for Liverpool Anglican Cathedral 1996, Gallery of Modern Art, Glasgow, 1996, Millennium Tower, Hamilton, 1997-98; work purchased by museums worldwide including Tate Gallery, London and MOMA, New York. New York Design Award for designs of six rugs in collaboration with Edinburgh Tapestry Workshop; has created limited edition books. Recreations: looking at pictures; cinema; family.

Withers, Professor Charles William John, BSc, PhD, FBA, FRSE, FRHistS, FRGS, FRSGS. Member, Academemea Europaea. Professor of Geography, Edinburgh University, since 1994, Emeritus, since 2019; Geographer Royal for Scotland, since 2015; b. 6.12.54, Edinburgh; m., Anne; 2 s.; 1 d. Educ. Daniel Stewart's College, Edinburgh; St. Andrews University; Cambridge University. Publications: author of 28 books and 200 academic articles. Recreations: reading; hill-walking; watercolour painting. Address: (b.) Institute of Geography, Edinburgh University, Drummond Street, Edinburgh; T.-0131-650 2559.

Withers, James. Chief Executive, Scotland Food & Drink, since 2011; Chief Executive, NFU Scotland, 2008-2011. Sits on the Scottish Government Board of Trade; Board member of the Scottish Tourism Alliance. Address: (b.) Scotland Food & Drink, 3, The Royal Highland Centre, Ingliston, Edinburgh EH28 8NB.

Witney, Eur. Ing. Professor Brian David, BSc, MSc, PhD, NDA, NDAgrE, CEng, CEnv, FIMechE, Hon.FIAgrE, MemASABE. Director, Land Technology Ltd., 1995-2013; Hon. Professor of Agricultural Engineering, Edinburgh University, since 1989; Professor of Terramechanics, Scottish Agricultural College, Edinburgh, 1994-95; b. 8.6.38, Edinburgh; m., Maureen M.I. Donnelly; 1 s.; 2 d. Educ. Daniel Stewart's College, Edinburgh; Edinburgh University; Durham University; Newcastle University. Senior Research Associate, Newcastle upon Tyne University, 1962-66; Research Fellow, US Army Research

Office, Duke Univ., 1966-67; Senior Scientific Officer, Military Engineering Experimental Establishment, Christchurch, 1967-70; Head, Agricultural Engineering Department, East of Scotland College of Agriculture, Edinburgh, 1970-86; Director, Scottish Centre of Agricultural Engineering, 1987-95, and Vice-Dean, Scottish Agricultural College, 1990-95. President, Institution of Agricultural Engineers, 1988-90; President, European Society of Agricultural Engineers, 1993-94; Managing Editor, Landwards, 1996-2007; Managing Editor, Land Technology, 1994-96; Editor and Chairman, Editorial Board, Journal of Agricultural Engineering Research, 1998-2001, Biosystems Engineering, 2002-07; Chairman, Douglas Bomford Trust, 1998-2003. EurAgEng Award for services to agricultural engineering, 2000. Publication: Choosing and Using Farm Machines. Address: (h.) 33 South Barnton Avenue, Edinburgh EH4 6AN.

Wolf, Professor Charles Roland, OBE, BSc, PhD, FRSE, FMedSci, FSA, FBTS. Founder and Chief Scientific Officer, CXR Biosciences Ltd., 2001-2012; Now Concept Life Sciences; b. 26.2.49, Sedgefield; m., Helga Loth; 1 s.; 1 d. Educ. Surrey University. Royal Society Fellow, Institute for Physiological Chemistry, University of Saarland, W. Germany 1976-77; Visiting Fellow, National Institute of Environmental Health Sciences, North Carolina, 1977-80; Visiting Scientist, ICI Central Toxicology Laboratories, Macclesfield, 1980-81; Head Scientist, Biochemistry Section, Institute of Toxicology, Mainz, W. Germany, 1981-82; Head, ICRF Molecular Pharmacology Group, Edinburgh University, 1982-92. Gerhard Zbinden Award, 2001. Publications; Molecular Genetics of Drug Resistance (Co-Editor), 1997; over 550 scientific papers and national and international awards including the James Black award from the Royal Society of Edinburgh. Recreations: weaving; piano playing; gardening; hiking; poetry. Address: (b.) Jacqui Wood Cancer Centre, Ninewells Hospital and Medical School, Dundee DD1 9SY; T.-01382 383134.

Wolffe, Rt. Hon. James, QC, FRSE. Lord Advocate, 2016-2021; Privy Counsellor, since 2016; Bencher, Middle Temple, since 2015; m., The Hon. Lady Wolffe; 2 s. Educ. University of Edinburgh; Balliol College, Oxford. Advocate, since 1992; Barrister, since 2013; First Standing Junior Counsel to the Scottish Ministers, 2002-07; QC since 2007; Advocate Depute, 2007-2010; Vice-Dean of the Faculty of Advocates, 2013-14; Dean, The Faculty of Advocates, 2014-16.

Wolffe, The Hon. Lady Wolffe (Sarah Wolffe), QC. Professor of Practice, University of Strathclyde, since 2021; Honorary Professor, Edinburgh Law School, since 2021; Senator of the College of Justice, 2014-2021; m., Rt. Hon. James Wolffe; 2 s. Career: qualified as a solicitor in 1992 and worked at the Bank of Scotland legal department, 1992-93; called to the bar in 1994 and until 2008 practised as a junior counsel, mainly in commercial and public law; standing junior counsel to the Department of Trade and Industry and its successor departments; ad hoc advocate depute, 2007-2014; appointed QC in 2008. As senior counsel, practised mainly in commercial and public law. Chancellor to the Bishop of the Argyll and Isles, 2004-2013; Chancellor to the Bishop of Edinburgh, 2007-2014; MacGillivray, Insurance Law, Scottish contributor to 10th and 11th editions; Mithani, Directors Disqualification, Scottish Editor for 2012 edition; Member: Disciplinary Tribunal of the Faculty of Advocates, 2005-2008, Police Appeals Tribunal, 2013-2014; CCEB Working Group on Insurance Law (appointed expert), 2013-2014; Faculty of Advocate's Law Reform Committee, 2013-2014; Commercial Court Consultative Committee, 2000-2004;

Canons Committee of the Scottish Episcopal Church, 1995-98. LLB with Distinction, University of Edinburgh, 1989; DipLP, University of Edinburgh, 1990; BA (Summa Cum Laude, Phi Beta Kappa), Dartmouth College, Hanover, NH, USA, 1984. Clubs: Dairymen's Country Club; Waverley Lawn Tennis, Squash and Sports Club. Scottish Civil Justice Council, Advocate Member, 2014. Emigrated to the United Kingdom in 1987.

Wood, Alex, BA (Hons), MLitt, MEd, MSc. Genealogical researcher, teacher and writer; b. 17.11.50, Dundee; m., Frances Kinnear; 2 d. Educ. Paisley Grammar School; New University of Ulster; Moray House College of Education; Edinburgh University; Stirling University; Strathclyde University. English Teacher, Craigroyston High School, 1973-75; Community Worker, Pilton Central Association, 1975-77; Remedial Teacher, Craigroyston High School, 1977-79; Principal Teacher, Learning Support, Craigroyston High School, 1979-90; Head of Centre, Millburn, Bathgate, 1990-96; Head Teacher, Kaimes School, 1996-99; Special Schools and Social Inclusion Manager, Edinburgh Education Department, 1999-2000; Principal and Head Teacher, Wester Hailes Education Centre, 2000-2011 (seconded Headteacher, Tynecastle High School, 2008-09). Edinburgh District Councillor, Pilton Ward, 1980-87; Parl. Candidate, Dumfriesshire, 1979 and West Edinburgh, 1984. Recreations: genealogy; reading; running. T.-0775 9898890.
E-mail: alexander.wood@blueyonder.co.uk
Web: www.alexwood.org.uk

Wood, Brian James, JP, BSc (Hons), FRSA. Rector, Hazlehead Academy, Aberdeen, 1993-2009 (retired); b. 6.12.49, Banff; m., Doreen A. Petrie; 1 s.; 1 d. Educ. Banff Academy; Aberdeen Academy; Aberdeen University; Aberdeen College of Education. Teacher of Physics, George Heriot's School, Edinburgh, 1972-75; Mackie Academy, 1975-89, latterly as Depute Rector; Rector, Mearns Academy, 1989-93. Deputy Convener of the Board of the Cairngorms National Park Authority (2010-2018); Justice of the Peace, Grampian Highland and Islands (1974-2019); Honorary Sheriff at Stonehaven; Member, University of Aberdeen Business Committee, 2012-2021; Director of The Cairngorms Trust; Chair of Braemar Community Council; Chair of St Margaret's Trust Braemar. Recreations: golf; fishing; reading; local history. Address: (h.) Downfield, 3 Broombank Terrace, Braemar; T.-013397 41407; e-mail: brian.j.wood@btinternet.com

Wood, Fergus, TD. Former Provost of Stirling (2008-2012); b. 10.09.42, Glasgow; m., Francesca; 2 s.; 1 d. Educ. Trinity College, Glenalmond. Trainee Journalist, Glasgow Herald, 1960-63; Scholarship in Communications, Norway, 1963-65; Journalist, Evening Times, Glasgow, 1965-69; PRO Phillips Phonographic Industries, Holland, 1969-72; Information Officer, Stirling University, 1972-80; Director, Scottish Woollen Industry, 1980-88; MD, Scottish Wool Centre Ltd., Aberfoyle, 1988-2008. Project Director, Scottish Fine Wool Producers, 1998-2005; Major in TA (TD in 1978); TA Service, 1960-90. Recreations: Celtic music (Band Leader, Kinlochard Ceilidh Band; Silver Discs, 2000 and 2003 from music industry). Address: (h.) Ledard Farm, Kinlochard, Stirling FK8 3TL; T.-01877 387219; e-mail: ceilidhband@btconnect.com

Wood, Graham Allan, MBChB, BDS, FDSRCPS, FRCS(Ed), FDSRCS(Ed), FDSRCS(Eng). Interim Professor in Oral Medicine, Royal Hospitals Trust and University of Belfast, 2011-15; Consultant Oral and Maxillofacial Surgeon, Southern General Hospital, Glasgow, 1995-2010; Past Vice Dean, Faculty of Dental Surgery, Royal College of Physicians and Surgeons of Glasgow; Honorary Clincial Senior Lecturer, University of Glasgow, since 1995; Clinical Professor, University of Texas, USA, 1990-2000; b. 15.8.46, Glasgow; m., Lindsay

Balfour; 1 s.; 1 d. Educ. Hillhead High School, Glasgow; University of Glasgow; University of Dundee. General dental practice, Glasgow, 1968-70; House Officer, Senior House Officer, Registrar, dental specialties, Glasgow Dental Hospital, Glasgow Victoria Infirmary and Canniesburn Hospital, 1970-72; Dental Surgeon, Grenfell Mission, Labrador, Canada, 1972-73; House Officer (plastic surgery), Dundee Royal Infirmary, 1978; Senior Registrar (oral and maxillofacial surgery), North Wales, 1979-83; Consultant, Oral and Maxillofacial Surgeon, North Wales, 1983-95. Fellow, International Association of Oral and Maxillofacial Surgeons; Fellow, British Association of Oral and Maxillofacial Surgeons; former Examiner, International Association of Oral and Maxillofacial Surgeons (retired). Recreations: hillwalking; golf; sailing; skiing. Address: (h.) Cambro, Gryffe Road, Kilmacolm PA13 4BB.

Wood, Sir Ian Clark, KT, GBE, CBE (1982), LLD, BSc, DBA, DTech, CBIM, FCIB, FRSE. Chairman and Chief Executive, John Wood Group PLC, 1967-2006, Chairman, 2007-2012; Chairman, J.W. Holdings, since 1982; Chancellor, Robert Gordon University, 2004-2021; Chairman, The Wood Foundation; Chairman, Opportunity North East (ONE), November 2015; Chairman, Energy Transition Zone (ETZ) Ltd, April 2021; b. 21.7.42, Aberdeen; m., Helen Macrae; 3 s. Educ. Robert Gordon's College, Aberdeen; Aberdeen University. Joined family business, John Wood & Sons, 1964; Chairman, Scottish Enterprise Board, 1997-2000; Fellow, Royal Society of Arts; Grampian Industrialist of the Year, 1978; Young Scottish Businessman of the Year, 1979; Scottish Free Enterprise Award, 1985; Scottish Business Achievement Award Trust - joint winner, 1992, corporate elite leadership award services category; Hon. LLD, 1984; Hon. DBA, 1998; HonDTech, 2002; Corporate Elite "World Player" Award, 1996; Scottish Business Insider Ambassador for Scotland, 2001; Fellow: Scottish Vocational Educational Council, Scottish Qualifications Authority; Business Achievement Award, Business Insider, 2002; Entrepreneurial Exchange Hall of Fame, 2002; Business Insider/PWC Scotland PLC Awards, CEO of the Year, 2003; Glenfiddich Spirit of Scotland Award for Business, 2003; Entrepreneurial Exchange Philanthropist of the Year, 2008; Inducted into Offshore Energy Centre's Hall of Fame, Houston, 2009; awarded Energy Institute's Cadman Medal, 2010; SCDI President's Award, November, 2011; Honorary Doctor of Engineering, Heriot Watt University, 2012; Honorary Doctor of Science, Strathclyde University, 2013; Lifetime Achievement Award, Oil & Gas UK, 2012; American Scottish Foundation's Wallace Award, 2012; Broadwalk UK Chairman of the Year Award, 2012; Royal Society of Edinburgh Royal Medal, 2013; Chairman of Commission of Developing Scotland's Young Workforce; Leader (appointed by UK Government) of a Review on maximising UKCS Oil & Gas recovery; Member of the Build Back Better Business Council, 2021; Board Member of NMIS, 2021; Founder Chairman, The Oil & Gas Technology Centre (OGTC), April 2016-March 2017; awarded Knighthood in the 1994 New Year Honours; awarded GBE (Knight Grand Cross) in Queen's Birthday Honours, June 2016; awarded The Knight of the Order of the Thistle (KT) in Queen's Birthday Honours, June 2018; Northern Star Business Awards Lifetime Achievement Award, 2014; Oil Council Lifetime Achievement Award, November 2014; Beacon Award for Philanthrophy, April 2015; Great London Scot Lifetime Achievement Award, November 2016; awarded Carnegie Medal of Philanthropy in 2019. Recreations: tennis; family; art. Address: (b.) J W Holdings Ltd, Blenheim House, Fountainhall Road, Aberdeen AB15 4DT; T.-01224 619842.

Wood, Jane Frances. Director of Membership and Nations, Business in the Community Scotland, since 2017; BT Group Nations and Regions Director, since 2018; formerly Chief Executive, Scottish Business in the Community (2009-2015); formerly Chair, Essential Edinburgh; b. 11.4.62, Oxford; m., Christopher Wood; 2 s.; 2 d. Educ. Madras College; Napier University. Marketing Manager, Scottish and Newcastle, 1987-89; Marketing Director, The Guinea Group, 1989-97; Director of Communications, GJW Public Affairs Europe, 1997-99; Head of Corporate Affairs, Alliance Boots, 1999-2009. CBI Scotland Council; Member, First Minister's National Economic Forum; Board Director, Institute of Directors Scotland; Member, Ministerial 20:20 Climate Change Delivery Group. Address: (h.) Port Lodge, 7 High Street, Dunbar, East Lothian EH42 1EA; T.-01368 865265. E-mail: janewood@sbcscot.com

Wood, Professor Robert Anderson, BSc, MB, ChB, FRCP Edin & Glas, FRCS Edin, FRCPsych; b. 26.5.39, Edinburgh; m., Dr. Sheila Pirie; 1 s.; 3 d. Educ. Edinburgh Academy; Edinburgh University. Postgraduate Dean and Professor of Clinical Medicine, Aberdeen University, 1992-99; Consultant Physician, Perth Royal Infirmary, 1972-92; Deputy Director of Postgraduate Medical Education, University of Dundee, 1985-91; Councillor, RCPE, 1990-92, Dean, 1992-95, Treasurer, 1999-2003, Trustee, 2004-2020; Director, MDDUS, 2004-09, previously Member of Council, 1992-2004; Member, Harveian Society (President, 1998-99); Her Majesty's Inspector of Anatomy for Scotland, 2007-2014; Member, Tribunal Service Criminal Injuries Compensation Appeals Tribunal, 2000-2011; Member, Advocates Discipline Tribunal, since 2000; Member, Royal and Ancient, Elie Golf House, Blairgowrie & Craigie Hill golf clubs. Address: (h.) Ballomill House, Abernethy, Perthshire PH2 9LD.

Woodfield, Professor Ruth, BA, MA, DPhil. Professor of Equalities and Organisation, University of St Andrews, since 2013, Co-Director of the Centre for Research into Equality, Diversity and Inclusion, Assistant Vice-Principal (Diversity), 2019-2021. Educ. University of Sussex. Career history: Professor of Sociology, University of Sussex, until 2013, held the roles of Head of Department (Sociology), School Director of Research and Knowledge Exchange (School of Law, Politics and Sociology), Sub-Dean of the School of Social Sciences; former Co-Head, School of Management, University of St Andrews. Published articles on a wide range of inequalities topics including: ethnicity and retention in higher education; student age and first destination employment; student attendance patterns and degree classification; also written monographs on women in computing, gendered occupational choice, and been commissioned to write HE sector reports on topics such as men's experiences of pastoral and academic support in higher education and retention and attainment patterns across the disciplines. Address: School of Management, University of St Andrews, The Gateway, North Haugh, St Andrews, Fife KY16 9RJ; T.-01334 461965. E-mail: rw57@st-andrews.ac.uk

Woodroffe, Wing Commander Richard John, MBE; b. 12.6.50, Newmarket; m., Elizabeth Clare; 3 s. Educ. Khormaksar, Changi, Rutlish and King Alfred's (Wantage) Grammar Schools; North Berkshire College. Purser Officer, P&O Lines Ltd., 1968; joined RAF, 1971: Pilot Officer, RAF St. Athan, 1972, Deputy Officer Commanding Accounts Flight, RAF Benson, 1973-74, Officer Commanding Personnel Services Flight, RAF Saxa Vord, 1974-75, promoted to Flying Officer, 1974, Operations Wing Adjutant and No. 3 (F) Squadron Intelligence Officer, RAF Germany Harrier Force, 1976-78, promoted to Flight Lieutenant, 1978, Officer Commanding Administration Flight, RAF Saxa Vord, 1979, Aide-de-Camp to Air Officer Commanding-in-Chief, Headquarters RAF Strike Command, 1980-82, Works Services and Airfield Survival Measures Project Officer, RAF Kinloss, 1982-84, promoted to Squadron Leader, 1984, College Secretariat 1 and College Press Liaison Officer, RAF College, Cranwell,

1984-86, Officer Commanding Personnel Management Squadron, RAF Bruggen, 1986-88, promoted to Wing Commander, 1988, assumed command of Administration Wing, RAF Leuchars, Fife, 1988-91, Air Member for Personnel's Management Planner and Briefer, MOD, 1991-93, Chairman of Boards, Officer and Aircrew Selection Centre, Cranwell, then Deputy President, Ground Boards, 1993-96; posted to NATO HQ Allied Forces Central (Brunssum, The Netherlands), 1996-2001; General Secretary, Royal British Legion Scotland, 2001-04; Thames Water Nevis, 2004-07; Trustee, Scottish Veterans' Garden City Association. Recreations: sub-aqua; fishing; flytying; rough shooting; social golf; rugby. Club: The Royal Air Force. Address: 15 Pitreavie Court, Dunfermline, Fife KY11 8UU; T.-01383 749630.

Woods, (Adrien) Charles, MA. Director, Scottish Universities Insight Institute, since 2012; Visiting Professor, University of Strathclyde, European Policies Research Centre, 2007-2013; formerly Senior Director, Strategy and Chief Economist, Scottish Enterprise; b. 22.9.55, London. Educ. St. Andrews University. Various posts, Scottish Development Agency, 1981-91; Scottish Enterprise: Director, Policy and Planning, 1991-92, Director, Operations, 1992-94; Chief Executive, Scotland Europa, 1994-97. Recreations: golf; cycling. Address: University of Strathclyde, Collins Building, 21 Richmond Street, Glasgow G1 1XQ.
E-mail: charlie.woods3@btinternet.com

Woods, Professor Philip John, BSc, PhD, CPhys, FInstP, FRSE. Professor of Nuclear Physics, Edinburgh University, since 2000, Head of Institute for Physics, 2005-09; b. 25.6.61, Lincoln; m., Claudia; 1 s.; 3 d. Educ. City Comprehensive School, Lincoln; Manchester University. Research Fellow, Birmingham University; Lecturer, then Reader, Edinburgh University, 1988-2000. Recreation: overseas travel. Address: (b.) School of Physics and Astronomy, University of Edinburgh, James Clerk Maxwell Building, Room 8203, Peter Guthrie Tait Road, Edinburgh EH9 3FD; T.-0131 650 5283; e-mail: phillip.j.woods@ed.ac.uk

Woolhouse, Professor Mark Edward John, OBE, MA, MSc, PhD, FRSE, FMEdSci. Chair of Infectious Disease Epidemiology, University of Edinburgh, since 1997; b. 25.4.59, Shrewsbury; m., Dr. Francisca Mutapi; 1 d. Educ. Tiffin School, Kingston, Surrey; New College, University of Oxford; University of York; Queen's University, Canada. Research Fellow: University of Zimbabwe, 1985-86, Imperial College, London, 1986-89, University of Oxford, 1989-97. Recreations: walking; fly-fishing. Address: (b.) Usher Institute, University of Edinburgh, Ashworth Laboratories, King's Buildings, Charlotte Auerbach Road, Edinburgh EH9 3FL; T.-0131 650 5456.

Woolman, The Hon. Lord (Stephen Woolman), Hon LLD. Senator of the College of Justice in Scotland, since 2008; Advocate, since 1987; b. 16.5.53, Edinburgh; m., Dr Helen Mackinnon; 2 d. Educ. George Heriot's School; Aberdeen University. Lecturer in Law, Edinburgh University, 1978-87; QC, 1998; Advocate Depute, 1999-2002; Deputy Chairman, Boundary Commission for Scotland, since 2009; Chairman of Council, St George's School for Girls, since 2011. Publication: Contract (4th edition), 2010. Keeper of the Advocates Library, 2004-08. Recreation: cinema. Address: (b.) Parliament House, Edinburgh EH1 1RF.

Wooton, Professor Ian, MA, MA, MPhil, PhD, FRSA. Professor of Economics, Strathclyde University, since 2003; Research Fellow, Centre for Economic Policy Research, London, since 1994; Fellow, CESifo Research Network, Munich, since 2006; b. 4.4.57, Kirkcaldy; 1 s.; 1 d.; Partner, Andrew Sawers. Educ. Kirkcaldy High School; St. Andrews University; Columbia University, New York. Associate Professor of Economics, University of Western Ontario, London, Canada, 1982-95; Bonar-Macfie Professor of Economics, Glasgow University, 1995-2003. Recreations: travel; architecture. Address: (b.) Department of Economics, Strathclyde Business School, University of Strathclyde, 199 Cathedral Street, Glasgow G4 0QU; T.-0141 548 3580; (h.) Flat 3/1, 26 Belhaven Terrace West, Glasgow G12 0UL; T.-0141-357 3708.
E-mail: ian.wooton@strath.ac.uk

Wotherspoon, James Robert Edwards, DL, WS, LLB. Senior Partner, Macandrew & Jenkins WS; Lord Lieutenant of Inverness, Lochaber, Badenoch & Strathspey, Inverness, since 2021; b. 17.3.55, Inverness; m., Mairi Fleming (nee Stewart); 2 s.; 1 d. Educ. Loretto School, Musselburgh; University of Aberdeen. LLB, Aberdeen; Apprenticeship, Patrick & James, WS, Edinburgh; joined MacAndrew & Jenkins, WS, Inverness in 1979. Recreations: golf; tennis; sailing; stalking; shooting; fishing. Address: (b.) 5 Drummond Street, Inverness IV1 1QF; T.-01463 723500.
E-mail: james@macandrewjenkins.co.uk

Wright, Andrew Paul Kilding, OBE, BArch, PPRIAS, FSA Scot, FFCS. Architectural Historian and Conservation Architect (retired); Partner, Law & Dunbar-Nasmith, 1981-2001; b. 11.2.47, Walsall; m., Jean Patricia; 1 s.; 2 d. Educ. Queen Mary's Grammar School, Walsall; Liverpool University School of Architecture. Practising architect, 1972-2020; President, Inverness Architectural Association, 1986-88; External Examiner, Robert Gordon University, 1990-2003; Council, Royal Institute of British Architects, 1988-94 and 1995-97; President, Royal Incorporation of Architects in Scotland, 1995-97 (Member, Council, RIAS, 1985-94, 1995-99); Diocesan Architect, Diocese of Moray, Ross and Caithness, 1989-98; Consultant Architect to National Trust for Scotland for Mar Lodge Estate, 1995-99; Board Director, Glasgow 1999 Festival Company, 1996-2003; Member, Ancient Monuments Board for Scotland, 1996-2003; Commissioner, Royal Fine Art Commission for Scotland, 1997-2005; Hon. Adviser, Historic Churches Scotland, since 1996; Member, Church of Scotland Committee on Artistic Matters, 1999-2005; Trustee, Clan MacKenzie Charitable Trust, 2018; Architectural Adviser, Holyrood Progress Group, Scottish Parliament, 2000-04; Conservation Adviser to Highland Historic Buildings Trust, since 2001; Conservation Advisory Panel to Hopetoun House Preservation Trust, 1997-2007; Member, Historic Environment Advisory Council for Scotland, 2003-09, Vice-Chair, 2003-06; Member, National Trust for Scotland Conservation Committee, 2007-2011; Trustee, Scottish Lime Centre Trust, since 2011; Member, Post Completion Advisory Group, Holyrood Building Project, 2004-06; Trustee: Cawdor Maintenance Trust, since 2010, Cawdor Heritage Charity, since 2010; Member, Historic Scotland Advisory Committee, 2012-15; Member, Historic Scotland/RCAHMS Transition Advisory Board, 2013-15; Trustee, Knockando Woolmill Trust, 2015-18; Trustee, Historic Scotland Foundation, since 2019. Recreations: music; railway history; fishing. Address: (b.) 16 Moy House Court, Forres IV36 2NZ; T.-07740 859005.

Wright, Charlotte. Chief Executive, Highlands and Islands Enterprise, 2017-2021 (Interim Chief Executive, 2016-17). Educ. Hookergate. Career history: held a number of roles in strategic planning and operational management, National Health Service in Tyneside; ran own small business in Fort William; Highlands and Islands Enterprise: appointed local enterprise company Chief Executive, Lochaber office in 2004; appointed as the agency's Regional Director for Highland in 2008, and as Director of Business and Sector Development in 2010.

Wright, Rev. David Livingston, MA, BD, FFCS. Minister of Religion, Church of Scotland, since 1957; b. 18.5.30, Aberdeen; m., Margaret Brown; 1 d.; 2 s. Educ. Robert Gordon's College, Aberdeen; King's College,

Aberdeen University. Organist and choirmaster, 1946-54; RAMC, 1949-51; Choirmaster of Youth for Christ, 1951-55; Minister: Cockenzie Chalmers Memorial, 1957-64, Forfar Lowson Memorial, 1964-71, Hawick Old, 1971-85, linked with Teviothead, 1972, Stornoway St Columba's Old Parish, 1985-98 and RAF chaplain. Former Moderator, Jedburgh and Lewis Presbyteries; convenor of Business Superintendance and World Mission committees; former Chairman, Scottish Reformation Society and National Church Association. Publications: reviews, articles, books - The Word Must Take Priority; The Way Forward for the Kirk; The Meaning of the Lord's Day; Reformed Book of Common Order (Contributor); Reformed and Evangelical (Editor); The Difference Christ Makes; Preaching the Word. Recreations: Cardiactive group; walking the dog; reading; playing piano and organ. Address: (h.) 84 Wyvis Drive, Nairn IV12 4TP; T.-01667 451613.

Wright, Professor Eric George, BSc, PhD, FRSB, FRCPath, FRSE. Emeritus Professor of Experimental Haematology, University of Dundee, since 2010; b. 11.1.49, Wolverhampton. Educ. Wolverhampton Grammar School; Sussex University, Manchester University. WHO Research Fellow, Sloan Kettering Cancer Center, New York; Research Fellow, Paterson Institute for Cancer Research, Manchester; Lecturer in Cellular Pathology, University of St. Andrews; senior scientific positions, Medical Research Council Radiation and Genome Stability Unit, Harwell; Honorary Professor, Brunel University, University of Reading; Fellow of the Higher Education Academy, 2007; Fellow of the British Institute of Radiology, 2007. David Anderson-Berry Medal, Royal Society of Edinburgh, 1999; Weiss Medal of the Association for Radiation Research, 2007; Bacq Alexander Award of the European Radiation Research Society, 2008; Sylvanus Thompson Medal of the British Institute of Radiology; Member, UK Department of Health Committee on Medical Effects of Radiation in the Environment, 1996-2007; Member of Steering Committee, Academic Clinical Oncology and Radiobiology Research Network, 2005-09. Publications: 200 scientific papers. Recreations: music; gardening; hillwalking. Address: (h.) Willowhill, Forgan, Newport on Tay, Fife DD6 8RA; e-mail: e.g.wright@dundee.ac.uk

Wright, George Gordon. Publisher, Writer and Photographer; b. 25.6.42, Edinburgh; m., Carmen Ilie; 1 s. Educ. Darroch Secondary School; Heriot Watt College. Started publishing as a hobby, 1969; left printing trade, 1973, to develop own publishing company; founder Member, Scottish General Publishers Association; Past Chairman, Scottish Young Publishers Society; Oliver Brown Award, 1994; Secretary/Treasurer, 200 Burns Club, since 1991. Photographic Exhibitions: Glisk: Photographs of the Scottish Literati, 1968-79, The Netherbow, 1979, The Write Stuff, Scottish Writers Through The Lens of Gordon Wright, National Library of Scotland, 2001. Publications: MacDiarmid: An Illustrated Biography, 1977; A Guide to the Royal Mile, 1979; Orkney From Old Photographs, 1981; A Guide to Holyrood Park and Arthur's Seat, 1987; 'A Great Idea at the Time' (Memoirs of a Scottish Publisher and Photographer), Vol. I. Growing Up in Edinburgh, 2013, Vol. II. A Precarious Occupation, 2015, Vol. III. Winners and Losers, 2015, Vol. IV. Highlights and Lowlights, 2015 (all Apple Books); The Dunedin Amateur Weight-Lifting Club, Edinburgh, 1932-1970; Larry Scott Under The Spotlight. A Posing Routine. Sixteen Photographs by Gordon Wright (Apple Book), 2016; Edinburgh: 300 Photographs of Things To See (Apple Book), 2016; The Man in the Library Lift & Other Poems, 2016; A Guide to the Royal Mile (Apple Book), 2019; Edinburgh's Holyrood Park & Arthur's Seat (Apple Book), 2019; The Book Club

for Bitter Hearts & Other Poems, 2020. Recreations: history of Edinburgh; photography; jazz. Address: (h.) 25 Mayfield Road, Edinburgh EH9 2NQ; T.-0131-667 1300.

Wright, Malcolm Robert, OBE, FRCGP, FRCPE, FRSA, Honorary Doctor, Paisley University, CIHSM. Director-General Health and Social Care and Chief Executive, NHS Scotland, 2019-20; Chief Executive, NHS Grampian, 2014-August 2018; Chief Executive, NHS Tayside, 2018; Chief Executive, NHS Education for Scotland, 2004-2014; b. 1.9.57, Blyth; 1 s.; 1 d. Educ. Kings School, Tynemouth; Penicuik High School. Hospital Manager, Great Ormond Street, London, 1989-92; Unit General Manager, Lothian Health Board, 1992-94; Chief Executive, Edinburgh and Sick Children's NHS Trust, 1994-99; Chief Executive, Dumfries and Galloway Acute and Maternity Hospitals NHS Trust, 1999-2001; Chief Executive, Dumfries and Galloway Health Board, 2001-04; Chair, Ministerial and Young People's Health Support Group, since 2000. Recreations: cycling; reading; theatre; opera; classical music; outdoor activity.

Wyatt, Daniel. Rector, Kelvinside Academy, since 2019; Executive Headmaster, Glasgow Schools Trust, since 2019. Educ. Exeter University; m., Norah; 2 c. Career history: PE and History Teacher, Dr Challoner's Grammar School, Amersham; moved north of the border in 2003; Deputy Rector, Kelvinside Academy, 2015-19. Address: Kelvinside Academy, 33 Kirklee Road, Glasgow G12 0SW; T.-0141 357 3376.

Wyke, John Anthony, MA, PhD, VetMB, HonFRCVS, FRSE, FMedSci. Emeritus Professor and Honorary Fellow, Glasgow University; b. 5.4.42, Cleethorpes. Educ. Dulwich College; Cambridge University; Glasgow University; London University. Leukemia Society of America Fellow, Universities of Washington and Southern California, 1970-72; Staff Scientist, Imperial Cancer Research Fund, 1972-85; Assistant Director of Research, 1985-87; Director, Beatson Institute for Cancer Research, 1987-2002. Research interests: mechanisms of cancer causation by viruses. Selected advisory positions; Governing body, AFRC Institute of Animal Health, 1988-1995; International Scientific Advisory Committee for the Danish Cancer Society, 1993-1996; Governing Body, Caledonian Research Foundation, 1994-2005; Chair, two capacity building programmes of the International Union against Cancer (UICC), Geneva, 1998-2002; Director, Scottish Cancer Foundation, 2002-2016 (Chairman, 2002-2010); Director, Association for International Cancer Research (now Worldwide Cancer Research), 2003-2016; Member of Council, Royal Veterinary College, 2008-2012; Trustee, RSE Scotland Foundation, 2012-2019. Address: (h.) 6 Ledcameroch Road, Bearsden, Glasgow G61 4AA; e-mail: johnwyke@hotmail.co.uk

Wylie, Jackie, MA. Artistic Director and Chief Executive, National Theatre of Scotland, since 2016; b. 1980, Edinburgh. Educ. University of Glasgow. Career history: worked in film and television production until 2004, then The Arches in Glasgow; worked under Andy Arnold as arts programmer, then became Artistic Director in 2008; created the Behaviour festival in 2009; co-commissioned large-scale performances by internationally established artists. Named a Clore Leadership Programme Fellow in 2016. Address: National Theatre of Scotland, Rockvilla, 125 Craighall Road, Glasgow G4 9TL; T.-0141 221 0970.

Wyllie, Gordon Malcolm, MStJ, LLB, DUniv (Glasgow), FSA Scot, NP, WS. Former Partner, Bird Semple (2012-2014); former Partner, Biggart Baillie LLP, Solicitors

510 WHO'S WHO IN SCOTLAND

(1980-2012); b. Newton Mearns. Educ. Dunoon Grammar School; Glasgow University. Clerk to General Commissioners of Inland Revenue, Glasgow North and South Divisions (1990-2009); Honorary Treasurer, Edinburgh Summer School in Ancient Greek, 1975-99; Director, Bailford Trustees Ltd., 1994-2012; Chairman, Britannia Panopticon Music Hall Trust, 1997-2005; Convener, Scottish Grant-Making Trusts Group, 2006-2010; Regional Chairman, now ambassador for Action Medical Research; Member, Council, Friends at the End, 2000-02, Convener, 2016-17; Chairman, Edinburgh Subscription Ball Committee; Freeman of Glasgow; Burgess of Edinburgh; Deacon, Incorporation of Hammermen of Edinburgh, 1996-99; Preses, Grand Antiquity Society of Glasgow, 2000-01; Boxmaster, Convenery of Trades of Edinburgh, 2000-03; Deacon Convener, Trades of Edinburgh, 2003-06; Clerk to the Trades House of Glasgow, 1987-2004; Governor, Trades Maiden Hospital of Edinburgh; Coordinator (2011-12) of first Edinburgh Convenery Exhibition of Incorporated Trades; Visitor, Incorporation of Maltmen of Glasgow, 2012-13; Chairman, Edinburgh West End Community Council, 2005-2013; Deacon, Inc. of Bonnetmakers and Dyers of Edinburgh, 2003-09; wrote Scottish contribution to International Bar Association's International Dictionary of Succession Terms; Elder, Church of Scotland, since 2005; Member, Trusts and Succession Committee of the Law Society of Scotland, since 2005 (Chairman, 2011-2020) and the European Commission's Group of Experts on Succession and Wills in the EU, 2005-08; Inaugural President, Burgess Association of Edinburgh, 2017-2020; Chairman, Glasgow Building Preservation Trust, since 2020. Recreations: music; history and the arts generally; country walks; foreign travel.

Wyllie, The Very Rev. Dr. Hugh Rutherford, MA, Hon.DD (Aberdeen), FCIBS. Minister, Old Parish Church of Hamilton, 1981-2000; Moderator, General Assembly of the Church of Scotland, 1992-93; b. 11.10.34, Glasgow; m., Eileen E. Cameron, MA (Hons); 2 d. Educ. Shawlands Academy; Hutchesons' Grammar School, Glasgow; Union Bank of Scotland, 1951-53 (MCIBS). National Service, RAF, 1953-55 (Air Radar Mechanic); University of Glasgow, 1956-62 (MA - The George Neilson Prize, The Ewing Prize, The Walter Scott Club Prize; Divinity - The Pitcairn Miller Frame Prizes, 1961 and 1962); President, Glasgow University Student Christian Movement, 1958; Chairman, SCM Scottish Council, 1958; Ordained Assistant Minister, Glasgow Cathedral, 1962-65; Minister, Dunbeth Church, Coatbridge, 1965-72; Minister, Cathcart South Church, Glasgow, 1972-81; Minister, The Old Parish Church of Hamilton, 1981-2000; Moderator, Presbytery of Hamilton, 1989-90; Convener, Business Committee, 1991-95; Chaplain: Royal British Legion, Hamilton, 1981-2001, Lanarkshire Burma Star Association, 1983-2001, Q Division, Strathclyde Police, 1984-2001; Founder, Hamilton Centre for Information for the Unemployed, 1983; introduced Dial-a-Fact on drugs and alcohol, 1986; established Hamilton Church History Project, 1984-87; Co-Founder, Hamilton and District Festival of Remembrance, 1983; Convener, General Assembly's Stewardship and Budget Committee, 1978-83; Convener, General Assembly's Stewardship and Finance Board, 1983-86; Convener, General Assembly's Assembly Council, 1987-91; Member, Board of Nomination to Church Chairs, 1985-91 and 1993-99; Member, General Assembly's Board of Practice and Procedure, 1991-95; Vice Chairman, Lanarkshire NHS Trust, 1996-99; Trustee, Lanarkshire Primary Care NHS Trust, 1999-2001; Lay Member, Scottish Executive's Working Party General Practitioners, 2000-02; Hon. Freeman, District of Hamilton, 1992; Hon. Doctor of Divinity (DD), Aberdeen, 1993; Hon. Fellow of the Chartered Insititute of Bankers in Scotland (FCIBS), 1997; George and Thomas Hutcheson Award, Hutchesons' Grammar School, Glasgow, 2002. Recreation: gardening. Address: 18 Chantinghall Road, Hamilton ML3 8NP.

Wyllie, James Hogarth, BA, MA. Professor (Emeritus), University of Aberdeen; Director of the Graduate Strategic Studies Degree Programmes, Aberdeen University, 1979-2021; b. 7.3.51, Dumfries; m., Claire Helen Beaton (deceased); 2 s. Educ. Sanquhar Academy; Dumfries Academy; Stirling University; Lancaster University. Research Officer, Ministry of Defence, 1974-75; Tutor in Politics, Durham University, 1975-77; Lecturer in Politics, University of East Anglia, 1977-79; freelance journalism; frequent current affairs comment and analysis, BBC Radio; Commonwealth Fellow, University of Calgary, 1988; International Affairs Analyst, Grampian Television, 1989-94; Specialist Correspondent, Jane's Intelligence Review, 1992-98. Selected publications: Influence of British Arms; European Security in the Nuclear Age; Economist Pocket Guide to Defence (Co-Author); International Politics since 1945 (Contributor); European Security in the New Political Environment; The Middle East and North Africa (Contributor); Issues in International Relations (Contributor). Member: International Institute for Strategic Studies; Royal United Services Institute for Defence Studies and German Council on Foreign Relations. Address: (b.) Department of Politics and International Relations, Aberdeen University, Aberdeen AB24 3QY. E-mail: j.h.wyllie@abdn.ac.uk; jameshwyllie@gmail.com

Wynd, Andrew H. D., MBE, MIoD. Chief Executive & Company Secretary, Spina Bifida Hydrocephalus Scotland. Address: (b.) The Dan Young Building, 6 Craighalbert Way, Cumbernauld, Glasgow G68 0LS; T.-01236 794500; e-mail: mail@sbhscotland.org.uk

Y

Yaqoob, Talat, BSc, MRes. Campaigner, writer and commentator; Director and Campaigner, Equate Scotland, 2016-2020. Educ. Heriot-Watt University; The University of Edinburgh. Career history: Campaigns and Events Assistant, The World Development Movement, 2008-09; National Union of Students (UK): Mental Health Campaigns Officer, 2009-11, Head of Membership Development, 2011; Campaigns Officer, White Ribbon Scotland, 2012-13; Consultant, 2013-15; External Engagement and Research Officer, The Scottish Parliament, 2015-16; Chair of the Board of Directors, First Aid Africa, 2011-17; Chair and Co-Founder, Women 5050, since 2014; Member of Board of Directors, Engender Scotland, since 2014. Winner of Outstanding Woman of the Year 2018 from Saltire Scotland.

Yeates, Damien. Chief Executive, Skills Development Scotland, since 2008. Previously Chief Executive of the Scottish University for Industry and the Govan Initiative; initiated a number of very successful programmes to promote skills and lifelong learning, including the establishment of the Digital Media Academy, the Community Technology Academy Network and the Blended Learning of Construction Skills (BLOCS) programme. Previously held directorships of the Scottish Urban Regeneration Forum and Realizations International Ltd. Address: (b.) 150 Broomielaw, Atlantic Quay, Glasgow G2 8LU.

Yellowlees, John, MA (Hons) (Cantab), MPhil (Edin), FCILT. Honorary Rail Ambassador; former External Relations Manager, Abellio Scotrail Ltd (retired). Career history: administrative civil servant in the Departments of the Environment and Transport for 17 years (headed branches responsible for client liaison on Scottish public buildings; policy on registration of merchant ships and fishing vessels; and coordination of transport programmes for London Docklands); joined railway industry in 1991 in Edinburgh (worked for ScotRail, the British Railways Board, Railtrack Scotland Zone, ScotRail Railways and First ScotRail, supporting the Head of Corporate Social Responsibility on development of its Adopt A Station policy and Community Rail strategy). Member: Executive Committee of the Scottish Transport Studies Group, the Industrial and Professional Advisory Committee of Napier University's School of the Built Environment and the Scottish advisers to the Railway Heritage Designation Advisory Board; Director of Transform Scotland, the Scottish campaign for a sustainable transport policy. Secretary of the Edinburgh Branch of the Saltire Society, since 2003; elected to Murrayfield Community Council in 2009, Chairman, since 2012.

Yellowlees, Professor Lesley Jane, CBE, HonFRSC, BSc, PhD, FRSE. Professor of Inorganic Electrochemistry, University of Edinburgh (Vice-Principal and Head of the College of Science & Engineering, 2011-17); President, Royal Society of Chemistry, 2012-2014; b. 31.8.53, London; m., Peter Yellowlees; 1 s.; 1 d. Educ. St Hilary's School, Edinburgh; University of Edinburgh. University of Edinburgh: Senior Lecturer, 1992, Reader, 1998, Personal Chair in Inorganic Electrochemistry, 2005-2010, Head of the School of Chemistry, 2005-2010. President, Royal Society of Chemistry Council, 2012-14; IUPAC 2011 Distinguished woman in Chemistry; DSc: Aberdeen, Bristol, Edinburgh Napier, Heriot-Watt, Huddersfield, Open, Queen's Belfast, St Andrews and Strathclyde Universities. Recreations: cooking; entertaining; reading;

walking. Address: (b.) College of Science & Engineering Office, University of Edinburgh, Weir Building, The King's Buildings, West Mains Road, Edinburgh EH9 3BF; T.-0131 650 5754; e-mail: l.j.yellowlees@ed.ac.uk

Young, Andrew, QC, LLB (Hons), DLP. Senator of the College of Justice, since 2022. Educ. University of Aberdeen; University of Glasgow. Career history: traineeship with Dundas & Wilson CS; called to the Scottish bar in 1992; served as standing junior counsel to the Foreign & Commonwealth Office, HM Customs & Excise and HM Revenue & Customs; appointed Queen's Counsel in 2007; part time chairman of the Police Appeals Tribunal, since 2013 and a part time chairman of the Competition Appeals Tribunal, since 2021. Publications: co-author of a textbook on commission & diligence, and has also been a contributor to two editions of Gloag & Henderson "The Law of Scotland". Address: Parliament House, Edinburgh EH1 1RQ.

Young, Chick. Football Correspondent, BBC Television and Radio, since 1988; b. 4.5.51, Glasgow. Educ. Glasgow High School; Bellahouston Academy, Glasgow. Daily Record, 1969-72; Carrick Herald, Girvan, 1972; Irvine Herald, 1972-73; Charles Buchan's Football Monthly, London, 1973-74; Editor, Scottish Football magazine, 1974-75; Scottish Daily News, 1975; Scottish Daily Express, 1976; Evening Times, Glasgow, 1977-88; Radio Clyde, 1977-95; BBC, since 1988; Sunday People, 1988-89; Scotland on Sunday, 1989-91; Columnist, Daily Star, since 1996; Columnist, Daily Express, since 2004; Columnist, BBC website, since 2002; Columnist, Paisley Daily Express, since 2012. Fraser Award, Young Journalist of the Year, 1973; British Provincial Sports Journalist of the Year, 1987; Sony Award, British Sports Broadcaster of the Year (Bronze), 1997; Scottish Sports Journalist of the Year Runner-up, 1997 and 2002; RTS Provincial Sports Reporter of the Year, 2000. Publications: Rebirth of the Blues; Mo. Address: (b.) BBC TV Sport, 40 Pacific Quay, Glasgow G51 1DA; e-mail: chick.young@bbc.co.uk

Young, David. Principal, Wester Hailes Education Centre, since 2016. Address: (b.) 5 Murrayburn Drive, Edinburgh EH14 2SU; T.-0131 442 2201.

Young, Jill, MBE. Lord Lieutenant, Dunbartonshire, since 2021; former Chief Executive, Golden Jubilee Foundation. The first female, and first non-military holder of the office of Lord Lieutenant.

Young, John Maclennan, OBE. Farmer, since 1949; Hon. Sheriff, Grampian, Highlands and Islands, 1995-2017; JP for Caithness, 1970-99; b. 6.6.33, Thurso. Educ. Thurso Miller Academy. Member, Caithness County Council, 1961-75 (Chairman, Housing Committee, 1968-73, Chairman, Planning Committee, 1973-75); Member, Highland Regional Council, 1974-90 (Chairman, Roads and Transport Committee, 1978-90); Provost of Caithness, 1995-99; Member, Caithness District Council, 1974-96 (Convener of the Council, 1974-96); Member, The Highland Council, 1995-99; President, Caithness Area Executive Commitee, NFU of Scotland, 1963 and 1964; Chairman, Scrabster Harbour Trust, 2001-03; Chairman, Wick Airport Consultative Committee, 1990-2002. Address: (b.) Sordale, Halkirk, Caithness KW12 6XB; T.-01847 831228.

Young, Laura. Environmental Educator and Ethical Influencer/Digital Freelance, Less Waste Laura, since 2018; Scotland COP26 Advocacy and Campaigns

Coordinator (Part-time), Tearfund, since 2020; Sky News Daily Climate Show contributor, since 2021. Educ. Kirkhill Primary School; Mearns Castle High School; University of Guelph; University of Dundee; University of Edinburgh. Career history: Front of House, Greene King, 2015-2018; Sustainability Auditor, 2018-19; Postgraduate Student, University of Edinburgh, 2018-19; Sustainability Intern, SP Energy Networks, 2019; Community Education Lead, Society Zero, 2018-2020; Member, Board of Trustees, Diamonds Scotland (Part-time), since 2021; Social Media Specialist, Bin Twinning (Part-time), since 2020; Content Creator, BBC The Social, since 2020; Youth and Emerging Generation Team Manager (Full-time), 2019-2021. Address: Tearfund, Suite 529-534 Baltic Chambers, 50 Wellington Street, Glasgow G2 6HJ; T.-0141 332 3621.

Young, Lesslie. Chief Executive, Epilespy Scotland, since 2009. Educ. Kirkcaldy High School. NHS: Charge Nurse, 1978-88, Quality Assurance Manager, 1988-89; set up a charity providing a home-based teaching system to children with learning disabilities and their families whilst also working as a partner in a home care business and an occupational health consultancy; joined Epilepsy Scotland's training department in 2006. Sits on the Criminal Justice Disability Advisory Group and presents annually at Dame Elish Angiolini's LLM Advocacy course; member of the Institute of Directors and the West of Scotland Vistage Group for CEOs. Address: Head Office, 48 Govan Road, Glasgow G51 1JL; T.-0141 427 4911.

Young, Mark Richard, BSc, PhD, FRES, FSBiol, CBiol. Emeritus Senior Lecturer, Aberdeen University; b. 27.10.48, Worcester; m., Jennifer Elizabeth Tully; 1 s.; 1 d. Educ. Kings School, Worcester; Birmingham University. Lecturer, Aberdeen University, 1973-89; Director of Teaching, School of Biological Sciences, 2004-2011; Academic Director, Centre for Learning and Teaching, 2007-2011. Member, North Board, Scottish Environment Protection Agency, 1996-2002; Member, Advisory Committee on SSSIs, 1998-2008. Recreations: natural history; walking; ball sports; visiting Hebridean islands; Samaritans. Address: (b.) School of Biological Sciences, University of Aberdeen, Tillydrone Avenue, Aberdeen AB24 2TZ; e-mail: m.young@abdn.ac.uk

Young, Mel, MBE. Chairman, sportscotland, since 2016 (previously Vice-Chairman); Board Member, UK Sport. Educ. Heriot-Watt University. Career history: worked as a journalist; Co-Founder, The Big Issue in Scotland Ltd, 1993-2004; President and co-founder of the Homeless World Cup, since 2003; co-founded the International Network of Street Papers (INSP) in 1995 and Social Entrepreneurs Network Scotland (Senscot) in 1999; set up City Lynx magazine and New Consumer Magazine; worked on a community newspaper in Wester Hailes in Edinburgh in the 1990s. Schwab Fellow of the World Economic Forum and a Senior Ashoka Fellow. Recipient of the 2016 Jackie Robinson Humanitarian Award; awarded an MBE in The Queen's Birthday Honours, 2017. Five Honorary Degrees from Scottish Universities. Publication: Goal: the story of the Homeless World Cup (Author). Recreation: lifelong supporter of Hibernian FC. Address: sportscotland, Doges, Templeton on the Green, 62 Templeton Street, Glasgow G40 1DA; T.-0141 534 6500.

Young, Meriel, BA, PGDipM, MCIM. Director, Promote A Route and Meriel Young Consulting, since 2006; Board Member, Loch Lomond and The Trossachs National Park Authority, 2002-2010; b. 10.01.73, Oban; m., Tim Hall; 2 s.; 1 d. Educ. Oban High School; Heriot

Watt University. Self-employed consultant and chartered marketer specialising in recreational and environmental management, communications and education; broad experience in project management across the public and private sector in community greenspace planning, urban forestry, transport and health policy; previously employed by City of Edinburgh Council (City Development), 1999-2003, and Woodland Trust Scotland, 1997-99; early freelance activities included running a day trips business, lecturing on environmental education and interpretation, and forestry contracting. Member of Central Scotland Regional Forestry Forum (FCS). Recreations: hillwalking; running; cycling; kayaking; sailing; yoga; travel; music; art. Address: 4 Kirkliston Road, South Queensferry, Edinburgh EH30 9LT.

Young, Rona Macdonald, BD, DipEd. Minister of Ayr: St Quivox Church, 2009-2015 (retired); Minister of Crosshouse Parish Church, 1991-2001; Minister of New Cumnock Parish Church, 2001-09 (Church returned to Full Status in 2004); b. 4.5.50, Giffnock, Glasgow; m., Thomas C. Young; 2 d.; 2 grandsons. Educ. Marr College, Troon; Craigie College, Ayr; Glasgow University. Primary School Teacher, Bentinck Primary, Kilmarnock, 1971-75; Minister of Crosshouse Parish Church, 1991-2001 (Church returned to Full Status in 1996). Recreations: reading; walking; town twinning. Address: (h.) 16 Macintyre Road, Prestwick, Ayrshire KA9 1BE; T.-01292 471982.

Young, Sheriff Principal Sir Stephen Stewart Templeton, QC, 3rd Bt. Sheriff Principal of Grampian, Highland and Islands, 2001-2012; b. 24.5.47; m.; 2 s. Educ. Rugby; Trinity College, Oxford; Edinburgh University. Sheriff, Glasgow and Strathkelvin, 1984; Sheriff of North Strathclyde at Greenock, 1984-2001.

Young, William Smith Geates, LLB (Hons), NP. Former Chairman, Brechin Tindal Oatts; b. 21.12.55, Girvan; m., Margot Glanville Jones. Educ. Girvan Academy; Glasgow University. Joined Tindal Oatts & Rodger, 1978; admitted Solicitor, 1980; Managing Partner, Tindal Oatts, 1993; Managing Partner, Brechin Tindal Oatts, 1997-2008. SFA Class 1 Referee List, 1990-2005; FIFA List of International Linesmen, 1992, 1993; FIFA List of International Referees, 1994-2000. Recreations: football; golf; after-dinner speaking.

Younger, Sir John (David) Bingham, KCVO (2012), LVO (2006). Lord-Lieutenant of Tweeddale, 1994-2014; b. 20.5.39, Doune; m., Anne Rosaleen Logan (deceased, 2012); 1 s.; 2 d. Educ. Eton College; Royal Military Academy, Sandhurst. Argyll and Sutherland Highlanders, 1957-69; Scottish and Newcastle Breweries, 1969-79; Founder and Managing Director, Broughton Brewery Ltd., 1979-95; Director, Broughton Ales, 1995-96. Deputy Lieutenant, Tweeddale, 1987, Vice Lord-Lieutenant, 1992. Chairman, Board of Governors, Belhaven Hill School Trust, 1988-94; Chairman, Scottish Borders Tourist Board, 1989; Member, A&SH Regimental Trust and Committee, 1985-96; Member, Queen's Bodyguard for Scotland (Royal Company of Archers), since 1969; Secretary, 1993-2007, Brigadier, 2002, Ensign, 2010; Vice President, RHASS, 1994; River Tweed Commissioner, 2002-2016; President: Lowland Reserve Forces and Cadets Association, 2006-2014, SSAFA (Borders), since 2006; Chairman, Bowmen Ltd, 2008-2015; Director, Eastgate Theatre and Arts Centre, Peebles, 2014, Chairman, 2015-18. Recreation: the countryside. Address: (h.) Mansemanet, Broughton, Peeblesshire ML12 6HF; T.-01899 830570.

Younger, Susan Emma, LLB, DipLP, WS, NP. Chairwoman, Cairn Mhor Childcare Partnership Ltd, 2017-19, Chief Executive, 2015-17; formerly Partner and Head of Banking, Morton Fraser (2002-2015); b. 12.4.64, Morpeth; m., Michael Younger; 3 d. Educ. St. Margarets,